Thorndike Barnhart

Children's Dictionary

by E. L. Thorndike/Clarence L. Barnhart

Scott Foresman - Addison Wesley

Editorial Offices: Glenview, Illinois • New York, New York
Sales Offices: Reading, Massachusetts • Duluth, Georgia • Glenview, Illinois
Carrollton, Texas • Menlo Park, California

http://www.sf.aw.com

This dictionary is also published under the title *Scott Foresman-Addison Wesley Beginning Dictionary.*

This dictionary includes a few entries that are registered trademarks in the United States at the time of this book's copyright; the entries are so identified, as a fact of reference. No judgment should be made or understood, however, as to the actual legal status of any word in the dictionary.

Feature Design:
Steven Curtis Design, Inc., Chicago: pp. 23A-B, 197A-B, 275A-B, 353A-B, 675A-B, 729A-B, 785A-B
Three Communication Design, Chicago: pp. 311A-B, 403A-B, 671A-B, 701A-B, 814-815, 822-823

Picture credits appear on pages iii-v.

ISBN 0-673-58933-1

Library of Congress Cataloging-in-Publication Data available upon request.

7 8 9 10 - DOW - 05 04

Art and Photo Credits

Cover Cover art (cheetah) Ron Kimball/Ron Kimball Studios

Front Matter Table of Contents Ron Kimball/Ron Kimball Studios **I-3** (zebra) SuperStock International **I-6** (bald eagle) SuperStock International

A Opener page (TL) SuperStock International (TR) ©PhotoDisc (C) Rich Stergulz **ablaze** Don Wilson **abreast** SuperStock International **abstract** Kandinsky, "Variation VI," Bauhaus Archive/E.T. Archive, London/SuperStock International **accessible** Mike Carroll **accumulate** SuperStock International **acrobat** Rob Barber **adapt** Stephen J. Krasemann/Photo Researchers, Inc. **adder** George Hamblin **admire** Bob Nonnemacher **adobe** SuperStock International **aerial** SuperStock International **affectionate** (L) Stephen J. Kraseman/DRK Photo (C) David C. Tomlinson/Tony Stone Images (R) Kim Heacox/Tony Stone Images **agile** LIFE Nature Library/THE PRIMATES Published by Time Life Books Inc. **ail** Joe Fournier **aircraft carrier** Sam Sargent/Gamma Liaison **albino** John Cancalosi/DRK Photo **alien** Rob Barber **alligator** SuperStock International **almond** John Zielinski **alpaca** Rich Stergulz **Alvin** Connie Mitchell **ameba** Mike Carroll **amphibian** John Zielinski **anaconda** Connie Mitchell **android** Kobal Collection **ankylosaurus** Gene Givan **ant** Dale R. Thompson/PNI/Bruce Coleman **anteater** Rich Stergulz **Ants** (spread) 23A-B (border) Peg Gerrity (BG) Peg Gerrity; 23A (BL) Tim Flach/Tony Stone Images (BC) Mantis Wildlife Films Oxford Scientific Films/Animals Animals (BR) K.G. Preston Mafham/Animals Animals; 23B (TL) Fritz Prenzel/Animals Animals **Appaloosa** Bobbi Tull **aqueduct** Gene Givan **ark** André Normil, "Noah's Ark"/SuperStock International **armadillo** John Zielinski **armor** Erich Lessing/Art Resource **artist** SuperStock International **ash[1]** SuperStock International **aster** Patti Murray/Animals Animals **astronaut** ©PhotoDisc **Atlas** David Lees/Corbis **attention** Leon Dishman/SuperStock International **auk** Jose Schell/Animals Animals **autumn** Donovan Reese/Tony Stone Images **avalanche** Itar-Tass/PNI/Sovfoto/Eastfoto **aviatior** SuperStock International **Aztec** Richard A. Cooke III/Tony Stone Images

B Opener page (TL) Maslowski/Visuals Unlimited (BL) SuperStock International (C) Connie Mitchell (TR) Rich Stergulz **backhand** Tom McCarthy/Photo Edit (R) Tom McCarthy/Photo Edit **bacteria** George Musil/Visuals Unlimited **bald eagle** SuperStock International **bamboo** Bobbi Tull **banjo** Dana White/Photo Edit **banner** Mike Dammer **bassoon** Spencer Grant/Photo Edit **bat[2]** Rich Stergulz **bazaar** John Pontier/Animals Animals **beehive** George Hamblin **beetle** David G. Campbell/Visuals Unlimited **bellows** John Zielinski **bend** LeeLee Brazeal **beret** SuperStock International **beseige** Patrick Piel/Gamma Liaison **bicycle** Gene Givan **bighorn** Joe McDonald/Animals Animals **biodiversity** SuperStock International **bison** Mickey Gibson/Animals Animals **blastoff** NASA **blimp** SuperStock International **bliss** Joe Fournier **blossom** William J. Weber/Visuals Unlimited **blowhole** (L) Stuart Westmoreland/Tony Stone Images (R) Daniel W. Gotshell/Visuals Unlimited **blue jay** Maslowski/Visuals Unlimited **boat** Connie Mitchell **bobsled** Mike Powell/AllSport USA **bongo** Spencer Grant/Photo Edit **boomerang** SuperStock International **botanical** Science VU/Visuals Unlimited **bouquet** SuperStock International **brachiosaurus** Connie Mitchell **Braille** Terry Vine/Tony Stone Images **break** Tony Freeman/Photo Edit **breaker** ©PhotoDisc **bridge** L. Linkhart/Visuals Unlimited **bristle** Michael & Barbara Reed/Animals Animals **broccoli** John Zielinski **brood** John Warden/Tony Stone Images **bubble** Claude Guillaumin/Tony Stone Images **bug** (TL) Lindholm/Visuals Unlimited (BL) Wm. S. Ormerod, Jr./Visuals Unlimited (R) Bill Beatty/Visuals Unlimited **bulldozer** Gene Givan **burn** E.R. Degginger/Animals Animals **burro** Walt Anderson/Visuals Unlimited **Butterflies** (spread) 89A-B; 89A (BL) SuperStock International (BC) Kjell B. Sandved/Visuals Unlimited (BR) Kjell B. Sandved/Visuals Unlimited (CR) Fred Hossler/Visuals Unlimited; 89B (C) SuperStock International (TR) Phyllis Greenberg/Animals Animals (BL) SuperStock International

C Opener page (TL) Ron Kimball/Ron Kimball Studios (TR) SuperStock International (BC) Mickey Gibson/Animals Animals (BR) Warren Marr/Panoramic Images **cactus** Gerald & Buff Corsi/Visuals Unlimited **calf[1]** Rich Stergulz **camouflage** Tony Stone Images **canary** John Zielinski **canoe** SuperStock International **canyon** Larry Ulrich/Tony Stone Images **Capitol** SuperStock International **caravan** Connie Mitchell **caribou** Art Wolfe/Tony Stone Images **carry** Peter Ryley/Oxford Scientific Films/Earth Scenes **cartwheel** SuperStock International **castle** SuperStock International **caterpillar** SuperStock International **caveman** Linda Howard **cello** David Young-Wolff/PhotoEdit **centipede** Gene Givan **chameleon** Art Wolfe/Tony Stone Images **chaps** Bobbi Tull **chat** Ellen Joy Sasaki **chauffeur** Tom McCarthy/PhotoEdit **cheer** George Hamblin **chess** Phil Borden/PhotoEdit **chimpanzee** Manoj Shah/Tony Stone Images **Chinese checkers** Tony Freeman/PhotoEdit **chip** SuperStock International **chopsticks** Michael Newman/PhotoEdit **chrysanthemum** Bobbi Tull **Civil War** Library of Congress **clam** E.C. Williams/Visuals Unlimited **claw** John Zielinski **cloud** (L) Jeffrey Howe/Visuals Unlimited (CR) SuperStock International (BR) Hugh Sitton/Tony Stone Images (TR) A.J. Copley/Visuals Unlimited **cluster** Will & Deni McIntyre/Tony Stone Images **cobra** John Zielinski **cockatoo** Ken Lucas/Visuals Unlimited **coconut** John Zielinski **collie** Rich Stergulz **colt** Renee Lynn/Tony Stone Images **comet** Bill & Sally Fletcher/Tom Stack & Associates **commencement** Tony Freeman/PhotoEdit **companion** SuperStock International **compass** Tony Freeman/PhotoEdit **computer** Tony Freeman/PhotoEdit **conch** SuperStock International **condor** Rich Stergulz **Conestoga wagon** SuperStock International **congestion** Will & Deni McIntyre/Tony Stone Images **conifer** Rich Stergulz **conservationist** Don Smetzer/Tony Stone Images **constellation** Bob Nonnemacher **consumer** Michael Newman/PhotoEdit **contestant** Tony Freeman/PhotoEdit **control tower** SuperStock International **convertible** Ron Kimball/Ron Kimball Studios **coral** Hal Beral/Visuals Unlimited **corn** Rob Barber **corral** ©PhotoDisc **costume** Paul Skillings/Tony Stone Images **cotton** Rich Stergulz **countless** Tony Stone Images **court** R. Moyer/Gamma Liaison **crane** Joe McDonald/Visuals Unlimited **crater** Allan E. Morton/Visuals Unlimited **creature** SuperStock International **crest** George Hamblin **crossbow** Gene Givan **crow's-nest** Gene Givan **crystal** (L) Mark A. Schneider/Visuals Unlimited (R) Dane S. Johnson/Visuals Unlimited **cuddle** Kjell B. Sandved/Visuals Unlimited **currency** SuperStock International **curtsy** Bobbi Tull **cyclone** Tony Arruza/Bruce Coleman Inc.

D Opener page (TL/TC) Stuart Westmoreland/Tony Stone Images (CR) SuperStock International (BR) SuperStock International **dancer** Hulton Getty/Tony Stone Images **dash** David Young-Wolff/PhotoEdit **dawdle** Joe Fournier **dead** Bobbi Tull **debris** Robert Ginn/PhotoEdit **deciduous** Alan Oddie/PhotoEdit **degree** George Hamblin **demolish** SuperStock International **derrick** SuperStock International **descent** Jose Carrillo/PhotoEdit **dessert** SuperStock International **detector** Mingasson/Gamma Liaison **dew** Myrleen Ferguson/PhotoEdit **different** LeeLee Brazeal **dipper** Bob Nonnemacher **dirty** Robert Ginn/PhotoEdit **disaster** Alon Reininger/Woodfin Camp & Associates **disguise** Warner Bros./©1997 D.C. Comics/Kobal Collection **disgusting** Joe Fournier **distance** Mike Dammer **distort** Tony Freeman/PhotoEdit **dive** David Leah/AllSport USA **DNA** George Hamblin **dolphin** SuperStock International **donkey** Rich Stergulz **dove[1]** John Zielinski **downy** SuperStock International **dragonfly** SuperStock International **Dragons** (spread) 197A-B (border) James Shaffer/PhotoEdit (BG) David Young-Wolff/PhotoEdit; 197A (CL) Janet L. Stone/National Audubon Society/Photo Researchers, Inc. (TR) The Charles Walker Collection/Stock Montage; 197B (T) Universal/Courtesy Kobal/Kobal Collection (BL) The Photo Library-Sydney/Geoff Higgins/Photo Researchers, Inc. (BC) Tom McHugh/Photo Researchers, Inc. (BR) Anthony Merceida/Photo Researchers, Inc. **drawbridge** Gene Givan **driftwood** Jo Prater/Visuals Unlimited **dromedary** John Zielinski **drum** (L) George Hunter/Tony Stone Images (LC) David E. Myers/Tony Stone Images (RC) Peter Rauter/Tony Stone Images (R) John Garrett/Tony Stone Images **dune** SuperStock International **dusk** Rocky Fry

E Opener page (TL) Larry Lee/Westlight (C) Manoj Shah/Tony Stone Images (TR) ©PhotoDisc (BR) The Granger Collection **earthquake** Michael Newman/PhotoEdit **eclipse** (BL) Gene Givan (TR) Joel Simon/Tony Stone Images **eel** Edward G. Lines, Jr./John G. Shedd Aquarium **egret** Bobbi Tull **elephant** (L) Manoj Shah/Tony Stone Images (R) Gerard Lacz/Animals Animals **emblem** courtesy of UNICEF **emperor** The Granger Collection **emu** Rich Stergulz **encourage** John Zielinski **engrave** Bard Wrisley/Gamma Liaison **enormous** Parker/Gamma Liaison **entertainment** Vic Bider/PhotoEdit equator Gene Givan **erupt** SuperStock International **estate** Geoff Johnson/Tony Stone Images **eucalyptus** Bonnie Kamin/PhotoEdit **excitement** Bill Aron/PhotoEdit **exercise** Jeff Greenberg/Visuals Unlimited **experiment** Brian Smith/Gamma Liaison **explore** NASA/National Geographic Society Image Collection **extend** Stephen Dalton/Animals Animals

F Opener page (TL) SuperStock International (TR) Peter Pearson/Tony Stone Images **falcon** Zig Leszczynski/Animals Animals **fangs** Schafer & Hill/Tony Stone Images **fawn** Rich Stergulz **feast** Tom McCarthy/PhotoEdit **feeler** George Hamblin **Ferris wheel** SuperStock International **fierce** R. Lindholm/Visuals Unlimited **fife** David Young-Wolff/PhotoEdit **figurehead** John Zielinski **fisherman** SuperStock International **flamingo** SuperStock International **flatfish** George Hamblin **flicker²** Rich Stergulz **flood** Rich Iwasaki/Tony Stone Images **floppy** Bobbi Tull **flourish** SuperStock International **flute** Kat Thacker **folk dance** Gary A. Conner/PhotoEdit **fool** The Granger Collection **footprint** Tom McCarthy/PhotoEdit **foreground** SuperStock International **forklift** Gene Givan **fossil** SuperStock International **fountain** Peter Pearson/Tony Stone Images **frame** SuperStock International **freighter** Gordon Fisher/Tony Stone Images **frigid** Barbara Gerlach/Visuals Unlimited **fulcrum** Yoshi Miyake **fungus** (L) SuperStock International (R) Laurie Campbell/Tony Stone Images **furrow** SuperStock International **futon** Milt & Joan Mann/Cameramann International, Ltd.

G Opener page (L) Henry Ausloon/Animals Animals (TR) © PhotoDisc (CR) Connie Mitchell (BR) Art Wolfe/Tony Stone Images **gallant** Corbis-Bettmann **galleon** Gene Givan **garter snake** Leonard Lee Rue III/Animals Animals **gavel** Rich Stergulz **gazelle** John Gerlach/Visuals Unlimited **genius** The Granger Collection **geodesic dome** Steve Vidler/Tony Stone Images **geyser** Alan Chapman/Visuals Unlimited **Giant Machines** (spread) 275A-B (BG) Lester Lefkowitz/Tony Stone Images; 275B (T) Arnold J. Karpoff/Visuals Unlimited (CL) A. J. Copley/Visuals Unlimited (CR) Joel Rogers/Tony Stone Images (BL) Vince Streano/Tony Stone Images **giraffe** Henry Ausloon/Animals Animals **glacier** SuperStock International **glider** Gene Givan **glowworm** John Zielinski **goalie** Al Bello/AllSport USA **gondola** Connie Mitchell **goose** Tom Edwards/Visuals Unlimited **gorilla** Art Wolfe/Tony Stone Images **gourd** gourds courtesy of Nan and Sid Simpson **graft** Bob Nonnemacher **Grand Canyon** Richard Kolar/Earth Scenes **grandfather clock** Photri **Great Dane** David Allan Brandt/Tony Stone Images **grin** SuperStock International **grotesque** (L) SuperStock International (R) SuperStock International **grumpy** Joe Fournier **guinea pig** Robert Maier/Animals Animals **gull** Rich Stergulz

H Opener page (L) Ralph A. Reinhold/Earth Scenes (BR) Anupe Manoj Shah/Animals Animals **haiku** Kjell B. Sandved/Visuals Unlimited **halo** Mark A. Schneider/Visuals Unlimited **hammock** Yoshi Miyake **handicraft** SuperStock International **hang glider** Mack Henley/Visuals Unlimited **hard hat** Michael P. Gadomski/Earth Scenes **hare** John Zielinski **harness** Connie Mitchell **hawk** Stephen Dalton/Animals Animals **headdress** (L) Tony Stone Images (R) David Young-Wolff/PhotoEdit **head-on** Wil Troyer/Visuals Unlimited **hedgehog** Rich Stergulz **helicopter** Ralph A. Reinhold/Earth Scenes **herb** Bobbi Tull **hero** (T/B) UPI-Corbis-Bettmann **hibernate** Rich Stergulz **Hidden Animals** (spread) 311A-B (BG) Michael P. Gadomski/Animals Animals; 311A (CL) SuperStock International (BL) Donald Specker/Animals Animals (TR) J. H. Robinson/Animals Animals (CR) Robert A. Lubeck/Animals Animals; 311B (TR) Ana Laura Gonzalez/Animals Animals (CR) Norbert Rosing/Animals Animals (CL) John Gerlach/Animals Animals (BL) Joe McDonald/Animals Animals **high jump** Walter Hodges/Tony Stone Images **hippopotamus** Anupe Manoj Shah/Animals Animals **hogan** John Zielinski **hollyhock** Bobbi Tull **honeycomb** William J. Weber/Visuals Unlimited **hoof** Rich Stergulz **horned toad** E. R. Degginger/Animals Animals **horseshoe** Leslye Borden/PhotoEdit **hot-air balloon** Tom Prettyman/PhotoEdit **howling** SuperStock International **humongous** Mike Dammer **husky** Marty Stouffer/Animals Animals **hyacinth** Bobbi Tull

I Opener page (L) © PhotoDisc (C) Anna E. Zukerman/PhotoEdit (R) FoodPix **identical twins** Myrleen Ferguson/PhotoEdit **igloo** Bobbi Tull **iguana** Rich Stergulz **immigrant** North Wind Picture Archives **impala** Kjell B. Sandved/Visuals Unlimited **impatiens** Connie Mitchell **improbable** Susan Hunt Yule **Inca** SuperStock International **Independence Day** Jose Carrillo/PhotoEdit **industrial** SuperStock International **infant** Bob Nonnemacher **ingredient** Jeff Greenberg/Visuals Unlimited **insignia** Bonnie Kamin/PhotoEdit **intercept** Richard Freeda/AllSport USA **interpreter** The Granger Collection **invasion** Frank Spooner/Gamma Liaison **invertebrate** SuperStock International **Irish setter** Franz Gorski/Peter Arnold, Inc. **irrigate** Inga Spence/Visuals Unlimited **ivy** Connie Mitchell

J Opener page (TR) Harry How/All Sport USA **jaguar** Michael Fogden/Animals Animals **jellyfish** James R. McCullagh/Visuals Unlimited **jet plane** Jim Stuart/Tony Stone Images **Jewelry and Gems** (spread) 353A-B (border) Felicia Martinez/PhotoEdit; 353A (TR/CR/BR) E. R. Degginger/Color-Pic Inc. (CL) Jason Laure/Laure Communications (BL) E. R. Degginger/Color-Pic Inc. (BC) Jason Laure/Woodfin Camp & Associates; 353B (TR) Adam Woolfit/Woodfin Camp & Associates (BC) John Drysdale/Woodfin Camp & Associates **jockey** Harry How/AllSport USA **joust** J. Nourok/PhotoEdit **jump rope** Tony Freeman/PhotoEdit **junk²** Sylvain Grandadam/Tony Stone Images

K Opener page (CL) National Portrait Gallery, London/SuperStock International (R) Myrleen Ferguson/PhotoEdit **kayak** Mark E. Gibson/Visuals Unlimited **kettle drum** Gene Givan **killer whale** Mickey Gibson/Animals Animals **kimono** Charles Preitner/Visuals Unlimited **king** National Portrait Gallery, London/SuperStock International **kite** George Hamblin **koala** Jane McAlonan/Visuals Unlimited

L Opener page (TL/TC) SuperStock International (TR) Connie Mitchell (BC) Rosemary Calvert/Tony Stone Images **labor union** Hulton Getty/Tony Stone Images **ladybug** Rosemary Calvert/Tony Stone Images **lamb** Rich Stergulz **lantern** Gene Givan **lark** Rich Stergulz **lasso** Tim Davis/Tony Stone Images **laundry** José Ortega **lavender** (L) SuperStock International (BR) Richard Shiell/Earth Scenes **leader** AP/Wide World Photos (Inset) UPI/Corbis-Bettmann **leash** Tony Freeman/PhotoEdit **leech** Cabisco/Visuals Unlimited **legendary** Kobal Collection **lemon** Connie Mitchell **leopard** Anupe Manoj Shah/Animals Animals **lettuce** Bobbi Tull **liberator** Hulton Getty/Tony Stone Images **lighthouse** SuperStock International **lilac** SuperStock International **lion** SuperStock International **litter** Fritz Prenzel/Animals Animals **llama** Gerald & Buff Corsi/Visuals Unlimited **lobster** George Hamblin **locomotive** Gary J. Benson **lollipop** Robert Brenner/PhotoEdit **longhorn** Connie Mitchell **loon** Rich Stergulz **lovebird** SuperStock International **luge** Clive Brunckill/AllSport USA **lynx** Len Rue Jr./Animals Animals

M Opener page (TL) Lee Boltin/Botin Picture Library (TR) Tony Stone Images **magnolia** (BL) B. Ormerod/Visuals Unlimited (R) Callahan/Visuals Unlimited **majestic** H. Richard Johnston/Tony Stone Images **makeup** Deborah Davis/PhotoEdit **mandolin** Gene Givan **mango** John Zielinski **mantis** Don W. Fawcett/Visuals Unlimited **marbles** Richard T. Nowitz **marionette** David Young-Wolff/PhotoEdit **Mars** (spread) 403A-B (border) Three Communications (BG) Jet Propulsion Laboratory; 403A (BR) NASA; 403B (TR) U.S. Geological Survey, Flagstaff, AZ (BL) NASA **mask** (L/LC/C/RC) Lee Boltin/Boltin Picture Library (R) Dave Rosenberg/Tony Stone Images **mastodon** Rich Stergulz **maternal** Bob Nonnemacher **maze** Jason Hawkes/Tony Stone Images **medieval** Bibliotheque Nationale, Paris/SuperStock International **Memorial Day** Richard Vogel/Gamma Liaison **menu** Connie Mitchell **mesa** Bill Kamin/Visuals Unlimited **microorganism** Andrew Syred/Science Photo Library/Photo Researchers, Inc. **mime** Archive Photos **miniature** David Young-Wolff/PhotoEdit **minuteman** Kindra Clineff/Tony Stone Images **miserable** Joe Fournier **mistletoe** John Zielinski **mitt** Rich Stergulz **mole** Linda Howard **mollusk** Carl Roessler/Animals Animals **monkey** Art Wolfe/Tony Stone Images **monster** Kobal Collection **moon** NASA **moose** Connie Mitchell **morning glory** Connie Mitchell **mosaic** Kjell B. Sandved/Visuals Unlimited **motocross** Tony Stone Images **mover** Ellen Joy Sasaki **mud** Roni Shepherd **mummy** Benton/Archive Photos **muralist** (L) Archive Photos (R) Florence Arquin /Archive Photos **mushroom** Michael Fogden/Earth Scenes **mutation** Ken Lucas/Visuals Unlimited

T **Opener page** (TL) John Zielinski (TR) MetaTools (C) Francis/Donna Caldwell/Visuals Unlimited (BR) Richard Hutchings/PhotoEdit **tadpole** Linda Howard **takeoff** George Herben/Visuals Unlimited **tangerine** John Zielinski **tarantula** Paul Freed/Animals Animals **target** Tony Garcia/Tony Stone Images **tassel** SuperStock International **taxicab** Liz Conrad **temple** Oliver Benn/Tony Stone Images **Temporary Structures** (spread) 701A-B; 701A (BL) L.L.T. Rhodes/Earth Scenes (CR) SuperStock International; 701B (BG) Mike Timo/Tony Stone Images (TC) Gary Connor/PhotoEdit (CR) Ralph A. Reinhold/Earth Scenes (BL) E.R. Degginger/Color-Pic, Inc. (BR) Jeff Greenberg/Unicorn Stock Photos **tepee** John Zielinski **terrarium** Linda Howard **test tube** Jeff J. Daly/Visuals Unlimited **tetherball** Yoshi Miyake **thatch** C. L. Smith/Visuals Unlimited **thesaurus** LeeLee Brazeal **thin** Ellen Joy Sasaki **thorn** Mark E. Gibson/Visuals Unlimited **throat** Mike Dammer **thrush** Maslowski/Visuals Unlimited **thyme** Linda Howard **tides** Carlyn Galati/Visuals Unlimited **tiger** Alfred B. Thomas/Animals Animals **tile** Gary Conner/PhotoEdit **time zone** Mapping Specialists **toad** John Zielinski. **toboggan** Cleo/PhotoEdit **tomatoes** D. Cavagnaro/Visuals Unlimited **tool** Gene Givan **topple** Lori Osiecki **tortoise** Jeff Greenberg/PhotoEdit **totem pole** SuperStock International **toucan** Francis/Donna Caldwell/Visuals Unlimited **tower** Bill Bachman/PhotoEdit **tow truck** Mike Dammer **tractor** A. Ramey/PhotoEdit **train** Connie Mitchell **transfusion** The Granger Collection **treasure** Connie Mitchell **Trees** (spread) 729A-B (border) Peg Garrity; 729A (CL) Jeff Gnass/Jeff Gnass Photography (CL Inset T) SuperStock International (CL Inset B-walnut) (CR) Jeff Foott/Jeff Foott Productions (CR Inset B-pine cone) (BL) Carol & Don Spencer/Visuals Unlimited (BL Inset T) Kevin Morris/Tony Stone Images (BR) Eising/StockFood America (BR Overlay) Cimbal/StockFood America; 729B (L-violin) (C-paper) (R) Peg Garrity **trellis** David Young-Wolff/PhotoEdit **triceratops** Rich Stergulz **tripod** Mark E. Gibson/Visuals Unlimited **trout** Ken Lucas/Visuals Unlimited **trunk** Mike Dammer **tuba** Richard Hutchings/PhotoEdit **tulip** (L) Timothy Kerr/Visuals Unlimited (BR) Bruce Gaylor/Visuals Unlimited **turkey** SuperStock International **twilight** Rocky Fry **typewriter** Corbis-Bettmann

U **Opener page** (L) David Young-Wolff/PhotoEdit (C) Musee de Cluny, Paris, France/SuperStock International **unconscious** Mary Jones **Underground Railroad** The Granger Collection **underwater** LeeLee Brazeal **unfold** Mike Dammer **unicorn** Musee de Cluny, Paris/SuperStock International **unicycle** David Young-Wolff/PhotoEdit **unnatural** Michael Newman/PhotoEdit **unravel** Myrleen Ferguson/PhotoEdit **uphill** Lori Adamski Peek/Tony Stone Images **upstream** Rich Stergulz **urn** The Lowe Art Museum, The University of Miami/SuperStock International

V **Opener page** (TL) David K. Crow/PhotoEdit (C) Sally Mayman/Tony Stone Images (R) Universal 193/Kobal Collection **valentine** The Granger Collection **vampire** Kobal Collection **vanilla** Linda Howard **velociraptor** Bob Nonnemacher **vertebra** Gene Givan **veterinarian** Kathi Lamm/Tony Stone Images **view** David Young-Wolff/PhotoEdit **Viking** Lance Paladino **violin** Bruce Berg/Visuals Unlimited **virtual reality** Lois & Bob Schlowsky/Tony Stone Images **volcano** Sally Mayman/Tony Stone Images **volleyball** David K. Crow/PhotoEdit **volunteer** Albert Copley/Visuals Unlimited **vulture** Bertram G. Murray/Animals Animals

W **Opener page** (TL) SuperStock (TC) Bruce Forster/Tony Stone Images (BR) Nada Pecnik/Visuals Unlimited **wagon** American Stock Photos/Archive Photos **walking stick** Donald Specker/Animals Animals **walnut** John Zielinski **walrus** Charles Krebs/Tony Stone Images **warbonnet** SuperStock International **warn** David Hiser/Tony Stone Images **wasp** Connie Mitchell **water lily** Tony Freeman/PhotoEdit **water ski** Jean-Francois Causse/Tony Stone Images **weasel** Rich Stergulz **weather vane** Felicia Martinez/PhotoEdit **weightless** NASA **well²** Bruce Forster/Tony Stone Images **werewolf** Museum of Modern Art Film Stills Archive, Courtesy Universal Pictures/Museum of Modern Art **wetland** David Young/Tom Stack & Associates **whelk** Linda Howard **whippoorwill** Connie Mitchell **whirl** Gamma Liaison International **White House** Everett Johnson/Tony Stone Images **whooping crane** Bobbi Tull **wigwam** John Zielinski **Wild Cats** (spread) 785A-B (border) Ron Kimball/Ron Kimball Studios (BG) Brian Hastings/Adventure Photo & Film; 785A (C) Ron Kimball/Ron Kimball Studios (BL) Ralph A. Clevinger/Westlight (BR) J. Sneesby/B. Wilkins/Tony Stone Images; 785B (TL) Jeanne Drake/Tony Stone Images (TC) R. Lindholm/Visuals Unlimited (TR) Tom Tietz/Tony Stone Images (C) Ron Kimball/Ron Kimball Studios (BC) John Livzey/Tony Stone Images (BL) Renee Stockdale/Animals Animals **willow** Sylvester Allred/Visuals Unlimited **wilt** Rob Barber **wingspan** E. R. Degginger/Animals Animals **winter** Chuck Pefley/Tony Stone Images **wish** Martin Chaffer/Tony Stone Images **wolf** SuperStock International **woodpecker** R. Lindholm/Visuals Unlimited **woolly mammoth** Rich Stergulz **workbench** Michael Newman/PhotoEdit **worm** Linda Howard **wrangler** Kathi Lamm/Tony Stone Images **wreath** SuperStock International **writer** The Granger Collection

X **Opener page** (TC) RNHRD NHS Trust/Tony Stone Images (BR) Dennis MacDonald/PhotoEdit

Y **Opener page** (TR) © PhotoDisc (BR) SuperStock International **yellow jacket** Bob Nonnemacher **yore** Connie Mitchell **yo-yo** ©PhotoDisc **yucca** Frederick Myers/Tony Stone Images

Z **Opener page** (TL) Dick Kern/Visuals Unlimited (C) Robert Frerck/Tony Stone Images (TR) Wide World (BR) SuperStock International **zinnia** Dick Keen/Visuals Unlimited **zoo** Linda Kelen

End Matter **809** SuperStock International **The Map of the United States** (spread) 810-811 Mapping Specialists Limited **The Map of the World** (spread) 812-813 Mapping Specialists Limited **Solar System** (spread) 814-815 (BG) Ebet Dudley; 843 (TR) Bill & Sally Fletcher/Tom Stack & Associates **Facts About the Fifty States** (spread) 816-819 Mapping Specialists Limited **Symbols That Make Us Proud** (spread) 820-821; 866 (L) SuperStock International (C) Paul Hurd/All Stock/PNI/AllStock, Inc.; 867 (R) SuperStock International **Weights and Measures** (spread) 822-823 (BR) Tony Freeman/PhotoEdit

Table of Contents

The Parts of a Dictionary Entry

1. The **entry word** is printed in large dark type. It shows how the word is spelled. The black dot or dots show where the syllables are in the word, if there is more than one. The dots also show how a word may be divided in writing.

2. **a.** The **pronunciation** is in parentheses. Letters and symbols in the pronunciation stand for special sounds.

   b. Vowel symbols, two-letter symbols, and the schwa are explained in the **pronunciation key** at the bottom of every right-hand page.

3. The **part-of-speech label** tells the part of speech of the entry word. It appears just after the pronunciation. When a word may function as more than one part of speech, a label appears after each definition number.

4. The **definition** of a word tells what it means. A word with more than one meaning has numbered definitions, one for each meaning.

5. An **example sentence** or **phrase** is printed in slanting type after the definition. It shows how the entry word may be used in a sentence or phrase.

6. **Special forms** of some entry words are printed in small dark type at the end of the entry:

   a. Noun plural forms appear if their spelling is unusual, or if there is a choice of forms.

a·corn (ā′kôrn), NOUN. the nut of an oak tree.

be·ret (bə rā′), NOUN. a soft, flat, round cap of wool or felt.

a	hat	ė	term	ô	order	ch	child	⎧a in about
ā	age	i	it	oi	oil	ng	long	e in taken
ä	far	ī	ice	ou	out	sh	she	ə⎨i in pencil
â	care	o	hot	u	cup	th	thin	o in lemon
e	let	ō	open	ù	put	ŦH	then	⎩u in circus
ē	equal	ò	saw	ü	rule	zh	measure	

cav·ern (kav′ərn), NOUN. a large cave.

A·mer·i·can (ə mer′ə kən),
1 ADJECTIVE. of or about the United States or its people; from the United States.
2 NOUN. someone born or living in the United States.
3 ADJECTIVE. of or about North America and South America or its people.
4 NOUN. someone born or living in North America or South America.

bare·ly (bâr′lē), ADVERB. with nothing to spare; only just: *I barely had time to catch my bus.*—(5)

cat·fish (kat′fish′), NOUN. a fish without scales and with long, slender feelers around the mouth that look something like a cat's whiskers. ❑ PLURAL **cat·fish** or **cat·fish·es.**

b. Adjective forms appear if you can add *-er* and *-est* to the main entry, and there is a spelling change.

c. Verb forms appear in order to show the way their different forms are spelled.

7. Sometimes other words made with **suffixes** are listed in small, dark type at the end of an entry. They are not defined, but their meanings combine with the meanings of the main entry words. An additional pronunciation is given if a vowel sound differs from the pronunciation of the main entry word.

8. A tiny number appears after and above words that have the same spelling.

9. An **idiom**, in red type, sometimes follows the rest of an entry. Idioms are word combinations with special definitions that cannot be understood from the meanings of the individual words.

10. A **cross-reference** directs you to another word in the dictionary; the target of a cross-reference is also printed in small dark type. Cross-references tell you where to find more information about a word, what words sound the same, other ways to spell a word, and so on.

11. A **usage label** shows that the use of a word or meaning is limited.

air·y (âr′ē), ADJECTIVE. breezy; filled with fresh air: *an airy room.* ❏ ADJECTIVE **air·i·er, air·i·est.** —⑥b

bash (bash), VERB. to strike with a smashing blow. ❏ VERB **bash·es, bashed, bash·ing.** —⑥c

ac·cuse (ə kyüz′), VERB. to charge with having done something wrong or illegal: *The driver was accused of speeding.* ❏ VERB **ac·cus·es, ac·cused, ac·cus·ing.** —**ac·cu·sa·tion** (ak′yə zā′shən), NOUN. —**ac·cus′er,** NOUN. —⑦

bark¹ (bärk), NOUN. the tough outside covering of the trunk and branches of trees and bushes.

bark² (bärk),
1 NOUN. the short, sharp sound that a dog makes.
2 VERB. to make this sound: *The dog barked.*
❏ VERB **barks, barked, bark·ing.**

clock (klok),
1 NOUN. a device for measuring and showing time.
2 VERB. to measure or record the time or speed of; time: *I clocked the runners with a stopwatch.*
❏ VERB **clocks, clocked, clock·ing.**
⑨— **around the clock,** IDIOM. every minute of the day; continuously: *They worked around the clock to repair the damage.*

ate (āt), VERB. the past tense of **eat:** *We ate our dinner. I ate too many cookies.* ■ Another word that sounds like this is **eight.**

bo·lo·gna (bə lō′nē), NOUN. a large sausage usually made of beef, veal, and pork. ❏ PLURAL **bo·lo·gnas.** Also spelled **baloney.** —⑩

⑪—

corn·y (kôr′nē), ADJECTIVE. (informal) silly and old-fashioned: *No one laughed at his corny jokes.* ❏ ADJECTIVE **corn·i·er, corn·i·est.**

Other material on a dictionary page can include pictures, which show you a visual image that can help you understand a definition. Special features in color bars give extra information about an entry word: its history, its synonyms, how to use it, and so on.

How to Use This Dictionary

Dictionary Entries

Dictionary information is divided into sections called entries. A dictionary entry often includes information about spelling, syllable spacing, pronunciation, meaning, usage, and history. A dictionary entry begins with an entry word, written in dark type. It may be a word, a phrase, an abbreviation, an acronym, or a proper name. Syllable division of an entry is shown by dots between syllables. This indicates where hyphens may be placed when a word needs to be written on two lines. (Usually, one-letter syllables are not hyphenated when writing.) An entry may include special inflected forms of nouns, pronouns, adjectives, and verbs. All entries are in a single alphabetical list.

Words that Aren't Entry Words

Some words are other forms of entry words, and are included in the entries for those base words. **Echoes, echoed,** and **echoing** are other forms of the verb entry word **echo.**

Other words are forms made up of the entry word plus a suffix. **Edgier** and **edgiest,** for example, are other forms of the adjective **edgy. Eagerly** and **eagerness,** for example, are adverb and noun forms made from the word **eager** and the suffixes *-ly* and *-ness.* Extra words like these are in small, dark type at or near the end of the entry word.

Alphabetical Order

Words are listed in a dictionary in alphabetical order. Spaces between word phrases are ignored for alphabetical purposes: **black eye** comes after **blacken.** Sometimes, two or more words have the same spelling, for historical reasons. These words have little numbers at the end. To find your word, you need to look at all the words spelled alike.

Guide Words

Guide words at the top of every page show what words are on the page. All words on the page come between the guide words in alphabetical order. For instance, the word **apatosaurus** is found on the page where the guide words are **anything** and **Appaloosa.**

Pronunciations

Pronunciations are provided for every entry word that is not pronounced somewhere else in this dictionary. They consist of key symbols that are mainly English letters, with a few marks above some letters. There is a single symbol for each separate sound in English. A short key to these marks appears at the bottom of every right-hand page. A complete table of all symbols appears on page I-9. Key words are shown with each pronunciation symbol. Each symbol should be pronounced as it is in its key word: **a** as in **hat, zh** as in **vision,** and so on.

A symbol that is not a letter is the schwa (ə). It is pronounced like the **a** in **about.** Pronunciations are divided into syllables. Syllable stress, or accent, is shown by the stress marks ′ (primary accent) or ′ (secondary accent), as in **butter** (but′ər), or **buttermilk** (but′ər milk′).

All pronunciations listed in this dictionary are considered correct by educated speakers. Some words have more than one acceptable pronunciation.

apatosaurus — about 70 feet long, including the tail

Definitions

The meanings of entry words are given in clear, easy-to-understand definitions. A definition is sometimes followed by a semicolon and a synonym. Example sentences or phrases sometimes follow a definition; they are written in slanted, or italic, type.

An entry word may have more than one meaning; if so, the definitions are numbered separately. Or an entry word may be used as more than one part of speech; in this case, each definition has a part of speech label.

Idioms

Sometimes a phrase that includes an entry word does not mean what it appears to mean, from the words that it contains. "To pull someone's leg" does not mean what it literally says. A phrase like this, called an idiom, is listed near the end of the entry for the main word in the phrase, in this case **leg.** Idioms are set in **red type.**

Usage Labels and Notes

Some words are only used in certain situations. The dictionary includes labels on these words. The label: "(informal)" goes with the word **goof,** indicating that the word is used in everyday talk and casual writing, but not in formal writing or speeches. The label: "(slang)" means that a word such as **nerd** is used in talk among friends, but not in writing except to imitate talk. The word **dungeon** is labeled "(earlier)." This means that the word was commonly used in the past, or is used today in stories written about the past.

Sometimes there is extra information about a word that it is useful to know. This information is set off from the entry by a small red star. There is one at the word **beware:**

be·ware (bi wâr′), *VERB.* to be on your guard against; be careful of: *You must beware of snakes here.* ★ **Beware** is used only in the present tense as a command or with helping verbs. This is why no forms of the verb are listed here.

Occasionally, a word's usage needs a longer explanation. You can see examples of these **Usage Note** features at **deaf** and **between.** These notes are printed at the end of the entry over a patch of color, and give more information about word usage.

Where Words Come From

Every word in English has a history. The word either is native to English, having been used since the earliest stage of English, or it was borrowed from another language, or it arose in one of a number of other ways. This dictionary includes brief histories, called Word Stories, for many words that have especially interesting stories to tell about how they came to be. Word Stories are printed with a color background to emphasize them.

Because of the large number of words that English has borrowed from other languages, there are lists of words given at the entries for many names of languages. This information has a color background and a title of its own: Word Source.

Other Features

There are several other kinds of information about words given in this dictionary, also printed over patches of color to make them stand out. They are included to help you choose the best word for an idea when you are writing something, or to give you useful information about a word, phrase, or idea.

A Synonym Study is a discussion of three or more words with similar meanings. It explains how similar words are used in different contexts. A Synonym Study gives a definition and an example sentence for each word.

Like a Synonym Study, a Word Bank can help you find words for your ideas. A Word Bank is a list of many words, all with meanings connected to one main subject.

Word Power is a feature that gives you added information about taking words apart and putting them back together. With the prefixes, suffixes, and combining forms listed in the Word Powers, it is easy to recognize ideas when you see them as word parts.

Another feature in this dictionary is called **Did You Know?** This includes interesting facts about a word or the physical thing it refers to. For example, at **flag** you learn how a worn-out American flag should be properly disposed of.

A feature entitled **Have You Heard?** explains some well-known sayings or idioms that you may have heard or run across in your reading.

Illustrations

Illustrations accompany many dictionary entries. They supply graphic details to the verbal definitions, as a help to understanding. Sizes of animals are included.

bald eagle — wingspread about 6½ feet

Words Not in This Dictionary

The English language contains well over half a million words. For the sake of convenience, this dictionary contains the words most often needed to be looked up by third, fourth, and fifth graders. Selection of these words is done on the basis of frequency counts of words in children's literature, and on observation of vocabulary that appears in classroom texts at these grade levels. However, it may happen that a less common word you are looking for is not in this dictionary. When this occurs, you need to use a larger dictionary. There are larger dictionaries of various sizes, and specialized dictionaries of many kinds that list biographical or geographical entries, or the vocabulary of particular subject areas. A reference librarian is a good person to ask which dictionary is the right one for you.

Help With English Spelling

Sometimes it is hard to find an unfamiliar word in the dictionary because you don't know the first letter. English spelling is a little irregular. The chart entitled Spellings of English Sounds on the following two pages can help you find the word you are looking for. On these pages are listed every English sound, and the different spellings that exist for each sound. For example, many words begin with the f-sound, but some are spelled *ph-*, as in **phrase.**

Spellings of English Sounds

This chart shows all the sounds of the English language, and it lists the ways in which each sound may be spelled. It can help you find words you can say but do not know how to spell.

The pronunciation symbols used in this dictionary are shown in the **blue** boxes. Each symbol represents a different sound.

Following each symbol are words showing different ways the sound may be spelled. The letters used to spell the sound are printed in **red** type. Common spellings are listed first.

Sometimes a word is used as an example in more than one list. This is because it is pronounced in more than one way.

Sound	Spelling and examples
a	at, plaid, half, laugh, Cheyenne
ā	age, aid, say, eight, vein, they, break, bouquet, straight, gauge, cafe, fiancé, beret
â	care, air, aerial, there, prayer, their, pear, heir
ä	father, heart, ah, calm, guard, yacht, baa, encore, reservoir
b	bad, rabbit
ch	child, future, watch, question, righteous, cello, Czech, catsup
d	did, filled, add
e	end, bread, any, said, friend, leopard, says, heifer, bury
ē	equal, happy, each, bee, ski, believe, either, key, algae, Phoenix, people, buoy
ėr	stern, turn, first, word, earth, journey, myrtle, err, whir, purr, herb, worry, colonel, chauffeur

Sound	Spelling and examples
f	fat, effort, phrase, laugh
g	go, egg, league, guest, ghost
gz	exact, exhibit, bangs
h	he, who, Gila monster, fajitas, Oaxaca
i	in, enough, hymn, manage, ear, build, sieve, busy, women, marriage, been, weird
ī	ice, sky, lie, high, rye, sign, eye, island, height, either, bayou, Cairo, aisle, aye, buy, geyser, coyote, annihilate
j	jam, gem, large, bridge, region, gradual, badger, soldier, exaggerate
k	kind, coat, back, chemist, ache, account, excite, quit, antique, liquor, acquire, khaki, zucchini
ks	parks, tactics, jacks, tax
l	land, tell, pale, medal, channel, lentil, kiln

Sound	Spelling and examples
m	me, common, calm, climb, solemn, phlegm
n	no, manner, knife, gnaw, pneumonia
ng	long, ink, tongue, handkerchief
o	odd, honest, knowledge
ō	old, oak, own, soul, toe, brooch, though, folk, bureau, oh, chauffeur, owe, sew, Seoul, depot
ȯ	all, auto, awful, ought, walk, taught, cough, awe, Utah, broad
ô	order, oar, mourn, quart, floor, war
oi	oil, boy, buoy, lawyer
ou	out, owl, bough, hour, Saudi, Laos
p	pay, happy
r	run, carry, wrong, rhythm
s	say, cent, tense, dance, miss, scent, listen, psychology, waltz, sword
sh	she, nation, special, mission, tension, machine, conscience, issue, ocean, schwa, sugar, nausea
t	tell, button, stopped, doubt, two, thyme, pterodactyl, pizza

Sound	Spelling and examples
th	thin
ŦH	then, breathe
u	under, other, trouble, flood, does
u̇	full, good, detour, wolf, should
ü	food, rule, move, soup, blue, threw, fruit, shoe, maneuver, through, lieutenant, buoy, Rwanda
v	very, have, of
w	will, wheat, quick, choir, croissant, Nahuatl
wu	one, was, won
y	yes, opinion, popular, piranha, hallelujah, azalea
yü	use, few, feud, cue, view, you, Houston, beauty, yule, queue
yu̇	uranium, Europe, your, vacuum
z	zero, has, buzz, scissors, fuse, xylophone, clothes, raspberry, asthma, czar
zh	division, measure, garage, azure, regime, equation, Rio de Janeiro
ə	occur, about, April, essential, cautious, circus, oxygen, bargain, dungeon, tortoise, pageant, authority

Full pronunciation key

The pronunciation of each word is shown just after the word, in this way: **ab·bre·vi·ate** (ə brē/vē āt).

The letters and signs used are pronounced as in the words below.

The mark / is placed after a syllable with primary or heavy stress, as in the example above.

The mark / after a syllable shows a secondary or lighter stress, as in **ab·bre·vi·a·tion** (ə brē/vē ā/shən).

a	hat, cap	p	paper, cup
ā	age, face	r	run, try
â	care, fair	s	say, yes
ä	father, far	t	tell, it
b	bad, rob	th	thin, both
ch	child, much	ŦH	then, smooth
d	did, red		
e	let, best	u	cup, butter
ē	equal, be	u̇	full, put
ėr	term, learn	ü	rule, move
f	fat, if	v	very, save
g	go, bag	w	will, woman
h	he, how	y	young, yet
i	it, pin	z	zero, breeze
ī	ice, five	zh	measure, seizure
j	jam, enjoy		represents:
k	kind, seek		a in about
l	land, coal	ə	e in taken
m	me, am		i in pencil
n	no, in		o in lemon
ng	long, bring		u in circus
o	hot, rock		
ō	open, go		
ȯ	all, caught		
ô	order, board		
oi	oil, voice		
ou	house, out		

Aa

anteater

A or **a¹** (ā), NOUN. the first letter of the English alphabet. ❑ PLURAL **A's** or **a's**.

a² (ə or ā), INDEFINITE ARTICLE.
 1 any: *Is there a pencil in the box?*
 2 one: *Please buy a dozen eggs.*
 3 every: *Thanksgiving comes once a year.*
 4 one kind of: *Chemistry is a science.*

aard·vark (ärd′värk), NOUN. an African animal with a long snout and strong claws. It digs up ants and catches them with its long, sticky tongue.

ab·a·cus (ab′ə kəs), NOUN. a frame with rows of beads or counters that slide back and forth. Abacuses are used for counting in China, Japan, and some other countries. ❑ PLURAL **ab·a·cus·es**.

ab·a·lo·ne (ab′ə lō′nē), NOUN. a tasty shellfish with a large, rather flat shell that has a pearly lining. ❑ PLURAL **ab·a·lo·nes**.

a·ban·don (ə ban′dən), VERB.
 1 to leave without intending to return to; desert:

The crew abandoned the sinking ship. ■ See the Synonym Study at **leave**.
 2 to give up entirely: *We abandoned the idea of a picnic because of the rain.*
 ❑ VERB **a·ban·dons, a·ban·doned, a·ban·don·ing.**
 –a·ban′don·ment, NOUN.

a·ban·doned (ə ban′dənd), ADJECTIVE. deserted: *The children played in the abandoned house.*

ab·bey (ab′ē), NOUN. the building or buildings where monks or nuns live. ❑ PLURAL **ab·beys**.

ab·bre·vi·ate (ə brē′vē āt), VERB. to make shorter: *We can abbreviate "hour" to "hr."* ❑ VERB **ab·bre·vi·ates, ab·bre·vi·at·ed, ab·bre·vi·at·ing.**

ab·bre·vi·a·tion (ə brē′vē ā′shən), NOUN. a shortened form: *"Wk." is an abbreviation for "week."*

ABC's, NOUN PLURAL.
 1 the alphabet: *We all must learn the ABC's.*
 2 the facts or skills to be learned first; basic rules: *I'm learning the ABC's of soccer.*

ab·di·cate (ab′də kāt), *VERB.* to give up office or authority; resign: *When the king abdicated his throne, his son became king.* ❑ *VERB* **ab·di·cates, ab·di·cat·ed, ab·di·cat·ing.** –**ab′di·ca′tion,** *NOUN.*

ab·do·men (ab′də mən), *NOUN.*
1 the part of the body that contains the stomach, the intestines, and other digestive organs; belly.
2 the last of the three parts of an insect's body.

ab·dom·i·nal (ab dom′ə nəl), *ADJECTIVE.* of the abdomen: *abdominal muscles.*

ab·duct (ab dukt′), *VERB.* to kidnap: *The bank president was abducted and held for ransom.* ❑ *VERB* **ab·ducts, ab·duct·ed, ab·duct·ing.**

ab·hor (ab hôr′), *VERB.* to feel disgust toward; hate very much: *He abhors snakes.* ❑ *VERB* **ab·hors, ab·horred, ab·hor·ring.**

a·bide (ə bīd′), *VERB.* to put up with; endure: *I can't abide their always being late.* ❑ *VERB* **a·bides, a·bid·ed, a·bid·ing.**

a·bil·i·ty (ə bil′ə tē), *NOUN.*
1 power: *Dogs do not have the ability to climb trees.*
2 skill or talent: *He has great ability in music.* ❑ *PLURAL* **a·bil·i·ties.**

a·blaze (ə blāz′), *ADJECTIVE.* on fire; blazing: *The forest was set ablaze by lightning.*

The forest was **ablaze.**

a·ble (ā′bəl), *ADJECTIVE.*
1 having enough power, skill, or means: *A cat is able to see in the dark.*
2 having more power or skill than usual; skillful: *She is an able teacher.* ❑ *ADJECTIVE* **a·bler, a·blest.**

Word Power   -able

The suffix **-able** is used to make adjectives. It means "able to be _____ed" or "likely to _____." An enjoy**able** party is a party that is **able to be** enjoy**ed**. A break**able** object is **likely to** break.

The suffix **-able** can also mean "suitable for _____ing" or "providing _____." An adopt**able** child is **suitable for** adopting. A comfort**able** chair is a chair **providing** comfort.

a·bly (ā′blē), *ADVERB.* in an able manner; with skill; well: *She did her job ably.*

ab·nor·mal (ab nôr′məl), *ADJECTIVE.* different from the ordinary or expected conditions; unusual: *We had an abnormal amount of rain and the stream flooded.* –**ab·nor′mal·ly,** *ADVERB.*

a·board (ə bôrd′), *ADVERB* or *PREPOSITION.* on board; in or on a ship, train, bus, or airplane: *"Is everyone aboard?" shouted the conductor. We had to be aboard the ship by noon.*

a·bol·ish (ə bol′ish), *VERB.* to do away with; put an end to: *Many people would like to abolish war.* ❑ *VERB* **a·bol·ish·es, a·bol·ished, a·bol·ish·ing.**

ab·o·li·tion (ab′ə lish′ən), *NOUN.* the act of putting an end to something: *The abolition of slavery in the United States occurred in 1865.*

Ab·o·li·tion·ist (ab′ə lish′ə nist), *NOUN.* someone who worked to put an end to slavery in the United States during the 1800s.

A-bomb (ā′bom′), *NOUN.* an atomic bomb.

a·bom·i·na·ble (ə bom′ə nə bəl), *ADJECTIVE.* causing disgust or horror: *Neglecting a pet is abominable. Murder is an abominable act.* –**a·bom′i·na·bly,** *ADVERB.*

Abominable Snowman, an apelike creature supposed to live high in the Himalayas.

Ab·o·rig·i·ne (ab′ə rij′ə nē′), *NOUN.* one of the earliest known people living in Australia. ❑ *PLURAL* **Ab·o·rig·i·nes.**

a·bort (ə bôrt′), *VERB.* to cause something to stop before it is completed: *They aborted the missile launch.* ❑ *VERB* **a·borts, a·bort·ed, a·bort·ing.**

a·bound (ə bound′), *VERB.* to be plentiful: *Fish abound in the ocean.* ❑ *VERB* **a·bounds, a·bound·ed, a·bound·ing.**

a·bout (ə bout′),
1 *PREPOSITION.* concerning; having something to do with: *"Black Beauty" is a story about a horse.*
2 *ADVERB* or *PREPOSITION.* approximately: *He weighs about 100 pounds. We arrived about 6:00 P.M.*
3 *PREPOSITION* or *ADVERB.* on all sides; around: *They gazed about the room in wonder.*

a·bove (ə buv′),
1 *ADVERB.* in or at a higher place; overhead: *The sky is above.*
2 *PREPOSITION.* higher than; over: *She kept her head above water. A captain is above a sergeant in rank.*
3 *PREPOSITION.* more than; better than: *Her grades were all above average.*

a·bove·board (ə buv′bôrd′), *ADJECTIVE.* in the open; honestly; without tricks: *Everything that the mayor did was open and aboveboard.*

ab·ra·ca·dab·ra (ab′rə kə dab′rə), *INTERJECTION.* a word used when performing a magic trick: *Abracadabra! I'm pulling a rabbit out of my hat!*

a·bra·sive (ə brā′siv),
1 *NOUN.* a substance that wears away, grinds, or polishes by friction. Sandpaper is an abrasive.
2 *ADJECTIVE.* harsh or crude: *He is an abrasive person.*

a·breast (ə brest′), *ADVERB or ADJECTIVE*.
1 side by side: *The soldiers marched six abreast.*
2 up with: *I like to keep abreast of the news.*

marching four **abreast**

a·bridge (ə brij′), *VERB*. to make shorter, especially by using fewer words: *A long story can be abridged by leaving out unimportant parts.* ❑ *VERB* **a·bridg·es, a·bridged, a·bridg·ing.**

a·broad (ə bròd′), *ADVERB*.
1 outside your country: *She is going abroad next year.*
2 far and wide; widely: *The news of the tornado damage was quickly spread abroad.*

a·brupt (ə brupt′), *ADJECTIVE*.
1 sudden: *The driver made an abrupt turn.*
2 sudden or rude in speech or manner: *She answered me with an abrupt remark and left.*

ab·scess (ab′ses), *NOUN*. a painful collection of pus in some part of the body. An abscess results from an infection. ❑ *PLURAL* **ab·scess·es.**

ab·sence (ab′səns), *NOUN*.
1 the condition or fact of being away: *My absence from school was caused by illness.*
2 the condition of not having something; lack: *Darkness is the absence of light.*

Have You Heard?

You may have heard the saying **"Absence makes the heart grow fonder."** This means that when someone is away, you think more about the good qualities of that person. It is often easier to like someone you don't see very much!

ab·sent (ab′sənt), *ADJECTIVE*.
1 away; missing: *Three students are absent.*
2 lacking; not existing: *In catfish, scales are absent.*

ab·sen·tee (ab′sən tē′), *NOUN*. someone who is away or remains away. ❑ *PLURAL* **ab·sent·ees.**

ab·sent-mind·ed (ab′sənt mīn′did), *ADJECTIVE*. forgetful; not paying attention to what is going on: *The absent-minded man put salt in his coffee.* —**ab′sent-mind′ed·ly,** *ADVERB*.

ab·so·lute (ab′sə lüt), *ADJECTIVE*.
1 complete; entire: *That is the absolute truth.*
2 not limited in any way: *The king had absolute power.*

ab·so·lute·ly (ab′sə lüt′lē), *ADVERB*.
1 completely: *My broken bike is absolutely useless.*
2 without doubt: *This is absolutely the best cake!*

ab·sorb (ab sôrb′), *VERB*.
1 to soak up: *The sponge absorbed the spilled milk.*
2 to take in without reflecting: *Rugs absorb sounds and make a house quieter.*
3 to take up all the attention of; interest very much: *Building a sand castle absorbed them for hours.*
❑ *VERB* **ab·sorbs, ab·sorbed, ab·sorb·ing.**

ab·sorb·ent (ab sôr′bənt), *ADJECTIVE*. able to take in moisture, light, heat, and so forth: *Absorbent paper towels are used to dry the hands.*

ab·sorb·ing (ab sôr′bing), *ADJECTIVE*. extremely interesting: *an absorbing TV program about dolphins.*

ab·sorp·tion (ab sôrp′shən), *NOUN*.
1 the action of taking in moisture, light, or heat: *A blotter dries ink by absorption.*
2 great interest: *Her absorption in the book was so complete that she did not hear the doorbell.*

ab·stain (ab stān′), *VERB*. to do without something; hold yourself back: *If you want to lose weight, abstain from eating candy and exercise more.*
❑ *VERB* **ab·stains, ab·stained, ab·stain·ing.**

ab·stract (ab′strakt), *ADJECTIVE*.
1 thought of as an idea, not as a real thing: *Sweetness is abstract; a sugar cube is concrete.*
2 not representing any actual object: *We saw many abstract paintings at the art museum.*

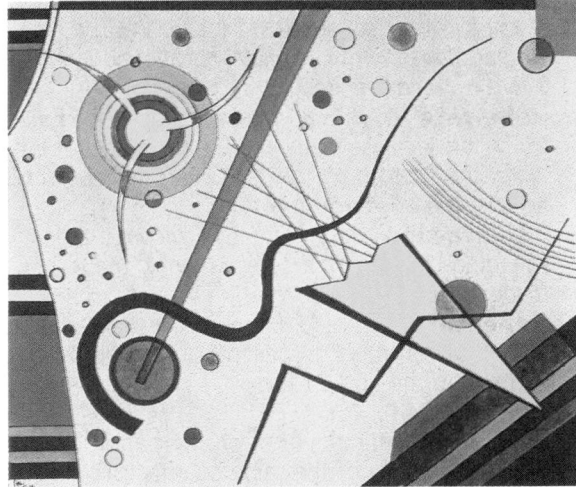
an **abstract** painting

a hat	ė term	ô order	ch child	⎧ a in about
ā age	i it	oi oil	ng long	⎪ e in taken
ä far	ī ice	ou out	sh she	ə ⎨ i in pencil
â care	o hot	u cup	th thin	⎪ o in lemon
e let	ō open	ù put	ᵺ then	⎩ u in circus
ē equal	ò saw	ü rule	zh measure	

ab·surd (ab sėrd′), ADJECTIVE. clearly not sensible; foolish: *Fear of the number 13 is absurd.*

ab·surd·i·ty (ab sėr′də tē), NOUN.
1 lack of sense; foolishness: *I could see the absurdity of his superstitions.*
2 something foolish or ridiculous.
❑ PLURAL **ab·surd·i·ties.**

a·bun·dance (ə bun′dəns), NOUN. great plenty; quantity that is more than enough: *There is an abundance of apples this year.*

a·bun·dant (ə bun′dənt), NOUN. more than enough; very plentiful: *The trapper had an abundant supply of food for the winter.* **–a·bun′dant·ly,** ADVERB.

a·buse (ə byüz′ for verb; ə byüs′ for noun),
1 VERB. to treat cruelly or roughly: *The children abused the dog by throwing rocks at it.*
2 NOUN. cruel or rough treatment: *verbal abuse.*
3 VERB. to use in a wrong or improper way: *The wicked king abused his power.*
❑ VERB **a·bus·es, a·bused, a·bus·ing.**

a·byss (ə bis′), NOUN. a very great depth; a very deep crack in the earth: *The castle overlooked an abyss two miles deep.* ❑ PLURAL **a·byss·es.**

a.c. or **a-c,** an abbreviation of **alternating current.**

ac·a·dem·ic (ak′ə dem′ik), ADJECTIVE.
1 of or for schools, colleges, and their studies: *The academic year usually begins in September.*
2 concerned with general education rather than commercial, technical, or professional education: *History and French are academic subjects; computer repair is a technical subject.*
–ac′a·dem′i·cal·ly, ADVERB.

a·cad·e·my (ə kad′ə mē), NOUN.
1 a private high school.
2 a school where some special subject can be studied: *West Point is a military academy.*
❑ PLURAL **a·cad·e·mies.**

ac·cel·e·rate (ak sel′ə rāt′), VERB. to go or cause to go faster; increase in speed: *The car accelerated when she stepped on the gas.* ❑ VERB **ac·cel·e·rates, ac·cel·e·rat·ed, ac·cel·e·rat·ing.**

ac·cel·e·ra·tion (ak sel′ə rā′shən), NOUN. the act of speeding up: *The rapid acceleration of the rocket made it soon disappear from view.*

ac·cel·e·ra·tor (ak sel′ə rā′tər), NOUN. the pedal or lever that controls the speed of an engine by controlling the flow of fuel.

ac·cent (ak′sent),
1 NOUN. a different manner of pronunciation heard in different parts of the same country, or in the speech of someone speaking a language not his or her own: *My father was born in Germany and still speaks English with a German accent.*
2 NOUN. the greater force or stronger tone of voice given to certain syllables or words: *In "letter," the accent is on the first syllable.*
3 NOUN. a mark (′) written or printed to show the spoken force of a syllable, as in *to·day* (tə dā′). Some words have two accents, a stronger accent (′) and a weaker accent (′), as in *ac·ci·den·tal* (ak′sə den′tl).
4 VERB. to pronounce or mark with an accent: *Should I accent "ally" on the first or second syllable?*
❑ VERB **ac·cents, ac·cent·ed, ac·cent·ing.**

ac·cept (ak sept′), VERB.
1 to take what is offered to you; agree to take: *The teacher accepted our gift.*
2 to say yes to: *I accepted the invitation to her birthday party.*
3 to take as true or satisfactory; believe: *The teacher accepted our excuse.*
❑ VERB **ac·cepts, ac·cept·ed, ac·cept·ing.**

ac·cept·a·ble (ak sep′tə bəl), ADJECTIVE.
1 likely to be gladly received; agreeable: *Flowers are an acceptable gift.*
2 good enough but not outstanding; satisfactory: *I got an acceptable grade.*

ac·cept·ance (ak sep′təns), NOUN.
1 a favorable reception; approval: *She was excited by the acceptance of her story by the magazine.*
2 the act of taking something offered or given: *Mom's delighted acceptance of our gift pleased us.*

ac·cess (ak′ses),
1 NOUN. the right to enter or use: *All students have access to the library during the afternoon.*
2 NOUN. an approach to places, things, or people: *Access to villages in the jungle is often difficult.*
3 VERB. to get information from a computer: *We accessed the student database for our mailing list.*
❑ VERB **ac·cess·es, ac·cessed, ac·cess·ing.**

ac·ces·si·ble (ak ses′ə bəl), ADJECTIVE. easy to get at; easy to use: *This theater is accessible by people with disabilities.*

ac·ces·sor·y (ak ses′ər ē), NOUN.
1 an extra thing added to help or improve something of more importance: *Her new car has many accessories, including a CD player.*

wheelchair **accessible**

2 someone who has helped someone else commit a crime or who does not report a crime.
❑ PLURAL **ac·ces·sor·ies.**

ac·ci·dent (ak′sə dənt), NOUN.
1 something harmful or unlucky that happens unexpectedly: *She was hurt in a car accident.*
2 something that happens without being planned or known in advance: *A series of lucky accidents led the scientists to the discovery.*

ac·ci·den·tal (ak′sə den′tl), *ADJECTIVE.* happening by chance: *Breaking the lamp was accidental; I did not do it on purpose.* −**ac′ci·den′tal·ly,** *ADVERB.*

ac·claim (ə klām′),
1 *VERB.* to welcome with loud approval; praise highly; applaud: *The crowd acclaimed the king.*
2 *NOUN.* a shout or show of approval; applause: *The astronaut was welcomed with great acclaim.*
□ *VERB* **ac·claims, ac·claimed, ac·claim·ing.**

ac·com·mo·date (ə kom′ə dāt), *VERB.*
1 to hold; have room for: *This airplane is large enough to accommodate 120 passengers.*
2 to help out: *I wanted change for a five-dollar bill, but no one could accommodate me.*
□ *VERB* **ac·com·mo·dates, ac·com·mo·dat·ed, ac·com·mo·dat·ing.**

ac·com·mo·da·tions (ə kom′ə dā′shənz), *NOUN.* a place to stay, and often a place to eat: *Can we find accommodations at a motel for tonight?*

ac·com·pa·ni·ment (ə kum′pə nē mənt), *NOUN.*
1 a part in music that helps or enriches the main part: *We sang with piano accompaniment.*
2 anything that goes along with something else: *The rain was a nasty accompaniment to our ride.*

ac·com·pa·ny (ə kum′pə nē), *VERB.*
1 to go along with: *I accompanied her on a walk.*
2 to play a musical accompaniment for: *She accompanied the singer on the piano.*
□ *VERB* **ac·com·pa·nies, ac·com·pa·nied, ac·com·pa·ny·ing.**

ac·com·plice (ə kom′plis), *NOUN.* someone who deliberately aids another in committing a crime or other wrong act: *The thief had an accomplice inside the building who unlocked the door.*

ac·com·plish (ə kom′plish), *VERB.* to complete; carry out: *She accomplished more today than anyone else.* □ *VERB* **ac·com·plish·es, ac·com·plished, ac·com·plish·ing.**

ac·com·plished (ə kom′plisht), *ADJECTIVE.* expert; skilled: *an accomplished tap dancer.*

ac·com·plish·ment (ə kom′plish mənt), *NOUN.* something done with knowledge, skill, or ability: *The pilot was proud of her accomplishments.*

ac·cord (ə kôrd′), *NOUN.* agreement: *Most people are in accord in their desire for peace.*

ac·cord·ing to (ə kôr′ding tü),
1 in agreement with: *He paid his debt according to his promise.*
2 in proportion to: *You will be paid according to the work you do.*
3 on the authority of: *According to the weather report, it is going to rain today.*

ac·cor·di·on (ə kôr′dē ən), *NOUN.* a wind instrument with a bellows, metal reeds, and a keyboard.

ac·count (ə kount′), *NOUN.*
1 a statement telling in detail about an event or thing; explanation: *She gave him an account of everything that happened on the class trip.*
2 value or importance: *She thought their out-of-date ideas were of little account.*
3 a statement of money received and spent; record of business dealings: *I decided to keep a written account of the way I spend my allowance.*

account for, *IDIOM.*
1 to tell what has been done with; answer for: *The treasurer had to account for the missing money.*
2 to explain: *Can you account for your absence?*
3 to be the cause of: *The flu accounted for his absence.*
□ *VERB* **ac·counts, ac·count·ed, ac·count·ing.**

on account of, *IDIOM.* because of; for the reason of: *The game was called off on account of rain.*

ac·count·ant (ə koun′tənt), *NOUN.* someone who examines or manages business accounts.

ac·cu·mu·late
(ə kyü′myə lāt), *VERB.*
to pile up; collect: *Dust and cobwebs had accumulated in the attic.*
□ *VERB* **ac·cu·mu·lates, ac·cu·mu·lat·ed, ac·cu·mu·lat·ing.**

ac·cu·mu·la·tion
(ə kyü′myə lā′shən), *NOUN.*
1 material collected; mass: *Their accumulation of old papers filled the attic.*
2 the act or process of collecting: *The accumulation of knowledge is one result of reading.*

Snow **accumulated** on the trees.

ac·cur·a·cy (ak′yər ə sē), *NOUN.* the condition of being without errors or mistakes; correctness; exactness: *This watch is noted for its accuracy.*

ac·cur·ate (ak′yər it), *ADJECTIVE.* exactly right; correct: *an accurate watch.* −**ac′cur·ate·ly,** *ADVERB.*

ac·cuse (ə kyüz′), *VERB.* to charge with having done something wrong or illegal: *The driver was accused of speeding.* □ *VERB* **ac·cus·es, ac·cused, ac·cus·ing.** −**ac·cu·sa·tion** (ak′yə zā′shən), *NOUN.* −**ac·cus′er,** *NOUN.*

ac·cus·tom (ə kus′təm), *VERB.* to make familiar by use or habit: *You can accustom yourself to almost any kind of food.* □ *VERB* **ac·cus·toms, ac·cus·tomed, ac·cus·tom·ing.**

a	hat	ė	term	ô	order	ch	child		a in about
ā	age	i	it	oi	oil	ng	long		e in taken
ä	far	ī	ice	ou	out	sh	she	ə	i in pencil
â	care	o	hot	u	cup	th	thin		o in lemon
e	let	ō	open	u̇	put	ŦH	then		u in circus
ē	equal	ȯ	saw	ü	rule	zh	measure		

ace (ās), NOUN.
1 a playing card with a single large heart, club, spade, or diamond in the middle. It is the highest card in most card games.
2 someone who is an expert at something: *She is an ace at baseball.*

ache (āk),
1 VERB. to suffer continuous dull pain: *My arms ache from carrying all these books.*
2 NOUN. a continuous dull pain: *I have a neck ache.*
3 VERB. to be eager; wish very much: *During the hot days of August we all ached to go swimming.*
❑ VERB **aches, ached, ach•ing.**

a•chieve (ə chēv′), VERB. to get by your own efforts; accomplish: *Did you achieve your goal?* ❑ VERB **a•chieves, a•chieved, a•chiev•ing.**

a•chieve•ment (ə chēv′mənt), NOUN.
1 something achieved; some plan or action carried out with courage or with unusual ability.
2 the act or fact of achieving: *The achievement of success is important to many people.*

ac•id (as′id),
1 NOUN. a chemical substance that unites with a base to form a salt. Acids can burn your skin.
2 ADJECTIVE. sour; sharp or biting to the taste: *Lemons are an acid fruit.*

acid rain, polluted rain caused by acids in the atmosphere from factories, cars, trucks, and buses. Acid rain harms plants and buildings.

ac•knowl•edge (ak nol′ij), VERB.
1 to admit to be true: *He acknowledged his error.*
2 to recognize publicly: *She acknowledged my contribution to the project.*
3 to make known that you received something: *She acknowledged the gift with a pleasant letter.*
❑ VERB **ac•knowl•edg•es, ac•knowl•edged, ac•knowl•edg•ing.**

ac•knowl•edg•ment (ak nol′ij mənt), NOUN. something done to show that you have received something: *The winner waved in acknowledgment of the cheers.*

ac•ne (ak′nē), NOUN. a disease in which oil glands in the skin become clogged, and pimples form.

a•corn (ā′kôrn), NOUN. the nut of an oak tree.

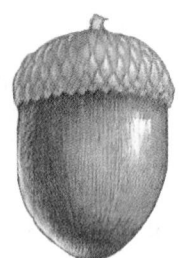
acorn

Have You Heard?

You may have heard someone say **"Great oaks from little acorns grow."** This means that big, successful things can come from small and unimportant beginnings.

a•cous•tic (ə kü′stik), ADJECTIVE.
1 of or about hearing or the organs of hearing.
2 of or about music or an instrument with sound that is not electrically amplified: *an acoustic guitar.*

ac•quaint•ance (ə kwān′təns), NOUN. someone known to you, but not a close friend: *We have many acquaintances in our town.*

ac•quaint•ed (ə kwān′tid), ADJECTIVE. **be acquainted with,** to know someone: *I have heard about your friend, but I'm not acquainted with him.*

ac•quire (ə kwīr′), VERB. to come to have; get as your own: *I acquired that chair at a yard sale and the table at an auction.* ❑ VERB **ac•quires, ac•quired, ac•quir•ing.**

ac•quit (ə kwit′), VERB. to declare someone not guilty after a trial; set free: *Both of the prisoners accused of the robbery were acquitted.* ❑ VERB **ac•quits, ac•quit•ted, ac•quit•ting.**

a•cre (ā′kər), NOUN. a unit of area equal to 43,560 square feet, used to measure land.

a•cre•age (ā′kər ij), NOUN. a number of acres: *The acreage of this park is over 800.*

ac•rid (ak′rid), ADJECTIVE. sharp, bitter, or stinging: *Smoke from burning plastics is acrid and bad for you.*

ac•ro•bat (ak′rə bat), NOUN. someone who can swing on a trapeze, do handsprings, and so on.

acrobat

ac•ro•bat•ic (ak′rə bat′ik), ADJECTIVE. of or like an acrobat: *He flipped backward with acrobatic skill.*

ac•ro•nym (ak′rə nim), NOUN. a word formed from the first letters or syllables of other words. EXAMPLE: *scuba (self-contained underwater breathing apparatus).*

Word Source

Acronym comes from Greek words meaning "tip" and "name." Many acronyms started as regular abbreviations, then developed pronunciations of their own. The words below are acronyms.

BASIC	NASA	scuba	UNICEF
laser	radar	sonar	ZIP (Code)

a•cross (ə kròs′), PREPOSITION.
1 from one side to the other of; over: *The cat walked across the lawn.*
2 on the other side of; beyond: *The woods are across the river.*

a·cryl·ic (ə kril′ik), NOUN. a strong plastic used to make fabrics, optical lenses, taillights, and the like.

act (akt),
1 NOUN. something done; deed: *Sharing the candy with your friends was a generous act.*
2 NOUN. the process of doing something: *I was caught in the act of hiding the presents.*
3 VERB. to do something: *The firemen acted promptly and saved the burning house.*
4 VERB. to pretend to be: *She's just acting angry to make you feel bad.*
5 NOUN. a feeling or emotion that is pretended, not real: *He's not angry; it's just an act.*
6 VERB. to behave: *I'm sorry I acted badly today.*
7 VERB. to perform on the stage, in movies, on TV, or on the radio: *He acts the part of a doctor on TV.*
8 NOUN. a main division in a play or opera: *This play has three acts.*
9 NOUN. one of several performances on a program: *We stayed to see the trained dog's act.*
10 NOUN. a law. An **act of Congress** is a bill that has been passed by Congress.
❏ VERB **acts, act·ed, act·ing.**
act up, IDIOM. to behave badly: *The children began to act up when the teacher left the room.*
clean up your act, IDIOM. to begin to behave better: *I'm not taking you to the movies unless you clean up your act.*

ac·tion (ak′shən), NOUN.
1 the act or process of doing something: *The quick action of the firemen saved the building.*
2 something done; act: *Finding the lost dog's owner was a kind action.*
3 combat in war: *My dad was wounded in action.*
4 **actions,** behavior: *Her actions were rude.*

ac·ti·vate (ak′tə vāt), VERB. to cause something to start working: *To activate the alarm, push here.*
❏ VERB **ac·ti·vates, ac·ti·vat·ed, ac·ti·vat·ing.**

ac·tive (ak′tiv), ADJECTIVE.
1 showing much action; moving rather quickly much of the time; lively: *Most children are more active than grown people.*
2 acting; working: *An active volcano may erupt at any time.*
—**ac′tive·ly,** ADVERB.

ac·tiv·i·ty (ak tiv′ə tē), NOUN.
1 the condition of being active; use of power; movement: *Children like physical activity.*
2 something to do: *Tennis is a popular activity.*
❏ PLURAL **ac·tiv·i·ties.**

ac·tor (ak′tər), NOUN. someone who performs on stage, in movies, on TV, or on radio.

ac·tress (ak′tris), NOUN. a woman or girl who performs on stage, in movies, on TV, or on radio.
❏ PLURAL **ac·tress·es.**

ac·tu·al (ak′chü əl), ADJECTIVE. real; existing as a fact: *What he told us wasn't a dream but an actual event.*

ac·tu·al·ly (ak′chü ə lē), ADVERB. really; in fact: *Are you actually going to Europe?*

ac·u·punc·ture (ak′yü pungk′chər), NOUN. an ancient Chinese practice of inserting needles into certain parts of the body. Acupuncture is used to treat some diseases and to relieve pain.

a·cute (ə kyüt′), ADJECTIVE.
1 sharp and severe: *A toothache can cause acute pain.*
2 keen; sharp: *Dogs have an acute sense of smell.*

acute angle, an angle smaller than a right angle.

ad (ad), NOUN. a short form of **advertisement.**
■ Another word that sounds like this is **add.**

A.D., after the birth of Christ. The year A.D. 100 is 100 years after the birth of Christ.

Ad·am's ap·ple (ad′əmz ap′əl), the slight lump in the front of your neck. It is formed by tough, elastic tissue in the upper end of your windpipe.

a·dapt (ə dapt′), VERB.
1 to change something to fit different conditions; adjust: *They adapted the barn for use as a studio.*
2 to change yourself; get used to something: *He adapted to the new school with no problem.*
❏ VERB **a·dapts, a·dapt·ed, a·dapt·ing.**
—**a·dapt′a·ble,** ADJECTIVE.

The seal's body has **adapted** to life in the water.

ad·ap·ta·tion (ad′ap tā′shən), NOUN.
1 the act or process of changing something to fit different conditions: *That species made a good adaptation to the drier climate.*
2 something changed to fit different forms or conditions: *This movie is an adaptation of a book.*

add (ad), VERB.
1 to find the sum of: *Add 3 and 4 and you have 7.*
2 to say further; go on to say or write: *She said good-bye and added that she had had a pleasant visit.*
3 to join one thing to another: *Add a stone to the pile.*
❏ VERB **adds, add·ed, add·ing.** ■ Another word that sounds like this is **ad.**

a	hat	ė	term	ô	order	ch	child	ə	a in about
ā	age	i	it	oi	oil	ng	long		e in taken
ä	far	ī	ice	ou	out	sh	she		i in pencil
â	care	o	hot	u	cup	th	thin		o in lemon
e	let	ō	open	ù	put	ᴛʜ	then		u in circus
ē	equal	ò	saw	ü	rule	zh	measure		

ad·dend (ad′end), NOUN. a number to be added to another: *In 2 + 3 = 5, the addends are 2 and 3.*

ad·der (ad′ər), NOUN. a kind of snake. The African and European adders are poisonous; the North American adder is not.

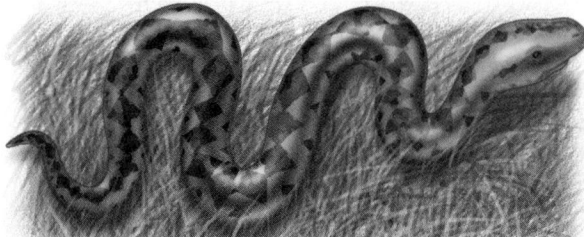

adder — 4 to 5 feet long

ad·dict (ad′ikt), NOUN. someone who has lost control of a habit: *A drug addict finds it very difficult to stop using drugs.*

ad·dict·ed (ə dik′tid), ADJECTIVE. uncontrollably following a habit: *addicted to drugs.*

ad·dic·tion (ə dik′shən), NOUN. the condition of following a habit uncontrollably: *She spoke about the harmful effects of drug addiction.*

ad·dic·tive (ə dik′tiv), ADJECTIVE. causing or tending to cause addiction: *Tobacco is addictive.*

ad·di·tion (ə dish′ən), NOUN.
1 the operation of adding one number to another: *2 + 3 = 5 is a simple addition.*
2 something added: *Whipped cream is a tasty addition to many desserts.*
3 a part added to a building: *We hope to put on a new addition.*

ad·di·tion·al (ə dish′ə nəl), ADJECTIVE. extra; more: *I need additional help.* **—ad·di′tion·al·ly,** ADVERB.

ad·di·tive (ad′ə tiv), NOUN. a substance combined with another substance to keep it from spoiling or make it work better.

ad·dress (ə dres′; *also* ad′res *for 1*),
1 NOUN. the place to which mail is directed: *Write your name and address on this envelope.*
2 VERB. to write on an envelope or package where it is to be sent: *Please address this letter for me.*
3 NOUN. a speech, especially one given to a large audience: *The President gave an address to the nation on television.*
4 VERB. to speak to or write to someone: *The king is addressed as "Your Majesty."*
❑ PLURAL **ad·dress·es;** VERB **ad·dress·es, ad·dressed, ad·dress·ing.**

ad·e·noids (ad′n oidz), NOUN PLURAL. the soft tissue in the upper part of the throat, at the back of the nose. Adenoids can swell up and make breathing and speaking difficult.

ad·e·quate (ad′ə kwit), ADJECTIVE. enough; sufficient; as much as is needed: *An adequate diet includes a variety of foods.* **—ad′e·quate·ly,** ADVERB.

ad·he·sive (ad hē′siv),
1 NOUN. glue, paste, or other substance for sticking things together.
2 ADJECTIVE. holding tight; sticky: *an adhesive label.*

adhesive tape, tape that is sticky on one side, used to hold bandages in place.

a·di·os (ä′dē ōs′ *or* ad′ē ōs′), INTERJECTION. good-bye.

ad·ja·cent (ə jā′snt), ADJECTIVE. close to; next: *The house adjacent to ours has been sold.*

ad·jec·tive (aj′ik tiv), NOUN. a word that describes more fully a person, place, or thing. In "a tiny ant," "The day is hot," "great joy," and "this pen," *tiny, hot, great,* and *this* are adjectives.

ad·journ (ə jėrn′), VERB. to put something off until a later time; postpone: *The meeting was adjourned until two o'clock.* ❑ VERB **ad·journs, ad·journed, ad·journ·ing.**

ad·just (ə just′), VERB.
1 to arrange; change to make fit: *He adjusted the chair.*
2 to get used to; become accustomed to: *Some wild animals never adjust to life in the zoo.*
❑ VERB **ad·justs, ad·just·ed, ad·just·ing.** **—ad·just′a·ble,** ADJECTIVE.

ad·just·ment (ə just′mənt), NOUN.
1 a means of adjusting: *All TVs have an adjustment for volume control.*
2 the act or process of getting used to something: *They were pleased with their daughter's adjustment to the new school.*

ad·lib (ad lib′), VERB. to make up what you are saying as you go along: *The actor forgot some of his lines and had to adlib his part.* ❑ VERB **ad·libs, ad·libbed, ad·lib·bing.**

ad·min·is·ter (ad min′ə stər), VERB.
1 to be in charge of something; manage; direct: *The mayor administers the city government.*
2 to give out; apply: *The coach administered first aid to the injured player.*
❑ VERB **ad·min·is·ters, ad·min·is·tered, ad·min·is·ter·ing.**

ad·min·is·tra·tion (ad min′ə strā′shən), NOUN.
1 the group of people in charge: *The principal and teachers are part of school's administration.*
2 **the Administration,** the President of the United States, the cabinet appointed by the President, and the departments of the government headed by cabinet members or other people appointed by the President.
3 the time during which a government holds office: *Franklin D. Roosevelt's administration lasted longer than that of any other president.*

ad·mir·a·ble (ad′mər ə bəl), ADJECTIVE. worth admiring; excellent: *His volunteer work is admirable.* **—ad′mir·a·bly,** ADVERB.

ad·mir·al (ad′mər əl), NOUN.
1 a military rank. See the chart on page 550.

2 any of several colorful butterflies, especially one kind having reddish streaks on its wings.

ad·mi·ra·tion (ad′mə rā′shən), *NOUN.* a feeling of wonder, pleasure, and approval: *I expressed my admiration for the artist's beautiful painting.*

ad·mire (ad mīr′), *VERB.*
1 to look at with wonder, pleasure, and approval: *We all admired the beautiful painting.*
2 to think highly of; respect: *I admire you.*
❑ *VERB* **ad·mires, ad·mired, ad·mir·ing. —ad·mir′er,** *NOUN.*

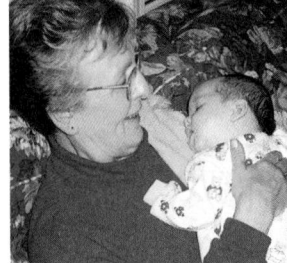
She **admires** her new grandchild.

ad·mis·sion (ad mish′ən), *NOUN.*
1 permission to enter; entrance: *Her brother has applied for admission to several colleges.*
2 the amount paid for the right to enter: *Admission to the movie is seven dollars.*
3 the act of admitting to be true; confession: *an admission of guilt.*

ad·mit (ad mit′), *VERB.*
1 to say that something is real or true; confess; acknowledge: *I admit now that I made a mistake.*
2 to allow to enter: *She was admitted to law school.*
❑ *VERB* **ad·mits, ad·mit·ted, ad·mit·ting.**

ad·mit·tance (ad mit′ns), *NOUN.* the right to enter; permission to enter: *No admittance!*

a·do·be (ə dō′bē),
1 *NOUN.* a building material made of clay baked in the sun.
2 *ADJECTIVE.* built or made of adobe: *Our friends in Arizona live in an adobe house.*

houses made of **adobe** and logs

ad·o·les·cence (ad′l es′ns), *NOUN.* the period of growth from childhood to adulthood; youth.

ad·o·les·cent (ad′l es′nt), *NOUN.* someone growing up from childhood to adulthood, especially someone from about 12 to about 20 years of age.

a·dopt (ə dopt′), *VERB.*
1 to take a child of other parents and bring up as your own: *They have adopted six children.*

2 to take something for your own or as your own choice; accept: *I liked your idea and adopted it. The members of the club voted to adopt the new rules.*
❑ *VERB* **a·dopts, a·dopt·ed, a·dopt·ing. —a·dopt′a·ble,** *ADJECTIVE.* **—a·dop·tion** (ə dop′shən), *NOUN.*

a·dor·a·ble (ə dôr′ə bəl), *ADJECTIVE.* attractive; delightful: *What an adorable kitten!*

a·dore (ə dôr′), *VERB.*
1 to love and admire someone very greatly: *She adores her mother.*
2 (informal) to like very much: *I just adored the movie!*
3 to worship: *"O! Come, let us adore Him," we sang.*
❑ *VERB* **a·dores, a·dored, a·dor·ing.**

a·dorn (ə dôrn′), *VERB.* to add beauty to; decorate.
❑ *VERB* **a·dorns, a·dorned, a·dorn·ing.**

a·drift (ə drift′), *ADJECTIVE.* drifting; floating without direction: *During the storm our boat was adrift.*

a·dult (ə dult′ or ad′ult),
1 *ADJECTIVE.* full-grown; grown-up; having full size and strength: *an adult person.*
2 *NOUN.* a fully grown person or other living thing.

Synonym Study

Adult means fully grown and developed: *Third graders cannot run as far as adult runners.*

Grown-up means adult but is used especially in contrast to something childish: *I like books for children more than ones for grown-up readers.*

Mature means fully grown and developed, especially mentally: *My cousin is only eight, but she is mature for her age.*

ANTONYMS: childish, immature.

a·dult·hood (ə dult′húd), *NOUN.* the condition or time of being an adult.

ad·vance (ad vans′),
1 *VERB.* to move forward: *The angry crowd advanced toward the building.*
2 *NOUN.* a forward movement; progress: *The army's advance was very slow.*
3 *NOUN.* money paid before it is due: *May I have an advance on next week's allowance?*
❑ *VERB* **ad·vanc·es, ad·vanced, ad·vanc·ing.**
in advance, *IDIOM.* ahead of time: *I paid for my ticket in advance.*

ad·vanced (ad vanst′), *ADJECTIVE.*
1 ahead of most others in knowledge, skill, progress, ideas, and so on: *We saw pictures of an advanced aircraft design.*
2 very old: *Grandpa lived to the advanced age of 91.*

a	hat	ė	term	ô	order	ch	child	⎧ a in about
ā	age	i	it	oi	oil	ng	long	⎪ e in taken
ä	far	ī	ice	ou	out	sh	she	ə ⎨ i in pencil
â	care	o	hot	u	cup	th	thin	⎪ o in lemon
e	let	ō	open	ù	put	₮H	then	⎩ u in circus
ē	equal	ȯ	saw	ü	rule	zh	measure	

ad·vance·ment (ad vans′mənt), NOUN.
1 the act or process of moving forward; improvement: *Advancements in the science of medicine have saved many lives.*
2 a promotion: *Good work won her advancement to a higher position.*

ad·van·tage (ad van′tij), NOUN. anything that is in your favor, or is a benefit; a help in getting something desired: *the advantages of education.*

take advantage of, IDIOM.
1 to use to help or benefit yourself: *We took advantage of the beautiful day by working in our garden.*
2 to behave unfairly towards someone: *He was so good-natured that people took advantage of him.*

ad·van·ta·geous (ad′vən tā′jəs), ADJECTIVE. favorable; helpful: *an advantageous agreement.*

ad·ven·ture (ad ven′chər), NOUN.
1 an unusual or exciting experience: *The trip to Alaska was quite an adventure for her.*
2 a bold and difficult undertaking, usually exciting and somewhat dangerous: *Sailing across the Pacific on a raft was a daring adventure.*

ad·ven·tur·ous (ad ven′chər əs), ADJECTIVE.
1 fond of adventures; ready to take risks: *The adventurous campers explored the cave.*
2 full of danger: *Sailing around the world in a small boat is an adventurous thing to do.*

ad·verb (ad′vėrb′), NOUN. a word that tells how, when, or where something happens. In "He walked slowly," "He came late," "I saw her there," and "She sings well," *slowly, late, there,* and *well* are adverbs. Adverbs also tell how much or how little is meant. In "This soup is very good" and "I am rather tired," *very* and *rather* are adverbs.

ad·ver·sar·y (ad′vər ser′ē), NOUN. a person or group on the other side in a contest or fight: *The two football teams were bitter adversaries.* ❏ PLURAL **ad·ver·sar·ies.**

ad·ver·si·ty (ad vėr′sə tē), NOUN. great difficulty; hardship: *The pioneers faced many adversities.* ❏ PLURAL **ad·ver·si·ties.**

ad·ver·tise (ad′vər tīz), VERB. to tell the public about a product, service, or need: *Stores often advertise on television.* ❏ VERB **ad·ver·tis·es, ad·ver·tised, ad·ver·tis·ing. —ad′ver·tis·er,** NOUN.

ad·ver·tise·ment (ad′vər tīz′mənt *or* ad vėr′tis mənt), NOUN. a paid announcement telling about some product, service, or need: *He put an advertisement in the paper to look for a job.*

ad·ver·tis·ing (ad′vər tī′zing), NOUN.
1 the business of preparing, designing, and publishing advertisements.
2 advertisements: *Billboards carry advertising.*

ad·vice (ad vīs′), NOUN. an opinion about what should be done: *My advice is that you study more.*

ad·vise (ad vīz′), VERB.
1 to give advice to: *He advised me to save my money.*
2 to inform: *We were advised that a storm was approaching, so we didn't go sailing.*
❏ VERB **ad·vis·es, ad·vised, ad·vis′ing. —ad·vis′er** *or* **ad·vi′sor,** NOUN.

ad·vi·sor·y (ad vī′zər ē),
1 ADJECTIVE. having power to advise: *The mayor appointed an advisory committee on pollution.*
2 NOUN. a bulletin or report to warn people about things that are expected to happen: *An advisory by the Weather Bureau warned of a storm.*
❏ PLURAL **ad·vi·sor·ies.**

ad·vo·cate (ad′və kāt *for verb;* ad′və kit *for noun*),
1 VERB. to speak in favor of; recommend publicly; support: *The mayor advocates building a new park.*
2 NOUN. someone who speaks in favor of something: *She is an advocate of animal rights.*
❏ VERB **ad·vo·cates, ad·vo·cat·ed, ad·vo·cat·ing.**

adz *or* **adze** (adz), NOUN. a tool somewhat like an ax, used for shaping heavy timbers. ❏ PLURAL **adz·es.**

an **aerial** view of Chicago

ad·verse (ad′vėrs′ *or* ad vėrs′), ADJECTIVE. unfavorable; harmful: *A poor diet and lack of sleep had an adverse effect on his health. He had an adverse reaction to the medication.*

aer·i·al (âr′ē əl),
1 ADJECTIVE. in or from the air: *This is an aerial photograph of the city.*
2 NOUN. See **antenna** (definition 2).

aer·o·bic (âr/ō/bik), ADJECTIVE.
1 living or growing only where there is oxygen: *aerobic bacteria.*
2 of or involving aerobics: *aerobic exercise.*

af·fec·tion·ate (ə fek/shə nit), ADJECTIVE. loving; fond; showing affection: *He gave the child an affectionate hug. I come from an affectionate family.* —**af·fec/tion·ate·ly,** ADVERB.

These animals seem very **affectionate.**

aer·o·bics (âr/ō/biks), NOUN. exercises that cause the body to use more oxygen and improve the heart, lungs, and circulation.

aer·o·nau·tics (âr/ə nȯ/tiks), NOUN. the science of the design and operation of aircraft.

aer·o·sol (âr/ə sol), NOUN. tiny particles of a solid or a liquid floating in air or other gas. Smoke and fog are aerosols.

aer·o·space (âr/ō spās),
1 NOUN. Earth's atmosphere and nearby outer space.
2 ADJECTIVE. of or about aircraft or spacecraft: *the aerospace industry.*

a·far (ə fär/), ADVERB. **from afar,** from far off; from a distance.

af·fair (ə fâr/), NOUN.
1 **affairs,** things that a person or business has to take care of; important matters: *Their lawyer looked after their affairs while they were gone.*
2 any thing, matter, or happening: *The costume party was a delightful affair.*

af·fect (ə fekt/), VERB.
1 to have an effect on; influence: *The small amount of rain last year affected the growth of crops.*
2 to touch the heart of; stir the feelings of: *The sad story affected me deeply.*
□ VERB **af·fects, af·fect·ed, af·fect·ing.**

Usage Note

Affect and **effect** are easily confused because they sound alike and their meanings are related. **Affect** means to influence someone or something: *The change in the law affected all the dog owners in the city.* **Effect** means the result of something that happens: *The effect of the anti-littering law was cleaner streets.*

af·fec·tion (ə fek/shən), NOUN. a friendly feeling; fondness; love. ■ See the Synonym Study at **love.**

af·firm (ə fėrm/), VERB. to say firmly; declare to be true; assert: *The prisoner affirmed his innocence.*
□ VERB **af·firms, af·firmed, af·firm·ing.**

af·firm·a·tive (ə fėr/mə tiv), ADJECTIVE. saying yes; affirming: *Her answer was affirmative.*

af·fix (af/iks), NOUN. a sound or group of sounds added to a word to change its meaning or use. Affixes are either prefixes like *un-* and *re-* or suffixes like *-ly, -s,* or *-ed.* □ PLURAL **af·fix·es.**

af·flict (ə flikt/), VERB. to cause pain to; trouble very much; distress: *She is afflicted with arthritis.* □ VERB **af·flicts, af·flict·ed, af·flict·ing.**

af·flic·tion (ə flik/shən), NOUN.
1 a condition of pain, trouble, or distress; misery: *The country suffered from the affliction of war.*
2 a cause of pain, trouble, or unhappiness: *Poverty is an affliction.*

af·flu·ent (af/lü ənt), ADJECTIVE. having a great deal of money; rich: *In that affluent community most of the homes have a swimming pool.*

af·ford (ə fôrd/), VERB.
1 to have the money, means, or time for: *Can we afford a new car? He cannot afford to waste time.*
2 to be able without difficulty or harm: *I can't afford to take the chance.*
□ VERB **af·fords, af·ford·ed, af·ford·ing.** —**af·ford/a·ble,** ADJECTIVE.

Af·ghan (af/gan),
1 NOUN. someone born or living in Afghanistan.
2 ADJECTIVE. of or about Afghanistan or its people.

Af·ghan·i·stan (af gan/ə stan), NOUN. a country in southwestern Asia.

a	hat	ė	term	ô	order	ch	child		a in about
ā	age	i	it	oi	oil	ng	long		e in taken
ä	far	ī	ice	ou	out	sh	she	ə⟨	i in pencil
â	care	o	hot	u	cup	th	thin		o in lemon
e	let	ō	open	ů	put	℔н	then		u in circus
ē	equal	ȯ	saw	ü	rule	zh	measure		

a·field (ə fēld′), ADVERB. away; away from home: *She wandered far afield in foreign lands.*

a·fire (ə fir′), ADVERB or ADJECTIVE. on fire; burning: *The lightning struck the building and set it afire.*

a·float (ə flōt′), ADVERB or ADJECTIVE. floating on the water or in the air: *It took two of us to get the heavy rowboat afloat.*

a·foot (ə füt′), ADVERB or ADJECTIVE. on foot; by walking: *The explorers abandoned their jeep and traveled afoot through the jungle. Some of the soldiers were on horses and some were afoot.*

a·fraid (ə frād′), ADJECTIVE.
1 frightened; feeling fear: *She was afraid of fire.*
2 sorry to have to say: *I'm afraid you are wrong.*

Synonym Study

Afraid means feeling fear: *I am afraid of snakes and spiders.*

Frightened means afraid: *The frightened deer leaped over the fence and ran away.*

Scared means the same as afraid but is less formal: *I am never scared of the dark.*

Alarmed means fearful and aware of danger: *We were alarmed when we heard the explosion.*

Terrified means feeling great fear: *The terrified children screamed when the tiger escaped.*

Petrified can mean feeling fear so strong that it makes you unable to move or think: *When the boy saw the rattlesnake he was petrified.*

See also the Synonym Studies at **fear** and **scare**.

ANTONYM: fearless.

Af·ri·ca (af′rə kə), NOUN. the continent south of Europe and east of the Atlantic Ocean. It is the second largest continent.

Af·ri·can (af′rə kən),
1 ADJECTIVE. of or about Africa or its people; from Africa.
2 NOUN. someone born or living in Africa.

African American,
1 an American of African descent.
2 of or about Americans of African descent.

African violet, a tropical houseplant with violet, white, or pink flowers.

Af·ro-A·mer·i·can (af′rō ə mer′ə kən), NOUN or ADJECTIVE. African American.

aft (aft), ADVERB. at or toward the rear of a ship, boat, or aircraft.

af·ter (af′tər),
1 PREPOSITION. later in time than: *After dinner we can go.*
2 PREPOSITION or ADVERB. following: *Day after day I waited for a letter from my friend.*

3 PREPOSITION or ADVERB. behind: *You come after me in the line. Jill came tumbling after.*
4 PREPOSITION. in search of; in pursuit of: *The dog ran after the rabbit.*
5 CONJUNCTION. later than the time that: *After he goes, we shall eat.*
6 PREPOSITION. in honor of; for: *She is named after her grandmother.*

af·ter·math (af′tər math), NOUN. a result, especially of something destructive: *The aftermath of the war was hunger and disease.*

af·ter·noon (af′tər nün′), NOUN. the part of the day between noon and evening.

af·ter·thought (af′tər thȯt′), NOUN. a second or later thought or explanation: *I ordered toast, and as an afterthought asked for it without butter.*

af·ter·ward (af′tər wərd), ADVERB. afterwards; later.

af·ter·wards (af′tər wərdz), ADVERB. later: *He went home first, but met us afterwards.*

a·gain (ə gen′), ADVERB. another time; once more: *Come again to play. Say that again.*

a·gainst (ə genst′), PREPOSITION.
1 in opposition to: *Our team will play against yours.*
2 upon or toward; in the opposite direction to: *Rain beat against the window. We sailed against the wind.*
3 in contact with: *The ladder is leaning against the tree.*
4 so as to defend or protect from: *An umbrella is protection against rain.*

ag·ate (ag′it), NOUN.
1 a kind of quartz with colored stripes or cloudy colors.
2 a marble used in games that looks like agate.

age (āj),
1 NOUN. time of life: *His age is ten.*
2 NOUN. the length of life: *Turtles live to a great age.*
3 NOUN. a particular period of life: *old age.*
4 NOUN. a period in history: *We live in the age of laptops and lasers.*
5 NOUN. **ages,** a long time: *I haven't seen you for ages!*
6 VERB. to grow old: *He is aging fast.*
7 VERB. to make old: *Worry can age you.*
❑ VERB **ag·es, aged, ag·ing** or **age·ing.**

a·ged (ā′jid for 1; ājd for 2), ADJECTIVE.
1 old; having lived a long time: *an aged woman.*
■ See the Synonym Study at **old.**
2 of the age of: *Children aged six must go to school.*

a·gen·cy (ā′jən sē), NOUN.
1 the office or business of some person or company that acts for another: *Employment agencies help people to get jobs.*
2 a special department of the government: *The Environmental Protection Agency is the agency that deals with pollution in the United States.*
❑ PLURAL **a·gen·cies.**

a·gen·da (ə jen′də), NOUN. a list of things that need to be dealt with: *The agenda for today's meeting is short.* ❑ PLURAL **a·gen·das.**

a·gent (āʹjənt), NOUN.
1 someone having the authority to act for another: *The real estate agent can sell your house quickly.*
2 something that produces an effect by its action: *Yeast is the agent that causes bread to rise.*

ag·gra·vate (agʹrə vāt), VERB.
1 to make worse; make more severe: *His headache was aggravated by the noise.*
2 to irritate: *She aggravated me with her questions.*
❑ VERB **ag·gra·vates, ag·gra·vat·ed, ag·gra·vat·ing.**

ag·gres·sion (ə greshʹən), NOUN. the first step in an attack or a quarrel: *A country that invades another country's territory is guilty of aggression.*

ag·gres·sive (ə gresʹiv), ADJECTIVE.
1 taking the first step in an attack or a quarrel; attacking: *The aggressive nation invaded two neighboring countries.*
2 forceful; energetic: *The police are waging an aggressive campaign against driving too fast.*

a·ghast (ə gastʹ), ADJECTIVE. struck with surprise or horror: *I was aghast when I saw the fire damage.*

ag·ile (ajʹəl), ADJECTIVE. able to move quickly and easily; nimble: *An acrobat has to be agile. You need an agile mind to solve puzzles.* **–agʹile·ly,** ADVERB.

an **agile** gibbon

ag·i·tate (ajʹə tāt), VERB. to shake or move violently; disturb; upset: *The wind agitated the surface of the river. News of his illness agitated me at first.* ❑ VERB **ag·i·tates, ag·i·tat·ed, ag·i·tat·ing.**

a·go (ə gōʹ),
1 ADJECTIVE. gone by; past: *I met her two years ago at a party.*
2 ADVERB. in the past: *He lived here long ago.*

ag·o·niz·ing (agʹə nīʹzing), ADJECTIVE. causing very great pain or suffering: *an agonizing loss.*

ag·o·ny (agʹə nē), NOUN. very great mental or physical suffering: *Nobody can stand for long the agony of a severe toothache.* ❑ PLURAL **ag·o·nies.**

a·gree (ə grēʹ), VERB.
1 to have the same feeling or opinion: *I agree that we should try to be more careful.*
2 to be in harmony; be the same as: *Your story agrees with mine.*
3 to say that you are willing; consent: *He agreed to go.* ■ See the Synonym Study at **promise.**
❑ VERB **a·grees, a·greed, a·gree·ing.**

a·gree·a·ble (ə grēʹə bəl), ADJECTIVE.
1 pleasant; pleasing: *He has an agreeable manner.* ■ See the Synonym Study at **good-natured.**
2 willing: *If she is agreeable, we can meet tonight.*

a·gree·ment (ə grēʹmənt), NOUN.
1 an understanding reached by two or more people, groups, or nations. Nations make treaties; people make contracts. Both are agreements.
2 harmony in feeling or opinion: *There was perfect agreement between the two friends.*

ag·ri·cul·tur·al (agʹrə kulʹchər əl), ADJECTIVE. of or about farming; of agriculture: *The Middle West is an important agricultural region.*

ag·ri·cul·ture (agʹrə kulʹchər), NOUN. the science of cultivating the soil to grow crops; farming.

a·ground (ə groundʹ), ADVERB or ADJECTIVE. stranded on the shore or on the bottom in shallow water: *The ship ran aground and stuck in the sand.*

A·guas·ca·lien·tes (äʹgwäs ka lyenʹtes), NOUN. a state in central Mexico.

ah (ä), INTERJECTION. an exclamation of pain, sorrow, regret, pity, admiration, surprise, contempt, or joy.

a·ha (ä häʹ), INTERJECTION. an exclamation of triumph, satisfaction, surprise, or joy.

a·head (ə hedʹ), ADVERB.
1 in front; before: *Walk ahead of me.*
2 forward: *Go ahead with this work for another week.*
3 in advance: *He was ahead of his class in reading.*
be ahead, IDIOM. to be winning: *Our team is ahead by six points.*

a·hoy (ə hoiʹ), INTERJECTION. a call used by sailors to call to a ship. They say, "Ship, ahoy!"

aid (ād),
1 VERB. to give support to someone; help: *The Red Cross aids flood victims.* ■ See the Synonym Study at **help.**
2 NOUN. help; assistance: *When my arm was broken, I could not dress without aid.*
❑ VERB **aids, aid·ed, aid·ing.**

aide (ād), NOUN. a helper; assistant: *a nurse's aide.*

AIDS (ādz), NOUN. a deadly disease caused by the HIV virus. This virus makes the body unable to resist other serious diseases.

ai·ki·do (ī kēʹdō), NOUN. a Japanese method of self-defense using no weapons. It uses holds and body movements to cause the attacker to lose balance.

a	hat	ė	term	ô	order	ch	child	⎧a in about
ā	age	i	it	oi	oil	ng	long	⎪e in taken
ä	far	ī	ice	ou	out	sh	she	ə⎨i in pencil
â	care	o	hot	u	cup	th	thin	⎪o in lemon
e	let	ō	open	u̇	put	ᴛʜ	then	⎩u in circus
ē	equal	ȯ	saw	ü	rule	zh	measure	

ail (āl), *VERB.*
1 to be the matter with; trouble: *What ails the child?*
2 to be ill; feel sick: *He has been ailing for a week.*
❑ *VERB* **ails, ailed, ail·ing.** ■ Another word that sounds like this is **ale.**

He is **ailing** with a bad cold.

ail·ment (āl′mənt), *NOUN.* an illness; sickness: *He has a serious heart ailment.*

aim (ām),
1 *VERB.* to point or direct something at a goal or target: *She aimed the arrow at the target. She aimed her comments at the tardy students.*
2 *NOUN.* the act of pointing or directing at something: *She hit the target because her aim was good.*
3 *VERB.* to try: *He aimed to please his teachers.*
4 *NOUN.* a purpose: *Her aim was to become a lawyer.*
❑ *VERB* **aims, aimed, aim·ing.**

aim·less (ām′lis), *ADJECTIVE.* without purpose; pointless: *He took a long, aimless walk around town.* **–aim′less·ly,** *ADVERB.*

ain't (ānt),
1 a contraction of **am not, is not,** or **are not.**
2 a contraction of **have not** or **has not.**

Usage Note

Ain't was often used in the 1600s and 1700s. During the 1800s it was criticized. Today, **ain't** is no longer acceptable in formal English. Even in informal speech, its use is not approved. However, it is often heard, especially in very casual speech. Careful speakers and writers do not use **ain't.**

air (âr),
1 *NOUN.* the invisible mixture of gases that surrounds the earth; the atmosphere. Air contains mostly nitrogen and oxygen.
2 *NOUN.* the space overhead; sky: *Birds fly in the air.*
3 *VERB.* to let fresh air in: *Open the windows and air the room.*
4 *VERB.* to be broadcast by radio or TV: *The program aired at 8:00 P.M.*
5 *NOUN.* a simple melody or tune.
6 *NOUN.* way; look; manner: *The diplomat had an air of importance.*
7 *NOUN.* **airs,** unnatural or showy manners: *Your friends will laugh if you put on airs.*
❑ *VERB* **airs, aired, air·ing.** ■ Another word that sounds like this is **heir.**
up in the air, *IDIOM.* not decided yet; uncertain: *Our plans are still up in the air.*

air bag, a device that protects passengers in a motor vehicle from being thrown forward in a crash. A plastic bag rapidly fills up with air and forms a cushion around the passenger.

air·borne (âr′bôrn′), *ADJECTIVE.*
1 off the ground: *The plane was quickly airborne.*
2 carried in aircraft: *airborne troops.*

air conditioning, a means of controlling the temperature and humidity of air and of removing dust. **–air′-con·di′tioned,** *ADJECTIVE.* **–air conditioner.**

air·craft (âr′kraft′), *NOUN.* a machine for flying. Airplanes, helicopters, and balloons are aircraft.
❑ *PLURAL* **air·craft.**

aircraft carrier, a large warship used as a floating base for aircraft. It has a large, flat deck on which to land or take off.

aircraft carrier

air·field (âr′fēld′), *NOUN.* a landing field for aircraft.

Air Force, the part of the armed forces of the United States that uses aircraft.

air·line (âr′līn′), *NOUN.* a company that carries passengers and freight by aircraft from one place to another.

air·mail (âr′māl′), *NOUN.*
1 mail sent by aircraft.
2 a system of sending mail by aircraft.

air·man (âr′mən), *NOUN.* any of several military ranks. See the chart on page 550. ❑ *PLURAL* **air·men.**

air·plane (âr′plān′), *NOUN.* an aircraft heavier than air, that has wings and is driven by a propeller or jet engine.

air·port (âr′pôrt′), *NOUN.* an area used regularly by aircraft to land and take off. An airport has buildings for passengers and for keeping and repairing aircraft.

air pressure, the pressure caused by the weight of the air.

Did You Know?

Although we do not feel it, the air presses down on everything on our planet all the time. At sea level, **air pressure** averages 14.7 pounds per square inch.

air·sick (âr′sik′), ADJECTIVE. sick as a result of the motion of aircraft. **–air′sick′ness,** NOUN.

air·strip (âr′strip′), NOUN. a paved or cleared area on which aircraft land and take off.

air·tight (âr′tit′), ADJECTIVE.
1 so tightly closed that no air or other gases can get in or out: *The food was packed in airtight containers so it would not spoil.*
2 having no weak points open to attack: *She presented an airtight argument.*

air·y (âr′ē), ADJECTIVE. breezy; filled with fresh air: *an airy room.* ❏ ADJECTIVE **air·i·er, air·i·est.**

aisle (īl), NOUN. a passage between rows of something, such as seats in a theater, shelves in a library, or counters in a store. ■ Other words that sound like this are **I'll** and **isle.**

a·jar (ə jär′), ADJECTIVE. slightly open: *Please leave the door ajar.*

AK, an abbreviation of **Alaska.**

a·kin (ə kin′), ADJECTIVE.
1 alike; similar: *His tastes in music seem akin to mine.*
2 belonging to the same family; related: *Your cousins are akin to you.*

Word Power   -al

The suffix **-al**[1] is used to make adjectives. It means "of," "like," or "as." Parental authority is the authority **of** a parent. An ornamental plate is a plate that is used **as** an ornament.

The suffix **-al**[2] is used to make nouns. It means "the act of _____ing." Refusal means **the act of** refusing. Arrival means **the act of** arriving.

AL, an abbreviation of **Alabama.**

Al·a·bam·a (al′ə bam′ə), NOUN. one of the southern states of the United States. *Abbreviation:* AL; *Capital:* Montgomery. **–Al′a·bam′an** or **Al′a·bam′i·an,** NOUN.

State Story **Alabama** was named for an American Indian tribe that once lived in the area. The tribe's name came from Indian words meaning "I clear the thicket."

A·lad·din (ə lad′n), NOUN. a boy in one of the stories in *The Arabian Nights.* He found a magic lamp and a magic ring. By rubbing either one of them he could call either of two powerful spirits to do whatever he asked.

à la mode or **a la mode** (ä′ lə mōd′ or al′ ə mōd′), served with ice cream: *pie à la mode.*

a·larm (ə lärm′),
1 NOUN. a bell or other device that makes a noise to warn or waken people: *a fire alarm.*
2 VERB. to make afraid; frighten: *The sudden noise alarmed me.* ■ See the Synonym Study at **scare.**
3 NOUN. sudden fear; excitement caused by fear: *The deer darted off in alarm.* ■ See the Synonym Study at **fear.**
❏ VERB **a·larms, a·larmed, a·larm·ing.**

alarm clock, a clock that can be set to ring or sound at a chosen time.

a·las (ə las′), INTERJECTION. a word expressing sorrow, grief, regret, or pity.

A·las·ka (ə las′kə), NOUN. one of the Pacific states of the United States, in the northwestern part of North America. Alaska is the largest state of the United States. *Abbreviation:* AK; *Capital:* Juneau. **–A·las′kan,** ADJECTIVE OR NOUN.

State Story **Alaska** got its name from a word used by people living on nearby islands. The word meant "mainland."

Al·ba·ni·a (al bā′nē ə), NOUN. a country in southeastern Europe. **–Al·ba′ni·an,** ADJECTIVE OR NOUN.

Al·ba·ny (ȯl′bə nē), NOUN. the capital of New York State.

al·ba·tross (al′bə tros), NOUN. a large sea bird that has webbed feet and very long wings. It can fly long distances. ❏ PLURAL **al·ba·tross·es.**

Al·ber·ta (al bėr′tə), NOUN. a province in western Canada. **–Al·ber′tan,** ADJECTIVE OR NOUN.

al·bi·no (al bī′nō), NOUN.
1 someone with very white or pale skin and hair, and pink eyes with red pupils.
2 an animal or plant that is white or pale.
❏ PLURAL **al·bi·nos.**

an **albino** baby alligator

a	hat	ė	term	ô	order	ch	child		a in about
ā	age	i	it	oi	oil	ng	long		e in taken
ä	far	ī	ice	ou	out	sh	she	ə {	i in pencil
â	care	o	hot	u	cup	th	thin		o in lemon
e	let	ō	open	u̇	put	ᴛʜ	then		u in circus
ē	equal	ȯ	saw	ü	rule	zh	measure		

al·bum (al′bəm), NOUN.
1 a book with blank pages for holding things like photographs, pictures, and stamps.
2 a recording on one or more records, tapes, or CDs: *Have you heard that singer's new album?*

al·co·hol (al′kə hȯl), NOUN. a colorless liquid in wine, beer, whiskey, rum, and vodka. Alcohol is used in medicines, in manufacturing, and as a fuel.

al·co·hol·ic (al′kə hȯ′lik),
1 ADJECTIVE. of or containing alcohol: *Whiskey and rum are alcoholic liquors.*
2 NOUN. someone who cannot control his or her need to drink alcohol.

al·co·hol·ism (al′kə hȯ liz′əm), NOUN. a disease in which people become unable to control their desire to drink alcohol.

al·cove (al′kōv), NOUN. a small room opening out of a larger room.

al·der (ȯl′dər), NOUN. a tree or shrub somewhat like a birch. Alders usually grow in wet land.

ale (āl), NOUN. a strong beer made from malt and hops. ■ Another word that sounds like this is **ail**.

a·lert (ə lèrt′),
1 ADJECTIVE. watchful; wide-awake: *The dog was alert to every sound.*
2 ADJECTIVE. quick to notice something and to take action: *Emergency room doctors have to always be alert.* ■ See the Synonym Study at **smart**.
3 NOUN. a signal warning of an attack by enemy aircraft, a hurricane, or other danger: *Our town has sirens for a tornado alert.*
4 VERB. to warn: *The siren alerted the town that a tornado had been sighted.*
❏ VERB **a·lerts**, **a·lert·ed**, **a·lert·ing**. −**a·lert′ness**, NOUN.

al·fal·fa (al fal′fə), NOUN. a plant with leaves like clover and bluish purple flowers. Alfalfa is grown as food for horses and cattle. Its deep roots contain bacteria that are good for the soil.

al·gae (al′jē), NOUN PLURAL. a group of living things, usually found in water, that can make their own food. Algae contain chlorophyll but lack true stems, roots, or leaves. ❏ SINGULAR **al·ga** (al′gə).

al·ge·bra (al′jə brə), NOUN. the branch of mathematics that deals with the relations between quantities. Algebra uses letters as symbols that can stand for many different numbers.

Al·ger·i·a (al jir′ē ə), NOUN. a country in northern Africa. −**Al·ger′i·an**, ADJECTIVE or NOUN.

a·li·as (ā′lē əs),
1 NOUN. a name other than your real name, used to hide who you are: *The spy's real name was Foster, but she went by the alias of Gray.*
2 ADVERB. otherwise called: *The police arrested a man named Johnson, alias Brown.*
❏ PLURAL **a·li·as·es**.

al·i·bi (al′ə bī), NOUN.
1 a claim that an accused person was somewhere else when a crime was committed: *His alibi was that he was in another city when the bank was robbed.*
2 an excuse: *What is your alibi for not doing your job?*
❏ PLURAL **al·i·bis**.

al·ien (ā′lyən),
1 NOUN. someone who is not a citizen of the country in which he or she lives.
2 NOUN. an imaginary creature from outer space: *The movie was about aliens landing on Earth.*
3 ADJECTIVE. strange; foreign: *Their customs are alien to ours.*

alien (definition 2)

a·light (ə līt′), VERB.
1 to get down; get off: *She alighted from the bus.*
2 to come down from the air; come down from flight: *The bird alighted on our windowsill.*
❏ VERB **a·lights**, **a·light·ed**, **a·light·ing**.

a·lign (ə līn′), VERB. to bring into line; arrange in a straight line: *A mechanic aligned the front wheels of our car.* ❏ VERB **a·ligns**, **a·ligned**, **a·lign·ing**.

a·like (ə līk′),
1 ADVERB. in the same way: *She and I think alike.*
2 ADJECTIVE. like one another; similar: *The children in that family are alike in many ways.*

al·i·men·tar·y ca·nal (al′ə men′tər ē kə nal′), the parts of the body through which food passes while it is being digested. The alimentary canal is a tube which begins at the mouth and ends where solid waste leaves the body.

a·live (ə līv′), ADJECTIVE.
1 having life; living: *Was the snake alive or dead?*
2 active: *Although our team played badly at first, we kept alive our hopes of winning.*

all (ȯl),
1 ADJECTIVE. every one of: *All the children came. You all know the teacher.*
2 PRONOUN. everyone: *All of us are going.*
3 PRONOUN. everything: *All is well.*
4 PRONOUN. the whole amount; the whole of: *All of the bread is gone. The mice ate all the cheese.*
5 ADVERB. wholly; entirely: *The cake is all gone.*
■ Another word that sounds like this is **awl**.

all in all, IDIOM. when everything has been taken into account: *All in all, I think you did a good job.*

at all, IDIOM. in any way: *Maybe he won't be able to go at all. She was not at all upset by his question.*

Al·lah (al′ə or ä′lə), NOUN. the Muslim name for God.

A

all·a·round (ȯl′ə round′), ADJECTIVE. able to do many things; useful in many ways: *She is an all-around athlete—she plays tennis, golfs, and swims well.*

al·lege (ə lej′), VERB. to declare; state: *Although he had no proof, the man alleged that she stole his watch.* ❑ VERB **al·leg·es, al·leged, al·leg·ing.**

al·leged (ə lejd′), ADJECTIVE. stated positively to be, but without proof: *the alleged burglar.*

Al·le·ghe·ny Moun·tains (al′ə gā′nē moun′tənz), a mountain range of the Appalachian Mountain system, in Pennsylvania, Maryland, Virginia, and West Virginia.

al·le·giance (ə lē′jəns), NOUN. loyalty; faithfulness: *I pledge allegiance to the flag.*

al·ler·gic (ə lèr′jik), ADJECTIVE.
1 having an allergy: *People who are allergic to cats sneeze if they are around them.*
2 caused by an allergy: *Hay fever is an allergic reaction to a kind of pollen.*

al·ler·gy (al′ər jē), NOUN. a physical reaction to certain things, such as certain kinds of pollen, food, or plants. Hay fever and hives are common signs of allergy. ❑ PLURAL **al·ler·gies.**

al·ley (al′ē), NOUN.
1 a narrow street behind buildings in a town.
2 See **bowling alley** (definition 1).
❑ PLURAL **al·leys.**

al·li·ance (ə lī′əns), NOUN. a union of persons, groups, or nations formed by agreement for some special purpose or benefit.

al·lied (ə līd′ or al′īd), ADJECTIVE. united by agreement: *France, Great Britain, Russia, and the United States were allied nations during World War II.*

al·li·ga·tor (al′ə gā′tər), NOUN. a large reptile with a thick, rough skin and strong jaws. It is like the crocodile but has a shorter and flatter head. Alligators live in the rivers and marshes of the warm parts of America and China.

Word Story

Alligator comes from Spanish words meaning "the lizard." When Spanish explorers came to America and saw alligators for the first time, they thought the animals looked like big lizards.

al·lot (ə lot′), VERB. to give to as a share; assign: *Each class was allotted a part in the school program.* ❑ VERB **al·lots, al·lot·ted, al·lot·ting.**

al·low (ə lou′), VERB.
1 to let someone do something; permit: *My parents won't allow us to swim in the river.*
2 to let someone have; give: *My parents allowed me a dollar to spend as I wish.*
3 to add or subtract to make up for something: *You ought to allow $50 for expenses on the trip.*
❑ VERB **al·lows, al·lowed, al·low·ing.**

al·low·ance (ə lou′əns), NOUN.
1 a sum of money given or set aside for expenses: *My weekly allowance is $5 if I do all my chores, and $2 if I don't.*
2 an amount subtracted to make up for something; discount: *The salesman offered us an allowance of $1500 on our old car when we bought a new one.*

al·loy (al′oi), NOUN. a metal made by melting and mixing two or more metals. Brass is an alloy of copper and zinc.

all right,
1 satisfactory: *The work was not done very well, but it was all right.*
2 in good health or condition; free from harm: *I dropped the bag, but the eggs are all right. The doctor says that I am all right.*
3 yes: *"Will you come with me?" "All right."*

all-star (ȯl′stär′), ADJECTIVE. made up of the best players or performers: *Two of our players have been named to the all-star team.*

al·ly (al′ī or ə lī′ for noun; ə lī′ for verb),
1 NOUN. a person, group, or nation united with another for some special purpose: *England and France were allies in World War II.*
2 VERB. to combine for some special purpose; unite by agreement. Small nations sometimes ally themselves with larger ones for protection.
❑ PLURAL **al·lies;** VERB **al·lies, al·lied, al·ly·ing.**

alligator — up to 12 feet long

al·ma·nac (ȯl′mə nak), NOUN.
1 a booklike calendar published every year that also gives information about the sun, moon, stars, tides, church days, and other facts, sometimes with weather predictions.
2 a reference book published yearly, with tables of facts and information on many subjects: *My almanac is out of date.*

a	hat	ė	term	ô	order	ch	child	⎧a in about
ā	age	i	it	oi	oil	ng	long	⎪e in taken
ä	far	ī	ice	ou	out	sh	she	ə⎨i in pencil
â	care	o	hot	u	cup	th	thin	⎪o in lemon
e	let	ō	open	u̇	put	ŦH	then	⎩u in circus
ē	equal	ȯ	saw	ü	rule	zh	measure	

al·might·y (ȯl mī′tē),
1 *ADJECTIVE.* possessing all power.
2 *NOUN.* **the Almighty,** God

al·mond (ä′mənd), *NOUN.* the tasty, oval-shaped nut of a tree growing in warm regions.

al·most (ȯl′mōst), *ADVERB.* nearly: *almost ten o'clock. I almost hit the ball.*

a·loft (ə lȯft′), *ADVERB.*
1 far above the earth; high up: *There were dozens of hot-air balloons aloft.*
2 high up among the sails and masts of a ship: *The sailor went aloft to get a better view of the shore.*

almond

a·lo·ha (ä lō′hä), *NOUN* or *INTERJECTION.* a Hawaiian word meaning:
1 greetings; hello.
2 good-bye; farewell.
❑ *PLURAL* **a·lo·has.**

a·lone (ə lōn′),
1 *ADJECTIVE* or *ADVERB.* without other people or things: *After my friends left, I was alone. One tree stood alone on the hill.*
2 *ADVERB.* without help from others: *I solved the problem alone.*
3 *ADJECTIVE.* only; not anyone else: *She alone can do this work.*
leave alone or **let alone,** *IDIOM.* to not bother; not meddle with: *Leave her alone so she can study.*

Synonym Study

Alone means being by yourself: *She is twelve now, old enough to stay home alone.*

Solitary means alone, often because you choose to be: *The boy went for a long, solitary walk.*

Isolated means alone and separated from others: *My mother grew up on an isolated farm, miles from the nearest town.*

Lone means alone. It is often used in stories and poems: *The ranchers wondered who the lone rider coming into Saddle Valley might be.*

a·long (ə lȯng′),
1 *PREPOSITION.* from one end to the other end of: *Trees are planted along the street.*
2 *ADVERB.* forward; onward: *March along quickly.*
3 *ADVERB.* together with someone or something: *We took our dog along.*
all along, *IDIOM.* all the time: *I knew the answer all along.*

a·long·side (ə lȯng′sīd′),
1 *ADVERB.* at the side; side by side: *They were sitting in the car when a truck pulled up alongside.*

2 *PREPOSITION.* by the side of; side by side with: *The boat was alongside the wharf.*

a·loof (ə lüf′), *ADJECTIVE.* tending to keep to yourself: *Her aloof manner kept her from making friends.*

a·loud (ə loud′), *ADVERB.* loud enough to be heard; not in a whisper: *She read the story aloud to the class before recess.*

al·pac·a (al pak′ə), *NOUN.* an animal of South America, closely related to the llama, but smaller. It is raised for its long, silky wool. ❑ *PLURAL* **al·pac·as** or **al·pac·a.**

alpaca — about 4 feet high at the shoulder

al·pha·bet (al′fə bet), *NOUN.* the letters of a language arranged in a fixed order, not as they are in words. The English alphabet is: a b c d e f g h i j k l m n o p q r s t u v w x y z.

Word Story

Alphabet comes from the names of the first two letters of the Greek alphabet: *alpha* A and *beta* B. The Romans came later and borrowed many words from the Greeks. They turned these two words into their Latin word *alphabetum.* English borrowed the Latin word over 500 years ago and shortened it to make our word.

al·pha·bet·i·cal (al′fə bet′ə kəl), *ADJECTIVE.* arranged by letters in the order of the alphabet: *Dictionary entries are listed in alphabetical order.* —**al′pha·bet′i·cal·ly,** *ADVERB.*

al·pha·bet·ize (al′fə bə tīz′), *VERB.* to arrange in alphabetical order: *The names in a telephone book have been alphabetized.* ❑ *VERB* **al·pha·bet·iz·es, al·pha·bet·ized, al·pha·bet·iz·ing.**

Alps (alps), *NOUN PLURAL.* a group of high mountains in southern Europe. The Alps are in Switzerland, France, Austria, and several other countries.

al·read·y (ȯl red′ē), *ADVERB.* by this time: *I've already finished my homework.*

al·so (ȯl′sō), *ADVERB.* too; in addition: *I like summer but I enjoy winter also.*

al·tar (ȯl′tər), NOUN. a table or stand used in religious worship in a church or temple: *The priest knelt in prayer before the altar.* ■ Another word that sounds like this is **alter.**

al·ter (ȯl′tər), VERB. to make or become different; change: *If this coat is too large, it can be altered.* ❑ VERB **al·ters, al·tered, al·ter·ing.** ■ Another word that sounds like this is **altar.**

al·ter·a·tion (ȯl′tə rā′shən), NOUN. a change: *We paneled the den and made other alterations. He bought a new suit but it needed alterations.*

al·ter·nate (ȯl′tər nāt *for verb;* ȯl′tər nit *for adjective and noun*),
1 VERB. to happen or be arranged by turns, first one and then the other. Squares and circles alternate in this row: ○ □ ○ □ ○ □ ○ □.
2 VERB. to take turns: *My brother and I will alternate in setting the table.*
3 ADJECTIVE. first one and then the other by turns: *Our flag has alternate stripes of red and white.*
4 ADJECTIVE. every other: *My friends and I go bowling on alternate Saturdays.*
5 ADJECTIVE. in place of another: *If it rains tomorrow, the fair will be held on an alternate day.*
6 NOUN. a substitute: *We have several alternates on our debating team.*
❑ VERB **al·ter·nates, al·ter·nat·ed, al·ter·nat·ing.** —**al′ter·nate·ly,** ADVERB.

alternating current, an electric current that reverses its direction at regular intervals.

al·ter·na·tive (ȯl tèr′nə tiv), NOUN.
1 a choice from among two or more things: *She had the alternatives of going to summer school or finding a summer job.*
2 one of the things to be chosen from: *She chose the first alternative and went to summer school.*

al·though (ȯl ᴛнō′), CONJUNCTION. in spite of the fact that; though: *Although it rained all day, they went on the hike.*

al·tim·e·ter (al tim′ə tər), NOUN. a device for measuring altitude. Altimeters work either by measuring air pressure or by using radar.

al·ti·tude (al′tə tüd), NOUN.
1 height above the earth's surface: *What altitude did the airplane reach?*
2 height above sea level: *The altitude of Denver is one mile.*

al·to (al′tō), NOUN.
1 the lowest singing voice in women and boys.
2 a singer or instrument with an alto range.
❑ PLURAL **al·tos.**

al·to·geth·er (ȯl′tə geᴛн′ər), ADVERB.
1 completely; entirely: *The house was altogether destroyed by fire.*
2 on the whole: *Altogether, he was pleased.*
3 all included: *Altogether there were 14 books.*

a·lu·mi·num (ə lü′mə nəm), NOUN. a very light, silver-white metal that does not tarnish easily. Aluminum is a chemical element. It is used to make tools, cans, airplane parts, and so on.

Al·vin (al′vin), NOUN. (trademark) an underwater vehicle used in ocean research.

Alvin

al·ways (ȯl′wāz), ADVERB.
1 every time; in each case: *Night always follows day.*
2 all the time; constantly; forever: *Their home is always open to others. We will always be friends.*

am (am), VERB. a present tense of **be:** *I am tired. I am going to school.*

a.m. or **A.M.,** before noon; in the time from midnight to noon: *School begins at 8:30 A.M.*

am·a·teur (am′ə chər *or* am′ə tər),
1 NOUN. someone who does something for pleasure, not for money: *Only amateurs can compete in college sports.*
2 NOUN. someone who does something rather poorly: *This painting is the work of an amateur; it shows very little skill.*
3 ADJECTIVE. of or by amateurs; by amateurs: *Our town has an amateur orchestra.*

a·maze (ə māz′), VERB. to surprise greatly; strike with sudden wonder: *She was amazed at how the strand of hair looked under a microscope.* ■ See the Synonym Study at **surprise.** ❑ VERB **a·maz·es, a·mazed, a·maz·ing.**

a·maze·ment (ə māz′mənt), NOUN. great surprise; sudden wonder: *I was filled with amazement when I first saw the ocean.*

a·maz·ing (ə mā′zing), ADJECTIVE. very surprising. —**a·maz′ing·ly,** ADVERB.

a	hat	ė	term	ô	order	ch	child	⎧ a in about
ā	age	i	it	oi	oil	ng	long	⎪ e in taken
ä	far	ī	ice	ou	out	sh	she	ə ⎨ i in pencil
â	care	o	hot	u	cup	th	thin	⎪ o in lemon
e	let	ō	open	ù	put	ᴛн	then	⎩ u in circus
ē	equal	ȯ	saw	ü	rule	zh	measure	

Am·a·zon (am′ə zon), *NOUN.* a river in northern South America. It is the largest river in the world.

am·bas·sa·dor (am bas′ə dər), *NOUN.* a representative of the highest rank sent by one government or ruler to another: *The United States ambassador to France lives in Paris.*

am·ber (am′bər),
1 *NOUN.* a hard, clear, yellow or yellowish brown substance, used for jewelry.
2 *ADJECTIVE* or *NOUN.* yellow or yellowish brown: *My cat has amber eyes.*

Did You Know?

Amber is what remains of the oily sap or resin of very ancient pine trees. After millions of years buried in the ground, the resin becomes something like a gem. You can often see insects that were trapped in the resin when the tree was still alive.

am·big·u·ous (am big′yü əs), *ADJECTIVE.* having more than one possible meaning. The sentence "After John hit Bob he ran away" is ambiguous because we cannot tell which boy ran away.

am·bi·tion (am bish′ən), *NOUN.*
1 a strong desire for fame or success; a longing for a high position or great power: *Because he was filled with ambition, he worked day and night.*
2 something for which you have a strong desire: *Her ambition is to be an astronaut.*

am·bi·tious (am bish′əs), *ADJECTIVE.* having ambition: *She was ambitious to become mayor and campaigned hard.* —**am·bi′tious·ly**, *ADVERB.*

am·bu·lance (am′byə ləns), *NOUN.* a vehicle equipped to carry sick or injured people.

am·bush (am′bush),
1 *NOUN.* a surprise attack on an enemy from some hiding place.
2 *NOUN.* a hidden place from which to attack: *The soldiers lay in ambush, waiting for a signal.*
3 *VERB.* to attack from a hiding place: *The bandits ambushed the stagecoach.*
❑ *PLURAL* **am·bush·es;** *VERB* **am·bush·es, am·bushed, am·bush·ing.**

a·me·ba (ə mē′bə), *NOUN.* a tiny one-celled living thing that moves by constantly changing its shape. Amebas are so small that they can be seen only with a microscope. ❑ *PLURAL* **a·me·bas.** Also spelled **amoeba.**

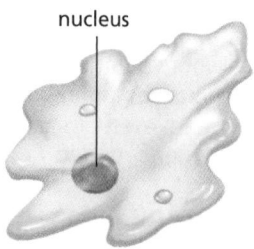

nucleus

ameba

a·men (ā′men′ or ä′men′), *INTERJECTION.* so be it; may it become true. *Amen* is said after a prayer, a wish, or a statement that you agree with.

a·mend (ə mend′), *VERB.*
1 to officially change: *The Constitution of the United States was amended so that women could vote.*
2 to change for the better; improve: *Officials made efforts to amend conditions in the crowded city.*
❑ *VERB* **a·mends, a·mend·ed, a·mend·ing.**

a·mend·ment (ə mend′mənt), *NOUN.* an official change: *The Constitution of the United States has over twenty amendments.*

Did You Know?

Two-thirds of Congress is needed to propose an **amendment** to the Constitution. Three-quarters of the states must approve of it before it becomes part of the Constitution.

a·mends (ə mendz′), *NOUN PLURAL.* **make amends,** to make up for some damage or mistake: *What can I do to make amends for being late?*

A·mer·i·ca (ə mer′ə kə), *NOUN.*
1 the United States of America.
2 North America.
3 North America and South America. The two continents are sometimes called **the Americas.**

Word Story

America is named after the Italian navigator **Amerigo Vespucci** (ə mer′ə gō ve spü′chē). A German map maker, believing that Vespucci was the first European to reach America, gave it his name in 1507.

A·mer·i·can (ə mer′ə kən),
1 *ADJECTIVE.* of or about the United States or its people; from the United States.
2 *NOUN.* someone born or living in the United States.
3 *ADJECTIVE.* of or about North America and South America or its people.
4 *NOUN.* someone born or living in North America or South America.

American Indian, one of the people who have lived in North or South America from long before the time of the first European settlers. ■ See the Usage Note at **Native American.**

Word Source

American Indian languages have given many words to English, because American Indians were the first to invent or see and name many things unknown to Europeans. The words below are some of the words that came into English from American Indian languages.

barbecue	iguana	poncho	squash[2]
cannibal	moccasin	potato	tomahawk
canoe	moose	powwow	totem pole
caribou	opossum	raccoon	wigwam
hammock	pecan	skunk	woodchuck

am·e·thyst (am′ə thist), *NOUN.* a purple or violet kind of quartz, used for jewelry.

a·mid (ə mid′), *PREPOSITION.* surrounded by; among: *Amid numerous foes, the knight fought bravely.*

a·midst (ə midst′), *PREPOSITION.* amid.

a·mi·go (ə mē′gō), *NOUN.* a friend. ❑ *PLURAL* **a·mi·gos.**

a·mi·no ac·id (ə mē′nō as′id), any of a group of complex organic compounds of nitrogen, hydrogen, carbon, and oxygen. Amino acids combine in various ways to form the proteins that make up living matter.

a·miss (ə mis′), *ADVERB* or *ADJECTIVE.* wrong; not the way it should be: *We knew something was amiss when the smoke alarm went off.*

am·mo·nia (ə mō′nyə), *NOUN.*
1 a colorless gas made up of nitrogen and hydrogen that has a strong smell. Ammonia is used in making fertilizers and plastics.
2 this gas dissolved in water. Ammonia is very useful for cleaning.

am·mu·ni·tion (am′yə nish′ən), *NOUN.* the bullets, shells, grenades, rockets, and bombs that can be exploded or fired from guns or other weapons.

am·ne·sia (am nē′zhə), *NOUN.* the loss of memory caused by injury to the brain, disease, or shock.

am·nes·ty (am′nə stē), *NOUN.* an official pardon for illegal acts. ❑ *PLURAL* **am·nes·ties.**

a·moe·ba (ə mē′bə), *NOUN.* another spelling of **ameba.** ❑ *PLURAL* **a·moe·bas.**

a·mong (ə mung′), *PREPOSITION.*
1 one of; in the group of: *The United States is among the largest countries in the world.*
2 with; in the company of: *They liked to spend time among friends.*
3 with a share for each of: *Divide the fruit among all of us.*
4 within the group of: *She had to choose from among the several law schools that accepted her.*
5 throughout: *Talk of revolution spread among the crowd.*
∎ See the Usage Note at **between.**

a·mount (ə mount′),
1 *NOUN.* the total sum: *What is the amount of the bill for the groceries?*
2 *NOUN.* a quantity or number of something: *No amount of coaxing made the dog leave its bone.*
3 *VERB.* to reach; add up: *The loss from the flood amounts to ten million dollars.*
4 *VERB.* to be equal to: *Keeping what belongs to another amounts to stealing.*
❑ *VERB* **a·mounts, a·mount·ed, a·mount·ing.**

amp (amp), *NOUN.*
1 an informal form of **amplifier.**
2 a short form of **ampere.**

am·pere (am′pir), *NOUN.* a unit for measuring the amount of an electric current.

am·phib·i·an (am fib′ē ən), *NOUN.*
1 any of many cold-blooded animals with backbones and moist skins without scales. Their young usually have gills and live in water until they develop lungs for living on land. Frogs and toads are amphibians.
2 a tank, truck, or other vehicle able to travel across land and water.

three kinds of **amphibians**

am·phib·i·ous (am fib′ē əs), *ADJECTIVE.* able to live both on land and in water: *Frogs are amphibious.*

am·phi·the·a·ter (am′fə thē′ə tər), *NOUN.* a circular or oval building with rows of seats around a central open space. Each row is higher than the one in front of it.

am·ple (am′pəl), *ADJECTIVE.*
1 more than enough: *We had ample time before the movie, so we stopped for a soda.*
2 large; roomy: *This house has ample closets.*
❑ *ADJECTIVE* **am·pler, am·plest.**

am·pli·fi·er (am′plə fī′ər), *NOUN.* a device in a radio, stereo, and so on, for strengthening electrical signals.

am·pli·fy (am′plə fī), *VERB.*
1 to make greater; make stronger: *amplified music.*
2 to add to; expand; enlarge: *Please amplify your description of the room by giving us more details.*
❑ *VERB* **am·pli·fies, am·pli·fied, am·pli·fy·ing.**

am·pu·tate (am′pyə tāt), *VERB.* to cut off all or part of an arm or leg. ❑ *VERB* **am·pu·tates, am·pu·tat·ed, am·pu·tat·ing. —am′pu·ta′tion,** *NOUN.*

am·u·let (am′yə lit), *NOUN.* some object worn as a magic charm against evil or harm: *The wizard gave him an amulet to protect him from dragons.*

a·muse (ə myüz′), *VERB.*
1 to cause to laugh or smile: *The clown's jokes and antics amused everyone.*

a	hat	ė	term	ô	order	ch	child	⎧ a in about
ā	age	i	it	oi	oil	ng	long	⎪ e in taken
ä	far	ī	ice	ou	out	sh	she	ə ⎨ i in pencil
â	care	o	hot	u	cup	th	thin	⎪ o in lemon
e	let	ō	open	u̇	put	ŦH	then	⎩ u in circus
ē	equal	ȯ	saw	ü	rule	zh	measure	

2 to keep pleasantly interested; entertain: *We amuse ourselves on rainy days with video games.*
❏ *VERB* **a•mus•es, a•mused, a•mus•ing.**

a•muse•ment (ə myüz′mənt), *NOUN.*
1 the condition of being amused: *The boy's amusement at the clowns was so great that we laughed with him.*
2 anything that amuses: *My parents' favorite amusement is going to the movies.*

amusement park, an outdoor place of entertainment with booths for games, various rides, and other amusements.

a•mus•ing (ə myü′zing), *ADJECTIVE.*
1 causing laughter or smiles: *The comedian told amusing jokes.* ■ See the Synonym Study at **funny.**
2 entertaining: *She read an amusing book.*

an (an), *INDEFINITE ARTICLE.*
1 any: *Is there an apple in the box?*
2 one: *I had an egg for breakfast.*
3 every: *He earns six dollars an hour.*
★ **An** is used in place of **a** before words that begin with vowels or that sound as if they begin with vowels.

anaconda — between 15 and 30 feet long

an•a•con•da (an′ə kon′də), *NOUN.* a very large South American snake that kills its prey by squeezing. Anacondas live in tropical forests and rivers and are the longest snakes in America, sometimes more than 30 feet long. ❏ *PLURAL* **an•a•con•das.**

Word Story

Anaconda comes from a mistake. About 300 years ago, European scientists learned this local name for a large snake of southeast Asia. About 200 years ago, a French scientist gave the name to a large snake he was studying, but his snake came from South America! So the name traveled thousands of miles and changed snakes in the process.

an•a•gram (an′ə gram), *NOUN.*
1 a word or phrase formed from another by rearranging the letters. *EXAMPLE:* roved—drove.
2 anagrams, *SINGULAR.* a game in which the players make words by changing and adding letters: *Anagrams is an interesting game.*

an•a•log (an′l og), *ADJECTIVE.* showing information with moving parts, instead of numbers: *an analog clock.*

a•nal•o•gy (ə nal′ə jē), *NOUN.*
1 likeness in some ways between things that are otherwise unlike; similarity: *The teacher made an analogy between the heart and a pump.*
2 a formal comparison between two parts that are related in the same way, such as, *"More is to less as loud is to soft."*
❏ *PLURAL* **a•nal•o•gies.**

a•nal•y•sis (ə nal′ə sis), *NOUN.*
1 separation of anything into its parts or elements to find out what it is made of. A chemical analysis of table salt shows that it is made up of two elements, sodium and chlorine.
2 a careful and detailed examination of something.
❏ *PLURAL* **a•nal•y•ses** (ə nal′ə sēz′).

an•a•lyze (an′l īz), *VERB.*
1 to examine carefully and in detail: *The newspaper article analyzed the results of the election.*
2 to separate anything into its parts or elements to find out what it is made of: *The chemistry teacher analyzed water into two gases, oxygen and hydrogen.*
❏ *VERB* **an•a•lyz•es, an•a•lyzed, an•a•lyz•ing.**

An•an•si or **An•an•se** (ä nän′sē), *NOUN.* (in west African myths) a tricky hero, often thought of as a spider.

an•ar•chy (an′ər kē), *NOUN.* the complete lack of a system of government and law.

a•nat•o•my (ə nat′ə mē), *NOUN.*
1 the science of the structure of living things. Anatomy is a part of biology.
2 the structure of a living thing: *The anatomy of an earthworm is much simpler than that of a dog. She studies plant anatomy.*
❏ *PLURAL* **a•nat•o•mies.**

an•ces•tor (an′ses′tər), *NOUN.* someone from whom you are directly descended. Your grandfathers and your grandmothers are ancestors.

an•ces•tral (an ses′trəl), *ADJECTIVE.* of or from ancestors: *England was the ancestral home of the Pilgrims.*

an•ces•try (an′ses′trē), *NOUN.* ancestors: *Many early settlers in California had Spanish ancestry.* ❏ *PLURAL* **an•ces•tries.**

an•chor (ang′kər),
1 *NOUN.* a heavy piece of iron or steel or other heavy weight, fastened to a chain or rope and dropped into the water to hold a ship or boat in place: *The anchor kept the boat from drifting.*
2 *VERB.* to hold in place with an anchor: *Can you anchor the boat in this storm?*
3 *VERB.* to set in place; attach firmly: *The campers anchored their tent to the ground.*
4 *NOUN.* someone on a television or radio program who announces news and coordinates reports from correspondents.
❏ *VERB* **an•chors, an•chored, an•chor•ing.**

an·cho·vy (an′chō vē), NOUN. a very small fish with a strong taste. Anchovies are often used as a pizza topping. ❑ PLURAL **an·cho·vies.**

an·cient (ān′shənt), ADJECTIVE.
1 belonging to times long past: *They found the ruins of an ancient temple built over 6000 years ago.*
2 of great age; very old: *Rome is an ancient city.*

Synonym Study

Ancient means very old. It is mostly used to describe things and people that existed a very long time ago: *Great temples and cities were built by the ancient Maya.*

Antique means of former times. It always describes things: *My parents like antique cars from the 1920s and 1930s.*

Outdated and **out-of-date** mean not in present use: *Outdated farm machinery was displayed at the museum. My address book has some out-of-date phone numbers in it.*

Old-fashioned means out-of-date in style, working, thinking, or behaving: *Old-fashioned plows were pulled by mules.*

Prehistoric means from the time before there was written history: *At the museum, we saw prehistoric tools made out of rocks.*

and (and), CONJUNCTION.
1 as well as; also: *Yesterday we went to the beach and to the zoo.*
2 added to; with: *4 and 2 make 6. I like ham and eggs.*
3 as a result: *The sun came out and the grass dried.*

An·des (an′dēz), NOUN PLURAL. a mountain range in western South America.

an·droid (an′droid), NOUN. a robot that resembles a human being.

an·ec·dote (an′ik dōt), NOUN. a short account of some interesting incident or event: *Many anecdotes are told about Abraham Lincoln.*

a·ne·mi·a (ə nē′mē ə), NOUN. a lack of red blood cells. Anemia causes people to feel weak and tired.

a·ne·mic (ə nē′mik), ADJECTIVE. having anemia.

an·e·mom·e·ter (an′ə mom′ə tər), NOUN. a device for measuring the speed of wind.

an·es·the·sia (an′əs thē′zhə), NOUN. loss of the ability to feel pain during an operation because of a drug that you are given.

an·es·thet·ic (an′əs thet′ik), NOUN. a substance that causes a loss of feeling in all or part of the body.

android

Dentists and surgeons use anesthetics so that patients will feel no pain.

a·new (ə nü′), ADVERB. again; once more: *I made so many mistakes that I had to begin my work anew.*

an·gel (ān′jəl), NOUN.
1 a messenger from God.
2 someone who is good, kind, or beautiful.

an·gel·fish (ān′jəl fish′), NOUN. a brightly colored tropical fish that has a thin body and long, pointed fins. ❑ PLURAL **an·gel·fish** or **an·gel·fish·es.**

an·gel·ic (an jel′ik), ADJECTIVE. like an angel; good, kind, or beautiful: *The baby had an angelic face.*

an·ger (ang′gər),
1 NOUN. the feeling that you have toward someone or something that hurts, upsets, or annoys: *His anger disappeared when she apologized.*
2 VERB. to feel or cause someone else to feel this way: *The girl's rudeness to her grandmother angered her parents.*
❑ VERB **an·gers, an·gered, an·ger·ing.**

an·gle (ang′gəl),
1 NOUN. the space between two lines or surfaces that meet.
2 NOUN. the figure formed by two such lines or surfaces.
3 VERB. to move or bend at an angle: *The road angles to the right here.*
4 NOUN. a point of view: *We are treating the problem from a new angle.*
❑ VERB **an·gles, an·gled, an·gling.**

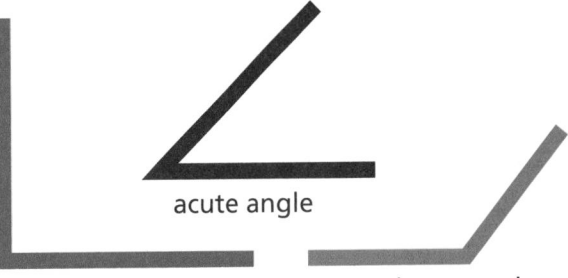

acute angle

right angle   obtuse angle

angles

An·go·la (ang gō′lə), NOUN. a country in southwest Africa. **−An·go′lan,** ADJECTIVE or NOUN.

an·gry (ang′grē), ADJECTIVE.
1 feeling or showing anger: *My parents were very angry when I disobeyed them.* ■ See the Synonym Study at **mad.**
2 stormy; threatening: *an angry sky, angry waves.*
❑ ADJECTIVE **an·gri·er, an·gri·est. −an′gri·ly,** ADVERB.

a	hat	ė	term	ô	order	ch	child		a in about
ā	age	i	it	oi	oil	ng	long		e in taken
ä	far	ī	ice	ou	out	sh	she	ə{	i in pencil
â	care	o	hot	u	cup	th	thin		o in lemon
e	let	ō	open	ů	put	ŦH	then		u in circus
ē	equal	ò	saw	ü	rule	zh	measure		

an·guish (ang′gwish), NOUN. very great pain or grief: *His broken leg caused great anguish.*

an·i·mal (an′ə məl), NOUN.
1 any living thing that contains many cells and that can move about. Most animals eat other living things, breathe oxygen, and have a nervous system. Dogs, birds, fish, snakes, flies, and worms are animals.
2 an animal other than a human being.

Word Bank

There are many special terms for groups of animals. You may already know that we say *herd* for groups of elephants, deer, camels, cattle, goats, oxen, seals, and some other animals. Here are some other terms that are special for a particular animal.

a colony of ants	a pride of lions
a swarm of bees	a crash of rhinoceroses
a murder of crows	a flock of sheep
a pack of dogs	a knot of toads
a school of fish	a pod of whales
a troop of kangaroos	a pack of wolves

an·i·mat·ed (an′ə mā′tid), ADJECTIVE. lively; full of life and spirit: *The class had an animated discussion.*

animated cartoon, a series of drawings arranged to be photographed and shown as a movie. Each drawing shows a slight change from the one before it. When they are shown in rapid sequence the figures appear to move.

an·i·mos·i·ty (an′ə mos′ə tē), NOUN. hatred; dislike: *The principals held an assembly to reduce the animosity between the rival schools.* ❑ PLURAL **an·i·mos·i·ties.**

an·ise (an′is), NOUN. a plant grown especially for its seeds, which taste like licorice.

an·kle (ang′kəl), NOUN. the joint that connects the foot with the leg.

an·ky·lo·saur (ang′kə lō sôr′), NOUN. a dinosaur that had bony plates and spikes covering its body. It had short legs and ate plants.

An·na·po·lis (ə nap′ə lis), NOUN. the capital of Maryland.

an·nex (ə neks′ *for verb;* an′eks *for noun*),
1 VERB. to join or add a smaller thing to a larger thing: *The United States annexed Texas in 1845.*
2 NOUN. something annexed; an added part, especially to a building: *We are building an annex to the school.* ❑ VERB **an·nex·es, an·nexed, an·nex·ing;** PLURAL **an·nex·es. —an′nex·a′tion,** NOUN.

an·ni·hi·late (ə nī′ə lāt), VERB. to destroy completely; wipe out of existence: *An avalanche annihilated the village.* ❑ VERB **an·ni·hi·lates, an·ni·hi·lat·ed, an·ni·hi·lat·ing. —an·ni′hi·la′tion,** NOUN.

an·ni·ver·sar·y (an′ə vėr′sər ē), NOUN. the yearly return of a special date: *Your birthday is an anniversary you like to have remembered.* ❑ PLURAL **an·ni·ver·sar·ies.**

an·nounce (ə nouns′), VERB.
1 to give public or formal notice of: *The teacher announced a spelling contest.*
2 to introduce programs, read news, and make announcements on radio or TV.
❑ VERB **an·nounc·es, an·nounced, an·nounc·ing.**

an·nounce·ment (ə nouns′mənt), NOUN. a public or formal notice: *The principal made an announcement at the assembly.*

an·nounc·er (ə noun′sər), NOUN. someone who makes announcements, introduces programs and reads news on radio or TV.

an·noy (ə noi′), VERB. to make somewhat angry; disturb: *Radio ads annoy me.* ❑ VERB **an·noys, an·noyed, an·noy·ing.**

an·noy·ance (ə noi′əns), NOUN.
1 a feeling of slight anger or impatience: *He showed his annoyance at us by slamming the door.*
2 something that annoys: *The heavy traffic on our street is an annoyance.*

an·nu·al (an′yü əl),
1 ADJECTIVE. coming once a year: *Your birthday is an annual event.*
2 ADJECTIVE. in a year; for a year: *For the last two years her annual salary has been $27,000.*
3 ADJECTIVE. living only one year or season: *Corn and beans are annual plants.*
4 NOUN. a plant that lives only one year or season. **—an′nu·al·ly,** ADVERB.

ankylosaur — about 30 feet long, including the tail

annual ring, any of the rings of wood seen when the trunk of a tree is cut through. Each ring shows one year's growth.

a·noint (ə noint′), VERB. to put oil on a person as part of a ceremony: *The bishop anointed the new king.* ❑ VERB **a·noints, a·noint·ed, a·noint·ing.**

A

a·non·y·mous (ə non′ə məs), *ADJECTIVE.* by or from someone whose name is not known or given: *an anonymous donor.* **—a·non′y·mous·ly,** *ADVERB.*

an·oth·er (ə nuᴛн′ər),
1 *ADJECTIVE* or *PRONOUN.* one more: *She ate a piece of candy and then asked for another.*
2 *ADJECTIVE.* different: *Show me another kind of hat.*
3 *PRONOUN.* a different one: *I don't like this book; give me another.*

an·swer (an′sər),
1 *VERB.* to say or write something when a question is asked: *She answered three questions out of four.*
2 *NOUN.* the words said or written when a question is asked: *I wrote the answers in ink.*
3 *VERB.* to do something when someone calls or knocks: *When the phone rang, I answered it.*
4 *NOUN.* the solution to a problem: *What is the correct answer to this arithmetic problem?*
5 *VERB.* to be responsible: *The bus driver must answer for the safety of the children in the bus.*
6 *VERB.* to agree with; correspond: *The dog we found answers to your description.*
   ❏ *VERB* **an·swers, an·swered, an·swer·ing.**

Synonym Study

Answer means something that you say or write when someone asks a question: *When the teacher asks a question about science, I nearly always give the right answer.*

Reply means an answer. It is a somewhat more formal word. It may suggest that the answer is a careful and complete one: *When his mother asked the prices of new cars, the salesman gave her a reply with exact figures.*

Response means an answer. It is used about actions and about words: *The firefighters' response to the alarm was so quick that their truck arrived in five minutes.*

ANTONYM: question.

answering machine, a device that answers telephone calls automatically, records messages, and plays the messages back when you want.

ant (ant), *NOUN.* any of many kinds of small crawling insects living in large colonies. Ants are black, brown, reddish, or yellowish. ■ Another word that can sound like this is **aunt.**
   —ant′like′, *ADJECTIVE.*

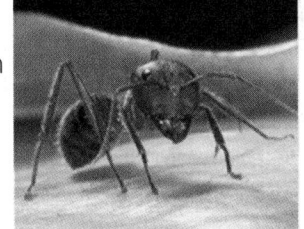

ant — less than an inch long

an·tag·o·nism (an tag′ə niz′əm), *NOUN.* active opposition; hostility: *During the argument, the boy's antagonism showed in his face.*

an·tag·o·nize (an tag′ə nīz), *VERB.* to make an enemy of; arouse dislike in: *Her unkind remarks antagonized people who had been her friends.*
   ❏ *VERB* **an·tag·o·niz·es, an·tag·o·nized, an·tag·o·niz·ing.**

ant·arc·tic (ant′ärk′tik or ant′är′tik),
1 *ADJECTIVE.* at or near the South Pole; of the south polar region.
2 *NOUN.* **the Antarctic,** the south polar region.

Ant·arc·ti·ca (ant′ärk′tə kə or ant′är′tə kə), *NOUN.* the continent around the South Pole.

Did You Know?

Antarctica is almost totally covered by ice. The world's lowest temperature was recorded in Antarctica in July 1983: 128.6 degrees Fahrenheit below zero!

ant·eat·er (ant′ē′tər), *NOUN.* a hairy animal about as big as a large dog. It has a long, narrow head and powerful claws. Anteaters dig up ants and termites and catch them with their long, sticky tongues.

anteater — about 6 feet long, including the tail

an·te·lope (an′tl ōp), *NOUN.*
1 an animal of Africa and Asia that chews its cud and has hoofs. It is like the deer in appearance, grace, and speed but is related to goats and cows.
2 an animal like this, found on the plains of western North America; pronghorn.
   ❏ *PLURAL* **an·te·lope** or **an·te·lopes.**

an·ten·na (an ten′ə), *NOUN.*
1 one of the long, slender feelers on the heads of insects, crabs, lobsters, and shrimp. ★ Another plural for this meaning is **an·ten·nae** (an ten′ē).
2 the device used in television or radio for sending out or receiving sounds and pictures; aerial. Antennas may be large dish-shaped structures, sets of narrow rods, or simple lengths of wire.
   ❏ *PLURAL* **an·ten·nas.**

an·them (an′thəm), *NOUN.* a song of praise or patriotism: *"The Star-Spangled Banner" is our national anthem. Some people want to change our anthem to "America the Beautiful."*

an·ther (an′thər), *NOUN.* the top part of the stamen of a flower. The anthers produce the pollen.

a hat	ė term	ô order	ch child
ā age	i it	oi oil	ng long
ä far	ī ice	ou out	sh she
â care	o hot	u cup	th thin
e let	ō open	ů put	ᴛн then
ē equal	ò saw	ü rule	zh measure

ə { a in about / e in taken / i in pencil / o in lemon / u in circus }

Ants

Ants are social insects that live in large groups called colonies. There are at least 20,000 kinds of ants throughout the world. They live in every area of the earth except for the coldest regions. Scientists believe that ants developed over 100 million years ago.

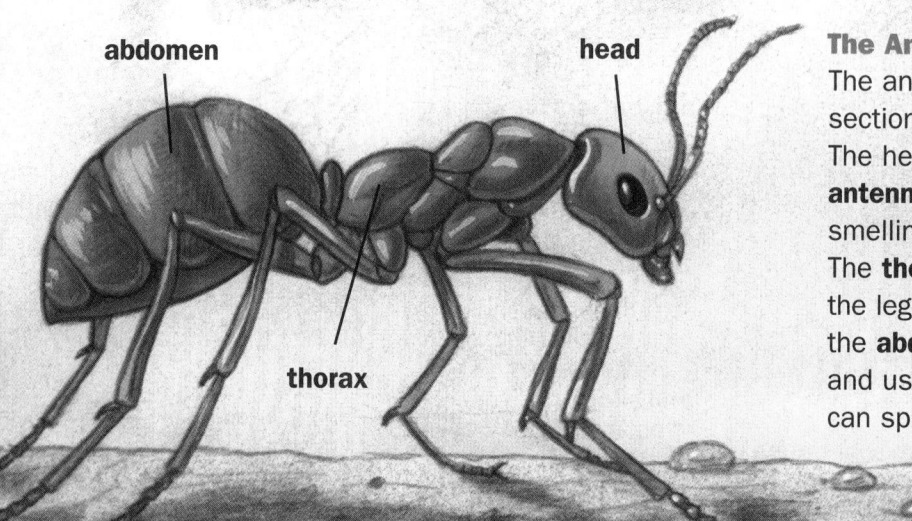

abdomen

head

thorax

The Ant's Body

The ant's body is divided into three sections, as all insect bodies are. The head contains the eyes and the **antennae,** which are organs used for smelling, tasting, and touching things. The **thorax** is the middle section, where the legs are attached. The final section, the **abdomen,** contains digestive organs and usually a stinger or a gland that can spray poison at an enemy.

Leafcutter ants of Central and South America chew off pieces of leaves, which they carry to their nests to use as gardening material to grow a kind of fungus that is their food.

Honey ants use some of their own worker ants as storage pots for honey. When an ant is hungry, it will come to one of the swollen storage ants clinging to the roof of the colony, and take a drink of honey from it.

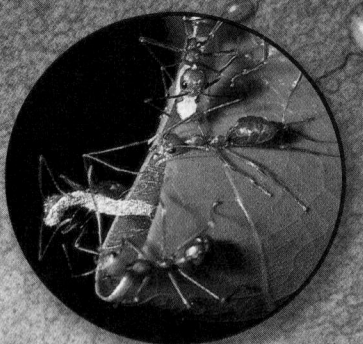

Weaver ants use the silk spun by their larvae to glue leaves together and make nests. These ants carry their larvae to the place where they are working. The larvae deposit sticky silk when the ants squeeze them.

The Ant's Home

Some ants create an underground nest by digging into the soil. They make rooms connected by tunnels. Each room has a special purpose.

A The queen lays her eggs and is fed by workers in this room.

B This room is used for the care and feeding of the larvae.

C This room is used for the care of pupae inside their cocoons.

D Worker ants rest in this room.

Gerrity-98

ant·hill (ant′hil′), NOUN. a heap of earth piled up by ants around the entrance to their tunnels.

an·thol·o·gy (an thol′ə jē), NOUN. a collection of poems, stories, or other writings, usually from various authors. ❑ PLURAL **an·thol·o·gies.**

an·thra·cite (an′thrə sīt), NOUN. a kind of coal that burns with very little smoke and flame; hard coal.

an·thro·pol·o·gy (an′thrə pol′ə jē), NOUN. the science or study of human beings, dealing especially with their fossil remains, physical characteristics, cultures, customs, and beliefs. **—an′thro·pol′o·gist,** NOUN.

Word Power   anti-

The prefix **anti-** means "against" or "preventing." **Antislavery** means **against** slavery. **Antifreeze prevents** freezing. **Antipollution** means **preventing** pollution.

an·ti·bi·ot·ic (an′ti bī ot′ik), NOUN. a substance produced that destroys or weakens germs.

an·ti·bod·y (an′ti bod′ē), NOUN. a substance in the blood that destroys or weakens germs and other harmful matter that enter the body. Antibodies help prevent infection. ❑ PLURAL **an·ti·bod·ies.**

an·tic·i·pate (an tis′ə pāt), VERB.
1 to look forward to; expect: *We are anticipating a good time at your party.*
2 to take care of ahead of time; consider in advance: *A good host anticipates his guests' wishes.* ❑ VERB **an·tic·i·pates, an·tic·i·pat·ed, an·tic·i·pat·ing.**

an·tic·i·pa·tion (an tis′ə pā′shən), NOUN. the act of looking forward to something. expectation: *In anticipation of a cold winter, they bought new gloves.*

an·tics (an′tiks), NOUN. funny gestures or actions: *The clown's antics amused the audience.*

an·ti·dote (an′ti dōt), NOUN. a medicine that acts against the harmful effects of a poison; remedy: *The doctor gave him the antidote quickly.*

an·ti·freeze (an′ti frēz′), NOUN. a substance added to the water in a car radiator to prevent freezing.

an·ti·gen (an′tə jən), NOUN. any substance from outside your body that causes the production of antibodies to protect you. Antigens can be bacteria, viruses, poisons, and so on.

an·ti·lock brakes (an′ti lok′ brāks′), brakes that help keep a car or truck from skidding. Antilock brakes are made so that brake pressure is applied to the wheels very briefly, over and over.

an·tique (an tēk′),
1 ADJECTIVE. of times long ago; from times long ago: *This antique chair was made in 1750.* ■ See the Synonym Study at **ancient.**
2 NOUN. something made long ago: *This carved chest is a genuine antique.* ❑ PLURAL **an·tiques.**

an·ti·sep·tic (an′tə sep′tik), NOUN. a substance that prevents the growth of germs that cause infection. Iodine and alcohol are antiseptics.

an·ti·tox·in (an′ti tok′sən), NOUN.
1 a kind of antibody that can prevent certain diseases, cure them, or make them milder.
2 a serum that contains an antitoxin. It is injected into people to protect them from a disease.

ant·ler (ant′lər), NOUN. a bony, branching growth on the head of a male deer, elk, or moose. Antlers grow in pairs and are shed once a year.

an·to·nym (an′tə nim), NOUN. a word that means the opposite of another word: *"True" is the antonym of "false" and "in" is the antonym of "out."*

an·vil (an′vəl), NOUN. an iron or steel block on which blacksmiths hammer and shape metal.

anx·i·e·ty (ang zī′ə tē), NOUN. uneasy thoughts or fears about what may happen; an uneasy feeling: *We were filled with anxiety when our airplane was caught in a storm.* ❑ PLURAL **anx·i·e·ties.**

anx·ious (angk′shəs), ADJECTIVE.
1 uneasy because of thoughts or fears of what may happen; troubled; worried: *The week of the flood was an anxious time for all of us.*
2 eager; wishing very much: *I was anxious to begin.* **—anx′ious·ly,** ADVERB.

an·y (en′ē),
1 ADJECTIVE. one out of many: *Choose any book you like from the books on the shelf.*
2 ADJECTIVE or PRONOUN. some: *I looked for fresh fruit, but I couldn't find any.*
3 ADJECTIVE. every: *Any child knows that.*
4 ADVERB. by some amount: *Has my singing improved any?*

an·y·bod·y (en′ē bud′ē or en′ē bə dē), PRONOUN. any person; anyone: *Has anybody been here?*

an·y·how (en′ē hou′), ADVERB. in any case; at any rate; anyway: *I can see as well as you can, anyhow.*

an·y·more (en′ē môr′), ADVERB. any longer; now: *He doesn't smoke anymore.* ■ See the Usage Note at **anyone.**

an·y·one (en′ē wun′), PRONOUN. any person; anybody: *Does anyone have an extra pencil?*

Usage Note

People sometimes confuse **anyone** and the two-word phrase **any one.** Anyone is written as one word when the accent is on **any:** *Can anyone tell me where they went?* It is written as two words when the accent is on **one:** *I'd like any one of those shirts.* The same is true of other words and phrases with **any,** including **anymore, anyplace, anything, anytime,** and **anyway.**

an·y·place (en′ē plās′), ADVERB. anywhere: *Put the book down anyplace.* ■ See the Usage Note at **anyone.**

an·y·thing (en′ē thing′),
  1 ADVERB. in any way or at all: *My bike isn't anything like yours.*
  2 PRONOUN. any thing: *Do you have anything to eat?*
  ■ See the Usage Note at **anyone**.

an·y·time (en′ē tīm′), ADVERB. at any time: *You are welcome to visit us anytime.* ■ See the Usage Note at **anyone**.

an·y·way (en′ē wā′), ADVERB. in any case: *I am coming anyway, no matter what you say.* ■ See the Usage Note at **anyone**.

an·y·where (en′ē wer′), ADVERB. in, at, or to any place: *I'll meet you anywhere you say.*

a·or·ta (ā ôr′tə), NOUN. the main artery that carries the blood from the left side of the heart to all parts of the body except the lungs. ❑ PLURAL **a·or·tas**.

A·pach·e (ə pach′ē), NOUN. a member of a tribe of American Indians living in the southwestern United States. ❑ PLURAL **A·pach·e** or **A·pach·es**.

a·part (ə pärt′), ADVERB.
  1 to pieces; in pieces; in separate parts: *She took the watch apart to see how it runs.*
  2 away from each other: *Keep the dogs apart.*
  tell apart, IDIOM. to see any difference between: *I can't tell the twins apart.*

a·part·ment (ə pärt′mənt), NOUN. a room or group of rooms to live in. An **apartment house** is a building with several apartments in it.

a·pat·o·sau·rus (ə pat′ə sôr′əs), NOUN. a huge, plant-eating dinosaur with a very long neck and a tail; brontosaurus. ❑ PLURAL **a·pat·o·sau·rus·es** or **a·pat·o·sau·ri** (ə pat′ə sôr′ī).

Word Story

Apatosaurus comes from Greek words meaning "to deceive" and "lizard," because its bones look like the bones of another dinosaur, and scientists were deceived when they first identified it. **Apatosaurus** is the scientific name because it was given by the first discoverer.

ape (āp),
  1 NOUN. a large, tailless animal like a monkey, with long arms. Chimpanzees and gorillas are apes.
  2 VERB. to imitate; mimic: *The children aped the way the TV star talked.*
  ❑ VERB **apes**, **aped**, **ap·ing**. **–ape′like′**, ADJECTIVE.

a·phid (ā′fid or af′id), NOUN. a very small insect that lives by sucking juices from plants.

a·piece (ə pēs′), ADVERB. for each one; each: *These apples cost fifty cents apiece.*

a·pol·o·gize (ə pol′ə jīz), VERB. to make an apology; say one is sorry: *I apologized for being so late.*
  ❑ VERB **a·pol·o·giz·es**, **a·pol·o·gized**, **a·pol·o·giz·ing**. **–a·pol′o·giz′er**, NOUN.

a·pol·o·gy (ə pol′ə jē), NOUN. words saying that you are sorry; explanation asking forgiveness. ❑ PLURAL **a·pol·o·gies**.

a·pos·tle or **A·pos·tle** (ə pos′əl), NOUN. one of the twelve special followers of Jesus. He chose them to spread His teachings everywhere.

a·pos·tro·phe (ə pos′trə fē), NOUN. a sign (′) used:
  1 to show the omission of one or more letters in contractions, as in *isn't* for *is not*, *tho′* for *though*.
  2 to show the possessive forms of nouns, as in *Lee's book*, *the lions′ den*.
  3 to form plurals of letters and numbers: *There are two o's in apology and four 9's in 959,990.*
  ❑ PLURAL **a·pos·tro·phes**.

Ap·pa·la·chian Moun·tains (ap′ə lā′chən moun′tənz), a group of mountains in the eastern United States and Canada.

ap·pall (ə pȯl′), VERB. to fill with horror or fear; dismay; terrify: *She was appalled by the violence.* ❑ VERB **ap·palls**, **ap·palled**, **ap·pall·ing**.

Ap·pa·loo·sa (ap′ə lü′sə), NOUN. a horse with dark spots, usually on the rump, on a white or gray background. ❑ PLURAL **Ap·pa·loo·sas**.

Appaloosa — about 5 feet high at the shoulder

apatosaurus — about 70 feet long, including the tail

a	hat		ė	term		ô	order		ch	child		⎧ a in about
ā	age		i	it		oi	oil		ng	long		⎪ e in taken
ä	far		ī	ice		ou	out		sh	she		ə ⎨ i in pencil
â	care		o	hot		u	cup		th	thin		⎪ o in lemon
e	let		ō	open		ù	put		ᴛʜ	then		⎩ u in circus
ē	equal		ȯ	saw		ü	rule		zh	measure		

ap·pa·ra·tus (ap′ə rā′təs or ap′ə rat′əs), NOUN. anything necessary to carry out a purpose or for a particular use: *A helmet is part of a firefighter's apparatus.* ❏ PLURAL **ap·pa·ra·tus** or **ap·pa·ra·tus·es.**

ap·par·el (ə par′əl), NOUN. clothing: *men's apparel.*

ap·par·ent (ə pâr′ənt), ADJECTIVE.
1 easy to see or understand: *It was apparent from the way she walked that she was very tired.*
2 seeming; appearing to be: *With half the votes counted, he was the apparent winner.*
—**ap·par′ent·ly,** ADVERB.

ap·peal (ə pēl′),
1 VERB. to make an earnest request; ask for help or sympathy: *When the children were in trouble they appealed to their parents for help.*
2 NOUN. an earnest request; call for help or sympathy: *An appeal for aid for the flood victims was broadcast on TV.*
3 VERB. to ask that a case be taken to a higher court or judge to be heard again: *When the judge ruled against them, they decided to appeal.*
4 NOUN. a request to have a case heard again before a higher court: *Their appeal was granted.*
5 VERB. to be attractive, interesting, or enjoyable: *Blue and red colors appeal to me.* ■ See the Synonym Study at **cute.**
6 NOUN. an attraction or interest: *Fads soon lose their appeal.*
❏ VERB **ap·peals, ap·pealed, ap·peal·ing.**

ap·pear (ə pir′), VERB.
1 to come into sight or presence: *One by one the stars appear. She suddenly appeared at the window.*
2 to seem; look: *The apple appeared sound on the outside, but it was rotten inside.*
3 to show or present yourself in public: *The singer will appear in concert today.*
❏ VERB **ap·pears, ap·peared, ap·pear·ing.**

ap·pear·ance (ə pir′əns), NOUN.
1 the act of coming into sight or presence: *His sudden appearance in the hall startled me.*
2 the act of coming before the public as a performer or author: *The singer made her first appearance in a concert in Paris.*
3 the way someone or something looks: *I knew from his appearance that he was ill.*

ap·pease (ə pēz′), VERB.
1 to satisfy: *A good dinner will appease your hunger.*
2 to make calm; quiet: *I tried to appease the crying child by giving him candy.*
❏ VERB **ap·peas·es, ap·peased, ap·peas·ing.**

ap·pen·di·ci·tis (ə pen′də sī′tis), NOUN. a soreness and swelling of the appendix.

ap·pen·dix (ə pen′diks), NOUN.
1 a slender, closed tube growing out of the large intestine.

2 an addition at the end of a book or document. ❏ PLURAL **ap·pen·dix·es** or **ap·pen·di·ces** (ə pen′də sēz′).

ap·pe·tite (ap′ə tīt), NOUN.
1 a desire for food: *Activity increases my appetite.*
2 a desire: *They have a great appetite for adventure.*

ap·pe·tiz·er (ap′ə tī′zər), NOUN. something that arouses the appetite, usually served before a meal. Pickles and olives are appetizers.

ap·pe·tiz·ing (ap′ə tī′zing), ADJECTIVE. arousing or exciting the appetite; pleasing to the taste: *Appetizing food always smells delicious.*

ap·plaud (ə plȯd′), VERB. to show approval by clapping hands or shouting: *The audience applauded at the end of the play.* ❏ VERB **ap·plauds, ap·plaud·ed, ap·plaud·ing.**

ap·plause (ə plȯz′), NOUN. approval shown by clapping the hands or shouting: *Applause for the singer's performance rang out from the audience.*

ap·ple (ap′əl), NOUN. a round, firm fruit that has white flesh, grown on a small tree. Apples may be red, yellow, green, or a combination of colors.

apple of someone's eye, IDIOM. someone or something that is loved very much: *His granddaughter is the apple of his eye.*

apple

Have You Heard?

You may have heard someone say that two things are **"like apples and oranges."** This means that the two things are so different that they cannot be compared in any useful way.

ap·ple·sauce (ap′əl sȯs′), NOUN. apples cooked with sugar, spices, and water until soft.

ap·pli·ance (ə plī′əns), NOUN. a device or machine designed for a particular purpose or operation. Blenders and refrigerators are appliances. ■ See the Synonym Study at **tool.**

ap·pli·ca·ble (ap′lə kə bəl), ADJECTIVE. capable of being applied; able to be put to practical use; appropriate; suitable: *The rule "Look before you leap" is almost always applicable.*

ap·pli·cant (ap′lə kənt), NOUN. someone who applies for something, such as a loan, a job, or admission to a school.

ap·pli·ca·tion (ap′lə kā′shēn), NOUN.
1 a request made in person or in writing: *I put in an application for a job at the supermarket.*
2 the act of putting to use: *The application of what you know will help you solve new problems.*

3 the act of applying; putting on: *The painter's careless application of paint spattered the floor.*

4 a computer program made for a particular use: *I bought a new graphing application.*

ap·ply (ə plī′), VERB.
1 to formally ask for: *He is applying for a job as clerk.*
2 to use: *I don't know how to apply this rule.*
3 to put on: *He applied two coats of paint to the table.*
4 to be useful or suitable; fit: *Does this rule apply?*
5 to set to work and stick to it: *She applied herself to learning to play the piano.*
❑ VERB **ap·plies, ap·plied, ap·ply·ing.**

ap·point (ə point′), VERB. to name for an office or position; officially choose: *The mayor appointed two new members to the school board.* ❑ VERB **ap·points, ap·point·ed, ap·point·ing.**

ap·point·ment (ə point′mənt), NOUN.
1 a meeting with someone at a certain time and place; engagement: *I have an appointment to see the doctor at four o'clock.*
2 the act of naming someone to an office or position; choosing: *The President announced the appointment of a new secretary of state.*

ap·praise (ə prāz′), VERB.
1 to estimate the value, amount, or quality of: *An employer should be able to appraise an employee's work.*
2 to set a price on; fix the value of: *The jeweler appraised the diamond ring at $2000.*
❑ VERB **ap·prais·es, ap·praised, ap·prais·ing.** —**ap·prais′er,** NOUN.

ap·pre·ci·ate (ə prē′shē āt), VERB.
1 to think highly of; recognize the worth of; value; enjoy: *Almost everybody appreciates good food. Most of us appreciate the importance of exercise.*
2 to be thankful for: *We appreciate your help.*
❑ VERB **ap·pre·ci·ates, ap·pre·ci·at·ed, ap·pre·ci·at·ing.**

ap·pre·ci·a·tion (ə prē′shē ā′shən), NOUN.
1 thankfulness; gratitude: *I showed my appreciation of her help by sending a letter of thanks.*
2 an understanding of the worth of something; recognition of something's value: *She has no appreciation of modern art.*

ap·pre·hend (ap′ri hend′), VERB.
1 to arrest; seize: *The burglars were apprehended by the police.*
2 to grasp with the mind; understand: *I could apprehend his meaning from his gestures alone.*
❑ VERB **ap·pre·hends, ap·pre·hend·ed, ap·pre·hend·ing.**

ap·pre·hen·sion (ap′ri hen′shən), NOUN.
1 fear; dread: *The roar of the hurricane filled us with apprehension.*
2 the act of seizing; arrest: *The appearance of the suspect's picture on TV led to her apprehension.*

ap·pren·tice (ə pren′tis),
1 NOUN. someone who is learning a trade or an art by working with a skilled worker.
2 VERB. to place or take as an apprentice: *Benjamin Franklin's father apprenticed him to a printer.*
❑ VERB **ap·pren·tic·es, ap·pren·ticed, ap·pren·tic·ing.**

ap·proach (ə prōch′),
1 VERB. to come near or nearer: *Walk softly as you approach the baby's crib. Winter is approaching.*
2 NOUN. the act of coming near or nearer: *Sirens warned us of the approach of the fire engine.*
3 NOUN. a way by which a place or person can be reached; access: *The approach to the house was a narrow path.*
4 NOUN. a method of starting work on a task or problem: *a good approach to the problem.*
❑ VERB **ap·proach·es, ap·proached, ap·proach·ing;** PLURAL **ap·proach·es.** —**ap·proach′a·ble,** ADJECTIVE.

ap·pro·pri·ate (ə prō′prē it *for adjective;* ə prō′prē āt *for verb*),
1 ADJECTIVE. suitable; proper: *Clean, comfortable clothes are appropriate for school.*
2 VERB. to set apart for some special use: *The state appropriated money for a new road into our town.*
❑ VERB **ap·pro·pri·ates, ap·pro·pri·at·ed, ap·pro·pri·at·ing.** —**ap·pro′pri·ate·ly,** ADVERB. —**ap·pro′pri·a·tion,** NOUN.

ap·prov·al (ə prü′vəl), NOUN.
1 a favorable opinion: *We all like others to show approval of what we do.*
2 permission: *Get your parents' approval for the trip. I had their approval to go.*

ap·prove (ə prüv′), VERB.
1 to have a favorable opinion of; be pleased with: *I do not approve of what you plan to do.*
2 to give permission for: *The school board approved next year's budget.*
❑ VERB **ap·proves, ap·proved, ap·prov·ing.**

ap·prox·i·mate (ə prok′sə mit *for adjective;* ə prok′sə māt *for verb*),
1 ADJECTIVE. nearly correct: *The approximate length of this room is 12 feet; the exact length is 12 feet 1 inch.*
2 VERB. to come near to; approach: *The crowd approximated a thousand people.*
❑ VERB **ap·prox·i·mates, ap·prox·i·mat·ed, ap·prox·i·mat·ing.**

ap·prox·i·mate·ly (ə prok′sə mit lē), ADVERB. nearly; about: *We are approximately 200 miles from home.*

Apr., an abbreviation of **April.**

a	hat	ė	term	ô	order	ch	child		a in about
ā	age	i	it	oi	oil	ng	long		e in taken
ä	far	ī	ice	ou	out	sh	she	ə {	i in pencil
â	care	o	hot	u	cup	th	thin		o in lemon
e	let	ō	open	ů	put	ⱦH	then		u in circus
ē	equal	ò	saw	ü	rule	zh	measure		

a·pri·cot (ā′prə kot *or* ap′rə kot), NOUN. a tasty, round, yellowish orange fruit that grows on a tree. Apricots are smaller than peaches.

A·pril (ā′prəl), NOUN. the fourth month of the year. It has 30 days.

April Fools' Day, April 1, a day on which tricks and jokes are played on people.

a·pron (ā′prən), NOUN. a piece of clothing worn over the front part of the body to cover or protect clothes: *I put on a kitchen apron when I started cooking.*

a·quar·i·um (ə kwâr′ē əm), NOUN.
1 a tank or glass bowl in which living fish or other water animals and water plants are kept.
2 a building used for showing collections of living fish, water animals, and water plants.

a·quat·ic (ə kwat′ik *or* ə kwät′ik), ADJECTIVE.
1 growing or living in water: *Water lilies are aquatic plants.*
2 taking place in or on water: *Swimming and sailing are aquatic sports.*

Ancient Roman aqueducts carried water from a river or spring in a channel along the top of the aqueduct. The water was delivered to public fountains, pipes, and pools in cities.

aqueduct

apt (apt), ADJECTIVE.
1 likely; inclined: *He is apt to make mistakes.*
2 quick to learn: *An apt student does well in school.*

ap·ti·tude (ap′tə tüd), NOUN. a natural tendency or talent; ability: *He has an aptitude for mathematics.*

aq·ua (ak′wə), ADJECTIVE *or* NOUN. light bluish green.
❑ PLURAL **a·quas.**

Word Story

The words **aqua, aquaculture, aquarium, aquatic, aqueduct,** and **aquifer** all come from a Latin word *aqua,* meaning "water." The English word **aqua** refers to the color of water. If you look up the other five words on this page, you can see how "water" is a part of their meanings too.

aq·ua·cul·ture (ak′wə kul′chər), NOUN. the science or business of growing plants, fish, or shellfish in water.

Aqua-Lung (ak′wə lung′), NOUN. (trademark) an underwater breathing device used in scuba diving.

aq·ue·duct (ak′wə dukt), NOUN. an artificial channel or large pipe for bringing water from a distance.

aq·ui·fer (ak′wə fər), NOUN. a wide layer of underground earth or rock that contains water. An aquifer supplies water to many wells.

AR, an abbreviation of **Arkansas.**

Ar·ab (ar′əb),
1 NOUN. someone born or living in Arabia.
2 NOUN. a member of a people living in southwestern and southern Asia and northern Africa.
3 ADJECTIVE. of or about the Arabs or Arabia.

A·ra·bi·a (ə rā′bē ə), NOUN. a large peninsula in southwestern Asia. —**A·ra′bi·an,** ADJECTIVE *or* NOUN.

Arabian Nights, a collection of stories from Arabia, Egypt, and India. They begin with the story of a king who marries a woman every night and kills her the next morning. One of his brides tells him a story so fascinating that he lets her live to finish it the next night. She tells him stories for one thousand and one nights. By then, the king has fallen in love with her and she is not killed.

Ar·a·bic (ar′ə bik),
1 NOUN. the language of the Arabs.
2 ADJECTIVE. of or about the Arabs or their language.

Word Source

Arabic has given a number of words to the English language, including the words below.

admiral	coffee	massage	syrup
albatross	crimson	satin	tambourine
alfalfa	giraffe	sofa	zero
algebra	hazard	spinach	
assassin	mask		

Arabic numerals, the figures 1, 2, 3, 4, 5, 6, 7, 8, 9, 0.

ar·bi·trar·y (är′bə trer′ē), ADJECTIVE. based on your own wishes, ideas, or will; not going by any rule or law: *The judge tried to be fair and did not make arbitrary decisions.* **–ar′bi·trar′i·ly,** ADVERB.

ar·bi·trate (är′bə trāt), VERB. to give a decision in a dispute; settle by arbitration: *The teacher arbitrated between the two girls in the quarrel.*
❏ VERB **ar·bi·trates, ar·bi·trat·ed, ar·bi·trat·ing.**

ar·bi·tra·tion (är′bə trā′shən), NOUN. a settlement of a dispute by someone chosen to judge matters affecting both sides: *Arbitration settled our dispute.*

ar·bor (är′bər), NOUN. a shaded place formed by trees or shrubs or by vines growing on a wooden frame.

arc (ärk), NOUN. any part of the curved line of a circle or of any curve. ▪ Another word that sounds like this is **ark.**

ar·cade (är kād′), NOUN.
1 a store in which customers pay to play games, especially video games.
2 passageway with an arched roof, often with shops along either side.

arch (ärch),
1 NOUN. a curved structure that bears the weight of the material above it. Arches often form the tops of doors, windows, and gateways.
2 VERB. to bend into an arch; curve: *The cat arched its back and hissed at the barking dog.*
3 NOUN. the lower part of the foot which makes a curve between the heel and the toes.
❏ PLURAL **arch·es;** VERB **arch·es, arched, arch·ing.**

ar·chae·ol·o·gy (är′kē ol′ə jē), NOUN. the study of the people, customs, and life of ancient times. Also spelled **archeology. –ar′chae·ol′o·gist,** NOUN.

arch·bish·op (ärch′bish′əp), NOUN. a bishop having the highest rank.

ar·che·ol·o·gy (är′kē ol′ə jē), NOUN. another spelling of **archaeology.**

arch·er (är′chər), NOUN. someone who shoots with a bow and arrow.

arch·er·y (är′chər ē), NOUN. the skill or sport of shooting with a bow and arrow.

ar·chi·pel·a·go (är′kə pel′ə gō), NOUN. a group of many islands. ❏ PLURAL **ar·chi·pel·a·gos** or **ar·chi·pel·a·goes.**

ar·chi·tect (är′kə tekt), NOUN. the person who designs and makes plans for buildings and sees that these plans are followed by the workers.

ar·chi·tec·ture (är′kə tek′chər), NOUN.
1 the science and art of designing buildings.
2 a style or special manner of building: *Greek architecture made much use of columns.*

arc·tic (ärk′tik or är′tik),
1 ADJECTIVE. at or near the North Pole; of the north polar region: *They explored the great arctic wilderness of northern Canada.*
2 NOUN. **the Arctic,** the north polar region.

Arctic Ocean, the ocean of the north polar region.

are (är), VERB. a present tense of **be:** *You are right. They are waiting. We are leaving.*

ar·e·a (âr′ē ə), NOUN.
1 the amount of surface; extent: *The area of this floor is 600 square feet.*
2 a region or district: *There are many farms in this area.*
3 a level, open space: *The city council decided to make a playground area here.*
4 a field of knowledge or interest: *There are many new techniques in the area of language teaching.*
❏ PLURAL **ar·e·as.**

area code, three numbers that are used before a phone number to direct a long-distance phone call to another telephone area.

a·re·na (ə rē′nə), NOUN. a space or building for contests, sports, or concerts. ❏ PLURAL **a·re·nas.**

aren't (ärnt), a contraction of **are not.**

Ar·gen·ti·na (är′jən tē′nə), NOUN. a country in southern South America. **–Ar·gen·tin·e·an** or **Ar·gen·tin·i·an** (är′jən tin′ē ən), ADJECTIVE or NOUN.

In **archeology,** important information is often buried in the earth.

a	hat	ė	term	ô	order	ch	child	⎧ a in about
ā	age	i	it	oi	oil	ng	long	⎪ e in taken
ä	far	ī	ice	ou	out	sh	she	ə⎨ i in pencil
â	care	o	hot	u	cup	th	thin	⎪ o in lemon
e	let	ō	open	ù	put	ᴛʜ	then	⎩ u in circus
ē	equal	ò	saw	ü	rule	zh	measure	

ar·gue (är′gyü), *VERB.*
1 to discuss with someone who disagrees: *He argued with his sister about who should wash the dishes.*
2 to give reasons for or against something: *One side argued for building a new school, and the other side argued against it.*
❏ *VERB* **ar·gues, ar·gued, ar·gu·ing.**

Synonym Study

Argue means to disagree strongly and give reasons for your point of view: *My cousins argued about whether to get a cat or a dog.*

Squabble means to argue childishly over small matters: *My little brother and sister squabble over who gets to sit in the front seat.*

Bicker means to squabble for a long period of time: *The twins bickered for months over who was the real owner of their cat.*

Quarrel means to argue noisily and angrily: *My parents are quarreling with our neighbors about the fence they put up.*

See also the Synonym Study at **fight.**

ar·gu·ment (är′gyə mənt), *NOUN.*
1 a discussion by people who disagree; dispute: *There was no argument over the results of the game.*
2 a reason or reasons offered for or against something: *Their arguments for a new school are convincing.*

ar·id (ar′id), *ADJECTIVE.* having very little rainfall; dry: *Desert lands are arid.*

a·rise (ə rīz′), *VERB.*
1 to rise up; get up: *They arose to greet us.* ■ See the Synonym Study at **rise.**
2 to move upward: *Smoke arises from the chimney.*
3 to come into being; come about: *Accidents often arise from carelessness.*
❏ *VERB* **a·ris·es, a·rose, a·ris·en** (ə riz′n), **a·ris·ing.**

ar·is·toc·ra·cy (ar′ə stok′rə sē), *NOUN.*
1 a class of people having a high position in society because of birth, rank, or title. Earls, duchesses, and princes belong to the aristocracy.
2 a class of people considered superior because of intelligence, culture, or wealth.
3 a form of government in which the nobles rule.
❏ *PLURAL* **ar·is·toc·ra·cies.**

a·ris·to·crat (ə ris′tə krat), *NOUN.*
1 someone who belongs to the aristocracy; a noble.
2 someone who has the tastes, opinions, and manners of a noble.
−**a·ris′to·crat′ic**, *ADJECTIVE.*

a·rith·me·tic (ə rith′mə tik), *NOUN.*
1 the branch of mathematics that deals with adding, subtracting, multiplying, and dividing.
2 the process of adding, subtracting, multiplying, or dividing; calculation: *There is a mistake in your arithmetic in that problem.*

Ar·i·zo·na (ar′ə zō′nə), *NOUN.* one of the southwestern states of the United States. *Abbreviation:* AZ; *Capital:* Phoenix. −**Ar′i·zo′nan** or **Ar′i·zo′ni·an**, *NOUN.*

State Story Arizona got its name from an American Indian word meaning "place of the small spring."

ark (ärk), *NOUN.* (in the Bible) the large boat in which Noah saved himself, his family, and a pair of each kind of animal from the Flood. ■ Another word that sounds like this is **arc.**

an artist's picture of Noah's **ark**

Ar·kan·sas (är′kən sȯ), *NOUN.* one of the southern states of the United States. *Abbreviation:* AR; *Capital:* Little Rock. −**Ar·kan·san** (är kan′zən), *NOUN.*

State Story Arkansas was named for an American Indian tribe that once lived in the area. This name came from an Indian word meaning "downstream people."

arm[1] (ärm), *NOUN.*
1 the part of the body between the shoulder and the hand.
2 something shaped or used like an arm. An armchair has two arms. An inlet is an arm of the sea. −**arm′like′**, *ADJECTIVE.*

twist someone's arm, *IDIOM.* to try hard to make someone do something: *He didn't want to come; I had to twist his arm.*

with open arms, *IDIOM.* in a warm, friendly way: *We welcomed her with open arms.*

Have You Heard?

You may have heard someone say that something "costs an arm and a leg." This means that something is very expensive: *Their vacation to Alaska cost an arm and a leg.*

arm² (ärm),
1 *VERB.* to supply with weapons: *During the Revolutionary War, the French helped arm the colonists.*
2 *NOUN.* **arms,** weapons of any kind. Guns, swords, axes, or sticks can be arms for defense or attack.
3 *VERB.* to supply with any means of defense or attack: *The lawyer entered court armed with the evidence to support his case.*
  ❑ *VERB* **arms, armed, arm·ing.**

ar·ma·da (är mä′də), *NOUN.* a large fleet of warships. ❑ *PLURAL* **ar·ma·das.**

ar·ma·dil·lo (är′mə dil′ō), *NOUN.* a small, burrowing animal that has a very hard shell made of bony plates. Armadillos are found in South America and some parts of southern North America. ❑ *PLURAL* **ar·ma·dil·los.**

Word Story

Armadillo comes from a Spanish word meaning "armed." Early Spanish explorers thought the animal's hard shell looked like and served as a kind of armor.

armadillo — 3 feet long, including the tail

ar·ma·ment (är′mə mənt), *NOUN.*
1 the weapons, ammunition, and equipment used by the military; war equipment and supplies.
2 the military forces of a country, including equipment and people.

arm·band (ärm′band′), *NOUN.* band of cloth worn around the upper arm as a symbol or badge: *a mourning armband of black cloth.*

arm·chair (ärm′châr′), *NOUN.* a chair with pieces at the side to support your arms or elbows.

armed forces, all the army, navy, marine, and air forces of a country.

Ar·me·ni·a (är mē′nē ə), *NOUN.* a country in southwestern Asia. **–Ar·me′ni·an,** *ADJECTIVE* or *NOUN.*

arm·ful (ärm′fùl), *NOUN.* as much as one or both arms can hold; armload: *I carried an armful of groceries.* ❑ *PLURAL* **arm·fuls.**

ar·mi·stice (är′mə stis), *NOUN.* a stop in warfare; temporary peace; truce.

arm·load (ärm′lōd′), *NOUN.* See **armful:** *I had an armload of firewood.*

ar·mor (är′mər), *NOUN.*
1 a covering, usually of metal or leather, worn to protect the body in fighting.
2 any kind of protective covering. The bony shell of an armadillo is armor.

ar·mored (är′mərd), *ADJECTIVE.* covered or protected with armor: *an armored car.*

arm·pit (ärm′pit′), *NOUN.* the hollow place under the arm at the shoulder; underarm.

arms (ärmz), *NOUN PLURAL.*
1 See **arm²** (definition 2).
2 fighting; war: *The colonists were quick to answer the call to arms.*

up in arms, *IDIOM.* very angry; in rebellion: *We were up in arms when the play was canceled.*

helmet
visor
shoulder piece
breastplate
mail²
thigh piece
knee piece
shinguard
shoe

armor of a 16th-century Austrian knight

ar·my (är′mē), *NOUN.*
1 a large, organized group of soldiers trained and armed for war.
2 often, **Army,** the military land forces of the United States.
3 any group of people organized for a purpose: *an army of research scientists.*
4 a very large number; multitude: *an army of ants.*
  ❑ *PLURAL* **ar·mies.**

a·ro·ma (ə rō′mə), *NOUN.* a strong, pleasant odor; fragrance: *Smell the aroma of the cake baking in the oven.* ❑ *PLURAL* **a·ro·mas.**

a·rose (ə rōz′), *VERB.* the past tense of **arise:** *She arose from her chair.*

a·round (ə round′),
1 *PREPOSITION.* in a circle about: *She has traveled around the world.*
2 *ADVERB.* in a circle: *The top spun around.*
3 *ADVERB.* in circumference: *The tree measures four feet around.*
4 *PREPOSITION.* on all sides of: *There were trees all around the lake.*
5 *PREPOSITION.* on the far side of; past: *The post office is around the corner.*
6 *PREPOSITION.* here and there; about: *We walked*

a hat	ė term	ô order	ch child	⎧ a in about
ā age	i it	oi oil	ng long	⎪ e in taken
ä far	ī ice	ou out	sh she	ə⎨ i in pencil
â care	o hot	u cup	th thin	⎪ o in lemon
e let	ō open	ù put	ŦH then	⎩ u in circus
ē equal	ò saw	ü rule	zh measure	

around to see the town. Don't leave your books around the house.

7 *ADVERB.* somewhere about; near: *We waited around for an hour.*

8 *ADVERB.* near in amount, number, or time to; about: *That shirt cost around $25. I'll be home around six o'clock.*

9 *PREPOSITION.* in the opposite direction: *Turn around! You are going the wrong way.*

a·rouse (ə rouz′), *VERB.*

1 to stir to action; excite: *The mystery story aroused my imagination.*

2 to awaken: *The sirens aroused me from my sleep.*

❏ *VERB* **a·rous·es, a·roused, a·rous·ing.**

ar·range (ə rānj′), *VERB.*

1 to put things in a certain order: *Please arrange the books on the library shelf.*

2 to plan; form plans: *Can you arrange to meet me this evening?*

3 to adapt; fit: *This music for the violin is also arranged for the piano.*

❏ *VERB* **ar·rang·es, ar·ranged, ar·rang·ing.** —**ar·rang′er,** *NOUN.*

ar·range·ment (ə rānj′mənt), *NOUN.*

1 the act of putting or the condition of being put in proper order: *Careful arrangement of books in a library makes them easier to find.*

2 the way or order in which things or people are put: *You can make six arrangements of the letters A, B, and C.*

3 something arranged in a particular way: *a flower arrangement, an arrangement for violin.*

4 arrangements, plans; preparations: *We made arrangements for our trip to Chicago.*

ar·ray (ə rā′),

1 *NOUN.* a display or collection of people or things: *The team had an impressive array of fine players.*

2 *VERB.* to put in a special order: *The general arrayed his troops for the battle.*

3 *NOUN.* (in mathematics) an orderly arrangement of objects or symbols in rows and columns.

❏ *VERB* **ar·rays, ar·rayed, ar·ray·ing.**

ar·rest (ə rest′),

1 *VERB.* to take someone to jail by authority of the law: *The police arrested the burglary suspect.*

2 *NOUN.* the act of seizing someone by authority of the law: *I saw the arrest of a murder suspect.*

3 *VERB.* to stop; check: *Filling a tooth arrests decay.*

❏ *VERB* **ar·rests, ar·rest·ed, ar·rest·ing.**

under arrest, *IDIOM.* held by the police: *He was under arrest for burglary.*

ar·riv·al (ə rī′vəl), *NOUN.*

1 an act of arriving; coming: *She is waiting for the arrival of the plane.*

2 someone or something that arrives: *We greeted the new arrivals at the door.*

ar·rive (ə rīv′), *VERB.*

1 to come to a place: *We arrived in Boston a week ago.* ■ See the Synonym Study at **come.**

2 to come: *Summer finally arrived.*

❏ *VERB* **ar·rives, ar·rived, ar·riv·ing.**

ar·ro·gant (ar′ə gənt), *ADJECTIVE.* too proud of yourself and too scornful of others: *Early success had made her vain and arrogant.* —**ar′ro·gant·ly,** *ADVERB.*

ar·row (ar′ō), *NOUN.*

1 a slender, pointed stick which is shot from a bow.

2 a sign (→) used to show direction or position in maps, on road signs, and in writing.

ar·row·head (ar′ō hed′), *NOUN.* the head or tip of an arrow.

ar·roy·o (ə roi′ō), *NOUN.* the dry bed of a stream, in the southwestern United States. ❏ *PLURAL* **ar·roy·os.**

ar·se·nal (är′sə nəl), *NOUN.* a building for storing or manufacturing weapons and ammunition.

an **arrowhead** made from chipped stone

ar·se·nic (är′sə nik), *NOUN.* a white, tasteless powder that is a deadly poison. It is used to make insecticides, weed killers, and certain medicines. Arsenic is a chemical element.

ar·son (är′sən), *NOUN.* the crime of intentionally setting fire to a building or other property.

art (ärt), *NOUN.*

1 the skills and methods of painting, drawing, and sculpture: *I am studying art and music.*

2 paintings, sculptures, and other works of art: *We went to an exhibit at the new museum of art.*

3 a set of principles or methods gained by experience; skill: *the art of making friends.*

ar·ter·y (är′tər ē), *NOUN.*

1 one of the blood vessels that carry blood from the heart to all parts of the body.

2 a main road; important channel: *Main Street is the major artery of traffic in our city.*

❏ *PLURAL* **ar·ter·ies.**

ar·thri·tis (är thrī′tis), *NOUN.* soreness and swelling of a joint or joints of the body.

ar·thro·pod (är′thrə pod), *NOUN.* any animal without a backbone that has a jointed body and jointed legs. Insects, spiders, and lobsters are arthropods.

Ar·thur (är′thər), *NOUN.* (in legends of the Middle Ages) the king of ancient Britain who gathered around him the knights of the Round Table.

ar·ti·choke (är′tə chōk), *NOUN.* the large flower bud of a plant with large, prickly leaves. Artichokes are cooked and eaten as a vegetable.

ar·ti·cle (är′tə kəl), NOUN.
1 a written composition that is part of a magazine, newspaper, or book: *This is a good article on fish.*
2 a section of a contract, treaty, or law.
3 a particular thing; item: *articles of clothing.* ▪ See the Synonym Study at **thing.**
4 one of the words *a, an,* or *the,* as in *a book, an egg, the boy. A* and *an* are **indefinite articles;** *the* is the **definite article.**

ar·tic·u·late (är tik′yə lāt), VERB. to speak distinctly; express in clear sounds and words: *The speaker articulated his words carefully so that everyone could understand him.* ❑ VERB **ar·tic·u·lates, ar·tic·u·lat·ed, ar·tic·u·lat·ing.**

ar·ti·fi·cial (är′tə fish′əl), ADJECTIVE.
1 made by human skill or labor; not natural: *Plastics are artificial substances that do not occur in nature.*
2 put on; pretended: *When nervous, he had an artificial laugh.*
–ar′ti·fi′cial·ly, ADVERB.

artificial intelligence, the ability of a computer to do things that require intelligence when done by human beings, such as playing chess.

artificial respiration, a way of restoring normal breathing to a person who has stopped breathing. Air is alternately forced into and out of the lungs.

ar·til·ler·y (är til′ər ē), NOUN.
1 very large guns that are moved around on wheels.
2 the part of an army that uses such guns.

ar·ti·san (är′tə zən), NOUN. someone skilled in a craft or trade; craftsman. Carpenters, masons, weavers, plumbers, and potters are artisans.

art·ist (är′tist), NOUN.
1 someone who paints or draws pictures.
2 someone who is skilled in any of the fine arts, such as sculpture, music, or literature.
3 a public performer, especially an actor or singer.

artist (definition 1)

as (az),
1 ADVERB. to the same degree: *I am as tall as you.*
2 PREPOSITION. doing the work of: *Who will act as teacher?*
3 CONJUNCTION. while; when: *As they were walking, it began to rain.*
4 CONJUNCTION. in the same way that: *Treat others as you wish them to treat you.*
5 CONJUNCTION. because: *As she was a skilled worker, she received good wages.*
6 PREPOSITION. like: *They treat him as an equal.* ▪ See the Usage Note at **like.**

7 PRONOUN. that which: *Do as I do and you'll learn this skill quickly.*
as if or **as though,** IDIOM. the way it would be if: *You sound as if you were angry.*
as is, IDIOM. in the present condition: *If we buy the house as is, it won't cost us very much.*
as of, IDIOM. from this time on: *As of September 1st, all students must wear the new uniform.*
as yet, IDIOM. up until now; so far: *We don't have any news as yet about the accident.*

as·bes·tos (as bes′təs), NOUN. a mineral that does not burn. Asbestos separates into fibers that are used in electrical insulation and fire-resistant clothing. The fibers are dangerous to inhale.

as·cend (ə send′), VERB. to go up; rise; climb: *She watched the airplane ascend quickly. A group of climbers is planning to ascend Mount Everest.*
▪ See the Synonym Studies at **climb** and **rise.**
❑ VERB **as·cends, as·cend·ed, as·cend·ing.**

as·cent (ə sent′), NOUN.
1 the act of going up; upward movement; rising: *The sudden ascent of the elevator made us dizzy.*
2 the act or process of climbing: *The ascent of Mount Everest is difficult.*
▪ Another word that sounds like this is **assent.**

ash¹ (ash), NOUN. what remains of a thing after it has been thoroughly burned: *Volcanic ash covered the valley after the volcano erupted.* ❑ PLURAL **ash·es.**

ash¹ — huge clouds of ash pouring from a volcano

ash² (ash), NOUN. a kind of shade tree that has silvery gray bark and small flowers. Its wood is used to make baseball bats. ❑ PLURAL **ash·es.**

a·shamed (ə shāmd′), ADJECTIVE.
1 feeling embarrassment; uncomfortable because

a	hat	ė	term	ô	order	ch	child		a in about
ā	age	i	it	oi	oil	ng	long		e in taken
ä	far	ī	ice	ou	out	sh	she	ə {	i in pencil
â	care	o	hot	u	cup	th	thin		o in lemon
e	let	ō	open	ů	put	ʈH	then		u in circus
ē	equal	ò	saw	ü	rule	zh	measure		

you have done something wrong, bad, or silly: *I was ashamed of the lies I had told.*

2 unwilling because of fear or shame: *I failed math and was ashamed to tell my parents.*

a·shore (ə shôr′), ADVERB. to the shore; on land: *The ship's crew went ashore. The sailor had been ashore for months.*

ash·tray (ash′trā′), NOUN. a holder for tobacco ashes.

Ash Wednesday, the first day of Lent; the seventh Wednesday before Easter.

A·sia (ā′zhə), NOUN. the largest continent, east of Europe and west of the Pacific Ocean. China, India, and Israel are countries in Asia. **–A′sian,** ADJECTIVE or NOUN.

Asian American,

1 an American of Asian descent.

2 of or about Americans of Asian descent.

a·side (ə sīd′), ADVERB.

1 to one side; away: *He stepped aside to let me pass in the hallway.*

2 out of your thoughts or consideration: *Swimming is easier if you can put your fears aside.*

aside from, IDIOM. except for: *Aside from arithmetic, I have finished my homework.*

as·i·nine (as′n īn), ADJECTIVE. obviously silly; foolish and stupid: *Wearing roller skates in the snow is asinine.* **–as′i·nine·ly,** ADVERB.

ask (ask), VERB.

1 to try to find out using questions: *Why don't you ask? She asked about our health. Ask directions.*

2 to seek the answer to: *Ask any questions you wish.*

3 to put a question to: *Ask him how old he is.*

4 to request something in words: *Ask them to sing. Ask for help if you need it.*

5 to invite: *I asked ten people to my birthday party. He asked them to dinner.*

6 to demand: *They were asking too high a price for their new video game.*

❏ VERB **asks, asked, ask·ing.**

Synonym Study

Ask means to try to find out information through a question: *I asked the hotel clerk about the arrangements for disabled people.*

Inquire means to ask in order to get detailed information: *The traveler inquired about the bus schedule at the ticket window.*

Quiz means to ask questions about what has been learned: *Our teacher will quiz us on today's spelling words.*

Question means to ask over and over again: *The principal questioned the class about what had happened at recess.*

ANTONYMS: answer, reply.

a·skew (ə skyü′), ADJECTIVE or ADVERB. turned or twisted to one side; out of the proper position: *Isn't that picture askew?*

a·sleep (ə slēp′),

1 ADJECTIVE. not awake; sleeping: *The cat is asleep in front of the fire.*

2 ADVERB. into a state of sleep: *The tired boy fell asleep before dinner.*

3 ADJECTIVE. numb: *My foot is asleep.*

as·par·a·gus (ə spar′ə gəs), NOUN. the tender, green shoots of a plant with scalelike leaves. Asparagus is cooked and eaten as a vegetable.

as·pect (as′pekt), NOUN.

1 one side or part or view of a subject: *We must consider each aspect of this plan before we decide.*

2 a look; appearance: *Before the storm, the sky had a gray, gloomy aspect.*

as·pen (as′pən), NOUN. a kind of poplar tree whose leaves tremble and rustle in the slightest breeze.

as·phalt (as′fôlt), NOUN.

1 a dark substance like tar, found in the ground or made from petroleum.

2 a smooth, hard mixture of this substance with crushed rock or sand. Asphalt is used to pave roads.

as·pire (ə spīr′), VERB. to have an ambition for something; desire earnestly; seek: *He aspired to be captain of the team.* ❏ VERB **as·pires, as·pired, as·pir·ing.**

as·pir·in (as′pər ən), NOUN. a drug used to relieve pain and reduce fever.

ass (as), NOUN.

1 See **donkey.**

2 a stupid, silly, or stubborn person; fool. ❏ PLURAL **ass·es.**

as·sas·sin (ə sas′n), NOUN. a murderer; someone who kills a well-known person by a sudden attack or from ambush.

as·sas·si·nate (ə sas′n āt), VERB. to murder, especially a well-known person, by a sudden attack or from ambush: *President Kennedy was assassinated in 1963.* ❏ VERB **as·sas·si·nates, as·sas·si·nat·ed, as·sas·si·nat·ing.** **–as·sas′si·na′tion,** NOUN.

as·sault (ə sôlt′),

1 NOUN. a sudden, vigorous attack: *The soldiers made an assault on the enemy fort.*

2 VERB. to make an attack on: *My friend barely escaped from the gang that tried to assault him.* ❏ VERB **as·saults, as·sault·ed, as·sault·ing.**

as·sem·ble (ə sem′bəl), VERB.

1 to gather or come together: *The principal assembled all the students in the auditorium.*

2 to put together; fit together: *Will you help me assemble my model airplane?* ■ See the Synonym Study at **make.**

❏ VERB **as·sem·bles, as·sem·bled, as·sem·bling.**

A

as·sem·bly (ə sem′blē), NOUN.
1 a group of people gathered for some purpose: *The principal addressed the school assembly.*
2 **Assembly,** the lower branch of the state legislature of some states of the United States.
3 the process of putting together something from parts: *The instructions said that assembly would take two hours.*
❏ PLURAL **as·sem·blies.**

assembly line, a row of workers and machines along which work is passed until the final product is made: *Most cars are made on an assembly line.*

as·sent (ə sent′), VERB. to express agreement; give consent: *Everyone assented to the plans for the picnic.* ❏ VERB **as·sents, as·sent·ed, as·sent·ing.**
∎ Another word that sounds like this is **ascent.**

as·sert (ə sėrt′), VERB.
1 to state positively; declare firmly: *She asserts that her story is absolutely true.*
2 to defend or insist on a right or claim: *It is necessary to assert your independence.*
❏ VERB **as·serts, as·sert·ed, as·sert·ing.**

as·sess (ə ses′), VERB.
1 to estimate the value of property or income for taxation: *The property was assessed at $100,000.*
2 to examine carefully and judge the value or quality of: *The school board met to assess the science program.*
❏ VERB **as·sess·es, as·sessed, as·sess·ing.**
—**as·sess′ment,** NOUN.

as·set (as′et), NOUN.
1 a valuable quality or possession; advantage: *The ability to get along with people is an asset.*
2 **assets,** things of value; property, such as a house, a car, stocks, bonds, or jewelry: *Their assets were sold at auction to pay their debts.*

as·sign (ə sīn′), VERB.
1 to give as a task to be done: *The teacher assigned the next ten problems.*
2 to fix; set: *The judge assigned a day for the trial.*
3 to give out; distribute: *The scoutmasters assigned a different tent area to each troop.*
❏ VERB **as·signs, as·signed, as·sign·ing.**

as·sign·ment (ə sīn′mənt), NOUN.
1 a task or amount of work to be done: *Today's assignment in arithmetic consists of ten examples.* ∎ See the Synonym Study at **job.**
2 the act of assigning: *Room assignments were made on the first day of school.*

as·sist (ə sist′),
1 VERB. to help; take part in: *She assisted the science teacher with the experiment.* ∎ See the Synonym Study at **help.**
2 NOUN. (in sports) a play that directly helps a teammate to score, such as a pass in basketball or hockey.
❏ VERB **as·sists, as·sist·ed, as·sist·ing.**

as·sist·ance (ə sis′təns), NOUN. help; aid: *I need your assistance.*

as·sist·ant (ə sis′tənt),
1 NOUN. a helper: *I was her assistant in the library.*
2 ADJECTIVE. helping; assisting: *an assistant teacher, an assistant coach.*

as·so·ci·ate (ə sō′shē āt for verb; ə sō′shē it for adjective),
1 VERB. to connect in thought: *We associate turkey with Thanksgiving.*
2 ADJECTIVE. joined with another or others: *I am an associate editor of the school paper.*
3 VERB. to join as a companion, partner, or friend: *She is associated with her brothers in business.*
❏ VERB **as·so·ci·ates, as·so·ci·at·ed, as·so·ci·at·ing.**

as·so·ci·a·tion (ə sō′sē ā′shən), NOUN.
1 a group of people joined together for some purpose: *Will you join the young people's association at our church?*
2 companionship or friendship: *They had enjoyed a close association over many years.*
3 an idea connected with another idea in thought: *Many people make the association of food with love. All of those old yearbooks have good associations for him.*

as·sort·ed (ə sôr′tid), ADJECTIVE. selected so as to be of different kinds; various: *They served assorted pies.*

as·sort·ment (ə sôrt′mənt), NOUN. a collection of various kinds: *These scarfs come in an assortment of colors.*

as·sume (ə süm′), VERB.
1 to take for granted without proof; suppose: *He assumed that the train would be on time.*
2 to pretend: *Although she was afraid, she assumed a confident manner.*
3 to take or claim something for yourself: *He assumed new responsibilities as coach.*
❏ VERB **as·sumes, as·sumed, as·sum·ing.**
—**as·sump·tion** (ə sump′shən), NOUN.

as·sur·ance (ə shùr′əns), NOUN.
1 a statement intended to make a person more certain or confident: *We gave her our assurance that we would not play in her yard again.*
2 security, certainty, or confidence: *We have the assurance of final victory.*

as·sure (ə shùr′), VERB.
1 to tell positively: *They assured us that the plane would be on time.*
2 to make sure: *I assured myself that I had all my books before leaving for school.*
❏ VERB **as·sures, as·sured, as·sur·ing.**

a	hat	ė	term	ô	order	ch	child		a in about
ā	age	i	it	oi	oil	ng	long		e in taken
ä	far	ī	ice	ou	out	sh	she	ə {	i in pencil
â	care	o	hot	u	cup	th	thin		o in lemon
e	let	ō	open	ù	put	ᴛʜ	then		u in circus
ē	equal	ò	saw	ü	rule	zh	measure		

as·ter (as′tər), NOUN. a common plant having daisylike flowers with white, pink, or purple petals around a yellow center.

aster

as·ter·isk (as′tə risk′), NOUN. a star-shaped mark (∗) used in printing and writing to tell a reader that there is more information at another place on the page. In computing, it is often used as a multiplication sign.

a·stern (ə stėrn′), ADVERB. at or toward the rear of a ship or boat; aft: *The captain went astern.*

as·ter·oid (as′tə roid′), NOUN. any of thousands of rocky objects smaller than 620 miles across, orbiting the sun. Most asteroids are between the orbits of Mars and Jupiter.

asth·ma (az′mə), NOUN. a disease that makes breathing difficult and causes wheezing and coughing.

a·stig·ma·tism (ə stig′mə tiz′əm), NOUN. a defect of an eye or of a lens that makes objects look fuzzy or that gives imperfect images, because light is not focused at one point.

a·stir (ə stėr′), ADJECTIVE. in motion; up and about: *Although it was late, the whole family was astir.*

as·ton·ish (ə ston′ish), VERB. to surprise greatly; amaze: *We were astonished at the force of the wind during the hurricane.* ▪ See the Synonym Study at **surprise**. ❑ VERB **as·ton·ish·es, as·ton·ished, as·ton·ish·ing.**

as·ton·ish·ment (ə ston′ish mənt), NOUN. great surprise; sudden wonder; amazement: *He stared at the Grand Canyon in astonishment.*

as·tound (ə stound′), VERB. to surprise greatly; amaze: *She was astounded by the news that she had won the contest.* ▪ See the Synonym Study at **surprise**. ❑ VERB **as·tounds, as·tound·ed, as·tound·ing.**

a·stray (ə strā′), ADVERB. out of the right way or place; wandering: *The gate is open and all the cows have gone astray.*

a·stride (ə strīd′), PREPOSITION. with one leg on each side of: *to sit astride a horse.*

Word Power   -astro

The combining form **astro-** means "star" or "space." **Astronomy** is the study of **stars** and **space.** An **astronaut** travels in **space.**

as·trol·o·gy (ə strol′ə jē), NOUN. the study of the influence that some people believe the sun, moon, stars, and planets have on lives and events here on earth.

as·tro·naut (as′trə nȯt), NOUN. a member of the crew of a spacecraft.

as·tron·o·mer (ə stron′ə mər), NOUN. someone who is an expert in astronomy.

as·tro·nom·i·cal (as′trə nom′ə kəl), ADJECTIVE.
1 of or about astronomy: *A telescope is an astronomical instrument.*
2 enormous; very great: *She has an astronomical sum of money.*
—**as′tro·nom′i·cal·ly,** ADVERB.

astronaut

As·tro·Turf (as′trō tėrf′), NOUN. (trademark) a synthetic material made of nylon and plastic. It is used instead of grass on playing fields and lawns.

as·tron·o·my (ə stron′ə mē), NOUN. the science that deals with the sun, moon, planets, stars, and other objects in outer space.

a·sy·lum (ə sī′ləm), NOUN.
1 (earlier) an institution for the care of the mentally ill or other people who needed care.
2 a refuge; shelter. Asylum is sometimes given by one nation to people of another nation.

a·sym·met·ri·cal (ā′si met′rə kəl), ADJECTIVE. having an unbalanced form or arrangement: *asymmetrical features, asymmetrical shapes.*
—**a′sym·met′ri·cal·ly,** ADVERB.

at (at, ət, *or* it), PREPOSITION.
1 in; on; by; near: *I will be at the store. There is someone at the front door.*
2 in the direction of; to; toward: *He threw it at me.*
3 on or near the time of: *She left at nine o'clock.*
4 in a condition of: *England and France were at war.*
5 for: *We bought two books at a dollar each.*

at bat or **at-bat** (at′bat′), NOUN. (in baseball) a team's turn or player's turn at batting.

ate (āt), VERB. the past tense of **eat**: *We ate our dinner. I ate too many cookies.* ▪ Another word that sounds like this is **eight.**

a·the·ist (ā′thē ist), NOUN. someone who believes that there is no God.

Ath·ens (ath′ənz), NOUN. the capital of Greece. Athens was famous in ancient times for its art and literature.

ath·lete (ath′lēt′), NOUN. someone trained in sports and exercises of physical strength, speed, and skill. Baseball players, gymnasts, and swimmers are athletes.

athlete's foot, a very contagious skin disease of the feet, caused by a fungus.

ath·let·ic (ath let′ik), ADJECTIVE.
1 of, like or suited to an athlete: *Dancers often have athletic skills.*
2 of or about active games and sports: *He joined an athletic association.*
3 strong and active: *She is an athletic girl and loves to hike and bike and swim.*
—**ath·let′i·cal·ly,** ADVERB.

ath·let·ics (ath let′iks), NOUN
1 PLURAL. sports and exercises that require physical strength and skill. Athletics include baseball, gymnastics, ice-skating, and tennis.
2 SINGULAR. the practice and principles of sports training: *Athletics is recommended for every pupil.*

Word Power   -ation

The suffix **-ation** is used to make nouns from verbs. It means the "act, condition, or result of _____ing." **Combination** means the **result of combining. Preparation** means the **act of preparing.**

At·lan·ta (at lan′tə), NOUN. the capital of the state of Georgia.

At·lan·tic (at lan′tik),
1 NOUN. the ocean east of North and South America. It extends to Europe and Africa.
2 ADJECTIVE. of, on, or near the Atlantic Ocean: *New York is on the Atlantic coast of North America.*

At·lan·tis (at lan′tis), NOUN. the legendary island in the Atlantic Ocean, said to have sunk beneath the sea.

at·las (at′ləs), NOUN. a book of maps. A big atlas has maps of every country. ❑ PLURAL **at·las·es.**

a statue of **Atlas**

Word Story

The word **atlas** comes from the name of Atlas, a giant in Greek myths. According to one story, he had to hold up the sky on his shoulders as a punishment. A picture showing this appeared as a first page in early books of maps. People began to call a book of maps an **atlas.**

ATM, automated teller machine: an electronic banking machine that gives out cash and takes deposits; cash machine.

at·mo·sphere (at′mə sfir), NOUN.
1 the air that surrounds the earth.
2 the mass of gases that surrounds a planet, star, or other object in outer space: *The atmosphere of Venus is cloudy.*
3 the air in any given place: *Plants grow rapidly in the moist atmosphere of a jungle.*
4 the surrounding conditions and mood of a place: *The peaceful atmosphere in the library helped me study.*

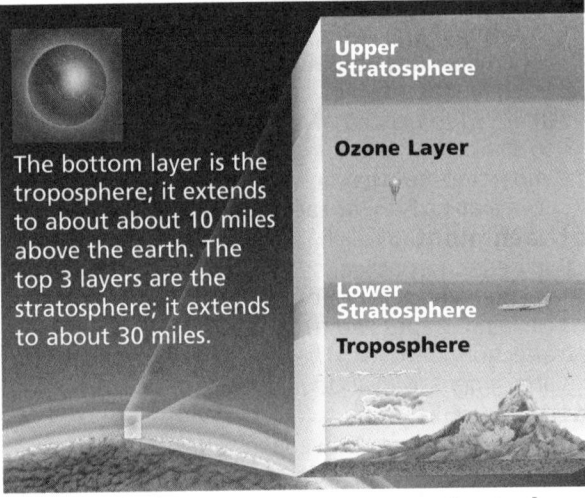

Upper Stratosphere
Ozone Layer
Lower Stratosphere
Troposphere

The bottom layer is the troposphere; it extends to about about 10 miles above the earth. The top 3 layers are the stratosphere; it extends to about 30 miles.

atmosphere

at·mo·spher·ic (at′mə sfir′ik), ADJECTIVE. of, in, or having something to do with the atmosphere: *Oxygen and nitrogen are atmospheric gases.*

at·oll (at′ol), NOUN. a coral island or group of islands forming a ring around a shallow lagoon.

a·tom (at′əm), NOUN. one of the tiny particles which make up all the matter in the universe.

a·tom·ic (ə tom′ik), ADJECTIVE.
1 of or about atoms: *atomic research.*
2 run by atomic energy: *an atomic submarine.*

atomic bomb, a bomb in which the splitting of atoms results in an explosion of tremendous force and heat, accompanied by a blinding light; A-bomb.

atomic energy, the energy that exists inside the nucleus of an atom; nuclear energy. Atomic energy can be released by splitting or combining the centers of some kinds of atoms.

a·top (ə top′), PREPOSITION. on the top of: *He had a hat atop his head.*

a·tri·um (ā′trē əm), NOUN.
1 either of the two upper chambers of the heart; auricle. An atrium receives blood from the veins and forces it into a lower chamber.

a	hat	ė	term	ô	order	ch	child		a in about
ā	age	i	it	oi	oil	ng	long		e in taken
ä	far	ī	ice	ou	out	sh	she	ə<	i in pencil
â	care	o	hot	u	cup	th	thin		o in lemon
e	let	ō	open	ů	put	ᴛʜ	then		u in circus
ē	equal	ò	saw	ü	rule	zh	measure		

2 in a modern building, a large room that is two or more stories tall, often containing trees and other plants.

a·tro·cious (ə trō′shəs), ADJECTIVE.
1 very cruel or brutal: *Kidnapping is an atrocious crime.*
2 very unpleasant: *The weather has been atrocious.*

a·troc·i·ty (ə tros′ə tē), NOUN. a very cruel or brutal act: *Many atrocities are committed in war.* ❑ PLURAL **a·troc·i·ties.**

at·tach (ə tach′), VERB.
1 to fasten: *I attached a rope to my sled.* ∎ See the Synonym Study at **join.**
2 to connect by love or affection: *She is very attached to her cousin.*
3 to think of as belonging to: *I did not attach much importance to what he said.*
❑ VERB **at·tach·es, at·tached, at·tach·ing.**

at·tach·ment (ə tach′mənt), NOUN.
1 something attached, such as an additional device. *Vacuum cleaners often have attachments for cleaning drapes and furniture.*
2 affection; devotion: *The children have a great attachment to their dog.*

at·tack (ə tak′),
1 VERB. to use force or weapons against; begin fighting against: *The dog attacked the cat. The enemy attacked at dawn.*
2 VERB. to talk or write against: *The candidate attacked his opponent's record as mayor.*
3 VERB. to go at with vigor: *The hungry hikers attacked dinner as soon as it was ready.*
4 NOUN. the act or process of attacking: *The enemy attack took us by surprise.*
5 NOUN. a sudden occurrence of illness: *an attack of flu, an attack of sneezing.*
❑ VERB **at·tacks, at·tacked, at·tack·ing. –at·tack·er,** NOUN.

at·tain (ə tān′), VERB.
1 to arrive at: *Grandpa has attained the age of 80.*
2 to gain by effort; accomplish: *She attained her goal.*
❑ VERB **at·tains, at·tained, at·tain·ing.**
–at·tain′a·ble, ADJECTIVE. **–at·tain′ment,** NOUN.

at·tempt (ə tempt′),
1 VERB. to try: *She attempted to climb the mountain.*
2 NOUN. a try; effort: *They made an attempt to climb the mountain.*
3 NOUN. an attack: *An assassin made an attempt upon the king's life.*
❑ VERB **at·tempts, at·tempt·ed, at·tempt·ing.**

at·tend (ə tend′), VERB.
1 to be present at: *I attended my cousin's wedding.*
2 to give care and thought; pay attention to: *Attend to your work.*
3 to go with; accompany: *Noble ladies attended the queen.*
❑ VERB **at·tends, at·tend·ed, at·tend·ing.**

at·tend·ance (ə ten′dəns), NOUN.
1 the fact of being present at a place: *Our class had perfect attendance today.*
2 the number of people present: *The attendance at the meeting was over 200.*

at·tend·ant (ə ten′dənt), NOUN. someone who waits on others: *The airplane had several flight attendants to care for the passengers.*

at·ten·tion (ə ten′shən), NOUN.
1 careful thinking, looking, or listening: *Give me your attention while I explain this math problem.*
2 care and thoughtfulness; consideration: *Dad shows our grandparents much attention.*
3 position of standing very straight with the arms at the sides, the heels together, and the eyes looking ahead: *The soldiers stood at attention during the inspection.*

These servicemen are standing at **attention.**

at·ten·tive (ə ten′tiv), ADJECTIVE. paying attention; observant: *The attentive pupil is most likely to learn.* ∎ See the Synonym Study at **interested.**
–at·ten′tive·ly, ADVERB.

at·tic (at′ik), NOUN. the space in a house just below the roof and above the other rooms.

Word Story

Attic comes from the words *attic story,* meaning "the top story of a building." It was called this because people used to build the top stories of their houses to look like the buildings of Attica (at′ə kə), a district of ancient Greece.

at·tire (ə tīr′),
1 NOUN. clothing or dress.
2 VERB. to clothe or dress: *The king was attired in a cloak trimmed with ermine.*
❑ VERB **at·tires, at·tired, at·tir·ing.**

at·ti·tude (at′ə tüd), NOUN. a way of thinking, acting, or feeling: *I used to dislike school but I've changed my attitude.* ∎ See the Synonym Study at **opinion.**

at·tor·ney (ə tėr′nē), NOUN. a lawyer. ❑ PLURAL **at·tor·neys.**

at·tract (ə trakt′), VERB.
1 to draw in or draw together; gather: *The magnet attracted the spilled pins. The famous musician attracted a crowd.*
2 to be pleasing to; win the attention and liking of: *Bright colors attract children.*
❑ VERB **at·tracts, at·tract·ed, at·tract·ing.**

at·trac·tion (ə trak′shən), NOUN.
1 something that draws in or gathers people: *The elephants were the chief attraction at the circus.*
2 the act or power of attracting: *The pins were drawn to the magnet by attraction. Sports have no attraction for me.*

at·trac·tive (ə trak′tiv), ADJECTIVE. winning attention and affection; pleasing: *an attractive young couple.*
▪ See the Synonym Study at **cute. –at·trac′tive·ly,** ADVERB. **–at·trac′tive·ness,** NOUN.

at·trib·ute (at′rə byüt), NOUN. a quality belonging to someone or something; characteristic: *Patience is an attribute of a good teacher.*

auc·tion (ȯk′shən),
1 NOUN. a public sale in which each thing is sold to the person who offers the most money for it.
2 VERB. to sell at an auction.
❑ VERB **auc·tions, auc·tioned, auc·tion·ing.**

auc·tion·eer (ȯk′shə nir′), NOUN. someone whose business is conducting auctions.

au·di·ble (ȯ′də bəl), ADJECTIVE. loud enough to be heard; able to be heard: *Her voice was barely audible.*

au·di·ence (ȯ′dē əns), NOUN.
1 a group of people gathered to hear or see something: *The audience enjoyed the play.*
2 the people who usually hear or see broadcasts on radio or TV: *This TV program has a large audience.*
3 a formal interview with someone of high rank: *He was granted an audience with the queen.*

au·di·o (ȯ′dē ō), ADJECTIVE. of or about sound: *We only recorded the audio part of the program.*

Word Power   audio-

The combining form **audio-** is used with other words or parts of words to add to their meaning. It describes something having to do with hearing or sound. An **audio**tape is a tape that records and plays back sound. **Audio**visual refers to something you hear as well as see.

au·di·o·tape (ȯ′dē ō tāp′), NOUN. magnetic tape that you can record sound onto.

au·di·o·vis·u·al (ȯ′dē ō vizh′ü əl), ADJECTIVE. of or affecting both hearing and sight. Schools use movies, slides, recordings, and other devices as audiovisual aids in teaching.

au·di·tion (ȯ dish′ən),
1 NOUN. a hearing to test the ability of a singer, actor, or other performer.
2 VERB. to perform at or give such a hearing: *Several of us auditioned for a part in a play.*
❑ VERB **au·di·tions, au·di·tioned, au·di·tion·ing.**

au·di·to·ri·um (ȯ′də tôr′ē əm), NOUN.
1 a large room for an audience in a theater, school, or the like; large hall.
2 a building especially designed for public meetings, concerts, and lectures.

au·di·to·ry (ȯ′də tôr′ē), ADJECTIVE. of hearing or the organs of hearing. The **auditory nerve** goes from the ear to the brain.

Aug., an abbreviation of **August.**

Au·gust (ȯ′gəst), NOUN. the eighth month of the year. It has 31 days.

Au·gus·ta (ȯ gus′tə), NOUN. the capital of Maine.

auk (ȯk), NOUN. a sea bird found in arctic regions that looks and acts like a penguin. Auks can fly but use their short wings mostly as paddles in swimming.

aunt (ant or änt), NOUN.
1 a sister of your father or mother.
2 the wife of your uncle.
▪ Another word that can sound like this is **ant.**

au·ri·cle (ȯr′ə kəl), NOUN.
1 the outer part of the ear.
2 See **atrium** (definition 1).

auk — 18 inches long

au·ro·ra (ȯ rôr′ə), NOUN. streamers or bands of light that appear in the sky at night, especially in polar regions. ❑ PLURAL **au·ro·ras.**

Aus·tin (ȯ′stən), NOUN. the capital of Texas.

Aus·tral·ia (ȯ strā′lyə), NOUN. the smallest continent, located southeast of Asia between the Pacific and Indian oceans. The country of Australia covers the whole continent. **–Aus·tral′ian,** ADJECTIVE or NOUN.

Aus·tri·a (ȯ′strē ə), NOUN. a country in central Europe. **–Aus′tri·an,** ADJECTIVE or NOUN.

au·then·tic (ȯ then′tik), ADJECTIVE. genuine; real: *That is her authentic signature.*

au·thor (ȯ′thər), NOUN.
1 someone who writes books, poems, stories, or articles; writer: *My favorite author is Dr. Seuss.*
2 someone who creates or begins anything: *Are you the author of this scheme?*

au·thor·i·ty (ə thôr′ə tē), NOUN.
1 the power or right to give commands and enforce obedience: *Parents have authority over their children. The police have the authority to give tickets.*
2 the authorities, the officials in control: *The authorities at city hall received many complaints about unpaved streets.*
3 an expert on some subject: *She is an authority on the Revolutionary War.*

a	hat	ė	term	ȯ	order	ch	child	⎧a in about
ā	age	i	it	oi	oil	ng	long	⎪e in taken
ä	far	ī	ice	ou	out	sh	she	ə⎨i in pencil
â	care	o	hot	u	cup	th	thin	⎪o in lemon
e	let	ō	open	u̇	put	ᴛʜ	then	⎩u in circus
ē	equal	ȯ	saw	ü	rule	zh	measure	

4 a source of information or advice: *A good dictionary is an authority on words.*
❑ PLURAL **au·thor·i·ties.**

Pumpkins are harvested in **autumn.**

au·thor·ize (o'thə rīz'), VERB. to give permission, approval, or right to: *The committee authorized us to proceed with our plan.* ❑ VERB **au·thor·iz·es, au·thor·ized, au·thor·iz·ing.** –**au'thor·i·za'tion,** NOUN.

au·to (o'tō), NOUN. a short form of **automobile.** See **car.** ❑ PLURAL **au·tos.**

Word Power   auto-

The combining form **auto-** is used with other words or parts of words to add to their meaning. **Auto-** means "by yourself" or "by itself." An **autobiography** is a biography written **by yourself.** An **autopilot** guides the plane **by itself.**

au·to·bi·og·ra·phy (o'tə bī og'rə fē), NOUN. the story of a person's life written by that person. ❑ PLURAL **au·to·bi·og·ra·phies.**

au·to·graph (o'tə graf),
1 NOUN. someone's signature: *Many people collect the autographs of celebrities.*
2 VERB. to write your name in or on something: *The basketball star autographed my shirt.*
❑ VERB **au·to·graphs, au·to·graphed, au·to·graph·ing.**

au·to·mate (o'tə māte), VERB. to convert to automation; operate by automation. ❑ VERB **au·to·mates, au·to·mat·ed, au·to·mat·ing.**

au·to·mat·ic (o'tə mat'ik),
1 ADJECTIVE. moving or acting by itself: *an automatic door.*
2 ADJECTIVE. done without thought or attention: *Breathing and swallowing are usually automatic.*
3 NOUN. a gun that throws out the empty shell and loads again by itself.

au·to·mat·i·cal·ly (o'tə mat'ik lē), ADVERB. in an automatic manner: *The door opened automatically.*

au·to·ma·tion (o'tə mā'shən), NOUN. the use of automatic controls in the operation of a machine or group of machines. In automation, machines do many of the tasks formerly performed by people.

au·to·mo·bile (o'tə mə bēl'), NOUN. See **car.**

au·top·sy (o'top sē), NOUN. a medical examination of a dead body to find the cause of death. ❑ PLURAL **au·top·sies.**

au·tumn (o'təm),
1 NOUN. the season of the year between summer and winter; fall.
2 ADJECTIVE. coming in autumn: *autumn leaves.*

aux·il·iar·y (og zil'yər ē),
1 ADJECTIVE. giving help or support; assisting: *Some sailboats have auxiliary engines.*
2 NOUN. someone or something that helps; aid: *The microscope is a useful auxiliary to the human eye.*
❑ PLURAL **aux·il·iar·ies.**

auxiliary verb, a kind of verb used with other verbs; helping verb. *Be, can, do, have, may, must, shall,* and *will* are auxiliary verbs. EXAMPLES: I *am* going; she *will* go; it *can* happen; we *must* leave; they *had* come.

a·vail·a·ble (ə vā'lə bəl), ADJECTIVE.
1 able to be used: *She is not available for the job; she is out of town.*
2 able to be had or gotten: *No tickets were available.*

av·a·lanche (av'ə lanch), NOUN.
1 a large mass of snow or rocks that suddenly slides or falls down the side of a mountain.
2 anything like an avalanche: *The reporters asked the governor an avalanche of questions.*

avalanche (definition 1)

Ave., an abbreviation of **avenue.**

a·venge (ə venj'), VERB. to get revenge for: *They fought to avenge the insult to their king.* ❑ VERB **a·veng·es, a·venged, a·veng·ing.** –**a·veng'er,** NOUN.

A

av·e·nue (av′ə nü), NOUN. a street, usually wide or bordered with trees. ❑ PLURAL **av·e·nues.**

av·er·age (av′ər ij),
1 NOUN. the quantity found by dividing the sum of all the quantities by the number of quantities. The average of 3 and 5 and 10 is 6 (because 3 + 5 + 10 = 18, and 18 ÷ 3 = 6).
2 VERB. to find the average of: *Will you average those numbers for me?*
3 ADJECTIVE. found by averaging: *The average temperature for the week was 82. The average grade on the test was an 85.*
4 VERB. to have as an average; amount on the average to: *The cost of our lunches at school averaged $6.50 a week.*
5 NOUN. the usual sort, amount, or kind: *The amount of rain this year has been below average.*
❑ VERB **av·er·ag·es, av·er·aged, av·er·ag·ing.**

a·vert (ə vėrt′), VERB.
1 to keep from happening; prevent; avoid: *She averted an accident by a quick turn of the wheel.*
2 to turn away; turn aside: *I averted my eyes from the car accident.*
❑ VERB **a·verts, a·vert·ed, a·vert·ing.**

a·vi·ar·y (ā′vē er′ē), NOUN. a place where many birds, especially wild birds, are kept. ❑ PLURAL **a·vi·ar·ies.**

a·vi·a·tion (ā′vē ā′shən), NOUN. the science of flying and navigating aircraft: *You must study aviation to become a pilot.*

a·vi·a·tor (ā′vē ā′tər), NOUN. someone who flies an aircraft; pilot.

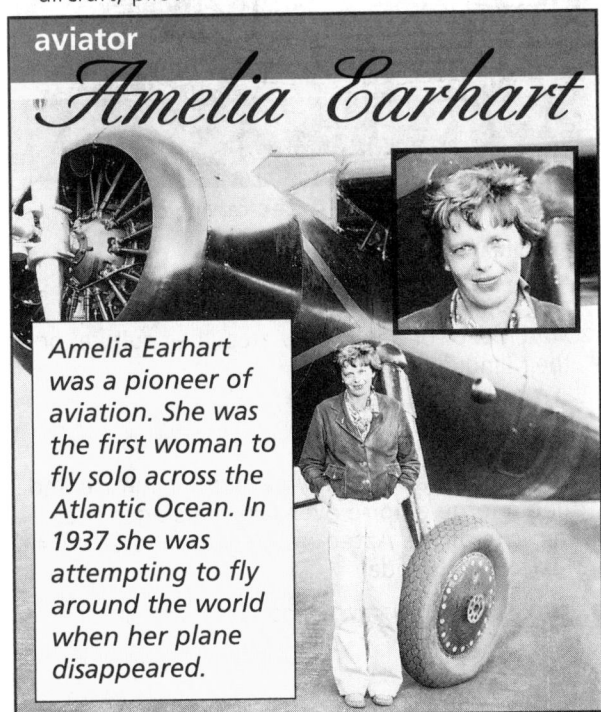

aviator

Amelia Earhart

Amelia Earhart was a pioneer of aviation. She was the first woman to fly solo across the Atlantic Ocean. In 1937 she was attempting to fly around the world when her plane disappeared.

av·o·ca·do (av′ə kä′dō), NOUN. a fruit with soft, green flesh, about the size and shape of a pear. It has thick green or black skin and a large, smooth seed. ❑ PLURAL **av·o·ca·dos.**

a·void (ə void′), VERB. to keep away from; keep out of the way of: *We avoided driving through large cities on our trip.* ❑ VERB **a·voids, a·void·ed, a·void·ing.** —**a·void′a·ble,** ADJECTIVE.

a·wait (ə wāt′), VERB. to wait for; look forward to: *I shall await your letter with eagerness.* ❑ VERB **a·waits, a·wait·ed, a·wait·ing.**

a·wake (ə wāk′),
1 VERB. to wake up; arouse: *I awoke from a sound sleep. The alarm clock awoke me.*
2 ADJECTIVE. roused from sleep; not asleep: *She is always awake early.*
❑ VERB **a·wakes, a·woke, a·wok·en** or **a·waked, a·wak·ing.**

a·wak·en (ə wā′kən), VERB. to wake up; stir up; arouse: *Birds awaken me each morning.* ❑ VERB **a·wak·ens, a·wak·ened, a·wak·en·ing.**

a·ward (ə wôrd′),
1 VERB. to give after careful consideration; grant: *A medal was awarded to the best speller in the class.*
2 NOUN. something given after careful consideration; prize: *That painting won the highest award at the art show.*
❑ VERB **a·wards, a·ward·ed, a·ward·ing.**

a·ware (ə wâr′), ADJECTIVE. having knowledge; realizing; conscious: *She was not aware of the danger she faced.* —**a·ware′ness,** NOUN.

a·way (ə wā′),
1 ADVERB. from a place; to a distance: *The car drove away quickly.*
2 ADJECTIVE or ADVERB. at a distance; a way off: *The sailor was far away from home. His home is miles away.*
3 ADJECTIVE. absent; not here: *My friend is away today.*
4 ADVERB. out of your possession, notice, or use: *He gave his boat away.*
5 ADVERB. out of existence: *The sounds died away.*
6 ADVERB. in another direction; aside: *She looked away suddenly.*

awe (ȯ),
1 NOUN. great fear and wonder; fear and great respect: *The sight of the waterfall filled us with awe.*
2 VERB. to cause to feel awe; fill with awe: *The majesty of the mountains awed us.*
❑ VERB **awes, awed, aw·ing.**

awe·some (ȯ′səm), ADJECTIVE.
1 causing great fear or wonder: *The fire was an awesome sight.*

a	hat	ė	term	ô	order	ch	child	ə {	a in about
ā	age	i	it	oi	oil	ng	long		e in taken
ä	far	ī	ice	ou	out	sh	she		i in pencil
â	care	o	hot	u	cup	th	thin		o in lemon
e	let	ō	open	ù	put	ᴛʜ	then		u in circus
ē	equal	ȯ	saw	ü	rule	zh	measure		

2 (informal) exceptionally good, desirable, or remarkable; terrific: *Where did you get those awesome shoes?*

awe·struck (ȯ′struk′), ADJECTIVE. filled with awe: *She was awestruck by the great beauty of the Grand Canyon.*

aw·ful (ȯ′fəl),

1 ADJECTIVE. causing fear; dreadful; terrible: *An awful storm with thunder and lightning came up.*
2 ADJECTIVE. very great: *I had an awful lot of work to do.*
3 ADJECTIVE. very bad: *I have an awful headache.*
▪ See the Synonym Study at **terrible.**
4 ADVERB. (informal) very: *I was awful mad.*

aw·ful·ly (ȯ′flē or ȯ′fə lē), ADVERB.

1 dreadfully; terribly: *The burn hurt awfully.*
2 very; truly; deeply: *I'm awfully sorry that I hurt your feelings.* ▪ See the Synonym Study at **very.**

a·while (ə hwīl′), ADVERB. for a short time: *We rested awhile after lunch.*

awk·ward (ȯk′wərd), ADJECTIVE.

1 clumsy; not graceful or skillful in movement: *Seals are very awkward on land, but graceful in the water.*
2 embarrassing: *He asked me such an awkward question that I did not know what to reply.* —**awk′ward·ly,** ADVERB. —**awk′ward·ness,** NOUN.

awl (ȯl), NOUN. a pointed tool used for making small holes in leather or wood. ▪ Another word that sounds like this is **all.**

awn·ing (ȯ′ning), NOUN. a piece of canvas, metal, wood, or plastic that forms a rooflike covering over a door, window, porch, or patio. Awnings are used for protection from the sun or rain.

a·woke (ə wōk′), VERB. the past tense of **awake**: *She awoke them at seven. We awoke early.*

a·wo·ken (ə wō′kən), VERB. a past participle of **awake**: *He has awoken late every day this week.*

ax or **axe** (aks), NOUN. a tool with a flat, sharp blade fastened on a handle, used for chopping, splitting, and shaping wood. ▪ PLURAL **ax·es.** —**ax′like′** or **axe′like′,** ADJECTIVE.

ax·is (ak′sis), NOUN.

1 a straight line around which an object turns or seems to turn. The axis of the earth is an imaginary line through the North Pole and the South Pole.
2 one of the main lines in a graph. Points are marked along an axis, and amounts of distance, time, weight, and so on can be recorded on it. ▪ PLURAL **ax·es** (ak′sēz′).

ax·le (ak′səl), NOUN. a bar or shaft on which a wheel turns. Some axles turn with the wheel.

aye or **ay** (ī),

1 ADVERB. yes: *Aye, aye, sir.*

2 NOUN. a vote or voter in favor of something: *The ayes won the vote.*
▪ PLURAL **ayes** or **ays.** ▪ Other words that sound like this are **eye** and **I.**

AZ, an abbreviation of **Arizona.**

a·zal·ea (ə zā′lyə), NOUN. a bush bearing many showy flowers. ▪ PLURAL **a·zal·eas.**

A·zer·bai·jan (ä′zər bī jän′), NOUN. a country in southeastern Europe. —**Az·er·bai·ja·ni** (ä′zər bī jä′nē), ADJECTIVE or NOUN.

an **Aztec** carving on a stone wall

Az·tec (az′tek),

1 NOUN. a member of an American Indian people of central Mexico.
2 ADJECTIVE. of or about the Aztec, their culture, or their language. ▪ PLURAL **Az·tec** or **Az·tecs.**

Did You Know?

The **Aztecs** had a highly developed culture and ruled a large empire over 400 years ago. The main city of the Aztec empire was where Mexico City is today.

az·ure (azh′ər), ADJECTIVE or NOUN. blue; blue like the sky.

butterfly

Bb

B or **b** (bē), *NOUN.* the second letter of the English alphabet. ❑ *PLURAL* **B's** or **b's.**

baa (bä *or* ba),
1 *NOUN.* the sound a sheep makes; bleat.
2 *VERB.* to make this sound; bleat.
   ❑ *PLURAL* **baas;** *VERB* **baas, baaed, baa·ing.**

bab·ble (bab′əl),
1 *VERB.* to make sounds like a baby: *My baby brother babbles in his crib.*
2 *NOUN.* talk that cannot be understood: *A confused babble filled the room.*
3 *VERB.* to talk foolishly: *She babbled on and on.*
4 *NOUN.* foolish talk.
   ❑ *VERB* **bab·bles, bab·bled, bab·bling.**

babe (bāb), *NOUN.* a baby.

ba·boon (ba bün′), *NOUN.* a large, fierce monkey with a doglike face. Baboons live in Africa and Arabia.

ba·by (bā′bē),
1 *NOUN.* a very young child; infant.
2 *NOUN.* the youngest of a family or group.
3 *ADJECTIVE.* young; small: *There were six baby hamsters in the cage.*
4 *ADJECTIVE.* of or for a baby: *baby shoes, a baby bottle.*
5 *ADJECTIVE.* like a baby; childish: *baby talk.*
6 *VERB.* to treat like a baby: *You are much too old to be babied.*
   ❑ *PLURAL* **ba·bies;** *VERB* **ba·bies, ba·bied, ba·by·ing.**

ba·by·ish (bā′bē ish), *ADJECTIVE.* like a baby; childish: *His round face and bald head gave him a babyish appearance.* **—ba′by·ish·ly,** *ADVERB.*

ba·by·sit (bā′bē sit′), *VERB.* to take care of a child or children while the parents are away for a while: *When my cousin baby-sits, she lets us stay up an extra hour.* ❑ *VERB* **ba·by-sits, ba·by-sat** (bā′bē sat′), **ba·by-sit·ting. —ba′by-sit′ter,** *NOUN.*

baby teeth, the first set of teeth.

bach·e·lor (bach′ə lər), *NOUN.* a man who is not married.

back (bak),

1 *NOUN.* the part of a body opposite to the front, including the spine.

2 *NOUN.* the side of anything away from the front; the rear or upper part: *a bruise on the back of my hand, the suitcase in the back of the closet.*

3 *ADJECTIVE.* at the back: *the back seat of the car.*

4 *NOUN.* the part of a chair, couch, or bench that supports the back of someone sitting down.

5 *VERB.* to support or help: *Her friends backed her plan.*

6 *VERB.* to move or cause to move backward: *I backed the car out of the driveway.*

7 *ADVERB.* behind in space or time: *Step back, please. Have you read the back issues of this magazine?*

8 *ADVERB.* in return: *They paid back the money.*

9 *ADVERB.* in the place from which something or someone came: *Put the books back.*

10 *NOUN.* a football player whose position is behind the line.
□ *VERB* **backs, backed, back·ing.** —**back′er,** *NOUN.* —**back′less,** *ADJECTIVE.*

back out or **back out of,** *IDIOM.* to break a promise to do something: *The village backed out of building a pool when the cost got too high.*

behind someone's back, *IDIOM.* without the person's knowing about it; secretly: *The cashier stole money behind the owner's back.*

turn your back on, *IDIOM.* to ignore, reject, or refuse to help someone or something: *I was upset when she turned her back on our project.*

back·ache (bak′āk′), *NOUN.* a continuous pain in the back.

back·board (bak′bôrd′), *NOUN.* (in basketball) the flat surface on which the basket is mounted.

back·bone (bak′bōn′), *NOUN.*

1 the main bone in the middle of the back in human beings, dogs, birds, snakes, frogs, fish, and many other animals; spine. The backbone is made up of many separate bones, called vertebrae, held together by muscles and tendons.

2 the most important part: *The Constitution is the backbone of our legal system.*

back·court (bak′kôrt′), *NOUN.*

1 the area of the court that a team defends.

2 the players who primarily defend and advance the ball in this part of the court; guards.

back·field (bak′fēld′), *NOUN.* the football players who start from behind the line.

back·fire (bak′fir′),

1 *NOUN.* an explosion of fuel vapor occurring at the wrong time or place in a gasoline engine.

2 *VERB.* to produce this kind of explosion: *The engine backfired.*

3 *VERB.* to have a result opposite to the expected result: *His plan backfired, and he lost his money.*
□ *VERB* **back·fires, back·fired, back·fir·ing.**

back·gam·mon (bak′gam′ən), *NOUN.* a game for two played on a special board with 12 spaces on each side. Each player has 15 pieces which are moved according to the throw of the dice.

back·ground (bak′ground′), *NOUN.*

1 past experience, knowledge, and training: *His early background included living on a farm.*

2 earlier conditions or events that help to explain some later condition or event: *The book gives the background of the Civil War.*

3 the part of a picture or scene toward the back: *There were two tall mountains in the background.*

4 the surface against which a thing or person is placed or shown: *The curtains had blue flowers on a white background.*

back·hand (bak′hand′), *NOUN.* a stroke in tennis and other games made with the back of the hand turned outward.

backhand

back·pack (bak′pak′),

1 *NOUN.* a pack worn on the back, held by shoulder straps; knapsack.

2 *VERB.* to go hiking or camping with a backpack.
□ *VERB* **back·packs, back·packed, back·pack·ing.** —**back′pack′er,** *NOUN.*

back·stage (bak′stāj′), *ADVERB* or *ADJECTIVE.* in the part of a theater not seen by the audience: *We went backstage after the play.*

back·up (bak′up′),

1 *NOUN.* someone or something that gives help or support when necessary: *The firefighters needed more fire trucks as backup to fight the fire.*

2 *NOUN.* a copy of something that will replace a lost original: *Make backups of all your computer files.*

3 *ADJECTIVE.* kept in reserve; extra: *a backup copy.*

back·ward (bak′wərd),

1 *ADVERB.* with the back first: *He fell backward.*

2 *ADVERB* or *ADJECTIVE.* toward the back: *Look backward! She gave us a backward look as she left.*

3 *ADVERB.* opposite to the usual way: *Can you count backward from twenty?*

4 *ADVERB.* from better to worse: *At first, living conditions improved; later they went backward.*

5 ADJECTIVE. slow in development: *a backward country.* ★ This meaning of **backward** is often considered offensive.

back·wards (bak′wərdz), ADVERB. See **backward** (definitions 1–4).

back·yard (bak′yärd′), NOUN. the yard behind a house or building.

ba·con (bā′kən), NOUN. salted and smoked meat from the back and sides of a pig.

bac·ter·i·a (bak tir′ē ə), NOUN PLURAL. very tiny and simple living things, so small that they can usually be seen only through a microscope. Some bacteria cause diseases such as pneumonia; others do useful things, such as turning cider into vinegar. ❑ SINGULAR **bac·ter·i·um** (bak tir′ē əm).

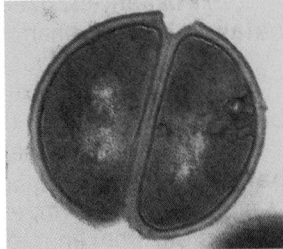

a pair of **bacteria** linked together

bad (bad), ADJECTIVE.
1 not good; not as it ought to be: *It was hard to read in the bad light. She made a bad guess.*
2 evil; wicked: *It is bad to hurt a helpless person.*
3 not friendly; cross; unpleasant: *He has a bad temper.*
4 causing sorrow: *I was very upset by the bad news.*
5 naughty; not behaving well: *The child was bad when she hit her playmate.*
6 severe: *A bad thunderstorm delayed the airplane.*
7 harmful; unhealthful: *Smoking is bad for you.*
8 rotten; spoiled: *Don't use that egg; it's gone bad.*
9 sorry: *I feel bad about losing your baseball.*
★ In formal English, only **bad** is used as an adjective. You should say *She feels bad* (She is sorry or sick), not *She feels badly* (Her sense of touch is out of order).
10 uncomfortable; sick: *Her cold made her feel bad.*
❑ ADJECTIVE **worse, worst. –bad′ness,** NOUN.

Synonym Study

Bad means not good or not as it ought to be: *He says the movie is bad because it bored him. Her skateboard has a bad wheel.*

Unsatisfactory means not good enough: *The student had to rewrite his unsatisfactory report.*

Poor can mean not good in quality: *The painters did a poor job, dripping paint all over.*

Inferior means worse than others or worse than it should be: *This TV is inferior to the one we have at home.*

See also the Synonym Studies at **naughty, terrible,** and **wicked.**

ANTONYMS: good, satisfactory.

bade (bad), VERB. a past tense of **bid:** *They bade her remain.* ★ **Bade** is used in very formal English and in stories.

badge (baj), NOUN. something worn to show that you belong to a certain job, school, class, or club.

badg·er (baj′ər),
1 NOUN. a gray, hairy animal about 2 feet long. Badgers feed at night and dig holes to live in.
2 VERB. to keep on annoying or teasing someone: *They badgered me with endless questions.*
❑ VERB **badg·ers, badg·ered, badg·er·ing.**

bad·ly (bad′lē), ADVERB.
1 in an unpleasant or awkward manner; poorly.
2 very much: *We need help badly.*
★ In formal English **badly** is used only to modify action verbs. SAY: *She sings badly.* NOT: *She sings bad.*

bad·min·ton (bad′min tən), NOUN. a game for two or four players who use lightweight rackets to hit a small object back and forth across a net. The point of the game is to keep the object in the air.

baf·fle (baf′əl), VERB. to be too hard for someone to understand or solve; bewilder: *This puzzle baffles me.* ❑ VERB **baf·fles, baf·fled, baf·fling.**

bag (bag), NOUN.
1 a container made of paper, cloth, or other soft material: *Vegetables are often sold in plastic bags.*
2 something used like a bag. Purses and suitcases are bags.
–bag′like′, ADJECTIVE.

ba·gel (bā′gəl), NOUN. a hard roll made of a ring of dough. It is simmered in water before baking.

bag·gage (bag′ij), NOUN. suitcases packed for traveling; luggage.

bag·gy (bag′ē), ADJECTIVE. hanging loosely: *The clown had baggy pants.* ❑ ADJECTIVE **bag·gi·er, bag·gi·est. –bag′gi·ness,** NOUN.

bag·pipe (bag′pip′), NOUN. a musical instrument made of a tube to blow through, a leather bag for pumping air, and four pipes.

bail¹ (bāl),
1 NOUN. money left with a court of law in order to free an accused person from jail until a trial is held: *They put up bail for their friend.*
2 VERB. to set an accused person free by offering this money: *They bailed their friend out of jail.*
❑ VERB **bails, bailed, bail·ing.** ∎ Another word that sounds like this is **bale.**

bail someone out, IDIOM. to help someone who is in trouble: *The teacher bailed him out when he forgot the answer.*

a	hat	ė	term	ô	order	ch	child		a in about
ā	age	i	it	oi	oil	ng	long		e in taken
ä	far	ī	ice	ou	out	sh	she	ə	i in pencil
â	care	o	hot	u	cup	th	thin		o in lemon
e	let	ō	open	u̇	put	ŦH	then		u in circus
ē	equal	ȯ	saw	ü	rule	zh	measure		

bail² (bāl), VERB. to throw water out of a boat using a bucket, pail, or other container: *She began to bail water out of the canoe.* ❑ VERB **bails, bailed, bail·ing.** ▪ Another word that sounds like this is **bale.**

bail out, IDIOM. to jump from an airplane by parachute: *The pilot bailed out of the burning plane.*

bait (bāt),
1 NOUN. anything, especially food, used to attract fish or other animals so that they may be caught.
2 VERB. to put bait on a hook or in a trap: *I baited my hook with a big, juicy worm.*
3 VERB. to torment someone by unkind or annoying remarks: *A noisy group kept baiting the speaker.* ❑ VERB **baits, bait·ed, bait·ing.**

Ba·ja Cal·i·for·nia Nor·te (bä′hä kä lē fôr′nyä nôr′tā), a state in northwestern Mexico.

Ba·ja Cal·i·for·nia Sur (bä′hä kä lē fôr′nyä sùr), a state in northwestern Mexico.

bake (bāk), VERB.
1 to cook food in the dry heat of an oven: *I am baking a cake for the party.*
2 to dry or harden by heat: *We baked the pots in a kiln.* ❑ VERB **bakes, baked, bak·ing.**

bak·er (bā′kər), NOUN. someone who makes or sells bread, pies, cakes, and pastries.

bak·er·y (bā′kər ē), NOUN. a place where bread, pies, cakes, and pastries are made or sold. ❑ PLURAL **bak·er·ies.**

baking powder, a mixture of chemicals used instead of yeast to cause biscuits or cakes to rise.

baking soda, a white powder used in cooking and medicine.

The surfer tries to keep his **balance.**

bal·ance (bal′əns),
1 NOUN. steady condition or position; equilibrium: *The gymnast lost her balance and fell.*
2 VERB. to put or keep something in a steady or stable condition: *He balanced a load of wood on his shoulder as he climbed the ladder. We will balance our diet by choosing a variety of healthy foods.*
3 NOUN. a device for weighing: *The chemist measured the compound's mass on a balance.*

4 VERB. to weigh two things against each other on scales, in your hands, or in your mind to see which is heavier or more important: *He balanced the two peaches in his hands and gave me the larger one. She balanced a trip to the mountains against a chance to go to summer camp.*
5 NOUN. the remainder left over after something is spent, used, or removed: *I had a balance of $200 in my account after I bought the old car.* ❑ VERB **bal·anc·es, bal·anced, bal·anc·ing.**

balance beam, a narrow bar or beam set about 4 feet above the floor, on which gymnasts perform balancing exercises.

balanced diet, a diet that has the right amount of food from each of the six nutrient groups.

bal·co·ny (bal′kə nē), NOUN.
1 an outside platform, enclosed by a railing, that sticks out from an upper floor of a building.
2 an upper floor in a theater, hall, or church that is built out over part of the lower floor. ❑ PLURAL **bal·co·nies.**

bald (bȯld), ADJECTIVE. wholly or partly without hair on the head. **—bald′ness,** NOUN.

bald eagle — wingspread about 6½ feet

bald eagle, a large, powerful, North American eagle with white feathers on its head, neck, and tail.

bale (bāl),
1 NOUN. a large bundle of material tightly wrapped for shipping or storage: *a bale of cotton.*
2 VERB. to make into bales: *That machine bales hay. Some businesses bale cardboard for recycling.* ❑ VERB **bales, baled, bal·ing.** ▪ Another word that sounds like this is **bail. —bal′er,** NOUN.

balk (bȯk), VERB. to stop short and stubbornly refuse to go on: *My horse balked at the fence.* ❑ VERB **balks, balked, balk·ing.**

ball¹ (bȯl), NOUN.
1 a round or somewhat oval object that is thrown, batted, kicked, rolled, or carried in various games. Different sizes and types of balls are used in tennis, baseball, football, and soccer.
2 a game in which some kind of ball is thrown, hit, or kicked, especially baseball.

B

3 anything round or roundish; something that is like a ball: *a ball of string, the ball of a foot.*

4 a baseball pitched too high, too low, or not over the plate, that the batter does not strike at. **—ball'-like'**, *ADJECTIVE.*

have a ball, *IDIOM.* to have a good time; enjoy yourself: *We all had a ball at the party.*

play ball, *IDIOM.* to agree to work together; cooperate: *We agreed agreed to play ball and help raise funds.*

ball² (bȯl), *NOUN.* a large, formal party with dancing.

bal·lad (bal'əd), *NOUN.*
1 a poem that tells a story. Ballads are often sung.
2 a romantic popular song.

ball-and-sock·et joint (bȯl'ən sok'it joint'), a joint in a skeleton formed by a ball or knob that fits into a socket, allowing circular motion. The shoulder and hip joints are ball-and-socket joints.

bal·last (bal'əst), *NOUN.* something heavy carried in a ship to steady it.

ball bearing, a part of a machine in which a metal bar turns upon a number of freely moving steel balls, called bearings. They are used to reduce friction.

bal·le·ri·na (bal'ə rē'nə), *NOUN.* a woman who dances in a ballet. □ *PLURAL* **bal·le·ri·nas.**

bal·let (bal'ā), *NOUN.* an elaborate dance by a group on a stage. A ballet usually tells a story through the movements of the dancing and the music.

ball·game (bȯl'gām'), *NOUN.* any game played with a ball, especially baseball.

bal·loon (bə lün'),
1 *NOUN.* an airtight bag filled with some gas lighter than air, so that it will float in the air. Some balloons carry people or scientific instruments.
2 *NOUN.* a child's toy made of thin rubber filled with air or some gas lighter than air.
3 *VERB.* to swell out like a balloon: *The sails of the boat ballooned in the wind.*
□ *VERB* **bal·loons, bal·looned, bal·loon·ing.**

bal·loon·ist (bə lü'nist), *NOUN.* someone who goes up in balloons.

bal·lot (bal'ət), *NOUN.* a piece of paper or other object used in voting: *Have you cast your ballot?*

ball·point pen (bȯl'point' pen'), a pen that writes with a small metal ball at the point.

ball·room (bȯl'rüm'), *NOUN.* a large room for dancing.

ba·lo·ney (bə lō'nē), *NOUN.*
1 nonsense: *That story is a lot of baloney and you shouldn't believe it.*
2 another spelling of **bologna.**
□ *PLURAL* **ba·lo·neys.**

bal·sa (bȯl'sə), *NOUN.* the strong, light wood of a tropical American tree, used in making model planes. □ *PLURAL* **bal·sas.**

Bal·tic Sea (bȯl'tik sē'), a sea in northern Europe.

bam·boo (bam bü'), *NOUN.* a woody grass with a very tall, stiff, hollow stem that has hard, thick joints. Bamboo is used for making canes, fishing poles, and even houses. □ *PLURAL* **bam·boos.**

bamboo

ban (ban),
1 *VERB.* to officially say that something must not be done: *Swimming is banned in this lake.*
2 *NOUN.* a law or order that bans something: *The city has a ban on parking in this busy street.*
□ *VERB* **bans, banned, ban·ning.**

ba·nan·a (bə nan'ə), *NOUN.* a curved, yellow tropical fruit with firm, tasty flesh. □ *PLURAL* **ba·nan·as.**

band¹ (band), *NOUN.*
1 a group of musicians performing together: *The school band played several marches.*
2 a number of people joined or acting together: *A band of robbers held up the train.*

band² (band),
1 *NOUN.* a thin, flat strip of material used to strengthen, bind, decorate, and so on: *Metal bands reinforced the wooden crate.*
2 *VERB.* to put a band on: *Scientists who study birds often band them so the birds can be identified later.*
3 *NOUN.* a stripe: *The white cup has a gold band.*
□ *VERB* **bands, band·ed, band·ing.**

band·age (ban'dij),
1 *NOUN.* a strip of cloth or other material used to wrap or cover a wound or injury.
2 *VERB.* to wrap or cover with a bandage.
□ *VERB* **band·ag·es, band·aged, band·ag·ing.**

ban·dan·na (ban dan'ə), *NOUN.* a large, colored handkerchief. □ *PLURAL* **ban·dan·nas.**

ban·dit (ban'dit), *NOUN.* a robber or thief.

bang (bang),
1 *NOUN.* a sudden, loud noise or blow: *We heard the bang of firecrackers.*
2 *VERB.* to make a sudden, loud noise: *The door banged as it blew shut.*
□ *VERB* **bangs, banged, bang·ing.**

Ban·gla·desh (bäng'glə desh'), *NOUN.* a country in southern Asia. **—Ban·gla·desh·i** (bäng'glə desh'ē), *ADJECTIVE or NOUN.*

a	hat	ė	term	ô	order	ch	child		a in about
ā	age	i	it	oi	oil	ng	long		e in taken
ä	far	ī	ice	ou	out	sh	she	ə {	i in pencil
â	care	o	hot	u	cup	th	thin		o in lemon
e	let	ō	open	ů	put	ᴙH	then		u in circus
ē	equal	ȯ	saw	ü	rule	zh	measure		

ban·gle (bang′gəl), NOUN.
1 a small ornament that hangs from a bracelet.
2 a bracelet.

bangs (bangz), NOUN PLURAL. hair cut short and worn over the forehead.

ban·ish (ban′ish), VERB. to force to leave a country; drive away: *The king banished his enemies. We banished her from the game for cheating.* ❑ VERB **ban·ish·es, ban·ished, ban·ish·ing.**
–**ban′ish·ment,** NOUN.

ban·is·ter (ban′ə stər), NOUN. the rail of a staircase and its row of supports: *Hold on to the banister on those steep stairs.*

ban·jo (ban′jō), NOUN. a musical instrument having four or five strings. The strings are plucked with the fingers or a pick.
❑ PLURAL **ban·jos.**

bank¹ (bangk),
1 NOUN. the ground bordering a river or lake; shore: *We fished from the bank.*
2 NOUN. a long pile or heap: *a bank of snow.*
3 VERB. to form a heap: *Tractors banked the snow.*
4 VERB. to bounce a basketball off the backboard into the basket.
❑ VERB **banks, banked, bank·ing.**

a five-string **banjo**

bank² (bangk),
1 NOUN. a place of business for keeping, lending, exchanging, and issuing money.
2 VERB. to keep or put money in a bank: *I bank the money I earn baby-sitting.*
3 NOUN. a small container with a slot through which coins can be dropped to save money.
4 NOUN. a place to keep reserve supplies: *a blood bank, a food bank.*
❑ VERB **banks, banked, bank·ing.**
  bank on, IDIOM. to depend on; count on: *I am banking on your help at the school carnival.*

bank account, money that you keep safe in a bank. You can take money out of it at any time.

bank·er (bang′kər), NOUN. someone who runs a bank.

bank·ing (bang′king), NOUN. the business of a bank or banker.

bank·rupt (bang′krupt),
1 ADJECTIVE. unable to pay your debts.
2 VERB. to make bankrupt: *Those expensive toys will bankrupt him.*
❑ VERB **bank·rupts, bank·rupt·ed, bank·rupt·ing.**

bank shot, a shot in basketball in which a player bounces the ball off the backboard into the basket.

ban·ner (ban′ər), NOUN. a flag or cloth with a design on it: *Our band has a special banner for parades.*

banner

ban·quet (bang′kwit), NOUN. a large meal with many courses, prepared for a special occasion; feast: *a wedding banquet.*

ban·ter (ban′tər),
1 NOUN. playful teasing; joking: *There was much banter going on at the party.*
2 VERB. to tease playfully; talk in a joking way: *The two friends bantered as they walked.*
❑ VERB **ban·ters, ban·tered, ban·ter·ing.**

Ban·tu (ban′tü), NOUN.
1 member of a large group of peoples living in central and southern Africa.
2 any of the languages of these peoples. Swahili is a Bantu language.
❑ PLURAL **Ban·tu** or **Bantus.**

Word Source

Bantu and other African languages have given a number of words to the English language. The words below are some of them:

banana	gnu	Kwanzaa	yam
banjo	jazz	okra	zombie
chimpanzee	jukebox	safari	

bap·tism (bap′tiz əm), NOUN. a ceremony in which someone is dipped in water or sprinkled with water, as a sign of washing away sin and of admission to the Christian church.

bap·tize (bap tīz′), VERB.
1 to dip someone into water or sprinkle with water as a sign of washing away sin and of admission into the Christian church.
2 to give a first name to someone at baptism; christen: *She was baptized Maria, but everyone calls her Missy.*
❑ VERB **bap·tiz·es, bap·tized, bap·tiz·ing.**

bar (bär),
1 NOUN. an evenly shaped piece of some solid, longer than it is wide or thick: *a bar of soap.*

2 *NOUN.* a pole or rod put across a door, gate, window, or across any opening to close it off: *The windows of the prison have iron bars.*

3 *VERB.* to put bars across; shut off: *Bar the door.*

4 *NOUN.* anything that blocks the way or prevents progress: *Shyness can be a bar to making friends.*

5 *VERB.* to block; obstruct: *Fallen trees bar the road.*

6 *VERB.* to keep out: *Dogs are barred from that store.*

7 *NOUN.* a band of color; stripe.

8 *NOUN.* a unit of rhythm in music, containing one or more notes or a rest; measure.

9 *NOUN.* the dividing line between two such units on a musical staff.

10 *NOUN.* a counter or place where drinks and sometimes food are served to customers.

11 *NOUN.* the whole group of practicing lawyers: *After passing my law exams, I was admitted to the bar.*
❏ *VERB* **bars, barred, bar·ring.**

barb (bärb), *NOUN.* a point sticking out and curving back from the point of an arrow or fishhook.

bar·bar·i·an (bär bâr′ē ən), *NOUN.* a member of a primitive, uncivilized people.

bar·be·cue (bär′bə kyü),
1 *NOUN.* an outdoor meal in which meat is cooked over an open fire.
2 *NOUN.* an open fireplace for cooking outside.
3 *NOUN.* meat cooked over an open fire.
4 *VERB.* to cook over an open fire or hot charcoal, often with a highly flavored sauce.
❏ *PLURAL* **bar·be·cues;** *VERB* **bar·be·cues, bar·be·cued, bar·be·cu·ing.**

barbed wire (bärbd′ wīr′), wire with sharp points on it every few inches, used for fences.

bar·ber (bär′bər), *NOUN.* someone whose work is cutting hair and shaving or trimming beards.

bar code, a set of short, vertical, thick and thin lines, often with numbers printed underneath. Bar codes are read by machines to find information about the coded items.

bare (bâr),
1 *ADJECTIVE.* without covering; not clothed; naked: *The sun burned his bare shoulders.*
2 *ADJECTIVE.* empty: *a room bare of furniture.*
3 *ADJECTIVE.* just enough and no more: *She earns only a bare living.*
4 *VERB.* to uncover something; reveal: *She bared her feelings. The dog bared its teeth.*
❏ *ADJECTIVE* **bar·er, bar·est;** *VERB* **bares, bared, bar·ing.**
▪ Another word that sounds like this is **bear.**

bare·back (bâr′bak′), *ADVERB* or *ADJECTIVE.* without a saddle; on a horse's bare back: *She likes to ride bareback. He is a bareback rider.*

bare·foot (bâr′fůt′), *ADJECTIVE* or *ADVERB.* wearing nothing on the feet: *I ran barefoot in the yard.*

bare·ly (bâr′lē), *ADVERB.* with nothing to spare; only just: *I barely had time to catch my bus.*

bar·gain (bär′gən),
1 *NOUN.* an agreement to trade or exchange: *You can't back out on our bargain.*
2 *NOUN.* something offered for sale cheap or bought cheap: *This hat is a bargain.*
3 *VERB.* to try to make a good deal: *I bargained with the owner and got the skates for only $15.*
❏ *VERB* **bar·gains, bar·gained, bar·gain·ing.** —**bar′gain·er,** *NOUN.*

barge (bärj), *NOUN.* a large boat with a flat bottom, used to carry freight on rivers and canals.

bar graph, a graph that shows amounts by parallel bars which differ in length in proportion to the difference in amount.

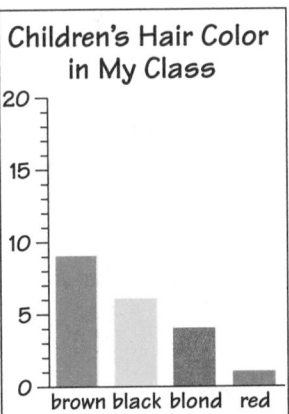
bar graph

bar·i·tone (bar′ə tōn), *NOUN.* a man's singing voice between tenor and bass.

bark¹ (bärk), *NOUN.* the tough outside covering of the trunk and branches of trees and bushes.

bark² (bärk),
1 *NOUN.* the short, sharp sound that a dog makes.
2 *VERB.* to make this sound: *The dog barked as I left.*
❏ *VERB* **barks, barked, bark·ing.**

Have You Heard?

You may have heard someone say **"His bark is worse than his bite."** This means that the person seems to be more upset or angry than he or she actually is.

bar·ley (bär′lē), *NOUN.* the grain of a kind of cereal grass. Barley is used as food for people and animals.

bar mitz·vah (bär′ mits′və), the ceremony or celebration held when a Jewish boy becomes thirteen years old. It means he has reached the age of religious responsibility.

barn (bärn), *NOUN.* a farm building for storing hay and grain and for sheltering animals and machinery. —**barn′like′,** *ADJECTIVE.*

bar·na·cle (bär′nə kəl), *NOUN.* a small, saltwater animal with a shell. It fastens itself to rocks, the timbers of docks, and the bottoms of ships.

barn·yard (bärn′yärd′), *NOUN.* the piece of ground around a barn.

a	hat	ė	term	ô	order	ch	child		a in about
ā	age	i	it	oi	oil	ng	long		e in taken
ä	far	ī	ice	ou	out	sh	she	ə	i in pencil
â	care	o	hot	u	cup	th	thin		o in lemon
e	let	ō	open	ů	put	ŦH	then		u in circus
ē	equal	ò	saw	ü	rule	zh	measure		

ba·rom·e·ter (bə rom′ə tər), *NOUN.* a device for measuring air pressure and predicting weather.

bar·on (bar′ən), *NOUN.*
1 a nobleman of the lowest rank.
2 a powerful person in industry: *a coal baron.*
■ Another word that sounds like this is **barren.**

bar·on·ess (bar′ə nis), *NOUN.*
1 the wife or widow of a baron.
2 a woman whose rank is equal to that of a baron.
❑ *PLURAL* **bar·on·ess·es.**

bar·racks (bar′əks), *NOUN PLURAL* or *SINGULAR.* a building or group of buildings for soldiers to live in, usually in a fort or camp.

bar·ra·cu·da (bar′ə kü′də), *NOUN.* a long, narrow fish with sharp teeth, found in salt water. ❑ *PLURAL* **bar·ra·cu·da** or **bar·ra·cu·das.**

bar·rel (bar′əl), *NOUN.*
1 a container with a round, flat top and bottom and sides that curve out slightly. Barrels are usually made of boards held together by hoops.
2 the amount that a barrel can hold: *They picked a barrel of apples.*
3 the metal tube of a gun through which a bullet is fired.

bar·ren (bar′ən), *ADJECTIVE.*
1 not able to bear seeds, fruit, or young: *a barren fruit tree; a barren animal.*
2 not able to produce or support much life: *a barren desert; a barren field.*
■ Another word that sounds like this is **baron.**

bar·rette (bə ret′), *NOUN.* a clip for holding the hair in place.

bar·ri·cade (bar′ə kād),
1 *NOUN.* a rough, hastily made barrier for defense: *The soldiers cut down trees to make a barricade.*
2 *VERB.* to block or close off with a barrier: *They barricaded the road with fallen trees.*
❑ *VERB* **bar·ri·cades, bar·ri·cad·ed, bar·ri·cad·ing.**

bar·ri·er (bar′ē ər), *NOUN.* something that stands in the way; something that stops progress or prevents movement: *The landslide created a barrier across the road.*

bar·ri·o (bär′ē ō), *NOUN.* the part of a city where mainly Spanish-speaking people live. ❑ *PLURAL* **bar·ri·os.**

bar·ter (bär′tər),
1 *VERB.* to trade by exchanging one kind of goods for other goods without using money; exchange: *The trapper bartered furs for supplies.*
2 *NOUN.* the act or process of exchanging goods.
❑ *VERB* **bar·ters, bar·tered, bar·ter·ing.**

base¹ (bās),
1 *NOUN.* the part on which anything stands or rests; bottom: *This big machine has a wide steel base.*
2 *NOUN.* a starting place; headquarters: *The base for our hike was the cabin.*

3 *VERB.* to use as a base or basis for: *This novel is based on the lives of famous people. He based his decision on the article he read in the newspaper.*
4 *NOUN.* the main or most important part of something: *This paint has an oil base.*
5 *NOUN.* the place that is a station or goal in certain games, such as baseball or hide-and-seek: *A home run doesn't count if you fail to touch a base.*
6 *NOUN.* a chemical compound that unites with an acid to form a salt. Ammonia and bleach contain bases.
7 *NOUN.* the line or surface on which a geometric shape is supposed to rest. Any side of a triangle can be its base.
8 *NOUN.* the form of a word to which prefixes and suffixes can be attached; root.
❑ *VERB* **bas·es, based, bas·ing.**

base² (bās), *ADJECTIVE.*
1 mean and cowardly: *To betray a friend is base.*
2 having little value when compared with something else, inferior: *Iron and lead are base metals; gold and silver are precious metals.*
❑ *ADJECTIVE* **bas·er, bas·est. –base′ness,** *NOUN.*

base·ball (bās′bȯl′), *NOUN.*
1 a game played with bat and ball by two teams of nine players, on a field with four bases; hardball. A batter who touches all the bases scores a run.
2 the ball used in this game; hardball.

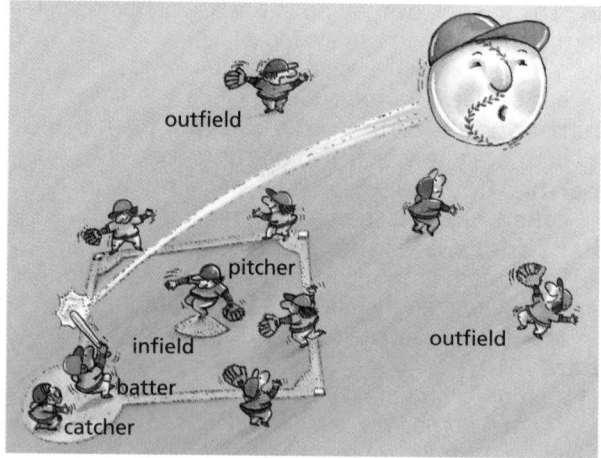

outfield

pitcher

infield

outfield

batter

catcher

baseball

base·man (bās′mən), *NOUN.* a baseball player guarding first, second, or third base. ❑ *PLURAL* **base·men.**

base·ment (bās′mənt), *NOUN.* the lowest story of a building, partly or wholly below ground.

bas·es¹ (bā′səz), *NOUN.* the plural of **base¹.**

ba·ses² (bā′sēz), *NOUN.* the plural of **basis.**

base word, a word from which other words are made. *Baby* is the base word of *babies, babied,* and *babying.*

bash (bash), *VERB.* to strike with a smashing blow.
❑ *VERB* **bash·es, bashed, bash·ing.**

bash·ful (bash′fəl), *ADJECTIVE*. uneasy in the presence of others; easily embarrassed; shy: *The child was too bashful to greet us.* ■ See the Synonym Study at **shy**. —**bash′ful·ly**, *ADVERB*.

ba·sic (bā′sik), *ADJECTIVE*. forming the basis or main part; fundamental: *Addition and division are two basic processes of arithmetic.*

BA·SIC (bā′sik), *NOUN*. a simple language used to give instructions to computers.

Word Story

BASIC comes from the first letters of five words: **B**eginner's **A**ll-purpose **S**ymbolic **I**nstruction **C**ode. The people who created the language gave it a name that says it is simple!

ba·si·cal·ly (bā′sik lē), *ADVERB*. mostly; usually: *I have a cold, but I am basically healthy.*

ba·sin (bā′sn), *NOUN*.
1 a wide, shallow bowl for holding liquids.
2 the amount that a basin can hold: *They have used up a basin of water.*
3 all the land drained by a river and the streams that flow into the river: *The Mississippi basin extends from the Appalachian Mountains to the Rockies.*

ba·sis (bā′sis), *NOUN*. the main part; foundation: *The basis of their friendship is a common interest in sports.* ❑ *PLURAL* **ba·ses**.

bask (bask), *VERB*. to warm yourself pleasantly: *I spent the evening basking in front of the fire.* ❑ *VERB* **basks, basked, bask·ing**.

bas·ket (bas′kit), *NOUN*.
1 a container made of twigs, grasses, or strips of wood woven together: *a picnic basket*.
2 the amount that a basket holds: *We bought a basket of peaches.*
3 anything that looks like or is used as a basket: *I bought a metal wastepaper basket.*
4 in basketball: **a** a metal hoop with an open net hanging from it, used as a goal. **b** a successful shot. —**bas·ket·like′**, *ADJECTIVE*.

bas·ket·ball (bas′kit bȯl′), *NOUN*.
1 a game played with a large, round ball between two teams of five players each. The players score points by tossing the ball through baskets hanging at either end of the court.
2 the ball used in this game.

bass¹ (bās), *NOUN*.
1 *NOUN*. the lowest singing voice of a man.
2 *NOUN*. the low part written for voice or instrument.
3 *NOUN*. See **double bass**.
4 *ADJECTIVE*. of or for the bass.
❑ *PLURAL* **bass·es**.

bass² (bas), *NOUN*.
1 a North American freshwater fish caught for food and for sport.

2 a saltwater fish caught for food and for sport.
❑ *PLURAL* **bass** or **bass·es**.

bass drum (bās′ drum′), a large drum that makes a deep, low sound when struck.

bas·soon (bə sün′), *NOUN*. a wind instrument that has a doubled wooden body and a curved metal pipe with a double reed. It has a deep tone.

baste¹ (bāst), *VERB*. to drip or pour melted fat or butter on food while roasting it: *Dad basted the turkey.*
❑ *VERB* **bastes, bast·ed, bast·ing**.

baste² (bāst), *VERB*. to sew with long, loose stitches. These stitches are removed after the final sewing. ❑ *VERB* **bastes, bast·ed, bast·ing**.

bassoon

bat¹ (bat),
1 *NOUN*. a sturdy wooden stick or metal club, used to hit the ball in baseball, cricket, and similar games.
2 *VERB*. to hit with a bat; hit: *He bats well at practice.*
❑ *VERB* **bats, bat·ted, bat·ting**.

at bat, *IDIOM*. having a turn at batting: *Our team is at bat.*

bat² (bat), *NOUN*. a flying mammal with a body like that of a mouse and wings covered by thin skin. Most bats are active only at night. There are over 900 kinds of bats. They live in all parts of the world except for the polar regions.

bat² — wingspread of about 12 inches

batch (bach), *NOUN*. a quantity of something made at the same time: *a batch of cookies, a batch of candy.* ❑ *PLURAL* **batch·es**.

a	hat	ė	term	ô	order	ch	child	⎧a in about
ā	age	i	it	oi	oil	ng	long	⎪e in taken
ä	far	ī	ice	ou	out	sh	she	ə⎨i in pencil
â	care	o	hot	u	cup	th	thin	⎪o in lemon
e	let	ō	open	u̇	put	ᴛʜ	then	⎩u in circus
ē	equal	ȯ	saw	ü	rule	zh	measure	

bath (bath), NOUN.
1 the act of washing the body, usually in a large tub of water: *I took a hot bath.*
2 water in a tub for a bath: *Your bath is ready.*
❏ PLURAL **baths** (baᴛʜz).

bathe (bāᴛʜ), VERB.
1 to take a bath or give a bath to: *I bathe regularly. We bathed our dog.*
2 to pour water or other liquid on or over: *She bathed her sore feet.*
3 to go swimming; go into a river, lake, or ocean for pleasure or to get cool.
❏ VERB **bathes, bathed, bath·ing.** –**bath′er,** NOUN.

bathing suit, clothing worn for swimming.

bath·robe (bath′rōb′), NOUN. a loose garment worn before and after a bath, or when resting.

bath·room (bath′rüm′), NOUN.
1 a room for taking baths or showers, usually equipped with a sink and a toilet.
2 a room containing a toilet.

bath·tub (bath′tub′), NOUN. a tub to bathe in.

bat mitz·vah (bät′ mits′və), the ceremony or celebration held when a Jewish girl becomes thirteen years old. It means she has reached the age of religious responsibility.

ba·ton (ba ton′), NOUN.
1 a light stick used by the conductor of a musical group to keep the beat and direct the performance.
2 a hollow metal rod that is twirled by a drum major or majorette for display.

Bat·on Rouge (bat′n rüzh′), the capital of Louisiana.

bat·tal·ion (bə tal′yən), NOUN. any large part of an army organized to act together. Two or more companies make a battalion.

bat·ter[1] (bat′ər), VERB. to strike with repeated blows so as to bruise, break, or get out of shape; pound: *The fireman battered down the door with an ax.*
∎ See the Word Story at **debate.** ❏ VERB **bat·ters, bat·tered, bat·ter·ing.**

bat·ter[2] (bat′ər), NOUN. a liquid mixture of flour, milk, and eggs that becomes solid when cooked. Cakes and muffins are made from batter.

bat·ter[3] (bat′ər), NOUN. the player at bat in a game.

bat·tered (bat′ərd), ADJECTIVE. damaged by hard use: *I found a battered old book in the office.*

battering ram, (earlier) a heavy wooden beam used for battering down walls and gates.

bat·ter·y (bat′ər ē), NOUN.
1 a single electric cell sealed in a metal case: *Batteries come in many different sizes.*
2 a set of two or more electric cells that produce electric current. Batteries provide the current that starts car and truck engines.
❏ PLURAL **bat·ter·ies.**

batting average, a three-digit decimal that shows the percentage of a batter's hits compared with the number of times at bat. 40 hits in 120 times at bat is a batting average of .333.

bat·tle (bat′l),
1 NOUN. a fight between armies, air forces, or navies: *The battle for the island lasted six months.*
2 NOUN. any fight or contest: *The candidates fought a battle of words during the campaign.*
3 VERB. to take part in a battle; fight; struggle: *The swimmer had to battle a strong current.* ∎ See the Synonym Study at **fight.**
❏ VERB **bat·tles, bat·tled, bat·tling.**

bat·tle·field (bat′l fēld′), NOUN. the place where a battle is fought or has been fought.

bat·tle·ment (bat′l mənt), NOUN. a low wall for defense at the top of a tower or wall.

bat·tle·ship (bat′l ship′), NOUN. a type of warship with the heaviest armor and the most powerful guns.

bawl (bȯl), VERB.
1 to weep loudly: *The baby fell and began to bawl.*
2 to shout or cry out in a noisy way: *"Attention!" bawled the sergeant.*
❏ VERB **bawls, bawled, bawl·ing.**

bay[1] (bā), NOUN. a part of a sea or lake partly surrounded by land. A bay is usually smaller than a gulf and larger than a cove.

bay[2] (bā), VERB. to bark with long, deep sounds: *to bay at the moon.* ❏ VERB **bays, bayed, bay·ing.**

bay·o·net (bā′ə nit), NOUN. a knife that can be attached to the front end of a rifle.

bay·ou (bī′ü), NOUN. a marshy, slow-moving stream that flows into or out of a lake, river, or gulf in the south central United States. ❏ PLURAL **bay·ous.**

ba·zaar (bə zär′), NOUN.
1 a street or streets full of small shops and booths, especially in Middle Eastern countries.
2 a sale of things, often held for some charity: *I bought this scarf at the church bazaar.*

bazaar (definition 1)

B.C., before Christ. The abbreviation B.C. is used for dates before the birth of Christ. The abbreviation A.D. is used for dates after the birth of Christ. 350

B.C. is 100 years earlier than 250 B.C. From 20 B.C. to A.D. 50 is 70 years.

be (bē), *VERB.*
1 **Be** is a very common verb that has several different forms. We say: I *am,* you (we, they) *are,* he (she, it) *is,* I (he, she, it) *was,* you (we, they) *were.*
2 to live; exist: *Could there be bears in this forest?*
3 to have a place or position: *The new bookcase is going to be in the bedroom.*
4 to happen; take place: *Where will the meeting be?*
5 to belong to the group of: *Whales are mammals.*
6 **Be** is used as a linking verb: *Can this jacket be yours? No, mine is yellow. Who is the librarian?*
7 **Be** is used to begin a command or a question: *Be careful. Is that so?*
8 **Be** is used as a helping verb to show present or past action: *Can he be sleeping this late? The room was painted last year.*
❏ *VERB* **am, are, is; was, were; been; be·ing.**
■ Another word that sounds like this is **bee.**

beach (bēch),
1 *NOUN.* an almost flat shore of sand or pebbles along the edge of a sea, lake, or big river.
2 *VERB.* to run onto the shore: *We beached the boat.*
❏ *PLURAL* **beach·es;** *VERB* **beach·es, beached, beach·ing.**
■ Another word that sounds like this is **beech.**

bea·con (bē′kən), *NOUN.*
1 a fire or light used as a signal to guide or warn.
2 a radio signal for guiding aircraft and ships through fogs and storms.

bead (bēd),
1 *NOUN.* a small ball or bit of glass, metal, or plastic with a hole through it, so that it can be strung on a thread with others like it.
2 *VERB.* to put beads on; ornament with beads.
❏ *VERB* **beads, bead·ed, bead·ing. —bead′like′, ADJECTIVE.**

bead·y (bē′dē), *ADJECTIVE.* small, round, and shiny: *The parakeet has beady eyes.* ❏ *ADJECTIVE* **bead·i·er, bead·i·est.**

bea·gle (bē′gəl), *NOUN.* a small hunting dog with smooth hair, short legs, and drooping ears.

beak (bēk), *NOUN.* the bill of a bird.

beak·er (bē′kər), *NOUN.* a thin glass or metal container used in laboratories. A beaker has a flat bottom, no handle, and a lip for pouring.

beam (bēm),
1 *NOUN.* a large, long piece of timber, iron, or steel. A beam is the main horizontal support of a ship.
2 *NOUN.* a ray of light: *the beam of a flashlight.*
3 *VERB.* to send out rays of light; shine: *The sun was beaming brightly.*
4 *VERB.* to look or smile brightly: *She beamed with joy.*
5 *NOUN.* a radio signal directed in a straight line, used to guide aircraft or ships.
❏ *VERB* **beams, beamed, beam·ing.**

bean (bēn), *NOUN.*
1 the smooth, somewhat flat seed of a bush or vine, eaten as a vegetable.
2 the long green or yellow pod containing such seeds, also used as a vegetable.
3 any seed shaped somewhat like a bean. Coffee beans are seeds of the coffee plant.

bean·ie (bē′nē), *NOUN.* a small cap. ❏ *PLURAL* **bean·ies.**

bear¹ (bâr), *VERB.*
1 to carry; hold up: *The ice is too thin to bear us.*
■ See the Synonym Study at **carry.**
2 to suffer; endure: *He cannot bear much pain.*
3 to bring forth; produce: *This tree bears fine apples.*
4 to give birth to: *Our cat will soon bear kittens.*
❏ *VERB* **bears, bore, borne** or **born, bear·ing.**
■ Another word that sounds like this is **bare.**
—bear′a·ble, ADJECTIVE.

bear down, *IDIOM.* to press down: *The lead will break if you bear down too hard on your pencil.*

bear² (bâr), *NOUN.* a large animal with thick, coarse fur and a very short tail. A bear walks flat on the soles of its feet. ■ Another word that sounds like this is **bare.**
—bear′like′, ADJECTIVE.

beard (bird), *NOUN.*
1 the hair growing on a man's chin and cheeks.
2 something like this. The long hair on the chin of a goat is a beard.

bear·ing
(bâr′ing), *NOUN.*
1 a way of standing, walking, and behaving; manner: *The dancer had a graceful bearing.*

bear² — about 8 feet long

2 a connection in thought or meaning; relation: *His questions had no bearing on our discussion.*
3 **bearings,** position in relation to other things; direction: *We had no compass, so we got our bearings from the stars.*
4 a part of a machine on which another part moves. A bearing supports the moving part and reduces friction by turning with the motion.

beast (bēst), *NOUN.* any four-footed animal. Lions, bears, cows, and horses are beasts. A **beast of burden** is an animal used for carrying loads.

beast·ly (bēst′lē), *ADJECTIVE.* like a beast; cruel; brutal. ❏ *ADJECTIVE* **beast·li·er, beast·li·est.**
—beast′li·ness, NOUN.

a	hat	ė	term	ô	order	ch	child		a in about
ā	age	i	it	oi	oil	ng	long		e in taken
ä	far	ī	ice	ou	out	sh	she	ə	i in pencil
â	care	o	hot	u	cup	th	thin		o in lemon
e	let	ō	open	ù	put	ŦH	then		u in circus
ē	equal	ò	saw	ü	rule	zh	measure		

beat (bēt),

1 *VERB.* to strike something again and again: *The baby beat the floor with the toy hammer.*
2 *NOUN.* a stroke or blow made again and again: *We heard the beat of a drum.*
3 *VERB.* to get the better of; defeat; win over: *Their team beat ours by a huge score.*
4 *VERB.* to mix by stirring rapidly with a fork or other utensil: *I helped make the cook by beating eggs.*
5 *NOUN.* a sound made by the regular action of the heart as it pumps blood.
6 *VERB.* to throb: *My heart beat fast with joy.*
7 *VERB.* to move up and down; flap: *The bird beat its wings.*
8 *NOUN.* the unit of time or accent in music: *A waltz has three beats to a measure.*
9 *NOUN.* a regular round or route taken by a police officer or guard: *The officers were friendly with the people on their beat.*
10 *ADJECTIVE.* (informal) tired; worn out: *I was beat after running the race.*
  ❑ *VERB* **beats, beat·en** or **beat, beat·ing.** ■ Another word that sounds like this is **beet.**

beat·en (bēt′n),

1 *ADJECTIVE.* traveled over a lot: *a beaten path.*
2 *ADJECTIVE.* defeated; overcome: *a beaten team.*
3 *VERB.* a past participle of **beat:** *We have beaten that school in soccer for the past three years.*

beat-up (bēt′up′), *ADJECTIVE.* (informal) worn out from long or hard use: *a beat-up car.*

beau·ti·ful (byü′tə fəl), *ADJECTIVE.* very pleasing to see or hear; delighting the mind or senses: *a beautiful park, beautiful music.* **–beau′ti·ful·ly,** *ADVERB.*

Synonym Study

Beautiful means delightful to see, hear, or think about: *In the fall the colors of some trees are beautiful.*

Pretty means pleasing to see or hear. It is often used to describe girls and women: *My cousin looks like her pretty mother.*

Handsome means pleasing to see. It is often used instead of beautiful or pretty to describe a man or boy: *That handsome cowboy rides a very fast horse.*

Good-looking means handsome or pretty: *My best friend's brother is very good-looking—and so is his sister.*

Lovely means especially beautiful and fine: *It was a lovely evening, with a sky full of stars.*

Gorgeous means very beautiful, and often very fancy or colorful: *The bride wore a gorgeous wedding dress.*

See also the Synonym Study at **cute.**

beau·ti·fy (byü′tə fī), *VERB.* to make beautiful: *Flowers beautify a room.* ❑ *VERB* **beau·ti·fies, beau·ti·fied, beau·ti·fy·ing.**

beau·ty (byü′tē), *NOUN.*

1 good looks: *The child had beauty and intelligence.*
2 the quality that pleases both the mind and the senses in art or nature.
3 something or someone beautiful: *the beauties of nature.*
  ❑ *PLURAL* **beau·ties.**

Have You Heard?

You may have heard people say **"Beauty is only skin deep."** This means that you should judge people by how they act, not by how they look. You can't know until you get to know them! The saying **"You can't judge a book by its cover"** means the same thing.

bea·ver (bē′vər), *NOUN.* an animal with soft fur, a broad, flat tail, webbed hind feet, and large front teeth. Beavers gnaw down trees and build dams and nests in streams.

be·came (bi kām′), *VERB.* the past tense of **become:** *The seed became a plant.*

be·cause (bi kòz′), *CONJUNCTION.* for the reason that; since: *Because we were late, we had to run home.*
because of, *IDIOM.* by reason of; on account of: *The game was called off because of rain.*

beck·on (bek′ən), *VERB.* to signal to someone by a motion of the head or hand: *She beckoned me to follow her.* ❑ *VERB* **beck·ons, beck·oned, beck·on·ing.**

be·come (bi kum′), *VERB.*

1 to come to be; grow to be: *It is becoming colder. You have become a good cook.*
2 to look well on; suit: *That blue sweater becomes you.*
  ❑ *VERB* **be·comes, be·came, be·come, be·com·ing.**
become of, *IDIOM.* to happen to: *What has become of the box of candy?*

be·com·ing (bi kum′ing), *ADJECTIVE.*

1 fitting; suitable: *the kindness and patience becoming to a teacher.*
2 attractive: *a very becoming new coat.*

bed (bed),

1 *NOUN.* anything to sleep or rest on. A bed is usually a wooden or metal frame that supports a mattress covered with sheets and blankets.
2 *NOUN.* any place where people or animals sleep or rest: *The cat made its bed by the fireplace.*
3 *VERB.* to provide with a bed; put to bed; go to bed: *She bedded the horse in the barn.*
4 *NOUN.* a flat base on which anything rests; foundation: *The flagpole stood in a bed of concrete.*
5 *NOUN.* the ground under a body of water: *The creek bed was soft and muddy.*

6 *NOUN.* a piece of ground in a garden in which plants are grown: *We planted a bed of tulips.*
❑ *VERB* **beds, bed•ded, bed•ding.**

bed•ding (bed′ing), *NOUN.*
1 sheets, blankets, or quilts.
2 material for animals' beds: *straw bedding.*

be•drag•gled (bi drag′əld), *ADJECTIVE.* wet or dirty, and hanging limp: *bedraggled hair.*

bed•rock (bed′rok′), *NOUN.*
1 the solid rock under the soil and under looser rocks.
2 foundation: *The bedrock of our business is quality.*

bed•room (bed′rüm′), *NOUN.* a room to sleep in.

bed•side (bed′sīd′), *NOUN.* the side of a bed: *The nurse sat by the patient's bedside.*

bed•spread (bed′spred′), *NOUN.* a cover for a bed that is spread over the blankets.

bed•time (bed′tīm′), *NOUN.* the time set for going to bed: *Her regular bedtime is nine o'clock.*

bee (bē), *NOUN.*
1 an insect with four wings and, usually, a stinger. Bees make honey from the nectar and pollen that they gather from flowers.
2 a gathering for work or amusement: *The teacher let us have a spelling bee in class today.*
❑ *PLURAL* **bees.** ■ Another word that sounds like this is **be.**

beech (bēch), *NOUN.* a tree with smooth, gray bark and glossy leaves. It bears a sweet nut and its wood is used for furniture. ❑ *PLURAL* **beech•es** or **beech.** ■ Another word that sounds like this is **beach.**

beef (bēf), *NOUN.* meat from a steer, cow, or bull.

bee•hive (bē′hīv′), *NOUN.*
1 a nest for a swarm of bees or a box built for them to live in; hive. Bees store honeycomb and raise their young in beehives.
2 a busy, swarming place: *a beehive of activity.*

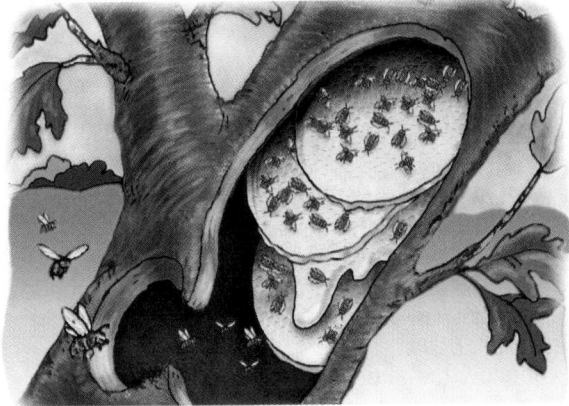
beehive (definition 1)

bee•line (bē′līn′), *NOUN.* the straightest way between two places, made like a bee's flight to its hive.

been (bin), *VERB.* the past participle of **be:** *I have been sick.* ■ Another word that sounds like this is **bin.**

beep (bēp),
1 *NOUN.* a sharp, short sound.
2 *VERB.* to make or cause to make sharp, short sounds: *My alarm beeps at 6:15 A.M. on school days. The driver beeped his horn to warn us.*
❑ *VERB* **beeps, beeped, beep•ing.**

beep•er (bē′pər), *NOUN.* a small electronic device that receives and transmits messages, especially phone numbers; pager. A beeper signals when a message is received by beeping or vibrating.

beer (bir), *NOUN.* an alcoholic drink made from malt flavored with hops.

bees•wax (bēz′waks′), *NOUN.* the wax made by bees, from which they make their honeycomb. The finest candles are made of beeswax.

beet (bēt), *NOUN.* the thick, fleshy root of a garden plant. Red beets are eaten as a vegetable. Sugar is made from white beets. ■ Another word that sounds like this is **beat.** —**beet′like′**, *ADJECTIVE.*

There are more than 300,000 kinds of **beetles.**

bee•tle (bē′tl), *NOUN.* an insect with two hard, shiny front wings that cover the delicate rear wings.

be•fore (bi fôr′),
1 *PREPOSITION.* earlier than: *Come before noon.*
2 *ADVERB.* earlier: *Come at five o'clock, not before.*
3 *ADVERB.* until now; in the past: *You were never late before.*
4 *PREPOSITION.* in front of, ahead of: *Walk before me.*
5 *ADVERB.* in front; ahead: *The scout went before to see if the trail was safe.*
6 *CONJUNCTION.* rather than; sooner than: *I'd starve before giving in.*
7 *CONJUNCTION.* earlier than the time when: *I would like to talk to you before you go.*

be•fore•hand (bi fôr′hand′), *ADVERB* or *ADJECTIVE.* ahead of time: *Get everything ready beforehand.*

a	hat	ė	term	ô	order	ch	child		a in about
ā	age	i	it	oi	oil	ng	long		e in taken
ä	far	ī	ice	ou	out	sh	she	ə	i in pencil
â	care	o	hot	u	cup	th	thin		o in lemon
e	let	ō	open	ů	put	ŦH	then		u in circus
ē	equal	ò	saw	ü	rule	zh	measure		

be·friend (bi frend′), VERB. to act as a friend to; help: *The children befriended the stray dog.* ❏ VERB **be·friends, be·friend·ed, be·friend·ing.**

beg (beg), VERB.
1 to ask for food, money, or clothes as a charity: *The hungry children begged for pennies.*
2 to ask a favor; ask earnestly or humbly: *The children begged for a ride on the pony.*
3 to ask politely and courteously: *I beg your pardon.*
❏ VERB **begs, begged, beg·ging.**

be·gan (bi gan′), VERB. the past tense of **begin:** *Snow began to fall.*

beg·gar (beg′ər), NOUN. someone who lives by begging.

Have You Heard?

You may have heard the saying **"Beggars can't be choosers."** This means that if you are asking for help, you have to accept whatever help is given. If you are unwilling to take what is offered, you may get nothing at all.

be·gin (bi gin′), VERB.
1 to do the first part; start: *When shall we begin? I began reading the book yesterday.*
2 to come into being: *The trouble began years ago.*
■ See the Synonym Study at **start.**
❏ VERB **be·gins, be·gan, be·gun, be·gin·ning.**

be·gin·ner (bi gin′ər), NOUN. someone who is doing something for the first time; someone who lacks skill and experience: *You skate well for a beginner.*

be·gin·ning (bi gin′ing), NOUN.
1 the time when anything begins: *The beginning of winter is usually on December 21st.*
2 the first part: *The beginning of the movie was dull.*
3 the starting point; source; origin: *The idea of the airplane had its beginning in the flight of birds.*

be·gun (bi gun′), VERB. the past participle of **begin:** *It has begun to rain.*

be·half (bi haf′), NOUN. side, interest, or favor: *A friend will act on my behalf while I'm away.*

be·have (bi hāv′), VERB.
1 to act; conduct yourself: *The children behaved politely. The ship behaves well even in a storm.*
2 to act properly; do what is right: *If you behave today, we can come here again.*
❏ VERB **be·haves, be·haved, be·hav·ing.**

be·hav·ior (bi hā′vyər), NOUN. a way of acting; conduct; actions: *Mean behavior showed her anger.*

be·head (bi hed′), VERB. to cut off the head of.
❏ VERB **be·heads, be·head·ed, be·head·ing.**

be·held (bi held′), VERB. the past tense of **behold:** *The boy beheld the approaching storm with fear.*

be·hind (bi hīnd′),
1 PREPOSITION. at the back of: *I hid behind a bush.*
2 ADVERB. at the back: *The dog's tail hung down behind.*

3 PREPOSITION. supporting: *Don't give up; we're all behind you.*
4 ADVERB. farther back: *The rest of the hikers are still quite a way behind.*
5 ADVERB. not on time; late: *I am behind in my work.*
6 ADVERB. in the place that has been or is being left: *When they went to New York, I stayed behind.*

be·hold (bi hōld′),
1 VERB. to look at; see: *Snow is a joy to behold.*
■ See the Synonym Study at **see.**
2 INTERJECTION. look! see! *Behold! the queen!*
❏ VERB **be·holds, be·held, be·hold·ing.**
—**be·hold′er,** NOUN.

beige (bāzh), ADJECTIVE. pale brown.

be·ing (bē′ing), NOUN.
1 a person; living creature: *a human being.*
2 life; existence: *The world came into being long ago.*

Bel·a·rus (bel′ə rüs′), NOUN. a country in eastern Europe.

be·lat·ed (bi lā′tid), ADJECTIVE. happening or coming late; delayed: *Your belated return worried us.*
—**be·lat′ed·ly,** ADVERB.

belch (belch),
1 VERB. to let out gas noisily from the stomach through the mouth; burp.
2 NOUN. an act of belching; burp.
❏ VERB **belch·es, belched, belch·ing;** PLURAL **belch·es.**

bel·fry (bel′frē), NOUN. a tower for a bell or bells.
❏ PLURAL **bel·fries.**

Bel·gium (bel′jəm), NOUN. a country in western Europe. —**Bel·gian** (bel′jən), NOUN or ADJECTIVE.

be·lief (bi lēf′), NOUN.
1 something thought to be true or real: *It was once a common belief that the earth is flat.* ■ See the Synonym Study at **opinion.**
2 acceptance as true or real: *His belief in ghosts makes him afraid of the dark.*
3 faith; trust: *She expressed her belief in people.*

be·lieve (bi lēv′), VERB.
1 to think something is true or real: *Who doesn't believe that the earth is round?*
2 to think somebody tells the truth: *I believe you.*
3 to have faith; trust: *We believe in our friends.*
4 to think; suppose: *I believe that a storm is coming.*
❏ VERB **be·lieves, be·lieved, be·liev·ing.**
—**be·liev′a·ble,** ADJECTIVE. —**be·liev′er,** NOUN.

Be·lize (bə lēz′), NOUN. a country in Central America.
—**Be·liz′e·an,** ADJECTIVE or NOUN.

bell (bel), NOUN.
1 a hollow metal object shaped like a cup, that makes a ringing musical sound when struck.
2 the stroke or sound of a bell: *Our teacher dismissed us five minutes before the bell.*
3 anything shaped like a bell: *the bell of a trumpet, the bell of a flower.*
—**bell′-like′,** ADJECTIVE.

bel·lig·er·ent (bə lij′ər ənt), ADJECTIVE.
1 eager to fight; warlike: *a belligerent gang of boys.*
2 at war; engaged in war; fighting: *Great Britain and Germany were belligerent powers in 1941.*
—**bel·lig′er·ent·ly,** ADVERB.

bel·low (bel′ō),
1 VERB. to make a loud, deep noise; roar: *He bellowed angrily at the children.*
2 NOUN. a loud, deep noise; roar.
❑ VERB **bel·lows, bel·lowed, bel·low·ing.**

bel·lows (bel′ōz), NOUN PLURAL or SINGULAR. a device for producing a strong current of air to make a fire hotter.

Bellows are worked by pushing the handles together and pulling them apart.

bellows

bel·ly (bel′ē), NOUN.
1 the lower front part of the body, below the chest; abdomen. It contains the stomach and intestines.
2 the under part of an animal's body.
3 the stomach: *I'm sleepy now that my belly is full.*
❑ PLURAL **bel·lies.**

bel·ly·but·ton (bel′ē but′n), NOUN. the mark or scar in the middle of the abdomen; navel. It is what remains after the cord connecting a newborn infant to its mother is cut.

be·long (bi lòng′), VERB. to be in the right place: *That book belongs on this shelf.*
❑ VERB **be·longs, be·longed, be·long·ing.**

belong to, IDIOM.
1 to be the property of: *Does this cap belong to you?*
2 to be a part of: *That top belongs to this box.*
3 to be a member of: *She belongs to the team.*

be·long·ings (bi lòng′ingz), NOUN PLURAL. things that someone owns; possessions.

be·lov·ed (bi luv′id *or* bi luvd′),
1 ADJECTIVE. dearly loved; dear: *my beloved puppy.*
2 NOUN. someone who is loved: *a note to my beloved.*

be·low (bi lō′),
1 ADVERB. in or to a lower place: *From the airplane we could see the fields below.*
2 PREPOSITION. lower than; under: *His room is below mine.*
3 PREPOSITION. less than: *It is four degrees below zero.*

belt (belt),
1 NOUN. a strip of leather or cloth, fastened around the waist to support clothes, tools, an so on.
2 VERB. to hit suddenly and hard: *She belted the ball over the fence.*
3 NOUN. an endless band that transfers motion from one wheel or pulley to another: *A belt connected to the engine turns the fan in a car.*
❑ VERB **belts, belt·ed, belt·ing.**

be·lu·ga (bə lü′gə), NOUN. a small, white whale that lives in arctic seas. ❑ PLURAL **be·lu·gas.**

bench (bench), NOUN.
1 a long seat, usually of wood or stone.
2 See **workbench.**
3 the judge or group of judges sitting in a court of law: *Bring the prisoner before the bench.*
❑ PLURAL **bench·es.**

bend (bend),
1 NOUN. a part that is not straight; curve; turn: *There is a sharp bend in the road here.*
2 VERB. to make or become crooked; curve: *bend a wire. The branch began to bend as I climbed along it.*
3 VERB. to stoop; bow: *She bent to pick a flower.*
❑ VERB **bends, bent, bend·ing.**

Synonym Study

Bend means to change shape, or to make something change shape: *The pull of the fish made the boy's pole bend.*

Curve means to go out of a straight line, or to make something go out of a straight line: *Her lips curved in a smile.*

Twist can mean to bend. It suggests something that bends many times: *This electric cord is all twisted.*

Wind[2] (wind) means to turn back and forth several times: *They drove down the winding road.*

The pole **bent** when he hooked a fish.

be·neath (bi nēth′),
1 ADVERB or PREPOSITION. in a lower place; below; underneath; under: *The apple fell to the ground beneath. The dog sat beneath the tree.*
2 PREPOSITION. not worthy of: *Your insulting remarks are beneath notice.*

a	hat	ė	term	ô	order	ch	child		
ā	age	i	it	oi	oil	ng	long		a in about
ä	far	ī	ice	ou	out	sh	she		e in taken
â	care	o	hot	u	cup	th	thin	ə	i in pencil
e	let	ō	open	ù	put	ŦH	then		o in lemon
ē	equal	ò	saw	ü	rule	zh	measure		u in circus

ben·e·fi·cial (ben′ə fish′əl), ADJECTIVE. favorable; helpful: *Daily exercise is beneficial to your health.* —**ben′e·fi·cial·ly**, ADVERB.

ben·e·fit (ben′ə fit),

1 NOUN. anything that is for the good of someone or something; advantage: *Good roads are of great benefit to travelers.*

2 VERB. to do good to; be good for: *Rest will benefit a sick person.*

3 VERB. to receive good; profit: *He benefited from the medicine.*

4 NOUN. **benefits,** money paid to a sick or disabled person by an insurance company or government. ❑ VERB **ben·e·fits, ben·e·fit·ed, ben·e·fit·ing.**

Be·nin (be nēn′), NOUN. a country in western Africa. —**Be·ni·nese** (bə ni nēz′), ADJECTIVE or NOUN.

bent (bent),

1 ADJECTIVE. not straight; crooked: *a bent nail.*

2 ADJECTIVE. determined: *He is bent on being a doctor.*

3 VERB. the past tense of **bend:** *I bent the wire.*

4 VERB. the past participle of **bend:** *Strong winds had bent the little tree to the ground.*

be·ret (bə rā′), NOUN. a soft, flat, round cap of wool or felt.

ber·ry (ber′ē), NOUN. any small, juicy fruit with many seeds. Strawberries and raspberries are berries. ❑ PLURAL **ber·ries.**
■ Another word that sounds like this is **bury.** —**ber′ry·like′,** ADJECTIVE.

berth (bėrth), NOUN.

1 a place to sleep on a ship or train: *I asked for an upper berth.*

2 a ship's place at a wharf.
■ Another word that sounds like this is **birth.**

beret

be·set (bi set′), VERB. to attack; attack from all sides: *Mosquitoes beset us all night.* ❑ VERB **be·sets, be·set, be·set·ting.**

be·side (bi sīd′), PREPOSITION. by the side of; close to; near: *Grass grows beside the fence. I sat beside them at lunch.*

beside yourself, IDIOM. very upset: *I'm beside myself with worry about them; they are three hours late!*
■ See the Synonym Study at **wild.**

be·sides (bi sīdz′),

1 ADVERB. more than that; moreover: *I won't go to the movies; besides, I have no money.*

2 PREPOSITION. in addition to: *Others came to the picnic besides our class.*

3 PREPOSITION. other than; except: *They spoke of no one besides you.*

be·siege (bi sēj′), VERB.

1 to surround and try to capture: *Enemy soldiers besieged the fortified town.*

2 to crowd around: *Admirers besieged the movie star.* ❑ VERB **be·sieg·es, be·sieged, be·sieg·ing.**

fans **besieging** a star

best (best),

1 ADJECTIVE. of the most valuable, excellent, or desirable quality: *I want to be one of the best students in the class.* ★ **Best** is the superlative of **good.**

2 ADVERB. in the most excellent way or to the greatest degree: *Who reads best? I like this book best.* ★ **Best** is the superlative of **well¹.**

3 NOUN. someone or something that is best: *He is the best in the class.*

best man, a man who accompanies the groom and stands with him at a wedding.

be·stow (bi stō′), VERB. to give something as a gift; give: *She bestowed money on the university.* ❑ VERB **be·stows, be·stowed, be·stow·ing.**

bet (bet),

1 NOUN. a promise between two people or groups that the one who is wrong will give something of value to the one who is right: *We made a two-dollar bet on who would win the game.*

2 VERB. to promise something of value to another if you are wrong; make a bet: *Which team did you bet on?*

3 NOUN. the money or thing promised: *My bet on the game was five dollars.*

4 VERB. to be very sure: *I bet you are wrong about that.* ❑ VERB **bets, bet, bet·ting.**

be·tray (bi trā′), VERB.

1 to hand over to an an enemy: *The traitor betrayed the general's plans to the enemy agent.*

2 to be unfaithful or disloyal to: *betray a promise.* ❑ VERB **be·trays, be·trayed, be·tray·ing.** —**be·tray′er,** NOUN.

be·tray·al (bi trā′əl), NOUN. the act of betraying.

bet·ter (bet′ər),

1 ADJECTIVE. more valuable, excellent, or desirable than another: *She left her old job for a better one.* ★ **Better** is the comparative of **good.**

2 *ADVERB.* in a more satisfactory way or to a greater degree: *Try to read better next time. I know my brother better than I know anyone else.* ★ **Better** is the comparative of **well**[1].

3 *NOUN.* a person or thing that is better: *Which is the better of these two dresses?*

4 *VERB.* to make something better; improve: *We can better that work by being more careful next time.*

5 *ADJECTIVE.* improved in health: *I feel better today.*

6 *VERB.* to do better than; surpass: *The other team could not better our score.*
❏ *VERB* **bet•ters, bet•ter•ed, bet•ter•ing.**

better off, *IDIOM.* in a better condition: *He is better off now that he has a new job.*

had better, *IDIOM.* ought to; should: *I had better go now.*

be•tween (bi twēn′),

1 *PREPOSITION* or *ADVERB.* in the space or time separating two objects or places: *The valley lay between two mountains. We don't go to school between Friday and Monday.*

2 *PREPOSITION.* in the range of: *Dogs usually give birth to between one and twelve puppies.*

3 *PREPOSITION.* connecting; joining: *There is a good highway between Chicago and Detroit.*

4 *PREPOSITION.* having to do with; involving: *A war between two countries can affect the whole world.*

5 *PREPOSITION.* either one or the other of: *We must choose between the two books.*

between you and me, *IDIOM.* as a secret; in confidence: *This is between you and me; don't tell anyone else.* ★ *Between you and I* is not correct in standard English.

Usage Note

Between is always used when there are only two of something: *The waitress divided the cake between the two girls.* **Among** is used when there are more than two of anything: *There were three children among the injured.*

bev•er•age (bev′ər ij), *NOUN.* a liquid used or made for drinking. Milk and tea are beverages.

be•ware (bi wâr′), *VERB.* to be on your guard against; be careful of: *You must beware of snakes here.* ★ **Beware** is used only in the present tense as a command or with helping verbs. This is why no forms of the verb are listed here.

be•wil•der (bi wil′dər), *VERB.* to confuse totally; puzzle: *I was bewildered by the confusing rules.*
❏ *VERB* **be•wil•ders, be•wil•dered, be•wil•der•ing.** **–be•wil′der•ment,** *NOUN.*

be•witch (bi wich′), *VERB.*

1 to put under a spell; use magic on: *In the story, a wicked fairy bewitched the princess.*

2 to charm; delight very much: *They were bewitched by their bright little grandchild.*
❏ *VERB* **be•witch•es, be•witched, be•witch•ing.**

be•yond (bi yond′),

1 *PREPOSITION.* on or to the farther side of; farther on than: *I live beyond those trees. I fell asleep on the bus and rode beyond my stop.*

2 *ADVERB.* farther away: *Beyond were the hills.*

3 *PREPOSITION.* later than; past: *I stayed up beyond my bedtime last night to watch the Olympics.*

4 *PREPOSITION.* out of the limit, range, or understanding of: *This shirt is so worn that it is beyond repair. The poem's meaning is beyond me.*

Bhu•tan (bü tän′), *NOUN.* a country in south central Asia.

Word Power bi-

The prefix **bi-** means "two" or "twice": **Bi**focals have **two** focus points. A **bi**annual event happens **twice** a year. A **bi**annual event can also happen every **two** years. Sometimes it's hard to know which meaning the writer is using.

bi•as (bī′əs),

1 *NOUN.* a tendency to favor or oppose someone or something unfairly: *An umpire should have no bias.*

2 *VERB.* to influence, usually unfairly: *Judges cannot let their feelings bias their decisions.*
❏ *PLURAL* **bi•as•es;** *VERB* **bi•as•es, bi•ased, bi•as•ing.**

bib (bib), *NOUN.* a cloth worn under the chin by babies to protect their clothing during meals: *The baby's bib was covered with mashed carrots.*

Bi•ble (bī′bəl), *NOUN.*

1 the book of sacred writings of the Christian religion containing the Old Testament and the New Testament.

2 the Hebrew Scriptures, sacred to Jews.

3 the book of the sacred writings of any religion.

Word Story

Bible comes from a Greek word meaning "book." In old times, the Bible was the only book most people ever saw. The Greek word originally meant "papyrus," the material on which people wrote before paper was invented.

bib•li•cal (bib′lə kəl), *ADJECTIVE.* of or from the Bible; having something to do with the Bible: *We read the biblical story of the Flood.*

bib•li•og•ra•phy (bib′lē og′rə fē), *NOUN.* a list of writings by a certain author or about a particular subject or person. ❏ *PLURAL* **bib•li•og•ra•phies.**

bi•ceps (bī′seps), *NOUN.* the large muscle in the front part of the upper arm. ❏ *PLURAL* **bi•ceps.**

a hat	ė term	ô order	ch child	a in about
ā age	i it	oi oil	ng long	e in taken
ä far	ī ice	ou out	sh she	ə i in pencil
â care	o hot	u cup	th thin	o in lemon
e let	ō open	ù put	ŦH then	u in circus
ē equal	ȯ saw	ü rule	zh measure	

bick·er (bik′ər), VERB. to take part in a noisy quarrel about something unimportant: *The children bickered about which TV show to watch and about who got the biggest ice-cream cone.* ∎ See the Synonym Study at **argue.** ❏ VERB **bick·ers, bick·ered, bick·er·ing.**

bi·coast·al (bī kō′stl), ADJECTIVE. of or between two coasts, especially the Atlantic and Pacific coasts of the United States: *bicoastal commuting.*

bi·cus·pid (bī kus′pid), NOUN. a tooth with two points. The bicuspids tear and grind food. Adult human beings have eight bicuspids.

bi·cy·cle (bī′sik′əl),
1 NOUN. a lightweight vehicle with two wheels, one behind the other. The wheels support a metal frame on which there is a seat. The rider pushes two pedals to turn the back wheel and steers with handlebars.
2 VERB. to ride a bicycle: *We bicycled 100 miles to raise money for cancer research.*
❏ VERB **bi·cy·cles, bi·cy·cled, bi·cy·cling.**

handlebars

frame

rim

spoke

hub

pedal

chain

bicycle

bi·cy·clist (bī′sik′list), NOUN. someone who rides a bicycle: *watch out for bicyclists.*

bid (bid),
1 VERB. to offer to pay a certain price: *She bid $15 for the table. He then bid $17.*
2 NOUN. an offer to pay a certain price: *She made a bid on the table. My bid was $12.*
3 VERB. to tell someone what to do or where to go; command: *The king bade his knights go forth and slay the dragon.*
4 VERB. to say; tell: *His friends bade him good-bye before he left.*
❏ VERB **bids, bade** or **bid, bid·den** or **bid, bid·ding.**

bid·den (bid′n), VERB. a past participle of **bid:** *The teacher had bidden them to be quiet.*

bi·fo·cals (bī fō′kəlz), NOUN PLURAL. glasses with two sections, the upper part for distant vision, the lower part for close vision.

big (big), ADJECTIVE. large; great in amount, size, or importance: *Rabbits are bigger than squirrels. The explosion was big news.* ❏ ADJECTIVE **big·ger, big·gest.**

Synonym Study

Big means that something has more than the usual size, number, or amount: *It was the biggest dragon Sir George had ever seen.*

Large means big. It often describes the space or amount of something: *The giant needed a very large house to live in.*

Great means large and out of the ordinary: *The great mountain peaks made us feel small.*

Bulky means big and awkward because of its size: *It was hard to get the bulky package through the narrow door.*

See also the Synonym Study at **huge.**

ANTONYMS: little, small.

Big·foot (big′fut), NOUN. a large, hairy creature something like a human being, believed to live in the mountains of the western United States.

big·horn (big′hôrn′), NOUN. a wild, grayish brown sheep of the Rocky Mountains, with large, curving horns. ❏ PLURAL **big·horn** or **big·horns.**

bighorn — about 3 feet high at the shoulder

bike (bīk),
1 NOUN. a bicycle.
2 VERB. to ride a bicycle.
❏ VERB **bikes, biked, bik·ing.**

bile (bīl), NOUN. a bitter, greenish yellow liquid produced by the liver. It helps digestion.

bi·lin·gual (bī ling′gwəl), ADJECTIVE.
1 speaking or knowing two languages well.
2 using two languages: *a bilingual dictionary.*

bill¹ (bil),
1 NOUN. a statement of money owed for work done or things supplied: *I had a $135 phone bill.*
2 VERB. to send a bill to: *The telephone company bills us each month.*
3 NOUN. a piece of paper money: *a dollar bill.*
4 NOUN. a written or printed statement; list of items. A **bill of rights** lists the basic rights belonging to the citizens of a country.
5 NOUN. a proposed law presented to a legislative group for its approval: *The Senate will vote on the new tax bill today.*
❏ VERB **bills, billed, bill·ing.**

bill² (bil), *NOUN.* the hard part of a bird's mouth; beak.

bill·board (bil′bôrd′), *NOUN.* a large board, usually outdoors, on which to display advertisements.

bill·fold (bil′fōld′), *NOUN.* a small, flat case for carrying paper money or cards in your pocket; wallet.

bil·liards (bil′yərdz), *NOUN.* a game played with three hard balls on a special table with a raised, cushioned edge. A long stick called a cue is used to hit the balls.

bil·lion (bil′yən), *NOUN or ADJECTIVE.* one thousand millions; 1,000,000,000.

bil·low (bil′ō),
1 *NOUN.* a great, swelling ocean wave.
2 *NOUN.* any great wave or mass of smoke, flame, or sound: *Billows of steam rose from the pot.*
3 *VERB.* to rise or roll in big waves: *Smoke billowed from the burning building.*
4 *VERB.* to swell out; bulge: *Sails billowed in the wind.*
❑ *VERB* **bil·lows, bil·lowed, bil·low·ing.**

bin (bin), *NOUN.* a box or enclosed place for holding or storing grain, coal, and so on. ■ Another word that sounds like this is **been.**

bi·nar·y sys·tem (bī′nər ē sis′təm), a system of writing numbers in which any amount can be written using only the figures 1 and 0. The binary system is used by computers.

bind (bīnd), *VERB.*
1 to tie together; hold tight; fasten: *She bound the package with string.*
2 to fasten sheets of paper into a cover; put a cover on a book: *The loose pages were bound into a book.*
3 to hold by a promise, duty, or law: *He wanted to stay longer, but felt bound by his promise to his parents that he would return early.*
4 to put a bandage on: *bind a wound.*
❑ *VERB* **binds, bound, bind·ing.**

bind·er (bīn′dər), *NOUN.* a cover for a loose-leaf notebook.

bin·go (bing′gō), *NOUN.* a game in which players cover numbers on cards as the numbers are called out. The first player to cover a row of numbers in any direction wins.

bi·noc·u·lars (bə nok′yə lərz), *NOUN PLURAL.* a double telescope made for use with both eyes. Binoculars make distant things appear nearer and larger.

Word Power   bio-

The combining form **bio-** is used with other words or parts of words to add to their meaning. It describes something having to do with life or living things. A **bio**graphy is the story of someone's life. **Bio**diversity is great variety of different living things.

bi·o·de·grad·a·ble (bī′ō di grā′də bəl), *ADJECTIVE.* able to be broken down by bacteria or other living things: *a biodegradable detergent.*

bi·o·di·ver·si·ty (bī′ō di vėr′sə tē), *NOUN.* a wide variety of species living together in one place.

Fish, coral, and plants show **biodiversity** in the ocean.

bi·o·graph·i·cal (bī′ə graf′ə kəl), *ADJECTIVE.* of or about someone's life: *biographical facts.*

bi·og·ra·phy (bī og′rə fē), *NOUN.* the written story of someone's life. ❑ *PLURAL* **bi·og·ra·phies.**

bi·o·haz·ard (bī′ō haz′ərd), *NOUN.* a living thing that would be a health threat if released into the environment. Germs produced in a laboratory and toxic chemicals are biohazards.

bi·o·log·i·cal (bī′ə loj′ə kəl), *ADJECTIVE.*
1 of living things: *biological studies.*
2 of or for biology: *a biological laboratory.*
−**bi·o·log′i·cal·ly,** *ADVERB.*

bi·ol·o·gy (bī ol′ə jē), *NOUN.* the science of living things. Biology studies the origin, structure, and activities of all forms of life. Botany, zoology, and ecology are branches of biology. −**bi·ol′o·gist,** *NOUN.*

bi·o·mass (bī′ō mas′), *NOUN.*
1 the total mass of all living things in a given space.
2 organic material, especially from plants and farm waste, considered as a source of energy.

bi·on·ic (bī on′ik), *ADJECTIVE.* having electronic parts that replace parts of the body.

bi·plane (bī′plān′), *NOUN.* an airplane with two wings on each side, one above the other.

birch (bėrch), *NOUN.* a tree that has hard wood, often used in making furniture. Its smooth bark may be peeled off in thin layers. ❑ *PLURAL* **birch·es.**

a	hat	ė	term	ô	order	ch	child	(a in about
ā	age	i	it	oi	oil	ng	long	e in taken
ä	far	ī	ice	ou	out	sh	she	ə ⎨ i in pencil
â	care	o	hot	u	cup	th	thin	o in lemon
e	let	ō	open	ů	put	ŦH	then	(u in circus
ē	equal	ȯ	saw	ü	rule	zh	measure	

bird (bėrd), NOUN. one of a group of warm-blooded animals that have a backbone, feathers, two legs, and wings. Birds lay eggs; most birds can fly. A **bird of prey** kills other animals for food. Eagles, hawks, vultures, and owls are birds of prey.

Have You Heard?

You may have heard someone say **"The early bird catches the worm."** This means that if you want to reach your goal, you should begin as soon as you can.

bird·ie (bėr′dē),
1 NOUN. a score of one less than par for any hole on a golf course.
2 VERB. to score one less than par in golf.
3 NOUN. See **shuttlecock**.
 ❏ PLURAL **bird·ies**.

bird·seed (bėrd′sēd′), NOUN. a mixture of small seeds often fed to birds.

birth (bėrth), NOUN.
1 the act of coming into life; being born: *At birth, the baby weighed 7 pounds, 8 ounces.*
2 the beginning; origin: *the birth of a nation.*
 ∎ Another word that sounds like this is **berth**.
 give birth to, IDIOM. to bring forth; bear: *The dog gave birth to four puppies.*

birth·day (bėrth′dā′), NOUN. the day on which someone was born or something began, usually celebrated yearly.

birth·mark (bėrth′märk′), NOUN. a mark on the skin that was present at birth.

birth·place (bėrth′plās′), NOUN.
1 the place where someone was born.
2 the place of origin: *Philadelphia is the birthplace of the United States.*

birth·right (bėrth′rīt′), NOUN. a right or privilege that someone is entitled to by birth: *Freedom of speech is a birthright in the United States.*

bis·cuit (bis′kit), NOUN. a small piece of baked bread dough that is made without yeast. Biscuits can be made with baking powder or baking soda.

bi·sect (bī′sekt), VERB. to divide an angle or a line segment into two equal parts. ❏ VERB **bi·sects, bi·sect·ed, bi·sect·ing.**

bish·op (bish′əp), NOUN.
1 a clergyman of high rank in some Christian churches.
2 one of the pieces in the game of chess. A bishop can move diagonally across empty squares.

Bis·marck (biz′märk), NOUN. the capital of North Dakota.

bi·son (bī′sn), NOUN. a large, wild animal of North America, related to cattle; buffalo. The bison has a big shaggy head and a hump above the shoulders. ❏ PLURAL **bi·son**.

bit¹ (bit), NOUN.
1 a small piece; small amount: *A pebble is a bit of rock.* ∎ See the Synonym Study at **piece**.
2 a short time: *Stay a bit.*
3 (informal) 12½ cents. A quarter is two bits.

bit² (bit), VERB.
1 the past tense of **bite**: *Our dog bit the dog next door.*
2 a past participle of **bite**: *I've just bit my tongue.*

bit³ (bit), NOUN.
1 a tool for boring or drilling that fits into a handle called a brace or into a drill.
2 the part of a bridle that goes in a horse's mouth.

bit⁴ (bit), NOUN. the smallest unit of information in a computer.

bite (bīt),
1 VERB. to seize, cut into, or cut off with the teeth: *She bit into the apple.*
2 NOUN. a piece bitten off; mouthful: *Eat the whole apple, not just a bite.*
3 NOUN. a light meal; snack: *Have a bite with me now or you'll get hungry later.*
4 VERB. to wound with teeth, fangs, or a sting: *My dog never bites. A mosquito bit me.*
5 NOUN. a wound made by biting or stinging: *Mosquito bites itch.*
6 VERB. to cause a sharp, smarting pain to: *The icy wind bit her nose and ears.*
7 VERB. to take a bait; be caught: *The fish are biting well today.*
 ❏ VERB **bites, bit, bit·ten** or **bit, bit·ing**. ∎ Another word that sounds like this is **byte**. **–bit′er,** NOUN.

bit·ing (bī′ting), ADJECTIVE. causing sharp pain or distress: *a biting wind, biting remarks.*

bit·ten (bit′n), VERB. a past participle of **bite**: *Finish the apple, now that you have bitten into it.*

bit·ter (bit′ər), ADJECTIVE.
1 having a sharp, harsh, unpleasant taste.
2 causing sharp pain or grief; hard to admit or bear: *His father's death was a bitter loss.*
3 showing pain or grief: *The lost child shed bitter tears.*
4 having feelings of hatred: *bitter enemies.*
 –bit′ter·ly, ADVERB. **–bit′ter·ness,** NOUN.

bison — about 6 feet high at the shoulder

B

bi·valve (bī′valv′), *NOUN.* any sea animal with soft body and a hinged shell that opens like a book. Oysters and clams are bivalves.

black (blak),
1 *NOUN.* the color of the ink this sentence is printed in.
2 *ADJECTIVE.* having this color: *a black sweater.*
3 *ADJECTIVE.* without any light; very dark: *The room was black as night.*
4 also, **Black, a** *NOUN.* someone whose ancestors belonged to the group of people who live in Africa south of the Sahara; in the United States, African American. **b** *ADJECTIVE.* of or about people of this background.
–**black′ness,** *NOUN.*

black out, *IDIOM.* to become unconscious; faint: *I blacked out because of all the smoke and fumes.*
❑ *VERB* **blacks, blacked, black·ing.**

black·ber·ry (blak′ber′ē), *NOUN.* a sweet, juicy, dark purple berry that grows on a thorny bush. It has many small seeds. ❑ *PLURAL* **black·ber·ries.**

black·bird (blak′bėrd′), *NOUN.* a group of North American birds, the male of which is mostly black.

black·board (blak′bôrd′), *NOUN.* a smooth, hard surface, used for writing or drawing on with chalk.

black·en (blak′ən), *VERB.*
1 to make or become black: *Soot blackened the snow.*
2 to speak evil of: *Enemies blackened his reputation.*
❑ *VERB* **black·ens, black·ened, black·en·ing.**

blacken someone's name, *IDIOM.* to ruin someone's reputation by saying bad things about them.

black eye, a dark purple bruise around an eye.

black hole, an astronomical object that is supposed to have been created by a collapsed star.

black·mail (blak′māl′),
1 *NOUN.* money gotten from someone by threats to tell something bad about him or her.
2 *VERB.* to get or try to get blackmail from.
❑ *VERB* **black·mails, black·mailed, black·mail·ing.**
–**black′mail′er,** *NOUN.*

black·out (blak′out′), *NOUN.*
1 a sudden loss of electrical power that causes lights to go off and appliances to stop working.
2 temporary blindness or loss of consciousness resulting from lack of blood circulation in the brain.

black·smith (blak′smith′), *NOUN.* someone who makes things out of iron by heating it in a forge and hammering it into shape on an anvil. Blacksmiths mend tools and shoe horses.

black·top (blak′top′), *NOUN.* asphalt mixed with crushed rock, used as paving material.

black widow, a small, poisonous North American spider. The female has a shiny, black body with a mark shaped like an hourglass on the underside.

blad·der (blad′ər), *NOUN.* a thin bag in the body that stores urine from the kidneys until you urinate.

blade (blād), *NOUN.*
1 the cutting part of anything like a knife or sword: *A carving knife should have a very sharp blade.*
2 a leaf of grass.
3 the flat, wide part of anything. An oar or a paddle has a blade at one end of the shaft.
4 the runner of an ice skate.

blame (blām),
1 *VERB.* to hold responsible for something bad or wrong: *The driver blamed the fog for the crash.*
2 *NOUN.* responsibility for something bad or wrong: *Carelessness gets the blame for many mistakes.*
3 *VERB.* to find fault with: *I don't blame her for asking.*
❑ *VERB* **blames, blamed, blam·ing.**

bland (bland), *ADJECTIVE.*
1 gentle; soothing: *a bland smile.*
2 smoothly agreeable and polite: *a bland manner.*
3 mild; not irritating: *a bland diet of baby food.*
–**bland′ly,** *ADVERB.* –**bland′ness,** *NOUN.*

blank (blangk),
1 *NOUN.* a space left empty or to be filled in: *Leave a blank if you can't answer the question.*
2 *ADJECTIVE.* not written or printed on: *blank paper.*
■ See the Synonym Study at **empty.**
3 *ADJECTIVE.* showing no emotion; vacant: *a blank look.*
4 *NOUN.* a cartridge with gunpowder but no bullet.
–**blank′ly,** *ADVERB.*

blan·ket (blang′kit),
1 *NOUN.* a soft, heavy covering woven from wool, cotton, nylon, or other material, used to keep people or animals warm.
2 *NOUN.* anything like a blanket: *a blanket of snow.*
3 *VERB.* to cover as if with a blanket: *Snow blanketed the trees.*
❑ *VERB* **blan·kets, blan·ket·ed, blan·ket·ing.**

blare (blâr),
1 *VERB.* to make a loud, harsh sound: *The horns blared.*
2 *NOUN.* a loud, harsh sound.
❑ *VERB* **blares, blared, blar·ing.**

blast (blast),
1 *VERB.* to blow something up with dynamite or other explosives: *The big boulders were blasted to clear the way for a new road.*
2 *NOUN.* an explosion: *We heard the blast a mile away.*
3 *NOUN.* a sound made by blowing a trumpet, horn, or whistle: *The blast of a bugle aroused the camp.*
4 *NOUN.* a strong, sudden rush of wind or air: *Last night we felt the icy blasts of winter.*
❑ *VERB* **blasts, blast·ed, blast·ing.** –**blast′er,** *NOUN.*

blast off, *IDIOM.* to take off into flight propelled by rockets: *The spacecraft blasts off tomorrow.*

a	hat	ė	term	ô	order	ch	child		a in about
ā	age	i	it	oi	oil	ng	long		e in taken
ä	far	ī	ice	ou	out	sh	she	ə	i in pencil
â	care	o	hot	u	cup	th	thin		o in lemon
e	let	ō	open	ù	put	ŦH	then		u in circus
ē	equal	ò	saw	ü	rule	zh	measure		

blast·off (blast′ȯf′), NOUN. the act of launching or taking off into rocket-propelled flight.

blastoff of the space shuttle

blaze¹ (blāz),
1 NOUN. a bright flame or fire: *We could see the blaze of the campfire across the beach.*
2 VERB. to burn with a bright flame: *A fire was blazing in the fireplace.*
3 VERB. to show bright colors or lights: *On New Year's Eve the big house blazed with lights.*
4 NOUN. a bright display: *Tulips made a blaze of color.*
□ VERB **blaz·es, blazed, blaz·ing.**

blaze² (blāz),
1 NOUN. a mark made on a tree by cutting off a piece of bark, to indicate a trail or boundary in a forest.
2 NOUN. a white spot on the face of a horse or cow.
3 VERB. to mark a trail by cutting blazes on trees.
□ VERB **blaz·es, blazed, blaz·ing.**

bleach (blēch),
1 VERB. to make white by exposing to sunlight or by using chemicals: *We bleached the towels in the wash.*
2 NOUN. any chemical used in bleaching: *She used bleach to wash the white sheets.*
□ VERB **bleach·es, bleached, bleach·ing;** PLURAL **bleach·es.**

bleach·ers (blē′chərz), NOUN PLURAL. benches for people attending games or other outdoor events. Bleachers have no roof and are the cheapest seats.

bleak (blēk),
1 ADJECTIVE. swept by winds; bare: *The rocky peaks of high mountains are bleak.*
2 ADVERB. without hope; dismal: *Prison life is bleak.* —**bleak′ly,** ADVERB.

bleat (blēt),
1 NOUN. the cry made by a sheep, goat, or calf.
2 VERB. to make a sound like this.
□ VERB **bleats, bleat·ed, bleat·ing.**

bled (bled), VERB.
1 the past tense of **bleed:** *The cut bled for an hour.*
2 the past participle of **bleed:** *He had bled on his shirt, so he washed it in cold water.*

bleed (blēd), VERB. to lose blood: *I'm bleeding from a scrape on my knee.* □ VERB **bleeds, bled, bleed·ing.**

blem·ish (blem′ish),
1 NOUN. something that spoils beauty; defect; flaw: *A pimple is a blemish on the skin.*
2 VERB. to injure; mar: *Scandal blemished the mayor's reputation.*
□ PLURAL **blem·ish·es;** VERB **blem·ish·es, blem·ished, blem·ish·ing.**

blend (blend),
1 VERB. to mix together; mix or become mixed so thoroughly that the things mixed cannot be distinguished or separated: *Blend the butter and sugar before adding the eggs and flour.* ■ See the Synonym Study at **mix.**
2 VERB. to shade into each other, little by little: *The colors of the rainbow blend into one another.*
3 NOUN. a mixture of several kinds: *This coffee is a blend.*
4 NOUN. two or more consonants that begin a syllable. The *sp* in *spell* and the *pl* in *replace* are blends.
5 NOUN. word made by combining two words, often with a syllable in common. EXAMPLE: *Motel* is a blend of *motor* and *hotel.*
□ VERB **blends, blend·ed, blend·ing.**

Word Source

A **blend** is a word that is made by combining two other words. In the list below, the blend at the left was formed by combining the words at the right.

BLEND	FORMED BY COMBINING	
bionics	biology	electronics
bit⁴	binary	digit
brunch	breakfast	lunch
chortle	chuckle	snort
motel	motor	hotel
smog	smoke	fog

blend·er (blen′der), NOUN. an electric kitchen appliance for grinding, mixing, or beating various foods.

bless (bles), VERB.
1 to make holy or sacred: *The bishop blessed the new church.*
2 to make happy or fortunate: *I have always been blessed with good health.*
□ VERB **bless·es, blessed** or **blest, bless·ing.**

bless·ed (bles′id or blest), ADJECTIVE.
1 holy; sacred.
2 fortunate; lucky.

bless·ing (bles′ing), NOUN.
1 a prayer asking God's kindness.
2 a wish for happiness or success: *When I left home, I received my family's blessing.*
3 anything that makes you happy and contented: *A good temper is a great blessing.*

B

blest (blest), *VERB.*
1 a past tense of **bless**: *The priest blest the baby.*
2 a past participle of **bless**: *blest with good health.*
blew (blü), *VERB.* the past tense of **blow²**: *The wind blew.* ▪ Another word that sounds like this is **blue.**
blight (blīt), *NOUN.*
1 a disease that causes plants or parts of plants to wither and die: *The crop was wiped out by blight.*
2 anything that destroys or ruins: *The garbage dump is a blight on the neighborhood.*
blimp (blimp), *NOUN.* a cigar-shaped, wingless aircraft. It is filled with gas that is lighter than air.

Did You Know?

Blimps used to be used for transportation. Now they are mainly used for taking aerial photographs and advertising products. Sometimes they are decorated in special ways.

This **blimp** is painted to look like a killer whale.

blind (blīnd),
1 *ADJECTIVE.* not able to see: *A blind person often uses a dog guide for help in getting around.*
2 *VERB.* to make someone unable to see: *The bright lights blinded me for a moment.*
3 *ADJECTIVE* or *ADVERB.* without the help of sight; by means of guidance systems: *flying blind in the fog.*
4 *ADJECTIVE.* without thought, judgment, or good sense: *I made a blind guess.*
5 *VERB.* to take away the power to understand or judge: *His strong opinions blinded him to the facts.*
6 *NOUN.* something that keeps out light or blocks sight. A window shade or shutter is a blind.
❑ *VERB* **blinds, blind·ed, blind·ing. –blind′ly,** *ADVERB.* **–blind′ness,** *NOUN.*
blind·fold (blīnd′fōld′),
1 *VERB.* to cover the eyes of: *We blindfolded her.*
2 *NOUN.* a piece of cloth that covers the eyes.
❑ *VERB* **blind·folds, blind·fold·ed, blind·fold·ing.**
blind spot, the area behind and to the side of a car that cannot be seen in the rearview or side mirrors.
blink (blingk), *VERB.*
1 to close and open the eyes quickly: *She blinked at the sudden light. We blink every few seconds.*

2 to shine with an unsteady light: *A little lantern blinked through the darkness.*
❑ *VERB* **blinks, blinked, blink·ing.**
on the blink, *IDIOM.* not working properly; broken: *That soda machine is always on the blink.*
blink·er (bling′kər), *NOUN.* a device with flashing lights used as a warning signal: *When her car broke down, the driver left the blinkers flashing.*
bliss (blis), *NOUN.* great happiness; perfect joy: *What bliss it is to relax in the pool on a hot day!*

She sat in the pool feeling total **bliss.**

bliss·ful (blis′fəl), *ADJECTIVE.* very happy; joyful.
blis·ter (blis′tər),
1 *NOUN.* a swelling in the skin filled with watery liquid. Blisters are caused by burns or rubbing.
2 *NOUN.* a similar swelling on the surface of a plant, on metal, on painted wood, or in glass.
3 *VERB.* to form or cause to form blisters: *Sunburn has blistered my back.*
❑ *VERB* **blis·ters, blis·tered, blis·ter·ing.**
bliz·zard (bliz′ərd), *NOUN.* a blinding snowstorm with very strong, cold winds.
bloat (blōt), *VERB.* to swell up; puff up: *Overeating bloated the cow's stomach.* ❑ *VERB* **bloats, bloat·ed, bloat·ing.**
blob (blob), *NOUN.* a small, soft drop; sticky lump: *Blobs of wax covered the candlestick.*
block (blok),
1 *NOUN.* a cube of wood, stone, and the like: *Infants often play with plastic blocks. Ancient Egyptians built huge pyramids with blocks of stone.*
2 *VERB.* to fill up so as to prevent passage or progress: *Heavy snow blocked the country roads.*
3 *VERB.* to put things in the way of; obstruct; hinder: *Illness blocked our vacation plans.*
4 *NOUN.* anything that keeps something from being done: *A block in traffic kept our car from moving on.*

a hat	ė term	ô order	ch child	⎧a in about
ā age	i it	oi oil	ng long	⎪e in taken
ä far	ī ice	ou out	sh she	ə⎨i in pencil
â care	o hot	u cup	th thin	⎪o in lemon
e let	ō open	u̇ put	ŦH then	⎩u in circus
ē equal	ȯ saw	ü rule	zh measure	

5 *NOUN.* the area in a city or town enclosed by four streets: *We walked around the block after dinner.*

6 *NOUN.* the length of one side of a block in a city or town: *Walk one block east.*

7 *VERB.* (in sports and games) to get in the way of or stop an opponent's play.

❑ *VERB* **blocks, blocked, block·ing.**

block·ade (blo kād′),

1 *NOUN.* the act of blocking a place by an army or navy to control who or what goes into or out of it.

2 *VERB.* to put under blockade.

❑ *VERB* **block·ades, block·ad·ed, block·ad·ing.**

blond or **blonde** (blond),

1 *ADJECTIVE.* light or pale gold in color: *blond hair, blond furniture.*

2 *ADJECTIVE.* having yellow or light brown hair and usually blue or gray eyes and fair skin.

3 *NOUN.* someone with hair, eyes, and skin like this. ★ A man or boy of this sort is usually called a **blond.** A woman or girl of this sort is usually called a **blonde.**

blood (blud), *NOUN.*

1 the red liquid in the veins, arteries, and capillaries of human beings and some other animals. Blood is pumped by the heart. It carries oxygen and digested food to all parts of the body and carries away waste materials.

2 relationship by descent from a single ancestor: *We are related by blood.*

in cold blood, *IDIOM.* cruelly or on purpose: *The gangsters shot down three men in cold blood.*

blood bank, a place where blood for use in transfusions is kept.

blood·hound (blud′hound′), *NOUN.* a large dog with a keen sense of smell, often used to find people.

blood pressure, the pressure of the blood against the inner walls of the arteries. Blood pressure changes according to your physical activity, excitement, health, and age.

blood·shed (blud′shed′), *NOUN.* the act of killing people; killing.

blood·stream (blud′strēm′), *NOUN.* the blood as it flows through the body.

blood vessel, any tube in the body through which the blood circulates. Arteries, veins, and capillaries are blood vessels.

blood·y (blud′ē), *ADJECTIVE.*

1 covered with blood; bleeding: *a bloody nose.*

2 accompanied by much killing: *a bloody battle.*

❑ *ADJECTIVE* **blood·i·er, blood·i·est.**

bloom (blüm),

1 *VERB.* to have flowers; open into flowers; blossom: *Many plants bloom in the spring.*

2 *NOUN.* a flower; blossom.

3 *NOUN.* the condition or time of flowering: *The garden is lovely when the roses are in bloom.*

4 *NOUN.* the condition or time of greatest health, vigor, or beauty: *the bloom of youth.*

❑ *VERB* **blooms, bloomed, bloom·ing. –bloom′er,** *NOUN.*

bloop·er (blü′pər), *NOUN.*

1 (informal) a foolish mistake; goof; blunder.

2 (in baseball) a fly ball that goes just beyond the infield.

blos·som (blos′əm),

1 *NOUN.* a flower, especially of a plant that produces fruit: *apple blossoms.*

2 *VERB.* to have flowers; open into flowers: *All the orchards blossom in spring.*

3 *VERB.* to open out; develop: *The shy child blossomed into an outgoing teenager.*

❑ *VERB* **blos·soms, blos·somed, blos·som·ing.**

an orange **blossom**

blot (blot),

1 *NOUN.* a spot of ink or stain of any kind.

2 *NOUN.* a blemish; disgrace: *The field of rusting cars was a blot on the landscape.*

3 *VERB.* to dry something with cloth or paper: *I blotted my face with a tissue.*

❑ *VERB* **blots, blot·ted, blot·ting.**

blotch (bloch), *NOUN.*

1 a large, irregular spot or stain.

2 a place where the skin is red or broken out.

❑ *PLURAL* **blotch·es.**

blot·ter (blot′ər), *NOUN.* (earlier) a soft paper used to dry writing by soaking up wet ink.

blouse (blous), *NOUN.*

1 a shirt worn by women and girls.

2 a military jacket: *a sailor's wool blouse.*

blow¹ (blō), *NOUN.*

1 a hard hit; knock; stroke: *The boxer struck his opponent a blow that knocked him down.*

2 a sudden happening that causes misfortune or loss; shock: *Her death was a great blow to him.*

blow² (blō), *VERB.*

1 to move rapidly or with power: *The wind blew in gusts.*

2 to drive or carry by a current of air: *The wind blew the curtain.*

3 to send forth a strong current of air: *You can blow on your hands to warm them.*

4 to empty or clear by forcing air through: *He sneezed twice, then blew his nose.*

5 to form or shape by air; swell with air: *I love to blow soap bubbles.*

6 to make a sound by a current of air or steam: *The whistle blows at noon.*

7 to break by an explosion: *The dynamite blew the wall to bits.*
❏ *VERB* **blows, blew, blown, blow·ing.**

blow a fuse, *IDIOM.*

1 to break the connection in an electrical fuse.

2 to lose your temper: *Dad blew a fuse when he found out what I had done.*

blow out, *IDIOM.* to put out or be put out by a current of air: *I blew out the candle.*

blow up, *IDIOM.*

1 to explode: *The ammunition ship blew up and sank when it hit the rocks.*

2 to fill something with air: *to blow up a bicycle tire.*

3 to become very angry: *I blew up at my sister for leaving our room in a mess.*

blow·hole (blō′hōl′), *NOUN.* a hole for breathing, in the top of the head of whales, porpoises, and dolphins.

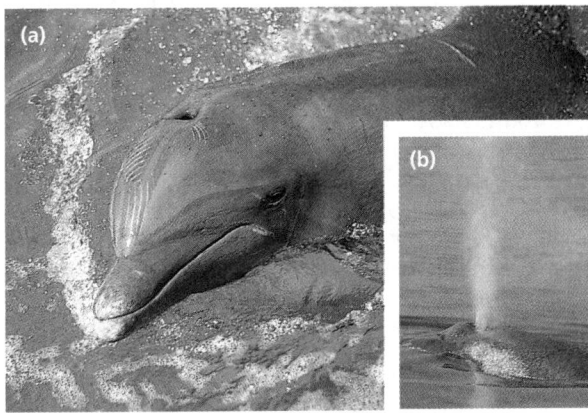

blowhole — of a porpoise (a) and of a whale (b)

blown (blōn), *VERB.* the past participle of **blow²**: *The wind has blown away my hat.*

blow·out (blō′out′), *NOUN.* the bursting of a tire: *A blowout caused the driver to lose control of the car.*

blow·torch (blō′tôrch′), *NOUN.* a device that shoots out a very hot flame. A blowtorch is used to cut metal and burn off paint. ❏ *PLURAL* **blow·torch·es.**

blub·ber (blub′ər), *NOUN.* the fat of whales and some other sea animals. Oil obtained from whale blubber was burned in lamps.

blue (blü),

1 *NOUN.* the color of the clear sky in daylight.

2 *ADJECTIVE.* having some shade of this color: *a blue flower, hands blue from cold.*

3 *ADJECTIVE.* sad; gloomy; discouraged: *She felt blue when her best friend moved away.*
❏ *PLURAL* **blues;** *ADJECTIVE* **blu·er, blu·est.** ■ Another word that sounds like this is **blew.**

out of the blue, *IDIOM.* completely unexpectedly: *Her visit came out of the blue.*

blue·ber·ry (blü′ber′ē), *NOUN.* a small, round, dark blue berry that grows on a bush. Blueberries are sweet and flavorful. They are often baked in pies or muffins. ❏ *PLURAL* **blue·ber·ries.**

blue·bird (blü′bėrd′), *NOUN.* a small blue songbird of North America, related to the robin.

blue·grass (blü′gras′), *NOUN.*

1 a grass with bluish green stems. It is valuable as food for horses and cattle, and is used for lawns.

2 a kind of country music, usually played on the fiddle, guitar, mandolin, and banjo.

blue jay, a North American bird with a crest and a blue back.

blue jay — about 12 inches long

blue jeans, jeans, usually made of blue denim.

blues (blüz), *NOUN.*

1 a slow, sad song or tune with jazz rhythm.

2 **the blues,** very sad feelings; low spirits: *Rainy days always give me the blues.*

blue whale, a blue-gray whale that can grow to be 100 feet long. It is the largest living animal.

bluff¹ (bluf), *NOUN.* a high, steep slope or cliff.

bluff² (bluf),

1 *VERB.* to fool or mislead someone by pretending to be confident about something: *She bluffed the robbers by yelling, "Here come the police!"*

2 *NOUN.* something said or done to fool others: *She pretended to have good cards, but it was a bluff.*
❏ *VERB* **bluffs, bluffed, bluff·ing.**

blu·ish (blü′ish), *ADJECTIVE.* somewhat blue.

a	hat	ė	term	ô	order	ch	child	
ā	age	i	it	oi	oil	ng	long	a in about
ä	far	ī	ice	ou	out	sh	she	e in taken
â	care	o	hot	u	cup	th	thin	ə i in pencil
e	let	ō	open	ů	put	₮H	then	o in lemon
ē	equal	ȯ	saw	ü	rule	zh	measure	u in circus

blun·der (blun′dər),
1 *NOUN.* a stupid mistake: *Misspelling the title of a book is a silly blunder to make in a book report.* ■ See the Synonym Study at **mistake.**
2 *VERB.* to make a stupid mistake: *Someone blundered in sending you to the wrong address.*
3 *VERB.* to move as if blind; stumble: *I blundered through the dark room.*
❏ *VERB* **blun·ders, blun·dered, blun·der·ing.**

blunt (blunt),
1 *ADJECTIVE.* without a sharp edge or point; dull: *a blunt knife.*
2 *VERB.* to make less sharp; make less keen: *Cutting wire blunted my scissors.*
3 *ADJECTIVE.* saying what you think very frankly, without trying to be polite; outspoken: *When I asked her if she liked my painting, her blunt answer was "No."*
❏ *VERB* **blunts, blunt·ed, blunt·ing.** –**blunt′ly,** *ADVERB.*

blur (blėr),
1 *VERB.* to make something less clear in form or outline: *Tears blurred my eyes.*
2 *NOUN.* something seen dimly or indistinctly: *When I don't have my glasses on, your face is just a blur.*
❏ *VERB* **blurs, blurred, blur·ring.**

blurb (blėrb), *NOUN.* advertisement or description, usually on the jacket of a book, album, and so on. Blurbs are usually full of high praise.

Word Story

Blurb is one of the few words that someone simply made up. Gelett Burgess, an American humorist, invented this word in 1907.

blur·ry (blėr′ē), *ADJECTIVE.* dim; indistinct: *The castle's blurry outline could barely be seen through the fog.* ❏ *ADJECTIVE* **blur·ri·er, blur·ri·est.**

blurt (blėrt), *VERB.* to say something suddenly or without thinking: *In his excitement he blurted out the secret.* ❏ *VERB* **blurts, blurt·ed, blurt·ing.**

blush (blush),
1 *VERB.* to become red in the face because of shame, confusion, or excitement: *The little boy blushed when everyone laughed at his mistake.*
2 *NOUN.* a sudden red color in your face caused by confusion, shame, or excitement.
❏ *VERB* **blush·es, blushed, blush·ing;** *PLURAL* **blush·es.**

blus·ter (blus′tər),
1 *VERB.* to storm noisily; blow violently: *The wind blustered outside the cozy house.*
2 *NOUN.* stormy noise and violence: *We could hear the bluster of the wind and rain.*
3 *VERB.* to talk noisily and violently: *They were very excited and angry, and blustered for a while.*
4 *NOUN.* noisy and threatening talk: *angry bluster.*
❏ *VERB* **blus·ters, blus·tered, blus·ter·ing.**

bo·a con·stric·tor (bō′ə kən strik′tər), a large nonpoisonous snake of the tropical parts of America, growing up to 15 feet long. It kills its prey by squeezing it to death.

boar (bôr), *NOUN.*
1 a male pig or hog.
2 a wild pig or hog.
❏ *PLURAL* **boars** or **boar.** ■ Another word that sounds like this is **bore.**

board (bôrd),
1 *NOUN.* a broad, thin piece of wood for use in building: *We used boards 10 inches wide, 1 inch thick, and 2 feet long for shelves.*
2 *VERB.* to cover something with such pieces of wood: *We boarded up the broken windows after the storm.*
3 *NOUN.* a flat piece of wood or other material used for one special purpose: *an ironing board.*
4 *NOUN.* a group of people managing something; council: *a school board, a board of directors.*
5 *VERB.* to get on a ship, train, bus, or airplane: *We board the school bus at the corner.*
6 *NOUN.* meals provided for pay: *The cost of going away to college includes room and board.*
7 *NOUN.* (in basketball) the backboard.
8 *NOUN.* **boards,** the low wooden fence around the edge of a hockey rink. Sheets of clear, hard plastic are usually mounted on top of this fence to protect spectators and to keep the puck in play.
❏ *VERB* **boards, board·ed, board·ing.**
on board, *IDIOM.* on a ship, train, bus, or airplane: *When everybody was on board, the ship sailed.*

board·er (bôr′dər), *NOUN.* someone who pays for meals, or for a room and meals, at someone else's house. ■ Another word that sounds like this is **border.**

boarding school, a school with buildings where the pupils live during the school term.

board·walk (bôrd′wȯk′), *NOUN.*
1 a sidewalk usually made of boards, along a beach or shore.
2 a narrow sidewalk made of boards, laid over wet spots along woods trails, in marshy areas, and so on.

boast (bōst),
1 *VERB.* to speak too highly of what you can do or what you own; brag: *He boasts about his grades and his wrestling trophies.*
2 *NOUN.* a statement speaking too highly of yourself; bragging words: *I don't believe her boast that she can run faster than I can.*
3 *VERB.* to have something to be proud of: *Our town boasts a beautiful new high school and a three-acre public park.*
❏ *VERB* **boasts, boast·ed, boast·ing.** –**boast′er,** *NOUN.*

boast·ful (bōst′fəl), *ADJECTIVE.* fond of bragging; boasting: *It is hard to listen to boastful people.* –**boast′ful·ly,** *ADVERB.* –**boast′ful·ness,** *NOUN.*

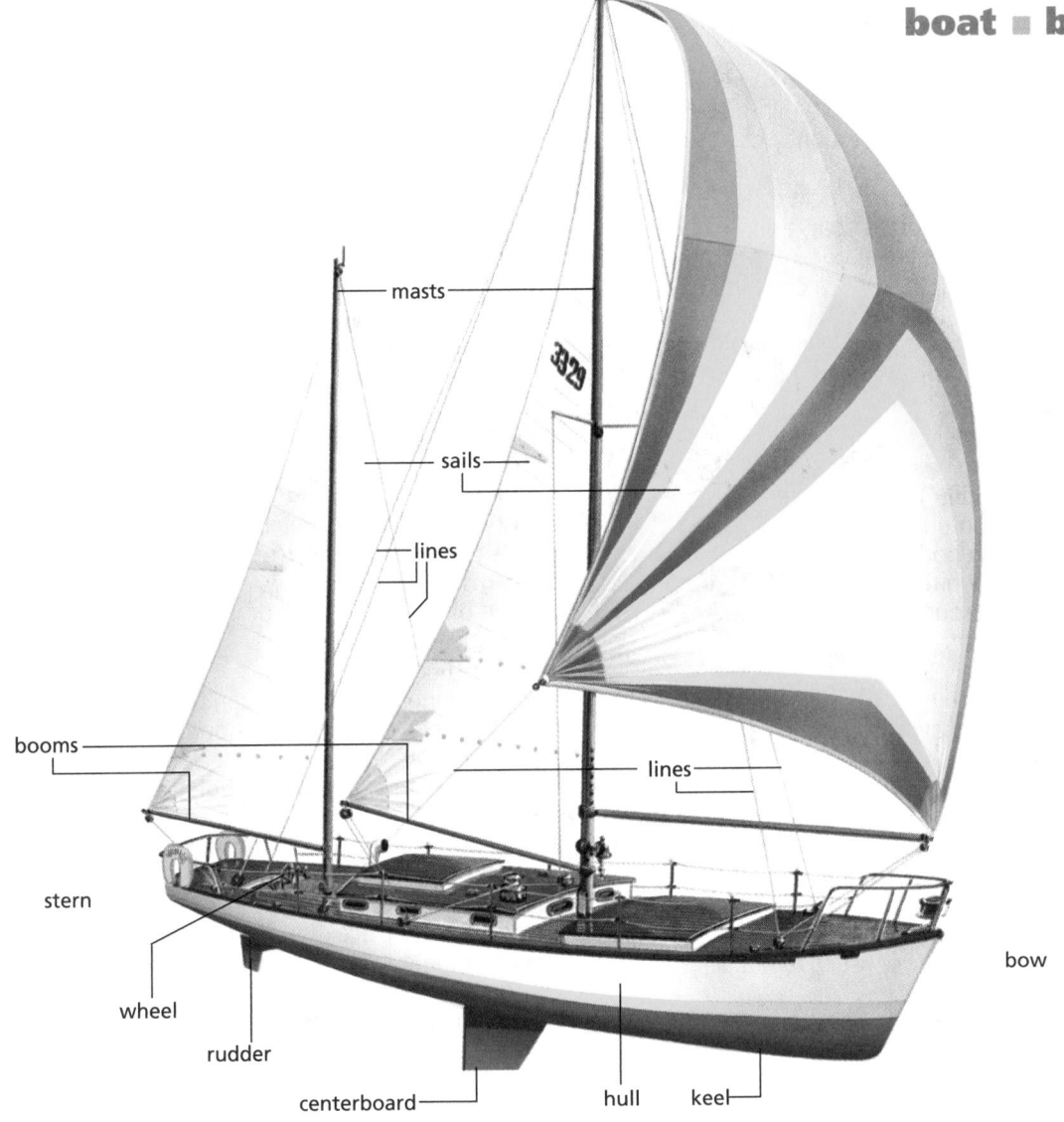

masts

sails

lines

booms

lines

stern

bow

wheel

rudder

centerboard

hull

keel

boat

boat (bōt), *NOUN.*
1 a small, open vessel for traveling on water, such as a sailboat, motorboat, or rowboat.
2 a large vessel, such as a freighter, passenger liner, or oil tanker; ship.
in the same boat, *IDIOM.* in the same situation: *If the storm hits, we'll all be in the same boat.*

Word Bank

There are many words used to talk about **boats.** If you want to learn more about boats you can start by looking these words up in this dictionary.

aft	cabin	helm	rigging
anchor	cargo	hull	rudder
ballast	crow's nest	keel	sail
beam	fore¹	knot	starboard
berth	frigate	mast	stern²
bow³	galley	oar	tiller
bridge	gunwale	port²	wake²

boat·ing (bō'ting), *NOUN.* the act or sport of going by boat, as in rowing or sailing.
bob¹ (bob),
1 *VERB.* to move up and down with short, quick motions: *The pigeon bobbed its head as it fed.*
2 *NOUN.* a short, quick motion up and down.
❑ *VERB* **bobs, bobbed, bob·bing.**
bob² (bob),
1 *NOUN.* a haircut that is about ear-level all around the head.
2 *VERB.* to cut hair short.
❑ *VERB* **bobs, bobbed, bob·bing.**
bob·bin (bob'ən), *NOUN.* a spool for holding thread, yarn, and the like. Bobbins are used in spinning, weaving, machine sewing, and making lace.

a	hat	ė	term	ô order	ch child	a in about
ā	age	i	it	oi oil	ng long	e in taken
ä	far	ī	ice	ou out	sh she	ə{ i in pencil
â	care	o	hot	u cup	th thin	o in lemon
e	let	ō	open	ů put	ᴛʜ then	u in circus
ē	equal	ȯ	saw	ü rule	zh measure	

bob·by pin (bob′ē pin′), a small, thin piece of metal with prongs that close tightly on the hair and hold it in place.

bob·cat (bob′kat′), NOUN. a wildcat of North America that has a spotted coat, a short tail, and pointed ears. Bobcats are about 3 feet long.

bob·o·link (bob′ə lingk), NOUN. a common North American songbird that lives in fields.

bob·sled (bob′sled′), NOUN. a long sled with two sets of runners. It has a steering wheel and brakes.

bob·white (bob′whīt′), NOUN. an American quail that has a grayish body with brown and white markings. Its call sounds like its name.

bobsled

bod·i·ly (bod′l ē), ADJECTIVE. of the body; in the body: *Athletes have bodily strength.*

bod·y (bod′ē), NOUN.
  1 the whole physical part of a human being or an animal: *I exercise to keep my body healthy.*
  2 the main part of an animal, apart from the head, limbs, or tail.
  3 a dead person or animal.
  4 a mass or group: *a body of water, the student body.*
  ❑ PLURAL **bod·ies.**

bod·y·guard (bod′ē gärd′), NOUN. a person or persons who guard someone: *A bodyguard usually accompanies the President.*

bog (bog), NOUN. an area of soft, wet, spongy ground; marsh; swamp.
  bog down, IDIOM. to make little or no progress; become unable to proceed: *I am bogged down with all this homework.* ❑ VERB **bogs, bogged, bog·ging.**

bo·gey·man (bŭg′ē man′ or bō′gē man′), NOUN. a frightening imaginary creature. ❑ PLURAL **bo·gey·men.**

bo·gus (bō′gəs), ADJECTIVE. not genuine; counterfeit: *a bogus $10 bill.*

boil¹ (boil), VERB.
  1 to bubble up and give off steam: *Water boils when heated.*
  2 to cause a liquid to boil by heating it: *Boil some water for tea.*
  3 to cook by boiling: *We boiled the eggs.*
  ❑ VERB **boils, boiled, boil·ing.**

boil² (boil), NOUN. a painful, red swelling on the skin caused by infection. A boil is hard and filled with pus.

boil·er (boi′lər), NOUN. a tank for making steam to heat buildings or drive engines.

boiling point, the temperature at which a liquid boils. The boiling point of water at sea level is 212 degrees Fahrenheit or 100 degrees Celsius.

Boi·se (boi′sē), NOUN. the capital of Idaho.

bois·ter·ous (boi′stər əs), ADJECTIVE. noisy, lively, and uncontrolled: *Boisterous laughter woke me.*

bold (bōld), ADJECTIVE.
  1 without fear; having or showing courage; brave: *The lion tamer was bold and fearless.* ■ See the Synonym Study at **brave.**
  2 rude; impudent: *The bold child made faces at us.*
  3 sharp and clear to the eye; striking: *The mountains stood in bold outline against the sky.*
  —**bold′ly,** ADVERB. —**bold′ness,** NOUN.

Bo·liv·i·a (bə liv′ē ə), NOUN. a country in western South America. —**Bo·liv′i·an,** ADJECTIVE or NOUN.

bo·lo·gna (bə lō′nē), NOUN. a large sausage usually made of beef, veal, and pork. ❑ PLURAL **bo·lo·gnas.** Also spelled **baloney.**

bol·ster (bōl′stər),
  1 NOUN. a long pillow or cushion for a couch or bed.
  2 VERB. to keep from falling; support; prop: *Her faith bolstered my confidence.*
  ❑ VERB **bol·sters, bol·stered, bol·ster·ing.**

bolt (bōlt),
  1 NOUN. a short metal rod with a head at one end and a screw thread for a nut at the other. Bolts are used to fasten things together or hold something in place.
  2 NOUN. a metal bar that slides to fasten shut a door or gate.
  3 NOUN. the part of a lock moved by a key.
  4 VERB. to fasten with a bolt: *We bolt the doors before going to bed.*
  5 NOUN. a flash of lightning.
  6 VERB. to dash off; run away: *The horse bolted.*
  ❑ VERB **bolts, bolt·ed, bolt·ing.**

bomb (bom),
  1 NOUN. a container filled with an explosive. A bomb is usually set off by the force with which it hits something or by an electric current.
  2 VERB. to attack with bombs; drop bombs on.
  ❑ VERB **bombs, bombed, bomb·ing.**

bom·bard (bom bärd′), VERB.
  1 to attack with bombs or heavy fire from big guns: *The artillery bombarded the enemy all day.*
  2 to keep attacking someone forcefully: *The lawyer bombarded the witness with questions.*
  ❑ VERB **bom·bards, bom·bard·ed, bom·bard·ing.**

Bom·bay (bom bā′), NOUN. a city in India.

bomb·er (bom′ər), NOUN. an airplane that drops bombs.

bond (bond),
  1 NOUN. a strong force or feeling that unites: *the bonds of affection between friends.*
  2 VERB. to bind together.
  ❑ VERB **bonds, bond·ed, bond·ing.**

B

bond·age (bon′dij), *NOUN.* the condition of being held against your will under the control or influence of some person or thing; lack of freedom.

bone (bōn),
1 *NOUN.* one of the pieces of the skeleton of an animal with a backbone: *the bones of the hand.*
2 *VERB.* to take bones out of: *We boned the fish before eating it.*
   ❑ *VERB* **bones, boned, bon·ing. –bone′like′,** *ADJECTIVE.*

bone marrow, the soft tissue that fills the hollow central part of most bones. Bone marrow produces both red and white blood cells.

bon·fire (bon′fīr′), *NOUN.* a large fire built outdoors: *We sat around the bonfire to keep warm.*

Word Story

Bonfire comes from the words **bone** and **fire.** It was called this because in the past, fires were made to burn old bones.

bon·go (bong′gō), *NOUN.* a small drum played with flattened hands. Bongos usually come in pairs and are held between the knees.
   ❑ *PLURAL* **bon·gos** or **bongoes.**

a pair of **bongos**

bon·net (bon′it), *NOUN.* (earlier) a covering for the head usually tied under the chin with strings or ribbons, worn by women and children.

bo·no·bo (bə nō′bō), *NOUN.* a small ape that lives in tropical Africa. It is closely related to the chimpanzee. ❑ *PLURAL* **bo·no·bos.**

bo·nus (bō′nəs), *NOUN.* something extra, given in addition to what is due: *The company gave each worker a bonus of $200.* ❑ *PLURAL* **bo·nus·es.**

bon·y (bō′nē), *ADJECTIVE.*
1 of bone: *the bony structure of the skull.*
2 full of bones: *a bony fish.*
3 having bones that stick out; very thin: *bony hands.*
   ❑ *ADJECTIVE* **bon·i·er, bon·i·est. –bon′i·ness,** *NOUN.*

boo (bü),
1 *NOUN* or *INTERJECTION.* a sound made to frighten or to show dislike: *I jumped out and shouted, "Boo!"*
2 *VERB.* to make such a sound; shout "boo" at: *He sang so badly that the audience booed him.*
   ❑ *PLURAL* **boos;** *VERB* **boos, booed, boo·ing.**

book (bük),
1 *NOUN.* sheets of paper, either blank or printed, bound together between covers: *I read the first two chapters of that book last night.*
2 *NOUN.* a number of similar things fastened together like a book: *a book of matches, a book of stamps.*
3 *NOUN.* a main division of a book: *Numbers is a book of the Old Testament.*
4 *VERB.* to reserve a seat on a plane, a hotel room, and so on: *He booked a flight to London.*
5 *VERB.* to officially charge someone with a crime: *At the police station, they booked the suspect.*
   ❑ *VERB* **books, booked, book·ing. –book′like′,** *ADJECTIVE.*

book·case (bük′kās′), *NOUN.* a piece of furniture with shelves for holding books.

book·keep·er (bük′kē′pər), *NOUN.* someone who keeps a record of business accounts.

book·let (bük′lit), *NOUN.* a little book; thin book. Booklets often have paper covers.

book·mark (bük′märk′), *NOUN.* a strip of cloth, paper, or the like, put between the pages of a book to mark the reader's place.

book·mo·bile (bük′mə bēl′), *NOUN.* a truck that serves as a traveling branch of a library.

book·store (bük′stôr′), *NOUN.* a store where books are sold.

boom¹ (büm),
1 *NOUN.* a deep hollow sound like the roar of cannon or of big waves: *We listened to the boom of the pounding surf.*
2 *VERB.* to make a deep hollow sound: *His voice boomed out above the rest.*
3 *NOUN.* a rapid growth: *The United States had a population boom after World War II.*
4 *VERB.* to grow rapidly: *Business is booming.*
   ❑ *VERB* **booms, boomed, boom·ing.**

boom² (büm), *NOUN.* a long pole or beam. A boom is used to extend the bottom of a sail or as the lifting arm of a derrick.

boo·me·rang (bü′mə rang′), *NOUN.* a curved piece of wood, used as a hunting weapon by the original people of Australia. Some kinds of boomerangs can be thrown so that they return to the thrower.

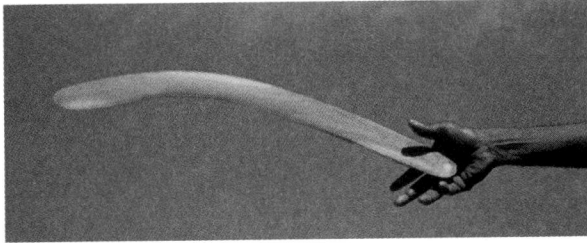

boomerang

a	hat	ė	term	ô	order	ch	child		a in about
ā	age	i	it	oi	oil	ng	long		e in taken
ä	far	ī	ice	ou	out	sh	she	ə {	i in pencil
â	care	o	hot	u	cup	th	thin		o in lemon
e	let	ō	open	ù	put	ᴛʜ	then		u in circus
ē	equal	ò	saw	ü	rule	zh	measure		

boost (büst),
1 NOUN. a lift or push that helps someone up or over something: *Give me a boost over the fence.*
2 VERB. to lift or push from below: *Her friend boosted her to the lowest branch of the apple tree.*
❑ VERB **boosts, boost·ed, boost·ing.**

boost·er (bü′stər), NOUN. a rocket or engine that provides part of the powerful upward lift to a spacecraft or missile, especially at lift-off.

booster shot, an additional dose of a vaccine or serum to continue the effect of a previous shot.

boot (büt),
1 NOUN. a leather or rubber covering for the foot and lower part of the leg.
2 NOUN. a kick: *She gave the ball a boot.*
3 VERB. to give a kick to: *Boot the ball to me!*
❑ VERB **boots, boot·ed, boot·ing.**

boot up, IDIOM. to start a computer or computer program.

boot·ee (bü′tē), NOUN. a baby's soft shoe, often knitted. ❑ PLURAL **boot·ees.** ■ Another word that sounds like this is **booty.**

booth (büth), NOUN.
1 a place where goods are sold or shown at a fair, market, or convention.
2 a small enclosed or partly enclosed place: *a voting booth, a phone booth, a booth in a diner.*
❑ PLURAL **booths** (büтнz or büths).

boo·ty (bü′tē), NOUN. things taken by force in war or during a robbery: *The pirates fought over how to divide the booty from the captured ship.*
■ Another word that sounds like this is **bootee.**

bor·der (bôr′dər), NOUN.
1 NOUN. the side, edge, or boundary of anything, or the part near it: *We camped on the border of the lake.*
2 VERB. to touch at the edge or boundary: *The United States borders on Canada and Mexico.*
3 NOUN. a strip on the edge of anything for strength or ornament: *a lace border.*
4 VERB. to put a border on: *to border a lawn with bushes.*
❑ VERB **bor·ders, bor·dered, bor·der·ing.** ■ Another word that sounds like this is **boarder.**

bore[1] (bôr), VERB.
1 to make a hole by means of a revolving tool: *I bored through my belt to make an extra hole.*
2 to make a hole by digging, chewing, or pushing: *Moles bore tunnels in lawns.*
❑ VERB **bores, bored, bor·ing.** ■ Another word that sounds like this is **boar.**

bore[2] (bôr),
1 VERB. to make someone weary by being dull and uninteresting: *This book bores me, so I won't finish it.*
2 NOUN. a dull, tiresome person or thing: *It is a bore to have to wash dishes three times a day.*
❑ VERB **bores, bored, bor·ing.** ■ Another word that sounds like this is **boar.**

bore[3] (bôr), VERB. the past tense of **bear**[1]: *She bore her loss bravely.* ■ Another word that sounds like this is **boar.**

bore·dom (bôr′dəm), NOUN. weariness caused by uninteresting people, events, or tasks: *Her boredom was evident during the speech.*

bor·ing (bôr′ing), ADJECTIVE. not interesting; dull.

born (bôrn), ADJECTIVE.
1 brought into life; brought forth: *We saw a newly born calf. He was born on December 30, 1900.*
2 by birth; by nature: *She could swim at such an early age, we believed she was a born athlete.*

borne (bôrn), VERB. a past participle of **bear**[1]: *I have borne the pack all day. She has borne three children.*

bor·ough (bėr′ō), NOUN. a town or a district within a city that has certain powers of government. ■ Other words that sound like this are **burro** and **burrow.**

bor·row (bor′ō), VERB.
1 to get something from another person by agreeing to return it later on: *I borrowed her book.*
2 to take and use something as your own; adopt; take: *The English word "kindergarten" was borrowed from German.*
❑ VERB **bor·rows, bor·rowed, bor·row·ing.**
—**bor′row·er,** NOUN.

Bos·ni·a-Her·ze·go·vi·na (boz′nē ə hėr′tsə gə vē′nə), NOUN. a country in southeastern Europe.

bos·om (bůz′əm),
1 NOUN. the upper, front part of the human body; breast: *She clasped the child to her bosom.*
2 ADJECTIVE. close and trusted: *bosom friends.*

boss (bȯs),
1 NOUN. someone who hires workers or tells them what to do; manager; foreman.
2 VERB. to be the boss of; direct; control: *He said that I was bossing him around.*
❑ VERB **boss·es, bossed, boss·ing;** PLURAL **boss·es.**

boss·y (bȯ′sē), ADJECTIVE. fond of telling others what to do: *Bossy people are seldom popular.* ❑ ADJECTIVE **boss·i·er, boss·i·est.**

Bos·ton (bȯ′stən), NOUN. the capital of Massachusetts.
—**Bos·to·ni·an** (bȯ stō′nē ən), NOUN or ADJECTIVE.

bo·tan·i·cal (bə tan′ə kəl), ADJECTIVE. of or about plants.

bot·a·ny (bot′n ē), NOUN. the science of plants; the study of plants and plant life. Botany is a branch of biology.
—**bot′a·nist,** NOUN.

studying plants in a **botanical** laboratory

both (bōth),
1 *ADJECTIVE*. the two; the one and the other: *Both houses are white.*
2 *PRONOUN*. the two together: *Both belong to her.*
3 *ADVERB* or *CONJUNCTION*. together; alike; equally: *She is both strong and healthy.*

both·er (boᴛн′ər),
1 *NOUN*. much fuss or worry; trouble: *What a lot of bother about nothing!*
2 *VERB*. to take trouble; concern yourself: *Don't bother to cook; we'll eat out.*
3 *NOUN*. someone or something that causes worry or trouble: *A door that will not shut is a bother.*
4 *VERB*. to annoy: *Hot weather bothers me.*
❑ *VERB* **both·ers, both·ered, both·er·ing.**

Bot·swa·na (bot swä′nə), *NOUN*. a country in southern Africa. **—Bot·swa′nan,** *NOUN* or *ADJECTIVE*.

bot·tle (bot′l),
1 *NOUN*. a container without handles for holding liquids, usually made of glass or plastic. Most bottles have narrow necks and caps or stoppers.
2 *NOUN*. the amount that a bottle can hold: *He drank a bottle of ginger ale.*
3 *VERB*. to put into bottles: *bottled water.*
❑ *VERB* **bot·tles, bot·tled, bot·tling. —bot′tler,** *NOUN*.

bot·tom (bot′əm),
1 *NOUN*. the lowest part: *These berries at the bottom of the basket are crushed.*
2 *NOUN*. the part on which anything rests; base: *The bottom of that glass is wet.*
3 *NOUN*. the ground under water: *Many wrecks lie at the bottom of the sea.*
4 *NOUN*. **bottoms,** pajama trousers.
5 *NOUN*. a seat: *This chair needs a new bottom.*
6 *ADJECTIVE*. lowest or last: *I see a robin on the bottom branch of that tree.*
7 *NOUN*. the buttocks.
—bot′tom·less, *ADJECTIVE*.
get to the bottom of something, *IDIOM*. to find out the truth about some mystery: *After the house was broken into a second time, we hired a detective to get to the bottom of things.*

bough (bou), *NOUN*. one of the main branches of a tree. ∎ Other words that sound like this are **bow[1]** and **bow[3]**.

bought (bȯt), *VERB*.
1 the past tense of **buy:** *We bought milk at the store.*
2 the past participle of **buy:** *I have bought two pens.*

boul·der (bōl′dər), *NOUN*. a large rock, rounded or worn down by the action of water and weather.

boul·e·vard (bùl′ə värd), *NOUN*. a broad street, often with a line of trees planted along its sides, or down the center.

bounce (bouns),
1 *VERB*. to spring into the air like a ball: *The baby likes to bounce up and down on the bed.*
2 *VERB*. to cause to bounce: *Bounce the ball to me.*
3 *NOUN*. the act of springing back: *I caught the ball on the first bounce.*
❑ *VERB* **bounc·es, bounced, bounc·ing.**

bounc·y (boun′sē), *ADJECTIVE*.
1 lively; eager: *She was bouncy and full of life.*
2 bouncing back; springing back: *He walks with a bouncy step.*
❑ *ADJECTIVE* **bounc·i·er, bounc·i·est.**

bound[1] (bound),
1 *ADJECTIVE*. under some obligation; having a duty to do something: *I feel bound by my promise.*
2 *ADJECTIVE*. certain; sure: *She is bound to succeed.*
3 *ADJECTIVE*. put in a cover: *a bound book.*
4 *VERB*. the past tense of **bind:** *She bound the package with string.*
5 *VERB*. the past participle of **bind:** *They have bound my hands.*

bound[2] (bound),
1 *VERB*. to leap or spring lightly along; jump: *Mountain goats can bound from rock to rock.*
∎ See the Synonym Study at **jump.**
2 *NOUN*. a jump: *With one bound the deer was gone, vanishing into the forest.*
❑ *VERB* **bounds, bound·ed, bound·ing.**

A stag **bounds** over a fallen tree.

bound[3] (bound), *VERB*. to form the boundary of; limit: *Canada bounds the United States on the north.* ❑ *VERB* **bounds, bound·ed, bound·ing.**
out of bounds, *IDIOM*. outside the area allowed by rules, custom, or law: *I kicked the ball out of bounds. The attic closet is out of bounds between Thanksgiving and Christmas.*

bound[4] (bound), *ADJECTIVE*. on the way; going: *The weary traveler was homeward bound at last.*

a	hat	ė	term	ô	order	ch	child		⎧ a in about
ā	age	i	it	oi	oil	ng	long		⎪ e in taken
ä	far	ī	ice	ou	out	sh	she	ə ⎨ i in pencil
â	care	o	hot	u	cup	th	thin		⎪ o in lemon
e	let	ō	open	ù	put	ᴛн	then		⎩ u in circus
ē	equal	ȯ	saw	ü	rule	zh	measure		

bound·ar·y (boun′dər ē), *NOUN.* a limiting line or thing; limit; border: *That fence marks the boundary between our yard and our neighbors' yard.* ❏ *PLURAL* **bound·ar·ies.**

bound·less (bound′lis), *ADJECTIVE.* not limited: *She has boundless energy.*

boun·ti·ful (boun′tə fəl), *ADJECTIVE.* more than enough; plentiful; abundant: *We put in enough plants for a bountiful supply of peas.* —**boun′ti·ful·ly,** *ADVERB.*

boun·ty (boun′tē), *NOUN.*
1 a reward: *There is no bounty for killing coyotes now.*
2 the quality of being generous; generosity. ❏ *PLURAL* **boun·ties.**

bou·quet (bō kā′ or bü kā′), *NOUN.* a bunch of flowers.

bout (bout), *NOUN.*
1 a trial of strength; contest: *Those are the two boxers who will appear in the main bout.*
2 a length of time that something unpleasant lasts: *I have just had a long bout of illness.*

a **bouquet** of flowers

bou·tique (bü tēk′), *NOUN.* a small shop that specializes in stylish clothes, especially for women. ❏ *PLURAL* **bou·tiques.**

bow¹ (bou),
1 *VERB.* to bend the head or body in greeting, respect, worship, or obedience: *The people bowed before the queen.*
2 *NOUN.* an act of bending the head or body in this way: *The men made a bow to the queen.* ❏ *VERB* **bows, bowed, bow·ing.** ■ Another word that sounds like this is **bough.**
bow to, *IDIOM.* to give in; yield: *The boy bowed to his parents' wishes.*

bow² (bō), *NOUN.*
1 a weapon for shooting arrows. A bow usually consists of a strip of flexible wood bent by a cord.
2 a slender wooden rod with horsehairs stretched on it, for playing a violin or similar instrument.
3 a knot that has loops: *She tied a big bow on the box.*

bow³ (bou), *NOUN.* the front of a ship, boat, or aircraft. ■ Another word that sounds like this is **bough.**

bow·els (bou′əlz), *NOUN PLURAL.*
1 the tube in the body into which food passes from the stomach; intestines.
2 the deep, inner part of anything: *Miners dig for coal in the bowels of the earth.* ❏ *SINGULAR* **bow·el.**

bowl¹ (bōl), *NOUN.*
1 a hollow, rounded dish, usually without handles: *a mixing bowl, a salad bowl.*

2 the amount that a bowl can hold: *She had a bowl of soup for lunch.*
3 the hollow, rounded part of anything: *The bowl of a pipe holds the tobacco.*
4 a special football game played when the season is over: *We went Florida to see the Orange Bowl.*

bowl² (bōl), *VERB.*
1 to play the game of bowling: *They bowl every Tuesday.*
2 to roll or throw the ball in the game of bowling: *You can bowl after me.* ❏ *VERB* **bowls, bowled, bowl·ing.**
bowl over, *IDIOM.* to strike with sudden wonder, surprise, or shock: *I was bowled over by the news.*

bow·leg·ged (bō′leg′id), *ADJECTIVE.* having the legs curved outward: *a bowlegged cowboy.*

bowl·ing (bō′ling), *NOUN.* a game played indoors, in which balls are rolled down an alley at bottle-shaped wooden pins.

bowling alley,
1 a long, narrow, wooden floor along which the ball is rolled in bowling; lane.
2 a building having many lanes for bowling.

box¹ (boks),
1 *NOUN.* a container, usually with four sides, a bottom, and a lid, to pack or put things in: *We packed the boxes full of books.*
2 *NOUN.* the amount that a box can hold: *I bought a box of soap.*
3 *VERB.* to pack in a box; put into a box: *She boxed up all her uncle's old ties.*
4 *NOUN.* an enclosed space, often with seats: *a jury box, a theater box.* ❏ *PLURAL* **box·es;** *VERB* **box·es, boxed, box·ing.** —**box′like′,** *ADJECTIVE.*

box² (boks), *VERB.*
1 to fight with the fists as a sport: *He had not boxed since he left school.*
2 to strike a blow with the open hand or fist: *I will box your ears if you yell at me again.* ❏ *VERB* **box·es, boxed, box·ing.**

box·car (boks′kär′), *NOUN.* an enclosed railroad freight car. It has a sliding door on each side.

box·er (bok′sər), *NOUN.*
1 a person who fights with the fists as a sport. Boxers wear padded gloves and follow special rules.
2 a medium-sized short-haired dog with a smooth brown coat. It is related to the bulldog.

box·ing (bok′sing), *NOUN.* the action or sport of fighting with the fists, usually while wearing padded leather gloves.

box office, the office or booth in a theater, hall, or stadium where tickets of admission are sold.

boy (boi), *NOUN.* a male child from birth to about eighteen. ■ Another word that can sound like this is **buoy.**

B

boy·cott (boi′kot),
1 *VERB.* to join together against and agree not to buy from, sell to, or have anything to do with a person, business, or nation. People boycott in order to force a change or to punish.
2 *NOUN.* the act of boycotting.
❑ *VERB* **boy·cotts, boy·cott·ed, boy·cott·ing.**

boy·friend (boi′frend′), *NOUN.* a girl's sweetheart or constant male companion.

boy·hood (boi′hůd), *NOUN.* the time of being a boy.

boy·ish (boi′ish), *ADJECTIVE.* like a boy: *boyish charm.*

reading **Braille**

boy scout, a member of an organization (the **Boy Scouts**) that seeks to develop character, citizenship, usefulness to others, and various skills.

brace (brās),
1 *NOUN.* something that holds parts together or in place, such as a timber used to strengthen a building or to support a roof.
2 *NOUN.* a device used to support a part of the body, such as a knee or wrist.
3 *NOUN.* **braces,** metal wires and bands used to straighten crooked teeth.
4 *VERB.* to give strength or firmness to something; support: *We braced the roof with four poles.*
5 *VERB.* to prepare yourself: *I braced myself for the crash.*
6 *NOUN.* the handle of a tool used for boring holes.
❑ *VERB* **brac·es, braced, brac·ing.**

brace·let (brās′lit), *NOUN.* a band or chain worn for ornament around the wrist or arm.

brach·i·o·sau·rus (brak′ē ə sôr′əs), *NOUN.* a giant, plant-eating dinosaur with a very long neck.
❑ *PLURAL* **brach·i·o·sau·rus·es.**

brack·et (brak′it),
1 *NOUN.* a flat piece of metal, wood, or plastic fastened to a wall to hold up a shelf.
2 *NOUN.* either of these signs [ ] used to enclose words or numbers.
3 *VERB.* to enclose within brackets: *The teacher bracketed the mistakes in my work.*
4 *NOUN.* any group thought of together: *I am the fastest swimmer in the 8-to-10 age bracket.*
❑ *VERB* **brack·ets, brack·et·ed, brack·et·ing.**

brag (brag), *VERB.* to speak too highly of yourself, what you have, or what you do; boast: *They bragged about their new car.* ❑ *VERB* **brags, bragged, brag·ging. –brag′ger,** *NOUN.*

braid (brād),
1 *NOUN.* a band formed by weaving together three or more strands of hair, ribbon, yarn, or the like: *She wore her hair in braids.*
2 *VERB.* to weave or twine together three or more strands of hair, ribbon, yarn, or the like: *She can braid her own hair.*
❑ *VERB* **braids, braid·ed, braid·ing.**

Braille or **braille** (brāl), *NOUN.* a system of writing and printing for people who cannot see. In Braille, letters and numbers are represented by different arrangements of raised dots and are read by touching them.

brain (brān), *NOUN.*
1 the part of the central nervous system in humans and many other animals. It is located in the head and consists of a soft mass of nerve cells. It controls almost all the functions of the body, and with it we can learn, think, and remember.
2 **brains,** intelligence: *Dogs have more brains than ants.*
–brain′less, *ADJECTIVE.*

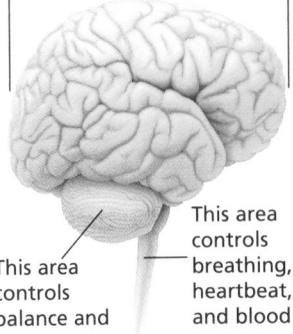

This large area controls thought and speech.

This area controls balance and movement.

This area controls breathing, heartbeat, and blood pressure.

the human **brain**

brachiosaurus — about 70 feet long, including the tail

a	hat	ė	term	ô	order	ch	child	⎰a in about
ā	age	i	it	oi	oil	ng	long	e in taken
ä	far	ī	ice	ou	out	sh	she	ə⎨i in pencil
â	care	o	hot	u	cup	th	thin	o in lemon
e	let	ō	open	ů	put	₮H	then	⎱u in circus
ē	equal	ò	saw	ü	rule	zh	measure	

brain·storm (brān′stôrm′), NOUN. a sudden idea or inspiration: *I've had a brainstorm; to make money, let's put on a play and charge admission.* ■ See the Synonym Study at **idea.**

brake (brāk),
1 NOUN. a device that presses or rubs against the wheels to slow or stop the motion of a vehicle.
2 VERB. to slow or stop by using a brake: *The driver braked the speeding car and it slid to a stop.*
❏ VERB **brakes, braked, brak·ing.** ■ Another word that sounds like this is **break.**

bram·ble (bram′bəl), NOUN. a bush with slender, drooping branches covered with little thorns. Blackberry and raspberry plants are brambles.

bran (bran), NOUN. the outer covering of grains like wheat and rye. When flour is made from these grains, the bran is often separated from the inner part. Bran is an important source of fiber in foods like bread and cereals.

branch (branch),
1 NOUN. a part of a tree growing out from the trunk; any large, woody part of a tree above the ground except the trunk.
2 NOUN. a division; part: *a branch of a river, a branch of a family. Biology is a branch of science.*
3 VERB. to divide into branches: *The road branches at the bottom of the hill.*
❏ PLURAL **branch·es;** VERB **branch·es, branched, branch·ing.**

brand (brand),
1 NOUN. a certain kind, grade, or make: *Do you like this brand of flour?*
2 NOUN. a name or mark that a company uses to distinguish its products from others; trademark.
3 NOUN. a mark made by burning the skin of an animal with a hot iron: *The cattle on this big ranch have a brand that shows who owns them.*
4 VERB. to mark by burning the skin with a hot iron.
❏ VERB **brands, brand·ed, brand·ing.**

brand-new (brand′nü′), ADJECTIVE. very new; entirely new: *Who took my brand-new bike?*
■ See the Synonym Study at **new.**

bran·dy (bran′dē), NOUN. a strong alcoholic drink made from wine or fermented fruit juice. ❏ PLURAL **bran·dies.**

brass (bras),
1 NOUN. a yellowish metal that is made of copper and zinc.
2 ADJECTIVE. made of brass: *brass candlesticks.*
3 NOUN PLURAL. **brass** or **brasses,** brass instruments.
❏ PLURAL **brass·es.**

brass instrument, a musical instrument made of metal. The trumpet, trombone, French horn, and tuba are brass instruments.

brat (brat), NOUN. a rude, annoying, or unpleasant child: *I won't baby-sit for that brat any more.*

brave (brāv),
1 ADJECTIVE. without fear; showing courage: *The brave girl went into the burning house to save a baby.*
2 VERB. to meet without fear; defy: *The early settlers braved the hardships of life in a new land.*
3 NOUN. an American Indian warrior.
❏ ADJECTIVE **brav·er, brav·est;** VERB **braves, braved, brav·ing.** –**brave′ly,** ADVERB.

Synonym Study

Brave means showing no fear or danger: *The brave girl rescued her sister from the fire.*

Courageous means brave and strong in spirit. A courageous person does what is right even when it is hard or dangerous: *It was courageous of my brother to admit that he had lied.*

Bold means willing and eager to face danger and take risks: *It's a movie about a bold girl with limited hearing who learns to fly a plane.*

Daring means bold: *My favorites were the daring women and men in the trapeze act.*

Heroic means very brave and noble. Heroic people put themselves in danger to help others: *A heroic lifeguard saved me from drowning.*

ANTONYM: cowardly.

brav·er·y (brā′vər ē), NOUN. courage; being brave: *I owe my life to the bravery of the firefighters.*

bray (brā),
1 NOUN. the loud, harsh cry or noise made by a donkey.
2 VERB. to make this sound.
❏ VERB **brays, brayed, bray·ing.**

Bra·zil (brə zil′), NOUN. a country in central South America. –**Bra·zil·ian** (brə zil′yən), NOUN or ADJECTIVE.

Brazil nut, the large, tasty nut of a tall tree growing in South America.

breach (brēch),
1 NOUN. an opening made by breaking down something solid; gap: *Cannon fire had made a breach in the wall of the fort.*
2 VERB. to break through; make an opening in: *Attacking troops breached the wall in several places.*
❏ PLURAL **breach·es;** VERB **breach·es, breached, breach·ing.**

bread (bred), NOUN.
1 a food made of flour or meal mixed with milk or water and baked. Most breads are made with yeast.
2 the things necessary for keeping alive, such as food: *How will you earn your daily bread?*
■ Another word that sounds like this is **bred.**

breadth (bredth), NOUN. the distance across something from one side to the other; width: *I traveled the length and breadth of the neighborhood looking for my lost dog.*

break (brāk),

1 *VERB.* to come apart or make come apart: *The plate broke into pieces when it fell. The winner broke the tape crossing the finish line.*

2 *NOUN.* a broken place; crack: *There was a break in the wall. The X ray showed a break in my leg.*

break (definition 1)

3 *VERB.* to damage: *She broke her watch by winding it too tightly.*

4 *VERB.* to crack the bone of: *He fell and broke his arm.*

5 *VERB.* to fail to keep or obey: *I hate to break a promise. People who break the law are punished.*

6 *VERB.* to force your way: *The lion broke out of its cage. The robbers broke into the warehouse.*

7 *NOUN.* the act of forcing your way out: *The prisoners made a break for freedom.*

8 *NOUN.* a short interruption in work or practice: *The coach told us to take a break for five minutes.*

9 *VERB.* to soften the force of: *The bushes broke her fall from the tree.*

10 *VERB.* to put an end to; stop: *to break a bad habit.*

11 *VERB.* to go beyond; do better than: *The speed of the new plane has broken all records.*

12 *NOUN.* (informal) a stroke of luck; fortune; chance: *Finding that money was a lucky break.*

  ❑ *VERB* **breaks, broke, bro·ken, break·ing.**
  ■ Another word that sounds like this is **brake.**
  —**break′a·ble,** *ADJECTIVE.*

break down, *IDIOM.*

1 to go out of order; stop working: *The car's engine broke down.*

2 to begin to cry: *He broke down when he heard the bad news.*

3 to separate or divide into parts or steps: *When food is digested, it is broken down into simpler forms that the body can use.*

break in, *IDIOM.*

1 to prepare for work, duty, or use: *break in a new salesperson, break in new shoes.*

2 to enter by force: *The thieves broke in through the basement.*

break into, *IDIOM.*

1 to enter by force: *A thief broke into the house.*

2 to begin suddenly: *She broke into a run.*

3 to interrupt: *He broke into their conversation.*

break off, *IDIOM.* to stop suddenly: *They broke off their conversation when they heard the crash.*

break out, *IDIOM.*

1 to start suddenly; begin: *A fire broke out in the hall.*

2 to have pimples or rashes appear on the skin: *The child broke out with measles.*

3 to leave by force; escape: *The thief broke out of jail.*

break up, *IDIOM.*

1 to scatter; separate into parts: *The fog is breaking up.*

2 to come or bring to an end: *The committee broke up its meeting early. Their marriage broke up.*

3 to laugh or cause to laugh: *The audience broke up at the comedian's jokes.*

Synonym Study

Break means to come apart suddenly or to force something to come apart: *The egg fell and broke. Mom broke the stick in two.*

Crack means to break, but not into pieces: *The stone cracked the window, but the glass did not fall out.*

Shatter means to break into many pieces: *The cup shattered when it hit the floor.*

Smash means to break something with great force: *The tornado smashed the farmhouse and the barn.*

Split means to break or to divide into parts: *We split several logs into firewood for the fireplace. The boy split his sandwich with his cousin.*

Fracture means to crack hard things, such as bones: *If you fall out of a tree, you may fracture your leg.*

See also the Synonym Studies at **destroy** and **harm.**

break·down (brāk′doun′), *NOUN.*

1 a failure to work: *The mechanic said there was a breakdown in the engine.*

2 a loss of health: *If you don't stop worrying, you will have a breakdown.*

break·er (brā′kər), *NOUN.* a wave that breaks into foam on the beach or on rocks.

Breakers pound rocks on the Pacific coast.

a	hat	ė	term	ô	order	ch	child		a in about
ā	age	i	it	oi	oil	ng	long		e in taken
ä	far	ī	ice	ou	out	sh	she	ə	i in pencil
â	care	o	hot	u	cup	th	thin		o in lemon
e	let	ō	open	ü	put	ŦH	then		u in circus
ē	equal	ò	saw	ü	rule	zh	measure		

break·fast (brek′fəst),
1 NOUN. the first meal of the day.
2 VERB. to eat breakfast: *I like to breakfast alone.*
❑ VERB **break·fasts, break·fast·ed, break·fast·ing.**

break·through (brāk′thrü′), NOUN. a discovery that solves a problem: *Vaccination was an important breakthrough in helping prevent disease.*

breast (brest), NOUN.
1 the upper, front part of the body between the shoulders and the stomach; chest.
2 a gland in females that gives milk.

breast·bone (brest′bōn′), NOUN. the thin, flat bone in the front of the chest to which the ribs are attached.

breast·plate (brest′plāt′), NOUN. a piece of armor that covers the chest and abdomen.

breast·stroke (brest′strōk′), NOUN. a stroke in swimming in which the swimmer lies face downward, draws both arms at one time from in front of the head to the sides, and kicks like a frog.

breath (breth), NOUN.
1 the air drawn into and forced out of the lungs: *Hold your breath a moment.*
2 the ability to breathe easily: *Running so fast made me lose my breath.*
3 a slight movement in the air: *Not a breath of air was stirring.*
catch your breath, IDIOM. to stop for breath; rest: *After the race we sat down to catch our breath.*
out of breath, IDIOM. short of breath; breathless: *At the end of the race the winner was out of breath.*
take someone's breath away, IDIOM. to amaze or delight: *The ocean view took her breath away.*
under your breath, IDIOM. in a whisper: *She was talking under her breath so no one could hear.*

breathe (brēᴛʜ), VERB.
1 to draw air into the lungs and force it out. You breathe through your nose or through your mouth.
2 to say softly; whisper: *He breathed a name in my ear.*
❑ VERB **breathes, breathed, breath·ing.**
—**breath′a·ble,** ADJECTIVE.

breath·less (breth′lis), ADJECTIVE.
1 out of breath: *Running fast made me breathless.*
2 unable to breathe freely because of fear, interest, or excitement: *breathless with terror.*
—**breath′less·ly,** ADVERB.

breath·tak·ing (breth′tā′king), ADJECTIVE. thrilling; exciting: *a breathtaking ride on the roller coaster.*

bred (bred), VERB.
1 the past tense of **breed:** *They bred cattle for market.*
2 the past participle of **breed:** *They have bred many prize-winning dogs.*
■ Another word that sounds like this is **bread.**

breech·es (brich′iz), NOUN.
1 short pants fastened below the knees.
2 pants; trousers.

breed (brēd),
1 VERB. to produce young: *Rabbits breed rapidly.*
2 VERB. to raise or grow: *That farmer breeds cattle for market.*
3 NOUN. a group of animals or plants looking much alike and having the same ancestry: *Collies and German shepherds are breeds of dogs.*
❑ VERB **breeds, bred, breed·ing.**

breed·ing (brē′ding), NOUN. training in good manners: *Politeness is a sign of good breeding.*

breeze (brēz),
1 NOUN. a light, gentle wind: *The breeze stirred the leaves on the trees.*
2 VERB. to move or work easily or briskly: *She breezed through her homework.*
❑ VERB **breez·es, breezed, breez·ing.**

breez·y (brē′zē), ADJECTIVE. with light winds blowing: *It was a breezy day.* ❑ ADJECTIVE **breez·i·er, breez·i·est.**

brew (brü), VERB.
1 to make beer or ale by soaking, boiling, and fermenting malt and hops: *That restaurant brews its own beer.*
2 to make a drink by soaking or boiling in water: *I brewed a pot of coffee.*
3 to plan; plot: *Those people whispering in the corner are brewing some mischief.*
4 to begin to form; gather: *Dark clouds show that a storm is brewing.*
❑ VERB **brews, brewed, brew·ing.**

brew·er·y (brü′ər ē), NOUN. a place where beer and ale are made. ❑ PLURAL **brew·er·ies.**

bri·ar (brī′ər), NOUN. another spelling of **brier.**

bribe (brīb),
1 NOUN. anything given or offered to get someone to do something wrong: *The speeding driver offered the police officer a bribe to let her go.*
2 VERB. to give or offer a bribe to: *A gambler bribed one of the boxers to lose the fight.*
❑ VERB **bribes, bribed, brib·ing.** —**brib′er,** NOUN.

brib·er·y (brī′bər ē), NOUN. the act of giving or taking a bribe: *The dishonest judge was arrested for bribery.* ❑ PLURAL **brib·er·ies.**

brick (brik),
1 NOUN. a block of clay baked by sun or fire. Bricks are used to build walls or houses and pave walks.
2 NOUN. these blocks used as building material: *Chimneys are usually built of brick. We used some old bricks and boards to make shelves.*
3 NOUN. anything shaped like a brick: *a brick of cheese.*
4 VERB. to cover or fill in with bricks: *The old window had been bricked up for many years.*
❑ VERB **bricks, bricked, brick·ing.**

brid·al (brī′dl), ADJECTIVE. of or for a bride or wedding: *a bridal shop, bridal gowns.* ■ Another word that sounds like this is **bridle.**

bride (brīd), *NOUN.* a woman just married or about to be married.

bride·groom (brīd′grüm′), *NOUN.* See **groom²**.

brides·maid (brīdz′mād′), *NOUN.* a young woman who attends the bride at a wedding: *She chose her sisters as her bridesmaids.*

bridge (brij),
1 *NOUN.* a structure built over a river, road, or railroad so that people or vehicles can get across.
2 *VERB.* to form a bridge over: *The log bridged the stream.*
3 *NOUN.* a platform above the deck of a ship for the officer in command: *The captain directed the course of the ship from the bridge.*
4 *NOUN.* the upper, bony part of the nose.
  ❑ *VERB* **bridg·es, bridged, bridg·ing.**
  bridge the gap, *IDIOM.* to bring two people, groups, or things closer together in some way: *A conversation and a handshake finally bridged the gap between the quarreling families.*

bridge (definition 1)

bri·dle (brī′dl),
1 *NOUN.* the part of a harness that fits around a horse's head, including the bit and reins.
2 *VERB.* to put a bridle on: *I saddled and bridled my horse.*
  ❑ *VERB* **bri·dles, bri·dled, bri·dling.** ■ Another word that sounds like this is **bridal.**

brief (brēf),
1 *ADJECTIVE.* lasting only a short time: *The meeting was brief. A brief shower fell in the afternoon.*
2 *ADJECTIVE.* using few words: *She made a brief announcement.*
3 *VERB.* to give detailed information to: *The forest ranger briefed the campers on fire prevention.*
  ❑ *VERB* **briefs, briefed, brief·ing. –brief′ly,** *ADVERB.*

brief·case (brēf′kās′), *NOUN.* a container with a handle for carrying papers, books, and the like.

bri·er (brī′ər), *NOUN.* a thorny or prickly plant or bush. The blackberry plant and the wild rose are often called briers. Also spelled **briar.**

bright (brīt), *ADJECTIVE.*
1 giving much light; shining: *The stars are bright, but sunshine is brighter.*
2 very light or clear: *It is a bright day. Dandelions are bright yellow.*
3 clever; intelligent: *A bright student learns quickly.* ■ See the Synonym Study at **smart.**
4 lively or cheerful: *a bright smile.*
  –bright′ly, *ADVERB.* **–bright′ness,** *NOUN.*

Synonym Study

Bright means giving a lot of light: *The bright sun caused me to blink.*

Shiny means reflecting a lot of light: *I scrubbed the pan until it was shiny.*

Brilliant means very bright: *The brilliant outdoor lights let us play ball after dark.*

Radiant means seeming full of light: *Mom's radiant smile showed how happy she was.*

Sunny means bright with sunshine: *Such a sunny place is perfect for a garden.*

Dazzling means bright enough to hurt the eyes: *Sunshine on snow is dazzling.*

ANTONYMS: dark, dim.

bright·en (brīt′n), *VERB.* to make or become bright or brighter: *Flowers brighten the fields in spring.*
  ❑ *VERB* **bright·ens, bright·ened, bright·en·ing.**

bril·liance (bril′yəns), *NOUN.*
1 great brightness; sparkle: *the brilliance of a fine diamond.*
2 great ability: *His brilliance as a pianist was soon recognized.*

bril·liant (bril′yənt), *ADJECTIVE.*
1 shining brightly; sparkling: *brilliant jewels, brilliant sunshine.* ■ See the Synonym Study at **bright.**
2 splendid; magnificent: *The singer gave a brilliant performance.*
3 having great ability or intelligence: *She is a brilliant mathematician.* ■ See the Synonym Study at **smart.**
  –bril′liant·ly, *ADVERB.*

brim (brim),
1 *NOUN.* an upper edge or a border; rim: *The glass was full to the brim.*
2 *VERB.* to fill to the brim; be full to the brim: *The pond was brimming with water after the heavy rain.*
3 *NOUN.* an edge that sticks out from the bottom of a hat: *The hat's wide brim shaded my eyes.*
  ❑ *VERB* **brims, brimmed, brim·ming.**

a hat	ė term	ô order	ch child	⎧a in about
ā age	i it	oi oil	ng long	⎪e in taken
ä far	ī ice	ou out	sh she	ə⎨i in pencil
â care	o hot	u cup	th thin	⎪o in lemon
e let	ō open	ů put	ᴛʜ then	⎩u in circus
ē equal	ò saw	ü rule	zh measure	

brine (brīn), NOUN. very salty water. Some pickles are kept in brine.

bring (bring), VERB.
1 to come with or carry some thing or person from another place: *The bus brought us home. Bring me a clean plate and take the dirty one away.*
2 to cause someone to come: *What brings you here?*
3 to cause something or someone to be in some condition: *She quickly brought the car to a stop.*
4 to sell for: *Tomatoes bring a high price in winter.*
❑ VERB **brings, brought, bring·ing.**

bring out, IDIOM.
1 to reveal; show: *The lawyer brought out new evidence at the trial.*
2 to offer to the public: *bring out a new product.*

bring up, IDIOM.
1 to care for in childhood; raise: *My grandparents brought up four children.*
2 to suggest for action or discussion; mention: *Please bring your plan up at the meeting.*

Usage Note

Bring is used when something is carried toward the person speaking: *Please bring me the can opener.* **Take** is used when something is carried away from the speaker: *Take the dress to the cleaners.*

brink (bringk), NOUN. the edge at the top of a steep place: *the brink of the cliff.*

on the brink of, IDIOM. close to; near: *Their business was on the brink of ruin.*

brisk (brisk), ADJECTIVE.
1 quick and active; lively: *a brisk walk.*
2 piercing; sharp: *a brisk wind.*
—**brisk′ly,** ADVERB.

bris·tle (bris′əl),
1 NOUN. one of the short, stiff hairs of some plants or animals. Hog bristles are often used in paintbrushes.
2 NOUN. a substitute for an animal bristle, often made of nylon.
3 VERB. to stand up straight: *The dog growled and its hair bristled.*
4 VERB. to make fur stand up straight: *The frightened kitten bristled when it saw the dog.*
❑ VERB **bris·tles, bris·tled, bris·tling.**

Brit·ain (brit′n), NOUN. England, Scotland, and Wales; Great Britain.

Brit·ish (brit′ish),
1 ADJECTIVE. of or about Great Britain or its people.
2 NOUN PLURAL. **the British,** the people of Great Britain.

British Columbia, a province in southwestern Canada, on the Pacific. —**British Columbian.**

brit·tle (brit′l), ADJECTIVE. very easily broken; breaking with a snap; apt to break: *Thin glass is brittle.* ❑ ADJECTIVE **brit·tler, brit·tlest.**

broad (brȯd), ADJECTIVE.
1 wide; large across: *Many cars can travel along that broad, new road.*
2 having wide range; extensive: *Our librarian has had broad experience with books.*
3 including only the most important parts; general: *Give the broad outlines of today's lesson.*
—**broad′ly,** ADVERB.

broad·cast (brȯd′kast′),
1 VERB. to send out by TV or radio: *Some stations broadcast twenty-four hours a day.*
2 NOUN. a program of speech, music, and the like, sent out by TV or radio: *The President's broadcast was televised from Washington, D.C.*
3 VERB. to make widely known: *Don't broadcast gossip.*
❑ VERB **broad·casts, broad·cast** or **broad·cast·ed, broad·cast·ing.** —**broad′cast′er,** NOUN.

broad·en (brȯd′n), VERB. to make or become broad or broader; widen: *The river broadens at its mouth. Travel broadens a person's experience.* ❑ VERB **broad·ens, broad·ened, broad·en·ing.**

bro·cade (brō kād′), NOUN. an expensive cloth with raised designs woven into it.

broc·co·li (brok′ə lē), NOUN. a vegetable with green branching stems and flower heads. It is related to cauliflower.

broccoli

broil (broil), VERB.
1 to cook directly over heat on a rack or under heat in a pan: *We often broil steaks.*
2 to be very hot: *You will broil in this hot sun.*
❑ VERB **broils, broiled, broil·ing.**

The frightened kitten **bristled** when she saw the dog.

broil·er (broi′lər), NOUN. a pan or rack for broiling.

broke (brōk),
1 VERB. the past tense of **break:** *She broke her glasses.*

2 *ADJECTIVE.* (informal) without money: *When we returned from vacation we were broke.* ■ See the Synonym Study at **poor.**

bro·ken (brō′kən),
1 *VERB.* the past participle of **break**: *The window was broken by a ball.*
2 *ADJECTIVE.* separated into parts by a break; in pieces: *a broken cup.*
3 *ADJECTIVE.* not in working condition; damaged: *a broken watch.*
4 *ADJECTIVE.* not kept: *a broken promise.*

bron·chi·al tubes (brong′kē əl tübz′), the two main branches of the windpipe, one going to each lung, and their many branches.

bron·chi·tis (brong kī′tis), *NOUN.* soreness and swelling of bronchial tubes. Bronchitis usually causes a deep cough.

bron·co (brong′kō), *NOUN.* a wild or partly tamed horse of the western United States. ❑ *PLURAL* **bron·cos.**

bron·to·sau·rus (bron′tə sôr′əs), *NOUN.* See **apatosaurus.** ❑ *PLURAL* **bron·to·sau·rus·es** or **bron·to·sau·ri** (bron′tə sôr′ī).

Word Story

Brontosaurus comes from two Greek words meaning "thunder" and "lizard." Because of its great size, the animal was thought of as making noise as loud as thunder when it moved around.

bronze (bronz),
1 *NOUN.* a dark yellow brown metal made of copper and tin.
2 *ADJECTIVE.* made of this metal: *He won a bronze medal in swimming.*
3 *VERB.* to make or become a dark yellow brown: *The lifeguard was bronzed by the sun.*
❑ *VERB* **bronz·es, bronzed, bronz·ing.**

Bronze Age, the period after the Stone Age when bronze tools and weapons were used. It was followed by the Iron Age.

brooch (brōch *or* brüch), *NOUN.* an ornamental pin having the point fastened with a clasp. Brooches are often made of metal. ❑ *PLURAL* **brooch·es.**

brood (brüd),
1 *NOUN.* the young birds hatched at one time in the nest or cared for together: *a brood of chicks, a brood of ducklings.*
2 *NOUN.* young animals or humans who share the same mother or are cared for by the same person: *Mothers always worry over their brood, no matter how old their children are.*
3 *VERB.* to sit on eggs in order to hatch them. Hens and other birds brood till the young are hatched.
4 *VERB.* to think or worry a long time about something: *The boy brooded over his lost dog.*
❑ *VERB* **broods, brood·ed, brood·ing.**

brook (brük), *NOUN.* a small stream.

broom (brüm), *NOUN.* a brush with a long handle for sweeping.

broom·stick (brüm′stik′), *NOUN.* the long handle of a broom.

broth (brôth), *NOUN.* a thin soup made from water in which meat, fish, or vegetables have been boiled. ❑ *PLURAL* **broths** (brôths *or* brôᴛʜz).

broth·er (bruᴛʜ′ər), *NOUN.*
1 the son of the same parents. A boy is a brother to the other children of his parents.
2 male member of the same group, club, union, and so on.

broth·er·hood (bruᴛʜ′ər húd), *NOUN.*
1 the bond between brothers; feeling of brother for brother: *Soldiers who are fighting together often have a strong feeling of brotherhood.*
2 an association of men with some common aim, interest, or profession.

broth·er·in·law (bruᴛʜ′ər in lò′), *NOUN.*
1 the brother of your husband or wife.
2 the husband of your sister.
❑ *PLURAL* **broth·ers·in·law.**

broth·er·ly (bruᴛʜ′ər lē), *ADJECTIVE.* of or like a brother; friendly; kindly: *The older boys gave me some brotherly advice.*

brought (brôt), *VERB.*
1 the past tense of **bring**: *She brought her lunch yesterday.*
2 the past participle of **bring**: *They have brought us a gift every time they visit.*

brow (brou), *NOUN.*
1 the part of the face above the eyes; forehead: *a wrinkled brow.*
2 the arch of hair over the eye; eyebrow: *He has heavy brows.*

a **brood** of ducklings

a	hat	ė	term	ô	order	ch	child		a in about
ā	age	i	it	oi	oil	ng	long		e in taken
ä	far	ī	ice	ou	out	sh	she	ə {	i in pencil
â	care	o	hot	u	cup	th	thin		o in lemon
e	let	ō	open	ù	put	ᴛʜ	then		u in circus
ē	equal	ò	saw	ü	rule	zh	measure		

brown (broun),
1 NOUN. the color of coffee and toast.
2 ADJECTIVE. having this color: *He has curly brown hair.*
3 VERB. to make or become brown: *She browned the onions in oil.* ❏ VERB **browns, browned, brown·ing.**

brown·ie (brou′nē), NOUN.
1 a small, flat, sweet chocolate cake, often containing nuts.
2 **Brownie,** a member of the junior division of the Girl Scouts.
3 (in stories) a good-natured elf or fairy, especially one supposed to help people secretly at night. ❏ PLURAL **brown·ies.**

brown·ish (brou′nish), ADJECTIVE. somewhat brown.

browse (brouz), VERB.
1 to feed on growing grass or leaves by nibbling and eating here and there; graze: *The sheep browsed in the meadow.*
2 to read or look here and there, as in a book, library, store, or on the World Wide Web: *She browsed through her new book. I spent the afternoon browsing the Web on my computer.* ❏ VERB **brows·es, browsed, brows·ing. –brows′er,** NOUN.

bruise (brüz),
1 NOUN. an injury to the body, caused by a fall or a blow, that does not break the skin: *The bruise turned black and blue.*
2 NOUN. an injury to the flesh of a fruit or vegetable.
3 VERB. to injure or be injured in a fleshy part: *Rough handling bruised the apples. My legs bruise easily.* ❏ VERB **bruis·es, bruised, bruis·ing.**

brunch (brunch), NOUN. a meal eaten late in the morning that combines breakfast and lunch. ❏ PLURAL **brunch·es**

bru·nette (brü net′),
1 ADJECTIVE. having dark brown or black hair.
2 NOUN. a woman or girl having hair of this color.

brush¹ (brush),
1 NOUN. a set of bristles, hair, or wires set in a stiff back or fastened to a handle. Brushes are used for sweeping, scrubbing, smoothing, or painting.
2 VERB. to sweep, scrub, smooth, or paint with a brush; use a brush on: *I brushed my hair.*
3 VERB. to wipe away; remove: *The child brushed the tears from his eyes.*
4 VERB. to touch lightly in passing: *His bumper brushed our fender but no damage was done.* ❏ PLURAL **brush·es;** VERB **brush·es, brushed, brush·ing.**

brush² (brush), NOUN.
1 the shrubs, bushes, and small trees growing thickly in the woods.
2 the branches broken or cut off: *After chopping down the tree, we burned the brush.*

Brus·sels sprouts (brus′əlz sprouts′), a vegetable that grows on a stalk in the form of many small heads. The heads look and taste like cabbages.

bru·tal (brü′tl), ADJECTIVE. cruel; inhuman: *a brutal beating.* **–bru′tal·ly,** ADVERB.

bru·tal·i·ty (brü tal′ə tē), NOUN. cruelty; brutal conduct. ❏ PLURAL **bru·tal·i·ties.**

brute (brüt), NOUN.
1 an animal; a creature without the ability to reason.
2 a cruel or coarse person.

bub·ble (bub′əl),
1 NOUN. a round, thin film of liquid enclosing air or gas: *soap bubbles.*
2 NOUN. a space filled with air or gas in a liquid or solid. Sometimes there are bubbles in ice or in glass.
3 VERB. to have bubbles; make bubbles; send up or rise in bubbles: *Boiling water bubbles in the pot.* ❏ VERB **bub·bles, bub·bled, bub·bling.**

burst someone's bubble, IDIOM. to make someone understand that a plan or hope they had is unrealistic or impossible: *I didn't want to burst her bubble, but I had to tell her that the concert had been canceled.*

blowing **bubbles**

bub·bly (bub′lē), ADJECTIVE. full of bubbles. ❏ ADJECTIVE **bub·bli·er, bub·bli·est.**

buck¹ (buk),
1 NOUN. a male deer, goat, hare, or rabbit.
2 VERB. to jump into the air with the back curved and come down with the front legs stiff: *My horse began to buck, but I managed to stay on.*
3 VERB. to fight against; work against: *I have to buck heavy traffic every Friday after work.* ❏ VERB **bucks, bucked, buck·ing.**

buck² (buk), NOUN. a dollar: *He'll do anything to make a buck.*

buck·et (buk′it), NOUN.
1 a container for carrying liquids, sand, or the like; pail.
2 the amount that a bucket can hold: *Pour in about four buckets of water.*

buck·le (buk′əl),
1 NOUN. a clasp used to hold together the ends of a belt, strap, or ribbon.
2 VERB. to fasten together with a buckle: *She buckled her belt.*

3 *VERB.* to bend out of shape; wrinkle: *The heavy snowfall caused the shed roof to buckle.*

4 *NOUN.* a bend or wrinkle: *a buckle in the roof.*
❑ *VERB* **buck·les, buck·led, buck·ling.**

buckle down, *IDIOM.* to force yourself to work hard: *I had to buckle down and study for the test.*

buck·skin (buk′skin′), *NOUN.* a strong, soft leather, yellowish or grayish in color, made from the skins of deer or sheep.

buck·toothed (buk′tütht′), *ADJECTIVE.* having upper front teeth that stick out beyond the other teeth.

buck·wheat (buk′wēt′), *NOUN.* the black or gray seeds of a plant with white flowers. Buckwheat flour is used in pancakes and noodles.

bud (bud),

1 *NOUN.* a small swelling on a plant that will grow into a flower, leaf, or branch: *Buds on the trees are a sign of spring.*

2 *NOUN.* a partly opened flower or leaf.

3 *VERB.* to put forth buds: *The tree has budded.*
❑ *VERB* **buds, bud·ded, bud·ding.**

nip something in the bud, *IDIOM.* to stop something before it starts to become worse: *Mom came over and nipped our argument in the bud.*

Bud·dha (bü′də), *NOUN.* the founder of Buddhism. The name means "The Enlightened One."

Bud·dhism (bü′diz əm), *NOUN.* a religion based on the teachings of Buddha.

Bud·dhist (bü′dist),

1 *NOUN.* someone who believes in and follows the teachings of Buddha.

2 *ADJECTIVE.* of or about Buddha, his followers, or the religion founded by him: *a Buddhist temple.*

bud·dy (bud′ē), *NOUN.* a close friend; pal. ❑ *PLURAL* **bud·dies.**

budge (buj), *VERB.* to move even a little: *The stone was so heavy that we couldn't budge it.* ❑ *VERB* **budg·es, budged, budg·ing.**

budg·et (buj′it),

1 *NOUN.* a plan of how you will spend money that you receive in a period of time. Governments, companies, schools, and families make budgets.

2 *VERB.* to make a plan for spending: *She budgeted her allowance for a tennis racket.*

3 *ADJECTIVE.* cheap; not expensive: *We stayed at a budget motel.*
❑ *VERB* **budg·ets, budg·et·ed, budg·et·ing.**

Bue·nos Ai·res (bwā′nəs âr′ēz), the capital of Argentina.

buff (buf), *VERB.* to polish; shine: *I buffed my shoes with a soft cloth.* ❑ *VERB* **buffs, buffed, buff·ing.**

buf·fa·lo (buf′ə lō), *NOUN.*

1 bison.

2 any of several kinds of large animals related to cattle, such as the water buffalo.
❑ *PLURAL* **buf·fa·lo, buf·fa·loes,** or **buf·fa·los.**

buf·fet (bu fā′), *NOUN.*

1 a piece of furniture with a flat top for dishes and shelves or drawers for silver and linen.

2 a meal at which guests serve themselves from food laid out on a table.

There are more than 25,000 kinds of **bugs.**

bug (bug),

1 *NOUN.* a crawling insect with a pointed beak for piercing and sucking; true bug.

2 *NOUN.* any insect somewhat like a true bug. Ants, spiders, beetles, and flies are often called bugs.

3 *NOUN.* a disease germ: *the flu bug.*

4 *NOUN.* a defect in the operation of a machine: *My car is running better now, but there are still a few bugs in it.*

5 *NOUN.* a mistake in the instructions given to a computer: *It took days to find the bug in the program.*

6 *NOUN.* a very small microphone hidden within a room, telephone, or other place, used to overhear conversations.

7 *VERB.* to hide a small microphone within a room, telephone, or other place for overhearing conversation: *The spy bugged enemy headquarters.*

8 *VERB.* (informal) to annoy; irritate: *His constant grumbling bugs me.*
❑ *VERB* **bugs, bugged, bug·ging. –bug′like′,** *ADJECTIVE.*

bug·gy (bug′ē), *NOUN.*

1 a baby carriage.

2 a light carriage with a single large seat, with or without a top, pulled by one horse.
❑ *PLURAL* **bug·gies.**

bu·gle (byü′gəl), *NOUN.* a musical instrument like a small trumpet without valves, made of brass.

bu·gler (byü′glər), *NOUN.* someone who blows a bugle.

a	hat	ė	term	ô	order	ch	child		a in about
ā	age	i	it	oi	oil	ng	long		e in taken
ä	far	ī	ice	ou	out	sh	she	ə	i in pencil
â	care	o	hot	u	cup	th	thin		o in lemon
e	let	ō	open	ů	put	ŦH	then		u in circus
ē	equal	ò	saw	ü	rule	zh	measure		

build (bild),
1 *VERB.* to make by putting materials together: *People build houses, bridges, ships, and machines. Birds build nests.* ■ See the Synonym Study at **make.**
2 *VERB.* to produce gradually; develop: *to build a business. Practice helped build a winning team.*
3 *NOUN.* a bodily shape: *He has a heavy build.*
❑ *VERB* **builds, built, build·ing. –build′er,** *NOUN.*

build·ing (bil′ding), *NOUN.*
1 something built. Barns, stores, factories, houses, and hotels are all buildings.
2 the business or process of making houses, stores, bridges, ships, and similar things.

built (bilt), *VERB.*
1 the past tense of **build:** *The bird built a nest in April.*
2 the past participle of **build:** *We have built a model of a castle.*

built-in (bilt′in′), *ADJECTIVE.* put in as part of something; not movable: *All the apartments have built-in dishwashers.*

bulb (bulb), *NOUN.*
1 a round, underground part from which certain plants grow. Onions and tulips grow from bulbs.
2 an object with a rounded, swelling part: *a light bulb.*

Bul·gar·i·a (bul gâr′ē ə), *NOUN.* a country in southeastern Europe. **–Bul·gar′i·an,** *ADJECTIVE or NOUN.*

bulge (bulj),
1 *VERB.* to swell outward: *His pockets bulged with toys.*
2 *NOUN.* an outward swelling: *The wallet made a bulge in his pocket.*
❑ *VERB* **bulg·es, bulged, bulg·ing.**

bulk (bulk), *NOUN.*
1 size, especially large size: *An elephant has great bulk.*
2 the largest part of: *The oceans form the bulk of the earth's surface.*

bulk·y (bul′kē), *ADJECTIVE.* large; hard to handle: *She was carrying a bulky package of groceries.*
❑ *ADJECTIVE* **bulk·i·er, bulk·i·est.** ■ See the Synonym Study at **big.**

bull (bul), *NOUN.*
1 the full-grown male of cattle.
2 the male of the whale, elephant, seal, and other large animals.

Have You Heard?

You may have heard the phrase **"take the bull by the horns."** This means to deal with a difficult problem bravely and directly.

bull·dog (bul′dog′), *NOUN.* a heavy, muscular dog of medium height. It has a large head, very short nose, strong jaws, and short hair.

bull·doz·er (bul′dō′zər), *NOUN.* a powerful tractor with a wide steel blade that pushes rocks and earth and knocks down small trees. Bulldozers are used to make rough ground level and to help build roads.

bul·let (bul′it), *NOUN.* a piece of metal shaped to be fired from a pistol or rifle.
bite the bullet, *IDIOM.* to do or accept something difficult or painful: *You might as well bite the bullet and apologize to her.*

bul·le·tin (bul′ə tən), *NOUN.*
1 a short statement of news: *Weather bulletins are broadcast on TV.*
2 a small magazine or newspaper that appears regularly: *Our club publishes a bulletin each month.*

bull·fight (bul′fit′), *NOUN.* a public entertainment in which people perform a series of dangerous movements with a bull, usually killing it at the end with a sword. Bullfights are popular in Spain, Mexico, and parts of South America.

bull·frog (bul′frog′), *NOUN.* a large frog that makes a loud, croaking noise.

bull·pen (bul′pen′), *NOUN.* (in baseball) a place close to the playing field where extra pitchers practice during a game.

bull's-eye (bulz′i′), *NOUN.*
1 the center of a target.
2 a shot that hits it.

bul·ly (bul′ē),
1 *NOUN.* someone who teases, threatens, or hurts smaller or weaker people.
2 *VERB.* to frighten someone with threats into doing something: *You can't bully me into doing that.*
❑ *PLURAL* **bul·lies;** *VERB* **bul·lies, bul·lied, bul·ly·ing.**

bum (bum), (informal)
1 *NOUN.* an idle person; tramp.
2 *VERB.* to beg: *We tried to bum a ride.*
3 *ADJECTIVE.* not working well; injured or damaged: *I've had a bum knee ever since the accident.*
❑ *VERB* **bums, bummed, bum·ming;** *ADJECTIVE* **bum·mer, bum·mest.**

bum·ble·bee (bum′bəl bē′), *NOUN.* a large bee with a thick, hairy body, usually banded with gold. Bumblebees make a loud, buzzing sound. ❑ *PLURAL* **bum·ble·bees.**

bulldozer

bump (bump),
1 *VERB.* to hit or strike against something solid or heavy: *The truck bumped our car.*
2 *NOUN.* a heavy blow: *The bump knocked over the chair.*
3 *NOUN.* a swelling caused by a blow: *I had a bump on my head from getting hit by a baseball.*
4 *NOUN.* a ridge or raised surface: *a bump in the road.*
❑ *VERB* **bumps, bumped, bump·ing.**

bump·er (bum′pər),
1 *NOUN.* a bar or bars of metal, rubber, or plastic across the front and back of a motor vehicle that protect it from being damaged if bumped.
2 *ADJECTIVE.* unusually large: *The farmer raised a bumper crop of wheat last year.*

bump·y (bum′pē), *ADJECTIVE.* rough or uneven; having or causing bumps: *We drove over the bumpy road.*
■ See the Synonym Study at **rough.** ❑ *ADJECTIVE* **bump·i·er, bump·i·est. –bump′i·ness,** *NOUN.*

bun (bun), *NOUN.*
1 a small, sweet, bread roll. Buns often have spices, raisins, or nuts in them.
2 hair coiled at the back of the head in a knot.

bunch (bunch),
1 *NOUN.* a group of things of the same kind growing, fastened, placed, or thought of together: *a bunch of grapes, a bunch of flowers.*
2 *NOUN.* (informal) a group of people: *a friendly bunch.*
3 *VERB.* to come together in one place: *The sheep were all bunched in the shed to keep warm.*
❑ *PLURAL* **bunch·es;** *VERB* **bunch·es, bunched, bunch·ing.**

bun·dle (bun′dl),
1 *NOUN.* a number of things tied or wrapped together; parcel: *a bundle of old newspapers.*
2 *VERB.* to tie or wrap together; make into a bundle: *We bundled all our old newspapers for the school's paper drive.*
❑ *VERB* **bun·dles, bun·dled, bun·dling.**

bun·ga·low (bung′gə lō), *NOUN.* a small one-story house.

bun·gee cord (bun′jē kôrd′), *NOUN.* an elastic cord with a hook on each end. Bungee cords are used to hold things in place. ❑ *PLURAL* **bun·gees.**

Did You Know?

Bungee jumping is a sport where people jump from high places with bungee cords hooked to straps on their bodies. The cords snap the jumpers back up before they hit the ground.

bun·gle (bung′gəl), *VERB.* to do or make something in a clumsy, unskilled way: *I tried to make a bookcase but I bungled the job.* ❑ *VERB* **bun·gles, bun·gled, bun·gling. –bun′gler,** *NOUN.*

bunk (bungk),
1 *NOUN.* a narrow bed, often stacked one above another: *I sleep in the top bunk.*

2 *VERB.* to sleep: *We bunked in the barn.*
❑ *VERB* **bunks, bunked, bunk·ing.**

bun·ny (bun′ē), *NOUN.* a rabbit. ❑ *PLURAL* **bun·nies.**

bunt (bunt),
1 *VERB.* to bat a pitched baseball so lightly that the ball goes only a short distance into the infield.
2 *NOUN.* a baseball hit in this way.
❑ *VERB* **bunts, bunt·ed, bunt·ing. –bunt′er,** *NOUN.*

bun·ting (bun′ting), *NOUN.*
1 a baby's warm, outer garment. It usually has a hood and is closed at the bottom.
2 a thin cloth used for flags.
3 long pieces of cloth having the colors and designs of a flag, used to decorate buildings and streets on holidays and special occasions.

buoy (bü′ē or boi), *NOUN.* an object floating on the water, kept in one place by an anchor. It warns against hidden rocks or shallow water and shows the safe part of a channel. ❑ *PLURAL* **buoys.**
■ Another word that can sound like this is **boy.**

bur (bėr), *NOUN.* a prickly, clinging cover of some fruits and seeds. Burs stick to cloth and fur. Also spelled **burr.**

bur·den (bėrd′n),
1 *NOUN.* something carried; load of things, care, duty, or sorrow: *the burden of housework.*
2 *NOUN.* a load too heavy to carry easily; heavy load: *Her debts are a burden that will bankrupt her.*
3 *VERB.* to put a load on; weigh down: *I don't want to burden you with my troubles.*
❑ *VERB* **bur·dens, bur·dened, bur·den·ing.**

bur·eau (byûr′ō), *NOUN.*
1 a piece of furniture with drawers for clothes and usually a mirror; dresser.
2 a business office, especially one at which facts of various kinds are available: *We asked about the airplane fares at the travel bureau.*
3 usually, **Bureau,** a division within a government department: *Bureau of Land Management, Bureau of Indian Affairs.*
❑ *PLURAL* **bur·eaus.**

burg·er (bėr′gər), *NOUN.* a short form of **hamburger.**

bur·glar (bėr′glər), *NOUN.* someone who breaks into a house or other building to steal things.

bur·glar·y (bėr′glər ē), *NOUN.* the act of breaking into a house or other building to steal things.
❑ *PLURAL* **bur·glar·ies.**

bur·i·al (ber′ē əl), *NOUN.* the act of putting a dead body in a grave, in a tomb, or in the sea; burying: *The sailor was given a burial at sea.*

a	hat	ė	term	ô	order	ch	child		a in about
ā	age	i	it	oi	oil	ng	long		e in taken
ä	far	ī	ice	ou	out	sh	she	ə	i in pencil
â	care	o	hot	u	cup	th	thin		o in lemon
e	let	ō	open	ů	put	ŦH	then		u in circus
ē	equal	ȯ	saw	ü	rule	zh	measure		

bur·ied (ber′ēd), VERB.
1 the past tense of **bury**: *The dog buried the bone.*
2 the past participle of **bury**: *The squirrels had buried many nuts by the first snowfall.*

Bur·ki·na Fa·so (bur′kē′nä fä′sō), NOUN. a country in western Africa.

bur·lap (bėr′lap), NOUN. a coarse fabric made from various fibers. Burlap is used to make sacks, curtains, wall coverings, and upholstery.

bur·ly (bėr′lē), ADJECTIVE. big and strong: *burly wrestlers.* ❑ ADJECTIVE **bur·li·er, bur·li·est.**

Bur·ma (bėr′mə), NOUN. the former name of **Myanmar.**

burn (bėrn),
1 VERB. to be on fire; be very hot: *The campfire burned all night.*
2 VERB. to use to produce heat: *Our furnace burns oil.*
3 VERB. to set on fire; destroy by fire: *Please burn those old papers.*
4 VERB. to injure by fire or heat: *The flame from the candle burned her finger.*
5 NOUN. an injury caused by fire or heat; burned place: *Hot oil can cause a bad burn.*
6 VERB. to make by fire or heat: *A spark from the fireplace burned a hole in the rug.*

The forest is **burning.**

7 VERB. to feel hot; give a feeling of heat to: *His forehead burns with fever.*
❑ VERB **burns, burned, burn·ing.**

burn down or **burn up**, IDIOM. to burn completely, so that nothing is left: *The fire department arrived too late, and the barn burned down.*

burn·er (bėr′nər), NOUN. the part of a lamp, stove, or furnace where the flame or heat is produced.

burnt (bėrnt), ADJECTIVE. damaged by fire or heat: *I don't like burnt toast.*

burp (bėrp), NOUN or VERB. See **belch**. ❑ VERB **burps, burped, burp·ing.**

burr (bėr), NOUN. another spelling of **bur**.

bur·ri·to (bu rē′tō), NOUN. a tortilla rolled around a seasoned filling, usually of beef, chicken, or beans. ❑ PLURAL **bur·ri·tos.**

Word Story

Burrito comes from a Mexican Spanish word and originally meant "little burro." People may have thought it was like a burro because the tortilla carries other food, or because its shape is like a burro's body.

bur·ro (bėr′ō), NOUN. a donkey used to carry loads or packs in the southwestern United States and Mexico. ❑ PLURAL **bur·ros**. ■ Other words that sound like this are **borough** and **burrow.**

burro — about 4 feet high at the shoulder

bur·row (bėr′ō),
1 NOUN. a hole dug in the ground by an animal for shelter or protection. Rabbits live in burrows.
2 VERB. to dig a hole in the ground: *The mole quickly burrowed out of sight.*
3 VERB. to work yourself into or under something: *She burrowed deeper into the blankets.*
❑ VERB **bur·rows, bur·rowed, bur·row·ing.** ■ Other words that sound like this are **borough** and **burro.** —**bur′row·er**, NOUN.

burst (bėrst),
1 VERB. to break open or be opened suddenly: *They burst the lock. The trees had burst into bloom.*
2 VERB. to fly apart suddenly with force; explode: *The balloon burst when he stuck a pin into it.*
3 VERB. to go, come, or do by force or suddenly: *Don't burst into the room without knocking.*
4 VERB. to be very full: *The barns were bursting with grain. She was bursting with joy.*
5 NOUN. a sudden release; outbreak: *In a burst of speed, she won the race at the last minute.*
❑ VERB **bursts, burst, burst·ing.**

Bu·run·di (bu rün′dē), NOUN. a country in central Africa.

bur·y (ber′ē), VERB.
1 to put a dead body in the earth, in a tomb, or in the sea: *The children buried the dead bird.*
2 to cover up; hide: *He dug up an ancient ruin that had been buried long ago.*
3 to put or sink deeply: *I buried myself in a book.*
❑ VERB **bur·ies, bur·ied, bur·y·ing.** ■ Another word that sounds like this is **berry.**

bus (bus),
1 NOUN. a large motor vehicle with seats inside. Buses carry passengers from one place to another along a certain route. A **double-decker bus** has seats on the top as well as inside.
2 VERB. to take or go by bus: *We are bused to school.*
❑ PLURAL **bus·es** or **bus·ses**; VERB **bus·es, bused, bus·ing** or **bus·ses, bussed, bus·sing.**

bush (bush), NOUN. a woody plant smaller than a tree. Bushes usually have with many separate branches starting from or near the ground.
❑ PLURAL **bush·es.**

beat around the bush, IDIOM. to avoid coming straight to the point: *Tell me the truth right now; don't beat around the bush.*

bush·el (bush'əl), NOUN.
1 a unit of measure for grain, fruit, vegetables, and other dry things, equal to 4 pecks.
2 a container that holds a bushel.

bush·y (bush'ē), ADJECTIVE. spreading out like a bush; growing thickly: *a bushy beard.* ❑ ADJECTIVE **bush·i·er, bush·i·est.**

bus·i·ly (biz'ə lē), ADVERB. in a busy manner; actively: *Bees were busily collecting nectar.*

busi·ness (biz'nis), NOUN.
1 work done to earn a living; occupation: *A carpenter's business is building.*
2 something that you have to do, deal with, or think about: *I am tired of the whole business.*
3 buying and selling; trade: *This hardware store does a lot of business in tools.*
4 a store, factory, or other place that makes or sells goods and services: *They own a bakery business.*
❑ PLURAL **busi·ness·es.**

mean business, IDIOM. to be serious or determined: *I guess she means business about moving to Utah.*

busi·ness·like (biz'nis līk'), ADJECTIVE. well managed; practical: *a businesslike manner.*

busi·ness·man (biz'nis man'), NOUN. a man who is in business or runs a business. ❑ PLURAL **busi·ness·men.**

busi·ness·wom·an (biz'nis wùm'ən), NOUN. a woman who is in business or runs a business.
❑ PLURAL **busi·ness·wom·en.**

bus·ing (bus'ing), NOUN. the practice of sending students by bus from one school district to another in order to achieve racial balance.

bust¹ (bust), NOUN.
1 a statue of a person's head, shoulders, and upper part of the chest.
2 a woman's breasts.

bust² (bust), VERB. informal:
1 to burst; break: *He dropped his watch and busted it.*
2 to arrest or put in jail: *He was busted for speeding.*
❑ VERB **busts, bust·ed, bust·ing.**

bus·tle (bus'əl),
1 VERB. to be noisily busy and in a hurry: *The children bustled to get ready for the party.*
2 NOUN. a noisy or excited activity: *There was a lot of bustle as the children got ready for the party.*
❑ VERB **bus·tles, bus·tled, bus·tling.**

bus·y (biz'ē),
1 ADJECTIVE. having plenty to do; working; active: *The principal of our school is a busy person.*
2 ADJECTIVE. full of work or activity: *Main Street is a busy place.*
3 VERB. to make busy; keep busy: *The children busied themselves with drawing pictures.*
4 ADJECTIVE. in use: *Her phone is still busy.*
❑ ADJECTIVE **bus·i·er, bus·i·est;** VERB **bus·ies, bus·ied, bus·y·ing.**

bus·y·bod·y (biz'ē bod'ē), NOUN. someone who is too involved in other people's private affairs.
❑ PLURAL **bus·y·bod·ies.**

but (but),
1 CONJUNCTION. on the other hand: *You may go, but you must come home at six o'clock.*
2 PREPOSITION. except: *I went swimming every day this week but Tuesday.*
3 CONJUNCTION. nevertheless; yet: *I wanted to go but I couldn't.*
4 ADVERB. yet: *The story was strange but true.*
■ Another word that sounds like this is **butt.**

butch·er (bùch'ər),
1 NOUN. someone who cuts up and sells meat.
2 VERB. to kill needlessly, cruelly, or in large numbers. ❑ VERB **butch·ers, butch·ered, butch·er·ing.**

but·ler (but'lər), NOUN. the head male servant in a household.

butt¹ (but), NOUN.
1 the thicker end of a weapon: *the butt of a gun.*
2 the end that is left; stub or stump: *a cigar butt.*
■ Another word that sounds like this is **but.**

butt² (but), NOUN. object of ridicule or scorn: *The new boy was the butt of jokes for several weeks.*
■ Another word that sounds like this is **but.**

butt³ (but),
1 VERB. to strike or push by knocking hard with the head or horns: *The male goats butted heads.*
2 NOUN. a push or blow with the head or horns.
❑ VERB **butts, butt·ed, butt·ing.** ■ Another word that sounds like this is **but.**

butt in, IDIOM. (informal) to enter into someone else's activities or conversation without being asked: *No one asked you to butt in!*

butte (byüt), NOUN. a steep hill that has a flat top and stands alone.

but·ter (but'ər),
1 NOUN. the solid yellowish fat separated from cream by churning.
2 VERB. to put butter on: *Please butter my bread.*
3 NOUN. a food that is cooked or ground fine so that it spreads like butter: *peanut butter, apple butter.*
❑ VERB **but·ters, but·tered, but·ter·ing.**

a	hat	ė	term	ô	order	ch	child		a in about
ā	age	i	it	oi	oil	ng	long		e in taken
ä	far	ī	ice	ou	out	sh	she	ə {	i in pencil
â	care	o	hot	u	cup	th	thin		o in lemon
e	let	ō	open	ù	put	₮H	then		u in circus
ē	equal	ò	saw	ü	rule	zh	measure		

Butterflies

Butterflies are beautiful insects. They live almost everywhere in the world. There are thousands and thousands of different kinds, or species. Each kind has its own special wing color and pattern.

How does a caterpillar change into a butterfly?

(1) Egg It all begins when a butterfly lays an egg on a plant. The egg hatches and becomes a caterpillar. The caterpillar eats the plant, growing so much that it sheds its skin several times.

(2) Chrysalis The caterpillar makes a sticky liquid that hardens into a shell, or chrysalis. Inside this shell, the caterpillar turns into a butterfly.

(3) Butterfly Finally, the shell breaks open, and the butterfly comes out. At first its wings are damp. After the wings dry and become stronger, the butterfly flies away. The chrysalis is left behind.

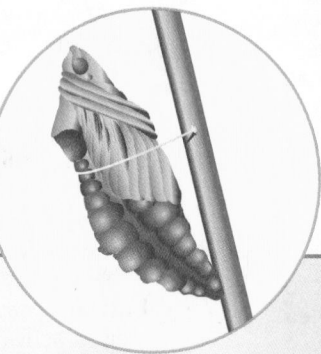

Colorful Wings

A butterfly's wings are covered with tiny scales. These scales give the wings their colors and patterns. Bright colors and patterns often protect butterflies by warning their enemies that they will taste bad.

Monarch Migration

Monarch butterflies are known for the long distances they travel. In the fall, they can migrate from as far north as Canada, southward to California, Florida, or Mexico. In the spring, they start back north, stopping along the way to lay eggs. The young butterflies continue the journey.

but·ter·cup (but′ər kup′), NOUN. a common plant with bright yellow flowers shaped like cups.

but·ter·fly (but′ər flī′), NOUN. an insect with a slender body and two pairs of large, usually brightly colored, wings. ❑ PLURAL **but·ter·flies.**

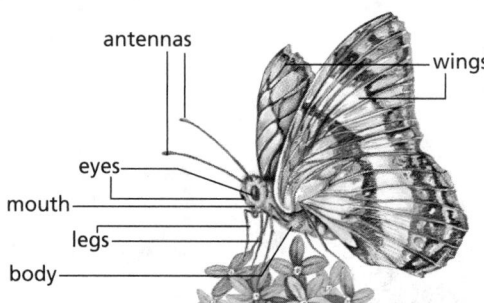

antennas — wings
eyes
mouth — legs
body

butterfly

but·ter·milk (but′ər milk′), NOUN. the salty liquid left over after butter has been made from cream.

but·ter·scotch (but′ər skoch′), NOUN. a candy or flavoring made from brown sugar and butter.

but·tocks (but′əks), NOUN PLURAL. the part of the body on which you sit; rump.

but·ton (but′n),
1 NOUN. a round, flat piece of plastic, metal, or wood sewn onto clothes as fastener or for decoration.
2 VERB. to fasten the buttons of: *Button your coat.*
3 NOUN. a knob pushed to make something work: *Push the button of the elevator to make it go up.*
❑ VERB **but·tons, but·toned, but·ton·ing.**

but·ton·hole (but′n hōl′), NOUN. a hole or slit through which a button is pushed.

buy (bī),
1 VERB. to get by paying money; purchase: *You can buy a pencil for ten cents.*
2 NOUN. a bargain: *That book was a real buy.*
❑ VERB **buys, bought, buy·ing.** ■ Another word that sounds like this is **by. –buy′er,** NOUN.

buzz (buz),
1 NOUN. the humming sound made by flies, mosquitoes, or bees.
2 NOUN. the low, humming sound of many people talking quietly: *the buzz of whispers.*
3 VERB. to make a steady, humming sound; hum loudly: *The radio should be fixed; it buzzes when you turn it on.*
4 VERB. to talk with enthusiasm or excitement: *The whole class buzzed with the news of the holiday.*
❑ VERB **buzz·es, buzzed, buzz·ing.**

buz·zard (buz′ərd), NOUN. any American vulture.

buzz·er (buz′ər), NOUN. an electrical device that makes a buzzing sound as a signal: *The buzzer went off, so I knew the cookies were ready.*

by (bī),
1 PREPOSITION. at the side of; near; beside: *The garden is by the house. Sit by me.*
2 PREPOSITION. along; over; through: *They went by the main road.*
3 PREPOSITION. through the means, use, or action of: *We traveled by airplane. The house was destroyed by fire. The story was written by our teacher.*
4 PREPOSITION. in the measure of: *They sell eggs by the dozen.*
5 PREPOSITION. as soon as; not later than: *Please try to be here by six o'clock.*
6 PREPOSITION. during: *The sun shines by day.*
7 PREPOSITION or ADVERB. past: *He walked by our house. The Pilgrims lived in days gone by. A car raced by.*
8 PREPOSITION. according to: *I like to play by the rules.*
9 PREPOSITION. combined with in arithmetic or measurement: *How many people can you fit in a room 4 feet by 9 feet?*
10 PREPOSITION. taken as steps in a series: *We'll review the schedule week by week.*
11 PREPOSITION. with a difference of: *We won the game by ten points.*
■ Another word that sounds like this is **buy.**

by and by, IDIOM. after a while; before long; soon: *Summer vacation will come by and by.*

by·gone (bī′gon′), ADJECTIVE. gone by; past; former: *Grandpa told us stories about bygone days.*

let bygones be bygones, IDIOM. to forget past quarrels or troubles: *Let's let bygones be bygones and be friends again.*

by·pass (bī′pas′),
1 NOUN. a road, channel, or pipe that avoids crowded or blocked conditions along the main passage: *Drivers use the bypass to avoid the city.*
2 VERB. to go around: *This road bypasses the city.*
❑ PLURAL **by·pass·es;** VERB **by·pass·es, by·passed, by·pass·ing.**

by·prod·uct (bī′prod′əkt), NOUN. something of value produced as the result of making something else: *Molasses is a by-product of sugar refining.*

by·stand·er (bī′stan′dər), NOUN. someone who stands near or looks on but does not take part; onlooker.

byte (bīt), NOUN. unit of computer information equal to eight bits. ■ Another word that sounds like this is **bite.**

castle

Cc

C or **c** (sē), *NOUN*. the third letter of the English alphabet. ❑ *PLURAL* **C's** or **c's.**

c or **c.,**
1 an abbreviation of **centimeter** or **centimeters.**
2 an abbreviation of **cubic.**

c. or **c,**
1 an abbreviation of **cent** or **cents.**
2 an abbreviation of **cup** or **cups.**

C or **C.,** an abbreviation of **Celsius.**

CA, an abbreviation of **California.**

cab (kab), *NOUN*.
1 a car with a driver that you pay to take you somewhere.
2 the covered part of a railroad engine, truck, tractor, or other machine where the driver or operator sits.

cab·bage (kab′ij), *NOUN*. a vegetable with thick, green or reddish purple leaves closely folded into a firm, round head.

cab·in (kab′ən), *NOUN*.
1 a small, roughly built house; hut: *a log cabin.*
2 a bedroom on a ship: *The 500 passengers occupied 200 cabins.*
3 the space for passengers, crew, or cargo in an aircraft or spacecraft: *The captain turned the lights on in the cabin.*

cab·i·net (kab′ə nit), *NOUN*.
1 a piece of furniture with shelves or drawers, used to hold articles such as dishes, jewels, or letters for use or display: *a medicine cabinet, a filing cabinet.*
2 **Cabinet,** a group of advisers chosen by the head of a nation to direct certain departments of the government.

ca·ble (kā′bəl), *NOUN*.
1 a strong, thick cord, usually made of wires twisted together: *A suspension bridge hangs from strong steel cables.*

2 an insulated bundle of wires that carries an electric current or electric signals. Cables carry telephone conversations, television signals, and telegraph messages.

3 See **cable TV.**

cable car,

1 a vehicle pulled along tracks by a moving cable.

2 a small enclosed car hanging from a cable that pulls it up mountains and across valleys.

cable TV, a system of sending television programs directly to viewers through electric cables for a fee.

ca·boose (kə büs′), NOUN. (earlier) a small railroad car for the use of the crew, usually the last car of a freight train.

ca·ca·o (kə kä′ō), NOUN. a tropical American tree that has large seeds from which cocoa and chocolate are made. ❏ PLURAL **ca·ca·os.**

cack·le (kak′əl),

1 NOUN. the loud clucking sound that a hen makes, especially after laying an egg.

2 VERB. to make this sound: *The hens started to cackle early in the morning.*

3 VERB. to laugh in a loud, harsh way: *The old man cackled at his own joke.*

❏ VERB **cack·les, cack·led, cack·ling.**

cac·tus (kak′təs), NOUN. a plant with a thick, fleshy stem that usually has spines but no leaves. Most cactuses grow in very hot, dry regions and have brightly colored flowers. ❏ PLURAL **cac·tus·es** or **cac·ti** (kak′tī).

Did You Know?

Most **cactuses** grow very slowly. Young cactuses may only grow an inch a year. But some can live to be 200 years old.

These **cactuses** are growing in a nursery.

ca·det (kə det′), NOUN. someone training to be an officer in the army, navy, or air force.

ca·fe or **ca·fé** (ka fā′), NOUN. a place to buy and eat a meal; a small restaurant. ❏ PLURAL **ca·fes** or **ca·fés.**

caf·e·ter·i·a (kaf′ə tir′ē ə), NOUN. a place to eat in a school, office building, or factory. You choose your food at a counter and carry it to your table. ❏ PLURAL **caf·e·ter·i·as.**

caf·feine (ka fēn′), NOUN. a slightly bitter drug found in coffee, tea, and some soft drinks.

cage (kāj),

1 NOUN. a frame or place closed in with wires, iron bars, or wood. Birds and wild animals are kept in cages.

2 VERB. to put or keep something in a cage: *After the lion was caught, it was caged.*

■ See the Word Story at **jail.** ❏ VERB **cag·es, caged, cag·ing.**

Cai·ro (kī′rō), NOUN. the capital of Egypt.

cake (kāk),

1 NOUN. a baked mixture of flour, sugar, eggs, flavoring and other things: *a chocolate birthday cake.*

2 NOUN. a flat, thin portion of dough, chopped potatoes, fish, and so on, baked or fried: *We had potato cakes for lunch.*

3 NOUN. a flat piece of something: *I carved a cake of soap into the shape of a dog.*

4 VERB. to become a solid shape; harden: *Mud cakes as it dries.*

❏ VERB **cakes, caked, cak·ing.**

cal or **cal.,** calorie or calories.

ca·lam·i·ty (kə lam′ə tē), NOUN. a terrible thing that happens, such as a flood, the loss of your sight or hearing, or the loss of your savings or property; disaster. ❏ PLURAL **ca·lam·i·ties.**

cal·ci·um (kal′sē əm), NOUN. a soft, white chemical element. It is a part of limestone, chalk, milk, teeth, and many other things. Calcium is needed for the growth of strong, healthy bones.

cal·cu·late (kal′kyə lāt), VERB.

1 to find a certain number by adding, subtracting, multiplying, or dividing: *They calculated the cost of building a house.*

2 to find out something by any process of reasoning; estimate: *Calculate the day of the week on which New Year's Day will fall.*

❏ VERB **cal·cu·lates, cal·cu·lat·ed, cal·cu·lat·ing.**

Word Story

Calculate comes from a Latin word meaning "pebble." In old times, people did arithmetic using piles of stones. If you have counted seventy stones into fourteen equal piles, you have calculated $70 \div 14 = 5$.

cal·cu·la·tion (kal′kyə lā′shən), NOUN.

1 the act or process of calculating to find a result.

2 the result found by calculating: *My calculation is that we will be home by noon.*

cal·cu·la·tor (kal′kyə lā′tər), NOUN. an electronic device that can do arithmetic and can solve some types of mathematical problems. A calculator has buttons with numbers and symbols and a display screen that shows the numbers entered and the answers. Most calculators are small enough to hold in one hand.

Cal·cut·ta (kal kut′ə), *NOUN.* a city in India.

cal·en·dar (kal′ən dər), *NOUN.*
1 a chart showing the months, weeks, and days of the year. A calendar shows the day of the week on which each day of the month falls.
2 a list or schedule: *The newspaper has a calendar of community events on page three.*

Did You Know?

The **calendar** we use today was introduced in 1582. In order to change to this new calendar, ten days were skipped in October. October 5 became October 15 that year.

calf[1] (kaf), *NOUN.*
1 a young cow or bull.
2 a young deer, elephant, whale, or seal.
□ *PLURAL* **calves.** **—calf′like′,** *ADJECTIVE.*

calf[1] (definition 1)

calf[2] (kaf), *NOUN.* the thick, muscular part of the back of the leg below the knee. □ *PLURAL* **calves.**

cal·i·co (kal′ə kō),
1 *NOUN.* a cotton cloth that usually has colored patterns printed on one side.
2 *ADJECTIVE.* spotted in colors: *a calico cat.*
□ *PLURAL* **cal·i·coes** or **cal·i·cos.**

Cal·i·for·nia (kal′ə fôr′nyə), *NOUN.* one of the Pacific coastal states of the United States. *Abbreviation:* CA; *Capital:* Sacramento.
—Cal′i·for′nian, *NOUN* OR *ADJECTIVE.*

State Story **California** is believed to come from the name of an imaginary island in a Spanish adventure story written about 1500. The story was still popular when Spanish explorers came to this part of the world.

call (kȯl),
1 *VERB.* to speak or say in a loud voice; shout or cry out: *He called from downstairs.* ■ See the Synonym Study at **shout.**
2 *NOUN.* a loud sound or shout: *a call for help.*
3 *NOUN.* the special noise or cry an animal or bird makes: *The call of a moose came from the forest.*
4 *VERB.* to make such a noise or cry: *The crows called to each other from the trees.*
5 *VERB.* to command or ask to come: *I called my dog with a loud whistle.*
6 *NOUN.* an invitation or command: *Many people answered the mayor's call for volunteer workers.*
7 *VERB.* to give a name to; name: *They called the new baby "Leslie."*
8 *VERB.* to talk to by telephone; communicate by telephone: *I called my parents to say I would be late. Did anyone call today?*
9 *NOUN.* communication by telephone: *Were there any calls for me while I was out?*
10 *VERB.* to make a short visit or stop: *The girl scouts called yesterday selling cookies.*
11 *NOUN.* a short visit or stop: *The rabbi made six calls.*
12 *VERB.* in sports: **a** *NOUN.* a decision or ruling made by a referee or umpire: *The batter was upset with the umpire's call of strike three.* **b** *VERB.* to make such a decision or ruling: *The umpire called the long fly a foul ball.* **c** *VERB.* to stop: *Our soccer game was called on account of heavy rain.*
□ *VERB* **calls, called, call·ing.**

call for, *IDIOM.*
1 to go and get; stop and get: *The cab called for her at the hotel.*
2 to need; require: *This recipe calls for two eggs.*
3 to request; demand: *The mayor called for an investigation of the warehouse fire.*

call off, *IDIOM.* to do away with; cancel: *We called off our trip.*

call up, *IDIOM.* to telephone: *Call me up at the office.*

close call, *IDIOM.* a narrow escape from trouble or danger: *I turned my homework in on time but it was a close call.*

on call, *IDIOM.* ready or available: *Doctors are expected to be on call day and night.*

call·er (kȯ′lər), *NOUN.*
1 someone who calls on the telephone.
2 someone who makes a short visit: *The doctor said that the patient could now have callers.*

cal·lig·ra·phy (kə lig′rə fē), *NOUN.* the art or practice of beautiful handwriting. You need a special kind of pen or brush to do calligraphy.

a	hat	ė	term	ô	order	ch	child		a in about
ā	age	i	it	oi	oil	ng	long		e in taken
ä	far	ī	ice	ou	out	sh	she	ə<	i in pencil
â	care	o	hot	u	cup	th	thin		o in lemon
e	let	ō	open	u̇	put	ᵷ	then		u in circus
ē	equal	ȯ	saw	ü	rule	zh	measure		

cal·lus (kal′əs), *NOUN.* a hard, thickened place on the skin, usually on the hands or feet. ❑ *PLURAL* **cal·lus·es.**

call waiting, a telephone service that tells you, when you are talking on the telephone, that there is another call coming in on the line. You may ignore the signal, or put the current call on hold to accept the new call. Afterward, the first call can be continued.

calm (käm),
1 *ADJECTIVE.* quiet; still; not stormy or windy: *a calm sea.*
2 *ADJECTIVE.* not excited; peaceful: *Although she was frightened, she answered in a calm voice.*
3 *NOUN.* quietness; stillness: *There was a sudden calm as the wind dropped.*
4 *VERB.* to make or become calm: *She calmed the baby.* ❑ *VERB* **calms, calmed, calm·ing.** —**calm′ly,** *ADVERB.* —**calm′ness,** *NOUN.*

cal·or·ie (kal′ər ē), *NOUN.* a unit that measures energy supplied by food. An ounce of sugar will produce about one hundred calories. ❑ *PLURAL* **cal·or·ies.**

Did You Know?

Children need to eat about 2000 **calories** a day to stay healthy. It is best to get these calories from vegetables, fruits, grains, meat, and dairy products instead of from junk foods and sweets. Calories from fatty junk foods and candy are often called **empty calories.**

calves (kavz), *NOUN.* the plural of **calf¹** and **calf².**

Cam·bo·di·a (kam bō′dē ə), *NOUN.* a country in southeastern Asia. —**Cam·bo′di·an,** *ADJECTIVE* or *NOUN.*

cam·cor·der (kam′kôr′dər), *NOUN.* a portable TV camera and video recorder combined.

came (kām), *VERB.* the past tense of **come:** *He came home early.*

cam·el (kam′əl), *NOUN.* either of two large, four-footed animals with long necks, used as beasts of burden in the desert. The camel of northern Africa has one hump; the camel of central Asia has two humps. Camels can go for a long time without drinking water.

Did You Know?

Camels are often used to carry heavy loads, but they are very unpredictable. All camels will kick, and Asian camels will spit at people. Sometimes camels will moan or groan when they get up with a heavy load.

cam·er·a (kam′ər ə), *NOUN.*
1 a device for taking photographs or movies. A camera lens focuses light rays through the dark inside part of the camera onto film, which records an image when the light hits it.
2 a device that changes images into electronic signals for television broadcasting. ❑ *PLURAL* **cam·er·as.**

Cam·er·oon (kam′ə rün′), *NOUN.* a country in west central Africa. —**Cam′er·oon′i·an,** *ADJECTIVE* or *NOUN.*

cam·ou·flage (kam′ə fläzh),
1 *NOUN.* a kind of covering that makes something look much like its surroundings. In nature, colors and patterns on skin, fur, feathers, and so on, help animals hide. People use paint, special clothing, and so on as camouflage.
2 *VERB.* to hide someone or something in this way: *The hunters were camouflaged with shrubbery so that they blended with the landscape.* ❑ *VERB* **cam·ou·flag·es, cam·ou·flaged, cam·ou·flag·ing.**

The owl's feathers are excellent **camouflage.**

camp (kamp),
1 *NOUN.* a place where a person or group lives outdoors, in a tent or tents or other shelter: *The travelers set up camp near the river.*
2 *VERB.* to live away from home for a time outdoors or in a tent or hut: *Our troop camped at the river.*
3 *NOUN.* a place where people, especially children, live and play outdoors for a time: *I hope to go to summer camp this year.* ❑ *VERB* **camps, camped, camp·ing.**

cam·paign (kam pān′),
1 *NOUN.* a number of connected activities to do or get something: *a campaign to build a new school.*
2 *VERB.* to take part or serve in a campaign: *She campaigned for mayor by giving speeches.* ❑ *VERB* **cam·paigns, cam·paigned, cam·paign·ing.**

Cam·pe·che (käm pā′chā), *NOUN.* a state in southeastern Mexico.

camp·er (kam′pər), *NOUN.*
1 someone who camps.
2 a trailer or motor vehicle equipped for camping.

camp·fire (kamp′fīr′), *NOUN.* an outdoor fire used for cooking, warmth, or social gatherings.

C

camp·site (kamp′sīt′), *NOUN.* a place where people camp.

cam·pus (kam′pəs), *NOUN.* the buildings and grounds of a college, school, hospital, business, and so on. ❑ *PLURAL* **cam·pus·es.**

can¹ (kan *or* kən), *HELPING VERB.*
1 to have the power to: *You can run fast.*
2 to know how to: *She can speak Spanish.*
3 to have the right to: *We can cross the street here. You can call me John.*
4 (informal) may: *Can I go now?*
❑ *PAST TENSE* **could.**

Usage Note

Can¹ is used in everyday speech and writing for both permission and ability: *Can I go now? They can run faster than I can.* In formal English, however, **can** means "to be able to" and **may** means "to have permission to": *He can walk with crutches. May I please speak with her?*

can² (kan),
1 *NOUN.* an airtight metal container in which food is stored: *a can of peaches.*
2 *NOUN.* a container of metal, usually with a cover or lid: *a paint can, a trash can.*
3 *NOUN.* the amount that a can holds: *Add three cans of water to make the orange juice.*
4 *VERB.* to put in an airtight can or jar to preserve: *We are going to can tomatoes.*
❑ *VERB* **cans, canned, can·ning.**

Can·a·da (kan′ə də), *NOUN.* a country in North America, north of the United States.

Canada Day, July 1, celebrated as a holiday in Canada in honor of the formation of the Dominion of Canada on that date in 1867.

Ca·na·di·an (kə nā′dē ən),
1 *ADJECTIVE.* of or about Canada or its people.
2 *NOUN.* someone born or living in Canada.

ca·nal (kə nal′), *NOUN.* a waterway dug across land for small ships or boats to travel through, or to carry water to places that need it.

ca·nar·y (kə nâr′ē), *NOUN.* a small green or yellow songbird, often kept as a pet. ❑ *PLURAL* **ca·nar·ies.**

can·cel (kan′səl), *VERB.*
1 to put an end to, set aside, or withdraw something; do away with: *She canceled her appointment with the dentist this morning. I canceled my plane reservations.*

canary — 6 to 8 inches long

2 to mark, stamp, or punch something so that it cannot be used again: *cancel a stamp.*
❑ *VERB* **can·cels, can·celed, can·cel·ing.** **–can′cel·la′tion,** *NOUN.*

cancel out, *IDIOM.* to have an opposite effect; to undo what has been done: *The extra costs of the fundraiser canceled out the money we made.*

can·cer (kan′sər), *NOUN.* a very harmful growth in the body. Cancer tends to spread and to destroy the healthy tissues and organs of the body.

can·di·date (kan′də dāt), *NOUN.* someone who seeks some office or honor or is suggested by others for it: *Voters choose the best candidate.*

Word Story

Candidate comes from a Latin word meaning "dressed in white." In ancient Rome, men trying to get elected wore white clothes to show their spotless records.

can·died (kan′dēd), *ADJECTIVE.* cooked in sugar; coated with sugar: *candied sweet potatoes.*

can·dle (kan′dl), *NOUN.* a stick of wax with a string, called a wick, through the center. As the wick burns, it gives light.

can·dle·stick (kan′dl stik′), *NOUN.* a holder for a candle.

can·dy (kan′dē),
1 *NOUN.* a sweet food made of sugar or syrup, often mixed with chocolate, fruit, nuts, or flavorings.
2 *VERB.* to cook or preserve a food by boiling it in sugar: *She candied the peaches for dessert.*
❑ *PLURAL* **can·dies;** *VERB* **can·dies, can·died, can·dy·ing.** **–can′dy·like′,** *ADJECTIVE.*

Did You Know?

Ancient Egyptians made the first **candies** by mixing nuts and fruit with honey. The first candy made with sugar was made in ancient India.

cane (kān), *NOUN.*
1 a slender stick used to help someone walk; walking stick.
2 any plant with a long, jointed stem. Sugarcane and bamboo are canes.

ca·nine (kā′nīn),
1 *NOUN.* a dog.
2 *ADJECTIVE.* of or like a dog: *canine faithfulness.*
3 *NOUN.* any of various animals related to dogs, including foxes, wolves, coyotes, and so on.
4 *NOUN.* one of the four pointed teeth next to the incisors.

a	hat	ė term	ô order	ch child	⎧a in about
ā	age	i it	oi oil	ng long	⎪e in taken
ä	far	ī ice	ou out	sh she	ə⎨i in pencil
â	care	o hot	u cup	th thin	⎪o in lemon
e	let	ō open	ů put	ŦH then	⎩u in circus
ē	equal	ò saw	ü rule	zh measure	

can·is·ter (kan′ə stər), NOUN. a small box or can, especially for tea, coffee, flour, or sugar.

can·ni·bal (kan′ə bəl), NOUN.
 1 someone who eats human flesh.
 2 an animal that eats others of its own kind: *Some fish are cannibals.*

can·non (kan′ən), NOUN. (earlier) a very large gun that fired explosive shells over long distances.
 ❑ PLURAL **can·non** or **can·nons.**

can·not (kan′ot or ka not′), VERB. another spelling of can not.

ca·noe (kə nü′),
 1 NOUN. a lightweight, narrow boat pointed at both ends and moved with a paddle.
 2 VERB. to paddle a canoe; go somewhere in a canoe: *We canoed to the campsite.*
 ❑ VERB **ca·noes, ca·noed, ca·noe·ing.**

These Native Americans are building a **canoe.**

can·o·py (kan′ə pē), NOUN.
 1 a covering fastened over a bed, throne, or entrance to a building.
 2 the uppermost layer of branches in forest trees.
 ❑ PLURAL **can·o·pies.**

can't (kant), a contraction of **cannot** or **can not.**

can·ta·loupe or **can·ta·loup** (kan′tl ōp), NOUN. a kind of melon with a hard, rough rind and sweet, juicy, orange flesh.

can·teen (kan tēn′), NOUN.
 1 a small container for carrying water or other drinks: *The scouts filled their canteens from the spring.*
 2 a store in a school, camp, factory, or hospital where you can buy food, drinks, and other things, often from vending machines.

can·ter (kan′tər),
 1 NOUN. a horse's slow gallop.
 2 VERB. to ride at a canter: *I cantered my horse down the road.*
 ❑ VERB **can·ters, can·tered, can·ter·ing.**

can·tor (kan′tər), NOUN. the person who leads the services in a Jewish religious service.

can·vas (kan′vəs), NOUN.
 1 a strong, heavy cloth made of cotton. It is used to make tents, sails, and certain articles of clothing, and for artists' paintings.
 2 a picture painted on canvas; oil painting: *The beautiful canvas was hanging in the art gallery.*
 ❑ PLURAL **can·vas·es. −can′vas·like′,** ADJECTIVE.

can·yon (kan′yən), NOUN. a narrow valley with high, steep sides, usually with a stream at the bottom.

canyon

cap (kap),
 1 NOUN. a soft covering for the head, having no brim or only a visor.
 2 NOUN. anything that covers or forms the top of something. The top of a jar, bottle, tube, marker, or pen is a cap.
 3 VERB. to put a cap on; cover the top of: *Snow capped the mountain peaks.*
 ❑ VERB **caps, capped, cap·ping.**

ca·pa·bil·i·ty (kā′pə bil′ə tē), NOUN. the ability to learn or do something; power: *A computer has the capability of solving mathematical problems very quickly.* ❑ PLURAL **ca·pa·bil·i·ties.**

ca·pa·ble (kā′pə bəl), ADJECTIVE. having the power or ability needed to do something; able: *He was such a capable student that everyone had great hopes for his future.* **−ca′pa·bly,** ADVERB.

capable of, IDIOM. having ability or power for: *This plane is capable of going 900 miles an hour.*

ca·pac·i·ty (kə pas′ə tē), NOUN.
 1 the amount of space inside; largest amount that a container can hold: *A 1-gallon container has a capacity of 4 quarts.*
 2 the ability to learn or do something: *A bright student has a great capacity for learning.*
 ❑ PLURAL **ca·pac·i·ties.**

cape[1] (kāp), NOUN. a piece of outer clothing, without sleeves, worn like a coat, often fastened at the neck.

cape[2] (kāp), NOUN. a point of land that sticks out into an ocean, bay, or other body of water.

ca·per (kā′pər), NOUN. a prank; trick: *She warned us not to try any capers while she was gone.*

cap·il·lar·y (kap′ə ler′e), *NOUN.* a very slender blood vessel, visible only through a microscope. Capillaries join the ends of arteries to the beginnings of veins. ❑ *PLURAL* **cap·il·lar·ies.**

cap·i·tal (kap′ə təl),
1 *NOUN.* a city where the government of a country, state, or province is located. See Usage Note at **Capitol.**
2 *NOUN.* a capital letter; an uppercase letter.
3 *ADJECTIVE.* punishable by death: *Murder is a capital crime in some countries.*
4 *NOUN.* money or property that companies or individuals use to increase their wealth: *The Smith Company has capital of $3,000,000.*
■ Another word that sounds like this is **Capitol.**

cap·i·tal·ism (kap′ə tə liz′əm), *NOUN.* a system of money and goods in which private individuals or groups of individuals own land, factories, and other means of production. Using the hired labor of other people, owners produce goods and services in competition for profits.

cap·i·tal·ize (kap′ə tə līz), *VERB.* to write or print with a capital letter: *You always capitalize the first letter of your name.* ❑ *VERB* **cap·i·tal·iz·es, cap·i·tal·ized, cap·i·tal·iz·ing. –cap′i·tal·i·za′tion,** *NOUN.*

capital letter, the large form of a letter; A, B, C, D, and so on, contrasted with a, b, c, d, and so on.

Usage Note

Capital letters are used at the beginnings of sentences or of proper names: *The girl's name is Jill.* Capital letters are sometimes used at the beginnings of words naming public officials. These words are capitalized when they are used as titles of address: *"What are your plans for the state, Governor?" asked a reporter.* They are also capitalized as part of a person's name: *Tonight's speaker will be Congresswoman Pat Pierce.* These words are usually not capitalized when they are used by themselves: *The mayor praised the district attorney's new program.*

Cap·i·tol (kap′ə təl), *NOUN.*
1 the building at Washington, D.C., in which Congress meets.
2 also, **capitol,** the building in which a state legislature meets.
■ Another word that sounds like this is **capital.**

Usage Note

Capitol and **capital** are often confused. **Capitol** is a building. **Capital** is a city: *There is a dome on the Capitol in Washington, D.C., the capital of the United States.*

cap·pu·ci·no (kap′ə chē′nō), *NOUN.* espresso coffee served with hot milk, often flavored with cinnamon.

cap·size (kap sīz′), *VERB.* to turn bottom side up in the water: *The sailboat nearly capsized in the high wind.* ❑ *VERB* **cap·siz·es, cap·sized, cap·siz·ing.**

cap·sule (kap′səl), *NOUN.*
1 a tiny dose of medicine in a gelatin case. A capsule dissolves easily in the stomach.
2 the front section of a rocket made to carry devices or astronauts into space.

cap·tain (kap′tən),
1 *NOUN.* the head of a group or team; leader or chief: *the captain of a basketball team.*
2 *NOUN.* the commander of a ship.
3 *NOUN.* a military rank. See the chart on page 550.
4 *VERB.* to lead or command as captain: *She will captain the softball team next season.*
❑ *VERB* **cap·tains, cap·tained, cap·tain·ing.**

cap·tion (kap′shən), *NOUN.* a title or words near a picture that tell what it is.

cap·tive (kap′tiv),
1 *NOUN.* a human being or an animal captured and held unwillingly; prisoner: *The pirates took many captives during raids along the coast.*
2 *ADJECTIVE.* made a prisoner; held unwillingly: *The enemy released the captive soldiers.*

cap·tiv·i·ty (kap tiv′ə tē), *NOUN.* the condition of being held against your will: *Some animals cannot stand captivity and die after a few weeks in a cage.*

cap·ture (kap′chər),
1 *VERB.* to make a prisoner of; take by force; seize: *We captured butterflies with a net.* ■ See the Synonym Study at **catch.**
2 *NOUN.* an act of capturing: *The capture of this ship took place off the coast of France.*
❑ *VERB* **cap·tures, cap·tured, cap·tur·ing.**

Capitol (definition 1)

a	hat	ė	term	ô	order	ch	child		a in about
ā	age	i	it	oi	oil	ng	long		e in taken
ä	far	ī	ice	ou	out	sh	she	ə	i in pencil
â	care	o	hot	u	cup	th	thin		o in lemon
e	let	ō	open	u̇	put	ŦH	then		u in circus
ē	equal	ȯ	saw	ü	rule	zh	measure		

car (kär), NOUN.
1 a passenger vehicle with four wheels and an engine, used for traveling; automobile: *They made the trip by car.*
2 any vehicle that moves on its wheels along tracks: *a subway car, a railroad car.*

car·a·mel (kar′ə məl *or* kär′məl), NOUN.
1 sugar browned or slightly burned over heat, used for coloring and flavoring food.
2 a chewy candy flavored with this sugar.

car·a·van (kar′ə van), NOUN. (earlier) a group of merchants, pilgrims, tourists, or the like, often traveling together for safety through difficult or dangerous country.

car·bu·re·tor (kär′bə rā′tər), NOUN. a device for mixing air with a liquid fuel to produce a mixture that burns easily. A lawnmower engine has a carburetor, but most cars now use a different method of delivering fuel to the engine.

card (kärd), NOUN.
1 a flat piece of stiff paper, thin cardboard, or plastic: *a birthday card, a library card, a credit card.*
2 **cards, a** a pack of cards with numbers and symbols, used in playing games. **b** a game or games played with such cards: *I like to play cards.*

card·board (kärd′bôrd′), NOUN. a stiff material made of layers of paper pulp pressed together, used to make cards, boxes, and so on.

a desert **caravan**

car·bo·hy·drate (kär′bō hī′drāt), NOUN. any of many related substances that contain carbon, hydrogen, and water. Carbohydrates are made from carbon dioxide and water by green plants in sunlight. Carbohydrates are one of the basic nutrient groups that your body needs for growth and health. Bread and rice are good sources of carbohydrates.

car·bon (kär′bən), NOUN. a very common chemical element that is in all living things. Coal and charcoal are mostly carbon. Diamonds and graphite are pure carbon in the form of crystals.

car·bon·at·ed (kär′bə nā′tid), ADJECTIVE. containing carbon dioxide under pressure. Carbonated soft drinks bubble and fizz when opened.

car·bon di·ox·ide (kär′bən dī ok′sīd), an odorless gas, present in the atmosphere and formed when any fuel containing carbon is burned. The air that is breathed out of an animal's lungs contains carbon dioxide. Plants absorb it from the air and use it to make plant tissue. Carbon dioxide is a greenhouse gas.

car·bon mon·ox·ide (kär′bən mə nok′sīd), a colorless, odorless, very poisonous gas, formed when carbon burns with too little air. It is part of the exhaust gases of motor vehicle engines and of cigarette smoke.

car·di·nal (kärd′n əl), NOUN.
1 one of the high officials of the Roman Catholic Church, appointed by the pope and ranking next below him. Cardinals wear red robes and red hats.
2 a North American songbird. The male has bright red feathers marked with a little gray and black.

cardinal number, a number which shows how many are meant. One, two, three, and so on, are cardinal numbers.

care (kâr),
1 NOUN. worry: *I haven't a care in the world.*
2 NOUN. attention: *A pilot's work requires great care.*
3 VERB. to feel interest: *Musicians care about music.*
4 NOUN. protection: *The little girl was left in her brother's care.*
5 VERB. to mind; object to: *Do you care if I leave early? I don't care if you leave as long as your work is done.*
❑ VERB **cares, cared, car·ing.**

take care of, IDIOM.
1 to take charge of; attend to: *She took care of all the children.*
2 to be careful with: *Take care of your money.*

ca·reer (kə rir′), NOUN. an occupation or profession: *I plan to make law my career.*

care·free (kâr′frē′), ADJECTIVE. without any worries; happy; cheerful: *The children spent a carefree summer sailing and swimming at the seashore.*

care·ful (kârʹfəl), ADJECTIVE.
1 thinking about what you say or do; watchful; cautious: *He is careful to tell the truth at all times. Be careful with my new bicycle!*
2 done with thought and attention: *Arithmetic requires careful work.*
–**careʹful·ly,** ADVERB.

care·giv·er (kârʹgiv/ər), NOUN. someone who looks after children, the elderly, or people with illnesses or disabilities: *My aunt is the caregiver for a woman who had a heart attack.*

caribou — about 4 feet high at the shoulder

care·less (kârʹlis), ADJECTIVE.
1 not thinking about what you say or do; not careful: *I was careless and broke the cup.*
2 done with little thought or effort; not exact or thorough: *Careless work often has to be done over.*
3 not caring; indifferent: *Some people are careless about their appearance.*
–**careʹless·ly,** ADVERB. –**careʹless·ness,** NOUN.

Synonym Study

Careless means not careful: *I was careless about shutting all the windows, and the curtains got soaked when it rained.*

Thoughtless means not thinking before doing something: *It was thoughtless of him to mention the party in front of the kid who wasn't invited.*

Inconsiderate means thoughtless of other people's feelings: *Our inconsiderate neighbors make a lot of noise at night.*

Reckless means not aware of possible danger: *The squirrels seem reckless, but they never fall from trees.*

ANTONYMS: careful, cautious, watchful.

ca·ress (kə resʹ),
1 NOUN. a touch showing affection; a light, tender stroke or embrace.

2 VERB. to touch or stroke tenderly; embrace gently.
❑ PLURAL **ca·ress·es;** VERB **ca·ress·es, ca·ressed, ca·ress·ing.** –**ca·ressʹa·ble,** ADJECTIVE.

care·tak·er (kârʹtā/kər), NOUN. a person who takes care of someone or of somebody else's house or property.

car·go (kärʹgō), NOUN. the load of goods carried by a ship, plane, or truck: *The freighter unloaded a cargo of wheat.* ❑ PLURAL **car·goes** or **car·gos.**

Car·ib·be·an (karʹə bēʹən or kə ribʹē ən), ADJECTIVE. of or about the Caribbean Sea or the islands in it.

Caribbean Sea, a sea bordered by Central America, the West Indies, and South America.

car·i·bou (karʹə bü), NOUN. a kind of large reindeer with branching antlers that lives in northern North America. ❑ PLURAL **car·i·bou** or **car·i·bous.**

car·jack·ing (kärʹjak/ing), NOUN. the act of stealing a car by forcing the driver to hand over the keys and get out.

car·na·tion (kär nāʹshən), NOUN. a red, white, or pink flower with a sweet, spicy smell, grown in gardens and greenhouses.

car·ni·val (kärʹnə vəl), NOUN. a place of amusement or a traveling show having mechanical rides and games where you can win prizes.

car·ni·vore (kärʹnə vôr), NOUN. any animal that feeds chiefly on the flesh of other animals. Carnivores have large, strong, sharp teeth.

car·niv·or·ous (kär nivʹər əs), ADJECTIVE. meat-eating; feeding chiefly on flesh. Cats, dogs, lions, tigers, and sharks are carnivorous animals.

car·ol (karʹəl),
1 NOUN. a song of joy sung at Christmas.
2 VERB. to sing carols: *At Christmas the children went from house to house, caroling.*
❑ VERB **car·ols, car·oled, car·ol·ing.** –**carʹo·ler** NOUN.

carp (kärp), NOUN. any of various large freshwater fishes that live in ponds and slow streams and feed mostly on plants. One kind is sometimes raised for food. ❑ PLURAL **carp** or **carps.**

car·pen·ter (kärʹpən tər), NOUN. someone whose work is building and repairing things made of wood.

car·pen·try (kärʹpən trē), NOUN. the work of a carpenter.

car·pet (kärʹpit),
1 NOUN. a heavy, woven fabric used for covering floors and stairs.
2 NOUN. anything like a carpet: *a carpet of grass.*
3 VERB. to cover something with a carpet: *The ground was carpeted with leaves.*
❑ VERB **car·pets, car·pet·ed, car·pet·ing.**

a	hat	ė	term	ô	order	ch	child	ə	a in about
ā	age	i	it	oi	oil	ng	long		e in taken
ä	far	ī	ice	ou	out	sh	she		i in pencil
â	care	o	hot	u	cup	th	thin		o in lemon
e	let	ō	open	ů	put	₮H	then		u in circus
ē	equal	ȯ	saw	ü	rule	zh	measure		

car phone, a portable phone for use in a car.

car·pool (kär′pül), NOUN. a group of people who take turns driving themselves and other people to and from a place: *The parents formed a carpool to take their children to school.*

car·port (kär′pôrt′), NOUN. a shelter for automobiles, usually attached to a house and open on at least one side.

car·riage (kar′ij), NOUN. a light, four-wheeled vehicle, often having a top that can be folded down. Some carriages are pulled by horses and are used to carry people. **Baby carriages** are small and portable, and can often be folded.

car·ri·er (kar′ē ər), NOUN. someone or some company that carries something. A postman is a mail carrier. Railroads, airlines, bus systems, and truck companies are carriers.

car·rot (kar′ət), NOUN. a long, narrow, orange vegetable that grows as a root. Carrots are eaten raw or cooked. ■ Another word that sounds like this is **karat.**

car·ry (kar′ē),

This woman is **carrying** fruits and vegetables.

1 VERB. to take something or someone from one place to another: *Railroads carry coal from the mines to the factories. The man carried the child home.*
2 VERB. to have with you: *I always carry an umbrella.*
3 VERB. to have a disease and pass it to someone or something else; spread: *Rats carry germs.*
4 VERB. to hold up; support: *Rafters carry the weight of the roof.*
5 VERB. to hold your body and head in a certain way: *The ballet dancer carries himself gracefully.*
6 VERB. to sing a melody or part with correct pitch: *I can't carry a tune.*
7 VERB. to keep in stock; sell: *This store carries toys and games.*
8 VERB. to transfer a number from one place or column in the sum to the next: *A 10 in the 1's column must be carried to the 10's column.*
9 NOUN. (in football) the act of running with the ball from scrimmage: *In three carries the speedy halfback made nearly 30 yards.*
❑ VERB **car·ries, car·ried, car·ry·ing.**

carry away, IDIOM. to arouse strong feeling in; influence beyond reason: *I was so carried away by the sad movie that I began to cry.*

carry on, IDIOM.
1 to do; manage; conduct: *She carried on a successful business.*
2 to keep going; not stop; continue: *We must carry on in our effort to establish world peace.*
3 to behave wildly or foolishly: *The children carried on at the party.*

carry out, IDIOM. to get done; do; complete: *They carried out the job well.*

Synonym Study

Carry[1] means to hold something while you move from one place to another: *"Please help me carry the mattress up to the attic," said my uncle. When the young child got tired, his mother carried him part of the way.*

Transport means to carry something in a ship, plane, car, truck, train, or other vehicle: *Trains no longer transport as many passengers as they once did.*

Bear[1] means to carry something, often something heavy: *"Will that small bike bear your weight?" asked the baby-sitter.*

Cart means to carry, in a cart or otherwise: *We use the van to cart the cans and bottles to the recycling center every Tuesday.*

Haul means to carry or drag. It suggests something heavy: *We hauled the new sofa into Grandma's apartment.*

car·ry-out (kar′ē out′), NOUN or ADJECTIVE. See **takeout.**

car seat, a protective seat for infants or young children. It attaches to the seat of a car with a seat belt. Car seats should always be placed in the back seat of a car if possible.

car·sick (kär′sik′), ADJECTIVE. sick to your stomach from the motion of a car, train, and so on.

Car·son Cit·y (kär′sən sit′ē), the capital of Nevada.

cart (kärt),
1 NOUN. a strong vehicle with two wheels, pulled by an animal, formerly used in farming and for carrying heavy loads.
2 NOUN. a light passenger vehicle for short trips, usually battery-powered: *a golf cart.*
3 NOUN. a small vehicle on wheels, usually pushed by hand: *a grocery cart.*
4 VERB. to carry in or as if in a cart: *We called them to cart the trash away.* ■ See the Synonym Study at **carry.**
❑ VERB **carts, cart·ed, cart·ing.**

Have You Heard?

You may have heard the phrase **"Don't put the cart before the horse."** This means that you shouldn't do things in the wrong order.

car·ti·lage (kär/tl ij), NOUN. a very tough, flexible tissue that is part of the skeleton of animals with backbones. Cartilage forms the nose, the ears, parts of the joints, and other body parts.

car·ton (kärt/n), NOUN.
1 a box made of cardboard or heavy paper: *Pack the books in large cartons.*
2 the amount that a carton holds: *The children drink a carton of milk at each meal.*

car·toon (kär tün/), NOUN.
1 a drawing that interests or amuses us by showing people or things in an exaggerated way. Cartoons are usually found in magazines and newspapers.
2 a comic strip.
3 See **animated cartoon.**

car·toon·ist (kär tü/nist), NOUN. someone who draws cartoons.

car·tridge (kär/trij), NOUN.
1 a case made of metal, plastic, or cardboard for holding gunpowder and a bullet or shot.
2 a container that holds a supply of material, made to be easily put into a larger device. Film, ink, and magnetic tape come in cartridges.
3 a small device with a plastic case and electronic circuits inside it. A cartridge put into a computer, a calculator, or an electronic game allows these machines to work in particular ways.

cart·wheel (kärt/wēl/), NOUN. a sideways handspring with the legs and arms kept straight.

This girl is turning a **cartwheel.**

carve (kärv), VERB. to cut something into slices or pieces: *I carved the meat at the dinner table.* ■ See the Synonym Study at **cut.** ❑ VERB **carves, carved, carv·ing. −carv/er,** NOUN.

carv·ing (kär/ving), NOUN. a carved work; carved decoration: *a wood carving.*

cas·cade (ka skād/),
1 NOUN. a small waterfall.
2 VERB. to fall, pour, or flow like a cascade: *The dishes went cascading to the floor.*
❑ VERB **cas·cades, cas·cad·ed, cas·cad·ing.**

case¹ (kās), NOUN.
1 an example or instance: *A case of chicken pox kept me away from school. Any case of cheating will be punished.*
2 the actual condition; real situation: *She said the work was done, but that was not the case.*
3 someone who has an injury or illness; patient: *I was the first case of poison ivy at camp.*
4 a matter for a court of law to decide: *The case will be brought before the court tomorrow.*
in case, IDIOM. it should happen that; if; supposing: *In case it rains, bring your umbrella.*
in case of, IDIOM. if there should be: *In case of fire, walk quietly to the nearest door.*

case² (kās), NOUN.
1 something that holds or covers something else: *Put your glasses in their case.*
2 a box: *There is a big case of books in the hall.*
3 the amount that a case can hold: *The children drank a case of ginger ale at the party.*

cash (kash),
1 NOUN. money in the form of coins and bills.
2 VERB. to give or get cash for: *The bank will cash your check.*
❑ VERB **cash·es, cashed, cash·ing.**

cash·ew (kash/ü), NOUN. the small, tasty nut of a tropical American tree.

Did You Know?

The **cashew** tree is related to poison ivy. Touching a cashew shell can sometimes cause blisters. However, the roasted nut has no poison and is completely safe.

cash·ier (ka shir/), NOUN. someone who has charge of money in a bank, or in any business.

cash machine. See **ATM.**

cash·mere (kash/mir), NOUN. a fine, soft wool, used in making sweaters or scarves.

cas·ket (kas/kit), NOUN. a coffin.

cas·se·role (kas/ə rōl/), NOUN.
1 a covered baking dish in which food can be both cooked and served.
2 food cooked and served in such a dish.

cas·sette (kə set/), NOUN.
1 a container holding magnetic tape for recording and playing back pictures, sound, or computer information.
2 a cartridge for film.

cast (kast),
1 VERB. to throw: *cast a stone, cast a fishing line.*

a	hat	ė	term	ô	order	ch	child		a in about
ā	age	i	it	oi	oil	ng	long		e in taken
ä	far	ī	ice	ou	out	sh	she	ə	i in pencil
â	care	o	hot	u	cup	th	thin		o in lemon
e	let	ō	open	ù	put	ᴛн	then		u in circus
ē	equal	ò	saw	ü	rule	zh	measure		

2 *VERB.* to throw off; cause to fall: *The snake cast its skin. The setting sun cast long shadows.*

3 *NOUN.* the distance a thing is thrown; throw: *The fisherman made a long cast with his line.*

4 *VERB.* to shape something by pouring it or squeezing it into a mold to harden. Metal is first melted and then cast.

5 *NOUN.* a hard or soft covering used to shape or support something: *My cousin's broken arm is in a plaster cast.*

6 *VERB.* to select someone for a part in a play: *The director cast her in the role of the heroine.*

7 *NOUN.* all the actors in a play: *The cast's biographies were listed on the program.*
❏ *VERB* **casts, cast, cast·ing.**

cast off, *IDIOM.* to let loose; set free: *We cast off the boat from its moorings.*

cas·ta·net (kas′tə net′), *NOUN.* one of a pair of wooden or plastic instruments held in the hand and clicked together in time to music.

cas·tle (kas′əl), *NOUN.*

1 a large stone building or group of buildings with thick walls, towers, and other defenses against attack. Most castles were built during the Middle Ages. Many were surrounded by water-filled ditches, or moats, for protection.

2 See **rook.**

castle (definition 1)

cas·u·al (kazh′ü əl), *ADJECTIVE.*

1 informal: *We dressed in casual clothes for the picnic. Her casual behavior was sometimes mistaken for rudeness.*

2 happening by chance; not planned or expected; accidental: *Our long friendship began with a casual meeting at a party.*

3 without plan or method; careless: *I didn't read the newspaper but gave it only a casual glance.*
—**cas′u·al·ly,** *ADVERB.*

cas·u·al·ty (kazh′ü əl tē), *NOUN.* someone who has been wounded, killed, or injured in battle or an accident: *The war produced many casualties. How many casualties are the result of drunk driving?*
❏ *PLURAL* **cas·u·al·ties.**

cat (kat), *NOUN.*

1 a small, furry animal with sharp teeth and claws. Cats are often kept as a pet or for catching mice and rats.

2 any animal of the group that includes house cats, lions, tigers, leopards, and jaguars.

cat·a·log (kat′l ȯg),

1 *NOUN.* a list. A library usually has a catalog of its books, arranged in alphabetical order. Many companies print catalogs showing pictures and prices of the things that they have to sell.

2 *VERB.* to make a list of; enter in the proper place in a list: *to catalog an insect collection.*
❏ *VERB* **cat·a·logs, cat·a·loged, cat·a·log·ing.**

cat·a·logue (kat′l ȯg), *NOUN* or *VERB.* another spelling of **catalog.** ❏ *PLURAL* **cat·a·logues;** *VERB* **cat·a·logues, cat·a·logued, cat·a·logu·ing.**

cat·a·pult (kat′ə pult),

1 *NOUN.* a weapon used in ancient times for throwing stones, arrows, and so on by means of a long wooden arm jerked by ropes.

2 *VERB.* to throw; hurl: *He stopped his bicycle so suddenly that he was catapulted over the handlebars.*
❏ *VERB* **cat·a·pults, cat·a·pult·ed, cat·a·pult·ing.**

cat·a·ract (kat′ə rakt′), *NOUN.*

1 a large, steep waterfall.

2 a disease of the eye in which the lens develops a cloudy film. A cataract makes you partly or entirely blind.

ca·tas·tro·phe (kə tas′trə fē), *NOUN.* a sudden, terribly bad thing that happens; very great misfortune. An earthquake, tornado, flood, or big fire is a catastrophe. ❏ *PLURAL* **ca·tas·tro·phes.**

cat·bird (kat′bėrd′), *NOUN.* a North American songbird with gray feathers. It makes a sound like a cat mewing.

catch (kach),

1 *VERB.* to take and hold something moving; seize: *Catch the ball with both hands. The children chased the puppy and caught it.*

2 *VERB.* to attract: *The huge sign caught my attention.*

3 *VERB.* to take or get: *Paper catches fire easily. Put on a warm coat or you will catch cold. I caught a glimpse of my mother waving as her plane took off.*

4 *VERB.* to reach or get to in time: *You have just five minutes to catch your train.*

5 *VERB.* to see, hear, or understand: *He spoke so rapidly that I didn't catch what he said.*

6 *VERB.* to become hooked or fastened: *My sweater caught in the door.*

7 *VERB.* to come upon suddenly; surprise: *Mother caught me just as I was hiding her birthday gift.*

8 *VERB.* to act as catcher in baseball: *He catches for our team.*

9 *NOUN.* the act of catching something: *She made a fine catch with one hand.*

10 *NOUN.* something that fastens: *The catch on that door is broken.*

11 *NOUN.* a thing or a group of things that has been caught: *A dozen fish is a good catch.*

12 *NOUN.* a game of throwing and catching a ball: *The children played catch on the lawn.*

13 *NOUN.* a hidden or tricky condition: *What's the catch?* ❏ *VERB* **catch•es, caught, catch•ing;** *PLURAL* **catch•es.**

catch on, *IDIOM.*

1 to get the idea; understand: *The second time the teacher explained the problem, I caught on.*

2 to be widely used or accepted: *That new song caught on quickly.*

catch up with, *IDIOM.* to come up even with someone or something while going the same way; overtake: *He was late, and had to run to catch up with me.*

Synonym Study

Catch means to get hold of someone or something that is moving: *The police tried to catch the man who grabbed my purse and ran away. Let's catch some fish for dinner.*

Trap means to catch and keep hold of an animal or person: *Workers at the zoo spent hours trying to trap the escaped leopard.*

Capture means to take by force: *The pirates captured the treasure ship.*

Seize means to take suddenly and by force: *King Richard's soldiers seized the enemy camp and soon won the battle.*

Grab means to seize, especially by hand: *I grabbed the cat before it got out the door.*

Snatch means to grab: *My brother's hat blew off, but he snatched it out of the air.*

catch•er (kach′ər), *NOUN.* the baseball player behind home plate who catches those balls thrown by the pitcher that are not hit by the batter.

catch•ing (kach′ing), *ADJECTIVE.* spread by infection; contagious: *Colds are catching.*

catch•y (kach′ē), *ADJECTIVE.* pleasing and easy to remember: *a catchy new song.* ❏ *ADJECTIVE* **catch•i•er, catch•i•est.**

cat•e•go•ry (kat′ə gôr′ē), *NOUN.* a group or general division in classification; class: *The library arranges their books according to categories.* ❏ *PLURAL* **cat•e•go•ries.**

ca•ter (kā′tər), *VERB.*

1 to provide food and supplies, service, and so on: *They run a restaurant and also cater weddings and parties.*

2 to provide what is needed or wanted: *The new store caters to tourists by selling souvenirs.* ❏ *VERB* **ca•ters, ca•tered, ca•ter•ing.**

cat•er•pil•lar (kat′ər pil′ər), *NOUN.* the wormlike larva of a butterfly or a moth. Caterpillars are often colorful, and many are furry or have bristles.

Word Story

Caterpillar comes from Latin words meaning "hairy cat." Many caterpillars have fuzz. No one knows for sure why they are named after cats—perhaps because some caterpillars arch their backs the way an angry cat does.

A **caterpillar's** body has 13 segments.

cat•fish (kat′fish′), *NOUN.* a fish without scales and with long, slender feelers around the mouth that look something like a cat's whiskers. ❏ *PLURAL* **cat•fish** or **cat•fish•es.**

ca•the•dral (kə thē′drəl), *NOUN.*

1 the official church of a bishop.

2 a large or important church.

Cath•o•lic (kath′ə lik),

1 *ADJECTIVE.* of or about the Christian church governed by the pope; Roman Catholic.

2 *NOUN.* a member of this church.

cat•nip (kat′nip), *NOUN.* a plant related to mint. Cats enjoy eating and smelling catnip.

CAT scan (kat′ skan′), an X-ray image of a cross section of the body created by a computer from a series of X-ray pictures. Doctors use CAT scans to locate disease in the body.

cat•sup (kech′əp or kach′əp), *NOUN.* another spelling of **ketchup.**

cat•tail (kat′tāl′), *NOUN.* a tall marsh plant that has a long, furry, brown spike and long, pointed leaves.

a	hat	ė	term	ô	order	ch	child	ə	a in about
ā	age	i	it	oi	oil	ng	long		e in taken
ä	far	ī	ice	ou	out	sh	she		i in pencil
â	care	o	hot	u	cup	th	thin		o in lemon
e	let	ō	open	ù	put	ᴛʜ	then		u in circus
ē	equal	ȯ	saw	ü	rule	zh	measure		

cat·tle (kat'l), NOUN PLURAL. animals that chew their cud, have hoofs, and are raised for meat, milk, and hides; cows, bulls, and steers.

caught (kȯt), VERB.
1 the past tense of **catch**: *I caught the ball.*
2 the past participle of **catch**: *We had caught seven trout by ten o'clock this morning.*

cau·li·flow·er (kȯ'lə flou'ər), NOUN. a vegetable that has a solid white head with green leaves around it. It is related to broccoli.

caulk (kȯk), VERB. to fill up a seam, crack, or joint so that it will not leak; make watertight.

cause (kȯz),
1 NOUN. a person, thing, or event that makes something else happen: *The flood was the cause of much damage.*
2 VERB. to make something happen; bring about: *A loud noise caused me to jump.*
3 NOUN. a reason for doing something: *Winning the contest was a cause for celebration.*
4 NOUN. something in which many people are interested and to which they give their support: *World peace is the cause she works for.*
❏ VERB **caus·es, caused, caus·ing.**

cau·tion (kȯ'shən),
1 NOUN. great care to avoid danger: *Use caution in crossing streets.*
2 VERB. to urge someone to be careful; warn: *I cautioned them against playing in the street.*
❏ VERB **cau·tions, cau·tioned, cau·tion·ing.**

cau·tious (kȯ'shəs), ADJECTIVE. very careful to avoid danger: *Cautious drivers obey the speed limits.* —**cau'tious·ly,** ADVERB.

cav·al·ry (kav'əl rē), NOUN. soldiers fighting on horseback or from tanks and other armored vehicles.

cave (kāv), NOUN. a hollow space underground, especially one with an opening in the side of a hill or mountain.
cave in, IDIOM.
1 to fall in; collapse: *The weight of the snow caused the roof of the cabin to cave in.*
2 to do something because of pressure from someone: *The president said he wouldn't cave in to the terrorist's demand for a jet.*
❏ VERB **caves, caved, cav·ing.**

cave-in (kāv'in'), NOUN.
1 the act or process of caving in; collapse: *a tunnel cave-in, the cave-in of a mine.*
2 a place where something has caved in.

cave·man (kāv'man'), NOUN. someone who lived in a cave in prehistoric times. ❏ PLURAL **cave·men.**

cav·ern (kav'ərn), NOUN. a large cave.

cave·wom·an (kāv'wum ən), NOUN. woman who lived in a cave in prehistoric times. ❏ PLURAL **cave·wo·men.**

cav·i·ty (kav'ə tē), NOUN. a hole or hollow place. Cavities in teeth are caused by decay. ❏ PLURAL **cav·i·ties.**

caw (kȯ),
1 NOUN. the harsh cry made by a crow or raven.
2 VERB. to make this cry.
❏ VERB **caws, cawed, caw·ing.**

cc, cc., or **c.c.,** an abbreviation of **cubic centimeter** or **cubic centimeters.**

CD. See **compact disc.**

CD-ROM (sē'dē'rom'), NOUN. a compact disc for use with a computer. It can produce text, pictures, movies, and sound.

cease (sēs), VERB. to stop: *The music ceased suddenly. We cease taking reservations after July 5.* See the Synonym Study at **stop.** ❏ VERB **ceas·es, ceased, ceas·ing.**

ce·dar (sē'dər), NOUN. an evergreen tree with widely spreading branches. Its fragrant, durable, reddish wood is used for making chests, pencils, posts, and shingles.

ceil·ing (sē'ling), NOUN.
1 the inside, top covering of a room.
2 the distance between the earth and the lowest clouds: *The weather report said that the ceiling was only 300 feet.*

cel·e·brate (sel'ə brāt), VERB.
1 to do something special in honor of a special person or day: *We celebrated my birthday with a party and cake and ice cream.*
2 to perform publicly with the proper ceremonies: *The priest celebrates Mass in church.*
❏ VERB **cel·e·brates, cel·e·brat·ed, cel·e·brat·ing.**

cel·e·bra·tion (sel'ə brā'shən), NOUN. the special services or activities in honor of a particular person, act, time, or day: *A Fourth of July celebration often includes fireworks.*

ce·leb·ri·ty (sə leb'rə tē), NOUN. a famous person; someone who is well known or often talked about. ❏ PLURAL **ce·leb·ri·ties.**

A family of **cavemen** may have lived like this.

cel·er·y (sel′ər ē), NOUN. a long, light green vegetable that separates into crisp stalks. Celery is eaten raw or cooked.

cell (sel), NOUN.
1 a small room in a prison, convent, or monastery.
2 any small, hollow place: *Bees store honey in the cells of a honeycomb.*
3 the basic unit of which all living things are made. Cells are usually extremely small and may form muscle, blood, wood, leaves, and so on. The cells of animals and plants have a nucleus near the center. They are enclosed by a **cell membrane.**
4 See **electric cell.**
■ Another word that sounds like this is **sell.**

cel·lar (sel′ər), NOUN. an underground room or rooms, usually under a building and often used for storage.

cel·lo (chel′ō), NOUN. a musical instrument like a violin, but very much larger and with a lower tone. It is held between the knees and played with a bow. ❏ PLURAL **cel·los.**

playing the **cello**

cel·lo·phane (sel′ə fān), NOUN. a clear, paperlike material made from cellulose. It is used as a wrapping to keep things fresh.

cel·lu·lose (sel′yə lōs), NOUN. a substance that forms the walls of plant cells. Cotton, flax, and hemp are largely cellulose.

Cel·si·us (sel′sē əs), ADJECTIVE. of, based on, or according to a scale for measuring temperature; centigrade. On the **Celsius scale,** 0 degrees is the temperature at which water freezes, and 100 degrees is the temperature at which water boils.

ce·ment (sə ment′),
1 NOUN. a fine, gray powder made by burning clay and limestone. Cement is mixed with water to make concrete and mortar.
2 NOUN. any soft substance which when it hardens makes things stick together: *rubber cement.*
3 VERB. to fasten or repair something with cement: *A cracked wall can be cemented. I cemented the handle back on the broken cup.*
❏ VERB **ce·ments, ce·ment·ed, ce·ment·ing.**

cem·e·ter·y (sem′ə ter/ē), NOUN. a place for burying the dead. ❏ PLURAL **cem·e·ter·ies.**

cen·sus (sen′səs), NOUN. an official count of the people of a country or district. It is taken to find out the number of people living there, their ages, what their jobs are, and so on. ❏ PLURAL **cen·sus·es.**

Did You Know?

The United States **census** is taken every ten years. The first one was done in 1790. The results of the census are very important. They determine how many representatives each state has in the House of Representatives.

cent (sent), NOUN. the smallest coin of the United States and Canada; penny. One hundred cents make one dollar. ■ Other words that sound like this are **scent** and **sent.**

cen·ten·ni·al (sen ten′ē əl),
1 ADJECTIVE. of or for a period of 100 years or a 100th anniversary.
2 NOUN. 100th anniversary: *the town's centennial.*

cen·ter (sen′tər),
1 NOUN. a point within a circle or round object equally distant from all points on the circle or on the surface of the object.
2 NOUN. the middle point, place, or part: *the center of a room.*
3 NOUN. a person, thing, or group that is the central point of attraction: *The Egyptian mummy was the center of the exhibit.*
4 NOUN. a place where people go for a certain purpose: *We went ice-skating yesterday at the recreation center.*
5 VERB. to place something in or at a center: *The bowl of fruit was centered on the table.*
6 VERB. to collect at a center: *The guests centered around the table.*
7 NOUN. a player in the middle of a forward group or line of players in football, hockey, basketball, and some other sports.
❏ VERB **cen·ters, cen·tered, cen·ter·ing.**

cen·ter·board (sen′tər bôrd), NOUN. a thin, flat piece of wood or metal that sticks out below the bottom of a boat. It keeps the boat steady as it moves.

center field, (in baseball) the section of the outfield between left field and right field. **−center fielder.**

Word Power centi-

The combining form **centi-** means "one hundred" or "one hundredth part." A **centipede** seems to have a hundred legs. A **centimeter** is one hundredth of a meter.

cen·ti·grade (sen′tə grād), ADJECTIVE. See **Celsius.**

cen·ti·gram (sen′tə gram), NOUN. a unit of weight or mass equal to 1/100 of a gram.

cen·ti·me·ter (sen′tə mē′tər), NOUN. a unit of length equal to 1/100 of a meter or about this long: ──────

a	hat	ė	term	ô	order	ch	child		a in about
ā	age	i	it	oi	oil	ng	long		e in taken
ä	far	ī	ice	ou	out	sh	she	ə {	i in pencil
â	care	o	hot	u	cup	th	thin		o in lemon
e	let	ō	open	ů	put	₮H	then		u in circus
ē	equal	ȯ	saw	ü	rule	zh	measure		

cen·ti·pede (sen′tə pēd′), *NOUN.* a flat, wormlike animal with many pairs of legs. Centipedes vary in length from an inch or so to nearly a foot. The bite of some centipedes is painful.

There are almost 3,000 kinds of **centipedes.**

cen·tral (sen′trəl), *ADJECTIVE.*
1 at the center; near the center: *The park is in the central part of the city.*
2 main; chief; principal: *The central library sends books to its branches.*

Central African Republic, a country in central Africa.

Central America, the part of North America between Mexico and South America.
—**Central American.**

central processing unit. See **CPU.**

cen·tur·y (sen′chər ē), *NOUN.*
1 each 100 years, counting from some special time, such as the birth of Jesus. The first century is 1 through 100; the twentieth century is 1901 through 2000.
2 a period of 100 years. From 1824 to 1924 is a century.
❑ *PLURAL* **cen·tur·ies.**

Usage Note

The name of a **century** is the number of its hundreds, plus one. The eighteen hundreds are the nineteenth century. The nineteen hundreds are the twentieth century. Dates B.C. are named in the same way. The two hundreds B.C. are the third century B.C., and so on.

ce·ram·ic (sə ram′ik), *ADJECTIVE.* of or about pottery or porcelain.

ce·ram·ics (sə ram′iks), *NOUN.* the art of making pottery or porcelain.

cer·e·al (sir′ē əl), *NOUN.*
1 a food made from grain. It is usually eaten with milk for breakfast.
2 any grass that produces grain used as a food. Wheat, rice, corn, oats, and barley are cereals.
■ Another word that sounds like this is **serial.**

ce·re·bral pal·sy (sə rē′ brəl pol′zē *or* ser′ə brəl pol′zē), a physical disability caused by damage to the brain before or at birth. People suffering from cerebral palsy have trouble controlling their muscles

cer·e·mo·ni·al (ser′ə mō′nē əl), *ADJECTIVE.* of or used in a ceremony: *ceremonial costumes.*

cer·e·mo·ni·ous (ser′ə mō′nē əs), *ADJECTIVE.* very formal; extremely polite: *a ceremonious bow.*

cer·e·mo·ny (ser′ə mō′nē), *NOUN.*
1 a special act or set of acts to be done on special occasions such as weddings, funerals, graduations, or holidays: *a graduation ceremony.*
2 very polite conduct; way of conducting yourself that follows the rules of polite social behavior: *Dinner was served with a great deal of ceremony.*
❑ *PLURAL* **cer·e·mo·nies.**

cer·tain (sėrt′n), *ADJECTIVE.*
1 sure: *I am certain that I will be home tonight.*
■ See the Synonym Study at **sure.**
2 some but not all: *Certain plants will not grow here.*

cer·tain·ly (sėrt′n lē), *ADVERB.* without a doubt; surely: *I will certainly be at the party.*

cer·tain·ty (sėrt′n tē), *NOUN.*
1 freedom from doubt; condition of being certain: *The man's certainty was surprising, for we could see that he was wrong.*
2 something certain; a sure fact: *The coming of spring and summer is a certainty.*
❑ *PLURAL* **cer·tain·ties.**

cer·tif·i·cate (sər tif′ə kit), *NOUN.* an official written or printed statement showing that something is a fact. Your birth certificate gives the date and place of your birth.

Chad (chad), *NOUN.* a country in central Africa.
—**Chad·i·an** (chad′ē ən), *ADJECTIVE* OR *NOUN.*

chafe (chāf), *VERB.* to rub until sore: *The new collar chafed his neck.* ❑ *VERB* **chafes, chafed, chaf·ing.**

chain (chān),
1 *NOUN.* a row of metal rings joined together: *The dog is fastened to a post by a chain.*
2 *NOUN.* a series of things linked together: *a chain of mountains, a chain of restaurants.*
3 *VERB.* to fasten something with a chain: *The dog was chained to a post.*
4 *NOUN.* anything that binds or restrains: *chains of duty.*
❑ *VERB* **chains, chained, chain·ing.** —**chain′like′,** *ADJECTIVE.*

chain saw, a portable power saw that has a loop of chain with sharp teeth. It is used to trim tree limbs, cut down small trees, and so on.

chair (châr), *NOUN.*
1 a seat that has a back and legs and, sometimes, arms, usually for one person.
2 a chairman or chairwoman.

chair·man (châr′mən), *NOUN.*
1 someone who is in charge of a meeting.
2 someone at the head of a committee or other official group.
❑ *PLURAL* **chair·men.**

chair·wom·an (châr′wům′ən), *NOUN.*
1 a woman in charge of a meeting.
2 a woman at the head of a committee or other official group.
❑ *PLURAL* **chair·wom·en.**

C

chalk (chȯk),
1 *NOUN.* a soft, white mineral used for writing or drawing. Chalk is made up mostly of very small fossil seashells.
2 *NOUN.* a white or colored substance used like chalk on a blackboard or chalkboard.
3 *VERB.* to mark, write, or draw with chalk.
❑ *VERB* **chalks, chalked, chalk·ing.** —**chalk′like′,** *ADJECTIVE.*

chalk up, *IDIOM.*
1 to give credit for: *I chalk up my success to hard work.*
2 to score: *Our team chalked up 12 points.*

chalk·board (chȯk′bôrd′), *NOUN.* a smooth, hard surface, used for writing or drawing on with chalk.

chal·lenge (chal′ənj),
1 *NOUN.* a call or invitation to a game, contest, or fight: *They accepted our team's challenge.*
2 *VERB.* to call or invite someone to a game, contest, or fight; dare: *The knight challenged his rival to fight a duel.*
3 *VERB.* to stop and question someone about an action: *When I tried to enter the building, the guard at the door challenged me.*
4 *VERB.* to call into question; doubt; dispute: *The teacher challenged my statement that Montana is a coastal state.*
5 *NOUN.* anything that tests your skill: *Fractions are a real challenge to me.*
6 *VERB.* to test your skills: *The duties of her job challenge her every day.*
❑ *VERB* **chal·leng·es, chal·lenged, chal·leng·ing.** —**chal′leng·er,** *NOUN.*

chal·lenged (chal′ənjd), *ADJECTIVE.* having special difficulties to overcome: *He is verbally challenged and works hard on his reading skills. Wheelchair access for the mobility-challenged is important for all public buildings.*

cham·ber (chām′bər), *NOUN.*
1 a room, especially a bedroom.
2 a hall where legislators meet: *the council chamber.*
3 a group of legislators: *The Congress of the United States has two chambers, the Senate and the House of Representatives.*
4 an enclosed space in the body of a living thing. *The heart has four chambers.*

cha·me·le·on (kə mē′lē ən), *NOUN.* a small lizard that can change the color of its skin to blend with the surroundings.

champ (champ), *NOUN.* a short form of **champion.**

cham·pi·on (cham′pē ən), *NOUN.* a person, animal, or thing that wins first place in a game or contest: *a swimming champion. Her steer was the champion at the county fair last year.*

cham·pi·on·ship (cham′pē ən ship), *NOUN.* the position of a champion; first place: *Our school won the championship in baseball.*

chance (chans), *NOUN.*
1 a good time to do something; opportunity: *I saw a chance to earn some money selling newspapers.*
2 an event that is possible; possibility: *There's a good chance that I will be elected class president.*
3 fate, fortune, or luck: *Chance led to the finding of gold in California.*
4 a risk: *You will be taking a chance if you swim there.*

by chance, *IDIOM.* accidentally; unintentionally: *I ran into her by chance yesterday.*

take a chance, *IDIOM.* to risk something; bet: *He took a chance that we'd be home and came over.*

chan·cel·lor (chan′sə lər), *NOUN.* a very high official. Chancellor is the title used for a very high official in governments, courts of law, and universities.

chan·de·lier (shan′də lir′), *NOUN.* a light that hangs from the ceiling, with branches for light bulbs or candles.

change (chānj),
1 *VERB.* to make or become different: *She changed the decoration of the room.*
2 *VERB.* to put or take something in place of another; substitute or exchange: *I changed seats with my brother.*
3 *NOUN.* the action of passing from one form or place to another: *Vacationing in the country is a pleasant change from city life.*
4 *NOUN.* variety; difference: *Let me lead for a change.*
5 *NOUN.* the money returned to you when you have paid a larger amount than the price of what you buy: *I handed the clerk a dollar for the apple, and he gave me fifty cents in change.*
6 *NOUN.* small coins: *He had a handful of change.*
7 *VERB.* to put different clothes on: *After swimming we went to the cabin and changed.*
❑ *VERB* **chang·es, changed, chang·ing.**

chameleon — most are between 7 and 10 inches long, including the tail

a	hat	ė	term	ȯ	order	ch	child	⎧a in about
ā	age	i	it	oi	oil	ng	long	⎪e in taken
ä	far	ī	ice	ou	out	sh	she	ə⎨i in pencil
â	care	o	hot	u	cup	th	thin	⎪o in lemon
e	let	ō	open	u̇	put	ŦH	then	⎩u in circus
ē	equal	ȯ	saw	ü	rule	zh	measure	

chan·nel (chan′l), NOUN.
1 a television station: *If you don't like this program, change to another channel.*
2 the way by which something moves or is carried: *The information came through secret channels.*
3 a body of water joining two larger bodies of water: *The English Channel lies between the North Sea and the Atlantic Ocean.*

chant (chant),
1 NOUN. a song in which several words or syllables are sung on one tone. Chants are sometimes used in religious services.
2 VERB. to sing: *The cantor chanted a prayer.*
3 VERB. to call out over and over again: *The football fans chanted, "Go, team, go!"*
❑ VERB **chants, chant·ed, chant·ing.**

Cha·nu·kah (hä′nə kə), NOUN. another spelling of Hanukkah.

cha·os (kā′os), NOUN. a condition of complete disorder and confusion: *The storm left the town in chaos.*

chap¹ (chap), VERB. to crack open; make or become rough: *My lips often chap in cold weather.* ❑ VERB **chaps, chapped, chap·ping.**

chap² (chap), NOUN. a fellow; man or boy: *He's a handsome chap.*

chap·el (chap′əl), NOUN.
1 a building for religious services, smaller than a church.
2 a small place for religious services in a larger building: *a hospital chapel, an airport chapel.*

chap·lain (chap′lən), NOUN. a member of the clergy serving a special group or place: *My uncle was a Navy chaplain.*

chaps (chaps), NOUN PLURAL. strong leather trousers without a back, worn over other trousers by cowboys.

chap·ter (chap′tər), NOUN.
1 a main division of a book, dealing with a particular part of the story or subject.
2 a local branch of a club or organization.

char·ac·ter (kar′ik tər), NOUN.
1 all the qualities or features of anything; kind; sort; nature: *The soil on the prairies is of a different character from that in the mountains.*
2 personality; the special way that someone feels, thinks, and acts: *She has an honest, dependable character.*
3 moral strength: *It takes character to endure hardship for very long.*

chaps with fringes

4 a person or animal in a play, poem, story, book, or movie: *My favorite character in "Charlotte's Web" is Wilbur, the pig.*
5 someone who attracts attention by being different or odd: *Ever since he shaved his head, people have thought of him as a real character.*
6 a letter, number, mark, or sign: *There are 52 characters in our alphabet, consisting of 26 small letters and 26 capital letters.*

char·ac·ter·is·tic (kar′ik tə ris′tik),
1 ADJECTIVE. typical; distinguishing one person or thing from others: *Bananas have a characteristic smell.*
2 NOUN. a typical quality or feature; whatever distinguishes one person or thing from others: *An elephant's trunk is its most noticeable characteristic.*

char·ac·ter·ize (kar′ik tə rīz′), VERB.
1 to describe the typical qualities or features of someone or something: *The story of "Red Riding Hood" characterizes the wolf as a cunning beast.*
2 to be a characteristic of something: *A camel is characterized by the humps on its back and its ability to go without water for several days.*
❑ VERB **char·ac·ter·iz·es, char·ac·ter·ized, char·ac·ter·iz·ing.**

char·coal (chär′kōl′), NOUN. a black, brittle form of carbon made by partly burning wood in a place where there is no air. Charcoal is used as fuel, in filters, and for drawing.

charge (chärj),
1 VERB. to ask as a price; demand in payment: *The store charges 99 cents a dozen for eggs.*
2 NOUN. a price; expense: *The delivery charge is $3.50.*
3 VERB. to ask to pay; request payment from: *Doctors charge their patients for treatment.*
4 VERB. to put down as a debt to be paid later: *We charged the table, so we'll get the bill later.*
5 NOUN. a debt to be paid: *"Cash or charge?" asked the clerk.*
6 VERB. to put an amount of electricity in: *Our car battery ran down and needed to be charged.*
7 NOUN. an amount of electricity stored in a battery.
8 VERB. to accuse someone officially: *The driver was charged with speeding.*
9 NOUN. an official or legal accusation: *He admitted the truth of the charge and paid a fine.*
10 VERB. to rush at; attack: *We charged the enemy fort.*
11 NOUN. an attack: *The charge drove the enemy back.*
❑ VERB **charg·es, charged, charg·ing.**
in charge, IDIOM. in command; responsible: *The mate is in charge when the captain leaves the ship.*
in charge of, IDIOM. having the care or management of; in command of; responsible for: *My mom is in charge of the art department.*

char·i·ot (char′ē ət), NOUN. a carriage with two wheels pulled by horses. The chariot was used in ancient times for fighting and racing.

char·i·ta·ble (char′ə tə bəl), *ADJECTIVE*.
1 ready to help or support; kindly: *a charitable man.*
2 dedicated to giving aid or charity to people in need: *We give money to many charitable organizations.*

char·i·ty (char′ə tē), *NOUN*.
1 the action of giving generously to the poor, or to organizations which look after the sick, the poor, and the helpless: *The charity of our citizens enabled the hospital to purchase new beds.*
2 a fund or organization for helping the sick, the poor, and the helpless: *She gives money to charity.*
3 kindness in judging people's faults.
❑ *PLURAL* **char·i·ties.**

Charles·ton (chärlz′tən), *NOUN*. the capital of West Virginia.

charm (chärm),
1 *NOUN*. the quality of pleasing or delighting someone: *The child's charm won our hearts.*
2 *VERB*. to please someone greatly; delight: *They were charmed by the seaside cottage.*
3 *NOUN*. a small ornament worn on a bracelet or chain.
4 *NOUN*. a word, verse, act, or thing supposed to have magic power to help or harm people.
❑ *VERB* **charms, charmed, charm·ing.**

2 *VERB*. to give a charter to: *The government chartered the new airline.*
3 *VERB*. to rent an entire bus, plane, and so on, for a group: *Our school chartered a bus for the trip.*
❑ *VERB* **char·ters, char·tered, char·ter·ing.**

chase (chās),
1 *VERB*. to run after to catch or kill: *Our cat chases mice. In that game, everyone chases the kid with the ball.*
2 *NOUN*. the act or process of running after to catch or kill: *The police caught up with the fleeing robbers after a long chase.*
3 *VERB*. to drive; drive away: *The blue jay chased the squirrel from its nest.*
4 *VERB*. to run after; follow: *I chased the ball.*
❑ *VERB* **chas·es, chased, chas·ing.**

chasm (kaz′əm), *NOUN*. a deep opening or crack in the earth.

chat (chat),
1 *NOUN*. easy, friendly talk: *We had a pleasant chat about old times.*
2 *VERB*. to talk in an easy, friendly way: *She and I often chat on the telephone.* ■ See the Synonym Study at **talk.** ❑ *VERB* **chats, chat·ted, chat·ting.**

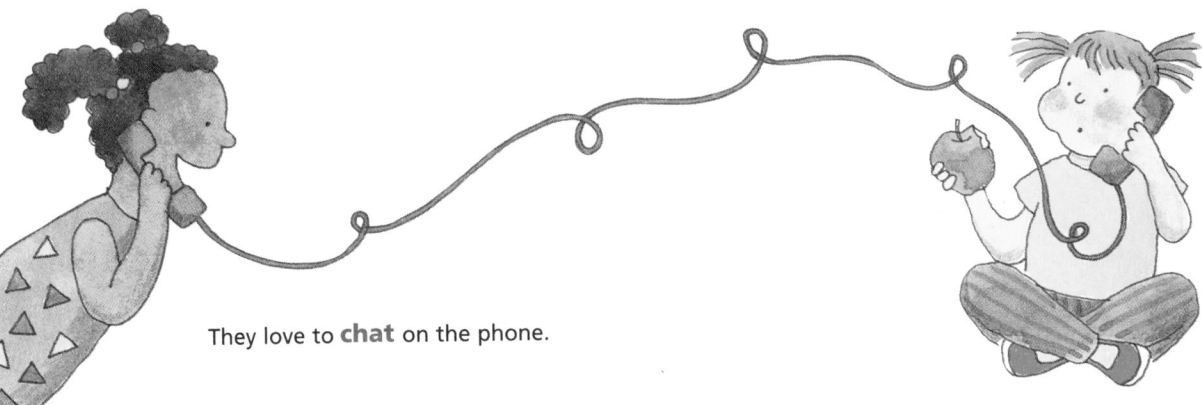

They love to **chat** on the phone.

charm·ing (chär′ming), *ADJECTIVE*. very pleasing; delightful; fascinating: *We saw a charming play.* ■ See the Synonym Study at **cute.**

chart (chärt),
1 *NOUN*. a map used by sailors to show the coasts, rocks, and shallow places of the sea.
2 *NOUN*. an arrangement of information in a form that makes it easy to understand, such as a picture, diagram, or table. There is a chart of United States presidents at the back of this book.
3 *VERB*. to make a map or chart of: *The navigator charted the course of the ship.*
❑ *VERB* **charts, chart·ed, chart·ing.**

char·ter (chär′tər),
1 *NOUN*. an official written statement that grants certain rights to people or a company: *The new airline must obtain a government charter.*

chat·ter (chat′ər),
1 *VERB*. to talk constantly and quickly, often about unimportant things: *The children chattered away on the bus.*
2 *NOUN*. constant, quick talk, often about unimportant things: *The pupils' chatter disturbed the classroom.*
3 *VERB*. to make quick, sharp sounds: *Monkeys chatter.*
4 *NOUN*. quick, sharp sounds: *She was awakened at dawn by the chatter of sparrows.*
5 *VERB*. to make a rattling sound: *My teeth sometimes chatter when I'm very cold.*
❑ *VERB* **chat·ters, chat·tered, chat·ter·ing.**

a	hat	ė	term	ô	order	ch	child	(a in about
ā	age	i	it	oi	oil	ng	long	e in taken
ä	far	ī	ice	ou	out	sh	she	ə ⟨ i in pencil
â	care	o	hot	u	cup	th	thin	o in lemon
e	let	ō	open	u̇	put	ᴛʜ	then	(u in circus
ē	equal	ȯ	saw	ü	rule	zh	measure	

chauf·feur (shō′fər *or* shō fèr′),
1 *NOUN.* someone whose work is driving a car for someone else.
2 *VERB.* to act as a chauffeur for someone.
□ *VERB* **chauf·feurs, chauf·feured, chauf·feur·ing.**

The **chauffeur** opens the door of the limousine.

cheap (chēp), *ADJECTIVE.*
1 low in price; not expensive: *Eggs are cheap out in the country. My sweaters are cheap, because my mother knits them herself.*
2 of low value; worth little: *My shoes were so cheap that they wore out in just a few weeks.*
3 unwilling to spend money; stingy: *Although he had the money, he was too cheap to buy a new suit.*
—**cheap′ly**, *ADVERB.* —**cheap′ness**, *NOUN.*

cheat (chēt),
1 *VERB.* to deceive or trick someone; do business or play in a way that is not honest: *I hate to play games with someone who cheats.*
2 *NOUN.* someone who is not honest and does things to deceive and trick other people: *I won't play with him anymore because he's a cheat.*
□ *VERB* **cheats, cheat·ed, cheat·ing.** —**cheat′er**, *NOUN.*

Synonym Study

Cheat means to do something dishonest while hoping others won't notice: *My sister never cheats at games, and she won't play with anyone who does.*

Trick means to cheat by misleading or fooling someone: *He tricked the man by selling him a repainted car and claiming it was new.*

Deceive means to make someone believe something that isn't true: *When the fish hide in the seaweed, their stripes deceive predators into thinking the fish aren't there.*

Swindle means to cheat someone, usually out of money: *A dishonest roofer swindled the church out of thousands of dollars.*

check (chek),
1 *VERB.* to examine something to see if it is correct, working properly, turned on, and so on: *Always check your answers.*
2 *VERB.* to seek information and advice from something: *I checked the dictionary to find out what the word meant.*
3 *VERB.* to mark something, often with a check: *The teacher checked the correct answers in red.*
4 *NOUN.* a mark (✓) to show that something has been looked at or compared. Often it shows that the thing looked at was found to be correct.
5 *NOUN.* a written order directing a bank to pay money to the person named: *My parents pay most of their bills by check.*
6 *NOUN.* a written statement of the amount owed in a restaurant: *After we finished eating, the waiter brought the check to our table.*
7 *VERB.* to leave or take something to be looked after: *We checked our suitcases at the airport.*
8 *NOUN.* a pattern made of squares: *Do you want a check or a stripe for your new shirt?*
9 *VERB.* to stop suddenly: *The tennis player checked her swing as the ball went out of bounds.*
10 *VERB.* to hold back; control: *He checked his anger.*
11 in chess: **a** *NOUN.* the position of a king in danger of being captured. **b** *INTERJECTION.* a word spoken to declare that your opponent's king is in danger of being captured.
12 in hockey: **a** *VERB.* to block the progress of an opposing player. **b** *NOUN.* the act of blocking the progress of an opposing player.
□ *VERB* **checks, checked, check·ing.**

check in, *IDIOM.* to arrive and register at a hotel, motel, and so on: *When did you check in?*

check out, *IDIOM.*
1 to pay the bill when leaving: *We checked out of the hotel before noon.*
2 to inspect or examine: *I checked out the apartment before deciding to rent it.*
3 to borrow from a library: *I checked out several books about skiing.*

Word Story

Check comes from a Persian word meaning "king." **Checkers** and **chess** come from the same word. The oldest meaning of **check** is definition 11a. All other meanings developed from that one.

check·er·board (chek′ər bôrd′), *NOUN.* a board marked in a pattern of 64 squares of two alternating colors, used in playing checkers or chess.

check·ers (chek′ərz), *NOUN.* a game played by two people, each with 12 flat, round pieces to move on a checkerboard. Each piece is called a **checker.**
■ See the Word Story at **check.**

C

check·mate (chek′māt′), in chess:

1 *NOUN.* the position of a king that cannot avoid being captured.

2 *INTERJECTION.* a word spoken to declare that your opponent's king cannot avoid being captured and that the game is over.

cheetah — about 6 feet long, including the tail

check·out count·er (check′out′ koun′tər), a counter in a store where you pay a cashier for what you bought.

check·up (chek′up′), *NOUN.*

1 a careful examination: *The mechanic gave my car a checkup to prepare it for the winter.*

2 a thorough examination by a doctor to see that you are healthy: *The doctor gave me a checkup.*

cheek (chēk), *NOUN.* the side of the face below either eye.

cheer (chir),

1 *NOUN.* a yell of encouragement and support or praise: *Three cheers for the winners!*

2 *VERB.* to call out or yell loudly to show that you like something: *We all cheered loudly.*

3 *VERB.* to urge on with cheers: *Everyone cheered our team.*

4 *NOUN.* good feelings; hope; joy: *The warmth of the fire brought us cheer.* ❑ *VERB* **cheers, cheered, cheer·ing.**

cheer·ful (chir′fəl), *ADJECTIVE.*

1 full of good feelings; joyful; glad: *She is a smiling, cheerful girl.*

2 pleasant; bringing cheer: *a cheerful, sunny room.* **–cheer′ful·ly,** *ADVERB.* **–cheer′ful·ness,** *NOUN.*

leading the crowd in a **cheer**

cheer·lead·er (chēr′lē′dər), *NOUN.* someone who leads a group in organized cheering, especially at school or athletic events.

cheer·y (chir′ē), *ADJECTIVE.* cheerful; pleasant; bright. ❑ *ADJECTIVE* **cheer·i·er, cheer·i·est. –cheer′i·ly,** *ADVERB.*

cheese (chēz), *NOUN.* a solid food made from the curds of milk. **–cheese′like′,** *ADJECTIVE.*

chee·tah (chē′tə), *NOUN.* a large cat with spots that is something like a leopard but smaller, found mainly in Africa. Cheetahs run very fast.

chef (shef), *NOUN.* a cook, especially the chief cook of a large restaurant.

chem·i·cal (kem′ə kəl),

1 *ADJECTIVE.* about or involving chemistry: *Chemical research has made possible many new products.*

2 *ADJECTIVE.* made by chemistry; used in chemistry: *The laboratory was full of chemical equipment.*

3 *NOUN.* any substance used in chemistry. Elements such as carbon and oxygen, and combinations of elements such as table salt, are chemicals. **–chem′i·cal·ly,** *ADVERB.*

chemical element. See **element** (definition 1).

chem·ist (kem′ist), *NOUN.* someone who is an expert in chemistry.

chem·is·try (kem′ə strē), *NOUN.* the science that deals with the different kinds of the most basic matter, called chemical elements. Chemistry studies the structure and actions of elements by themselves and combined with each other to make different substances.

che·mo·ther·a·py (kē′mō ther′ə pē), *NOUN.* the treatment of disease, especially cancer, by using special drugs.

cher·ish (cher′ish), *VERB.* to care for someone tenderly; treat with affection; aid or protect: *Parents cherish their children.* ❑ *VERB* **cher·ish·es, cher·ished, cher·ish·ing.**

Cher·o·kee (cher′ə kē′), *NOUN.* a member of a tribe of American Indians of the southeastern United States, now living mostly in Oklahoma. ❑ *PLURAL* **Cher·o·kee** or **Cher·o·kees.**

cher·ry (cher′ē), *NOUN.* a small, round, juicy fruit with a stone or pit inside. Cherries grow on trees. ❑ *PLURAL* **cher·ries.**

Did You Know?

Most **cherries** in the United States are grown in California, Michigan, Oregon, and Washington. **Sweet cherries** are usually eaten raw. **Sour cherries** are often used to make pies.

a	hat	ė	term	ô	order	ch	child		a in about
ā	age	i	it	oi	oil	ng	long		e in taken
ä	far	ī	ice	ou	out	sh	she	ə	i in pencil
â	care	o	hot	u	cup	th	thin		o in lemon
e	let	ō	open	u̇	put	ŦH	then		u in circus
ē	equal	ȯ	saw	ü	rule	zh	measure		

chess (ches), NOUN. a game played by two people, each with 16 pieces. The pieces can be moved in various ways on a checkerboard. ▪ See the Word Story at **check**.

Only a few moves have been made in this game of **chess**.

chest (chest), NOUN.
1 the front part of the body between the neck and the stomach.
2 a large box with a lid, used for holding things: *a tool chest; a toy chest.*
3 a piece of furniture with drawers.

chest·nut (ches'nut),
1 NOUN. a sweet nut that grows on a tree. Chestnuts are eaten after roasting.
2 ADJECTIVE or NOUN. reddish brown.

chew (chü), VERB. to crush or grind something with the teeth: *Chew your food more slowly.* ❑ VERB **chews, chewed, chew·ing.**

chewing gum, gum sweetened and flavored for chewing.

chew·y (chü'ē), ADJECTIVE. requiring much chewing: *chewy caramels.* ❑ ADJECTIVE **chew·i·er, chew·i·est.**

Chey·enne (shī an'), NOUN.
1 the capital of Wyoming.
2 a member of a tribe of American Indians living in Montana and Oklahoma.

Chi·a·pas (chē ä'päs), NOUN. a state in eastern Mexico.

Chi·ca·go (shə kò'gō or shə kä'gō), NOUN. a city in Illinois. **–Chi·ca'go·an,** NOUN.

Chi·ca·na (chi kä'nä), NOUN. a female American of Mexican descent. ❑ PLURAL **Chi·ca·nas.**

Chi·ca·no (chi kä'nō), NOUN. an American of Mexican descent; Mexican American. ❑ PLURAL **Chi·ca·nos.**

chick (chik), NOUN. a young bird, especially a chicken.

chick·a·dee (chik'ə dē'), NOUN. a small bird with black, white, and gray feathers. Its call sounds something like its name. ❑ PLURAL **chick·a·dees.**

chick·en (chik'ən),
1 NOUN. a bird raised for food; hen or rooster.
2 NOUN. the meat of a chicken used for food: *We often have roast chicken for dinner.*
3 ADJECTIVE. (informal) afraid of danger: *She didn't want them to think she was chicken.*

chick·en pox (chik'ən poks'), a mild, contagious disease. It causes fever and a skin rash. Most people who get chicken pox are children.

chick·pea (chik'pē'), NOUN. the pale brown seed of a plant related to green peas; garbanzo. Chickpeas are larger than green peas and must be cooked.

chief (chēf),
1 NOUN. the head of a group; leader; someone who is highest in rank or authority: *a chief of police.*
2 ADJECTIVE. at the head; leading: *the chief engineer of a building project.* ▪ See the Synonym Study at **main**.
3 ADJECTIVE. most important; main: *The chief thing on my mind was dinner.*

chief·ly (chēf'lē), ADVERB.
1 mainly; mostly: *a sauce made chiefly of tomatoes.*
2 first of all; especially: *We visited Washington chiefly to see the Capitol and the White House.*

chief·tain (chēf'tən), NOUN. the head of a clan or group; leader: *a Scottish chieftain.*

Chi·hua·hua (chē wä'wä), NOUN. a very small dog of an old Mexican breed.

child (chīld), NOUN.
1 a young boy or girl.
2 a son or daughter.
3 a baby: *I expect my child will be born today.*
❑ PLURAL **chil·dren. –child'less,** ADJECTIVE.

child·hood (chīld'hud), NOUN. the time during which you are a child.

child·ish (chīl'dish), ADJECTIVE.
1 of or like a child: *She spoke in a high, childish voice.*
2 not proper for a grown person; silly: *Crying for things you can't have is childish.*
–child'ish·ly, ADVERB. **–child'ish·ness,** NOUN.

child·proof (chīld'prüf'), ADJECTIVE. not able to be opened, used, or hurt by a child because of its design.

chil·dren (chil'drən), NOUN PLURAL.
1 young boys and girls.
2 sons and daughters: *Their children are still in school.*

Chil·e (chil'ē), NOUN. a country in southwestern South America.
–Chil'e·an, ADJECTIVE or NOUN.

chil·i (chil'ē), NOUN.
1 a highly seasoned dish of chopped meat and hot peppers. Chili is often made with beans.
2 a pod of green or red pepper with a hot, spicy taste. Chilies are used to flavor food and to make sauces.
❑ PLURAL **chil·ies** or **chil·is.**
▪ Another word that sounds like this is **chilly.**

chili (definition 2)

chill (chil),
1 *NOUN.* an unpleasant coldness: *There's a chill in the air today.*
2 *ADJECTIVE.* unpleasantly cold: *A chill wind blew across the lake.*
3 *VERB.* to make or become cold: *The icy wind chilled us to the bone.*
4 *NOUN.* a sudden coldness of the body with shivering: *I had a chill yesterday and still feel too sick to go to school today.*
❑ *VERB* **chills, chilled, chill·ing.**

chill·y (chil′ē), *ADJECTIVE.*
1 cold; unpleasantly cool: *It is a rainy, chilly day.* ∎ See the Synonym Study at **cold.**
2 cold in manner; unfriendly: *She has been chilly to me since our quarrel.*
❑ *ADJECTIVE* **chill·i·er, chill·i·est.** ∎ Another word that sounds like this is **chili.**

chime (chīm),
1 *NOUN.* a set of bells, pipes, or pieces of glass or metal that make a musical sound when struck or moved.
2 *NOUN.* the musical sound produced by such an instrument.
3 *VERB.* to ring out musically: *The bells chime at noon.*
❑ *VERB* **chimes, chimed, chim·ing.**

chim·ney (chim′nē), *NOUN.* a tall, hollow column, usually made of brick, to carry away smoke from a fireplace or furnace. A person who cleans these is called a **chimney sweep.** ❑ *PLURAL* **chim·neys.**

chimp (chimp), *NOUN.* a short form of **chimpanzee.**

chim·pan·zee (chim′pan zē′ or chim pan′zē), *NOUN.* an African ape smaller than a gorilla; chimp. Chimpanzees are very intelligent. ❑ *PLURAL* **chim·pan·zees.**

chin (chin), *NOUN.* the part of your face below your mouth.

chin yourself, *IDIOM.* to hang by your hands from an overhead bar and pull up until your chin reaches the bar. ❑ *VERB* **chins, chinned, chin·ning.**

chi·na (chī′nə), *NOUN.*
1 a fine, white pottery made of clay baked by a special process, first used in China.
2 dishes, vases, or other things made of china.

Chi·na (chī′nə), *NOUN.* a large country in eastern Asia.

chin·chil·la (chin chil′ə), *NOUN.* a small South American animal that looks something like a squirrel. It has very valuable soft, bluish gray fur. ❑ *PLURAL* **chin·chil·las.**

chimpanzee — 3½ to 5½ feet tall

Chi·nese (chī nēz′),
1 *ADJECTIVE.* of or about China, its people, or their language.
2 *NOUN PLURAL.* **the Chinese,** people born or living in China.
3 *NOUN.* the language of China.

Word Source

Chinese has given some words to the English language. The following words are from Chinese: **ketchup, kung fu, soy sauce, tea, typhoon,** and **wok.**

Chinese checkers, a game for two to six players using marbles on a star-shaped board with small holes in which the marbles rest. The object is to move all your marbles by steps or jumps to the opposite side of the board.

This game of **Chinese checkers** is about to begin.

chink (chingk), *NOUN.* a narrow opening; crack: *The chinks in the log cabin let in wind and snow.*

Chi·nook (shə nùk′ or chə nùk′), *NOUN.* a member of a group of American Indian tribes that live in the state of Washington.

chin-up (chin′up′), *NOUN.* the exercise of chinning yourself.

chip (chip),
1 *NOUN.* a small, thin piece that has been cut or broken off something: *They used chips of wood to light a fire.* ∎ See the Synonym Study at **piece.**
2 *NOUN.* a place where a small, thin piece has been cut or broken off: *This cup has a chip in the rim.*
3 *VERB.* to cut or break off a small thin piece of something: *I chipped the cup when I knocked it off the table.*
4 *NOUN.* a small, thin piece of food or candy: *potato chips, chocolate chips.*

a	hat	ė	term	ô	order	ch	child		a in about
ā	age	i	it	oi	oil	ng	long		e in taken
ä	far	ī	ice	ou	out	sh	she	ə	i in pencil
â	care	o	hot	u	cup	th	thin		o in lemon
e	let	ō	open	ù	put	ᴛʜ	then		u in circus
ē	equal	ò	saw	ü	rule	zh	measure		

5 *NOUN.* a very small, thin piece of silicon or similar material that holds a very complicated set of tiny electronic devices; microchip. Chips are used in computers, video games, televisions, and other electronic

chip (definition 5)

machines. A chip can control thousands of electric signals in a space smaller than your fingernail.
  ❏ *VERB* **chips, chipped, chip·ping.**

chip in, *IDIOM.* to join with others in giving money or help: *We all chipped in to buy Dad a gift for his fortieth birthday.*

Have You Heard?

You may have heard someone say **"He has a chip on his shoulder."** This means that a person is very touchy and easy to make angry.

chip·munk (chip′mungk), *NOUN.* a small, striped North American animal something like a squirrel. It lives in a burrow in the ground

chi·ro·prac·tor (kī′rə prak′tər), *NOUN.* someone who is trained to treat diseases by pressing and adjusting the position of bones and muscles.

chirp (chėrp),
  1 *NOUN.* the short, sharp sound made by some small birds and insects: *I heard the chirp of a sparrow.*
  2 *VERB.* to make a chirp: *The crickets chirped outside the house.*
  ❏ *VERB* **chirps, chirped, chirp·ing.**

chis·el (chiz′əl),
  1 *NOUN.* a metal tool with a sharp edge at the end of a strong blade. Chisels are used for cutting and shaping wood, stone, or metal.
  2 *VERB.* to cut or shape something with a chisel: *The sculptor was at work chiseling a statue.*
  ❏ *VERB* **chis·els, chis·eled, chis·el·ing.**

chiv·al·ry (shiv′əl rē), *NOUN.* very polite behavior toward women.

chlo·rine (klôr′ēn′), *NOUN.* a greenish yellow, bad-smelling, poisonous gas. Chlorine is a chemical element used in bleach and to make water pure.

chlo·ro·phyll (klôr′ə fil), *NOUN.* the substance in green plants that gives them their color. Plants use chlorophyll and light to make their own food from water and carbon dioxide.

choc·o·late (chȯk′lit *or* chȯk′ə lit),
  1 *NOUN.* a powder or syrup made from roasted and ground cacao beans.
  2 *NOUN.* a candy made of chocolate.
  3 *NOUN.* a drink made of chocolate with sugar and hot milk or water.

4 *ADJECTIVE.* made of or flavored with chocolate: *chocolate cake, chocolate milk.*

choice (chois),
  1 *NOUN.* the act of picking something out of a group: *I was careful in my choice of a pet.*
  2 *NOUN.* the power or opportunity to choose: *I have my choice between a radio and a camera.*
  3 *NOUN.* someone or something picked or selected: *This camera is my choice.*
  4 *NOUN.* a quantity and variety to pick from: *We found a wide choice of vegetables in the market.*
  5 *ADJECTIVE.* excellent; of the best quality: *The choicest fruit had the highest price.*
  ❏ *ADJECTIVE* **choic·er, choic·est.**

choir (kwīr), *NOUN.* a group of singers who perform together, often in a church service.

choke (chōk), *VERB.*
  1 to prevent someone from breathing by squeezing or blocking the throat; strangle: *Dad's shirt was too small, and the top button almost choked him.*
  2 to be unable to breathe: *I choked on a bite of pie.*
  3 to fill up or block something: *Sand is choking the river.*
  ❏ *VERB* **chokes, choked, chok·ing.**

cho·les·te·rol (kə les′tə rol′), *NOUN.* a white, fatty substance found in the blood and tissues of the body. Eggs, cheese, and meat contain cholesterol.

choose (chüz), *VERB.*
  1 to pick out or select someone or something from a group: *Choose a book. She chose wisely.*
  2 to decide to do something: *I chose not to go.*
  ❏ *VERB* **choos·es, chose, cho·sen, choos·ing.**

Synonym Study

Choose means to decide to take something: *My little brother always chooses the yellow cup.*

Pick[1] means to choose just what you want from many things: *When they chose sides, each captain tried to pick the best players.*

Select means to choose from many things after thinking carefully: *It was time to select which charity the class would raise money for.*

Elect means to choose one person from others by voting: *The fifth grade elects class officers.*

chop (chop),
  1 *VERB.* to cut by hitting with something sharp: *You can chop wood with an ax. Chop down the tree.*
  2 *VERB.* to cut into small pieces: *Mom asked me to chop some walnuts for the brownies.*
    ▪ See the Synonym Study at **cut.**
  3 *NOUN.* a cutting blow or stroke: *He split the log with one chop of his ax.*
  4 *NOUN.* a slice of meat, especially of lamb, veal, or pork that usually contains a piece of rib bone.
  ❏ *VERB* **chops, chopped, chop·ping.**

C

chop·py (chop′ē), ADJECTIVE.
1 jerky: *The speaker made nervous, choppy gestures.*
2 moving in short, irregular, broken waves: *The strong west wind made the water very choppy.*
❑ ADJECTIVE **chop·pi·er, chop·pi·est.**

chop·sticks (chop′stiks′), NOUN PLURAL. a pair of small, thin sticks held in one hand, used to lift food to the mouth. The Chinese, Japanese, and other Asians use chopsticks.

These girls are eating with **chopsticks.**

chord[1] (kôrd), NOUN. a combination of three or more notes of music played at the same time. ∎ Another word that sounds like this is **cord.**

chord[2] (kôrd), NOUN. a straight line that connects two points on a curve. ∎ See the illustration at **circle.** ∎ Another word that sounds like this is **cord.**

chore (chôr), NOUN.
1 a small task or easy job that you have to do regularly: *Feeding the pets is my daily chore.* ∎ See the Synonym Study at **job.**
2 a difficult or disagreeable thing to do: *Painting the house is a real chore.*

chor·tle (chôr′tl),
1 NOUN. a gleeful chuckle or snort.
2 VERB. to chuckle or snort with glee: *He chortled at the joke.* ❑ VERB **chor·tles, chor·tled, chor·tling.**

cho·rus (kôr′əs), NOUN.
1 a group of singers who sing together, such as a choir: *Our school chorus gave a holiday concert.*
2 the repeated part of a song coming after each verse: *We all knew the chorus of the song by heart.*
3 a group of singers and dancers. ❑ PLURAL **cho·rus·es.**

chose (chōz), VERB. the past tense of **choose:** *She chose the red dress.*

cho·sen (chō′zn),
1 VERB. the past participle of **choose:** *Have you chosen a book from the library?*
2 ADJECTIVE. picked out; selected from a group: *Six chosen scouts marched at the front of the parade.*

chow·der (chou′dər), NOUN. a thick soup made of clams or fish with potatoes and vegetables.

Christ (krīst), NOUN. Jesus, the founder of the Christian religion.

chris·ten (kris′n), VERB.
1 to give someone a first name at baptism: *The child was christened Maria.*
2 to give something a name in a special ceremony: *The new ship was christened and then launched.*
❑ VERB **chris·tens, chris·tened, chris·ten·ing.**

Chris·tian (kris′chən),
1 NOUN. someone who believes in Christ and follows His teachings.
2 ADJECTIVE. believing in or belonging to the religion of Christ: *the Christian church, Christian countries.*
3 ADJECTIVE. of or about Christ, His teachings, or His followers: *the Christian faith.*

Chris·ti·an·i·ty (kris′chē an′ə tē), NOUN. the religion based on the teachings of Christ as they appear in the Bible.

Christ·mas (kris′məs), NOUN. the yearly celebration of the birth of Christ; December 25. ❑ PLURAL **Christ·mas·es.**

Christmas tree, a real or artificial evergreen tree hung with decorations for Christmas.

chrome (krōm), NOUN.
1 the shiny, silvery metal parts of a car, bus, boat, and so on.
2 chromium.

chro·mi·um (krō′mē əm), NOUN. a grayish, brittle metal that does not rust easily. Chromium is a chemical element that is usually mixed with other metals. It is used to make a shiny, silvery coating on parts of cars, toasters, and other things.

Did You Know?

Chromium is used to make stainless steel. Stainless steel does not rust easily and is often used to make kitchen utensils and pots and pans.

chro·mo·some (krō′mə sōm), NOUN. one of the very long chains of special chemical compounds within a cell nucleus. Chromosomes contain sections called genes. Genes control the physical characteristics passed on to the offspring of a plant or animal.

chron·ic (kron′ik), ADJECTIVE. lasting a long time because it is difficult to cure: *a chronic disease.*

chron·i·cle (kron′ə kəl), NOUN. a written record of happenings in the order in which they happened; history: *Columbus kept a chronicle of his voyages.*

chron·o·log·i·cal (kron′ə loj′ə kəl), ADJECTIVE. arranged in the order of the time in which things happened: *In telling a story, you usually follow chronological order.*

a	hat	ė	term	ô	order	ch	child	a in about
ā	age	i	it	oi	oil	ng	long	e in taken
ä	far	ī	ice	ou	out	sh	she	ə { i in pencil
â	care	o	hot	u	cup	th	thin	o in lemon
e	let	ō	open	ů	put	ᴛʜ	then	u in circus
ē	equal	ȯ	saw	ü	rule	zh	measure	

chrys·a·lis (kris′ə lis), *NOUN.*
1 a stage in the development of a butterfly from a caterpillar; pupa. The caterpillar becomes a chrysalis when it develops a hard shell around itself. During the time inside the shell, the chrysalis changes into a butterfly.
2 the shell in which this occurs.
❏ *PLURAL* **chrys·a·lis·es.**

chry·san·the·mum (krə san′thə məm), *NOUN.* a round flower with many petals, which blooms in many different colors in the fall.

chrysanthemum

Did You Know?

The **chrysanthemum** has been the symbol of the emperor of Japan since 797 A.D. People in Japan celebrate the Feast of the Chrysanthemums in October.

chub·by (chub′ē), *ADJECTIVE.* round and plump: *chubby cheeks.* ❏ *ADJECTIVE* **chub·bi·er, chub·bi·est.**

chuck·le (chuk′əl),
1 *VERB.* to laugh softly or quietly: *She chuckled to herself.* ■ See the Synonym Study at **laugh.**
2 *NOUN.* a soft laugh; gentle laughter.
❏ *VERB* **chuck·les, chuck·led, chuck·ling.**

chug (chug),
1 *NOUN.* a short, loud burst of sound: *We heard the chug of a steam engine.*
2 *VERB.* to make sounds like this while moving: *The old truck chugged along the road.*
❏ *VERB* **chugs, chugged, chug·ging.**

chum (chum), *NOUN.* (earlier) a very close friend.

chunk (chungk), *NOUN.* a thick piece or lump: *He put another chunk of wood on the campfire.* ■ See the Synonym Study at **piece.**

chunk·y (chung′kē), *ADJECTIVE.* short and thick; chubby: *The child had a chunky build.* ❏ *ADJECTIVE* **chunk·i·er, chunk·i·est.**

church (chėrch), *NOUN.*
1 a building for public Christian worship: *The church was full on Sunday morning.*
2 public worship of God in a church: *Don't be late for church.*
3 **Church,** a group of Christians with the same beliefs and under the same authority: *the Greek Orthodox Church, the Roman Catholic Church.*
❏ *PLURAL* **church·es.**

churn (chėrn),
1 *NOUN.* a container or machine in which butter is made from cream by beating and shaking it.
2 *VERB.* to beat and shake cream in a churn.

3 *VERB.* to move as if beaten and shaken: *The water churns in the rapids.*
❏ *VERB* **churns, churned, churn·ing.**

chute (shüt), *NOUN.* a steep slide or passageway that goes down. There are chutes for carrying mail, soiled clothes, and coal to a lower level.

ci·ca·da (sə kā′də), *NOUN.* a large insect with a wide head and two pairs of thin, transparent wings. The male makes a shrill sound in hot, dry weather.
❏ *PLURAL* **ci·ca·das.**

Word Power   -cide

The combining form **-cide** is used with other words or parts of words to mean "killing" or "killer." An insecti**cide** **kills** insects. Sui**cide** is the act of **killing** yourself.

ci·der (sī′dər), *NOUN.* the juice pressed out of apples, used as a drink and in making vinegar.

ci·gar (si gär′), *NOUN.* a tight roll of tobacco leaves for smoking.

cig·a·rette (sig′ə ret′), *NOUN.* a small tube of finely cut tobacco rolled in a thin sheet of paper for smoking.

ci·lan·tro (si lan′trō), *NOUN.* an herb related to parsley. Its leaves and seeds are used as flavoring.

cil·i·a (sil′ē ə), *NOUN PLURAL.* the very small, hairlike parts growing from certain cells. Cilia in the nose, throat, and lungs remove mucus, dust, and germs with their waving motion. Some microscopic living things use cilia to move around in liquid.
❏ *SINGULAR* **cil·i·um** (sil′ē əm).

cinch (sinch), *NOUN.*
1 a strong strap for fastening a saddle or pack on a horse.
2 (informal) something that is easy to do, or that is sure to happen: *It's a cinch once you learn how.*
❏ *PLURAL* **cinch·es.**

cin·der (sin′dər), *NOUN.*
1 a piece of wood or coal partly burned and no longer flaming.
2 **cinders,** wood or coal partly burned but no longer in flames: *I removed the cinders from the fireplace.*

cin·e·ma (sin′ə mə), *NOUN.*
1 a movie theater.
2 **the cinema,** movies.
❏ *PLURAL* **cin·e·mas.**

cin·na·mon (sin′ə mən), *NOUN.* a spice made from the inner bark of a tropical tree.

cir·cle (sėr′kəl),
1 *NOUN.* a perfectly round line. Every point on a circle is the same distance from the center.

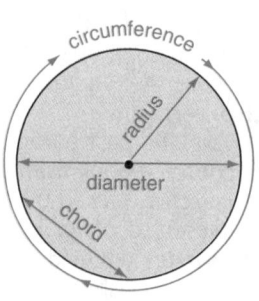
circle

2 *NOUN.* a figure bounded by such a line. *You can draw circles with a compass.*

3 *NOUN.* anything shaped like a circle; ring: *We sat in a circle around the teacher.*

4 *VERB.* to go around in a circle: *The plane circled until the fog lifted and it was able to land.*

5 *VERB.* to form or make a circle around something: *I circled the wrong answer.*

6 *NOUN.* a group of people with the same interests: *She has a large circle of friends.*
❏ *VERB* **cir·cles, cir·cled, cir·cling.**

circle graph. See **pie chart.**

cir·cuit (sėr′kit), *NOUN.*

1 the act of going around: *Earth takes a year to make its circuit of the sun.*

2 the path through which an electric current flows.

circuit breaker, a switch that automatically breaks an electric circuit when the current gets too strong.

cir·cu·lar (sėr′kyə lər),

1 *ADJECTIVE.* round like a circle: *The full moon has a circular shape.*

2 *ADJECTIVE.* moving in a circle: *The hands of a clock follow a circular path.*

3 *NOUN.* a letter, notice, or advertisement sent to each one of a number of people.

cir·cu·late (sėr′kyə lāt), *VERB.*

1 to go around or to send around: *Open windows allowed air to circulate through the building. A memo from the principal was circulated throughout our school.*

2 to flow from the heart through the arteries and veins back to the heart: *Blood circulates all through your body.*
❏ *VERB* **cir·cu·lates, cir·cu·lat·ed, cir·cu·lat·ing.**

cir·cu·la·tion (sėr′kyə lā′shən), *NOUN.*

1 the act or process of going around; the action of circulating: *Open windows increase the circulation of air in a room.*

2 the flow of the blood from the heart through the arteries and veins and back to the heart.

3 the number of copies of a newspaper or magazine that are sent out during a certain time: *That newspaper has a daily circulation of 500,000.*

cir·cu·la·to·ry (sėr′kyə lə tôr′ē), *ADJECTIVE.* of or about circulation. The **circulatory system** of the human body includes the heart and the blood vessels. It moves blood through the body.

cir·cum·fer·ence (sər kum′fər əns), *NOUN.*

1 the round line of a circle. Every point on the circumference of a circle is the same distance from the center.

2 the distance around a circle: *The circumference of the earth at the equator is almost 25,000 miles.*

cir·cum·stance (sėr′kəm stans), *NOUN.* a condition that goes along with some fact or event: *What were the circumstances of the accident?*

cir·cus (sėr′kəs), *NOUN.* a traveling show of acrobats, clowns, horses, riders, and wild animals. ❏ *PLURAL* **cir·cus·es.**

cir·rus cloud (sir′əs kloud′), a cloud formation made up of thin, featherlike white clouds of ice crystals formed very high in the air.

cite (sīt), *VERB.* to quote a passage, book, or author, especially as an authority: *She cited the Constitution to prove her statement.* ❏ *VERB* **cites, cit·ed, cit·ing.** ■ Other words that sound like this are **sight** and **site.**

cit·i·zen (sit′ə zən), *NOUN.*

1 someone who by birth or immigration is a member of a nation. A citizen owes loyalty to that nation and is given certain rights by it: *Many immigrants have become citizens of the United States.*

2 someone who lives in a city or town: *We are all citizens of Los Angeles, and must work together.*

cit·i·zen·ship (sit′ə zən ship), *NOUN.* the duties, rights, and privileges of a citizen.

cit·rus (sit′rəs), *ADJECTIVE.* of or about a group of trees that grow in warm climates and produce fruit that is high in vitamin C. Lemons, oranges, and grapefruit are **citrus fruits.**

cit·y (sit′ē), *NOUN.* a large, important center of population and business activity. New York, Buenos Aires, London, Cairo, and Shanghai are major cities of the world. ❏ *PLURAL* **cit·ies.**

civ·ic (siv′ik), *ADJECTIVE.*

1 of or about a city: *She is interested in civic affairs and will be a candidate for mayor.*

2 of or about citizens or citizenship. A person's civic duties include such things as obeying the laws, voting, and paying taxes.

civ·ics (siv′iks), *NOUN.* the study of the duties, rights, and privileges of citizens.

civ·il (siv′əl), *ADJECTIVE.*

1 of the government, state, or nation: *Police departments are civil institutions to protect citizens.*

2 polite; courteous: *It was hard for me to give a civil answer to their rude question.*

ci·vil·ian (sə vil′yən),

1 *NOUN.* someone who is not a member of any of the armed forces or police.

2 *ADJECTIVE.* of or for civilians; not military or naval: *Soldiers on leave usually wear civilian clothes.*

civ·i·li·za·tion (siv′ə lə zā′shən), *NOUN.*

1 an advanced way of life that usually includes towns, written forms of language, and special kinds of work for people.

a	hat	ė	term	ô	order	ch	child		
ā	age	i	it	oi	oil	ng	long		a in about
ä	far	ī	ice	ou	out	sh	she		e in taken
â	care	o	hot	u	cup	th	thin	ə	i in pencil
e	let	ō	open	ů	put	₮H	then		o in lemon
ē	equal	ȯ	saw	ü	rule	zh	measure		u in circus

2 the ways of living of a people or nation: *There are differences between Chinese civilization and that of the United States.*

civ·i·lize (siv′ə līz), VERB. to change from a primitive way of life to a life of civilization. □ VERB **civ·i·liz·es, civ·i·lized, civ·i·liz·ing.**

civ·i·lized (siv′ə līzd), ADJECTIVE.
1 living in a state of civilization: *The ancient Greeks were a civilized people.*
2 showing culture and good manners; refined: *civilized behavior, a civilized attitude.*

civil rights, the rights of every citizen of the United States, of whatever race, color, religion, or sex.

civil service, the branch of government service concerned with affairs other than military, naval, legislative, or judicial. Forest rangers and postal service employees belong to the civil service.

civil war,
1 a war between opposing groups in one nation.
2 Civil War, the war between the northern and southern states of the United States from 1861 to 1865.

a battle of the **Civil War**

clack (klak),
1 VERB. to make a short, sharp sound: *The train clacked over the rails.*
2 NOUN. a short, sharp sound: *We could hear the clack of her bracelets as she walked along.*
□ VERB **clacks, clacked, clack·ing.**

clad (klad), ADJECTIVE. covered in; clothed: *In summer, the woods are clad in green.*

claim (klām),
1 VERB. to demand something as your own or your right: *The settlers claimed the land as theirs.*
2 NOUN. a demand for something as your own or your right: *Both drivers filed insurance claims for repairs.*
3 NOUN. a right or title to something: *a legal claim.*
4 NOUN. a piece of land which someone claims: *The miner worked his claim, but found little gold.*
5 VERB. to say that something is a fact: *She claimed that her answer was correct.*
6 NOUN. a declaration that something is true: *Careful*

study showed that the claims that the vaccine would prevent polio were correct.
□ VERB **claims, claimed, claim·ing.**

clam (klam),
1 NOUN. a shellfish with a soft body and a shell in two hinged halves. Clams burrow in sand along the seashore, or at the edges of rivers and lakes. Many kinds are good to eat.
2 VERB. to go out after clams; dig for clams.
□ VERB **clams, clammed, clam·ming.**

This giant **clam** grows up to 4 feet long.

clam·ber (klam′bər), VERB. to climb something, using your hands and feet; scramble: *We clambered up the cliff.* □ VERB **clam·bers, clam·bered, clam·ber·ing.**

clam·my (klam′ē), ADJECTIVE. cold, damp, and sticky: *The walls of the cellar were clammy.* ■ See the Synonym Study at **damp.** □ ADJECTIVE **clam·mi·er, clam·mi·est. –clam′mi·ness,** NOUN.

clam·or (klam′ər),
1 NOUN. a loud noise, especially of voices; continuous noise: *the clamor of the crowd.*
2 VERB. to make a loud or continuous noise.
□ VERB **clam·ors, clam·ored, clam·or·ing.**

clamp (klamp),
1 NOUN. a device for holding things tightly together: *I used a clamp to hold the arm on the chair until the glue dried.*
2 VERB. to fasten the parts of something together with a clamp; strengthen with clamps: *The wood is clamped together while the glue is drying.*
□ VERB **clamps, clamped, clamp·ing.**

clan (klan), NOUN. a group of related families that claim they descended from a common ancestor.

clang (klang),
1 NOUN. a loud, harsh, ringing sound like metal being hit: *The clang of the fire bell woke us.*
2 VERB. to make or cause to make a loud, harsh, ringing sound: *The fire bell clanged.*
□ VERB **clangs, clanged, clang·ing.**

clank (klangk),
1 NOUN. a sharp, harsh sound like the rattle of a heavy chain: *the clank of heavy machinery.*
2 VERB. to make or cause to make a sharp, harsh sound: *The steel door clanked shut.*
□ VERB **clanks, clanked, clank·ing.**

clap (klap),
1 VERB. to strike together loudly: *The teacher clapped his hands to get us to pay attention.*
2 VERB. to applaud by striking your hands together: *When the show was over, we all clapped.*

3 NOUN. a sudden noise, such as a single burst of thunder, the sound of the hands struck together, or the sound of a loud slap.

4 VERB. to slap lightly, but without anger: *My friend clapped me on the back.*

5 NOUN. a light slap, not given in anger: *I gave my friend a clap on the shoulder.*
❏ VERB **claps, clapped, clap·ping.**

clap·per (klap′ər), NOUN. the movable part inside a bell that strikes the outer part of the bell and makes it ring.

clar·i·fy (klar′ə fī), VERB. to make something clearer; explain: *The teacher's explanation clarified the difficult instructions.* ❏ VERB **clar·i·fies, clar·i·fied, clar·i·fy·ing.** –**clar′i·fi·ca′tion,** NOUN.

clar·i·net (klar′ə net′), NOUN. a wooden or plastic wind instrument played with keys and holes for the fingers and a reed mouthpiece.

clar·i·ty (klar′ə tē), NOUN. clearness: *He expresses his ideas with great clarity.*

clash (klash),
1 VERB. to disagree strongly; come into conflict: *The children clashed over whose turn it was.*
2 NOUN. a strong disagreement; conflict: *a clash of wills.*
3 VERB. to not go well together: *That red sweater clashes with your green skirt.*
4 NOUN. a loud, harsh sound like that of two things running into each other or of striking metal: *As the band approached, we heard the clash of cymbals.*
❏ VERB **clash·es, clashed, clash·ing;** PLURAL **clash·es.**

clasp (klasp),
1 NOUN. something to fasten two parts or pieces together. A buckle on a belt is one kind of clasp.
2 VERB. to fasten something together with a clasp.
3 VERB. to hold something or someone closely with the arms; embrace: *She clasped the kitten tenderly.*
4 VERB. to grip something firmly with the hand; grasp: *I clasped the railing as I climbed the stairs.*
❏ VERB **clasps, clasped, clasp·ing.**

class (klas),
1 NOUN. a group of pupils taught together: *My class meets in room 202.*
2 NOUN. a meeting of such a group: *She was sick and missed a great many classes.*
3 NOUN. all pupils entering a school together and graduating in the same year: *the class of 2007.*
4 NOUN. a group of people or things alike in some way; kind; sort: *Pet owners make up a large class of people in this country.*
5 NOUN. a rank of society: *the upper class, the middle class, the lower class.*
6 VERB. to put people or things in a class; classify: *She is classed among the best swimmers in school.*
7 NOUN. grade or quality: *The travel guide describes hotels of various classes.*
❏ PLURAL **class·es;** VERB **class·es, classed, class·ing.**

clas·sic (klas′ik),
1 NOUN. a book or painting of the highest quality: *"Alice in Wonderland" is a classic.*
2 ADJECTIVE. of the highest quality; excellent: *"Sleeping Beauty" is a classic children's story.*
3 NOUN. a very fine author or artist: *Dickens is a classic.*
4 NOUN. **the classics,** the literature of ancient Greece and Rome.

clas·si·cal (klas′ə kəl), ADJECTIVE.
1 of or about the literature, art, and life of ancient Greece and Rome: *Classical languages include ancient Greek and the Latin of the ancient Romans.*
2 of high musical quality. Symphonies, concertos, and operas are considered classical music.

clas·si·fi·ca·tion (klas′ə fə kā′shən), NOUN. the arrangement of things into classes or groups: *The classification of books in a library helps you to find the books you want.*

clas·si·fy (klas′ə fī), VERB. to arrange things into groups or classes: *In the post office, mail is classified according to the places where it is to go.*
❏ VERB **clas·si·fies, clas·si·fied, clas·si·fy·ing.**

class·mate (klas′māt′), NOUN. a member of the same class in school.

class·room (klas′rüm′), NOUN. a room in which classes are held; schoolroom.

clat·ter (klat′ər),
1 NOUN. a loud, rattling noise like that of many plates being struck together: *The clatter in the school cafeteria made it hard to hear him talk.*
■ See the Synonym Study at **noise.**
2 VERB. to move or fall with a loud, rattling noise: *The horse's hoofs clattered over the stones.*
❏ VERB **clat·ters, clat·tered, clat·ter·ing.**

clause (klȯz), NOUN. a part of a sentence having a subject and a verb. In the sentence "They came before we left," both "They came" and "before we left" are clauses.

claw (klȯ),
1 NOUN. a sharp, hooked nail on the foot of a bird or animal.
2 NOUN. the pincers of a lobster, crab, crayfish, and the like.

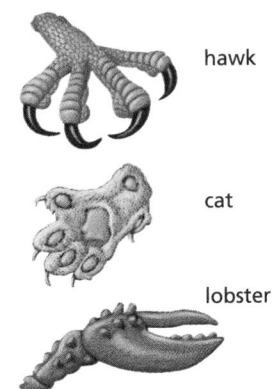

hawk

cat

lobster

claw (definitions 1 and 2)

a	hat	ė	term	ô	order	ch	child	⎧a in about
ā	age	i	it	oi	oil	ng	long	⎪e in taken
ä	far	ī	ice	ou	out	sh	she	ə⎨i in pencil
â	care	o	hot	u	cup	th	thin	⎪o in lemon
e	let	ō	open	ů	put	ŦH	then	⎩u in circus
ē	equal	ȯ	saw	ü	rule	zh	measure	

3 *VERB.* to scratch, tear, seize, or pull something with the claws or the hands: *The kitten was clawing the screen door.*

❑ *VERB* **claws, clawed, claw·ing.**

clay (klā), *NOUN.* a sticky kind of earth that can be easily shaped when wet and hardens when it is dried or baked. Bricks and dishes are made from various kinds of clay.

clean (klēn),

1 *ADJECTIVE.* free from dirt or filth; not soiled or stained: *He wore clean clothes.*

2 *ADJECTIVE.* having clean habits: *Cats are clean animals.*

3 *VERB.* to make something free from dirt or filth: *I'm going to clean the house today.*

4 *ADVERB.* by the rules; in a fair way: *Both teams played the game clean, in spite of their fierce rivalry.*

5 *ADVERB.* completely: *The horse jumped clean over the brook.*

❑ *VERB* **cleans, cleaned, clean·ing. —clean′ness,** *NOUN.*

come clean, *IDIOM.* to tell the truth about something: *We came clean and admitted that we were responsible for the mess.*

clean·er (klē′nər), *NOUN.*

1 someone whose work is keeping buildings, windows, or other objects clean.

2 anything that removes dirt, grease, or stains: *We use a special cleaner on the rug.*

clean·li·ness (klen′lē nis), *NOUN.* the condition of being clean.

clean·ly (klēn′lē), *ADVERB.* in a clean or precise manner: *The butcher's knife cut cleanly through the meat.*

cleanse (klenz), *VERB.* to make clean: *The doctor cleansed the wound before bandaging it.* ❑ *VERB* **cleans·es, cleansed, cleans·ing.**

cleans·er (klen′zər), *NOUN.* a substance for cleaning, especially a powder for scrubbing: *Use cleanser on the bathtub.*

clear (klir),

1 *ADJECTIVE.* bright; not cloudy, misty, or hazy; light: *A clear sky is free of clouds.*

2 *VERB.* to become clear: *It rained and then it cleared.*

3 *ADJECTIVE.* easy to see through; transparent: *I looked through the clear glass.*

4 *ADJECTIVE.* easily heard, seen, or understood; plain: *The witness gave a clear account of the accident. It is clear that it is going to rain.*

5 *ADJECTIVE.* open; not blocked: *When the snowplows come, the road will soon be clear.*

6 *VERB.* to remove something to make a space clear: *After dinner, we cleared the table. We cleared out the attic and turned it into a playroom.*

7 *VERB.* to pass by or over something without touching it: *The horse cleared the fence.*

8 *ADJECTIVE.* free from blame or guilt; innocent: *The man did nothing wrong and had a clear conscience.*

9 *ADVERB.* in a clear manner; completely; entirely: *We could see clear to the bottom of the lake.*

❑ *VERB* **clears, cleared, clear·ing. —clear′ly,** *ADVERB.* **—clear′ness,** *NOUN.*

steer clear, *IDIOM.* to avoid someone or something: *I get scared easily, so I steer clear of horror movies. Steer clear of her when she's in a bad mood.*

Have You Heard?

Clear as a bell, clear as day, and **clear as crystal** all mean that something is easy to understand. However, if something is not easy to understand, you can also use a phrase with the word *clear*—**clear as mud.**

clear·ance (klir′əns), *NOUN.*

1 permission for a vehicle to do something: *The pilot circled the airfield, waiting for clearance to land.*

2 a clear space: *There was only a foot of clearance between the top of the truck and the tunnel roof.*

clear·ing (klir′ing), *NOUN.* an open space of cleared land in a forest.

cleat (klēt), *NOUN.* a piece of metal, wood, stiff leather, or plastic that sticks out from the sole or heel of a shoe to keep you from slipping.

cleav·er (klē′vər), *NOUN.* a tool with a heavy blade and a short handle, used for cutting through meat or bone.

clef (klef), *NOUN.* a sign in music that shows the pitch of the notes on a staff. The **treble clef** shows that the notes on the staff are all above middle C. The **bass clef** shows that the notes on the staff are below middle C.

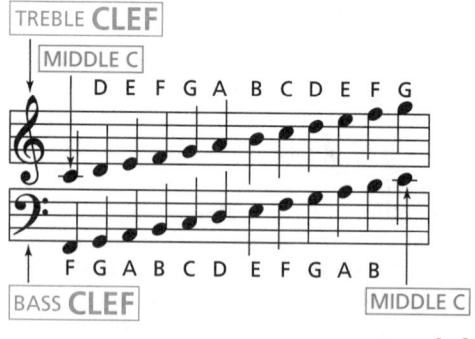

clef

cleft (kleft),

1 *ADJECTIVE.* split; divided: *a cleft stick.*

2 *NOUN.* a space or opening made by splitting; crack: *a cleft in the rocks.*

clem·en·tine (klem′ən tīn), *NOUN.* a sweet, round, orange citrus fruit about as big as an egg. Clementines are a cross between a tangerine and an orange.

clench (klench), VERB.
1 to close tightly together: *She clenched her teeth and refused to take the medicine.*
2 to grasp something firmly: *I clenched the bat.*
❏ VERB **clench·es, clenched, clench·ing.**

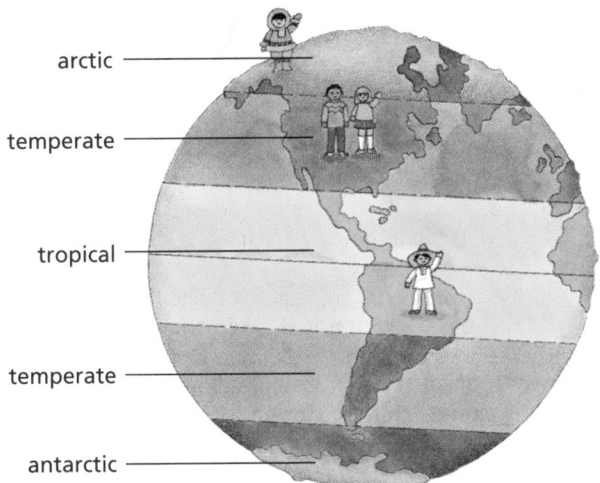

arctic
temperate
tropical
temperate
antarctic

climate (definition 2)

cler·gy (klėr′jē), NOUN PLURAL. people trained to do religious work, such as ministers, priests, mullahs, and rabbis.

cler·gy·man (klėr′jē mən), NOUN. a member of the clergy; a minister, priest, mullah, or rabbi. ❏ PLURAL **cler·gy·men.**

cler·gy·wom·an (klėr′jē wům ən), NOUN. a woman member of the clergy. ❏ PLURAL **cler·gy·wom·en.**

cler·i·cal (kler′ə kəl), ADJECTIVE.
1 of or for a clerk or clerks: *Keeping records and typing letters are clerical jobs in an office.*
2 of the clergy: *clerical robes, clerical duties.*

clerk (klėrk), NOUN.
1 someone hired to sell goods in a store; salesperson.
2 someone hired in an office to file records or keep accounts.

clev·er (klev′ər), ADJECTIVE.
1 bright; intelligent; having a quick mind: *She is the cleverest person in our class.* ■ See the Synonym Study at **smart.**
2 showing skill or intelligence: *a clever trick.*
−clev′er·ly, ADVERB. **−clev′er·ness,** NOUN.

click (klik),
1 NOUN. a short, sharp sound like a key turning in a lock: *I heard a click as the dime went in the slot.*
2 VERB. to make such a sound: *The key clicked in the lock.*
3 VERB. to press and release a button on a computer mouse, in order to give an instruction to the computer.
❏ VERB **clicks, clicked, click·ing.**

cli·ent (klī′ənt), NOUN.
1 someone who uses and pays for the services or advice of a lawyer, accountant, or other person.
2 a customer.

cliff (klif), NOUN. a very steep, rocky slope.

cli·mate (klī′mit), NOUN.
1 the kind of weather a place has. Climate includes conditions of temperature, rainfall, wind, and so on.
2 a region with a certain climate: *We went to a warmer climate on our winter vacation.*

cli·max (klī′maks), NOUN. the most exciting part of a story or an experience: *A visit to the Grand Canyon was the climax of our trip.* ❏ PLURAL **cli·max·es.**

climb (klīm),
1 VERB. to go up, especially by using your hands or feet, or both: *She climbed the stairs quickly.*
2 VERB. to go in any direction, especially with the help of the hands: *We climbed over the fence.*
3 VERB. to grow upward. A vine climbs by twining about a support of some kind.
4 NOUN. the action of going up: *Our climb up the mountain took ten hours.*
5 VERB. to move upward; rise: *The price of gasoline climbed last year.*
6 NOUN. a place to be climbed: *The path ended in a difficult climb.*
❏ VERB **climbs, climbed, climb·ing. −climb′er,** NOUN.

Synonym Study

Climb means to go up, mainly by using hands and feet: *Dad will climb a ladder to take down the window screen.*

Ascend means to go up or move up to the top of something: *We ascended the mountain.*

Mount[1] can mean to get up on something: *The cowboy mounted the horse and galloped off.*

Scale[3] can mean to climb up something. It suggests great effort: *The explorers scaled the high cliff and found a hidden lake below.*

See also the Synonym Study at **rise.**

clinch (klinch), VERB. to settle something definitely: *A deposit of five dollars clinched the bargain.*
❏ VERB **clinch·es, clinched, clinch·ing.**

cling (kling), VERB.
1 to hold on tightly to someone: *He clung to his grandfather's hand.*
2 to stick or hold fast to something: *A vine clings to its support. Wet clothes cling to the body.*
❏ VERB **clings, clung, cling·ing.**

a	hat	ė	term	ô	order	ch	child		a in about
ā	age	i	it	oi	oil	ng	long		e in taken
ä	far	ī	ice	ou	out	sh	she	ə<	i in pencil
â	care	o	hot	u	cup	th	thin		o in lemon
e	let	ō	open	ů	put	ᴛʜ	then		u in circus
ē	equal	ȯ	saw	ü	rule	zh	measure		

clin·ic (klin′ik), NOUN. a place where people can receive special medical treatment, such as surgery, dental care, and so on. A clinic is often connected with a hospital or medical school.

clink (klingk),
1 NOUN. a light, sharp, ringing sound, like that of glasses hitting together.
2 VERB. to make a sound like this: *The spoon clinked in the glass.*
❑ VERB **clinks, clinked, clink·ing.**

clip¹ (klip),
1 VERB. to cut; cut short; trim with scissors or clippers: *The barber clipped my bangs too short.*
2 VERB. to cut something out of a newspaper or magazine: *She clipped the cartoon for me.*
■ See the Synonym Study at **cut.**
3 NOUN. a fast pace or speed: *The bus passed at quite a clip.*
❑ VERB **clips, clipped, clip·ping.**

clip² (klip),
1 VERB. to hold things tight; fasten: *I clipped the papers together.*
2 NOUN. something used for clipping things together: *a hair clip, a paper clip.*
❑ VERB **clips, clipped, clip·ping.**

clip·per (klip′ər), NOUN.
1 a tool for cutting: *hair clippers, a nail clipper.*
2 a fast sailing ship: *American clippers used to sail all over the world.*

clip·ping (klip′ing), NOUN. a piece cut out of a newspaper or magazine.

cloak (klōk),
1 NOUN. a long, loose piece of clothing for outdoor wear, usually without sleeves.
2 NOUN. anything that covers or hides something: *They hid their dislike behind a cloak of friendship.*
3 VERB. to cover something up: *I cloaked my fear by pretending to be unafraid.*
❑ VERB **cloaks, cloaked, cloak·ing.**

clob·ber (klob′ər), VERB. to hit something hard or beat it severely: *A falling branch clobbered me.*
❑ VERB **clob·bers, clob·bered, clob·ber·ing.**

clock (klok),
1 NOUN. a device for measuring and showing time.
2 VERB. to measure or record the time or speed of; time: *I clocked the runners with a stopwatch.*
❑ VERB **clocks, clocked, clock·ing.**
around the clock, IDIOM. every minute of the day; continuously: *They worked around the clock to repair the damage.*

Word Story

Clock comes from a Latin word meaning "bell." The first mechanical clocks were invented in the Middle Ages and had only bells to mark the hours, no numbers or hands.

clock·wise (klok′wīz′), ADVERB or ADJECTIVE. in the direction in which the hands of a clock move; around from left to right: *Turn the key clockwise to unlock the door.*

clockwise

clog (klog),
1 VERB. to block: *Hair and grease clogged the drain. An accident clogged traffic.*
2 NOUN. a shoe with a thick, wooden sole.
❑ VERB **clogs, clogged, clog·ging.**

clone (klōn),
1 NOUN. a living thing that grows from a very small amount of bodily material taken from one parent. A clone and its parent are always exactly alike.
2 VERB. to produce from a single parent.
❑ VERB **clones, cloned, clon·ing.**

close¹ (klōz),
1 VERB. to shut: *Close the door. Close your eyes.*
2 VERB. to come or bring to an end: *The meeting closed with a speech by the president.* ■ See the Synonym Study at **end.**
3 VERB. to not be open for business any longer: *The bank closes at 2:30 on Wednesdays.*
4 NOUN. an end: *She spoke at the close of the meeting.*
❑ VERB **clos·es, closed, clos·ing.** ■ Another word that sounds like this is **clothes.**

close² (klōs),
1 ADJECTIVE. with little space between; near together; near: *The two parks are very close.*
2 ADJECTIVE. known or loved very well: *a close friend.*
3 ADJECTIVE. careful; strict: *Pay close attention.*
4 ADJECTIVE. nearly equal: *a close contest.*
5 ADVERB. near: *The two farms lie close together.*
❑ ADJECTIVE **clos·er, clos·est. —close′ly,** ADVERB. **—close′ness,** NOUN.

clos·et (kloz′it), NOUN. a small room used for storing clothes or household supplies.

close-up (klōs′up′), NOUN. a picture taken with a camera at close range: *We took a close-up of the monument so that the names would show.*

clot (klot),
1 NOUN. a moist, half-solid lump: *a blood clot.*
2 VERB. to form into clots: *Blood clots when it is exposed to the air.*
❑ VERB **clots, clot·ted, clot·ting.**

cloth (klòth), NOUN.
1 a woven or knitted material made from wool, cotton, silk, rayon, or other fiber.
2 a piece of cloth used for a special purpose: *I bought a new cloth for the kitchen table.*
❑ PLURAL **cloths** (klòᴛнz or klòths).

clothe (klōтн), *VERB.*
1 to put clothes on; cover with clothes; dress: *I clothed the child warmly in a heavy sweater and pants.*
2 to provide with clothes: *feed and clothe your family.*
❑ *VERB* **clothes, clothed** or **cloth·ing.**

clothes (klōz), *NOUN PLURAL.* coverings for the body: *I bought a jacket, jeans, and other clothes.*
■ Another word that sounds like this is **close¹.**

clothes·pin (klōz′pin′), *NOUN.* a wooden or plastic clip to hold clothes that are drying on a line.

cloth·ing (klō′тнing), *NOUN.* coverings for the body: *This store sells men's clothing.*

cloud (kloud),
1 *NOUN.* a white or gray mass floating high in the sky. Clouds are made up of tiny drops of water or ice crystals.
2 *NOUN.* a mass of smoke or dust in the air.
3 *VERB.* to cover with a cloud or as if with a cloud: *Mist clouded our view.*
4 *VERB.* to grow cloudy: *My eyes clouded with tears.*
❑ *VERB* **clouds, cloud·ed, cloud·ing. –cloud′less,** *ADJECTIVE.* **–cloud′like′,** *ADJECTIVE.*

stratus

cumulus

cumulonimbus

cirrus

clouds

cloud·burst (kloud′bėrst′), *NOUN.* a sudden, heavy rain.

cloud·y (klou′dē), *ADJECTIVE.*
1 covered with clouds; having clouds in it: *I took an umbrella because the sky was cloudy.*
2 not clear: *The stream is cloudy with mud.*
❑ *ADJECTIVE* **cloud·i·er, cloud·i·est.**

clove¹ (klōv), *NOUN.* usually, **cloves,** the strong, fragrant, dried flower bud of a tropical tree, used as a spice.

clove² (klōv), *NOUN.* a small, separate section of a plant bulb such as garlic.

clo·ver (klō′vər), *NOUN.* a plant that has small, fragrant flowers in round bunches and three leaves at the end of its stems. Clover attracts bees with its nectar, provides food for cattle, and enriches the soil with nitrogen from its roots. **Four-leaf clovers** are rare and considered a sign of good luck.

clown (kloun),
1 *NOUN.* a performer who makes people laugh by wearing funny costumes and makeup and by playing tricks and jokes: *The clowns in the circus were very funny.*
2 *VERB.* to act like a clown; play tricks and jokes; act silly: *Quit clowning and be serious.*
3 *NOUN.* someone who acts like a clown; silly person: *He is the class clown.*
❑ *VERB* **clowns, clowned, clown·ing.**

club (klub),
1 *NOUN.* a heavy stick of wood, thicker at one end, used as a weapon.
2 *NOUN.* a wooden or metal stick with a long handle, used in some games to hit a ball: *golf clubs.*
3 *VERB.* to beat or hit with a club or something similar.
4 *NOUN.* a group of people joined together for some special purpose: *My parents belong to a tennis club.*
5 *NOUN.* a figure shaped like this: ♣
6 *NOUN.* a playing card with one or more figures shaped like this.
❑ *VERB* **clubs, clubbed, club·bing.**

club·house (klub′hous′), *NOUN.*
1 a building used by a club.
2 a shack, room, or other place used by children for meetings and play: *The children built a clubhouse.*
❑ *PLURAL* **club·hous·es** (klub′hou′ziz).

cluck (kluk),
1 *NOUN.* the sound that a hen makes when calling to her chicks, looking for food, and so on.
2 *VERB.* to make this sound.
❑ *VERB* **clucks, clucked, cluck·ing.**

clue (klü), *NOUN.* something which helps to solve a mystery or problem: *The police could find no fingerprints or other clues to help them find the thief.* ❑ *PLURAL* **clues. –clue′less,** *ADJECTIVE.*

clump (klump),
1 *NOUN.* a number of things of the same kind growing or grouped together; cluster: *a clump of trees.*
2 *NOUN.* a lump or mass: *a clump of earth.*
3 *VERB.* to walk in a heavy, clumsy, noisy manner: *The hiker clumped along in heavy boots.*
❑ *VERB* **clumps, clumped, clump·ing.**

a hat	ė term	ô order	ch child	
ā age	i it	oi oil	ng long	a in about
ä far	ī ice	ou out	sh she	e in taken
â care	o hot	u cup	th thin	ə ⟨ i in pencil
e let	ō open	ù put	тн then	o in lemon
ē equal	ò saw	ü rule	zh measure	u in circus

clum·sy (klum′zē), ADJECTIVE. awkward in moving: *The cast on my broken leg made me clumsy.*
❑ ADJECTIVE **clum·si·er, clum·si·est.** –**clum′si·ly,** ADVERB. –**clum′si·ness,** NOUN.

clung (klung), VERB.
1 the past tense of **cling**: *The child clung to his sister.*
2 the past participle of **cling**: *Mud had clung to my boots.*

clus·ter (klus′tər),
1 NOUN. a number of things of the same kind, growing or grouped together: *a little cluster of houses in the valley.*
2 VERB. to form into a cluster; gather in a group: *The children clustered around their teacher.*
❑ VERB **clus·ters, clus·tered, clus·ter·ing.**

The children **cluster** around their teacher.

clutch (kluch),
1 VERB. to grasp something tightly: *I clutched the railing to keep from falling.*
2 VERB. to snatch; seize eagerly: *I clutched at the rail.*
3 NOUN. a device for connecting or disconnecting the engine and the gears in a motor vehicle.
❑ VERB **clutch·es, clutched, clutch·ing;** PLURAL **clutch·es.**

clut·ter (klut′ər),
1 NOUN. many things lying around in disorder; litter: *It was hard to find the lost pen in the clutter.*
2 VERB. to litter with things: *Her desk was cluttered with papers and books.*
❑ VERB **clut·ters, clut·tered, clut·ter·ing.**

cm or **cm.,** an abbreviation of **centimeter** or **centimeters.**

Word Power   co-

The prefix **co-** means "with" or "together." A **co**pilot is someone who pilots **with** you. **Co**operation is working **together.**

CO, an abbreviation of **Colorado.**

coach (kōch),
1 NOUN. someone who teaches or trains an athlete, a performer, or athletic teams: *He is my tennis coach.*
2 VERB. to train or teach someone: *She coaches runners.*
3 NOUN. a railroad car with seats for passengers.
4 NOUN. a kind of passenger seating and service on an airplane that is cheaper than traveling first-class.
5 NOUN. (earlier) a large, usually closed carriage with seats inside and often on top. In former times, most coaches carried passengers along a regular run, stopping for meals and fresh horses.
❑ PLURAL **coach·es;** VERB **coach·es, coached, coach·ing.**

co·ag·u·late (kō ag′yə lāt), VERB. to change from a liquid to a thickened mass; thicken: *Blood coagulates when it is exposed to the air.* ❑ VERB **co·ag·u·lates, co·ag·u·lat·ed, co·ag·u·lat·ing.**

Coa·hui·la (kwä wē′lä), NOUN. a state in northern Mexico.

coal (kōl), NOUN.
1 a black mineral that is mostly carbon. Coal is formed from partly decayed plants under great pressure for millions of years in the earth. It is burned as fuel.
2 a piece of burning wood or coal: *The big log had burned down to a few glowing coals.*

coarse (kôrs), ADJECTIVE.
1 made up of fairly large parts; not fine: *coarse sand.*
2 rough: *Burlap is a coarse cloth.*
❑ ADJECTIVE **coars·er, coars·est.** ■ Another word that sounds like this is **course.** –**coarse′ly,** ADVERB. –**coarse′ness,** NOUN.

coast (kōst),
1 NOUN. the land along the sea; seashore: *Many ships were wrecked on that rocky coast.*
2 VERB. to slide down a hill or ride without using effort or power: *You can coast downhill on a sled.*
❑ VERB **coasts, coast·ed, coast·ing.**

coast·al (kō′stl), ADJECTIVE. at or along a coast: *Coastal waters are often dangerous for ships.*

coast·er (kō′stər), NOUN. a small tray or mat placed under a glass or bottle: *Use a coaster when you put down your drink so you don't hurt the table.*

Coast Guard, the branch of the armed forces of the United States that protects lives and property and combats smuggling along our coasts.

coat (kōt),
1 NOUN. a piece of outer clothing with long sleeves: *It is cold enough today for your winter coat.*
2 NOUN. any outer covering: *a dog's coat of hair.*
3 NOUN. a thin layer: *a coat of paint.*
4 VERB. to cover something with a thin layer of a substance: *The floor is coated with varnish. The shelves were coated with dust.*
❑ VERB **coats, coat·ed, coat·ing.**

coat·ing (kō′ting), NOUN. a layer of any substance spread over a surface: *a coating of dust on the shelf.*

coat of arms, a design or pattern, usually on a shield, that in former times was a symbol for a knight or lord. Some families, schools, and other groups now have coats of arms. ❑ PLURAL **coats of arms.**

coax (kōks), VERB. to talk someone into doing something by using gentle words and kindness: *She coaxed me into letting her use my bike.* ❑ VERB **coax·es, coaxed, coax·ing.**

cob (kob), NOUN. See **corncob.**

co·balt (kō′bȯlt), NOUN. a silver-white metal chemical element used in making steel and paint.

cob·bler¹ (kob′lər), *NOUN.* someone whose work is mending or making shoes.

cob·bler² (kob′lər), *NOUN.* a fruit pie baked in a deep dish, usually with a crust only on the top.

cob·ble·stone (kob′əl stōn′), *NOUN.* a rounded stone formerly used to pave streets.

co·bra (kō′brə), *NOUN.* any of several very poisonous snakes of Asia and Africa. When excited, a cobra flattens its neck so that its head seems to have a hood. ❑ *PLURAL* **co·bras.**

cob·web (kob′web′), *NOUN.* a spider's web, or the stuff it is made of.

co·caine (kō kān′ or kō′kān), *NOUN.* a drug formerly used to deaden pain, now used as a stimulant. It can cause addiction.

cobra — between 6 and 18 feet long

cock¹ (kok),
1 *NOUN.* a male bird, especially a rooster.
2 *VERB.* to pull back the hammer of a gun so that it is ready to fire: *The sheriff cocked his revolver.* ❑ *VERB* **cocks, cocked, cock·ing.**

cock² (kok), *VERB.* to stick up, or tilt to one side: *The puppy cocked its ears at the strange sound.* ❑ *VERB* **cocks, cocked, cock·ing.**

cock·a·too (kok′ə tü), *NOUN.* any of several large parrots of Australia and nearby areas, with a crest that it can raise and lower. ❑ *PLURAL* **cock·a·toos.**

cock·pit (kok′pit′), *NOUN.* the place where the pilot sits in an airplane or spacecraft.

cock·roach (kok′rōch′), *NOUN.* a small, brownish or yellowish insect often found in kitchens and around water pipes. Cockroaches usually feed at night. ❑ *PLURAL* **cock·roach·es.**

cockatoo — about 16 inches long

cock·y (kok′ē), *ADJECTIVE.* too sure of yourself; conceited: *He was a cocky fellow who thought he knew everything.* ❑ *ADJECTIVE* **cock·i·er, cock·i·est.**

co·coa (kō′kō), *NOUN.*
1 a powder made by roasting and grinding the seeds of the cacao tree and removing some of the fat.
2 a drink made from this powder with sugar and milk or water.

co·co·nut (kō′kə nut′), *NOUN.* a large, round fruit with a hard shell. Coconuts grow on a tree called the **coconut palm.** Coconuts contain a white liquid called **coconut milk.** Its sweet, white, tough meat is shredded for use in desserts.

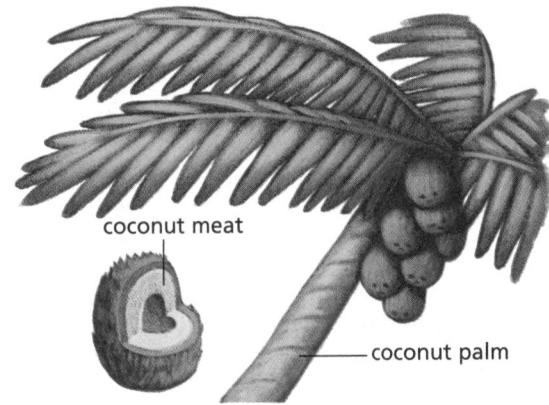
coconut meat
coconut palm
coconut

co·coon (kə kün′), *NOUN.* the silky case spun by caterpillars to live in while they are turning into adult insects. **–co·coon′like′,** *ADJECTIVE.*

cod (kod), *NOUN.* an important food fish found in the cold parts of northern oceans; codfish. ❑ *PLURAL* **cod** or **cods.**

code (kōd),
1 *NOUN.* a system of secret writing; an arrangement of words or figures to keep a message short or secret: *The army tried to figure out the code that the enemy used to write messages.*
2 *VERB.* to change into a code: *The spy coded a message to headquarters.*
3 *NOUN.* a collection of laws or rules: *The building code requires the inspection of electrical wiring. Running in the halls is against the school code.*
4 *NOUN.* a system of signals for sending messages. Flags or blinking lights are used to send messages between ships.
5 *NOUN.* any set of signals or symbols used with computers or other machines.
❑ *VERB* **codes, cod·ed, cod·ing. –cod′er,** *NOUN.*

cod·fish (kod′fish′), *NOUN.* See **cod.** ❑ *PLURAL* **cod·fish** or **cod·fish·es.**

cof·fee (kô′fē), *NOUN.* a dark brown drink made from the seeds of the coffee plant. These seeds, called **coffee beans,** are roasted and ground to make coffee.

cof·fin (kô′fən), *NOUN.* a box into which a dead person is put to be buried.

a	hat	ė	term	ô	order	ch	child	⎧a in about
ā	age	i	it	oi	oil	ng	long	⎪e in taken
ä	far	ī	ice	ou	out	sh	she	ə⎨i in pencil
â	care	o	hot	u	cup	th	thin	⎪o in lemon
e	let	ō	open	ù	put	ŦH	then	⎩u in circus
ē	equal	ò	saw	ü	rule	zh	measure	

cog (kog), NOUN. one of a series of teeth on the edge of a gear. —**cog′like′**, ADJECTIVE.

coil (koil),
1 VERB. to wind around and around, forming a pile, a tube, or a curl: *The wire spring was tightly coiled.*
2 NOUN. anything that is coiled. One wind or turn of a coil is a single coil.
❑ VERB **coils, coiled, coil·ing.**

coin (koin),
1 NOUN. a flat, round piece of metal used as money. Pennies, nickels, dimes, and quarters are coins.
2 VERB. to make coins from metal: *The mint coins millions of nickels and dimes each year.*
3 VERB. to make up a new word or phrase: *We often coin new words to name new products.*
❑ VERB **coins, coined, coin·ing.**

co·in·ci·dence (kō in′sə dəns), NOUN. the accidental happening of two things at the same time: *It is a coincidence that my cousin and I were born on the very same day.*

co·la (kō′lə), NOUN. a bubbly soft drink flavored with a nut from a tropical tree.

cold (kōld),
1 ADJECTIVE. much less warm than your body: *Snow and ice are cold.*
2 ADJECTIVE. less warm than it usually is: *The weather is cold for April.*
3 ADJECTIVE. feeling cold or chilly: *Put on a sweater, or you will be cold.*
4 NOUN. absence of heat; coldness: *Warm clothes protect against the cold of winter.*
5 NOUN. a common sickness that causes a runny nose, coughing, and sneezing.
6 ADJECTIVE. not kind and cheerful; unfriendly: *Since our argument she has been cold to me.*
—**cold′ness**, NOUN.

catch cold or **catch a cold**, IDIOM. to become sick with a cold.

out in the cold, IDIOM. ignored; abandoned; left alone by others: *They all went to the movies and left him out in the cold.*

Synonym Study

Cold means having or feeling no warmth: *Cold and clear, it was a beautiful day for ice-skating. My toes are cold.*

Cool means somewhat cold, in a pleasant way: *The weather was cool and comfortable.*

Chilly means unpleasantly cold: *It is too chilly to go swimming this morning.*

Freezing means so cold that people are very uncomfortable: *Shut the door, please; it's freezing outside.*

ANTONYMS: hot, warm.

cold-blood·ed (kōld′blud′id), ADJECTIVE.
1 having blood that is about the same temperature as the air or water around the animal. The blood of such animals is colder in winter than in summer. Turtles are cold-blooded; dogs are warm-blooded.
2 lacking in feeling; cruel: *a cold-blooded murderer.*

cold snap, a short period of cold weather.

cole·slaw (kōl′slò′), NOUN. a salad made of shredded raw cabbage.

Co·li·ma (kō lē′mä), NOUN. a state in southwestern Mexico.

col·i·se·um (kol′ə sē′əm), NOUN. a large building or stadium for games, contests, and so on.

col·lab·o·rate (kə lab′ə rāt′), VERB. to work together to get something done: *My friend and I collaborated on a report on whales.* ❑ VERB **col·lab·o·rates, col·lab·o·rat·ed, col·lab·o·rat·ing.**

col·lage (kə läzh′), NOUN. a picture made by pasting things such as colored paper, parts of photos and newspapers, and small objects onto a background.

collage

col·lapse (kə laps′),
1 VERB. to fall down or cave in: *The roof of our barn collapsed under the heavy snow.*
2 NOUN. the act of falling down or caving in: *A heavy flood caused the collapse of the bridge.*
3 VERB. to break down; fail suddenly: *The business collapsed because it was run poorly.*
4 VERB. to fold or push together: *This table collapses.*
❑ VERB **col·laps·es, col·lapsed, col·laps·ing.**
—**col·laps′i·ble**, ADJECTIVE.

col·lar (kol′ər),
1 NOUN. the part of a coat, a dress, or a shirt that goes around or just below the neck.
2 NOUN. a leather or plastic band or a metal chain for the neck of a dog or other pet animal.
3 VERB. (informal) to arrest someone; capture.
❑ VERB **col·lars, col·lared, col·lar·ing.**

col·lar·bone (kol′ər bōn′), NOUN. the bone that joins the breastbone and the shoulder blade.

col·league (kol′ēg′), NOUN. a fellow worker: *His colleagues taught his classes while he was ill.*
❑ PLURAL **col·leagues.**

col·lect (kə lekt′), VERB.
1 to bring things together; gather together: *Our teacher collected our homework this morning.*
2 to come together into a group: *A crowd soon collected around the artist.*
❑ VERB **col·lects, col·lect·ed, col·lect·ing.**

col·lect·i·ble (kə lek′tə bəl), NOUN. anything that is collected or might be collected, especially something that is unusual or out of date. Old dolls and old bicycles are collectibles.

col·lec·tion (kə lek′shən), NOUN. a group of things gathered from many places and belonging together: *Our library has a large collection of books.*

col·lec·tor (kə lek′tər), NOUN.
1 someone or something that collects: *I am a stamp collector.*
2 someone hired to collect money owed: *He works for the government as a tax collector.*

col·lege (kol′ij), NOUN. a school where you can study after high school that gives degrees or diplomas: *After I finish high school, I plan to go to college to become a teacher.*

col·lide (kə līd′), VERB. to crash; hit against or strike hard together: *I collided with my sister in the dark hall.* ❑ VERB **col·lides, col·lid·ed, col·lid·ing.**

col·lie (kol′ē), NOUN. a large, long-haired dog. Collies are used for tending sheep and as pets. ❑ PLURAL **col·lies.**

collie — about 2½ feet high at the shoulder

col·li·sion (kə lizh′ən), NOUN. a crash; hitting against or striking hard together: *The car was badly damaged in the collision. Did anyone see what caused the collision?*

Co·lom·bi·a (kə lum′bē ə), NOUN. a country in northwestern South America. **—Co·lom′bi·an,** ADJECTIVE or NOUN.

co·lon¹ (kō′lən), NOUN. a mark (:) of punctuation. Colons are used before explanations, lists, and long quotations to set them off from the rest of the sentence.

co·lon² (kō′lən), NOUN. the lower part of the large intestine.

colo·nel (kėr′nl), NOUN. a military rank. See the chart on page 550. ■ Another word that sounds like this is **kernel.**

co·lo·ni·al (kə lō′nē əl), ADJECTIVE.
1 of or about a colony or colonies: *She studies French colonial government.*

2 of or about the thirteen British colonies which became the United States of America.

col·o·nist (kol′ə nist), NOUN. someone who lives in a colony; settler: *Early colonists in New England suffered from cold and hunger.*

col·o·nize (kol′ə nīz), VERB. to set up a colony or colonies in: *The English colonized New England.* ❑ VERB **col·o·niz·es, col·o·nized, col·o·niz·ing.** **—col′o·ni·za′tion,** NOUN. **—col′o·niz′er,** NOUN.

col·o·ny (kol′ə nē), NOUN.
1 a group of people who leave their own country and go to settle in another land, but who still remain citizens of their own country: *The Pilgrim colony came from England to America in 1620.*
2 the settlement made by such a group of people: *The Pilgrims founded a colony at Plymouth, Massachusetts.*
3 **the Colonies,** the thirteen British colonies that became the United States of America; New Hampshire, Massachusetts, Rhode Island, Connecticut, New York, New Jersey, Pennsylvania, Delaware, Maryland, Virginia, North Carolina, South Carolina, and Georgia.
4 a territory distant from the country that governs it: *Singapore used to be a British colony.*
5 a group of living things of the same kind that grow or live together: *a colony of ants.* ❑ PLURAL **col·o·nies.**

col·or (kul′ər),
1 NOUN. red, yellow, blue, or any combination of them. Green is a combination of yellow and blue; purple is a combination of red and blue.
2 VERB. to give color to something; put color on: *I colored a picture with crayons.*
3 NOUN. something that provides color; a stain or dye: *Sunlight faded the colors of the bedspread.*
4 NOUN. the appearance of the skin; complexion: *She has a healthy color.* ❑ VERB **col·ors, col·ored, col·or·ing. —col′or·less,** ADJECTIVE.

Col·o·rad·o (kol′ə rad′ō or kol′ə rä′dō), NOUN.
1 one of the Rocky Mountain states of the United States. *Abbreviation:* CO; *Capital:* Denver.
2 a river in the western United States and Mexico. **—Col′o·rad′an,** NOUN.

State Story **Colorado** comes from a Spanish word meaning "red." The Colorado River runs through canyons of red stone and carries red mud in its water. The state was named for the river.

a	hat	ė	term	ô	order	ch	child		
ā	age	i	it	oi	oil	ng	long	⎧	a in about
ä	far	ī	ice	ou	out	sh	she		e in taken
â	care	o	hot	u	cup	th	thin	ə⎨	i in pencil
e	let	ō	open	ů	put	ŦH	then		o in lemon
ē	equal	ò	saw	ü	rule	zh	measure	⎩	u in circus

col·or-blind (kul′ər blīnd′), ADJECTIVE. unable to tell certain colors apart; unable to see certain colors. Some color-blind people may see both red and green as the same shade of brown.

col·or·ful (kul′ər fəl), ADJECTIVE.
1 interesting or exciting: *Her letters describe her colorful travels.*
2 having many or bright colors: *She bought a colorful red and yellow scarf.*
—**col′or·ful·ly**, ADVERB.

col·or·ing (kul′ər ing), NOUN.
1 the way in which someone or something is colored: *Our cat has a tan coloring.*
2 a substance used to color: *I added some yellow food coloring to the cake frosting.*

co·los·sal (kə los′əl), ADJECTIVE. of amazing size; gigantic: *Skyscrapers are colossal buildings.*

colt (kōlt), NOUN. a young, male horse, donkey, or zebra. A male horse is a colt until it is four or five years old.

This young **colt** stays near his mother.

Co·lum·bi·a (kə lum′bē ə), NOUN. the capital of South Carolina.

Co·lum·bus (kə lum′bəs), NOUN. the capital of Ohio.

col·umn (kol′əm), NOUN.
1 a tall, slender structure something like a large post; pillar. Columns are usually made of stone, wood, or metal, and used as supports or ornaments to a building.
2 anything that seems tall and slender like a column: *A column of smoke rose from the fire.*
3 a line of persons or things following one behind another.
4 a narrow division of a page reading from top to bottom, kept separate by lines or by blank spaces. This page has two columns.
5 a part of a newspaper used for a special subject or written by a special writer: *the sports column, the advice column.*

co·ma (kō′mə), NOUN. a long period of deep unconsciousness. A coma may be caused by disease, injury, or poison. ❑ PLURAL **co·mas.**

comb (kōm),
1 NOUN. a piece of plastic, metal, or the like, with teeth, used to arrange the hair or to hold it in place.
2 NOUN. anything shaped or used like a comb. One kind of comb cleans and untangles wool.
3 VERB. to take out the tangles in something; arrange with a comb: *Please comb your hair.*
4 VERB. to search through something: *We combed the neighborhood to find our lost dog.*
5 NOUN. the thick, red, fleshy piece on the top of the head of chickens and some other fowls.
❑ VERB **combs, combed, comb·ing.**

com·bat (kəm bat′ or kom′bat *for verb;* kom′bat *for noun),*
1 VERB. to fight against something; struggle with: *Doctors combat disease.*
2 NOUN. a fight with weapons; battle: *The soldier was wounded in combat.*
3 NOUN. any fight or struggle.
❑ VERB **com·bats, com·bat·ted, com·bat·ting.**

com·bi·na·tion (kom′bə nā′shən), NOUN.
1 one single thing made by joining or mixing two or more different things: *The color purple is a combination of red and blue.*
2 a series of numbers or letters used in opening a certain kind of lock: *He forgot his combination.*

com·bine (kəm bīn′), VERB. to join two or more things together; unite: *Our club combined the offices of secretary and treasurer. Two atoms of hydrogen combine with one atom of oxygen to form water.* ■ See the Synonym Study at **join.**
❑ VERB **com·bines, com·bined, com·bin·ing.**

com·bin·ing form (kəm bīn′ing fôrm′), a word part added to other word parts or words to create a new meaning. *Auto-, -graphy,* and *geo-* are combining forms.

com·bus·ti·ble (kəm bus′tə bəl), ADJECTIVE. capable of catching fire and burning; easy to burn: *Gasoline is highly combustible.*

com·bus·tion (kəm bus′chən), NOUN. the act or process of burning.

come (kum), VERB.
1 to move toward: *Come this way. One boy came toward me; the other boy went away from me.*
2 to arrive: *The girls will come home tomorrow.*
3 to reach; extend: *The drapes come to the floor.*
4 to be born; be from: *She comes from a musical family. The word "coma" comes from a Greek word.*
5 to turn out to be; become: *My wish came true.*
6 to be available or be sold: *This soup comes in a can.*
❑ VERB **comes, came, come, com·ing.**

come across, IDIOM. to meet or find by chance: *She came across an old doll while cleaning her closet.*

come around, IDIOM.
1 to change to a different way of thinking: *I knew she'd come around and let me go to the concert.*

2 to happen regularly: *Her birthday's coming around again; let's have a surprise party.*

come out, *IDIOM.*

1 to be offered to the public: *The singer's new recording will come out next fall.*

2 to put in an appearance; turn out: *How many people came out to cheer the team?*

come to, *IDIOM.*

1 to become conscious again: *He came to slowly after the accident.*

2 to be equal in amount: *The bill comes to $45.*

come up with, *IDIOM.* to think of something new; suggest something new: *He came up with a great idea for our science project.*

how come, *IDIOM.* (informal) why; for what reason: *How come he gets to stay up late tonight?*

Synonym Study

Come means to get to a place: *The bus hasn't come yet, and I'm going to be late for school.*

Arrive means to get to a place, usually after a trip of some length: *Everyone was delighted when Grandpa arrived from Atlanta.*

Reach means to get to a place, often after a lot of work: *After hiking all day, we reached camp.*

Show up means to come somewhere. It suggests a strong chance of not coming there: *I didn't think she would attend my party, but she showed up at the last moment.*

ANTONYMS: leave.

co·me·di·an (kə mē′dē ən), *NOUN.* someone who acts in comedies or who amuses an audience with funny talk and actions.

co·me·di·enne (kə mē′dē en′), *NOUN.* a woman who acts in comedies or who amuses an audience with funny talk and actions.

com·e·dy (kom′ə dē), *NOUN.* an amusing play or show having a happy ending. ❑ *PLURAL* **com·e·dies.**

com·et (kom′it), *NOUN.* a very large object in space that looks like a star with a cloudy tail of light. Comets are made of ice, dust, and gases and shine by reflecting sunlight. They move very slowly across the sky as they travel in a path around the sun.

Word Story

Comet comes from a Greek word meaning "long-haired star." It was called this because the tail of a comet looks like long, flowing hair.

com·fort (kum′fərt),

1 *VERB.* to ease the grief or pain of someone: *She comforted the crying child.*

2 *NOUN.* someone or something that lessens sorrow or makes life easier: *You were a great comfort to me while I was sick.*

3 *NOUN.* a feeling of pleasure and happiness; freedom from pain or hardship: *It's nice to have enough money to live in comfort.*
❑ *VERB* **com·forts, com·fort·ed, com·fort·ing.**

com·fort·a·ble (kum′fər tə bəl), *ADJECTIVE.*

1 giving comfort: *A soft, warm bed is comfortable.*

2 feeling nice and relaxed; free from pain or hardship: *We felt comfortable in the warm house.*
—com′fort·a·bly, *ADVERB.*

Synonym Study

Comfortable means giving or feeling comfort and pleasure: *She always sits in the same comfortable chair to read.*

Cozy means comfortable, warm, and giving or feeling friendly happiness: *The brightly colored pillows made the room cheerful and cozy.*

Snug means comfortable and sheltered, usually in a small space: *The sleeping bag kept him warm and snug during the cold night.*

Easy can mean comfortable and free from care or worry: *My uncle's easy manner makes us feel at home when we stay with him.*

ANTONYM: uncomfortable.

com·ic (kom′ik),

1 *ADJECTIVE.* very funny; causing laughter or smiles: *I enjoy writing comic poems for my friends.*

2 *NOUN.* a comedian.

3 *ADJECTIVE.* of or about comedy; in comedies: *a comic actor.*

4 *NOUN.* **comics,** comic strips.

comic book, a magazine containing comic strips.

comet

a hat	ė term	ô order	ch child	⎧ a in about
ā age	i it	oi oil	ng long	⎪ e in taken
ä far	ī ice	ou out	sh she	ə ⎨ i in pencil
â care	o hot	u cup	th thin	⎪ o in lemon
e let	ō open	u̇ put	ᴛʜ then	⎩ u in circus
ē equal	ȯ saw	ü rule	zh measure	

comic strip, a group of cartoons that tell a funny or exciting story.

com·ma (kom′ə), NOUN. a punctuation mark (,) usually used where a pause would be made in speaking a sentence aloud. Commas are used to separate ideas, parts of a sentence, or things in a series. ❑ PLURAL **com·mas.**

com·mand (kə mand′),
1 VERB. to give an order to someone; order; direct: *The queen commanded the admiral to set sail at once.*
2 NOUN. an order; direction: *The admiral obeyed the queen's command.*
3 VERB. to be in control of something; have power or authority over: *A captain commands a ship.*
4 NOUN. control; power; authority: *When the fire started, she took command and led us to safety.*
5 VERB. to deserve something and get it: *She is a person who commands our respect.*
6 NOUN. the soldiers or ships or a region under someone who has the right to command them: *The captain knew every person in his command.*
7 NOUN. the ability to use something skillfully: *Although she lived in Mexico until she was ten, she now has an excellent command of English.*
❑ VERB **com·mands, com·mand·ed, com·mand·ing.**

com·mand·er (kə man′dər), NOUN.
1 someone who commands or is in charge: *The commander of the rebel forces led a daring raid.*
2 a military rank. See the chart on page 550.

com·mand·ment (kə mand′mənt), NOUN.
1 (in the Bible) one of the ten rules for living and for worship, called the **Ten Commandments,** given by God to the Jews.
2 any command or official order.

com·mem·o·rate (kə mem′ə rāt), VERB. to honor the memory of someone: *The Vietnam War Memorial commemorates those Americans who died in that war.* ❑ VERB **com·mem·o·rates, com·mem·o·rat·ed, com·mem·o·rat·ing.**

com·mence (kə mens′), VERB. to begin; start: *The play will commence at ten o'clock.* ■ See the Synonym Study at **start.** ❑ VERB **com·menc·es, com·menced, com·menc·ing.**

com·mence·ment (kə mens′mənt), NOUN.
1 a beginning; start: *We are eagerly waiting for the commencement of spring.*
2 the ceremony during which colleges and schools give diplomas to the students who have finished their studies.

commencement

com·ment (kom′ent),
1 NOUN. a short statement, note, or remark that explains, praises, or finds fault with someone or something: *The teacher had written helpful comments on the last page of my composition.*
2 VERB. to make a comment or comments: *Everyone commented on my new coat.*
❑ VERB **com·ments, com·ment·ed, com·ment·ing.**

com·merce (kom′ərs), NOUN. the buying and selling of goods in large amounts; trade: *The United States has a great deal of commerce with other countries.*

com·mer·cial (kə mėr′shəl),
1 ADJECTIVE. of or about trade or business: *My uncle owns a store and several other commercial establishments.*
2 NOUN. an advertising message on TV or radio, broadcast between or during programs: *Have you seen the commercial for that new toy?*

com·mis·sion (kə mish′ən),
1 NOUN. a written order giving someone certain powers, rights, and duties. In the army a person who is appointed to the rank of lieutenant or higher receives a commission.
2 VERB. to give someone the right, the power, or the duty to do something: *They commissioned a real estate agent to sell their house.*
3 NOUN. a group of people appointed or elected with authority to do certain things: *a commission to investigate the rise in crime.*
4 NOUN. the act of doing something wrong: *He was arrested for the commission of a series of crimes.*
5 NOUN. the money paid to a salesperson for some amount of business done: *She gets a commission of 10 percent on all the sales that she makes.*
6 VERB. to put a ship into active service: *A new ship is commissioned when it has the officers, crew, and supplies needed for a trip.*
❑ VERB **com·mis·sions, com·mis·sioned, com·mis·sion·ing.**

out of commission, IDIOM. not in good working order: *A broken chain put my bicycle out of commission.*

com·mis·sion·er (kə mish′ə nər), NOUN. an official in charge of some department of a government: *a police commissioner, a health commissioner.*

com·mit (kə mit′), VERB.
1 to do or perform some action, usually something wrong: *A person who steals commits a crime.*
2 to put under the care of a jail or hospital: *Mentally ill people are sometimes committed to hospitals.*
❑ VERB **com·mits, com·mit·ted, com·mit·ting.**

commit yourself, IDIOM. to promise that you will do something; devote yourself to something: *I have committed myself to finishing this project and I must keep my promise.*

com·mit·tee (kə mit′ē), NOUN. a group of people chosen or elected to do some special thing: *Our teacher appointed a committee of five pupils to plan the class picnic.* ❑ PLURAL **com·mit·tees.**

com·mod·i·ty (kə mod′ə tē), NOUN. anything that is bought and sold: *Corn, wood, and gold are commodities.* ❑ PLURAL **com·mod·i·ties.**

com·mon (kom′ən),
1 ADJECTIVE. often seen or found; usual: *Snow is common in cold countries.*
2 ADJECTIVE. general; of all; by all: *By common consent of the class, she was chosen for president.*
3 ADJECTIVE. belonging equally to all: *The house is the common property of the three brothers.*
4 NOUN. also, **commons,** land owned or used by all the people of a village or town.

common denominator, a number that can be divided, without a remainder, by the denominators of two or more fractions. 15 is a common denominator of ⅗ and ⅔ because 15 can be divided by both 5 and 3 without a remainder. When ⅗ and ⅔ are written using this common denominator, they become ⁹⁄₁₅ and ¹⁰⁄₁₅.

> 12 is a **common denominator** of ½, ¼, ⅓, and ⅙.
> ½ = ⁶⁄₁₂   ¼ = ³⁄₁₂   ⅓ = ⁴⁄₁₂   ⅙ = ²⁄₁₂

common factor, a number that will divide into each of two or more other numbers without a remainder: *A common factor of 9 and 12 is 3.*

com·mon·ly (kom′ən lē), ADVERB. usually; generally: *Multiplication facts are commonly taught in third grade.*

common noun, name for any one of a class or group of people, places or things. *Boy* and *city* are common nouns.

com·mon·place (kom′ən plās′), ADJECTIVE. ordinary; not fancy or interesting: *The white daisy is a commonplace flower.*

common sense, good sense in everyday affairs; practical intelligence: *He was not a good student, but he had a lot of common sense.*

com·mon·wealth (kom′ən welth′), NOUN.
1 a nation in which the people have the right to make the laws; republic: *Brazil, Australia, the United States, and Germany are commonwealths.*
2 any state of the United States, especially Kentucky, Massachusetts, Pennsylvania, and Virginia.

com·mo·tion (kə mō′shən), NOUN. a noisy, violent disturbance: *Their fight in the playground caused quite a commotion!*

com·mu·ni·ca·ble (kə myü′nə kə bəl), ADJECTIVE. able to be passed along to other people; contagious: *Colds are communicable.*

com·mu·ni·cate (kə myü′nə kāt), VERB. to give or exchange information or news: *When my brother is away at school, I communicate with him by*

e-mail. *She communicated her wishes to me in a letter.* ❑ VERB **com·mu·ni·cates, com·mu·ni·cat·ed, com·mu·ni·cat·ing.** —**com·mu′ni·ca′tor,** NOUN.

com·mu·ni·ca·tion (kə myü′nə kā′shən), NOUN.
1 the act or process of giving or exchanging information or news: *American Sign Language is an important means of communication for the deaf.*
2 the information or news given; message which gives information or news: *Your communication came in time to change all my plans.*
3 **communications,** the various methods of exchanging information used in everyday life, including the telephone, radio, computers, and so on: *A network of communications links all parts of the civilized world.*

com·mun·ion (kə myü′nyən), NOUN. an exchange of thoughts and feelings; fellowship: *There was a close communion among the three sisters.*

com·mu·nism (kom′yə niz′əm), NOUN. a system of government in which all property, the means of production, and the system of distribution are owned or controlled by the state. Goods are shared by all.

com·mu·nist (kom′yə nist), NOUN. someone who supports communism.

com·mu·ni·ty (kə myü′nə tē), NOUN.
1 all the people living in the same place; the people of any district or town: *This lake provides water for six communities.*
2 a neighborhood; the place, district, or area where people live, work, and play: *There are a few stores and a bank in our community, but not a theater.*
3 a group of people living together or sharing common interests: *the scientific community.*
4 all the living things in any one place.
❑ PLURAL **com·mu·ni·ties.**

community center, building where the people of a community meet for recreation or social and educational purposes: *Twice a week I play volleyball at the community center.*

com·mu·ta·tive prop·er·ty (kom′yə tā′tiv prop′ər tē), the rule in mathematics stating that the order in which numbers are added or multiplied will not change the result. EXAMPLE: 2 + 3 will give the same result as 3 + 2.

com·mute (kə myüt′), VERB. to travel regularly to and from work by train, bus, or car. ❑ VERB **com·mutes, com·mut·ed, com·mut·ing.**

com·mut·er (kə myü′tər), NOUN. someone who travels regularly to and from work by train, bus, or car.

a	hat	ė	term	ô	order	ch	child		
ā	age	i	it	oi	oil	ng	long		a in about
ä	far	ī	ice	ou	out	sh	she		e in taken
â	care	o	hot	u	cup	th	thin	ə	i in pencil
e	let	ō	open	ů	put	ŦH	then		o in lemon
ē	equal	ò	saw	ü	rule	zh	measure		u in circus

com·pact¹ (kəm pakt′ or kom′pakt *for adjective;* kom′pakt *for noun*),
1 *ADJECTIVE.* closely and firmly packed together: *The leaves of a cabbage are folded into a compact head.*
2 *ADJECTIVE.* smaller than usual in order to save space: *a compact, portable TV, a compact car.*
3 *NOUN.* a small case containing face powder and a mirror.
4 *NOUN.* an car smaller than most models.

com·pact² (kom′pakt), *NOUN.* an agreement: *The United Nations is a result of a compact among nearly all nations of the world.*

compact disc (kom′pakt disk′), a small, thin plastic disk that contains music, computer programs, and other kinds of information; CD.

com·pan·ion (kəm pan′yən), *NOUN.* someone who goes along with or spends time with you; someone who shares in what you are doing: *The twins were companions in work and play.*

These **companions** are smiling for the camera.

com·pan·ion·ship (kəm pan′yən ship), *NOUN.* friendly feeling between companions; fellowship: *I enjoy the companionship of my friends.*

com·pa·ny (kum′pə nē), *NOUN.*
1 a business firm: *That company makes clothing.*
2 a group of people joined together for some purpose: *a company of actors.*
3 one or more guests; visitors: *company for dinner.*
4 a companion or companions: *You are known by the company you keep.*
5 companionship: *I have enjoyed your company.*
❑ *PLURAL* **com·pa·nies.**

com·pa·ra·ble (kom′pər ə bəl), *ADJECTIVE.* able to be compared; similar: *The two students are of comparable ability.* —**com′pa·ra·bly,** *ADVERB.*

com·par·a·tive (kəm par′ə tiv),
1 *ADJECTIVE.* based on comparison; involving comparison: *a comparative study of bees and wasps.*
2 *ADJECTIVE.* measured by comparison with something else; relative: *Although next-door neighbors, they are comparative strangers.*

3 *NOUN.* (in grammer) a form of a word or a combination of words showing a greater degree or amount of something. *Fuller* is the comparative of *full. Better* is the comparative of *good. More quickly* is the comparative of *quickly.*
—**com·par′a·tive·ly,** *ADVERB.*

com·pare (kəm pâr′), *VERB.*
1 to find out or point out how people or things are alike and how they are different: *I compared my answers with the teacher's and found a mistake in my addition.*
2 to say that something is like something else; liken: *The fins of a fish may be compared to the wings of a bird; both are used in moving.*
3 to be considered like or equal: *Canned fruit cannot compare with fresh fruit.*
❑ *VERB* **com·pares, com·pared, com·par·ing.**

com·par·i·son (kəm par′ə sən), *NOUN.*
1 the act of comparing two or more people or things: *The teacher's comparison of the heart to a pump helped us understand how the heart works.*
2 close similarity: *There is no comparison between these two cameras; one is much better than the other.*

com·part·ment (kəm pärt′mənt), *NOUN.* a part or section of anything, set off by walls or partitions: *Many refrigerators have separate compartments for vegetables and fruit.*

com·pass (kum′pəs), *NOUN.*
1 a device for showing directions, with a magnetic needle that always points to the north.
2 a tool used for drawing circles and curved lines and for measuring distances.
❑ *PLURAL* **com·pass·es.**

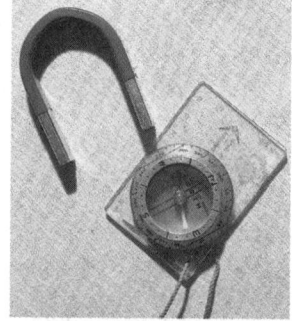

compass (definition 1)

com·pas·sion (kəm pash′ən), *NOUN.* a feeling of being sorry for someone else's hardship and wanting to help; sympathy: *Compassion for the flood victims brought many large contributions.*

com·pas·sion·ate (kəm pash′ə nit), *ADJECTIVE.* wishing to help those who suffer; full of compassion: *The compassionate doctor gave free treatment to the poor.*

com·pat·i·ble (kəm pat′ə bəl), *ADJECTIVE.* able to exist or get along well with someone else; in harmony: *My new roommate and I are quite compatible.* —**com·pat′i·bil′i·ty,** *NOUN.*

com·pel (kəm pel′), *VERB.* to force someone to do something: *Rain compelled us to stop our ballgame.* ❑ *VERB* **com·pels, com·pelled, com·pel·ling.**

C

com·pen·sate (kom′pən sāt), *VERB.*
1 to give something to someone in order to make up for something lost or taken away: *The children mowed our lawn to compensate us for the window they broke playing ball.*
2 to pay: *They compensated her for her extra work.*
❑ *VERB* **com·pen·sates, com·pen·sat·ed, com·pen·sat·ing. –com′pen·sa′tion,** *NOUN.*

com·pete (kəm pēt′), *VERB.* to try to win a contest or get something wanted by other people: *She competed against many fine athletes for the gold medal. Will you compete for that job?* ❑ *VERB* **com·petes, com·pet·ed, com·pet·ing.**

com·pe·tent (kom′pə tənt), *ADJECTIVE.* properly qualified; able: *She is a competent driver who has never caused an accident.* **–com′pe·tent·ly,** *ADVERB.*

com·pe·ti·tion (kom′pə tish′ən), *NOUN.*
1 the act of trying to win a contest or get something wanted by other people.
2 a contest.

com·pet·i·tive (kəm pet′ə tiv), *ADJECTIVE.*
1 involving competition: *Tennis and baseball are competitive sports.*
2 eager to compete: *Our athletes are full of competitive spirit.*

com·pet·i·tor (kəm pet′ə tər), *NOUN.* someone who tries hard to win or get something wanted by other people; opponent: *There are many competitors for the golf championship.*

com·pile (kəm pīl′), *VERB.* to collect in a list or account: *I compiled a list of books written on the subject of glaciers.* ❑ *VERB* **com·piles, com·piled, com·pil·ing.**

com·plain (kəm plān′), *VERB.*
1 to say that you are unhappy, annoyed, or upset about something: *We complained that it was too cold.*
2 to report than you are not well: *He complained about his leg pain.*
❑ *VERB* **com·plains, com·plained, com·plain·ing. –com·plain′er,** *NOUN.*

Synonym Study

Complain means to say that you are unhappy about something that is wrong: *"This store never has any good candy," she complained.*

Grumble means to complain in a growling, angry way: *My uncle grumbles about his job.*

Whine can mean to complain in a sad voice about unimportant things: *When my baby sister is tired, she whines about everything.*

Gripe means to complain in a continuous, annoying way: *If you don't stop griping, you won't get any dessert at all.*

Squawk can mean to complain loudly. This use is informal: *"It's my turn!" he squawked.*

com·plaint (kəm plānt), *NOUN.*
1 a statement that something makes you unhappy, annoyed, or upset: *Her letter is filled with complaints about the food at camp.*
2 a cause for complaining: *Her main complaint is that she has too much work to do.*
3 an accusation; charge: *The judge heard the complaint and ordered an investigation.*

com·ple·ment (kom′plə ment), *VERB.* to supply what is missing; complete: *The salty flavor of the olives and pickles complemented the blandness of the cheese.* ■ Another word that can sound like this is **compliment.** ❑ *VERB* **com·ple·ments, com·ple·ment·ed, com·ple·ment·ing.**

com·plete (kəm plēt′),
1 *ADJECTIVE.* having all the necessary parts; whole; entire: *My grandparents live in the country and have a complete set of garden tools.*
2 *ADJECTIVE.* perfect; thorough: *The birthday party was a complete surprise to me.*
3 *ADJECTIVE.* finished; done: *I am not allowed to go out with my friends until all my homework is complete.*
4 *VERB.* to finish something: *She completed her homework early in the evening.* ■ See the Synonym Study at **end.**
❑ *VERB* **com·pletes, com·plet·ed, com·plet·ing.**

com·plete·ly (kəm plēt′lē), *ADVERB.*
1 in every way; entirely; wholly: *The film was completely ruined when I held it up to the light.*
2 thoroughly; perfectly: *The birthday party completely surprised me.*

com·ple·tion (kəm plē′shən), *NOUN.*
1 the act of finishing; completing: *After the completion of the job, she went home.*
2 the condition of being finished: *The work is near completion.*
3 (in football) a pass caught by a receiver.

com·plex (kəm pleks′ *or* kom′pleks), *ADJECTIVE.*
1 made up of a number of parts that work together: *A computer is a complex device.*
2 hard to understand: *The instructions for our new computer game were so complex that they were hard to follow.*

com·plex·ion (kəm plek′shən), *NOUN.* the color and general appearance of the skin, especially of the face: *The child has a healthy complexion.*

com·plex·i·ty (kəm plek′sə tē), *NOUN.* quality or condition of being complex: *The complexity of the road map puzzled him.*

a hat	ė term	ô order	ch child	⎧a in about
ā age	i it	oi oil	ng long	⎪e in taken
ä far	ī ice	ou out	sh she	ə⎨i in pencil
â care	o hot	u cup	th thin	⎪o in lemon
e let	ō open	ù put	ᴛʜ then	⎩u in circus
ē equal	ò saw	ü rule	zh measure	

com·pli·cate (kom′plə kāt), VERB. to make something complex or hard to understand: *Too many rules complicate a game.* □ VERB **com·pli·cates, com·pli·cat·ed, com·pli·cat·ing.**

com·pli·cat·ed (kom′plə kā′tid), ADJECTIVE.
1 complex or hard to understand: *The directions for assembling this toy are too complicated.*
2 made up of many parts that work together: *A jet engine is a complicated machine.*

He invented a **complicated** toothbrush.

com·pli·ca·tion (kom′plə kā′shən), NOUN. something that makes whatever you are doing more difficult: *Various complications delayed the start of our trip.*

com·pli·ment (kom′plə mənt *for noun;* kom′plə ment *for verb*),
1 NOUN. something nice said about you; something said in praise of your work: *She received many compliments on her science project.*
2 VERB. to pay a compliment to someone; congratulate: *Our coach complimented the winner.* □ VERB **com·pli·ments, com·pli·ment·ed, com·pli·ment·ing.** ■ Another word that can sound like this is **complement.**

com·pli·men·tar·y (kom′plə men′tər ē), ADJECTIVE.
1 expressing a compliment; praising: *I like to receive complimentary remarks about my work.*
2 given free: *We received two complimentary tickets to the circus.*

com·ply (kəm plī′), VERB. to do what you have been asked or told to do: *I will comply with your wishes.* □ VERB **com·plies, com·plied, com·ply·ing.**

com·po·nent (kəm pō′nənt), NOUN.
1 something that goes together with other things to make a whole: *Music is an important component of a child's education.*
2 a part of an electronic or mechanical system: *The CD player is a new component in our sound system.*

com·pose (kəm pōz′), VERB.
1 to make up: *Oxygen and nitrogen compose most of the air that we breathe. Our party was composed of three adults and four children.*

2 to put a work of art together, using words, sounds, colors, and so on. To compose a story or poem is to construct it from words. To compose a piece of music is to invent the melody and write down the notes.
□ VERB **com·pos·es, com·posed, com·pos·ing.**

com·pos·er (kəm pō′zər), NOUN. someone who writes music.

com·pos·ite (kəm poz′it), ADJECTIVE. made up of various parts: *She made a composite photograph by putting together parts of several others.*

com·po·si·tion (kom′pə zish′ən), NOUN.
1 something that has been composed. A symphony, poem, or painting is a composition.
2 the process of putting something together. Writing sentences, making pictures, and setting type in printing are all forms of composition.
3 a short essay written as a school exercise: *I wrote a composition about my dog.*
4 the separate parts that make up something and the way they are put together: *Scientists are studying the composition of the meteorite.*

com·post (kom′pōst), NOUN. a mixture of decaying leaves, grass, manure, and so on, for fertilizing soil.

com·pound (kom′pound),
1 NOUN. a word made up of two or more words. *Steamship* is a compound made up of the two words *steam* and *ship.*
2 ADJECTIVE. made up of more than one part: *Blackboard is a compound word.*
3 NOUN. a mixture: *Many medicines are compounds.*
4 NOUN. a substance formed by chemical combination of two or more elements: *Water is a compound of hydrogen and oxygen.*

com·pre·hend (kom′pri hend′), VERB. to understand something: *If you can use a word correctly, you comprehend it.* □ VERB **com·pre·hends, com·pre·hend·ed, com·pre·hend·ing.**

com·pre·hen·sion (kom′pri hen′shən), NOUN. the act or power of understanding something: *Arithmetic is beyond the comprehension of a baby.*

com·pre·hen·sive (kom′pri hen′siv), ADJECTIVE. including whatever is necessary; covering a broad range: *The school term ended with a comprehensive review. They offered a comprehensive insurance policy.* **–com′pre·hen′sive·ly,** ADVERB.

com·press (kəm pres′ *for verb;* kom′pres *for noun*),
1 VERB. to press together; make smaller by pressure: *Cotton is compressed into bales.*
2 NOUN. a pad of cloth applied to a part of the body to stop bleeding or to reduce soreness and swelling: *I put a cold compress on my forehead to relieve my headache.*
□ VERB **com·press·es, com·pressed, com·press·ing;** PLURAL **com·press·es. –com·press′i·ble,** ADJECTIVE.

C

com·pro·mise (kom′prə mīz),
1 *VERB.* to settle an argument by agreeing that each side will give up a part of what it demands: *We all wanted the game, so we compromised by sharing it.*
2 *NOUN.* a settlement of an argument in which each side agrees to give up a part of what it demands: *Our compromise was to take turns with the toy.*
   ❑ *VERB* **com·pro·mis·es, com·pro·mised, com·pro·mis·ing.** **—com′pro·mis′er,** *NOUN.*

com·pute (kəm pyüt′), *VERB.* to find out something by using arithmetic; calculate: *We computed the cost of our trip.* ❑ *VERB* **com·putes, com·put·ed, com·put·ing.** **—com′put·a·ble,** *ADJECTIVE.* **—com′pu·ta′tion,** *NOUN.*

com·put·er (kəm pyü′tər), *NOUN.* an electronic machine that can store, recall, and work with various kinds of information. A computer performs these tasks according to instructions that the user gives it. Computers keep files, play games, solve mathematical problems, and control the operations of other machines.

Word Bank

Computers have their own vocabulary, much of it very new. If you want to learn more about computers, you can start by looking up these words in this dictionary.

BASIC	gigabyte	mouse
bit[4]	hard drive	PC
bug	home page	personal
CD-ROM	hypertext	computer
CPU	kilobyte	printer
chip	Internet	RAM
cursor	laptop	ROM
database	laser disc	scroll
desktop	megabyte	software
download	modem	trackball
e-mail	monitor	World Wide Web
floppy disk		

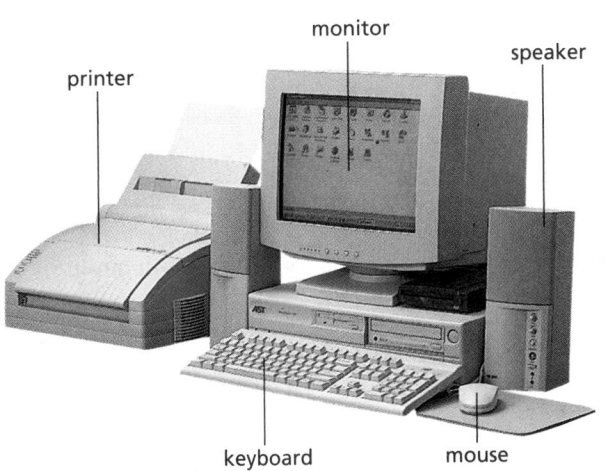

printer

monitor

speaker

keyboard

mouse

computer

computer graphics,
1 the use of computers to produce pictures, diagrams, and other images.
2 images produced by computers.

com·put·er·ize (kəm pyü′tə rīz′), *VERB.*
1 to equip with computers: *Our school library has been computerized.*
2 to enter or process information in a computer: *Next year, the store will computerize all of its financial records.*
   ❑ *VERB* **com·put·er·iz·es, com·put·er·ized, com·put·er·iz·ing.**

com·rade (kom′rad), *NOUN.* a close companion and friend, especially one who shares in what you are doing.

con·cave (kon kāv′), *ADJECTIVE.* hollow and curved in like the inside of a bowl or a spoon.

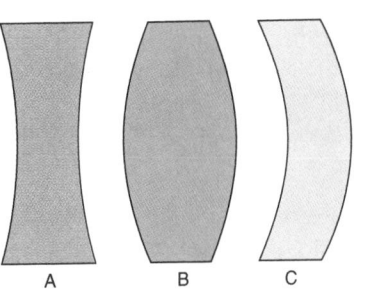

concave and **convex**
A. both concave
B. both convex
C. concave and convex

A   B   C

concave and **convex**

con·ceal (kən sēl′), *VERB.* to put or keep something out of sight; hide: *Dad concealed the surprise gift in the closet behind the winter scarves.*
   ❑ *VERB* **con·ceals, con·cealed, con·ceal·ing.** **—con·ceal′ment,** *NOUN.*

con·cede (kən sēd′), *VERB.* to admit that something is true: *I conceded that I had made a mistake. The candidate conceded defeat in the election.* ❑ *VERB* **con·cedes, con·ced·ed, con·ced·ing.**

con·ceit (kən sēt′), *NOUN.* too high an opinion of yourself or of your ability to do things.

con·ceit·ed (kən sē′tid), *ADJECTIVE.* having too high an opinion of yourself or of your ability to do things.

con·ceive (kən sēv′), *VERB.*
1 to imagine in your mind; think up: *He conceived of his million-dollar invention at age twelve.*
2 to have a particular idea or feeling about something: *Most people cannot conceive of life without cars and TV.*
   ❑ *VERB* **con·ceives, con·ceived, con·ceiv·ing.** **—con·ceiv′a·ble,** *ADJECTIVE.*

a hat	ė term	ô order	ch child	a in about
ā age	i it	oi oil	ng long	e in taken
ä far	ī ice	ou out	sh she	ə i in pencil
â care	o hot	u cup	th thin	o in lemon
e let	ō open	u̇ put	ᴛʜ then	u in circus
ē equal	ȯ saw	ü rule	zh measure	

con·cen·trate (kon′sən trāt), VERB.
1 to pay close attention: *I concentrated on my reading so that I would understand the story.* ■ See the Synonym Study at **think**.
2 to bring or come together in one place: *A magnifying glass can concentrate enough sunlight to burn paper. The audience at the music festival concentrated around the stage.*
❏ VERB **con·cen·trates, con·cen·trat·ed, con·cen·trat·ing.**

concentration camp, a prison camp where political enemies, prisoners of war, or members of minority groups are held by government order.

con·cen·tra·tion (kon′sən trā′shən), NOUN.
1 close attention: *When he gave the problem his full concentration, he figured out the answer.*
2 a group brought together in one place: *There is a large concentration of fish in the lake.*

con·cept (kon′sept), NOUN. a thought; idea: *We believe in the concept that a person is innocent until proven guilty.* ■ See the Synonym Study at **idea**.

con·cep·tion (kən sep′shən), NOUN. a thought; idea: *Her conception of the problem was different from mine.*

con·cern (kən sèrn′),
1 VERB. to be the business or affair of; interest: *The school play concerns every member of the class.*
2 NOUN. anything that relates to your work or your interests; business; affair: *The party decorations are my concern; you pay attention to food.*
3 NOUN. worry: *Their concern over their sick child kept them awake all night.*
4 VERB. to cause someone to worry; trouble: *We didn't want to concern you with the bad news.*
❏ VERB **con·cerns, con·cerned, con·cern·ing.**

con·cerned (kən sèrnd′), ADJECTIVE.
1 worried about something; troubled: *My aunt is very concerned about her health.*
2 interested: *Concerned citizens make use of their right to vote.*

con·cern·ing (kən sèr′ning), PREPOSITION. about; relating to: *The reporter asked many questions concerning the accident.*

con·cert (kon′sərt), NOUN. a musical performance in which one or more musicians take part: *The school orchestra gave a free concert.*

con·cer·to (kən cher′tō), NOUN. a piece of music to be played by one or more principal instruments, such as a violin or piano, accompanied by an orchestra. ❏ PLURAL **con·cer·tos.**

con·ces·sion (kən sesh′ən), NOUN.
1 anything allowed in order to have agreement: *The teacher made a special concession and postponed the test.*
2 a right or space leased for a specific purpose: *Our concession at the school fair sold lemonade.*

conch (kongk or konch), NOUN.
1 a sea animal with a soft body and a large spiral shell.
2 a shell of such an animal.
❏ PLURAL **conchs** (kongks) or **conch·es** (kon′chiz).

conch (definition 2)

con·clude (kən klüd′), VERB.
1 to end: *The play concluded with a song.* ■ See the Synonym Study at **end**.
2 bring to an end; finish: *After we concluded our business at the bank, we went to lunch.*
3 to reach certain decisions or opinions after careful thought: *From its tracks, we concluded that the animal must have been very large.*
❏ VERB **con·cludes, con·clud·ed, con·clud·ing.**

con·clu·sion (kən klü′zhən), NOUN.
1 the end: *I couldn't wait to read the conclusion of the story.*
2 a decision or opinion reached after careful thought: *She came to the conclusion that she would have to work harder to finish on time.*

con·coct (kon kokt′), VERB.
1 to prepare: *He concocted a drink made of grape juice and ginger ale.*
2 make up; think up; invent: *They concocted an excuse for being late to school.*
❏ VERB **con·cocts, con·coct·ed, con·coct·ing.**

Con·cord (kong′kərd), NOUN. the capital of New Hampshire.

con·crete (kon′krēt′ or kon krēt′),
1 NOUN. a mixture of cement, sand or gravel, and water that hardens as it dries. Concrete is used for foundations, buildings, roads, dams, and bridges.
2 ADJECTIVE. existing as an actual object; real: *A painting is concrete, but its beauty is not.*

con·cus·sion (kən kush′ən), NOUN. an injury to the brain caused by a blow or fall.

con·demn (kən dem′), VERB.
1 to say that something or someone is very bad or evil: *We condemn cruelty to animals.*
2 to give a punishment to someone; sentence: *The spy was condemned to death.*
3 to declare something is unsafe: *This house was condemned because the roof has fallen in.*
❏ VERB **con·demns, con·demned, con·demn·ing.**
—**con·dem·na·tion,** (kon′dem nā′shən), NOUN.

con·den·sa·tion (kon′den sā′shən), NOUN.
1 something condensed; condensed mass. A cloud is a condensation of water vapor in the atmosphere.
2 something that has been shortened: *The magazine printed a condensation of the book.*

con·dense (kən dens′), VERB.
1 to make a liquid thicker: *Cream condenses when it is cooked.*
2 to change from a gas or a vapor to a liquid. If warm air touches a cold surface, it condenses into tiny drops of water.
3 to say or write something in fewer words: *A long story can often be condensed.*
❏ VERB **con·dens·es, con·densed, con·dens·ing.**

con·di·tion (kən dish′ən),
1 NOUN. the state in which someone or something is found: *My room was in a messy condition.*
2 NOUN. a state of physical fitness; good health: *The athlete was in excellent condition.*
3 VERB. to put in a state of fitness: *Exercise conditions your muscles.*
4 NOUN. **conditions,** set of circumstances: *Icy roads cause bad driving conditions.*
5 NOUN. something that must happen before something else can happen: *One condition of the peace treaty was the return of all prisoners.*
❏ VERB **con·di·tions, con·di·tioned, con·di·tion·ing.**

con·di·tion·er (kən dish′ə nər), NOUN. a substance that is used to improve something: *Since my hair is too dry, I use a conditioner after I shampoo it.*

con·do (kon′dō), NOUN. a short form of condominium. ❏ PLURAL **con·dos.**

con·do·min·i·um (kon′də min′ē əm), NOUN.
1 an apartment house in which each apartment is owned rather than rented.
2 an apartment in a building like this.

con·dor (kon′dər), NOUN. a large vulture with a bare neck and head. Condors live on high mountains in South America and California.

con·duct (kon′dukt for noun; kən dukt′ for verb),
1 NOUN. a way of acting; behavior thought of as good or bad: *Her conduct was rude.*
2 VERB. to direct the playing of a group of musicians in a performance.
3 VERB. to go along with as a leader; guide: *She conducts tours through the museum.*
4 VERB. to transmit: *Metals conduct heat well.*
❏ VERB **con·ducts, con·duct·ed, con·duct·ing.**

con·duc·tor (kən duk′tər), NOUN.
1 someone who directs the playing of a group of musicians.

condor — about 4½ feet long

2 someone in charge of a train and its passengers. The conductor often collects tickets or fares.
3 something that transmits heat, electricity, light, or sound: *Copper wire is used as a conductor of electricity.*

cone (kōn), NOUN.
1 a solid object with a flat, round base that narrows to a point at the top.
2 anything shaped like a cone: *an ice-cream cone.*
3 a cone-shaped cluster of seeds. Pines, cedars, and many other evergreen trees have cones.

Con·es·to·ga wag·on (kon′ə stō′gə wag′ən), a covered wagon with large, narrow wheels. American pioneers used them for traveling across the prairie with their belongings.

Did You Know?
Conestoga wagons were pulled by teams of horses or oxen. The wheels of the wagon could be taken off and the wagon could be used as a boat.

Conestoga wagon

con·fed·er·a·cy (kən fed′ər ə sē), NOUN.
1 a union of countries or states; group of people joined together for a special purpose.
2 **the Confederacy,** the group of 11 southern states that left the United States in 1860 and 1861.
❏ PLURAL **con·fed·er·a·cies.**

con·fed·er·ate (kən fed′ər it),
1 NOUN. a person or country joined with another for a special purpose; ally: *The thief and his confederates escaped to another city.*
2 ADJECTIVE. joined together for a special purpose; allied.
3 **Confederate, a** ADJECTIVE. of or belonging to the Confederacy. **b** NOUN. someone who lived in, supported, or fought for the Confederacy.

a	hat	ė	term	ô	order	ch	child	⎧a in about
ā	age	i	it	oi	oil	ng	long	⎪e in taken
ä	far	ī	ice	ou	out	sh	she	ə ⎨i in pencil
â	care	o	hot	u	cup	th	thin	⎪o in lemon
e	let	ō	open	ù	put	ŦH	then	⎩u in circus
ē	equal	ò	saw	ü	rule	zh	measure	

con·fed·e·ra·tion (kən fed/ə rā/shən), NOUN. a group joined together for a special purpose: *The United States was originally a confederation of 13 colonies.*

con·fer (kən fėr/), VERB.
1 to talk things over; exchange ideas: *His parents conferred with the teacher about his schoolwork.*
2 to give; bestow: *The university conferred an honorary degree on the scientist.*
❏ VERB **con·fers, con·ferred, con·fer·ring.**

con·fer·ence (kon/fər əns), NOUN. a meeting of interested people to discuss a particular subject: *Parent conferences will be held next week.*

con·fess (kən fes/), VERB.
1 to admit that you have done something wrong: *I confessed to eating all the cookies.*
2 to tell sins to a priest in order to obtain God's forgiveness.
❏ VERB **con·fess·es, con·fessed, con·fess·ing.**

con·fes·sion (kən fesh/ən), NOUN.
1 an act of confessing; telling your mistakes: *The burglary suspect made a full confession.*
2 an act of telling your sins to a priest in order to obtain forgiveness.

con·fet·ti (kən fet/ē), NOUN. bits of colored paper thrown about at weddings, parades, or other celebrations: *We threw confetti at the bride and groom as they left the church.*

Word Story

Confetti comes from an Italian word meaning "candies." Italians used to celebrate carnivals by throwing candies wrapped in colored paper. In other countries, people threw just the paper.

con·fide (kən fīd/), VERB. to tell someone a secret: *He confided his troubles to his sister.* ❏ VERB **con·fides, con·fid·ed, con·fid·ing.**

con·fi·dence (kon/fə dəns), NOUN.
1 a firm belief or trust in someone or something: *I have complete confidence in his honesty.*
2 a firm belief in yourself and your abilities: *Early successes have given him great confidence.*
3 a feeling of trust that someone will not tell other people what is said: *The secret was told to me in strict confidence.*

con·fi·dent (kon/fə dənt), ADJECTIVE. firmly believing; certain; sure: *I feel confident that our team will win.* ■ See the Synonym Study at **sure.**
—**con/fi·dent·ly,** ADVERB.

con·fi·den·tial (kon/fə den/shəl), ADJECTIVE. secret; not to be published or talked about: *This story is confidential; you must never repeat it.*
—**con/fi·den/tial·ly,** ADVERB.

con·fine (kən fīn/), VERB.
1 to keep someone in; hold in: *A cold confined her to the house.*
2 to keep within limits; restrict: *She confined her reading to biography.*
❏ VERB **con·fines, con·fined, con·fin·ing.**
—**con·fine/ment,** NOUN.

con·firm (kən fėrm/), VERB.
1 to make clear that something is true or correct; make certain: *The newspaper confirmed the story.*
2 to tell someone that something is approved or definite: *The hotel telephoned to confirm the reservation I had made last week.*
3 to approve; agree to: *The Senate confirmed the President's appointments to the Cabinet.*
❏ VERB **con·firms, con·firmed, con·firm·ing.**

con·fir·ma·tion (kon/fər mā/shən), NOUN.
1 the act of making sure of something by getting more information or evidence: *I telephoned the restaurant for confirmation of our reservations.*
2 something that confirms; proof: *Don't believe rumors that lack confirmation.*
3 Confirmation, the holy ceremony of admitting someone to full membership in a church or synagogue after required study and preparation.

con·fis·cate (kon/fə skāt), VERB. to take or seize with authority: *The teacher confiscated my comic books.* ❏ VERB **con·fis·cates, con·fis·cat·ed, con·fis·cat·ing.**

con·flict (kon/flikt for noun; kən flikt/ for verb),
1 NOUN. a fight, struggle, or war, especially a long one: *The conflict between them lasted for years.*
2 NOUN. a strong disagreement: *A conflict of opinion arose over where to go on our vacation.*
3 VERB. to disagree strongly: *Her report of the accident conflicted with mine.*
❏ VERB **con·flicts, con·flict·ed, con·flict·ing.**

con·form (kən fôrm/), VERB. to act according to law or rule: *Members must conform to the rules of our club.* ❏ VERB **con·forms, con·formed, con·form·ing.**

con·front (kən frunt/), VERB.
1 to face something boldly; meet courageously: *We encouraged her to confront her problems.*
2 to bring someone face to face with something; place something directly before someone: *The teacher confronted me with my failing grade.*
❏ VERB **con·fronts, con·front·ed, con·front·ing.**

con·fuse (kən fyüz/), VERB.
1 to mix up: *So many questions at once confused me.*
2 to mistake one thing or person for another: *People often confuse this girl with her twin sister.*
❏ VERB **con·fus·es, con·fused, con·fus·ing.**

con·fu·sion (kən fyü/zhən), NOUN.
1 a condition of disorder and uncontrolled action: *In the confusion after the accident, I forgot to get the name of the witness.*
2 the condition of being perplexed or bewildered: *His confusion over the exact address caused him to go to the wrong house.*

con·ges·tion
(kən jes′chən), NOUN.
1 a crowded condition: *I was caught in Sunday's traffic congestion and got home late.*
2 too much blood or mucus in a part of the body: *nasal congestion.*

congestion on a city sidewalk

Con·go (kong′gō), NOUN. a country in west central Africa.
−Con·go·lese (kong′gə ləz′), ADJECTIVE or NOUN.

con·grat·u·late (kən grach′ə lāt), VERB. to tell someone that you are pleased by his or her happiness or good fortune: *Everyone congratulated the winner of the race.* ❑ VERB **con·grat·u·lates, con·grat·u·lat·ed, con·grat·u·lat·ing.**

con·grat·u·la·tions (kən grach′ə lā′shənz), NOUN.
1 pleasure at someone else's happiness or good fortune: *We yelled our congratulations to the winners.*
2 a word used to express such pleasure: *Congratulations on your high grades.*

con·gre·gate (kong′grə gāt), VERB. to come together in a crowd or group. ❑ VERB **con·gre·gates, con·gre·gat·ed, con·gre·gat·ing.**

Word Story

Congregate comes from a Latin word meaning "to flock together." Some animals, such as sheep, geese, and horses, always group themselves together into a flock or a herd. They are never alone. People often flock together by choice.

con·gre·ga·tion (kong′grə gā′shən), NOUN.
1 the people gathered together for religious worship or instruction.
2 a gathering of people or things; assembly.

con·gress (kong′gris), NOUN.
1 the legislative body of a nation, especially of a republic.
2 **Congress,** the national legislative body of the United States. Congress has two parts, the Senate and the House of Representatives. Members of Congress are elected from every state.
❑ PLURAL **con·gress·es.**

con·gress·man (kong′gris mən), NOUN. a member of Congress, especially of the House of Representatives. ❑ PLURAL **con·gress·men.**

con·gress·wom·an (kong′gris wùm′ən), NOUN. a woman member of Congress, especially of the House of Representatives. ❑ PLURAL **con·gress·wom·en.**

con·i·fer (kon′ə fər or kō′nə fər), NOUN. a tree or bush, usually an evergreen such as the pine or spruce, that has cones.

Did You Know?

Conifers are one of the oldest groups of plants. Fossils of conifers have been found that are more than 300 million years old. Conifers live a long time, too. One conifer, the **bristlecone pine** (bris′l kōn′ pīn′), can live to be more than 4000 years old.

The bristlecone pine is a kind of **conifer.**

con·junc·tion (kən jungk′shən), NOUN. a word that connects words, phrases, clauses, or sentences. *And, but, or, though,* and *if* are conjunctions.

con·nect (kə nekt′), VERB.
1 to join one thing to another; fasten together: *Connect the hose to a faucet.* ■ See the Synonym Study at **join.**
2 to think of something in relation to something else: *We usually connect spring with flowers.*
3 to plug into an electrical or telephone circuit: *The speaker doesn't work because it's not connected.*
❑ VERB **con·nects, con·nect·ed, con·nect·ing.**
−con·nec′tor or **con·nect′er,** NOUN.

Con·nect·i·cut (kə net′ə kət), NOUN. one of the northeastern states of the United States. *Abbreviation:* CT; *Capital:* Hartford.

State Story **Connecticut** comes from an American Indian word meaning "on the long tidal river." The Connecticut River runs through the center of the state into Long Island Sound. Where it meets the sea, its water rises and falls with the tides.

a	hat	ė	term	ô	order	ch	child		a in about
ā	age	i	it	oi	oil	ng	long		e in taken
ä	far	ī	ice	ou	out	sh	she	ə	i in pencil
â	care	o	hot	u	cup	th	thin		o in lemon
e	let	ō	open	ù	put	ŦH	then		u in circus
ē	equal	ò	saw	ü	rule	zh	measure		

con·nec·tion (kə nek′shən), NOUN.
1 something that connects; connecting part: *The connection between the radiator and the furnace is a pipe that comes through the floor.*
2 any kind of relation; association: *There is a strong connection between Thanksgiving and pie.*
3 the scheduling of trains, ships, buses, or airplanes so that passengers can change from one to the other without delay: *The bus arrived late at the airport and we missed our airplane connection.*

con·quer (kong′kər), VERB.
1 to win in war; get by fighting: *The evil knights conquered the defenseless kingdom.*
2 to overcome someone or something; get the better of: *His desire to be an actor conquered his shyness.*
❏ VERB **con·quers, con·quered, con·quer·ing.**

con·quer·or (kong′kər ər), NOUN. someone who conquers.

con·quest (kon′kwest), NOUN.
1 the action or process of conquering: *to gain a country by conquest.*
2 something conquered: *Mexico and Peru were important Spanish conquests.*

con·science (kon′shəns), NOUN. the ideas and feelings within you that tell you when you are doing right and warn you of what is wrong: *I couldn't tell her a lie because my conscience would bother me.*

con·scious (kon′shəs), ADJECTIVE.
1 having knowledge; aware of what is going on: *I was conscious of a sharp pain.*
2 awake: *About five minutes after fainting he became conscious again.*
−**con′scious·ly,** ADVERB.

con·scious·ness (kon′shəs nis), NOUN.
1 the condition of being conscious; awareness: *The injured woman lost consciousness.*
2 all of someone's thoughts and feelings.

con·sec·u·tive (kən sek′yə tiv), ADJECTIVE. following one right after another: *Monday, Tuesday, and Wednesday are consecutive days of the week.*
−**con·sec′u·tive·ly,** ADVERB.

con·sent (kən sent′),
1 VERB. give approval or permission: *My parents would not consent to my staying out overnight.*
2 NOUN. approval; permission: *We have our mother's consent to go swimming.*
❏ VERB **con·sents, con·sent·ed, con·sent·ing.**

con·se·quence (kon′sə kwens), NOUN. a result: *The consequence of the fall was a broken leg.*

con·ser·va·tion (kon′sər vā′shən), NOUN.
1 protection from loss, waste, or being used up: *Conservation of energy saves fuel.*
2 the official protection and care of forests, rivers, and other natural resources.

con·ser·va·tion·ist (kon′sər vā′shə nist), NOUN. someone who wants to preserve and protect the forests, rivers, and other natural resources of a country.

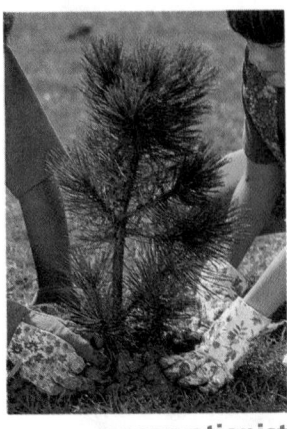
conservationist

con·serv·a·tive (kən sėr′və tiv),
1 ADJECTIVE. wanting to keep things as they are or were in the past; opposed to change in established traditions.
2 NOUN. someone opposed to change.
3 ADJECTIVE. not inclined to take risks; cautious: *This company uses conservative business methods.*

con·serve (kən sėrv′), VERB. to protect something from loss or from being used up; preserve: *Try to conserve your strength for the end of the race.*
❏ VERB **con·serves, con·served, con·serv·ing.**

con·sid·er (kən sid′ər), VERB.
1 to think about something in order to decide: *Before you act, consider the problem.*
2 to think someone to be: *I consider him cute.*
3 to keep in mind; take into account: *This watch runs very well, when you consider how old it is.*
4 to be thoughtful of others and their feelings: *A kind person considers the feelings of others.*
❏ VERB **con·sid·ers, con·sid·ered, con·sid·er·ing.**

con·sid·er·a·ble (kən sid′ər ə bəl), ADJECTIVE. large; important: *$50,000 is a considerable sum of money.*

con·sid·er·ate (kən sid′ər it), ADJECTIVE. thoughtful of other people and their feelings: *It was considerate of you to call and let me know that you would be late.* −**con·sid′er·ate·ly,** ADVERB.

con·sid·er·a·tion (kən sid′ə rā′shən), NOUN.
1 careful thought about things in order to decide: *Give careful consideration to your answers.*
2 something that you think about when you make a decision: *Price is a consideration in buying a car.*
3 thoughtfulness toward others and their feelings: *Playing loud music at night shows a lack of consideration for the neighbors.*

con·sist (kən sist′), VERB. to be made up: *A week consists of seven days.* ❏ VERB **con·sists, con·sist·ed, con·sist·ing.**

con·sist·en·cy (kən sis′tən sē), NOUN.
1 the degree of firmness or stiffness of something: *Frosting for a cake must be of the right consistency to spread easily without dripping.*
2 the quality of keeping to the same kinds of action: *You show very little consistency if you are always changing your mind.*
❏ PLURAL **con·sist·en·cies.**

con·sist·ent (kən sis′tənt), *ADJECTIVE.* always acting or thinking in the same way as you did before. —**con·sist′ent·ly,** *ADVERB.*

con·sole (kən sōl′), *VERB.* to help an unhappy person feel better: *The policeman consoled the lost child by promising to find his parents.* ❑ *VERB* **con·soles, con·soled, con·sol·ing.** —**con·so·la·tion** (kon′sə lā′shən), *NOUN.* —**con·sol′er,** *NOUN.*

con·sol·i·date (kən sol′ə dāt), *VERB.* to join several things into one thing; unite; combine: *The three companies consolidated and formed a single large company.* ❑ *VERB* **con·sol·i·dates, con·sol·i·dat·ed, con·sol·i·dat·ing.** —**con·sol′i·da′tion,** *NOUN.*

con·so·nant (kon′sə nənt), *NOUN.*
1 any letter of the alphabet that is not a vowel. The letters *b, c, d,* and *f* are consonants.
2 a sound represented by such a letter or combination of letters. The two consonants in *ship* are spelled by the letters *sh* and *p.*

con·spic·u·ous (kən spik′yü əs), *ADJECTIVE.*
1 very easy to see: *A traffic light should be placed where it is conspicuous.*
2 attracting attention; remarkable: *The soldier received a medal for conspicuous bravery.* —**con·spic′u·ous·ly,** *ADVERB.*

con·spir·a·cy (kən spir′ə sē), *NOUN.* a secret plan with other people to do something wrong or unlawful; plot: *There was a conspiracy to overthrow the government.* ❑ *PLURAL* **con·spir·a·cies.**

con·spire (kən spīr′), *VERB.* to plan secretly with other people to do something wrong or unlawful; plot: *The spies conspired to steal the documents.* ❑ *VERB* **con·spires, con·spired, con·spir·ing.**

con·stant (kon′stənt), *ADJECTIVE.*
1 never stopping; continuous: *Three days of constant rain caused flooding.*
2 always the same; not changing: *The ship held a constant course due north.* —**con′stant·ly,** *ADVERB.*

con·stel·la·tion (kon′stə lā′shən), *NOUN.* a group of stars that forms a pattern.

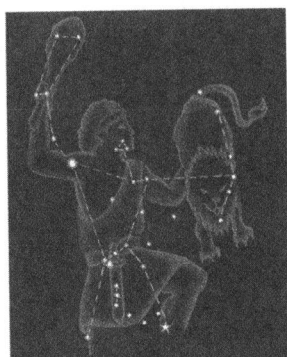

constellation

Did You Know?

The word **constellation** is also used to mean an area of the sky where stars can be seen. The sky is divided into 88 constellations. People at the equator can see all of the constellations. People farther north and south can only see some of them.

con·sti·pa·ted (kon′stə pā′tid), *ADJECTIVE.* not able to move your bowels easily.

con·stit·u·ent (kən stich′ü ənt), *NOUN.* one of the voters represented by an elected official: *Senators are eager to hear from their constituents.*

con·sti·tute (kon′stə tüt), *VERB.* to make up something; form: *Seven days constitute a week.* ❑ *VERB* **con·sti·tutes, con·sti·tut·ed, con·sti·tut·ing.**

con·sti·tu·tion (kon′stə tü′shən), *NOUN.*
1 a system of basic rules according to which a nation, state, or group is governed.
2 the Constitution, the written set of basic rules by which the United States is governed.

con·sti·tu·tion·al (kon′stə tü′shə nəl), *ADJECTIVE.* of, in, or according to the constitution of a nation, state, or group: *The Supreme Court must decide whether this law is constitutional.*

con·struct (kən strukt′), *VERB.* to put something together; build: *We constructed a raft of logs fastened with rope.* ■ See the Synonym Study at **make.** ❑ *VERB* **con·structs, con·struct·ed, con·struct·ing.**

con·struc·tion (kən struk′shən), *NOUN.*
1 the act of putting something together; building: *The construction of the bridge took nearly a year.*
2 the way in which something is put together: *Cracks and leaks are signs of poor construction.*
3 something built or put together: *The doll's house was a construction of wood and cardboard.*

construction paper, a kind of heavy paper, often brightly colored, used to make things, especially in schools: *We made pictures by gluing beans to construction paper.*

con·struc·tive (kən struk′tiv), *ADJECTIVE.* helping to improve; useful: *During my report the teacher gave some constructive suggestions that helped me think of ideas I had overlooked.* —**con·struc′tive·ly,** *ADVERB.* —**con·struc′tive·ness,** *NOUN.*

con·sul (kon′səl), *NOUN.* an officer appointed by a government to live in some foreign city in order to look after its business interests and to protect its citizens who are traveling or living there.

con·sult (kən sult′), *VERB.* to seek information or advice from someone or something; refer to: *You can consult travelers, books, or maps for help in planning a trip abroad. If you are sick you should consult a doctor.* ❑ *VERB* **con·sults, con·sult·ed, con·sult·ing.** —**con·sul·ta·tion** (kon′səl tā′shən), *NOUN.*

a	hat	ė	term	ô	order	ch	child		a in about
ā	age	i	it	oi	oil	ng	long		e in taken
ä	far	ī	ice	ou	out	sh	she	ə	i in pencil
â	care	o	hot	u	cup	th	thin		o in lemon
e	let	ō	open	u̇	put	ᴛʜ	then		u in circus
ē	equal	ȯ	saw	ü	rule	zh	measure		

con·sult·ant (kən sult′nt), NOUN. someone hired to give advice on how to run a business, keep computers working, and so on.

con·sume (kən süm′), VERB.
1 to use up; spend: *Rockets consume large quantities of fuel when they take off.*
2 to eat or drink up: *We will each consume at least two sandwiches on our hike.* ■ See Synonym study at **eat.**
3 to destroy completely: *The fire consumed the house.*
❑ VERB **con·sumes, con·sumed, con·sum·ing.**

con·sum·er (kən sü′mər), NOUN.
1 someone who buys and uses food, clothing, or anything grown or made by someone else.
2 any living thing that has to eat in order to stay alive. Animals are consumers, but plants make their own food.

consumers selecting a product

con·sump·tion (kən sump′shən), NOUN.
1 the act or process of using something up: *We took along fruit for consumption on the trip.*
2 the amount used up: *Our gas consumption on the trip was 120 gallons.*

con·tact (kon′takt),
1 NOUN. the condition or fact of touching; touching together: *A magnet will draw pieces of iron or steel into contact with it.*
2 NOUN. communication: *The control tower lost radio contact with the airplane pilot.*
3 VERB. to get in touch with someone; make a connection with: *I've been trying to contact you for two days.*
4 NOUN. See **contact lens.**
❑ VERB **con·tacts, con·tact·ed, con·tact·ing.**

contact lens, a very small, thin, plastic lens worn directly on the front of the eyeball to improve vision. Contact lenses are used instead of glasses.

con·ta·gious (kən tā′jəs), ADJECTIVE.
1 spreading by contact with people who already have the illness; catching: *Mumps is contagious.*
2 easily spreading from one person to another: *Yawning is often contagious.*

3 able to pass a sickness on to someone else: *She had to stay home because she is still contagious.*

con·tain (kən tān′), VERB.
1 to have something inside itself: *My wallet contains two dollars. Books contain information.*
2 to be equal to: *A pound contains 16 ounces.*
3 to control your feelings: *She could not contain her excitement over winning the contest.*
❑ VERB **con·tains, con·tained, con·tain·ing.**

con·tain·er (kən tā′nər), NOUN. a box, can, jar, or anything used to hold or store something.

con·tam·i·nate (ken tam′ə nāt), VERB. to make something impure or spoil it by mixing it with something else; pollute: *The water was contaminated by sewage.* ❑ VERB **con·tam·i·nates, con·tam·i·nat·ed, con·tam·i·nat·ing.** —**con·tam′i·na′tion,** NOUN.

con·tem·po·rar·y (kən tem′pə rer′ē),
1 ADJECTIVE. of or in the present time; modern: *I have a book of contemporary children's stories.*
2 NOUN. someone who lives in the same period of time as another person: *Abraham Lincoln and Robert E. Lee were contemporaries.*
3 ADJECTIVE. belonging to the same period of time: *The computer and the laser were contemporary inventions.*
❑ PLURAL **con·tem·po·rar·ies.**

con·tempt (kən tempt′), NOUN.
1 the feeling that someone or something is shameful and disgraceful; scorn: *He felt contempt for the thief.*
2 the condition of being despised; disgrace: *The traitor was held in contempt.*

con·tempt·i·ble (kən temp′tə bəl), ADJECTIVE. deserving contempt or scorn: *Cruelty to animals is contemptible.*

con·tend (ken tend′), VERB.
1 to fight; struggle: *The first settlers in New England had to contend with harsh winters, sickness, and lack of food.*
2 to take part in a contest; compete: *Five runners were contending in the first race.*
3 to declare something to be true: *Doctors contend that cigarette smoking is dangerous to your health.*
❑ VERB **con·tends, con·tend·ed, con·tend·ing.** —**con·tend′er,** NOUN.

con·tent[1] (kon′tent), NOUN.
1 **contents,** all the things inside a box, a house, and so on: *An old chair and a bed were the only contents of the room.*
2 chapters or sections in a book. A **table of contents** gives a list of these.
3 what is written in a book; what is said in a speech: *I didn't understand the content of his speech.*
4 the amount of something in a substance: *Maple syrup has a high sugar content.*

con·tent² (kən tent′),
1 *VERB.* to satisfy; please: *Nothing contents me when I am sick.*
2 *ADJECTIVE.* satisfied; pleased: *Will you be content to wait till tomorrow?*
  ❏ *VERB* **con·tents, con·tent·ed, con·tent·ing.**
  —**con·tent′ment,** *NOUN.*

con·tent·ed (kən ten′tid), *ADJECTIVE.* satisfied: *A contented person is happy with things as they are.*
  —**con·tent′ed·ly,** *ADVERB.* —**con·tent′ed·ness,** *NOUN.*

con·test (kon′test), *NOUN.*
1 a trial of skill to see who can win. A game or race is a contest.
2 a fight, struggle, or dispute for power: *The two students took part in a fierce contest for class president.*

con·test·ant (kən tes′tənt), *NOUN.* someone who takes part in a contest: *My sister was a contestant in the 100-yard dash.*

These **contestants** are running a hurdles race.

con·text (kon′tekst), *NOUN.* the part directly before and after a word or sentence that influences its meaning. You can often tell the meaning of a word from its use in context.

con·ti·nent (kon′tə nənt), *NOUN.* one of the seven great masses of land on the earth. The continents are North America, South America, Europe, Africa, Asia, Australia, and Antarctica.

con·ti·nent·al (kon′tə nen′tl), *ADJECTIVE.* of, about, or like a continent.

con·tin·u·al (kən tin′yü əl), *ADJECTIVE.*
1 repeated many times; very frequent: *I can't study with these continual interruptions.*
2 never stopping: *Farmers depend on the continual flow of the river.*
  —**con·tin′u·al·ly,** *ADVERB.*

con·tin·ue (kən tin′yü), *VERB.*
1 to keep up; keep on; go on: *The rain continued all day. We continued walking after asking for directions.*
2 to go on with something after stopping for a while: *The story will be continued next week.*

3 to stay; remain: *The children must continue in school till the end of June.*
  ❏ *VERB* **con·tin·ues, con·tin·ued, con·tin·u·ing.**
  —**con·tin′u·a′tion,** *NOUN.*

con·tin·u·ous (kən tin′yü əs), *ADJECTIVE.* without a stop: *a continuous sound, a continuous line of cars.*
  —**con·tin′u·ous·ly,** *ADVERB.*

con·tour (kon′tùr), *NOUN.* the line formed by the edge or outside of some shape or mass: *The contour of the coast here is very irregular.*

con·tract (kon′trakt *for noun;* kon′trakt *or* kən trakt′ *for 2;* kən trakt′ *for 3-5;*),
1 *NOUN.* an agreement, usually in writing, by which two or more people promise to do or not to do certain things. A contract can be enforced by law.
2 *VERB.* to make a contract: *The builder contracted to build a new house for a certain price.*
3 *VERB.* to catch; get: *She contracted the flu, but soon got well again.*
4 *VERB.* to shorten a word or phrase by omitting some of the letters or sounds: *In talking and writing we often contract "do not" to "don't."*
5 *VERB.* to draw together; make or become shorter or smaller: *The earthworm contracted its body. A balloon contracts when the air is let out of it.*
  ❏ *VERB* **con·tracts, con·tract·ed, con·tract·ing.**

con·trac·tion (kən trak′shən), *NOUN.*
1 something contracted; shortened form: *"Can't" is a contraction of "cannot."*
2 action of contracting: *Cold causes the contraction of substances; heat causes their expansion.*

con·trac·tor (kon′trak tər), *NOUN.* someone who agrees to supply materials or to do a job for a certain price: *My family hired a contractor to build our new house.*

con·tra·dict (kon′trə dikt′), *VERB.*
1 to say the opposite of what someone has said: *Not only did she contradict him, she said that he was not telling the truth.*
2 to be opposite to something; disagree with: *Your story and her story contradict each other.*
  ❏ *VERB* **con·tra·dicts, con·tra·dict·ed, con·tra·dict·ing.**

con·tra·dic·tion (kon′trə dik′shən), *NOUN.*
1 a statement that contradicts another: *His story was a direct contradiction of yours.*
2 the act of denying what has been said: *The expert spoke without fear of contradiction.*

con·tra·ry (kon′trer ē *for 1 and 2;* kən trer′ē *for 3*),
1 *ADJECTIVE.* opposite; completely different: *Her taste in music is contrary to mine.*

a hat	ė term	ô order	ch child	⎧a in about
ā age	i it	oi oil	ng long	e in taken
ä far	ī ice	ou out	sh she	ə⎨i in pencil
â care	o hot	u cup	th thin	o in lemon
e let	ō open	ù put	ŦH then	⎩u in circus
ē equal	ò saw	ü rule	zh measure	

2 NOUN. the opposite: *After promising to come early, she did the contrary and came late.*

3 ADJECTIVE. stubborn: *The contrary boy often refused to do what was suggested.*

on the contrary, IDIOM. exactly opposite to what has been said: *He is not stingy; on the contrary, no one could be more generous.*

con·trast (kon′trast *for noun;* kən trast′ *for verb*),

1 NOUN. a great difference: *There is a clear contrast between life now and life years ago.*

2 NOUN. someone or something that shows differences when compared with another: *Her dark hair is a sharp contrast to her brother's light hair.*

3 VERB. to compare two things in order to show their differences: *The science book contrasts birds and fish.*

4 VERB. to be different from something else when compared with it: *Her interest in sports contrasts with her brother's liking for books.*

❑ VERB **con·trasts, con·trast·ed, con·trast·ing.**

con·trib·ute (kən trib′yüt), VERB.

1 to give money, help, advice, and so on, along with other people: *Everyone was asked to contribute suggestions for the party.*

2 to write articles or stories for a newspaper or magazine.

❑ VERB **con·trib·utes, con·trib·ut·ed, con·trib·ut·ing.** –**con·trib′u·tor,** NOUN.

contribute to, IDIOM. to help bring about: *A poor diet contributed to the child's bad health.*

con·tri·bu·tion (kon′trə byü′shən), NOUN. money, help, advice, and so on that is given; gift: *Our contribution to the picnic was the lemonade.*

con·trol (kən trōl′),

1 VERB. to have power or authority over something; direct: *The government controls the printing of money.*

2 NOUN. power to decide things; authority; direction: *Children are under their parents' control.*

3 VERB. to keep from showing your feelings too much so that you can act calmly: *Sometimes it's necessary to control your temper.*

4 NOUN. the ability to keep from showing your feelings too much: *You must gain control of temper.*

5 NOUN. a device on or connected to a machine that starts, stops, or adjusts its operation: *This control starts the dishwasher.*

6 NOUN. **the controls,** the devices by which an aircraft, car, or other machine is operated: *The pilot sat down at the controls.*

❑ VERB **con·trols, con·trolled, con·trol·ling.** –**con·trol′ler,** NOUN.

control tower, a tower at an airfield for controlling the taking off and landing of aircraft.

con·tro·ver·sial (kon′trə vėr′shəl), ADJECTIVE. causing argument or disagreement: *The possibility of keeping school open all year is a controversial topic.*

con·tro·ver·sy (kon′trə vėr′sē), NOUN. a dispute; long argument: *The controversy between the company and the union ended after the strike was settled.* ❑ PLURAL **con·tro·ver·sies.**

con·va·les·cent (kon′və les′nt),

1 ADJECTIVE. getting your health and strength back after an illness.

2 NOUN. someone who is getting better after being sick for a while.

con·vene (kən vēn′), VERB. to gather together; assemble: *Congress convenes at least once a year.* ❑ VERB **con·venes, con·vened, con·ven·ing.**

con·ven·ience (kən vē′nyəns), NOUN.

1 the quality of being simple or easy to use, reach, get, and so on: *The convenience of packaged goods increases their sale.*

2 comfort; advantage: *Many national parks have camping places for the convenience of tourists.*

3 something that saves trouble or work: *A folding table is a convenience in a small room.*

con·ven·ient (kən vē′nyənt), ADJECTIVE.

1 easy to use; saving trouble; well arranged: *It's convenient to have a garage attached to your house.*

2 easily done; not troublesome: *Will it be convenient for you to bring your lunch to school?* –**con·ven′ient·ly,** ADVERB.

con·vent (kon′vent), NOUN.

1 a group of nuns living together.

2 the building or buildings in which they live.

con·ven·tion (kən ven′shən), NOUN.

1 a meeting arranged for some particular purpose: *Political parties hold conventions every four years to choose candidates for President.*

2 behavior that most people agree on: *Using the right hand to shake hands is a convention.*

con·ven·tion·al (kən ven′shə nəl), ADJECTIVE. following usual, customary behavior: *"Good morning" is a conventional greeting.*

an air traffic controller at work in a **control tower**

con·ver·sa·tion (kon′vər sā′shən), NOUN. friendly talk between two or more people; exchange of thoughts by talking informally together.

con·verse (kən vėrs′), *VERB.* to talk together. ❑ *VERB* **con·vers·es, con·versed, con·vers·ing.**

con·ver·sion (kən vėr′zhən), *NOUN.*
1 the act or process of changing something into a different state or form: *Heat causes the conversion of water into steam.*
2 a change from one religious belief to another.
3 (in football) one or two extra points scored after a touchdown.

con·vert (kən vėrt′ *for verb;* kon′vėrt′ *for noun*),
1 *VERB.* to change something into a different form: *The generators at the dam convert water power into electricity.*
2 *VERB.* to cause someone to change from one religious belief to another: *Missionaries tried to convert the villagers.*
3 *NOUN.* someone who has been converted to a different belief.
❑ *VERB* **con·verts, con·vert·ed, con·vert·ing.**

con·vert·i·ble (kən vėr′tə bəl),
1 *NOUN.* a car with a folding top.
2 *NOUN.* a sofa that can be unfolded and used as a bed.
3 *ADJECTIVE.* able to be converted: *A dollar bill is convertible into ten dimes.*

convertible (definition 1)

con·vex (kon veks′ *or* kon′veks), *ADJECTIVE.* curved out, like the outside of a bowl: *Headlights are convex on the outside.* ■ See the illustration at **concave.**

con·vey (kən vā′), *VERB.* to take someone or something from one place to another; carry; bring: *A bus conveyed the passengers to the airport. A wire conveys an electric current.* ❑ *VERB* **con·veys, con·veyed, con·vey·ing.**

con·vey·or belt or **con·vey·er belt** (kən vā′ər belt′), a mechanical device that carries things from one place to another by means of a moving, endless belt.

con·vict (kən vikt′ *for verb;* kon′vikt *for noun*),
1 *VERB.* to prove or find someone guilty: *The jury convicted the accused woman of stealing.*
2 *NOUN.* someone serving a prison sentence for a crime.
❑ *VERB* **con·victs, con·vict·ed, con·vict·ing.**

con·vic·tion (kən vik′shən), *NOUN.*
1 the act of proving or finding someone guilty: *The trial resulted in the conviction of the accused man.*
2 a strong belief: *It's my conviction that he is right.*

con·vince (kən vins′), *VERB.* to make someone believe something: *The mistakes she made convinced me that she had not studied her lesson.* ❑ *VERB* **con·vinc·es, con·vinced, con·vinc·ing.**

con·voy (kon′voi), *NOUN.* a group of ships or motor vehicles traveling together for protection or convenience.

con·vul·sion (kən vul′shən), *NOUN.* a powerful, uncontrolled shaking of your entire body, caused by illness.

cook (kůk),
1 *VERB.* to make food ready to eat by using heat. Boiling, frying, broiling, roasting, and baking are some ways to cook.
2 *VERB.* to be cooked: *Let the meat cook slowly.*
3 *NOUN.* someone who cooks.
■ See the Word Story at **kitchen** ❑ *VERB* **cooks, cooked, cook·ing.**

cook·ie (kůk′ē), *NOUN.* a small, flat, sweet cake. ❑ *PLURAL* **cook·ies.**

Word Story

The word **cookie** looks as if it came from the word *cook.* Actually it comes from a Dutch word meaning "little cake."

cook·out (kůk′out′), *NOUN.* a meal where you cook food outdoors on a grill: *We served hot dogs, hamburgers, and corn at our cookout.*

cool (kül),
1 *ADJECTIVE.* somewhat cold; more cold than hot: *Yesterday was a cool day.* ■ See the Synonym Study at **cold.**
2 *VERB.* to make or become cool: *The ground cools off after the sun goes down.*
3 *ADJECTIVE.* not very friendly: *My former friend gave me a cool greeting.*
4 *ADJECTIVE.* not excited; calm: *Everyone kept cool when paper in the wastebasket caught fire.*
5 *NOUN.* (informal) calmness; presence of mind: *He was so upset by the accident that he lost his cool completely.*
6 *ADJECTIVE.* (informal) very good; excellent: *That movie was so cool that it was worth seeing twice.* ❑ *VERB* **cools, cooled, cool·ing.** –**cool′ly,** *ADVERB.* –**cool′ness,** *NOUN.*

cool·er (kü′lər), *NOUN.* a container that cools food or drinks, or keeps them cool.

a	hat	ė	term	ô	order	ch	child		a in about
ā	age	i	it	oi	oil	ng	long		e in taken
ä	far	ī	ice	ou	out	sh	she	ə ⟨ i in pencil
â	care	o	hot	u	cup	th	thin		o in lemon
e	let	ō	open	ů	put	ŦH	then		u in circus
ē	equal	ò	saw	ü	rule	zh	measure		

coop (küp), *NOUN.* a small cage or pen for chickens, rabbits, or other small animals.

 coop up, *IDIOM.* to keep someone or something in a space that is too small: *Don't coop up a big dog in a little yard.* ❑ *VERB* **coops, cooped, coop·ing.**

co-op (kō′op′), *NOUN.* a short form of **cooperative.**

co·op·er·ate (kō op′ə rāt′), *VERB.* to work together: *Everyone cooperated in helping to clean up after the class party.* ❑ *VERB* **co·op·e·rates, co·op·e·rat·ed, co·op·e·rat·ing.**

co·op·e·ra·tion (kō op′ə rā′shən), *NOUN.* the act or process of working together: *Cooperation can accomplish things that no person could do alone.*

co·op·er·a·tive (kō op′ər ə tiv),
 1 *ADJECTIVE.* willing to work together with others: *Most of the pupils were helpful and cooperative.*
 2 *NOUN.* a business, store, or apartment building owned by the people who work or live there; co-op. Cooperatives usually provide their members with goods or services at a reduced price. **—co·op′er·a·tive·ly,** *ADVERB.*

co·or·di·nate (kō ôrd′n āt *for verb;* kō ôrd′n it *for noun*),
 1 *VERB.* to work or cause something to work together in the proper way: *Coordinating the movements of the arms and legs is the hardest part of learning to swim.*
 2 *NOUN.* any of a set of numbers that give the position of a point by reference to fixed lines. ❑ *VERB* **co·or·di·nates, co·or·di·nat·ed, co·or·di·nat·ing. —co·or′di·na′tor,** *NOUN.*

coordinate grid, a graph made of a grid of numbered horizontal and vertical lines. An ordered pair of numbers gives the location of any point on the graph.

coordinating conjunction, a word, such as *and* or *but,* that joins words, phrases, or clauses of equal grammatical importance. In "John and I are friends," *and* is a coordinating conjunction.

co·or·di·na·tion (kō ôrd′n ā′shən), *NOUN.* the action of working together in a smooth way: *Muscular coordination is important to an athlete.*

cope (kōp), *VERB.* to deal with something successfully: *She was busy but was still able to cope with the extra work.* ❑ *VERB* **copes, coped, cop·ing.**

cop·i·er (kop′ē ər), *NOUN.* See **photocopier.**

co·pi·lot (kō′pī′lət), *NOUN.* the assistant pilot in an aircraft.

cop·per (kop′ər),
 1 *NOUN.* a soft, reddish brown metal. Copper is a chemical element. It is an excellent conductor of heat and electricity.
 2 *ADJECTIVE.* made of this metal: *a copper kettle.*

cop·per·head (kop′ər hed′), *NOUN.* a poisonous snake of eastern North America. It has a copper-colored head.

cop·y (kop′ē),
 1 *NOUN.* something made to look just like something else. A written page, a picture, or a dress can be an exact copy of another.
 2 *VERB.* to make a copy of something: *Copy this page.*
 3 *VERB.* to follow someone's example; imitate: *She copied her aunt's way of dressing.*
 4 *NOUN.* one of a number of books, magazines, newspapers, or pictures made at the same printing: *Please pick up six copies of today's paper.* ❑ *PLURAL* **cop·ies;** *VERB* **cop·ies, cop·ied, cop·y·ing.**

cop·y·cat (kop′ē kat′), *NOUN.* someone who imitates someone else.

co·ral (kôr′əl),
 1 *NOUN.* a hard substance formed from the skeletons of tiny sea animals. These animals live in large colonies. One kind of coral is used to make jewelry.
 2 *ADJECTIVE or NOUN.* deep pink; yellowish red.

Did You Know?

Many islands in the Pacific Ocean started as large piles of living and dead **coral.** Soil is trapped on top of the piles and plants begin to grow. In time, an entire island is formed.

coral reef

coral reef, a ridge of coral and mineral deposits at or near the surface of the sea. Coral reefs support many kinds of living things.

coral snake, a small, poisonous American snake. Coral snakes have bodies banded by alternating rings of red, yellow, and black.

cord (kôrd), *NOUN.*
 1 a thick string; very thin rope: *He tied the package with a cord.*
 2 a length of flexible, electrical wire covered with plastic. It has a plug at one end that connects an electrical appliance to an outlet.
 3 a structure like a cord in an animal body. The spinal cord is in the backbone.
 ■ Another word that sounds like this is **chord.**

cor·dial (kôr′jəl), ADJECTIVE. sincerely friendly; hearty; warm: *My friends gave me a cordial welcome.* **–cor′dial·ly,** ADVERB.

cor·du·roy (kôr′də roi′), NOUN. a thick cotton cloth with close, raised ridges that run lengthwise along the cloth.

core (kôr),
1 NOUN. the hard, central part containing the seeds of apples and pears: *After eating the apple, he threw the core away.*
2 NOUN. the central or most important part of something: *He is honest to the core. The core of her speech was that we must not waste resources.*
3 VERB. to take out the core of fruit: *Core the apples.* ❑ VERB **cores, cored, cor·ing.** ■ Another word that sounds like this is **corps.**

cork (kôrk), NOUN.
1 the light, thick, outer bark of a kind of oak tree. Cork is used for bottle stoppers, floats for fishing lines, and floor coverings.
2 a bottle stopper made of cork or other material.

Did You Know?

A **cork tree** has to grow for twenty years before its bark can be removed. After that, the bark can be taken again about every ten years.

cork·screw (kôrk′skrü′), NOUN. a tool that can be screwed into corks to remove them from bottles. A corkscrew is a long, twisted piece of metal with a sharp point and a handle.

corn¹ (kôrn), NOUN. a yellow or white vegetable that grows on ears on a tall, green plant; maize. Corn is used as food for people and farm animals.

She loves **corn** best.

corn² (kôrn), NOUN. a hard thickening of the skin, usually on a toe. Shoes that rub or fit too tightly can cause painful corns.

corn·bread (kôrn′bred′), NOUN. a bread made of cornmeal.

corn·cob (kôrn′kob′), NOUN. the central, woody part of an ear of corn, on which the kernels grow; cob.

cor·ne·a (kôr′nē ə), NOUN. the transparent part of the outer coat of the eyeball. It covers the iris and the pupil. ❑ PLURAL **cor·ne·as.**

cor·ner (kôr′nər),
1 NOUN. the place where two lines or surfaces meet; angle: *A chair sits in the corner of the room. Write your name in the upper right corner of the paper.*
2 NOUN. the place where two streets meet: *There is a traffic light at the corner.*
3 ADJECTIVE. at or on a corner: *I went to the corner store to buy some milk.*
4 VERB. to drive something into a corner: *Workers at the zoo cornered the lion in the alley and returned it to its cage.*
❑ VERB **cor·ners, cor·nered, cor·ner·ing.**
just around the corner, IDIOM. about to happen; happening soon: *Christmas is just around the corner.*

cor·ner·back (kôr′nər bak′), NOUN. (in football) a member of the defensive backfield.

cor·net (kôr net′), NOUN. a wind instrument like a trumpet, usually made of brass.

corn·meal (kôrn′mēl′), NOUN. coarsely ground dried corn.

corn·row (kôrn′rō′), NOUN.
1 a narrow hair braid laid flat against the scalp.
2 a hairdo in which the hair is arranged in rows of flat braids.

corn·y (kôr′nē), ADJECTIVE. (informal) silly and old-fashioned: *No one laughed at his corny jokes.* ❑ ADJECTIVE **corn·i·er, corn·i·est.**

co·ro·na·tion (kôr′ə nā′shən), NOUN. the ceremony of crowning a king, queen, emperor, or empress.

cor·por·al (kôr′pər əl), NOUN. a military rank. See the chart on page 550.

cor·po·ra·tion (kôr′pə rā′shən), NOUN. a large business company. A corporation can manufacture products, buy and sell, and own property, according to law.

corps (kôr), NOUN.
1 a group of soldiers trained for special military service: *the Medical Corps, the Signal Corps.*
2 a group of people with special training, organized for working together: *a corps of nurses.*
❑ PLURAL **corps** (kôrz). ■ Another word that sounds like this is **core.**

corpse (kôrps), NOUN. a dead human body.

cor·pus·cle (kôr′pus′əl), NOUN. any of the cells that form a large part of the blood. Red corpuscles carry oxygen from the lungs to various parts of the body; some white corpuscles destroy germs.

a	hat	ė	term	ô	order	ch	child		a in about
ā	age	i	it	oi	oil	ng	long		e in taken
ä	far	ī	ice	ou	out	sh	she	ə {	i in pencil
â	care	o	hot	u	cup	th	thin		o in lemon
e	let	ō	open	u̇	put	ŦH	then		u in circus
ē	equal	ȯ	saw	ü	rule	zh	measure		

cor·ral (kə ral′),
1 NOUN. a fenced-in place for keeping horses, cattle, and other animals.
2 VERB. to drive animals into or keep them in a corral: *The cowboys corralled the herd of wild ponies.*
3 VERB. to surround someone: *The reporters corralled the mayor and began asking questions.*
❏ VERB **cor·rals, cor·ralled, cor·ral·ling.**

corral (definition 1)

cor·rect (kə rekt′),
1 ADJECTIVE. without any mistakes; right: *She gave the correct answer.*
2 VERB. to mark the mistakes in something; remove the mistakes from: *The teacher corrected our tests and returned them to us.*
3 VERB. to change something to a better condition or to agree with some standard: *Braces will correct crooked teeth.*
4 ADJECTIVE. agreeing with an accepted standard of good behavior; proper: *correct manners.*
❏ VERB **cor·rects, cor·rect·ed, cor·rect·ing.**
—**cor·rect′ly,** ADVERB. —**cor·rect′ness,** NOUN.

cor·rec·tion (kə rek′shən), NOUN. a change that corrects an error or mistake: *Write your corrections in neatly so I can read them.*

cor·re·spond (kôr′ə spond′), VERB.
1 to be alike; be the same as something else: *Her answers correspond with mine.*
2 to be similar: *The fins of a fish correspond to the wings of a bird.*
3 to exchange letters with someone: *Will you correspond with me while I am away?*
❏ VERB **cor·re·sponds, cor·re·spond·ed, cor·re·spond·ing.**

cor·re·spond·ence (kôr′ə spon′dəns), NOUN.
1 close similarity; agreement: *Your account of the accident has little correspondence with the story the other witness told.*
2 an exchange of letters; letter writing: *The boy kept up a correspondence with his friend from Europe after she returned home.*

cor·re·spond·ent (kôr′ə spon′dənt), NOUN.
1 someone who exchanges letters with another person: *My cousin and I are correspondents.*
2 someone hired to send news from a distant place: *There was a report on the news tonight from the correspondent in China.*

cor·ri·dor (kôr′ə dər), NOUN. a long hallway into which rooms open: *Our classroom is at the end of a corridor.*

cor·rode (kə rōd′), VERB. to wear or eat away gradually: *Moisture corrodes iron.* ❏ VERB **cor·rodes, cor·rod·ed, cor·rod·ing.**

cor·ru·gat·ed (kôr′ə gā′tid), ADJECTIVE. bent or shaped into wavy folds or ridges: *The carton was made of corrugated cardboard.*

cor·rupt (kə rupt′),
1 ADJECTIVE. influenced by bribes; dishonest: *The editorial criticized the corrupt judge.*
2 VERB. to influence someone by bribes; make dishonest; bribe: *That judge cannot be corrupted.*
❏ VERB **cor·rupts, cor·rupt·ed, cor·rupt·ing.**
—**cor·rup′tion,** NOUN. —**cor·rupt′ly,** ADVERB.

cor·sage (kôr säzh′), NOUN. a small bouquet worn on the waist or shoulder of a woman's clothes, or on her wrist.

cor·set (kôr′sit), NOUN. (earlier) a stiff, close-fitting piece of underwear worn about the waist and hips to support or shape the body.

cos·met·ic (koz met′ik), NOUN. a preparation for beautifying the skin or hair. Powder and lipstick are cosmetics.

cos·mic (koz′mik), ADJECTIVE. of or about the whole universe: *Cosmic forces produce stars and planets.*

cos·mo·naut (koz′mə nôt), NOUN. a Russian astronaut.

cos·mo·pol·i·tan (koz′mə pol′ə tən), ADJECTIVE.
1 feeling at home in all parts of the world: *Diplomats are usually cosmopolitan people.*
2 belonging to all parts of the world; not limited to any one country or its people; widely spread: *Music is a cosmopolitan art.*

cost (kôst),
1 NOUN. the price paid for something: *The cost of this watch was $75.*
2 VERB. to have a price of: *This watch costs $75.*
3 NOUN. a loss; sacrifice: *The fox escaped from the trap at the cost of a leg.*
4 VERB. to cause the loss or sacrifice of something: *A thoughtless remark almost cost me a friend.*
❏ VERB **costs, cost, cost·ing.**

Cos·ta Ri·ca (kos′tə rē′kə), a country in Central America. —**Costa Rican.**

cost·ly (kôst′lē), ADJECTIVE.
1 having great value: *costly jewels.*
2 causing great loss: *He made a costly mistake.*
❏ ADJECTIVE **cost·li·er, cost·li·est.**

cos·tume (kos′tüm), NOUN.
1 clothes that are worn at a particular time, or in a particular place: *The kimono is part of the national costume of Japan.*
2 clothes that someone can put on to look like someone else: *The actors wore colonial costumes.*

Word Story

Costume comes from a Latin word meaning "custom." **Custom** comes from the same Latin word. When people have a custom, or habit, of wearing one particular kind of clothing, it becomes the costume of their country or time.

cot (kot), NOUN. a narrow bed, sometimes made of canvas stretched on a frame that folds up.

cot·tage (kot′ij), NOUN.
1 a small house: *They lived in a cottage in the woods.*
2 a house at a summer resort.

cottage cheese, a soft, white cheese made from sour skim milk.

cot·ton (kot′n), NOUN.
1 the soft, white fibers that grow in fluffy bunches on the cotton plant.
2 cloth made from cotton fibers: *I like to wear cotton in hot weather.*

the **cotton** plant

cot·ton·mouth (kot′n mouth′), NOUN. See **water moccasin.**
❑ PLURAL **cot·ton·mouths** (kot′n mouthz′).

cot·ton·tail (kot′n tāl′), NOUN. a common American wild rabbit with a fluffy white tail.

couch (kouch), NOUN. a long, comfortable seat for two or more people, built with cushions and springs and having a back and arms; sofa. ❑ PLURAL **couch·es. —couch′like′,** ADJECTIVE.

cou·gar (kü′gər), NOUN. See **mountain lion.**

cough (kȯf),
1 VERB. to force air out of your throat with a loud noise: *Dust in the air can make you cough.*
2 NOUN. the act or sound of coughing.
3 NOUN. a mild illness that causes repeated coughing.
❑ VERB **coughs, coughed, cough·ing.**

cough up, IDIOM. to give someone something they need or that you owe, especially money: *I couldn't cough up the five dollars I owed him.*

could (kůd), HELPING VERB.
1 the past tense form of **can¹**: *She could ski and swim very well.*
2 might be able to: *Perhaps I could go tomorrow.*
3 may: *Could I have a glass of milk? It could snow today.*

could·n't (kůd′nt), a contraction of **could not.**

These actors are wearing colonial **costumes.**

coun·cil (koun′səl), NOUN.
1 a group of people called together to give advice and to discuss or settle questions.
2 a group of people elected by citizens to make laws for and manage a city or town.
■ Another word that sounds like this is **counsel.**

coun·sel (koun′səl),
1 NOUN. ideas and suggestions; advice: *good counsel.*
2 NOUN. a lawyer or group of lawyers: *Each side of a case in a court of law has its own counsel.*
3 VERB. to give advice to someone; advise: *My teacher counseled me to join the school band.*
❑ VERB **coun·sels, coun·seled, coun·sel·ing.**
■ Another word that sounds like this is **council.**

coun·se·lor (koun′sə lər), NOUN.
1 someone who gives advice; adviser.
2 a lawyer.
3 an instructor or leader in a summer camp.

count¹ (kount),
1 VERB. to name numbers in order: *count from one to ten.*
2 VERB. to add something up; find the number of: *I counted the books and found there were fifty.*
3 NOUN. an act of adding up: *The count showed more than 5000 votes had been cast.*
4 NOUN. the total number; amount: *The exact count was 5170 votes.*
5 VERB. to have an influence; be of account or value: *Every vote counts in an election.*
❑ VERB **counts, count·ed, count·ing.**

count on, IDIOM.
1 to expect; allow for: *I hadn't counted on your coming so early; I'm not ready yet.*
2 to depend; rely: *We count on your help.*

count someone out, IDIOM. to not include someone: *After hearing his plans, I told him to count me out.*

a	hat	ė	term	ô	order	ch	child		a in about
ā	age	i	it	oi	oil	ng	long		e in taken
ä	far	ī	ice	ou	out	sh	she	ə	i in pencil
â	care	o	hot	u	cup	th	thin		o in lemon
e	let	ō	open	ů	put	th	then		u in circus
ē	equal	ȯ	saw	ü	rule	zh	measure		

count² (kount), NOUN. a European nobleman about equal in rank to an English earl.

count·down (kount′doun′), NOUN. the act or practice of calling out of the minutes or seconds left before the launching of a missile, rocket, or the like. This is done by counting backwards from a certain time to zero.

count·er¹ (koun′tər), NOUN.
1 a long, flat, raised surface on which food is prepared or eaten, goods are displayed and sold, money is counted, and the like: *The pies were set on the counter to cool.*
2 something used for counting: *Use your counters to find the answer to 12 plus 7.*

coun·ter² (koun′tər),
1 ADVERB or ADJECTIVE. opposed; contrary; in the opposite way: *He acted counter to his promise. Your plans are counter to ours.*
2 VERB. to act or go against; oppose: *He countered my plan with one of his own.*
❏ VERB **coun·ters, coun·tered, coun·ter·ing.**

Word Power   counter-

The prefix **counter-** means "against" or "opposite." **Counter**clockwise means the direction **opposite** clockwise. A **counter**spy works **against** other spies.

coun·ter·clock·wise (koun′tər klok′wīz′), ADVERB or ADJECTIVE. in the direction opposite to that in which the hands of a clock go; around from right to left. ■ See the illustration at **clockwise.**

coun·ter·feit (koun′tər fit),
1 VERB. to copy something in order to cheat people: *They were arrested for counterfeiting twenty-dollar bills.*
2 NOUN. something copied and passed as genuine: *This bill looks genuine, but it is a counterfeit.*
3 ADJECTIVE. not genuine: *a counterfeit stamp.*
❏ VERB **coun·ter·feits, coun·ter·feit·ed, coun·ter·feit·ing. –coun′ter·feit′er,** NOUN.

coun·ter·part (koun′tər pärt′), NOUN. someone or something that looks a lot like someone or something else: *She is the counterpart of her twin sister.*

count·ess (koun′tis), NOUN.
1 the wife or widow of a count or an earl.
2 a woman whose rank is equal to that of a count or an earl.
❏ PLURAL **count·ess·es.**

count·less (kount′lis), ADJECTIVE. a great many: *There were countless sunflowers in the field.*
■ See the Synonym Study at **many.**

coun·try (kun′trē),
1 NOUN. land; region: *The country here is rough and hilly.*
2 NOUN. the land of a group of people united under the same government and usually speaking the same language: *France is a country in Europe.*
3 NOUN. the land where someone was born or where he or she is a citizen: *The United States is my country.*
4 NOUN. the people of a nation: *The whole country cheered when the war ended.*
5 NOUN. the land outside of cities and towns: *She likes the farms and fields of the country.*
6 ADJECTIVE. of or in the country: *He likes hearty country food and fresh country air.*
❏ PLURAL **coun·tries.**

coun·try·side (kun′trē sīd′), NOUN. the land outside of cities and towns: *I saw many cows and horses in the countryside.*

coun·ty (koun′tē), NOUN. one of the districts into which a state or country is divided for purposes of government. ❏ PLURAL **coun·ties.**

cou·ple (kup′əl),
1 NOUN. two things of the same kind that go together; pair: *She bought a couple of tires for her bike.*
2 NOUN. a man and woman who are married, engaged, or dance partners.
3 NOUN. a small number; a few: *a couple of days.*
4 VERB. to join two or more things together: *The workers coupled the freight cars.*
❏ VERB **cou·ples, cou·pled, cou·pling.**

cou·pon (kü′pon), NOUN. a small piece of paper or part of a package or advertisement that gives the person who holds it a gift or a price reduction: *He saved coupons from cereal boxes and got a free toy.*

cour·age (kėr′ij), NOUN. the ability to meet danger instead of running away from it; fearlessness: *The pioneers faced the hardships of their westward journey with courage.*

cou·ra·geous (kə rā′jəs), ADJECTIVE. full of courage; fearless. ■ See the Synonym Study at **brave.**
–cou·ra′geous·ly, ADVERB.

There are **countless** sunflowers in the field.

course (kôrs), NOUN.
1 the direction taken: *Our course was straight to the north.*

2 onward movement; forward progress: *Our history book traces the course of human development from the cave to modern city living.*

3 a series of classes on a particular subject: *Each course in mathematics lasts one year.*

4 a part of a meal served at one time: *The first course was chicken soup.*

5 a place for races or games: *a golf course.*
∎ Another word that sounds like this is **coarse.**

of course, IDIOM. surely; certainly: *Of course we can go!*

on course for, IDIOM. likely to do, reach, or get something: *She is on course for the tennis championship this year.*

court (kôrt),

1 NOUN. a place where a judge decides questions of law, or where trials are held.

2 NOUN. officials, including a judge or judges, and often a jury, who decide legal cases or issues.

3 NOUN. a place where games such as tennis and basketball are played.

4 NOUN. a ruler and his or her advisers, followers, and household: *the court of Queen Elizabeth I.*

5 NOUN. an assembly held by a king, queen, or other ruler: *The queen held court to hear her advisers.*

6 NOUN. a space partly or wholly enclosed by walls or buildings: *The four apartment houses were built around a central grass court.*

7 VERB. to try to win the love of; pay loving attention to: *He courted her by bringing her flowers every day.* ❏ VERB **courts, court·ed, court·ing.**

a royal **court** in Indonesia

cour·te·ous (kėr′tē əs), ADJECTIVE. polite and showing respect: *The clerks are courteous at this store.* **–cour′te·ous·ly,** ADVERB.

cour·te·sy (kėr′tə sē), NOUN.

1 polite behavior; thoughtfulness toward other people: *It is a sign of courtesy to give your seat to an old person on a bus.*

2 a courteous act or expression: *Thanks for all your courtesies.* ❏ PLURAL **cour·te·sies.**

court·house (kôrt′hous′), NOUN.

1 a building in which law courts meet.

2 a building used for the government of a county. ❏ PLURAL **court·hous·es** (kôrt′hou′ziz).

court·yard (kôrt′yärd′), NOUN. a space enclosed by walls, in or near a large building.

cous·in (kuz′n), NOUN. a son or daughter of your uncle or aunt. First cousins have the same grandparents; second cousins have the same great-grandparents.

cove (kōv), NOUN. a small, sheltered bay.

cov·er (kuv′ər),

1 VERB. to put something over someone or something else: *I covered the child with a blanket.*

2 VERB. to spread over something: *Snow covered the ground.*

3 NOUN. anything that protects, shelters, or hides something: *Get under cover before the storm hits!*

4 VERB. to go over; travel: *On our trip we covered 400 miles a day by car.*

5 VERB. to include something: *The math review covers everything we've studied this term.*

6 VERB. to report or photograph an event, meeting, or the like: *A reporter covered the football game for the newspaper.* ❏ VERB **cov·ers, cov·ered, cov·er·ing.**

covered wagon, a wagon having a canvas cover that can be taken off.

cov·et (kuv′it), VERB. to want something that belongs to someone else: *Her friends coveted her new bicycle.* ❏ VERB **cov·ets, cov·et·ed, cov·et·ing.**

cow (kou), NOUN.

1 the full-grown female of farm cattle, raised for its milk.

2 the female of the buffalo, moose, whale, and other large animals that nurse their young: *an elephant cow.*

cow·ard (kou′ərd), NOUN. someone who lacks courage or is easily made afraid; someone who runs from danger.

cow·ard·ice (kou′ər dis), NOUN. a lack of courage; failure to do your duty because of fear: *The officer was guilty of cowardice in the presence of danger.*

cow·ard·ly (kou′ərd lē), ADJECTIVE. without courage; like a coward.

cow·boy (kou′boi′), NOUN. a man who works on a cattle ranch or at rodeos.

cow·girl (kou′gėrl′), NOUN. a woman who works on a cattle ranch or at rodeos.

cow·hand (kou′hand′), NOUN. someone who works on a cattle ranch.

a	hat	ė	term	ô	order	ch	child		a in about
ā	age	i	it	oi	oil	ng	long		e in taken
ä	far	ī	ice	ou	out	sh	she	ə	i in pencil
â	care	o	hot	u	cup	th	thin		o in lemon
e	let	ō	open	u̇	put	ᴛʜ	then		u in circus
ē	equal	ȯ	saw	ü	rule	zh	measure		

cow·hide (kou′hīd′), NOUN.
1 the hide of a cow.
2 leather made from the hide of cattle.

cowl (koul), NOUN.
1 a monk's cloak with a hood.
2 the hood itself.

co-work·er (kō′wėr′kər), NOUN. someone who works with another person: *You should try very hard to get along with your co-workers.*

coy·o·te (kī ō′tē or kī′ōt), NOUN. a small wolflike animal living in many parts of western North America. Coyotes have light yellow fur. ❑ PLURAL **coy·o·tes** or **coy·o·te.**

co·zy (kō′zē), ADJECTIVE. warm and comfortable; snug: *The cat lay in a cozy corner near the fireplace.* ■ See the Synonym Study at **comfortable.** ❑ ADJECTIVE **co·zi·er, co·zi·est.**

CPR, a technique used to revive victims of heart attack, drowning, and other kinds of heart failure. It includes both mouth-to-mouth breathing and rhythmical pressure on the breastbone that forces the victim's heart to pump.

CPU, central processing unit: the part of a computer that carries out instructions and processes data.

crab (krab), NOUN. a shellfish with eight jointed legs, two claws, and a broad, flat shell. Many kinds of crabs are good to eat.
—crab′like′, ADJECTIVE.

crab apple, a small, sour apple used to make jelly.

Most **crabs** live in or near the ocean.

crack (krak),
1 NOUN. a split or opening made by breaking without separating into parts: *There is a crack in this cup.*
2 VERB. to break something without separating it into parts: *You have cracked the window.* ■ See the Synonym Study at **break.**
3 NOUN. a narrow opening: *I can see between the cracks in the old wood floor.*
4 NOUN. a sudden, sharp noise like that made by loud thunder, a whip, or something breaking.
5 VERB. to make or cause to make a sudden, sharp noise: *The lion tamer cracked his whip.*
6 VERB. to break something open with a sudden, sharp noise: *We cracked the nuts.*
7 NOUN. a hard, sharp blow: *The falling branch gave me a crack on the head.*
❑ VERB **cracks, cracked, crack·ing.**

crack·er (krak′ər), NOUN. a thin, crisp piece of baked bread dough that is made without yeast.

crack·le (krak′əl),
1 VERB. to make slight, sharp sounds: *A fire crackled in the fireplace.*

2 NOUN. a slight, sharp sound, such as paper makes when it is crumpled.
❑ VERB **crack·les, crack·led, crack·ling.**

cra·dle (krā′dl),
1 NOUN. a small bed for a baby, usually one that can rock from side to side.
2 VERB. to hold someone or something as if in a cradle: *I cradled the baby in my arms.*
3 NOUN. a place where anything begins its growth: *The sea is thought to have been the cradle of life.*
❑ VERB **cra·dles, cra·dled, cra·dling.**

craft (kraft), NOUN.
1 a special skill: *The carpenter shaped and fitted the wood with great craft.*
2 a trade, art, or activity requiring skilled work, usually by hand: *Carpentry is a craft. Embroidery is a craft.*
3 skill in deceiving other people; slyness; sly tricks: *By craft the gambler won the card game.*
4 PLURAL. boats or ships: *Craft of all kinds come into New York every day.*

crafts·man (krafts′mən), NOUN. someone skilled in a craft or trade. ❑ PLURAL **crafts·men.**

craft·y (kraf′tē), ADJECTIVE. skillful in deceiving other people: *The crafty girl tricked her brother into doing all her chores.* ❑ ADJECTIVE **craft·i·er, craft·i·est. −craft′i·ly,** ADVERB. **−craft′i·ness,** NOUN.

cram (kram), VERB.
1 to force something into a space that is too small; stuff: *I crammed all my clothes into a suitcase.*
2 to crowd too many people into a space: *The bus was crammed, with many people standing.* ■ See the Synonym Study at **full.**
❑ VERB **crams, crammed, cram·ming.**

cramp (kramp),
1 NOUN. a sudden, painful contracting of muscles, often from chill or strain: *The swimmer suffered a cramp and had to be helped from the pool.*
2 VERB. to shut in a small space; limit: *In only three rooms, the family was cramped for space.*
❑ VERB **cramps, cramped, cramp·ing.**

cran·ber·ry (kran′ber′ē), NOUN. a firm, sour, dark red berry used in making sauce, juice, and jelly. ❑ PLURAL **cran·ber·ries.**

crane (krān),
1 NOUN. a machine with a long, swinging arm, for lifting and moving heavy objects.
2 NOUN. a large wading bird with long legs, neck, and bill.

crane — about 3 feet long

3 *VERB.* to stretch the neck up or forward, in order to see better: *She craned her neck to get a better view.*
❏ *VERB* **cranes, craned, cran·ing.**

crank (krangk),
1 *NOUN.* a part or handle connected to a machine, that you turn in a circle to set the machine motion: *I turned the crank of the pencil sharpener.*
2 *VERB.* to work or start something with a crank.
3 *NOUN.* (informal) someone who has strange ideas or habits.
❏ *VERB* **cranks, cranked, crank·ing.**

crank·y (krang′kē), *ADJECTIVE.* very easily annoyed; grouchy. ■ See the Synonym Study at **cross.**
❏ *ADJECTIVE* **crank·i·er, crank·i·est.**

crash (krash),
1 *NOUN.* a sudden, loud noise like many dishes falling and breaking: *a crash of thunder.*
2 *VERB.* to make a sudden, loud noise: *The thunder crashed loudly.*
3 *VERB.* to fall, hit, and be damaged or destroyed with force and a loud noise: *The airplane lost power and crashed.*
4 *NOUN.* a falling, hitting, and being damaged or destroyed with force and a loud noise: *The pilot brought down the damaged plane without a crash.*
5 *NOUN.* the violent striking of one solid thing against another: *I was not hurt in the car crash.*
6 *VERB.* (of computers) to stop working because of a problem in the equipment or an error in the computer program.
7 *VERB.* to strike another object with violence: *The car crashed into a stop sign.*
❏ *VERB* **crash·es, crashed, crash·ing.**

crate (krāt),
1 *NOUN.* a large frame or box made of strips of wood, for shipping glass, china, fruit, or furniture.
2 *VERB.* to pack in a crate: *to crate a mirror for moving.*
❏ *VERB* **crates, crat·ed, crat·ing.**

cra·ter (krā′tər), *NOUN.*
1 a hole in the ground shaped like a bowl: *This crater was made by a meteorite.*
2 the opening at the top of a volcano.

crave (krāv), *VERB.* to want something very much: *The thirsty hiker craved water.* ❏ *VERB* **craves, craved, crav·ing.**

crav·ing (krā′ving), *NOUN.* a strong desire for something: *I had a craving for something sweet.*

craw·fish (krȯ′fish′), *NOUN.* See **crayfish.** ❏ *PLURAL* **craw·fish** or **craw·fish·es.**

crawl (krȯl),
1 *VERB.* to move slowly on the hands and knees, or with the body close to the ground: *Babies crawl before they begin to walk. Worms, snakes, and lizards crawl.*
2 *VERB.* to move slowly: *The heavy traffic crawled through the narrow tunnel.*

3 *NOUN.* a slow movement: *Traffic slowed to a crawl.*
4 *VERB.* to be covered with crawling things: *The ground was crawling with ants.*
5 *NOUN.* a fast way of swimming with overarm strokes and rapid kicking of the feet.
❏ *VERB* **crawls, crawled, crawl·ing.**

cray·fish (krā′fish′), *NOUN.* a freshwater animal that looks a lot like a small lobster; crawfish. Crayfish are often boiled and eaten. ❏ *PLURAL* **cray·fish** or **cray·fish·es.**

cray·on (krā′on or krā′ən), *NOUN.* a stick or pencil of colored wax used for drawing or writing.

craze (krāz), *NOUN.* a temporary, popular interest in doing some one thing: *The craze for flying kites was replaced by a craze for skateboards.*

cra·zy (krā′zē), *ADJECTIVE.*
1 foolish: *It was crazy to jump out of that tree.*
2 very enthusiastic: *crazy about horses.*
3 having a sick mind; mentally ill; insane.
❏ *ADJECTIVE* **cra·zi·er, cra·zi·est.** —**cra′zi·ly,** *ADVERB.* —**cra′zi·ness,** *NOUN.*

Usage Note

Crazy is not a polite word to describe a person with mental illness. Careful writers and speakers do not use *crazy, mad,* or similar words except to mean "very foolish or unreasonable."

creak (krēk),
1 *VERB.* to squeak loudly: *The hinges on the door creaked because they needed oiling.*
2 *NOUN.* a loud squeaking noise: *The creak of the stairs in the old house was scary.*
❏ *VERB* **creaks, creaked, creak·ing.** ■ Other words that sound like this are **creek** and **Creek.**

crater (definition 1)

a hat	ė term	ô order	ch child	⎧a in about
ā age	i it	oi oil	ng long	⎪e in taken
ä far	ī ice	ou out	sh she	ə⎨i in pencil
â care	o hot	u cup	th thin	⎪o in lemon
e let	ō open	u̇ put	ᴛʜ then	⎩u in circus
ē equal	ȯ saw	ü rule	zh measure	

cream (krēm), NOUN.
1 the thick, yellowish part of milk. Cream rises to the top when milk as it comes from the cow is allowed to stand. Butter is made from cream.
2 any preparation like cream that is put on the skin: *shaving cream, skin cream.*
3 the best part of anything: *The cream of a class is made up of the best students.*

cream·y (krē'mē), ADJECTIVE. like cream; smooth and soft: *pie with a rich, creamy filling.* ❑ ADJECTIVE **cream·i·er, cream·i·est.**

crease (krēs), NOUN. a line on cloth, paper, and so on, made by folding or wrinkling; fold: *Her slacks have a sharp crease down the front.*

cre·ate (krē āt'), VERB.
1 to make something which has not been made before: *Composers create music.*
2 to cause something to happen: *The noise created a disturbance.*
❑ VERB **cre·ates, cre·at·ed, cre·at·ing.**

cre·a·tion (krē ā'shən), NOUN.
1 the act or process of making a thing which has not been made before: *The gasoline engine led to the creation of the modern car.*
2 all things created; the world and everything in it; the universe: *They thought their house by the ocean was the nicest spot in all creation.*
3 something produced by intelligence or skill, usually something important or original: *A poem is a creation of the imagination.*

cre·a·tive (krē ā'tiv), ADJECTIVE. having the power to create things or ideas: *He has a very creative mind, always full of new ideas.* **–cre·a'tive·ly,** ADVERB. **–cre·a'tive·ness,** NOUN.

cre·a·tor (krē ā'tər), NOUN.
1 someone who creates something.
2 **the Creator,** God.

crea·ture (krē'chər), NOUN.
1 any living person or animal: *We fed the lost dog because the poor creature was starving.*
2 an imaginary, frightening being: *I dreamed I was captured by creatures from outer space.*

cred·it (kred'it),
1 NOUN. belief in the truth of something; faith; trust: *I put great credit in what he says.*
2 VERB. to believe in the truth of something: *I can credit all that you are telling me.*
3 NOUN. trust in someone's ability and intention to pay: *This store will extend credit to customers.*

creature from another planet

4 NOUN. reputation in money matters: *If you pay your bills on time, your credit will be good.*
5 NOUN. praise; honor: *Whoever does the work should get the credit.*
❑ VERB **cred·its, cred·it·ed, cred·it·ing.**

credit card, a plastic card that allows someone to charge the cost of goods or services instead of paying cash.

Cree (krē), NOUN. a member of a tribe of American Indians living in Canada and Montana.

creed (krēd), NOUN.
1 a brief statement of the main points of religious belief of some church.
2 any statement of faith, belief, or opinion: *"Honesty is the best policy" was their creed.*

creek (krēk or krik), NOUN. a small stream. ▪ Another word that sounds like this is **creak.**

Creek (krēk), NOUN. a member of a group of American Indians tribes living mostly in Oklahoma. ▪ Another word that sounds like this is **creak.**

creep (krēp),
1 VERB. to move slowly with the body close to the ground or floor; crawl: *The cat crept toward the mouse.*
2 VERB. to move slowly: *Traffic creeps along in rush hour.*
3 VERB. to grow along the ground or on a wall: *Ivy crept up the wall of the old house.*
4 NOUN. **the creeps,** a feeling of fear or horror, as if things were creeping over your skin: *Movies about ghosts give me the creeps.*
❑ VERB **creeps, crept, creep·ing.**

creep·y (krē'pē), ADJECTIVE. causing a feeling of horror, as if things were creeping over your skin; scary. ❑ ADJECTIVE **creep·i·er, creep·i·est.**

crepe (krāp), NOUN. a very thin pancake, usually served folded around a filling.

crepe paper, a thin, crinkled tissue paper used for making decorations.

crept (krept), VERB.
1 the past tense of **creep:** *The cat crept toward the mouse.*
2 the past participle of **creep:** *We had crept up on them in the dark.*

cres·cent (kres'nt), NOUN.
1 the shape of the moon when it is small and thin
2 anything that curves in a similar way.

crest (krest), NOUN.
1 a small growth of feathers or fur on the head of a bird or animal
2 the top part: *the crest of a wave, the crest of the hill.*

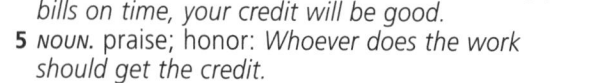

a blue jay's **crest**

crev·ice (krev′is), NOUN. a narrow split or crack: *Tiny ferns grew in crevices in the stone wall.*

crew (krü), NOUN. a group of people who work together: *It takes a crew of ten to sail that ship.*

crib (krib), NOUN.
1 a small bed with high sides to keep a baby from falling out.
2 a building or bin for storing grain: *Rats damaged much of the corn in the crib.*

crick·et¹ (krik′it), NOUN. a common black or brown insect related to the grasshopper. The male cricket makes a chirping noise by rubbing its front wings together.

crick·et² (krik′it), NOUN. an English outdoor game played by two teams of eleven players each, with a ball, bats, and wickets.

crime (krīm), NOUN.
1 a very wrong deed that is against the law: *Murder is a crime.*
2 criminal activity: *Police forces combat crime.*
3 an evil or wrong act: *It is a crime to ignore child abuse.*

crim·i·nal (krim′ə nəl),
1 NOUN. someone who has committed a crime: *The criminal was sentenced to prison for theft.*
2 ADJECTIVE. of or about crime or its punishment: *A criminal court hears criminal cases.*
3 ADJECTIVE. like a crime; very wrong: *It is criminal to neglect a pet.*

crim·son (krim′zən), ADJECTIVE or NOUN. deep red.

cringe (krinj), VERB. to shrink from danger or pain; crouch in fear: *The kitten cringed when it saw the dog come into the yard.* ❏ VERB **cring·es, cringed, cring·ing.**

crin·kle (kring′kəl), VERB.
1 to make or become wrinkled.
2 to make a crackling or rustling sound: *Paper crinkles when it is crushed.*
❏ VERB **crin·kles, crin·kled, crin·kling.**

crip·ple (krip′əl),
1 NOUN. a human being or an animal that cannot use an arm or leg properly because of injury or birth defect. ★ Many people object to the use of **cripple** to describe a person. Careful writers and speakers avoid this use of the word. It is wise to use **disabled,** or to give details.
2 VERB. to cause someone or something to be disabled: *A broken hip crippled my dog for several months.*
3 VERB. to damage something: *The ship was crippled by the storm.*
❏ VERB **crip·ples, crip·pled, crip·pling.**

cri·sis (krī′sis), NOUN.
1 a serious situation that may become worse: *A shortage of oil could produce an energy crisis.*
2 the worst time in a disease: *After the fever broke, the doctor said the crisis was over.*
❏ PLURAL **cri·ses** (krī′sēz′).

crisp (krisp), ADJECTIVE.
1 hard and thin; easy to break: *Dry toast is crisp. Fresh celery is crisp.*
2 cool and fresh: *The air this morning was crisp.*
3 quick and to the point: *"Sit down!" was her crisp command.*
−**crisp′ly,** ADVERB. −**crisp′ness,** NOUN.

criss·cross (kris′krós′),
1 VERB. to mark or cover something with crossed lines: *Little cracks crisscrossed the wall.*
2 VERB. to come and go across something: *Buses and cars crisscross the city.*
3 ADJECTIVE. made or marked with crossed lines: *Plaids have a crisscross pattern.*
❏ VERB **criss·cross·es, criss·crossed, criss·cross·ing.**

crit·ic (krit′ik), NOUN.
1 someone whose job is to say what is good, bad, or interesting about books, music, movies, and so on: *We read what the critics had to say about the new play in the newspaper.*
2 someone who disapproves or finds fault with someone or something: *I tried to please him, but he was my worst critic.*

crit·i·cal (krit′ə kəl), ADJECTIVE.
1 tending to find fault or disapprove: *She was so critical of people's mistakes that no one liked her.*
2 of or like a crisis: *Help arrived at the critical moment.*
3 dangerous: *The patient was in a critical condition.*
−**crit′i·cal·ly,** ADVERB.

crit·i·cism (krit′ə siz′əm), NOUN.
1 unfavorable remarks: *Criticism usually annoys people.*
2 the act of criticizing something: *She writes a weekly column of theater criticism.*

crit·i·cize (krit′ə sīz), VERB.
1 to blame someone; find fault with: *Do not criticize her until you know the facts.*
2 to judge something as a critic: *He criticized the novel in great detail.*
❏ VERB **crit·i·ciz·es, crit·i·cized, crit·i·ciz·ing.**

croak (krōk),
1 NOUN. the deep, hoarse sound made by a frog or a crow.
2 VERB. to make this sound.
❏ VERB **croaks, croak·ed, croak·ing.** −**croak′er,** NOUN.

Cro·a·tia (krō ā′shə), NOUN. a country in southeastern Europe. −**Cro·a′tian,** ADJECTIVE or NOUN.

cro·chet (krō shā′), VERB. to make sweaters, lace, and other things by looping thread or yarn into links with a single hooked needle. Crocheting is similar to knitting. ❏ VERB **cro·chets** (krō shāz′), **cro·cheted** (krō shād′), **cro·chet·ing** (krō shā′ing).

a	hat	ė	term	ô	order	ch	child		a in about
ā	age	i	it	oi	oil	ng	long		e in taken
ä	far	ī	ice	ou	out	sh	she	ə<	i in pencil
â	care	o	hot	u	cup	th	thin		o in lemon
e	let	ō	open	ù	put	∓H	then		u in circus
ē	equal	ò	saw	ü	rule	zh	measure		

croc·o·dile (krok′ə dīl), *NOUN.* a large animal with a long body, four short legs, a thick skin, a long, tapering head, and a long tail. Crocodiles look a lot like alligators. They live in the rivers and marshes of warm parts of the world.

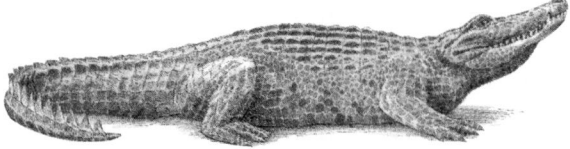

crocodile — between 12 and 20 feet long

cro·cus (krō′kəs), *NOUN.* a small plant that blooms very early in the spring and has white, yellow, or purple flowers. ❑ *PLURAL* **cro·cus·es.**

crois·sant (krə sänt′ or kwä sänt′), *NOUN.* a small roll of bread shaped like a crescent.

crook (krúk),
1 *VERB.* to make a hook or curve in something; bend: *I crooked my leg around the branch.*
2 *NOUN.* a hooked, curved, or bent part: *I carry my books in the crook of my arm.*
3 *NOUN.* a dishonest person; thief: *The crook stole all my money.*
   ❑ *VERB* **crooks, crook·ed, crook·ing.**

crook·ed (krúk′id), *ADJECTIVE.*
1 not straight; bent; full of curves: *The crooked road twisted and turned through the hills.*
2 not honest: *a crooked scheme.*
   —**crook′ed·ly,** *ADVERB.*

crop (krop),
1 *NOUN.* plants grown by farmers for food: *Wheat and corn are two major crops in the United States.*
2 *NOUN.* the amount of any grain, fruit, or vegetable which is grown in one season: *The drought made the potato crop very small this year.*
3 *VERB.* to cut short or bite off the top of: *Sheep had cropped the grass closely.*
4 *NOUN.* a baglike swelling of a bird's food passage. In the crop, digestion of food begins.
   ❑ *VERB* **crops, cropped, crop·ping.**

cro·quet (krō kā′), *NOUN.* a lawn game played by knocking wooden balls through small wire hoops with mallets.

Word Power   cross-

The combining form **cross-** is used with other words or parts of words to add to their meaning. **Cross-** can mean "across" or "crossing." **Cross-**country means **across** the country. A **cross**walk is used for **crossing** the street.

Cross- can also mean "opposing" or "opposite." **Cross-**examination is examination of witnesses by the **opposing** side in a court case.

cross (krós),
1 *VERB.* to move or go across to the other side of something: *He crossed the street. The bridge crosses the river.*
2 *VERB.* to go across each other: *Main Street crosses Market Street.*
3 *NOUN.* a straight line with another line across it to form a T, an X, or a +.
4 *NOUN.* something with this shape: *She wears a gold cross around her neck.*
5 *NOUN.* **the Cross,** the wooden cross on which Jesus died.
6 *VERB.* to draw a line across something: *In writing you cross the letter "t." She crossed out the wrong word.*
7 *VERB.* to put or lay one over another: *He crossed his arms.*
8 *ADJECTIVE.* lying or going across; crossing: *I saw you standing at the intersection of the cross streets.*
9 *ADJECTIVE.* in a bad temper: *People are often cross when they don't feel well.*
10 *VERB.* to mix kinds or breeds of living things: *A new plant can be made by crossing two others.*
11 *NOUN.* a mixture of kinds of living things: *My dog is a cross between a collie and a poodle.*
   ❑ *VERB* **cross·es, crossed, cross·ing;** *PLURAL* **cross·es.**
   —**cross′ly,** *ADVERB.*

Synonym Study

Cross means in a bad mood: *She is cross today because she lost her favorite hat.*

Cranky means becoming angry easily and grumbling a lot: *The cranky child threw down his toys and wouldn't play with them.*

Grumpy and **grouchy** mean having a bad temper and complaining: *The reason I'm grumpy is that I have a bad headache, so leave me alone. When the headache stops, I won't be grouchy anymore.*

Ornery means always in a bad mood, mean, and hard to get along with: *The ornery woman who works in the grocery store has no friends.*

Surly means in a bad mood and acting rudely because of it: *She was surly after I refused to share my homework, and she wouldn't walk home with me.*

See also the Synonym Study at **mad.**

ANTONYM: cheerful.

cross·bar (krós′bär′), *NOUN.* a bar, line, or stripe going from side to side.

cross·bones (krós′bōnz′), *NOUN PLURAL.* two bones placed in an X shape, usually below a skull, to mean death: *The pirates raised a black flag with a white skull and crossbones on it.*

cross·bow (krȯs′bō′), NOUN. (earlier) a weapon for shooting arrows, made of a bow fastened across a wooden body with a groove in it to aim the arrows.

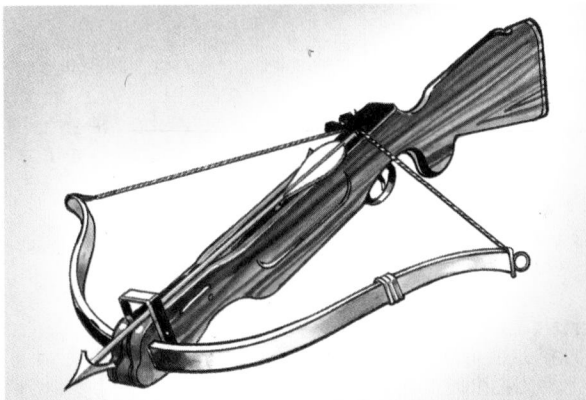

crossbow

cross-coun·try (krȯs′kun′trē), ADJECTIVE.
1 across fields or open country: *Do you enjoy cross-country skiing?*
2 across an entire country: *She took a cross-country flight from Maine to Oregon.*

cross-ex·am·ine (krȯs′eg zam′ən), VERB. to question a witness for the opposing side of a case in court. Lawyers often do this in order to make the jury doubt someone's testimony. ❑ VERB **cross-ex·am·ines, cross-ex·am·ined, cross-ex·am·in·ing. –cross′-ex·am′in·a′tion,** NOUN.

cross-eyed (krȯs′id′), ADJECTIVE. having one or both eyes turned in toward the nose, and unable to focus on the same point.

cross·ing (krȯ′sing), NOUN.
1 the place where railroad tracks cross a road.
2 the place where a street or river may be crossed: *White lines mark the crossing.*
3 an act of going across, especially a voyage across water: *The ship's crossing of the Atlantic took two weeks.*

cross-ref·er·ence (krȯs′ref′ər əns), NOUN. a reference from one part of a book or index to another part. In this book, the word **grouchy** has a cross-reference to the Synonym Study at **cross.**

cross·road (krȯs′rōd′), NOUN.
1 a road that crosses another road.
2 **crossroads,** place where roads cross: *At the crossroads we stopped and read the signs.*

cross section,
1 a cut made directly through the middle of something: *I sliced the tomatoes by making a series of cross sections.*
2 a piece cut in this way.
3 a small selection of people, animals, or things with the same qualities as the entire group; sample.

cross·walk (krȯs′wȯk′), NOUN. an area marked with lines, used by people walking across a street.

cross·word puz·zle (krȯs′wėrd′ puz′əl), a puzzle with sets of numbered squares to be filled in with words, one letter in each square. The words may be read both across and down. Clues are given with numbers that match the numbers of the squares.

Did You Know?

Crossword puzzles first appeared in a New York newspaper in 1913. Today, crossword puzzles are created in many languages. Competitions are held all around the world to solve very difficult puzzles or to solve a puzzle the fastest.

crotch (kroch), NOUN. the area of the body between the legs. ❑ PLURAL **crotch·es.**

crouch (krouch),
1 VERB. to stoop over with the legs bent: *The cat crouched in the corner, waiting for the mouse to come out of its hole.*
2 NOUN. a crouching position.
❑ VERB **crouch·es, crouched, crouch·ing;** PLURAL **crouch·es.**

crow¹ (krō),
1 NOUN. the loud cry of a rooster.
2 VERB. to make this cry: *The cock crowed as the sun rose.*
3 VERB. to boast; show your happiness and pride: *The winning team crowed over its victory.*
❑ VERB **crows, crowed, crow·ing.**

crow² (krō), NOUN. a large, shiny, black bird with a loud cry.

as the crow flies, IDIOM. in a perfectly straight line: *The park is only two miles away as the crow flies.*

This **cross section** of a garden shows the many things that live beneath the surface.

a	hat	ė	term	ô	order	ch	child	⎧a in about
ā	age	i	it	oi	oil	ng	long	⎪e in taken
ä	far	ī	ice	ou	out	sh	she	ə⎨i in pencil
â	care	o	hot	u	cup	th	thin	⎪o in lemon
e	let	ō	open	ú	put	ŦH	then	⎩u in circus
ē	equal	ȯ	saw	ü	rule	zh	measure	

crow·bar (krō′bär′), NOUN. a bar of iron or steel used to lift things or pry them apart.

crowd (kroud),
1 NOUN. a large number of people together: *A crowd gathered at the scene of the fire.*
2 NOUN. a group of people often found together: *Our crowd wasn't invited to the party.*
3 VERB. to collect or gather in large numbers: *The children crowded around the edge of the swimming pool to hear the instructor.*
4 VERB. to fill something too full: *Christmas shoppers crowded the store.* ■ See the Synonym Study at **full**.
❑ VERB **crowds, crowd·ed, crowd·ing.**

crown (kroun),
1 NOUN. a head covering of precious metal and jewels, worn by a king or queen.
2 NOUN. **the Crown**, royal power; supreme governing power in a country ruled by a king or queen: *The Crown granted lands in colonial America to William Penn.*
3 VERB. to make someone king or queen: *The prince was crowned in London.*
4 VERB. to honor someone; reward: *Her hard work was crowned with success.*
5 NOUN. the top; highest part: *the crown of a hat, the crown of a mountain.*
6 VERB. to be on top of something; cover the highest part of: *A fort crowns the hill.*
7 NOUN. the part of a tooth which appears above the gum, or an artificial substitute for it.
❑ VERB **crowns, crowned, crown·ing.**

crow's-nest (krōz′nest′), NOUN. a platform near the top of a ship's mast.

cru·cial (krü′shəl), ADJECTIVE. very important: *This was the crucial game that would decide the championship.* —**cru·cial·ly**, ADVERB.

crude (krüd), ADJECTIVE.
1 in a natural or raw state. **Crude oil** is oil pumped from wells before it is refined and prepared for use.
2 not carefully made; rough: *He lived in a crude hut made of straw.*
3 lacking good manners: *crude behavior.*
❑ ADJECTIVE **crud·er, crud·est.** —**crude′ly**, ADVERB.

cru·el (krü′əl), ADJECTIVE.
1 ready to hurt others or to enjoy their suffering: *The cruel man kicked his dog.*
2 causing pain or suffering: *War is cruel.*
—**cru′el·ly**, ADVERB.

a lookout standing in the **crow's-nest**

cru·el·ty (krü′əl tē), NOUN.
1 cruel behavior.
2 a cruel act or acts: *That organization seeks to prevent cruelty to animals.*
❑ PLURAL **cru·el·ties.**

cruise (krüz),
1 VERB. to sail about from place to place; sail over or about: *We cruised through the Greek islands on our vacation. The Coast Guard cruised along the shore.*
2 NOUN. a voyage for pleasure: *We went for a cruise on the Great Lakes last summer.* ■ See the Synonym Study at **trip**.
3 VERB. to travel from place to place: *The taxi cruised the city streets in search of passengers.*
❑ VERB **cruis·es, cruised, cruis·ing.**

cruis·er (krü′zər), NOUN.
1 a warship with less armor and more speed than a battleship.
2 a motorboat having a cabin so that people can live on board.
3 a police car.

crumb (krum), NOUN. a very small piece of bread or cake broken from a larger piece: *I fed crumbs to the birds.* ■ See the Synonym Study at **piece**.

crum·ble (krum′bəl), VERB. to break into small pieces or crumbs: *Do not crumble your bread on the table.* ❑ VERB **crum·bles, crum·bled, crum·bling.**

crum·bly (krum′blē), ADJECTIVE. tending to crumble; easily crumbled: *These cookies are very crumbly.*
❑ ADJECTIVE **crum·bli·er, crum·bli·est.**

crum·ple (krum′pəl), VERB.
1 to crush something together; wrinkle: *She crumpled the paper into a ball.*
2 to fall down: *He crumpled to the floor in a faint.*
❑ VERB **crum·ples, crum·pled, crum·pling.**

crunch (krunch),
1 VERB. to chew something noisily: *She crunched a carrot.*
2 VERB. to make or move with a crunching noise: *The children crunched through the snow.*
3 NOUN. the act or sound of crunching.
❑ VERB **crunch·es, crunched, crunch·ing;** PLURAL **crunch·es.**

crunch·y (krun′chē), ADJECTIVE. hard or crisp so that it crunches when chewed: *crunchy candy.*
❑ ADJECTIVE **crunch·i·er, crunch·i·est.**

cru·sade (krü sād′),
1 NOUN. **Crusade**, any one of eight Christian military expeditions between the years 1096 and 1272 to take Palestine from the Muslims.
2 NOUN. a strong movement against a public evil or in favor of some new idea: *Everyone was asked to join the crusade against cancer.*
3 VERB. to take part in a crusade: *They are crusading against smoking.*
❑ VERB **cru·sades, cru·sad·ed, cru·sad·ing.**

cru·sad·er (krü sā′dər), NOUN. someone who takes part in a crusade.

crush (krush),
1 VERB. to squeeze something together so hard that it breaks or bruises it: *The car door slammed and crushed her fingers.*
2 VERB. to wrinkle something or crease it by pressure or rough handling: *My suitcase was so full that my clothes were crushed.*
3 VERB. to break something into fine pieces by grinding, pounding, or pressing it: *We crushed ice for the drinks.*
4 VERB. to defeat something totally, using great force: *The revolt was crushed.*
5 NOUN. a sudden, strong liking for someone: *I once had a crush on my third-grade teacher.*
□ VERB **crush·es, crushed, crush·ing;** PLURAL **crush·es. —crush′er,** NOUN.

crust (krust), NOUN.
1 the outside part of bread.
2 dough rolled out thin and baked for the bottom and top coverings of pies.
3 any hard outside covering: *The crust of the snow was thick enough to walk on.*
4 the solid outside part of the earth.

crus·ta·cean (krus′tā′shən), NOUN. any of a group of animals with hard shells that mostly live in water. Crabs, lobsters, and shrimp are crustaceans.

crutch (kruch), NOUN. a support to help a disabled or injured person walk. It is a stick with a padded bar at the top that fits under the person's arm and supports part of his or her weight in walking.
□ PLURAL **crutch·es.**

cry (krī),
1 VERB. to shed tears: *My little sister cried when she broke her favorite toy.*
2 VERB. to call loudly; shout: *"Wait!" she cried from behind me.* ■ See the Synonym Study at **shout.**
3 NOUN. a loud call; shout: *We heard his cry for help and rushed to find him.*
4 NOUN. the act of shedding tears: *Sometimes you feel much better after a good cry.*
□ VERB **cries, cried, cry·ing;** PLURAL **cries.**

Have You Heard?

You may have heard people say **"He has cried wolf once too often."** To *cry wolf* means to give a false alarm. This phrase comes from an old fable. In the fable, a shepherd boy calls for help to save his sheep from a wolf. When the other shepherds come to help him, he tells them it was a joke. After he has done this several times, a wolf really does attack. But people don't believe the boy anymore and no one comes to help him.

crys·tal (kris′tl), NOUN.
1 a hard, solid piece of some substance that is naturally formed of flat surfaces and angles. Crystals can be small, like grains of salt, or large, like some kinds of stone.
2 a very clear glass from which drinking glasses, vases, and other things are made: *They have a collection of fine crystal.*
3 a clear, transparent mineral that looks like ice. It is a kind of quartz.
4 the transparent glass or plastic over the face of a watch.

crystals (definition 1)

CT, an abbreviation of **Connecticut.**

cu or **cu.,** an abbreviation of **cubic.**

cub (kub), NOUN. a baby bear, fox, or lion.

Cu·ba (kyü′bə), NOUN. an island country in the West Indies, south of Florida. **—Cu′ban,** ADJECTIVE or NOUN.

cub·by (kub′ē), NOUN. a short form of **cubbyhole.**
□ PLURAL **cub·bies.**

cub·by·hole (kub′ē hōl′), NOUN.
1 a small compartment for storing things; cubby: *The children leave their boots and gloves in their cubbyholes.*
2 a very small room: *I keep my computer desk in a cubbyhole next to the kitchen.*

cube (kyüb),
1 NOUN. a solid object with 6 square sides that are equal in size.
2 NOUN. anything shaped like a cube: *ice cubes, a cube of sugar.*
3 VERB. to make or form something into the shape of a cube: *The beets were cubed instead of sliced.*
4 NOUN. the sum when a number is multiplied by itself twice: *8 is the cube of 2, because 2 × 2 × 2 = 8.*
□ VERB **cubes, cubed, cub·ing.**

cu·bic (kyü′bik), ADJECTIVE. having length, width, and thickness. A cubic foot is the volume of a cube whose edges are each one foot long.

a	hat	ė	term	ô	order	ch	child		ə	a in about
ā	age	i	it	oi	oil	ng	long			e in taken
ä	far	ī	ice	ou	out	sh	she			i in pencil
â	care	o	hot	u	cup	th	thin			o in lemon
e	let	ō	open	ù	put	ᴛʜ	then			u in circus
ē	equal	ò	saw	ü	rule	zh	measure			

cub scout, a member of an organization (the **Cub Scouts**) that seeks to develop character, citizenship, usefulness to others, and various skills.

cuck·oo (kü′kü),
1 *NOUN.* a bird whose call sounds much like its name. The European cuckoo lays its eggs in the nests of other birds instead of hatching them itself.
2 *ADJECTIVE.* (informal) silly; foolish.
❑ *PLURAL* **cuck·oos.**

cu·cum·ber (kyü′kum bər), *NOUN.* a long, green, firm vegetable that grows on a vine. Cucumbers are eaten raw in salads or made into pickles.

cud (kud), *NOUN.* a mouthful of food brought back from the stomach of cattle or similar animals for a slow second chewing.

cud·dle (kud′l), *VERB.*
1 to hold closely and lovingly in your arms or lap: *I cuddled the kitten.*
2 to lie close and comfortably; curl up: *The two puppies cuddled together in front of the fire.*
❑ *VERB* **cud·dles, cud·dled, cud·dling.**

These kittens have **cuddled** up for a nap.

cue¹ (kyü),
1 *NOUN.* a signal to an actor, musician, or other performer that it is time to do something: *The crash of cymbals was his cue to fall down.*
2 *NOUN.* a hint as to what should be done: *Take your cue from me at the party about leaving.*
3 *VERB.* to give someone a cue: *Cue me when I'm supposed to start singing.*
❑ *PLURAL* **cues;** *VERB* **cues, cued, cu·ing** or **cue·ing.**
∎ Another word that sounds like this is **queue.**

cue² (kyü), *NOUN.* a long, wooden stick used for striking the ball in the game of billiards or pool.
❑ *PLURAL* **cues.** ∎ Another word that sounds like this is **queue.**

cuff (kuf), *NOUN.*
1 a band of material attached to a sleeve and worn around the wrist: *The collar and cuffs of a shirt are the first parts to wear out.*
2 the turned-up fold around the bottom of a leg of a pair of trousers.

cul·ti·vate (kul′tə vāt), *VERB.*
1 to prepare and use land to raise crops by plowing it, planting seeds, and taking care of the growing plants.
2 to help plants grow by work and care: *My uncle cultivates roses.*
3 to improve or develop by study or training: *She cultivated her mind by reading good books.*
❑ *VERB* **cul·ti·vates, cul·ti·vat·ed, cul·ti·vat·ing.**

cul·ti·va·tion (kul′tə vā′shən), *NOUN.*
1 the process of preparing land and growing crops by plowing, planting, and necessary care: *Better cultivation of soil will result in better crops.*
2 the process of improving or developing by study or training: *The cultivation of good study habits can lead to better grades.*

cul·ti·va·tor (kul′tə vā′tər), *NOUN.* a tool or machine used to loosen the ground and destroy weeds.

cul·tur·al (kul′chər əl), *ADJECTIVE.* of or about culture: *I enjoy going to symphony concerts, ballets, plays, and other cultural events.*

cul·ture (kul′chər), *NOUN.*
1 the beliefs, customs, arts, and tools of a nation or people at a certain time: *Our textbook includes a chapter on the culture of the Romans.*
2 interest in and activities that involve art, music, and literature.
3 growth of bacteria or other tiny living things in a laboratory for medical or scientific use.

cum·ber·some (kum′bər səm), *ADJECTIVE.* hard to move or manage; clumsy: *The armor worn by knights was often so cumbersome they had to be helped onto their horses.*

cu·mu·lo·nim·bus cloud (kyü′myə lō nim′bəs kloud′), a very large cloud formation with very tall peaks that sometimes flatten at the top; thundercloud.

cu·mu·lus cloud (kyü′myə ləs kloud′), a fluffy white cloud with a flat bottom, seen in fair weather.

cun·ning (kun′ing), *ADJECTIVE.* clever in deceiving; sly: *The cunning fox outwitted the dogs and got away.* —**cun′ning·ly,** *ADVERB.*

cup (kup),
1 *NOUN.* a container to drink from. Most cups have handles.
2 *NOUN.* as much as a cup holds: *She drank a cup of milk.*
3 *NOUN.* a unit of volume for liquids, equal to 8 fluid ounces.
4 *NOUN.* anything shaped like a cup: *A silver cup was awarded to the winner of the race.*
5 *VERB.* to place your hands in the shape of a cup: *He cupped his cold hands around the mug of hot chocolate to warm them.*
❑ *VERB* **cups, cupped, cup·ping.** —**cup′like′,** *ADJECTIVE.*

cup·board (kub′ərd), NOUN. a set of shelves closed in by a door, for dishes and food.

cup·cake (kup′kāk′), NOUN. a small cake about the same size as a cup.

cup·ful (kup′fúl), NOUN. as much as a cup can hold. ❏ PLURAL **cup·fuls.**

curb (kėrb),
1 NOUN. a raised border of concrete or stone along the edge of a sidewalk or street: *The driver parked the car close to the curb.*
2 VERB. to control: *Try to curb your anger.*
❏ VERB **curbs, curbed, curb·ing.**

curd (kėrd), NOUN. usually, **curds,** the thick part of milk that separates from the watery part when the milk sours. Cheese is made from curds.

cur·dle (kėr′dl), VERB. to form into curds: *Milk curdles when it is kept too long in a warm place.*
❏ VERB **cur·dles, cur·dled, cur·dling.**

cure (kyúr),
1 VERB. to bring someone back to health; make well: *The medicine cured the sick child.*
2 NOUN. something that can make a sick person better; remedy: *The scientist hoped to find a cure for the common cold.*
3 VERB. to keep meat from spoiling by drying, salting, smoking, or other means.
❏ VERB **cures, cured, cur·ing.**

cur·few (kėr′fyü), NOUN. a set time in the evening when you are required to be off the streets or at home: *Children in this town must be home before curfew.*

Word Story

The word **curfew** comes from old French words meaning "to cover the fire." In the Middle Ages fires were put out at night, in order to reduce the danger to wooden houses. Night was also the time for people to be off the streets, safe at home. The same word was used to express both these ideas.

cur·i·os·i·ty (kyúr′ē os′ə tē), NOUN.
1 a strong desire to know something: *She satisfied her curiosity about animals by visiting the zoo every week.*
2 a strange, unusual, or rare thing: *One of the curiosities we saw was a basket made of an armadillo shell.*
❏ PLURAL **cur·i·os·i·ties.**

cur·i·ous (kyúr′ē əs), ADJECTIVE.
1 eager to know: *Small children are very curious, and they ask many questions.*
2 strange; odd; unusual: *I found a curious old box in the attic.*
—**cur′i·ous·ly,** ADVERB.

curl (kėrl),
1 VERB. to twist into rings; roll into coils: *The baby's hair curls naturally.*

2 VERB. to curve or twist out of shape: *Paper curls as it burns.*
3 NOUN. a curled lock of hair: *The child's hair hung down in long curls.*
4 NOUN. anything curled or bent into a curve: *Curls of smoke rose from the fire.*
❏ VERB **curls, curled, curl·ing.** —**cur′li·ness,** NOUN.

curl·y (kėr′lē), ADJECTIVE.
1 curling or tending to curl: *curly hair.*
2 having curls or curly hair: *a curly head.*
❏ ADJECTIVE **curl·i·er, curl·i·est.**

cur·rant (kėr′ənt), NOUN.
1 a small, sweet raisin used in cakes and buns.
2 a small, sour, red, black, or white berry that is used for jelly.
■ Another word that sounds like this is **current.**

cur·ren·cy (kėr′ən sē), NOUN. the money in actual use in a country: *Coins and paper money are currency in the United States.* ❏ PLURAL **cur·ren·cies.**

Many countries have their own **currency.**

cur·rent (kėr′ənt),
1 NOUN. a flow or stream of water, electricity, air, or any fluid: *The current swept the stick down the river. The current went off when the storm hit.*
2 ADJECTIVE. of or about the present time.
■ Another word that sounds like this is **currant.**

cur·rent·ly (kėr′ənt lē), ADVERB. at the present time; now: *The flu is currently going around school and many people are absent.*

cur·ry (kėr′ē), NOUN.
1 a spicy or hot sauce or powder. Curry is a popular seasoning in India.
2 a food flavored with this seasoning.
❏ PLURAL **cur·ries.**

curse (kėrs),
1 VERB. to say rude or bad words; swear: *I cursed when I shut the door on my finger.*

a	hat	ė	term	ô	order	ch	child	⎧a in about
ā	age	i	it	oi	oil	ng	long	⎪e in taken
ä	far	ī	ice	ou	out	sh	she	ə⎨i in pencil
â	care	o	hot	u	cup	th	thin	⎪o in lemon
e	let	ō	open	ú	put	ᵺ	then	⎩u in circus
ē	equal	ò	saw	ü	rule	zh	measure	

2 *NOUN.* the words used in swearing: *Their talk was full of curses.*

3 *NOUN.* the words that someone says when wishing that harm will come to someone else: *The witch uttered a long curse with many strange words in it.*

4 *VERB.* to bring evil or harm on; trouble greatly; torment: *The farmers were cursed with dust storms.*

5 *NOUN.* something that causes a great deal of harm or trouble: *Rabbits can be a curse to gardeners.*
❑ *VERB* **curs·es, cursed, curs·ing.**

cur·sive (kėr′siv), *ADJECTIVE.* written with the letters joined together. Most people use cursive letters when signing their name or taking notes.

cur·sor (kėr′sər), *NOUN.* a movable mark on a computer screen. It shows where the next typed letter will appear, or where the mouse is pointing.

curt (kėrt), *ADJECTIVE.* rudely brief when you say something to someone: *The impatient clerk gave a curt reply.* −**curt′ly,** *ADVERB.* −**curt′ness,** *NOUN.*

cur·tain (kėrt′n), *NOUN.*
1 a cloth hung across a window or other space to shut out light, to give privacy, or for decoration.
2 (in a theater) a cloth that hangs between the stage or movie screen and the audience.

curt·sy (kėrt′sē),
1 *NOUN.* a bow of respect or greeting by women and girls, made by bending the knees and lowering the body.
2 *VERB.* to make a curtsy: *The actress curtsied when the audience applauded.*
❑ *PLURAL* **curt·sies;** *VERB* **curt·sies, curt·sied, curt·sy·ing.**

The ballerina **curtsies** at the end of her dance.

curve (kėrv),
1 *NOUN.* a line that has no straight part. A circle is a closed curve.
2 *NOUN.* a bend in a road: *The cars had to slow down to go around the curves.*
3 *VERB.* to bend so as to form a line that has no straight part: *The highway curved to the right in a sharp turn.* ■ See the Synonym Study at **bend.**
4 *NOUN.* a baseball thrown to swerve just before it reaches the batter.
❑ *VERB* **curves, curved, curv·ing.**

cush·ion (kush′ən),
1 *NOUN.* a soft pillow or pad used to sit, lie, or kneel on: *The chair has a cushion on the seat.*
2 *NOUN.* anything that is like a cushion by being soft: *I fell on a cushion of deep snow.*
3 *VERB.* to soften or ease the effects of: *Nothing could cushion the shock of my friend's death.*
❑ *VERB* **cush·ions, cush·ioned, cush·ion·ing.**

cus·tard (kus′tərd), *NOUN.* a baked, boiled, or frozen dessert made with eggs, milk, and sugar.

cus·to·di·an (ku stō′dē ən), *NOUN.*
1 someone who looks after something: *He is the custodian of the library's collection of rare books.*
2 a janitor: *a school custodian.*

cus·to·dy (kus′tə dē), *NOUN.* the official duty of looking after someone; care: *Parents have the custody of their young children.*

cus·tom (kus′təm),
1 *NOUN.* any usual action; habit: *It was her custom to get up early.*
2 *NOUN.* an old or popular way of doing things: *The social customs of many countries differ from ours.*
3 *ADJECTIVE.* made especially for one customer: *He wore custom suits made for him by an expert tailor.*
4 *NOUN.* **customs, a** taxes paid to the government on things brought in from a foreign country: *I paid $4 in customs on the $100 Swiss watch.* **b** an office at a seaport, airport, or border-crossing point where imported goods are checked.
■ See the Word History at **costume.**

cus·tom·ar·y (kus′tə mer′ē), *ADJECTIVE.* usual: *My customary bedtime is ten o'clock.*
−**cus′tom·ar′i·ly,** *ADVERB.*

cus·tom·er (kus′tə mər), *NOUN.* someone who buys goods or services: *Just before the holidays the store was full of customers.*

cus·tom·ize (kus′tə mīz), *VERB.* to build, alter, or remodel according to the instructions of the buyer: *customize a kitchen, customize a car.* ❑ *VERB* **cus·tom·iz·es, cus·tom·ized, cus·tom·iz·ing.**

cus·tom-made (kus′təm mād′), *ADJECTIVE.* made especially for a customer: *a custom-made suit.*

cut (kut),
1 *VERB.* to divide, separate, open, or remove with something sharp: *I cut the meat with a knife. He cut a hole through the wall with an axe.*
2 *VERB.* to hurt with something sharp: *She cut her finger on the broken glass.*
3 *NOUN.* an opening made by something sharp: *I put a bandage on my leg to cover the cut.*
4 *NOUN.* a piece that has been cut off or cut out: *A leg of lamb is a tasty cut of meat.*
5 *VERB.* to have teeth grow through the gums: *The baby is cutting her first tooth.*
6 *VERB.* to make something smaller; reduce; decrease: *We must cut our expenses to save money.*
7 *VERB.* to cut short; trim: *The barber cut my hair.*
8 *NOUN.* an act of making something shorter or smaller: *The speech was too long, so cuts were made.*
9 *VERB.* to cross: *A brook cuts through that field.*
10 *VERB.* to make a recording on: *cut a record, cut a tape.*
11 *VERB.* to stay away from on purpose: *The principal called my parents when I cut two classes.*
❑ *VERB* **cuts, cut, cut·ting.**

a cut above the rest, IDIOM. much better than other things of the same kind: *That new game is a cut above the rest.*

cut back, IDIOM. to make something less: *We cut back our heating bill by turning down the thermostat.*

cut down, IDIOM. to make something happen less often; to do or have less of something: *He cut down on candy.*

cut in, IDIOM.
1 to break in; interrupt: *She cut in suddenly with a remark while I was talking.*
2 to interrupt a dancing couple to take the place of one of them.
3 to move a vehicle suddenly into a line of moving traffic: *The driver cut in, just missing another car.*

cut off, IDIOM.
1 to stop something: *Their electricity was cut off when they didn't pay the bill.*
2 to separate someone or something from others: *The whole town was cut off by the flood.*

Synonym Study

Cut means to divide or to remove with something sharp: *"Will you cut the cake?" she asked. I cut the ribbon from the package.*

Trim means to cut off parts that are not needed or not neat: *Mom trimmed my bangs because I could hardly see.*

Shave means to cut off hair with a razor: *He shaves with an electric razor.*

Snip means to cut something off with a small, quick stroke: *I snipped a thread that was hanging from my sleeve.*

Shear means to remove something, especially wool, using shears, scissors, or clippers: *Ranchers shear their sheep in the spring.*

Clip[1] can mean to cut something out of a magazine or newspaper: *She clipped a picture from the magazine to illustrate her report on hurricanes.*

Carve and **slice** mean to cut something by moving a knife back and forth through it: *She carved the turkey. Then she sliced some bread.*

Split means to cut, usually from end to end: *He split the loaf of Italian bread and spread butter and garlic powder on it.*

Saw[1] means to cut with short back-and-forth strokes: *He sawed at the rope with a knife.*

Chop means to cut something up by hitting it with a sharp tool: *The man used an ax to chop wood for the fire.*

cute (kyüt), ADJECTIVE.
1 sweetly pretty: *a cute baby.*
2 handsome; good-looking: *The new boy was cute.*
❑ ADJECTIVE **cut•er, cut•est. —cute′ness,** NOUN.

Synonym Study

Cute means pleasing or good-looking. It is commonly used to show liking and approval: *His little brother is cute. What a cute dress she is wearing. The puppies were all so cute it was hard to decide which one to pick.*

Attractive means pleasing to look at and interesting: *The second-grade room is very attractive. That attractive young man is my cousin.*

Appealing means attractive and enjoyable: *He has a good sense of humor and is very appealing.*

Charming means pleasant and fascinating: *I enjoyed meeting your charming cousin.*

See also the Synonym Studies at **beautiful** and **good-natured.**

cut•lass (kut′ləs), NOUN. a short, heavy, slightly curved sword. ❑ PLURAL **cut•lass•es.**

cut•ter (kut′ər), NOUN.
1 a tool or machine for cutting: *a wire cutter, a cookie cutter.*
2 someone who cuts: *A garment cutter cuts out pieces of fabric to be made into clothes.*

cut•ting (kut′ing),
1 NOUN. a small shoot cut from a plant to grow a new plant.
2 ADJECTIVE. able to cut; sharp: *Be careful to avoid the cutting edge of a saw.*
3 ADJECTIVE. hurting the feelings: *He was offended by her cutting remark.*

cy•ber•space (sī′bər spās′), NOUN.
1 a visual space in three dimensions created by computer graphics. A user can move objects pictured in this space or change the space.
2 an imaginary space in which computers work. Anything done with a computer can be said to happen in cyberspace: *My notes were lost in cyberspace when my computer crashed.*

cy•cle (sī′kəl),
1 NOUN. any series of events which repeats itself in the same order over and over again.
2 VERB. to ride a bicycle, tricycle, or motorcycle: *We cycled around the park this morning.*
❑ VERB **cy•cles, cy•cled, cy•cling.**

a	hat	ė	term	ô	order	ch	child		a in about
ā	age	i	it	oi	oil	ng	long		e in taken
ä	far	ī	ice	ou	out	sh	she	ə	i in pencil
â	care	o	hot	u	cup	th	thin		o in lemon
e	let	ō	open	ů	put	ŦH	then		u in circus
ē	equal	ò	saw	ü	rule	zh	measure		

cy·clist (sī′klist), NOUN. someone who rides a bicycle or motorcycle.

cy·clone (sī′klōn), NOUN.
1 a very violent windstorm with very strong winds. During a cyclone, the winds blow in a large circular pattern.
2 a small, intense cyclone with a funnel that extends down from the clouds and may touch the ground; tornado.

One special kind of cyclone is called a tornado. It is much smaller but more intense. This kind of cyclone is usually only several hundred feet wide, but the whirling winds can reach speeds of 300 miles an hour.

cyclone (definition 2)

cyl·in·der (sil′ən dər), NOUN. a hollow or solid object shaped like a round pole or tube. Tin cans and rollers are cylinders.

Word Story

Cylinder comes from a Greek word meaning "to roll." In ancient times, the only way to move heavy objects such as building stones was on rollers, usually wooden ones. Anything shaped like a round log was also called a roller.

cy·lin·dri·cal (sə lin′drə kəl), ADJECTIVE. shaped like a cylinder. Cans of fruit, candles, and water pipes are usually cylindrical.

cym·bal (sim′bəl), NOUN. a round brass plate used as a musical instrument. Cymbals are often used in pairs and make a loud, ringing noise when struck against each other. ▪ Another word that sounds like this is **symbol.**

cy·press (sī′prəs), NOUN.
1 an evergreen tree with small, dark green leaves like scales.
2 a tree of the southern United States that loses its leaves each autumn. The wood of this cypress is used for boards and shingles.
❏ PLURAL **cy·press·es.**

Cy·prus (sī′prəs), NOUN. an island country in the Mediterranean Sea.

cy·to·plasm (sī′tə plaz′əm), NOUN. the living substance or part of the protoplasm of a cell that remains outside the cell's nucleus.

czar (zär), NOUN. an emperor. When Russia had an emperor, his title was czar.

cza·ri·na (zä rē′nə), NOUN.
1 the wife of a czar.
2 a Russian ruler; empress.
❏ PLURAL **cza·ri·nas.**

Czech (chek),
1 NOUN. someone born or living in the Czech Republic.
2 NOUN. the language of the Czech Republic.
3 ADJECTIVE. of or about the Czech Republic, its people, or their language.

Czech Republic, a country in central Europe.

dragonfly

Dd

D or **d** (dē), *NOUN.* the fourth letter of the English alphabet. ❑ *PLURAL* **D's** or **d's**.

dab (dab),
1 *VERB.* to touch lightly; stroke gently: *I dabbed my lips with a napkin.*
2 *VERB.* to put on with light strokes: *She dabbed paint on the canvas.*
3 *NOUN.* a small soft or moist mass: *dabs of butter. Put a dab of paint on this spot you missed.*
❑ *VERB* **dabs, dabbed, dab·bing.**

dab·ble (dab'əl), *VERB.*
1 to dip something in and out of water; splash: *We sat and dabbled our feet in the pool.*
2 to work at something without your full effort: *He dabbled at painting but soon gave it up.*
❑ *VERB* **dab·bles, dab·bled, dab·bling.**

dachs·hund (däks'hund' *or* däk'sənd), *NOUN.* a small dog with a long body, drooping ears, and very short legs.

dad (dad), *NOUN.* (informal) father.

dad·dy (dad'ē), *NOUN.* (informal) father. ❑ *PLURAL* **dad·dies.**

dad·dy-long·legs (dad'ē long'legz'), *NOUN.* an insect that looks much like a spider, but does not bite. It has a small, round body and long, thin legs. ❑ *PLURAL* **dad·dy-long·legs.**

daf·fo·dil (daf'ə dil), *NOUN.* a plant with long, slender leaves and yellow flowers that bloom early in the spring. Daffodils grow from bulbs.

dag·ger (dag'ər), *NOUN.* (earlier) a small weapon with a short, pointed blade.
look daggers at, *IDIOM.* to glare at someone.

dai·ly (dā'lē),
1 *ADJECTIVE.* done, happening, or appearing every day: *a daily visit, a daily paper.*
2 *ADVERB.* every day; day by day: *She rides her bike daily.*
3 *NOUN.* a newspaper printed every day, or every day but Sunday. ❑ *PLURAL* **dai·lies.**

dain·ti·ly (dān′tl ē), ADVERB. in a dainty way.

dain·ty (dān′tē), ADJECTIVE. having delicate beauty; fresh and pretty: *She wore a dainty cotton dress.* ❑ ADJECTIVE **dain·ti·er, dain·ti·est. –dain′ti·ness,** NOUN.

dair·y (dâr′ē),
1 NOUN. a place where milk and cream are kept and made into butter and cheese.
2 NOUN. a company that sells milk, cream, butter, cheese, yogurt, ice cream, and so on.
3 ADJECTIVE. of or about milk and products made from milk: *dairy cattle, the dairy industry.*
❑ PLURAL **dair·ies.**

dai·sy (dā′zē), NOUN. a wildflower having white, pink, or yellow petals around a yellow center.
❑ PLURAL **dai·sies. –dai′sy·like′,** ADJECTIVE.

Da·ko·ta (də kō′tə), NOUN.
1 **the Dakotas,** North and South Dakota.
2 the Sioux, especially those living in the eastern section of their lands. ▪ See the Usage Note at **Sioux.**
★ The plural for this meaning is **Dakota.**
–Da·ko′tan, ADJECTIVE or NOUN.

dale (dāl), NOUN. a valley.

Dal·las (dal′əs), NOUN. a city in Texas.

Dal·ma·tian (dal mā′shən), NOUN. a large, short-haired dog, usually white with black spots.

dam (dam),
1 NOUN. a wall built to hold back the water of a stream or river.
2 VERB. to put up a dam; block up with a dam: *Beavers had dammed the stream.*
❑ VERB **dams, dammed, dam·ming.**

dam·age (dam′ij),
1 NOUN. harm or injury that lessens the value or usefulness of something: *The accident did some damage to the car.*
2 VERB. to harm or injure so as to lessen value or usefulness; hurt: *An early fall frost damaged the apple crops.* ▪ See the Synonym Study at **harm.**
❑ VERB **dam·ag·es, dam·aged, dam·ag·ing.**

damp (damp),
1 ADJECTIVE. a little wet; moist: *This house is damp in rainy weather.*
2 NOUN. moisture: *When it's foggy you can feel the damp in the air.*
–damp′ness, NOUN.

Synonym Study

Damp means slightly wet, often in an unpleasant way: *Who left this damp towel here?*

Moist means slightly wet, often in a pleasant way: *I prefer moist cake to a dry one.*

Humid means having a lot of moisture in the air: *Today it is 90 degrees and very humid.*

Clammy means cold and damp: *They shivered in the dark, clammy basement.*

See also the Synonym Study at **wet.**

damp·en (dam′pən), VERB.
1 to make or become damp: *He sprinkled water over the clothes to dampen them before ironing.*
2 to depress; discourage: *The sad news dampened our spirits.*
❑ VERB **damp·ens, damp·ened, damp·en·ing.**

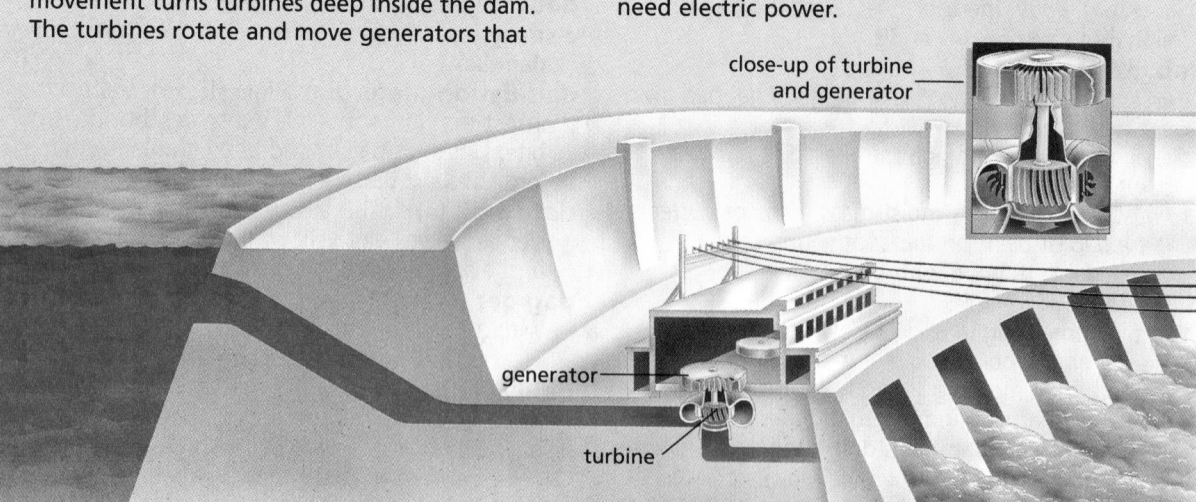

This dam uses the force of a flowing river to produce electricity. The water in the river must pass through the dam. As it flows through, its movement turns turbines deep inside the dam. The turbines rotate and move generators that cause large amounts of electric energy to flow into the wires. From there, the electricity is sent to homes, schools, stores, and other places that need electric power.

close-up of turbine and generator

generator

turbine

This **dam** is using flowing water to produce electricity.

D

dance (dans),
1 *VERB.* to move in rhythm, especially to music: *She can dance very well.*
2 *NOUN.* movement in rhythm with music: *Ballet is a well-known form of dance.*
3 *NOUN.* some special group of steps: *The waltz is a dance that is easy to learn.*
4 *NOUN.* a party where people dance.
5 *VERB.* to jump up and down; move around in a lively way: *The children danced with delight.*
  ❑ *VERB* **danc·es, danced, danc·ing.** **–danc′er,** *NOUN.*

dancer

Martha Graham

Martha Graham was an American dancer and teacher. She was a pioneer of modern dance. She developed a style of teaching dance that is used all over the world.

dan·de·li·on (dan′dl ī′ən), *NOUN.* a plant that grows as a weed in lawns and fields. It has yellow flowers.
dan·druff (dan′drəf), *NOUN.* small, white flakes of dead skin that fall from the scalp.
dan·dy (dan′dē),
1 *NOUN.* an excellent or very impressive thing: *That new bike is a dandy.*
2 *ADJECTIVE.* excellent; first-rate: *I got a dandy new bike.*
  ❑ *PLURAL* **dan·dies;** *ADJECTIVE* **dan·di·er, dan·di·est.**
Dane (dān), *NOUN.* someone born or living in Denmark.
dan·ger (dān′jər), *NOUN.*
1 the strong possibility that something bad or harmful will happen: *The trip through the jungle was full of danger.*
2 something that may cause harm: *Hidden rocks are a danger to ships.*
dan·ger·ous (dān′jər əs), *ADJECTIVE.* not safe; likely to harm you: *Shooting off firecrackers is dangerous.* **–dan′ger·ous·ly,** *ADVERB.*

dan·gle (dang′gəl), *VERB.*
1 to hang and swing loosely: *The mountain climber dangled from a rope.*
2 to hold or carry something so that it swings loosely: *The cat played with the string that I dangled in front of it.*
  ❑ *VERB* **dan·gles, dan·gled, dan·gling.**
Dan·ish (dā′nish),
1 *ADJECTIVE.* of Denmark, its people, or their language.
2 *NOUN PLURAL.* **the Danish,** the people of Denmark.
3 *NOUN.* the language of Denmark.
4 *NOUN.* also, **danish,** a kind of rich pastry, usually eaten for breakfast.
dare (dâr),
1 *VERB.* to be brave or bold enough: *The children dared to explore the haunted house.*
2 *VERB.* to challenge someone: *I dare you to jump the puddle.*
3 *NOUN.* a challenge: *I took his dare to jump.*
  ❑ *VERB* **dares, dared, dar·ing.**
dare·dev·il (dâr′dev′əl),
1 *NOUN.* a reckless person.
2 *ADJECTIVE.* recklessly daring: *The motorist's daredevil driving caused an accident.*
dar·ing (dâr′ing),
1 *NOUN.* the courage to take risks; boldness: *The lifeguard's daring saved a swimmer's life.*
2 *ADJECTIVE.* bold; fearless: *a daring trapeze act.*
  ▪ See the Synonym Study at **brave.**
dark (därk),
1 *ADJECTIVE.* with little or no light: *A night without a moon is dark.*
2 *ADJECTIVE.* nearly black in color: *Her eyes are brown and very dark.*
3 *ADJECTIVE.* gloomy: *It was a dark day, rainy and cold.*
4 *NOUN.* darkness: *Don't be afraid of the dark.*
5 *NOUN.* night; nightfall: *Hurry to get home before dark.*
  –dark′ness, *NOUN.*
in the dark, *IDIOM.* in ignorance: *He said nothing, leaving me in the dark about his plans.*
dark·en (där′kən), *VERB.* to make or become dark or darker: *The sky darkened as the storm came nearer.*
  ❑ *VERB* **dark·ens, dark·ened, dark·en·ing.**
dar·ling (där′ling),
1 *NOUN.* someone who is very dear to you: *He is a darling.*
2 *ADJECTIVE.* very dear; much loved: *"My darling daughter," her letter began.*
3 *ADJECTIVE.* (informal) pleasing or attractive: *What a darling little puppy!*

a	hat	ė	term	ô	order	ch	child		a in about
ā	age	i	it	oi	oil	ng	long		e in taken
ä	far	ī	ice	ou	out	sh	she	ə {	i in pencil
â	care	o	hot	u	cup	th	thin		o in lemon
e	let	ō	open	u̇	put	ŦH	then		u in circus
ē	equal	ȯ	saw	ü	rule	zh	measure		

darn (därn), VERB. to mend a hole by making rows of stitches back and forth across it. ❑ VERB **darns, darned, darn·ing.**

dart (därt),

1 NOUN. a slender, pointed object usually thrown by hand.

2 NOUN. **darts,** an indoor game in which darts are thrown at a target: *Darts is Dad's favorite game.*

3 VERB. to move suddenly and swiftly: *The deer saw us and darted away.*

❑ VERB **darts, dart·ed, dart·ing.**

dash (dash),

1 VERB. to rush: *We dashed down the street to catch the bus.*

2 NOUN. a rush: *We made a dash for the bus.*

3 VERB. to ruin: *My hopes were dashed by the news.*

4 NOUN. a small amount: *Put in just a dash of pepper.*

5 NOUN. a short race: *He won the fifty-yard dash.*

6 NOUN. a mark (—) used in writing or printing. A dash shows that there is a pause in thought.

❑ VERB **dash·es, dashed, dash·ing.**

dash (definition 5)

dash off, IDIOM. to do, make, write, and so on, quickly: *He dashed off a letter to his friend.*

dash·board (dash'bôrd'), NOUN. a panel below the windshield of a car or truck. It contains the speedometer and other dials that show whether the car or truck is working properly.

da·shi·ki (də shə'kē), NOUN. a loose shirt of African origin, colorfully printed or embroidered. ❑ PLURAL **da·shi·kis.**

da·ta (dā'tə or dat'ə), NOUN PLURAL.

1 facts; information: *Names, ages, and other data about the class are written in the teacher's book.*

2 information in electronic form that can be used or processed by a computer. ★ This sense of **data** is often used with a singular verb: *The new data is needed by Friday at the latest.*

da·ta·base (dā'tə bās' or dat'ə bās'), NOUN. a large collection of information, stored and made available by a computer or computers. Databases include such items as newspaper stories, airplane schedules, or inventory lists.

date¹ (dāt),

1 NOUN. the time when something happens or happened: *July 4, 1776, is the date of the signing of the Declaration of Independence.*

2 NOUN. the day of the month: *What is Friday's date?*

3 VERB. to put a date on something: *I dated the letter.*

4 VERB. to find out the date of something; give a date to: *The scientist was unable to date the fossil.*

5 VERB. to belong to a certain period of time: *The oldest house in town dates from the 1780s.*

6 NOUN. an appointment for a certain time: *Don't forget our lunch date on Friday!*

7 VERB. to go out with someone for friendship or companionship: *They have been dating one another for several months.*

8 NOUN. someone that you go out with: *He was her date for the school dance last Friday.*

❑ VERB **dates, dat·ed, dat·ing.**

out of date, IDIOM. old-fashioned: *I refused to wear the suit because it was out of date.*

up to date, IDIOM.

1 in fashion; modern: *His clothes are always up to date.*

2 up to the present time: *The teacher entered our latest grades on our report cards to bring them up to date.*

date² (dāt), NOUN. the sweet fruit of a kind of palm tree.

daugh·ter (do'tər), NOUN. a female child. A girl or woman is the daughter of her father and mother.

daugh·ter-in-law (do'tər in lo'), NOUN. the wife of your son. ❑ PLURAL **daugh·ters-in-law.**

daw·dle (do'dl), VERB. to waste time; be idle: *Don't dawdle so long over your work.* ❑ VERB **daw·dles, daw·dled, daw·dling.** —**daw'dler,** NOUN.

dawdling

dawn (don),

1 NOUN. the beginning of day; the first light in the east.

2 NOUN. the beginning: *Dinosaurs roamed our planet long before the dawn of human life.*

3 VERB. to grow light in the morning: *The day was dawning when I awoke.*

❑ VERB **dawns, dawned, dawn·ing.**

day (dā), NOUN.

1 the time of light between sunrise and sunset: *Days are longer in summer than in winter.*

2 the 24 hours of day and night: *There are seven days in a week.*

3 the hours for work: *Our office has a seven-hour day.*

4 a time; period: *In the days of old, they used candles.*

make someone's day, IDIOM. to make someone happy or pleased: *Their thanks made my day.*

day·break (dā′brāk′), NOUN. the time when it first begins to get light in the morning; dawn.

day camp, a summer camp where children play sports, open during the daytime.

day-care cen·ter (dā′kâr′ sen′tər), a place where small children are cared for during the day while their parents are at work.

day·dream (dā′drēm′),
1 NOUN. the act of thinking in a dreamlike way.
2 VERB. to think about pleasant things in a dreamlike way.
❑ VERB **day·dreams, day·dreamed, day·dream·ing.**

day·light (dā′līt′), NOUN.
1 the light of day: *Some colors look better in daylight.*
2 dawn; daybreak: *He was up at daylight.*

day·light-sav·ing time (dā′līt′sā′ving tīm′), time that is one hour ahead of standard time. It gives more daylight after working hours. Daylight-saving time begins on the first Sunday in April and ends on the last Sunday in October.

day·time (dā′tīm′), NOUN. the time between dawn and sunset: *Babies sleep even in the daytime.*

day-to-day (dā′tə dā′), ADJECTIVE.
1 happening every day or most days: *We all have day-to-day chores. She does the day-to-day shopping.*
2 only for today, not for the future: *During our vacation we lived a day-to-day life.*

daze (dāz),
1 VERB. to make someone unable to think clearly; stun: *A blow on the head dazed him so that he could not keep playing.*
2 NOUN. a condition of mental confusion: *She was in a daze after falling from her horse and could not understand what was happening.*
❑ VERB **daz·es, dazed, daz·ing.**

daz·zle (daz′əl), VERB.
1 to hurt the eyes with too much light: *It dazzles the eyes to look straight at bright headlights.*
∎ See the Synonym Study at **bright.**
2 to amaze someone: *We were dazzled by the richness of the palace.*
❑ VERB **daz·zles, daz·zled, daz·zling.**

DC, an abbreviation of **District of Columbia.**

d.c., an abbreviation of **direct current.**

Word Power   de-

The prefix **de-** has several meanings. **De-** can mean "to do the opposite of." **De**segregate means to **do the opposite of** segregate.

De- can mean "down" or "lower." A **de**pressant slows **down** normal activity.

De- can mean "to take away" or "to remove." **De**frost means to **remove the** frost.

DE, an abbreviation of **Delaware.**

dea·con (dē′kən), NOUN.
1 an officer of a church who helps the minister with duties other than preaching.
2 a member of the clergy next below a priest or minister in rank.

dead (ded),
1 ADJECTIVE. not alive; no longer living: *The roses in my garden are dead.*
2 NOUN PLURAL. **the dead,** people who are no longer alive: *We remember our war dead on Memorial Day.*
3 ADJECTIVE. without life: *The surface of the moon is dead.*
4 ADJECTIVE. dull; quiet; not active: *This beach is crowded now, but in the winter it's dead.*

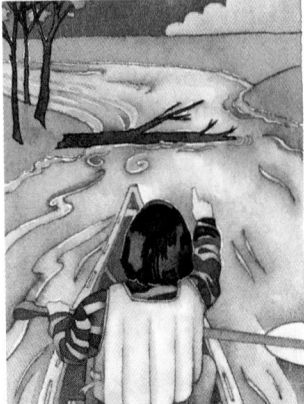
There is a log **dead ahead!**

5 ADJECTIVE. without force, power, or activity: *The car won't start because the battery is dead.*
6 ADJECTIVE. very tired; exhausted: *I was dead when I finished the six-mile hike.*
7 ADJECTIVE. out of play: *a dead ball.*
8 ADJECTIVE. sure; certain: *a dead shot with a rifle.*
9 ADVERB. completely; absolutely: *I was dead tired after the long hike.*
10 NOUN. the time when there is the least life stirring: *A loud noise woke us in the dead of night.*
dead ahead, IDIOM. directly in front of: *A floating log lay dead ahead of our canoe.*

dead·beat (ded′bēt′), NOUN. (informal) someone who avoids paying bills.

dead·en (ded′n), VERB.
1 to make something dull or weak; lessen the force of: *Some medicines deaden pain.*
2 to make something soundproof: *Thick walls deaden the noises from the street.*
❑ VERB **dead·ens, dead·ened, dead·en·ing.**

dead end, a street that is closed at one end.

dead·line (ded′līn′), NOUN. the latest possible time to do something: *Friday afternoon is the deadline for handing in our book reports.*

dead·ly (ded′lē), ADJECTIVE.
1 causing death; likely to cause death; fatal: *a deadly disease, deadly toadstools.*
2 filled with hatred: *deadly enemies.*
❑ ADJECTIVE **dead·li·er, dead·li·est.**

a	hat	ė	term	ô	order	ch	child	a in about
ā	age	i	it	oi	oil	ng	long	e in taken
ä	far	ī	ice	ou	out	sh	she	ə ⟨ i in pencil
â	care	o	hot	u	cup	th	thin	o in lemon
e	let	ō	open	ù	put	ᴛʜ	then	u in circus
ē	equal	ò	saw	ü	rule	zh	measure	

deaf (def), ADJECTIVE.
1 also, **Deaf,** not able, or only partly able, to hear: *Some deaf people use American Sign Language.*
2 not willing to listen to something: *He is deaf to any criticism of his work.*
　—deaf′ness, NOUN.

Usage Note

Deaf is not the only word to describe people who cannot hear or who do not hear well. Some people prefer to use **hearing-impaired,** and it is wise to be careful. If in doubt, ask!

deaf·en (def′ən), VERB.
1 to make someone deaf: *A hard blow on the ear can deafen someone for life.*
2 to stun someone with a powerful noise: *A sudden explosion deafened us for a moment.* ■ See the Synonym Study at **loud.**
　❏ VERB **deaf·ens, deaf·ened, deaf·en·ing.**

deal (dēl),
1 VERB. to work or be concerned with: *Arithmetic deals with numbers.*
2 VERB. to act or behave: *Deal kindly with them so you don't hurt their feelings.*
3 VERB. to handle or manage; take action about: *Mother dealt with the leak until the plumber came.*
4 VERB. to carry on business; buy and sell: *This business deals in sports equipment.*
5 NOUN. a bargain: *He got a good deal on a TV set.*
6 VERB. to give with the intention of harming or punishing: *One fighter dealt the other a hard blow.*
7 VERB. to hand out: *It's my turn to deal the cards.*
8 NOUN. an arrangement; plan: *I have a deal to trade some old books with her.*
　❏ VERB **deals, dealt, deal·ing.**
a good deal or **a great deal,** IDIOM. a large part, portion, or amount: *A great deal of her money goes for rent.*

deal·er (dē′lər), NOUN.
1 someone who makes a living by buying and selling things: *a used-car dealer.*
2 someone who deals the cards in a card game.

dealt (delt), VERB.
1 the past tense of **deal:** *The principal's talk dealt with fire drills.*
2 the past participle of **deal:** *The cards have been dealt.*

dear (dir),
1 ADJECTIVE. much loved; precious: *His sister was very dear to him.*
2 NOUN. a darling; dear one: *"Come, my dear," said her grandfather.*
3 ADJECTIVE. highly respected. *Dear Sir* or *Dear Madam* is the usual polite way to begin a letter.
4 INTERJECTION. an exclamation of surprise, worry, or trouble: *Oh, dear! I lost my pencil.*
　■ Another word that sounds like this is **deer.**

dear·ly (dir′lē), ADVERB. very much: *We love our parents dearly.*

death (deth), NOUN.
1 the act or fact of dying; the end of life: *The old man's death was calm and peaceful.*
2 any ending that is like dying: *the death of hope.*
3 the condition of being dead: *In death he looked peaceful.*

de·bate (di bāt′),
1 VERB. to think over the reasons for and against something: *I am debating buying a new car.*
2 NOUN. a discussion, often public, of reasons for and against something: *There has been much debate about building a new school.*
3 VERB. to discuss a question or topic according to certain rules: *The two candidates debated the need to build a new expressway.*
　❏ VERB **de·bates, de·bat·ed, de·bat·ing.**
　—de·bat′er, NOUN.

Word Story

Debate comes from a Latin word meaning "to beat." **Batter**[1] comes from the same Latin word. People used to debate with swords; now they debate with words.

de·bris (də brē′), NOUN. scattered pieces or bits of something that has been torn down or blown up, left by a flood, or the like.

Debris littered the beach.

debt (det), NOUN.
1 something owed to someone else: *He paid back all his debts.*
2 the condition of owing something to someone: *The loan from the bank has put her in debt.*

debt·or (det′ər), NOUN. someone who owes something to another person: *If I borrow a dollar from you, I am your debtor.*

de·bug (dē bug′), VERB. to find and correct the mistakes in a computer program: *It took hours to debug his homework assignment.* ❏ VERB **de·bugs, de·bugged, de·bug·ging.**

Dec., an abbreviation of **December.**

dec·ade (dek′ād), NOUN. a period of ten years. From 1989 to 1999 is a decade. ■ See the Word Story at **December.**

de·caf·fein·at·ed (di kaf′ə nā′tid), ADJECTIVE. having the caffeine removed: *decaffeinated coffee.*

de·cay (di kā′),
1 VERB. to become rotten; rot: *The old apples got moldy and decayed.*
2 NOUN. the action or process of rotting: *The decay of the pier was made worse by the storm.*
3 VERB. to grow less in power, strength, wealth, or beauty: *Empires grow great and then decay.*
4 NOUN. the process of growing less in power, strength, wealth, or beauty: *the decay of a nation's strength.*
❏ VERB **de·cays, de·cayed, de·cay·ing.**

de·ceased (di sēst′),
1 ADJECTIVE. dead: *a deceased writer.*
2 NOUN. **the deceased,** a particular dead person or persons: *The deceased had been a famous writer.*

de·ceit (di sēt′), NOUN.
1 the act of making someone believe that something false is true: *He was a truthful person, incapable of deceit.*
2 the quality that makes someone tell lies or cheat: *The dishonest trader was full of deceit.*

de·ceit·ful (di sēt′fəl), ADJECTIVE.
1 ready or willing to deceive or lie: *a deceitful person.*
2 meant to deceive: *a deceitful story.*
—de·ceit′ful·ly, ADVERB. **—de·ceit′ful·ness,** NOUN.

de·ceive (di sēv′), VERB. to make someone believe something is true that is actually false; mislead: *The magician deceived her audience into thinking she had really pulled a rabbit from a hat.* ■ See the Synonym Study at **cheat.** ❏ VERB **de·ceives, de·ceived, de·ceiv·ing. —de·ceiv′er,** NOUN.

De·cem·ber (di sem′bər), NOUN. the 12th and last month of the year. It has 31 days.

Word Story

December came from a Latin word meaning "ten." In the ancient Roman calendar, December was the tenth month of the year, which began in March.

The words **decade, decimal,** and **dime** also come from the Latin word for ten.

de·cen·cy (dē′sn sē), NOUN. the quality of being decent; proper behavior: *Common decency requires that you pay for the window you broke.*

de·cent (dē′snt), ADJECTIVE.
1 proper and right: *The decent thing to do is to pay for the damage you have done.*
2 good enough; pretty good: *I usually get decent grades at school.*
—de′cent·ly, ADVERB.

de·cep·tion (di sep′shən), NOUN. the act of misleading or lying to someone; deceiving: *The twins' deception in exchanging places fooled us.*

de·cep·tive (di sep′tiv), ADJECTIVE. tending to deceive: *the deceptive warmth of winter sunlight, deceptive advertising.* **—de·cep′tive·ly,** ADVERB.

de·cide (di sīd′), VERB.
1 to make up your mind about something; resolve: *She decided to be a scientist.*
2 to settle a question or dispute: *Fighting is not the best way to decide an argument.*
3 to give a judgment or decision: *The jury heard the evidence and decided on a verdict of not guilty.*
❏ VERB **de·cides, de·cid·ed, de·cid·ing.**

de·cid·u·ous (di sij′ü əs), ADJECTIVE. having leaves that drop off each fall season. Maples, oaks, and locusts are deciduous trees.

deciduous trees

dec·i·mal (des′ə məl),
1 NOUN. a fraction like .04 or $\frac{4}{100}$, or .2 or $\frac{2}{10}$.
2 NOUN. a number like 75.24, 3.062, .7, or .091.
3 ADJECTIVE. of or based on the number ten: *The metric system is a decimal system of measurement.* ■ See the Word Story at **December.**

decimal fraction, a fraction whose denominator is ten or a multiple of ten, expressed by placing a decimal point to the left of the numerator.
EXAMPLES: .04 = $\frac{4}{100}$, .2 = $\frac{2}{10}$

decimal point, a period placed before a decimal fraction, as in 2.03 or .623.

decimal system, a system of numbering that is based on units of 10.

de·ci·sion (di sizh′ən), NOUN. the act of making up your mind about something: *I have not yet come to a decision about buying that bicycle.*

a	hat	ė	term	ô	order	ch	child
ā	age	i	it	oi	oil	ng	long
ä	far	ī	ice	ou	out	sh	she
â	care	o	hot	u	cup	th	thin
e	let	ō	open	ù	put	ᴛʜ	then
ē	equal	ò	saw	ü	rule	zh	measure

ə { a in about / e in taken / i in pencil / o in lemon / u in circus

de·ci·sive (di sī′siv), ADJECTIVE.
1 having or giving a clear result; settling something beyond question: *The team won by 20 points, which was a decisive victory.*
2 showing firmness and determination: *She was known for her decisive manner in the classroom.*
—**de·ci′sive·ly**, ADVERB. —**de·ci′sive·ness**, NOUN.

deck (dek),
1 NOUN. one of the floors of a ship that divide it into different levels.
2 NOUN. a part or floor that resembles a ship's deck: *Carpenters built a deck on the back of our house.*
3 NOUN. a pack of playing cards: *He shuffled the deck.*
4 VERB. to decorate; trim: *Deck the halls with holly.*
❏ VERB **decks, decked, deck·ing.**

Word Story

Deck comes from an early Dutch word meaning "roof" or "covering." The change in meaning from roof or covering to floor took place in English. The deck of a ship is a covering over the space below and also serves as a floor for the space you are on.

dec·la·ra·tion (dek′lə rā′shən), NOUN.
1 a public statement; official announcement: *The royal declaration was announced in every city and town.*
2 the act of officially declaring something: *The soldiers rejoiced at the declaration of a truce.*

Declaration of Independence, the public statement adopted by the Second Continental Congress on July 4, 1776, in which the American colonies declared themselves free and independent of Great Britain.

Declaration of Independence

de·clar·a·tive sen·tence (di klar′ə tiv sen′təns), a sentence that makes a statement. "I'm eating" and "The dog has four legs" are declarative sentences.

de·clare (di klâr′), VERB.
1 to announce something publicly or formally: *Congress has the power to declare war.* ■ See the Synonym Study at **say.**
2 to say something openly or strongly: *I declared that I would never do anything so foolish again.*
❏ VERB **de·clares, de·clared, de·clar·ing.**

de·cline (di klīn′),
1 VERB. to refuse to do or accept something: *They declined to do as they were told.*
2 VERB. to grow less in power, strength, wealth, or beauty: *Great nations have risen and declined.*
3 NOUN. the process of growing worse: *Lack of money led to a decline in the condition of the school.*

4 NOUN. the act of falling to a lower level; sinking: *a decline in prices.*
❏ VERB **de·clines, de·clined, de·clin·ing.**

de·code (dē kōd′), VERB.
1 to translate secret writing from code into ordinary language that you can understand.
2 to change computer information from some unreadable form into a readable text.
❏ VERB **de·codes, de·cod·ed, de·cod·ing.**
—**de·cod′er**, NOUN.

de·com·pose (dē′kəm pōz′), VERB. to decay; rot: *Lettuce and oranges decompose quickly in the heat.* ❏ VERB **de·com·pos·es, de·com·posed, de·com·pos·ing.**

de·com·pos·er (dē′kəm pō′zər), NOUN. a living thing that acts on dead animals and plants and puts the material stored in them back into the soil. Mushrooms and bacteria are decomposers.

de·com·po·si·tion (dē′kom pə zish′ən), NOUN. the act or process of decay; rotting: *Topsoil is created by the decomposition of grass and leaves.*

dec·o·rate (dek′ə rāt′), VERB.
1 to make something beautiful by adding ornaments: *We decorated the Christmas tree.*
2 to paint or wallpaper a room: *The old rooms looked like new after they had been decorated.*
3 to give a badge, ribbon, or medal to someone: *The general decorated the soldier for his brave act.*
❏ VERB **dec·o·rates, dec·o·rat·ed, dec·o·rat·ing.**

dec·o·ra·tion (dek′ə rā′shən), NOUN.
1 something used to decorate; ornament: *We put holiday decorations up in the classroom.*
2 a badge, ribbon, or medal given as an honor.
3 the act of decorating: *Decoration of the gymnasium took most of the day before the dance.*

dec·o·ra·tor (dek′ə rā′tər), NOUN. someone who decorates. An **interior decorator** plans and arranges the furniture and decorations for a house or other building.

de·coy (dē′koi or di koi′),
1 VERB. to lead someone by tricky methods: *The bird decoyed us away from her nest by dragging a drooping wing.*
2 NOUN. an artificial bird used to attract birds into a trap or near the hunter.
3 NOUN. any person or thing used to lead or tempt someone into a dangerous situation.
❏ VERB **de·coys, de·coyed, de·coy·ing.**

de·crease (di krēs′ *for verb;* dē′krēs *for noun*),
1 VERB. to make or become less: *The driver decreased the speed of the car.*
2 NOUN. the process of becoming less: *Toward nightfall there was a decrease in temperature.*
3 NOUN. the amount by which something becomes less: *The decrease in temperature was 10 degrees.*
❏ VERB **de·creas·es, de·creased, de·creas·ing.**

de·cree (di krē′),
1 *NOUN.* an official decision; order with the force of a law: *The new state holiday was declared by a decree of the Governor.*
2 *VERB.* to order or settle by authority: *The city council decreed that all dogs must be licensed.*
❑ *PLURAL* **de·crees;** *VERB* **de·crees, de·creed, de·cree·ing.**

ded·i·cate (ded′ə kāt), *VERB.* to set something apart for a purpose: *The library was dedicated to the memory of a great writer.* ❑ *VERB* **ded·i·cates, ded·i·cat·ed, ded·i·cat·ing.**

ded·i·ca·tion (ded′ə kā′shən), *NOUN.*
1 the act of setting something apart for a purpose: *I was present at the dedication of the new park.*
2 great and constant interest in something: *He showed true dedication to his work.*

de·duct (di dukt′), *VERB.* to take away; subtract: *When I broke the window, my parents deducted its cost from my allowance.* ❑ *VERB* **de·ducts, de·duct·ed, de·duct·ing.** –**de·duct′i·ble,** *ADJECTIVE.*

de·duc·tion (di duk′shən), *NOUN.*
1 the act or process of taking away; subtraction: *When I broke the window, my parents made a deduction from my allowance to pay for it.*
2 an amount that is deducted: *There was a deduction of $20 from the price of the damaged chair.*

deed (dēd), *NOUN.*
1 something done; an act; an action: *To feed the hungry is a good deed.*
2 a written or printed statement of ownership. *The buyer of land receives a deed to the property from the former owner.*

dee·jay (dē′jā′), *NOUN.* See **disc jockey.**

deep (dēp),
1 *ADJECTIVE.* going a long way down from the top or surface: *a deep cut, a deep pond.*
2 *ADVERB.* far down; far on: *They dug deep before they found water.*
3 *ADJECTIVE.* low in pitch: *He has a deep voice.*
4 *ADJECTIVE.* hard to understand; needing much time for thought: *a deep subject, deep thoughts.*
5 *ADJECTIVE.* strong; very intense; extreme: *She fell into a deep sleep. Deep feeling is hard to put into words.*
6 *ADJECTIVE.* rich and dark in color: *deep red roses.*
7 *ADJECTIVE.* from front to back; in depth: *Our playground at school is 100 feet deep.*
8 *NOUN.* **the deep,** the sea: *Long ago, frightened sailors thought they saw monsters from the deep.*
–**deep′ly,** *ADVERB.*

deep·en (dē′pən), *VERB.* to make or become deeper: *We deepened the hole.* ❑ *VERB* **deep·ens, deep·ened, deep·en·ing.**

deer (dir), *NOUN.* an animal that has long legs, hoofs, and a long neck. Deer are swift forest animals related to the moose and elk. The male grows new antlers every year. ❑ *PLURAL* **deer.**
■ Another word that sounds like this is **dear.**
–**deer′like′,** *ADJECTIVE.*

de·face (di fās′), *VERB.* to spoil how something looks: *Scribbling and underlining deface a book's pages.* ❑ *VERB* **de·fac·es, de·faced, de·fac·ing.**

de·feat (di fēt′),
1 *VERB.* to win a victory over: *to defeat the enemy in battle, to defeat another softball team.*
2 *VERB.* to cause something to fail; make useless: *The prince defeated the duke's wicked plan.*
3 *NOUN.* the act of defeating: *The crowd cheered the home team's defeat of the visiting team.*
4 *NOUN.* the condition of being defeated: *We were unhappy about our team's defeat.*
❑ *VERB* **de·feats, de·feat·ed, de·feat·ing.**

de·fect (dē′fekt *or* di fekt′), *NOUN.* something missing or broken that prevents a thing from being perfect; imperfection: *The cloth had holes and other defects.*

de·fec·tive (di fek′tiv), *ADJECTIVE.* not perfect; not working properly: *This watch is defective; it does not keep the correct time.* –**de·fec′tive·ness,** *NOUN.*

de·fend (di fend′), *VERB.*
1 to keep something safe; guard from attack or harm; protect: *The soldiers defended the fort.*
2 to act, speak, or write in favor of: *The newspapers defended the governor's action.*
❑ *VERB* **de·fends, de·fend·ed, de·fend·ing.** –**de·fend′er,** *NOUN.*

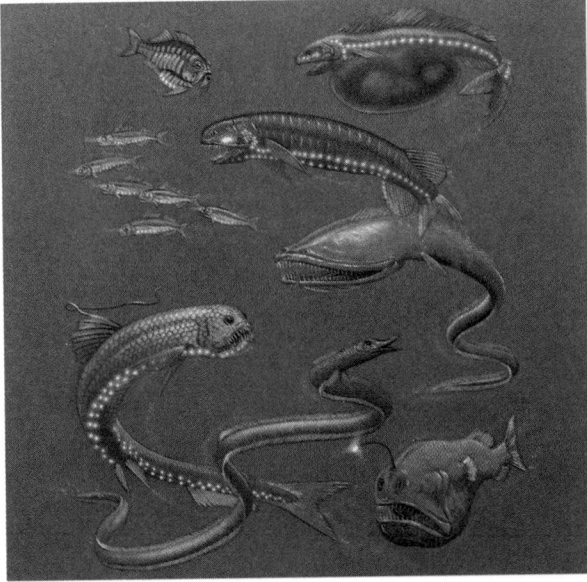

These creatures live very **deep** in the ocean.

a hat	ė term	ô order	ch child	⎧ a in about
ā age	i it	oi oil	ng long	⎪ e in taken
ä far	ī ice	ou out	sh she	ə ⎨ i in pencil
â care	o hot	u cup	th thin	⎪ o in lemon
e let	ō open	ù put	ᵺ then	⎩ u in circus
ē equal	ò saw	ü rule	zh measure	

de·fense (di fens′ for 1 and 2; di fens′ or dē′fens for 3), NOUN.
1 any thing or act that defends, guards, or protects something: *A wall was the city's only defense.*
2 the act of guarding something against attack or harm; protecting: *The armed forces are responsible for the defense of the country.*
3 the team or team members who try to keep their opponents from scoring points: *Our football team has a good defense.*
—**de·fense′less**, ADJECTIVE.

de·fen·sive (di fen′siv), ADJECTIVE.
1 used for protection; meant to defend: *Knights wore defensive armor in battle.*
2 (in sports) defending the team's goal: *Their team has some great defensive players.*
—**de·fen′sive·ly**, ADVERB. —**de·fen′sive·ness**, NOUN.

de·fer¹ (di fėr′), VERB. to put something off until a later time; delay: *The test was deferred because so many students were sick.* ❑ VERB **de·fers, de·ferred, de·fer·ring.** —**de·fer′rer**, NOUN.

de·fer² (di fėr′), VERB. to give in to someone else's opinion or judgment: *The children deferred to their parents' wishes.* ❑ VERB **de·fers, de·ferred, de·fer·ring.** —**de·fer′rer**, NOUN.

de·fi·ance (di fī′əns), NOUN. the act of standing up against authority and refusing to recognize or obey it: *She refused to obey the rules and was punished for her defiance.*

de·fi·ant (di fī′ənt), ADJECTIVE. disobedient; showing defiance: *She told us in a defiant manner that she was against our plans.* —**de·fi′ant·ly**, ADVERB.

de·fi·cien·cy (di fish′ən sē), NOUN. a lack or absence of something needed: *A deficiency of calcium in your diet can cause soft bones and teeth.* ❑ PLURAL **de·fi·cien·cies.**

de·fi·cient (di fish′ənt), ADJECTIVE. lacking something needed; not complete: *His diet was deficient in calcium.*

de·fine (di fīn′), VERB.
1 to make clear the meaning of something; explain: *A dictionary defines words.*
2 to show or mark the limits of something: *The boundary between the United States and Canada is defined by treaty.*
❑ VERB **de·fines, de·fined, de·fin·ing.** —**de·fin′a·ble**, ADJECTIVE. —**de·fin′er**, NOUN.

def·i·nite (def′ə nit), ADJECTIVE.
1 clear; exact; not vague: *Say "Yes" or "No," or give me some definite answer.*
2 certain; without doubt: *Is it definite that they will go?* —**def′i·nite·ly**, ADVERB.

definite article, the article *the.* "A dog" means "any dog"; "the dog" means "a particular dog."

def·i·ni·tion (def′ə nish′ən), NOUN. a clear statement of the meaning of a word or phrase.

One definition of "home" is "the place where a person or a family lives."

de·flate (di flāt′), VERB. to let air or gas out of a balloon, tire, ball, and so on: *A nail had deflated the tire.* ❑ VERB **de·flates, de·flat·ed, de·flat·ing.**

de·fo·rest·a·tion (dē fôr′i stā′shən), NOUN. the act or process of removing the trees from an area of land.

de·form (di fôrm′), VERB. to spoil how something is shaped or how it looks: *Shoes that are too tight may deform your feet.* ❑ VERB **de·forms, de·formed, de·form·ing.**

de·frost (di frȯst′), VERB.
1 to thaw something: *I defrosted the fish for dinner.*
2 to remove frost or ice from something: *We defrosted the refrigerator.*
❑ VERB **de·frosts, de·frost·ed, de·frost·ing.** —**de·frost′er**, NOUN.

deft (deft), ADJECTIVE. quick and skillful in action: *The fingers of a violinist must be deft.* —**deft′ly**, ADVERB.

de·fy (di fī′), VERB. to disobey authority; resist boldly: *The American Colonies defied many British laws.* ❑ VERB **de·fies, de·fied, de·fy·ing.**

de·grade (di grād′), VERB. to bring shame or disrespect upon someone; dishonor: *Students who cheat degrade themselves.* ❑ VERB **de·grades, de·grad·ed, de·grad·ing.**

de·gree (di grē′), NOUN.
1 a unit for measuring temperature. The freezing point of water is 32 degrees Fahrenheit (32° F). This is equal to 0 degrees Celsius (0° C).
2 a unit for measuring an angle or a part of a circle. There are 90 degrees in a right angle (90°) and 360 degrees (360°) in the circumference of a circle.
3 a rank or title given by a college or university to a student who graduates or to a famous person as an honor: *My mother has a degree in physics.*
4 a step in a series; stage in a process: *By degrees I became better at tennis.*
5 an amount; extent: *To what degree are you interested in reading?* ❑ PLURAL **de·grees.**

This thermometer shows **degrees** Fahrenheit and Celsius.

de·hy·drate (dē hī′drāt), VERB. to take water or moisture from; dry: *High fever dehydrates the body.* ❑ VERB **de·hy·drates, de·hy·drat·ed, de·hy·drat·ing.** —**de′hy·dra′tion**, NOUN.

dei·non·y·chus (dī non′ə kəs), *NOUN.* a swift, meat-eating dinosaur about 9 feet long, with huge claws. It ran upright and resembled a velociraptor. ❑ PLURAL **dei·non·y·chus·es.**

deinonychus — about 9 feet long

de·i·ty (dē′ə tē), *NOUN.*
1 a god or goddess: *The ancient Romans had many deities.*
2 the Deity, God.
❑ PLURAL **de·i·ties.**

de·ject·ed (di jek′tid), *ADJECTIVE.* sad; discouraged: *He became dejected when he couldn't find a job.* **—de·ject′ed·ly,** *ADVERB.*

Del·a·ware (del′ə wâr), *NOUN.* one of the southern states of the United States. *Abbreviation:* DE; *Capital:* Dover. **—Del′a·war′e·an,** *NOUN.*

State Story **Delaware** was named for the Delaware River. The river was named for Baron De La Warr, who lived from 1577 to 1618. He was the first governor of the colony of Virginia.

de·lay (di lā′),
1 *VERB.* to put something off till a later time: *We will delay our lunch date for a week.*
2 *NOUN.* the act of putting something off till a later time: *The delay upset our plans.*
3 *VERB.* to make something late; keep waiting: *The accident delayed the train for two hours.*
4 *NOUN.* the period of time that something is put off or held up: *After a delay of one hour, the plane took off.*
❑ VERB **de·lays, de·layed, de·lay·ing.**

del·e·gate (del′ə git or del′ə gāt *for noun;* del′ə gāt *for verb*),
1 *NOUN.* someone who is given power or authority to act for others; a representative: *Our club sent two delegates to the meeting.*
2 *VERB.* to appoint someone to do something: *Her team delegated her to buy the new baseball bat.*
❑ VERB **del·e·gates, del·e·gat·ed, del·e·gat·ing.**

del·e·ga·tion (del′ə gā′shən), *NOUN.* a group of delegates: *Each club sent a delegation to the meeting.*

de·lete (di lēt′), *VERB.* to strike out or take out anything written or printed. ❑ VERB **de·letes, de·let·ed, de·let·ing.**

del·i (del′ē), *NOUN.* a short form of **delicatessen.** ❑ PLURAL **del·is.**

de·lib·er·ate (di lib′ər it *for adjective;* di lib′ə rāt′ *for verb*),
1 *ADJECTIVE.* done on purpose; carefully thought over before acting: *Their excuse was a deliberate lie.*
2 *ADJECTIVE.* slow; very careful: *The old man walked with deliberate steps.*
3 *VERB.* to think over carefully; consider: *I am deliberating where to put up my new picture.*
❑ VERB **de·lib·er·ates, de·lib·er·at·ed, de·lib·er·at·ing. —de·lib′er·ate·ly,** *ADVERB.*

de·lib·e·ra·tion (di lib′ə rā′shən), *NOUN.*
1 careful thought: *After long deliberation, he said "No."*
2 slowness and care: *She drove the car across the icy bridge with great deliberation.*

del·i·ca·cy (del′ə kə sē), *NOUN.* a special or rare kind of food. Lobster is a delicacy. ❑ PLURAL **del·i·ca·cies.**

del·i·cate (del′ə kit), *ADJECTIVE.*
1 fragile; thin; easily torn: *a delicate spider web.*
2 requiring care, skill, or tact: *Choosing between my two friends put me in a delicate situation.*
3 pleasing to see, touch, or taste; mild or soft: *delicate foods, delicate colors.*
4 very quickly responding to slight changes of condition; sensitive: *The surgeon used delicate instruments for the eye operation.*
—del′i·cate·ly, *ADVERB.*

del·i·ca·tes·sen (del′ə kə tes′n), *NOUN.* a store that sells prepared foods, such as cooked meats, smoked fish, cheese, salads, and sandwiches.

de·li·cious (di lish′əs), *ADJECTIVE.* very pleasing or satisfying; delightful, especially to the taste or smell: *a delicious cake.* **—de·li′cious·ly,** *ADVERB.*

de·light (di līt′),
1 *NOUN.* great pleasure; joy: *The children took great delight in their toys.*
2 *NOUN.* something that gives great pleasure: *Swimming is her delight.*
3 *VERB.* to please greatly: *The circus delighted us.*
❑ VERB **de·lights, de·light·ed, de·light·ing.**

de·light·ful (di līt′fəl), *ADJECTIVE.* giving joy; very pleasing: *a delightful visit from her friends.* **—de·light′ful·ly,** *ADVERB.*

a	hat	ė	term	ô	order	ch	child		a in about
ā	age	i	it	oi	oil	ng	long		e in taken
ä	far	ī	ice	ou	out	sh	she	ə	i in pencil
â	care	o	hot	u	cup	th	thin		o in lemon
e	let	ō	open	ù	put	ᴛʜ	then		u in circus
ē	equal	ò	saw	ü	rule	zh	measure		

de·lir·i·ous (di lir′ē əs), ADJECTIVE.
1 not able to speak or think clearly because of fever, shock, and so on: *The patient was delirious.*
2 wildly excited: *The students were delirious with joy when their team won the tournament.*
—**de·lir′i·ous·ly,** ADVERB.

de·liv·er (di liv′ər), VERB.
1 to take something to someone's house, office, and so on: *The mail carrier delivered our mail early.*
2 to make a speech: *She delivered a talk on her travels in Africa. The minister delivered the sermon.*
3 to set free; rescue; save: *Deliver us from temptation.* ■ See the Synonym Study at **save.**
❑ VERB **de·liv·ers, de·liv·ered, de·liv·er·ing.**

de·liv·er·y (di liv′ər ē), NOUN.
1 the act of taking something to someone's house, office, and so on: *Mail delivery here is at noon.*
2 a manner of speaking or singing: *The speaker had an excellent delivery.*
❑ PLURAL **de·liv·er·ies.**

del·ta (del′tə), NOUN. a flat area of earth and sand that collects at the mouth of some rivers and is usually shaped like a triangle. ❑ PLURAL **del·tas.**

del·uge (del′yüj), NOUN.
1 a great flood: *After the dam broke, the deluge washed away the bridge.*
2 a heavy fall of rain: *We were caught in a deluge.*

de·mand (di mand′),
1 VERB. to ask for with authority or as a right: *The landlord demanded payment of the overdue rent.*
2 VERB. to call for; require; need: *Training a puppy demands patience.*
3 NOUN. something that is demanded; claim: *Parents have many demands upon their time.*
4 NOUN. an act of demanding: *a demand for a bigger allowance.*
5 NOUN. the desire and ability to buy: *Because of the large crop, the supply of apples is greater than the demand this year.*
❑ VERB **de·mands, de·mand·ed, de·mand·ing.**

de·moc·ra·cy (di mok′rə sē), NOUN.
1 a government that is run by the people who live under it. In a democracy either the people rule through meetings that all may attend, such as a town meeting in New England, or they elect representatives to take care of the business of government.
2 a country or town in which the government is a democracy.
❑ PLURAL **de·moc·ra·cies.**

Dem·o·crat (dem′ə krat), NOUN. a member of the Democratic Party.

dem·o·crat·ic (dem′ə krat′ik), ADJECTIVE.
1 of a democracy; like a democracy.
2 treating other people as your equals: *The queen's democratic ways made her dear to her people.*

3 **Democratic,** of the Democratic Party.
—**dem′o·crat′i·cal·ly,** ADVERB.

Democratic Party, one of the two main political parties in the United States.

de·mol·ish (di mol′ish), VERB. to tear something down; blow up; destroy: *The hurricane demolished many seaside buildings.* ■ See the Synonym Study at **destroy.** ❑ VERB **de·mol·ish·es, de·mol·ished, de·mol·ish·ing.**

They **demolished** the old building with explosives.

de·mon (dē′mən), NOUN. a devil; evil spirit.

dem·on·strate (dem′ən strāt), VERB.
1 to show something clearly; prove: *The pianist demonstrated her musical skill.*
2 to explain something by the use of examples: *The coach demonstrated how to dribble a basketball.*
3 to show how something works: *The saleswoman played a CD to demonstrate the stereo for us.*
4 to take part in a parade or meeting to protest something, or to make demands: *An angry crowd demonstrated in front of the mayor's office.*
❑ VERB **dem·on·strates, dem·on·strat·ed, dem·on·strat·ing.**

dem·on·stra·tion (dem′ən strā′shən), NOUN.
1 clear proof: *The ease with which she solved the problem was a demonstration of her ability in math.*
2 the act of explaining by the use of examples: *A compass was used in a demonstration of the earth's magnetism.*
3 the act of showing how something works: *The store offered a free demonstration of the vacuum cleaner.*
4 a parade or meeting to protest something or to make demands.

dem·on·stra·tor (dem′ən strā′tər), NOUN. someone who takes part in a parade or meeting to protest or make demands.

de·mote (di mōt′), VERB. to put someone back to a lower grade; reduce in rank: *The corporal was demoted to private.* ❑ VERB **de·motes, de·mot·ed, de·mot·ing.** —**de·mo′tion,** NOUN.

den (den), NOUN.
1 a wild animal's home or resting place: *The bear's den was in a cave.*
2 a private room for reading and work, usually small and cozy.

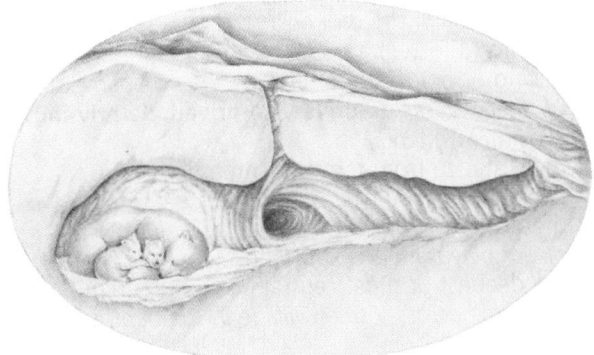

Polar bears sleep in their **den.**

de·ni·al (di nī′əl), NOUN. a statement that something is not true: *Galileo was forced to make a public denial of his belief that the earth goes around the sun.*

den·im (den′əm), NOUN. a heavy, coarse cotton cloth used for jeans, overalls, jackets, and so on.

Den·mark (den′märk), NOUN. a country in northwestern Europe.

de·nom·i·na·tion (di nom′ə nā′shən), NOUN.
1 a religious group: *There are many Protestant denominations.*
2 a kind of thing with a stated name or value: *The only denominations I have are five-dollar bills and tens.*

de·nom·i·na·tor (di nom′ə nā′tər), NOUN. the number below or to the right of the line in a fraction. In ¾, 4 is the denominator, and 3 is the numerator.

de·note (di nōt′), VERB.
1 to mean: *The word "density" denotes thickness.*
2 to be a sign of something; indicate: *A fever usually denotes sickness.*
❑ VERB **de·notes, de·not·ed, de·not·ing.**

de·nounce (di nouns′), VERB. to speak out against something; express strong disapproval of; condemn: *The king denounced the traitors.* ❑ VERB **de·nounc·es, de·nounced, de·nounc·ing.**

dense (dens), ADJECTIVE. closely packed together; thick: *We could not see to steer the boat through the dense fog.* ❑ ADJECTIVE **dens·er, dens·est.**
—**dense′ly,** ADVERB.

den·si·ty (den′sə tē), NOUN.
1 the condition of being crowded, thick, or dense: *The density of the forest prevented us from seeing more than a little way ahead.*
2 the amount of matter in a unit of volume: *The density of lead is greater than the density of wood.*
❑ PLURAL **den·si·ties.**

dent (dent),
1 NOUN. a hollow place on a surface made by a blow or pressure: *What made this dent on my fender?*
2 VERB. to make or get a dent or dents: *The movers dented the table. Soft wood dents easily.*
❑ VERB **dents, dent·ed, dent·ing.**

den·tal (den′tl), ADJECTIVE. of or for the teeth: *Proper dental care can prevent tooth decay.*

dental floss, a strong, often waxed thread for cleaning between the teeth.

den·tal hy·gien·ist. See **hygienist.**

den·tin (den′tən), NOUN. the hard, bony material beneath the enamel of a tooth. It forms the main part of a tooth.

den·tist (den′tist), NOUN. a doctor whose work is the care of teeth. A dentist fills cavities in teeth and cleans, straightens, or replaces them.

den·tist·ry (den′tə strē), NOUN. the work of a dentist.

Den·ver (den′vər), NOUN. the capital of Colorado.

de·ny (di nī′), VERB.
1 to say something is not true: *The prisoners denied the charges against them.*
2 to refuse to give something: *I could not deny the stray cat some milk.*
❑ VERB **de·nies, de·nied, de·ny·ing.**

de·o·dor·ant (dē ō′dər ənt), NOUN. a spray, cream, powder, and so on, that prevents bad odors on your body.

de·part (di pärt′), VERB. to go away; leave: *The train departs at 6:15.* ■ See the Synonym Study at **leave.** ❑ VERB **de·parts, de·part·ed, de·part·ing.**

de·part·ment (di pärt′mənt), NOUN. a separate part of a business, government, university, and so on: *Our city government has a fire department and a police department.*

department store, a large store that sells many different kinds of products in separate departments.

de·par·ture (di pär′chər), NOUN. the act of going away; act of leaving: *Their sudden departure took us by surprise.*

de·pend (di pend′), VERB.
1 to be a result of: *The success of our picnic will depend on the weather.*
2 to have as a support; get help from; rely on: *Children depend upon their parents for food and clothing. I depend on my alarm clock to wake me in time for school.*
❑ VERB **de·pends, de·pend·ed, de·pend·ing.**

a hat	ė term	ô order	ch child	(a in about
ā age	i it	oi oil	ng long	e in taken
ä far	ī ice	ou out	sh she	ə⟨ i in pencil
â care	o hot	u cup	th thin	o in lemon
e let	ō open	u̇ put	ᴛʜ then	(u in circus
ē equal	ȯ saw	ü rule	zh measure	

de·pend·a·ble (di pen′də bəl), ADJECTIVE. reliable; trustworthy: *My friend works hard and is dependable.* **–de·pend′a·bil·i·ty,** NOUN.

de·pend·ence (di pen′dəns), NOUN.
1 the action or habit of trusting or relying on another for support or help: *I am going to work so that I can end my dependence on my parents.*
2 the condition of being controlled by something else: *We learned about the dependence of crops on good weather.*

de·pend·ent (di pen′dənt),
1 ADJECTIVE. trusting in or relying on another person or thing for support or help: *A child is dependent on its parents.*
2 NOUN. a person who is supported by someone else.

dependent clause, a group of words that has a subject and a verb but cannot stand alone as a sentence. It needs some added statement to complete its thought or idea. The phrases *because it rained, when I practice,* and *that you are kind* are dependent clauses.

de·pict (di pikt′), VERB. to show something in a picture, a drawing, a story, and so on: *The artist tried to depict the magnificence of the sunset.* ❑ VERB **de·picts, de·pict·ed, de·pict·ing.** **–de·pic′tion,** NOUN.

de·plet·ion (di plē′shən), NOUN. the act or process of reducing the amount of something: *Irrigation can result in depletion of the underground water supply.*

de·port (di pôrt′), VERB. to officially force someone to leave. When a person is deported he or she is sent back to his or her native land. ❑ VERB **de·ports, de·port·ed, de·port·ing.**

de·pos·it (di poz′it),
1 NOUN. money paid as a promise to do something or to pay more later: *I put a $25 deposit on the coat.*
2 NOUN. something put in a certain place to be kept safe. When you put money put in the bank, you make a deposit.
3 VERB. to put in a place to be kept safe: *Deposit your money in the bank.*
4 VERB. to put something down; lay down; leave lying: *She deposited her heavy and bulky bundles on the table.*
5 NOUN. a mass of some mineral in rock or in the ground: *deposits of coal.*
❑ VERB **de·pos·its, de·pos·it·ed, de·pos·it·ing.**

de·pos·i·tor (di poz′ə tər), NOUN. someone who deposits money in a bank.

de·pot (dē′pō), NOUN. a railroad or bus station.

de·press (di pres′), VERB. to make someone sad or gloomy: *The bad news depressed me.* ❑ VERB **de·press·es, de·pressed, de·press·ing.**

de·pres·sant (di pres′nt), NOUN. a drug that slows down the normal activity of the nervous system: *Alcohol is a depressant.*

de·pres·sion (di presh′ən), NOUN.
1 low spirits; sadness: *Failure can bring on depression.*
2 a time when business activity is very slow and many people are out of work.
3 a low place; hollow: *Rain formed puddles in the depressions in the ground.*

de·prive (di prīv′), VERB. to keep someone from having or doing something: *Worrying deprived me of sleep.* ❑ VERB **de·prives, de·prived, de·priv·ing.**

depth (depth), NOUN.
1 the distance from the top to the bottom: *The depth of the well is about 25 feet.*
2 the distance from front to back: *The depth of our playground is 250 feet.*
3 the deepest or most central part of anything: *We came across a small village in the depths of the jungle.*

dep·u·ty (dep′yə tē), NOUN. someone selected to help with the work of or to take the place of another person: *A sheriff's deputies help him or her enforce the law.* ❑ PLURAL **dep·u·ties.**

de·rail (dē rāl′), VERB. to run or cause to run off the rails: *The train was derailed just north of Boston.* ❑ VERB **de·rails, de·rail·ed, de·rail·ing.**

der·by (dėr′bē), NOUN.
1 a horse race: *His horse won the Kentucky Derby.*
2 a stiff hat with a rounded crown and narrow brim. ❑ PLURAL **der·bies.**

de·rive (di rīv′), VERB. to get something from some source: *She derives much pleasure from reading.* ❑ VERB **de·rives, de·rived, de·riv·ing.**

de·rog·a·to·ry (di rog′ə tôr′ē), ADJECTIVE. not favorable: *We don't like to hear derogatory remarks about our school.*

der·rick (der′ik), NOUN.
1 a machine for lifting and moving heavy objects. A derrick has a long arm that swings at an angle from the base of an upright post or frame.
2 a framework like a tower over an oil well that holds the drilling and hoisting machinery.

derrick (definition 2)

de·scend (di send′), VERB.
1 to move down from a higher to a lower place: *I descended the stairs to the basement. The river descends from the mountains to the sea.*
2 to be a descendant of: *Both of my parents descend from pioneers.*
❑ VERB **de·scends, de·scend·ed, de·scend·ing.**

de·scend·ant or **de·scend·ent** (di sen′dənt), NOUN.
1 someone born of a certain family or group: *a descendant of the Pilgrims.*
2 an offspring; child, grandchild, great-grandchild, and so on. You are a direct descendant of your parents, grandparents, and great-grandparents.

de·scent (di sent′), NOUN.
1 the act or process of moving down from a higher to a lower place: *The descent of the balloon was more rapid than its rise had been.*
2 your family origin; ancestors: *We are of Italian descent.*

descent (definition 1)

de·scribe (di skrib′), VERB. to tell in words how someone looks, feels, or acts, or to record the important things about a place, a thing, or an event: *The reporter described the accident in detail.* ❑ VERB **de·scribes, de·scribed, de·scrib·ing.**

de·scrip·tion (di skrip′shən), NOUN. the words that describe how someone looks, feels, or acts, or that record the important things about a place, a thing, or an event: *a description of the missing child, a vivid description of the fire.*

de·scrip·tive (di skrip′tiv), ADJECTIVE. showing in words the most interesting or important things about something; describing: *A descriptive booklet tells about the places to be seen on the trip.*
—**de·scrip′tive·ly,** ADVERB.

de·seg·re·gate (dē seg′rə gāt), VERB. to stop the separation of people in schools, stores, and public places according to their race. ❑ VERB **de·seg·re·gates, de·seg·re·gat·ed, de·seg·re·gat·ing.** —**de·seg′re·ga′tion,** NOUN.

des·ert[1] (dez′ərt),
1 NOUN. a dry, sandy region without water and trees: *In the Southwest there is a desert called the Mojave.*
2 ADJECTIVE. having no people: *a desert island.*

de·sert[2] (di zèrt′), VERB. to go away and leave a person or a place, especially one that should not be left: *A husband should not desert his family. A soldier who deserts is punished.* ❑ VERB **de·serts, de·sert·ed, de·sert·ing.** —**de·sert′er,** NOUN.

de·serve (di zèrv′), VERB. to have a right to something; be worthy of: *A hard worker deserves good pay.* ❑ VERB **de·serves, de·served, de·serv·ing.**

de·sign (di zīn′),
1 NOUN. a sketch, drawing, or plan made to serve as a pattern from which to work: *The design showed how to build the machine.*
2 NOUN. the arrangement of details, form, and color in painting, weaving, or building: *We chose a wallpaper design with tan and white stripes.*
3 VERB. to make a first sketch of; plan out; arrange the form and color of: *My mother designed my coat and my grandmother made it.*
4 VERB. to set apart; intend; plan: *My parents designed his room to be a study.*
❑ VERB **de·signs, de·signed, de·sign·ing.**
—**de·sign′er,** NOUN.

des·ig·nate (dez′ig nāt), VERB.
1 to point out; mark; show: *Red lines designate main roads on this map.*
2 to select someone for an office; appoint: *She has been designated by the mayor as chief of police.*
3 to name: *Historians designate the period A.D. 500 to A.D. 1500 as the Middle Ages.*
❑ VERB **des·ig·nates, des·ig·nat·ed, des·ig·nat·ing.**

designated hitter, (in baseball) a player who does not play in the field but is designated at the start of a game to bat in place of the pitcher.

de·sir·a·ble (di zī′rə bəl), ADJECTIVE. worth wishing for; worth having; pleasing: *The creek valley was a desirable location for the state park.*
—**de·sir′a·bil′i·ty,** NOUN.

de·sire (di zīr′),
1 NOUN. a strong wish: *My desire is to travel.*
2 VERB. to want something very badly: *The people in the warring nations desired peace.*
❑ VERB **de·sires, de·sired, de·sir·ing.**

desk (desk), NOUN. a piece of furniture with a flat top on which to write or study.

desk·top (desk′top′), ADJECTIVE.
1 small enough to fit on a desk: *Dad just got a desktop copier.*
2 done with office computers: *Mom works in desktop publishing.*

Des Moines (də moin′), the capital of Iowa.

des·o·late (des′ə lit), ADJECTIVE.
1 not lived in; deserted: *a desolate house.*
2 destroyed; ruined: *We visited the desolate ruins.*
3 unhappy; miserable: *The lost child was desolate.*

des·o·la·tion (des′ə lā′shən), NOUN.
1 destruction; ruin: *The people mourned the desolation of their town by a tornado.*
2 sadness; lonely sorrow: *He felt great desolation when his best friend moved away.*

de·spair (di spâr′),
1 NOUN. the complete loss of hope; a dreadful feeling that nothing good can happen to you: *Despair seized us as we felt the boat sinking.*

a	hat	ė	term	ô	order	ch	child		a in about
ā	age	i	it	oi	oil	ng	long		e in taken
ä	far	ī	ice	ou	out	sh	she	ə	i in pencil
â	care	o	hot	u	cup	th	thin		o in lemon
e	let	ō	open	ů	put	ŦH	then		u in circus
ē	equal	ò	saw	ü	rule	zh	measure		

2 *VERB.* to lose hope: *By the third day, we despaired of ever finding our lost dog.*
❑ *VERB* **de·spairs, de·spaired, de·spair·ing.**

des·per·ate (des′pər it), *ADJECTIVE.*
1 ready to try anything because of hopelessness: *The prisoner leaped from the moving car in a desperate attempt to escape.*
2 having little chance for hope or cure; very dangerous: *a desperate illness.*
3 extremely or hopelessly bad: *People in the slums live in desperate conditions.*
—**des′per·ate·ly,** *ADVERB.*

des·pe·ra·tion (des′pə rā′shən), *NOUN.* a hopeless and reckless feeling; willingness to try anything: *In desperation he jumped out the window when he saw the stairs were on fire.*

de·spise (di spīz′), *VERB.* to hate someone or something very much: *Many people despise snakes.* ❑ *VERB* **de·spis·es, de·spised, de·spis·ing.**

des·sert (di zėrt′), *NOUN.* pie, cake, ice cream, cheese, fruit, and so on served at the end of a meal.

des·ti·na·tion (des′tə nā′shən), *NOUN.* the place to which a person or thing is going or is being sent.

des·ti·ny (des′tə nē), *NOUN.* the things that will happen to you; your fate or fortune: *She felt it was her destiny to be a writer.* ❑ *PLURAL* **des·ti·nies.**

de·stroy (di stroi′), *VERB.* to damage something very badly; ruin: *A tornado destroyed the house. The rain destroyed all hope of a picnic.* ❑ *VERB* **de·stroys, de·stroyed, de·stroy·ing.**

Synonym Study

Destroy means to put an end to something, often by breaking or pulling it to pieces: *We destroyed our sand castle before the ocean waves could wash it away.*

Demolish means to smash or pull something to pieces: *A bulldozer can demolish brick walls.*

Wreck means to damage badly or completely: *Two cars were wrecked in the accident.*

Ruin means to make something worthless or useless: *Bugs that eat leaves can ruin a garden.*

Spoil means to ruin: *Paint spilled on his drawing and spoiled it.*

See also the Synonym Studies at **break** and **harm**.

ANTONYMS: create, make.

de·stroy·er (di stroi′ər), *NOUN.* a small, fast warship with guns, torpedoes, and missiles.

de·struc·tion (di struk′shən), *NOUN.*
1 great damage; ruin: *The storm left destruction behind it.*
2 the act or process of destroying: *A bulldozer was used in the destruction of the old barn.*

de·struc·tive (di struk′tiv), *ADJECTIVE.* damaging; causing destruction: *Fires and earthquakes are destructive.* —**de·struc′tive·ness,** *NOUN.*

de·tach (di tach′), *VERB.* to unfasten something and remove it; separate: *I detached a key from the chain.* ❑ *VERB* **de·tach·es, de·tached, de·tach·ing.** —**de·tach′a·ble,** *ADJECTIVE.*

de·tail (di tāl′ *or* dē′tāl),
1 *NOUN.* a single fact or bit of information: *Her report was complete; it didn't leave out any details.*
2 *NOUN.* a particular part of some greater whole: *The plan has been approved, but a few details remain to be worked out.*
3 *VERB.* to tell fully; tell even the small and unimportant parts of something: *They detailed to us all the things they had done on their vacation.*
❑ *VERB* **de·tails, de·tailed, de·tail·ing.**

de·tain (di tān′), *VERB.*
1 to keep someone from moving forward; delay: *The heavy traffic detained us for almost an hour.*
2 to officially hold someone as a prisoner; keep in custody: *Police detained the suspected burglar for questioning.*
❑ *VERB* **de·tains, de·tained, de·tain·ing.**

de·tect (di tekt′), *VERB.* to discover something that is hard to notice: *Could you detect any odor in the room?* ❑ *VERB* **de·tects, de·tect·ed, de·tect·ing.** —**de·tect′a·ble,** *ADJECTIVE.* —**de·tec′tion,** *NOUN.*

de·tec·tive (di tek′tiv), *NOUN.* a member of a police force or other person whose work is investigating crimes, catching criminals, and so on.

de·tec·tor (di tek′tər), *NOUN.* a device that discovers something, especially something that is harmful: *Every home should have a smoke detector.*

An airport security guard uses a metal **detector.**

dessert

de·ten·tion (di ten'shən), NOUN.
1 the act of keeping someone after school: *Detention is a common punishment in our school.*
2 in detention, held until a trial or for some unspecified period of time: *The protesters have been in detention since June.*

de·ter·gent (di tėr'jənt), NOUN. a liquid or powder used for cleaning. Many detergents are chemical compounds that act like soap.

de·ter·mi·na·tion (di tėr'mə nā'shən), NOUN. great firmness in doing what you have planned to do in spite of difficulty: *The boy's determination was not weakened by disappointment or hardships.*

de·ter·mine (di tėr'mən), VERB.
1 to find out exactly what the facts are: *The pilot determined how far she was from the airport.*
2 to make up your mind very firmly: *He determined to become the best player on the team.*
3 to be the deciding fact in reaching a certain result; settle: *Tomorrow's weather will determine whether we go to the beach or stay home.*
❑ VERB **de·ter·mines, de·ter·mined, de·ter·min·ing.**

de·ter·mined (di tėr'mənd), ADJECTIVE. with your mind made up: *Her determined look showed that she had decided what to do.* **—de·ter'mined·ly,** ADVERB.

de·test (di test'), VERB. to dislike someone or something very much; hate; despise: *I detest cheaters.* ❑ VERB **de·tests, de·test·ed, de·test·ing.**
—de·test'a·ble, ADJECTIVE.

de·tour (dē'tùr),
1 NOUN. a road that is used when the main or direct road cannot be traveled: *Our bus had to take a detour because the road was blocked.*
2 VERB. to use a detour: *We detoured around the bridge that had been washed out.*
❑ VERB **de·tours, de·toured, de·tour·ing.**

de·tract (di trakt'), VERB. to take away or reduce something important or valuable: *The ugly frame detracts from the beauty of the picture.* ❑ VERB **de·tracts, de·tract·ed, de·tract·ing.**

De·troit (di troit'), NOUN. a city in Michigan.

dev·as·tate (dev'ə stāt), VERB. to destroy completely; make a place totally unfit to live in: *A tornado devastated miles of countryside.* ❑ VERB **dev·as·tates, dev·as·tat·ed, dev·as·tat·ing.**
—dev'as·ta'tion, NOUN.

de·vel·op (di vel'əp), VERB.
1 to grow; bring or come into being or activity: *Plants develop from seeds. Scientists have developed many new drugs to fight disease.*
2 to make or become bigger, better, more useful, and so on: *Exercise develops the muscles. His business developed very slowly.*
3 to use chemicals on a photographic film or plate to bring out the picture.
❑ VERB **de·vel·ops, de·vel·oped, de·vel·op·ing.**

de·vel·op·ment (di vel'əp mənt), NOUN.
1 the process of developing; growth: *We watched the development of the seeds into plants.*
2 a recent event or happening: *The newspaper told about the latest developments in the elections.*
3 a group of similar houses or apartment buildings built in one area and usually by the same builder.
—de·vel'op·ment'al, ADJECTIVE.
—de·vel'op·ment'al·ly, ADVERB.

de·vice (di vīs'), NOUN. something invented for a particular use: *Our gas stove has a device for lighting it automatically.* ∎ See the Synonym Study at **tool.**

dev·il (dev'əl), NOUN.
1 the Devil, in the Jewish and Christian religions, the supreme evil spirit; Satan.
2 any evil spirit.
3 a wicked or cruel person.

de·vi·ous (dē'vē əs), ADJECTIVE.
1 not straightforward: *They were engaged in a devious scheme for finding out the test questions in advance.*
2 out of the direct way; winding: *We took a devious route through side streets to avoid the crowded main streets.*
—de'vi·ous·ly, ADVERB. **—de'vi·ous·ness,** NOUN.

de·vise (di vīz'), VERB. to think up some way of doing something; invent: *The kids are trying to devise a way to earn money during vacation.* ❑ VERB **de·vis·es, de·vised, de·vis·ing.**

de·vote (di vōt'), VERB. to give your money, time, or effort to some person or purpose: *She devoted herself to her studies. Many people devoted their efforts to cleaning up the neighborhood.* ❑ VERB **de·votes, de·vot·ed, de·vot·ing.**

de·vot·ed (di vō'tid), ADJECTIVE. very loyal; faithful: *Dogs are often devoted companions.*
—de·vot'ed·ly, ADVERB. **—de·vot'ed·ness,** NOUN.

de·vo·tion (di vō'shən), NOUN.
1 a strong feeling of loyalty and affection: *the devotion of parents to their children.* ∎ See the Synonym Study at **love.**
2 devotions, prayers.

de·vour (di vour'), VERB.
1 to eat something hungrily or greedily: *The lion devoured the gnu.* ∎ See the Synonym Study at **eat.**
2 to consume; destroy: *The fire devoured the forest.*
❑ VERB **de·vours, de·voured, de·vour·ing.**

de·vout (di vout'), ADJECTIVE. active in worship and prayer; very religious: *a devout Muslim, a devout Christian, a devout Jew.* **—de·vout'ly,** ADVERB.

a	hat	ė	term	ô	order	ch	child		a in about
ā	age	i	it	oi	oil	ng	long		e in taken
ä	far	ī	ice	ou	out	sh	she	ə	i in pencil
â	care	o	hot	u	cup	th	thin		o in lemon
e	let	ō	open	ù	put	ᴛʜ	then		u in circus
ē	equal	ò	saw	ü	rule	zh	measure		

dew (dü), NOUN. the moisture from the air that collects in small drops on cool surfaces during the night: *In the early morning, the grass is often wet with dew.* ■ Other words that sound like this are **do¹** and **due.**

morning **dew**

dew·drop (dü′drop′), NOUN. a drop of dew.

di·a·be·tes (dī′ə bē′tis), NOUN. a disease in which a person's body cannot properly absorb normal amounts of sugar and starch.

di·ag·nose (dī′əg nōs′), VERB. to find out by tests or examination: *The doctor diagnosed the disease as measles.* ❑ VERB **di·ag·nos·es, di·ag·nosed, di·ag·nos·ing.**

di·ag·no·sis (dī′əg nō′sis), NOUN. the act or process of finding out what disease a person or animal has by examination and careful study of the symptoms: *The doctor used X rays in her diagnosis.* ❑ PLURAL **di·ag·no·ses** (dī′əg nō′sēz′).

di·ag·o·nal (dī ag′ə nəl),
1 ADJECTIVE. slanting; going from one side to the other at an angle: *My blue tie has red diagonal stripes.*
2 NOUN. a straight line that cuts across in a slanting direction, often from corner to corner. **–di·ag′o·nal·ly,** ADVERB.

di·a·gram (dī′ə gram),
1 NOUN. a drawing or sketch showing clearly what a thing is, how it works, or what it looks like. A plan of a house or an airplane is a diagram.
2 VERB. to put on paper or on a chalkboard in the form of a drawing or sketch; make a diagram of something: *Our teacher diagramed how we should leave the building during a fire drill.*
❑ VERB **di·a·grams, di·a·gramed, di·a·gram·ing.**

di·al (dī′əl),
1 NOUN. the front surface or face of a measuring instrument. A dial has numbers, letters, or marks over which a pointer moves. The pointer indicates amount, speed, pressure, time, direction, or the like. The face of a clock, a compass, or a thermostat is a dial.

2 NOUN. a knob or other device of a radio or television set with numbers and letters on it for tuning in to a radio or television station.
3 NOUN. the round, movable part of some older telephones used in making telephone calls.
4 VERB. to call a phone number: *She dialed the wrong number the first time she tried to call us.* ❑ VERB **di·als, di·aled, di·al·ing.**

Word Story

Dial probably comes from a Latin word meaning "day." The face of a sundial or clock was called "the wheel of day," and people started using the word for other marked circles.

di·a·lect (dī′ə lekt), NOUN. a form of a language spoken in a certain region or by a certain group of people: *A dialect of French is spoken in Louisiana by descendants of French Canadians.*

di·a·logue or **di·a·log** (dī′ə lòg), NOUN. a conversation in a book, play, movie, or TV show, either spoken or written out: *That book has a good plot and much clever dialogue.*

dial tone, a buzzing sound heard when you pick up a telephone. It means you can dial a number.

di·am·e·ter (dī am′ə tər), NOUN.
1 a straight line that goes from one side of a circle or sphere through the center to the other side. ■ See the illustration at **circle.**
2 the length of such a line; width; thickness: *The tree trunk was almost 2 feet in diameter.*

di·a·mond (dī′mənd), NOUN.
1 a precious stone, usually colorless, that is formed of pure carbon in crystals. It is used to make jewelry and in industry.
2 a figure shaped like this: ◇
3 a playing card with a figure shaped like this.
4 (in baseball) the area inside the square formed by home plate and the three bases; infield.

Did You Know?

Diamond is the hardest substance known. Diamonds cannot be hurt by acid, but they can be destroyed by high heat. If a diamond is burned without oxygen, it turns into the soft lead, or graphite, that is used in pencils.

di·a·per (dī′pər), NOUN. a piece of cloth or other soft material folded and used as underpants for a baby.

di·a·phragm (dī′ə fram), NOUN. a layer of muscles and tendons separating the cavity of the chest from the cavity of the abdomen. Its movement helps to control your breathing.

di·ar·rhe·a (dī′ə rē′ə), NOUN. the condition of having bowel movements that are frequent and liquid.

di·ar·y (dī′ər ē), NOUN.
1 a record, written down each day, of what has

D

happened to you, or what you have done or thought, during that day: *I kept a diary while I was on vacation.*
2 a book for keeping such a daily record.
❏ *PLURAL* **di·ar·ies.**

dice (dīs),
1 *NOUN PLURAL.* small cubes with from one to six spots on each side. Dice are used in playing some games.
2 *VERB.* to cut into small cubes: *Carrots are sometimes diced before being cooked.*
❏ *VERB* **dic·es, diced, dic·ing.**

dic·tate (dik′tāt), *VERB.*
1 to say or read something aloud for another person to write down, or for a machine to record: *The teacher dictated a list of books to us.*
2 to make others do what you tell them to do; give orders: *Big nations sometimes dictate to little ones.*
❏ *VERB* **dic·tates, dic·tat·ed, dic·tat·ing.** **–dic·ta′tion,** *NOUN.*

dic·ta·tor (dik′tā tər), *NOUN.* a leader who takes complete power over a country and allows no criticism of his or her rule.

dic·tion·ar·y (dik′shə ner′ē), *NOUN.* a book that lists the words of a language in alphabetical order. You can use this dictionary to find out the meaning, pronunciation, and spelling of a word. ❏ *PLURAL* **dic·tion·ar·ies.**

did (did), *VERB.* the past tense of **do:** *Did he go to school? Yes, he did.*

did·n't (did′nt), a contraction of **did not.**

die¹ (dī), *VERB.*
1 to stop living; become dead: *The flowers in the garden died from frost.*
2 to stop working: *The engine sputtered and died.*
3 to lose force: *After a while the wind died down.*
4 (informal) to want very much: *I was dying for an ice-cream cone.*
❏ *VERB* **dies, died, dy·ing.** ▪ Another word that sounds like this is **dye.**

die off, *IDIOM.* to die one after another until all are dead: *The entire herd of cows died off during the drought.*

die² (dī), *NOUN.*
1 a tool used to shape or cut metal. Dies are used to stamp coins and medals, to shape or punch holes in metal sheets, and to make threads on screws and bolts.
2 one of a pair of dice.
▪ Another word that sounds like this is **dye.**

die·sel en·gine (dē′zəl en′jən), an engine that burns oil with heat produced by compressing air.

di·et (dī′ət),
1 *NOUN.* the kind of food and drink that you usually eat: *My diet is made up of meat, fish, vegetables,* grains, fruits, water, and milk. Grass is a large part of a cow's diet.
2 *NOUN.* special foods eaten because you are sick, or to lose or gain weight: *While I was sick I was on a liquid diet.*
3 *VERB.* to eat special food as a part of a doctor's treatment, or to lose or gain weight.
4 *ADJECTIVE.* having fewer calories: *diet sodas.*
❏ *VERB* **di·ets, di·et·ed, di·et·ing.** **–di′et·er,** *NOUN.*

dif·fer (dif′ər), *VERB.*
1 to be different: *My answer to the math problem differed from hers, so we asked the teacher for the right answer.*
2 to have different opinions; disagree: *The two of us differ about what to buy Mom.*
❏ *VERB* **dif·fers, dif·fered, dif·fer·ing.**

dif·fer·ence (dif′ər əns), *NOUN.*
1 the condition of being unlike something else: *There are a few differences between baseball and softball.*
2 way in which people or things are different: *The only difference between the twins is that John weighs five pounds more than Bob.*
3 what is left after subtracting one number from another: *The difference between 6 and 15 is 9.*
4 a quarrel; dispute: *We had a difference over a name for the puppy.*

make a difference, *IDIOM.* to be important; matter: *Your vote will make a difference in the election.*

dif·fer·ent (dif′ər ənt), *ADJECTIVE.*
1 not alike; not like something else: *We saw different kinds of animals at the zoo.*
2 not the same; separate; distinct: *She won three different swimming contests.*
3 unusual: *That story was really different; I've never read one like it.*
–dif′fer·ent·ly, *ADVERB.*

They planted seeds of **different** vegetables.

a	hat	ė	term	ô	order	ch	child	ʃ a in about
ā	age	i	it	oi	oil	ng	long	e in taken
ä	far	ī	ice	ou	out	sh	she	ə ⎨ i in pencil
â	care	o	hot	u	cup	th	thin	o in lemon
e	let	ō	open	u̇	put	ŦH	then	u in circus
ē	equal	ȯ	saw	ü	rule	zh	measure	

dif·fi·cult (dif′ə kult), ADJECTIVE.
1 hard to do or understand: *Arithmetic is difficult for some pupils.*
2 hard to deal with or get along with; not easy to please: *My cousin is difficult and is always unhappy.*

dif·fi·cul·ty (dif′ə kul′tē), NOUN.
1 the condition or quality of being difficult: *The difficulty of the job kept us from finishing it on time.*
2 hard work; much effort: *I walked with difficulty after I sprained my ankle.*
3 something that stands in the way of getting things done; something that is hard to do or understand: *Lack of time was the main difficulty.*
❑ PLURAL **dif·fi·cul·ties.**

dig (dig), VERB.
1 to use a shovel, spade, hands, claws, or snout to make a hole or turn over soil: *Dogs bury bones and dig for them later.*
2 to make something by digging: *The workers dug a cellar.*
3 to get something by digging: *to dig potatoes.*
4 to make a thrust or stab into: *The cat dug its claws into my hand.*
❑ VERB **digs, dug, dig·ging. –dig′ger,** NOUN.

dig up, IDIOM. to get or find, especially by a careful search or by study: *You can probably dig up the information you need in the school library.*

di·gest (də jest′ *for verb;* dī′jest *for noun*),
1 VERB. to change food in the stomach and intestines, so that the body can use it: *The body digests fat slowly.*
2 NOUN. a brief statement or a shortened form of what is in a longer book or article.
❑ VERB **di·gests, di·gest·ed, di·gest·ing. –di·gest′i·ble,** ADJECTIVE.

di·ges·tion (də jes′chən), NOUN. the process of digesting food: *Proper digestion is necessary for good health.*

di·ges·tive (də jes′tiv), ADJECTIVE. of or for digestion: *Saliva is one of the digestive juices.*

digestive system, the system of the body that digests food; alimentary canal. It includes the mouth, stomach, intestine, and other organs.

dig·it (dij′it), NOUN.
1 any of the figures 0, 1, 2, 3, 4, 5, 6, 7, 8, 9. Sometimes 0 is not called a digit.
2 a finger or toe.

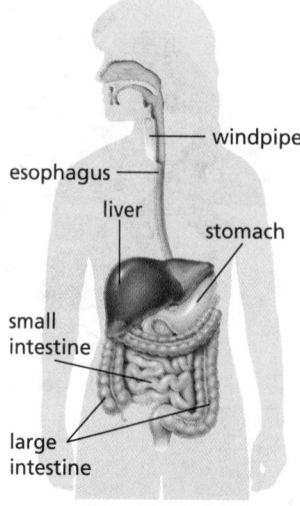

windpipe
esophagus
liver
stomach
small intestine
large intestine

digestive system

dig·i·tal (dij′ə təl), ADJECTIVE. showing time, temperature, or other information by digits, rather than by the positions of hands on a dial: *a digital clock.* **–dig′it·al·ly,** ADVERB.

dig·ni·fied (dig′nə fid), ADJECTIVE. noble; stately; having dignity: *The queen has a dignified manner.*

dig·ni·ty (dig′nə tē), NOUN.
1 a proud and self-respecting manner or appearance: *The candidate kept her dignity during the noisy debate.*
2 a quality of character or ability that makes other people respect you: *A judge should maintain the dignity of his or her position.*

dike (dīk), NOUN. a bank of earth or a dam built as a defense against flooding by a river or the sea.

di·lap·i·dat·ed (də lap′ə dā′tid), ADJECTIVE. falling to pieces; partly ruined or decayed through neglect: *No one had lived in the dilapidated old house for years.*

dil·i·gent (dil′ə jənt), ADJECTIVE. working hard and being very careful; not lazy: *The diligent student kept on working until he had finished his homework.* **–dil′i·gent·ly,** ADVERB.

dill (dil), NOUN. a plant whose seeds or leaves are used to flavor pickles and other foods.

di·lute (də lüt′), VERB. to make something weaker or thinner by adding water or some other liquid: *I diluted the frozen orange juice with several cans of water.* ❑ VERB **di·lutes, di·lut·ed, di·lut·ing.**

dim (dim),
1 ADJECTIVE. not bright; without much light: *With the blinds drawn, the room was dim.*
2 ADJECTIVE. not clearly seen, heard, or understood: *We could see only the dim outline of the mountain in the distance.*
3 ADJECTIVE. not seeing, hearing, or understanding clearly: *My grandmother's eyesight is getting dimmer.*
4 VERB. to make or become less bright: *She dimmed the car's headlights as the other car approached.*
❑ ADJECTIVE **dim·mer, dim·mest;** VERB **dims, dimmed, dim·ming. –dim′ly,** ADVERB. **–dim′ness,** NOUN.

dime (dīm), NOUN. a coin of the United States and Canada equal to 10 cents. Ten dimes make one dollar. ∎ See the Word Story at **December.**

di·men·sion (də men′shən), NOUN. a measurement of length, width, or thickness: *I need wallpaper for a room of the following dimensions: 16 feet long, 12 feet wide, and 8 feet high.*

di·min·ish (də min′ish), VERB. to make or become smaller in size, amount, or importance: *A sound diminishes as you get farther and farther away from it.* ❑ VERB **di·min·ish·es, di·min·ished, di·min·ish·ing.**

di·min·u·tive (də min′yə tiv), ADJECTIVE. very small; tiny. **–di·min′u·tive·ly,** ADVERB.

dim·ple (dim′pəl), NOUN. a small hollow place, usually in the cheek or chin.

din (din), *NOUN.* a loud, unpleasant noise that lasts a long time: *The din of the crowd was deafening.*

dine (dīn), *VERB.* to eat dinner: *We dine at six o'clock.*
❑ *VERB* **dines, dined, din·ing.** ∎ See the Synonym Study at **eat.**

din·er (dī′nər), *NOUN.*
1 someone who is eating dinner.
2 a small, casual restaurant. Diners are often open all night.
3 a railroad car in which meals are served.

din·ghy (ding′ē), *NOUN.* a small rowboat. ❑ *PLURAL* **din·ghies.**

din·gy (din′jē), *ADJECTIVE.* dirty-looking; lacking brightness or freshness; dull: *Dingy curtains covered the windows of the dusty old room.*
❑ *ADJECTIVE* **din·gi·er, din·gi·est.** ∎ See the Synonym Study at **dirty. −din′gi·ness,** *NOUN.*

dining room, a room in which dinner and other meals are served.

din·ner (din′ər), *NOUN.*
1 the main meal of the day: *What's for dinner?*
2 a formal meal in honor of some person or occasion: *They gave a dinner to honor the mayor.*

di·no·saur (dī′nə sôr), *NOUN.* one of a group of extinct reptiles that lived many millions of years ago. Some dinosaurs were bigger than elephants. Some were smaller than cats.

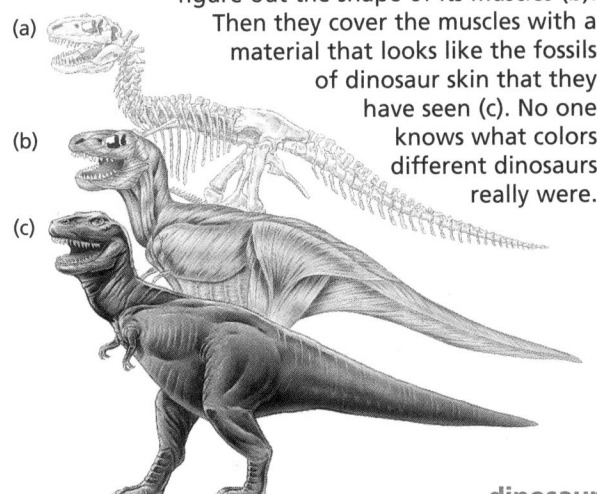

By studying a dinosaur's bones (a), scientists can figure out the shape of its muscles (b). Then they cover the muscles with a material that looks like the fossils of dinosaur skin that they have seen (c). No one knows what colors different dinosaurs really were.

dinosaur

di·o·cese (dī′ə sis), *NOUN.* the church district under the authority of a bishop.

dip (dip),
1 *VERB.* to put something under water or any liquid and lift it quickly out again: *He dipped his hand into the pool to see how cold the water was.*
2 *NOUN.* a quick plunge into and out of water; short swim: *She felt cool after a dip in the ocean.*

3 *VERB.* to take up in the hollow of the hand or with a pail, pan, or other container: *They dipped water from the bucket.*
4 *NOUN.* a creamy mixture of foods eaten by scooping it up with a cracker, potato chip, or the like: *a cheese dip, onion dip.*
5 *VERB.* to lower and raise again quickly: *The ship's flag was dipped as a salute.*
6 *VERB.* to slope downward: *The road dips into the valley.*
7 *NOUN.* a sudden slope or drop: *The dip in the road made the car bounce.*
❑ *VERB* **dips, dipped, dip·ping.**

diph·thong (dif′thong), *NOUN.* a vowel sound made up of two vowel sounds pronounced in one syllable, such as *oi* in *noise* or *ou* in *out.*

di·plo·ma (də plō′mə), *NOUN.* a written or printed paper, given by a school or college, which says that someone has completed certain courses, or has received a degree. ❑ *PLURAL* **di·plo·mas.**

dip·lo·mat (dip′lə mat), *NOUN.*
1 someone whose work is to handle the relations of his or her country with other nations.
2 someone who is skillful in dealing with people.

dip·lo·mat·ic (dip′lə mat′ik), *ADJECTIVE.* skillful in dealing with people: *I gave a diplomatic answer to avoid hurting her feelings.*
−dip′lo·mat′i·cal·ly, *ADVERB.*

dip·per (dip′ər), *NOUN.*
1 a cup-shaped object with a long handle, used to scoop up water or other liquids.
2 The **Big Dipper** and **Little Dipper** are two groups of stars in the northern sky that look something like a dipper.

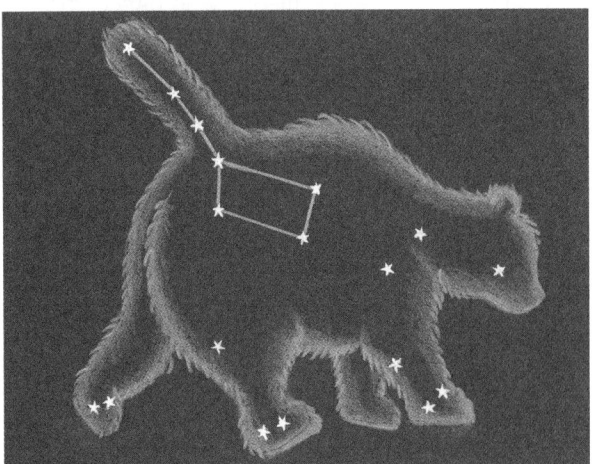

The **Big Dipper** is part of a larger group of stars that people thought looked like a bear.

a	hat	ė	term	ô	order	ch	child	⎧ a in about
ā	age	i	it	oi	oil	ng	long	⎪ e in taken
ä	far	ī	ice	ou	out	sh	she	ə⎨ i in pencil
â	care	o	hot	u	cup	th	thin	⎪ o in lemon
e	let	ō	open	u̇	put	ᴛʜ	then	⎩ u in circus
ē	equal	ȯ	saw	ü	rule	zh	measure	

di·rect (də rekt′),

1 *VERB.* to be in charge of something; manage; control: *The teacher directs the work of the class.*
2 *VERB.* to order; command: *The police officer directed traffic at the busy intersection.*
3 *VERB.* to tell or show someone the way: *The signpost directed us to turn left.*
4 *VERB.* to point or aim: *The firefighters directed the hose at the flames.*
5 *ADJECTIVE.* straight; without a stop or turn: *A bee makes a direct flight to the hive.*
6 *ADJECTIVE.* truthful; honest: *She gave direct answers to all the questions.*
7 *ADVERB.* directly: *This airplane goes to Los Angeles direct, without stopping.*
❑ *VERB* **di·rects, di·rect·ed, di·rect·ing.**

direct current, an electric current that flows in one direction. The current from all batteries is direct current.

di·rec·tion (də rek′shən), *NOUN.*

1 management; guidance; control: *The school is under the direction of the principal.*
2 **directions,** instructions about what to do, how to do something, or where to go: *He needs directions to the post office.*
3 any way in which you may face, point, or go: *School is in one direction and the mall is in another.*

di·rect·ly (də rekt′lē), *ADVERB.*

1 in a direct line or manner; straight: *This road runs directly into the center of town.*
2 with nothing in between: *Our apartment is directly above a flower shop.*

di·rec·tor (də rek′tər), *NOUN.* someone who directs an activity, especially someone who directs the performance of a play, a movie, or a show on television or radio.

di·rec·tor·y (də rek′tər ē), *NOUN.* a book or list of names and addresses. A telephone book is a directory with telephone numbers. ❑ *PLURAL* **di·rec·tor·ies.**

dir·i·gi·ble (dir′ə jə bəl *or* də rij′ə bəl), *NOUN.* an aircraft made with a rigid framework. It is filled with gas that is lighter than air.

dirk (dėrk), *NOUN.* (earlier) a dagger: *Scottish warriors used to fight with dirks.*

dirt (dėrt), *NOUN.*

1 anything that makes something unclean, such as mud, grease, or dust.
2 earth; soil: *Before I planted my garden I had to take lots of stones out of the dirt.*

dirt bike, a lightweight motorcycle built especially for travel on trails or dirt roads.

dirt-cheap (dėrt′chēp′), *ADJECTIVE.* very cheap: *He bought his bike dirt-cheap at an auction.*

dirt-poor (dėrt′pùr′), *ADJECTIVE.* very poor: *He said that they were poor, but not dirt-poor.*

dirt·y (dėr′tē),

1 *ADJECTIVE.* not clean; soiled by mud, grease, dust, and so on: *I got dirty working on the car.*
2 *ADJECTIVE.* not fair, decent, or acceptable: *To say that you would meet me and then not show up was a dirty trick.*
3 *VERB.* to make dirty; soil: *Don't dirty your hands in the mud.*
❑ *ADJECTIVE* **dirt·i·er, dirt·i·est;** *VERB* **dirt·ies, dirt·ied, dirt·y·ing.** —**dirt′i·ness,** *NOUN.*

getting **dirty** in a puddle of mud

Word Power   dis-

The prefix **dis-** means "the opposite of" or "the lack of." **Dis**honest means not honest, or **the opposite of** honest. **Dis**comfort means the **lack of** comfort.

In verbs, **dis-** can mean "to not do" or "to undo." **Dis**approve means to **not** approve. **Dis**connect means to **undo** a connection.

dis·a·bil·i·ty (dis′ə bil′ə tē), *NOUN.*

1 a lack of ability to do or use something: *His disability was due to illness.*
2 something that disables: *Severe arthritis can be a disability.*
❑ *PLURAL* **dis·a·bil·i·ties.**

dis·a·ble (dis ā′bəl), *VERB.* to make unable to do or use something; cripple: *A sprained wrist disabled the tennis player for three weeks.* ❑ *VERB* **dis·a·bles, dis·a·bled, dis·a·bling.**

dis·a·bled (dis ā′bəld), *ADJECTIVE.* having an illness or condition that prevents someone from being able to do certain things that most people can do. People who are **learning disabled,** for example, are often very intelligent but have problems using language or numbers.

dis·ad·van·tage (dis′əd van′tij), *NOUN.* something that may make someone less successful than other people: *Shyness can be a disadvantage in school.*

dis·a·gree (dis′ə grē′), *VERB.*

1 to argue; quarrel: *The two neighbors stopped being friendly after they disagreed about their boundary line.*
2 to have different opinions; differ: *Doctors sometimes disagree about the proper method of treating a patient.*
3 be different from something; to fail to agree: *My account of the accident disagrees with hers.*
4 to have a bad effect on someone: *I can't eat strawberries because they disagree with me.*
❑ *VERB* **dis·a·grees, dis·a·greed, dis·a·gree·ing.**

dis·a·gree·a·ble (dis′ə grē′ə bəl), ADJECTIVE.
1 unpleasant; not to your liking: *Our hike in the rain was a disagreeable experience.*
2 not friendly; grouchy: *People often become disagreeable when they are tired.*

dis·a·gree·ment (dis′ə grē′mənt), NOUN.
1 a quarrel; dispute: *Their disagreement led to the end of their friendship.*
2 a failure to agree about something; difference of opinion: *The disagreement that existed among members of the jury led to a new trial.*

dis·ap·pear (dis′ə pir′), VERB.
1 to pass out of sight; leave: *The little dog disappeared around the corner.*
2 to vanish completely; stop existing: *When spring comes, the snow disappears.*
❑ VERB **dis·ap·pears, dis·ap·peared, dis·ap·pear·ing.**

dis·ap·pear·ance (dis′ə pir′əns), NOUN. the act of disappearing: *The disappearance of the airplane brought about a search of the entire mountain.*

dis·ap·point (dis′ə point′), VERB. to fail to satisfy someone's desire, expectation, or hope: *The circus disappointed him, for there was no elephant.* ❑ VERB **dis·ap·points, dis·ap·point·ed, dis·ap·point·ing.**

dis·ap·point·ment (dis′ə point′mənt), NOUN.
1 the feeling you have when you do not get what you expected or hoped for: *When she did not get a new bicycle, her disappointment was very great.*
2 someone or something that causes disappointment: *The boring movie was a disappointment.*

dis·ap·prov·al (dis′ə prü′vəl), NOUN. a bad opinion of something; dislike: *She did not hesitate to express her disapproval of our noisy game.*

dis·ap·prove (dis′ə prüv′), VERB. to have or express a bad opinion of something: *My parents disapprove of rough games in the house.* ❑ VERB **dis·ap·proves, dis·ap·proved, dis·ap·prov·ing.**

dis·arm (dis ärm′), VERB.
1 to take away someone's weapons: *The police captured the robbers and disarmed them.*
2 to stop having armed forces or to reduce their size: *The nations agreed to disarm.*
❑ VERB **dis·arms, dis·armed, dis·arm·ing.**

dis·as·ter (də zas′tər), NOUN. a sudden event that causes great suffering or loss. A flood, fire, or earthquake is a disaster.

The earthquake was **a disaster.**

dis·be·lief (dis′bi lēf′), NOUN. a strong feeling that something is not true: *When we heard the rumor, we immediately expressed disbelief.*

disc (disk), NOUN.
1 See **compact disc.**
2 another spelling of **disk.**
3 (earlier) a phonograph record.

dis·card (dis kärd′), VERB. to give up something that is useless or worn out: *I discarded my torn sweater.*
❑ VERB **dis·cards, dis·card·ed, dis·card·ing.**

dis·charge (dis chärj′ for verb; dis′chärj for noun),
1 VERB. to officially send someone away from a place: *The doctor discharged her patient from the hospital.*
2 NOUN. an official release or sending away: *My cousin received his discharge from the army last month.*
3 VERB. to unload cargo or passengers from a ship, train, bus, or airplane: *The ship discharged its passengers at the dock.*
4 NOUN. something that leaks or flows out: *There was a watery discharge from her eyes.*
❑ VERB **dis·charg·es, dis·charged, dis·charg·ing.**

dis·ci·ple (də sī′pəl), NOUN.
1 a believer in the thought and teaching of any leader; follower.
2 one of the followers of Jesus.

dis·ci·pline (dis′ə plin),
1 NOUN. training that helps someone learn to obey rules and control his or her behavior: *Children who have had no discipline are often hard to teach.*
2 NOUN. the quality of having learned to obey rules: *The pupils show good discipline during fire drills.*
3 VERB. to train someone; bring under control: *The teacher was unable to discipline the unruly class.*
4 NOUN. punishment: *A little discipline would do them good.*
5 VERB. to punish: *She disciplined her child fairly.*
❑ VERB **dis·ci·plines, dis·ci·plined, dis·ci·plin·ing.**

disc jockey, an announcer for a radio program that consists chiefly of recorded popular music; deejay.

dis·close (dis klōz′), VERB. to make something known that was hidden; reveal: *He disclosed my secret.* ❑ VERB **dis·clos·es, dis·closed, dis·clos·ing.**

dis·col·or (dis kul′ər), VERB. to change or spoil the color of something; stain: *Smoke had discolored the building.* ❑ VERB **dis·col·ors, dis·col·ored, dis·col·or·ing.**

dis·com·fort (dis kum′fərt), NOUN.
1 uneasiness; lack of comfort: *Embarrassing questions cause discomfort.*
2 a thing that causes discomfort: *Mud and cold were the discomforts the campers minded most.*

a	hat	ė	term	ô	order	ch	child		a in about
ā	age	i	it	oi	oil	ng	long		e in taken
ä	far	ī	ice	ou	out	sh	she	ə<	i in pencil
â	care	o	hot	u	cup	th	thin		o in lemon
e	let	ō	open	ů	put	ᵺ	then		u in circus
ē	equal	ò	saw	ü	rule	zh	measure		

dis·con·nect (dis′kə nekt′), *VERB.* to undo or break the connection of: *I disconnected the fan by pulling out the plug.* ❑ *VERB* **dis·con·nects, dis·con·nect·ed, dis·con·nect·ing.**

dis·con·tent (dis′kən tent′), *NOUN.* a feeling of not being satisfied and wanting something different: *Low pay and long hours of work caused discontent among the factory workers.*

dis·con·tent·ed (dis′kən ten′tid), *ADJECTIVE.* not satisfied; disliking what you have and wanting something different: *The discontented workers went on strike.* **–dis′con·tent′ed·ly,** *ADVERB.*

dis·con·tin·ue (dis′kən tin′yü), *VERB.* to put an end to something; stop: *The network discontinued my favorite TV show.* ■ See the Synonym Study at **stop.** ❑ *VERB* **dis·con·tin·ues, dis·con·tin·ued, dis·con·tin·u·ing.**

dis·cord (dis′kôrd), *NOUN.* angry disagreement: *Arguments caused discord that spoiled the trip.*

dis·count (dis′kount),
1 *VERB.* to take off a certain amount from the price of something: *The store discounts all clothes ten percent.*
2 *NOUN.* the amount taken off a price: *We bought our new TV set on sale at a 20 percent discount.* ❑ *VERB* **dis·counts, dis·count·ed, dis·count·ing. –dis′count·er,** *NOUN.*

dis·cour·age (dis kėr′ij), *VERB.*
1 to take away someone's courage; destroy someone's hopes: *Failing over and over discourages anyone.*
2 to try to persuade someone not to do something: *All her friends discouraged her from trying such a dangerous swim.* ❑ *VERB* **dis·cour·ag·es, dis·cour·aged, dis·cour·ag·ing. –dis·cour′age·ment,** *NOUN.*

dis·cour·te·ous (dis kėr′tē əs), *ADJECTIVE.* not polite; rude: *It is discourteous to interrupt someone who is talking.* **–dis·cour′te·ous·ly,** *ADVERB.* **–dis·cour′te·ous·ness,** *NOUN.*

dis·cov·er (dis kuv′ər), *VERB.*
1 to find out something that you need to know about: *I discovered that I had left my ID at home.*
2 to find out something that was not known before: *Radium was discovered in 1898.* ■ See the Synonym Study at **find.** ❑ *VERB* **dis·cov·ers, dis·cov·ered, dis·cov·er·ing. –dis·cov′er·er,** *NOUN.*

dis·cov·er·y (dis kuv′ər ē), *NOUN.*
1 something found out: *One of Benjamin Franklin's discoveries was that lightning is electricity.*
2 the act of seeing or learning of something for the first time: *Balboa's discovery of the Pacific Ocean occurred in 1513.* ❑ *PLURAL* **dis·cov·er·ies.**

dis·crim·i·nate (dis krim′ə nāt), *VERB.*
1 to show an unfair difference in your treatment of people or groups: *It is wrong to discriminate against people because of their race, religion, nationality, or sex.*
2 to make or see a difference between things; distinguish: *People who are color-blind usually cannot discriminate between red and green.* ❑ *VERB* **dis·crim·i·nates, dis·crim·i·nat·ed, dis·crim·i·nat·ing.**

dis·crim·i·na·tion (dis krim′ə nā′shən), *NOUN.*
1 the act of showing an unfair difference in your treatment of people or groups: *Racial discrimination in hiring is against the law.*
2 the ability to make good choices; good judgment: *My uncle showed lack of discrimination in his choice of a business partner.*

dis·cus (dis′kəs), *NOUN.* a heavy, circular plate of wood with a metal rim. It is used in an athletic contest to see who can throw it farthest. ❑ *PLURAL* **dis·cus·es.**

dis·cuss (dis kus′), *VERB.* to talk about something with other people: *The class discussed the story.* ■ See the Synonym Study at **talk.** ❑ *VERB* **dis·cuss·es, dis·cussed, dis·cuss·ing.**

dis·cus·sion (dis kush′ən), *NOUN.* the action of talking something over with other people: *After hours of discussion, we came to a decision.*

dis·ease (də zēz′), *NOUN.* a sickness; illness; condition in which a bodily system, organ, or part does not work properly: *Diabetes is a disease.*

dis·grace (dis grās′),
1 *NOUN.* the loss of honor or respect; shame: *Being caught cheating was a disgrace.*
2 *VERB.* to cause disgrace to someone; bring shame upon: *The traitor disgraced his family and friends.*
3 *NOUN.* someone or something that causes dishonor or shame: *These slums are a disgrace to our city.* ❑ *VERB* **dis·grac·es, dis·graced, dis·grac·ing.**

dis·grace·ful (dis grās′fəl), *ADJECTIVE.* causing dishonor or loss of respect; shameful: *Their rude behavior was disgraceful.* **–dis·grace′ful·ly,** *ADVERB.*

dis·guise (dis gīz′),
1 *VERB.* to make changes in your clothes or appearance so that you look like someone else: *On Halloween I disguised myself as a pirate.*
2 *NOUN.* the clothes or actions used in making these changes: *Glasses and a wig formed the spy's disguise.*
3 *VERB.* to hide what something really is; make something seem like something else: *She disguised her voice on the telephone.*
❑ *VERB* **dis·guis·es, dis·guised, dis·guis·ing.**

wearing a **disguise**

dis·gust (dis gust′),
1 *NOUN.* a strong feeling of dislike.
2 *VERB.* to cause a feeling of dislike in: *The smell of rotten eggs disgusts people.*
❑ *VERB* **dis·gusts, dis·gust·ed, dis·gust·ing.**

dis·gust·ing (dis gus′ting), *ADJECTIVE.* extremely unpleasant: *Spoiled food can taste disgusting.*

The garbage smells **disgusting.**

dish (dish), *NOUN.*
1 anything to serve food in. Plates, platters, bowls, cups, and saucers are all dishes.
2 the amount served in a dish: *two dishes of ice cream.*
3 food that is prepared and served: *Macaroni and cheese is the dish I like best.*
❑ *PLURAL* **dish·es.**

dis·hon·est (dis on′ist), *ADJECTIVE.* not honest; tending to cheat or lie: *Someone who lies or steals is dishonest.* **–dis·hon·est·ly,** *ADVERB.*

dis·hon·es·ty (dis on′ə stē), *NOUN.* a lack of honesty: *The article exposed the mayor's dishonesty.*

dis·hon·or (dis on′ər),
1 *NOUN.* loss of reputation or honor; shame; disgrace: *Cheating brought dishonor to the team.*
2 *VERB.* to bring disgrace or shame upon: *Don't dishonor the flag by letting it touch the ground.*
❑ *VERB* **dis·hon·ors, dis·hon·ored, dis·hon·or·ing.**

dis·hon·or·a·ble (dis on′ər ə bəl), *ADJECTIVE.* causing disgrace or shame; without honor: *The police officer was accused of taking bribes and other dishonorable acts.* **–dis·hon′or·a·bly,** *ADVERB.*

dish·wash·er (dish′wäsh′ər), *NOUN.* a machine for washing dishes, pots, and glasses.

dis·in·fect (dis′in fekt′), *VERB.* to clean something by using something that kills germs. ❑ *VERB* **dis·in·fects, dis·in·fect·ed, dis·in·fect·ing.**

dis·in·fect·ant (dis′in fek′tənt), *NOUN.* a substance used to destroy disease germs. Alcohol and iodine are disinfectants.

dis·in·te·grate (dis in′tə grāt), *VERB.* to break up into small parts or bits: *The old papers had disintegrated into dust.* ❑ *VERB* **dis·in·te·grates, dis·in·te·grat·ed, dis·in·te·grat·ing.**

dis·in·ter·est·ed (dis in′tər ə stid), *ADJECTIVE.* able to judge something fairly because you have nothing to gain from it: *Umpires make disinterested decisions.*

disk (disk), *NOUN.*
1 a flat, thin, round object shaped like a coin.
2 a round, flat plate made of metal or plastic and with a magnetic surface, used to store information and instructions for computers.

disk drive, an electronic device that transfers information and instructions back and forth between a computer and magnetic storage disks.

disk·ette (dis ket′), *NOUN.* a small plastic disk used to store information and instructions for computers; floppy disk.

dis·like (dis līk′),
1 *VERB.* to not like something or someone: *He dislikes studying and would rather play soccer.*
2 *NOUN.* a feeling of not liking: *a dislike of spicy food.*
❑ *VERB* **dis·likes, dis·liked, dis·lik·ing.**

dis·lo·cate (dis′lō kāt), *VERB.* to force a bone out of its proper position: *He dislocated his shoulder when he fell.* ❑ *VERB* **dis·lo·cates, dis·lo·cat·ed, dis·lo·cat·ing. –dis′lo·ca′tion,** *NOUN.*

dis·lodge (dis loj′), *VERB.* to force something out of a place or position: *Use a crowbar to dislodge that stone.* ❑ *VERB* **dis·lodg·es, dis·lodged, dis·lodg·ing.**

dis·loy·al (dis loi′əl), *ADJECTIVE.* unfaithful; not loyal: *He was disloyal to his friends, often talking about them behind their backs.* **–dis·loy′al·ly,** *ADVERB.*

dis·mal (diz′məl), *ADJECTIVE.* dark; gloomy: *A cold, rainy day can seem quite dismal.* **–dis′mal·ly,** *ADVERB.*

Word Story

Dismal comes from Latin words meaning "evil days." In old times, people thought certain days were unlucky, as some people now think Friday the 13th is unlucky. People expected those days to be dark and gloomy.

dis·may (dis mā′),
1 *NOUN.* a sudden helpless fear of what is about to happen or what has happened: *I was filled with dismay when the basement began to flood.*
2 *VERB.* to trouble someone greatly; make afraid: *The thought that she might fail the test dismayed her.*
❑ *VERB* **dis·mays, dis·mayed, dis·may·ing.**

dis·miss (dis mis′), *VERB.*
1 to send someone away; allow to go: *At noon the teacher dismissed the class for lunch.*
2 to remove from office or service; force to leave: *We dismissed the painters because they were sloppy.*
❑ *VERB* **dis·miss, dis·missed, dis·miss·ing.**

a hat	ė term	ô order	ch child	a in about
ā age	i it	oi oil	ng long	e in taken
ä far	ī ice	ou out	sh she	ə = i in pencil
â care	o hot	u cup	th thin	o in lemon
e let	ō open	u̇ put	ᴛʜ then	u in circus
ē equal	ȯ saw	ü rule	zh measure	

dis·miss·al (dis mis′əl), NOUN.
1 the act of dismissing: *The dismissal of those five workers caused a strike.*
2 the condition or fact of being dismissed: *The company refused to announce the reason for the workers' dismissal.*

dis·mount (dis mount′), VERB. to get off something, such as a horse or a bicycle: *She dismounted and let her horse graze.* ❑ VERB **dis·mounts, dis·mount·ed, dis·mount·ing.**

dis·o·be·di·ence (dis′ə bē′dē əns), NOUN. failure to do what you are told to do: *The child was punished for disobedience.*

dis·o·be·di·ent (dis′ə bē′dē ənt), ADJECTIVE. failing to follow orders or rules; refusing to obey: *The disobedient child would not go to bed when her parents told her to.* ■ See the Synonym Study at **naughty.**

dis·o·bey (dis′ə bā′), VERB. to fail to do what you are told to do; refuse to obey orders: *The student who disobeyed the teacher was punished.* ❑ VERB **dis·o·beys, dis·o·beyed, dis·o·bey·ing.**

dis·or·der (dis ôr′dər), NOUN.
1 a condition in which things are not where or as they should be; confusion: *The room was in disorder after the birthday party.*
2 a sickness; disease: *a stomach disorder.*

dis·or·der·ly
(dis ôr′dər lē), ADJECTIVE.
1 not neat; untidy: *I can never find anything in this disorderly closet.*
2 causing noisy public disorder: *The disorderly crowd pushed and shoved to get on the bus.* ■ See the Synonym Study at **wild.**
—dis·or·der·li·ness, NOUN.

dis·or·gan·ized
(dis ôr′gə nīzd),
ADJECTIVE. thrown into great confusion: *The airline schedules were disorganized because of bad weather.*

a **disorderly** bedroom

dis·patch (dis pach′),
1 VERB. to send someone or something off to some place or for some purpose: *Extra fire trucks were dispatched to the site of the blaze.* ■ See the Synonym Study at **send.**
2 NOUN. a written message, such as special news or government business: *The reporter in Paris rushed dispatches to her newspaper in New York.*
❑ VERB **dis·patch·es, dis·patched, dis·patch·ing;** PLURAL **dis·patch·es. —dis·patch′er,** NOUN.

dis·pel (dis pel′), VERB. to make something go away; get rid of: *Talking with the pilot helped dispel my fear of flying.* ❑ VERB **dis·pels, dis·pelled, dis·pel·ling.**

dis·pense (dis pens′), VERB.
1 to give something out; distribute: *The Red Cross dispensed food and clothing to the flood victims.*
2 to prepare something and give it out: *Pharmacists must dispense medicine with the greatest care.*
❑ VERB **dis·pens·es, dis·pensed, dis·pens·ing.**

dis·pens·er (dis pen′sər), NOUN. a device or machine that gives out some item of general use: *a soap dispenser.*

dis·perse (dis pėrs′), VERB. to move or scatter something in all directions: *The fog dispersed after the sun rose.* ❑ VERB **dis·pers·es, dis·persed, dis·pers·ing.**

dis·place (dis plās′), VERB.
1 to move something from its usual place or position: *The war displaced thousands of people.*
2 to take the place of something: *The car has displaced the horse and buggy.*
❑ VERB **dis·plac·es, dis·placed, dis·plac·ing.**

dis·play (dis plā′),
1 VERB. to put something out where people can easily see it: *The store displayed the new game.* ■ See the Synonym Study at **show.**
2 NOUN. a public showing; exhibit: *Have you seen the library's display of new books?*
3 NOUN. a computer's screen, the window in a hand-held calculator, or the lighted numbers in a digital clock, VCR, and so on, which show important information.
❑ VERB **dis·plays, dis·played, dis·play·ing.**

dis·please (dis plēz′), VERB. to annoy or anger someone: *The teacher is displeased by students who are late for class.* ❑ VERB **dis·pleas·es, dis·pleased, dis·pleas·ing.**

dis·pos·a·ble (dis pō′zə bəl), ADJECTIVE. made or meant to be thrown away after use: *disposable diapers, disposable cups.*

dis·pos·al (dis pō′zəl), NOUN.
1 the act of getting rid of something: *The city takes care of the disposal of garbage.*
2 an electric device installed under a sink to grind up kitchen waste and dispose of it down the drain.

dis·pose (dis pōz′), VERB. **dispose of,**
1 to get rid of: *Please dispose of that rubbish.*
2 to take care of important matters: *The committee disposed of all its business in an hour.*
❑ VERB **dis·pos·es, dis·posed, dis·pos·ing.**

dis·po·si·tion (dis′pə zish′ən), NOUN.
1 someone's natural way of acting toward other people: *His cheerful disposition made him popular.*
2 tendency; inclination: *A considerate person has a disposition to be helpful.*

dis·prove (dis prüv′), VERB. to prove that something is false or incorrect: *She disproved my claim that I had less candy by weighing both boxes.* ❑ VERB **dis·proves, dis·proved, dis·prov·ing.**

dis·pute (dis pyüt′),
1 VERB. to give reasons or facts for or against something; argue: *Congress disputed over the need for new taxes.*
2 NOUN. an angry argument or quarrel: *There is a dispute over where to build the new school.*
3 VERB. to say that something is false or doubtful; disagree with: *The insurance company disputed his claim for damages to his car.*
   ❑ VERB **dis·putes, dis·put·ed, dis·put·ing.**

dis·qual·i·fy (dis kwäl′ə fī), VERB. to officially say that someone is unfit or unable to do something: *The principal disqualified two members of the swimming team because they had low grades.*
   ❑ VERB **dis·qual·i·fies, dis·qual·i·fied, dis·qual·i·fy·ing.**

dis·re·gard (dis′ri gärd′),
1 VERB. to pay no attention to something; ignore: *We disregarded the cold weather and went camping as planned.*
2 NOUN. lack of attention; neglect: *Her disregard of traffic signs caused her to have an accident.*
   ❑ VERB **dis·re·gards, dis·re·gard·ed, dis·re·gard·ing.**

dis·rep·u·ta·ble (dis rep′yə tə bəl), ADJECTIVE. having a bad reputation; not respectable: *Police closed the disreputable tavern after many complaints about the noise.*

dis·re·spect (dis′ri spekt′), NOUN. rudeness; lack of respect: *I meant no disrespect by my remark.*

dis·re·spect·ful (dis′ri spekt′fəl), ADJECTIVE. rude; impolite: *Making fun of the elderly is disrespectful.*
   —**dis′re·spect′ful·ly,** ADVERB.

dis·rupt (dis rupt′), VERB. to keep something from working or going on in its usual way: *The storm disrupted electrical power and telephone service throughout the area.* ❑ VERB **dis·rupts, dis·rupt·ed, dis·rupt·ing.**

dis·sat·is·fac·tion (dis′sat i sfak′shən), NOUN. a feeling of not being pleased with something: *Low pay often causes job dissatisfaction.*

dis·sat·is·fied (dis sat′i sfīd), ADJECTIVE. not happy; disappointed: *The dissatisfied workers voted to strike for higher pay.*

dis·sent (di sent′),
1 VERB. to disagree with an opinion that other people have about something: *Two of the judges dissented from the decision of the other three.*
2 NOUN. a difference of opinion; disagreement: *Dissent among the members broke up the meeting.*
   ❑ VERB **dis·sents, dis·sent·ed, dis·sent·ing.**
   —**dis·sent′er,** NOUN.

dis·solve (di zolv′), VERB.
1 to become liquid by being put into a liquid: *Salt or sugar will dissolve in water.*
2 to bring to an end: *They dissolved the club because they disagreed about the rules.*
   ❑ VERB **dis·solves, dis·solved, dis·solv·ing.**

dis·tance (dis′təns), NOUN.
1 the amount of space between two things: *The distance from our house to school is two miles.*
2 a place far away: *She saw a light in the distance.*

A map shows the **distance** between places.

dis·tant (dis′tənt), ADJECTIVE.
1 far away in space: *The sun is distant from the earth.*
2 far apart in time: *We plan a trip to Europe in the distant future.*
3 not closely related: *A third cousin is a distant relative.*
   —**dis′tant·ly,** ADVERB.

dis·taste (dis tāst′), NOUN. a feeling of dislike: *His distaste for cabbage showed clearly on his face.*

dis·taste·ful (dis tāst′fəl), ADJECTIVE. unpleasant; disagreeable: *Cleaning out garbage cans is a distasteful task.* —**dis·taste′ful·ness,** NOUN.

dis·till (dis til′), VERB. to make a liquid pure by heating it and turning it into a vapor and then cooling it by itself into liquid form again: *Water is distilled to remove minerals and other impurities. Gasoline is distilled from crude oil.* ❑ VERB **dis·tills, dis·tilled, dis·till·ing.** —**dis′til·la′tion,** NOUN.

dis·tinct (dis tingkt′), ADJECTIVE.
1 clearly different; not the same: *She asked me about it three distinct times. Mice are distinct from rats.*
2 easily seen, heard, or understood: *Large, distinct print is easy to read.*
   —**dis·tinct′ly,** ADVERB.

a hat	ė term	ô order	ch child	a in about
ā age	i it	oi oil	ng long	e in taken
ä far	ī ice	ou out	sh she	ə i in pencil
â care	o hot	u cup	th thin	o in lemon
e let	ō open	u̇ put	ᴛʜ then	u in circus
ē equal	ȯ saw	ü rule	zh measure	

dis·tinc·tion (dis tingk′shən), NOUN.
1 difference: *The distinction between hot and cold is easily noticed.*
2 the act of making a difference: *They treated all their children alike without distinction.*
3 something that makes you especially worthy or well known; honor: *The judge served on the court for many years with distinction.*

dis·tinc·tive (dis tingk′tiv), ADJECTIVE. clearly showing a difference from others; special: *Police officers wear a distinctive uniform.*
—**dis·tinc′tive·ly**, ADVERB. —**dis·tinc′tive·ness**, NOUN.

dis·tin·guish (dis ting′gwish), VERB.
1 to see the differences between things; tell apart: *Can you distinguish silk from nylon?*
2 to see or hear something clearly: *On a clear, bright day you can distinguish things far away.*
3 to be a quality or feature of something that makes it clearly different from other similar things: *The elephant's trunk distinguishes it from all other animals.*
4 to make yourself famous or well-known: *He distinguished himself by winning the spelling bee.*
❑ VERB **dis·tin·guish·es, dis·tin·guished, dis·tin·guish·ing.**

dis·tort (dis tôrt′), VERB.
1 to pull or twist something out of shape; change the normal appearance of: *Rage distorted his face.*
2 to change from the truth: *The driver distorted the facts of the accident to keep from getting a ticket.*
❑ VERB **dis·torts, dis·tort·ed, dis·tort·ing.**

The mirror **distorts** the boy's face.

dis·tract (dis trakt′), VERB. to draw someone's attention away from something: *Noise distracts me when I am trying to study.*
❑ VERB **dis·tracts, dis·tract·ed, dis·tract·ing.**

dis·tress (dis tres′),
1 NOUN. great pain or suffering; anxiety; trouble: *The loss of our kitten caused us much distress.*
2 VERB. to cause pain or suffering; make someone unhappy: *Your tears distress me.*
❑ VERB **dis·tress·es, dis·tressed, dis·tress·ing.**

dis·trib·ute (dis trib′yüt), VERB.
1 to give some to each person in a group: *He distributed the candy among his friends.*
2 to spread or scatter something: *A painter should distribute the paint evenly over the wall.*
❑ VERB **dis·trib·utes, dis·trib·ut·ed, dis·trib·ut·ing.**
—**dis·trib′u·tor**, NOUN.

dis·tri·bu·tion (dis′trə byü′shən), NOUN.
1 the action of distributing: *After the contest the distribution of prizes to the winners took place.*
2 a way of being distributed: *If some get more than others, there is an uneven distribution.*

dis·trib·u·tive prop·er·ty (dis trib′yə tiv prop′ər tē), NOUN. (in mathematics) a rule stating that multiplication produces the same result when performed on a set of numbers or on the numbers individually. EXAMPLE: $3(4 + 5) = (3 \times 4) + (3 \times 5)$.

dis·trict (dis′trikt), NOUN. a part of a country, a state, or a city, marked off for some special purpose: *a business district, a school district.*

District of Columbia, a district in the southeastern United States that is entirely occupied by the city of Washington, the capital of the United States. *Abbreviation:* DC

Word Story   **District of Columbia** comes from the name of Christopher Columbus.

dis·trust (dis trust′),
1 VERB. to not trust someone or something; doubt: *Everyone should distrust shaky ladders.*
2 NOUN. a feeling that you cannot trust someone or something: *I could not explain my distrust of the stranger.* ∎ See the Synonym Study at **doubt.**
❑ VERB **dis·trusts, dis·trust·ed, dis·trust·ing.**

dis·turb (dis tėrb′), VERB.
1 to bother someone by talking or by being noisy; interrupt: *Please don't disturb me; I'm studying.*
2 to make someone very sad or troubled: *He was disturbed to hear of his friend's illness.*
3 to destroy the peace or quiet of something: *Truck traffic disturbed the neighborhood all day long.*
4 to put out of normal order: *Someone has disturbed my books; I can't find the one I want.*
❑ VERB **dis·turbs, dis·turbed, dis·turb·ing.**

dis·turb·ance (dis tėr′bəns), NOUN.
1 the act of disturbing or the condition of being disturbed: *Car alarms often cause disturbances.*
2 something that disturbs: *Turn off the TV so it won't be a disturbance.*
3 violent, public disorder: *The police were called to quiet the disturbance at the street corner.*

ditch (dich),
1 NOUN. a long, narrow hole dug in the earth. Ditches are usually used to carry off water.
2 VERB. (informal) to get rid of something: *The bank robbers ditched the car they had stolen and fled.*
❑ PLURAL **ditch·es;** VERB **ditch·es, ditched, ditch·ing.**

dit·to mark (dit′ō märk′), a small mark (″) used to avoid repeating something written immediately above. Ditto marks are often used on long lists, bills, tables, and so on. EXAMPLE:

```
6 lb. apples at 75¢ . . . . .$4.50
4 ″  grapes ″  ″  ″. . . . .  3.00
```

D

dive (dīv),
1 *VERB.* to jump headfirst into water, with arms stretched out above the head: *He dived into the pool with a small splash.*
2 *NOUN.* the action of diving: *The young man made a graceful back dive off the diving board.*
3 *VERB.* to go down or out of sight suddenly: *The gopher dived into its hole and disappeared.*
4 *VERB.* to drop quickly out of the sky or through the water at a steep angle: *The hawk dived straight at the field mouse. The submarine dived toward the bottom.*
□ *VERB* **dives, dived** or **dove, dived, div·ing.**

He **dived** into the pool with a small splash.

div·er (dī′vər), *NOUN.*
1 someone who dives.
2 someone whose job is to work under water, wearing special equipment.

di·verse (də vėrs′), *ADJECTIVE.* various; differing; different: *A great many diverse opinions were expressed at the meeting.*

di·ver·sion (də vėr′zhən), *NOUN.*
1 something that occupies your attention while you are trying to watch something else: *A magician's talk creates a diversion so that we don't see how the tricks are done.*
2 a relief from work or care; amusement; pastime; entertainment: *Watching television is a popular diversion.*

di·ver·si·ty (də vėr′sə tē), *NOUN.* variety; difference: *We celebrate the great diversity of people here in the United States.*

di·vert (də vėrt′), *VERB.*
1 to turn something in another direction: *We dug a ditch to divert water from the stream into the fields.*
2 to turn someone's attention to something else: *The siren of the fire engine diverted the audience's attention from the play.*
3 to amuse; entertain: *Listening to music diverted him after a hard day's work.*
□ *VERB* **di·verts, di·vert·ed, di·vert·ing.**

di·vide (də vīd′), *VERB.*
1 to separate into parts: *A brook divides the field. The path divides at the pond.*
2 to separate something into equal parts: *When you divide 8 by 2, you get 4.*
3 to give out as a share to each person: *We divided the candy.*
4 to disagree or cause to disagree: *The question of a shorter lunch hour divided the school board and the students.*
□ *VERB* **di·vides, di·vid·ed, di·vid·ing.**

div·i·dend (div′ə dend), *NOUN.*
1 a number to be divided by another: *In 728 ÷ 16, 728 is the dividend.*
2 the profit earned by a company and divided among the owners of the company and people who own stock in the company.

di·vine (də vīn′), *ADJECTIVE.*
1 of God or a god: *The Bible describes the creation of the world as a divine act.*
2 given by or coming from God: *The king believed that his power to rule was a divine right.*
3 to or for God; sacred; holy: *Services for divine worship are held daily.*
—**di·vine′ly,** *ADVERB.*

diving board, a flexible board at the side of a pool that sticks out over the water. Divers use this to spring into the air before diving.

di·vis·i·ble (də viz′ə bəl), *ADJECTIVE.* able to be divided: *The number 12 is divisible by 4.*

di·vi·sion (də vizh′ən), *NOUN.*
1 the operation of dividing one number by another: *26 ÷ 2 = 13 is a simple division.*
2 one of the parts into which something is divided; section: *the research division of a drug company.*
3 the action of giving some to each; sharing: *The division of his property among his children was ordered by his will.*
4 the action of dividing or the condition of being divided: *the division of land into lots for houses.*
5 something that divides: *This fence is the division between your property and mine.*

di·vi·sor (də vī′zər), *NOUN.* a number by which another number is divided: *In 728 ÷ 16, 16 is the divisor.*

di·vorce (də vôrs′),
1 *NOUN.* the legal ending of a marriage.
2 *VERB.* to legally end a marriage: *They were divorced last year.*
□ *VERB* **di·vorc·es, di·vorced, di·vorc·ing.**

div·ot (div′ət), *NOUN.* a small clump of grass or dirt dug up when a golfer's club strikes the ball.

di·vulge (də vulj′), *VERB.* to tell; reveal; make known: *The traitor divulged secret government plans to the enemy.* □ *VERB* **di·vulg·es, di·vulged, di·vulg·ing.**

a	hat	ė	term	ô	order	ch	child		a in about
ā	age	i	it	oi	oil	ng	long		e in taken
ä	far	ī	ice	ou	out	sh	she	ə	i in pencil
â	care	o	hot	u	cup	th	thin		o in lemon
e	let	ō	open	ů	put	⊤H	then		u in circus
ē	equal	ȯ	saw	ü	rule	zh	measure		

diz·zy (diz'ē), ADJECTIVE.
1 likely to fall, stagger, or spin around; not steady: *When you spin round and round, and stop suddenly, you feel dizzy.*
2 likely to make someone dizzy; causing dizziness: *The airplane climbed to a dizzy height.*
❑ ADJECTIVE **diz·zi·er, diz·zi·est. –diz'zi·ness,** NOUN.

Word Story

Dizzy comes from an old English word meaning "foolish." When you are very dizzy, you may feel and act foolish.

Dji·bou·ti (ji bü'tē), NOUN. a country in eastern Africa.
DNA, the large, complex molecules found in all living cells. DNA is the substance that contains genes. It is mainly responsible for the transmission of inherited characteristics from parents to their offspring.

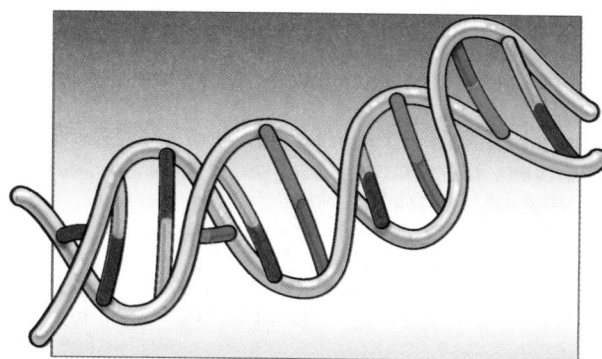

a short section of **DNA**

do¹ (dü), VERB.
1 to carry through to an end any action or piece of work; carry out; perform: *Do your work well.*
2 to take care of; do work on: *Who does the dishes at your house?*
3 to act; behave: *You did very well today.*
4 to be satisfactory: *That hat will do.*
5 to work out; solve: *do an arithmetic problem.*
6 **Do** is used as a helping verb: **a** to ask questions: *Do you like milk?* **b** to make what one says stronger: *I do want to go.* **c** to stand for another word already used: *My dog goes where I do. Her brother walks just as she does.* **d** in expressions that contain *not: People talk; animals do not.*
7 to get along; manage: *I am doing well in my new job.*
❑ VERB **does, did, done, do·ing.** ∎ Other words that sound like this are **dew** and **due. –do'a·ble,** ADJECTIVE.

do away with, IDIOM.
1 to put an end to; abolish: *do away with a rule.*
2 to kill: *The trap did away with the rat.*

do without, IDIOM. to get along without: *We can't do without a car, now that we live in the country.*

make do, IDIOM. to get along; manage: *We'll make do with these old costumes.*
do² (dō), NOUN. (in music) the first and last tone of a scale. *Do, re, mi, fa, sol, la, ti, do* are the names of the tones of a scale. ❑ PLURAL **dos.** ∎ Other words that sound like this are **doe** and **dough.**
Do·ber·man pin·scher (dō'bər mən pin'shər), a large slender dog with short, dark hair.
doc·ile (dos'əl), ADJECTIVE. easy to control or train; obedient: *People who are just learning to ride should choose a docile horse.* **–doc'ile·ly,** ADVERB.
dock (dok),
1 NOUN. a platform built on the shore or out from the shore; wharf; pier. Ships load and unload beside a dock.
2 VERB. to bring a ship to dock: *The crew docked the ship and began to unload it.*
3 NOUN. a platform for loading and unloading trucks or railroad cars.
4 VERB. to join two spacecraft to each other while in space.
❑ VERB **docks, docked, dock·ing.**
doc·tor (dok'tər),
1 NOUN. someone who is trained to treat diseases. Physicians, dentists, and veterinarians are doctors.
2 VERB. to treat disease in someone: *My mother doctored me when I had a cold.*
❑ VERB **doc·tors, doc·tored, doc·tor·ing.**
doc·trine (dok'trən), NOUN. what is taught as true by a church, nation, or group; belief: *religious doctrine. The Constitution states the doctrine of freedom of speech.*
doc·u·ment (dok'yə mənt), NOUN. something written or printed that gives information and can often be used as proof of some fact. Letters, maps, and pictures are documents.
dodge (doj), VERB.
1 to move or jump quickly to one side: *As I looked, he dodged behind a bush.*
2 to move quickly in order to get away from a person, a blow, or something thrown: *She dodged the Frisbee as it came flying at her.*
3 to avoid something that you do not want to deal with: *She dodged our question by changing the subject.*
❑ VERB **dodg·es, dodged, dodg·ing. –dodg'er,** NOUN.
do·do (dō'dō), NOUN. a large, clumsy bird that could not fly. Dodos lived on several islands in the Indian Ocean until the last ones died about 300 years ago. ❑ PLURAL **do·dos** or **do·does.**
doe (dō), NOUN. a female deer, antelope, rabbit, or hare. ∎ Other words that sound like this are **do²** and **dough.**
does (duz), VERB. a present tense of **do:** *She does all her work. Does he sing well?*
does·n't (duz'nt), a contraction of **does not.**

boxer

German shepard

collie

retriever

spaniel

various kind of **dogs**

dog (dȯg),
1 *NOUN.* a four-legged animal closely related to the wolf. Dogs are kept as pets and for hunting and guarding property.
2 *VERB.* to hunt or follow like a dog: *Bill collectors dogged them for over a month.*
❑ *VERB* **dogs, dogged, dog·ging. –dog′like′,** *ADJECTIVE.*

Have You Heard?

You may have heard someone say **"You can't teach an old dog new tricks."** This means that it can be hard to get people to try new things, especially if they have been doing things the same way for a long time.

dog guide, a dog that has been trained to lead or guide someone with impaired sight or hearing.
dog·wood (dȯg′wu̇d′), *NOUN.* a tree with large white or pinkish blossoms in the spring.
doi·ly (doi′lē), *NOUN.* a small piece of linen, lace, paper, or plastic used under a dish or vase as a decoration or to protect the surface beneath it.
❑ *PLURAL* **doi·lies.**
do·ings (dü′ingz), *NOUN PLURAL.* activities; actions; events: *There were dances, parties, and lots of doings over the holidays.*
dole (dōl), *VERB.* to give out in small portions: *Mom doled out a few raisins as a snack.* ❑ *VERB* **doles, doled, dol·ing.**
doll (dol), *NOUN.* a child's toy made to look like a baby, a child, or a grown person. **–doll′-like′,** *ADJECTIVE.*
dol·lar (dol′ər), *NOUN.* a unit of money in the United States and Canada equal to 100 cents. $1.00 means one dollar.
dol·phin (dol′fən), *NOUN.* a sea animal similar to a small whale. It has a long, rounded snout and is very intelligent.
do·main (dō mān′), *NOUN.* the lands under the control of one ruler or government: *The brave knight was given the best land in the queen's domain.*
dome (dōm), *NOUN.* a large, rounded roof usually found on a church or government building.

do·mes·tic (də mes′tik),
1 *ADJECTIVE.* of or about the home, the household, or family affairs: *A housekeeper is a domestic worker.*
2 *ADJECTIVE.* living with or cared for by human beings; not wild; tame. Horses, dogs, cats, cows, and pigs are **domestic animals.**
3 *ADJECTIVE.* of, about, or made in your own country; not foreign: *domestic products.*
4 *NOUN.* a servant in a household. A butler or a maid is a domestic.
–do·mes′ti·cal·ly, *ADVERB.*
dom·i·nant (dom′ə nənt), *ADJECTIVE.* most powerful; controlling; having most influence: *The principal was the dominant person at the meeting.*
dom·i·nate (dom′ə nāt), *VERB.* to control or rule someone or something by strength or power: *She is very outspoken and tends to dominate our club meetings.* ❑ *VERB* **dom·i·nates, dom·i·nat·ed, dom·i·nat·ing. –dom′i·na′tion,** *NOUN.*
Do·min·i·can Re·pub·lic (də min′ə kən ri pub′lik), a country in the West Indies.
do·min·ion (də min′yən), *NOUN.*
1 the power or right to control people or nations.
2 the lands under the control of one ruler or government.
dom·i·no (dom′ə nō), *NOUN.* one of a set of small, flat pieces of wood or plastic marked with spots. When you play **dominoes,** you try to match the blanks or the number of spots with the piece played previously. ❑ *PLURAL* **dom·i·noes** or **dom·i·nos.**
do·nate (dō′nāt), *VERB.* to give money or help; contribute: *I donated ten dollars to charity.* ❑ *VERB* **do·nates, do·nat·ed, do·nat·ing.**
do·na·tion (dō nā′shən), *NOUN.* a gift of money or help; contribution: *He gave a donation to charity.*

dolphin — up to 13 feet long

a hat	ė term	ô order	ch child	⎧ a in about
ā age	i it	oi oil	ng long	⎪ e in taken
ä far	ī ice	ou out	sh she	ə ⎨ i in pencil
â care	o hot	u cup	th thin	⎪ o in lemon
e let	ō open	u̇ put	ŦH then	⎩ u in circus
ē equal	ȯ saw	ü rule	zh measure	

done (dun),
1 ADJECTIVE. finished; completed; ended: *She is done with her homework.*
2 ADJECTIVE. cooked: *I like my steak well done.*
3 VERB. the past participle of **do**: *Have you done all of the problems?*

don·key (dong′kē), NOUN. an animal something like a small horse but with longer ears and a shorter mane; ass. ❑ PLURAL **don·keys.**

donkey — about 4 feet high at the shoulder

do·nor (dō′nər), NOUN. someone who donates. A blood donor is a person who gives blood.

don't (dōnt), a contraction of **do not.**

Usage Note

Don't is sometimes used with *he, she,* or *it* in speech instead of **doesn't.** This use is not accepted in writing or in standard or formal speech. SAY: *She doesn't like our new teacher.* NOT: *She don't like our new teacher.*

doo·dle (dü′dl), VERB. to draw or make marks in an absent-minded way while talking or thinking.
❑ VERB **doo·dles, doo·dled, doo·dling.**

doom (düm),
1 NOUN. a terrible fate; ruin; death: *As the ship sank, the voyagers faced their doom.*
2 VERB. to sentence someone to an unhappy or terrible fate: *The prisoner was doomed to death.*
3 VERB. to ruin your hopes or chance of success: *The weather doomed our picnic.*
❑ VERB **dooms, doomed, doom·ing.**

door (dôr), NOUN.
1 a movable part to close an opening in a wall, cabinet, vehicle, or the like. A door turns on hinges or slides open and shut.
2 a doorway: *I walked into the hall through the door.*

door·bell (dôr′bel′), NOUN. a bell that you ring to let people inside a house or apartment know you are there.

door·step (dôr′step′), NOUN. a step leading from an outside door to the ground.

door·way (dôr′wā′), NOUN. an opening in a wall where a door opens and closes.

dope (dōp), NOUN. (informal)
1 a very foolish person.
2 a narcotic or other drug, such as heroin or marijuana.

dor·mant (dôr′mənt), ADJECTIVE. not active: *Many volcanoes are dormant. Bears and other animals that hibernate are dormant during the winter.*

dor·mi·to·ry (dôr′mə tôr′ē), NOUN. a building with many rooms to sleep and study in. Many colleges have dormitories for students whose homes are somewhere else. ❑ PLURAL **dor·mi·to·ries.**

dor·mouse (dôr′mous′), NOUN. a small European animal something like a squirrel. It sleeps during cold weather. ❑ PLURAL **dor·mice** (dôr′mīs′).

dose (dōs),
1 NOUN. the amount of a medicine to be taken at one time: *a dose of cough medicine.*
2 VERB. to give medicine to someone: *The doctor dosed the sick child with penicillin.*
❑ VERB **dos·es, dosed, dos·ing.**

dot (dot),
1 NOUN. a tiny, round mark; point: *Put a dot over each* i.
2 NOUN. a small spot: *a blue necktie with white dots.*
3 VERB. to mark with a dot or dots: *Dot your* i*'s and* j*'s.*
❑ VERB **dots, dot·ted, dot·ting.**

dote (dōt), VERB. **dote on,** to be foolishly fond of; be too fond of: *He dotes on his grandchildren.* ❑ VERB **dotes, dot·ed, dot·ing.**

dou·ble (dub′əl),
1 ADJECTIVE. twice as much, as large, or as strong: *They were given double pay for working on Sunday.*
2 VERB. to make or become twice as much or twice as many: *They doubled their investment in ten years.*
3 ADJECTIVE. made of two parts that are alike; in a pair: *double doors.*
4 ADJECTIVE. having two meanings. The spelling b-e-a-r has a double meaning: *to carry* and *an animal.*
5 ADVERB. two instead of one: *It is dangerous to ride double on a bicycle.*
6 NOUN. someone or something just like another: *Her twin sister is her double.*
7 VERB. to fold something over: *She doubled the slice of bread to make a sandwich.*
8 in baseball: **a** NOUN. a hit by which the batter gets to second base safely. **b** VERB. to make such a hit: *I doubled in the second inning.*
9 NOUN. **doubles,** a game played with two people on each side, especially in tennis.
❑ VERB **dou·bles, dou·bled, dou·bling.**

dou·ble bass (dub′əl bās′), a musical instrument nearly as tall as a person, shaped like a violin and having a very deep tone.

dou·ble-click (dub′əl klik′), VERB. to press on a computer mouse button twice rapidly to get the

D

computer to do something or to find some information. ❑ *VERB* **dou·ble-clicks, dou·ble-clicked, dou·ble-click·ing.**

dou·ble-cross (dub′əl kròs′), *VERB.* to promise to do one thing and then do something else that cheats or harms the person you made the promise to. ❑ *VERB* **dou·ble-cross·es, dou·ble-crossed, dou·ble-cross·ing. —dou′ble-cross′er,** *NOUN.*

dou·ble-head·er (dub′əl hed′ər), *NOUN.* two baseball games played one right after another.

dou·ble-park (dub′əl pärk′), *VERB.* to park a car in a driving lane beside another car that is parked by a curb. ❑ *VERB* **dou·ble-parks, dou·ble-park·ed, dou·ble-park·ing.**

double play, (in baseball) a play in which two runners are put out.

doubt (dout),
1 *VERB.* to feel uncertain; not believe; not be sure: *She doubted if her watch was correct. I doubt that I will be able to play this week.*
2 *NOUN.* a lack of belief; feeling of uncertainty: *My doubts vanished when she won the race.*
❑ *VERB* **doubts, doubt·ed, doubt·ing.**

Synonym Study

Doubt means a feeling of not believing something or not being sure: *His doubt grew as he listened to their excuses. They have doubts about whether to buy a new car.*

Uncertainty means a feeling of not being sure of someone or something: *Uncertainty about the weather caused them to cancel the picnic.*

Suspicion means a feeling of not trusting someone. This word is often used in connection with a crime or bad deed: *He finished the mystery and learned that his suspicion of the cook was correct.*

Mistrust means suspicion or lack of trust: *The diver looked at the sharks with mistrust.*

Distrust means strong suspicion or a serious lack of trust: *The guard saw the woman hide something, so he watched her with distrust.*

ANTONYMS: **belief, certainty.**

doubt·ful (dout′fəl), *ADJECTIVE.* full of doubt; not sure; not certain: *We are doubtful about the weather for tomorrow.* **—doubt′ful·ly,** *ADVERB.*

doubt·less (dout′lis), *ADVERB.* without doubt; surely: *Since the autumn has been so cold, winter will doubtless come early.* **—doubt′less·ly,** *ADVERB.*

dough (dō), *NOUN.* a soft, thick mixture of flour, liquid, and other things from which bread, biscuits, cake, and pie crust are made. ■ Other words that sound like this are **do²** and **doe.** **—dough′like′,** *ADJECTIVE.*

dough·nut (dō′nut′), *NOUN.* a small cake of sweetened dough cooked in deep fat. A doughnut is usually made in the shape of a ring.

dove¹ (duv), *NOUN.* a bird with a thick body and short legs; pigeon. The dove is often a symbol of peace.

dove² (dōv), *VERB.* a past tense of **dive:** *She dove deep into the water looking for sunken treasure.*

Do·ver (dō′vər), *NOUN.* the capital of Delaware.

dove¹ — about 11 inches long

down¹ (doun),
1 *ADVERB.* from a higher to a lower place or condition: *They ran down the hill. The temperature has gone down.*
2 *ADVERB.* in a lower place or condition: *Down in the valley the fog still lingers. The sun is down.*
3 *ADVERB.* from an earlier time to a later time: *The story has come down through many years.*
4 *PREPOSITION.* down along: *You can ride down a hill, sail down a river, or walk down a street.*
5 *ADJECTIVE.* going or pointed down: *We waited for a down elevator.*
6 *VERB.* to drink something quickly: *She downed the medicine with one swallow.*
7 *ADJECTIVE.* sick; ill: *She is down with a cold.*
8 *ADJECTIVE.* out of order: *Our computer is down.*
9 in football: **a** *NOUN.* a play from scrimmage. A team has four downs to gain at least ten yards. **b** *ADJECTIVE.* no longer in play: *Officials marked the ball down at the 15-yard line.*
10 *ADVERB* or *ADJECTIVE.* in cash when bought: *You can pay $10 down and the rest later. We made a down payment on a new car.*
❑ *VERB* **downs, downed, down·ing.**

down² (doun), *NOUN.* soft feathers: *the down of a young bird.*

down·cast (doun′kast′), *ADJECTIVE.*
1 turned downward: *She stood with downcast eyes, avoiding my look.*
2 sad; discouraged: *After all our plans failed, we felt very downcast.*

down·hill (doun′hil′),
1 *ADVERB.* down the slope of a hill; downward: *I ran downhill.*
2 *ADJECTIVE.* going or sloping downward: *a downhill race, downhill skiing.*

a	hat	è	term	ô	order	ch	child	⎧a in about
ā	age	i	it	oi	oil	ng	long	⎪e in taken
ä	far	ī	ice	ou	out	sh	she	ə⎨i in pencil
â	care	o	hot	u	cup	th	thin	⎪o in lemon
e	let	ō	open	ù	put	ᴛʜ	then	⎩u in circus
ē	equal	ò	saw	ü	rule	zh	measure	

Dragons

Dragons are mythical beasts that are part of the folklore of many European and Asian cultures. While European dragons are scary monsters, Asian dragons are friendly and bring good fortune.

Komodo Dragon

Many lizards big and small have been given the name "dragon." The biggest lizard in the world is the Komodo dragon. They live on the island of Komodo in Indonesia, and they can grow to be more than 10 feet long. They eat deer, pigs, and even water buffalo.

St. George

The most famous European story about dragons is the story of St. George. He rescued a princess from a dragon by killing it with his lance. He is the patron saint of England.

Scary Dragons

In European stories, dragons have scaly skin, bat wings, and sometimes breathe fire. They are known to have huge hoards of gold, and they like to eat princesses.

Friendly Dragons

In Asian stories, dragons have long and colorful bodies, small horns, and often beards. They are friendly and wise. Some dragons have the power to control the weather. Some dragons can become very big or very small, or become invisible.

Have you seen any real dragons lately?

Like the Komodo dragon, other lizards have reminded people of the legendary dragons. Which one of the lizards below do you think looks the most like a dragon?

bearded dragon

flying dragon

water dragon

down·load (doun′lōd′), *VERB.* to transfer computer information from one computer to another smaller one, or from a computer to another device such as a printer. ❑ *VERB* **down·loads, down·load·ed, down·load·ing.**

down·pour (doun′pôr′), *NOUN.* a sudden heavy rain.

down·right (doun′rīt′),
  1 *ADJECTIVE.* thorough; complete: *a downright lie.*
  2 *ADVERB.* thoroughly; completely: *downright rude.*

down·size (doun′sīz′), *VERB.* to make a business company smaller by reducing the number of people who work there. ❑ *VERB* **down·siz·es, down·sized, down·siz·ing.**

down·stairs (doun′stârz′),
  1 *ADVERB* or *ADJECTIVE.* on or to a lower floor: *I looked downstairs for my book. The downstairs room is dark.*
  2 *NOUN.* the lower floor or floors: *The entire downstairs was flooded after the heavy rain.*

down·stream (doun′strēm′), *ADVERB* or *ADJECTIVE.* in the direction of the current of a stream; down a stream: *It is easy to swim or row downstream.*

down·town (doun′toun′),
  1 *ADJECTIVE.* of or in the main part of a town, where most shops and offices are: *a downtown theater.*
  2 *ADVERB.* to or into the downtown area: *My parents went downtown shopping.*

down·ward (doun′wərd), *ADVERB* or *ADJECTIVE.* toward a lower place or position: *The bird swooped downward. The downward trip was a lot faster than the climb.*

down·wards (doun′wərdz), *ADVERB.* downward.

down·y (dou′nē),
  ADJECTIVE. covered with soft feathers; like soft feathers: *a downy chick.*
  ❑ *ADJECTIVE* **down·i·er, down·i·est.**

dow·ry (dou′rē), *NOUN.* (in some societies) the money or property that a woman brings to the man she marries.
  ❑ *PLURAL* **dow·ries.**

two **downy** ducklings

doz., an abbreviation of **dozen.**

doze (dōz), *VERB.* to sleep lightly; be half asleep: *After dinner he dozed on the couch.* ❑ *VERB* **doz·es, dozed, doz·ing. —doz′er,** *NOUN.*

doz·en (duz′n), *NOUN.* group of 12; 12: *We will need three dozen eggs and a dozen rolls.* ❑ *PLURAL* **doz·ens** or (after a number) **doz·en.**

Dr., an abbreviation of **Doctor.**

drab (drab), *ADJECTIVE.* dull; not interesting: *The smoky mining town was full of drab houses.*
  ❑ *ADJECTIVE* **drab·ber, drab·best. —drab′ness,** *NOUN.*

draft (draft),
  1 *NOUN.* an unwanted current of air: *Close the window; there is a draft.*
  2 *NOUN.* a rough copy, plan, or sketch: *She made two different drafts of her book report before she handed it in in final form.*
  3 *VERB.* to write out a rough copy, plan, or sketch of something: *We drafted a new set of rules.*
  4 *NOUN.* the selection of people for a special purpose. Men needed as soldiers are sometimes supplied to the army by draft.
  5 *VERB.* to select someone for some special purpose: *If no one volunteers, I will draft someone for the job.*
  ❑ *VERB* **drafts, draft·ed, draft·ing.**

draft·y (draf′tē), *ADJECTIVE.* having unwanted currents of air: *The room was drafty, so I closed the window.* ❑ *ADJECTIVE* **draft·i·er, draft·i·est.**

drag (drag),
  1 *VERB.* to pull or move something along heavily or slowly; pull along the ground: *A team of horses dragged the big log out of the forest.* ∎ See the Synonym Study at **pull.**
  2 *VERB.* to trail along the ground: *The little girl's blanket dragged behind her as she walked.*
  3 *VERB.* to go too slowly: *Time drags when you are bored.*
  4 *VERB.* to pull nets or hooks over or along for some purpose: *They dragged the bay for oysters.*
  5 *NOUN.* (informal) a boring person or situation: *You're a real drag; you never want to have any fun.*
  ❑ *VERB* **drags, dragged, drag·ging.**

drag·on (drag′ən), *NOUN.* a huge, fierce animal in old stories, supposed to look like a winged lizard with scales and claws, and often supposed to breathe out fire and smoke.

drag·on·fly (drag′ən flī′), *NOUN.* a large, harmless insect with a long, slender body and two pairs of long wings. It flies about very rapidly to catch flies, mosquitoes, and other insects. ❑ *PLURAL* **drag·on·flies.**

There are more than 4,000 kinds of **dragonfies.**

drain (drān),
 1 *VERB.* to draw off or flow off slowly: *The water drains into the river.*
 2 *VERB.* to draw water or other liquid from something; empty or dry out by draining: *The farmers drained the swamps to get more land for crops. Set the dishes here to drain.*
 3 *NOUN.* a channel or pipe for carrying off water or waste of any kind: *The bathtub drain was clogged.*
 4 *VERB.* to use up little by little: *The long war drained both nations of food, fuel, and other resources.*
 5 *NOUN.* the process of using up little by little: *A long illness can be a drain on your strength.*
 ❑ *VERB* **drains, drained, drain·ing.**

drain·age (drā′nij), *NOUN.* the action or process of drawing off water: *The drainage of swamps improved the land near the river.*

drake (drāk), *NOUN.* a male duck.

dra·ma (drä′mə or dram′ə), *NOUN.*
 1 a play with a serious theme, usually presented in a theater; a story written to be performed by actors.
 2 the art of writing and producing plays: *He is studying drama.*
 3 a movie with a serious story or theme.
 4 a part of real life that seems to have been planned like a story: *The history of the United States is a great and thrilling drama.*
 ❑ *PLURAL* **dra·mas.**

dra·mat·ic (drə mat′ik), *ADJECTIVE.* exciting; full of action or feeling: *The runner scored a dramatic win in a close race.* —**dra·mat′i·cal·ly,** *ADVERB.*

dram·a·tist (dram′ə tist), *NOUN.* someone who writes plays.

dram·a·tize (dram′ə tīz), *VERB.*
 1 to arrange or present in the form of a play: *The children dramatized the story of Rip Van Winkle.*
 2 to make something seem exciting and thrilling: *The speaker dramatized her story with her hands and voice.*
 ❑ *VERB* **dram·a·tiz·es, dram·a·tized, dram·a·tiz·ing.** —**dram′a·ti·za′tion,** *NOUN.*

drank (drangk), *VERB.* the past tense of **drink**: *I drank four glasses of milk yesterday.*

drape (drāp),
 1 *VERB.* to cover or hang something with cloth falling loosely in folds, especially as a decoration: *The buildings were draped with red, white, and blue cloth.*
 2 *VERB.* to arrange something so that it hangs loosely in folds: *I draped the cape around my shoulders.*
 3 *NOUN.* **drapes,** cloth hung in folds: *There are drapes on the large windows in the living room.*
 ❑ *VERB* **drapes, draped, drap·ing.**

dras·tic (dras′tik), *ADJECTIVE.* extreme; very forceful or severe: *During the drought the city took the drastic step of turning the water off at certain times.* —**dras′ti·cal·ly,** *ADVERB.*

draw (drȯ),
 1 *VERB.* to make a picture or likeness of anything with pen, pencil, or chalk: *Draw a circle.*
 2 *VERB.* to attract: *A parade always draws crowds.*
 3 *VERB.* to move; come: *The car drew near.*
 4 *VERB.* to cause something to move by pulling it; drag; haul: *The horses drew the wagon.*
 5 *VERB.* to pull something out; cause to come out: *She drew her gun from its holster.*
 6 *NOUN.* the action of pulling something out: *The sheriff was quick on the draw and shot the villain.*
 7 *VERB.* to breathe in; inhale: *Draw a deep breath.*
 8 *VERB.* to bring about as a response to something: *Their performance drew cheers from the audience.*
 9 *NOUN.* a game in which both teams score the same number of runs, points, and so on; tie.
 ❑ *VERB* **draws, drew, drawn, draw·ing.**

draw out, *IDIOM.* to make long or longer: *His speech was too drawn out.*

draw·back (drȯ′bak′), *NOUN.* anything that makes a situation or experience less complete or satisfying: *Constant rain was the only drawback on our trip.*

draw·bridge (drȯ′brij′), *NOUN.* a bridge that can be entirely or partly lifted, lowered, or moved to one side. In castles, drawbridges were lifted to keep out enemies. A drawbridge over a river is raised to let boats pass underneath.

a raised **drawbridge**

drawer (drȯr), *NOUN.* a box with handles, built to slide in and out of a table, desk, or bureau.

draw·ing (drȯ′ing), *NOUN.*
 1 a picture, sketch, plan, or design done with pen, pencil, or crayon.
 2 the act or process of making such a sketch, plan, or design: *She is good at drawing and painting.*

a	hat	ė	term	ô	order	ch	child		a in about
ā	age	i	it	oi	oil	ng	long		e in taken
ä	far	ī	ice	ou	out	sh	she	ə{	i in pencil
â	care	o	hot	u	cup	th	thin		o in lemon
e	let	ō	open	u̇	put	ŦH	then		u in circus
ē	equal	ȯ	saw	ü	rule	zh	measure		

drawl (drȯl),
1 *VERB.* to talk in a slow way, drawing out the vowels.
2 *NOUN.* the speech of someone who talks this way.
❏ *VERB* **drawls, drawled, drawl•ing.**

drawn (drȯn), *VERB.* the past participle of **draw:** *That old horse has drawn many loads.*

draw•string (drȯ′string′), *NOUN.* a string or cord threaded through the folded edge of a bag, jacket, and so on, so that it can be opened or closed.

dread (dred),
1 *VERB.* to fear greatly what is to come: *My dog dreads his weekly bath.*
2 *NOUN.* fear, especially fear of something that will happen, or may happen: *They lived in dread of another great earthquake.*
3 *ADJECTIVE.* causing great fear; frightening: *AIDS is a dread disease.*
❏ *VERB* **dreads, dread•ed, dread•ing.**

dread•ful (dred′fəl), *ADJECTIVE.*
1 causing dread; terrible; fearful: *The fairy tale was about a dreadful dragon.*
2 very bad; very unpleasant: *I have a dreadful cold.*
−**dread′ful•ly,** *ADVERB.*

dream (drēm),
1 *NOUN.* thoughts, feelings, and mental images during sleep: *I had a bad dream last night.*
2 *NOUN.* something like a dream; daydream; wish: *Sometimes I sit at my desk and have dreams of becoming a famous scientist.*
3 *VERB.* to think, feel, hear, or see during sleep; have dreams: *The little boy dreamed that he was flying.*
4 *VERB.* to imagine; think of as possible: *The sky was so clear that I never dreamed it would rain.*
❏ *VERB* **dreams, dreamed** or **dreamt, dream•ing.**
−**dream′er,** *NOUN.* −**dream′less,** *ADJECTIVE.*
−**dream′like′,** *ADJECTIVE.*

Word Story

Dream may come from an old English word meaning "joy" or "music." Clearly, people had good dreams then! We still call something wonderful "a dream."

dreamt (dremt), *VERB.*
1 a past tense of **dream:** *She dreamt of flying.*
2 a past participle of **dream:** *I have always dreamt of meeting the President.*

dream•y (drē′mē), *ADJECTIVE.*
1 like a dream; vague; dim: *His vacation at the seashore soon became just a dreamy memory.*
2 fond of daydreaming: *She is a dreamy person.*
❏ *ADJECTIVE* **dream•i•er, dream•i•est.**

drear•y (drir′ē), *ADJECTIVE.* dull; depressing; gloomy: *A cold, rainy day is dreary.* ❏ *ADJECTIVE* **drear•i•er, drear•i•est.** −**drear′i•ness,** *NOUN.*

dredge (drej),
1 *NOUN.* a machine with a scoop or a suction pipe for cleaning out or deepening a harbor or channel.
2 *VERB.* to clean out or deepen a harbor or channel with a dredge. ❏ *VERB* **dredg•es, dredged, dredg•ing.**

dregs (dregz), *NOUN PLURAL.* any small bits that settle to the bottom of a liquid: *I rinsed the dregs out of my cup.*

drench (drench), *VERB.* to wet something thoroughly; soak: *A heavy rain drenched the campers.* ■ See the Synonym Study at **wet.** ❏ *VERB* **drench•es, drenched, drench•ing.**

dress (dres),
1 *NOUN.* a piece of clothing worn by women and girls. A dress is a top and skirt made as one piece or sewed together.
2 *NOUN.* clothes; clothing: *They went to the dance in formal dress.*
3 *VERB.* to put clothes on someone: *Please dress the baby.*
4 *VERB.* to wear clothes properly and attractively: *Some people don't know how to dress.*
5 *VERB.* to comb, brush, and arrange hair.
6 *VERB.* to put medicine or bandages on a wound or sore.
❏ *PLURAL* **dress•es;** *VERB* **dress•es, dressed, dress•ing.**

dress up, *IDIOM.*
1 to put on your best clothes: *They dressed up for the party.*
2 to put on a costume or unusual clothes: *I dressed up like a pirate for Halloween.*

dress•er (dres′ər), *NOUN.* a piece of furniture with drawers for clothes; bureau.

dress•ing (dres′ing), *NOUN.*
1 a sauce for salads or other foods.
2 a mixture of bread crumbs and seasoning used to stuff chickens or turkeys.
3 a medicine or a bandage, put on a wound or sore.

drew (drü), *VERB.* the past tense of **draw:** *She drew a picture of her home.*

drib•ble (drib′əl),
1 *VERB.* to flow or let flow in drops or small amounts; trickle: *Gasoline dribbled from the nozzle.*
2 *NOUN.* a drop; trickle: *There's a dribble of milk running down your chin.*
3 *VERB.* to move a ball along by bouncing it or giving it short kicks: *to dribble a basketball or soccer ball.*
❏ *VERB* **drib•bles, drib•bled, drib•bling.**

dried (drīd), *VERB.*
1 the past tense of **dry:** *I dried my hands.*
2 the past participle of **dry:** *I have already dried the dishes.*

dri•er (drī′ər), *ADJECTIVE.* more dry: *This towel is drier than that one.* ■ Another word that sounds like this is **dryer.**

dries (drīz), *VERB.* a present tense of **dry:** *Dad usually dries the dishes.*

dri·est (drī′ist), ADJECTIVE. most dry: *Which is the driest towel?*

drift (drift),
1 VERB. to carry or be carried along by currents of air or water: *A raft drifts if it is not steered.*
2 NOUN. the movement caused by currents of air or water: *the drift of an iceberg.*
3 VERB. to go along without knowing or caring where you are going: *Some people have a purpose in life, but others just drift.*
4 VERB. to pile up or be piled up by the wind: *The wind is so strong that it's drifting the snow.*
5 NOUN. snow or sand heaped up by the wind: *After the heavy snow there were deep drifts in the yard.*
❑ VERB **drifts, drift·ed, drift·ing. —drift′er,** NOUN.

drift·wood (drift′wůd′), NOUN. wood floating in the water or that has washed ashore.

driftwood on a beach

drill (dril),
1 NOUN. a tool or machine for boring holes.
2 VERB. to bore a hole with a drill; use a drill: *Several wells were drilled before oil was found.*
3 VERB. to teach by having the learner practice something over and over: *The sergeant drilled the new recruits.*
4 NOUN. the process of teaching or training by having the students practice something over and over: *The class had plenty of drill in arithmetic.*
❑ VERB **drills, drilled, drill·ing. —drill′er,** NOUN.

drink (dringk),
1 VERB. to swallow anything liquid, such as water or milk: *A person must drink water to stay alive.*
2 NOUN. a liquid that you swallow: *Water is a good drink when you are thirsty.*
3 NOUN. a portion of a liquid: *May I have a drink of milk?*
4 VERB. to suck up; absorb: *The dry soil drank up the rain.*
5 NOUN. alcoholic liquor.
6 VERB. to drink alcoholic liquor: *It's against the law to drink and drive.*
❑ VERB **drinks, drank, drunk, drink·ing.**
—drink′a·ble, ADJECTIVE. **—drink′er,** NOUN.

drip (drip),
1 VERB. to fall or let fall in drops: *Rain drips from an umbrella.*
2 NOUN. the action of falling in drops: *The drip of water from a leaking faucet annoys me.*
3 VERB. to be so wet that drops fall: *After exercising, my forehead was dripping with sweat.*
❑ VERB **drips, dripped, drip·ping.**

drive (drīv),
1 VERB. to control the movement of a car or other vehicle: *Are you old enough to drive?*
2 VERB. to go or carry in a car or other vehicle: *We want to drive through the mountains on the way home.*
3 NOUN. a trip in a car or other vehicle: *On Sunday we took a drive in the country.*
4 NOUN. a road: *We went along the drive that follows the seashore.*
5 VERB. to force someone or something to go somewhere: *Drive the dog away.*
6 VERB. to supply the power that makes a machine or vehicle go: *Steam used to drive most locomotives.*
7 NOUN. a strong force; push; pressure: *She has enough drive to succeed.*
8 VERB. to force someone into a certain condition: *Mosquitoes drove us crazy at the park.*
9 VERB. to force something into: *She drove several nails into the board.*
10 NOUN. an organized effort to do something: *The town held a drive to get money for charity.*
11 VERB. to force someone to work hard: *The workers said that their boss drove them too hard.*
12 in sports: **a** VERB. to hit a ball or opposing player very hard: *He drove the golf ball over 300 yards.* **b** NOUN. a very hard hit: *The batter's drive went into deep left field.* **c** NOUN. a series of plays that moves the ball, puck, and so on, toward the goal: *Our determined drive resulted in a touchdown.*
13 NOUN. See **disk drive.**
❑ VERB **drives, drove, driv·en, driv·ing.**

drive-in (drīv′in′), NOUN. a restaurant, bank, or movie arranged and equipped so that customers may drive in and be served or entertained while staying in their cars.

driv·en (driv′ən), VERB. the past participle of **drive:** *Mom has just driven to work.*

driv·er (drī′vər), NOUN.
1 someone who drives a car or other vehicle.
2 a golf club used to hit the ball from the tee.

drive·way (drīv′wā′), NOUN. a private road leading from a house or garage to the street.

a	hat	ė	term	ô	order	ch	child		a in about
ā	age	i	it	oi	oil	ng	long		e in taken
ä	far	ī	ice	ou	out	sh	she	ə { i in pencil
â	care	o	hot	u	cup	th	thin		o in lemon
e	let	ō	open	ů	put	ᴛʜ	then		u in circus
ē	equal	ò	saw	ü	rule	zh	measure		

driz·zle (driz′əl),
1 *VERB.* to rain gently, in very small drops like mist.
2 *NOUN.* very small drops of rain like mist.
□ *VERB* **driz·zles, driz·zled, driz·zling.**

drom·e·dar·y (drom′ə der′ē), *NOUN.* a camel with one hump, used as a beast of burden in Arabia and northern Africa. □ *PLURAL* **drom·e·dar·ies.**

Word Story

Dromedary comes from a Greek word meaning "running." Dromedaries that have been bred for racing may reach speeds of 40 miles per hour.

dromedary — 6 to 7 feet high at the shoulder

drone (drōn),
1 *NOUN.* a male bee that fertilizes the queen. Drones have no stings, and do no work.
2 *VERB.* to make a deep, continuous humming sound: *Bees droned among the flowers.*
3 *NOUN.* a deep, continuous humming sound: *the drone of machinery, the drone of mosquitoes.*
4 *VERB.* to talk or speak in a dull, monotonous voice: *We almost fell asleep as the speaker droned on.*
□ *VERB* **drones, droned, dron·ing.**

drool (drül), *VERB.* to let saliva run from the mouth as a baby does. □ *VERB* **drools, drooled, drool·ing.**

droop (drüp), *VERB.*
1 to hang down; bend down: *Flowers soon droop if they are not put in water.*
2 to become weak, tired, or discouraged; lose strength and energy: *The children were drooping by the end of their walk in the hot sun.*
□ *VERB* **droops, drooped, droop·ing.**

drop (drop),
1 *VERB.* to fall or let fall, especially suddenly: *The acrobat dropped from the high rope into the net below. The price of sugar may drop soon.*
2 *NOUN.* a sudden fall: *a drop in temperature.*
3 *NOUN.* the distance down; length of a fall: *From the top of the cliff to the water is a drop of 200 feet.*
4 *NOUN.* a small amount of liquid in a round shape: *a drop of rain, a drop of blood.*

5 *NOUN.* a small amount of something shaped like a drop: *a cough drop.*
6 *NOUN.* **drops,** liquid medicine given in drops: *eye drops, nose drops.*
7 *VERB.* to fall or let fall in very small amounts; drip: *Rain dropped from the trees.*
8 *VERB.* to let go; dismiss: *Members who do not pay their dues will be dropped from the club.*
9 *VERB.* to leave out; omit: *Drop the "e" in "drive" before adding "ing."*
10 *VERB.* to stop thinking or talking about something: *The question is not important; let it drop.*
11 *VERB.* to send: *Drop me a note from camp.*
□ *VERB* **drops, dropped, drop·ping.**

drop in, *IDIOM.* to visit informally: *Drop in and see me tomorrow.*

drop off, *IDIOM.*
1 to deliver someone or something: *Drop me off at the next corner, please.*
2 to go to sleep: *I dropped off soon after going to bed.*

drop out, *IDIOM.* to leave school before completing a course or term.

drop·let (drop′lit), *NOUN.* a tiny drop.

drop·per (drop′ər), *NOUN.* a narrow glass or plastic tube open at one end with a hollow rubber cap at the other end. It is used to put drops of liquid into the eyes, nose, or throat.

drought (drout), *NOUN.* a long period of dry weather.

drove¹ (drōv), *VERB.* the past tense of **drive:** *We drove two hundred miles today.*

drove² (drōv), *NOUN.*
1 a group of cattle, sheep, or hogs moving or driven along together; herd; flock: *The rancher shipped a drove of cattle to market.*
2 usually, **droves,** many people moving along together; crowd: *People rushed to the main square in droves.*

drown (droun), *VERB.* to die or cause to die under water or other liquid because of lack of air to breathe: *We almost drowned when our boat overturned. The flood drowned many cattle in the lowlands.* □ *VERB* **drowns, drowned, drown·ing.**

drown out, *IDIOM.* to keep another sound from being heard by being louder than it: *The traffic's noise drowned out my mother's voice.*

drow·sy (drou′zē), *ADJECTIVE.* sleepy; half asleep: *Sitting at my desk after a big lunch, I began to feel drowsy.* □ *ADJECTIVE* **drow·si·er, drow·si·est.** —**drow′si·ness,** *NOUN.*

drudg·er·y (druj′ər ē), *NOUN.* any work that is hard, uninteresting, or disagreeable: *I think that washing dishes is drudgery.*

drug (drug),
1 *NOUN.* a substance used to prevent, treat, or cure disease or pain. Penicillin and aspirin are drugs.

2 *NOUN.* a substance taken for its effect and not for medical reasons. Drugs like cocaine and alcohol speed up or slow down the activity of the body or affect the senses.

3 *VERB.* to give drugs to someone, often drugs that are harmful or cause sleep: *The spy drugged the guard and then stole the secret code.*
 ❑ *VERB* **drugs, drugged, drug·ging.**

drug·gist (drug′ist), *NOUN.* (earlier) a pharmacist.

drug·store (drug′stôr′), *NOUN.* a store that sells drugs and other medicines and often such things as soft drinks, cosmetics, and magazines.

drum (drum),

1 *NOUN.* a musical instrument that makes a sound when you beat it. A drum is hollow with a cover stretched tight over the ends.

2 *VERB.* to play the drum: *My sister drums in a rock band*

3 *VERB.* to beat, tap, or strike again and again: *Stop drumming on the table with your fingers; it's very annoying.*

4 *NOUN.* a barrel or container shaped something like a drum: *an oil drum.*
 ❑ *VERB* **drums, drummed, drum·ming.**
 −drum′mer, *NOUN.*

dry (drī),

1 *ADJECTIVE.* not wet; not moist: *Dust is dry. The paint is dry now.*

2 *VERB.* to make or become dry: *We washed and dried the dishes after dinner. Clothes dry in the sun.*

3 *ADJECTIVE.* having little rain: *Arizona has a dry climate.*

4 *ADJECTIVE.* empty of water or other liquid: *That pond is dry in the summer.*

5 *ADJECTIVE.* thirsty; wanting a drink: *I am very dry after that hike.*

6 *ADJECTIVE.* not under, in, or on water: *He was glad to be on dry land and away from the swamp.*
 ❑ *ADJECTIVE* **dri·er, dri·est;** *VERB* **dries, dried, dry·ing.**
 −dry′ly, *ADVERB.* **−dry′ness,** *NOUN.*

dry cell, a small battery in which the chemicals producing the electric current are made into a paste. A flashlight battery is a dry cell.

dry-clean (drī′klēn′), *VERB.* to clean clothes or fabrics with a chemical cleaning fluid instead of water. Silk, wool, and rayon are often dry-cleaned.
 ❑ *VERB* **dry-cleans, dry-cleaned, dry-clean·ing.**
 −dry cleaner. −dry cleaning.

dry·er (drī′ər), *NOUN.* a machine that removes water by heat or air: *a clothes dryer, a hair dryer.*
 ■ Another word that sounds like this is **drier.**

drums from many lands: (a) Kenya, (b) China, (c) Alaska, (d) Italy

drum major, a man who leads a marching band, often twirling a baton.

drum ma·jor·ette (drum′ mā′jə ret′), a girl or woman who leads parades, twirling a baton.

drum·stick (drum′stik′), *NOUN.*

1 a stick for beating a drum.

2 the lower half of the leg of a cooked chicken or turkey.

drunk (drungk),

1 *ADJECTIVE.* having had too many alcoholic drinks; intoxicated. People who are drunk have trouble speaking, thinking, or acting normally.

2 *NOUN.* someone who often drinks too much alcoholic liquor.

3 *VERB.* the past participle of **drink:** *He has drunk several glasses of milk already.*

du·al (dü′əl), *ADJECTIVE.* made of two parts; double: *The airplane had dual controls, one set for the learner and one for the teacher.* ■ Another word that sounds like this is **duel.**

du·bi·ous (dü′bē əs), *ADJECTIVE.* doubtful; uncertain: *Our picnic tomorrow is looking dubious because of the weather.* **−du′bi·ous·ly,** *ADVERB.*

duch·ess (duch′is), *NOUN.*

1 the wife or widow of a duke.

2 a woman who has a rank equal to that of a duke.
 ❑ *PLURAL* **duch·ess·es.**

a	hat	ė	term	ô	order	ch	child		a in about
ā	age	i	it	oi	oil	ng	long		e in taken
ä	far	ī	ice	ou	out	sh	she	ə	i in pencil
â	care	o	hot	u	cup	th	thin		o in lemon
e	let	ō	open	ù	put	ŦH	then		u in circus
ē	equal	ò	saw	ü	rule	zh	measure		

duck¹ (duk), *NOUN.*
1 a wild or tame swimming bird with a flat bill, short neck, short legs, and webbed feet.
2 a female duck. The male is called a drake.

duck² (duk), *VERB.*
1 to lower your head or bend your body quickly to keep from being hit or seen: *She ducked to avoid a low branch.*
2 to push someone's head or body suddenly under water and out again; dunk: *The children in the pool were ducking each other.*
3 to get or keep away from; avoid; dodge: *He ducked the blow. She ducked my question.*
❑ *VERB* **ducks, ducked, duck·ing.**

duck·billed plat·y·pus (duk′bild′ plat′ə pəs), *NOUN.* See **platypus.**

duck·ling (duk′ling), *NOUN.* a young duck.

duct (dukt), *NOUN.*
1 a tube, pipe, or channel that air or liquid flows through.
2 a tube in the body that a bodily fluid flows through: *tear ducts.*

dud (dud), *NOUN.*
1 a shell or bomb that fails to explode.
2 a failure: *The new movie was a complete dud.*

due (dü),
1 *ADJECTIVE.* owed as a debt; to be paid as a right: *The money due her for her work was paid today. Respect is due to older people.*
2 *NOUN.* what someone has a right to: *Courtesy is his due while he is your guest.*
3 *NOUN.* **dues,** the amount of money it costs to be a member of a club; a fee or tax for some purpose: *Members who do not pay dues will be suspended from the club.*
4 *ADJECTIVE.* promised to come or be ready; expected: *Your report is due tomorrow.*
5 *ADVERB.* straight; directly: *The ship sailed due west.* ▪ Other words that sound like this are **dew** and **do¹.**

due to, *IDIOM.*
1 caused by: *The accident was due to the bad fog.*
2 (informal) because of: *The game was called off due to rain.*

du·el (dü′əl),
1 *NOUN.* a formal fight between two people armed with pistols or swords. Duels were fought to settle quarrels or avenge insults. They took place in the presence of two witnesses.
2 *NOUN.* any fight or contest between two opponents: *The last game of the season was a duel between two very good teams.*

duck¹ — about 18 inches long

3 *VERB.* to fight a duel: *The two rivals dueled at dawn.*
❑ *VERB* **du·els, du·eled, du·el·ing.** ▪ Another word that sounds like this is **dual. –du′el·er,** *NOUN.*

du·et (dü et′), *NOUN.*
1 a piece of music for two voices or instruments.
2 two singers or players performing together.

dug (dug), *VERB.*
1 the past tense of **dig:** *The dog dug a hole in the yard.*
2 the past participle of **dig:** *I have dug the potatoes.*

dug·out (dug′out′), *NOUN.*
1 a boat made by hollowing out a large log.
2 a small shelter at the side of a baseball field, used by players not on the field.
3 a rough shelter or dwelling formed by digging into the side of a hill or trench.

duke (dük), *NOUN.* a nobleman ranking just below a prince.

dull (dul),
1 *ADJECTIVE.* not interesting; boring: *a dull book.*
2 *ADJECTIVE.* not sharp or pointed: *a dull knife.*
3 *ADJECTIVE.* not bright or clear: *a dull color, a dull, overcast sky.*
4 *ADJECTIVE.* slow in understanding; not learning easily: *a dull mind. A dull person often fails to get the joke.*
5 *ADJECTIVE.* not felt sharply: *the dull pain of a bruise.*
6 *VERB.* to make or become dull: *Chopping wood dulled the blade of the ax.*
❑ *VERB* **dulls, dulled, dull·ing. –dull′ness,** *NOUN.* **–dul′ly,** *ADVERB.*

Synonym Study

Dull means not interesting: *She told a dull story in which nothing happened.*

Uninteresting means too common and ordinary to hold your interest: *With only three players, the game was pretty uninteresting.*

Boring means so dull that it makes you unhappy: *When something is boring, five minutes can seem like half an hour.*

Monotonous means boring and always the same: *The scenery was monotonous when we drove across the empty prairie.*

ANTONYMS: interesting, fascinating.

dumb (dum), *ADJECTIVE.*
1 not able to speak: *Even intelligent animals are dumb.*
2 unwilling to speak; silent; not speaking.
3 not intelligent; silly: *Forgetting your homework is a dumb thing to do.*

Usage Note

Dumb is not used by careful writers and speakers today to mean "unable to speak," because the word's other meanings have made it sound unfriendly.

dumb·bell (dum′bel′), *NOUN.* a short bar of wood or iron with large, heavy, round ends. Dumbbells are often used in pairs and are lifted or swung around to exercise the muscles of the arms or back.

dum·my (dum′ē),
1 *NOUN.* a life-size model of a person used to display clothing in store windows.
2 *NOUN.* (informal) a foolish person.
3 *ADJECTIVE.* made to look like the real thing; imitation: *We had a fight with dummy swords made of wood.*
❑ *PLURAL* **dum·mies.**

dump (dump),
1 *VERB.* to empty something out; throw down in a pile: *The truck dumped the gravel in the yard.*
2 *NOUN.* a place for throwing trash: *Garbage is taken to the city dump.*
3 *VERB.* to throw something away that you don't want anymore: *We dumped some soggy newspapers in the trash bin.*
❑ *VERB* **dumps, dumped, dump·ing.**

Have You Heard?

You may have heard someone say that they are "down in the dumps." This means they are very sad and depressed.

dump·ling (dump′ling), *NOUN.* a rounded piece of dough, boiled or steamed, often served with meat.

dunce (duns), *NOUN.* a very foolish, ignorant person or one who is not willing to learn.

dune (dün), *NOUN.* a mound or ridge of sand piled up by the wind.

dunes in the Sahara desert

dun·ga·ree (dung′gə rē′), *NOUN.*
1 a coarse cotton cloth, used for work clothes.
2 **dungarees,** trousers or clothing made of this cloth.

dun·geon (dun′jən), *NOUN.* (earlier) a dark underground room or cell to keep prisoners in.

dunk (dungk),
1 *VERB.* to dip food into a liquid: *She likes to dunk doughnuts in coffee.*

2 in basketball: **a** *VERB.* to throw the ball down through the basket from above the rim. **b** *NOUN.* a shot made in this way: *He had seven dunks in one game.*
❑ *VERB* **dunks, dunked, dunk·ing.**

du·pli·cate (dü′plə kit *for adjective and noun;* dü′plə kāt *for verb*),
1 *ADJECTIVE.* exactly like something else: *We have duplicate keys for the front door.*
2 *NOUN.* one of two things that are exactly alike; exact copy: *He mailed the letter, but kept a duplicate.*
3 *VERB.* to make an exact copy of something: *Duplicate the picture so that we can both have copies of it.*
❑ *VERB* **du·pli·cates, du·pli·cat·ed, du·pli·cat·ing.**

du·pli·ca·tion (dü′plə kā′shən), *NOUN.* the act of duplicating or the condition of being duplicated: *Duplication of effort is a waste of time.*

dur·a·ble (dùr′ə bel), *ADJECTIVE.* able to last a long time even if used or worn a lot: *Work clothes are made of durable fabric.* **–dur′a·bil′i·ty,** *NOUN.*

Du·ran·go (dù rang′gō), *NOUN.* a state in northwestern Mexico.

du·ra·tion (dù rā′shən), *NOUN.* the time that something lasts: *The storm was sudden and of short duration.*

dur·ing (dùr′ing), *PREPOSITION.*
1 through the time of: *We played inside during the storm.*
2 at some time in; in the course of: *Come to see me during my office hours.*

dusk (dusk), *NOUN.* the time just before dark: *We saw the evening star at dusk.*

a cloudy sky at **dusk**

dust (dust),
1 *NOUN.* fine, dry, powdery earth: *Dust lay thick on the road.*

a	hat	ė	term	ô	order	ch	child	⎧ a in about
ā	age	i	it	oi	oil	ng	long	⎪ e in taken
ä	far	ī	ice	ou	out	sh	she	ə⎨ i in pencil
â	care	o	hot	u	cup	th	thin	⎪ o in lemon
e	let	ō	open	ù	put	ŦH	then	⎩ u in circus
ē	equal	ò	saw	ü	rule	zh	measure	

2 *NOUN.* tiny particles of dirt and fluff that collect on floors, furniture, and so on: *The old books were covered with dust.*

3 *VERB.* to brush or wipe the dust from something: *I dusted the furniture.*

❑ *VERB* **dusts, dust·ed, dust·ing.**

dust·y (dus′tē), *ADJECTIVE.* covered or filled with dust: *I found some dusty old books in the attic.*

❑ *ADJECTIVE* **dust·i·er, dust·i·est. –dust′i·ness,** *NOUN.*

Dutch (duch),

1 *ADJECTIVE.* of or about the Netherlands, its people, or their language.

2 *NOUN PLURAL.* **the Dutch,** the people of the Netherlands.

3 *NOUN.* the language spoken by the Dutch.

Word Source

Dutch is the official language of the Netherlands. The following words have come into English from Dutch:

boss	dock	pickle	slim
cookie	easel	skate¹	spook
cruise	gruff	sled	spool
deck	iceberg	sleigh	

du·ti·ful (dü′tə fəl), *ADJECTIVE.* doing everything that you are supposed to do; obedient: *Dutiful children always help their parents.* **–du′ti·ful·ly,** *ADVERB.*

du·ty (dü′tē), *NOUN.*

1 the thing that is right and proper to do; what you ought to do: *It is your duty to obey the laws.*

2 the thing that you must do in your work: *Her duties at the post office are to sort and weigh packages.*

3 a tax, especially on articles brought into a country: *There is a duty on perfume brought into the United States.*

❑ *PLURAL* **du·ties.**

on duty, *IDIOM.* working at your job or position.

dwarf (dwôrf),

1 *NOUN.* a person, animal, or plant that is much smaller than the usual size for its kind.

2 *NOUN.* (in fairy tales) an ugly little man who often has magic power.

3 *VERB.* to cause something to seem smaller; tower over: *A tall oak dwarfed all the other trees on the block.*

❑ *PLURAL* **dwarfs** or **dwarves** (dwôrvz); *VERB* **dwarfs, dwarfed, dwarf·ing.**

dwell (dwel), *VERB.* to live in; make your home in: *They dwell in the country but work in the city.*

■ See the Synonym Study at **live.** ❑ *VERB* **dwells, dwelt** or **dwelled, dwell·ing. –dwell′er,** *NOUN.*

dwell on, *IDIOM.* to think, speak, or write about something for a long time: *I try not to dwell on my problems.*

dwell·ing (dwel′ing), *NOUN.* the place in which someone lives.

dwelt (dwelt), *VERB.*

1 a past tense of **dwell:** *We dwelt there for a long time.*

2 a past participle of **dwell:** *We have dwelt in the country for years.*

dwin·dle (dwin′dl), *VERB.* to become smaller and smaller; shrink: *During the blizzard the campers' supply of food dwindled day by day.* ❑ *VERB* **dwin·dles, dwin·dled, dwin·dling.**

dye (dī),

1 *NOUN.* something that can be mixed with water and used to color cloth, hair, and other things.

2 *VERB.* to color or stain permanently: *I dyed my shirt red.* ❑ *VERB* **dyes, dyed, dye·ing.** ■ Another word that sounds like this is **die. –dy′er,** *NOUN.*

dy·ing (dī′ing), *ADJECTIVE.*

1 about to die; near death: *a dying old man.*

2 coming to an end: *the dying year.*

dy·nam·ic (dī nam′ik), *ADJECTIVE.* very active; having a lot of energy: *a dynamic leader.*

dy·na·mite (dī′nə mit),

1 *NOUN.* a powerful explosive most commonly used in blasting rocks or tree stumps, and in building tunnels.

2 *VERB.* to blow something up with dynamite.

❑ *VERB* **dy·na·mites, dy·na·mit·ed, dy·na·mit·ing.**

Word Story

Dynamite comes from a Greek word meaning "power." The word was made up by Alfred Nobel, the Swedish chemist who invented this explosive.

dy·na·mo (dī′nə mō), *NOUN.* a machine that makes electricity; generator. ❑ *PLURAL* **dy·na·mos.**

dy·nas·ty (dī′nə stē), *NOUN.* a series of rulers who belong to the same family. ❑ *PLURAL* **dy·nas·ties.**

dys·lex·i·a (dis lek′sē ə), *NOUN.* a difficulty in reading because of the brain's difficulty in recognizing different letters. People with dyslexia sometimes see a word's letters in the wrong order.

emperor

E or **e** (ē), *NOUN.* the fifth letter of the English alphabet.
  ❑ *PLURAL* **E's** or **e's.**

E or **E.,**
  1 an abbreviation of **east.**
  2 an abbreviation of **eastern.**

each (ēch),
  1 *ADJECTIVE.* every: *Each child has a desk.*
  2 *PRONOUN.* every one: *Each of the students has a pencil.*
  3 *ADVERB.* for each one; apiece: *These pens are a quarter each.*

each other, each of two persons or things doing something that affect the other: *The two friends saw each other at the playground. The boats hit each other in the fog.*
  ★ **Each other** should be used in speaking or writing about two people: *She and I have known each other since second grade.* **One another** should be used about three or more people: *The triplets are often mistaken for one another.*

ea·ger (ē′gər), *ADJECTIVE.* wanting very much: *We are eager to go to the picnic. He is eager to meet with you about the plans for the new park.* —**ea′ger·ly,** *ADVERB.* —**ea′ger·ness,** *NOUN.*

eager beaver, (informal) someone who is too hard-working, ambitious, or enthusiastic: *We have too many eager beavers who want to work on the school play and not enough for them to do.*

ea·gle (ē′gəl), *NOUN.* a large bird with very good vision and strong sharp claws for hunting. Eagles have large, powerful wings.

ea·gle-eyed (ē′gəl īd′), *ADJECTIVE.*
  1 able to see far and clearly: *He was an eagle-eyed scout so the general sent him on the mission.*
  2 paying close attention to detail: *Our eagle-eyed accountant found the error.*

Eagle Scout, the highest rank that can be achieved in the Boy Scouts.

ea·glet (ē′glit), *NOUN.* a young eagle.

ear¹ (ir), *NOUN.*
1 the organ of the body with which people and animals hear. It has inner and outer parts.
2 the sense of hearing: *Her voice is pleasing to the ear.*
play by ear, *IDIOM.* to be able to play an instrument without needing written notes as a guide.
play it by ear, *IDIOM.* to go ahead with your plans and be ready to change them as other things change.

Have You Heard?

You may have heard someone say that something went **"in one ear and out the other."** This means that the person who heard it did not pay any attention and will not remember what was said.

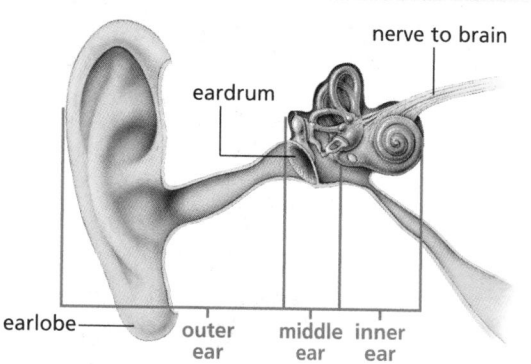

ear¹

ear² (ir), *NOUN.* the part of certain plants, such as corn, on which grains grow.
ear·drum (ir′drum′), *NOUN.* a thin layer of tissue that stretches across the middle ear. It vibrates when sound waves strike it.
earl (érl), *NOUN.* a British nobleman.
ear·lobe (ir′lōb′), *NOUN.* the soft, rounded lower tip of the outer part of the ear.
ear·ly (ér′lē), *ADVERB* or *ADJECTIVE.*
1 in the beginning; in the first part: *The sun is not too hot early in the day.*
2 before the usual time: *We have an early dinner today. Please come early.*
  ❑ *ADJECTIVE* **ear·li·er, ear·li·est.**
ear·muffs (ir′mufs′), *NOUN PLURAL.* a pair of coverings worn over the ears in cold weather to keep them warm.
earn (érn), *VERB.*
1 to get money in return for work or service; be paid: *She earns $175 a week.*
2 to get something that you deserve: *Her hard work earned her the respect of her teachers.*
  ❑ *VERB* **earns, earned, earn·ing.** ▪ Another word that sounds like this is **urn. –earn′er,** *NOUN.*
ear·nest (ér′nist), *ADJECTIVE.* eager and serious about what you are doing: *The earnest pupil tried very hard to do his best.* **–ear′nest·ly,** *ADVERB.*

earn·ings (ér′ningz), *NOUN PLURAL.* money that someone has earned; salary; profits.
ear·phones (ir′fōnz′), *NOUN PLURAL.* two small speakers held against the ears by a curved piece of plastic or metal. Earphones carry sound directly from a radio, portable CD player, and so on.
ear·ring (ir′ring′), *NOUN.* a piece of jewelry worn as an ornament on the ear.
earth (érth), *NOUN.*
1 also, **Earth,** the planet on which we live.
2 the land surface of the earth: *Our environment is made up of the earth, the sea, and the sky.*
3 dirt: *The earth in the garden is soft.*
earth·en (ér′thən), *ADJECTIVE.*
1 made of baked clay: *Earthen jugs were dug up at the site of the ancient town.*
2 made of earth: *The old cabin had an earthen floor.*
earth·ly (érth′lē), *ADJECTIVE.* being or belonging here on earth; not heavenly: *She left all her earthly goods to her niece.*
earth·quake (érth′kwāk′), *NOUN.* a violent shaking or shifting motion of the ground, caused by the sudden movement of rock far beneath the earth's surface.

Did You Know?

Earthquakes are measured using the **Richter scale** (rik′tər skāl′). An earthquake less than 2.0 on this scale can't be felt by people. Each number up on the scale is ten times greater than the number it follows. Thus, a 3.0 earthquake is 10 times stronger than a 2.0 earthquake, and a 4.0 earthquake is 100 times stronger than a 2.0 earthquake. A 5.0 earthquake is 1000 times stronger than a 2.0 earthquake, and so on. Earthquakes that measure more than 7.0 on the Richter scale can cause a huge amount of damage.

This building was destroyed in an **earthquake.**

earth·worm (érth′wérm′), *NOUN.* a long, narrow, reddish brown worm. Earthworms help loosen and enrich the soil.

ease (ēz),
1 *NOUN.* freedom from pain or trouble; comfort: *When school is out, I am going to live a life of ease for a whole week.*
2 *VERB.* to make free from pain or trouble: *Her kind words eased my worried mind.*
3 *VERB.* to move slowly and carefully: *He eased the big box through the narrow door.*
❏ *VERB* **eas·es, eased, eas·ing.**

ea·sel (ē′zəl), *NOUN.* a frame for holding a picture or blackboard.

eas·i·ly (ē′zə lē), *ADVERB.*
1 without trying hard; with little effort: *The simple tasks were easily done.*
2 surely; without question: *He is easily the best player on the field.*

east (ēst),
1 *NOUN.* the direction of the sunrise.
2 *ADVERB.* toward the east; farther toward the east: *Walk east to find the road.*
3 *ADJECTIVE.* coming from the east: *an east wind.*
4 *ADJECTIVE.* in the east: *the east wing of a house.*
5 *NOUN.* **the East, a** the eastern part of the United States; the region from Maine through Maryland. **b** the countries in Asia: *China and Japan are in the East.*
east of, *IDIOM.* further east than: *Ohio is east of Indiana.*

Eas·ter (ē′stər), *NOUN.* the yearly Christian celebration of Christ's rising from the dead. Easter comes on a Sunday between March 22 and April 25.

Word Story

Easter comes from **east.** The old English goddess of the dawn and her holiday were named for the direction where the sun rises. When the Christian celebration replaced this holiday, people kept using the name they were used to.

east·er·ly (ē′stər lē), *ADJECTIVE.*
1 toward the east: *I walked in an easterly direction.*
2 from the east: *An easterly wind was blowing.*

east·ern (ē′stərn), *ADJECTIVE.*
1 toward the east: *There is a camping area at the eastern end of the mountain.*
2 from the east: *eastern tourists.*
3 of or in the east: *eastern schools.*
4 Eastern, a of or in the eastern part of the United States. **b** of or in the countries in Asia.

East Germany, a former country in Europe.

East In·dies (ēst′ in′dēz), the islands off the coast of southeast Asia.

east·ward (ēst′wərd), *ADVERB* or *ADJECTIVE.* toward the east; east: *to walk eastward, an eastward slope.*

east·wards (ēst′wərdz), *ADVERB.* See **eastward.**

eas·y (ē′zē), *ADJECTIVE.*
1 not hard to do or get: *Washing dishes is easy work.*
2 free from pain, difficulty, or worry; pleasant: *The wealthy family led an easy life.* ■ See the Synonym Study at **comfortable.**
3 not strict or harsh: *My teacher is an easy grader.*
❏ *ADJECTIVE* **eas·i·er, eas·i·est. —eas′i·ness,** *NOUN.*

eat (ēt), *VERB.*
1 to chew and swallow food: *Cows eat grass and grain.*
2 to have a meal: *Where shall we eat?*
3 to destroy or wear something away: *Rust ate away part of the car's fender.*
❏ *VERB* **eats, ate, eat·en, eat·ing. —eat′er,** *NOUN.*

Synonym Study

Eat means to put food into the mouth and swallow it: *We ate lunch outside yesterday. He doesn't like to eat soup on hot days.*

Consume can mean to eat or drink up: *Many cases of soda and bags of chips were consumed at the party.*

Dine means to eat dinner: *The truck driver stopped to dine at the Friendly Restaurant.*

Devour means to eat hungrily or greedily: *The hungry lion devoured the meat. He devoured three sandwiches.*

Snack means to eat between meals: *She likes to snack on fruit when she gets home from school.*

Nibble means to eat in small bites: *My little sister is nibbling a cracker.*

Gobble[1] means to eat quickly, in large bites or gulps: *He told them not to gobble their food.*

eat·en (ēt′n), *VERB.* the past participle of **eat:** *Have you eaten yet?*

eaves (ēvz), *NOUN PLURAL.* the lower edge of a roof that extends over the side of a building.

eaves·drop (ēvz′drop′), *VERB.* to listen secretly to someone else's conversation: *He eavesdropped on the two girls in the next room.* ❏ *VERB* **eaves·drops, eaves·dropped, eaves·drop·ping. —eaves′drop·per,** *NOUN.*

Word Story

Eavesdrop was formed from *eavesdropper,* in the earlier meaning "one who stands under the eaves to listen." The image is that of a person pressed up against a house listening to conversation inside.

a	hat	ė	term	ô	order	ch	child	a in about
ā	age	i	it	oi	oil	ng	long	e in taken
ä	far	ī	ice	ou	out	sh	she	i in pencil
â	care	o	hot	u	cup	th	thin	o in lemon
e	let	ō	open	ù	put	ᵀH	then	u in circus
ē	equal	ò	saw	ü	rule	zh	measure	

ebb (eb),
1 NOUN. the flow of the ocean's tide away from the shore.
2 VERB. to flow out: *We waded out as the tide ebbed.*
3 VERB. to grow less or weaker: *Her courage ebbed as she climbed to the high diving board.*
□ VERB **ebbs, ebbed, ebb·ing.**

E·bo·la vi·rus (i bō′lə vir′əs), kind of virus that causes serious or deadly bleeding in human beings. It was identified in 1976 in Africa.

eb·on·y (eb′ə nē), NOUN. a hard, heavy, black wood. Black piano keys are sometimes made of ebony.

ec·cen·tric (ek sen′trik),
1 ADJECTIVE. behaving in an unusual or peculiar way; odd: *Wearing a fur coat summer is eccentric.*
2 NOUN. someone who behaves in an unusual manner.

ec·cen·tric·i·ty (ek′sen tris′ə tē), NOUN.
1 something out of the ordinary; oddity: *It is an eccentricity to carry around an open umbrella on sunny days.*
2 an eccentric condition; being unusual or out of the ordinary: *The clock's eccentricity became noticeable when it struck thirteen.*
□ PLURAL **ec·cen·tric·i·ties.**

ech·o (ek′ō),
1 NOUN. a repeated sound. You hear an echo when a sound you make bounces back from a distant hill or wall so that you hear it again.
2 VERB. to be heard again: *The shot echoed through the valley.*
3 VERB. to say or do what someone else says or does: *Small children sometimes echo their parents' words and actions.*
□ VERB **ech·oes, ech·oed, ech·o·ing;** PLURAL **ech·oes.**

ech·o·lo·ca·tion (ek′ō lō kā′shən), NOUN.
1 a method of locating distant or unseen objects by measuring the time it takes for sound waves echoed off the objects to return to the waves' source.
2 a method used by bats, dolphins, and other animals to locate objects by making high-pitched sounds that echo off the objects.

e·clair or **é·clair** (ā klâr′), NOUN. an oblong piece of pastry filled with whipped cream or custard and covered with icing. □ PLURAL **e·clairs** or **é·clairs.**

e·clipse (i klips′),
1 NOUN. the process of complete or partial blocking of light passing from one object in outer space to another. A **solar eclipse** occurs when the moon passes between the sun and the earth. A **lunar eclipse** occurs when the earth passes between the sun and the moon.
2 VERB. to make dim by comparison; surpass: *He eclipsed his older brother in sports.*
□ VERB **e·clips·es, e·clipsed, e·clips·ing.**

Word Power   eco-

The combining form **eco-** means "environment." **Ecology** is the science of the environment. An **ecosystem** is a physical environment with a community of living things.

ec·o·log·i·cal (ē′kə loj′ə kəl or ek′ə loj′ə kəl), ADJECTIVE. of or about ecology: *ecological studies.*

e·col·o·gy (ē kol′ə jē), NOUN. the science that deals with the relation of living things to their environment and to each other. Ecology is a branch of biology. **—e·col′o·gist,** NOUN.

e·co·nom·ic (ē′kə nom′ik or ek′ə nom′ik), ADJECTIVE. of or about economics: *Growing unemployment caused serious economic problems.*

e·co·nom·i·cal (ē′kə nom′ə kəl or ek′ə nom′ə kəl), ADJECTIVE. avoiding waste; thrifty: *An economical shopper tries to buy things on sale.* **—e′co·nom′i·cal·ly,** ADVERB.

e·co·nom·ics (ē kə nom′iks or ek′ə nom′iks), NOUN. the science that studies how money, goods, and services are produced, distributed, and used.

e·con·o·mize (i kon′ə mīz), VERB. to cut down on expenses; thrifty: *We can economize by turning off lights when we don't need them.* □ VERB **e·con·o·miz·es, e·con·o·mized, e·con·o·miz·ing.**

e·con·o·my (i kon′ə mē), NOUN.
1 the business affairs of a country or area: *Under the new administration, the country's economy improved greatly.*
2 the act or process of making the most of what you have; thrift; the use of something without any waste: *By thinking about economy in buying food, we were able to save enough money for a vacation.*
□ PLURAL **e·con·o·mies.**

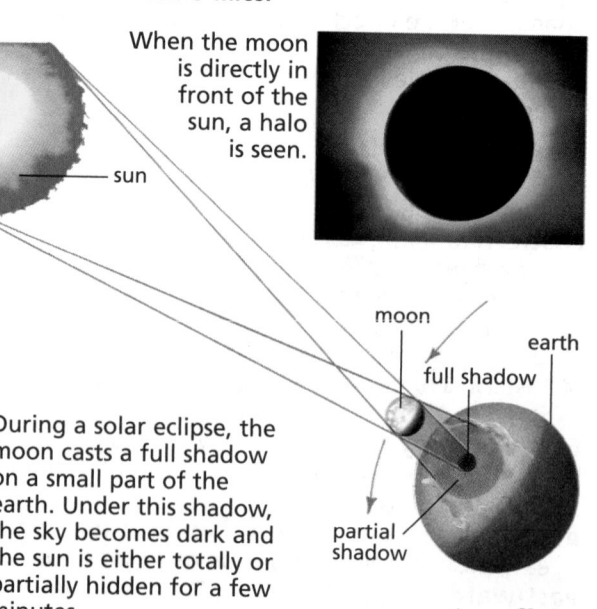

When the moon is directly in front of the sun, a halo is seen.

sun

moon

earth

full shadow

partial shadow

During a solar eclipse, the moon casts a full shadow on a small part of the earth. Under this shadow, the sky becomes dark and the sun is either totally or partially hidden for a few minutes.

a solar **eclipse**

An **ecosystem** is created by many different forms of life.

e·co·sys·tem (ē′kō sis′təm *or* ek′ō sis′təm), *NOUN.* a physical environment with its community of living things, and their relationship with each other. An ecosystem may be a lake, a desert, and so on.

ec·sta·sy (ek′stə sē), *NOUN.* a feeling of very great joy; thrilling or overwhelming delight: *The little girl was speechless with ecstasy over her birthday present.* ❑ *PLURAL* **ec·sta·sies.**

Ec·ua·dor (ek′wə dôr), *NOUN.* a country in northwestern South America. —**Ec′ua·do′ran, Ec′ua·do′re·an,** or **Ec′ua·do′ri·an,** *ADJECTIVE* or *NOUN.*

edge (ej),
1 *NOUN.* the line or place where something begins or ends; side: *This page has four edges.*
2 *NOUN.* the thin side of a blade that cuts: *The knife had a very sharp edge.*
3 *VERB.* to move little by little: *She edged her way through the crowd.*
4 *VERB.* to put a border on; form an edge on: *The gardener edged the bed of tulips and daffodils with white stones.*
❑ *VERB* **edg·es, edged, edg·ing.**

on edge, *IDIOM.* nervous; anxious: *He was really on edge about the test.*

ed·i·ble (ed′ə bəl), *ADJECTIVE.* safe or good to eat: *Toadstools are not edible.*

ed·it (ed′it), *VERB.*
1 to prepare a piece of writing, a book, and so on, for publication by correcting errors and checking facts: *My older brother edits books.*
2 to be in charge of a publication and decide what will be printed in it: *Two girls were chosen to edit the school paper.*
❑ *VERB* **ed·its, ed·it·ed, ed·it·ing.**

e·di·tion (i dish′ən), *NOUN.*
1 all the copies of a book, newspaper, or magazine printed exactly alike and at the same time: *The third edition of the book included many new maps.*
2 the form in which a book is printed: *This edition of "Alice in Wonderland" has large print and pictures.*

ed·i·tor (ed′ə tər), *NOUN.*
1 someone who edits.
2 someone who decides what will be printed in a newspaper or magazine.

ed·i·to·ri·al (ed′ə tôr′ē əl),
1 *NOUN.* an article in a newspaper or magazine giving the editor's or publisher's opinion about something.
2 *ADJECTIVE.* of or by an editor: *editorial work.*

ed·u·cate (ej′ə kāt), *VERB.* to teach, train, or provide schooling for: *The job of teachers is to educate people.* ❑ *VERB* **ed·u·cates, ed·u·cat·ed, ed·u·cat·ing.**

ed·u·ca·tion (ej′ə kā′shən), *NOUN.*
1 the act or process of training someone; schooling: *In the United States, public schools offer an education to all children.*
2 the knowledge and abilities gained through study and training: *A person with education knows how to speak, write, and read well.*

ed·u·ca·tion·al (ej′ə kā′shə nəl), *ADJECTIVE.*
1 of or for education: *The educational goals of our school are high.*

a hat	ė term	ô order	ch child	a in about
ā age	i it	oi oil	ng long	e in taken
ä far	ī ice	ou out	sh she	ə i in pencil
â care	o hot	u cup	th thin	o in lemon
e let	ō open	u̇ put	ᴛʜ then	u in circus
ē equal	ȯ saw	ü rule	zh measure	

2 providing education: *Our science class saw an educational movie about wild animals.*

Word Power   -ee

The suffix **-ee** means "a person who." An employee is a **person who** is employed. An absentee is a **person who** is absent.

eel — up to 6 feet long

eel (ēl), NOUN.
1 a long fish without scales that looks like a snake. There are many kinds of eels. Most live in the ocean, but one kind, the **common eel,** can live in both salt and fresh water.
2 one of a number of fishes that are similar to eels, such as the electric eel.
❑ PLURAL **eel** or **eels. —eel′like′,** ADJECTIVE.

Did You Know?

All freshwater **eels** begin their lives in an area of the Atlantic Ocean called the **Sargasso Sea** (sär gas′ō sē′). They breed and lay their eggs there.

eer·ie (ir′ē), ADJECTIVE. causing fear because of strangeness or weirdness: *A dark, eerie old house stood at the end of the driveway. The eerie music made the movie scarier.* ❑ ADJECTIVE **eer·i·er, eer·i·est. —eer′i·ly,** ADVERB.

ef·fect (ə fekt′), NOUN. something made to happen; result: *The medicine had the effect of reducing pain.*
■ Another word that sounds like this is **affect.**
for effect, IDIOM. for show; to impress others: *He said that only for effect; he really didn't mean it.*
in effect, IDIOM. in force or operation; active: *That law has been in effect for two years.*
take effect, IDIOM. to operate; become active: *That pill takes effect as soon as you swallow it.*

ef·fec·tive (ə fek′tiv), ADJECTIVE.
1 producing the desired result; getting results: *Aspirin is a very effective medicine for fever.*
2 in operation; active: *The new rule about tardiness becomes effective next Monday.*
—ef·fec′tive·ly, ADVERB. **—ef·fec′tive·ness,** NOUN.

ef·fi·cien·cy (ə fish′ən sē), NOUN. the ability to do things without waste of time or energy: *The skilled carpenter worked with great efficiency.*

ef·fi·cient (ə fish′ənt), ADJECTIVE. able to produce the desired effect without waste of time, energy, or materials; capable: *An efficient worker makes good use of his or her skills.* **—ef·fi′cient·ly,** ADVERB.

ef·fort (ef′ərt), NOUN.
1 the use of concentration and energy to do something; trying hard: *Climbing a steep hill takes effort.*
2 an attempt to do something: *She did not win the race, but she made an effort.*
—ef′fort·less, ADJECTIVE.

egg¹ (eg), NOUN.
1 the round or oval object which is laid by the female of birds, insects, many reptiles and fish, and other types of animals. Young animals develop and hatch from these eggs.
2 the contents of an egg, especially a hen's egg, used as food: *I like two scrambled eggs on toast for breakfast.*
3 an egg cell.

egg² (eg), VERB. **egg on,** to urge: *We egged the team on to victory.* ❑ VERB **eggs, egged, egg·ing.**

Word Story

Egg² comes from an old word used in Iceland to mean "edge." An early meaning of our word was "to sharpen" or "to give an edge to." When we egg someone on, we sharpen that person's willingness to do what we want.

egg cell, a cell in a female plant or animal for producing offspring. After an egg cell combines with a sperm cell, a new living thing starts to grow.

egg·plant (eg′plant′), NOUN. a large, purple, somewhat pear-shaped vegetable.

e·gret (ē′gret), NOUN. a wading bird with a long neck and a long bill. Egrets are usually white. They are a type of heron.

E·gypt (ē′jipt), NOUN. a country in northeastern Africa.

E·gyp·tian (i jip′shən),
1 ADJECTIVE. of or about Egypt or its people.
2 NOUN. someone born or living in Egypt.

egret — about 2½ feet long

eight (āt), NOUN or ADJECTIVE. one more than seven; 8.
■ Another word that sounds like this is **ate.**

eight·een (ā′tēn′), NOUN or ADJECTIVE. eight more than ten; 18.

eight·eenth (ā′tēnth′), ADJECTIVE or NOUN.
1 next after the 17th.
2 one of 18 equal parts.

eighth (ātth), ADJECTIVE or NOUN.
1 next after the seventh; last in a series of eight.
2 one of eight equal parts.

eight·i·eth (ā′tē ith), ADJECTIVE or NOUN.
1 next after the 79th; last in a series of 80.
2 one of 80 equal parts.

eight·y (ā′tē), NOUN or ADJECTIVE. eight times ten; 80.
□ PLURAL **eight·ies.**

ei·ther (ē′ʈʜər or ī′ʈʜər),
1 CONJUNCTION. one of the two possibilities mentioned: *Either you or I will call her.*
2 ADJECTIVE or PRONOUN. one or the other of two: *You may read either book. Choose either of the videos.*
3 ADJECTIVE or PRONOUN. each of two: *There are farms on either side of the river.*
4 ADVERB. also; likewise: *If I don't go, he won't either.*

e·ject (i jekt′), VERB.
1 to throw someone or something out; turn out; drive out: *The city council ejected him from the meeting when he began shouting.*
2 to release a cassette, videotape, or the like from a tape player or similar machine.
□ VERB **e·jects, e·ject·ed, e·ject·ing.**

el (el), NOUN. See **elevated** (definition 2).

e·lab·or·ate (i lab′ər it), ADJECTIVE. worked out with great care; having many details; complicated: *Her parents made elaborate plans for the birthday party.* —**e·lab′or·ate·ly,** ADVERB.

e·las·tic (i las′tik),
1 ADJECTIVE. able to spring back to its original shape after being stretched: *Rubber bands are elastic.*
2 NOUN. a tape or cloth woven partly out of an elastic material: *His shorts have a band of elastic at the top.*

el·bow (el′bō),
1 NOUN. the joint between the upper and lower arm.
2 NOUN. any bend or corner having the same shape as a bent arm. A bent joint for connecting pipes or a sharp turn in a river may be called an elbow.
3 VERB. to push someone with your elbow: *He elbowed me off the sidewalk.*
□ VERB **el·bows, el·bowed, el·bow·ing.**

eld·er (el′dər),
1 ADJECTIVE. older: *The young man in the picture is my elder brother.*
2 NOUN. an older person: *As an only child, she spent a lot of her time with her elders.*

eld·er·ly (el′dər lē), ADJECTIVE. past middle age; somewhat old: *Several elderly people work as teachers' aides at our school.* ■ See the Synonym Study at **old.**

eld·est (el′dist), ADJECTIVE. oldest: *Their eldest daughter graduated from high school last year.*

e·lect (i lekt′), VERB. to choose or select someone for political office by voting: *Americans elect a President every four years.* ■ See the Synonym Study at **choose.** □ VERB **e·lects, e·lect·ed, e·lect·ing.**

e·lec·tion (i lek′shən), NOUN.
1 an act of choosing by vote: *In our city we have an election for mayor every two years.*
2 the condition of being chosen or selected for an office by vote: *The candidate's excellent record and honest campaign resulted in her election.*

Word Bank

Elections have their own vocabulary with many special words. If you want to know more about them, you can begin by looking up these words in this dictionary.

ballot	district	platform	primary
campaign	landslide	poll	vote
convention	mandate	precinct	ward
delegation	nomination		

e·lec·tric (i lek′trik), ADJECTIVE. of or using electricity: *an electric light, an electric current.*

e·lec·tri·cal (i lek′trə kəl), ADJECTIVE. electric: *electrical energy, an electrical storm.* —**e·lec′tri·cal·ly,** ADVERB.

electric cell, a container holding materials that produce electricity by chemical action. A battery consists of one or more electric cells.

electric eel, a long South American freshwater fish that looks like an eel but is related to the catfish and carp. It can give strong electric shocks.

e·lec·tri·cian (i lek′trish′ən), NOUN. someone whose work is installing or repairing electric wiring, lights, or motors.

e·lec·tric·i·ty (i lek′tris′ə tē), NOUN.
1 a form of energy that can produce light, heat, or motion. Electricity is produced by machines called generators, by batteries, and by solar cells. Electricity makes light bulbs shine, televisions and radios work, cars start, and subways run.
2 an electric current: *The storm damaged the wires carrying electricity to the house.*

Word Story

Electricity comes from a Greek word meaning "amber." If amber is rubbed with a cloth, it becomes charged with electricity and attracts straws or hair. The ancient Greeks were the first to record this fact and give it a name.

a	hat	ė	term	ô	order	ch	child	a in about
ā	age	i	it	oi	oil	ng	long	e in taken
ä	far	ī	ice	ou	out	sh	she	ə ⎨ i in pencil
â	care	o	hot	u	cup	th	thin	o in lemon
e	let	ō	open	ù	put	ʈʜ	then	u in circus
ē	equal	ò	saw	ü	rule	zh	measure	

Word Power   electro-

The combining form **electro-** means "electric" or "electricity." **Electro**cution is the act of killing someone with **electricity**. An **electron** is a particle with an **electric** charge.

e·lec·tro·cute (i lek′trə kyüt), *VERB*. to kill someone by a strong electric shock. ❑ *VERB* **e·lec·tro·cutes, e·lec·tro·cut·ed, e·lec·tro·cut·ing.** —**e·lec′tro·cu′tion,** *NOUN*.

e·lec·tro·mag·net (i lek′trō mag′nit), *NOUN*. a piece of iron that becomes a strong magnet when an electric current is passing through wire coiled around it.

e·lec·tro·mag·net·ic (i lek′trō mag net′ik), *ADJECTIVE*. of or caused by an electromagnet.

e·lec·tron (i lek′tron), *NOUN*. a very tiny particle having the smallest unit of negative electrical charge found in nature. All atoms have one or more electrons in motion outside a nucleus. Electricity is the result of the flow of many electrons through a conductor.

e·lec·tron·ic (i lek·tron′ik), *ADJECTIVE*.
1 containing silicon chips, transistors, and so on, that control the flow of electric current: *electronic devices.*
2 working or controlled by electronic devices: *an electronic oven, an electronic timer.* —**e·lec′tron′i·cal·ly,** *ADVERB*.

African elephant
9 to 11 feet high
at the shoulder

Indian elephant
8 to 10 feet high
at the shoulder

electronic mail. See **e-mail.**

e·lec·tron·ics (i lek′tron′iks), *NOUN*.
1 *SINGULAR*. the branch of physics that studies the way electrons act in various materials, in magnetic fields, and so on.
2 *PLURAL*. appliances and equipment, such as microwave ovens, computers, televisions, and radar, that work by means of electronic devices.

el·e·gance (el′ə gəns), *NOUN*. good taste; grace and beauty: *We admired the elegance of the clothes worn to the formal dinner.*

el·e·gant (el′ə gənt), *ADJECTIVE*. showing good taste; graceful; beautiful: *Their house had elegant furniture.* —**el′e·gant·ly,** *ADVERB*.

el·e·ment (el′ə mənt), *NOUN*.
1 one of the basic substances from which all other things are made; chemical element. An element is formed of only one kind of atom. Elements combine in molecules to form more complicated substances. Gold, iron, oxygen, carbon, and tin are elements.
2 one of the parts of which anything is made up: *I like a story that has an element of surprise in it. We need to learn the elements of arithmetic.*
3 **the elements,** the forces of the atmosphere, especially in bad weather: *The barn was gray because it had been exposed to the elements for years.*

el·e·men·tar·y (el′ə men′tər ē), *ADJECTIVE*. of or dealing with the simple, necessary parts to be learned first: *elementary arithmetic.*

elementary school,
1 a school having grades kindergarten through fourth or fifth, followed by middle school.
2 a school having grades kindergarten through sixth, followed by junior high school.
3 a school having grades kindergarten through eighth, followed by a four-year high school.

el·e·phant (el′ə fənt), *NOUN*. either of two huge mammals, the largest living land animals. The elephant has ivory tusks and a long, flexible snout called a trunk. **African elephants** have large ears, and both the males and females have tusks. **Indian elephants** have smaller ears, and the females often have no tusks.

Have You Heard?

You may have heard something described as a **"white elephant."** A white elephant is anything useless that you don't want because it is hard to find a place for or take care of.

el·e·vate (el′ə vāt), *VERB*.
1 to raise or lift someone or something up: *The doctor told me to elevate my injured foot.*
2 to raise someone in rank or position: *The company elevated her to the position of manager.* ❑ *VERB* **el·e·vates, el·e·vat·ed, el·e·vat·ing.**

el·e·vat·ed (el′ə vā′tid),
1 *ADJECTIVE*. lifted up; raised: *an elevated platform.*
2 *NOUN*. an electric railroad raised above street level, allowing traffic to pass underneath; el.

el·e·va·tion (el′ə vā′shən), *NOUN*.
1 height above the earth's surface: *The airplane flew at an elevation of 20,000 feet.*
2 height above sea level: *The elevation of Denver is 5280 feet.*
3 a raised place; a high place. A hill is an elevation.

el·e·va·tor (el′ə vā′tər), NOUN.
1 a moving room, platform, or cage to carry people and things up and down in a building, mine, and so on.
2 a tall, narrow building for storing grain.

e·lev·en (i lev′ən), NOUN or ADJECTIVE. one more than ten; 11.

e·lev·enth (i lev′ənth), ADJECTIVE or NOUN.
1 next after the tenth.
2 one of 11 equal parts.

elf (elf), NOUN. (in stories) a tiny creature that plays tricks on people. ❏ PLURAL **elves.**

el·i·gi·ble (el′ə jə bəl), ADJECTIVE. able or allowed to do something or to have something; properly qualified: *Pupils had to pass all subjects to be eligible to play sports.* −**el′i·gi·bil′i·ty,** NOUN.

e·lim·i·nate (i lim′ə nāt), VERB. to get rid of something; remove: *Losing the game eliminated our team from the finals.* ❏ VERB **e·lim·i·nates, e·lim·i·nat·ed, e·lim·i·nat·ing.** −**e·lim′i·na′tion,** NOUN.

elk (elk), NOUN. a large deer of North America. ❏ PLURAL **elk** or **elks.**

el·lipse (i lips′), NOUN. a figure shaped like an oval with both ends alike.

elm (elm), NOUN. a tall shade tree with high, spreading branches.

El Ni·ño (el nē′nyō), a rise in the surface temperature of the Pacific Ocean, occurring unpredictably every few years. It can cause major weather changes around the world.

e·lope (i lōp′), VERB. to run away secretly together to get married. ❏ VERB **e·lopes, e·loped, e·lop·ing.**

El Sal·va·dor (el sal′və dôr), a country in Central America.

else (els),
1 ADJECTIVE. other than the person, place, or thing mentioned; different: *Will somebody else speak? What else could I say?*
2 ADJECTIVE. in addition; more: *Did you ask anyone else?*
3 ADVERB. differently: *How else can it be done?*
4 ADVERB. **or else,** otherwise; if not: *Hurry and eat your breakfast, or else you will be late.*

else·where (els′wâr), ADVERB. in, at, or to some other place: *Next year we'll go elsewhere for our vacation.*

e·lude (i lüd′), VERB. to escape from someone by quickness or cleverness; slip away from: *The fox eluded the dogs.* ❏ VERB **e·ludes, e·lud·ed, e·lud·ing.**

elves (elvz), NOUN. the plural of **elf.**

e-mail (ē′māl), NOUN. electronic mail:
1 a system of sending messages using computers linked by telephone wires or radio signals.
2 a message sent by such a system. ❏ PLURAL **e-mails.**

e·man·ci·pate (i man′sə pāt), VERB. to set someone free from slavery; release: *Women have been emancipated from many former restrictions.* ❏ VERB **e·man·ci·pates, e·man·ci·pat·ed, e·man·ci·pat·ing.** −**e·man′ci·pa′tion,** NOUN.

Emancipation Proclamation, a proclamation issued by Abraham Lincoln on January 1, 1863. It declared that all slaves in any state rebelling against the United States were free.

em·bank·ment (em bangk′mənt), NOUN. a raised bank of earth or stones, used to hold back water or support a roadway or railroad.

em·bark (em bärk′), VERB.
1 to go on board a ship or an aircraft: *We embarked for Europe in New York.*
2 to set out on something new or important; start: *After leaving college, the young woman embarked upon a business career.*
❏ VERB **em·barks, em·barked, em·bark·ing.**

em·bar·rass (em bar′əs), VERB. to make someone uneasy and ashamed; make self-conscious: *She embarrassed me by asking me if I really liked her.*
❏ VERB **em·bar·rass·es, em·bar·rassed, em·bar·rass·ing.**

em·bar·rassed (em bar′əst), ADJECTIVE. uneasy and ashamed; self-conscious: *When I realized that I had given the wrong answer, I was embarrassed.*

em·bar·rass·ment (em bar′əs mənt), NOUN. shame; an uneasy feeling: *I blushed in embarrassment at my stupid mistake.*

em·bed (em bed′), VERB. to stick something firmly in something else: *Precious stones are often found embedded in rock.* ❏ VERB **em·beds, em·bed·ded, em·bed·ding.**

em·ber (em′bər), NOUN. a piece of wood or coal still glowing in the ashes of a fire.

em·bez·zle (em bez′əl), VERB. to secretly take money that belongs to the business where you work: *The cashier embezzled $50,000 from the bank.* ❏ VERB **em·bez·zles, em·bez·zled, em·bez·zling.** −**em·bez′zler,** NOUN. −**em·bez′zle·ment,** NOUN.

em·blem (em′bləm), NOUN. something that stands for an idea, company, family, and so on; symbol: *The dove is an emblem of peace.*

em·bod·y (em bod′ē), VERB. to put an idea into a form that can be seen: *A building embodies the idea of its architect.* ❏ VERB **em·bod·ies, em·bod·ied, em·bod·y·ing.**

This is the **emblem** of an organization that helps feed children around the world.

a	hat	ė	term	ô	order	ch	child		a in about
ā	age	i	it	oi	oil	ng	long		e in taken
ä	far	ī	ice	ou	out	sh	she	ə	i in pencil
â	care	o	hot	u	cup	th	thin		o in lemon
e	let	ō	open	ù	put	ŦH	then		u in circus
ē	equal	ò	saw	ü	rule	zh	measure		

em·brace (em brās′),

1 *VERB.* to hug someone; hold in your arms to show love or friendship: *I embraced my old friend.*
2 *NOUN.* a hug: *My friend gave me a fond embrace.*
3 *VERB.* to take up; accept: *He eagerly embraced the offer of a trip to Europe.*
❑ *VERB* **em·brac·es, em·braced, em·brac·ing.**

em·broi·der (em broi′dər), *VERB.* to decorate cloth or leather with a pattern of stitches: *I embroidered the shirt with a colorful design.* ❑ *VERB*
em·broi·ders, em·broi·dered, em·broi·der·ing.

em·broi·der·y (em broi′dər ē), *NOUN.*

1 the act or art of embroidering.
2 embroidered work or material.

em·bry·o (em′brē ō), *NOUN.* an animal or plant in its very early stages of development, especially before it can be recognized as a definite animal or plant.
❑ *PLURAL* **em·bry·os.**

em·er·ald (em′ər əld),

1 *NOUN.* a bright green precious stone.
2 *ADJECTIVE* or *NOUN.* bright green.

Did You Know?

Emeralds are mined in Colombia, India, Russia, South Africa, and Zimbabwe. Emeralds have even been found in the United States, in North Carolina. Perfect emeralds are very rare and can be more expensive than diamonds.

e·merge (i mėrj′), *VERB.* to come into view; come up; to come out: *The sun emerged from behind a cloud. Many facts emerged as a result of a second investigation.* ❑ *VERB* **e·merg·es, e·merged, e·merg·ing.**

e·mer·gen·cy (i mėr′jən sē),

1 *NOUN.* a situation that calls for immediate action: *I keep tools in my car for use in an emergency.*
2 *ADJECTIVE.* for use during a time of sudden need: *She pulled the emergency brake and stopped the car.*
❑ *PLURAL* **e·mer·gen·cies.**

em·i·grant (em′ə grənt), *NOUN.* someone who leaves his or her own country to settle in another country: *My grandparents were emigrants from Japan.*

em·i·grate (em′ə grāt), *VERB.* to leave your own country to settle in another country: *My uncle emigrated to Ireland from the United States.*
❑ *VERB* **em·i·grates, em·i·grat·ed, em·i·grat·ing.**
−**em·i·gra·tion** (em′ə grā′shen), *NOUN.*

em·i·nent (em′ə nənt), *ADJECTIVE.* standing above all others in rank; famous; outstanding: *an eminent poet.* −**em′i·nent·ly,** *ADVERB.*

e·mis·sions (i mish′ənz), *NOUN PLURAL.* gases released into the air from an engine, smokestack, and so on.

e·mit (i mit′), *VERB.* to send out; give off: *The sun emits light and heat.* ❑ *VERB* **e·mits, e·mit·ted, e·mit·ting.**

e·mo·tion (i mō′shən), *NOUN.* a strong feeling of any kind. Joy, grief, fear, hate, love, anger, and excitement are emotions.

e·mo·tion·al (i mō′shə nəl), *ADJECTIVE.*

1 of or about the emotions: *A person who is always afraid may have emotional problems.*
2 with strong feeling; appealing to the emotions: *The speaker made an emotional plea for money to help disabled children.*
3 easily excited or upset: *Emotional people are likely to cry if they hear sad music or read sad stories.*
−**e·mo′tion·al·ly,** *ADVERB.*

em·per·or (em′pər ər), *NOUN.* a man who is the ruler of an empire.

em·pha·sis (em′fə sis), *NOUN.*

1 special importance or attention given to something: *That school puts emphasis on arithmetic and reading.*
2 greater loudness or accent put on particular words or syllables: *In reading, our teacher puts emphasis upon the most important words.*
❑ *PLURAL* **em·pha·ses** (em′fə sēz′).

a Chinese **emperor** of long ago

em·pha·size (em′fə sīz), *VERB.*

1 to call attention to; give special importance to: *The principal emphasized the importance of a good breakfast before a test.*
2 to say with extra force: *He emphasized her name as he read the list of winners.*
❑ *VERB* **em·pha·siz·es, em·pha·sized, em·pha·siz·ing.**

em·pire (em′pīr), *NOUN.*

1 a group of nations or states under one ruler or government: *The Roman Empire lasted for hundreds of years.*
2 a country ruled by an emperor or an empress.

em·ploy (em ploi′), *VERB.* to pay someone to work for you: *That big factory employs many workers.*
❑ *VERB* **em·ploys, em·ployed, em·ploy·ing.**

em·ploy·ee (em ploi′ē), *NOUN.* someone who works for a person, a company, the government, and so on. ❑ *PLURAL* **em·ploy·ees.**

em·ploy·er (em ploi′ər), *NOUN.* a person, a company, the government, and so on, that employs one or more people.

em·ploy·ment (em ploi′mənt), *NOUN.*

1 a person's regular work; job: *She had no difficulty finding employment.*

2 the act of employing or condition of being employed: *A large office requires the employment of many people.*

em·press (em′pris), *NOUN.*
1 a woman who is the ruler of an empire.
2 the wife of an emperor.
❑ *PLURAL* **em·press·es.**

emp·ty (emp′tē),
1 *ADJECTIVE.* with nothing or no one in it: *The birds had gone and their nest was left empty.*
2 *VERB.* to make or become empty; make empty: *He emptied his glass. The hall emptied after the meeting.*
3 *ADJECTIVE.* not real; without meaning: *An empty threat has no force behind it.*
❑ *ADJECTIVE* **emp·ti·er, emp·ti·est;** *VERB* **emp·ties, emp·tied, emp·ty·ing.** **–emp′ti·ness,** *NOUN.*

Synonym Study

Empty means with nothing in it: *It's hard to study on an empty stomach. When our neighbors moved away, their house remained empty.*

Vacant means with nothing on it or in it. It is used mostly to describe places: *Nothing but weeds grew in the vacant lot.*

Blank means with nothing on it. It is used mostly to describe flat things: *He gave each student a blank piece of paper.*

Hollow means empty inside: *I climbed into the hollow tree trunk. Tennis balls are hollow.*

ANTONYM: full.

e·mu (ē′myü), *NOUN.* a Australian bird like an ostrich, but smaller. Emus cannot fly, but they can run very fast. ❑ *PLURAL* **e·mus.**

emu — about 5½ feet high

Word Power -en

The suffix **-en** means "to make or become" or "to give or get." To black**en** something is to **make it** black. To strength**en** something is to **give it** strength.

en·a·ble (en ā′bəl), *VERB.* to make someone or something able to do something: *Airplanes enable people to travel great distances rapidly.* ❑ *VERB* **en·a·bles, en·a·bled, en·a·bling.**

en·act (en akt′), *VERB.* to make something into law: *Congress enacted a bill to lower taxes.* ❑ *VERB* **en·acts, en·act·ed, en·act·ing. –en·act′ment,** *NOUN.*

e·nam·el (i nam′əl),
1 *NOUN.* a glasslike substance melted and then cooled to make a smooth, hard surface. Different colors of enamel are used to cover or decorate metal, glass, pottery, and so on.
2 *NOUN.* a paint used to make a smooth, hard, glossy surface.
3 *NOUN.* the smooth, hard, glossy outer layer that covers and protects a tooth.
4 *VERB.* to cover or decorate something with enamel.
❑ *VERB* **e·nam·els, e·nam·eled, e·nam·el·ing.**

en·chant (en chant′), *VERB.*
1 to put someone under a magic spell: *The witch had enchanted the princess.*
2 to delight someone greatly; charm: *The music enchanted us all.*
❑ *VERB* **en·chants, en·chant·ed, en·chant·ing. –en·chant′er,** *NOUN.*

en·chant·ment (en chant′mənt), *NOUN.*
1 the use of magic spells: *In "The Wizard of Oz" Dorothy finds herself at home again by the enchantment of the Good Witch.*
2 something that delights or charms: *We felt the enchantment of the moonlight on the lake.*

en·cir·cle (en sėr′kəl), *VERB.* to form a circle around something; surround: *Trees encircled the pond.*
❑ *VERB* **en·cir·cles, en·cir·cled, en·cir·cling.**

en·close (en klōz′), *VERB.*
1 to shut something in on all sides; surround completely: *Tall buildings enclose the tiny park.*
2 to put a wall or fence around: *We are going to enclose our backyard to enjoy more privacy.*
3 to put something in an envelope along with a letter: *He enclosed a check with the order form.*
❑ *VERB* **en·clos·es, en·closed, en·clos·ing.**

en·clo·sure (en klō′zhər), *NOUN.*
1 an enclosed place, such as a pen or corral: *This farm keeps the geese and ducks in one enclosure.*
2 something enclosed: *The envelope contained a card and $5 as an enclosure.*

en·code (en kōd′), *VERB.* to put information or a message into code: *The spy encoded his message.*
❑ *VERB* **en·codes, en·cod·ed, en·cod·ing. –en·cod′er,** *NOUN.*

a	hat	ė	term	ô	order	ch	child		a in about
ā	age	i	it	oi	oil	ng	long		e in taken
ä	far	ī	ice	ou	out	sh	she	ə	i in pencil
â	care	o	hot	u	cup	th	thin		o in lemon
e	let	ō	open	ù	put	ᴛʜ	then		u in circus
ē	equal	ò	saw	ü	rule	zh	measure		

en·core (äng′kôr or än′kôr), NOUN.
1 a demand, which an audience makes by shouting "Encore!" and by clapping, for a person or group to give an extra performance: *The singer received several encores and many bouquets.*
2 an extra song, appearance, and so on, given because of the applause of the audience.

en·coun·ter (en koun′tər),
1 VERB. to meet someone or something unexpectedly: *What if we should encounter a bear?*
2 NOUN. an unexpected meeting: *A fortunate encounter brought the two friends back together.*
3 VERB. to have to deal with something; experience: *She encountered many problems in her new job.*
❑ VERB **en·coun·ters, en·coun·tered, en·coun·ter·ing.**

en·cour·age (en kėr′ij), VERB.
1 to give someone courage or confidence; urge on: *We encouraged our team with loud cheers.*
2 to give help to something; help to cause: *Sunlight encourages the growth of green plants.*
❑ VERB **en·cour·ag·es, en·cour·aged, en·cour·ag·ing.**

The cheers of her friends **encouraged** the runner.

en·cour·age·ment (en kėr′ij mənt), NOUN.
1 the condition of feeling encouraged: *The singer drew her encouragement from the crowd.*
2 something that gives hope, courage, or confidence: *The teacher's praise of his drawings was his only encouragement.*

en·cy·clo·pe·di·a (en sī′klə pē′dē ə), NOUN. a book or set of books giving information on all branches of knowledge, with its articles arranged alphabetically. ❑ PLURAL **en·cy·clo·pe·di·as.**

end (end),
1 NOUN. the last part: *He read to the end of the book.*
2 NOUN. the part where something begins or where it stops: *Every stick has two ends. Skip to the end.*
3 VERB. to finish something: *Let us end this fight.*
4 NOUN. a goal that someone has: *She had this end in mind—to do her work without a mistake.*

5 NOUN. (in football) an offensive or defensive player at either end of the line.
❑ VERB **ends, end·ed, end·ing.**

Synonym Study

End means to come to the last part of something or to bring it to its last part: *The game ended in a tie. My brother ended his performance with a somersault.*

Finish and **complete** mean to end what you started to do. These words suggest that you have done everything necessary: *I finished painting the picture yesterday. He completed the statue in time to enter it in the art show.*

Conclude is a formal word that means to end: *The principal concluded the assembly by awarding the prize for the best work of art.*

Close[1] (klōz) can mean to bring something to an end: *The school chorus closed the talent show by singing "America the Beautiful."*

See also the Synonym Studies at **last**[1] and **stop.**

ANTONYMS: begin, start.

en·dan·ger (en dān′jər), VERB. to put someone or something in danger: *Fire endangered the barn.*
❑ VERB **en·dan·gers, en·dan·gered, en·dan·ger·ing.**

endangered species, a kind of plant, animal, or other living thing that may soon become extinct.

en·deav·or (en dev′ər), VERB. to try very hard to do something; make an effort: *Each time she endeavored to do better than before.* ❑ VERB **en·deav·ors, en·deav·ored, en·deav·or·ing.**

end·ing (en′ding), NOUN.
1 the last part of something; end: *The story has a sad ending.*
2 a letter or syllable added to a word to change its meaning; suffix. The most common plural endings are "s" or "es."

end·less (end′lis), ADJECTIVE.
1 lasting or going on forever; having no end: *the endless revolution of planets around the sun.*
2 joined in a circle; without ends: *The back wheel of a bicycle is turned by an endless chain.*
—**end′less·ly,** ADVERB.

en·dorse (en dôrs′), VERB.
1 to write your name on the back of a check: *He endorsed the check so that the bank would cash it.*
2 to approve something; support: *Parents endorsed the plan for a school playground.*
❑ VERB **en·dors·es, en·dorsed, en·dors·ing.** —**en·dorse′ment,** NOUN. —**en·dors′er,** NOUN.

en·dow (en dou′), VERB. to give money or property to provide an income for: *The rich man endowed his old college.* ❑ VERB **en·dows, en·dowed, en·dow·ing.**

end·point (end′point′), NOUN. the point where a line segment begins or ends.

en·dur·ance (en dùr′əns), NOUN. the power or ability to keep on doing something in spite of pain or difficulties: *A runner must have great endurance to run 10 miles.*

en·dure (en dùr′), VERB.
1 to remain in existence; last; keep on: *Metal and stone endure for a long time.*
2 to put up with something; bear; stand: *The pioneers endured many hardships.*
❑ VERB **en·dures, en·dured, en·dur·ing.**

end zone, the part of a football field between the goal line and the end of the field. It is ten yards deep.

en·e·my (en′ə mē), NOUN.
1 a person or group that hates and tries to harm another: *They have few enemies.*
2 a country, army, or force that your country is at war with: *The enemy has crossed our borders.*
3 anything harmful: *Drought is an enemy of farmers.*
❑ PLURAL **en·e·mies.**

en·er·get·ic (en′ər jet′ik), ADJECTIVE. lively and active; full of energy: *Cool autumn days make me feel energetic.* **–en·er·get′i·cal·ly,** ADVERB.

en·er·gy (en′ər jē), NOUN.
1 the strength and ability to do things and be physically active: *I was so full of energy that I could not keep still.*
2 the power or ability to do work, such as lifting or moving an object. Light, heat, and electricity are different forms of energy. All of these can be used as sources of power to do work.
❑ PLURAL **en·er·gies.**

en·force (en fôrs′), VERB. to force obedience to a rule or law: *The police will enforce the laws of the city.* ❑ VERB **en·forc·es, en·forced, en·forc·ing.** **–en·force′a·ble,** ADJECTIVE. **–en·forc′er,** NOUN. **–en·force′ment,** NOUN.

en·gage (en gāj′), VERB.
1 to take part in something; be active in: *They engaged in conversation.*
2 to keep someone busy: *Work engages his time.*
❑ VERB **en·gag·es, en·gaged, en·gag·ing.**

en·gaged (en gājd′), ADJECTIVE. promised to marry: *A party was given for the engaged couple.*

en·gage·ment (en gāj′mənt), NOUN.
1 a promise to marry: *Their parents announced the young couple's engagement.*
2 a meeting with someone at a certain time; an appointment: *I have a dinner engagement tonight.*

en·gine (en′jən), NOUN.
1 a machine that changes energy from fuel, steam, water pressure, and so on, into motion and power. An engine is used to apply power to some work, such as running other machines.
2 See **locomotive.**

en·gi·neer (en′jə nir′), NOUN.
1 someone who is an expert in engineering.
2 someone who runs a locomotive.

en·gi·neer·ing (en′jə nir′ing), NOUN. the science, work, or profession of building or managing engines, machines, roads, bridges, railroads, mines, electrical systems, and so on: *The Golden Gate bridge is a triumph of engineering.*

Eng·land (ing′glənd), NOUN. the largest division of Great Britain, in the southern part of the island.

Eng·lish (ing′glish),
1 ADJECTIVE. of or about England, its people, or their language.
2 NOUN PLURAL. **the English,** the people of England.
3 NOUN. the language of England. English is also spoken in Australia, Canada, the United States, and many other places around the world.

Did You Know?

English has more words than any other language. The largest dictionaries of English have more than 600,000 words. This dictionary has more than 35,000 words.

English Channel, the narrow body of water between England and France.

en·grave (en grāv′), VERB. to carve words, pictures, designs, and so on, into a surface: *The jeweler engraved the boy's initials on the back of the watch. She engraved her name and phone number on her bike in case it was stolen.* ❑ VERB **en·graves, en·graved, en·grav·ing.** **–en·grav′er,** NOUN.

engraving in metal

en·grav·ing (en grā′ving), NOUN.
1 a picture made from an engraved metal plate:
2 the art or act of someone who engraves.

en·gulf (en gulf′), VERB. to overwhelm someone or something with a lot of material, water, and so on: *A wave engulfed the small boat. The crowd engulfed the stadium.* ❑ VERB **en·gulfs, en·gulfed, en·gulf·ing.**

en·hance (en hans′), VERB. to improve the value, taste, importance, and so on, of something: *Spices enhance the taste of many foods. The gardens enhanced the beauty of the house.* ❑ VERB **en·hanc·es, en·hanced, en·hanc·ing.**

a	hat	ė	term	ô	order	ch	child	⎧a in about
ā	age	i	it	oi	oil	ng	long	⎪e in taken
ä	far	ī	ice	ou	out	sh	she	ə⎨i in pencil
â	care	o	hot	u	cup	th	thin	⎪o in lemon
e	let	ō	open	ủ	put	ᴛʜ	then	⎩u in circus
ē	equal	ò	saw	ü	rule	zh	measure	

en·joy (en joi′), VERB.
1 to have or use something with pleasure; like: *The children enjoyed their visit to the museum.*
2 to have something as an advantage or benefit: *He enjoys good health.*
❑ VERB **enjoys, enjoyed, enjoy·ing. –en·joy′a·ble,** ADJECTIVE.

en·joy·ment (en joi′mənt), NOUN. pleasure; joy; delight: *The children found great enjoyment in their visit to the museum.*

en·large (en lärj′), VERB. to make or become larger: *I enlarged a photograph.* ❑ VERB **en·larg·es, en·larged, en·larg·ing. –en·larg′er,** NOUN.

en·large·ment (en lärj′mənt), NOUN. a photograph that has been made larger.

en·light·en (en lit′n), VERB. to provide truth and knowledge to someone; inform; instruct: *The book enlightened me on the subject of medicine.*
❑ VERB **en·light·ens, en·light·ened, en·light·en·ing.**

en·list (en list′), VERB.
1 to join a branch of the armed forces: *She enlisted in the navy.*
2 to get the help of: *We enlisted my sister and her friends in building our new clubhouse.*
❑ VERB **en·lists, en·list·ed, en·list·ing.**

en·liv·en (en li′vən), VERB. to make lively, active, or cheerful: *Bright curtains enliven a dull room.*
❑ VERB **en·liv·ens, en·liv·en·ed, en·liv·en·ing.**

e·nor·mous (i nôr′məs), ADJECTIVE. very, very large; huge: *Cleaning the garage will be an enormous task. Long ago enormous animals lived on the earth.* ■ See the Synonym Study at **huge.** **–e·nor′mous·ly,** ADVERB.

an **enormous** chocolate bar

e·nough (i nuf′),
1 ADJECTIVE. as much or as many as you need or want; sufficient: *Are there enough seats for everybody?* ★ The adjective **enough** may be used before or after the noun it describes: *There is room enough for three. Is there enough room for your suitcase?*
2 NOUN. an amount needed or wanted: *Has he had enough to eat?*
3 ADVERB. until no more is needed or wanted; sufficiently: *Have you eaten enough?*

en·rage (en rāj′), VERB. to make someone very angry; fill with rage: *Teasing enraged the dog.*
❑ VERB **en·rag·es, en·raged, en·rag·ing.**

en·rich (en rich′), VERB.
1 to improve the quality of something: *The illustrations enrich the book.*
2 to make someone or something rich or richer: *A good education enriches your mind.*
❑ VERB **en·rich·es, en·riched, en·rich·ing. –en·rich′ment,** NOUN.

en·roll (en rōl′), VERB. to make or become a member of a class, club, and so on: *He enrolled his daughter and son in a music school. I enrolled in a ballet class.* ❑ VERB **en·rolls, en·rolled, en·roll·ing.**

en·roll·ment (en rōl′mənt), NOUN.
1 the number of students enrolled: *The school has an enrollment of 200 students.*
2 the act or process of enrolling: *Enrollment took place in the fall.*

en route (än rüt′), on the way: *We shall stop at Hartford en route from New York to Boston.*

en·sign (en′sən), NOUN. a military rank. See the chart on page 550.

en·slave (en slāv′), VERB. to take away freedom from someone. ❑ VERB **en·slaves, en·slaved, en·slav·ing.**

en·sure (en shùr′), VERB. to make something sure or certain: *Careful planning and hard work ensured the success of the party.* ❑ VERB **en·sures, en·sured, en·sur·ing.**

en·tan·gle (en tang′gəl), VERB.
1 to get twisted up and caught: *The fly was entangled in the spider's web.*
2 to involve; get into difficulty: *Do not entangle us in your schemes.*
❑ VERB **en·tan·gles, en·tan·gled, en·tan·gling.**

en·ter (en′tər), VERB.
1 to go into; come in: *He entered the house. Let them enter.*
2 to join; become a part or member of: *She entered the contest.*
3 to write or print in a book or list: *Words are entered alphabetically in a dictionary.*
❑ VERB **en·ters, en·tered, en·ter·ing.**

en·ter·prise (en′tər priz), NOUN. a plan to be tried, especially one that is important, difficult, or dangerous: *A trip into space is a daring enterprise.* ■ See the Synonym Study at **plan.**

en·ter·tain (en′tər tān′), VERB.
1 to keep someone pleasantly interested or amused: *The clown entertained the children and the adults at the party.*
2 to have as a guest or have guests: *They entertained ten people at dinner.*
❑ VERB **en·ter·tains, en·ter·tained, en·ter·tain·ing.**

en·ter·tain·er (en′tər tā′nər), NOUN. a singer, musician, and so on, who performs in public: *They hired entertainers to perform at their party.*

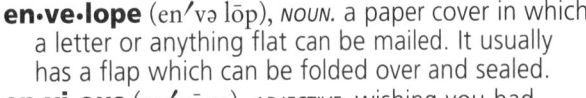

E

en·ter·tain·ment
(en′tər tān′mənt), NOUN.
1 something that interests, pleases, or amuses people, such as a show or a circus.
2 the act of entertaining: *We devoted ourselves to the entertainment of our guests.*
3 amusement: *I played the piano for their entertainment.*

en·thu·si·asm
(en thü′zē az′əm), NOUN. an eager interest in doing something: *There is a lot of enthusiasm for swimming on a hot day.*

The water slide was great **entertainment.**

en·thu·si·as·tic (en thü′zē as′tik), ADJECTIVE. eagerly interested; full of enthusiasm: *My little brother is enthusiastic about going to kindergarten.*
—**en·thu′si·as′ti·cal·ly,** ADVERB.

en·tire (en tīr′), ADJECTIVE. whole; complete: *The entire class behaved very well on the trip.*
—**en·tire′ly,** ADVERB.

en·ti·tle (en tī′tl), VERB.
1 to give someone a claim or right to something: *The one who wins is entitled to first prize.*
2 to give a title to a book, play, and so on; name: *I entitled my story "Looking for Treasure."*
❑ VERB **en·ti·tles, en·ti·tled, en·ti·tling.**

en·trance¹ (en′trəns), NOUN.
1 the way into a place; door or passageway: *The entrance to the hotel was blocked with baggage.*
2 the act of entering: *The actor's entrance was greeted with applause.*

en·trance² (en trans′), VERB. to capture someone's complete attention with pleasure or great interest: *The singer's voice entranced the audience.* ❑ VERB **en·tranc·es, en·tranced, en·tranc·ing.**

en·trust (en trust′), VERB. to hand someone or something over to another person for protection: *They entrusted their child to her grandparents.*
❑ VERB **en·trusts, en·trust·ed, en·trust·ing.**

en·try (en′trē), NOUN.
1 the action of entering: *His sudden entry startled me.*
2 a place by which to enter; way to enter. An entrance hall is an entry.
3 something written or printed in a book or list, or in a computer. Each word explained in a dictionary is an entry or **entry word.**
❑ PLURAL **en·tries.**

en·vel·op (en vel′əp), VERB. to wrap or cover something; surround: *The baby was enveloped in blankets.* ❑ VERB **en·vel·ops, en·vel·oped, en·vel·op·ing.**

en·ve·lope (en′və lōp), NOUN. a paper cover in which a letter or anything flat can be mailed. It usually has a flap which can be folded over and sealed.

en·vi·ous (en′vē əs), ADJECTIVE. wishing you had what someone else has: *He was envious of his brother's success in sports.* —**en′vi·ous·ly,** ADVERB.

en·vi·ron·ment (en vī′rən mənt), NOUN.
1 all the surrounding things, conditions, and influences affecting the growth of living things, especially air, water, and soil.
2 surroundings: *She grew up in an environment of poverty.*
—**en·vi′ron·men′tal,** ADJECTIVE.

en·vy (en′vē),
1 NOUN. the feeling of wanting what someone else has: *All of us were filled with envy when we saw her new bicycle.*
2 NOUN. the cause of this feeling: *Their new car was the envy of the neighborhood.*
3 VERB. to want what someone else has: *He envied her success.*
❑ VERB **en·vies, en·vied, en·vy·ing.**

Word Story

Envy comes from Latin words meaning "at" or "against" and "to look." Envy often occurs when a person watches someone else succeed and feels resentment against that success.

en·zyme (en′zīm), NOUN. any substance produced in living cells that influences a chemical reaction within a living thing. Enzymes in saliva begin to break down food so that it can be digested.

ep·ic (ep′ik),
1 NOUN. a long poem that tells the adventures of one or more great heroes.
2 ADJECTIVE. of or like an epic; grand; heroic: *The first flight over the Atlantic was an epic deed.*

ep·i·dem·ic (ep′ə dem′ik), NOUN. the rapid spread of a disease that causes many people to have it at the same time: *Doctors warned that a flu epidemic was possible.*

ep·i·lep·sy (ep′ə lep′sē), NOUN. a condition of the brain that may cause convulsions and periods of unconsciousness.

ep·i·sode (ep′ə sōd), NOUN.
1 a single happening or group of happenings in real life or a story: *Being elected class president was an important episode in her life at school.*
2 one part of a story that is published or broadcast in several parts, one at a time.

a hat	ė term	ô order	ch child	⎧ a in about
ā age	i it	oi oil	ng long	e in taken
ä far	ī ice	ou out	sh she	ə⎨ i in pencil
â care	o hot	u cup	th thin	o in lemon
e let	ō open	u̇ put	ŦH then	⎩ u in circus
ē equal	ȯ saw	ü rule	zh measure	

e·qual (ē′kwəl),
1 ADJECTIVE. the same in amount, size, number, value, or rank: *Ten dimes are equal to one dollar. Everyone is considered equal before the law.*
2 VERB. to be the same as: *Two times five equals ten.*
3 NOUN. someone or something that is equal: *In spelling she had no equal.*
❑ VERB **e·quals, e·qual·ed, e·qual·ing. —e′qual·ly,** ADVERB.

e·qual·i·ty (i kwäl′ə tē), NOUN. the condition of being equal, especially referring to political and economic rights and responsibilities.

equal sign, the sign (=), showing that what follows is the same in value, amount, meaning, and so on, as what came before: $7 + 8 = 15.$

e·qua·tion (i kwā′zhən), NOUN. a statement that two quantities are equal. EXAMPLE: $4 + 5 = 9.$

e·qua·tor (i kwā′tər),
NOUN. an imaginary circle around the middle of the earth, halfway between the North Pole and the South Pole. The equator divides the earth into the Northern Hemisphere and the Southern Hemisphere.

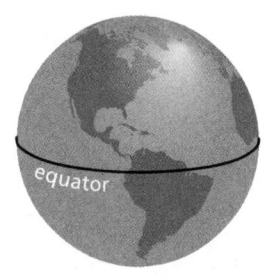

equator

e·qua·to·ri·al
(ē′kwə tôr′ē əl), ADJECTIVE. of or near the equator: *Ecuador is an equatorial country.*

Equatorial Guinea, a country in western Africa.

Word Power   equi-

The combining form **equi-** means "equal" or "equally." An **equi**lateral triangle has three **equal** sides. All the sides are **equally** long. **Equi**distant means **equally** distant.

e·qui·dis·tant (ē′kwə dis′tənt), ADJECTIVE. equally distant: *All points of the circumference of a circle are equidistant from the center.*

e·qui·lat·er·al tri·an·gle (ē′kwə lat′ər əl trī′ang′gəl), a triangle that has three equal sides.

e·qui·lib·ri·um (ē′kwə lib′rē əm), NOUN. See **balance** (definition 1).

e·qui·nox (ē′kwə noks), NOUN. either of the two times in the year when day and night are of equal length everywhere on earth. An equinox occurs when the sun passes directly above the earth's equator, about March 21 and September 22.
❑ PLURAL **e·qui·nox·es.**

e·quip (i kwip′), VERB. to supply someone or something with something that is needed or wanted; supply with all that is needed: *The scouts equipped themselves with canteens and food for the hike.* ❑ VERB **e·quips, e·quipped, e·quip·ping.**

e·quip·ment (i kwip′mənt), NOUN. what someone or something is equipped with; outfit; supplies: *camping equipment.*

e·quiv·a·lent (i kwiv′ə lənt),
1 ADJECTIVE. equal: *Nodding your head is equivalent to saying yes.*
2 NOUN. something equivalent: *Five pennies are the equivalent of a nickel.*

Word Power   -er

The suffix **-er**[1] means "someone or something that _____s." A follow**er** is **someone who** follows. A dispens**er** is **something that** dispenses.

The suffix **-er**[2] means "more." Soft**er** means **more** soft. Slow**er** means **more** slow.

er·a (ir′ə), NOUN. a period of time or history: *We live in the era of space exploration.* ❑ PLURAL **er·as.**

e·rase (i rās′), VERB.
1 to get rid of something by rubbing it out: *He erased the wrong answer and wrote in the right one.*
2 to remove something recorded from a tape: *She erased one of my favorite videotapes.*
❑ VERB **e·ras·es, e·rased, e·ras·ing. —e·ras′a·ble,** ADJECTIVE.

Word Story

Erase comes from Latin words meaning "scrape away." Before Europeans learned about rubber, they erased writing by scraping it off with a sharp knife. Rubbing is easier, and that is how **rubber** got its name.

e·ras·er (i rā′sər), NOUN. something used to erase marks made with pencil, ink, or chalk: *His pencil had a worn-out eraser.*

e·rect (i rekt′),
1 ADJECTIVE. straight up; not bent over: *erect posture.*
2 VERB. to put something straight up; set upright: *They erected a TV antenna on the roof.*
3 VERB. to put up; build: *That house was erected forty years ago.*
❑ VERB **e·rects, e·rect·ed, e·rect·ing. —e·rect′ly,** ADVERB. **—e·rect′or,** NOUN.

Er·ie (ir′ē), NOUN. **Lake,** one of the Great Lakes.

Er·i·tre·a (er′ə trē′ə), NOUN. a country in northeastern Africa. **—Er′i·tre′an,** ADJECTIVE or NOUN.

er·mine (ėr′mən), NOUN. a weasel that is brown in summer but white with a black tip on its tail in winter. White ermine fur was often worn by royalty. ❑ PLURAL **er·mine** or **er·mines.**

e·ro·sion (i rō′zhən), NOUN. the process of wearing away or being worn away little by little by water, air, and so on: *In geography, we study the erosion of the earth by wind and water.*

err (ėr or er), VERB. to make a mistake: *Everyone errs at some time or other.* ❑ VERB **errs, erred, err·ing.**

er·rand (er′ənd), NOUN.
1 a short trip that you take to do something: *She has gone on an errand to the store.*
2 something you do on a trip like this: *I did six errands in one trip.* ■ See the Synonym Study at **job.**

er·rat·ic (ə rat′ik), ADJECTIVE.
1 uncertain; irregular: *An erratic alarm clock is not dependable.*
2 unusual; odd: *I liked his erratic ideas.*

er·ror (er′ər), NOUN.
1 a mistake; something done that is wrong: *I failed my test because of errors in spelling.* ■ See the Synonym Study at **mistake.**
2 (in baseball) a fielder's mistake that either allows a batter to reach first, or a runner to advance one or more bases.

e·rupt (i rupt′), VERB.
1 to burst or flow forth violently: *Lava and ashes erupted from the volcano.*
2 to violently send out steam, lava, and so on: *The volcano erupted twice last year.*
❑ VERB **e·rupts, e·rupt·ed, e·rupt·ing.**
—**e·rup′tion,** NOUN.

Lava and steam **erupt** from the volcano.

es·ca·la·tor (es′kə lā′tər), NOUN. a moving stairway: *The store had both an elevator and an escalator.*

es·cape (e skāp′),
1 VERB. to get out and away from someplace; get free: *The bird escaped from its cage.*
2 VERB. to keep free or safe from: *We all escaped the flu.*
3 NOUN. the act or fact of getting away: *Their escape was aided by the thick fog.*
❑ VERB **es·capes, es·caped, es·cap·ing.**

es·cort (es′kôrt *for noun;* e skôrt′ *for verb*),
1 NOUN. a person or group going with another person to give protection, or to show honor: *An escort of officials accompanied the famous visitor.*
2 NOUN. a person who goes on a date with another person: *Her escort to the party was a tall young man.*
3 VERB. to go with someone as an escort: *Police cars escorted the governor during the Memorial Day parade.* ❑ VERB **es·corts, es·cort·ed, es·cort·ing.**

Es·ki·mo (es′kə mō),
1 NOUN. a member of a people living in the arctic regions of North America and northeastern Asia; Inuit; Inupiaq.
2 NOUN. the language of the Eskimo.
3 ADJECTIVE. of or about the Eskimo or their language.
❑ PLURAL **Es·ki·mo** or **Es·ki·mos.**

Usage Note

Eskimo is a word disliked by many members of the people who have been called by that name. They prefer **Inuit** or **Inupiaq** as names for themselves and their language. Others use these names in respect for this preference. However, **Eskimo** remains common. It is a good idea to consider the feelings of others. If in doubt, ask!

e·soph·a·gus (ē sof′ə gəs), NOUN. the tube that carries food from the throat to the stomach.
❑ PLURAL **e·soph·a·gus·es** or **e·soph·a·gi** (i sof′ə jī).

es·pe·cial·ly (e spesh′ə lē), ADVERB.
1 in a special way; chiefly: *This book is designed especially for students.*
2 very: *The weather is especially nice today.*

es·pres·so (e spres′ō), NOUN. a very strong coffee made from beans roasted black. Espresso is brewed in a special machine.

es·say (es′ā), NOUN. a short written composition on a particular subject, explaining a subject, expressing an opinion, and so on.

es·sence (es′ns), NOUN. the most important or identifying part of something: *Being considerate is the essence of politeness.*

es·sen·tial (ə sen′shəl),
1 ADJECTIVE. absolutely necessary; extremely important: *Good food is essential to good health.*
2 ADJECTIVE. most typical: *Generosity is the essential part of his character.*
3 NOUN. **essentials,** absolutely necessary elements or qualities: *Learn the essentials first, then learn the details.*
—**es·sen′tial·ly,** ADVERB.

Word Power   -est

The suffix **-est** means "most." Warm**est** means most warm. Slow**est** means most slow.

es·tab·lish (e stab′lish), VERB.
1 to set something up and keep it going for a long

a	hat	ė	term	ô	order	ch	child		a in about
ā	age	i	it	oi	oil	ng	long		e in taken
ä	far	ī	ice	ou	out	sh	she	ə	i in pencil
â	care	o	hot	u	cup	th	thin		o in lemon
e	let	ō	open	ů	put	ŦH	then		u in circus
ē	equal	ò	saw	ü	rule	zh	measure		

time: *establish a government, establish a business. The English established colonies in America.*

2 to show something beyond any doubt; prove: *He established his client's alibi by calling several witnesses.*
❏ *VERB* **es·tab·lish·es, es·tab·lished, es·tab·lish·ing.**

es·tab·lish·ment (e stab′lish mənt), *NOUN.*
1 the act or process of establishing something: *The establishment of the business took several years.*
2 something established. A household, business, church, or army is an establishment.

es·tate (e stāt′), *NOUN.*
1 a large piece of land in the country, usually with a large house built on it.
2 money and property that someone owns; possessions: *an estate of $2,000,000.*

There were beautiful gardens on the **estate**.

es·teem (e stēm′),
1 *VERB.* to think highly of someone or something; respect: *We esteem courage.*
2 *NOUN.* a very favorable opinion of someone or something; respect: *Courage is held in great esteem.*
❏ *VERB* **es·teems, es·teemed, es·teem·ing.**

es·ti·mate (es′tə mit *for noun;* es′tə māt *for verb*),
1 *NOUN.* a judgment or careful guess about amount, size, value, and so on: *Her estimate of the length of the fish was 15 inches.*
2 *VERB.* to form a judgment or opinion about something: *We estimate the job will take several days to complete.*
❏ *VERB* **es·ti·mates, es·ti·mat·ed, es·ti·mat·ing.**
—**es′ti·ma′tor,** *NOUN.*

Es·to·ni·a (e stō′nē ə), *NOUN.* a country in northeastern Europe. —**Es·to′ni·an,** *ADJECTIVE or NOUN.*

etc., an abbreviation of the Latin words *et cetera,* which mean "and all the rest." When you read this word aloud, you usually read "and so forth" or "and so on." When *etc.* is used at the end of a series of words, it means that what has been said about the mentioned words is also true of similar things.

etch (ech), *VERB.* to engrave a design on a metal plate or on glass using an acid that eats away the lines. When filled with ink, the lines of the design reproduce a copy on paper. ❏ *VERB* **etchs, etch·ed, etch·ing.**

etch·ing (ech′ing), *NOUN.* a picture or design printed from an etched plate.

e·ter·nal (i tėr′nl), *ADJECTIVE.*
1 without beginning or ending; lasting forever: *the eternal darkness of outer space.*
2 seeming to go on forever: *When will we have an end to this eternal noise?*
—**e·ter′nal·ly,** *ADVERB.*

e·ter·ni·ty (i tėr′nə tē), *NOUN.*
1 all time; all the past and all the future.
2 a period of time that seems endless: *I waited in the dentist's office for an eternity.*
❏ *PLURAL* **e·ter·ni·ties.**

Word Power   -eth

The suffix **-eth** means "number ____ in a series." **Sixtieth** means **number** sixty **in a series.** It is only used with numbers that end in -y: *thirtieth, fortieth.* See also the Word Power at **-th.**

e·ther (ē′thər), *NOUN.* a liquid chemical that causes you to become unconscious when you inhale its fumes. It used to be used in operations so that a person would not feel pain.

eth·i·cal (eth′ə kəl), *ADJECTIVE.*
1 morally right: *Our school demands ethical conduct from all students and teachers.*
2 following formal or professional rules of right and wrong: *It is not ethical for a doctor to gossip about a patient.*
—**eth′i·cal·ly,** *ADVERB.*

E·thi·o·pi·a (ē′thē ō′pē ə), *NOUN.* a country in eastern Africa. —**E′thi·o′pi·an,** *ADJECTIVE or NOUN.*

eth·nic (eth′nik), *ADJECTIVE.* of or about a group of people who have the same race, nationality, or culture: *ethnic festivals, ethnic foods.*

et·i·quette (et′ə ket), *NOUN.* the usual rules for polite behavior in society: *Etiquette requires that we eat peas with a fork, not a knife.*

Word Power   -ette

The suffix **-ette** means "little." A **kitchenette** is a **little** kitchen. ★ Sometimes **-ette** has been used to mean "female." An **usherette** is a **female** usher. This use is often considered offensive. It is better to use the more general word, like *usher,* instead of an *-ette* word.

et·y·mol·o·gy (et′ə mol′ə jē), *NOUN.* an explanation of the origin and history of a word; word story. There is an interesting etymology at the word **erase** on page 222. ❏ *PLURAL* **et·y·mol·o·gies.**

eu·ca·lyp·tus
(yü/kə lip/təs), NOUN. a very tall tree that grows mainly in Australia. Eucalyptus oil is used in flavorings and perfumes. ❑ PLURAL **eu·ca·lyp·tus·es.**

a **eucalyptus** tree

Eur·a·sia (yùr ā/zhə), NOUN. Europe and Asia, thought of as a single continent.

Eur·ope (yùr/əp), NOUN. the continent west of Asia and east of the Atlantic Ocean. Only one continent, Australia, is smaller than Europe. France, Italy, and Greece are countries in Europe.

Eur·o·pe·an (yùr/ə pē/ən),
1 ADJECTIVE. of or about Europe or its people; from Europe.
2 NOUN. someone born or living in Europe. Danes, Germans, and Spaniards are Europeans.

e·vac·u·ate (i vak/yü āt), VERB. to get everyone out of a dangerous place or situation: *People quickly evacuated the burning building. Efforts were made to evacuate all civilians from the war zone.* ❑ VERB **e·vac·u·ates, e·vac·u·at·ed, e·vac·u·at·ing. –e·vac/u·a/tion,** NOUN.

e·vade (i vād/), VERB. to get away from someone or something by trickery; avoid by cleverness: *The thief evaded the police.* ❑ VERB **e·vades, e·vad·ed, e·vad·ing.**

e·val·u·ate (i val/yü āt), VERB. to find out how much something is worth, how well something is working, and so on: *An expert will evaluate the old paintings you wish to sell.* ❑ VERB **e·val·u·ates, e·val·u·at·ed, e·val·u·at·ing. –e·val/u·a/tion,** NOUN.

e·vap·o·rate (i vap/ə rāt/), VERB.
1 to turn into a vapor or a gas: *Boiling water evaporates rapidly.*
2 to disappear: *My good resolutions evaporated soon after New Year's Day.*
❑ VERB **e·vap·o·rates, e·vap·o·rat·ed, e·vap·o·rat·ing. –e·vap/o·ra/tion,** NOUN.

eve (ēv), NOUN. the evening or day before some holiday or special day: *Christmas Eve.*

e·ven (ē/vən),
1 ADJECTIVE. flat; level; smooth: *The country is even, with no high hills.*
2 ADJECTIVE. at the same level: *The snow was even with the windowsill.*
3 ADJECTIVE. staying about the same; regular: *an even temper, an even temperature.*
4 ADJECTIVE. equal; no more or less than: *They divided the money into even shares.*

5 VERB. to make equal or level: *She evened the edges by trimming them.*
6 ADJECTIVE. able to be divided by 2 without a remainder. 2, 4, 6, 8, and 10 are **even numbers.**
7 ADVERB. though you would not expect it: *Even the weather service was fooled by the sudden snowstorm. He is ready, even eager, to go.*
8 ADVERB. still; yet: *You can read even better if you try.*
❑ VERB **e·vens, e·vened, e·ven·ing. –e/ven·ly,** ADVERB.

eve·ning (ēv/ning), NOUN. the time between sunset and bedtime: *We spent the evening at the lake.*

Did You Know?

An **evening star** is any planet that can be seen after the sun goes down. Mercury and Venus are most often seen as evening stars. When they are seen at dawn they are called **morning stars.**

e·vent (i vent/), NOUN.
1 a happening, especially an important happening: *Newspapers report current events.*
2 one item in a program of sports: *The 100-yard dash was the last event.*
in any event, IDIOM. in any case; whatever happens.

e·ven·tu·al (i ven/chü əl), ADJECTIVE. coming at the end of or as a result of something: *After several failures, his eventual success surprised us.*

e·ven·tu·al·ly (i ven/chü ə lē), ADVERB. finally; in the end: *We searched a long time for the key and eventually we found it.*

ev·er (ev/ər), ADVERB.
1 at any time: *Is she ever at home?*
2 at all times; always: *She is ever ready to accept a new challenge.*
3 in any way; at all: *How did you ever move that table by yourself?*

Ev·er·est (ev/ər ist), NOUN. **Mount,** the mountain in the Himalayas between Tibet and Nepal, 29,028 feet high. It is the highest mountain in the world.

Ev·er·glades (ev/ər glādz/), NOUN PLURAL. a very large swampy region in southern Florida.

ev·er·green (ev/ər grēn/),
1 ADJECTIVE. having green leaves all year round.
2 NOUN. an evergreen plant. Pine, spruce, cedar, ivy, and rhododendrons are evergreens.

ev·er·last·ing (ev/ər las/ting), ADJECTIVE.
1 lasting forever; eternal: *the everlasting beauty of nature.*
2 lasting too long; tiresome: *Their everlasting complaints annoyed me.*

a	hat	ė	term	ô	order	ch	child	ə	a in about
ā	age	i	it	oi	oil	ng	long		e in taken
ä	far	ī	ice	ou	out	sh	she		i in pencil
â	care	o	hot	u	cup	th	thin		o in lemon
e	let	ō	open	ù	put	₮н	then		u in circus
ē	equal	ò	saw	ü	rule	zh	measure		

eve·ry (ev′rē), ADJECTIVE.
1 each single: *Read every word on the page. Every student must have a book.*
2 each period of time: *The subway stops here every twenty minutes.*
every now and then, IDIOM. from time to time: *Every now and then we have a frost that ruins the crop.*
every other, IDIOM. every second: *I wash my hair every other day.*

eve·ry·bod·y (ev′rē bud′ē or ev′rē bə dē), PRONOUN. every person; everyone: *Everybody likes the new principal.*

eve·ry·day (ev′rē dā′), ADJECTIVE.
1 happening every day; daily: *Accidents are everyday occurrences.*
2 for every ordinary day; common; not for Sundays or holidays: *She wears everyday clothes to work.*

eve·ry·one (ev′rē wun′), PRONOUN. each one; everybody: *Everyone in the class is here.*

ev·o·lu·tion (ev′ə lü′shən), NOUN.
1 the process in which slight physical changes are passed from living things to their young, adding up to larger changes over a number of generations: *According to Darwin's scientific ideas, all forms of life are the results of evolution from earlier forms of life.*
2 the gradual development of something: *the evolution of transportation from horse and buggy to jet aircraft.*

e·volve (i volv′), VERB.
1 to develop gradually into a different form of life as the result of many small changes happening over many thousands of years: *The modern horse evolved from a prehistoric animal that was only as big as a dog.*
2 to develop gradually: *The modern automobile evolved from the horse and buggy.*
❑ VERB **e·volves, e·volved, e·volv·ing.**

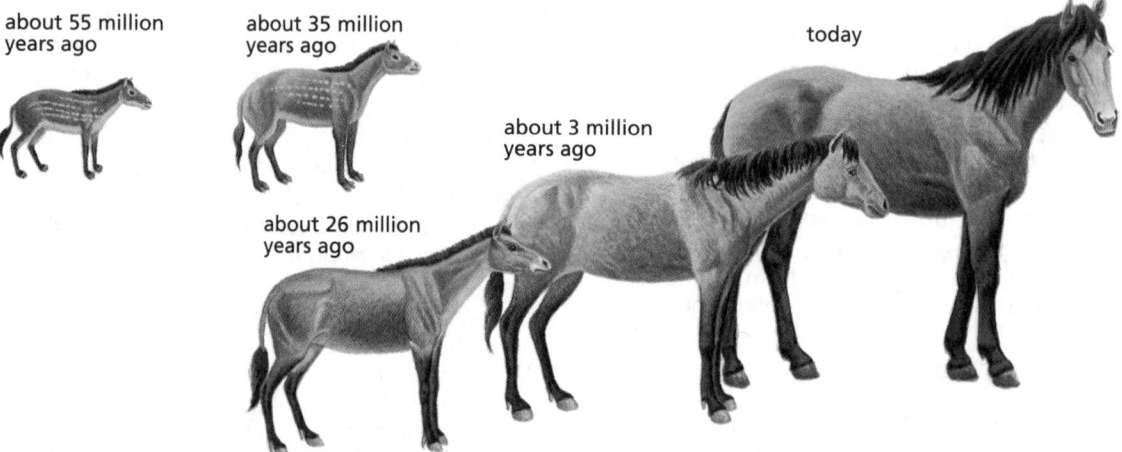

about 55 million years ago

about 35 million years ago

about 26 million years ago

about 3 million years ago

today

The modern horse has **evolved** over millions of years from a very small ancestor.

eve·ry·thing (ev′rē thing′), PRONOUN. all things; every thing: *She did everything she could to help her friend.*

eve·ry·where (ev′rē wâr′), ADVERB. in every place; in all places or lands: *We looked everywhere for our lost dog.*

ev·i·dence (ev′ə dəns), NOUN. anything that shows what has happened; facts; proof: *The evidence showed that he had caused the accident.*

ev·i·dent (ev′ə dənt), ADJECTIVE. easy to see or understand; clear; plain: *It was evident that the broken vase could never be fixed.* **—ev′i·dent·ly,** ADVERB.

e·vil (ē′vəl),
1 ADJECTIVE. causing harm; bad; wrong: *an evil plan, the evil effects of war.*
2 NOUN. bad or evil quality; wickedness: *Their thoughts were full of evil.*
3 NOUN. something causing harm: *Crime and poverty are some of the evils of society.*

ewe (yü), NOUN. a female sheep. ■ Other words that sound like this are **yew** and **you.**

Word Power   ex-

The prefix **ex-** means "former" or "formerly." An **ex-**president is a **former** president. An **ex-**Marine is a **former** Marine. An **ex-**wife is a **former** wife.

ex·act (eg zakt′), ADJECTIVE. without any mistake; accurate; precise: *I gave her the exact amount. Please be exact in your estimate of the cost.* **—exact′ness,** NOUN.

ex·act·ly (eg zakt′lē), ADVERB.
1 without any error; precisely: *Her calculation was exactly right. I know exactly where the cat is.*
2 in every way: *He always does exactly as he pleases.*

ex·ag·ge·rate (eg zaj′ə rāt′), VERB. to say or think something is larger or greater than it is: *The little boy was exaggerating when he said he had more*

than a thousand video games. ❑ VERB
ex·ag·ge·rates, ex·ag·ge·rat·ed, ex·ag·ge·rat·ing.

ex·ag·ge·ra·tion (eg zaj/ə rā/shən), NOUN. a statement that goes beyond the truth: *It is an exaggeration to say that you would rather die than touch a snake.*

ex·am (eg zam/), NOUN. a short form of **examination.**

ex·am·i·na·tion (eg zam/ə nā/shən), NOUN.
1 an act or process of examining; exam: *The doctor made a careful examination of my eyes.*
2 a test of knowledge or ability; exam: *Our teacher gave us an examination in arithmetic.*

ex·am·ine (eg zam/ən), VERB.
1 to look at something closely and carefully: *The doctor examined the wound.*
2 to ask someone questions about what he or she knows: *The lawyer examined the witness.*
❑ VERB **ex·am·ines, ex·am·ined, ex·am·in·ing.**
—**ex·am/in·er,** NOUN.

ex·am·ple (eg zam/pəl), NOUN.
1 one of a group of persons or things mentioned to show what the others are like: *New York is an example of a busy city.*
2 someone or something to be imitated or copied; a model; pattern: *He is an example to younger kids.*
3 a problem or question where the answer is shown to help you solve others of the same kind.

ex·as·pe·rate (eg zas/pə rāt/), VERB. to make someone very annoyed or angry: *The pupils' constant noise exasperated their teacher.* ❑ VERB **ex·as·pe·rates, ex·as·pe·rat·ed, ex·as·pe·rat·ing.** —**ex·as/per·a/tion,** NOUN.

ex·ca·vate (ek/skə vāt/), VERB.
1 to dig something out and remove it; scoop out: *Big machines excavate the dirt and load it into trucks.*
2 to uncover by digging: *Scientists have excavated many fossil dinosaur bones.*
❑ VERB **ex·ca·vates, ex·ca·vat·ed, ex·ca·vat·ing.**

ex·ca·va·tion (ek/skə vā/shən), NOUN.
1 act or process of digging something out: *The excavation for the new basement took three days.*
2 a hole made by digging: *The excavation for the new building was 150 feet across.*

ex·ceed (ek sēd/), VERB. to be more or greater than something, especially a legal limit: *Drivers should not exceed the speed limit.* ❑ VERB **ex·ceeds, ex·ceed·ed, ex·ceed·ing.**

ex·ceed·ing·ly (ek sē/ding lē), ADVERB. extremely; very: *Yesterday was an exceedingly hot day.*
■ See the Synonym Study at **very.**

ex·cel (ek sel/), VERB. to be better at something than other people; be very good at something: *She excels in arithmetic.* ❑ VERB **ex·cels, ex·celled, ex·cel·ling.**

ex·cel·lence (ek/sə ləns), NOUN. extremely good quality: *We praised him for the excellence of his report.*

ex·cel·lent (ek/sə lənt), ADJECTIVE. of extremely good quality; better than others; very, very good: *Excellent work deserves high praise.*
—**ex/cel·lent·ly,** ADVERB.

ex·cept (ek sept/),
1 PREPOSITION. leaving out; not including: *He works every day except Sunday.*
2 CONJUNCTION. but; were it not for the fact that: *We could have gone today except for the rain.*

ex·cep·tion (ek sep/shən), NOUN. something that is different from what is usual or the rule: *He comes on time every day; today is an exception.*

ex·cep·tion·al (ek sep/shə nəl), ADJECTIVE. unusual; out of the ordinary: *an exceptional student. This warm weather is exceptional for January.*
—**ex·cep/tion·al·ly,** ADVERB.

ex·cess (ek ses/ for noun; ek/ses for adjective),
1 NOUN. a larger amount of something than is necessary or allowed; part that is too much: *I ate most of my cake and fed the excess to the birds.*
2 ADJECTIVE. extra: *Passengers must pay for excess baggage taken on an airplane.*
❑ PLURAL **ex·ces·ses.**

ex·ces·sive (ek ses/iv), ADJECTIVE. too much; too great; extreme: *We moved because the rent was excessive.* —**ex·ces/sive·ly,** ADVERB.

ex·change (eks chānj/),
1 VERB. to give something to someone in return for something else; trade: *He exchanged the tight coat for one that was a size larger.*
2 VERB. to give and take things of the same kind: *We exchanged test papers to check our answers.*
3 NOUN. an act of giving and taking: *Ten pennies for a dime is a fair exchange. After the war there was an exchange of prisoners.*
4 NOUN. a place where people buy, sell, or trade things. A stock exchange is a place to do business in stocks.
❑ VERB **ex·chang·es, ex·changed, ex·chang·ing.**

ex·cite (ek sīt/), VERB. to cause strong, lively feelings in someone: *Plans for a field trip excited the students very much.* ❑ VERB **ex·cites, ex·cit·ed, ex·cit·ing.**

ex·cit·ed (ek sī/tid), ADJECTIVE. having very strong, lively feelings about something that you like: *The excited mob rushed into the mayor's office. We were all very excited about going to the zoo.*
—**ex·cit/ed·ly,** ADVERB.

a	hat	ė	term	ô	order	ch	child		a in about
ā	age	i	it	oi	oil	ng	long		e in taken
ä	far	ī	ice	ou	out	sh	she	ə	i in pencil
â	care	o	hot	u	cup	th	thin		o in lemon
e	let	ō	open	ù	put	ŦH	then		u in circus
ē	equal	ò	saw	ü	rule	zh	measure		

ex·cite·ment
(ek sīt′mənt), NOUN.
1 an excited condition: *The birth of twins caused great excitement in the family.*
2 something that excites someone: *Riding the roller coaster was too much excitement for me.*

ex·cit·ing (ek sī′ting), ADJECTIVE. causing strong lively feelings; thrilling: *We read an exciting story about pirates and buried treasure.*

ex·claim (ek sklām′), VERB. to cry out with strong feelings: *"That's wonderful!" she exclaimed.* ❏ VERB **ex·claims, ex·claimed, ex·claim·ing.**

The crowd was filled with **excitement.**

ex·cla·ma·tion (ek′sklə mā′shən), NOUN. something said suddenly or loudly as the result of surprise or strong feeling. *Oh!, Hooray!, Well!, Look!,* and *Listen!* are common exclamations.

exclamation mark or **exclamation point,** a mark (!), used after a word, phrase, or sentence to show that it was exclaimed: *Wow! That dog is huge!*

ex·clude (ek sklüd′), VERB. to keep someone from joining or taking part in something: *The club's rules exclude from membership anyone who lives out of town.* ❏ VERB **ex·cludes, ex·clud·ed, ex·clud·ing.**

ex·clu·sive (ek sklü′siv), ADJECTIVE.
1 used by only one person or thing; not divided or shared with others: *exclusive use of the driveway.*
2 keeping out certain people or groups: *an exclusive golf course.*

ex·cur·sion (ek skėr′zhən), NOUN. a short trip taken for fun, often by a number of people together: *Our club went on an excursion to the mountains.*

ex·cuse (ek skyüs′ for noun; ek skyüz′ for verb),
1 NOUN. a reason for doing or not doing something: *He had many excuses for being late for school.*
2 VERB. to be a reason or explanation for something: *Sickness excuses absence from school.*
3 VERB. to pardon; forgive: *Please excuse my lateness.*
4 VERB. to free someone from the responsibility of doing something: *Those who passed the first test will be excused from the second one.*
5 NOUN. a note saying that someone should be excused for something or from something: *If you are late, your parents must write you an excuse.*
❏ VERB **ex·cus·es, ex·cused, ex·cus·ing.**

ex·e·cute (ek′sə kyüt), VERB.
1 to put someone to death according to law: *The murderer was executed.*
2 to put into effect; enforce: *Congress makes the laws; the President executes them.*
❏ VERB **ex·e·cutes, ex·e·cut·ed, ex·e·cut·ing.**

ex·e·cu·tion (ek′sə kyü′shən), NOUN. the act of putting someone to death according to law.

ex·e·cu·tion·er (ek′sə kyü′shə nər), NOUN. someone who puts criminals to death according to law.

ex·ec·u·tive (eg zek′yə tiv),
1 NOUN. someone who manages a business, a department of a government, and so on: *The president of the company is the top executive there.*
2 ADJECTIVE. having the duty and power of putting laws into effect: *The President is the head of the executive branch of government.*

ex·empt (eg zempt′),
1 VERB. to free someone from a duty, obligation, rule, and so on; release: *Students who get high grades all year are exempted from final exams.*
2 ADJECTIVE. freed from a duty, obligation, or rule: *School property is exempt from taxes.*
❏ VERB **ex·empts, ex·empt·ed, ex·empt·ing.**

ex·er·cise (ek′sər sīz),
1 NOUN. the active use of the body to improve it: *Physical exercise is good for your health.*
2 VERB. to do a series of movements that work your muscles: *I exercise for ten minutes each morning.*
3 VERB. to make active use of: *It is wise to exercise caution in crossing the street.*
4 NOUN. something that gives practice and training or causes improvement or develops a skill: *Study the lesson, and then do the exercises.*
❏ VERB **ex·er·cis·es, ex·er·cised, ex·er·cis·ing.**

This boy is **exercising** his arms and chest.

ex·ert (eg zėrt′), VERB. to put a power or skill to full use: *A gymnast exerts both strength and skill. A ruler exerts authority.* ❏ VERB **ex·erts, ex·ert·ed, ex·ert·ing.** —**ex·er′tion,** NOUN.

ex·hale (eks hāl′), VERB. to breathe out: *After taking a deep breath, she exhaled slowly.* ❏ VERB **ex·hales, ex·haled, ex·hal·ing.**

ex·haust (eg zȯst′),
1 VERB. to tire someone out completely; wear out: *The long, hard climb up the hill exhausted us.*
2 VERB. to use something up completely: *The dry summer nearly exhausted the city's supply of water from the reservoir.*

3 NOUN. the burned gases that escape from an engine: *Automobile exhaust is poisonous.*
❑ VERB **ex·hausts, ex·haust·ed, ex·haust·ing.**

ex·haust·ed (eg zȯ′stid), ADJECTIVE.
1 worn out; very tired: *The exhausted hikers stopped to rest.* ▪ See the Synonym Study at **tired.**
2 completely used up: *Our patience was exhausted by all the quarreling.*

ex·haus·tion (eg zȯs′chən), NOUN. the condition of being exhausted; great tiredness: *The hikers were suffering from extreme exhaustion.*

ex·hib·it (eg zib′it),
1 VERB. to show something publicly; put on display: *She hopes to exhibit her paintings in New York.* ▪ See the Synonym Study at **show.**
2 VERB. to show something; reveal: *Both of their children exhibit a talent for music.*
3 NOUN. public showing; exhibition: *Our school gave an exhibit of student science projects.*
❑ VERB **ex·hib·its, ex·hib·it·ed, ex·hib·it·ing.**
—**ex·hib′i·tor,** NOUN.

ex·hi·bi·tion (ek′sə bish′ən), NOUN.
1 a public show: *The art school holds an exhibition of paintings every year.*
2 an act of showing; display: *Pushing and shoving in line is an exhibition of bad manners.*

ex·ile (eg′zil or ek′sil),
1 VERB. to force someone to leave his or her country, often by law as a punishment; banish: *The traitors were exiled from their country for life.*
2 NOUN. someone sent into exile: *She has been an exile since the end of the war.*
3 NOUN. the condition of being exiled: *He was sent into exile for life.*
❑ VERB **ex·iles, ex·iled, ex·il·ing.**

ex·ist (eg zist′), VERB.
1 to have being; be; be a reality: *The possibility of space travel has existed for only a few years. She believes that ghosts exist.*
2 to live; have life: *A person cannot exist without air.*
3 to be found; occur: *That butterfly exists only in North America.*
❑ VERB **ex·ists, ex·ist·ed, ex·ist·ing.**

ex·ist·ence (eg zis′təns), NOUN.
1 the condition of being: *Dinosaurs disappeared from existence millions of years ago.*
2 the condition of being real: *Most people no longer believe in the existence of ghosts.*

ex·it (eg′zit or ek′sit),
1 NOUN. a way out of a room, building, and so on: *The theater had six exits.*
2 NOUN. an act of leaving; departure: *When the cat came in, the mice made a hasty exit.*
3 VERB. to go out; leave: *Please exit by the doors at the rear of the room.*
❑ VERB **ex·its, ex·it·ed, ex·it·ing.**

ex·o·skel·e·ton
(ek′sō skel′ə tən), NOUN. any hard, external covering that protects or supports an animal body. Insects, lobsters, and turtles have exoskeletons.

The turtle's shell is an **exoskeleton.**

ex·ot·ic (eg zot′ik), ADJECTIVE. strange and unusual, often coming from a different country: *We saw many exotic birds at the zoo.*

Word Story

Exotic comes from a Greek word meaning "outside." Exotic things come from outside the country, or outside people's usual experience.

ex·pand (ek spand′), VERB. to make or grow larger; swell up: *A balloon expands when it is blown up. Metal expands when it is heated.* ❑ VERB **ex·pands, ex·pand·ed, ex·pand·ing.** —**ex·pand′er,** NOUN.

ex·panse (ek spans′), NOUN. a very large area: *The Pacific Ocean is a vast expanse of water.*

ex·pan·sion (ek span′shən), NOUN.
1 the act or process of becoming larger: *Heat causes the expansion of gases.*
2 an expanded part or form: *That book is an expansion of a magazine article.*

ex·pect (ek spekt′), VERB.
1 to think that something will probably happen; look forward to: *I expect to take a vacation in May.*
2 to count on something because it is necessary or right: *I expect you to pay for the damage you did.*
❑ VERB **ex·pects, ex·pect·ed, ex·pect·ing.**

ex·pec·ta·tion (ek′spek tā′shən), NOUN.
1 expectations, good reasons for expecting something: *They have expectations of money from a rich aunt.*
2 act of expecting or condition of being expected; anticipation: *The farmer bought a new truck in expectation of a good harvest.*

ex·pe·di·tion (ek′spə dish′ən), NOUN.
1 a long, well-planned trip for a special purpose, such as exploration or scientific study: *an expedition to the moon.* ▪ See the Synonym Study at **trip.**
2 the people, ships, and so on, that make such a trip.

ex·pel (ek spel′), VERB.
1 to officially remove someone from a school, club, and so on: *A pupil who cheats or steals may be expelled from school.*

a	hat	ė	term	ô	order	ch	child		a in about
ā	age	i	it	oi	oil	ng	long		e in taken
ä	far	ī	ice	ou	out	sh	she	ə {	i in pencil
â	care	o	hot	u	cup	th	thin		o in lemon
e	let	ō	open	ù	put	ᴛH	then		u in circus
ē	equal	ȯ	saw	ü	rule	zh	measure		

2 to force something out: *The lifeguard pressed on the drowning victim's chest to expel water from his lungs.*
❏ *VERB* **ex·pels, ex·pelled, ex·pel·ling.**

ex·pense (ek spens′), *NOUN.*
1 the money that you spend on something: *The expense of the trip was small.*
2 a cause of spending; something that you spend money on: *Supporting a child at college is an expense for parents.*

ex·pen·sive (ek spen′siv), *ADJECTIVE.* costing a lot of money; having a high price: *My uncle has an expensive car.*

ex·per·i·ence (ek spir′ē əns),
1 *NOUN.* things that are seen, done, or lived through: *We had several pleasant experiences on our trip. People learn by experience.*
2 *NOUN.* knowledge or skill gained by seeing, doing, or living through things: *I've gained valuable experience from working with computers.*
3 *VERB.* to have happen to you; feel: *to experience great pain.*
❏ *VERB* **ex·per·i·enc·es, ex·per·i·enced, ex·per·i·enc·ing.**

ex·per·i·ment (ek sper′ə ment *for verb;* ek sper′ə mənt *for noun*),
1 *VERB.* to try something using some kind of careful method in order to find out about it: *I wanted to experiment with some new colors for my painting.*
2 *NOUN.* a carefully planned trial or test to find out something: *We made an experiment to learn the weight of the air in a basketball.*
❏ *VERB* **ex·per·i·ments, ex·per·i·ment·ed, ex·per·i·ment·ing. —ex·per′i·men·ta′tion,** *NOUN.* **—ex·per′i·ment′er,** *NOUN.*

These girls are performing a science **experiment.**

ex·per·i·men·tal (ek sper′ə men′tl), *ADJECTIVE.*
1 based on or resulting from experiments: *Chemistry is an experimental science.*
2 still being tested or tried: *Development of new computers is still in an experimental stage. He saw an experimental car at the auto show.*
—ex·per′i·men′tal·ly, *ADVERB.*

ex·pert (ek′spėrt′ *for noun;* ek spėrt′ *or* ek′spėrt′ *for adjective*),
1 *NOUN.* someone who has great skill or who knows a great deal about some special thing: *She is an expert at fishing.*
2 *ADJECTIVE.* having or showing special skill or knowledge: *She is an expert painter.*
—ex·pert′ly, *ADVERB.*

ex·pi·ra·tion (ek′spə rā′shən), *NOUN.* the fact or process of coming to an end: *We shall move at the expiration of our lease.*

ex·pire (ek spīr′), *VERB.*
1 to no longer be good or usable: *Your library card has expired.*
2 to die: *The king expired at the stroke of midnight.*
❏ *VERB* **ex·pires, ex·pired, ex·pir·ing.**

ex·plain (ek splān′), *VERB.*
1 to tell about something so that people are able to understand it: *The teacher explained multiplication to the class.*
2 to give reasons for something; tell what the cause of something is: *Can you explain your friend's absence from class?*
❏ *VERB* **ex·plains, ex·plained, ex·plain·ing.**

ex·pla·na·tion (ek′splə nā′shən), *NOUN.*
1 the act or process of making something clear; giving reasons for something: *He did not understand the teacher's explanation of multiplication.*
2 something that explains: *This diagram is a good explanation of how a car's engine works.*

ex·plan·a·to·ry (ek splan′ə tôr′ē), *ADJECTIVE.* helping to explain something; helping to make things clear: *Read the explanatory part of the lesson before you try to do the problems.*

ex·plic·it (ek splis′it), *ADJECTIVE.* clearly expressed; exact: *She gave such explicit directions that everyone understood them.* **—ex·plic′it·ly,** *ADVERB.*

ex·plode (ek splōd′), *VERB.*
1 to blow up; burst with a loud noise: *The building was destroyed when the gas furnace exploded.*
2 to cause to explode: *Some people explode firecrackers on the Fourth of July.*
3 to burst forth noisily: *The speaker's mistake was so funny the audience exploded with laughter.*
❏ *VERB* **ex·plodes, ex·plod·ed, ex·plod·ing.**

ex·ploit (ek sploit′ *for verb;* ek′sploit *for noun*),
1 *VERB.* to treat unfairly for your own advantage: *Nations used to exploit their colonies, taking as much wealth out of them as they could.*
2 *VERB.* to make good use of something; use to your advantage: *A mine is exploited for its minerals.*
3 *NOUN.* a very brave or skillful act: *This book tells about the exploits of Robin Hood.*
❏ *VERB* **ex·ploits, ex·ploit·ed, ex·ploit·ing.** **—ex′ploi·ta′tion,** *NOUN.*

ex·plo·ra·tion (ek/splə rā/shən), *NOUN.* the act or process of traveling in unknown lands or seas, or in outer space in order to discover new things.

ex·plore (ek splôr/), *VERB.*
1 to travel over unknown lands or seas, or in outer space in order to discover new things: *A small vehicle has explored the surface of Mars.*
2 to go over something carefully; examine: *The children explored the new house from attic to cellar.*
□ *VERB* **ex·plores, ex·plored, ex·plor·ing.**
—**ex·plor/er,** *NOUN.*

An astronaut **explores** the surface of the moon.

Explorer Scout, a person between 14 and 20 years old who is in the exploring program of the Boy Scouts, which focuses on work or hobby interests.

ex·plo·sion (ek splō/zhən), *NOUN.*
1 the action of blowing up; bursting with a loud noise: *The explosion of the bomb shook the whole neighborhood.*
2 a noisy outburst: *explosions of anger, an explosion of laughter.*
3 a very sudden or rapid increase or growth: *The explosion of the world's population has led to a shortage of food in many countries.*

ex·plo·sive (ek splō/siv),
1 *ADJECTIVE.* able to explode; likely to explode: *Gunpowder is explosive.*
2 *NOUN.* something that is able or likely to explode. *Dynamite is an explosive.*

ex·po·nent (ek spō/nənt), *NOUN.* a small number written above and to the right of a symbol or quantity to show how many times the symbol or quantity is to be used as a factor. EXAMPLES: $2^2 = 2 \times 2$; $a^3 = a \times a \times a$.

ex·port (ek spôrt/ or ek/spôrt *for verb;* ek/spôrt *for noun*),
1 *VERB.* to send goods out of one country for sale and use in another country: *The United States exports corn. China exports cotton.* ■ See the Synonym Study at **send.**

2 *NOUN.* something exported: *Cotton is an important export of the United States.*
3 *NOUN.* the act or fact of exporting: *the export of oil from the Arab nations.*
□ *VERB* **ex·ports, ex·port·ed, ex·port·ing.**

ex·pose (ek spōz/), *VERB.*
1 to uncover something so that it can be seen: *While we fished, our arms were exposed to the hot sun.* ■ See the Synonym Study at **show.**
2 to put someone in contact with a contagious disease: *The whole class has been exposed to the flu.*
3 to make something known; reveal: *They exposed the plot to the police.*
□ *VERB* **ex·pos·es, ex·posed, ex·pos·ing.**

ex·po·sure (ek spō/zhər), *NOUN.*
1 an act or fact of exposing something, especially something hidden: *The exposure of the real criminal cleared the innocent suspect.*
2 the fact or condition of being exposed: *Exposure to the rain has ruined this machinery.*

ex·press (ek spres/),
1 *VERB.* to put your thoughts or feelings into words: *Try to express your idea clearly in your first paragraph.* ■ See the Synonym Study at **say.**
2 *VERB.* to show something by your look, voice, or action: *A smile expresses joy.*
3 *NOUN.* a train, bus, or elevator that goes direct from one point to another without making intermediate stops: *I took the express to Phoenix.*
4 *ADJECTIVE.* traveling quickly from one main station to another without making stops in between: *The express train sped past our small town's station.*
□ *VERB* **ex·press·es, ex·pressed, ex·press·ing;** *PLURAL* **ex·press·es.**

ex·pres·sion (ek spresh/ən), *NOUN.*
1 a word or group of words with a particular meaning: *"Nerd" is a slang expression.*
2 an act of showing by your look, voice, or action: *A sigh is often an expression of sadness.*
3 a look that shows what you are feeling: *The winners all had happy expressions on their faces.*

ex·pres·sive (ek spres/iv), *ADJECTIVE.* showing clearly what someone thinks or feels: *Actors usually have expressive faces.* —**ex·pres/sive·ly,** *ADVERB.* —**ex·pres/sive·ness,** *NOUN.*

ex·press·way (ek spres/wā/), *NOUN.* a wide highway built for high-speed, long-distance travel; thruway.

ex·qui·site (ek/skwi zit or ek skwiz/it), *ADJECTIVE.* very lovely; unusually beautiful: *The violet is an exquisite flower. That is an exquisite poem.* —**ex/qui·site·ly,** *ADVERB.*

a	hat	ė	term	ô	order	ch	child		a in about
ā	age	i	it	oi	oil	ng	long		e in taken
ä	far	ī	ice	ou	out	sh	she	ə	i in pencil
â	care	o	hot	u	cup	th	thin		o in lemon
e	let	ō	open	ů	put	ᴛʜ	then		u in circus
ē	equal	ò	saw	ü	rule	zh	measure		

ex·tend (ek stend′), VERB.
1 to stretch something out; hold out: *to extend your hand.*
2 to continue; reach; go on: *This beach extends for miles in both directions.*
3 to increase or enlarge: *They plan to extend their research in that field.*
4 to give; grant: *This organization extends help to poor people.*
❏ VERB **ex·tends, ex·tend·ed, ex·tend·ing.**

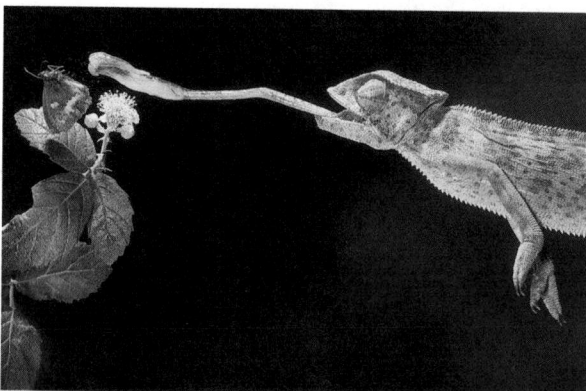

The chameleon **extends** its tongue to catch its dinner.

ex·ten·sion (ek sten′shən), NOUN.
1 extra time for getting something done: *The teacher gave me an extension on my report because I had been so sick.*
2 an addition: *The new extension to our school will make room for more students.*
3 an extra telephone connected with the main telephone: *I picked up the extension before I knew you were on the phone.*

ex·ten·sive (ek sten′siv), ADJECTIVE. large; having a wide influence or effect: *an extensive park, extensive changes.* **−ex·ten′sive·ly,** ADVERB.

ex·tent (ek stent′), NOUN. the size, space, length, amount, or degree to which a thing extends: *a vast extent of prairie. The extent of a judge's power is limited by law.*

ex·te·ri·or (ek stir′ē ər),
1 NOUN. the outside of something: *I saw only the exterior of the house, not the interior.*
2 ADJECTIVE. outer: *The skin of an apple is its exterior covering.*

ex·ter·mi·nate (ek ster′mə nāt), VERB. to kill or destroy completely: *This poison will exterminate rats.* ❏ VERB **ex·ter·mi·nates, ex·ter·mi·nat·ed, ex·ter·mi·nat·ing. −ex·ter′mi·na′tion,** NOUN.

ex·ter·nal (ek ster′nl), ADJECTIVE. on the outside of something; outer: *An ear of corn has an external husk.* **−ex·ter′nal·ly,** ADVERB.

ex·tinct (ek stingkt′), ADJECTIVE.
1 no longer existing: *Dinosaurs are extinct.*
2 no longer active: *an extinct volcano.*

ex·tinc·tion (ek stingk′shən), NOUN.
1 the act or process of destroying something totally or bringing something to an end: *Doctors are working for the extinction of diseases.*
2 the condition of being extinct: *Many endangered species face extinction.*

ex·tin·guish (ek sting′gwish), VERB. to stop a light or fire from burning; put out: *Water extinguished the fire.* ❏ VERB **ex·tin·guish·es, ex·tin·guished, ex·tin·guish·ing. −ex·tin′guish·er,** NOUN.

ex·tra (ek′strə),
1 ADJECTIVE or ADVERB. more than what is usual, expected, or needed: *extra pay.*
2 NOUN. anything more than what is usual, expected, or needed: *He bought a new car with many extras.* ❏ PLURAL **ex·tras.**

Word Power   extra-

The prefix **extra-** means "outside" or "beyond." An **extra**terrestrial is supposed to come from a place **outside** our planet. Something **extra**ordinary is **beyond** what is ordinary or expected.

ex·tract (ek strakt′ *for verb;* ek′strakt *for noun*),
1 VERB. to pull something out, usually with some effort; take out: *The dentist decided to extract a tooth.*
2 NOUN. something taken out of something else: *Vanilla extract is made from vanilla beans.*
❏ VERB **ex·tracts, ex·tract·ed, ex·tract·ing.**

ex·traor·di·nar·y (ek strôr′də ner′ē), ADJECTIVE. very unusual; remarkable; special: *Eight feet is an extraordinary height for a human being.* **−ex·traor′di·nar′i·ly,** ADVERB.

ex·tra·ter·res·tri·al (ek′strə tə res′trē əl),
1 NOUN. an imaginary creature from outer space.
2 ADJECTIVE. beyond or outside the earth or its atmosphere.

ex·trav·a·gance (ek strav′ə gəns), NOUN. careless and wasteful spending of money or use of things: *Their extravagance kept them in debt.*

ex·trav·a·gant (ek strav′ə gənt), ADJECTIVE. spending money or using things carelessly and wastefully: *It is extravagant to buy a second TV when you have not finished paying for the first one.* **−ex·trav′a·gant·ly,** ADVERB.

ex·treme (ek strēm′),
1 ADJECTIVE. much more than usual; very great: *She drove with extreme caution during the snowstorm.*
2 ADJECTIVE. at the very end; farthest possible: *He lives in the extreme western part of town.*
3 NOUN. two things that are as different as possible from each other: *Joy and grief are two extremes of feeling.*

ex·treme·ly (ek strēm′lē), ADVERB. severely; very: *It is extremely cold in the Arctic.* ■ See the Synonym Study at **very.**

ex·trem·i·ty (ek strēm′ə tē), NOUN.
1 the very end; the tip: *Florida is at the southeastern extremity of the United States.*
2 **extremities,** the hands and feet.
  ❑ PLURAL **ex·trem·i·ties.**

eye (ī),
1 NOUN. the part of the body that people and animals use for seeing.
2 NOUN. the colored part of the eye; iris: *She has brown eyes.*
3 VERB. to watch; observe: *The child eyed the monkey with great interest.*
4 NOUN. often, **eyes,** a way of thinking; view; opinion: *Stealing is a crime in the eyes of the law.*
5 NOUN. something like an eye or that suggests an eye. The little spots on potatoes, the hole in a needle, and the loop into which a hook fastens are all called eyes.
6 NOUN. the calm, clear area at the center of a hurricane.
  ❑ VERB **eyes, eyed, ey·ing** or **eye·ing.** ■ Other words that sound like this are **ay, aye,** and **I.**
keep an eye on, IDIOM. to look after; watch carefully: *Keep an eye on the baby.*
see eye to eye, IDIOM. to agree entirely: *My parents and I do not see eye to eye on my allowance.*
eye·ball (ī′bȯl′), NOUN. the eye without the surrounding lids and bony socket. It contains the lens, the retina, and nerves and is filled with fluids.
eye·brow (ī′brou′), NOUN. the hair that grows along the bony ridge just above the eye.

eye·glass·es (ī′glas′əz), NOUN PLURAL. a pair of glass or plastic lenses, mounted in a frame, used to help someone see better; glasses; spectacles.
eye·lash (ī′lash′), NOUN. one of the protective hairs on the edge of the eyelid. ❑ PLURAL **eye·lash·es.**

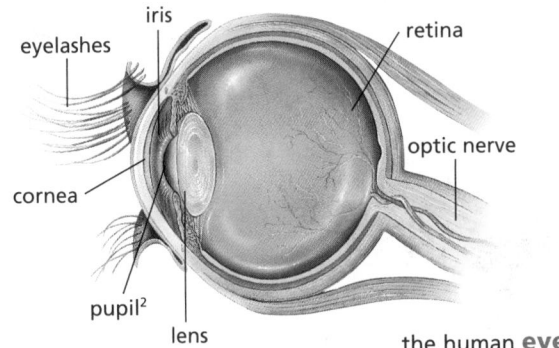

the human **eye**

eye·lid (ī′lid′), NOUN. the movable covers of skin, upper or lower, by means of which we can shut and open our eyes.
eye·piece (ī′pēs′), NOUN. the lens or set of lenses in a telescope or microscope that is closest to the eye of the user.
eye·sight (ī′sīt′), NOUN. the power of seeing; sight: *A hawk has keen eyesight. Grandpa's eyesight has improved a lot since his operation.*
eye·wit·ness (ī′wit′nis), NOUN. someone who has actually seen something happen and so can tell about it.

flamingo

fountain

F or **f** (ef), *NOUN.* the sixth letter of the English alphabet. ❑ *PLURAL* **F's** or **f's.**

F or **F.,** an abbreviation of **Fahrenheit.**

fa (fä), *NOUN.* (in music) the fourth tone of a scale. ❑ *PLURAL* **fas.**

fa·ble (fā′bəl), *NOUN.*
 1 a story that is made up to teach a lesson. Fables are often about animals who can talk.
 2 a story that is not true.

fab·ric (fab′rik), *NOUN.* a woven or knitted material cloth. Velvet, denim, and linen are fabrics.

fab·u·lous (fab′yə ləs),
 1 wonderful; exciting: *They had a fabulous trip.*
 2 not believable; amazing: *The painting was sold at a fabulous price.*
  —fab′u·lous·ly, *ADVERB.*

face (fās),
 1 *NOUN.* the front part of the head. Your eyes, nose, and mouth are parts of your face.

 2 *NOUN.* a look; expression: *His face was sad.*
 3 *NOUN.* an ugly or funny look made by twisting up your face: *I made a face at my brother.*
 4 *NOUN.* the front or important side of something: *The symbols and numbers are on the face of a playing card.*
 5 *VERB.* to have the face or front toward: *The house faces the street. Please face the camera.*
 6 *VERB.* to meet bravely or boldly: *It is always better to face a challenge than to avoid one.*
  ❑ *VERB* **fac·es, faced, fac·ing.**
 keep a straight face, *IDIOM.* to look serious; keep from laughing: *He managed to keep a straight face even when the clown squirted him.*

face·off (fās′ôf′), *NOUN.* (in hockey or lacrosse) the act of putting the puck or ball in play when the referee drops it between two opposing players.

fa·cial (fā′shəl), *ADJECTIVE.* of or for the face: *She wiped off the lipstick with a facial tissue.*

fa·cil·i·ty (fə sil′ə tē), NOUN.
1 **facilities,** rooms, equipment, and so on that make an action easier or provide a special service: *The laundry facilities in our building are out of order.*
2 the power to do something easily and quickly; skill in using the hands or mind: *She has the facility to become a fine violinist.*
❑ PLURAL **fa·cil·i·ties.**

fact (fakt), NOUN.
1 something that is known to be true; something known to have happened: *It is a fact that the Pilgrims sailed to America in 1620.*
2 what is true; truth: *The fact is that I did not want to go to the dance.*

fac·tor (fak′tər), NOUN.
1 a cause of something: *The low price was a factor in my decision to buy this car.*
2 often **factors,** numbers that are multiplied together to produce another number: *The factors of 10 are the numbers 2 and 5.*

fac·tor·y (fak′tər ē), NOUN. a building or group of buildings where people make things. ❑ PLURAL **fac·tor·ies.**

fac·tu·al (fak′chü əl), ADJECTIVE. based on facts; containing facts: *I wrote a factual account of our field trip for the school paper.* **—fac′tu·al·ly,** ADVERB.

fac·ul·ty (fak′əl tē), NOUN.
1 the teachers at a school, college, or university.
2 **faculties,** powers of the mind or body: *Although 100 years old now, she still has all her faculties.*
3 the power or ability to do some special thing: *She has a great faculty for arithmetic.*
❑ PLURAL **fac·ul·ties.**

fad (fad), NOUN. something that interests almost everyone for a short time; fashion or craze.

Cabbage Patch dolls were a big **fad.**

fade (fād), VERB.
1 to lose or cause to lose color: *Sunlight faded the sofa.*
2 to lose freshness or strength; wither: *Our garden flowers faded at the end of the summer.*

3 to die away; disappear little by little: *The sound of the train slowly faded away after it went by.*
❑ VERB **fades, fad·ed, fad·ing.**

Fahr·en·heit (far′ən hīt), ADJECTIVE. of, based on, or according to a scale for measuring temperature. On the **Fahrenheit scale,** 32 degrees is the temperature at which water freezes, and 212 degrees is the temperature at which water boils.

fail (fāl), VERB.
1 to not be able to do something; to not succeed: *He tried to stay awake all night, but he failed.*
2 to not do what should be done; neglect: *She failed to follow our advice.*
3 to not be of any use to someone when needed: *When I needed their help, they failed me.*
4 to lose strength; grow weak; die away: *The patient's heart was failing.*
5 to receive a failing grade: *You failed the test because you didn't study.*
6 to give a failing grade to a student.
❑ VERB **fails, failed, fail·ing.**

fail·ure (fā′lyər), NOUN.
1 a lack of success: *My first song was a failure.*
2 the act of not doing something; neglecting: *Failure to follow directions may cause errors.*
3 the process or condition of losing strength; becoming weak: *heart failure, kidney failure.*
4 someone or something that has failed: *The picnic was a failure because it rained.*

faint (fānt),
1 ADJECTIVE. not clear or plain; dim: *a faint image.*
2 ADJECTIVE. weak; feeble: *a faint voice.*
3 VERB. to suddenly become unconscious for a short time: *After the car accident the driver fainted.*
4 ADJECTIVE. about to faint; dizzy and weak: *I felt faint from hunger.*
❑ VERB **faints, faint·ed, faint·ing. —faint′ly,** ADVERB.

DID YOU KNOW?

Fainting usually only lasts a few minutes. A person who has fainted should be placed flat on his or her back. If you feel you may faint, you should lie down, or sit down with your head between your knees.

fair[1] (fâr),
1 ADJECTIVE. giving the same treatment to all; honest; just: *Try to be fair to everyone.*
2 ADJECTIVE. according to the rules: *It isn't fair to peek when you're playing hide-and-seek.*
3 ADJECTIVE. not good and not bad; average: *That movie wasn't one of my favorites; it was only fair.*

a	hat	ė	term	ô	order	ch	child	⎛a in about
ā	age	i	it	oi	oil	ng	long	e in taken
ä	far	ī	ice	ou	out	sh	she	ə⎨i in pencil
â	care	o	hot	u	cup	th	thin	o in lemon
e	let	ō	open	ù	put	ŦH	then	⎝u in circus
ē	equal	ȯ	saw	ü	rule	zh	measure	

4 _ADJECTIVE._ light; not dark: _A blond person has fair hair and skin._

5 _ADJECTIVE._ clear; sunny; not cloudy or stormy: _We had fair weather for the picnic._

6 _ADVERB._ in a fair manner; honestly: _The team played fair._

7 _ADJECTIVE._ beautiful: _our fair city._

8 _ADJECTIVE._ (in baseball) falling within the base lines; not being a foul: _a fair ball._

■ Another word that sounds like this is **fare.**
—**fair′ness,** _NOUN._

fair² (fâr), _NOUN._

1 an outdoor show of farm animals and other things: _I won the prize for the best quilt at the county fair._

2 a gathering of buyers and sellers, often held at the same time and place every year: _a trade fair, an art fair._

3 a sale of some kind: _Our school held a fair to raise money for new library books._

■ Another word that sounds like this is **fare.**

fair·ly (fâr′lē), _ADVERB._

1 in a just and honest manner: _All contestants will be treated fairly._

2 in some amount; rather; somewhat: _She is a fairly good pupil, about average._

fair·y (fâr′ē), _NOUN._ (in stories) a tiny, make-believe person, very lovely and delicate, who can help or harm human beings. ❑ _PLURAL_ **fair·ies.**

faith (fāth), _NOUN._

1 a firm belief in someone; trust; confidence: _We have faith in our friends._

2 a belief in God.

3 a religion: _the Islamic faith, the Christian faith._

faith·ful (fāth′fəl), _ADJECTIVE._

1 worthy of trust; loyal: _A faithful friend will keep your secret._

2 true to fact; accurate: _The witness gave a faithful account of what happened._
—**faith′ful·ly,** _ADVERB._ —**faith′ful·ness,** _NOUN._

faith·less (fāth′lis), _ADJECTIVE._ not loyal: _faithless friends._ —**faith′less·ly,** _ADVERB._ —**faith′less·ness,** _NOUN._

fa·ji·tas (fə hē′təz), _NOUN PLURAL._ thin strips of meat soaked in flavoring, then broiled or grilled and served with tortillas.

fake (fāk),

1 _ADJECTIVE._ intended to deceive; not real; false: _fake fur, fake money._

2 _VERB._ to make something false appear to be real in order to deceive: _to fake someone's signature._

3 _NOUN._ something false that seems real: _The diamond was a fake._

4 _VERB._ to pretend: _He faked being sick._
❑ _VERB_ **fakes, faked, fak·ing.** —**fak′er,** _NOUN._

fa·la·fel (fə lä′fəl), _NOUN._ a small ball or patty made from ground chickpeas and spices, then fried in oil. Falafel is often eaten with pita bread.

fal·con (fȯl′kən or fal′kən), _NOUN._ a swift hawk having a short, curved bill and long claws and wings. Falcons are sometimes trained to hunt and kill birds and small game.

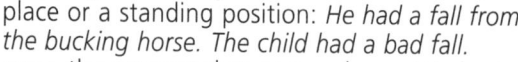

falcon — between 8 and 20 inches long

fall (fȯl),

1 _VERB._ to drop or come down from a higher place: _Snow is falling fast. Her hat fell off._

2 _NOUN._ the act of dropping from a higher place or a standing position: _He had a fall from the bucking horse. The child had a bad fall._

3 _NOUN._ the amount that comes down: _We had a heavy fall of snow last weekend._

4 _NOUN._ **falls,** a waterfall: _Niagara Falls. We enjoyed visiting the falls._

5 _VERB._ to come down suddenly from a standing position: _A baby who is learning to walk often falls._

6 _NOUN._ destruction; end: _the fall of an empire._

7 _VERB._ to lose position, power, or dignity: _The ruler fell from the people's favor._

8 _VERB._ to be captured, overthrown, or destroyed: _The fort fell after the enemy's violent attack._

9 _VERB._ to pass into some condition or state: _He fell sick. The baby fell asleep. The boy and girl fell in love._

10 _VERB._ to happen; take place: _This year my birthday falls on a Monday._

11 _VERB._ to become lower or less: _Prices are falling. The water in the river has fallen two feet._

12 _NOUN._ a season of the year between summer and winter; autumn.

13 _ADJECTIVE._ of, occurring in, or suitable for the fall: _fall clothes, fall plowing._
❑ _VERB_ **falls, fell, fall·en, fall·ing.**

fall back on, _IDIOM._ to turn to someone or something when other things fail: _When it started pouring we fell back on our plan to go to the movies._

fall·en (fȯl′ən),

1 _ADJECTIVE._ down on the ground; down flat: _The road was blocked by a fallen tree._

2 _VERB._ the past participle of **fall:** _Much rain has fallen._

fall·out (fȯl′out′), _NOUN._ the radioactive particles that fall to the earth after a nuclear explosion.

false (fȯls), _ADJECTIVE._

1 not true; not correct; wrong. A **false note** is wrong in pitch. A **false step** is a mistake.

2 not loyal; deceitful: _a false friend._

3 not real; artificial: _false teeth._
❑ _ADJECTIVE_ **fals·er, fals·est.** —**false′ly,** _ADVERB._

false·hood (fȯls′hud′), _ADJECTIVE._ a false statement; a lie.

fal·ter (fȯl′tər), VERB.
1 to become unsteady in movement; stumble; totter: *The horse faltered on the rocky lane.*
2 to hesitate; lose courage; waver: *I faltered for a moment before I jumped.*
❑ VERB **fal·ters, fal·tered, fal·ter·ing.**

fame (fām), NOUN. the fact or condition of being very well known: *He was surprised by his sudden fame.*

fa·mil·iar (fə mil′yər), ADJECTIVE.
1 well-known; common: *a familiar face.*
2 having a good or thorough knowledge of: *She is familiar with French and English.*
3 close; personal; intimate: *She spent her vacation visiting old and familiar friends.*
–**fa·mil′iar·ly**, ADVERB.

fam·i·ly (fam′ə lē), NOUN.
1 parents or a parent and child or children: *Many families came to our neighborhood fair.*
2 the children of a father and mother: *They are raising a family.*
3 all a person's relatives: *a family reunion.*
4 a group of related living things. Lions, tigers, and leopards belong to the cat family.
❑ PLURAL **fam·i·lies.**

family tree, a diagram showing how all the members and ancestors of a family are related.

fam·ine (fam′ən), NOUN. almost total lack of food in a region or among a group of people; a time of starvation: *The famine was prevented by shipments of food from many countries.*

fa·mous (fā′məs), ADJECTIVE. very well known; noted: *The famous singer was greeted by a large crowd.*

fan¹ (fan),
1 NOUN. a device with rotating blades turned by an electric motor. It makes a breeze to cool a room, a car's engine, and so on.
2 NOUN. a piece of stiff paper, attached to a handle, waved back and forth to make a breeze.
3 VERB. to stir, blow, or move air on toward: *Fan the fire to make it burn faster. She fanned herself.*
4 NOUN. anything that is flat and spread out like an open fan: *The peacock spread out its tail into a beautiful fan.*
❑ VERB **fans, fanned, fan·ning.** –**fan′like**′, ADJECTIVE.

fan² (fan), NOUN. someone extremely interested in something, such as a sport, a television series, or a performer: *Mom is a real fan of that singer and has all his CDs.*

Word Story

Fan² is short for **fanatic,** which comes from a Latin word meaning "temple." A football fan may go to the stadium with the same devotion that ancient Romans went to their temples. When the word lost its ending, it also dropped the negative sense of its meaning.

fa·nat·ic (fə nat′ik),
1 NOUN. someone whose feelings or beliefs are unreasonably strong: *My friend is a fanatic about fresh air and always has her windows open.*
2 ADJECTIVE. enthusiastic beyond reason; too great or unreasonable: *He has a fanatic interest in golf.*
▪ See the Word Story at **fan².** –**fa·nat′i·cal·ly,** ADVERB.

fan·cy (fan′sē),
1 ADJECTIVE. not plain or simple; decorated; having special added parts: *fancy embroidery, a fancy dinner for guests.*
2 ADJECTIVE. of high quality or unusual kind: *fancy strawberries.*
3 VERB. to like; be fond of: *She fancies bright colors, but he prefers the softer ones.*
❑ ADJECTIVE **fan·ci·er, fan·ci·est;** VERB **fan·cies, fan·cied, fan·cy·ing.**

fang (fang), NOUN. a long, pointed tooth of a dog, snake, and so on.

fan·tas·tic (fan tas′tik), ADJECTIVE.
1 very odd; unreal; strange and wild in shape or manner: *The fire cast weird, fantastic shadows on the walls.*
2 causing admiration, wonder, or surprise: *Our science project was a fantastic success.*
–**fan·tas′ti·cal·ly,** ADVERB.

sharp **fangs**

fan·ta·sy (fan′tə sē), NOUN. a product of the imagination; something that exists only in your mind: *She had a fantasy in which she won five million dollars.* ❑ PLURAL **fan·ta·sies.**

far (fär),
1 ADVERB. a long way; a long way off: *They live far from town. Far in the future, we may visit other worlds.*
2 ADJECTIVE. not near; distant: *They live in a far country. The moon is far from the earth.*
3 ADJECTIVE. more distant: *We live on the far side of the hill.*
4 ADVERB. much: *It is far better to go by train.*
❑ ADVERB **far·ther, far·thest** or **fur·ther, fur·thest;** ADJECTIVE **far·ther, far·thest** or **fur·ther, fur·thest.**

so far, IDIOM. until now: *So far this week we've enjoyed fine weather.*

far·a·way (fär′ə wā′), ADJECTIVE. distant; far away: *He read of faraway places in geography books.*

a	hat	ė	term	ô	order	ch	child	ə	a in about
ā	age	i	it	oi	oil	ng	long		e in taken
ä	far	ī	ice	ou	out	sh	she		i in pencil
â	care	o	hot	u	cup	th	thin		o in lemon
e	let	ō	open	u̇	put	ҭн	then		u in circus
ē	equal	ȯ	saw	ü	rule	zh	measure		

fare (fâr),
1 *NOUN.* the money that someone pays to ride in a taxi, bus, train, airplane, and so on.
2 *VERB.* to get along; get on; do: *She is faring well in school.*
❑ *VERB* **fares, fared, far•ing.** ■ Another word that sounds like this is **fair.**

Far East, China, Japan, and other parts of eastern Asia. **–Far Eastern.**

fare•well (fâr/wel/),
1 *INTERJECTION.* good-bye: *Farewell! Have a good trip!*
2 *NOUN.* good wishes when saying good-bye: *We said our farewells at the station.*
3 *ADJECTIVE.* parting; last: *a farewell kiss. The singer gave a farewell performance.*

farm (färm),
1 *NOUN.* a piece of land where someone raises crops or animals.
2 *NOUN.* a place where someone raises a certain kind of thing: *a turnip farm, a mink farm.*
3 *VERB.* to raise crops or animals: *He farms for a living.*
❑ *VERB* **farms, farmed, farm•ing.**

Many animals live on a farm.

farm•er (fär/mər), *NOUN.* someone who raises crops or animals on a farm.

farm•ing (fär/ming), *NOUN.* the business of raising crops or animals on a farm; agriculture.

far•sight•ed (fär/sī/tid), *ADJECTIVE.* seeing distant things more clearly than near ones. Some farsighted people wear glasses to read.

far•ther (fär/ᴛʜər),
1 *ADJECTIVE.* more distant: *My house is farther from school than yours is.*
2 *ADVERB.* to a greater distance: *We walked farther than we meant to.*
★ **Farther** is a comparative of **far.**

far•thest (fär/ᴛʜist),
1 *ADJECTIVE.* most distant: *Ours is the house farthest down the road.*
2 *ADVERB.* to or at the greatest distance: *He hit the ball farthest.*

3 *ADVERB.* most: *Their ideas were the farthest advanced at that time.*
★ **Farthest** is a superlative of **far.**

fas•ci•nate (fas/n āt), *VERB.* to interest greatly; charm: *The designs and colors in African art fascinate me.* ■ See the Synonym Study at **interested.** ❑ *VERB* **fas•ci•nates, fas•ci•nat•ed, fas•ci•nat•ing. –fas/ci•na/tion,** *NOUN.*

fash•ion (fash/ən), *NOUN.*
1 the current custom in dress, manners, or speech; style: *the latest fashion in shoes.*
2 the way something is shaped, made, or done; manner: *He walks in a peculiar fashion.*

fash•ion•a•ble (fash/ə nə bəl), *ADJECTIVE.* following the fashion; in fashion; stylish: *They replaced their old clothes with fashionable new outfits.*

fast¹ (fast),
1 *ADJECTIVE.* quick; rapid; swift: *She is a fast runner.* ■ See the Synonym Study at **quick.**
2 *ADVERB.* quickly; rapidly; swiftly: *Airplanes go fast.*
3 *ADJECTIVE.* showing a time ahead of the real time: *That clock is fast.*
4 *ADJECTIVE.* firm; loyal: *They have been fast friends for years.*

fast² (fast),
1 *VERB.* to go without food; eat little or nothing; go without certain kinds of food: *Some people fast for religious reasons.*
2 *NOUN.* the act or time of fasting.
❑ *VERB* **fasts, fast•ed, fast•ing.**

fas•ten (fas/n), *VERB.*
1 to tie, lock, or cause to hold together: *fasten a door, fasten a seat belt.* ■ See the Synonym Study at **join.**
2 to fix; direct: *The dog fastened its eyes on me.*
❑ *VERB* **fas•tens, fas•tened, fas•ten•ing.**

fas•ten•er (fas/n ər), *NOUN.* a device used to make two parts or pieces stay together. A zipper is a fastener.

fast-food (fast/füd/), *ADJECTIVE.* of or serving food that is prepared and served quickly, such as hamburgers, pizza, fried chicken, and so on: *fast-food restaurants.*

fat (fat),
1 *NOUN.* a white or yellow oily substance formed in the body of animals. Fat is a nutrient. Fat is also found in plants, especially in some seeds.
2 *ADJECTIVE.* having a lot of this: *fat meat.*
3 *ADJECTIVE.* having much flesh; plump; weighing a lot more than usual: *The dog is too fat.*
❑ *ADJECTIVE* **fat•ter, fat•test.**

fa•tal (fā/tl), *ADJECTIVE.*
1 causing someone's death: *Most fatal car accidents involve alcohol or drugs.*
2 causing destruction or ruin: *The loss of all our money was fatal to our plans.*

fate (fāt), NOUN.
1 the power that is often believed to control what is to happen in the future.
2 the things that happen to a person or group; someone's fortune: *History shows that the fate of many nations is the same.*

fate·ful (fāt′fəl), ADJECTIVE. having a great effect on what is to come; decisive: *a fateful battle.*

fat-free (fat′frē′), ADJECTIVE. made without fat or oil. Some people with special health problems eat fat-free food.

fa·ther (fä′тнər), NOUN.
1 a male parent.
2 a man who did important work as a maker or leader: *Washington is called the father of his country.*
3 the Father, God.
4 Father, a title of respect for a priest.
—**fa′ther·ly,** ADVERB.

fa·ther-in-law (fä′тнər in lò′), NOUN. the father of your husband or wife. ❑ PLURAL **fa·thers-in-law.**

fath·om (faтн′əm), NOUN. a unit of length equal to 6 feet. It is used in measuring the depth of water and the length of the ropes and cables on ships.

fa·tigue (fə tēg′), NOUN. a tired feeling caused by hard work or effort: *I felt extreme fatigue after studying all day.*

fa·tigued (fə tēgd′), ADJECTIVE. tired; weary: *I was fatigued by the long journey.*

fat·ten (fat′n), VERB.
1 to make something fat: *fatten pigs for market.*
2 to become fat: *The pigs fattened on corn.*
❑ VERB **fat·tens, fat·tened, fat·ten·ing.**

fat·ty (fat′ē), ADJECTIVE. of or containing fat: *You should avoid fatty foods.* ❑ ADJECTIVE **fat·ti·er, fat·ti·est.**

fau·cet (fò′sit), NOUN. a device for turning on or off the flow of water; tap.

fault (fòlt), NOUN.
1 a cause for blame; responsibility: *Whose fault is it?*
2 a weakness or defect; a failing: *Carelessness is her greatest fault.*
—**fault′less,** ADJECTIVE.

fault·y (fòl′tē), ADJECTIVE. not working properly; defective: *The leak in the tire was caused by a faulty valve.* ❑ ADJECTIVE **fault·i·er, fault·i·est.**

faun (fòn), NOUN. (in Roman myths) a creature like a man, but with the ears, horns, tail, and legs of a goat. ■ Another word that sounds like this is **fawn.**

fau·na (fò′nə), NOUN. animals as a group: *The fauna of Australia is unique.* ❑ PLURAL **fau·nas.**

fa·vor (fā′vər),
1 NOUN. an act of kindness: *Will you do me a favor?*
2 VERB. to like; approve: *We favor his plan.*
3 VERB. to give more than is fair to: *The teacher favors you.*
4 VERB. to treat gently: *The dog favors its sore foot when it walks.*
5 NOUN. a small gift given to every guest at a party: *Paper hats and bags of candy were used as favors at the birthday party.*
❑ VERB **fa·vors, fa·vored, fa·vor·ing.**

in favor of, IDIOM. on the side of: *The referee's decision was in favor of the other team, and they won the game.*

fa·vor·a·ble (fā′vər ə bəl), ADJECTIVE.
1 showing approval: *"Yes" is a favorable answer to a request.*
2 to your advantage; helping; promising: *A favorable wind made the boat go faster.*
—**fa′vor·a·bly,** ADVERB.

fa·vor·ite (fā′vər it),
1 ADJECTIVE. liked better than others: *What is your favorite flower?*
2 NOUN. someone or something that you like better than other people or things: *He is a favorite with everybody.*

fa·vor·it·ism (fā′vər ə tiz′əm), NOUN. the act of giving better treatment to some people than to others: *A teacher or coach should not show favoritism.*

fawn (fòn), NOUN. a deer that is less than a year old. ■ Another word that sounds like this is **faun.**
—**fawn′like′,** ADJECTIVE.

fawn

fax (faks),
1 VERB. to send printed matter and photographs over telephone lines, reproducing exact copies on the receiving end.
2 NOUN. the exact copy made made in this way.
❑ VERB **fax·es, faxed, fax·ing;** PLURAL **fax·es.**

fax machine, an electronic device for sending and receiving copies over telephone lines.

a	hat	ė	term	ô	order	ch	child		
ā	age	i	it	oi	oil	ng	long	⎧ a	in about
ä	far	ī	ice	ou	out	sh	she	⎪ e	in taken
â	care	o	hot	u	cup	th	thin	ə⎨ i	in pencil
e	let	ō	open	ů	put	тн	then	⎪ o	in lemon
ē	equal	ò	saw	ü	rule	zh	measure	⎩ u	in circus

fear (fir),
1 NOUN. a feeling that danger or something bad is near: *I have a fear of heights.*
2 VERB. to be afraid of: *Our cat fears big dogs.*
3 VERB. to have an uneasy feeling or idea about something: *I fear that I am late.*
❑ VERB **fears, feared, fear·ing.**

Synonym Study

Fear means the feeling of being scared: *The animals rushed out of the collapsing barn in fear.*

Fright means sudden fear: *Waking up to the sound of a siren gave me a terrible fright.*

Alarm means fright caused by danger: *The rabbit hopped away in alarm when we got too close to it.*

Terror means very great fear: *People in the burning building shouted in terror.*

Horror means terror and a creepy feeling: *The ghost story filled us with horror.*

See also the Synonym Studies at **afraid** and **scare.**

fear·ful (fir′fəl), ADJECTIVE.
1 causing fear; terrible; dreadful: *a fearful dragon.*
2 feeling fear of something; frightened: *The child was fearful of the dark.*
−**fear′ful·ly,** ADVERB.

fear·less (fir′lis), ADJECTIVE. without fear; afraid of nothing; brave: *a fearless lion tamer.* −**fear′less·ly,** ADVERB. −**fear′less·ness,** NOUN.

fear·some (fir′səm), ADJECTIVE. causing fear; frightful: *The monster in the movie was a fearsome sight*

feast (fēst),
1 NOUN. a big meal for some special occasion and for a number of guests; banquet: *We went to the wedding feast.*
2 VERB. to eat a big meal; have a feast: *We feast on turkey and pumpkin pie at Thanksgiving.*
❑ VERB **feasts, feast·ed, feast·ing.**

The entire family gathered for the Thanksgiving **feast.**

feat (fēt), NOUN. an act that shows great skill, strength, or daring. ∎ Another word that sounds like this is **feet.**

feath·er (feᴛн′ər), NOUN. one of the many light, flat growths that cover a bird's skin. −**feather′like′,** ADJECTIVE.

feath·er·y (feᴛн′ər ē), ADJECTIVE. like feathers; soft and light: *feathery clouds.*

fea·ture (fē′chər),
1 NOUN. a part of the face. The eyes, nose, mouth, chin, and forehead are features.
2 NOUN. a distinct part or quality; thing that stands out and attracts your attention: *Your plan has many good features.*
3 VERB. to give special attention to something: *The local newspapers featured the mayor's speech.*
❑ VERB **fea·tures, fea·tured, fea·tur·ing.**

Feb., an abbreviation of **February.**

Feb·ru·ar·y (feb′rü er′ē), NOUN. the second month of the year. It has 28 days except in leap years, when it has 29.

Word Story

February comes from the name of an ancient Roman ceremony of purification that was held on February 15. On this day Romans repented and made up for their bad deeds.

fed (fed), VERB.
1 the past tense of **feed:** *We fed the birds.*
2 the past participle of **feed:** *Have they been fed yet?*
fed up, IDIOM. bored, impatient, or disgusted with something: *I became fed up with waiting and left.*

fed·er·al (fed′ər əl), ADJECTIVE.
1 formed by an agreement between states setting up a central government: *The United States became a nation by federal union.*
2 of or for the central government of the United States, not of any state or city alone: *Coining money is a federal power.*

fed·e·ra·tion (fed′ə rā′shən), NOUN. a union of states, nations, clubs, and so on: *Each member of the federation controls its own affairs.*

fee (fē), NOUN.
1 money that you pay to get in to see something; charge: *an admission fee.*
2 money that you pay to a doctor, lawyer, and so on, for something they do for you: *Doctors and lawyers receive fees for their services.*
❑ PLURAL **fees.**

fee·ble (fē′bəl), ADJECTIVE. very weak: *A sick person is often feeble. A feeble attempt is liable to fail.*
❑ ADJECTIVE **fee·bler, fee·blest.** −**fee′bly,** ADVERB.

feed (fēd),
1 VERB. to give food to: *We feed babies because they cannot feed themselves.*

F

2 *VERB.* to give as food: *We feed hay to cows.*

3 *VERB.* to eat: *Starlings feed in our lawn after it rains.*

4 *NOUN.* food for animals: *Give the chickens their feed.*
❑ *VERB* **feeds, fed, feed·ing. –feed′er,** *NOUN.*

feed·back (fēd′bak′), *NOUN.*

1 the process by which a system, machine, and so on, regulates itself by sending back to itself information about what it is doing.

2 a reaction to or advice about how you are doing something: *She improved the organization of her report after feedback from the teacher.*

feel (fēl),

1 *VERB.* to touch something in order to see what it is like: *Feel this cloth.*

2 *NOUN.* the way something seems to the touch; feeling: *I like the feel of silk.*

3 *VERB.* to be aware of something: *I felt the cool breeze on my face.*

4 *VERB.* to be; have the feeling of being: *He feels angry. We felt hot.*

5 *VERB.* to seem to be; have the feeling of: *The air feels cold.*

6 *VERB.* to have an idea or an opinion about something: *I feel that we can count on their help.*

7 *VERB.* to have a feeling of: *They feel pity. I felt pain.* ★ In this sense, formal English uses **bad,** not **badly:** *The mayor feels bad about missing the press conference.*

8 *VERB.* to have pity or sympathy: *We feel for people who suffer.*
❑ *VERB* **feels, felt, feel·ing.**

feel·er (fē′lər), *NOUN.* a special part of an animal's body used for finding out about things by touching them. Insects, crabs, lobsters, and shrimp have feelers on their heads.

feelers

feel·ing (fē′ling), *NOUN.*

1 how you feel about something. Joy, love, fear, and anger are feelings.

2 **feelings,** the emotional part of your nature: *You hurt my feelings when you yelled at me.*

feeler

3 an awareness; sensation: *I had a feeling that someone was watching me.*

4 the sense of touch. By feeling something we tell whether it is hard or soft, hot or cold, and so on.

5 an opinion: *I have no feeling about the plan, one way or the other.*

feet (fēt), *NOUN.* the plural of **foot:** *A dog has four feet. I am five feet tall.* ■ Another word that sounds like this is **feat.**

fe·line (fē′līn),

1 *ADJECTIVE.* of or about a cat: *a feline disease.*

2 *NOUN.* a cat.

3 *NOUN.* any animal belonging to a group of meat-eating mammals including domestic cats, lions, tigers, cheetahs, and so on.

fell¹ (fel), *VERB.* the past tense of **fall:** *Snow fell last night.*

fell² (fel), *VERB.* to cause something to fall; knock, cut, or strike down: *They had to fell many trees to clear the land.* ❑ *VERB* **fells, felled, fell·ing.**

fel·low (fel′ō),

1 *NOUN.* a man or boy.

2 *NOUN.* someone; anybody: *What can a fellow do?*

3 *ADJECTIVE.* being in a similar situation, group, and so on: *fellow classmates, fellow workers.*

fel·low·ship (fel′ō ship), *NOUN.*

1 a feeling of companionship; friendliness: *I enjoy the fellowship of my classmates.*

2 group of people having similar tastes, interests, beliefs, aims, and so on.

felt¹ (felt), *VERB.*

1 the past tense of **feel:** *I felt the cat's soft fur.*

2 the past participle of **feel:** *I have never felt so sad.*

felt² (felt), *NOUN.* a cloth that is made by rolling and pressing together fibers such as wool, nylon, or fur, instead of being woven.

fe·male (fē′māl),

1 *ADJECTIVE.* of or about women or girls.

2 *NOUN.* a woman or girl.

3 *ADJECTIVE.* belonging to the sex that can give birth to young or lay eggs. Cows are female animals.

4 *NOUN.* an animal belonging to this sex.

fem·i·nine (fem′ə nən), *ADJECTIVE.* of, for, or like women or girls: *feminine clothing styles.*

fem·i·nism (fem′ə niz′əm), *NOUN.*

1 the belief that women should have the same economic, political, legal, and social rights as men; the belief that men and women are equal.

2 a movement to get these rights and to encourage equal treatment of men and women.

fence (fens),

1 *NOUN.* a wooden or metal railing or wall put around a yard, garden, or field. A fence shows where some space ends or keeps things in or out.

2 *VERB.* to put a fence around something.

3 *VERB.* to fight with long slender swords or foils.
❑ *VERB* **fenc·es, fenced, fenc·ing. –fenc′er,** *NOUN.*

on the fence, *IDIOM.* undecided; without a definite opinion: *He is on the fence about the new schools plan.*

a	hat	ė	term	ô	order	ch	child		a in about
ā	age	i	it	oi	oil	ng	long		e in taken
ä	far	ī	ice	ou	out	sh	she	ə	i in pencil
â	care	o	hot	u	cup	th	thin		o in lemon
e	let	ō	open	ù	put	ᴛʜ	then		u in circus
ē	equal	ò	saw	ü	rule	zh	measure		

fenc·ing (fen′sing), NOUN. the art or sport of fighting with thin, light swords.

fend·er (fen′dər), NOUN. a curved piece of metal that fits over the wheel of a car, truck, or bicycle. The fender protects the wheel and reduces splashing in wet weather.

fer·ment (fər ment′), VERB. to undergo or produce a gradual chemical change in which yeast, bacteria, or chemicals change sugar into alcohol and carbon dioxide. Grape juice ferments into wine. ❑ VERB **fer·ments, fer·ment·ed, fer·ment·ing.** —**fer′men·ta′tion,** NOUN.

fern (fėrn), NOUN. a kind of plant that has roots, stems, and feathery leaves, but no flowers or seeds. Cells called spores grow in the little brown dots on the backs of the leaves. Each spore can develop into a new plant.

fe·ro·cious (fə rō′shəs), ADJECTIVE. very cruel; fierce; savage: *The bear's ferocious growl was terrifying.*

fer·ret (fer′it),
1 NOUN. a small animal with a long body and short legs. It is a kind of weasel. Ferrets are sometimes kept as pets.
2 VERB. to find out by searching hard for a long time: *The detective was able to ferret out important evidence.*
❑ VERB **fer·rets, fer·ret·ed, fer·ret·ing.**

Fer·ris wheel (fer′is wēl′), a large revolving wheel with seats. People pay to ride on them at carnivals, amusements parks, and fairs.

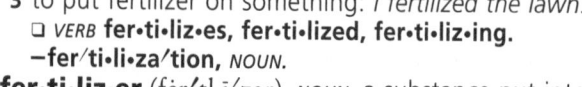

fer·ry (fer′ē),
1 VERB. to carry people, vehicles, and goods across a river, lake, or other stretch of water.
2 NOUN. a boat that carries people, vehicles, and goods on a trip like this.
3 VERB. to carry back and forth in an airplane, truck, and so on.
❑ VERB **fer·ries, fer·ried, fer·ry·ing; PLURAL fer·ries.**

Ferris wheel

fer·tile (fėr′tl), ADJECTIVE.
1 able to bear seeds, fruit, or young.
2 able to grow into a new, adult living thing: *Chicks hatch from fertile eggs.*
3 able to produce good crops easily: *This area has fertile soil.*

fer·ti·lize (fėr′tl īz), VERB.
1 to make fertile; to make a living thing able to produce offspring.
2 to unite with an egg cell in fertilization.

3 to put fertilizer on something: *I fertilized the lawn.*
❑ VERB **fer·ti·liz·es, fer·ti·lized, fer·ti·liz·ing.** —**fer′ti·li·za′tion,** NOUN.

fer·ti·liz·er (fėr′tl ī′zər), NOUN. a substance put into or on the soil to make it produce more crops.

fer·vent (fėr′vənt), ADJECTIVE. showing great emotion; very earnest: *She made a fervent plea for food and medicine for the earthquake victims.*

fer·vor (fėr′vər), NOUN. great emotion; enthusiasm: *The patriot spoke with such fervor that his voice trembled.*

fes·ti·val (fes′tə vəl), NOUN.
1 a day or special time of rejoicing or feasting, often in memory of some great happening: *Hanukkah is a Jewish festival.*
2 a program of entertainment, often held annually: *a summer music festival.*

fes·tive (fes′tiv), ADJECTIVE. of or suitable for a feast, festival, or holiday; merry: *A birthday is a festive occasion.* —**fes′tive·ly,** ADVERB.

fes·tiv·i·ty (fe stiv′ə tē), NOUN. festive activity; something done to celebrate: *wedding festivities, holiday festivities.* ❑ PLURAL **fes·tiv·i·ties.**

fetch (fech), VERB.
1 to go and get something; bring: *Fetch me my glasses.*
2 to sell for: *These eggs will fetch a good price.*
❑ VERB **fetch·es, fetched, fetch·ing.**

feud (fyüd),
1 NOUN. a long and angry quarrel between families or groups.
2 VERB. to carry on a long and angry quarrel: *Those neighbors have feuded for years.*
❑ VERB **feuds, feud·ed, feud·ing.**

Did You Know?

One of the most famous **feuds** in America took place in the Appalachian Mountains between two families, the Hatfields and the McCoys. Their feud started in 1860 and lasted for thirty years. Twenty people died because of the feud.

feu·dal·ism (fyü′dl iz′əm), NOUN. the social system of Europe during the Middle Ages. Under this system, people provided military service, farm labor, and part of their crops to their lord in return for his protection and the use of land.

fet·ter (fet′ər),
1 NOUN. usually, **fetters,** chains for the feet: *Fetters prevented the prisoner's escape.*
2 VERB. to bind with chains; chain the feet of.
❑ VERB **fet·ters, fet·tered, fet·ter·ing.**

fe·ver (fē′vər), NOUN.
1 a body temperature that is higher than normal. Normal human temperature is 98.6 degrees Fahrenheit or 37.0 degrees Celsius.
2 a sickness that causes or is accompanied by fever: *scarlet fever, typhoid fever.*

fe·ver·ish (fē′vər ish), ADJECTIVE.
1 having fever.
2 excited; restless: *I packed my bags in feverish haste.*
—**fe′ver·ish·ly,** ADVERB.

few (fyü),
1 ADJECTIVE. not many: *Few people came to the meeting because of the storm.*
2 NOUN. a small number: *We don't have many videos, only a few.*

fi·an·cé (fē′än sā′), NOUN. a man engaged to be married: *He is her fiancé.* ❑ PLURAL **fi·an·cés.**

fi·an·cée (fē′än sā′), NOUN. a woman engaged to be married: *She is his fiancée.* ❑ PLURAL **fi·an·cées.**

fib (fib),
1 NOUN. a lie about something that doesn't matter very much.
2 VERB. to tell a lie like this.
❑ VERB **fibs, fibbed, fib·bing.** —**fib′ber,** NOUN.

fi·ber (fī′bər), NOUN.
1 a thread; threadlike part. A muscle is made up of many fibers.
2 a substance made up of threads or threadlike parts: *Hemp fiber can be spun or woven.*
3 any part of vegetable food that cannot be digested. Fiber speeds the movement of food and waste products through the intestines.

fiber optics, a branch of physics that studies how sounds, pictures, and computer data can be sent by laser light. This light travels through very thin clear fibers of glass or plastic. The fibers carry large amounts of information very quickly.
—**fi·ber-op·tic** (fī′bər op′tik), ADJECTIVE.

fic·tion (fik′shən), NOUN.
1 a story that is not fact. Short stories and novels are fiction.
2 something made up that is presented as truth: *She exaggerates her experiences so much that it is hard to separate fact from fiction.*

fid·dle (fid′l),
1 NOUN. a violin.
2 VERB. to play a violin.
3 VERB. to make absent-minded movements with something: *Please stop fiddling with that paper.*
❑ VERB **fid·dles, fid·dled, fid·dling.**

fidg·et (fij′it), VERB. to move about restlessly: *Children sometimes fidget if they have to sit still too long.* ❑ VERB **fidg·ets, fidg·et·ed, fidg·et·ing.**

field (fēld),
1 NOUN. a piece of land with few or no trees; open country: *They saw a field of wild flowers.*
2 NOUN. piece of land used for crops or for pasture: *a soybean field, a corn field.*
3 NOUN. a piece of land used for some special purpose: *a baseball field, oil fields, coal fields.*
4 NOUN. a range of interest; area of activity or occupation: *Her field is medicine.*

5 VERB. (in baseball and softball) to stop or catch a batted ball.
❑ VERB **fields, field·ed, field·ing.** —**field′er,** NOUN.

field goal,
1 (in football) a play that scores three points, made by a place kick through the goalposts.
2 (in basketball) a basket scored while the ball is in play, counting either two or three points.

field trip, a trip away from school to give students an opportunity to learn by seeing things in person: *The class went on a field trip to the zoo.*

fiend (fēnd), NOUN.
1 a devil; evil spirit.
2 a very wicked or cruel person.
3 someone who spends a lot of time in some game or activity: *a tennis fiend.*

fiend·ish (fēn′dish), ADJECTIVE. very cruel or wicked: *They heard the fiendish laughter of a wicked witch.*
—**fiend′ish·ly,** ADVERB. —**fiend′ish·ness,** NOUN.

fierce (firs), ADJECTIVE.
1 wild and frightening; dangerous: *The hunter was attacked by a fierce lion.*
2 very great or strong; intense: *fierce anger, a fierce wind, fierce waves.*
❑ ADJECTIVE **fierc·er, fierc·est.** —**fierce′ly,** ADVERB. —**fierce′ness,** NOUN.

a **fierce** expression

fie·ry (fī′ə rē *or* fī′rē), ADJECTIVE.
1 like fire; very hot; glowing: *fiery red, fiery heat.*
2 full of feeling or spirit: *The mayor made a fiery speech defending his school reform plan.*
❑ ADJECTIVE **fie·ri·er, fie·ri·est.**

fi·es·ta (fē es′tə), NOUN.
1 a religious festival, especially in a Spanish-speaking country or area.
2 holiday or festivity.
❑ PLURAL **fi·es·tas.**

a	hat	ė	term	ô	order	ch	child		
ā	age	i	it	oi	oil	ng	long		a in about
ä	far	ī	ice	ou	out	sh	she		e in taken
â	care	o	hot	u	cup	th	thin	ə	i in pencil
e	let	ō	open	u̇	put	ŦH	then		o in lemon
ē	equal	ȯ	saw	ü	rule	zh	measure		u in circus

fife (fīf), NOUN. a small, musical instrument like a flute, played by blowing into it. Fifes are used with drums to make music for marching.

fif·teen (fif'tēn'), NOUN or ADJECTIVE. five more than ten; 15.

fif·teenth (fif'tēnth'), ADJECTIVE or NOUN.
1 next after the 14th.
2 one of 15 equal parts.

fifth (fifth), ADJECTIVE or NOUN.
1 next after the fourth; last in a series of five.
2 one of five equal parts.

fif·ti·eth (fif'tē ith), ADJECTIVE or NOUN.
1 next after the 49th; last in a series of 50.
2 one of 50 equal parts.

fif·ty (fif'tē), NOUN or ADJECTIVE. five times ten; 50.
❏ PLURAL **fif·ties.**

fifty-fifty, IDIOM. evenly; in half: *We split the money from our paper route fifty-fifty.*

fig (fig), NOUN. a small, soft, sweet fruit about the size of a plum. It grows on a tree in warm regions. Figs are usually dried like raisins.

fight (fīt),
1 NOUN. a violent struggle using fists or weapons; combat. A fight ends when one side gives up.
2 NOUN. an angry dispute; quarrel: *Their fights were always over money.*
3 VERB. to carry on or take part or in a violent struggle, quarrel, combat, or the like; have a fight: *to fight a battle. Enemy countries fight with armies.*
4 VERB. to argue or disagree with someone: *My sister and I often fight over which TV show to watch.*
5 VERB. to take part in a struggle against: *to fight disease, to fight your fear of the dark.*
6 VERB. to get or make by struggling: *She had to fight her way through the crowd.*
❏ VERB **fights, fought, fight·ing. —fight'er,** NOUN.

Synonym Study

Fight means to oppose someone or something with actions or words: *The puppies fight a lot, but they never hurt each other. If I ask to stay up late, Mom will fight me over it.*

Struggle means to fight with difficulty: *He struggled to get his stubborn calf back inside the gate.*

Battle means to fight for a period of time: *Her team battled all summer for first place.*

War means to fight strongly for a long time: *After years of warring with the British, Americans won their independence.*

See also the Synonym Study at **argue.**

fig·ment (fig'mənt), NOUN. something imagined; a made-up story: *I don't believe it; it's just a figment of your imagination.*

These **fife** players are wearing 18th-century costumes.

fig·ure (fig'yər),
1 NOUN. a symbol for a number. 1, 2, 3, 4, and so on, are figures.
2 VERB. to use numbers to find out the answer to some problem; calculate: *Can you figure the cost of painting this room?*
3 NOUN. **figures,** arithmetic: *He is very good at figures.*
4 NOUN. a form partially or completely enclosing a surface or space. Squares, triangles, cubes, and other shapes are called figures.
5 NOUN. someone's body shape: *a slender figure.*
6 NOUN. a form or shape: *In the darkness she saw dim figures moving.*
7 NOUN. a person: *The governor is a well-known figure throughout the state.*
❏ VERB **fig·ures, fig·ured, fig·ur·ing.**

figure out, IDIOM. to think out; understand: *We couldn't figure out where our dog had gone.*

fig·ure·head (fig'yər hed'), NOUN.
1 someone who is a leader in name only, without real authority.
2 (earlier) a carved human figure placed for decoration on the front of a ship.

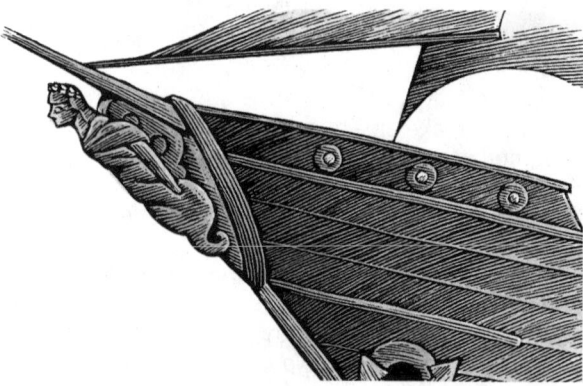
a ship's **figurehead**

figure of speech, an expression in which words are used out of their ordinary meaning to add beauty or force. When we say someone has "the eye of an eagle," we are using a figure of speech.

file¹ (fil),

1 *NOUN.* a container, drawer, or folder for keeping memos, letters, or other papers in order.

2 *NOUN.* a set of papers kept in order: *a file of bills.*

3 *VERB.* to put things away in a certain order: *Please file those letters.*

4 *NOUN.* information or instructions that a computer keeps together under a single name. A file can be placed in memory, recalled from memory, or processed all at once.

5 *VERB.* to march or move in a row, one behind the other: *The pupils filed out of the room.*

6 *NOUN.* a row of persons or things one behind another: *The file of soldiers marched in time.*

7 *VERB.* to place an official document among the records of a court, public office, or the like: *The deed to our house is filed with the county clerk.*
□ *VERB* **files, filed, fil·ing.**

file² (fil),

1 *NOUN.* a steel tool with many small ridges or teeth on it. Its rough surface is used to smooth rough materials or wear away hard substances.

2 *VERB.* to smooth something or wear it away with a file.
□ *VERB* **files, filed, fil·ing.**

Fil·i·pi·no (fil′ə pē′nō), *NOUN.* someone born or living in the Philippines. □ *PLURAL* **Fil·i·pi·nos.**

fill (fil), *VERB.*

1 to make or become full: *Fill this cup with milk.*

2 to take up all the space in; spread throughout: *The crowd filled the hall.*

3 to supply what is needed or wanted: *The pharmacist filled the doctor's prescription.*

4 to fill a hole or crack in something by putting something in it: *The dentist filled my tooth.*

5 to hold and do the duties of a position or office: *We want you to fill the office of treasurer.*
□ *VERB* **fills, filled, fill·ing.**

fil·let (fi lā′ or fil′ā),

1 *NOUN.* a slice of meat or fish without bones or fat.

2 *VERB.* to cut fish or meat into such slices.
□ *VERB* **fil·lets, fil·leted, fil·let·ing.**

fill·ing (fil′ing), *NOUN.* something put in a hole, gap, or crack to fill it: *a filling in a tooth.*

fil·ly (fil′ē), *NOUN.* a young female horse, donkey, or zebra; mare that is less than four or five years old.
□ *PLURAL* **fil·lies.**

film (film),

1 *NOUN.* a roll or sheet of thin material covered with a coating that is changed by light, used to take photographs: *He bought two rolls of film.*

2 *NOUN.* a movie: *We saw a film about animals.*

3 *NOUN.* a very thin surface or coating, often of liquid: *Oil on water will spread and make a film.*

4 *VERB.* to make a movie of a book or story: *They filmed "The Wizard of Oz."*
□ *VERB* **films, filmed, film·ing.**

fil·ter (fil′tər),

1 *NOUN.* a device for passing water, other liquids, or air, through cloth, paper, sand, charcoal, and so on. This is done in order to remove impurities.

2 *NOUN.* a material through which the liquid or air passes in a filter.

3 *VERB.* to pass or flow very slowly: *Water filters through the sandy soil and into the well.*

4 *VERB.* to put through a filter: *We filter this water for drinking.*

5 *VERB.* to remove by using a filter: *Filter the dirt out of the water.*
□ *VERB* **fil·ters, fil·tered, fil·ter·ing.**

filth (filth), *NOUN.* any foul, disgusting dirt: *The alley was filled with garbage and filth.*

filth·y (fil′thē), *ADJECTIVE.* very dirty; foul: *a filthy shirt.* □ *ADJECTIVE* **filth·i·er, filth·i·est.**

fin (fin), *NOUN.*

1 one of the movable winglike or fanlike parts of a fish's or other sea animal's body.

2 something shaped or used like a fin. Fins are used in scuba diving and snorkeling.

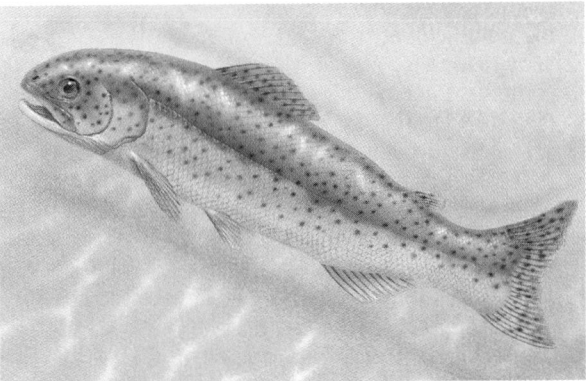

By moving its **fins,** a fish can swim and balance itself in the water.

fi·nal (fi′nl),

1 *ADJECTIVE.* at the end; coming last: *The book was interesting from the first to the final chapter.*
■ See the Synonym Study at **last.**

2 *ADJECTIVE.* not able to be changed; allowing no more discussion: *The person with the highest authority makes the final decisions.*

3 *NOUN.* **finals,** the last or deciding set in a series of games or examinations.

fi·na·le (fə nal′ē or fə nä′lē), *NOUN.* the last part of a piece of music or a play. □ *PLURAL* **fi·na·les.**

fi·nal·ly (fi′nl ē), *ADVERB.* at the end; at last: *The school bus finally came.*

a	hat	ė	term	ô	order	ch	child		a in about
ā	age	i	it	oi	oil	ng	long		e in taken
ä	far	ī	ice	ou	out	sh	she	ə	i in pencil
â	care	o	hot	u	cup	th	thin		o in lemon
e	let	ō	open	ù	put	ᵀʜ	then		u in circus
ē	equal	ò	saw	ü	rule	zh	measure		

fi·nance (fə nans′ or fi′nans),
1 NOUN. the management or control of money, including banking and investments.
2 NOUN. **finances,** money; income; revenues: *Her finances did not permit her to buy new CDs.*
3 VERB. to provide money for something: *A part-time job helped finance her college education.*
❑ VERB **fi·nances, fi·nanced, fi·nanc·ing.**

fi·nan·cial (fə nan′shəl or fi nan′shəl), ADJECTIVE. of or about money or the management of money: *Our financial affairs are in good order.*
—**fi·nan′cial·ly,** ADVERB.

fin·an·cier (fin′ən sir′ or fi′nən sir′), NOUN. someone who is skilled in managing and investing money. Bankers are financiers.

finch (finch), NOUN. a small songbird with a bill shaped like a cone. Sparrows, cardinals, and canaries are finches.
❑ PLURAL **finch·es.**

find (find),
1 VERB. to come upon; discover: *I found a dime.*
2 VERB. to look for something and get it: *Please find my hat for me.*
3 VERB. to learn: *We found that he could not swim.*
4 VERB. to decide and declare: *The jury found the woman guilty.*
5 NOUN. something found: *This old car is a real find at such a low price.*
❑ VERB **finds, found, find·ing.**
find out, IDIOM. to learn about; discover.

female

male

finch — about 4 inches long

Synonym Study

Find means to come upon something: *He found a dollar on the street.*

Discover means to find something that has not been known or that has been hidden: *I discovered some baby birds in a nest.*

Locate can mean to find the position of something: *The museum was easy to locate.*

Spot can mean to locate: *We spotted Monkey Island on the zoo map.*

ANTONYMS: lose, misplace.

find·ing (fin′ding), NOUN. the act of discovering; discovery: *The finding of a cure for the disease was a welcome event.*

fine¹ (fin),
1 ADJECTIVE. very good; excellent: *Everyone praised his fine singing. She is a fine student.*
2 ADJECTIVE. in good health; well: *I'm fine, thank you.*
3 ADJECTIVE. very small or thin: *Thread is finer than rope. Sand is finer than gravel.*
4 ADJECTIVE. delicate: *The tablecloth and napkins were made of fine linen.*
5 ADVERB. very well; excellently: *I'm doing fine.*
❑ ADJECTIVE **fin·er, fin·est.** —**fine′ly,** ADVERB.

fine² (fin),
1 NOUN. money that someone has to pay as punishment for breaking a law or regulation.
2 VERB. to make someone pay money in this way: *The judge fined her $50.*
❑ VERB **fines, fined, fin·ing.**

fin·ger (fing′gər),
1 NOUN. one of the five end parts of the hand, especially the four besides the thumb.
2 NOUN. anything shaped or used like a finger: *a long finger of land.*
3 VERB. to touch or handle with the fingers: *He absent-mindedly fingered the paper clips.*
❑ VERB **fin·gers, fin·gered, fin·ger·ing.**

fin·ger·nail (fing′gər nāl′), NOUN. the thin, hard layer that covers the tip of a finger.

fin·ger·print (fing′gər print′),
1 NOUN. the pattern of very fine lines and circles that the tip of a finger or thumb makes when you press it against something; mark made by the fleshy tip of a finger.
2 VERB. to take someone's fingerprints.
❑ VERB **fin·ger·prints, fin·ger·print·ed, fin·ger·print·ing.**

Did You Know?

Your **fingerprints** can be used to identify you because everyone's fingerprints are different. Everyone's earprints and footprints are also different. But people touch more things with their fingers than with their ears or bare feet, so fingerprints are used more often.

fin·ick·y (fin′ə kē), ADJECTIVE. too hard to please; fussy: *He is a finicky eater.* —**fin′ick·i·ness,** NOUN.

fin·ish (fin′ish),
1 VERB. to get to the end of something; complete: *to finish a book, to finish painting a picture.*
■ See the Synonym Study at **end.**
2 NOUN. an end: *She led the race right to the finish.*
3 VERB. to use something up completely: *I finished the bottle of milk at lunch.*
4 NOUN. the way in which a surface is prepared: *a smooth finish on furniture.*
5 VERB. to prepare the surface of something in some way: *to finish metal with a dull surface.*
❑ VERB **fin·ish·es, fin·ished, fin·ish·ing;** PLURAL **fin·ish·es.**

Fin·land (fin′lənd), NOUN. a country in northern Europe.

Finn (fin), NOUN. someone born or living in Finland.

Finn·ish (fin′ish),
1 *ADJECTIVE.* of Finland, its people, or their language.
2 *NOUN.* the language of Finland.
fiord (fyôrd), *NOUN.* another spelling of **fjord.**

fire drill, the practice of what to do in case of fire. In a fire drill, people practice leaving a building in an orderly way, and firefighters practice using their equipment.

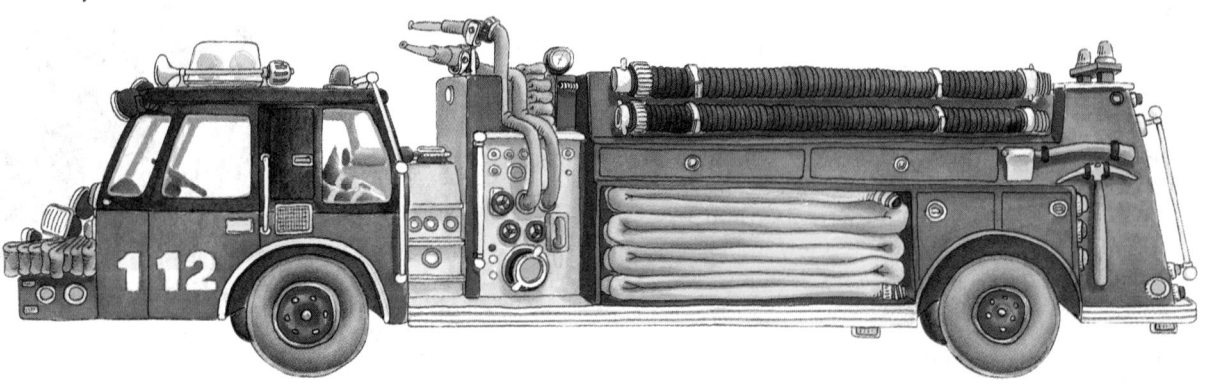

fire engine

fir (fėr), *NOUN.* an evergreen tree that has soft, flat needles and upright cones. Small firs are often used for Christmas trees. ■ Another word that sounds like this is **fur.**

fire (fir),
1 *NOUN.* the flame, heat, and light caused by something burning: *Fire from the burning cabin destroyed many trees nearby.*
2 *NOUN.* something burning: *Lightning may start a fire in a dry forest.*
3 *VERB.* to dry and harden something with heat; bake: *Bricks are fired to make them hard.*
4 *NOUN.* enthusiasm; excitement: *Their hearts were full of patriotic fire.*
5 *VERB.* to arouse someone; excite: *Stories of adventure fire the imagination.*
6 *NOUN.* the act of shooting guns or other weapons: *The enemy's fire forced the troops to take shelter in the ravine.*
7 *VERB.* to shoot: *I fired at the target.*
8 *VERB.* to dismiss from a job: *The manager fired two salespeople last week.*
❑ *VERB* **fires, fired, fir·ing.**
play with fire, *IDIOM.* to behave in a risky or dangerous way: *I told him skating without a helmet was playing with fire.*

Have You Heard?

You may have heard someone say **"Fight fire with fire!"** This means that you should use the same methods or the same amount of effort as your opponent.

fire·arm (fir′ärm′), *NOUN.* a portable gun. Pistols, rifles, and shotguns are firearms.
fire·crack·er (fir′krak′ər), *NOUN.* a small tube of paper containing gunpowder and a fuse. Firecrackers explode with a loud noise when lit.

fire engine, a truck with equipment for pumping and spraying water to put out fires; fire truck.
fire escape, a stairway or ladder used when a building is on fire.
fire ex·tin·guish·er (fir′ ek sting′gwish ər), a container filled with chemicals that can be sprayed on a small fire to put it out.
fire·fight·er (fir′fī′tər), *NOUN.* someone whose work is putting out fires.
fire·fly (fir′flī′), *NOUN.* a small insect that gives off flashes of light when it flies at night; lightning bug. ❑ *PLURAL* **fire·flies.**
fire·house (fir′hous′), *NOUN.* a building where fire engines are kept, and where firefighters are on duty. ❑ *PLURAL* **fire·hous·es** (fir′hou′ziz).
fire·man (fir′mən), *NOUN.*
1 a firefighter.
2 someone whose work is looking after fires in a furnace, boiler, and so on.
❑ *PLURAL* **fire·men.**
fire·place (fir′plās′), *NOUN.* a structure built to hold a fire. Indoor fireplaces are usually made of brick or stone. Fireplaces can burn wood or natural gas A chimney leads the smoke outside, usually up through the roof.
fire·proof (fir′prüf′),
1 *ADJECTIVE.* almost impossible to burn; very resistant to fire: *Steel and concrete are fireproof.*
2 *VERB.* to make something fireproof: *State law required us to fireproof the theater curtain.*
❑ *VERB* **fire·proofs, fire·proofed, fire·proof·ing.**

a	hat	ė	term	ô	order	ch	child	⎧ a in about
ā	age	i	it	oi	oil	ng	long	⎪ e in taken
ä	far	ī	ice	ou	out	sh	she	ə ⎨ i in pencil
â	care	o	hot	u	cup	th	thin	⎪ o in lemon
e	let	ō	open	ú	put	ᴛʜ	then	⎩ u in circus
ē	equal	ò	saw	ü	rule	zh	measure	

fire·side (fĭr′sīd′), NOUN.
1 the part of a room around a fireplace or hearth.
2 home; hearth: *The weary travelers longed to be back at their own fireside.*

fire truck. See **fire engine.**

fire·wood (fĭr′wŭd′), NOUN. wood to make a fire.

fire·works (fĭr′wėrks′), NOUN PLURAL. firecrackers and other things that make a loud noise or go up high in the air and burst in a shower of stars and sparks. ❑ SINGULAR **fire·work.**

firm¹ (fėrm), ADJECTIVE.
1 not soft or yielding when pressed: *a firm mattress.*
2 not easily moved or shaken; securely in place: *She made the shelf firm by screwing it to the wall.*
3 not easily changed; determined; positive: *a firm character, a firm belief, a firm voice.*
  —firm′ly, ADVERB. **—firm′ness,** NOUN.

firm² (fėrm), NOUN. a company or other business organization.

first (fėrst),
1 ADJECTIVE. coming before all others: *He is first in the class.*
2 ADVERB. before anything else; before all others: *We eat first and then feed the cat.*
3 NOUN. someone, something, or someplace that is first: *We were the first to get here.*
4 NOUN. the beginning: *At first I did not like school.*
5 ADVERB. for the first time: *When we first met, we were both in grade school.*

first aid, emergency treatment that someone gives to an injured or sick person before a doctor sees the person.

first-class (fėrst′klas′),
1 ADJECTIVE. of the highest class or best quality; excellent: *a first-class teacher.*
2 ADVERB. by the best and most expensive seating and service offered by ship, airplane, or train: *We could not afford to travel first-class.*

first·hand (fėrst′hand′), ADJECTIVE or ADVERB. direct; from the original source: *firsthand information.*

first person, the form of a pronoun or verb used to refer to the speaker or writer and those with whom he or she is included. *I, me, we,* and *us* are pronouns of the first person.

first-rate (fėrst′rāt′), ADJECTIVE. of the highest class; excellent; very good: *We had a first-rate summer.*

fish (fish),
1 NOUN. one of a very large group of cold-blooded animals that live in water and have gills instead of lungs. Fish are usually covered with scales and have fins for swimming.
2 NOUN. the flesh of fish used for food.
3 VERB. to catch fish; try to catch fish.
4 VERB. to search: *I fished in my pocket for a dime.*
  ❑ VERB **fish·es, fished, fish·ing;** PLURAL **fish** or **fish·es.**

fish·er·man (fish′ər mən), NOUN. someone who makes a living by catching fish. ❑ PLURAL **fish·er·men.**

fish·er·y (fish′ər ē), NOUN. place for catching or breeding fish. ❑ PLURAL **fish·er·ies.**

fish·hook (fish′hŭk′), NOUN. a hook used for catching fish.

a **fisherman** at work

fish·y (fish′ē), ADJECTIVE.
1 like a fish in smell, taste, or shape.
2 doubtful; unlikely: *I don't believe that fishy story.*
  ❑ ADJECTIVE **fish·i·er, fish·i·est.**

fis·sion (fish′ən), NOUN. the splitting apart of atomic nuclei to produce tremendous amounts of energy; nuclear fission.

fist (fist), NOUN. a tightly closed hand: *He shook his fist at me.*

fit¹ (fit),
1 ADJECTIVE. having the necessary qualities; suitable: *Grass is food for cows; it is not fit for people.*
2 ADJECTIVE. in good physical condition; healthy and strong: *Proper exercise and good food help keep us fit.*
3 VERB. to be right, proper, or suitable for something: *a punishment that fits the crime.*
4 VERB. to make something right, proper, or suitable; suit: *She fitted the words to the music.*
5 VERB. to have the right size or shape for your body or a part of your body: *Does this glove fit?*
6 VERB. to make the right size or shape; adjust: *I had my new jacket fitted at the store.*
7 NOUN. the way that something fits: *The coat had a nice fit; it was not too tight.*
  ❑ ADJECTIVE **fit·ter, fit·test;** VERB **fits, fit** or **fit·ted, fit·ting. —fit′ly,** ADVERB.

fit² (fit), NOUN.
1 a sudden, violent outburst of feeling: *In a fit of anger, she punched her brother.*
2 a short period of doing some one thing; spell: *a fit of coughing, a fit of laughing.*

fit·ness (fit′nis), NOUN. the condition of being healthy and strong: *physical fitness.*

fit·ting (fit′ing), ADJECTIVE. right; proper; suitable: *a fitting reward.* **—fit′ting·ly,** ADVERB.

five (fiv), NOUN or ADJECTIVE. one more than four; 5.

fix (fiks), VERB.
1 to mend; repair: *He fixed my watch.*
2 to put in order; set right; arrange: *Fix your hair.*
3 to prepare a meal or food: *I'll fix dinner now.*
4 to make firm; fasten in place: *I fixed the post in the ground.*

5 to direct or hold your eyes, attention, and so on, steadily: *We fixed our eyes on the board.*

6 to pay someone money in advance to arrange a result: *to fix a jury, to fix a race.*
❑ VERB **fix·es, fixed, fix·ing.** –**fix′a·ble,** ADJECTIVE. –**fix′er,** NOUN.

fix up, IDIOM. to get something for someone: *He fixed us up with concert tickets.*

in a fix, IDIOM. in a difficult position; in trouble: *We're in a fix! The car is out of gas.* ❑ PLURAL **fix·es.**

fix·ture (fiks′chər), NOUN. something put in place to stay: *There are light fixtures along the wall.*

fizz (fiz),
1 VERB. to make a hissing sound.
2 NOUN. a hissing, bubbling sound.
❑ VERB **fizz·es, fizzed, fizz·ing;** PLURAL **fizz·es.**

fjord (fyôrd), NOUN. a long, narrow bay bordered by steep cliffs.

Word Story

We borrowed **fjord** from the Norwegian word for such a bay. There are hundreds of fjords along the rocky west coast of Norway.

FL, an abbreviation of **Florida.**

flab·ber·gast·ed (flab′ər gas′tid), ADJECTIVE. speechless with surprise; greatly astonished: *We were flabbergasted when we saw his costume.*

flab·by (flab′ē), ADJECTIVE. without firmness; soft; weak: *His muscles were flabby after his three-month illness.* ❑ ADJECTIVE **flab·bi·er, flab·bi·est.** –**flab′bi·ness,** NOUN.

flag (flag),
1 NOUN. a piece of cloth, usually with square corners, with a picture or pattern that stands for some country: *We salute the United States flag.*
2 NOUN. a cloth or banner, often used as a signal: *a red flag of danger.*
3 VERB. to stop or signal someone or something with or as if with a flag: *We tried to flag a cab.*
❑ VERB **flags, flagged, flag·ging.**

Did You Know?

When an American **flag** is no longer usable because it is dirty or torn, it is not thrown away. Instead, it is burned.

flag·pole (flag′pōl′), NOUN. the pole that a flag flies from.

flair (flâr), NOUN. a natural ability: *The poet had a flair for making clever rhymes.* ■ Another word that sounds like this is **flare.**

flake (flāk),
1 NOUN. a small, flat, thin piece: *flakes of rust.*
2 VERB. to come off something in flakes: *Spots showed where the paint had flaked off.*
❑ VERB **flakes, flaked, flak·ing.**

flame (flām),
1 NOUN. the part of a fire that you can see shoot up into the air: *a candle's flame.*
2 VERB. to rise up in flames; burn; blaze: *The dry logs flamed up in the fireplace.*
3 NOUN. the condition of burning with flames; blaze: *The dying fire suddenly burst into flame.*
❑ VERB **flames, flamed, flam·ing.**

fla·min·go (flə ming′gō), NOUN. a tropical wading bird with very long legs and neck and a curved beak. Its feathers vary from rosy pink to bright red. ❑ PLURAL **fla·min·gos** or **fla·min·goes.**

flamingo — between 3 and 5 feet tall

Did You Know?

Flamingos are not born pink. Their feathers get their color from the shellfish and algae they eat. Baby flamingos are a grayish white.

flam·ma·ble (flam′ə bəl), ADJECTIVE. easily set on fire; inflammable: *Paper is flammable.*
■ See the Usage Note at **inflammable.**

flank (flangk),
1 NOUN. the side of an animal or a human being between the ribs and the hip.
2 VERB. to be at the side of something: *A garage flanked the house.*
3 NOUN. the far right or the far left side of an army, fort, fleet, or formation.
4 VERB. to attack or get around the flanks.
❑ VERB **flanks, flanked, flank·ing.**

flan·nel (flan′l), NOUN. a soft, warm cloth.

flap (flap),
1 VERB. to swing or sway about loosely and with some noise: *The sails flapped in the wind.*
2 VERB. to move wings, arms, and the like, up and down: *The goose flapped its wings but could not fly.*
3 VERB. to strike noisily with something broad and flat: *The clown's big shoes flapped on the ground.*
4 NOUN. a piece hanging or fastened at only one edge of something: *The coat had flaps on the pockets. I sealed the flap on the envelope.*
❑ VERB **flaps, flapped, flap·ping.**

a	hat	ė	term	ô	order	ch	child		a in about
ā	age	i	it	oi	oil	ng	long		e in taken
ä	far	ī	ice	ou	out	sh	she	ə<	i in pencil
â	care	o	hot	u	cup	th	thin		o in lemon
e	let	ō	open	ů	put	ᴛʜ	then		u in circus
ē	equal	ȯ	saw	ü	rule	zh	measure		

flap·jack (flap′jak′), NOUN. See **pancake**.

flare (flâr),

1 VERB. to flame up briefly or unsteadily: *The damp logs flared up briefly; then the fire went out.*

2 NOUN. a blaze; bright, brief flame: *In the flare of the match I was able to find the light switch.*

3 NOUN. a device that produces a dazzling light that burns for a short time, used for signaling, lighting up an area, or as a warning: *The Coast Guard ship responded to the lifeboat's flare.*

4 VERB. to burst out into open anger or violence: *Her temper flared at the insult.*

5 VERB. to spread out in the shape of a bell: *These pants flare at the bottom.*
  ❏ VERB **flares, flared, flar·ing.** ■ Another word that sounds like this is **flair.**

flare up, IDIOM. to become very intense or serious: *The disagreement between them flared up at the game.*

flash (flash),

1 NOUN. a sudden, brief light or flame: *a flash of lightning.*

2 VERB. to give out a light or flame like this: *Lightning flashed across the sky.*

3 VERB. to come suddenly; pass quickly: *A thought flashed across my mind.*

4 NOUN. a very short time: *It all happened in a flash.*

5 VERB. to give out or send out something like a flash: *Her eyes flashed defiance.*

6 VERB. to send by computer, satellite, television, or the like: *They flashed the news across the country.*

7 NOUN. a brief news report that includes only a few details of what happened.
  ❏ PLURAL **flash·es;** VERB **flash·es, flashed, flash·ing.**

flash·bulb (flash′bulb′), NOUN. an electric bulb that gives out a brilliant flash of light for a very short time. It is used in taking photographs at night or indoors.

flash·card (flash′kärd′), NOUN. a card with a letter, word, number, simple problem, or picture on it. As a drill, the teacher displays a flashcard briefly and the student gives a quick answer.

flash·light (flash′lit′), NOUN. a portable electric light, powered by batteries.

flash·y (flash′ē), ADJECTIVE. likely to attract attention; too bright or dazzling to be in good taste: *His coat was a little too flashy.* ❏ ADJECTIVE **flash·i·er, flash·i·est. −flash′i·ness,** NOUN.

flask (flask), NOUN. a glass or metal bottle, especially one with a narrow neck.

flat (flat),

1 ADJECTIVE. smooth and level; even: *flat land.*

2 ADJECTIVE. horizontal; lying at full length: *The storm left the trees flat on the ground.*

3 NOUN. the flat part: *The flat of your hand is your palm.*

4 NOUN. often **flats,** land that is flat and level: *mud flats.*

5 ADJECTIVE. wide but not very deep or thick. Plates are flat.

6 ADJECTIVE. with very little air in it: *A nail or sharp stone can cause a flat tire.*

7 NOUN. a tire with very little air in it: *Our car got a flat when we drove over a nail.*

8 ADJECTIVE. not to be changed: *We pay a flat rate.*

9 ADJECTIVE. without much life, interest, or flavor; dull: *Plain food tastes flat.*

10 ADJECTIVE. not shiny or glossy: *We used flat paint on the walls and enamel on the woodwork.*

11 ADJECTIVE or ADVERB. below the true pitch in music: *The singer's high notes were flat. Try not to sing flat.*

12 NOUN. a tone one half step below natural pitch: *Play a B flat.*

13 NOUN. the sign in music (♭) that shows this.

14 ADVERB. in a flat manner: *He fell flat on the floor.*
  ❏ ADJECTIVE **flat·ter, flat·test. −flat′ness,** NOUN.

flat·fish (flat′fish′), NOUN. a fish that has a flat body and swims on its side. Flatfish have both eyes on the upper side of their bodies. Halibut, flounder, and sole are kinds of flatfish. ❏ PLURAL **flat·fish** or **flat·fish·es.**

Flounders are a kind of **flatfish**.

flat·ten (flat′n), VERB. to make or become flat: *Use a rolling pin to flatten the pie dough.* ❏ VERB **flat·tens, flat·tened, flat·ten·ing.**

flat·ter (flat′ər), VERB.

1 to praise someone too much or exaggerate in order to please someone: *He was only flattering me when he said I sang well.*

2 to show someone to be more beautiful or better looking than what is true: *This picture flatters me.*
  ❏ VERB **flat·ters, flat·tered, flat·ter·ing. −flat′ter·er,** NOUN.

flat·ter·y (flat′ər ē), NOUN. praise, usually untrue or exaggerated: *Some people use flattery to get favors.*

fla·vor (flā′vər),

1 NOUN. the special taste that a food has: *Chocolate and vanilla have different flavors.*

2 VERB. to give added taste to something; season: *The onion flavors the whole stew.*
  ❏ VERB **fla·vors, fla·vored, fla·vor·ing.**

fla·vor·ful (flā′vər fəl), ADJECTIVE. having a lot of flavor.

fla·vor·ing (flā′vər ing), NOUN. something used to give a particular taste to food or drink: *chocolate flavoring, vanilla flavoring.*

flaw (flȯ), NOUN. a slight defect; blemish; fault: *A flaw in the cup caused it to break.* **—flaw′less,** ADJECTIVE.

flax (flaks), NOUN. a slender, upright plant with narrow leaves and blue flowers. Linen is woven from the threadlike parts of flax stems.

flea (flē), NOUN. a small, jumping insect without wings. Fleas live on the bodies of dogs, cats, and other animals, and feed on their blood. ❑ PLURAL **fleas.** ∎ Another word that sounds like this is **flee.**

fled (fled), VERB.
1 the past tense of **flee**: *We fled the burning house.*
2 the past participle of **flee**: *The prisoner has fled.*

fledg·ling (flej′ling), NOUN.
1 a young bird that has just grown the feathers needed for flying.
2 a young, inexperienced person: *a fledgling lawyer.*

flee (flē), VERB. to run away in order to escape: *The robbers tried to flee, but they were caught.* ❑ VERB **flees, fled, flee·ing.** ∎ Another word that sounds like this is **flea.**

fleece (flēs),
1 NOUN. the coat of wool that covers a sheep. The wool shorn from one sheep is called a fleece.
2 VERB. to take money from someone, either by charging too much for something bought, or by cheating the buyer. ❑ VERB **fleec·es, fleeced, fleec·ing.**

fleet¹ (flēt), NOUN.
1 a group of warships under one command: *the United States fleet.*
2 a group of ships, airplanes, motor vehicles, or the like, moving or working together: *a fleet of trucks.*

fleet² (flēt), ADJECTIVE. swiftly moving; quick: *The fleet horse won the race.*

flesh (flesh), NOUN.
1 the soft part of the body that covers the bones and is covered by skin. Flesh is made up mostly of muscles and fat.
2 meat: *Lions eat the flesh of zebras.*
3 the soft part of fruits or vegetables; the part of fruits that can be eaten: *The flesh of apples is white.*

flesh·y (flesh′ē), ADJECTIVE. having a lot of flesh; plump; fat. ❑ ADJECTIVE **flesh·i·er, flesh·i·est.** **—flesh′i·ness,** NOUN.

flew (flü), VERB. the past tense of **fly²**: *The bird flew away.* ∎ Other words that sound like this are **flu** and **flue.**

flex (fleks), VERB. to bend: *She flexed her stiff arm slowly.* ❑ VERB **flex·es, flexed, flex·ing.**

flex·i·ble (flek′sə bəl), ADJECTIVE.
1 easily bent; not stiff; bending without breaking: *Leather, rubber, and wire are flexible.*

2 able to change easily to fit different conditions: *I have a flexible work schedule.* **—flex′i·bil′i·ty,** NOUN.

flick (flik),
1 NOUN. a sudden, snapping stroke or movement: *She threw the dart with a flick of the wrist.*
2 VERB. to hit or move something with a quick snapping motion: *The children flicked wet towels at each other.* ❑ VERB **flicks, flicked, flick·ing.**

flick·er¹ (flik′ər),
1 VERB. to shine or burn with an unsteady light: *The candle flickered in the breeze.*
2 NOUN. an unsteady light or flame: *a candle's flicker.*
3 VERB. to move slightly: *A smile flickered across his face when he saw her.*
4 NOUN. a quick, light movement: *I knew he was not sleeping by the flicker of his eyelids.* ❑ VERB **flick·ers, flick·ered, flick·er·ing.**

flick·er² (flik′ər), NOUN. a large woodpecker of North America, with yellow markings on the wings and tail, and a spotted breast.

flied (flīd), VERB.
1 the past tense of **fly²** (for definition 9): *The batter flied to center field.*
2 a past participle of **fly²** (for definition 9): *She has flied out twice.*

fli·er (flī′ər), NOUN.
1 someone or something that flies: *That eagle is a high flier.*
2 an airplane pilot; aviator.

flicker² — about 10½ inches long

flies¹ (flīz), NOUN. the plural of **fly¹** and **fly²**: *There are many flies on the window. Both batters hit flies to the outfield.*

flies² (flīz), VERB. a present tense of **fly²**: *A bird flies. He flies an airplane.*

flight¹ (flīt), NOUN.
1 a trip in an aircraft: *We had an enjoyable flight.*
2 the act or manner of flying: *the flight of a bird.*
3 the distance a bird, bullet, airplane, and so on can fly: *The flight of the arrow was over 100 yards.*
4 a group of things flying through the air together: *a flight of pigeons.*
5 a set of stairs from one landing or one story of a building to the next.

a	hat	ė	term	ô	order	ch	child	(	a in about
ā	age	i	it	oi	oil	ng	long		e in taken
ä	far	ī	ice	ou	out	sh	she	ə<	i in pencil
â	care	o	hot	u	cup	th	thin		o in lemon
e	let	ō	open	ù	put	ᴛʜ	then	(	u in circus
ē	equal	ȯ	saw	ü	rule	zh	measure		

flight² (flīt), NOUN. the act of running away; escape: *The flight of the prisoners was discovered.*

flight attendant, someone employed by an airline to look after passengers during an airplane flight.

flim·sy (flim′zē), ADJECTIVE.
1 easily torn or broken; not strongly made: *She accidentally tore the flimsy paper.*
2 not convincing; not easy to believe: *Their excuse was so flimsy that no one believed it.* ❑ ADJECTIVE **flim·si·er, flim·si·est. −flim′si·ness,** NOUN.

flinch (flinch), VERB. to draw back quickly from difficulty, danger, or pain: *She flinched when she touched the hot radiator.* ❑ VERB **flinch·es, flinched, flinch·ing.**

fling (fling),
1 VERB. to throw something with force: *to fling a stone.* ■ See the Synonym Study at **throw.**
2 NOUN. a throw.
❑ VERB **flings, flung, fling·ing.**

flint (flint), NOUN. a very hard stone that makes a spark when struck against steel.

flip (flip),
1 VERB. to cause something or someone to spin end over end in the air: *to flip a coin. He flipped me over his shoulder, and I landed on my feet.*
2 NOUN. an act of flipping; a toss: *The winner was picked by the flip of a coin.*
3 VERB. to move something with a snap or a jerk: *Please flip that light switch for me.*
4 VERB. to turn something over: *The cook flipped the pancake over in the frying pan.*
❑ VERB **flips, flipped, flip·ping.**

flip·per (flip′ər), NOUN.
1 one of the broad, flat body parts used for swimming by animals such as seals and walruses.
2 a molded rubber shoe used to help you swim.

flirt (flèrt),
1 VERB. to pay attention to someone in a romantic way without being serious about it.
2 NOUN. someone who flirts.
❑ VERB **flirts, flirt·ed, flirt·ing.**

float (flōt),
1 VERB. to move along slowly on top of the water or in the air. A cork will float, but a stone sinks.
2 NOUN. anything that stays up or holds up something else in water. A raft is a float.
3 VERB. to rest or move in a liquid, the air, and the like: *Clouds floated in the sky.*
4 NOUN. a low, flat car that carries something to show in a parade: *The king of the parade rode on a beautiful float covered with flowers.*
❑ VERB **floats, float·ed, float·ing.**

flock (flok),
1 NOUN. a group of animals of the same kind, staying, feeding, or traveling together: *a flock of sheep, a flock of birds.*
2 NOUN. a large group or number; crowd: *Visitors came in flocks to the zoo to see the new gorilla.*
3 VERB. to stay in a group; crowd: *The children flocked around the ice-cream stand.*
❑ VERB **flocks, flocked, flock·ing.**

floe (flō), NOUN. a large sheet of floating ice. ❑ PLURAL **floes.** ■ Another word that sounds like this is **flow.**

flood (flud),
1 NOUN. a great flow of water over an area that is usually dry land: *The heavy rains caused a serious flood near the river.*
2 VERB. to flow over; cover or fill with water: *The river flooded the fields.*
3 NOUN. **the Flood,** (in the Bible) the water that covered the earth in the time of Noah.
4 NOUN. a great flow of anything: *She apologized in a flood of words.*
5 VERB. to fill, cover, or overcome like a flood: *In the morning, my room is flooded with sunlight.*
❑ VERB **floods, flood·ed, flood·ing.**

There was a **flood** in our town last year.

flood·light (flud′līt′), NOUN. a lamp that gives a broad beam of light.

floor (flôr),
1 NOUN. the surface of a room that you walk on: *The floor of this room is made of wood.*
2 NOUN. a story of a building: *I live on the top floor.*
3 NOUN. a flat surface at the bottom of something: *They dropped their net to the floor of the ocean.*
4 VERB. to knock down: *The boxer floored his opponent with one blow.*
❑ VERB **floors, floored, floor·ing.**

flop (flop),
1 VERB. to move loosely or clumsily: *The fish flopped helplessly on the deck.*
2 VERB. to drop or sit down heavily or clumsily: *The tired girl flopped down into a chair.*
3 NOUN. a failure: *The party was a flop.*
4 VERB. to fail: *Their first business venture flopped.*
❑ VERB **flops, flopped, flop·ping.**

flop·py (flop′ē),
1 *ADJECTIVE.* soft and flexible: *Her hat has a floppy brim.*
2 *NOUN.* See **floppy disk.**
□ *ADJECTIVE* **flop·pi·er, flop·pi·est.**

floppy disk, a small plastic disk with a magnetic surface, used to store information and instructions for computers; diskette.

She wore a hat with a **floppy** brim.

flo·ra (flôr′ə), *NOUN.* plants as a group: *the floras of the two islands.* □ *PLURAL* **flo·ras.**

Flo·ri·da (flôr′ə də), *NOUN.* one of the southern states of the United States. *Abbreviation:* FL; *Capital:* Tallahassee. **—Flo·rid′i·an,** *NOUN.*

State Story **Florida** comes from a Spanish phrase meaning "many flowers" and "Easter." Juan Ponce de León, the Spanish explorer, gave the area this name when he first sighted it, on Easter of 1513.

floss (flȯs),
1 *NOUN.* See **dental floss.**
2 *VERB.* to use dental floss, or use dental floss on: *I floss my teeth in the morning and at night.*
3 *NOUN.* a fine silk or cotton thread. Floss is often dyed bright colors and used for embroidery and crafts.
□ *VERB* **floss·es, flossed, floss·ing.**

floun·der[1] (floun′dər), *VERB.*
1 to move clumsily and with difficulty: *After the blizzard, we found cattle floundering in the snow.*
2 to be confused and make mistakes: *I was so nervous I floundered through my speech.*
□ *VERB* **floun·ders, floun·dered, floun·der·ing.**

floun·der[2] (floun′dər), *NOUN.* a large group of saltwater flatfish, important as a source of food. Flounder swim on the side of their bodies and have both eyes on the upper side. See the picture at **flatfish.** □ *PLURAL* **floun·der** or **floun·ders.**

flour (flour),
1 *NOUN.* the fine powder or meal made by grinding and sifting wheat or other grain.
2 *VERB.* to cover or sprinkle something with flour.
□ *VERB* **flours, floured, flour·ing.**

flour·ish (flėr′ish),
1 *VERB.* to grow or develop well; thrive: *Your radishes are flourishing.*
2 *VERB.* to wave something in the air: *She flourished the letter at us.*
3 *NOUN.* an act of waving about in the air: *The magician removed his cape with a flourish.*
□ *VERB* **flour·ish·es, flour·ished, flour·ish·ing;** *PLURAL* **flour·ish·es.**

flow (flō),
1 *VERB.* to run like water; move in a stream or current: *Blood flows through our bodies.*
2 *NOUN.* a stream; current: *There is a constant flow of water from the spring.*
3 *VERB.* to pour; move steadily: *The crowd flowed out of the town hall and down the main street.*
4 *NOUN.* any smooth movement: *the flow of traffic.*
5 *NOUN.* the act or process of pouring out: *A tight bandage should stop the flow of blood.*
□ *VERB* **flows, flowed, flow·ing.** ▪ Another word that sounds like this is **floe.**

flow·er (flou′ər),
1 *NOUN.* a part of a plant or tree that produces the seed; blossom. Flowers are often very fragrant and beautifully colored or shaped.
2 *NOUN.* a plant that is grown for its blossoms.
3 *VERB.* to have or produce flowers; bloom: *Many fruit trees flower in the spring.*
□ *VERB* **flow·ers, flow·ered, flow·er·ing.** **—flow′er·like′,** *ADJECTIVE.*

flown (flōn), *VERB.* the past participle of **fly**[2]: *The flag is flown on all national holidays.*

flu (flü), *NOUN.* a contagious disease much like a very bad cold; influenza. ▪ Other words that sound like this are **flew** and **flue. —flu′·like′,** *ADJECTIVE.*

Word Story

Flu is a shortened form of **influenza,** which comes from a Latin word meaning "influence." The disease was thought to occur because of the influence of bad stars on its victims.

flue (flü), *NOUN.* a pipe or tube that allows smoke or hot air to escape. A chimney has a flue. □ *PLURAL* **flues.** ▪ Other words that sound like this are **flew** and **flu.**

The flowers are **flourishing** in this park.

a	hat	ė	term	ô	order	ch	child		a in about
ā	age	i	it	oi	oil	ng	long		e in taken
ä	far	ī	ice	ou	out	sh	she	ə	i in pencil
â	care	o	hot	u	cup	th	thin		o in lemon
e	let	ō	open	u̇	put	⊤H	then		u in circus
ē	equal	ȯ	saw	ü	rule	zh	measure		

fluff (fluf),
1 *NOUN.* soft, light particles, such as hair, tiny feathers, or bits of wool.
2 *NOUN.* a soft, light mass: *The kitten is a ball of fluff.*
3 *VERB.* to shake or puff something out into a soft, light mass: *I fluffed my pillow.*
❏ *VERB* **fluffs, fluffed, fluff·ing.**

fluff·y (fluf′ē), *ADJECTIVE.*
1 soft and light: *She wore a bright fluffy scarf. Whipped cream is fluffy.* ■ See the Synonym Study at **soft.**
2 covered with soft, light feathers or hair: *The baby chicks were fluffy.*
❏ *ADJECTIVE* **fluff·i·er, fluff·i·est. –fluff′i·ness,** *NOUN.*

flu·id (flü′id),
1 *NOUN.* any liquid or gas; something that will flow. Water, mercury, air, and oxygen are fluids.
2 *ADJECTIVE.* like a liquid or a gas; flowing: *We poured the fluid mass of hot fudge into a pan.*

flum·mox (flum′əks), *VERB.* (informal) to confuse; bewilder: *The problem had me flummoxed.* ❏ *VERB* **flum·mox·es, flum·moxed, flum·mox·ing.**

flung (flung), *VERB.*
1 the past tense of **fling:** *I flung my coat on the chair.*
2 the past participle of **fling:** *They have flung all the boots into the closet.*

flunk (flungk), *VERB.*
1 to fail in schoolwork: *I flunked the spelling test.*
2 to give someone a failing grade: *The teacher flunked him.*
❏ *VERB* **flunks, flunked, flunk·ing.**

fluo·res·cent (flȯ res′nt *or* flù res′nt), *ADJECTIVE.* glowing or able to give off light when exposed to X rays or other kinds of radiation.

fluo·ride (flȯr′īd *or* flùr′īd), *NOUN.* a chemical substance that is added to drinking water and toothpaste to prevent cavities.

fluor·ine (flùr′ēn), *NOUN.* a pale yellow, poisonous gas that occurs naturally only in combination with other substances. Fluorine is a chemical element.

flur·ry (flėr′ē), *NOUN.*
1 a sudden gust: *A flurry of wind upset the small boat.*
2 a light fall of rain or snow: *snow flurries.*
3 a sudden commotion: *There was a flurry of alarm when the fire broke out.*
❏ *PLURAL* **flur·ries.**

flush (flush),
1 *VERB.* to blush; glow: *Her face flushed when they laughed at her.*
2 *NOUN.* a rosy glow or blush: *The sky glowed with the flush of sunrise. A sudden flush showed his embarrassment.*
3 *VERB.* to send a sudden rush of water over or through something to clean or empty it: *I flushed the toilet. The gutters were flushed to clean them.*
❏ *VERB* **flush·es, flushed, flush·ing;** *PLURAL* **flush·es.**

flus·ter (flus′tər), *VERB.* to make someone nervous and excited; confuse: *The honking of horns flustered the driver, and he stalled his car.* ❏ *VERB* **flus·ter, flus·tered, flus·ter·ing.**

flute (flüt), *NOUN.* a long, slender, musical instrument made of a tube of metal. A flute is played by blowing across a hole near one end. Different notes are made by covering different holes along its length with the fingers or with keys.

playing a wooden **flute**

flut·ter (flut′ər),
1 *VERB.* to wave back and forth quickly and lightly: *The flag fluttered in the breeze.*
2 *NOUN.* a quick, light, flapping movement: *I watched the flutter of our curtains in the breeze.*
3 *VERB.* to flap the wings: *The chickens fluttered excitedly when they saw the dog.*
4 *VERB.* to move through the air with a quick, wavy motion: *The falling leaves fluttered to the ground.*
5 *VERB.* to beat a little faster than usual: *My heart fluttered when I rose to give my speech.*
6 *NOUN.* a feeling of excitement: *The appearance of the queen caused a great flutter in the crowd.*
❏ *VERB* **flut·ters, flut·tered, flut·ter·ing.**

fly¹ (flī), *NOUN.*
1 any of a large group of insects that have two wings, especially the housefly.
2 a fishhook with feathers, silk, or tinsel on it to make it look like a fly.
❏ *PLURAL* **flies.**

fly² (flī),
1 *VERB.* to move through the air with wings: *These birds fly long distances.*
2 *VERB.* to float or wave in the air: *Our flag flies every day.*
3 *VERB.* to cause something to float or wave in the air: *The children are flying kites.*
4 *VERB.* to travel by aircraft; to carry by aircraft: *We flew to Hawaii. The government flew food and supplies to the flooded city.*
5 *VERB.* to pilot an aircraft: *My cousin flies his plane for fun. He flies planes for a living.*
6 *VERB.* to rush; move swiftly: *When the phone rang, I flew to answer it.*
7 *NOUN.* a flap to cover buttons or a zipper on clothing.
8 *NOUN.* also, **fly ball,** a baseball batted high in the air: *The batter hit a fly ball to left field.*
9 *VERB.* to bat a baseball high in the air. ★ The past tense and past participle for this meaning is **flied:** *The batter flied to the outfield.*
❏ *VERB* **flies, flew, flown, fly·ing;** *PLURAL* **flies.**

flying fish, a tropical fish that has fins like wings and can leap and sail through the air.

flying fish — about 18 inches long

flying saucer, a disk-shaped object that many people say they have seen in the sky; UFO.

foal (fōl), NOUN. a young horse, donkey, or zebra; colt or filly.

foam (fōm),
1 NOUN. a mass of very small bubbles.
2 VERB. to form or gather into a mass of bubbles: *The soda foamed over the glass.*
3 NOUN. a spongy, flexible, or stiff material made from plastics, rubber, and so on.
❑ VERB **foams, foamed, foam·ing.**

fo·cus (fō′kəs),
1 NOUN. a point at which rays of light or heat meet after being reflected from a mirror or bent by a lens.
2 VERB. to bring rays of light or heat to a focus: *The lens focused the sun's rays on the paper.*
3 NOUN. the distance from a lens or mirror to the point where rays from it meet: *A near-sighted eye has a shorter focus than a normal eye.*
4 NOUN. the correct adjustment of a lens, or of the eye, to make a clear image: *If the camera is not brought into focus, the photo will be blurred.*
5 VERB. to adjust a lens or the eye to make a clear image: *A near-sighted person cannot focus accurately on distant objects.*
6 NOUN. a central point of attraction, attention, or activity: *The baby was the focus of everyone's attention.*
7 VERB. to concentrate; direct: *I focused all my attention on the teacher.*
❑ PLURAL **fo·cus·es;** VERB **fo·cus·es, fo·cused, fo·cus·ing.**

fod·der (fod′ər), NOUN. any coarse food for horses, cattle, and sheep. Hay and straw are fodder.

foe (fō), NOUN. an enemy.

fog (fog),
1 NOUN. a cloud of fine drops of water that floats in the air just above the earth's surface; thick mist.
2 VERB. to cover something with fog or vapor: *The steam in the bathroom fogged the mirror.*
3 NOUN. a confused or puzzled condition: *My mind was in a fog from lack of sleep.*
❑ VERB **fogs, fogged, fog·ging.**

fog·gy (fog′ē), ADJECTIVE.
1 covered with fog; misty: *a foggy morning.*
2 not clear; dim; blurred: *a foggy photo.*
❑ ADJECTIVE **fog·gi·er, fog·gi·est.**

fog·horn (fog′hôrn′), NOUN. a deep, loud horn that warns ships in foggy weather.

foil[1] (foil), VERB. to prevent someone from carrying out their plans: *Quick thinking by the bank clerk foiled the robbers, and they were captured.* ❑ VERB **foils, foiled, foil·ing.**

foil[2] (foil), NOUN. a very thin sheet of metal: *Candy is sometimes wrapped in foil to keep it fresh.*

fold (fōld),
1 VERB. to bend or double over on itself: *to fold paper.*
2 NOUN. a mark or line made by folding something: *Cut along this fold.*
3 VERB. to bend close to the body: *She folded her arms.*
4 VERB. to hold someone closely in your arms: *He folded the crying child in his arms.*
❑ VERB **folds, folded, fold·ing.**

fold·er (fōl′dər), NOUN. a holder for papers made by folding a piece of stiff paper once.

fo·li·age (fō′lē ij), NOUN. the leaves of a plant or plants.

folk (fōk),
1 NOUN. people of a particular kind: *Most city folk know very little about farming.*
2 ADJECTIVE. of or coming from the common people: *folk music, a folk singer.*
3 NOUN. **folks, a** people: *Most folks enjoy eating.*
b (informal) relatives: *How are all your folks?*
c parents: *My folks aren't home tonight.*
❑ PLURAL **folk** or **folks.**

folk dance,
1 a traditional dance handed down from generation to generation.
2 the music for it.

a Mexican **folk dance**

a	hat	ė	term	ô	order	ch	child		a in about
ā	age	i	it	oi	oil	ng	long		e in taken
ä	far	ī	ice	ou	out	sh	she	ə	i in pencil
â	care	o	hot	u	cup	th	thin		o in lemon
e	let	ō	open	ù	put	ŦH	then		u in circus
ē	equal	ò	saw	ü	rule	zh	measure		

folk·lore (fōk′lôr′), NOUN. the beliefs, stories, legends, and customs of a people: *Stories about Johnny Appleseed are part of American folklore.*

folk song, a song created by and handed down among the common people.

folk·tale (fōk′tāl′), NOUN. a story or legend created by and handed down among the common people.

fol·li·cle (fol′ə kəl), NOUN. a small cavity or sac in the body. Hair grows from follicles in the skin.

fol·low (fol′ō), VERB.
1 to go or come after: *Night follows day. You lead and we'll follow.*
2 to come after as a result: *Floods followed the heavy rain.*
3 to go along the course of: *Follow this road.*
4 to use; obey; take as a guide: *Follow her advice.*
5 to watch something closely; keep in view: *I followed the bird's flight.*
6 to keep the mind on something; understand: *Could you explain how to solve that math problem again? I couldn't follow it all.*
☐ VERB **fol·lows, fol·lowed, fol·low·ing.**

fol·low·er (fol′ō ər), NOUN.
1 someone who follows the ideas or beliefs of another: *Christians are followers of Christ.*
2 someone or something that follows: *That student is a leader, not a follower.*

fol·low·ing (fol′ō ing),
1 NOUN. a group of followers or fans: *That team has quite a following.*
2 ADJECTIVE. coming right after; next after: *If that was Sunday, then the following day must have been Monday.*

fol·ly (fol′ē), NOUN.
1 a lack of sense; unwise conduct: *Her folly led her deep into debt.*
2 a foolish act, practice, or idea; something silly: *It was folly to leave your bike unlocked in the street.*
☐ PLURAL **fol·lies** for 2.

fond (fond), ADJECTIVE. loving or liking: *She gave her daughter a fond look.* ∎ See the Synonym Study at **love. −fond′ly,** ADVERB. **−fond′ness,** NOUN.

food (füd), NOUN. anything that living things eat, drink, or take in that makes them live and grow.

food chain, several kinds of living things that are linked because each kind uses another kind as food. Cats, birds, caterpillars, and plants are a food chain because each living thing eats the next named living thing.

food poisoning, an illness caused by eating foods that contain harmful bacteria or poisonous chemicals.

food processor, a small electric kitchen appliance with a covered plastic container and rotating knives. It is used for quickly chopping, slicing, grating, or mixing foods.

fool (fül),
1 NOUN. someone without any sense; someone who acts unwisely: *He's a fool to drive so fast.*
2 NOUN. a clown formerly kept by a king, queen, or other noble to amuse people.
3 VERB. to joke, tease, or pretend: *I'm not really hurt; I was only fooling.*
4 VERB. to make a fool of someone; deceive; trick: *You can't fool me.* ☐ VERB **fools, fooled, fool·ing.**

fool (definition 2)

fool·har·dy (fül′här′dē), ADJECTIVE. foolishly bold; reckless. ☐ ADJECTIVE **fool·har·di·er, fool·har·di·est.**

fool·ish (fü′lish), ADJECTIVE. without any sense; unwise: *It is foolish to cross the street without looking both ways.* **−fool′ish·ly,** ADVERB. **−fool′ish·ness,** NOUN.

fool·proof (fül′prüf′), ADJECTIVE. so safe, simple, or well made that anyone can use or do it: *My plan is foolproof; nothing can go wrong.*
∎ See the Synonym Study at **perfect.**

The white arrows point from the thing being eaten to those that do the eating. The food chain starts with the plants, which store food energy from the sun.

food chain in a freshwater lake

foot (fut), NOUN.
1 the part of the body at the end of the leg; part that a person, animal, or thing stands on.
2 the part opposite the head of something: *I keep an extra blanket at the foot of my bed.*

F

3 the lowest part; the bottom; base: *the foot of a column, the foot of a hill, the foot of a page.*
4 a unit of length equal to 12 inches. 3 feet = 1 yard. ❏ PLURAL **feet.**

put your foot down, IDIOM. to make up your mind and act firmly: *If you don't go to bed right now, I'll have to put my foot down.*

Have You Heard?

There are many idioms that use the word **foot.** If you **"put your foot in your mouth,"** you have said something that offends or upsets the person you were talking to, and you feel embarrassed. When you **"shoot yourself in the foot,"** you have done or said something foolish that causes problems for you. If you **"get off on the wrong foot,"** you have made a bad start at something.

foot·ball (fut′bȯl′), NOUN.
1 a game played by two teams of eleven players each, on a field with a goal at each end; Teams score by advancing a ball across the opposing team's goal line by a run or pass, or by kicking it through the goalposts.
2 the inflated leather ball used in this game.

foot·ing (fut′ing), NOUN.
1 a firm position of the feet: *I lost my footing and fell.*
2 a place to put a foot; support for the feet: *The steep cliff gave us no footing.*
3 condition; relationship: *The United States and Canada are on a friendly footing.*

foot·note (fut′nōt′), NOUN. a note at the bottom of a page about something written on the page.

foot·print (fut′print′), NOUN. a mark made by a foot.

foot·step (fut′step′), NOUN.
1 someone's step: *a baby's first footsteps.*
2 the sound of someone's steps: *I heard footsteps.*
follow in someone's footsteps, IDIOM. to do as someone else has done.

footprints on a wet beach

for (fôr), PREPOSITION.
1 in place of: *We used boxes for chairs.*
2 in support of: *He stands for honest government.*
3 at the price of: *These apples are eight for a dollar.*
4 because of: *We thanked him for his kindness.*
5 with the object or purpose of: *He went for a walk.*
6 in order to become, have, keep, or get to: *He ran for his life. She is hunting for her cat. They left for New York yesterday.*
7 meant to be used by or with; suited to: *a box for gloves, books for children.*

8 meant to belong to: *This gift is for you.*
9 with regard or respect to: *It is warm for April. Eating too much is bad for your health.*
10 because of; by reason of: *I was punished for talking.*
11 in honor of: *A party was given for her.*
12 as far as: *We walked for a mile.*
13 as long as: *We worked for an hour.*
14 as being: *They know it for a fact.*
15 to the amount of: *a check for $20.*
■ Other words that sound like this are **fore** and **four.**

fo·rage (fôr′ij),
1 NOUN. hay, grain, or other food for horses, cattle, or other domestic animals.
2 VERB. to hunt or search for food: *Rabbits forage in our garden.*
3 VERB. to hunt; search about: *We foraged for old lumber to build a tree house.*
❏ VERB **fo·rag·es, fo·raged, fo·rag·ing.**

for·bad (fər bad′), VERB. a past tense of **forbid.**
★ **Forbad** is an old use: *The king forbad his knights to challenge the dragon.*

for·bade (fər bad′), VERB. a past tense of **forbid:** *My parents forbade me to stay out past ten o'clock.*

for·bid (fər bid′), VERB.
1 to make a rule against; prohibit: *The city forbids skateboarding in the parks.*
2 to order someone not to do something: *My mother has forbidden me to swim alone.*
❏ VERB **for·bids, for·bade** or **for·bad, for·bid·den, for·bid·ding.**

for·bid·den (fər bid′n),
1 ADJECTIVE. not allowed; against the law or the rules: *Chewing gum is forbidden in the classroom.*
2 VERB. the past participle of **forbid:** *My parents have forbidden me to swim in the river.*

force (fôrs),
1 NOUN. power; strength: *The falling tree hit the ground with great force.*
2 NOUN. strength used against someone or something; violence: *We had to use force to break it open.*
3 VERB. to make you act against your will: *Give it to me at once, or I will force you to.*
4 VERB. to get or take by strength or violence: *He forced his way in.*
5 VERB. to break something open; break through: *I had to force the lock to get into my suitcase.*
6 NOUN. a group of people who work together: *our office force, the police force.*
7 NOUN. any cause that produces, changes, or stops the motion of an object: *the force of gravitation.*
❏ VERB **for·ces, forced, forc·ing.**

a	hat	ė	term	ô	order	ch	child		a	in about
ā	age	i	it	oi	oil	ng	long		e	in taken
ä	far	ī	ice	ou	out	sh	she	ə	i	in pencil
â	care	o	hot	u	cup	th	thin		o	in lemon
e	let	ō	open	u̇	put	ᴛʜ	then		u	in circus
ē	equal	ȯ	saw	ü	rule	zh	measure			

force·ful (fôrs'fəl), *ADJECTIVE.* having much force; vigorous; strong: *I admired her frank and forceful manner.* –**force'ful·ly,** *ADVERB.* –**force'ful·ness,** *NOUN.*

for·ceps (fôr'seps), *NOUN SINGULAR* or *PLURAL.* small pincers or tongs used by surgeons or dentists for seizing and holding. Dentists use forceps for pulling teeth.

ford (fôrd),
1 *NOUN.* a place where a river or stream is not too deep to cross by walking or driving through it.
2 *VERB.* to cross a river or stream by walking or driving through it.
□ *VERB* **fords, ford·ed, ford·ing.**

Word Power   fore-

The prefix **fore-** means "front" or "before." A **fore**foot is a **front** foot. To **foresee** means to see something **before** it happens.

fore¹ (fôr), *ADJECTIVE.* at the front; toward the beginning or front; forward: *The fore section of a ship is called the bow.* ■ Other words that sound like this are **for** and **four.**

fore² (fôr), *INTERJECTION.* (in golf) a shout of warning to people ahead of you on the course. They may be in danger from a ball that you hit toward them. ■ Other words that sound like this are **for** and **four.**

fore·arm (fôr'ärm'), *NOUN.* the part of the arm between the elbow and the wrist.

fore·cast (fôr'kast'),
1 *VERB.* to tell what is going to happen: *Cooler weather is forecast for tomorrow.*
2 *NOUN.* a statement of what is going to happen: *What is the weather forecast?*
□ *VERB* **fore·casts, fore·cast** or **fore·cast·ed, fore·cast·ing.** –**fore'cast·er,** *NOUN.*

fore·fa·ther (fôr'fä'ᴛʜər), *NOUN.* an ancestor: *My forefathers were pioneers.*

fore·fin·ger (fôr'fing'gər), *NOUN.* the finger next to the thumb; index finger.

fore·foot (fôr'fut'), *NOUN.* one of the front feet of an animal having four or more feet. □ *PLURAL* **fore·feet.**

fore·ground (fôr'ground'), *NOUN.* the part of a picture or scene closest to the person looking at it: *The cottage stands in the foreground with the mountains in the background.*

fore·head (fôr'id or fôr'hed'), *NOUN.* the part of the face above the eyes.

fo·reign (fôr'ən), *ADJECTIVE.*
1 outside your own country: *She has traveled a lot in foreign countries.*
2 coming from outside your own country: *a foreign ship, a foreign language, foreign money.*
3 of, for, or with other countries: *foreign trade.*

fo·reign·er (fôr'ə nər), *NOUN.* someone from another country.

fore·leg (fôr'leg'), *NOUN.* one of the front legs of an animal having four or more legs.

fore·man (fôr'mən), *NOUN.*
1 someone in charge of a group of workers or of part of a factory.
2 someone chosen to be the leader of a jury.
□ *PLURAL* **fore·men.**

fore·most (fôr'mōst), *ADJECTIVE.* the most famous; leading: *He is regarded as one of the foremost scientists of this century.*

fore·run·ner (fôr'run'ər), *NOUN.* something that is a sign or warning that something is coming: *Black clouds and high winds are forerunners of a storm.*

fore·see (fôr sē'), *VERB.* to see or know beforehand: *She could foresee that the job would take all day, so she canceled her afternoon plans.* □ *VERB* **fore·sees, fore·saw** (fôr sò'), **fore·seen** (fôr sēn'), **fore·see·ing.** –**fore·see'a·ble,** *ADJECTIVE.*

fore·sight (fôr'sīt'), *NOUN.* the ability to see or imagine what is likely to happen and get ready for it: *She had the foresight to wear a warm coat.*

fo·rest (fôr'ist), *NOUN.* a large area with many tall trees; thick woods: *Many animals live in the forest.*

fo·rest·er (fôr'ə stər), *NOUN.* someone who is in charge of planting and taking care of a forest.

fo·rest·ry (fôr'ə strē), *NOUN.* the science and practice of planting and taking care of forests.

There is a house with a garden in the **foreground** of this mountain scene.

fore·tell (fôr tel'), *VERB.* to tell about something before it happens: *Who can foretell the future?* □ *VERB* **fore·tells, fore·told** (fôr tōld'), **fore·tell·ing.**

for·ev·er (fər ev'ər), *ADVERB.*
1 without ever coming to an end; for all time: *Nobody lives forever.*
2 always; all the time: *My older brother is forever talking on the phone.*

F

fore·word (fôr′wėrd′), *NOUN.* a brief introduction or preface to a book or speech. ■ Another word that sounds like this is **forward.**

for·feit (fôr′fit),
1 *VERB.* to lose something or have to give it up because of your own act, neglect, or fault: *Some of our players were sick, so we had to forfeit the game.*
2 *NOUN.* something lost or given up because of some act, neglect, or fault: *The forfeit of the game cost us the championship.*
❏ *VERB* **for·feits, for·feit·ed, for·feit·ing.**

for·gave (fər gāv′), *VERB.* the past tense of **forgive:** *She forgave my mistake.*

forge¹ (fôrj),
1 *NOUN.* a kind of small hearth or fireplace where metal is heated until it is slightly soft and then hammered into shape.
2 *NOUN.* a blacksmith's shop.
3 *VERB.* to heat metal until it is very soft and then hammer it into shape: *The blacksmith forged a bar of iron into a big hook.*
4 *VERB.* to make; shape; form: *Leaders of the two governments forged a new trade agreement.*
5 *VERB.* to make or write something false in order to to deceive someone: *Forging checks is a serious crime.*
❏ *VERB* **forg·es, forged, forg·ing.**

forge² (fôrj), *VERB.* to move forward slowly but steadily: *One runner forged ahead of the others and won the race.* ❏ *VERB* **forg·es, forged, forg·ing.**

for·get (fər get′), *VERB.*
1 to be unable to remember; fail to recall: *I forgot my lines in the play.*
2 to fail to remember to do, take, or notice: *I forgot to call the dentist.*
❏ *VERB* **for·gets, for·got, for·got·ten, for·get·ting.**

for·get·ful (fər get′fəl), *ADJECTIVE.* liable to forget; having a poor memory: *If I get too tired, I become forgetful.* **—for·get′ful·ness,** *NOUN.*

for·get-me-not (fər get′mē not′), *NOUN.* a plant that has clusters of small blue or white flowers.

for·give (fər giv′), *VERB.* to not have angry feelings toward someone; pardon: *She forgave me for breaking her tennis racket.* ❏ *VERB* **for·gives, for·gave, for·giv·en** (fər giv′ən), **for·giv·ing.**

for·give·ness (fər giv′nis), *NOUN.* the act of forgiving; pardon.

for·got (fər got′), *VERB.* the past tense of **forget:** *He was so busy that he forgot to eat his lunch.*

for·got·ten (fər got′n), *VERB.* the past participle of **forget:** *I have forgotten my lunch money!*

fork (fôrk),
1 *NOUN.* a tool that you eat with. It has a handle and several long points at one end.
2 *NOUN.* a tool that has long, sharp points for lifting and throwing hay; pitchfork.
3 *NOUN.* anything shaped like a fork: *the fork of a tree, the fork of a road.*
4 *VERB.* to divide into two branches: *There is a garage where the road forks.*
❏ *VERB* **forks, forked, fork·ing.**

fork·lift (fôrk′lift′),
NOUN. a device attached to one end of a truck or small heavy vehicle. It has horizontal metal arms that can be inserted under a load to lift or lower it.

forklift

for·lorn (fôr lôrn′), *ADJECTIVE.* sad and lonely from being left all alone. **—for·lorn′ly,** *ADVERB.*

form (fôrm),
1 *NOUN.* a shape: *Circles are simple forms.*
2 *VERB.* to make in a certain shape: *Bakers form dough into loaves.*
3 *VERB.* to take shape: *Clouds form in the sky.*
4 *VERB.* to become: *Water forms ice when it freezes.*
5 *VERB.* to organize; establish: *We formed a club.*
6 *VERB.* to develop: *She formed the good habit of doing her homework before watching TV.*
7 *NOUN.* a kind: *Ice and steam are forms of water.*
8 *NOUN.* a way of doing something; manner; method: *He is a fast runner, but his form is bad.*
9 *NOUN.* a piece of printed paper with blank spaces to be filled in: *We filled out a form to get a license for our dog.*
10 *NOUN.* any of the ways in which a word is spelled to show its different meanings. *Toys is the plural form of toy.*
❏ *VERB* **forms, formed, form·ing.**

for·mal (fôr′məl),
1 *ADJECTIVE.* not relaxed and friendly; not familiar and homelike: *a formal greeting.*
2 *ADJECTIVE.* according to set customs or rules: *The President made a formal visit to Japan.*
3 *NOUN.* a dance, party, or other social affair at which women and men wear fancy clothing.
4 *NOUN.* a long, fancy dress worn to such a social affair: *She wore a new formal to the dance.*
—for·mal·ly, *ADVERB.*

for·mat (fôr′mat),
1 *NOUN.* the shape, size, and general arrangement of a book, magazine, and so on.

a	hat	ė	term	ô	order	ch	child	⟨ a in about
ā	age	i	it	oi	oil	ng	long	e in taken
ä	far	ī	ice	ou	out	sh	she	ə⟨ i in pencil
â	care	o	hot	u	cup	th	thin	o in lemon
e	let	ō	open	ů	put	ᴛH	then	⟨ u in circus
ē	equal	ò	saw	ü	rule	zh	measure	

2 NOUN. the design, plan, arrangement, or manner of anything: *the format of a TV show.*

3 VERB. (in computers) to make a diskette ready for use.
❑ VERB **for·mats, for·mat·ted, for·mat·ting.**

for·ma·tion (fôr mā′shən), NOUN.

1 the act or process of forming, making, or shaping something: *the formation of a new club.*

2 the way in which something is arranged; arrangement; order: *Football players line up in various formations for their plays.*

3 something that is formed: *Clouds are formations of tiny drops of water in the sky.*

for·mer (fôr′mər), ADJECTIVE.

1 the first of two: *Given a choice between a telescope and a camera, she chose the former because of her interest in astronomy.*

2 earlier; past: *In former times, cooking was done in fireplaces instead of stoves.*

for·mer·ly (fôr′mər lē), ADVERB. in an earlier time; some time ago: *Our teacher formerly taught math.*

for·mu·la (fôr′myə lə), NOUN.

1 a set of directions for preparing a mixture: *a formula for making soap.*

2 a mixture of milk, water, sugar, and other nutrients for feeding babies that are not nursed.

3 a combination of symbols used in chemistry to show what is in a compound: *The formula for water is H_2O.*

4 a combination of symbols used in mathematics to state a rule or principle. The formula for the area of a rectangle is A = lw (in which A stands for area and lw for length times width).
❑ PLURAL **for·mu·las.**

for·syth·i·a (fôr sith′ē ə), NOUN. a shrub having many bell-shaped, yellow flowers in early spring before its leaves come out. ❑ PLURAL **for·syth·i·as.**

fort (fôrt), NOUN. a strong building or place that can easily be defended against an enemy.

forth (fôrth), ADVERB.

1 forward: *From this day forth I'll try to do better.*

2 out; into view: *The sun came forth.*
■ Another word that sounds like this is **fourth.**

for·ti·eth (fôr′tē ith), ADJECTIVE or NOUN.

1 next after the 39th; last in a series of 40.

2 one of 40 equal parts.

for·ti·fi·ca·tion (fôr′tə fə kā′shən), NOUN. a wall or fort built to make a place too strong to attack easily.

for·ti·fy (fôr′tə fī), VERB.

1 to build forts or walls to protect a place against attack; strengthen against attack.

2 to enrich something with vitamins and minerals: *Some dairies fortify their milk.*
❑ VERB **for·ti·fies, for·ti·fied, for·ti·fy·ing.**

fort·night (fôrt′nīt), NOUN. two weeks.

for·tress (fôr′tris), NOUN. a place built with thick walls and strong defenses. ❑ PLURAL **for·tress·es.**

for·tu·nate (fôr′chə nit), ADJECTIVE. having or bringing good luck; lucky: *You are fortunate in having such a fine family.* —**for′tu·nate·ly,** ADVERB.

for·tune (fôr′chən), NOUN.

1 a great deal of money or property; riches; wealth: *The family made a fortune in oil.*

2 luck; good luck: *Fortune was against us and we lost.*

3 what is going to happen to someone; fate: *No one can really tell you your fortune.*

for·tune·tell·er (fôr′chən tel′ər), NOUN. someone who claims to be able to tell what is going to happen to people before it happens.

for·ty (fôr′tē), ADJECTIVE or NOUN. four times ten; 40.
❑ PLURAL **for·ties.**

fo·rum (fôr′əm), NOUN.

1 a meeting to discuss questions of public interest: *An open forum was held to discuss the city budget.*

2 the public square or marketplace of an ancient Roman city, where business was done and courts and public assemblies were held.

for·ward (fôr′wərd),

1 ADVERB. onward; ahead: *Forward, march! From this time forward we shall be friends.*

2 ADVERB or ADJECTIVE. to the front; toward the front: *The magician asked for a helper from the audience to come forward.*

3 ADJECTIVE. at the front; near the front: *Our cabin was in the forward part of the ship.*

4 VERB. to send something on farther: *Please forward my mail to my new address.*

5 ADJECTIVE. too sure of yourself; bold: *Don't be so forward as to interrupt the speaker.*

6 NOUN. a player in basketball, soccer, and some other games who plays in the front line.
❑ VERB **for·wards, for·ward·ed, for·ward·ing.**
■ Another word that sounds like this is **foreword.**

for·wards (fôr′wərdz), ADVERB. forward.

fos·sil (fos′əl), NOUN. a part or print of a plant or animal that lived a long time ago. Fossils of dinosaurs that lived many millions of years ago have been found all over the world.

the **fossil** of an ancient fish

fossil fuel, a fuel found in the earth and formed from the remains of things that lived millions of years ago. Coal, oil, and natural gas are fossil fuels.

fos·ter (fô′stər),
1 *ADJECTIVE.* belonging to a family, but not related by birth or adoption. A **foster child** is a child brought up by people who are not the parents by birth or adoption. A **foster father, foster mother,** or **foster parents** are people who bring up foster children in a **foster home.**
2 *VERB.* to help the growth or development of something; encourage: *His parents fostered his interest in reading by giving him many books.*
□ *VERB* **fos·ters, fos·tered, fos·ter·ing.**

fought (fôt), *VERB.*
1 the past tense of **fight:** *They fought for their rights.*
2 the past participle of **fight:** *Many battles have been fought there.*

foul (foul),
1 *ADJECTIVE.* very dirty; nasty; smelly: *foul air.*
2 *VERB.* to make something dirty: *Oil fouled the harbor.*
3 *ADJECTIVE.* very wicked or cruel: *Murder is a foul crime.*
4 *ADJECTIVE.* unfair; against the rules: *The boxer received a foul punch after the bell ended the round.*
5 in sports: **a** *NOUN.* an unfair play; thing done against the rules. **b** *VERB.* to make an unfair play against someone: *The defender fouled him as he dribbled toward the basket.*
6 in baseball: **a** *NOUN.* a ball hit outside the foul lines. **b** *ADJECTIVE.* outside the foul lines. **c** *VERB.* to hit a ball outside the foul lines.
□ *VERB* **fouls, fouled, foul·ing.** ■ Another word that sounds like this is **fowl.**

foul line,
1 (in baseball) either one of the two straight lines that go from home plate through first base and third base to the end of the playing field.
2 (in basketball) a line 15 feet in front of each basket from which free throws are attempted.

found¹ (found), *VERB.*
1 the past tense of **find:** *We found the lost toy behind the couch.*
2 the past participle of **find:** *The lost child has been found.*

found² (found), *VERB.* to set up; establish: *The Pilgrims founded a colony at Plymouth.* □ *VERB* **founds, found·ed, found·ing. –found′er,** *NOUN.*

foun·da·tion (foun dā′shən), *NOUN.*
1 a part that other parts rest on for support; base: *The foundation of a house is built first.*
2 a basis: *This report has no foundation in fact.*
3 a charitable organization that provides money, especially for research.

Founding Father,
1 one of the men who planned and wrote the Constitution of the United States.

2 **founding father,** someone who sets up a business, company, or institution.

found·ry (foun′drē), *NOUN.* a place where metal is melted and molded into various shapes. □ *PLURAL* **found·ries.**

foun·tain (foun′tən), *NOUN.*
1 water flowing or rising into the air in a stream or spray.
2 a device from which a person can get a drink of water: *Every floor here has a drinking fountain.*
3 a good source: *My friend is a fountain of information about football.*

fountain (definition 1)

fountain pen, a pen for writing in which the ink flows from a tube inside.

four (fôr), *NOUN* or *ADJECTIVE.* one more than three; 4. ■ Other words that sound like this are **for** and **fore.**

four-foot·ed (fôr′fut′id), *ADJECTIVE.* having four feet: *A dog is a four-footed animal.*

Four-H clubs or **4-H clubs** (fôr′āch′ klubz′), a group of clubs that teach farm and home skills to children, mainly in rural areas.

four·teen (fôr′tēn′), *NOUN* or *ADJECTIVE.* four more than ten; 14.

four·teenth (fôr′tēnth′), *ADJECTIVE* or *NOUN.*
1 next after the 13th.
2 one of 14 equal parts.

fourth (fôrth), *ADJECTIVE* or *NOUN.*
1 next after the third.
2 quarter; one of four equal parts. ■ Another word that sounds like this is **forth.**

Fourth of July, a holiday in honor of the adoption of the Declaration of Independence on July 4, 1776; Independence Day.

a	hat	ė	term	ô	order	ch	child		a in about
ā	age	i	it	oi	oil	ng	long		e in taken
ä	far	ī	ice	ou	out	sh	she	ə ⟨	i in pencil
â	care	o	hot	u	cup	th	thin		o in lemon
e	let	ō	open	ů	put	₮H	then		u in circus
ē	equal	ò	saw	ü	rule	zh	measure		

fowl (foul), NOUN. any of several kinds of large birds used for food. Chickens, ducks, pheasants, and turkeys are fowl. ❑ PLURAL **fowl** or **fowls.** ∎ Another word that sounds like this is **foul.**

fox (foks), NOUN. a wild animal that looks something somewhat like a small dog, with a pointed snout and a bushy tail. ❑ PLURAL **fox•es** or **fox. –fox′like**′, ADJECTIVE.

frac•tion (frak′shən), NOUN.
1 one or more of the equal parts of a whole number or thing. ½, ⅓, and ⅘ are fractions.
2 a very small part; not all of something: *I had time to do only a fraction of my homework.* ∎ See the Synonym Study at **part.**

frac•ture (frak′chər),
1 NOUN. a break or crack in bone or cartilage: *She suffered a fracture in her leg.*
2 VERB. to break; crack: *I fell and fractured my arm.* ∎ See the Synonym Study at **break.** ❑ VERB **frac•tures, frac•tured, frac•tur•ing.**

frag•ile (fraj′əl), ADJECTIVE. easily broken; delicate: *Be careful; that thin glass is fragile.* **–fra•gil•i•ty** (frə jil′ə tē), NOUN.

frag•ment (frag′mənt), NOUN. a part broken off something; piece of something broken: *I glued the fragments of the broken vase back together.* ∎ See the Synonym Study at **piece.**

fra•grance (frā′grəns), NOUN. a sweet smell; pleasing odor: *the fragrance of flowers.*

fra•grant (frā′grənt), ADJECTIVE. having a sweet smell or odor: *These roses are very fragrant.*

frail (frāl), ADJECTIVE. slender and not very strong; weak: *a frail and sickly child.*

frame (frām),
1 NOUN. a support over which something is built: *The frame of the house was finally completed.*
2 NOUN. the body: *She is a thin person with a small frame.*
3 NOUN. something in which something else is set: *The painting was set in a plain black frame. The window frames are made of aluminum.*
4 VERB. to put a border around something: *I framed a photo of my best friend.*
5 VERB. to make someone seem guilty by some false arrangement: *The murderer tried to frame the neighbor by planting false evidence.* ❑ VERB **frames, framed, fram•ing.**

frame•work (frām′werk′), NOUN.
1 a structure that gives shape or support to something: *The bridge has a steel framework.*
2 the way in which something is put together; structure; system: *The framework of government has not changed in over 200 years.*

France (frans), NOUN. a large country in western Europe.

frank (frangk), ADJECTIVE. honest and free in expressing your real thoughts and feelings; not afraid to say what you think: *She was frank in telling me that she thought the plan would not work.* **–frank′ly,** ADVERB. **–frank′ness,** NOUN.

Frank•fort (frangk′fərt), NOUN. the capital of Kentucky.

frank•furt•er (frangk′fər tər), NOUN. a reddish sausage made of beef and pork, or just of beef, usually eaten on a bun; hot dog; wiener.

fran•tic (fran′tik), ADJECTIVE. very excited; wild with rage, fear, pain, or grief: *The trapped animal made frantic efforts to escape.* **–fran′ti•cal•ly,** ADVERB.

fraud (frȯd), NOUN.
1 the use of dishonesty to trick or cheat someone: *The person who sold us fake insurance was charged with fraud.*
2 someone who is not what he or she pretends to be: *The fortuneteller was a fraud; she had no knowledge of the future.*

fray (frā), VERB. to separate into threads; become ragged or worn along the edge: *Long wear had frayed the collar of his old shirt.* ❑ VERB **frays, frayed, fray•ing.**

freak (frēk), NOUN.
1 something very odd or unusual: *Snow in summer would be called a freak of nature.*
2 (informal) a person who is especially interested in or devoted to something: *a movie freak.*

freck•le (frek′əl), NOUN. one of the small, light brown spots that some people have on their skin.

The **frame** of the house was finally completed.

free (frē),
1 ADJECTIVE. not under someone else's control or rule; not enslaved: *a free person, a free nation.*
2 ADJECTIVE. not fastened or shut up; loose: *They set free the bear cub caught in the trap.*
3 ADJECTIVE. not kept from acting or thinking as you please: *She was free to do as she liked.*
4 ADJECTIVE. not busy: *She will call you when she is free.*
5 VERB. to let something loose: *We freed the bird from the cage. She freed her foot from a tangled vine.*

6 *ADJECTIVE* or *ADVERB.* not costing anything: *These tickets are free. We were admitted to the play free.* ❏ *ADJECTIVE* **fre•er, fre•est;** *VERB* **frees, freed, free•ing.** —**free′ly,** *ADVERB.*

Word Power   -free

The suffix **-free** is used to make adjectives. It means "without ____." Someone who is care**free** is **without** care. Sometimes **-free** is used with a hyphen. Something that is **salt-free** is **without** salt.

free•bie (frē′bē), *NOUN.* (informal) something given or received free of charge, such as a ticket to a ball game. ❏ *PLURAL* **free•bies.**

free•dom (frē′dəm), *NOUN.*
1 the condition of being free: *The American colonists gained freedom from England.*
2 the power to do, say, or think as you please: *freedom of speech, freedom of religion.*

free throw, (in basketball) a shot awarded to a player who has been fouled by a member of the opposing team. Each successful attempt is worth one point.

free•way (frē′wā′), *NOUN.* a highway for fast driving on which no tolls are charged.

freeze (frēz),
1 *VERB.* to become hard from cold; turn into a solid: *The raindrops froze into ice crystals.*
2 *VERB.* to make or become very cold: *The north wind froze the spectators. We froze at the football game.*
3 *VERB.* to kill or injure something by frost; be killed or injured by frost: *A drop in temperature froze the tomato plants.*
4 *NOUN.* a period during which there is freezing weather: *An early freeze damaged many gardens and orchards.*
5 *VERB.* to become unable to move: *I froze on the high diving board, afraid to jump into the water.* ❏ *VERB* **freez•es, froze, fro•zen, freez•ing.**

freeze-dry (frēz′drī′), *VERB.* to dry food by freezing and evaporating the liquid content in a vacuum. Freeze-dried food keeps well without being refrigerated. ❏ *VERB* **freeze-dries, freeze-dried, freeze-dry•ing.**

freez•er (frē′zər), *NOUN.* a refrigerator or a part of a refrigerator in which the temperature is well below the freezing point. Foods are frozen and kept from spoiling in freezers.

freezing point, the temperature at which a liquid freezes. The freezing point of water at sea level is 32 degrees Fahrenheit or 0 degrees Celsius.

freight (frāt), *NOUN.*
1 the goods that a train, truck, ship, or aircraft carries.
2 a system of carrying goods on a train, ship, aircraft, or truck: *He sent the box by freight.*

freight•er (frā′tər), *NOUN.* a ship that carries freight.

freighter

French (french),
1 *ADJECTIVE.* of or about France, its people, or their language.
2 *NOUN PLURAL.* **the French,** the people of France.
3 *NOUN.* the language of France. It is also spoken in Belgium, Switzerland, Canada, and other countries.

Word Source

French has given many words to the English language, including the words below:

amateur	cafe	kerchief	spaniel
ambulance	collage	lawn	supper
baboon	curfew	pansy	turquoise
barber	dandelion	plateau	utilize
bribe	garage	poach²	Vermont
butcher	grudge	restaurant	vinegar

French fries, potatoes cut into thin strips and fried in deep fat until crisp on the outside.

French Gui•an•a (french′ gē an′ə), a French territory in northern South America.

French horn, a brass wind instrument that is made of a long, narrow tube coiled in a circular shape. It produces a mellow tone.

fren•zy (fren′zē), *NOUN.*
1 a frantic condition; near madness: *They were in a frenzy after hearing that their child was missing.*
2 a very great excitement: *The crowd was in a frenzy after the home team scored the winning goal.* ❏ *PLURAL* **fren•zies.**

a	hat	ė	term	ô	order	ch	child	a in about
ā	age	i	it	oi	oil	ng	long	e in taken
ä	far	ī	ice	ou	out	sh	she	ə i in pencil
â	care	o	hot	u	cup	th	thin	o in lemon
e	let	ō	open	ů	put	ŦH	then	u in circus
ē	equal	ò	saw	ü	rule	zh	measure	

.quen·cy (frē′kwən sē), NOUN.
1 the number of times something happens within a certain amount of time: *The flashes of light came with a frequency of three per minute.*
2 frequent occurrence: *The frequency of their visits annoyed us.*
❑ PLURAL **fre·quen·cies.**

fre·quent (frē′kwənt), ADJECTIVE. happening or appearing often: *In my part of the country, storms are frequent in March.*

fre·quent·ly (frē′kwənt lē), ADVERB. often; time after time: *The twins are frequently mistaken for each other.*

fresh¹ (fresh), ADJECTIVE.
1 just made, grown, or gathered: *fresh coffee, fresh flowers.* ■ See the Synonym Study at **new.**
2 new; recent: *Is there any fresh news from home?*
3 another; new: *After her failure she made a fresh start.*
4 not salty: *We looked for a source of fresh water.*
5 not spoiled; not stale: *Is this milk fresh?*
6 not artificially preserved: *Fresh foods often have better flavor than canned foods.*
7 not tired out: *After a nap, she felt fresh and rested.*
8 vigorous; lively: *After a shower, I felt fresh and ready to go.*
—**fresh′ly,** ADVERB. —**fresh′ness,** NOUN.

fresh² (fresh), ADJECTIVE. rude; disrespectful: *She often got into trouble for making fresh remarks to her teachers.*

fresh·man (fresh′mən), NOUN. a student in the first year of high school or college. ❑ PLURAL **fresh·men.**

fresh·wa·ter (fresh′wȯ′tər), ADJECTIVE. of or living in water that is not salty: *The catfish is a freshwater fish.*

fret (fret), VERB. to be unhappy or worried about something; be restless: *Don't fret over your mistakes. The baby frets in hot weather.* ❑ VERB **frets, fret·ted, fret·ting.**

fret·ful (fret′fəl), ADJECTIVE. unhappy or worried; restless: *Babies are fretful when they are cutting teeth.*

Fri., an abbreviation of **Friday.**

fri·ar (frī′ər), NOUN. a man who belongs to one of the religious brotherhoods of the Roman Catholic Church. Friars own no property and keep very few possessions.

fric·tion (frik′shən), NOUN.
1 the resistance to motion of surfaces that touch: *A sled moves more easily on smooth ice than on rough ground because there is less friction.*
2 the act of rubbing one thing against another: *Matches are lighted by friction.*
3 disagreements or arguments between people or groups that have differing ideas or opinions: *Constant friction between the two nations brought them dangerously close to war.*

Fri·day (frī′dē), NOUN. the sixth day of the week; the day after Thursday.

Word Story

Friday comes from an old English word meaning "Frigg's day." Frigg (frig) was the old English goddess of love, and her day was considered the luckiest day of the week.

fridge (frij), NOUN. an informal form of **refrigerator.**

fried (frīd),
1 ADJECTIVE. cooked in hot fat: *I love fried eggs on toast.*
2 VERB. the past tense of **fry:** *I fried the ham.*
3 VERB. the past participle of **fry:** *The potatoes have been fried already.*

friend (frend), NOUN.
1 someone you like and who likes you: *I was glad to call her my friend.*
2 someone who supports something: *He was a generous friend of the art museum.*
—**friend′less,** ADJECTIVE.

friend·ly (frend′lē), ADJECTIVE.
1 like a friend; kind: *a friendly teacher.* ■ See the Synonym Study at **good-natured.**
2 like a friend's: *I gave her a friendly greeting.*
❑ ADJECTIVE **friend·li·er, friend·li·est.**
—**friend′li·ness,** NOUN.

friend·ship (frend′ship), NOUN.
1 the condition of being friends: *Our friendship lasted for many years.*
2 friendly feeling or behavior; friendliness: *We tried to help show friendship to the foreign visitors.*

frieze (frēz), NOUN. a band of decoration around a room, building, or mantel.

frig·ate (frig′it), NOUN. a fast sailing warship of medium size. Frigates have three masts and were especially in use from 1750 to 1850.

fright (frīt), NOUN. sudden fear; sudden terror: *The loud howl filled me with fright.* ■ See the Synonym Study at **fear.**

fright·en (frīt′n), VERB.
1 to scare someone or something; make afraid: *Thunder frightened the puppy.* ■ See the Synonym Studies at **scare** and **afraid.**
2 to cause someone or something to do something out of fear: *The sudden noise frightened the deer back into the woods.*
❑ VERB **fright·ens, fright·ened, fright·en·ing.**

fright·ful (frīt′fəl), ADJECTIVE.
1 causing fear or terror: *Being lost in the forest was a frightful experience.*
2 terrible to think about; shocking: *The frightful destruction caused by the fire stretched for miles.*
—**fright′ful·ly,** ADVERB.

frig·id (frij′id), ADJECTIVE.
1 very cold: *Arctic regions have a frigid climate.*
2 very unfriendly: *After our argument, he gave me a frigid stare whenever we met.*

The baby seal seems comfortable in the **frigid** Arctic.

fringe (frinj), NOUN.
1 a border or trimming made of threads or cords, either hanging loose or tied together in small bunches: *a fringe of yarn.*
2 anything like this; border: *A fringe of hair hung over her forehead.*

Fris·bee (friz′bē), NOUN. (trademark) a saucer-shaped disk of colored plastic tossed back and forth in play. ❏ PLURAL **Fris·bees.**

frisk·y (fris′kē), ADJECTIVE. full of energy; playful; lively: *The horse was so frisky that the rider could barely stay on it.* ❏ ADJECTIVE **frisk·i·er, frisk·i·est.** **–frisk′i·ness,** NOUN.

frit·ter¹ (frit′ər), VERB. to waste time: *Don't fritter away the day watching TV.* ❏ VERB **frit·ters, frit·tered, frit·ter·ing.**

frit·ter² (frit′ər), NOUN. sliced fruit, vegetables, meat, or fish covered with batter and fried. ❏ VERB **frit·ters, frit·tered, frit·ter·ing.**

frog (frog), NOUN. a small animal with smooth green or spotted skin and webbed feet. Most frogs live near water and use their strong back legs for hopping and swimming. **–frog′like′,** ADJECTIVE.

frog·man (frog′man′), NOUN. someone trained and equipped for working underwater. ❏ PLURAL **frog·men.**

frol·ic (frol′ik), VERB. to play about joyously; have fun together: *The children frolicked with the puppy.* ❏ VERB **frol·ics, frol·icked, frol·ick·ing.**

from (frum), PREPOSITION.
1 out of: *I took a quarter from my pocket. Steel is made from iron.*
2 out of the possession of: *Take the book from her.*
3 starting at; beginning with: *We took a train from New York. I start two weeks from today.*
4 because of: *I am suffering from a cold.*
5 coming from: *oil from Alaska, a word from Spanish.*

6 as compared to: *I can tell apples from oranges.*
7 given, sent, or caused by: *a letter from a friend. The cut on his finger was from a knife.*
8 off: *He took a book from the table.*

frond (frond), NOUN. a leaf of a fern or palm.

front (frunt),
1 NOUN. the part of anything that faces forward; forward part: *the front of a car, the front of a coat.*
2 NOUN. the first part; beginning: *in the front of a book.*
3 NOUN. the place where fighting is going on during a war: *Wounded soldiers were sent home from the front.*
4 NOUN. the land facing a street or a body of water: *We have a house on the lake front.*
5 ADJECTIVE. on or in the front; at the front: *a front door.*
6 VERB. to have the front toward; face: *My house fronts on the park.*
7 NOUN. the area where two large air masses of different temperature meet. A **cold front** is the edge of a mass of cold air. A **warm front** is the edge of a mass of warm air.
❏ VERB **fronts, front·ed, front·ing.**

There are about 3,500 kinds of **frogs.**

fron·tier (frun tir′), NOUN.
1 the farthest edge of settled country, where the wilderness begins.
2 the farthest limits of something: *I admire people who explore the frontiers of science.*
3 the part of one country that touches the edge of another country; boundary line between two countries: *Border guards patrolled the frontier between the two countries.*

a	hat	ė	term	ô	order	ch child	(a in about
ā	age	i	it	oi	oil	ng long	e in taken
ä	far	ī	ice	ou	out	sh she	ə { i in pencil
â	care	o	hot	u	cup	th thin	o in lemon
e	let	ō	open	ů	put	ŦH then	(u in circus
ē	equal	ô	saw	ü	rule	zh measure	

265

frost (fròst),
1 NOUN. a freezing condition; temperature below the point at which water freezes: *The first frost came early last winter.*
2 NOUN. feathery crystals of ice that have formed when water vapor in the air condenses at a temperature below freezing: *frost on the grass.*
3 VERB. to cover something with frost or something that suggests frost: *The cold frosted the trees.*
4 VERB. to cover something with frosting: *The cook frosted the cake.*
❑ VERB **frosts, frost·ed, frost·ing.**

frost·bite (fròst′bīt′), NOUN. an injury to a part of the body caused by freezing: *The victim's fingers and toes were numb from frostbite.*

frost·bit·ten (fròst′bit′n), ADJECTIVE. injured by freezing: *My ears were frostbitten.*

frost·ing (frò′sting), NOUN. a flavored, sweet mixture of sugar, butter or margarine, egg whites, and other things, used to cover cakes and other baked goods; icing.

frost·y (frò′stē), ADJECTIVE.
1 cold enough for frost: *a frosty morning.*
2 covered with frost: *The glass is frosty.*
3 unfriendly: *a frosty stare, a frosty manner.*
❑ ADJECTIVE **frost·i·er, frost·i·est.**

froth (fròth),
1 NOUN. foam: *the froth on a chocolate soda.*
2 VERB. to give out froth; foam: *The soda frothed up.*
❑ VERB **froths, frothed, froth·ing.**

frown (froun),
1 NOUN. an act of wrinkling your forehead to show that you are angry or do not like something: *We could see a frown on her face.*
2 VERB. to wrinkle your forehead to show disapproval or anger; look displeased or angry: *My teacher frowned when I came in late.*
3 VERB. to look with disapproval: *The principal frowned on our plan for a picnic just before exams.*
❑ VERB **frowns, frowned, frown·ing.**

froze (frōz), VERB. the past tense of **freeze**: *The water in the pond froze last week.*

fro·zen (frō′zn),
1 ADJECTIVE. hardened with cold; turned into ice: *frozen sherbet.*
2 ADJECTIVE. very cold: *I need a parka; I'm frozen.*
3 ADJECTIVE. kept from spoiling by freezing: *frozen food.*
4 ADJECTIVE. killed or injured by frost: *frozen plants.*
5 VERB. the past participle of **freeze**: *The water has frozen.*

fru·gal (frü′gəl), ADJECTIVE.
1 not wasteful; saving; using just enough: *A frugal person always shops for bargains.*
2 costing just a little; barely enough: *He ate a frugal supper of bread and milk.*
—**fru·gal·i·ty** (frü gal′ə tē), NOUN.

fruit (früt), NOUN.
1 a juicy or fleshy product of a tree, bush, shrub, or vine, usually sweet and good to eat. Apples, oranges, bananas, and berries are fruit.
2 the part of a plant where the seeds are. Pea pods, acorns, and grains of wheat are fruits.
❑ PLURAL **fruit** or **fruits.**

frus·trate (frus′trāt), VERB.
1 to keep something from happening that you have planned; block: *Rain frustrated our plan for a picnic.*
2 to make someone feel angry or hopeless because they cannot do something: *It frustrates her not to be able to swim.*
❑ VERB **frus·trates, frus·trat·ed, frus·trat·ing.**
—**frus·tra′tion**, NOUN.

fry (frī), VERB. to cook something in hot fat: *We fried the potatoes.* ❑ VERB **fries, fried, fry·ing.**

frying pan. See skillet.

ft., an abbreviation of **foot** or **feet.**

fudge (fuj), NOUN. soft candy made of sugar, milk, chocolate, and butter.

fu·el (fyü′əl), NOUN. anything that you can burn that gives heat or power. Coal, wood, oil, and natural gas are kinds of fuel.

fu·gi·tive (fyü′jə tiv), NOUN. someone who is running away or has run away: *He is a fugitive from justice.*

Word Power -ful

The suffix **-ful** is used to make adjectives and nouns. It means "full of _____," "showing _____," or "enough to fill a _____." Cheerful means **full of** cheer. Careful means **showing** care. Cupful means **enough to fill** a cup.

ful·crum (ful′krəm), NOUN. the support on which a lever turns in moving or lifting something.

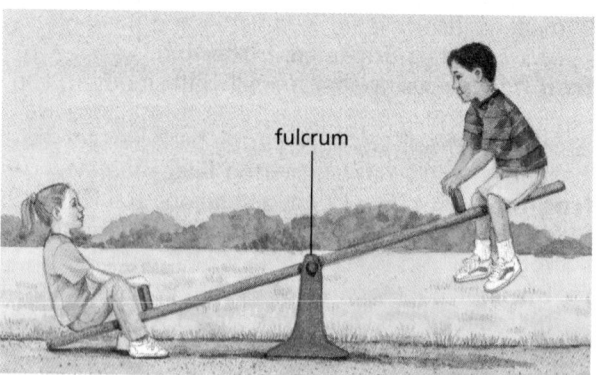

fulcrum

A seesaw pivots on the **fulcrum** in the middle of the board.

ful·fill (fùl fil′), VERB.
1 to keep or carry out a promise or an agreement: *He did not fulfill his promise to be home by ten.*
2 to do a duty, obey a command, and so on: *She fulfilled all the teacher's requests.*
❑ VERB **ful·fills, ful·filled, ful·fill·ing.**

full (fùl),
1 *ADJECTIVE*. not able to hold any more. Something is full when it holds all that it is intended to hold.
2 *ADJECTIVE*. having eaten enough to fill you up: *Aren't you full yet?*
3 *ADJECTIVE*. complete; entire: *I ran a full mile.*
4 *ADVERB*. completely: *Fill the pail full.*
—**full′ness**, *NOUN*.

Synonym Study

Full means holding as much as possible: *Parents' Day was a full day at school, with one event after another.*

Crowded means filled with people: *We were squashed in the crowded elevator.*

Packed can mean filled tightly: *The championship finals were played at a packed stadium.*

Stuffed can mean filled so tightly that it is hard to get things out: *The mailbox was stuffed with bills and junk mail.*

Jammed and **crammed** can mean filled more tightly than should be: *The party was so jammed there was no room to dance. I tried to force one more tape into the video store's crammed drop box.*

ANTONYM: empty.

full·back (fùl′bak′), *NOUN*.
1 (in football) a member of the offensive backfield.
2 (in soccer) a player who primarily defends the area near his or her own goal.

full-grown (fùl′grōn′), *ADJECTIVE*. fully grown.

full moon, the moon seen from the earth as a whole circle.

full-time (fùl′tīm′), *ADJECTIVE* or *ADVERB*. for all of the usual time: *She is looking for a full-time job. I work full-time.*

ful·ly (fùl′ē), *ADVERB*. completely; entirely: *I am fully satisfied. The gymnasium was fully equipped with bars, ropes, and rings.*

fum·ble (fum′bəl),
1 *VERB*. to search awkwardly for something; feel around clumsily: *I fumbled for the light switch.*
2 *VERB*. to let a ball drop instead of catching and holding it: *The quarterback fumbled the ball, and the other team recovered it.*
3 *NOUN*. an awkward attempt to find or handle something.
❑ *VERB* **fum·bles, fum·bled, fum·bling.** —**fum′bler,** *NOUN*.

fume (fyüm),
1 *NOUN*. often, **fumes,** gas, smoke, or vapor, especially if harmful, strong, or giving out odor: *The fumes from the truck's exhaust nearly choked me.*
2 *VERB*. to let off anger or annoyance in angry comments: *She fumed about the slow train.*
❑ *VERB* **fumes, fumed, fum·ing.**

fu·mi·gate (fyü′mə gāt), *VERB*. to expose to fumes that will kill mice, rats, insects, and so on. ❑ *VERB* **fu·mi·gates, fu·mi·gat·ed, fu·mi·gat·ing.**

fun (fun),
1 *NOUN*. a good time; enjoyment: *They had a lot of fun at the party.*
2 *ADJECTIVE*. enjoyable; pleasant; entertaining: *We had a fun day at the beach.* ★ Many people consider **funner** and **funnest** to be too informal.
❑ *ADJECTIVE* **fun·ner, fun·nest.**

func·tion (fungk′shən),
1 *NOUN*. the proper work or purpose of something: *The function of the stomach is to digest food.*
2 *VERB*. to work; act: *The old elevator no longer functions.*
3 *NOUN*. a formal public or social gathering for some purpose: *The hotel ballroom is often used for weddings and other functions.*
❑ *VERB* **func·tions, func·tioned, func·tion·ing.**

fund (fund),
1 *NOUN*. a sum of money set aside for a special purpose: *Our school has a fund of $2,000 for books.*
2 *NOUN*. **funds,** money ready to use: *We took $20 from the club's funds to buy a flag.*
3 *NOUN*. a stock or store ready for use: *There is a fund of information in our new library.*
4 *VERB*. to provide money for something: *The city funded a summer recreation program.*
❑ *VERB* **funds, fund·ed, fund·ing.**

fun·da·men·tal (fun′də men′tl),
1 *ADJECTIVE*. basic; essential; forming a basis: *Reading is a fundamental skill.*
2 *NOUN*. something basic; essential part: *We are taught the fundamentals of grammar in English class.*
—**fun′damen·tal·ly,** *ADVERB*.

fun·da·men·tal·ism (fun′də men′tl iz′əm), *NOUN*. the belief that the words of the Bible were inspired by God and should be believed and followed literally.

fund·rais·er (fund′rā′zər), *NOUN*. an event, such as a special sale, dinner, or performance, put on by or for a nonprofit organization to raise money: *A candy sale is this year's band fundraiser.*
—**fund′rais′ing,** *ADJECTIVE*.

fu·ner·al (fyü′nər əl), *NOUN*. the ceremonies held at the burial of a dead person. A funeral usually includes a religious service and the process of taking the body to the place where it is buried or burned.

a hat	ė term	ô order	ch child	a in about
ā age	i it	oi oil	ng long	e in taken
ä far	ī ice	ou out	sh she	ə i in pencil
â care	o hot	u cup	th thin	o in lemon
e let	ō open	ù put	₮H then	u in circus
ē equal	ò saw	ü rule	zh measure	

fun·gus (fung′gəs), NOUN. any living thing that is like a plant but has no leaves, flowers, or green coloring matter, and cannot make its own food as plants do. Mushrooms, toadstools, molds, and yeast are fungi. ❑ PLURAL **fun·gi** (fun′jī or fun′gī) or **fun·gus·es**.

two kinds of **fungus:** (a) a poisonous mushroom, (b) a tree fungus

fun·nel (fun′l), NOUN.
1 a utensil that has a narrow tube at the bottom and a cone with a wide mouth at the top. A funnel is used to pour liquid, powder, or grain into a small opening without spilling.
2 a smokestack or chimney on a steamship or steam engine.

fun·ny (fun′ē), ADJECTIVE.
1 causing laughter; amusing: *funny jokes.*
2 strange; odd: *It's funny that they are so late.*
❑ ADJECTIVE **fun·ni·er, fun·ni·est.**

Synonym Study

Funny means causing people to laugh or to be amused: *Her funny story caused laughter all over the room.*

Amusing means mildly funny: *She always starts her letters with amusing stories.*

Witty means funny in a clever way: *The teacher often makes witty comments that students enjoy.*

Humorous means meant to be funny: *I like humorous comic books better than scary comics.*

Hilarious means very funny: *The hilarious movie made everyone laugh out loud.*

See also the Synonym Study at **laugh.**

ANTONYM: serious.

fur (fėr), NOUN.
1 the soft, thick hair that covers the skin of many animals.
2 skin with such hair on it.
3 usually, **furs,** clothes made of fur: *dressed in furs.*
■ Another word that sounds like this is **fir.**

fur·i·ous (fyùr′ē əs), ADJECTIVE.
1 very angry; full of wild, fierce anger: *The owner was furious when she saw the broken window.*
■ See the Synonym Study at **mad.**
2 very strong; powerful: *a furious rush of activity, a furious blizzard.*
−**fur′i·ous·ly,** ADVERB.

fur·lough (fėr′lō), NOUN. a period of time when you do not have to be on official duty: *The soldier has two weeks furlough.*

fur·nace (fėr′nis), NOUN. an enclosed space for a very hot fire. Furnaces are used to heat buildings, melt metals, and make glass.

fur·nish (fėr′nish), VERB.
1 to supply what is necessary; provide: *furnish an army with blankets. The sun furnishes heat.*
2 to supply a room, house, or office with furniture or equipment: *We furnished the second bedroom with used furniture.*
❑ VERB **fur·nish·es, fur·nished, fur·nish·ing.**

fur·ni·ture (fėr′nə chər), NOUN. movable articles needed in a room, house, or office. Beds, chairs, tables, and desks are furniture.

fur·row (fėr′ō), NOUN.
1 a long, narrow groove or track, cut into the earth by a plow.
2 a wrinkle: *His brow was lined with furrows of worry.*

fur·ry (fėr′ē), ADJECTIVE.
1 covered with fur: *Bears are furry animals.*
2 soft like fur: *The rock was covered with furry moss.*
❑ ADJECTIVE **fur·ri·er, fur·ri·est.** −**fur′ri·ness,** NOUN.

furrows (definition 1)

fur·ther (fėr′ᴛʜər),
1 ADJECTIVE. more distant: *on the further side.*
2 ADVERB. to a more advanced point: *She inquired further into the matter.*
3 ADJECTIVE. more: *Do you need further help?*
4 VERB. to help something forward: *Let us further the cause of peace.*
5 ADVERB. also; in addition: *My parents told me to clean my room and said further that I must vacuum it.*
★ **Further** is a comparative of **far.** ❑ VERB **fur·thers, fur·thered, fur·ther·ing.**

fur·ther·more (fėr′ᴛʜər môr), ADVERB. in addition; also; besides: *Be sure to arrive on time; furthermore, don't forget to bring your bathing suit.*

fur·thest (fėr′ᴛʜist),
1 ADJECTIVE. most distant: *To make you unhappy was the furthest thing from my mind.*

2 *ADVERB.* to or at the greatest distance: *He hit the ball furthest.*

3 *ADVERB.* most: *Their ideas were the furthest advanced at that time.*

★ **Furthest** is a superlative of **far.**

fur·y (fyùr′ē), *NOUN.*
1 wild, fierce anger; rage: *She was in a fury because I had dropped her camera.*
2 violence; fierceness: *the fury of a hurricane.*
❑ *PLURAL* **fur·ies.**

fuse¹ (fyüz), *NOUN.* a slow-burning wick or mechanical device used to set off a shell, bomb, or blast of gunpowder.

fuse² (fyüz),
1 *NOUN.* a wire or strip of metal in an electric circuit that melts and breaks the circuit if the current becomes dangerously strong.
2 *VERB.* to melt or join together by melting: *Copper and zinc are fused to make brass.*
3 *VERB.* to blend; unite: *The intense heat fused the rocks together.*
❑ *VERB* **fus·es, fused, fus·ing.**

blow a fuse, *IDIOM.* to lose your temper; become angry: *When he saw the mess he blew a fuse.*

fu·se·lage (fyü′sə läzh *or* fyü′sə lij), *NOUN.* the body of an airplane, to which the wings and tail are fastened. The fuselage holds the passengers, crew, and cargo.

fu·sion (fyü′zhən), *NOUN.*
1 the act of melting together; fusing: *Bronze is made by the fusion of copper and tin.*
2 the combining of atomic nuclei to produce tremendous amounts of energy. The heat and light of the sun and stars are the results of nuclear fusion.

fuss (fus),
1 *NOUN.* much trouble over small matters; useless talk and worry: *My parents made a great fuss because I didn't tell them that I'd be late.*
2 *VERB.* to make a fuss: *There's no need to fuss over the broken cup.*
❑ *VERB* **fuss·es, fussed, fuss·ing.**

fuss·y (fus′ē), *ADJECTIVE.* hard to please; never satisfied: *When you are sick you may be fussy about food.*
❑ *ADJECTIVE* **fuss·i·er, fuss·i·est. −fuss′i·ness,** *NOUN.*

fu·tile (fyü′tl), *ADJECTIVE.* useless; never successful: *He fell down after making futile attempts to keep his balance.* **−fu′tile·ly,** *ADVERB.*

fu·ton (fü′ton), *NOUN.* a padded sleeping mat, often placed directly on the floor. Futons were originally used in Japan but are now common in the United States and Canada. ❑ *PLURAL* **fu·tons** *or* **fu·ton.**

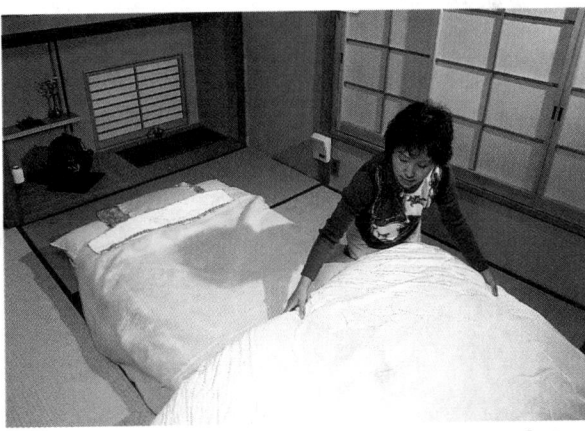
futon

fu·ture (fyü′chər),
1 *NOUN.* all time to come; what is to come; what will be: *You cannot change the past, but you can do better in the future.*
2 *ADJECTIVE.* coming; about to be: *We hope your future years will all be happy.*
3 *ADJECTIVE.* expressing something expected to happen or exist in time to come: *the future tense of a verb.*

fuzz (fuz), *NOUN.* loose, light fibers or hairs; fine down: *the fuzz on a caterpillar, the fuzz on a peach.*

fuzz·y (fuz′ē), *ADJECTIVE.*
1 like or covered with fuzz: *Peaches are fuzzy.*
2 not clear; blurred: *This photograph is too fuzzy for me to identify the people in it.*
❑ *ADJECTIVE* **fuzz·i·er, fuzz·i·est. −fuzz′i·ness,** *NOUN.*

Word Power   -fy

The suffix **-fy** means "to make or become ____." **Simplify** means to **make** simple. **Beautify** means to **make** beautiful. **Solidify** means to **become** solid.

gondola

Gg

G or **g** (jē), _NOUN._ the seventh letter of the English alphabet. ❏ _PLURAL_ **G's** or **g's.**

G, General (a rating for a movie that is recommended for all age groups).

g or **g.,** an abbreviation of **gram** or **grams.**

GA, an abbreviation of **Georgia.**

gab (gab), (informal)
1 _VERB._ to talk about unimportant things; chatter: _We gabbed for twenty minutes on the phone._
2 _NOUN._ conversation about unimportant things. ❏ _VERB_ **gabs, gabbed, gab·bing.**

ga·ble (gā′bəl), _NOUN._ the triangular piece of wall between two sloping surfaces of a roof.

Ga·bon (gä bȯn′), _NOUN._ a country in west central Africa. **—Gab·o·nese** (gab′ə nēz′), _ADJECTIVE_ or _NOUN._

gadg·et (gaj′it), _NOUN._ a small tool or device that you use to do a certain task: _Can openers and cookie cutters are kitchen gadgets._ ▪ See the Synonym Study at **tool.**

gag (gag),
1 _NOUN._ something put in a person's mouth to keep him or her from talking or crying out.
2 _VERB._ to stop up someone's mouth with a gag: _The robbers tied the man's arms and gagged him._
3 _VERB._ to choke and feel the need to throw up: _I gagged on the bad-tasting medicine._
4 _NOUN._ a joke: _The comedian's gags made us laugh._
❏ _VERB_ **gags, gagged, gag·ging.**

gai·ly (gā′lē), _ADVERB._
1 happily; merrily: _Excited by the good news, she danced gaily around the room._
2 brightly: _gaily dressed in colorful costumes._

gain (gān),
1 _VERB._ to come to have something; get; obtain; win: _The farmer gained possession of more land. I've worked hard to gain his respect._
2 _NOUN._ an increase, addition, or advantage: _I've had a noticeable gain in weight this past year._

3 *VERB.* to get as an increase, addition, or advantage: *The car gained speed.*
❑ *VERB* **gains, gained, gain·ing.**

gait (gāt), *NOUN.* a manner of walking or running: *A gallop is one of the gaits of a horse.* ■ Another word that sounds like this is **gate.**

gal., an abbreviation of **gallon** or **gallons.**

ga·la (gā′lə), *ADJECTIVE.* festive: *Thanksgiving is a gala day for our family.*

gal·ax·y (gal′ək sē), *NOUN.*
1 a group of billions of stars forming one system. Earth and the sun are in the Milky Way galaxy.
2 the Galaxy. See **Milky Way.**
❑ *PLURAL* **gal·ax·ies.**

Did You Know?

Astronomers think that there are about 100 billion galaxies in the universe. Large galaxies have more than a trillion stars. Small galaxies have less than one billion. Almost all galaxies seem to be moving away from the earth. The ones that are the farthest away seem to be moving the fastest.

gale (gāl), *NOUN.*
1 a very strong wind: *The boat was sunk in the gale.*
2 a noisy outburst: *We heard gales of laughter.*

gall (gȯl), *NOUN.*
1 a bitter liquid made in the liver; bile.
2 too great boldness.

gal·lant (gal′ənt), *ADJECTIVE.* noble in spirit or in conduct; brave: *She was praised for her gallant rescue of the drowning child.* **—gal′lant·ly,** *ADVERB.*

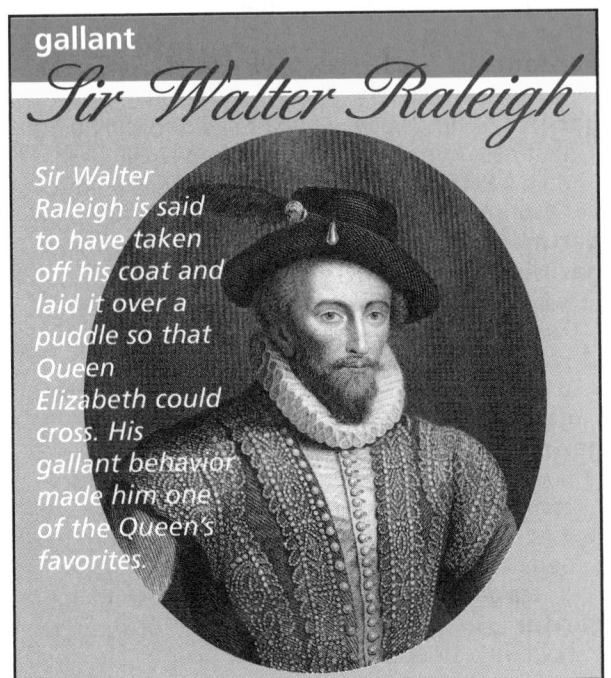

gallant

Sir Walter Raleigh

Sir Walter Raleigh is said to have taken off his coat and laid it over a puddle so that Queen Elizabeth could cross. His gallant behavior made him one of the Queen's favorites.

gall bladder, a small sac attached to the liver, where bile is stored for digestion.

gal·le·on (gal′ē ən), *NOUN.* a large, high ship of former times, usually with several decks.

galleon

gal·ler·y (gal′ər ē), *NOUN.*
1 a room or building used to show collections of pictures and statues.
2 the highest balcony of a theater.
❑ *PLURAL* **gal·ler·ies.**

gal·ley (gal′ē), *NOUN.*
1 a long, narrow ship of former times having oars and sails. Galleys were often rowed by enslaved people or convicts.
2 the kitchen of a ship or airplane.
❑ *PLURAL* **gal·leys.**

gal·lon (gal′ən), *NOUN.* a unit for measuring liquids, equal to four quarts.

gal·lop (gal′əp),
1 *NOUN.* the fastest gait of a horse or of many other four-footed animals. In a gallop, all four feet are off the ground at the same time in each leap.
2 *VERB.* to ride or go at a gallop: *The wild horse galloped off when it saw us.*
❑ *VERB* **gal·lops, gal·loped, gal·lop·ing.**

gal·lows (gal′ōz), *NOUN.* a wooden frame made of a horizontal bar on two upright posts, used for hanging criminals by a rope. ❑ *PLURAL* **gal·lows.**

Gam·bi·a (gam′bē ə), *NOUN.* The, a country in western Africa. **—Gam′bi·an,** *ADJECTIVE* or *NOUN.*

gam·ble (gam′bəl),
1 *VERB.* to play games of chance for money; bet: *Some people gamble on horse races.*
2 *VERB.* to take a risk: *The firefighters gambled with their lives to rescue the child.*

a	hat	ė	term	ô	order	ch	child	⎧ a in about
ā	age	i	it	oi	oil	ng	long	e in taken
ä	far	ī	ice	ou	out	sh	she	ə⎨ i in pencil
â	care	o	hot	u	cup	th	thin	o in lemon
e	let	ō	open	u̇	put	ŦH	then	⎩ u in circus
ē	equal	ȯ	saw	ü	rule	zh	measure	

3 NOUN. a risky act or plan: *Putting money into a new business is often a gamble.*
  ❑ VERB **gam·bles, gam·bled, gam·bling.**
  —gam′bler, NOUN.

game (gām), NOUN.

1 an organized way of playing; something with rules that is done for fun: *Tag is a game that we enjoy.*
  ∎ See the Synonym Study at **play.**

2 a contest with certain rules, in which one person or side tries to win: *a football game, a game of checkers.*

3 a set of objects, such as dice, cards, round pieces of wood or plastic, and a board, used in playing certain kinds of games. Checkers and backgammon are games.

4 wild animals, birds, or fish hunted or caught for sport or for food.

Word Bank

There are many different kinds of **games,** with many different names. If you want to learn more about them, you can begin by looking up these words in this dictionary.

backgammon	dominoes	poker²
billiards	hide-and-seek	pool²
bingo	hopscotch	tag²
checkers	horseshoes	tetherball
chess	kickball	tick-tack-toe
Chinese checkers	leapfrog	tug-of-war
croquet	marbles	video game
darts	Ping-Pong	

gan·der (gan′dər), NOUN. a male goose.

gang (gang), NOUN.

1 a group of people working or going around together: *A gang of workers repaired the road. A whole gang of us went swimming.*

2 a group engaged in wrongdoing: *Members of a gang were arrested for stealing cars.*

  gang up on, IDIOM. to get together with others to oppose or attack someone: *Some girls ganged up on her and pushed her down in the snow.*
  ❑ VERB **gangs, ganged, gang·ing.**

gang·ster (gang′stər), NOUN. a member of a gang of criminals.

gap (gap), NOUN.

1 a broken place; opening: *The cows got out of the field through a gap in the fence.*

2 an unfilled space; empty part; blank: *The story is not complete; there are several gaps in it.*

gape (gāp), VERB.

1 to stare with your mouth open: *The crowd gaped at the daring tricks of the tightrope walkers.*

2 to open wide: *A deep hole in the earth gaped before us.*
  ❑ VERB **gapes, gaped, gap·ing. —gap′er,** NOUN.

ga·rage (gə räzh′ *or* gə räj′), NOUN.

1 a place where cars, trucks, and buses are kept.

2 a shop for repairing cars, trucks, and so on.

garb (gärb),

1 NOUN. the way you are dressed; kind of clothing: *stylish garb, official garb.*

2 VERB. to clothe: *The bride was garbed in white.*
  ❑ VERB **garbs, garbed, garb·ing.**

Word Story

Garb comes from an Italian word meaning "elegance." Because clothing is so important to an elegant appearance, that meaning took over.

gar·bage (gär′bij), NOUN. scraps, especially scraps of food, to be thrown away.

gar·ban·zo (gär bän′zō), NOUN. See **chickpea.**
  ❑ PLURAL **gar·ban·zos.**

gar·den (gärd′n),

1 NOUN. a piece of ground used for growing vegetables, flowers, or fruits.

2 VERB. to take care of a garden: *I garden as a hobby.*
  ❑ VERB **gar·dens, gar·dened, gar·den·ing.**

gar·den·er (gärd′nər), NOUN.

1 someone employed to take care of a garden, lawn, and so on.

2 someone who gardens.

gar·de·nia (gär dē′nyə), NOUN. a fragrant, white flower with smooth petals. ❑ PLURAL **gar·de·nias.**

gar·gle (gär′gəl), VERB. to rinse your throat out with warm salt water or liquid medicine. ❑ VERB **gar·gles, gar·gled, gar·gling.**

gar·goyle (gär′goil), NOUN. an ornamental stone carving in the shape of a strange animal or a human being.

gar·land (gär′lənd), NOUN. a wreath of flowers or leaves.

gar·lic (gär′lik), NOUN. a plant related to the onion that has a small bulb with a strong smell. Each bulb has sections called cloves. Garlic is used to flavor meats, sauces, salad dressing, and so on.

gar·ment (gär′mənt), NOUN. any piece of clothing.

gar·nish (gär′nish),

1 NOUN. something that you use to decorate food: *The turkey was served with a garnish of parsley.*

2 VERB. to decorate food before you serve it.
  ❑ PLURAL **gar·nish·es;** VERB **gar·nish·es, gar·nished, gar·nish·ing.**

gar·ri·son (gar′ə sən),

1 NOUN. a group of soldiers stationed in a fort or town to defend it.

2 VERB. to station soldiers in a fort or town to defend it.
  ❑ VERB **gar·ri·sons, gar·ri·soned, gar·ri·son·ing.**

gar·ter (gär′tər), NOUN. an elastic band or strap to hold up a stocking or sock.

garter snake, a very common, harmless snake. It is brown or green with long yellow stripes.

Did You Know?

Garter snakes have live babies instead of laying eggs. They usually have about 18 babies at one time, but could have as many as 80. Some baby garter snakes eat earthworms.

garter snake — about 2½ feet long

gas (gas),
1 *NOUN.* a substance that is not a solid or a liquid. A gas has no shape or size of its own and can expand without limit. Air is a mixture of gases.
2 *NOUN.* any mixture of gases that can be burned. Gas is used for cooking and heating.
3 *NOUN.* a gas that poisons, suffocates, or stuns.
4 *VERB.* to kill or injure someone or something with poisonous gas.
5 *NOUN.* gasoline.
   ❏ *PLURAL* **gas•es;** *VERB* **gas•ses, gassed, gas•sing.**

gas•e•ous (gas′ē əs), *ADJECTIVE.* in the form of or like gas: *Steam is water in a gaseous condition.*

gash (gash),
1 *NOUN.* a long, deep cut or wound: *A piece of ice put a gash in his hand when he slipped off the sled.*
2 *VERB.* to make a long, deep cut or wound in something: *I gashed my foot on a broken shell.*
   ❏ *PLURAL* **gash•es;** *VERB* **gash•es, gashed, gash•ing.**

gas mask, a mask that covers your mouth and nose to keep out poisonous gas and smoke. It has a filter that allows only air to pass through.

gas•o•hol (gas′ə hȯl), *NOUN.* a fuel made of ninety percent gasoline and ten percent alcohol. Gasohol may be used in cars, trucks, and so on.

gas•o•line (gas′ə lēn′ *or* gas′ə lēn′), *NOUN.* a colorless liquid made from petroleum. It evaporates and burns very easily. Gasoline is used to run cars, trucks, and so on.

gasp (gasp),
1 *VERB.* to try hard to get your breath with an open mouth. A person gasps when out of breath or surprised.

2 *NOUN.* the act of trying hard to get your breath with your mouth open: *After the race she found it hard to talk between gasps for breath.*
3 *VERB.* to say something with gasps: *"Help!" gasped the drowning man.*
   ❏ *VERB* **gasps, gasped, gasp•ing.**

gas station, a place where gasoline and oil for motor vehicles are sold; service station.

gate (gāt), *NOUN.* a door in a wall or fence that turns on hinges or slides open and shut: *Someone left the gate open and the dog got out.* ■ Another word that sounds like this is **gait.**

Word Power   -gate

The suffix **-gate** is used to describe some scandal or criminal activity. It is an unusual suffix because it does not really mean anything specific. It is used to give an catchy name to some suspicious happening: *The confusion over the missing cookie sale money was called Cookiegate in the newspaper.* The suffix comes from *Watergate,* the name of an office building in Washington, D.C. A burglary there led to a famous political scandal in the 1970s.

gate•way (gāt′wā′), *NOUN.*
1 an opening in a wall or fence for a gate.
2 a way to go in or out; way to get to something: *A good education can be a gateway to success.*

gath•er (gaᴛʜ′ər), *VERB.*
1 to bring or come together in one place; collect: *A crowd gathered to hear the speech.*
2 to get or gain little by little: *The train gathered speed as it left the station.*
3 to understand from what you have seen or heard: *I gather from the excitement that we won!*
   ❏ *VERB* **gath•ers, gath•ered, gath•er•ing.**
   —**gath′er•er,** *NOUN.*

gath•er•ing (gaᴛʜ′ər ing), *NOUN.* a group of people who have gotten together; meeting: *We had a large family gathering at our house last Sunday.*

gaud•y (gȯ′dē), *ADJECTIVE.* too colorful or bright: *He wore a gaudy tie.* ❏ *ADJECTIVE* **gaud•i•er, gaud•i•est.**
   —**gaud′i•ness,** *NOUN.*

gauge (gāj),
1 *NOUN.* a device for measuring: *I'll use a gauge to see if my bicycle tires need more air.*
2 *NOUN.* a standard measure or a scale of standard measurements. There are gauges of the thickness of wire, the inside diameter of a shotgun barrel, and so on.

G

a	hat	ė	term	ô	order	ch	child		a in about
ā	age	i	it	oi	oil	ng	long		e in taken
ä	far	ī	ice	ou	out	sh	she	ə {	i in pencil
â	care	o	hot	u	cup	th	thin		o in lemon
e	let	ō	open	ù	put	ᴛʜ	then		u in circus
ē	equal	ȯ	saw	ü	rule	zh	measure		

3 *VERB.* to measure something accurately: *Barometers are used to gauge air pressure.*
❑ *VERB* **gaug·es, gauged, gaug·ing.**

gaunt (gȯnt), *ADJECTIVE.* very thin and bony; with hollow eyes and a starved look: *Hunger had made him gaunt.* ❑ *ADJECTIVE* **gaunt·er, gaunt·est.**

gaunt·let (gȯnt′lit), *NOUN.* an iron glove which was part of a knight's armor.

gauze (gȯz), *NOUN.* a very thin, light cloth, easily seen through. Gauze is often used for bandages. **—gauze′like′,** *ADJECTIVE.*

gave (gāv), *VERB.* the past tense of **give:** *She gave me some of her candy.*

gav·el (gav′əl), *NOUN.* a small wooden hammer used in a meeting or in court to signal for attention or order: *The chairman rapped on the table twice with his gavel.*

gawk (gȯk), *VERB.* to stare at someone or something in a rude way; gape: *People driving by gawked at the accident but did not stop to help.* ❑ *VERB* **gawks, gawked, gawk·ing.**

gavel

gay (gā), *ADJECTIVE.*
1 happy and full of fun; merry: *The children were cheerful and gay on the day of the first snowfall.*
2 bright; showy: *She wore a gay red and yellow scarf.*

gaze (gāz),
1 *VERB.* to look long and steadily at someone or something: *For hours we sat gazing at the stars.*
■ See the Synonym Study at **look.**
2 *NOUN.* a long, steady look.
❑ *VERB* **gaz·es, gazed, gaz·ing. —gaz′er,** *NOUN.*

ga·zelle (gə zel′), *NOUN.* a small, graceful, deerlike animal of Africa and Asia. ❑ *PLURAL* **ga·zelles** or **ga·zelle.**

gazelle — about 2½ feet high at the shoulder

gear (gir),
1 *NOUN.* a wheel having teeth that fit into the teeth of another wheel, so that one wheel can turn the other. Gears pass motion from one part of a machine to another.
2 *NOUN.* the equipment needed for some purpose: *Fishing gear includes a line, a pole, and hooks.*
3 *VERB.* to make something fit; adjust; adapt: *The classes were geared to the needs of the students.*
❑ *VERB* **gears, geared, gear·ing.**

gear·shift (gir′shift′), *NOUN.* a device for changing from one set of gears to another in a car or other motor vehicle.

geese (gēs), *NOUN.* the plural of **goose.**

Gei·ger count·er (gī′gər koun′tər), a device that detects and measures radioactivity.

gel·a·tin (jel′ə tən), *NOUN.* a substance like glue or jelly obtained by boiling the bones, hoofs, and other waste parts of animals. Gelatin is used in making desserts, glue, medicine capsules, and film.

gem (jem), *NOUN.*
1 a precious stone, especially when cut or polished; jewel. Diamonds and rubies are gems.
2 someone or something that is very beautiful or precious: *The gem of her collection was a rare Italian stamp.*

gen·der (jen′der), *NOUN.* sex: *the female gender.*

gene (jēn), *NOUN.* a section of the special chemical chains called chromosomes in the nucleus of a cell. Genes control the characteristics inherited from parents, such as the color of your hair and eyes, the shapes of flowers, and so on.

gen·er·a (jen′ər ə), *NOUN.* a plural of **genus.**

gen·er·al (jen′ər əl),
1 *ADJECTIVE.* common to many or most; not limited to a few; widespread: *In our school there is a general interest in sports.*
2 *ADJECTIVE.* including the main features, not the details, of something: *An owner's manual gives general instructions on looking after your car.*
3 *NOUN.* any of several military ranks. See the chart on page 550.

gen·er·al·ize (jen′ər ə līz), *VERB.* to make into a general rule after examining particular facts: *If you know that cats, lions, leopards, pumas, and tigers eat meat, you can generalize that all members of the cat family eat meat.* ❑ *VERB* **gen·er·al·iz·es, gen·er·al·ized, gen·er·al·iz·ing.**

gen·er·al·ly (jen′ər ə lē), *ADVERB.*
1 in most cases; usually: *They are generally on time.*
2 commonly; widely: *It was once generally believed that the earth is flat.*

gen·e·rate (jen′ə rāt′), *VERB.* to cause something to be; produce: *The force of running water can be used to generate electricity.* ❑ *VERB* **gen·e·rates, gen·e·rat·ed, gen·e·rat·ing.**

gen·e·ra·tion (jen′ə rā′shən), NOUN.
1 all the people born in about the same time. Your parents and their friends belong to one generation; you and your friends belong to the next generation.
2 about twenty-five years, or the average time from the birth of one generation to the birth of the next generation.
3 one stage in the history of a family: *The picture showed four generations—great-grandmother, grandmother, mother, and baby.*
4 the act or process of producing: *Steam and water power are used for the generation of electricity.*

genius

Albert Einstein is considered one of the greatest scientific geniuses ever. He created the theory of relativity, which made it possible to develop nuclear energy.

gen·e·ra·tor (jen′ə rā′tər), NOUN. a machine for producing electricity. Generators use flowing water, steam, wind, or other sources of energy to produce electricity.

ge·ner·ic (jə ner′ik), ADJECTIVE. not sold under a trademark or brand name: *generic drugs.*

gen·e·ros·i·ty (jen′ə ros′ə tē), NOUN. willingness to share what you have; unselfishness: *That wealthy family is known for its generosity.*

gen·er·ous (jen′ər əs), ADJECTIVE. willing to share what you have; unselfish: *Our teacher is always generous with his time.* **—gen′er·ous·ly,** ADVERB.

ge·net·ic (jə net′ik), ADJECTIVE. of or about a gene or genes: *a genetic disorder.* **—ge·net′i·cal·ly,** ADVERB.

genetic code, the order in which many special chemical compounds are linked together into genes in the DNA molecule. A specific order creates a pattern that tells a cell how to make some substance necessary for life and growth.

genetic engineering, the alteration of the genes of a living thing by scientists. Genetic engineering can change the way a cell works or what features a parent passes on to its offspring.

ge·net·i·cist (jə net′ə sist), NOUN. an expert in genetics.

ge·net·ics (jə net′iks), NOUN. the branch of biology that studies the principles of heredity and physical changes in living things.

gen·ial (jē′nyəl), ADJECTIVE. pleasant; cheerful and friendly: *She was glad to see us again and gave us a genial welcome.* **—gen′ial·ly,** ADVERB.

ge·nie (jē′nē), NOUN. an imaginary spirit that can take human form and do magical things: *When Aladdin rubbed his lamp, the genie appeared.* ❑ PLURAL **ge·nies.**

gen·ius (jē′nyəs), NOUN.
1 very great mental skill and ability: *Important discoveries are often made by people of genius.*
2 someone having such power: *Benjamin Franklin and Albert Einstein were geniuses.* ❑ PLURAL **gen·ius·es.**

gen·tile or **Gen·tile** (jen′til),
1 NOUN. someone who is not Jewish.
2 ADJECTIVE. not Jewish.

gen·tle (jen′tl), ADJECTIVE.
1 not rough or violent; tender: *A gentle rocking motion put the baby to sleep.*
2 gradual; not harsh or extreme: *a gentle slope.*
3 friendly; kind: *She has a gentle disposition.* ❑ ADJECTIVE **gen·tler, gen·tlest. —gen′tle·ness,** NOUN.

gen·tle·man (jen′tl mən), NOUN.
1 a man with a well-known family and high social position: *He was a respected gentleman from an old, wealthy family.*
2 any man that has good manners: *A gentleman does not push into line ahead of others.*
3 a polite term for any man. "Gentlemen" is often used in speaking or writing to a group of men. ❑ PLURAL **gen·tle·men.**

gent·ly (jent′lē), ADVERB.
1 in a gentle way; tenderly; softly: *Handle the baby gently.*
2 gradually: *a gently sloping hillside.*

gen·u·ine (jen′yü ən), ADJECTIVE.
1 real; true: *This wallet is genuine leather.*
2 sincere; honest: *We felt genuine regret when our neighbors moved away.* **—gen′u·ine·ly,** ADVERB.

ge·nus (jē′nəs), NOUN. a group of related living things. Wolves, coyotes, and dogs belong to the same genus. ❑ PLURAL **gen·er·a** or **ge·nus·es.**

a hat	ė term	ô order	ch child	⎧a in about
ā age	i it	oi oil	ng long	e in taken
ä far	ī ice	ou out	sh she	ə⎨i in pencil
â care	o hot	u cup	th thin	o in lemon
e let	ō open	ù put	℠H then	⎩u in circus
ē equal	ò saw	ü rule	zh measure	

G

Word Power   geo-

The combining form **geo-** means "earth" or "of the earth." **Geology** is the science of the earth. A **geographer** is someone who studies the earth.

ge·o·de·sic dome
(jē′ə des′ik dōm′), a dome held up by a lightweight framework of connected triangles.

a **geodesic dome**

ge·og·ra·pher
(jē og′rə fər), NOUN. someone who is an expert in geography.

ge·o·graph·ic
(jē′ə graf′ik), ADJECTIVE. geographical.

ge·o·graph·i·cal
(jē′ə graf′ə kəl), ADJECTIVE. of or about geography. **−ge′o·graph′i·cal·ly,** ADVERB.

ge·og·ra·phy (jē og′rə fē), NOUN.
1 the study of the earth's surface, climate, continents, countries, peoples, natural resources, and industries.
2 the surface features of a place or region: *We studied the geography of New England.*

ge·o·log·ic (jē′ə loj′ik), ADJECTIVE. geological: *geologic time.*

ge·o·log·i·cal (jē′ə loj′ə kəl), ADJECTIVE. of or about geology: *a geological survey.* **−ge′o·log′i·cal·ly,** ADVERB.

ge·ol·o·gy (jē ol′ə jē), NOUN. the science that studies the composition and history of the earth. **−ge·ol′o·gist,** NOUN.

ge·o·met·ric (jē′ə met′rik), ADJECTIVE.
1 of or about geometry.
2 made up of straight lines, circles, and other simple shapes; regular and evenly balanced: *I wore a sweater with colorful geometric patterns.* **−ge′o·met′ri·cal·ly,** ADVERB.

ge·om·e·try (jē om′ə trē), NOUN. the branch of mathematics that measures and compares points, lines, angles, surfaces, and solids.

Geor·gia (jôr′jə), NOUN.
1 one of the southern states of the United States. *Abbreviation:* GA; *Capital:* Atlanta.
2 a country in southwestern Europe. **−Geor′gian,** ADJECTIVE OR NOUN.

State Story The state of Georgia was named for George II. He was king of England when Georgia was founded as a colony.

ge·ra·ni·um (jə rā′nē əm), NOUN. a plant with showy flowers of red, pink, or white, often grown in pots for window plants.

ger·bil (jėr′bəl), NOUN. an animal something like a mouse with long hind legs.

Did You Know?

Pet **gerbils** are descended from wild gerbils captured in central Asia and sent to Japan. They were then sent to the United States for research. They were so cute that people wanted them for pets.

germ (jėrm), NOUN.
1 a very tiny, simple living thing that often causes disease. Viruses and bacteria are germs.
2 the earliest form of a living thing; seed or bud.

Ger·man (jėr′mən),
1 ADJECTIVE. of or about Germany, its people, or their language.
2 NOUN. someone born or living in Germany.
3 NOUN. the language of Germany, Austria, and part of Switzerland.

Word Source

German has given a number of words to the English language, including the words below.

accordion	frankfurter	knob	poodle
dachshund	hamburger	muffin	pumpernickel
delicatessen	hamster	noodle	waltz
fife	kindergarten	plump	wiener

German shepherd, a large, strong, intelligent dog, often trained to work with soldiers and police or to guide blind people.

Ger·ma·ny (jėr′mə nē), NOUN. a large country in central Europe. From 1949 to 1990 Germany was divided into West Germany and East Germany.

ger·mi·nate (jėr′mə nāt), VERB. to start growing or developing; sprout: *Seeds germinate in the spring.*
❑ VERB **ger·mi·nates, ger·mi·nat·ed, ger·mi·nat·ing. −ger′mi·na′tion,** NOUN.

a **germinating** seed

ges·ture (jes′chər),
1 NOUN. a meaningful movement of your hands, arms, or any part of your body. Gestures can be

used instead of words or with words to help express an idea or feeling.

2 *NOUN.* any action done for effect or to impress others: *Her refusal was merely a gesture; she really wanted to go to the party with us.*

3 *VERB.* to make gestures; use gestures: *She gestured at me to be silent.*
❏ *VERB* **ges·tures, ges·tured, ges·tur·ing.**

Ge·sund·heit (gə zùnt′hīt), *INTERJECTION.* a German word for health. It is often said when someone has just sneezed.

get (get), *VERB.*
1 to acquire; obtain; receive: *I got a present.*
2 to reach; arrive: *I got home early last night.*
3 to cause to be or do: *Get the windows open.*
4 to become: *It is getting colder.*
5 to bring: *Please get me a drink of water.*
6 to persuade; influence: *Try to get them to come, too.*
7 to hit; strike: *The ball got the batter on the arm.*
8 to understand: *The teacher explained the math problem again, but I still didn't get it.*
❏ *VERB* **gets, got, got** or **got·ten, get·ting.**

get along with or **get along,** *IDIOM.* to be friendly: *He gets along with all his classmates. Can't you two try to get along?*

get away with, *IDIOM.* to take or do something and escape safely: *They got away with the jewels.*

get in, *IDIOM.*
1 to go in: *I had hoped to get in without being seen.*
2 to put in: *He kept talking, and I couldn't get in a word.*
3 to arrive: *Our train should get in at 9 P.M.*

get on, *IDIOM.*
1 to go up on or into: *We got on a train.*
2 to put on: *Get on your boots; we have to go out in the snow.*
3 to grow old: *Our cat is getting on in years.*
■ See the Synonym Study at **old.**
4 to succeed: *How are you getting on in your new job?*
5 to agree: *I get on well with my roommate.*

get out, *IDIOM.*
1 to go out: *Let's get out of here!*
2 to become known: *The secret got out.*

get out of, *IDIOM.* to escape; avoid doing: *She's always trying to get out of doing the dishes.*

get over, *IDIOM.* to recover from: *He finally got over his cold.*

get to, *IDIOM.* to be allowed to: *I got to stay up late last night.*

get together, *IDIOM.*
1 to come together; meet: *Let's get together soon and have lunch.*
2 to come to an agreement: *The jury was unable to get together.*

get up, *IDIOM.*
1 to arise: *She got up at six o'clock.*
2 to stand up: *I fell on the ice and couldn't get up.*

gey·ser (gī′zər), *NOUN.* a spring that sends up fountains or jets of hot water or steam every so often.

Gha·na (gä′nə), *NOUN.* a country in western Africa. —**Gha·nai·an** (gä′nē ən or gä nä′ən), *ADJECTIVE* or *NOUN.*

ghast·ly (gast′lē), *ADJECTIVE.*
1 horrible: *The destruction caused by the forest fire was a ghastly sight.*
2 very bad: *a ghastly failure.*
❏ *ADJECTIVE* **ghast·li·er, ghast·li·est.**

a spouting **geyser**

ghet·to (get′ō), *NOUN.* a part of a city where any particular racial group or nationality lives. People usually live in ghettos for economic or other reasons rather than by choice. ❏ *PLURAL* **ghet·tos.**

ghost (gōst), *NOUN.* (in stories) the spirit of a dead person, supposed to appear to living people as a pale, dim, faint form. —**ghost′like′,** *ADJECTIVE.*

ghost·ly (gōst′lē), *ADJECTIVE.* like a ghost; pale, dim, and faint: *A ghostly form walked across the stage.*
❏ *ADJECTIVE* **ghost·li·er, ghost·li·est.**

ghost town, a once lively town where nobody lives now.

gi·ant (jī′ənt),
1 *NOUN.* an imaginary being like a huge person.
2 *NOUN.* a person of great size or very great power.
3 *ADJECTIVE.* huge: *He grew a giant pumpkin for the state fair.*

giant sequoia, a very large evergreen tree of California; sequoia. Giant sequoias are the heaviest trees in the world, although they are not the tallest.

gib·bon (gib′ən), *NOUN.* a small, pale brown ape of southeastern Asia. Gibbons have very long arms and live in trees.

gid·dy (gid′ē), *ADJECTIVE.* dizzy; having a whirling feeling in the head: *I was giddy from riding the merry-go-round.* ❏ *ADJECTIVE* **gid·di·er, gid·di·est.** —**gid′di·ness,** *NOUN.*

gift (gift), *NOUN.*
1 something given; present: *a birthday gift.*
2 a natural talent; special ability: *a gift for painting.*

gift·ed (gif′tid), *ADJECTIVE.* extremely talented; having special ability: *a gifted musician.*

G

a	hat	ė	term	ô	order	ch	child	⎰a in about
ā	age	i	it	oi	oil	ng	long	⎰e in taken
ä	far	ī	ice	ou	out	sh	she	ə⎰i in pencil
â	care	o	hot	u	cup	th	thin	⎰o in lemon
e	let	ō	open	ù	put	ᴛʜ	then	⎱u in circus
ē	equal	ò	saw	ü	rule	zh	measure	

Giant Machines

In our cities and towns and all along our highways, the land has been shaped to suit our needs. The metals and other materials that we use to build our world have been dug up from the earth. The power to shape the land and to get the materials we need is provided by these giant machines: they dig, shape, lift, and carry things too large for the human body alone.

This mining machine scoops up tons of coal and drops it into a giant truck.

Only a large diesel truck is powerful enough to haul this huge tree trunk to the sawmill.

A special kind of tractor with a scraping blade smooths the surface of a roadway.

A crane hoists sections of a building higher and higher as the building grows taller.

A worker washes mud off a large bit that drills deep into the earth to find oil.

gig·a·byte (gig′ə bīt′), NOUN. one billion bytes. A gigabyte is a measurement of computer storage capacity.

gi·gan·tic (jī gan′tik), ADJECTIVE. like a giant; very large or powerful; huge: *Some dinosaurs were gigantic.* ∎ See the Synonym Study at **huge.**

gig·gle (gig′əl),
1 VERB. to laugh in a silly or uncontrolled way. ∎ See the Synonym Study at **laugh.**
2 NOUN. a silly or uncontrolled laugh.
□ VERB **gig·gles, gig·gled, gig·gling.**

Gi·la mon·ster (hē′lə mon′stər), a large, poisonous lizard with a thick tail and heavy body, covered with beadlike orange and black scales. It is found in the southwestern United States and northern Mexico.

gild (gild), VERB. to cover with a thin layer of gold. □ VERB **gilds, gild·ed, gild·ing.** ∎ Another word that sounds like this is **guild.**

gill (gil), NOUN. a specially formed part of the body of a fish, tadpole, crab, or other water animal by which the animal gets oxygen from water.

gim·mick (gim′ik), NOUN. a clever or tricky idea, stunt, or device: *The toys given to kids at that restaurant are a gimmick to attract families.*

gin·ger (jin′jər), NOUN. a spice made from the root of a tropical plant.

gin·ger·bread (jin′jər bred′), NOUN. a kind of cake flavored with ginger. Gingerbread is often made in fancy shapes.

gin·ger·ly (jin′jər lē), ADVERB. with extreme care or caution: *He walked gingerly across the ice.*

gink·go (ging′ko), NOUN. a large ornamental tree with fan-shaped leaves. □ PLURAL **gink·goes.**

gi·raffe (jə raf′), NOUN. a large African animal that has a very long neck and long legs, and a spotted skin. Giraffes are the tallest living animals.

giraffe — up to 18 feet tall

gird·er (gèr′dər), NOUN. a strong beam of steel, concrete, or wood. The weight of a floor is usually supported by girders. A tall building or big bridge often has steel girders for its frame.

girl (gèrl), NOUN. a female child from birth to about eighteen.

Usage Note

Using **girl** to mean a woman over the age of eighteen is considered unfriendly by some people. Others say that it is meant as a compliment. Careful writers and speakers avoid using the word with this meaning in most circumstances. If in doubt, ask!

girl·friend (gèrl′frend′), NOUN.
1 a boy's sweetheart or constant female companion.
2 a female friend.

girl·hood (gèrl′hùd), NOUN. the time of being a girl.

girl·ish (gèr′lish), ADJECTIVE.
1 of or like a girl: *girlish laughter.*
2 like a girl's; suitable for a girl: *girlish clothes.*

girl scout, a member of an organization (the **Girl Scouts**) that seeks to develop character, citizenship, usefulness to others, and various skills.

give (giv),
1 VERB. to hand over as a present; make a gift of: *My parents gave me ice skates for my birthday.*
2 VERB. to hand over: *Give me that pencil.*
3 VERB. to pay: *She gave three dollars for the used CD.*
4 VERB. to let have; cause to have: *She gave us permission to go. Don't give him any trouble.*
5 VERB. to cause someone to feel something: *Loud noises give me a headache.*
6 VERB. to offer; present: *We gave a full report.*
7 VERB. to put forth; utter: *He gave a cry of pain.*
8 VERB. to supply; produce: *Lamps give light.*
9 VERB. to yield to force: *The lock gave when they pushed hard against the door.*
10 NOUN. the ability to stretch or bend without breaking; flexibility: *a fabric with a lot of give.*
□ VERB **gives, gave, giv·en, giv·ing. –giv′er,** NOUN.

give and take, IDIOM. cooperation: *We need lots of give and take here to make our plan a success.*

give away, IDIOM.
1 to give as a present: *She gave away her best toy.*
2 to present a bride to a bridegroom at a wedding: *The bride was given away by her father.*
3 to cause to be known; reveal; betray: *The spy gave away secrets to the enemy.*

give in, IDIOM. to surrender; yield under pressure; admit defeat: *A stubborn person will never give in.*

give or take, IDIOM. plus or minus: *He will be here at noon, give or take a few minutes.*

give out, IDIOM.
1 to distribute: *The answers will be given out today.*
2 to make known: *Who gave out this information?*
3 to become used up or worn out: *My strength gave out after the long climb.*

give up, *IDIOM.*
1 to hand over; surrender: *When the troops saw that they were surrounded, they gave up.*
2 to stop having or doing: *We gave up the search when it got dark. My dad gave up smoking.*
3 to stop trying: *Don't give up so soon; try again!*

giv·en (giv′ən),
1 *ADJECTIVE.* limited; stated: *You must finish the test in a given time.*
2 *ADJECTIVE.* inclined; disposed: *He is given to boasting.*
3 *VERB.* the past participle of **give:** *Our teacher has given us too much homework this week.*

gla·cial (glā′shəl), *ADJECTIVE.* of ice or glaciers; having a great amount of ice or many glaciers: *During the glacial period, much of the Northern Hemisphere was covered with great ice sheets.*

The **glacier** is slowly moving into the sea.

gla·cier (glā′shər), *NOUN.* a great mass of ice moving very slowly down a mountain or along a valley, or spreading very slowly over a land area. Glaciers are formed from snow on high ground wherever winter snowfall exceeds summer melting for many years.

Did You Know?

There are two kinds of **glaciers. Continental glaciers,** or icecaps, are found near the North and South poles. They are broad sheets of ice. **Valley glaciers** are narrow fingers of ice that fill mountain valleys. Most glaciers move a foot a day, but some glaciers can move 100 feet a day.

glad (glad), *ADJECTIVE.*
1 happy; pleased: *She is glad to see us.* ■ See the Synonym Study at **happy.**
2 bringing joy; pleasant: *She brought glad news.* ❏ *ADJECTIVE* **glad·der, glad·dest. −glad′ly,** *ADVERB.* **−glad′ness,** *NOUN.*

glad·den (glad′n), *VERB.* to make glad; become glad: *We were gladdened by the good news.* ❏ *VERB* **glad·dens, glad·dened, glad·den·ing.**

glade (glād), *NOUN.* a small open space in a wood or forest.

glad·i·a·tor (glad′ē ā′tər), *NOUN.* a captive, enslaved person, or professional fighter who fought at the public shows in the arenas in ancient Rome.

glad·i·o·lus (glad′ē ō′ləs), *NOUN.* a plant with spikes of large, handsome flowers in various colors.
❏ *PLURAL* **glad·i·o·li** (glad′ē ō′lī), **glad·i·o·lus,** or **glad·i·o·lus·es.**

glam·or·ous (glam′ər əs), *ADJECTIVE.* exciting and fascinating; charming: *a glamorous job overseas.*

glam·our (glam′ər), *NOUN.* a mysterious, exciting quality that attracts other people; charm: *the glamour of movie stars.*

glance (glans),
1 *NOUN.* a quick look: *She gave the pictures only a glance.*
2 *VERB.* to look quickly: *I glanced out of the window.* ■ See the Synonym Study at **look.**
3 *VERB.* to hit something and go off at a slant: *The bullet glanced off the stone.*
❏ *VERB* **glanc·es, glanced, glanc·ing.**

gland (gland), *NOUN.* an organ in the body that makes some substance that the body needs. Glands produce saliva and tears. Females have glands that make milk.

glare (glâr),
1 *NOUN.* a strong, unpleasant light.
2 *VERB.* to shine strongly or unpleasantly; shine so brightly as to hurt the eyes: *Bright sunlight glared off the water at the beach.*
3 *NOUN.* an angry stare.
4 *VERB.* to stare angrily at someone or something.
❏ *VERB* **glares, glared, glar·ing.**

glar·ing (glâr′ing), *ADJECTIVE.*
1 shining so brightly that it hurts the eyes.
2 easily seen: *a glaring mistake.*
3 staring angrily.

glass (glas),
1 *NOUN.* a hard, transparent substance that breaks easily. Windows and lenses are made of glass.
2 *NOUN.* something to drink from made of glass: *He filled the glass with water.*
3 *NOUN.* the amount that a glass can hold: *Drink a glass of water.*
4 *NOUN.* **glasses,** a pair of glass or plastic lenses set in a frame, used to help someone see better.
5 *ADJECTIVE.* made of glass: *a glass dish, glass beads.*
❏ *PLURAL* **glass·es. −glass′like′,** *ADJECTIVE.*

glass·y (glas′ē), *ADJECTIVE.* like glass; smooth; easily seen through: *With no wind, the small pond had a glassy surface.* ❏ *ADJECTIVE* **glass·i·er, glass·i·est.**

a	hat	ė	term	ô	order	ch	child		a in about
ā	age	i	it	oi	oil	ng	long		e in taken
ä	far	ī	ice	ou	out	sh	she	ə	i in pencil
â	care	o	hot	u	cup	th	thin		o in lemon
e	let	ō	open	ù	put	₮H	then		u in circus
ē	equal	ò	saw	ü	rule	zh	measure		

glaze (glāz),
1 *VERB.* to put glass into or onto something, such as a window or picture frame; cover with glass.
2 *NOUN.* a smooth, glassy surface or glossy coating: *the glaze on a china cup.*
3 *VERB.* to cover with a shiny, smooth coating: *The pottery is glazed at the factory.*
4 *VERB.* to become shiny: *The sick man's eyes were glazed with fever.*
❑ *VERB* **glaz·es, glazed, glaz·ing.** **–glaz′er,** *NOUN.*

gleam (glēm),
1 *NOUN.* a flash or beam of light: *We saw the gleam of headlights through the rain.*
2 *VERB.* to send out a flash or beam of light; shine: *A candle gleamed in the dark.*
❑ *VERB* **gleams, gleamed, gleam·ing.**

glee (glē), *NOUN.* a feeling of lively joy; great delight: *The children at the party laughed with glee at the clown's antics.*

glee·ful (glē′fəl), *ADJECTIVE.* filled with glee; merry; joyous. **–glee′ful·ly,** *ADVERB.*

glen (glen), *NOUN.* a small, narrow valley.

glide (glīd),
1 *VERB.* to move along smoothly, evenly, and easily: *Birds, ships, dancers, and skaters glide.*
2 *NOUN.* a smooth, even, easy movement.
3 *VERB.* to come down smoothly without using a motor: *The paper airplane glided to the floor.*
❑ *VERB* **glides, glid·ed, glid·ing.**

glid·er (glī′dər), *NOUN.* an aircraft without an engine. Rising air currents keep it up in the air.

Did You Know?

Most **gliders** are launched by being towed by an airplane. The airplane releases the glider when they reach 2000 to 3000 feet. Some gliders can be pulled into the air like kites by a car.

glider

glim·mer (glim′ər),
1 *NOUN.* a faint, unsteady light.
2 *VERB.* to shine with a faint, unsteady light: *The moon glimmered through the clouds after the storm.*

3 *NOUN.* a vague idea; dim notion; faint glimpse: *A few clouds gave us a glimmer of hope that rain might come and end the drought.*
❑ *VERB* **glim·mers, glim·mered, glim·mer·ing.**

glimpse (glimps),
1 *NOUN.* a very quick look: *I caught a glimpse of the falls as our train went by.*
2 *VERB.* to get a quick look at something: *I glimpsed the falls as our train went by.*
❑ *VERB* **glimps·es, glimpsed, glimps·ing.**

glint (glint),
1 *NOUN.* a gleam; flash: *The glint in her eye showed that she was angry.*
2 *VERB.* to gleam; flash: *Sunlight glinted on the rain puddles.*
❑ *VERB* **glints, glint·ed, glint·ing.**

glis·ten (glis′n), *VERB.* to shine from being wet: *Her eyes glistened as she told us of her cat's death.*
❑ *VERB* **glis·tens, glis·tened, glis·ten·ing.**

glitch (glich), *NOUN.* any sudden or unexpected problem, technical difficulty, or breakdown: *a computer glitch.* ❑ *PLURAL* **glitch·es.**

Word Story

Glitch comes from a Yiddish word meaning "a slip" or "a skid." When something develops a glitch, it's as if it slips off its tracks.

glit·ter (glit′ər),
1 *VERB.* to shine with a bright, sparkling light: *The jewels and new coins glittered.*
2 *NOUN.* a bright, sparkling light: *We enjoyed the glitter of the bright lights at the mall.*
3 *NOUN.* tiny, sparkling objects such as tinsel or spangles, used for decoration.
❑ *VERB* **glit·ters, glit·tered, glit·ter·ing.**

Have You Heard?

You may have heard someone say "All that **glitters is not gold.**" This means that something or someone may *look* good but not be good.

gloat (glōt), *VERB.* to feel or show great satisfaction over what you have done, or over someone else's failures: *She gloated over her success in the race.*
❑ *VERB* **gloats, gloat·ed, gloat·ing.**

glob (glob), *NOUN.* a shapeless mass; small lump: *The passing car spattered me with globs of mud.*

glob·al (glō′bəl), *ADJECTIVE.* of or involving the whole world; worldwide: *The threat of global war has decreased.* **–glob′al·ly,** *ADVERB.*

global warming, the warming of the earth's atmosphere, which could result in worldwide changes in climate. Global warming is believed to be caused by too much carbon dioxide and water vapor in the air.

globe (glōb), NOUN.
1 a sphere with a map of the earth on it.
2 the earth; world.
3 anything round like a ball.

gloom (glüm), NOUN.
1 darkness; deep shadow; dim light: *We peered into the gloom of the old, dark barn.*
2 sad thoughts and feelings; sadness: *A feeling of gloom came over us as we said good-bye.*

gloom·y (glü′mē), ADJECTIVE.
1 dark; dim: *a gloomy winter day.*
2 in low spirits; sad: *a gloomy mood.*
3 dismal; causing gloom; discouraging: *There were gloomy predictions of flooding.*
❏ ADJECTIVE **gloom·i·er, gloom·i·est.** –**gloom′i·ly,** ADVERB. –**gloom′i·ness,** NOUN.

glo·ri·fy (glôr′ə fī), VERB.
1 to give glory to; make glorious: *glorify a hero.*
2 to worship; praise: *We sang hymns glorifying God.*
❏ VERB **glo·ri·fies, glo·ri·fied, glo·ri·fy·ing.** –**glo′ri·fi·ca′tion,** NOUN.

glo·ri·ous (glôr′ē əs), ADJECTIVE.
1 magnificent; splendid: *What a glorious day!*
2 giving glory: *Our team won a glorious victory.*
3 having or deserving glory: *a glorious hero.* –**glo′ri·ous·ly,** ADVERB.

glo·ry (glôr′ē), NOUN.
1 great praise and honor; fame: *His heroic act won him glory.*
2 something that brings praise and honor; source of pride and joy: *America's great men and women are its glory.*
3 great beauty and magnificence: *the glory of the royal palace.*
❏ PLURAL **glo·ries.**

glory in, IDIOM. to be very proud of something: *The teacher gloried in her class's achievements.* ❏ VERB **glo·ries, glo·ried, glo·ry·ing.**

gloss (glôs), NOUN. a smooth, shiny surface on anything: *Varnished furniture has a high gloss.*
❏ PLURAL **gloss·es.**

glos·sar·y (glos′ər ē), NOUN. a list of important words with explanations. Most textbooks have glossaries at the end. ❏ PLURAL **glos·sar·ies.**

gloss·y (glô′sē), ADJECTIVE. smooth and shiny: *She brushed the kitten's fur until it was glossy.*
❏ ADJECTIVE **gloss·i·er, gloss·i·est.**

glove (gluv), NOUN. a covering for the hand, with places for each of the four fingers and the thumb. Gloves are worn to keep the hands warm or clean. Boxers and baseball and hockey players use special padded gloves for protection.

glow (glō),
1 VERB. to shine because of heat; be red-hot or white-hot: *Embers still glowed in the fireplace after the fire had died down.*
2 NOUN. the shine from something that is red-hot or white-hot: *the glow of molten steel.*
3 VERB. to give off light without heat: *Some clocks glow in the dark.*
4 NOUN. a bright, warm color: *We watched the glow of sunset.*
5 NOUN. the warm feeling or color of the body: *the glow of health on her cheeks.*
6 VERB. to show a warm color; look warm: *His cheeks glowed as he jogged.*
❏ VERB **glows, glowed, glow·ing.**

glow·worm (glō′werm′), NOUN. an insect that glows in the dark.

glu·cose (glü′kōs), NOUN. a special form of sugar that is found in the tissues of most living things. Glucose is the main source of energy for the body.

The wingless females of some kinds of fireflies are called **glowworms.**

glue (glü),
1 NOUN. a substance used to stick things together.
2 VERB. to stick things together with glue: *We glued the parts of the model racing car together.*
❏ PLURAL **glues;** VERB **glues, glued, glu·ing.**

gm or **gm.,** an abbreviation of **gram** or **grams.**

gnarled (närld), ADJECTIVE. rough and twisted; having knots: *the gnarled roots of a tree.*

gnat (nat), NOUN. a small fly with two wings. Most gnats bite, and their bites itch.

Spelling Note   gn-

The letters **gn-** are used to spell the beginnings of some English words in which the *g* is not pronounced. Hundreds of years ago, the *g* was pronounced in many of these words. The word **gnat,** for instance, was pronounced gə nat′.

gnaw (nȯ), VERB. to bite at and wear away: *A mouse has gnawed right through the cover of this box.*
❏ VERB **gnaws, gnawed, gnaw·ing.**

gnome (nōm), NOUN. (in stories) a dwarf that lives in the earth and guards treasures of precious metals and stones.

Did You Know?

In the Middle Ages, people believed that **gnomes** existed and could swim through the ground as a fish swims through water.

a hat	ė term	ô order	ch child	a in about
ā age	i it	oi oil	ng long	e in taken
ä far	ī ice	ou out	sh she	ə { i in pencil
â care	o hot	u cup	th thin	o in lemon
e let	ō open	u̇ put	ᴛʜ then	u in circus
ē equal	ȯ saw	ü rule	zh measure	

G

gnu (nü), NOUN. a large African antelope with a mane and beard, curved horns, and a long tail; wildebeest. ❑ PLURAL **gnu** or **gnus.** ■ Other words that sound like this are **knew** and **new.**

go (gō), VERB.
1 to move along: *Cars go on the road.*
2 to move away; leave: *Don't go yet.*
3 to be in motion or action; act; work; run: *Electricity makes the washing machine go.*
4 to stay in a certain condition: *to go hungry.*
5 to proceed; advance: *I went to New York.*
6 to take part in the activity of: *to go skiing, to go swimming.*
7 to pass: *Vacation goes quickly.*
8 to be given: *First prize goes to you.*
9 to have its place; belong: *This book goes on the top shelf.*
10 to make a certain sound: *The cork went "pop!"*
11 to be sold: *Those cards go for $5 each because they're rare.*
12 to have certain words; be said: *How does that song go?*
❑ VERB **goes, went, gone, go•ing.**

go off, IDIOM.
1 to leave; depart: *My sister has gone off to college.*
2 to explode; be fired: *The pistol went off unexpectedly.*
3 to start to ring; sound: *I was already awake when the alarm went off.*

go on, IDIOM.
1 to go ahead; continue: *After a pause he went on reading.*
2 to happen: *What's going on here?*

go out, IDIOM.
1 to go to a party or show: *We went out last night.*
2 to stop burning: *Don't let the candle go out.*

goad (gōd), VERB. to drive or urge on; act as a spur to: *Extreme hunger goaded her to steal food.*
❑ VERB **goads, goad•ed, goad•ing.**

goal (gōl), NOUN.
1 the place where a race ends.
2 the place or object that players try to advance the ball or puck to in certain games in order to score.
3 the point or points scored by advancing the ball or puck into this place or object.
4 something desired: *Her goal was to be a scientist.*

goal•ie (gō′lē), NOUN. a player who tries to keep the puck or ball from entering the goal in hockey, soccer, and some other sports; goalkeeper.
❑ PLURAL **goal•ies.**

goal•keep•er (gōl′kē′pər), NOUN. See **goalie.**

goal line, a line marking the front part of a goal in football, hockey, and some other games.

goal•post (gōl′pōst), NOUN. one of a pair of posts with a bar across them, forming a goal in football, soccer, hockey, and some other sports.

goat (gōt), NOUN. an animal with horns, a beard, and hoofs. They are raised for their milk and their hides. **—goat′like′,** ADJECTIVE.

get someone's goat, IDIOM. to annoy or anger someone: *He really gets my goat with his dumb jokes and pranks.*

gob•ble¹ (gob′əl), VERB. to eat very quickly. ■ See the Synonym Study at **eat.** ❑ VERB **gob•bles, gob•bled, gob•bling.**

gob•ble² (gob′əl),
1 NOUN. the noise a turkey makes.
2 VERB. to make this noise or one like it.
❑ VERB **gob•bles, gob•bled, gob•bling.**

gob•lin (gob′lən), NOUN. (in stories) a mean dwarf.

god (god), NOUN.
1 a being thought to have powers greater than those of human beings and considered worthy of worship.
2 a likeness or image; idol.

God (god), NOUN. an all-powerful being worshiped in most religions as the maker and ruler of the world.

god•child (god′child′), NOUN. a child whom a grown-up person sponsors at his or her baptism.
❑ PLURAL **god•chil•dren.**

god•dess (god′is), NOUN. a female god. ❑ PLURAL **god•dess•es.**

god•fa•ther (god′fä′ᵺər), NOUN. a man who sponsors a child when it is baptized. The godfather promises to help the child to be a good Christian.

god•moth•er (god′muᵺ′ər), NOUN. a woman who sponsors a child when it is baptized. The godmother promises to help the child to be a good Christian.

This **goalie** is making a save.

god•par•ent (god′pâr′ənt), NOUN. a godfather or godmother.

goes (gōz), VERB. a present tense of **go:** *He goes to work.*

gog•gles (gog′əlz), NOUN PLURAL. eyeglasses that fit tightly against the forehead. They are worn to protect the eyes from light, water, dust, and so on.

gold (gōld),
1 *NOUN.* a shiny, bright yellow, precious metal that is a chemical element. Gold is used in making coins, watches, and other jewelry.
2 *ADJECTIVE.* made of this metal; golden: *She was given a gold watch as a graduation present.*
3 *ADJECTIVE* or *NOUN.* bright yellow.

Did You Know?

South Africa mines the most **gold,** followed by the United States and Australia. The biggest gold deposit in the United States is in the town of Lead (lēd), South Dakota.

gold·fish (gōld′fish′), *NOUN.* a small orange or golden fish, kept as a pet in garden pools or in glass bowls indoors. Goldfish are a kind of carp.
❏ *PLURAL* **gold·fish** or **gold·fish·es.**

golf (golf),
1 *NOUN.* an outdoor game played with a small, hard ball and a set of long-handled clubs with metal or wooden heads. Players try to hit the ball into a series of holes with as few strokes as possible.
2 *VERB.* to play this game.
❏ *VERB* **golfs, golfed, golf·ing.** —**golf′er,** *NOUN.*

golf course, a place where golf is played. Most golf courses have either 9 or 18 holes.

gondola (definition 1)

gold·en (gōl′dən), *ADJECTIVE.*
1 made of gold: *The queen wore a golden crown.*
2 shining like gold; bright yellow: *golden hair.*
3 very good; extremely favorable, valuable, or important: *a golden opportunity.*

Have You Heard?

You may have heard people say **"Do unto others as you would have them do unto you."** This is called the **Golden Rule.** It means that you should always treat people as you would like them to treat you.

gold·en·rod (gōl′dən rod′), *NOUN.* a wild plant with tall stalks of small yellow flowers. It blooms in the fall.

Did You Know?

Many people think that **goldenrod** pollen causes hay fever and allergies. But goldenrod pollen is too wet and heavy to float through the air. Most allergies are caused by other plants.

gold·finch (gōld′finch′), *NOUN.* a small yellow songbird marked with black on its head, wings, and tail. It is sometimes called the **wild canary** because of its color and song. ❏ *PLURAL* **gold·finch·es.**

gon·do·la (gon′dl ə), *NOUN.*
1 a long, narrow boat with a high peak at each end, used on the canals of Venice.
2 a car or basket that hangs under a balloon and holds the passengers and equipment.
3 an enclosed car, hung from a cable, that carries passengers up a ski slope or mountain.
❏ *PLURAL* **gon·do·las.**

gone (gon),
1 *ADJECTIVE.* away: *They are gone on their vacation.*
2 *ADJECTIVE.* passed away; dead: *Great-grandmother is gone now.*
3 *ADJECTIVE.* used up; consumed: *Is all the candy gone?*
4 *VERB.* the past participle of **go:** *She has gone to the movies.*

gong (gong), *NOUN.* a piece of metal shaped like a bowl or saucer. It makes a loud noise when struck.

goo (gü), *NOUN.* (informal) thick, sticky matter.

good (gùd),
1 *ADJECTIVE.* having high quality; well done: *The teacher said my report was good.*

a	hat	ė	term	ô	order	ch	child	⎧a in about
ā	age	i	it	oi	oil	ng	long	⎪e in taken
ä	far	ī	ice	ou	out	sh	she	ə⎨i in pencil
â	care	o	hot	u	cup	th	thin	⎪o in lemon
e	let	ō	open	ù	put	ᴛʜ	then	⎩u in circus
ē	equal	ò	saw	ü	rule	zh	measure	

2 *ADJECTIVE.* right; as it ought to be: *good health, good weather.*

3 *ADJECTIVE.* behaving well; doing what is right: *You have been a very good boy.*

4 *ADJECTIVE.* kind; friendly: *Say a good word for me.*

5 *ADJECTIVE.* proper; desirable: *This is a good book for children.*

6 *ADJECTIVE.* reliable; dependable: *She showed good judgment.*

7 *ADJECTIVE.* pleasant; enjoyable: *Have a good time.*

8 *ADJECTIVE.* useful: *What drugs are good for a fever?*

9 *NOUN.* benefit: *What I told you was for your own good.*

10 *ADJECTIVE.* tasting good; satisfying: *a good meal.*

11 *NOUN.* that which is good: *I always try to find the good in people.*

12 *NOUN.* **goods, a** personal property; belongings: *household goods.* **b** things for sale.
❑ *ADJECTIVE* **bet·ter, best.**

as good as, *IDIOM.* almost; practically: *The battle was as good as won.*

for good, *IDIOM.* forever; finally; permanently: *They have moved out for good.*

make good, *IDIOM.*
1 to make up for; pay for: *The boys made good the damage they had done.*
2 to succeed: *He made good in business.*

no good, *IDIOM.* bad: *That game is no good—this one is much more fun.*

Usage Note

Good is an adjective, and so it is commonly used with linking verbs such as **feel, look,** and **smell:** *After a long vacation, he feels good and he looks good.* It is common in speech to use **good** with other verbs, as if it were an adverb, but careful writers and speakers use **well¹** instead: *This soap smells good and cleans well.*

good-by (gu̇d/bī/), *INTERJECTION or NOUN.* another spelling of **good-bye.** ❑ *PLURAL* **good-bys.**

good-bye (gu̇d/bī/), *INTERJECTION or NOUN.* an expression that people say when they leave, or hang up the telephone: *He waved and called "Good-bye!" as he drove off. We said good-bye at the airport.* ❑ *PLURAL* **good·byes.**

Word Story

Good-bye comes from words of farewell, "God be with you." Because people said this often, they tended to shorten it. Because they also said "good day" and "good evening," they tended to begin this farewell with "good."

Good Friday, the Friday before Easter.

good-look·ing (gu̇d/lu̇k/ing), *ADJECTIVE.* nice to look at; handsome or beautiful. ■ See the Synonym Study at **beautiful.**

good-na·tured (gu̇d/nā/chərd), *ADJECTIVE.* easy to be with, work with, and so on; pleasant; kind. **—good/-na/tured·ly,** *ADVERB.*

Synonym Study

Good-natured means having a kind and pleasant personality: *He is good-natured and often helps his friends.*

Agreeable means pleasant and fun to be with: *He is a very agreeable person, and we like to visit him.*

Likable means pleasant and easy to like: *She is a likable girl, and I voted for her for class president.*

Friendly means pleasant and liking other people: *He is friendly to everyone in the class.*

Kind¹ and **nice** mean friendly and full of sympathy: *He is a kind person and always tries to help people. People are nice to him in return.*

Sympathetic means able to understand how other people feel: *Her sympathetic nature makes her an excellent nurse.*

Thoughtful can mean kind and considerate of others: *It was thoughtful of him to hold the elevator door for the lady in the wheelchair.*

ANTONYMS: nasty, unpleasant.

good·ness (gu̇d/nis), *NOUN.* kindness; the quality of being good.

good·will (gu̇d/wil/), *NOUN.*
1 kindly or friendly feeling.
2 the good reputation a business has with its customers.

good·y (gu̇d/ē),
1 *NOUN.* usually **goodies,** something good to eat, such as candy.
2 *INTERJECTION.* an exclamation of pleasure: *Oh, goody!* ❑ *PLURAL* **good·ies.**

goo·ey (gü/ē), *ADJECTIVE.* soft and sticky: *I like gooey candy.* ❑ *ADJECTIVE* **goo·i·er, goo·i·est.**

goof (güf), (informal)
1 *VERB.* to make a stupid mistake; blunder: *She goofed when she mailed the letter without a stamp.*
2 *NOUN.* a stupid mistake; blunder.
❑ *VERB* **goofs, goofed, goof·ing.**

goof off, *IDIOM.* (informal) to waste time; avoid work: *They spent the afternoon goofing off.*

goof-off (güf/òf/), *NOUN.* (informal) someone who wastes time or avoids work.

goof·y (gü/fē), *ADJECTIVE.* silly; foolish: *He has such goofy ideas!* ❑ *ADJECTIVE* **goof·i·er, goof·i·est.**

goop (güp), *NOUN.* (informal) a thick, sticky substance; goo: *What will wash this goop off my sweater?*

goose (güs), NOUN.
1 a tame or wild bird like a duck, but larger and with a longer neck. A goose has webbed feet.
2 a female goose. The male is called a gander.
3 the flesh of a goose used for food.
❑ PLURAL **geese.**

goose·ber·ry (güs′ber′ē), NOUN. a sour, green berry a little smaller than a grape. It grows in bunches on a thorny bush. Gooseberries are used to make pies, tarts, or jam. ❑ PLURAL **goose·ber·ries.**

goose — about 2 feet long

goose·bumps (güs′bumps′), NOUN PLURAL. a rough condition of the skin, like that of a plucked goose, caused by cold or fear; goose pimples.

goose pimples. See **goosebumps.**

go·pher (gō′fər), NOUN. a ratlike animal of North America with large cheek pouches. Gophers dig long tunnels in the ground to live in.

gore¹ (gôr), NOUN. blood that is spilled; thick blood: *The battlefield was covered with gore.*

gore² (gôr), VERB. to wound with a horn or tusk: *The bull gored the farmer.* ❑ VERB **gores, gored, gor·ing.**

gorge (gôrj),
1 NOUN. a deep, narrow valley, usually steep and rocky.
2 VERB. to eat greedily; stuff yourself with food.
❑ VERB **gorg·es, gorged, gorg·ing.**

gor·geous (gôr′jəs), ADJECTIVE.
1 very beautiful: *She has a gorgeous smile.*
2 richly colored; splendid: *a gorgeous sunset.*
■ See the Synonym Study at **beautiful.**
–**gor′geous·ly,** ADVERB.

go·ril·la (gə ril′ə), NOUN. the largest and most powerful ape. Gorillas are similar to chimpanzees, but much larger. They live in the forests of central Africa. ❑ PLURAL **go·ril·las.** ■ Another word that sounds like this is **guerrilla.**

Did You Know?

Gorillas look fierce but they are usually shy and friendly. They need attention and companionship. The first gorillas kept in zoos alone did not live very long. It is thought that they died from loneliness.

gor·y (gôr′ē), ADJECTIVE. bloody. ❑ ADJECTIVE **gor·i·er, gor·i·est.**

gosh (gosh), INTERJECTION. an exclamation: *Gosh, it's cold today!*

gos·ling (goz′ling), NOUN. a young goose.

gos·pel (gos′pəl), NOUN.
1 the teachings of Jesus and the Apostles.
2 Gospel, any one of the first four books of the New Testament. They tell about the life and teachings of Jesus.
3 anything that you believe is the absolute truth: *They took the doctor's words as gospel.*

Word Story

Gospel comes from an old English word meaning "good news." The teachings of Jesus and the Apostles have often been described this way.

gos·sip (gos′ip),
1 NOUN. idle talk, not always true, about other people and their private lives: *I won't listen to gossip.*
2 VERB. to repeat what you know or have heard about other people and their private lives: *The two of them were gossiping about the new girl.*
3 NOUN. someone who gossips a good deal: *He knows everyone and is the biggest gossip in town.*
❑ VERB **gos·sips, gos·siped, gos·sip·ing.**
–**gos′sip·er,** NOUN.

got (got), VERB.
1 the past tense of **get:** *We got the letter yesterday.*
2 a past participle of **get:** *We had got tired of waiting.*

got·ten (got′n), VERB. a past participle of **get:** *It has gotten to be quite late.*

gouge (gouj),
1 NOUN. a tool with a curved, hollow blade. Gouges are used for cutting round grooves or holes in wood.
2 VERB. to cut something with a gouge or other sharp object: *I gouged my leg on the fence.*
3 NOUN. a groove or hole made by gouging.
❑ VERB **goug·es, gouged, goug·ing.** –**goug′er,** NOUN.

gorilla — up to 6 feet tall when standing

a	hat	ė	term	ô	order	ch	child	⎧a in about
ā	age	i	it	oi	oil	ng	long	⎪e in taken
ä	far	ī	ice	ou	out	sh	she	ə⎨i in pencil
â	care	o	hot	u	cup	th	thin	⎪o in lemon
e	let	ō	open	ù	put	ᴛʜ	then	⎩u in circus
ē	equal	ò	saw	ü	rule	zh	measure	

gourd (gôrd), *NOUN.* the fruit of a vine closely related to the pumpkin. Its hard, dried shell is used for cups, bowls, or ladles. There are many kinds of gourds. —**gourd′like′**, *ADJECTIVE.*

decorated **gourds**

gour·met (gur′mā), *NOUN.* someone who is expert in judging and choosing foods, wines, and the like.

gov·ern (guv′ərn), *VERB.*
1 to rule; control; manage: *The election determined which party would govern.*
2 to influence or guide: *What governed his decision?*
❑ *VERB* **gov·erns, gov·erned, gov·ern·ing.**

gov·ern·ment (guv′ərn mənt), *NOUN.*
1 a group of people who rule or manage a country, state, district, or city at any time. The government of the United States consists of the President and the cabinet, the Congress, and the Supreme Court.
2 a system of ruling: *The United States has a democratic form of government.*
3 the act or process of running a country, state, district, or city.
—**gov′ern·men′tal**, *ADJECTIVE.*

Word Bank

There are many kinds of **government,** and many words to write and talk about them. If you want to learn more about this subject, you can begin by looking up these words in the dictionary. See also the Word Bank at **election.**

Cabinet	dictator	prime minister
Capitol	executive	Representative
citizen	governor	republic
civil service	legislature	Senator
Congress	mayor	socialism
constituent	monarchy	state
constitution	parliament	Supreme Court
communism	President	Vice-President
democracy		

gov·er·nor (guv′ər nər), *NOUN.*
1 an official elected as the head of a state of the United States. The governor of a state carries out the laws made by the state legislature.
2 an official appointed to rule a province or colony.

gown (goun), *NOUN.*
1 a woman's dress, especially a long fancy dress worn at parties.
2 a loose outer piece of clothing worn by graduating college students, judges, and others; robe.

grab (grab),
1 *VERB.* to take suddenly; snatch: *I grabbed my coat and ran for the bus.* ■ See the Synonym Study at **catch.**

2 *NOUN.* the act of taking something suddenly: *She made a grab for the ball.*
❑ *VERB* **grabs, grabbed, grab·bing.**
up for grabs, *IDIOM.* easily gotten; able to be had by anyone: *Several seats in Congress are up for grabs in this year's election.*

grace (grās),
1 *NOUN.* beauty of form or movement: *The ballerina danced with wonderful grace.*
2 *NOUN.* a short prayer of thanks given before or after a meal.
3 *VERB.* to give grace or honor to: *The queen graced the ball with her presence.*
❑ *VERB* **grac·es, graced, grac·ing.**
in someone's good graces, *IDIOM.* favored or liked by: *I like being in the teacher's good graces.*

grace·ful (grās′fəl), *ADJECTIVE.* beautiful in form or movement: *a graceful dancer.* —**grace′ful·ly,** *ADVERB.*

gra·cious (grā′shəs), *ADJECTIVE.* pleasant and kind; courteous: *He welcomed his guests in such a gracious manner that they felt at home.*
—**gra′cious·ly,** *ADVERB.* —**gra′cious·ness,** *NOUN.*

grade (grād),
1 *NOUN.* a class in school: *I'm in the fifth grade.*
2 *NOUN.* a degree in rank, quality, or value: *The best grade of milk is grade A.*
3 *VERB.* to sort; place according to class: *These apples are graded by size.*
4 *NOUN.* a number or letter that shows how well you have done: *My grade in English is B.*
5 *VERB.* to give a grade to: *The teacher graded the papers.*
6 *NOUN.* the slope of a road or railroad track: *The trucks moved slowly up the steep grade.*
❑ *VERB* **grades, grad·ed, grad·ing.**
make the grade, *IDIOM.* to succeed: *No one expected her to even make the grade, but she beat the school record.*

grad·er (grā′dər), *NOUN.*
1 someone who is in a certain grade at school: *a fifth grader, a first grader.*
2 someone or something that grades: *My teacher is an easy grader.*

grade school, an elementary school.

grad·u·al (graj′ü əl), *ADJECTIVE.* happening slowly, by small steps or degrees; moving little by little: *This low hill has a gradual slope.* —**grad′u·al·ly,** *ADVERB.*

grad·u·ate (graj′ü āt *for verb;* graj′ü it *for noun*),
1 *VERB.* to finish the course of studies of a school or college and be given a diploma or paper saying so.
2 *NOUN.* someone who has graduated and has a diploma.
❑ *VERB* **grad·u·ates, grad·u·at·ed, grad·u·at·ing.**

grad·u·a·tion (graj′ü ā′shən), *NOUN.*
1 the act of graduating from a school or college.
2 the ceremony of graduating; graduating exercises.

graf·fi·ti (grə fē′tē), *NOUN.* drawings or writings scratched or scribbled on a wall or other surface: *We removed the graffiti on our school's walls.*

graft (graft),
1 *VERB.* to fasten a shoot or bud from one tree or plant in a slit in another tree or plant, so it will grow there as a part of it.
2 *NOUN.* a shoot or bud used in grafting. A graft from a fine apple tree may be put on a poor one to improve it.
3 *VERB.* to take a piece of skin or bone from one person or part of the body and put it in someone else's body, so that it will grow there permanently.
4 *NOUN.* a piece of skin or bone moved from one person's body to another.
□ *VERB* **grafts, graft·ed, graft·ing.**

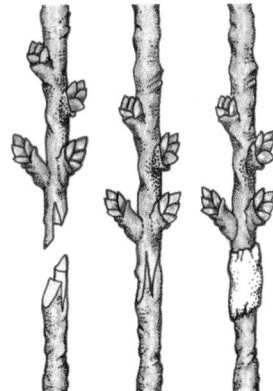

A **graft** joining parts of two different plants.

gra·ham crack·ers (grā′əm krak′ərz), crackers made from whole-wheat flour.

grain (grān), *NOUN.*
1 the seed of wheat, oats, corn, rice, and other cereal grasses.
2 the plants that these seeds grow on.
3 one of the tiny bits of which sand, sugar, or salt is made up.
4 the little lines and other markings in wood, marble, and so on: *That mahogany table has a fine grain.*
go against the grain, *IDIOM.* to be very difficult to accept or do because of your principles or beliefs: *It goes against the grain for him to work on Sundays.*

gram (gram), *NOUN.* a unit of weight or mass in the metric system. A paper clip weighs about one gram.

Word Power   -gram

The suffix **-gram** means "_____ grams" or "_____ of a gram." A kilo**gram** is a thousand grams. A centi**gram** is one hundredth of a gram.

gram·mar (gram′ər), *NOUN.*
1 the rules about the forms and uses of words in sentences. We study grammar to help us speak and write in a way that others can understand.
2 the use of words according to these rules: *My teacher's grammar is excellent.*

grammar school, an elementary school.

gram·mat·i·cal (grə mat′ə kəl), *ADJECTIVE.* of or according to the rules of grammar: *Our French teacher speaks grammatical English but has a French accent. "You should have saw it" is a grammatical mistake.* **–gram·mat′i·cal·ly,** *ADVERB.*

grand (grand), *ADJECTIVE.*
1 large and wonderful to look at: *a grand palace.*
2 of very high or noble quality; dignified: *grand music, a grand old man.*
3 great; important; main: *The grand prize was a car.*
4 excellent; very good: *I had a grand time at the party.*

Grand Canyon, a very large and deep canyon of the Colorado River, in northern Arizona. The Grand Canyon is about 1 mile deep and is 277 miles long. It was made a National Park in 1919.

a view of the **Grand Canyon**

grand·child (grand′child′), *NOUN.* a child of your son or daughter. □ *PLURAL* **grand·chil·dren** (grand′chil′drən).

grand·daugh·ter (grand′dȯ′tər), *NOUN.* a daughter of your son or daughter.

grand·fa·ther (grand′fä′ᴛʜər), *NOUN.* the father of your father or mother.

grandfather clock, a clock in a tall, wooden case, which stands on the floor.

grand·ma (grand′mä′), *NOUN.* (informal) grandmother. □ *PLURAL* **grand·mas.**

grand·moth·er (grand′muᴛʜ′ər), *NOUN.* the mother of your mother or father.

grand·pa (grand′pä′), *NOUN.* (informal) grandfather. □ *PLURAL* **grand·pas.**

grandfather clock

a	hat	ė	term	ô	order	ch	child		a in about
ā	age	i	it	oi	oil	ng	long		e in taken
ä	far	ī	ice	ou	out	sh	she	ə {	i in pencil
â	care	o	hot	u	cup	th	thin		o in lemon
e	let	ō	open	u̇	put	ᴛʜ	then		u in circus
ē	equal	ȯ	saw	ü	rule	zh	measure		

G

grand·par·ent (grand'pâr'ənt), *NOUN.* a grandfather or grandmother.

grand slam, (in baseball) a home run with three runners on base.

grand·son (grand'sun'), *NOUN.* a son of your son or daughter.

grand·stand (grand'stand'), *NOUN.* a section of seats, often covered by a roof, for people watching baseball games or other outdoor events.

gran·ite (gran'it), *NOUN.* a very hard, gray or pink rock used for buildings and monuments. Granite is made of crystals of several different minerals.

gran·ny (gran'ē), *NOUN.* (informal) a grandmother.
❑ *PLURAL* **gran·nies.**

gra·no·la (grə nō'lə), *NOUN.* a dry breakfast cereal of rolled oats, flavored with other things such as honey, chopped dried fruit, and nuts.

grant (grant),
1 *VERB.* to give what is asked for; allow: *The principal granted our request for a party after school.*
2 *VERB.* to admit that something is true; accept without proof: *I grant that you are right so far.*
3 *NOUN.* a gift, especially land or money given by the government: *The professor received a research grant of $80,000.*
❑ *VERB* **grants, grant·ed, grant·ing.**

take for granted, *IDIOM.* to believe to be true; suppose: *We took for granted that the sailor could swim.*

grape (grāp), *NOUN.* a small, round, juicy berry, usually red, purple, or pale green. Grapes grow in bunches on vines. They are eaten raw or made into raisins, jelly, or wine.

Have You Heard?

You may have heard the phrase "sour grapes." This comes from a fable about a fox who wanted a bunch of grapes but couldn't reach them. To make himself feel better, the fox decided the grapes were probably sour. In the same way, someone who can't have something may claim not to want it: *She said she didn't want to go to the party anyway—sounds like sour grapes to me.*

grape·fruit (grāp'früt'), *NOUN.* a large, juicy, yellow citrus fruit. Grapefruit may have pale yellow or pink flesh. ❑ *PLURAL* **grape·fruit** or **grape·fruits.**

grape·vine (grāp'vīn'), *NOUN.* a vine that grapes grow on.

graph (graf),
1 *NOUN.* a line or drawing that shows information, especially how one quantity is related to another quantity. You could draw a graph to show the change in your height as you have gotten older.
2 *VERB.* to make a graph of something.
❑ *VERB* **graphs, graphed, graph·ing.**

Word Power -graph

The combining form **-graph** or **-graphy** can mean "something written or recorded." An auto**graph** is someone's **written** name. A bio**graphy** is the **record** of someone's life.

graph·ics (graf'iks), *NOUN PLURAL.* pictures or diagrams made by a computer or video game: *The graphics in my new video game are terrific.*

graph·ite (graf'it), *NOUN.* a soft, black form of pure carbon, used for lead in pencils.

grasp (grasp),
1 *VERB.* to grab and hold something tightly by closing your fingers around it: *I grasped the sleeve of her coat as I fell.*
2 *NOUN.* the act of grabbing and holding onto something; clasp of the hand: *I almost lost my grasp on the rope.*
3 *NOUN.* the ability to reach or gain something: *Success is within his grasp.*
4 *VERB.* to understand something: *He grasped my meaning at once.*
5 *NOUN.* an understanding: *She has a good grasp of arithmetic.*
❑ *VERB* **grasps, grasped, grasp·ing.**

grass (gras), *NOUN.*
1 plants with green blades that cover fields, lawns, and pastures. Horses, cows, and sheep eat grass.
2 a plant that has jointed stems and long, narrow leaves. Wheat, corn, and sugar cane are grasses.
3 land covered with grass; lawn: *The children played on the grass.*
❑ *PLURAL* **grass·es. —grass'like',** *ADJECTIVE.*

grass·hop·per (gras'hop'ər), *NOUN.* an insect with wings and strong hind legs for jumping.

grass·y (gras'ē), *ADJECTIVE.* covered with grass.
❑ *ADJECTIVE* **grass·i·er, grass·i·est.**

grass·land (gras'land'), *NOUN.* land with grass on it. A prairie is a kind of grassland.

grasshopper — up to 4 inches long

grate¹ (grāt), *NOUN.*
1 a frame of iron bars to hold burning fuel in a furnace or fireplace.
2 See **grating.**
■ Another word that sounds like this is **great.**

grate² (grāt),
1 *VERB.* to wear something down or grind it off in small pieces: *The cook grated the cheese before melting it.*
2 *VERB.* to rub against something with a harsh, jarring noise: *The door grated on its old, rusty hinges.*

3 *VERB.* to have an annoying or unpleasant effect on someone: *Their loud voices grate on my nerves.*
❑ *VERB* **grates, grat·ed, grat·ing.** ■ Another word that sounds like this is **great.**

grate·ful (grāt′fəl), *ADJECTIVE.* feeling thankful because someone has done something for you: *I am grateful for your help.* **–grate′ful·ly,** *ADVERB.*

grat·i·fy (grat′ə fī), *VERB.* to give pleasure or satisfaction to; please: *I was gratified to hear that you liked the scarf I knitted for you.* ❑ *VERB* **grat·i·fies, grat·i·fied, grat·i·fy·ing.**

gra·ting (grā′ting), *NOUN.* a framework of parallel or crossed bars; grate. Windows in a prison, bank, or ticket office often have gratings over them.

grat·i·tude (grat′ə tüd), *NOUN.* a feeling of being grateful; thankfulness.

grave¹ (grāv), *NOUN.*
1 a hole dug in the ground where a dead body is to be buried.
2 any place of burial: *a watery grave.*

grave² (grāv), *ADJECTIVE.* important; serious; critical: *a grave decision, a grave illness.* ❑ *ADJECTIVE* **grav·er, grav·est. –grave′ly,** *ADVERB.*

grav·el (grav′əl), *NOUN.* pebbles and pieces of rock that are larger than grains of sand. Gravel is used for roads and paths.

grave·yard (grāv′yärd′), *NOUN.* a place where dead people are buried; cemetery.

grav·i·ta·tion (grav′ə tā′shən), *NOUN.* the force that makes all objects in the universe attract one another. Gravitation keeps the planets in their orbits around the sun. **–grav′i·ta′tion·al,** *ADJECTIVE.*

grav·i·ty (grav′ə tē), *NOUN.*
1 the natural force that causes objects to move or tend to move toward the center of the earth. Gravity causes objects to have weight.
2 seriousness; importance: *The gravity of the situation was greatly increased by threats of war.*

gra·vy (grā′vē), *NOUN.* a sauce for meat, potatoes, or other food. It is made from the juice that comes out of meat during cooking. ❑ *PLURAL* **gra·vies.**

gray (grā),
1 *NOUN.* a color that is a mixture of black and white.
2 *ADJECTIVE.* having this color: *gray hair.*
3 *ADJECTIVE.* dark; gloomy; dismal: *a gray, rainy day.*

gray·ish (grā′ish), *ADJECTIVE.* somewhat gray.

graze¹ (grāz), *VERB.* to feed on grass that is growing: *Cattle were grazing in the field.* ❑ *VERB* **graz·es, grazed, graz·ing.**

graze² (grāz), *VERB.*
1 to scrape lightly against something while passing it: *The car grazed the garage door.*
2 to scrape the skin from a part of your body: *She grazed her knee when she fell.*
❑ *VERB* **graz·es, grazed, graz·ing.**

grease (grēs),
1 *NOUN.* soft, melted animal fat.
2 *NOUN.* any thick, oily substance.
3 *VERB.* to put grease on; lubricate: *I greased my bike chain.*
❑ *VERB* **greas·es, greased, greas·ing. –grease′less,** *ADJECTIVE.*

greas·y (grē′sē or grē′zē), *ADJECTIVE.*
1 having grease on it: *a greasy rag.*
2 containing much grease; oily: *Greasy food is hard to digest.*
❑ *ADJECTIVE* **greas·i·er, greas·i·est.**

great (grāt), *ADJECTIVE.*
1 very big or large: *a great forest, a great crowd.* ■ See the Synonym Study at **big.**
2 much; more than is usual: *great kindness, great pain.*
3 important; remarkable; famous: *a great singer, a great event, a great picture.*
4 very good; fine: *We had a great time at your birthday party.*
■ Another word that sounds like this is **grate.** **–great′ness,** *NOUN.*

Great Britain, England, Scotland, and Wales. Great Britain is the largest island of Europe.

Great Dane, a very large, powerful, short-haired dog.

Great Dane — about 3 feet high at shoulder

great-grand·child (grāt′grand′child′), *NOUN.* a child of your grandchild. ❑ *PLURAL* **great-grand·chil·dren** (grāt′grand′chil′dren).

great-grand·fa·ther (grāt′grand′fä′ᴛʜər), *NOUN.* the father of your grandparent.

great-grand·moth·er (grāt′grand′muᴛʜ′ər), *NOUN.* the mother of your grandparent.

great-grand·par·ent (grāt′grand′pâr′ənt), *NOUN.* a great-grandfather or a great-grandmother.

a	hat	ė	term	ô	order	ch	child		a in about
ā	age	i	it	oi	oil	ng	long		e in taken
ä	far	ī	ice	ou	out	sh	she	ə	i in pencil
â	care	o	hot	u	cup	th	thin		o in lemon
e	let	ō	open	ù	put	ᴛʜ	then		u in circus
ē	equal	ò	saw	ü	rule	zh	measure		

G

Great Lakes, five very large lakes between the United States and Canada. The Great Lakes are named Ontario, Erie, Huron, Michigan, and Superior.

great·ly (grāt′lē), ADVERB. very much: *Your help was greatly appreciated.*

Great Plains, a region just east of the Rocky Mountains in the United States and Canada. It is mostly pasture land.

Greece (grēs), NOUN. a country in southeastern Europe.

greed (grēd), NOUN. a very strong desire to have more than your share of something: *Their greed for money and success was never satisfied.*

greed·y (grē′dē), ADJECTIVE. wanting more than your share of something: *The dictator was greedy for power and money.* ❑ ADJECTIVE **greed·i·er, greed·i·est. —greed′i·ly,** ADVERB.

Greek (grēk),
1 ADJECTIVE. of or about Greece, its people, or their language.
2 NOUN. someone born or living in Greece.
3 NOUN. the language of Greece.

Word Source

Ancient **Greek** is the source of hundreds of English words, especially many of the terms we use in science. The following words came from Greek:

alphabet	crocodile	licorice	planet
astronaut	cyclone	marmalade	pope
Bible	dinosaur	melon	rhinoceros
church	galaxy	meteorite	skeleton
comet	helicopter	octopus	xylophone

green (grēn),
1 NOUN. the color of most growing plants, grass, and the leaves of trees in summer.
2 ADJECTIVE. having this color: *green paint.*
3 ADJECTIVE. covered with growing plants, grass, or leaves: *green fields.*
4 ADJECTIVE. not ripe; not fully grown: *Most green fruit is not good to eat.*
5 ADJECTIVE. without experience or training: *Several of the players were green at the start of the season.*
6 NOUN. **greens,** leaves and stems eaten as a vegetable: *beet greens, mustard greens.*
7 NOUN. the very smooth, grassy area around the hole into which a player putts a golf ball.

green·house (grēn′hous′), NOUN. a building with a glass or plastic roof and sides, kept warm and full of light for growing plants. ❑ PLURAL **green·hous·es** (grēn′hou′ziz).

greenhouse effect, the effect of carbon dioxide, water vapor, and some other gases in the atmosphere. They act to trap the sun's heat just as the glass of a greenhouse does, causing warming. With increasing carbon dioxide from fossil fuels, this effect could cause a change in global climate.

greenhouse gas, any of the gases in the atmosphere, such as carbon dioxide, that trap the sun's heat and cause the greenhouse effect.

green·ish (grē′nish), ADJECTIVE. somewhat green.

Green·land (grēn′lənd), NOUN. an arctic island northeast of North America. It is the largest island in the world and belongs to Denmark.

Word Story

Greenland got its name because when it was first explored 1,000 years ago, its climate was warmer. Viking explorers and the settlers they brought from Iceland saw fields of green grass.

green thumb, a remarkable ability to grow flowers and vegetables: *You certainly must have a green thumb to have such a beautiful garden.*

greet (grēt), VERB.
1 to speak or write to someone in a friendly, polite way; address in welcome: *She greeted us at the door.*
2 to respond to: *His speech was greeted with cheers.*
❑ VERB **greets, greet·ed, greet·ing. —greet′er,** NOUN.

greet·ing (grē′ting), NOUN.
1 the actions or words of someone who greets somebody; welcome.
2 **greetings,** friendly wishes on a special occasion.

gre·nade (grə nād′), NOUN. a small bomb which is thrown by hand or fired from a rifle.

grew (grü), VERB. the past tense of **grow**: *It grew colder as the sun went down.*

grey (grā), NOUN or ADJECTIVE. another spelling of **gray.**

grey·hound (grā′hound′), NOUN. a tall, slender dog with a long nose and smooth coat. Greyhounds can run very fast.

grid (grid), NOUN. a group of squares formed by two sets of lines that run both across and up and down. Grids are used on maps to locate places.

grid·dle (grid′l), NOUN. a heavy, flat metal pan or surface on which to cook pancakes, bacon, hamburgers, and so on.

The yellow arrows show trapped heat reflected back to the earth.

greenhouse effect

grief (grēf), NOUN. great sadness caused by trouble or loss; deep sorrow.

grieve (grēv), VERB. to be very sad; make someone very sad: *The children grieved over their kitten's death. The news of your illness grieved us.* ❑ VERB **grieves, grieved, griev·ing.**

grill (gril),
1 NOUN. a device with parallel bars for cooking something directly over a fire. It is used to hold meat, fish, sausages, and so on.
2 VERB. to cook something on a grill; broil.
3 VERB. to question someone thoroughly for a long time: *The detectives grilled several suspects concerning the crime.*
❑ VERB **grills, grilled, grill·ing.**

grim (grim), ADJECTIVE.
1 not smiling; serious: *My parents looked grim when they heard about the broken windows.*
2 not giving up: *Near exhaustion, the runner kept on with grim determination.*
❑ ADJECTIVE **grim·mer, grim·mest. —grim'ly,** ADVERB.

gri·mace (grim'is),
1 NOUN. a twisted expression of the face: *a grimace caused by pain.*
2 VERB. to make faces: *The clown grimaced at me.*
❑ VERB **gri·mac·es, gri·maced, gri·mac·ing.**

grime (grīm), NOUN. thick dirt that is rubbed deeply and firmly into a surface: *Soap and water removed only a little of the grime on our hands.*

grim·y (grī'mē), ADJECTIVE. covered with thick dirt; very dirty: *grimy hands, grimy floor.* ❑ ADJECTIVE **grim·i·er, grim·i·est. —grim'i·ness,** NOUN.

grin (grin),
1 VERB. to smile with your teeth showing: *She grinned and said, "Hello."*
2 NOUN. a wide smile with your teeth showing: *He gave me a friendly grin.*
❑ VERB **grins, grinned, grin·ning.**

grind (grīnd), VERB.
1 to crush or cut something into small bits or powder: *That mill grinds wheat into flour.*

She has a charming **grin.**

2 to sharpen or smooth something, or wear it away by rubbing it on something rough: *He sharpened the ax by grinding it on a grindstone.*
3 to make a harsh sound by rubbing; grate: *My sister grinds her teeth while she sleeps.*
❑ VERB **grinds, ground, grind·ing.**

grind·stone (grīnd'stōn'), NOUN. a flat, round stone set in a frame and turned by hand, foot, or a motor. It is used to sharpen tools, such as axes and knives, or to smooth and polish things.

grip (grip),
1 NOUN. a tight grasp; firm hold: *The dog had a firm grip on the bone, and would not let go.*
2 VERB. to take firm hold of something: *She gripped the railing.*
3 NOUN. a part to take hold of; handle.
4 NOUN. firm control; power: *The country was in the grip of a severe drought.*
❑ VERB **grips, gripped, grip·ping.**

gripe (grīp), VERB. to complain: *He was always griping about something.* ❑ VERB **gripes, griped, grip·ing.**

grit (grit),
1 NOUN. very fine bits of gravel or sand.
2 NOUN. bravery; courage; endurance.
3 VERB. to close tightly together: *She gritted her teeth and jumped into the cold water.*
❑ VERB **grits, grit·ted, grit·ting.**

grits (grits), NOUN PLURAL. coarsely ground corn, with the outer covering removed. Grits are eaten boiled.

grit·ty (grit'ē), ADJECTIVE. of or containing grit; like grit; sandy. ❑ ADJECTIVE **grit·ti·er, grit·ti·est.**

griz·zled (griz'əld), ADJECTIVE. grayish; gray: *a grizzled beard.*

griz·zly (griz'lē), NOUN. a short form of **grizzly bear.**
❑ PLURAL **griz·zlies.**

grizzly bear, a very large, fierce, brownish gray bear of western North America.

groan (grōn),
1 NOUN. a sound made down in the throat that shows grief, pain, or disapproval; deep moan.
2 VERB. to give a groan or groans: *The movers groaned as they lifted the piano.*
❑ VERB **groans, groaned, groan·ing.** ■ Another word that sounds like this is **grown. —groan'er,** NOUN.

gro·cer (grō'sər), NOUN. someone who sells food and household supplies.

gro·cer·y (grō'sər ē), NOUN.
1 a small store that sells food and household items.
2 **groceries,** articles of food that you buy in a grocery or supermarket.
❑ PLURAL **gro·cer·ies.**

grog·gy (grog'ē), ADJECTIVE.
1 weak, shaky, and not able to think clearly: *A blow on the head made me groggy.*
2 not yet completely awake: *I was groggy after my nap.*
❑ ADJECTIVE **grog·gi·er, grog·gi·est.**

groom¹ (grüm),
1 VERB. to take care of your appearance; make neat and tidy: *He was always perfectly groomed.*
2 VERB. to feed, rub down, brush, and generally take care of horses.

G

a	hat	ė	term	ô	order	ch	child	ə	a in about
ā	age	i	it	oi	oil	ng	long		e in taken
ä	far	ī	ice	ou	out	sh	she		i in pencil
â	care	o	hot	u	cup	th	thin		o in lemon
e	let	ō	open	ů	put	ᴛʜ	then		u in circus
ē	equal	ò	saw	ü	rule	zh	measure		

3 *NOUN.* someone whose work is taking care of horses. ❑ *VERB* **grooms, groomed, groom·ing.**

groom² (grüm), *NOUN.* a man who has just married or who is about to be married; bridegroom.

groove (grüv), *NOUN.* a long, narrow cut channel, especially one made by a tool: *My desk has a groove for pencils.*

grope (grōp), *VERB.*
1 to feel about for something with your hands: *He groped for a flashlight when the lights went out.*
2 to find by feeling about with your hands; feel your way slowly: *I groped my way across the dark room.*
❑ *VERB* **gropes, groped, grop·ing.**

gross (grōs),
1 *ADJECTIVE.* with nothing taken out; total; whole; entire. Gross receipts are all the money taken in before costs are deducted.
2 *ADJECTIVE.* coarse; disgusting: *gross manners.*
3 *NOUN.* twelve dozen; 144.
4 *ADJECTIVE.* very easily seen; glaring: *gross errors.*
5 *ADJECTIVE.* extreme; excessive: *gross inequality.*
❑ *PLURAL* **gross. —gross'ly,** *ADVERB.*

gro·tesque (grō tesk'), *ADJECTIVE.* ugly or unnatural in shape, appearance, or manner: *The book had pictures of hideous dragons and other grotesque monsters.* **—gro·tesque'ly,** *ADVERB.*

carvings of **grotesque** creatures

grouch (grouch), *NOUN.* someone who is often grumbling and complaining. ■ See the Word Story at **grudge.** ❑ *PLURAL* **grouch·es.**

grouch·y (grou'chē), *ADJECTIVE.* tending to grumble or complain. ■ See the Synonym Study at **cross.**
❑ *ADJECTIVE* **grouch·i·er, grouch·i·est.**

ground¹ (ground),
1 *NOUN.* the soil or dirt on the surface of the earth: *The ground was hard and rocky.*
2 *NOUN.* any piece of land or region used for some purpose: *The band practices on the parade ground.*
3 *NOUN.* **grounds, a** the land, lawns, and gardens around a house or school. **b** the small bits that sink to the bottom of a drink such as coffee or tea; dregs; sediment.

4 *VERB.* (in baseball) to hit a ball so that it rolls or bounces along the ground.
5 *VERB.* to run aground; hit the bottom or shore: *The boat grounded in shallow water.*
6 *NOUN.* often **grounds,** the basis for what is said, thought, claimed, or done; reason: *What are your grounds for that statement?*
7 *VERB.* to connect an electric wire from a circuit to the earth so that a dangerous current can be safely absorbed.
8 *VERB.* to keep a pilot or an aircraft from flying: *The pilot was grounded by injury.*
9 *VERB.* to keep a child or teenager from going out of the home for entertainment, as punishment: *My brother was grounded for coming home late.*
❑ *VERB* **grounds, ground·ed, ground·ing.**

common ground, *IDIOM.* an area of agreement, especially between people who often disagree.

ground² (ground), *VERB.*
1 the past tense of **grind:** *I ground the corn into meal.*
2 the past participle of **grind:** *The wheat was ground to make flour.*

ground ball, (in baseball) a batted ball that bounces or rolls along the ground.

ground·hog (ground'hòg'), *NOUN.* See **woodchuck.**

Groundhog Day, February 2, the day when groundhogs are believed to come out of their holes. If the sun is shining, and the groundhogs see their shadows, it is believed that they go back in their holes and that winter continues for six more weeks.

group (grüp),
1 *NOUN.* a number of people or things together: *A group of children were playing tag.*
2 *NOUN.* a number of people or things belonging or classed together: *Wheat, rye, and oats belong to the grain group.*
3 *VERB.* to gather into a group or groups: *Group the numbers to form three columns.*
❑ *VERB* **groups, grouped, group·ing.**

grouse (grous), *NOUN.* a small, plump bird that looks something like a chicken. Grouse are mostly brown, with some black or white feathers, and are hunted for food. ❑ *PLURAL* **grouse.**

grove (grōv), *NOUN.* a group of trees standing together. An orange grove is an orchard of orange trees.

grow (grō), *VERB.*
1 to become bigger; increase: *Plants grow from seeds. Her business has grown fast.*
2 to live and become big: *Few trees grow in the desert.*
3 to plant and raise: *We grow cotton in the southern part of the United States.*
4 to become: *It grew cold when the sun went down.*
❑ *VERB* **grows, grew, grown, grow·ing.**

grow up, *IDIOM.* to become full-grown; become an adult: *What will you be when you grow up?*

growl (groul),
1 *VERB*. to make a deep, low, angry sound: *The dog growled at the stranger.*
2 *NOUN*. a sound like that made by a fierce dog; deep, warning snarl.
❏ *VERB* **growls, growled, growl·ing.** –**growl′er,** *NOUN*.

grown (grōn),
1 *ADJECTIVE*. arrived at full growth. A grown person is an adult.
2 *VERB*. the past participle of **grow**: *The corn has grown very tall.*
■ Another word that sounds like this is **groan.**

grown-up (grōn′up′),
1 *ADJECTIVE*. adult: *a grown-up person.* ■ See the Synonym Study at **adult.**
2 *ADJECTIVE*. of, like, or suitable for adults: *She has very grown-up manners for an eight-year-old.*
3 *NOUN*. an adult: *The grown-ups helped the children decorate the room for the birthday party.*

growth (grōth), *NOUN*.
1 the process of growing; development.
2 something that has grown or is growing: *A thick growth of bushes covered the ground.*

grub (grub),
1 *NOUN*. a soft, thick, wormlike larva of beetles and some other kinds of insects.
2 *VERB*. to dig or dig up: *Pigs grub for roots.*
3 *NOUN*. (informal) food.
❏ *VERB* **grubs, grubbed, grub·bing.**

grub·by (grub′ē), *ADJECTIVE*. very dirty; grimy: *I put on grubby clothes to clean out the garage.*
❏ *ADJECTIVE* **grub·bi·er, grub·bi·est.**

grudge (gruj),
1 *NOUN*. an angry feeling against someone; dislike lasting a long time: *Our neighbors have had a grudge against us since we asked them to keep their dog out of our yard.*
2 *VERB*. to feel jealousy or anger toward someone over what they have possession of: *He grudged me my prize even though he had won two.*
❏ *VERB* **grudg·es, grudged, grudg·ing.**

Word Story

Grudge comes from a French word meaning "to grumble quietly." **Grouch** comes from the same word. A grouch with a grudge is sure to grumble.

gru·el·ing (grü′ə ling), *ADJECTIVE*. very tiring; exhausting: *Mountain climbing can be grueling.*

grue·some (grü′səm), *ADJECTIVE*. horrible to look at or think about: *a gruesome crime.*
–**grue′some·ly,** *ADVERB*.

gruff (gruf), *ADJECTIVE*.
1 deep and harsh: *a gruff voice.*
2 unfriendly; grouchy: *a gruff manner.*
–**gruff′ly,** *ADVERB*.

grum·ble (grum′bəl),
1 *VERB*. to complain in a quietly angry way; find fault: *The students are always grumbling about the cafeteria's food.* ■ See the Synonym Study at **complain.**
2 *NOUN*. a quietly angry complaint.
❏ *VERB* **grum·bles, grum·bled, grum·bling.** –**grum′bler,** *NOUN*.

grump·y (grum′pē), *ADJECTIVE*. grouchy and likely to complain about things: *I went to bed late last night and woke up this morning feeling grumpy.*
■ See the Synonym Study at **cross.** ❏ *ADJECTIVE* **grump·i·er, grump·i·est.** –**grump′i·ly,** *ADVERB*.

a **grumpy** expression

grunt (grunt),
1 *NOUN*. the deep, hoarse sound that a hog makes.
2 *NOUN*. a sound like this: *She lifted the heavy box with a grunt.*
3 *VERB*. to make this sound: *I grunted as I lifted the box.*
❏ *VERB* **grunts, grunt·ed, grunt·ing.**

gua·ca·mo·le (gwä′kə mō′lē), *NOUN*. a dip made of mashed avocado, tomato, onion, and spices.

Guam (gwäm), *NOUN*. an island in the western Pacific. It belongs to the United States.
–**Gua·ma·ni·an** (gwä mä′nē ən), *ADJECTIVE* or *NOUN*.

Gua·na·jua·to (gwä′nä hwä′tō), *NOUN*. a state in central Mexico.

guar·an·tee (gar′ən tē′),
1 *NOUN*. a promise or pledge to replace or repair a purchased product or to return the money paid if something is not as it should be: *We have a one-year guarantee on our new car.*
2 *VERB*. to promise to repair or replace something if it is not as it should be: *This clock is guaranteed.*
3 *VERB*. to promise to do something: *The store guaranteed to deliver my purchase by Friday.*

a	hat	ė	term	ô	order	ch	child		a in about
ā	age	i	it	oi	oil	ng	long		e in taken
ä	far	ī	ice	ou	out	sh	she	ə {	i in pencil
â	care	o	hot	u	cup	th	thin		o in lemon
e	let	ō	open	ù	put	ᴛʜ	then		u in circus
ē	equal	ò	saw	ü	rule	zh	measure		

4 *NOUN.* something that makes sure that something will happen as a result: *Failure to study is practically a guarantee of failure to learn.*
❏ PLURAL **guar·an·tees**; *VERB* **guar·an·tees, guar·an·teed, guar·an·tee·ing.**

guard (gärd),
1 *VERB.* to watch over someone or something; keep safe; defend: *The dog guarded the child.*
2 *VERB.* to keep someone from getting out; hold back: *Guard the prisoners.*
3 *NOUN.* a person or group that protects or watches. A soldier or group of soldiers protecting a person or place is a guard.
4 *VERB.* to take precautions against something: *Guard against cavities by brushing your teeth and flossing often.*
5 *NOUN.* anything that gives someone or something protection from harm: *A helmet is a guard against head injuries.*
6 *VERB.* to try to keep an opposing player from scoring or playing well in basketball and some other sports.
7 *NOUN.* (in football) an offensive player at either side of the center.
8 *NOUN.* (in basketball) a member of the backcourt.
❏ *VERB* **guards, guard·ed, guard·ing.**

guard·i·an (gär′dē ən), *NOUN.*
1 someone who takes care of another person or of some special thing.
2 a person appointed by law to take care of the affairs of someone who is young or who cannot take care of his or her own affairs.
–guard′i·an·ship, *NOUN.*

Gua·te·ma·la (gwä′tə mä′lə), *NOUN.* a country in Central America. **–Gua′te·ma′lan,** *ADJECTIVE or NOUN.*

gua·va (gwä′və), *NOUN.* the small, yellow or red fruit of a tropical American evergreen tree or bush, used for jelly, jam, and so on.
❏ PLURAL **gua·vas.**

Guer·re·ro (gə rer′ō), *NOUN.* a state in southern Mexico.

guer·ril·la (gə ril′ə), *NOUN.* a member of a band of fighters who attack the enemy by sudden raids, ambushes, and so on. Guerrillas are not part of a regular army. ■ Another word that sounds like this is **gorilla.**

guava

guess (ges),
1 *VERB.* to form an opinion about something when you do not know the facts: *Are you sure or are you just guessing?*

2 *NOUN.* an opinion formed without really knowing: *My guess is that it will rain tomorrow.*
3 *VERB.* to get the answer to something by guessing: *Can you guess the answer to that riddle?*
4 *VERB.* to think; suppose: *I guess I won't go with you after all.*
❏ *VERB* **guess·es, guessed, guess·ing;** PLURAL **guess·es. –guess′er,** *NOUN.*

guest (gest), *NOUN.*
1 a person who is received and entertained at someone else's home, club, and so on; visitor.
2 a person staying at a hotel or motel.
3 a well-known person invited to appear at a single performance of a radio or TV show, concert, and the like: *The senator was a guest on the talk show.*

guid·ance (gīd′ns), *NOUN.* helpful advice or instruction: *Under her mother's guidance, she learned how to swim.*

guide (gīd),
1 *VERB.* to show someone how to get somewhere or how to do something: *The scout guided us through the wilderness. The counselor guided him in the choice of a career.*
2 *NOUN.* someone or something that shows the way: *Tourists sometimes hire guides.*
❏ *VERB* **guides, guid·ed, guid·ing.**

guide word, a word put at the top of a page as a guide to the contents of the page. Guide words tell what are the first and last entries on the page. The guide words for this page are **guard** and **guilty.**

guild (gild), *NOUN.* an association formed by people having the same interests, work, and so on, for some useful or common purpose: *The author is a member of the Writers Guild.* ■ Another word that sounds like this is **gild.**

guil·lo·tine (gil′ə tēn′), *NOUN.* a machine for cutting off someone's head with a heavy blade that slides down between two posts.

Word Story

The **guillotine** was named for Joseph Guillotin (jō′zef′ gē′ȯ tan′). He was a French doctor who suggested the use of this machine as a faster, more merciful way to execute criminals than hanging. It was first used in 1792 during the French Revolution.

guilt (gilt), *NOUN.*
1 the fact or condition of having broken a law or rule: *The evidence proved their guilt.*
2 a feeling of having done something wrong: *Even though no one had seen him take the money, his guilt made him put it back.*
–guilt′less, *ADJECTIVE.*

guilt·y (gil′tē), *ADJECTIVE.*
1 having done something wrong; deserving to be blamed and punished: *The jury found her guilty.*

2 knowing or showing that you have done something wrong: *a guilty conscience, a guilty look.* ❑ ADJECTIVE **guilt•i•er, guilt•i•est.** –**guilt′i•ly,** ADVERB.

Guin•ea (gin′ē), NOUN. a country in western Africa. –**Guin′e•an,** ADJECTIVE or NOUN.

Guin•ea-Bis•sau (gin′ē bi sou′), NOUN. a country in northwestern Africa.

guinea pig, a small, fat animal that has short ears and a short tail or no tail. Guinea pigs are kept as pets and used in scientific experiments.

Did You Know?

Guinea pigs are not related to pigs. They are rodents, like squirrels, rabbits, and mice. Guinea pigs are pets in the United States, but are used for food in some parts of South America.

guinea pig — about 1 foot long

gui•tar (gə tär′), NOUN. a musical instrument that usually has six strings, played with the fingers or with a pick.

gulch (gulch), NOUN. a very deep, narrow valley with steep sides. ❑ PLURAL **gulch•es.**

gulf (gulf), NOUN.
1 a large part of an ocean or sea with land around most of it: *The Gulf of Mexico is between Florida and Mexico.*
2 a great lack of understanding: *The quarrel left a gulf between the old friends.*

gull (gul), NOUN. a graceful, gray and white bird that lives near large bodies of water. A gull has long wings, webbed feet, and a thick, strong beak.

gul•li•ble (gul′ə bəl), ADJECTIVE. too ready to believe whatever people say, and thus easy to cheat or trick. –**gul•li•bil•i•ty,** (gul′ə bil′ə tē), NOUN.

gul•ly (gul′ē), NOUN. a ditch made by heavy rains or running water. ❑ PLURAL **gul•lies.**

gulp (gulp),
1 VERB. to swallow something eagerly or greedily: *The hungry girl gulped down the bowl of soup.*
2 NOUN. the act of swallowing: *He ate it all in one gulp.*
3 NOUN. the amount swallowed at one time; mouthful: *She took a gulp of milk.*

4 VERB. to make a swallowing sound in your throat: *The thought of riding the roller coaster made me gulp.* ❑ VERB **gulps, gulped, gulp•ing.**

gum[1] (gum), NOUN.
1 a sticky substance produced by some seaweeds, plants, and trees. Gum is used to make glue for stamps, keep whipped cream fluffy, and so on.
2 See **chewing gum.**

gum[2] (gum), NOUN. often, **gums,** the soft, pink flesh that your teeth grow out of.

gum•drop (gum′drop′), NOUN. a chewy, jellylike piece of candy.

gun (gun),
1 NOUN. weapon with a metal tube for shooting bullets or shells. Rifles and pistols are guns.
2 NOUN. anything resembling a gun in use or shape: *a spray gun.*
3 VERB. to shoot something or someone with a gun; hunt with a gun: *The soldiers were gunned down.*
4 VERB. to make something go faster; increase the speed of: *He gunned the engine to get up the hill.* ❑ VERB **guns, gunned, gun•ning.**

stick to your guns, IDIOM. to stand by your opinion; to refuse to give up: *He stuck to his guns and refused to sing the different lyrics.*

gun•pow•der (gun′pou′dər), NOUN. an explosive that is used in guns and fireworks.

gun•wale (gun′l), NOUN. the upper edge of a ship's or boat's side.

gup•py (gup′ē), NOUN. a very small fish of tropical fresh water, often kept in aquariums. The female gives birth to live young instead of laying eggs. ❑ PLURAL **gup•pies.**

gull — between 1 and 2 feet long

gur•gle (gėr′gəl),
1 VERB. to flow or run with a bubbling sound: *Water often gurgles when it is poured out of a bottle.*

a	hat	ė	term	ô	order	ch	child		a in about
ā	age	i	it	oi	oil	ng	long		e in taken
ä	far	ī	ice	ou	out	sh	she	ə	i in pencil
â	care	o	hot	u	cup	th	thin		o in lemon
e	let	ō	open	ù	put	₮н	then		u in circus
ē	equal	ò	saw	ü	rule	zh	measure		

2 *NOUN.* a bubbling sound.

3 *VERB.* to make bubbling sounds: *The baby gurgled happily.*

❑ *VERB* **gur·gles, gur·gled, gur·gling.**

gush (gush),

1 *VERB.* to flow out suddenly; pour out: *Oil gushed from the new well.*

2 *NOUN.* a sudden flow of water or other liquid: *If you get a deep cut, there usually is a gush of blood.*

3 *VERB.* to talk in a fast, silly way about your interests or feelings.

❑ *VERB* **gush·es, gushed, gush·ing;** *PLURAL* **gush·es.**

gust (gust), *NOUN.* a sudden, violent rush of wind: *A gust upset the small sailboat.*

gut (gut), *NOUN.*

1 the whole alimentary canal or one of its parts, such as the intestines or stomach.

2 a string made from the intestines of animals. Gut is used for violin strings and tennis rackets.

bust a gut, *IDIOM.* (informal) to work very hard.

spill your guts, *IDIOM.* (informal) to tell everything about something secret.

gut·ter (gut′ər), *NOUN.*

1 a channel or ditch along the side of a street or road to carry off water; low part of a street beside the sidewalk.

2 a channel or trough along the lower edge of a roof to carry off rain water.

guy (gī), *NOUN.* a man or boy; fellow.

Guy·an·a (gī an′ə), *NOUN.* a country in northern South America. **—Guy·a·nese** (gī′ə nēz′), *ADJECTIVE* or *NOUN.*

gym (jim), *NOUN.*

1 a short form of **gymnasium.**

2 a class in which students are taught how to exercise and take care of the body; physical education.

gym·na·si·um (jim nā′zē əm), *NOUN.* a room or building that has equipment for physical exercises or training and for indoor athletic sports.

Word Story

Gymnasium comes from a Greek word meaning "naked." In ancient times athletes trained and exercised with no clothes on.

gym·nast (jim′nast), *NOUN.* an expert in gymnastics.

a **gymnast** performing on a balance beam

gym·nas·tics (jim nas′tiks), *NOUN.*

1 *PLURAL.* exercises for developing the muscles, such as the ones done in a gymnasium.

2 *SINGULAR.* a sport in which very difficult physical exercises are performed.

gyp·sy (jip′sē),

1 *NOUN.* also, **Gypsy,** someone belonging to a wandering group of people who came from India long ago.

2 *ADJECTIVE.* of the gypsies: *gypsy music.*

❑ *PLURAL* **gyp·sies.**

gypsy moth, a brownish or white moth whose caterpillars cause great damage to trees by eating their leaves.

gy·rate (jī′rāt), *VERB.* to go in a circle or spiral; whirl; rotate: *A spinning top gyrates.* ❑ *VERB* **gy·rates, gy·rat·ed, gy·rat·ing. —gy·ra′tion,** *NOUN.*

gy·ro·scope (jī′rə skōp), *NOUN.* a heavy wheel mounted on an axle inside a frame. When the wheel spins, it resists any change in either direction in which its axle points. Large gyroscopes help to keep ships and aircraft exactly on course. Small gyroscopes are toys.

hummingbird

H or **h** (āch), *NOUN.* the eighth letter of the English alphabet. ❑ *PLURAL* **H's** or **h's.**

ha (hä), *INTERJECTION.*
1 a cry of surprise, joy, or triumph: *"Ha! I caught you!"*
2 the sound of a laugh: *"Ha! ha!" laughed the boys.*

hab·it (hab′it), *NOUN.*
1 something you do over and over, sometimes without thinking: *I have a habit of biting my nails.*
2 the clothing worn by members of some religious orders. Monks and nuns often wear habits.

hab·i·tat (hab′ə tat), *NOUN.* the particular kind of place where a living thing is naturally found: *The jungle is the habitat of monkeys.*

ha·bit·u·al (hə bich′ü əl), *ADJECTIVE.*
1 done because it is a habit: *a habitual smile.*
2 regular: *A habitual reader reads a great deal.*
—**ha·bit′u·al·ly,** *ADVERB.*

ha·ci·en·da (hä′sē en′də), *NOUN.* (in Latin America) a ranch or country house. ❑ *PLURAL* **ha·ci·en·das.**

hack (hak), *VERB.*
1 to cut or chop something with hard blows: *She hacked the meat into small pieces.*
2 to cough in a loud, painful way.
❑ *VERB* **hacks, hacked, hack·ing.**

hack·er (hak′ər), *NOUN.*
1 someone who is especially interested in computers and skilled in using them.
2 someone who illegally accesses other people's computer systems.

had (had), *VERB.*
1 the past tense of **have:** *She had a party to celebrate her graduation.*
2 the past participle of **have:** *We have had pizza for dinner three times this week.*

had·n't (had′nt), a contraction of **had not.**

Hai·da (hī′də), *NOUN.* a member of a tribe of American Indians living in western Canada and southern Alaska. ❑ *PLURAL* **Hai·da** or **Hai·das.**

297

hai·ku (hī′kü), *NOUN.* a three-line poem having five syllables in the first line, seven in the second, and five in the third. ❑ *PLURAL* **hai·ku.**

The butterfly lands
on a beautiful flower,
sips a summer meal.

haiku

hail¹ (hāl),
1 *NOUN.* small, roundish, frozen raindrops that fall from the clouds in a shower. A single piece of hail is called a **hailstone** (hāl′stōn′).
2 *VERB.* to fall in hail. ❑ *VERB* **hails, hailed, hail·ing.**

hail² (hāl),
1 *VERB.* to greet; cheer; shout in welcome to: *The crowd hailed the winner of the race.*
2 *INTERJECTION.* greetings! welcome!: *Hail to the winner!*
3 *VERB.* to call out or signal to: *I hailed a taxi.*
❑ *VERB* **hails, hailed, hail·ing.**

hair (hâr), *NOUN.*
1 a fine threadlike growth from the skin of people and animals.
2 a mass of such growths: *I combed my hair.*
∎ Another word that sounds like this is **hare.**
—**hair′less,** *ADJECTIVE.* —**hair′like′,** *ADJECTIVE.*

Did You Know?

The average person has about 100,000 **hairs** on their head. People normally lose about 70 to 100 hairs every day as new hair grows in.

hair·cut (hâr′kut′), *NOUN.* the act or style of cutting the hair.

hair·do (hâr′dü′), *NOUN.* a way of arranging the hair. ❑ *PLURAL* **hair·dos.**

hair·y (hâr′ē), *ADJECTIVE.* covered with hair; having a lot of hair: *I have hairy arms.* ❑ *ADJECTIVE* **hair·i·er, hair·i·est.** —**hair′i·ness,** *NOUN.*

Hai·ti (hā′tē), *NOUN.* a country in the West Indies. —**Hai·tian** (hā′shən), *ADJECTIVE or NOUN.*

half (haf),
1 *NOUN.* one of two equal parts: *Half of four is two.*
2 *ADJECTIVE.* being one of two equal parts: *a half hour.*
3 *ADVERB.* to a half of the full amount or degree: *a glass half full of milk.*
4 *NOUN.* one of the two equal periods of play in some games, such as football, basketball, or soccer.

5 *ADVERB.* partly; not completely: *half cooked.*
❑ *PLURAL* **halves.**

half·back (haf′bak′), *NOUN.* (in football) a member of the offensive backfield.

half brother, a brother related through one parent only.

half·heart·ed (haf′här′tid), *ADJECTIVE.* without any real interest or enthusiasm: *I made a halfhearted attempt to study.* —**half′heart′ed·ly,** *ADVERB.*

half-mast (haf′mast′), *NOUN.* a position halfway or part way down from the top of a mast or staff. A flag is lowered to half-mast as a mark of respect for someone who has died.

half sister, a sister related through one parent only.

half·time (haf′tīm′), *NOUN.* the time between two halves of a game, such as football or basketball.

half·way (haf′wā′),
1 *ADVERB.* half the way: *The ladder reached only halfway.*
2 *ADVERB.* partially; not completely: *I am halfway done.*
3 *ADJECTIVE.* midway: *Chicago was the halfway point in our trip from New York to Denver.*
4 *ADJECTIVE.* not going far enough; incomplete: *Fires cannot be prevented by halfway measures.*

hal·i·but (hal′ə bət), *NOUN.* a food fish related to the flounder. Some halibut weigh several hundred pounds. ❑ *PLURAL* **hal·i·but** or **hal·i·buts.**

hall (hȯl), *NOUN.*
1 a way for going through a buildings; hallway: *A hall ran the length of the upper floor of the house.*
2 a passage or room at the entrance to a building; hallway: *Leave your umbrella in the hall.*
3 a large room for holding meetings, parties, or banquets: *No hall in town was large enough for the crowd gathered to hear the famous singer.*
∎ Another word that sounds like this is **haul.**

hal·le·lu·jah (hal′ə lü′yə), *INTERJECTION.* praise the Lord.

hal·lowed (hal′ōd), *ADJECTIVE.* made holy or sacred: *"Hallowed be your name."*

Hal·low·een or **Hal·low·e'en** (hal′ō ēn′), *NOUN.* the evening of October 31, when children dress up in costumes and ask for treats at other people's houses.

hall·way (hȯl′wā′), *NOUN.* See **hall** (definitions 1 and 2).

ha·lo (hā′lō), *NOUN.*
1 a ring of light around the sun, moon, or other shining body.
2 a golden circle or disk of light around the head of a saint or angel in pictures or statues.
❑ *PLURAL* **ha·los** or **ha·loes.**

the moon with a **halo**

halt (hȯlt),
1 *VERB.* to stop for a while: *The store halted deliveries during the strike.* ■ See the Synonym Study at **stop.**
2 *NOUN.* a temporary stop: *Work came to a halt at noon.*
❏ *VERB* **halts, halt·ed, halt·ing.**

hal·ter (hȯl′tər), *NOUN.*
1 a rope or strap for leading or tying an animal.
2 a blouse worn by women and girls which fastens behind the neck and across the back and leaves the arms and back bare.

halve (hav), *VERB.*
1 to divide something into two equal parts; share equally: *He and I agreed to halve expenses on our trip.*
2 to reduce the amount of something to half of what it was: *The new machine will halve our costs.*
❏ *VERB* **halves, halved, halv·ing.** ■ Another word that sounds like this is **have.**

halves (havz), *NOUN.* the plural of **half.**

ham (ham), *NOUN.* meat from the upper part of a hog's hind leg, usually salted and smoked.

ham·burg·er (ham′bėr′gər), *NOUN.* ground beef, usually shaped into round flat cakes and fried or broiled and served on a bun; burger. A hamburger with a slice of melted cheese on top of the meat is called a **cheeseburger** (chēz′bėr′gər).

ham·mer (ham′ər),
1 *NOUN.* a tool with a metal head fastened to a handle. Hammers are used to pound nails into wood.
2 *VERB.* to pound something with a hammer.
3 *VERB.* to hit something again and again: *The teacher hammered on the desk with a ruler.*
❏ *VERB* **ham·mers, ham·mered, ham·mer·ing.**

ham·mock (ham′ək), *NOUN.* a bed or couch made of canvas or a net of cord that is strung between two trees or poles.

relaxing in a **hammock**

ham·per¹ (ham′pər), *VERB.* to make it difficult for someone to do something: *Wet wood hampered our efforts to start the campfire.* ❏ *VERB* **ham·pers, ham·pered, ham·per·ing.**

ham·per² (ham′pər), *NOUN.* a large basket with a cover: *a picnic hamper, a laundry hamper.*

ham·ster (ham′stər), *NOUN.* a furry, burrowing animal something like a mouse, but larger. Hamsters have a short tail and large cheek pouches. They are often kept as pets.

hand (hand),
1 *NOUN.* the part of the body at the end of the arm, which takes and holds things. The hand has four fingers and a thumb.
2 *NOUN.* something like a hand: *The hands of my watch have stopped moving.*
3 *NOUN.* a hired worker who uses his or her hands: *a factory hand.*
4 *VERB.* to give something with the hand; pass: *Please hand me a spoon.*
5 *NOUN.* **hands,** possession; control: *This property is no longer in my hands.*
6 *NOUN.* a part or share in doing something: *She had no hand in the matter.*
7 *NOUN.* a side: *There was a small table on my left hand.*
8 *NOUN.* a round of applause or clapping: *The crowd gave the winner a big hand.*
9 *NOUN.* a promise of marriage: *He asked the king for his daughter's hand.*
10 *NOUN.* the breadth of a hand; 4 inches: *This horse is 18 hands high.*
11 *ADJECTIVE.* of, for, by, or in the hand: *a hand mirror, hand weaving, a hand pump.*
12 *NOUN.* the cards held by a player in one round of a card game.
❏ *VERB* **hands, hand·ed, hand·ing.**

at hand, *IDIOM.* within reach; near: *When I type I always keep an eraser at hand.*

by hand, *IDIOM.* by using the hands, not machinery: *Shoes were once made by hand, but today most of them are made by machine.*

give someone a hand or **lend someone a hand,** *IDIOM.* to help someone: *Please give me a hand with this box.*

hand down, *IDIOM.* to pass along: *Great-grandmother's ring is handed down to the oldest child in the family.*

hand out, *IDIOM.* to give out; distribute: *Who would like to help me hand out our new dictionaries?*

have your hands full, *IDIOM.* to be very busy; have all you can do: *Our teacher has her hands full with us.*

on hand, *IDIOM.*
1 within reach; near: *Try to be on hand when I need you.*
2 ready: *We have bandages on hand just in case.*

out of hand, *IDIOM.* out of control: *Don't let your temper get out of hand.*

a	hat	ė	term	ô	order	ch	child		a in about
ā	age	i	it	oi	oil	ng	long		e in taken
ä	far	ī	ice	ou	out	sh	she	ə ⟨	i in pencil
â	care	o	hot	u	cup	th	thin		o in lemon
e	let	ō	open	u̇	put	ŦH	then		u in circus
ē	equal	ȯ	saw	ü	rule	zh	measure		

H

hand·bag (hand′bag′), NOUN. a woman's small bag for money, keys, and cosmetics; purse.

hand·ball (hand′bȯl′), NOUN.
1 a game played by hitting a small rubber ball against a wall with the hand.
2 a rubber ball used in this game

hand·book (hand′bùk′), NOUN. a small book of information or directions: *a handbook on birds.*

hand·cuff (hand′kuf′),
1 NOUN. **handcuffs,** a pair of two steel rings joined by a short chain and locked around a prisoner's wrists.
2 VERB. to put handcuffs on someone.
□ VERB **hand·cuffs, hand·cuffed, hand·cuff·ing.**

Word Power

-handed -headed -hearted

The combining forms **-handed, -headed,** and **-hearted** are all used to describe what kind of hand, head, or heart someone has or uses. Left-**handed** means using your left hand. Bald-**headed** means having a bald head. Kind**hearted** means having a kind heart. Many other body parts can be used the same way. Can you think of words that end in **-footed** or **-legged** or **-eared**?

hand·ful (hand′fùl), NOUN.
1 as much or as many as you can hold in your hand: *a handful of candy.*
2 a small number or quantity: *Only a handful of fans came to the game.*
□ PLURAL **hand·fuls.**

hand·i·cap (han′dē kap′),
1 NOUN. something that makes it harder to do what you want to do: *A sore throat is a handicap in singing.*
2 VERB. to make it harder for someone to do something: *The swimmer was handicapped by a sore arm.*
□ VERB **hand·i·caps, hand·i·capped, hand·i·cap·ping.**

hand·i·capped (han′dē kapt′), ADJECTIVE. having a physical or mental disability.

hand·i·craft
(han′dē kraft′), NOUN.
1 a trade or art requiring skill with the hands. Weaving baskets is a handicraft.
2 something made by hand: *The bazaar sold handicrafts.*

hand·ker·chief
(hang′kər chif), NOUN. a soft, usually square piece of cloth used for wiping your nose, face, or hands.

handicraft (definition 1)

han·dle (han′dl),
1 NOUN. the part of something that you hold onto with your hand. Spoons, pitchers, hammers, and pails have handles.
2 VERB. to touch, feel, or use something with the hand: *I handled the old book carefully to avoid tearing the pages.*
3 VERB. to manage something; direct: *The rider handled the horse well.*
4 VERB. to behave or act when handled: *This car handles easily.*
5 VERB. to deal with something: *The teacher handled discipline problems with ease.*
□ VERB **han·dles, han·dled, han·dling.**

han·dle·bar (han′dl bär′), NOUN. often, **handlebars,** the curved bar on a bicycle or motorcycle that the rider holds and steers by.

hand·made (hand′mād′), ADJECTIVE. made by hand, not by machine: *handmade pottery.*

hand·out (hand′out′), NOUN. food, clothing, or money given to someone: *The beggar asked for a handout.*

hand·shake (hand′shāk′), NOUN. the act of clasping and shaking each other's hands in friendship, agreement, or greeting.

hand·some (han′səm), ADJECTIVE.
1 good-looking; pleasing in appearance. We usually say that a man is handsome, but that a woman is pretty or beautiful. ∎ See the Synonym Study at **beautiful.**
2 generous: *They gave the school a handsome gift of two hundred dollars.*
□ ADJECTIVE **hand·som·er, hand·som·est.**

hand·spring (hand′spring′), NOUN. a somersault made by springing onto the hands, flipping the body over backwards, and landing on the feet.

hand·stand (hand′stand′), NOUN. the act of balancing on your hands with your feet in the air.

hand·writ·ing (hand′rī′ting), NOUN.
1 writing done by hand, with a pen or pencil: *The entire novel was in the author's own handwriting; none of it was typewritten.*
2 a manner or style of writing: *He recognized his mother's handwriting on the envelope.*

hand·y (han′dē), ADJECTIVE.
1 easy to reach or use; useful: *There were handy shelves near the kitchen sink.*
2 skillful with the hands: *She is handy with tools and was able to fix our broken faucet.*
□ ADJECTIVE **hand·i·er, hand·i·est.**

hang (hang), VERB.
1 to be held from above on a hook, branch, and so on: *Hang your hat on the hook. The swing hangs from a tree.*
2 to fasten or be fastened so as to leave swinging freely: *to hang a door on its hinges.*

3 to put someone to death by hanging with a rope around the neck. ★ The past tense and past participle for this meaning is **hanged.**

4 to droop; bend down: *She hung her head in shame.*

5 to depend: *His future hangs on their decision.*
❑ *VERB* **hangs, hung, hang·ing.**

get the hang of, *IDIOM.* to learn the way of using or doing something: *After practicing volleyball serves for an hour, I began to get the hang of it.*

hang·ar (hang′ər), *NOUN.* a very large building where aircraft are kept.

hang·er (hang′ər), *NOUN.* something that you hang clothes on, made of wire, wood, or plastic: *a coat hanger.*

hang glider, a device like a large kite, used to glide through the air from a high place. A harness holds the rider in place. **–hang gliding.**

hang glider

hang·nail (hang′nāl′), *NOUN.* a bit of skin that hangs partly loose near a fingernail.

Ha·nuk·kah (hä′nə kə), *NOUN.* a yearly Jewish festival that lasts eight days, mostly in December. It celebrates the recapture of the holy Jewish Temple many centuries ago.

hap·haz·ard (hap′haz′ərd),

1 *ADJECTIVE.* not planned; random: *haphazard answers.*

2 *ADVERB.* by chance; at random: *Papers were scattered haphazard on the desk.*

hap·pen (hap′ən), *VERB.*

1 to take place; occur: *What happened in class today?*

2 to be or take place by chance: *Accidents will happen.*
❑ *VERB* **hap·pens, hap·pened, hap·pen·ing.**

hap·pen·ing (hap′ə ning), *NOUN.* something that happens; event: *The evening newscast reviewed the happenings of the day.*

hap·pi·ly (hap′ə lē), *ADVERB.*

1 in a happy manner: *We played happily together.*

2 by luck; with good fortune: *Happily, I found my lost wallet.*

hap·py (hap′ē), *ADJECTIVE.*

1 feeling as you do when you are well and are having a good time; glad; pleased; contented: *She is happy in her work.*

2 showing that you are glad: *a happy smile.*
❑ *ADJECTIVE* **hap·pi·er, hap·pi·est. –hap′pi·ness,** *NOUN.*

Synonym Study

Happy means feeling good and being pleased: *She was happy to have made the softball team.*

Cheerful means happy and in good spirits: *He is still as cheerful as ever, even though he faces a serious operation.*

Glad means feeling pleasure because of something good: *I was glad to be invited to the party.*

ANTONYMS: sad, unhappy.

hap·py-go-luck·y (hap′ē gō′luk′ē), *ADJECTIVE.* not worrying about what may happen; carefree: *The happy-go-lucky student was not interested in getting high grades.*

har·ass (har′əs *or* hə ras′), *VERB.* to annoy or bother greatly: *The heat and the flies harassed us on the journey.* ❑ *VERB* **har·ass·es, har·assed, har·ass·ing. –har′ass·ment** *or* **har·ass′ment,** *NOUN.*

har·bor (här′bər),

1 *NOUN.* an area of quiet water where ships are safe: *Boats headed for the harbor when the storm began.*

2 *VERB.* to give shelter to: *The dog's shaggy hair harbors fleas.*

3 *VERB.* to have and keep in your mind: *It's never good to harbor a grudge.*
❑ *VERB* **har·bors, har·bored, har·bor·ing.**

hard (härd),

1 *ADJECTIVE.* solid and firm to the touch; not soft: *a hard nut.*

2 *ADVERB.* firmly: *Don't squeeze my hand so hard.*

3 *ADJECTIVE.* taking a lot of work or energy; difficult: *Cleaning out the garage was a hard job.*

4 *ADVERB.* with difficulty: *The swimmer was breathing hard after he finished the race.*

5 *ADJECTIVE.* acting with energy; industrious; energetic: *He is a hard worker and gets a lot done.*

6 *ADVERB.* with effort: *I worked hard on this project.*

7 *ADVERB.* with great force or vigor: *It is raining hard.*

8 *ADJECTIVE.* very cold and stormy: *We had a hard winter last year.*
–hard′ness, *NOUN.*

hard of hearing, *IDIOM.* somewhat deaf.

hard·ball (härd′bôl′), *NOUN.* See **baseball.**

hard-boiled (härd′boild′), *ADJECTIVE.* boiled until hard: *I like hard-boiled eggs.*

a	hat	ė	term	ô	order	ch	child	⎧ a in about
ā	age	i	it	oi	oil	ng	long	e in taken
ä	far	ī	ice	ou	out	sh	she	ə ⎨ i in pencil
â	care	o	hot	u	cup	th	thin	o in lemon
e	let	ō	open	ù	put	ŦH	then	⎩ u in circus
ē	equal	ò	saw	ü	rule	zh	measure	

hard copy, printed copy that can be read without the use of any special equipment. Computer printouts are hard copy.

hard drive, a computer disk drive used for storing computer data. Hard drives are not usually moved in and out of a computer by the user.

hard·en (härd′n), VERB. to make or become hard: *As the candy cooled, it hardened.* ❑ VERB **hard·ens, hard·ened, hard·en·ing.**

hard hat, a helmet worn by construction workers as protection against falling objects.

hard·ly (härd′lē), ADVERB.
1 only just; barely: *We hardly had time to wash.*
2 probably not: *They are hardly likely to come in this rain.*

hard hat

hard·ship (härd′ship), NOUN. something that makes life difficult: *Hunger and sickness were among the hardships of pioneer life.*

hard·ware (härd′wâr′), NOUN.
1 articles made from metal. Locks, hinges, nails, screws, knives, and so on are hardware.
2 a computer and any machine used with it, such as a disk drive or printer.

hard·wood (härd′wüd′), NOUN. a hard, dense wood such as oak, cherry, ebony, and mahogany.

har·dy (här′dē), ADJECTIVE. able to stand up under difficult conditions; strong: *Cold weather does not kill hardy plants.* ■ See the Synonym Study at **strong.** ❑ ADJECTIVE **har·di·er, har·di·est.** —**har′di·ness,** NOUN.

hare (hâr), NOUN. a small animal about as big as a cat, with soft fur and long ears. Hares have long back legs and can hop very fast. They are related to rabbits.
❑ PLURAL **hares** or **hare.**
■ Another word that sounds like this is **hair.**

hare — about 2 feet long

Did You Know?

How can you tell a **hare** from a **rabbit?** They look a lot alike, but hares are bigger and have longer ears and legs. It is easy to tell if you see their babies. Baby hares are hopping around in just a few hours, but baby rabbits are helpless and blind at birth. Both hares and rabbits hide their nests well, so your best chance to see their babies may be at a zoo.

harm (härm),
1 VERB. to damage; injure; hurt: *Do not pick or harm the flowers in the park.*
2 NOUN. something that hurts you or causes pain or loss; injury; damage: *He slipped and fell down but suffered no harm.*
❑ VERB **harms, harmed, harm·ing.**

Synonym Study

Harm means to cause pain or injury to someone or something: *Pollution harms the environment.*

Hurt and **injure** mean to wound someone or something: *He hurt the other team's player when they ran into each other. She injured her knee when she tripped on the stairs.*

Damage means to harm something in a way that lessens its value: *My bicycle was badly damaged when a delivery truck backed into it.*

See also the Synonym Studies at **break** and **destroy.**

ANTONYM: help.

harm·ful (härm′fəl), ADJECTIVE. causing harm; causing injury: *Smoking is harmful to your health.* —**harm′ful·ly,** ADVERB. —**harm′ful·ness,** NOUN.

harm·less (härm′lis), ADJECTIVE. causing no harm; not harmful: *It's only a harmless spider.* —**harm′less·ly,** ADVERB. —**harm′less·ness,** NOUN.

har·mon·i·ca (här mon′ə kə), NOUN. a small musical instrument shaped like a thick candy bar, with metal reeds. It is played by breathing in and out through openings. ❑ PLURAL **har·mon·i·cas.**

har·mo·ni·ous (här mō′nē əs), ADJECTIVE.
1 agreeing in feelings, ideas, or actions; getting on well together: *The children played together in a harmonious group.*
2 going well together: *A beautiful picture has harmonious colors.*
3 sweet-sounding; musical: *I love the harmonious sounds of a choir.*

har·mo·nize (här′mə nīz), VERB.
1 to be in harmony or agreement: *The colors of the furniture and the rug harmonized perfectly.*
2 to sing or play in harmony: *We like to get together and harmonize before choir practice.*
❑ VERB **har·mo·niz·es, har·mo·nized, har·mo·niz·ing.**

har·mo·ny (här′mə nē), NOUN.
1 agreement in feelings, ideas, or actions; getting on well together: *The neighbors lived in harmony with each other.*
2 the sounding of two or more musical tones that go well together.
❑ PLURAL **har·mo·nies.**

har·ness (här′nis),
1 *NOUN.* the leather straps, bands, and other pieces used to hitch a horse or other animal to a carriage, wagon, or plow.
2 *VERB.* to put a harness on: *I harnessed the horses.*
3 *VERB.* to control something in order to put it to use: *Solar cells harness the power of the sun to make electricity.*
❑ *PLURAL* **har·ness·es;** *VERB* **har·ness·es, har·nessed, har·ness·ing.**

harness (definition 1)

harp (härp), *NOUN.* a large, stringed instrument. It is played by plucking the strings with the fingers.
harp·ist (här′pist), *NOUN.* someone who plays a harp.
har·poon (här pün′),
1 *NOUN.* a spearlike weapon with a rope tied to it. It is used for catching whales and other sea animals.
2 *VERB.* to strike, catch, or kill with a harpoon.
❑ *VERB* **har·poons, har·pooned, har·poon·ing.**
harp·si·chord (härp′sə kôrd), *NOUN.* a musical instrument with a keyboard like a piano. When you press the keys, the strings are plucked by leather or quill points.
Har·ris·burg (har′is bèrg′), *NOUN.* the capital of Pennsylvania.
har·row (har′ō),
1 *NOUN.* a heavy farm tool with iron teeth or upright disks. Harrows are used to break up the soil into fine pieces before planting seeds.
2 *VERB.* to pull a harrow over land: *After plowing and harrowing the field, we sow the wheat.*
❑ *VERB* **har·rows, har·rowed, har·row·ing.**
harsh (härsh), *ADJECTIVE.*
1 rough to the touch, taste, eye, or ear: *a harsh voice.* ■ See the Synonym Study at **rough.**
2 cruel; severe: *a harsh judge.*
3 unpleasant but real: *harsh facts.*
—**harsh′ly,** *ADVERB.* —**harsh′ness,** *NOUN.*
Hart·ford (härt′fərd), *NOUN.* the capital of Connecticut.

har·vest (här′vist),
1 *NOUN.* the act of reaping and gathering grain and other food crops.
2 *VERB.* to gather crops: *to harvest wheat.*
3 *NOUN.* the ripe crops that are picked after the growing season is over: *The potato harvest was small this year.*
❑ *VERB* **har·vests, har·vest·ed, har·vest·ing.** —**har′vest·er,** *NOUN.*
harvest moon, the full moon at harvest time or about September 23.
has (haz), *VERB.* a present tense of **have:** *Who has my book? He has been sick.*
hash (hash), *NOUN.* a mixture of cooked meat, potatoes, and other vegetables, chopped into small pieces and fried or baked.
has·n't (haz′nt), a contraction of **has not.**
has·sle (has′əl),
1 *NOUN.* a bother; trouble: *the hassle of fixing a broken bicycle.*
2 *VERB.* to bother someone; annoy; harass: *He doesn't repay loans unless you hassle him.*
❑ *VERB* **has·sles, has·sled, has·sling.**
haste (hāst), *NOUN.* the act of hurrying; trying to be quick: *All my haste was of no use; I missed the bus anyway.*

Have You Heard?

You may have heard the phrase **"Haste makes waste."** This means that if you do something too quickly, you may have to do it over again. And that's a waste of time and energy.

has·ten (hā′sn), *VERB.*
1 to be quick; go fast: *She hastened to explain that she had not meant to be rude.*
2 to cause to be quick; speed; hurry: *Medicine and rest hastened my recovery from the flu.*
❑ *VERB* **has·tens, has·tened, has·ten·ing.**
hast·y (hā′stē), *ADJECTIVE.*
1 quick; hurried: *He gave his watch a hasty glance and ran for the train.* ■ See the Synonym Study at **quick.**
2 in too big a hurry; not well thought out: *A hasty decision may cause unhappiness.*
❑ *ADJECTIVE* **hast·i·er, hast·i·est.** —**hast′i·ly,** *ADVERB.* —**hast′i·ness,** *NOUN.*
hat (hat), *NOUN.* a covering for your head, usually worn outdoors. —**hat′less,** *ADJECTIVE.*
keep something under your hat, *IDIOM.* to keep something a secret: *Keep the plans for the party under your hat!*

a	hat	ė	term	ô	order	ch	child	a in about
ā	age	i	it	oi	oil	ng	long	e in taken
ä	far	ī	ice	ou	out	sh	she	ə { i in pencil
â	care	o	hot	u	cup	th	thin	o in lemon
e	let	ō	open	ủ	put	ŦH	then	u in circus
ē	equal	ò	saw	ü	rule	zh	measure	

H

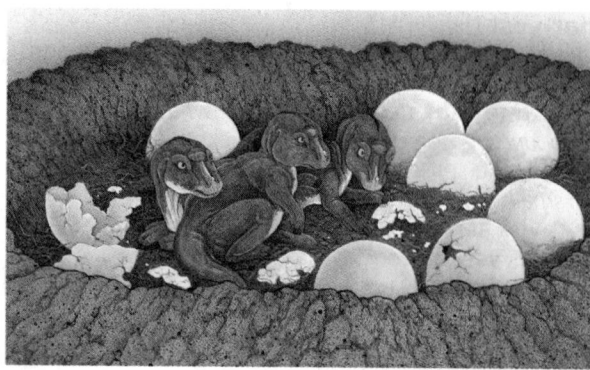

Baby dinosaurs **hatched** from eggs.

hatch¹ (hach), *VERB.*
 1 to come out of an egg: *The chickens hatched today.*
 2 to bring forth young; open: *The eggs will probably hatch tomorrow.*
 3 to plan something secretly; plot: *The spies hatched a scheme to steal government secrets.*
 ❑ *VERB* **hatch•es, hatched, hatch•ing.**

Have You Heard?

You may have heard the phrase **"Don't count your chickens before they hatch."** This means that you shouldn't assume that you will get what you want or need before you actually have it in your hand.

hatch² (hach), *NOUN.*
 1 an opening in a ship's deck or in the floor or roof of a building. Goods are loaded through the **cargo hatch.** The **escape hatch** in an airplane permits passengers to get out in an emergency.
 2 a trap door covering such an opening.
 ❑ *PLURAL* **hatch•es.**

hatch•er•y (hach′ər ē), *NOUN.* a place for hatching eggs, especially of fish and chickens. ❑ *PLURAL* **hatch•er•ies.**

hatch•et (hach′it), *NOUN.* a small ax with a handle about a foot long, for use with one hand.
 bury the hatchet, *IDIOM.* to forget an argument and become friends again: *Why don't you two bury the hatchet?*

hate (hāt),
 1 *VERB.* to not like someone or something at all; dislike very much: *Cats usually hate dogs.*
 2 *NOUN.* a very strong dislike: *to feel hate toward your enemies.*
 ❑ *VERB* **hates, hat•ed, hat•ing.**

hate•ful (hāt′fəl), *ADJECTIVE.*
 1 causing hate: *hateful behavior.*
 2 feeling hate; showing hate: *a hateful comment.*
 –hate′ful•ly, *ADVERB.* **–hate′ful•ness,** *NOUN.*

ha•tred (hā′trid), *NOUN.* a very strong dislike; hate.

hat trick, (in hockey) the act of scoring three goals in a single game by one player.

haugh•ty (hȯ′tē), *ADJECTIVE.* too proud of yourself and unfriendly toward other people: *A haughty person is often unpopular.* ❑ *ADJECTIVE* **haugh•ti•er, haugh•ti•est. –haugh′ti•ly,** *ADVERB.* **–haugh′ti•ness,** *NOUN.*

haul (hȯl),
 1 *VERB.* to pull or drag something heavy with force: *The logs were hauled to the mill by horses.*
 ■ See the Synonym Study at **pull.**
 2 *VERB.* to carry a load of something: *Trucks, trains, and ships haul freight.* ■ See the Synonym Study at **carry.**
 3 *NOUN.* the distance that a load is hauled: *Long hauls cost more than short ones.*
 4 *NOUN.* the amount won or taken at one time; catch: *The fishing boats made a good haul and came back fully loaded.*
 ❑ *VERB* **hauls, hauled, haul•ing.** ■ Another word that sounds like this is **hall. –haul′er,** *NOUN.*

haunch (hȯnch), *NOUN.*
 1 the part of the body around the hips: *The dog sat on its haunches.*
 2 the leg and loin of an animal, used for food: *We froze the haunch of venison.*
 ❑ *PLURAL* **haunch•es.**

haunt (hȯnt),
 1 *VERB.* (of a ghost) to visit a place or appear somewhere frequently: *People say ghosts haunt that old house.*
 2 *VERB.* to visit often: *He haunts the video arcade.*
 3 *NOUN.* a place often gone to or visited: *The lake was their favorite haunt on hot summer days.*
 4 *VERB.* to be often with; come often to: *Memories of his youth haunted the old man.*
 ❑ *VERB* **haunts, haunted, haunt•ing.**

have (hav), *VERB.*
 1 to hold in your hand or in your possession: *I have a stick in my hand. They have a big house and farm.*
 2 to contain or include as a part of something: *The house has several upstairs windows.*
 3 to cause somebody to do something or something to be done: *Please have the store deliver the suit.*
 4 to take; get: *Have a seat. You need to have a rest.*
 5 to eat or drink: *We always have breakfast at home.*
 6 to go through; experience: *Have a good time at the party tonight.*
 7 to allow; permit: *She won't have any noise while she is reading.*
 8 to be ill with; suffer from: *I've had a very bad headache all day.*
 9 to hold in the mind: *I have an idea.*
 10 to be related to someone: *She has three brothers.*
 11 to be in a relationship with someone: *I have three good friends.*
 12 to give birth to: *She had a girl.*
 13 to be the parent or parents of: *They have three children.*

14 Have is used as a helping verb before past participles (words like *asked, been, broken, done,* and *called*) to express completed action: *They have eaten. She had gone before. I have called him. They will have left by Sunday afternoon.*

15 Have is used as a helping verb before the word *to* and a verb to express an idea that must be done: *We have to go. They have to read several books this month.*

❑ *VERB* **has, had, hav·ing.** ■ Another word that sounds like this is **halve.**

have to do with, *IDIOM.* to relate to; deal with: *Botany has to do with the study of plants.*

Usage Note

In spoken English, **have** is sometimes confused with **of** in verb phrases because they can sound alike. People sometimes make this mistake in writing. SAY: *I would have gone if you asked me.* NOT: *I would of gone if you asked me.*

ha·ven (hā′vən), *NOUN.*
1 a place of shelter and safety: *The warm cabin was a haven from the storm.*
2 a harbor; port.

have·n't (hav′ənt), a contraction of **have not.**

Ha·wai·i (hə wī′ē), *NOUN.*
1 a state of the United States in the northern Pacific, made up of the **Hawaiian Islands.** *Abbreviation:* HI; *Capital:* Honolulu.
2 the largest of the Hawaiian islands.

State Story **Hawaii** comes from the Hawaiian name of the largest island in the group. According to legend, it was also the name of the place from which the first settlers came.

Ha·wai·ian (hə wī′yən),
1 *ADJECTIVE.* of or about Hawaii or its people.
2 *NOUN.* someone born or living in Hawaii.
3 *NOUN.* the original language of Hawaii.

hawk¹ (hok), *NOUN.* a bird of prey with a strong, hooked beak, and large curved claws. There are many kinds of hawks. **–hawk′like′,** *ADJECTIVE.*

hawk² (hok), *VERB.* to carry various goods around and offer them for sale to people that walk by: *Peddlers hawked their wares in the street.* ❑ *VERB* **hawks, hawked, hawk·ing.**

hawk¹ — about 8½ inches long

haw·thorn (ho′thôrn), *NOUN.* a thorny shrub or small tree that has clusters of fragrant white, red, or pink flowers and small, red berries.

hay (hā), *NOUN.* grass, alfalfa, or clover, cut and dried as food for cattle and horses. ■ Another word that sounds like this is **hey.**

hay fever, an allergy caused by the pollen of ragweed and other plants. Hay fever often causes sneezing, a runny nose, and itchy eyes and nose.

hay·loft (hā′lôft′), *NOUN.* a place in a stable or barn where hay is stored.

hay·ride (hā′rīd′), *NOUN.* an outing in a wagon partly filled with hay.

hay·stack (hā′stak′), *NOUN.* a large pile of hay stored outside.

haz·ard (haz′ərd),
1 *NOUN.* something that may cause damage or injury: *Mountain climbing is full of hazards.*
2 *VERB.* to take a chance with; risk: *I won't even hazard a guess.*
❑ *VERB* **haz·ards, haz·ard·ed, haz·ard·ing.**

haz·ard·ous (haz′ər dəs), *ADJECTIVE.* dangerous; risky.

haze (hāz), *NOUN.* a small amount of mist or smoke in the air: *It was hard to see clearly through the haze.*

ha·zel (hā′zəl),
1 *NOUN.* a shrub or small tree whose light brown nuts are good to eat.
2 *ADJECTIVE.* light brown.

ha·zy (hā′zē), *ADJECTIVE.*
1 misty; smoky; dim: *a hazy sky.*
2 not distinct; obscure: *It was so long ago, I have only a hazy memory of what happened.*
❑ *ADJECTIVE* **ha·zi·er, ha·zi·est. –ha′zi·ly,** *ADVERB.*

H-bomb (āch′bom′), *NOUN.* See **hydrogen bomb.**

he (hē),
1 *PRONOUN.* the boy, man, or male animal spoken about: *He works hard, but his work pays him well.*
2 *NOUN.* a male: *Is your dog a he or a she?*
3 *PRONOUN.* anyone: *He who hesitates is lost.*
❑ *PRONOUN PLURAL* **they.**

head (hed),
1 *NOUN.* the top section of the human body or the front part of most animal bodies where the eyes, ears, nose, mouth, and brain are.
2 *NOUN.* the mind; understanding; intelligence: *She can do that math problem in her head.*
3 *NOUN.* the top part of anything: *the head of a pin.*
4 *NOUN.* the front part of anything: *the head of a line, the head of a comet.*
5 *NOUN.* the part opposite the foot of something: *the head of a bed.*
6 *VERB.* to be at the front or the top of something: *to head a parade.*

a	hat	ė	term	ô	order	ch	child	⎧ a in about
ā	age	i	it	oi	oil	ng	long	⎪ e in taken
ä	far	ī	ice	ou	out	sh	she	ə⎨ i in pencil
â	care	o	hot	u	cup	th	thin	⎪ o in lemon
e	let	ō	open	ů	put	ŦH	then	⎩ u in circus
ē	equal	o	saw	ü	rule	zh	measure	

7 VERB. to move toward; face toward: *Our ship headed south.*

8 NOUN. the chief person; leader: *A principal is the head of a school.*

9 ADJECTIVE. chief; leading: *the head nurse.*

10 VERB. to be the head or chief of something; lead: *Who will head the team?*

11 NOUN. anything rounded like a head: *a head of cabbage.*

12 NOUN. the striking or cutting part of a tool or implement: *You hit the nail with the head of a hammer.*

13 NOUN. **heads,** the top side of a coin.

14 NOUN. the part of a tape recorder or disk drive that produces, detects, or erases magnetic signals on the tape or disk.
❑ PLURAL **heads;** VERB **heads, head·ed, head·ing.**

head off, IDIOM. to get in front of; check: *She tried to head off the runaway horse.*

keep your head, IDIOM. to stay calm and controlled.

lose your head, IDIOM. to get excited; lose your self-control.

over someone's head, IDIOM. too hard to understand: *Chemistry is way over my head.*

Have You Heard?

You may have heard someone say that **"Two heads are better than one."** This means that two people working together to solve a problem is better than one person working alone.

head·ache (hed′āk′), NOUN. a pain in the head.

head·band (hed′band′), NOUN. a band worn around the head.

head·dress (hed′dres′), NOUN. a covering or decoration for the head: *On special occasions members of the tribe wore headdresses made of feathers and beads.* ❑ PLURAL **head·dress·es.**

headdresses: (a) North American, (b) Chinese

head·first (hed′fėrst′), ADVERB.
1 with the head first: *He fell headfirst down the stairs.*
2 hastily; rashly.

head·ing (hed′ing), NOUN. something written or printed at the top of a page or at the beginning of a chapter or letter. A name and address at the top of a letter is a heading.

head·light (hed′līt′), NOUN. a bright light, usually one of a pair, at the front of a motor vehicle or railroad engine.

head·line (hed′līn′), NOUN. the words printed in heavy type at the top of a newspaper article telling what it is about.

head·long (hed′lòng), ADVERB or ADJECTIVE.
1 with the head first: *He took a headlong dive into the pool.*
2 in too great a rush; without stopping to think: *The boy ran headlong across the busy streets.*

head·mas·ter (hed′mas′tər), NOUN. the man in charge of a private school; principal.

head·mis·tress (hed′mis′tris), NOUN. the woman in charge of a private school; principal. ❑ PLURAL **head·mis·tress·es.**

head·on (hed′on′), ADJECTIVE or ADVERB. with the head or front first: *a head-on collision, to collide head-on.*

young gnus butting **head-on**

head·phones (hed′fōnz′), NOUN PLURAL. earphones held against both ears by a band over the head.

head·quar·ters (hed′kwôr′tərz), NOUN PLURAL or SINGULAR.
1 the place from which the chief or commanding officer of an army or police force sends out orders.
2 the main office; the center of operations or of authority: *The headquarters of the American Red Cross is in Washington.*

head·rest (hed′rest′), NOUN. a support for the head, built as part of a seat. Dentists' chairs, airplane seats, and car seats have headrests.

head start, an advantage or lead allowed to a person at the start of a race, a course of study, and so on.

head·stone (hed′stōn′), NOUN. a stone, often carved with a name and dates, set at the head of a grave.

head·strong (hed′stróng′), ADJECTIVE. foolishly determined to have your own way; hard to control or manage: *a headstrong horse.*

head·way (hed′wā′), NOUN. progress: *Science has made much headway in fighting disease.*

heal (hēl), VERB. to make or become well; return to health; cure: *The cut healed quickly. The medicine healed my sore throat quickly.* ❏ VERB **heals, healed, heal·ing.** ■ Other words that sound like this are **heel** and **he'll.**

Word Story

Heal comes from an old English word meaning "whole." The English word **health** comes from the same root. If someone is healed, or has good health, that person is whole, or sound.

health (helth), NOUN.
1 the condition of being well or not sick; freedom from illness of any kind: *Food, sleep, and exercise are important to your health.*
2 the condition of the body or mind: *That young athlete is in excellent health.*

health food, any food believed to be especially good for you. Health foods come from living things raised or prepared without chemicals.

health·ful (helth′fəl), ADJECTIVE. giving health; good for the health: *a healthful diet, healthful exercise.*

health·y (hel′thē), ADJECTIVE.
1 having good health: *a healthy baby.*
2 giving health; good for the health: *healthy diet.* ❏ ADJECTIVE **health·i·er, health·i·est.**

heap (hēp),
1 NOUN. a pile of many things thrown or lying together: *a heap of stones.*
2 VERB. to form things into a pile; gather in piles: *I heaped the dirty clothes beside the washer.*
3 NOUN. a large amount: *a heap of trouble.*
4 VERB. to give something generously or in large amounts: *to heap praise on someone.*
5 VERB. to fill something full or more than full: *to heap a plate with food.*
❏ VERB **heaps, heaped, heap·ing.**

hear (hir), VERB.
1 to take in a sound or sounds through the ear: *We couldn't hear in the back. I can hear my watch tick.*
2 to listen to: *You must hear what he has to say.*
3 to get news or information about something: *Have you heard from your sister in Trenton?*
❏ VERB **hears, heard, hear·ing.** ■ Another word that sounds like this is **here.** **–hear′er,** NOUN.

heard (hėrd), VERB.
1 the past tense of **hear:** *I heard the noise.*
2 the past participle of **hear:** *That was heard next door!*
■ Another word that sounds like this is **herd.**

hear·ing (hir′ing), NOUN.
1 the power to hear; sense by which sound is perceived: *The doctor tested my hearing.*
2 the act or process of perceiving sound, of listening, or of receiving information: *Hearing the good news made us happy.*
3 a formal or official meeting to hear facts or arguments: *The judge gave both sides a hearing.*
4 the distance that a sound can be heard: *I must stay within hearing of the telephone.*

hearing aid, a small, electronic device that makes sounds louder for people who cannot hear well.

hear·ing-im·paired (hir′ing im pârd′), ADJECTIVE. not able to hear as well as most other people can; having a weak sense of hearing.

hear·say (hir′sā′), NOUN. common talk; gossip.

heart (härt), NOUN.
1 the hollow organ inside your chest that pumps blood to the rest of your body.
2 the part of yourself that feels, loves, hates, and desires: *He has a kind heart. She knew in her heart that she was wrong.*
3 love; affection: *I gave my heart to you.*
4 courage; enthusiasm: *The losing team still had plenty of heart.*
5 the middle; center: *in the heart of the forest.*
6 the main part; most important part: *the very heart of the matter.*
7 a figure shaped somewhat like this: ♥
8 a playing card with one or more figures shaped like this.
by heart, IDIOM. by memory: *learn a poem by heart.*

Did You Know?

In one day, your **heart** pumps almost 2000 gallons of blood. If you live to be 70 you will have had about 2½ billion heartbeats.

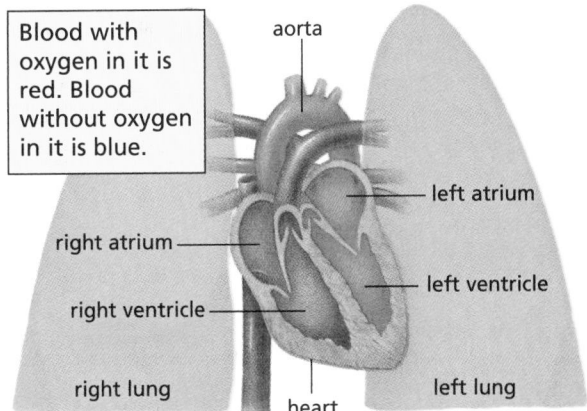

Blood with oxygen in it is red. Blood without oxygen in it is blue.

aorta
left atrium
right atrium
left ventricle
right ventricle
right lung
heart
left lung

the human **heart**

a	hat	ė	term	ô	order	ch	child	a in about
ā	age	i	it	oi	oil	ng	long	e in taken
ä	far	ī	ice	ou	out	sh	she	ə{ i in pencil
â	care	o	hot	u	cup	th	thin	o in lemon
e	let	ō	open	ù	put	ŦH	then	u in circus
ē	equal	ȯ	saw	ü	rule	zh	measure	

heart attack, a sudden failure of the heart to work properly, sometimes resulting in death.

heart·beat (härt/bēt/), NOUN. a single beat of the heart as it pumps blood. It can be felt as a pulse at the wrist.

heart·bro·ken (härt/brō/kən), ADJECTIVE. very sad; filled with sorrow or grief.

hearth (härth), NOUN. the stone or brick floor of a fireplace.

heart·less (härt/lis), ADJECTIVE. very cruel; without sympathy. —**heart/less·ly,** ADVERB. —**heart/less·ness,** NOUN.

heart·y (här/tē), ADJECTIVE.
1 warm and friendly; full of feeling; sincere: *We gave our old friends a hearty welcome.*
2 with a lot of food; nourishing: *A hearty meal satisfied her appetite.*
    ❑ ADJECTIVE **heart·i·er, heart·i·est.** —**heart/i·ly,** ADVERB. —**heart/i·ness,** NOUN.

heat (hēt),
1 NOUN. the condition of being hot; great warmth: *the heat of a fire.*
2 VERB. to make or become warm or hot: *We heated the soup. The soup is heating slowly.*
3 NOUN. hot weather: *Many people dislike the heat of summer.*
4 NOUN. the form of energy that flows from a hotter object to a colder one and causes both objects to change temperature. The sun's heat warms up the water in a swimming pool.
5 NOUN. one trial in a race: *I won the first heat, but lost the final race.*
    ❑ VERB **heats, heat·ed, heat·ing.**

heat·er (hē/tər), NOUN. a device that gives heat or warmth, such as a stove, furnace, or radiator.

heath (hēth), NOUN. open land with heather or low bushes growing on it; moor. A heath has few or no trees.

hea·then (hē/ᴛʜən),
1 NOUN. someone who does not believe in the God of the Bible; someone who is not a Christian, Jew, or Moslem; a pagan.
2 NOUN. people who are heathens.
3 ADJECTIVE. of or about heathens; not Christian, Jewish, or Muslim; pagan.
    ❑ PLURAL **hea·thens** or **hea·then.**

heath·er (heᴛʜ/ər), NOUN. a low, evergreen shrub that grows in Scotland and England.

heat·stroke (hēt/strōk/), NOUN. a sudden illness with fever and dry skin, caused by too much heat.

heave (hēv),
1 VERB. to lift something with force or effort: *She heaved the heavy box onto the truck.*
2 VERB. to lift and throw something: *We heaved the old carpet out the back door.* ■ See the Synonym Study at **throw.**

3 VERB. to give out a sigh or groan with a deep, heavy breath: *We heaved a sigh of relief when the test was over.*
4 VERB. to rise and fall alternately: *The waves heaved in the storm.*
5 NOUN. the act of heaving; throw: *With a mighty heave my friends and I pushed the boat into the water.*
    ❑ VERB **heaves, heaved, heav·ing.**

heav·en (hev/ən), NOUN.
1 (in Christian and some other religious use) the place where God and the angels are.
2 a place or condition of great happiness.
3 **heavens, a** the sky: *Clouds floated lazily in the heavens.* **b** outer space: *Thousands of stars were shining in the heavens.*

heav·en·ly (hev/ən lē), ADJECTIVE.
1 of or in heaven: *heavenly angels.*
2 very beautiful or excellent; pleasing: *It was a heavenly day for a hike in the woods.*
3 of or in the heavens: *The sun, the moon, and the stars are heavenly objects.*

heav·y (hev/ē), ADJECTIVE.
1 hard to lift or carry; weighing a lot: *The washing machine was a heavy load for us to carry.*
2 of more than usual weight for its kind: *The costume was made of heavy silk.*
3 of great amount or force; greater than usual; large: *a heavy rain, a heavy meal.*
4 serious; deep; grave: *a heavy discussion.*
    ❑ ADJECTIVE **heav·i·er, heav·i·est.** —**heav/i·ly,** ADVERB. —**heav/i·ness,** NOUN.

He·brew (hē/brü),
1 NOUN. the ancient language of the Jews, in which the Old Testament was written. Citizens of Israel speak a modern form of Hebrew.
2 NOUN. a Jew; descendant of one of the desert tribes led by Moses that settled in Palestine.
3 ADJECTIVE. Jewish.

Word Source

Hebrew is one of the oldest languages still spoken today. The following words came into English from Hebrew: **amen, Hanukkah, Jehovah, kosher, pita, rabbi, Sabbath,** and **Satan.**

hec·tare (hek/tār), NOUN. a unit of area in the metric system, equal to 10,000 square meters or about 2½ acres.

hec·tic (hek/tik), ADJECTIVE. very busy and exciting: *The children had a hectic time getting to school after the big snowstorm.* —**hec/ti·cal·ly,** ADVERB.

he'd (hēd),
1 a contraction of **he had.**
2 a contraction of **he would.**
    ■ Another word that sounds like this is **heed.**

hedge (hej), NOUN. a thick row of bushes or small trees planted as a fence.

hedge·hog (hej′hog′), NOUN. a small animal of Europe, Asia, and Africa, with spines on its back. When attacked, a hedgehog rolls up into a bristling ball.

hedgehog — about 9 inches long

heed (hēd),
1 VERB. to give careful attention to; take notice of: *Now heed what I say.*
2 NOUN. careful attention; notice: *Pay heed to her instructions.*
❑ VERB **heeds, heed·ed, heed·ing.** ■ Another word that sounds like this is **he'd. —heed′less,** ADJECTIVE.

heel (hēl),
1 NOUN. the back part of your foot, below the ankle.
2 NOUN. the part of a sock, stocking, or shoe that covers your heel.
3 NOUN. the part of a shoe or boot that is under the heel or that raises the heel: *The heels on these shoes are too high.*
4 NOUN. anything shaped, used, or placed at an end like a heel, such as an end crust of bread.
5 VERB. to follow closely at your heels: *The dog was trained to heel.*
❑ VERB **heels, heeled, heel·ing.** ■ Other words that sound like this are **heal** and **he'll.**

heif·er (hef′ər), NOUN. a young cow that has not had a calf.

height (hīt), NOUN.
1 a measurement from top to bottom; how tall or high someone or something is: *What is the height of that mountain?*
2 the quality of being tall: *She used her height to advantage in sports.*
3 a distance up; altitude: *the height of a plane in the sky.*
4 the highest point; greatest degree: *Fast driving on icy roads is the height of foolishness.*

height·en (hīt′n), VERB. to make or become stronger or greater; increase: *The wind whistling in the trees outside heightened the suspense of the ghost story.* ❑ VERB **height·ens, height·ened, height·en·ing.**

Heim·lich ma·neu·ver (hīm′lik mə nü′vər), a method used to save someone who is choking. You grasp the victim from behind, beneath the ribs, and squeeze hard with both hands clasped together. This will clear the person's windpipe.

heir (âr), NOUN. someone who has the right to somebody's property or title after the death of its owner. ■ Another word that sounds like this is **air.**

heir·ess (âr′is), NOUN. an heir who is a woman or girl. ❑ PLURAL **heir·ess·es.**

heir·loom (âr′lüm′), NOUN. a valuable possession handed down from generation to generation: *This old clock is a family heirloom.*

held (held), VERB.
1 the past tense of **hold**[1]: *He held the kitten gently.*
2 the past participle of **hold**[1]: *The swing is held by strong ropes.*

Hel·e·na (hel′ə nə), NOUN. the capital of Montana.

hel·i·cop·ter (hel′ə kop′tər), NOUN. an aircraft that flies without wings. It has large blades that spin rapidly to raise the aircraft and make it move.

Did You Know?

Helicopters cannot fly as fast or as far as airplanes, and they need more fuel. A helicopter can fly only about 600 miles before needing more fuel. But helicopters can land without a runway, which airplanes can't do.

helicopter

he·li·um (hē′lē əm), NOUN. a very light gas that will not burn, often used in hot-air balloons. Helium is a chemical element.

hell (hel), NOUN. (in Christian and some other religious use) the place where wicked people are punished after death.

he'll (hēl),
1 a contraction of **he will.**

a	hat	ė	term	ô	order	ch	child		a in about
ā	age	i	it	oi	oil	ng	long		e in taken
ä	far	ī	ice	ou	out	sh	she	ə {	i in pencil
â	care	o	hot	u	cup	th	thin		o in lemon
e	let	ō	open	ů	put	₮H	then		u in circus
ē	equal	ò	saw	ü	rule	zh	measure		

2 a contraction of **he shall.**

■ Other words that sound like this are **heal** and **heel.**

hel·lo (he lō′ *or* hə lō′), INTERJECTION. a call of greeting or surprise. We usually say "hello" when we call or answer a call on the telephone.

helm (helm), NOUN. a handle or wheel controlling the rudder, by which a ship is steered.

hel·met (hel′mit), NOUN. a covering to protect the head. Knights wore helmets as part of their armor. Soldiers wear steel helmets; football players wear plastic helmets.

help (help),

1 VERB. to give or do what is needed or useful: *My parents helped me with my homework.*

2 NOUN. the act of helping someone; aid: *I need some help with my homework.*

3 NOUN. someone or something that helps: *A sewing machine is a help in making clothes.*

4 VERB. to make something better: *This medicine will help your cough.*

5 NOUN SINGULAR *or* PLURAL. a person or group of people hired to do something: *Many companies hire temporary summer help.*

6 VERB. to keep from doing something; keep from: *I can't help yawning.*

❑ VERB **helps, helped, help·ing.** —**help′er,** NOUN.

help yourself to, IDIOM. to take for or serve yourself: *Help yourself to the milk.*

Synonym Study

Help means to do part of the work that someone else has to do: *Everyone helped get ready for the surprise party.*

Assist means to help someone do something by working with him or her: *Teachers' aides often assist teachers in the classroom.*

Aid means to give help that is needed: *A librarian aided me in my search for the book.*

help·ful (help′fəl), ADJECTIVE. giving help; useful: *Mom tries to be helpful when I have a problem.* —**help′ful·ly,** ADVERB. —**help′ful·ness,** NOUN.

help·ing (hel′ping), NOUN. the amount of food served to someone at one time.

helping verb, a verb used with another word to make a complete verb phrase. Some helping verbs are *am, be, can, do, have, may, must, shall,* and *will.* EXAMPLES: I **am** going; she **will** go; they **are** lost; **can** you help?

help·less (help′lis), ADJECTIVE. not able to help or look after yourself: *Babies are completely helpless when they are first born.* —**help′less·ly,** ADVERB. —**help′less·ness,** NOUN.

hem (hem),

1 NOUN. a border or edge on a piece of clothing, made by folding the cloth over and sewing it down.

2 VERB. to fold over and sew down the edge of cloth: *to hem a skirt.*

❑ VERB **hems, hemmed, hem·ming.**

hem·i·sphere (hem′ə sfir), NOUN.

1 a half of a sphere or globe.

2 a half of the earth's surface. North and South America are in the **Western Hemisphere;** Europe, Asia, and Africa are in the **Eastern Hemisphere.** All the countries north of the equator are in the **Northern Hemisphere;** those south of the equator are in the **Southern Hemisphere.**

hem·lock (hem′lok), NOUN.

1 an evergreen tree with flat needles, small cones, and reddish bark.

2 a poisonous plant with spotted stems, finely divided leaves, and small white flowers.

he·mo·glo·bin (hē′mə glō′bən), NOUN. a substance in the red blood cells that carries oxygen from the lungs to the tissues of the body. Hemoglobin contains iron and gives blood its red color.

hemp (hemp), NOUN. a tall plant of Asia whose tough fibers are made into heavy string, rope, and coarse cloth. It grows wild in the United States.

hen (hen), NOUN. a full-grown female bird, especially a chicken.

hence (hens), ADVERB. for this reason: *The king died, and hence his son became king.* ★ **Hence** is used mostly in formal writing and speaking.

her (her),

1 PRONOUN. *She* and *her* mean the girl or woman or female animal spoken about: *She is not here. Have you seen her? Please try to find her.*

2 ADJECTIVE. of or belonging to her; done by her: *She has left her book. The cat protects her kittens.*

her·ald (her′əld),

1 NOUN. (long ago) someone who carried messages between rulers, and made public announcements.

2 VERB. to bring news of something; announce: *The first robin heralded the coming of spring.*

❑ VERB **her·alds, her·ald·ed, her·ald·ing.**

herb (ėrb), NOUN. a plant whose leaves and stems are used for medicine and seasoning. Sage, mint, and parsley are herbs.

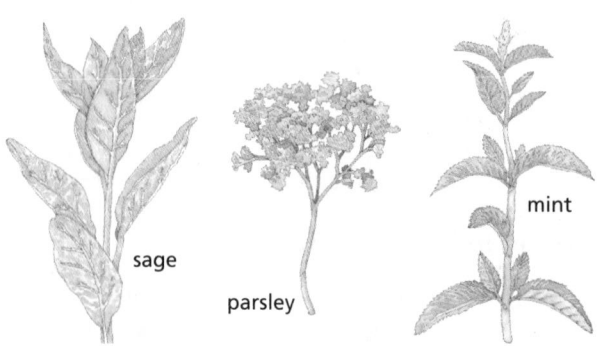

sage

parsley

mint

herbs

her·bi·cide (ėr′bə sīd *or* hėr′bə sīd), *NOUN.* a poisonous chemical used to kill weeds.

her·bi·vore (ėr′bə vôr *or* hėr′bə vôr), *NOUN.* any animal that feeds mainly on plants.

herd (hėrd),
1 *NOUN.* a group of animals of one kind, especially large animals, keeping, feeding, or moving together: *a herd of cows, a herd of elephants.*
2 *VERB.* to drive or guide a herd or group in a particular direction: *The farmer herded the cows home. We were herded through the museum.*
3 *VERB.* to tend or take care of cattle or sheep.
❑ *VERB* **herds, herd·ed, herd·ing.** ∎ Another word that sounds like this is **heard. —herd′er,** *NOUN.*

here (hir),
1 *ADVERB.* in this place; at this place or point: *We will stop here. Here the speaker paused.*
2 *ADVERB.* to this place: *Bring them here for their lesson.*
3 *NOUN.* this place: *Where do we go from here?*
4 *INTERJECTION.* an answer showing that you are present when roll is called.
5 *INTERJECTION.* an exclamation used to call attention to someone or something: *"Here! Take this away."* ∎ Another word that sounds like this is **hear.**

he·red·i·tar·y (hə red′ə ter′ē), *ADJECTIVE.* passed on or caused by heredity: *Eye color is hereditary.*

he·red·i·ty (hə red′ə tē), *NOUN.* the passing of physical or mental characteristics from one generation of living things to the next.

here's (hirz), a contraction of **here is.**

her·it·age (her′ə tij), *NOUN.* traditions, skills, and so on, that are handed down from one generation to the next; inheritance: *Freedom is our most precious heritage.*

her·mit (hėr′mit), *NOUN.* someone who goes away from other people and lives alone.

he·ro (hir′ō), *NOUN.*
1 someone admired for his or her bravery, great deeds, or noble qualities.
2 the most important person in a story, play, or poem.
3 a short form of **hero sandwich.** See **submarine sandwich.**
❑ *PLURAL* **her·oes.**

he·ro·ic (hi rō′ik), *ADJECTIVE.*
1 like a hero; very brave; great; noble: *The lifeguard made a heroic rescue.* ∎ See the Synonym Study at **brave.**
2 of or about heroes: *a heroic poem.*
—he·ro′i·cal·ly, *ADVERB.*

her·o·in (her′ō ən), *NOUN.* a poisonous, addictive, narcotic drug.

her·o·ine (her′ō ən), *NOUN.*
1 a girl or woman admired for her bravery, great deeds, or noble qualities. ★ This use of **heroine** is often considered old-fashioned. The word **hero** is now used to describe any brave person.

2 the most important female person in a story, play, or poem.

her·on (her′ən), *NOUN.* a wading bird with a long neck, a long bill, and long legs.

hero sandwich. See **submarine sandwich.**

her·ring (her′ing), *NOUN.* a small food fish of the northern Atlantic Ocean. ❑ *PLURAL* **her·rings** or **her·ring.**

hers (hėrz), *PRONOUN.* the one or ones belonging to her: *My books are new; hers are old.*

her·self (hər self′), *PRONOUN.*
1 **Herself** is used to make a statement stronger: *She herself did it. She herself brought the book.*
2 **Herself** is used instead of *she* or *her* in cases like: *She hurt herself. She did it by herself.*
3 her real or true self: *She is not herself today.*

he's (hēz),
1 a contraction of **he is.**
2 a contraction of **he has.**

hero/heroine Rosa Parks

In 1955, Rosa Parks refused to give up her seat on a bus to a white passenger in Alabama. She was arrested, and other African Americans boycotted the bus system.

hes·i·tate (hez′ə tāt), *VERB.*
1 to be unwilling to do or say something because you have not yet made up your mind: *I hesitated about taking his side in the argument until I knew the whole story.*
2 to stop for an instant; pause.
❑ *VERB* **hes·i·tates, hes·i·tat·ed, hes·i·tat·ing. —hes′i·ta′tion,** *NOUN.*

a	hat	ė	term	ô	order	ch	child	a in about
ā	age	i	it	oi	oil	ng	long	e in taken
ä	far	ī	ice	ou	out	sh	she	ə i in pencil
â	care	o	hot	u	cup	th	thin	o in lemon
e	let	ō	open	ů	put	ŦH	then	u in circus
ē	equal	ò	saw	ü	rule	zh	measure	

Hidden Animals

The animal world is tough. Animals are always on the lookout for the bigger, faster, meaner predator that wants them for lunch.

Some animals, like the impala, run away from danger. Some animals, like the porcupine and armadillo, passively protect themselves from attack. Rattlesnakes and bees fight back. The animals on this page hide in plain sight. Some hide to avoid being eaten. Others hide so that they can sneak up on their prey. Can you find them in these pictures?

The **moth** and **frog** blend in and hide against the bark. They blend in perfectly. This keeps them from being a bird's dinner.

The **dead-leaf butterfly** and **walking stick** look like parts of the plants they rest on. They try to look like dry, dead leaves and twigs instead of like tasty bugs.

Predators have camouflage too. Lions are the color of the dry grass they lurk in, waiting for prey. The polar bear looks like another drift of snow as he looks for an unlucky seal or bird.

The **snowshoe hare** and the **chameleon** change their camouflage. The snowshoe hare is brown in the summer to blend into the woods, and white in the winter to hide against the snow. The chameleon changes much faster. It is green against leaves but turns brown when against bark or on the ground.

hex·a·gon (hek′sə gon), NOUN. a figure having six angles and six sides.

hey (hā), INTERJECTION. a sound made to attract attention, express surprise or other feeling, or ask a question: *"Hey! Stop!" "Hey? What did you say?"*
■ Another word that sounds like this is **hay.**

hi (hī), INTERJECTION. a call of greeting; hello.
■ Another word that sounds like this is **high.**

HI, an abbreviation of **Hawaii.**

hi·ber·nate (hī′bər nāt), VERB. to spend all winter sleeping or resting, such as woodchucks and some other wild animals do. □ VERB **hi·ber·nates, hi·ber·nat·ed, hi·ber·nat·ing. —hi′ber·na′tion,** NOUN.

Bears **hibernate** in the winter.

hic·cup (hik′up),
1 NOUN. a sudden, repeated intake of breath with a muffled clicking sound.
2 NOUN. **the hiccups,** a condition of having one hiccup after another.
3 VERB. to have the hiccups.
□ VERB **hic·cups, hic·cupped, hic·cup·ping.**

hick·or·y (hik′ər ē), NOUN. a North American tree with nuts that are good to eat. Its hard wood is used to make handles for axes, hammers, and so on. □ PLURAL **hick·or·ies.**

hid (hid), VERB.
1 the past tense of **hide¹**: *The dog hid the bone.*
2 a past participle of **hide¹**: *They have hid the money in a safe place.*

Hi·dal·go (ē ᴛʜäl′gō *or* hi dal′gō), NOUN. a state in central Mexico.

hid·den (hid′n),
1 ADJECTIVE. put or kept out of sight; secret: *The story is about hidden treasure.*
2 VERB. a past participle of **hide¹**: *Where have you hidden the candy?*

hide¹ (hīd), VERB.
1 to put or keep something out of sight: *Hide it where no one else can find it.*
2 to cover something up: *Clouds hide the sun.*

3 to keep something secret: *I tried to hide my disappointment.*
□ VERB **hides, hid, hid·den** or **hid, hid·ing.**

hide² (hīd), NOUN. an animal's skin. Leather is made from hide.

hide-and-seek (hīd′n sēk′), NOUN. a game in which one player tries to find the other players who have hidden.

hid·e·ous (hid′ē əs), ADJECTIVE. very ugly; frightful; horrible: *hideous monsters.* **—hid′e·ous·ly,** ADVERB.

hide·out (hīd′out′), NOUN. a place for hiding: *The spy had a hideout on the border.*

high (hī),
1 ADJECTIVE. tall: *The mountain is over 20,000 feet high.*
2 ADJECTIVE. up above the ground: *We saw an airplane high in the air.*
3 ADJECTIVE. greater, stronger, or better than usual; great: *High winds tore the roof off our barn.*
4 ADJECTIVE. not low in pitch; sharp; shrill: *A soprano can sing high notes.*
5 ADJECTIVE. above other people in rank or importance: *She is a high government official.*
6 ADJECTIVE. happily excited: *high spirits.*
7 ADVERB. at or to a high point, place, amount, pitch, and so on: *The price of gas has gone too high.*
8 NOUN. a high point, level, or position: *Food prices reached a new high last month.*
9 NOUN. an arrangement of gears to give a motor vehicle its greatest speed.
■ Another word that sounds like this is **hi.**

high jump, a contest to determine how high each contestant can jump over a horizontal bar set at higher and higher levels. **—high jumper.**

high jump

high·land (hī′lənd), NOUN. a country or region that is higher and hillier than the neighboring country.

high·ly (hī′lē), ADVERB.
1 in a high degree; very; very much: *highly recommended.* ■ See the Synonym Study at **very.**
2 very favorably: *He spoke highly of his best friend.*
3 at a high rate: *She is highly paid.*

High·ness (hī′nis), *NOUN.* a title of honor given to members of royal families: *Address the prince as "Your Highness."* ❏ *PLURAL* **High·ness·es.**

high-rise (hī′rīz′),
1 *ADJECTIVE.* having many stories; very tall: *a high-rise apartment building.*
2 *NOUN.* a building having many stories.

high school, a school attended after middle school or junior high school.

high seas, the open ocean. The high seas are outside the authority of any country.

high-strung (hī′strung′), *ADJECTIVE.* very nervous; easily excited: *We are always quiet around our uncle, because he is very high strung.*

high-tech (hī′tek′), *ADJECTIVE.* made or working by advanced modern technology such as lasers, computer chips, or genetic engineering; very complex and modern in methods and materials: *high-tech toys, high-tech virtual reality systems.*

high tide, the time when the ocean comes up highest on the shore. High tides occur twice daily.

high·way (hī′wā′), *NOUN.* a main public road.

hi·jack (hī′jak′), *VERB.* to take over a vehicle or aircraft by force from the driver or pilot. ❏ *VERB* **hi·jacks, hi·jacked, hi·jack·ing.** —**hi′jack′er,** *NOUN.*

hike (hīk),
1 *VERB.* to take a long walk; tramp; march: *We hiked five miles today.*
2 *NOUN.* a long walk; tramp or march: *It was a four-mile hike through the forest to the camp.* ❏ *VERB* **hikes, hiked, hik·ing.** —**hik′er,** *NOUN.*

hi·lar·i·ous (hə lâr′ē əs), *ADJECTIVE.* very funny; noisy and cheerful: *We saw a hilarious movie.*
■ See the Synonym Study at **funny.**

hill (hil), *NOUN.*
1 a high piece of ground, not as big as a mountain.
2 a little heap or pile: *Ants and moles make hills.*

hill·side (hil′sīd′), *NOUN.* the side of a hill.

hill·y (hil′ē), *ADJECTIVE.* having many hills: *hilly country.* ❏ *ADJECTIVE* **hill·i·er, hill·i·est.**

hilt (hilt), *NOUN.* the handle of a sword or dagger.

him (him), *PRONOUN. He* and *him* mean the boy or man or male animal spoken about: *Take him home. Give him a drink. Go to him.* ■ Another word that sounds like this is **hymn.**

Him·a·la·yas (him′ə lā′əz *or* hə mä′lyəz), *NOUN PLURAL.* a group of high mountains in southern Asia. Several of the highest mountains in the world are in the Himalayas.

him·self (him self′ *or* im self′), *PRONOUN.*
1 **Himself** is used to make a statement stronger: *He himself did it. Did you see Roy himself?*
2 **Himself** is used instead of *he* or *him* in cases like: *He cut himself. He asked himself what he really wanted. He kept the toy for himself.*
3 his real or true self: *He feels like himself again.*

hind (hīnd), *ADJECTIVE.* back; rear: *a dog's hind legs.*

Hin·du (hin′dü),
1 *NOUN.* someone who believes in Hinduism.
2 *ADJECTIVE.* of or about the Hindus, their language, or their religion.
❏ *PLURAL* **Hin·dus.**

Hin·du·ism (hin′dü iz′əm), *NOUN.* the religion and social system of the Hindus.

hinge (hinj), *NOUN.* a joint on which a door, gate, cover, or lid moves back and forth so that it can open and close.

hinged (hinjd), *ADJECTIVE.* opening and closing with or as if with a hinge.

hint (hint),
1 *NOUN.* a clue that helps you know or figure out something: *Don't give me any hints; I want to solve the riddle on my own.*
2 *VERB.* to make something known in an indirect way: *She hinted that she was tired by yawning.*
❏ *VERB* **hints, hint·ed, hint·ing.**

hip (hip), *NOUN.*
1 the part that sticks out on each side of the body below a person's waist where the leg joins the body.
2 a similar part in animals, where the hind leg joins the body.

hip·po (hip′ō), *NOUN.* a short form of **hippopotamus.** ❏ *PLURAL* **hip·pos.**

hip·po·pot·a·mus (hip′ə pot′ə məs), *NOUN.* a huge, thick-skinned, almost hairless animal found near the rivers of Africa; hippo. Hippopotamuses feed on plants and can stay underwater for a long time. ❏ *PLURAL* **hip·po·pot·a·mus·es** *or* **hip·po·pot·a·mi** (hip′ə pot′ə mī).

hippopotamus — about 5 feet high at the shoulder

hire (hīr),
1 *VERB.* to pay for the use of something or the work or services of someone: *She hired a car for the trip.*

a	hat	ė	term	ô	order	ch	child	⎧ a in about
ā	age	i	it	oi	oil	ng	long	e in taken
ä	far	ī	ice	ou	out	sh	she	ə ⎨ i in pencil
â	care	o	hot	u	cup	th	thin	o in lemon
e	let	ō	open	ů	put	ŦH	then	⎩ u in circus
ē	equal	ò	saw	ü	rule	zh	measure	

2 NOUN. payment for the use of a thing or the work or services of a person: *Are these boats for hire?* ❑ VERB **hires, hired, hir·ing.**

his (hiz),
1 ADJECTIVE. of or belonging to him; done by him: *His name is Bill. This is his book. He has finished his work.*
2 PRONOUN. the one or ones belonging to him: *My books are new; his are old.*

His·pan·ic (hi span′ik),
1 ADJECTIVE. Spanish.
2 ADJECTIVE. Latin American.
3 NOUN. someone of Spanish-speaking descent.

hiss (his),
1 VERB. to make a sound like *ss,* or like a drop of water on a hot stove. Geese and snakes hiss.
2 NOUN. a sound like *ss: Hisses were heard from many who disliked what the speaker was saying.*
3 VERB. to show disapproval of by hissing: *The audience hissed the boring play.*
❑ VERB **hiss·es, hissed, hiss·ing;** PLURAL **hiss·es.**

his·to·ri·an (hi stôr′ē ən), NOUN. someone who writes about history; expert in history.

his·to·ric (hi stôr′ik), ADJECTIVE. famous or important in history: *Plymouth Rock and Bunker Hill are historic sites. Our town gives tours of our historic houses.*

his·to·ri·cal (hi stôr′ə kəl), ADJECTIVE.
1 of or about history: *historical documents.*
2 based on history: *He likes historical novels.*
3 known to be real or true; in history, not in legend: *Is the story of King Arthur myth or historical fact.*
—his·to′ri·cal·ly, ADVERB.

his·to·ry (his′tər ē), NOUN.
1 the story or record of important past events connected with a person or a nation: *We studied the history of Mexico.*
2 the branch of knowledge that deals with past events: *My favorite subject in school is history.*
3 all past events considered together; course of human affairs: *the lessons of history.*
❑ PLURAL **his·tor·ies.**

hit (hit),
1 VERB. to give a blow to; strike; knock: *I hit the ball with a bat. The ball hit the window.*
2 NOUN. a blow; stroke: *I drove the stake into the ground with one hit.*
3 VERB. to get to what is aimed at: *The second arrow hit the bull's-eye.*
4 NOUN. the act of striking what is aimed at: *a direct hit.*
5 NOUN. a successful performance: *The new play is the hit of the season.*
6 NOUN. the act of successfully hitting a baseball so that the batter gets at least to first base.
❑ VERB **hits, hit, hit·ting. —hit′ter,** NOUN.

hit it off, IDIOM. to get along well together: *The two friends hit it off from the start.*

hitch (hich),
1 VERB. to tie or fasten something with a hook, ring, rope, or strap: *She hitched her horse to a post.*
2 VERB. to move or pull something with a jerk: *He hitched his chair nearer to the fire.*
3 NOUN. a short, sudden pull or jerk: *He gave his pants a hitch.*
4 NOUN. something that causes a delay or makes things more difficult: *A hitch in their plans made them miss the train.*
❑ VERB **hitch·es, hitched, hitch·ing;** PLURAL **hitch·es.**
get hitched, IDIOM. (informal) to get married.

hitch·hike (hich′hīk′), VERB. to travel by asking for free rides from passing motor vehicles. ❑ VERB **hitch·hikes, hitch·hiked, hitch·hik·ing. —hitch′hik′er,** NOUN.

HIV, the virus that causes AIDS.

hive (hīv), NOUN.
1 See **beehive** (definition 1).
2 a large number of bees that make a honeycomb and raise their young: *The whole hive was busy.*

hives (hīvz), NOUN PLURAL. an allergic reaction in which the skin itches and becomes red.

hoard (hôrd),
1 VERB. to save something up and store it away: *The squirrel hoarded nuts for the winter.*
2 NOUN. something that is saved and stored away: *The squirrel kept its hoard of nuts in a tree.*
❑ VERB **hoards, hoard·ed, hoard·ing.** ■ Another word that sounds like this is **horde. —hoard′er,** NOUN.

hoarse (hôrs), ADJECTIVE.
1 sounding rough and deep: *the hoarse sound of a frog.*
2 having a rough voice: *His cold made him hoarse.*
❑ ADJECTIVE **hoars·er, hoars·est.** ■ Another word that sounds like this is **horse. —hoarse′ly,** ADVERB. **—hoarse′ness,** NOUN.

hoax (hōks), NOUN. a mischievous trick, especially a made-up story passed off as true: *The report of men from Mars was a hoax.* ❑ PLURAL **hoax·es.**

hob·ble (hob′əl), VERB. to walk awkwardly; limp: *The hiker hobbled along with a sprained ankle.*
❑ VERB **hob·bles, hob·bled, hob·bling.**

hob·by (hob′ē), NOUN. something a person likes to do in his or her free time; pastime: *Our teacher's hobby is gardening.* ■ See the Synonym Study at **play.** ❑ PLURAL **hob·bies.**

hock·ey (hok′ē), NOUN. a game played by two teams on ice, a field, pavement, and so on. The players hit a puck or ball with curved sticks to drive it into the other team's goal.

hoe (hō),
1 NOUN. a tool with a thin blade set across the end of a long handle, used for loosening soil or cutting small weeds.
2 VERB. to loosen, dig, or cut with a hoe.
❑ PLURAL **hoes;** VERB **hoes, hoed, hoe·ing.**

hog (hog),
1 *NOUN.* a full-grown pig, raised for food.
2 *VERB.* (informal) to take more than your share of something: *Don't hog the cookies!*
❑ *VERB* **hogs, hogged, hog·ging.**

ho·gan (hō'gän'), *NOUN.* a dwelling used by the Navaho Indians of North America. Hogans are built with logs and covered with earth.

a Navaho **hogan**

hog·gish (hog'ish), *ADJECTIVE.*
1 very selfish or greedy.
2 dirty, filthy.

hoist (hoist), *VERB.* to raise or lift something up, often with ropes and pulleys: *We hoisted the flag up the pole.* ❑ *VERB* **hoists, hoist·ed, hoist·ing.**

hold¹ (hōld),
1 *VERB.* to pick up and keep something in your hands or arms: *Please hold my hat. Hold my watch while I play.* ■ See the Synonym Study at **keep.**
2 *NOUN.* a grasp or grip: *Take a good hold of this rope.*
3 *NOUN.* something to hold onto: *The face of the cliff had enough holds for a good climber.*
4 *VERB.* to keep something in a place or position; support: *Hold the dish level.*
5 *VERB.* to stay strong or secure; not break, loosen, or give way: *The dike held during the flood.*
6 *VERB.* to keep someone from leaving: *Police held the burglary suspect for questioning.*
7 *VERB.* to have space inside for something; contain: *This theater holds 500 people.*
8 *VERB.* to have: *We held a meeting of the club last week. She held the office of mayor for four years.*
❑ *VERB* **holds, held, hold·ing.**

get hold of, *IDIOM.* to contact or reach, especially by telephone: *I can't get hold of anyone in my class.*

hold out, *IDIOM.* to continue; last: *The food will only hold out two days more.*

hold up, *IDIOM.*
1 to keep from falling; support: *The roof is held up by pillars.*
2 to stop; delay: *I don't want to hold you up if you're in a hurry.*

3 to stop by force and rob: *Bandits held up the stagecoach when it was three miles out of town.*

hold² (hōld), *NOUN.* the space inside a ship or airplane where the cargo is carried.

hold·er (hōl'dər), *NOUN.* something that you use to hold onto something else with. Pads of cloth are used as holders for lifting hot dishes.

hold·ing (hōl'ding), *NOUN.* a piece of land or property: *The government has vast holdings in the West that are used as national parks.*

hold·up (hōld'up'), *NOUN.*
1 the act of robbing: *a bank holdup.*
2 a delay: *I was late because of a holdup in traffic.*

hole (hōl), *NOUN.*
1 an open place: *There's a hole in my sock.*
2 a hollow place in something solid: *Rabbits dig holes in the ground to live in.*
3 a small, round, hollow place on a golf course, into which a golf ball is hit.
4 one of the parts of a golf course.
■ Another word that sounds like this is **whole.**

hol·i·day (hol'ə dā), *NOUN.* a day when you do not go to work; a day for having fun or celebrating: *The Fourth of July is a national holiday in the United States.*

ho·li·ness (hō'lē nis), *NOUN.*
1 the quality of being holy or sacred.
2 **Holiness,** a title used in speaking to or of the pope. The pope is addressed as "Your Holiness" and spoken of as "His Holiness."

Hol·land (hol'ənd), *NOUN.* another name for the **Netherlands. –Hol'land·er,** *NOUN.*

hol·ler (hol'ər),
1 *VERB.* to cry or shout loudly: *"Come quick," she hollered from the yard.*
2 *NOUN.* a loud cry or shout: *She gave a holler.*
❑ *VERB* **hol·lers, hol·lered, hol·ler·ing.**

hol·low (hol'ō),
1 *ADJECTIVE.* having nothing, or only air, inside; empty; with a hole inside; not solid: *A tube or pipe is hollow.* ■ See the Synonym Study at **empty.**
2 *NOUN.* a hollow place; hole: *Water collected in the hollows in the road.*
3 *VERB.* to take out the inside parts: *We hollowed out the pumpkin to make a jack-o'-lantern.*
4 *NOUN.* a low place between hills; valley: *They built their house in a hollow.*
❑ *VERB* **hol·lows, hol·lowed, hol·low·ing.**

hol·ly (hol'ē), *NOUN.* an evergreen bush or tree that has bright red berries and shiny green leaves with sharp points. ❑ *PLURAL* **hol·lies.**

a hat	ė term	ô order	ch child	a in about
ā age	i it	oi oil	ng long	e in taken
ä far	ī ice	ou out	sh she	ə i in pencil
â care	o hot	u cup	th thin	o in lemon
e let	ō open	ů put	ᴛʜ then	u in circus
ē equal	ȯ saw	ü rule	zh measure	

hol·ly·hock (hol′ē hok), NOUN. a tall plant grown in gardens for its clusters of large, showy flowers of various colors.

hol·o·caust (hol′ə kȯst), NOUN.
1 complete destruction by fire, especially of animals or human beings.
2 **the Holocaust,** the systematic killing by the Nazis of about six million European Jews during World War II.

hol·o·gram (hol′ə gram or hō′lə gram), NOUN. a kind of photograph showing an object in three dimensions. A hologram shows an image that appears to be solid.

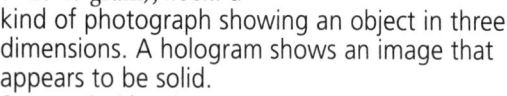

hollyhock

hol·ster (hōl′stər), NOUN. a leather case for a pistol, worn on a belt or under the shoulder.

ho·ly (hō′lē), ADJECTIVE.
1 given or belonging to God; set apart for God's service: *the Holy Bible.*
2 leading a life like a saint: *a holy man.*
❑ ADJECTIVE **ho·li·er, ho·li·est.** ■ Another word that sounds like this is **wholly.**

home (hōm),
1 NOUN. the place where a person or family lives; your own house: *Her home is at 25 South Street.*
2 NOUN. the place where you were born or brought up; your town or country: *His home is Texas.*
3 NOUN. the place where something is specially common: *Africa is the home of lions.*
4 NOUN. a place where people who are homeless, poor, old, sick, or blind may live and be looked after: *Grandpa lives in a home for the aged.*
5 ADJECTIVE. of or for your home; domestic: *I really enjoy home cooking.*
6 ADJECTIVE. (in sports) played in a team's home town: *a home game.*
7 ADVERB. at or to your home or country: *I want to go home.*
8 NOUN. the goal in many games.
9 ADVERB. to the place or thing aimed at: *The spear struck home. I drove the nail home.*
−**home′less,** ADJECTIVE. −**home′like′,** ADJECTIVE.
at home, IDIOM. at ease; comfortable: *Feel at home.*

home·land (hōm′land′), NOUN. the country that is someone's home; native land.

home·ly (hōm′lē), ADJECTIVE. not good-looking: *a homely face.* ❑ ADJECTIVE **home·li·er, home·li·est.**

home·made (hōm′mād′), ADJECTIVE. made at home: *homemade bread.*

home page, the opening page of a web site; web site.

home plate, a hard rubber slab that a baseball player stands beside to bat the ball. A player must touch the other three bases and then home plate in order to score a run.

hom·er (hō′mər), NOUN. a home run in baseball.

home·room (hōm′rüm′), NOUN. a classroom where members of a class meet to do such things as answer roll call and hear announcements.

home run, a hit in baseball that allows the batter to run all the bases and score a run.

home·sick (hōm′sik′), ADJECTIVE. very sad because you are far away from home.

home·spun (hōm′spun′), NOUN. a cloth made of yarn spun at home.

home·stead (hōm′sted′), NOUN.
1 a house with its land and other buildings; farm with its buildings.
2 public land granted to a settler by the United States government.

home·ward (hōm′wərd), ADVERB or ADJECTIVE. toward home: *We turned homeward.*

home·work (hōm′wėrk′), NOUN. a lesson to be studied or worked on outside the classroom.

hom·i·cide (hom′ə sīd), NOUN. the act of killing a human being.

ho·mog·e·nize (hə moj′ə nīz), VERB. to mix something completely so that all parts of it are the same: *homogenized milk.* ❑ VERB **ho·mog·e·niz·es, ho·mog·e·nized, ho·mog·e·niz·ing.**

hom·o·graph (hom′ə graf), NOUN. a word having the same spelling as another word, but a different history and meaning. *Bass* (bas), meaning "a kind of fish," and *bass* (bās), meaning "a male singing voice," are homographs. They may or may not be pronounced the same.

hom·o·nym (hom′ə nim), NOUN. a word having the same pronunciation and often the same spelling as another word. Homonyms have different histories and meanings. *Mail,* meaning "letters," *mail,* meaning "armor," and *male,* meaning "masculine," are homonyms.

hom·o·phone (hom′ə fōn), NOUN. a word having the same sound as another, but a different spelling, history, and meaning. *Ate* and *eight* are homophones.

Hon·dur·as (hon dur′əs), NOUN. a country in Central America. −**Hon·dur′an,** ADJECTIVE or NOUN.

hon·est (on′ist), ADJECTIVE.
1 telling the truth; truthful; not lying, cheating, or stealing: *They are honest people.*
2 gotten without lying, cheating, or stealing: *They made an honest profit. He lived an honest life.*
3 not hiding your real nature; frank; open: *She is honest about her feelings.*
−**hon′est·ly,** ADVERB.

hon·es·ty (on′ə stē), *NOUN.* the quality of being honest and fair; doing and saying what is right and true: *She shows honesty in her work.*

hon·ey (hun′ē), *NOUN.*
1 a thick, sweet, yellow or golden liquid that is good to eat. Bees make honey out of the drops of juice they collect from flowers.
2 darling; dear: *"Is that you, honey?" she called.*
❑ *PLURAL* **hon·eys.**

hon·ey·bee (hun′ē bē′), *NOUN.* a bee that makes honey. ❑ *PLURAL* **hon·ey·bees.**

hon·ey·comb
(hun′ē kōm′), *NOUN.* a structure of wax made up of rows of six-sided cells. It is made by honeybees to store their honey, pollen, and eggs.

hon·ey·moon
(hun′ē mün′),
1 *NOUN.* a holiday spent together by a newly married couple.
2 *VERB.* to spend or have a honeymoon.

honeycomb

❑ *VERB* **hon·ey·moons, hon·ey·mooned, hon·ey·moon·ing. –hon′ey·moon′er,** *NOUN.*

hon·ey·suck·le (hun′ē suk′əl), *NOUN.* a climbing plant with fragrant white, yellow, or red flowers.

honk (hongk),
1 *NOUN.* the cry of a wild goose.
2 *NOUN.* a sound like the blare of a trumpet: *the honk of a car horn.*
3 *VERB.* to make this sound: *We honked as we drove by.*
❑ *VERB* **honks, honked, honk·ing.**

Hon·o·lu·lu (hon′ə lü′lü), *NOUN.* the capital of Hawaii.

hon·or (on′ər),
1 *NOUN.* a sense of knowing what is right or proper and always doing it: *A person of honor always keeps his or her promises.*
2 *NOUN.* respect and praise from other people: *My grandfather had the honor of being elected a judge.*
3 *VERB.* to show respect to someone: *We honor our country's dead soldiers on Memorial Day.*
4 *NOUN.* a special right to do something; privilege: *The mayor had the honor of introducing the governor before the parade started.*
5 *NOUN.* **Honor,** a title of respect used in speaking to a judge, mayor, governor, or senator: *Please join us, your Honor.*
❑ *VERB* **hon·ors, hon·ored, hon·or·ing.**
–hon′or·a·ble, *ADJECTIVE.*

hon·or·ar·y (on′ə rer′ē), *ADJECTIVE.* given as an honor to someone who has done great or important things: *The university awarded honorary degrees to three famous scientists.*

hood (húd), *NOUN.*
1 a soft, cloth covering for the head and neck, either separate or as part of a coat.
2 anything like a hood in shape or use.
3 a hinged metal covering over the engine of a car.

hood·lum (húd′ləm), *NOUN.* a criminal or gangster.

hoof (húf), *NOUN.* the hard part of the foot of horses, cattle, sheep, pigs, and some other animals. ❑ *PLURAL* **hoofs** or **hooves.**

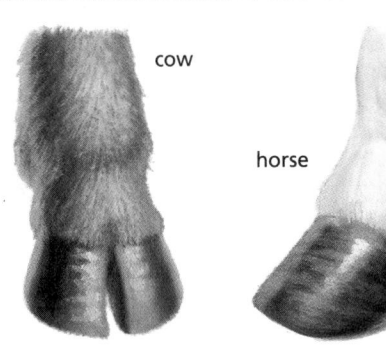
cow

horse

hoof

hook (húk),
1 *NOUN.* a curved piece of metal, wood, or plastic used to hang things on: *Hang your coat on that hook.*
2 *VERB.* to catch fish with a hook: *I hooked three trout when I went fishing yesterday.*
3 *VERB.* to fasten with a hook or hooks: *Will you hook my dress for me?*
4 *NOUN.* a curved piece of wire, usually with a barb at the end, for catching fish.
5 *NOUN.* anything curved or bent like a hook: *His nose has a slight hook.*
❑ *VERB* **hooks, hooked, hook·ing.**

hook up, *IDIOM.* to connect a piece of electronic equipment to another component.

hooked (húkt), *ADJECTIVE.* curved or bent like a hook.

hoop (húp *or* hüp), *NOUN.*
1 a ring or flat band in the form of a circle: *a hoop for holding embroidery, a basketball hoop.*
2 a large wooden, iron, or plastic ring used as a toy, especially for spinning around the body.
3 **hoops,** (informal) basketball.
■ Another word that can sound like this is **whoop.**

hoo·ray (hú rā′), *INTERJECTION or NOUN.* a shout of joy, approval, and so on: *"Hooray!" they shouted as the team scored again. Give a hooray for the team!*

hoot (hüt),
1 *NOUN.* the sound that an owl makes.
2 *VERB.* to make this sound or one like it.
3 *NOUN.* a shout to show disapproval or scorn.

a	hat	ė	term	ô	order
ā	age	i	it	oi	oil
ä	far	ī	ice	ou	out
â	care	o	hot	u	cup
e	let	ō	open	ù	put
ē	equal	ò	saw	ü	rule

ch	child
ng	long
sh	she
th	thin
ŦH	then
zh	measure

ə ⎧ a in about
  ⎪ e in taken
  ⎨ i in pencil
  ⎪ o in lemon
  ⎩ u in circus

4 *VERB.* to shout disapproval of or scorn for: *The audience hooted the speaker's plan.*
❑ *VERB* **hoots, hoot·ed, hoot·ing.**

hooves (hůvz), *NOUN.* a plural of **hoof.**

hop (hop),
1 *VERB.* to jump, or move by jumping, on one foot: *How far can you hop on your right foot?* ■ See the Synonym Study at **jump.**
2 *VERB.* to jump, or move by jumping, with both or all feet at once: *The kangaroo hopped away.*
3 *VERB.* to jump over: *I hopped the ditch and ran home.*
4 *NOUN.* a jump or leap: *I came up each step with a hop.*
❑ *VERB* **hops, hopped, hop·ping.**

hope (hōp),
1 *NOUN.* a feeling that what you want to happen will happen: *Her encouragement gave me hope.*
2 *VERB.* to wish for something and expect it to happen: *I hope to do well in school this year.*
3 *NOUN.* something hoped for: *It is my hope that we win.*
4 *NOUN.* a cause of hope: *You are our only hope for winning the race.*
❑ *VERB* **hopes, hoped, hop·ing.**

hope·ful (hōp′fəl), *ADJECTIVE.*
1 feeling or showing hope; expecting to receive what you want: *We were hopeful that the weather would improve.*
2 causing or giving hope: *The news from my doctor was hopeful.*

hope·ful·ly (hōp′fə lē), *ADVERB.*
1 in a hopeful manner: *He smiled hopefully at the judges.*
2 it is hoped that: *Hopefully, business will improve soon.*

hope·less (hōp′lis), *ADJECTIVE.*
1 feeling no hope: *Our attempts to get help failed so often that we became hopeless.*
2 giving no hope: *He has a hopeless illness.*
—**hope′less·ly,** *ADVERB.* —**hope′less·ness,** *NOUN.*

Ho·pi (hō′pē), *NOUN.* a member of a tribe of American Indians living in northern Arizona.
❑ *PLURAL* **Ho·pi** or **Ho·pis.**

hop·scotch (hop′skoch′), *NOUN.* a game in which the players hop over lines drawn on the ground.

horde (hôrd), *NOUN.* a multitude; crowd; swarm: *Hordes of grasshoppers destroyed the crops.*
■ Another word that sounds like this is **hoard.**

ho·ri·zon (hə rī′zn), *NOUN.* the line where earth and sky seem to meet. You cannot see beyond the horizon.

ho·ri·zon·tal (hôr′ə zon′tl), *ADJECTIVE.* parallel to the horizon; at right angles to a vertical line; level and flat: *A table top is a horizontal surface.*
—**ho′ri·zon′tal·ly,** *ADVERB.*

horizontal axis, the main line that runs from left to right in a graph. An axis has points separated by equal spaces marked on it.

hor·mone (hôr′mōn), *NOUN.* a substance formed in certain glands, which enters the bloodstream and affects or controls the activity of some organ or tissue. —**hor·mo′nal,** *ADJECTIVE.*

horn (hôrn), *NOUN.*
1 a hard, hollow, permanent growth on the heads of cattle, sheep, goats, and some other animals. Horns are usually curved and pointed.
2 the substance or material of horns. A person's fingernails, the beaks of birds, the hoofs of horses, and tortoise shells are all made of horn.
3 a musical instrument that you play by blowing into it. It was once made of horn, but now it is made of brass or other metal.
4 something that makes a signal of danger: *He honked his horn to warn us that he was coming.*

horned toad (hôrnd′ tōd′), a small lizard with a broad, flat body, short tail, and many hornlike spines.

horned toad — between 2½ and 6½ inches long

hor·net (hôr′nit), *NOUN.* a large insect that can give a very painful sting.

hor·ri·ble (hôr′ə bəl), *ADJECTIVE.*
1 causing horror; frightful; shocking: *AIDS is a horrible disease.*
2 extremely unpleasant: *What is that horrible smell?*
■ See the Synonym Study at **terrible.**
—**hor′ri·bly,** *ADVERB.*

hor·rid (hôr′id), *ADJECTIVE.*
1 very unpleasant: *What a horrid color!* ■ See the Synonym Study at **terrible.**
2 causing great fear; frightful: *A horrid fire!*

hor·ri·fy (hôr′ə fī), *VERB.*
1 to cause someone to feel horror: *The child was horrified by the large, snarling dog.* ■ See the Synonym Study at **scare.**
2 to shock someone very much: *We were horrified by such rude behavior.*
❑ *VERB* **hor·ri·fies, hor·ri·fied, hor·ri·fy·ing.**

hor·ror (hôr′ər), *NOUN.*
1 a feeling of very great fear. ■ See the Synonym Study at **fear.**

2 a very strong dislike: *I have a horror of guns.*

3 something that causes great fear: *For the soldier, war was a horror.*

horse (hôrs), NOUN.

1 a large, four-legged animal with hoofs, and a mane and tail of long hair. Horses are used for riding and for carrying and pulling loads.

2 a padded piece of gymnasium equipment, supported by legs. It is used in jumping exercises and for gymnastics.
■ Another word that sounds like this is **hoarse.**

horse around, IDIOM. to fool around; get into mischief. ❏ VERB **hors·es, horsed, hors·ing.**

Have You Heard?

You may have heard someone say "You can lead a horse to water, but you can't make him drink." This means that you can give someone an opportunity, but you can't make them take advantage of it.

horse·back (hôrs′bak′),

1 NOUN. the back of a horse: *We went to the mountains on horseback.*

2 ADVERB. on the back of a horse: *to ride horseback.*

horse·fly (hôrs′flī′), NOUN. a large fly that bites people and animals, especially horses, to suck their blood. ❏ PLURAL **horse·flies.**

horse·hair (hôrs′hâr′), NOUN. hair from the mane or tail of a horse.

horse·man (hôrs′mən), NOUN.

1 someone who rides on horseback: *Three horsemen galloped down the road.*

2 someone who is skilled in riding or managing horses: *The horse show was put on by a group of horsemen.*
❏ PLURAL **horse·men.**

horse·play (hôrs′plā′), NOUN. rough, boisterous fun: *Stop the horseplay before you ruin the sofa.*

horse·pow·er
(hôrs′pou′ər), NOUN. a measure of the power of an engine. One horsepower is the power to lift 550 pounds one foot in one second.

horse·shoe (hôrsh′shü′), NOUN.

1 a flat piece of metal shaped like a U, nailed to the bottom of a horse's hoof to protect it.

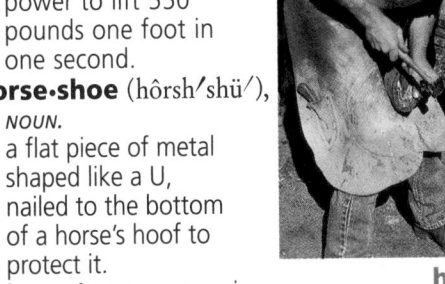
horseshoe

2 horseshoes, a game in which the players try to throw horseshoes against or near a stake 40 feet away.

horse·wom·an (hôrs′wùm′ən), NOUN.

1 a woman who rides on horseback.

2 a woman who is skilled in riding or managing horses.
❏ PLURAL **horse·wom·en.**

hor·ti·cul·ture (hôr′tə kul′chər), NOUN.

1 the study of garden plants, flowers, fruits, and vegetables.

2 the cultivation of a garden; hobby of gardening.

hose (hōz),

1 NOUN. a flexible tube of rubber or plastic for carrying a liquid or a gas. Hoses are used to water lawns and to fill tires with air.

2 NOUN PLURAL. stockings or socks.

ho·sier·y (hō′zhər ē), NOUN. hose; stockings or socks: *The company made hosiery for children.*

hos·pice (hos′pis), NOUN. a nursing home or similar place where people with terminal illness go for medical and emotional help before they die.

hos·pi·tal (hos′pi təl), NOUN. a place where doctors and nurses care for sick or injured people.

hos·pi·tal·i·ty (hos′pə tal′ə tē), NOUN. the generous treatment of guests or strangers.

hos·pi·tal·ize (hos′pi tə līz), VERB. to put someone in a hospital for treatment: *She was hospitalized after the accident.* ❏ VERB **hos·pi·tal·iz·es, hos·pi·tal·ized, hos·pi·tal·iz·ing.** —**hos′pi·tal·i·za′tion,** NOUN.

host¹ (hōst), NOUN.

1 someone who receives another person as a guest: *Before we left the party, we thanked our hosts.*

2 a living thing in or on which a parasite lives: *The oak tree is the host of the mistletoe that grows on it.*

host² (hōst), NOUN. a large number: *As it grew dark, a few stars appeared, then a host.*

hos·tage (hos′tij), NOUN. a person who is held as a prisoner until some demand is agreed to: *The convicts took guards as hostages until they were promised better living conditions.*

hos·tel (hos′tl), NOUN. a cheap place to spend the night, especially one for young people; inn.
■ Another word that sounds like this is **hostile.**

host·ess (hō′stis), NOUN.

1 a woman who receives another person as her guest.

2 a woman employed in a restaurant, hotel, and so on, to greet and attend to customers.
❏ PLURAL **host·ess·es.**

hos·tile (hos′tl), ADJECTIVE. unfriendly; showing dislike or hatred: *She did hostile things such as telling lies about me.* ■ Another word that sounds like this is **hostel.**

a	hat	ė	term	ô	order	ch	child	⎧a in about
ā	age	i	it	oi	oil	ng	long	⎪e in taken
ä	far	ī	ice	ou	out	sh	she	ə⎨i in pencil
â	care	o	hot	u	cup	th	thin	⎪o in lemon
e	let	ō	open	ù	put	ᴛʜ	then	⎩u in circus
ē	equal	ò	saw	ü	rule	zh	measure	

hos·til·i·ty (ho stil′ə tē), NOUN.
1 unfriendliness; dislike or hatred: *They showed signs of hostility toward our plan.*
2 **hostilities,** acts of war; warfare; fighting: *The peace treaty brought hostilities to an end.*
❏ PLURAL **hos·til·i·ties.**

hot (hot), ADJECTIVE.
1 having much heat; very warm: *Fire is hot.*
2 warmer than usual: *This weather is hot for May.*
3 feeling hot or warm: *The long run made me hot.*
4 having a sharp, burning taste: *Pepper is hot.*
5 violent; fiery: *He has a hot temper.*
6 new; fresh: *I just got some hot news. The trail is still hot, so the police expect to catch the criminal.*
❏ ADJECTIVE **hot·ter, hot·test.**

hot-air bal·loon (hot′âr′ bə lün′), a balloon made of very light fabric, filled with air heated by a gas burner. The heated air inside the balloon causes it to rise into the air. Hot-air balloons can carry a number of people.

hot-air balloon

hot dog. See **frankfurter.**

ho·tel (hō tel′), NOUN. a place where people traveling away from home can rent a room to sleep in.

hound (hound),
1 NOUN. a dog of any of various breeds, most of which use the sense of smell to hunt. Hounds have large, drooping ears and short hair.
2 NOUN. any dog.
3 VERB. to pester someone to do something: *The children hounded their parents to buy a color TV.*
❏ VERB **hounds, hound·ed, hound·ing.**

hour (our), NOUN.
1 one of the 12 equal periods of time between noon and midnight, or between midnight and noon; 60 minutes; ¹/₂₄ of a day.
2 the time of day: *This clock strikes the hours.*
3 the time for anything: *Our breakfast hour is at eight.*
4 **hours,** time for work or study: *What are the dentist's office hours?*
■ Another word that sounds like this is **our.**

hour·glass (our′glas′), NOUN. a device for measuring time, made up of two glass bulbs connected by a narrow neck. It takes an hour for sand in the top bulb to pass through the neck to the bottom bulb. ❏ PLURAL **hour·glass·es.**

hour·ly (our′lē),
1 ADJECTIVE. done, happening, or counted every hour: *There are hourly reports of the news and weather on this radio station.*

2 ADJECTIVE. for each hour: *an hourly wage.*
3 ADVERB. every hour: *Give two doses of the medicine hourly.*

house (hous *for noun;* houz *for verb*),
1 NOUN. a building in which people live.
2 NOUN. the people living in a house; household: *The noise woke up the whole house.*
3 NOUN. a building used for any purpose: *a tool house, a movie house.*
4 VERB. to take or put into a house; shelter: *Where can we house all these children?*
❏ PLURAL **hous·es** (hou′ziz); VERB **hous·es, housed, hous·ing.**
on the house, IDIOM. free; without charge: *This hamburger is on the house.*

house·boat (hous′bōt′), NOUN. a boat that can be used as a place to live in.

house·fly (hous′flī′), NOUN. a fly that lives around and in houses, feeding on food, garbage, and so on. ❏ PLURAL **house·flies.**

house·hold (hous′hōld), NOUN.
1 all the people living in a house: *Everyone in our household helps with the chores.*
2 a home and its affairs: *a well-run household.*

house·keep·er (hous′kē′pər), NOUN.
1 someone who takes care of a household or who does housework.
2 someone who is hired to manage or do housework in a home or hotel.

House of Representatives, the lower house of Congress.

house·plant (hous′plant′), NOUN. any plant in a pot or box, kept inside the house. African violets are popular houseplants.

house·wife (hous′wif′), NOUN. a married woman who manages a home and its affairs for her family. ❏ PLURAL **house·wives** (hous′wivz′).

house·work (hous′wėrk′), NOUN. the work to be done in managing a house, such as washing, ironing, cleaning, or cooking.

hous·ing (hou′zing), NOUN. houses or other places to live in: *The university built more housing for its students.*

Hous·ton (hyü′stən), NOUN. a city in Texas.

hov·er (huv′ər), VERB.
1 to stay in or near one place in the air: *The two birds hovered over their nest.*
2 to stay in or near one place; wait nearby: *The dogs hovered around the kitchen door, hoping to be fed.*
❏ VERB **hov·ers, hov·ered, hov·er·ing.**

how (hou),
1 ADVERB *or* CONJUNCTION. in what way; by what means: *Please tell me how to do it.*
2 ADVERB. to what degree or amount: *How tall is she? How hot is it?*

3 *ADVERB* or *CONJUNCTION.* in what condition: *How are you today? How do I look?*

4 *ADVERB.* for what reason; why: *How is it you are late?*

how come, *IDIOM.* why: *How come you didn't call me?*

how·ev·er (hou ev′ər),

1 *CONJUNCTION.* nevertheless; yet; in spite of that: *I was late for dinner; however, there was plenty left.*

2 *ADVERB.* to whatever degree or amount; no matter how: *I'll come however busy I am.*

3 *ADVERB.* in whatever way; by whatever means: *However did you get so dirty?*

howl (houl),

1 *VERB.* to give a long, loud, sad cry: *Our dog often howls at night.*

2 *NOUN.* a long, loud, sad cry: *the howl of a wolf.*

3 *VERB.* to give a long, loud cry of pain or rage.

4 *NOUN.* a loud cry of pain or rage.

5 *NOUN.* a yell or shout: *We heard howls of laughter.*

6 *VERB.* to yell or shout: *howl with laughter.*

❑ *VERB* **howls, howled, howl·ing.**

a **howling** coyote

hr., an abbreviation of **hour** or **hours.**

hub (hub), *NOUN.*

1 the central part of a wheel.

2 a center of interest, importance, or activity: *Malls are the hubs of suburban life.*

huck·le·ber·ry (huk′əl ber′ē), *NOUN.* a small berry that grows on a shrub. Huckleberries are like blueberries but are darker in color. ❑ *PLURAL* **huck·le·ber·ries.**

hud·dle (hud′l),

1 *VERB.* to crowd close: *The sheep huddled together in a corner. We huddled under the covers.*

2 *NOUN.* a grouping of football players behind the line of scrimmage to get ready for the next play. ❑ *VERB* **hud·dles, hud·dled, hud·dling.**

hue (hyü), *NOUN.* a color or a shade of color: *The room was painted in several hues of green.* ❑ *PLURAL* **hues.**

huff (huf),

1 *NOUN.* a fit of anger or annoyance: *We had a heated argument, and she left in a huff.*

2 *VERB.* to puff; blow: *I huffed and puffed up the stairs with the heavy package.*

❑ *VERB* **huffs, huffed, huff·ing.**

hug (hug),

1 *VERB.* to put your arms around something or someone and hold tight: *I hugged my new puppy.*

2 *NOUN.* a tight squeeze with the arms: *She gave the puppy a hug.*

❑ *VERB* **hugs, hugged, hug·ging.**

huge (hyüj), *ADJECTIVE.* very large in size or amount: *A whale is a huge animal. He won a huge sum of money.* ❑ *ADJECTIVE* **hug·er, hug·est.** **–huge′ly,** *ADVERB.*

Synonym Study

Huge means very big: *The great white shark has huge jaws.*

Enormous means much larger than normal: *The enormous gorilla was one of the greatest attractions at the zoo.*

Vast means covering a very wide area: *The Sahara is a vast desert in northern Africa.*

Immense means so big that it is hard to measure: *The Pacific Ocean is immense.*

Gigantic means very much larger than other things of the same kind: *The gigantic shopping mall has over two hundred stores.*

See also the Synonym Study at **big.**

ANTONYM: **tiny.**

hulk (hulk), *NOUN.* a big, clumsy person or thing: *The wrestler was a hulk of a man.*

hull (hul), *NOUN.*

1 the body or frame of a ship. Masts, sails, and rigging are not part of the hull.

2 the outer covering of a seed.

hum (hum),

1 *VERB.* to make a steady sound like the noise of a bee or of a spinning top: *The old fan hummed loudly.*

2 *NOUN.* a continuous, murmuring sound: *the hum of bees, the hum of the city streets.*

3 *VERB.* to sing with closed lips, not saying any words: *She was humming a tune.*

4 *VERB.* to be busy and active: *Things really hummed at campaign headquarters just before the election.* ❑ *VERB* **hums, hummed, hum·ming.** **–hum′mer,** *NOUN.*

hu·man (hyü′mən),

1 *ADJECTIVE.* of or relating to people: *Language is a human characteristic.*

a	hat	ė	term	ô	order	ch child	⎧a in about
ā	age	i	it	oi	oil	ng long	⎪e in taken
ä	far	ī	ice	ou	out	sh she	ə⎨i in pencil
â	care	o	hot	u	cup	th thin	⎪o in lemon
e	let	ō	open	ů	put	ŦH then	⎩u in circus
ē	equal	ò	saw	ü	rule	zh measure	

2 *ADJECTIVE.* having the form or qualities of people: *Men, women, and children are human beings.*

3 *NOUN.* a person; human being: *Humans walk upright.*

hu·mane (hyü mān′), *ADJECTIVE.* kind; not cruel or brutal: *I believe in the humane treatment of animals.* **–hu·mane′ly,** *ADVERB.*

hu·man·i·ty (hyü man′ə tē), *NOUN.*

1 human beings as a group; everyone: *All humanity will be helped by advances in medical science.*

2 kindness: *Treat animals with humanity.*

hum·ble (hum′bəl),

1 *ADJECTIVE.* not proud; modest: *She is very humble, in spite of her success in sports.*

2 *ADJECTIVE.* low in position or condition; not grand: *a humble job, a humble shack.*

3 *VERB.* to make humble; make lower in position, condition, or pride: *The team that bragged they would win was humbled by a big defeat.*
❑ *ADJECTIVE* **hum·bler, hum·blest;** *VERB* **hum·bles, hum·bled, hum·bling. –hum′bly,** *ADVERB.*

hu·mid (hyü′mid), *ADJECTIVE.* moist; damp: *We found that the air was very humid near the sea.*
▪ See the Synonym Study at **damp.**

hu·mid·i·ty (hyü mid′ə tē), *NOUN.* the amount of moisture in the air: *High humidity is uncomfortable.*

hu·mil·i·ate (hyü mil′ē āt), *VERB.* to lower someone's pride, dignity, or self-respect: *They humiliated me by criticizing me in front of my friends.* ❑ *VERB* **hu·mil·i·ates, hu·mil·i·at·ed, hu·mil·i·at·ing. –hu·mil′i·a′tion,** *NOUN.*

hummingbird — between 2 and 8 inches long

hum·ming·bird (hum′ing bėrd′), *NOUN.* a very small, brightly colored American bird with a long, narrow bill and narrow wings that move so fast they make a humming sound in the air.

hu·mon·gous (hyü mung′gəs *or* hyü mong′gəs), *ADJECTIVE.* (informal) huge; extraordinarily large: *A humongous snowstorm closed all the schools.*

hu·mor (hyü′mər),

1 *NOUN.* a funny or amusing quality: *I see no humor in your tricks.*

2 *NOUN.* the ability to see or show the funny or amusing side of things: *Her sense of humor enabled her to joke about her problems.*

3 *NOUN.* a state of mind; mood; temper: *Is the teacher in a good humor this morning?*

4 *VERB.* to give in to someone's wishes; agree with: *They humored the sick child by allowing her to eat ice cream.* ❑ *VERB* **hu·mors, hu·mored, hu·mor·ing.**

hu·mor·ist (hyü′mər ist), *NOUN.* a humorous talker; writer of jokes and funny stories.

hu·mor·ous (hyü′mər əs), *ADJECTIVE.* full of humor; funny; amusing: *We all laughed at the humorous story.* ▪ See the Synonym Study at **funny. –hu′mor·ous·ly,** *ADVERB.*

hump (hump), *NOUN.* a rounded lump that sticks up: *Some camels have two humps on their backs.* **–hump′like′,** *ADJECTIVE.*

hump·back whale (hump′bak′ wāl′), a large whale with a rounded back, a humplike fin, and long, narrow flippers. It is known for its songs.

hu·mus (hyü′məs), *NOUN.* a dark brown part of the soil formed from decayed leaves and other plant matter. Humus contains valuable plant foods.

hunch (hunch),

1 *NOUN.* a feeling or suspicion: *I had a hunch that it would rain, so I took along an umbrella.*

2 *NOUN.* a hump.

3 *VERB.* to raise, bend, or form into a hump: *She sat hunched up with her chin on her knees.*
❑ *PLURAL* **hunch·es;** *VERB* **hunch·es, hunched, hunch·ing.**

hun·dred (hun′drəd), *NOUN or ADJECTIVE.* ten times ten; 100. There are one hundred cents in a dollar.

hun·dredth (hun′drədth), *ADJECTIVE or NOUN.*

1 next after the 99th; last in a series of 100.

2 one of 100 equal parts.

hung (hung), *VERB.*

1 the past tense of **hang:** *He hung up his cap.*

2 the past participle of **hang:** *Your dress has hung here all day.*

A **humongous** pumpkin won first prize in the gardening contest.

Hun·gar·i·an (hung gâr′ē ən),
1 *ADJECTIVE.* of or about Hungary, its people, or their language.
2 *NOUN.* someone born or living in Hungary.
3 *NOUN.* the language of Hungary.

Hun·gar·y (hung′gər ē), *NOUN.* a country in central Europe.

hun·ger (hung′gər),
1 *NOUN.* pain or weakness caused by having had nothing to eat.
2 *NOUN.* a desire or need for food: *I ate an apple to satisfy my hunger.*
3 *NOUN.* a lack of food; shortage of food: *Hunger takes many lives each year.*
4 *NOUN.* a strong desire: *a hunger for knowledge.*
5 *VERB.* to have a strong desire; crave; long: *The neglected child hungered for love and attention.*
❑ *VERB* **hun·gers, hun·gered, hun·ger·ing.**

hun·gry (hung′grē), *ADJECTIVE.*
1 feeling a need to eat: *I missed breakfast and was hungry all morning.*
2 showing hunger: *The stray cat had a hungry look.*
3 eager: *A person who longs to read and study is hungry for knowledge.*
❑ *ADJECTIVE* **hun·gri·er, hun·gri·est. –hun′gri·ly,** *ADVERB.*

hunk (hungk), *NOUN.* a big lump or piece of something: *I ate a hunk of cheese.*

hunt (hunt),
1 *VERB.* to go after wild birds or other animals in order to catch or kill them for food or for sport: *They went to the woods to hunt deer.*
2 *NOUN.* the act of hunting: *I went on a duck hunt with my brothers.*
3 *VERB.* to look for something; try to find: *I hunted for my lost book for hours.*
4 *NOUN.* an attempt to find something or someone: *Everyone joined in the hunt for the lost child.*
❑ *VERB* **hunts, hunt·ed, hunt·ing.**

hunt·er (hun′tər), *NOUN.*
1 someone who hunts.
2 a horse or dog trained for hunting.

hur·dle (hėr′dl),
1 *NOUN.* a barrier for people or horses to jump over in a race.
2 *VERB.* to jump over: *The horse hurdled both the fence and the ditch.*
3 *NOUN.* something that stands in the way; problem or difficulty: *Getting my parents' consent was the last hurdle before I could join the football team.*
❑ *VERB* **hur·dles, hur·dled, hur·dling. –hur′dler,** *NOUN.*

hurl (hėrl), *VERB.* to throw something with great force: *She hurled a stone into the river.* ∎ See the Synonym Study at **throw.** ❑ *VERB* **hurls, hurled, hurl·ing.**

Hur·on (hyür′ən), *NOUN.* **Lake,** one of the Great Lakes.

hur·rah (hə rä′), *INTERJECTION* or *NOUN.* another spelling of **hooray.**

hur·ray (hə rä′), *INTERJECTION* or *NOUN.* another spelling of **hooray.**

hur·ri·cane (hėr′ə kān), *NOUN.* a fierce storm with very strong, dangerous winds and, usually, very heavy rain. The wind in a hurricane blows at more than 75 miles per hour.

hur·ried (hėr′ēd), *ADJECTIVE.* done or made in a hurry; hasty: *a hurried escape, a hurried reply.* **–hur′ried·ly,** *ADVERB.*

hur·ry (hėr′ē),
1 *VERB.* to move or act more quickly than usual; rush: *She hurried to get to work on time. They hurried the sick child to the doctor.*
2 *NOUN.* a hurried movement or action: *In his hurry he dropped the bag of groceries.*
3 *NOUN.* eagerness to have or do something quickly: *She was in a hurry to meet her friends.*
4 *VERB.* to urge someone to go faster or to do something faster: *Don't hurry the driver.*
❑ *VERB* **hur·ries, hur·ried, hur·ry·ing.**

hurt (hėrt), *VERB.*
1 to cause pain or injury to: *The stone hurt my foot.* ∎ See the Synonym Study at **harm.**
2 to feel pain: *My hand hurts.*
3 to do damage or harm to something: *Large price increases can hurt sales.*
4 to cause emotional pain to someone: *Did I hurt your feelings?*
❑ *VERB* **hurts, hurt, hurt·ing.**

hus·band (huz′bənd), *NOUN.* a man who is married.

hush (hush),
1 *VERB.* to stop making a noise; make or become silent or quiet: *The wind has hushed. Hush your dog.*
2 *NOUN.* silence; quiet; stillness: *In the hush after the storm, a bird began to sing.*
3 *INTERJECTION.* stop the noise! be silent!
❑ *VERB* **hush·es, hushed, hush·ing;** *PLURAL* **hushes.**

husk (husk),
1 *NOUN.* the dry outer covering of certain seeds or fruits. An ear of corn has a husk.
2 *VERB.* to remove the husk from; shuck: *Husk the corn before cooking it.*
❑ *VERB* **husks, husked, husk·ing.**

husk·y[1] (hus′kē), *ADJECTIVE.*
1 big and strong: *He was a husky young man.*
2 sounding rough and deep; hoarse: *Her voice was husky because she had a cold.*
❑ *ADJECTIVE* **husk·i·er, husk·i·est. –husk′i·ly,** *ADVERB.* **–husk′i·ness,** *NOUN.*

a	hat	ė	term	ô	order	ch	child		a in about
ā	age	i	it	oi	oil	ng	long		e in taken
ä	far	ī	ice	ou	out	sh	she	ə	i in pencil
â	care	o	hot	u	cup	th	thin		o in lemon
e	let	ō	open	ů	put	₮ℋ	then		u in circus
ē	equal	ò	saw	ü	rule	zh	measure		

husk·y² or **Hus·ky** (hus′kē), NOUN. a strong, medium-sized dog used to pull sleds in arctic regions. A husky usually has a thick coat and a bushy tail. ❑ PLURAL **hus·kies** or **Hus·kies.**

husky² — a team of huskies

hus·tle (hus′əl),
1 VERB. to move quickly and energetically; hurry: *I had to hustle to get the lawn mowed before it rained.*
2 VERB. to push or shove someone roughly: *Security guards hustled the demonstrators away from the mayor's office.*
3 NOUN. hurried movement: *The family prepared for the holidays with much hustle and bustle.*
❑ VERB **hus·tles, hus·tled, hus·tling.**

hut (hut), NOUN. a small, roughly built cabin or house.

hutch (huch), NOUN. a box or pen for small animals. Rabbits are kept in hutches. ❑ PLURAL **hutch·es.**

hy·a·cinth (hī′ə sinth), NOUN. a spring plant that grows from a bulb and has many small, fragrant flowers along its stem.

hy·brid (hī′brid),
1 NOUN. the offspring of two living things of different kinds or species.
2 ADJECTIVE. bred from two different kinds or species: *A mule is a hybrid animal produced from a female horse and a male donkey.*

hyacinth

hy·drant (hī′drənt), NOUN. a large water pipe that sticks up out of the ground. It has places where firefighters can connect hoses.

Word Power   hydro-

The combining form **hydro-** means "having to do with water." **Hydro**electric power comes from moving water. **Hydro**ponics uses only **water** to grow plants.

hy·dro·e·lec·tric (hī′drō i lek′trik), ADJECTIVE. producing electricity by using the power of moving water: *hydroelectric power.*

hy·dro·gen (hī′drə jən), NOUN. a colorless gas that burns easily. Hydrogen is a chemical element that weighs less than any other known substance. It combines with oxygen to form water.

hydrogen bomb, a bomb in which the combining of atoms of hydrogen produces an explosion of tremendous force; H-bomb. It is much more powerful than the atomic bomb.

hy·dro·pon·ics (hī′drə pon′iks), NOUN. the process of growing plants without soil by the use of water containing the necessary nutrients.

hy·e·na (hī ē′nə), NOUN. a wild animal of Africa and Asia that feeds on other animals at night. Hyenas look something like dogs, with spotted coats, long front legs, and short hind legs. ❑ PLURAL **hy·e·nas.**

hy·giene (hī′jēn′), NOUN. the rules and practices that help people stay well. Keeping your body and surroundings clean is an important part of hygiene.

hy·gien·ist (hī jē′nist), NOUN. a person who helps a dentist by examining and cleaning patients' teeth and by taking X rays.

hymn (him), NOUN. a song of praise, especially in honor of God. ■ Another word that sounds like this is **him.**

hym·nal (him′nəl), NOUN. a book of hymns.

hy·per (hī′pər), ADJECTIVE. (informal) very nervous, jumpy, or irritable: *He's so hyper he can't sit still.*

Word Power   hyper-

The prefix **hyper-** means "more than usual." **Hyper**active means more than usually active. **Hyper**text gives you more than the usual text.

hy·per·ac·tive (hī′pər ak′tiv), ADJECTIVE. very active, especially to an abnormal or unhealthy degree.

hy·per·text (hī′pər tekst′), NOUN. a way of showing and storing data on a computer that lets you make connections to related information by selecting a word or phrase to explore further. Words and phrases that are connected to more information are often shown in a different color.

hy·phen (hī′fən), NOUN. a mark (-) used to show that two or more words have been combined into a single term, as in *left-handed.* A hyphen also shows that a word has been divided at the end of a line.

hy·phen·ate (hī′fə nāt), VERB. to join words or to divide a word by using a hyphen. In this dictionary, the dots between syllables show where to hyphenate a word that doesn't fit on one line.
❑ VERB **hy·phen·ates, hy·phen·at·ed, hy·phen·at·ing. –hy′phen·a′tion,** NOUN.

hyp·no·tize (hip′nə tīz), *VERB.* to put someone into a state similar to sleep, but more active. A hypnotized person tends to follow spoken suggestions and may feel no pain or other kinds of stimulation. ❏ *VERB* **hyp·no·tiz·es, hyp·no·tized, hyp·no·tiz·ing.**

hy·poc·ri·sy (hi pok′rə sē), *NOUN.* the act or fact of pretending to be what you are not, especially claiming to be very good or religious but not acting that way.

hyp·o·crite (hip′ə krit), *NOUN.* someone who pretends to be what he or she is not, especially someone who claims to be very good or religious but does not act that way.

hy·pot·e·nuse (hī pot′n üs), *NOUN.* the side of a right triangle opposite the right angle.

hy·poth·e·sis (hī poth′ə sis), *NOUN.* something assumed to be true because it seems likely; theory: *The detective's hypothesis was that the robbery was an inside job.* ❏ *PLURAL* **hy·poth·e·ses** (hī poth′ə sēz′).

hys·ter·i·cal (hi ster′ə kəl), *ADJECTIVE.*
1 unnaturally excited; emotional: *hysterical sobs.*
2 showing an extreme lack of self-control; unnaturally excited: *The hysterical child was unable to stop crying.*
3 very funny: *Isn't that cartoon hysterical?*
—**hys·ter′i·cal·ly,** *ADVERB.*

H

impala

iceberg

Ii

I or **i** (ī), *NOUN.* the ninth letter of the English alphabet. ❏ *PLURAL* **I's** or **i's**.

I (ī), *PRONOUN.* the person who is speaking or writing: *The boy said, "I am ten years old." I like my dog.* ■ Other words that sound like this are **aye, ay,** and **eye.**

IA, an abbreviation of **Iowa.**

i·bex (ī′beks), *NOUN.* a wild goat that lives in the mountains of Europe, Asia, and Africa. Both male and female ibexes have long, curving horns. ❏ *PLURAL* **i·bex** or **i·bex·es.**

ice (īs),
1 *NOUN.* frozen water; water made solid by cold.
2 *VERB.* to cover with frosting: *Mom let me ice the cake.*
3 *NOUN.* a frozen dessert, usually one made of sweetened fruit juice.
4 *VERB.* to put ice in or around: *The coach told me to ice my swollen ankle.* ❏ *VERB* **ic·es, iced, ic·ing.**

break the ice, *IDIOM.* to make people feel comfortable: *We played a party game to break the ice.*

ice over, *IDIOM.* to turn to ice; freeze: *This lake ices over in winter.*

on thin ice, *IDIOM.* in a dangerous situation: *He's on thin ice talking back like that.*

Ice Age, a long period of time when much of the northern part of the earth was covered with glaciers. The most recent Ice Age took place about 10,000 years ago.

ice·berg (īs′bėrg′), *NOUN.* a large mass of ice floating in the sea. Icebergs break off the lower ends of glaciers.

ice·cap (īs′kap′), *NOUN.* a permanent covering of ice over a large area, sloping down on all sides from a high center. Greenland has an icecap.

ice cream, a smooth, frozen dessert made of various milk products, sweetened and flavored. —**ice-cream** (īs′krēm′), *ADJECTIVE.*

ice cube, a small piece of ice used to cool drinks. Ice cubes are usually in the shape of a cube.

Ice·land (īs′lənd), *NOUN*. an island country in the northern Atlantic Ocean.

Ice·lan·dic (īs lan′dik),

1 *ADJECTIVE*. of Iceland, its people, or their language.

2 *NOUN*. language of Iceland.

Word Source

Icelandic has given many words to the English language, including the words below.

anger	odd	skirt	Viking
calf²	outlaw	sky	weak
egg¹	ransack	tatter	wheeze
egg²	reindeer	tight	window

ice skate, a shoe with a metal runner attached for skating on ice.

ice-skate (īs′skāt′), *VERB*. to skate on ice. ❑ *VERB* **ice-skates, ice-skat·ed, ice-skat·ing. –ice skater.**

i·ci·cle (ī′si kəl), *NOUN*. a pointed, hanging stick of ice formed by the freezing of dripping water.

ic·ing (ī′sing), *NOUN*. See **frosting.**

i·con (ī′kon), *NOUN*.

1 a small picture on a computer screen that stands for a file, program, or software command that you can select with a cursor.

2 a picture or image of Jesus, an angel, or a saint.

i·cy (ī′sē), *ADJECTIVE*.

1 covered with ice; slippery: *I skidded on the icy street.*

2 like ice; very cold: *icy fingers.*

3 made of or mixed with ice: *an icy snowball.*

4 cold and unfriendly: *She gave me an icy stare.*
❑ *ADJECTIVE* **i·ci·er, i·ci·est. –i′ci·ly,** *ADVERB*.

I'd (īd), a contraction of **I should, I would,** or **I had.**

ID, an abbreviation of **Idaho.**

identical twins

I·da·ho (ī′də hō), *NOUN*. one of the Rocky Mountain states of the United States. *Abbreviation:* ID; *Capital:* Boise. **–I′da·ho′an,** *NOUN*.

State Story **Idaho** may have come from an Apache word for the Comanche (kə man′chē) Indians.

i·de·a (ī dē′ə), *NOUN*.

1 a belief, plan, or picture in the mind: *Swimming is her idea of fun.*

2 a thought; fancy; opinion: *I had no idea that the job would be so hard.*

3 the point or purpose: *The idea of a vacation is to get a rest.*
❑ *PLURAL* **i·de·as.**

Synonym Study

Idea means a picture or plan in your mind: *I have an idea about what to do after school this afternoon.*

Notion means an idea. It is often used for an idea that is not fully formed: *He had a notion that a class picnic might be fun.*

Concept means a general idea of something: *"What is your concept of democracy?" was the first question on our exam.*

Thought means an idea about something: *I offered some thoughts on where to hold the picnic.*

Brainstorm means a sudden, very good idea: *We just had a brainstorm—a picnic at the amusement park!*

See also the Synonym Studies at **opinion** and **think.**

i·de·al (ī dē′əl),

1 *NOUN*. a perfect type; model to be imitated; what you would wish to be: *Her mother is her ideal.*

2 *ADJECTIVE*. perfect; just as you would wish: *A warm, sunny day is ideal for a picnic.* ■ See the Synonym Study at **perfect.**

i·den·ti·cal (ī den′tə kəl), *ADJECTIVE*. exactly alike: *My sister and I have identical bikes.*
–i·den′ti·cal·ly, *ADVERB*.

i·den·ti·fi·ca·tion (ī den′tə fə kā′shən), *NOUN*. something used to prove who someone is or what something is: *She offered her driver's license as identification.*

i·den·ti·fy (ī den′tə fī), *VERB*. to recognize, tell, or prove who something is or what something is: *He identified the wallet as his by telling what it looked like and what was in it.* ❑ *VERB* **i·den·ti·fies, i·den·ti·fied, i·den·ti·fy·ing. –i·den′ti·fi′a·ble,** *ADJECTIVE*.

i·den·ti·ty (ī den′tə tē), *NOUN*. who or what you are: *The writer concealed her identity by signing her stories with a pen name.* ❑ *PLURAL* **i·den·ti·ties.**

a	hat	ė term	ô order	ch child
ā	age	i it	oi oil	ng long
ä	far	ī ice	ou out	sh she
â	care	o hot	u cup	th thin
e	let	ō open	ù put	ŦH then
ē	equal	ò saw	ü rule	zh measure

ə { a in about / e in taken / i in pencil / o in lemon / u in circus }

id·i·om (id′ē əm), *NOUN.* a phrase or expression that has a meaning that cannot be understood from the ordinary meanings of the words in it. "Hold your tongue" is an English idiom meaning to keep quiet.

id·i·ot (id′ē ət), *NOUN.* a very foolish person or someone who has done something foolish: *What an idiot I was to forget my keys!*

id·i·ot·ic (id′ē ot′ik), *ADJECTIVE.* very foolish: *What an idiotic idea!*

i·dle (i′dl),

1 *ADJECTIVE.* doing nothing; not busy; not working: *Give me some help; don't just stand there idle.*

2 *ADJECTIVE.* lazy; not willing to do things: *Some idle students do very little schoolwork.*

3 *ADJECTIVE.* not in operation; not working or being used: *idle factories.*

4 *VERB.* to do nothing; spend or waste time: *It's pleasant to idle away hours lying in a hammock.*

5 *VERB.* to run slowly without transmitting power. A motor idles when it is out of gear.
❑ *ADJECTIVE* **i·dler, i·dlest;** *VERB* **i·dles, i·dled, i·dling.** **–i′dler,** *NOUN.* **–i′dly,** *ADVERB.*

i·dol (i′dl), *NOUN.*

1 someone or something that you love or admire very much: *That movie star is my idol.*

2 an image or object that is worshiped as a god.

if (if), *CONJUNCTION.*

1 on the condition that; in case: *Come if you can. If it rains tomorrow, we shall stay at home.*

2 whether: *I wonder if he will go?*

3 although; even though: *It was a welcome, if unexpected, visit.*

Usage Note

When **if** is used about things that are not the fact or that cannot be true, it is followed by **were:** *If I were the President, I would have vetoed the bill.*

In sentences that do not contain an untrue statement, **if** is followed by **was:** *If her last performance was Sunday, she will be home today.*

green iguana — up to 6 feet long

if·fy (if′ē), *ADJECTIVE.* having unknown qualities or conditions; doubtful: *an iffy undertaking.*
❑ *ADJECTIVE* **if·fi·er, if·fi·est.**

ig·loo (ig′lü), *NOUN.* a house made of hard blocks of snow. Some Inuit used to live in igloos in the winter. ❑ *PLURAL* **ig·loos.**

igloo

ig·ne·ous rock (ig′nē əs rok′), *NOUN.* rock formed by the cooling and hardening of melted rock and minerals deep inside the earth. Lava and granite are igneous rocks.

ig·nite (ig nīt′), *VERB.*

1 to set something on fire: *A spark from the campfire ignited the dry grass.*

2 to catch fire; begin to burn: *Gasoline vapor ignites easily.*
❑ *VERB* **ig·nites, ig·nit·ed, ig·nit·ing.**

ig·ni·tion (ig nish′ən), *NOUN.* the electrical device in a vehicle that starts the engine with power from the battery.

ig·nor·ance (ig′nər əns), *NOUN.* a lack of knowledge; condition of being ignorant.

ig·nor·ant (ig′nər ənt), *ADJECTIVE.*

1 knowing little or nothing: *People who live in the city are often ignorant of farm life.*

2 uninformed; unaware: *He was ignorant of the fact that Paris is the capital of France.*

ig·nore (ig nôr′), *VERB.* to pay no attention to something or someone: *The driver ignored the traffic light and almost hit another car.* ❑ *VERB* **ig·nores, ig·nored, ig·nor·ing.**

i·gua·na (i gwä′nə), *NOUN.* a large lizard with a row of spines along its back. It is found in tropical America. ❑ *PLURAL* **i·gua·nas.**

Did You Know?

The **green iguana** is becoming extinct in some areas of Central and South America. The iguana is such a popular pet that too many have been taken from those places.

Word Power   il-

The prefix **il-** means "not." **Il**legal means **not** legal. This prefix is used instead of **in-** before words that begin with the letter **l**.

IL, an abbreviation of **Illinois.**

ill (il),
1 *ADJECTIVE.* sick; having some disease; not well: *She was ill with a fever.*
2 *NOUN.* often, **ills,** evil; harm; trouble: *Poverty and hunger are among the ills of our society.*
3 *ADJECTIVE.* not good: *ill health.*
❑ *ADJECTIVE* **worse, worst.**

I'll (il),
1 a contraction of **I will.**
2 a contraction of **I shall.**
■ Other words that sound like this are **aisle** and **isle.**

il·le·gal (i lē′gəl), *ADJECTIVE.*
1 against the law: *It is illegal to drive without wearing a seat belt.*
2 (in sports) against the rules.
—**il·le′gal·ly,** *ADVERB.*

il·leg·i·ble (i lej′ə bəl), *ADJECTIVE.* very hard or impossible to read: *The ink had faded so that many words were illegible.*

Il·li·nois (il′ə noi′), *NOUN.* one of the Midwestern states of the United States. *Abbreviation:* IL; *Capital:* Springfield. —**Il′li·nois′an,** *NOUN.*

State Story   Illinois got its name from the way French explorers wrote the name of the Indians living in the area. The Indian name meant "men."

il·lit·er·ate (i lit′ər it), *ADJECTIVE.* not knowing how to read and write. Most people in the Middle Ages were illiterate.

ill·ness (il′nis), *NOUN.* sickness; disease: *Cancer is a serious illness.* ❑ *PLURAL* **ill·ness·es.**

il·lu·mi·nate (i lü′mə nāt), *VERB.* to light something up: *Four large lamps illuminated the room.* ❑ *VERB* **il·lu·mi·nates, il·lu·mi·nat·ed, il·lu·mi·nat·ing.** —**il·lu′mi·na′tion,** *NOUN.*

il·lu·sion (i lü′zhən), *NOUN.*
1 something that appears to be different from what it actually is: *The long, straight highway gave the illusion of becoming narrower in the distance.*
2 a false idea or belief: *Many people have the illusion that wealth is the chief cause of happiness.*

il·lus·trate (il′ə strāt), *VERB.*
1 to provide a book with pictures, diagrams, or maps that explain or decorate it: *This book is well illustrated.*
2 to make something clear or explain it by stories, examples, or comparisons: *The way that a pump works is used to illustrate how the heart sends blood around the body.*
❑ *VERB* **il·lus·trates, il·lus·trat·ed, il·lus·trat·ing.**

il·lus·tra·tion (il′ə strā′shən), *NOUN.*
1 a picture, diagram, or map used to explain or decorate something.
2 a story, example, or comparison used to make clear or explain something: *An apple cut into four equal parts is a good illustration of what ¼ means.*

il·lus·tra·tor (il′ə strā′tər), *NOUN.* an artist who makes pictures to be used as illustrations.

ill will, dislike; unkind or unfriendly feeling: *She bears ill will toward the people who cheated her.*

Word Power   im-

The prefix **im-** means "not." **Im**possible means **not** possible. **Im**patient means **not** patient. **Im**mature means **not** mature. This prefix is used instead of **in-** before words that begin with **m** or **p.**

I'm (īm), a contraction of **I am.**

im·age (im′ij), *NOUN.*
1 a picture in the mind: *I can shut my eyes and see images of things and people.*
2 a likeness of an object or person produced by a mirror or through a lens.
3 a statue; likeness made of stone, wood, or some other material: *The store sold little images of birds.*
4 a likeness or copy: *She is the image of her mother.*

i·mag·i·nar·y (i maj′ə ner′ē), *ADJECTIVE.* not real; existing only in the imagination: *The equator is an imaginary circle around the earth.*

i·mag·i·na·tion (i maj′ə nā′shən), *NOUN.*
1 the power to make pictures or ideas in the mind of things not present to the senses. A poet, artist, or inventor must have imagination to create new things or ideas or to combine old ones in new forms.
2 something that is imagined: *Is it my imagination, or did I just see a mouse?*

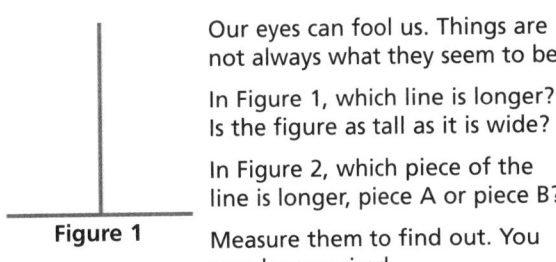

Our eyes can fool us. Things are not always what they seem to be.

In Figure 1, which line is longer? Is the figure as tall as it is wide?

In Figure 2, which piece of the line is longer, piece A or piece B? Measure them to find out. You may be surprised.

Figure 1

Figure 2

optical **illusions**

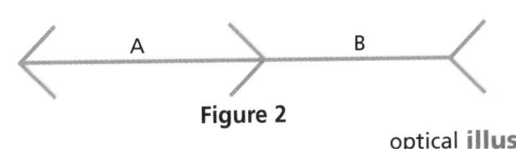

a	hat	ė	term	ô	order	ch	child		a in about
ā	age	i	it	oi	oil	ng	long		e in taken
ä	far	ī	ice	ou	out	sh	she	ə ⎨	i in pencil
â	care	o	hot	u	cup	th	thin		o in lemon
e	let	ō	open	ù	put	ᴛʜ	then		u in circus
ē	equal	ò	saw	ü	rule	zh	measure		

i·mag·i·na·tive (i maj′ə nə tiv), *ADJECTIVE*. having or showing a good imagination: *an imaginative child, imaginative fairy tales.*

i·mag·ine (i maj′ən), *VERB*.
1 to make a picture or idea of something in your mind: *We can hardly imagine life without cars.*
2 to guess: *I imagine it will rain tomorrow.*
    ❑ *VERB* **i·mag·ines, i·mag·ined, i·mag·in·ing.** —**i·mag′in·a·ble,** *ADJECTIVE*.

i·mam (i mäm′), *NOUN*. a Muslim leader of prayer or religious leader.

im·i·tate (im′ə tāt), *VERB*.
1 to try to be like someone else: *The little boy imitates his older brother.*
2 to act like something else: *He amused the class by imitating a duck, a monkey, and a bear.*
3 to be like or look like something else: *Wood is sometimes painted to imitate stone.*
    ❑ *VERB* **im·i·tates, im·i·tat·ed, im·i·tat·ing.** —**im′i·ta′tor,** *NOUN*.

im·i·ta·tion (im′ə tā′shən),
1 *NOUN*. something that imitates something else: *He does a good imitation of a rooster crowing.*
2 *ADJECTIVE*. not real: *imitation pearls.*
3 *NOUN*. the act or process of imitating: *We learn many things by imitation.*

im·mac·u·late (i mak′yə lit), *ADJECTIVE*. without a spot or stain; absolutely clean: *The newly washed shirts were immaculate.*

im·ma·ture (im′ə chùr′ or im′ə tùr′), *ADJECTIVE*.
1 not mature; not ripe; not full-grown.
2 acting in a childish way; not showing the good sense expected at your age: *It is immature to expect to get your own way all the time.*
    —**im′ma·ture′ly,** *ADVERB*.

im·me·di·ate (i mē′dē it), *ADJECTIVE*.
1 coming at once; right away: *When you dial 911, you get an immediate reply.*
2 closest; nearest: *Your immediate neighbors live next door.*

Word Story

Immediate comes from Latin words meaning "not in the middle." The word describes things that are as close as possible in time or space, with nothing else coming between.

im·me·di·ate·ly (i mē′dē it lē), *ADVERB*. at once; right away: *I answered his letter immediately.*

im·mense (i mens′), *ADJECTIVE*. very big; huge; vast: *An ocean is an immense body of water.* ∎ See the Synonym Study at **huge.**

im·mense·ly (i mens′lē), *ADVERB*. very much: *We enjoyed the party immensely.*

im·merse (i mèrs′), *VERB*.
1 to put something completely into a liquid: *He immersed his aching feet in a bucket of hot water.*

2 to involve yourself deeply in something: *The young pianist immersed herself in practice six hours a day.*
    ❑ *VERB* **im·mers·es, im·mersed, im·mers·ing.**

im·mi·grant (im′ə grənt), *NOUN*. someone who comes into a country or region to live there: *Canada has many immigrants from Europe.*

These **immigrants** entered the United States from Europe in 1901.

im·mi·grate (im′ə grāt), *VERB*. to come into a foreign country or region to live there. ❑ *VERB* **im·mi·grates, im·mi·grat·ed, im·mi·grat·ing.** —**im′mi·gra′tion,** *NOUN*.

im·mo·ral (i môr′əl), *ADJECTIVE*. morally wrong: *Lying and stealing are immoral.*

im·mor·tal (i môr′tl), *ADJECTIVE*.
1 living forever; never dying: *The Greeks believed their gods were immortal.*
2 remembered or famous forever: *A truly great artist gains immortal fame.*

im·mune (i myün′), *ADJECTIVE*.
1 protected from disease; having immunity: *Vaccination makes a person practically immune to polio.*
2 not affected by something bad: *Nobody is immune to criticism.*

immune system, the system of antibodies and special white blood cells in a person or animal that recognize, attack, and destroy germs and other foreign material that enter the body.

im·mu·ni·ty (i myü′nə tē), *NOUN*. resistance to disease: *One attack of measles usually gives a person immunity to that disease.*

im·mu·nize (im′yə nīz), *VERB*. to protect someone from disease; give immunity to: *Vaccination immunizes you against smallpox.* ❑ *VERB* **im·mu·niz·es, im·mu·nized, im·mu·niz·ing.** —**im′mu·ni·za′tion,** *NOUN*.

im·pact (im′pakt), *NOUN*.
1 the action of one thing hitting against another; collision: *The impact of the heavy stone against the windowpane shattered the glass.*
2 a strong or dramatic effect that something has on someone: *Her speech about kids living in poverty had an impact on the audience.*

im·pair (im pâr′), VERB. to make something worse; damage; harm; weaken: *Poor eating habits impaired his health.* ❏ VERB **im·pairs, im·paired, im·pair·ing.** —**im·pair′ment,** NOUN.

im·paired (im pârd′), ADJECTIVE. weakened; damaged; injured: *impaired hearing, visually impaired.*

im·pa·la (im pä′lə), NOUN. a reddish brown African antelope noted for its speed and its long leaps. The male impala has long, curved horns. ❏ PLURAL **im·pa·las.**

impala — about 3 feet high at the shoulder

im·par·tial (im pär′shəl), ADJECTIVE. fair; just; not supporting either side of an argument or dispute: *A judge should be impartial.* —**im·par′tial·ly,** ADVERB.

im·pa·tience (im pā′shəns), NOUN. a lack of patience: *My impatience grew as I waited for the game to start.*

im·pa·tiens (im pā′shənz), NOUN. a plant with pink, orange, yellow, purple, or white flowers. The seed pods of the impatiens burst open and shoot out seeds when they are ripe.

impatiens

im·pa·tient (im pā′shənt), ADJECTIVE. not patient; not willing to put up with delay, annoyance, pain, or bother: *He is impatient with his little brother's whining.* —**im·pa′tient·ly,** ADVERB.

im·peach (im pēch′), VERB. to accuse a public official of wrong conduct while in office. Charges are brought before a special kind of court, and the official is removed from office if found guilty. ❏ VERB **im·peach·es, im·peached, im·peach·ing.** —**im·peach′ment,** NOUN.

im·per·a·tive (im per′ə tiv),
1 ADJECTIVE. very important to do; necessary: *It is imperative that this very sick child should stay in bed.*
2 ADJECTIVE. of or about a verb form that makes a command or request.

3 NOUN. (in grammar) the form of a verb that expresses this. In "Try to be quiet" and "Please take me to the park," *try* and *take* are imperatives.

im·per·fect (im pėr′fikt), ADJECTIVE. not perfect; having a defect: *A crack in the cup made it imperfect.* —**im′per·fec′tion,** NOUN. —**im·per′fect·ly,** ADVERB.

im·per·i·al (im pir′ē əl), ADJECTIVE. of or about an empire or its ruler: *We visited the imperial palace.*

im·per·son·al (im pėr′sə nəl), ADJECTIVE. without emotion: *a cold, impersonal response to angry words.*

im·per·son·ate (im pėr′sə nāt), VERB. to pretend to be someone else; copy the voice, appearance, and manners of: *She impersonated a well-known movie star to amuse us.* ❏ VERB **im·per·son·ates, im·per·son·at·ed, im·per·son·at·ing.** —**im·per′son·a′tion,** NOUN.

im·per·ti·nent (im pėrt′n ənt), ADJECTIVE. rude; disrespectful: *Talking back to older people is impertinent.* —**im·per′ti·nent·ly,** ADVERB.

im·pet·u·ous (im pech′ü əs), ADJECTIVE. likely to act quickly, without thinking enough about it first: *He often does sudden impetuous things.*

im·plant (im plant′ for verb; im′plant for noun),
1 VERB. to set a piece of tissue or material, a device, and so on, into the body by surgery: *Artificial teeth are implanted into the jaw.*
2 NOUN. something set into the body by surgery: *The pacemaker is an implant that regulates the heartbeat.*
❏ VERB **im·plants, im·plant·ed, im·plant·ing.**

im·ple·ment (im′plə mənt), NOUN. a useful piece of equipment; tool. *Plows and axes are implements.*

im·ply (im plī′), VERB. to mean something without saying it outright; suggest: *The teacher's smile implied that she had forgiven us.* ❏ VERB **im·plies, im·plied, im·ply·ing.**

im·po·lite (im′pə līt′), ADJECTIVE. not polite; having or showing bad manners; rude. —**im′po·lite′ness,** NOUN.

im·port (im pôrt′ or im′pôrt for verb; im′pôrt for noun),
1 VERB. to bring something in from a foreign country for sale or use: *The United States imports coffee.*
2 NOUN. something brought into a country for sale or use: *Rubber is a useful import.*
❏ VERB **im·ports, im·port·ed, im·port·ing.** —**im′por·ta′tion,** NOUN.

Usage Note

Import and **export** sometimes get confused. **Import** means to bring something into a country. **Export** means to send something out of a country: *The United States imports bananas and exports corn.*

a	hat	ė	term	ô	order	ch	child		a in about
ā	age	i	it	oi	oil	ng	long		e in taken
ä	far	ī	ice	ou	out	sh	she	ə	i in pencil
â	care	o	hot	u	cup	th	thin		o in lemon
e	let	ō	open	u̇	put	ᴛʜ	then		u in circus
ē	equal	ȯ	saw	ü	rule	zh	measure		

im·por·tance (im pôrt′ns), NOUN. quality of being important; value: *We can all see the importance of good health.*

im·por·tant (im pôrt′nt), ADJECTIVE.
1 having great meaning or value: *It is important that you learn to read well.*
2 having power or being famous: *Our mayor is an important person in our town.*
—**im·por′tant·ly**, ADVERB.

im·pose (im pōz′), VERB. to put a burden, punishment, or tax on someone: *The judge imposed fines on each guilty person.* ❑ VERB **im·pos·es, im·posed, im·pos·ing.**

im·pos·ing (im pō′zing), ADJECTIVE. impressive because of its size, appearance, or dignity: *The Capitol at Washington, D.C., is imposing.*

im·pos·si·bil·i·ty (im pos′ə bil′ə tē), NOUN.
1 the condition of being impossible: *We all realize the impossibility of living long without food.*
2 something impossible: *Holding your breath for an hour is an impossibility.*
❑ PLURAL **im·pos·si·bil·i·ties.**

im·pos·si·ble (im pos′ə bəl), ADJECTIVE.
1 not able to be or happen: *It is impossible to have an outdoor picnic when it's raining.*
2 very hard to put up with: *Spending the entire summer indoors would be impossible.*
—**im·pos′si·bly**, ADVERB.

im·pos·tor (im pos′tər), NOUN. someone who pretends to be someone else in order to fool or cheat other people.

im·prac·ti·cal (im prak′tə kəl), ADJECTIVE. not making sense; not practical: *It was impractical to try to have a garden in such poor soil.*

im·press (im pres′), VERB.
1 to have a strong effect on someone's mind or feelings: *The movie about the pioneers impressed us with their courage.*
2 to make someone understand how important something is: *The teacher tried to impress on us the value of a quiet place to study.*
❑ VERB **im·press·es, im·pressed, im·press·ing.**

im·pres·sion (im presh′ən), NOUN.
1 an effect produced on someone: *The giraffe in the zoo made a great impression on the child.*
2 an idea; notion: *I have a vague impression that I left the front door unlocked.*
3 an imitation; impersonation: *The comedian did impressions of several movie stars.*

im·pres·sive (im pres′iv), ADJECTIVE. able to impress someone's mind, feelings, or conscience: *The actors gave an impressive performance.*
—**im·pres′sive·ly**, ADVERB.

im·print (im′print *for noun;* im print′ *for verb*),
1 NOUN. a mark made by something pressed on a soft surface: *Your foot made an imprint in the sand.*

2 NOUN. a strong influence; effect: *Many buildings in the American Southwest show the imprint of Spanish architecture.*
3 VERB. to put something on a surface by pressing: *He imprinted a kiss on his grandmother's cheek.*
❑ VERB **im·prints, im·print·ed, im·print·ing.**

im·pris·on (im priz′n), VERB. to put or keep someone in prison. ❑ VERB **im·pris·ons, im·pris·oned, im·pris·on·ing.** —**im·pris′on·ment**, NOUN.

im·prob·a·ble (im prob′ə bəl), ADJECTIVE. not probable; not likely to be true: *They told an improbable story of seeing a ghost.*

A horse on a bicycle is an **improbable** sight.

im·prop·er (im prop′ər), ADJECTIVE.
1 wrong; incorrect: *That driver made an improper turn into a one-way street.*
2 not suitable: *A damp basement is an improper place to store books.*
3 not decent; morally wrong: *Reading another person's mail is improper.*
—**im·prop′er·ly**, ADVERB.

improper fraction, a fraction with a numerator that is equal to or greater than the denominator. $\frac{3}{2}$, $\frac{5}{3}$, $\frac{7}{4}$, $\frac{21}{12}$, and $\frac{8}{8}$ are improper fractions.

im·prove (im prüv′), VERB. to make or become better: *Try to improve your spelling. His health is improving.* ❑ VERB **im·proves, im·proved, im·prov·ing.**

im·prove·ment (im prüv′mənt), NOUN.
1 the act of making better or becoming better: *Her class work shows much improvement since last fall.*
2 a change or addition to something that adds value to it: *The improvements to our house were costly.*
3 someone or something that is better than a previous one; advance: *Our new computer is an improvement over our old one.*

im·pro·vise (im′prə vīz′), VERB.
1 to make up music or poetry on the spur of the moment; sing or speak without preparation: *She likes to improvise melodies on the piano.*

2 to make or do something with whatever you have to work with: *The children improvised a tent out of blankets and poles.*
❑ VERB **im·pro·vis·es, im·pro·vised, im·pro·vis·ing.** **—im′pro·vis′er,** NOUN.

im·pru·dent (im prüd′nt), ADJECTIVE. not wise or prudent; rash: *an imprudent answer.*

im·pu·dent (im′pyə dənt), ADJECTIVE. shamelessly bold; very rude and disrespectful: *The impudent child made faces at us.* **—im′pu·dent·ly,** ADVERB.

im·pulse (im′puls), NOUN. a sudden desire to do something; urge: *I had a strong impulse to call him.*

im·pul·sive (im pul′siv), ADJECTIVE. acting upon impulse; tending to do things suddenly without very much thought: *Impulsive people often buy things they don't need.* **—im·pul′sive·ly,** ADVERB. **—im·pul′sive·ness,** NOUN.

im·pure (im pyür′), ADJECTIVE. not pure; dirty: *The air in cities is often impure.*

im·pur·i·ty (im pyür′ə tē), NOUN. usually, **impurities,** things that make something else impure: *Filtering the water removed some of its impurities.* ❑ PLURAL **im·pur·i·ties.**

in (in),
1 PREPOSITION. within; not outside: *We live in the city.*
2 PREPOSITION. during: *It rained in the afternoon.*
3 PREPOSITION. at the end of; after: *I'll be ready in an hour.*
4 PREPOSITION. into: *Go in the house.*
5 PREPOSITION. using; by means of: *She wrote in pencil. I paid in cash.*
6 PREPOSITION. out of: *one in a hundred.*
7 PREPOSITION. to or at the position or condition of; affected by: *Is your brother in trouble?*
8 ADVERB. in or into some place; on the inside: *Come in. Lock the dog in.*
9 ADVERB. present, especially in your home or office: *The doctor is not in today.*
■ Another word that sounds like this is **inn.**

ins and outs, IDIOM.
1 turns and twists: *She knows the ins and outs of the road because she has traveled it so often.*
2 different parts; details: *The manager knows the ins and outs of the business better than the owner.*

Word Power   in-

The prefix **in-** means "not" or "without." **In**correct means **not** correct. An **in**justice is **without** justice. **In**attentive means **not** attentive.

in., an abbreviation of **inch** or **inches.**
IN, an abbreviation of **Indiana.**
in·a·bil·i·ty (in′ə bil′ə tē), NOUN. a lack of ability, means, or power.
in·ac·cur·ate (in ak′yər it), ADJECTIVE. not accurate; containing mistakes: *There was inaccurate information in the book.* **—in·ac′cur·ate·ly,** ADVERB.

in·ad·e·quate (in ad′ə kwit), ADJECTIVE. not enough; not so much as is required: *Inadequate nutrition can cause disease.* **—in·ad′e·quate·ly,** ADVERB.

in·ap·pro·pri·ate (in′ə prō′prē it), ADJECTIVE. not appropriate; not suitable. **—in′ap·pro′pri·ate·ly,** ADVERB.

in·at·ten·tive (in′ə ten′tiv), ADJECTIVE. not attentive; negligent; careless. **—in′at·ten′tive·ly,** ADVERB.

in·au·gu·rate (in ȯ′gyə rāt′), VERB.
1 to install someone in office with a ceremony: *A President of the United States is inaugurated every four years.*
2 to open a building for public use with a ceremony or celebration: *The new city hall was inaugurated with a parade and speeches.*
❑ VERB **in·au·gu·rates, in·au·gu·rat·ed, in·au·gu·rat·ing.**

in·au·gu·ra·tion (in ȯ′gyə rā′shən), NOUN.
1 the act or ceremony of installing someone in office: *The inauguration of a President of the United States takes place on January 20.*
2 the opening of a building for public use with a ceremony or celebration: *The inauguration of the new city hall began with a parade.*

in·born (in′bôrn′), ADJECTIVE. natural; already present when someone is born: *The artist had an inborn talent for drawing.*

In·ca (ing′kə), NOUN. a member of an ancient people of South America. The Inca ruled a large empire in Peru and other parts of South America. This empire fell to the Spaniards in the 1500s.
❑ PLURAL **In·ca** or **In·cas.**

in·can·ta·tion (in′kan tā′shən), NOUN. the use of a set of words spoken as a magic charm or to cast a magic spell.

an **Inca** drinking cup

in·ca·pa·ble (in kā′pə bəl), ADJECTIVE. having very little ability; not capable; not efficient: *An employer cannot afford to hire incapable workers.*

in·cense (in′sens), NOUN. a substance that gives off a sweet smell when burned.

in·ces·sant (in ses′nt), ADJECTIVE. never stopping; continual: *The incessant noise from the factory kept me awake all night.* **—in·ces′sant·ly,** ADVERB.

a	hat	ė	term	ô	order	ch	child	⎧a in about
ā	age	i	it	oi	oil	ng	long	⎪e in taken
ä	far	ī	ice	ou	out	sh	she	ə⎨i in pencil
â	care	o	hot	u	cup	th	thin	⎪o in lemon
e	let	ō	open	ù	put	ᴛʜ	then	⎩u in circus
ē	equal	ȯ	saw	ü	rule	zh	measure	

inch (inch),
1 *NOUN.* a unit of length equal to ¹⁄₁₂ of a foot.
2 *VERB.* to move slowly or little by little: *We inched along with the rest of the heavy traffic.*
❑ *PLURAL* **inch•es;** *VERB* **inch•es, inched, inch•ing.**

inch•worm (inch′wėrm′), *NOUN.* a small green or brown caterpillar with an unusual way of moving. It brings its back half forward to form a loop in its body, and then it moves its front half forward.

in•ci•dent (in′sə dənt), *NOUN.* something that happens; event: *I saw a funny incident on the playground today.*

in•ci•den•tal•ly (in′sə den′tl ē), *ADVERB.* by the way: *Incidentally, are you coming to the concert tonight?*

in•cin•e•ra•tor (in sin′ə rā′tər), *NOUN.* a furnace or other device that burns trash and other things.

in•ci•sor (in sī′zər), *NOUN.* a tooth with a sharp edge for cutting; one of the front teeth. Human beings have eight incisors.

in•cli•na•tion (in′klə nā′shən), *NOUN.* a natural fondness for doing something: *She has an inclination for sports.*

in•cline (in klīn′ *for verb;* in′klīn *for noun*),
1 *VERB.* to slope or slant: *The street inclines upward.*
2 *NOUN.* a sloping surface; slope; slant. The side of a hill is an incline.
❑ *VERB* **in•clines, in•clined, in•clin•ing.**

in•clined (in klīnd′), *ADJECTIVE.*
1 willing; tending: *I am inclined to agree with you.*
2 sloping; slanting: *an inclined surface.*

inclined plane, a plank or other plane surface placed at an angle to the ground and used to move heavy weights to a higher level with little force. It is a simple machine.

Giant blocks of stone were dragged up an
inclined plane to build a pyramid.

in•clude (in klüd′), *VERB.*
1 to contain: *Their farm includes a small pond.*
2 to be part of a total: *The price of the property includes the land, house, and furniture.*
❑ *VERB* **in•cludes, in•clud•ed, in•clud•ing.**

in•come (in′kum′), *NOUN.* the money that someone earns: *A person's yearly income is all the money earned in a year.*

income tax, a government tax on a person's income.

in•com•ing (in′kum′ing), *ADJECTIVE.* coming in: *the incoming tide.*

in•com•par•a•ble (in kom′pər ə bəl), *ADJ.* without equal; *My mother is a woman of incomparable beauty.* —**in•com′par•a•bly,** *ADVERB.*

in•com•pat•i•ble (in′kəm pat′ ə bəl), *ADJECTIVE.*
1 not able to live or act together peaceably: *My cat and dog are incompatible.*
2 (in electronics) not able to be used with another item or items: *The two computers have incompatible software.*
—**in′com•pat′i•bil′i•ty,** *NOUN.* —**in′com•pat′i•bly,** *ADVERB.*

in•com•pe•tent (in kom′pə tənt), *ADJECTIVE.* not able to do something well: *an incompetent mechanic.*

in•com•plete (in′kəm plēt′), *ADJECTIVE.* not complete; unfinished: *His book report was incomplete.* —**in′com•plete′ly,** *ADVERB.*

in•con•sid•er•ate (in′kən sid′ər it), *ADJECTIVE.* not thoughtful of other people and their feelings; thoughtless. ▪ See the Synonym Study at **careless.** —**in′con•sid′er•ate•ly,** *ADVERB.*

in•con•spic•u•ous (in′kən spik′yü əs), *ADJECTIVE.* not easily seen; not attracting very much attention: *They live in a small, inconspicuous house.* —**in′con•spic′u•ous•ly,** *ADVERB.*

in•con•ven•ient (in′kən vē′nyənt), *ADJECTIVE.* causing problems or difficulty: *Shelves that are too high to reach easily are inconvenient.* —**in′con•ven′ient•ly,** *ADVERB.*

in•cor•po•rate (in kôr′pə rāt′), *VERB.*
1 to make something a part of something else: *We will incorporate your suggestion into the plan.*
2 to form a business into a corporation: *When the business became large, the owners incorporated it.*
❑ *VERB* **in•cor•po•rates, in•cor•po•rat•ed, in•cor•po•rat•ing.** —**in•cor′po•ra′tion,** *NOUN.*

in•cor•rect (in′kə rekt′), *ADJECTIVE.* not correct; wrong; not true: *The newspaper gave an incorrect account of the accident.* —**in′cor•rect′ly,** *ADVERB.*

in•crease (in krēs′ *for verb;* in′krēs *for noun*),
1 *VERB.* to make or become greater in number, amount, size, and so on: *The racecar driver steadily increased the speed of his car.*
2 *NOUN.* a gain in size or numbers; growth: *There has been a great increase in accidents this year.*
3 *NOUN.* an amount added; addition: *Gasoline prices reflect an increase of five cents a gallon.*
❑ *VERB* **in•creas•es, in•creased, in•creas•ing.**

in•cred•i•ble (in kred′ə bəl), *ADJECTIVE.*
1 impossible to believe; unbelievable: *The hurricane's power was incredible.*
2 very good: *What an incredible day it was!* —**in•cred′i•bly,** *ADVERB.*

in·cu·bate (ing′kyə bāt), *VERB*. to sit on eggs in order to hatch them: *Birds incubate their eggs.* ❑ *VERB* **in·cu·bates, in·cu·bat·ed, in·cu·bat·ing.**

in·cu·ba·tor (ing′kyə bā′tər), *NOUN*.
1 a box or chamber that keeps eggs warm until they hatch.
2 any similar device or machine. Very small babies and babies that are born too early are sometimes kept for a time in hospital incubators.

in·cur·a·ble (in kyûr′ə bəl), *ADJECTIVE*. not able to be cured: *an incurable disease.* –**in·cur′a·bly,** *ADVERB*.

in·debt·ed (in det′id), *ADJECTIVE*. owing money or being grateful to someone or something: *We are indebted to science for many of the comforts in our lives.*

in·deed (in dēd′), *ADVERB*. in fact; in truth; really; surely: *War is indeed terrible.*

in·def·i·nite (in def′ə nit), *ADJECTIVE*.
1 not exact; vague: *"Maybe" is a very indefinite answer.*
2 not limited: *We have an indefinite time to finish.*
3 not yet decided; uncertain: *Our plans are indefinite.*
–**in·def′i·nite·ly,** *ADVERB*.

indefinite article, the article *a* or *an*. "A dog" or "an animal" means "any dog" or "any animal"; "the dog" means "a certain or particular dog."

in·dent (in dent′), *VERB*. to begin a line farther in from the left margin than the other lines: *The first line of a paragraph is usually indented.* ❑ *VERB* **in·dents, in·dent·ed, in·dent·ing.**

in·de·pend·ence (in′di pen′dəns), *NOUN*. freedom to make your own decisions about things; freedom from the control, support, influence, or help of others: *The American colonies won independence from England.*

Independence Day, a holiday in honor of the adoption of the Declaration of Independence on July 4, 1776; Fourth of July.

in·de·pend·ent (in′di pen′dənt), *ADJECTIVE*.
1 thinking or acting for yourself; not influenced by other people: *an independent voter.*
2 guiding, ruling, or governing oneself; not under another country's rule: *The United States is an independent country.*
–**in′de·pend′ent·ly,** *ADVERB*.

independent clause, a group of words that has a subject and a verb and can stand alone as a complete sentence. An independent clause expresses a whole, complete thought. *She fixed my computer, I am hungry,* and *it works* are independent clauses.

in·dex (in′deks), *NOUN*. a list of people, places, and things that are mentioned in a book. An index gives the page numbers where each of these can be found. It is arranged in alphabetical order at the end of the book. ❑ *PLURAL* **in·dex·es.**

index finger, the finger next to the thumb; forefinger.

In·di·a (in′dē ə), *NOUN*. a country in southern Asia.
In·di·an (in′dē ən),
1 *NOUN*. a Native American. ■ See the Usage Note at **Native American.**
2 *ADJECTIVE*. of or for Native Americans.
3 *ADJECTIVE*. of, living in, or belonging to India or the East Indies: *Indian elephants, Indian temples.*
4 *NOUN*. someone born or living in India or the East Indies.

Word Story

When Christopher Columbus arrived in the New World, he thought he had reached an island near India so he called the people he met there **Indians.** People soon knew that the islands weren't near India but the name stuck.

ready for the **Independence Day** parade

In·di·an·a (in′dē an′ə), *NOUN*. one of the Midwestern states of the United States. *Abbreviation:* IN; *Capital:* Indianapolis.
–**In′di·an′an** or **In′di·an′i·an,** *ADJECTIVE* or *NOUN*.

State Story Indiana comes from the word **Indian** (definition 1). When the name was first used, mostly American Indians lived there.

a	hat	ė	term	ô	order	ch child
ā	age	i	it	oi	oil	ng long
ä	far	ī	ice	ou	out	sh she
â	care	o	hot	u	cup	th thin
e	let	ō	open	ù	put	ŦH then
ē	equal	ò	saw	ü	rule	zh measure

ə {
a in about
e in taken
i in pencil
o in lemon
u in circus

In·di·a·nap·o·lis (in′dē ə nap′ə lis), NOUN. the capital of Indiana.

Indian Ocean, an ocean south of Asia, east of Africa, and west of Australia.

in·di·cate (in′də kāt), VERB.
1 to show something or point it out: *The arrow on a sign indicates the right way to go.*
2 to be a sign of something: *Fever indicates illness.*
❏ VERB **in·di·cates, in·di·cat·ed, in·di·cat·ing.**

in·di·ca·tion (in′də kā′shən), NOUN. something that shows or points something out; sign: *There was no indication that the house was occupied.*

in·dif·fer·ence (in dif′ər əns), NOUN. not caring; lack of interest or attention: *The child's indifference to food worried his parents.*

in·dif·fer·ent (in dif′ər ənt), ADJECTIVE. not caring one way or the other: *I was indifferent to their insults.* **−in·dif′fer·ent·ly,** ADVERB.

in·di·ges·tion (in′də jes′chən), NOUN. pain in your stomach or abdomen because you are having difficulty in digesting your food: *Eating too much and too fast may cause indigestion.*

in·dig·nant (in dig′nənt), ADJECTIVE. angry at something you feel is unfair or mean. **−in·dig′nant·ly,** ADVERB.

in·dig·na·tion (in′dig nā′shən), NOUN. the feeling of being angry at something unfair or mean; anger mixed with scorn: *Cruelty to animals aroused his indignation.*

in·di·go (in′də gō),
1 ADJECTIVE or NOUN. deep violet blue.
2 NOUN. a blue dye that can be obtained from various plants. It is now usually made artificially.
3 NOUN. a plant from which indigo was obtained.
❏ PLURAL **in·di·gos** or **in·di·goes.**

in·di·rect (in′də rekt′), ADJECTIVE.
1 not direct; not straight: *We walk to town by a road that is indirect, but very pleasant.*
2 not saying something clearly; not going straight to the point: *Silence can be an indirect way of saying you don't like something.*
3 not directly caused by something: *An increase in traffic was an indirect result of higher bus fares.* **−in′di·rect·ly,** ADVERB.

in·dis·tinct (in′dis tingkt′), ADJECTIVE. not clearly seen, heard, or remembered; not distinct: *an indistinct memory.* **−in′dis·tinct·ly,** ADVERB.

in·di·vid·u·al (in′də vij′ü əl),
1 NOUN. a person: *He is the tallest individual in his family.*
2 NOUN. a single object or living thing: *We saw a herd of giraffes containing 30 individuals.*
3 ADJECTIVE. single; for one person only: *Benches are for several people; chairs are individual seats.*
4 ADJECTIVE. belonging to one person or thing specially: *I can always identify her drawings because of their individual style.*

in·di·vid·u·al·ly (in′də vij′ü ə lē), ADVERB. personally; one at a time; as individuals: *Sometimes our teacher helps us individually.*

in·di·vis·i·ble (in′də viz′ə bəl), ADJECTIVE. not able to be divided: *"One nation under God, indivisible, with liberty and justice for all."*

In·do·ne·sia (in′də nē′zhə), NOUN. a country made up of many islands off the coast of southeastern Asia. **−In′do·ne′sian,** ADJECTIVE or NOUN.

in·door (in′dôr′), ADJECTIVE. done or used in a house or building: *indoor tennis.*

in·doors (in′dôrz′ or in dôrz′), ADVERB. in or into a house or building: *Go indoors.*

in·dulge (in dulj′), VERB.
1 to let yourself have, use, or do what you want: *Every so often he indulges in a chocolate soda.*
2 to let someone else do what he or she wants: *We often indulge a sick person.*
❏ VERB **in·dulg·es, in·dulged, in·dulg·ing.**

in·dus·tri·al (in dus′trē əl), ADJECTIVE.
1 of, used in, or produced by industry: *industrial products, industrial robots.*
2 having highly developed industries: *The United States and Great Britain are industrial nations.*

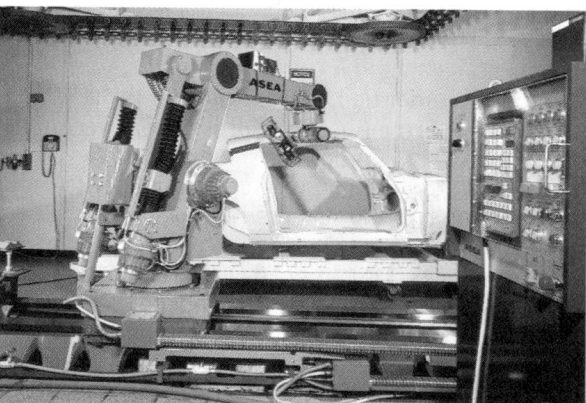
Industrial robots are used in factories.

in·dus·tri·al·ize (in dus′trē ə līz), VERB. to develop large industries in a country. ❏ VERB **in·dus·tri·al·iz·es, in·dus·tri·al·ized, in·dus·tri·al·iz·ing. −in·dus′tri·al·i·za′tion,** NOUN.

in·dus·tri·ous (in dus′trē əs), ADJECTIVE. working hard and steadily: *An industrious student usually has good grades.* **−in·dus′tri·ous·ly,** ADVERB.

in·dus·try (in′də strē), NOUN.
1 the production of all kinds of goods, especially in factories or plants: *Mexican industry is expanding.*
2 a kind of business that makes a particular product: *My mother works in the automobile industry.*
❏ PLURAL **in·dus·tries.**

in·ed·i·ble (in ed′ə bəl), ADJECTIVE. not fit to eat: *Toadstools are inedible.*

in·ef·fec·tive (in′ə fek′tiv), *ADJECTIVE.* not producing the desired effect: *An ineffective medicine fails to cure a disease or relieve pain.* —**in′ef·fec′tive·ly,** *ADVERB.*

in·ef·fi·cient (in′ə fish′ənt), *ADJECTIVE.* not able to produce a result without wasting time, money, or energy; not efficient; wasteful: *A machine that uses too much fuel is inefficient.* —**in′ef·fi′cient·ly,** *ADVERB.*

in·e·qual·i·ty (in′i kwol′ə tē), *NOUN.* a lack of equality; condition or case of being unequal in amount, size, value, or rank: *There is a great inequality between the salaries of a bank president and a bank clerk.* ❑ *PLURAL* **in·e·qual·it·ies.**

in·er·tia (in ėr′shə), *NOUN.* the tendency of all objects and matter to stay still, or if moving, to go on moving in the same direction, unless acted on by some force.

in·ev·i·ta·ble (in ev′ə tə bəl), *ADJECTIVE.* sure to happen; certain to come: *Death is inevitable.* —**in·ev′i·ta·bil′i·ty,** *NOUN.* —**in·ev′i·ta·bly,** *ADVERB.*

in·ex·pen·sive (in′ik spen′siv), *ADJECTIVE.* not costing a lot of money; having a low price: *I bought an inexpensive car* —**in′ex·pen′sive·ly,** *ADVERB.*

in·ex·per·i·enced (in′ik spir′ē ənst), *ADJECTIVE.* lacking the skill and knowledge gained from experience.

in·fan·cy (in′fən sē) *NOUN.*
1 the time of being a baby; early childhood.
2 an early stage of anything: *Space travel is still in its infancy.*

in·fant (in′fənt),
1 *NOUN.* a baby; very young child.
2 *ADJECTIVE.* of or for an infant: *an infant blanket, infant food.*

a smiling **infant**

Word Story

Infant comes from two Latin words meaning "not speaking." Babies and very small children who can't yet talk are called *infants.*

in·fan·try (in′fən trē), *NOUN.* soldiers that are trained, equipped, and organized to fight on foot.

in·fect (in fekt′), *VERB.* to cause disease by bringing a living thing into contact with germs, viruses, and so on: *Dirt can infect an open cut. If you have a bad cold, you may infect the people around you.* ❑ *VERB* **in·fects, in·fect·ed, in·fect·ing.**

in·fec·tion (in fek′shən), *NOUN.*
1 the act or process of causing disease in people and other living things by bringing them into contact with germs, viruses, and so on.

2 a disease caused in this manner, especially one that can spread from one person to another.

in·fec·tious (in fek′shəs), *ADJECTIVE.* spread by infection: *Malaria is an infectious disease that is spread by the bite of certain mosquitoes.*

in·fer·i·or (in fir′ē ər), *ADJECTIVE.*
1 not as good as most others: *This cloth is inferior to real silk.* ■ See the Synonym Study at **bad.**
2 lower in position or rank: *A lieutenant is inferior to a captain.*

in·fer·tile (in fėr′tl), *ADJECTIVE.*
1 not able to bear seeds, fruit, or young: *an infertile cow.*
2 not able to produce good crops: *an infertile field.*

in·fest (in fest′), *VERB.* to spread in great numbers throughout an area and cause harm or damage: *Mosquitoes infest swamps.* ❑ *VERB* **in·fests, in·fest·ed, in·fest·ing.** —**in′fes·ta′tion,** *NOUN.*

in·field (in′fēld′), *NOUN.*
1 the part of a baseball field that is inside the lines connecting the bases; diamond.
2 the first, second, and third basemen and shortstop of a baseball team.

in·field·er (in′fēl′dər), *NOUN.* a baseball player who plays in the infield.

in·fi·nite (in′fə nit), *ADJECTIVE.* without limits or bounds; endless: *the infinite expanse of outer space.*

in·fin·i·tive (in fin′ə tiv), *NOUN.* a verb in its simplest form, often preceded by "to." Infinitives do not show who is doing the action of the verb nor when the action is taking place. In "I want to buy milk," and "We must go now," *to buy* and *go* are infinitives.

in·flamed (in flāmd′), *ADJECTIVE.* unnaturally warm, red, sore, or swollen: *eyes inflamed from smoke.*

in·flam·ma·ble (in flam′ə bəl), *ADJECTIVE.* easily set on fire: *Paper is inflammable.*

Usage Note

Inflammable and **flammable** mean the same thing. It is better to use *flammable* since the prefix **in-** often means "not," and could confuse your reader.

in·flam·ma·tion (in′flə mā′shən), *NOUN.* heat, redness, swelling, and pain in a part of the body, caused by infection: *Boils are inflammations of the skin.*

in·flate (in flāt′), *VERB.* to force air or gas into a balloon, tire, or some other hollow thing, causing it to swell up. ❑ *VERB* **in·flates, in·flat·ed, in·flat·ing.** —**in·flat′a·ble,** *ADJECTIVE.*

a	hat	ė	term	ô	order	ch	child		a in about
ā	age	i	it	oi	oil	ng	long		e in taken
ä	far	ī	ice	ou	out	sh	she	ə⟨	i in pencil
â	care	o	hot	u	cup	th	thin		o in lemon
e	let	ō	open	u̇	put	ᴛʜ	then		u in circus
ē	equal	ȯ	saw	ü	rule	zh	measure		

in·fla·tion (in flā′shən), NOUN. a sudden or steady increase in the price of goods.

in·flict (in flikt′), VERB. to give or cause a blow, wound, or pain to someone: *A knife can inflict a bad wound.* ❑ VERB **in·flicts, in·flict·ed, in·flict·ing.**

in·flu·ence (in′flü əns),
1 NOUN. the power of getting other people to do something or to think in a certain way: *Use your influence to persuade your friends to join our club.*
2 NOUN. someone or something that has this power: *Her older sister has a good influence on her.*
3 VERB. to have some power or influence on: *What we read influences our thinking.*
❑ VERB **in·flu·enc·es, in·flu·enced, in·flu·enc·ing.**

in·flu·en·tial (in′flü en′shəl), ADJECTIVE. having influence: *Influential friends helped him get a job.*

in·flu·en·za (in′flü en′zə), NOUN. See **flu.**

in·form (in fôrm′), VERB.
1 to give knowledge, facts, or news to someone: *Her letter informed us of when she expected to arrive.*
2 to give information about someone else's wrongdoing to the police: *The criminal who was caught informed against the other robbers.*
❑ VERB **in·forms, in·formed, in·form·ing.**

in·for·mal (in fôr′məl), ADJECTIVE.
1 not formal; not according to rules: *an informal meeting.*
2 used in everyday, common talk, but not used in formal talking or writing. A word like *kids* (meaning "children") is informal.
—**in·for′mal·ly,** ADVERB.

in·for·ma·tion (in′fər mā′shən), NOUN. knowledge given or received of some fact or event; news: *A encyclopedia contains much information. We have just received information of the astronauts' safe landing.*

in·fur·i·ate (in fyur′ē āt), VERB. to make someone very angry or furious: *Their insults infuriated us.*
❑ VERB **in·fur·i·ates, in·fur·i·at·ed, in·fur·i·at·ing.**

in·gen·ious (in jē′nyəs), ADJECTIVE.
1 clever at making or inventing things: *The ingenious girls made a folding ladder for their tree house.*
2 cleverly made: *He made an ingenious bird feeder from an old tin can and some wire.*

in·gre·di·ent
(in grē′dē ənt), NOUN. one of the parts of a mixture: *The ingredients of a cake usually include eggs, sugar, flour, and flavoring.*

measuring **ingredients**

in·hab·it (in hab′it), VERB. to live in: *Fish inhabit the sea.* ❑ VERB **in·hab·its, in·hab·it·ed, in·hab·it·ing.** —**in·hab′it·a·ble,** ADJECTIVE.

in·hab·it·ant (in hab′ə tənt), NOUN. someone who lives in a place: *Our town has ten thousand inhabitants.*

in·hale (in hāl′), VERB. to breathe air, gas, tobacco smoke, and so on, into the lungs. ❑ VERB **in·hales, in·haled, in·hal·ing.**

in·hal·er (in hā′ler), NOUN. a device for breathing in a healing vapor, especially to relieve nasal congestion.

in·her·ent (in hir′ənt), ADJECTIVE. existing; belonging naturally to a person or thing: *Her inherent curiosity about flowers led her to study plants.*

in·her·it (in her′it), VERB.
1 to get something after the former owner dies; receive as an heir: *After Grandfather's death, Mother inherited all his property.*
2 to get from your parents or ancestors through heredity: *I inherited my mother's dark hair.*
❑ VERB **in·her·its, in·her·it·ed, in·her·it·ing.** —**in·her′i·tor,** NOUN.

in·her·it·ance (in her′ə təns), NOUN. anything inherited: *The house was his inheritance.*

in·hos·pit·a·ble (in hos′pi tə bəl *or* in′ho spit′ə bəl), ADJECTIVE. not hospitable; not making visitors comfortable: *Our inhospitable neighbor never offers visitors any refreshments.*

in·hu·man (in hyü′mən), ADJECTIVE. without kindness, mercy, or tenderness; cruel: *He has an inhuman lack of concern for the suffering of others.*

i·ni·tial (i nish′əl),
1 ADJECTIVE. happening at the beginning of something; first; earliest: *His initial effort at skating was a failure.*
2 NOUN. the first letter of a word: *The initials U.S. stand for United States.*
3 VERB. to mark or sign something with your initials: *Lee Ann Wong initialed the note "L.A.W."*
❑ VERB **i·ni·tials, i·ni·tialed, i·ni·tial·ing.**

i·ni·ti·ate (i nish′ē āt), VERB.
1 to start something; begin: *This year we shall initiate a series of free concerts.*
2 to admit someone with formal ceremonies into a group or society: *The old members initiated the new members.*
❑ VERB **i·ni·ti·ates, i·ni·ti·at·ed, i·ni·ti·at·ing.**

i·ni·ti·a·tion (i nish′ē ā′shən), NOUN. the ceremonies by which someone is admitted to a group or society: *Everyone in the club attended the initiation of the new members.*

i·ni·ti·a·tive (i nish′ə tiv), NOUN. the ability to decide what to do, without needing to be told by someone else: *She shows a lot of initiative in planning class projects.*

in·ject (in jekt′), *VERB.* to put liquid into someone's body through a hollow needle: *The doctor injected penicillin into my arm.* ❑ *VERB* **in·jects, in·ject·ed, in·ject·ing. –in·ject′a·ble,** *ADJECTIVE.*

in·jec·tion (in jek′shən), *NOUN.*
1 a liquid injected: *The nurse prepared the injection.*
2 the act or process of injecting: *The medicine was given by injection rather than by mouth.*

in·jure (in′jər), *VERB.* to harm or hurt a person or an animal: *He was injured in a car accident.* ■ See the Synonym Study at **harm.** ❑ *VERB* **in·jures, in·jured, in·jur·ing.**

in·jur·y (in′jər ē), *NOUN.* physical harm to a person or an animal: *She escaped from the train wreck without injury.* ❑ *PLURAL* **in·jur·ies.**

in·jus·tice (in jus′tis), *NOUN.*
1 lack of justice: *We were angry at the injustice of her decision to punish the entire class for one student's bad behavior.*
2 an unjust act: *It is a great injustice to send an innocent person to jail.*

ink (ingk),
1 *NOUN.* a liquid used for writing or printing. These words are written in black ink.
2 *VERB.* to put ink on something; stain with ink.
❑ *VERB* **inks, inked, ink·ing.**

Did You Know?

It is easy to make **invisible ink.** Try writing on white paper with milk or lemon juice. Then expose your paper to heat. (Ask an adult if you can use a hair dryer.) Your secret writing should turn brown on the paper.

in·land (in′lənd),
1 *ADJECTIVE.* away from the coast or the border; in the interior: *Illinois is an inland state.*
2 *ADVERB.* in or toward the interior: *He traveled inland from New York to Chicago.*

in-law (in′lò′), *NOUN.* someone related by marriage.

in·let (in′let), *NOUN.* a narrow strip of water that runs from a larger body of water into the land or between islands: *The fishing village was on a small inlet of the sea.*

in-line skates (in′lin′ skāts′), special boots with wheels or rollers attached in a single line, instead of in pairs side by side.

inn (in), *NOUN.*
1 a place where travelers can get meals and a room to sleep in.
2 a restaurant or tavern.
■ Another word that sounds like this is **in.**

in-line skates

in·ner (in′ər), *ADJECTIVE.* farther in; inside: *an inner room.*

inner ear, the deepest part of the ear. It contains the organs of balance and the organs that change sound into nerve messages.

in·ning (in′ing), *NOUN.* the division of a baseball game during which each team has a turn at bat.

inn·keep·er (in′kē′pər), *NOUN.* someone who owns or manages an inn.

in·no·cence (in′ə səns), *NOUN.* freedom from guilt; the condition of being innocent.

in·no·cent (in′ə sənt), *ADJECTIVE.* free from sin or wrong; not guilty of a crime: *In the United States a person is presumed innocent until proved guilty.* **–in′no·cent·ly,** *ADVERB.*

in·oc·u·late (in ok′yə lāt), *VERB.* to inject with a preparation made from killed or weakened germs. This causes a mild form of a disease, and the body builds up protection against the disease. ❑ *VERB* **in·oc·u·lates, in·oc·u·lat·ed, in·oc·u·lat·ing. –in·oc′u·la′tion,** *NOUN.*

in·put (in′pùt′),
1 *VERB.* to put information into a computer.
2 *NOUN.* any information that is put into a computer.
3 *NOUN.* someone's comments or opinion: *We asked for input from all the members of the staff.*
❑ *VERB* **in·puts, in·put, in·put·ting.**

in·quire (in kwir′), *VERB.* to try to find out by asking questions; ask: *The detective went from house to house, inquiring if anyone had seen anything suspicious.* ■ See the Synonym Study at **ask.** ❑ *VERB* **in·quires, in·quired, in·quir·ing. –in·quir′er,** *NOUN.*

in·quir·y (in kwi′rē *or* in′kwər ē), *NOUN.* the act or process of searching for truth, information, or knowledge: *His inquiry into the town's history led him to many interesting stories.* ❑ *PLURAL* **in·quir·ies.**

in·quis·i·tive (in kwiz′ə tiv), *ADJECTIVE.* asking many questions; curious: *Children are often inquisitive.* **–in·quis′i·tive·ly,** *ADVERB.* **–in·quis′i·tive·ness,** *NOUN.*

in·sane (in sān′), *ADJECTIVE.*
1 mentally ill. ★ **Insane** is now used to mean "mentally ill" only in legal discussions.
2 for mentally ill people: *an insane asylum.*
3 extremely foolish: *People used to think that plans for a flying machine were insane.*

in·san·i·ty (in san′ə tē), *NOUN.*
1 mental illness: *The lawyer claimed that the prisoner had attacked the guard during a fit of temporary insanity.*
2 a complete lack of common sense; foolishness: *It is insanity to drive a car without any brakes.*

a	hat	ė	term	ô	order	ch	child		a in about
ā	age	i	it	oi	oil	ng	long		e in taken
ä	far	ī	ice	ou	out	sh	she	ə	i in pencil
â	care	o	hot	u	cup	th	thin		o in lemon
e	let	ō	open	ù	put	ŦH	then		u in circus
ē	equal	ò	saw	ü	rule	zh	measure		

in·scribe (in skrīb′), VERB. to write, engrave, or mark something on a surface: *The ring was inscribed with her name.* ❑ VERB **in·scribes, in·scribed, in·scrib·ing.**

in·scrip·tion (in skrip′shən), NOUN. something inscribed: *the inscription on a tombstone.*

in·sect (in′sekt), NOUN.
1 any of a group of very small animals without bones, with bodies divided into three parts. Insects have three pairs of legs and one or two pairs of wings. Flies, mosquitoes, butterflies, beetles, and bees are insects.
2 any similar small animal, especially one without wings and with four pairs of legs. Spiders and centipedes are often called insects.
–in′sect·like′, ADJECTIVE.

Did You Know?

There are more than one million different kinds of **insects,** and almost 10,000 new kinds are discovered every year. Some scientists believe that there are more than one million kinds yet to be discovered.

in·sec·ti·cide (in sek′tə sīd), NOUN. a substance for killing insects.

in·se·cure (in′si kyur′), ADJECTIVE.
1 not confident about yourself; timid: *He is so insecure that he has trouble talking to other children.*
2 not safe from danger or harm: *During an earthquake, people in tall buildings are in an insecure position.*

in·sert (in sėrt′ for verb; in′sėrt′ for noun),
1 VERB. to put something inside something else: *She inserted the key into the lock.*
2 NOUN. something put inside something else: *The book contained an insert of several pages of pictures.*
❑ VERB **in·serts, in·sert·ed, in·sert·ing.**

in·side (in′sīd′ or in′sīd′),
1 NOUN. the inner surface of something: *The inside of the box was lined with colored paper.*
2 NOUN. the inner space of something: *The inside of the house was glowing with light.*
3 ADJECTIVE. on or by the inner side: *an inside seat, an inside pocket.*
4 ADVERB. in or into the inner part: *Please step inside. It is too nice a day to stay inside.*
5 PREPOSITION. within; in: *The nut is inside the shell.*
inside out, IDIOM.
1 so that what should be inside is outside; with the inside showing: *He turned his pockets inside out.*
2 completely; thoroughly: *She knew the rules inside out.*

in·sight (in′sīt′), NOUN. deep understanding in dealing with people or with facts: *We study science to gain insight into the world we live in.*

in·sig·ni·a (in sig′nē ə), NOUN. a medal, badge, and so on, that shows someone's rank or membership in an organization: *The crown is the insignia of royalty.* ❑ PLURAL **in·sig·ni·a** or **in·sig·ni·as.**

These Brownies wear **insignia** on their sashes.

in·sig·nif·i·cant (in′sig nif′ə kənt), ADJECTIVE. of little use or importance: *A penny is an insignificant amount of money.*

in·sin·cere (in′sin sir′), ADJECTIVE. not sincere; deceitful: *He never intended to keep his insincere promises.* **–in′sin·cere′ly,** ADVERB.

in·sist (in sist′), VERB.
1 to say over and over again that something is true: *After her arrest she insisted on her innocence.*
2 to demand: *She insists that we should all learn to ski.*
❑ VERB **in·sists, in·sist·ed, in·sist·ing.**

in·so·lent (in′sə lənt), ADJECTIVE. rude; without respect: *They were insolent to walk away while you were talking to them.* **–in′so·lent·ly,** ADVERB.

in·som·ni·a (in som′nē ə), NOUN. an inability to sleep; sleeplessness.

in·spect (in spekt′), VERB.
1 to look at something carefully; examine: *You should inspect yourself for ticks after walking in the woods.*
2 to examine something formally or officially: *Government officials inspect factories and mines to make sure that they are safe for workers.*
❑ VERB **in·spects, in·spect·ed, in·spect·ing.**

in·spec·tion (in spek′shən), NOUN.
1 the act or process of inspecting; examination: *An inspection of the roof showed no leaks.*
2 a formal or official examination: *The firefighters lined up for their daily inspection by their officers.*

in·spec·tor (in spek′tər), NOUN. someone whose job is to inspect something: *The city building inspector told the landlord to fix the fire escape.*

in·spi·ra·tion (in′spə rā′shən), NOUN.
1 something that has a strong effect on what you feel or do, especially something good: *Some people get inspiration from sermons, some from nature.*
2 someone who causes people to feel good, work harder, and so on: *The teacher was an inspiration to her students.*
3 a sudden, brilliant idea.

in·spire (in spīr′), VERB.
1 to cause someone to do something good: *His poor grade inspired him to study harder for the next test.*
2 to cause a good thought or a good feeling in someone: *The leader's courage inspired confidence in others.*

3 to fill someone with excitement: *The speaker inspired the crowd.*
❑ *VERB* **in·spires, in·spired, in·spir·ing.**

in·stall (in stȯl′), *VERB.* to put something in place where it can be used: *The new owner of the house had a telephone installed.* ❑ *VERB* **in·stalls, in·stalled, in·stall·ing. –in·stall′er,** *NOUN.*

in·stall·ment (in stȯl′mənt), *NOUN.* one of a series of payments for something you buy, usually paid monthly: *The table cost $1,000; we paid in two monthly installments of $500 each.*

in·stance (in′stəns), **for instance,** for example: *In the computer industry, for instance, new jobs are being created every year.*

in·stant (in′stənt),
1 *NOUN.* a very short amount of time: *He paused for an instant.*
2 *NOUN.* a particular moment: *Stop this instant!*
3 *ADJECTIVE.* without delay; happening immediately: *The medicine gave instant relief from pain.*
4 *ADJECTIVE.* prepared beforehand and requiring little or no cooking, mixing, or additional ingredients: *instant coffee, instant pudding.*

in·stant·ly (in′stənt lē), *ADVERB.* at once.

in·stead (in sted′), *ADVERB.* in place of someone or something else: *She stayed home, and her sister went riding instead.*
instead of, *IDIOM.* rather than; in place of: *Instead of studying, I watched TV.*

in·stinct (in′stingkt), *NOUN.*
1 an animal's ability to know how to do something without learning how to do it: *Birds have an instinct for building nests.*
2 a natural tendency or ability; talent: *Even as a child, the artist had an instinct for drawing.*

in·stinc·tive (in stingk′tiv), *ADJECTIVE.* born in an animal or person, not learned: *The spinning of webs is instinctive in spiders.* **–in·stinc′tive·ly,** *ADVERB.*

in·sti·tute (in′stə tüt),
1 *NOUN.* an organization for some special purpose. An art institute teaches or displays art. A technical school is often called an institute.
2 *VERB.* to set something up; begin: *After the accident, the police instituted an investigation into its causes.*
❑ *VERB* **in·sti·tutes, in·sti·tut·ed, in·sti·tut·ing.**

in·sti·tu·tion (in′stə tü′shən), *NOUN.*
1 a club, society, or any organization set up for some special purpose. A church, school, college, hospital, or prison is an institution.
2 an established law or custom: *Marriage is an institution among most of the world's people.*

in·struct (in strukt′), *VERB.*
1 to show someone how to do something; teach; educate: *We have one teacher who instructs us in reading, arithmetic, and science.*

2 to give directions or orders to someone: *The owner of the house instructed her agent to sell it.*
❑ *VERB* **in·structs, in·struct·ed, in·struct·ing.**

in·struc·tion (in struk′shən), *NOUN.*
1 teaching; training; education: *He devoted his life to the instruction of children.*
2 **instructions,** directions or orders: *The teacher's instructions were clearly understood.*

in·struc·tor (in struk′tər), *NOUN.* a teacher, especially in college or in a sport: *tennis instructor, physics instructor.*

in·stru·ment (in′strə mənt), *NOUN.*
1 a tool used to do something; mechanical device: *A forceps and a drill are two instruments used by dentists.* ■ See the Synonym Study at **tool.**
2 a device for producing musical sounds: *wind instruments, stringed instruments. A violin, cello, and piano were the instruments in the trio.*
3 a device for measuring, recording, or controlling something. A thermometer is an instrument for measuring temperature.

musical **instruments**

in·stru·men·tal (in′strə men′tl), *ADJECTIVE.* played on or written for musical instruments: *Some people prefer instrumental music to listening to a choir.*

in·suf·fi·cient (in′sə fish′ənt), *ADJECTIVE.* not enough: *The police had insufficient evidence to arrest the thief.* **–in′suf·fi′cient·ly,** *ADVERB.*

in·su·late (in′sə lāt), *VERB.* to cover or line something so that electricity, heat, or sound can neither get in or out: *My winter boots are insulated. Telephone wires are often insulated by a covering of rubber.* ❑ *VERB* **in·su·lates, in·su·lat·ed, in·su·lat·ing.**

in·su·la·tion (in′sə lā′shən), *NOUN.* a material used to insulate something: *Rubber is a common insulation for electric wires.*

a	hat	ė	term	ô	order	ch	child	⎧ a in about
ā	age	i	it	oi	oil	ng	long	e in taken
ä	far	ī	ice	ou	out	sh	she	ə ⎨ i in pencil
â	care	o	hot	u	cup	th	thin	o in lemon
e	let	ō	open	u̇	put	ᴛʜ	then	⎩ u in circus
ē	equal	ȯ	saw	ü	rule	zh	measure	

in·su·lin (in′sə lən), NOUN. a substance produced by the pancreas and necessary for the body to use sugar. The lack of insulin is a cause of diabetes.

in·sult (in sult′ *for verb;* in′sult *for noun*),
1 VERB. to say or do something very rude or disrespectful to someone: *She insulted me by calling me a liar.*
2 NOUN. something you say or do that is very rude or disrespectful: *It is an insult to call someone ugly or stupid.*
❑ VERB **in·sults, in·sult·ed, in·sult·ing.**

Word Story

Insult comes from a Latin word meaning "to jump at." Later on, the meaning changed from the idea of a physical attack to the idea of an attack with words.

in·sur·ance (in shùr′əns), NOUN.
1 the act or business of insuring property, persons, or lives. Fire insurance, burglary insurance, accident insurance, life insurance, and health insurance are some of the many kinds.
2 the amount of money for which someone or something is insured.

in·sure (in shùr′), VERB.
1 to make something or someone safe against loss or harm by paying money to an insurance company: *She insured her car against accident, theft, and fire.*
2 to agree to pay money if certain kinds of harm or loss happen to something or someone. An insurance company will insure your property, health, or life.
❑ VERB **in·sures, in·sured, in·sur·ing.**

in·tact (in takt′), ADJECTIVE. not broken; uninjured; whole: *The missing bicycle was found and returned intact.*

in·take (in′tāk′), NOUN.
1 the place where water, air, or gas enters a channel, pipe, or other narrow opening.
2 the act or process of taking something in: *Your intake of food must be enough to provide extra energy when you play football.*

in·te·ger (in′tə jər), NOUN. any number that does not include a fraction; whole numbers.

in·te·grate (in′tə grāt), VERB.
1 to put or bring two or more parts of something together: *The committee will try to integrate the different ideas into a single plan.*
2 to make schools, parks, and other public facilities equally available to people of all races: *to integrate a neighborhood.*
❑ VERB **in·te·grates, in·te·grat·ed, in·te·grat·ing.**

in·te·gra·tion (in′tə grā′shən), NOUN. the act or process of including people of all races equally in schools, parks, neighborhoods, and the like.

in·teg·ri·ty (in teg′rə tē), NOUN. honesty; sincerity: *I respect people with integrity.*

in·tel·lect (in′tə lekt), NOUN. the power of knowing; understanding; intelligence: *To learn math or spelling, you must use your intellect.*

in·tel·lec·tu·al (in′tə lek′chü əl), ADJECTIVE. using or needing intelligence: *A good discussion requires intellectual effort.*

in·tel·li·gence (in tel′ə jəns), NOUN.
1 the ability to learn and know something; understanding; mind: *A dolphin has more intelligence than a shark. Intelligence tests are given in many schools.*
2 information, especially secret information, about an enemy: *Spies supply our government with intelligence.*

in·tel·li·gent (in tel′ə jənt), ADJECTIVE. having or showing a great ability to learn and know things; quick at learning: *Elephants are intelligent animals.*
■ See the Synonym Study at **smart.**
—**in·tel′li·gent·ly,** ADVERB.

in·tend (in tend′), VERB. to have something in mind as a purpose; plan: *We intend to go home soon.*
❑ VERB **in·tends, in·tend·ed, in·tend·ing.**

in·tense (in tens′), ADJECTIVE.
1 very much; very great; very strong: *Intense heat melts iron. A bad burn causes intense pain.*
2 having or showing strong feelings. An intense person feels things very deeply.
—**in·tense′ly,** ADVERB.

in·ten·si·ty (in ten′sə tē), NOUN. the quality of being strong or of having a strong effect on something; force: *The intensity of tropical sunlight made us squint.* ❑ PLURAL **in·ten·si·ties.**

in·ten·sive (in ten′siv), ADJECTIVE. very thorough; done with a lot of hard work and attention to detail: *New laws were passed following an intensive study of the causes of pollution.*

in·tent (in tent′), NOUN. a purpose; intention: *I'm sorry I hurt you; that wasn't my intent.* —**in·tent′ly,** ADVERB.

intent on, IDIOM. having your eyes or thoughts directed at someone or something; attentive: *an intent look.*

in·ten·tion (in ten′shən), NOUN. a plan, goal, or purpose that you have: *Our intention is to travel next summer.*

in·ten·tion·al (in ten′shə nəl), ADJECTIVE. done on purpose; meant; planned: *The kick she gave me under the table was intentional; it was a signal to be quiet.* —**in·ten′tion·al·ly,** ADVERB.

in·ter·ac·tive (in′tər ak′tiv), ADJECTIVE. allowing two-way communication between a user and a computer, television, or other device. An interactive system allows the user to ask and answer questions that control the information shown and heard.

in·ter·cept (in′tər sept′), *VERB.* to take, grab, or stop something on its way from one place to another: *to intercept a letter, to intercept a football pass.* ❑ *VERB* **in·ter·cepts, in·ter·cept·ed, in·ter·cept·ing.**

in·ter·change·a·ble (in′tər chān′jə bəl), *ADJECTIVE.* able to be put or used in each other's place; able to be switched: *interchangeable parts.*

intercepting a pass

in·ter·com (in′tər kom′), *NOUN.* a system of microphones and loudspeakers by which people can talk to each other from different parts of a building, aircraft, ship, and so on.

in·ter·est (in′tər ist),
1 *NOUN.* a feeling of wanting to know, see, do, own, or take part in something: *He has an interest in collecting stamps.*
2 *VERB.* to arouse this kind of feeling in; make someone curious: *A good mystery interests most people.*
3 *NOUN.* the power of arousing this kind of feeling: *A dull book lacks interest.*
4 *NOUN.* something in which someone has a share or part. Any business, activity, or pastime can be an interest.
5 *NOUN.* the money paid for the use of someone else's money: *The interest on the loan was 7 percent a year.*
❑ *VERB* **in·ter·ests, in·ter·est·ed, in·ter·est·ing.**

in·ter·est·ed (in′tər ə stid), *ADJECTIVE.* feeling or showing interest: *an interested spectator.*

Synonym Study

Interested means paying attention because you want to: *Her report kept the whole class interested.*

Attentive means paying attention: *She learns quickly because she is so attentive.*

Absorbed means very interested: *I was absorbed all afternoon in the space adventure story.*

Fascinated means so interested by something that it is hard to turn your attention away from it: *I am fascinated by the colorful insects in my science teacher's collection.*

ANTONYM: **bored.**

in·ter·est·ing (in′tər ə sting), *ADJECTIVE.* holding someone's attention: *Stories about travel and adventure are interesting to many people.*

in·ter·fere (in′tər fir′), *VERB.*
1 to get in the way of something: *I will come Saturday if nothing interferes with my plans.*
2 to get mixed up in other people's business: *He is always interfering in other people's business.*
❑ *VERB* **in·ter·feres, in·ter·fered, in·ter·fer·ing.**

in·ter·fer·ence (in′tər fir′əns), *NOUN.*
1 the act or process of interfering: *Your interference spoiled our fun.*
2 the act of illegally blocking an opposing player in football, hockey, and some other sports.

in·ter·i·or (in tir′ē ər),
1 *NOUN.* the inside of something; inner surface or space: *The interior of the house was beautifully decorated.*
2 *ADJECTIVE.* inner; on or for the inside: *The interior walls of the house were painted last year.*
3 *NOUN.* the part of a region or country away from the coast or border: *There are deserts in the interior of Asia.*

in·ter·jec·tion (in′tər jek′shən), *NOUN.* a written or spoken word that expresses emotion or sensation. *Ouch! oh! alas!* and *hurrah!* are interjections.

in·ter·me·di·ate (in′tər mē′dē it), *ADJECTIVE.* happening between other things: *Classes are offered in beginning, intermediate, and advanced lifesaving.*

in·ter·mis·sion (in′tər mish′ən), *NOUN.* the time between parts of a play, concert, and so on: *The concert was from 8 to 10:30 with an intermission at 9 o'clock.*

in·tern (in′tėrn′), *NOUN.* a doctor who is working at a hospital where she or he is studying medicine.

in·ter·nal (in tėr′nl), *ADJECTIVE.* on the inside of your body: *The accident caused internal injuries.*
—**in·ter′nal·ly,** *ADVERB.*

in·ter·na·tion·al (in′tər nash′ə nəl), *ADJECTIVE.* between or among two or more countries: *A treaty is an international agreement.*

In·ter·net (in′tər net′), *NOUN.* an extremely large computer network, including many smaller networks of university, government, business, and private computers, linked by telephone lines. Using the Internet, people can exchange messages and information all over the world.

in·ter·plan·e·tar·y (in′tər plan′ə ter′ē), *ADJECTIVE.* between the planets: *interplanetary travel.*

in·ter·pret (in tėr′prit), *VERB.*
1 to explain the meaning of something: *to interpret a hard passage in a book, to interpret a dream.*

a	hat	ė	term	ô	order	ch	child	⎧a in about
ā	age	i	it	oi	oil	ng	long	⎪e in taken
ä	far	ī	ice	ou	out	sh	she	ə⎨i in pencil
â	care	o	hot	u	cup	th	thin	⎪o in lemon
e	let	ō	open	ù	put	ᵺ	then	⎩u in circus
ē	equal	ȯ	saw	ü	rule	zh	measure	

2 to bring out the meaning of: *The actress interpreted the part of the queen with great skill.*
3 to work as an interpreter.
❏ *VERB* **in·ter·prets, in·ter·pret·ed, in·ter·pret·ing.**

in·ter·pre·ta·tion (in tėr′prə tā′shən), *NOUN.*
1 the act of interpreting; explanation: *People often give different interpretations to the same facts.*
2 the act of bringing out the meaning: *His interpretation of that song was very sad.*

in·ter·pret·er (in tėr′prə tər), *NOUN.* someone whose work is changing words spoken in one language into the words of another language: *Because my parents do not speak Spanish, their guide in Mexico acted as their interpreter also.*

interpreter **Sacajawea**

Sacajawea was an American Indian woman who acted as an interpreter for the explorers Lewis and Clark in what is now the Northwest U.S.

in·ter·ra·cial (in′tər rā′shel), *ADJECTIVE.* between or involving different racial groups: *interracial cooperation.*

in·ter·ro·gate (in ter′ə gāt), *VERB.* to ask someone questions in a very careful, thorough manner: *The lawyers interrogated the witness.* ❏ *VERB* **in·ter·ro·gates, in·ter·ro·gat·ed, in·ter·ro·gat·ing.** **–in·ter′ro·ga′tion,** *NOUN.*

in·ter·rog·a·tive (in′tə rog′ə tiv), *ADJECTIVE.*
1 asking a question; having the form of a question: *an interrogative sentence.*
2 (in grammar) used in asking a question. *Where, when, why* are **interrogative adverbs.** *Who* and *what* are **interrogative pronouns.**

in·ter·rupt (in′tə rupt′), *VERB.*
1 to break in upon someone who is talking, working, resting, and so on: *Please don't interrupt me until I've finished talking on the phone.*

2 to stop something that is happening: *A fire drill interrupted the lesson.*
❏ *VERB* **in·ter·rupts, in·ter·rupt·ed, in·ter·rupt·ing.**

in·ter·rup·tion (in′tə rup′shən), *NOUN.* the act of interrupting or condition of being interrupted: *The rain continued without interruption all day.*

in·ter·sect (in′tər sekt′), *VERB.* to cross each other; cross: *Streets usually intersect at right angles. Find the point where the two lines intersect on the graph.* ❏ *VERB* **in·ter·sects, in·ter·sect·ed, in·ter·sect·ing.**

in·ter·sec·tion (in′tər sek′shən), *NOUN.* a place where one thing crosses another: *My house is near the intersection of Main Street and Pine Avenue.*

in·ter·state (in′tər stāt′), *NOUN.* a road that connects different states: *You take Interstate 94 from Detroit to Chicago.*

in·ter·val (in′tər vəl), *NOUN.*
1 a period of time between things: *There is an interval of six days between Christmas and New Year's Day.*
2 space between things: *Trees were planted with intervals of 25 feet between each two trees.*

in·ter·view (in′tər vyü),
1 *NOUN.* a meeting, generally of people face to face, to talk something over: *My parents had an interview with the teacher about my work.*
2 *VERB.* to ask someone questions at an interview: *Reporters from the newspaper interviewed the mayor.*
❏ *VERB* **in·ter·views, in·ter·viewed, in·ter·view·ing. –in′ter·view′er,** *NOUN.*

in·tes·tine (in tes′tən), *NOUN.*
1 the part of the digestive system that extends below the stomach. Food from the stomach passes into the intestine, where digestion is completed and water is absorbed. In adult human beings, the narrow **small intestine** is about 25 feet long; the wider **large intestine** is about 5 feet long.
2 intestines, the intestine.

in·ti·mate (in′tə mit), *ADJECTIVE.*
1 having a very close, friendly relationship with someone; closely acquainted: *They have been intimate friends since childhood.*
2 personal; private: *A diary is a very intimate book.* **–in′ti·mate·ly,** *ADVERB.*

in·to (in′tü), *PREPOSITION.*
1 to the inside of; toward and inside: *Come into the house.*
2 to the condition or form of: *Divide the apple into three parts. Cold weather turns water into ice.*
3 against: *In the dark, she walked into the closet door.*
4 divided into: *Five into twenty is four.*

in·tol·er·a·ble (in tol′ər ə bəl), *ADJECTIVE.* too hard or painful to stand: *The pain was intolerable.*

in·tol·er·ant (in tol′ər ənt), ADJECTIVE. not willing to let others act as they choose. **−in·tol′er·ant·ly**, ADVERB.

in·tox·i·cate (in tok′sə kāt), VERB.
1 to make someone drunk: *Wine can intoxicate people.*
2 to excite someone greatly: *The joy of victory intoxicated the team.*
□ VERB **in·tox·i·cates, in·tox·i·cat·ed, in·tox·i·cat·ing. −in·tox′i·ca′tion,** NOUN.

in·tri·cate (in′trə kit), ADJECTIVE. with many twists and turns; puzzling: *A mystery story often has a very intricate plot.* **−in′tri·cate·ly,** ADVERB.

in·trigue (in trēg′),
1 VERB. to excite someone's curiosity and interest: *The book's unusual title intrigued me.*
2 NOUN. a crafty plot; secret scheme: *The general took part in the intrigue to take over the country.*
□ VERB **in·trigues, in·trigued, in·tri·guing;** PLURAL **in·trigues.**

in·tro·duce (in′trə düs′), VERB.
1 to tell people each other's names when they don't know each other: *I introduced her to my new friend.*
2 to bring into use, notice, or knowledge: *The new kid introduced different slang into our classroom.*
3 to begin: *He introduced his speech by telling a joke.*
□ VERB **in·tro·duc·es, in·tro·duced, in·tro·duc·ing.**

in·tro·duc·tion (in′trə duk′shən), NOUN.
1 the beginning of a speech, a piece of music, or a book.
2 the process of being introduced: *She was confused by her introduction to so many new people.*
3 the act of introducing: *The introduction of steel made tall buildings easier to build.*

in·trude (in trüd′), VERB. to force yourself into some place where you are not wanted: *He intrudes on the privacy of his neighbors.* □ VERB **in·trudes, in·trud·ed, in·trud·ing. −in·trud′er,** NOUN.

In·u·it (in′ü it *or* in′yü it),
1 NOUN. the people living mainly in the arctic regions of Canada and Greenland; the Eskimo people.
2 NOUN. the language of this people; Eskimo.
3 ADJECTIVE. of or about this people or their language.
∎ See the Usage Note at **Eskimo.** □ PLURAL **In·u·it** or **In·u·its.**

I·nu·pi·aq (i nü′pē ak′),
1 NOUN. the people living mainly in the arctic regions of Alaska; the Eskimo people.
2 NOUN. the language of this people; Eskimo.
3 ADJECTIVE. of this people or their language.
∎ See the Usage Note at **Eskimo.** □ PLURAL **I·nu·pi·aq**

in·vade (in vād′), VERB.
1 to enter another country with force or as an enemy; attack: *Soldiers invaded the country.*
2 to enter some place as if to take possession of it: *Tourists invaded the city.*
□ VERB **in·vades, in·vad·ed, in·vad·ing. −in·vad′er,** NOUN.

in·va·lid[1] (in′və lid),
1 NOUN. someone who is weak because of sickness or injury.
2 ADJECTIVE. not well; weak and sick.

in·val·id[2] (in val′id), ADJECTIVE. not good; not legal: *Unless a check is signed, it is invalid.*

in·val·u·a·ble (in val′yü ə bəl), ADJECTIVE. having great value: *Good health is an invaluable blessing.*

in·va·sion (in vā′zhən), NOUN. the act or process of entering another country as an enemy; attack.

invasion

in·vent (in vent′), VERB.
1 to make something for the first time; think up something new: *The telephone was invented in 1876.*
2 to make up an excuse, story, and so on: *Since they had no good reason for being late, they invented one.*
□ VERB **in·vents, in·vent·ed, in·vent·ing. −in·ven′tor,** NOUN.

in·ven·tion (in ven′shən), NOUN. something new that someone makes or thinks of: *Television is a twentieth-century invention.*

in·ven·to·ry (in′vən tôr′ē),
1 NOUN. a complete list of things. An inventory of property or goods tells how many there are of each thing and what they are worth.
2 NOUN. all the things listed or to be listed: *The store is having a sale to reduce its inventory.*
3 VERB. to make a detailed list of things; enter in a list: *Some stores inventory their stock once a month.*
□ PLURAL **in·ven·to·ries;** VERB **in·ven·to·ries, in·ven·to·ried, in·ven·to·ry·ing.**

in·vert (in vėrt′), VERB.
1 to turn something upside down: *Remove the cake from the pan by inverting it onto a rack.*
2 to turn the other way; change to the opposite; reverse the position, direction, or order of things: *If you invert "I can," you have "Can I?"*
□ VERB **in·verts, in·vert·ed, in·vert·ing.**

a	hat	ė	term	ô	order	ch	child		a in about
ā	age	i	it	oi	oil	ng	long		e in taken
ä	far	ī	ice	ou	out	sh	she	ə	i in pencil
â	care	o	hot	u	cup	th	thin		o in lemon
e	let	ō	open	ů	put	∓H	then		u in circus
ē	equal	ȯ	saw	ü	rule	zh	measure		

in·ver·te·brate (in vėr′tə brit),
1 NOUN. an animal without a backbone. Worms and insects are invertebrates; fishes and mammals are vertebrates.
2 ADJECTIVE. without a backbone: *invertebrate animals.*

These colorful sea worms are **invertebrates.**

in·vest (in vest′), VERB.
1 to use money to buy something which will produce a profit or an income: *Some people invest money in land.*
2 to spend time or energy in order to make or discover something: *Much time and energy have been invested in the crusade against smoking.* ❑ VERB **in·vests, in·vest·ed, in·vest·ing.** —**in·ves′tor,** NOUN.

in·ves·ti·gate (in ves′tə gāt), VERB. to examine something thoroughly in order to find out all about it: *The detectives investigated the crime to find out who committed it. Scientists are investigating the causes of blindness.* ❑ VERB **in·ves·ti·gates, in·ves·ti·gat·ed, in·ves·ti·gat·ing.** —**in·ves′ti·ga′tor,** NOUN.

in·ves·ti·ga·tion (in ves′tə gā′shən), NOUN. a careful examination: *An investigation of the accident by the police put the blame on both drivers.*

in·vest·ment (in vest′mənt), NOUN.
1 something bought which is expected to yield money as interest or profit or both: *She has a good income from wise investments.*
2 an investing; laying out of money: *Getting an education is a wise investment of time and money.*
3 an amount of money invested: *His investments amount to thousands of dollars.*

in·vis·i·ble (in viz′ə bəl), ADJECTIVE. not able to be seen; not visible: *Thought is invisible. Germs are invisible to the naked eye.*

in·vi·ta·tion (in′və tā′shən), NOUN.
1 a polite request asking someone to come to some place or to do something: *The children received invitations to the party at the community center.*
2 the act of inviting someone to do something.

in·vite (in vīt′), VERB. to ask someone politely to come to some place or to do something: *I invited some friends to a party.* ❑ VERB **in·vites, in·vit·ed, in·vit·ing.**

in·vit·ing (in vī′ting), ADJECTIVE. attractive; tempting: *The warm glow of the fire was inviting after a long hike in the snow.*

in·vol·un·tar·y (in vol′ən ter′ē), ADJECTIVE.
1 not controlled by the will: *Breathing is mainly involuntary.*
2 not done of your own free will; unwilling: *Taking gym was involuntary on my part; the school requires it.*

in·volve (in volv′), VERB.
1 to have as a necessary part; include: *Housework involves cooking, washing dishes, sweeping, and cleaning.*
2 to get someone into difficulty or danger: *One foolish mistake can involve you in a good deal of trouble.*
3 to take up the attention of; absorb: *She was involved in working out a puzzle.* ❑ VERB **in·volves, in·volved, in·volv·ing.** —**in·volve′ment,** NOUN.

in·volved (in volvd′), ADJECTIVE. difficult to understand because there are so many parts: *an involved sentence, an involved explanation.*

in·ward (in′wərd), ADVERB. toward the inside: *a passage leading inward.*

i·o·dine (ī′ə dīn), NOUN.
1 a substance used in medicine, in photography, and in making dyes. Iodine is a chemical element. It is added to most table salt because people need small amounts of it for proper growth.
2 a brown liquid containing iodine, put on wounds to kill germs and prevent infection.

Word Power   -ion

The suffix **-ion** means "the act or result of _____ing", or "the condition of being _____."
An eruption is the **act of** erupting. Corruption is the **condition of being** corrupt.

IOU (ī′ō′yü′), NOUN. an informal written promise to pay a debt: *I gave my friend an IOU for two dollars.* ❑ PLURAL **IOUs** or **IOU's.**

I·o·wa (ī′ə wə), NOUN. one of the Midwestern states of the United States. *Abbreviation:* IA; *Capital:* Des Moines. —**I′o·wan,** NOUN.

State Story Iowa comes from the name of a Native American tribe. It was the name another tribe used to make fun of them, and meant "the sleepy ones."

I·ran (i ran′ *or* i rän′), NOUN. a country in southwestern Asia. —**I·ra·ni·an** (i rā′nē ən *or* i rä′nē ən), ADJECTIVE *or* NOUN.

I·raq (i rak′ *or* i räk′), *NOUN.* a country in southwestern Asia. **—I·raq·i** (i rak′ē *or* i räk′ē), *ADJECTIVE* or *NOUN.*

Ire·land (ir′lənd), *NOUN.*
1 an island in the Atlantic Ocean, west of Great Britain. It is divided into the Republic of Ireland and Northern Ireland.
2 **Republic of Ireland,** a country in southern and central Ireland.

i·ris (ī′ris), *NOUN.*
1 a plant with large, showy flowers, and leaves shaped like swords.
2 the colored part of the eye around the pupil.
❑ *PLURAL* **i·ris·es.**

I·rish (ī′rish),
1 *ADJECTIVE.* of or about Ireland or its people.
2 *NOUN PLURAL.* **the Irish,** the people of Ireland.

Irish setter, a hunting dog with long, silky, reddish brown hair.

Irish setter — about 2 feet high at the shoulder

i·ron (ī′ərn),
1 *NOUN.* the commonest and most useful metal, from which tools and machinery are made. Steel is made from iron. Iron is a chemical element.
2 *ADJECTIVE.* made of iron: *an iron fence.*
3 *NOUN.* an implement with a flat surface which is heated and used to press clothing.
4 *VERB.* to press with a heated iron: *She ironed her dress before school.*
❑ *VERB* **i·rons, i·roned, i·ron·ing.**

Have You Heard?

You may have heard someone say **"Strike while the iron is hot!"** Iron can be hammered into the desired shape only when it is hot. Lots of other things can only be done successfully if you do them right away. If you wait too long the iron will be cold and you can't work with it. Your opportunity has been lost.

Iron Age, the period after the Bronze Age, when people used iron tools and weapons.

i·ron·ic (ī ron′ik), *ADJECTIVE.*
1 expressing one thing and meaning the opposite: *Her ironic laugh showed that she wasn't the least bit amused.*
2 contrary to what would naturally be expected: *It was ironic that the man was hit by his own car.*

i·ro·ny (ī′rə nē), *NOUN.* a way of speaking or writing in which the ordinary meaning of the words is the opposite of the thought in the speaker's mind: *The tallest person was called "Shorty" in irony.*

Ir·o·quois (ir′ə kwoi), *NOUN.* a member of a powerful confederacy of American Indian tribes. They lived mostly in what is now New York State.
❑ *PLURAL* **Ir·o·quois.**

ir·reg·u·lar (i reg′yə lər), *ADJECTIVE.*
1 not regular; not according to custom or rule: *irregular behavior.*
2 not in normal rhythm: *The doctor listened to the sick child's irregular breathing.*
—ir·reg′u·lar·ly, *ADVERB.*

ir·rel·e·vant (i rel′ə vənt), *ADJECTIVE.* not to the point; off the subject: *A question about science is irrelevant in a music lesson.* **—ir·rel′e·vant·ly,** *ADVERB.*

ir·re·sist·i·ble (ir′i zis′tə bəl), *ADJECTIVE.* not able to be fought against; very great: *I had an irresistible desire for ice cream.* **—ir′re·sist′i·bly,** *ADVERB.*

ir·re·spon·si·ble (ir′i spon′sə bəl), *ADJECTIVE.* doing things that are careless or dangerous without thinking about the possible results: *It is irresponsible to drive when you have been drinking alcohol.*

ir·ri·gate (ir′ə gāt), *VERB.* to supply land with water by using ditches or by sprinkling so that crops will grow. ❑ *VERB* **ir·ri·gates, ir·ri·gat·ed, ir·ri·gat·ing.** **—ir′ri·ga′tion,** *NOUN.*

The sprinkler **irrigates** the crops.

a	hat	ė	term	ô	order	ch	child		a in about
ā	age	i	it	oi	oil	ng	long		e in taken
ä	far	ī	ice	ou	out	sh	she	ə	i in pencil
â	care	o	hot	u	cup	th	thin		o in lemon
e	let	ō	open	ù	put	ŦH	then		u in circus
ē	equal	ȯ	saw	ü	rule	zh	measure		

ir·ri·ta·ble (ir/ə tə bəl), ADJECTIVE. easily made angry: *When the rain spoiled her plans, she was irritable for the rest of the day.* **–ir/ri·ta·bly,** ADVERB.

ir·ri·tate (ir/ə tāt), VERB.
1 to arouse someone to impatience or anger; annoy: *Their constant interruptions irritated me.*
2 to make a part of your body more sensitive than is natural or normal: *Sunburn irritates the skin.*
❑ VERB **ir·ri·tates, ir·ri·tat·ed, ir·ri·tat·ing.**

ir·ri·ta·tion (ir/ə tā/shən), NOUN. something that annoys you: *Constant loud noise can be an irritation if you are trying to rest.*

is (iz), VERB. a present tense of **be:** *The earth is round. He is at school. It is going to rain. Flour is sold by the pound.*

Word Power   -ish

The suffix **-ish** means "somewhat" or "like." **Sweet**ish means **somewhat** sweet. **Child**ish means **like** a child. **Green**ish means **somewhat** green.

Is·lam (is/ləm), NOUN.
1 the religion based on the teachings of Muhammad as they appear in the Koran; religion of the Muslims.
2 Muslims as a group.
–Is·lam/ic, ADJECTIVE.

is·land (ī/lənd), NOUN.
1 a body of land surrounded by water: *Hawaii is made up of a group of islands.*
2 something that is similar to a piece of land surrounded by water. A platform in the middle of crowded streets is called a **safety island.**

isle (īl), NOUN. a small island. ■ Other words that sound like this are **aisle** and **I'll.**

is·let (ī/lit), NOUN. a very small island.

is·n't (iz/nt), a contraction of **is not.**

i·so·late (ī/sə lāt), VERB. to keep someone or something away from other people or things: *People with contagious diseases should be isolated to keep the diseases from spreading.*
❑ VERB **i·so·lates, i·so·lat·ed, i·so·lat·ing.**
–i/so·la/tion, NOUN.

i·sos·ce·les tri·an·gle (ī sos/ə lēz/ trī/ang/gəl), a triangle that has two equal sides.

Is·ra·el (iz/rē əl), NOUN.
1 a country in southwestern Asia on the eastern Mediterranean sea.
2 an ancient Jewish kingdom in northern Palestine.

Is·rae·li (iz rā/lē),
1 NOUN. someone born or living in the country of Israel.
2 ADJECTIVE. of or about Israel or its people.
❑ PLURAL **Is·rae·lis.**

is·sue (ish/ü),
1 VERB. to send out; put forth: *This magazine is issued every week.*
2 NOUN. something printed and sent out for sale: *That newsstand sells the latest issues of all the popular magazines and newspapers.*
3 NOUN. a point to be debated; problem: *The voters had four issues to settle.*
❑ VERB **is·sues, is·sued, is·su·ing;** PLURAL **is·sues.**

Word Power   -ist

The suffix **-ist** has many meanings. It means "someone who is an expert in _____." A **botan**ist is **an expert in** botany. It also means "someone who plays a _____." A **trombon**ist is **someone who plays** a trombone.

The suffix **-ist** can also mean "someone who works in or with _____." A **journal**ist is **someone who works in** journalism.

Is·tan·bul (is/tän bül/), NOUN. a city in Turkey.

isth·mus (is/məs), NOUN. a narrow strip of land, with water on both sides, that connects two larger bodies of land: *The Isthmus of Panama connects North America and South America.*
❑ PLURAL **isth·mus·es.**

it (it),
1 PRONOUN. the object, person, or living thing spoken about: *Look at it carefully. What is it you want? It's my turn now.*
2 PRONOUN. the subject of the verb in some special kinds of sentences: *It is raining. It is hard to believe that she gone.*
3 NOUN. (in games) the player who must catch, find, guess, and so on: *If I tag you, you're it.*
❑ PRONOUN PLURAL **they.**

I·tal·ian (i tal/yən),
1 ADJECTIVE. of or about Italy, its people, or their language.
2 NOUN. someone born or living in Italy.
3 NOUN. the language of Italy.

Word Source

The **Italian** language developed from Latin. The words listed below have come into English from Italian, but many can be traced back to Latin:

balcony	lasagna	pizza	soprano
baritone	macaroni	quarantine	spaghetti
concerto	oboe	salami	trombone
duet	opera	solo	umbrella
gondola	piano	sonata	zucchini

i·tal·ic (i tal/ik), NOUN. **italics,** printed letters that slant to the right: *These words are in italics.*
★ In writing and typing, italics are shown by single underline.

i·tal·i·cize (i tal/ə sīz), VERB.
1 to print in letters that slope to the right: *This sentence is italicized.*

2 to underline written words with a single line. We italicize expressions that we wish to emphasize. ❑ *VERB* **i·tal·i·ciz·es, i·tal·i·cized, i·tal·i·ciz·ing.**

It·a·ly (it′l ē), *NOUN.* a country in southern Europe.

itch (ich),
1 *NOUN.* a feeling in the skin that makes you want to scratch.
2 *VERB.* to cause this feeling: *Mosquito bites itch.*
3 *VERB.* to feel this way in the skin: *My nose itches.*
4 *NOUN.* a strong feeling or desire for something: *She has an itch to travel.*
❑ *PLURAL* **itch·es;** *VERB* **itch·es, itched, itch·ing.**

itch·y (ich′ē), *ADJECTIVE.* itching: *My nose was itchy all morning.* ❑ *ADJECTIVE* **itch·i·er, itch·i·est.**

i·tem (ī′təm), *NOUN.*
1 a separate thing or article: *The list had twelve items on it. I need to get a few items at the store.*
■ See the Synonym Study at **thing.**
2 a piece of news: *There were several interesting items in yesterday's newspaper.*

it'll (it′l), a contraction of **it will.**

its (its), *ADJECTIVE.* of or belonging to something just mentioned: *The dog wagged its tail.*

Usage Note

The possessive pronoun **its** is always written without an apostrophe: *The frog opened its eyes.* Only the contraction **it's,** meaning "it is" or "it has" is written with an apostrophe: *It's almost time for dinner. It's been a long day.*

it's (its),
1 a contraction of **it is.**
2 a contraction of **it has.**
■ See the Usage Note above.

it·self (it self′), *PRONOUN.*
1 a form of *it* used to make a statement stronger: *The land itself is worth the money, without the house.*
2 a form used instead of *it, him,* or *her* in cases like: *The horse tripped and hurt itself.*

Word Power   -ity

The suffix **-ity** means "the state or condition of being _____." **Timidity** means **the state of being** timid.

The form **-ty** is often used instead of **-ity,** as in safety.

I've (īv), a contraction of **I have.**

i·vor·y (ī′vər ē), *NOUN.*
1 a hard, white substance that makes up the tusks of elephants or walruses. Ivory was used for piano keys, knife handles, and jewelry.
2 creamy white.

Did You Know?

The demand for **ivory** has led to the illegal killing of hundreds of thousands of African elephants by poachers. In 1989, all trade in ivory and other elephant products was banned.

Ivory Coast, a country in western Africa.

i·vy (ī′vē), *NOUN.*
1 a climbing plant with smooth, shiny evergreen leaves.
2 any of various other climbing plants, as poison ivy.
❑ *PLURAL* **i·vies.**

The old brick wall was covered with **ivy.**

jockey

Jj

J or **j** (jā), *NOUN.* the tenth letter of the English alphabet. □ *PLURAL* **J's** or **j's.**

jab (jab),
1 *VERB.* to stab with something pointed: *He jabbed his fork into the potato.*
2 *NOUN.* a poke with something pointed: *She gave him a jab with her elbow. I woke him up with a jab of my pencil.*
□ *VERB* **jabs, jabbed, jab·bing.**

jab·ber (jab′ər),
1 *VERB.* to talk in a very fast, excited way; chatter.
2 *NOUN.* very fast, excited talk; chatter.
□ *VERB* **jab·bers, jab·bered, jab·ber·ing.**

jack (jak), *NOUN.*
1 a tool or machine for lifting or pushing up heavy things a short distance off the ground: *He raised the car with a jack to change the flat tire.*
2 a playing card with the picture of a servant or soldier on it.
3 a small six-pointed piece of metal used in the game of jacks.
4 **jacks,** a game played with jacks and a small rubber ball. Each player bounces the ball and picks up the jacks in between bounces.

jack up, *IDIOM.* to lift something with a jack: *She jacked up the car to change the flat tire. They jacked up the house to fix the foundation.*
□ *VERB* **jacks, jacked, jack·ing.**

jack·al (jak′əl), *NOUN.* a wild animal of Africa and Asia somewhat like a dog. Jackals are hunters but will often follow a lion or a leopard and eat what is left of the prey it kills.

jack·et (jak′it), *NOUN.*
1 a short coat.
2 an outer covering: *a book jacket.*

jack-in-the-box (jak′in ᴛнə boks′), *NOUN.* a toy figure that jumps up from a box when the lid is opened. □ *PLURAL* **jack-in-the-box·es.**

jack·knife (jak′nīf′), NOUN.
1 a large, strong pocketknife. A jackknife may have several blades of different sizes that fold into the handle.
2 a kind of dive in which a diver touches the feet with the hands while in the air, and straightens out before entering the water.
❑ PLURAL **jack·knives** (jak′nīvz′).

jack-o'-lan·tern (jak′ə lan′tərn), NOUN. a pumpkin hollowed out and cut to look like a face, used as a lantern at Halloween.

jack·pot (jak′pot′), NOUN. the biggest prize of a game.
hit the jackpot, IDIOM.
1 to get the big prize.
2 to have very good luck.

jack·rab·bit (jak′rab′it), NOUN. a large hare of western North America, with very long legs and ears.

Jack·son (jak′sən), NOUN. the capital of Mississippi.

jade (jād), NOUN. a hard stone used for jewelry and ornaments. Most jade is green.

jag·ged (jag′id), ADJECTIVE. having a ragged, uneven edge with many sharp points: *We cut our bare feet on the jagged rocks.* **–jag′ged·ness,** NOUN.

jag·uar (jag′wär), NOUN. a large cat with spots, much like a leopard but more heavily built. Jaguars live in forests in tropical America.

jaguar — about 8 feet long, including the tail

jail (jāl),
1 NOUN. a place where people are put when they break the law. People in jail are locked in.
2 VERB. to put someone in jail; keep in jail: *The police arrested and jailed the suspected thief.*
❑ VERB **jails, jailed, jail·ing.**

Word Story

Jail comes from a Latin word meaning "coop." **Cage** comes from the same word. A coop is a cage for birds, and prisoners are sometimes called "jailbirds."

Ja·kar·ta (jə kär′ tə), NOUN. the capital of Indonesia.

ja·la·pe·ño (hä′lə pā′nyō), NOUN. a very spicy, hot pepper. Jalapeños are often used in Mexican food.
❑ PLURAL **ja·la·pe·ños.**

Ja·lis·co (hä lēs′kō *or* hə lis′kō), NOUN. a state in central Mexico.

jam¹ (jam),
1 VERB. to push something into a tight place with force: *I tried to jam one more book into the box.*
2 VERB. to be stuck or caught so that it cannot work: *The window has jammed; I cannot open it.*
3 VERB. to press or squeeze things or people tightly together: *They jammed us all into one bus.*
■ See the Synonym Study at **full.**
4 NOUN. a crowded group of things that cannot move freely: *She was delayed by the traffic jam.*
5 VERB. to bruise or crush by squeezing: *I jammed my fingers in the door.*
6 VERB. to fill or block up the way by crowding: *Floating logs jammed the river.*
7 NOUN. a difficulty or tight spot: *I was in a jam.*
❑ VERB **jams, jammed, jam·ming.**

jam² (jam), NOUN. fruit boiled with sugar until thick: *raspberry jam, plum jam.*

Ja·mai·ca (jə mā′kə), NOUN. an island country in the West Indies. **–Ja·mai′can,** ADJECTIVE *or* NOUN.

Jan., an abbreviation of **January.**

jan·gle (jang′gəl),
1 VERB. to make or cause to make an unpleasant ringing sound: *Pots and pans jangled in the kitchen. The boy jangled the keys.*
2 NOUN. an unpleasant ringing sound: *the jangle of the telephone.*
3 VERB. to have an unpleasant effect on: *The noise jangled my nerves.*
❑ VERB **jan·gles, jan·gled, jan·gling.**

jan·i·tor (jan′ə tər), NOUN. someone whose work is taking care of a building or offices. Janitors do cleaning and make some repairs.

Jan·u·ar·y (jan′yü er′ē), NOUN. the first month of the year. It has 31 days.

Word Story

January comes from *Janus,* the ancient Roman god of gates and doors and of beginnings and endings. He was shown with two faces, one looking forward and one looking backward. January is the time for looking back at the year just ended, and forward to the year beginning.

Ja·pan (jə pan′), NOUN. a country made up of four large islands and many smaller ones in the western Pacific, along the eastern coast of Asia.

Jap·a·nese (jap′ə nēz′),
1 ADJECTIVE. of or about Japan, its people, or their language.

a hat	ė term	ô order	ch child	⎧ a in about
ā age	i it	oi oil	ng long	⎪ e in taken
ä far	ī ice	ou out	sh she	ə ⎨ i in pencil
â care	o hot	u cup	th thin	⎪ o in lemon
e let	ō open	ù put	ᴛʜ then	⎩ u in circus
ē equal	ò saw	ü rule	zh measure	

2 *NOUN.* someone born or living in Japan.

3 *NOUN.* the language of Japan.
❑ *PLURAL* **Jap·a·nese.**

Word Source

Some Japanese words that have come into the English language are **haiku, judo, karate, kimono,** and **obi.**

jar¹ (jär), *NOUN.*
1 a short, wide bottle used to hold things. Many jars are made of glass: *We made pickles and put them up in jars.*
2 the amount that a jar can hold: *They ate a jar of peanut butter.*

jar² (jär), *VERB.*
1 to shake or rattle something so that it moves suddenly: *Your heavy footsteps jar my table.*
2 to have a harsh, unpleasant effect on something or someone: *The kids' screaming jarred my nerves.*
❑ *VERB* **jars, jarred, jar·ring.**

jas·mine (jaz'mən *or* jas'mən), *NOUN.* a shrub or vine with very fragrant yellow or white flowers.

jaunt (jȯnt), *NOUN.* a short journey, especially for fun: *We went on a one-day jaunt to the seashore and back.*

jave·lin (jav'lən), *NOUN.* a lightweight spear thrown for distance in track and field contests.

jaw (jȯ), *NOUN.*
1 the upper or lower bone or set of bones that together form the framework of the mouth. The lower jaw is movable.
2 jaws, the parts in a tool or machine that bite or grasp.

jay (jā), *NOUN.* See **blue jay.**

jay·walk (jā'wȯk'), *VERB.* to walk across a street without paying attention to traffic rules. ❑ *VERB* **jay·walks, jay·walked, jay·walk·ing.**
—**jay'walk'er,** *NOUN.*

jazz (jaz),
1 *NOUN.* a kind of music with a strong beat. Many jazz melodies are created by the musicians as they play.
2 *ADJECTIVE.* of or related to jazz: *a jazz band.*

jeal·ous (jel'əs), *ADJECTIVE.*
1 feeling angry or afraid that somebody you love may love someone else better, or may prefer someone else to you: *The child was jealous when anyone paid attention to the new baby.*
2 unhappy because someone has something that you want to have: *He is jealous of his brother's good grades.*
—**jeal'ous·ly,** *ADVERB.*

jeal·ous·y (jel'ə sē), *NOUN.* the feeling of being jealous: *She could not hide her jealousy when her brother got a new bicycle.*

jeans (jēnz), *NOUN PLURAL.* pants made of a strong cotton cloth.

jeep (jēp), *NOUN.* a small but powerful motor vehicle often used in areas where there are rough roads or no roads.

Word Story

Jeep probably comes from a fast way of pronouncing *G.P.,* the abbreviation for General Purpose Car. That was the name by which this type of vehicle was known in the United States Army during World War II.

jeer (jir),
1 *VERB.* to make fun of or laugh at someone: *Do not jeer at the mistakes or misfortunes of others.*
2 *NOUN.* an insulting remark or yell: *The mayor's speech asking for higher taxes was interrupted by jeers from the audience.*
❑ *VERB* **jeers, jeered, jeer·ing.**

Jef·fer·son Cit·y (jef'ər sən sit'ē), the capital of Missouri.

Je·ho·vah (ji hō'və), *NOUN.* one of the names for God in the Old Testament.

jel·ly (jel'ē), *NOUN.* fruit juice boiled with sugar and then cooked until firm: *toast and jelly.* ❑ *PLURAL* **jel·lies.** —**jel'ly·like',** *ADJECTIVE.*

jel·ly·bean (jel'ē bēn'), *NOUN.* a bean-shaped piece of candy made of boiled and flavored sugar.

jel·ly·fish (jel'ē fish'), *NOUN.* a sea animal like a lump of jelly. Most jellyfish have long, trailing tentacles that can sometimes sting. ❑ *PLURAL* **jel·ly·fish** or **jel·ly·fish·es.**

jellyfish — up to 6½ feet wide

jeop·ar·dy (jep'ər dē), *NOUN.* **in jeopardy,** in danger: *Many lives were in jeopardy during the forest fire.*

jerk (jėrk),
1 *VERB.* to pull or twist suddenly: *If the water is too hot, you jerk your hand out.*
▪ See the Synonym Study at **pull.**
2 *NOUN.* a sudden, sharp pull, twist, or jump forward: *The old car started with a jerk.*
3 *VERB.* to move with a jerk: *The old wagon jerked along the rutted dirt road.*
❑ *VERB* **jerks, jerked, jerk·ing.**

jerk·y¹ (jėr′kē), ADJECTIVE. with sudden starts and stops: *We went on a jerky hayride through the fields.* ❏ ADJECTIVE **jerk·i·er, jerk·i·est.**

jerk·y² (jėr′kē), NOUN. strips of dried meat, often beef.

jer·sey (jėr′zē), NOUN.
1 a soft, knitted cloth used for clothing.
2 a shirt that is pulled on over your head, made of this cloth: *Our soccer team wears red jerseys.* ❏ PLURAL **jer·seys.**

Je·ru·sa·lem (jə rü′sə ləm), NOUN. the capital of Israel, in the eastern part. It is a holy city to Jews, Christians, and Muslims.

jest (jest),
1 NOUN. a joke: *His jests weren't very funny.*
2 VERB. to joke: *I was just jesting, but they thought I meant what I said.*
❏ VERB **jests, jest·ed, jest·ing.**

jest·er (jes′tər), NOUN. someone who jests. In the Middle Ages, kings and queens often had jesters to amuse them with tricks, antics, and jokes.

Je·sus (jē′zəs), NOUN. the founder of the Christian religion.

a **jet plane** with twin engines

jet (jet),
1 NOUN. also, **jet plane,** an aircraft driven by one or more jet engines.
2 VERB. to fly by such an aircraft: *to jet to Europe.*
3 NOUN. a stream of water, steam, gas, and so on, forced from a small opening: *A fountain sends up a jet of water.*
❏ VERB **jets, jet·ted, jet·ting.**

Word Story

Jet comes from a Latin word meaning "to throw." A jet of water is thrown hard from the spout, and a jet engine throws an airplane fast through the air.

jet engine, an engine that shoots out a jet of exhaust gases forcefully from the rear of the engine. The force of the jet drives the engine forward.

jet stream, a very large current of air moving at a very high speed, six to eight miles above the ground.

Jew (jü), NOUN.
1 someone who is descended from the people led by Moses, who settled in Palestine and now live in Israel and many other countries.
2 someone whose religion is Judaism.

jew·el (jü′əl), NOUN.
1 a precious stone; gem.
2 a valuable ornament to be worn, often made of gold or silver and set with gems: *The princess wore all her finest jewels at the ceremony.*

jew·el·er (jü′ə lər), NOUN. someone who makes, sells, or repairs jewelry and watches.

jew·el·ry (jü′əl rē), NOUN. rings, bracelets, necklaces, or other ornaments to be worn, usually set with real or imitation gems and made of silver or gold.

Jew·ish (jü′ish), ADJECTIVE. of, about, or being a member of the Jews or their religion: *the Jewish faith.*

jif·fy (jif′ē), NOUN. **in a jiffy,** in a very short time: *I was on my bike in a jiffy, pedaling down the drive.*

jig (jig),
1 NOUN. a lively dance.
2 NOUN. the music for this dance.
3 VERB. to dance a jig.
❏ VERB **jigs, jigged, jig·ging.**

jig·gle (jig′əl),
1 VERB. to move or shake something from side to side; jerk slightly: *Don't jiggle the desk when I'm trying to write.*
2 NOUN. a slight shake; light jerk.
❏ VERB **jig·gles, jig·gled, jig·gling.**

jig·saw puz·zle (jig′sȯ′ puz′əl), a picture glued onto cardboard or wood and sawed into small, differently shaped pieces that can be fitted together again.

jin·gle (jing′gəl),
1 NOUN. a sound like that of little bells, or of coins or keys striking together.
2 VERB. to make or cause to make a sound like this: *He jingled the coins in his pocket.*
3 NOUN. a simple tune, often with words, used to advertise products on television or radio.
❏ VERB **jin·gles, jin·gled, jin·gling.**

jinx (jingks), NOUN. someone or something that brings you bad luck. ❏ PLURAL **jinx·es.**

jit·ters (jit′ərz), NOUN. usually, **the jitters,** the feeling of extreme nervousness: *I had a bad case of the jitters when I had to sing in public.*

a	hat	ė	term	ô	order	ch	child		a in about
ā	age	i	it	oi	oil	ng	long		e in taken
ä	far	ī	ice	ou	out	sh	she	ə	i in pencil
â	care	o	hot	u	cup	th	thin		o in lemon
e	let	ō	open	ů	put	ŦH	then		u in circus
ē	equal	ȯ	saw	ü	rule	zh	measure		

Jewelry and Gems

cubic zirconia

Gems are precious stones, minerals, or other materials used in making jewelry and other ornaments. Diamonds, rubies, opals, and pearls are all gems.

Glittering Gems

Most gems are mined, and gems are found all over the world. Diamonds come mostly from Australia, Africa, and Russia. The best rubies and sapphires are found in Myanmar and Thailand. The best emeralds come from Colombia. Most pearls are found in the waters of the Persian Gulf. Turquoise is found in the United States.

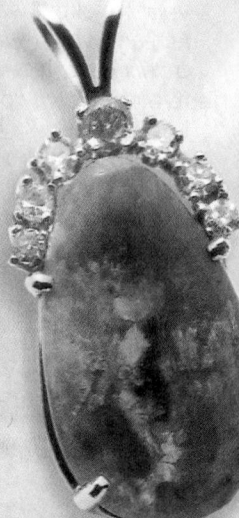

black opal

sapphire and rubies

jade

mined diamonds

From Gems to Jewelry

After the gems are mined, they need to be polished and cut. The way a gem is cut causes it to look brilliant and reflect light. The most popular shapes have many facets, especially for diamonds and other transparent stones. Gems can also be polished smooth, without cut facets.

Basic Gem Shapes

brilliant

emerald

oval

pear

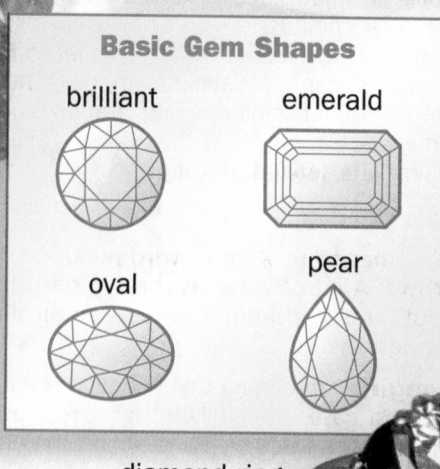

diamond ring

Birthstones

January
Garnet

February
Amethyst

March
Aquamarine

April
Diamond

May
Emerald

June
Alexandrite

July
Ruby

August
Peridot

September
Sapphire

October
Rose Zircon

November
Topaz

December
Blue Zircon

Precious Symbols

Certain gems have special meanings for people. For instance, diamonds are used in engagement rings to symbolize eternity, since diamonds are the hardest gems. Many people wear jewelry that contains their birthstone.

Rings and Things

Once a gem is cut, it can be placed into a setting for rings, bracelets, earrings, necklaces, or even crowns. Settings are usually made of gold or other precious metals.

jit·ter·y (jit′ər ē), ADJECTIVE. feeling nervous; jumpy: *I was a little jittery before my first airplane ride.*

job (job), NOUN.
1 the work that you do for money: *My sister is looking for a job.*
2 anything a person has to do: *I'm not going to wash the dishes; this week that's your job.*
3 a definite amount of work done for a fixed price: *They will do the remodeling job for $2,500.*

Synonym Study

Job means work to do: *I will be lucky to find a summer job that pays well.*

Task means a certain amount of assigned work to be done: *Our task was to unwind string as the kite rose.*

Chore means a regular task: *My chores include setting the table and taking out the garbage.*

Assignment means a certain amount of required work, especially schoolwork: *In science class, we have a written homework assignment every day.*

Errand means a job that includes making a trip: *Now that Mom works late at the hospital, we buy groceries and do the other errands.*

See also the Synonym Study at **work**.

jock·ey (jok′ē), NOUN. someone who rides horses in races as a job. ❑ PLURAL **jock·eys.**

The **jockey** urges the horse to run faster.

jog (jog),
1 VERB. to run slowly and steadily: *I jog several miles every day for exercise.*
2 NOUN. a slow, steady run: *We went for a jog.*
3 VERB. to shake with a push or jerk: *She jogged my elbow to get my attention.*
4 VERB. to stir up your own or someone else's memory with something: *He tied a string around his finger to jog his memory.*
❑ VERB **jogs, jogged, jog·ging.**

jog·ger (jog′ər), NOUN. someone who jogs for exercise.

join (join), VERB.
1 to unite with; come together with: *Join us as soon as you can. The stream joins the river just below the mill.*
2 to become a member of some kind of group: *She joined a tennis club.*
3 to bring or put things together; connect, fasten, or clasp together: *They joined hands. The island was joined to the mainland by a bridge.*
4 to make or become one; combine; unite: *The minister joined the young couple in marriage. The two clubs joined forces during the campaign.*
5 to take part with others in doing something: *We all joined in the song.*
❑ VERB **joins, joined, join·ing.**

Synonym Study

Join means to put or bring things together: *The two wagon trains joined to cross the prairie together. Everyone in the game joined hands and formed a circle.*

Connect means to join things together, often so they touch at one place: *"Please connect the keyboard to the computer," directed the teacher.*

Fasten means to make things touching each other stay in place: *"Fasten your mittens to your sleeves, please," Mom said.*

Attach means to fasten: *We attached a long tail to the kite.*

Combine means to put things or people together for a special purpose: *The combined efforts of 60 people made the show a success.*

Unite means to join into a single thing: *More than two hundred years ago, thirteen colonies united to form one country.*

See also the Synonym Study at **mix**.

joint (joint),
1 NOUN. the place in the body where two bones join. There is usually motion at a joint.
2 NOUN. one of the parts of which a jointed thing is made up: *the middle joint of a finger.*
3 NOUN. the place at which two things or parts are joined together. A pocketknife has a joint to fold the blade inside the handle.
4 ADJECTIVE. done by two or more people: *By our joint efforts we managed to push the car back on the road.*
5 ADJECTIVE. sharing: *My sister and I are joint owners of this dog.*

joint·ed (join′tid), ADJECTIVE. having a joint or joints: *Lobsters have jointed legs.*

joke (jōk),
1 *NOUN.* a short, funny story you tell to make people laugh.
2 *VERB.* to make jokes; say or do something as a joke: *As it got colder, we joked about having snow in July.*
❑ *VERB* **jokes, joked, jok·ing.**

jol·ly (jol′ē), *ADJECTIVE.* very cheerful; full of fun: *She is a jolly person who laughs and jokes a lot.*
❑ *ADJECTIVE* **jol·li·er, jol·li·est.**

These knights are **jousting** for sport.

jolt (jōlt),
1 *VERB.* to shake someone or something suddenly; jar: *The old wagon jolted us on the rough road.*
2 *NOUN.* a sudden jerking movement: *He put his brakes on suddenly, and the car stopped with a jolt.*
3 *NOUN.* a sudden surprise or shock: *News of the plane crash gave them a jolt.*
❑ *VERB* **jolts, jolt·ed, jolt·ing.**

jon·quil (jong′kwəl), *NOUN.* a plant with yellow or white flowers that is much like a daffodil. Jonquils grow from bulbs.

Jor·dan (jôrd′n), *NOUN.* a country in southwestern Asia, east of Israel. **—Jor·da·ni·an** (jor dā′nē ən), *ADJECTIVE* or *NOUN.*

josh (josh), *VERB.* (informal) to tease someone in a friendly way. ❑ *VERB* **josh·es, joshed, josh·ing.**

jos·tle (jos′əl), *VERB.* to shove, push, or crowd against someone roughly: *We were jostled by the big crowd at the entrance to the circus.* ❑ *VERB* **jos·tles, jos·tled, jos·tling.**

jot (jot), *VERB.* to write something down briefly or in haste: *The waiter jotted down our order.* ❑ *VERB* **jots, jot·ted, jot·ting.**

jounce (jouns), *VERB.* to bounce; bump; jolt: *The old car jounced along the rough road.* ❑ *VERB* **jounc·es, jounced, jounc·ing.**

jour·nal (jėr′nl), *NOUN.*
1 a newspaper or magazine, especially one that deals with a special subject: *I subscribe to a weekly sports journal.*
2 a daily record. A diary is a journal of what a person does, thinks, and feels.

jour·nal·ism (jėr′nl iz′əm), *NOUN.* the work of gathering, writing, and presenting news in newspapers and magazines or on TV or radio.

jour·nal·ist (jėr′nl ist), *NOUN.* someone who works in journalism. Reporters are journalists.

jour·ney (jėr′nē),
1 *NOUN.* a long trip from one place to another: *I'd like to take a journey around the world.*
■ See the Synonym Study at **trip.**
2 *VERB.* to travel; take a trip: *I journeyed through Asia.*
❑ *PLURAL* **jour·neys;** *VERB* **jour·neys, jour·neyed, jour·ney·ing.**

joust (joust), in the Middle Ages:
1 *VERB.* to fight with lances on horseback. Knights used to joust with each other for sport.
2 *NOUN.* combat between two knights in armor on horseback, armed with lances.
❑ *VERB* **jousts, joust·ed, joust·ing.**

jowl (joul), *NOUN.* a fold of flesh hanging from or under the lower jaw.

joy (joi), *NOUN.*
1 a feeling of great happiness; gladness: *She jumped for joy when she saw the new puppy.*
2 something that causes gladness or happiness: *On a hot day, a cool swim is a joy.*

joy·ful (joi′fəl), *ADJECTIVE.* causing or showing joy; glad; happy: *joyful news, joyful looks.* **—joy′ful·ly,** *ADVERB.*

joy·ous (joi′əs), *ADJECTIVE.* filled with joy; glad; happy: *The birth of their first child was a joyous occasion.* **—joy′ous·ly,** *ADVERB.*

joy·stick (joi′stik′), *NOUN.* an upright rod used to control video games and computer games. It can be moved in all directions.

jr. or **Jr.,** an abbreviation of **Junior.**

ju·bi·lant (jü′bə lənt), *ADJECTIVE.* very happy; joyful: *We were jubilant when we won the game.*

Ju·da·ism (jü′dē iz′əm), *NOUN.* the religion of the Jews, based on the teachings of the Old Testament.

judge (juj),
1 *NOUN.* a public official who hears and decides cases in a court of law.
2 *VERB.* to act as a judge in a court of law: *No one knows yet who will judge the case.*
3 *NOUN.* someone chosen to settle a dispute or to decide who wins a race or contest.
4 *VERB.* to decide who or what wins a contest: *A teacher from a different school will judge our science projects and award the first prize.*
5 *NOUN.* someone who can decide how good a thing is: *She is a good judge of character.*

a	hat	ė	term	ô	order	ch	child		a in about
ā	age	i	it	oi	oil	ng	long		e in taken
ä	far	ī	ice	ou	out	sh	she	ə	i in pencil
â	care	o	hot	u	cup	th	thin		o in lemon
e	let	ō	open	ù	put	ŦH	then		u in circus
ē	equal	ȯ	saw	ü	rule	zh	measure		

6 *VERB.* to form an opinion about someone or something: *The librarian judged the merits of the new book.*
❑ *VERB* **judg·es, judged, judg·ing.**

judg·ment (juj′mənt), *NOUN.*
1 an opinion; estimate: *In my judgment, she is the best singer.* ■ See the Synonym Study at **opinion.**
2 the power to judge well; good sense: *Since she has judgment in such matters, we will ask her.*

ju·di·cial (jü dish′əl), *ADJECTIVE.* of or by judges; of or about a court of law or the administration of justice: *The judicial branch of the government enforces the laws.*

ju·do (jü′dō), *NOUN.* a method of fighting or self-defense without weapons. In judo you use the strength and weight of your opponent to your advantage.

jug (jug), *NOUN.* a large, deep container that holds liquids. A jug usually has a spout and a handle.

jug·gle (jug′əl), *VERB.* to keep several objects in the air at the same time by quickly tossing them up one at a time and catching them: *She can juggle four balls at once.* ❑ *VERB* **jug·gles, jug·gled, jug·gling.** –**jug′gler,** *NOUN.*

juice (jüs), *NOUN.* the liquid part of fruits, vegetables, and meats: *lemon juice, apple juice, carrot juice.*

juic·y (jü′sē), *ADJECTIVE.* full of juice: *a juicy orange.*
❑ *ADJECTIVE* **juic·i·er, juic·i·est.** –**juic′i·ness,** *NOUN.*

juke·box (jük′boks′), *NOUN.* an automatic, coin-operated record or compact disc player. ❑ *PLURAL* **juke·box·es.**

Ju·ly (jü lī′), *NOUN.* the seventh month of the year. It has 31 days.

Word Story

July was named in honor of the Roman leader Julius Caesar (jü′lyəs sē′zər), who was born in this month.

jum·ble (jum′bəl),
1 *NOUN.* a mess; confusion: *The broken radio was a jumble of wires and parts.*
2 *VERB.* to mix things up thoroughly: *She jumbled up everything in her drawer while hunting for the sock.*
❑ *VERB* **jum·bles, jum·bled, jum·bling.**

jum·bo (jum′bō), *ADJECTIVE.* very big: *a jumbo soda.*

Word Story

Jumbo comes from the name of a very large elephant exhibited by P. T. Barnum (bär′nəm). No one knows how the elephant got its name.

jumbo jet, a large airplane holding about 500 passengers.

jump (jump),
1 *VERB.* to throw yourself up into the air by using your legs; leap: *How high can you jump?*

2 *NOUN.* the action of jumping in this way; a leap: *The horse made a fine jump.*
3 *VERB.* to leap over or across something: *The speeding car jumped the curb and crashed.*
4 *VERB.* to give a sudden movement or jerk: *He jumped when the loud noise startled him.*
5 *VERB.* to rise suddenly: *The price of orange juice jumped when the orange crop was ruined.*
6 *NOUN.* a sudden rise: *a jump in the cost of living.*
❑ *VERB* **jumps, jumped, jump·ing.**

Synonym Study

Jump means to move suddenly through the air: *I jumped over the puddle.*

Leap means to jump high into the air: *My dog always leaps into my arms when I whistle.*

Bound² means to move quickly with many jumps: *The deer bounded across the meadow and into the woods.*

Skip means to move quickly, jumping on one foot after another: *They skipped down the street.*

Hop means to jump on one foot, or on both feet together: *A robin hopped along the window ledge and looked in our kitchen.*

jump ball, (in basketball) the upward toss of a ball by the referee between two opposing players. Each player jumps up for the ball and tries to tap it to a teammate, putting it into play.

jump·er¹ (jum′pər), *NOUN.* someone or something that jumps.

jump·er² (jum′pər), *NOUN.* a sleeveless dress that you wear over a blouse.

jump rope,
1 a children's game or a form of exercise in which you jump over a rope as it is swung under your feet and over your head.
2 a rope with handles on each end used for this game or exercise.

jump shot, (in basketball) a shot made while jumping, especially when the player is at the highest point of the jump.

playing **jump rope**

jump·y (jum′pē), *ADJECTIVE.* feeling nervous; easily excited or frightened: *I felt jumpy after the scary TV show.* ❑ *ADJECTIVE* **jump·i·er, jump·i·est.**

junc·tion (jungk′shən), *NOUN.* a place where things come together. A railroad junction is a place where railroad lines meet or cross.

June (jün), *NOUN.* the sixth month of the year. It has 30 days.

Word Story

June comes from **Juno** (jü′nō), the Roman goddess who was queen of the gods. She was also the goddess of marriage, and June is a favorite time for weddings.

Ju·neau (jü′nō), *NOUN.* the capital of Alaska.

jun·gle (jung′gəl), *NOUN.* a kind of thick forest where many bushes, vines, and trees grow. Jungles are hot and humid.

jungle gym, a framework of steel bars for children to climb or swing on for fun; monkey bars.

jun·ior (jü′nyər),
1 *ADJECTIVE.* the younger. The word *junior* is used of a son having the same name as his father: *Hunter Smith, Junior, is the son of Hunter Smith, Senior.*
2 *ADJECTIVE.* of or for younger people: *They are playing in the junior chess tournament.*
3 *ADJECTIVE.* of lower position; of less standing than some others: *a junior officer, a junior accountant.*
4 *NOUN.* a student in the third year of high school or college.
5 *ADJECTIVE.* of or referring to these students: *The junior class held a dance.*

junior high school, a school that includes grades seven, eight, and sometimes six or nine. It is followed by high school.

ju·ni·per (jü′nə pər), *NOUN.* an evergreen shrub or tree with tiny bluish cones that look like berries.

junk¹ (jungk), *NOUN.* old, worn-out things that nobody wants anymore; trash; rubbish.

junk² (jungk), *NOUN.* a kind of Chinese sailing ship.

junk²

junk food, food that contains calories and a lot of flavor, but has little other value.

junk mail, printed matter that is mostly catalogs and advertising, sent to many addresses.

junk·yard (jungk′yärd′), *NOUN.* a place where old cars, machinery, and so on, are collected and sold.

Ju·pi·ter (jü′pə tər), *NOUN.*
1 the largest planet. Jupiter is more than ten times bigger than Earth. It is the fifth in distance from the sun.
2 the chief god of the ancient Romans. The Greeks called him Zeus.

jur·or (jür′ər), *NOUN.* a member of a jury.

jur·y (jür′ē), *NOUN.*
1 a group of people that hear evidence in a case brought before a court of law. A jury listens to evidence and decides whether someone is innocent or guilty.
2 any group of people chosen to give a judgment or to decide who is the winner: *The jury of teachers gave her poem the first prize.*
❑ *PLURAL* **jur·ies.**

just (just),
1 *ADVERB.* a very little while ago: *Is he here? No, he just left.*
2 *ADVERB.* barely: *I just caught the train.*
3 *ADVERB.* truly: *The weather is just glorious.*
4 *ADVERB.* only; merely: *He went just because his friend was going.*
5 *ADVERB.* exactly: *That is just a pound.*
6 *ADVERB.* nearly; almost exactly: *See the picture just above.*
7 *ADJECTIVE.* right; fair: *We felt that $100 was not a just price for our old car.*
8 *ADJECTIVE.* good; honest: *The man led a just life.*

jus·tice (jus′tis), *NOUN.*
1 fairness; rightness; quality of being just: *She never doubted the justice of her cause.*
2 a judge. The Supreme Court has nine justices.

jus·ti·fy (jus′tə fi), *VERB.*
1 to give a good reason for something: *The fine quality of this cloth justifies its high cost.*
2 to show that something is just or right: *Can you justify your act?*
3 to clear someone of blame or guilt for doing something: *The court ruled that he was justified in hitting the man in self-defense.*
❑ *VERB* **jus·ti·fies, jus·ti·fied, jus·ti·fy·ing.**

jut (jut), *VERB.* to stick out from something: *The pier jutted out from the shore into the water.* ❑ *VERB* **juts, jut·ted, jut·ting.**

ju·ve·nile (jü′və nəl *or* jü′və nīl),
1 *ADJECTIVE.* of or for boys and girls: *juvenile books.*
2 *NOUN.* a young person, especially someone under 18 years old.

a	hat	ė	term	ô	order	ch	child	⟨a in about
ā	age	i	it	oi	oil	ng	long	e in taken
ä	far	ī	ice	ou	out	sh	she	ə⟨i in pencil
â	care	o	hot	u	cup	th	thin	o in lemon
e	let	ō	open	ů	put	℔	then	u in circus
ē	equal	ò	saw	ü	rule	zh	measure	

king

Kk

K or **k** (kā), *NOUN.* the 11th letter of the English alphabet. ❑ *PLURAL* **K's** or **k's.**

K (kā), *NOUN.*
1 a short form of **kilobyte.**
2 a thousand dollars: *The advertised salary for the job is 38K.*
❑ *PLURAL* **K.**

kale (kāl), *NOUN.* a garden vegetable with loose, curled, dark green leaves. Kale is related to cabbage.

ka·lei·do·scope (kə lī′də skōp), *NOUN.* a tube containing bits of colored glass and two mirrors. As you turn it, you see continually changing patterns.

kan·ga·roo (kang′gə rü′), *NOUN.* an Australian animal that has small front legs and very strong hind legs, which give it great leaping power. It uses its tail for balance. The female kangaroo has a pouch in front in which she carries her young.
❑ *PLURAL* **kan·ga·roos** or **kan·ga·roo.**

Kan·sas (kan′zəs), *NOUN.* one of the midwestern states of the United States. *Abbreviation:* KS; *Capital:* Topeka. —**Kan·san** (kan′zən), *NOUN.*

State Story **Kansas** was named for an American Indian tribe that once lived in the area. The name may have come from a native word of the Sioux Indians, meaning "people of the south wind."

Ka·ra·chi (kə rä′ chē), *NOUN.* a city in Pakistan.

kar·at (kar′ət), *NOUN.* 1/24 part gold. A gold ring of 18 karats is 18 parts pure gold and 6 parts other metals. ■ Another word that sounds like this is **carrot.**

ka·ra·te (kə rä′tē), *NOUN.* a Japanese method of fighting or self-defense without weapons by striking with the hands, elbows, knees, and feet at the opponent's body.

ka·ty·did (kā′tē did′), *NOUN.* a large green insect something like a grasshopper. The male makes a shrill noise by rubbing its front wings together. The noise sounds like its name.

Kau·ai (kou′ī), NOUN. the fourth largest island of Hawaii.

kay·ak (kī′ak), NOUN.
1 an Eskimo canoe made of animal skins stretched over a light frame of wood or bone with an opening in the middle that you sit in.
2 a lightweight canoe similar to this, made of other material.

Ka·zakh·stan (kə zäk′stän), NOUN. a country in central Asia.

kayak (definition 2)

ka·zoo (kə zü′), NOUN. a toy musical instrument that makes a buzzing sound when the player hums into it. ❑ PLURAL **ka·zoos**.

keel (kēl), NOUN. the main timber or steel piece that runs along the length of the bottom of a ship or boat.
keel over, IDIOM.
1 to upset; turn upside down: *The sailboat keeled over in the storm.*
2 to fall over suddenly: *He keeled over in a faint.*
❑ VERB **keels, keeled, keel·ing.**

keen (kēn), ADJECTIVE.
1 having a sharp edge for cutting something: *It is easier to cut meat with a keen blade.*
2 quickly and clearly aware; able to work quickly and carefully: *She has a keen mind.*
3 full of enthusiasm; eager: *He is keen about soccer.*
–**keen′ly,** ADVERB.

keep (kēp),
1 VERB. to have something as your own: *You may keep this book.*
2 VERB. to hear something and not tell anyone else: *Can you keep a secret?*
3 VERB. to take care of something and protect it; guard: *The bank keeps money for people.*
4 VERB. to prevent something from happening: *Keep the dog from getting out of the yard.*
5 VERB. to stay or cause something to stay in good condition; preserve: *Milk does not keep long in hot weather. A refrigerator keeps food fresh.*
6 VERB. to stay or cause something to stay the same as it is; continue: *Keep the fire burning.*
7 VERB. to do what you said you would do: *Mom kept her promise to take us to the movies.*
8 NOUN. food and a place to sleep: *Part of her earnings pays for her keep.*
❑ VERB **keeps, kept, keep·ing.**
for keeps, IDIOM.
1 for the winner to keep what he or she has won: *We were playing marbles for keeps.*

2 forever; permanently: *They have moved to Florida for keeps.*
keep up with, IDIOM. to go or move as fast as: *You walk so fast that I cannot keep up with you.*

Synonym Study

Keep means to have and not get rid of something: *My sister keeps shoes long after they wear out.*

Withhold means to keep back and refuse to give. It is a formal word: *I shall withhold part of your allowance to pay for the broken window.*

Hold[1] can mean to take and keep in your hands or arms to help someone else: *Please hold these books until I get my locker open.*

Save can mean to keep and put away: *I am saving money for a new game cartridge.*

keep·er (kē′pər), NOUN. someone who watches, guards, or takes care of people, animals, or things: *He is the keeper of the lighthouse.*

keep·ing (kē′ping), NOUN. the care or protection of someone: *The children were left in their grandparents' keeping.*

keep·sake (kēp′sāk′), NOUN. something kept in order to remind you of someone: *Before she moved away, I asked for her picture as a keepsake.*

keg (keg), NOUN. a small barrel: *a keg of beer.*

kelp (kelp), NOUN. a large, tough, brown seaweed.

ken·nel (ken′l), NOUN.
1 a house for a dog.
2 often, **kennels,** a place where dogs are raised or are left by their owners to be looked after.

Ken·tuck·y (kən tuk′ē), NOUN. one of the south central states of the United States. *Abbreviation:* KY; *Capital:* Frankfort. –**Ken·tuck′i·an,** NOUN.

State Story Kentucky may have come from a Cherokee Indian word meaning "meadow land."

Ken·ya (ken′yə *or* kē′nyə), NOUN. a country in eastern Africa. –**Ken′yan,** ADJECTIVE or NOUN.

kept (kept), VERB.
1 the past tense of **keep:** *He kept the book I gave him.*
2 the past participle of **keep:** *I have kept your books here for you overnight.*

ker·chief (kėr′chif), NOUN. a piece of cloth worn over the head or around the neck.

ker·nel (kėr′nl), NOUN.
1 the softer part inside the hard shell of a nut or inside the stone of a fruit.

a	hat	ė	term	ô	order	ch	child		a in about
ā	age	i	it	oi	oil	ng	long		e in taken
ä	far	ī	ice	ou	out	sh	she	ə	i in pencil
â	care	o	hot	u	cup	th	thin		o in lemon
e	let	ō	open	ů	put	ŦH	then		u in circus
ē	equal	ȯ	saw	ü	rule	zh	measure		

2 a grain or seed like that of wheat or corn.
- ■ Another word that sounds like this is **colonel.**

ker·o·sene (ker′ə sēn′), NOUN. a kind of fuel made from petroleum. It is used in lamps, stoves, and some kinds of engines.

ketch·up (kech′əp), NOUN. a sauce to use with meat, fish, and so on. Tomato ketchup is made of tomatoes, onions, salt, sugar, and spices.

ket·tle (ket′l), NOUN. a metal pot for boiling liquids or cooking fruit and vegetables.

ket·tle·drum
(ket′l drum′), NOUN. a large brass or copper drum with a round bottom and a skin called parchment stretched over the top.

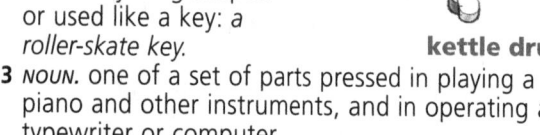

kettle drum

key¹ (kē),
1 NOUN. a small metal tool for opening and closing a lock.
2 NOUN. anything shaped or used like a key: *a roller-skate key.*
3 NOUN. one of a set of parts pressed in playing a piano and other instruments, and in operating a typewriter or computer.
4 VERB. also, **key in.** See **keyboard** (definition 2).
5 NOUN. an answer to a puzzle or problem; guide to a solution: *the key to a crossword puzzle, the key to a mystery story.*
6 NOUN. a list or book of answers to questions.
7 NOUN. a list that explains abbreviations or symbols, used in a dictionary, map, graph, and so on. There is a pronunciation key in this dictionary at the bottom of the next page.
8 ADJECTIVE. very important: *the key industries of a nation, the key facts.*
9 NOUN. an important or essential part of something: *A common interest in music is the key to their friendship.*
10 NOUN. a scale or system of notes in music related to one another in a special way and based on a particular note: *a song written in the key of C.*
- ❑ PLURAL **keys**; VERB **keys, keyed, key·ing.**

key² (kē), NOUN. a low island or reef. There are keys south of Florida. ❑ PLURAL **keys.**

key·board (kē′bôrd′),
1 NOUN. the set of keys in a piano, organ, typewriter, computer, and so on.
2 VERB. to type information into a computer, word processor, calculator, and so on.
- ❑ VERB **key·boards, key·board·ed, key·board·ing.**

key·pad (kē′pad′), NOUN. a group of keys that is usually part of a computer keyboard. The keys are arranged like the keys of a calculator.

key·stone (kē′stōn′), NOUN. the middle stone at the top of an arch, holding the other stones or pieces in place.

kg or **kg.,** an abbreviation of **kilogram** or **kilograms.**

khak·i (kak′ē or kä′kē),
1 ADJECTIVE or NOUN. dull yellowish brown.
2 NOUN. a heavy cloth of this color, used a lot for soldiers' uniforms.
3 NOUN. **khakis, a** a uniform made of this cloth: *Khakis will be worn in the parade.* **b** pants made of khaki cloth.
- ❑ PLURAL **khak·is.**

kick (kik),
1 VERB. to strike or strike out at something with the foot: *That horse kicks when anyone comes near it.*
2 VERB. to move something by kicking it: *to kick a ball along the ground, to kick off your shoes.*
3 VERB. to score by kicking: *to kick a field goal.*
4 NOUN. the act of kicking: *lined up for the kick.*
5 NOUN. a blow with the foot: *The horse's kick knocked me down.*
6 NOUN. a movement of the feet while you are swimming.
7 NOUN. a thrill; excitement: *The children got a kick out of going to the circus.*
- ❑ VERB **kicks, kicked, kick·ing.**

kick off, IDIOM.
1 (in football and soccer) to put the ball in play with a kick at the beginning of each half and after a score has been made.
2 (informal) to begin; start: *The sale will kick off the store's new hours.*

kick·ball (kik′bôl′), NOUN. a game something like baseball. You roll the ball instead of throwing it, and you kick it instead of hitting it with a bat.

kick·off (kik′ôf′), NOUN. (in football and soccer) a kick that puts the ball in play at the beginning of each half and after a score has been made.

kick·stand (kik′stand′), NOUN. a metal rod or other device fastened to the frame or rear axle of a bicycle or motorcycle. It holds up a vehicle that is not being used.

kid¹ (kid),
1 NOUN. (informal) a child.
2 ADJECTIVE. (informal) younger: *They are playing in the yard with my kid brother.*
3 NOUN. a young goat.
4 NOUN. leather made from the skin of a young goat, used for gloves and shoes.

kid² (kid), VERB. to tease someone in a playful way: *Those two love to kid one another.* ❑ VERB **kids, kid·ded, kid·ding.** –**kid′der,** NOUN.

kid·nap (kid′nap), VERB. to take someone away by force and hold him or her captive. ❑ VERB **kid·naps, kid·napped, kid·nap·ping** or **kidnaps, kid·naped, kid·nap·ing.** –**kid′nap·per** or **kid′nap·er,** NOUN.

kid·ney (kid′nē), NOUN. one of the pair of organs in the body that separate waste matter and waste water from the blood. The waste is passed off to the bladder as urine. □ PLURAL **kid·neys.**

kidney bean, a large, red bean, shaped like a kidney and used in soups, chili, and so on.

kill (kil),
1 VERB. to cause someone or something to die: *The car accident killed three people.*
2 NOUN. the act of killing someone or something.
3 NOUN. an animal or animals that have been killed: *The hunters brought home their kill.*
4 VERB. to put an end to something; get rid of: *We use baking soda to kill odors in the refrigerator.*
5 VERB. to use up time: *We killed an hour at the zoo.*
□ VERB **kills, killed, kill·ing.** –**kil′ler,** NOUN.

kill·deer (kil′dir′), NOUN. a North American bird that has two black bands across its breast. It has a loud, shrill cry. □ PLURAL **kill·deers** or **kill·deer.**

killer whale, a small whale that kills and eats large fish, seals, and even other whales; orca. Killer whales travel in groups.

killer whale — between 20 and 30 feet long

kill·joy (kil′joi′), NOUN. someone who spoils other people's fun.

kiln (kil or kiln), NOUN. a furnace or oven for burning, baking, or drying something. Bricks are baked in a kiln.

ki·lo (kē′lō or kil′ō), NOUN.
1 a short form of **kilogram.**
2 a short form of **kilometer.**
□ PLURAL **ki·los.**

Word Power   kilo-

The combining form **kilo-** is used to mean "one thousand." It is used mostly with measurements. A **kilometer** is 1000 meters. A **kilowatt** is 1000 watts.

kil·o·byte (kil′ə bīt′), NOUN.
1 a unit of computer information, equal to 1024 bytes.
2 1000 bytes.

kil·o·gram (kil′ə gram′), NOUN. the basic unit of weight or mass in the metric system, equal to 1000 grams.

ki·lom·e·ter (kə lom′ə tər or kil′ə mē′tər), NOUN. a unit of length, equal to 1000 meters.

kil·o·watt (kil′ə wot′), NOUN. a unit of electrical power, equal to 1000 watts.

kilt (kilt), NOUN. a pleated skirt, reaching to the knees, worn by men in parts of Scotland.

ki·mo·no (kə mō′nə), NOUN. (in Japan) a long, loose outer coat that both men and women wear, held in place by a sash. □ PLURAL **ki·mo·nos.**

kimono

kin (kin), NOUN. someone's family or relatives: *All our kin came to the family reunion.*

next of kin, IDIOM. nearest living relative.

kind¹ (kīnd), ADJECTIVE. friendly; nice; doing good rather than harm: *A kind person tries to help others. Sharing your lunch with the student who had none was a kind thing to do.* ■ See the Synonym Study at **good-natured.**

kind² (kīnd), NOUN. a group of things that are alike in some way; sort; type: *I like many kinds of food. A kilt is a kind of skirt.*

kind of, IDIOM. (informal) nearly; almost; somewhat: *The room was kind of dark.*

kin·der·gar·ten (kin′dər gärt′n), NOUN. a school for children from about 4 to 6 years old. The children are educated by means of games, toys, and pleasant activities. Kindergarten is the year of school before first grade.

Word Story

Kindergarten comes from German words meaning "children" and "garden." People thought that children should grow in this class like flowers grow in a garden.

kind·heart·ed (kīnd′här′tid), ADJECTIVE. having or showing a kind heart; kindly; sympathetic: *The kindhearted man rescued the kitten.*

kin·dle (kin′dl), VERB.
1 to set something on fire; light: *I used a match to kindle the wood.*

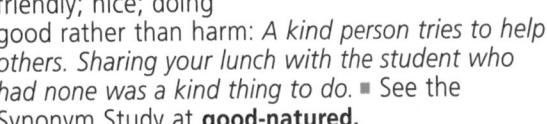

a hat	ė term	ô order	ch child	a in about
ā age	i it	oi oil	ng long	e in taken
ä far	ī ice	ou out	sh she	ə i in pencil
â care	o hot	u cup	th thin	o in lemon
e let	ō open	u̇ put	ŦH then	u in circus
ē equal	o̊ saw	ü rule	zh measure	

2 to stir someone's feelings up; arouse: *The unfairness of the punishment kindled my anger.* ❑ VERB **kin•dles, kin•dled, kin•dling.**

kin•dling (kind′ling), NOUN. small pieces of wood for starting a fire.

kind•ly (kīnd′lē),
1 ADJECTIVE. kind; friendly: *kindly faces, a kindly smile.*
2 ADVERB. in a kind or friendly way: *They thanked him kindly for the help.*
3 ADVERB. please: *Kindly help me lift this box of books.* ❑ ADJECTIVE **kind•li•er, kind•li•est.** –**kind′li•ness,** NOUN.

kind•ness (kīnd′nis), NOUN.
1 a kind nature; quality of being kind: *We admire his kindness.*
2 a kind act: *They showed me many kindnesses during my visit.* ❑ PLURAL **kind•ness•es.**

kin•dred (kin′drid), ADJECTIVE. like; similar; related: *We are studying about dew, frost, and kindred facts of nature.*

ki•net•ic en•er•gy (kin net′ik en′ər jē), the energy of an object in motion.

king (king), NOUN.
1 a man who rules a country and its people.
2 something or someone that is the best in its class: *The lion is often called the king of the beasts.*
3 an important piece in the game of chess. A king can move one square in any direction. The object of chess is to capture your opponent's king.
4 a piece that has moved entirely across the board in checkers. It can move in any direction.
5 a playing card with the picture of a king on it.

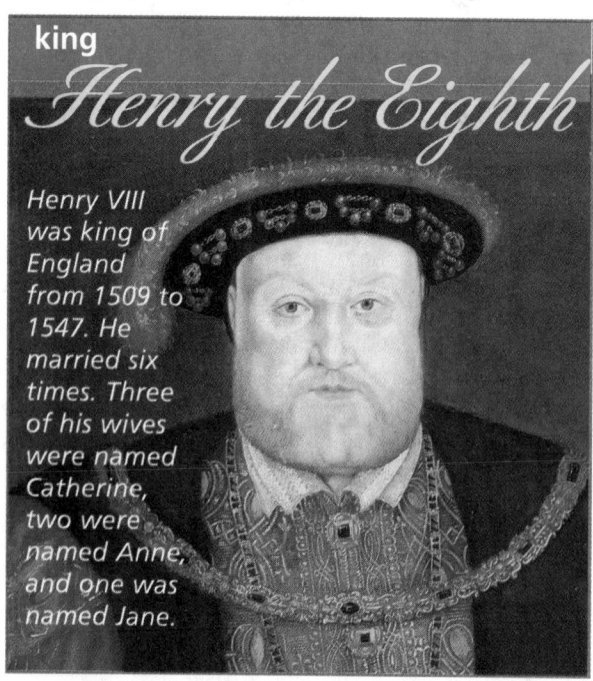

king

Henry the Eighth

Henry VIII was king of England from 1509 to 1547. He married six times. Three of his wives were named Catherine, two were named Anne, and one was named Jane.

king•dom (king′dəm), NOUN.
1 a country that is ruled by a king or a queen.
2 the basic category used in classifying living things. Mice belong to the animal kingdom, maple trees to the plant kingdom, and mushrooms to the kingdom of fungi.

king•fish•er (king′fish′ər), NOUN. a brightly colored bird with a large head, a crest, and a strong beak. Kingfishers eat fish and insects.

king•ly (king′lē), ADJECTIVE.
1 of or like a king; royal; noble: *kingly pride.*
2 fit for a king: *He wore kingly robes.* ❑ ADJECTIVE **king•li•er, king•li•est.**

king-size (king′sīz′), ADJECTIVE. larger than usual; the largest of its type: *a king-size mattress.*

kink (kingk),
1 NOUN. a twist or curl in thread, rope, or hair.
2 VERB. to form a kink or kinks; make kinks in: *The rope kinked as she rolled it up.*
3 NOUN. a pain or stiffness in a muscle; cramp: *a kink in the back, a kink in the leg.* ❑ VERB **kinks, kinked, kink•ing.**

kins•man (kinz′mən), NOUN. a male relative. ❑ PLURAL **kins•men.**

kins•wo•man (kinz′wùm′ən), NOUN. a female relative. ❑ PLURAL **kins•wom•en.**

Ki•o•wa (kī′ə wə), NOUN. a member of an American Indian tribe living in Oklahoma.

kiss (kis),
1 VERB. to touch someone or something with your lips as a sign of love, greeting, or respect.
2 NOUN. a touch with your lips as a sign of love, greeting, or respect. ❑ VERB **kiss•es, kissed, kiss•ing;** PLURAL **kiss•es.**

kit (kit), NOUN.
1 a package of all the parts of something that you put together to make something: *My uncle bought me a model airplane kit.*
2 a set of tools or supplies: *a first aid kit.*

kitch•en (kich′ən), NOUN. a room where food is cooked or prepared.

kitch•en•ette (kich′ə net′), NOUN. a very small kitchen.

kite (kīt), NOUN.
1 a light wooden frame that is covered with paper, cloth, or plastic. Kites are flown in the air on the end of a long string.
2 a kind of hawk with long, pointed wings and often a long, forked tail.

kite (definition 1)

kit•ten (kit′n), NOUN. a young cat.

kit•ty (kit′ē), NOUN. a pet name for a cat or kitten. ❑ PLURAL **kit•ties.**

ki·wi (kē′wē), NOUN.
1 a bird of New Zealand with shaggy feathers, tiny undeveloped wings, and a long flexible bill. Kiwis cannot fly.
2 a sweet green fruit shaped like an egg. Kiwis are covered by brown, fuzzy skins.
 ❑ PLURAL **ki·wis.**

km or **km.,** an abbreviation for **kilometer** or **kilometers.**

knack (nak), NOUN. a special skill; power to do something easily: *She has a real knack for drawing and painting.*

Spelling Note   kn-

Why are some words spelled with **kn-** but pronounced with only *n*? In old days, the *k* was pronounced, too. **Knack** was pronounced (kə nak′). Because this is harder to say than just (nak), the pronunciation changed. However, the spelling stayed the same.

knap·sack (nap′sak′), NOUN. a cloth bag with two shoulder straps, used for carrying food, clothes, and so on; backpack.

knead (nēd), VERB.
1 to press or mix together dough or clay into a soft mass: *The baker was kneading dough to make bread.*
2 to press and squeeze a part of the body with your hands; massage: *Kneading the muscles in a stiff shoulder helps to take away the stiffness.*
 ❑ VERB **kneads, knead·ed, knead·ing.** ■ Another word that sounds like this is **need.**

knee (nē), NOUN. the part of your leg that bends; the joint between the thigh and the lower leg.

knee·cap (nē′kap′), NOUN. the flat, movable bone at the front of your knee.

kneel (nēl), VERB. to go down on your knee or knees; rest on your knees: *I knelt down to pull a weed from the garden.* ❑ VERB **kneels, knelt** or **kneeled, kneel·ing.**

knell (nel),
1 NOUN. the sound of a bell rung slowly after a death or at a funeral.
2 VERB. to ring slowly.
3 VERB. to give a warning sound.
 ❑ VERB **knells, knell·ed, knell·ing.**

knelt (nelt), VERB.
1 a past tense of **kneel:** *They knelt and prayed.*
2 a past participle of **kneel:** *They have knelt and prayed every day this week.*

knew (nü), VERB. the past tense of **know:** *She knew the right answer.* ■ Other words that sound like this are **gnu** and **new.**

knick·ers (nik′ərz), NOUN PLURAL. (earlier) short, loose trousers gathered in at the knee.

knick·knack (nik′nak′), NOUN. a small object of little value used as an ornament.

knife (nīf),
1 NOUN. a thin, flat metal blade with a handle, used to cut or spread something.
2 VERB. to cut or stab someone with a knife.
 ❑ PLURAL **knives;** VERB **knifes, knifed, knif·ing.**
 –knife′like′, ADJECTIVE.

knight (nīt),
1 NOUN. (in the Middle Ages) a soldier who rode a horse and fought for a king or lord. Knights often wore metal suits called armor when fighting.
2 NOUN. (in modern times) a man raised to a high, honored rank because of great achievement or service. A man named John Smith becomes Sir John Smith, or Sir John, as a knight.
3 VERB. to raise someone to the rank of knight: *He was knighted by the queen.*
4 NOUN. one of the pieces in the game of chess.
 ❑ VERB **knights, knight·ed, knight·ing.** ■ Another word that sounds like this is **night.**

a **knight** in armor

knight·hood (nīt′hùd), NOUN. the rank of a knight.
knit (nit), VERB.
1 to make an article of clothing by looping yarn or thread together with long needles, or by machinery which forms loops instead of weaving: *My mother is going to teach me how to knit.*

a	hat	ė	term	ô	order	ch	child		a in about
ā	age	i	it	oi	oil	ng	long		e in taken
ä	far	ī	ice	ou	out	sh	she	ə	i in pencil
â	care	o	hot	u	cup	th	thin		o in lemon
e	let	ō	open	ù	put	ᴛʜ	then		u in circus
ē	equal	ò	saw	ü	rule	zh	measure		

2 to join people closely and firmly together: *The players were all knit into a team that played together smoothly.*

3 to grow together: *The doctor fixed his arm so that the broken bone would knit.*
❑ VERB **knits, knit** or **knit·ted, knit·ting.** –**knit′ter,** NOUN.

knives (nīvz), NOUN. the plural of **knife.**

knob (nob), NOUN.
1 a rounded lump: *Dad's walking stick has a large knob at the top.*
2 a handle, object, or part often shaped like a rounded lump: *I accidentally pulled the knob off one of my dresser drawers.* –**knob′like′,** ADJECTIVE.

knock (nok),
1 VERB. to give a hard blow or blows to; hit: *She knocked the ball over the fence.*
2 VERB. to hit something and cause it to fall: *The speeding car knocked over a sign.*
3 VERB. to hit something with your closed fist: *She knocked on the door.*
4 NOUN. the sound of a hard object hitting against something: *I heard a knock at the door.*
5 NOUN. a blow: *That knock on my head really hurt.*
6 VERB. to make a noise, especially a rattling or pounding noise: *The engine is knocking.*
7 NOUN. the sound caused by loose parts or improper burning of fuel: *I told the mechanic that there was a knock in an engine.*
❑ VERB **knocks, knocked, knock·ing.**

knock out, IDIOM. to hit so hard as to make helpless or unconscious: *She was knocked out by the fall.*

knock·er (nok′ər), NOUN. a swinging metal knob, ring, and so on, fastened on a door so that you can knock with it.

knoll (nōl), NOUN. a small rounded hill; mound.

knot (not),
1 NOUN. a fastening made by tying or twining together pieces of one or more ropes, strings, or cords: *a square knot, a slip knot.*
2 VERB. to tie or twine something together in a knot: *He knotted two ropes together.*
3 NOUN. a tangled mass of hair: *Try to comb out the knots in your hair.*
4 NOUN. a small group of people: *A knot of students stood talking outside the classroom.*
5 NOUN. a hard, roundish place in a tree where a branch grows out.
6 NOUN. a unit of speed used on ships and aircraft, equal to 6076 feet per hour: *The ship's speed is 20 knots.*
❑ VERB **knots, knot·ted, knot·ting.** ▪ Another word that sounds like this is **not.**

knot·hole (not′hōl′), NOUN. a hole in a board formed when a knot falls out.

knot·ty (not′ē), ADJECTIVE.
1 full of knots: *knotty wood.*
2 hard to figure out; difficult; puzzling: *a knotty math problem.*
❑ ADJECTIVE **knot·ti·er, knot·ti·est.**

know (nō), VERB.
1 to have the facts about something: *She knows arithmetic. My new science teacher really knows his subject.*
2 to be completely certain about some fact or facts: *We know that 2 and 2 are 4. She was there at the time; she will know.*
3 to have knowledge of how to do something: *I know from experience how to bake a cake.*
4 to have met and spoken to; be friends with: *I know her very well, but I don't know her sister.*
5 to recognize something: *You will know his house by the red roof.*
❑ VERB **knows, knew, known, know·ing.** ▪ Another word that sounds like this is **no.**

Synonym Study

Know means to have facts about something or someone: *My sister knows how to speak two languages. I know that our new neighbor just moved here from the Philippines.*

Realize means to know that something is true: *They realized that they had wandered far from the village.*

Recognize can mean to realize: *I recognize that I hurt her feelings, and I'm sorry.*

know-how (nō′hou′), NOUN. the ability to do something: *It takes a lot of know-how to operate such a complicated machine.*

knowl·edge (nol′ij), NOUN.
1 what you know: *Gardeners have a great knowledge of flowers.*
2 the fact of knowing: *The knowledge of our victory caused great joy.*

known (nōn),
1 VERB. the past participle of **know:** *George Washington is known as the father of his country.*
2 ADJECTIVE. familiar to all; well-known: *He is a man of known kindness.*

knuck·le (nuk′əl), NOUN. a joint in a finger, especially one of the joints between your finger and the rest of your hand.

knuckle down, IDIOM. to work hard: *He knuckled down to the job.*

knuckle under, IDIOM. to give in; yield: *She would not knuckle under to their demands.* ❑ VERB **knuck·les, knuck·led, knuck·ling.**

knuck·le·ball (nuk′əl bôl′), NOUN. a slow, unpredictable baseball pitch thrown with the tips of the fingers, having little speed or spin.

ko·a·la (kō ä′lə), *NOUN.* a gray, furry animal of Australia that looks something like a small bear and carries its young in a pouch. Koalas live in trees.
❑ *PLURAL* **ko·a·las.**

Ko·mo·do drag·on (kə mō′dō drāg′ən), a very large lizard found on certain islands of Indonesia. It is the largest living lizard.

koala — about 2½ feet long

kook·y (kü′kē), *ADJECTIVE.* (slang) odd; foolish.
❑ *ADJECTIVE* **kook·i·er, kook·i·est.**

Ko·ran (kə ran′ *or* kə rän′), *NOUN.* the sacred book of the Islamic religion.

Ko·re·a (kô rē′ə), *NOUN.* a former country on a peninsula in eastern Asia, now divided into North Korea and South Korea. **–Ko·re′an,** *ADJECTIVE* or *NOUN.*

ko·sher (kō′shər), *ADJECTIVE.*
1 prepared according to Jewish law: *kosher meat.*
2 (informal) right; proper; correct: *It's not kosher to change the rules in the middle of the game.*

KS, an abbreviation of **Kansas.**

kud·zu (kŭd′zü), *NOUN.* a vine originally found in Japan and China, now growing widely in the southern United States. Kudzu grows quickly and can become a nuisance.

kung fu (kŭng′ fü′), a Chinese form of fighting or self-defense. It is similar to karate.

Ku·wait (kù wāt′), *NOUN.* a country in southwestern Asia, on the peninsula of Arabia. **–Ku·wai·ti** (kù wā′tē), *ADJECTIVE* or *NOUN.*

Kwan·zaa or **Kwan·za** (kwän′zə), *NOUN.* an African American celebration that commemorates various African festivals, especially one for the new planting season. It lasts from December 26 to January 1.

KY, an abbreviation of **Kentucky.**

Kyr·gyz·stan (kir gēz′stän), *NOUN.* a country in central Asia.

K

lighthouse

Ll

L or **l** (el), *NOUN.* the 12th letter of the English alphabet. ❑ *PLURAL* **L's** or **l's.**

l or **L.,** an abbreviation of **liter** or **liters.**

la (lä), *NOUN.* (in music) the sixth tone of a scale. ❑ *PLURAL* **las.**

LA, an abbreviation of **Louisiana.**

lab (lab), *NOUN.* a short form of **laboratory.**

la·bel (lā′bəl),

1 *NOUN.* a piece of paper or cloth that is sewed, glued, or fastened to something. A label tells what something is, who it belongs to, or who made it.

2 *VERB.* to put or write a label on something: *The bottle is labeled "Poison." She labeled her backpack with her name and address.*

3 *VERB.* to describe someone or something with a special word or phrase: *The new governor was labeled a liberal.*

❑ *VERB* **la·bels, la·beled, la·bel·ing.**

la·bor (lā′bər),

1 *NOUN.* work; toil: *The carpenter was well paid for his labor.* ■ See the Synonym Study at **work.**

2 *NOUN.* workers as a group: *Labor wants safer working conditions.*

3 *VERB.* to do work; work hard; toil: *The farmers labored all day in the fields.*

4 *VERB.* to move slowly and with great effort: *The ship labored in the heavy seas. The old car labored as it climbed the steep hill.*

❑ *VERB* **la·bors, la·bored, la·bor·ing. —la′bor·er,** *NOUN.*

lab·o·ra·to·ry (lab′rə tôr′ē), *NOUN.* a room or building with special equipment where scientists work and do tests and experiments: *The drug was tested on animals in the laboratory.* ❑ *PLURAL* **lab·o·ra·to·ries.**

Labor Day, the first Monday in September. Labor Day is a legal holiday throughout the United States in honor of working people.

labor union, a group of workers joined together to protect and promote their interests.

labor union **Cesar Chavez**

Cesar Chavez was a great American labor organizer. He founded the United Farm Workers and led national boycotts of grapes and other produce from nonunion farms.

lace (lās),
1 *NOUN.* very thin threads that are woven together to make fine thread in an ornamental pattern.
2 *NOUN.* a cord, string, or leather strip for pulling and holding something together: *These shoes need new laces.*
3 *VERB.* to pull or hold something together with a lace or laces: *Lace up your shoes.*
❑ *VERB* **lac·es, laced, lac·ing. –lace′like′,** *ADJECTIVE.*

lack (lak),
1 *NOUN.* the condition of being without: *Lack of a fire made him cold.*
2 *VERB.* to not have; be without: *Some guinea pigs lack tails.*
3 *VERB.* to not have enough; need: *This book lacks excitement.*
4 *NOUN.* a shortage; not having enough: *Lack of rest made them tired.*
❑ *VERB* **lacks, lacked, lack·ing.**

lac·quer (lak′ər),
1 *NOUN.* a liquid coating put on metals, wood, or paper. It dries to a hard, shiny finish.
2 *VERB.* to coat something with lacquer.
❑ *VERB* **lac·quers, lac·quered, lac·quer·ing.**

la·crosse (lə krós′), *NOUN.* a game played with a ball and basketlike rackets by two teams, usually of 10 players each. The players carry the ball in the rackets, trying to hurl it into the other team's goal.

lad (lad), *NOUN.* a boy or young man.

lad·der (lad′ər), *NOUN.* a wooden or metal device used for climbing up or down. A ladder has two long side pieces with steps or rungs fastened between them.

lad·en (lād′n), *ADJECTIVE.* loaded; burdened: *The camels were laden with bundles of silk.*

la·dle (lā′dl), *NOUN.* a large, cup-shaped spoon with a long handle, used for dipping liquids from pots or vats.

la·dy (lā′dē), *NOUN.*
1 a polite term for any woman. "Ladies" is often used in speaking or writing to a group of women.
2 a woman of well-known family and high social position: *a lady by birth.*
3 a woman having good manners.
4 **Lady,** a title used in writing or speaking about women of certain high ranks in Great Britain: *Lord and Lady Grey attended the Queen's reception.*
❑ *PLURAL* **la·dies.**

Word Story

Lady comes from old English words meaning "loaf" and "to knead." In old times, bread was baked at home by the woman in charge of the house. The idea of the woman in charge led to the meaning of a woman of high rank.

la·dy·bug (lā′dē bug′), *NOUN.* a small, round, reddish beetle with black spots. It eats certain insects that are harmful to plants.

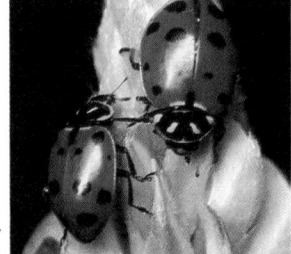

ladybug — about ¼ inch long

lag (lag),
1 *VERB.* to move too slowly; fall behind: *They lagged because they were tired.*
2 *NOUN.* an amount of time between two events; delay: *There was a long lag in forwarding mail to us after we moved.*
❑ *VERB* **lags, lagged, lag·ging. –lag′ger,** *NOUN.*

la·goon (lə gün′), *NOUN.* a pond or small lake, usually connected with a larger body of water.

Word Story

Lagoon comes from a Latin word meaning "hole" or "pit." A pit in the ground soon fills with water, so the Latin word was also used to mean "pond."

La·gos (lä′gōs *or* lā′gos), *NOUN.* a city in Nigeria.

a hat	ė term	ô order	ch child	⎧a in about
ā age	i it	oi oil	ng long	e in taken
ä far	ī ice	ou out	sh she	ə⎨i in pencil
â care	o hot	u cup	th thin	o in lemon
e let	ō open	ù put	ᴛʜ then	⎩u in circus
ē equal	ò saw	ü rule	zh measure	

L

laid (lād), *VERB.*
1 the past tense of **lay¹**: *He laid down the heavy bundle.*
2 the past participle of **lay¹**: *Those eggs were laid this morning.*

lain (lān), *VERB.* the past participle of **lie²**: *The snow has lain on the ground a week.* ■ Another word that sounds like this is **lane.**

lair (lâr), *NOUN.* a den or resting place of a wild animal.

lake (lāk), *NOUN.* a body of water with land all around it. A lake is larger than a pond and usually contains fresh water.

La·ko·ta (lə kō′tə), *NOUN.* the Sioux, especially those living in the western sections of their land. ■ See the Usage Note at **Sioux.** ❑ *PLURAL* **La·ko·ta.**

lamb (lam), *NOUN.*
1 a young sheep.
2 the meat from a lamb: *roast lamb.*

Spelling Note   -mb

Some English words, such as *lamb* and *climb,* are spelled with **-mb,** where the *b* is not pronounced. Hundreds of years ago, the *b* was pronounced, but it is much easier to leave it out, so people did. The spelling survived, but the sound did not.

lamb

lame (lām),
1 *ADJECTIVE.* not able to walk properly; having a hurt leg or foot: *He limps because he has been lame since birth.*
2 *ADJECTIVE.* stiff and sore: *My arm is lame from playing ball.*
3 *VERB.* to make someone unable to walk properly: *The accident lamed her for life.*
4 *ADJECTIVE.* poor; not very good: *Stopping to play is a lame excuse for being late to school.* ★ This meaning of **lame** is often considered offensive when used about people.
❑ *ADJECTIVE* **lam·er, lam·est;** *VERB* **lames, lamed, lam·ing.**

lamp (lamp), *NOUN.* a device that gives light. A gas or electric light is called a lamp. Oil lamps hold oil and a wick by which the oil is burned.

La·nai (lä nī′), *NOUN.* an island in the central part of the Hawaiian islands.

lance (lans),
1 *NOUN.* a long wooden spear with a sharp iron or steel head: *The knights carried lances.*
2 *VERB.* to cut part of the body open with a small, very sharp knife: *The doctor lanced the dog's infected leg.*
❑ *VERB* **lanc·es, lanced, lanc·ing.**

land (land),
1 *NOUN.* the solid part of the earth's surface: *After many weeks at sea, the sailors sighted land.*
2 *VERB.* to come to land; bring to land: *The ship landed at the pier.*
3 *VERB.* to come down from the air; come to rest: *The plane landed safely. The eagle landed on a rock.*
4 *VERB.* to go on shore from a ship or boat: *The passengers landed.*
5 *NOUN.* ground; soil: *This is good land for a garden.*
6 *NOUN.* a country; region: *Switzerland is a mountainous land.*
❑ *VERB* **lands, land·ed, land·ing.**

land·fill (land′fil′), *NOUN.* the place where garbage is buried to get rid of it.

land·form (land′fôrm′), *NOUN.* a shape formed on the surface of the land. Mountains, hills, and plains are three kinds of landforms.

land·ing (lan′ding), *NOUN.*
1 the act of coming to land: *There are millions of takeoffs and landings at the nation's airports each year.*
2 a place where people or goods are landed from a ship or helicopter. A wharf, dock, or pier is a landing for boats.
3 a platform between flights of stairs.

land·la·dy (land′lā′dē), *NOUN.* a woman who owns a building or land that is rented to other people: *We called our landlady to have the sink fixed.*
❑ *PLURAL* **land·la·dies.**

land·lord (land′lôrd′), *NOUN.* someone who owns a building or land that is rented to other people: *Our landlord came by to fix the dripping faucet.*

land·mark (land′märk′), *NOUN.*
1 something familiar or easily seen, used as a guide: *The hiker did not lose her way in the forest because the rangers' high tower served as a landmark.*
2 any important fact or event; any happening that stands out above others: *The invention of the telephone was a landmark in the history of communication.*
3 a place that is important or interesting: *That old building is a historical landmark.*

land·scape (land′skāp),
1 *NOUN.* a view of scenery from one place: *The two hills with the valley formed a beautiful landscape.*
2 *NOUN.* a picture showing a view like this.
3 *VERB.* to arrange trees, shrubs, or flowers in order

to make an area of land more pleasant to look at: *This park has been carefully landscaped.*
❑ *VERB.* **land·scapes, land·scaped, land·scap·ing.** —**land′scap·er,** *NOUN.*

land·slide (land′slīd′), *NOUN.*
1 a mass of earth or rock that slides down a steep slope.
2 an election victory by a great majority over the other candidates.

lane (lān), *NOUN.*
1 a narrow path or road, often between grass, bushes, or fences.
2 a course or route used by cars, ships, or aircraft going in the same direction.
3 See **bowling alley** (definition 1).
■ Another word that sounds like this is **lain.**

lan·guage (lang′gwij), *NOUN.*
1 words that people write or speak; human speech: *Civilization would be impossible without language.*
2 the speech of one nation, tribe, or other large group of people: *the French language.*
3 the expression of thoughts and feelings in ways other than by words: *sign language.*
4 a system of words, numbers, symbols, and abbreviations that stand for information and instructions in a computer.

Did You Know?

There are more than six thousand **languages** spoken in the world today. Only about 200 languages have more than a million speakers. English, Arabic, and Japanese are a few of the 23 languages that are spoken by more than 50 million people each.

language arts, reading, writing, spelling, speech, and other subjects that develop skill in using language.

lank·y (lang′kē), *ADJECTIVE.* very long and thin; tall and ungraceful: *He was a lanky teenager.*
❑ *ADJECTIVE* **lank·i·er, lank·i·est.**

Lan·sing (lan′sing), *NOUN.* the capital of Michigan.

lan·tern (lan′tərn), *NOUN.* a portable lamp with a transparent covering around it to protect it from wind and rain.

La·os (lous *or* lä′ōs), *NOUN.* a country in southeastern Asia. —**La·o·tian** (lā ō′shən *or* lou′shən), *ADJECTIVE or NOUN.*

lap¹ (lap), *NOUN.* the upper legs and hips of someone who is sitting down: *I held the baby on my lap.*

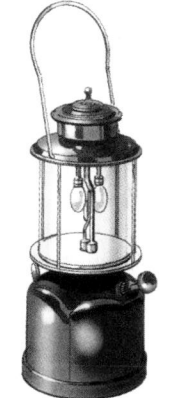

lantern

lap² (lap),
1 *VERB.* to partly cover and stick out beyond something else; overlap: *The shingles lapped over each other.*
2 *NOUN.* the part that laps over another part.
3 *NOUN.* the entire length of something, such as a racetrack or a swimming pool: *I swam three laps before breakfast.*
❑ *VERB.* **laps, lapped, lap·ping.**

lap³ (lap), *VERB.*
1 to drink by taking liquid up with the tongue; lick: *Cats and dogs lap up water.*
2 to move or beat gently against a surface with a lapping sound; splash gently: *Little waves lapped against the boat.*
❑ *VERB.* **laps, lapped, lap·ping.**

la·pel (lə pel′), *NOUN.* either of the two front parts of a coat folded back just below the collar.

lapse (laps),
1 *NOUN.* a slight mistake or error: *Due to a lapse of memory, I could not remember his name.*
2 *NOUN.* the passage of time: *After a lapse of 10 years, he returned to the family farm.*
3 *VERB.* to slip back; sink down: *I tried to be tidy, but soon lapsed into my old sloppy ways.*
❑ *VERB.* **laps·es, lapsed, laps·ing.**

lap·top (lap′top′), *NOUN.* a small portable computer, easily balanced and used on your lap.

lard (lärd), *NOUN.* the fat of hogs, melted for use in cooking: *The cook uses lard in making pies.*

lar·der (lär′dər), *NOUN.*
1 a pantry; place where food is kept: *Are there any onions in the larder?*
2 a stock of food: *The hunter's larder included flour, bacon, and deer meat.*

large (lärj), *ADJECTIVE.* of more than the usual size, amount, or number; big: *There was a large crowd at the game. A million dollars is a large sum of money.* ■ See the Synonym Study at **big.**
❑ *ADJECTIVE* **larg·er, larg·est.**

at large, *IDIOM.*
1 at liberty; free: *Is the escaped prisoner still at large?*
2 as a whole; altogether: *The mayor's popularity is high among the people at large.*

large intestine, the lower part of the intestine. It removes water from the waste material that it receives from the small intestine.

large·ly (lärj′lē), *ADVERB.* mostly; mainly: *The Sahara Desert consists largely of sand.*

lar·i·at (lar′ē ət), *NOUN.* See **lasso.**

a	hat	ė	term	ô	order	ch	child		a in about
ā	age	i	it	oi	oil	ng	long		e in taken
ä	far	ī	ice	ou	out	sh	she	ə	i in pencil
â	care	o	hot	u	cup	th	thin		o in lemon
e	let	ō	open	u̇	put	ᴛʜ	then		u in circus
ē	equal	ȯ	saw	ü	rule	zh	measure		

lark (lärk), NOUN. a small songbird of Europe, Asia, America, and northern Africa that sings while soaring in the air. The skylark is one kind of lark.

lark·spur (lärk′spėr′), NOUN. a plant with a tall stalk of thickly growing blue, pink, or white flowers.

lark — about 6½ inches long

lar·va (lär′və), NOUN. the wormlike form of an insect from the time it leaves the egg until it becomes a pupa. A caterpillar is the larva of a butterfly or moth. ❑ PLURAL **lar·vae** (lär′vē).

Word Story

Larva comes from a Latin word meaning "a mask." This stage of an insect's life was called a mask because it does not look like its adult form.

lar·yn·gi·tis (lar′ən jī′tis), NOUN. soreness and swelling of the larynx. Laryngitis usually causes a loss of voice for a time.

lar·ynx (lar′ingks), NOUN. the lower part of your throat, where the vocal cords are. ❑ PLURAL **la·ryn·ges** (lə rin′jēz) or **lar·ynx·es**.

la·sa·gna (lə zä′nyə), NOUN. a food made of chopped meat, cheese, and tomato sauce, baked in layers with wide noodles. Lasagna is often made with a vegetable like spinach instead of with meat.

la·ser (lā′zər), NOUN. a device that makes a very narrow, extremely strong beam of light. Laser beams are used to cut hard materials, remove body tissues, and send television signals.

Word Story

Laser comes from the words **l**ight **a**mplification by **s**timulated **e**mission of **r**adiation. It was formed by using the first letter of most of these words. It is easier to understand how this word was formed than to understand how lasers are formed.

laser disc, a thin, metal disc coated with plastic, about twice as wide as a compact disc. Movies, pictures, music, and computer information can be recorded on laser discs.

lash¹ (lash),

1 NOUN. the part of a whip that is not the handle: *The leather lash cut the side of the horse.*

2 NOUN. a stroke or blow with a whip: *The horse was cut by a lash of the whip.*

3 VERB. to strike with a whip: *The driver of the team lashed her horses on.*

4 VERB. to beat back and forth: *The lion lashed its tail. The wind lashes the sails.*

5 NOUN. one of the tiny hairs on the edge of your eyelid; eyelash.
❑ PLURAL **lash·es;** VERB **lash·es, lashed, lash·ing.**

lash² (lash), VERB. to tie or fasten things with a rope: *We lashed logs together to make a raft.* ❑ VERB **lash·es, lashed, lash·ing.**

lass (las), NOUN. a girl or young woman. ❑ PLURAL **lass·es.**

las·so (las′ō),

1 NOUN. a long rope with a loop at the end, used for catching horses and cattle; lariat.

2 VERB. to catch an animal with a lasso.
❑ PLURAL **las·sos** or **las·soes;** VERB **las·sos, las·soed, las·so·ing.**

last¹ (last),

1 ADJECTIVE. coming after all others: *Z is the last letter; A is the first.*

2 ADVERB. after all the others: *She ran last in line.*

3 ADJECTIVE. most recent: *I saw him last week.*

4 ADVERB. most recently: *When did you see him last?*

5 ADJECTIVE. most unlikely: *Fighting is the last thing I would do.*

6 ADJECTIVE. being the only left: *I ate the last apple.*

7 NOUN. the end: *Be faithful to the last.*

8 NOUN. someone or something that is last: *The last of the leaves have fallen.*

at last, IDIOM. finally: *At last the baby fell asleep.*

The cowboy uses a **lasso** to catch a wild horse.

Synonym Study

Last¹ means after all others, or coming at the end: *She ate the last apple, leaving the bowl empty. The last month of the year is December.*

Final means last. It emphasizes that there are no more to come: *He scored the winning points in the final second of the game. This is my final warning: It's time to go to bed!*

Latest can mean most recent or last up to this time: *Have you seen their latest music video? This is the latest model of the sports car.*

Ultimate means last, especially as part of a process: *She is learning to play the piano because her ultimate goal is to write songs.*

See also the Synonym Studies at **end** and **stop.**

last² (last), VERB.

1 to go on; continue in time: *The play lasted three hours. How long will the snow last?*

2 to continue to be in good condition: *I hope these shoes last for another year.*
❑ *VERB* **lasts, last·ed, last·ing.**

last·ing (las′ting), *ADJECTIVE.* existing for a long time; permanent: *The voyage had a lasting effect on me.*

latch (lach),
1 *NOUN.* something that keeps a door, gate, or window closed. It consists of a movable piece of metal or wood that fits into an opening.
2 *VERB.* to fasten something with a latch: *Latch the door.*
❑ *VERB* **latch·es, latched, latch·ing;** *PLURAL* **latch·es.**

late (lāt),
1 *ADJECTIVE* or *ADVERB.* after the usual time that something happens: *We had a late supper because we went to a 6 o'clock movie.*
2 *ADJECTIVE* or *ADVERB.* near the end: *It was late in the day, but not completely dark yet.*
3 *ADJECTIVE.* not long past; recent: *My parents just bought a late model car.* ■ See the Synonym Study at **last**[1].
4 *ADJECTIVE.* recently dead: *The late Mary Lee was a skilled surgeon.*
❑ *ADJECTIVE* **lat·er** or **lat·ter, lat·est** or **last;** *ADVERB* **lat·er, lat·est** or **last. —late′ness,** *NOUN.*

Have You Heard?

You may have heard the phrase **"Better late than never."** This means that it is better to do something after you were supposed to than to never do it at all.

late·ly (lāt′lē), *ADVERB.* recently: *He has not been looking well lately.*

lat·er·al (lat′ər əl), *ADJECTIVE.* of, at, from, or toward the side: *A lateral fin of a fish grows from its side.* **—lat′er·al·ly,** *ADVERB.*

la·tex (lā′teks), *NOUN.* a milky liquid found in some plants. It hardens in the air, and is used to make rubber and other products.

lathe (lāŦH), *NOUN.* a machine that holds pieces of wood or metal. It turns them rapidly against a cutting tool which shapes them.

lath·er (laŦH′ər),
1 *NOUN.* the foam made from soap and water.
2 *VERB.* to put lather on something: *He lathers his face before shaving.*
3 *VERB.* to form a lather: *This soap lathers well.*
4 *NOUN.* the foam formed in sweating: *The horse was covered in lather after the race.*
❑ *VERB* **lath·ers, lath·ered, lath·er·ing.**

Lat·in (lat′n),
1 *NOUN.* the language of the ancient Romans. Latin was used by scholars in Europe throughout the Middle Ages.
2 *ADJECTIVE.* of Latin; in Latin: *Latin poetry.*
3 *ADJECTIVE.* of the peoples (Italians, French, Spanish, and Portuguese) whose languages have come from Latin.

Word Source

Latin was the language of ancient Rome. Here is a small sample of the hundreds of words that came into English from Latin:

author	human	motor	student
aviation	insect	muscle	stupid
binoculars	insult	obey	unicorn
bus	journey	offend	vaccine
cereal	language	porpoise	vertebra
dolphin	lava	pupil	video
education	liberty	republic	virus
fossil	map	rotate	volcano
hospital	menu	salute	

La·ti·na (lə tē′nə *or* la tē′nə), *NOUN.* a girl or woman of Hispanic descent. ❑ *PLURAL* **La·ti·nas.**

Latin America, South America, Central America, Mexico, and most of the West Indies.

Latin American,
1 of or from Latin America.
2 someone born or living in Latin America.

La·ti·no (la tē′nō), *NOUN.* a boy or man of Hispanic descent. ❑ *PLURAL* **La·ti·nos.**

lat·i·tude (lat′ə tüd), *NOUN.*
1 the distance north or south of the equator, measured in degrees. A degree of latitude is about 69 miles.
2 freedom to do and say what you want to: *The children are allowed much latitude in spending their allowances.*

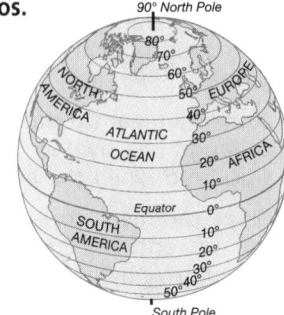

There are 10 degrees of **latitude** between each pair of lines.

Word Story

Latitude comes from a Latin word meaning "wide." The earliest maps were flat, not round, and were wider than they were long. Lines of latitude were drawn across the width of the map. See also the Word Story at **longitude.**

lat·ter (lat′ər), *ADJECTIVE.*
1 the second of two: *Canada and the United States are in North America; the former lies north of the latter.*
2 more recent; later; toward the end: *Friday comes in the latter part of the week.*

Lat·vi·a (lat′vē ə), *NOUN.* a country in northeastern Europe. **—Lat′vi·an,** *ADJECTIVE* or *NOUN.*

a	hat	ė	term	ô	order	ch	child
ā	age	i	it	oi	oil	ng	long
ä	far	ī	ice	ou	out	sh	she
â	care	o	hot	u	cup	th	thin
e	let	ō	open	ù	put	ŦH	then
ē	equal	ò	saw	ü	rule	zh	measure

ə { a in about / e in taken / i in pencil / o in lemon / u in circus }

laugh (laf),
1 *VERB.* to make the sounds and movements that show you are happy or amused: *We all laughed at the clown's funny tricks.*
2 *NOUN.* sounds made when someone laughs: *She gave a hearty laugh at the joke.*
 ❑ *VERB* **laughs, laughed, laugh·ing.**
have the last laugh, *IDIOM.* to get the better of someone after you seem to have lost: *In the race between the hare and the tortoise, the tortoise had the last laugh.*
laugh at, *IDIOM.* to make fun of: *They laughed at their friend for believing in ghosts.*
laugh off, *IDIOM.* to get out of by laughing; treat as a joke: *I just laugh off their nasty comments.*

Synonym Study

Laugh means to show joy or amusement by making certain sounds and movements: *She laughs at all of my jokes. I laughed at the silly hat.*

Chuckle means to laugh very quietly or softly: *They chuckled as they read the comic strip.*

Giggle means to laugh in a silly way, with short, high-pitched sounds: *All the children giggled when they saw the goofy puppets.*

Snicker means to laugh but try to cover it up, or laugh in a sly way: *The villain in the TV show snickered when the hero was trapped.*

Roar can mean to laugh loudly, in uncontrolled amusement: *The circus crowd roared as more and more clowns tumbled out of the tiny car.*

See also the Synonym Study at **funny.**

laugh·a·ble (laf'ə bəl), *ADJECTIVE.* so foolish or so bad that it is almost funny: *a laughable mistake.* —**laugh'a·bly,** *ADVERB.*
laugh·ter (laf'tər), *NOUN.* the sounds or action of laughing: *Laughter filled the room.*
launch[1] (lònch),
1 *VERB.* to put a boat or ship into the water; set afloat: *The new ship was launched at the shipyard.*
2 *VERB.* to send something out into the air with force: *The satellite was launched in a rocket.*
3 *NOUN.* the act of launching a rocket, missile, aircraft, or ship: *The launch of the first space vehicle was a historic event.*
4 *VERB.* to start; get going: *Our friends helped us launch our business by lending us money.*
 ❑ *VERB* **launch·es, launched, launch·ing;** *PLURAL* **launch·es.** —**launch'er,** *NOUN.*
launch[2] (lònch), *NOUN.* a small, open motorboat for pleasure trips. ❑ *PLURAL* **launch·es.**
launch pad or **launching pad,** the surface or platform from which a rocket or spacecraft is shot into the air.

Laun·dro·mat (lòn'drə mat), *NOUN.* (trademark) a self-service laundry that has coin-operated washing machines and dryers.
laun·dry (lòn'drē), *NOUN.*
1 clothes, towels, and so on, that have been washed or need to be washed.
2 a room or building where clothes and linens are washed and ironed.
 ❑ *PLURAL* **laun·dries.**

laundry drying on the line

lau·rel (lôr'əl), *NOUN.*
1 a small evergreen tree with smooth, shiny leaves.
2 any tree or shrub like this. The mountain laurel has pale pink clusters of flowers.
3 **laurels,** high honor; fame.
la·va (lä'və), *NOUN.*
1 the hot, melted rock flowing from a volcano.
2 the rock formed by the cooling of this melted rock. Some lavas are hard and glassy; others are light and porous.
 ❑ *PLURAL* **la·vas.**
lav·a·to·ry (lav'ə tôr'ē), *NOUN.* a bathroom; toilet.
 ❑ *PLURAL* **lav·a·to·ries.**
lav·en·der (lav'ən dər),
1 *NOUN.* a small shrub with stalks of thickly growing fragrant, pale purple flowers. Lavender is used to make perfumes. Bags of dried lavender are often put in drawers and closets to give clothes a nice smell.
2 *ADJECTIVE* or *NOUN.* pale purple.

lavender (definition 1)

lav·ish (lav′ish),
1 *ADJECTIVE.* too much; more than is needed: *She served me a lavish helping of ice cream.*
2 *VERB.* to give or spend something very freely or too freely: *We lavished kindness on our sick friend.*
❑ *VERB* **lav·ish·es, lav·ished, lav·ish·ing.**
–lav′ish·ly, *ADVERB.*

law (lȯ), *NOUN.*
1 a rule made by the government of a country or state for all the people who live there: *Good citizens obey the laws. There is a law against spitting in public.*
2 a system of rules formed to protect society: *Criminal law deals with crimes.*
3 the study of such a system of rules; profession of a lawyer: *This student is planning a career in law.*
4 any rule or principle: *Scientists study natural laws.*
–law′less, *ADJECTIVE.*

lay down the law, *IDIOM.*
1 to give orders that must be obeyed: *There is no official to lay down the law on this question.*
2 to give a scolding: *The teacher laid down the law to the noisy class.*

take the law into your own hands, *IDIOM.* to protect your rights or punish a crime without appealing to courts of law: *In the early days of the American West, settlers often took the law into their own hands.*

law·ful (lȯ′fəl), *ADJECTIVE.* allowed by law; legal: *a lawful trial, lawful arrests.* **–law′ful·ly,** *ADVERB.*

lawn (lȯn), *NOUN.* a piece of land covered with grass kept closely cut, especially near or around a house.

lawn·mow·er (lȯn′mō′ər), *NOUN.* a machine with revolving blades for cutting the grass on a lawn.

law·suit (lȯ′süt′), *NOUN.* a case in a court of law started by one person to claim something from another; suit.

law·yer (lȯ′yər *or* loi′yer), *NOUN.* someone who has studied law and gives advice about matters of law or acts for other people in a court of law.

lay[1] (lā), *VERB.*
1 to put something down: *Lay your hat on the table.*
2 to place someone in a lying-down position: *Lay the baby down gently.*
3 to put something flat in place: *to lay bricks. They laid the carpet on the floor.* ■ See the Synonym Study at **put.**
4 to produce an egg or eggs: *Birds, fish, and reptiles lay eggs. All the hens were laying well.*
❑ *VERB* **lays, laid, lay·ing.** ■ Another word that sounds like this is **lei.**

lay aside *or* **lay away,** *IDIOM.* to save: *I laid away a dollar a week toward buying a bicycle.*

lay off, *IDIOM.*
1 to put out of work: *During the slack season many workers were laid off.*

2 to mark off: *The coach laid off the boundaries of the tennis court.*
3 to stop teasing or interfering with: *Lay off! I'm trying to study.*

Usage Note

Lay[1] and **lie**[2] are sometimes confused, because the past tense of **lie**[2] is **lay**[2] : *He lay on the couch.* **Lay**[1] means "to put down": *Lay your hat there. She laid her book on the desk.* Don't use **lay** to mean "rest flat." Use **lie:** *The wallet was lying in the street. I want to lie down.*

lay[2] (lā), *VERB.* the past tense of **lie**[2]: *I lay down for a rest.* ■ Another word that sounds like this is **lei.**

lay·er (lā′ər),
1 *NOUN.* a thickness of some material: *There are about six layers of paint on this wall. The runner wore a warm layer of clothing next to her skin.*
2 *VERB.* to cut hair in layers.
❑ *VERB* **lay·ers, lay·ered, lay·er·ing.**

lay·off (lā′ȯf′), *NOUN.* the act of putting people out of work temporarily.

lay-up *or* **lay·up** (lā′up′), *NOUN.* (in basketball) a shot made close to the basket.

la·zy (lā′zē), *ADJECTIVE.*
1 not willing to work or move fast: *He lost his job because he was lazy.*
2 moving slowly: *A lazy stream winds through the meadows.*
❑ *ADJECTIVE* **la·zi·er, la·zi·est. –la′zi·ly,** *ADVERB.* **–la′zi·ness,** *NOUN.*

lb., an abbreviation of **pound**[1]. ❑ *PLURAL* **lb.** or **lbs.**

Word Story

Why is **lb.** the abbreviation for **pound?** The Latin word for pound is *libra* (lē′brə). In old England, most people who could write knew Latin. They were used to the abbreviation **lb.** from Latin, and they borrowed it for the English word with the same meaning.

lead[1] (lēd),
1 *VERB.* to show the way by going along with someone or by being in front of someone: *The teacher led the children down the sidewalk to the park.*
2 *VERB.* to be first; go first: *Our team was leading when the bell rang.*
3 *VERB.* to be a way to get somewhere: *This road leads to the lake. Hard work leads to success.*
4 *VERB.* to pass or spend time in some special way: *He leads a quiet life in the country.*

a	hat	ė	term	ô	order	ch	child	⎧a in about
ā	age	i	it	oi	oil	ng	long	e in taken
ä	far	ī	ice	ou	out	sh	she	ə ⎨ i in pencil
â	care	o	hot	u	cup	th	thin	o in lemon
e	let	ō	open	u̇	put	ŦH	then	⎩u in circus
ē	equal	ȯ	saw	ü	rule	zh	measure	

lead² ■ leak

5 *VERB.* to direct: *A general leads an army. She leads the community orchestra. I led the singing.*
6 *NOUN.* the place of a leader; place in front: *He always takes the lead when we plan to do anything.*
7 *NOUN.* the main part in a play or other performance.
8 *NOUN.* the amount that one is ahead: *He had a lead of 3 yards in the race.*
9 *NOUN.* a suggestion; clue: *He was not sure where to look for the information, but the librarian gave him several good leads.*
❑ *VERB* **leads, led, lead·ing.**

lead off, *IDIOM.*
1 to begin; start: *The teacher led off the class discussion with a question.*
2 (in baseball) the first player of the batting order or the first to come to bat in an inning.

lead on, *IDIOM.* to persuade or trick someone into doing something foolish or illegal: *He admitted throwing the rocks, but said his friends had led him on.*

lead² (led),
1 *NOUN.* a heavy, easily melted, bluish gray metal, used to make pipe, bullets, and paint. Lead is a chemical element.
2 *ADJECTIVE.* made of lead: *a lead pipe.*
3 *NOUN.* the gray material in the middle of a pencil that you write with. Pencil lead is pure carbon.
■ Another word that sounds like this is **led.**

lead·er (lē′dər), *NOUN.* someone who shows the way; someone who goes first: *He was the leader on our hike. She is a born leader.*

leader Martin Luther King, Jr.

The Reverend Martin Luther King, Jr., was an American minister who led a nonviolent movement to end racial discrimination in the United States. He was assassinated in 1968.

lead·er·ship (lē′dər ship), *NOUN.*
1 the act of being a leader.
2 the ability to lead: *Leadership is an asset to an officer.*

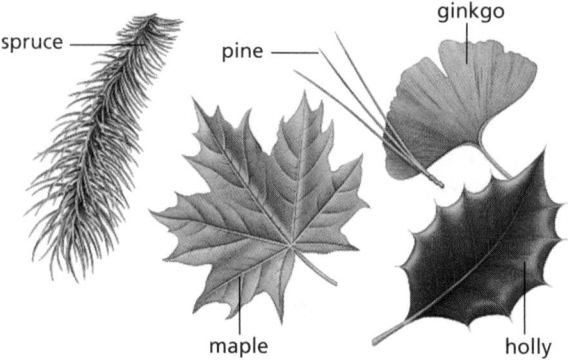

spruce pine ginkgo maple holly

various kinds of **leaves**

leaf (lēf),
1 *NOUN.* one of the thin, flat, green parts of a tree or other plant. Leaves grow on the stem or grow up from the roots.
2 *VERB.* to grow leaves: *The trees along the river leaf earlier than those on the hill.*
3 *NOUN.* a thin sheet or piece: *a leaf of a book.*
4 *VERB.* to turn the pages: *to leaf through a book.*
5 *NOUN.* a flat movable piece in the top of a table: *We put two extra leaves in the table for the party.*
❑ *PLURAL* **leaves;** *VERB* **leafs, leafed, leaf·ing.**
—**leaf′less,** *ADJECTIVE.* —**leaf′like′,** *ADJECTIVE.*

Have You Heard?

You may have heard someone say **"He has turned over a new leaf."** This means that someone has decided to start over and to do better in the future.

leaf·let (lēf′lit), *NOUN.*
1 a small flat or folded sheet of paper with printing on it: *She handed out advertising leaflets at the mall.*
2 a small or young leaf.

leaf·y (lē′fē), *ADJECTIVE.* having many leaves; covered with leaves: *Cabbage and kale are green, leafy vegetables.* ❑ *ADJECTIVE* **leaf·i·er, leaf·i·est.**
—**leaf′i·ness,** *NOUN.*

league (lēg), *NOUN.*
1 a group of people, parties, or nations formed to help one another.
2 an association of sports clubs or teams: *a baseball league, the National Football League.*
❑ *PLURAL* **leagues.**

leak (lēk),
1 *NOUN.* a hole or crack that should not be there. A leak lets something in or out.
2 *VERB.* to go in or out through a hole or crack, or in ways suggesting a hole or crack: *Water leaked into the basement. The news leaked out.*

3 *VERB*. to let something in or out which is meant to stay where it is: *My boat leaks and lets water in. That pipe leaks gas.*
❑ *VERB* **leaks, leaked, leak·ing.** ■ Another word that sounds like this is **leek.**

leak·y (lē′kē), *ADJECTIVE*. having a leak or leaks; leaking: *The drip of the leaky faucet kept me awake all night.* ❑ *ADJECTIVE* **leak·i·er, leak·i·est.**

lean[1] (lēn), *VERB*.
1 to bend; stand in a slanting position: *The small tree leans over in the wind.*
2 to rest against something or someone for support: *Lean against me.*
3 to set or put something in a leaning position: *Lean the ladder against the wall.*
❑ *VERB* **leans, leaned, lean·ing.**

lean[2] (lēn), *ADJECTIVE*.
1 not fat; thin: *We fed the lean and hungry stray dog.* ■ See the Synonym Study at **thin.**
2 producing little; not plentiful: *We had a lean harvest.*
−lean′ness, *NOUN*.

leap (lēp),
1 *NOUN*. a jump.
2 *VERB*. to jump: *The basketball player leaped high to block his opponent's shot.* ■ See the Synonym Study at **jump.**
3 *VERB*. to jump over something: *She leaped the wall.*
❑ *VERB* **leaps, leaped** or **leapt, leap·ing. −leap′er,** *NOUN*.

leap·frog (lēp′frog′), *NOUN*. a game in which one player leaps over another player, who is bending over.

leapt (lept *or* lēpt), *VERB*.
1 a past tense of **leap:** *The dog leapt over the fence.*
2 a past participle of **leap:** *The frogs have leapt into the pond.*

leap year, a year having 366 days. The extra day is February 29. A leap year happens every 4 years. The year 2000 is a leap year.

learn (lėrn), *VERB*.
1 to gain knowledge or skill: *Some people learn slowly.*
2 to memorize something: *to learn a poem by heart.*
3 to find out; come to know: *He learned about the new house being built on the corner.*
4 to become able by study or practice: *In school we learn to read.*
❑ *VERB* **learns, learned, learn·ing. −learn′er,** *NOUN*.

Usage Note

Some people use **learn** when they mean **teach.** This is not correct standard usage. You should avoid it, especially when you are writing.

learn·ed (lėr′nid), *ADJECTIVE*. having a great deal of knowledge; scholarly: *a learned professor.*

learn·ing (lėr′ning), *NOUN*. knowledge gained by study; scholarship: *a scholar of great learning.*

learning disability, any of several conditions that make it difficult for someone to learn a specific skill, such as reading or writing. Learning disabilities can affect people of great intelligence.

lease (lēs),
1 *NOUN*. a written statement saying for how long a certain property is rented and how much money shall be paid for it.
2 *NOUN*. length of time for which a lease is made: *a two-year lease.*
3 *VERB*. to rent: *We leased an apartment for a year.*
❑ *VERB* **leas·es, leased, leas·ing.**

leash (lēsh),
1 *NOUN*. a leather or rope strap, or chain for holding an animal in check: *He led the dog on a leash.*
2 *VERB*. to hold in your feelings with a leash; control: *She leashed her anger and did not say a harsh word.*
❑ *VERB* **leash·es, leashed, leash·ing;** *PLURAL* **leash·es.**

He walked the dog on a **leash.**

least (lēst),
1 *ADJECTIVE*. less than any other; smallest: *Ten cents is a little money; five cents is less; one cent is least.* ★ **Least** is a superlative of **little.**
2 *NOUN*. the smallest amount; smallest thing: *The least you can do is to thank him.*
3 *ADVERB*. to the smallest extent or degree: *She liked that book least of all. Corn is the vegetable he likes least.* ★ **Least** is the superlative of **little.**

at least, *IDIOM*.
1 not less than: *Brush your teeth at least twice a day.*
2 at any rate; in any case: *Even if you don't want to swim, at least you can come to the lake with me.*

leath·er (leŦH′ər), *NOUN*. the skin of an animal that has been cleaned and colored in a special way. Leather is used to make shoes, gloves, jackets, saddles, and so on.

leave[1] (lēv), *VERB*.
1 to go away; go away from: *We leave tonight. They left the room.*
2 to stop living in, belonging to, or working at or for: *to leave the country, to leave your job.*
3 to go without taking something away with you; let stay behind: *I left my book on the table.*
4 to let something stay in a certain condition: *We'll leave a light on for you. Please leave me alone.*

a	hat	ė	term	ô	order	ch	child		a	in about
ā	age	i	it	oi	oil	ng	long		e	in taken
ä	far	ī	ice	ou	out	sh	she	ə	i	in pencil
â	care	o	hot	u	cup	th	thin		o	in lemon
e	let	ō	open	ù	put	ŦH	then		u	in circus
ē	equal	ò	saw	ü	rule	zh	measure			

5 to give money or property to someone, often by a will, when a person dies: *She left a large fortune to her children.*

6 to give or hand over something to someone else to do: *I left the driving to my sister.*

7 to not do something: *I'll leave my homework till tomorrow.*

8 to have as a remainder after subtraction: *4 from 10 leaves 6.*
  ❑ *VERB* **leaves, left, leav·ing.**

leave off, *IDIOM.* to stop: *Continue the story from where I left off.*

leave out, *IDIOM.*
1 to not say, do, or put in: *She left out two words when she read the sentence.*
2 to neglect; forget: *Since everyone was busy, he felt that he was left out.*

Synonym Study

Leave means to go away from where you are: *A commuter train to Chicago leaves from this station every hour.*

Depart means to leave. It is a formal word: *The President departs for Washington today.*

Withdraw means to leave, often because you have to: *Under heavy attack from the enemy, the soldiers withdrew.*

Desert² (di zėrt′) means to leave when it is wrong to leave: *Just when our band got a job, the drummer deserted.*

Abandon can mean to leave suddenly. It suggests going away from a problem with no idea of returning: *We abandoned the farm after the third year with no rain. We abandoned the idea of a ski trip when we saw what it would cost.*

ANTONYM: arrive.

leave² (lēv), *NOUN.*
1 permission to be absent from duty. A **leave of absence** is an official permission to stay away from your work, school, or military duty.
2 the length of time for which you have a leave of absence: *The soldier went home on a ten-day leave.*

leaves (lēvz),
1 *NOUN.* the plural of **leaf.**
2 *VERB.* a present tense of **leave¹**: *I cry every time she leaves for summer camp.*

Leb·a·non (leb′ə nən), *NOUN.* a country in southwestern Asia, on the Mediterranean.
  —Leb·a·nese (leb′ə nēz′), *ADJECTIVE or NOUN.*

lec·ture (lek′chər),
1 *NOUN.* a planned speech or talk on a chosen subject given before an audience.
2 *VERB.* to give a lecture: *The professor lectured on American history.*

3 *NOUN.* the act of criticizing someone for doing something wrong: *My parents give me a lecture when I come home late.*
4 *VERB.* to criticize someone for doing something wrong; scold: *My parents lectured me when they found out I had lied.*
  ❑ *VERB* **lec·tures, lec·tured, lec·tur·ing.**
  —lec′tur·er, *NOUN.*

led (led), *VERB.*
1 the past tense of **lead¹**: *She led her dog home.*
2 the past participle of **lead¹**: *We were led through the cavern by a guide.*
  ∎ Another word that sounds like this is **lead²**.

ledge (lej), *NOUN.*
1 a narrow shelf: *a window ledge.*
2 a shelf or ridge of rock.

lee (lē), *NOUN.* the side or part sheltered from the wind: *The wind was so fierce that we huddled in the lee of the boat.*

leech (lēch), *NOUN.* a worm living in ponds and streams that sucks the blood of animals. ❑ *PLURAL* **leech·es.**

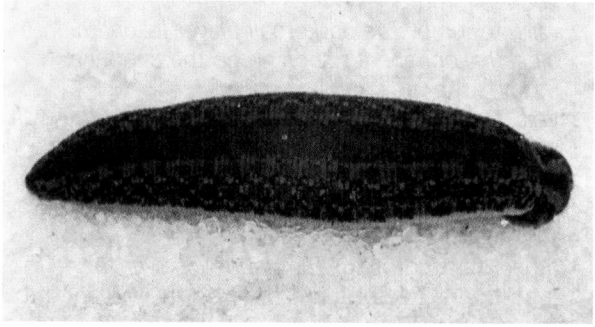

leech — up to 8 inches long

leek (lēk), *NOUN.* a vegetable somewhat like a long, thick, green onion; scallion. ∎ Another word that sounds like this is **leak.**

left¹ (left),
1 *ADJECTIVE.* belonging to the side of this dictionary entry where the definition numbers appear; of the side of a keyboard where the letter *A* appears: *A person has a right hand and a left hand.*
2 *ADJECTIVE.* on this side when viewed from the front: *Take a left turn at the next light.*
3 *ADVERB.* on or to the left side: *Turn left.*
4 *NOUN.* the left side or hand: *He sat at my left.*

left² (left), *VERB.*
1 the past tense of **leave¹**: *He left his hat in the hall.*
2 the past participle of **leave¹**: *She should have left at four o' clock.*

left field, (in baseball) the section of the outfield beyond third base. **—left fielder.**

left-hand (left′hand′), *ADJECTIVE.*
1 on or to the left: *the upper left-hand corner of a page.*
2 of, for, or with the left hand: *a left-hand glove.*

left-hand·ed (left′han′did), ADJECTIVE.
1 using the left hand more easily and readily than the right.
2 done with the left hand: *a left-handed tennis serve.*
3 made to be used with the left hand: *a left-handed baseball glove.*
—**left′-hand′ed·ness,** NOUN.

Have You Heard?

You may have heard someone say that a person gave a **"left-handed compliment."** This is a compliment that is really an insult, such as "That was a good catch for someone as clumsy as you!" Why *left-handed?* Because most people are more skillful with their right hand than their left hand.

left·o·ver (left′ō′vər),
1 NOUN. usually, **leftovers,** things that are left. Scraps of food from a meal are leftovers.
2 ADJECTIVE. uneaten or unused; remaining: *I made some sandwiches with the leftover sliced turkey.*

leg (leg), NOUN.
1 the part of the body between the hip and the foot. People and animals stand on their legs.
2 the part of a piece of clothing that covers your leg: *I fell and tore my pants' leg.*
3 anything that is shaped or used like a leg: *a table leg.*
4 one of the parts or stages of any trip, process, or activity: *We are on the last leg of our vacation.*
pull someone's leg, IDIOM. to fool, trick, or make fun of someone: *He believed me, but I was only pulling his leg.*

le·gal (lē′gəl), ADJECTIVE.
1 according to law; lawful: *Hunting is legal only during certain seasons.*
2 of or about law or lawyers: *legal advice.*
—**le′gal·ly,** ADVERB.

leg·end (lej′ənd), NOUN.
1 a story coming down from the past, which many people have believed: *The stories about Robin Hood are legends, not history.*
2 the words accompanying a picture, diagram, or map: *The legend underneath the picture tells us that the city is Rome.*

leg·end·ar·y (lej′ən der′ē), ADJECTIVE. of or described in a legend or legends; not historical: *Robin Hood was a legendary person.*

Robin Hood was a **legendary** person.

leg·gings (leg′ingz), NOUN PLURAL.
1 tight, stretchy pants: *She wore black leggings and a sweater.*
2 extra outer coverings of cloth or leather for the legs, for use out of doors.

leg·i·ble (lej′ə bəl), ADJECTIVE. easy to read; plain and clear: *Her handwriting is quite large and legible.* —**leg′i·bil′i·ty,** NOUN. —**leg′i·bly,** ADVERB.

le·gion (lē′jən), NOUN.
1 a large group of soldiers; army.
2 a great many; very large number: *Legions of grasshoppers destroyed the crops.*

leg·is·late (lej′ə slāt), VERB. to make a law or laws: *Congress legislates for the United States.* ❑ VERB **leg·is·lates, leg·is·lat·ed, leg·is·lat·ing.**

leg·is·la·tion (lej′ə slā′shən), NOUN.
1 the act or process of making laws: *Congress has the power of legislation.*
2 a law or laws: *Important legislation is reported in today's newspaper.*

leg·is·la·tive (lej′ə slā′tiv), ADJECTIVE.
1 involving the making of laws: *Congress passed many legislative reforms this month.*
2 having the duty and power of making laws: *Congress is a legislative body.*

leg·is·la·tor (lej′ə slā′tər), NOUN. an elected official who makes laws; member of a group that makes laws. Senators and Representatives are legislators.

leg·is·la·ture (lej′ə slā′chər), NOUN. a group of elected officials that has the duty and power of making laws for a state or country. Each state of the United States has a legislature.

le·git·i·mate (lə jit′ə mit), ADJECTIVE.
1 allowed or admitted by law; rightful; lawful: *a legitimate ruler.*
2 valid; acceptable: *Sickness is a legitimate reason for a child's absence from school.*
—**le·git′i·mate·ly,** ADVERB.

leg·ume (leg′yüm *or* li gyüm′), NOUN. any of many plants that bear pods containing a number of seeds. Beans and peas are legumes. Legumes release nitrogen from their roots, fertilizing the soil they grow in.

lei (lā), NOUN. a wreath of flowers or leaves worn as an ornament around the neck or on the head. ❑ PLURAL **leis.** ■ Another word that sounds like this is **lay.**

lei·sure (lē′zhər), NOUN. the time when you are not at work or studying, when you may rest, amuse yourself, and do the things you like to do: *She's been too busy to have much leisure.*

a hat	ė term	ô order	ch child	⟨a in about
ā age	i it	oi oil	ng long	e in taken
ä far	ī ice	ou out	sh she	ə⟨ i in pencil
â care	o hot	u cup	th thin	o in lemon
e let	ō open	ů put	ŦH then	⟨u in circus
ē equal	ȯ saw	ü rule	zh measure	

lei·sure·ly (lē′zhər lē), *ADJECTIVE.* in no hurry; taking plenty of time: *I took a leisurely strool to the lake.*

lem·on (lem′ən),

1 *NOUN.* a sour, yellow citrus fruit about as big as an egg. Lemon juice is often used for flavoring and cooking.

2 *ADJECTIVE.* flavored with lemon.

3 *NOUN.* (informal) something or someone that is worthless or unpleasant: *This car is a lemon.*

lemon
(definition 1)

lem·on·ade (lem′ə nād′), *NOUN.* a drink made of lemon juice, sugar, and water.

le·mur (lē′mər), *NOUN.* a small mammal something like a monkey, but with a foxlike face and woolly fur. Lemurs live in trees and are active mostly at night.

lend (lend), *VERB.*

1 to let someone have something or use something for a while, until you get it back: *Will you lend me your bicycle for an hour?*

2 to make a loan or loans: *Banks lend money and charge interest.*
  ❑ *VERB* **lends, lent, lend·ing. –lend′er,** *NOUN.*

length (lengkth), *NOUN.*

1 how long something is: *the length of a room, eight inches in length.*

2 how long something lasts in time: *the length of a visit.*

length·en (lengk′thən), *VERB.* to make or become longer: *The tailor can lengthen those pants.* ❑ *VERB* **length·ens, length·ened, length·en·ing.**

length·wise (lengkth′wīz′), *ADVERB* or *ADJECTIVE.* in the direction of the length: *She cut the cloth lengthwise.*

length·y (lengk′thē), *ADJECTIVE.* lasting a long time; too long: *His story was so lengthy that I lost interest.* ❑ *ADJECTIVE* **length·i·er, length·i·est.**

len·ient (lē′nyənt), *ADJECTIVE.* not harsh when judging or punishing someone: *a lenient judge.* **–len′ient·ly,** *ADVERB.*

lens (lenz), *NOUN.*

1 a curved piece of glass or plastic that will bring closer together or send wider apart the rays of light passing through it. The lenses of a telescope make things look larger and nearer.

2 the part of the eye that focuses light rays upon the retina.
  ❑ *PLURAL* **lens·es.**

lent (lent), *VERB.*

1 the past tense of **lend:** *I lent you my pencil.*

2 the past participle of **lend:** *He had lent me his knife.*

Lent (lent), *NOUN.* the forty weekdays before Easter, observed in many Christian churches as a time for giving up certain habits, favorite foods, and so on.

len·til (len′tl), *NOUN.* a vegetable much like a very small bean. Lentils are often eaten in soup.

leop·ard (lep′ərd), *NOUN.* a large cat of Africa and Asia, having a dull yellowish fur spotted with black. Black leopards are called panthers.

leopard — from 6 to 8 feet long, including the tail

le·o·tard (lē′ə tärd), *NOUN.* a tight-fitting piece of clothing, with or without sleeves. Dancers and gymnasts wear leotards.

Word Story

Leotard comes from the name of Jules Léotard (zhül′ lā′ō tär), a famous French trapeze artist of the 1800s. So many people saw him perform in this garment that they named it after him.

lep·re·chaun (lep′rə kän), *NOUN.* (in Irish legends) an elf resembling a little old man, believed to own hidden gold.

less (les),

1 *ADJECTIVE.* smaller: *of less width, less importance.*

2 *ADJECTIVE.* not so much; not so much of: *to have less rain, to eat less meat.*

3 *NOUN.* a smaller amount or quantity: *He refused to take less than $5.*

4 *ADVERB.* to a smaller extent or degree; not so; not so well: *less important, less known.*
  ★ **Less** is the comparative of **little.**

Word Power   -less

The suffix **-less** means "without." **Doubtless** means **without** doubt. **Homeless** means **without** a home.

less·en (les′n), *VERB.* to make or become less: *The fever lessened during the night.* ❑ *VERB* **less·ens, less·ened, less·en·ing.** ▪ Another word that sounds like this is **lesson.**

less·er (les′ər), *ADJECTIVE.* less; smaller: *When asked to choose between the mile and the half-mile races, she chose to run the lesser distance.*

les·son (les′n), *NOUN.* something that you study and learn; something you have been taught: *Children* *study many different lessons in school.* ■ Another word that sounds like this is **lessen.**

let (let), *VERB.*
1 to not stop someone or something from doing something; allow; permit: *Let the dog have a bone. They let the visitor on board the ship.*
2 Let is used in giving suggestions and commands: *"Let's go fishing"* means "I suggest that we go fishing." *"Let all members do their duty"* means all members must do their duty.
☐ *VERB* **lets, let, let·ting.**

let down, *IDIOM.*
1 to lower: *We let the heavy box down from the roof very slowly.*
2 to disappoint: *Don't let us down today; we're counting on you to win.*

let off, *IDIOM.* to permit to go free: *I was let off with a warning to do better in the future.*

let on, *IDIOM.* to allow to be known; reveal your knowledge of: *He didn't let on that he knew their secret.*

let out, *IDIOM.*
1 to make larger: *You've grown so much, I'll have to let out the waist on this skirt.*
2 to dismiss or be dismissed: *Our school lets out at three o'clock.*

let up, *IDIOM.* to stop; pause: *They never let up in the fight.*

Usage Note

People sometimes mix up **let** and **leave¹. Let** means not to stop something from happening. **Leave** means to go away. In writing and in most speech, you should use sentences such as *"Let her be"* or *"Let him go if he wants to."* Except in very relaxed conversation, you should not use **leave** in those sentences or others like them. In *"Leave me alone,"* of course, the meaning is "go away!"

let's (lets), a contraction of **let us.**

let·ter (let′ər),
1 *NOUN.* a written or printed message: *He told me about his vacation in a letter.*
2 *NOUN.* a part of the alphabet; mark or sign that stands for one of the sounds that make up words. There are 26 letters in our alphabet.
3 *VERB.* to mark or write with letters: *Please letter a new sign.*
☐ *VERB* **let·ters, let·tered, let·ter·ing.**

letter carrier, someone who delivers mail.

let·ter·ing (let′ər ing), *NOUN.*
1 letters that are drawn, painted, or stamped.
2 the act of making letters.

let·ter-per·fect (let′ər pėr′fikt), *ADJECTIVE.* knowing your part or lesson perfectly: *I practiced my part in the play until I was letter-perfect.*

let·tuce (let′is), *NOUN.* a garden plant grown for its large leaves, used in salads and sandwiches. There are many kinds of lettuce.

Most kinds of **lettuce** are green.

leu·ke·mi·a (lü kē′mē ə), *NOUN.* a form of cancer in which there are too many white blood cells in the blood.

lev·ee (lev′ē), *NOUN.*
1 a bank of earth built to keep a river from overflowing: *There are levees in many places along the lower Mississippi River.*
2 a landing place for boats along a river.
☐ *PLURAL* **lev·ees.** ■ Another word that sounds like this is **levy.**

lev·el (lev′əl),
1 *ADJECTIVE.* flat and even; having the same height everywhere: *a level floor.*
2 *ADJECTIVE.* of equal height or importance: *The table is level with the sill of the window.*
3 *NOUN.* a device for showing whether a surface is level.
4 *VERB.* to make something level: *The builder leveled the ground with a bulldozer.*
5 *VERB.* to lay low; bring to the level of the ground; to knock down: *The tornado leveled our house.*
6 *NOUN.* how high something is; height: *The flood rose to a level of 60 feet.*
7 *NOUN.* a stage of learning or achievement; position; rank: *She reads at a high level for her class.*
☐ *VERB* **lev·els, lev·eled, lev·el·ing.**

on the level, *IDIOM.* fair; honest: *I don't think that business is on the level.*

lev·er (lev′ər *or* lē′vər), *NOUN.*
1 a bar used for lifting a weight at one end by pushing down at the other end. It must be supported at any point in between by a fixed part called a fulcrum. The lever is a simple machine.

a	hat	ė	term	ô	order	ch	child		a in about
ā	age	i	it	oi	oil	ng	long		e in taken
ä	far	ī	ice	ou	out	sh	she	ə	i in pencil
â	care	o	hot	u	cup	th	thin		o in lemon
e	let	ō	open	u̇	put	ᴛʜ	then		u in circus
ē	equal	ȯ	saw	ü	rule	zh	measure		

2 a bar or handle that you use to operate a machine.

lev·y (lev′ē),
1 VERB. to officially collect a sum of money: *The government levies taxes to pay its expenses.*
2 NOUN. money collected by authority or force.
❑ VERB **lev·ies, lev·ied, lev·y·ing;** PLURAL **lev·ies.**
■ Another word that sounds like this is **levee.**

li·a·ble (lī′ə bəl), ADJECTIVE.
1 likely: *That glass is liable to break.*
2 legally responsible; bound by law to pay: *The Postal Service is not liable for damage to a parcel unless it is insured.*

li·ar (lī′ər), NOUN. someone who tells lies.

lib·er·al (lib′ər əl),
1 ADJECTIVE. generous: *A liberal giver gives much.*
2 ADJECTIVE. willing to accept the ideas of other people; tolerant: *a liberal thinker.*
3 NOUN. someone who believes in progress and reforms.
—**lib′er·al·ly,** ADVERB.

lib·e·rate (lib′ə rāt′), VERB. to set someone free: *In 1865, the United States liberated all people who had been enslaved.* ❑ VERB **lib·e·rates, lib·e·rat·ed, lib·e·rat·ing.** —**lib′e·ra′tion,** NOUN. —**lib′e·ra′tor,** NOUN.

liberator
Simón Bolívar

Simón Bolívar was a great Venezuelan general and politician. He led fights for freedom from Spanish rule in South America. Bolivia is named after him.

Li·ber·i·a (lī bir′ē ə), NOUN. a country in western Africa. Liberia was founded in 1821 by people who had been freed from slavery in the United States. —**Li·ber′i·an,** ADJECTIVE or NOUN.

lib·er·ty (lib′ər tē), NOUN.
1 freedom: *In 1865, the United States granted liberty to all people who were enslaved.*

2 the right or power to do as one pleases; power or opportunity to do something: *Americans enjoy basic liberties under the Bill of Rights.*
❑ PLURAL **lib·er·ties.**

at liberty, IDIOM. allowed; permitted: *You are at liberty to make any choice you please.*

li·brar·i·an (lī brer′ē ən), NOUN. someone who directs or helps to manage a library.

li·brar·y (lī′brer′ē), NOUN. a room or building where a collection of books, magazines, films, or recordings is kept for public use and borrowing.
❑ PLURAL **li·brar·ies.**

Lib·y·a (lib′ē ə), NOUN. a country in northern Africa. —**Lib′y·an,** ADJECTIVE or NOUN.

lice (līs), NOUN. the plural of **louse.**

li·cense (lī′sns),
1 NOUN. a paper, card, or plate showing official permission to do something: *The policeman asked the reckless driver for his license.*
2 VERB. to give a license to; permit by law: *A doctor is licensed to practice medicine.*
❑ VERB **li·cens·es, li·censed, li·cens·ing.**

li·chen (lī′kən), NOUN. a living thing that looks somewhat like moss. It grows in patches on rocks, trees, and other surfaces. ■ Another word that sounds like this is **liken.**

lick (lik),
1 VERB. to move your tongue over something: *I licked the stamp and stuck it on the envelope.*
2 VERB. to lap something up with the tongue: *The kids licked their ice cream cones.*
3 NOUN. the act of moving your tongue over something: *She gave the spoon a big lick.*
4 VERB. (informal) to defeat in a fight or contest; conquer: *Our team always licks theirs.*
❑ VERB **licks, licked, lick·ing.**

lic·or·ice (lik′ər is *or* lik′ər ish), NOUN. a sweet substance obtained from the dried root of a plant. Licorice is used in medicine and candy.

lid (lid), NOUN. a cover that can be taken off something; top: *the lid of a box, the lid of a jar.*

lie¹ (lī),
1 NOUN. something said or written that is not true; something that is not true said to deceive: *He told a lie about the broken window.*
2 VERB. to say or write something that is not true; tell a lie: *He lied about the broken window.*
❑ VERB **lies, lied, ly·ing.** ■ Another word that sounds like this is **lye.**

lie² (lī), VERB.
1 to have your body in a flat position along the ground or other surface: *to lie on the grass, to lie in bed.*
2 to be flat on a surface: *The book was lying on the table.*
3 to be; exist: *The lake lies to the south of us. We could see a ship lying offshore at anchor.*

4 to be buried; be in a grave: *Here lie the fallen soldiers of many wars.*
■ See the Usage Note at **lay**[1]. ❑ *VERB* **lies, lay, lain, ly·ing.** ■ Another word that sounds like this is **lye.**

lieu·ten·ant (lü ten′ənt), *NOUN.*
1 a military rank. See the chart on page 550.
2 a police or fire department officer, usually ranking next below a captain and next above a sergeant.
3 a person who acts in the place of someone higher in authority: *The scoutmaster used the two boys as his lieutenants.*

life (līf), *NOUN.*
1 the condition of living or being alive. People, animals, plants, bacteria, and all living things have life; rocks and metals do not.
2 the time that someone or something is alive: *During her life she was an outstanding doctor.*
3 a living being; person: *Five lives were lost in the fire.*
4 living things: *The desert island had almost no animal or vegetable life.*
5 a way of living: *a country life, a dull life.*
6 an account of someone's life: *Several lives of Lincoln have been written.*
7 spirit; vigor: *Put more life into your work.*
❑ *PLURAL* **lives.**

life-and-death (līf′ən deth′), *ADJECTIVE.*
1 involving life or death; critical: *It was a life-and-death medical emergency.*
2 extremely important; vital: *Good business at holiday season is a life-and-death matter for many stores.*

life·boat (līf′bōt′), *NOUN.* a strong, open boat with oars, specially built for escaping from sinking ships.

life cycle, all the stages of development that a living thing passes through during its life.

life·guard (līf′gärd′), *NOUN.* someone employed at a beach or pool to help in case of accident or danger to swimmers.

life jacket, a sleeveless jacket filled with a lightweight material or with air, worn as a life preserver.

life·less (līf′lis), *ADJECTIVE.*
1 without life: *The spaceship made an emergency landing on the lifeless planet.*
2 dead: *The lifeless body floated ashore.*
—**life′less·ly,** *ADVERB.*

life·like (līf′līk′), *ADJECTIVE.* looking exactly like a real person or thing: *He painted a lifelike portrait.*

life·long (līf′lông′), *ADJECTIVE.* lasting all your life: *They had formed a lifelong friendship.*

life preserver, a wide belt, ring, or vest made of plastic or cork, used to keep someone afloat in the water.

life·sav·ing (līf′sā′ving), *NOUN.* the skills and actions used in saving lives, especially to save someone from drowning.

life-size (līf′sīz′), *ADJECTIVE.* having the same size as the living thing: *a life-size statue.*

life·span (līf′span′), *NOUN.* the length of time something can be expected to live: *The lifespan of a wild elephant is about 65 years.*

life-support system (līf′sə pôrt′ sis′tem), equipment that helps or replaces a life process, such as breathing, for a person who would not otherwise survive: *She was on a life-support system while she waited for a kidney transplant.*

life·time (līf′tīm′), *NOUN.* the time during which a life lasts: *My grandparents have seen many changes in their lifetime.*

life·work (līf′wėrk′), *NOUN.* work that takes or lasts a whole lifetime; main work in life: *Excavating the ruined temple was her lifework.*

lift (lift),
1 *VERB.* to raise something up higher; raise into the air; pick up: *Please help me lift this heavy box.*
2 *VERB.* to raise someone's feelings, thoughts, and the like: *The good news lifted our spirits.*
3 *VERB.* to rise and go; go away: *The fog lifted at dawn.* ■ See the Synonym Study at **rise.**
4 *VERB.* to go up; be raised: *The lid to the CD player lifts up when you press a button.*
5 *NOUN.* a happier feeling about something: *Mother's promotion gave her a big lift.*
6 *NOUN.* the act of lifting: *She showed surprise with a lift of her eyebrows.*
7 *NOUN.* a ride in a vehicle: *Can you give me a lift home?*
❑ *VERB* **lifts, lift·ed, lift·ing.**

lift-off (lift′ôf′), *NOUN.* the exact moment when a rocket is launched.

lig·a·ment (lig′ə mənt), *NOUN.* a band of strong tissue that connects bones or holds organs of the body in place.

The ligaments are shown in white.

ligaments

light[1] (līt),
1 *NOUN.* energy in the form of radiation that the eye can see. It travels at a speed of 186,282 miles per second in a vacuum: *The sun gives light to the earth.*
2 *NOUN.* something that gives light: *Please turn off the lights when you leave.*

a	hat	ė	term	ô	order	ch	child		a in about
ā	age	i	it	oi	oil	ng	long		e in taken
ä	far	ī	ice	ou	out	sh	she	ə{	i in pencil
â	care	o	hot	u	cup	th	thin		o in lemon
e	let	ō	open	u̇	put	ᴛʜ	then		u in circus
ē	equal	ȯ	saw	ü	rule	zh	measure		

3 VERB. to cause something to give light: *She lit the lamp.*

4 VERB. to give light to; fill with light: *The room was lit by six candles.*

5 ADJECTIVE. bright; clear: *The moon made the night as light as day.*

6 NOUN. brightness; clearness: *a dim light, bright light.*

7 VERB. to make bright or clear: *Her face was lit by a smile.*

8 ADJECTIVE. not dark; pale in color: *I have light brown hair and light blue eyes.*

9 VERB. to set fire to: *I lit the candles.*

10 VERB. to catch fire: *Matches light when you scratch them.*

❑ VERB **lights, lit** or **light·ed, light·ing.** —**light'ness,** NOUN.

see the light, IDIOM. to understand something: *I've had trouble learning to use my computer, but I'm really beginning to see the light now.*

shed light on or **throw light on,** IDIOM. to make clear; explain something: *The police found evidence that shed light on several neighborhood burglaries.*

light² (līt), ADJECTIVE.

1 not weighing very much; not heavy: *a light load.*

2 having less than usual weight or thickness: *a light jacket.*

3 less than usual in amount or force: *a light sleep, a light rain, a light meal.*

4 easy to bear or do: *light punishment, a light task.*

5 moving easily: *She had a light step.*

light³ (līt), VERB. to come down from flight: *A bird lit on the branch.* ❑ VERB **lights, lit** or **light·ed, light·ing.**

light·en¹ (līt'n), VERB. to brighten; become brighter: *The sky lightens before the dawn.* ❑ VERB **light·ens, light·ened, light·en·ing.**

light·en² (līt'n), VERB.

1 to reduce the load of; make or become lighter: *Your help lightened our work.*

2 to make or become more cheerful: *The good news lightened our hearts.*

❑ VERB **light·ens, light·ened, light·en·ing.**

lighten up, IDIOM. (informal) to become less serious; to relax and be more cheerful: *We told her to lighten up about the schedule.*

light·head·ed (līt'hed'id), ADJECTIVE. feeling dizzy: *The fever made me feel light-headed.*

light·heart·ed (līt'här'tid), ADJECTIVE. happy; cheerful: *The warm, sunny weather made us feel lighthearted.* —**light'heart'ed·ly,** ADVERB.

light·house (līt'hous'), NOUN. a tall building like a tower that has a strong, bright light that shines far out over the water. Lighthouses are located on or near the shore to guide ships and warn of danger. ❑ PLURAL **light·hous·es** (līt'hou'ziz).

light·ing (lī'ting), NOUN. the way in which lights are arranged: *overhead lighting.*

light·ly (līt'lē), ADVERB.

1 with little weight or force: *A robin perched lightly on the branch.*

2 to a small degree or extent; not much: *The children were lightly clad due to the heat.*

3 quickly; easily: *She jumped lightly aside.*

light·ning (līt'ning), NOUN. a flash of electricity in the sky. The sound that it makes is thunder.

lightning bug. See **firefly.**

light pen, a device like a pen which produces an electrical signal when it is pointed at light. It is used for directing a computer to add, remove, or change information shown on its display screen.

light·weight (līt'wāt'), ADJECTIVE. not heavy; light in weight: *We packed the food in lightweight containers. Bring a lightweight jacket on the field trip to the park.*

lik·a·ble (lī'kə bəl), ADJECTIVE. having qualities that make someone popular: *She is very likable.*
■ See the Synonym Study at **good-natured.**

like¹ (līk),

1 PREPOSITION or ADJECTIVE. much the same as; similar to: *Our house is like theirs.*

2 PREPOSITION. what you would expect of: *Isn't it just like them to be late?*

3 PREPOSITION. in the right condition for: *I feel like working.*

4 CONJUNCTION. (informal) in the same way as; as: *Snakes attract him like puppies and kittens attract most people.*

Usage Note

Like¹ is used with nouns and pronouns: *She looks like her mother and talks like her too.* **As** is used with verbs: *He didn't behave as he should.* Many people feel that using **like** with a verb is wrong. Others feel that this use is only informal.

lighthouse

like² (līk),
1 *VERB.* to be pleased with something or someone; be attracted by: *Cats like milk.*
2 *VERB.* to have a kindly or friendly feeling for: *I like my friends and they like me.*
3 *VERB.* to desire; wish for something: *I would like more time to finish this. Come whenever you like.*
4 *NOUN.* **likes,** likings; preferences: *You know all my likes and dislikes.*
□ *VERB* **likes, liked, lik·ing.**

Word Power   -like

The suffix **-like** means "similar to" or "like." **Cloudlike** means **similar to** a cloud. Bell-**like** means **like** a bell.

like·li·hood (līk′lē hùd), *NOUN.* a strong chance that something will happen: *Is there any likelihood of rain today?*

like·ly (līk′lē),
1 *ADJECTIVE.* probable: *One likely result of this heavy rain is the rising of the river.*
2 *ADVERB.* probably: *I shall very likely be home all day.*
3 *ADJECTIVE.* to be expected: *It's likely to be hot in July.*
□ *ADJECTIVE* **like·li·er, like·li·est.**

lik·en (lī′kən), *VERB.* to compare something to something else: *The young woman's voice was likened to that of a famous singer.* □ *VERB* **lik·ens, lik·ened, lik·en·ing.** ■ Another word that sounds like this is **lichen.**

like·ness (līk′nis), *NOUN.*
1 being alike; similarity: *The boy's likeness to his father was striking.*
2 a picture: *This photo is a good likeness of you.*
□ *PLURAL* **like·ness·es.**

like·wise (līk′wīz′), *ADVERB.*
1 the same: *See what I do. Now you do likewise.*
2 also; moreover; too: *I must go home now, and you likewise.*

lik·ing (lī′king), *NOUN.* the fact of enjoying or being fond of something: *a liking for apples.*

li·lac (lī′lək),
1 *NOUN.* a bush with clusters of tiny, fragrant, pale pinkish purple or white flowers.
2 *ADJECTIVE* or *NOUN.* pale pinkish purple.

a beautiful **lilac**

Word Story

Lilac comes from a Persian word meaning "blue." Often colors are named for plants, but this is a plant named for a color.

lil·y (lil′ē), *NOUN.* a plant with tall, thin stems and large, showy, bell-shaped flowers. Lilies grow from bulbs. □ *PLURAL* **lil·ies. –lil′y·like′,** *ADJECTIVE.*

lily of the valley, a plant having tiny, fragrant, trumpet-shaped white flowers arranged along a single flower stem. □ *PLURAL* **lilies of the valley.**

Li·ma (lē′mə), *NOUN.* the capital of Peru.

li·ma bean (lī′mə bēn′), a broad, flat, pale green bean, used as a vegetable.

limb (lim), *NOUN.*
1 a large branch: *They sawed the dead limb off the tree before it fell.*
2 a leg, arm, or wing.

lim·ber (lim′bər), *ADJECTIVE.* bending easily; flexible: *A piano player must have limber fingers.*

lime¹ (līm), *NOUN.* a powdery white substance made by burning limestone, shells, or bones. Lime is used in making cement and on fields to improve the soil.

lime² (līm), *NOUN.* a sour, green citrus fruit a little smaller than a lemon. Limes are used for flavoring and cooking.

lim·er·ick (lim′ər ik), *NOUN.* a kind of humorous verse of five lines.

lime·stone (līm′stōn′), *NOUN.* a rock used for building and for making lime.

lim·it (lim′it),
1 *NOUN.* the farthest possible point or edge; where something ends or must end: *the limit of your vision. I have reached the limit of my patience.*
2 *NOUN.* **limits,** boundary: *Keep within the limits of the school grounds.*
3 *VERB.* to set a limit to something; restrict: *We must limit our expenses to $100.*
□ *VERB* **lim·its, lim·it·ed, lim·it·ing.** **–lim′i·ta′tion,** *NOUN.*

off limits, *IDIOM.* forbidden; not allowed: *You know that Dad's workshop is off limits because of the dangerous tools.*

lim·it·ed (lim′ə tid), *ADJECTIVE.* not a very great amount or number: *limited space, a limited number of seats.*

lim·o (lim′ō), *NOUN.* a short form of **limousine.**
□ *PLURAL* **lim·os.**

lim·ou·sine (lim′ə zēn′ *or* lim′ə zēn′), *NOUN.*
1 a large car with comfortable seating for a number of passengers; limo. Limousines are often hired for special trips or occasions.
2 a large car or small bus used to take passengers to or from an airport, railway, or bus station, and so on; limo.

a hat	ė term	ô order	ch child	⎧a in about
ā age	i it	oi oil	ng long	⎪e in taken
ä far	ī ice	ou out	sh she	ə⎨i in pencil
â care	o hot	u cup	th thin	⎪o in lemon
e let	ō open	ù put	ŦH then	⎩u in circus
ē equal	ò saw	ü rule	zh measure	

limp¹ (limp),
  1 *NOUN.* a painful, uneven step or walk because of an injury or disease.
  2 *VERB.* to walk with a painful step: *After my fall, I limped for a few days.*
    ❑ *VERB* **limps, limped, limp·ing.**
limp² (limp), *ADJECTIVE.* not stiff; easy to bend: *Spaghetti gets limp when cooked.*
Lin·coln (ling′kən), *NOUN.* the capital of Nebraska.
lin·den (lin′dən), *NOUN.* a shade tree with heart-shaped leaves and clusters of small, fragrant yellowish flowers.
line¹ (lin),
  1 *NOUN.* a long narrow mark: *Draw two lines here.*
  2 *NOUN.* anything that is like a long narrow mark: *Wrinkles appear as lines on your skin.*
  3 *VERB.* to mark with lines: *Please line your paper with a pencil and ruler.*
  4 *NOUN.* a single row of words on a page or in a newspaper column: *two lines of text.*
  5 *NOUN.* (in mathematics) the path traced by a moving point. It has length, but no thickness.
  6 *NOUN.* a piece of string, rope, cord, or wire: *Father put new line on my fishing pole.*
  7 *NOUN.* an edge or boundary: *My dad chalks the lines of our neighborhood soccer field.*
  8 *NOUN.* a row of people or things: *A long line of people waited outside the theater.*
  9 *VERB.* to form a line along: *Trees line both sides of our street.*
  10 *NOUN.* a short letter; note: *Drop me a line.*
  11 *NOUN.* a connected series of people or things following one another in time: *She is the latest in a long line of gifted athletes in my family.*
  12 *NOUN.* a system of transportation: *a bus line, a subway line.*
  13 *NOUN.* **lines,** words that an actor speaks in a play: *I almost forgot my lines.*
  14 *NOUN.* a single verse of poetry.
  15 *NOUN.* in football: **a** the line of scrimmage. **b** the players along the line of scrimmage at the start of a play.
  16 *NOUN.* a telephone connection: *I'm sorry, the line is busy.*
    ❑ *VERB* **lines, lined, lin·ing.**
  hold the line, *IDIOM.* to stand firm; maintain a position: *The librarians sometimes let us stay a little late, but when it comes to eating in the library, they really hold the line.*
  in line, *IDIOM.* in agreement: *His plan for our science project is in line with mine.*
  line up, *IDIOM.* to form a line; form into a line: *Please line up near the door.*
  out of line, *IDIOM.* uncalled-for; not suitable or proper: *They can disagree, but name-calling is out of line.*

line² (lin), *VERB.* to put a layer of paper, cloth, or felt on the inside surface of something: *Her boots are lined with fur.* ❑ *VERB* **lines, lined, lin·ing.**
line·back·er (lin′bak′ər), *NOUN.* (in football) a defensive player who plays directly behind the defensive linemen.
line drive, a baseball hit so hard that it goes in an almost straight line.
line graph, a graph in which points that stand for quantities are marked on a diagram and then connected by a series of short straight lines.
line·man (lin′mən), *NOUN.*
  1 someone who sets up or repairs telephone or electric power lines.
  2 (in football) a player in the line; a center, guard, tackle, or end.
    ❑ *PLURAL* **line·men.**
lin·en (lin′ən), *NOUN.*
  1 cloth or thread made from flax.
  2 **linens,** articles made of linen or similar cloth. Tablecloths, napkins, sheets, towels, and shirts are linens.
line of scrimmage, (in football) an imaginary line running across the field at the point where the ball is placed after a play has ended.
lin·er (li′nər), *NOUN.* something that lines or serves as a lining: *My coat has a fleece liner for extra warmth.*
line·up (lin′up′), *NOUN.*
  1 (in sports) a list of the players taking part in a game.
  2 a formation of people or things into a line. A police lineup is an arrangement of a group of people for identification.
lin·ger (ling′gər), *VERB.* to stay somewhere as if you are unwilling to leave: *She lingered after the others had left.* ❑ *VERB* **lin·gers, lin·gered, lin·ger·ing.**
lin·go (ling′gō), *NOUN.* the language or talk used and understood only by people in a certain kind of work, activity, sport, and so on: *baseball lingo, computer lingo.* ❑ *PLURAL* **lin·goes.**
lin·ing (li′ning), *NOUN.* a layer of material that covers the inner surface of something: *The lining in my coat is torn.*
link (lingk),
  1 *NOUN.* any ring or loop of a chain.
  2 *NOUN.* someone or something that joins or connects as a link does: *Our elders are links to the past.*
  3 *VERB.* to join people or things as a link does; unite or connect: *Don't try to link me with this scheme.*
    ❑ *VERB* **links, linked, link·ing.**
linking verb, a verb that connects a noun or pronoun subject with a following adjective or noun. In "The trees are maples" and "He is a student," *are* and *is* are linking verbs.
li·no·le·um (lə nō′lē əm), *NOUN.* a hard, smooth, shiny floor covering.
lint (lint), *NOUN.* tiny bits of thread or fluff from cloth.

li·on (lī′ən), NOUN. a large cat of Africa and southern Asia that has a dull yellowish coat. The male has a long mane of thick hair.

Have You Heard?

You may have heard the phrase **"the lion's share."** This means an unfairly large part of something. The phrase comes from a fable. In the fable, a lion, a wolf, a fox, and a jackal hunt together. After the hunt, the lion refuses to share with the other animals. When the fable was written the lion's share meant all of something. Now it means the biggest part.

li·on·ess (lī′ə nes), NOUN. a female lion. ❑ PLURAL **li·on·ess·es.**

lip (lip), NOUN.
1 either one of the two fleshy, movable edges of the mouth.
2 the top edge of a container: *the lip of a pitcher.*

lip reading, understanding what someone says by watching the movements of the speaker's lips.

lip·stick (lip′stik′), NOUN. a small stick of a waxlike substance, used for coloring the lips.

liq·uid (lik′wid),
1 NOUN. any substance that is not a solid or a gas; substance that flows freely like water or syrup.
2 ADJECTIVE. in the form of a liquid: *My family has been using liquid soap lately.*

liq·uor (lik′ər), NOUN. an alcoholic drink, such as brandy, vodka, or whiskey.

lisp (lisp),
1 VERB. to say the sounds of *th* as in *thin* and *then* instead of *s* or *z* in speaking: *A person who lisps might say, "Thing a thong" for "Sing a song."*
2 NOUN. the act of saying a *th* sound for *s* and *z*: *I used to speak with a lisp.*
❑ VERB **lisps, lisped, lisp·ing.**

list (list),
1 NOUN. words, names, numbers, and so on that are written one below the other: *a grocery list.*
2 VERB. to make a list of something; enter in a list: *A dictionary lists words in alphabetical order.*
❑ VERB **lists, list·ed, list·ing.**

lis·ten (lis′n), VERB.
1 to try to hear someone or something: *We listened for the sound of their car. I like to listen to music.*
2 to pay attention to someone: *Sometimes it helps to listen to someone who has had more experience.*
❑ VERB **lis·tens, lis·tened, lis·ten·ing.** —**lis′ten·er,** NOUN.

lit[1] (lit), VERB.
1 a past tense of **light**[1]: *She lit a match.*
2 a past participle of **light**[1]: *Have you lit the candles?*

lit[2] (lit), VERB.
1 a past tense of **light**[3]: *Two birds lit on my window sill.*
2 a past participle of **light**[3]: *The butterfly had lit upon the flower.*

lion — from 7 to 9 feet long, including the tail

lite (līt), ADJECTIVE. (informal) having fewer calories than similar food or drinks: *lite yogurt.*

li·ter (lē′tər), NOUN. a unit of volume in the metric system, used for measuring liquids. A liter is a little more than a quart.

lit·er·a·cy (lit′ər ə sē), NOUN.
1 the ability to read and write.
2 an understanding of the basic facts of a particular area of knowledge: *computer literacy.*

lit·er·al (lit′ər əl), ADJECTIVE.
1 following the exact words of the original: *The student made a literal translation into English of the letter written in Spanish.*
2 true to fact: *She wrote a literal account of the speech.*

lit·er·al·ly (lit′ər ə lē), ADVERB.
1 word for word; without exaggeration: *Tell the story literally as you heard it.*
2 actually: *The earthquake literally destroyed hundreds of homes.*

lit·er·ate (lit′ər it), ADJECTIVE. able to read and write.

lit·er·a·ture (lit′ər chùr *or* lit′ər ə chər), NOUN.
1 something that has been written in a beautiful and thoughtful way. Stories, poems, and plays are kinds of literature: *Shakespeare is a great name in English literature.*
2 printed matter of any kind: *campaign literature.*

Lith·u·a·ni·a (lith′ü ā′nē ə), NOUN. a country in northeastern Europe, bordering on Poland. Lithuania was formerly part of the Soviet Union. —**Lith′u·a′ni·an,** ADJECTIVE *or* NOUN.

lit·mus pa·per (lit′məs pā′pər), paper treated with a special chemical. Blue litmus paper will turn red if put into an acid. Red litmus paper will turn blue if put into a base.

a	hat	ė	term	ô	order	ch	child	ə	a in about
ā	age	i	it	oi	oil	ng	long		e in taken
ä	far	ī	ice	ou	out	sh	she		i in pencil
â	care	o	hot	u	cup	th	thin		o in lemon
e	let	ō	open	ù	put	ᴛʜ	then		u in circus
ē	equal	ò	saw	ü	rule	zh	measure		

lit·ter (lit′ər),
1 *NOUN.* little bits of things left scattered around in disorder: *We picked up the litter.*
2 *VERB.* to scatter things around; leave stuff lying around; make a room or other space untidy: *I've littered my room with dirty laundry.*
3 *NOUN.* the young animals born at one time: *Our dog just had a litter of puppies.*
4 *NOUN.* a stretcher for carrying a sick or hurt person.
❑ *VERB* **lit·ters, lit·tered, lit·ter·ing.** **—lit′ter·er,** *NOUN.*

a **litter** of kittens with their mother

lit·tle (lit′l),
1 *ADJECTIVE.* not big or large; small. A grain of sand or the head of a pin is little.
2 *ADJECTIVE.* short; not long in time or in distance: *Wait a little while and I'll go a little way with you.*
3 *ADJECTIVE.* not much: *We have very little milk left.*
4 *NOUN.* a small amount: *Move a little to the left.*
5 *NOUN.* not much; not enough: *Little is being done to aid the victims of the hurricane.*
6 *ADVERB.* to a small extent: *The teacher read from a book that was little known to us.*
❑ *ADJECTIVE* **less** or **less·er, least** or **lit·tler, lit·tlest;** *ADVERB* **less, least.**
little by little, *IDIOM.* slowly; gradually: *Little by little she improved her writing skills.*

Synonym Study

Little means not big, or less than normal in size: *In the dollhouse she saw a little chair like the big chairs in her own house.*

Small means little: *This small glass holds only five ounces of water. Some people consider him small for his age.*

Short can mean not tall: *I am not too short to reach that high shelf.*

Skimpy means too little to be enough: *The skimpy snack left us hungry.*

See also the Synonym Study at **tiny.**

ANTONYMS: big, large.

Little League, a group of baseball teams organized for children from eight to twelve years of age.
Little Rock, the capital of Arkansas.
liv·a·ble (liv′ə bəl), *ADJECTIVE.* fit to live in: *a livable house.*
live¹ (liv), *VERB.*
1 to make your home in a place; dwell: *Who lives in this house?*
2 to be alive; exist: *All human beings have an equal right to live.*
3 to remain alive: *Grandfather lived until last year.*
4 to feed: *Lions live upon other animals.*
5 to pass life: *live a life of ease, live well.*
❑ *VERB* **lives, lived, liv·ing.**
live with, *IDIOM.*
1 to live in the same place with; share a home with: *I live with two friends, and we share expenses.*
2 to accept quietly; tolerate; put up with: *I like some of my classmates; others I just live with.*

Synonym Study

Live¹ means to have a home in a certain place: *We live on Maple Street. Where does your family live?*

Dwell is a formal word that means to live: *Some desert people dwell in tents.*

Reside is also a formal word. It means to live in one place over a period of time: *The President resides in the White House while in office.*

Stay can mean to live somewhere for a while as a guest: *My mom stays in hotels when she travels on business.*

Lodge means to live in a place for a short time: *My sister lodged with a French family on her trip to Paris.*

live² (līv), *ADJECTIVE.*
1 alive; living: *a live dog.*
2 burning or glowing: *live coals.*
3 carrying an electric current: *a live wire.*
4 not previously recorded on tape or film; broadcast during the actual performance: *They broadcast a live performance of the play.*
live·li·hood (līv′lē hùd), *NOUN.* See **living** (definition 3).
live·ly (līv′lē),
1 *ADJECTIVE.* full of life and spirit; active: *Our neighbor has a very lively dog.*
2 *ADJECTIVE.* bright; vivid: *lively colors.*
3 *ADJECTIVE.* cheerful: *a lively conversation.*
4 *ADVERB.* in a lively manner: *Please step lively.*
❑ *ADJECTIVE* **live·li·er, live·li·est. —live′li·ness,** *NOUN.*
liv·er (liv′ər), *NOUN.*
1 the large, reddish brown organ in people and animals that makes bile and helps the body digest food.
2 the liver of an animal used as food.

live·stock (liv'stok'), *NOUN.* farm animals. Cows, horses, sheep, and pigs are examples of livestock.

liv·ing (liv'ing),
1 *ADJECTIVE.* having life; being alive: *a living plant.*
2 *NOUN.* the condition of being alive: *The young people were filled with the joy of living.*
3 *NOUN.* a means of keeping alive; livelihood: *She earns her living as a reporter.*
4 *NOUN.* manner of life: *We enjoy country living.*
5 *ADJECTIVE.* full of life; vigorous; strong; active: *The community leader has a living set of beliefs.*

living room, a room for general family use; sitting room.

liz·ard (liz'ərd), *NOUN.* a reptile that has scaly skin, four legs, and a narrow body. **—liz'ard·like',** *ADJECTIVE.*

lla·ma (lä'mə), *NOUN.* a South American animal something like a camel, but smaller and without a hump. Llamas have woolly hair and are used as beasts of burden. ❏ *PLURAL* **lla·mas** or **lla·ma.**

load (lōd),
1 *NOUN.* something that is being carried: *The truck carried a load of lumber.*
2 *NOUN.* the amount that usually is carried at one time: *We asked them to deliver four loads of sand.*
3 *VERB.* to put what is to be carried into or onto something: *We loaded our camping equipment into the car trunk.*
4 *VERB.* to put film into a camera: *He loaded the camera.*
5 *VERB.* of computers: **a** to move data or a program from a disk, tape, and so on, into a computer's main memory: *As soon as the graphics software is loaded, we can start.* **b** to put a floppy disk or a tape into a computer drive: *I just finished creating my document, and now I'm loading a backup disk.*
6 *VERB.* (in baseball) to put runners on first, second, and third bases: *That walk has loaded the bases.*
❏ *VERB* **loads, load·ed, load·ing. —load'er,** *NOUN.*

loaf[1] (lōf), *NOUN.*
1 bread that is baked as one piece.
2 anything made into the shape of a loaf. Meat loaf is meat chopped and mixed with other things and then baked.
❏ *PLURAL* **loaves.**

Have You Heard?

You may have heard someone say **"Half a loaf is better than none."** This means that it is better to take what you can get rather than risk getting nothing.

loaf[2] (lōf), *VERB.* to spend time doing nothing very important: *I can loaf all day Saturday.* ❏ *VERB* **loafs, loafed, loaf·ing. —loaf'er,** *NOUN.*

loam (lōm), *NOUN.* rich, fertile earth; earth in which decaying leaves and other plant matter are mixed with clay and sand.

loan (lōn),
1 *VERB.* to make someone a loan; lend: *Her friend loaned her the money.*
2 *NOUN.* anything that is lent, especially money: *He asked his brother for a small loan.*
3 *NOUN.* the act of lending something: *She asked for a loan of his pen.*
❏ *VERB* **loans, loaned, loan·ing.** ■ Another word that sounds like this is **lone.**

loaves (lōvz), *NOUN.* the plural of **loaf**[1].

lob·by (lob'ē), *NOUN.* an entrance hall; passageway: *A hotel lobby usually has chairs and couches to sit on.* ❏ *PLURAL* **lob·bies.**

llama — about 4 feet high at the shoulder

lobe (lōb), *NOUN.* a rounded part that sticks out or down. The lobe of the ear is the lower rounded end.

lob·ster (lob'stər), *NOUN.* a tasty shellfish having five pairs of legs, with large claws on the front pair.

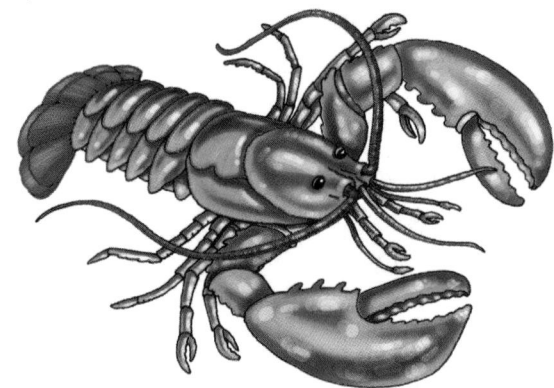

lobster — body about 8 inches long

lo·cal (lō'kəl),
1 *ADJECTIVE.* about a certain place, especially nearby, not far away: *I go to a local doctor. The local news is on at 10:00.*

a	hat	ė	term	ô	order	ch	child		a in about
ā	age	i	it	oi	oil	ng	long		e in taken
ä	far	ī	ice	ou	out	sh	she	ə {	i in pencil
â	care	o	hot	u	cup	th	thin		o in lemon
e	let	ō	open	ů	put	ŦH	then		u in circus
ē	equal	ò	saw	ü	rule	zh	measure		

2 *ADJECTIVE.* having an effect on only one part of your body: *My dentist gave me a local anesthetic before he pulled my tooth.*

3 *ADJECTIVE.* making all, or almost all, stops: *a local train.*

4 *NOUN.* a train, bus, subway, or the like, that makes all, or almost all, of the stops on its route.

The **locomotive** pulls a long freight train.

lo·cate (lō′kāt), *VERB.*

1 to find out exactly where something is: *We followed the stream until we located its source.* ■ See the Synonym Study at **find.**

2 to set up or build something in a place: *They located their new store on Oak Street.*

3 to state or show the position of: *Can you locate Africa on the globe?*

❑ *VERB* **lo·cates, lo·cat·ed, lo·cat·ing.**

lo·ca·tion (lō kā′shən), *NOUN.* a position or place: *The camp was in a bad location, with no water nearby.*

lock¹ (lok),

1 *NOUN.* something that keeps doors, boxes, windows, and similar things closed. Many locks must be opened with keys.

2 *VERB.* to fasten something with a lock: *Lock the door.*

3 *VERB.* to shut something in or out or up: *We lock up jewels in a safe.*

4 *VERB.* to join, fit, or link together: *The girls locked arms and walked down the street together.*

5 *NOUN.* the part of a canal, river, or dock where the level of the water can be changed by letting water in or out, to raise or lower ships.

❑ *VERB* **locks, locked, lock·ing.**

lock² (lok), *NOUN.* a curl of hair.

lock·er (lok′ər), *NOUN.* a small closet or cupboard that can be locked.

locker room, a room for changing clothes, with lockers for storing clothes and sports equipment. There are usually locker rooms in or near gymnasiums, swimming pools, health clubs, and so on.

lock·et (lok′it), *NOUN.* a little ornamental case that holds someone's picture or a lock of their hair. A locket is usually worn around the neck on a chain or necklace.

lock·jaw (lok′jò′), *NOUN.* See **tetanus.**

lock·smith (lok′smith′), *NOUN.* someone who makes or repairs locks and keys.

lo·co·mo·tive (lō′kə mō′tiv), *NOUN.* a large engine that moves from place to place under its own power, used to pull railroad trains.

lo·cust (lō′kəst), *NOUN.*

1 a kind of grasshopper that travels with others in great swarms, destroying crops.

2 a tree with small, rounded leaflets and clusters of fragrant white flowers.

lodge (loj),

1 *VERB.* to live in a place for a time: *We lodged in motels on our trip.* ■ See the Synonym Study at **live¹.**

2 *NOUN.* a house, especially a small house or cabin: *My aunt and uncle rent a lodge in the mountains for the summer.*

3 *VERB.* to get caught or stuck somewhere: *My kite lodged in the branches of a big tree.*

❑ *VERB* **lodg·es, lodged, lodg·ing.**

lodg·ing (loj′ing), *NOUN.*

1 a place where someone is living only for a short time: *a lodging for the night.*

2 **lodgings,** a rented room or rooms in someone's house.

loft (lòft), *NOUN.*

1 the room under the roof of a barn: *This loft is full of hay.*

2 a balcony in a church or hall: *a choir loft.*

loft·y (lòf′tē), *ADJECTIVE.*

1 very high: *lofty mountains.*

2 proud; haughty: *He had a lofty contempt for others.*

❑ *ADJECTIVE* **loft·i·er, loft·i·est.**

log (lòg),

1 *NOUN.* a long piece of wood, cut from a tree trunk or a large branch.

2 *ADJECTIVE.* made of logs: *a log cabin.*

3 *VERB.* to cut down trees, cut them into logs, and get them out of the forest: *The government does not allow logging in this park.*

4 *NOUN.* the daily record of a ship's voyage.

5 *VERB.* to enter information in a ship's log.

❑ *VERB* **logs, logged, log·ging.**

log in or **log on,** *IDIOM.* to begin use of a computer or communication with a computer network: *She logs on to check her e-mail.*

log off or **log out,** *IDIOM.* to finish use of a computer or communication with a computer network: *He didn't log off until eleven o'clock.*

log·ger (lòg′ər), *NOUN.* someone whose work is logging.

log·ic (loj′ik), *NOUN.* proper use of argument; forceful reasoning; a way of convincing or proving: *The logic of his argument convinced us.*

log·i·cal (loj′ə kəl), ADJECTIVE.
1 of, about, or using logic: *logical reasoning.*
2 reasoning correctly: *a clear and logical mind.*
–**log′i·cal·ly,** ADVERB.

loin (loin), NOUN.
1 usually, **loins,** the part of the body of an animal or human being between the ribs and the hip.
2 a piece of meat from this part of an animal: *a loin of pork.*

loi·ter (loi′tər), VERB. to hang around a place when you have no reason to be there: *The sign at the convenience store says "No loitering."* ❏ VERB **loi·ters, loi·tered, loi·ter·ing.** –**loi′ter·er,** NOUN.

lol·li·pop (lol′ē pop), NOUN. a piece of hard candy, usually on the end of a small stick.

a giant **lollipop**

Lon·don (lun′dən), NOUN. a city in England. London is the capital of the United Kingdom. –**Lon′don·er,** NOUN.

lone (lōn), ADJECTIVE. without others; alone; single: *The lone traveler was glad to reach home.*
■ See the Synonym Study at **alone.**
■ Another word that sounds like this is **loan.**

lone·ly (lōn′lē), ADJECTIVE.
1 sad because you are alone and need company or friends: *He was lonely while his brother was away.*
2 without many people: *a lonely road.*
3 by itself: *a lonely tree.*
❏ ADJECTIVE **lone·li·er, lone·li·est.** –**lone′li·ness,** NOUN.

lone·some (lōn′səm), ADJECTIVE.
1 feeling lonely: *I was lonesome while you were away.*
2 making you feel lonely: *a lonesome journey.*
–**lone′some·ness,** NOUN.

long¹ (lòng),
1 ADJECTIVE. measuring a great distance or amount from the beginning to the end of something: *A year is a long time. I read a long story.*
2 ADJECTIVE. in length: *My table is three feet long.*
3 ADJECTIVE. having a long, narrow shape: *a long shelf.*
4 NOUN. a long time: *Summer will come before long.*
5 ADJECTIVE. lasting for some time: *I went on a long trip.*
6 ADVERB. for a long time: *I can't stay long.*
7 ADVERB. for its whole length: *I read all day long.*
8 ADVERB. at a point of time far distant from the time indicated: *long before, long after.*
9 ADJECTIVE. (of vowels) not short. A **long vowel** is a vowel like *a* in *late* (lāt), *e* in *be* (bē), or *o* in *note* (nōt).
❏ ADJECTIVE **long·er** (lòng′gər), **long·est** (lòng′gist).

long² (lòng), VERB. to wish very much for something: *She longed to see her good friend.* ❏ VERB **longs, longed, long·ing.**

long·hand (lòng′hand′), NOUN. ordinary writing, not typed.

long·horn (lòng′hôrn′), NOUN. a kind of cattle with very long horns, formerly common in the southwestern United States.

longhorn — about 5 feet high at the shoulder

long·ing (lòng′ing),
1 NOUN. a strong desire: *a longing for home.*
2 ADJECTIVE. having or showing strong desire: *a child's longing look at a window full of toys.*
–**long′ing·ly,** ADVERB.

lon·gi·tude (lon′jə tüd), NOUN. distance east or west on the earth's surface, measured in degrees from a line that runs north and south through Greenwich (gren′ich), England. This line marks 0° longitude.

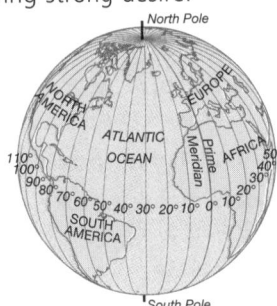

There are ten degrees of **longitude** between each pair of lines.

Word Story

Longitude comes from a Latin word meaning "long." The earliest maps were flat, not round. The length of a map is the distance from top to bottom. Lines of longitude were drawn in that direction. See also the Word History at **latitude.**

long jump, a contest in which each contestant takes a running start and then jumps to cover as much ground as possible.

a	hat	ė	term	ô	order	ch	child	⎧ a in about
ā	age	i	it	oi	oil	ng	long	⎪ e in taken
ä	far	ī	ice	ou	out	sh	she	ə ⎨ i in pencil
â	care	o	hot	u	cup	th	thin	⎪ o in lemon
e	let	ō	open	ù	put	ᴛʜ	then	⎩ u in circus
ē	equal	ò	saw	ü	rule	zh	measure	

look (lùk),

1 _VERB._ to turn your eyes toward something; see; try to see: _Look at the pictures._
2 _VERB._ to try to find something; search: _I looked everywhere for my keys._
3 _NOUN._ a glance; seeing: _I took a quick look at the book._
4 _VERB._ to face: _My bedroom looks onto the garden._
5 _VERB._ to seem; appear to be a certain way: _She looks pale._
6 _NOUN._ appearance: _The old house had a spooky look._
7 _NOUN._ **looks,** personal appearance: _He has his mother's good looks._
❑ _VERB_ **looks, looked, look·ing.**

look after, _IDIOM._ to attend to; take care of: _Will you look after my bird while I'm away?_

look down on, _IDIOM._ to despise: _The miser looked down on all beggars._

look forward to, _IDIOM._ to expect with pleasure: _The children are looking forward to the picnic._

look into, _IDIOM._ to examine; investigate: _The president of our club is looking into the problem._

look out, _IDIOM._ to be careful; watch out: _Look out for cars as you cross the street._

look up, _IDIOM._

1 to find: _He looked up the unfamiliar word in a dictionary._
2 to call on; visit: _Look me up when you come to town._
3 to get better; improve: _Things are looking up for me since I got the new job._

look up to, _IDIOM._ to respect: _The students looked up to their teacher._

Synonym Study

Look means to take in with your eyes: _Look at the size of the fish I just caught!_

Watch means to look at for a period of time: _We watched the jugglers perform with hoops and balls._

Glance means to look quickly: _I glanced in his direction, but he didn't notice me._

View means to watch or look at something, especially information or entertainment on a screen: _We viewed a video about travel in Asia._

Gaze means to watch steadily. It is used to show a strong attraction to what is watched: _The baby gazed in wonder at the butterfly._

Stare means to watch steadily and directly, usually without blinking: _The children stared at the dinosaur skeleton in the natural history museum._

See also the Synonym Study at **see.**

looking glass, a mirror.

look·out (lùk′out′), _NOUN._

1 a careful watch for someone to come or for something to happen: _Be on the lookout for her car._

2 a place from which to watch: _a scenic lookout._
3 someone who has the duty of watching: _The lookout cried, "Land!"_

loom¹ (lüm), _NOUN._ a machine for weaving cloth.

loom² (lüm), _VERB._ to appear suddenly or dimly as a large and dangerous shape: _An iceberg loomed out of the fog._ ❑ _VERB_ **looms, loomed, loom·ing.**

loon (lün), _NOUN._ a large diving bird with webbed feet that eats fish. Loons have a loud, wild cry.

loon — about 30 inches long

loon·y (lü′nē), _ADJECTIVE._ (informal) foolish or silly. ❑ _ADJECTIVE_ **loon·i·er, loon·i·est. –loon′i·ness,** _NOUN._

loop (lüp),

1 _NOUN._ the part of a curved string, ribbon, bent wire, or cord that crosses itself.
2 _NOUN._ a line, path, or motion shaped like this. In handwriting, _b_ and _g_ and _h_ and _l_ have loops. _The road makes a wide loop around the lake._
3 _VERB._ to form a loop or loops: _The plane looped twice in the air above the crowd._
4 _NOUN._ a set of instructions that a computer carries out more than once.
❑ _VERB_ **loops, looped, loop·ing.**

loop·hole (lüp′hōl′), _NOUN._ a means of escape: _A loophole in the law saved the lawyer's client._

loose (lüs), _ADJECTIVE._

1 not fastened: _a loose thread._
2 not tight: _loose clothing._
3 not firmly set or fastened in: _a loose tooth._
4 free; not shut in or up: _The dog has been loose all day._
❑ _ADJECTIVE_ **loos·er, loos·est. –loose′ly,** _ADVERB._ **–loose′ness,** _NOUN._

loose-leaf (lüs′lēf′), _ADJECTIVE._ having pages or sheets that can be taken out and replaced: _I bought three new loose-leaf notebooks for school._

loos·en (lü′sn), _VERB._ to make or become loose; untie; unfasten: _After our picnic we had to loosen our belts._ ❑ _VERB_ **loos·ens, loos·ened, loos·en·ing.**

loot (lüt),

1 _VERB._ to steal things by force, especially during war, riot, or natural disaster: _Rioters looted supermarkets and liquor stores._

2 *NOUN.* things or money stolen; booty; spoils: *Police later found the burglar's hidden loot.*
❏ *VERB.* **loots, loot·ed, loot·ing.** ■ Another word that sounds like this is **lute.** —**loot′er,** *NOUN.*

lope (lōp), *VERB.* to run with a long, easy stride: *The horse loped along the trail in an easy gallop.*
❏ *VERB* **lopes, loped, lop·ing.**

lop·sid·ed (lop′sī′did), *ADJECTIVE.* larger or heavier on one side than the other. —**lop′sid′ed·ly,** *ADVERB.* —**lop′sid′ed·ness,** *NOUN.*

lord (lôrd), *NOUN.*
1 (in the Middle Ages) an owner, ruler, or master of land and the people who lived on the land.
2 Lord, a God. **b** Christ: *the year of our Lord 1251.*
3 Lord, a title used in writing or speaking about men of certain high ranks in Great Britain: *Lord and Lady Grey attended the reception.*

Word Story

Lord comes from old English words meaning "loaf" and "guard." A man in charge of a house in ancient times had to defend the household food if necessary. The idea of a man in charge led to the meaning of a ruler.

Los An·ge·les (lòs an′jə ləs), a city in California. —**Los An·ge·le·no** (lòs an′jə lē′nō), *NOUN.*

lose (lüz), *VERB.*
1 to be defeated; not win: *Our team lost.*
2 to be unable to find: *I've lost my math book.*
3 to have something taken away from you by accident, carelessness, parting, or death: *My great-grandfather lost his life in World War II.*
4 to fail to keep, preserve, or maintain something: *I try not to lose my temper with my little brother.*
5 to waste; spend or let go by without any result: *to lose time waiting, to lose a chance to go to college.*
❏ *VERB* **los·es, lost, los·ing.**

los·er (lü′zər), *NOUN.* someone or something that loses or suffers loss: *Our team was the loser.*

loss (lòs), *NOUN.*
1 the fact of losing or having lost something: *The loss of your health is serious, but the loss of a pencil is not.*
2 losses, the value of the thing or things lost: *The losses from the fire were $10,000.*
3 a defeat: *Our team had only two losses this season.*
4 the sad feeling you have when you lose something important to you: *Having to move away was a great loss to him.*
❏ *PLURAL* **loss·es.**

lost (lòst),
1 *VERB.* the past tense **lose:** *I lost my new pencil.*
2 *VERB.* the past participle of **lose:** *She has lost her best friend.*
3 *ADJECTIVE.* no longer possessed; no longer to be found: *lost friendships, lost books.*

4 *ADJECTIVE.* not won: *a lost battle, a lost prize.*
5 *ADJECTIVE.* not sure about where you are: *They became lost after missing the turn on the trail.*
6 *ADJECTIVE.* not used to good purpose; wasted: *It was a lost morning; I dozed in bed until noon.*

lot (lot),
1 *NOUN.* a number of people or things considered as a group; collection: *This lot of oranges is better than the last one I bought.*
2 *NOUN.* a plot of ground: *an empty lot.*
3 *NOUN.* one of a set of objects, such as bits of paper, wood, or the like, used to decide something by chance.
4 *NOUN.* such a method of deciding: *It was settled by lot.*
5 *NOUN.* someone's fate or fortune: *It was his lot later to become president.*
6 *ADVERB.* **a lot** or **lots,** a great deal; much: *I feel a lot better.*
a lot of or **lots of,** *IDIOM.* a great many; much: *Our library has a lot of books. Some athletes make lots of money.* ■ See the Synonym Study at **many.**

lo·tion (lō′shən), *NOUN.* a liquid containing medicine. Lotions are applied to the skin to relieve pain, to heal, to clean, or to soften the skin.

lot·ter·y (lot′ər ē), *NOUN.* a scheme for distributing prizes by lot or chance. In a lottery a large number of tickets are sold, only a few of which win prizes. ❏ *PLURAL* **lot·ter·ies.**

loud (loud),
1 *ADJECTIVE.* not quiet or soft; making a great sound: *The door slammed with a loud noise.*
2 *ADJECTIVE.* noisy: *I cannot study in a loud place.*
3 *ADVERB.* in a loud manner: *We called loud and long for our dog.*
—**loud′ly,** *ADVERB.* —**loud′ness,** *NOUN.*

Synonym Study

Loud means having or making a big sound: *She doesn't like loud music.*

Noisy means with a lot of loud, harsh sounds: *The noisy traffic bothered his father.*

Deafening means loud enough to hurt the ears: *She plugged her ears to block out the deafening sound of the fireworks.*

Thunderous can mean with a loud noise that sounds like thunder: *We heard the thunderous waterfall before we saw it.*

See also the Synonym Studies at **noise** and **shout.**

ANTONYM: quiet.

a	hat	ė	term	ô	order	ch	child		a in about
ā	age	i	it	oi	oil	ng	long		e in taken
ä	far	ī	ice	ou	out	sh	she	ə	i in pencil
â	care	o	hot	u	cup	th	thin		o in lemon
e	let	ō	open	ù	put	₮H	then		u in circus
ē	equal	ò	saw	ü	rule	zh	measure		

loud·speak·er (loud′spē′kər), NOUN. a device for making sounds louder, especially in a public-address system; speaker.

Lou·i·si·an·a (lù ē′zē an′ə), NOUN. one of the southern states of the United States. *Abbreviation:* LA; *Capital:* Baton Rouge. **–Lou·i′si·an′i·an** or **Lou·i′si·an′an,** NOUN.

State Story Louisiana was named for Louis XIV, king of France. French explorers named the entire Mississippi River valley after him. The name survived in the state where the river ends.

lounge (lounj),
1 VERB. to stand, sit, or lie at ease in a lazy way: *He lounged in an old chair.*
2 NOUN. a comfortable and informal room in which you can be at ease: *a theater lounge.*
❑ VERB **loung·es, lounged, loung·ing. –loung′er,** NOUN.

louse (lous), NOUN. a small, wingless insect that lives on the bodies of people and animals and sucks their blood. ❑ PLURAL **lice.**

lous·y (lou′zē), ADJECTIVE.
1 bad; poor; of low quality: *a lousy movie.*
2 infested with lice.
❑ ADJECTIVE **lous·i·er, lous·i·est.**

lov·a·ble (luv′ə bəl), ADJECTIVE. easy to love: *She was a most lovable person, always kind and thoughtful.*

love (luv),
1 NOUN. a deep, tender feeling for someone or something: *love for your family, love for a sweetheart.*
2 VERB. to have such a feeling for someone or something: *I love my parents. I love my country.*
3 NOUN. someone who is loved; sweetheart.
4 VERB. to like something very much; take great pleasure in: *He loves music.*
❑ VERB **loves, loved, lov·ing.**
fall in love, IDIOM. to begin to love; come to feel love.
in love, IDIOM. feeling love for someone or something.

Synonym Study

Love means a strong and tender feeling of liking or being fond of someone: *This picture of my family shows the love we feel for each other.*

Affection means a kind, warm feeling for someone or something. It is not as strong a word as love: *She shows affection for her dog by playing with him and caring for him.*

Fondness means liking or affection: *He and his grandparents share a fondness for ranchero music.*

Devotion means a very loyal feeling of love, either for someone or something: *Her devotion to gymnastics leaves her little time for other sports.*

ANTONYMS: hate, hatred.

love·bird (luv′bėrd′), NOUN. any of several small parrots that show great affection for their mates. They are often kept in cages as pets.

lovebirds — about 6 inches long

love·ly (luv′lē), ADJECTIVE.
1 beautiful in appearance or character; lovable: *They are the loveliest children we know.* ■ See the Synonym Study at **beautiful.**
2 very pleasing; delightful: *We all had a lovely holiday.* ■ See the Synonym Study at **nice.**
❑ ADJECTIVE **love·li·er, love·li·est. –love′li·ness,** NOUN.

lov·er (luv′ər), NOUN.
1 someone who is in love with another person.
2 someone having a strong liking for something: *a lover of books.*

lov·ing (luv′ing), ADJECTIVE. feeling or showing love; affectionate; fond: *The orphan was adopted into a loving family.* **–lov′ing·ly,** ADVERB.

low (lō),
1 ADJECTIVE. not high or tall: *This stool is very low.*
2 ADJECTIVE. in a low place; near the ground: *a low shelf, a low jump.*
3 ADJECTIVE. below others; inferior: *a low grade of beef, to rise from a low position as clerk to president of a company.*
4 ADJECTIVE. small; less than usual: *a low price, low, temperature, low speed.*
5 ADJECTIVE. not high in the musical scale: *a low note.*
6 ADJECTIVE. not loud; soft: *a low whisper.*
7 ADJECTIVE. sad; depressed: *low in spirit.*
8 ADVERB. at or to a low point, place, amount, or pitch: *The sun sank low. Supplies are running low.*
9 NOUN. a low point, level, position, and so on: *The low for tonight will be near freezing.*
–low′ness, NOUN.

low·er (lō′ər),
1 VERB. to let something down or haul it down: *We lower the flag at night.*
2 VERB. to make or become less: *Lower the volume on the radio. Prices lowered somewhat during the winter.*

3 *ADJECTIVE* or *ADVERB*. not as high: *Prices were lower last year than this.*
❑ *VERB* **low·ers, low·ered, low·er·ing.**

low·er·case (lō′ər kās′), in printing:
1 *NOUN*. small letters, not capitals.
2 *ADJECTIVE*. in small letters, not capitals.

low·land (lō′lənd), *NOUN*. land that is lower and flatter than the neighboring country.

low tide, the time when the ocean is lowest on the shore. Low tides occur two times a day.

loy·al (loi′əl), *ADJECTIVE*. true and faithful to someone or something: *Loyal friends don't desert you. She is a loyal citizen of this country.* —**loy′al·ly,** *ADVERB*.

loy·al·ty (loi′əl tē), *NOUN*. loyal feeling or behavior; faithfulness: *The knights pledged their loyalty to the king.* ❑ *PLURAL* **loy·al·ties.**

lu·bri·cant (lü′brə kənt), *NOUN*. a slippery substance, such as oil or grease, for putting on parts of machines that move against each other. A lubricant reduces friction by making the parts slippery so that they will work together easily.

lu·bri·cate (lü′brə kāt), *VERB*. to make parts of machinery smooth and easy to work together by putting on oil, grease, or the like. ❑ *VERB* **lu·bri·cates, lu·bri·cat·ed, lu·bri·cat·ing.** —**lu′bri·ca′tion,** *NOUN*.

luck (luk), *NOUN*. something that just seems to happen to you; chance; fortune: *I won the game by luck, not by skill.*

out of luck, *IDIOM*. having bad luck; unlucky: *The tornado missed the city, but the camp was out of luck.*

try your luck, *IDIOM*. to see what you can do: *She decided to try her luck at acting.*

luck·i·ly (luk′ə lē), *ADVERB*. by good luck; fortunately: *Luckily I found my lost ring.*

luck·y (luk′ē), *ADJECTIVE*. having or bringing good luck: *a lucky person, a lucky hat.* ❑ *ADJECTIVE* **luck·i·er, luck·i·est.**

lug (lug), *VERB*. to pull something along or carry it with effort; drag: *We lugged the carpet to the yard to clean it.* ❑ *VERB* **lugs, lugged, lug·ging.**

luge (lüzh),
1 *NOUN*. a racing sled, used by one or two people.
2 *VERB*. to race on a luge.
❑ *VERB* **luges, luged, lug·ing** or **luge·ing.** —**lug′er,** *NOUN*.

lug·gage (lug′ij), *NOUN*. suitcases or handbags that a traveler carries on a trip.

racing a **luge**

luke·warm (lük′wôrm′), *ADJECTIVE*.
1 slightly warm: *I like soup hot, not lukewarm.*
2 not very excited about something; halfhearted: *I gave him a lukewarm greeting.*

lull (lul),
1 *VERB*. to make calm; quiet; soothe: *Their confidence lulled my fears. The music lulled me to sleep.*
2 *NOUN*. a period of calm or quiet: *a lull in a storm.*
❑ *VERB* **lulls, lulled, lull·ing.**

lul·la·by (lul′ə bī), *NOUN*. a soft song that quiets a baby so that it falls asleep. ❑ *PLURAL* **lul·la·bies.**

lum·ber (lum′bər), *NOUN*. wood that has been cut into boards or planks, and prepared for use.

lum·ber·jack (lum′bər jak′), *NOUN*. someone whose work is cutting down trees and hauling out the logs.

lum·ber·man (lum′bər mən), *NOUN*. See **lumberjack.** ❑ *PLURAL* **lum·ber·men.**

lu·mi·nous (lü′mə nəs), *ADJECTIVE*. shining by its own light: *The sun and stars are luminous bodies.*

lump (lump),
1 *NOUN*. a small, solid chunk of something that has no special shape: *He doesn't like lumps in his oatmeal.* ■ See the Synonym Study at **piece.**
2 *NOUN*. a swelling; bump: *There is a lump on my head where I bumped it.*
3 *VERB*. to put different kinds of things together: *A credit card allows you to lump a month's expenses and pay with just one check.*
4 *ADJECTIVE*. not in parts; whole: *I was given a lump sum of money for all my living expenses for the school year.*
❑ *VERB* **lumps, lumped, lump·ing.**

lump·y (lum′pē), *ADJECTIVE*. full of lumps: *Mashed potatoes shouldn't be lumpy.* ❑ *ADJECTIVE* **lump·i·er, lump·i·est.** —**lump′i·ness,** *NOUN*.

lu·nar (lü′nər), *ADJECTIVE*. of or like the moon: *a lunar eclipse, a lunar landscape.*

lunch (lunch),
1 *NOUN*. a meal eaten in the middle of the day; the meal between breakfast and dinner: *We usually have lunch at noon.*
2 *VERB*. to eat lunch: *We lunched in the park.*
❑ *VERB* **lunch·es, lunched, lunch·ing;** *PLURAL* **lunch·es.**

lunch·eon (lun′chən), *NOUN*. a lunch, especially one for a group of people, for a special occasion: *Our club is having a luncheon on Sunday.*

lunch·room (lunch′rüm′), *NOUN*. a room in a school, office building, and so on, where meals are served or lunches brought from home can be eaten.

a	hat	ė	term	ô	order	ch	child		a in about
ā	age	i	it	oi	oil	ng	long		e in taken
ä	far	ī	ice	ou	out	sh	she	ə ⟨	i in pencil
â	care	o	hot	u	cup	th	thin		o in lemon
e	let	ō	open	ù	put	ŦH	then		u in circus
ē	equal	ò	saw	ü	rule	zh	measure		

lung (lung), *NOUN.* either one of a pair of organs in the chest of human beings and other animals that breathe. Lungs give the blood the oxygen it needs and take away carbon dioxide.

lunge (lunj),
1 *NOUN.* any sudden forward movement: *I made a lunge for the ball as it went by me.*
2 *VERB.* to move suddenly forward: *The dog lunged at the stranger.*
❑ *VERB* **lung·es, lunged, lung·ing.**

lurch (lėrch),
1 *NOUN.* a sudden leaning or roll to one side, like that of a ship, a car, or someone staggering: *The boat gave a lurch and began to sink.*
2 *VERB.* to make a lurch; stagger: *The injured animal lurched forward.*
❑ *VERB* **lurch·es, lurched, lurch·ing;** *PLURAL* **lurch·es.**

lure (lùr),
1 *NOUN.* something that attracts or tempts: *Gold was the lure that brought miners to California in 1849.*
2 *VERB.* to attract someone or something by offering something desirable: *Bees are lured by the scent of flowers.*
3 *NOUN.* the bait, especially the artificial bait, used in fishing: *I used a shiny lure to catch the fish.*
❑ *VERB* **lures, lured, lur·ing.**

lurk (lėrk), *VERB.* to wait around somewhere without being noticed; wait out of sight: *A tiger was lurking in the jungle outside the village.* ❑ *VERB* **lurks, lurked, lurk·ing.**

lus·cious (lush′əs), *ADJECTIVE.* very pleasing to see, taste, smell, hear, or feel: *My sister entered a painting full of luscious colors for the art fair.*

lush (lush), *ADJECTIVE.* tender and juicy; growing thick and green: *Lush grass grows along the river banks.* **—lush′ly,** *ADVERB.* **—lush′ness,** *NOUN.*

lus·ter (lus′tər), *NOUN.* a bright shine on the surface of something: *the luster of pearls.*

lus·trous (lus′trəs), *ADJECTIVE.* shining; glossy: *lustrous satin.*

lute (lüt), *NOUN.* a stringed instrument of former times. It is something like a large mandolin and is played by plucking the strings. ■ Another word that sounds like this is **loot.**

lux·ur·i·ous (lug zhùr′ē əs), *ADJECTIVE.* very comfortable and beautiful: *They live in a luxurious apartment with expensive furniture.* **—lux·ur′i·ous·ly,** *ADVERB.*

lux·ur·y (luk′shər ē or lug′zhər ē), *NOUN.*
1 the comforts and beauties of life beyond what are really necessary: *They were a wealthy family who could afford to live in luxury.*
2 something that is pleasant but not necessary: *Candy is a luxury.*
❑ *PLURAL* **lux·ur·ies.**

Word Power   -ly

The suffix **-ly**[1] means "in a _____ way or manner." Cheerful**ly** means **in a** cheerful **way.** Soft**ly** means **in a** soft **manner.**

The suffix **-ly**[2] can mean "like a _____." Ghost**ly** means **like a** ghost. Brother**ly** means **like a** brother. It can also mean "of each or every _____" or "that happens or appears every_____." A month**ly** visit **happens every** month. A dai**ly** newspaper **appears every** day.

lye (lī), *NOUN.* a strong solution used to make soap and in cleaning. ■ Another word that sounds like this is **lie.**

ly·ing (lī′ing), *NOUN.* the act of telling a lie; habit of telling lies: *Lying just got me into more trouble.*

Lyme dis·ease (līm də zēz′), a serious disease spread by ticks.

lymph (limf), *NOUN.* a nearly colorless liquid in the tissues of the body, somewhat like blood without the red corpuscles. Lymph nourishes the tissues and fights infection.

lynch (linch), *VERB.* to put an accused person to death by hanging without a lawful trial: *An angry mob lynched the stranger.* ❑ *VERB* **lynch·es, lynched, lynch·ing.**

lynx (lingks), *NOUN.* a kind of wildcat of the northern United States and Canada. It has a short tail and rather long legs. ❑ *PLURAL* **lynx** or **lynx·es.**

lynx — about 4 feet long, including the tail

lyre (līr), *NOUN.* an ancient stringed instrument somewhat like a small harp.

lyr·ic (lir′ik), *NOUN.* **lyrics,** the words for a song.

lyr·i·cal (lir′ə kəl), *ADJECTIVE.* expressing strong emotion in a beautiful manner, as in poetry; poetic: *She became almost lyrical when she described the scenery.* **—lyr′i·cal·ly,** *ADVERB.*

motorcycle

Mm

M or **m** (em), *NOUN.* the 13th letter of the English alphabet. ❑ *PLURAL* **M's** or **m's.**

m or **m.,** an abbreviation of **meter²** or **meters.**

m. or **m,**
  1 an abbreviation of **mile** or **miles.**
  2 an abbreviation of **minute** or **minutes.**

ma (mä), *NOUN.* (informal) mamma; mother.

MA, an abbreviation of **Massachusetts.**

ma'am (mam), *NOUN.* a contraction of **madam.**

mac·a·ro·ni (mak′ə rō′nē), *NOUN.* a mixture of flour and water that has been dried, usually in the form of hollow tubes, to be cooked for food. Macaroni is a form of pasta.

mac·a·roon (mak′ə rün′), *NOUN.* a very sweet cookie made of egg whites, sugar, and ground almonds or coconut.

ma·caw (mə kȯ′), *NOUN.* a large parrot of South and Central America, with a long tail and brilliant feathers. Macaws can learn to imitate human speech.

ma·chet·e (mə shet′ē *or* mə chet′ē), *NOUN.* a large, heavy knife, used in South America, Central America, and the West Indies. Machetes are used as cutting tools and as weapons. ❑ *PLURAL* **ma·chet·es.**

ma·chine (mə shēn′), *NOUN.*
  1 a device containing an arrangement of fixed and moving parts that does work, powered by electricity or fuel. Cars, washers, and computers are machines.
  2 See **simple machine.**

machine gun, a gun that fires bullets continuously with one pull of the trigger.

ma·chin·er·y (mə shē′nər ē), *NOUN.*
  1 machines: *A factory often contains a lot of expensive machinery. She repairs lawn mowers and other small machinery.*
  2 the working parts of a machine: *The machinery of a computer should be kept clean.*

ma·chin·ist (mə shē′nist), NOUN. a worker who shapes metal by using machines and power tools.

mack·er·el (mak′ər əl), NOUN. a saltwater fish of the North Atlantic, used for food. ❑ PLURAL **mack·er·el** or **mack·er·els.**

mac·ro (mak′rō), NOUN. a set of computer commands stored together. Using a macro is faster than entering each command separately. ❑ PLURAL **mac·ros.**

mad (mad), ADJECTIVE.
1 very angry: *The insult made me mad.*
2 foolish; unwise: *Trying to row across the ocean is a mad undertaking.*
3 unreasonably fond: *She is mad about soccer.*
4 mentally ill.
5 having rabies. A mad dog often foams at the mouth and may bite people.
❑ ADJECTIVE **mad·der, mad·dest.** —**mad′ly,** ADVERB.

Synonym Study

Mad means feeling anger: *My father gets mad if I forget to do my chores.*

Angry means the same as mad: *I will be angry if she reveals my secret.*

Sore can mean mad: *My cousin is sore at me because I got her new skirt dirty.*

Irritated means bothered or made somewhat angry: *Dad became irritated when he had to wait a long time in the cafeteria line.*

Furious means wildly angry: *Getting stung by the bees made the grizzly bear furious. I was furious when I saw the mess.*

See also the Synonym Study at **cross.**

Mad·a·gas·car (mad′ə gas′kər), NOUN. an island country in the Indian Ocean, off the coast of Africa.

mad·am (mad′əm), NOUN. a polite title used in writing or speaking to any woman: *May I help you, madam?*

mad·ame (mad′əm or mä däm′), NOUN. a French word meaning "Mrs." or "madam." ❑ PLURAL **mes·dames.**

mad·den (mad′n), VERB. to make someone very angry or excited: *The crowd was maddened by the umpire's decision.* ❑ VERB **mad·dens, mad·dened, mad·den·ing.**

made (mād),
1 VERB. the past tense of **make:** *Dad made the cake with chocolate icing and lots of nuts.*
2 VERB. the past participle of **make:** *I have made lots of money mowing lawns this summer.*
3 ADJECTIVE. built; constructed; formed: *a strongly made swing.*
■ Another word that sounds like this is **maid.**

made-up (mād′up′), ADJECTIVE.
1 not real; imaginary: *a made-up story.*
2 wearing makeup: *The clowns had made-up faces.*

mad·house (mad′hous′), NOUN. a place of noise and confusion: *The arena was a madhouse after the team won the game.* ❑ PLURAL **mad·hous·es** (mad′hou′ziz).

Mad·i·son (mad′ə sən), NOUN. the capital of Wisconsin.

mad·man (mad′man′), NOUN. someone who is mentally ill: *The explosion was probably the work of a madman.* ❑ PLURAL **mad·men.**

mad·ness (mad′nis), NOUN.
1 the condition of being mentally ill.
2 foolish activity: *It would be madness to try to sail a boat in this storm.*

mag·a·zine (mag′ə zēn′), NOUN. a publication that appears regularly, containing stories and articles by various writers. Most magazines are published either weekly or monthly.

Word Story

Magazine comes from an Arabic word meaning "warehouse." A printed magazine is like a warehouse of information, pictures, ideas, and notices of things to buy.

mag·got (mag′ət), NOUN. the wormlike larva of a young fly just hatched from its egg.

mag·ic (maj′ik),
1 NOUN. (in stories) the art of using secret words, acts, or objects to make unnatural things happen: *The fairy's magic changed the brothers into swans.*
2 NOUN. the skill of seeming to make things appear, disappear, or change into something else; performing tricks that seem to be impossible: *The magician made rabbits appear out of the hat by magic.*
3 ADJECTIVE. done by magic or as if by magic: *A magic palace stood in place of their hut.*

mag·i·cal (maj′ə kəl), ADJECTIVE. done by magic or as if by magic: *The waving of the magician's wand produced a magical effect.* —**mag′i·cal·ly,** ADVERB.

ma·gi·cian (mə jish′ən), NOUN.
1 (in stories) someone who can use magic: *The wicked magician cast a spell over the princess.*
2 someone who entertains people by doing magic tricks: *The magician pulled—not one, but three rabbits out of his hat!*

mag·ma (mag′mə), NOUN. hot melted rock beneath the surface of the earth.

Word Story

Magma comes from a Greek word meaning "to squeeze in the hands." Magma oozes and spreads as dough or clay does if you squeeze it.

mag·ne·si·um (mag nē′zē əm), NOUN. a very light, silver-white metal that burns with a dazzling white light. It is a chemical element, used for fireworks and combined with other metals to make strong, lightweight parts for spacecraft and cars.

mag·net (mag′nit), NOUN. a piece of metal that pulls bits of iron or steel to it.

Did You Know?

Every **magnet** has a south pole and a north pole. A north pole always attracts a south pole, and a south pole always attracts a north pole. But a south pole will push away another south pole, and a north pole will push away another north pole. Opposite poles attract, and like poles push away.

mag·net·ic (mag net′ik), ADJECTIVE.
1 of or about magnets or their force: *A pocket compass has a magnetic needle.*
2 very attractive: *She has a magnetic personality.* —**mag·net′i·cal·ly,** ADVERB.

magnetic field, the space around a magnet or electric current in which magnetic force occurs.

magnetic pole,
1 one of the two places opposite each other on a magnet where its magnetic force is strongest.
2 **Magnetic Pole,** one of the two places on the earth's surface toward which a compass needle points. The **North Magnetic Pole** is in the Arctic; the **South Magnetic Pole** is in Antarctica.

magnetic tape, a plastic tape, coated with a magnetic substance, used to record sounds, pictures, or information.

mag·net·ism (mag′nə tiz′əm), NOUN.
1 the force of magnets that attracts iron or steel.
2 the power to attract or charm: *A person with magnetism has many friends and admirers.*

magnet school, a school with special programs in certain subjects where students from all parts of a city or district may attend.

mag·nif·i·cence (mag nif′ə səns), NOUN. richness of material, color, and ornament; grand beauty: *We were dazzled by the magnificence of the scenery.*

mag·nif·i·cent (mag nif′ə sənt), ADJECTIVE. wonderful to look at; richly colored or decorated; grand; splendid: *a magnificent palace, a magnificent view.* —**mag·nif′i·cent·ly,** ADVERB.

mag·ni·fy (mag′nə fī), VERB.
1 to cause something to look larger than it really is: *A microscope magnifies bacteria so that you can see them and study them.*
2 to go beyond the truth in telling about something; exaggerate: *Was the fish really that big, or are you magnifying its size?*
❑ VERB **mag·ni·fies, mag·ni·fied, mag·ni·fy·ing.** —**mag′ni·fi·ca′tion,** NOUN.

magnifying glass, a piece of curved glass, called a lens, or a combination of lenses, that causes things to look larger than they really are.

mag·ni·tude (mag′nə tüd), NOUN.
1 greatness of size: *The magnitude of the destruction caused by the hurricane had to be seen to be believed.*
2 importance: *The war brought problems of very great magnitude to many nations.*

mag·nol·ia (mag nō′lyə), NOUN. a North American tree or shrub with large white, pink, or purplish flowers. There are several kinds. ❑ PLURAL **mag·nol·ias.**

magnolia trees in bloom

mag·pie (mag′pī), NOUN. a black and white bird with a long tail and short wings and a noisy call. ❑ PLURAL **mag·pies.**

ma·hog·a·ny (mə hog′ə nē),
1 NOUN. a tree that grows in tropical America.
2 NOUN. its dark reddish brown wood. Because mahogany takes a very high polish, it is often used in making furniture.
3 ADJECTIVE or NOUN. dark reddish brown.

maid (mād), NOUN.
1 a girl or woman whose job is doing housework.
2 (earlier) a girl or woman who has not married.
■ Another word that sounds like this is **made.**

maid·en (mād′n),
1 NOUN. (earlier) a girl or young woman who has not married; maid.
2 ADJECTIVE. never married: *a maiden aunt.*
3 ADJECTIVE. done or made for the first time: *a ship's maiden voyage.*

maiden name, a woman's last name before marriage: *My maiden name is Smith, but my married name is Rogers.*

a	hat	ė	term	ô	order	ch	child		a in about
ā	age	i	it	oi	oil	ng	long		e in taken
ä	far	ī	ice	ou	out	sh	she	ə	i in pencil
â	care	o	hot	u	cup	th	thin		o in lemon
e	let	ō	open	ù	put	℟H	then		u in circus
ē	equal	ò	saw	ü	rule	zh	measure		

mail¹ (māl),
1 *NOUN.* letters, postcards, magazines, packages, and so on, sent by a postal service.
2 *NOUN.* the system by which such mail is sent: *You can pay most bills by mail.*
3 *VERB.* to send by way of the post office; put in a mailbox: *Should I mail that letter for you?* ■ See the Synonym Study at **send.**
4 *NOUN.* See **e-mail.**
❑ *VERB* **mails, mailed, mail·ing.** ■ Another word that sounds like this is **male.**

mail² (māl), *NOUN.* armor made of metal rings, small loops of chain linked together, or plates, for protecting the body against arrows or spears.
■ Another word that sounds like this is **male.**

mail·box (māl′boks′), *NOUN.*
1 a box or large container where mail is placed for collection by the post office.
2 a private box at your home or business where which mail is delivered.
❑ *PLURAL* **mail·box·es.**

mail carrier, someone who carries or delivers mail; mailman; postman.

mail·man (māl′man′), *NOUN.* See **mail carrier.**
❑ *PLURAL* **mail·men.**

maim (mām), *VERB.* to hurt someone so seriously that a body part is damaged or lost: *The lawn mower maimed him so badly that he lost three toes.* ❑ *VERB* **maims, maimed, maim·ing.**

main (mān), *ADJECTIVE.* most important; largest: *the main dish at dinner, the main street of a town.*
■ Another word that sounds like this is **mane.**

Synonym Study

Main means most important: *One main switch controls all the lights in this building.*

Major means more important than most others: *Major roads carry thousands of cars every hour.*

Chief means leading, or first in rank: *Who is the chief justice of the Supreme Court?*

Principal means first in order of importance: *The principal character in the movie "Home Alone" saves his family's house from burglars.*

Maine (mān), *NOUN.* one of the northeastern states of the United States. *Abbreviation:* ME; *Capital:* Augusta. —**Main′er,** *NOUN.*

State Story **Maine** probably comes from a phrase, "the main," meaning "mainland." Explorers may have used that phrase about the coast of Maine to separate it from the many nearby islands.

main·land (mān′land′), *NOUN.* the main part of a continent or country, not including islands or small peninsulas along the shores.

main·ly (mān′lē), *ADVERB.* for the most part; chiefly; mostly: *He is interested mainly in art.*

main·tain (mān tān′), *VERB.*
1 to keep up; carry on in the same way: *You must maintain your footing when you play tug-of-war.*
2 to keep something supplied, equipped, or in good repair: *They employ her to maintain the machinery.*
3 to declare something to be true: *He maintains that he was innocent.*
❑ *VERB* **main·tains, main·tained, main·tain·ing.**

main·te·nance (mān′tə nəns), *NOUN.*
1 the act or process of keeping something in good repair.
2 the condition of being maintained; support: *A government collects taxes to pay for its maintenance.*

maize (māz), *NOUN.* See **corn¹.** ■ Another word that sounds like this is **maze.**

ma·jes·tic (mə jes′tik), *ADJECTIVE.* looking very impressive; grand: *Majestic, snowcapped mountains towered above us.* —**ma·jes′ti·cal·ly,** *ADVERB.*

the **majestic** beauty of wilderness

maj·es·ty (maj′ə stē), *NOUN.*
1 great beauty; impressive appearance: *the majesty of the Andes Mountains.*
2 **Majesty,** a title used in speaking to or about a king, queen, emperor, or the like: *Your Majesty, His Majesty, Her Majesty.*
❑ *PLURAL* **Maj·es·ties** for 2.

ma·jor (mā′jər),
1 *ADJECTIVE.* more important; larger; greater: *The major part of a little baby's life is spent in sleeping.* ■ See the Synonym Study at **main.**
2 *ADJECTIVE.* important, great, or serious: *a major illness, a major improvement.*
3 *NOUN.* a military rank. See the chart on page 550.

ma·jor·i·ty (mə jôr′ə tē), *NOUN.* the larger number; greater part; more than half: *A majority of the children chose red covers for the books they had made.* ❑ *PLURAL* **ma·jor·i·ties.**

make (māk),

1 *VERB.* to put together or build something; form; shape: *to make a new dress, to make a fire.*

2 *NOUN.* kind; brand: *What make of car is this?*

3 *VERB.* to have the qualities needed for: *Wood makes a good fire.*

4 *VERB.* to cause something to happen; bring about: *to make trouble, to make a noise, to make peace.*

5 *VERB.* to force someone to do something: *We made him go home.*

6 *VERB.* to cause to be or become: *A fire will make the room warm. She made a fool of herself.*

7 *VERB.* to become; turn out to be: *He will make a good lawyer.*

8 *VERB.* to get or earn: *to make good grades.*

9 *VERB.* to do; perform: *make a speech, make an error.*

10 *VERB.* to amount to; add up to: *2 and 3 make 5.*
  ❑ *VERB* **makes, made, mak·ing. –ma′ker,** *NOUN.*

make believe, *IDIOM.* to pretend: *The girl liked to make believe she was an airplane pilot.*

make do, *IDIOM.* to get along; manage: *We must try to make do with what we have.*

make it, *IDIOM.* to succeed: *We always knew she would make it as an actress.*

make out, *IDIOM.*

1 to write out: *She made out a shopping list.*

2 to see; recognize: *I can barely make out this picture.*

make up, *IDIOM.*

1 to put together: *to make up cloth into a shirt.*

2 to invent: *to make up a story.*

3 to give or do in place of: *to make up for lost time.*

4 to become friends again after a quarrel: *We were always fighting and then making up.*

5 to compose; consist of; form: *Children made up the audience.*

6 to decide: *Make up your mind.*

Synonym Study

Make means to put something together or to give form to something: *Make me a sandwich, please. They made a fancy sand castle.*

Shape means to make something by giving it a form: *This machine takes clay and shapes it into bricks for another machine to bake.*

Build and **construct** mean to make something from materials and according to a plan: *Carpenters build houses, and engineers construct bridges.*

Manufacture means to create something from materials, over and over: *My mom works for a company that manufactures artificial arms and legs.*

Assemble can mean to make an object by fitting parts where they belong: *I assembled the model car by following the diagram.*

make-be·lieve (māk′bi lēv′), *ADJECTIVE.* not real; imaginary; pretend: *Some children have make-believe playmates.*

make·shift (māk′shift′), *ADJECTIVE.* used as a temporary substitute when you don't have exactly what you need: *When the tent blew down, we used blankets as a makeshift shelter.*

make·up or **make-up** (māk′up′), *NOUN.*

1 the lipstick, powder, rouge, and the like, put on the face; cosmetics.

2 the cosmetics an actor uses in order to look the part.

3 the way in which a thing is put together: *The makeup of the class includes children from different parts of the town.*

an actor putting on **makeup**

ma·lar·i·a (mə lâr′ē ə), *NOUN.* a disease that causes chills, fever, and sweating. Malaria is transmitted by mosquitoes that have bitten infected persons.

Ma·la·wi (mə lä′wē), *NOUN.* a country in southeastern Africa. **–Ma·la′wi·an,** *ADJECTIVE* or *NOUN.*

Ma·lay (mā′lā), *NOUN.* the language spoken in Malaysia and nearby areas.

Word Source

Malay is the official language of Malaysia, and is also spoken on nearby islands. The following words came into English from Malay: **bamboo, cockatoo, gong, ketchup, launch[2], orangutan,** and **paddy**

Ma·lay·sia (mə lā′zhə), *NOUN.* a country in southeastern Asia. **–Ma·lay′sian,** *ADJECTIVE* or *NOUN.*

a	hat	ė	term	ô	order	ch	child		a in about
ā	age	i	it	oi	oil	ng	long		e in taken
ä	far	ī	ice	ou	out	sh	she	ə	i in pencil
â	care	o	hot	u	cup	th	thin		o in lemon
e	let	ō	open	u̇	put	ᵺ	then		u in circus
ē	equal	ȯ	saw	ü	rule	zh	measure		

male (māl),

1 *NOUN.* a man or boy.
2 *ADJECTIVE.* of or about men or boys.
3 *ADJECTIVE.* belonging to the sex that can fertilize eggs and be the father of young. Bucks, bulls, and roosters are male animals.
4 *NOUN.* an animal belonging to this sex.
■ Another word that sounds like this is **mail.**

Ma·li (mä′lē), *NOUN.* a country in western Africa. **—Ma′li·an,** *ADJECTIVE or NOUN.*

ma·lig·nant (mə lig′nənt), *ADJECTIVE.* very harmful; able to cause death: *A cancer is a malignant growth.*

mall (mȯl), *NOUN.*

1 a shopping center with stores, shops, restaurants, and so on, that open onto a wide walking area or passageway.
2 a wide walking area or passageway, especially one in a shopping center.
■ Another word that sounds like this is **maul.**

mal·lard (mal′ərd), *NOUN.* a kind of duck of Europe, northern Asia, and North America. The male has a greenish black head and a white band around its neck. □ *PLURAL* **mal·lard** or **mal·lards.**

mallard — about 16 inches long

mal·let (mal′it), *NOUN.* a hammer with a large head. Rubber mallets are used to pound out dents in metal. Wooden mallets with long handles are used to play croquet and polo.

mal·nu·tri·tion (mal′nü trish′ən), *NOUN.* a weak, poorly nourished condition of your body: *People suffer from malnutrition because of eating the wrong kinds of food as well as from lack of food.*

malt (mȯlt), *NOUN.* grain, usually barley, soaked in water until it sprouts and tastes sweet. Malt is used in making beer and ale.

malt·ed milk (mȯl′tid milk′), a drink prepared by mixing a powder made of dried milk, malt, and wheat flour with milk, flavoring, and often ice cream.

mal·treat (mal trēt′), *VERB.* to treat someone roughly or cruelly; abuse: *There are state laws against maltreating animals.* □ *VERB* **mal·treats, mal·treat·ed, mal·treat·ing. —mal·treat′ment,** *NOUN.*

ma·ma or **mam·ma** (mä′mə), *NOUN.* (informal) mother. □ *PLURAL* **ma·mas** or **mam·mas.**

mam·mal (mam′əl), *NOUN.* one of a large group of warm-blooded animals with backbones, usually having hair. Mammals feed their young with milk from the mother's breasts. Human beings, cattle, dogs, cats, and whales are all mammals.

Did You Know?

Most **mammals** give birth to live young. But two kinds of mammals lay eggs instead. They are the spiny anteater and the platypus.

mam·moth (mam′əth),

1 *NOUN.* a large elephant with a hairy skin and long curved tusks. The last mammoth died thousands of years ago.
2 *ADJECTIVE.* huge; gigantic: *Building the Panama Canal was a mammoth undertaking.*

man (man),

1 *NOUN.* an grown-up male person. When a boy grows up, he becomes a man.
2 *NOUN.* a human being; person: *No man can be certain of the future.*
3 *NOUN.* the human race; mankind: *Man has existed for thousands of years.*
4 *VERB.* to supply with a crew: *We can man ten ships.* □ *PLURAL* **men;** *VERB* **mans, manned, man·ning.**

Word Power -man

The suffix **-man** means "man from a certain place" or "person who deals with _____ or is part of _____." A French**man** is a man **from** France. A fire**man** is a person who **deals with** fire. A police**man** is **part of** the police.

Many people now find words ending with **-man** offensive because they feel that such words leave out women. Careful writers and speakers use **firefighter, police officer,** and other words that avoid the ending **-man.**

man·age (man′ij), *VERB.*

1 to control or guide something; handle; direct: *Good riders manage their horses well. They hired someone to manage the business.*
2 to succeed in doing something: *I shall manage to keep warm with this blanket.*
□ *VERB* **man·ag·es, man·aged, man·ag·ing. —man′age·a·ble,** *ADJECTIVE.*

man·age·ment (man′ij mənt), *NOUN.*

1 the act or process of managing or handling; control; direction: *Bad management caused the bank's failure.*
2 the people that manage a business or an institution: *The management of the store decided to hire more employees.*

man·ag·er (man′ə jər), NOUN. someone who controls the daily workings of an office, store, project, and so on: *She is the manager of the restaurant.*

man·a·tee (man′ə tē′), NOUN. a large plant-eating water mammal with flippers and a flat, oval tail. Manatees live in warm, shallow water in the Americas and West Africa. ❑ PLURAL **man·a·tees.**

man·dar·in (man′dər ən), NOUN. a small, sweet citrus fruit with a thin, orange, very loose skin and sections that separate easily. It tastes something like a tangerine.

man·date (man′dāt), NOUN.
1 a command or official order.
2 the power or authority given to a government by the votes of the people in an election: *The governor had a mandate to increase taxes.*

man·do·lin (man′də lin′), NOUN. a musical instrument with a pear-shaped body and four to six pairs of metal strings.

mane (mān), NOUN. the long, heavy hair on the back of the neck of a horse, or around the face and neck of a male lion.
■ Another word that sounds like this is **main.**

mandolin

ma·neu·ver (mə nü′vər),
1 NOUN. a planned movement of troops or warships: *Every year the armed forces hold maneuvers for practice.*
2 NOUN. a skillful plan; clever trick: *He used a series of maneuvers to get us to use his plan.*
3 VERB. to plan something skillfully; use clever tricks; scheme: *Scheming people always maneuver to get what they want.*
4 VERB. to move something or handle it skillfully: *She maneuvered the car through the traffic with ease.*
❑ VERB **ma·neu·vers, ma·neu·vered, ma·neu·ver·ing. –ma·neu′ver·a·bil′i·ty,** NOUN. **–ma·neu′ver·a·ble,** ADJECTIVE.

man·ga·nese (mang′gə nēz′), NOUN. a hard, brittle, grayish white metal. Manganese is a chemical element, often used mixed with other metals.

man·ger (mān′jər), NOUN. a box or trough that you put hay or other food in for horses or cows.

man·gle (mang′gəl), VERB.
1 to cut or tear something roughly: *The bear's paw was badly mangled by the jaws of the steel trap.*
2 to do or play badly; ruin: *The child mangled the music because it was too difficult for her to play.*
❑ VERB **man·gles, man·gled, man·gling.**

man·go (mang′gō), NOUN. the sweet, juicy, oval fruit of a tropical tree. Mangoes have a thick, yellowish red rind.
❑ PLURAL **man·goes** or **man·gos.**

man·hole (man′hōl′), NOUN. a hole in a street with a metal cover. Through a manhole, a worker can enter a sewer, or get at electrical wiring or telephone lines, in order to repair them.

mango

man·hood (man′hùd), NOUN.
1 the condition or time of being a man: *The boy was about to enter manhood.*
2 the character or qualities of a man.

ma·ni·ac (mā′nē ak), NOUN. a wildly excited person who may be violent or destructive.

man·i·cure (man′ə kyùr),
1 NOUN. professional care for the fingernails including trimming, cleaning, and polishing.
2 VERB. to give the fingernails a manicure.
❑ VERB **man·i·cures, man·i·cured, man·i·cur·ing.**

Ma·nil·a (mə nil′ə), NOUN. the capital of the Philippines.

Man·i·to·ba (man′ə tō′bə), NOUN. a province in south central Canada. **–Man′i·to′ban,** ADJECTIVE or NOUN.

man·kind (man′kīnd′ for 1; man′kīnd′ for 2), NOUN.
1 the human race; all human beings: *Mankind has populated most areas of the earth.*
2 men as a group: *Mankind and womankind both like praise.*

man·ly (man′lē), ADJECTIVE. having qualities that are thought to be typical of men: *a manly show of strength and courage.* ❑ ADJECTIVE **man·li·er, man·li·est. –man′li·ness,** NOUN.

man-made (man′mād′), ADJECTIVE. made by people; artificial: *a man-made satellite.*

manned (mand), ADJECTIVE. occupied or controlled by one or more people: *a manned space vehicle.*

man·ner (man′ər), NOUN.
1 a way of doing or happening: *The manner of their meeting makes a good story.*
2 a way of acting or behaving: *She has a kind manner.*
3 **manners,** polite ways of behaving: *People with manners say "Please" and "Thank you."*
■ Another word that sounds like this is **manor.**

man-of-war (man′ə wôr′), NOUN. a kind of warship used in former times. ❑ PLURAL **men-of-war.**

a	hat	ė	term	ô	order	ch	child		a in about
ā	age	i	it	oi	oil	ng	long		e in taken
ä	far	ī	ice	ou	out	sh	she	ə	i in pencil
â	care	o	hot	u	cup	th	thin		o in lemon
e	let	ō	open	ù	put	ᴛH	then		u in circus
ē	equal	ȯ	saw	ü	rule	zh	measure		

man·or (man′ər), NOUN.
1 (in the Middle Ages) a large estate, part of which was set aside for the lord and the rest divided among the peasants. The peasants paid the lord rent in goods, services, or money.
2 a large estate in the country.
■ Another word that sounds like this is **manner**.

man·sion (man′shən), NOUN. a large, expensive house.

man·slaugh·ter (man′slȯ′tər), NOUN. (in law) a killing that is accidental, or that is not planned.

man·tel (man′tl), NOUN. a shelf above a fireplace.
■ Another word that sounds like this is **mantle**.

man·tis (man′tis), NOUN. an insect like a long, thin grasshopper that eats other insects; praying mantis. The mantis holds its front legs doubled up as if praying. ❑ PLURAL **man·tis·es**.

mantis — up to 5 inches long

man·tle (man′tl), NOUN.
1 a loose coat without sleeves; cloak.
2 the layer of the earth lying beneath the crust and above the core.
■ Another word that sounds like this is **mantel**.

man·u·al (man′yü əl),
1 ADJECTIVE. of or done with the hands: *Performing surgery requires manual skill. Digging a trench with a shovel is manual labor.*
2 NOUN. a small book that helps its readers to understand and use something; handbook: *A manual came with my pocket calculator.*
—**man′u·al·ly**, ADVERB.

man·u·fac·ture (man′yə fak′chər), VERB.
1 to make things by hand or machine. A big factory manufactures goods in large quantities by using machines and dividing the work up among many people. ■ See the Synonym Study at **make**.
2 to invent or make up: *Students who are late sometimes manufacture excuses.*
❑ VERB **man·u·fac·tures**, **man·u·fac·tured**, **man·u·fac·tur·ing**. —**man′u·fac′tur·er**, NOUN.

ma·nure (mə nùr′), NOUN. animal waste, especially when put in or on the ground to make the soil rich in order to grow better crops.

man·u·script (man′yə skript), NOUN. a book or article that comes directly from a writer, before it is worked on by an editor. Manuscripts are sent to publishers to be made into printed books, magazine articles, and the like.

man·y (men′ē),
1 ADJECTIVE. a great number of; numerous: *many years ago. There are many children in the city.*
2 NOUN or PRONOUN. a large number of people or things: *There were many at the dance.*
❑ ADJECTIVE **more, most**.

Synonym Study

Many means made up of a large number: *There were many apples on the tree before the harvest.*

Numerous means many. It emphasizes the large number: *At the library, I saw numerous books about space travel, and I checked out two.*

Countless means so many that they can hardly be counted: *In the summer night, countless fireflies flew about, flickering in the dark.*

Quite a few means many: *Quite a few people were at the movie, but we still found seats.*

A lot of and **lots of** mean a great number or amount of. They are informal phrases: *There were a lot of fans at last night's ball game, and lots of them stayed for the fireworks.*

ANTONYM: **few**.

Ma·o·ri (mou′rē),
1 NOUN. a member of the Polynesian people who were the original inhabitants of New Zealand.
2 NOUN. their language.
3 ADJECTIVE. of or about the Maori or their language. ❑ PLURAL **Ma·o·ri** or **Ma·o·ris**.

map (map),
1 NOUN. a drawing of the earth's surface or of part of it, showing countries, cities, rivers, seas, lakes, and mountains.
2 VERB. to make a map of; show on a map: *Explorers have mapped most of the earth.*
❑ VERB **maps**, **mapped**, **map·ping**.

map out, IDIOM. to plan something; arrange in detail: *Each Monday we map out the week's work.*

Word Story

Map comes from a Latin word meaning "napkin" or "cloth." Early maps were drawn on cloth. See also the Word Stories at **latitude** and **longitude**.

ma·ple (mā′pəl), NOUN. a tree grown for shade, ornament, wood, or its sap. There are many kinds of maples. They all have leaves with deep notches and winged seeds that grow in pairs.

maple syrup, syrup made by boiling the sap of maples.

mar (mär), VERB. to spoil the beauty of something; damage; injure: *Weeds mar a garden. A nail in my shoe marred the floor.* ❏ VERB **mars, marred, mar·ring.**

Mar., an abbreviation of **March.**

mar·a·thon (mar′ə thon),
1 NOUN. a foot race of 26 miles, 385 yards.
2 ADJECTIVE. lasting a very long time: *a marathon spelling bee.*

Word Story

Marathon was first used as the name of a race at the first modern Olympic Games in 1896, in memory of a famous run from Marathon to Athens in Greece. People began to use the word about any long physical activity, in phrases like *dance marathon.* Today people combine the last part of *marathon* with other words to make new words like *bikeathon* (bik′ə thon) and *walkathon* (wȯk′ə thon).

mar·ble (mär′bəl), NOUN.
1 a hard rock formed from limestone by heat and pressure under the ground.
2 a small, usually colored glass ball, used in children's games.
3 **marbles,** a children's game. Players take turns shooting a marble with a flick of the thumb to knock other marbles out of a ring. Marbles is easy to learn.

playing **marbles**

Did You Know?

Marble is mined all over the world. It may be white or colored, plain or patterned, and can be polished to be smooth and shiny. Some of the fanciest marble comes from Italy. Marble that comes from Vermont is often white and marble that comes from Tennessee can be pink. Marble is used for statues and in buildings.

march (märch),
1 VERB. to walk in a group in line, with everyone taking equal steps: *The members of the band marched in the parade to the beat of the drums.*
2 NOUN. the act of marching: *The band began their march at the town library.*
3 NOUN. music with a steady beat, composed for marching or for its pleasing rhythm: *She enjoys playing marches on the piano.*
4 VERB. to walk or move steadily: *He marched to the front of the room and began his speech.*
   ❏ VERB **march·es, marched, march·ing;** PLURAL **march·es. —march′er,** NOUN.

March (märch), NOUN. the third month of the year. It has 31 days.

Word Story

March comes from a Latin word meaning "of Mars." Mars was the Roman god of war. The Greeks called him **Ares** (âr′ēz).

mare (mâr), NOUN. a female horse, donkey, or zebra.

mar·gar·ine (mär′jər ən *or* mär′jər ēn′), NOUN. a soft food like butter, made from vegetable oils.

mar·gin (mär′jən), NOUN.
1 the blank space around the writing or printing on a page: *Do not write in the margin.*
2 an extra amount; amount beyond what is necessary: *We try to allow a margin of 15 minutes in catching a train.*

mar·i·gold (mar′ə gōld), NOUN. a garden plant with yellow, orange, or red flowers.

mar·i·jua·na (mar′ə wä′nə), NOUN. the dried leaves and flowers of the hemp plant. Marijuana is a drug which is sometimes smoked for its effect.

ma·ri·na (mə rē′nə), NOUN. a small harbor with a dock where small boats may tie up, buy fuel and supplies, and so on. ❏ PLURAL **ma·ri·nas.**

ma·rine (mə rēn′),
1 ADJECTIVE. of or found in the sea: *marine animals.*
2 ADJECTIVE. of the sea; for use at sea: *marine law, marine power, marine supplies.*
3 NOUN. also, **Marine,** someone serving in the Marine Corps.

Marine Corps, a branch of the armed forces of the United States with its own sea, air, and land units.

mar·i·o·nette (mar′ē ə net′), NOUN. a puppet that is moved by strings or wires, often on a little stage.

mar·i·time (mar′ə tīm), ADJECTIVE.
1 of or about the sea; of shipping and sailing: *Ships and sailors are governed by maritime law.*
2 on the sea; living on or near the sea: *Maritime peoples engage in boating and fishing.*

marionette

a hat	ė term	ô order	ch child	(a in about
ā age	i it	oi oil	ng long	e in taken
ä far	ī ice	ou out	sh she	ə { i in pencil
â care	o hot	u cup	th thin	o in lemon
e let	ō open	ù put	ŦH then	(u in circus
ē equal	ȯ saw	ü rule	zh measure	

M

Mars

The Red Planet

For thousands of years, people have been looking into the night sky at the planet Mars and wondering what might be there. Mars looks reddish because a large part of its surface is rocks and soil that contain rust.

Mars has been known as "The Red Planet" for so long that people have connected it in their minds with warfare and bloodshed. The planet was named for Mars, the Roman god of war.

Is there life on Mars?

In 1996, scientists discovered a small meteorite that they believe had been blasted into space from beneath the surface of Mars thousands of years ago. Within the meteorite, they found evidence that suggests that life may have existed on Mars.

Inside the rock were shapes that look like fossils of bacteria but are much smaller. The evidence is still being studied, so no one knows yet whether or not there ever was life on Mars— but there is a possibility.

Is Mars like Earth?

Mars is the planet most like Earth in its surface conditions. Mars has the same four seasons that we know on Earth.

Scientists believe that large amounts of water once flowed over the surface of the planet. Water is a basic need of living things, and if there was life on Mars at one time, water would have been necessary.

There are also gigantic volcanoes on Mars. The largest of these is more than 15 miles high — the tallest volcano known.

Mars has mountains, craters, valleys, rocky deserts, and canyons. The biggest canyon, shown below, is about 3,000 miles long, 90 miles wide, and 6 miles deep. On Earth, it would extend from New York to Los Angeles.

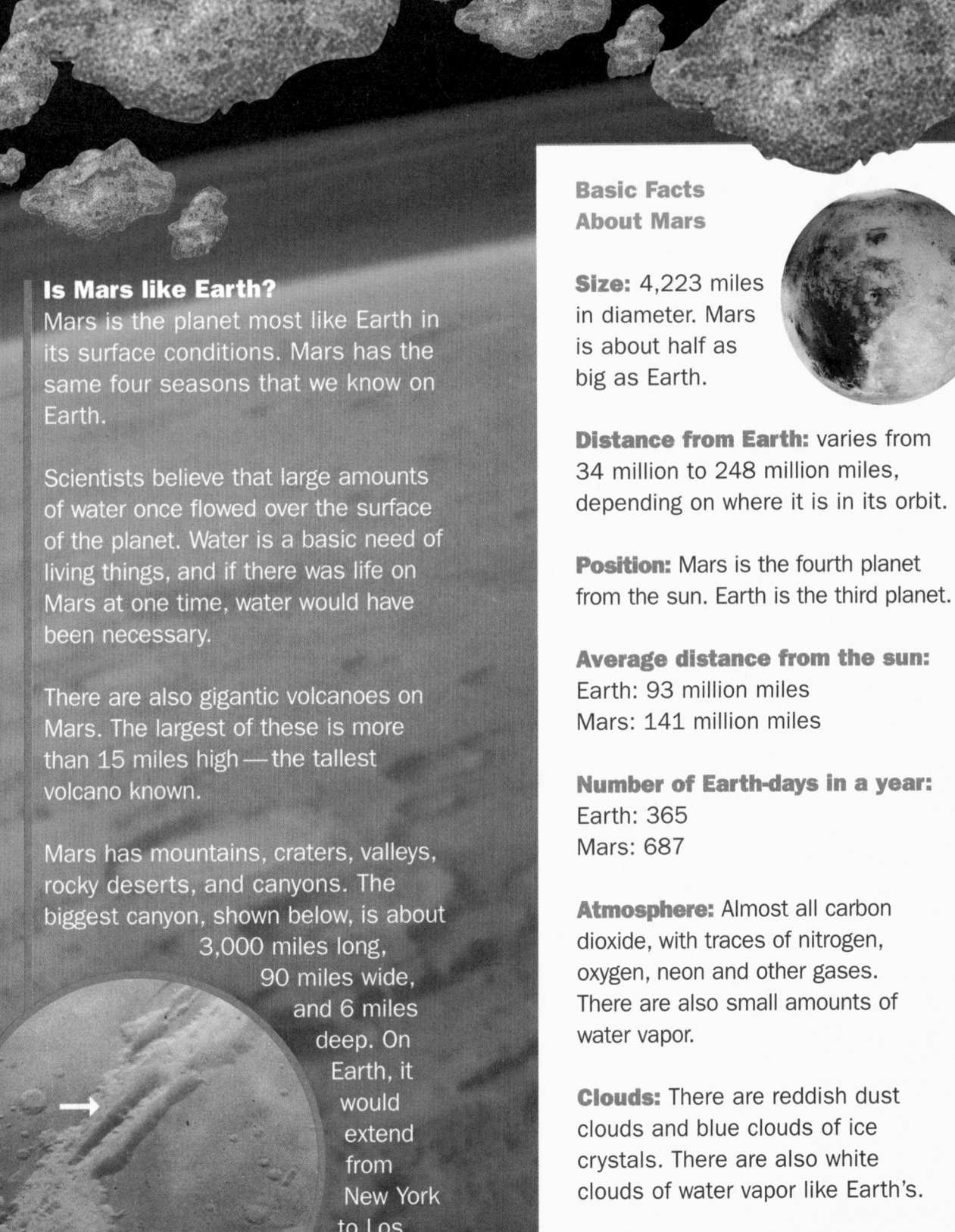

Basic Facts About Mars

Size: 4,223 miles in diameter. Mars is about half as big as Earth.

Distance from Earth: varies from 34 million to 248 million miles, depending on where it is in its orbit.

Position: Mars is the fourth planet from the sun. Earth is the third planet.

Average distance from the sun:
Earth: 93 million miles
Mars: 141 million miles

Number of Earth-days in a year:
Earth: 365
Mars: 687

Atmosphere: Almost all carbon dioxide, with traces of nitrogen, oxygen, neon and other gases. There are also small amounts of water vapor.

Clouds: There are reddish dust clouds and blue clouds of ice crystals. There are also white clouds of water vapor like Earth's.

Temperature:
Hottest: 63 F (17 C)
Coldest: −225 F (−143 C)

mark (märk),

1 NOUN. a line, dot, and so on, made on something.

2 NOUN. a line or dot that shows a point or position: *This mark shows how far you jumped.*

3 NOUN. a sign or indication of something: *Saying "thank you" is a mark of good manners.*

4 NOUN. a letter or number to show how well you have done; grade: *My mark in arithmetic was B.*

5 VERB. to put grades on: *The teacher marked our examination papers.*

6 VERB. to make a mark on something: *Be careful not to mark the table.*

7 VERB. to put in a pin or make a line to show where a place is: *Mark all the rivers on this map.*

8 VERB. to show something clearly; be a sign of: *A tall pine marks the beginning of the trail. A frown marked her unhappiness.*
□ VERB **marks, marked, mark·ing.** —**mark′er,** NOUN.

make your mark, IDIOM. to succeed; become well known: *That girl is a hard worker; she'll make her mark.*

mark down, IDIOM.

1 to write down; note down.

2 to mark for sale at a lower price: *By January, most winter coats had been marked down.*

mark up, IDIOM.

1 to damage; spoil the appearance of: *Don't mark up the desks.*

2 to mark for sale at a higher price.

mar·ket (mär′kit),

1 NOUN. an open space or covered building where people buy and sell food, cattle, or other things.

2 VERB. to sell something: *The farmer cannot market all of his wheat.*

3 NOUN. a store for the sale of food: *a meat market.*

4 NOUN. a particular area or group to which goods may be sold: *The United States is a large market for South American coffee.*

5 NOUN. the demand for something; price offered: *The drought created a high market for corn.*
□ VERB **mar·kets, mar·ket·ed, mar·ket·ing.** —**mar′ket·er,** NOUN.

mar·ket·place (mär′kət plās′), NOUN.

1 a place where a market is held.

2 the business world in general.

mark·ing (mär′king), NOUN. a pattern of marks: *The bird had beautiful markings.*

mar·lin (mär′lən), NOUN. a large sea fish related to the swordfish. □ PLURAL **mar·lin** or **mar·lins.**

mar·ma·lade (mär′mə lād), NOUN. a spread similar to jam, made of oranges or of other fruit. The peel is usually sliced up and boiled with the fruit.

ma·roon¹ (mə rün′), ADJECTIVE or NOUN. very dark brownish red.

ma·roon² (mə rün′), VERB. to leave someone in a lonely, helpless position: *The snowstorm marooned*

us in a cabin miles from town. □ VERB **ma·roons, ma·rooned, ma·roon·ing.**

mar·riage (mar′ij), NOUN.

1 the condition of living together as husband and wife; married life: *We wished the bride and groom a happy marriage.*

2 the ceremony of being married; wedding.

mar·ried (mar′ēd), ADJECTIVE.

1 living together as husband and wife: *a married couple.*

2 having a husband or wife: *a married man.*

mar·row (mar′ō), NOUN. See **bone marrow.**

mar·ry (mar′ē), VERB.

1 to take someone as a husband or a wife: *He plans to marry her soon.*

2 to become married: *She married late in life.*

3 to join as husband and wife: *The minister married them.*
□ VERB **mar·ries, mar·ried, mar·ry·ing.**

Mars (märz), NOUN.

1 the planet next beyond Earth. It is the fourth in distance from the sun.

2 the Roman god of war.

marsh (märsh), NOUN. low, soft land covered at times by water, where grasses and reeds but not trees grow. □ PLURAL **marsh·es.** —**marsh′like′,** ADJECTIVE.

mar·shal (mär′shəl), NOUN.

1 an officer of various kinds, especially a police officer. A United States marshal is an officer of a federal court whose duties are like a sheriff's.

2 a person in charge of a parade or ceremony: *She is our parade marshal.*
■ Another word that sounds like this is **martial.**

marsh·mal·low (märsh′mal′ō or märsh′mel′ō), NOUN. a soft, white, spongy candy, covered with powdered sugar.

marsh·y (mär′shē), ADJECTIVE. soft and wet like a marsh: *a marshy field.* □ ADJECTIVE **marsh·i·er, marsh·i·est.** —**marsh′i·ness,** NOUN.

mar·su·pi·al (mär sü′pē əl), NOUN. an animal that carries its young in a pouch. Kangaroos and opossums are marsupials.

mar·tial (mär′shəl), ADJECTIVE. of or about war; suitable for war: *the martial arts.* ■ Another word that sounds like this is **marshal.** —**mar′tial·ly,** ADVERB.

Mar·tian (mär′shən),

1 NOUN. (in stories) someone who lives on the planet Mars.

2 ADJECTIVE. of or about the planet Mars: *The Martian atmosphere has little oxygen.*

mar·tin (märt′n), NOUN. a large swallow with a short beak and a forked tail.

Martin Luther King Day, the third Monday in January, celebrated as a holiday in some states of the United States in honor of King's birth.

mar·tyr (mär′tər),
1 *NOUN.* someone who is put to death or is made to suffer greatly because of his or her religion or other beliefs. *Many of the early Christians were martyrs.*
2 *VERB.* to put someone to death or torture because of his or her religion or other beliefs.
❑ *VERB* **mar·tyrs, mar·tyred, mar·tyr·ing.**

mar·vel (mär′vəl),
1 *NOUN.* something that fills you with wonder: *The airplane is one of the marvels of science.*
2 *VERB.* to be filled with wonder: *She marveled at the beautiful sunset.*
❑ *VERB* **mar·vels, mar·veled, mar·vel·ing.**

mar·vel·ous (mär′və ləs), *ADJECTIVE.*
1 wonderful: *The walk on the moon was a marvelous event.*
2 great; fine: *We had a marvelous time.*
—**mar′vel·ous·ly,** *ADVERB.*

Mar·y (mâr′ē), *NOUN.* the mother of Jesus.

Mar·y·land (mer′ə lənd), *NOUN.* one of the southern states of the United States. *Abbreviation:* MD; *Capital:* Annapolis. —**Mar′y·land·er,** *NOUN.*

State Story Charles I, who was the king of England, named **Maryland** in 1632 in honor of his queen, **Henrietta Maria** (hen′rē et′ə mə rē ə).

mas·cot (mas′kot), *NOUN.* an animal, person, or thing supposed to bring good luck to a team, organization, and so on: *The children kept the stray dog as their family mascot.*

mas·cu·line (mas′kyə lin), *ADJECTIVE.*
1 of or about men or boys.
2 like a man; manly: *a deep, masculine voice.*

mash (mash), *VERB.* to crush or smash something into a soft mass: *I'll mash the potatoes.* ❑ *VERB* **mash·es, mashed, mash·ing.**

ma·son (mā′sn), *NOUN.* someone who builds with stone or brick.

ma·son·ry (mā′sn rē), *NOUN.* a wall, foundation, or part of a building made of brick or stone.

mas·que·rade (mas′kə rād′),
1 *VERB.* to disguise yourself: *The king masqueraded as a beggar to find out if his people really liked him.*
2 *NOUN.* a party where masks and costumes are worn.
❑ *VERB* **mas·que·rades, mas·que·rad·ed, mas·que·rad·ing.**

mass¹ (mas),
1 *NOUN.* a lump: *a mass of dough.*
2 *NOUN.* a large quantity: *a mass of flowers.*
3 *VERB.* to gather together in quantity; collect into a mass: *Many people massed in the square.*
4 *NOUN.* the majority; greater part: *The great mass of the world's population wants to live in peace.*
5 *ADJECTIVE.* of or by many people: *a mass protest.*
6 *NOUN.* **the masses,** the common people.
7 *NOUN.* the amount of matter anything contains. The mass of an object is always the same, whether on earth, on another planet, or in outer space. Its weight, which depends on the force of gravity, can vary.
❑ *PLURAL* **mass·es;** *VERB* **mass·es, massed, mass·ing.**

Mass or **mass²** (mas), *NOUN.* the main service of worship in the Roman Catholic Church and in some other churches. ❑ *PLURAL* **Mass·es** or **mass·es.**

Mas·sa·chu·setts (mas′ə chü′sits), *NOUN.* one of the northeastern states of the United States. *Abbreviation:* MA; *Capital:* Boston.

State Story **Massachusetts** comes from the name of an American Indian tribe living near Boston. The name probably meant "at the big hills," which are south of where the city is now.

M

Alaska   Indonesia   Japan   Zaïre   United States

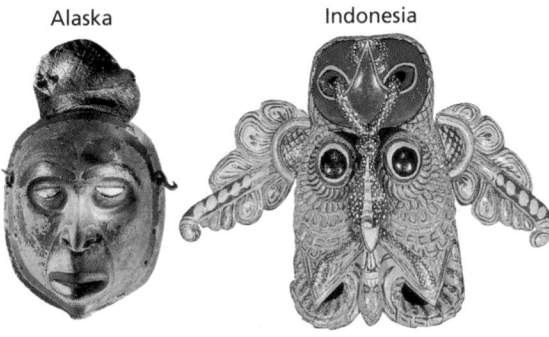

masks from many lands

mask (mask),
1 *NOUN.* a covering that hides or protects your face: *The firefighter wore a gas mask.*
2 *VERB.* to cover your face with a mask: *I didn't recognize them because they were masked.*
3 *VERB.* to hide or disguise something: *A smile masked his disappointment.*
❑ *VERB* **masks, masked, mask·ing.**

mas·sa·cre (mas′ə kər),
1 *NOUN.* the act of savagely killing people or animals.

a	hat	ė	term	ô	order	ch	child		a in about
ā	age	i	it	oi	oil	ng	long		e in taken
ä	far	ī	ice	ou	out	sh	she	ə {	i in pencil
â	care	o	hot	u	cup	th	thin		o in lemon
e	let	ō	open	ù	put	ŦH	then		u in circus
ē	equal	ò	saw	ü	rule	zh	measure		

2 *VERB.* to kill many people or animals needlessly or cruelly: *European hunters massacred thousands of African wild animals.*
❑ *VERB* **mas·sa·cres, mas·sa·cred, mas·sa·cring.**

mas·sage (mə säzh′),
1 *NOUN.* the action of rubbing and pressing the muscles and joints to increase the circulation of the blood: *A massage feels good when you are tired.*
2 *VERB.* to give a massage to someone: *Let me massage your back for you.*
❑ *VERB* **mas·sag·es, mas·saged, mas·sag·ing.**

mas·sive (mas′iv), *ADJECTIVE.* big and heavy; bulky: *A massive boulder blocked the road.*
—**mas′sive·ly,** *ADVERB.*

mast (mast), *NOUN.* a long pole of wood or steel set upright on a ship to support the sails and rigging.

mas·ter (mas′tər),
1 *NOUN.* someone who has power or authority over people or tame animals: *The dog ran away from its master.*
2 *NOUN.* an expert, such as a great artist or skilled worker.
3 *ADJECTIVE.* very skilled: *She is a master painter.*
4 *ADJECTIVE.* main; controlling: *a master plan, a master switch.*
5 *VERB.* to become the master of something: *She learned to master her temper.*
6 *VERB.* to learn how to do something: *He has mastered riding his bicycle.*
❑ *VERB* **mas·ters, mas·tered, mas·ter·ing.**
—**mas′ter·ly,** *ADVERB.*

mas·ter·ful (mas′tər fəl), *ADJECTIVE.* expert; skillful; masterly: *The violinist gave a masterful performance.* —**mas′ter·ful·ly,** *ADVERB.*

mas·ter·piece (mas′tər pēs′), *NOUN.*
1 something done or made with wonderful skill.
2 someone's greatest piece of work.

mas·ter·y (mas′tər ē), *NOUN.* very great skill or knowledge: *The biologist showed a mastery of her field.*

mas·to·don (mas′tə don), *NOUN.* one of a group of extinct animals much like mammoths and modern elephants.

mat (mat),
1 *NOUN.* a small rug of cloth, woven straw, rubber, and so on, used to protect a floor: *Please wipe your feet on the mat before you enter.*
2 *VERB.* to tangle together like a mat: *The swimmer's wet hair was matted.*
3 *NOUN.* a large, thick pad covered with canvas or plastic that is spread on the floor for use in exercising, tumbling, wrestling, or relaxing.
❑ *VERB* **mats, mat·ted, mat·ting.**

mat·a·dor (mat′ə dôr), *NOUN.* the chief performer in a bullfight. The matador usually kills the bull with a sword at the end.

match¹ (mach), *NOUN.* a short, slender piece of wood or stiff paper. A match has a tip that catches fire when you rub it against something rough.
❑ *PLURAL* **match·es.**

match² (mach),
1 *NOUN.* someone or something equal to another or much like another: *A child is not a match for an adult.*
2 *VERB.* to be equal to someone in a contest: *No one could match the skill of the unknown archer.*
3 *VERB.* to be alike; go well together: *My hat and scarf match.*
4 *VERB.* to find the equal of something or one exactly like it: *Until I can match this wool, I won't be able to finish knitting the sweater.*
5 *NOUN.* a game or contest: *a boxing match, a tennis match.*
6 *VERB.* to try your skill or strength against; oppose: *She matched her skill against mine.*
❑ *PLURAL* **match·es;** *VERB* **match·es, matched, match·ing.** —**match′less,** *ADJECTIVE.*

mate (māt),
1 *NOUN.* one of a pair of things: *Where is the mate to this glove?*
2 *VERB.* to join as a couple including a male and a female in order to produce young: *Birds mate in the spring.*
3 *NOUN.* either the male or female of a pair of breeding animals.
4 *NOUN.* someone's husband or wife.
❑ *VERB* **mates, mat·ed, mat·ing.**

ma·ter·i·al (mə tir′ē əl),
1 *NOUN.* what a thing is made from or used for: *Wood and steel are building materials.*
2 *NOUN.* cloth: *I chose a colorful material for the curtains.*
3 *ADJECTIVE.* of or about matter or things; physical: *the material world.*
4 *NOUN.* **materials,** tools or other things needed for making or doing something. Writing materials include paper, pens, and pencils.

mastodon — between 8 and 9 feet high at the shoulder

ma·ter·i·al·ize (mə tir′ē ə līz), *VERB.* to appear or cause to appear in bodily form: *A spirit materialized from the smoke of the magician's fire.* ❑ *VERB* **ma·ter·i·al·iz·es, ma·ter·i·al·ized, ma·ter·i·al·iz·ing.**

ma·ter·nal (mə tèr′nl), *ADJECTIVE.*
1 of or like a mother; motherly: *maternal feelings, maternal joy.*
2 related on the mother's side of the family: *Our maternal grandparents visit us every Thanksgiving.*
—**ma·ter′nal·ly,** *ADVERB.*

ma·ter·ni·ty (mə tèr′nə tē),
1 *NOUN.* condition of being a mother.
2 *ADJECTIVE.* for a woman who will have a baby soon: *maternity clothes.*

maternal pride

math (math), *NOUN.* a short form of **mathematics.**

math·e·mat·i·cal (math′ə mat′ə kəl), *ADJECTIVE.* of or about mathematics: *mathematical problems.*

math·e·ma·ti·cian (math′ə mə tish′ən), *NOUN.* someone who is an expert in mathematics.

math·e·mat·ics (math′ə mat′iks), *NOUN.* the science that studies the measurement and relationships of quantities. Arithmetic is one part of mathematics.

mat·ri·mo·ny (mat′rə mō′nē), *NOUN.* the condition of being married.

mat·ter (mat′ər),
1 *NOUN.* what things are made of; material; substance. Matter occupies space, has weight, and can exist as a solid, liquid, or gas.
2 *NOUN.* a topic, question, or problem that needs to be thought about and dealt with: *Mother met with her boss to discuss business matters.*
3 *NOUN.* things that are written or printed: *reading matter.*
4 *NOUN.* trouble: *"What's the matter?" she asked.*
5 *VERB.* to be important: *Nothing seems to matter when you are very sick.*
❑ *VERB* **mat·ters, mat·tered.**

as a matter of fact, *IDIOM.* in truth; in reality; actually: *Did you like the movie? As a matter of fact, I did.*

no matter, *IDIOM.* regardless of: *No matter how long it takes, I'm going to finish this project.*

Did You Know?

There are three forms or states of **matter: liquid, solid,** and **gas.** Water exists in all three states. Water is a liquid, ice is a solid, and steam is a gas.

mat·ter-of-fact (mat′ər əv fakt′), *ADJECTIVE.* sticking to the facts; not emotional.

mat·tress (mat′ris), *NOUN.* a covering of strong cloth stuffed with cotton, foam rubber, or some other material, and sometimes containing springs. It is used on a bed or as a bed. ❑ *PLURAL* **mat·tress·es.**

Word Story

Mattress comes from an Arabic word meaning "to throw." Before there were mattresses, people used to sleep on cushions thrown on the floor.

ma·ture (mə chùr′ *or* mə tùr′),
1 *ADJECTIVE.* ripe or full grown: *Grain is harvested when it is mature.*
2 *VERB.* to ripen; come to full growth: *These apples are maturing fast.*
3 *ADJECTIVE.* mentally or physically like an adult: *He is very mature for one so young.* ■ See the Synonym Study at **adult.**
❑ *VERB* **ma·tures, ma·tured, ma·tur·ing.**

ma·tur·i·ty (mə chùr′ə tē *or* mə tùr′ə tē), *NOUN.* the condition of being mature.

mat·zo (mät′sə), *NOUN.* a thin, flat piece of baked bread dough that is made without yeast. It is eaten especially during the Jewish holiday of Passover. ❑ *PLURAL* **mat·zos.**

Mau·i (mou′ē), *NOUN.* the second largest island of Hawaii.

maul (mòl),
1 *NOUN.* a very heavy hammer or mallet.
2 *VERB.* to injure someone seriously using claws and teeth: *The lion mauled its keeper badly.*
❑ *VERB* **mauls, mauled, maul·ing.** ■ Another word that sounds like this is **mall.**

Mau·ri·ta·ni·a (môr′ə tā′nē ə), *NOUN.* a country in western Africa. —**Mau′ri·ta′ni·an,** *ADJECTIVE* OR *NOUN.*

max·i·mum (mak′sə məm),
1 *NOUN.* the largest or highest amount; greatest possible amount: *Sixteen miles in a day was the maximum that any of our club walked last summer.*
2 *ADJECTIVE.* greatest possible: *The maximum score on this test is 100.*

may (mā), *HELPING VERB.*
1 to be permitted or allowed to: *May I go now? You may have an apple.*
2 to be possible that it will: *It may rain tomorrow. The train may be late.*
3 it is hoped that: *May you have a pleasant trip.*
❑ *PAST TENSE* **might.**

a	hat	ė	term	ô	order	ch	child		a in about
ā	age	i	it	oi	oil	ng	long		e in taken
ä	far	ī	ice	ou	out	sh	she	ə	i in pencil
â	care	o	hot	u	cup	th	thin		o in lemon
e	let	ō	open	ù	put	ᴛʜ	then		u in circus
ē	equal	ȯ	saw	ü	rule	zh	measure		

May (mā), *NOUN*. the fifth month of the year. It has 31 days.

Word Story

May comes from a Latin word meaning "of Maia." *Maia* (mī'ə) was a Roman goddess and wife of *Vulcan* (vul'kən), the Roman god of fire.

Ma·ya (mī'ə), *NOUN*. a member of an American Indian tribe that lived in central America and Mexico. The Maya had a highly developed culture from about A.D. 350 to about A.D. 800. ❏ *PLURAL* **Ma·ya** or **Ma·yas**. —**Ma'yan**, *ADJECTIVE* or *NOUN*.

may·be (mā'bē), *ADVERB*. it may be; possibly; perhaps: *Maybe you'll have better luck next time.*
★ **Maybe** is an adverb. It goes with verbs: *Maybe it will be sunny tomorrow.* **May be** is a verb phrase: *It may be sunny tomorrow.*

may·on·naise (mā'ə nāz'), *NOUN*. a dressing made of egg yolks, vegetable oil, vinegar or lemon juice, and seasoning, beaten together until thick.

may·or (mā'ər), *NOUN*. the person who is at the head of a city or town government.

maze (māz), *NOUN*. a system of paths built so that it is hard to find your way through it: *A guide led us through the maze of caves.* ■ Another word that sounds like this is **maize**.

a **maze** cut into thick shrubbery

MD, an abbreviation of **Maryland.**

M.D., Doctor of Medicine.

me (mē), *PRONOUN*. I and me mean the person speaking: *She said, "Give the dog to me. It likes me."* ■ Another word that sounds like this is **mi.**

ME, an abbreviation of **Maine.**

mead·ow (med'ō), *NOUN*. a piece of grassy land, especially one used for growing hay or as a pasture for grazing animals.

mead·ow·lark (med'ō lärk'), *NOUN*. a bird of North America about as big as a robin. It has a thick body, short tail, and a yellow breast marked with black.

mea·ger (mē'gər), *ADJECTIVE*. not very large: *I was still hungry after the meager meal.* —**mea'ger·ly,** *ADVERB*.

meal¹ (mēl), *NOUN*.
1 breakfast, lunch, dinner, or supper.
2 the food eaten or served at any one time: *We enjoyed each meal at the hotel.*

meal² (mēl), *NOUN*. seeds of wheat, oats, corn, or the like that have been ground up.

mean¹ (mēn), *VERB*.
1 to say the same thing as something else. The word *car* means *automobile.*
2 to be a sign of; indicate: *Red means stop.*
3 to have a certain amount of importance or value; matter: *Good friends mean a lot to a person.*
4 to plan; have in mind; intend: *Do you think they mean to visit us? I mean to have the chops for dinner.*
❏ *VERB* **means, meant, mean·ing.**

mean² (mēn), *ADJECTIVE*.
1 unkind; cruel: *It is mean to spread gossip about your friends. Never be mean to animals.*
2 (informal) very impressive; surprising in force or effect: *He makes a mean bowl of chili.*

mean³ (mēn),
1 *ADJECTIVE*. halfway between two extremes; average: *The mean number between 3 and 9 is 6.*
2 *NOUN*. **means, a** the method used to bring something about: *We won the game by fair means.* **b** wealth: *He is a man of means.*
by all means, *IDIOM*. certainly; in any possible way; at any cost: *By all means stop in to see us.*
by no means, *IDIOM*. certainly not: *I shall by no means miss the chance to see her while she is in town.*

me·an·der (mē an'dər), *VERB*.
1 to follow a winding course: *A brook meanders through the meadow.*
2 to wander aimlessly: *We meandered through the park.*
❏ *VERB* **me·an·ders, me·an·dered, me·an·der·ing.**

a **meandering** river

mean·ing (mē'ning), *NOUN*. what a word, phrase, or sentence means: *The meaning of that sentence is clear.* —**mean'ing·less,** *ADJECTIVE*.

mean·ing·ful (mē'ning fəl), *ADJECTIVE*. full of meaning; significant: *a meaningful discussion.*

meant (ment), *VERB*.
1 the past tense of **mean¹**: *He explained what he meant.*
2 the past participle of **mean¹**: *I have meant to talk to you about that all day.*

mean·time (mēn′tīm′), NOUN. the time between: *Dinner isn't ready yet; in the meantime, let's set the table.*

mean·while (mēn′hwīl′), ADVERB.
1 in the time between: *I have to leave in an hour; meanwhile, I'm going to rest.*
2 at the same time: *The children got lost at the zoo; meanwhile, their parents were searching for them.*

mea·sles (mē′zəlz), NOUN SINGULAR or PLURAL.
1 a contagious disease most often of children that causes a bad cold, fever, and small red spots on the skin. Vaccination can prevent measles.
2 a milder disease with similar red spots.

meas·ure (mezh′ər),
1 VERB. to find the size or amount of something; find how long, wide, deep, large, or much something is: *We measured the amount of water in the pail and found that it was two liters.*
2 VERB. to mark something off, in inches, meters, pounds, liters, or some other unit: *Measure off 2 yards of this silk.*
3 VERB. to be of a certain size or amount: *Buy some paper that measures 20 by 25 centimeters.*
4 NOUN. a size or amount: *His waist measure is 30 inches.*
5 NOUN. something that you measure things with. A yardstick, a measuring tape, and a cup are common measures.
6 NOUN. a bar of music.
❑ VERB **meas·ures, meas·ured, meas·ur·ing.**

meas·ure·ment (mezh′ər mənt), NOUN. a size or amount found by measuring: *The measurements of the room are 10 by 15 feet.*

meat (mēt), NOUN.
1 animal flesh used for food. Beef and pork are kinds of meat. Fish and poultry are not usually called meat.
2 the part of anything that can be eaten: *The meat of the walnut is tasty.*
■ Another word that sounds like this is **meet.**

me·chan·ic (mə kan′ik), NOUN. someone whose job is fixing machines: *an automobile mechanic.*

me·chan·i·cal (mə kan′ə kəl), ADJECTIVE.
1 of or involving a machine or machinery: *She is good at solving mechanical problems.*
2 made or worked by machinery: *a mechanical doll.*
3 without expression: *His performance was very mechanical.*
—**me·chan′i·cal·ly,** ADVERB.

mech·a·nism (mek′ə niz′əm), NOUN. a machine or its working parts: *the mechanism of a watch.*

mech·a·nize (mek′ə nīz), VERB. to do something using machinery, rather than by hand: *Much housework has been mechanized.* ❑ VERB **mech·a·niz·es, mech·a·nized, mech·a·niz·ing.**

med·al (med′l), NOUN. a piece of metal like a coin, given as a prize or award. A medal usually has a picture or words stamped on it: *She received the gold medal for winning the race.* ■ Another word that sounds like this is **meddle.**

me·dal·lion (mə dal′yən), NOUN. a large medal.

med·dle (med′l), VERB. to busy yourself with or in other people's things or affairs without being asked or needed: *Don't meddle with my books or my toys.* ❑ VERB **med·dles, med·dled, med·dling.** ■ Another word that sounds like this is **medal.** —**med′dler,** NOUN.

med·dle·some (med′l səm), ADJECTIVE. meddling; interfering; likely to meddle in other people's affairs.

me·di·a (mē′dē ə), NOUN.
1 often, **the media,** television, newspapers, magazines, radio, and other such means of communication: *The media has a great influence on the modern world.*
2 a plural of **medium** (definitions 3-5).
3 See **medium** (definition 4).

Usage Note

Media was originally a plural of **medium.** Because people often think of all forms of mass communication together, **media** has become a common singular noun. Some people still use it as a plural, however.

me·di·an (mē′dē ən),
1 NOUN. the middle number of a series. The median of 1, 3, 4, 8, 9 is 4. The median of 8, 12, 16, 20 is 14.
2 ADJECTIVE. in the middle: *the median vein of a leaf.*

me·di·ate (mē′dē āt), VERB. to help bring about an agreement between persons or sides in a dispute or quarrel: *to mediate between a company and its striking employees.* ❑ VERB **me·di·ates, me·di·at·ed, me·di·at·ing.** —**me′di·a′tion,** NOUN. —**me′di·a·tor,** NOUN.

med·i·cal (med′ə kəl), ADJECTIVE. of or about healing or the science and art of medicine: *My older sister is in medical school.* —**med′i·cal·ly,** ADVERB.

med·i·ca·tion (med′ə kā′shən), NOUN. See **medicine** (definition 1).

med·i·cine (med′ə sən), NOUN.
1 a substance, such as a drug, used to treat or prevent disease: *While I was sick I had to take my medicine three times a day.*
2 the science of treating, preventing, or curing disease and improving health: *You must study medicine for several years to become a doctor.*

medicine man. See **shaman.**

a	hat	ė	term	ô	order	ch	child		a in about
ā	age	i	it	oi	oil	ng	long		e in taken
ä	far	ī	ice	ou	out	sh	she	ə	i in pencil
â	care	o	hot	u	cup	th	thin		o in lemon
e	let	ō	open	ù	put	ᴛʜ	then		u in circus
ē	equal	ȯ	saw	ü	rule	zh	measure		

me·di·e·val (mē dē′vəl *or* med ē′vəl), *ADJECTIVE.* of or belonging to the Middle Ages (the years from about A.D. 500 to about 1450).

a painting of a **medieval** city

me·di·o·cre (mē′dē ō′kər), *ADJECTIVE.* of average or lower than average quality; ordinary; neither good nor bad: *He is a mediocre student.*

med·i·tate (med′ə tāt), *VERB.* to become peaceful and think quietly. ❑ *VERB* **med·i·tates, med·i·tat·ed, med·i·tat·ing.** ■ See the Synonym Study at **think.** —**med′i·ta′tion,** *NOUN.*

Med·i·ter·ra·ne·an Sea (med′ə tə rā′nē ən sē′), a large sea bordered by Europe, Asia, and Africa.

Word Story

Mediterranean comes from a Latin word meaning "middle of the world." When this sea was named, people didn't know very much about geography.

me·di·um (mē′dē əm),
1 *ADJECTIVE.* having a middle position, quality, or condition: *He is of medium height. She wears a medium size.*
2 *NOUN.* that which is in the middle; neither one extreme nor the other; middle condition: *They have found a happy medium between city and country life.* ★ The only plural form for this meaning is **mediums.**
3 *NOUN.* something or someone through which anything acts; means: *Money is a medium of exchange. Copper wire is a medium for conducting electricity.*
4 *NOUN.* a means of communication, especially to large numbers of people; media: *Television is the favorite medium for many advertisers.*
5 *NOUN.* a substance in which something can live; environment: *Water is the only medium in which fish can live.*
❑ *PLURAL* **me·di·ums** *or* **me·di·a.**

med·ley (med′lē), *NOUN.* a piece of music made up of several songs played or sung one right after another. ❑ *PLURAL* **med·leys.**

meek (mēk), *ADJECTIVE.* giving up too easily; too shy or humble: *Don't be meek about asking for the job.* —**meek′ly,** *ADVERB.*

meet (mēt),
1 *VERB.* to come face to face with someone at a certain time or place: *We met last week at the game.*
2 *VERB.* to be introduced to: *Have you met my sister?*
3 *VERB.* to get together with someone: *I'll meet my friend at the library.*
4 *VERB.* to come together; join: *Two roads met near the bridge.*
5 *VERB.* to be somewhere to welcome and help others when they arrive: *They met us at the airport.*
6 *NOUN.* a gathering for athletic competition: *Our first track meet is next Saturday.*
❑ *VERB* **meets, met, meet·ing.** ■ Another word that sounds like this is **meat.**

meet with, *IDIOM.*
1 to find by chance; encounter: *We met with bad weather.*
2 to have; get: *The plan met with approval.*

meet·ing (mē′ting), *NOUN.*
1 any gathering or assembly of people: *Our club held a meeting.*
2 the act of getting together: *Meeting my friend after school was fun.*
3 a gathering or assembly of people for worship: *a Quaker meeting, a prayer meeting.*

meg·a·byte (meg′ə bīt′), *NOUN.* a unit of computer information. One megabyte is equal to one million bytes.

mel·an·chol·y (mel′ən kol′ē),
1 *NOUN.* a very sad feeling; depression; sadness.
2 *ADJECTIVE.* sad; gloomy: *a melancholy evening.*

mel·low (mel′ō),
1 *ADJECTIVE.* soft and rich in sound or color: *a violin with a mellow tone, velvet with a mellow color.*
2 *ADJECTIVE.* made gentle and wise by age and experience: *He has grown mellow with the passing years.*
3 *VERB.* to make or become mellow: *His temper has mellowed as he has gotten older.*
❑ *VERB* **mel·lows, mel·lowed, mel·low·ing.** —**mel′low·ness,** *NOUN.*

me·lo·di·ous (mə lō′dē əs), *ADJECTIVE.*
1 pleasing to the ear; musical: *a melodious voice.*
2 producing melody: *melodious birds.* —**me·lo′di·ous·ness,** *NOUN.*

mel·o·dy (mel′ə dē), *NOUN.* a pleasing or easily remembered series of musical notes; tune. Music has melody, harmony, and rhythm. ❑ *PLURAL* **mel·o·dies.** —**me·lod·ic** (mə lod′ik), *ADJECTIVE.*

mel·on (mel′ən), NOUN. a large, sweet, juicy fruit with a thick, hard skin. Melons grow on vines. Cantaloupes and watermelons are kinds of melons.

a military graveyard on **Memorial Day**

melt (melt), VERB.
1 to turn something from a solid into a liquid by heating it. Ice becomes water when it melts.
2 to dissolve: *Sugar melts in water.*
❏ VERB **melts, melt·ed, melt·ing.**

melting point, the temperature at which a solid substance melts. Different substances have different melting points. The melting point of water is 32 degrees Fahrenheit or 0 degrees Celsius.

mem·ber (mem′bər), NOUN.
1 a person, animal, or thing belonging to a group: *Every member of the family was home for the holidays. The club has one hundred members.*
2 a part of a plant, animal, or human body, especially a leg, arm, or wing.

mem·ber·ship (mem′bər ship), NOUN.
1 the fact or condition of being a member of a club, group, and the like: *Do you enjoy your membership in the Boy Scouts?*
2 the members: *All of the club's membership was present.*

mem·brane (mem′brān), NOUN. a very thin, soft layer or sheet of tissue that lines or covers a living thing, a part of a living thing, or a cell.

me·men·to (mə men′tō), NOUN. something that reminds you of something in the past; souvenir: *These postcards are mementos of our trip.* ❏ PLURAL **me·men·tos** or **me·men·toes.**

mem·o (mem′ō), NOUN. a short form of **memorandum.** ❏ PLURAL **mem·os.**

mem·or·a·ble (mem′ər ə bəl), ADJECTIVE. worth remembering; not to be forgotten: *Graduation is a memorable occasion.* **–mem′or·a·bly,** ADVERB.

mem·o·ran·dum (mem′ə ran′dəm), NOUN. a message, note, or report, usually written as a reminder: *I sent him a memorandum suggesting a meeting tomorrow.* ❏ PLURAL **mem·o·ran·dums** or **mem·o·ran·da** (mem′ə ran′də).

me·mo·ri·al (mə môr′ē əl), NOUN. something that is a reminder of some event or person, such as a statue, an arch or column, a book, or a holiday.

Memorial Day, a holiday for remembering and honoring members of the United States armed services who have died in war. In most states, it is on the last Monday in May.

mem·o·rize (mem′ə rīz′), VERB. to learn something by heart: *We have all memorized the alphabet.*
❏ VERB **mem·o·riz·es, mem·o·rized, mem·o·riz·ing.**
–mem·or·i·za·tion (mem′ə ri zā′tion), NOUN.

mem·or·y (mem′ər ē), NOUN.
1 the ability to remember things or keep things in your mind: *She has a good memory, so she will recall when that happened.*
2 a person, thing, or event that you can remember: *My seventh birthday party is a favorite memory.*
3 all that you can remember: *This is the hottest summer within my memory.*
4 the part of a computer in which information and instructions are stored; storage.
❏ PLURAL **mem·or·ies.**

men (men), NOUN PLURAL.
1 the plural of **man.**
2 human beings; people in general: *"All men are created equal."*

men·ace (men′is),
1 NOUN. a threat: *That vicious dog is a menace!*
2 VERB. to threaten something: *Floods menaced the valley towns with destruction.*
❏ VERB **men·ac·es, men·aced, men·ac·ing.**

mend (mend),
1 VERB. to put something in good condition again; repair: *to mend a broken doll, to mend clothing.*
2 NOUN. a place that has been mended: *The mend in your shirt scarcely shows.*
3 VERB. to get better from an illness or injury; get back your health: *My sprained ankle has mended.*
❏ VERB **mends, mend·ed, mend·ing.**

me·no·rah (mə nôr′ə), NOUN. a candlestick with eight branches used during the Jewish festival of Hanukkah.

Word Power   -ment

The suffix **-ment** can mean "the act of _____ing." Enjoyment is the **act of** enjoying something. It can also mean "the condition of being _____ed." Amazement is the **condition of** being amazed. The suffix -ment also means "the result of _____ing." A measurement is the **result of** measuring.

a	hat	ė	term	ô	order	ch	child		
ā	age	i	it	oi	oil	ng	long		a in about
ä	far	ī	ice	ou	out	sh	she		e in taken
â	care	o	hot	u	cup	th	thin	ə	i in pencil
e	let	ō	open	ů	put	ŦH	then		o in lemon
ē	equal	ȯ	saw	ü	rule	zh	measure		u in circus

M

men·tal (men′tl), ADJECTIVE.
1 of, by, or for the mind: *mental illness, mental arithmetic.*
2 having a mental disease or disorder; for people having a mental disease or disorder: *a mental patient, a mental hospital.*

men·tal·ly (men′tl ē), ADVERB. with the mind; in the mind: *Grandmother is still strong physically and mentally.*

men·tion (men′shən),
1 VERB. to tell or speak about something: *I mentioned your idea to the group that is planning the picnic.*
2 NOUN. a short statement: *No mention of the game appeared in the newspaper.*
❑ VERB **men·tions, men·tioned, men·tion·ing.**

men·u (men′yü), NOUN.
1 a list of the food for sale in a restaurant.
2 a list of things to choose from, shown by a computer to the user: *You can play any game on the menu.*
❑ PLURAL **men·us.**

menu

Word Story

Menu comes from a Latin word meaning "made small." The idea here is that a menu is a listing of all the small details of a meal, or a list of all the meals that a customer can choose from.

me·ow (mē ou′),
1 NOUN. a sound made by a cat or kitten; mew.
2 VERB. to make this sound.
❑ VERB **me·ows, me·owed, me·ow·ing.**

mer·ce·nar·y (mėr′sə ner′ē),
1 ADJECTIVE. working for money only; acting with money as the motive.
2 NOUN. a soldier serving for pay in a foreign army.
❑ PLURAL **mer·ce·nar·ies.**

mer·chan·dise (mėr′chən dīz), NOUN. goods for sale: *Most drugstores sell books, games, pencils, and other kinds of merchandise as well as medicines.*

mer·chant (mėr′chənt),
1 NOUN. someone who buys and sells goods for a living: *Some merchants do most of their business with foreign countries.*
2 ADJECTIVE. of or about trade; commercial: *merchant ships.*

mer·ci·ful (mėr′si fəl), ADJECTIVE. showing or feeling mercy toward other people. **—mer′ci·ful·ly,** ADVERB.

mer·ci·less (mėr′si lis), ADJECTIVE. showing no mercy toward other people: *merciless cruelty.*
—mer′ci·less·ly, ADVERB.

mer·cur·y (mėr′kyər ē), NOUN. a heavy, silver-white metal that is liquid at ordinary temperatures. Mercury is a chemical element. It is used in thermometers.

Did You Know?

Mercury is the only metal that is liquid at room temperature. This is why it is used in thermometers. However, it is very poisonous, so some thermometers use alcohol instead.

Mer·cur·y (mėr′kyər ē), NOUN.
1 the planet closest to the sun.
2 in Roman myths, the god who served as messenger for the other gods.

mer·cy (mėr′sē), NOUN. more kindness than justice requires: *The judge showed mercy to the young offender.* ❑ PLURAL **mer·cies.**

mere (mir), ADJECTIVE. nothing else than; only: *The cut was the merest scratch.* ★ **Mere** does not have a comparative. The superlative of **mere** is **merest.**

mere·ly (mir′lē), ADVERB. simply; only; and nothing more; and that is all: *I am merely a member of the club, not one of the officers.*

merge (mėrj), VERB. to join several things into one; combine; unite: *The big company merged various small businesses.* ■ See the Synonym Study at **mix.**
❑ VERB **merg·es, merged, merg·ing.**

me·rid·i·an (mə rid′ē ən), NOUN.
1 any imaginary circle that goes around the earth and passes through the North and South Poles.
2 one half of such a circle, running from the North to the South Pole. All the places on one meridian have the same longitude.

mer·it (mer′it),
1 NOUN. goodness or value that deserves reward or praise: *You will be marked according to the merit of your work.*
2 VERB. to deserve: *Your excellent work merits praise.*
3 NOUN. **merits,** the real facts or qualities, whether good or bad: *I approve of your plan on its merits, not just because you are my friend.*
❑ VERB **mer·its, mer·it·ed, mer·it·ing.**

mer·maid (mėr′mād′), NOUN. (in stories) a creature of the sea, with the head and body of a woman and the tail of a fish.

mer·ry (mer′ē), ADJECTIVE. joyful: *We had a merry holiday.* ❑ ADJECTIVE **mer·ri·er, mer·ri·est.**
—mer′ri·ly, ADVERB.

mer·ry-go-round (mer′ē gō round′), NOUN. a machine that goes around and around. It usually has carved wooden horses and other animals that you can ride on.

me·sa (mā′sə), NOUN. a high, steep hill that has a flat top and stands by itself. A mesa is usually larger and steeper than a butte. ❏ PLURAL **me·sas.**

mes·dames (mā däm′), NOUN. the plural of **madame.**

mesh (mesh),
1 NOUN. material that has been woven from threads or thin wires: *Some insects are so small that they can pass through the mesh of a window screen.*
2 VERB. to fit closely together. Gears are made so that the teeth of one can mesh with the teeth of another.
❏ PLURAL **mesh·es;** VERB **mesh·es, meshed, mesh·ing.**

me·squite (me skēt′), NOUN. a tree or bush common in the southwestern United States and Mexico. Mesquite bears pods that are used as food for cattle. Smoke from burning mesquite is used to flavor foods.

mess (mes),
1 NOUN. a place or group of things that is not clean or neat: *Please clean up the mess in your room.*
2 VERB. to make a failure of something; spoil: *He messed up his chances of winning the race.*
3 NOUN. an unpleasant, difficult, or unsuccessful situation: *I made a mess of the test.*
❏ PLURAL **mess·es;** VERB **mess·es, messed, mess·ing.**

mes·sage (mes′ij), NOUN.
1 the words sent or delivered from one person or group to another: *a telephone message.*
2 a formal political speech: *the President's message to Congress.*

mes·sen·ger (mes′n jər), NOUN. someone who carries a message or goes on an errand.

mess·y (mes′ē), ADJECTIVE. not neat or clean; in a mess; untidy: *The attic was so messy it took two days to clean it.* ❏ ADJECTIVE **mess·i·er, mess·i·est.** —**mess′i·ly,** ADVERB. —**mess′i·ness,** NOUN.

mesa

me·tab·o·lism (mə tab′ə liz′əm), NOUN. the processes by which all living things turn food into energy and living tissue. Life and growth depend on metabolism.

met·al (met′l),
1 NOUN. a hard substance such as iron, gold, silver, steel, or aluminum. Metals are usually shiny and are found underground in the form of ore. Metals can be melted, and they can usually be hammered into thin sheets. Metals carry heat and electricity well.
2 ADJECTIVE. made of a metal or of a mixture of metals: *a metal chair.*

me·tal·lic (mə tal′ik), ADJECTIVE.
1 of or containing metal: *a metallic substance.*
2 like metal: *This fabric has a metallic gleam.*

met·a·mor·phic rock (met′ə môr′fik rok), rock that has been changed by heat and pressure in the earth's crust. Slate is a metamorphic rock that is formed from shale, a sedimentary rock.

met·a·mor·pho·sis (met′ə môr′fə sis), NOUN. a change of bodily form in the life cycle of some animals and insects. ❏ PLURAL **met·a·mor·pho·ses** (met′ə môr′fə sēz′).

Tadpoles become frogs by metamorphosis; they lose their tails and grow legs.

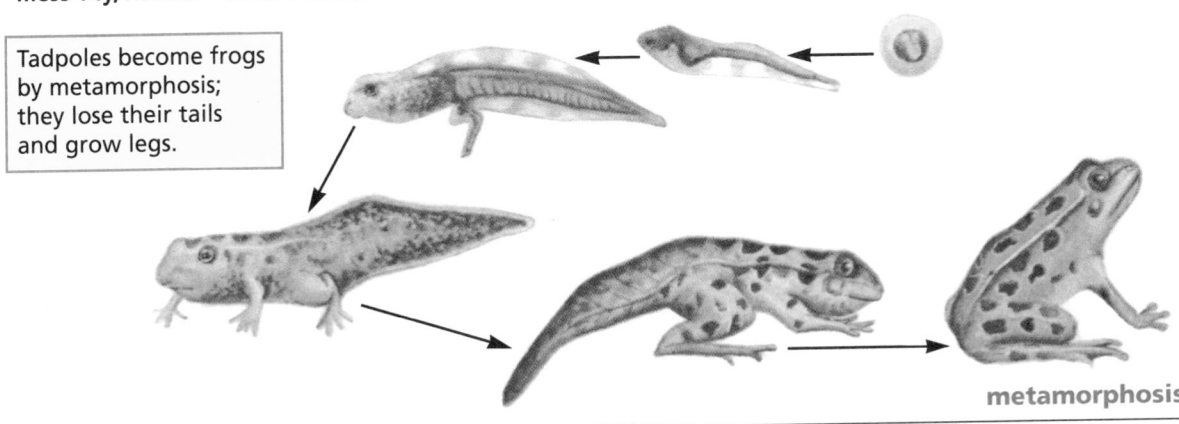

metamorphosis

met (met), VERB.
1 the past tense of **meet:** *We met at school.*
2 the past participle of **meet:** *We were met at the gate by our three dogs.*

a	hat	ė	term	ô	order	ch	child	⎧a in about
ā	age	i	it	oi	oil	ng	long	⎪e in taken
ä	far	ī	ice	ou	out	sh	she	ə⎨i in pencil
â	care	o	hot	u	cup	th	thin	⎪o in lemon
e	let	ō	open	ů	put	ŦH	then	⎩u in circus
ē	equal	ȯ	saw	ü	rule	zh	measure	

met·a·phor (met′ə fôr), NOUN. a spoken or written expression in which something is described by comparing it to something else, without using the words *like* or *as*. "A heart of stone" is a metaphor.

Usage Note

Metaphor compares things without using *like* or *as*: *I have a mountain of work to do.* **Simile** compares things using *like* or *as*: *He is as strong as an ox.* Some metaphors are so common that they are now standard phrases, including *head of government, career path,* and *window of opportunity.*

me·te·or (mē′tē ər), NOUN. a mass of stone and metal that comes toward the earth from outer space with enormous speed; shooting star. Meteors become so hot from rushing through the air that they glow and often burn up.

me·te·or·ite (mē′tē ə rīt′), NOUN. a mass of stone and metal that has fallen from outer space to a planet or moon; a fallen meteor.

me·te·or·ol·o·gy (mē′tē ə rol′ə jē), NOUN. the science that studies weather and the atmosphere. Meteorology includes the study of atmospheric conditions such as wind, moisture, and temperature. Weather forecasts are also part of meteorology. —**me′te·or·ol′o·gist**, NOUN.

Word Power   -meter

The combining form **-meter** means "a device for measuring." A speed**ometer** is a **device for measuring** speed. It is also used in metric system measurements. A kilo**meter** is one thousand **meters.**

me·ter¹ (mē′tər), NOUN.
1 any kind of poetic rhythm; the arrangement of beats or accents in a line of poetry. The meter of "Jack and Jill went up the hill" is not the meter of "One, two, buckle my shoe."
2 the arrangement of beats in music; rhythm.

me·ter² (mē′tər), NOUN. the basic unit of length in the metric system. A meter is about three inches longer than a yard.

me·ter³ (mē′tər), NOUN. a device that measures, or measures and records: *Mother put two quarters in the parking meter.*

meth·ane (meth′ān), NOUN. a colorless, odorless, flammable gas. Methane occurs in marshes, oil wells, volcanoes, and coal mines.

meth·od (meth′əd), NOUN. a particular way of doing something: *Frying is one method of cooking eggs.*

meth·od·i·cal (mə thod′ə kəl), ADJECTIVE.
1 done according to a method; orderly: *a methodical check of your work.*

2 acting according to a method: *A scientist is usually a methodical person.*
—**me·thod′i·cal·ly**, ADVERB.

met·ric (met′rik), ADJECTIVE. of or about the metric system: *I bought my dad a set of metric wrenches for Christmas.*

metric system, a system of measurement which counts by tens. Its basic unit of length is the meter, and its basic unit of weight or mass is the kilogram. A common unit of volume in the metric system is the liter.

metric ton, a unit of weight or mass in the metric system, equal to 1000 kilograms.

met·ro·nome (met′rə nōm), NOUN. a device like a clock that can be adjusted to tick at different speeds. People practicing music sometimes use a metronome to help them keep time.

metronome

me·trop·o·lis (mə trop′ə lis), NOUN. a large, important city: *Boston is a busy metropolis.* ❑ PLURAL **me·trop·o·lis·es.**

met·ro·pol·i·tan (met′rə pol′ə tən), ADJECTIVE. of, about, or belonging to a large city. A **metropolitan area** is the area or region including a large city and its suburbs.

mew (myü),
1 NOUN. the sound made by a cat or kitten; meow.
2 VERB. to make this sound: *Our kitten mews when it gets hungry.*
❑ VERB **mews, mewed, mew·ing.**

Mex·i·can (mek′sə kən),
1 ADJECTIVE. of or about Mexico or its people.
2 NOUN. someone born or living in Mexico.

Mexican Spanish, the Spanish language as it is spoken in Mexico.

Word Source

Mexican Spanish combines traditional Spanish with many words from Native American languages, especially Nahuatl. It has given a number of words to the English language, including those listed below. Words that were originally Nahuatl words are marked with a star.

abalone	canyon	jalapeño	stampede
avocado*	chaps	mesquite*	taco
bronco	chili*	mustang	tamale*
burrito	chocolate*	ocelot*	tomato*
cacao*	coyote*	quetzal*	
cafeteria	guacamole*		

Mex·i·co (mek′sə kō), NOUN.
1 a country in North America, just south of the western United States.
2 **Gulf of Mexico,** a gulf of the Atlantic Ocean between the southeastern United States and Mexico.

Mé·xi·co (me′hē kō), NOUN. a state in south central Mexico.

Mexico City, the capital of Mexico.

mez·za·nine (mez′n ēn′), NOUN. a low story, usually extending above part of the main floor to form a balcony.

mg or **mg.,** an abbreviation of **milligram** or **milligrams.**

mi (mē), NOUN. (in music) the third tone of a scale.
❑ PLURAL **mis.** ■ Another word that sounds like this is **me.**

mi., an abbreviation of **mile** or **miles.**

MI, an abbreviation of **Michigan.**

mi·ca (mī′kə), NOUN. a mineral that divides into thin, partly transparent layers. Mica is used as insulation, especially in small electrical appliances such as toasters.

mice (mīs), NOUN.
1 the plural of **mouse** (definition 1).
2 a plural of **mouse** (definition 2).

Mich·i·gan (mish′ə gən), NOUN.
1 one of the Midwestern states of the United States. *Abbreviation:* MI; *Capital:* Lansing.
2 **Lake Michigan,** one of the Great Lakes.
—**Mich·i·gan·der** (mish′i gan′der) or **Mich·i·gan·ite** (mish′i gə nīt), NOUN.

State Story **Michigan** got its name from Lake Michigan. This name came from an American Indian word meaning "the big lake."

Mi·cho·a·cán (mē′chō ä kän′), NOUN. a state in southwestern Mexico.

Word Power micro-

The combining form **micro-** is used to add the meaning "very small" to another word or part of a word. Microfilm is used to make **very small** photographs. A **microscope** is used to see **very small** things.

mi·crobe (mī′krōb), NOUN. See **microorganism.**

mi·cro·chip (mī′krō chip′), NOUN. See **chip** (definition 5).

mi·cro·com·pu·ter (mī′krō kəm pyü′tər), NOUN. See **personal computer.**

mi·cro·fiche (mī′krō fēsh′), NOUN. a small sheet of microfilm showing many pages of a book or other printed work. ❑ PLURAL **mi·cro·fiche** or **mi·cro·fich·es** (mī′krō fēsh′).

mi·cro·film (mī′krō film′), NOUN. very small photographs of pages from a book, newspaper, and so on. Microfilm is made into a long strip that is wound on a reel like a roll of tape. You can read microfilm on a machine in most libraries.

mi·cro·or·gan·ism (mī′krō ôr′gə niz′əm), NOUN. any living thing that can only be seen with a microscope; microbe. Bacteria are microorganisms.

Slimy masses of these **microorganisms,** called pond scum, float on the surface of ponds.

mi·cro·phone (mī′krə fōn), NOUN. an electrical device that makes your voice sound louder. Television and radio stations use microphones for broadcasting.

mi·cro·scope
(mī′krə skōp), NOUN. a device with a curved piece of glass called a lens, or a combination of lenses, for making small things look larger. Things that you cannot see with the naked eye are clearly visible through a microscope.

mi·cro·scop·ic
(mī′krə skop′ik), ADJECTIVE. not able to be seen without using a microscope: *microscopic germs.* ■ See the Synonym Study at **tiny.**

microscope

mi·cro·wave (mī′krō wāv′),
1 NOUN. an electromagnetic wave, with a wavelength between one millimeter and 30 centimeters.
2 VERB. to cook or heat food in a microwave oven.
3 NOUN. an oven that uses microwaves to cook food quickly: *Heat this in the microwave for a minute.*
❑ VERB **mi·cro·waves, mi·cro·waved, mi·cro·wav·ing.**

a	hat	ė	term	ô	order	ch	child		a in about
ā	age	i	it	oi	oil	ng	long		e in taken
ä	far	ī	ice	ou	out	sh	she	ə<	i in pencil
â	care	o	hot	u	cup	th	thin		o in lemon
e	let	ō	open	ú	put	ᴛʜ	then		u in circus
ē	equal	ȯ	saw	ü	rule	zh	measure		

mid (mid), ADJECTIVE. a short form of **middle**.

mid·day (mid′dā′), NOUN. the middle of the day; noon.

mid·dle (mid′l),
1 NOUN. the point or part that is the same distance from each end or side; center: *the middle of the road, the middle of the day.*
2 ADJECTIVE. halfway between; in the center; at the same distance from either end or side: *the middle house in the row.*

mid·dle-aged (mid′l ājd′), ADJECTIVE. of middle age; between youth and old age.

Middle Ages, the period in European history between ancient and modern times, from about A.D. 500 to about 1450.

middle class, the class of people between the very wealthy class and the class of poor people. The middle class includes business and professional people, office workers, and many skilled workers. **—mid′dle-class′,** ADJECTIVE.

middle ear, a hollow space between the eardrum and the inner ear. In human beings, it contains three small bones which pass on sound waves from the eardrum to the inner ear.

Middle East, a region from the eastern Mediterranean to Iran. Egypt, Israel, Turkey, and Iraq are some of the countries in the Middle East. Also, **Mideast. —Middle Eastern,** ADJECTIVE.

middle school, a school between elementary school and high school, usually including grades six through eight.

Middle West. See **Midwest. —Middle Western,** ADJECTIVE. **—Middle Westerner,** NOUN.

Mid·east (mid′ēst′), NOUN. See **Middle East. —Mid′east′ern,** ADJECTIVE.

mid·get (mij′it), NOUN. someone very much smaller than normal but shaped the same as other people.

mid·night (mid′nīt′), NOUN. 12 o'clock at night; the middle of the night.

midst (midst), NOUN. **in the midst of,** in the middle of; during; surrounded by: *in the midst of the storm.*

mid·sum·mer (mid′sum′ər), NOUN. the middle of summer.

mid·way (mid′wā′), ADVERB or ADJECTIVE. in the middle of something; halfway: *midway between these trees and the lake, a midway position.*

Mid·way (mid′wā′), NOUN. a small group of islands in the central Pacific. It belongs to the United States.

Mid·west (mid′west′), NOUN. a region of the United States. Illinois, Indiana, Iowa, Kansas, Michigan, Minnesota, Missouri, Nebraska, North Dakota, Ohio, South Dakota, and Wisconsin are the states in this region. Also, **Middle West. —Mid′west′ern,** ADJECTIVE. **—Mid′wes′ter·ner,** NOUN.

mid·win·ter (mid′win′tər),
1 NOUN. the middle of winter.
2 ADJECTIVE. in the middle of winter.

might[1] (mīt), HELPING VERB.
1 the past tense of **may:** *Mother said that we might play in the barn.*
2 possibly did: *I thought he might have missed the train.*
3 possibly would: *She might like basketball if she were taller.*
■ Another word that sounds like this is **mite.**

might[2] (mīt), NOUN. great power; strength: *We had to pull with all our might to move the bookcase.*
■ Another word that sounds like this is **mite.**

might·y (mī′tē),
1 ADJECTIVE. powerful; strong: *a mighty ruler, mighty force.*
2 ADJECTIVE. very great: *a mighty oak tree.*
3 ADVERB. (informal) very: *a mighty long time.*
■ See the Synonym Study at **very.**
❑ ADJECTIVE **might·i·er, might·i·est. —might′i·ly,** ADVERB. **—might′i·ness,** NOUN.

mi·grant (mī′grənt),
1 ADJECTIVE. migrating: *a migrant worker.*
2 NOUN. a human being or an animal that migrates.

mi·grate (mī′grāt), VERB.
1 to move from one place to settle in another place: *Many pioneers from New England migrated to other parts of the United States.*
2 to go from one region to another when the seasons change: *Most birds migrate to warmer areas in the winter.*
❑ VERB **mi·grates, mi·grat·ed, mi·grat·ing.**

mi·gra·tion (mī grā′shən), NOUN. the act of migrating: *Some kinds of birds travel thousands of miles on their migrations.*

mike (mīk), NOUN. an informal form of **microphone.**

mild (mīld), ADJECTIVE.
1 gentle; kind: *He has a mild disposition.*
2 not harsh or severe; warm; calm; temperate: *This has been a mild winter.*
3 soft or sweet to the senses; not sharp, sour, bitter, or strong in taste: *I like mild cheese.*
—mild′ly, ADVERB.

mil·dew (mil′dü), NOUN. a kind of fungus that appears on plants or on paper, clothes, or leather during damp weather: *These wet clothes smell like mildew.*

mile (mīl), NOUN. a unit for measuring length or distance. It is equal to 5280 feet.

mile·age (mī′lij), NOUN.
1 the miles traveled: *Our car's mileage last year was 10,000 miles.*
2 miles traveled for each gallon of gas used by a car or truck: *What kind of mileage does your new car get? Ours gets about 25.*

mile·stone (mil′stōn′), NOUN.
1 an important event: *The invention of printing was a milestone in education.*
2 a stone set up on a road to show the distance in miles to a certain place.

mil·i·tar·y (mil′ə ter′ē),
1 ADJECTIVE. of or about armed forces or war: *military government, military regulations.*
2 ADJECTIVE. done by soldiers: *military maneuvers.*
3 NOUN. **the military,** the armed forces.

mi·li·tia (mə lish′ə), NOUN. an army of citizens who are not regular soldiers but who are trained for war and other emergencies. Every state of the United States has a militia called the National Guard. ❑ PLURAL **mi·li·tias.**

milk (milk), NOUN.
1 the rich, white liquid from cows, which we drink and use in cooking.
2 a similar liquid produced by the adult females of many other animals as food for their young ones.
–**milk′like′,** ADJECTIVE.

Have You Heard?

You may have heard someone say **"Don't cry over spilt milk."** This means that you shouldn't be upset about something that has already happened and that you can't change.

milk shake, a drink prepared by shaking or blending together milk, flavoring, and ice cream.

milk·y (mil′kē), ADJECTIVE.
1 like milk; white as milk.
2 of or containing milk.
❑ ADJECTIVE **milk·i·er, milk·i·est.**

Milky Way, a broad band of faint light that stretches across the sky at night; the Galaxy. The Milky Way is the galaxy in which our sun is located. It is made up of countless stars, most of which are too far away to be seen separately without a telescope.

Milky Way

mill (mil),
1 NOUN. a building containing a machine that grinds grain into flour or meal.
2 NOUN. any machine for crushing or grinding beans, nuts, seeds, and the like: *a coffee mill, a pepper mill.*
3 VERB. to grind something up very fine.
4 NOUN. a building where machines are used to make things: *Cotton cloth is made in a cotton mill.*

5 VERB. to move about in a confused way: *The frightened cattle began to mill around.*
❑ VERB **mills, milled, mill·ing.**

mil·len·ni·um (mə len′ē əm), NOUN. a period of a thousand years: *The world is many millenniums old.* ❑ PLURAL **mil·len·ni·ums** or **mil·len·ni·a** (mə len′ē ə).

Did You Know?

The next **millennium** actually starts January 1, 2001. This is because there was no "year zero." Some people disagree and call 2000 the start of the new millenium. To be sure, you might want to celebrate on December 31, 1999 *and* on December 31, 2000!

mil·let (mil′it), NOUN. the very small grain of a kind of cereal grass, grown for food or hay.

Word Power   milli-

The combining form **milli-** is used to mean "one thousandth part of." A milliliter is **one thousandth** of a liter. A millimeter is **one thousandth** of a meter.

mil·li·gram (mil′ə gram), NOUN. a unit of weight equal to 1/1000 of a gram.

mil·li·li·ter (mil′ə lē′tər), NOUN. a unit of volume equal to 1/1000 of a liter.

mil·li·me·ter (mil′ə mē′tər), NOUN. a unit of length equal to 1/1000 of a meter.

mil·lion (mil′yən), NOUN or ADJECTIVE. one thousand thousand; 1,000,000.

mil·lion·aire (mil′yə nâr′), NOUN. someone whose wealth adds up to a million or more dollars or other unit of money.

mil·lionth (mil′yənth), NOUN or ADJECTIVE.
1 next after the 999,999th.
2 one of a million equal parts.

mime (mīm),
1 NOUN. an actor who performs silently. Mimes use body movements and facial expressions instead of speech.
2 VERB. to act without using words; act in a pantomime: *He mimed walking against the wind.*
❑ VERB **mimes, mimed, mim·ing.**

You can imagine a shovel in this **mime's** hands.

a	hat	ė	term	ô	order	ch	child		a in about
ā	age	i	it	oi	oil	ng	long		e in taken
ä	far	ī	ice	ou	out	sh	she	ə	i in pencil
â	care	o	hot	u	cup	th	thin		o in lemon
e	let	ō	open	ù	put	ᴛʜ	then		u in circus
ē	equal	ò	saw	ü	rule	zh	measure		

mim·ic (mim′ik),
1 VERB. to make fun of by imitating: *The children tried to annoy the baby-sitter by mimicking her accent.*
2 NOUN. someone or something that imitates.
3 VERB. to copy closely; imitate: *A parrot can mimic voices.*
4 VERB. to resemble something closely in form or color.
❑ VERB **mim·ics, mim·icked, mim·ick·ing.**

mince (mins), VERB. to chop something up into very small pieces. ❑ VERB **minc·es, minced, minc·ing.**

mind (mīnd),
1 NOUN. the part of a person that knows, remembers, thinks, feels, chooses, and so on.
2 VERB. to look after; take care of: *Please mind the baby. Why don't you mind your own business?*
3 VERB. to obey: *Mind your father and mother.*
4 NOUN. what you think or feel; opinion; view: *I used to like that TV program, but I have changed my mind.*
5 VERB. to feel bad about: *Some people don't mind cold weather.*
❑ VERB **minds, mind·ed, mind·ing.**

keep in mind, IDIOM. to give your attention to; remember: *Please keep my suggestions in mind.*

make up your mind, IDIOM. to decide: *I made up my mind to study harder and get better grades.*

never mind, IDIOM. it doesn't matter; don't worry: *Never mind; we'll be able to go tomorrow instead of today.*

on your mind, IDIOM. in your mind; in your thoughts: *With all this work I must do, I've got a lot on my mind.*

out of your mind, IDIOM. very foolish; senseless.

mind·less (mīnd′lis), ADJECTIVE. without intelligence; stupid: *mindless behavior, mindless activity.*

mine¹ (mīn), PRONOUN. the one or ones belonging to me: *This book is mine.*

mine² (mīn),
1 NOUN. a large hole or space dug in the earth to get out ores, precious stones, coal, salt, or anything valuable: *a coal mine, a gold mine.*
2 VERB. to get something from a mine: *to mine coal, to mine gold.*
3 NOUN. a rich source: *The book proved to be a mine of information about computers.*
4 NOUN. a small bomb placed in or under water, or buried just beneath the ground, to explode and destroy enemy shipping, troops, or equipment.
5 VERB. to put mines underground or underwater: *The enemy secretly mined the mouth of the harbor, and many ships were destroyed.*
❑ VERB **mines, mined, min·ing.**

min·er (mī′nər), NOUN. someone who works in a mine. ■ Another word that sounds like this is **minor.**

min·er·al (min′ər əl), NOUN.
1 a solid substance, usually dug from the earth. Minerals often form crystals. Coal, gold, sand, and mica are minerals. Some minerals, such as iron, sodium, and zinc, are nutrients.
2 any substance that is not a plant, an animal, or another living thing. Sand is a mineral.

min·gle (ming′gəl), VERB.
1 to mix things together; combine: *The flavors of garlic and the other spices mingled in the stew.*
■ See the Synonym Study at **mix.**
2 to meet and talk with various people at a meeting, party, and so on: *I tried to mingle with everyone at the party.*
❑ VERB **min·gles, min·gled, min·gling.**

min·i (min′ē), ADJECTIVE. small or short for its kind: *Our weekend in New York was a mini vacation.*

min·i·a·ture
(min′ē ə chùr),
1 NOUN. a very small copy of something: *In the museum there is a miniature of the ship "Mayflower."*
2 ADJECTIVE. done or made on a very small scale; tiny: *miniature cars, miniature furniture.* ■ See the Synonym Study at **tiny.**

The doll's house is filled with **miniature** furniture.

min·i·bike
(min′ē bīk′), NOUN. a small motorcycle.

min·i·cam (min′ē kam), NOUN. a miniature camera, especially a television or video camera.

min·i·mize (min′ə mīz), VERB. to make something seem smaller, less important, and so on, than it actually is: *She minimized the work involved in order to get me to do the job.* ❑ VERB **min·i·mized, or min·i·miz·ing.**

min·i·mum (min′ə məm),
1 NOUN. the least possible amount; lowest amount: *Each of the children had to drink some milk at breakfast; half a glass was the minimum.*
2 ADJECTIVE. least possible; lowest: *Eighteen is the minimum age for voting in the United States.*

min·ing (mī′ning), NOUN.
1 the work or business of getting ores, coal, or other minerals from mines.
2 the act or process of laying bombs underground or underwater.

min·is·ter (min′ə stər),
1 NOUN. the spiritual leader of a church; pastor.
2 VERB. to be of service to someone; be helpful: *He ministered to the needs of his sick friend.*
❑ VERB **min·is·ters, min·is·tered, min·is·ter·ing.**

min·is·try (min′ə strē), NOUN. the office, duties, or time of service of a minister. ❑ PLURAL **min·is·tries.**

min·i·van (min′ē van′), NOUN. a small passenger van.

mink (mingk), NOUN. an animal like a weasel that lives in water part of the time. The fur of the mink is very valuable.

Min·ne·so·ta (min′ə sō′tə), NOUN. one of the Midwestern states of the United States. *Abbreviation:* MN; *Capital:* St. Paul.
—**Min′ne·so′tan,** NOUN.

State Story **Minnesota** was named for the Minnesota River. This name came from American Indian words meaning "sky-colored water."

min·now (min′ō), NOUN. a very small freshwater fish. ❑ PLURAL **min·nows** or **min·now.**

mi·nor (mī′nər),
1 ADJECTIVE. smaller; lesser; less important: *Correct the important errors in your paper before you bother with the minor ones.*
2 NOUN. someone under 18 or 21 years, the legal age when you become an adult.
■ Another word that sounds like this is **miner.**

mi·nor·i·ty (mə nôr′ə tē), NOUN.
1 the smaller number or part of a group of people or things; less than half: *A minority of the children wanted a party, but the majority chose a picnic.*
2 a group within a country, state, or other area that is different from the larger part of the population in some way, such as race or religion.
❑ PLURAL **mi·nor·i·ties.**

min·strel (min′strəl), NOUN. a singer or musician in the Middle Ages who entertained people by singing or reciting poems.

mint¹ (mint), NOUN.
1 a fragrant plant used for flavoring. Peppermint and spearmint are kinds of mint.
2 a piece of candy flavored with mint.

mint² (mint),
1 NOUN. a place where money is coined by the government.
2 VERB. to coin money: *The government has not minted many silver dollars lately.*
3 NOUN. a large amount: *That car must have cost a mint.*
4 ADJECTIVE. as good as new; spotless: *That car is still in mint condition, although it is ten years old.*
❑ VERB **mints, mint·ed, mint·ing.**

min·u·et (min′yü et′), NOUN.
1 a slow, graceful dance popular in the 1600s and 1700s.
2 the music for it, often composed for listening rather than dancing.

mi·nus (mī′nəs),
1 PREPOSITION. less; decreased by: *12 minus 3 leaves 9.*
2 PREPOSITION. without something that should be there: *The library book was returned minus its cover.*

3 ADJECTIVE. less than: *B minus is not so high a mark as B.*
4 NOUN. **minus sign,** the sign (–) meaning that the quantity following it is to be subtracted.
5 ADJECTIVE. below zero: *Yesterday the temperature was –10 degrees.*
❑ PLURAL **mi·nus·es.**

min·ute¹ (min′it), NOUN.
1 one of the 60 equal periods of time that make up an hour; 60 seconds.
2 a short time; an instant: *I'll be there in a minute.*
3 an exact point of time: *The minute you see them, call me.*
4 **minutes,** an official written account of what was said and what was decided at a meeting.

mi·nute² (mī nüt′), ADJECTIVE. very small: *Even a minute speck of dust makes him sneeze.* ■ See the Synonym Study at **tiny.**

minute hand, the hand on a clock or watch that indicates minutes. It moves around the whole dial once in an hour.

min·ute·man
(min′it man′), NOUN. a member of the American militia just before and during the Revolutionary War. The minutemen kept themselves ready for military service at a minute's notice. ❑ PLURAL **min·ute·men.**

a memorial to the **minutemen**

mir·a·cle (mir′ə kəl), NOUN.
1 a wonderful happening that is beyond the known laws of nature: *It would be a miracle if your dog learned to talk.*
2 something marvelous or almost unbelievable that happens: *It's a miracle you weren't hurt in that fall.*

mi·rac·u·lous (mə rak′yə ləs), ADJECTIVE.
1 going against the laws of nature: *The miraculous fountain of youth was supposed to make old people young again.*
2 wonderful; marvelous: *Firefighters carried out many injured people in a miraculous rescue from a burning building.*
—**mi·rac′u·lous·ly,** ADVERB.

mi·rage (mə räzh′), NOUN. something that you think you see that is not really there, usually in the desert, at sea, or in the distance along a paved road.

mire (mīr), NOUN. soft, deep mud; slush.

a	hat	ė	term	ô	order	ch	child		a in about
ā	age	i	it	oi	oil	ng	long		e in taken
ä	far	ī	ice	ou	out	sh	she	ə	i in pencil
â	care	o	hot	u	cup	th	thin		o in lemon
e	let	ō	open	ů	put	ᴛʜ	then		u in circus
ē	equal	ò	saw	ü	rule	zh	measure		

mired (mīrd), *ADJECTIVE*. stuck or bogged down: *The truck was mired in deep snow.*

mir·ror (mir′ər),
1 *NOUN*. a smooth glass or polished metal surface that you can see yourself in.
2 *VERB*. to reflect as a mirror does: *The still water mirrored the trees along the bank.*
❑ *VERB* **mir·rors, mir·rored, mir·ror·ing.**

Word Power mis-

The prefix **mis-** means "bad" or "badly" or "wrong" or "wrongly." Misbehavior means **bad** behavior. To misbehave means to behave **badly**. The misuse of a word means the **wrong** use of a word. To misspell means to spell **wrongly.**

mis·be·have (mis′bi hāv′), *VERB*. to behave badly: *Some of the children misbehaved at the picnic.*
❑ *VERB* **mis·be·haves, mis·be·haved, mis·be·hav·ing.**

mis·cel·la·ne·ous (mis′ə lā′nē əs), *ADJECTIVE*. made up of many different kinds of things; varied: *He had a miscellaneous collection of stones, butterflies, stamps, and many other things.*

mis·chief (mis′chif), *NOUN*.
1 a way of acting that causes harm or trouble, often without your meaning it: *Playing with matches is mischief that may cause a fire.*
2 harm or injury done by someone: *Spreading gossip can do a lot of mischief.*

mis·chie·vous (mis′chə vəs), *ADJECTIVE*.
1 full of mischief; naughty: *The mischievous child poured honey all over the kitchen.* ■ See the Synonym Study at **naughty.**
2 full of playful tricks and teasing fun: *My friends were feeling mischievous and hid my glasses as a joke.*
—**mis′chie·vous·ly,** *ADVERB*. —**mis′chie·vous·ness,** *NOUN*.

Pronunciation Note

Mischievous is sometimes pronounced as if it were spelled with an *i* after the *v.* This pronunciation and spelling are not accepted in standard English, and it is wise to avoid them.

mi·ser (mī′zər), *NOUN*. someone who loves money for its own sake and doesn't spend very much.

mis·er·a·ble (miz′ər ə bəl), *ADJECTIVE*.
1 very unhappy: *The sick child was often miserable.*
2 causing trouble or unhappiness: *The weather has been miserable all week.*
—**mis′er·a·bly,** *ADVERB*.

mis·er·y (miz′ər ē), *NOUN*. great unhappiness or suffering caused by being poor, worried, or in pain: *Think of the misery of having no home or friends.* ❑ *PLURAL* **mis·er·ies.**

mis·fit (mis′fit′), *NOUN*. someone who does not get along very well in a job or a group.

mis·for·tune (mis fôr′chən), *NOUN*.
1 bad luck: *She had the misfortune to break her arm.*
2 a piece of bad luck: *The flood was a great misfortune for the people in the town.*

mis·giv·ing (mis giv′ing), *NOUN*. a feeling of doubt or worry about something: *We started off through the storm with some misgivings.*

mis·guid·ed (mis gī′did), *ADJECTIVE*. led into mistakes or wrongdoing; misled: *You were misguided when you let him copy your paper.*

mis·hap (mis′hap), *NOUN*. an unlucky accident: *He had a terrible mishap while riding his bicycle.*

mis·laid (mis lād′), *VERB*.
1 the past tense of **mislay**: *She mislaid her books.*
2 the past participle of **mislay**: *I have mislaid my pen.*

mis·lay (mis lā′), *VERB*. to put something somewhere and then forget where it is: *I am always mislaying my gloves.* ❑ *VERB* **mis·lays, mis·laid, mis·lay·ing.**

mis·lead (mis lēd′), *VERB*.
1 to cause someone to go in the wrong direction: *Our guide misled us, and we got lost.*
2 to lead someone to think something that is not true: *Some advertisements can mislead people.*
❑ *VERB* **mis·leads, mis·led, mis·lead·ing.**

mis·led (mis led′), *VERB*.
1 the past tense of **mislead**: *You misled me when you told me that your house was easy to find.*
2 the past participle of **mislead**: *My mother's advice has never misled me.*

mis·place (mis plās′), *VERB*. to put something somewhere and then forget where it is: *I misplaced my glasses.* ❑ *VERB* **mis·plac·es, mis·placed, mis·plac·ing.**

mis·print (mis′print′), *NOUN*. a mistake in printing.

mis·pro·nounce (mis′prə nouns′), *VERB*. to pronounce something incorrectly: *Some people mispronounce the word "mischievous."* ❑ *VERB* **mis·pro·nounc·es, mis·pro·nounced, mis·pro·nounc·ing.**

a **miserable** way to ride

mis·read (mis rēd′), VERB.
1 to read incorrectly: *I misread the sign.*
2 to misunderstand; interpret incorrectly: *You misread my joke if you think it was meant as an insult.*
❑ VERB **mis·reads, mis·read** (mis red′), **mis·read·ing.**

miss (mis),
1 VERB. to fail to hit something: *I swung at the ball and missed.*
2 NOUN. a failure to hit or reach something: *I had four hits and two misses at target practice.*
3 VERB. to fail to find, get, or meet something; fail to do: *I set out to meet my father, but in the dark I missed him.*
4 VERB. to let something pass by; not seize: *I missed my only chance of a ride to town.*
5 VERB. to fail to catch: *I missed the bus and was late to school.*
6 VERB. to fail to do or answer something correctly: *I missed three words in today's spelling lesson.*
7 VERB. to fail to keep, do, or be present at: *I missed my music lesson today.*
8 VERB. to feel the absence of: *I missed you!*
❑ VERB **miss·es, missed, miss·ing;** PLURAL **miss·es.**

Miss (mis), NOUN.
1 a title used before the name of a young girl or an unmarried woman: *Miss Brown, the Misses Brown, the Miss Browns.*
2 **miss,** a girl or young unmarried woman.
3 **miss,** a way to politely address a young woman whose name you do not know: *Oh, miss, may I see a menu, please?*
❑ PLURAL **Miss·es** for 1, **mis·ses** for 2.

mis·sile (mis′əl), NOUN. a rocket that delivers a bomb to a target.

miss·ing (mis′ing), ADJECTIVE.
1 lacking or wanting; absent: *It was a good cake but something was missing. Four children were missing from class today.*
2 lost; gone; out of its usual place: *The missing ring was found under the dresser.*

mis·sion (mish′ən), NOUN.
1 an errand or task that people are sent somewhere to do: *He was sent on a mission to find the pilot of the jet that crashed.*
2 a group of people sent out on some special business: *She was an important member of the mission sent by our government to France.*
3 a center or headquarters for religious or social work: *The church set up a mission with a soup kitchen to help local homeless people.*

mis·sion·ar·y (mish′ə ner′ē), NOUN. someone sent to a foreign country by a church to preach and do helpful things: *Missionaries helped start churches, schools, and hospitals in many places.* ❑ PLURAL **mis·sion·ar·ies.**

Mis·sis·sip·pi (mis′ə sip′ē), NOUN.
1 one of the southern states of the United States. *Abbreviation:* MS; *Capital:* Jackson.
2 a very long river in the central United States.
—**Mis′sis·sip′pi·an,** NOUN.

State Story **Mississippi** comes from an American Indian word meaning "big river." The state got its name from the river.

Mis·sour·i (mə zùr′ē or mə zùr′ə), NOUN.
1 one of the Midwestern states of the United States. *Abbreviation:* MO; *Capital:* Jefferson City.
2 a long river in the northern United States.
—**Mis·sour′i·an,** NOUN.

State Story **Missouri** comes from the name of an American Indian tribe who lived near the place where the Missouri and Mississippi Rivers meet. The name probably meant "people of the big canoes." The state got its name from the river.

mis·spell (mis spel′), VERB. to write or say the wrong letters when you are spelling a word.
❑ VERB **mis·spells, mis·spelled, mis·spell·ing.**

mist (mist),
1 NOUN. a cloud of very fine drops of water in the air; fog.
2 VERB. to come down in mist; rain in very fine drops: *It is only misting, so you don't need an umbrella.*
❑ VERB **mists, mist·ed, mist·ing.**

mis·take (mə stāk′),
1 NOUN. something that is not right or is not done the way it should be done; an error: *I made a mistake in adding these numbers. I'm sorry that I used your towel by mistake.*
2 VERB. to misunderstand what you see or hear: *We mistook her polite words for friendliness.*
❑ VERB **mis·takes, mis·took, mis·tak·en, mis·tak·ing.**

Synonym Study

Mistake means something you do wrong: *It was a mistake to leave the cake where the dog could get it.*

Error means a mistake: *She made no errors on her geography test.*

Slip[1] can mean a mistake, especially in speaking: *In a slip of the tongue, I called Dad, "Dab."*

Blunder means a careless or stupid mistake: *Putting the wrong date on the party invitations was a real blunder.*

a	hat	ė	term	ô	order	ch	child		a in about
ā	age	i	it	oi	oil	ng	long		e in taken
ä	far	ī	ice	ou	out	sh	she	ə<	i in pencil
â	care	o	hot	u	cup	th	thin		o in lemon
e	let	ō	open	ù	put	ŦH	then		u in circus
ē	equal	ò	saw	ü	rule	zh	measure		

M

mis·tak·en (mə stā′kən),
1 ADJECTIVE. wrong: *I saw I was mistaken and admitted my error.*
2 VERB. the past participle of **mistake**: *They have mistaken me for someone else.*
—**mis·tak′en·ly**, ADVERB.

Mis·ter (mis′tər), NOUN.
1 Mr., a title put before a man's name or the name of his office: *Mr. Stein, Mr. President.*
2 **mister,** a polite way to address a man whose name you do not know: *Do you need directions, mister?*

mis·tle·toe (mis′əl tō),
NOUN. an evergreen bush with white berries that grows on other trees. It is used as a Christmas decoration.

mistletoe

mis·took (mis tùk′), VERB. the past tense of **mistake**: *I mistook you for your sister yesterday.*

mis·treat (mis trēt′), VERB. to treat a human being or an animal badly: *It is cruel to mistreat animals.* ❑ VERB **mis·treats, mis·treat·ed, mis·treat·ing.** —**mis·treat′ment**, NOUN.

mis·tress (mis′tris), NOUN. a woman who owns or controls something: *The kitten greeted its mistress with loud meows.* ❑ PLURAL **mis·tress·es.**

mis·trust (mis trust′),
1 VERB. to feel no confidence in something or someone; doubt: *I mistrusted my ability to learn to swim.*
2 NOUN. a lack of trust or confidence; suspicion: *He looked with mistrust at the stranger.* ■ See the Synonym Study at **doubt**.
❑ VERB **mis·trusts, mis·trust·ed, mis·trust·ing.**

mist·y (mis′tē), ADJECTIVE.
1 covered with mist: *misty hills.*
2 not clearly seen; vague; indistinct: *We had only a misty view of the skyline.*
❑ ADJECTIVE **mist·i·er, mist·i·est.**

mis·un·der·stand (mis′un′dər stand′), VERB. to think that you understand something when you actually don't understand it: *I misunderstood the meaning of the poem.* ❑ VERB **mis·un·der·stands, mis·un·der·stood** (mis′un′dər stùd′), **mis·un·der·stand·ing.**

mis·un·der·stand·ing (mis′un′dər stan′ding), NOUN.
1 a failure to understand what something really means.
2 a minor quarrel or disagreement: *After their misunderstanding they spoke to each other very little.*

mis·use (mis yüz′ for verb; mis yüs′ for noun),
1 VERB. to use something for the wrong purpose: *He misuses his screwdriver by using it to open cans.*
2 VERB. to treat someone or something badly; abuse: *The children misused their dog by trying to ride on its back.*

3 NOUN. a wrong use: *I notice a misuse of the word "who" in your letter.*
❑ VERB **mis·us·es, mis·used, mis·us·ing.**

mite (mīt), NOUN. anything very small; little bit: *There was not a mite of dust anywhere in the house.*
■ Another word that sounds like this is **might.**

mitt (mit), NOUN. a large leather glove with a big pad over the palm and fingers, used by baseball players: *a catcher's mitt.*

mit·ten (mit′n), NOUN. a kind of winter glove that covers the four fingers together and the thumb separately.

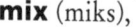
a catcher's **mitt**

mix (miks),
1 VERB. to put things together and blend them well: *We mixed butter, sugar, milk, flour, eggs, and flavoring for a cake.*
2 VERB. to be mixed; blend together: *Oil and water will not mix.*
3 VERB. to get along well together; make friends easily: *She likes people and mixes well in almost any group.*
4 NOUN. a mixture: *A strange mix of people attended the opening of the play.*
❑ VERB **mix·es, mixed, mix·ing;** PLURAL **mix·es.**

mix up, IDIOM.
1 to confuse: *I was so mixed up that I did very badly on the test.*
2 to involve: *They were mixed up in a dishonest scheme to cheat people.*

Synonym Study

Mix means to put two or more things together: *There is always a bowl of mixed candies in Grandma's living room.*

Mingle means to mix, especially many things together: *The flavors of the meat, vegetables, and spices mingle in the stew.*

Blend means to mix thoroughly: *She blended the flour and eggs and other ingredients to make a cake.*

Merge means to become completely mixed with something else: *The two toy manufacturers merged into one large company.*

See also the Synonym Study at **join.**

mixed (mikst), ADJECTIVE. formed of different kinds: *He bought a pound of mixed nuts.*

mixed number, a whole number and a fraction, such as 3⅝ and 28¾.

mix·ture (miks′chər), NOUN.
1 something that has been mixed: *Orange is a mixture of yellow and red.*
2 a mixed condition: *At the end of the movie I felt a mixture of relief and disappointment.*

mix-up (miks′up′), NOUN. a misunderstanding: *Our books arrived late because of a mix-up in the orders.*

ml or **ml.,** an abbreviation of **milliliter** or **milliliters.**

mL or **mL.,** an abbreviation of **milliliter** or **milliliters.**

mm or **mm.,** an abbreviation of **millimeter** or **millimeters.**

MN, an abbreviation of **Minnesota.**

MO, an abbreviation of **Missouri.**

mo., an abbreviation of **month** or **months.**

moan (mōn),
1 NOUN. a long, low sound expressing pain or grief.
2 VERB. to make moans: *The sick man moaned.*
❑ VERB **moans, moaned, moan·ing.** ■ Another word that sounds like this is **mown.**

moat (mōt), NOUN.
1 a deep, wide ditch, usually filled with water, dug around a castle. A moat was used as a protection against enemies in the Middle Ages.
2 a similar ditch used in zoos to separate animals from the people.

Word Story

Moat comes from a French word meaning "a mound." Early castles were built on hills made by digging dirt and piling it up. The ditch where the dirt came from often filled up with water. People saw that the ditches were a good defense, so they began to make them on purpose and borrowed the name.

mob (mob),
1 NOUN. an angry, possibly violent crowd.
2 NOUN. a large number of people; crowd: *There was a mob of shoppers at the mall today.*
3 VERB. to crowd around, especially in curiosity or anger: *The eager children mobbed the ice-cream truck the moment it appeared.*
❑ VERB **mobs, mobbed, mob·bing.**

mo·bile (mō′bəl *for adjective;* mō′bēl *for noun*),
1 ADJECTIVE. movable; easy to move: *Several mobile classrooms were brought to the crowded school.*
2 NOUN. a kind of sculpture hanging from wires and balanced so that it moves in a slight breeze.

mobile home, a house trailer, especially a large one set on a more or less permanent site.

mo·bil·i·ty (mō bil′ə tē), NOUN. the ability to move or be moved.

moc·ca·sin (mok′ə sən), NOUN.
1 a soft leather shoe or sandal, often without an attached heel. Many American Indians wore moccasins, often made of deer hide.
2 See **water moccasin.**

mock (mok),
1 VERB. to laugh at or make fun of someone or something: *Rude people in the audience mocked the new play.*
2 VERB. to make fun of someone by copying or imitating him or her: *Some classmates mocked the way I hobbled around on my sore foot.*
3 ADJECTIVE. not real; imitation: *The troops took part in a mock battle.*
❑ VERB **mocks, mocked, mock·ing.**

mock·ing·bird (mok′ing bėrd′), NOUN. a grayish songbird that imitates the calls of other birds.

mode (mōd), NOUN. the way or manner in which something is done; method: *Riding a donkey is a slow mode of travel.*

mod·el (mod′l),
1 NOUN. a small copy of something: *A globe is a model of the earth. His hobby is making models of sailing ships.*
2 VERB. to make or shape out of something soft: *In art class I modeled a kitten in clay.*
3 NOUN. the way in which something is made; design; style: *Our car is a new model.*
4 NOUN. someone or something to be copied or imitated: *Your mother is a fine person; make her your model.*
5 ADJECTIVE. just right or perfect; ideal: *They tried very hard to be model parents.*
6 NOUN. someone who poses for artists and photographers.
7 NOUN. someone employed by a clothing store to wear clothes that are for sale, so that customers can see how they look.
8 VERB. to be a model: *Would you like to model for a department store?*
❑ VERB **mod·els, mod·eled, mod·el·ing.**

mobile (definition 2)

a	hat	ė	term	ô	order	ch	child		a in about
ā	age	i	it	oi	oil	ng	long		e in taken
ä	far	ī	ice	ou	out	sh	she	ə	i in pencil
â	care	o	hot	u	cup	th	thin		o in lemon
e	let	ō	open	ů	put	ᵺ	then		u in circus
ē	equal	ȯ	saw	ü	rule	zh	measure		

mo·dem (mō′dəm), NOUN. an electronic device that enables a computer to send or receive information or instructions over the telephone.

mod·er·ate (mod′ər it *for adjective;* mod′ə rāt′ *for verb*),
1 ADJECTIVE. reasonable; not extreme: *The bus traveled at moderate speed.*
2 VERB. to make or become less extreme or violent: *The wind is moderating.*
❑ VERB **mod·er·ates, mod·er·at·ed, mod·er·at·ing. —mod′er·ate·ly,** ADVERB.

mod·er·a·tion (mod′ə rā′shən), NOUN. **in moderation,** without going to extremes: *It is all right to eat candy in moderation.*

mod·ern (mod′ərn), ADJECTIVE.
1 of or relating to the present time; of times not long past: *Television is a modern invention.*
■ See the Synonym Study at **new.**
2 having new ideas about things; not old-fashioned: *They are young and have modern views on life.*

mod·ern·ize (mod′ər nīz), VERB. to make or become modern: *We plan to modernize our kitchen.* ❑ VERB **mod·ern·iz·es, mod·ern·ized, mod·ern·iz·ing. —mod′ern·i·za′tion,** NOUN.

mod·est (mod′ist), ADJECTIVE.
1 not thinking too highly of yourself; not vain: *In spite of many honors, the scientist remained a modest person.*
2 using only what is proper or polite in speech, clothing, and so on.
3 unwilling to call attention to yourself; not bold: *Some professional athletes are quite modest about their unusual skills.* ■ See the Synonym Study at **shy.**
4 not very large or impressive: *a modest house.* **—mod′est·ly,** ADVERB.

mod·est·y (mod′ə stē), NOUN. the quality of not thinking too highly of yourself; humble.

mod·i·fy (mod′ə fī), VERB.
1 to change something in order to make it better or different: *They have modified the design of that car.*
2 to limit the meaning of a word or phrase: *In "red rose," the adjective "red" modifies "rose."*
❑ VERB **mod·i·fies, mod·i·fied, mod·i·fy·ing. —mod′i·fi·ca′tion,** NOUN.

mod·ule (moj′ül), NOUN. a unit or system complete in itself which is part of a larger system and is designed for a particular use: *The astronauts landed on the moon in the spacecraft's lunar module.*

Mo·ham·med (mō ham′id), NOUN. another spelling of **Muhammad.**

Mo·hawk (mō′hòk), NOUN. a member of a tribe of American Indians living in New York, Ontario, and Quebec. ❑ PLURAL **Mo·hawk** or **Mo·hawks.**

moist (moist), ADJECTIVE. slightly wet; damp: *You should apply the polish with a moist cloth.* ■ See the Synonym Study at **damp.**

mois·ten (mois′n), VERB. to make or become moist: *His eyes moistened with tears.* ❑ VERB **mois·tens, mois·tened, mois·ten·ing.**

mois·ture (mois′chər), NOUN. water or other liquid spread in very small drops in the air or on a surface.

Mo·ja·ve (mō hä′vē), NOUN. a large desert in California.

mo·lar (mō′lər), NOUN. one of the large back teeth with a broad surface for grinding. Adult human beings have twelve molars.

mo·las·ses (mə las′iz), NOUN. a sweet, brown syrup. Molasses is produced during the process of making sugar from sugar cane.

mold¹ (mōld),
1 NOUN. a hollow container that you pour something into. When the soft material hardens, it will have the shape of the container.
2 VERB. to make or form something into shape: *We molded the dough into loaves to be baked.*
❑ VERB **molds, mold·ed, mold·ing.**

mold² (mōld),
1 NOUN. a fuzzy growth, often greenish in color, that appears on food and other things when they are left too long in a warm, moist place. Mold is a fungus.
2 VERB. to become covered with mold: *This food will mold unless you refrigerate it.*
❑ VERB **molds, mold·ed, mold·ing.**

mold·ing (mōl′ding), NOUN. a strip, usually of wood, around the upper or lower walls of a room, or around doorways or window frames.

Mol·do·va (mòl dō′və), NOUN. a country in southeastern Europe.

mold·y (mōl′dē), ADJECTIVE.
1 covered with mold: *moldy cheese.*
2 musty; stale: *The closet had a moldy smell.*
❑ ADJECTIVE **mold·i·er, mold·i·est. —mold′i·ness,** NOUN.

mole¹ (mōl), NOUN. a spot on the skin, usually brown.

mole² (mōl), NOUN. a small animal that lives underground most of the time. Moles have soft, smooth fur and very small eyes that cannot see well.

mole² — from 5 to 8 inches long, including the tail

mol·e·cule (mol′ə kyül), NOUN. the smallest particle into which a substance can be divided without changing it into a different substance. Molecules are made of atoms bonded together.

mole·hill (mōl′hil′), NOUN. a small mound or ridge of dirt raised up by moles burrowing underground.

mol·lusk (mol′əsk), NOUN. an animal with a soft body, sometimes protected with a shell. Snails, oysters, clams, octopuses, and squid are mollusks.

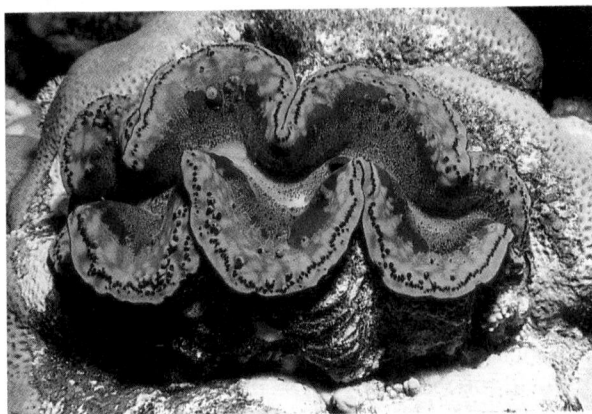

This giant clam is a kind of **mollusk.**

Mo·lo·kai (mō′lō kī′), NOUN. the fifth largest island of Hawaii.

molt (mōlt), VERB. to shed the feathers, skin, hair, or shell before a new growth. Birds, snakes, and insects molt. ❑ VERB **molts, molt·ed, molt·ing.**

mol·ten (mōlt′n), ADJECTIVE. melted: *Molten rock is called lava.*

mom (mom), NOUN. (informal) mother.

mo·ment (mō′mənt), NOUN.
1 a very short amount or length of time; instant: *I'll be with you in a moment.*
2 a particular point of time: *I started the very moment I got your message.*

mo·men·tar·i·ly (mō′mən ter′ə lē), ADVERB.
1 for a moment: *She hesitated momentarily.*
2 in a moment; very soon: *I'll finish my homework momentarily.*

mo·men·tar·y (mō′mən ter′ē), ADJECTIVE. lasting only a very short time: *There was a momentary hesitation before she spoke.*

mo·men·tous (mō men′təs), ADJECTIVE. very important: *Choosing between peace and war is a momentous decision.*

mo·men·tum (mō men′təm), NOUN. the force with which an object moves: *A falling object gains momentum as it falls. The momentum of the racing cars carried them far beyond the finish line.*

mom·ma (mom′ə), NOUN. (informal) mother.
❑ PLURAL **mom·mas.**

mom·my (mom′ē), NOUN. (informal) mother.
❑ PLURAL **mom·mies.**

Mon., an abbreviation of **Monday.**

mon·arch (mon′ərk), NOUN.
1 a king, queen, emperor, or other ruler.
2 a large, orange and black butterfly.

Word Story

Monarch comes from a Greek word meaning "alone." In old times, a monarch ruled alone, and a country has only one monarch at a time.

mon·ar·chy (mon′ər kē), NOUN.
1 government by a monarch.
2 a nation governed by a monarch.
❑ PLURAL **mon·ar·chies.**

mon·as·ter·y (mon′ə ster′ē), NOUN. a building or buildings where monks live and work together.
❑ PLURAL **mon·as·ter·ies.**

Mon·day (mun′dā′), NOUN. the second day of the week; the day after Sunday.

Word Story

Monday comes from an earlier English word meaning "the moon's day." It was called this because it follows Sunday, that is, the sun's day.

mon·ey (mun′ē), NOUN.
1 coins and paper that you can buy and sell things with.
2 wealth: *He is a man of money.*

Word Story

Money comes from a Latin word meaning "she who protects." This was a description of the goddess *Juno* (jü′nō). The Romans made coins in Juno's temple. **Mint**[2] comes from the same Latin word.

Mon·go·li·a (mong gō′lē ə), NOUN. a country in central Asia.

mon·goose (mong′güs), NOUN. a slender animal of Africa and Asia. It is famous for its ability to kill poisonous snakes. ❑ PLURAL **mon·goos·es.**

mon·grel (mung′grəl or mong′grəl), NOUN. an animal or plant of mixed breed, especially a dog.

mon·i·tor (mon′ə tər),
1 NOUN. a pupil in school who has special duties, such as taking attendance.
2 NOUN. a receiver or other device that is used to listen to or watch something: *Most banks have TV monitors to observe customers and to prevent holdups.*
3 VERB. to listen to or watch something, using a receiver or other device: *Police monitor traffic by using cars equipped with radar.*

a	hat	ė	term	ô	order	ch	child
ā	age	i	it	oi	oil	ng	long
ä	far	ī	ice	ou	out	sh	she
â	care	o	hot	u	cup	th	thin
e	let	ō	open	u̇	put	ŦH	then
ē	equal	ȯ	saw	ü	rule	zh	measure

ə { a in about / e in taken / i in pencil / o in lemon / u in circus

M

4 NOUN. a screen on which a computer shows information or instructions. A television set may be used as a monitor with some computers.
❑ VERB **mon·i·tors, mon·i·tored, mon·i·tor·ing.**

monk (mungk), NOUN. a man who gives up everything else for religion and enters a monastery to live.

mon·key (mung′kē),
1 NOUN. one of the many smaller animals of the group most like human beings, not a gorilla or other large ape. Monkeys have long tails, and hands and feet that can hold things.
2 VERB. often, **monkey around,** to play around with or fool with something: *Don't monkey around with the computer.*
❑ PLURAL **mon·keys;** VERB **mon·keys, mon·keyed, mon·key·ing.**

South American spider **monkeys**

monkey bars. See **jungle gym.**

monkey wrench, a wrench with a movable jaw that can be adjusted to fit different sizes of nuts.

mon·o·cle (mon′ə kəl), NOUN. (earlier) a glass lens for one eye.

mon·o·gram (mon′ə gram), NOUN. someone's initials combined in one design. Monograms are used on note paper, table linen, clothing, jewelry, and so on.

mon·o·logue (mon′l ȯg), NOUN.
1 a long speech by one person in a group.
2 a part of a play in which a single actor speaks alone.
❑ PLURAL **mon·o·logues.**

mon·o·plane (mon′ə plān), NOUN. an airplane with only one pair of wings. Most modern airplanes are monoplanes.

mo·nop·o·lize (mə nop′ə līz), VERB.
1 to have or get complete possession or control of a product or service: *One company monopolized the telephone service in our area.*
2 to keep other people from sharing in something: *Don't monopolize your teacher's time.*
❑ VERB **mo·nop·o·liz·es, mo·nop·o·lized, mo·nop·o·liz·ing.**

mo·nop·o·ly (mə nop′ə lē), NOUN.
1 the complete control of a product or service: *The electric company has a monopoly on providing electrical service in the area it serves.*
2 a person or company with complete control of a product or service.
❑ PLURAL **mo·nop·o·lies.**

mon·o·rail (mon′ə rāl), NOUN.
1 a single rail serving as a complete track for the vehicles that are either balanced on it or that hang from it.
2 a railway in which cars run on a single rail, either balancing on it or hanging from it.

mon·o·syl·la·ble (mon′ə sil′ə bəl), NOUN. a word of one syllable. *Yes* and *no* are monosyllables.

mon·o·tone (mon′ə tōn), NOUN. a way of speaking without changing the pitch of your voice: *Don't read in a monotone; use expression.*

mo·not·o·nous (mə not′n əs), ADJECTIVE.
1 speaking always with the same tone: *She spoke in a monotonous voice.*
2 tiring or boring because of its sameness: *Sorting mail is monotonous work. Eating the same thing for lunch every day becomes monotonous.*
■ See the Synonym Study at **dull.**
—**mo·not′o·nous·ly,** ADVERB.
—**mo·not′o·nous·ness,** NOUN.

mo·not·o·ny (mə not′n ē), NOUN. lack of variety; tiring or boring sameness: *Some people complain about the monotony of the desert landscape.*

mon·soon (mon sün′), NOUN.
1 a powerful wind of the Indian Ocean and southern Asia. It blows from the southwest from April to October and from the northeast during the rest of the year.
2 a season during which this wind blows from the southwest, usually bringing heavy rains.

mon·ster (mon′stər),
1 NOUN. a make-believe person or animal that is scary. Dragons, zombies, and werewolves are monsters.
2 ADJECTIVE. huge: *The movie was a monster success. We made a monster snowman.*
3 NOUN. a huge creature or thing.

monster from an old movie

mon·stros·i·ty
(mon stros′ə tē), NOUN. something that is huge, ugly, shocking, or horrible: *That new building is a monstrosity.* ❑ PLURAL **mon·stros·i·ties.**

mon·strous (mon′strəs), ADJECTIVE.
1 horrible; dreadful: *Murder is a monstrous crime.*
2 huge; enormous: *A monstrous wave sank the tiny fishing boat.*

Mon·tan·a (mon tan′ə), NOUN. one of the Rocky Mountain states of the United States. *Abbreviation:* MT; *Capital:* Helena. —**Mon·tan′an,** NOUN.

State Story **Montana** comes from a Spanish word meaning "region having many mountains."

Mont·gom·er·y (mont gum/ər ē), NOUN. the capital of Alabama.

month (munth), NOUN. one of the twelve periods of time into which a year is divided. April, June, September, and November have 30 days; February has 28 days except in leap years; all the other months have 31 days.

Word Story

Month comes from an old English word related to **moon**. The time from one full moon to the next is about a month long—which is probably why we have months at all.

month·ly (munth/lē),
1 ADJECTIVE. of or for a month; lasting a month: *a monthly supply, a monthly salary.*
2 ADJECTIVE. done, happening, or paid once a month: *a monthly meeting, a monthly examination.*
3 ADVERB. once a month; every month: *Some magazines come monthly.*
4 NOUN. a magazine published once a month.
❑ PLURAL **month·lies.**

Mont·pel·ier (mont pē/lyər), NOUN. the capital of Vermont.

Mon·tre·al (mon/trē ȯl/), NOUN. a city in Canada.

mon·u·ment (mon/yə mənt), NOUN.
1 something set up to honor a person or an event; anything that keeps alive the memory of a person or an event. A monument may be a building, pillar, arch, statue, tomb, or stone.
2 something recognized as an excellent example of its type: *Her novel is a monument of literature.*

mon·u·men·tal (mon/yə men/tl), ADJECTIVE.
1 serving as a monument: *a monumental chapel.*
2 lasting; important: *The Constitution of the United States is a monumental document.*

moo (mü),
1 NOUN. the sound made by a cow.
2 VERB. to make this sound.
❑ PLURAL **moos;** VERB **moos, mooed, moo·ing.**

moose — about 7 feet high at the shoulder

mood (müd), NOUN. the way someone is feeling: *I am in the mood to play now; I don't want to study.*

mood·y (mü/dē), ADJECTIVE.
1 likely to have changes of mood, often becoming sad or depressed: *She has been moody ever since she lost her job.*
2 quietly sad; gloomy: *He sat in moody silence.*
❑ ADJECTIVE **mood·i·er, mood·i·est. —mood/i·ness,** NOUN.

moon (mün), NOUN.
1 the large shining object in the night sky. It revolves around the earth once in about 29½ days. The moon looks bright because it reflects the sun's light.
2 any object that, like our moon, revolves around another planet: *the moons of Jupiter.*
3 the American Indian month of about 29½ days.

moon

Have You Heard?

You may have heard the phrase **"once in a blue moon."** Something that happens once in a blue moon means that it happens very rarely or hardly ever.

moon·light (mün/lit/), NOUN. the light of the moon.

moor¹ (mur), VERB. to put or keep a boat or ship in place by means of ropes or chains fastened to the shore or to anchors: *We moored the boat to the dock.* ❑ VERB **moors, moored, moor·ing.**

moor² (mur), NOUN. an open wasteland, usually covered with heather: *Sheep are raised on the moors of Scotland.*

Moor (mur), NOUN. someone who was born or lived in northwestern Africa. The Moors were Muslims who spoke Arabic. In the A.D. 700s the Moors invaded and conquered Spain. They were driven out in 1492.

moose (müs), NOUN. an animal that looks like a very large deer, living in Canada, the northern part of the United States, and Eurasia. The male has a large head and broad antlers. ❑ PLURAL **moose.**

mop (mop),
1 NOUN. a bundle of coarse yarn or cloth, or a sponge, fastened at the end of a long handle and used to clean floors, dishes, and other things.
2 VERB. to wash or wipe up the floor with a mop.

a	hat	ė	term	ô	order	ch	child		a in about
ā	age	i	it	oi	oil	ng	long		e in taken
ä	far	ī	ice	ou	out	sh	she	ə	i in pencil
â	care	o	hot	u	cup	th	thin		o in lemon
e	let	ō	open	ù	put	ᴛʜ	then		u in circus
ē	equal	ȯ	saw	ü	rule	zh	measure		

3 VERB. to wipe tears or sweat from: *She mopped her brow with a handkerchief.*
❑ VERB **mops, mopped, mop·ping.**

mope (mōp), VERB. to be sad and feel sorry for yourself: *He has been moping indoors all afternoon.* ❑ VERB **mopes, moped, mop·ing.**

mo·ral (môr′əl),
1 ADJECTIVE. good in character or conduct; behaving according to traditional standards of right and wrong; right; just: *a moral person.*
2 NOUN. **morals,** character or behavior in matters of right and wrong: *a person of excellent morals.*
3 ADJECTIVE. of or about the difference between right and wrong: *Whether to keep a large sum of money you have found or to turn it over to the police is a moral question.*
4 NOUN. the lesson or teaching of a fable, a story, or an event: *The moral of the story was "Look before you leap."*

mo·rale (mə ral′), NOUN. the confidence or enthusiasm of a person or group: *The morale of the team was low after its defeat.*

Usage Note

Morale and **moral** look alike, and they both come from a Latin word meaning "customs." So it is easy to confuse them. One way to remember the difference is that **morale** ends in e, for energy, efficiency, and enthusiasm.

mo·ral·i·ty (mə ral′ə tē), NOUN.
1 the rightness or wrongness of an action: *They spent the evening arguing about the morality of war.*
2 good actions; virtue: *high standards of morality.*

mo·ral·ly (môr′ə lē), ADVERB.
1 in a moral manner: *to behave morally.*
2 from a moral point of view: *What they did was morally wrong.*

mo·ray (môr′ā), NOUN. a fierce, often brightly colored eel found in warm seas.

mor·bid (môr′bid), ADJECTIVE. horrible; gruesome: *the morbid details of a murder.* **–mor′bid·ly,** ADVERB.

more (môr),
1 ADJECTIVE. greater in amount, degree, or number: *more humid, more people. A foot is more than an inch.* ★ **More** is the comparative of **much** and **many.**
2 NOUN. a greater or additional amount, degree, or number: *Tell me more about your camping trip.*
3 ADVERB. to a greater degree or extent: *A burn hurts more than a scratch does.* ★ **More** is the comparative of **much.**
4 ADVERB. in addition; farther: *Take one step more.*
5 ADJECTIVE. further; additional: *This plant needs more sun.*
6 ADVERB. *More* is part of the comparative form of most adverbs, and of most adjectives longer than one syllable: *more easily, more truly, more careful.*

more or less, IDIOM.
1 somewhat: *Most people are more or less honest.*
2 about; approximately: *The distance is 50 miles, more or less.*

Mo·re·los (mō re′lōs *or* mə rā′ləs), NOUN. a state in south central Mexico.

more·o·ver (môr ō′vər), ADVERB. also; besides: *I don't want to go skating; moreover, it's too cold.*

morn·ing (môr′ning), NOUN. the early part of the day, ending at noon. ■ Another word that sounds like this is **mourning.**

morning glory, a climbing vine that has funnel-shaped blue, lavender, pink, or white flowers. Its flowers open early in the morning but close later in the sunlight. ❑ PLURAL **morn·ing glo·ries.**

morning glory

Mo·roc·co (mə rok′ō), NOUN. a country in northern Africa. **–Mo·roc′can,** ADJECTIVE *or* NOUN.

morph (môrf), VERB.
1 to change one picture into another one, so that the process of change is either invisible or very smooth, using a computer: *He morphed the picture of a baby's face into a picture of a kitten's face.*
2 to change in this way from one appearance to another: *The alien morphed from lizard form to tiger form.*
❑ VERB **morphs, morphed, morph·ing.**

Morse code (môrs′ kōd′), a system by which letters are expressed by dots, dashes, and spaces or by long and short sounds or flashes of light. Morse code is now rarely used.

mor·sel (môr′səl), NOUN. a small piece or amount, especially of food: *I was so hungry I ate every morsel on my plate.*

mor·tal (môr′tl),
1 ADJECTIVE. sure to die sometime: *All of us are mortal.*
2 NOUN. a human being: *No mortal could have survived the fire.*
3 ADJECTIVE. causing death: *a mortal illness.*
4 ADJECTIVE. lasting until death: *a mortal enemy.*
5 ADJECTIVE. very great; extreme: *mortal terror.* **–mor′tal·ly,** ADVERB.

mor·tar (môr'tər), NOUN. a mixture of lime, dry cement, sand, and water for holding bricks or stones together.

mort·gage (môr'gij), NOUN. a loan given to the buyer of a building, or of land, used to pay for the property. The lender holds a claim to the property until the loan is repaid.

mo·sa·ic (mō zā'ik), NOUN. a picture or design made by setting small pieces of stone, glass, or tile into a flat surface. Mosaics are used in the floors, walls, or ceilings of some fine buildings.

a **mosaic** from 7th-century Jerusalem

Mos·cow (mos'kou), NOUN. the capital of Russia and formerly of the Soviet Union.

Mos·lem (moz'ləm), NOUN or ADJECTIVE. another spelling of **Muslim.**

mosque (mosk), NOUN. a Muslim place of worship. ❑ PLURAL **mosques.**

mo·squi·to (mə skē'tō), NOUN. a small, slender insect with two wings. The female bites and sucks blood from people and animals, causing itching. There are many kinds of mosquitoes; one kind transmits malaria; another transmits yellow fever. ❑ PLURAL **mo·squi·toes** or **mo·squi·tos.**

moss (mȯs), NOUN. the very small, soft, flat, green plants that grow close together like a carpet on the ground, on rocks, or on trees. ❑ PLURAL **moss·es.**

moss·y (mȯ'sē), ADJECTIVE. covered with moss: *a mossy bank.* ❑ ADJECTIVE **moss·i·er, moss·i·est.**

most (mōst),
1 ADJECTIVE. greatest in amount, degree, or number: *The winner gets the most money.* ★ **Most** is the superlative of **much** and **many.**
2 NOUN. the greatest amount, degree, or number: *We did most of the work around the house.*
3 ADVERB. in the highest degree; to the greatest extent: *This tooth hurts most. They were most kind to me.* ★ **Most** is the superlative of **much.**
4 ADJECTIVE. almost all: *Most people like ice cream.*

5 ADVERB. *Most* helps to make the superlative form of almost all adverbs, and of almost all adjectives longer than one syllable: *most easily, most truly, most careful.*

most·ly (mōst'lē), ADVERB. almost all; for the most part; mainly; chiefly: *The work is mostly done.*

mo·tel (mō tel'), NOUN. a hotel along or near a highway where motorists can rent a room to sleep in.

moth (môth), NOUN.
a winged insect like a butterfly, but having a thicker body and flying mostly at night. There are over 100,000 kinds of moths. One kind lays eggs in cloth and fur, and its larvae eat holes in the material. Some moth larvae, such as silkworms, are useful to people. ❑ PLURAL **moths** (mȯᴛʜz or mȯths).

The smallest **moths** have a ⅛ inch wingspread. The largest moths can have a wingspread of 12 inches.

moth·er (muᴛʜ'ər),
1 NOUN. a woman who has a child or children.
2 VERB. to take care of someone as a mother does: *She mothers her baby sister.*
3 NOUN. the cause or source of anything: *Necessity is the mother of invention.*
4 ADJECTIVE. native: *English is our mother tongue.* ❑ VERB **moth·ers, moth·ered, moth·er·ing.** —**moth'er·less,** ADJECTIVE.

moth·er-in-law (muᴛʜ'ər in lȯ'), NOUN. the mother of your husband or wife. ❑ PLURAL **moth·ers-in-law.**

moth·er·ly (muᴛʜ'ər lē), ADJECTIVE. like a mother; kind: *a motherly person, a motherly smile.* —**moth'er·li·ness,** NOUN.

moth·er-of-pearl (muᴛʜ'ər əv pėrl'), NOUN. the hard, smooth, shiny lining of some seashells. It changes colors when moved or turned in the light. It is used to make buttons and ornaments.

mo·tion (mō'shən),
1 NOUN. movement; moving; change of position or place. Anything is in motion which is not still: *Can you feel the motion of the ship?*
2 NOUN. a movement of the hand, the head, and so on, to send someone a message.
3 VERB. to make a movement, as of the hand or head, to get someone to do something: *She motioned to us to come over to her side of the room.*
4 NOUN. a formal suggestion made in a meeting, to be voted on: *I made a motion to adjourn.* ❑ VERB **mo·tions, mo·tioned, mo·tion·ing.**

a	hat	ė	term	ô	order	ch	child		a in about
ā	age	i	it	oi	oil	ng	long		e in taken
ä	far	ī	ice	ou	out	sh	she	ə {	i in pencil
â	care	o	hot	u	cup	th	thin		o in lemon
e	let	ō	open	u̇	put	ᴛʜ	then		u in circus
ē	equal	ȯ	saw	ü	rule	zh	measure		

go through the motions, IDIOM. to do something required, without enthusiasm or effort: *Although I did not want to see his snapshots, I went through the motions of looking at them.*

mo·tion·less (mō'shən lis), ADJECTIVE. not moving.

motion picture. See **movie.**

mo·tive (mō'tiv), NOUN. a thought or feeling that makes you do something: *My motive in going was a wish to travel.*

mo·to·cross (mō'tō cros'), NOUN. a motorcycle race run over rugged trails with hills and curves, rather than on a flat paved track. ❑ PLURAL **mo·to·cross·es.**

racing in a **motocross**

mo·tor (mō'tər),
1 NOUN. an engine that makes a machine work: *an electric motor.*
2 ADJECTIVE. run by a motor: *a motor vehicle.*
3 ADJECTIVE. causing motion. Motor nerves arouse muscle contraction.

mo·tor·boat (mō'tər bōt'), NOUN. a boat that is powered by a motor.

mo·tor·cy·cle (mō'tər sī'kəl), NOUN. a motor vehicle with two wheels. It looks like a bicycle but is heavier and larger.

mo·tor·ist (mō'tər ist), NOUN. someone who drives or travels in a car.

motor vehicle, any vehicle run by a motor, which travels on wheels on roads and highways. Cars, trucks, buses, and motorcycles are motor vehicles.

mot·to (mot'ō), NOUN.
1 a brief sentence adopted as a rule of conduct: *"Think before you speak" is my motto.*
2 a sentence, word, or phrase that shows the beliefs or ideals of a person, group, school and so on. It is usually written or engraved on some object. ❑ PLURAL **mot·toes** or **mot·tos.**

mound (mound), NOUN.
1 a bank or pile of earth, stones, or other material: *a mound of hay.*
2 the slightly elevated area that a baseball pitcher pitches from.

mount¹ (mount),
1 VERB. to go up something: *to mount a hill, to mount a ladder.*
2 VERB. to get up on an animal that you are going to ride: *to mount a horse.* ■ See the Synonym Study at **climb.**
3 NOUN. a horse for riding: *The riding instructor had an excellent mount.*
4 VERB. to rise; increase; rise in amount: *The cost of living mounts steadily.*
5 VERB. to fasten something in a setting, backing, or support: *to mount a picture on cardboard.* ❑ VERB **mounts, mount·ed, mount·ing.**

mount² (mount), NOUN. a mountain; high hill. *Mount* is often used before the names of mountains, as in *Mount Everest.*

moun·tain (moun'tən), NOUN.
1 a very high hill.
2 a very large heap or pile of anything: *There is a mountain of dirty laundry in my room.*
3 a huge amount: *She overcame a mountain of difficulties.*

Have You Heard?

You may have heard someone say **"Don't make a mountain out of a molehill."** This means that you are acting as if something is very important when really it is very small.

moun·tain·eer (moun'tə nir'), NOUN. someone skilled in mountain climbing.

mountain goat, a white, goatlike antelope of the Rocky Mountains. It has black horns and a beard.

mountain lion, a large cat with brownish yellow fur, that lives in parts of North and South America; puma; cougar; panther.

moun·tain·ous (moun'tə nəs), ADJECTIVE.
1 covered with mountain ranges: *mountainous country.*
2 huge: *a mountainous wave.*

mountain range, a row of mountains; large group of mountains.

mourn (môrn), VERB. to feel very sad and show sorrow over: *They mourned their daughter's death.* ❑ VERB **mourns, mourned, mourn·ing. –mourn'er,** NOUN.

mourn·ing (mor'ning), NOUN. sign of sorrow for someone's death, such as the wearing of black clothing or the flying of flags at half-mast. ■ Another word that sounds like this is **morning.**

in mourning, IDIOM. feeling great sadness or grief about someone's death.

mouse (mous), NOUN.
1 a small animal with soft fur, a pointed snout, and a long, thin tail. Some kinds of mice live in people's houses. Other kinds live in fields and meadows.

2 a rounded box small enough to fit in one hand, connected to a computer by an electric cord, usually with a button or buttons for giving commands. Moving it across a flat surface controls the movement of a pointer on the computer screen. ★ Another plural form for this meaning is **mous·es** (mou′siz).
❏ PLURAL **mice. –mouse′like′**, ADJECTIVE.

mous·tache (mus′tash), NOUN. another spelling of **mustache.**

mouth (mouth), NOUN.
1 the opening in the face of a human being or an animal where food is taken in.
2 the opening to something that looks like a mouth: *the mouth of a cave, the mouth of a bottle.*
3 the part of a river where its waters flow into some other body of water.
❏ PLURAL **mouths** (mouᴛʜz).

mouth·ful (mouth′fůl), NOUN. as much as the mouth can easily hold. ❏ PLURAL **mouth·fuls.**

mouth·piece (mouth′pēs′), NOUN. the part of a musical instrument, telephone, pipe, or the like, that is placed in or against someone's mouth.

mouth·wash (mouth′wäsh′), NOUN. a flavored liquid used to rinse your mouth and teeth.
❏ PLURAL **mouth·wash·es.**

mov·a·ble (mü′və bəl), ADJECTIVE.
1 able to be moved, or to be carried from place to place: *movable furniture.*
2 changing from one date to another in different years: *Thanksgiving is a movable holiday.*

move (müv),
1 VERB. to put something in a different place: *Move your chair to the table.*
2 VERB. to change place or position: *The child moved in his sleep.*
3 VERB. to change the place where you live: *We move to the country next week.*
4 VERB. to put or keep something in motion; shake; stir: *The wind moves the leaves.*
5 VERB. to make progress; go: *The train moved slowly.*
6 NOUN. the act of moving; movement: *an impatient move of the head.*
7 NOUN. an action taken to bring about some result: *Our next move was to earn some money.*
8 VERB. (in games) to change to a different square according to the rules: *to move a pawn in chess.*
9 NOUN. the act of moving a piece in chess and other games: *That was a good move.*
10 VERB. (in a meeting) to suggest or propose something: *Madam Chairman, I move that the report of the treasurer be adopted.*
❏ VERB **moves, moved, mov·ing.**

move in, IDIOM. to move yourself, your family, and your belongings into a new place to live: *The new couple is moving in next week.*

move out, IDIOM. to move yourself, your family, and your belongings out of the place where you have been living: *We have to move out by the end of the month.*

Synonym Study

Move means to change the position of something: *She moved her chair closer to the table.*

Shift means to move something to a different place or position, especially one nearby: *She shifted on the cushion, trying to get comfortable.*

Transfer means to change the position of something: *He transferred his loose change from one pocket to the other.*

Remove means to move something from one place to another: *I removed the cake carefully from the oven.*

See also the Synonym Studies at **pull** and **push.**

move·ment (müv′mənt), NOUN.
1 the act or fact of moving: *We run by movements of the legs.*
2 the moving parts of a machine. The movement of a watch consists of many little wheels.
3 the efforts and results of a group of people working together to reach a common goal: *The civil rights movement was responsible for many new laws.*
4 one of the separate sections of a musical composition such as a symphony, sonata, and so on.

mov·er (mü′vər), NOUN. a person or company whose work is moving furniture from one house or place to another.

Movers work very hard.

a	hat	ė	term	ô	order	ch	child		a in about
ā	age	i	it	oi	oil	ng	long		e in taken
ä	far	ī	ice	ou	out	sh	she	ə<	i in pencil
â	care	o	hot	u	cup	th	thin		o in lemon
e	let	ō	open	ů	put	ᴛʜ	then		u in circus
ē	equal	ò	saw	ü	rule	zh	measure		

M

mov·ie (mü′vē), NOUN.
1 a series of pictures shown on a screen quickly enough that the images seem to be moving; motion picture.
2 **the movies,** a showing of such a story: *I like to go to the movies.*
❑ PLURAL **mov·ies.**

mov·ing (mü′ving), ADJECTIVE.
1 changing or able to change place or position: *a moving car.*
2 stirring pity, tender feelings, or other emotions: *a moving story.*

mow (mō), VERB. to cut down grass or grain with a machine or a scythe: *to mow grass, to mow a field of alfalfa.* ❑ VERB **mows, mowed** or **mown, mow·ing.** —**mow′er,** NOUN.

mown (mōn), VERB. a past participle of **mow:** *Harvesters have mown down wheat in all the nearby fields.* ■ Another word that sounds like this is **moan.**

Mo·zam·bique (mō′zam bēk′), NOUN. a country in southeastern Africa. —**Mo·zam·bi·can** (mō′zam bē′kən), ADJECTIVE or NOUN.

mph or **m.p.h.,** miles per hour.

Mr. (mis′tər), a title used before a man's name or the name of his position: *Mr. Stern, Mr. Speaker.*

MRI, an image of parts of the body made without using X rays.

Mrs. (mis′iz), a title used before a married woman's name: *Mrs. Jackson.*

MS, an abbreviation of **Mississippi.**

Ms. or **Ms** (miz), a title used before a woman's name: *Ms. Karen Hansen.*

Usage Note

Ms. is used by both married and unmarried women. **Mrs.** is used by married women. **Miss** is used by unmarried women, and sometimes in speaking to a woman whose name is not known. **Ms.** is often used when writing to a woman if you do not know whether she is married or not. In speaking or referring to someone in person, it is wise to ask which title she prefers.

MT, an abbreviation of **Montana.**

Mt., an abbreviation of **mount²** or **mountain.**
❑ PLURAL **Mts.**

much (much),
1 ADJECTIVE. in great amount or degree: *much rain, much pleasure, not much money.*
2 NOUN. a great amount: *I did not hear much of the talk. Too much of this cake will make you sick. Don't make too much of a fuss about it.*
3 ADVERB. to a high degree; greatly: *much better weather. I was much pleased with the toy.*
4 ADVERB. nearly; about: *This is much the same as the others.*
❑ ADJECTIVE **more, most;** ADVERB **more, most.**

how much, IDIOM.
1 what price: *How much is that shirt?*
2 what amount of: *How much ice cream did you eat?*

muck (muk), NOUN. wet, sloppy dirt or filth.

mu·cus (myü′kəs), NOUN. a slimy substance that moistens and protects the linings of the body. A cold in the head causes mucus to flow freely.

mud (mud), NOUN. very wet earth that is soft and sticky: *mud on the ground after rain.*

mud·dle (mud′l),
1 VERB. to mix things up into a real mess: *Somebody really muddled that job.*
2 VERB. to think or act in a confused, blundering way: *to muddle through a difficulty.*
3 NOUN. a mess; disorder; confusion: *After the party the room was in a muddle.*
❑ VERB **mud·dles, mud·dled, mud·dling.**

playing in the **mud**

mud·dy (mud′ē),
1 ADJECTIVE. having a lot of mud; covered with mud: *a muddy road.*
2 ADJECTIVE. clouded with, or as is with, mud: *muddy water, a muddy color.*
3 VERB. to make or become muddy: *His boots muddied the floor when he came into the house. She muddied her clothes digging in the garden.*
❑ ADJECTIVE **mud·di·er, mud·di·est;** VERB **mud·dies, mud·died, mud·dy·ing.** —**mud′di·ness,** NOUN.

muff (muf),
1 NOUN. (earlier) a covering of fur or other material for keeping both hands warm. One hand is put in at each end.
2 VERB. to do something badly or awkwardly: *He muffed his chance to get the job.*
❑ VERB **muffs, muffed, muff·ing.**

muf·fin (muf′ən), NOUN. a small, round cake made of wheat flour, cornmeal, or the like. Muffins are often served hot.

muf·fle (muf′əl), VERB.
1 to make a sound quieter or softer: *The strong wind muffled our voices.*
2 to wrap or cover something up in order to keep it warm and dry: *I muffled up in a warm scarf.*
❑ VERB **muf·fles, muf·fled, muf·fling.**

muf·fler (muf′lər), NOUN.
1 anything used to make a sound quieter or softer. A car muffler fastened to the exhaust pipe deadens the sound of the engine's exhaust.
2 a scarf worn around the neck for warmth.

mug (mug),
1 *NOUN.* a heavy china or metal drinking cup with a handle.
2 *NOUN.* the amount a mug holds: *drink a mug of milk.*
3 *VERB.* to attack someone, usually in order to rob him or her.
❑ *VERB* **mugs, mugged, mug·ging.**

mug·gy (mug′ē), *ADJECTIVE.* warm and humid: *Yesterday the weather was muggy.* ❑ *ADJECTIVE* **mug·gi·er, mug·gi·est. –mug′gi·ness,** *NOUN.*

Mu·ham·mad (mù ham′əd), *NOUN.* A.D. 570?-632, Arab prophet, founder of Islam, the religion of the Muslims. Also spelled **Mohammed.**

mul·ber·ry (mul′ber′ē), *NOUN.*
1 a tree with small, berrylike fruit that can be eaten. The leaves of one kind of mulberry are used for feeding silkworms.
2 its sweet, usually dark purple fruit.
❑ *PLURAL* **mul·ber·ries.**

mulch (mulch),
1 *NOUN.* a loose material, such as straw, decaying leaves, or sawdust, that you spread on the ground around trees or plants. Mulch is used to protect the roots from cold or heat and to prevent the soil from drying out. It also makes the soil richer.
2 *VERB.* to cover plants with straw or leaves.
❑ *PLURAL* **mulches;** *VERB* **mulch·es, mulched, mulch·ing.**

mule (myül), *NOUN.* an animal which is the offspring of a male donkey and a female horse. It has the shape and size of a horse, but the large ears, small hoofs, and tail of a donkey.

mul·lah (mul′ə), *NOUN.* a title of respect for someone who is learned in Islamic law; a religious scholar or leader.

mul·let (mul′it), *NOUN.* a fish that lives close to the shore in warm waters. **Gray mullet** are larger, live close to shore, and are good to eat. **Red mullet** are small and brightly colored. ❑ *PLURAL* **mul·let** or **mul·lets.**

mul·ti·cul·tur·al (mul′ti kul′chər əl), *ADJECTIVE.* having or representing many different cultures: *a multicultural society.*

mul·ti·me·di·a (mul′ti mē′dē ə), *ADJECTIVE.* using a combination of different media, such as tapes, films, CDs, and photographs, to entertain, communicate, or teach.

mul·ti·ple (mul′tə pəl),
1 *ADJECTIVE.* of, having, or involving many parts: *She is a person of multiple interests.*
2 *NOUN.* a number that can be divided by another number without a remainder: *12 and 6 are multiples of 3.*

mul·ti·ple scle·ro·sis (mul′ti pəl sklə rō′sis), a disease of the nervous system that attacks the brain and the spinal cord.

mul·ti·pli·cand (mul′tə plə kand′), *NOUN.* a number to be multiplied by another: *In 497 multiplied by 5, the multiplicand is 497.*

mul·ti·pli·ca·tion (mul′tə plə kā′shən), *NOUN.* the operation of multiplying one number by another: $12 \times 3 = 36$ *is a simple multiplication.*

multiplication sign, the symbol × or a centered dot, used to show the operation of multiplying. EXAMPLES: $2 \times 2 = 4$; $2 \cdot 2 = 4$.

mul·ti·pli·er (mul′tə pli′ər), *NOUN.* a number by which another number is to be multiplied: *In* 83×5, *5 is the multiplier.*

mul·ti·ply (mul′tə pli), *VERB.*
1 to add a number a stated number of times: *To multiply 6 by 3 means to add 6 three times, making 18.*
2 to increase in number: *As we climbed up the mountain, the dangers and difficulties multiplied.*
❑ *VERB* **mul·ti·plies, mul·ti·plied, mul·ti·ply·ing.**

mul·ti·tude (mul′tə tüd), *NOUN.* a great many; crowd: *a multitude of difficulties, a multitude of enemies.*

mum·ble (mum′bəl),
1 *VERB.* to speak unclearly, as you do when your lips are partly closed: *She mumbled something about not being able to come to the party.*
2 *NOUN.* speech or sound that is unclear; mutter: *There was a mumble of protest from the team against the umpire's decision.*
❑ *VERB* **mum·bles, mum·bled, mum·bling. –mum′bler,** *NOUN.*

mum·my (mum′ē), *NOUN.* a dead body preserved from decay. Egyptian mummies have lasted more than 3000 years.
❑ *PLURAL* **mum·mies.**

mummy

mumps (mumps), *NOUN.* a contagious disease most often of children. It causes your neck and face to swell and makes it hard for you to swallow. Vaccination can prevent mumps.

munch (munch), *VERB.* to chew steadily and vigorously: *The horse munched its oats.* ❑ *VERB* **munch·es, munched, munch·ing.**

M

a	hat	ė	term	ô	order	ch	child		a in about
ā	age	i	it	oi	oil	ng	long		e in taken
ä	far	ī	ice	ou	out	sh	she	ə	i in pencil
â	care	o	hot	u	cup	th	thin		o in lemon
e	let	ō	open	ù	put	ŦH	then		u in circus
ē	equal	ò	saw	ü	rule	zh	measure		

mu·nic·i·pal (myü nis′ə pəl), *ADJECTIVE*. of or about the affairs of a city or town: *the municipal police.*

mur·al (myùr′əl), *NOUN*. a large picture painted on a wall.

mur·al·ist (myür′ə list), *NOUN*. someone who paints murals.

muralist **Diego Rivera**

Diego Rivera was a Mexican artist. He painted murals about Mexican history and culture. His murals often had bright colors and simple figures. Some of his murals can be found in the United States.

mur·der (mėr′dər),
1 *NOUN*. the unlawful killing of a human being when it is planned beforehand.
2 *VERB*. to kill a human being intentionally.
❏ *VERB* **mur·ders, mur·dered, mur·der·ing.**

mur·der·er (mėr′dər ər), *NOUN*. someone who murders somebody.

mur·der·ous (mėr′dər əs), *ADJECTIVE*.
1 able to kill: *a murderous blow.*
2 ready or eager to murder: *a murderous villain.*

murk·y (mėr′kē), *ADJECTIVE*. dark; gloomy: *a murky prison.* ❏ *ADJECTIVE* **murk·i·er, murk·i·est.**
—**murk′i·ness,** *NOUN*.

mur·mur (mėr′mər),
1 *NOUN*. a soft, steady sound that rises and falls a little and goes on without breaks: *the murmur of a stream.*
2 *VERB*. to make such a soft, steady sound: *The brook murmured on its way down the mountain.*
❏ *VERB* **mur·murs, mur·mured, mur·mur·ing.**

mus·cle (mus′əl), *NOUN*.
1 the tissue in the bodies of people and animals made of fibers that can be tightened or loosened to make the body move.
2 a special bundle of such tissue which moves some particular bone or part: *Feel the muscles in my arm!*
▪ Another word that sounds like this is **mussel.**

mus·cu·lar (mus′kyə lər), *ADJECTIVE*.
1 of or affecting the muscles: *a muscular strain.*
2 having well-developed muscles; strong: *She has very muscular arms.*
—**mus′cu·lar·ly,** *ADVERB*.

mus·cu·lar dys·tro·phy (mus′kyə lər dis′trə fē), a disease in which the muscles slowly get weaker and weaker.

muse (myüz), *VERB*. to think about things in a relaxed way: *She spent the whole afternoon musing.* ❏ *VERB* **mus·es, mused, mus·ing.**

mu·se·um (myü zē′əm), *NOUN*. a building for displaying a collection of objects illustrating science, ancient life, art, or other subjects.

mush (mush), *NOUN*.
1 cornmeal boiled in water or milk.
2 a soft, thick mass: *After the heavy rain the old dirt road turned to mush.*
❏ *PLURAL* **mush·es.**

mush·room (mush′rüm), *NOUN*. a small fungus shaped like an umbrella, that grows very fast. Some mushrooms are good to eat, but many can poison you.

mush·y (mush′ē), *ADJECTIVE*. like mush; soft and wet: *I don't like mushy vegetables.* ▪ See the Synonym Study at **soft.** ❏ *ADJECTIVE* **mush·i·er,** or **mush·i·est.**

mushroom

mu·sic (myü′zik), *NOUN*.
1 the art of making sounds that are beautiful, and putting them together into beautiful or interesting arrangements. Music usually has melody, harmony, and rhythm.
2 beautiful, pleasing, or interesting arrangements of sounds.
3 written or printed signs for musical tones: *Can you read music?*
4 any pleasant sound: *the music of a bubbling brook.*

Word Bank

Music has a large vocabulary of its own, with many different words. If you want to learn more about music, you can begin by looking up these words in this dictionary.

accompaniment	blues	jazz	rock'n'roll
air	classical	lullaby	serenade
anthem	concerto	march	sonata
ballad	folk song	opera	symphony
bluegrass	hymn	overture	

mu·si·cal (myü′zə kəl),
1 ADJECTIVE. of or producing music: *a musical instrument, a musical composer.*
2 ADJECTIVE. sounding beautiful or pleasing; like music: *musical speech.*
3 ADJECTIVE. set to music or accompanied by music: *a musical performance.*
4 ADJECTIVE. fond of or skilled in music: *My neighbor is very musical; she plays the guitar and sings.*
5 NOUN. a play or movie with songs and dances.
—**mu′si·cal·ly,** ADVERB.

music box, a box or case with a device inside that plays music.

mu·si·cian (myü zish′ən), NOUN. someone skilled in music, especially someone who sings, plays, writes, or conducts music as a profession or business: *An orchestra is composed of many musicians.*

mus·ket (mus′kit), NOUN. a kind of old gun with a long barrel. A musket fires a large lead ball instead of a bullet.

mus·ket·eer (mus′kə tir′), NOUN. (earlier) a soldier armed with a musket.

musk·mel·on (musk′mel′ən), NOUN. a small, juicy melon with orange pulp and a hard rind. The cantaloupe is a muskmelon.

musk ox (musk′ oks′), an animal of Greenland and northern North America that chews its cud and has hoofs and a shaggy coat. It looks something like a bison.

This snake has two heads because of a **mutation.**

musk·rat (musk′rat′), NOUN. a water animal of North America somewhat like a rat, but larger.
❑ PLURAL **musk·rat** or **musk·rats.**

Mus·lim (muz′ləm *or* mùz′ləm),
1 NOUN. someone who believes in and follows the teachings of Muhammad.
2 ADJECTIVE. of or about Muhammad, his followers, or the religion of Islam.

muss (mus), VERB. to get someone's clothes, hair, or things messed up or untidy: *The wind mussed up her hair.* ❑ VERB **muss·es, mussed, muss·ing.**

mus·sel (mus′əl), NOUN. a shellfish that has two hinged parts to its shell. Mussels look like clams and are found in both fresh and salt water. ■ Another word that sounds like this is **muscle.**

must (must), HELPING VERB.
1 to have to; be forced to: *You must eat to live.*
2 ought to; should: *You must read this story.*
3 to be likely or certain: *You must be joking. I must seem very rude. They must have left already.*
❑ PAST TENSE **must.**

mus·tache (mus′tash), NOUN. the hair that grows on a man's upper lip. Also spelled **moustache.**

mus·tang (mus′tang), NOUN. a small wild or half-wild horse of the North American plains.

Word Story

Mustang comes from a Latin word meaning "mixed." That turned into a Spanish word meaning "a group of mixed animals." Spanish-speaking people in the United States used a form of that word to mean "a stray horse," likely to turn up in such a group.

mus·tard (mus′tərd), NOUN. a yellow powder or paste with a sharp, hot taste, made from the seeds of a plant. Mustard is used as a seasoning.

must·n't (mus′nt), a contraction of **must not.**

mus·ty (mus′tē), ADJECTIVE. smelling or tasting moldy or damp; moldy: *a musty room, musty crackers.*
❑ ADJECTIVE **mus·ti·er, mus·ti·est.**

mu·tant (myüt′nt), NOUN. a new variety of living thing that results from mutation.

mu·ta·tion (myü tā′shən), NOUN.
1 a change within a gene or genes, resulting in a new feature or character that appears suddenly in a living thing and that can be inherited.
2 a new feature or character.

mute (myüt),
1 ADJECTIVE. silent; not making a sound: *The child stood mute with embarrassment.*
2 NOUN. someone who cannot speak.
3 NOUN. a clip or pad put on a musical instrument to soften its sound.
4 VERB. to put this device on a musical instrument: *She muted the strings of her violin.*
❑ VERB **mutes, mut·ed, mut·ing.** —**mute′ly,** ADVERB.

mu·ti·late (myü′tl āt), VERB.
1 to injure someone badly by cutting or tearing off a part of the body: *Several passengers were mutilated in the train wreck.*

a	hat	ė	term	ô	order	ch	child		a in about
ā	age	i	it	oi	oil	ng	long		e in taken
ä	far	ī	ice	ou	out	sh	she	ə {	i in pencil
â	care	o	hot	u	cup	th	thin		o in lemon
e	let	ō	open	ù	put	ŦH	then		u in circus
ē	equal	ò	saw	ü	rule	zh	measure		

Mysterious

Ancient civilizations in many places created structures that are mysterious to us in the modern world. It is often hard for us today to understand why they built these things. It is also sometimes very hard to figure out how they built them.

The Pyramids of Egypt There are 35 major pyramids still standing near the Nile River in Egypt. They were built more than 4,500 years ago without machines or iron tools as tombs for Egyptian kings. Some of the pyramids are more than 450 feet high and cover more than 13 acres.

The Great Spinx has a human head and a lion's body. It is 240 feet long and 66 feet high. The head and body were carved from one giant rock.

Stonehenge One of the most mysterious structures in the world is Stonehenge, in England. It is a group of huge stones set in circles between 2800 and 1500 B.C. Some of the stones are 22 feet tall and weigh up to 40 tons. Stonehenge was probably used as a religious center and gathering place until the Romans conquered Britain in 43 A.D.

Structures

Easter Island This small island in the Pacific Ocean contains more than 600 huge stone heads, some over 40 feet tall. They weigh as much as 90 tons.

Machu Picchu In what is now Peru, Machu Picchu was built by the Incas, probably as a home for the royal family.

Chichén Itzá The pyramid at Chichén Itzá was built so that the setting sun during the equinoxes would cast the shadow of a snake on the steps of the pyramid. This had religious significance for the ancient Maya.

2 to destroy or ruin some part of something: *The book was badly mutilated by someone who had torn out some pages.*
□ *VERB* **mu·ti·lates, mu·ti·lat·ed, mu·ti·lat·ing.** —**mu′ti·la′tion,** *NOUN.*

mu·ti·ny (myüt′n ē),
1 *NOUN.* a violent attempt by soldiers or sailors to take the control of a military unit or ship from its officers.
2 *VERB.* to take part in a mutiny; rebel.
□ *PLURAL* **mu·ti·nies;** *VERB* **mu·ti·nies, mu·ti·nied, mu·ti·ny·ing.**

mutt (mut), *NOUN.* a dog, especially a mongrel.

mut·ter (mut′ər), *VERB.*
1 to speak or utter words unclearly, with your lips partly closed; mumble: *He muttered a rude remark.*
2 to complain; grumble: *The shoppers muttered about the high price of meat.*
□ *VERB* **mut·ters, mut·tered, mut·ter·ing.**

mut·ton (mut′n), *NOUN.* the meat from a fully grown sheep.

mu·tu·al (myü′chü əl), *ADJECTIVE.*
1 done, said, or felt by each toward the other; given and received: *mutual affection, mutual dislike.*
2 each to the other: *mutual enemies.*
3 belonging to each of several: *We are happy to have him as our mutual friend.*
—**mu′tu·al·ly,** *ADVERB.*

muz·zle (muz′əl),
1 *NOUN.* the part of an animal's head that sticks forward and includes the nose, mouth, and jaws. Dogs and horses have muzzles.
2 *NOUN.* a cover or cage of leather straps or wires to put over an animal's head to keep it from biting someone or from eating.
3 *VERB.* to put a muzzle on: *to muzzle a dog.*
4 *NOUN.* the open front end of a gun or pistol.
□ *VERB* **muz·zles, muz·zled, muz·zling.**

MVP, (in a game, sport, or league) most valuable player.

my (mī), *ADJECTIVE.* of or belonging to me: *I learned my lesson. My house is around the corner.*

My·an·mar (mī än′mär), *NOUN.* a country in southeastern Asia. Its former name was Burma.

myr·i·ad (mir′ē əd), *NOUN.* a very great number: *There are myriads of stars.*

myr·tle (mėr′tl), *NOUN.*
1 an evergreen shrub of the southern part of Europe, with shiny leaves and fragrant white flowers and dark blue berries.
2 a low, creeping evergreen vine found in Canada and the United States. It has blue flowers.

my·self (mī self′), *PRONOUN.*
1 Myself is used to make a statement stronger: *I myself will go.*
2 Myself is used instead of *I* or *me* in cases like: *I can cook for myself. I hurt myself.*
3 my real self: *I am not myself today.*

mys·te·ri·ous (mi stir′ē əs), *ADJECTIVE.* hard to explain or understand; full of mystery: *The mysterious call echoed across the lake.*
—**mys·ter′i·ous·ly,** *ADVERB.*

mys·ter·y (mis′tər ē), *NOUN.*
1 something that is hidden or unknown: *Astronomers investigate the mysteries of the universe.*
2 a novel or other story about a mysterious event or events which are not explained until the end, so as to keep the reader in suspense.
□ *PLURAL* **mys·ter·ies.**

Synonym Study

Mystery means something that has not been explained or cannot be completely understood: *One of the great mysteries of science is why dinosaurs became extinct.*

Problem can mean a difficult question or a mystery: *The police have solved the problem of where the money was hidden.*

Puzzle means a baffling or challenging problem: *The principal faced a puzzle—where was the missing mascot?*

Riddle[1] means a trick question that requires clever thinking to answer: *The princess had to solve the wizard's riddle before she could enter the magic forest.*

Secret can mean a mystery or something hidden from your knowledge: *She wanted to know the secret of how a chameleon changes color.*

mys·ti·fy (mis′tə fī), *VERB.* to confuse someone completely; puzzle: *The magician's tricks totally mystified us.* □ *VERB* **mys·ti·fies, mys·ti·fied, mys·ti·fy·ing.**

myth (mith), *NOUN.*
1 a legend or story, usually one that attempts to explain something in nature: *According to Greek myth, lightning is the weapon of Zeus, chief of the gods.*
2 a made-up person or thing: *Her trip to Europe was a myth invented to impress the other girls.*

myth·i·cal (mith′ə kəl), *ADJECTIVE.* of or like a myth; in myths: *mythical monsters.* —**myth′i·cal·ly,** *ADVERB.*

my·thol·o·gy (mi thol′ə jē), *NOUN.* a collection of myths: *Greek mythology.* □ *PLURAL* **my·thol·o·gies.**

necklace

Nn

N or **n** (en), *NOUN.* the 14th letter of the English alphabet. ◻ *PLURAL* **N's** or **n's.**

N or **N.,**
1 an abbreviation of **north** or **North.**
2 an abbreviation of **northern** and **Northern.**

na·cho (nä′chō), *NOUN.* a baked tortilla chip, often with a topping of cheese, beans, and hot peppers. ◻ *PLURAL* **na·chos.**

nag[1] (nag), *VERB.* to annoy someone by complaining about something that needs to be done: *I will clean up my room if you will stop nagging me.* ◻ *VERB* **nags, nagged, nag·ging.** —**nag′ger,** *NOUN.*

nag[2] (nag), *NOUN.* an old or inferior horse.

Na·hua·tl (nä′wä tl), *NOUN.* the language of the Aztec and other American Indians of central Mexico and Central America.

nail (nāl),
1 *NOUN.* a slender piece of metal that has a point at one end and usually a flat or rounded head at the other end. You hammer nails through pieces of wood to hold them together.
2 *VERB.* to fasten something with a nail or nails: *I nailed the poster to the wall.*
3 *NOUN.* the hard part at the end of a finger or toe. ◻ *VERB* **nails, nailed, nail·ing.**

na·ked (nā′kid), *ADJECTIVE.*
1 with no clothes on: *Your naked shoulders will get sunburned if you aren't careful.*
2 without the addition of anything else; plain: *The naked truth sometimes hurts.* —**na′ked·ness,** *NOUN.*

naked eye, the eye without the help of a telescope or microscope: *Bacteria are tiny organisms, invisible to the naked eye.*

name (nām),
1 *NOUN.* the word or words used to speak about a person, animal, place, or thing: *Our cat's name is Mitten. "The Beehive State" is a name for Utah.*

2 *VERB.* to give someone or something a name: *What shall we name the baby?*

3 *VERB.* to call by name; mention by name: *Three persons were named in the report.*

4 *VERB.* to identify something by name: *Can you name these flowers?*

5 *NOUN.* reputation: *She made a name for herself as a writer.*

6 *VERB.* to choose someone: *He was named captain of the team.*

❑ *VERB* **names, named, nam·ing.**

name·less (nām′lis), *ADJECTIVE.*

1 having no name: *We fed the nameless kitten.*

2 not marked with a name: *a nameless grave.*

name·ly (nām′lē), *ADVERB.* that is to say: *We visited two cities—namely, Boston and Springfield.*

name·sake (nām′sāk′), *NOUN.* someone named after another person: *My brother, Abraham, is the namesake of Abraham Lincoln.*

Na·mib·i·a (nä mib′ē ə), *NOUN.* a country in southwestern Africa. **—Na·mib′i·an,** *ADJECTIVE or NOUN.*

nan·ny (nan′ē), *NOUN.* a child's nurse. ❑ *PLURAL* **nan·nies.**

nap (nap),

1 *NOUN.* a short sleep: *The baby takes a nap after lunch.*

2 *VERB.* to sleep for a short time: *Grandfather naps in his armchair.*

❑ *VERB* **naps, napped, nap·ping.**

nape (nāp), *NOUN.* the back of the neck.

nap·kin (nap′kin), *NOUN.* a piece of cloth or paper used at meals to protect your clothing or to wipe your lips or fingers.

nar·cot·ic (när kot′ik), *NOUN.* any drug that causes sleep and dulls pain.

National parks preserve our country's wilderness.

nar·rate (nar′āt), *VERB.* to tell the story of something: *I narrated the story while my friend acted it out.* ❑ *VERB* **nar·rates, nar·rat·ed, nar·rat·ing. —nar·ra′tion,** *NOUN.* **—nar′ra·tor,** *NOUN.*

nar·ra·tive (nar′ə tiv), *NOUN.* a story; tale: *a thrilling narrative.* ■ See the Synonym Study at **story[1].**

nar·row (nar′ō),

1 *ADJECTIVE.* not wide; not far from one side of something to the other side: *A path that is only 12 inches wide is narrow.*

2 *ADJECTIVE.* small; limited: *a narrow circle of friends.*

3 *VERB.* to become smaller in width; make or become narrow: *The road narrows here.*

4 *ADJECTIVE.* close; with a small margin: *a narrow escape.*

❑ *VERB* **nar·rows, nar·rowed, nar·row·ing. —nar′row·ly,** *ADVERB.*

nar·row-mind·ed (nar′ō mīn′did), *ADJECTIVE.* not willing to consider new ideas or the opinions of other people.

NASA (nas′ə), *NOUN.* National Aeronautics and Space Administration: an agency of the United States government that directs civilian research and development in aerospace technology.

na·sal (nā′zəl), *ADJECTIVE.* of, in, or for the nose: *Mother bought some nasal spray for my cold.*

Nash·ville (nash′vil), *NOUN.* the capital of Tennessee.

na·stur·tium (nə stėr′shəm), *NOUN.* a plant with yellow, orange, or red flowers. Some people eat the bitter seeds and leaves in salads.

nas·ty (nas′tē), *ADJECTIVE.*

1 mean; cruel; hateful: *Several nasty people threw rocks at the birds on the lake.*

2 very unpleasant: *a nasty scratch. The nasty weather ruined our plans for a picnic.* ■ See the Synonym Study at **terrible.**

3 dirty; filthy: *Dead fish and garbage covered the surface of the nasty creek.*

❑ *ADJECTIVE* **nas·ti·er, nas·ti·est.**

na·tion (nā′shən), *NOUN.* a group of people living in one country, united under the same government, and usually speaking the same language: *The United States and France are nations.*

na·tion·al (nash′ə nəl), *ADJECTIVE.* of or about a nation; belonging to a whole nation: *national laws. The flood was declared a national disaster.*

na·tion·al·i·ty (nash′ə nal′ə tē), *NOUN.* the fact or condition of belonging to a nation. Citizens of the same country have the same nationality. ❑ *PLURAL* **na·tion·al·i·ties.**

na·tion·al·ly (nash′ə nə lē), *ADVERB.* throughout the nation: *The President's speech was broadcast nationally.*

national park, land kept by the national government for people to enjoy because of its beautiful scenery or historical interest.

na·tion·wide (nā'shən wīd'), ADJECTIVE. taking place throughout the nation: a nationwide election.

na·tive (nā'tiv),
1 NOUN. someone born in a certain place or country.
2 ADJECTIVE. born in a certain place or country: She is a native daughter of Kansas.
3 ADJECTIVE. belonging to someone because of that person's birth: The United States is my native land.
4 ADJECTIVE. learned first because that is what your parents spoke: English is my native language.
5 NOUN. one of the people originally living in a place or country and found there by explorers or settlers.
6 NOUN. a living thing that originated in a place: The kangaroo is a native of Australia.
—**na'tive·ly**, ADVERB.

Native American, one of the people who have lived in America from long before the time of the first European settlers; American Indian.

Usage Note

Some members of this group prefer the term **American Indian.** Other members prefer the term **Native American.** This term emphasizes the fact that these people were the first to settle America. It avoids the word Indian, which comes from Columbus's mistaken belief that he had sailed to Asia. The best solution is to use the precise name, such as Cherokee or Hopi, whenever you can.

nat·ur·al (nach'ər əl),
1 ADJECTIVE. belonging to the nature a living thing is born with: It is natural for ducks to swim.
2 ADJECTIVE. normal; expected: natural feelings and actions, a natural death.
3 ADJECTIVE. not artificial; not made by human beings: Coal and oil are natural products.
4 ADJECTIVE. like nature; true to life: The picture looked natural.
5 ADJECTIVE. (in music) neither sharp nor flat; not changed in pitch by a sharp or a flat.
6 NOUN. someone who is especially suited for something because of his or her inborn talent or ability: He is a natural on the saxophone.
—**nat'ur·al·ness**, NOUN.

natural gas, a gas formed naturally in the earth. Natural gas is used for cooking and heating.

nat·ur·al·ist (nach'ər ə list), NOUN. someone who studies living things.

nat·ur·al·ize (nach'ər ə līz), VERB. to make someone a citizen who was born somewhere in another country. ❑ VERB **nat·ur·al·iz·es, nat·ur·al·ized, nat·ur·al·iz·ing. —nat'ur·al·i·za'tion,** NOUN.

nat·ur·al·ly (nach'ər ə lē), ADVERB.
1 in a natural way: Speak naturally; don't try to imitate someone else.

2 by nature: She was a naturally athletic child.
3 as you might expect; of course: She offered me some candy; naturally, I took it.

natural resources, materials found in nature that are useful or necessary for life. Land, water, minerals, and forests are natural resources.

natural science, any science that studies the facts of nature or the physical world. Biology, geology, and physics are natural sciences.

na·ture (nā'chər), NOUN.
1 everything in the world not made by people. Plants, animals, the air, water, oceans, mountains, and people are part of nature.
2 the basic characteristics born in a person or animal and always present there; character: It is the nature of birds to fly. It is against his nature to be unkind.
3 life without artificial things: Wild animals live in a state of nature.
4 kind; type: books of a scientific nature.

naught (not), NOUN.
1 nothing: All my studying came to naught; I failed the test.
2 zero; 0.

naugh·ty (no'tē), ADJECTIVE. bad; not behaving well: The naughty child refused to pick up her toys. ❑ ADJECTIVE **naugh·ti·er, naugh·ti·est. —naugh'ti·ness,** NOUN.

Synonym Study

Naughty means not behaving well or not nice: My brother was naughty at dinner, so he was sent from the table without dessert.

Bad can mean not behaving well: When her dog chews on her shoes, she calls him a bad dog.

Disobedient means not obeying or not willing to obey: The disobedient girl did not do as she was told.

Mischievous means taking pleasure from behaving badly: The mischievous child pulled the cat's tail.

See also the Synonym Study at **wicked.**

ANTONYMS: well-behaved, nice.

nau·se·a (no'zē ə or no'shə), NOUN. the feeling that you are about to vomit.

nau·se·ate (no'zē āt or no'shē āt), VERB. to make or become sick; feel that you are about to vomit. ❑ VERB **nau·se·ates, nau·se·at·ed, nau·se·at·ing.**

a hat	ė term	ô order	ch child	a in about
ā age	i it	oi oil	ng long	e in taken
ä far	ī ice	ou out	sh she	ə i in pencil
â care	o hot	u cup	th thin	o in lemon
e let	ō open	ù put	₮H then	u in circus
ē equal	o saw	ü rule	zh measure	

nau·ti·cal (nȯ′tə kəl), ADJECTIVE. of or about ships, sailors, or navigation: *nautical charts*.

Nav·a·jo or **Nav·a·ho** (nav′ə hō), NOUN. a member of a tribe of American Indians living mainly in New Mexico, Arizona, and Utah. ❑ PLURAL **Nav·a·jo** or **Nav·a·jos; Nav·a·ho** or **Nav·a·hos.**

na·val (nā′vəl), ADJECTIVE. of, for, or about warships or the navy: *naval supplies, a naval officer, a great naval power.*

na·vel (nā′vəl), NOUN. See **belly button**.

nav·i·ga·ble (nav′ə gə bəl), ADJECTIVE. able to be traveled on by boats: *The Mississippi River is a navigable river.* —**nav′i·ga·bil′i·ty,** NOUN.

nav·i·gate (nav′ə gāt), VERB.
1 to sail, manage, or steer a ship, aircraft, or rocket: *She navigated the sailboat through the choppy waters.*
2 to sail on or over a sea or river: *The steamboat captain navigated the Mississippi for twenty years.* ❑ VERB **nav·i·gates, nav·i·gat·ed, nav·i·gat·ing.**

nav·i·ga·tion (nav′ə gā shən), NOUN.
1 the skill or process of finding a ship's or aircraft's position and course.
2 the act or process of navigating: *Navigation was difficult during the storm.*

nav·i·ga·tor (nav′ə gā′tər), NOUN.
1 someone who has command of the navigating of a ship or aircraft.
2 (long ago) an explorer of the seas: *The Polynesians were great navigators.*

2 NOUN. a vote of "no": *The yeas outnumber the nays, so the plan is approved.*
▪ Another word that sounds like this is **neigh.**

Na·ya·rit (nī ə rēt′), NOUN. a state in western Mexico.

Na·zi (nä′tsē or nat′sē), NOUN. a brutal political party that ruled Germany from 1933 until 1945, when Germany was defeated in World War II. ❑ PLURAL **Na·zis.**

NC, an abbreviation of **North Carolina.**

ND, an abbreviation of **North Dakota.**

NE or **N.E.,**
1 an abbreviation of **northeast** or **Northeast.**
2 an abbreviation of **northeastern** or **Northeastern.**

NE, an abbreviation of **Nebraska.**

near (nir),
1 ADVERB or ADJECTIVE. close; not far; to or at a short distance: *They searched far and near for their lost dog. The holiday season is drawing near. The post office is quite near.*
2 PREPOSITION. close to; not far away from: *Our house is near the river.*
3 VERB. to come near something: *The train slowed as it neared the station.*
4 ADJECTIVE. close in feeling or relationship: *We went on a vacation to the mountains with some near and dear friends.*
5 ADJECTIVE. by a close margin; narrow: *a near miss.* ❑ VERB **nears, neared, near·ing.** —**near′ness,** NOUN.

navigator

Ferdinand Magellan

Ferdinand Magellan was a Portuguese navigator. Although he was killed in the Philippine islands in 1521, his ship was the first to sail around the world, arriving back in Spain in 1522. The Pacific Ocean was named by Magellan. He called it "Pacific," which means "peaceful," because it was calmer than the rough Atlantic.

na·vy (nā′vē), NOUN.
1 a large, organized group of men and ships trained and equipped for war.
2 often, **Navy,** the military sea forces of the United States. ❑ PLURAL **na·vies.**

navy blue, a dark blue.

nay (nā),
1 ADVERB. (formerly) no.

near·by (nir′bī′), ADJECTIVE or ADVERB. near; not far away: *We rode the horses at a nearby farm.*

near·ly (nir′lē), ADVERB. not quite; almost: *It is nearly bedtime. I nearly broke my leg when I fell.*

near·sight·ed (nir′sī′tid), ADJECTIVE. seeing nearby things more clearly than things far away. Some nearsighted people wear glasses or contact lenses. —**near′sight′ed·ness,** NOUN. —**near′sight′ed·ly,** ADVERB.

neat (nēt), ADJECTIVE.
1 clean and orderly: *a neat desk, a neat room.*
2 able and willing to keep things in order: *a neat child.*
3 skillful; clever: *a neat trick.*
4 (informal) very nice; wonderful: *It was a neat party.*
—**neat′ly**, ADVERB. —**neat′ness**, NOUN.

Synonym Study

Neat means clean and in order: *After she put away her toys and clothes, the room was neat. Her baseball uniform always looks neat before a game.*

Orderly means neat: *If he kept his desk orderly, he could find things more easily.*

Tidy means neat and arranged in a pleasing way: *Grandma's room at the nursing home is tidy and bright.*

ANTONYM: messy.

Ne·bras·ka (nə bras′kə), NOUN. one of the Midwestern states of the United States. *Abbreviation:* NE; *Capital:* Lincoln.
—**Ne·bras′kan**, NOUN.

State Story **Nebraska** comes from a word in a language related to Sioux, meaning "flat water." This was a name for the **Platte River** (plat′riv′ər). *Platte* comes from a French word meaning "flat." The Platte River is mostly slow and smooth.

neb·u·la (neb′yə lə), NOUN. a mass of dust particles and gases in outer space. A nebula may either be dark or appear as a glowing haze scattered with stars. ❑ PLURAL **neb·u·las** or **neb·u·lae** (neb′yə lē′).

nec·es·sar·i·ly (nes′ə ser′ə lē), ADVERB.
1 always; of necessity: *Babies are not necessarily cute.*
2 as a logical result: *War necessarily causes misery and waste.*

nec·es·sar·y (nes′ə ser′ē), ADJECTIVE. needing to be done: *The repairs to the car were necessary.*

ne·ces·si·ty (nə ses′ə tē), NOUN.
1 something which cannot be done without: *Food and water are necessities.*
2 the fact of being necessary: *He understood the necessity of eating the proper foods.*
❑ PLURAL **ne·ces·si·ties.**

neck (nek), NOUN.
1 the part of your body between your head and your shoulders.
2 the part of a piece of clothing that fits the neck: *the neck of a shirt.*
3 any narrow part like a neck: *the neck of a bottle.*
neck and neck, IDIOM. equal or even in a race or contest.
stick your neck out, IDIOM. to do or say something that may be risky or dangerous: *When other kids made fun of my friend's old shoes, I stuck my neck out and told them that was unkind.*

neck·lace (nek′lis), NOUN. a kind of jewelry worn around the neck. Necklaces may be made of gold, silver, or beads.

neck·tie (nek′tī′), NOUN. a narrow strip of colorful cloth worn around the neck; tie. A necktie is worn under the collar of a shirt, tied in front.

nec·tar (nek′tər), NOUN. a sweet liquid found in many flowers. Bees gather nectar and make it into honey.

American Indian **necklace** made of beads

nec·ta·rine (nek′tə rēn′), NOUN. a kind of peach without any fuzz on its skin.

need (nēd),
1 VERB. to be unable to do without something; lack: *I need a new hat. Plants need water.*
2 NOUN. something that has to be; necessity: *There is no need to hurry. In the desert their need was water.*
3 NOUN. a lack of something useful or desired: *You are in need of new shoes.*
4 NOUN. a lack of money; being poor: *This family's need was so great the children did not have shoes.*
5 VERB. must; should; have to; ought to: *He need not go. She needs to go.*
❑ VERB **needs, need·ed, need·ing.** ■ Another word that sounds like this is **knead. —need′less,** ADJECTIVE. —**need′less·ly,** ADVERB.

nectarine

Have You Heard?

You may have heard the phrase **"A friend in need is a friend indeed."** This means that a friend who helps you when you are really in trouble is a true friend.

nee·dle (nē′dl),
1 NOUN. a very slender tool used in sewing. A needle is sharp at one end, and has a small hole or eye to pass a thread through.

a hat	ė term	ô order	ch child	ʃa in about
ā age	i it	oi oil	ng long	e in taken
ä far	ī ice	ou out	sh she	ə⟨i in pencil
â care	o hot	u cup	th thin	o in lemon
e let	ō open	u̇ put	ŦH then	u in circus
ē equal	ȯ saw	ü rule	zh measure	

2 *NOUN.* a slender rod used in knitting.

3 *NOUN.* a thin steel pointer in a compass, dial, and the like, that shows amount, speed, and so on.

4 *NOUN.* a very thin steel tube with a sharp point at one end. It is used for giving shots, taking blood from the body, and so on.

5 *VERB.* to annoy or tease someone: *They kept needling me about my new glasses.*

6 *NOUN.* the needle-shaped leaf of a fir or pine tree.

7 *NOUN.* the very small, pointed device in a record player. It fits into grooves in the record and picks up sounds recorded there. ❑ *VERB* **nee·dles, nee·dled, nee·dling. −nee′dle·like′,** *ADJECTIVE.*

Have You Heard?

You may have heard someone say **"It's like looking for a needle in a haystack."** This means that something is almost impossible to find.

nee·dle·point (nē′dl point′), *NOUN.* embroidery made on a canvas cloth. Needlepoint usually covers an entire surface such as a small pillow.

Needlepoint creates a work of art with a needle and thread.

need·n't (nēd′nt), a contraction of **need not.**

need·y (nē′dē), *ADJECTIVE.* very poor; not having enough to live on: *a needy family.* ■ See the Synonym Study at **poor.** ❑ *ADJECTIVE* **need·i·er, need·i·est.**

neg·a·tive (neg′ə tiv),

1 *ADJECTIVE.* saying no: *A shake of the head is a negative answer.*

2 *NOUN.* a word or statement that says no. "I won't" is a negative.

3 *ADJECTIVE.* not positive; not hopeful: *Negative suggestions are not helpful.*

4 *ADJECTIVE.* less than zero; minus: *−5 is a negative number.*

5 *ADJECTIVE.* of the kind of electricity that electrons carry. Negative electricity travels along wires and is used for power.

6 *NOUN.* a photographic image in which light and dark are reversed. Prints are made from it.

7 *ADJECTIVE.* showing the absence of a particular disease or germ: *Her test for the infection was negative.*

ne·glect (ni glekt′),

1 *VERB.* to give too little care or attention to something: *Don't neglect your health.*

2 *VERB.* to fail to do something: *She neglected to tell us what happened.*

3 *NOUN.* a lack of care or attention: *The car has been ruined by years of neglect.*

❑ *VERB* **ne·glects, ne·glect·ed, ne·glect·ing.**

neg·li·gence (neg′lə jəns), *NOUN.* a lack of proper care or attention; carelessness; neglect: *Negligence was the cause of the accident.*

neg·li·gent (neg′lə jənt), *ADJECTIVE.* showing neglect; careless: *The negligent driver caused the accident.* **−neg′li·gent·ly,** *ADVERB.*

ne·go·ti·ate (ni gō′shē āt), *VERB.*

1 to talk something over in order to come to an agreement: *Both countries are negotiating for an end to the war.*

2 to agree to something: *They finally negotiated a peace treaty. The baseball player negotiated a new contract.*

❑ *VERB* **ne·go·ti·ates, ne·go·ti·at·ed, ne·go·ti·at·ing. −ne·go′ti·a·tor,** *NOUN.*

ne·go·ti·a·tion (ni gō′shē ā′shən), *NOUN.* often, **negotiations,** the act or process of negotiating: *Both sides waited anxiously as the negotiations for peace went on for months.*

Ne·gro (nē′grō),

1 *NOUN.* someone whose ancestors belonged to the group of people living in Africa south of the Sahara; Black; in the United States, African American.

2 *ADJECTIVE.* of or about people of this background. ★ Most people prefer to use **African American** or **Black** instead of **Negro,** which is considered offensive by some people. ❑ *PLURAL* **Ne·groes.**

A photographic **negative** (a) is used to make a positive print (b).

neigh (nā),
1 *NOUN.* a sound that a horse makes.
2 *VERB.* to make a sound like this.
❑ *VERB* **neighs, neighed, neigh·ing.** ■ Another word that sounds like this is **nay.**

neigh·bor (nā′bər),
1 *NOUN.* someone who lives next door or nearby.
2 *NOUN.* someone or something that is near or next to another: *The big tree brought down several of its smaller neighbors as it fell.*
3 *VERB.* to be near or next to: *Canada neighbors the United States.*
❑ *VERB* **neigh·bors, neigh·bored, neigh·bor·ing.**

neigh·bor·hood (nā′bər hùd),
1 *NOUN.* the streets and houses surrounding the place where you live: *We have a school and a park in our neighborhood.*
2 *NOUN.* people living near one another: *The whole neighborhood came to the big party.*
3 *ADJECTIVE.* of or for a neighborhood: *I like to read our neighborhood newspaper.*

neigh·bor·ly (nā′bər lē), *ADJECTIVE.* kind; friendly: *It was neighborly of them to help us move in.*
—**neigh′bor·li·ness,** *NOUN.*

nei·ther (nē′ŦHər *or* nī′ŦHər),
1 *CONJUNCTION, ADJECTIVE,* or *PRONOUN.* not either: *Neither you nor I will go. Neither statement is true. Neither of the statements is true.*
2 *CONJUNCTION.* nor: *They didn't go; neither did we.*

ne·on (nē′on), *NOUN.* a colorless, odorless gas, forming a very small part of the air. Neon is a chemical element. It glows when electricity is passed through it in electric lights and signs.

Ne·pal (nə pòl′), *NOUN.* a country in south central Asia. —**Nep·a·lese** (nep′ə lēz′), *ADJECTIVE* or *NOUN.*

neph·ew (nef′yü), *NOUN.* a son of your brother or sister; son of your spouse's brother or sister.

Nep·tune (nep′tün), *NOUN.*
1 the fourth largest planet and the eighth in distance from the sun. Neptune cannot be seen without a telescope.
2 the Roman god of the sea.

nerd (nėrd), *NOUN.* (slang) someone who spends so much time on an interest that there is little time for social contact: *a computer nerd.*

nerve (nėrv), *NOUN.*
1 a kind of tissue that connects the brain or spinal cord with the other parts of the body. Nerves carry messages to and from the brain.
2 mental strength; courage: *Don't lose your nerve.*
3 boldness; disrespect: *They had a lot of nerve to say that we were talking too loud.*

get on someone's nerves, *IDIOM.* to annoy or irritate someone: *His whistling gets on my nerves.*

nerve cell, one of the special cells of the body that are able to send and receive electrical impulses.

nerv·ous (nėr′vəs), *ADJECTIVE.*
1 easily frightened or upset: *My sister is nervous and doesn't like to be alone at night.*
2 restless or uneasy: *Thunder and lightning make me nervous.*
3 of or about the nerves: *a nervous disorder, nervous energy.*
—**nerv′ous·ly,** *ADVERB.* —**nerv′ous·ness,** *NOUN.*

nervous system, a system of nerve fibers, nerve cells, and other nerve tissue in a person or animal. Your nervous system includes the brain and spinal cord, and controls all your body activities.

Word Power   -ness

The suffix **-ness** means "the quality of being _____" or "a _____ action." Sweet**ness** is the quality of being sweet. Kind**ness** is kind action.

nest (nest),
1 *NOUN.* a kind of home that birds build out of twigs, leaves, mud, and the like. Birds lay their eggs and protect their young ones in nests.
2 *NOUN.* a place used by insects, fishes, turtles, rabbits, or the like, to live in.

a robin's **nest** with eggs

3 *NOUN.* a snug resting place: *The little boy made a cozy nest among the sofa cushions and took a nap.*
4 *VERB.* to build and use a nest: *The bluebirds are nesting here now.*
❑ *VERB* **nests, nest·ed, nest·ing.**

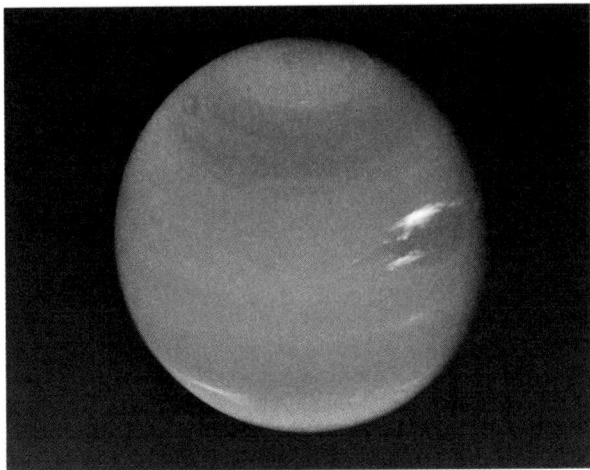

Neptune (definition 1)

a	hat	ė	term	ô	order	ch	child		a in about
ā	age	i	it	oi	oil	ng	long		e in taken
ä	far	ī	ice	ou	out	sh	she	ə {	i in pencil
â	care	o	hot	u	cup	th	thin		o in lemon
e	let	ō	open	ù	put	ŦH	then		u in circus
ē	equal	ò	saw	ü	rule	zh	measure		

nes·tle (nesʹəl), VERB.
1 to settle yourself comfortably: *She nestled down into the big chair.*
2 to hold someone in a loving way: *Father nestled my baby sister in his arms.*
❑ VERB **nes·tles, nes·tled, nes·tling.**

net¹ (net),
1 NOUN. a kind of cloth, large with open squares, made of string tied together.
2 NOUN. anything made of net. Nets are used to catch butterflies, birds, and fish, to keep your hair in place, and to separate opposing players in games such as tennis and volleyball.
3 VERB. to catch in a net: *I netted a big fish. She netted a butterfly.*
❑ VERB **nets, net·ted, net·ting.** —**netʹlikeʹ**, ADJECTIVE.

net² (net),
1 ADJECTIVE. what is left after deductions. The net weight of a glass jar of candy is the weight of the candy itself.
2 VERB. to gain: *The sale netted me a good profit.*
❑ VERB **nets, net·ted, net·ting.**

net³ (net), NOUN. **the Net,** the Internet: *She spends hours exploring the Net.*

Neth·er·lands (neᴛʜʹər ləndz), NOUN. **the,** a country in northwestern Europe. —**Neth·er·land·er** (neᴛʜʹər lanʹdər), NOUN.

Word Story

Netherlands is an English translation of a very similar Dutch word meaning "lowlands." The country is lower than the land around it—in fact, much of it is actually below sea level.

net·tle (netʹl), NOUN. a kind of plant having sharp leaf hairs that sting the skin when you touch them.

net·work (netʹwẻrkʹ), NOUN.
1 any system of lines, wires, roads, and the like, that cross: *a network of highways, a network of railroads.*
2 a group of TV or radio stations that work together, so that what is broadcast by one station may be broadcast by all of them.

neu·tral (nüʹtrəl),
1 ADJECTIVE. not on either side in a quarrel or war: *Switzerland was neutral during World War II.*
2 ADJECTIVE. having little or no color: *White and gray are neutral colors.*
3 ADJECTIVE. (in chemistry) neither an acid nor a base.
4 NOUN. the position of gears when they do not transmit motion from the engine to the wheels or other working parts.
—**neuʹtral·ly**, ADVERB.

neu·tral·ize (nüʹtrə liz), VERB. to cancel the effect of something: *An open container of vinegar will neutralize unpleasant odors in a closet.* ❑ VERB **neu·tral·iz·es, neu·tral·ized, neu·tral·iz·ing.**

neu·tron (nüʹtron), NOUN. a tiny particle that is neither positive nor negative electrically. Neutrons occur in the nucleus of all atoms except hydrogen.

Ne·vad·a (nə vadʹə *or* nə väʹdə), NOUN. one of the Rocky Mountain states of the United States. *Abbreviation:* NV; *Capital:* Carson City.
—**Ne·vadʹan**, NOUN.

State Story **Nevada** comes from a Spanish word meaning "snowy." The state has many snowcapped mountains.

nev·er (nevʹər), ADVERB. not ever; at no time: *She has never been to New York.*

nev·er·more (nevʹər môrʹ), ADVERB. never again.

nev·er·the·less (nevʹər ᴛʜə lesʹ), ADVERB. however; none the less; in spite of it: *She was very tired; nevertheless, she kept on working.*

new (nü), ADJECTIVE.
1 never made or thought of before; just recently made, known, felt, or discovered: *She invented a new machine. That's a new idea.*
2 recently grown or made; not old: *a new bud.*
3 not used yet; not worn or used up: *We bought some new furniture.*
4 beginning again: *Sunrise marks a new day.*
5 just come; having recently come to a new place or job: *Our class has a new teacher. She is new in town.*
6 later; modern; recent: *We are learning the new dances in gym class.*
7 not familiar: *Algebra is new to me.*
■ Other words that sound like this are **gnu** and **knew.** —**newʹness**, NOUN.

Synonym Study

New means very recently made or become known: *A new movie starring the Fantastic Frogs has just been made.*

Brand-new means very new: *He hasn't even worn his brand-new sweater yet.*

Fresh¹ means newly picked or made and not yet affected by time or use: *She loves the taste of fresh corn in the summer. Start over with a fresh sheet of paper.*

Original can mean new or of a new kind: *He likes to make up original poems.*

Modern means of the present time or not far in the past: *Modern clothes are not like the clothes of a hundred years ago. Modern cars have many safety features.*

Up-to-date means keeping up with new styles, ideas, or methods: *She wants an up-to-date book about computers.*

ANTONYM: old.

new·born (nü′bôrn′),
ADJECTIVE. recently or
only just born: *a
newborn baby.*

New Bruns·wick
(nü′ brunz′wik), a
province in
southeastern Canada.
–New Brunswicker.

new·com·er
(nü′kum′ər), NOUN.
someone who has just
come to a place.

New Del·hi (nü del′ē),
NOUN. the capital of
India.

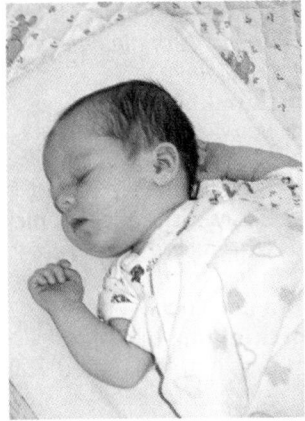

a **newborn** baby

New England, the northeastern part of the United
States. Maine, New Hampshire, Vermont,
Massachusetts, Rhode Island, and Connecticut are
the New England states.

New·found·land (nü′fənd lənd *or* nü found′land),
NOUN. a province in eastern Canada.
–New′found·land·er, NOUN.

New Hamp·shire (nü′ hamp′shər), one of the
northeastern states of the United States.
Abbreviation: NH; *Capital:* Concord. **–New
Hampshirite.**

State Story   New Hampshire was named in
1629 for *Hampshire,* a county in England.

New Jer·sey (nü′ jėr′zē), one of the northeastern
states of the United States. *Abbreviation:* NJ;
Capital: Trenton. **–New Jerseyite.**

State Story   New Jersey was named in 1664
for the British island of *Jersey.*

new·ly (nü′lē), ADVERB. lately; recently: *newly
discovered, newly painted walls.*

New Mexico, one of the southwestern states of
the United States. *Abbreviation:* NM; *Capital:*
Santa Fe. **–New Mexican.**

State Story   New Mexico is a translation of the
Spanish name *Nuevo México.* A Spanish explorer
gave this name to the area in 1564 to suggest
that it would be as rich as the country of Mexico.

new moon, the moon when seen as a thin
crescent or when it is almost invisible.

news (nüz), NOUN.
1 information about something which has just
happened or will soon happen: *The news that
our teacher was leaving made us sad.*
2 a report in a newspaper, on TV, or radio about
what is happening in the world.
3 newscast: *I saw it on the 10 o'clock news.*

news·cast (nüz′kast′), NOUN. a TV or radio program
that reports current events and news bulletins.

news·pa·per (nüz′pā′pər), NOUN. sheets of paper
printed every day or week, telling the news,
carrying advertisements, pictures, articles, and
useful information.

news·reel (nüz′rēl′), NOUN. (earlier) a short movie
showing current events. Before television, movies
in theaters would be accompanied by cartoons
and a newsreel.

news·stand (nüz′stand′), NOUN. a place where
newspapers and magazines are sold.

newt (nüt), NOUN. a small salamander that lives in
water part of the time.

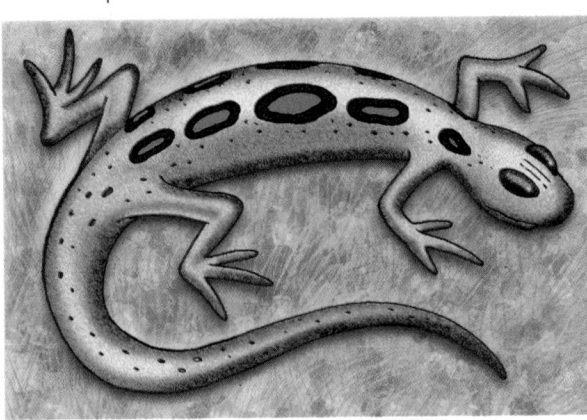

newt — about 4 inches long, including the tail

New Testament, the Christian scriptures in the
Bible, which contain the life and teachings of
Jesus recorded by His followers, together with
their own experiences and teachings.

New World, North America and South America.

New Year or **New Year's,** January 1; the first day
or days of the year.

New Year's Day, January 1.

New Year's Eve, the eve of New Year's Day;
December 31. New Year's Eve is often celebrated
with parties and public festivities.

New York (nü′ yôrk′),
1 one of the northeastern states of the United
States. *Abbreviation:* NY; *Capital:* Albany.
2 a city in this state. New York is the largest city in
the United States.
–New Yorker.

State Story   The state of New York was
named in 1664 in honor of the Duke of
York, who lived from 1633 to 1701. It was
given this name by his brother Charles II,
king of England.

a	hat	ė	term	ô	order	ch	child	(a in about
ā	age	i	it	oi	oil	ng	long	e in taken
ä	far	ī	ice	ou	out	sh	she	ə⟨ i in pencil
â	care	o	hot	u	cup	th	thin	o in lemon
e	let	ō	open	ù	put	ᴛʜ	then	(u in circus
ē	equal	ȯ	saw	ü	rule	zh	measure	

N

New Zea·land (nü′ zē′lənd), an island country in the southern Pacific Ocean. **–New Zealander.**

next (nekst),
 1 *ADJECTIVE.* nearest: *The phone is in the next room.*
 2 *ADJECTIVE.* following at once: *The next day after Sunday is Monday.*
 3 *ADVERB.* the first time after this: *When you next visit me, bring it.*
 4 *ADVERB.* in the place, time, or position that is nearest: *His name comes next on the list.*

next door, in or at the next house or apartment: *He lives next door.*

next-door (nekst′dôr′), *ADJECTIVE.* in or at the next house or apartment: *my next-door neighbor.*

Nez Perce (nez′ pėrs′), a member of a North American Indian tribe living in Idaho, Oregon, and Washington. ❏ *PLURAL* **Nez Perce** or **Nez Perc·es.**

NH, an abbreviation of **New Hampshire.**

Ni·ag·ar·a Falls (ni ag′rə fôlz′), a very high, wide waterfall on the boundary between the United States and Canada.

nib·ble (nib′əl),
 1 *VERB.* to eat with quick small bites. Mice and rats nibble. ■ See the Synonym Study at **eat.**
 2 *VERB.* to bite something gently or lightly: *A fish nibbles at the bait.*
 3 *NOUN.* the act of nibbling; small bite.
 ❏ *VERB* **nib·bles, nib·bled, nib·bling. –nib′bler,** *NOUN.*

Nic·a·ra·gua (nik′ə rä′gwə), *NOUN.* a country in Central America. **–Nic′a·ra′guan,** *ADJECTIVE* or *NOUN.*

nice (nīs), *ADJECTIVE.*
 1 good or pleasing; agreeable; satisfactory: *a nice day, a nice ride, a nice child.*
 2 friendly and kind: *They were nice to me.* ■ See the Synonym Study at **good-natured.**
 3 showing care or skill; very fine: *a nice piece of writing, a nice shot, a nice try.*
 ❏ *ADJECTIVE* **nic·er, nic·est. –nice′ly,** *ADVERB.*

Synonym Study

Nice means pleasing or good. It is a general word: *It was nice of him to remember my birthday.*

Pleasant means giving pleasure and enjoyment: *She spent a pleasant day in the park.*

Enjoyable means giving a feeling of enjoyment and happiness: *This is an enjoyable movie.*

Lovely can mean pleasing and delightful: *We had a lovely time at summer camp.*

Wonderful means very enjoyable: *They had a wonderful time skating at the rink.*

niche (nich), *NOUN.*
 1 a hollow place in a wall for a statue or vase.
 2 (in biology) the relationship of a particular species to the other living things in an environment: *The cat's original niche was as a predator of small animals.*

nick (nik),
 1 *NOUN.* a place where a small bit has been cut or broken out: *She cut nicks in a stick to keep score.*
 2 *VERB.* to make a nick or nicks in something.
 ❏ *VERB* **nicks, nicked, nick·ing.**
 in the nick of time, *IDIOM.* just in time: *We reached home in the nick of time; a minute later there was a downpour.*

nick·el (nik′əl), *NOUN.*
 1 a coin in the United States and Canada worth five cents.
 2 a hard, silvery metal that is often mixed with other metals to make durable objects. Nickel is a chemical element.

nick·name (nik′nām′),
 1 *NOUN.* a name used instead of someone's real name: *"Ed" is a nickname for "Edward."*
 2 *VERB.* to give a nickname to someone: *They nicknamed the redheaded girl "Rusty."*
 ❏ *VERB* **nick·names, nick·named, nick·nam·ing.**

nic·o·tine (nik′ə tēn′), *NOUN.* a poison contained in the leaves, roots, and seeds of tobacco. When someone smokes, breathing in nicotine makes the heart work harder.

niece (nēs), *NOUN.* a daughter of your brother or sister; daughter of your spouse's brother or sister.

Ni·ger (nī′jər), *NOUN.* a country in western Africa.

Ni·ger·i·a (nī jir′ē ə), *NOUN.* a country in western Africa. **–Ni·ger′i·an,** *ADJECTIVE* or *NOUN.*

night (nīt), *NOUN.* the time between evening and morning; time from sunset to sunrise, especially when it is dark. ■ Another word that sounds like this is **knight.**

night·fall (nīt′fôl′), *NOUN.* the coming of night.

night·gown (nīt′goun′), *NOUN.* a long, loose garment worn by women in bed.

night·in·gale (nīt′n gāl′), *NOUN.* a small, reddish brown bird of Europe. The nightingale sings sweetly at night as well as in the daytime.

nightingale — about 6 inches long

Word Story

Nightingale comes from old English words meaning "to sing" and "night." The male nightingale sings night and day, but because few other birds sing at night, its beautiful song can be heard most clearly then.

night·ly (nīt′lē),
1 *ADJECTIVE*. done, happening, or appearing every night: *I like to watch the nightly news on TV.*
2 *ADVERB*. every night or at night: *Performances are given nightly except on Sunday.*

night·mare (nīt′mâr′), *NOUN*.
1 a very frightening dream: *I had a nightmare about falling off a high building.*
2 a very frightening experience: *The hurricane was a nightmare.*

night·time (nīt′tīm′), *NOUN*. the time between evening and morning.

Nile (nīl), *NOUN*. a river in Africa. The Nile is the longest river in the world.

nim·ble (nim′bəl), *ADJECTIVE*. active, light, and quick; unlikely to stumble: *The nimble goat leaped from ledge to ledge on the mountain.*
❑ *ADJECTIVE* **nim·bler, nim·blest. −nim′bly,** *ADVERB*.

nine (nīn), *NOUN or ADJECTIVE*. one more than eight; 9.

nine·teen (nīn′tēn′), *NOUN or ADJECTIVE*. nine more than ten; 19.

nine·teenth (nīn′tēnth′), *ADJECTIVE or NOUN*.
1 next after the 18th.
2 one of 19 equal parts.

nine·ti·eth (nīn′tē ith), *ADJECTIVE or NOUN*.
1 next after the 89th.
2 one of 90 equal parts.

nine·ty (nīn′tē), *NOUN or ADJECTIVE*. ten more than eighty; nine times ten; 90. ❑ *PLURAL* **nine·ties.**

nin·ja (nin′jə), *NOUN*. someone trained in the martial arts developed by a group active in Japan hundreds of years ago. ❑ *PLURAL* **nin·ja** or **nin·jas.**

ninth (ninth),
1 *ADJECTIVE or NOUN*. next after the eighth.
2 *NOUN*. one of nine equal parts.

nip (nip),
1 *VERB*. to squeeze something hard and quickly; pinch; bite: *The crab nipped my toe.*
2 *NOUN*. a tight squeeze; pinch; sudden bite.
3 *VERB*. to take something off by biting, pinching, or snipping it: *Grandma nipped the loose thread from my sleeve.*
4 *VERB*. to have a sharp, biting effect on a part of the body: *A cold wind nipped our ears.*
5 *NOUN*. a sharp cold; chill: *There is a nip in the air this frosty morning.*
❑ *VERB* **nips, nipped, nip·ping.**

nip·ple (nip′əl), *NOUN*.
1 the dark, roundish part of the front of the breast. Infants and baby animals suck milk from the female nipple.
2 the rubber cap of a baby's bottle, through which the baby gets milk and other liquids.

ni·tro·gen (nī′trə jən), *NOUN*. a gas without color, taste, or odor which forms about four fifths of the air. Nitrogen is a chemical element.

NJ, an abbreviation of **New Jersey.**

NM, an abbreviation of **New Mexico.**

no (nō),
1 *ADVERB*. a word used to say that you can't or won't do something, that an answer is wrong, and so on: *Will you come? No. Can a cow fly? No.*
2 *ADJECTIVE*. not any: *Dogs have no wings.*
3 *ADVERB*. not at all: *He is no better.*
■ Another word that sounds like this is **know.**

no. or **No.,** an abbreviation of **number.**

No·bel Peace Prize (nō bel′ pēs′ priz′), a prize awarded every year to a person who has done important work for peace. There are also Nobel prizes in physics, chemistry, medicine, literature, and economics. The Nobel prizes were set up by Alfred Nobel, who was a Swedish chemist. He invented dynamite.

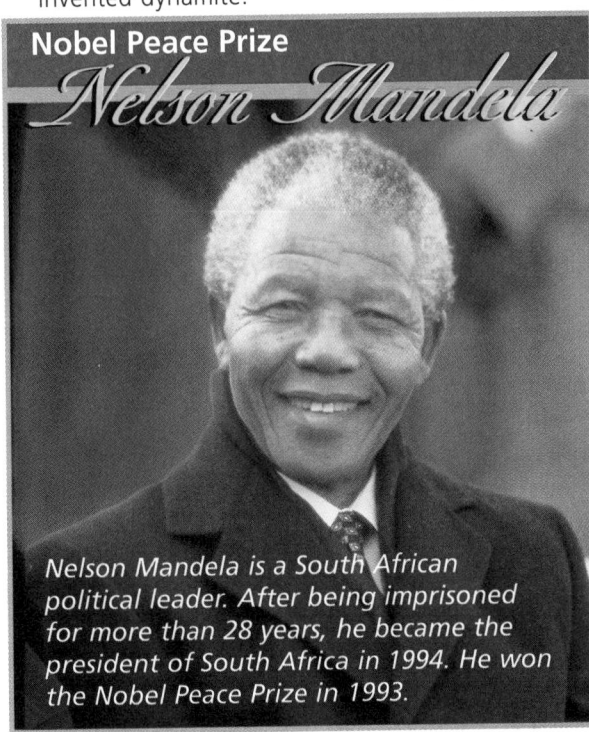

Nobel Peace Prize
Nelson Mandela

Nelson Mandela is a South African political leader. After being imprisoned for more than 28 years, he became the president of South Africa in 1994. He won the Nobel Peace Prize in 1993.

no·bil·i·ty (nō bil′ə tē), *NOUN*.
1 people of high rank, title, or birth in society. Kings, dukes, and so on, belong to the nobility.
2 noble character: *the nobility of a great deed.*

no·ble (nō′bəl),
1 *ADJECTIVE*. showing greatness of mind and character; good: *a noble person, a noble deed.*
2 *ADJECTIVE*. excellent; fine; splendid; magnificent: *Niagara Falls is a noble sight.*

a	hat	ė	term	ô	order	ch	child	(	a in about
ā	age	i	it	oi	oil	ng	long		e in taken
ä	far	ī	ice	ou	out	sh	she	ə⟨	i in pencil
â	care	o	hot	u	cup	th	thin		o in lemon
e	let	ō	open	ů	put	ŦH	then		u in circus
ē	equal	ȯ	saw	ü	rule	zh	measure	(	

3 *ADJECTIVE.* belonging to the nobility: *a noble family.*

4 *NOUN.* someone belonging to the nobility: *Nobles who opposed the king plotted against him.* ❑ *ADJECTIVE* **no·bler, no·blest. —no′bly,** *ADVERB.*

no·ble·man (nō′bəl mən), *NOUN.* a man of noble rank, title, or birth. ❑ *PLURAL* **no·ble·men.**

no·ble·wom·an (nō′bəl wǔm′ən), *NOUN.* a woman of noble rank, title, or birth. ❑ *PLURAL* **no·ble·wom·en.**

no·bod·y (nō′bud′ē or nō′bə dē),

1 *PRONOUN.* no one; no person: *Nobody helped me.*

2 *NOUN.* someone of no importance: *I was ignored and made to feel like a nobody.* ❑ *PLURAL* **no·bod·ies.**

noc·tur·nal (nok tėr′nl), *ADJECTIVE.*

1 active in the night: *The owl is a nocturnal bird.*

2 of or happening at night: *Grandfather sometimes takes nocturnal walks.* **—noc·tur′nal·ly,** *ADVERB.*

Most owls are **nocturnal.**

nod (nod),

1 *VERB.* to bow your head slightly and raise it again quickly.

2 *VERB.* to say yes by moving your head in this way: *Father quietly nodded his consent.*

3 *NOUN.* the act of nodding the head: *She gave us a nod as she passed.*

4 *VERB.* to let your head fall forward and bob about when you are sleepy or falling asleep. ❑ *VERB* **nods, nod·ded, nod·ding.**

No·el (nō el′), *NOUN.* Christmas.

Word Story

Noel comes from a French word meaning "Christmas." In French, the word is spelled *Noël.* As a first name for either boys or girls, this name was often given to children born on Christmas Day.

no-hit·ter (nō′hit′ər), *NOUN.* a baseball game in which a pitcher gives up no base hits to the opposing team.

noise (noiz), *NOUN.*

1 an unpleasant or disturbing sound: *The noise kept me awake.*

2 any sound: *the noise of rain on the roof.*

Synonym Study

Noise usually means an unpleasant sound: *The noise of traffic woke me up. What's making that noise?*

Clatter means the noise of things hitting each other: *Can't you wash the pots without all that clatter?*

Racket[1] means a clattering, banging noise: *The carpenter hammering nails couldn't help making a racket. The kids running up and down the stairs made a terrible racket.*

Uproar can mean the loud yelling of a crowd: *There was an uproar when the umpire called the runner out on a close play at third base.*

See also the Synonym Studies at **loud** and **shout.**

ANTONYM: silence.

noise·mak·er (noiz′mā′kər), *NOUN.*

1 someone or something who makes too much noise.

2 something that makes noise, especially a horn, rattle, and so on, used to make noise at a party.

nois·y (noi′zē), *ADJECTIVE.*

1 making a lot of noise: *a noisy crowd, a noisy machine.*

2 full of noise: *a noisy street, a noisy house, the noisy city.* ■ See the Synonym Study at **loud.** ❑ *ADJECTIVE* **nois·i·er, nois·i·est. —nois′i·ly,** *ADVERB.*

no·mad (nō′mad), *NOUN.* a member of a group of people that moves from place to place to find food or somewhere for its animals to graze: *Many Inuit are nomads.*

no·mad·ic (nō mad′ik), *ADJECTIVE.* of or about nomads or their life: *Nomadic people often live in tents.*

nom·i·nate (nom′ə nāt), *VERB.*

1 to name someone as a candidate for an office: *He was nominated for president, but chose not to run.*

2 to appoint someone to an office in government: *Presidents nominate their cabinet members.* ❑ *VERB* **nom·i·nates, nom·i·nat·ed, nom·i·nat·ing.**

nom·i·na·tion (nom′ə nā′shən), *NOUN.*

1 the act of naming a candidate for office: *The nominations for president of the club were written on the blackboard.*

2 a selection of someone for office; appointment to office: *Her nomination as Ambassador to France was approved by the Senate.*

nom·i·nee (nom′ə nē′), *NOUN.* someone nominated for an office or to be a candidate for election to an office. ❑ *PLURAL* **nom·i·nees.**

Word Power   non-

The prefix **non-** means "not" or "not a." It also means "the opposite of" or "lack of." Nonpoisonous means **not** poisonous. Nonfiction means **not a** work of fiction. Nonviolence means **the opposite of** or **lack of** violence.

The prefix **non-** is so useful that it gets added to many words, with a hyphen or without one, whichever way seems easier to read.

none (nun), *PRONOUN.*
1 not any: *We have none of that paper left.*
2 no one; not one: *None of these is mine.*
3 no people: *None have arrived.*
  ▪ Another word that sounds like this is **nun.**

non·fic·tion (non fik′shən), *NOUN.* writing that is not fiction. Nonfiction deals with real people and events rather than imaginary ones.

non·poi·son·ous (non poi′zn əs), *ADJECTIVE.* containing no poison.

non·prof·it (non prof′it), *ADJECTIVE.* not for profit; without profit: *a nonprofit organization.*

non·sense (non′sens), *NOUN.* words or ideas that don't make sense; plan or suggestion that is foolish: *That tale about the ghost that haunts the old mansion is nonsense.*

non·stop (non′stop′), *ADJECTIVE* or *ADVERB.* without stopping: *We took a nonstop flight from Boston to Richmond. He flew nonstop from Denver to Miami.*

non·un·ion (non yü′nyən), *ADJECTIVE.* not recognizing or favoring trade unions: *nonunion farms, a nonunion shop.*

non·vi·o·lence (non vi′ə ləns), *NOUN.* the belief in the use of peaceful methods to achieve any goal; opposition to any form of violence.

noo·dle (nü′dl), *NOUN.* a mixture of flour, water, and eggs, dried into hard flat strips.

nook (nùk), *NOUN.*
1 a cozy little corner: *The cat likes to sleep in a nook by the furnace.*
2 a hidden, sheltered place: *There is a wonderful nook in the woods behind our house.*

noon (nün), *NOUN.* 12 o'clock in the daytime; the middle of the day.

no one, no person; nobody.

noose (nüs), *NOUN.* a loop at the end of a rope with a knot through which the rope can slip to tighten the loop. Nooses are used in lassos.

nor (nôr), *CONJUNCTION.* and no; and not: *We had neither food nor water with us. I have not gone there, nor will I ever go.*

nor·mal (nôr′məl),
1 *ADJECTIVE.* usual; regular: *The normal temperature of the human body is 98.6 degrees.*
2 *NOUN.* the usual state or level: *After the heavy rains, the river was 10 feet above normal.*
3 *ADJECTIVE.* healthy in your body or mind: *Your tonsils look normal. It is not normal to feel sad all the time.*
  —**nor′mal·ly,** *ADVERB.*

Norse (nôrs),
1 *ADJECTIVE.* of or about ancient Scandinavia, its people, or their language.
2 *NOUN PLURAL.* **the Norse,** the people of ancient Scandinavia.
3 *NOUN.* the language of these people.

nonviolence
Mohandas Gandhi

Mohandas Gandhi was an Indian leader who led a nonviolent movement that won India's independence from Great Britain. He was assassinated in 1948.

north (nôrth),
1 *ADJECTIVE.* the direction to the right as you face the setting sun; the direction a compass needle points.
2 *ADJECTIVE* or *ADVERB.* toward the north; farther toward the north: *We live on the north side of town. Drive north for a mile.*
3 *ADJECTIVE.* coming from the north: *a north wind.*
4 *ADJECTIVE.* in the north: *the north window of a house.*
5 *NOUN.* the part of any country toward the north.
6 *NOUN.* **the North,** the northern part of the United States, the states north of Maryland, the Ohio River, and Missouri. These states formed most of the Union in the Civil War.

north of, *IDIOM.* further north than: *Iowa is north of Missouri.*

a	hat	ė	term	ô	order	ch	child		a in about
ā	age	i	it	oi	oil	ng	long		e in taken
ä	far	ī	ice	ou	out	sh	she	ə ⟨	i in pencil
â	care	o	hot	u	cup	th	thin		o in lemon
e	let	ō	open	ù	put	ᴛʜ	then		u in circus
ē	equal	ò	saw	ü	rule	zh	measure		

N

North America, a continent northwest of South America and west of the Atlantic Ocean. It is the third largest continent; only Asia and Africa are larger. The United States, Canada, and Mexico are countries in North America. **–North American.**

North Car·o·li·na (nôrth′ kar′ə li′nə), one of the southern states of the United States. *Abbreviation:* NC; *Capital:* Raleigh. **–North Carolinian** (nôrth′ kâr′ə lin′ē ən).

State Story **North Carolina** was named in honor of Charles I, king of England, who lived from 1600 to 1649. His name in Latin is *Carolus.*

North Da·ko·ta (nôrth′ də kō′tə), one of the Midwestern states of the United States. *Abbreviation:* ND; *Capital:* Bismarck. **–North Dakotan.**

State Story **North Dakota** was named for the Sioux Indians. The Sioux call themselves *Dakota* or *Lakota,* meaning "allies" or "friends."

north·east (nôrth′ēst′),
1 *ADJECTIVE.* halfway between north and east; in the northeast: *The northeast route is the shortest.*
2 *NOUN.* a northeast direction.
3 *NOUN.* a place that is in the northeast part or direction.
4 *ADVERB.* toward the northeast: *At this point the road turns northeast.*
5 *ADJECTIVE.* coming from the northeast: *a northeast wind.*
6 *NOUN.* **the Northeast,** the northeastern part of the United States, including New England, New York, Pennsylvania, and New Jersey.

north·east·ern (nôrth′ē′stərn), *ADJECTIVE.*
1 toward the northeast: *the northeastern sky.*
2 from the northeast.
3 of or in the northeast: *a northeastern climate.*
4 **Northeastern,** of or in the northeastern part of the United States.

north·er·ly (nôr′ℱHər lē), *ADJECTIVE* or *ADVERB.*
1 facing or toward the north: *The storm traveled northerly and passed us by.*
2 from the north: *a northerly wind.*

north·ern (nôr′ℱHərn), *ADJECTIVE.*
1 toward the north: *the northern side of a building.*
2 from the north: *a northern breeze.*
3 of or in the north: *They have lived in northern climates.*
4 **Northern,** of or in the northern part of the United States: *Boston is a Northern city.*

north·ern·er (nôr′ℱHər nər), *NOUN.*
1 someone born or living in the north.
2 **Northerner,** someone born or living in the northern part of the United States.

Northern Ireland, the northern part of Ireland. It is associated with Great Britain.

northern lights, bands of light that appear in the night sky in northern regions. The light is created by the earth's magnetic field.

northern lights

North Korea, a country in eastern Asia. **–North Korean.**

North Pole, the northern end of the earth's axis.

north·ward (nôrth′wərd), *ADJECTIVE* or *ADVERB.* toward the north; north: *I walked northward. The wheat field is on the northward slope of the hill.*

north·wards (nôrth′wərdz), *ADVERB.* See **northward.**

north·west (nôrth′west′),
1 *ADJECTIVE.* halfway between north and west; in the northwest: *the northwest district.*
2 *NOUN.* a northwest direction.
3 *NOUN.* a place that is in the northwest part or direction.
4 *ADVERB.* toward the northwest: *The road from here on runs northwest.*
5 *ADJECTIVE.* coming from the northwest: *a northwest wind.*
6 *NOUN.* **the Northwest,** the northwestern part of the United States, including Washington, Oregon, and Idaho.

north·west·ern (nôrth′wes′tərn), *ADJECTIVE.*
1 toward the northwest: *the northwestern sky.*
2 from the northwest.
3 of or in the northwest: *a northwestern climate.*
4 **Northwestern,** of or in the northwestern part of the United States.

Northwest Territories, a division of northern Canada, east of the Yukon Territory.

Nor·way (nôr′wā), *NOUN.* a country in northern Europe.

Nor·we·gian (nôr wē′jən),
1 *ADJECTIVE.* of or relating to Norway, its people, or their language.
2 *NOUN.* someone born or living in Norway.
3 *NOUN.* the language of Norway.

nose (nōz),
1 *NOUN.* the part of the face sticking out above the mouth, used for breathing and smelling.

2 *NOUN.* the sense of smell: *That dog has a good nose for hunting.*

3 *VERB.* to smell; investigate or discover by smell: *The hounds nosed the scent of the fox.*

4 *VERB.* to touch, rub, or push with the nose: *The cat nosed its kittens.*

5 *NOUN.* a part that sticks out, especially at the front of something: *the nose of an airplane.*
❑ *VERB* **nos·es, nosed, nos·ing.**

under your nose, *IDIOM.* in plain sight: *I lost my pencil, but found it again right under my nose.*

Have You Heard?

You may have heard someone say **"Don't cut off your nose to spite your face."** This means that you shouldn't do something that will hurt you a lot just to make someone else mad or upset.

nose·bleed (nōz'blēd'), *NOUN.* a flow of blood from the nose.

nos·tril (nos'trəl), *NOUN.* either of the two openings in the nose. Air is breathed into the lungs, and smells come into the sensitive parts of the nose, through the nostrils.

nos·y (nō'zē), *ADJECTIVE.* too curious about other people's business: *Our nosy neighbors were always asking questions about our family.* ❑ *ADJECTIVE* **nos·i·er, nos·i·est. –nos'i·ness,** *NOUN.*

not (not), *ADVERB.* a word that says no: *Cold is not hot. Six and two do not make ten.* ■ Another word that sounds like this is **knot.**

no·ta·ble (nō'tə bəl), *ADJECTIVE.* worth noticing; remarkable; important: *Last week's eruption of the volcano was a notable event.*

Notable events interest everyone.

no·ta·tion (nō tā'shən), *NOUN.*

1 a set of signs or symbols that stand for numbers or other things. Mathematics and music each have special systems of notation.

2 a note to help your memory: *I made a notation in the margin of the book.*

notch (noch),

1 *NOUN.* a nick or cut shaped like a V, made in an edge or on a curving surface: *People used to cut notches on a stick to keep count of numbers.*

2 *VERB.* to make a notch or notches in something.
❑ *VERB* **notch·es, notched, notch·ing;** *PLURAL* **notch·es.**

note (nōt),

1 *NOUN.* a short sentence, phrase, or single word, written down to remind one of what was in a book, a speech, or an agreement: *Sometimes our teacher has us take notes on what we read.*

2 *NOUN.* a very short letter: *a note of thanks.*

3 *VERB.* to write down something to be remembered: *Our class notes the weather daily on a chart.*

4 *NOUN.* a piece of information added to a word or a passage in a book, often to help pupils in studying the book: *A footnote is a note at the bottom of the page about something on the page.*

5 *NOUN.* greatness; fame: *a person of note.*

6 *VERB.* to notice; give attention to: *Please note what I do next.*

7 *NOUN.* (in music) a written sign that shows what sound to make.

8 *NOUN.* a single musical sound: *Sing this note for me.*
❑ *VERB* **notes, not·ed, not·ing.**

note·book (nōt'bùk'), *NOUN.* a book of blank or lined paper in which to write notes of things to learn or remember.

not·ed (nō'tid), *ADJECTIVE.* well-known; famous: *She is a noted author.*

noth·ing (nuth'ing),

1 *PRONOUN.* not anything: *Nothing arrived by mail.*

2 *NOUN.* something or someone of no value or importance: *Don't worry, it's nothing.*

3 *NOUN.* zero.

4 *ADVERB.* not at all: *She looks nothing like her sister.*

no·tice (nō'tis),

1 *NOUN.* attention; observation: *A sudden movement caught his notice.*

2 *VERB.* to look at; see: *I noticed a hole in my sock.* ■ See the Synonym Study at **see.**

3 *NOUN.* information or warning about something that is going to happen: *The whistle blew to give notice that the boat was about to leave.*

4 *NOUN.* a written or printed announcement, sign, or message: *There's a notice in the newspaper about their wedding. We posted notices about our yard sale.*

5 *NOUN.* the act of telling that you are leaving or must leave rented quarters or a job at a given time: *I gave two weeks' notice when I quit my job.*
❑ *VERB* **no·tic·es, no·ticed, no·tic·ing.**

a	hat	ė	term	ô	order	ch	child		a in about
ā	age	i	it	oi	oil	ng	long		e in taken
ä	far	ī	ice	ou	out	sh	she	ə	i in pencil
â	care	o	hot	u	cup	th	thin		o in lemon
e	let	ō	open	ù	put	ŦH	then		u in circus
ē	equal	ò	saw	ü	rule	zh	measure		

no·tice·a·ble (nō′ti sə bəl), ADJECTIVE. easily seen or noticed: *The class has made a noticeable improvement in spelling since the last test.*
—**no′tice·a·bly**, ADVERB.

no·ti·fi·ca·tion (nō′tə fə kā′shən), NOUN. a notice: *She received a notification of the meeting.*

no·ti·fy (nō′tə fī), VERB. to let someone know something; announce to; inform: *Our teacher notified us that there would be a test on Monday.*
❑ VERB **no·ti·fies, no·ti·fied, no·ti·fy·ing.**

no·tion (nō′shən), NOUN.
1 an opinion; belief: *People have different notions about how children should be raised.* ■ See the Synonym Study at **idea.**
2 a desire or thought that suddenly occurs to someone: *I had a notion to give them a call.*

no·to·ri·ous (nō tôr′ē əs), ADJECTIVE. well-known, especially because of something bad: *Our neighbors are notorious for giving noisy parties.*
—**no·to′ri·ous·ly**, ADVERB.

not·with·stand·ing (not′wiтн stan′ding or not′with stan′ding),
1 PREPOSITION. in spite of: *I bought it notwithstanding the high price.*
2 ADVERB. nevertheless: *It is raining; but I shall go, notwithstanding.*

Blackbeard was a **notorious** pirate.

noun (noun), NOUN. a word that names a person, place, thing, quality, or event. Words like *Lisa, Boston, kindness, book,* and *party* are nouns.

nour·ish (nėr′ish), VERB.
1 to make someone or something grow; keep alive and well, with food; feed: *Milk nourishes a baby.*
2 to support or encourage something: *Getting a letter published in the newspaper nourished her hopes of being a writer.*
❑ VERB **nour·ish·es, nour·ished, nour·ish·ing.**

nour·ish·ment (nėr′ish mənt), NOUN. what is necessary for healthy life and growth; food: *They were ill from lack of proper nourishment.*

Nov., an abbreviation of **November.**

No·va Sco·tia (nō′və skō′shə), a province in southeastern Canada. —**Nova Scotian.**

nov·el (nov′əl),
1 NOUN. a long, made-up story with characters and a plot. Novels are usually about people, scenes, and happenings like the ones you might meet in real life.
2 ADJECTIVE. unusual; strange; new: *Peanut butter and ham was a novel idea for a sandwich.*

nov·el·ist (nov′ə list), NOUN. someone who writes novels.

nov·el·ty (nov′əl tē), NOUN.
1 the quality of being unusual or new; newness: *After the novelty of the game wore off, we didn't want to play it any more.*
2 a new or unusual thing: *Staying up late was a novelty to the children.*
3 novelties, small, unusual articles, such as toys or inexpensive jewelry.
❑ PLURAL **nov·el·ties.**

No·vem·ber (nō vem′bər), NOUN. the 11th month of the year. It has 30 days.

Word Story

November came from a Latin word meaning "nine." In the ancient Roman calendar, November was the ninth month of the year, which began in March.

nov·ice (nov′is), NOUN.
1 a beginner; someone who is new to something: *Novices are likely to make some mistakes.*
2 someone who is not yet a monk or nun, but is in a period of trial and preparation.

now (nou),
1 ADVERB. at this time: *He is here now. Most people do not believe in ghosts now. Do it now!*
2 ADVERB. by this time: *She must be home now.*
3 NOUN. this time: *by now, until now, from now on.*
4 ADVERB. as things are; as it is: *Now I can never believe you again.*
5 ADVERB. *Now* is used in many sentences where it makes very little difference in the meaning: *Now what do you mean? Oh, come now! Now, you knew that was wrong, didn't you?*

now and then or **now and again,** IDIOM. from time to time; once in a while: *I see him now and then, but not often.*

now that, IDIOM. since: *Now that you mention it, I do remember.*

now·a·days (nou′ə dāz′), ADVERB. at the present day; in these times: *Nowadays people travel in cars rather than carriages.*

no·where (nō′wâr),
1 ADVERB. in no place; at no place; to no place: *The lost watch was nowhere to be seen.*
2 NOUN. a place that is not well-known or is far from everything else: *Our car broke down in the middle of nowhere.*

noz·zle (noz′əl), NOUN. a short length of metal tube put on a hose or pipe so that you can change the amount of liquid that comes out: *He adjusted the nozzle so that the water came out in a fine spray.*

nub (nub), NOUN. the point or main idea of anything: *Now we've reached the nub of the problem.*

nu·cle·ar (nü′klē ər), ADJECTIVE.
1 of or about a nucleus, especially the nucleus of an atom: *Neutrons and protons are nuclear particles.*
2 of or about atoms, atomic energy, or atomic weapons; atomic: *a nuclear reactor, the nuclear age.*

Pronunciation Note

Nuclear is pronounced as nü kyə lər by many people. Many other people feel that this pronunciation is wrong, but it is so common that it will probably be accepted into the language.

nuclear energy, the energy that exists inside the nucleus of an atom; atomic energy. Nuclear energy can be released by splitting or combining the centers of some kinds of atoms.

nuclear fission. See **fission.**

nuclear reactor. See **reactor.**

nu·cle·us (nü′klē əs), NOUN.
1 a central part or thing around which other parts or things are collected: *A dictionary and a dozen novels formed the nucleus of the classroom library.*
2 the central part of an atom, consisting of protons and neutrons. The nucleus forms a core around which electrons orbit.
3 a special part found in most living cells which controls their growth and their division to form new cells.
❑ PLURAL **nu·cle·i** (nü′klē ī) or **nu·cle·us·es.**

nude (nüd), ADJECTIVE. with no clothes on; naked.

nudge (nuj),
1 VERB. to push someone slightly to attract attention: *She nudged me with her elbow when it was my turn.* ■ See the Synonym Study at **push.**
2 NOUN. a slight push.
❑ VERB **nudg·es, nudged, nudg·ing.**

Nue·vo Le·ón (nwā′vō lā ōn′), NOUN. a state in northern Mexico.

nug·get (nug′it), NOUN. a small, rough piece of valuable metal ore: *gold nuggets.*

nui·sance (nü′sns), NOUN. something or someone that annoys you, or is disagreeable: *Flies are a nuisance.*

numb (num),
1 ADJECTIVE. not able to feel anything: *numb with cold.*
2 VERB. to make a part of the body numb: *The dentist gave me a shot to numb my jaw.*
3 VERB. to dull someone's feelings: *The news of her death numbed them with grief.*
❑ VERB **numbs, numbed, numb·ing. —numb′ness,** NOUN.

num·ber (num′bər),
1 NOUN. the total or sum of a group of things or people; amount: *The number of students in our class is twenty.*
2 NOUN. a word that tells exactly how many. Two, thirteen, twenty-one, and one hundred are such numbers.

3 NOUN. a word that tells rank or place in a series. Second and thirteenth are such numbers.
4 NOUN. a figure or group of figures that stands for a number; numeral. 2, 7, and 9 are numbers.
5 VERB. to give a number to: *The pages of this book are numbered.*
6 VERB. to be or amount to a given number: *The states in the Union number 50.*
7 NOUN. one of a numbered series, often a particular numeral identifying a someone or something: *a telephone number, a house number, a locker number.*
8 VERB. to limit; fix the number of: *Our old dog's days are numbered.*
9 NOUN. (in grammar) a word form or ending which shows whether one or more is meant. *Girl, child,* and *this* are in the singular number; *girls, children,* and *these* are in the plural number.
❑ VERB **num·bers, num·bered, num·ber·ing.**

Word Power   Number Prefixes

People often want to know "how many?" This is why each **number** has a prefix that answers that question. Look up these words in this dictionary to answer these questions: How many wheels does a **uni**cycle have? How many points does a **bi**cuspid have? How many angles does a **tri**angle have? How many brothers or sisters does a **quad**ruplet, **quint**uplet, **sext**uplet, or **sept**uplet have? How many sides does an **oct**agon have? How many years are in a **dec**ade?

num·ber·less (num′bər lis), ADJECTIVE. very numerous; too many to count: *There are numberless fish in the sea.*

number line, a line divided into equal segments by points marked with numbers in order.

nu·mer·al (nü′mər əl), NOUN. a figure or group of figures standing for a number. 7, 25, 463, iv, and XIX are numerals.

nu·mer·a·tor (nü′mə rā′tər), NOUN. the number above or to the left of the line in a fraction, which shows how many equal parts of the whole make up the fraction. In ⅜, 3 is the numerator and 8 is the denominator.

nu·mer·i·cal (nü mer′ə kəl), ADJECTIVE. of or about a number or numbers; in or by numbers: *My Oozewoman comic books are arranged in numerical order by issue number.* **—nu·mer′i·cal·ly,** ADVERB.

nu·mer·ous (nü′mər əs), ADJECTIVE. a great many: *The child asked numerous questions.* ■ See the Synonym Study at **many.**

a hat	ė term	ô order	ch child	⎰a in about
ā age	i it	oi oil	ng long	e in taken
ä far	ī ice	ou out	sh she	ə⎨i in pencil
â care	o hot	u cup	th thin	o in lemon
e let	ō open	u̇ put	ᴛʜ then	⎱u in circus
ē equal	ȯ saw	ü rule	zh measure	

nun (nun), NOUN. a woman who lives a life devoted to religion. Nuns often live together in groups that teach or care for the poor and sick. ■ Another word that sounds like this is **none**.

nurse (nėrs),
1 NOUN. someone who is trained to take care of the sick, the injured, or the very old. Nurses often work with doctors in hospitals.
2 VERB. to take care of the sick: *They nursed their children through the flu.*
3 VERB. to cure or try to cure something: *She nursed a bad cold by going to bed.*
4 NOUN. a woman who cares for and brings up other people's young children or babies.
5 VERB. to treat something with special care: *He nursed his sore arm by using it very little.*
6 VERB. to give milk to a baby at the breast.
7 VERB. to suck milk from the breast of a mother.
❑ VERB **nurs·es, nursed, nurs·ing.**

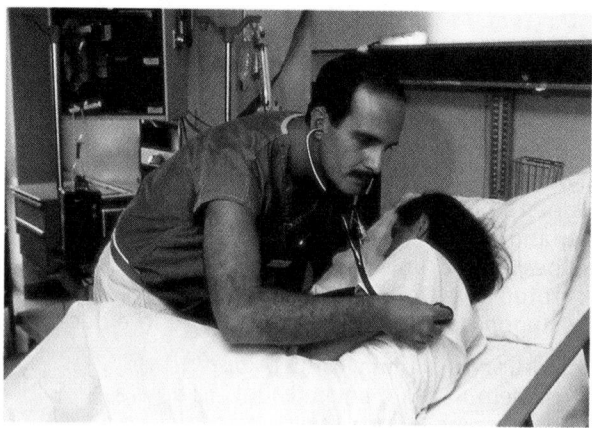

This **nurse** is checking his patient's lungs.

nurs·er·y (nėr′sər ē), NOUN.
1 a room set apart for the use and care of babies.
2 a place where babies and small children are cared for during the day: *a private nursery.*
3 a piece of ground or place where young plants are raised for transplanting or sale.
❑ PLURAL **nurs·er·ies.**

nursery school, a school for children not old enough to go to kindergarten.

nursing home, a place for the care of very old people or anyone who needs nursing care over a long period of time.

nur·ture (nėr′chər), VERB. to bring up and care for a child: *They nurtured the child as if she were their own.* ❑ VERB **nur·tures, nur·tured, nur·tur·ing.**

nut (nut), NOUN.
1 a dry fruit or seed with a hard shell and a kernel inside. The kernel is often good to eat. Most nuts grow on trees.
2 the kernel of a nut: *The recipe calls for chopped nuts.*

3 a small piece of metal or plastic with a hole in the center containing a screw thread. It screws on to a bolt to hold the bolt in place.
4 informal: **a** an odd or silly person. **b** a devoted fan: *a baseball nut.*
—**nut′like**′, ADJECTIVE.

nut·crack·er (nut′krak′ər), NOUN. a device for cracking the shells of nuts.

nut·meg (nut′meg), NOUN. a hard, spicy seed, about as big as a large marble, of a tropical tree. The seed is grated and used for flavoring food.

nu·tri·ent (nü′trē ənt), NOUN. any substance that is required by living things for energy, growth, and repair of tissues: *Vegetables are good sources of vitamins, minerals, and other nutrients.*

nu·tri·tion (nü trish′ən), NOUN. food; nourishment: *A balanced diet provides nutrition for your body.*

nutcracker

nu·tri·tious (nü trish′əs), ADJECTIVE. nourishing; valuable as food: *Eggs are nutritious.*
—**nu·tri′tious·ly,** ADVERB.

nuts (nuts), ADJECTIVE. (informal) extremely foolish: *He's nuts to try a dangerous stunt like that.*

be nuts about, IDIOM. (informal) to like very much: *She's nuts about water-skiing.*

nut·ty (nut′ē), ADJECTIVE.
1 like nuts; tasting like nuts: *a nutty flavor.*
2 (informal) odd or silly: *We did nutty things like jumping into the pool with our clothes on.*
❑ ADJECTIVE **nut·ti·er, nut·ti·est.**

nuz·zle (nuz′əl), VERB. to rub your nose against someone in a gentle, loving way. ❑ VERB **nuz·zles, nuz·zled, nuz·zling.**

NV, an abbreviation of **Nevada.**

NW or **N.W.,**
1 an abbreviation of **northwest** or **Northwest.**
2 an abbreviation of **northwestern** or **Northwestern.**

NY, an abbreviation of **New York.**

ny·lon (nī′lon), NOUN.
1 a synthetic substance that is very strong and somewhat elastic. Clothing, tents, stockings, and brushes are made of nylon.
2 **nylons,** stockings made of nylon.

orchid

O or **o** (ō), *NOUN.* the 15th letter of the English alphabet. ❏ *PLURAL* **O's** or **o's.**

O., an abbreviation of **Ohio.**

O·a·hu (ō ä′hü), *NOUN.* the third largest island of Hawaii. Honolulu, the capital of Hawaii, is on Oahu.

oak (ōk), *NOUN.* a tree that produces extremely hard wood, used for furniture and floors. There are many kinds of oaks, found in most parts of the world. Acorns are the seeds of oaks.

oar (ôr), *NOUN.* a long pole with one end that is broad and flat, used in rowing. ■ Other words that sound like this are **or** and **ore.** —**oar′like′,** *ADJECTIVE.*

o·a·sis (ō ā′sis), *NOUN.* a place in the desert where there is water and where trees and plants can grow. ❏ *PLURAL* **o·a·ses** (ō ā′sēz′).

oath (ōth), *NOUN.* a statement swearing that something is true: *I gave an oath that I would tell the truth.* ❏ *PLURAL* **oaths** (ōthz or ōths).

oat·meal (ōt′mēl′), *NOUN.*
1 oats that are partially ground up and flattened into small flakes.
2 a cooked cereal made from this: *We often have oatmeal with cream and sugar for breakfast.*

oats (ōts), *NOUN PLURAL* or *SINGULAR.* the grain of a kind of cereal grass, or the plant that it grows on. The grain is used to make oatmeal and as a food for horses and other farm animals.

Oa·xa·ca (wä hä′kə), *NOUN.* a state in southeastern Mexico.

o·be·di·ence (ōbē′dē əns), *NOUN.* the act or habit of doing what you are told to do: *Some parents demand complete obedience from their children.*

o·be·di·ent (ō bē′dē ənt), *ADJECTIVE.* doing what one is told to do; willing to obey: *The obedient dog came running over at its owner's whistle.* —**o·be′di·ent·ly,** *ADVERB.*

o·bese (ō bēs′), *ADJECTIVE.* very fat.

o·bey (ō bā′), VERB.
1 to do what someone tells you to do; follow orders: *The dog obeyed its owner and went home.*
2 to do what the law or a rule tells you to do: *A good citizen obeys the laws.*
❑ VERB **o·beys, o·beyed, o·bey·ing.**

o·bi (ō′bē), NOUN. a long, broad sash worn like a belt around the waist of a kimono. ❑ PLURAL **o·bis.**

ob·ject (ob′jikt),
1 NOUN. anything solid that you can see or touch; thing: *What is that object by the fence?* ■ See the Synonym Study at **thing.**
2 NOUN. someone or something that a person directs his or her feeling, thought, or action toward: *He is the object of my affection.*
3 NOUN. something that a person intends to do; purpose; goal: *My object in coming here was to help you.*
4 NOUN. (in grammar) a word or group of words that receives the action of a verb, or that follows a preposition. In "He threw the ball to his sister," *ball* is the object of the verb *threw*, and *sister* is the object of the preposition *to.*
5 VERB. to feel or express dislike for something; be opposed to: *Many people object to loud noise. I object to your remarks about my dog.*
❑ VERB **ob·jects, ob·ject·ed, ob·ject·ing.**
—**ob·jec′tor,** NOUN.

ob·jec·tion (əb jek′shən), NOUN.
1 something offered as a reason or argument against something: *One of the objections to the new plan was that it would cost too much.*
2 a feeling of dislike: *He has no objection to hard work.*

ob·jec·tion·a·ble (əb jek′shə nə bəl), ADJECTIVE. unpleasant: *I smell an objectionable odor.*

ob·jec·tive (əb jek′tiv),
1 NOUN. something that a person intends to do; goal; purpose: *My objective this summer will be learning to play tennis better.*
2 ADJECTIVE. not influenced by your personal thoughts or feelings; not subjective: *The witness gave an objective report of the accident.*
—**ob·jec′tive·ly,** ADVERB.

ob·li·gate (ob′lə gāt), VERB. to make someone feel strongly that he or she must do something: *A witness in court is obligated to tell the truth.*
❑ VERB **ob·li·gates, ob·li·gat·ed, ob·li·gat·ing.**

ob·li·ga·tion (ob′lə gā′shən), NOUN. a duty to do something because of a law or because you feel you should: *We have an obligation to help our friends.*

o·blige (ə blij′), VERB.
1 to make someone do something: *I am obliged to leave early to catch my train.*
2 to make someone grateful by doing him or her a favor: *I'm very much obliged for your offer to help.*
❑ VERB **o·blig·es, o·bliged, o·blig·ing.**

ob·long (ob′lòng), ADJECTIVE. longer than it is wide: *Most loaves of bread are oblong.*

ob·nox·ious (əb nok′shəs), ADJECTIVE. very disagreeable: *Their rudeness made them obnoxious to me. That toy makes such an obnoxious noise.*
—**ob·nox′ious·ly,** ADVERB.

o·boe (ō′bō), NOUN. a wind instrument in which a thin, high tone is produced by a mouthpiece with two reeds.

ob·scene (əb sēn′), ADJECTIVE. offending modesty or decency: *obscene language, an obscene phone call.*

ob·scure (əb skyùr′),
1 ADJECTIVE. hard to understand or distinguish; not clear: *an obscure message, an obscure shape, obscure sounds.*
2 ADJECTIVE. not well known: *an obscure little village, an obscure poet.*
3 VERB. to hide something from view: *Clouds obscure the sun.*
❑ VERB **ob·scures, ob·scured, ob·scur·ing.**
—**ob·scure′ly,** ADVERB.

oboe

ob·scu·ri·ty (əb skyùr′ə tē), NOUN.
1 difficulty in being understood: *The obscurity of the book caused an argument over its meaning.*
2 the condition of being unknown: *Abraham Lincoln rose from obscurity to fame.*

ob·serv·ance (əb zėr′vəns), NOUN. the act of paying attention to or keeping laws or customs: *Observance of the traffic laws is the sign of a good driver.*

ob·serv·ant (əb zėr′vənt), ADJECTIVE. quick to notice things: *If you are observant in the woods, you will find many unusual flowers.*

ob·ser·va·tion (ob′zər vā′shən), NOUN.
1 the act, habit, or power of seeing and noting something: *By trained observation, a doctor can tell much about the condition of a patient.*
2 something seen and noted: *During science experiments she kept careful records of her observations.*
3 the fact or condition of being seen: *The spy avoided observation.*
4 a remark or comment about something: *Dad made an observation about the mess in my room.*

ob·serv·a·to·ry (əb zėr′və tôr′ē), NOUN. a building equipped with telescopes and other devices for studying the stars, planets, weather conditions, and so on. ❑ PLURAL **ob·serv·a·to·ries.**

ob·serve (əb zėrv′), VERB.
1 to see and note; notice: *I didn't observe anything different. Did you observe anything strange about her?* ■ See the Synonym Study at **see.**

2 to look at something carefully in order to learn about it; study: *An astronomer observes the stars.*

3 to remark; comment: *"Bad weather ahead," she observed.*

4 to obey a law, rule, and the like: *We observed the rule about not walking on the grass.*

5 to celebrate: *to observe the Sabbath.*
□ *VERB* **ob·serves, ob·served, ob·serv·ing.** —**ob·serv′er,** *NOUN.*

ob·so·lete (ob′sə lēt), *ADJECTIVE.* no longer in use; out-of-date: *You can see examples of obsolete machinery in museums.*

ob·sta·cle (ob′stə kəl), *NOUN.* something that keeps something from happening by getting in the way: *She overcame many obstacles to become a doctor.*

The fallen trees created an **obstacle** on the tracks.

ob·sti·nate (ob′stə nit), *ADJECTIVE.* stubborn. —**ob′sti·nate·ly,** *ADVERB.*

ob·struct (əb strukt′), *VERB.*

1 to block a path, road, and so on, so that is hard to pass through: *Fallen trees from the storm obstructed the highway.*

2 to get in the way of: *Trees obstruct our view of the ocean.*
□ *VERB* **ob·structs, ob·struct·ed, ob·struct·ing.**

ob·struc·tion (əb struk′shən), *NOUN.*

1 something that is in the way; obstacle: *The old path was blocked by such obstructions as boulders and fallen trees.*

2 the act or process of blocking or stopping: *Obstruction of justice is a crime.*

ob·tain (əb tān′), *VERB.* to get something through effort: *We obtain knowledge in school.* □ *VERB* **ob·tains, ob·tained, ob·tain·ing.** —**ob·tain′a·ble,** *ADJECTIVE.*

ob·tuse an·gle (əb tüs′ ang′gəl), an angle greater than a right angle.

ob·vi·ous (ob′vē əs), *ADJECTIVE.* easy to see or understand: *It was obvious that she was angry.* —**ob′vi·ous·ly,** *ADVERB.*

oc·ca·sion (ə kā′zhən), *NOUN.*

1 a particular time: *We have met them on several occasions.*

2 a special event: *The coronation was an impressive occasion.*

3 a good chance; opportunity: *The trip we took gave us an occasion to get to know each other better.*

A birthday party is a happy **occasion.**

oc·ca·sion·al (ə kā′zhə nəl), *ADJECTIVE.* happening sometimes or once in a while: *We had fine weather all summer except for an occasional thunderstorm.*

oc·ca·sion·al·ly (ə kā′zhə nə lē), *ADVERB.* every so often; now and then; once in a while: *We get together with our cousins occasionally.*

oc·cu·pant (ok′yə pənt), *NOUN.* someone who occupies or lives in something: *The occupants of the cabin stepped out as I approached.*

oc·cu·pa·tion (ok′yə pā′shən), *NOUN.*

1 the work someone does regularly or to earn a living: *Caring for the sick is a nurse's occupation.*

2 the invasion and physical possession of something: *The town endured the occupation by enemy troops for over a year.*

oc·cu·py (ok′yə pī), *VERB.*

1 to live in: *Two families occupy the house next door.*

2 to take possession of something: *The enemy army occupied the capital city.*

3 to have; hold: *A judge occupies an important position.*

4 to take up space; fill: *The building occupies an entire block.*

5 to keep busy doing something: *Composing music occupied her attention.*
□ *VERB* **oc·cu·pies, oc·cu·pied, oc·cu·py·ing.**

oc·cur (ə kėr′), *VERB.*

1 to happen; take place: *Storms often occur in winter.*

a	hat	ė	term	ô	order	ch	child		a in about
ā	age	i	it	oi	oil	ng	long		e in taken
ä	far	ī	ice	ou	out	sh	she	ə<	i in pencil
â	care	o	hot	u	cup	th	thin		o in lemon
e	let	ō	open	ù	put	ŦH	then		u in circus
ē	equal	ò	saw	ü	rule	zh	measure		

2 to be found; exist: *"E" occurs in print more often than any other letter.*

3 to come into your mind: *Has it occurred to you to close the windows?* ❏ *VERB* **oc·curs, oc·curred, oc·cur·ring.**

oc·cur·rence (ə kėr′əns), *NOUN.* something that happens; an event: *Her visit was an unexpected occurrence.*

o·cean (ō′shən), *NOUN.*
1 the great body of salt water that covers almost three fourths of the earth's surface; the sea.
2 any of its four main parts—the Atlantic, Pacific, Indian, and Arctic oceans.

o·cean·og·ra·phy (ō′shə nog′rə fē), *NOUN.* the science that studies the oceans and seas and the living things in them.

oc·e·lot (os′ə lot), *NOUN.* a large cat with spots, somewhat like a leopard but much smaller. It is found from Texas through Mexico and into parts of South America.

o'clock (ə klok′), *ADVERB.* of or by the clock: *one o'clock.*

Oct., an abbreviation of **October.**

oc·ta·gon (ok′tə gon), *NOUN.* a figure having eight angles and eight sides.

oc·tave (ok′tiv), *NOUN.*
1 the eight tones in a musical scale. The tones from one C to the next tone called C include one octave.
2 the eighth tone above (or below) a given tone, having twice (or half) as many vibrations per second.

Oc·to·ber (ok tō′bər), *NOUN.* the tenth month of the year. It has 31 days.

Word Story

October came from a Latin word meaning "eight." In the ancient Roman calendar, October was the eighth month of the year, which began in March.

oc·to·pus (ok′tə pəs), *NOUN.* a sea animal having a soft, thick body and eight arms with suckers on them. There are about 100 kinds of octopus. ❏ *PLURAL* **oc·to·pus·es** or **oc·to·pi** (ok′tə pī).

Word Story

Octopus comes from a Greek word meaning "having eight feet." We define the octopus as having eight arms. In earlier times these arms were thought of as looking like legs with feet.

odd (od), *ADJECTIVE.*
1 acting strange or doing something strange: *We think our dog is odd because she loves vegetables.*
2 strange; peculiar; unusual: *What an odd house; it has no windows.*
3 having one left over when divided by 2; uneven. Three, five, and seven are **odd numbers.**
4 being only one of a pair of things: *an odd sock.*

5 occasional: *He could not find regular work and had to take odd jobs.*

odd·i·ty (od′ə tē), *NOUN.* a strange, unusual, or peculiar person or thing. ❏ *PLURAL* **odd·i·ties.**

odd·ly (od′lē), *ADVERB.* in a strange or unusual manner: *an oddly shaped cup.*

ocelot — about 4 feet long, including the tail

odds (odz), *NOUN PLURAL.* the chance that something is true or that it will happen, often expressed in numbers; advantage: *The odds are in our favor and we should win.*

at odds, *IDIOM.* quarreling; disagreeing: *The two brothers were often at odds.*

odds and ends, *IDIOM.* things left over; extra bits: *He went about the house picking up the odds and ends.*

o·dor (ō′dər), *NOUN.* scent or smell: *the odor of roses, the odor of garbage.* **−o′dor·less,** *ADJECTIVE.*

od·ys·sey (od′ə sē), *NOUN.* a long series of wanderings and adventures: *Her odyssey in sports competitions took her all the way to the Olympic games.* ❏ *PLURAL* **od·ys·seys.**

The smallest kind of **octopus** measures about 1 inch from the tip of one arm to the tip of its opposite arm. The largest measures up to 20 feet from tip to tip.

of (uv or ov), *PREPOSITION.*
1 belonging to: *the children of my aunt, the news of the day, the driver of the car, the causes of the war.*
2 made from: *a house of bricks, castles of sand.*
3 having; with: *a house of six rooms.*

4 with a certain quality: *a word of praise, a look of pity.*
5 away from; from: *north of Boston.*
6 about; concerning: *My teacher thinks well of me.*
7 as a result of using something; out of; owing to: *We expect much of the new medicine.*
8 from among: *Many of my classmates were at the party.*

off (òf),
1 ADVERB. from the usual or correct position or condition: *I took off my hat.*
2 PREPOSITION. from; away from: *He pushed me off my seat. We are miles off the main road.*
3 ADVERB. away; at a distance: *to go off on a journey. Christmas is only five weeks off.*
4 PREPOSITION. subtracted from: *The store took $25 off the regular price.*
5 ADVERB. so as to stop or reduce something: *Turn off the water.*
6 ADJECTIVE. no longer planned; canceled: *The game is off.*
7 PREPOSITION or ADJECTIVE. not on: *The electricity is off. That book is off the shelf.*
8 ADVERB or ADJECTIVE. without work: *take off an afternoon. She likes to read during off hours.*
9 ADJECTIVE. in error; wrong: *Your answer is way off.*
 off and on, IDIOM. at some times and not at others; now and then: *He has lived in Europe off and on for ten years.*

of·fend (ə fend′), VERB. to hurt someone's feelings; upset: *My friend was offended by my laughter.*
 ❑ VERB **of·fends, of·fend·ed, of·fend·ing.**
 —of·fen′der, NOUN.

of·fense (ə fens′ for 1; ò′fens for 2), NOUN.
1 the act of breaking the law; crime. Offenses against the law are punished by fines or imprisonment.
2 the team that has the ball, puck, and so on, in a game: *Our football team has a good offense.*
 take offense, IDIOM. to be offended: *I didn't take offense when he called me by my brother's name.*

of·fen·sive (ə fen′siv),
1 ADJECTIVE. rude and insulting: *"Shut up" is an offensive remark.*
2 ADJECTIVE. unpleasant; disagreeable; disgusting: *The rotten eggs had an offensive odor.*
3 ADJECTIVE. used for attack; relating to attack: *offensive weapons, an offensive war for conquest.*
4 ADJECTIVE. (in sports) of or relating to scoring or offense: *an offensive squad.*
5 NOUN. a military attack: *Planes bombed the enemy lines on the night before the offensive.*
 —of·fen′sive·ly, ADVERB.

of·fer (ò′fər),
1 VERB. to hand something to someone, to see if it will be taken or not: *to offer your hand, to offer a handkerchief.*
2 VERB. to say that you are willing to do or give something: *I offered to wash the dishes.*
3 VERB. to bring a thought to someone's mind; suggest: *She offered a few ideas to improve the plan. He offered a good price for the car.*
4 NOUN. a statement that offers something: *an offer of money, an offer to sing.*
5 NOUN. something that is offered: *She made an offer of $90,000 for the house.*
 ❑ VERB **of·fers, of·fered, of·fer·ing.**

off·hand (òf′hand′ for adverb; òf′hand′ for adjective),
1 ADVERB. at once; without previous thought of preparation: *The carpenter could not tell offhand the cost of his work.*
2 ADJECTIVE. done or made without previous thought or preparation; casual: *Her offhand opinion turned out to be quite accurate.*

of·fice (ò′fis), NOUN.
1 a place where people do the work of a business or profession: *The doctor's office is on the third floor.*
2 the staff of people carrying on work in such a place: *Half the office is on vacation.*
3 a position, especially a public position: *The President holds the highest public office in the United States.*

of·fi·cer (ò′fə sər), NOUN.
1 someone who commands other people in the armed forces. Majors, generals, captains, and admirals are officers.
2 someone who holds an important job in business or in government: *She is the chief financial officer of the company.*
3 a police officer.

an army **officer**

of·fi·cial (ə fish′əl),
1 NOUN. someone who holds an office; officer: *The mayor is a public official.*
2 ADJECTIVE. of or for a position of authority: *an official uniform, official business.*
3 ADJECTIVE. having authority: *An official announcement is expected next week.*
 —of·fi′cial·ly, ADVERB.

off·lim·its (òf′lim′its), ADJECTIVE. not to be used or entered by anyone; prohibited: *The street is off-limits for play.*

a	hat	ė	term	ô	order	ch	child		a in about
ā	age	i	it	oi	oil	ng	long		e in taken
ä	far	ī	ice	ou	out	sh	she	ə	i in pencil
â	care	o	hot	u	cup	th	thin		o in lemon
e	let	ō	open	ù	put	ŦH	then		u in circus
ē	equal	ò	saw	ü	rule	zh	measure		

off·set (óf′set′), VERB. to make up for: *A good offense helps offset a weak defense in sports.*
❑ VERB **off·sets, off·set, off·set·ting.**

off·shoot (óf′shüt′), NOUN. a shoot from a main stem; branch: *an offshoot of a plant.*

off·shore (óf′shôr′), ADJECTIVE or ADVERB. off or away from the shore: *The wind was blowing offshore. We saw offshore oil wells along the coast.*

off·side (óf′sīd′), ADVERB or ADJECTIVE. (in sports) illegally ahead of the ball or puck: *The play was ruled offside. Which player was offside?*

An **oil painting** can create a bright scene.

off·spring (óf′spring′), NOUN. the young of a living thing; descendant: *All their offspring had red hair.*
❑ PLURAL **off·spring.**

off-the-cuff (óf′ŦHə kuf′), ADJECTIVE. not planned or rehearsed: *an off-the-cuff remark.*

off-the-wall (óf′ŦHə wòl′), ADJECTIVE. (informal) very foolish; highly unusual: *an off-the-wall suggestion.*

of·ten (ò′fən or óf′tən), ADVERB. many times; frequently: *We often go to the beach on Saturdays.*

o·gre (ō′gər), NOUN. (in fairy tales) a giant or monster that eats people.

oh (ō), INTERJECTION. a word used to express surprise, joy, pain, and other feelings: *Oh, dear me!*
■ Another word that sounds like this is **owe.**

OH, an abbreviation of **Ohio.**

O·hi·o (ō hī′ō), NOUN.
1 one of the Midwestern states of the United States. *Abbreviation:* OH; *Capital:* Columbus.
2 a river in the United States.
—**O·hi′o·an,** NOUN.

State Story   Ohio got its name from the Ohio River. It may have come from an Iroquois Indian word meaning "fine" or "beautiful."

oil (oil),
1 NOUN. any of many kinds of thick, fatty or greasy liquids that are lighter than water, often burn easily, and will not mix with water. Mineral oils, such as kerosene, are used for fuel; animal fats, such as lard, and vegetable oils, such as olive oil, are used in cooking.
2 NOUN. See **petroleum.**
3 VERB. to put oil on or in something: *She oiled the squeaking hinges of the basement door.*
4 NOUN. an oil paint or an oil painting.
❑ VERB **oils, oiled, oil·ing.**

strike oil, IDIOM.
1 to find petroleum by boring a hole in the earth.
2 to find something very profitable: *He really struck oil with his bike repair shop.*

oil paint, a paint made by mixing coloring matter with oil.

oil painting, a picture painted with oil paints.

oil·y (oi′lē), ADJECTIVE.
1 containing oil: *oily salad dressing.*
2 covered or soaked with oil: *oily rags.*
3 like oil; smooth; slippery: *an oily liquid.*
❑ ADJECTIVE **oil·i·er, oil·i·est.** —**oil′i·ness,** NOUN.

oint·ment (oint′mənt), NOUN. any greasy substance used on your skin to heal it or to make it soft. Ointments often contain medicine.

OK or **O.K.** (ō′kā′),
1 ADJECTIVE or ADVERB or INTERJECTION. all right: *The new schedule was OK. "OK, OK!" he yelled.*
2 VERB. to say that something is all right; approve: *The principal has to OK my class schedule.*
3 NOUN. an approval: *She gave the plan her OK.*
❑ VERB **OK's, OK'd, OK'ing** or **O.K.'s, O.K.'d, O.K.'ing;** PLURAL **OK's** or **O.K.'s.** Also spelled **okay.**

Word Story

OK comes from a funny misspelling of *all correct.* The letters were used as a presidential campaign slogan in 1840. Now it is hard to imagine that people ever didn't say **OK.**

OK, an abbreviation of **Oklahoma.**

o·kay (ō′kā′), ADJECTIVE, ADVERB, INTERJECTION, VERB or NOUN. another spelling of **OK.** ❑ VERB **o·kays, o·kayed, o·kay·ing.**

O·kla·ho·ma (ō′klə hō′mə), NOUN. one of the southwestern states of the United States. *Abbreviation:* OK; *Capital:* Oklahoma City.
—**O′kla·ho′man,** ADJECTIVE or NOUN.

State Story   Oklahoma comes from Choctaw (chok′tò) words meaning "red people." The name was created by a Choctaw leader for his people's land in this area. It was then used for the railroad stop that became Oklahoma City, and then for the whole state.

Oklahoma City, the capital of Oklahoma.

o·kra (ō′krə), NOUN. a vegetable with sticky pods used in soups and stews. Okra is grown in warm regions of the United States and other countries.

old (ōld), *ADJECTIVE*.
1 not young or new; having lived or existed for a long time: *old people, an old oak tree, an old violin.*
2 of age; in age: *The baby is ten months old.*
3 nearly worn out by age or use: *an old coat.*
4 over a long period of time: *We are old friends.*
5 former: *An old pupil came back to visit our teacher.*
❑ *ADJECTIVE* **old·er, old·est** or **eld·er, eld·est.**
of old, *IDIOM.* of a time long ago; of the past: *the knights of old.*

Synonym Study

Old means having lived for a long time: *The old woman can remember when cars and phones were very rare.*

Aged (ā'jid) means having lived a very long time: *My aged grandparents live with us.*

Elderly means somewhat old: *The elderly women have been friends for many years.*

Getting on in years is an idiom that means old: *Grandfather is getting on in years, so he exercises to stay strong and fit.*

See also the Synonym Study at **ancient.**

ANTONYM: young.

old·en (ōl'dən), *ADJECTIVE.* old; of old; ancient: *In olden times very few people lived to old age.*

old-fash·ioned (ōld'fash'ənd), *ADJECTIVE*.
1 out-of-date; of an old style: *old-fashioned clothing.* ∎ See the Synonym Study at **ancient.**
2 preferring old ways or ideas: *My grandparents are quite old-fashioned.*

Old Testament, the Christian term for Hebrew Scriptures. The Old Testament contains the religious and social laws of the Jews, their history, important works of their literature, and writings of their prophets.

old-tim·er (ōld'tī'mər), *NOUN.* someone who has lived a long time or been a member of a group for a long time: *The neighborhood old-timers remember when the streets were not paved.*

Old World, Europe, Asia, and Africa.

ol·ive (ol'iv),
1 *NOUN.* the small oval fruit of an evergreen tree that grows in warm regions. Olives are eaten green or ripe, and are used to make olive oil.
2 *ADJECTIVE* or *NOUN.* dark yellowish green; yellowish brown.

olive oil, oil pressed from olives, used in cooking.

O·lym·pi·a (ō lim'pē ə), *NOUN.* the capital of Washington.

O·lym·pic (ō lim'pik),
1 *ADJECTIVE.* of or about the Olympic games: *an Olympic athlete.*
2 *NOUN.* **Olympics,** See **Olympic games.**

These women do not feel **old.**

Olympic games, international athletic contests held every four years in a different country; Olympics. Separate summer and winter games are held, alternating every two years.

Word Story

The modern **Olympic games** take their name from contests in athletics, poetry, and music, held every four years by the ancient Greeks. **Olympic** comes from *Olympia,* the Greek name of the plain where the contests were held.

O·man (ō män'), *NOUN.* a country in southeastern Arabia. **–O·ma·ni** (ō mä'nē), *ADJECTIVE* or *NOUN.*

ome·let (om'lit), *NOUN.* eggs beaten with milk or water, fried or baked, and then folded over, often around a filling.

Have You Heard?

You may have heard someone say **"You can't make an omelet without breaking eggs."** This means that it is hard to get an important job done without doing unpleasant things.

o·men (ō'mən), *NOUN.* something supposed to be a sign of what is to happen; object or event that is believed to mean good or bad fortune: *A red sunrise is said to be an omen of bad weather.*

om·i·nous (om'ə nəs), *ADJECTIVE.* threatening: *The dark skies looked ominous.* **–om'i·nous·ly,** *ADVERB.*

o·mis·sion (ō mish'ən), *NOUN.* something left out: *His song was the only omission from the program.*

o·mit (ō mit'), *VERB.* to leave something out: *I make most of my spelling mistakes when I omit letters.*
❑ *VERB* **o·mits, o·mit·ted, o·mit·ting.**

a	hat	ė	term	ô	order	ch	child		a in about
ā	age	i	it	oi	oil	ng	long		e in taken
ä	far	ī	ice	ou	out	sh	she	ə	i in pencil
â	care	o	hot	u	cup	th	thin		o in lemon
e	let	ō	open	ú	put	ᵵн	then		u in circus
ē	equal	ò	saw	ü	rule	zh	measure		

om·ni·vore (om'nə vôr'), NOUN. a human being or an animal that eats any kind of food.

on (on),

1 PREPOSITION. above and supported by: *This book is on the table.*

2 PREPOSITION. touching something so as to cover it or be around it: *I put the ring on my finger.*

3 PREPOSITION. close to: *We have a house on the shore.*

4 PREPOSITION. in the direction of; toward: *The protesters marched on the Capitol.*

5 PREPOSITION. fastened to: *The picture is on the wall.*

6 ADVERB. farther; onwards: *March on, soldiers!*

7 PREPOSITION. by means of; by the use of: *I just talked to her on the phone.*

8 PREPOSITION. in the condition of: *She is on duty.*

9 ADJECTIVE. taking place: *The race is on.*

10 ADJECTIVE. in use; operating: *The radio is on.*

11 PREPOSITION. at the time of; during: *They greeted us on our arrival.*

12 PREPOSITION. being broadcast by: *The game is on TV.*

13 ADVERB. from a time; forward: *later on, from that day on.*

14 PREPOSITION. about: *I read a book on animals.*

15 PREPOSITION. for the purpose of: *I went on an errand.*

16 PREPOSITION. among: *I am not on the committee that is considering new members for our club.*

and so on, IDIOM. and more of the same: *Fruits such as oranges, lemons, grapefruit, and so on contain a vitamin that we need daily.*

once (wuns),

1 ADVERB. one time: *Read it once more.*

2 NOUN. a single time: *Once is enough.*

3 ADVERB. at some time in the past; formerly: *That small town was once the capital of the state.*

4 CONJUNCTION. when: *Most people like to swim, once they have learned how.*

at once, IDIOM.

1 immediately: *You must come at once.*

2 at the same time: *All three children spoke at once.*

once in a while, IDIOM. now and then; not very often: *We see our cousins once in a while.*

once upon a time, IDIOM. long ago: *Once upon a time there were dinosaurs.*

on·com·ing (on'kum'ing), ADJECTIVE. coming toward you: *oncoming traffic.*

one (wun),

1 NOUN. the number 1.

2 ADJECTIVE. a single: *one person, one apple.*

3 NOUN. a single person or thing: *I like the red ones.*

4 ADJECTIVE. some: *One day you will be sorry.*

5 PRONOUN. someone or something: *Two of you may go, but one must stay.*

6 PRONOUN. any person, standing for people in general: *One does not like to be left out.*

■ Another word that sounds like this is **won.**

—one'ness, NOUN.

one by one, IDIOM. one after another: *They came out the door one by one.*

one another, each other: *The losing team looked at one another.*

one-celled (wun'seld'), ADJECTIVE. having only one cell: *Bacteria are one-celled living things.*

one·self (wun self'), PRONOUN. one's own self: *At the age of seven one ought to dress oneself.*

one-sid·ed (wun'sī'did), ADJECTIVE. unfair; seeing only one side of a question: *The umpire seemed one-sided in his decisions, favoring the home team.*

one-way (wun'wā'), ADJECTIVE. moving or allowing movement in only one direction: *a one-way street, a one-way ticket.*

on·ion (un'yən), NOUN. a vegetable with a strong flavor, eaten raw or used in cooking. Onions grow as underground bulbs. **—on'ion·like',** ADJECTIVE.

onion

on-line or **on·line** (on'līn'), ADJECTIVE.

1 available or communicating by computer, especially through e-mail or the Internet: *an on-line dictionary. My aunt just went on-line and sent me three messages.*

2 controlled by a computer.

3 connected to a computer.

on·look·er (on'lŭk'ər), NOUN. someone who watches something without taking part in it; spectator: *Only a few children were actually playing; the rest were onlookers.*

on·ly (ōn'lē),

1 ADJECTIVE. by itself or by themselves; and no more: *Water is her only drink. These are the only roads along the shore.*

2 ADVERB. with nothing else; merely: *She sold only two.*

3 ADVERB. and no one else; alone: *Only he remained.*

4 ADVERB. for no other reason; simply: *I did it only for friendship.*

5 CONJUNCTION. except that; but: *He would have started, only it rained.*

6 ADJECTIVE. best; finest: *Chocolate is the only flavor for me!*

if only, IDIOM. I wish: *If only the sun would shine!*

Usage Note

Only should go right in front of the word it describes: *I saw only six ducks.* You didn't see any more. *I only saw six ducks.* You didn't hear them, just saw them. In everyday speech, people often put **only** near the verb of a sentence, no matter what it is supposed to describe. Careful writers and speakers do this only rarely.

on·o·mat·o·poe·ia (on′ə mat′ə pē′ə), NOUN. the formation of a word or name by imitating the sound associated with the thing, as in *buzz, hum, slap,* and *splash.*

on·set (on′set′), NOUN. the beginning: *The onset of this disease is gradual.*

On·tar·i·o (on târ′ē ō), NOUN.
1 a province in Canada, north of the Great Lakes.
2 **Lake Ontario,** one of the Great Lakes.
—**On·tar′i·an,** ADJECTIVE or NOUN.

on·to (on′tü), PREPOSITION. on to; to a position on: *to throw a ball onto the roof, to get onto a horse, a boat driven onto the rocks.*

on·ward (on′wərd), ADVERB or ADJECTIVE. on; further on; toward the front; forward: *The crowd around the store window began to move onward. After circling once, the helicopter resumed its onward course.*

on·wards (on′wərdz), ADVERB. See **onward.**

ooze (üz), VERB. to flow out little by little: *Blood still oozed from the cut.*
❑ VERB **ooz·es, oozed, ooz·ing.**

o·pal (ō′pəl), NOUN. a gem that shows beautiful changes of color. Opals are often white with streaks of different colors.

an **opal** before it has been cut and polished

Did You Know?

The elements that make up an **opal** are also found in ordinary sand. But opals have a special structure that causes light to bend inside them and flash the colors of the rainbow.

o·paque (ō pāk′), ADJECTIVE. not letting light pass through; not transparent: *A brick wall is opaque.*

o·pen (ō′pən),
1 ADJECTIVE. not closed; so that things or people can get in or out; not shut: *She climbed in through the open window.*
2 ADJECTIVE. not closed up, fastened, or tied: *The drawer was open. Your dress is open in the back.*
3 ADJECTIVE. not closed in: *the open sea, an open field.*
4 ADJECTIVE. ready for customers to enter: *The bank is open from 9 to 3 on Tuesdays.*
5 NOUN. **the open, a** an open or clear space; open air: *They slept out in the open.* **b** public view or knowledge: *The town's terrible secret is now out in the open.*
6 ADJECTIVE. unfilled; not taken: *The position is still open.*
7 ADJECTIVE. able to be entered, used, shared, or attended by everyone, or by a certain group: *The meeting is open to the public. The race is open to ten-year-old girls.*
8 ADJECTIVE. not covered or protected; exposed: *an open fire, an open jar.*

9 ADJECTIVE. ready to listen to new ideas and judge them fairly: *She has an open mind.*
10 ADJECTIVE. frank and sincere: *Please be open with me.*
11 VERB. to make or become open: *Open the window. The door opened.*
12 VERB. to be an opening into a place: *This door opens into the dining room.*
13 VERB. to spread out or unfold: *to open a book, to open a letter.*
14 VERB. to start something or set it up: *My uncle opened a new store.*
15 VERB. to begin: *School opens in September.*
❑ VERB **o·pens, o·pened, o·pen·ing.**

open to, IDIOM. ready to take; willing to consider: *I am open to suggestions.*

open air, the outdoors: *Children like to play in the open air.*

o·pen-and-shut (ō′pən ən shut′), ADJECTIVE. simple and direct; obvious; straightforward: *It seemed to be an open-and-shut case of murder.*

o·pen·er (ō′pə nər), NOUN.
1 something that is used to open closed containers: *Where is the can opener?*
2 (in sports) the first game of a scheduled series.

o·pen·hand·ed (ō′pən han′did), ADJECTIVE. generous; liberal: *She made an openhanded donation to our school's technology fund.*
—**o′pen·hand′ed·ly,** ADVERB.
—**o′pen·hand′ed·ness,** NOUN.

o·pen·heart·ed (ō′pən här′tid), ADJECTIVE. free in expressing your real thoughts, opinions, and feelings; frank: *We had an openhearted discussion about moving to a new city.*

o·pen·ing (ō′pə ning),
1 NOUN. a hole, gap, or clear space in something: *an opening in a wall, an opening in the forest.*
2 NOUN. the first part; the beginning: *The opening of the story took place in New York.*
3 ADJECTIVE. first; beginning: *We couldn't hear the opening words of her speech.*
4 NOUN. a formal beginning: *The opening of the art exhibit will be at three o'clock.*
5 NOUN. a job that is open or vacant: *an opening for a teller in a bank.*
6 NOUN. a favorable opportunity to do something: *I kept waiting for an opening to ask for a new bike.*

o·pen·ly (ō′pən lē), ADVERB. in an open manner; not secretly: *I discussed my problem openly.*

o·pen-mind·ed (ō′pən mīn′did), ADJECTIVE. willing to listen to other people's ideas; open to new arguments or ideas.

a	hat	ė	term	ô	order	ch	child	ə	a in about
ā	age	i	it	oi	oil	ng	long		e in taken
ä	far	ī	ice	ou	out	sh	she		i in pencil
â	care	o	hot	u	cup	th	thin		o in lemon
e	let	ō	open	ů	put	ŦH	then		u in circus
ē	equal	ȯ	saw	ü	rule	zh	measure		

op·er·a (op′ər ə), NOUN. a special kind of play written with music to go along with most of the story. In opera, the actors usually sing instead of speaking their lines, and an orchestra provides music for each part of the story. ❑ PLURAL **op·er·as.**

Singers perform a duet in an **opera.**

op·e·rate (op′ə rāt′), VERB.
1 to be at work; run: *The machinery operates night and day.*
2 to keep at work; manage: *He operates an elevator. The company operates three factories.*
3 to try to cure a sick or hurt person by cutting into his or her body; do surgery: *The doctor operated on the injured man.*
❑ VERB **op·e·rates, op·e·rat·ed, op·e·rat·ing.**

op·e·ra·tion (op′ə rā′shən), NOUN.
1 the act or process of working or causing something to operate: *The operation of an airline requires many people.*
2 the way something works: *The operation of this machine is simple.*
3 the act or process of cutting into a sick or hurt part of the body by a doctor to make it better; surgery: *Taking out an inflamed appendix is a common operation.*
4 a series of planned actions to reach a goal: *They planned a rescue operation to save the lost hikers.*
5 (in mathematics) something done to one or more numbers or quantities according to specific rules. Addition, subtraction, multiplication, and division are the four most common operations in arithmetic.

op·e·ra·tor (op′ə rā′tər), NOUN. someone who runs a machine or other device: *a forklift operator, a telephone operator.*

o·pin·ion (ə pin′yən), NOUN.
1 what you think about something; ideas: *In my opinion, their plan will never succeed.*
2 a judgment of what something or someone is worth: *I had a good opinion of his ability.*

3 a formal judgment by an expert; professional advice: *He wanted the doctor's opinion about the cause of his leg pain.*

Synonym Study

Opinion means what someone thinks about something: *Opinions may be supported by facts, but they still can be questioned.*

View can mean a personal opinion: *His view that sign language is easy is based on using it with his brother.*

Belief means what someone holds to be true. It is a stronger word than opinion: *She shares her sister's belief that recycling is important.*

Judgment means an opinion based on considering and deciding: *In my judgment, the soccer team needs to practice kicking goals.*

Attitude means the way that someone thinks and feels about something: *She has a positive attitude about going to a new school and expects to do well there.*

See also the Synonym Study at **idea.**

o·pos·sum (ə pos′əm), NOUN. a small animal that lives in trees and carries its young in a pouch; possum. When it is attacked, it becomes limp and appears to be dead. ❑ PLURAL **o·pos·sums** or **o·pos·sum.**

opossum — about 3 feet long, including the tail

op·po·nent (ə pō′nənt), NOUN. someone who is on the other side in a fight, contest, or discussion: *She defeated her opponent in the election.*

op·por·tu·ni·ty (op′ər tü′nə tē), NOUN. a good chance to do something; convenient occasion: *I had an opportunity to earn some money baby-sitting.* ❑ PLURAL **op·por·tu·ni·ties.**

op·pose (ə pōz′), VERB. to be against some idea, plan, goal, and so on; resist: *Many people opposed building a new highway because of the cost.* ❑ VERB **op·pos·es, op·posed, op·pos·ing.**

op·pos·ing (ə pō′zing), ADJECTIVE. in opposition to; on the other side; competing: *My best friend plays for our opposing team today.*

op·po·site (op′ə zit),
1 ADJECTIVE. placed directly across from something else; face to face or back to back: *The house straight across the street is opposite to ours.*
2 ADJECTIVE. as different from each other as they can be: *North and south are opposite directions.*

3 *NOUN.* someone or something as different as it can be: *Night is the opposite of day.*

op·po·si·tion (op/ə zish/ən), *NOUN.*
1 the act of opposing something; resistance: *There was some opposition to the new school tax.*
2 (in sports) an opposing team.

op·press (ə pres/), *VERB.* to govern harshly, unjustly, and cruelly: *The people were oppressed by the invaders.* ❑ *VERB* **op·press·es, op·pressed, op·press·ing. —op·pres·sion** (ə presh/ən), *NOUN.* **—op·pres/sor,** *NOUN.*

op·pres·sive (ə pres/iv), *ADJECTIVE.*
1 hard to stand: *The great heat was oppressive.*
2 harsh; cruel; unjust: *Oppressive measures were taken to crush the rebellion.*
—op·pres/sive·ly, *ADVERB.*

op·tic (op/tik), *ADJECTIVE.* of or relating to the eye or the sense of sight. The **optic nerve** goes from the eye to the brain.

op·ti·cal (op/tə kəl), *ADJECTIVE.*
1 of or relating to the eye or the sense of sight; visual: *Being nearsighted is an optical defect.*
2 made to help you see better: *Telescopes and microscopes are optical devices.*

optical fiber, a very thin, transparent thread of glass or plastic, able to carry light from end to end without loss or change. Optical fibers are used to send images, voices, and data.

op·ti·cian (op tish/ən), *NOUN.* someone who makes or sells eyeglasses and contact lenses.

op·ti·mist (op/tə mist), *NOUN.* someone who thinks that things usually turn out all right.

op·ti·mis·tic (op/tə mis/tik), *ADJECTIVE.* sure that things will turn out well; cheerful: *She is an optimistic person.* **—op/ti·mis/ti·cal·ly,** *ADVERB.*

op·tion (op/shən), *NOUN.*
1 the right or freedom of choice: *Students in our school have the option of taking Spanish, French, or German.*
2 something that can be chosen; a choice: *Power windows are an option on many new cars.*

op·tion·al (op/shə nəl), *ADJECTIVE.* left up to you; not required: *Attendance at the school dance is optional.*

op·tom·e·trist (op tom/ə trist), *NOUN.* someone who is trained and licensed to examine the eyes and prescribe eyeglasses.

or (ôr), *CONJUNCTION.*
1 Or is used to suggest a choice. It connects words, and sometimes groups of words, of equal importance in a sentence: *You can go or stay. Is it sweet or sour? Take a dime or two nickles.*
2 Or may state the only choice left: *Either eat this or go hungry.*
3 Or may state what will happen if the first does not happen: *Hurry, or you will be late.*

4 Or may explain that two things are the same: *an igloo or Eskimo snow house.*
■ Other words that sound like this are **oar** and **ore.**

Word Power   -or

The suffix **-or** means "someone or something that _____s." Act**or** means **someone who** acts. Generat**or** means **something that** generates.

OR, an abbreviation of **Oregon.**

o·ral (ôr/əl), *ADJECTIVE.*
1 spoken; using speech: *An oral agreement is not enough; we must have a written promise.*
2 of or in the mouth: *Flossing your teeth is important to good oral hygiene.*
—o/ral·ly, *ADVERB.*

o·range (ôr/inj),
1 *NOUN.* a round, reddish yellow citrus fruit about as big as a baseball. Oranges are eaten whole or squeezed to make juice.
2 *ADJECTIVE* or *NOUN.* reddish yellow.

Oranges are tasty and refreshing.

o·rang·u·tan (ə rang/ə tan/), *NOUN.* an ape with very long arms and long, reddish hair, somewhat larger than a chimpanzee. Orangutans live in the forests of islands off southeast Asia.

This young **orangutan** may grow to 4½ feet tall.

a	hat	ė	term	ô	order	ch	child		a in about
ā	age	i	it	oi	oil	ng	long		e in taken
ä	far	ī	ice	ou	out	sh	she	ə	i in pencil
â	care	o	hot	u	cup	th	thin		o in lemon
e	let	ō	open	ù	put	ŦH	then		u in circus
ē	equal	ò	saw	ü	rule	zh	measure		

or·bit (ôr′bit),
1 *NOUN.* the path of an astronomical object around another larger object: *Gravity keeps the earth in its orbit around the sun.*
2 *VERB.* to travel around the earth or some other astronomical object in an orbit: *Some artificial satellites can orbit the earth in less than an hour.* ❏ *VERB* **or·bits, or·bit·ed, or·bit·ing.**

or·ca (ôr′kə), *NOUN.* See **killer whale.** ❏ *PLURAL* **or·cas.**

or·chard (ôr′chərd), *NOUN.* a piece of ground on which fruit trees grow.

or·ches·tra (ôr′kə strə), *NOUN.* a group of musicians playing strings, brass, woodwinds, and percussion instruments. An orchestra is usually led by a conductor. ❏ *PLURAL* **or·ches·tras.**

or·chid (ôr′kid), *NOUN.* a plant with flowers that often have unusual shapes and colors.

There are over 20,000 different kinds of **orchids.**

or·dain (ôr dān′), *VERB.* to appoint officially as a minister, priest, or rabbi in a formal ceremony: *My aunt was ordained as a minister last week.* ❏ *VERB* **or·dains, or·dain·ed, or·dain·ing.**

or·deal (ôr dēl′), *NOUN.* a very unpleasant experience: *Going to the dentist is an ordeal for me.*

or·der (ôr′dər),
1 *VERB.* tell someone what to do; command; bid: *The teacher ordered the class to sit down.*
2 *NOUN.* a command: *Our parents expect us to obey their orders.*
3 *VERB.* to ask for something to be brought to your table in a restaurant: *I ordered fish for dinner.*
4 *NOUN.* a spoken or written request for something: *We telephoned an order for two pizzas to be delivered.*
5 *NOUN.* the thing or things that you asked to be delivered: *When will you be able to deliver our order?*
6 *NOUN.* the way one thing follows another: *Our names are listed in alphabetical order.*
7 *NOUN.* the condition in which every part or piece is in its right place: *After the movers left, we placed the furniture in order.*

8 *NOUN.* the peaceful condition of things in which everyone obeys the law and there is no trouble: *Order was established after the riot.*
9 *NOUN.* a portion or serving of food in a restaurant, delicatessen, and so on.
10 *NOUN.* often, **Order,** a society of monks, friars, or nuns: *He is a member of the Order of Saint Francis.* ❏ *VERB* **or·ders, or·dered, or·der·ing.**

in order to, *IDIOM.* as a means to; with a view to; for the purpose of: *She worked hard in order to win the prize.*

out of order, *IDIOM.*
1 not working right: *My watch is out of order.*
2 in the wrong arrangement or condition: *He listed the states alphabetically, but Texas was out of order.*

ordered pair, (in mathematics) any two numbers that locate a point on a coordinate grid.

or·der·ly (ôr′dər lē),
1 *ADJECTIVE.* neatly arranged; in order: *an orderly arrangement of dishes on shelves.* ■ See the Synonym Study at **neat.**
2 *ADJECTIVE.* well-behaved: *an orderly class.*
3 *NOUN.* someone who works in a hospital, keeping things clean and in order. ❏ *PLURAL* **or·der·lies. –or·der·li·ness,** *NOUN.*

or·di·nal num·ber (ôrd′n əl num′bər), a number that shows order or position in a series. First, second, third, and so on, are ordinal numbers.

or·di·nance (ôrd′n əns), *NOUN.* a rule or law made by local government; decree: *Some cities have ordinances forbidding the burning of leaves.*

or·di·nar·i·ly (ôrd′n er′ə lē), *ADVERB.* usually; commonly; normally: *We ordinarily go to the movies on Saturday.*

or·di·nar·y (ôrd′n er′ē), *ADJECTIVE.*
1 usual; regular; normal: *My ordinary lunch is soup, a sandwich, and milk.*
2 not special; average: *Most of our neighbors are ordinary people.*

out of the ordinary, *IDIOM.* unusual; not regular: *Such a long delay is out of the ordinary.*

ore (ôr), *NOUN.* a mineral or rock containing enough metal or metals to make mining it profitable: *Gold ore was discovered in California in 1848.* ■ Other words that sound like this are **oar** and **or.**

o·reg·a·no (ə reg′ə nō), *NOUN.* a fragrant herb with leaves that are used for seasoning food.

O·re·gon (ôr′ə gon *or* ôr′ə gən), *NOUN.* one of the Pacific states of the United States. *Abbreviation:* OR; *Capital:* Salem.
–O·re·go·ni·an (ôr′ə gō′nē ən), *NOUN.*

State Story Oregon is a mystery. It may come from a French word meaning "hurricane," once used as the name of the Columbia River. It may come from a Spanish word meaning "big ears," describing people who lived there. It may simply be a mistake in spelling on a map.

or·gan (ôr′gən), NOUN.
1 any part of a living thing that does a special job. The eyes, ears, stomach, heart, and skin are organs of the body. Stamens are organs of flowers.
2 a musical instrument that produces tones when air is forced through pipes of different sizes. The organ has a keyboard like a piano.
3 a similar instrument whose tones are produced electronically.

or·gan·ic (ôr gan′ik), ADJECTIVE.
1 of or from living things. Decaying grass and animal manure are organic fertilizers.
2 grown without artificial pesticides or fertilizers.
—**or·gan′i·cal·ly**, ADVERB.

or·gan·ism (ôr′gə niz′əm), NOUN. an individual animal, plant, or other living thing.

O·ri·en·tal (ôr′ē en′tl),
1 ADJECTIVE. of or about the Orient; Eastern: *Oriental customs, Oriental food.*
2 NOUN. someone born or living in the East, especially the Far East.
3 NOUN. someone with ancestors that came from the Far East.

Usage Note

The noun **Oriental** is considered offensive by some people. Whenever possible, use the specific nationality of your subject, such as Japanese or Cambodian. If you don't know a person's country of origin or are speaking of people from more than one country, say or write **Asian.**

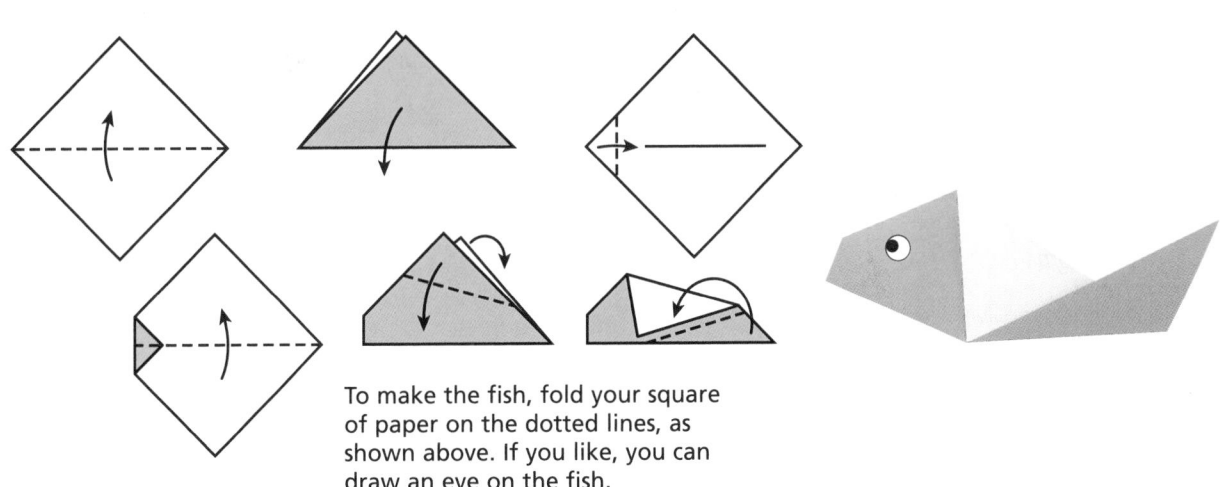

To make the fish, fold your square of paper on the dotted lines, as shown above. If you like, you can draw an eye on the fish.

origami

or·gan·i·za·tion (ôr′gə nə zā′shən), NOUN.
1 a group of people united for some purpose. Churches, clubs, and political parties are organizations.
2 the way in which something's parts are arranged to work together: *The organization of the human body is very complicated.*

or·gan·ize (ôr′gə nīz), VERB.
1 to plan something and get it working: *Let's organize a volleyball team.*
2 to combine people in a labor union or political party: *They worked hard to organize the miners.*
❑ VERB **or·gan·iz·es, or·gan·ized, or·gan·iz·ing.**
—**or′gan·iz′er,** NOUN.

o·ri·ent (ôr′ē ənt), NOUN.
1 the east.
2 **the Orient,** the East; Eastern countries. The Orient usually includes Asia and countries east and southeast of the Mediterranean.

o·ri·ga·mi (ôr′ə gä′mē), NOUN. the Japanese art of folding paper to make objects, such as birds, animals, flowers, as decorations.

o·ri·gin (ôr′ə jin), NOUN.
1 the place or point where something comes from; beginning: *I don't recall the origin of the quarrel.*
2 descent; birth: *She is of Mexican origin.*

o·rig·i·nal (ə rij′ə nəl),
1 ADJECTIVE. first; earliest: *They were the original owners of that house. The hat has been marked down from its original price.*
2 ADJECTIVE. not copied or imitated from something; new; fresh: *She wrote an original poem.* ■ See the Synonym Study at **new.**

a	hat	ė	term	ô	order	ch	child		a in about
ā	age	i	it	oi	oil	ng	long		e in taken
ä	far	ī	ice	ou	out	sh	she	ə	i in pencil
â	care	o	hot	u	cup	th	thin		o in lemon
e	let	ō	open	u̇	put	ᴛʜ	then		u in circus
ē	equal	ȯ	saw	ü	rule	zh	measure		

3 *ADJECTIVE.* able to do, make, or think something new: *Edison had an original mind.*

4 *NOUN.* something that has been copied, imitated, or translated: *The original of this picture is in Rome.*

o·rig·i·nal·i·ty (ə rij′ə nal′ə tē), *NOUN.* newness; freshness: *I was impressed by the play's originality.*

o·rig·i·nal·ly (ə rij′ə nə lē), *ADVERB.*
1 by origin: *He is originally from Canada. It was originally her idea.*
2 at first; in the first place: *This house was originally quite small.*

o·rig·i·nate (ə rij′ə nāt), *VERB.* to come or cause to come into being; begin: *Where did that story originate?* ❑ *VERB* **o·rig·i·nates, o·rig·i·nat·ed, o·rig·i·nat·ing.** **−o·rig′i·na·tor,** *NOUN.*

o·ri·ole (ôr′ē ōl or ôr′ē əl), *NOUN.* an American songbird having yellow and black or orange and black feathers.

or·na·ment (ôr′nə mənt) *NOUN.* something that adds beauty to something else: *Lace, jewels, vases, and statues are ornaments.*

or·na·men·tal (ôr′nə men′tl), *ADJECTIVE* for ornament; as decoration: *There were ornamental tiles around the fireplace.*

or·nate (ôr nāt′), *ADJECTIVE.* having a lot of decoration: *an ornate design.*

or·ner·y (ôr′nər ē), *ADJECTIVE.* (informal) mean and grouchy: *Our next-door neighbor is an ornery person.* ■ See the Synonym Study at **cross.** ❑ *ADJECTIVE* **or·ner·i·er, or·ner·i·est.**

oriole — about 7 inches long

Word Story

Ornery comes from **ordinary.** Writers spelled the word a new way to show how people were pronouncing it. The new spelling developed a new meaning. Something just ordinary isn't very good. People used **ornery** to mean "not good, unpleasant, annoying," and then "mean."

or·ni·thol·o·gy (ôr′nə thol′ə jē), *NOUN.* a branch of zoology dealing with the study of birds. **−or′ni·thol′o·gist,** *NOUN.*

or·phan (ôr′fən),
1 *NOUN.* a child whose parents are dead.
2 *VERB.* to cause someone to become an orphan: *The war orphaned the child.*
❑ *VERB* **or·phans, or·phaned, or·phan·ing.**

or·phan·age (ôr′fə nij), *NOUN.* a home for orphans.

or·tho·don·tist (ôr′thə don′tist), *NOUN.* a dentist whose work is straightening teeth.

or·tho·dox (ôr′thə doks), *ADJECTIVE.*
1 following traditional views or opinions, especially in religion.
2 generally accepted; approved by tradition; customary: *My parents have very orthodox ideas about education.*

os·ten·ta·tious (os′ten tā′shəs), *ADJECTIVE.* intended to get attention or to show off: *She wore ostentatious jewels fit for a queen.*

os·trich (os′trich), *NOUN.* a large bird of Africa that can run fast but cannot fly. Ostriches are the largest birds. ❑ *PLURAL* **os·trich·es.**

ostrich — about 8 feet tall

Did You Know?

As many as five female **ostriches** lay their eggs in a single nest. One dominant female watches the eggs and keeps them warm during the day. A male ostrich keeps them warm at night.

oth·er (uᴛн′ər),
1 *ADJECTIVE.* remaining: *I am home, but the other members of the family are away.*
2 *ADJECTIVE.* additional: *I have no other place to go.*
3 *ADJECTIVE.* not the same thing or person already mentioned: *It wasn't my friend that got hurt but some other boy.*
4 *PRONOUN.* the other one: *Each praises the other for their hard work.*
5 *PRONOUN.* another person or thing: *There are others to consider.*

every other, *IDIOM.* every second; alternate: *We have spelling every other day.*

the other day *IDIOM.* recently: *I saw her the other day at the mall.*

oth·er·wise (uᴛн′ər wīz),
1 *ADVERB.* in a different way; differently: *I could not act otherwise.*
2 *ADVERB* or *ADJECTIVE.* different: *It might have been otherwise.*
3 *ADVERB.* in other ways: *It is windy, but otherwise a nice day.*
4 *CONJUNCTION.* or else; if not: *Come at once; otherwise you will be too late.*

Ot·ta·wa (ot′ə wə), *NOUN.* the capital of Canada. Ottawa is in Ontario. ❑ *PLURAL* **Ot·ta·wa** or **Ot·ta·was.**

ot·ter (ot′ər), *NOUN.* an animal like a large weasel that lives near water. Otters have thick, glossy, brown fur and webbed paws. ❑ *PLURAL* **ot·ter** or **ot·ters.**

Did You Know?

Otters live everywhere except Australia and Antarctica. The **giant otter** of South America can grow to be seven feet long!

otter — about 4 feet long, including the tail

ouch (ouch), *INTERJECTION.* an exclamation expressing sudden pain.

ought (ȯt), *HELPING VERB.*
1 to have a duty; should: *You ought to obey your parents. I ought to be home by ten.*
2 to be right or suitable: *Cruelty ought not to be allowed.*
3 to be very likely: *It ought to be a fine day tomorrow.*
★ **Ought** only exists in the present tense. **Ought** is used in the negative with **not** or as the contraction **oughtn't.** Careful writers and speakers avoid such phrases as *shouldn't ought* or *hadn't ought.* ❑ *VERB* **oughts, ought·ed, ought·ing.**

ought·n't (ȯt′nt), a contraction of **ought not.**

ounce (ouns), *NOUN.*
1 a unit of weight equal to ¹⁄₁₆ of a pound.
2 a unit for measuring liquids; fluid ounce. 16 ounces = 1 pint.
3 a very small amount: *An ounce of prevention is worth a pound of cure.*

Word Story

Ounce comes from a Latin word meaning "a twelfth." In old measuring systems, an ounce was a twelfth of a pound. The word still means a part of a pound, but today that part is usually a sixteenth of a pound.

our (our), *ADJECTIVE.* of or for us; belonging to us: *Our classes were interesting. We need our coats now.* ▪ Another word that sounds like this is **hour.**

ours (ourz), *PRONOUN.* the one or ones belonging to us: *This garden is ours. Ours is a large house.*

our·selves (our selvz′), *PRONOUN PLURAL.*
1 **Ourselves** is used to make a statement stronger: *We ourselves will do the work.*
2 **Ourselves** is used instead of *we* or *us* in cases like: *We cook for ourselves. We help ourselves.*
3 our real or true selves: *We were not ourselves after the accident.*

Word Power   -ous

The suffix **-ous** means "full of _____" or "like _____." Joy**ous** means **full of** joy. Furi**ous** means **full of** fury. Thunder**ous** means **like** thunder. Carnivor**ous** means **like** a carnivore.

oust (oust), *VERB.* to force out; drive out: *The sparrows have ousted the bluebirds from their nest.* ❑ *VERB* **ousts, oust·ed, oust·ing.**

out (out),
1 *ADVERB.* away; forth: *The water will rush out.*
2 *ADJECTIVE.* not in use, action, control, or fashion: *The fire is out. The election results show that our present mayor is out. That style is out this year.*
3 *ADVERB.* outside: *It's raining out.*
4 *ADVERB.* not at home; away from your office, work, and so on: *My mother is out just now.*
5 in baseball: **a** *ADJECTIVE.* not successful in reaching base or advancing from one base to another: *The outfielder caught the fly and the batter was out.* **b** *NOUN.* the condition of being put out or the act of putting a player out. A team's turn at bat lasts until three outs are made.
6 *ADVERB.* off: *Turn the light out.*
7 *PREPOSITION.* through to the outside; out of: *She went out the door.*
8 *ADVERB.* into the open; made public; made known: *The secret is out now. The new book will be out next month.*
9 *ADVERB.* to or at an end: *Let them talk their problems out. We can work it out.*
10 *ADVERB.* aloud; plainly: *Speak out so that all can hear.*
11 *ADVERB.* from among others: *Pick out an apple for me.*
12 *ADJECTIVE.* not possible; not to be considered: *I have no money, so going to the movies is out.*

out of, *IDIOM.*
1 from within: *He came out of the house.*
2 not within: *He is out of town.*
3 away from; beyond: *The airplane was soon out of sight. This style went out of fashion.*
4 without: *I am out of work. We are out of coffee.*

a hat	ė term	ô order	ch child	⎧a in about
ā age	i it	oi oil	ng long	⎪e in taken
ä far	ī ice	ou out	sh she	ə⎨i in pencil
â care	o hot	u cup	th thin	⎪o in lemon
e let	ō open	u̇ put	ŦH then	⎩u in circus
ē equal	ȯ saw	ü rule	zh measure	

5 from: *My dress is made out of silk.*

6 from among: *She saw three out of four patients who called. We picked our puppy out of that litter.*

7 because of: *I went only out of curiosity.*

Word Power   out-

The prefix **out-** means "outward," "outside," "more than," or "better than." An **out**stretched arm is stretched **outward**. An **out**lying suburb lies **outside** the city. To **out**weigh someone is to weigh **more than** someone. To **out**do someone is to do **better than** someone.

out·age (ou′tij), NOUN. an unexpected loss of electrical power.

out·board mo·tor (out′bôrd′ mō′tər), a small motor attached to the rear of a boat or canoe.

out·break (out′brāk′), NOUN. a sudden start of something bad: *There has been an outbreak of disease in the area.*

out·burst (out′bėrst′), NOUN. the action of bursting forth: *There was an outburst of laughter when the clowns stumbled.*

out·cast (out′kast′), NOUN. someone who is driven away from home and friends: *The criminal was an outcast.*

out·come (out′kum′), NOUN. something that happens, especially as a result: *What was the outcome of the race?*

out·cry (out′krī′), NOUN. a strong expression of disapproval; protest: *The raising of taxes caused a public outcry.* ❑ PLURAL **out·cries.**

out·dat·ed (out dā′tid), ADJECTIVE. out-of-date; old-fashioned: *He is a person with outdated ideas.*

out·do (out dü′), VERB. to do more or better than someone else; surpass: *She's such a good tennis player that I know I won't be able to outdo her.*
❑ VERB **out·does, out·did** (out did′), **out·done** (out dun′), **out·do·ing.**

This typewriter is an **outdated** version.

out·door (out′dôr′), ADJECTIVE. done, used, or living outdoors: *Tag is an outdoor game.*

out·doors (out′dôrz′),

1 ADVERB. outside; not indoors: *Let's go outdoors to play ball.*

2 NOUN. the world outside; the open air: *a day of hiking in the great outdoors.*

out·er (ou′tər), ADJECTIVE. farther out; on the outside: *Shingles are used as an outer covering for many roofs.*

outer space, the space beyond the earth's atmosphere: *The moon is in outer space.*

out·field (out′fēld′), NOUN.

1 the part of a baseball field beyond the diamond or infield.

2 the three players in the outfield.

out·field·er (out′fēl′dər), NOUN. a baseball player who plays in the outfield.

out·fit (out′fit),

1 NOUN. a set of clothes that match or go well together: *That jacket and dress make a lovely outfit.*

2 NOUN. all the things necessary for any activity: *the outfit for a camping trip.*

3 VERB. to furnish someone with everything necessary for any activity; equip: *The store outfitted us for our camping trip.*

4 NOUN. a group working together, such as a group of soldiers: *His father and mine were in the same outfit during the war.*
❑ VERB **out·fits, out·fit·ted, out·fit·ting.**

out·go·ing (out′gō′ing), ADJECTIVE.

1 leaving a position or an office: *the outgoing president.*

2 friendly and helpful to others: *An outgoing person makes friends easily.*

out·grow (out grō′), VERB.

1 to grow too large for something: *I have outgrown my shoes twice this year.*

2 to grow or mature so that you are no longer interested in something: *He outgrew his interest in toy cars.*

3 to grow faster or taller than someone else: *By the time he was ten, he had outgrown his father.*
❑ VERB **out·grows, out·grew** (out grü′), **out·grown** (out grōn′), **out·grow·ing.**

out·ing (ou′ting), NOUN. a short pleasure trip with other people: *On Sunday we went on an outing to the beach.* ■ See the Synonym Study at **trip.**

out·land·ish (out lan′dish), ADJECTIVE. not familiar; strange or ridiculous: *an outlandish orange wig.*

out·last (out last′), VERB. to last longer than something else: *These shoes have outlasted all my others.* ❑ VERB **out·lasts, out·last·ed, out·last·ing.**

out·law (out′lò′),

1 NOUN. (formerly) a criminal.

2 VERB. to make or declare something illegal: *Several states have agreed to outlaw gambling.* ❑ VERB **out·laws, out·lawed, out·law·ing.**

out·let (out′let), NOUN.

1 an opening for letting something out: *We had to replace the outlet on our hot water heater.*

$5,000 REWARD

JESSE JAMES

For Train Robbery

Notify AUTHORITIES
LIBERTY, MISSOURI

outlaw (definition 1)

2 a way of expressing your ideas, feelings, or abilities: *Running is an outlet for his energies.*

3 a place in a wall for putting in an electric plug.

out·line (out′līn′),

1 *NOUN.* a line around the outside of something that shows its shape: *The outline of Italy suggests a boot.*

2 *NOUN.* a drawing or style of drawing that gives only outer lines: *Make an outline of the scene before you paint it.*

3 *VERB.* to draw the outer line of something: *Outline a map of America.*

4 *NOUN.* a brief plan; rough draft: *Make an outline before trying to write a composition.*

❑ *VERB* **out·lines, out·lined, out·lin·ing.**

out·live (out liv′), *VERB.* to live longer than someone or something; survive; outlast: *She outlived her older sister. This old shirt has outlived its usefulness.*

❑ *VERB* **out·lives, out·lived, out·liv·ing.**

out·look (out′lùk′), *NOUN.*

1 a way of thinking about things; point of view: *She has a cheerful outlook on life.*

2 what seems likely to happen: *The outlook for our picnic is not very good; it looks as if it will rain.*

out·ly·ing (out′lī′ing), *ADJECTIVE.* lying far from the center; remote: *an outlying suburb.*

out·num·ber (out num′bər), *VERB.* to be larger in number than: *They outnumbered us three to one.*

❑ *VERB* **out·num·bers, out·num·bered, out·num·ber·ing.**

out-of-bounds (out′əv boundz′), *ADJECTIVE* or *ADVERB.* outside the boundary line; out of play: *an out-of-bounds ball. He kicked the ball out-of-bounds.*

out-of-date (out′əv dāt′), *ADJECTIVE.* old-fashioned; not in present use: *A horse and buggy is an out-of-date means of traveling.* ■ See the Synonym Study at **ancient.**

out·pa·tient (out′pā′shənt), *NOUN.* a patient who receives treatment at a hospital or clinic but does not stay there.

out·post (out′pōst′), *NOUN.*

1 a guard, or small number of soldiers, placed at some distance from an army or camp, to prevent a surprise attack.

2 the place where these soldiers are stationed.

out·put (out′pùt′),

1 *NOUN.* an amount of something that is produced: *What is the daily output of cars at this factory?*

2 *NOUN.* information that is produced by a computer.

3 *VERB.* to produce information: *His program outputs the date in Roman and Arabic numerals.*

❑ *VERB* **out·puts, out·put·ted** or **out·put, out·put·ting.**

out·rage (out′rāj′),

1 *NOUN.* an act of violence that shows no regard for the rights or feelings of others: *Setting the house on fire was an outrage.*

2 *NOUN.* the anger caused by an act like this.

3 *VERB.* to offend someone greatly: *The British government outraged the colonists by taxing them unfairly.*

❑ *VERB* **out·rag·es, out·raged, out·rag·ing.**

out·ra·geous (out rā′jəs), *ADJECTIVE.* very bad or insulting; shocking: *outrageous language.* —**out·ra′geous·ly,** *ADVERB.*

out·ran (out ran′), *VERB.* the past tense of **outrun:** *He outran me easily.*

out·rig·ger (out′rig′ər), *NOUN.* a framework that sticks out from the side of a light boat or canoe to keep it from turning over.

a canoe with a lightweight **outrigger**

out·right (out′rīt′),

1 *ADJECTIVE.* complete; total; absolute: *That is an outright lie!*

2 *ADVERB.* altogether; entirely; not gradually: *They sold their entire stamp collection outright.*

3 *ADVERB.* openly: *We laughed outright.*

out·run (out run′), *VERB.* to run faster than someone or something: *She can outrun her older sister.* ❑ *VERB* **out·runs, out·ran, out·run, out·run·ning.**

out·side (out′sīd′),

1 *NOUN.* the side or surface that is out; outer part: *to polish the outside of a car, the outside of a house.*

2 *ADJECTIVE.* on the outside; outer: *The outside covering of a nut is called the hull.*

3 *ADVERB.* on or to the outside; outdoors: *Run outside and play.*

4 *PREPOSITION.* out of: *Stay outside the house. My cousins live outside the city.*

5 *ADJECTIVE.* from another person or place: *We may need some outside help on this project.*

a	hat	ė	term	ô	order	ch child	⎧a in about
ā	age	i	it	oi	oil	ng long	⎪e in taken
ä	far	ī	ice	ou	out	sh she	ə⎨i in pencil
â	care	o	hot	u	cup	th thin	⎪o in lemon
e	let	ō	open	ù	put	₮H then	⎩u in circus
ē	equal	ò	saw	ü	rule	zh measure	

outside chance, IDIOM. a very small possibility: *There is an outside chance that our team might win.*

out·sid·er (out′si′dər), NOUN. someone not belonging to a particular group, company, or the like.

out·skirts (out′skèrts′), NOUN PLURAL. the outer parts or edges of a town or district; outlying parts: *They have a farm on the outskirts of town.*

out·smart (out smärt′), VERB. to get the better of someone by being clever or smarter: *I outsmarted everyone and won the game.* ❑ VERB **out·smarts, out·smart·ed, out·smart·ing.**

out·spo·ken (out′spō′kən), ADJECTIVE. speaking frankly and honestly: *Your own family is likely to be outspoken in its remarks about you.*

out·stand·ing (out stan′ding), ADJECTIVE.
1 remarkable; very impressive: *She is an outstanding student.*
2 not paid; unpaid: *outstanding debts.*

out·stretched (out′strecht′), ADJECTIVE. stretched out: *He welcomed his old friend with outstretched arms.*

out·ward (out′wərd),
1 ADJECTIVE. toward the outside: *She gave one outward glance.*
2 ADVERB. on or toward the outside; outwards: *The coat was turned with the lining outward.*
3 ADJECTIVE. able to be seen; plain to see: *Her outward behavior was calm and quiet.*

out·wards (out′wərdz), ADVERB. See **outward.**

out·weigh (out wā′), VERB.
1 to be more valuable or important than something else: *The advantages of the plan outweigh its disadvantages.*
2 to weigh more than: *He outweighs me by ten pounds.* ❑ VERB **out·weighs, out·weighed, out·weigh·ing.**

out·wit (out wit′), VERB. to get the better of someone by being clever: *She usually outwits me and wins at checkers.* ❑ VERB **out·wits, out·wit·ted, out·wit·ting.**

o·val (ō′vəl), ADJECTIVE.
1 shaped like an egg.
2 shaped like an ellipse.

o·var·y (ō′vər ē), NOUN.
1 the part of a female animal in which eggs develop.
2 the part of a plant that holds new seeds. ❑ PLURAL **o·var·ies.**

ov·en (uv′ən), NOUN. the part of a stove used for baking, roasting, and sometimes broiling food.

o·ver (ō′vər),
1 PREPOSITION or ADVERB. above: *the sky over our heads.*
2 PREPOSITION. above and to the other side of; across: *to leap over a wall. Can you climb over that hill?*
3 ADVERB. down; out and down from an edge: *If you go too near the edge, you may fall over.*
4 PREPOSITION. out and down from; down from the edge of: *The ball rolled over the side of the porch.*

5 ADVERB. so as to cover the surface: *The river has frozen over.*
6 PREPOSITION. on, about, or upon, so as to cover: *Spread the canvas over the new cement. Farms are spread all over this valley.*
7 ADVERB. again: *I had to write my paper over.*
8 PREPOSITION. during: *We were out of town over the weekend.*
9 ADJECTIVE. at an end: *The play is over.*
10 PREPOSITION. about; concerning: *I was upset over our argument.*
11 PREPOSITION. more than: *It cost over $10.*
12 ADVERB. too; besides: *I ate two apples and had one left over.*
13 ADVERB. so that the other side is up or showing; upside down: *Turn over a page.*
14 ADVERB. more than: *Over 50 people came to his birthday party.*
15 ADVERB. in a place for a period of time: *We stayed over in New York City until Monday.*
16 ADVERB. at your home: *Can they sleep over?*

over and over, IDIOM. again and again: *Practice the song over and over until you do it right.*

Word Power   over-

The prefix **over-** means "above," "across," "too much," and "extra." **Over**head means **above** the head. **Over**seas means **across** the seas. **Over**do means to do **too much.** **Over**time means **extra** time.

o·ver·alls (ō′vər ôlz′), NOUN PLURAL. loose trousers with a piece covering the chest. Overalls are usually worn over clothes to keep them clean.

o·ver·arm (ō′vər ärm′), ADJECTIVE. with the arm raised above the shoulder; overhand.

o·ver·ate (ō′vər āt′), VERB. the past tense of **overeat:** *I have a stomach ache because I overate.*

o·ver·bite (ō′vər bīt′), NOUN. a condition in which someone's upper teeth stick out over the lower teeth when the mouth is closed.

o·ver·board (ō′vər bôrd′), ADVERB. over the side of a ship or boat into the water: *He fell overboard.*

go overboard, IDIOM. to go too far in an effort because of extreme enthusiasm.

o·ver·came (ō′vər kām′), VERB. the past tense of **overcome:** *I finally overcame my fear.*

o·ver·cast (ō′vər kast′), ADJECTIVE. covered with clouds; dark; gloomy: *The sky was overcast before the storm.*

o·ver·charge (ō′vər chärj′), VERB. to charge too high a price for something: *The store overcharged you for the eggs.* ❑ VERB **o·ver·charg·es, o·ver·charged, o·ver·charg·ing.**

o·ver·come (ō′vər kum′), VERB.
1 to get the better of someone; win the victory over; conquer; defeat: *to overcome an enemy, to overcome difficulties, to overcome a fault.*

2 to make someone weak or helpless: *The child was overcome by weariness and fell asleep.*
❏ VERB **o•ver•comes, o•ver•came, o•ver•come, o•ver•com•ing.**

o•ver•cooked (ō/vər kŭkt), ADJECTIVE. cooked too much or too long

o•ver•do (ō/vər dü/), VERB.
1 to do more than you should: *When getting over an illness you mustn't overdo it.*
2 to cook something too much: *The vegetables were overdone.*
❏ VERB **o•ver•does, o•ver•did** (ō/vər did/), **o•ver•done** (ō/vər dun/), **o•ver•do•ing.**

o•ver•dose (ō/vər dōs/), NOUN. too big a dose: *An overdose of medicine can harm you.*

o•ver•dress (ō/vər dres/), VERB. to wear clothes that are too fancy or formal: *My sister hopes that she didn't overdress for the party.* ❏ VERB **o•ver•dress•es, o•ver•dressed, o•ver•dress•ing.**

o•ver•due (ō/vər dü/), ADJECTIVE. due some time ago but not yet arrived, returned, or paid: *The plane is overdue. These library books are a week overdue.*

o•ver•eat (ō/vər ēt/), VERB. to eat too much. ❏ VERB **o•ver•eats, o•ver•ate, o•ver•eat•en** (ō/vər ēt/n), **o•ver•eat•ing.**

o•ver•flow (ō/vər flō/ for verb; ō/vər flō/ for noun),
1 VERB. to flow over or beyond normal limits: *Rivers often overflow in the spring.*
2 VERB. to cover; flood: *The river overflowed my garden.*
3 VERB. to extend out beyond; be too many for: *The crowd overflowed the small room and filled the hall.*
4 NOUN. the act of overflowing; excess: *The overflow from the cup ran onto the table.*
❏ VERB **o•ver•flows, o•ver•flowed, o•ver•flown** (ō/vər flōn/), **o•ver•flow•ing.**

o•ver•grow (ō/vər grō/), VERB. to grow over: *Ivy overgrew the wall.* ❏ VERB **o•ver•grows, o•ver•grew** (ō/vər grü/), **o•ver•grown, o•ver•grow•ing.**

o•ver•grown (ō/vər grōn/),
1 ADJECTIVE. grown too big or too fast: *Linemen have trimmed branches from the overgrown tree.*
2 VERB. the past participle of **overgrow**: *The vines have overgrown the wall.*

o•ver•hand (ō/vər hand/), ADJECTIVE or ADVERB. with the hand raised above the shoulder: *an overhand throw, to pitch overhand.*

o•ver•hang (ō/vər hang/), VERB. to hang over; stick out over: *Trees overhang the street.* ❏ VERB **o•ver•hangs, o•ver•hung, o•ver•hang•ing.**

o•ver•haul (ō/vər hȯl/ for verb; ō/vər hȯl/ for noun),
1 VERB. to examine something completely in order to make necessary repairs or changes: *Once a year we overhaul our boat.*
2 NOUN. the act or process of overhauling: *We give our boat an annual overhaul.*
❏ VERB **o•ver•hauls, o•ver•hauled, o•ver•haul•ing.**

o•ver•head (ō/vər hed/ for adverb; ō/vər hed/ for adjective and noun),
1 ADVERB. over the head; on high; above: *the stars overhead.*
2 ADJECTIVE. placed above; placed high up: *overhead pipes.*
3 NOUN. the regular expenses of running a business, such as rent, lighting, heating, taxes, and repairs.

o•ver•hear (ō/vər hir/), VERB. to hear something you are not meant to hear: *They spoke so loud that I could not help overhearing what they said.* ❏ VERB **o•ver•hears, o•ver•heard** (ō/vər hėrd/), **o•ver•hear•ing.**

o•ver•heat (ō/vər hēt/), VERB. to make or become too hot, especially beyond the point of safety or comfort: *My car overheated when we drove through the mountains.* ❏ VERB **o•ver•heats, o•ver•heat•ed, o•ver•heat•ing.**

o•ver•hung (ō/ver hung/), VERB.
1 the past tense of **overhang**: *A big awning overhung the sidewalk.*
2 the past participle of **overhang**: *Trees have overhung our roof for years and kept our house cool in summer.*

o•ver•joyed (ō/vər joid/), ADJECTIVE. very happy; delighted.

o•ver•laid (ō/vər lād/), VERB.
1 the past tense of **overlay**: *The workmen overlaid the dome with gold.*
2 the past participle of **overlay**: *Someone has overlaid that beautiful wood floor with carpet.*

o•ver•land (ō/vər land/), ADVERB or ADJECTIVE. on land; by land: *an overland route, to travel overland from Maine to Texas.*

Part of this house **overhangs** a waterfall.

a	hat	ė	term	ô	order	ch	child		a in about
ā	age	i	it	oi	oil	ng	long		e in taken
ä	far	ī	ice	ou	out	sh	she	ə{	i in pencil
â	care	o	hot	u	cup	th	thin		o in lemon
e	let	ō	open	u̇	put	ᴛʜ	then		u in circus
ē	equal	ȯ	saw	ü	rule	zh	measure		

o·ver·lap (ō′vər lap′), VERB. to partly cover something and extend beyond it: *Shingles are laid to overlap each other.* ❑ VERB **o·ver·laps, o·ver·lapped, o·ver·lap·ping.**

o·ver·lay (ō′vər lā′ for verb; ō′vər lā′ for noun),
1 VERB. to lay or place one thing over or upon something else.
2 NOUN. something laid over something else, especially an ornamental layer: *an overlay of gold on a statue.*
❑ VERB **o·ver·lays, o·ver·laid, o·ver·lay·ing.**

o·ver·load (ō′vər lōd′ for verb; ō′vər lōd′ for noun),
1 VERB. to load too heavily: *to overload a boat.*
2 NOUN. too heavy a load: *The overload of electric current caused the power to go off.*
❑ VERB **o·ver·loads, o·ver·load·ed, o·ver·load·ing.**

This truck is **overloaded** with furniture.

o·ver·look (ō′vər lük′), VERB.
1 to fail to notice something: *Here are some letters which you overlooked.*
2 to excuse someone for doing something bad: *I will overlook your bad behavior this time.*
3 to have a view of something from above: *This high window overlooks half the city.*
❑ VERB **o·ver·looks, o·ver·looked, o·ver·look·ing.**

o·ver·night (ō′vər nīt′ for adverb; ō′vər nīt′ for adjective),
1 ADVERB. during the night: *She likes to stay overnight with friends.*
2 ADJECTIVE. for the night: *overnight guests.*
3 ADVERB. immediately; at once: *Change will not come overnight.*

o·ver·pass (ō′vər pas′), NOUN. a bridge over a road, railroad, or canal. ❑ PLURAL **o·ver·pass·es.**

o·ver·pow·er (ō′vər pou′ər), VERB.
1 to defeat or conquer someone because you are stronger: *The wrestler overpowered his opponent.*
2 to be much greater or stronger than something: *The smell from the factory overpowered all others.*
❑ VERB **o·ver·pow·ers, o·ver·pow·ered, o·ver·pow·er·ing.**

o·ver·ran (ō′vər ran′), VERB. the past tense of **overrun:** *Vines overran the garden.*

o·ver·rate (ō′vər rāt′), VERB. to rate or estimate too highly: *I overrated my strength and had to ask for help.* ❑ VERB **o·ver·rates, o·ver·rat·ed, o·ver·rat·ing.**

o·ver·rule (ō′vər rül′), VERB. to rule or decide against someone's argument, objection, or the like: *The president overruled my plan.* ❑ VERB **o·ver·rules, o·ver·ruled, o·ver·rul·ing.**

o·ver·run (ō′vər run′), VERB.
1 to spread over and spoil or harm in some way: *Rats overran the stable.*
2 to defeat and occupy something: *Enemy troops overran the fort.*
3 to spread over: *Vines overran the wall.*
4 to run or go beyond something: *She overran second base and was tagged out.*
❑ VERB **o·ver·runs, o·ver·ran, o·ver·run, o·ver·run·ning.**

o·ver·saw (ō′vər so′), VERB. the past tense of **oversee:** *Father oversaw the construction of our new garage.*

o·ver·seas (ō′vər sēz′ for adverb; ō′vər sēz′ for adjective),
1 ADVERB. across the sea; beyond the sea; abroad: *I want to travel overseas.*
2 ADJECTIVE. done, used, or serving overseas: *My aunt did overseas military duty last year.*
3 ADJECTIVE. of or from countries across the sea; foreign: *He made a fortune in overseas trade.*

o·ver·see (ō′vər sē′), VERB. to look after and direct work or workers; manage; supervise: *to oversee a factory.* ❑ VERB **o·ver·sees, o·ver·saw, o·ver·seen** (ō′vər sēn′), **o·ver·see·ing.**

o·ver·se·er (ō′vər sē′ər), NOUN. someone who oversees others or their work: *The overseer forced the workers in the fields to pick faster.*

o·ver·shad·ow (ō′vər shad′ō), VERB. to be more important than: *Preparations for the school play soon overshadowed other student activities. She felt overshadowed by her older sister.* ❑ VERB **o·ver·shad·ows, o·ver·shad·owed, o·ver·shad·ow·ing.**

o·ver·shoe (ō′vər shü′), NOUN. a waterproof shoe or boot, made of rubber or plastic, worn over another shoe to keep the foot dry and warm. ❑ PLURAL **o·ver·shoes.**

o·ver·shoot (ō′vər shüt′), VERB.
1 to shoot over: *The archer overshot the target.*
2 to go beyond or past: *The plane overshot the runway.*
❑ VERB **o·ver·shoots, o·ver·shot** (ō′vər shot′), **o·ver·shoot·ing.**

o·ver·sight (ō′vər sīt′), NOUN. a mistake, such as failure to notice something or think of something: *Through an oversight, the cat got no supper last night.*

o•ver•sized (ō′vər sīzd′), ADJECTIVE. too big; larger than the ordinary size: *an oversized book.*

o•ver•sleep (ō′vər slēp′), VERB. to sleep beyond a certain hour; sleep too long. ❑ VERB **o•ver•sleeps, o•ver•slept** (ō′vər slept′), **o•ver•sleep•ing.**

o•ver•spread (ō′vər spred′), VERB. to spread over something: *Ivy overspreads our cottage.* ❑ VERB **o•ver•spreads, o•ver•spread, o•ver•spread•ing.**

an **oversized** pumpkin

o•ver•step (ō′vər step′), VERB. to go beyond some rule or limit; exceed: *He overstepped the rules.* ❑ VERB **o•ver•steps, o•ver•stepped, o•ver•step•ping.**

o•ver•take (ō′vər tāk′), VERB.
1 to catch up with someone or something: *The blue car overtook ours.*
2 to come upon suddenly: *A storm overtook us.* ❑ VERB **o•ver•takes, o•ver•took, o•ver•tak•en** (ō′vər tā′kən), **o•ver•tak•ing.**

o•ver•throw (ō′vər thrō′ *for verb;* ō′vər thrō′ *for noun*),
1 VERB. to take away the power of; defeat: *The people overthrew the government.*
2 NOUN. defeat; upset: *the overthrow of the king.*
3 VERB. to throw a ball past the place where it should go: *The shortstop overthrew third base.* ❑ VERB **o•ver•throws, o•ver•threw** (ō′vər thrü′), **o•ver•thrown** (ō′vər thrōn′), **o•ver•throw•ing.**

o•ver•ture (ō′vər chər), NOUN.
1 a musical composition played by the orchestra as an introduction to an opera or other long musical composition.
2 an attempt to make an agreement with an opponent: *After twenty years of war, the enemy is making peace overtures..*

o•ver•turn (ō′vər tėrn′), VERB. to turn something upside down: *The boat overturned.* ❑ VERB **o•ver•turns, o•ver•turned, o•ver•turn•ing.**

o•ver•weight (ō′vər wāt′), ADJECTIVE. having too much weight: *I am overweight for my height.*

o•ver•whelm (ō′vər hwelm′), VERB. to overcome completely: *The parents of the dead child were overwhelmed with sadness.* ❑ VERB **o•ver•whelms, o•ver•whelmed, o•ver•whelm•ing.**

o•ver•work (ō′vər wėrk′ *for noun;* ō′vər wėrk′ *for verb*),
1 NOUN. too much or too hard work: *He is exhausted from overwork.*
2 VERB. to cause someone or something to work too hard or too long: *She overworks her staff.* ❑ VERB **o•ver•works, o•ver•worked, o•ver•work•ing.**

owe (ō), VERB.
1 to have to pay someone; be in debt to: *I owe her $2.*
2 to have to give: *I really think you owe me an apology for what you just said.*
3 to be indebted for something: *We owe a great deal to our parents.* ❑ VERB **owes, owed, ow•ing.** ■ Another word that sounds like this is **oh.**

ow•ing (ō′ing), ADJECTIVE. due; owed: *I must pay what is owing.*

owing to, IDIOM. on account of; because of: *Owing to the bad weather, we canceled our trip.*

barred owl

barn owl

great gray owl

eagle owl

four kinds of **owls**

o•ver•time (ō′vər tīm′),
1 NOUN. extra time; time beyond the regular hours: *I was paid for the overtime I worked.*
2 ADVERB. beyond the regular hours: *They worked overtime.*
3 NOUN. an extra period of time at the end of a sport event that is tied: *The game is in overtime.*

o•ver•took (ō′vər túk′), VERB. the past tense of **overtake.**

owl (oul), NOUN. a bird with a big head, big eyes, and a hooked beak. Owls hunt mice and small birds at night. There are almost 150 kinds of owls. **—owl′like′,** ADJECTIVE.

a hat	ė term	ô order	ch child	⟨a in about
ā age	i it	oi oil	ng long	e in taken
ä far	ī ice	ou out	sh she	ə⟨i in pencil
â care	o hot	u cup	th thin	o in lemon
e let	ō open	ú put	ᴛʜ then	u in circus
ē equal	ò saw	ü rule	zh measure	

own (ōn),
1 *VERB.* to have or keep something because it belongs to you; possess: *I own many books.*
2 *ADJECTIVE.* belonging to you: *This is my own book.*
❑ *VERB* **owns, owned, own·ing.**

of your own, *IDIOM.* belonging to oneself: *You have a good mind of your own.*

on your own, *IDIOM.* not ruled or directed by someone else: *As a young man, he traveled around the world on his own.*

own up, *IDIOM.* to admit to; confess: *He owned up to picking her flowers.*

own·er (ō′nər), *NOUN.* someone who owns something: *Who is the owner of this dog?*

own·er·ship (ō′nər ship), *NOUN.* the condition of being an owner; right of possession: *She claimed ownership of the abandoned car.*

ox (oks), *NOUN.* the full-grown male of cattle that cannot father young. Oxen are used for farm work or for beef. ❑ *PLURAL* **ox·en. −ox′like′,** *ADJECTIVE.*

ox·cart (oks′kärt′), *NOUN.* a cart drawn by oxen.

ox·i·dize (ok′sə dīz), *VERB.* to combine with oxygen. When a substance burns or rusts, it oxidizes. ❑ *VERB* **ox·i·diz·es, ox·i·dized, ox·i·diz·ing.**

ox·y·gen (ok′sə jən), *NOUN.* an invisible gas that forms about one fifth of the air and about one third of water. Oxygen is a chemical element.

Animals cannot live without oxygen. Fire will not burn without oxygen.

oys·ter (oi′stər), *NOUN.* a shellfish with a rough, irregular shell in two halves. They are found in shallow water along the coasts. Many kinds are good to eat and some kinds produce pearls.

oz., an abbreviation of **ounce** or **ounces.** ❑ *PLURAL* **oz.**

o·zone (ō′zōn), *NOUN.* a form of oxygen with a sharp smell, produced by electricity and present in the air especially after a thunderstorm. Ozone is a poisonous gas often found in smog.

oxen — about 5 feet high at the shoulder

ozone layer, a part of the upper atmosphere containing large amounts of ozone. It is 10 to 30 miles above the earth's surface. It shields the earth from unhealthy amounts of ultraviolet radiation.

paramecium

Pp

P or **p** (pē), *NOUN.* the 16th letter of the English alphabet. ❑ *PLURAL* **P's** or **p's.**

p., an abbreviation of **page¹.**

pa (pä), *NOUN.* (informal) papa; father; daddy. ❑ *PLURAL* **pas.**

PA,
1 an abbreviation of **Pennsylvania.**
2 See **public-address system.**

pace (pās),
1 *NOUN.* a step: *He took three paces into the room.*
2 *VERB.* to walk with regular steps: *The tiger paced back and forth in its cage.*
3 *NOUN.* the length of a step in walking; about 2½ feet: *There were perhaps ten paces between me and the bear.*
4 *VERB.* to measure by paces: *We paced off the distance and found it to be 69 paces.*
5 *NOUN.* rate; speed: *to walk at a fast pace.*
❑ *VERB* **pac·es, paced, pac·ing.**

pace·mak·er (pās′mā′kər), *NOUN.*
1 someone or something that sets the pace.
2 an electronic device implanted in the chest wall to maintain or restore the normal rhythm of the heartbeat.

Pa·cif·ic (pə sif′ik),
1 *NOUN.* an ocean west of North and South America. It extends to Asia and Australia.
2 *ADJECTIVE.* of, along, or located in the Pacific Ocean. California, Oregon, Washington, Alaska, and Hawaii are the Pacific states: *The Pacific coast of the United States has very beautiful scenery.*

pac·i·fi·er (pas′ə fi′ər), *NOUN.* a rubber or plastic nipple or ring given to a baby to suck so that he or she will not cry.

pac·i·fist (pas′ə fist), *NOUN.* someone who opposes war and believes that all disputes between nations should be settled by peaceful means.

pac·i·fy (pas′ə fī), *VERB.* to make someone calm; quiet down; give peace to: *We tried to pacify our angry neighbor.* ❑ *VERB* **pac·i·fies, pac·i·fied, pac·i·fy·ing.** –**pac′i·fi·ca′tion,** *NOUN.*

pack (pak),

1 *VERB.* to put things together in a bundle, box, bale, or other container: *Pack your books in this box.*
2 *VERB.* to fill with things; put your things into: *Pack your trunk.*
3 *NOUN.* a small package, usually containing a certain number of items: *I bought a pack of gum.*
4 *NOUN.* a backpack: *The hikers carried heavy packs.*
5 *VERB.* to press or crowd closely together: *A hundred people were packed into one small room.*
6 *VERB.* to fill a space with all that it will hold: *A large audience packed the small theater.* ∎ See the Synonym Study at **full.**
7 *NOUN.* a number of animals of the same kind hunting together: *Wolves hunt in packs; tigers hunt alone.*
❑ *VERB* **packs, packed, pack·ing.**

pack off, *IDIOM.* to send away: *The child was packed off to bed.*

pack·age (pak′ij),

1 *NOUN.* a bundle of things tightly packed or wrapped together; box or bag with things packed in it; parcel.
2 *VERB.* to put something in a package.
3 *NOUN.* a box, carton, and so on, with something packed inside: *We ate a whole package of cookies.*
❑ *VERB* **pack·ages, pack·aged, pack·ag·ing.** –**pack′ag·er,** *NOUN.*

pack·et (pak′it), *NOUN.* a small package; parcel: *Grandma saved a packet of letters from her aunt.*

pact (pakt), *NOUN.* a formal agreement: *The three nations signed a peace pact.*

pad (pad),

1 *NOUN.* a piece of something soft, such as cotton or foam rubber, used for comfort, protection, or stuffing; cushion: *The baby's carriage has a pad.*
2 *VERB.* to fill with something soft; stuff: *to pad a chair.*
3 *NOUN.* a soft part on the underside of the feet of dogs, foxes, and some other animals.
4 *NOUN.* a number of sheets of paper fastened together at one edge; tablet.
5 *NOUN.* the large floating leaf of the water lily.
6 *NOUN.* See **launch pad.**
❑ *VERB* **pads, pad·ded, pad·ding.**

pad·ding (pad′ing), *NOUN.* any material used to pad something with, such as cotton or foam rubber.

pad·dle[1] (pad′l),

1 *NOUN.* a short oar with a broad blade at one end or both ends, usually held with both hands in rowing a boat or canoe.
2 *VERB.* to move a boat or a canoe by pulling a paddle or paddles through the water.
3 *NOUN.* a broad piece of wood with a handle at one end, used for stirring, for mixing, for beating rugs, and in other ways.
4 *NOUN.* a nearly round wooden object with a short handle, used to hit the ball in table tennis.
5 *VERB.* to beat someone with a paddle; spank.
6 *NOUN.* an electronic device used to control video games and computer games. It is a flat handle containing a wheel and a button.
❑ *VERB* **pad·dles, pad·dled, pad·dling.** –**pad′dle·like′,** *ADJECTIVE.* –**pad′dler,** *NOUN.*

pad·dle[2] (pad′l), *VERB.* to move the hands or feet about in water: *Children love to paddle around in the pool.* ❑ *VERB* **pad·dles, pad·dled, pad·dling.**

paddle wheel, a wheel with large flat boards fastened around it. They move a ship through the water.

an old-fashioned steamboat with a **paddle wheel**

pad·dy (pad′ē), *NOUN.* a flooded area with raised banks around its sides, for growing rice. ❑ *PLURAL* **pad·dies.**

pad·lock (pad′lok′),

1 *NOUN.* a lock that can be put on and removed. It hangs by a curved bar, hinged at one end and snapped shut at the other.
2 *VERB.* to fasten something shut with a padlock.
❑ *VERB* **pad·locks, pad·locked, pad·lock·ing.**

pa·gan (pā′gən),

1 *NOUN.* someone who is not a Christian, Jew, or Muslim; someone who worships many gods or no god; a heathen. The ancient Romans were pagans.
2 *ADJECTIVE.* of or about pagans; heathen: *pagan customs, pagan religions.*

Word Story

Pagan comes from a Latin word meaning "village." People in country villages continued to worship many gods long after people in Rome and other cities had become Christians.

page[1] (pāj), *NOUN.* one side of a sheet or piece of paper: *My story is three pages long.*

page² (pāj),
1 *NOUN.* someone who runs errands or delivers messages. Pages at hotels usually wear uniforms.
2 *VERB.* to try to find someone in a public place by having his or her name called out.
3 *VERB.* to call someone to the telephone by means of a beeper: *Page me when you are ready to be picked up.*
4 *NOUN.* (in the Middle Ages) a youth who was preparing to be a knight.
❑ *VERB* **pag·es, paged, pag·ing.**

pag·eant (paj′ənt), *NOUN.* a public show that represents scenes from history, legend, or the like: *Our school gave a pageant of the coming of the Pilgrims to America.*

pag·er (pā′jər), *NOUN.* See **beeper.**

pa·go·da (pə gō′də), *NOUN.* a temple having many stories, with a roof curving upward from each story. There are pagodas in India, Japan, and China. ❑ *PLURAL* **pa·go·das.**

2 feelings of great sadness: *The death of someone we love causes us pain.*
■ Another word that sounds like this is **pane.**

pain·ful (pān′fəl), *ADJECTIVE.* causing pain; hurting: *They both suffered painful injuries in the accident.* —**pain′ful·ly,** *ADVERB.*

pain·less (pān′lis), *ADJECTIVE.* without pain; causing no pain. —**pain′less·ly,** *ADVERB.*

pains·tak·ing (pānz′tā′king), *ADJECTIVE.* very careful: *He trimmed the boards with painstaking care.*

paint (pānt),
1 *NOUN.* a liquid that you spread on a surface to color and protect it. Paint comes in many different colors.
2 *VERB.* to cover or decorate something with paint: *We painted the house last summer.*
3 *VERB.* to make a picture of something, using paint: *The artist painted animals.*
❑ *VERB* **paints, paint·ed, paint·ing.**

paint·brush (pānt′brush′), *NOUN.* a brush for putting on paint. ❑ *PLURAL* **paint·brush·es.**

painter — Juan Gris/Mary Cassatt/René Magritte

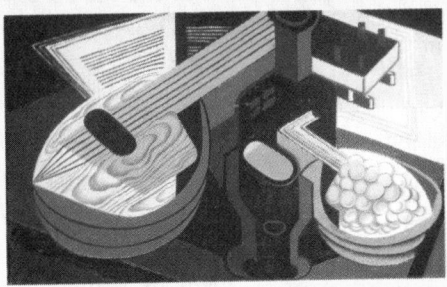

◀ *Juan Gris was a Spanish painter who painted in the modern style called cubism. He often painted objects using rich, strong colors.*

©1999 C.Herscovici, Brussels/Artist's Rights Society (A.R.S.), New York

Mary Cassatt was an American ▶ painter who painted in France. She painted scenes of people doing ordinary, everyday things, especially loving scenes of mothers and children. Her paintings are often very peaceful.

▲ *René Magritte was a Belgian painter. He often painted scenes that contained a combination of elements that do not usually go together. His paintings sometime seem like dreams.*

paid (pād), *VERB.*
1 the past tense of **pay:** *He paid his bill in full.*
2 the past participle of **pay:** *I have paid my bills.*

pail (pāl), *NOUN.*
1 a round container with a handle, used for carrying liquids, sand, and so on; bucket.
2 the amount that a pail holds.
■ Another word that sounds like this is **pale.**

pain (pān), *NOUN.*
1 a feeling of being hurt; suffering: *A cut gives pain. A toothache is a pain.*

paint·er (pān′tər), *NOUN.*
1 someone who paints pictures; artist. *Georgia O'Keeffe, Pablo Picasso, and René Magritte are all famous 20th-century painters.*
2 someone who paints rooms, houses, or other buildings.

a hat	ė term	ô order	ch child	a in about
ā age	i it	oi oil	ng long	e in taken
ä far	ī ice	ou out	sh she	ə i in pencil
â care	o hot	u cup	th thin	o in lemon
e let	ō open	ù put	ŦH then	u in circus
ē equal	ò saw	ü rule	zh measure	

paint·ing (pān′ting), NOUN.
1 a picture; something that is or was painted.
2 the act of someone who paints.

Word Bank

Painting has a large vocabulary. If you want to know more about painting, you can begin by looking up these words in this dictionary.

abstract	landscape	palette	portrait
canvas	mural	perspective	sketch
easel	oil painting	pigment	watercolor

pair (pâr),
1 NOUN. a set of two things; two things that go together: *I bought a new pair of shoes.*
2 NOUN. two animals or human beings that work or play together: *A pair of horses pulled the carriage. Several pairs of dancers were practicing on stage.*
3 VERB. to arrange or be arranged in pairs: *My socks are neatly paired in a drawer.*
4 NOUN. a single thing with two parts that work together: *Where's my pair of scissors?*
5 VERB. to join in a pair; mate: *Some animals pair for life.*
❑ PLURAL **pairs** or **pair**; VERB **pairs, paired, pair·ing.**
▪ Other words that sound like this are **pare** and **pear.**
pair off, IDIOM. to arrange in pairs; form into pairs: *The campers paired off and started the hike.*

Pai·ute (pī yüt′ or pī′yüt), NOUN.
1 a member of a tribe of American Indians living in Arizona, Nevada, Utah, California, and Oregon.
2 the language of this tribe.
❑ PLURAL **Pai·ute** or **Pai·utes.**

pa·ja·ma (pə jä′mə or pə jam′ə), ADJECTIVE. of or in pajamas: *pajama tops, pajama party.*

pa·ja·mas (pə jä′məz or pə jam′əz), NOUN PLURAL. clothing to sleep in, made up of a shirt and loose trousers.

Word Story

Pajamas comes from Persian words meaning "leg" and "clothing." People in Persia and India wore loose trousers as daytime clothes. Europeans began wearing these trousers to sleep in, with a loose shirt, and called both parts **pajamas.**

Pak·i·stan (pak′ə stan), NOUN. a country in southern Asia. —**Pak·i·stan·i** (pak′ə stan′ē), ADJECTIVE or NOUN.

pal (pal),
1 NOUN. a close friend; playmate.
2 VERB. to be on very friendly terms with someone: *We palled around together for years.*
❑ VERB **pals, palled, pal·ling.**

pal·ace (pal′is), NOUN. a very large, grand house, especially the official home of a king or queen.

pal·ate (pal′it), NOUN. the roof of the mouth. The bony part in front is the **hard palate,** and the fleshy part in back is the **soft palate.** ▪ Another word that sounds like this is **palette.**

pale (pāl),
1 ADJECTIVE. without much color: *When you have been ill, your face is sometimes pale.*
2 ADJECTIVE. not bright; dim: *a pale blue. The bright stars are surrounded by hundreds of pale ones.*
3 VERB. to turn pale: *Their faces paled at the bad news.*
❑ ADJECTIVE **pal·er, pal·est;** VERB **pales, paled, pal·ing.** ▪ Another word that sounds like this is **pail.** —**pale′ness,** NOUN.

pa·le·on·tol·o·gy (pā′lē on tol′ə jē), NOUN. the science that studies the forms of life existing in prehistoric time by examining fossil animals and plants. —**pa′le·on·tol′o·gist,** NOUN.

Pal·es·tine (pal′ə stīn), NOUN. a region in southwestern Asia on the Mediterranean Sea. It is now divided chiefly between Israel and Jordan.

pal·ette (pal′it), NOUN. a thin board, usually oval or oblong, with a thumb hole at one end, used by artists to mix paints on. ▪ Another word that sounds like this is **palate.**

pal·in·drome (pal′in drōm), NOUN. a word, verse, sentence, or number which reads the same backward or forward: "Never odd or even" is a palindrome; "9449" is a palindrome.

palm¹ (päm),
1 NOUN. the inside of the hand between the wrist and the fingers.
2 VERB. to conceal something in your hand: *The magician palmed the nickel.*
❑ VERB **palms, palmed, palm·ing.**
palm off, IDIOM. to get someone to buy or take something that isn't worth anything by pretending it is valuable: *He palmed off that broken game on me by saying it could be fixed easily.*

palm² (päm), NOUN. a tree that has a tall trunk, no branches, and many large leaves at the top. Palms grow in warm climates.

palm²

Palm Sunday, the Sunday before Easter.

pal·o·mi·no (pal′ə mē′nō), NOUN. a cream colored or golden tan horse. Its mane and tail are usually lighter colored.
❑ PLURAL **pal·o·mi·nos.**

pal·try (pȯl′trē), ADJECTIVE. almost worthless; petty: *I sold my old, rusted bicycle for a paltry sum of money.* ❑ ADJECTIVE **pal·tri·er, pal·tri·est.**

pam•pas (pam′pəz), *NOUN PLURAL.* the vast, grassy, treeless plains of South America.

pam•per (pam′pər), *VERB.* to treat someone too well; give someone too many gifts or too much attention: *Grandparents often pamper their grandchildren.* ❑ *VERB* **pam•pers, pam•pered, pam•per•ing.**

pam•phlet (pam′flit), *NOUN.* a booklet with a few pages.

pan (pan),
1 *NOUN.* a flat utensil to cook food in. Pans are usually broad, shallow, and have no cover.
2 *NOUN.* anything like this. Gold and other metals are sometimes obtained by washing ore in pans.
3 *VERB.* to wash gravel or sand in a pan to separate the gold: *He panned for gold in the stream.*
❑ *VERB* **pans, panned, pan•ning.**

pan out, *IDIOM.* to succeed; work out: *Her scheme panned out.*

Have You Heard?

You may have heard someone say **"out of the frying pan, into the fire."** This means that the person has gone from a bad situation to one that is even worse.

Pan•a•ma (pan′ə mä), *NOUN.*
1 an isthmus or narrow neck of land that connects North and South America.
2 a country in Central America on the Isthmus of Panama.
—**Pan•a•ma•ni•an** (pan′ə mā′nē ən), *ADJECTIVE* or *NOUN.*

Panama Canal, a canal cut across the Isthmus of Panama to connect the Atlantic and Pacific oceans.

Pan-A•mer•i•can (pan′ə mer′ə kən), *ADJECTIVE.* of or about all the people or countries of North, Central, and South America.

pan•cake (pan′kāk′), *NOUN.* a flat, round kind of bread made of liquid batter and fried in a pan; flapjack.

pan•cre•as (pan′krē əs), *NOUN.* a large gland near the stomach. It produces insulin and helps the body to digest food. ❑ *PLURAL* **pan•cre•as•es.**

pan•da (pan′də), *NOUN.*
1 a bearlike animal of Asia, mostly white with black legs, often called the **giant panda.** Few pandas are alive today.
2 a reddish brown animal somewhat like a raccoon, called the **lesser panda.** It lives in the mountains of India. ❑ *PLURAL* **pan•das.**

panda — between 5 and 6 feet long

pane (pān), *NOUN.* a single sheet of glass or plastic in part of a window or a door: *Big hailstones and sudden gusts of wind broke several panes of glass.*
■ Another word that sounds like this is **pain.**

Word Story

Pane comes from a Latin word meaning "cloth." **Panel** comes from the same word. Before glass was easy to get, people filled their windows with cloth thin enough to let light in.

pan•el (pan′l),
1 *NOUN.* a flat sheet of wood, glass, or plastic, that makes up part of a surface. A panel is often sunk below or raised above the rest, and used for a decoration. Panels may be in a door or other woodwork or on large pieces of furniture.
2 *VERB.* to furnish or decorate something with panels: *The walls were paneled with oak.*
3 *NOUN.* a group of people picked to discuss or decide something: *A panel of experts gave its opinion on ways to solve the traffic problem.*
4 *NOUN.* the board containing the devices, controls, or dials used in operating a car, aircraft, computer, or other mechanism.
■ See the Word Story above. ❑ *VERB* **pan•els, pan•eled, pan•el•ing.**

pang (pang), *NOUN.*
1 a sudden, short, sharp pain: *She suffered from pangs of a toothache.*
2 a sudden painful emotion: *A pang of pity moved my heart.*

pan•ic (pan′ik),
1 *NOUN.* sudden uncontrollable feeling of fear that causes a person or group to lose self-control and do things that don't make sense: *When the theater caught fire, there was a panic, and everyone tried to get out the door at once.*
2 *VERB.* to suffer from a feeling of panic: *The audience panicked when the fire broke out.*
❑ *VERB* **pan•ics, pan•icked, pan•ick•ing.**

Word Story

Panic comes from a Greek word meaning "of Pan." Pan was a Greek god whose appearance was thought to cause terror among people who saw him.

pan•ick•y (pan′ə kē), *ADJECTIVE.* feeling panic: *When fire broke out in the theater, I became panicky.*

pan•ic-strick•en (pan′ik strik′ən), *ADJECTIVE.* frightened out of your wits.

a hat	ė term	ô order	ch child	ə = a in about
ā age	i it	oi oil	ng long	e in taken
ä far	ī ice	ou out	sh she	i in pencil
â care	o hot	u cup	th thin	o in lemon
e let	ō open	u̇ put	ᴛʜ then	u in circus
ē equal	ȯ saw	ü rule	zh measure	

P

pan·o·ram·a (pan/ə ram/ə), NOUN. a view of a large area: *We looked out on a panorama of beach and sea.* ❏ PLURAL **pan·o·ram·as.**

pan·sy (pan/zē), NOUN. a flower somewhat like a violet but much larger and having flat petals usually of several colors. ❏ PLURAL **pan·sies.**

Word Story

Pansy comes from an old French word meaning "thought." The flower was called this because it was considered the symbol of thought or remembrance.

pant (pant), VERB. to breathe hard and quickly: *He is panting from playing tennis.* ❏ VERB **pants, pant·ed, pant·ing.**

pan·ther (pan/thər), NOUN.
1 a leopard, most often a black leopard.
2 See **mountain lion.**
❏ PLURAL **pan·thers** or **pan·ther.**

pan·ties (pan/tēz), NOUN PLURAL. a kind of underwear without legs worn by women or children.

pan·to·mime (pan/tə mīm), NOUN. a play in which the actors make motions and bodily movements but do not speak.

pan·try (pan/trē), NOUN. a small room in which food, dishes, silverware, or table linen is kept.
❏ PLURAL **pan·tries.**

pants (pants), NOUN PLURAL. clothing worn to cover the legs, from the waist to the ankles; trousers.

pa·pa (pä/pə), NOUN. father; daddy. ❏ PLURAL **pa·pas.**

pa·pa·ya (pə pä/yə), NOUN. the oval-shaped fruit of a tropical American tree. Papayas have yellowish pulp, and are good to eat. ❏ PLURAL **pa·pa·yas.**

pa·per (pā/pər),
1 NOUN. a material used for writing, printing, drawing, wrapping packages, and covering walls. Paper is made in thin sheets from wood pulp, rags, and straw.
2 NOUN. a single piece of paper.
3 NOUN. a newspaper: *I like to read the Sunday paper.*
4 NOUN. **papers,** official documents telling who or what you are.
5 NOUN. an article; essay: *The professor read a paper on the teaching of English.*
6 ADJECTIVE. made of paper: *paper dolls.*
–pa/per·like/, ADJECTIVE.

pa·per·back (pā/pər bak/), NOUN. a book with a paper binding or cover.

paper clip, a flat, bent piece of wire used for holding papers together.

pa·poose (pa püs/), NOUN. a North American Indian baby. ★ **Papoose** is often considered offensive.

Pap·u·a New Gui·nea (pap/yü ə nü gin/ē or pä/pü ä/ nü gin/ē), a country in the southwestern Pacific.

pa·py·rus (pə pī/rəs), NOUN. a tall water plant from which the ancient Egyptians, Greeks, and Romans made a kind of paper to write on. ❏ PLURAL **pa·py·rus·es** or **pa·py·ri** (pə pī/rī).

par (pär), NOUN. an average or normal amount, degree, or condition: *After his cold he felt below par.*

par·a·ble (par/ə bəl), NOUN. a brief story used to teach some truth or moral lesson.

par·a·chute (par/ə shüt),
1 NOUN. a huge piece of cloth like a big umbrella. It is used in jumping from an aircraft.
2 VERB. to come down by parachute: *The pilot of the burning plane parachuted safely to the ground.*
❏ VERB **par·a·chutes, par·a·chut·ed, par·a·chut·ing.**

Parachutes are made of thin, strong cloth.

pa·rade (pə rād/),
1 NOUN. a group of people marching together in rows down a street. Parades often have bands playing music.
2 VERB. to march in a procession; walk proudly as if in a parade: *The teams paraded around the stadium.*
3 VERB. to show something off: *to parade your wealth.*
❏ VERB **pa·rades, pa·rad·ed, pa·rad·ing.**

par·a·dise (par/ə dīs), NOUN.
1 heaven.
2 a place or condition of great happiness: *The summer camp was a paradise for her.*

par·a·graph (par/ə graf), NOUN. a group of sentences that are about one main idea.

A paragraph begins on a new line and usually has some space before the first word.

Par·a·guay (par′ə gwā *or* par′ə gwī), NOUN. a country in central South America. —**Par′a·guay′an,** ADJECTIVE *or* NOUN.

par·a·keet (par′ə kēt), NOUN. a bird with brightly colored feathers and a long tail. It is a kind of small parrot.

par·a·le·gal (par′ə lē′gəl), NOUN. someone trained to assist a lawyer.

par·al·lel (par′ə lel),
1 ADJECTIVE. being the same distance apart throughout their length, like the two rails of a railroad track.
2 VERB. to be at the same distance from throughout their length: *The street parallels the railroad.*
3 NOUN. a parallel line, curve, or surface.
4 NOUN. any of the imaginary parallel circles around the earth that mark degrees of latitude.
5 NOUN. a comparison to show likeness: *to draw a parallel between this winter and last winter.*
6 VERB. to be or find a case which is similar or parallel to: *Can you parallel that for friendliness?*
❑ VERB **par·al·lels, par·al·leled, par·al·lel·ing.**

par·al·lel·o·gram (par′ə lel′ə gram), NOUN. a figure with four sides. The opposite sides of a parallelogram are parallel and of equal length.

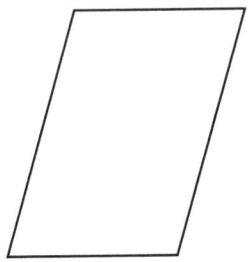

This **parallelogram** has no right angles.

pa·ral·y·sis (pə ral′ə sis), NOUN. a loss of part or all of the ability to move or feel in part of the body: *Injury to the spinal cord can cause paralysis.*

par·a·lyze (par′ə līz), VERB.
1 to cause a loss of part or all of the power to move or feel in any part of the body: *His arm was paralyzed.*
2 to make someone or something powerless or helpless: *Fear paralyzed my mind.*
❑ VERB **par·a·lyz·es, par·a·lyzed, par·a·lyz·ing.**

par·a·me·ci·um (par′ə mē′sē əm), NOUN. a very small one-celled living thing shaped like a slipper. Paramecia live in fresh water. They are not animals or plants but another kind of life, called protists.
❑ PLURAL **par·a·me·ci·a** (par′ə mē′sē ə).

par·a·med·ic (par′ə med′ik), NOUN. someone who is trained to give medical treatment at the scene of an emergency.

par·a·mount (par′ə mount), ADJECTIVE. most important; supreme: *Truth is of paramount importance.*

par·a·site (par′ə sīt), NOUN. a living thing that spends its life on or in another living thing, from which it gets its food, often harming the other in the process. Lice and fleas are parasites.

par·a·sit·ic (par′ə sit′ik), ADJECTIVE. of or like a parasite; living on others.

par·a·sol (par′ə sȯl), NOUN. a lightweight umbrella used as a protection from the sun.

par·a·troop·er (par′ə trü′pər), NOUN. a soldier trained to use a parachute for dropping from an aircraft into a battle area.

par·cel (pär′səl), NOUN.
1 a bundle of things wrapped or packed together; package: *I had my arms filled with parcels.*
2 a piece: *The farmer sold two parcels of land.*

parch (pärch), VERB. to make or become hot and dry or thirsty: *I am parched with the heat.* ❑ VERB **parch·es, parched, parch·ing.**

parch·ment (pärch′mənt), NOUN. the skin of sheep or goats, prepared for use as a writing material. Parchment was used for books before paper was invented.

par·don (pärd′n),
1 VERB. to set someone free from punishment: *The governor pardoned the prisoner.*
2 NOUN. an official paper that sets someone free from punishment: *The governor's pardon freed the innocent man.*
❑ VERB **par·dons, par·doned, par·don·ing.**
I beg your pardon, IDIOM. please excuse me: *I beg your pardon, but I didn't hear you.*

pare (pâr), VERB.
1 to cut, trim, or shave off the outer part of something; peel: *I pared the apple before eating it.*
2 to gradually reduce: *We pared down our expenses.*
❑ VERB **pares, pared, par·ing.** ■ Other words that sound like this are **pair** and **pear.**

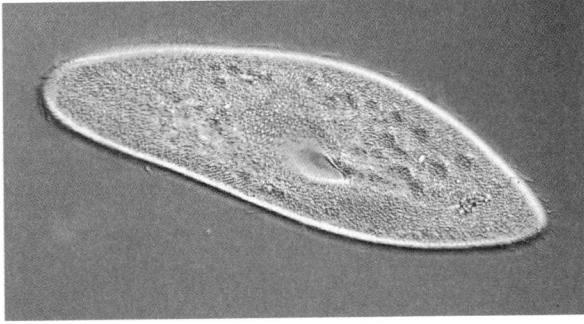

a **paramecium** photographed through a microscope

par·ent (pâr′ənt), NOUN.
1 a father or mother.
2 any living thing that produces offspring.

pa·ren·tal (pə ren′tl), ADJECTIVE. of or about a parent or parents: *The teenager resented parental advice.*

a	hat	ė	term	ô	order	ch	child	⎧a in about
ā	age	i	it	oi	oil	ng	long	e in taken
ä	far	ī	ice	ou	out	sh	she	ə⎨i in pencil
â	care	o	hot	u	cup	th	thin	o in lemon
e	let	ō	open	ù	put	ᴛʜ	then	⎩u in circus
ē	equal	ȯ	saw	ü	rule	zh	measure	

P

483

parental leave, a leave of absence from work to care for a new baby or a recently adopted child. Parental leave is usually without pay.

pa·ren·the·sis (pə ren′thə sis), NOUN. either of two curved lines ( ) used to set off a word, phrase, or sentence inserted within a sentence to explain or qualify something. The pronunciations in this dictionary are enclosed in parentheses. ❑ PLURAL **pa·ren·the·ses** (pə ren′thə sēz′).

Did You Know?

Combining **parentheses** and punctuation can be confusing. Here are some simple rules to make it easier. If the parentheses occur within a sentence, then you should put the punctuation outside of the parentheses. *I will send you the new book (if you don't have it already).* If the parentheses hold a complete sentence, then the punctuation goes inside the parentheses. *I love her new book. (She is my favorite author.)*

par·ent·ing (pâr′ən ting), NOUN. the acts and duties of being a father or mother; the raising of children.

Par·is (par′is), NOUN. the capital of France.

par·ish (par′ish), NOUN.
1 a district that has its own church and priest or minister.
2 (in Louisiana) a county.
❑ PLURAL **par·ish·es.**

park (pärk),
1 NOUN. an area of land with grass and trees. People use parks for walking and playing.
2 NOUN. a field or stadium, especially for sports events.
3 VERB. to leave a motor vehicle someplace for a time.
❑ VERB **parks, parked, park·ing.**

par·ka (pär′kə), NOUN. a heavy waterproof coat or jacket with a hood, originally worn in the Arctic and made of skins. ❑ PLURAL **par·kas.**

parking lot, an open area used for parking motor vehicles, often for a fee.

park·way (pärk′wā′), NOUN. a wide road that has spaces planted with grass, trees, or flowers along the edges of the road or in the center.

par·lia·ment (pär′lə mənt), NOUN. the highest legislative body in some countries, including Canada and Great Britain. ■ See the Word Story at **parlor.**

par·lor (pär′lər), NOUN.
1 (formerly) a room for receiving or entertaining guests; sitting room.
2 a store or kind of business that offers a service; shop: *A new ice-cream parlor opened downtown.*

Word Story

Parlor comes from a French word meaning "to talk." **Parliament** comes from the same word. A **parlor** was used mostly for conversation. **Parliament** is where politicians make speeches.

pa·ro·chi·al school (pə rō′kē əl skül′), an elementary or secondary school run by a church or religious organization.

pa·role (pə rōl′),
1 VERB. to grant a prisoner an early release from jail before the full term is served: *He was paroled after serving two years of a three-year sentence.*
2 NOUN. the release of a prisoner from jail before the full term is served.
❑ VERB **pa·roles, pa·roled, pa·rol·ing.**

par·rot (par′ət),
1 NOUN. a brightly colored bird with a stout, hooked bill. Some parrots can imitate sounds and repeat words and sentences.
2 VERB. to repeat something without really understanding it: *The student parroted the difficult, unfamiliar words.* ❑ VERB **par·rots, par·roted, par·rot·ing. –par′rot·like′,** ADJECTIVE.

parrot — up to 40 inches long, including the tail

par·sley (pär′slē), NOUN. a garden plant with finely divided, fragrant leaves. Parsley is used to flavor and decorate platters of food.

par·snip (pär′snip), NOUN. the long, tapering, whitish root of a garden plant, eaten as a vegetable.

par·son (pär′sən), NOUN. a Protestant clergyman.

part (pärt),
1 NOUN. something less than the whole; not all: *He ate part of an apple.*
2 NOUN. something that helps to make up a whole thing: *An engine has many parts.*
3 NOUN. a share: *I had a big part in planning the picnic.*
4 NOUN. someone's side in a dispute or contest: *She always takes her sister's part.*
5 NOUN. a character in a play or movie; role: *He played the part of the king.*
6 VERB. to pull something apart or to come apart: *She parted the curtains and looked out. Her lips parted as she gazed at the picture.*
7 VERB. to go apart; separate: *They parted at the door.*
8 NOUN. a dividing line left in combing your hair.
9 NOUN. one of the voices or instruments in music. The four parts in singing are soprano, alto, tenor, and bass.
10 NOUN. music for one voice or instrument: *the alto part.*
11 ADJECTIVE. less than the whole; partial: *She and two cousins own a business; each is a part owner.*
12 ADVERB. partly; not entirely: *My aunt is part Irish.*
❑ VERB **parts, part·ed, parting.**

part with, IDIOM. to give up; let go: *He wouldn't part with his dog for anything.*

take part, *IDIOM.* to take or have a share: *She took no part in the discussion.*

Synonym Study

Part means some piece or amount that is less than the whole: *The sheep are grazing in part of the field.*

Portion means a part: *They each got a portion of the prize money. Cut the meat loaf so that there is a portion for everyone.*

Section means a part, especially one that can be considered or handled by itself: *This section of his yard looks like a Japanese garden.*

Segment means a section. It often suggests that something has parts naturally and in each case: *Each segment of a grapefruit has a thin skin.*

Fraction means a distinct part of a whole: *We will read only a fraction of the play this week..*

Share means the part that belongs to each person: *She wants to do her fair share of the work.*

See also the Synonym Study at **piece.**

par·tial (pär′shəl), *ADJECTIVE.*
1 not complete; not total: *My parents made a partial payment on our new car.*
2 inclined to favor one more than another: *Parents should not be partial to any one of their children.*
3 having a liking for something: *I am partial to sports.*

par·tial·ly (pär′shə lē), *ADVERB.* not completely: *partially awake.*

par·tic·i·pate (pär tis′ə pāt), *VERB.* to take part with other people in something: *The teacher participated in the children's games.* □ *VERB* **par·tic·i·pates, par·tic·i·pat·ed, par·tic·i·pat·ing.** —**par·tic′i·pa′tion,** *NOUN.* —**par·tic′i·pa′tor,** *NOUN.*

par·ti·ci·ple (pär′tə sip′əl), *NOUN.* a form of a verb which may also be used as an adjective. In the sentence *The girl writing at the blackboard is Sue, writing* is a present participle. In the sentence *The police found the stolen silver, stolen* is a past participle.

par·ti·cle (pär′tə kəl), *NOUN.* a very little piece of something: *I got a particle of dust in my eye.*

par·tic·u·lar (pər tik′yə lər),
1 *ADJECTIVE.* this one here, not any other; specific: *That particular car is already sold.*
2 *ADJECTIVE.* different from others; unusual; special: *He is a particular friend of mine.*
3 *NOUN.* an individual part; detail: *All the particulars of the accident are now known.*

par·tic·u·lar·ly (pər tik′yə lər lē), *ADVERB.* especially: *I am particularly fond of him.*

part·ing (pär′ting), *ADJECTIVE.* given, taken, or done as you are leaving: *a parting request.*

par·ti·tion (pär tish′ən),
1 *NOUN.* a screen or wall between rooms or spaces.
2 *VERB.* to divide something into parts: *The new owners partitioned the attic into three bedrooms.* □ *VERB* **par·ti·tions, par·ti·tioned, par·ti·tion·ing.**

part·ly (pärt′lē), *ADVERB.* in part; not completely: *They are partly to blame.*

part·ner (pärt′nər), *NOUN.*
1 a member of a company who shares the risks and profits of the business.
2 a companion in a dance.
3 a player on the same team or side in a game. —**part′ner·ship,** *NOUN.*

part of speech, any of the groups into which words are divided according to their use in sentences. The parts of speech are the noun, pronoun, adjective, verb, adverb, preposition, conjunction, and interjection.

par·tridge (pär′trij), *NOUN.* a wild bird that is hunted and used for food. Grouse and quail are sometimes called partridges. □ *PLURAL* **par·tridge** or **par·tridg·es.**

part-time (pärt′tīm′), *ADJECTIVE.* for only part of the usual work or study time: *a part-time job.*

par·ty (pär′tē), *NOUN.*
1 a social event where a group of people have a good time: *She invited her friends to a party.*
2 a group of people doing something together: *a dinner party, a search party.*
3 a group of people organized to gain political influence and win elections: *the Democratic Party.* □ *PLURAL* **par·ties.**

pass (pas),
1 *VERB.* to go by; move past: *The parade passed. We passed a truck. They pass our house every day.*
2 *VERB.* to move on: *The days pass quickly. The salesman passed from house to house.*
3 *VERB.* to hand something from one person to another: *Please pass the butter.*
4 in sports: **a** *VERB.* to throw or hit a ball or puck to another player. **b** *NOUN.* the transfer of a ball or puck to another player.
5 *VERB.* to approve or be approved: *Congress passed the new tax bill. The bill passed by only three votes.*

This quarterback has just thrown a **pass.**

a	hat	ė	term	ô	order	ch	child	(a in about
ā	age	i	it	oi	oil	ng	long	e in taken
ä	far	ī	ice	ou	out	sh	she	ə { i in pencil
â	care	o	hot	u	cup	th	thin	o in lemon
e	let	ō	open	u̇	put	ᴛʜ	then	u in circus
ē	equal	ȯ	saw	ü	rule	zh	measure	

6 *VERB.* to succeed in a course: *She passed Spanish.*

7 *NOUN.* written permission: *No one can get in the fort without a pass.*

8 *NOUN.* a free ticket: *She won a pass to the circus.*

9 *NOUN.* a narrow road or path: *A dangerous pass crosses the mountains.*
   ❏ *VERB* **pass·es, passed, pass·ing;** *PLURAL* **pass·es.** —**pass'er,** *NOUN.*

pass away, *IDIOM.* to come to an end; die.

pass on, *IDIOM.* to die.

pass out, *IDIOM.*
1 to hand something out, distribute: *Please pass out this test to the members of the class.*
2 to faint; lose consciousness: *We carried him home after he passed out.*

pas·sage (pas'ij), *NOUN.*
1 a hall or way through a building; passageway.
2 an opening through a body part: *nasal passages.*
3 the act or fact of passing or moving along: *Our tastes can change with the passage of time.*
4 a short part of a piece of writing or music: *The author read a passage from his latest book.*
5 a journey by ship; voyage: *We had a stormy passage across the Atlantic.*
6 the act of making a bill into law by a favoring vote of a legislature: *the passage of a bill.*

pas·sage·way (pas'ij wā'), *NOUN.* a hallway, alley, or tunnel that you can use to get somewhere.

pas·sen·ger (pas'n jər), *NOUN.* someone who rides in an aircraft, bus, ship, train, or car: *The bus carried 30 passengers.*

pass·er·by (pas'ər bi'), *NOUN.* someone who passes by: *A passerby saw the accident.* ❏ *PLURAL* **pass·ers·by.**

pass·ing (pas'ing),
1 *ADJECTIVE.* going by; moving past: *We waved at the people in the passing train.*
2 *ADJECTIVE.* done quickly or carelessly; hurried: *She gave the book only a passing glance.*
3 *ADJECTIVE.* not lasting very long; brief: *He made a passing mention of his last visit to us.*
4 *ADJECTIVE.* enough to be able to pass a course or examination: *A 75 is a passing grade.*

pas·sion (pash'ən), *NOUN.*
1 a very strong feeling: *Hate and anger are passions.*
2 romantic love.
3 something that you like a lot: *Music is her passion.*

pas·sion·ate (pash'ə nit), *ADJECTIVE.* having or showing strong feelings: *She is a passionate believer in equal rights for all.*

pas·sive (pas'iv), *ADJECTIVE.* not active; allowing things to happen to you: *a passive attitude.* —**pas'sive·ly,** *ADVERB.*

passive smoking, the breathing in of tobacco smoke by someone who is not smoking, because someone nearby is smoking.

Pass·o·ver (pas'ō'vər), *NOUN.* a yearly Jewish holiday in memory of the escape of the Hebrews from Egypt. Passover is celebrated during eight days in March or April with special meals and prayers.

pass·port (pas'pôrt), *NOUN.* a small book giving you official permission to travel in a foreign country, under the protection of your own government.

pass·word (pas'wėrd'), *NOUN.* a secret word that allows the person using it to enter an area that is under guard, or to enter a computer system.

past (past),
1 *ADJECTIVE.* gone by; ended: *Summer is past. Our troubles are past.*
2 *ADJECTIVE.* just gone by: *The past year was great.*
3 *NOUN.* all the time that has gone by: *Life began far back in the past. History is a study of the past.*
4 *NOUN.* the past life or history of someone or something: *a nation with a glorious past. I cannot change my past.*
5 *PREPOSITION.* beyond: *It is half past two. The children ran past the house.*
6 *ADJECTIVE.* having formerly served in an office or position: *She is a past president of the club.*
7 *ADVERB.* by; beyond: *The train sped past.*
8 *ADJECTIVE.* expressing something that happened or existed in time gone by: *The past tense of the verb "laugh" is "laughed."*

Usage Note

Past began as another way of spelling **passed.** Then people used the different spellings for different meanings. Now **passed** is used only as a verb: *She passed him. Has the bus passed my stop?* **Past** is used as an adjective, adverb, noun, and preposition — but not as a verb.

pas·ta (pä'stə), *NOUN.* any of several kinds of food, such as macaroni, spaghetti, or noodles. Pasta is made of flour, water, and sometimes milk or eggs. Dry pasta comes in many different shapes.
■ See the Word Story at **paste.**

some different kinds of pasta

paste (pāst),

1 *NOUN.* a mixture you use to stick things together. It is often made of flour and water boiled together.
2 *VERB.* to stick things together with paste.
3 *NOUN.* any food that has been cooked to a soft, thick mass: *tomato paste, anchovy paste.*
❏ *VERB* **pastes, past·ed, past·ing.**

Word Story

Paste comes from a Greek word meaning "porridge." **Pasta** and **pastry** come from the same word. Flour and water make paste, and they also make pasta or pastry. The difference between the words is just a difference in recipe.

pas·tel (pa stel′),

1 *NOUN.* a kind of chalklike crayon used in drawing.
2 *NOUN.* a drawing made with these crayons.
3 *ADJECTIVE.* soft and pale: *pastel blue.*

pas·teur·ize (pas′chə rīz′), *VERB.* to heat milk or other liquids hot enough and long enough to kill certain harmful germs. ❏ *VERB* **pas·teur·iz·es, pas·teur·ized, pas·teur·iz·ing. –pas′teur·i·za′tion,** *NOUN.*

Word Story

Pasteurize was formed from the name of Louis Pasteur (lwē′ pa stėr′), who lived from 1822 to 1895. He was a French scientist who invented this way of keeping milk from spoiling.

pas·time (pas′tīm′), *NOUN.* a pleasant way of spending your time; amusement; recreation. Games and sports are pastimes. ■ See the Synonym Study at **play.**

pas·tor (pas′tər), *NOUN.* a minister or priest who is in charge of a church.

pas·try (pā′strē), *NOUN.*

1 pies, tarts, or other baked food made with dough rich in butter or other shortening.
2 the dough for this kind of food.
3 one piece of such baked food.
■ See the Word Story at **paste.** ❏ *PLURAL* **pas·tries.**

pas·ture (pas′chər),

1 *NOUN.* a grassy field where cattle, sheep, or horses can feed.
2 *NOUN.* grass and other growing plants: *These lands supply good pasture.*
3 *VERB.* to put cattle, sheep, or horses out to pasture: *The farmer pastured his cattle near the stream.*
❏ *VERB* **pas·tures, pas·tured, pas·tur·ing.**

pat (pat),

1 *VERB.* to strike or tap gently with something flat: *He patted the dough into a flat cake.*
2 *VERB.* to tap lightly with your hand as a sign of sympathy, approval, or affection: *She patted the dog.*
3 *NOUN.* a light stroke or tap with the hand or with something flat.

4 *NOUN.* a small lump, especially of butter.
❏ *VERB* **pats, pat·ted, pat·ting.**

have pat or **have down pat,** *IDIOM.* to have perfectly; know thoroughly.

pat on the back, *IDIOM.* a compliment; praise.

stand pat, *IDIOM.* to hold to things as they are and refuse to change.

patch (pach),

1 *NOUN.* a piece put on something to mend a hole or a tear in it, or as a decoration.
2 *NOUN.* a cloth pad put over a hurt eye to protect it.
3 *VERB.* to put a patch or patches on; mend: *I patched the hole in the knee of my jeans.*
4 *NOUN.* a small piece of ground that is different from what surrounds it: *There were several brown patches on the lawn. We have a strawberry patch in our garden.*
❏ *PLURAL* **patch·es;** *VERB* **patch·es, patched, patch·ing. –patch′a·ble,** *ADJECTIVE.*

patch up, *IDIOM.* to put an end to; settle: *We finally patched up our quarrel.*

patch·work (pach′wėrk′), *NOUN.* pieces of cloth of various colors or shapes sewed together.

a **patchwork** quilt

pat·ent (pat′nt),

1 *NOUN.* a government document which says that a person or company can make, use, or sell a new invention for a certain number of years.
2 *VERB.* to get a patent for: *She patented her new invention.*
❏ *VERB* **pat·ents, pat·ent·ed, pat·ent·ing.**

pa·ter·nal (pə tėr′nl), *ADJECTIVE.*

1 of or like a father; fatherly: *Their uncle has taken a paternal interest in their welfare since their father died.*

a	hat	ė	term	ô	order	ch	child	⎧ a in about
ā	age	i	it	oi	oil	ng	long	⎪ e in taken
ä	far	ī	ice	ou	out	sh	she	ə ⎨ i in pencil
â	care	o	hot	u	cup	th	thin	⎪ o in lemon
e	let	ō	open	u̇	put	ŦH	then	⎩ u in circus
ē	equal	ȯ	saw	ü	rule	zh	measure	

2 related on the father's side of the family: *Both of his paternal grandparents are still living.*

path (path), NOUN.
1 a track made when people or animals travel over the same ground a lot. It is usually too narrow for cars or wagons.
2 the line along which someone or something moves; route: *The moon has a regular path through the sky.*
❑ PLURAL **paths** (paᴛʜz or paths).

pa·thet·ic (pə thet′ik), ADJECTIVE. pitiful; causing pity: *The stray dog was a pathetic sight.* —**pa·thet′i·cal·ly**, ADVERB.

pa·tience (pā′shəns), NOUN. the ability to wait quietly for something you want or to put up with something difficult or annoying: *He showed great patience with the quarreling children.* ★ Do not confuse **patience** with **patients.**

pa·tient (pā′shənt),
1 ADJECTIVE. able to wait quietly for something that you want: *We need to be patient while we are standing in line.*
2 NOUN. someone who is being treated by a doctor. —**pa′tient·ly**, ADVERB.

pat·i·o (pat′ē ō), NOUN. a paved part of a yard next to a house, used for outdoor meals, relaxation, and the like. ❑ PLURAL **pat·i·os.**

pa·tri·ot (pā′trē ət), NOUN. someone who loves his or her country and gives it loyal support.

pa·tri·ot·ic (pā′trē ot′ik), ADJECTIVE. having or showing love and loyal support for your country: *It is patriotic to fly the American flag on the Fourth of July.* —**pa′tri·ot′i·cal·ly**, ADVERB.

pa·tri·ot·ism (pā′trē ə tiz′əm), NOUN. love and loyal support for your country.

pa·trol (pə trōl′),
1 VERB. to go around in a building or an area watching out for trouble and criminal acts: *The police patrolled once every hour.*
2 NOUN. people who patrol: *The patrol was changed at midnight.*
3 NOUN. the act of patrolling an area: *They were on patrol all evening.*
❑ VERB **pa·trols, pa·trolled, pa·trol·ling.**

pa·trol·man (pə trōl′mən), NOUN. a policeman who keeps watch over a certain area in a city, a part of a road, and so on.

pa·tron (pā′trən), NOUN.
1 a regular customer; someone who shops at a store or goes to a hotel or restaurant regularly.
2 someone who supports some person, art, cause, or task: *A well-known patron of art, she has helped many young painters.*

pa·tron·ize (pā′trə nīz or pat′rə nīz), VERB.
1 to be a regular customer of: *We patronize our neighborhood stores.*

2 to act as a patron toward; support or protect: *We patronize the ballet.*
3 to treat someone as if you were superior to them: *She felt the older girls were patronizing her.*
❑ VERB **pa·tron·iz·es, pa·tron·ized, pa·tron·iz·ing.**

pat·ter (pat′ər),
1 VERB. to make rapid taps: *The rain pattered on the windowpane.*
2 VERB. to move with a rapid tapping sound: *Bare feet pattered along the hard floor.*
3 NOUN. a series of quick taps or the sound they make: *the patter of raindrops.*
❑ VERB **pat·ters, pat·tered, pat·ter·ing.**

pat·tern (pat′ərn),
1 NOUN. the way the same colors or shapes appear over and over again in order on cloth, printed paper, and so on; design: *The wallpaper had a striped pattern.*
2 NOUN. a guide for something that you are making: *I used a paper pattern in cutting the cloth for my coat.*
3 VERB. to make something according to a model: *They patterned the new contract on last year's contract.*
4 NOUN. the regular way that things are done or that things happen: *The migration patterns of birds are studied by many scientists.*
❑ VERB **pat·terns, pat·terned, pat·tern·ing.**

patriotic Nathan Hale/Patrick Henry

Nathan Hale was an American patriot who was hanged as a spy by the British. Before he was hanged he said, "I only regret that I have but one life to lose for my country."

Patrick Henry was an American patriot and political leader. He is remembered for the saying "Give me liberty or give me death."

pat·ty (pat′ē), NOUN. a small, round, flat piece of cooked meat: *We bought hamburger patties for the barbecue.* ❑ PLURAL **pat·ties.**

pau·per (pȯ′pər), NOUN. a very poor person.

pause (pȯz),
1 _VERB._ to stop somewhere for a short time; wait: _I paused for a moment to look in a store window._
2 _NOUN._ a short stop or rest: _After a pause for lunch we returned to work._
❑ _VERB_ **paus·es, paused, paus·ing.**

pave (pāv), _VERB._ to cover a street, sidewalk, driveway, or parking lot with concrete or asphalt.
❑ _VERB_ **paves, paved, pav·ing.**

pave·ment (pāv′mənt), _NOUN._
1 a covering or surface for streets, sidewalks, driveways, or parking lots, made of concrete or asphalt.
2 a paved road.

pa·vil·ion (pə vil′yən), _NOUN._
1 a light building, usually with open sides, used for shelter or pleasure: _The swimmers took shelter from the storm in the beach pavilion._
2 a large tent with a floor raised on posts.
3 any building that houses an exhibition at a fair.

paw (pȯ),
1 _NOUN._ the foot of a four-footed animal having claws. Cats, dogs, and bears have paws.
2 _VERB._ to strike or scrape with the paws or feet: _The cat pawed the mouse it had caught. The horse pawed the ground, eager to be going again._
❑ _VERB_ **paws, pawed, paw·ing.**

pawn¹ (pȯn), _VERB._ to leave something of value with another person who lends you money. When you pay back the money, you get the object back.
❑ _VERB_ **pawns, pawned, pawn·ing.**

pawn² (pȯn), _NOUN._
1 the least important piece in the game of chess.
2 an unimportant person or thing used by somebody to gain an advantage.

pawn·bro·ker (pȯn′brō′kər), _NOUN._ someone who lends you money in return for something of value. The pawnbroker keeps what you leave until you repay the money.

Paw·nee (pȯ nē′), _NOUN._ a member of a tribe of American Indians that once lived in Nebraska and Kansas, and now lives in Oklahoma. ❑ _PLURAL_ **Paw·nee** or **Paw·nees.**

pay (pā),
1 _VERB._ to give money to someone for things or for work: _Pay the doctor._
2 _NOUN._ the money given to someone for things or work: _He gets his pay every Friday._
3 _VERB._ to give money for something: _Have you paid the phone bill?_
4 _VERB._ to give someone what is owed: _We have to pay our debts._
5 _VERB._ to give or offer: _to pay attention, to pay a compliment._
6 _VERB._ to be worthwhile: _It pays to be polite._
❑ _VERB_ **pays, paid, pay·ing. —pay′a·ble,** _ADJECTIVE._ **—pay′er,** _NOUN._

pay back, _IDIOM._
1 to return borrowed money.
2 to give the same treatment as received: _I hope to be able to pay back her help._

pay off, _IDIOM._
1 to give all the money that is owed; pay in full: _He used the money to pay off his loan._
2 to have a good result: _Years of practice paid off, and she is now a successful violinist._

pay·load (pā′lōd′), _NOUN._ load carried by a vehicle. The payload of a rocket is contained in the nose cone, and may be machines or astronauts.

pay·ment (pā′mənt), _NOUN._
1 the act of paying: _I handle the payment of our bills._
2 the amount of money paid for something: _We have a monthly payment of $250 on our car._
3 something paid; pay: _The pleasure of helping you is payment enough._

pay-per-view (pā′pər vyü′), _NOUN._ a cable TV system that charges you only for those movies, games, and so on, that you have watched.

pay·roll (pā′rōl′), _NOUN._
1 a list of people to be paid and the amount that each one is to receive: _Her store has ten people on the payroll._
2 the total amount of wages to be paid to them: _As the company grew, the payroll got larger._

PC, an abbreviation of **personal computer.**

pea (pē), _NOUN._ one of the round seeds, eaten as a vegetable, that are inside the long, green pod of a garden plant.
❑ _PLURAL_ **peas.**

fresh **peas**

peace (pēs), _NOUN._
1 freedom from war: _He works for world peace._
2 freedom from quarreling or disagreement; condition of quiet, order, and calm: _It was nice to have peace in the house._
■ Another word that sounds like this is **piece.**

peace·a·ble (pē′sə bəl), _ADJECTIVE._ peaceful.
—peace′a·bly, _ADVERB._

peace·ful (pēs′fəl), _ADJECTIVE._
1 quiet; calm; full of peace: _It was peaceful in the mountains._
2 liking peace; keeping peace: _peaceful neighbors._
—peace′ful·ly, _ADVERB._ **—peace′ful·ness,** _NOUN._

a	hat	ė	term	ô	order	ch	child	⎧a in about
ā	age	i	it	oi	oil	ng	long	⎪e in taken
ä	far	ī	ice	ou	out	sh	she	ə⎨i in pencil
â	care	o	hot	u	cup	th	thin	⎪o in lemon
e	let	ō	open	u̇	put	ᴛʜ	then	⎩u in circus
ē	equal	ȯ	saw	ü	rule	zh	measure	

peace pipe, a pipe smoked by North American Indians as a sign or pledge of peace.

peach (pēch),

1 *NOUN.* a juicy, round fruit with fuzzy yellow and red skin and a rough stone called a pit. Peaches grow on trees in warm climates.

2 *ADJECTIVE* or *NOUN.* yellowish pink.

❏ *PLURAL* **peach·es.**

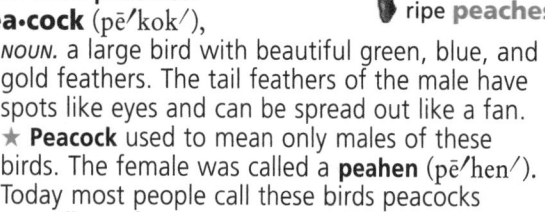

ripe **peaches**

pea·cock (pē′kok′), *NOUN.* a large bird with beautiful green, blue, and gold feathers. The tail feathers of the male have spots like eyes and can be spread out like a fan.

★ **Peacock** used to mean only males of these birds. The female was called a **peahen** (pē′hen′). Today most people call these birds peacocks regardless of sex. ❏ *PLURAL* **pea·cocks** or **pea·cock.**

The **peacock's** body is about 2½ feet long. Its feathers are about 5 feet long.

peak (pēk),

1 *NOUN.* the pointed top of a mountain or hill: *We saw the snowy peaks in the distance.*

2 *NOUN.* any pointed end or top: *the peak of a roof.*

3 *NOUN.* the highest point: *That famous scientist has reached the peak of his profession.*

4 *NOUN.* the front part or the brim of a cap, which stands out.

5 *ADJECTIVE.* in the highest or best state; prime: *peak condition, peak performance.*

■ Another word that sounds like this is **peek.**

peal (pēl),

1 *NOUN.* a loud, long sound: *I heard a peal of thunder and realized the storm was near.*

2 *NOUN.* the loud ringing of bells.

3 *VERB.* to sound out in a long, loud sound or ring: *The bells pealed forth their message of joy.*

❏ *VERB* **peals, pealed, peal·ing.** ■ Another word that sounds like this is **peel.**

pea·nut (pē′nut′), *NOUN.* the nutlike seed of a plant. Peanuts grow in pods that ripen underground. They are roasted and used as food or pressed to get an oil for cooking.

peanut butter, a food made of peanuts that are ground up until soft and smooth. It is spread on bread or crackers.

pear (pâr), *NOUN.* a sweet, juicy, green or yellowish fruit rounded at one end and smaller toward the stem end. Pears grow on trees and are related to apples. ■ Other words that sound like this are **pair** and **pare.**

pearl (pėrl), *NOUN.* a white or nearly white gem that has a soft shine like satin. Pearls are sometimes found inside the shell of a kind of oyster, or in other similar shellfish. **–pearl′like′,** *ADJECTIVE.*

Word Story

Pearl comes from a Latin word meaning "ham." In ancient times pearls were most often found in a kind of shellfish shaped like a ham.

pearl·y (pėr′lē), *ADJECTIVE.* like a pearl in color or luster: *She had pearly white teeth.* ❏ *ADJECTIVE* **pearl·i·er, pearl·i·est.**

peas·ant (pez′nt), *NOUN.* a poor farmer that lives and works on a small farm or portion of land in Europe, Asia, and Latin America.

peat (pēt), *NOUN.* partly rotted moss and plants that is found in marshes and swamps. It is used as garden compost or, when dried, as fuel.

peb·ble (peb′əl), *NOUN.* a small stone, usually worn smooth and round by being rolled about by water.

pe·can (pi kän′ *or* pi kan′), *NOUN.* a nut that has a smooth shell shaped like a large olive. Pecans grow on trees in the southern United States. They are eaten raw or cooked in pies, cookies, and other desserts.

peck[1] (pek),

1 *VERB.* to strike at something and pick it up with the beak: *The hen pecked corn.*

2 *NOUN.* a stroke made with the beak: *The canary gave me a peck.*

3 *VERB.* to make by striking with the beak: *The woodpecker pecked holes in the trees.*

4 *NOUN.* a light, quick kiss.

❏ *VERB* **pecks, pecked, peck·ing.**

peck[2] (pek), *NOUN.* a unit of measure for grain, fruit, vegetables, and other dry things, equal to 8 quarts or one fourth of a bushel: *We bought a peck of potatoes.*

pe·cul·iar (pi kyü′lyər), *ADJECTIVE.* strange; odd; unusual: *He wore a peculiar tie that looked like a fish.* **–pe·cul′iar·ly,** *ADVERB.*

ped·al (ped′l),
1 *NOUN.* a lever moved by the foot; the part on which the foot is placed to move any kind of machinery. The two pedals of a bicycle, pushed down one after the other, make it go.
2 *VERB.* to move something by pushing its pedals: *I pedaled my bicycle slowly up the hill.*
❏ *VERB* **ped·als, ped·aled, ped·al·ing.** ■ Another word that sounds like this is **peddle.**

ped·dle (ped′l), *VERB.* to carry things from place to place and sell them: *The salesman peddled brushes from house to house.* ❏ *VERB* **ped·dles, ped·dled, ped·dling.** ■ Another word that sounds like this is **pedal.**

ped·dler (ped′lər), *NOUN.* someone who travels around selling things carried in a pack or in a truck, wagon, or cart.

ped·es·tal (ped′i stəl), *NOUN.* a base on which a column or a statue stands.
place on a pedestal or **put on a pedestal,** *IDIOM.* to admire greatly: *She put her older brother on a pedestal—everything he did was right.*

pe·des·tri·an (pə des′trē ən), *NOUN.* someone who walks or is walking: *Pedestrians have to watch for cars turning corners.*

pe·di·a·tri·cian (pē′dē ə trish′ən), *NOUN.* a doctor who treats sick infants and children and studies their diseases.

ped·i·gree (ped′ə grē′), *NOUN.* a list of ancestors of a human being or an animal; family tree. ❏ *PLURAL* **ped·i·grees.**

peek (pēk),
1 *VERB.* to look quickly at something or someone: *You must not peek while you are counting in hide-and-seek.*
2 *NOUN.* a quick look: *I took a peek into the oven to see what we were having for dinner.*
❏ *VERB* **peeks, peeked, peek·ing.** ■ Another word that sounds like this is **peak.**

peel (pēl),
1 *NOUN.* the outer covering of fruit or vegetables: *orange peel, potato peels.*
2 *VERB.* to cut the skin, rind, or bark from something: *He peeled the orange.*
3 *VERB.* to pull off something that is stuck on: *I peeled the tape off my hand.*
4 *VERB.* to come off in little pieces: *The paint on the shed is peeling.*
❏ *VERB* **peels, peeled, peel·ing.** ■ Another word that sounds like this is **peal.**

peep¹ (pēp),
1 *VERB.* to look quickly through a hole, crack, and the like: *My kid sister peeped through the curtains at the guests.*
2 *NOUN.* a quick or secret look: *When no one was around, he took a peep at his birthday presents.*

3 *VERB.* to look out, as if peeping; come partly out: *Violets peeped among the leaves.*
❏ *VERB* **peeps, peeped, peep·ing.**

peep² (pēp),
1 *NOUN.* the cry of a young bird or chicken; a chirp.
2 *VERB.* to make such a sound; chirp: *We could hear the birds peeping in their nest.*
❏ *VERB* **peeps, peeped, peep·ing.**

peer¹ (pir), *NOUN.* someone who has the same rank, ability, or qualities as another person; equal: *She is such a fine singer that it is hard to find her peer.*
■ Another word that sounds like this is **pier.**
—**peer′less,** *ADJECTIVE.*

peer² (pir), *VERB.* to look closely at something in order to see it clearly. ❏ *VERB* **peers, peered, peer·ing.**
■ Another word that sounds like this is **pier.**

peg (peg), *NOUN.* a pin or small bolt of wood or metal used to fasten parts together, to hang things on, to plug a hole, to tie a rope or string on to, or to mark the score in a game.

Have You Heard?

You may have heard the phrase **"a square peg in a round hole."** This means that something or someone doesn't fit where they are or in what they are doing.

Pe·king·ese (pē′kə nēz′), *NOUN.* a small dog with long hair and a broad, flat face. ❏ *PLURAL* **Pe·king·ese.**

pel·i·can (pel′ə kən), *NOUN.* a very large sea bird with a pouch under its very large bill. A pelican scoops up fish into its pouch for food.

pel·let (pel′it), *NOUN.* a little ball of mud, paper, hail, snow, food, medicine, and the like.

pelt¹ (pelt), *VERB.*
1 to throw things at someone; attack: *We pelted each other with snowballs.*
2 to beat heavily: *The rain came pelting down.* ❏ *VERB* **pelts, pelted, pelt·ing.**

pelt² (pelt), *NOUN.* the skin of a sheep, goat, or other small animal that has fur, before it is tanned.

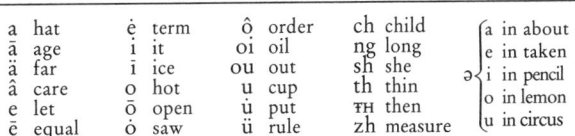

pelican — about 3½ feet long

a	hat	ė	term	ô	order	ch	child	⎧a in about
ā	age	i	it	oi	oil	ng	long	⎪e in taken
ä	far	ī	ice	ou	out	sh	she	ə⎨i in pencil
â	care	o	hot	u	cup	th	thin	⎪o in lemon
e	let	ō	open	ů	put	ŦH	then	⎩u in circus
ē	equal	ȯ	saw	ü	rule	zh	measure	

pen¹ (pen),
1 *NOUN.* a tool you use when you write or draw with ink.
2 *VERB.* to write: *I penned a brief note.*
❑ *VERB* **pens, penned, pen·ning.**

pen² (pen),
1 *NOUN.* a small, fenced yard for cows, sheep, pigs, chickens, or other farm animals.
2 *VERB.* to shut something up in a pen.
❑ *VERB* **pens, penned, pen·ning.**

pe·nal·ize (pē′nl īz), *VERB.*
1 to declare that something is punishable by law or by rule: *Speeding is penalized.*
2 to punish a player or a team with a penalty: *Our team was penalized for interference.*
❑ *VERB* **pe·nal·iz·es, pe·nal·ized, pe·nal·iz·ing.**

pen·al·ty (pen′l tē), *NOUN.*
1 punishment: *The penalty for speeding in our town is a large fine.*
2 (in sports) a disadvantage placed on a team or player for breaking a rule.
❑ *PLURAL* **pen·al·ties.**

penalty box, a seating area to the side of a hockey rink where players are sent after receiving a penalty.

pen·cil (pen′səl),
1 *NOUN.* a pointed tool to write or draw with. It is made of a thin rod of soft carbon, called graphite, inside a wood or metal tube.
2 *VERB.* to mark or write something with a pencil: *I penciled in the appointment on my calendar.*
❑ *VERB* **pen·cils, pen·ciled, pen·cil·ing.**

pend·ant (pen′dənt), *NOUN.* a hanging ornament, such as a locket.

pen·du·lum (pen′jə ləm), *NOUN.* a weight hung from a point in a large clock so that it is free to swing back and forth.

pen·e·trate (pen′ə trāt), *VERB.*
1 to get into or through something: *A falling tree branch penetrated the garage roof.*
2 to see into; understand: *I could not penetrate the mystery.*
❑ *VERB* **pen·e·trates, pen·e·trat·ed, pen·e·trat·ing.**
—**pen′e·tra′tion,** *NOUN.*

pen·guin (pen′gwin), *NOUN.* a sea bird that dives and swims with flippers but does not fly. Penguins live in the Antarctic and other cold areas of the Southern Hemisphere.

penguin — up to 4 feet tall

Did You Know?

When a **penguin** is molting, or changing its feathers, it cannot eat. Because penguins dive underwater to catch fish for their food, they can't eat when they are losing their feathers. Without their waterproof feathers, they would freeze in the icy antarctic water before they caught a single fish. Luckily, penguins only molt for a few weeks every year.

pen·i·cil·lin (pen′ə sil′ ən), *NOUN.* a very powerful drug used to kill the bacteria that cause certain diseases. It is made from a kind of mold.

pe·nin·su·la (pə nin′sə lə), *NOUN.* an area of land with water lying almost all the way around it. Florida is a peninsula. ❑ *PLURAL* **pe·nin·su·las.**

pen·i·ten·tiar·y (pen′ə ten′shər ē), *NOUN.* a prison for criminals. ❑ *PLURAL* **pen·i·ten·tiar·ies.**

pen·knife (pen′nīf′), *NOUN.* a small pocketknife. ❑ *PLURAL* **pen·knives** (pen′nīvz′).

pen·man·ship (pen′mən ship), *NOUN.* the art or skill of writing by hand with pen or pencil.

pen name, a name used by a writer instead of his or her real name.

pen·nant (pen′ənt), *NOUN.*
1 a flag, usually long and narrow, used on ships, in signaling, or as a school banner.
2 a flag that indicates championship, especially of a professional baseball league season.

pen·ni·less (pen′ē lis), *ADJECTIVE.* without a cent of money; very poor: *I've lost all my money and now I'm penniless.* ■ See the Synonym Study at **poor.**

Penn·syl·van·ia (pen′səl vā′nyə), *NOUN.* one of the northeastern states of the United States. *Abbreviation:* PA; *Capital:* Harrisburg.
—**Penn′syl·van′ian,** *NOUN.*

State Story Pennsylvania, meaning "Penn's woods," was formed by combining the name "Penn" with a Latin word meaning "woods." It was named by King Charles II of England in 1681 in honor of the father of the colony's founder, **William Penn.**

pen·ny (pen′ē), *NOUN.*
1 a cent; coin of the United States and Canada. One hundred pennies make one dollar.
2 a British coin. One hundred pennies make one pound.
❑ *PLURAL* **pen·nies.**

Have You Heard?

You may have heard the phrase **"penny-wise and pound-foolish."** The pound in this phrase is the unit of money used in Great Britain and other places. This phrase is used about someone who is very careful about small expenses, but who is wasteful about big ones.

pen pal, someone with whom you exchange letters regularly. Pen pals often live in different countries and have never met.

pen·sion (pen′shən), NOUN. a regular payment by a company or government to someone who is either retired or disabled.

peppers (definition 2)

pen·ta·gon (pen′tə gon), NOUN. a figure having five angles and five sides.

pe·o·ny (pē′ə nē), NOUN. a garden plant with large and fragrant red, pink, or white flowers. ❑ PLURAL **pe·o·nies.**

peo·ple (pē′pəl),
1 NOUN PLURAL. men, women, and children; persons: *There were twelve people present.* ★ The singular for this form is **person.**
2 NOUN. a race; nation: *Asian peoples, the American people.* ★ The plural for this meaning is **peoples.**
3 NOUN PLURAL. persons in general; the public: *A democracy is a government of the people.*
4 NOUN PLURAL. someone's family or relatives: *He spends his holidays with his people.*
5 VERB. to fill a land or an area with people: *Many nations helped people America.* ❑ VERB **peo·ples, peo·pled, peo·pling.**

peonies in bloom

Usage Note

People is a plural noun except when it means "one population group, considered among many groups." This is definition 2, and it is a singular noun. It has a plural form, **peoples,** meaning "several population groups, considered as groups." If the groups have their own names and clear identities, they are peoples. But most of the time, human beings are people.

pep (pep), NOUN. high energy: *She seems full of pep today.*
pep up, IDIOM. to fill or inspire someone with energy; put new life into: *A brisk walk after dinner will pep you up.* ❑ VERB **peps, pepped, pep·ping.**
pep·per (pep′ər),
1 NOUN. a seasoning with a hot, spicy taste, used for soups, meats, or vegetables. Pepper is made by grinding the berries of a vine grown in parts of Asia.
2 NOUN. any of several hollow, crisp, red or green vegetables with many seeds and mild or hot taste. They are eaten raw, cooked, or pickled.
3 VERB. to hit someone with many small objects thrown rapidly: *We peppered them with snowballs.* ❑ VERB **pep·pers, pep·pered, pep·per·ing.**
pep·per·mint (pep′ər mint), NOUN.
1 a kind of mint grown for its oil which is used in medicine and candy.
2 a candy flavored with peppermint oil.
pep·pe·ro·ni (pep′ə rō′nē), NOUN. a very spicy Italian sausage. It is often used as a pizza topping.
per (pər or pėr), PREPOSITION. for each: *Apples cost one dollar per pound.* ■ Another word that can sound like this is **purr.**
per·ceive (pər sēv′), VERB.
1 to be aware of something by means of your senses; see, hear, taste, smell, or feel something: *Many animals do not perceive colors as we do.* ■ See the Synonym Study at **see.**
2 to realize; understand: *I soon perceived that the baby was hungry.* ❑ VERB **per·ceives, per·ceived, per·ceiv·ing.**
per·cent (pər sent′), NOUN. the number of parts in each hundred; hundredths. The symbol for percent is %: *Five percent of 100 is 5.*
per·cent·age (pər sen′tij), NOUN.
1 a rate or proportion of each hundred; part of each hundred: *What percentage of children were absent last Friday?*
2 a part; proportion: *A large percentage of cars now have air bags.*
per·cep·tion (pər sep′shən), NOUN.
1 understanding: *She had a clear perception of the problem, and soon solved it.*
2 the act of being aware of something: *My perception of time became confused when I flew from New York to Hawaii.*
perch[1] (pėrch),
1 NOUN. a bar, branch, rod, and so on, that a bird can land on.

a hat	ė term	ô order	ch child	(a in about
ā age	i it	oi oil	ng long	e in taken
ä far	ī ice	ou out	sh she	ə⟨ i in pencil
â care	o hot	u cup	th thin	o in lemon
e let	ō open	ů put	ŦH then	(u in circus
ē equal	ò saw	ü rule	zh measure	

2 *VERB.* to come to rest on something; settle; sit: *A robin perched on the branch.*

3 *VERB.* to sit up rather high on something: *He perched on a stool in the kitchen.*
❑ *PLURAL* **perch•es;** *VERB* **perch•es, perched, perch•ing.**

perch² (pėrch), *NOUN.*

1 a small freshwater fish, used for food.

2 a similar saltwater fish.
❑ *PLURAL* **perch** or **perch•es.**

per•cus•sion (pər kush′ən), *NOUN.*

1 the action of striking one object against another with force; blow.

2 the sound or shock made by the forceful striking of one object against another.

3 See **percussion instrument.**

percussion instrument, a musical instrument that produces sound when a part of it is struck. The drums and the piano are percussion instruments.

pe•ren•ni•al (pə ren′ē əl),

1 *ADJECTIVE.* living more than two years: *perennial garden plants.*

2 *NOUN.* a perennial plant. Roses are perennials.

per•fect (pėr′fikt *for adjective;* pər fekt′ *for verb*),

1 *ADJECTIVE.* without any faults or mistakes: *a perfect spelling test, a perfect apple.*

2 *VERB.* to remove all faults from something; make complete: *to perfect an invention. The artist was perfecting his picture.*

3 *ADJECTIVE.* having all its parts there; complete: *The set was perfect; nothing was missing or broken.*

4 *ADJECTIVE.* exact: *a perfect copy, a perfect circle.*
❑ *VERB* **per•fects, per•fect•ed, per•fect•ing.**
—**per′fect•ly,** *ADVERB.*

Synonym Study

Perfect means having no faults or being the best: *Today is a perfect day. She turned in a perfect paper.*

Flawless and **faultless** mean not having any faults: *This new computer program is flawless. The gymnast's performance was faultless in every way.*

Foolproof means made so that nothing can go wrong: *She gave me her foolproof recipe for a chocolate cake.*

Ideal means perfect in every way: *This meadow is the ideal spot for our picnic.*

per•fec•tion (pər fek′shən), *NOUN.* the condition of being perfect; highest excellence: *Her goal was to achieve perfection in her work.*

per•fo•rate (pėr′fə rāt′), *VERB.*

1 to make a hole or holes through something: *The target was perforated by bullets.*

2 to make a row or rows of holes through something: *Sheets of postage stamps are perforated.*
❑ *VERB* **per•fo•rates, per•fo•rat•ed, per•fo•rat•ing.**

per•form (pər fôrm′), *VERB.*

1 to do an action or a piece of work: *Perform your duties well. The surgeon performed an operation.*

2 to act, play, sing, or do tricks in public: *We went to the circus to see the animals perform.*
❑ *VERB* **per•forms, per•formed, per•form•ing.**

per•form•ance (pər fôr′məns), *NOUN.*

1 the act of carrying out; doing: *The firefighter was injured in the performance of his duties.*

2 a play, circus, or other show: *The orchestra's performance is at 8 o'clock.*

per•form•er (pər fôr′mər), *NOUN.* someone who performs, especially someone who performs to entertain other people. Singers, dancers, and magicians are performers.

This **performer** is a singer and a dancer.

per•fume (pėr′fyüm *for noun;* pər fyüm′ *for verb*),

1 *NOUN.* a liquid with a pleasant smell that you put on your skin: *She wore a perfume that smelled like apple blossoms.*

2 *NOUN.* a sweet smell: *the perfume of the flowers.*

3 *VERB.* to fill with sweet odor: *Flowers perfume the air.*
❑ *VERB* **per•fumes, per•fumed, per•fum•ing.**

Word Story

Perfume comes from Latin words meaning "through" and "smoke." In old times, people often gave rooms a sweet smell by burning incense. Other kinds of sweet-smelling substances were named for that smoke.

per•haps (pər haps′), *ADVERB.* it may be; possibly: *Perhaps a letter will come to you today.*

per•il (per′əl), *NOUN.* the danger of harm, injury, or death: *This bridge is not safe; cross it at your peril.*

pe•rim•e•ter (pə rim′ə tər), *NOUN.* the distance around an area or around a figure such as a square, triangle, or oval.

per·i·od (pir′ē əd), NOUN.
1 a length of time: *She visited us for a short period.*
2 a certain time: *the period of World War II.*
3 one of the portions that a game is divided into: *Our team led until the third period.*
4 one of the portions of time that a school day is divided into.
5 the dot (.) marking the end of most sentences or showing an abbreviation, as in Mr. or Dec.

per·i·od·ic (pir′ē od′ik), ADJECTIVE. occurring, appearing, or done again and again at regular times: *The coming of the new moon is a periodic event.* —**per′i·od′i·cal·ly**, ADVERB.

per·i·od·i·cal (pir′ē od′ə kəl), NOUN. a magazine that is published at regular times, less often than daily: *This periodical comes out monthly.*

per·i·scope (per′ə skōp), NOUN. a device that allows people in a submarine to see something on the surface. It is a tube with an arrangement of prisms or mirrors that reflect light rays down the tube.

per·ish (per′ish), VERB. to be destroyed; die: *Many people perished in the fire.* ❑ VERB **per·ish·es, per·ished, per·ish·ing.**

per·ish·a·ble (per′i shə bəl), ADJECTIVE. likely to spoil or decay: *Bananas are perishable.*

per·jur·y (per′jər ē), NOUN. the act of swearing in a law court that something is true when you know that it is false.

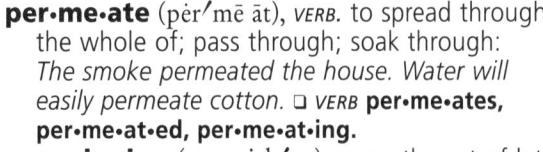

The **periscope** can be pulled back inside the submarine.

perk (perk), VERB. to raise quickly: *The dog perked up its ears when it heard its owner.* ❑ VERB **perks, perked, perk·ing.**

perk up, IDIOM. to brighten up; become more cheerful and lively: *Perk up; things will get better.*

perk·y (per′kē), ADJECTIVE. lively and alert: *a perky squirrel.* ❑ ADJECTIVE **perk·i·er, perk·i·est.** —**perk′i·ness,** NOUN.

per·ma·nent (per′mə nənt), ADJECTIVE. meant to last; not for a short time only: *I have only two permanent fillings in my teeth. After doing odd jobs for a month, I got a permanent position as a clerk in a store.* —**per′ma·nent·ly,** ADVERB.

permanent teeth, the new teeth that grow when your first teeth fall out during your childhood. Permanent teeth can last the rest of your life.

per·me·ate (per′mē āt), VERB. to spread through the whole of; pass through; soak through: *The smoke permeated the house. Water will easily permeate cotton.* ❑ VERB **per·me·ates, per·me·at·ed, per·me·at·ing.**

per·mis·sion (pər mish′ən), NOUN. the act of letting someone do something; consent: *She asked the teacher's permission to leave early.*

per·mit (pər mit′ *for verb;* per′mit *for noun*),
1 VERB. to let someone do something; allow: *My parents will not permit me to stay up late.*
2 NOUN. a license or written order giving someone permission to do something: *Do you have a permit to fish in this lake?*
❑ VERB **per·mits, per·mit·ted, per·mit·ting.**

per·pen·dic·u·lar (per′pən dik′yə lər), ADJECTIVE.
1 straight up and down; vertical: *We turned back when we came to a perpendicular cliff.*
2 at right angles. One line is perpendicular to another when it makes a square corner with another. The floor of a room is perpendicular to the side walls and parallel to the ceiling.

per·pe·trate (per′pə trāt), VERB. to do or commit a crime, fraud, trick, or anything bad or foolish: *They were arrested for perpetrating a robbery.*
❑ VERB **per·pe·trates, per·pe·trat·ed, per·pe·trat·ing.** —**per′pe·tra′tor,** NOUN.

per·pet·u·al (pər pech′ü əl), ADJECTIVE.
1 continuous; never stopping: *The waters of the river go over the falls with a perpetual roar.*
2 eternal; lasting forever: *the perpetual hills.* —**per·pet′u·al·ly,** ADVERB.

per·pet·u·ate (pər pech′ü āt), VERB. to cause to continue; keep from being forgotten: *The statue perpetuates the memory of those who died in the war.* ❑ VERB **per·pet·u·ates, per·pet·u·at·ed, per·pet·u·at·ing.**

per·plex (pər pleks′), VERB. to trouble someone with doubt; puzzle; confuse: *He was perplexed by the complex problem.* ❑ VERB **per·plex·es, per·plexed, per·plex·ing.**

per·se·cute (per′sə kyüt), VERB. to treat someone badly, especially because of his or her beliefs: *The ancient Romans persecuted Christians.* ❑ VERB **per·se·cutes, per·se·cut·ed, per·se·cut·ing.** —**per′se·cu′tor,** NOUN. —**per′se·cu′tion,** NOUN.

per·se·vere (per′sə vir′), VERB. to keep on doing something that is hard to do; persist. ❑ VERB **per·se·veres, per·se·vered, per·se·ver·ing.**

Per·sia (per′zhə), NOUN. an ancient empire in southwestern Asia.

a	hat	ė	term	ô	order	ch	child		a in about
ā	age	i	it	oi	oil	ng	long		e in taken
ä	far	ī	ice	ou	out	sh	she	ə	i in pencil
â	care	o	hot	u	cup	th	thin		o in lemon
e	let	ō	open	ù	put	ŦH	then		u in circus
ē	equal	ò	saw	ü	rule	zh	measure		

P

Per·sian (pėr′zhən), NOUN. the language spoken in Iran.

Word Source

Persian is the official language of Iran, and one of the official languages of Afghanistan. Some words that have come into English from Persian are:

bazaar	khaki	mummy	shawl
candy	lemon	orange	tulip
caravan	lilac	pajamas	turban
jackal	magic	pistachio	

per·sim·mon (pər sim′ən), NOUN. a round, yellowish orange fruit about the size of a plum. Persimmons are very bitter when green, but sweet and good to eat when very ripe.

per·sist (pər sist′), VERB.
1 to keep on doing something; refuse to stop: *In spite of our warnings, she persisted in teasing the dog.*
2 to last a long time: *On some very high mountains snow persists throughout the year.*
❑ VERB **per·sists, per·sist·ed, per·sist·ing.**

per·sist·ence (pər sis′təns), NOUN. the act or quality of refusing to give up: *Her persistence was rewarded by a part in the school play.*

per·sist·ent (pər sis′tənt), ADJECTIVE.
1 refusing to stop or give up: *The child was persistent in her demands for cookies and candy.*
2 lasting; continuing: *I had a persistent headache that lasted for three days.*
—**per·sist′ent·ly,** ADVERB.

per·son (pėr′sən), NOUN.
1 a man, woman, or child; human being: *Any person who wishes may come to the fair.*
2 the human body: *The person of the king was well guarded.*
3 (in grammar) a form of pronouns or verbs used to show the person speaking, the person spoken to, or the person or thing spoken of. *I* and *we* are used for the first person; *you,* for the second person; *he, she, it,* and *they,* for the third person.
in person, IDIOM. personally: *The author will appear in person.*

per·son·al (pėr′sə nəl), ADJECTIVE.
1 belonging to someone; private: *a personal letter.*
2 directly by yourself, not through others or by letter or telephone: *The author made personal appearances at several bookstores to autograph her books.*
3 of or about the body: *personal cleanliness.*

personal computer, a computer designed to fit on a desk top, used in offices, schools, and homes; microcomputer.

per·son·al·i·ty (pėr′sə nal′ə tē), NOUN.
1 the personal or individual quality that makes someone different from another person: *Her warm, friendly personality makes her popular.*

2 a well-known person: *I collect autographs of famous personalities in the entertainment world.*
❑ PLURAL **per·son·al·i·ties.**

per·son·al·ly (pėr′sə nə lē), ADVERB.
1 as far as you are concerned: *Personally, I like apples better than oranges.*
2 by yourself; not by the aid of others: *The owner of this store deals personally with customers.*
3 as a person: *I don't know her personally, but I've been told she is a talented writer.*
4 as being meant for yourself: *Don't take what I said personally; I didn't mean to insult you.*

per·son·nel (pėr′sə nel′), NOUN. the people employed in any work, business, or service: *The factory did not have enough personnel to complete the large order on time.*

per·spec·tive (pər spek′tiv), NOUN.
1 the art of picturing objects on a flat surface in order to give the appearance of distance.
2 a particular way of understanding things; mental point of view: *Many problems seem less important when viewed in their proper perspective.*

per·spi·ra·tion (pėr′spə rā′shən), NOUN.
1 sweat: *Her neck is damp with perspiration.*
2 the process of sweating: *Perspiration helps the body to cool itself.*

per·spire (pər spīr′), VERB. to sweat: *The room was so hot I began to perspire.* ❑ VERB **per·spires, per·spired, per·spir·ing.**

per·suade (pər swād′), VERB. to get someone to do something or to believe something: *I knew I should study, but he persuaded me to go to the movies.* ❑ VERB **per·suades, per·suad·ed, per·suad·ing.**

per·sua·sion (pər swā′zhən), NOUN. the act or process of persuading: *All our attempts at persuasion were useless; she would not come with us.*

per·sua·sive (pər swā′siv), ADJECTIVE. able or likely to persuade: *Your persuasive argument convinced me.*
—**per·sua′sive·ly,** ADVERB. —**per·sua′sive·ness,** NOUN.

per·tain (pər tān′), VERB. to be about something; refer; be related: *My question pertains to yesterday's homework.* ❑ VERB **per·tains, per·tained, per·tain·ing.**

Pe·ru (pə rü′), NOUN. a country in western South America. —**Pe·ru·vi·an** (pə rü′vē ən), ADJECTIVE or NOUN.

pes·ky (pes′kē), ADJECTIVE. annoying; troublesome: *A pesky mosquito kept buzzing around my head.*
❑ ADJECTIVE **pes·ki·er, pes·ki·est.**

pe·so (pā′sō), NOUN. the basic unit of money in various countries of Latin America and in the Philippines. ❑ PLURAL **pe·sos.**

pes·si·mis·tic (pes′ə mis′tik), ADJECTIVE. expecting the worst thing or things to happen: *I was pessimistic about passing the test because I hadn't studied.* —**pes′si·mis′ti·cal·ly,** ADVERB.

pest (pest), NOUN.
1 an insect or animal that is harmful or destructive: *garden pests.*
2 someone or something that is annoying; nuisance: *Don't be such a pest!*

pes·ter (pes′tər), VERB. to annoy someone: *Flies pester us. Don't pester me with foolish questions.*
❑ VERB **pes·ters, pes·tered, pes·ter·ing.**

pes·ti·cide (pes′tə sīd), NOUN. something used to kill pests. Farmers often use pesticides to kill insects that damage their crops.

pet (pet),
1 NOUN. an animal that you take care of and treat with love.
2 ADJECTIVE. treated as a pet: *a pet rabbit.*
3 VERB. to stroke or pat lovingly and gently: *The kitten purred softly while she petted it.*
4 NOUN. a darling or favorite: *He is the teacher's pet.*
❑ VERB **pets, pet·ted, pet·ting.**

pet·al (pet′l), NOUN. one of the soft, thin parts of a flower that are usually colored. **–pet′al·like′,** ADJECTIVE.

pe·ti·tion (pə tish′ən),
1 NOUN. a letter that many people sign to ask for something to be added or changed: *The residents on our street signed a petition asking the city council for a new sidewalk.*
2 VERB. to make a request to someone: *We petitioned the principal to improve school lunches and lengthen recess.*
❑ VERB **pe·ti·tions, pe·ti·tioned, pe·ti·tion·ing.**

a chunk of **petrified** wood

pet·ri·fy (pet′rə fī), VERB.
1 to turn into stone or a substance like stone: *Ancient tree trunks that have petrified can be seen in Arizona.*
2 to paralyze someone with fear, horror, or surprise: *I was petrified when lightning struck our house.*
■ See the Synonym Study at **afraid.**
❑ VERB **pet·ri·fies, pet·ri·fied, pet·ri·fy·ing.**

pe·tro·le·um (pə trō′lē əm), NOUN. a dark, thick, oily liquid that is found in the earth; oil. Gasoline, kerosene, and many other products are made from petroleum.

pet·ti·coat (pet′ē kōt), NOUN. a skirt worn beneath a dress or outer skirt by women and girls.

pet·ty (pet′ē), ADJECTIVE. having very little importance or value: *Don't let petty quarrels upset you.*
❑ ADJECTIVE **pet·ti·er, pet·ti·est. –pet′ti·ness,** NOUN.

pet·ty of·fi·cer (pet′ē ò′fə sər), a military rank. See the chart on page 550.

pe·tun·ia (pə tü′nyə), NOUN. a common garden plant that has white, pink, and purple flowers shaped like funnels. ❑ PLURAL **pe·tun·ias.**

petunias

pew (pyü), NOUN. a bench with a high back for people to sit on in church. Pews are fastened to the floor.

pew·ter (pyü′tər), NOUN. a metal made by combining tin with lead. Pewter is used to make dishes and other utensils.

Spelling Note **ph**

Words that use **ph** for the sound of *f* come from Greek. The ancient Greeks spelled this sound with a letter in their alphabet that is not in the Roman alphabet. The Romans decided to use *ph* to represent this sound. Since we borrowed so many Greek words from the Romans, we used the Roman spelling.

phan·tom (fan′təm),
1 NOUN. a vague or dim appearance of something or someone; ghost.
2 ADJECTIVE. like a ghost; unreal: *She thought she saw a phantom ship gliding through the fog.*

phar·aoh (fâr′ō), NOUN. the title given to the kings of ancient Egypt.

phar·ma·cist (fär′mə sist), NOUN. someone who is trained and licensed to fill doctors' prescriptions.

the golden mask of a **pharaoh**

a	hat	ė	term	ô	order	ch	child		a in about
ā	age	i	it	oi	oil	ng	long		e in taken
ä	far	ī	ice	ou	out	sh	she	ə	i in pencil
â	care	o	hot	u	cup	th	thin		o in lemon
e	let	ō	open	ů	put	ŦH	then		u in circus
ē	equal	ò	saw	ü	rule	zh	measure		

P

phar·ma·cy (fär′mə sē), NOUN. See **drugstore**.
❏ PLURAL **phar·ma·cies**.

phase (fāz), NOUN.
1 one of the changing stages of development of someone or something: *At present his voice is changing; that is a phase all boys go through.*
2 one side, part, or view of something: *What phase of arithmetic are you studying now?*
3 the shape of the lighted part of the moon or a planet at a certain time.
phase in, IDIOM. to start something new one step at a time: *The school phased in a new dress code.*
phase out, IDIOM. to stop something one step at a time: *We phased out the old requirements.*
❏ VERB **phas·es, phased, phas·ing**.

pheas·ant (fez′nt), NOUN. a kind of bird with a long tail and brightly colored feathers that is hunted and used for food. Wild pheasants live in many parts of Europe and America. ❏ PLURAL **pheas·ants** or **pheas·ant**.

The male **pheasant** is about 3 feet long, including the tail.

phe·nom·e·na (fə nom′ə nə), NOUN. a plural of **phenomenon**.

phe·nom·e·nal (fə nom′ə nəl), ADJECTIVE. extraordinary: *She has a phenomenal memory.*

phe·nom·e·non (fə nom′ə non), NOUN.
1 a fact or event that can be observed: *Lightning is an electrical phenomenon.*
2 someone or something that is extraordinary or remarkable: *The fond parents think their child is a phenomenon.* ★ The correct plural form for this meaning is **phenomena**.
❏ PLURAL **phe·nom·e·na** or **phe·nom·e·nons**.

Phil·a·del·phi·a (fil′ə del′fē ə), NOUN. a city in Pennsylvania. —**Phil′a·del′phi·an**, ADJECTIVE or NOUN.

Phil·ip·pines (fil′ə pēnz′), NOUN PLURAL. a country made up of over 7000 islands in the Pacific Ocean southeast of Asia. —**Phil′ip·pine**, ADJECTIVE or NOUN.

phil·o·den·dron (fil′ə den′drən), NOUN. a climbing plant with green and yellow leaves, often grown as a houseplant. There are many different kinds of philodendron.

phi·los·o·pher (fə los′ə fər), NOUN. someone who studies philosophy a great deal.

phil·o·soph·i·cal (fil′ə sof′ə kəl), ADJECTIVE.
1 of or about philosophy or philosophers.
2 wise, calm, and reasonable: *I try to be philosophical about my troubles.*
—**phil′o·soph′i·cal·ly**, ADVERB.

phi·los·o·phy (fə los′ə fē), NOUN.
1 the study that attempts to understand the basic nature of knowledge and reality.
2 a system of beliefs for guiding your own life: *the philosophy of a Puritan.*
❏ PLURAL **phi·los·o·phies**.

phlegm (flem), NOUN. the thick mucus that forms in the lungs, nose, and throat during a cold.

Phoe·nix (fē′niks), NOUN. the capital of Arizona.

Word Story

Phoenix was named for a mythical bird, the phoenix. The phoenix was said to live for 500 or 600 years. Then it burnt itself and rose from the ashes for another long life. Traces of an ancient American Indian settlement were found at the site, and the new inhabitants hoped that it would rise again like the phoenix and become a great city.

phone (fōn), NOUN or VERB. a short form of **telephone**. ❏ VERB **phones, phoned, phon·ing**.

Word Power   -phone

The combining form **-phone** means "sound" or "device for sound." A homo**phone** is a word with the same **sound** as another word. A tele**phone** is a **device** for sending and receiving **sound**.

pho·net·ic (fə net′ik), ADJECTIVE. representing sounds made with the voice. Phonetic symbols are marks used to show pronunciation. We use ō as the phonetic symbol for the sound of *o* in *photo*.

phon·ics (fon′iks), NOUN. a system of teaching the sounds of letters and groups of letters in words. Phonics is used to teach reading.

pho·no·graph (fō′nə graf), NOUN. See **record player**.

pho·ny (fō′nē),
1 ADJECTIVE. not genuine; fake: *The jeweler told her that the diamond was phony.*
2 NOUN. a fake; pretender: *The doctor turned out to be a phony who had no medical training.*
❏ ADJECTIVE **pho·ni·er, pho·ni·est**; PLURAL **pho·nies**.
—**pho′ni·ness**, NOUN.

Word Story

Phony may come from an Irish word meaning "a ring." Criminals used to cheat people with rings that looked like gold, but were actually phony.

phos·phor·us (fos′fər əs), NOUN. a chemical element present in all plant and animal tissue. It combines with other chemicals to form a great variety of substances essential to life.

pho·to (fō′tō), NOUN. a short form of **photograph**. ❑ PLURAL **pho·tos**.

Word Power   photo-

The combining form **photo-** means "light" or "photography." **Photo**synthesis makes **light** into food. A **photo**copy is a copy made by **photo**graphy.

pho·to·cop·i·er (fō′tō kop′ē ər), NOUN. a machine that makes copies of documents using a special kind of photography; copier.

pho·to·cop·y (fō′tō kop′ē),
1 NOUN. a special kind of photographic copy.
2 VERB. to produce a photocopy of something.
❑ PLURAL **pho·to·cop·ies**; VERB **pho·to·cop·ies, pho·to·cop·ied, pho·to·cop·y·ing**.

photo finish,
1 a finish in a race so close that a photograph is necessary to decide the winner.
2 any contest decided by a close difference.

pho·to·gen·ic (fō′tə jen′ik), ADJECTIVE. having features that photograph very well: *He has a photogenic face.*

pho·to·graph (fō′tə graf),
1 NOUN. a picture you make with a camera.
2 VERB. to take a photograph of.
❑ VERB **pho·to·graphs, pho·to·graphed, pho·to·graph·ing**.

pho·tog·ra·pher (fə tog′rə fər), NOUN.
1 someone who takes photographs.
2 someone whose business is taking photographs.

a **photographer** working outdoors

pho·to·graph·ic (fō′tə graf′ik), ADJECTIVE. used in or produced by photography: *He bought some photographic supplies. I made a photographic record of our trip.* —**pho′to·graph′i·cal·ly**, ADVERB.

pho·tog·ra·phy (fə tog′rə fē), NOUN. the art or process of taking photographs: *My photography is improving.*

pho·to·syn·the·sis (fō′tō sin′thə sis), NOUN. the process by which green plants use the energy of light to make their own food from carbon dioxide and water.

phrase (frāz),
1 NOUN. two or more words that have a meaning but do not contain a subject and verb, and do not form a complete sentence. *"At school," "in the house,"* and *"hoping to see you soon"* are phrases.
2 NOUN. a short group of words that expresses a familiar or popular idea. *"All for one and one for all"* is a phrase.
3 VERB. to express something in a particular way: *I tried to phrase my excuse politely.*
❑ VERB **phras·es, phrased, phras·ing**.

phys·i·cal (fiz′ə kəl),
1 ADJECTIVE. of or for the body: *I enjoy physical exercise. She has great physical strength.*
2 NOUN. a medical examination by a doctor: *I had to have a physical before I could go to summer sports camp.*
3 ADJECTIVE. of or about the world that you can touch and see and measure, not the world of thought or ideas: *The ocean tide is a physical force.* —**phys′i·cal·ly**, ADVERB.

physical education, instruction in how to exercise and take care of your body, especially as a course at a school or college.

physical therapy, treatment of diseases and injuries by remedies such as exercise and massage, rather than by drugs.

phy·si·cian (fə zish′ən), NOUN. a doctor of medicine.

phys·i·cist (fiz′ə sist), NOUN. someone who is an expert in physics.

phys·ics (fiz′iks), NOUN. the science that studies matter and energy and their relationships to each other. Physics includes the study of motion, heat, light, sound, electricity, magnetism, and atomic energy.

phys·i·ol·o·gy (fiz′ē ol′ə jē), NOUN. the science that studies the normal working of living things or their parts: *animal physiology, human physiology.*

phy·sique (fə zēk′), NOUN. body; bodily structure: *The swimmer had a beautiful physique.* ❑ PLURAL **phy·siques**.

pi (pī), NOUN. the Greek letter π, used as the symbol for the ratio of the circumference of any circle to its diameter: π is equal to about 3.1416.
∎ Another word that sounds like this is **pie**.

pi·an·ist (pē an′ist or pē′ə nist), NOUN. someone who plays the piano.

a hat	ė term	ô order	ch child	⎰a in about
ā age	i it	oi oil	ng long	e in taken
ä far	ī ice	ou out	sh she	ə⎨i in pencil
â care	o hot	u cup	th thin	o in lemon
e let	ō open	ù put	₮H then	⎱u in circus
ē equal	ò saw	ü rule	zh measure	

pi·an·o (pē an′ō), NOUN. a large musical instrument that you play with your fingers. Its tones come from steel wires called strings. When you strike the keys, small hammers hit the strings and produce sounds. ❑ PLURAL **pi·an·os.**

Word Story

Piano was shortened from *pianoforte*, which comes from two Italian words meaning "soft" and "loud." The piano was called this because of the many different tones that can be played on it.

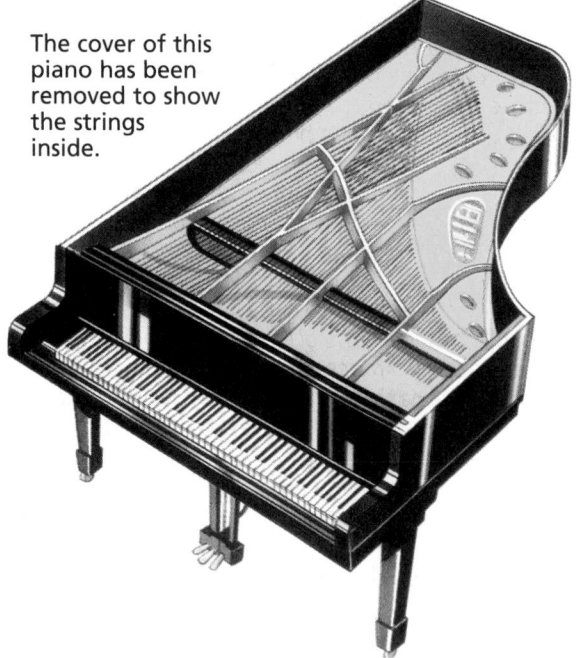

The cover of this piano has been removed to show the strings inside.

This **piano** is used for concerts. It can be up to 9 feet long.

pic·co·lo (pik′ə lō), NOUN. a musical instrument that looks like a small flute but produces sounds an octave higher. ❑ PLURAL **pic·co·los.**

pick¹ (pik),
1 VERB. to take the one you want from a group; choose; select: *I picked a blue shirt to go with my jeans.* ∎ See the Synonym Study at **choose.**
2 NOUN. a choice or selection: *This red rose is my pick.*
3 VERB. to pull or take something off with the fingers; gather: *We pick fruit.*
4 VERB. to use something pointed to remove things: *It's not polite to pick your teeth in public.*
5 VERB. to open something with a pointed device or wire: *The burglar picked the lock on the garage.*
6 VERB. to pluck the strings of a musical instrument.
7 NOUN. a thin, flat piece of plastic or metal used to pluck the strings of a musical instrument.
8 VERB. to try to start a fight or quarrel with someone: *Don't pick a quarrel with them.*
❑ VERB **picks, picked, pick·ing.**

pick on, IDIOM. to annoy; tease: *My older brother and sister are always picking on me.*
pick up, IDIOM.
1 to take up; lift: *She picked up a hammer.*
2 to take into a vehicle or ship; give a ride to: *The bus stopped at the corner to pick up passengers.*
3 to get and take along with you: *I picked up a pizza on my way home.*
4 to make greater; increase: *The bus picked up speed on its way down the hill.*
5 to succeed in seeing or hearing: *She picked up a radio broadcast from Paris.*
6 to tidy up; put in order: *I picked up my room.*

pick² (pik), NOUN.
1 a tool with a heavy metal bar pointed at one or both ends, having a long wooden handle; pickax. It is used for breaking up hard soil or rocks.
2 a tool with a sharp point. Ice is broken into pieces with a pick.

pick·ax (pik′aks′), NOUN. See **pick²** (definition 1). ❑ PLURAL **pick·ax·es.**

pick·er·el (pik′ər əl), NOUN. a freshwater fish that is smaller than the pike and has a long, pointed head. It is used for food. ❑ PLURAL **pick·er·el** or **pick·er·els.**

pick·et (pik′it),
1 NOUN. a pointed stake or peg placed upright to make a fence or driven into the ground to tie a horse to.
2 NOUN. someone stationed by a labor union near a factory or store where there is a strike. Pickets try to prevent employees from working or customers from buying.
3 NOUN. someone who demonstrates to support a cause or to protest something.
4 VERB. to walk about or stand near as a picket: *to picket a factory during a strike.*
❑ VERB **pick·ets, pick·et·ed, pick·et·ing.**

pick·le (pik′əl),
1 NOUN. a cucumber or other vegetable preserved in a spicy liquid containing salt water, vinegar, and so on.
2 NOUN. salt water, vinegar, or other liquid in which meat and vegetables can be preserved.
3 VERB. to preserve something in pickle: *We pickled several quarts of beets yesterday.*
❑ VERB **pick·les, pick·led, pick·ling.**

pick·pock·et (pik′pok′it), NOUN. someone who steals from other people's pockets or purses.

pick·up (pik′up′), NOUN.
1 the act of picking something up: *the daily pickup of mail.*
2 the ability to go faster quickly: *Although our car is ten years old, it still has good pickup.*
3 See **pickup truck.**

pickup truck, a small, light truck with an open back, used for light hauling; pickup.

pick·y (pik/ē), *ADJECTIVE.* hard to please; particular: *Some customers are very picky about their shoes.*
❏ *ADJECTIVE* **pick·i·er, pick·i·est. –pick/i·ness,** *NOUN.*

pic·nic (pik/nik),
1 *NOUN.* a party with a meal outdoors: *We had a picnic at the beach.*
2 *VERB.* to have a picnic or go on a picnic: *Our family often picnics at the beach.*
❏ *VERB* **pic·nics, pic·nicked, pic·nick·ing.
–pic/nick·er,** *NOUN.*

pic·to·graph (pik/tə graf), *NOUN.* a chart or diagram showing facts or information by using pictures of different colors, sizes, and so on.
–pic/to·graph/ic, *ADJECTIVE.*

Eggs Laid by Animals	
Python	◐◐◐◖
Turtle	◐◐◐◐◐◐◐◐◐
Frog	◐◐◐◐◐◐
Salamander	◐◖
Each symbol stands for 10 eggs. So, a frog lays 60 eggs.	Key ◐ = 10 eggs

pictograph

pic·ture (pik/chər),
1 *NOUN.* a drawing, painting, portrait, or photograph of someone or something; printed copy of any of these: *The book contains a good picture of a tiger.*
2 *VERB.* to draw or paint someone or something; make into a picture: *The artist pictured life in the old West.*
3 *NOUN.* a close likeness; image: *He is the picture of his father.*
4 *VERB.* to form a picture of something in your mind; imagine: *It is hard to picture life 200 years ago.*
5 *NOUN.* a vivid description: *The speaker gave us a good picture of life in the old West.*
6 *NOUN.* a movie.
7 *NOUN.* the image on a television set.
❏ *VERB* **pic·tures, pic·tured, pic·tur·ing.**

Have You Heard?

You may have heard someone say **"A picture is worth a thousand words."** This means that one picture can easily show something that would be difficult to describe in words. Try to describe in detail the expression on someone's face and you'll know why sometimes a picture is worth a thousand words!

pic·tur·esque (pik/chə resk/), *ADJECTIVE.*
1 interesting or pretty enough to be used as the subject of a picture: *I saw a picturesque old mill.*
2 making a picture for the mind; vivid: *This author uses very picturesque language.*

pie (pī), *NOUN.* a kind of food made of fruit, meat, and so on, baked in a crust: *We had apple pie for dessert.* ■ Another word that sounds like this is **pi.**

Have You Heard?

You may have heard it said that someone had to **"eat humble pie."** This means that the person was wrong and had to apologize, even though he or she really didn't want to. Another phrase that means the same thing is **"eat crow."**

piece (pēs),
1 *NOUN.* one of the parts into which something is divided or broken; bit: *The cup broke in pieces.*
2 *NOUN.* a small quantity of something: *a piece of land containing two acres, a piece of bread.*
3 *NOUN.* a single thing of a set or class: *This set of china has 144 pieces.*
4 *NOUN.* an individual work of art: *Have you heard his latest piece?*
5 *NOUN.* a coin: *A nickel is a five-cent piece.*
6 *VERB.* to make or repair something by adding or joining pieces: *to piece a quilt.*
❏ *VERB* **piec·es, pieced, piec·ing.** ■ Another word that sounds like this is **peace.**

Synonym Study

Piece means a small part of something larger, or one thing among others like it: *I picked up the pieces of the jigsaw puzzle. A chess game begins with 32 pieces on the board.*

Fragment means a part that has been broken off: *Our dog dug up a fragment of a bowl.*

Bit[1] means a small piece of something larger: *He found two whole crackers and another one broken into bits.*

Crumb means a tiny piece of bread or cake, broken from a larger piece: *After dinner there were some crumbs on the table.*

Scrap[1] means a little bit, especially of something that is left over: *The quilt was made from scraps of cloth that Grandma had saved.*

Lump means a small, solid piece of material: *Our snowman's eyes are lumps of coal.*

Chunk means a thick lump: *I threw a chunk of wood into the campfire.*

Chip means a thin small piece: *A chip of paint fell off the wall in your room.*

See also the Synonym Study at **part.**

a hat	ė term	ô order	ch child
ā age	i it	oi oil	ng long
ä far	ī ice	ou out	sh she
â care	o hot	u cup	th thin
e let	ō open	u̇ put	ᴛʜ then
ē equal	ȯ saw	ü rule	zh measure

ə { a in about / e in taken / i in pencil / o in lemon / u in circus }

pie chart, a circular chart divided into sections like slices of a pie; circle graph. The size of a section shows the amount it stands for.

pier (pir), NOUN. a structure built out over the water, used as a walk or a dock.
   ▪ Another word that sounds like this is **peer.**

Children's Hair Color in My Class

30% black
20% blond
5% red
45% brown

pie chart

pierce (pirs), VERB.
1 to go into or go through something: *A tunnel pierces the mountain.*
2 to make a hole in something; bore into or through: *A nail pierced the tire of our car.*
   ❑ VERB **pierc·es, pierced, pierc·ing.**

Pierre (pir), NOUN. the capital of South Dakota.

pig (pig), NOUN. an animal with a fat body, short legs, hoofs, and a broad snout. It is raised for its meat. **—pig′like′,** ADJECTIVE.

pig out, IDIOM. (informal) to stuff yourself with food; eat too much: *Mom doesn't let us pig out on junk food.* ❑ VERB **pigs, pigged, pig·ging.**

pig — up to 4 feet high at the shoulder

pig·eon (pij′ən), NOUN. a kind of bird with a plump body and short tail and legs; dove.

pig·gy·back (pig′ē bak′), ADJECTIVE or ADVERB. on the back: *Father gave me a piggyback ride.*

pig·gy bank (pig′ē bangk′), a small container in the shape of a pig, with a slot in the top for coins.

pig·let (pig′lit), NOUN. a little pig.

pig·ment (pig′mənt), NOUN.
1 a coloring material, especially a powdered dry substance. Paint and dyes are made by mixing pigments with liquid.
2 the substance that occurs in and colors the tissues of a living thing. The color of a person's hair, skin, and eyes is produced by pigments.

pig·pen (pig′pen′), NOUN. a pen where pigs are kept; pigsty; sty.

pig·skin (pig′skin′), NOUN.
1 the skin of a pig.
2 leather made from it.
3 (informal) a football.

pig·sty (pig′stī), NOUN. See **pigpen.** ❑ PLURAL **pig·sties.**

pig·tail (pig′tāl′), NOUN. a braid of hair that hangs down from the back of the head.

pike (pīk), NOUN. a large freshwater fish with a long pointed head. ❑ PLURAL **pike** or **pikes.**

pile¹ (pīl),
1 NOUN. a stack of things: *I gathered a pile of wood.*
2 NOUN. a mound or hill of something: *We need to move that pile of dirt.*
3 VERB. to make into a pile or stack: *The campers piled the extra wood in a corner.*
4 NOUN. a large amount: *I have a pile of work to do.*
5 VERB. to cover with large amounts of something: *to pile a plate with food.*
   ❑ VERB **piles, piled, pil·ing.**

pile² (pīl), NOUN. a heavy beam driven upright into the ground or the bed of a river. Piles can help support a bridge, wharf, or building.

pil·grim (pil′grəm), NOUN.
1 someone who goes on a journey to a sacred or holy place as an act of religious devotion.
2 a traveler; wanderer.
3 Pilgrim, one of the English settlers who founded Plymouth, Massachusetts, in 1620.

pill (pil), NOUN. medicine that is made into a tiny ball that you can swallow easily.

pil·lar (pil′ər), NOUN. a slender upright support; column. Pillars are usually made of stone, wood, or metal and used as supports or ornaments for a building.

pil·low (pil′ō), NOUN. a soft bag that you put your head on when you rest or sleep. Pillows are filled with feathers or other soft material.

pi·lot (pī′lət),
1 NOUN. someone trained to operate the controls of an aircraft or spacecraft in flight.
2 NOUN. someone whose business is to steer ships in or out of a harbor or through dangerous waters. A ship takes on a pilot before coming into a harbor.
3 NOUN. someone who steers a ship or boat.
4 VERB. to act as a pilot of an aircraft, ship, or spacecraft; steer: *to pilot an airplane.*
   ❑ VERB **pi·lots, pi·lot·ed, pi·lot·ing.**

pim·ple (pim′pəl), NOUN. a small, sore, red swelling under the skin.

pin (pin),
1 NOUN. a short thin piece of wire with a point at one end and a head at the other, used to fasten things together.
2 NOUN. a badge or an ornament with a pin or clasp to fasten it to clothing: *She wore her class pin.*

3 *NOUN.* a peg made of wood, metal, or plastic, used to fasten things together, hold something, or hang things on.

4 *VERB.* to fasten something with a pin or pins; put a pin through: *I pinned a notice on the bulletin board.*

5 *VERB.* to hold something fast in one position: *When the tree fell, it pinned the lumberjack's leg to the ground.*

6 *NOUN.* a bottle-shaped piece of wood used in the game of bowling.
❑ *VERB* **pins, pinned, pin•ning.**

Have You Heard?

You may have heard someone say that they are **"on pins and needles."** This means that they are very nervous or excited. People often say this when they are waiting to see if something will happen the way they want it to.

pi•ña•ta (pē nyä′tə), *NOUN.* a pot filled with candy, fruit, and small toys, hung at Christmas time in Mexico and other Latin American countries. Blindfolded children swing sticks in order to break the pot to get what is inside.
❑ *PLURAL* **pi•ña•tas.**

pin•cers (pin′sərz), *NOUN PLURAL* or *SINGULAR.*

1 a tool for gripping things tightly, made like scissors but with jaws instead of blades.

2 the large claw with which crabs, lobsters, and crayfish pinch or nip; pair of claws.

piñata

pinch (pinch),

1 *VERB.* to squeeze something between your thumb and forefinger or between two hard things: *I pinched my hand when the door closed too quickly.*

2 *NOUN.* a squeeze between your thumb and forefinger or between two hard things: *He gave me a pinch on the arm to keep me awake.*

3 *VERB.* to press on something so that it hurts; squeeze: *These new shoes pinch my feet.*

4 *NOUN.* a sharp pressure that hurts; a squeeze: *the pinch of tight shoes.*

5 *VERB.* to cause to shrink or become thin: *a face pinched by hunger.*

6 *NOUN.* a time of special need; emergency: *I will help you in a pinch.*

7 *NOUN.* as much as can be taken up with the tips of finger and thumb; very small amount: *a pinch of salt.*
❑ *VERB* **pinch•es, pinched, pinch•ing;** *PLURAL* **pinch•es.**

pinch-hit (pinch′hit′), *VERB.* (in baseball) to bat for another player, especially when a hit is badly needed. ❑ *VERB* **pinch-hits, pinch-hit, pinch-hit•ting. –pinch hitter.**

pine¹ (pīn), *NOUN.* a tree that bears cones and has evergreen leaves shaped like needles. Pines are of value for lumber, tar, and turpentine. There are about 100 kinds of pine trees.

pine² (pīn), *VERB.* **pine for,** to miss someone or something very badly: *The homesick children were pining for their parents.* ❑ *VERB* **pines, pined, pin•ing.**

pine•ap•ple (pī′nap′əl), *NOUN.* the large, juicy fruit of a tropical plant with slender, stiff leaves.

pineapple

ping (ping),

1 *NOUN.* a sound like that of something hard whistling through the air or striking something metal.

2 *VERB.* to make this sound.
❑ *VERB* **pings, pinged, ping•ing.**

Ping-Pong (ping′pong′), *NOUN.* (trademark) a game played on a large table marked something like a tennis court, using small wooden paddles and a light, hollow, plastic ball; table tennis.

pink (pingk),

1 *NOUN.* a color that is made by mixing red and white; very light or pale red.

2 *ADJECTIVE.* very pale red.

3 *NOUN.* a garden plant with fragrant flowers of various colors, mostly white, pink, and red. A carnation is one kind of pink.
–pink′ness, *NOUN.*

pink•eye (pingk′ī′), *NOUN.* a contagious disease that causes redness and soreness of the inner eyelids and the front of the eyeball.

pink•ish (ping′kish), *ADJECTIVE.* somewhat pink.

pin•point (pin′point′),

1 *VERB.* to aim at something accurately; locate it exactly: *The pilot was trying to pinpoint a place for landing.*

2 *NOUN.* something very small or sharp: *A pinpoint of light sparkled against the deep blue sky.*

3 *NOUN.* the point of a pin.
❑ *VERB* **pin•points, pin•point•ed, pin•point•ing.**

pint (pīnt), *NOUN.* a unit of volume for measuring liquids, equal to ½ a quart; 16 fluid ounces.

a	hat	ė	term	ô	order	ch	child		a in about
ā	age	i	it	oi	oil	ng	long		e in taken
ä	far	ī	ice	ou	out	sh	she	ə	i in pencil
â	care	o	hot	u	cup	th	thin		o in lemon
e	let	ō	open	ů	put	ŦH	then		u in circus
ē	equal	ò	saw	ü	rule	zh	measure		

P

pin·to (pin′tō), NOUN. a spotted, white and black or white and brown horse. ❑ PLURAL **pin·tos.**

pin·wheel (pin′wēl′), NOUN.
1 a toy made of a wheel fastened to a stick by a pin so that it revolves in the wind.
2 a kind of firework that revolves when lighted.

pioneer
Elizabeth Blackwell

Elizabeth Blackwell was the first American woman to become a doctor. She was rejected from 29 medical schools because she was a woman. She and her sister later started their own medical school.

pi·o·neer (pī′ə nir′),
1 NOUN. someone who settles in a part of a country preparing it for other settlers to come later.
2 NOUN. someone who goes first, or does something first, and so prepares a way for other people: *Elizabeth Blackwell was a pioneer in medicine.*
3 VERB. to prepare something or open it up for other people: *Astronauts are pioneering space exploration.*
❑ VERB **pi·o·neers, pi·o·neered, pi·o·neer·ing.**

Word Story

Pioneer comes from a Latin word meaning "foot." Groups of foot soldiers used to go ahead of an army to make roads and build bridges, preparing the way for others, as later pioneers prepared for settlements.

pi·ous (pī′əs), ADJECTIVE. religious; having or showing deep respect for God: *She is a pious woman who goes to church every morning.* —**pi′ous·ly,** ADVERB.

pipe (pīp),
1 NOUN. a tube through which a liquid or gas flows.
2 VERB. to carry or move a liquid or gas by means of a pipe or pipes: *Water is piped from the reservoir.*
3 NOUN. a tube of clay, wood, or other material, with a bowl at one end, that you smoke tobacco in.

4 NOUN. a musical instrument with a single tube into which the player blows.
5 VERB. to play music on a pipe: *The shepherd piped a strange melody.*
6 NOUN. any one of the tubes in an organ.
7 VERB. to make a shrill noise; speak or sing in a shrill voice: *The child piped, "I'm hungry!"*
❑ VERB **pipes, piped, pip·ing.**

pipe·line (pīp′līn′), NOUN. a series of pipes that moves or carries oil or gas, usually over a great distance.

pip·er (pī′pər), NOUN. someone who plays on a pipe or bagpipe.

pip·ing (pī′ping), ADJECTIVE. **piping hot,** very hot; boiling.

pi·ra·cy (pī′rə sē), NOUN. robbery on the sea.

pi·ra·nha (pi rä′nyə or pə rä′nə), NOUN. a small South American freshwater fish with very sharp teeth. Piranhas in groups will attack even large animals. ❑ PLURAL **pi·ra·nha** or **pi·ra·nhas.**

pi·rate (pī′rit), NOUN. someone who attacks and robs ships at sea.

pis·ta·chi·o (pi stash′ē ō or pi stä′shē ō), NOUN. a small, greenish nut that tastes something like an almond. ❑ PLURAL **pis·ta·chi·os.**

pis·til (pis′tl), NOUN. the part of a flower that produces seeds.

pis·tol (pis′tl), NOUN. a small, short gun held and fired with one hand.

pis·ton (pis′tən), NOUN. a short, solid cylinder, or a flat, round piece of metal, fitting closely inside a larger cylinder. It moves rapidly back and forth, powered by the force of exploding gasoline vapor, steam, or liquid. Pistons are used in pumps and engines.

pit¹ (pit),
1 NOUN. a hole in the ground. A mine or the shaft of a mine is a pit.
2 NOUN. a little hollow place or scar. Acne sometimes leaves pits in the skin.
3 VERB. to mark something with small pits or scars: *The old car's fenders and doors were pitted with rust spots.*
4 VERB. to put someone into a contest with someone else: *She was pitted against her best friend in the last round of the tennis match.*
❑ VERB **pits, pit·ted, pit·ting.**

pit² (pit),
1 NOUN. the hard seed of a cherry, peach, olive, date, or similar fruit; stone.
2 VERB. to remove the pits from fruit: *I pitted cherries to make a cherry pie.*
❑ VERB **pits, pit·ted, pit·ting.**

pi·ta (pē′tə), NOUN. a flat, round bread commonly eaten in the Middle East. It is now very popular in this country. ❑ PLURAL **pi·tas.**

pit bull, a dog known for its strength and willingness to fight.

pitch¹ (pich),
1 *VERB.* to throw; toss: *They pitched pebbles into the lake.* ▪ See the Synonym Study at **throw.**
2 in baseball: **a** *VERB.* to throw a ball to the batter. **b** *NOUN.* the act of pitching: *The first pitch was a strike.*
3 *VERB.* to set firmly in the ground: *to pitch a tent.*
4 *VERB.* to fall or plunge forward: *I lost my balance and pitched down the stairs.*
5 *VERB.* to plunge with the bow rising and then falling: *The ship pitched about in the storm.*
6 *NOUN.* degree of highness or lowness of a sound.
7 *NOUN.* a talk, argument, plan, or offer used to persuade, as in selling: *The clerk had developed a strong sales pitch.*
   ❑ *VERB* **pitch·es, pitched, pitch·ing;** *PLURAL* **pitch·es.**

pitch² (pich), *NOUN.* a black, sticky substance made from tar or turpentine, used to cover the seams of wooden ships, to cover roofs, or to make pavements. ❑ *PLURAL* **pitch·es.**

pitch·er¹ (pich′ər), *NOUN.*
1 a container made of china, glass, or silver, with a lip at one side and a handle at the other. Pitchers are used for holding and pouring out liquids.
2 the amount that a pitcher holds: *He drank a pitcher of milk.*

pitch·er² (pich′ər), *NOUN.* a player on a baseball team who pitches to the catcher. The batter tries to hit the ball before it gets to the catcher.

pitch·fork (pich′fôrk′), *NOUN.* a large fork with a long handle for lifting and throwing hay.

pit·i·ful (pit′i fəl), *ADJECTIVE.*
1 to be pitied; deserving pity: *The fox caught in the trap was a pitiful sight.*
2 deserving contempt: *She gave us a pitiful excuse.*
   —**pit′i·ful·ly,** *ADVERB.*

a **pitcher** getting ready to pitch

pit·y (pit′ē),
1 *NOUN.* sympathy for someone else's suffering or distress: *We felt pity for the lost, hungry puppy.*
2 *VERB.* to feel pity for someone or something: *I pitied the homeless puppy.*
3 *NOUN.* something to be sorry for: *It is a pity to be kept in the house in fine weather.*
   ❑ *VERB* **pit·ies, pit·ied, pit·y·ing.**

piv·ot (piv′ət),
1 *NOUN.* a shaft, pin, or point on which something turns. The pin of a hinge is a pivot.

2 *VERB.* to turn on a pivot or as if on a pivot: *The basketball player pivoted on one foot.*
   ❑ *VERB* **piv·ots, piv·ot·ed, piv·ot·ing.**

pix·el (pik′səl), *NOUN.* any one of the many tiny points, each of varying color and brightness, that make up an electronic image.

pix·ie (pik′sē), *NOUN.* (in stories) a fairy or an elf.
   ❑ *PLURAL* **pix·ies.**

piz·za (pē′tsə), *NOUN.* a kind of food made by baking a large flat layer of bread dough covered with cheese, tomato sauce, mushrooms, and so on.
   ❑ *PLURAL* **piz·zas.**

pj's or **p.j.'s** (pē′jāz′), *NOUN PLURAL.* an abbreviation of **pajamas.**

pl., an abbreviation of **plural.**

plac·ard (plak′ärd *or* plak′ərd), *NOUN.* a notice that is posted in a public place; poster.

place (plās),
1 *NOUN.* the space where someone or something is: *This should be a nice, quiet place to rest.*
2 *NOUN.* a city, town, village, district, island, and so on: *This town seems like a very busy place.*
3 *NOUN.* a building or spot used for some particular purpose: *A store or office is a place of business.*
4 *NOUN.* a house; dwelling: *They have a beautiful place in the country.*
5 *NOUN.* a point that you have reached in reading: *Don't lose your place.*
6 *NOUN.* the right or usual position for something: *There is a time and place for everything. Each book is in its place on the shelf.*
7 *NOUN.* a rank; position: *She won first place in the contest. She has a high place in government.*
8 *NOUN.* the position of a digit in a number: *In the number 365, the figure 3 is in the hundreds place.*
9 *NOUN.* a space or seat for someone: *We took our places at the table.*
10 *VERB.* to put something in a particular position or condition: *Place the books on the table.* ▪ See the Synonym Study at **put.**
11 *VERB.* to identify by remembering the place, time, or situation in which someone or something was known before: *I know that person's face, but I can't place her.*
12 *VERB.* to finish in a certain position in a race or competition: *I placed third in the swimming meet.*
   ❑ *VERB* **plac·es, placed, plac·ing.**
in place of, *IDIOM.* instead of: *Use water in place of milk in that recipe.*
take place, *IDIOM.* to happen; occur: *Where did the accident take place?*

a	hat	ė	term	ô	order	ch	child	(a	in about
ā	age	i	it	oi	oil	ng	long	e	in taken
ä	far	ī	ice	ou	out	sh	she	ə ⟨ i	in pencil
â	care	o	hot	u	cup	th	thin	o	in lemon
e	let	ō	open	ù	put	ᴛʜ	then	(u	in circus
ē	equal	ò	saw	ü	rule	zh	measure		

place kick, the act of kicking a ball placed or held on the ground in football, soccer, and some other sports.

place value, the value given to the place each digit has in a number. In 438, the place value of 4 is hundreds; the place value of 3 is tens; the place value of 8 is ones.

plac·id (plas′id), ADJECTIVE. pleasantly calm or peaceful; quiet: *We fished in the placid stream.*

plague (plāg),
1 NOUN. a very dangerous disease that spreads rapidly from one person to another and often causes death.
2 NOUN. someone or something that annoys or is disagreeable: *Weeds are a plague to a gardener.*
3 VERB. to bother or annoy someone: *Mosquitoes plague us in the summer.*
   ❑ PLURAL **plagues;** VERB **plagues, plagued, pla·guing.**

plaid (plad),
1 NOUN. any cloth with a pattern of crossed stripes of different widths and colors.
2 ADJECTIVE. having a pattern of checks or stripes: *She wore a plaid dress.*

plain (plān),
1 ADJECTIVE. easy to hear, see, or understand; clear: *The meaning is plain.*
2 ADJECTIVE. without ornament or decoration: *All the girls wore plain white dresses to graduation.*
3 ADJECTIVE. not rich or highly seasoned: *plain food.*
4 ADJECTIVE. common; ordinary; simple in manner: *They were plain, hard-working people.*
5 ADJECTIVE. not pretty or handsome: *a plain face.*
6 NOUN. a flat area of land: *Cattle wandered over the western plains.*
   ∎ Another word that sounds like this is **plane.**
   −plain′ly, ADVERB. **−plain′ness,** NOUN.

Plains Indian, a member of any of the American Indian tribes that lived on the Great Plains.

plain·spo·ken (plān′spō′kən), ADJECTIVE. plain or frank in speech: *a plain-spoken man, a plain-spoken criticism.*

plain·tive (plān′tiv), ADJECTIVE. sad; gloomy: *He wrote a plaintive song about lost love. The dog gave a plaintive howl.*

plan (plan),
1 NOUN. something you have thought about and expect to do: *Our summer plans were upset by mother's illness.*
2 VERB. to think out in advance how something is to be made or done: *Have you planned your trip?*
3 VERB. to have in your mind as a purpose; intend: *I plan to go to New York next week.*
4 NOUN. a drawing or diagram that shows how the parts of something fit together: *floor plans, building plans.*
   ❑ VERB **plans, planned, plan·ning. −plan′ner,** NOUN.

Synonym Study

Plan means a carefully thought-out way of doing or making something: *I like his plan for surprising our teacher on her birthday.*

Program can mean a plan going from one step or event to the next: *Our city's program for cleaning up dump sites went smoothly.*

Undertaking means a plan of great imagination, danger, or difficulty: *Feeding our neighbor's six dogs was quite an undertaking for us.*

Enterprise means a bold undertaking: *This business enterprise will cost me lots of money if it fails.*

Scheme means a plan of carefully chosen details: *He has a scheme to save on groceries by growing his own vegetables.*

Plot means a secret plan, especially to do something evil: *Police uncovered a plot to rob the bank.*

See also the Synonym Studies at **idea** and **think.**

plane¹ (plān),
1 NOUN. any flat or level surface: *the plane of a table.*
2 ADJECTIVE. flat; level: *a plane surface.*
3 NOUN. a short form of **airplane.**
   ∎ Another word that sounds like this is **plain.**

plane² (plān),
1 NOUN. a tool with a blade for smoothing wood.
2 VERB. to smooth wood with a plane: *The carpenter planed the boards.*
   ❑ VERB **planes, planed, plan·ing.** ∎ Another word that sounds like this is **plain.**

plan·et (plan′it), NOUN. one of the nine large astronomical objects that move around the sun. Mercury, Venus, Earth, Mars, Jupiter, Saturn, Uranus, Neptune, and Pluto are planets.

using a **plane**

Did You Know?

People have come up with lots of phrases that help you remember the order of the **planets.** (The first letter of each word in the phrase is the first letter of the name of the planet.) Here are two: *My Very Easy Method—Just Set Up Nine Planets. My Very Esteemed Mother Just Served Us Nine Pizzas.*

plan·e·tar·i·um (plan′ə ter′ē əm), NOUN. a building with special equipment for showing the

movements of the sun, moon, planets, stars, and comets. These movements are shown by projecting lights on the inside of a dome.
❑ PLURAL **plan·e·tar·i·ums.**

plan·e·tar·y (plan′ə ter′ē), ADJECTIVE. of a planet; having something to do with planets.

plank (plangk), NOUN. a long, flat piece of sawed wood that is thicker than a board.
 walk the plank, IDIOM. to be put to death by being forced to walk off a plank extending from a ship's side over the water. Pirates used to make their prisoners do this.

plant·er (plan′tər), NOUN.
 1 someone who owns or runs a plantation.
 2 a box or other container for plants to grow in.

plaque (plak), NOUN.
 1 a thin film containing germs, which forms on the teeth. Plaque can cause tooth decay.
 2 an ornamental tablet of metal, porcelain, or the like, often with writing carved on it.
 ❑ PLURAL **plaques.**

plas·ma (plaz′mə), NOUN. the clear, almost colorless, liquid part of blood, in which the corpuscles or blood cells float.

There are two types of **plankton.** One type is simple algae. The other type is microscopic protozoans and sea animals, such as jellyfish.

Some plankton spend their whole lives as plankton, but other plankton are the eggs and immature forms of animals that live on the bottom of the ocean. These eggs and immature forms drift along with the other plankton near the surface of the ocean until they mature and sink to the bottom.

Plankton are carried around by currents in the water. Some plankton can swim but they cannot swim fast or hard enough to avoid the currents.

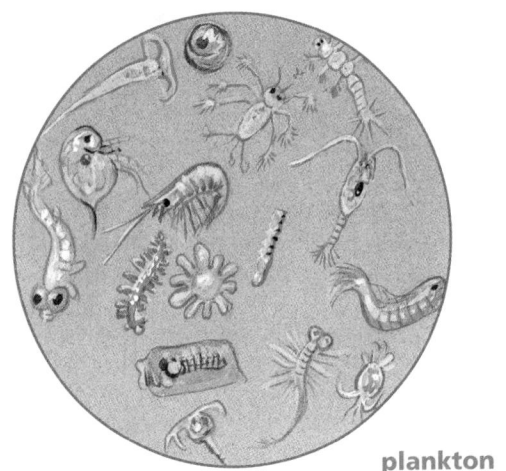
plankton

plank·ton (plangk′tən), NOUN. the very small living things that float or drift in water, especially at or near the surface. Plankton provides food for many fish in oceans and lakes.

plant (plant),
 1 NOUN. any living thing that can make its own food from sunlight, air, and water. Plants cannot move about by themselves. Trees, bushes, vines, grass, vegetables, and seaweed are all plants.
 2 VERB. to put something in the ground to grow: *She planted sunflower seeds in the backyard.*
 3 VERB. to set something firmly in or on: *The climbers planted a flag on the top of the mountain. She planted her feet on the rock.*
 4 NOUN. a building, machinery, and tools used in manufacturing some article or in producing something.
 ❑ VERB **plants, plant·ed, plant·ing. –plant′like′,** ADJECTIVE.

plan·tain (plan′tən), NOUN. a kind of long, very starchy banana. It is eaten cooked.

plan·ta·tion (plan tā′shən), NOUN. a large farm or estate on which cotton, tobacco, sugarcane, or rubber trees are grown. The work on a plantation is done by workers who live there.

plas·ter (plas′tər),
 1 NOUN. a soft mixture of lime, sand, and water that hardens as it dries. Plaster is used for covering some walls or ceilings.
 2 VERB. to cover a wall or ceiling with plaster.
 3 VERB. to spread with anything thickly: *His shoes were plastered with mud.*
 ❑ VERB **plas·ters, plas·tered, plas·ter·ing.**
 –plas′ter·er, NOUN.

plas·tic (plas′tik),
 1 NOUN. a kind of material that can be shaped or molded when hot and become hard when cooled. Some plastics are very tough. Many dishes, toys, combs, and so on, are made of plastic.
 2 ADJECTIVE. made of plastic: *a plastic bottle.*

plate (plāt),
 1 NOUN. a dish that is almost flat and usually round. Our food is served on plates.
 2 NOUN. the portion of food served on a dish at a meal: *The waitress served me a plate of stew.*

a	hat	ė	term	ô	order	ch	child		a in about
ā	age	i	it	oi	oil	ng	long		e in taken
ä	far	ī	ice	ou	out	sh	she	ə	i in pencil
â	care	o	hot	u	cup	th	thin		o in lemon
e	let	ō	open	u̇	put	ŦH	then		u in circus
ē	equal	ȯ	saw	ü	rule	zh	measure		

P

3 *VERB.* to cover something with a thin layer of silver, gold, or some other metal: *The spoon was plated with silver.*

4 *NOUN.* a thin, flat sheet or piece of metal: *The warship was covered with steel plates.*

5 *NOUN.* a thin, flat piece of metal on which something is stamped or engraved: *a license plate.*

6 *NOUN.* the plate. See **home plate**.
■ See the Word Story below. ❑ *VERB* **plates, plat·ed, plat·ing.**

pla·teau (pla tō′), *NOUN.* a large, flat area in the mountains or high above sea level. ❑ *PLURAL* **pla·teaus** or **pla·teaux** (pla tōz′).

Word Story

A **plateau** is a flat area of land. Its name comes from an older French word meaning "flat." Another English word from the same source is **plate**.

plat·form (plat′fôrm), *NOUN.*
1 a raised level surface for people to stand or sit on: *There is a platform beside the track at the railroad station. The hall has a platform for speakers.*
2 a plan of action or statement of beliefs of a group: *The platform of the new political party demands lower taxes.*

plat·i·num (plat′n əm), *NOUN.* a precious metal that looks like silver. Platinum does not tarnish or melt easily. It is used for making chemical and industrial equipment and in jewelry. It is a chemical element.

pla·toon (plə tün′), *NOUN.* the part of an army commanded by a lieutenant. Two or more squads make a platoon.

plat·ter (plat′ər), *NOUN.* a large, shallow dish longer than it is wide. Platters are used for holding or serving food, especially meat and fish.

plat·y·pus (plat′ə pəs), *NOUN.* a small mammal of Australia that lays eggs; duckbilled platypus. It lives in the water and has webbed feet and a bill something like a duck's. Platypuses have a coat of thick, brown fur. ❑ *PLURAL* **plat·y·pus·es.**

The platypus uses its broad, flat bill to scoop up worms, shellfish, and other small, freshwater animals.

platypus — about 2 feet long, including the tail

play (plā),
1 *NOUN.* fun; sport; something done to amuse yourself: *We have time for play after school.*
2 *VERB.* to have fun; take part in jokes or tricks: *The kitten plays with its tail. He played a joke on his sister.*
3 *VERB.* to take part in a game: *Children play tag and ball.*
4 *VERB.* to take part in a game against another team: *Our team played the sixth-grade team.*
5 *NOUN.* a turn, move, or action in a game: *It's your play next.*
6 *VERB.* to put into action in a game: *Play your card.*
7 *NOUN.* a story acted out on the stage: *"Romeo and Juliet" is a famous play.*
8 *NOUN.* the performance of such a story on television, radio, or the stage: *The play lasted two hours.*
9 *VERB.* to act a part on stage: *The famous actress played Juliet.*
10 *VERB.* to act in a certain way: *to play sick, to play the fool, to play fair.*
11 *VERB.* to perform on a musical instrument: *He plays the piano very well.*
12 *VERB.* to cause to produce recorded or broadcast sound or pictures: *to play a CD, to play the radio.*
13 *VERB.* to act carelessly; do foolish things: *Don't play with matches.*
❑ *VERB* **plays, played, play·ing.**

Synonym Study

Play means anything you do for enjoyment with your body or your mind: *Recess is time for play between classes.*

Fun means a good time or amusement: *We all had fun at the county fair.*

Game means anything played for fun: *I prefer a game of tag to hide-and-seek.*

Sport means any game or contest that requires skill and practice. A sport usually has set rules: *Her favorite sport is hockey.*

Pastime means anything you do to enjoy yourself by passing time pleasantly: *My mother's favorite pastime is knitting.*

Hobby means something that interests you a lot and that you do because you enjoy it: *His hobby is collecting baseball cards.*

play·er (plā′ər), *NOUN.*
1 someone who plays an instrument, game, and so on: *a flute player, a baseball player.*
2 a device that plays something: *A phonograph is a record player.*

play·ful (plā′fəl), *ADJECTIVE.*
1 full of fun; fond of playing: *a playful puppy.*
2 joking; not serious: *a playful remark.*
–play′ful·ly, *ADVERB.* **–play′ful·ness,** *NOUN.*

play·ground (plā′ground′), NOUN. a place to play outdoors.

play·house (plā′hous′), NOUN. a small house for a child to play in. ❏ PLURAL **play·hous·es** (plā′hou′ziz).

playing card, one of a set of cards to play games with.

play·mate (plā′māt′), NOUN. someone that you play with.

play·off or **play-off** (plā′ȯf′), NOUN. a game or a series of games played after the regular season to decide a championship.

play·pen (plā′pen′), NOUN. a small folding enclosure for a baby or young child to play in.

play·room (plā′rüm′), NOUN. a room for children to play in.

play·thing (plā′thing′), NOUN. something to play with; toy.

play·wright (plā′rit′), NOUN. someone who writes plays.

plaz·a (plaz′ə or plä′zə), NOUN.
1 a public square in a city or town.
2 a shopping center.
❏ PLURAL **plaz·as.**

plea (plē), NOUN.
1 the act of asking for something in a very serious way: *The homeless people made a plea for help.*
2 an answer made by a defendant to a charge in a court of law: *a plea of innocent.*

plead (plēd), VERB.
1 to ask for something in a genuine, serious way: *When the rent was due, the poor family pleaded for more time.*
2 to reply to a charge in a court of law: *An accused person has the choice of pleading guilty or not guilty.*
❏ VERB **pleads, plead·ed** or **pled, plead·ing.**

pleas·ant (plez′nt), ADJECTIVE.
1 pleasing; enjoyable: *We took a pleasant walk through the park this afternoon.* ■ See the Synonym Study at **nice.**
2 friendly; easy to get along with: *She is a pleasant person.*
3 fair; not stormy: *Today is a pleasant day.*
—**pleas′ant·ly,** ADVERB.

please (plēz),
1 ADVERB. a polite word you use when you ask someone for something: *Would you please answer the phone. Please come here.*
2 VERB. to give pleasure to: *Toys please children.*
3 VERB. to be satisfactory: *Such a fine meal cannot fail to please.*
4 VERB. to wish; think fit: *Do what you please.*
❏ VERB **pleas·es, pleased, pleas·ing.**

pleas·ing (plē′zing), ADJECTIVE. giving pleasure; pleasant: *a very pleasing young man, a pleasing smile.* —**pleas′ing·ly,** ADVERB.

pleas·ure (plezh′ər), NOUN.
1 a feeling of being happy: *His pleasure in the gift was obvious.*
2 something that pleases; cause of joy or delight: *It is a great pleasure to see you again.*

pleat (plēt),
1 NOUN. a flat, usually narrow, double fold made in cloth: *My new skirt has many pleats.*
2 VERB. to fold or arrange in pleats: *a pleated skirt, a pleated fan.*
❏ VERB **pleats, pleat·ed, pleat·ing.**

The **pleats** in this fan let you fold it up.

pled (pled), VERB.
1 a past tense of **plead:** *The lawyer pled her case.*
2 a past participle of **plead:** *The accused burglar has pled innocent to the charges.*

pledge (plej),
1 NOUN. an serious promise: *They signed a pledge to give money to charity.*
2 VERB. to promise something seriously: *We pledge allegiance to the flag.* ■ See the Synonym Study at **promise.**
3 NOUN. something given to another person as a guarantee of good faith or of a future action; security: *She left jewelry as a pledge for the loan.*
❏ VERB **pledg·es, pledged, pledg·ing.**

plen·ti·ful (plen′ti fəl), ADJECTIVE. more than enough: *We had a plentiful supply of food.*
—**plen′ti·ful·ly,** ADVERB.

plen·ty (plen′tē), NOUN. all that you need: *You have plenty of time to catch the train.*

pli·ers (plī′ərz), NOUN PLURAL. a tool with pincers for holding small objects firmly, or for bending or cutting wire.

plod (plod), VERB.
1 to walk slowly and heavily: *The old man plodded wearily along the road.*
2 to proceed in a slow, patient way: *He plods away at his lessons until he learns them.*
❏ VERB **plods, plod·ded, plod·ding.** —**plod′der,** NOUN.

plop (plop),
1 NOUN. a sound like that of a flat object striking water without a splash.
2 VERB. to make this sound.
3 VERB. to fall or drop: *She plopped her books down on the table.*
❏ VERB **plops, plopped, plop·ping.**

a	hat	ė	term	ô	order	ch	child		a in about
ā	age	i	it	oi	oil	ng	long		e in taken
ä	far	ī	ice	ou	out	sh	she	ə	i in pencil
â	care	o	hot	u	cup	th	thin		o in lemon
e	let	ō	open	ù	put	ᴛʜ	then		u in circus
ē	equal	ȯ	saw	ü	rule	zh	measure		

plot (plot),
1 *NOUN.* a secret plan, especially to do something wrong: *They hatched a plot to rob the bank.*
▪ See the Synonym Study at **plan.**
2 *VERB.* to plan secretly with other people to do something wrong: *The rebels plotted against the government.*
3 *NOUN.* the main story of a play, novel, or poem: *I like plots filled with action and adventure, with a little romance.*
4 *NOUN.* a small piece of ground: *a garden plot.*
5 *VERB.* to make a map or diagram of something: *The pilot plotted the plane's course.*
❏ *VERB* **plots, plot·ted, plot·ting.**

plough (plou), *NOUN.* or *VERB.* another spelling of **plow.**
❏ *VERB* **ploughs, ploughed, plough·ing.**

plow (plou),
1 *NOUN.* a large piece of farm equipment pulled by a tractor or farm animals. Plows are used for turning up the soil before planting seeds.
2 *VERB.* to turn up the soil with a plow: *to plow a field.*
3 *NOUN.* a snowplow.
4 *VERB.* to move snow: *They plowed all the driveways on our street after the snow fell.*
5 *VERB.* to move through anything like a plow does; advance slowly and with effort: *The ship plowed through the waves.*
❏ *VERB* **plows, plowed, plow·ing.**

pluck (pluk),
1 *VERB.* to pick or pull something off: *He plucked flowers in the garden.*
2 *NOUN.* the act of picking or pulling.
3 *VERB.* to play a musical instrument by pulling on its strings: *She was plucking the banjo softly.*
4 *VERB.* to pull the feathers or hair off of something or someone: *We plucked the chicken before cooking it. She plucks her eyebrows.*
❏ *VERB* **plucks, plucked, pluck·ing.**

plug (plug),
1 *NOUN.* a device at the end of a wire to make an electrical connection by fitting into a socket.
2 *NOUN.* a piece of wood, rubber, or other substance used to fill a hole: *I pulled the plug to drain the water from the bathtub.*
3 *VERB.* to fill something up with a plug: *They plugged the hole with cement.*
❏ *VERB* **plugs, plugged, plug·ging.**

plum (plum), *NOUN.* a round, sweet, juicy fruit with smooth skin and a stone inside. Plums grow on trees and are green, purple, or yellow. ▪ See the Word Story at **prune[1].**

plum·age (plü′mij), *NOUN.* the feathers of a bird.

plumb·er (plum′ər), *NOUN.* someone whose work is putting in and repairing water pipes, sinks, bathtubs, and so on, in buildings: *When the water pipe froze, we called a plumber.*

plumb·ing (plum′ing), *NOUN.*
1 the water pipes, sinks, bathtubs, and so on, in a building: *bathroom plumbing.*
2 the work or trade of a plumber.

plume (plüm), *NOUN.* a large, long feather.

plump (plump), *ADJECTIVE.* pleasantly round and full: *The young child had plump cheeks.*

plunge (plunj),
1 *VERB.* to throw something or thrust it with force into a liquid: *Plunge your hand into the water.*
2 *VERB.* to throw yourself into something suddenly: *She plunged into the lake to save the drowning swimmer.*
3 *VERB.* to fall or move suddenly downward: *The kite plunged toward the ground.*
4 *NOUN.* a jump or dive: *The diver made a sudden plunge from the cliff into the sea.*
❏ *VERB* **plung·es, plunged, plung·ing.**

plung·er (plun′jər), *NOUN.* a rubber suction cup on a long stick, used for unplugging drains and toilets that are stopped up.

plur·al (plúr′əl),
1 *ADJECTIVE.* more than one in number. *Cat* is singular; *cats* is plural.
2 *NOUN.* the form of a word that shows it means more than one. *Books* is the plural of *book; men* is the plural of *man; we* is the plural of *I; these* is the plural of *this.*

plus (plus),
1 *PREPOSITION.* added to: *3 plus 2 equals 5.*
2 *PREPOSITION.* and also: *The work of an engineer requires intelligence plus experience.*
3 *ADJECTIVE.* and more: *Her grade was B plus.*
4 *NOUN.* the sign (+) meaning that the quantity following it is to be added.
5 *NOUN.* a positive quality or item; something favorable, welcome, or helpful: *Her sense of humor is a real plus.*
❏ *PLURAL* **plus·es** or **plus·ses.**

These African lovebirds have colorful **plumage.**

plush (plush), NOUN. a fabric like velvet but thicker and softer. Many stuffed toys are covered with plush.

Plu·to (plü′tō), NOUN.
1 the smallest planet and the one farthest from the sun.
2 the Greek and Roman god of the region of the dead.

plu·to·ni·um (plü tō′nē əm), NOUN. a radioactive chemical element usually produced artificially from uranium. It is used as a source of atomic energy.

Plym·outh (plim′əth), NOUN. a town in southeastern Massachusetts, founded by the Pilgrims.

ply·wood (plī′wúd′), NOUN. a board or boards made of several thin layers of wood glued together.

p.m. or **P.M.,** the time from noon to midnight: *Our school day ends at 3 P.M.*

pneu·mo·nia (nü mō′nyə), NOUN. a serious disease that can cause fluid in the lungs, high fever, and difficulty in breathing. Pneumonia often follows a bad cold or other disease.

P.O. or **p.o.,** an abbreviation of **post office.**

poach[1] (pōch), VERB.
1 to hunt or fish illegally.
2 to go illegally onto someone else's land, especially to hunt or fish.
❑ VERB **poach·es, poached, poach·ing. –poach′er,** NOUN.

poach[2] (pōch), VERB. to cook an egg by breaking it into boiling water. ❑ VERB **poach·es, poached, poach·ing.**

pock (pok), NOUN. a pimple, mark, or pit left on the skin by smallpox and certain other diseases.

pock·et (pok′it),
1 NOUN. a small piece of cloth sewed into clothing to carry things.
2 VERB. to put something in your pocket: *I pocketed the change.*
3 ADJECTIVE. small enough to go in a pocket: *I was given a pocket camera for my birthday.*
4 NOUN. any of the hollow places at the corners and sides of a pool table that the balls are driven into.
❑ VERB **pock·ets, pock·et·ed, pock·et·ing.**

pock·et·book (pok′it búk′), NOUN.
1 a wallet; billfold.
2 a woman's purse.

pock·et·knife (pok′it nīf′), NOUN. a small knife with one or more blades that fold into the handle.
❑ PLURAL **pock·et·knives** (pok′it nīvz′).

pod (pod), NOUN. a long, narrow part of a plant in which seeds grow. Beans, peas, and okra grow in pods.

po·em (pō′əm), NOUN. a piece of writing that expresses the writer's imagination. In a poem, the patterns made by the sounds of the words have special importance.

po·et (pō′it), NOUN. someone who writes poems.

po·et·ic (pō et′ik), ADJECTIVE. of or like poems or poets: *She told the story in poetic language.*
–po·et′i·cal·ly, ADVERB.

po·et·ry (pō′i trē), NOUN. poems: *Have you read much poetry?*

po·go stick (pō′gō stik), a toy consisting of a stick that contains a spring, and has a small platform for each foot near the bottom and a handle at the top. You can hop from place to place by jumping up and down on the platforms, while holding the handle.

poin·set·ti·a (poin set′ə or poin set′ē ə), NOUN. a plant with large scarlet leaves that look like flower petals. Poinsettias are used as Christmas decorations.
❑ PLURAL **poin·set·ti·as.**

hopping on a **pogo stick**

point (point),
1 NOUN. a sharp end: *the point of a needle.*
2 NOUN. a period in writing; a decimal point in numbers.
3 NOUN. (in mathematics) something that has position without length or width. Two lines meet or cross at a point.
4 NOUN. a place; spot: *Stop at this point.*
5 NOUN. a degree; stage: *the freezing point, the boiling point.*
6 NOUN. a small part of a series of ideas or thoughts: *The speaker replied to the argument point by point.*
7 NOUN. a special quality or feature of someone: *Courage and endurance were her good points.*
8 NOUN. the main idea of something: *I did not get the point of the joke.*
9 VERB. to aim: *The archer pointed the arrow at the target.*
10 VERB. to show the position or direction of something with your finger: *He pointed the way to the village over the hills.*
11 NOUN. a piece of land with a narrow part that sticks out into the water; cape.
12 NOUN. a unit for keeping score in a game: *We won the game by three points.*
❑ VERB **points, point·ed, point·ing.**

beside the point, IDIOM. having nothing to do with the subject; not appropriate: *Her remark was careless and beside the point.*

a	hat	ė	term	ô	order	ch	child		a in about
ā	age	i	it	oi	oil	ng	long		e in taken
ä	far	ī	ice	ou	out	sh	she	ə	i in pencil
â	care	o	hot	u	cup	th	thin		o in lemon
e	let	ō	open	ù	put	ŦH	then		u in circus
ē	equal	ò	saw	ü	rule	zh	measure		

P

make a point of, IDIOM. to insist on: *I made a point of arriving on time.*

point out, IDIOM. to show or call attention to; indicate: *Please point out my mistakes.*

to the point, IDIOM. on the subject; relevant: *His speech was brief and to the point.*

point·ed (poin′tid), ADJECTIVE.
1 having a point or points: *a pointed roof.*
2 sharp; piercing: *She has a pointed wit.*

point·er (poin′tər), NOUN.
1 a long, narrow stick used to point things out on a map, blackboard, and the like.
2 a hint; suggestion: *She gave him some pointers on improving his tennis.*
3 the hand of a clock, gauge, or dial.
4 a short-haired hunting dog. A pointer is trained to show where an animal is by standing still with its head and body pointing toward it.
5 someone or something that points.

point·less (point′lis), ADJECTIVE. without any meaning or purpose: *This is a pointless argument.*

point of view, an attitude of mind: *Sometimes it's hard to understand another person's point of view.*

poise (poiz),
1 NOUN. calm; self-confidence: *She has great poise and never seems embarrassed.*
2 VERB. to balance something: *The athlete poised the weight in the air before throwing it.*
□ VERB **pois·es, poised, pois·ing.**

poi·son (poi′zn),
1 NOUN. anything that is very dangerous to your life or health if you swallow it or breathe it in. Arsenic and lead are poisons.
2 VERB. to kill or harm someone or something with poison.
3 VERB. to put poison in or on something: *to poison food, to poison arrows.*
4 VERB. to have a very harmful effect on something: *Jealousy poisoned their friendship.*
□ VERB **poi·sons, poi·soned, poi·son·ing.**
—**poi′son·er,** NOUN.

poison ivy, a climbing plant that looks like ivy. It causes a painful rash on the skin of most people who touch it.

poi·son·ous (poi′zn əs), ADJECTIVE. containing poison; very harmful to life or health: *The rattlesnake's bite is poisonous.*

poke (pōk),
1 VERB. to push with force against someone or something: *He poked me in the ribs with his elbow.*
2 VERB. to thrust or push: *The dog poked its head out of the car window.*
3 NOUN. the act or fact of poking: *During the game she got an accidental poke in the eye.*
□ VERB **pokes, poked, pok·ing.**

pok·er[1] (pō′kər), NOUN. a metal rod for stirring a fire.

po·ker[2] (pō′kər), NOUN. a card game in which the players bet on the value of the cards that they hold in their hands.

Po·land (pō′lənd), NOUN. a country in central Europe, on the eastern border of Germany.

po·lar (pō′lər), ADJECTIVE. of or near the North or South Pole: *It is very cold in the polar regions.*

polar bear, a large white bear of the arctic regions.

polar bear — up to 11 feet long

Pole (pōl), NOUN. someone born or living in Poland.

pole[1] (pōl), NOUN. a long, slender, usually round piece of wood or metal: *a fishing pole, a totem pole. The flag in front of our school flies on a pole.*
∎ Another word that sounds like this is **poll.**

pole[2] (pōl), NOUN.
1 either end of the earth's axis. The North Pole and the South Pole are opposite each other.
2 either end of a battery or magnet. The magnetic or electrical force at one pole is opposite to the force at the other pole.
∎ Another word that sounds like this is **poll.**

pole vault, an athletic contest in which people try to jump over a horizontal bar using a long pole.
—**pole′-vault′er,** NOUN.

po·lice (pə lēs′),
1 NOUN. an organization of people hired to protect us and our things, and to make sure that everyone obeys the laws. Police may arrest people who break the law.
2 VERB. to keep something orderly and safe for everyone: *The neighbors police the streets.*
□ VERB **po·lic·es, po·liced, po·lic·ing.**

po·lice·man (pə lēs′mən), NOUN. a member of the police. □ PLURAL **po·lice·men.**

police officer, a member of the police.

po·lice·wom·an (pə lēs′wùm′ən), NOUN. a woman who is a member of the police. □ PLURAL **po·lice·wom·en.**

pol·i·cy[1] (pol′ə sē), NOUN. a plan of action; way of management: *It is a poor policy to promise more than you can do.* □ PLURAL **pol·i·cies.**

pol·i·cy² (pol′ə sē), *NOUN.* a written agreement about insurance. An insurance policy makes clear when money will be paid, and how much. ❑ *PLURAL* **pol·i·cies.**

po·li·o (pō′lē ō), *NOUN.* a disease most often of children that causes fever, paralysis of various muscles, and sometimes death. Polio is now very rare.

pol·ish (pol′ish),
1 *VERB.* to make something smooth and shiny: *to polish wood, to polish silverware.*
2 *NOUN.* a substance used to put a shine on something: *silver polish, shoe polish.* ❑ *VERB* **pol·ish·es, pol·ished, pol·ish·ing;** *PLURAL* **pol·ish·es.**
polish off, *IDIOM.*
1 to get done with; finish: *He polished off his homework in an hour.*
2 to eat or drink up greedily: *They polished off the entire pie between them.*

Pol·ish (pō′lish),
1 *ADJECTIVE.* of or about Poland, its people, or their language.
2 *NOUN.* the language of Poland.

po·lite (pə līt′), *ADJECTIVE.* behaving in a nice, friendly way; having good manners: *The polite girl gave the old man her seat on the bus.* ❑ *ADJECTIVE* **po·lit·er, po·lit·est. –po·lite′ly,** *ADVERB.* **–po·lite′ness,** *NOUN.*

po·lit·i·cal (pə lit′ə kəl), *ADJECTIVE.*
1 of or about citizens or government: *Treason is a political offense.*
2 of or about politicians or their methods: *a political party, political meetings.* **–po·lit′i·cal·ly,** *ADVERB.*

pol·i·ti·cian (pol′ə tish′ən), *NOUN.* someone whose occupation or chief activity is government: *Politicians are busy near election time.*

pol·i·tics (pol′ə tiks), *NOUN.*
1 *SINGULAR.* the work of government; management of public business: *The senator was engaged in politics for many years.*
2 *PLURAL.* political principles or opinions: *Her politics are very liberal.*

pol·ka (pōl′kə *or* pō′kə), *NOUN.*
1 a kind of lively dance.
2 the music for it. ❑ *PLURAL* **pol·kas.**

pol·ka dot (pō′kə dot′), one of a number of large dots that form a pattern on cloth.

poll (pōl),
1 *NOUN.* the act of voting; collection of votes: *The class had a poll to decide where it would have its picnic.*
2 *NOUN.* **polls,** a place where votes are cast and counted: *The polls will be open all day.*
3 *NOUN.* a survey of public opinion about a particular subject.

4 *VERB.* to ask people for their opinions; question: *She polled the students to learn how many liked the cafeteria food.* ❑ *VERB* **polls, polled, poll·ing.**
■ Another word that sounds like this is **pole.**

pol·len (pol′ən), *NOUN.* a fine powder released from the anthers of flowers and the cones of some trees. It fertilizes the female cells of plants.

pol·li·nate (pol′ə nāt), *VERB.* to carry pollen to a plant. Many flowers are pollinated by bees. ❑ *VERB* **pol·li·nates, pol·li·nat·ed, pol·li·nat·ing. –pol′li·na′tion,** *NOUN.*

Bees **pollinate** flowers as they fly from one blossom to another.

pol·li·wog (pol′ē wog), *NOUN.* See **tadpole.**

pol·lu·tant (pə lüt′nt), *NOUN.* something that pollutes: *The leftover oil from a factory is a pollutant of the stream it flows into.*

pol·lute (pə lüt′), *VERB.* to make air, water, or soil dirty and harmful to people: *The water at the beach was polluted by water released from the factory.* ❑ *VERB* **pol·lutes, pol·lut·ed, pol·lut·ing.**

pol·lu·tion (pə lü′shən), *NOUN.*
1 the act or process of dirtying any part of the environment, especially with waste material: *Exhaust from cars causes air pollution.*
2 anything that dirties an environment, especially waste material: *Pollution in the lake killed many fish.*

po·lo (pō′lō), *NOUN.* a game similar to hockey, played on horseback with long-handled mallets and a wooden ball.

pol·y·gon (pol′ē gon), *NOUN.* a figure with three or more straight sides and angles.

Pol·y·ne·sia (pol′ə nē′zhə), *NOUN.* a very large group of small islands in the Pacific between South America and Australia. **–Pol′y·ne′sian,** *ADJECTIVE* or *NOUN.*

a	hat	ė	term	ô	order	ch	child	⎧ a in about
ā	age	i	it	oi	oil	ng	long	e in taken
ä	far	ī	ice	ou	out	sh	she	ə⎨ i in pencil
â	care	o	hot	u	cup	th	thin	o in lemon
e	let	ō	open	u̇	put	ᴛʜ	then	⎩ u in circus
ē	equal	ȯ	saw	ü	rule	zh	measure	

P

pol·yp (pol′ip), NOUN.
1 a simple form of water animal consisting largely of a stomach with tentacles around the edge to gather in food. Polyps often grow in colonies, with their bases connected. Coral is made by polyps.
2 a small, usually harmless growth in the body. Polyps that grow in the nose or intestine can block those passages and must be removed by surgery.

poodle — about 1½ feet high at the shoulder

pome·gran·ate (pom′ə gran′it), NOUN. the reddish yellow fruit of a small tree. Pomegranates have thick skin, tasty red pulp, and many seeds.

pomp (pomp), NOUN. a stately or showy display; magnificence: *The new ruler was crowned with great pomp.*

pom·pom (pom′pom), NOUN.
1 a colored, fluffy ball of feathers, silk, wool, or the like, worn on clothing or worn by fans and cheerleaders at football or basketball games.
2 an ornamental tuft or ball of feathers, silk, or the like, worn on a hat, dress, or shoe.

pomp·ous (pom′pəs), ADJECTIVE. acting too proudly: *The leader of the band bowed in a pompous manner.* **–pomp′ous·ly,** ADVERB.

pon·cho (pon′chō), NOUN. a large piece of cloth or other material, often waterproof, with a slit in the middle for the head to go through. Ponchos are worn in South America as cloaks. Waterproof ponchos are used in the armed forces and by hikers and campers. ❑ PLURAL **pon·chos.**

pond (pond), NOUN. a body of still water, smaller than a lake: *a duck pond.*

pon·der (pon′dər), VERB. to think something over carefully: *to ponder a problem.* ❑ VERB **pon·ders, pon·dered, pon·der·ing.**

pon·toon (pon tün′), NOUN. either of two boat-shaped parts of an airplane, used for landing on or taking off from water.

po·ny (pō′nē), NOUN. a kind of small horse. Ponies are usually less than 5 feet tall at the shoulder. ❑ PLURAL **po·nies.**

pony express, a system of carrying letters and small packages in the western United States in 1860 and 1861 by riders on fast ponies or horses.

po·ny·tail (pō′nē tāl′), NOUN. a hair style in which the hair is pulled back and tied, with the ends falling free from the where the hair is tied.

poo·dle (pü′dl), NOUN. an intelligent dog with thick, curly hair.

Word Story

Poodle comes from a German word meaning "puddle." Poodles were bred as hunting dogs, and they used to run into water to retrieve birds that had fallen there.

pool¹ (pül), NOUN.
1 a tank of water to swim in: *a swimming pool.*
2 a small pond: *a forest pool.*
3 a puddle: *a pool of grease under a car.*

pool² (pül),
1 NOUN. a game played with 16 hard, numbered balls on a special table with six pockets. Players try to drive the balls into the pockets with long sticks called cues.
2 VERB. to put things or money together for common advantage: *We pooled our money to buy food.*
3 NOUN. a system or arrangement in which money, vehicles, people with a specific skill, and the like, can be shared: *The hikers put all their supplies in a pool for everyone to use.*
❑ VERB **pools, pooled, pool·ing.**

poor (pùr),
1 ADJECTIVE. having very little money: *The children were so poor that they had no shoes.*
2 NOUN PLURAL. **the poor,** people who have little or nothing.
3 ADJECTIVE. not good in quality; lacking something: *poor soil, a poor crop, a poor cook.* ■ See the Synonym Study at **bad.**
4 ADJECTIVE. deserving pity; unfortunate: *This poor child is hurt.*

Synonym Study

Poor means having little or no money: *A poor person may not have a lot of clothes to wear.*

Penniless means without any money, even if only for a short time: *She was penniless after spending the last cent of her allowance.*

Broke is an informal word that can mean without money: *I am too broke to go to a movie.*

Needy means poor and not having enough to live on: *The needy family receives food stamps from the government.*

ANTONYMS: rich, wealthy.

poor·ly (pùr′lē), *ADVERB.* not enough; badly: *The desert is poorly supplied with water. The student did poorly on the test.*

pop¹ (pop),
1 *VERB.* to make a short, quick, bursting sound: *The firecrackers popped in bunches.*
2 *NOUN.* a short, quick, bursting sound: *The bottle opened with a pop.*
3 *VERB.* to burst open; cause to burst open: *The balloon popped. We popped some popcorn.*
4 *VERB.* to move, go, or come suddenly or unexpectedly: *Our neighbor popped in for a short chat.*
5 *VERB.* to thrust or put suddenly: *She popped her head out through the window.*
6 *NOUN.* a bubbly soft drink: *strawberry pop.*
7 *VERB.* (in baseball) to hit a short, high ball over the infield.
❑ *VERB* **pops, popped, pop·ping.**

pop² (pop), *NOUN.* papa; father.

pop·corn (pop′kôrn′), *NOUN.* a kind of corn that bursts open noisily and puffs out when you heat it.

pope or **Pope** (pōp), *NOUN.* the head of the Roman Catholic Church.

pop fly, (in baseball) a short, high fly ball.

pop·lar (pop′lər), *NOUN.* a tree that grows rapidly and produces light, soft wood.

pop·py (pop′ē), *NOUN.* a plant with delicate, showy red, yellow, or white flowers. ❑ *PLURAL* **pop·pies.**

Pop·si·cle (pop′sə kəl), *NOUN.* (trademark) a flavored, colored, sweetened ice that is molded onto a stick.

pop-top (pop′top′), *ADJECTIVE.* having a metal tab that can be bent and pushed into the top of a can to make an opening.

pop·u·lace (pop′yə lis), *NOUN.* the common people: *The king addressed the populace on his birthday and promised fewer taxes.*

pop·u·lar (pop′yə lər), *ADJECTIVE.*
1 liked by most people: *a popular song.*
2 liked by acquaintances or associates: *His good nature makes him the most popular boy in the school.*
3 widespread among many people; common: *It is a popular belief that black cats bring bad luck.*
4 of or for the people; by the people; representing the people: *The United States has a popular government.*
—**pop′u·lar·ly,** *ADVERB.*

pop·u·lar·i·ty (pop′yə lar′ə tē), *NOUN.* the fact or condition of someone or something being liked by most people.

pop·u·late (pop′yə lāt), *VERB.* to furnish an area with inhabitants: *Europe helped populate America.*
❑ *VERB* **pop·u·lates, pop·u·lat·ed, pop·u·lat·ing.**

pop·u·la·tion (pop′yə lā′shən), *NOUN.*
1 the people of a city, country, or district.
2 the number of people living in a place.

3 all the living things of one kind that live in a place: *The river's trout population is growing.*

pop·u·lous (pop′yə ləs), *ADJECTIVE.* full of people; having many people per square mile: *California is the most populous state of the United States.*

por·ce·lain (pôr′sə lin), *NOUN.* a very fine kind of pottery; china. Porcelain may be so thin that light shines through it.

porch (pôrch), *NOUN.* a platform with a roof along the outside of a house, without walls or with walls having many windows: *Our house has a big front porch.* ❑ *PLURAL* **porch·es.**

porcupine — about 3 feet long, including the tail

por·cu·pine (pôr′kyə pin), *NOUN.* a small animal that is covered with coarse hair and sharp spines called quills.

Word Story

Porcupine comes from Latin words meaning "pig" and "thorn." **Porpoise** comes from the Latin words meaning "pig" and "fish." Many things reminded Romans of pigs. With the porcupine, it was probably shape and size. With the porpoise, it was the snout.

pore¹ (pôr), *VERB.* to look at or study something steadily and carefully: *I pored over the book trying to find the answer.* ❑ *VERB* **pores, pored, por·ing.**
▪ Another word that sounds like this is **pour.**

pore² (pôr), *NOUN.* a very small opening. Sweat comes through the pores in the skin. ▪ Another word that sounds like this is **pour.**

pork (pôrk), *NOUN.* the meat of a pig used for food.

po·rous (pôr′əs), *ADJECTIVE.* full of pores through which liquids or gases can pass: *Cloth is porous. Aluminum is not porous.*

a hat	ė term	ô order	ch child	a in about
ā age	i it	oi oil	ng long	e in taken
ä far	ī ice	ou out	sh she	ə i in pencil
â care	o hot	u cup	th thin	o in lemon
e let	ō open	u̇ put	ᴛʜ then	u in circus
ē equal	ȯ saw	ü rule	zh measure	

P

por·poise (pôr′pəs), NOUN. a sea animal with a blunt, rounded snout. Porpoises are related to dolphins and whales. ❏ PLURAL **por·poise** or **por·pois·es.**

porpoise — from 4 to 7 feet long

por·ridge (pôr′ij), NOUN. oatmeal or other grain boiled in water or milk until it thickens.

port¹ (pôrt), NOUN.
1 a place where ships and boats can be sheltered from storms; harbor.
2 a place where ships and boats can load and unload; city or town with a harbor: *New York City is an important port.*

port² (pôrt), NOUN. the side of a ship, boat, or aircraft to your left when you are facing the front, when you are aboard.

por·ta·ble (pôr′tə bəl), ADJECTIVE. able to be carried or moved; easily carried: *I have a portable radio.*

por·ter (pôr′tər), NOUN.
1 someone employed to carry burdens or baggage: *Give your bags to the porter.*
2 an attendant in a sleeping car of a passenger train.

port·hole (pôrt′hōl′), NOUN. an opening in a ship's side to let in light and air.

por·tion (pôr′shən),
1 NOUN. a part or share: *A portion of each school day is devoted to arithmetic.* ■ See the Synonym Study at **part.**
2 NOUN. an amount of food served to someone at one time: *I can't eat such a large portion.*
3 VERB. to divide something into parts or shares: *The money was portioned out among the children.*
❏ VERB **por·tions, por·tioned, por·tion·ing.**

port·ly (pôrt′lē), ADJECTIVE. fat or large in a dignified way. ❏ ADJECTIVE **port·li·er, port·li·est.**
–**port′li·ness,** NOUN.

por·trait (pôr′trit), NOUN. a picture of someone, especially of his or her face.

por·tray (pôr trā′), VERB.
1 to draw or paint someone or something; make a picture of: *to portray a historical scene.*
2 to describe something or someone in words: *The story portrayed the way of life of the Plains Indians.*

3 to act the part of someone in a play or movie: *The actor portrayed a doctor in a soap opera.*
❏ VERB **por·trays, por·trayed, por·tray·ing.**

Por·tu·gal (pôr′chə gəl), NOUN. a country in southwestern Europe.

Por·tu·guese (pôr′chə gēz′),
1 ADJECTIVE. of or about Portugal, its people, or their language.
2 NOUN PLURAL. **the Portuguese,** the people of Portugal.
3 NOUN. the language of Portugal and Brazil.
❏ PLURAL **Por·tu·guese.**

Word Source

The following words have come into English from **Portuguese:**

albino	flamingo	macaw	piranha
cobra	jaguar	mandarin	zebra
dodo	junk²	mango	

pose (pōz),
1 NOUN. a way of holding your body: *a natural pose, a pose taken in exercising.*
2 VERB. to hold your body in one position: *She posed an hour for her portrait.*
3 NOUN. a way of behaving that is not sincere: *Her interest in people is real; it isn't just a pose.*
4 VERB. to pretend to be something or someone: *They posed as a rich couple although they had little money.*
❏ VERB **pos·es, posed, pos·ing.**

po·si·tion (pə zish′ən),
1 NOUN. the place where something or someone is: *The flowers grew in a sheltered position behind the house.*
2 NOUN. a way of being placed: *a comfortable position.*
3 NOUN. a job: *He has a position in a bank.*
4 NOUN. a way of thinking; set of opinions: *What is your position on this question?*
5 VERB. to put something or someone into a certain position: *The police positioned themselves around the suspect's house.*
❏ VERB **po·si·tions, po·si·tioned, po·si·tion·ing.**

pos·i·tive (poz′ə tiv), ADJECTIVE.
1 without question or doubt; sure: *We have positive evidence that the planets move around the sun.* ■ See the Synonym Study at **sure.**
2 too sure; too confident: *A positive manner annoys some people.*
3 able to do or add something; practical: *Don't just make a negative criticism; give us some positive help.*
4 showing your agreement or approval: *a positive answer to a question.*
5 showing that a particular disease, condition, germ, and so on, is present: *The test was positive.*
6 of the kind of electricity that protons carry.
7 greater than zero: *Five above zero is a positive quantity.*

pos·i·tive·ly (poz′ə tiv lē), ADVERB.
 1 in a positive way: *The audience reacted positively to our play.*
 2 absolutely; very: *I was positively furious at them for being so rude.*

pos·se (pos′ē), NOUN. a group of citizens called together by a sheriff to help maintain law and order: *The posse chased the bandits across the prairie.* ❑ PLURAL **pos·ses.**

pos·sess (pə zes′), VERB. to own or have something: *My aunt possesses great intelligence and determination.* ❑ VERB **pos·sess·es, pos·sessed, pos·sess·ing.** –**pos·ses′sor,** NOUN.

pos·ses·sion (pə zesh′ən), NOUN.
 1 the act or fact of possessing or having; ownership: *Those books are in my possession.*
 2 **possessions,** things possessed; property: *Please move your possessions from my room.*

pos·ses·sive (pe zes′iv),
 1 ADJECTIVE. showing possession. *My, your, his,* and *our* are possessive adjectives because they indicate who possesses or owns.
 2 NOUN. word showing possession. In "your book," *your* is a possessive.
 3 ADJECTIVE. selfish with your belongings: *She is very possessive of her books and will not lend them.* –**pos·ses′sive·ly,** ADVERB. –**pos·ses′sive·ness,** NOUN.

pos·si·bil·i·ty (pos′ə bil′ə tē), NOUN.
 1 the condition of being possible: *There is a possibility that the train may be late.*
 2 a possible thing, person, or event: *A whole week of rain is a possibility.* ❑ PLURAL **pos·si·bil·i·ties.**

pos·si·bly (pos′ə blē), ADVERB.
 1 no matter what happens: *I cannot possibly go.*
 2 perhaps: *Possibly you are right.*

pos·sum (pos′əm), NOUN. a short form of **opossum.** ❑ PLURAL **pos·sums** or **pos·sum.**

Word Power   post-

The prefix **post-** means "after." **Post**war means **after** the war. A **post**script is written **after** the rest of the letter.

post¹ (pōst),
 1 NOUN. a piece of wood, metal, plastic, and so on, set in the ground to hold something up: *the posts of a door, a hitching post.*
 2 VERB. to fasten a notice up in a place where everyone can see it: *The list of winners will be posted soon.*
 ❑ VERB **posts, post·ed, post·ing.**

post² (pōst),
 1 NOUN. a place where a soldier, police officer, guard, and so on, is stationed.
 2 NOUN. a military base where soldiers are stationed.
 3 VERB. to place someone at a post: *They posted guards at the door.*
 4 NOUN. a job or position: *the post of secretary, a diplomatic post.*
 ❑ VERB **posts, post·ed, post·ing.**

post³ (pōst), VERB. to supply with up-to-date information; inform: *Keep me posted about your new job.* ❑ VERB **posts, post·ed, post·ing.**

post·age (pō′stij), NOUN. the amount paid on anything sent by mail.

a collection of **postage stamps**

pos·si·ble (pos′ə bəl), ADJECTIVE.
 1 able to be done: *It is possible to cure tuberculosis. Space travel is now possible.*
 2 not true for sure, but perhaps true: *It is possible that they left without us.*
 3 able to be done or chosen properly: *That is the only possible action. He is the only possible candidate.*

postage stamp, an official stamp placed on mail to show that postage has been paid; stamp: *My friend has a large postage stamp collection.*

a	hat	ė	term	ô	order	ch	child	⎧ a in about
ā	age	i	it	oi	oil	ng	long	e in taken
ä	far	ī	ice	ou	out	sh	she	ə ⎨ i in pencil
â	care	o	hot	u	cup	th	thin	o in lemon
e	let	ō	open	ù	put	ᵺ	then	⎩ u in circus
ē	equal	ȯ	saw	ü	rule	zh	measure	

post·al (pō′stəl), *ADJECTIVE.* of or about mail and post offices: *postal regulations, a postal clerk.*

postal card,

1 an officially produced card sold by a post office, that has a government postage stamp printed on it and is used to send a message by mail.

2 See **postcard.**

Postal Service, an independent agency of the United States government that provides mail services, sells postage stamps, and so on.

post·card (pōst′kärd′), *NOUN.* a card, usually about 3½ inches by 5½ inches, for sending a message by mail; postal card. Postcards often have a picture on one side.

post·er (pō′stər), *NOUN.* a large printed picture or message put up on a wall.

pos·ter·i·ty (po ster′ə tē), *NOUN.* all the people that will live in the future: *He photographed the event for posterity.*

post·man (pōst′mən), *NOUN.* See **mail carrier.**
❑ *PLURAL* **post·men.**

post·mark (pōst′märk′), *NOUN.* an official mark stamped on mail to cancel the postage stamp and record the place and date of mailing.

post·mas·ter (pōst′mas′tər), *NOUN.* the person in charge of a post office.

post office, a place where workers take in and send out mail and sell postage stamps.

post·pone (pōst pōn′), *VERB.* to put something off till later; delay: *The ballgame was postponed because of rain.* ❑ *VERB* **post·pones, post·poned, post·pon·ing. —post·pone′ment,** *NOUN.*

post·script (pōst′skript), *NOUN.* a short note added to a letter, written below the writer's name.

pos·ture (pos′chər), *NOUN.* a position of the body; way of holding the body: *Good posture is important to health.*

post·war (pōst′wôr′), *ADJECTIVE.* after the war: *There was a postwar increase in the number of births.*

pot (pot),

1 *NOUN.* a round, deep pan used for cooking. There are many different kinds and shapes of pots.

2 *NOUN.* the amount a pot will hold: *She brought a small pot of beans.*

3 *NOUN.* a round plant holder, usually made of plastic or clay: *The flower pots were full of daisies.*

4 *VERB.* to put something into a pot: *I potted the young tomato plants.*
❑ *VERB* **pots, pot·ted, pot·ting.**

Have You Heard?

You may have heard someone say **"that's the pot calling the kettle black!"** This means that you are criticizing another person for a fault you have yourself.

po·tas·si·um (pə tas′ē əm), *NOUN.* a soft, silver-white metal. Potassium is used in making soap and fertilizers. It is a chemical element.

po·ta·to (pə tā′tō), *NOUN.* a round or oval, hard, starchy vegetable with a thin skin. It is one of the most widely used vegetables in Europe and America. Potatoes grow underground.
❑ *PLURAL* **po·ta·toes.**

Word Story

Potato comes from a word in a Native American language of the Caribbean, meaning "sweet potato." Europeans learned the word but applied it to the unsweet potato.

potato chips, thin slices of potato fried in deep fat.

po·ten·tial (pə ten′shəl),

1 *ADJECTIVE.* capable of happening; coming into being: *There is a potential danger of being bitten when playing with a strange dog.*

2 *NOUN.* an ability or skill that may develop in the future: *She has a lot of potential as a basketball player.*
—po·ten·tial·ly, *ADVERB.*

pot·hole (pot′hōl′), *NOUN.* a deep hole in the surface of a street or road. Potholes are caused by ice that freezes and swells in small cracks.

po·tion (pō′shən), *NOUN.* a drink, especially one used as a medicine or poison, or in magic.

Word Story

Potion comes from a Latin word meaning "to drink." **Poison** comes from the same Latin word. In old times, people believed in the power of special drinks to heal illness, to work magic, to attract love — or to kill.

pot·ter (pot′ər), *NOUN.* someone who makes pots, dishes, or vases out of clay.

pot·ter·y (pot′ər ē), *NOUN.* pots, dishes, or vases made from clay and baked until they are hard.

pouch (pouch), *NOUN.*

1 a bag or sack: *a tobacco pouch.*

2 a part of some animals that is like a bag or pocket. A kangaroo has a pouch on the stomach for carrying its young. A chipmunk has cheek pouches for carrying food. ❑ *PLURAL* **pouch·es.**

This **potter** shapes wet clay as it spins on a special kind of plate.

poul·try (pōl′trē), *NOUN.* birds that people raise for their meat or eggs. Chickens, turkeys, geese, and ducks are poultry.

pounce (pouns), *VERB.* to jump on something suddenly and seize it: *The cat pounced upon the mouse.* ❑ *VERB* **pounc·es, pounced, pounc·ing.**

pound¹ (pound), *NOUN.*
1 a unit of weight equal to 16 ounces.
2 a unit of money in Great Britain equal to 100 pennies. £1 means one pound.
❑ *PLURAL* **pounds** or **pound.**

pound² (pound), *VERB.*
1 to hit something hard again and again; hit heavily: *She pounded the door with her fist.*
2 to beat hard; throb: *After running fast you can feel your heart pound.*
3 to make something into a powder or pulp by pounding it: *They pounded the grains of corn into meal.*
❑ *VERB* **pounds, pound·ed, pound·ing.**

pound³ (pound), *NOUN.* a place where stray animals are kept and cared for: *I found my lost dog at the pound.*

pour (pôr), *VERB.*
1 to flow or cause something to flow in a steady stream: *I poured the milk from the bottle into the cups. The crowd poured out of the theater.*
2 to rain heavily: *It poured all day.*
❑ *VERB* **pours, poured, pour·ing.** ■ Another word that sounds like this is **pore.**

pout (pout), *VERB.* to show that you are unhappy by pushing out your lips or looking angry or sulky: *He pouted when he didn't the new toy.* ❑ *VERB* **pouts, pout·ed, pout·ing.**

pov·er·ty (pov′ər tē), *NOUN.* the condition of being poor: *Their ragged clothes showed their poverty.*

pow·der (pou′dər),
1 *NOUN.* very tiny bits of things ground as fine as dust: *baking powder, baking powder.*
2 *VERB.* to sprinkle or cover something with powder: *She powdered her face.*
3 *NOUN.* gunpowder: *Soldiers used to carry their powder in a powder horn.*
❑ *VERB* **pow·ders, pow·dered, pow·der·ing.**

pow·der·y (pou′dər ē), *ADJECTIVE.* like powder; in the form of powder: *powdery snow.*

pow·er (pou′ər),
1 *NOUN.* strength or force: *Penicillin is a medicine of great power.*
2 *NOUN.* the ability to do or act: *I will give you all the help in my power.*
3 *NOUN.* authority or the right to do something: *Congress has power to declare war.*
4 *NOUN.* someone or something that has authority or influence; important nation: *The five powers held a peace conference.*
5 *NOUN.* energy or force that can do work: *Running water can produce electric power.*
6 *VERB.* to provide something with power or energy: *a boat powered by an outboard motor.*
7 *ADJECTIVE.* operated by a motor; equipped with its own motor: *a power drill.*
❑ *VERB* **pow·ers, pow·ered, pow·er·ing.**

pow·er·ful (pou′ər fəl), *ADJECTIVE.* having great power or force; strong: *a powerful person, a powerful medicine, a powerful nation.* ■ See the Synonym Study at **strong.** **–pow′er·ful·ly,** *ADVERB.*

pow·er·less (pou′ər lis), *ADJECTIVE.* without power; helpless: *The mouse was powerless in the cat's claws.* **–pow′er·less·ness,** *NOUN.*

power plant, a building with machinery for generating electric power.

power surge, a large, sudden, brief increase in the amount of current in an electric circuit. A power surge can damage electrical equipment.

pow·wow (pou′wou′), *NOUN.*

1 a spiritual ceremony of the North American Indians, usually accompanied by feasting and dancing, performed for the cure of disease, success in hunting, or for other purposes.
2 a council or conference of or with North American Indians.
3 any conference or meeting.

a young dancer at a **powwow**

Word Story

Powwow comes from an American Indian word meaning "to tell the future by dreams." American Indian spiritual leaders often used their dreams this way, especially during ceremonies and conferences.

pp., an abbreviation of **pages¹.**
pr., an abbreviation of **pair.**
PR, an abbreviation of **Puerto Rico.**
prac·ti·cal (prak′tə kəl), *ADJECTIVE.*
1 suitable for an actual situation; useful: *An outdoor swimming pool is more practical in Florida than in Minnesota.*
2 having good sense: *A practical person does not spend time and money foolishly.*

a	hat	ė	term	ô	order	ch	child	⎧a in about
ā	age	i	it	oi	oil	ng	long	⎪e in taken
ä	far	ī	ice	ou	out	sh	she	ə⎨i in pencil
â	care	o	hot	u	cup	th	thin	⎪o in lemon
e	let	ō	open	ů	put	ᴛн	then	⎩u in circus
ē	equal	ò	saw	ü	rule	zh	measure	

practical joke, a trick or joke played on someone.

prac·ti·cal·ly (prak'tik lē), ADVERB.

1 almost; nearly: *Our house is around the corner, so we are practically home.*

2 really: *She is only a clerk, but she is in the store so much that she practically runs the business.*

3 in a practical way; in a useful way: *You must stop wishing and start thinking practically.*

prac·tice (prak'tis),

1 VERB. to do some act again and again to learn to do it well: *She practiced pitching the ball. I practice on the piano every day.*

2 NOUN. an action done many times over to gain skill: *Practice makes perfect.*

3 NOUN. a skill gained by experience or exercise: *He was out of practice at batting.*

4 VERB. to do usually; make a custom of: *Practice what you preach.*

5 NOUN. the usual way; custom: *It is the practice at weddings to toss rice or birdseed at the newly married couple.*

6 VERB. to work at a profession, art, or occupation: *to practice medicine.*

7 NOUN. the act of working at a profession: *She is engaged in the practice of law.*

8 NOUN. the business of a doctor or a lawyer: *The old doctor sold his practice to a younger doctor.*
❑ VERB **prac·tic·es, prac·ticed, prac·tic·ing.**

prair·ie (prâr'ē), NOUN. a large area of level or rolling land with grass but few or no trees. PLURAL **prair·ies.**

prairie dog, an animal like a woodchuck but smaller, usually about 12 to 20 inches long. Prairie dogs live in large burrows that they dig. A colony of them often contains hundreds of animals.

prairie schooner, a large covered wagon used in crossing the plains of North America before the railroads were built.

prairie dog — up to 20 inches long, including the tail

praise (prāz),

1 NOUN. the act of saying that someone or something is good: *Everyone heaped praise upon the winning team.*

2 VERB. to speak well of someone: *The coach praised the team for its fine playing.*

3 VERB. to worship in words or song: *to praise God.*
❑ VERB **prais·es, praised, prais·ing.**

praise·wor·thy (prāz'wėr'ᴛʜē), ADJECTIVE. deserving praise: *praiseworthy deeds.*

prance (prans), VERB.

1 to spring about on the hind legs: *Horses prance when they feel lively.*

2 to move or jump around proudly: *The children pranced about in their new Halloween costumes.*
❑ VERB **pranc·es, pranced, pranc·ing. –pranc'er,** NOUN.

prank (prangk), NOUN. a playful trick: *His favorite prank is to unplug all the lamps in the living room.*

pray (prā), VERB. to ask for something from God; speak to God in worship: *They prayed for God's help.* ❑ VERB **prays, prayed, pray·ing.** ■ Another word that sounds like this is **prey.**

prayer (prâr), NOUN.

1 the act of praying: *We knelt in prayer.*

2 words used in praying: *the Lord's Prayer.*

praying mantis. See **mantis.**

Word Power   pre-

The prefix **pre-** means "before" or "in advance." Prewar means **before** a war. To prepay means to pay **in advance.**

preach (prēch), VERB.

1 to speak on a religious subject; deliver a sermon: *Our minister preaches on Sunday morning.*

2 to persuade people that something is good or should be done: *The coach was always preaching about getting enough sleep, vegetables, exercise, and fresh air.*
❑ VERB **preach·es, preached, preach·ing.**

preach·er (prē'chər), NOUN. someone who preaches; minister.

pre·cau·tion (pri kȯ'shən), NOUN. something you do to keep something bad from happening: *Locking doors is a precaution against thieves.*

pre·cede (prē sēd'), VERB. to go or come before: *The letter A precedes B in the alphabet. The band preceded the floats in the parade.* ❑ VERB **pre·cedes, pre·ced·ed, pre·ced·ing.**

pre·ced·ing (prē sē'ding), ADJECTIVE. going before or coming before: *Turn back and look on the preceding page for the answer.*

pre·cinct (prē'singkt), NOUN. a part or district of a city: *a police precinct, an election precinct.*

pre·cious (presh'əs), ADJECTIVE.

1 having great value. Gold and silver are often called **precious metals.** Diamonds and rubies are **precious stones.**

2 loved a great deal; dear: *He is my precious child.*

pre·cip·i·ta·tion (pri sip'ə tā'shən), NOUN.

1 the water that falls to the earth in the form of rain, snow, sleet, or hail: *The forecast is for some precipitation this afternoon.*

2 the amount of water that falls from the air in a certain time.

pre·cise (pri sīs′), ADJECTIVE. exact; accurate; definite: *Their precise directions helped us find our way easily.* —**pre·cise·ly,** ADVERB.

pre·ci·sion (pri sizh′ən), NOUN. the condition of being exact; accuracy: *The archer shoots with precision.*

pred·a·tor (pred′ə tər), NOUN. an animal that lives by killing and eating other animals. Tigers, bears, hawks, and wolves are predators.

This **predator** is chasing his lunch.

pred·a·to·ry (pred′ə tôr′ē), ADJECTIVE. living by killing and eating other animals.

pre·dic·a·ment (pri dik′ə mənt), NOUN. an unpleasant or difficult situation: *She was in a predicament when she missed the last bus home.*

pred·i·cate (pred′ə kit), NOUN. the word or words in a sentence that tell what is said about the subject. In "Dogs bark," "The dogs dug holes," and "The dogs are beagles," *bark, dug holes,* and *are beagles* are all predicates.

pre·dict (pri dikt′), VERB. to tell about something before it happens; forecast: *The Weather Service predicts rain for tomorrow.* ❑ VERB **pre·dicts, pre·dict·ed, pre·dict·ing.** —**pre·dict′a·ble,** ADJECTIVE.

pre·dic·tion (pri dik′shən), NOUN. something predicted; prophecy: *The official predictions about the weather often come true.*

pre·dom·i·nant (pri dom′ə nənt), ADJECTIVE.
1 having more power, authority, or influence than others; superior: *The United States has become the predominant nation in the Western Hemisphere today.*
2 most noticeable: *Green was the predominant color in the forest.*
—**pre·dom′i·nant·ly,** ADVERB.

pref·ace (pref′is), NOUN. an introduction to a book or speech: *My history book has a preface written by the author.*

pre·fer (pri fėr′), VERB. to like something better: *She prefers swimming to fishing. I will come later, if you prefer.* ❑ VERB **pre·fers, pre·ferred, pre·fer·ring.**

pref·er·a·ble (pref′ər ə bəl), ADJECTIVE. more desirable. —**pref′er·a·bly,** ADVERB.

pref·er·ence (pref′ər əns), NOUN.
1 the act or attitude of liking one thing better than another: *My preference is for roast beef rather than leg of lamb.*
2 something preferred; your first choice: *My preference in reading is a mystery story.*

pre·fix (prē′fiks), NOUN. a syllable, syllables, or word put at the beginning of a word to change its meaning or make another word. Some examples are *pre-* in *prepaid, under-* in *underline, dis-* in *disappear, un-* in *unlike,* and *re-* in *reopen.* ❑ PLURAL **pre·fix·es.**

preg·nant (preg′nənt), ADJECTIVE. having one or more unborn babies growing inside the body.

pre·his·to·ric (prē′hi stôr′ik), ADJECTIVE. of or belonging to times before histories were written: *Prehistoric peoples used stone tools.* ■ See the Synonym Study at **ancient.**

prej·u·dice (prej′ə dis), NOUN.
1 an unreasonable dislike of someone because of his or her race, religion, gender, and so on.
2 an opinion formed without taking time and care to judge fairly: *Your dislike of broccoli is just prejudice; you've never even tried it.*

pre·lim·i·nar·y (pri lim′ə ner′ē), ADJECTIVE. coming before the main business; leading to something more important: *After some preliminary announcements, the speaker was introduced.*

pre·ma·ture (prē′mə chùr′ or prē′mə tùr′), ADJECTIVE. before the proper time; too soon: *The baby was premature. Their arrival an hour before the party began was premature.* —**pre′ma·ture′ly,** ADVERB.

prem·is·es (prem′ə səz), NOUN PLURAL. a house or building with its grounds.

pre·mi·um (prē′mē əm), NOUN.
1 a reward; prize: *Some magazines give premiums for getting new subscriptions.*
2 the money paid for insurance: *I pay premiums on my life insurance four times a year.*

pre·oc·cu·pied (prē ok′yə pīd), ADJECTIVE. having your attention focused on one thing so that you don't notice other things: *She was too preoccupied to hear the doorbell.*

pre·paid (prē pād′), VERB.
1 the past tense of **prepay:** *We prepaid our airline tickets.*
2 the past participle of **prepay:** *I have prepaid the bill for the books we ordered.*

a	hat	ė	term	ô	order	ch	child		a in about
ā	age	i	it	oi	oil	ng	long		e in taken
ä	far	ī	ice	ou	out	sh	she	ə ⟨	i in pencil
â	care	o	hot	u	cup	th	thin		o in lemon
e	let	ō	open	ù	put	ᴛʜ	then		u in circus
ē	equal	ò	saw	ü	rule	zh	measure		

P

prep·a·ra·tion (prep/ə rā/shən), NOUN.
1 the act of getting something ready: *I sharpened the knife in preparation for carving the meat.*
2 something done to get ready: *Our preparations for the game included a lot of practice.*
3 a specially made medicine, food, or mixture of any kind: *There is a new preparation for removing rust.*

pre·pare (pri pâr/), VERB. to get something ready; to get yourself ready for doing something: *We all helped prepare a picnic lunch. When the bell rings, we all prepare to go outside.* ❑ VERB **pre·pares, pre·pared, pre·par·ing.**

pre·pay (prē pā/), VERB. to pay for something in advance: *to prepay a bill.* ❑ VERB **pre·pays, pre·paid, pre·pay·ing. –pre·pay/ment,** NOUN.

prep·o·si·tion (prep/ə zish/ən), NOUN. a word that shows the relationship between a noun and some other word, such as a verb, adjective, or noun. In the following sentence, *from, to, by,* and *for* are prepositions: *Go from weak to strong by exercising for just a few minutes each day.*

Usage Note

Some people believe that sentences should not end with **prepositions.** Although many famous writers disagree with this rule, it is a good idea to follow it in formal writing. Wait until you are famous to break it.

pre·school (prē/skül/),
1 ADJECTIVE. before the age of going to regular school: *This toy is good for preschool children.*
2 NOUN. a school for children below the age of five: *My three-year-old sister is in preschool.*

pre·scribe (pri skrib/), VERB. to say or write down what medicine or treatment someone who is sick should have: *The doctor prescribed penicillin.*
❑ VERB **pre·scribes, pre·scribed, pre·scrib·ing.**

pre·scrip·tion (pri skrip/shən), NOUN.
1 a doctor's written order for preparing and using a medicine: *The doctor wrote a prescription for my cough.*
2 a medicine prescribed by a doctor and prepared by a pharmacist.

pres·ence (prez/ns), NOUN.
1 the fact or condition of being present somewhere: *I just learned of their presence in the city.*
2 the place where someone is: *The messenger was admitted to the king's presence.*

pres·ent[1] (prez/nt),
1 ADJECTIVE. here; not absent: *Every member of the class was present. Oxygen is present in the air.*
2 ADJECTIVE. at this time: *the present ruler, present prices.*
3 NOUN. **the present,** now; this time: *That is enough for the present.*
4 ADJECTIVE. expressing something happening or existing now: *the present tense of a verb.*

pre·sent[2] (pri zent/ *for verb;* prez/nt *for noun*),
1 VERB. to give: *We presented flowers to our teacher.*
2 NOUN. a gift; something given: *a birthday present.*
3 VERB. to introduce someone to a person or to a group: *Ms. Smith, may I present Mr. Brown?*
4 VERB. to show, tell, read, or act out something: *Our class wrote and presented a play.*
❑ VERB **pre·sents, pre·sent·ed, pre·sent·ing.**

presenting flowers to a medal winner

pres·en·ta·tion (prez/n tā/shən *or* prē/zen tā/shən), NOUN.
1 the act of giving; delivering: *the presentation of a gift.*
2 something that is presented to an audience: *I gave a presentation to the class about my trip to Mexico.*

pres·ent·ly (prez/nt lē), ADVERB.
1 at the present time; now: *She is presently in fourth grade.*
2 before long; soon: *I will do the dishes presently.*

pres·er·va·tion (prez/ər vā/shən), NOUN.
1 the act of preserving something or keeping it safe: *Doctors work for the preservation of our health.*
2 the condition of being preserved: *Egyptian mummies have been in a state of preservation for thousands of years.*

pre·serv·a·tive (pri zėr/və tiv), NOUN. any substance that will prevent decay or injury: *Paint is a preservative for wood surfaces.*

pre·serve (pri zėrv/),
1 VERB. to keep something from harm or change; protect: *Good nutrition helps to preserve your health.*
2 VERB. to prepare food to keep it from spoiling. Boiling with sugar, salting, smoking, and pickling are different ways of preserving food.
3 NOUN. **preserves,** fruit cooked with sugar and sealed from the air: *homemade plum preserves.*
4 NOUN. a place where wild animals, fish, or trees and plants are protected: *People are not allowed to hunt in that preserve.*
❑ VERB **pre·serves, pre·served, pre·serv·ing. –pre·serv/er,** NOUN.

pre·side (pri zīd′), VERB. to be in charge of a meeting: *Our principal will preside at our election of school officers. When the principal cannot attend the meeting, the assistant principal presides.* ❑ VERB **pre·sides, pre·sid·ed, pre·sid·ing.**

pres·i·den·cy (prez′ə dən sē), NOUN.
1 the office of president: *She was elected to the presidency of the Junior Club.*
2 the time during which a president is in office: *The United States entered World War II in the presidency of Franklin D. Roosevelt.* ❑ PLURAL **pres·i·den·cies.**

Did You Know?

Grover Cleveland was the only person to hold the **presidency** of the United States two different times. He was elected in 1884 and again in 1892. Benjamin Harrison was elected in 1888. This makes Grover Cleveland the 22nd and the 24th President of the United States.

pres·i·dent (prez′ə dənt), NOUN.
1 the chief officer of a company, college, society, or club.
2 **President,** the highest officer of a republic.

Word Story

President comes from a Latin word meaning "to sit in front." If a group is seated together at a public event, the leaders will be sitting at the front.

pres·i·den·tial (prez′ə den′shəl), ADJECTIVE. of or about a president or presidency: *a presidential election, a presidential candidate.*

Presidents' Day, the third Monday in February, celebrated as a holiday in some states to commemorate the birthdays of Abraham Lincoln and George Washington.

Presidents' Day

press (pres),
1 VERB. to push something with steady force: *Press the button to ring the bell.*
2 VERB. to squeeze; squeeze out: *Press all the juice from the oranges.*

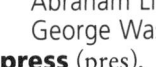

3 VERB. to make something smooth with a hot iron: *I pressed my shirt to get the wrinkles out.*
4 VERB. to hold someone or something close to you; hug: *I pressed the puppy to my chest.*
5 NOUN. pressure; push: *The press of many duties keeps the principal very busy.*
6 NOUN. a machine for pressing, squeezing, and so on: *a cider press.*
7 NOUN. a printing press.
8 NOUN PLURAL. **the press,** newspapers, magazines, radio, and TV, and the people who report for them: *The mayor's speech was reported by the press.*
9 VERB. to keep asking somebody to do something: *We pressed our guests to stay until the snow stopped.*
10 NOUN. (in basketball) a defensive system in which players guard their opponents very closely. ❑ VERB **press·es, pressed, press·ing;** PLURAL **press·es.**

press·ing (pres′ing), ADJECTIVE. needing immediate action or attention; urgent: *A person with a broken leg is in pressing need of a doctor's help.*

pres·sure (presh′ər),
1 NOUN. the continued action of a weight or force: *The small box was flattened by the pressure of the heavy book on it.*
2 NOUN. the force per unit of area: *There is a pressure of 20 pounds to the square inch on this tire.*
3 NOUN. stress or strain: *Some people don't work well under pressure.*
4 NOUN. a strong influence: *I was under pressure from the others to change my mind.*
5 VERB. to force or urge someone to do something: *The car dealer tried to pressure my parents into buying a car.* ❑ VERB **pres·sures, pres·sured, pres·sur·ing.**

pres·tige (pre stēzh′), NOUN. reputation or respect that someone gets because of what is known about his or her abilities or achievements: *Her prestige rose when her classmates learned that she knew how to ski.*

pre·sume (pri züm′), VERB. to suppose that something is true without proving it: *You'll play out of doors, I presume, if there is sunshine.* ❑ VERB **pre·sumes, pre·sumed, pre·sum·ing.**

pre·tend (pri tend′),
1 VERB. to make believe something, just for fun: *Let's pretend that we are grown-ups.*
2 VERB. to claim falsely that something is true when it is not: *I pretended to like the meal so that my host would be pleased.*
3 ADJECTIVE. imaginary; make-believe: *The child had a pretend horse.* ❑ VERB **pre·tends, pre·tend·ed, pre·tend·ing.** —**pre·tend′er,** NOUN.

pre·text (prē′tekst), NOUN. a false reason concealing the real reason; misleading excuse: *She did not go, on the pretext of being too busy.*

a	hat	ė	term	ô	order	ch	child	⎧a in about
ā	age	i	it	oi	oil	ng	long	e in taken
ä	far	ī	ice	ou	out	sh	she	ə⎨i in pencil
â	care	o	hot	u	cup	th	thin	o in lemon
e	let	ō	open	ů	put	₮H	then	⎩u in circus
ē	equal	ȯ	saw	ü	rule	zh	measure	

P

pret·ty (prit′ē),
1 ADJECTIVE. pleasing; attractive; good to see or hear: *a pretty dress, a pretty face.* ■ See the Synonym Study at **beautiful.**
2 ADVERB. fairly; rather: *It is pretty late.*
❑ ADJECTIVE **pret·ti·er, pret·ti·est. −pret′ti·ly,** ADVERB. **−pret′ti·ness,** NOUN.

pret·zel (pret′səl), NOUN. a kind of bread, usually in the shape of a knot or stick, salted on the outside.

Word Story

Pretzel comes from a Latin word meaning "an arm." The knot-shaped pretzel looks like a pair of crossed arms. The English word came from a German form of the Latin, so it looks German.

prev·a·lent (prev′ə lənt), ADJECTIVE. widespread; in general use; common: *Colds are prevalent in the winter.*

pre·vent (pri vent′), VERB.
1 to keep someone from doing something: *Illness prevented me from doing my work.* ■ See the Synonym Study at **stop.**
2 to keep something from happening: *Vaccination prevents smallpox.*
❑ VERB **pre·vents, pre·vent·ed, pre·vent·ing.** **−pre·vent′a·ble** or **pre·vent′i·ble,** ADJECTIVE.

pre·ven·tion (pri ven′shən), NOUN. the act of preventing: *the prevention of fire.*

pre·ven·tive (pri ven′tiv), ADJECTIVE. able to prevent something: *Preventive measures were taken to stop the spread of the disease.*

pre·view (prē′vyü′),
1 NOUN. an advance showing of scenes from a movie, play, or television show.
2 VERB. to view something ahead of time: *My teacher previewed the movie before showing it to the class.*
❑ VERB **pre·views, pre·viewed, pre·view·ing.**

pre·vi·ous (prē′vē əs), ADJECTIVE. happening or being before some act or event; earlier: *Our team had more wins in the previous season.*
−pre′vi·ous·ly, ADVERB.

pre·writ·ing (prē′rī′ting), NOUN. the creation and organization of ideas before beginning your story or essay.

prey (prā), NOUN.
1 an animal that is hunted or seized for food by another animal: *Mice and birds are the prey of cats.*
2 the habit of hunting and killing other animals for food: *Hawks are birds of prey.*
❑ PLURAL **prey.** ■ Another word that sounds like this is **pray.**

prey on or **prey upon,** IDIOM. to hunt or kill animals for food: *Cats prey on mice.*

price (prīs),
1 NOUN. the amount of money someone must pay to buy something; cost: *The price of this cap is $8.*

2 VERB. to put a price on something: *The hat was priced at $18.*
3 VERB. to find out the price of something: *Mother is pricing cars.*
4 NOUN. what must be given or done to get something else: *The Pilgrims paid a heavy price for coming to America; half of them died during the first winter.*
❑ VERB **pric·es, priced, pric·ing.**

price·less (prīs′lis), ADJECTIVE. extremely valuable: *Many museums have collections of priceless works of art.*

a **priceless** painting

prick (prik),
1 NOUN. a little hole or mark in something that is made by a sharp point.
2 VERB. to make a little hole or mark on something with a sharp point: *I pricked my finger on a thorn.*
3 NOUN. a sharp pain from something pricking you.
❑ VERB **pricks, pricked, prick·ing.**

prick·le (prik′əl),
1 NOUN. a small, sharp point; thorn.
2 VERB. to feel a prickly or tingling feeling: *My skin prickled as I listened to the scary story.*
❑ VERB **prick·les, prick·led, prick·ling.**

prick·ly (prik′lē), ADJECTIVE.
1 having many sharp points or thorns: *a prickly nettle, a prickly porcupine.*
2 sharp and stinging: *a prickly skin rash.*
❑ ADJECTIVE **prick·li·er, prick·li·est. −prick′li·ness,** NOUN.

prickly pear, the pear-shaped fruit of a kind of cactus. Prickly pears are eaten by people and cattle.

prickly pear

pride (prīd), NOUN.
1 a sense of your own worth; self-respect.
2 the pleasure or satisfaction in something that you have done: *I take pride in a hard job well done.*
3 too high an opinion of yourself: *Pride goes before a fall.*
■ Another word that sounds like this is **pried.**

pride yourself on, IDIOM. to be proud of: *I pride myself on being a good student.* ❑ VERB **prides, prid·ed, prid·ing.**

pried (prīd), VERB.
1 the past tense of **pry:** *I pried the window open with a screwdriver.*

2 the past participle of **pry:** *The window has been pried open.*
■ Another word that sounds like this is **pride.**

priest (prēst), NOUN. a clergyman or minister of some Christian churches.

pri·mar·i·ly (prī mer′ə lē), ADVERB. above all; chiefly; principally: *That student is primarily interested in science.*

pri·mar·y (prī′mer′ē),
1 ADJECTIVE. chief; first in importance: *The primary reason for eating a balanced diet is good health.*
2 NOUN. an election in which members of a political party choose candidates for office. Primaries are held before the regular election.
❏ PLURAL **pri·mar·ies.**

primary accent or **primary stress,**
1 the strongest accent in the pronunciation of a word.
2 a mark (′) used to show this.

primary color, any of a group of colors which, when mixed together, can produce all other colors. Red, yellow, and blue are primary colors.

primary school, the first three or four grades of elementary school.

primary teeth, the first teeth you get as a baby. Between the ages of five and seven, permanent teeth take the place of primary teeth.

pri·mate (prī′māt), NOUN. one of a group of mammals that have the most highly developed brains and hands with thumbs that can be used to hold on to things. Apes, monkeys, and human beings are primates.

prime[1] (prīm), ADJECTIVE.
1 first in rank; chief: *The town's prime need is a new school.*
2 first in quality; first-rate; excellent: *We had a piece of prime beef for dinner.*

prime[2] (prīm), NOUN. the best part; best time; best condition: *A person of forty is in the prime of life.*

prime[3] (prīm), VERB. to prepare something by putting something in it or on it. Wood is primed with a special first coat of paint so that the final coat will not soak in. ❏ VERB **primes, primed, prim·ing. –prim′er,** NOUN.

prime minister, the chief official in some governments. Canada and Great Britain have prime ministers.

prime number, a number that can be divided without a remainder only by itself and 1. The numbers 2, 3, 5, 7, and 11 are prime numbers.

prime time, the hours during the evening, usually thought to be from 7 to 11 P.M., when the greatest number of people are watching television.

prim·i·tive (prim′ə tiv), ADJECTIVE.
1 of or about times long ago: *Primitive people often lived in caves.*

2 very simple, such as was common early in human history: *A primitive way of making fire is by rubbing two sticks together.*
–prim′i·tive·ness, NOUN.

prim·rose (prim′rōz′), NOUN. a plant having bell-shaped or funnel-shaped flowers of various colors, often yellow or pink.

prince (prins), NOUN. a son of a king or queen; son of a king's or queen's son. **–prince′ly,** ADVERB.

Prince Ed·ward Is·land (prins′ ed′wərd ī′lənd), a province in eastern Canada. **–Prince Edward Islander.**

prin·cess (prin′ses or prin′sis), NOUN.
1 a daughter of a king or queen; daughter of a king's or queen's son.
2 a wife or widow of a prince.
❏ PLURAL **prin·cess·es.**

princess
Princess Diana

Princess Diana was not a storybook princess. She worked tirelessly for charity, including helping AIDS patients and working to ban land mines.

prin·ci·pal (prin′sə pəl),
1 NOUN. someone who is the head of a school.
2 ADJECTIVE. main; chief; most important: *Chicago is the principal city of Illinois.* ■ See the Synonym Study at **main.**
3 NOUN. a sum of money on which interest is paid. ■ See the Usage Note at **principle.**

prin·ci·pal·ly (prin′sə pə lē), ADVERB. for the most part; above all; chiefly.

a hat	ė term	ô order	ch child	⎧a in about
ā age	i it	oi oil	ng long	⎪e in taken
ä far	ī ice	ou out	sh she	ə⎨i in pencil
â care	o hot	u cup	th thin	⎪o in lemon
e let	ō open	ú put	₮H then	⎩u in circus
ē equal	ȯ saw	ü rule	zh measure	

P

prin·ci·ple (prin′sə pəl), NOUN.
1 a basic truth or law; truth that is a foundation for other truths: *the principle of free speech.*
2 a rule of action or conduct: *I make it a principle to save some money each week.*
3 a law of science explaining how something works: *the principle of an electric motor.*

Usage Note

Principle and **principal** are often confused because they sound alike. They are spelled similarly because they both come from the same Latin word that **prince** does. A way to remember how to spell them is from their meanings, **principle**, means a basic truth or rule, and it ends in *-le* like *rule.* All other possible meanings—important, chief person, head of a school, money—are spelled the other way, **principal**, and end in *-al.*

print (print),
1 VERB. to use a machine that makes many copies of words, pictures, diagrams, and the like, on paper. Books, magazines, newspapers, and pamphlets are printed.
2 VERB. See **publish.**
3 NOUN. words, pictures, or the like transferred onto paper: *The book had very large print.*
4 VERB. to make letters the way they look in print instead of connecting them: *Please print clearly.*
5 NOUN. a kind of cloth with a pattern pressed on it: *She has two dresses made of print.*
6 NOUN. a picture made in a special way; printed picture or design.
7 NOUN. a picture that is copied by photography from a painting.
8 NOUN. a footprint or fingerprint.
9 NOUN. a photograph produced from a negative.
   ❑ VERB **prints, print·ed, print·ing.**
in print, IDIOM.
1 in printed form: *She was excited to see her name in print in the magazine.*
2 still available for purchase from the publisher: *Check to see if that book is still in print.*
out of print, IDIOM. no longer sold by the publisher: *That book is out of print; check a used bookstore.*
print out, IDIOM. (of computers) to produce or display information in printed or readable form: *They needed to print out the database entries.*

print·er (prin′tər), NOUN.
1 someone whose business or work is printing.
2 a machine that prints, controlled by a computer.

print·ing (prin′ting), NOUN.
1 the production of books, newspapers, magazines, or pamphlets.
2 printed words, letters, and so on.
3 letters made like those in print.

printing press, a machine for printing, using large rollers and ink.

print·out (print′out′), NOUN. the printed output of a computer: *This printout lists the name and age of everyone in the class.*

pri·or (prī′ər), ADJECTIVE. coming before; earlier: *I can't go because I have a prior engagement.*

pri·or·i·ty (prī ôr′ə tē), NOUN.
1 something given attention before anything else: *The young couple's first priority was to find a decent place to live.*
2 quality of coming before in order or importance: *Fire engines, police cars, and ambulances have priority over other traffic.*
   ❑ PLURAL **pri·or·i·ties.**

prism (priz′əm), NOUN. a transparent solid object that separates white light into the colors of the rainbow.

pris·on (priz′n), NOUN. a public building in which people who have broken laws are locked up: *The convicted killer was sentenced to prison for life.* **−pris′on·like′,** ADJECTIVE.

prism

pris·on·er (priz′n ər), NOUN.
1 someone who is under arrest or held in a jail or prison.
2 someone taken by the enemy in war.

pris·sy (pris′ē), ADJECTIVE. too careful; too fussy.
   ❑ ADJECTIVE **pris·si·er, pris·si·est.**

pri·va·cy (prī′və sē), NOUN.
1 the condition of being away from other people: *in the privacy of your home.*
2 secrecy: *He told me his reasons in strict privacy.*

pri·vate (prī′vit),
1 ADJECTIVE. not for the public; for one person only or for a few special people: *a private road, a private house, a private letter.*
2 ADJECTIVE. personal; not public: *the private life of a king, a private opinion.*
3 ADJECTIVE. secret; confidential: *News reached her through private channels.*
4 ADJECTIVE. having no public office: *After many years as mayor, he enjoyed being a private citizen.*
5 NOUN. a military rank. See the chart on page 550.
   −pri′vate·ly, ADVERB.
in private, IDIOM. secretly: *The rebels met in private to plot against the government.*

pri·va·teer (prī′və tir′), NOUN. an armed ship owned by civilians. Formerly, the United States government commissioned privateers to attack and capture enemy ships.

priv·i·lege (priv′ə lij), NOUN. a special right, advantage, or favor that someone has: *My sister has the privilege of driving the family car.*

prize¹ (prīz),
1 NOUN. something you win for doing something well; reward: *Prizes will be given for the best stories.*
2 ADJECTIVE. given as a prize: *He saved the prize money for his college education.*
3 ADJECTIVE. worthy of a prize: *prize vegetables.*

prize² (prīz), VERB. to value something highly: *She prizes her new bicycle.* ❑ VERB **priz·es, prized, priz·ing.**

pro (prō), NOUN or ADJECTIVE. a short form of **professional.** ❑ PLURAL **pros.**

Word Power   pro-

The prefix **pro-** means "in favor of" or "supporting." A **prodemocracy** movement is in favor of democracy. A **pro-bicycle** rally is supporting bicycles and bicycle riders.

prob·a·bil·i·ty (prob′ə bil′ə tē), NOUN.
1 the quality or fact of being likely or probable; good chance: *There is a probability of rain.*
2 something that is likely to happen: *A storm is a probability for tomorrow.*
❑ PLURAL **prob·a·bil·i·ties.**

prob·a·ble (prob′ə bəl), ADJECTIVE.
1 likely to happen: *Cooler weather is probable after this shower.*
2 likely to be true: *Something he ate is the probable cause of his upset stomach.*

prob·a·bly (prob′ə blē), ADVERB. more likely than not.

pro·ba·tion (prō bā′shən), NOUN.
1 the system of letting criminals out of prison early as long as they stay out of trouble: *He can't leave the state while he is on probation.*
2 a time for testing, especially for new employees who are on probation so that employers can make sure that he or she is the right person for the job.

probe (prōb),
1 VERB. to examine something thoroughly; investigate: *I probed my memory for her name.*
2 NOUN. a thorough examination; investigation: *The governor ordered a probe of illegal gambling.*
3 NOUN. a slender device for exploring something. A doctor or dentist uses a probe to explore the depth or direction of a wound or cavity.
4 VERB. to examine something with a probe.
5 NOUN. a spacecraft carrying scientific devices to record or report back information about planets or other objects in outer space: *a lunar probe.*
❑ VERB **probes, probed, prob·ing.**

prob·lem (prob′ləm), NOUN.
1 a question or situation, especially a difficult one: *Poverty is a national problem. I have a problem with my foot.* ■ See the Synonym Study at **mystery.**

2 something you have to work out the answer for: *I have two more math problems to do.*

pro·ce·dure (prə sē′jər), NOUN. a way of doing something: *What's your procedure for making bread?*

pro·ceed (prə sēd′), VERB.
1 to keep on doing something, especially after pausing for a short time: *I'm sorry about the interruption; please proceed with your story.*
2 to carry on any activity: *I proceeded to light the fire.*
❑ VERB **pro·ceeds, pro·ceed·ed, pro·ceed·ing.**

pro·ceed·ings (prə sē′dingz), NOUN.
1 the action in a case in a court of law.
2 a record of what was done at the meetings of a society or club.

pro·ceeds (prō′sēdz′), NOUN PLURAL. the money you get from a sale or some other activity: *The proceeds from the school play will be used to buy a new curtain for the stage.*

proc·ess (pros′es or prō′ses),
1 NOUN. the act of doing or making something by following a set of steps in order to achieve a desired result: *By what process is cloth made from wool?*
2 VERB. to treat or prepare something by some special method: *This cloth has been processed to make it waterproof.*
❑ PLURAL **proc·ess·es;** VERB **proc·ess·es, proc·essed, proc·ess·ing.**

pro·ces·sion (prə sesh′ən), NOUN. things or people that are marching or riding forward: *Traffic was held up to let a funeral procession go by.*

proc·es·sor (pros′es ər or prō′ses ər), NOUN.
1 the central processing unit of a computer, especially the part of this unit in which data are examined, compared, changed, and the like.
2 someone or something that processes: *She works as an order processor for a large company.*

a space **probe** high above the earth

a hat	ė term	ô order	ch child
ā age	i it	oi oil	ng long
ä far	ī ice	ou out	sh she
â care	o hot	u cup	th thin
e let	ō open	u̇ put	ŦH then
ē equal	ȯ saw	ü rule	zh measure

ə { a in about / e in taken / i in pencil / o in lemon / u in circus }

pro·claim (prə klām'), *verb.* to make something known publicly and officially; declare publicly: *The President proclaimed this week National Dog Week.*
❑ *verb* **pro·claims, pro·claimed, pro·claim·ing.**

proc·la·ma·tion (prok'lə mā'shən), *noun.* an official announcement: *The queen issued a proclamation that the war was over.*

pro·cure (prə kyür'), *verb.* to get something by effort: *to procure a position in a bank. The lawyer procured the prisoner's release.* ❑ *verb* **pro·cures, pro·cured, pro·cur·ing.**

prod (prod),
1 *verb.* to poke or jab with something pointed: *He prodded the donkey gently to get it to move.*
2 *verb.* to try to encourage someone to do something: *My parents keep prodding me to clean my room.*
3 *noun.* a poke; thrust: *That prod in the ribs hurt.*
4 *noun.* a stick with a sharp point; goad.
❑ *verb* **prods, prod·ded, prod·ding.**

prod·i·gy (prod'ə jē), *noun.* someone gifted with amazing brilliance or talent. ❑ *plural* **prod·i·gies.**

pro·duce (prə düs' *for verb;* prō'düs *for noun*),
1 *verb.* to make something out of raw materials: *This factory produces stoves.*
2 *verb.* to bring about; cause: *Hard work produces success.*
3 *verb.* to grow or bring forth something: *Some farmers produce wheat, corn, and soybeans. Hens produce eggs.*
4 *verb.* to bring something out into view; show: *Produce your proof. Our class produced a play.*
5 *noun.* farm products, especially fruits and vegetables.
❑ *verb* **pro·duc·es, pro·duced, pro·duc·ing.**

pro·duc·er (prə dü'sər), *noun.*
1 someone who produces, especially someone who makes or grows things or who provides a service.
2 someone in charge of presenting a play, a movie, or a TV or radio show.
3 a living thing that can make its own food from minerals, water, and sunlight. All green plants and some bacteria are producers.

prod·uct (prod'əkt), *noun.*
1 something that someone makes or grows. Cloth is a factory product. Grain is a farm product.
2 a number you get when you multiply two or more numbers together: *40 is the product of 5 and 8.*

pro·duc·tion (prə duk'shən), *noun.*
1 the act or process of producing; manufacture: *the production of cars.*
2 something that is produced: *the yearly production of a farm.*

pro·fes·sion (prə fesh'ən), *noun.*
1 an occupation that requires special education, such as law, medicine, teaching, or the ministry.

2 the people engaged in an occupation like this: *The medical profession favors this law.*

pro·fes·sion·al (prə fesh'ə nəl),
1 *adjective.* of or about a profession: *The surgeon showed great professional skill during the operation.*
2 *adjective.* working at a profession: *A lawyer or a doctor is a professional person.*
3 *noun.* someone who works at a profession; a professional man or woman: *This conference is for accountants and other finance professionals.*
4 *adjective.* making a business or trade of something that others do for pleasure: *They are professional musicians.*
—pro·fes'sion·al·ly, *adverb.*

pro·fes·sor (prə fes'ər), *noun.* a teacher of the highest rank in a college or university.

pro·fi·cient (prə fish'ənt), *adjective.* very skilled or talented in any art, science, or subject; expert: *She is very proficient in music.*

pro·file (prō'fīl), *noun.*
1 a side view, especially of the human face.
2 a brief description of someone or something: *The newspaper printed a profile on the new mayor.*

Do you recognize these **profiles**?

prof·it (prof'it),
1 *noun.* the money that someone who runs a business has left after all the bills and salaries are paid.
2 *verb.* to make a profit.
3 *noun.* an advantage; benefit: *What profit is there in worrying?*
4 *verb.* to benefit from something: *A wise person profits from mistakes.*
❑ *verb* **prof·its, prof·it·ed, prof·it·ing.** ■ Another word that sounds like this is **prophet.**
—prof'it·less, *adjective.*

prof·it·a·ble (prof'ə tə bəl), *adjective.*
1 yielding profit: *The sale held by the Girl Scouts was very profitable.*
2 useful: *We spent a profitable afternoon in the library working on our research projects. They didn't find the class profitable.*

pro·found (prə found′), ADJECTIVE.
1 felt strongly; very great: *profound despair, profound sympathy.*
2 going far deeper than what is easily understood: *a profound book, profound thoughts.*

pro·fuse (prə fyüs′), ADJECTIVE.
1 very abundant: *I gave profuse thanks for the help.*
2 spending or giving freely; extravagant: *He was profuse in his praise of the book.*

pro·gram (prō′gram),
1 NOUN. a list of items or events together with a list of those who appear in a performance.
2 NOUN. the items included in a performance: *The entire program was delightful.*
3 NOUN. what you see on television or hear on the radio: *a news program.*
4 NOUN. a plan for what is going to be done: *a business program, a government program.* ■ See the Synonym Study at **plan.**
5 NOUN. a set of instructions that tells a computer how to do a certain job.
6 VERB. to prepare a set of instructions for a computer, so that it will do a certain job.
❏ VERB **pro·grams, pro·grammed, pro·gram·ming.**

pro·gram·mer (prō′gram′ər), NOUN. someone who prepares a computer program or programs.

prog·ress (prog′res *for noun;* prə gres′ *for verb*),
1 NOUN. an advance or growth; improvement: *the progress of science. The class showed rapid progress in its studies.*
2 VERB. to get better at doing something; advance; improve: *We progress in learning step by step.*
3 NOUN. the act or process of moving forward: *We made rapid progress on our trip to Utah.*
4 VERB. to move forward; go ahead: *The building of the new school progressed quickly during the summer.*
❏ VERB **pro·gress·es, pro·gressed, pro·gress·ing.**

pro·gres·sion (prə gresh′ən), NOUN. the act or process of moving forward in steps or stages: *The exercises form a progression from easy to very hard.*

pro·gres·sive (prə gres′iv), ADJECTIVE.
1 making progress; advancing to something better: *a progressive nation.*
2 working for improvement or reform in government, religion, or business.
–**pro·gres′sive·ly,** ADVERB.

pro·hib·it (prō hib′it), VERB.
1 to not allow something by law or authority: *Picking flowers in the park is prohibited.*
2 to prevent: *Rainy weather and fog prohibited flying.*
❏ VERB **pro·hib·its, pro·hib·it·ed, pro·hib·it·ing.**

pro·hi·bi·tion (prō′ə bish′ən), NOUN.
1 the act of not allowing something: *The prohibition of swimming in the city's reservoirs is sensible.*
2 often, **Prohibition,** a law or laws against making or selling liquor.

proj·ect (proj′ekt *for noun;* prə jekt′ *for verb*),
1 NOUN. a plan for doing something; scheme: *The mayor proposed a project for better sewage disposal.*
2 NOUN. a special assignment: *a computer project.*
3 VERB. to make an image that can be seen on a surface: *Motion pictures are projected on the screen. The tree projects a shadow on the grass.*
4 VERB. to stick out: *The rocky cliff projects far out over the water.*
5 NOUN. a group of apartment buildings built and run as a unit, especially with government support: *They live in a big housing project.*
❏ VERB **pro·jects, pro·ject·ed, pro·ject·ing.**

His hands **project** a shadow that looks like a bird.

pro·jec·tile (prə jek′təl), NOUN. any object that can be thrown, hurled, or shot, such as a stone, a bullet, or a rocket.

pro·jec·tion (prə jək′shən), NOUN. a part that sticks out from something: *rocky projections on the face of a cliff.*

pro·jec·tor (prə jek′tər), NOUN. a device for projecting movies or a picture on a screen.

pro·long (prə lȯng′), VERB. to make something longer; extend: *Good health care may prolong a sick person's life.* ❏ VERB **pro·longs, pro·longed, pro·long·ing.**

prom (prom), NOUN. a formal dance given by a college or high school class.

prom·i·nent (prom′ə nənt), ADJECTIVE.
1 well-known; important: *a prominent citizen.*
2 easy to see: *I hung the picture in a prominent place in the living room.*
3 sticking out: *Frogs have prominent eyes.*
–**prom′i·nent·ly,** ADVERB.

a	hat	ė	term	ô	order	ch	child		
ā	age	i	it	oi	oil	ng	long		a in about
ä	far	ī	ice	ou	out	sh	she		e in taken
â	care	o	hot	u	cup	th	thin	ə	i in pencil
e	let	ō	open	u̇	put	ŦH	then		o in lemon
ē	equal	ȯ	saw	ü	rule	zh	measure		u in circus

prom·ise (prom′is),

1 *NOUN.* words that you say or write that tell someone that you will do or will not do something: *You can count on her to keep her promise.*

2 *VERB.* to say or write that you will do or will not do something: *They promised to stay till we came.*

3 *NOUN.* something that gives hope of success in the future: *She shows promise as a musician.*

4 *VERB.* to give people reason to expect something: *The rainbow promises fair weather.*

❏ *VERB* **prom·is·es, prom·ised, prom·is·ing.**

Synonym Study

Promise means to give your word to someone that you will or will not do something: *I promise to go to the zoo with you next Saturday.*

Agree can mean to promise to do something that someone else wants: *I agreed to play tennis with her.*

Pledge means to promise something in a sincere, solemn way: *She pledged twenty dollars to the animal shelter.*

Vow means to pledge with special seriousness: *I vowed never to forget her birthday again.*

Swear can mean to make a serious pledge or vow. The word often is used about a person who makes an official oath: *A person under oath swears to tell only the truth.*

prom·is·ing (prom′ə sing), *ADJECTIVE.* giving people hope that something or someone will turn out well: *The promising young painter has a great deal of talent. The weather looks promising for our trip to the beach.*

pro·mote (prə mōt′), *VERB.*

1 to raise someone to the next grade or level of importance: *Pupils who pass this test will be promoted to the next higher grade.*

2 to help something or someone grow or develop: *A kindly feeling toward other countries will promote peace.*

3 to try to sell something by advertising it: *A series of commercials promoted the new soap.*

❏ *VERB* **pro·motes, pro·mot·ed, pro·mot·ing.**

pro·mo·tion (prə mō′shən), *NOUN.*

1 an advance to a higher rank or level: *The clerk was given a promotion and an increase in salary.*

2 the act of helping something to grow or develop toward success: *They are active in the promotion of better health care.*

prompt (prompt),

1 *ADJECTIVE.* done at once; made without delay: *She gave the teacher a prompt answer.*

2 *ADJECTIVE.* quick to do something: *My science teacher is prompt in grading our exams.*

3 *VERB.* to cause someone to do something: *His curiosity prompted him to ask questions.*

4 *VERB.* to remind a speaker or actor of the next words if he or she forgets them: *Please prompt me if I forget my lines.*

❏ *VERB* **prompts, prompt·ed, prompt·ing.**
—prompt′ly, *ADVERB.* **—prompt′ness,** *NOUN.*

prone (prōn), *ADJECTIVE.*

1 likely or apt to do something: *He is prone to forget to do his chores.*

2 lying down, usually with the face down: *He lay prone on the bed, sound asleep.*

prong (prȯng), *NOUN.* one of the pointed ends of a fork or antler.

prong·horn (prȯng′hôrn′), *NOUN.* a very fast animal that looks like an antelope, found on the plains of western North America. ❏ *PLURAL* **prong·horn** or **prong·horns.**

pronghorn — up to 3½ feet high at the shoulder

pro·noun (prō′noun), *NOUN.* a word that takes the place of a noun or nouns. In "John and Mary did not go because they were sick," *they* is a pronoun used in the second part of the sentence to avoid repeating *John and Mary.*

pro·nounce (prə nouns′), *VERB.*

1 to say or make the sounds of a word; speak: *Pronounce your words clearly.*

2 to state something in a positive or official way: *The doctor pronounced her cured.*

❏ *VERB* **pro·nounc·es, pro·nounced, pro·nounc·ing.**

pro·nounced (prə nounst′), *ADJECTIVE.* very strong: *She has pronounced opinions on politics.*

pron·to (pron′tō), *ADVERB.* quickly; immediately; promptly: *They got the job done pronto.*

pro·nun·ci·a·tion (prə nun′sē ā′shən), *NOUN.*

1 a way of pronouncing. This book gives the pronunciation of each main word.

2 the act of saying or making the sounds of words; speaking.

proof (prüf),
1 *NOUN.* a way or means of showing that something is true: *Is what you say a guess or do you have proof?*
2 *ADJECTIVE.* of tested value against something: *This fabric is wrinkle-proof.*

Word Power   -proof

The suffix **-proof** means "safe from" or "able to resist." A fire**proof** box is **safe from** fire. A child**proof** bottle is **able to resist** a child's attempts to open it.

proof·read (prüf′rēd′),
VERB. to read something and mark mistakes like spelling errors that you need to correct. ❏ *VERB* **proof·reads, proof·read** (prüf′red′), **proof·read·ing.**
–**proof′read′er,** *NOUN.*

Proofreading Marks

≡ Make a capital.
/ Make a small letter.
∧ Add something.
ℓ Take out something.
⊙ Add a period.
New paragraph.

prop (prop),
1 *VERB.* to hold something up by placing a support under or against it or by leaning it against something: *He propped his skis against the garage wall. He was propped up in bed with pillows.*
2 *NOUN.* something or someone used to support something or someone else: *I used the book as a prop behind my painting.*
❏ *VERB* **props, propped, prop·ping.**

prop·a·gan·da (prop′ə gan′də), *NOUN.*
1 organized efforts to spread information that is often biased or inaccurate, in order to influence public opinion: *Government propaganda is most effective when there is no freedom of the press.*
2 information spread in this way: *During the war, the enemies spread propaganda.*

pro·pel (prə pel′), *VERB.* to drive or push something forward: *propelled by ambition. Rowers propel a boat with oars.* ■ See the Synonym Study at **push.**
❏ *VERB* **pro·pels, pro·pelled, pro·pel·ling.**

pro·pel·lant (prə pel′ənt), *NOUN.* explosive fuel that drives a rocket forward or upward when it is ignited.

pro·pel·ler (prə pel′ər), *NOUN.* the metal blades that turn rapidly on a shaft, making boats and aircraft move.

propeller beanie, a small cap with a propeller attached to the top. The propeller usually does not have a motor.

prop·er (prop′ər), *ADJECTIVE.*
1 right for the occasion; fitting: *Night is the proper time to sleep.*
2 in the strict sense of the word: *Puerto Rico is not part of the United States proper.*
3 decent; respectable: *proper conduct.*

proper fraction, a fraction with a numerator that is less than the denominator. For example, ¾ is a proper fraction.

prop·er·ly (prop′ər lē), *ADVERB.* in a proper, correct, or suitable manner: *Eat properly.*

proper noun, a word that names a particular person, place, or thing. *Maria, George, Chicago,* and *Monday* are proper nouns. Proper nouns always begin with capital letters.

prop·er·ty (prop′ər tē), *NOUN.*
1 something that someone owns; possession or possessions: *This house is her property.*
2 a piece of land: *He owns some property in Ohio.*
3 a special power that something has, or something that it can do. Since wood floats, we say that wood has the property of floating.
❏ *PLURAL* **prop·er·ties.**

proph·e·cy (prof′ə sē), *NOUN.* something told about the future, especially something believed to be directed by God. ❏ *PLURAL* **proph·e·cies.**

proph·e·sy (prof′ə sī), *VERB.*
1 to speak when or as if directed by God.
2 to tell what will happen in the future; foretell; predict: *The fortuneteller prophesied that I would have good luck in the future.*
❏ *VERB* **proph·e·sies, proph·e·sied, proph·e·sy·ing.**

proph·et (prof′it), *NOUN.*
1 a religious leader who claims to speak as directed by God: *the prophets of the Old Testament.*
2 someone who tells what will happen: *Don't be such a gloomy prophet.*
■ Another word that sounds like this is **profit.**

pro·por·tion (prə pôr′shən), *NOUN.*
1 the relation of two things; a size, number, or amount compared to another: *Mix water and orange juice in the proportions of three to one by adding three measures of water to every measure of orange juice.*
2 a proper relation between parts of something: *The dog's short legs were not in proportion to its long body.*
3 a part; portion: *A large proportion of Nevada is desert.*
4 **proportions, a** size; extent: *Canada has forests of huge proportions.* **b** dimensions: *The proportions of the furniture are too big for this small room.*

pro·pos·al (prə pō′zəl), *NOUN.*
1 a plan for doing something; scheme; suggestion: *The club will now hear this member's proposal.*
2 an offer of marriage: *She turned down the wicked prince's proposal.*

a	hat	ė	term	ô	order	ch	child	⟨ a in about
ā	age	i	it	oi	oil	ng	long	e in taken
ä	far	ī	ice	ou	out	sh	she	ə ⟨ i in pencil
â	care	o	hot	u	cup	th	thin	o in lemon
e	let	ō	open	u̇	put	ŦH	then	⟨ u in circus
ē	equal	o̊	saw	ü	rule	zh	measure	

P

pro·pose (prə pōz′), VERB.
1 to suggest a plan for doing something: *She proposed that we take turns using the computer.*
2 to intend to do something; plan: *She proposes to save half of all she earns.*
3 to make an offer of marriage to someone.
❏ VERB **pro·pos·es, pro·posed, pro·pos·ing.**

prop·o·si·tion (prop′ə zish′ən), NOUN. a plan to be considered; proposal: *She made a proposition to buy out her partner's interest in the store.*

pro·pri·e·tor (prə prī′ə tər), NOUN. an owner.

pro·pul·sion (prə pul′shən), NOUN.
1 a force or impulse that drives something forward: *Most large aircraft are powered by propulsion of jet engines.*
2 the act of driving something forward or onward.

prose (prōz), NOUN. the ordinary form of written language; language that is not poetry.

Word Story

Prose comes from a Latin word meaning "straightforward" or "direct." **Poetry,** in Latin as in English, often uses words in fancy or complicated ways. **Prose** is more direct, like a straight road compared to a winding one.

pros·e·cute (pros′ə kyüt), VERB. to bring someone before a court of law to face a criminal charge: *Reckless drivers will be prosecuted.* ❏ VERB
pros·e·cutes, pros·e·cut·ed, pros·e·cut·ing.

pros·e·cu·tion (pros′ə kyü′shən), NOUN.
1 the act or process of carrying on a lawsuit: *The prosecution will be stopped if the stolen money is returned.*
2 the lawyers who bring official charges against someone accused of a crime in a court of law.

pros·e·cu·tor (pros′ə kyü′tər), NOUN. the lawyer who takes charge of the government's side of a case against an accused person.

pros·pect (pros′pekt),
1 NOUN. the act of looking forward to something: *The prospect of a vacation in Hawaii is a very exciting one.*
2 NOUN. chance of getting something in the future: *Without a high school education the prospect of getting a good job is poor.*
3 VERB. to search or look for something: *They prospected for gold in California.*
4 NOUN. someone who may become a customer, buyer, or candidate: *The sales representative called on several prospects before she finally made a sale.*
❏ VERB **pros·pects, pros·pect·ed, pros·pect·ing.**

pro·spec·tive (prə spek′tiv), ADJECTIVE. expected; probable; likely to be: *a prospective customer, a prospective raise in pay.*

pros·pec·tor (pros′pek tər), NOUN. someone who explores or examines a region, looking for gold, oil, uranium, or other valuable resources.

pros·per (pros′pər), VERB. to be successful or wealthy. ❏ VERB **pros·pers, pros·pered, pros·per·ing.**

pros·per·i·ty (pros per′ə tē), NOUN. success; wealth: *a time of peace and prosperity.*

a lucky **prospector**

pros·per·ous (pros′pər əs), ADJECTIVE. successful; wealthy: *His mother is a prosperous banker.*

pro·tect (prə tekt′), VERB. to keep someone or something safe from harm or danger; defend; guard: *Proper food protects a person's health.*
▪ See the Synonym Study at **safe.** ❏ VERB **pro·tects, pro·tect·ed, pro·tect·ing.** —**pro·tec′tor,** NOUN.

pro·tec·tion (prə tek′shən), NOUN.
1 the act of keeping someone or something safe from harm; defense: *We have a large dog for our protection.*
2 something or someone that prevents damage: *A hat offers protection from the sun.*

pro·tec·tive (prə tek′tiv), ADJECTIVE.
1 protecting; defensive: *The hard protective covering of a turtle saves it from being eaten.*
2 preventing injury to nearby people: *Do not remove the protective device on this machine.*
—**pro·tec′tive·ness,** NOUN.

pro·tein (prō′tēn), NOUN. one of the substances that are necessary as nutrients for the growth and repair of the cells of animals and plants. Enzymes, hormones, and antibodies are proteins.

pro·test (prō′test *for noun;* prə test′ *for verb*),
1 NOUN. a strong statement that objects to something you think is bad or unfair: *They yielded only after protest.*
2 VERB. to make strong objections to something: *I protested against having to wash the dishes.*
3 VERB. to state firmly that something is true: *The accused speeder protested her innocence.*
❏ VERB **pro·tests, pro·test·ed, pro·test·ing.**
—**pro·test′er** or **pro·tes′tor,** NOUN.

Prot·es·tant (prot′ə stənt),
1 NOUN. a member of any of certain Christian churches that left the Roman Catholic Church.
2 ADJECTIVE. of or about Protestants or their religion.

pro·tist (prō′tist), NOUN. a living thing that has characteristics both of animals and of plants. Protists are usually one-celled. Amebas and many algae are protists.

pro·ton (prō′ton), NOUN. a tiny particle that carries a single positive electric charge. Protons are an essential part of the nuclei of all atoms.

pro·to·plasm (prō′tə plaz′əm), NOUN. living matter; the living substance of all plant, animal, and other cells. Protoplasm contains fats, proteins, and other complex molecules in a thick fluid.

pro·to·zo·an (prō′tə zō′ən), NOUN. a living thing that is like an animal but has only one cell. Protozoans cannot be seen without a microscope. Most protozoans live in water. They are not animals or plants but another kind of life called protists. Amebas and paramecia are protozoans. ❑ PLURAL **pro·to·zo·ans** or **pro·to·zo·a** (prō′tə zō′ə).

pro·trac·tor (prō trak′tər), NOUN. a tool for drawing or measuring angles. It is shaped like a half circle.

proud (proud), ADJECTIVE.
1 having pride in yourself or your achievements.
2 feeling pleasure or satisfaction in something that you have done: *I am proud to have been chosen to be class president.*
–proud′ly, ADVERB.

proud of, IDIOM. thinking well of yourself or of people or things that have something to do with you: *I am proud of my family. I am proud of my country.*

prove (prüv), VERB.
1 to show that something is true: *Prove your statement.*
2 to turn out to be: *The book proved interesting.* ❑ VERB **proves, proved, proved** or **prov·en, prov·ing.**

prov·en (prü′vən),
1 ADJECTIVE. known to be true, accurate, or good enough: *proven results, a proven leader.*
2 VERB. a past participle of **prove**: *You have proven me wrong.*

prov·erb (prov′ėrb′), NOUN. a short, wise saying used for a long time by many people. "Haste makes waste" is a proverb.

pro·vide (prə vīd′), VERB.
1 to give something that is needed or wanted; supply; furnish: *The school provides inexpensive lunches for students.*
2 to make plans for the future: *They saved and invested money to provide for their old age.*
3 to state something that must be done or happen: *Our club's rules provide that dues must be paid monthly.*
❑ VERB **pro·vides, pro·vid·ed, pro·vid·ing.**
–pro·vid′er, NOUN.

pro·vid·ed (prə vī′did), CONJUNCTION. on the condition that; if: *She will go provided her friends can go also.*

Prov·i·dence (prov′ə dəns), NOUN. the capital of Rhode Island.

prov·ince (prov′əns), NOUN. one of the main divisions of a country. Canada is divided into provinces instead of into states.

pro·vi·sion (prə vizh′ən), NOUN.
1 a statement that makes a condition: *Our apartment lease has a provision that no pets are allowed.*
2 the act of providing something; preparation: *They made provision for their children's education.*
3 **provisions,** a supply of food: *After a long winter the settlers were low on provisions.*

pro·voke (prə vōk′), VERB.
1 to make someone angry: *My comments provoked him.*
2 to bring about or cause something: *The senator's speech provoked much discussion.*
❑ VERB **pro·vokes, pro·voked, pro·vok·ing.**

prow (prou), NOUN. the pointed front part of a ship or boat; bow.

prowl (proul), VERB. to go about quietly and secretly, like an animal hunting or a thief looking for something to steal: *Many wild animals prowl at night.* ❑ VERB **prowls, prowled, prowl·ing.**
–prowl′er, NOUN.

a **prowling** cheetah

pru·dent (prüd′nt), ADJECTIVE. planning in a careful way; sensible: *Prudent people save part of their wages.* **–pru′dent·ly,** ADVERB.

prune[1] (prün), NOUN. a kind of sweet plum that is dried: *We had stewed prunes for breakfast.*

Word Story

Prune[1] comes from a Greek word meaning "plum." **Plum** comes from the same Greek word. Greeks thought of fresh plums and dried plums as the same thing, but in English different words developed for the different forms of this fruit.

a hat	ė term	ô order	ch child	⎧a in about
ā age	i it	oi oil	ng long	⎪e in taken
ä far	ī ice	ou out	sh she	ə⎨i in pencil
â care	o hot	u cup	th thin	⎪o in lemon
e let	ō open	ů put	ŦH then	⎩u in circus
ē equal	ȯ saw	ü rule	zh measure	

prune² (prün), *VERB.* to cut off parts of a tree or bush: *We pruned several branches from the top of our apple tree.* ❑ *VERB* **prunes, pruned, prun·ing.**

pry (prī), *VERB.* to raise or move something by force using a lever of some kind: *I used a large screwdriver to pry open the window.* ❑ *VERB* **pries, pried, pry·ing.**

P.S., an abbreviation of **postscript.**

psalm (säm), *NOUN.* a sacred song or poem, especially one of the Psalms of the Old Testament.

psy·chi·a·trist (sī kī/ə trist), *NOUN.* a doctor who treats mental illness and emotional disorders.

psy·cho·log·i·cal (sī/kə loj/ə kəl), *ADJECTIVE.* of or about the mind: *Doctors think his problem is psychological, not physical.* **–psy/cho·log/i·cal·ly,** *ADVERB.*

psy·chol·o·gy (sī kol/ə jē), *NOUN.* the science of the mind. Psychology deals with personal actions, emotions, and thoughts. **–psy·chol/o·gist,** *NOUN.*

pt., an abbreviation of **pint.** ❑ *PLURAL* **pt.** or **pts.**

ptar·mi·gan (tär/mə gən), *NOUN.* a plump bird that looks somewhat like a chicken, found in mountainous and cold regions. ❑ *PLURAL* **ptar·mi·gan** or **ptar·mi·gans.**

pter·o·dac·tyl (ter/ə dak/təl), *NOUN.* a flying reptile that had wings something like a bat's. Pterodactyls are extinct.

pterodactyl — wingspread up to 40 feet

pub·lic (pub/lik),
1 *NOUN.* everyone; all the people: *The public should be informed when there is danger of an epidemic.*
2 *ADJECTIVE.* of or for everyone; belonging to the people: *a public meeting, public libraries.*
3 *ADJECTIVE.* working in government in the service of the people: *a public official.*
4 *ADJECTIVE.* known to many or all; not private: *Though he tried to keep it secret, the actor's illness soon became public knowledge.*

public-address system, a set of devices made up of one or more microphones, amplifiers, and loudspeakers so that a large audience, as on a street or in an auditorium, can hear.

pub·li·ca·tion (pub/lə kā/shən), *NOUN.*
1 a book, newspaper, or magazine; anything that is published: *This newspaper is a weekly publication.*
2 the act of printing and selling books, newspapers, or magazines.

pub·lic·i·ty (pub lis/ə tē), *NOUN.* information given to the public so that they will know about something: *The new movie received favorable publicity in newspapers and on TV.*

pub·lic·ly (pub/lik lē), *ADVERB.*
1 in a public manner; openly: *The mayor admitted her error publicly.*
2 by the public: *The new park is a publicly supported project.*

public school, a free school supported by taxes.

pub·lish (pub/lish), *VERB.* to prepare and offer for sale a book, newspaper, magazine, or other printed material. ❑ *VERB* **pub·lish·es, pub·lished, pub·lish·ing.**

pub·lish·er (pub/li shər), *NOUN.* a person or company whose business is to produce and sell books, newspapers, magazines, or other printed material.

puck (puk), *NOUN.* the hard, black rubber disk that players use in the game of ice hockey.

puck·er (puk/ər), *VERB.* to pull something up into wrinkles or folds: *to pucker your brow, to pucker cloth in sewing.* ❑ *VERB* **puck·ers, puck·ered, puck·er·ing.**

pud·ding (pùd/ing), *NOUN.* a soft, cooked food that is usually sweet: *chocolate pudding, rice pudding.*

pud·dle (pud/l), *NOUN.*
1 a small pool of water, especially dirty water: *I stepped in a puddle of rain water.*
2 a small pool of any liquid: *a puddle of ink.*

pudg·y (puj/ē), *ADJECTIVE.* short and fat or thick: *The plump baby had pudgy little hands.* ❑ *ADJECTIVE* **pudg·i·er, pudg·i·est. –pudg/i·ness,** *NOUN.*

Pueb·la (pwe/blä), *NOUN.* a state in southeastern Mexico.

pueb·lo (pweb/lō), *NOUN.*
1 an Indian village in which homes are grouped together to form a large building which is several stories high. Pueblos are built of baked clay bricks and stone and usually have flat roofs.
2 **Pueblo,** a member of any Indian tribe in the southwestern United States and northern Mexico who live in pueblos.
❑ *PLURAL* **pueb·los.**

Word Story

Pueblo comes from a Spanish word meaning "village" and "people." When Spanish explorers found American Indians living in villages of impressive buildings, the explorers called these people after the villages.

Puer·to Ri·can (pwer′tə rē′kən),
  1 of or about Puerto Rico or its people.
  2 a person born or living in Puerto Rico.
Puer·to Ri·co (pwer′tə rē′kō), an island in the eastern part of the West Indies. It is protected by the United States, but it makes its own laws. *Abbreviation:* PR; *Capital:* San Juan.

Word Story

Puerto Rico comes from Spanish words meaning "port" and "rich." **Puerto Rico** was used at first for the island's main city and its harbor, because Spanish settlers hoped to become wealthy. Later on, people started calling the whole island Puerto Rico.

puff (puf),
  1 *VERB.* to breathe fast and hard: *She puffed as she climbed the stairs.*
  2 *VERB.* to give out short, quick blasts of air, smoke, and so on: *The steam engine puffed black smoke high into the air. Please don't puff smoke toward me.*
  3 *NOUN.* a short, quick blast: *A puff of wind blew my hat off.*
  4 *VERB.* to smoke: *He puffed a cigar.*
  5 *VERB.* to swell up: *My broken toe puffed up to twice its usual size.*
  ❑ *VERB* **puffs, puffed, pu·**

puf·fin (puf′ən), *NOUN.* a sea bird of northern waters, having a thick body, a large head, and a bill of several colors.

puff·y (puf′ē), *ADJECTIVE.* puffed out; swollen: *My eyes were puffy from crying.* ❑ *ADJECTIVE* **puff·i·er, puff·i·est.** **–puff′i·ness,** *NOUN.*

puffin — 12 to 15 inches long

pull (pul),
  1 *VERB.* to move something toward you, using force: *Pull the door open; don't push it.*
  2 *VERB.* to take hold of something with your fingers or a tool and tug it out: *to pull someone's hair, to pull at someone's sleeve.*
  3 *VERB.* to take hold of something with your fingers or a tool and take it from where it was: *She pulled out the nails with the claw of a hammer.*
  4 *VERB.* to move, especially with great effort: *Slowly the runner pulled ahead of the others in the race.*
  5 *VERB.* to tear or rip something: *The baby pulled the toy to pieces.*
  6 *VERB.* to stretch too far; strain: *I pulled a muscle in my leg while skiing.*
  7 *NOUN.* the act of pulling; tug: *The boy gave a pull at the rope.*

  8 *NOUN.* an effort of pulling; effort: *It was a hard pull to get up the hill.*
  ❑ *VERB* **pulls, pulled, pull·ing.**
pull in, *IDIOM.* to arrive: *They pulled in this morning.*
pull off, *IDIOM.* to do something successfully; succeed in: *No one thought he could pull off that dive, but he did!*
pull out, *IDIOM.* to leave: *What time does the train pull out? It pulled out of the station an hour ago.*
pull through, *IDIOM.* to get through a difficult or dangerous situation: *The doctor thinks that the patient will pull through.*
pull yourself together, *IDIOM.* to get control of your mind or energies: *I stopped crying and started to pull myself together.*

Synonym Study

Pull means to make something move toward you, or follow along behind you: *The tractor pulls a plow.*

Tug means to pull hard, sometimes stopping to rest between pulls: *She tugged at the door that was stuck.*

Jerk means to pull quickly and suddenly: *He jerked his arm away from the cage when the tiger came close.*

Drag means to pull something along the ground or floor: *I dragged the heavy chair across the room.*

Haul means to pull something big or heavy for a long distance: *A locomotive must be very powerful to haul that long line of boxcars.*

Tow means to pull something along behind a car or whatever you're riding in: *They towed a boat behind their car.*

See also the Synonym Study at **move**.

ANTONYM: push.

pul·ley (pul′ē), *NOUN.*
  1 a wheel with a groove in which a rope fits, that you can lift weights with. The pulley is a simple machine: *Our flag is raised to the top of a pole by a rope and two pulleys.*
  2 a set of such wheels used to increase the power applied.
  ❑ *PLURAL* **pul·leys.**

pull·o·ver (pul′ō′vər), *NOUN.* a sweater or shirt that you put on by pulling it over your head and shoulders.

a	hat	ė	term	ô	order	ch	child	a in about
ā	age	i	it	oi	oil	ng	long	e in taken
ä	far	ī	ice	ou	out	sh	she	ə { i in pencil
â	care	o	hot	u	cup	th	thin	o in lemon
e	let	ō	open	ù	put	ŦH	then	u in circus
ē	equal	ò	saw	ü	rule	zh	measure	

pulp (pulp), NOUN.
1 any soft, wet mass. Paper is made from wood that has been ground to a pulp.
2 the soft, juicy part of any fruit or vegetable.
3 the soft inner part of a tooth. It contains blood vessels and nerves.

pul·pit (pùl'pit), NOUN. a platform in a church where the minister stands to preach.

pul·sate (pul'sāt), VERB. to beat or throb. ❑ VERB **pul·sates, pul·sat·ed, pul·sat·ing. –pul·sa'tion,** NOUN.

pulse (puls), NOUN.
1 the beating of the arteries caused by the rush of blood that the heart pumps into them.
2 any regular, measured beat: *the pulse of an engine.*

pul·ve·rize (pul'və rīz'), VERB. to grind something to powder or dust. ❑ VERB **pul·ve·riz·es, pul·ve·rized, pul·ve·riz·ing.**

pu·ma (pyü'mə), NOUN. a large cat with brownish yellow fur. Pumas live in parts of North and South America. Other names for it are mountain lion, cougar, and panther. ❑ PLURAL **pu·mas.**

puma — up to 8 feet long, including the tail

pum·ice (pum'is), NOUN. a light, glassy rock having many tiny holes in it. Pumice comes from volcanoes and is used for grinding and polishing things.

pump (pump),
1 NOUN. a machine or device for making liquids or gases go into, through, or out of things. A gas pump makes gas flow from an underground storage tank into the tank of a vehicle.
2 VERB. to move liquids or gases with a pump: *We pump water from a well in our yard.*
3 VERB. to move like a pump does: *The heart pumps blood to all parts of the body.*
4 VERB. to pump air into: *Pump up the car's tires.*
❑ VERB **pumps, pumped, pump·ing.**

pum·per·nick·el (pum'pər nik'əl), NOUN. a kind of rye bread. It is dark and firm.

pump·kin (pump'kin), NOUN. a large, roundish, orange fruit that grows on a vine. Pumpkins are used for making pies and for jack-o'-lanterns.

pun (pun),
1 NOUN. the humorous use of a word where it can have different meanings. "We must all hang together or we shall all hang separately" is a famous pun by Benjamin Franklin.
2 VERB. to make a pun or puns.
❑ VERB **puns, punned, pun·ning.**

Word Story

Pun is a short word with a clear meaning, and you might expect it to have a simple word story. In fact, it appeared in English suddenly, about 300 years ago. No one knows where it came from.

punch¹ (punch),
1 VERB. to hit someone with your fist: *She punched him in the arm.*
2 NOUN. a quick blow: *He took a punch to the jaw.*
3 NOUN. a tool for making holes in something: *a leather punch.*
4 VERB. to make a hole in something: *The bus driver punched our tickets.*
❑ VERB **punch·es, punched, punch·ing;** PLURAL **punch·es. –punch'er,** NOUN.

punch² (punch), NOUN. a drink made of different liquids, often fruit juices, mixed together. ❑ PLURAL **punch·es.**

punching bag, a leather or plastic bag, usually hung from the ceiling. Punching bags are hit with the fists for exercise or to develop boxing skills.

punc·tu·al (pungk'chü əl), ADJECTIVE. prompt; exactly on time: *He is always punctual.* **–punc'tu·al·ly,** ADVERB.

punc·tu·ate (pungk'chü āt), VERB. to use periods, commas, and other marks in writing or printing to help make the meaning clear. ❑ VERB **punc·tu·ates, punc·tu·at·ed, punc·tu·at·ing. –punc'tu·a'tion** NOUN.

punctuation mark, a mark used in writing or printing to help make the meaning clear. Periods, commas, question marks, semicolons, and colons are punctuation marks.

punc·ture (pungk'chər),
1 NOUN. a hole made by something pointed: *A puncture made by a nail caused the flat tire.*
2 VERB. to make a hole in something: *A sharp rock punctured the bottom of the canoe.*
❑ VERB **punc·tures, punc·tured, punc·tur·ing.**

pun·ish (pun'ish), VERB. to cause pain or unhappiness to someone who did something wrong: *Pupils who don't behave in class may be punished by the teacher.* ❑ VERB **pun·ish·es, pun·ished, pun·ish·ing.**

pun·ish·a·ble (pun'i shə bəl), ADJECTIVE. requiring punishment: *Illegal parking is punishable by a fine of $10.*

pun·ish·ment (pun′ish mənt), NOUN. a penalty for doing something wrong or unlawful: *Her punishment for stealing was a year in prison.*

punk (pungk), NOUN. (informal)
1 a young hoodlum.
2 a young person who enjoys unusual behavior, hair styles, makeup, and clothing.

punt (punt),
1 VERB. (in football and soccer) to kick a ball before it touches the ground after dropping it.
2 NOUN. a kick made this way.
❏ VERB **punts, punt·ed, punt·ing. –punt′er,** NOUN.

pu·ny (pyü′nē), ADJECTIVE. weak; of less than usual size or strength: *One of the newborn puppies was so puny we feared it might not live.* ❏ ADJECTIVE **pu·ni·er, pu·ni·est. –pu′ni·ness,** NOUN.

pup (pup), NOUN.
1 a young dog; puppy.
2 a young fox, wolf, coyote, or seal.

pu·pa (pyü′pə), NOUN. the form of an insect while it is changing from a wormlike larva into an adult; chrysalis. Many pupae are enclosed in a tough case or cocoon and can't move about. A caterpillar becomes a pupa and then a butterfly or moth. ❏ PLURAL **pu·pae** (pyü′pē) or **pu·pas.**

pu·pil¹ (pyü′pəl), NOUN. someone who is learning in school or that someone else is teaching.

pu·pil² (pyü′pəl), NOUN. the center of the eye that looks like a black spot. Light enters your eyes through your pupils.

Word Story

Pupil² comes from a Latin word meaning "a little doll." The center of the eye was called this because when you look into the eye of another person you can see a tiny image of yourself.

pup·pet (pup′it), NOUN. a figure that looks like a person or animal. It is moved by wires, strings, or the hands.

pup·py (pup′ē), NOUN. a young dog; a baby dog.
❏ PLURAL **pup·pies.**

How many **puppies** do you see?

pur·chase (pėr′chəs),
1 VERB. to buy something: *We purchased a new car.*
2 NOUN. something that is bought: *That hat was a very good purchase.*
❏ VERB **pur·chas·es, pur·chased, pur·chas·ing. –pur′chas·er,** NOUN.

pure (pyür), ADJECTIVE.
1 not mixed with anything else; genuine: *He has a sweater made of pure wool.*
2 perfectly clean; not dirty: *pure water, pure air.*
3 nothing else than; mere: *They won by pure luck.*
4 with no evil; without sin: *a pure mind.*
❏ ADJECTIVE **pur·er, pur·est. –pure′ly,** ADVERB.

pur·i·fy (pyür′ə fī), VERB. to make pure: *Filters are used to purify water.* ❏ VERB **pur·i·fies, pur·i·fied, pur·i·fy·ing. –pur′i·fi·ca′tion,** NOUN.

Pur·i·tan (pyür′ə tən), NOUN. (in the 1500s and 1600s) a member of a religious group that wanted simpler forms of worship and stricter morals than other Protestants did. Many Puritans settled in New England.

pur·i·ty (pyür′ə tē), NOUN.
1 freedom from dirt or other substances; cleanness: *They tested the purity of the town's drinking water.*
2 freedom from evil; innocence: *Mother Teresa was a person of great goodness and purity.*

pur·ple (pėr′pəl),
1 NOUN. a dark color that is a mixture of red and blue.
2 ADJECTIVE. having this color: *purple grapes.*

pur·plish (pėr′plish), ADJECTIVE. somewhat purple.

pur·pose (pėr′pəs), NOUN. a reason for something that someone wants to do: *Her purpose in coming to see us was to ask for a donation to the hospital fund.*

on purpose, IDIOM. with a purpose; not by accident: *He tripped me on purpose.*

purr (pėr),
1 NOUN. a low, murmuring sound that a cat makes when it is pleased.
2 VERB. to make this sound.
❏ VERB **purrs, purred, purr·ing.** ▪ Another word that can sound like this is **per.**

purse (pėrs), NOUN.
1 a woman's handbag.
2 a small bag or container to hold coins, usually carried in a handbag or pocket.

pur·sue (pər sü′), VERB.
1 to follow something or someone in order to catch or catch up to it; chase: *The dogs pursued the rabbit.*
2 to keep on doing or trying to do something: *She pursued the study of music for four years.* ❏ VERB **pur·sues, pur·sued, pur·su·ing. –pur·su′er,** NOUN.

a	hat	ė	term	ô	order	ch	child	(	a in about
ā	age	i	it	oi	oil	ng	long		e in taken
ä	far	ī	ice	ou	out	sh	she	ə {	i in pencil
â	care	o	hot	u	cup	th	thin		o in lemon
e	let	ō	open	u̇	put	ᴛʜ	then		u in circus
ē	equal	ȯ	saw	ü	rule	zh	measure	(	

P

pur·suit (pər süt′), NOUN.
 1 the act of pursuing; chase: *The dog is in pursuit of the cat.*
 2 an occupation or recreation that you spend a lot of time doing: *Fishing is his favorite pursuit.*

pus (pus), NOUN. a thick, yellowish white liquid found in infected sores.

push (pùsh),
 1 VERB. to move something away from you with force: *Push the door; don't pull it.*
 2 VERB. to force your way through something: *We pushed through the crowd.*
 3 VERB. to urge someone to do something faster; make go forward: *Please push the drivers to get all these packages delivered today.*
 4 VERB. to urge the use or purchase of: *That manufacturer is pushing its small cars this year.*
 5 NOUN. the act of pushing: *Give the door a push.*
 ❑ VERB **push·es, pushed, push·ing;** PLURAL **push·es.**

Synonym Study

Push means to move something away from you: *While she tugged on the reins, he tried to push the stubborn mule from behind.*

Nudge means push gently: *I nudged her with my elbow to get her attention.*

Shove means to push hard against something or someone: *He shoved the dirty clothes into his laundry bag.*

Thrust means to push hard and quickly: *The firefighters thrust open the doors of the burning house.*

Propel means to push forward with a steady force: *Rockets propel a spacecraft as it lifts off a launching pad.*

See also the Synonym Study at **move.**

push·o·ver (pùsh′ō′vər), NOUN. someone who is very easy to beat in a game or race.

push·up (pùsh′up′), NOUN. an exercise done by lying face down and raising your body with your arms while keeping your back straight and your toes on the ground.

push·y (pùsh′ē), ADJECTIVE. bossy; aggressive.
 ❑ ADJECTIVE **push·i·er, push·i·est.** −**push′i·ness,** NOUN.

puss (pùs), NOUN. a cat. ❑ PLURAL **puss·es.**

pus·sy (pùs′ē), NOUN. a cat. ❑ PLURAL **pus·sies.**

pus·sy·cat (pùs′ē kat′), NOUN. a cat: *Here, pussycat.*

pussy willow, a small North American willow with furry gray flowers that look like tiny bits of cat fur. Pussy willows bloom in early spring.

put (pùt), VERB.
 1 to place or set something somewhere: *I put sugar in my tea. Put away your toys.*
 2 to cause something to be a certain way: *Put your room in order. I put myself under the care of a doctor.*
 3 to say or express something in a certain way: *The teacher puts things clearly.*
 ❑ VERB **puts, put, put·ting.**

put down, IDIOM.
 1 to put an end to: *The rebellion was soon put down.*
 2 to write down.
 3 to say unkind things about someone: *She never puts anyone down.*

put off, IDIOM. to lay aside; make wait: *We put off our meeting for a week.*

put on, IDIOM.
 1 to present on a stage; produce: *We put on a play.*
 2 to take on or add to yourself: *He put on weight.*
 3 to pretend: *I put on an expression of innocence.*
 4 to dress yourself: *Put on your gloves; it's cold out.*

put out, IDIOM.
 1 to make stop burning; extinguish: *The firefighters put out the fire.*
 2 to provoke; offend: *I was put out by her rudeness.*

put up, IDIOM.
 1 to offer: *They put up their house for sale.*
 2 to give or show: *She put up a brave front.*
 3 to build: *Several new houses were put up across the street from ours.*
 4 to provide lodging and food for: *They put us up for the night.*

put up with, IDIOM. to bear with patience; endure.

Synonym Study

Put means to move something to some place: *Please put the flowers in this vase. He put his crutches on the floor next to his chair.*

Place means to put something in a certain spot: *She placed the heavy dish very carefully in the center of the table.*

Set means to put something in a certain position: *The furniture movers carefully set the piano next to the wall.*

Lay¹ means to put something in a horizontal or lying-down position: *My brother and I helped my uncle lay the new carpet.*

doing a **pushup**

putt (put),
1 *VERB.* to strike a golf ball gently and carefully in an effort to make it roll into the hole.
2 *NOUN.* a light stroke given to a golf ball: *A good putt requires control.*
❑ *VERB* **putts, putt·ed, putt·ing.**

put·ter[1] (put′ər), *VERB.* to keep yourself busy doing unimportant things: *I like to putter around the garden.* ❑ *VERB* **put·ters, put·tered, put·ter·ing.**

putt·er[2] (put′ər), *NOUN.* a golf club used in putting.

put·ty (put′ē),
1 *NOUN.* a soft material that can be molded and hardens as it dries. Putty is used to fasten glass in window frames.
2 *VERB.* to use putty in window frames.
❑ *VERB* **put·ties, put·tied, put·ty·ing.**

puz·zle (puz′əl),
1 *NOUN.* a hard problem: *How to get all my things into one suitcase is a puzzle.* ▪ See the Synonym Study at **mystery.**
2 *NOUN.* a game that you play by fitting together pieces of wood or cardboard to create a picture, design, or special shape: *A famous Chinese puzzle has seven pieces of wood to fit together.*
3 *VERB.* to make it hard for someone to understand something, confuse: *How the cat got out puzzled us.*
❑ *VERB* **puz·zles, puz·zled, puz·zling.**

puzzle over, *IDIOM.* to think hard about; try hard to do or work out: *I puzzled over the math problem for a long time before I got the right answer.*

Pyg·my (pig′mē), *NOUN.*
1 one of a group of people living in Africa who are less than 5 feet tall.

2 **pygmy,** very small. Some smaller varieties of animals are the **pygmy chimpanzee** and the **pygmy hippopotamus.**
❑ *PLURAL* **Pyg·mies** or **pyg·mies.**

pyr·a·mid (pir′ə mid), *NOUN.*
1 a solid figure with a base and with triangular sides that meet in a point.
2 anything having the form of a pyramid.
3 **Pyramids,** the huge, massive stone pyramids, serving as royal tombs, built by the ancient Egyptians.

three of the largest **Pyramids** in Egypt

py·thon (pī′thon), *NOUN.* a very large snake of Asia, Africa, and Australia that kills its prey by squeezing it.

P

quartz

quetzel

Q or **q** (kyü), *NOUN.* the 17th letter of the English alphabet. *Q* is followed by *u* in most English words. ❏ *PLURAL* **Q's** or **q's.**

Qa·tar (kä′tär), *NOUN.* a country in eastern Arabia.

qt., an abbreviation of **quart.** ❏ *PLURAL* **qt** or **qts.**

quack¹ (kwak),
1 *NOUN.* the sound that a duck makes.
2 *VERB.* to make this sound.
❏ *VERB* **quacks, quacked, quack·ing.**

quack² (kwak), *NOUN.* someone who pretends to be a doctor.

quad·ri·lat·er·al (kwäd′rə lat′ər əl), *NOUN.* a figure having four sides and four angles. Squares and rectangles are quadrilaterals.

quad·ru·ped (kwäd′rə ped), *NOUN.* an animal that has four feet. Bears, horses, and cats are quadrupeds.

qua·dru·plet (kwä drü′plit), *NOUN.* one of four children born at the same time to the same mother.

quail¹ (kwāl), *NOUN.* a plump, wild bird that is hunted and used for food. A bobwhite is one kind of quail. ❏ *PLURAL* **quail** or **quails.**

quail² (kwāl), *VERB.* to be afraid; lose courage; shrink back with fear: *They quailed at the sight of the rattlesnake.* ❏ *VERB* **quails, quailed, quail·ing.**

quaint (kwānt), *ADJECTIVE.* strange or odd in an interesting, pleasing, or amusing way: *Many old photos seem quaint to us today.* —**quaint′ly,** *ADVERB.*

quake (kwāk),
1 *VERB.* to shake; tremble: *They quaked with fear.*
2 *NOUN.* a short form of **earthquake.**
❏ *VERB* **quakes, quaked, quak·ing.**

Quak·er (kwā′kər), *NOUN.* a member of a Christian group which observes simple religious services. Quakers are opposed to war and to taking oaths.

qual·i·fi·ca·tion (kwäl′ə fə kā′shən), *NOUN.*
1 a quality, skill, or ability that makes someone fit for a job, task, office, or function: *A knowledge of*

trails is one qualification for a guide. *She has all the qualifications for the position of sales director.*

2 something added to a statement that changes of limits it: *I can recommend the book with only one qualification: it's very long.*

qual·i·fy (kwäl′ə fī), VERB.
1 to make or become fit for a job, task, office, or function: *He qualified for a driver's license.*
2 to add something to a statement that limits it: *Qualify your statement that dogs are loyal by adding "usually."*
  ❑ VERB **qual·i·fies, qual·i·fied, qual·i·fy·ing.**

qual·i·ty (kwäl′ə tē), NOUN.
1 something special about a someone or something that makes it what it is: *One quality of sugar is sweetness. She has many fine qualities.*
2 a degree of excellence: *I avoid restaurants where the food or service is of poor quality.*
  ❑ PLURAL **qual·i·ties.**

qualm (kwäm *or* kwòm), NOUN. a sudden uneasy feeling in your mind because you are not sure you are doing the right thing: *I had no qualms about playing tennis instead of working on such a sunny day.*

quan·ti·ty (kwän′tə tē), NOUN. an amount or number: *Use equal quantities of nuts and raisins in the cake.* ❑ PLURAL **quan·ti·ties.**

quar·an·tine (kwôr′ən tēn′ *or* kwär′ən tēn′),
1 VERB. to keep a person, animal, or plant away from others for a period of time to prevent the spread of a contagious disease: *People with smallpox were quarantined.*
2 NOUN. the condition of being quarantined: *The ship was in quarantine because the crew had smallpox.*
  ❑ VERB **quar·an·tines, quar·an·tined, quar·an·tin·ing.**

Word Story

Quarantine comes from a Latin word meaning "forty." In old times, some ships were forbidden to unload for forty days after reaching port, to prevent disease.

quar·rel (kwôr′əl *or* kwär′əl),
1 NOUN. a fight with words; angry talk with someone who does not agree with you about something; argument: *The children had a quarrel over which TV show to watch.*
2 VERB. to fight with words; speak angrily to each other about something; argue: *The two friends quarreled three weeks ago and they haven't spoken to each other since then.* ■ See the Synonym Study at **argue.**
  ❑ VERB **quar·rels, quar·reled, quar·rel·ing.**

quar·rel·some (kwôr′əl səm *or* kwär′əl səm), ADJECTIVE. too ready to quarrel; fond of fighting: *A quarrelsome person has few friends.*

quar·ry (kwôr′ē *or* kwär′ē), NOUN. a place where stone is dug, cut, or blasted out for use in putting up buildings. ❑ PLURAL **quar·ries.**

quart (kwôrt), NOUN.
1 a unit for measuring liquids, equal to one fourth of a gallon: *a quart of milk, a quart of orange juice.*
2 a unit for measuring dry things, equal to one eighth of a peck: *a quart of berries.*

quar·ter (kwôr′tər),
1 NOUN. one of four equal parts; half of a half; one fourth: *a quarter of an apple, a quarter of an hour.*
2 VERB. to divide something into four equal parts: *She quartered the apple.*
3 NOUN. a coin of the United States and Canada equal to 25 cents. Four quarters make one dollar.
4 NOUN. one of four equal periods of play in some games, such as football and basketball.
5 NOUN. one of the four periods of the moon, lasting about 7 days each.
6 NOUN. **quarters,** a place to live or stay in: *The circus travels around the country much of the year, but has its winter quarters in the South.*
  ❑ VERB **quar·ters, quar·tered, quar·ter·ing.**

quar·ter·back (kwôr′tər bak′), NOUN. (in football) a member of the offensive backfield. The quarterback directs a team's offense.

quar·ter·fi·nal (kwôr′tər fī′nəl),
1 ADJECTIVE. of or about the four games, matches, or rounds that come before the semifinals and finals in a tournament.
2 NOUN. often, **quarterfinals,** these four games.

quar·ter·ly (kwôr′tər lē),
1 ADJECTIVE. four times a year: *Dad makes quarterly payments on our insurance.*
2 ADVERB. once each quarter of a year: *Some magazines are published quarterly.*

quar·tet (kwôr tet′), NOUN.
1 a group of four singers or players performing together.
2 any group of four things or people.

quartz (kwôrts), NOUN. a very hard kind of rock. **Common quartz** is colorless and transparent, but agate, flint, and many other kinds of quartz are colored.

transparent **quartz** from Arkansas

Q

a	hat	ė	term	ô	order	ch	child	⎧a in about
ā	age	i	it	oi	oil	ng	long	⎪e in taken
ä	far	ī	ice	ou	out	sh	she	ə⎨i in pencil
â	care	o	hot	u	cup	th	thin	⎪o in lemon
e	let	ō	open	ů	put	ᵺ	then	⎩u in circus
ē	equal	ò	saw	ü	rule	zh	measure	

qua·sar (kwā′sär *or* kwā′zär), *NOUN.* any of many astronomical objects that look like stars but give off as much radiation as whole galaxies. Quasars are thought to be the centers of extremely distant galaxies.

qua·ver (kwā′vər),
1 *VERB.* to shake; tremble: *His voice quavered with fear.*
2 *NOUN.* a trembling of the voice: *After the accident the driver spoke with a quaver.*
❏ *VERB* **qua·vers, qua·vered, qua·ver·ing.**

quea·sy (kwē′zē), *ADJECTIVE.* feeling mild nausea; slightly sick at your stomach. ❏ *ADJECTIVE* **quea·si·er, quea·si·est. –quea′si·ness,** *NOUN.*

Que·bec (kwi bek′), *NOUN.* a province in eastern Canada. **–Que·beck′er,** *NOUN.*

Quech·ua (kech′wä), *NOUN.* an American Indian language spoken by the people who once ruled the Inca empire in South America. **–Quech′uan,** *ADJECTIVE.*

Word Source

Quechua is still spoken in the Andes Mountains region of South America. The following words have come into English from Quechua: **alpaca, condor, llama, pampas,** and **puma.**

queen (kwēn), *NOUN.*
1 a woman who rules a country and its people.
2 the wife of a king.
3 a woman who is very beautiful or important, or the best at what she does: *She is the queen of mystery writers.*
4 a female bee or ant that lays eggs. There is usually only one queen in a hive of bees.
5 a playing card with the picture of a queen on it.
6 the most powerful piece in chess. A queen can move in any straight or diagonal row across any number of empty squares.

Queen Elizabeth I of England

queer (kwir), *ADJECTIVE.* strange; odd; peculiar: *That was a queer remark for her to make.*

quench (kwench), *VERB.*
1 to satisfy: *Cold lemonade quenched our thirst.*
2 to drown something out: *We quenched the fire with water.*
❏ *VERB* **quench·es, quenched, quench·ing.**

Que·ré·ta·ro (ke re′tä rō′), *NOUN.* a state in central Mexico.

quer·y (kwir′ē),
1 *NOUN.* a question: *She had a query about the high cost of our trip.*

2 *VERB.* to ask; ask about; inquire into: *The teacher queried my reason for being late.*
3 *VERB.* to express doubt about: *Some of us queried the accuracy of the vote.*
❏ *PLURAL* **quer·ies;** *VERB* **quer·ies** *or* **quer·ied, quer·y·ing.**

quest (kwest), *NOUN.* a search for something; hunt: *She went to the library on a quest for something entertaining to read.*

ques·tion (kwes′chən),
1 *NOUN.* something asked in order to find out something: *The teacher answered the children's questions about the story.*
2 *VERB.* to ask someone in order to find out something: *Then the teacher questioned the children about what happened in the story.*
■ See the Synonym Study at **ask.**
3 *NOUN.* a feeling of doubt or disagreement about something: *A question arose about who owned the football.*
4 *VERB.* to doubt something: *I question the truth of their story.*
5 *NOUN.* something to be talked over, investigated, or considered: *Mother raised the question of whether we need a new car.*
❏ *VERB* **ques·tions, ques·tioned, ques·tion·ing.**

out of the question, *IDIOM.* impossible; not to be considered: *Our teacher said that postponing the test was out of the question. Chocolate cake for breakfast is out of the question!*

ques·tion·a·ble (kwes′chə nə bəl), *ADJECTIVE.* open to question; doubtful; uncertain: *Whether your statement is true is questionable.*

question mark, a punctuation mark (?) put after a question in writing or printing.

ques·tion·naire (kwes′chə nâr′), *NOUN.* a written or printed list of questions used to gather information from people or to get a sample of popular opinion.

quet·zal (ket säl′), *NOUN.* a Central American bird with brilliant golden, green, and scarlet feathers. The male has long, flowing tail feathers.

queue (kyü), *NOUN.* a number of people, vehicles, or computer instructions waiting their turn in a line.
❏ *PLURAL* **queues.**
■ Another word that sounds like this is **cue.**

quetzal — up to 4 feet long, including the tail

quiche (kēsh), *NOUN.* a pie crust filled with beaten eggs and cream, cheese, onion, bacon, or other ingredients, then baked.

quick (kwik),
1 *ADJECTIVE.* fast and sudden; swift: *The cat made a quick jump onto the sofa. We made a quick trip to the store.*
2 *ADJECTIVE.* lively; ready; active: *She has a quick wit.*
3 *ADJECTIVE.* able to learn or understand things fast: *She has a quick mind.*
4 *ADVERB.* quickly: *Find a bandage quick!*
5 *NOUN.* the tender, sensitive flesh under a fingernail or toenail: *Some people bite their nails down to the quick.*
—**quick′ly,** *ADVERB.* —**quick′ness,** *NOUN.*

Synonym Study

Quick means moving, happening, or done in a short time: *With a quick turn, the driver avoided hitting the other car.*

Fast[1] means moving with much speed: *Our track team has many fast runners, so our school wins most races.*

Rapid means very quick. It is used mostly to describe motion: *We began to walk at a rapid pace when we heard the bell.*

Speedy means very quick. It is often used for things that you want to happen or be finished: *He was very sick, but he made a speedy recovery.*

Swift means very fast: *She fielded the ball and threw to first base in one swift motion.*

Hasty means quick and with not enough time or thought: *His hasty decision caused us many problems later.*

ANTONYM: slow.

quick·en (kwik′ən), *VERB.*
1 to move more quickly: *Quicken your pace.*
2 to become more active or alive: *His pulse quickened as the footsteps grew louder.*
❑ *VERB* **quick·ens, quick·ened, quick·en·ing.**

quick·sand (kwik′sand′), *NOUN.* a very deep, soft, wet sand that will not hold up your weight. Quicksand may swallow up people and animals.

qui·et (kwī′ət),
1 *ADJECTIVE.* making no sound; not noisy: *quiet footsteps, a quiet room.*
2 *ADJECTIVE.* at rest; not busy: *We enjoyed a quiet evening at home.*
3 *ADJECTIVE.* not talking; silent: *It was a very quiet audience.*
4 *NOUN.* the condition of being quiet; peace: *I like to read in quiet.*
5 *VERB.* to make or become quiet: *Soft words quieted the frightened child. The wind quieted down.*
❑ *VERB* **qui·ets, qui·et·ed, qui·et·ing.** —**qui′et·ly,** *ADVERB.* —**qui′et·ness,** *NOUN.*

writing with a **quill** dipped in ink

quill (kwil), *NOUN.*
1 a large stiff feather.
2 (earlier) a pen made from a feather.
3 a stiff sharp hair or spine like the end of a feather. A porcupine has quills on its back.

quilt (kwilt),
1 *NOUN.* a soft covering for a bed, usually made of two pieces of cloth with a soft pad between them, held in place by stitching.
2 *VERB.* to make quilts, usually with colorful patterns: *Our sewing group quilts on Wednesday afternoon.*
3 *VERB.* to stitch fabric together with a soft lining: *Grandma is quilting me a jacket.*
❑ *VERB* **quilts, quilt·ed, quilt·ing.**

a patchwork **quilt**

a	hat	ė	term	ô	order	ch	child		a in about
ā	age	i	it	oi	oil	ng	long		e in taken
ä	far	ī	ice	ou	out	sh	she	ə	i in pencil
â	care	o	hot	u	cup	th	thin		o in lemon
e	let	ō	open	ů	put	ᴛʜ	then		u in circus
ē	equal	ȯ	saw	ü	rule	zh	measure		

Q

Quin·ta·na Roo (kēn tä′nä rō′), *NOUN.* a state in southeastern Mexico.

quin·tet (kwin tet′), *NOUN.*
1 a group of five singers or players performing together.
2 any group of five things or people.

quin·tu·plet (kwin tup′lit *or* kwin tü′plit), *NOUN.* one of five children born at the same time to the same mother.

quit (kwit), *VERB.*
1 to stop doing something: *They quit work at five.*
2 to leave something; give up: *She quit her job. He quit college after one year.*
❑ *VERB* **quits, quit, quit·ting.**
call it quits, *IDIOM.* to abandon an attempt to do something: *The roads were so icy we called it quits and went back home.*

quite (kwīt), *ADVERB.*
1 completely; entirely: *I am quite alone.*
2 really; truly: *There has been quite a change in the weather.*
3 very: *It is quite hot.*
quite a few, *IDIOM.* many; a good many: *Quite a few of us went to the game.*

quit·ter (kwit′ər), *NOUN.* someone who gives up a game, a project, or a challenge whenever it becomes difficult; someone unwilling to try hard.

quiv·er¹ (kwiv′ər),
1 *VERB.* to shake all over: *The puppy quivered with excitement.*
2 *NOUN.* the act of shaking: *A quiver of his lips showed that he was about to cry.*
❑ *VERB* **quiv·ers, quiv·ered, quiv·er·ing.**

quiv·er² (kwiv′ər), *NOUN.* a case that holds arrows, worn slung over one shoulder.

quiz (kwiz),
1 *NOUN.* a short or informal test: *Each week the teacher gives us a quiz in spelling.*

2 *VERB.* to examine someone by asking questions; test the knowledge of: *Each week our teacher quizzes us in spelling.* ■ See the Synonym Study at **ask.**
❑ *PLURAL* **quiz·zes;** *VERB* **quiz·zes, quizzed, quiz·zing.**

quiz·zi·cal (kwiz′ə kəl), *ADJECTIVE.* showing that you are puzzled or bewildered; baffled: *She had a quizzical expression on her face.* **–quiz′zi·cal·ly,** *ADVERB.*

quo·ta (kwō′tə), *NOUN.* the share of a total due from or to a particular district, state, or person: *Each class had its quota of tickets to sell for the school fair.*

quo·ta·tion (kwō tā′shən), *NOUN.* somebody's words repeated exactly by another person; passage quoted from a book or speech.

quotation mark, one of a pair of marks (" ") put at the beginning and end of a quotation.

Usage Note

A period or comma goes before a closing **quotation mark.** *"Yes," he said, "I can."* A colon or semicolon goes after a closing quotation mark. A question mark or exclamation point may go before or after a closing quotation mark. They go before a closing quotation mark if they are part of what is being quoted. If not, they go after: *Who shouted "Help!"?*

quote (kwōt),
1 *VERB.* to repeat exactly the words of another person or a passage from a book: *The newspaper quoted the mayor.*
2 *NOUN.* a short form of **quotation.**
❑ *VERB* **quotes, quot·ed, quot·ing.**

quo·tient (kwō′shənt), *NOUN.* a number you get by dividing one number by another. If you divide 26 by 2, the quotient is 13.

rainbow

Rr

R or **r** (är), *NOUN.* the 18th letter of the English
alphabet. ❑ *PLURAL* **R's** or **r's.**

rab·bi (rab′ī), *NOUN.* a teacher of the Jewish religion;
leader of a Jewish congregation. ❑ *PLURAL* **rab·bis.**

rab·bit (rab′it), *NOUN.*
1 a small animal, about as big as a cat, with soft fur
and long ears. Rabbits have long back legs and
can hop very fast. They are related to hares.
2 its fur.
  —**rab′bit·like′,** *ADJECTIVE.*

ra·bies (rā′bēz), *NOUN.* a disease that causes
damage to brain cells and paralyzes muscles.
Human beings usually get rabies from the bite
of an infected animal. Unless it is treated with a
serum, rabies causes death. ■ See the Word Story
at **rage.**

rac·coon (ra kün′), *NOUN.* a small, grayish animal
with thick fur. Its tail is long and has rings of
different colors. Raccoons look for food at night.

race¹ (rās),
1 *NOUN.* a contest to see who can do something the
fastest: *The Kentucky Derby is a horse race. Every
year our town holds a boat race.*
2 *NOUN.* **races,** a series of races run in one day: *Have
you been to the races this year?*
3 *VERB.* to run a race with someone; try to beat in a
contest of speed: *I'll race you home.*
4 *VERB.* to run, move, or go fast: *I raced home
from school.*
  ❑ *VERB* **rac·es, raced, rac·ing.**

race² (rās), *NOUN.*
1 a major group of human beings that pass on
certain physical characteristics from one
generation to another.
2 any group with similar characteristics or ancestry:
All people belong to the human race.

race·car (rās′kär), *NOUN.* a car used for racing.

race·course (rās′kôrs′). *NOUN.* See **racetrack.**

rac·er (rā′sər), NOUN.
1 a person, animal, boat, or car that takes part in races.
2 a large, harmless North American snake that can move very rapidly.

race·track (rās′trak′), NOUN. a track laid out for racing. It is usually round or oval.

ra·cial (rā′shəl), ADJECTIVE.
1 of or about a race of people: *racial traits.*
2 of or involving races: *racial discrimination.*
—**ra′cial·ly,** ADVERB.

rac·ism (rā′siz′əm), NOUN.
1 the belief that one race, especially your own, is superior to other races.
2 the unfair treatment of people of a certain race or races based on this belief.

rac·ist (rā′sist),
1 NOUN. someone who believes in or practices racism.
2 ADJECTIVE. influenced by racism: *racist opinions.*

rack (rak), NOUN. a frame with bars, shelves, hooks, or pegs to hold, arrange, or keep things on: *a bike rack, a clothes rack, a tool rack.*

rack up, IDIOM. (informal) to score: *We racked up 28 points in ten minutes.* ❑ VERB **racks, racked, rack·ing.**

rack·et¹ (rak′it), NOUN.
1 loud noise; loud talk: *Don't make a racket when others are reading.* ■ See the Synonym Study at **noise.**
2 a dishonest scheme for getting money from people, often by threatening to hurt them or what belongs to them.

rack·et² (rak′it), NOUN. an oval wooden or metal frame with a network of strings and a handle. It is used to hit the ball in games like tennis.

Word Story

Racket² comes from an Arabic word meaning "the palm of the hand." A racket is held with its handle resting against the palm of the hand

using a tennis **racket**

rac·quet (rak′it), NOUN. another spelling of **racket².**

rac·quet·ball (rak′it bȯl′), NOUN. a game played in a court with four walls, using a hollow rubber ball and a racket with a short handle.

ra·dar (rā′där), NOUN. an electronic device for determining the position and speed of unseen objects by the reflection of radio waves.

Word Story

Radar comes from the words **ra**dio **d**etecting **and r**anging. See the Word Source at **acronym.**

ra·di·ant (rā′dē ənt), ADJECTIVE.
1 shining; bright; beaming: *A radiant smile lit up her face.* ■ See the Synonym Study at **bright.**
2 sent off in rays from some source; radiated: *A fire produces radiant heat.*
—**ra′di·ant·ly,** ADVERB.

radiant energy, energy in the form of waves. Heat, light, X rays, and radio waves are forms of radiant energy.

ra·di·ate (rā′dē āt), VERB.
1 to give out rays of: *The sun radiates light and heat.*
2 to come out in rays: *Heat radiates from hot steam pipes.*
❑ VERB **ra·di·ates, ra·di·at·ed, ra·di·at·ing.**

ra·di·a·tion (rā′dē ā′shən), NOUN.
1 the process of giving off energy in the form of invisible rays such as light or heat.
2 the rays sent out or given off.
3 the rays or tiny particles that are given off by the atoms of a radioactive substance; radioactivity. This sort of radiation is often harmful to cells.

ra·di·a·tor (rā′dē ā′tər), NOUN.
1 a device for heating a room, made up of pipes filled with hot water or steam.
2 a device for cooling water. The radiator of a car gives off heat quickly and thus keeps the engine from overheating.

rad·i·cal (rad′ə kəl),
1 ADJECTIVE. basic; fundamental: *To lose weight I had to make radical changes in my eating habits.*
2 ADJECTIVE. extreme; favoring extreme changes or reforms: *Her ideas about state taxes are radical.*
3 NOUN. someone who favors extreme changes or reforms; someone with extreme opinions.
—**rad′i·cal·ly,** ADVERB.

ra·di·i (rā′dē ī), NOUN. a plural of **radius.**

ra·di·o (rā′dē ō),
1 NOUN. a method of sending and receiving sounds without using wires to connect the sender and the receiver: *Music is broadcast by radio.*
2 NOUN. the device on which these sounds may be heard or from which they may be sent.
3 VERB. to send out by radio: *The ship radioed a call for help.*
❑ PLURAL **ra·di·os;** VERB **ra·di·os, ra·di·oed, ra·di·o·ing.**

ra·di·o·ac·tive (rā′dē ō ak′tiv), ADJECTIVE. of, having, or caused by radioactivity. Radium and uranium are radioactive metals.

ra·di·o·ac·tiv·i·ty (rā′dē ō ak tiv′ə tē), NOUN.
1 the property that certain metals have of giving off rays or tiny particles from their atomic nuclei.
2 the rays or particles, such as electrons or neutrons, given off.

rad·ish (rad′ish), NOUN. the small, crisp, red or white root of a garden plant. Radishes have a sharp taste and are eaten raw. ❑ PLURAL **rad·ish·es.**

ra·di·um (rā′dē əm), NOUN. a radioactive metal, used in treating cancer. Radium is a chemical element.

ra·di·us (rā′dē əs), NOUN.
1 any line going straight from the center to the outside of a circle or a sphere. See the illustration at **circle.**
2 a circular area measured by the length of its radius: *The explosion could be heard within a radius of ten miles.*
❑ PLURAL **ra·di·i** or **ra·di·us·es.**

ra·don (rā′don), NOUN. a dangerous, radioactive gas that sometimes leaks into basements from the soil. Radon is a chemical element.

raf·fle (raf′əl),
1 NOUN. a kind of lottery in which many people each pay a small sum for a chance to win a prize.
2 VERB. to give something as a prize in a raffle.
❑ VERB **raf·fles, raf·fled, raf·fling.**

raft (raft), NOUN. something made of wood or rubber that can carry people and things on water. A raft is flat and can be moved by a pole or paddles.

raft·er (raf′tər), NOUN. one of the slanting timbers that hold up a roof.

rag (rag), NOUN.
1 a torn or worn piece of cloth, often made from a scrap of old or torn material: *Use a clean rag to dry your hands.*
2 **rags,** tattered or worn-out clothes: *The beggar was dressed in rags.*

rage (rāj),
1 NOUN. violent anger: *His voice quivered with rage.*
2 VERB. to talk or act violently: *She raged against injustice.*
3 VERB. to happen with great force or violence: *A storm is raging.*
❑ VERB **rag·es, raged, rag·ing.**

Word Story

Rage comes from a Latin word meaning "violent anger." **Rabies** comes from the same Latin word. A dog that obviously has rabies is often called a "mad dog."

rag·ged (rag′id), ADJECTIVE.
1 worn or torn into rags: *He wore ragged clothes.*
2 wearing torn or badly worn-out clothing: *Ragged children begged for food in the ruined city.*
3 having loose shreds or bits: *a ragged bit of fabric.*
—**rag′ged·ness,** NOUN.

rag·weed (rag′wēd′), NOUN. a weed whose leaves have a ragged appearance. Its pollen is a common cause of hay fever.

raid (rād),
1 NOUN. a sudden attack: *The pirates planned a raid on the harbor.*
2 VERB. to attack suddenly: *The enemy raided our camp.*
❑ VERB **raids, raid·ed, raid·ing. —raid′er,** NOUN.

rail (rāl), NOUN.
1 a bar of wood or metal fastened to upright supports. A rail separates things or keeps you from falling off the edge of something. There are stair rails, fence rails, and deck rails on a ship.
2 one of a pair of steel bars laid parallel on ties as a track for a train.
3 a railroad: *We travel first by rail and then by boat.*

rail·ing (rā′ling), NOUN. a kind of fence or barrier of upright supports and a rail across the top. It is used as a support or a barrier.

rail·road (rāl′rōd′), NOUN.
1 a road or track with two parallel steel rails on which the wheels of trains run.
2 the tracks, stations, trains, and the people who manage them.

Word Bank

If you want to learn about **railroads,** you can start by looking up these words in this dictionary.

boxcar	elevated	locomotive	tie
caboose	engine	rail	timetable
conductor	engineer	roundhouse	track
depot	express	station	transfer
diner	first-class	subway	
el	freight		

The transcontental **railroad** was completed in 1869.

a	hat	ė	term	ô	order	ch	child		a in about
ā	age	i	it	oi	oil	ng	long		e in taken
ä	far	ī	ice	ou	out	sh	she	ə	i in pencil
â	care	o	hot	u	cup	th	thin		o in lemon
e	let	ō	open	ù	put	ᴛʜ	then		u in circus
ē	equal	ò	saw	ü	rule	zh	measure		

R

rail·way (rāl'wā'), NOUN.
1 a railroad.
2 a track made of rails.

rain (rān),
1 NOUN. the water that falls in drops from the clouds: *The rain spattered the windows.*
2 NOUN. the fall of such drops: *A hard rain began to come down.*
3 VERB. to fall in drops of water: *It rained all day.*
4 VERB. to fall like rain: *Sparks rained down from the burning building.*
❑ VERB **rains, rained, rain·ing.** ■ Other words that sound like this are **reign** and **rein**.
rained out, IDIOM. delayed or canceled because of rain: *Today's game was rained out, and will be played tomorrow.*

Have You Heard?

You may have heard someone say **"It never rains but it pours."** This means that sometimes it seems that when one bad thing happens, other bad things happen to make things worse.

rain·bow (rān'bō'), NOUN. a curved band of many colors in the sky. A rainbow often appears when the sun shines right after it rains. The seven colors of the rainbow are violet, indigo, blue, green, yellow, orange, and red. Rainbows occur when the sun's rays are bent and reflected by drops of water.

a beautiful **rainbow**

rain·coat (rān'kōt'), NOUN. a waterproof coat that protects you from rain.
rain·drop (rān'drop'), NOUN. a drop of rain.

Did You Know?

Raindrops fall at different speeds depending on their size. Large raindrops can fall as fast as 30 feet per second. Small raindrops can fall as slowly as 7 feet per second.

rain·fall (rān'fol'), NOUN.
1 a shower of rain.
2 the amount of water in the form of rain, sleet, or snow that falls within a certain time: *Yearly rainfall in New York is much greater than in Arizona.*

rain·fo·rest or **rain fo·rest** (rān'fôr'ist), NOUN. a very thick forest in a place where rain is very heavy throughout the year. Rainforests are usually in tropical areas.

rain·storm (rān'stôrm'), NOUN. a storm with a lot of rain.

rain·y (rā'nē), ADJECTIVE.
1 having a lot of rain: *April is a rainy month.*
2 wet with rain: *The cars moved slowly on the rainy streets.*
❑ ADJECTIVE **rain·i·er, rain·i·est.**

raise (rāz),
1 VERB. to lift something up; put up: *We raised the flag. Raise your hand if you know the answer.*
2 VERB. to cause something to rise: *The cars raised a cloud of dust. Yeast raises bread dough.*
3 VERB. to make something higher or larger; increase in degree, amount, or price: *That store has raised its prices again. Don't raise your voice when the baby is sleeping.*
4 NOUN. an increase in amount, especially in wages, salary, or allowance.
5 VERB. to bring or gather something together: *We helped to raise money for a hospital.*
6 VERB. to look after plants or animals so that they will grow: *The farmer raises chickens and corn.*
7 VERB. to bring up: *Parents raise their children.*
8 VERB. to build; build up; set up: *They raised a monument to the famous poet.*
❑ VERB **rais·es, raised, rais·ing.** ■ Another word that sounds like this is **raze**.

rai·sin (rā'zn), NOUN. a small, sweet, dried grape.

ra·jah or **ra·ja** (rä'jə), NOUN. a ruler or chief in India, and in some other Eastern countries. ❑ PLURAL **ra·jahs** or **ra·jas.**

rake (rāk),
1 NOUN. a long-handled tool having a bar at one end with teeth in it. A rake is used for smoothing the soil or gathering together loose leaves, hay, or straw.
2 VERB. to move something with a rake: *She raked the leaves off the grass.*
3 VERB. to search carefully: *She raked the newspaper ads, hoping to find a bicycle for sale.*
❑ VERB **rakes, raked, rak·ing.**
rake in, IDIOM. (informal) to get a lot of something easily: *Their new business is raking in money.*

Ra·leigh (ro'lē), NOUN. the capital of North Carolina.

ral·ly (ral'ē),
1 VERB. to bring a group of people together again: *The commander was able to rally the fleeing troops.*

2 *VERB.* to come together for a common purpose or action: *The people rallied to rebuild the dike before the river flooded their homes.*

3 *VERB.* to come to help someone: *She rallied to the side of her injured friend.*

4 *VERB.* to recover health and strength: *My sick friend has begun to rally.*

5 *NOUN.* a meeting of many people for a particular purpose: *We all attended the rally in support of the candidate for president.*

6 *VERB.* (in sports) to come from behind in scoring: *We rallied in the fourth quarter to win the semifinal game.*
❑ *VERB* **ral·lies, ral·lied, ral·ly·ing;** *PLURAL* **ral·lies.**

ram (ram),

1 *NOUN.* a male sheep.

2 *VERB.* to crash hard against something; strike violently; strike head-on: *One ship rammed the other ship.*

3 *VERB.* to push something down or in by heavy blows: *He rammed the fence post into the ground.*

4 *NOUN.* a machine or part of a machine that strikes heavy blows.

ram (definition 1)

❑ *VERB* **rams, rammed, ram·ming.**

RAM, random access memory: a form of temporary computer memory in which all data are equally available and can be put in or taken out at any time.

Ram·a·dan (räm′ə dän′), *NOUN.* the ninth month of the Muslim year. Muslims fast every day during Ramadan from dawn until sunset.

ram·ble (ram′bəl),

1 *VERB.* to wander about: *We rambled here and there through the woods.*

2 *VERB.* to talk or write in a confused way without sticking to the subject.

3 *NOUN.* a walk for pleasure, not to go to any special place.
❑ *VERB* **ram·bles, ram·bled, ram·bling.**

ram·bling (ram′bling), *ADJECTIVE.*

1 wandering about.

2 going from one thing to another without clear connections: *The rambling speech bored us.*

3 growing or extending in irregular ways and various directions: *They live in a rambling old house. Rambling roses frame the front porch.*

ramp (ramp), *NOUN.* a sloping way that connects two different levels, especially of a building or road; slope: *The passengers walked up the ramp to board their plane.*

ram·page (ram′pāj′ *for noun;* ram pāj′ *for verb*),

1 *NOUN.* a fit of rushing wildly about; violent behavior.

2 *VERB.* to rush wildly about; behave violently.
❑ *VERB* **ram·pag·es, ram·paged, ram·pag·ing.**

ram·part (ram′pärt), *NOUN.* a wide bank of earth, often with a wall on top, built around a fort to help defend it.

ram·rod (ram′rod′), *NOUN.*

1 (earlier) a rod for ramming down the ammunition in a gun that is loaded from the muzzle.

2 a rod for cleaning the barrel of a gun.

ran (ran), *VERB.* the past tense of **run:** *The dog ran after the cat.*

ranch (ranch),

1 *NOUN.* a very large farm and its buildings. Sheep, cattle, or horses are raised on ranches.

2 *VERB.* to work on a ranch; manage a ranch.
❑ *PLURAL* **ranch·es;** *VERB* **ranch·es, ranched, ranch·ing.**

ranch·er (ran′chər), *NOUN.* someone who owns or manages a ranch.

ran·dom (ran′dəm), *ADJECTIVE.* by chance; without any plan: *I don't know the answer, but I'll take a random guess.*

at random, *IDIOM.* by chance; without a plan or without making a choice: *She took a book at random from the shelf.*

rang (rang), *VERB.* the past tense of **ring²:** *I jumped when the telephone rang.*

range (rānj),

1 *NOUN.* the distance between certain limits; extent: *A dog has a greater range of hearing than a person.*

2 *NOUN.* variety; number: *There is wide range of colors to choose from.*

3 *VERB.* to vary between certain limits: *The prices ranged from $5 to $20.*

4 *NOUN.* the greatest distance at which something can operate or go: *This missile has a range of 1500 miles.*

5 *NOUN.* an open space used for grazing.

6 *VERB.* to wander over; rove; roam: *Dinosaurs once ranged the earth.*

7 *NOUN.* a row or line of mountains: *The Allegheny Mountains form a range of the Appalachian Mountains.*

8 *NOUN.* a stove for cooking: *We have a gas range in our kitchen.*
❑ *VERB* **rang·es, ranged, rang·ing.**

rang·er (rān′jər), *NOUN.*

1 someone employed to guard a forest.

2 one of a body of armed troops employed to travel around through a region to police it.

a	hat	ė	term	ô	order	ch	child		a in about
ā	age	i	it	oi	oil	ng	long		e in taken
ä	far	ī	ice	ou	out	sh	she	ə<	i in pencil
â	care	o	hot	u	cup	th	thin		o in lemon
e	let	ō	open	u̇	put	ŦH	then		u in circus
ē	equal	ô	saw	ü	rule	zh	measure		

R

★★★★ Ranks in the United States Armed Services

ARMY	NAVY	AIR FORCE	MARINE CORPS
General	Admiral	General	General
Lieutenant General	Vice Admiral	Lieutenant General	Lieutenant General
Major General	Rear Admiral (upper)	Major General	Major General
Brigadier General	Rear Admiral (lower)	Brigadier General	Brigadier General
Colonel	Captain	Colonel	Colonel
Lieutenant Colonel	Commander	Lieutenant Colonel	Lieutenant Colonel
Major	Lieutenant Commander	Major	Major
Captain	Lieutenant	Captain	Captain
First Lieutenant	Lieutenant Junior Grade	First Lieutenant	First Lieutenant
Second Lieutenant	Ensign	Second Lieutenant	Second Lieutenant
Chief Warrant Officer	Chief Warrant Officer		Chief Warrant Officer
Warrant Officer	Warrant Officer		Warrant Officer
Sergeant Major	Master Chief Petty Officer	Chief Master Sergeant	Sergeant Major; Master Gunnery Sergeant
First Sergeant; Master Sergeant	Senior Chief Petty Officer	Senior Master Sergeant	First Sergeant; Master Sergeant
Sergeant First Class; Specialist 7	Chief Petty Officer	Master Sergeant	Gunnery Sergeant
Staff Sergeant; Specialist 6	Petty Officer First Class	Technical Sergeant	Staff Sergeant
Sergeant; Specialist 5	Petty Officer Second Class	Staff Sergeant	Sergeant
Corporal; Specialist 4	Petty Officer Third Class	Sergeant	Corporal
Private First Class	Seaman	Airman First Class	Lance Corporal
Private Second Class	Seaman Apprentice	Airman	Private First Class
Private	Seaman Recruit	Airman Basic	Private

rank¹ (rangk),
1 *NOUN.* a row or line, usually of soldiers, placed side by side.
2 *VERB.* to arrange things or people in a particular order: *The author's first book was highly ranked by the newspaper reviewer.*
3 *NOUN.* a position; grade; class: *The rank of major is higher than the rank of captain.*
4 *VERB.* to have a certain place or position in relation to other persons or things: *I ranked high on the test.*
❏ *VERB* **ranks, ranked, rank·ing.**

rank² (rangk), *ADJECTIVE.* having an unpleasant, strong smell or taste: *rank meat, rank tobacco.*

ran·sack (ran′sak), *VERB.*
1 to search thoroughly through something: *We ransacked the house for my lost ring.*
2 to violently search through and rob a place: *The army ransacked the city and carried off its gold.*
❏ *VERB* **ran·sacks, ran·sacked, ran·sack·ing.**

ran·som (ran′səm),
1 *NOUN.* the price paid or demanded before a captured or kidnapped person is set free: *The robber held the travelers for ransom.*
2 *VERB.* to get the freedom of a captured or kidnapped person by paying a price: *They ransomed the kidnapped child with a great sum of money.*
❏ *VERB* **ran·soms, ran·somed, ran·som·ing.**

rap¹ (rap),
1 *NOUN.* a light, sharp knock: *a rap on the window.*
2 *VERB.* to knock sharply on something: *The chairman rapped on the table for order.*
❏ *VERB* **raps, rapped, rap·ping.** ■ Another word that sounds like this is **wrap.**

rap² (rap), *NOUN.* a kind of popular music with a strong beat, no melody, and rhymed lyrics that are chanted, not sung. ■ Another word that sounds like this is **wrap.**

rap·id (rap′id),
1 *ADJECTIVE.* very quick; fast: *a rapid walk, a rapid worker.* ■ See the Synonym Study at **quick.**
2 *NOUN.* **rapids,** a part of a river where the water moves fast over rocks lying near the surface.
—**rap′id·ly,** *ADVERB.*

rap·per (rap′ər), *NOUN.* a rap musician.

rap·ture (rap′chər), *NOUN.* joy or extreme happiness: *The children watched the magician in rapture.*

rare¹ (râr), *ADJECTIVE.* not often seen or found; very unusual: *rare coins.* ❏ *ADJECTIVE* **rar·er, rar·est.**

rare² (râr), *ADJECTIVE.* not cooked very much: *a rare steak.* ❏ *ADJECTIVE* **rar·er, rar·est.**

rare·ly (râr′lē), *ADVERB.* seldom; not often: *A person who is usually on time is rarely late.*

ras·cal (ras′kəl), *NOUN.*
1 a mischievous person: *That little rascal ate my pie!*
2 a bad, dishonest person.

rash¹ (rash), *ADJECTIVE.* careless; reckless; taking too much risk: *It is rash to cross the street without looking both ways.* —**rash′ly,** *ADVERB.*

rash² (rash), *NOUN.* a sudden appearance of many small red spots on the skin. Scarlet fever causes a rash.

rasp (rasp),
1 *VERB.* to make a harsh, grating sound: *The file rasped as she worked.*
2 *NOUN.* a harsh, grating sound: *The rasp in his voice was due to a sore throat.*
❏ *VERB* **rasps, rasped, rasp·ing.**

rasp·ber·ry (raz′ber′ē), NOUN. a small, tasty, black or red berry. Raspberries grow on prickly bushes. ❑ PLURAL **rasp·ber·ries.**

rat (rat), NOUN.
1 a gnawing animal with a long tail that looks like a mouse, but larger.
2 (slang) a hateful, disloyal person.
—**rat′like**′, ADJECTIVE.

raspberry

smell a rat, IDIOM. to suspect a trick or scheme.

rate (rāt),
1 NOUN. the quantity, amount, or degree, stated in relation to some other measurement: *The car was going at the rate of 40 miles an hour.*
2 NOUN. the number of times something happens in a period of time; frequency: *The restaurant was selling burgers at the rate of 150 an hour.*
3 VERB. to put a value on something: *We rated the house at $90,000.*
4 NOUN. a price: *We pay the regular rate.*
❑ VERB **rates, rat·ed, rat·ing.**

rath·er (raTH′ər), ADVERB.
1 more willingly: *I would rather go on Friday.*
2 more truly or correctly: *We arrived late Monday night, or rather, Tuesday morning.*
3 to some extent; somewhat; more than a little: *After working so long he was rather tired.*

rat·i·fy (rat′ə fī), VERB. to approve; confirm: *The Senate ratified the treaty.* ❑ VERB **rat·i·fies, rat·i·fied, rat·i·fy·ing.** —**rat′i·fi·ca′tion,** NOUN.

rat·ing (rā′ting), NOUN.
1 a score or mark given to someone as a measure of his or her skill: *The judges gave the skater a high rating.*
2 **ratings,** the level of popularity of television programs as determined by a count of how many people watch them.

Did You Know?

Movie ratings are voluntary. Movie makers put ratings on movies so that parents can know what movies are suitable for children. The ratings are:

G General Audiences. Movies for all ages.
PG Parental Guidance suggested.
PG-13 Parental Guidance. Not appropriate for children under 13.
R Restricted. Under 17 only with parent or guardian.
NC-17 No one under 17 admitted.

ra·ti·o (rā′shē ō), NOUN.
1 the relation between two numbers or quantities meant when we say *times as many* or *times as much.* "They have sheep and cows in the ratio of 10 to 2″ means that they have ten sheep for every two cows, or five times as many sheep as cows.
2 a quotient. The ratio between two quantities is the number of times one contains the other. The ratio of 3 to 6 is ³⁄₆ or ½; the ratio of 6 to 3 is ⁶⁄₃ or 2. The ratios of 3 to 5 and 6 to 10 are the same. ❑ PLURAL **ra·ti·os.**

ra·tion (rash′ən or rā′shən),
1 NOUN. the daily allowance of food for a person or animal when supplies are scarce.
2 VERB. to allow people to use only certain amounts of something because it is scarce: *Food was rationed during the war.*
❑ VERB **ra·tions, ra·tioned, ra·tion·ing.**

ra·tion·al (rash′ə nəl), ADJECTIVE.
1 able to think and reason clearly: *Human beings are rational animals.*
2 of or based on reasoning: *a rational explanation.*
—**ra′tion·al·ly,** ADVERB.

rat·tle (rat′l),
1 VERB. to make or cause to make a number of short, sharp sounds: *The wind made the door rattle.*
2 NOUN. a number of short, sharp sounds: *We could hear the rattle of hailstones on the sidewalk.*
3 NOUN. a toy that makes a noise when you shake it: *The baby shook the rattle.*
4 NOUN. the series of tough, hollow rings at the tip of a rattlesnake's tail.
5 VERB. to say something quickly: *She rattled off the names of all the planets.*
6 VERB. to confuse or upset someone: *I was so rattled that I forgot my speech.*
❑ VERB **rat·tles, rat·tled, rat·tling.**

rat·tler (rat′lər), NOUN. an informal form of **rattlesnake.**

rat·tle·snake (rat′l snāk′), NOUN. a poisonous snake with a thick body and a broad head, that makes a buzzing noise with rattles at the end of its tail; rattler.

rattlesnake — up to 7½ feet long

a hat	ė term	ô order	ch child	ʃa in about
ā age	i it	oi oil	ng long	e in taken
ä far	ī ice	ou out	sh she	ə⟨i in pencil
â care	o hot	u cup	th thin	o in lemon
e let	ō open	ú put	ᴛʜ then	ʟu in circus
ē equal	ò saw	ü rule	zh measure	

R

rau·cous (rȯ′kəs), ADJECTIVE. hoarse; having a harsh sound: *We heard the raucous caw of a crow.*

rave (rāv), VERB.
1 to talk in a wild, excited way. Someone with a fever may rave.
2 to talk about something with great enthusiasm: *They raved about the food.*
❑ VERB **raves, raved, rav·ing.**

ra·ven (rā′vən), NOUN. a large black bird related to the crow but even larger.

rav·en·ous (rav′ə nəs), ADJECTIVE. very hungry: *I hadn't eaten all day and was ravenous.*

ra·vine (rə vēn′), NOUN. a long, deep, narrow valley: *The river had worn a ravine between the two hills.*

rav·i·o·li (rav′ē ō′lē), NOUN SINGULAR or PLURAL. small, square pieces of dough filled with chopped meat, cheese, and so on. Ravioli is boiled in water and served with a tomato sauce. ❑ PLURAL **rav·i·o·li** or **rav·i·o·lis.**

rav·ish·ing (rav′i shing), ADJECTIVE. very beautiful; lovely: *jewels of ravishing beauty.*

raw (rȯ), ADJECTIVE.
1 not cooked: *People should not eat raw meat.*
2 in its natural state; not prepared in any way: *Raw milk has not been pasteurized.*
3 with the skin worn or rubbed until it is sore: *There was a raw spot on the horse under the saddle.*
4 damp and cold: *A raw wind was blowing from the ocean.*

raw·hide (rȯ′hīd′), NOUN.
1 the skin of cattle that has not been tanned.
2 a rope or whip made of this.

raw material, anything that comes from mines, farms, forests, or the like before it is prepared for use in factories, mills, and similar places. Coal, coffee beans, iron ore, and cotton are raw materials.

ray[1] (rā), NOUN.
1 a line or beam of light: *rays of the sun.*
2 a line or stream of heat, light, or other radiant energy.
3 a thin line or part coming out from a center. The petals of a daisy and the arms of a starfish are rays.
4 a slight trace; faint gleam: *A ray of hope pierced the gloom.*
5 a part of a line stretching from a fixed point on the line but having no end point.
■ Another word that sounds like this is **re.**

ray[1] (definition 3)

ray[2] (rā), NOUN. a fish with a wide, flat body and very wide fins. ■ Another word that sounds like this is **re.**

ray·on (rā′on), NOUN. an artificial fiber or fabric made from cellulose, and used instead of silk, cotton, and other natural fabrics.

raze (rāz), VERB. to tear something down or destroy it completely: *The old factory was razed, and a new one was built on the same site.* ❑ VERB **raz·es, razed, raz·ing.** ■ Another word that sounds like this is **raise.**

ra·zor (rā′zər), NOUN. a tool with one or more sharp blades used for shaving.

re (rā), NOUN. (in music) the second tone of a scale. ❑ PLURAL **res.** ■ Another word that sounds like this is **ray.**

Word Power re-

The prefix **re-** means "again" or "back." To **re**open means to open **again.** To **re**pay means to pay **back.**

reach (rēch),
1 VERB. to get to someone or something: *Your letter reached me yesterday. We reached an agreement.* ■ See the Synonym Study at **come.**
2 VERB. to stretch out or hold out a hand or an arm: *He reached out in the dark and turned on the lights.*
3 VERB. to touch: *I cannot reach the top of the wall. The anchor reached bottom.*
4 VERB. to stretch out your arm and hand to touch or grab something; try to get: *I reached for the rope.*
5 VERB. to get in touch with someone: *I could not reach you by telephone.*
6 NOUN. the act of stretching out; act of reaching: *With a long reach, the drowning man grasped the rope.*
7 NOUN. the extent or distance of reaching: *Food and water were left within reach of the sick dog.*
❑ VERB **reach·es, reached, reach·ing;** PLURAL **reach·es.**

re·act (rē akt′), VERB.
1 to act in response: *Dogs react to kindness by showing affection.*
2 to experience unpleasant effects because of something: *to react to a medicine with hives.*
3 to act chemically. Hydrogen reacts with oxygen to form water.
❑ VERB **re·acts, re·act·ed, re·act·ing.**

re·ac·tion (rē ak′shən), NOUN. an action in response to some influence: *Our reaction to a joke is to laugh. The doctor carefully watched the patient's reactions to the tests.*

re·ac·tor (rē ak′tər), NOUN. a device for splitting the nuclei of atoms to produce atomic energy without causing an explosion; nuclear reactor.

read (rēd), VERB.
1 to look at and understand written or printed words: *I read the book. The blind read by touching special raised print with the tips of their fingers.*
2 to learn about something from writing or print: *I read of the event in the paper.*

3 to say out loud the words of writing or print: *Please read this story to me.*
4 to show something by letters, figures, or signs: *The thermometer reads 70 degrees.*
5 to get the meaning of something; understand: *She seemed to read my thoughts.*
□ *VERB* **reads, read** (red), **read·ing.** ■ Another word that sounds like this is **reed. —read′a·ble,** *ADJECTIVE.*

read into, *IDIOM.* to interpret in a certain way, often attributing more than intended: *He read into the remark an insult.*

read up on, *IDIOM.* to study or learn about something by reading.

read·er (rē′dər), *NOUN.*
1 someone who reads.
2 a book for learning and practicing reading.

read·i·ly (red′l ē), *ADVERB.*
1 quickly: *The student, who had done all the homework, answered readily.*
2 easily; without difficulty: *This information can be readily located in your science book.*

read·ing (rē′ding), *NOUN.*
1 the act or process of looking at and understanding the meaning of written or printed words.
2 the written or printed matter that has been read or that is to be read: *I have a lot of reading to do this weekend for school.*
3 the act of speaking written or printed words out loud; public recital.
4 the amount shown on the scale of a scientific instrument: *The reading on the thermometer was 96 degrees.*

read·y (red′ē),
1 *ADJECTIVE.* all set to do something: *Dinner is ready. We were ready to start at nine.*
2 *ADJECTIVE.* willing: *I am ready to forget our argument.*
3 *ADJECTIVE.* eager; liable: *Don't be so ready to find fault.*
4 *ADJECTIVE.* easy to get at: *We always keep some ready money in the house.*
5 *VERB.* to make something ready; prepare: *The expedition readied itself during the summer.*
□ *ADJECTIVE* **read·i·er, read·i·est;** *VERB* **read·ies, read·ied, read·y·ing.**

read·y-made (red′ē mād′), *ADJECTIVE.* ready for sale and immediate use: *This store sells ready-made hats.*

re·al (rē′əl),
1 *ADJECTIVE.* not make-believe; not made up; actually existing. Pandas are real, but unicorns are not real.
2 *ADJECTIVE.* not imitation; genuine: *This bracelet is made of real gold.*
3 *ADVERB.* (informal) very; really: *Come again real soon.*

real estate, land together with the buildings, fences, trees, water, and minerals that belong with it.

re·al·is·tic (rē′ə lis′tik), *ADJECTIVE.*
1 like the real thing; lifelike: *The speaker gave a very realistic picture of life a hundred years ago.*
2 seeing things or facts as they really are: *She wanted to buy a car, but decided to be realistic and save her money for college.*
—re′al·is′ti·cal·ly, *ADVERB.*

re·al·i·ty (rē al′ə tē), *NOUN.*
1 actual existence; true state of affairs: *I doubt the reality of what I saw; I must have dreamed it.*
2 a real thing; actual fact: *Storms and cold temperatures are two realities of winter.*
□ *PLURAL* **re·al·i·ties.**

re·al·i·za·tion (rē′ə lə zā′shən), *NOUN.*
1 a clear understanding; full awareness; perception: *The explorers had full realization of the dangers that they were to face.*
2 the act of making or becoming real: *Winning an Olympic medal was the realization of all her hopes.*

re·al·ize (rē′ə līz), *VERB.*
1 to understand something clearly: *I realize how hard you worked.*
2 to make something real: *Her scholarship made it possible for her to realize the dream of going to college.*
□ *VERB* **re·al·iz·es, re·al·ized, re·al·iz·ing.**

re·al·ly (rē′ə lē), *ADVERB.*
1 truly; in fact: *We all should learn to accept things as they really are.*
2 very: *It's a really cold winter this year.*

realm (relm), *NOUN.*
1 a kingdom: *The power of the realm was in the king's hands.*
2 a particular interest or area of study: *the realm of biology, the realm of poetry.*

reap (rēp), *VERB.*
1 to cut grain.
2 to gather in a crop.
3 to get something as a return or reward for doing something: *Kind acts often reap happy smiles.*
□ *VERB* **reaps, reaped, reap·ing.**

reap·er (rē′pər), *NOUN.* a machine that cuts grain or gathers in a crop.

re·ap·pear (rē′ə pir′), *VERB.* to come into sight again: *The moon reappeared from behind the cloud.* □ *VERB* **re·ap·pears, re·ap·peared, re·ap·pear·ing.**

rear¹ (rir),
1 *NOUN.* the side of anything that is opposite the front side; back part; back: *The kitchen is in the rear of the house.*

a hat	ė term	ô order	ch child	⎧a in about
ā age	i it	oi oil	ng long	e in taken
ä far	ī ice	ou out	sh she	ə⎨i in pencil
â care	o hot	u cup	th thin	o in lemon
e let	ō open	u̇ put	ŦH then	⎩u in circus
ē equal	ò saw	ü rule	zh measure	

2 *ADJECTIVE.* at the back; in the back: *Please leave by the rear door of the bus.*

rear² (rir), *VERB.*
1 to bring someone up; help to grow: *They reared their children in a peaceful home.*
2 to raise; lift up: *The buffalo reared its head.*
3 (of an animal) to rise on its hind legs.
❏ *VERB* **rears, reared, rear·ing.**

rear admiral, a military rank. See the chart on page 550.

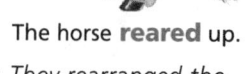

The horse **reared** up.

re·ar·range (rē′ə ranj′), *VERB.* to arrange again or in a new or different way: *They rearranged the furniture for the party. I rearranged my schedule to meet them.* ❏ *VERB* **re·ar·rang·es, re·ar·ranged, re·ar·rang·ing.** —**re′ar·range′ment,** *NOUN.*

rear·view mir·ror (rir′vyü′ mir′ər), a mirror mounted above the windshield or outside the door of a motor vehicle It allows the driver to see traffic on the road behind.

rea·son (rē′zn),
1 *NOUN.* whatever explains why something happened or why someone did something: *I have a good reason for doing it this way.*
2 *VERB.* to think things out; solve new problems: *Most animals can't reason.* ■ See the Synonym Study at **think.**
3 *NOUN.* the ability or power to think: *He was so angry he temporarily lost his reason.*
4 *VERB.* to argue or try to persuade someone to do something: *If you reason with them, they may change their minds.*
❏ *VERB* **rea·sons, rea·soned, rea·son·ing.**

rea·son·a·ble (rē′zn ə bəl), *ADJECTIVE.*
1 according to reason; sensible; not foolish: *When I am angry, I do not always act in a reasonable way.*
2 not asking too much; fair; just: *He is a very reasonable person.*
3 not high in price; inexpensive: *We bought this computer for a very reasonable price.*
—**rea′son·a·bly,** *ADVERB.*

rea·son·ing (rē′zn ing), *NOUN.*
1 the process of thinking things out and solving problems.
2 reasons; arguments.

re·as·sure (rē′ə shùr′), *VERB.* to make someone feel more calm or confident about something: *The calmness of the crew during the storm reassured the passengers.* ❏ *VERB* **re·as·sures, re·as·sured, re·as·sur·ing.**

re·bate (rē′bāt),
1 *NOUN.* a return of part of the money paid for something; partial refund.
2 *VERB.* to return part of the money paid for something.
❏ *VERB* **re·bates, re·bat·ed, re·bat·ing.**

reb·el (reb′əl *for noun;* ri bel′ *for verb*),
1 *NOUN.* someone who resists or fights against authority instead of obeying: *The rebels armed themselves against the government.*
2 *VERB.* to resist or fight against law or authority: *Unfair taxes forced the colonists to rebel.*
❏ *VERB* **reb·els, re·belled, re·bel·ling.**

re·bel·lion (ri bel′yən), *NOUN.*
1 a fight against your own government: *The American colonists came to be in rebellion against the British king.*
2 an act of fighting against any control: *The prisoners rose in rebellion against their guards.*

re·bel·lious (ri bel′yəs), *ADJECTIVE.*
1 fighting against authority; acting like a rebel: *The rebellious troops marched on the capital.*
2 hard to manage; disobedient: *The rebellious child would not obey the rules.*
—**re·bel′lious·ly,** *ADVERB.* —**re·bel′lious·ness,** *NOUN.*

re·boot (ri büt′), *VERB.* to start a computer again by loading the program that controls its basic operations. ❏ *VERB* **re·boots, re·boot·ed, re·boot·ing.**

re·bound (ri bound′ *for verb;* rē′bound′ *for noun*),
1 *VERB.* to bounce back: *The outfielder caught the ball as it rebounded off the fence.*
2 *NOUN.* in basketball: **a** *NOUN.* a ball that bounces back off the backboard or the rim of the basket after a shot attempt. **b** *VERB.* to catch a rebound.
❏ *VERB* **re·bounds, re·bound·ed, re·bound·ing.**

re·buff (ri buf′),
1 *NOUN.* a blunt or sudden refusal to someone who makes advances, offers help, or makes a request: *Her offer to help met with a rebuff.*
2 *VERB.* to give a sudden refusal to: *The friendly dog was rebuffed by a kick.*
❏ *VERB* **re·buffs, re·buffed, re·buff·ing.**

re·build (rē bild′), *VERB.* to build something again.
❏ *VERB* **re·builds, re·built, re·build·ing.**

re·built (rē bilt′), *VERB.*
1 the past tense of **rebuild:** *Workers rebuilt our house after it burned down.*
2 the past participle of **rebuild:** *Our house was rebuilt last year.*

re·buke (ri byük′),
1 *VERB.* to scold: *The teacher rebuked the child for throwing paper on the floor.*
2 *NOUN.* an expression of disapproval; scolding: *The child feared the teacher's rebuke.*
❏ *VERB* **re·bukes, re·buked, re·buk·ing.**

re·bus (rē′bəs), NOUN. a puzzle in which pictures, numbers, and so on, stand for syllables or words. A picture of a cat on a log is a rebus for catalog. ❑ PLURAL **re·bus·es.**

Word Story

Rebus comes from Latin words meaning "by means of objects." In order to read a rebus, you need to know the names of the objects pictured.

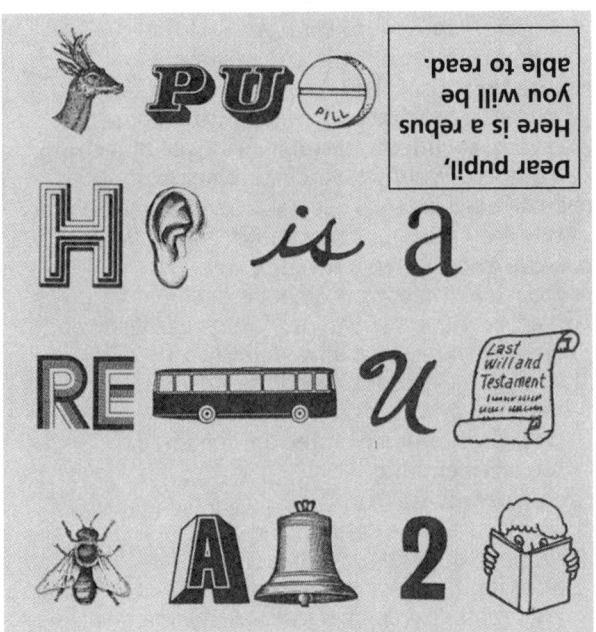

Can you read this **rebus**?

re·call (ri kȯl′ for verb; ri kȯl′ or rē′kȯl′ for noun),
1 VERB. to call something back to mind; remember: *I can recall stories read to me when I was very young.* ■ See the Synonym Study at **remember.**
2 VERB. to call back a vehicle or other product in order to replace or repair a defective part.
3 NOUN. the act of calling something back: *The manufacturer ordered the recall of several thousand cars that had faulty headlights.* ❑ VERB **re·calls, re·called, re·call·ing.**

re·cap·ture (rē kap′chər), VERB. to capture again; have again: *The soldiers recaptured the fort.* ❑ VERB **re·cap·tures, re·cap·tured, re·cap·tur·ing.**

re·cede (ri sēd′), VERB. to go or move backward: *When the tide receded, we dug for clams.* ❑ VERB **re·cedes, re·ced·ed, re·ced·ing.**

re·ceipt (ri sēt′), NOUN.
1 a written statement that money, a package, or a letter has been received: *Sign the receipt for this parcel.*
2 **receipts,** money received or taken in from sales, services, and so on: *Our expenses were less than our receipts.*

3 the act of receiving or the condition of being received: *He smiled upon receipt of the good news.*

re·ceive (ri sēv′), VERB.
1 to take or get something that someone gives you or sends you: *It's nice to receive a gift. He received a letter today.*
2 to let someone into your house; welcome: *The neighbors were glad to receive the new couple.* ❑ VERB **re·ceives, re·ceived, re·ceiv·ing.**

re·ceiv·er (ri sē′vər), NOUN.
1 someone who receives something: *The receiver of a gift should thank the giver.*
2 something that receives: *Public telephones have coin receivers for nickels, dimes, and quarters.*
3 the part of the telephone that you hold next to your ear.
4 a device that receives sounds, or sounds and pictures, sent by radio waves: *a radio receiver, a television receiver.*
5 (in football) an offensive player eligible to receive a forward pass.

a **receiver** catching a pass

re·cent (rē′snt), ADJECTIVE.
1 done or made not long ago: *This chair is a recent purchase.*
2 not long past; modern: *The recent period of history includes several wars.*
—**re′cent·ly,** ADVERB.

re·cep·tion (ri sep′shən), NOUN.
1 a welcome or greeting: *She got a warm reception from her friend.*
2 a party or gathering to welcome people: *Our school gave a reception for our new principal.*
3 the quality of the sound in a radio or sound and picture in a television set: *Reception was poor because we were so far from the transmitter.*
4 (in football) a catch of a forward pass.

re·cep·tion·ist (ri sep′shə nist), NOUN. someone employed to talk to customers in a place of business, take telephone calls, and so on: *The receptionist directed me to the right office.*

re·cess (rē′ses or ri ses′),
1 NOUN. a short time during which classroom work stops: *Our school has an hour's recess at noon.*

R

a	hat	ė	term	ô	order	ch	child	⎧a in about
ā	age	i	it	oi	oil	ng	long	⎪e in taken
ä	far	ī	ice	ou	out	sh	she	ə⎨i in pencil
â	care	o	hot	u	cup	th	thin	⎪o in lemon
e	let	ō	open	u̇	put	ᵺ	then	⎩u in circus
ē	equal	ȯ	saw	ü	rule	zh	measure	

2 *VERB.* to take a break; interrupt work for a time: *The committee recessed for lunch.*

3 *NOUN.* a hollow place in part of a wall or other flat surface: *The bench was in a recess of the wall.*
❑ *VERB* **re·cess·es, re·cessed, re·cess·ing.**

re·charge (rē chärj′), *VERB.* to charge again with electric power: *I recharged the battery.* ❑ *VERB* **re·charg·es, re·charged, re·charg·ing.** —**re·charge′a·ble,** *ADJECTIVE.*

rec·i·pe (res′ə pē), *NOUN.* a set of written directions that show you how to fix something to eat: *Please give me your recipe for bread.* ❑ *PLURAL* **rec·i·pes.**

re·cit·al (ri sī′tl), *NOUN.* a musical performance, usually given by a single performer: *My music teacher will give a recital Tuesday afternoon.*

re·cite (ri sīt′), *VERB.*
1 to say something from memory, especially in front of an audience: *He recited several poems.*
2 to tell about something in detail: *She recited the day's adventures.*
❑ *VERB* **re·cites, re·cit·ed, re·cit·ing.** —**rec·i·ta·tion** (res′ə tā′shən), *NOUN.*

reck·less (rek′lis), *ADJECTIVE.* behaving or acting in a careless way, regardless of possible dangerous effects or results: *Reckless driving causes many accidents.* ■ See the Synonym Study at **careless.** —**reck′less·ly,** *ADVERB.* —**reck′less·ness,** *NOUN.*

reck·on (rek′ən), *VERB.*
1 (informal) to think or suppose: *I reckon he'll be late.*
2 to find the number or value of; count: *Reckon the cost before you decide.*
❑ *VERB* **reck·ons, reck·oned, reck·on·ing.**

re·claim (ri klām′), *VERB.*
1 to bring something back to a useful, good condition: *The city reclaimed the old dump site by covering it up with soil and then planting grass.* ■ See the Synonym Study at **save.**
2 to get something valuable from things that have been thrown out: *That company reclaims rubber from old tires.*
❑ *VERB* **re·claims, re·claimed, re·claim·ing.** —**rec·la·ma·tion** (rek′lə mā′shən), *NOUN.*

re·cline (ri klīn′), *VERB.* to lean back; lie down.
❑ *VERB* **re·clines, re·clined, re·clin·ing.**

re·clin·er (ri klī′nər), *NOUN.* a comfortable armchair with a seat and back that can change position so that a person can lean back comfortably.

rec·og·ni·tion (rek′əg nish′ən), *NOUN.*
1 the act of recognizing or the condition of being recognized: *With a good disguise he escaped recognition.*
2 favorable attention; acceptance: *The actor soon won recognition from the public.*
3 the act of accepting or admitting that something is true: *We insisted on complete recognition of our rights.*

rec·og·nize (rek′əg nīz), *VERB.* to realize that you have seen or known someone or something before: *You have grown so much that I scarcely recognized you.* ❑ *VERB* **rec·og·niz·es, rec·og·nized, rec·og·niz·ing.** —**rec′og·niz′a·ble,** *ADJECTIVE.*

re·coil (ri koil′),
1 *VERB.* to pull yourself back; shrink back: *Many people recoil at the sight of a snake.*
2 *VERB.* to spring back: *The gun recoiled after I fired it.*
3 *NOUN.* the action of springing back: *The recoil of the shotgun hurt my shoulder.*
❑ *VERB* **re·coils, re·coiled, re·coil·ing.**

rec·ol·lect (rek′ə lekt′), *VERB.* to remember: *As I recollect, I had measles when I was about four.*
❑ *VERB* **rec·ol·lects, rec·ol·lect·ed, rec·ol·lect·ing.**
■ See the Synonym Study at **remember.**

rec·ol·lec·tion (rek′ə lek′shən), *NOUN.* memory: *It was the hottest summer within recollection.*

rec·om·mend (rek′ə mend′), *VERB.*
1 to speak in favor of someone or something: *The teacher recommended her for the job. Can you recommend a good adventure story?*
2 to advise: *The doctor recommended that the patient stay in bed for several days.*
❑ *VERB* **rec·om·mends, rec·om·mend·ed, rec·om·mend·ing.**

rec·om·men·da·tion (rek′ə men dā′shən), *NOUN.*
1 words of advice: *What is the doctor's recommendation for a fever?*
2 anything that recommends someone or something: *My brother's employer from last summer wrote him a recommendation for a job at the pool.*

rec·on·cile (rek′ən sīl), *VERB.*
1 to make two or more people friends again: *My mom reconciled my quarreling sisters with a quiet conversation.*
2 to bring ideas, stories, and so on, into harmony or agreement: *It is impossible to reconcile their story with the facts.*
❑ *VERB* **rec·on·ciles, rec·on·ciled, rec·on·cil·ing.**

rec·on·cil·i·a·tion (rek′ən sil′ē ā′shən), *NOUN.* the act of bringing or coming together again in friendship.

re·con·struct (rē′kən strukt′), *VERB.* to build something again; rebuild: *After the earthquake, many buildings had to be reconstructed.* ❑ *VERB* **re·con·structs, re·con·struct·ed, re·con·struct·ing.**

re·cord (ri kôrd′ *for verb;* rek′ərd *for noun*),
1 *VERB.* to put something into writing or some other permanent form for future use: *Record what the speaker says. We record history in books.*
2 *NOUN.* something written down and kept for future reference: *I kept a record of my expenses on the trip.*
3 *NOUN.* a thin, flat disk with grooves from which a record player can produce music, words, or other sounds that were previously copied.

4 *VERB.* to copy music, words, or pictures, usually on a magnetic tape, for future use.

5 *NOUN.* the known facts about what someone or something has done: *She has a fine record at school.*

6 *NOUN.* the highest score, rate, or speed yet reached: *Who holds the record for the high jump?*
❏ *VERB* **re·cords, re·cord·ed, re·cord·ing.**

off the record, *IDIOM.* not to be recorded or quoted: *He agreed to talk as long as it was off the record.*

on record, *IDIOM.* recorded, especially publicly: *He is on record as opposing the new school plan.*

re·cord·er (ri kôr′dər), *NOUN.*
1 someone whose business is to make and keep records.
2 See **tape recorder.**
3 a wooden musical instrument something like a flute.

re·cord·ing (ri kôr′ding), *NOUN.* a phonograph record, magnetic tape, compact disc, laser disc, and the like, on which sound or pictures and sound have been recorded.

record player, a device that produces sounds when you play records on it; phonograph.

listening to one of the first **record players**

re·count¹ (ri kount′), *VERB.* to tell about something in detail: *He recounted all the events of the day.*
❏ *VERB* **re·counts, re·count·ed, re·count·ing.**

re·count² or **re-count** (rē kount′ *for verb;* rē′kount′ *for noun*),
1 *VERB.* to count something again: *I recounted the money to make certain it was the right amount.*
2 *NOUN.* a second count: *The defeated candidate demanded a recount of the votes.*
❏ *VERB* **re·counts, re·count·ed, re·count·ing.**

re·cov·er (ri kuv′ər), *VERB.*
1 to get well again: *She is recovering from a cold.*
2 to get back something lost or stolen: *The police recovered the missing car.*
❏ *VERB* **re·cov·ers, re·cov·ered, re·cov·er·ing.**

re·cov·er (rē kuv′ər), *VERB.* to put a new cover on something: *We had our couch re-covered.* ❏ *VERB* **re·cov·ers, re·cov·ered, re·cov·er·ing.**

re·cov·er·y (ri kuv′ər ē), *NOUN.* the act or process of coming back to health: *She had a rapid recovery after surgery.*
❏ *PLURAL* **re·cov·er·ies.**

rec·re·a·tion (rek′rē ā′shən), *NOUN.* play; fun; amusement. Gardening, sports, games, and reading are all forms of recreation.

re·cruit (ri krüt′),
1 *NOUN.* a newly enlisted member of one of the armed forces.
2 *VERB.* to get men and women to join one of the armed forces.
3 *NOUN.* a new member of any group or class: *The Nature Club needs recruits.*
4 *VERB.* to get new members; get people to join: *We recruited some great new players for the team.*
❏ *VERB* **re·cruits, re·cruit·ed, re·cruit·ing.**
—**re·cruit′er,** *NOUN.* —**re·cruit′ment,** *NOUN.*

rec·tan·gle (rek′tang′gəl), *NOUN.* a four-sided figure with four right angles.

rec·tan·gu·lar (rek tang′gyə lər), *ADJECTIVE.* shaped like a rectangle.

re·cu·pe·rate (ri kü′pə rāt′), *VERB.* to recover from sickness, exhaustion, and so on: *It took us a few days to recuperate after the long trip.* ❏ *VERB* **re·cu·pe·rates, re·cu·pe·rat·ed, re·cu·pe·rat·ing.**
—**re·cu′pe·ra′tion,** *NOUN.*

re·cur (ri kėr′), *VERB.* to happen again; occur again: *Leap year recurs every four years.* ❏ *VERB* **re·curs, re·curred, re·cur·ring.**

re·cy·cle (rē sī′kəl), *VERB.* to treat or process something so that it can be used again. Paper, aluminum, and glass products are commonly recycled. ❏ *VERB* **re·cy·cles, re·cy·cled, re·cy·cling.**
—**re·cy′cla·ble,** *ADJECTIVE.*

red (red),
1 *NOUN.* the color of blood.
2 *ADJECTIVE.* having this color: *a red rose.*
—**red′ness,** *NOUN.*

in the red, *IDIOM.* in debt; losing money: *Their business is still in the red after two years.*

red blood cell, a cell in the blood that carries oxygen from the lungs to various parts of the body. Red blood cells give fresh blood its red color.

Basketball is a popular form of **recreation.**

a	hat	ė	term	ô	order	ch	child	⎧a in about
ā	age	i	it	oi	oil	ng	long	⎪e in taken
â	far	ī	ice	ou	out	sh	she	ə⎨i in pencil
â	care	o	hot	u	cup	th	thin	⎪o in lemon
e	let	ō	open	ù	put	ﬕ	then	⎩u in circus
ē	equal	ò	saw	ü	rule	zh	measure	

R

red·coat (red′kōt′), NOUN. (long ago) a British soldier.

Red Cross, an international organization that cares for the sick and wounded in war, and relieves suffering caused by floods, fires, earthquakes, and other disasters. Its badge is a red cross on a white background.

red·dish (red′ish), ADJECTIVE. somewhat red.

re·deem (ri dēm′), VERB.
1 to turn in coupons or trading stamps for something valuable.
2 to make up for something: *The singer's final solo helped redeem a poor performance.*
❑ VERB **re·deems, re·deemed, re·deem·ing.**

red·head (red′hed′), NOUN. someone who has red hair: *Our class has ten blonds, fifteen brunettes, and three redheads.*

red·head·ed (red′hed′id), ADJECTIVE. having red hair.

red·hot (red′hot′), ADJECTIVE. hot enough to glow with red light: *a red-hot coal.*

re·dis·cov·er (rē′dis kuv′ər), VERB. to discover someone or something again: *I rediscovered an old friend at the game.* ❑ VERB **re·dis·cov·ers, re·dis·cov·er·ed, re·dis·cov·er·ing.**

re·duce (ri düs′), VERB.
1 to make something less; make smaller: *We have reduced expenses this year.*
2 to lose weight: *His doctor advised him to reduce.*
3 to change something to another form: *The chalk was reduced to powder. If you reduce 3 feet, 6 inches to inches you have 42 inches.*
❑ VERB **re·duc·es, re·duced, re·duc·ing.** —**re·duc′i·ble,** ADJECTIVE.

re·duc·tion (ri duk′shən), NOUN.
1 the act of reducing or the condition of being reduced: *The new rules against pollution resulted in a reduction of smog.*
2 the amount by which something is reduced: *The reduction in cost was $5.*

red·wood (red′wùd′), NOUN. a very large evergreen tree of California and Oregon coastal regions; sequoia. Redwoods are the tallest living trees, many reaching a height of over 300 feet. Their soft, durable wood is often used for siding and outdoor furniture.

Redwood trees grow up to 300 feet tall.

reed (rēd), NOUN.
1 a kind of tall grass that grows in wet places. Reeds have hollow, jointed stalks.
2 a thin piece of wood, metal, or plastic in a musical instrument that produces sound when air is blown over it.
∎ Another word that sounds like this is **read.**

reed instrument, a musical instrument that makes sound by means of a vibrating reed or reeds. Oboes, clarinets, English horns, and saxophones are reed instruments.

reef (rēf), NOUN. a narrow ridge of rocks, sand, or coral at or near the surface of the water.

reek (rēk),
1 VERB. to have a strong, unpleasant smell: *The beach reeks of dead fish.*
2 NOUN. a strong, unpleasant smell: *We noticed the reek of cooked cabbage as we entered the hall.*
❑ VERB **reeks, reeked, reek·ing.** ∎ Another word that sounds like this is **wreak.**

reel¹ (rēl), NOUN.
1 a roller or spool for winding up fishing line, wire, hose, film, and so on.
2 something wound up on a reel: *two reels of film.*
reel in, IDIOM. to pull something in with a reel or by winding: *She reeled in a fish.*
reel off, IDIOM. to say, write, or make in a quick, easy way: *He can reel off stories by the hour.*
❑ VERB **reels, reeled, reel·ing.**

reel² (rēl),
1 VERB. to suddenly sway or stagger from a blow or shock: *She reeled when the ball struck her.*
2 VERB. to be dizzy: *My head was reeling after the fast dance.*
3 NOUN. a lively dance, or the music for it.
❑ VERB **reels, reeled, reel·ing.**

re·e·lect (rē′i lekt′), VERB. to elect someone again.
❑ VERB **re·e·lects, re·e·lect·ed, re·e·lect·ing.** —**re′e·lec′tion,** NOUN.

re·en·ter (rē en′tər), VERB. to enter again; go in again: *The rocket reentered the earth's atmosphere.*
❑ VERB **re·en·ters, re·en·tered, re·en·ter·ing.**

re·en·try (rē en′trē), NOUN. the act or process of entering again or returning, especially of a rocket or spacecraft into the earth's atmosphere.
❑ PLURAL **re·en·tries.**

ref (ref), NOUN. an informal form of **referee.**

re·fer (ri fėr′), VERB.
1 to send someone to a source of information or help: *Our teacher referred us to the librarian for some help with our questions.*
2 to turn to something for information or help: *I refer to a dictionary to find the meaning of words.*
3 to mention or speak about something or someone: *The speaker referred to the Bible.*
❑ VERB **re·fers, re·ferred, re·fer·ring.**

ref·e·ree (ref′ə rē′),
1 *NOUN.* someone who makes sure that players follow the rules in some games and sports: *The referee blew her whistle.*
2 *VERB.* to act as a referee.
❑ *PLURAL* **ref·e·rees;** *VERB* **ref·e·rees, ref·e·reed, ref·e·ree·ing.**

ref·er·ence (ref′ər əns), *NOUN.*
1 the act of calling someone's attention to something: *The report contained many references to newspaper articles.*
2 a statement, page number, and so on, that directs a reader to other information: *You will find that reference on page 16.*
3 someone who can give information about someone else's character or ability: *He gave his principal as a reference.*
4 a statement about someone's character or ability: *When she left the company, she received an excellent reference from her boss.*

reference book, a book containing helpful facts or information: *A dictionary is a reference book.*

re·fill (rē fil′ *for verb;* rē′fil′ *for noun*),
1 *VERB.* to fill something again: *I refilled my glass with milk.*
2 *NOUN.* something used to refill something else: *Refills can be bought for some kinds of pens and pencils.*
3 *NOUN.* the act of replacing something that has been used up, such as medicine: *a refill for my prescription.*
❑ *VERB* **re·fills, re·filled, re·fill·ing.**

re·fine (ri fin′), *VERB.*
1 to make something pure. Sugar, oil, and metals are refined before they are used.
2 to make something better or more exact: *She worked to refine her skill in writing.*
❑ *VERB* **re·fines, re·fined, re·fin·ing.**

re·fin·er·y (ri fi′nər ē), *NOUN.* a building and machinery for purifying sugarcane, petroleum, or other things. ❑ *PLURAL* **re·fin·er·ies.**

re·flect (ri flekt′), *VERB.*
1 to give back light, heat, or sound; bounce back: *A white roof reflects the heat of the sun.*
2 to give back an image: *The mirror reflects my face.*
3 to think carefully about something: *Take time to reflect before making a decision.*
4 to bring praise or blame on someone: *The children's spoiled behavior reflected on their parents.*
❑ *VERB* **re·flects, re·flect·ed, re·flect·ing.**

re·flec·tion (ri flek′shən), *NOUN.*
1 a reflected likeness; image: *I looked at my reflection in the mirror.*
2 something that is reflected: *The reflection of the car's headlights in the rearview mirror blinded me.*

3 the act of reflecting or the condition of being reflected: *The reflection of sunlight by sand and water can cause a sunburn.*
4 careful thinking about something: *On reflection, the plan seemed too dangerous.*
5 a remark or action that brings praise or blame on someone: *The children's kindness is a reflection on their parents.*

The squirrel seems to be staring at its **reflection.**

re·flec·tor (ri flek′tər), *NOUN.* any surface or device that reflects light, heat, sound, and so on. Specially shaped pieces of glass or metal are often used as reflectors on cars, bridges, road signs, and so on.

re·flex (rē′fleks), *NOUN.* a reaction in your body that takes place without your thinking about it. Sneezing and shivering are reflexes. ❑ *PLURAL* **re·flex·es.**

re·form (ri fôrm′),
1 *VERB.* to make something or someone better: *Some prisons try to reform criminals instead of just punishing them.*
2 *VERB.* to become better: *They promised to reform if given another chance.*
3 *NOUN.* an improvement: *The new government made many reforms.*
❑ *VERB* **re·forms, re·formed, re·form·ing.**
—**ref·or·ma·tion** (ref′ər mā′shən), *NOUN.*

re·frain (ri frān′), *NOUN.* a phrase or verse repeated several times in a song or poem. In "Deck the Halls" the refrain is "fa la la la la, la la la la."

re·fresh (ri fresh′), *VERB.* to make someone or something fresh again; renew: *His bath refreshed him. She refreshed her memory by a glance at the book.* ❑ *VERB* **re·fresh·es, re·freshed, re·fresh·ing.**

re·fresh·ing (ri fresh′ing), *ADJECTIVE.* able to refresh: *a cool, refreshing drink.*

a	hat	ė	term	ô	order	ch	child	⟨a in about
ā	age	i	it	oi	oil	ng	long	e in taken
ä	far	ī	ice	ou	out	sh	she	ə⟨i in pencil
â	care	o	hot	u	cup	th	thin	o in lemon
e	let	ō	open	ů	put	ᴛʜ	then	⟨u in circus
ē	equal	ȯ	saw	ü	rule	zh	measure	

R

re·fresh·ments (ri fresh′mənts), NOUN. food or drink: *Cake and lemonade were the refreshments at our party.*

re·frig·e·rate (ri frij′ə rāt′), VERB. to make or keep something cold: *Milk, meat, fish, and fruit juice must be refrigerated to prevent spoiling.*
❏ VERB **re·frig·e·rates, re·frig·e·rat·ed, re·frig·e·rat·ing. –re·frig′e·ra′tion,** NOUN.

re·frig·e·ra·tor (ri frij′ə rā′tər), NOUN. an electrical appliance that keeps food or other things cold; fridge.

ref·uge (ref′yüj), NOUN. shelter or protection from danger or trouble.

ref·u·gee (ref′yə jē′), NOUN. someone who flees to another country for safety from war or from persecution: *Refugees from the war were cared for in neighboring countries.* ❏ PLURAL **ref·u·gees.**

re·fund (ri fund′ or rē′fund for verb; rē′fund for noun),
1 VERB. to pay money back: *If the refrigerator doesn't work, the store will refund your money.*
2 NOUN. a return of money paid: *The show was canceled, and refunds were given to ticket holders.*
3 NOUN. the money paid back: *I put my tax refund in a savings account.*
❏ VERB **re·funds, re·fund·ed, re·fund·ing.**

re·fus·al (ri fyü′zəl), NOUN. the act of refusing: *I was disappointed by his refusal to lend me money.*

re·fuse[1] (ri fyüz′), VERB.
1 to say no to someone or something: *I refused the offer. She refused me permission to leave class early.*
2 to say that you will not do, give, or allow something: *They refuse to obey.*
❏ VERB **re·fus·es, re·fused, re·fus·ing.**

Word Story

Refuse[1] comes from a Latin word meaning "to pour back." If someone said no to a drink, it was poured back into the jar. Something that everyone said no to became known as **refuse[2]**.

ref·use[2] (ref′yüs), NOUN. trash; rubbish: *The city sanitation department took away all refuse from the streets.*

re·gain (ri gān′), VERB. to get something back again; recover: *After the illness, she regained her health quickly.* ❏ VERB **re·gains, re·gained, re·gain·ing.**

re·gal (rē′gəl), ADJECTIVE. belonging to or fit for a king or queen; splendid; magnificent: *A regal banquet was given for visiting world leaders.*

re·gard (ri gärd′),
1 VERB. to think of; consider: *We regard our school band as the best in the state.*
2 VERB. to show respect for something: *Please regard the rights of others.*
3 NOUN. thoughtfulness for other people and their feelings; care: *Have regard for the feelings of other people.*

4 VERB. to look closely at something; watch: *The cat regarded me anxiously when I picked up her kittens.*
5 NOUN. a good opinion; respect: *The teacher has high regard for your ability.*
6 NOUN. **regards,** good wishes; greetings: *She sends her regards.*
❏ VERB **re·gards, re·gard·ed, re·gard·ing.**

re·gard·ing (ri gär′ding), PREPOSITION. about; concerning: *A letter regarding the field trip to the museum was sent to parents.*

re·gard·less (ri gärd′lis), ADJECTIVE. in spite of: *The bridge will be built, regardless of the cost.*

reg·gae (reg′ā), NOUN. a kind of popular music that began in the West Indies. Reggae has a strong, lively rhythm and uses the same instruments used in blues and rock'n'roll.

re·gime (ri zhēm′ or rā zhēm′), NOUN. a system of government or rule: *the Communist regime in China.*

reg·i·ment (rej′ə mənt), NOUN. the part of an army commanded by a colonel. A regiment is made up of two or more battalions.

re·gion (rē′jən), NOUN.
1 any place, space, or area: *Bighorn sheep live in mountainous regions.*
2 any large part of the earth's surface: *It is very cold in the polar regions.*

The city's trucks collect our **refuse.**

re·gion·al (rē′jə nəl), ADJECTIVE. of or in a particular region: *I checked the newspaper for our regional weather forecast.*

Usage Note

Regional word choices can be quite different. If you live in a part of the country where a soft drink is called a *soda,* someone who asks for a can of *pop* will sound odd to you. Do you call a big sandwich on a roll a *submarine,* or *hero,* or something else? From these and other regional word choices, an expert in language can figure out where you're from, without even meeting you.

reg·is·ter (rej′ə stər),
1 *VERB.* to write something in a list or record: *The teacher registered the names of the new pupils.*
2 *VERB.* to have your name written in a list or record: *You must register before you can vote.*
3 *NOUN.* a book in which a list or record is kept: *After we signed the motel register, we went to our rooms.*
4 *NOUN.* something that records numbers, quantities, and so on. A **cash register** shows the amount of money taken in.
5 *VERB.* to show figures on a gauge or dial; record: *The thermometer registers 90 degrees.*
6 *VERB.* to show surprise, joy, anger, or other feeling by the expression on your face or by your reactions: *The child's eyes registered surprise at the gift of a new bicycle.*
❑ *VERB* **reg·is·ters, reg·is·tered, reg·is·ter·ing.**

registered nurse, someone who has graduated from a nursing school and who has a state license.

reg·is·tra·tion (rej′ə strā′shən), *NOUN.*
1 the act or process of registering: *Registration of new students is next Monday.*
2 a document that shows that something is registered: *The police officer asked to see our car registration.*

re·gret (ri gret′),
1 *VERB.* to feel sorry for or about something: *We regretted his absence.*
2 *NOUN.* a feeling of sorrow; sense of loss: *I left my friends behind with deep regret.*
3 *NOUN.* **regrets,** a polite reply that says no to an invitation: *She could not come, to the party but she sent her regrets.*
❑ *VERB* **re·grets, re·gret·ted, re·gret·ting.**

reg·u·lar (reg′yə lər), *ADJECTIVE.*
1 following a custom or rule; usual: *Six o'clock was her regular hour of rising.*
2 doing the same thing often: *He's a regular customer at the show store.*
3 even in size, spacing, or speed: *regular teeth, regular breathing.*
−reg′u·lar·ly, *ADVERB.*

reg·u·late (reg′yə lāt), *VERB.*
1 to control something by rule, principle, or system: *The government regulates the coining of money.*
2 to keep something at a stated level, amount, or rate; control; adjust: *A thermostat regulates the temperature of the room.*
❑ *VERB* **reg·u·lates, reg·u·lat·ed, reg·u·lat·ing.**

reg·u·la·tion (reg′yə lā′shən), *NOUN.*
1 a rule; law: *traffic regulations.*
2 the act of controlling or the condition of being controlled by rule, principle, or system: *The regulation of air travel is carried out by the government.*

reg·u·la·tor (reg′yə lā′tər), *NOUN.* a device used to control the flow of something. A regulator is used in scuba diving to control the flow of oxygen from the air tank.

re·ha·bil·i·tate (rē′hə bil′ə tāt), *VERB.*
1 to restore something to a good condition; make useful again: *The school is to be rehabilitated.*
2 to restore someone to a condition of good health or to useful activity, by means of medical treatment and therapy.
❑ *VERB* **re·ha·bil·i·tates, re·ha·bil·i·tat·ed, re·ha·bil·i·tat·ing. −re′ha·bil′i·ta′tion,** *NOUN.*

re·hears·al (ri hėr′səl), *NOUN.* the act of rehearsing; process of preparing for a performance: *The rehearsal for the show was a disaster, but the actual performance was great.*

re·hearse (ri hėrs′), *VERB.* to practice something for a performance: *We rehearsed our parts for the play.* ❑ *VERB* **re·hears·es, re·hearsed, re·hears·ing.**

reign (rān),
1 *NOUN.* the period of power of a ruler: *The queen's reign lasted fifty years.*
2 *VERB.* to rule: *A king reigns over his kingdom.*
3 *VERB.* to exist everywhere: *During a heavy snowstorm silence reigns.*
❑ *VERB* **reigns, reigned, reign·ing.** ■ Other words that sound like this are **rain** and **rein.**

rein (rān),
1 *NOUN.* usually, **reins,** long, narrow straps fastened to a bridle or bit, used to guide and control an animal.
2 *VERB.* to guide and control something: *She reined her horse hard to the left to miss a low branch.*
3 *NOUN.* usually, **reins,** a means of control and direction: *When the President was ill, the Vice-President took the reins of government.*
❑ *VERB* **reins, reined, rein·ing.** ■ Other words that sound like this are **rain** and **reign.**

rein·deer (rān′dir′), *NOUN.* a large deer with branching antlers that lives in arctic regions. Reindeer living in North America are called caribou. ❑ *PLURAL* **rein·deer.**

reindeer — between 3 and 4 feet high at the shoulder

a	hat	ė	term	ô	order	ch	child	⟨a in about
ā	age	i	it	oi	oil	ng	long	e in taken
ä	far	ī	ice	ou	out	sh	she	ə ⟨ i in pencil
â	care	o	hot	u	cup	th	thin	o in lemon
e	let	ō	open	u̇	put	ᴛ̇ʜ	then	⟨u in circus
ē	equal	ȯ	saw	ü	rule	zh	measure	

R

re·in·force (rē′in fôrs′), VERB. to strengthen something with new force, materials, arguments, and so on: *More supports were added to reinforce the bridge. Scientists reinforce theories with new discoveries.* ❑ VERB **re·in·forc·es, re·in·forced, re·in·forc·ing.** —**re′in·force′ment**, NOUN.

re·in·vent (rē′in vent′), VERB. to invent again or in a new way. ❑ VERB **re·in·vents, re·in·vent·ing, re·in·vent·ing.**

Have You Heard?

You may have heard someone say **"Let's not reinvent the wheel."** This means that you shouldn't spend a lot of time and energy working on something that isn't any better than what already exists.

re·ject (ri jekt′), VERB.
1 to refuse to take or accept something; turn down: *She rejected our help. He tried to join the army but was rejected because of poor health.*
2 to throw away: *Reject all tomatoes with soft spots.*
❑ VERB **re·jects, re·ject·ed, re·ject·ing.**

re·jec·tion (ri jek′shən), NOUN. the act of rejecting or the condition of being rejected: *The inspector ordered the rejection of the faulty parts.*

re·joice (ri jois′), VERB. to be glad or happy; be filled with joy: *I rejoiced to hear of her success.* ❑ VERB **re·joic·es, re·joiced, re·joic·ing.**

re·join (rē join′), VERB. to join again; unite again: *After my telephone conversation, I rejoined my friends in the kitchen.* ❑ VERB **re·joins, re·joined, re·join·ing.**

re·lapse (ri laps′ *for verb;* rē′laps *or* ri laps′ *for noun*),
1 VERB. to slip back into a former condition: *After one cry of surprise, he relapsed into silence.*
2 NOUN. the act of slipping back into a former condition, especially being sick: *She seemed to be getting over her illness but then had a relapse after being caught in the rain.*
❑ VERB **re·laps·es, re·lapsed, re·laps·ing.**

re·late (ri lāt′), VERB.
1 to connect things in thought or meaning: *"Better" and "best" are related to "good."*
2 to tell about something: *The traveler related the story of her adventures.*
❑ VERB **re·lates, re·lat·ed, re·lat·ing.**

re·lat·ed (ri lā′tid), ADJECTIVE. belonging to the same family: *Cousins are related.*

re·la·tion (ri lā′shən), NOUN.
1 a connection in thought or meaning: *Your answer has no relation to the question.*
2 the connection or dealings between people, groups, or countries: *Our firm has business relations with their firm.*
3 someone who belongs to the same family as someone else; relative.

re·la·tion·ship (ri lā′shən ship), NOUN.
1 the condition of belonging to the same family.
2 the condition that exists between people or groups that deal with each other: *I have good relationships with all of my teachers this year.*

rel·a·tive (rel′ə tiv), NOUN. someone who belongs to the same family as somebody else, such as a father, brother, aunt, nephew, or cousin.

re·lax (ri laks′), VERB.
1 to spend time away from work; do things that are easy and fun: *We relaxed during the holidays.*
2 to loosen something up; make or become less stiff: *Relax your muscles to rest them.*
3 to make or become less strict or severe: *Discipline is relaxed on the last day of school.*
❑ VERB **re·lax·es, re·laxed, re·lax·ing.**

re·lax·a·tion (rē′lak sā′shən), NOUN. relief from work or effort; recreation: *Walking and reading are my favorite relaxations.*

re·lay (rē′lā *for noun;* rē′lā *or* ri lā′ *for verb*),
1 VERB. to pass something along: *Please relay this message to your parents.*
2 NOUN. a fresh supply: *A new relay of firefighters was rushed in to fight the huge blaze.*
❑ VERB **re·lays, re·layed, re·lay·ing.**

re·lease (ri lēs′),
1 VERB. to let someone go; set free: *Prisoners were released after the war.*
2 NOUN. the act of letting someone go; setting free: *The end of the war brought the release of the prisoners.*
3 VERB. to free someone from an obligation: *She released him from his promise.*
❑ VERB **re·leas·es, re·leased, re·leas·ing.**

rel·e·vant (rel′ə vənt), ADJECTIVE. connected with the matter in hand; to the point: *Please ask only relevant questions.*

re·li·a·ble (ri lī′ə bəl), ADJECTIVE. able to be depended on: *Send her to the bank for the money; she is reliable and honest.* —**re·li′a·bil′i·ty**, NOUN. —**re·li′a·bly**, ADVERB.

rel·ic (rel′ik), NOUN. something left over from the past: *Scientists look for relics from the daily lives of our ancestors.*

re·lief (ri lēf′), NOUN.
1 something that frees someone from pain, burden, or difficulty; aid; help: *Relief in the form of food and blankets was quickly sent to the tornado victims.*
2 the act or process of freeing someone from a pain, burden, or difficulty: *A person with a toothache expects relief when he goes to the dentist.*
3 freedom from a period of duty: *The nurse was on duty all day with only a short period of relief.*
4 someone who relieves someone else from duty: *The watchman's relief arrives at seven.*

relief map, a map that shows depths and heights of a surface by using shading, colors, or solid materials such as clay.

This **relief map** of California shows its mountains and valleys.

re·lieve (ri lēv′), VERB.
1 to reduce the pain or trouble of something: *What will relieve a headache? We telephoned to relieve our parents' uneasiness.*
2 to set someone free from hardship: *Your coming relieves me of writing a long letter.*
3 to free someone on duty by taking his or her place: *The cashier waited for someone to relieve him so that he could eat lunch.*
❑ VERB **re·lieves, re·lieved, re·liev·ing.**

re·li·gion (ri lij′ən), NOUN.
1 belief in and worship of God or gods.
2 a particular system of faith and worship: *the Christian religion, the Muslim religion.*

re·li·gious (ri lij′əs), ADJECTIVE.
1 of or about religion: *religious meetings, religious books, religious differences.*
2 believing in and paying attention to religion: *They are a religious family; they pray before each meal.*
—**re·li′gious·ly,** ADVERB.

re·lin·quish (ri ling′kwish), VERB. to give up; let go: *The small dog relinquished its bone to the big dog.*
❑ VERB **re·lin·quish·es, re·lin·quished, re·lin·quish·ing.**

rel·ish (rel′ish),
1 NOUN. something that adds flavor to food. Olives and pickles are relishes.
2 VERB. to like the taste of something; enjoy: *We all relished the lime sherbet.*
❑ VERB **rel·ish·es, rel·ished, rel·ish·ing.**

re·load (rē lōd′), VERB. to load again. ❑ VERB **re·loads, re·load·ed, re·load·ing.**

re·lo·cate (rē lō′kāt), VERB. to move to a new place: *Next year our school will relocate to a new building.* ❑ VERB **re·lo·cates, re·lo·cat·ed, re·lo·cat·ing.** —**re′lo·ca′tion,** NOUN.

re·luc·tance (ri luk′təns), NOUN. unwillingness; slowness in action because of unwillingness: *She took part in the game with reluctance.*

re·luc·tant (ri luk′tənt), ADJECTIVE. unwilling; not really wanting to do something: *Our dog is reluctant to go out in very cold weather.*
—**re·luc′tant·ly,** ADVERB.

re·ly (ri lī′), VERB. to depend on something or someone; trust: *I am relying on you. Rely on your own efforts.* ❑ VERB **re·lies, re·lied, re·ly·ing.**

re·main (ri mān′),
1 VERB. to stay in or at a place: *We shall remain at the lake till September.*
2 VERB. to stay in the same condition: *The town remains the same year after year.*
3 VERB. to be left: *A few apples remain on the tree.*
4 NOUN. **remains, a** what is left: *The remains of the meal were fed to the dog.* **b** a dead body: *Washington's remains are buried at Mount Vernon.*
❑ VERB **re·mains, re·mained, re·main·ing.**

re·main·der (ri mān′dər), NOUN. the part left over; rest: *If you take 2 from 9, the remainder is 7. After studying an hour, she spent the remainder of the afternoon playing.*

re·make (rē māk′ *for verb;* rē′māk *for noun),*
1 VERB. to make something again; make over: *We remade the garage to hold two cars.*
2 NOUN. something made again, especially a newer version of a movie.
❑ VERB **re·makes, re·made** (rē mād′), **re·mak·ing.**

re·mark (ri märk′),
1 VERB. to say something in a few words; state; comment: *She remarked that it was a beautiful day for a picnic.*
2 NOUN. something said in a few words; short statement: *The principal made a few remarks.*
❑ VERB **re·marks, re·marked, re·mark·ing.**

re·mark·a·ble (ri mär′kə bəl), ADJECTIVE. worth noticing because it is unusual: *He has a remarkable memory for names and faces.*
—**re·mark′a·bly,** ADVERB.

re·mar·riage (rē mar′ij), NOUN. any marriage after your first marriage.

re·match (rē′mach′), NOUN. a second match, game, series, and so on, between two opponents or teams. ❑ PLURAL **re·match·es.**

rem·e·dy (rem′ə dē),
1 NOUN. a medicine, treatment, or procedure for injuries or diseases; cure: *Aspirin is used as a remedy for headaches.*
2 VERB. to cure or relieve something: *A nap remedied my weariness.*
❑ PLURAL **rem·e·dies;** VERB **rem·e·dies, rem·e·died, rem·e·dy·ing.**

R

a	hat	ė	term	ô	order	ch	child		a in about
ā	age	i	it	oi	oil	ng	long		e in taken
ä	far	ī	ice	ou	out	sh	she	ə {	i in pencil
â	care	o	hot	u	cup	th	thin		o in lemon
e	let	ō	open	ů	put	ᴛʜ	then		u in circus
ē	equal	ò	saw	ü	rule	zh	measure		

re·mem·ber (ri mem′bər), *VERB.*
1 to call something back to your mind: *I can't remember that man's name.*
2 to keep something in mind; take care not to forget: *Remember me when I am gone.*
❏ *VERB* **re·mem·bers, re·mem·bered, re·mem·ber·ing.**

Synonym Study

Remember means to call something back to mind: *"Do you remember the name of the book you told me about?" he asked.*

Recall means to remember. It is often used when you make an effort to think of something: *I couldn't recall where I had left my glasses; then I realized they were on top of my head.*

Recollect means to recall something, especially something from long ago: *My grandmother can recollect her childhood as if it were yesterday.*

ANTONYM: forget.

re·mind (ri mīnd′), *VERB.* to make someone think of something: *This picture reminds me of a story I once heard.* ❏ *VERB* **re·minds, re·minded, re·mind·ing.**

re·mind·er (ri mīn′dər), *NOUN.* something to help you remember: *The notes taped to my mirror are reminders of things I need to do.*

re·mod·el (rē mod′l), *VERB.* to make changes in the shape or structure of a house or building: *They remodeled the old barn into a house.* ❏ *VERB* **re·mod·els, re·mod·eled, re·mod·el·ing.**

re·morse (ri môrs′), *NOUN.* a deep, painful regret that you feel for having done something wrong: *I felt remorse for hurting my friend's feelings.*

re·mote (ri mōt′), *ADJECTIVE.*
1 far away; far off: *The North Pole is a remote part of the world.*
2 distant: *She is a remote relative; a third cousin, to be exact.*
3 slight; faint: *I haven't the remotest idea what you mean.*
❏ *ADJECTIVE* **re·mot·er, re·mot·est. —re·mote′ly,** *ADVERB.*

remote control, a device used to control a television set or other electronic equipment from a distance.

re·mov·al (ri mü′vəl), *NOUN.* the act of removing something; act of taking away: *We made arrangements for the removal of the dead tree.*

re·move (ri müv′), *VERB.*
1 to move something from a place or position; take off; take away: *Please remove your hat.*
■ See the Synonym Study at **move.**
2 to get rid of something; put an end to: *The demonstration removed any doubts we had about the invention's usefulness.*

3 to dismiss someone from an office or position: *The mayor removed the chief of police for corruption.*
❏ *VERB* **re·moves, re·moved, re·mov·ing.**

Ren·ais·sance (ren′ə säns), *NOUN.*
1 the great revival of art and learning in Europe during the 1300s, 1400s, and 1500s.
2 the period of time when this revival occurred.

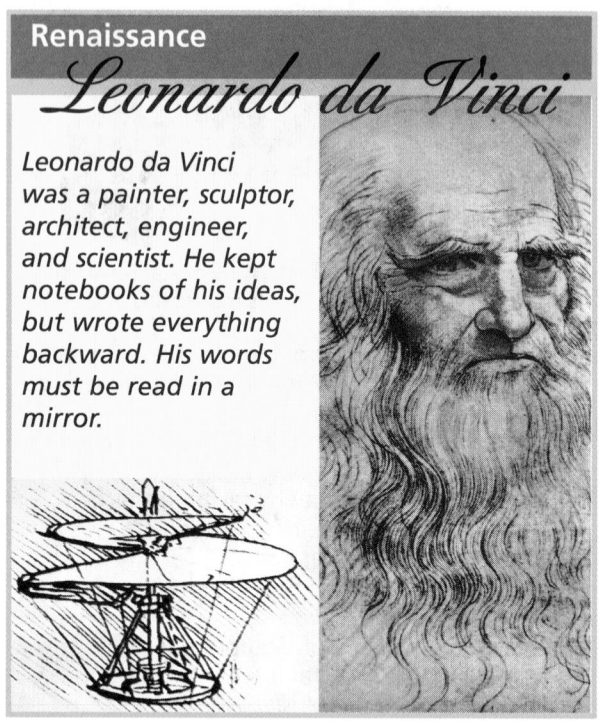

Renaissance

Leonardo da Vinci

Leonardo da Vinci was a painter, sculptor, architect, engineer, and scientist. He kept notebooks of his ideas, but wrote everything backward. His words must be read in a mirror.

re·name (rē nām′), *VERB.* to give a new name to something or someplace; name again: *They bought a used boat and renamed it "Sea Gull."*
❏ *VERB* **re·names, re·named, re·nam·ing.**

re·new (ri nü′), *VERB.*
1 to make something like new; restore: *Rain renews the green of the fields.*
2 to begin something again; say, do, or give again: *She renewed her efforts to fix the broken bicycle.*
3 to replace something with new material or a new thing of the same sort; fill again: *He asked the doctor to renew his prescription.*
4 to give or get again for a new period of time: *We renewed our lease for another year.*
❏ *VERB* **re·news, re·newed, re·new·ing.**
—re·new′a·ble, *ADJECTIVE.*

re·new·al (ri nü′əl), *NOUN.* the act of renewing or the condition of being renewed: *Hot weather brings a renewal of interest in swimming.*

ren·o·vate (ren′ə vāt), *VERB.* to make something like new; restore to good condition: *It's time to renovate our kitchen.* ❏ *VERB* **ren·o·vates, ren·o·vat·ed, ren·o·vat·ing. —ren′o·va′tion,** *NOUN.* **—ren′o·va′tor,** *NOUN.*

rent (rent),

1 *NOUN.* the money paid for the use of property: *My apartment is small, but the rent is low.*

2 *VERB.* to pay for the use of property: *Her parents rented a video for her party.*

3 *VERB.* to accept money for the use of property: *The hardware store rents some tools.*

❑ *VERB* **rents, rent·ed, rent·ing.** —**rent′er,** *NOUN.*

for rent, *IDIOM.* available in return for rent paid: *That vacant apartment is for rent.*

rent·al (ren′tl), *NOUN.* an amount received or paid as rent: *The yearly rental of her house is $7,200.*

re·o·pen (rē ō′pən), *VERB.*

1 to open again: *School will reopen in September.*

2 to begin a discussion again: *I want to reopen the discussion of our plans.*

❑ *VERB* **re·o·pens, re·o·pened, re·o·pen·ing.**

re·or·gan·ize (rē ôr′gə nīz), *VERB.* to organize something again; arrange in a new way: *Classes will be reorganized after the first few days of school.* ❑ *VERB* **re·or·gan·iz·es, re·or·gan·ized, re·or·gan·iz·ing.** —**re·or′gan·i·za′tion,** *NOUN.*

re·paid (ri pād′), *VERB.*

1 the past tense of **repay:** *I repaid the money I had borrowed.*

2 the past participle of **repay:** *They have repaid all their debts.*

re·pair (ri pâr′),

1 *VERB.* to put something in good condition again; mend: *He repairs shoes.*

2 *NOUN.* the act or work of repairing: *After the storm, repair of the roof was necessary.*

3 *NOUN.* the condition or shape that something is in: *The house was in very bad repair.*

❑ *VERB* **re·pairs, re·paired, re·pair·ing.** —**re·pair′a·ble,** *ADJECTIVE.*

re·pair·man (ri pâr′man′), *NOUN.* someone whose work is repairing something. ❑ *PLURAL* **re·pair·men.**

re·pay (ri pā′), *VERB.*

1 to pay back; give back: *When can you repay me? She repaid the money she had borrowed.*

2 to do something in return for something received: *No thanks can repay such kindness.*

3 to do in return for someone: *The student's success repaid the teacher for his efforts.*

❑ *VERB* **re·pays, re·paid, re·pay·ing.** —**re·pay′a·ble,** *ADJECTIVE.* —**re·pay′ment,** *NOUN.*

re·peal (ri pēl′),

1 *VERB.* to put an official end to a law; cancel: *The city council repealed several laws.*

2 *NOUN.* the act of repealing: *He voted for the repeal of that law.*

❑ *VERB* **re·peals, re·pealed, re·peal·ing.**

re·peat (ri pēt′ *for verb;* rē′pēt′ *or* ri pēt′ *for noun),*

1 *VERB.* to say something again: *She repeated her statement for emphasis.*

2 *VERB.* to do or make something again: *I try not to repeat my mistakes.*

3 *VERB.* to say over; recite: *She can repeat many poems from memory.*

4 *VERB.* to tell to someone else or to other people: *I promised not to repeat the secret.*

5 *NOUN.* something repeated: *a TV repeat.*

❑ *VERB* **re·peats, re·peat·ed, re·peat·ing.** —**re·peat′a·ble,** *ADJECTIVE.* —**re·peat′er,** *NOUN.*

re·peat·ed (ri pē′tid), *ADJECTIVE.* said, done, or made over and over: *Her repeated efforts at last resulted in success.* —**re·peat′ed·ly,** *ADVERB.*

re·pel (ri pel′), *VERB.*

1 to force something back; drive back: *They repelled the enemy's attack.*

2 to keep something off or out: *Rubber repels water.*

3 to force something apart or away: *The like poles of two magnets repel each other.*

4 to cause violent dislike for something in someone: *Spiders and worms repel me.*

❑ *VERB* **re·pels, re·pelled, re·pel·ling.**

re·pel·lent (ri pel′ənt), *NOUN.* anything that repels something: *We sprayed ourselves with insect repellent to protect ourselves from the mosquitoes.*

re·pent (ri pent′), *VERB.* to feel sorry for doing something wrong and wish that you had not done it: *She repented for yelling at her little brother.*

❑ *VERB* **re·pents, re·pent·ed, re·pent·ing.**

rep·e·ti·tion (rep′ə tish′ən), *NOUN.*

1 something repeated; repeated occurrence.

2 the act of repeating; doing again; saying again: *Any repetition of the offense will be punished.*

re·place (ri plās′), *VERB.*

1 to put something back in its proper place again: *Replace the books on the shelves.*

2 to take the place of someone: *A substitute replaced our teacher.*

3 to put something in place of something else: *I will replace the cup I broke.*

❑ *VERB* **re·plac·es, re·placed, re·plac·ing.**

re·place·ment (ri plās′mənt), *NOUN.*

1 someone or something that replaces: *She is a replacement for our usual shortstop.*

2 the act of replacing or the condition of being replaced: *The law required the replacement of all wooden freight cars by steel cars.*

re·plant (rē plant′), *VERB.* to place new plants or trees in an area, replacing previous ones: *After the city finished repairing the sidewalk, all the neighbors brought flowers to replant along the path.* ❑ *VERB* **re·plants, re·plant·ed, re·plant·ing.**

a	hat	ė	term	ô	order	ch	child		a in about
ā	age	i	it	oi	oil	ng	long		e in taken
ä	far	ī	ice	ou	out	sh	she	ə	i in pencil
â	care	o	hot	u	cup	th	thin		o in lemon
e	let	ō	open	ù	put	ŦH	then		u in circus
ē	equal	ò	saw	ü	rule	zh	measure		

R

re·play (rē plā′ *for verb;* rē′plā′ *for noun*),
  1 VERB. to play something again.
  2 NOUN. something, such as a game, that is played again.
  3 NOUN. a videotape recording of a part of a game broadcast on television: *We saw the touchdown again on the replay.*
  ❑ VERB **re·plays, re·played, re·play·ing.**

rep·li·ca (rep′lə kə), NOUN. an exact copy; reproduction: *A replica of the famous painting is on display.* ❑ PLURAL **rep·li·cas.**

re·ply (ri plī′),
  1 VERB. to answer someone by words or action: *He replied with a shout.*
  2 NOUN. something said or done as an answer; response: *I didn't hear your reply to the question.*
  ■ See the Synonym Study at **answer.**
  ❑ VERB **re·plies, re·plied, re·ply·ing;** PLURAL **re·plies.**

re·port (ri pôrt′),
  1 NOUN. words that are said or written to tell about something, especially in a public or formal way: *My mother wrote a report for her company on how to increase sales.*
  2 VERB. to make a report of something; tell: *The radio reports the news and weather.*
  3 VERB. to present yourself somewhere: *Report for work at eight o'clock.*
  ❑ VERB **re·ports, re·port·ed, re·port·ing.**

report card, a written report sent regularly by the school to your parents or guardians, giving information on your work and behavior.

re·port·er (ri pôr′tər), NOUN. someone who gathers and reports news for a newspaper, magazine, or television or radio station.

re·pose (ri pōz′),
  1 NOUN. rest; sleep: *I lay down for a short repose*
  2 VERB. to lie at rest: *The cat reposed upon the cushion with her sleeping kittens.*
  ❑ VERB **re·pos·es, re·posed, re·pos·ing.**

reporter

rep·re·sent (rep′ri zent′), VERB.
  1 to stand for something; be a sign or symbol of.
  2 to act in place of someone; speak and act for: *Elected officials represent the voters.*
  3 to show something in a picture; portray: *This painting represents the signing of the Declaration of Independence.*
  ❑ VERB **rep·re·sents, rep·re·sent·ed, rep·re·sent·ing.**

rep·re·sen·ta·tion (rep′ri zen tā′shən), NOUN.
  1 the act of representing something.
  2 the condition or fact of being represented: *"Taxation without representation is tyranny."*

rep·re·sent·a·tive (rep′ri zen′tə tiv),
  1 NOUN. someone elected to act or speak for other people: *He is our representative at the meeting.*
  2 NOUN. **Representative,** a member of the House of Representatives.
  3 ADJECTIVE. having its citizens represented by people who have been elected: *a representative government.*
  4 ADJECTIVE. serving as an example of; typical: *Oak and maple are representative American hardwoods.*

re·pro·duce (rē′prə düs′), VERB.
  1 to make a close copy of something: *Can you reproduce my handwriting?*
  2 to produce offspring: *Most plants reproduce by seeds.*
  ❑ VERB **re·pro·duc·es, re·pro·duced, re·pro·duc·ing. –re′pro·duc′i·ble,** ADJECTIVE.

re·pro·duc·tion (rē′prə duk′shən), NOUN.
  1 a copy: *a reproduction of a famous painting.*
  2 the process by which living things produce offspring.
  3 the act or process of reproducing: *Music fans expect a high quality of sound reproduction from their CD players.*

re·proof (ri prüf′), NOUN. words of blame or disapproval; blame.

rep·tile (rep′til), NOUN. one of a group of cold-blooded animals that have backbones and lungs and are usually covered with scales. Snakes, lizards, turtles, alligators, and dinosaurs are reptiles.

Word Story

Reptile comes from a Latin word meaning "to crawl." Many reptiles have short legs and move with their stomach close to the ground; snakes move with their bellies right on the ground.

re·pub·lic (ri pub′lik), NOUN.
  1 a government in which the citizens elect representatives to manage the government. It is usually headed by a president.
  2 a nation or state that has such a government. The United States and Mexico are republics.

re·pub·li·can (ri pub′lə kən),
  1 ADJECTIVE. of or like that of a republic: *Many countries have a republican form of government.*
  2 NOUN. someone who favors a republic: *The republicans fought to overthrow the king.*
  3 **Republican, a** ADJECTIVE. of the Republican Party. **b** NOUN. a member of the Republican Party.

Republican Party, one of the two main political parties in the United States.

re·pul·sive (ri pul′siv), ADJECTIVE. causing disgust or strong dislike: *the repulsive smell of a skunk.* **–re·pul′sive·ness,** NOUN.

rep·u·ta·tion (rep/yə tā/shən), NOUN. what people think and say about the character or quality of someone or something: *This store has an excellent reputation for service. Cheating in games ruined his reputation.*

re·quest (ri kwest/),
1 VERB. to ask for something from someone, an office, and so on: *She requested a loan from her bank.*
2 NOUN. the act of asking for something: *Your request for a ticket was made too late.*
3 NOUN. something that is asked for: *She granted my request.*
❑ VERB **re·quests, re·quest·ed, re·quest·ing.**

re·quire (ri kwīr/), VERB.
1 to need: *Gardens require sunshine.*
2 to say that you have to do something: *The rules required us all to be present.*
❑ VERB **re·quires, re·quired, re·quir·ing.**

re·quire·ment (ri kwīr/mənt), NOUN.
1 a need; something needed: *Patience is a requirement in teaching.*
2 a demand; something demanded: *That school has a requirement that students wear uniforms.*

re·read (rē rēd/), VERB. to read something again: *I would like to reread that book someday.* ❑ VERB **re·reads, re·read** (rē red/), **re·read·ing.**

re·run (rē run/ *for verb;* rē/run/ *for noun*),
1 VERB. to run something again: *We had to rerun the race because it was a tie.*
2 NOUN. a television show or movie that is shown again. ❑ VERB **re·runs, re·ran** (rē ran/), **re·run, re·run·ning.**

res·cue (res/kyü),
1 VERB. to save someone from danger, capture, or harm; free; deliver: *She rescued the man from drowning.* ■ See the Synonym Study at **save.**
2 NOUN. the act of saving or freeing someone from harm or danger: *The fireman was praised for his brave rescue of the children in the burning house.*
❑ VERB **res·cues, res·cued, res·cu·ing;** PLURAL **res·cues. —res/cu·er,** NOUN.

rescued from sharks

re·search (ri serch/ *or* rē/serch/),
1 NOUN. the act of seeking facts or truth in books, by means of experiments, and so on; investigation: *Medical research helps find cures for diseases.*
2 VERB. to seek facts or truth about something; investigate: *My father is researching the history of our family.*
❑ PLURAL **re·search·es;** VERB **re·search·es, re·searched, re·search·ing. —re·search/er,** NOUN.

re·sem·blance (re zem/bləns), NOUN. similar appearance; likeness: *Cousins often show some resemblance to each other.*

re·sem·ble (ri zem/bəl), VERB. to look like or be similar to someone or something: *Our house resembles yours, but the colors of the rooms are very different.* ❑ VERB **re·sem·bles, re·sem·bled, re·sem·bling.**

re·sent (ri zent/), VERB. to feel bitter and angry about something: *I resent the lies you have been telling about me.* ❑ VERB **re·sents, re·sent·ed, re·sent·ing.**

re·sent·ment (ri zent/mənt), NOUN. the angry or bitter feeling that you have if you are injured or insulted: *Everyone feels resentment at being treated unfairly.*

res·er·va·tion (rez/ər vā/shən), NOUN.
1 usually, **reservations,** an arrangement to have a room, a seat, or the like, held in advance for your use later on: *We made dinner reservations at our favorite restaurant.*
2 land set aside by the government for a special purpose: *an Indian reservation.*
3 a feeling of doubt that you have about something: *She didn't mention them, but she had reservations about their plan.*

re·serve (ri zerv/),
1 VERB. to save something for use later: *Reserve enough money for your fare home.*
2 VERB. to arrange to have something set aside for someone's use: *We reserved a table at our favorite restaurant.*
3 NOUN. something kept back for future use; store: *a reserve of food, a reserve of energy, a reserve of money.*
4 NOUN. **reserves,** members of the armed forces not assigned to duty, but ready to serve when needed.
❑ VERB **re·serves, re·served, re·serv·ing.**

re·served (ri zervd/), ADJECTIVE.
1 set apart for someone's use: *We had reserved seats at the football game.*

R

a	hat	ė	term	ô	order	ch	child		a in about
ā	age	i	it	oi	oil	ng	long		e in taken
ä	far	ī	ice	ou	out	sh	she	ə	i in pencil
â	care	o	hot	u	cup	th	thin		o in lemon
e	let	ō	open	u̇	put	ŦH	then		u in circus
ē	equal	ȯ	saw	ü	rule	zh	measure		

2 tending to keep to yourself; quiet: *A reserved person does not make friends easily.*

res·er·voir (rez′ər vwär), NOUN. a place where water is collected and stored for use.

re·side (ri zīd′), VERB. to live in or at a place for a long time: *This family has resided in our town for many years.* ∎ See the Synonym Study at **live**. ❑ VERB **re·sides, re·sid·ed, re·sid·ing.**

res·i·dence (rez′ə dəns), NOUN. a house or home; the place where a person lives: *The Governor's residence is just outside the state capital.*

res·i·dent (rez′ə dənt), NOUN. someone living in a place, not just a visitor: *The residents of the town are proud of its new library.*

res·i·den·tial (rez′ə den′shəl), ADJECTIVE. of or suitable for homes or residences: *They live in a large residential district outside the city.*

res·i·due (rez′ə dü), NOUN. what remains after a part is taken; remainder: *The syrup had dried up, leaving a sticky residue.* ❑ PLURAL **res·i·dues.**

re·sign (ri zīn′), VERB. to give up a job, office, or position: *She resigned her position on the school paper.* ❑ VERB **re·signs, re·signed, re·sign·ing.**

resign yourself, IDIOM. to submit quietly to something that you don't like; adapt yourself: *He resigned himself to a week in bed when he hurt his back.*

res·ig·na·tion (rez′ig nā′shən), NOUN.
1 a written statement giving notice that you resign.
2 the act of resigning: *There have been many resignations from the committee.*

re·signed (ri zīnd′), ADJECTIVE. accepting something that is unpleasant without complaining about it.

res·in (rez′n), NOUN. a sticky, yellow or brown substance that flows from some trees. Some resin is made artificially. Resin is used in medicine and in varnishes and plastics.

re·sist (ri zist′), VERB.
1 to fight against something; oppose: *She resisted the plan to close our neighborhood library.*
2 to try to keep from doing something that you want to do: *I could not resist laughing.*
3 to not give in to the action or effect of something: *A healthy body resists disease.* ❑ VERB **re·sists, re·sist·ed, re·sist·ing.**

re·sist·ance (ri zis′təns), NOUN.
1 the act of resisting: *The bank clerk offered no resistance to the robbers.*
2 the power to resist illness: *Some people have great resistance to disease.*

re·sist·ant (ri zis′tənt), ADJECTIVE. not willing to accept something: *She was resistant to changes.*

res·o·lu·tion (rez′ə lü′shən), NOUN.
1 a firm decision to do or not to do something: *He made a resolution to get up early.*
2 the quality of having strong determination: *The pioneers' resolution overcame their hardships.*

re·solve (ri zolv′),
1 VERB. to make up your mind about something: *I resolved to do better work in the future.*
2 VERB. to explain and clarify something: *Their letter resolved all our doubts.*
3 NOUN. firm determination; resolution. ❑ VERB **re·solves, re·solved, re·solv·ing.**

res·o·nant (rez′n ənt), ADJECTIVE. full and rich in sound: *The singer's resonant voice filled the auditorium.*

re·sort (ri zôrt′),
1 NOUN. a place people go to, usually for recreation: *There are many summer resorts in the mountains.*
2 VERB. to use something as a method when other methods have failed: *When discussion doesn't solve a problem, some nations resort to war.*
3 NOUN. someone or something turned to for help: *Friends and family are the best resort in a time of crisis or trouble.* ❑ VERB **re·sorts, re·sort·ed, re·sort·ing.**

re·sound (ri zound′), VERB.
1 to be filled with sound; echo: *The room resounded with the children's shouts.*
2 to echo: *The hills resounded when we shouted.* ❑ VERB **re·sounds, re·sound·ed, re·sound·ing.**

re·source (ri sôrs′ or rē′sôrs), NOUN. something that will meet a need. We have resources of money, of knowledge, and of strength.

re·spect (ri spekt′),
1 NOUN. a feeling of honor and admiration: *The children show great respect for their parents.*
2 VERB. to feel or show special thoughts for someone; honor: *We respect honest people.*
3 NOUN. a careful attitude toward things: *We should show respect for school buildings, parks, and other public property.*
4 VERB. to be careful or thoughtful about something: *Respect the ideas and feelings of others.*
5 NOUN. **respects,** polite expressions: *Give them my respects.*
6 NOUN. a particular feature or detail: *The plan is unwise in many respects.* ❑ VERB **re·spects, re·spect·ed, re·spect·ing.**

These people are bowing to show their **respect.**

re·spect·a·ble (ri spek′tə bəl), ADJECTIVE.
1 very well thought of; having a good reputation: *They are very respectable people.*
2 fairly good: *His schoolwork is respectable, but never brilliant.*

re·spect·ful (ri spekt′fəl), ADJECTIVE. showing respect; polite: *I always try to be respectful to other people.* —**re·spect′ful·ly**, ADVERB.

re·spec·tive (ri spek′tiv), ADJECTIVE. belonging to each separate person or thing that is mentioned: *The classes went to their respective rooms.*

re·spec·tive·ly (ri spek′tiv lē), ADVERB. each separately or in the order mentioned: *The three children are 6, 8, and 10 years old, respectively.*

res·pi·ra·tion (res′pə rā′shən), NOUN. the act or process of breathing in and out: *A bad cold can make respiration difficult.*

res·pir·a·to·ry (res′pər ə tôr′ē), ADJECTIVE. of or about breathing: *Dust in the air causes respiratory problems.*

respiratory system, the system of the body that takes in oxygen from the air and gets rid of carbon dioxide. The nasal passages, bronchial tubes, and lungs are parts of the respiratory system.

respiratory system

re·spond (ri spond′), VERB.

1 to say or write something as an answer; reply: *He responded briefly to the question.*

2 to react to something: *A dog responds to kind treatment by loving its owner.*

3 to get better after taking medicine: *She responded quickly to the medicine and was well in a few days.*
❑ VERB **re·sponds, re·spond·ed, re·spond·ing.**

re·sponse (ri spons′), NOUN. an answer by saying, writing, or doing something: *Her response to my letter was prompt. She laughed in response to his joke.* ▪ See the Synonym Study at **answer.**

re·spon·si·bil·i·ty (ri spon′sə bil′ə tē), NOUN.

1 the act or fact of being responsible; duty: *We agreed to share responsibility for planning the birthday party.*

2 something or someone that you are responsible for: *Keeping my room clean and feeding the cat are my responsibilities.*
❑ PLURAL **re·spon·si·bil·i·ties.**

re·spon·si·ble (ri spon′sə bəl), ADJECTIVE.

1 expected to take care of someone or something: *You are responsible for keeping your room cleaned up.*

2 being the cause of something, especially something bad or unpleasant: *Rain was responsible for the small attendance.*

3 able to be trusted; reliable: *The class chose a responsible pupil to take care of its money.*
—**re·spon′si·bly**, ADVERB.

rest[1] (rest),

1 NOUN. sleep: *The children had a good night's rest.*

2 VERB. to be still or quiet; sleep: *Lie down and rest.*

3 NOUN. a short pause to be quiet after working or playing hard: *After mowing the lawn, I needed rest. I left the swimming pool for a short rest.*

4 VERB. to be free from work, effort, care, or trouble: *Most people like to rest on weekends.*

5 NOUN. the condition of being still: *The ball came to rest at her feet.*

6 VERB. to give rest to; refresh by rest: *Stop and rest your feet.*

7 VERB. to place or be placed for support; lie; lay something: *He rested his rake against the fence. The roof of the porch rests on columns.*

8 VERB. (of the eyes) to look directly at someone or something: *Our eyes rested on the open book.*

9 NOUN. in music: **a** a pause of definite length. **b** a mark that shows this pause.
❑ VERB **rests, rest·ed, rest·ing.** ▪ Another word that sounds like this is **wrest.**

lay to rest, IDIOM. to bury: *lay a body to rest.*

rest[2] (rest),

1 NOUN. what is left: *The sun was out in the morning but it rained for the rest of the day.*

2 NOUN. those that are left: *One horse was running ahead of the rest.*

3 VERB. to continue to be; remain: *The final decision rests with you.*
❑ VERB **rests, rest·ed, rest·ing.** ▪ Another word that sounds like this is **wrest.**

res·tau·rant (res′tə ränt′ or res′tər ənt), NOUN. a place to buy and eat a meal.

Word Story

The word **restaurant** was borrowed from a French word. It can be traced back to a Latin word meaning "to restore." The idea is that in a restaurant you can restore your strength by eating. The English word **restore** comes from the same Latin word.

rest·less (rest′lis), ADJECTIVE.

1 unable to rest; not still or quiet; uneasy: *The dog was restless, as if it sensed some danger.*

2 without rest or sleep: *The sick child passed a restless night.*
—**rest′less·ly**, ADVERB. —**rest′less·ness**, NOUN.

res·to·ra·tion (res′tə rā′shən), NOUN. something that has been restored: *The house we slept in was a restoration of a colonial mansion.*

a	hat	ė	term	ô	order	ch	child
ā	age	i	it	oi	oil	ng	long
ä	far	ī	ice	ou	out	sh	she
â	care	o	hot	u	cup	th	thin
e	let	ō	open	ù	put	ŦH	then
ē	equal	ò	saw	ü	rule	zh	measure

ə { a in about / e in taken / i in pencil / o in lemon / u in circus }

R

re·store (ri stôr′), *VERB.*
1 to bring something back to a former condition or to a normal condition: *They have almost completely restored the old house.*
2 to give something back that had been taken away: *She restored the money she had found to its owner.* ❑ *VERB* **re·stores, re·stored, re·stor·ing.** **–re·stor′a·ble,** *ADJECTIVE.* **–re·stor′er,** *NOUN.*

re·strain (ri strān′), *VERB.* to hold something or someone back: *I could not restrain my curiosity to see what was in the box.* ❑ *VERB* **re·strains, re·strained, re·strain·ing.**

re·strict (ri strikt′), *VERB.* to keep something within limits; confine: *Our club membership is restricted to only twelve people.* ❑ *VERB* **re·stricts, re·strict·ed, re·strict·ing.**

re·stric·tion (ri strik′shən), *NOUN.* a rule or law that restricts something: *The restrictions on the use of the playground are: no fighting; no littering.*

rest·room or **rest room** (rest′rüm′), *NOUN.* a washroom or bathroom in a public building.

re·sult (ri zult′),
1 *NOUN.* something that happens because of something else; what is caused: *The result of my fall was a broken leg.*
2 *VERB.* to happen because of something: *Sickness often results from eating spoiled food.* ❑ *VERB* **re·sults, re·sult·ed, re·sult·ing.**
result in, *IDIOM.* to cause something to happen: *Eating spoiled food often results in sickness.*

re·sume (ri züm′), *VERB.*
1 to begin doing something again: *Let's resume reading where we left off.*
2 to take again: *Those standing may resume their seats.* ❑ *VERB* **re·sumes, re·sumed, re·sum·ing.**

res·ur·rec·tion (rez′ə rek′shən), *NOUN.*
1 the act of coming to life again; rising from the dead.
2 **Resurrection,** (in Christian belief) the rising again of Jesus after His death and burial.

re·tail (rē′tāl),
1 *NOUN.* the sale of goods in stores or shops directly to the user.
2 *ADJECTIVE.* of or about the sale of goods in small quantities: *The wholesale price of this coat is $40; the retail price is $60.*
3 *VERB.* to sell or be sold directly to users: *They retail these jackets at $60 each.* ❑ *VERB* **re·tails, re·tailed, re·tail·ing.** **–re′tail·er,** *NOUN.*

re·tain (ri tān′), *VERB.*
1 to continue to have or hold something; keep: *A china teapot retains heat for quite a long time. Our baseball team retained a lead throughout the game.*
2 to keep in mind; remember: *She retained the tune but not the words of the song.* ❑ *VERB* **re·tains, re·tained, re·tain·ing.**

re·tain·er (ri tā′nər), *NOUN.* a metal and plastic device worn in your mouth to hold your teeth in place. You wear a retainer on your teeth after they have been straightened by wearing braces.

re·tard·ed (ri tär′did), *ADJECTIVE.* slow in mental development.

ret·i·na (ret′n ə), *NOUN.* the lining at the back of the eyeball. It is sensitive to light and receives the images of things looked at. ❑ *PLURAL* **ret·i·nas.**

re·tire (ri tīr′), *VERB.*
1 to give up an office or occupation, usually at a certain age: *Our teachers retire at 65.*
2 to go to bed: *We retire early.*
3 to put out a batter, side, and so on, in baseball and cricket. ❑ *VERB* **re·tires, re·tired, re·tir·ing.** **–re·tire′ment,** *NOUN.*

re·tired (ri tīrd′), *ADJECTIVE.* no longer working, usually because of age: *a retired teacher.*

re·tir·ing (ri tī′ring), *ADJECTIVE.* shrinking from society or publicity; shy: *He is a quiet, retiring person.*

re·trace (ri trās′), *VERB.* to go back over your steps, a path, and so on: *We retraced our steps to where we started.* ❑ *VERB* **re·trac·es, re·traced, re·trac·ing.**

re·treat (ri trēt′),
1 *VERB.* to move back: *The enemy retreated before the advance of our soldiers.*
2 *NOUN.* the act of moving back: *The army's retreat was orderly.*
3 *NOUN.* a safe, quiet place for rest or relaxation: *She went to her mountain retreat for the weekend.* ❑ *VERB* **re·treats, re·treat·ed, re·treat·ing.**

re·trieve (ri trēv′), *VERB.*
1 to get something back again; recover: *I lost my notebook and never retrieved it.*
2 to find and carry back to someone: *A dog can be trained to retrieve a ball.* ❑ *VERB* **re·trieves, re·trieved, re·triev·ing.**

re·triev·er (ri trē′vər), *NOUN.* a dog that can be trained to find killed or wounded game and bring it back to a hunter.

retriever — about 2 feet high at the shoulder

re·turn (ri tèrn′),
1 *VERB.* to go back; come back; happen again: *Return home at once. My sister will return this summer.*
2 *NOUN.* the act of going or coming back; happening again: *We look forward all winter to our return to the country.*
3 *VERB.* to bring back; send something back: *You need to return that book to the library.*
4 *NOUN.* often, **returns,** profit: *The returns from the sale were more than a hundred dollars.*

5 *NOUN.* an official report, especially of an election; account: *The returns are in, and the mayor has been reelected.*

6 *VERB.* to report or announce something officially: *The jury returned a verdict of guilty.*

7 in football: **a** *VERB.* to run a kick, fumble, or intercepted pass back toward your opponent's goal. **b** *NOUN.* the runback of a kick, fumble, or intercepted pass.
❑ *VERB* **re•turns, re•turned, re•turn•ing.**

re•turn•a•ble (ri tėr′nə bəl), *ADJECTIVE.* meant or required to be returned: *returnable bottles and cans.*

re•un•ion (rē yü′nyən), *NOUN.* the act of coming together again: *We have a family reunion at Thanksgiving.*

re•u•nite (rē′yü nīt′), *VERB.* to bring together again; come together again: *The two friends were reunited after a long separation.* ❑ *VERB* **re•u•nites, re•u•nit•ed, re•u•nit•ing.**

re•us•a•ble (rē yü′zə bəl), *ADJECTIVE.* able to be used over and over: *reusable containers.*

re•veal (ri vēl′), *VERB.*
1 to make something known: *I promised never to reveal her secret.*
2 to display or show something: *His smile revealed his even white teeth.*
❑ *VERB* **re•veals, re•vealed, re•veal•ing.**

rev•e•la•tion (rev′ə lā′shən), *NOUN.*
1 something that is made known: *Her true nature was a revelation to me.*
2 the act of making something known: *We all waited for the revelation of the winner's name.*

re•venge (ri venj′), *NOUN.* the act of doing harm to someone who has done harm to you: *If you embarrass him, he will get revenge.*

rev•e•nue (rev′ə nü), *NOUN.* money that comes from sales or from taxes. ❑ *PLURAL* **rev•e•nues.**

rev•er•ence (rev′ər əns), *NOUN.* a feeling of deep respect, mixed with wonder, fear, and love.

Rev•er•end (rev′ər ənd), *ADJECTIVE.* a title for members of the clergy: *The Reverend John Smith.*

re•verse (ri vėrs′),
1 *ADJECTIVE.* turned backward; opposite or contrary in position or direction: *Play the reverse side of that phonograph record.*
2 *NOUN.* the opposite of what is usual or expected: *I found the reverse of what I thought I would find.*
3 *NOUN.* the back: *What is on the reverse of the coin?*
4 *VERB.* to turn inside out; turn upside down: *He reversed his coat when it started to rain.*
5 *NOUN.* an arrangement of gears that reverses the movement of machinery: *Put the car in reverse and back up.*
6 *VERB.* to change something to its opposite; repeal: *The higher court reversed the lower court's decision.*
❑ *VERB* **re•vers•es, re•versed, re•vers•ing.**

re•view (ri vyü′),
1 *VERB.* to look at something again; study again: *Review today's lesson for tomorrow.*
2 *NOUN.* the act of looking at or studying again: *We had a review of the past year's major events.*
3 *NOUN.* an official inspection or examination: *A review of the troops will be held during the general's visit.*
4 *NOUN.* an opinion or judgment of a book, play, concert, movie, and so on, published in a newspaper or magazine.
5 *VERB.* to examine and give an opinion of something: *She reviews books for a living.*
❑ *VERB* **re•views, re•viewed, re•view•ing.**
—**re•view′er,** *NOUN.*

re•vise (ri vīz′), *VERB.*
1 to read over something carefully in order to correct and improve it: *She has revised the story to make it shorter.*
2 to change something: *I revised my plan.*
❑ *VERB* **re•vis•es, re•vised, re•vis•ing.**

re•viv•al (ri vī′vəl), *NOUN.*
1 the act or process of bringing or coming back to style or use: *a revival of interest in folk music.*
2 special services or efforts made to awaken or increase interest in religion.

re•vive (ri vīv′), *VERB.*
1 to bring back or come back to life or consciousness: *The lifeguard revived the half-drowned swimmer.*
2 to restore; make or become fresh: *Hot cocoa revived us after a long, cold walk.*
3 to bring something back to popular notice or use again: *A local theater is trying to revive some old movies.*
❑ *VERB* **re•vives, re•vived, re•viv•ing.**

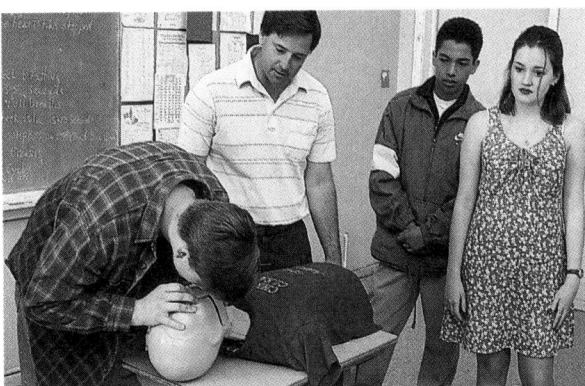

These students are learning how to **revive** someone by practicing on a dummy.

a	hat	ė	term	ô	order	ch	child	⎧a in about
ā	age	i	it	oi	oil	ng	long	⎪e in taken
ä	far	ī	ice	ou	out	sh	she	ə⎨i in pencil
â	care	o	hot	u	cup	th	thin	⎪o in lemon
e	let	ō	open	ů	put	∓H	then	⎩u in circus
ē	equal	ò	saw	ü	rule	zh	measure	

re·voke (ri vōk′), *VERB.* to cancel; repeal; withdraw: *After his third ticket for speeding, his driver's license was revoked.* ❑ *VERB* **re·vokes, re·voked, re·vok·ing.**

re·volt (ri vōlt′),
1 *NOUN.* the act or condition of rising against the authority of the government: *One cause of the revolt was unfair taxes.*
2 *VERB.* to rise up against the authority of the government: *The people revolted against the dictator.*
3 *VERB.* to cause someone to feel disgust: *Senseless cruelty revolts me.*
❑ *VERB* **re·volts, re·volt·ed, re·volt·ing.**

rev·o·lu·tion (rev′ə lü′shən), *NOUN.*
1 a movement in a circle or curve around some point: *One revolution of the earth around the sun takes a year.*
2 the act or fact of turning around a center: *The wheel of the motor turns at a rate of more than one thousand revolutions a minute.*
3 a complete change in government, usually caused by violent force: *The American Revolution gave independence to the colonies.*
4 a complete change of some kind: *The automobile caused a revolution in the way people traveled.*

rev·o·lu·tion·ar·y (rev′ə lü′shə ner′ē), *ADJECTIVE.*
1 of or about a political revolution: *revolutionary speeches, revolutionary leaders.*
2 bringing about or causing great changes: *Radio and television were two revolutionary inventions of this century.*

Revolutionary War, the war fought by the American colonies from 1775 to 1783 to gain their independence from England.

rev·o·lu·tion·ize (rev′ə lü′shə nīz), *VERB.* to change completely; produce a very great change in: *Computers have revolutionized people's lives.* ❑ *VERB* **rev·o·lu·tion·iz·es, rev·o·lu·tion·ized, rev·o·lu·tion·iz·ing.**

re·volve (ri volv′), *VERB.*
1 to move in a circle around something: *The moon revolves around the earth.*
2 to turn around a center: *The wheels of a moving car revolve.*
■ See the Synonym Study at **turn.** ❑ *VERB* **re·volves, re·volved, re·volv·ing.**

re·volv·er (ri vol′vər), *NOUN.* a small gun that can be fired several times without being loaded again.

re·ward (ri wôrd′),
1 *NOUN.* something you get in return for something that you have done: *A summer at camp was her reward for high grades.*
2 *NOUN.* money that is given or offered for something. Rewards are given for information that leads to the capture of criminals and the return of lost property.
3 *VERB.* to give a reward to someone: *They rewarded me for finding their lost dog.*
❑ *VERB* **re·wards, re·ward·ed, re·ward·ing.**

re·wind (rē wīnd′ for verb; rē′wīnd for noun),
1 *VERB.* to wind recording tape backward, toward the beginning: *After watching the movie, she rewound the tape and took it out of the VCR.*
2 *NOUN.* the act or process of rewinding tape.
❑ *VERB* **re·winds, re·wound, re·wind·ing.**

re·word (rē wėrd′), *VERB.* to put something in other words. ❑ *VERB* **re·words, re·word·ed, re·word·ing.**

re·wound (rē wound′), *VERB.*
1 the past tense of **rewind:** *I rewound the tape and listened to the message again.*
2 the past participle of **rewind:** *That videotape has been rewound.*

re·write (rē rīt′), *VERB.* to write something over again; write in a different form. ❑ *VERB* **re·writes, re·wrote** (rē rōt′), **re·writ·ten** (rē rit′n), **re·writ·ing.**

Reye's syn·drome (rīz′ sin′drōm or rāz′ sin′drōm), a rare and often fatal disease that occurs in children, most often after infections caused by viruses.

rheu·mat·ic fe·ver (rü mat′ik fē′vər), a disease most often of children that causes fever, pain in the joints, and often damage to the heart.

rheu·ma·tism (rü′mə tiz′əm), *NOUN.* a condition that causes soreness, swelling, and stiffness of the joints or muscles.

Rhine (rīn), *NOUN.* a river in western Europe.

rhi·no (rī′nō), *NOUN.* a short form of **rhinoceros.**
❑ *PLURAL* **rhi·no** or **rhi·nos.**

rhi·noc·er·os (rī nos′ər əs), *NOUN.* a large, thick-skinned animal of Africa and Asia with hoofs and with one or two upright horns above its nose. Rhinoceroses eat grass and other plants.
❑ *PLURAL* **rhi·noc·er·os·es** or **rhi·noc·er·os.**

This kind of **rhinoceros** has two horns and is about 5½ feet high at the shoulder.

Rhode Is·land (rōd′ ī′lənd), one of the northeastern states of the United States. *Abbreviation:* RI; *Capital:* Providence. **—Rhode Islander.**

State Story   Rhode Island probably got its name from **Rhodes** (rōdz), an island in the eastern Mediterranean Sea. The name was originally given to the largest island in **Narragansett Bay** (nar′ə gan′sit bā′). This island was thought to be about the size of the island of Rhodes.

rho·do·den·dron (rō′də den′drən), NOUN. an evergreen shrub with tough leaves and clusters of bright pink, purple, or white flowers.

rhom·bus (rom′bəs), NOUN. a parallelogram with equal sides. A rhombus usually has angles that are greater or less than a right angle. ❑ PLURAL **rhom·bus·es.**

rhu·barb (rü′bärb), NOUN. the sour stalks of a garden plant with very large, poisonous leaves. The stalks are used for making sauce or pies.

rhyme (rīm),
1 VERB. to have words or lines that end in the same sound: *"Long" and "song" rhyme. "Go to bed" rhymes with "sleepy head."*
2 NOUN. a word or line that ends in the same sound as another word or line: *"Have you any wool?" and "Three bags full" are rhymes.*
3 NOUN. a poem or song that has rhymes like this.
4 NOUN. an agreement in the last sounds of words or lines.
5 VERB. to use a word with another word that rhymes with it: *She rhymed "love" with "dove."* ❑ VERB **rhymes, rhymed, rhym·ing.**

without rhyme or reason, IDIOM. having no system or sense: *Their new plan is without rhyme or reason—it will never work!*

rhythm (riŦH′əm), NOUN. the natural strong beat that some music or poetry has. Rhythm makes you want to clap your hands to keep time.

rhyth·mic (riŦH′mik), ADJECTIVE. rhythmical: *the rhythmic beat of the heart.*

rhyth·mi·cal (riŦH′mə kəl), ADJECTIVE. having rhythm: *the rhythmical sound of the music.* **—rhyth′mi·cal·ly,** ADVERB.

RI, an abbreviation of **Rhode Island.**

rib (rib), NOUN.
1 one of the curved bones that go from the backbone around the heart and lungs to the front of the body.
2 something like a rib. The curved timbers in a ship's frame are called ribs. An umbrella has ribs.

rib·bon (rib′ən), NOUN.
1 a narrow piece of cloth or paper used for decorating and tying things: *The gift was tied with a big red ribbon.*

2 anything like such a strip: *The flag was torn to ribbons by the windstorm.* **—rib′bon·like′,** ADJECTIVE.

rice (rīs), NOUN. the grain of a kind of cereal grass, or the plant that it grows on. Rice is grown in warm climates and is an important food in India, China, and Japan.

At least half the people in the world eat **rice** every day.

rich (rich),
1 ADJECTIVE. having a great deal of money, land, goods, or other property: *That movie star is a very rich man.*
2 NOUN PLURAL. **the rich,** rich people.
3 ADJECTIVE. having a lot of something; well supplied: *Kuwait is a country rich in oil.*
4 ADJECTIVE. producing a lot of something: *a rich soil, a rich mine.*
5 ADJECTIVE. containing plenty of butter, eggs, cream, and flavoring: *a rich cake, a rich sauce.*
6 ADJECTIVE. valuable; worthy: *a rich harvest, a rich suggestion.*
7 ADJECTIVE. deep; full: *My favorite dress is made of rich red velvet. That famous singer is known for his rich tone.* **—rich′ly,** ADVERB. **—rich′ness,** NOUN.

rich·es (rich′iz), NOUN PLURAL. a great deal of money or property; wealth.

Rich·mond (rich′mənd), NOUN. the capital of Virginia.

rick·et·y (rik′ə tē), ADJECTIVE. liable to fall or break down: *There were two rickety chairs in the room.*

ric·o·chet (rik′ə shā′), VERB. to skip or glance off a surface in a different direction: *The bullet struck a rock and ricocheted through the air.* ❑ VERB **ric·o·chets, ric·o·cheted** (rik′ə shād′), **ric·o·chet·ing** (rik′ə shā′ing).

a	hat	ė	term	ô	order	ch	child	⎧a in about
ā	age	i	it	oi	oil	ng	long	⎪e in taken
ä	far	ī	ice	ou	out	sh	she	ə⎨i in pencil
â	care	o	hot	u	cup	th	thin	⎪o in lemon
e	let	ō	open	ů	put	ŦH	then	⎩u in circus
ē	equal	ò	saw	ü	rule	zh	measure	

R

rid (rid), VERB. to remove something harmful or annoying from a place: *What will rid a house of mice?* ❏ VERB **rids, rid** or **rid·ded, rid·ding.**
get rid of, IDIOM.
1 to get free from: *I can't get rid of this cold.*
2 to cause something to disappear: *Poison will get rid of the ants.*

rid·den (rid′n), VERB. the past participle of **ride:** *I had ridden my bicycle all day.*

rid·dle[1] (rid′l), NOUN. a puzzle that asks a question. EXAMPLE: When is a door not a door? ANSWER: When it is ajar. ■ See the Synonym Study at **mystery.**

rid·dle[2] (rid′l), VERB. to fill with many holes: *Insects had riddled the old tree stump.* ❏ VERB **rid·dles, rid·dled, rid·dling.**

ride (rīd),
1 VERB. to sit on something and make it go: *to ride a horse, to ride a bicycle.*
2 VERB. to be carried along in something: *to ride on a train, to ride in a car.*
3 VERB. to be carried along or on something: *The eagle rides the wind. The raft rode the waves.*
4 NOUN. a trip on horseback, in a car, on a bike, train, or on anything else that carries you: *On Sundays we take a ride into the country.*
5 NOUN. a machine that people ride on for fun at a carnival or amusement park: *The carnival had a roller coaster, a Ferris wheel, and other rides.*
❏ VERB **rides, rode, rid·den, rid·ing.**
let ride, IDIOM. to leave undisturbed or undecided: *Let it ride until later.*
ride out, IDIOM. to survive successfully: *The small boat rode out the storm without damage.*

rid·er (rī′dər), NOUN. someone who rides on or in something: *The riders were thrown forward when the train made a sudden stop.*

ridge (rij), NOUN.
1 a long, narrow chain of hills or mountains: *We camped for a week on the Blue Ridge of the Appalachian Mountains.*
2 any raised narrow strip: *the ridges in plowed ground, the ridges on corduroy cloth.*
3 a line where two sloping surfaces meet: *He squatted near the ridge of the roof as he laid shingles.*

rid·i·cule (rid′ə kyül),
1 VERB. to laugh at or make fun or someone: *The cruel children ridiculed her old clothes.*
2 NOUN. words or actions that make fun of somebody or something: *I was hurt by the ridicule of my classmates.*
❏ VERB **rid·i·cules, rid·i·culed, rid·i·cul·ing.**

ri·dic·u·lous (ri dik′yə ləs), ADJECTIVE. completely silly; laughable: *It would be ridiculous to walk backward all the time.* —**ri·dic′u·lous·ly,** ADVERB.

ri·fle (rī′fəl), NOUN. a gun with a long barrel. A rifle is usually fired from the shoulder.

rig (rig),
1 NOUN. heavy equipment used for drilling into the earth: *My uncle works on an oil rig.*
2 VERB. to arrange something in a dishonest, unfair way: *The race was rigged.*
3 NOUN. a truck or other large motor vehicle: *His mother drives a big rig.*
4 VERB. to equip a ship with masts, sails, and ropes: *It took us 20 minutes to rig our sailboat.*
5 NOUN. the arrangement of masts and sails on a ship.
❏ VERB **rigs, rigged, rig·ging.**
rig up, IDIOM. to put something together in a hurry, using whatever is lying around: *The girls rigged up a tent in the yard with a rope and a blanket.*

an offshore oil **rig**

rig·ging (rig′ing), NOUN. the ropes, chains, and cables that support and control a ship's masts and sails.

right (rīt),
1 ADJECTIVE. good; just; lawful: *She did the right thing when she told the truth.*
2 ADVERB. in a way that is good, just, or lawful: *He acted right when he told the truth.*
3 NOUN. whatever is right, just, good, true: *Do right, not wrong.*
4 NOUN. something that is due to you: *Each member of the club has a right to vote. I demanded my rights.*
5 ADJECTIVE. correct; true: *the right answer.*
6 ADVERB. correctly; truly: *She guessed right.*
7 ADJECTIVE. fitting; proper: *Learn to say the right thing at the right time.*
8 ADVERB. properly; well: *It's faster to do a job right the first time.*
9 ADJECTIVE. well: *I don't feel right; I think I'm getting the flu.*
10 ADJECTIVE. meant to be seen; most important: *the right side of cloth, right side up.*
11 VERB. to make something right: *He worked to right a wrong.*

12 *VERB.* to put right; get into the proper position: *The boys righted the boat. The ship righted itself after the big wave passed.*

13 *ADJECTIVE.* in the direction toward the last word on this line; opposite of left. You have a right hand and a left hand.

14 *ADVERB.* on or to the right side: *Turn right when you get to the corner.*

15 *NOUN.* the right-hand side: *Turn to your right.*

16 *ADVERB.* exactly: *Your cap is right where you left it.*

17 *ADVERB.* at once; immediately: *Stop playing right now.*

18 *ADVERB.* directly: *Look me right in the eye.*
> ❑ *VERB* **rights, right·ed, right·ing.** ■ Other words that sound like this are **rite** and **write.**
> **—right′ness,** *NOUN.*

right away, *IDIOM.* at once; immediately.

right angle, an angle of 90 degrees. The angles in a square are right angles.

right·eous (rī′chəs), *ADJECTIVE.*

1 doing right; virtuous; morally good: *A righteous person treats others with kindness.*

2 proper; just; right: *righteous anger.*
> **—right′eous·ness,** *NOUN.*

right field, (in baseball) the section of the outfield beyond first base. **—right fielder.**

right·ful (rīt′fəl), *ADJECTIVE.*

1 according to law; by right: *the rightful owner of this dog.*

2 just and right; proper: *I took my rightful place alongside the others.*
> **—right′ful·ly,** *ADVERB.*

right-hand (rīt′hand′), *ADJECTIVE.*

1 on or to the right: *At this corner, you should make a right-hand turn.*

2 of, for, or with the right hand: *a right-hand glove, a right-hand throw.*

3 most helpful or useful: *He is the scoutmaster's right-hand man.*

right-hand·ed (rīt′han′did), *ADJECTIVE.* using your right hand more easily and more readily than your left. Most people are right-handed.
> **—right′-hand′ed·ness,** *NOUN.*

right·ly (rīt′lē), *ADVERB.*

1 in a just manner; fairly: *She was quite rightly upset by their behavior.*

2 correctly: *She guessed rightly that it would rain.*

right triangle, a triangle with one right angle.

rig·id (rij′id), *ADJECTIVE.*

1 stiff; firm; not bending: *a rigid metal bar.*

2 severe and not changing: *In our home, it is a rigid rule to wash your hands before eating.*
> **—rig′id·ly,** *ADVERB.*

rim (rim), *NOUN.* an edge or border that is on or around anything: *the rim of a wheel, the rim of a cup.*

rind (rīnd), *NOUN.* a tough outer covering on oranges, lemons, limes, melons, and cheese.

ring¹ (ring),

1 *NOUN.* a thin circle of metal or other material: *a wedding ring, a key ring, a napkin ring.*

2 *NOUN.* a circle or something in a circular shape: *You can tell the age of a tree by counting the number of rings in its wood; one ring grows every year. The children danced in a ring.*

3 *VERB.* to put or grow in a ring or closed shape around something; enclose: *Trees ringed the backyard.*

4 *NOUN.* an enclosed space for races or games: *a circus ring, a boxing ring.*
> ❑ *VERB* **rings, ringed, ring·ing.** ■ Another word that sounds like this is **wring.**

ring² (ring),

1 *VERB.* to make a clear sound, as a bell does: *Did the telephone ring?*

2 *VERB.* to cause something to give forth a clear, ringing sound: *Ring the bell.*

3 *NOUN.* the sound of a bell: *Did you hear a ring?*

4 *NOUN.* a sound something like that of a bell: *On a cold night we can hear the ring of skates on ice.*

5 *VERB.* to hear a sound like that of a bell ringing: *My ears ring when I have a fever.*

6 *NOUN.* a call on the telephone: *I'll give you a ring tonight.*
> ❑ *VERB* **rings, rang, rung, ring·ing.** ■ Another word that sounds like this is **wring.**

ring a bell, *IDIOM.* be familiar; to remind you of something: *I can't remember your name but your face rings a bell.*

ring up, *IDIOM.* to record a specific amount on a cash register: *He rang up my groceries in a hurry.*

ring·lead·er (ring′lē′dər), *NOUN.* someone who leads other people in opposition to authority or law: *The ringleaders of the mutiny were placed in irons.*

ring·worm (ring′wėrm′), *NOUN.* a contagious skin disease caused by a fungus. Ringworm causes ring-shaped patches on the scalp or other areas.

rink (ringk), *NOUN.*

1 a sheet of ice for ice-skating.

2 a smooth floor for roller-skating.

rinse (rins),

1 *VERB.* to wash something with clean water: *Rinse all the soap out of your hair after you wash it.*

2 *VERB.* to wash something lightly: *Rinse your mouth with warm water.*

3 *NOUN.* the act of rinsing: *Give the plate a final rinse in hot water.*
> ❑ *VERB* **rins·es, rinsed, rins·ing.**

Ri·o de Ja·nei·ro (rē′ō dā zhə ner′ō), a city in Brazil.

R

a	hat	ė	term	ô	order	ch	child		a in about
ā	age	i	it	oi	oil	ng	long		e in taken
ä	far	ī	ice	ou	out	sh	she	ə	i in pencil
â	care	o	hot	u	cup	th	thin		o in lemon
e	let	ō	open	ů	put	ŦH	then		u in circus
ē	equal	o	saw	ü	rule	zh	measure		

ri·ot (rī′ət),
1 *NOUN.* a wild, violent disturbance by a lot of people: *There was a riot in the prison over bad food.*
2 *VERB.* to behave in a wild, disorderly way.
3 *NOUN.* (informal) a very funny person or performance: *She was a riot at the party.*
❑ *VERB* **ri·ots, ri·ot·ed, ri·ot·ing.** —**ri′ot·er,** *NOUN.*

ri·ot·ous (rī′ə təs), *ADJECTIVE.*
1 taking part in a riot: *The leaders of the riotous mob were arrested.*
2 noisily cheerful; wild: *Sounds of riotous glee came from the playhouse.*
—**ri′ot·ous·ly,** *ADVERB.*

rip (rip),
1 *VERB.* to cut or pull something off in a rough way; tear off: *I ripped the cover off the box.*
2 *NOUN.* a torn place, especially a torn seam in a piece of clothing: *Please sew up this rip in my sleeve.*
3 *VERB.* to move fast or violently: *Fire ripped through the building.*
❑ *VERB* **rips, ripped, rip·ping.**

ripe (rīp), *ADJECTIVE.* full-grown and ready to be picked and eaten: *a ripe piece of fruit, ripe grain, ripe vegetables.* ❑ *ADJECTIVE* **rip·er, rip·est.**

rip·en (rī′pən), *VERB.* to become ripe; make ripe: *Tomatoes ripen quickly in the sun.* ❑ *VERB* **rip·ens, rip·ened, rip·en·ing.**

rip·ple (rip′əl),
1 *NOUN.* a very little wave: *I threw a stone into still water and watched the ripples spread in rings.*
2 *NOUN.* anything that seems like a tiny spreading wave: *a ripple of laughter in the crowd.*
3 *VERB.* to make little ripples on something: *A breeze rippled the water.*
❑ *VERB* **rip·ples, rip·pled, rip·pling.**

Ripples spread where the pebble dropped.

rise (rīz),
1 *VERB.* to get up from a lying, sitting, or kneeling position; stand up; get up: *Please rise from your seat when you say your lines.*
2 *VERB.* to get up from sleep or rest: *I rise at 7 o'clock every morning.*
3 *VERB.* to go up; come up: *Mercury rises in a thermometer on a hot day.*
4 *VERB.* to go higher; increase: *Prices have begun to rise a little.*
5 *NOUN.* the act or process of going up; increase: *a rise in prices, a rise in temperature.*
6 *VERB.* to advance in importance or rank: *He rose from office clerk to president of the company.*
7 *VERB.* to slope upward: *Hills rise in the distance.*
8 *NOUN.* an upward slope: *The house is situated on a slight rise.*
9 *VERB.* to come above the horizon: *The sun rises in the morning.*
10 *VERB.* to revolt; rebel: *The peasants rose against the nobles.*
11 *VERB.* to grow larger and lighter; swell: *Yeast makes dough rise.*
❑ *VERB* **ris·es, rose, ris·en, ris·ing.**

Synonym Study

Rise means to get up or go up: *She rose from her chair to open the door. When my aunt gets mad, her voice rises.*

Arise means to get up, usually from a seat or a bed. It is a formal word: *The President arises before dawn.*

Ascend means to go upward steadily: *The plane ascended into the clouds and disappeared.*

Lift can mean to go up slowly: *The crowd watched the hot-air balloons lift into the sky.*

See also the Synonym Study at **climb.**

ris·en (riz′n), *VERB.* the past participle of **rise:** *The sun had risen long before I woke up.*

risk (risk),
1 *NOUN.* a chance of harm, loss, or danger: *There is less risk of getting sick if you eat properly.*
2 *VERB.* to expose something to the chance of harm or loss: *You'll risk your neck climbing that tree.*
3 *VERB.* to take a chance on something bad happening: *They risked defeat in fighting the larger army.*
❑ *VERB* **risks, risked, risk·ing.**

risk·y (ris′kē), *ADJECTIVE.* full of risk; dangerous.
❑ *ADJECTIVE* **risk·i·er, risk·i·est.** —**risk′i·ness,** *NOUN.*

rite (rīt), *NOUN.* a solemn ceremony. Most religions have rites for marriage and burial. ▪ Other words that sound like this are **right** and **write.**

rit·u·al (rich′ü əl), *NOUN.* a set or system of rites. The rites of marriage and burial are part of the ritual of most religions.

ri·val (rī′vəl),
1 *NOUN.* someone who wants and tries to get the same thing as you do: *She and I were rivals for the same class office.*

2 *ADJECTIVE.* wanting the same thing as someone else: *The rival supermarkets both cut their prices.*

3 *VERB.* to equal; match: *The sunset rivaled the sunrise in beauty.*

❑ *VERB* **ri·vals, ri·valed, ri·val·ing**

ri·val·ry (rī′vəl rē), *NOUN.* an effort to obtain something that someone else wants; competition: *There is rivalry among business firms for trade.*

❑ *PLURAL* **ri·val·ries.**

riv·er (riv′ər), *NOUN.*

1 a large natural stream of water that flows into a lake, ocean, or the like.

2 a large stream or flow of material: *Rivers of mud and lava flowed from the volcano.*

riv·er·bed (riv′ər bed′), *NOUN.* the channel or bed in which a river flows.

riv·er·boat (riv′ər bōt′), *NOUN.* a boat for use on a river, usually having a flat bottom.

riv·et (riv′it),

1 *NOUN.* a metal bolt with a head at one end. The end opposite the head is hammered to form another head after it is passed through the things to be joined. Rivets are often used to fasten heavy pieces of steel together.

2 *VERB.* to fasten something with a rivet or rivets.

3 *VERB.* to have your interest focused on something: *Their attention was riveted on the speaker.*

❑ *VERB* **riv·ets, riv·et·ed, riv·et·ing.**

riv·u·let (riv′yə lit), *NOUN.* a very small stream.

R.N., an abbreviation of **registered nurse.**

roach (rōch), *NOUN.* a short form of **cockroach.**

❑ *PLURAL* **roach·es.**

road (rōd), *NOUN.*

1 a smooth surface made for cars, trucks, and the like, to travel on.

2 a way: *the road to ruin, the road to peace.*
■ Another word that sounds like this is **rode.**

road·bed (rōd′bed′), *NOUN.* the foundation for a road or for railroad tracks.

road map, a drawing of a part of the earth's surface showing roads for motor vehicle travel.

road·run·ner (rōd′run′ər), *NOUN.* a bird of the deserts of the southwestern United States. It has a long tail and a crest and can run very fast.

road·side (rōd′sīd′), *NOUN.* the side of a road: *Flowers grew along the roadside.*

road·way (rōd′wā′), *NOUN.* the part of a road used by motor vehicles.

roam (rōm), *VERB.* to walk around with no special plan or aim; wander: *to roam through the fields.*

❑ *VERB* **roams, roamed, roam·ing.**

roan (rōn), *NOUN.* a horse with a red, brown, or black coat with white hairs mixed in.

roar (rôr),

1 *VERB.* to make a loud deep sound; make a loud noise: *The lion roared.*

2 *NOUN.* a loud deep sound; loud noise: *the roar of the cannon, a roar of laughter.*

3 *VERB.* to laugh loudly: *The audience roared at the clown's sad face and tiny hat.* ■ See the Synonym Study at **laugh.**

4 *VERB.* to move with a roar: *The locomotive roared past the crossing.*

❑ *VERB* **roars, roared, roar·ing.**

roast (rōst),

1 *VERB.* to cook something with the dry heat of an oven, an open fire, or hot charcoal: *Roast the meat for an hour. Coffee beans are roasted and ground to make coffee.*

2 *NOUN.* a piece of meat cooked by roasting.

3 *ADJECTIVE.* roasted: *roast beef, roast pork.*

4 *VERB.* to make or become very hot: *I am roasting in this heavy coat.*

❑ *VERB* **roasts, roast·ed, roast·ing.**

rob (rob), *VERB.* to take by force something that does not belong to you: *Thieves robbed the bank of thousands of dollars.* ❑ *VERB* **robs, robbed, rob·bing. —rob′ber,** *NOUN.*

rob·ber·y (rob′ər ē), *NOUN.* the act of robbing; theft; stealing: *a bank robbery.* ❑ *PLURAL* **rob·ber·ies.**

robe (rōb), *NOUN.*

1 a long, loose, piece of clothing like a coat: *I wore a robe over my pajamas.*

2 an article of clothing that shows rank or office: *a judge's black robe, the queen's robes of state, a choir robe.*

rob·in (rob′ən), *NOUN.* a North American songbird with a reddish breast and gray back and tail. Robins are often considered a sign of spring.

robin — between 9 and 11 inches long

a hat	ė term	ô order	ch child	⎧ a in about
ā age	i it	oi oil	ng long	e in taken
ä far	ī ice	ou out	sh she	ə ⎨ i in pencil
â care	o hot	u cup	th thin	o in lemon
e let	ō open	u̇ put	ᴛʜ then	⎩ u in circus
ē equal	ȯ saw	ü rule	zh measure	

R

ro·bot (rō′bot or rō′bət), NOUN. a machine with moving parts controlled by a computer. The computer makes it possible for the machine to perform complicated tasks, over and over, without a person to control it. Robots are sometimes built to look like human beings, but they can have any shape or size.

Word Story

Robot comes from a Czech word meaning "forced labor." A play about machines shaped like people made the word widely known. Most people still think of robots as mechanical people.

ro·bot·ics (rō bot′iks), NOUN. the study, design, construction, and use of robots.

ro·bust (rō bust′ or rō′bust), ADJECTIVE. strong and healthy; sturdy: *He is a robust young man.* ■ See the Synonym Study at **strong.**

rock¹ (rok), NOUN.
1 any piece of stone: *She threw a rock in the lake.*
2 a large mass of stone: *The ship was wrecked on the rocks.*
3 any hard mineral matter that is not metal; stone. The earth's crust is made up of rock under a layer of soil. —**rock′like**′, ADJECTIVE.

rock² (rok),
1 VERB. to move backward and forward, or from side to side; sway: *My chair rocks. The waves rocked the ship.*
2 NOUN. a rocking movement.
3 NOUN. See **rock′n′roll.**
❏ VERB **rocks, rocked, rock·ing.**

rock·er (rok′ər), NOUN.
1 one of the curved pieces on which a cradle or rocking chair rocks.
2 See **rocking chair.**

rock·et (rok′it),
1 NOUN. a device consisting of a tube open at one end in which a fuel is rapidly burned. The burning fuel creates gases that escape from the open end and force the tube and whatever is attached to it upward or forward. Rockets are used for fireworks, space exploration, warfare, and so on.
2 VERB. to move very, very fast like a rocket: *The singing group rocketed to fame with its first hit record. The racing car rocketed across the finish line.*
❏ VERB **rock·ets, rock·et·ed, rock·et·ing.**

Rock·ies (rok′ēz), NOUN PLURAL. See **Rocky Mountains.**

rocking chair, a chair mounted on rockers, or on springs, so that it can rock back and forth.

rocking horse, a toy horse on rockers or on springs for children to ride.

rock′n′roll (rok′ən rōl′), NOUN. a kind of popular music with a strong beat and simple melody. It uses electric guitars, bass, and drums.

rock·y (rok′ē), ADJECTIVE. full of rocks: *a rocky shore.*
❏ ADJECTIVE **rock·i·er, rock·i·est.**

Rocky Mountains, a group of high mountains in western North America. The Rocky Mountains are the longest mountain system in North America. They extend from Alaska to New Mexico.

Rocky Mountains

Rocky Mountain States, the states located along either side of the Rocky Mountains. Montana, Colorado, Wyoming, Utah, and Nevada are the Rocky Mountain States.

rod (rod), NOUN.
1 a thin straight pole or bar of wood, metal, or plastic: *a fishing rod, a curtain rod.*
2 a stick used to beat or punish someone.

rode (rōd), VERB. the past tense of **ride:** *We rode ten miles yesterday.* ■ Another word that sounds like this is **road.**

ro·dent (rōd′nt), NOUN. any of a group of mammals with large front teeth that are used for gnawing. Rats, mice, and squirrels are rodents.

ro·de·o (rō′dē ō or rō dā′ō), NOUN. a contest or show in which cowboys and cowgirls show their skills. They ride wild horses, steers, and bulls, and rope cattle. ❏ PLURAL **ro·de·os.**

rogue (rōg), NOUN.
1 a tricky or dishonest person; rascal.
2 a mischievous person: *The little rogue ate my pie!*
3 an animal with a savage nature that lives apart from the herd: *A rogue elephant is dangerous.*
❏ PLURAL **rogues.**

role (rōl), NOUN.
1 an actor's part in a play: *a leading role in the play.*
2 a job or function that someone has: *My aunt has the role of baby-sitter whenever my parents are busy.*
■ Another word that sounds like this is **roll.**

roll (rōl),
1 *VERB*. to move along by turning over and over: *The ball rolled away.*
2 *VERB*. to wind or wrap something into a round shape; wrap: *She rolled the string into a ball.*
3 *NOUN*. something rolled up: *a roll of film, a roll of paper.*
4 *NOUN*. a rounded mass: *a roll of cookie dough.*
5 *VERB*. to move or be moved on wheels: *The car rolled along.*
6 *VERB*. to move with a side-to-side motion: *I rolled my eyes. The ship rolled in the waves.*
7 *NOUN*. the act of rolling; motion from side to side: *The ship's roll made some of the crew sick.*
8 *VERB*. to turn over, or over and over: *The horse rolled in the dust.*
9 *VERB*. to make something flat or smooth with a rolling pin: *Roll the dough thin for these cookies.*
10 *NOUN*. a deep, loud sound: *the roll of thunder.*
11 *NOUN*. a list of names; list: *I will call the roll to find out who is absent.*
12 *NOUN*. a kind of bread or cake: *a sweet roll.*
  ■ Another word that sounds like this is **role.**
  ❑ *VERB* **rolls, rolled, roll·ing.**
on a roll, *IDIOM.* having great success which seems likely to continue.
roll call, the act of calling a list of names to find out who is present.
roll·er (rō′lər), *NOUN.*
1 a cylinder on which something is rolled along or rolled up. Window shades go up and down on rollers. Hair is curled on rollers.
2 a cylinder of metal, stone, wood, or other material used for smoothing, spreading, pressing, or crushing: *A heavy roller was used to smooth the tennis court. The paint was applied with a small roller.*
3 something that rolls, especially a small wheel:
Roll·er·blades (rō′lər blādz′), *NOUN PLURAL.* (trademark) in-line skates.
roller coaster, a ride at an amusement park, made up of inclined tracks along which trains of small cars roll and make steep drops and sudden turns.
roller skate, a shoe or metal base with four small wheels, used for skating on a smooth, dry surface.
roll·er-skate (rō′lər skāt′), *VERB.* to move on roller skates: *The children roller-skated to the park.* ❑ *VERB* **roll·er-skates, roll·er-skat·ed, roll·er-skat·ing.**
rolling pin, a cylinder of wood, plastic, or glass with a handle at each end, for rolling out dough.
ro·ly-po·ly (rō′lē pō′lē), *ADJECTIVE.* short and plump: *He was a roly-poly baby.*
ROM, read-only memory: a part of a computer in which information and instructions are stored permanently. Everything stored there can be copied and used, but nothing can be added to this memory or removed from it

Ro·man (rō′mən),
1 *ADJECTIVE.* of or about ancient or modern Rome or its people.
2 *NOUN.* someone born or living in Rome.
3 *NOUN.* a citizen of ancient or modern Rome.
4 *ADJECTIVE.* of or about the Roman Catholic Church.
5 *NOUN.* **roman,** the upright style of type most used in printing and typing. This sentence is in roman.
Roman Catholic,
1 of or belonging to the Christian church that recognizes the pope as the supreme head.
2 a member of this church.
ro·mance (rō mans′), *NOUN.*
1 a love affair: *"Cinderella" is the story of the romance between a beautiful girl and a prince.*
2 a story or poem telling of heroes and marvelous adventures: *They loved reading the romances about King Arthur and his knights.*
3 real happenings that are like stories of heroes and are full of love, excitement, or noble deeds: *The children dreamed of traveling in search of romance.*
Ro·ma·ni·a (rō mā′nē ə), *NOUN.* a country in southeastern Europe. **—Ro·ma′ni·an,** *ADJECTIVE* or *NOUN.*
Roman numerals, the numerals like XXIII, LVI, and MDCCLX, in which I = 1, V = 5, X = 10, L = 50, C = 100, D = 500, and M = 1000.

Did You Know?

Here are some tips to help you figure out those confusing **Roman numerals.**

1 Remember that when a letter is repeated, its value is repeated: XXX = 30 (10+10+10).
2 When a smaller letter follows a bigger letter, the two values are added: XI = 11 (10 + 1).
3 When a smaller letter comes before a bigger letter, subtract the smaller one from the bigger one: IV = 4 (5-1).

This clock uses **Roman numerals** to mark the hours.

R

a hat	ė term	ô order	ch child	a in about
ā age	i it	oi oil	ng long	e in taken
ä far	ī ice	ou out	sh she	ə i in pencil
â care	o hot	u cup	th thin	o in lemon
e let	ō open	u̇ put	ŦH then	u in circus
ē equal	ȯ saw	ü rule	zh measure	

ro·man·tic (rō man′tik), ADJECTIVE.
1 bringing to mind thoughts of love: *The band played soft, romantic music.*
2 having ideas or feelings filled with thoughts of love: *The old couple remembered the days when they were young and romantic.*
3 full of love, adventure, mystery, or marvels: *He likes to read romantic tales of love and war.*
—**ro·man′ti·cal·ly**, ADVERB.

Rome (rōm), NOUN. the capital of Italy. Rome was the capital of an ancient empire whose language and culture have greatly influenced the modern world.

Have You Heard?

Rome was the most important city in the world for more than a thousand years. Two of the many sayings about it follow:

"Rome was not built in a day." means that you shouldn't try to do a big or important job too quickly. Another phrase you may have heard is

"When in Rome, do as the Romans do." This means that you should follow the customs of the people you are visiting.

romp (romp),
1 VERB. to play in a rough, noisy way; rush, tumble, and jump around in play: *On rainy days the children liked to romp in the basement.*
2 NOUN. rough, lively play: *The children had a romp on the beach.*
❑ VERB **romps, romped, romp·ing.**

roof (rüf), NOUN.
1 the top covering of a building.
2 something like this: *the roof of a cave, the roof of a car.*
3 the inside, upper surface inside your mouth: *She had a sore on the roof of her mouth.*
❑ PLURAL **roofs.** —**roof′less**, ADJECTIVE. —**roof′like**′, ADJECTIVE.

raise the roof, IDIOM. (informal) to make a disturbance; create an uproar or confusion: *All the cousins in one house can really raise the roof.*

rook (rúk), NOUN. a piece in the game of chess; castle. A rook can move in a straight line across any number of empty squares.

rook·ie (rúk′ē), NOUN.
1 a player in his or her first year of professional sports.
2 an inexperienced person; beginner.
❑ PLURAL **rook·ies.**

room (rüm),
1 NOUN. a part of a house, or other building, with walls of its own: *a dining room, the living room.*
2 NOUN. the people in a room: *The whole room laughed.*
3 NOUN. an amount of space that something takes up: *The cars did not have room to move in the crowded street.*
4 NOUN. an opportunity: *There is room for improvement in her work.*
5 VERB. to live in a room with someone: *Three girls from our town roomed together at college.*
❑ VERB **rooms, roomed, room·ing.**

room·mate (rüm′māt′), NOUN. someone who shares a room with another person or persons.

room·y (rü′mē), ADJECTIVE. large; having plenty of room: *Her new apartment is quite roomy.* ❑ ADJECTIVE **room·i·er, room·i·est.** —**room′i·ness**, NOUN.

roost (rüst),
1 NOUN. a bar or perch on which birds rest or sleep.
2 VERB. to sit as birds do on a roost; settle for the night.
❑ VERB **roosts, roost·ed, roost·ing.**

roost·er (rü′stər), NOUN. a full-grown male chicken.

rooster — about 8½ pounds

root¹ (rüt),
1 NOUN. the part of a plant that grows underground. It holds the plant in place, absorbs water and food from the soil, and often stores food.
2 NOUN. something like a root in shape, position, or use: *the root of a tooth, the roots of the hair.*
3 NOUN. a part from which other things grow and develop; cause; source: *Let's get to the root of this problem.*
4 VERB. to become fixed in the ground; send out roots and begin to grow: *Some plants root more quickly than others.*
5 NOUN. a word that other words are made from. *Friend* is the root of *friendless, friendly,* and *friendship.*
❑ VERB **roots, root·ed, root·ing.** ■ Another word that can sound like this is **route.** —**root′like**′, ADJECTIVE.

Have You Heard?

You may have heard someone say **"The love of money is the root of all evil."** People say this when they want to say that greed has caused a particular problem. This proverb comes from the Bible.

root² (rüt), VERB.
1 to dig with the snout: *The pigs rooted up the garden.*
2 to search through something in a rough way: *She rooted through the closet looking for her old shoes.*
❑ VERB **roots, root·ed, root·ing.** ■ Another word that can sound like this is **route.**

root³ (rüt), *VERB.* to cheer or support a team or a member of a team enthusiastically. ❑ *VERB* **roots, root·ed, root·ing.** ■ Another word that can sound like this is **route.**

root beer, a bubbly soft drink flavored with the juice of the roots of certain plants.

rope (rōp),
1 *NOUN.* a strong thick line or cord made by twisting smaller cords together.
2 *VERB.* to tie, bind, or fasten something with a rope: *He roped the horse to a post.*
3 *VERB.* to enclose or mark something off with a rope: *In winter, they rope off the entrance to the beach.*
4 *VERB.* to catch a horse, calf, or other animal with a rope that has a loop at the end.
❑ *VERB* **ropes, roped, rop·ing.**

know the ropes, *IDIOM.* (informal) to know about a business or activity: *He agreed to stay and help until I got to know the ropes.*

rope in, *IDIOM.* (informal) to get or lead in by tricking: *She roped me in to going shopping by promising we'd only be at the mall for a little while.*

ro·sar·y (rō′zər ē), *NOUN.* a string of beads for keeping count in saying a series of prayers, used by Roman Catholics. ❑ *PLURAL* **ro·sar·ies.**

rose¹ (rōz),
1 *NOUN.* a flower that grows on a thorny bush. Roses are red, pink, white, or yellow and usually smell very sweet.
2 *ADJECTIVE* or *NOUN.* pinkish red: *Her dress was rose.*

rose² (rōz), *VERB.* the past tense of **rise:** *The cat rose and stretched.*

rose·bud (rōz′bud′),
NOUN. the bud of a rose.

Rosh Ha·sha·nah
(rosh′ hə shä′nə), the Jewish New Year. It usually occurs in September.

ros·in (roz′n), *NOUN.* a hard, yellow substance that is made from pine resin. Rosin is rubbed on violin bows and the shoes of acrobats and ballet dancers to keep them from slipping.

ros·y (rō′zē), *ADJECTIVE.*
1 like a rose; pinkish red: *rosy cheeks.*
2 promising hope or success: *a rosy future.*
❑ *ADJECTIVE* **ros·i·er, ros·i·est. –ros′i·ness,** *NOUN.*

rot (rot),
1 *VERB.* to become or cause to become rotten; decay; spoil: *So much rain will make the fruit rot.*
2 *NOUN.* the process of rotting; decay.
3 *NOUN.* any of many different diseases of plants and animals.
❑ *VERB* **rots, rot·ted, rot·ting.**

ro·tar·y (rō′tər ē), *ADJECTIVE.*
1 turning like a top or a wheel; rotating: *rotary motion.*
2 having parts that rotate: *a rotary engine.*

ro·tate (rō′tāt), *VERB.*
1 to move around a center or axis; turn in a circle; revolve. Wheels, tops, and the earth rotate. ■ See the Synonym Study at **turn.**
2 to change in a regular order; cause to take turns: *Farmers rotate their crops in order to keep the soil healthy.*
❑ *VERB* **ro·tates, ro·tat·ed, ro·tat·ing. –ro′ta·tor,** *NOUN.*

Word Story

Rotate comes from a Latin word meaning "wheel." Other English words from the same Latin root include **rotation, rotor, rodeo, roll,** and **roly-poly.**

ro·ta·tion (rō tā′shən), *NOUN.* the act of turning round a center; turning in a circle: *The earth's rotation causes night and day.*

ro·tor (rō′tər), *NOUN.*
1 the part of a machine that spins.
2 a system of spinning blades by which a helicopter is able to fly.

rot·ten (rot′n), *ADJECTIVE.*
1 no longer fit to eat; spoiled: *a rotten egg.*
2 not in good condition: *rotten beams in a floor.*
3 bad; nasty: *The weather was rotten yesterday. He had a rotten cold all last week.* ■ See the Synonym Study at **terrible.**

rouge (rüzh), *NOUN.* a red powder, paste, or liquid for coloring the cheeks.

rough (ruf),
1 *ADJECTIVE.* with an uneven surface; not smooth: *rough boards, the rough bark of oak trees.*
2 *ADJECTIVE.* stormy: *rough weather, a rough sea.*
3 *ADJECTIVE.* filled with pain or difficulty: *She had a rough time recovering from the accident.*
4 *ADJECTIVE.* likely to be violent; not gentle: *Football can be a rough game.*
5 *ADVERB.* roughly: *Those older boys play too rough for me.*
6 *ADJECTIVE.* not completed; shown without details: *a rough drawing, a rough idea.*
7 *ADJECTIVE.* coarse and tangled: *rough fur, a dog with a rough coat of hair.*
–rough′ness, *NOUN.*

rough it, *IDIOM.* to live without comforts and conveniences: *They have been roughing it in the woods this summer.*

rose¹ (definition 1)

a	hat	ė	term	ô	order	ch	child	a in about
ā	age	i	it	oi	oil	ng	long	e in taken
ä	far	ī	ice	ou	out	sh	she	i in pencil
â	care	o	hot	u	cup	th	thin	o in lemon
e	let	ō	open	ů	put	ᴙH	then	u in circus
ē	equal	ȯ	saw	ü	rule	zh	measure	

R

rough up, IDIOM.

1 to make something rough: *A strong wind roughed up the waves.*

2 to beat; treat roughly: *The angry mob roughed up the accused traitor.*

❑ VERB **roughs, roughed, rough·ing.**

Synonym Study

Rough means having a surface that is not smooth: *All this gardening has made my hands rough and dry.*

Uneven means not smooth or level: *The plowed field was uneven and hard to walk across.*

Bumpy means having a lot of bumps: *The sidewalk is bumpy with snow and ice.*

Harsh means unpleasantly rough to the touch: *Sandpaper feels harsh if you rub your hand over it.*

Rugged means having a rough, uneven surface: *The mountain country was so rugged that once we even had to drive through a stream.*

ANTONYM: smooth.

rough·house (ruf′hous′), VERB. to act in a rough, noisy way: *The children were roughhousing in the backyard.* ❑ VERB **rough·hous·es, rough·housed, rough·hous·ing.**

rough·ly (ruf′lē), ADVERB.

1 in a rough manner: *They pushed him roughly out the door.*

2 about; approximately: *My house is roughly a thousand miles from here.*

round (round),

1 ADJECTIVE. shaped like a ball or a circle: *Oranges are round. A ring is round.*

2 ADJECTIVE. plump: *The baby had round cheeks.*

3 VERB. to make or become curved: *The carpenter rounded the corners of the table.*

4 ADVERB or PREPOSITION. around: *Wheels go round. They built a fence round the yard.*

5 VERB. to go around a corner or a curve: *The car rounded the corner at high speed.*

6 NOUN. **rounds,** a series of visits to places or people while at work: *The watchman makes his rounds of the building.*

7 NOUN. a series of duties or events: *a round of duties.*

8 NOUN. a section of a game or sport: *a round in a boxing match, a round of cards.*

9 NOUN. a complete game or unit: *They played a round of golf this morning.*

10 NOUN. a bullet; a single shot: *Three rounds of ammunition were left in the rifle.*

11 NOUN. a short song sung by several persons or groups beginning one after the other. "Row, Row, Row Your Boat" is a round.

12 VERB. to change a number to the nearest hundredth, tenth, ten, hundred, and so on. 7578 rounded to the nearest hundred is 7600.

❑ VERB **rounds, round·ed, round·ing.**
—**round′ness,** NOUN.

round up, IDIOM. to drive or bring together: *The cowboys rounded up the cattle.*

round·house (round′hous′), NOUN. (earlier) a circular building where locomotives were repaired or stored. It was built around a platform that turned around. ❑ PLURAL **round·hous·es** (round′hou′ziz).

This locomotive has come to the **roundhouse** for repairs.

round·ish (roun′dish), ADJECTIVE. somewhat round.

round number, a number in even tens, hundreds, thousands, and so on. 3874 in round numbers would be 3900 or 4000.

Round Table, the table used by King Arthur and his knights. It was made round to show that all who sat at it were of equal rank.

round trip, a trip to someplace and back again. —**round′-trip′,** ADJECTIVE.

round·up (round′up′), NOUN.

1 the act of driving or bringing cattle together from long distances.

2 the act of gathering or picking up suspects: *There was a police roundup of burglary suspects.*

3 a summary of information on television or radio: *Let's listen to the weather roundup.*

rouse (rouz), VERB.

1 to wake someone up: *I was roused by the ring of the telephone.*

2 to excite or stir someone up: *She was roused to anger by the insult.*

❑ VERB **rous·es, roused, rous·ing.**

rout (rout),

1 NOUN. the flight of a defeated army in disorder: *The enemy's retreat soon became a rout.*

2 VERB. to cause someone to run away from a battle: *Our soldiers routed the enemy.*

3 *VERB.* to defeat someone completely: *The baseball team routed its opponents by a score of ten to one.*
4 *NOUN.* a complete defeat: *The baseball game ended in a rout.*
❑ *VERB* **routs, rout·ed, rout·ing.** ■ Another word that can sound like this is **route.**

route (rüt *or* rout),
1 *NOUN.* a way that you choose to get somewhere: *Will you go to the coast by the northern route?*
2 *VERB.* to send someone by a certain way or road: *The signs routed us to a side road around the flood.*
3 *NOUN.* a fixed, regular course or area of a person making deliveries or sales: *a newspaper route, a mail route.*
❑ *VERB* **routes, rout·ed, rout·ing.** ■ Other words that can sound like this are **root** and **rout.**

rou·tine (rü tēn′),
1 *NOUN.* a regular or usual method of doing things: *Brushing my teeth is part of my nightly routine.*
2 *ADJECTIVE.* regular: *I get a routine medical checkup every year.*
–rou·tine′ly, *ADVERB.*

rove (rōv), *VERB.* to wander; wander about; roam: *She loved to rove through the woods near her house.* ❑ *VERB* **roves, roved, rov·ing. –rov′er,** *NOUN.*

row¹ (rō), *NOUN.* a straight line of people or things: *The children stood in a row. Corn is planted in rows.*
in a row, *IDIOM.* one after another; in succession: *They won the state championship three years in a row.*

row² (rō),
1 *VERB.* to use oars to move a boat. When you row, you sit backward, and pull the oars through the water.
2 *VERB.* to carry someone in a rowboat: *Row us to the island.*
3 *NOUN.* a trip in a rowboat: *It's a short row to the island.*
❑ *VERB* **rows, rowed, row·ing. –row′er,** *NOUN.*

row³ (rou), *NOUN.* a noisy quarrel; noise: *The two brothers had a row over the bicycle. What's all this row about?*

row·boat (rō′bōt′), *NOUN.* a boat moved by oars.

row·dy (rou′dē),
1 *ADJECTIVE.* rough; noisy: *The gym was full of a rowdy group of kids.* ■ See the Synomyn Study at **wild.**
2 *NOUN.* a rough, noisy person: *The rowdies were asked to leave the gym.*
❑ *ADJECTIVE* **row·di·er** *or* **row·di·est;** *PLURAL* **row·dies. –row′di·ness,** *NOUN.*

roy·al (roi′əl), *ADJECTIVE.*
1 of or about someone who has inherited power to rule; of or about kings and queens: *the royal family.*
2 belonging to a king or queen or a kingdom: *royal power, a royal palace, a royal navy.*
3 suitable for a king or queen; splendid: *a royal welcome, a royal feast.*
–roy′al·ly, *ADVERB.*

roy·al·ty (roi′əl tē), *NOUN.*
1 a royal person; royal persons. Kings, queens, princes, and princesses are royalty.
2 the rank or dignity of a king or queen; royal power: *The crown is the symbol of royalty.*
3 Usually, **royalties,** a share of the receipts or profits paid to the writer of a book or a piece of music.

rpm *or* **r.p.m.,** revolutions per minute: the number of complete turns something makes in one minute. A 45 rpm record makes 45 complete turns on the turntable in one minute.

rte., an abbreviation of **route.**

rub (rub),
1 *VERB.* to move something back and forth against something else: *Rub your hands to warm them.*
2 *VERB.* to push and press along the surface of something: *The nurse rubbed my sore back.*
3 *VERB.* to clean, smooth, or polish by moving one thing firmly against another: *Rub the silver with a soft cloth.*
4 *NOUN.* the act of rubbing someone or something: *Mom gave me a back rub.*
❑ *VERB* **rubs, rubbed, rub·bing.**

rub it in, *IDIOM.* to keep on mentioning something unpleasant: *I didn't mind losing as much as I minded her rubbing it in that she won.*

a **rowing** crew

a	hat	ė	term	ô	order	ch	child		a in about
ā	age	i	it	oi	oil	ng	long		e in taken
ä	far	ī	ice	ou	out	sh	she	ə {	i in pencil
â	care	o	hot	u	cup	th	thin		o in lemon
e	let	ō	open	ů	put	ŦH	then		u in circus
ē	equal	ò	saw	ü	rule	zh	measure		

rub·ber (rub′ər),
1 *NOUN.* an elastic material made from the juice of certain tropical plants or by a chemical process. Rubber will not let air or water through.
2 *NOUN.* **rubbers,** overshoes made of rubber.
3 *ADJECTIVE.* made of rubber: *a rubber tire.*
■ See the Word Story at **eraser.**

rubber band, a circular strip of rubber, used to hold things together.

rubber stamp, a stamp made of rubber, used with ink to print dates, signatures, pictures, or designs on paper, letters, and so on.

rub·bish (rub′ish), *NOUN.* worthless or useless stuff; trash; junk: *Pick up the rubbish and burn it.*

rub·ble (rub′əl), *NOUN.* rough broken stone or bricks from a building or wall that has been knocked down.

ru·by (rü′bē),
1 *NOUN.* a clear, hard, deep red precious stone.
2 *ADJECTIVE.* deep, glowing red: *ruby lips, ruby wine.*
❑ *PLURAL* **ru·bies.**

rud·der (rud′ər), *NOUN.*
1 a movable flat piece of wood or metal at the rear of a boat or ship to steer it by.
2 a similar piece on an aircraft.

rud·dy (rud′ē), *ADJECTIVE.* having a fresh, healthy, red look: *ruddy cheeks.* ❑ *ADJECTIVE* **rud·di·er, rud·di·est.**

rude (rüd), *ADJECTIVE.*
1 with bad manners; impolite: *It is rude to stare.*
2 rough; coarse; roughly made or done: *Prehistoric people made rude tools from stone.*
❑ *ADJECTIVE* **rud·er, rud·est. —rude′ly,** *ADVERB.*
—rude′ness, *NOUN.*

ruf·fle (ruf′əl),
1 *VERB.* to make the surface of something rough or uneven: *A breeze ruffled the lake.*
2 *NOUN.* a strip of cloth, ribbon, or lace gathered along one edge and used for trimming.
❑ *VERB* **ruf·fles, ruf·fled, ruf·fling.**

rug (rug), *NOUN.* a heavy floor covering made of heavy fabric or fibers. Rugs usually cover only part of a room's floor.

rug·ged (rug′id), *ADJECTIVE.*
1 covered with rough edges; rough and uneven: *rugged rocks, rugged ground.* ■ See the Synonym Study at **rough.**
2 sturdy and vigorous; able to do and endure a lot: *Pioneers were rugged people.*
3 strong and irregular: *rugged features.*
4 stormy: *rugged weather.*
—rug′ged·ness, *NOUN.*

ru·in (rü′ən),
1 *NOUN.* often, **ruins,** what is left after a building, wall, or the like has fallen to pieces: *We visited the ruins of an ancient city.*
2 *NOUN.* very great damage; destruction: *The ruin of property caused by the earthquake was enormous.*
3 *NOUN.* the condition of being completely damaged or fallen down: *The abandoned house had gone to ruin.*
4 *VERB.* to destroy or spoil something completely: *The rain ruined our picnic.* ■ See the Synonym Study at **destroy.**
5 *VERB.* to cause someone to lose all his or her money: *She was ruined by making bad investments.*
❑ *VERB* **ru·ins, ru·ined, ru·in·ing.**

ruins of a great Greek temple

Did You Know?

The **ruins** on the bottom of the opposite page were built nearly 2,500 years ago in Athens, Greece. What remains is the city's main temple, the **Parthenon** (pär′thə non). It was dedicated to **Athena** (ə thē′nə), the goddess of wisdom. It has been admired and copied by builders all over the world.

ru·in·ous (rü′ə nəs), *ADJECTIVE.* causing destruction: *The frost in late spring was ruinous to the crops.*

rum·ble (rum′bəl),

1 *VERB.* to make a deep, heavy, continuous sound: *Thunder rumbled in the distance.*

2 *NOUN.* a deep, heavy, continuous sound:

❑ *VERB* **rum·bles, rum·bled, rum·bling.**

rum·mage (rum′ij), *VERB.* to search through something thoroughly by moving things around: *I rummaged in my drawer for a clean pair of socks.*

❑ *VERB* **rum·mag·es, rum·maged, rum·mag·ing.**

rummage sale, a sale of odds and ends or old clothing, usually held to raise money for charity.

You can find useful and interesting objects at a **rummage sale.**

rule (rül),

1 *NOUN.* something that tells what we must do or what we must not do: *We have to obey the rules of the game.*

2 *VERB.* to make a decision in favor of one side and against another: *My parents ruled in my favor in the dispute between my sister and me. The judge ruled against them.*

3 *VERB.* to control a country and its people; govern: *The majority rules in a democracy.*

4 *NOUN.* control; government: *We believe in the rule of the majority.*

5 *NOUN.* something that usually happens or is done; what is usually true: *Fair weather is the rule in June.*

6 *VERB.* to mark something with lines: *She used a ruler to rule the paper.*

❑ *VERB* **rules, ruled, rul·ing.**

as a rule, *IDIOM.* usually: *As a rule, hail falls in summer rather than in winter.*

rul·er (rü′lər), *NOUN.*

1 someone who rules or governs: *Kings and queens are rulers.*

2 a straight strip of wood, metal, or plastic used to measure how long something is. Rulers also help you draw straight lines.

rum (rum), *NOUN.* a strong alcoholic drink made from sugar cane or molasses.

ru·mor (rü′mər),

1 *NOUN.* a statement or information passed along from one person to another that may be true or not: *The rumor spread that a new school would be built here.*

2 *VERB.* to tell or spread rumors: *It was rumored that the government was going to increase the gasoline tax.*

❑ *VERB* **ru·mors, ru·mored, ru·mor·ing.**

rump (rump), *NOUN.* the rear part of the body of an animal, where the legs join the back.

rum·ple (rum′pəl), *VERB.* to make something wrinkled, crumpled, or messy: *to rumple sheets of paper, to rumple a suit.* ❑ *VERB* **rum·ples, rum·pled, rum·pling.**

run (run),

1 *VERB.* to move your legs very fast, so that you have both feet off the ground at the same time: *A horse can run faster than a person.*

2 *VERB.* to go somewhere in a hurry: *Run for help.*

3 *VERB.* to make a quick trip: *Let's run over to the lake for the weekend.*

R

a	hat	ė	term	ô	order	ch	child	(a in about
ā	age	i	it	oi	oil	ng	long	e in taken
ä	far	ī	ice	ou	out	sh	she	ə { i in pencil
â	care	o	hot	u	cup	th	thin	o in lemon
e	let	ō	open	u̇	put	⊤H	then	u in circus
ē	equal	ȯ	saw	ü	rule	zh	measure	

Impalas can **run** very fast.

4 NOUN. a quick trip: *Let's take a run over to the lake this afternoon.*

5 VERB. to run away from something in order to escape danger; flee: *Run for your life!*

6 VERB. to do something by running or rushing: *She ran errands all morning.*

7 VERB. to travel between places: *This train runs from Chicago to St. Louis.*

8 NOUN. a trip, especially a regular trip over a certain route: *The train makes a run of nearly a hundred miles in two hours.*

9 VERB. to reach; extend: *Shelves run along the walls. The road runs from New York to Atlanta.*

10 VERB. to flow out of or over something: *Blood runs from a cut.*

11 VERB. to have mucus flow from your nose: *My nose runs whenever I have a cold.*

12 VERB. to dissolve and spread: *The color ran when the shirt was washed.*

13 VERB. to continue; last: *Our lease runs for one more year.*

14 VERB. to take part in a race or contest: *She's looking forward to running in the race tomorrow.*

15 NOUN. the act of running: *Dad took part in a five-mile run.*

16 VERB. to be a candidate for election: *He will run for President.*

17 VERB. to operate or cause to operate: *The engine ran smoothly all day without overheating. Can you run this machine?*

18 VERB. to be in charge of something; manage: *to run a business.*

19 NOUN. a score in baseball: *Our team made three runs in the third inning of the game.*

20 NOUN. a series of regular performances: *This play has had a run of two years.*

21 NOUN. a place where threads have slipped out of fabric: *a run in a stocking.*

22 VERB. to get past or through: *Enemy ships tried to run the blockade.*

23 VERB. to be suffering from: *I'm running a fever this morning.*

24 VERB. to do something as a test: *My doctor wants to run some tests to see if I'm allergic to dust.*

25 VERB. to publish in a newspaper or magazine: *She ran an ad for a used bicycle in good condition.*

26 VERB. to take something somewhere: *Please run this recipe over to the neighbor's house.*

❏ VERB **runs, ran, run, run·ning.**

in the long run, IDIOM. on the whole; in the end: *In the long run we will have to investigate the mystery.*

run across, IDIOM. to meet by chance: *I ran across an old friend in town today.*

run down, IDIOM.

1 to stop going or working: *The clock has run down.*

2 to say bad things about: *to run someone down, to run down the food at a restaurant.*

3 to make tired or ill: *She is run down from working too hard.*

run into, IDIOM.

1 to meet by chance: *I ran into an old friend at the library.*

2 to crash into: *A large steamship ran into the tugboat.*

run out, IDIOM. to come to an end: *After three minutes his time ran out on the telephone call.*

run out of, IDIOM. to use up; have no more: *Mother ran out of eggs and sent me to the store for more.*

run over, IDIOM.

1 to ride or drive over: *The car ran over some glass.*

2 to overflow: *The waiter filled my cup too full and the coffee ran over onto the table.*

run a risk, IDIOM. to expose yourself to some danger: *We ran the risk of catching cold by playing in the rain.*

run·a·way (run′ə wā′),

1 NOUN. a person or animal that has run away.

2 ADJECTIVE. running with nobody to guide or stop it; out of control: *a runaway horse.*

run·back (run′bak′), NOUN. (in football) a run made by a player after catching a kick, intercepting a pass, or recovering an opponent's fumble.

run-down (run′doun′), ADJECTIVE.

1 tired; sick: *A run-down student won't do well in her studies.*

2 falling to pieces; partly ruined: *They bought a run-down old building and fixed it up.*

rung¹ (rung), VERB. the past participle of **ring²**: *The bell has rung.* ▪ Another word that sounds like this is **wrung.**

rung² (rung), NOUN.

1 a bar used as a step of a ladder.

2 a bar set between the legs of a chair or as part of the back or arm of a chair.

▪ Another word that sounds like this is **wrung.**

run·ner (run′ər), NOUN.

1 a person, animal, or thing that runs; racer: *A runner arrived out of breath.*

2 (in baseball) a player on the team at bat who either is on base or is running to the next base.

3 one of the narrow pieces that a sleigh, sled, or ice skate slides on.

4 a long narrow strip of fabric: *We have a runner of carpet in our hall.*

5 a slender stem that takes root along the ground, producing new plants in this way. *Strawberry plants spread by runners.*

run·ner-up (run′ər up′), *NOUN.* a player or team that wins second place in a contest.

running (run′ing),

1 *NOUN.* the act of a person, animal, or thing that runs: *Running is good exercise.*

2 *ADJECTIVE.* flowing: *Our cabin has running water.*

3 *ADJECTIVE.* going on continuously: *She made running comments as she showed the slides of her vacation trip.*

4 *ADJECTIVE.* done with or during a run: *I made a running jump off the bank into the river.*

in the running, *IDIOM.* having a chance to win.

out of the running, *IDIOM.* having no chance to win.

running mate, the person chosen by candidates for president to be vice president if they win the election.

run·ny (run′ē), *ADJECTIVE.*

1 nearly or almost melted: *Some people like runny ice cream.*

2 tending to drip mucus: *A runny nose and watering eyes are symptoms of a cold.*

❑ *ADJECTIVE* **run·ni·er, run·ni·est.**

run·off (run′óf′), *NOUN.*

1 a final, deciding election, race, or contest: *There will be a runoff next month if no candidate receives a majority of the votes cast in today's election.*

2 something that runs off, such as rain that flows from fields into streams.

runt (runt), *NOUN.* an animal or plant that is smaller than the usual size.

run·way (run′wā′), *NOUN.* a smooth, level strip of land on which aircraft land and take off.

runway

rup·ture (rup′chər),

1 *VERB.* to break; burst: *There was a bluish mark on his thigh where a blood vessel had ruptured.*

2 *NOUN.* the act of breaking or the condition of being broken: *The rupture of a blood vessel usually causes a bruise.*

❑ *VERB* **rup·tures, rup·tured, rup·tur·ing.**

rur·al (rür′əl), *ADJECTIVE.* in the country; belonging to the country; like that of the country: *a rural school, rural roads.*

ruse (rüz), *NOUN.* a trick or plan to mislead others.

rush[1] (rush),

1 *VERB.* to move with speed or force: *Firefighters rushed to put out the fire. The flooding river rushed past.*

2 *VERB.* to send, push, or force something or someone with speed or haste: *Rush this order, please. The injured pedestrian was rushed to the hospital.*

3 *VERB.* to go somewhere or do something very quickly: *They rush into things without knowing anything about them.*

4 *NOUN.* a big hurry: *The rush of city life can be exciting. What is your rush? Wait a minute.*

5 *NOUN.* the act of rushing: *The rush of the flood swept everything before it.*

6 *NOUN.* a great or sudden effort of many people to go somewhere or get something: *The Christmas rush is the busiest time of year for stores.*

7 *ADJECTIVE.* needing to be done fast: *A rush order must be filled at once.*

8 *VERB.* to attack with much speed and force: *The soldiers rushed the enemy.*

❑ *VERB* **rush·es, rushed, rush·ing;** *PLURAL* **rush·es.**

making a basket from **rushes**

rush[2] (rush), *NOUN.* a grasslike plant with a hollow stem that grows in wet soil or marshy places. The seats of chairs are sometimes made from the stems of rushes. ❑ *PLURAL* **rush·es.**

a	hat	ė	term	ô	order	ch	child
ā	age	i	it	oi	oil	ng	long
ä	far	ī	ice	ou	out	sh	she
â	care	o	hot	u	cup	th	thin
e	let	ō	open	ủ	put	ᵀH	then
ē	equal	ò	saw	ü	rule	zh	measure

ə { a in about / e in taken / i in pencil / o in lemon / u in circus }

R

587

Driving can be difficult during **rush hour.**

rush hour, the time of day when traffic is heaviest or when trains and buses are most crowded: *Rush hour traffic made me late.*

Rus·sia (rush′ə), NOUN.
1 a country in eastern Europe and northwestern Asia. It was formerly a large part of the Soviet Union.
2 See **Soviet Union.**

Rus·sian (rush′ən),
1 ADJECTIVE. of or about Russia, its people, or their language.
2 NOUN. someone born or living in Russia.
3 NOUN. the chief language of Russia.

Word Source

Russian has given many words to the English language. The following words are some of them: **czar, mammoth, parka, shaman, Soviet, steppe, tundra,** and **vodka.**

rust (rust),
1 NOUN. the reddish brown or orange coating that forms on iron or steel when it is open to air or moisture.
2 VERB. to become covered with this: *Don't leave the tools our in the rain or they will rust.*
3 NOUN. a plant disease that causes brown spots on leaves and stems.
❑ VERB **rusts, rust·ed, rust·ing.**

rus·tic (rus′tik), ADJECTIVE. belonging to or suitable for the country; rural: *The play had a rustic setting.*

rus·tle (rus′əl),
1 NOUN. a light, soft sound of things gently rubbing together: *The breeze caused a rustle of the leaves.*
2 VERB. to make or cause to make this sound: *Leaves rustled in the breeze. The wind rustled the papers.*
3 VERB. to steal cattle or horses: *The sheriff arrested the men who had rustled the cattle from the Bar-None ranch.*
❑ VERB **rus·tles, rus·tled, rus·tling.**

rus·tler (rus′lər), NOUN. a cattle thief.

rust·y (rus′tē), ADJECTIVE.
1 covered with rust; rusted: *Don't cut the apple with that rusty knife.*
2 no longer good or skillful from lack of use or practice: *My skating is rusty because I haven't skated all year.*
❑ ADJECTIVE **rust·i·er, rust·i·est.**

rut (rut),
1 NOUN. a track made in the ground by wheels: *A car went over the curb and made ruts in our lawn.*
2 NOUN. a way of acting or living that has become tiresome and uninteresting: *Some people become so set in their ways that they get in a rut.*

ruth·less (rüth′lis), ADJECTIVE. having no pity; showing no mercy; cruel: *a ruthless dictator.*
—**ruth′less·ly,** ADVERB. —**ruth′less·ness,** NOUN.

Rwan·da (rü än′də), NOUN. a country in central Africa. —**Rwan′dan,** ADJECTIVE or NOUN.

rye (rī),
1 NOUN. the grain of a kind of cereal grass, or the plant that it grows on. Rye grows in cool climates and is used for making flour and as food for farm animals.
2 ADJECTIVE. made mainly from rye grain or flour: *rye bread.*
3 NOUN. a bread made from rye flour: *She ordered a ham sandwich on rye.*
▪ Another word that sounds like this is **wry.**

squid

S s

S or **s** (es), *NOUN.* the 19th letter of the English alphabet. ❑ *PLURAL* **S's** or **s's.**

S or **S.,**
1 an abbreviation of **south.**
2 an abbreviation of **southern.**

Sab·bath (sab′əth), *NOUN.* the day of the week used for rest and worship by some religious groups, usually Sunday or Saturday.

sa·ber (sā′bər), *NOUN.* (earlier) a heavy, curved sword with a sharp edge, used by soldiers on horseback.

sa·ber-toothed ti·ger (sā′bər tütht′ tī′gər), a large, prehistoric animal something like a tiger. Two of its upper front teeth were very long and curved.

sa·ble (sā′bəl), *NOUN.* a flesh-eating animal something like a weasel but larger. It has valuable, dark brown, glossy fur.

sab·o·tage (sab′ə täzh),
1 *NOUN.* damage done to property, machinery, bridges, railroads, or the like, especially by enemy agents.
2 *VERB.* to damage or destroy something deliberately: *The spy sabotaged the truck so that he could escape.* ❑ *VERB* **sab·o·tag·es, sab·o·taged, sab·o·tag·ing.**

sac (sak), *NOUN.* a part like a bag inside an animal or plant, often one that holds liquids. ■ Another word that sounds like this is **sack. –sac′like′,** *ADJECTIVE.*

sack¹ (sak),
1 *NOUN.* a large bag made of coarse cloth. Sacks are used for holding grain, flour, potatoes, and so on.
2 *NOUN.* a paper or plastic bag: *What's in the sack?* ❑ *VERB* **sacks, sacked, sack·ing.** ■ Another word that sounds like this is **sac. –sack′like′,** *ADJECTIVE.*

sack² (sak), *VERB.* to rob a captured city by force: *The soldiers sacked the town.* ❑ *VERB* **sacks, sacked, sack·ing.** ■ Another word that sounds like this is **sac.**

Sac·ra·men·to (sak′rə men′tō), *NOUN.* the capital of California.

sa·cred (sā′krid), ADJECTIVE.
1 belonging to or dedicated to God; holy: *A church is a sacred building.*
2 connected with religion; religious: *sacred music.*

sac·ri·fice (sak′rə fīs),
1 NOUN. the act of offering something to a god.
2 NOUN. something that is offered: *The ancient Hebrews killed animals on altars as sacrifices to God.*
3 VERB. to give or offer something to a god.
4 NOUN. the act of giving up one thing for another: *Our teacher does not approve of any sacrifice of studies to sports.*
5 VERB. to give something up: *The soldier sacrificed his life for his comrades.*
6 NOUN. (in baseball) a bunt that helps a base runner to advance, or a fly that allows a base runner to score, although the batter is put out.
❑ VERB **sac·ri·fic·es, sac·ri·ficed, sac·ri·fic·ing.**

sad (sad), ADJECTIVE.
1 unhappy; full of sorrow: *I felt sad when we moved.*
2 causing unhappy feelings: *A pet's death is a sad loss.*
❑ ADJECTIVE **sad·der, sad·dest. –sad′ly,** ADVERB. **–sad′ness,** NOUN.

sad·dle (sad′l),
1 NOUN. a seat for a rider on a horse's back, or on a bicycle or motorcycle.
2 VERB. to put a saddle on something: *Saddle the horse.*
❑ VERB **sad·dles, sad·dled, sad·dling.**

sa·fa·ri (sə fär′ē), NOUN. a journey or hunting expedition in eastern Africa. ❑ PLURAL **sa·fa·ris.**

safe (sāf),
1 ADJECTIVE. out of danger; secure: *We feel safe with the dog in the house.*
2 ADJECTIVE. not causing harm or danger: *Is it safe to leave the house unlocked? This toy is safe for babies.*
3 ADJECTIVE. free from being stolen: *Keep your money in a safe place.*
4 ADJECTIVE. careful: *My parents are safe drivers.*
5 ADJECTIVE. (in baseball) reaching a base without being put out.
6 NOUN. a steel or iron box for money, jewels, papers, and so on.
❑ ADJECTIVE **saf·er, saf·est. –safe′ly,** ADVERB.

Synonym Study

Safe means out of any danger: *I try to stay safe on my bicycle by always wearing a helmet and following traffic rules.*

Secure means safe and without fear: *The lion cubs felt secure when close to their mother.*

Protected means kept safe from danger: *Many of the ants are outside the anthill, but the queen is protected inside.*

Snug means safe and comfortable: *The mountain lion keeps her cubs snug in their den.*

safe·guard (sāf′gärd′),
1 VERB. to keep something safe; guard against hurt or danger; protect: *Food laws safeguard our health.*
2 NOUN. something that gives protection; defense: *Keeping clean is a safeguard against disease.*
❑ VERB **safe·guards, safe·guard·ed, safe·guard·ing.**

safe·ty (sāf′tē), NOUN.
1 freedom from harm or danger: *There is a lifeguard at the swimming pool to assure your safety.*
2 in football: **a** a play in which an offensive player downs the ball, or is downed, behind the offensive goal line. A safety counts two points for the defensive team. **b** a defensive player who plays closest to the defensive goal line.
❑ PLURAL **safe·ties.**

safety belt. See **seat belt.**

safety pin, a pin bent back on itself to form a kind of spring. A guard covers the point of the pin and keeps it from opening accidentally.

sag (sag), VERB.
1 to sink or hang down under weight or pressure: *The wooden bridge sagged in the middle as the travelers crossed it.*
2 to become weaker: *Our courage sagged.*
❑ VERB **sags, sagged, sag·ging.**

a **sagging** bridge

sa·ga (sä′gə), NOUN. any story of heroic deeds.
❑ PLURAL **sa·gas.**

sage[1] (sāj),
1 NOUN. a wise man.
2 ADJECTIVE. very wise: *The king received sage advice.*

sage[2] (sāj), NOUN. the dried leaves of a plant, used as a seasoning in food.

sage·brush (sāj′brush′), NOUN. a grayish green, bushy plant, common on the dry plains of western North America.

Sa·har·a (sə hâr′ə *or* sə här′ə), NOUN. a very large desert in northern Africa. **–Sa·har′an,** ADJECTIVE or NOUN.

Did You Know?

The **Sahara** is the world's biggest desert. It is just about as big as the United States.

said (sed),
1 *ADJECTIVE.* named or mentioned before: *the said witness, the said sum of money.*
2 *VERB.* the past tense of **say:** *He said he would come.*
3 *VERB.* the past participle of **say:** *She had said "No" every time.*

Most **salamanders** are about 5 inches long, including the tail. The largest can be over 5 feet long.

sail (sāl),
1 *NOUN.* a piece of cloth that catches the wind to make a ship move on the water.
2 *VERB.* to travel on water by the action of wind on sails.
3 *VERB.* to travel on water in a ship or boat.
4 *VERB.* to move smoothly like a ship with sails: *The dancers sailed across the room.*
5 *VERB.* to manage a ship or boat: *The boys are learning to sail.*
6 *VERB.* to begin a trip by water: *She sailed from New York to Europe.*
□ *VERB* **sails, sailed, sail·ing.** ■ Another word that sounds like this is **sale. −sail′like′,** *ADJECTIVE.*

sail·board (sāl′bôrd′), *NOUN.* a surfboard that is attached to a mast and a hand-held sail. Speed and direction are controlled by moving the sail.

sail·boat (sāl′bōt′), *NOUN.* a boat that is moved by sails.

sail·or (sā′lər), *NOUN.*
1 someone whose work is handling a ship or boat.
2 a member of a ship's crew. Members of the United States Navy who are not officers are called sailors.

saint (sānt), *NOUN.*
1 a very holy person, especially someone declared to be a saint by a church.
2 someone who is very humble, patient, or like a saint in other ways.

Saint Ber·nard (sānt′ bər närd′), a big, brown and white dog with a large head. This dog was first bred by monks to rescue travelers lost in snow in the Swiss Alps.

sake (sāk), *NOUN.*
1 cause or interest: *Don't go to any trouble for my sake.*
2 purpose: *We moved to the country for the sake of peace and quiet.*

sal·ad (sal′əd), *NOUN.* raw green vegetables, such as lettuce and celery, served with a dressing. Often meat, fish, eggs, cooked vegetables, or fruits are used with, or instead of, the raw green vegetables.

sal·a·man·der (sal′ə man′dər), *NOUN.* an animal shaped like a lizard, but belonging to the same group as frogs and toads. Salamanders live in damp places.

sa·la·mi (sə lä′mē), *NOUN.* a kind of thick sausage, often flavored with garlic. It is usually sliced and eaten cold. □ *PLURAL* **sa·la·mis.**

sal·ar·y (sal′ər ē), *NOUN.* money that you get paid for work that you do: *Her yearly salary was $30,000.* □ *PLURAL* **sal·ar·ies.**

Word Story

Salary comes from a Latin word meaning "salt." Roman soldiers were given money to buy salt to preserve their food with. Even now, people who are good at their jobs are said to be "worth their salt."

sale (sāl), *NOUN.*
1 the act of selling something; exchange of goods for money: *The sale of a house usually involves a lawyer.*
2 **sales,** the amount sold: *Today's sales were larger than yesterday's.*
3 the act of selling something at lower prices than usual: *This store is having a sale on suits.*
■ Another word that sounds like this is **sail.**
for sale, *IDIOM.* to be sold: *That car is for sale.*
on sale, *IDIOM.* for sale at lower prices than usual: *Coffee is on sale today.*

Sa·lem (sā′ləm), *NOUN.* the capital of Oregon.

sales·man (sālz′mən), *NOUN.* someone whose job is selling. □ *PLURAL* **sales·men.**

sales·per·son (sālz′pėr′sən), *NOUN.* someone whose job is selling things, especially in a store. □ *PLURAL* **sales·peo·ple** or **sales·per·sons.**

sales tax, a tax based on the price of things you buy in a store, restaurant, and so on.

sales·wom·an (sālz′wüm′ən), *NOUN.* a woman whose job is selling. □ *PLURAL* **sales·wom·en.**

sa·li·va (sə lī′və), *NOUN.* the liquid produced by glands in the mouth to keep it moist, help in chewing, and start digestion.

salm·on (sam′ən), *NOUN.* a large food fish with silvery scales and yellowish pink flesh. □ *PLURAL* **salm·on.**

S

a	hat	ė	term	ô	order	ch	child		a in about
ā	age	i	it	oi	oil	ng	long		e in taken
ä	far	ī	ice	ou	out	sh	she	ə	i in pencil
â	care	o	hot	u	cup	th	thin		o in lemon
e	let	ō	open	ù	put	ŦH	then		u in circus
ē	equal	ȯ	saw	ü	rule	zh	measure		

sal·mo·nel·la (sal/mə nel/ə), NOUN. one of a group of bacteria that cause food poisoning, typhoid fever, and other dangerous diseases. □ PLURAL **sal·mo·nel·lae** (sal/mə nel/ē) or **sal·mo·nel·las.**

sal·sa (säl/sə), NOUN. a spicy sauce made with onions, tomatoes, and hot peppers.

salt (sȯlt),
1 NOUN. a white material found in the earth and in sea water. Salt makes food taste better and keeps it from spoiling.
2 ADJECTIVE. containing salt: *The ocean is a great body of salt water.*
3 VERB. to put salt on food to make it taste better: *We salted the popcorn before eating it.*
4 VERB. to scatter salt on; apply salt to: *to salt roads to melt ice and snow.*
5 NOUN. a chemical compound formed by the reaction of an acid and a base. Baking soda is a salt.
□ VERB **salts, salt·ed, salt·ing.**

salt of the earth, IDIOM. the best people.

take something with a grain of salt, IDIOM. to treat something as unreliable or uncertain: *He took her description of the accident with a grain of salt, since she had exaggerated before.*

Salt Lake City, the capital of Utah.

salt·wa·ter (sȯlt/wȯ/tər), ADJECTIVE.
1 made up of or containing salt water: *I gargle with a warm saltwater solution.*
2 living in the sea or in water like the sea: *saltwater fish.*

salt·y (sȯl/tē), ADJECTIVE. tasting of salt. Sweat and tears are salty. □ ADJECTIVE **salt·i·er, salt·i·est.**
—**salt/i·ness,** NOUN.

sal·u·ta·tion (sal/yə tā/shən), NOUN. something said, written, or done to salute. You begin a letter with a salutation, such as "Dear Mr. Johnson" or "Dear Sue."

sa·lute (sə lüt/),
1 VERB. to show your respect to something or someone by raising your right hand to your forehead, by firing guns, or by lowering flags: *The soldier saluted the officer.*
2 NOUN. the act of saluting; sign of welcome or respect: *The queen gracefully acknowledged the salutes of the crowd.*
□ VERB **sa·lutes, sa·lut·ed, sa·lut·ing.**

sal·vage (sal/vij),
1 NOUN. the rescue of property from fire, flood, or shipwreck.
2 VERB. to save property or goods from fire, flood, or shipwreck.
□ VERB **sal·vag·es, sal·vaged, sal·vag·ing.**
—**sal/vage·a·ble,** ADJECTIVE. —**sal/vag·er,** NOUN.

sal·va·tion (sal vā/shən), NOUN.
1 someone or something that saves: *The down coat was my salvation during the blizzard.*
2 (in Christian use) the act or process of saving the soul.

salve (sav), NOUN. a soft, greasy substance put on wounds and sores; healing ointment: *Is this salve good for insect bites?*

same (sām),
1 ADJECTIVE. not another; not different: *We came back the same way we went.*
2 ADJECTIVE. just alike; not different: *Her name and mine are the same.*
3 ADJECTIVE. not changed: *It is the same beautiful place we saw last summer.*
4 PRONOUN. the same person or thing.
5 ADVERB. **the same,** in the same manner; alike: *"Sea" and "see" are pronounced the same.*
—**same/ness,** NOUN.

sam·ple (sam/pəl),
1 NOUN. a small part of something that shows what the rest is like: *paint samples, free samples.*
2 VERB. to taste a part of something to see how it is: *We sampled the cake and found it very good.*
□ VERB **sam·ples, sam·pled, sam·pling.**

sam·u·rai (sam/u rī/), NOUN. (in the Middle Ages) a Japanese warrior. □ PLURAL **sam·u·rai.**

San An·to·ni·o (san/ an tō/nē ō), a city in Texas.

san·a·to·ri·um (san/ə tôr/ē əm), NOUN. a place for treating people who are recovering from illness. □ PLURAL **san·a·to·ri·ums.** Also spelled **sanitarium.**

samurai

sanc·tion (sangk/shən),
1 NOUN. permission with authority; support; approval: *You need the owner's sanction to cross this property.*
2 VERB. to authorize; approve; allow: *Her conscience does not sanction stealing.*
3 NOUN. a punishment, such as a blockade, limits on trade, or the like, carried out by one or more countries against another country. Sanctions are used to enforce international law.
□ VERB **sanc·tions, sanc·tioned, sanc·tion·ing.**

sanc·tu·ar·y (sangk/chü er/ē), NOUN.
1 a sacred place. A church is a sanctuary.
2 a place where you can find safety or protection: *We found sanctuary from the storm in a cave.*
3 a place where birds or animals may not be hunted: *We visited the new wildlife sanctuary.*
□ PLURAL **sanc·tu·ar·ies.**

sand (sand),
1 NOUN. tiny grains of broken rock. Sand is found along beaches and in deserts.

2 VERB. to spread sand on a frozen surface: *The highway department sanded the icy road.*

3 VERB. to make something smooth by rubbing it with sand or sandpaper: *I sanded the edges of a piece of wood.*
❑ VERB **sands, sand·ed, sand·ing. −sand′er,** NOUN.

san·dal (san′dl), NOUN. a kind of shoe fastened to your foot by straps.

sand·bar (sand′bär′), NOUN. a ridge of sand in a river or along a shore, made by tides or currents.

sand·box (sand′boks′), NOUN. a shallow box that contains sand, especially for children to play in.
❑ PLURAL **sand·box·es.**

sand castle, a pile of sand shaped like a castle. Sand castles are made by people playing at the beach.

San Di·e·go (san′ dē ā′gō), a city in California.

sand·pa·per (sand′pā′pər),
1 NOUN. sturdy paper with sand glued on it, used for smoothing, cleaning, or polishing.
2 VERB. to rub something with sandpaper.
❑ VERB **sand·pa·pers, sand·pa·pered, sand·pa·per·ing.**

sand·pip·er (sand′pīpər), NOUN. a small bird with a long bill, living on sandy shores.

sand·stone (sand′stōn′), NOUN. a kind of rock that is made mostly of sand.

sand·wich (sand′wich),
1 NOUN. two or more slices of bread with meat, jelly, cheese, or some other food between them.
2 VERB. to put someone or something in between two things: *I was sandwiched between two large boxes in the back seat of the car.*
❑ PLURAL **sand·wich·es;** VERB **sand·wich·es, sand·wiched, sand·wich·ing.**

Word Story

Sandwich comes from the name of the Earl of Sandwich, a British nobleman of the 1700s, who supposedly invented it so that he would not have to leave a card game to eat.

sand·y (san′dē), ADJECTIVE.
1 containing sand; made up of sand: *sandy soil.*
2 covered with sand: *Most of the shore is rocky, but there is a sandy beach.*
❑ ADJECTIVE **sand·i·er, sand·i·est. −sand′i·ness,** NOUN.

sane (sān), ADJECTIVE.
1 having a healthy mind; not mentally ill.
2 showing good sense; reasonable: *A person with a sane attitude toward driving doesn't take chances.*
❑ ADJECTIVE **san·er, san·est. −sane′ly,** ADVERB.

sang (sang), VERB. a past tense of **sing**: *The bird sang for us yesterday.*

san·i·tar·i·um (san′ə ter′ē əm), NOUN. another spelling of **sanatorium.**

san·i·tar·y (san′ə ter′ē), ADJECTIVE.

1 of or about health; preventing disease: *There are sanitary regulations in hospitals and schools.*
2 free from dirt and filth: *Food should be kept in a sanitary place.*

san·i·ta·tion (san′ə tā′shən), NOUN. the act or process of protecting the health of the public by inspecting food supplies and disposing of waste matter.

san·i·ty (san′ə tē), NOUN.
1 the condition of having good mental health.
2 the ability to think in a reasonable way.

We spent the day making a **sand castle.**

San Juan (san′ wän′), the capital of Puerto Rico.

sank (sangk), VERB. a past tense of **sink**: *The ship sank before help reached it.*

San Lu·is Po·to·sí (sän′ lwēs′ pō tō sē′), NOUN. a state in central Mexico.

San·skrit (san′skrit), NOUN. the ancient written language of India.

Word Source

Sanskrit has given many words to the English language. The words below are some of them.

Buddha	loot	punch[2]	sugar
cheetah	mandarin	sapphire	thug
jungle	pagoda		

San·ta Claus (san′tə klöz′), the saint of Christmas giving. He is pictured as a fat, jolly, old man with a white beard, dressed in a red suit trimmed with fur.

San·ta Fe (san′tə fā′), the capital of New Mexico.

São Pau·lo (soun′ pou′lù), a city in Brazil.

sap (sap), NOUN. the liquid that circulates through a plant, carrying water and food as blood does in animals.

sap·ling (sap′ling), NOUN. a young tree.

a	hat	ė	term	ô	order	ch	child		⎧a in about
ā	age	i	it	oi	oil	ng	long		⎪e in taken
ä	far	ī	ice	ou	out	sh	she	ə⎨ i in pencil
â	care	o	hot	u	cup	th	thin		⎪o in lemon
e	let	ō	open	ù	put	ŦH	then		⎩u in circus
ē	equal	ò	saw	ü	rule	zh	measure		

S

sap·phire (saf′ir), *NOUN.* a hard, clear, bright blue precious stone.

Did You Know?

The largest cut **sapphire** was mined in Australia. It was carved into a head of Abraham Lincoln.

sar·cas·tic (sär kas′tik), *ADJECTIVE.* making fun of something in a bitter or sneering way: *"Don't hurry!" was my brother's sarcastic comment as I slowly dressed.* **−sar·cas′ti·cal·ly,** *ADVERB.*

sar·dine (sär dēn′), *NOUN.* a small fish preserved in oil for food. ❑ *PLURAL* **sar·dine** or **sar·dines.**

sa·ri (sär′ē), *NOUN.* a long piece of cotton or silk worn wound around the body with one end thrown over the head or shoulder. It is the outer garment of Hindu women. ❑ *PLURAL* **sa·ris.**

sash¹ (sash), *NOUN.* a long, broad strip of cloth or ribbon, worn as an ornament around the waist or over one shoulder. ❑ *PLURAL* **sash·es.**

a **sari** from India

sash² (sash), *NOUN.* a frame for the glass or plastic pane in a window or door. ❑ *PLURAL* **sash·es.**

Sa·skatch·e·wan (sa skach′ə wän), *NOUN.* a province in south central Canada.

sat (sat), *VERB.*
1 the past tense of **sit:** *I sat at the end of the table.*
2 the past participle of **sit:** *I never have sat there before.*

Sat., an abbreviation of **Saturday.**

Sa·tan (sāt′n), *NOUN.* (in the Jewish and Christian religions) the supreme evil spirit; the Devil.

satch·el (sach′əl), *NOUN.* a small bag, especially one for carrying clothes or books.

sat·el·lite (sat′l īt), *NOUN.*
1 an astronomical object that revolves around a planet; a moon. The moon is a satellite of Earth.
2 an artificial object shot by a rocket into an orbit around the earth or other astronomical object. Such satellites are used to send weather and other scientific information back to earth; they also transmit television programs across the earth.

sat·in (sat′n), *NOUN.* a silk or rayon cloth with one very smooth, shiny side.

sat·is·fac·tion (sat′i sfak′shən), *NOUN.* the condition of being satisfied, or pleased and contented: *She felt satisfaction at having done well.*

sat·is·fac·to·ry (sat′i sfak′tər ē), *ADJECTIVE.* good enough to meet a need or purpose; acceptable: *If your work is satisfactory, you will pass.*

sat·is·fy (sat′i sfi), *VERB.*
1 to give enough of something to someone: *He satisfied his hunger with a sandwich and milk.*
2 to set someone free from doubt; convince: *She is satisfied that it was an accident.*
❑ *VERB* **sat·is·fies, sat·is·fied, sat·is·fy·ing.**

sat·u·rate (sach′ə rāt′), *VERB.* to soak something completely or thoroughly; fill full: *During the fog, the air was saturated with moisture.* ❑ *VERB* **sat·u·rates, sat·u·rat·ed, sat·u·rat·ing.**

Sat·ur·day (sat′ər dē), *NOUN.* the seventh day of the week; the day after Friday.

Word Story

Saturday comes from **Saturn** and the old English word meaning "day." It is the only day with a name that comes from a Latin word.

Sat·urn (sat′ərn), *NOUN.*
1 the second largest planet. Saturn has a system of many rings around it.
2 the Roman god of agriculture.

sauce (sòs), *NOUN.*
1 something, usually a liquid, served with or on food to make it taste better.
2 stewed fruit: *cranberry sauce.*

Have You Heard?

You may have heard the saying **"What's sauce for the goose is sauce for the gander."** This means that what is the rule for one person should be the rule for others, so that people can be treated fairly and equally.

sauce·pan (sòs′pan′), *NOUN.* a small pan or pot with a handle, used for stewing and boiling foods.

sau·cer (sò′sər), *NOUN.* a small, flat dish to set a cup on. **−sau′cer·like′,** *ADJECTIVE.*

Sau·di (sou′dē *or* sò′dē),
1 *ADJECTIVE.* of or about Saudi Arabia.
2 *NOUN.* someone born or living in Saudi Arabia.
❑ *PLURAL* **Sau·dis.**

Saudi Arabia, a country in southwestern Asia. **−Saudi Arabian.**

Sauk (sòk), *NOUN.* a member of a tribe of American Indians living in Iowa, Kansas, and Oklahoma. ❑ *PLURAL* **Sauk** or **Sauks.**

sau·na (sou′nə *or* sò′nə), *NOUN.*
1 a steam bath made by throwing water on hot stones.
2 a building or room used for such a steam bath. ❑ *PLURAL* **sau·nas.**

saun·ter (sòn′tər), *VERB.* to walk along slowly and happily; stroll: *People sauntered through the park.* ❑ *VERB* **saun·ters, saun·tered, saun·ter·ing.**

sau·sage (sò′sij), *NOUN.* chopped pork, beef, or other meats, seasoned and stuffed into a tube made of very thin skin.

sav·age (sav′ij),
1 *ADJECTIVE.* fierce; cruel; ready to fight: *a savage dog.*
2 *NOUN.* someone who is fierce, brutal, or cruel.
3 *NOUN.* a member of a primitive, uncivilized people.
★ This meaning of **savage** is considered offensive.
−**sav′age·ly,** *ADVERB.*

sa·van·na or **sa·van·nah** (sə van′ə), *NOUN.* a grassy plain with few or no trees, especially one in the southern United States or near the tropics.
❑ *PLURAL* **sa·van·nas** or **sa·van·nahs.**

a **savanna** in Africa

save (sāv),
1 *VERB.* to make or keep someone or something safe from harm, danger, loss, and so on; rescue: *The dog saved the boy's life.*
2 *VERB.* to keep something that you want to use in the future: *to save money, to save rubber bands.*
■ See the Synonym Study at **keep.**
3 *VERB.* to keep from spending or wasting something: *We took the shortcut to save time.*
4 *VERB.* to copy computer data to a protected form, either in another file or on another device.
5 *NOUN.* (in sports) the act of preventing an opponent's shot from entering your goal.
❑ *VERB* **saves, saved, sav·ing.** −**sav′a·ble** or **save′a·ble,** *ADJECTIVE.* −**sav′er,** *NOUN.*

Synonym Study

Save means to make safe or to keep safe from danger: *The mayor saved the historic building.*

Rescue means to save with quick or strong actions: *The boat rescued the swimmers before the sharks reached them.*

Deliver can mean to save from a danger or suffering: *A heavy rain delivered the town from the advancing forest fire.*

Reclaim means to save by bringing back to a good, useful condition: *The injured athlete reclaimed her skills through long workouts.*

sav·ings (sā′vingz), *NOUN PLURAL.* all the money that you have saved.

saw¹ (sȯ),
1 *NOUN.* a tool for cutting, made of a thin, metal blade with sharp teeth on the edge.
2 *VERB.* to cut something with a saw: *I sawed the wood in two.* ■ See the Synonym Study at **cut.**
❑ *VERB* **saws, sawed, sawed** or **sawn, saw·ing.**

saw² (sȯ), *VERB.* the past tense of **see:** *I saw a robin yesterday.*

saw·dust (sȯ′dust′), *NOUN.* particles of wood that fall when you cut wood with a saw.

saw·mill (sȯ′mil′), *NOUN.* a building where machines saw timber into planks or boards.

sawn (sȯn), *VERB.* a past participle of **saw¹**: *At the sawmill, workers have sawn dozens of redwood logs.*

sax·o·phone (sak′sə fōn), *NOUN.* a brass musical wind instrument with keys for the fingers and a reed mouthpiece.

say (sā),
1 *VERB.* to speak: *What did you say? "Thank you," I said.*
2 *VERB.* to put thoughts or ideas into words; tell: *Say what you think.*
3 *VERB.* to recite; repeat: *Say your prayers.*
4 *VERB.* to show or indicate information: *My watch says it's noon.*
5 *NOUN.* a chance to say something or give your opinion: *If you have all had your say, we will vote now.*
6 *NOUN.* power to decide something; authority: *Who has the final say in this matter?*
❑ *VERB* **says, said, say·ing.**

Synonym Study

Say means to put an idea or feeling into words: *"I'm ready," I said. What did she say in her card?*

Tell can mean to give information by speech or writing: *Don't tell anyone where we're going. Does the poster tell what the movie is about?*

Voice means to say something, usually about your feelings: *She often voices strong opinions.*

Declare can mean to say something firmly and openly: *"This is the best cake I ever ate," declared the little boy.*

State means to say something in a formal way: *The manager stated that the contest was over.*

Express means to say or to show exactly what you mean: *Grandma's smile expressed her thanks.*

See also the Synonym Study at **talk.**

S

a	hat	ė	term	ô	order	ch	child		a in about
ā	age	i	it	oi	oil	ng	long		e in taken
ä	far	ī	ice	ou	out	sh	she	ə<	i in pencil
â	care	o	hot	u	cup	th	thin		o in lemon
e	let	ō	open	u̇	put	ŦH	then		u in circus
ē	equal	ȯ	saw	ü	rule	zh	measure		

say·ing (sā′ing), NOUN. something that people say often; proverb: *"Haste makes waste" is a saying.*

says (sez), VERB. a present tense of **say**: *He says he'll be late.*

SC, an abbreviation of **South Carolina.**

scab (skab), NOUN. a hard layer of dried blood and tissue that forms over a cut or sore as it heals: *A scab formed on my scraped knee.*

scaf·fold (skaf′əld), NOUN.
1 a temporary wooden or metal structure next to a building, that workers and their materials stand on when they are working on the building.
2 a raised platform on which criminals are put to death, usually by hanging.

scald (skȯld), VERB.
1 to burn with hot liquid or steam: *I scalded myself with hot grease.*
2 to heat almost to boiling, but not quite: *In some recipes, you have to scald the milk.*
❏ VERB **scalds, scald·ed, scald·ing.**

scale¹ (skāl), NOUN.
1 a device for weighing: *I stood on the bathroom scale to weigh myself.*
2 usually, **scales,** a balance for weighing: *She weighed some meat on the scales.*

scale² (skāl),
1 NOUN. one of the thin, flat, hard plates that form the outer covering of some fish and reptiles.
2 VERB. to remove scales from something: *She scaled the fish with a knife.*
❏ VERB **scales, scaled, scal·ing.** —**scale′like′,** ADJECTIVE.

scale³ (skāl),
1 NOUN. a system or plan for measuring or comparing things: *The salary scale for this job ranges from $25,000 now to $40,000 after ten years.*
2 NOUN. a series of marks made along a line with regular distances between them, to use in measuring something. A thermometer is marked with a scale.
3 NOUN. the size of a plan, map, drawing, or model compared with the actual size of what it represents: *This map is drawn to the scale of one inch for each 100 miles.*
4 NOUN. (in music) a series of tones going up or down in pitch: *She practices scales on the piano.*
5 VERB. to climb something: *They scaled the wall by ladders.* ∎ See the Synonym Study at **climb.**
❏ VERB **scales, scaled, scal·ing.**

sca·lene tri·an·gle (skā′lēn′ trī′ang′gəl), a triangle that has three sides unequal.

scal·lion (skal′yən), NOUN.
1 a young onion.
2 See **leek.**

scal·lop (skal′əp or skäl′əp), NOUN. a shellfish something like a small clam. In some kinds the muscle that opens and closes the shell is good to eat.

scal·loped (skal′əpt or skäl′əpt), ADJECTIVE. baked with sauce and bread crumbs in a dish: *scalloped oysters, scalloped potatoes.*

scalp (skalp),
1 NOUN. the skin on the top and back of the head, usually covered with hair.
2 VERB. to cut or tear part of the scalp from someone.
❏ VERB **scalps, scalped, scalp·ing.**

scal·pel (skal′pəl), NOUN. a small, straight knife used by surgeons.

scal·y (skā′lē), ADJECTIVE. covered with scales: *Snakes are scaly creatures.* ❏ ADJECTIVE **scal·i·er, scal·i·est.**

scam (skam), (informal)
1 NOUN. a clever but dishonest trick; fraud.
2 VERB. to trick someone or to get something in a clever but dishonest way: *He scammed two tickets by claiming to know the band's drummer.*
❏ VERB **scams, scammed, scam·ming.**

scam·per (skam′pər), VERB. to run quickly: *The mice scampered away when the cat came.* ❏ VERB **scam·pers, scam·pered, scam·per·ing.**

scan (skan),
1 VERB. to look at or examine something with great care: *You should scan every word of the contract before you sign it.*
2 VERB. to glance at; look over hastily.
3 VERB. to examine automatically by using a device such as a scanner: *The clerk scanned the groceries and gave us the total bill.*
4 NOUN. the picture or other information provided by a scanner: *a brain scan.*
❏ VERB **scans, scanned, scan·ning.**

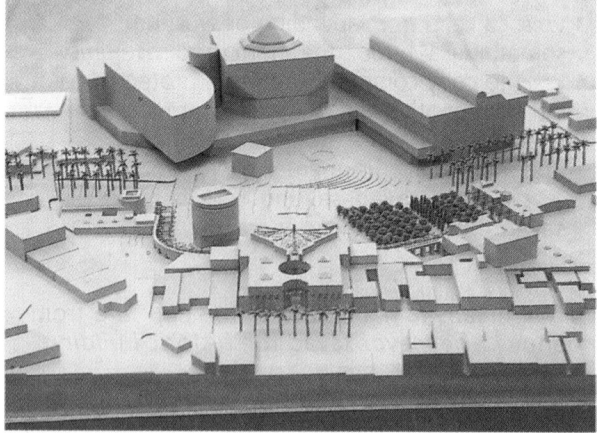

What is the **scale** of this model?

scan·dal (skan′dl), NOUN.
1 something that brings disgrace or shocks public opinion: *It was a scandal for the city treasurer to take tax money for personal use.*
2 public talk about someone that will hurt that person's reputation.

Scan·di·na·vi·a (skan′də nā′vē ə), *NOUN.* a region of northwestern Europe that includes Norway, Sweden, Denmark, and sometimes Finland and Iceland.

Scan·di·na·vi·an (skan′də nā′vē ən),
1 *ADJECTIVE.* of or about Scandinavia, its people, or their languages.
2 *NOUN.* someone born or living in Scandinavia.
3 *NOUN.* the languages of Denmark, Iceland, Norway, and Sweden.

Word Source

Scandinavian languages gave many words to English. Here are some of the words that have come from Scandinavian:

anger	geyser	reindeer	sky
calf[2]	guest	saga	troll
clip[1]	husband	scale[1]	ugly
egg[1]	loft	scare	weak
egg[2]	low	sister	window
fjord	nag[1]	ski	wing
flaw	nay	skirt	wrong
floe	odd	skull	
get	outlaw		

scan·ner (skan′ər), *NOUN.*
1 a medical device that can find tumors, fractures, and so on. It works by sending radiation or sound waves through tissue to create an image of a part of the body.
2 a device that uses a laser to read the vertical lines of a bar code.
3 a device that examines printed text, images, photographs, and the like, and creates electronic images of them.

scant·y (skan′tē), *ADJECTIVE.* barely enough; meager: *Drought caused a scanty harvest.* ❑ *ADJECTIVE* **scant·i·er, scant·i·est.**

scape·goat (skāp′gōt′), *NOUN.* someone or something blamed for the mistakes of others.

scar (skär),
1 *NOUN.* a mark left by a healed cut, wound, burn, or sore: *My vaccination scar is small.*
2 *NOUN.* any mark like this: *See the scars that your shoes have made on the chair rungs.*
3 *VERB.* to mark something with a scar: *He scarred the wood with the hammer when he missed the nail.*
❑ *VERB* **scars, scarred, scar·ring.**

Word Story

Scar comes from a Greek word meaning "fireplace." A fireplace always shows traces of old fires. The Greeks also used the word to mean the marks that fire left on burned skin.

scarce (skârs), *ADJECTIVE.* hard to get; rare: *Very old stamps are scarce.* ❑ *ADJECTIVE* **scarc·er, scarc·est.**

scarce·ly (skârs′lē), *ADVERB.* not quite; barely: *We could scarcely see the ship through the thick fog.*

scare (skâr),
1 *VERB.* to make someone feel that something bad might happen; frighten: *The lightning scared us badly.* ■ See the Synonym Study at **afraid.**
2 *NOUN.* a feeling of fear; fright: *I had a sudden scare when I saw a dog running toward me.*
3 *NOUN.* fright or panic that many people experience: *There was a bomb scare at the airport.*
❑ *VERB* **scares, scared, scar·ing.**

scare away or **scare off,** *IDIOM.* to frighten away; drive off: *The watchdog scared away the robber with its loud barking.*

Synonym Study

Scare means to make someone afraid: *It scares me when cars drive by too fast.*

Frighten means to fill someone with sudden fear: *My dog mask frightened the cat.*

Alarm means to cause worry about possible danger: *It alarms my parents if the phone rings late at night.*

Horrify means to make someone sick with fear: *It's horrifying to think that the plane nearly crashed.*

Terrify means to fill someone with very great fear: *The landslide terrified the climbers.*

See also the Synonym Studies at **afraid** and **fear.**

The boy loved to **scare** his cat.

scare·crow (skâr′krō′), *NOUN.* a figure of a person dressed in old clothes, set up in a field to frighten birds away from crops.

a	hat	ė	term	ô	order	ch	child		a in about
ā	age	i	it	oi	oil	ng	long		e in taken
ä	far	ī	ice	ou	out	sh	she	ə	i in pencil
â	care	o	hot	u	cup	th	thin		o in lemon
e	let	ō	open	ů	put	ŦH	then		u in circus
ē	equal	ò	saw	ü	rule	zh	measure		

scarf (skärf), NOUN. a long, broad piece of cloth worn around the neck, shoulders, or head. ❏ PLURAL **scarves** (skärvz) or **scarfs**.

scar·let (skär′lit), ADJECTIVE. very bright red.

scar·y (skâr′ē), ADJECTIVE. making someone feel afraid: *We watched a scary movie.* ❏ ADJECTIVE **scar·i·er, scar·i·est. –scar′i·ness,** NOUN.

scat·ter (skat′ər), VERB.
1 to throw a little bit of something here and some more over there; sprinkle: *I scattered salt on the sidewalk to melt the ice.*
2 to separate and drive off in different directions: *The police scattered the disorderly crowd.*
3 to separate and go in different directions: *The pigeons scattered when the dog ran toward them.*
❏ VERB **scat·ters, scat·tered, scat·ter·ing.**

scav·en·ger (skav′ən jər), NOUN.
1 an animal that feeds on dead and decaying animals or plants. Vultures are scavengers.
2 someone who picks up junk or waste material to recycle it.

These vultures are **scavengers**.

scavenger hunt, a game in which each person or team is given a list of various objects to collect without buying them. The winner is whoever first returns to the starting point with all the objects on the list.

scene (sēn), NOUN.
1 the time, place, and circumstances of a play, story, movie, or television show: *The scene of the book is laid in Boston in the year 1775.*
2 the place where something bad happened: *An ambulance hurried to the scene of the accident.*
3 a beautiful sight to look at; view: *The white sailboats in the blue water made a pretty scene.*
4 a part of an act of a play: *The king comes to the castle in Act I, Scene 2.*
5 a show of strong feeling in front of other people: *The child kicked and screamed and made a dreadful scene.*
   ■ Another word that sounds like this is **seen**.

scen·er·y (sē′nər ē), NOUN.
1 what you see when you look around outside. Scenery can include mountains, valleys, forests, and so on.
2 the painted hangings or screens used on a stage to show where the action of a play is taking place: *The scenery shows a garden in the moonlight.*

scen·ic (sē′nik), ADJECTIVE.
1 of or about natural scenery: *The scenic views in Yellowstone National Park are famous.*
2 having a lot of fine scenery: *We drove along the scenic highway.*
   –scen′i·cal·ly, ADVERB.

scent (sent),
1 NOUN. a nice smell: *The scent of roses filled the air.*
2 VERB. to smell something: *The dog scented a rabbit and ran off after it.*
3 NOUN. a smell left by an animal that passes by: *The dogs followed the fox by its scent.*
4 NOUN. perfume: *She used too much scent.*
   ❏ VERB **scents, scent·ed, scent·ing.** ■ Other words that sound like this are **cent** and **sent**.

sched·ule (skej′ül or skej′əl),
1 NOUN. a written or printed statement of when things will take place: *a TV program schedule.*
2 VERB. to plan or arrange something for a definite time or date: *We scheduled our vacation for August.*
3 NOUN. the time at which something is supposed to be done, or when vehicles are to arrive or leave: *The bus was an hour behind schedule.*
   ❏ VERB **sched·ules, sched·uled, sched·ul·ing.**

scheme (skēm),
1 NOUN. a plan for doing something: *He has a scheme for extracting salt from sea water.*
   ■ See the Synonym Study at **plan**.
2 NOUN. a plot or plan to do something illegal: *She had a scheme to cheat the government.*
3 VERB. to plot or plan something that is illegal: *They were scheming steal the jewels.*
4 NOUN. a system that you use to arrange how something works or how it looks: *The color scheme of the room is blue and gold.*
   ❏ VERB **schemes, schemed, schem·ing. –schem′er,** NOUN.

schol·ar (skol′ər), NOUN. someone whose regular work is study or research: *The professor was a famous scholar.* **–schol′ar·ly,** ADJECTIVE.

schol·ar·ship (skol′ər ship), NOUN.
1 knowledge gained by study; quality of learning and knowledge.
2 money given to help a student continue his or her studies: *The college offered her a scholarship of one thousand dollars.*

school¹ (skül),
1 NOUN. a place where you learn things in a group: *Children go to school to learn and to have fun.*

2 *NOUN.* learning in school; instruction: *Most children start school when they are about five years old.*

3 *NOUN.* all the students and teachers in a school: *Our school will be in a new building next fall.*

4 *NOUN.* a particular department or group in a university: *a medical school, a law school.*

5 *VERB.* to teach someone: *He was schooled in computer repair.*
  ❑ *VERB* **schools, schooled, school·ing.**

Word Story

School¹ comes from a Greek word meaning "leisure." In ancient Greece, most children were put to work early. Only people with enough money for leisure could continue their educations.

school² (skül), *NOUN.* a large number of the same kind of fish or water animals swimming together: *a school of mackerel.*

school·ing (skü′ling), *NOUN.* instruction in school; education received at school.

school·room (skül′rüm′), *NOUN.* a room in which pupils are taught.

school·teach·er (skül′tē′chər), *NOUN.* someone who teaches in a school.

school·work (skül′wėrk′), *NOUN.* a student's lessons and assignments.

school·yard (skül′yärd′), *NOUN.* a piece of ground around or near a school, used for play or games.

scientist G̲eorge W̲ashington C̲arver

George Washington Carver was born into slavery shortly before its abolition. He became a research scientist in agriculture. He developed more than 300 products from the peanut plant, and gained great international recognition for his research.

schoon·er (skü′nər), *NOUN.* a ship with two or more masts and sails set lengthwise.

schwa (shwä), *NOUN.*
1 an unstressed vowel sound such as *a* in *about* or *o* in *lemon.*
2 the symbol ə, used to represent this sound.
  ❑ *PLURAL* **schwas.**

sci·ence (sī′əns), *NOUN.*
1 the process of gathering knowledge based on observed facts and tested truths.
2 a branch of such knowledge. Biology, chemistry, physics, and astronomy are **natural sciences.** Economics is a **social science.**

Word Bank

The vocabulary of **science** includes a large number of combining forms, prefixes, and suffixes. When scientists make new discoveries and need new words, they often form them by combining these word parts that are already in use. For instance, if someone invented a method for recording the sounds of living things from far away, it might be called "biotelephonography." Among the many combining forms, prefixes, and suffixes of science are these:

astro-	geo-	-ist	photo-
bio-	-graph	micro-	-scope
electro-	hydro-	-phone	thermo-

science fiction, stories, books, movies, and television shows that combine science and imagination. Science fiction deals with life in the future, on other planets, and so on.

sci·en·tif·ic (sī′ən tif′ik), *ADJECTIVE.*
1 using the facts and laws of science: *scientific methods, scientific farming.*
2 of or used in science: *scientific instruments.*
  —**sci′en·tif′i·cal·ly,** *ADVERB.*

sci·en·tist (sī′ən tist), *NOUN.* someone who has expert knowledge of some branch of science.

sci-fi (sī′fī′), (informal)
1 *NOUN.* a short form of **science fiction.**
2 *ADJECTIVE.* of or about science fiction.

scis·sors (siz′ərz), *NOUN PLURAL* or *SINGULAR.* a tool for cutting things. It has has two sharp blades fastened in the middle and handles at one end held with your fingers.

scold (skōld), *VERB.* to speak to someone in an angry way: *She scolded the kids for making such a mess.*
  ❑ *VERB* **scolds, scold·ed, scold·ing.**

S

a	hat	ė	term	ô	order	ch	child	a in about
ā	age	i	it	oi	oil	ng	long	e in taken
ä	far	ī	ice	ou	out	sh	she	ə ⎰ i in pencil
â	care	o	hot	u	cup	th	thin	o in lemon
e	let	ō	open	ů	put	ŦH	then	u in circus
ē	equal	ȯ	saw	ü	rule	zh	measure	

scoop (sküp),
1 *NOUN.* a tool like a small shovel used to dip up things. A cuplike scoop is used to dish up ice cream.
2 *NOUN.* the amount picked up at one time by a scoop: *Use two scoops of flour and one of sugar.*
3 *VERB.* to pick up with a scoop, or the way a scoop does: *You scoop up snow with your hands to make snowballs.*
4 *NOUN.* the part of a dredge or power shovel that picks up or holds coal, sand, and so on.
5 *VERB.* to hollow out or make by scooping: *The children scooped holes in the sand.*
❑ *VERB* **scoops, scooped, scoop·ing. –scoop′er,** *NOUN.*

scoot (süt), *VERB.* to go quickly; dart: *He scooted out the door.* ❑ *VERB* **scoots, scoot·ed, scoot·ing.**

scoot·er (skü′tər), *NOUN.* a child's vehicle made of a board for the feet between two wheels, one in front of the other, steered by an upright handlebar.

scope (skōp), *NOUN.* the extent or range of understanding or mental activity: *The scope of the child's interests was enlarged from reading many books.*

Word Power   -scope

The combining form **-scope** means "a device for viewing or examining." A telescope is a **device for viewing** distant objects. A stethoscope is a **device for examining** the lungs and heart.

scorch (skôrch), *VERB.*
1 to burn something slightly: *I scorched the cake.*
2 to dry up; wither: *The strong sun scorched our lawn.*
❑ *VERB* **scorch·es, scorched, scorch·ing.**

score (skôr),
1 *NOUN.* the points made in a game, contest, or test: *The score was 9 to 2 in favor of our school.*
2 *VERB.* to make points in a game, contest, or test: *She scored 85 percent on the spelling test.*
3 *NOUN.* a group or set of twenty: *four score and seven years ago.* ★ The plural for this meaning is **score.**
4 *NOUN.* a written or printed piece of music arranged for different instruments or voices: *She was studying the score of the piece she was learning to play.*
❑ *VERB* **scores, scored, scor·ing. –score′less,** *ADJECTIVE.* **–scor′er,** *NOUN.*

score·board (skôr′bôrd′), *NOUN.* a large board on which the scores of the teams at a sporting event are recorded and displayed.

score·keep·er (skôr′kē′pər), *NOUN.* someone who keeps score, especially in sports.

scorn (skôrn),
1 *VERB.* to have no respect for someone or something; despise: *Most people scorn cheaters.*
2 *NOUN.* a feeling of great disrespect for someone; contempt: *Most people feel scorn for liars.*
❑ *VERB* **scorns, scorned, scorn·ing.**

scorn·ful (skôrn′fəl), *ADJECTIVE.* showing contempt; full of scorn: *They spoke of our old car in a scornful way.* **–scorn′ful·ly,** *ADVERB.*

scor·pi·on (skôr′pē ən), *NOUN.* a small animal related to the spider but much larger. It has a poisonous stinger in its tail.

scorpion — up to 8 inches long, including the tail

Scot (skot), *NOUN.* someone born or living in Scotland.

Scotch (skoch),
1 *NOUN.* a kind of whiskey made in Scotland.
2 *ADJECTIVE* or *NOUN.* Scottish. ★ The people of Scotland do not like this term. They prefer **Scottish.**

Scot·land (skot′lənd), *NOUN.* the division of Great Britain that is north of England.

Scot·tish (skot′ish),
1 *ADJECTIVE.* of or about Scotland, its people, or their language.
2 *NOUN PLURAL.* **the Scottish,** the people of Scotland.
3 *NOUN.* the form of English spoken by the people of Scotland.

scoun·drel (skoun′drəl), *NOUN.* a very bad person; villain; rascal: *Some scoundrels set fire to the barn.*

scour¹ (skour), *VERB.* to clean something by rubbing it very hard: *I scoured the sink with cleanser.* ❑ *VERB* **scours, scoured, scour·ing.**

scour² (skour), *VERB.* to search someplace carefully: *We scoured the house for my pet snake.* ❑ *VERB* **scours, scoured, scour·ing.**

scout (skout),
1 *NOUN.* someone sent to find out what the enemy is doing. A scout usually wears a uniform; a spy does not.
2 *NOUN.* something that acts as a scout. Some ships and airplanes are scouts.
3 *VERB.* to act as a scout; hunt around to find something: *We scouted for firewood.*
4 *NOUN.* someone belonging to the Boy Scouts or Girl Scouts.
❑ *VERB* **scouts, scout·ed, scout·ing.**

scout·mas·ter (skout′mas′tər), *NOUN.* an adult in charge of a troop of Boy Scouts.

scowl (skoul),
1 *VERB.* to look at someone in an angry way; frown: *She scowled at the man who stepped on her toes.*
2 *NOUN.* an angry look; frown.
❑ *VERB* **scowls, scowled, scowl·ing. –scowl′er,** *NOUN.*

scrag·gly (skrag′lē), *ADJECTIVE.* rough or irregular; ragged: *The man had a scraggly beard.* ❑ *ADJECTIVE* **scrag·gli·er, scrag·gli·est.**

scram·ble (skram′bəl),

1 *VERB.* to make your way, especially by climbing or crawling quickly: *We scrambled up the steep, rocky hill, trying to follow the guide.*

2 *NOUN.* a quick climb or walk over rough ground: *It was a long scramble over rocks to the top of the hill.*

3 *VERB.* to struggle with other people, players, and so on, for something: *The players scrambled to get the ball.*

4 *NOUN.* a struggle to get something for yourself: *Some people enjoy the scramble for wealth and power.*

5 *VERB.* to change an electronic signal so that a special receiver is needed to understand transmitted messages. Government agencies sometimes scramble signals that carry secret information.

6 *VERB.* to cook eggs with the whites and yolks mixed together.

❑ *VERB* **scram·bles, scram·bled, scram·bling.**

scrap[1] (skrap),

1 *NOUN.* a small piece; little bit; small part left over: *Put the scraps of paper in the wastebasket.*

■ See the Synonym Study at **piece.**

2 *VERB.* to throw aside as useless or worn out: *They scrapped the old machinery.*

❑ *VERB* **scraps, scrapped, scrap·ping.**

scrap[2] (skrap),

1 *NOUN.* a brief fight, quarrel, or struggle: *The dogs growled and then got into a scrap over a bone.*

2 *VERB.* to fight, quarrel, or struggle: *Those two dogs are always scrapping.*

❑ *VERB* **scraps, scrapped, scrap·ping. —scrap′per,** *NOUN.*

scrap·book (skrap′bůk′), *NOUN.* a book with blank pages that you can keep or paste pictures or clippings in.

scrape (skrāp),

1 *VERB.* to rub something with something sharp or rough to make it smooth or clean: *Scrape your muddy shoes with this old knife.*

2 *VERB.* to remove something by rubbing it off with something sharp or rough: *We need to scrape the old peeling paint off the house before we repaint it.*

3 *VERB.* to scratch a part of your body by rubbing it against something rough: *She fell and scraped her knee on the sidewalk.*

4 *NOUN.* a scraped place: *My scrape is healing.*

5 *VERB.* to rub against something with a harsh sound: *The branch scraped against the window.*

6 *NOUN.* a difficulty; position hard to get out of: *Children often get into scrapes.*

❑ *VERB* **scrapes, scraped, scrap·ing.**

scrape by or **scrape through,** *IDIOM.* to get through something with difficulty: *My grade was just high enough to scrape by.*

scrape together, *IDIOM.* to collect something with great difficulty: *I've finally scraped together enough money for a bicycle.*

scrap·er (skrā′pər), *NOUN.* a tool for scraping: *We removed the loose paint with a scraper.*

scratch (skrach),

1 *VERB.* to make a mark on something by using something sharp or rough: *Your boots have scratched the wood floor.*

2 *NOUN.* a mark made by something sharp: *There are deep scratches on this desk.*

3 *VERB.* to make marks on the skin with the nails or claws: *The cat scratched me.*

4 *NOUN.* a very slight cut: *That scratch on your hand will soon be well.*

5 *VERB.* to rub or scrape something that itches with your fingernails: *Don't scratch your mosquito bites.*

6 *NOUN.* the sound of scratching: *The only noise was the soft scratch of her pen.*

7 *VERB.* to rub with a harsh noise: *Twigs scratched against the windows when the wind blew.*

❑ *VERB* **scratch·es, scratched, scratch·ing;** *PLURAL* **scratch·es. —scratch′er,** *NOUN.*

from scratch, *IDIOM.*

1 from the beginning: *I lost my notes and had to start my paper from scratch.*

2 using fresh ingredients; not from a package: *I baked a cake from scratch.*

scratch·y (skrach′ē), *ADJECTIVE.* likely to scratch or scrape: *He wore a scratchy wool sweater.*

❑ *ADJECTIVE* **scratch·i·er, scratch·i·est.**

scrawl (skról),

1 *VERB.* to write or draw in a careless way: *She scrawled her name on her paper.*

2 *NOUN.* careless handwriting: *She signed the letter with a scrawl.*

❑ *VERB* **scrawls, scrawled, scrawl·ing.**

scraw·ny (skró′nē), *ADJECTIVE.* very thin; skinny: *Turkeys have scrawny necks.* ❑ *ADJECTIVE* **scraw·ni·er, scraw·ni·est.**

scream (skrēm),

1 *VERB.* to make a loud, sharp cry. People scream when they are frightened, angry, or excited.

■ See the Synonym Study at **shout.**

2 *NOUN.* a loud, sharp cry.

❑ *VERB* **screams, screamed, scream·ing. —scream′er,** *NOUN.*

screech (skrēch),

1 *VERB.* to cry out sharply in a high voice; shriek: *Someone screeched, "Help! Help!"*

2 *NOUN.* a shrill, harsh scream or sound: *The loud screeches brought the police.*

❑ *VERB* **screech·es, screeched, screech·ing;** *PLURAL* **screech·es.**

a hat	ė term	ô order	ch child	a in about
ā age	i it	oi oil	ng long	e in taken
ä far	ī ice	ou out	sh she	i in pencil
â care	o hot	u cup	th thin	o in lemon
e let	ō open	ů put	ᴛʜ then	u in circus
ē equal	ò saw	ü rule	zh measure	

S

screen (skrēn),
1 *NOUN.* a flat, white surface on which movies or slides are shown.
2 *NOUN.* movies; the movie industry: *She was a great star of stage and screen.*
3 *NOUN.* a glass surface on which television pictures, computer information, or video game diagrams appear.
4 *NOUN.* the information shown by a computer at any particular moment, or any particular diagram shown by a video game machine.
5 *NOUN.* wire woven together with small openings in between: *We have screens in our windows.*
6 *NOUN.* a covered frame that hides, protects, or separates. There are often screens between hospital beds.
7 *VERB.* to shelter, protect, or hide something with a screen: *We screened our porch to keep out bugs.*
❑ *VERB* **screens, screened, screen•ing.**

screw (skrü),
1 *NOUN.* a slender piece of metal like a nail with a ridge twisted evenly around its length. It has a slot in its flat or rounded head for a screwdriver to fit into, and a sharp point at the other end.
2 *VERB.* to turn something the way you turn a screw; twist: *He screwed the lid tightly on the jar.*
3 *VERB.* to fasten or tighten something with a screw or screws: *Dad screwed the hinges to the door.*
❑ *VERB* **screws, screwed, screw•ing.**

screw•driv•er (skrü/dri/vər), *NOUN.* a tool for putting in or taking out screws.

scrib•ble (skrib/əl),
1 *VERB.* to write or draw something carelessly or hastily: *I scribbled a note to let them know we would be late.*
2 *NOUN.* something that has been scribbled.
❑ *VERB* **scrib•bles, scrib•bled, scrib•bling.**

scribe (skrīb), *NOUN.* (long ago) someone whose job was making copies of written things. Before printing was invented, there were many scribes.

scrim•mage (skrim/ij), *NOUN.* (in football) the play that takes place when the ball is passed back by the center and which continues until the official's whistle calls the play over.

scrimp (skrimp), *VERB.* to spend as little money as possible: *They scrimped and saved to buy a new motorboat.* ❑ *VERB* **scrimps, scrimped, scrimp•ing.**

script (skript), *NOUN.*
1 the manuscript of a play, movie, or radio or television broadcast.
2 handwriting; written letters, figures, signs, or characters.

Scrip•ture (skrip/chər), *NOUN.*
1 the Bible.
2 **the Scriptures,** the Bible.
3 **scripture,** any sacred writing.

scroll (skrōl),
1 *NOUN.* a roll of parchment or paper, especially one with writing on it.
2 *VERB.* to move across a computer screen in a horizontal or vertical direction.
❑ *VERB* **scrolls, scrolled, scroll•ing.**

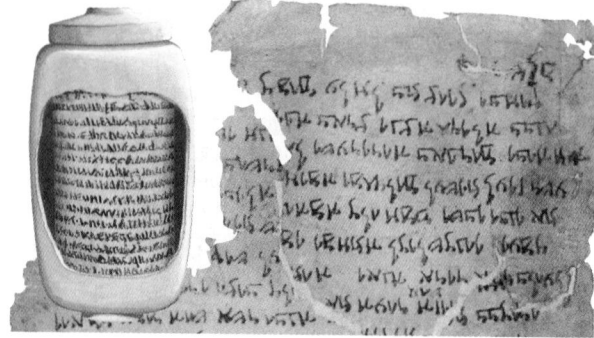

Ancient **scrolls** were often stored in clay jars.

scrub (skrub),
1 *VERB.* to rub something hard in order clean it: *We scrubbed the floor with a brush and soap.*
2 *NOUN.* the act of scrubbing: *Give your face and hands a good scrub.*
❑ *VERB* **scrubs, scrubbed, scrub•bing. —scrub/ber,** *NOUN.*

scruff (skruf), *NOUN.* the skin at the back of the neck.

scruf•fy (skruf/ē), *ADJECTIVE.* messy; untidy: *scruffy clothes.* ❑ *ADJECTIVE* **scruf•fi•er, scruf•fi•est.**

scrump•tious (skrump/shəs), *ADJECTIVE.* very pleasing or satisfying, especially to the taste or smell; delightful: *We enjoyed a scrumptious meal at their restaurant.*

scrunch (skrunch), *VERB.*
1 to crumple or squeeze something: *He scrunched the wad of paper in his fist.*
2 to crouch: *He scrunched down in his seat.*
❑ *VERB* **scrunch•es, scrunched, scrunch•ing.**

scrunch•y (skrun/chē), *NOUN.* an elastic band, usually covered with cloth. Scrunchies are used to hold hair in place. ❑ *PLURAL* **scrunch•ies.**

scru•ple (skrü/pəl), *NOUN.* usually, **scruples,** a feeling of uneasiness that keeps someone from doing something: *She has scruples about lying.*

scru•pu•lous (skrü/pyə ləs), *ADJECTIVE.*
1 very careful to do what is right.
2 very careful about small details: *A restaurant has to be scrupulous about cleanliness.*
—scru/pu•lous•ly, *ADVERB.*

scu•ba (skü/bə),
1 *NOUN.* portable equipment used to breathe underwater, including tanks of compressed air, a mouthpiece with valves to regulate the flow of air, a face mask, fins, and so on.
2 *ADJECTIVE.* using or made up of such equipment: *a scuba class, scuba gear.*
■ See the Word Source at **acronym.**

scuba diving, the act of swimming underwater with scuba gear.

Scuba diving requires special equipment.

scuff (skuf), *VERB.* to wear or injure the surface of something by hard use: *I've scuffed my new shoes.* ❑ *VERB* **scuffs, scuffed, scuff·ing.**

scuf·fle (skuf′əl),
1 *VERB.* to struggle or fight briefly over something: *The children were scuffling over the ball.*
2 *NOUN.* a brief struggle or fight: *I lost my hat in the scuffle.* ❑ *VERB* **scuf·fles, scuf·fled, scuf·fling.**

scull (skul),
1 *NOUN.* an oar worked from side to side over the end of a boat to move it forward.
2 *NOUN.* one of a pair of oars used, one on each side, by a single rower.
3 *VERB.* to move a boat forward by a scull or by sculls. ❑ *VERB* **sculls, sculled, scull·ing.** ■ Another word that sounds like this is **skull.**

sculp·tor (skulp′tər), *NOUN.* an artist who makes things by cutting or shaping them. Sculptors make statues of marble, bronze, and so on.

sculp·ture (skulp′chər),
1 *NOUN.* the art of carving or modeling figures. Sculpture includes the cutting of statues from blocks of marble, stone, or wood, casting in bronze, and modeling in clay or wax.
2 *VERB.* to make figures in this way; carve or model.
3 *NOUN.* a figure made in this way: *There are many famous sculptures in the museums.* ❑ *VERB* **sculp·tures, sculp·tured, sculp·tur·ing.**

scum (skum), *NOUN.* a thin layer that rises to the top of a liquid: *Green scum floated on the pond.*

scur·ry (skėr′ē), *VERB.* to run quickly; hurry: *We could hear the mice scurry about in the walls.* ❑ *VERB* **scur·ries, scur·ried, scur·ry·ing.**

scur·vy (skėr′vē), *NOUN.* a disease caused by a lack of vitamin C. It causes bleeding gums, weakness, and spots that look like bruises on the skin. Scurvy used to be common among sailors when they had little to eat except bread and salt meat.

scut·tle (skut′l), *VERB.* to scamper; scurry: *The crabs scuttled across the sand.* ❑ *VERB* **scut·tles, scut·tled, scut·tling.**

scuz·zy (sku′zē), *ADJECTIVE.* (slang) dirty or unpleasant in appearance or character: *He wears scuzzy clothes.* ❑ *ADJECTIVE* **scuz·zi·er, scuz·zi·est.**

scythe (sīⱦH), *NOUN.* a long, slightly curved blade on a long handle, used for cutting grass, grain, and so on.

SD, an abbreviation of **South Dakota.**

SE or **S.E.,**
1 an abbreviation of **southeast.**
2 an abbreviation of **southeastern.**

sea (sē), *NOUN.*
1 the great body of salt water that covers almost three fourths of the earth's surface; the ocean.
2 any large body of salt water, smaller than an ocean: *the North Sea, the Mediterranean Sea.*
3 a very large amount or number: *There was a sea of people at the mall.* ❑ *PLURAL* **seas.** ■ Another word that sounds like this is **see.**

at sea, *IDIOM.* out on the sea: *We were at sea out of sight of land for ten days.*

go to sea, *IDIOM.* to become a sailor: *The captain had gone to sea when he was barely seventeen.*

put to sea, *IDIOM.* to begin a voyage: *The cruise ship put to sea at ten o'clock this morning.*

sea a·nem·o·ne (sē′ ə nem′ə nē), a small, flowerlike sea animal with a fleshy, cylindrical body and a mouth surrounded by many tentacles.

sea·board (sē′bôrd′), *NOUN.* the land near the sea: *New Jersey is on the Atlantic seaboard.*

sea·far·ing (sē′fâr′ing), *ADJECTIVE.* going, traveling, or working on the sea: *a hardy seafaring people.*

sea·food (sē′füd′), *NOUN.* any saltwater fish or shellfish that is good to eat. Tuna, lobster, and oysters are all kinds of seafood.

sea·go·ing (sē′gō′ing), *ADJECTIVE.* made for going to sea: *a seagoing tugboat.*

sea gull, any gull, especially one living on or near the sea.

sea horse, a small fish that has a head that looks something like a horse's head.

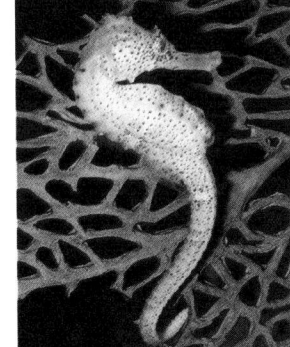

Most **sea horses** are about 6 inches long. Some may be up to 12 inches long.

a	hat	ė	term	ô	order	ch	child		a in about
ā	age	i	it	oi	oil	ng	long		e in taken
ä	far	ī	ice	ou	out	sh	she	ə	i in pencil
â	care	o	hot	u	cup	th	thin		o in lemon
e	let	ō	open	ů	put	ⱦH	then		u in circus
ē	equal	ô	saw	ü	rule	zh	measure		

S

seal¹ (sēl),
1 *NOUN.* a design or pattern used to show ownership or authority. Seals are stamped into important government papers to show that they are genuine.
2 *NOUN.* (formerly) a piece of wax, paper, metal, or the like, on which the design is stamped.
3 *VERB.* to close something very tightly; fasten: *Seal the letter before mailing it.*
4 *NOUN.* the part of a top or lid on a container that shows it has not been opened: *The jar of instant coffee was covered with a seal.*
5 *NOUN.* a special kind of stamp: *Christmas seals.*
❑ *VERB* **seals, sealed, seal·ing. —seal'a·ble,** *ADJECTIVE.* **—seal'er,** *NOUN.*

seal² (sēl), *NOUN.* a sea mammal with large flippers, usually living in cold regions. Some kinds have very valuable fur. ❑ *PLURAL* **seals** or **seal.**
—seal'like', *ADJECTIVE.*

Did You Know?

A **seal** can hold its breath underwater for as long as 28 minutes. The average person can hold his or her breath for only a minute.

sea level, the altitude at the surface of the sea. Mountains, plains, and ocean beds are measured in feet or meters above or below sea level.

sea lion, a large seal of the Pacific coast.

seam (sēm), *NOUN.* the line formed by sewing together two pieces of cloth, canvas, leather, and the like: *the seams of a coat.* ■ Another word that sounds like this is **seem. —seam'less,** *ADJECTIVE.*

sea·man (sē'mən), *NOUN.*
1 a sailor.
2 a military rank. See the chart on page 550.
❑ *PLURAL* **sea·men.**

seam·stress (sēm'stris), *NOUN.* a woman whose work is sewing. ❑ *PLURAL* **seam·stress·es.**

sea·plane (sē'plān'), *NOUN.* an airplane that can take off and land on water.

sea·port (sē'pôrt'), *NOUN.* a city, port, or harbor on the coast that ships can reach from the sea: *New York is a seaport.*

sear (sir), *VERB.*
1 to burn the surface of: *The hot iron seared my hand.*
2 to cook meat quickly over high heat.
❑ *VERB* **sears, seared, sear·ing.**

search (sėrch),
1 *VERB.* to look through; go over carefully; examine, especially for something hidden: *The police searched the prisoners to see if they had weapons.*
2 *VERB.* to try to find something by looking for it; seek: *We searched all day for the lost kitten.*
3 *NOUN.* the act of searching; examination: *She found her book after a long search.*
❑ *VERB* **search·es, searched, search·ing;** *PLURAL* **search·es. —search'a·ble,** *ADJECTIVE.* **—search'er,** *NOUN.*

in search of, *IDIOM.* trying to find; looking for: *The children went in search of their lost dog.*

search·light (sėrch'līt'), *NOUN.* a device that can throw a very bright beam of light in any direction.

sea·shell (sē'shel'), *NOUN.* the shell of any shellfish, such as an oyster or clam.

sea·shore (sē'shôr'), *NOUN.* the land at the edge of a sea; seaside; shore.

sea·sick (sē'sik'), *ADJECTIVE.* sick and dizzy from the effects of a ship's motion. **—sea'sick'ness,** *NOUN.*

sea·side (sē'sīd'), *NOUN.* See **seashore.**

sea·son (sē'zn),
1 *NOUN.* one of the four periods of the year; spring, summer, autumn, or winter.
2 *NOUN.* any period of time marked by something special: *the holiday season, basketball season.*
3 *VERB.* to make something taste better: *Season your egg with salt.*
❑ *VERB* **sea·sons, sea·soned, sea·son·ing.**

in season, *IDIOM.* in the time or condition for eating, hunting, and so on: *Cherries are in season in June.*
out of season, *IDIOM.* not in season.

sea·son·al (sē'zn əl), *ADJECTIVE.* happening at regular intervals: *Heavy rains are seasonal in Asia and Africa.*

sea·son·ing (sē'zn ing), *NOUN.* something that improves flavor: *Salt and spices are seasonings.*

seat (sēt),
1 *NOUN.* something to sit on. Chairs, benches, and stools are seats.
2 *NOUN.* a place to sit: *Can you find a seat on the bus?*
3 *NOUN.* a place in which you have the right to sit. If someone has a seat in Congress, it means that person is a member of Congress.
4 *NOUN.* the part of a chair, bench, stool, and the like, on which you sit: *This bench has a broken seat.*
5 *NOUN.* the part of the body on which you sit, or the clothing covering it: *The seat of her jeans is patched. Those trousers are too tight across the seat.*
6 *VERB.* to set or place someone on a seat: *Please seat yourself in a comfortable chair.*
7 *VERB.* to have seats for: *Our school auditorium seats one thousand pupils.*
❑ *VERB* **seats, seat·ed, seat·ing.**

Have You Heard?

You may have heard the phrase **"flying by the seat of your pants."** This means that you are guessing your way through something difficult or dangerous. People say this when they think someone does not have enough knowledge or experience to do what they are trying to do.

seat belt, a belt or set of belts fastened to the seat of a car or airplane, used to hold someone in the seat in case there is a crash, jolt, or bump; safety belt.

sea urchin, a small, round sea animal with a spiny shell.

sea urchin — from 2 to 5 inches in diameter

sea·weed (sē′wēd′), NOUN. any plant or any living thing like a plant growing in the sea.

se·cede (si sēd′), VERB. to officially withdraw from a group or country: *Some southern states seceded from the United States during the Civil War.* ❑ VERB **se·cedes, se·ced·ed, se·ced·ing.**

se·clud·ed (si klü′did), ADJECTIVE. completely away from other people; private: *We rented a secluded cottage in the woods.* **—se·clud′ed·ness,** NOUN.

sec·ond[1] (sek′ənd),
1 ADJECTIVE. next after the first: *the second seat from the front, a second child.*
2 ADJECTIVE. another; other: *Give me a second chance.*
3 ADVERB. in the second group, division, rank, or place: *I finished second in the tennis finals.*
4 NOUN. someone or something that is second: *You won the first prize; I won the second.*
5 NOUN. **seconds,** a second portion of food: *After I finished eating what was on my plate, I went back for seconds.*

sec·ond[2] (sek′ənd), NOUN. one of the 60 very short equal periods of time that make up a minute.

sec·ond·ar·y (sek′ən der′ē), ADJECTIVE. next after the first in importance, order, time, and so on: *In nutrition, good health is primary; attractive appearance is secondary.* **—sec′ond·ar′i·ly,** ADVERB.

secondary accent or **secondary stress,**
1 an accent in a word that is stronger than no accent but weaker than the strongest accent. The second syllable of *ab·bre′vi·a′tion* has a secondary accent.
2 the mark (′) used to show this.

secondary school, a school that you go to after elementary school or junior high school; high school.

sec·ond-class (sek′ənd klas′), ADJECTIVE. of inferior grade, quality, or position: *second-class goods.*

second hand, the hand on a clock or watch, pointing to the seconds. It moves around the whole dial once in a minute.

sec·ond·hand (sek′ənd hand′), ADJECTIVE.
1 not new; used already by someone else: *They bought a secondhand car.*
2 not original; gotten from someone else: *He had to rely on secondhand information.*
3 buying and selling used goods: *a secondhand store.*

secondhand smoke, smoke from a cigarette, cigar, or pipe that is inhaled by someone other than the person smoking.

sec·ond·ly (sek′ənd lē), ADVERB. in the second place.

sec·ond-rate (sek′ənd rāt′), ADJECTIVE. poor in quality; not of the highest class: *They didn't rehearse enough, and gave a second-rate performance.*

se·cre·cy (sē′krə sē), NOUN. the condition of being secret or being kept secret: *Plans for the birthday party were made in the greatest secrecy.*

se·cret (sē′krit),
1 ADJECTIVE. kept from the knowledge of others: *a secret errand, a secret weapon.* ■ See the Synonym Study at **mystery.**
2 ADJECTIVE. working or acting in secret: *the secret police, a secret agent.*
3 NOUN. something that you don't tell anyone: *Can you keep a secret?*
4 NOUN. a hidden cause or reason: *I wish I knew the secret of her success.*
—se′cret·ly, ADVERB.

in secret, IDIOM. secretly; privately; not openly: *I have said nothing in secret that I would not say openly.*

sec·re·tar·y (sek′rə ter′ē), NOUN.
1 someone who works in an office, doing word processing and keeping records for a person, company, club, committee, and so on: *Our club has a secretary who takes notes at the meeting.*
2 someone who is in charge of a department of the government. The Secretary of the Treasury is the head of the Treasury Department.
❑ PLURAL **sec·re·tar·ies.**

Word Story

Secretary comes from a Latin word meaning "a secret." Secretaries are expected to keep the secrets of the people or organizations they work for.

se·crete (si krēt′), VERB. to produce something liquid, so that it flows: *Glands in the mouth secrete saliva.* ❑ VERB **se·cretes, se·cret·ed, se·cret·ing.**

sect (sekt), NOUN. a group of people having the same religious beliefs or opinions: *Each religious sect in the town had its own church.*

a	hat	ė	term	ô	order	ch	child	⟨a in about
ā	age	i	it	oi	oil	ng	long	e in taken
ä	far	ī	ice	ou	out	sh	she	ə⟨i in pencil
â	care	o	hot	u	cup	th	thin	o in lemon
e	let	ō	open	u̇	put	ᴛʜ	then	⟨u in circus
ē	equal	ȯ	saw	ü	rule	zh	measure	

S

sec·tion (sek′shən), NOUN.
1 a part cut off from something; division; slice: *Cut the pie into eight equal sections.* ■ See the Synonym Study at **part.**
2 a part of a book, newspaper, law, and so on: *Our arithmetic book has several sections on dividing fractions.*
3 a region; part of a country, city, or community: *His office is in the business section of town.*

se·cure (si kyur′),
1 ADJECTIVE. safe from loss, attack, escape, or danger: *This is a secure hiding place.* ■ See the Synonym Study at **safe.**
2 VERB. to make something or someone safe; protect: *You cannot secure yourself against all risks and dangers.*
3 ADJECTIVE. free from care or fear: *He hoped for a secure old age.*
4 ADJECTIVE. firmly fastened; not liable to give way: *Is there a secure lock on the rear window?*

This baby chimp is **secure** in its mother's arms.

5 VERB. to tie something up tightly: *She secured the rowboat to the dock.*
❑ VERB **se·cures, se·cured, se·cur·ing.** —**se·cure′ly,** ADVERB.

se·cur·i·ty (si kyur′ə tē), NOUN.
1 freedom from danger, care, or fear; feeling or condition of being safe: *It gave us a sense of security to have the lifeguard nearby while we swam.*
2 something given to another person as a guarantee of good faith that something will be done in the future: *She used her car title as security for the loan.*

se·dan (si dan′), NOUN. a closed car seating four or more people.

sed·a·tive (sed′ə tiv), NOUN. a medicine that reduces pain or excitement.

sed·i·ment (sed′ə mənt), NOUN.
1 any material that settles to the bottom of a liquid: *Sediment collects at the bottom of lakes and rivers.*
2 the earth and stones left by water, wind, or ice. When a river overflows, it leaves sediment on the land it covers.

sed·i·men·tar·y rock (sed′ə men′tər ē rok′), rock formed from minerals, dead plants and animals, and so on, that have gradually been compressed over thousands of years. Coal and limestone are kinds of sedimentary rock.

see (sē), VERB.
1 to become aware of something by looking at it: *See that black cloud?*
2 to have the power of sight: *The blind do not see.*
3 to understand something that is said or written: *I see what you mean.*
4 to find something out: *I will see what needs to be done.*
5 to live through or experience something: *I've never seen such a terrible storm before.*
6 to go with; attend; escort: *She saw her friend home safely.*
7 to pay a visit to someone: *I went to see a friend.*
8 to go to someone for advice or information: *She needs to see a doctor about her cough.*
❑ VERB **sees, saw, seen, see·ing.** ■ Another word that sounds like this is **sea.**

see about, IDIOM. to consider and decide later: *Dad said he'd see about taking us to the zoo.*

see off, IDIOM. to go with someone to the starting place of a trip: *We saw them off at the airport.*

see through, IDIOM.
1 to understand the real character or hidden purpose of: *I saw through their excuses.*
2 to go through with; finish: *I mean to see this job through.*

see to, IDIOM. to look after; take care of: *They saw to it that their children had good educations.*

Synonym Study

See means to know something's appearance with your eyes: *From this hill you can see the lake.*

Behold means to see. It is an older word, often found in stories: *The weary and thirsty desert travelers beheld a lifesaving pool of water.*

Observe means to see and give attention to: *The biologist made notes on everything he observed in the bird's nest, then wrote his report.*

Notice means to observe: *Notice how close to the ground that plane is flying.*

Perceive can mean to see and understand. It is a formal word: *Do you perceive the difference between the shapes of those clouds?*

See also the Synonym Study at **look.**

seed (sēd),
1 NOUN. the part of a plant that grows into a new plant. A seed has a protective outer coat and contains a tiny new plant with a supply of food for early growth: *We planted seeds in the garden.*

2 *VERB.* to scatter seeds over a place: *The farmer seeded the field with corn.*
❑ *VERB* **seeds, seed·ed, seed·ing;** *PLURAL* **seeds** or **seed. −seed′less,** ADJECTIVE. **−seed′like′,** ADJECTIVE.

seed·ling (sēd′ling), *NOUN.* a young plant grown from a seed: *I dug up the seedlings and transplanted them into the garden.*

seek (sēk), *VERB.*
1 to try to find something; look for; hunt; search: *We are seeking a new home.*
2 to try to get something: *Some people seek wealth.*
3 to try; attempt: *Nations are seeking to make peace.*
❑ *VERB* **seeks, sought, seek·ing. −seek′er,** NOUN.

seem (sēm), *VERB.*
1 to appear to be: *Does this room seem hot to you?*
2 to appear to be true or to be the case: *It seems likely to rain.*
❑ *VERB* **seems, seemed, seem·ing.** ■ Another word that sounds like this is **seam.**

seen (sēn), *VERB.* the past participle of **see:** *Have you seen my parents?* ■ Another word that sounds like this is **scene.**

seep (sēp), *VERB.* to flow very slowly through something; trickle; ooze: *Water seeped through the tent roof.* ❑ *VERB* **seeps, seeped, seep·ing.**

seer·suck·er (sir′suk′ər), *NOUN.* a cloth with alternate stripes of plain and crinkled material.

see·saw (sē′sȯ′),
1 *NOUN.* a plank resting on a support near its middle so that the ends can move up and down. Children sit at the opposite ends and move up and down.
2 *VERB.* to move up and down on such a plank: *The two children seesawed in the playground.*
❑ *VERB* **see·saws, see·sawed, see·saw·ing.**

seg·ment (seg′mənt), *NOUN.* a piece or part of a whole that is cut off, marked off, or broken off; division; section: *A tangerine is easily pulled apart into its segments. A line can be divided into segments.* ■ See the Synonym Study at **part.**

seg·re·gate (seg′rə gāt), *VERB.* to separate people of different races from each other by having separate schools, restaurants, theaters, and so on. ❑ *VERB* **seg·re·gates, seg·re·gat·ed, seg·re·gat·ing.**

seg·re·ga·tion (seg′rə gā′shən), *NOUN.* the separation of people of different races from each other, especially in schools and other public places.

seis·mo·graph (sīz′mə graf), *NOUN.* a device for measuring and recording the strength of earthquakes.

seize (sēz), *VERB.*
1 to take something and hold onto it with force; clutch; grasp: *In my fright I seized her arm.*
2 to take possession of something by force: *The soldiers seized the city.*
■ See the Synonym Study at **catch.** ❑ *VERB* **seiz·es, seized, seiz·ing.**

sei·zure (sē′zhər), *NOUN.*
1 a sudden attack of disease: *The seizures caused by epilepsy can be controlled with medication.*
2 the act of seizing: *the seizure of property.*

sel·dom (sel′dəm), *ADVERB.* rarely; not often: *She is seldom ill.*

se·lect (si lekt′),
1 *VERB.* to pick out from a group; choose: *Select the book you want.* ■ See the Synonym Study at **choose.**
2 *ADJECTIVE.* picked out as the best; carefully chosen: *I am one of a select group of skiers chosen to compete.*
❑ *VERB* **se·lects, se·lect·ed, se·lect·ing.**

se·lec·tion (si lek′shən), *NOUN.*
1 a group of things to choose from; choice: *This library has a good selection of mystery stories.*
2 a person, thing, or group that is chosen: *This book of stories is my selection.*
3 the condition of being chosen: *Her selection as a candidate was certain.*

self (self), *NOUN.*
1 your own person: *his very self, my very self.*
2 the character of a person; nature of a person or thing: *She does not seem like her former self.*
❑ *PLURAL* **selves.**

Word Power   self-

The prefix **self-** has many meanings. It can mean "of or over yourself." **Self**-control means control **over yourself.**

It can mean "by or in yourself." **Self**-confidence means confidence **in yourself.**

It can mean "to or for yourself." **Self**-addressed means addressed **to yourself.**

The prefix **self-** can also mean "automatic" or "automatically." A **self**-winding watch is a watch that winds itself **automatically.**

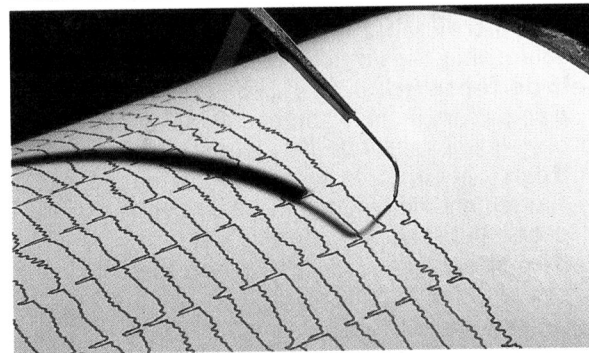

The lines made by the **seismograph** show the motion of the earth during an earthquake.

a	hat	ė	term	ô	order	ch	child		a in about
ā	age	i	it	oi	oil	ng	long		e in taken
ä	far	ī	ice	ou	out	sh	she	ə {	i in pencil
â	care	o	hot	u	cup	th	thin		o in lemon
e	let	ō	open	u̇	put	ᴛʜ	then		u in circus
ē	equal	ȯ	saw	ü	rule	zh	measure		

self-ad·dressed (self′ə drest′), ADJECTIVE. addressed to yourself: *a self-addressed stamped envelope.*

self-con·fi·dence (self′kon′fə dəns), NOUN. a belief in your own ability, power, or judgment; confidence in yourself.

self-con·fi·dent (self′kon′fə dənt), ADJECTIVE. believing in your own ability, power, judgment, and so on. —**self′con·fi·dent·ly**, ADVERB.

self-con·scious (self′kon′shəs), ADJECTIVE. embarrassed, especially by the presence of other people or by the opinions you believe other people have of you; shy: *I always feel self-conscious when I'm among people I don't know.*

3 to be on sale; be sold: *Strawberries sell at a high price in January. These T-shirts and posters sell for ten dollars each.*

4 to be bought by a great many people: *The new computers are really selling this season.*
❑ VERB **sells, sold, sell·ing.** ■ Another word that sounds like this is **cell.** —**sell′er**, NOUN.

selves (selvz), NOUN. the plural of **self:** *She has two selves—one that likes to save money and one that likes to spend it.*

sem·a·phore (sem′ə fôr), NOUN. a system for sending signals. Hand-held flags in different positions represent each letter of the alphabet.

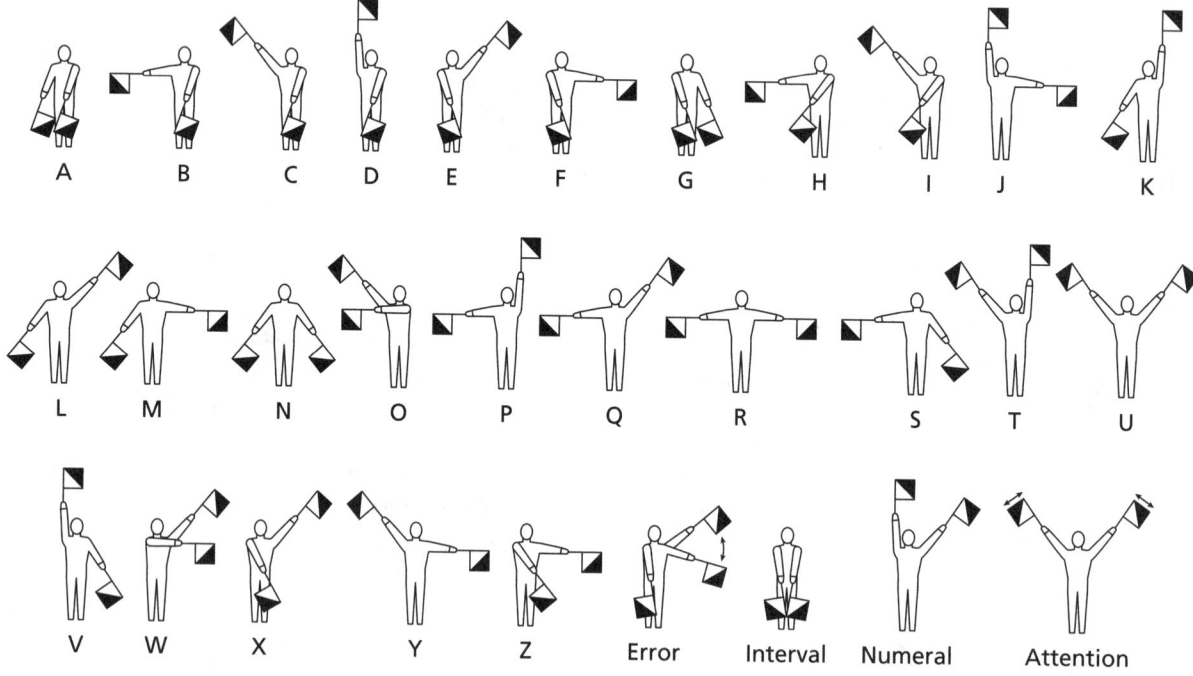

the **semaphore** alphabet

self-con·trol (self′kən trōl′), NOUN. the control of your own actions or feelings.

self-de·fense (self′di fens′), NOUN. defense of your own person, property, or reputation: *After he'd been hit, he fought back in self-defense.*

self·ish (sel′fish), ADJECTIVE. caring too much for yourself and not enough for other people. Selfish people put their own interests first.

self-re·spect (self′ri spekt′), NOUN. respect for yourself; proper pride.

self-serv·ice (self′sėr′vis), ADJECTIVE. of or describing a place where you serve yourself: *a self-service gas station, a self-service cafeteria.*

sell (sel), VERB.

1 to exchange something for money or other payment: *We plan to sell our house.*

2 to have goods of some kind for sale: *The bakery sells bread, cakes, and pies.*

se·mes·ter (sə mes′tər), NOUN. one of the main parts of a school year: *My brother will graduate from college at the end of the spring semester.*

Word Power   semi-

The prefix **semi-** can mean "half," "partly," or "twice." A semicircle is **half** a circle. A semisolid is **partly** solid. Semimonthly means **twice** a month.

sem·i·cir·cle (sem′i sėr′kəl), NOUN. a half of a circle: *We sat in a semicircle around the fire.*

sem·i·co·lon (sem′i kō′lən), NOUN. a mark of punctuation (;) that shows a shorter pause than a period does, but longer than a comma does. EXAMPLE: *We got to the pool very late; that left us almost no time left for swimming.*

sem·i·fi·nal (sem′i fī′nl for adjective; sem′i fī′nl for noun),

1 ADJECTIVE. of or about the two games, rounds, or

matches that come before the final one in a tournament: *Our team lost in the semifinal game.*

2 NOUN. often, **semifinals,** one of these two games: *Our team was defeated in the semifinals.*

sem·i·nar·y (sem′ə ner′ē), NOUN. a school or college that trains students to be priests, ministers, or rabbis. ❑ PLURAL **sem·i·nar·ies.**

Sem·i·nole (sem′ə nōl), NOUN. a member of a tribe of American Indians that settled in Florida in the 1700s. The Seminole now live in the Florida Everglades and in Oklahoma. ❑ PLURAL **Sem·i·nole** or **Sem·i·noles.**

sen·ate (sen′it), NOUN. the upper branch of an assembly that makes laws. The Congress of the United States is the Senate and the House of Representatives.

sen·a·tor (sen′ə tər), NOUN.
1 a member of a senate.
2 **Senator,** a member of the United States Senate.

send (send), VERB.
1 to cause someone to go from one place to another: *Mom sent us to the lake for a swim. The teacher sent me on an errand.*
2 to cause something to be carried: *We sent the package by air mail.*
3 to cause to come, occur, or be: *Please send help at once.*
❑ VERB **sends, sent, send·ing.** —**send′er,** NOUN.

send for, IDIOM.
1 to tell or order to come: *We asked him to send for help.*
2 to order to be delivered, usually by mail: *The ad said where to send for a catalog. We sent for a pizza with extra cheese.*

Synonym Study

Send means to cause something to move from one place to another: *Teams of scientists and engineers have sent rockets into outer space.*

Ship means to send by ship or some other vehicle: *We shipped clothes and books in a trunk to our relatives in Poland.*

Mail[1] means to send by the post office and letter carriers: *If you mail the invitations today, they will arive on Friday.*

Export means to send something out of the country to be sold in another country: *China exports silk garments to the United States.*

Transmit can mean to send signals or programs: *Weather forecasters transmit storm warnings by radio and TV.*

Dispatch means to send quickly: *The company dispatched a bicycle messenger with the package.*

Sen·e·gal (sen′ə gȯl′ or sen′ə gäl), NOUN. a country in western Africa. —**Sen·e·ga·lese** (sen′ə gə lēz′), ADJECTIVE or NOUN.

se·nile (sē′nil), ADJECTIVE. showing the loss of mental and physical abilities caused by various diseases that can occur in old age.

sen·ior (sē′nyər),
1 ADJECTIVE. the older of two people. The word *senior* is used of a father whose son has the same name: *John Parker, Senior, is the father of John Parker, Junior.*
2 ADJECTIVE. of or for older people: *My grandmother plays in the senior golf tournament.*
3 NOUN. an older person: *I am my sister's senior by seven years.*
4 ADJECTIVE. higher in rank or longer in service: *Mr. Johnson is the senior member of the firm of Johnson and Brown.*
5 NOUN. a student who is a member of the graduating class of a high school or college.
6 ADJECTIVE. of or for the last year of high school or college: *the senior class, the senior prom.*

senior citizen, an older person, especially someone who is old enough to receive a pension.

se·ñor (sen yôr′), NOUN. a Spanish word meaning:
1 Mr. or sir.
2 a man.
❑ PLURAL **se·ño·res** (sen yô′res).

se·ño·ra (sen yôr′ä), NOUN. a Spanish word meaning:
1 Mrs. or madam.
2 a married woman.
❑ PLURAL **se·ño·ras.**

se·ño·ri·ta (sen′yô rē′tä), NOUN. a Spanish word meaning:
1 Miss.
2 an unmarried girl or woman.
❑ PLURAL **se·ño·ri·tas.**

sen·sa·tion (sen sā′shən), NOUN.
1 the power to see, hear, feel, taste, or smell: *Blindness is the loss of the sensation of sight.*
2 a feeling: *I have a sensation of dizziness when I walk along cliffs.*
3 an excited feeling in a large group of people: *The announcement of peace caused a sensation throughout the nation.*

sen·sa·tion·al (sen sā′shə nəl), ADJECTIVE.
1 very good or exciting; outstanding; spectacular: *The sensational catch made the crowd cheer.*
2 trying to stir up strong or excited feeling about something: *It was a sensational newspaper story.* —**sen·sa′tion·al·ly,** ADVERB.

a	hat	ė	term	ô	order	ch	child		a	in about
ā	age	i	it	oi	oil	ng	long		e	in taken
ä	far	ī	ice	ou	out	sh	she	ə	i	in pencil
â	care	o	hot	u	cup	th	thin		o	in lemon
e	let	ō	open	u̇	put	ᴛʜ	then		u	in circus
ē	equal	ȯ	saw	ü	rule	zh	measure			

S

sense (sens),

1 NOUN. a power of a living thing to know what happens outside itself. Sight, smell, taste, hearing, and touch are the physical senses: *A dog has a very keen sense of smell.*

2 NOUN. a feeling: *The extra lock on the door gives us a sense of security.*

3 VERB. to feel that something is true: *I sense that you would rather not go.*

4 NOUN. an understanding: *Everyone thinks he has a good sense of humor.*

5 NOUN. the power to think in a clear and wise way; intelligence: *She had the good sense to stay out of the argument.*

6 NOUN. what something means; meaning: *What sense does the word have in each sentence?*
□ VERB **sens•es, sensed, sens•ing.**

make sense, IDIOM. to have a meaning; be reasonable: *"Cow cat bless Monday" doesn't make sense.*

sense•less (sens′lis), ADJECTIVE.

1 unconscious: *A hard blow on the head knocked him senseless.*

2 foolish; stupid: *a senseless idea.*
—**sense′less•ness,** NOUN.

sense organ, a part of the body by which sensation is received. Your nose, eyes, ears, and skin are sense organs.

sen•si•ble (sen′sə bəl), ADJECTIVE. having good sense; showing good judgment: *She is far too sensible to do anything foolish.* —**sen′si•bly,** ADVERB.

sen•si•tive (sen′sə tiv), ADJECTIVE.

1 able to sense something quickly: *The eye is sensitive to light.*

2 easily affected or influenced by something: *Thermometers are sensitive to changes in temperature.*

3 easily hurt or offended: *My aunt is sensitive about her weight.*

4 aware of the feelings and needs of other people.
—**sen′si•tive•ly,** ADVERB. —**sen′si•tive•ness,** NOUN.

sen•sor (sen′sər), NOUN. any device that reacts to heat, light, pressure, and so on, and transmits a signal. A thermostat is a heat sensor.

sen•sor•y (sen′sər ē), ADJECTIVE. of or about sensation or the senses.

sent (sent), VERB.

1 the past tense of **send:** *I sent the letter last week.*

2 the past participle of **send:** *They have already sent the presents.*
∎ Other words that sound like this are **cent** and **scent.**

sen•tence (sen′təns),

1 NOUN. a word or group of words that makes a statement, a request, a question, a command, or an exclamation. Written sentences begin with capital letters and end with a period, a question mark, or an exclamation mark.

EXAMPLES: The books are heavy. Please hand me a pencil. Is this yours? Come in. Good morning, class. Ouch!

2 NOUN. the punishment given to someone who is found guilty of a crime: *The thief received a sentence of five years in prison.*

3 VERB. to give a punishment to someone: *The judge sentenced the thief to five years in prison.*
□ VERB **sen•tenc•es, sen•tenced, sen•tenc•ing.**

sen•ti•ment (sen′tə mənt), NOUN.

1 a mixture of thought and feeling. Admiration, patriotism, and loyalty are sentiments.

2 a feeling, especially a tender feeling: *Her letter expressed sentiments of friendship and sympathy.*

sen•ti•men•tal (sen′tə men′tl), ADJECTIVE.

1 having or showing a great deal of tender feeling: *He writes sentimental poetry.*

2 easily affected by tender emotions: *He is a sentimental person.*

3 of or dependent on sentiment: *These old family photographs have sentimental value.*
—**sen′ti•men′tal•ly,** ADVERB.

sen•try (sen′trē), NOUN. a soldier who keeps watch and guards against surprise attacks: *The sentry at the gate saluted the officer and let him pass.* □ PLURAL **sen•tries.**

sentries guarding a palace in England

Seoul (sōl), NOUN. the capital of South Korea.

se•pal (sē′pəl), NOUN. one of the leaflike parts which make up the outer covering of a flower. In most flowers, the sepals make a green cup at the base of the flower.

sep•a•rate (sep′ə rāt′ for verb; sep′ər it for adjective),

1 VERB. to keep two things apart; divide: *The Atlantic Ocean separates America from Europe.*

2 VERB. to go or come apart: *The children separated and ran in all directions.*

3 VERB. to move some things away from other things: *Separate your books from mine.*

4 VERB. to live apart from each other. A husband and wife may separate by agreement or by order of a court.

5 ADJECTIVE. away from others; apart: *a separate room, separate seats.*

6 ADJECTIVE. individual; single: *the separate parts of a machine.*
□ VERB **sep•a•rates, sep•a•rat•ed, sep•a•rat•ing.**
—**sep′ar•ate•ly,** ADVERB. —**sep′a•ra′tion,** NOUN.

Sept., an abbreviation of **September.**

Sep·tem·ber (sep tem′bər), *NOUN.* the ninth month of the year. It has 30 days.

Word Story

September came from a Latin word meaning "seven." The month was called this because it was the seventh month in the ancient Roman calendar.

sep·tu·plet (sep tup′lit), *NOUN.* one of seven children born at the same time to the same mother.

se·quel (sē′kwəl), *NOUN.* a complete story that continues an earlier story about the same characters: *I didn't like the movie's sequel.*

se·quence (sē′kwəns), *NOUN.*
1 the order in which things come, or need to be put: *Arrange the names in alphabetical sequence.*
2 a connected series of things: *The teacher planned a sequence of lessons on one subject.*

se·quoi·a (si kwoi′ə), *NOUN.*
1 See **giant sequoia.**
2 See **redwood.**
  ❑ *PLURAL* **se·quoi·as.**

se·ra·pe (se rä′pē), *NOUN.* a shawl or blanket, often having bright colors, worn in Latin America.
  ❑ *PLURAL* **se·ra·pes.**

Ser·bi·a (sėr′bē ə), *NOUN.* a country in southeastern Europe. —**Ser′bi·an,** *ADJECTIVE* or *NOUN.*

ser·e·nade (ser′ə nād′),
1 *NOUN.* music played or sung outdoors at night, especially by a lover under someone's window.
2 *VERB.* to sing or play to someone in this way.
  ❑ *VERB* **ser·e·nades, ser·e·nad·ed, ser·e·nad·ing.** —**ser′e·nad·er,** *NOUN.*

se·rene (sə rēn′), *ADJECTIVE.* peaceful or calm: *She sat on the beach with a serene smile, listening to the waves.* —**se·rene′ly,** *ADVERB.*

a **serene** landscape

se·ren·i·ty (sə ren′ə tē), *NOUN.* peace and quiet; calmness: *the serenity of the quiet woods.*

serf (sėrf), *NOUN.* (in the Middle Ages) an enslaved farm worker who could not be sold off the land but passed from one owner to another with the land. ▪ Another word that sounds like this is **surf.**

ser·geant (sär′jənt), *NOUN.*
1 a military rank. See the chart on page 550.
2 a police officer who ranks just above an ordinary policeman.

ser·i·al (sir′ē əl), *NOUN.* a story published in installments in a magazine or newspaper, or televised as a series of individual programs. ▪ Another word that sounds like this is **cereal.**

serial number, a number given to one of a series of people, things, and the like, as a means of easy identification: *All of the computers in the school have serial numbers.*

ser·ies (sir′ēz), *NOUN.*
1 a number of similar things that follow one another in a row: *A series of rainy days spoiled their vacation.*
2 a television program shown at a regular time: *We watched the new mystery series last night.*
  ❑ *PLURAL* **ser·ies.**

ser·i·ous (sir′ē əs), *ADJECTIVE.*
1 not fooling; sincere: *Are you joking or serious?*
2 thoughtful; not humorous: *a serious face, a serious discussion of the problem.*
3 important; needing careful thought: *Choice of your life's work is a serious matter.*
4 important because of the harm it may do; dangerous: *The patient was in serious condition.*
—**ser′i·ous·ly,** *ADVERB.* —**ser′i·ous·ness,** *NOUN.*

ser·mon (sėr′mən), *NOUN.*
1 a talk on religion or something connected with religion, usually given as part of a church service.
2 a serious talk about how you should act or what you should do: *The children got a sermon on their table manners.*

ser·pent (sėr′pənt), *NOUN.* a snake, especially a big snake.

ser·rat·ed (ser′ā tid), *ADJECTIVE.* notched like the edge of a saw: *Use a serrated knife to cut the tomatoes.*

ser·um (sir′əm), *NOUN.* a liquid used to prevent or cure a disease, obtained from the blood of an animal that has been made immune to the disease. Polio vaccine is a serum.

serv·ant (sėr′vənt), *NOUN.* someone hired to work in someone else's house as a cook, maid, and so on.

a	hat	ė	term	ô	order	ch	child		a in about
ā	age	i	it	oi	oil	ng	long		e in taken
ä	far	ī	ice	ou	out	sh	she	ə	i in pencil
â	care	o	hot	u	cup	th	thin		o in lemon
e	let	ō	open	ù	put	ᴛʜ	then		u in circus
ē	equal	ò	saw	ü	rule	zh	measure		

S

serve (sèrv),
1 *VERB.* to work for someone; give service to: *to serve a worthwhile cause, to serve customers in a store, to serve in the army.*
2 *VERB.* to bring food to someone: *The waiter served us.*
3 *VERB.* to put food or drink on the table: *The waitress served the soup. Dinner is served.*
4 *VERB.* to supply enough for: *One pie will serve six persons.*
5 *VERB.* to be used in some way: *Boxes can serve as seats.*
6 *VERB.* to spend: *The thief served a term in prison.*
7 *VERB.* to put the ball in play by hitting it in volleyball and in games played with a racket, such as tennis.
8 *NOUN.* the act of serving the ball in volleyball and in games played with a racket, such as tennis; service.
❏ *VERB* **serves, served, serv·ing. –serv′er,** *NOUN.*

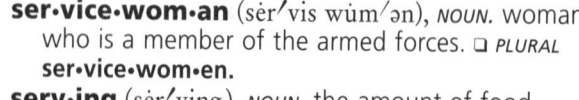

serve (definition 7)

serve someone right, *IDIOM.* to be just what someone deserves: *The punishment served him right.*

serv·ice (sèr′vis),
1 *NOUN.* a helpful act or acts: *They performed many services for their community.*
2 *NOUN.* a business or system that supplies something useful or necessary: *Bus service was good.*
3 *NOUN.* a department of government or public employment, or the people working in it: *the diplomatic service.*
4 *NOUN.* the army, navy, or air force: *We were in the service together.*
5 *NOUN.* often **services,** a religious meeting; religious ceremony: *They attend services on Friday evening. The marriage service will be performed on Saturday.*
6 *NOUN.* the manner of serving food or the food served: *The service in this restaurant is excellent.*
7 *VERB.* to repair or maintain a motor vehicle, appliance, and the like: *The mechanic serviced our car.*
8 *NOUN.* See **serve** (definition 8).
❏ *VERB* **serv·ic·es, serv·iced, serv·ic·ing.**

serv·ice·man (sèr′vis man′), *NOUN.*
1 a member of the armed forces.
2 someone who repairs or maintains machinery or equipment: *We called a serviceman to fix our dryer.*
❏ *PLURAL* **serv·ice·men.**

service station. See **gas station.**

ser·vice·wom·an (sèr′vis wùm′ən), *NOUN.* woman who is a member of the armed forces. ❏ *PLURAL* **ser·vice·wom·en.**

serv·ing (sèr′ving), *NOUN.* the amount of food served to someone at one time; helping.

ses·a·me (ses′ə mē), *NOUN.* the small seeds of a tropical plant. They are used in bread, candy, and other foods, and in making a tasty oil.

ses·sion (sesh′ən), *NOUN.*
1 a meeting of a court, council, or legislature: *We attended one session of the trial.*
2 the time of meetings like this: *This year's session of Congress was unusually long.*
3 the meeting of a group for a special purpose: *The singer was late for the recording session.*
in session, *IDIOM.* meeting: *Congress is now in session.*

set (set),
1 *VERB.* to put something in some place; put; place: *Set the box on its end.* ■ See the Synonym Study at **put.**
2 *VERB.* to put something in the right place, position, or condition for use; arrange; put in proper order: *Please set the table for dinner. The doctor set my broken leg.*
3 *VERB.* to cause to be: *A spark set the woods on fire.*
4 *VERB.* to decide on something: *The teacher set a time limit for the test.*
5 *ADJECTIVE.* decided: *My family has a set time for dinner.*
6 *ADJECTIVE.* ready: *I am all set to try again.*
7 *ADJECTIVE.* stubborn; unwilling to change: *They are set in their ways and will not compromise.*
8 *VERB.* to go down below the horizon: *The sun sets in the west.*
9 *NOUN.* a group of things or people that go together: *They bought a new set of dishes.*
10 *NOUN.* the scenery of a play, a movie, or the like.
11 *NOUN.* a device for receiving radio or television signals that turns them into sounds and pictures: *We have a television set in the basement.*
12 *NOUN.* a group of numbers or other items which are alike in some way. All even numbers form a set, and any number that can be divided by 2 is a member of this set.
❏ *VERB* **sets, set, set·ting.**

set aside, *IDIOM.*
1 to put to one side: *He set the fragile vase aside.*
2 to keep for later use: *He set a few cookies aside for after dinner.*
set forth, *IDIOM.*
1 to make known; put; place: *She set forth her opinions on the subject.*
2 to start to go: *He set forth on a trip around the world.*
set off, *IDIOM.*
1 to explode: *She set off a string of firecrackers.*
2 to start to go: *We set off for home.*

3 to cause something to start to ring, buzz, and so on: *Something burning set off the smoke alarm.*

set on or **set upon**, IDIOM. to attack: *They were set on by a pack of dogs.*

set out, IDIOM.
1 to start to go: *They set out on a hike.*
2 to spread out to show, sell, or use: *Set out tables and chairs for the party. The merchant set out his wares.*
3 to plant: *We set out tomato plants in the spring.*

set up, IDIOM.
1 to build: *to set up a monument.*
2 to begin; start: *He sold his old business and set up a new one.*

set·ter (set′ər), NOUN. a long-haired hunting dog, trained to stand motionless and point its nose toward the birds that it finds by smell.

setter — about 2 feet high at the shoulder

set·ting (set′ing), NOUN.
1 a frame or other thing in which something is set. The gold that holds a jewel is a setting.
2 the place and time of a story, play, or movie: *The setting was a garden in England in the 1860s.*

set·tle (set′l), VERB.
1 to agree on something; decide: *Let's settle this argument.*
2 to put or be put in order; arrange: *I must settle all my affairs before going away for the summer.*
3 to go to live in a new country or place: *Our cousin intends to settle in California.*
4 to set up the first towns and farms in an area: *The English settled New England.*
5 to come to rest in a particular place: *A heavy fog settled over the airport.*
6 to get into a comfortable position: *The cat settled itself in the chair for a nap.*
❏ VERB **set·tles, set·tled, set·tling.**

settle down, IDIOM. to calm down; become quiet: *The children began to settle down for a nap.*

settle for, IDIOM. to accept something less than what was expected: *The runner had to settle for second place.*

settle up, IDIOM. to pay your bill: *We settled up at the hotel desk before we left.*

set·tle·ment (set′l mənt), NOUN.
1 an agreement or arrangement to settle a dispute: *The striking workers finally reached a contract settlement with their employers.*
2 the act or process of settling people in a new country: *The settlement of the English along the Atlantic coast began in the 1600s.*
3 a place where people have come to live; colony: *England had many settlements in America.*

set·tler (set′lər), NOUN. someone who settles in a new country.

sev·en (sev′ən), NOUN or ADJECTIVE. one more than six; 7.

sev·en·teen (sev′ən tēn′), NOUN or ADJECTIVE. seven more than ten; 17.

sev·en·teenth (sev′ən tēnth′), ADJECTIVE or NOUN.
1 next after the 16th.
2 one of 17 equal parts.

sev·enth (sev′ənth), ADJECTIVE or NOUN.
1 next after the sixth.
2 one of seven equal parts.

sev·en·ti·eth (sev′ən tē ith), ADJECTIVE or NOUN.
1 next after the 69th.
2 one of 70 equal parts.

sev·en·ty (sev′ən tē), NOUN or ADJECTIVE. seven times ten; 70. ❏ PLURAL **sev·en·ties.**

sev·er·al (sev′ər əl), ADJECTIVE or PRONOUN PLURAL. more than two or three but not many; some; a few: *He gained several pounds over the holidays. Several have given their consent.*

se·vere (sə vir′), ADJECTIVE.
1 very strict; stern; harsh: *The judge gave a severe sentence to the guilty criminal.*
2 painful; violent: *I have a severe headache.*
3 serious; dangerous: *She had a severe illness.*
❏ ADJECTIVE **se·ver·er, se·ver·est. –se·vere′ly,** ADVERB.

sew (sō), VERB.
1 to push a needle and thread through pieces of cloth, skin, and so on, in order to join them together.
2 to fasten something with stitches: *She sewed on a button. I sewed a hem on the dress.*
❏ VERB **sews, sewed, sewed** or **sewn, sew·ing.**
▪ Other words that sound like this are **so** and **sow**[1].

sew·age (sü′ij), NOUN. the waste matter that flows from house toilets through sewers.

sew·er (sü′ər), NOUN. an underground drain that carries away waste water and refuse.

sewing machine, a machine for sewing or stitching cloth.

a	hat	ė	term	ô	order	ch	child		a in about
ā	age	i	it	oi	oil	ng	long		e in taken
ä	far	ī	ice	ou	out	sh	she	ə	i in pencil
â	care	o	hot	u	cup	th	thin		o in lemon
e	let	ō	open	u̇	put	ᴛH	then		u in circus
ē	equal	ȯ	saw	ü	rule	zh	measure		

S

sewn (sōn), *VERB.* a past participle of **sew**: *She has sewn patches on her jeans.* ■ Another word that sounds like this is **sown**.

sex (seks), *NOUN.*
1 either of the two basic kinds of human beings and many other living things. The two sexes are males and females.
2 the condition of being male or female: *The list of members of the club was arranged by age and by sex.*
❑ *PLURAL* **sex•es.**

sex•tu•plet (seks tup′lit), *NOUN.* one of six children born at the same time to the same mother.

shab•by (shab′ē), *ADJECTIVE.*
1 worn out and dirty: *His old suit looks shabby.*
2 run-down: *The apartment building was in a shabby neighborhood.*
❑ *ADJECTIVE* **shab•bi•er, shab•bi•est.**

shack (shak), *NOUN.* a roughly built hut or little house: *We built a shack of old boards in the backyard.*

shack•le (shak′əl),
1 *NOUN.* a metal band fastened around the ankle or wrist of a prisoner or enslaved person. Shackles are usually fastened to each other, the wall, or the floor by chains.
2 *VERB.* to put shackles on someone.
3 *NOUN.* anything that prevents freedom of action or thought: *Fear and prejudice are shackles.*
❑ *VERB* **shack•les, shack•led, shack•ling.**

shade (shād),
1 *NOUN.* a place out of the sunshine where something blocks the light: *Let's sit in the shade.*
2 *NOUN.* something that shuts out light: *Pull down the shades of the windows.*
3 *VERB.* to keep light from: *A big hat shades the eyes.*
4 *NOUN.* lightness or darkness of color: *I want to see silks in all shades of blue.*
5 *NOUN.* **shades,** (informal) sunglasses.
6 *VERB.* to make a part of something darker than the rest; use black in a picture to color in an area: *The teacher shaded part of the circle to explain fractions.*
❑ *VERB* **shades, shad•ed, shad•ing.**

shad•ow (shad′ō),
1 *NOUN.* the shade made by some person, animal, or thing. Sometimes your shadow is much longer than you are, and sometimes it is much shorter.
2 *NOUN.* often, **shadows,** darkness; partial shade: *There was someone lurking in the shadows.*
3 *VERB.* to follow someone closely, usually secretly: *The detective shadowed the suspected burglar.*
❑ *VERB* **shad•ows, shad•owed, shad•ow•ing.** —**shad′ow•like′,** *ADJECTIVE.*

shad•ow•y (shad′ō ē), *ADJECTIVE.* like a shadow; dim; faint: *We stared at the shadowy outline in the pale moonlight.*

shad•y (shā′dē), *ADJECTIVE.*
1 in the shade: *We sat in a shady spot.*
2 giving shade: *We sat under a shady tree.*
3 not honest: *They were involved in a shady deal.*
❑ *ADJECTIVE* **shad•i•er, shad•i•est.** —**shad′i•ness,** *NOUN.*

shaft (shaft), *NOUN.*
1 a bar to support parts of a machine that turn, or to help move turning parts.
2 a deep tunnel down into the earth. The entrance to a mine is called a shaft.
3 a hollow passage that goes from the bottom of a building to the top: *an elevator shaft.*
4 the long, thin part of an arrow, spear, or lance.
5 the long, straight handle of a hammer, ax, golf club, and so on.

shag•gy (shag′ē), *ADJECTIVE.*
1 covered with a thick, rough mass of hair or wool: *The pony was shaggy in the winter.*
2 long, thick, and rough: *Dad has shaggy eyebrows.*
❑ *ADJECTIVE* **shag•gi•er, shag•gi•est.** —**shag′gi•ness,** *NOUN.*

shake (shāk),
1 *VERB.* to move something quickly back and forth, up and down, or from side to side: *The baby shook the rattle. The branches of the old tree shook in the wind.*
2 *VERB.* to throw off or scatter by movement: *She shook the snow off her clothes.*
3 *VERB.* to clasp someone's hand when you say hello to him or her: *to shake hands.*
4 *VERB.* to tremble or make tremble: *The kitten was shaking with cold.*
5 *VERB.* to shock or disturb; upset: *His lie shook my faith in his honesty.*
6 *NOUN.* the act of shaking: *Her answer was a shake of her head.*
7 *NOUN.* See **milk shake.**
❑ *VERB* **shakes, shook, shak•en, shak•ing.**
■ Another word that can sound like this is **sheik.**

shake up, *IDIOM.*
1 to shake hard: *Shake up a mixture of oil and vinegar for the salad.*
2 to shock or make nervous: *I was shaken up by the experience.*

shadow (definition 1)

shak·er (shā′kər), NOUN. a container for salt, pepper, and so on, having a top with holes in it.

shak·y (shā′kē), ADJECTIVE.
1 weak or unsteady: *He spoke in a shaky voice.*
2 liable to break down: *The abandoned old house had a shaky porch.*
  ❑ ADJECTIVE **shak·i·er, shak·i·est. –shak′i·ness,** NOUN.

shale (shāl), NOUN. a rock formed from hardened clay or mud in thin layers that split easily.
  –shale′like′, ADJECTIVE.

shall (shal), HELPING VERB.
1 **Shall** is used to express future time, command, obligation, and necessity: *They shall come soon. You shall go to the party, I promise you.*
2 **Shall** is also used when you ask a question that is a suggestion: *Shall I open the windows? Shall we go home now?*
  ❑ PAST TENSE **should.**

shal·low (shal′ō), ADJECTIVE. not deep: *shallow water, a shallow dish, a shallow mind.* ❑ ADJECTIVE **shal·low·er, shal·low·est. –shal′low·ness,** NOUN.

sham (sham), NOUN. something that is not true: *Their claim to be descended from British royalty is a sham.*

sha·man (shä′mən, shā′mən or sham′ən), NOUN. a man in American Indian tribes believed to have close contact with the spirit world, and to be skilled in curing diseases; medicine man.

sham·ble (sham′bəl), VERB. to walk awkwardly or unsteadily: *The exhausted hikers shambled into camp.* ❑ VERB **sham·bles, sham·bled, sham·bling.**

sham·bles (sham′bəlz), NOUN. mess: *They made a shambles of the clean room.*

shame (shām),
1 NOUN. a painful feeling that you have done something wrong or improper: *Remembering her angry outburst caused her to blush with shame.*
2 VERB. to cause someone to feel shame: *My silly mistake shamed me.*
3 VERB. to force someone to do something by shame: *I was shamed into cleaning my room after guests saw it.*
4 NOUN. loss of honor; disgrace: *He didn't want to bring shame to his family.*
5 VERB. to bring disgrace upon someone: *She never shamed her family.*
6 NOUN. something to feel sorry about: *What a shame you can't come to the party!*
  ❑ VERB **shames, shamed, sham·ing.**

shame·ful (shām′fəl), ADJECTIVE. causing shame: *We were shocked by his shameful behavior.*
  –shame′ful·ly, ADVERB.

shame·less (shām′lis), ADJECTIVE. without shame; not feeling disgrace: *Everyone knows that he is a shameless liar.* **–shame′less·ly,** ADVERB.
  –shame′less·ness, NOUN.

sham·poo (sham pü′),
1 NOUN. a liquid soap or detergent, often scented, used to wash the hair.
2 VERB. to wash your hair with shampoo.
  ❑ PLURAL **sham·poos;** VERB **sham·poos, sham·pooed, sham·poo·ing.**

sham·rock (sham′rok), NOUN. any of several plants with bright green leaves divided into three parts. The shamrock is the national emblem of Ireland.

Shang·hai (shang′hī′), NOUN. a city in China.

shan't (shant), a contraction of **shall not.**

shan·ty (shan′tē), NOUN. a roughly built hut or cabin. ❑ PLURAL **shan·ties.**

shamrock

shape (shāp),
1 NOUN. the way something looks; the form something takes: *An apple is different in shape from a banana.*
2 VERB. to form something into a certain shape: *The child shaped clay into balls.* ■ See the Synonym Study at **make.**
3 NOUN. physical condition: *Athletes exercise to keep themselves in good shape.*
  ❑ VERB **shapes, shaped, shap·ing. –shape′less,** ADJECTIVE. **–shap′er,** NOUN.

shape up, IDIOM.
1 to take on a certain form or appearance; develop: *Our school project is shaping up well.*
2 to behave properly; do what is expected: *You will have to shape up if you expect to get a good grade in this subject.*

take shape, IDIOM. to have or take on a definite form: *The general outline of the novel began to take shape.*

shape·ly (shāp′lē), ADJECTIVE. having a pleasing shape. ❑ ADJECTIVE **shape·li·er, shape·li·est.**

share (shâr),
1 NOUN. the part of something that belongs to one person; portion: *You've done more than your share of the work.* ■ See the Synonym Study at **part.**
2 VERB. to let someone use something along with you: *The sisters share the same room.*
3 VERB. to have a share; take part: *Everyone shared in making the picnic a success.*

S

a hat	ė term	ô order	ch child	⌐a in about
ā age	i it	oi oil	ng long	⎧e in taken
ä far	ī ice	ou out	sh she	ə⎨i in pencil
â care	o hot	u cup	th thin	⎩o in lemon
e let	ō open	ů put	ŦH then	⌐u in circus
ē equal	ȯ saw	ü rule	zh measure	

4 *NOUN.* each of the equal parts into which the ownership of a company or corporation is divided: *The ownership of this railroad is divided into several million shares.*
❏ *VERB* **shares, shared, shar·ing.**

shark (shärk), *NOUN.* a large sea fish that eats other fish. There are about 370 kinds of sharks. Certain kinds are dangerous to humans.
—shark′like′, *ADJECTIVE.*

shark — up to 40 feet long

sharp (shärp),
1 *ADJECTIVE.* having a thin edge that can cut, or having a fine point: *It's easy to cut meat with a sharp knife.*
2 *ADJECTIVE.* having an edge or point; not rounded: *Watch out for the sharp corner on that table.*
3 *ADJECTIVE.* with a sudden change: *a sharp turn, a sharp drop in temperature.*
4 *ADJECTIVE.* intelligent; clever: *She is a sharp lawyer.*
5 *ADJECTIVE.* harsh; severe: *sharp words, a sharp wind.*
6 *ADJECTIVE.* with a strong taste or odor: *sharp cheese.*
7 *ADJECTIVE.* clear; distinct: *That was sharp contrast between black and white in the photo.*
8 *ADJECTIVE.* watchful; alert: *The eagle has sharp eyes.*
9 *ADVERB.* promptly; exactly: *Come at one o'clock sharp.*
10 *ADVERB.* in a careful, alert way: *Look sharp!*
11 *ADVERB.* above the true pitch in music: *He sang sharp.*
12 *NOUN.* a tone one half step above natural pitch.
—sharp′ly, *ADVERB.* **—sharp′ness,** *NOUN.*

sharp·en (shär′pən), *VERB.* to make something sharp: *Please sharpen the pencil.* ❏ *VERB* **sharp·ens, sharp·ened, sharp·en·ing. —sharp′en·er,** *NOUN.*

shat·ter (shat′ər), *VERB.*
1 to break something suddenly into small pieces: *A stone shattered the window.* ■ See the Synonym Study at **break.**
2 to destroy something: *Our hopes for a picnic were shattered by the rain.*
❏ *VERB* **shat·ters, shat·tered, shat·ter·ing.**

shave (shāv),
1 *VERB.* to cut hair off the face, chin, or some other part of the body with a razor: *The actor shaved his head in order to play a bald man.* ■ See the Synonym Study at **cut.**

2 *NOUN.* the act of cutting off hair with a razor.
3 *VERB.* to cut something off in very thin slices: *She shaved the chocolate to decorate the cake.*
❏ *VERB* **shaves, shaved, shaved** or **shav·en, shav·ing.**

close shave, *IDIOM.* a narrow miss or escape: *The car missed her, but it was a close shave.*

shav·en (shā′vən),
1 *ADJECTIVE.* shaved: *He has a clean-shaven face.*
2 *VERB.* a past participle of **shave:** *He had shaven an hour earlier.*

shav·er (shā′vər), *NOUN.*
1 someone who shaves.
2 a tool for shaving.

shav·ing (shā′ving), *NOUN.*
1 usually, **shavings,** very thin pieces or slices: *Shavings of wood littered the garage floor.*
2 the act or process of cutting hair from the face, chin, or some other part of the body with a razor: *He washed his face after shaving.*

shawl (shȯl), *NOUN.* a square or long piece of cloth worn about the shoulders or head.

she (shē),
1 *PRONOUN.* the girl, woman, or female animal spoken about or mentioned before: *My sister says she likes to read and her reading helps her in school.*
2 *PRONOUN.* anything thought of as female and spoken about or mentioned before: *She was a fine old ship.*
3 *NOUN.* a female: *Is the baby a he or a she?*
❏ *PRONOUN PLURAL* **they;** *NOUN PLURAL* **shes.**

shear (shir), *VERB.* to cut the wool or fleece from: *to shear sheep.* ■ See the Synonym Study at **cut.**
❏ *VERB* **shears, sheared, sheared** or **shorn, shear·ing.**
■ Another word that sounds like this is **sheer.**

shears (shirz), *NOUN PLURAL.* any cutting device that looks like heavy scissors: *Where are the kitchen shears?*

sheath (shēth), *NOUN.* a case or covering for the blade of a sword, dagger, or knife. ❏ *PLURAL* **sheaths** (shēᴛʜz or shēths).

shed¹ (shed), *NOUN.* a building used for the shelter or storage of goods or vehicles, usually having only one story: *The rake is in the tool shed.*

shed² (shed), *VERB.*
1 to pour out; let flow: *to shed tears, to shed blood.*
2 to let hair or fur fall off: *Our dog sheds a lot.*
3 to keep liquid from coming through: *The umbrella sheds water.*
❏ *VERB* **sheds, shed, shed·ding.**

she'd (shēd),
1 a contraction of **she had.**
2 a contraction of **she would.**

sheen (shēn), *NOUN.* brightness; shine: *Satin and polished silver have a sheen.*

sheep (shēp), *NOUN.* an animal with a thick coat and hoofs that chews its cud. Sheep are related to goats, and are raised for wool, meat, and skin. ❑ *PLURAL* **sheep.**

Sheep have warm coats of wool.

sheep·dog (shēp′dȯg′), *NOUN.* a collie or other dog trained to help a shepherd watch and tend sheep.

sheep·ish (shē′pish), *ADJECTIVE.* shy or embarrassed: *He gave her a sheepish smile.* **—sheep′ish·ly,** *ADVERB.* **—sheep′ish·ness,** *NOUN.*

sheer (shir), *ADJECTIVE.*
1 complete; absolute: *His excuse was sheer nonsense.*
2 straight up and down; steep: *I came to a sheer cliff.*
3 very thin; almost transparent: *Those sheer curtains will let the light through.*
   ■ Another word that sounds like this is **shear.**
   —sheer′ly, *ADVERB.*

sheet (shēt), *NOUN.*
1 a large piece of cloth, usually of linen or cotton, used on a bed to sleep on or under.
2 a single piece of paper.
3 a broad, thin piece of anything: *a sheet of glass.*
4 a broad, flat surface: *There was a sheet of ice on the windshield.*

sheik (shēk *or* shāk), *NOUN.* an Arab chief or head of a family, village, or tribe. ■ Another word that can sound like this is **shake.**

shelf (shelf), *NOUN.* a thin, flat piece of wood, stone, metal, or other material, fastened to a wall or frame to hold things, such as books or dishes. ❑ *PLURAL* **shelves.**

shell (shel),
1 *NOUN.* the hard outside covering of some animals. Oysters, turtles, snails, and beetles all have shells.
2 *NOUN.* the hard outside covering of a nut, seed, or fruit.
3 *NOUN.* the hard outside covering of an egg.
4 *VERB.* to take something out of a shell: *He shelled a handful of peanuts.*
5 *NOUN.* a cartridge for a rifle, pistol, or shotgun.

6 *NOUN.* a metal container fired by artillery. It explodes when it hits the ground.
7 *VERB.* to fire shells at something: *The enemy shelled the town.*
   ❑ *VERB* **shells, shelled, shell·ing. —shell′-like′,** *ADJECTIVE.*

she'll (shēl),
1 a contraction of **she shall.**
2 a contraction of **she will.**

shel·lac (shə lak′),
1 *NOUN.* a kind of varnish made from resin dissolved in alcohol. Shellac dries rapidly to give wood and other materials a shiny appearance, and protection from air and moisture.
2 *VERB.* to put shellac on: *We shellacked the picnic table and the lawn chairs.*
   ❑ *VERB* **shel·lacs, shel·lacked, shel·lack·ing.**

shell·fish (shel′fish′), *NOUN.* a water animal with a shell. Oysters, crabs, lobsters, and crayfish are shellfish. ❑ *PLURAL* **shell·fish** or **shell·fish·es.**

shel·ter (shel′tər),
1 *NOUN.* something that covers or protects you from weather, danger, or attack: *Trees provide shelter from the sun.*
2 *VERB.* to protect or hide someone: *Grandma sheltered the fugitives.*
3 *NOUN.* protection or refuge: *We took shelter from the storm in a barn.*
   ❑ *VERB* **shel·ters, shel·tered, shel·ter·ing.**

shelve (shelv), *VERB.*
1 to put something on a shelf: *My job is shelving books at the library.*
2 to lay something aside: *Let us shelve that argument.*
   ❑ *VERB* **shelves, shelved, shelv·ing.**

shelves (shelvz), *NOUN.* the plural of **shelf.**

shep·herd (shep′ərd),
1 *NOUN.* someone who takes care of sheep.
2 *VERB.* to guide or direct: *The teacher shepherded the class safely out of the burning building.*
   ❑ *VERB* **shep·herds, shep·herd·ed, shep·herd·ing.**

shep·herd·ess (shep′ər dis), *NOUN.* a woman who takes care of sheep. ❑ *PLURAL* **shep·herd·ess·es.**

sher·bet (shėr′bət), *NOUN.* a frozen dessert made of fruit juice, sugar, and water or milk.

sher·iff (sher′if), *NOUN.* the most important law enforcement officer of a county. A sheriff appoints deputies who help keep order.

she's (shēz),
1 a contraction of **she is.**
2 a contraction of **she has.**

a	hat	ė	term	ô	order	ch	child		
ā	age	i	it	oi	oil	ng	long	⎧	a in about
ä	far	ī	ice	ou	out	sh	she		e in taken
â	care	o	hot	u	cup	th	thin	ə ⎨ i in pencil
e	let	ō	open	ù	put	ᵺ	then		o in lemon
ē	equal	ȯ	saw	ü	rule	zh	measure	⎩ u in circus

S

Shet·land po·ny (shet'lənd pō'nē), a small, sturdy pony with a rough coat.

Shetland pony — between 3 and 4 feet high at the shoulder

shied (shīd), VERB.
1 the past tense of **shy:** *The horse shied and threw the rider.*
2 the past participle of **shy:** *It had never shied like that before.*

shield (shēld),
1 NOUN. a piece of metal, leather, or plastic carried on your arm to protect your body from being struck.
2 NOUN. anything used to protect: *I turned up my collar as a shield against the cold wind.*
3 NOUN. something shaped like a shield. A police officer's badge is called a shield.
4 VERB. to protect or defend someone: *They shielded me from unjust punishment.*
❑ VERB **shields, shield·ed, shield·ing.**

shift (shift),
1 VERB. to move or change something from one place, position, or person, to another; change: *He shifted the heavy bag from one hand to the other.* ■ See the Synonym Study at **move.**
2 NOUN. a change of direction, position, or attitude: *The President carried out a shift in foreign policy.*
3 NOUN. a group of workers who work during the same time period: *In the factory where Dad works, the night shift begins at 12:30 A.M.*
4 NOUN. the time during which a group like this works: *She is on the night shift this week.*
5 VERB. to change the position of gears, as in a car.
❑ VERB **shifts, shift·ed, shift·ing.**

shift·y (shif'tē), ADJECTIVE. tricky; not straightforward: *The burglary suspect gave shifty answers to the police.* ❑ ADJECTIVE **shift·i·er, shift·i·est.**

shil·ling (shil'ing), NOUN. a former British coin equal to 12 pennies: *Twenty shillings made one pound.*

shim·mer (shim'ər), VERB. to gleam faintly: *Both the sea and the sand shimmered in the moonlight.*
❑ VERB **shim·mers, shim·mered, shim·mer·ing.**

shin (shin), NOUN. the front part of the leg from the knee to the ankle.

shine (shīn),
1 VERB. to give off a bright light; reflect light; glow: *The sun shines. His face is shining with soap and water.*
2 VERB. to cause to shine: *I shined my flashlight in the direction of the noise.*
3 NOUN. the condition of being shiny; polish.
4 NOUN. fair weather; sunshine: *We'll be there rain or shine.*
5 VERB. to make something bright; polish: *I have to shine my shoes.*
❑ VERB **shines, shone** or **shined, shin·ing.**

shin·gle (shing'gəl),
1 NOUN. a thin piece of wood, asbestos, or other material, laid in rows to cover roofs and walls.
2 VERB. to cover something with these pieces: *We shingled the roof last summer.*
❑ VERB **shin·gles, shin·gled, shin·gling.**

shin·guard (shin'gärd'), NOUN.
1 a protective covering for the shins and sometimes the knees, worn by soccer players, hockey players, and baseball catchers.
2 the part of a suit of armor that protects the shin and lower leg.

shin·y (shī'nē), ADJECTIVE. giving off or reflecting a bright light; bright: *A new penny is shiny.* ■ See the Synonym Study at **bright.** ❑ ADJECTIVE **shin·i·er, shin·i·est.** —**shin'i·ness,** NOUN.

ship (ship),
1 NOUN. a very large boat that travels on oceans and deep waterways. Freighters, passenger liners, and oil tankers are some kinds of ships.
2 NOUN. an aircraft or spacecraft.
3 VERB. to send or carry something from one place to another by ship, train, truck, or airplane: *Did he ship it by express or by freight?* ■ See the Synonym Study at **send.**
❑ VERB **ships, shipped, ship·ping.**

Word Power   -ship

The suffix **-ship** means "the office, position, or occupation of _____." Governor**ship** means **the office of** governor.

It also means "the quality or condition of being _____." Partner**ship** means **the condition of being** a partner.

The suffix **-ship** can also mean "the act, power, or skill of _____." Workman**ship** means **the skill of** a workman.

ship·ment (ship'mənt), NOUN.
1 the act of shipping goods: *The oranges were crated for shipment.*
2 the goods sent at one time to a person or company: *We received two shipments of paper.*

ship·ping (ship′ing), NOUN.
1 the act or business of sending goods by ship, train, truck, or airplane.
2 ships: *Much of the world's shipping passes through the Panama Canal each year.*

ship·shape (ship′shāp′), ADJECTIVE. very neat; tidy: *I made my room shipshape before Grandma arrived.*

ship·wreck (ship′rek′), NOUN.
1 the destruction or loss of a ship: *Only two people were saved from the shipwreck.*
2 a wrecked ship: *At low tide several old shipwrecks could be seen.*

shipwreck (definition 2)

ship·wrecked (ship′rekt′), ADJECTIVE. having suffered loss or destruction of a ship.

ship·yard (ship′yärd′), NOUN. a place near the water where ships are built or repaired.

shirk (shėrk), VERB. to avoid or get out of doing something you should be doing: *You will lose your job if you continue to shirk responsibility.* ❑ VERB **shirks, shirked, shirk·ing. –shirk′er,** NOUN.

shirt (shėrt), NOUN. a piece of clothing for your arms and chest. A shirt usually has a collar, sleeves, and an opening in the front that is closed by buttons.

shish ke·bab (shish′ kə bäb′), small pieces of seasoned meat, tomatoes, peppers, and so on, roasted and served on a skewer.

shiv·er (shiv′ər),
1 VERB. to shake with cold, fear, or excitement: *I shivered in the cold wind.*
2 NOUN. the act of shaking from cold, fear, or excitement: *A shiver of fear ran down my back during the movie.*
❑ VERB **shiv·ers, shiv·ered, shiv·er·ing.**

shoal (shōl), NOUN. a place in a sea, lake, or river where the water is shallow: *The ship was wrecked on the shoals.*

shock¹ (shok),
1 NOUN. something that suddenly upsets you: *Her death was a great shock to her family.*

2 NOUN. a sudden, violent shake, blow, or crash: *Earthquake shocks are often felt in Japan. The two trains collided with a terrible shock.*
3 VERB. to cause someone to feel surprise, horror, or disgust: *That child's bad manners shocked me.*
4 NOUN. the feeling or physical effects caused by an electric current passing through your body.
5 VERB. to give an electric shock to someone: *That lamp shocked me when I touched it with my wet hands.*
6 NOUN. a dangerous bodily condition that sometimes causes a person to become unconscious. Shock may set in after a severe injury or loss of blood.
❑ VERB **shocks, shocked, shock·ing.**

shock² (shok), NOUN. a group of stalks of corn or bundles of grain set up on end together.

shock³ (shok), NOUN. a thick, bushy mass: *An untidy shock of red hair stuck out from under his cap.*

shock·ing (shok′ing), ADJECTIVE.
1 causing very painful feelings or surprise: *We heard the shocking news of the airplane crash.*
2 causing disgust or horror: *The crimes of the convicted murderers were shocking.*
–shock′ing·ly, ADVERB.

shod (shod), VERB.
1 a past tense of **shoe**: *The cowboy shod his horse.*
2 the past participle of **shoe**: *He has shod several of the horses already.*

shoe (shü),
1 NOUN. an outer covering for a person's foot. Shoes are often made of leather and usually have a stiff sole and a heel.
2 NOUN. a short form of **horseshoe**.
3 VERB. to furnish with a shoe or shoes: *A blacksmith shoes horses.*
❑ VERB **shoes, shod** or **shoed, shoe·ing.** ▪ Another word that sounds like this is **shoo. –shoe′less,** ADJECTIVE.

shoe·lace (shü′lās′), NOUN. a cord or a strip of leather or other material for fastening a shoe; shoestring.

shoe·string (shü′string′), NOUN. See **shoelace.**

shone (shōn), VERB.
1 a past tense of **shine**: *The sun shone all last week.*
2 a past participle of **shine**: *It has not shone since.*
▪ Another word that sounds like this is **shown.**

shoo (shü),
1 INTERJECTION. an exclamation used to scare or drive something away animals or small children: *"Shoo! You children get away from that cake!"*

a hat	ė term	ô order	ch child	⎧a in about
ā age	i it	oi oil	ng long	e in taken
ä far	ī ice	ou out	sh she	ə⎨i in pencil
â care	o hot	u cup	th thin	o in lemon
e let	ō open	u̇ put	ŦH then	⎩u in circus
ē equal	ȯ saw	ü rule	zh measure	

2 VERB. to scare or drive something away: *Shoo those pesky flies away.*
❑ VERB **shoos, shooed, shoo•ing.** ■ Another word that sounds like this is **shoe.**

shook (shùk), VERB. the past tense of **shake:** *They shook hands.*

shoot (shüt),
1 VERB. to hit, wound, or kill something or someone with a bullet, an arrow, and so on: *He shot a rabbit.*
2 VERB. to fire a gun: *She shot her rifle at the target.*
3 VERB. to send swiftly: *A bow shoots an arrow. She shot question after question at us.*
4 VERB. to move suddenly and rapidly: *A speeding car shot by us.*
5 VERB. to send a ball, puck, or the like toward the goal while scoring or trying to score: *We went to the gym and shot baskets.*
6 VERB. to take a picture with a camera; photograph: *I shot several views of the mountains.*

shooting a basket

7 VERB. to come forth from the ground; grow; grow rapidly: *Buds shoot forth in the spring.*
8 NOUN. a new part growing out; young branch: *See the new shoots on that bush.*
❑ VERB **shoots, shot, shoot•ing. —shoot′er,** NOUN.

shooting star, a meteor seen falling through the sky at night.

shop (shop),
1 VERB. to visit stores to look at or to buy things: *We shopped all morning for a coat.*
2 NOUN. a place where things are made or repaired or certain kinds of work are done: *a barber's shop, a carpenter's shop.*
3 NOUN. a place where things are sold; store: *My aunt runs a small dress shop.*
❑ VERB **shops, shopped, shop•ping. —shop′per,** NOUN.

shop•keep•er (shop′kē/pər), NOUN. someone who owns or manages a shop or store.

shop•lift (shop′lift/), VERB. to steal things from a store while pretending to be a customer. ❑ VERB **shop•lifts, shop•lift•ed, shop•lift•ing. —shop′lift/er,** NOUN.

shopping center, a group of stores built as a unit on or near a main road. Most shopping centers have large areas for parking cars.

shore (shôr), NOUN. the land at the edge of a sea, lake, or large river.
off shore, IDIOM. in or on the water, not far from the shore: *The yacht was anchored off shore.*

shorn (shôrn), VERB. a past participle of **shear:** *They have shorn 20 sheep this morning.*

short (shôrt),
1 ADJECTIVE. not of great length from the beginning to the end; not long: *a short rope, a short street.*
2 ADJECTIVE. not lasting very long: *We heard a short talk by the principal today.*
3 ADJECTIVE. not tall: *a short man, short grass.* ■ See the Synonym Study at **little.**
4 ADJECTIVE. not having enough: *We are short of food.*
5 ADJECTIVE. so brief that it is rude: *She was so short with me that I felt hurt.*
6 ADVERB. not quite reaching the point aimed at: *The arrows landed just short of the target.*
7 ADJECTIVE. (of vowels). A **short vowel** is a vowel like *a* in *hat, e* in *leg, i* in *it, o* in *hot,* or *u* in *hut.*
8 NOUN. **shorts, a** short pants that do not reach the knees. **b** a similar kind of men's or boys' underwear.
9 See **short circuit.**
for short, IDIOM. in order to make shorter: *Robert was called Rob for short.*
in short, IDIOM. briefly: *I will give you the details later; in short, the party has been canceled.*
run short, IDIOM.
1 to not have enough: *Let me know if you run short of money before then.*
2 to not be enough: *Our food supply ran short before the end of the camping trip.*
short for, IDIOM. a shortened form of: *The word "phone" is short for "telephone."*
short of, IDIOM. not up to; less than: *Nothing short of your best work will satisfy me.*

short•age (shôr′tij), NOUN. too small an amount; lack: *a shortage of grain after the drought.*

short circuit, an electrical problem that happens when insulation wears off wires so that they touch each other. A short circuit may cause a fire.

short•cut (shôrt′kut/), NOUN. a quicker way to get somewhere or do something: *To save time we took a shortcut through a vacant lot.*

short•en (shôrt′n), VERB. to make or become shorter: *The new highway shortens the trip.*
❑ VERB **short•ens, short•ened, short•en•ing.**

short•en•ing (shôrt′n ing), NOUN. butter, lard, vegetable oil, or other fat, used to make pastry or cake crisp or crumbly.

short•ly (shôrt′lē), ADVERB. in a short time; before long; soon: *I will be with you shortly.*

short·sight·ed (shôrt′sī′tid), ADJECTIVE.
1 nearsighted; not able to see far.
2 not thinking carefully about the future: *It was shortsighted of us not to bring food for the hike.*
—**short′sight′ed·ness,** NOUN.

short·stop (shôrt′stop′), NOUN. a baseball player who plays between second and third base.

shot¹ (shot), NOUN.

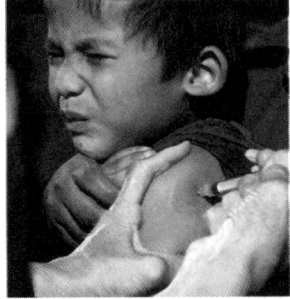

shot (definition 6)

1 the act or sound of firing a gun or other weapon: *We heard two shots.*
2 the balls of lead or steel fired from a shotgun, gun, or cannon. ★ The plural for this meaning is **shot**.
3 an attempt to hit something by shooting at it: *That was a good shot, and it hit the mark.*
4 someone who shoots: *He is a good shot.*
5 a kick, throw, or hit in some games, made in order to score points.
6 a dose of medicine placed under the skin with a hollow needle: *I was given a shot of penicillin.*
7 an attempt; try: *I think I'll take a shot at that job.*

shot² (shot), VERB.
1 the past tense of **shoot**: *I shot the gun.*
2 the past participle of **shoot**: *I have shot three times and missed.*

shot·gun (shot′gun′), NOUN. a long gun that fires very small shot instead of bullets.

should (shùd), HELPING VERB.
1 the past tense of **shall**.
2 ought to: *You should try to make fewer mistakes.*
3 **Should** is used to express uncertainty: *If it should rain, I won't go.*
4 **Should** is used to ask for an opinion about a past action: *Should I have asked her to the party?*

shoul·der (shōl′dər),
1 NOUN. the part of the body between the neck and the arms.
2 NOUN. the part of a piece of clothing that covers a shoulder: *I tore the shoulder of my jacket.*
3 NOUN. **shoulders,** the two shoulders and the upper part of the back: *The man carried a trunk on his shoulders.*
4 NOUN. the edge of a road: *When a tire went flat, we pulled onto the shoulder to fix it.*
5 VERB. to take on the job of doing something that requires effort, expense, and so on: *She shouldered the responsibility of raising her niece.*
❑ VERB **shoul·ders, shoul·dered, shoul·der·ing.**

cry on someone's shoulder, IDIOM. to tell someone your troubles or worries: *I came to cry on her shoulder about losing the race.*

give someone the cold shoulder, IDIOM. to show dislike for; avoid: *He has given me the cold shoulder ever since our argument.*

shoulder blade, the flat bone of either shoulder, in the upper back.

should·n't (shùd′nt), a contraction of **should not.**

shout (shout),
1 VERB. to call or yell loudly: *I shouted for help when the boat sank. Somebody shouted, "Fire!"*
2 NOUN. a loud call or yell: *I heard their shouts for help.*
❑ VERB **shouts, shout·ed, shout·ing.** —**shout′er,** NOUN.

Synonym Study

Shout means to speak out in a loud voice to get the attention of someone: *I shouted, "I'm over here."*

Call means to speak in a louder voice than usual: *She called to her friend on the front step next door.*

Yell means to shout as loud as you can when you are excited: *"That's my boy!" Mom yelled when my brother hit a home run.*

Cry means to call out, with or without words: *When the ball hit him, he cried, "Ow!"*

Scream means to cry out in a very loud voice. You scream when you are angry, afraid, or excited: *We all screamed at the monster in the movie.*

Shriek means to scream: *Shrieking with joy, the children ran into the ocean.*

See also the Synonym Studies at **loud** and **noise.**

shove (shuv),
1 VERB. to push something forward by force from behind: *Help me shove this bookcase into place.*
■ See the Synonym Study at **push.**
2 VERB. to push roughly or rudely: *The people shoved to get on the crowded car.*
3 NOUN. a push: *We gave the boat a shove which sent it far out into the water.*
❑ VERB **shoves, shoved, shov·ing.**

shov·el (shuv′əl),
1 NOUN. a tool with a broad scoop, used to dig a hole or to scoop something up: *a snow shovel.*
2 VERB. to lift and throw something with this tool: *She shoveled the snow from the walk.*
3 VERB. to throw or lift something as if you were using a shovel: *The hungry girl shoveled the food into her mouth.*
❑ VERB **shov·els, shov·eled, shov·el·ing.**

a	hat	ė	term	ô	order	ch	child	⎧a in about
ā	age	i	it	oi	oil	ng	long	⎪e in taken
ä	far	ī	ice	ou	out	sh	she	ə⎨i in pencil
â	care	o	hot	u	cup	th	thin	⎪o in lemon
e	let	ō	open	ù	put	ᴛʜ	then	⎩u in circus
ē	equal	ò	saw	ü	rule	zh	measure	

S

show (shō),
1 *VERB.* to bring or put something so that you can see it: *She showed me her rock collection.*
2 *VERB.* to be in sight; appear; be seen: *Amusement showed in his face.*
3 *VERB.* to explain or to point out something to someone: *She showed us the way to town.*
4 *VERB.* to guide someone: *Please show them to the door.*
5 *VERB.* to make something clear to someone: *The teacher showed me how to do the problem.*
6 *NOUN.* a place where special things are shown to the public: *a flower show, a boat show.*
7 *NOUN.* a play, movie, or television program: *We saw a good show on TV last night.*
8 *VERB.* to grant; give: *The governor was asked to show mercy and pardon the criminal.*
9 *NOUN.* a display: *The jewels made a fine show.*
10 *NOUN.* a display for effect: *He put on a show of learning to impress us.*
❏ *VERB* **shows, showed, shown** or **showed, show•ing.**

for show, *IDIOM.* to attract attention; for effect: *That fancy car is just for show.*

show off, *IDIOM.* to make a show of; display your good points or abilities: *He showed off his new clothes. My little sister likes to show off by doing cartwheels when we have company.*

show up, *IDIOM.* to put in an appearance: *We were going to play ball, but the other team didn't show up.* ∎ See the Synonym Study at **come.**

Synonym Study

Show means to cause something to be seen: *She showed her friends how well she could use her artificial hand.*

Display means to show things in a way that gets people's attention: *Our champion pumpkin was displayed at the county fair.*

Exhibit can mean to show something publicly: *On Visitors' Day, the school classes exhibited drawings they had done.*

Expose can mean to show openly where anyone can see: *When the wall of the building was torn down, the rooms inside were all exposed.*

ANTONYMS: conceal, hide[1].

show business, the entertainment industry.
show•er (shou′ər),
1 *NOUN.* a bath in which you stand under running water.
2 *VERB.* to take a bath like this: *I shower every night.*
3 *NOUN.* rain that lasts only a short time.
4 *VERB.* to wet with a shower; sprinkle; spray: *Water from the broken hose showered us.*

5 *NOUN.* anything like a fall of rain: *We saw a shower of sparks fall from the engine.*
❏ *VERB* **show•ers, show•ered, show•er•ing.**

It was the best pumpkin in the garden **show.**

shown (shōn), *VERB.* a past participle of **show:** *She has shown us how to play many games.*
∎ Another word that sounds like this is **shone.**

show-off (shō′ôf′), *NOUN.* someone who shows off in an effort to attract attention: *Some people are terrible show-offs.*

show•y (shō′ē), *ADJECTIVE.*
1 making a display; likely to attract attention: *Peonies are showy flowers.*
2 too bright and flashy to be in good taste: *I didn't like that showy dress.*
❏ *ADJECTIVE* **show•i•er, show•i•est. —show′i•ness,** *NOUN.*

shrank (shrangk), *VERB.* a past tense of **shrink:** *My shirt shrank in the wash.*

shred (shred),
1 *NOUN.* a very small piece that has been torn off or cut off from something; very narrow, ragged strip: *The wind tore the sail to shreds. We picked up the shreds of leftover cloth.*
2 *NOUN.* a very little bit; scrap: *There's not a shred of evidence that he took the money.*
3 *VERB.* to tear or cut something into small pieces: *He shredded lettuce for the salad.*
❏ *VERB* **shreds, shred•ded, shred•ding. —shred′der,** *NOUN.*

shrew (shrü), *NOUN.* a small animal like a mouse, that has a long snout and brownish fur. Shrews eat insects and worms. **—shrew′like′,** *ADJECTIVE.*

shrewd (shrüd), *ADJECTIVE.* good at making decisions; clever: *She is a shrewd store manager with a talent for knowing what the public wants to buy.* **—shrewd′ly,** *ADVERB.* **—shrewd′ness,** *NOUN.*

shriek (shrēk),
1 *VERB.* to make a loud, sharp, shrill sound. People sometimes shriek because of terror, anger, pain, or joy. ∎ See the Synonym Study at **shout.**
2 *NOUN.* a loud, sharp, shrill sound: *Shrieks of laughter greeted the clown's tricks.*
❏ *VERB* **shrieks, shrieked, shriek•ing.**

shrill (shril), *ADJECTIVE.* high and sharp in sound; piercing: *Crickets and katydids make shrill noises.*

shrimp (shrimp), NOUN. a small shellfish with a long tail. There are about 2,000 kinds of shrimp. Some kinds are used for food. ❑ PLURAL **shrimp** or **shrimps.** —**shrimp′like′**, ADJECTIVE.

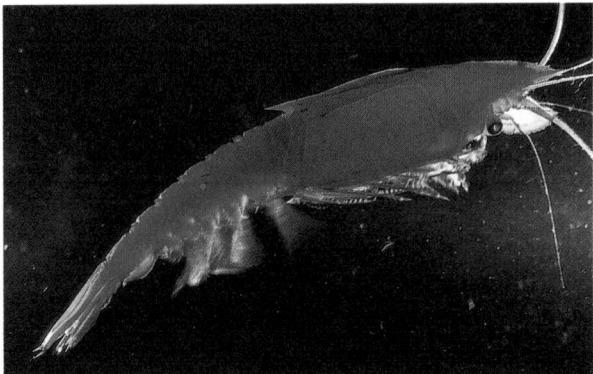

shrimp — up to 12 inches long.

shrine (shrīn), NOUN. a sacred place; place where sacred things are kept. A shrine may be the tomb of a saint, an altar, or a place for a holy object.

shrink (shringk), VERB.
1 to pull back: *I shrank from the snake in its cage.*
2 to make or become smaller: *The dryer shrank my socks. I've shrunk my essay to five pages.*
❑ VERB **shrinks, shrank** or **shrunk, shrunk** or **shrunk·en, shrink·ing.**

shriv·el (shriv′əl), VERB. to dry up, shrink, and wrinkle: *The hot sunshine shriveled the grass.*
❑ VERB **shriv·els, shriv·eled, shriv·el·ing.**

shroud (shroud),
1 NOUN. something that covers or conceals something: *The fog was a shroud over the city.*
2 VERB. to cover or conceal something: *The earth is shrouded in darkness.*
❑ VERB **shrouds, shroud·ed, shroud·ing.**

shrub (shrub), NOUN. a woody plant smaller than a tree, usually with many separate stems starting from or near the ground; bush.

shrub·ber·y (shrub′ər ē), NOUN. a group of shrubs: *Shrubbery hid the house from the street.*

shrug (shrug),
1 VERB. to raise your shoulders as an expression of doubt or lack of interest: *He shrugged his shoulders when I asked him for the time.*
2 NOUN. the act of raising your shoulders in this way: *She replied with a shrug.*
❑ VERB **shrugs, shrugged, shrug·ging.**

shrunk (shrungk), VERB. a past participle of **shrink:** *These socks have shrunk and I can't get them on.*

shrunk·en (shrung′kən), ADJECTIVE.
1 grown smaller; shriveled: *I threw away the shrunken orange.*
2 a past participle of **shrink:** *You have shrunken my best sweater in the dryer!*

shuck (shuk), VERB. to remove the outer covering from something: *I shucked the corn before cooking it.* ❑ VERB **shucks, shucked, shuck·ing.**

shud·der (shud′ər),
1 VERB. to shake all over with horror, fear, or cold: *I shudder at the sight of snakes.*
2 NOUN. the act of shaking: *A shudder went through me when I saw the snake.*
❑ VERB **shud·ders, shud·dered, shud·der·ing.**

shuf·fle (shuf′əl),
1 VERB. to scrape or drag your feet while walking: *We shuffled along the slippery sidewalk.*
2 NOUN. the act of scraping or dragging your feet.
3 VERB. to mix cards in order to change their order.
❑ VERB **shuf·fles, shuf·fled, shuf·fling.**

shun (shun), VERB. to keep away from something; avoid: *She shuns housework.* ❑ VERB **shuns, shunned, shun·ning.**

shush (shush),
1 VERB. to stop making noise; hush: *The librarian asked the noisy kids to shush.*
2 INTERJECTION. hush! stop the noise!
❑ VERB **shush·es, shushed, shush·ing.**

shut (shut),
1 VERB. to close something or put a cover on something: *to shut a box, to shut a window.*
2 VERB. to close something by bringing parts of it together: *Shut your eyes. Shut the book.*
3 VERB. to become closed: *The baby's mouth shut and she refused to eat any more.*
4 VERB. to close something up securely: *The canary was shut in its cage.*
5 ADJECTIVE. not open; closed: *I keep my bedroom door shut when I'm not home.*
❑ VERB **shuts, shut, shut·ting.**

shut down, IDIOM. to close a factory or the like for a time; stop work: *We've got to shut down until there is a demand for our product.*

shut out, IDIOM.
1 to keep from coming in: *The curtains shut out the light.*
2 to defeat a team without allowing it to score: *The pitcher shut out the other team, limiting them to three hits.*

shut up, IDIOM.
1 to shut the doors and windows of.
2 to stop talking: *It was rude of you to tell me to shut up.* ★ Most people feel that saying "Shut up!" is not polite.

shut·out (shut′out′), NOUN. a defeat of a team without allowing it to score at all.

a	hat	ė	term	ô	order	ch	child	⎧a in about
ā	age	i	it	oi	oil	ng	long	⎪e in taken
ä	far	ī	ice	ou	out	sh	she	ə⎨i in pencil
â	care	o	hot	u	cup	th	thin	⎪o in lemon
e	let	ō	open	ù	put	ᴛʜ	then	⎩u in circus
ē	equal	ò	saw	ü	rule	zh	measure	

S

shut·ter (shut′ər), NOUN.
1 a device in a camera that opens and closes to allow light to reach the film and produce a picture.
2 a movable cover for a window: *We closed the shutters as the storm came near.*

shut·tle (shut′l),
1 NOUN. a device used in weaving that carries the thread back and forth across the piece being woven.
2 VERB. to move quickly back and forth: *We shuttled between our old house and our new house many times on moving day.*
3 NOUN. a bus, train, or airplane that runs regularly back and forth over a short distance.
4 NOUN. **the shuttle.** See **space shuttle.**
❏ VERB **shut·tles, shut·tled, shut·tling.**

shut·tle·cock (shut′l kok′), NOUN. the small object hit back and forth in the game of badminton; birdie. A shuttlecock was originally a cork with feathers stuck in one end, but now is often made of plastic.

shy (shī),
1 ADJECTIVE. not feeling comfortable around people; bashful: *He is shy and dislikes parties.*
2 ADJECTIVE. easily frightened; timid: *A deer is a shy animal.*
3 VERB. to jump back or to the side suddenly in fear or surprise: *The horse shied at the newspaper blowing along the ground.*
❏ ADJECTIVE **shy·er, shy·est** or **shi·er, shi·est;** VERB **shies, shied, shy·ing.** —**shy′ly,** ADVERB. —**shy′ness,** NOUN.

Synonym Study

Shy means lacking confidence and uneasy in the presence of others: *Shy people feel uncomfortable talking to strangers.*

Bashful means shy and easily embarrassed: *She was so bashful that she wouldn't even look at me.*

Timid means shy and frightened: *He is a timid child, but he made a good speech at the school assembly.*

Modest can mean unwilling to draw attention to yourself: *She is so modest that she lets other people get the praise for her work.*

Si·a·mese cat (sī′ə mēz′ kat′), a short-haired, blue-eyed cat, usually with a light tan body and dark face, ears, feet, and tail.

Si·ber·i·a (sī bir′ē ə), NOUN. a region in northern Asia. It is part of Russia. —**Si·ber′i·an,** ADJECTIVE or NOUN.

sick (sik),
1 ADJECTIVE. not feeling well; having some disease; ill.
2 ADJECTIVE. vomiting or feeling as though about to vomit: *The motion of the boat made me sick.*
3 NOUN. **the sick,** sick people: *The sick need special care.*
4 ADJECTIVE. weary; tired: *I'm sick of school.*

5 ADJECTIVE. feeling angry or upset about something: *It makes me sick to think he won first prize.*

sick·en (sik′ən), VERB. to make or become sick: *The sight of blood sickens some people.* ❏ VERB **sick·ens, sick·ened, sick·en·ing.**

sick·en·ing (sik′ə ning), ADJECTIVE. causing nausea or disgust.

sick·le (sik′əl), NOUN. a tool with a curved blade on a short handle, used to cut grass, grain, and so on.

sick·ly (sik′lē), ADJECTIVE.
1 often sick; not healthy: *The baby was sickly and required a lot of medical care.*
2 of or reminding you of sickness: *a sickly yellow.*
❏ ADJECTIVE **sick·li·er, sick·li·est.**

sick·ness (sik′nis), NOUN. illness; feeling sick; disease: *a terrible sickness.* ❏ PLURAL **sick·ness·es.**

side (sīd),
1 NOUN. a surface that extends from the top to the bottom of something: *A square has four sides. There is a door at the side of the house.*
2 NOUN. either of the two surfaces of paper or cloth: *Write only on one side of the paper.*
3 NOUN. a particular surface: *We only see the side of the moon facing the earth.*
4 NOUN. either the right or the left part of something; either part or region beyond a central line: *the east side of a city, our side of the street.*
5 NOUN. either the right or the left part of the body: *I felt a sharp pain in my side.*
6 NOUN. a group of people who oppose another group: *We'll choose sides for a game of softball.*
7 NOUN. a point of view that is opposed to others: *Let's hear your side of the argument.*
8 NOUN. a part of a family line: *He is English on his mother's side and Spanish on his father's side.*
9 ADJECTIVE. at, toward, from, or on one side: *a side door, the side aisles of a theater, a side view.*

side with, IDIOM. to take the part of one person or group: *The sisters always side with each other.*

take sides, IDIOM. to join with one person or group against another: *I never take sides in an argument.*
❏ VERB **sides, sid·ed, sid·ing.**

Siamese cat — about 10 inches high at the shoulder

side·burns (sīd'bėrnz'), *NOUN PLURAL.* a strip of whiskers growing down each cheek in front of the ears.

side effect, an additional effect of a drug, usually one that is unpleasant: *Some drugs produce side effects such as an upset stomach.*

side·line (sīd'līn'), *NOUN.*
1 a line that marks the side of a playing field.
2 **sidelines,** the space just outside one of these lines: *We all watched the game from the sidelines.*

long **sideburns**

side·long (sīd'lông'), *ADJECTIVE.* to one side; toward the side: *He gave a sidelong glance to see if they were still there.*

side·show (sīd'shō'), *NOUN.* a small show in connection with a main one at a fair or circus.

side·step (sīd'step'), *VERB.*
1 to step aside: *I sidestepped the puddle of water.*
2 to avoid something you do not want to do: *She would never sidestep a responsibility.* □ *VERB* **side·steps, side·stepped, side·step·ping.**

side·track (sīd'trak'), *VERB.* to draw someone's attention away from what he or she was thinking or talking about: *Don't sidetrack me with pointless questions.* □ *VERB* **side·tracks, side·tracked, side·track·ing.**

side·walk (sīd'wòk'), *NOUN.* a place to walk along the side of a street, usually paved with concrete.

side·ways (sīd'wāz'), *ADVERB* or *ADJECTIVE.*
1 to one side; toward one side: *a sideways motion.*
2 with one side toward the front: *to stand sideways.*

sid·ing (sī'ding), *NOUN.* boards, shingles, and the like, that form the outside walls of a wooden building.

siege (sēj), *NOUN.*
1 the act or process of surrounding a fortified place with an army trying to capture it: *The castle was under siege for ten days before its defenders gave up.*
2 any long attack: *Grandma had a terrible siege of arthritis last winter.*

si·er·ra (sē er'ə), *NOUN.* a chain or ridge of jagged hills or mountains. □ *PLURAL* **si·er·ras.**

Si·er·ra Le·o·ne (sē er'ə lē ō'nē), a country in western Africa. —**Sierra Leonean.**

si·es·ta (sē es'tə), *NOUN.* a nap or rest taken at noon or in the afternoon. □ *PLURAL* **si·es·tas.**

sieve (siv), *NOUN.* a kitchen tool having holes that let only liquids and smaller pieces pass through: *Shaking flour through a sieve removes lumps.*

sift (sift), *VERB.*
1 to separate large pieces from small pieces by shaking them through a sieve: *Sift the gravel and remove the larger stones.*
2 to put something through a sieve: *Sift powdered sugar onto the top of the cake.*
3 to examine something very carefully: *The jury sifted the evidence before making its decision.* □ *VERB* **sifts, sift·ed, sift·ing.** —**sift'er,** *NOUN.*

sigh (sī),
1 *VERB.* to let out a very long, deep breath because you are sad, tired, or free from worry: *We heard her sigh with relief.*
2 *NOUN.* the act or sound of sighing: *a sigh of relief.*
3 *VERB.* to make a sound like a sigh: *The wind sighed through the trees.* □ *VERB* **sighs, sighed, sigh·ing.**

sight (sīt),
1 *NOUN.* the power or sense of seeing; vision: *Birds have better sight than dogs.*
2 *NOUN.* the act of seeing; look: *We caught our first sight of the sea.*
3 *NOUN.* the distance that someone can see: *Land was in sight.*
4 *NOUN.* something seen; view: *Some people can't stand the sight of blood.*
5 *NOUN.* something worth seeing: *Niagara Falls is one of the great sights of the world.*
6 *NOUN.* (informal) something that looks bad or odd: *Your room is a sight.*
7 *VERB.* to see: *The lifeboat drifted for several days before the survivors sighted land.*
8 *NOUN.* a device to guide your eye when you take aim at something: *the sights on a rifle.*
∎ Other words that sound like this are **cite** and **site.** □ *VERB* **sights, sight·ed, sight·ing.** —**sight'less,** *ADJECTIVE.*

Have You Heard?

You may have heard someone say **"out of sight, out of mind."** This means that it is easy to forget about something you have not seen for a while.

sight·ing (sī'ting), *NOUN.* the act of seeing or the condition of being seen: *The newspaper reported the sighting of a new comet.*

a	hat	ė	term	ô	order	ch	child	
ā	age	i	it	oi	oil	ng	long	a in about
ä	far	ī	ice	ou	out	sh	she	e in taken
â	care	o	hot	u	cup	th	thin	ə i in pencil
e	let	ō	open	ù	put	₮H	then	o in lemon
ē	equal	ò	saw	ü	rule	zh	measure	u in circus

S

sight·see·ing (sīt′sē′ing), NOUN. the act of going around to see interesting things or places: *a weekend of sightseeing.* —**sight′se′er,** NOUN.

sign (sīn),
1 NOUN. a mark or words that tell you what to do or what not to do: *The sign reads "Keep off the grass." The signs for addition, subtraction, multiplication, and division are +, −, ×, and ÷.*
2 VERB. to write your name on something. A person signs a letter or a check.
3 NOUN. a motion or gesture used to stand for or point out something: *A nod is a sign of agreement.*
4 NOUN. something that shows activity, existence, and so on: *There are no signs of life about the house.*
❑ VERB **signs, signed, sign·ing. —sign′er,** NOUN.

sign off, IDIOM. to stop broadcasting: *That radio station signs off at midnight.*

sign up, IDIOM. to enlist or join by written agreement: *I signed up as a member of the scouts.*

Do you know what these **signs** mean?

sig·nal (sig′nəl),
1 NOUN. something that warns you about something, or that points something out: *A red light is a signal to stop.*
2 VERB. to make a signal or signals to: *She signaled the taxi to stop by raising her hand.*
3 VERB. to make something known by using a signal or signals: *A bell signals the end of a school period.*
4 NOUN. an electrical wave or current that carries sounds and pictures to be received by a radio, television set, or the like.
❑ VERB **sig·nals, sig·naled, sig·nal·ing.**

sig·na·ture (sig′nə chər), NOUN. a person's name written by that person.

sig·nif·i·cance (sig nif′ə kəns), NOUN.
1 importance; seriousness: *The principal wants to see you on a matter of significance.*
2 the meaning of something: *I understood the significance of her look.*

sig·nif·i·cant (sig nif′ə kənt), ADJECTIVE. very important: *The invention of writing was a significant event in human history.* —**sig·nif′i·cant·ly,** ADVERB.

sign language, a language in which motions, especially of the fingers, hands, and arms, stand for words and ideas.

sign·post (sīn′pōst′), NOUN. a post that has signs, notices, or directions on it.

si·lence (sī′ləns),
1 NOUN. an absence of sound or noise; stillness: *The teacher asked for silence.*
2 NOUN. the act or condition of keeping still: *His silence made us believe he agreed with our plan.*
3 VERB. to make someone or something be silent; quiet: *Please silence that barking dog.*
❑ VERB **si·lenc·es, si·lenced, si·lenc·ing.**

si·lent (sī′lənt), ADJECTIVE.
1 without any noise; quiet; still: *a silent house.*
2 without speaking; saying little or nothing: *Students must be silent during the study hour.*
3 not spoken; not said out loud: *The "e" in "time" is a silent letter.*
—**si′lent·ly,** ADVERB.

sil·hou·ette (sil′ü et′),
1 NOUN. a dark image outlined against a lighter background: *The silhouette of a man could be seen against the movie screen.*
2 NOUN. a picture that is cut out of black paper or filled in with some single color to form an outline.
3 VERB. to show something in outline.
❑ VERB **sil·hou·ettes, sil·hou·et·ted, sil·hou·et·ting.**

sil·i·con (sil′ə kən), NOUN. a very common chemical element found in the earth's crust. Sand and most rocks and soils contain silicon. It is used in computer chips, transistors, and other products.

silk (silk), NOUN.
1 a fine, soft thread spun by silkworms.
2 a soft, smooth cloth made from this thread.
3 anything like silk. The glossy threads at the end of an ear of corn are called **corn silk.**
—**silk′like′,** ADJECTIVE.

Did You Know?

The Chinese were the first to discover methods of making **silk.** They made so much money selling silk that they threatened to execute anyone who revealed the secret of these methods. They kept the secret for 3000 years.

silk·en (sil′kən), ADJECTIVE.
1 made of silk: *The king wore silken robes.*
2 like silk; smooth, soft, and shiny: *The princess had long, silken hair.*

silk·worm (silk′wėrm′), NOUN. a special kind of caterpillar that spins silk to make a cocoon.

silk·y (sil′kē), ADJECTIVE. like silk; smooth, soft, and shiny: *My kitten has silky fur.* ■ See the Synonym Studies at **smooth** and **soft.** ❑ ADJECTIVE **silk·i·er, silk·i·est. −silk′i·ness,** NOUN.

sill (sil), NOUN. a piece of wood or stone at the bottom of a door or window frame.

sil·ly (sil′ē), ADJECTIVE. not making sense; not serious; foolish; ridiculous: *It's silly to be afraid of harmless insects like moths.* ❑ ADJECTIVE **sil·li·er, sil·li·est.**

si·lo (sī′lō), NOUN. a tall, cylinder-shaped, airtight building in which grain or other food for farm animals can be stored without spoiling. ❑ PLURAL **si·los.**

silo

silt (silt), NOUN. very fine particles of earth and sand carried by moving water: *The harbor is being choked with silt.*

sil·ver (sil′vər),
1 NOUN. a shining white precious metal that is a chemical element. Silver is used to make coins, jewelry, spoons, knives, and forks.
2 NOUN. coins made of this or a similar metal: *He pulled a handful of silver out of his pocket.*
3 NOUN. knives, forks, spoons, or dishes made of or coated with silver: *I polished the silver so it could be used for Thanksgiving dinner.*
4 ADJECTIVE. made of or covered with silver: *He sugared the tea with a silver spoon.*
5 ADJECTIVE. having the color of silver: *She wore a silver jacket over her dress.*

Have You Heard?

You may have heard someone say **"He was born with a silver spoon in his mouth."** This means that the person comes from a wealthy family. People sometimes use this phrase to show that they disapprove of someone because they think that person didn't have to work very hard for successes.

sil·ver·smith (sil′vər smith′), NOUN. someone who makes or repairs things made of silver.

sil·ver·ware (sil′vər wâr′), NOUN. knives, forks, or spoons made of silver or some other metal.

sil·ver·y (sil′vər ē), ADJECTIVE. like silver; like that of silver: *He polished the metal to a silvery gleam.*

sim·i·lar (sim′ə lər), ADJECTIVE. almost alike in some way; alike: *The children in that family are very similar in appearance.* **−sim′i·lar·ly,** ADVERB.

sim·i·lar·i·ty (sim′ə lar′ə tē), NOUN.
1 the condition of being similar; resemblance: *There is a remarkable similarity between your handwriting and hers.*
2 **similarities,** points of resemblance.
  ❑ PLURAL **sim·i·lar·i·ties.**

sim·i·le (sim′ə lē), NOUN. a figure of speech you use to compare two different things or ideas using the words *like* or *as. A face like marble* and *as brave as a lion* are similes. ■ See the Usage Note at **metaphor.** ❑ PLURAL **sim·i·les.**

sim·mer (sim′ər), VERB.
1 to cook food just below the boiling point: *The soup should simmer for a few hours to improve its taste.*
2 to be nearly at the point of breaking out in anger, fighting, and so on: *Rebellion simmered throughout the summer. He was simmering with anger.*
  ❑ VERB **sim·mers, sim·mered, sim·mer·ing.**

sim·ple (sim′pəl), ADJECTIVE.
1 easy to do or understand: *a simple problem.*
2 not fancy or showy; plain: *simple clothing.*
3 having few parts; not complex: *A pair of pliers is a simple device.*
  ❑ ADJECTIVE **sim·pler, sim·plest.**

simple machine, a basic mechanical device which increases force or changes its direction. The lever, wedge, and screw are simple machines.

sim·plic·i·ty (sim plis′ə tē), NOUN.
1 freedom from difficulty; clearness: *The simplicity of that book makes it suitable for children.*
2 plainness: *Hospital rooms are furnished with simplicity.*

sim·pli·fy (sim′plə fī), VERB. to make something plainer or simpler; easier: *The rules of the game were simplified for younger children.* ❑ VERB **sim·pli·fies, sim·pli·fied, sim·pli·fy·ing.**

sim·ply (sim′plē), ADVERB.
1 in a simple manner: *The teacher tried to explain the problem simply.*
2 merely; only: *We simply need a little information.*
3 absolutely: *The day was simply perfect for hiking.*

si·mul·ta·ne·ous (sī′məl tā′nē əs), ADJECTIVE. done or happening at the same time: *The two simultaneous shots sounded like one.*

a	hat	ė	term	ô	order	ch	child		a in about
ā	age	i	it	oi	oil	ng	long		e in taken
ä	far	ī	ice	ou	out	sh	she	ə	i in pencil
â	care	o	hot	u	cup	th	thin		o in lemon
e	let	ō	open	u̇	put	ŦH	then		u in circus
ē	equal	ȯ	saw	ü	rule	zh	measure		

S

sin (sin),
1 *NOUN.* the act of breaking a religious law on purpose.
2 *VERB.* to break a religious law.
3 *NOUN.* wrongdoing of any kind; immoral act. *Lying, stealing, dishonesty, and cruelty are sins.*
□ *VERB* **sins, sinned, sin•ning.**

Si•na•lo•a (sē′nä lō′ä), *NOUN.* a state in western Mexico.

Sin•bad (sin′bad), *NOUN.* a sea captain in *The Arabian Nights* who went on seven extraordinary voyages.

since (sins),
1 *PREPOSITION.* from a past time till now: *The sun has been up since five.*
2 *CONJUNCTION.* after the time that: *He has been home only once since he went to New York.*
3 *ADVERB.* from then till now: *I caught cold Saturday and have been in bed ever since.*
4 *ADVERB.* at some time between then and now: *He at first refused the position, but has since accepted it.*
5 *CONJUNCTION.* because: *Since you feel tired, you should rest.*

sin•cere (sin sir′), *ADJECTIVE.* meaning what you say or do; honest: *I made a sincere effort to pass the test.*
□ *ADJECTIVE* **sin•cer•er, sin•cer•est. —sin•cere′ly,** *ADVERB.*

sin•cer•i•ty (sin ser′ə tē), *NOUN.* honesty; truthfulness: *We doubted the sincerity of his apology.*

sin•ew (sin′yü), *NOUN.* a very tough cord that joins muscle to bone; tendon.

sing (sing), *VERB.*
1 to make music with your voice: *You sing that song very well.*
2 to make pleasant sounds that are like music: *Birds sing as day begins.*
□ *VERB* **sings, sang** or **sung, sung, sing•ing. —sing′er,** *NOUN.*

sing

Sing•a•pore (sing′ə pôr), *NOUN.* an island country off the coast of southeastern Asia.

singe (sinj), *VERB.* to burn something slightly: *A spark from the fireplace singed the rug.* □ *VERB* **sing•es, singed, singe•ing.**

sin•gle (sing′gəl),
1 *ADJECTIVE.* only one: *The spider hung by a single thread.*
2 *ADJECTIVE.* for only one person: *The sisters share one room with two single beds in it.*
3 *ADJECTIVE.* not married: *a single man.*
4 *NOUN.* **singles,** a game played with only one person on each side: *In tennis, she likes to play singles rather than doubles.*
5 in baseball: **a** *NOUN.* a hit that allows the batter to reach first base only. **b** *VERB.* to make such a hit.
□ *VERB* **sin•gles, sin•gled, sin•gling.**

single out, *IDIOM.* to choose one person out of a group: *She was singled out for praise.*

sin•gle-hand•ed (sing′gəl han′did), *ADJECTIVE* or *ADVERB.* done by one person, without help from others. **—sin′gle-hand′ed•ly,** *ADVERB.*

single parent, a parent who is raising a child or children without the other parent.

sin•gu•lar (sing′gyə lər),
1 *ADJECTIVE.* one in number. *Dog is singular; dogs is plural.*
2 *NOUN.* a form of a word to show that it means no more than one. *Ox is the singular of oxen.*

sin•is•ter (sin′ə stər), *ADJECTIVE.*
1 bad; evil; dishonest: *a sinister plan.*
2 showing bad intentions; threatening: *a sinister look.*

Word Story

Sinister comes from a Latin word meaning "on the left side." The ancient Romans tried to predict the future by omens—events that people thought were signs of what would happen. Their omens included birds in flight or a bolt of lightning. Omens on the left side were thought to mean bad luck, so the Latin word also meant "unlucky." In English the meaning is even more negative.

sink (singk),
1 *VERB.* to go down; fall slowly; go lower and lower: *The sun is sinking in the west.*
2 *VERB.* to go or make something go under: *The ship sank. The submarine sank two ships.*
3 *NOUN.* a shallow basin or tub with a pipe to drain it: *The dishes are in the kitchen sink.*
4 *VERB.* to make or become lower or weaker: *Her voice sank to a whisper.*
5 *VERB.* to go deeply: *Let this lesson sink into your mind.*
□ *VERB* **sinks, sank** or **sunk, sunk, sink•ing. —sink′a•ble,** *ADJECTIVE.*

si•nus (sī′nəs), *NOUN.* one of the spaces inside the bones in the front of the skull. The sinuses connect with the nose and may become infected by cold germs. □ *PLURAL* **si•nus•es.**

Sioux (sü), NOUN. a group of American Indian tribes living on the plains of the northern United States and southern Canada; Dakota; Lakota. ❑ PLURAL **Sioux** (sü *or* süz).

Usage Note

Many **Sioux** prefer the name **Dakota** or **Lakota** instead of **Sioux**. These names mean "allies" in their own language. The name **Sioux** is believed to come from an a different tribe's word meaning "foreigner" or "enemy."

sit (definition 4)

sip (sip),
1 VERB. to drink a little bit at a time: *I sipped my tea.*
2 NOUN. a very small drink of something: *I took a sip.*
❑ VERB **sips, sipped, sip·ping.**

si·phon (si′fən),
1 NOUN. a bent tube through which liquid can be made to flow. Air pressure will push the liquid from one container into another at a lower level.
2 VERB. to move liquid through a siphon: *They siphoned some gasoline from their car to ours.*
❑ VERB **si·phons, si·phoned, si·phon·ing.**

sir (sėr), NOUN.
1 a polite title used in writing or speaking to any man: *"Thank you for helping me, sir."*
2 **Sir,** the title of a knight: *Sir Walter Raleigh.*

sire (sir), NOUN. a title of respect formerly used to a great noble and now used to a king: *"Good morning, Sire,"* said the page to the king.

si·ren (si′rən), NOUN. a device that makes a loud, shrill, warning sound: *A police car went past, siren wailing and lights flashing.*

sis·ter (sis′tər), NOUN.
1 a daughter of the same parents. A girl is a sister to the other children of her parents.
2 a female member of the same group, club, union, or religious organization.

sis·ter·hood (sis′tər hůd), NOUN.
1 an affectionate relationship between sisters; feeling of sister for sister.

2 an association of women with a common aim, interest, or profession.

sis·ter-in-law (sis′tər in lò′), NOUN.
1 the sister of your husband or wife.
2 the wife of your brother.
❑ PLURAL **sis·ters-in-law.**

sit (sit), VERB.
1 to rest on the lower part of your body, with your knees bent and your weight off your feet: *She sat in a chair.*
2 to seat someone: *I sat the child in the chair.*
3 to be somewhere; remain: *The clock has sat on that shelf for years.*
4 to cover eggs so that they will hatch; brood: *The hen will sit until the eggs are ready to hatch.*
5 See **baby-sit.**
6 to pose: *sit for a portrait.*
❑ VERB **sits, sat, sit·ting.**

sit in or **sit in on,** IDIOM. to take part in a game, meeting, or the like: *He sat in on our class.*

sit up, IDIOM.
1 to raise the body to a sitting position: *Stop slumping and sit up on your chair.*
2 to stay in a sitting position: *The sick man was able to sit up while eating.*
3 to stay up instead of going to bed: *They sat up talking all night.*

sit·com (sit′kom), NOUN. a short form of **situation comedy.**

site (sit), NOUN. the position or place of something: *The site for the new school has been chosen.* ■ Other words that sound like this are **cite** and **sight.**

sit·ter (sit′ər), NOUN. a baby-sitter.

sit·ting (sit′ing), NOUN.
1 a meeting or session of a court of law, legislature, commission, and so on: *The hearing lasted through six sittings.*
2 the time of remaining seated: *He read five chapters at one sitting.*

sitting room. See **living room.**

sit·u·ate (sich′ü āt), VERB. to place something in a certain place: *The school is situated near the noisy road.* ❑ VERB **sit·u·ates, sit·u·at·ed, sit·u·at·ing.**

sit·u·a·tion (sich′ü ā′shən), NOUN. the condition in which someone or something is at a certain time: *It is a very disagreeable situation to be alone and without money in a strange city.*

situation comedy, a comedy, especially a weekly TV series, about the same character or group of characters in various funny situations; sitcom.

a	hat	ė	term	ô	order	ch	child		a in about
ā	age	i	it	oi	oil	ng	long		e in taken
ä	far	ī	ice	ou	out	sh	she	ə	i in pencil
â	care	o	hot	u	cup	th	thin		o in lemon
e	let	ō	open	ů	put	ᴛʜ	then		u in circus
ē	equal	ò	saw	ü	rule	zh	measure		

S

sit-up (sit′up′), NOUN. an exercise done by lying on your back and then sitting up without raising your feet: *She does 30 sit-ups every morning.*

six (siks), NOUN or ADJECTIVE. one more than five; 6. ❑ PLURAL **six·es.**

Have You Heard?

You may have heard the phrase **"Six of one and half a dozen of the other."** People say this when they want describe two things as just about equal.

six·teen (sik′stēn′), NOUN or ADJECTIVE. six more than ten; 16.

six·teenth (sik′stēnth′), ADJECTIVE or NOUN.
1 next after the 15th.
2 one of 16 equal parts.

sixth (siksth), ADJECTIVE or NOUN.
1 next after the fifth.
2 one of six equal parts.

six·ti·eth (sik′stē ith), ADJECTIVE or NOUN.
1 next after the 59th.
2 one of 60 equal parts.

six·ty (sik′stē), NOUN or ADJECTIVE. six times ten; 60. ❑ PLURAL **six·ties.**

siz·a·ble (sī′zə bəl), ADJECTIVE. fairly large: *By the time she was forty she had a sizable fortune.*

size (sīz), NOUN.
1 how big or how small something is: *The two boys are the same size.*
2 an amount, number, or quantity of something: *The city's population has grown in size.*
3 one of a set of numbers that tells how big clothes or shoes are: *His collar size is fourteen.*

size up, IDIOM. to form an opinion of someone or something: *We sized up the candidates before we voted.*
❑ VERB **siz·es, sized, siz·ing.**

siz·zle (siz′əl),
1 VERB. to make a hissing sound, like fat when it is frying or burning.
2 NOUN. a hissing sound.
❑ VERB **siz·zles, siz·zled, siz·zling.**

skate¹ (skāt),
1 NOUN. an ice skate, a roller skate, or an in-line skate.
2 VERB. to glide or roll along on skates.
❑ VERB **skates, skat·ed, skat·ing. —skat′er,** NOUN.

skate² (skāt), NOUN. a broad, flat fish with very wide fins. ❑ PLURAL **skate** or **skates.**

skate·board (skāt′bôrd′),
1 NOUN. a narrow board with roller-skate wheels attached to each end, used for gliding or moving on any hard surface.
2 VERB. to ride on a skateboard.
❑ VERB **skate·boards, skate·board·ed, skate·board·ing. —skate′board′er,** NOUN.

skel·e·ton (skel′ə tən), NOUN.
1 the framework of bones inside the body that supports the muscles and organs of any animal having a backbone.
2 a frame: *the steel skeleton of a building.*

skeleton in the closet, IDIOM. a secret source of embarrassment, grief, or shame, especially to a family: *The skeleton in their closet was that their son was in prison.*

a friendly **skeleton**

Word Story

Skeleton comes from a Greek word meaning "dried up." The Greeks used this same word to mean "a mummy" or "a skeleton."

skep·ti·cal (skep′tə kəl), ADJECTIVE. tending to doubt; questioning the truth of theories and apparent facts. **—skep′ti·cal·ly,** ADVERB.

sketch (skech),
1 NOUN. a rough, quickly done drawing, painting, or design.
2 VERB. to make a sketch of something; draw roughly.
3 NOUN. a short description, story, or play.
❑ VERB **sketch·es, sketched, sketch·ing;** PLURAL **sketch·es.**

sketch·y (skech′ē), ADJECTIVE. incomplete; done very roughly: *The first news bulletins gave only a sketchy account of the disaster.* ❑ ADJECTIVE **sketch·i·er, sketch·i·est. —sketch′i·ness,** NOUN.

skew·er (skyü′ər),
1 NOUN. a long pin of wood or metal stuck through chunks of meat and vegetables to hold them together while they are cooking.
2 VERB. to fasten with a skewer or skewers.
❑ VERB **skew·ers, skew·ered, skew·er·ing.**

ski (skē),
1 NOUN. one of a pair of long, flat, narrow pieces of hard wood, plastic, or metal, that is fastened to shoes or boots so that you can glide over snow.
2 NOUN. a similar device used to glide over water; water ski.
3 VERB. to glide over snow or water on skis.
❑ PLURAL **skis;** VERB **skis, skied, ski·ing. —ski′er,** NOUN.

skid (skid),
1 VERB. to slip or slide to one side while moving: *The car skidded on the slippery road.*
2 NOUN. a sideways slip or slide to one side: *The car went into a skid on the icy road.*
❑ VERB **skids, skid·ded, skid·ding.**

skies (skīz), NOUN. the plural of **sky:** *cloudy skies.*

skill (skil), NOUN.
1 an ability to do something well, especially an ability you get from practice or knowledge: *It takes great skill to tune a piano.*
2 an art or craft: *Weaving and drawing are skills.*

skilled (skild), ADJECTIVE.
1 having skill; trained; experienced: *a skilled worker.*
2 showing or requiring skill: *Welding is skilled labor.*

skil·let (skil′it), NOUN. a shallow pan with a handle, used for frying.

skill·ful (skil′fəl), ADJECTIVE.
1 having skill; expert: *a skillful surgeon.*
2 showing skill: *That is a skillful piece of work.*
—skill′ful·ly, ADVERB. **—skill′ful·ness,** NOUN.

skim (skim), VERB.
1 to remove something from the top of a liquid: *The cook skims the fat from the soup.*
2 to move or cause to move lightly over something: *Dragonflies skimmed over the water.*
3 to read something hastily: *I didn't read it carefully; I just skimmed the book.*
❑ VERB **skims, skimmed, skim·ming.**

skim milk or **skimmed milk,** milk from which the cream has been removed.

skimp·y (skim′pē), ADJECTIVE. too small; not enough: *a skimpy lunch.* ■ See the Synonym Study at **little.**
❑ ADJECTIVE **skimp·i·er, skimp·i·est.**

skin (skin),
1 NOUN. the outer covering of human and animal bodies, plants, fruits, and seeds: *Their skin was tanned from being in the sun. Peach skins are fuzzy.*
2 NOUN. an animal skin that leather is made from.
3 VERB. to hurt yourself by scratching or tearing some of your skin: *She fell and skinned her knee.*
❑ VERB **skins, skinned, skin·ning. —skin′like′,** ADJECTIVE.

by the skin of your teeth, IDIOM. very narrowly; barely: *She escaped by the skin of her teeth.*

skin·ny (skin′ē), ADJECTIVE. very thin; too thin: *a skinny kid.* ■ See the Synonym Study at **thin.**
❑ ADJECTIVE **skin·ni·er, skin·ni·est.**

skip (skip), VERB.
1 to hop first on one foot and then the other foot: *The children skipped merrily down the street.* ■ See the Synonym Study at **jump.**
2 to jump quickly over something: *They skipped rope.*
3 to pass over or not do something: *Skip any questions you can't answer.*
4 to send or go bounding along a surface; skim: *I like to skip stones on the lake.*
❑ VERB **skips, skipped, skip·ping.**

skip·per (skip′ər), NOUN. the captain of a ship.

skirt (skėrt),
1 NOUN. a piece of women's clothing that hangs from the waist.
2 NOUN. the part of a dress that hangs from the waist.

3 VERB. to pass along the border or edge of a place: *The new highway skirts the city.*
❑ VERB **skirts, skirt·ed, skirt·ing.**

skit (skit), NOUN. a short play that is often humorous.

skull (skul), NOUN. the bony framework of the head and face in human beings and other animals with backbones. The skull encloses and protects the brain. ■ Another word that sounds like this is **scull.**

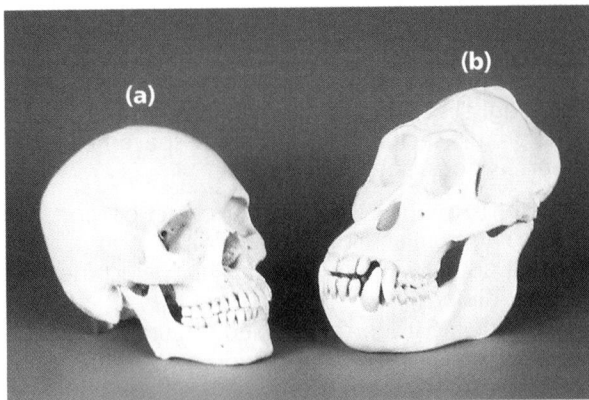

skulls of a human (a) and of an orangutan (b)

skunk (skungk), NOUN.
1 an animal of North America about the size of a cat, with black and white stripes along the back and a bushy tail. Skunks spray out a strong, stinking liquid when they are frightened or attacked.
2 (informal) a mean, unpleasant person.

Did You Know?

The **skunk** is one of the few woodland animals that doesn't blend into its surroundings. The skunk's dramatic black and white coloring scares enemies so much that a skunk rarely has to spray.

skunk — between 20 and 34 inches long, including the tail

a hat	ė term	ô order	ch child	ə { a in about
ā age	i it	oi oil	ng long	e in taken
ä far	ī ice	ou out	sh she	i in pencil
â care	o hot	u cup	th thin	o in lemon
e let	ō open	ů put	ŦH then	u in circus
ē equal	ò saw	ü rule	zh measure	

S

sky (skī), NOUN. the space overhead that seems to cover the earth; the area where clouds form: *a blue sky, a cloudy sky.* ❏ PLURAL **skies.**

Did You Know?

Why is the **sky** blue? Sunlight interacting with the atmosphere makes the sky look blue. The sun's light is made up of light waves of many different wavelengths. Each wavelength is seen as a different color. The blue wavelengths bounce off the particles in the atmosphere more than the other colors do. More of the blue light is scattered and becomes visible. Astronauts see blackness in outer space because there is no atmosphere.

sky·div·ing (skī'dī'ving), NOUN. the act or sport of jumping from an airplane and dropping for a great distance before opening your parachute. —**sky'div'er,** NOUN.

sky·lark (skī'lärk'), NOUN. a kind of European lark.

sky·light (skī'līt'), NOUN. a window in a roof or ceiling.

sky·line (skī'līn'), NOUN.
1 the line where earth and sky seem to meet; horizon.
2 the outline of buildings, mountains, or trees, as seen against the sky: *the New York skyline.*

sky·rock·et (skī'rok'it),
1 NOUN. a kind of firework that goes up high in the air and explodes in a shower of stars and sparks.
2 VERB. to rise suddenly: *The price of honey has skyrocketed.*
❏ VERB **sky·rock·ets, sky·rock·et·ed, sky·rock·et·ing.**

sky·scrap·er (skī'skrā'pər), NOUN. a very tall building.

slab (slab), NOUN. a broad, flat, thick piece of stone, wood, meat, or anything else that is solid: *This sidewalk is made of slabs of concrete.*

slack (slak), ADJECTIVE. not tight or firm; loose: *She tightened the slack rope.*

slacks (slaks), NOUN PLURAL. long pants worn especially for relaxing.

slain (slān), VERB. the past participle of **slay:** *Bears have slain a few sheep.*

slam (slam),
1 VERB. to shut or close something with great force and noise: *She slammed the door shut.*
2 VERB. to throw or hit something with great force: *That car slammed into a truck.*
3 NOUN. the act or sound of slamming: *The door blew shut with a slam.*
❏ VERB **slams, slammed, slam·ming.**

slam-dunk (slam'dungk'), VERB or NOUN. See **dunk** (definition 2). ❏ VERB **slam-dunks, slam-dunked, slam-dunk·ing.**

slan·der (slan'dər),
1 NOUN. a false statement meant to harm someone's reputation: *The candidate for mayor accused his opponent of slander.*
2 VERB. to talk falsely about someone.
❏ VERB **slan·ders, slan·dered, slan·der·ing.** —**slan'der·er,** NOUN.

slang (slang), NOUN. words, phrases, or meanings not used when speaking or writing formal English. Slang is often very lively and expressive and is used in talk between friends, but it is not usually proper in school writing. Slang is mostly made up of new words or meanings that are popular for only a short time.

slant (slant),
1 VERB. to be higher at one end than at the other; lean to one side or the other; slope: *Most handwriting slants to the right.*
2 NOUN. a sloping direction, position, or movement: *The roof has a sharp slant.*
❏ VERB **slants, slant·ed, slant·ing.**

slap (slap),
1 NOUN. a blow with the open hand or with something flat.
2 VERB. to strike something with the open hand or with something flat: *He slapped the fly with a folded newspaper.*
3 VERB. to put or throw something with force: *She slapped the book down on the table.*
❏ VERB **slaps, slapped, slap·ping.** —**slap'per,** NOUN.

slap shot, (in hockey) a fast shot made with a swinging stroke of the stick at the puck.

slash (slash),
1 VERB. to cut something with a sweeping blow of a sword, knife, or whip: *She slashed the vines and tall weeds to clear a path.*
2 NOUN. a cutting stroke: *the slash of a sword.*
3 NOUN. a cut or wound made by a stroke like this; gash: *When the screwdriver slipped, it made a deep slash on his thumb.*
4 VERB. to reduce a great deal: *Salaries were slashed when business became bad.*
5 NOUN. a great reduction: *a slash in prices.*
❏ VERB **slash·es, slashed, slash·ing;** PLURAL **slash·es.** —**slash'er,** NOUN.

slat (slat), NOUN. a long, thin, narrow piece of wood, metal, or plastic: *the slats of a Venetian blind.*

slate (slāt), NOUN. a bluish gray rock that splits easily into thin, smooth layers. Slate is used to cover roofs and for blackboards. —**slate'like',** ADJECTIVE.

slaugh·ter (slö'tər),
1 NOUN. the act of killing an animal or animals for food: *the slaughter of a steer.*
2 NOUN. the act of cruelly killing a great number of people: *The battle resulted in a frightful slaughter of men and horses.*

3 *VERB.* to kill an animal or animals for food; butcher: *Cattle and sheep are slaughtered.*
4 *VERB.* to kill brutally or cruelly.
❑ *VERB* **slaugh·ters, slaugh·tered, slaugh·ter·ing.**

slave (slāv),
1 *NOUN.* someone who is owned by another person.
2 *NOUN.* someone who is controlled or ruled by a desire, habit, or influence: *a slave of drink, a slave to your emotions.*
3 *VERB.* to work very hard: *We slaved all day cooking.*
❑ *VERB* **slaves, slaved, slav·ing.**

slav·er·y (slā′vər ē), *NOUN.*
1 the condition of being owned and having to work for someone else.
2 the custom of owning people and making them work.
3 hard work like that of a slave.

slay (slā), *VERB.* to kill someone or something violently: *Jack slew the giant.* ❑ *VERB* **slays, slew, slain, slay·ing.** ■ Another word that sounds like this is **sleigh.**

sled (sled),
1 *NOUN.* a framework on runners used for sliding on snow or ice. Sleds pulled by dogs are often used in the Arctic.
2 *VERB.* to ride or coast on a sled.
❑ *VERB* **sleds, sled·ded, sled·ding.**

having fun in **sleds**

sledge·ham·mer (slej′ham′ər), *NOUN.* a large, heavy hammer, usually swung with both hands.

sleek (slēk), *ADJECTIVE.*
1 soft and shiny; smooth: *sleek hair.*
2 having smooth, soft skin, hair, or fur: *a sleek cat.*
—sleek′ness, *NOUN.*

sleep (slēp),
1 *VERB.* to rest your body and mind in a state without thought or awareness: *We sleep at night.*
2 *NOUN.* a resting condition of your body and mind that happens naturally and regularly: *Many people need eight hours of sleep a night.*
❑ *VERB* **sleeps, slept, sleep·ing. —sleep′like′,** *ADJECTIVE.*

sleep in, *IDIOM.* to sleep later than usual, on purpose: *It was Saturday, so I could sleep in.*

sleep over, *IDIOM.* (informal) to stay the night at someone else's home: *She was allowed to sleep over after the party.*

sleeping bag, a long, warmly lined or padded cloth bag, used for sleep when camping.

sleep·less (slēp′lis), *ADJECTIVE.* without sleep; restless: *a sleepless night in hot weather.*
—sleep′less·ness, *NOUN.*

sleep·ov·er (slēp′ō vər), *NOUN.* a party where the guests spend the night at the home of the person giving the party.

sleep·y (slē′pē), *ADJECTIVE.*
1 ready to go to sleep: *He never gets enough rest and is always sleepy.* ■ See the Synonym Study at **tired.**
2 quiet; not active: *There was very little to do in the sleepy little mountain town.*
❑ *ADJECTIVE* **sleep·i·er, sleep·i·est. —sleep′i·ly,** *ADVERB.* **—sleep′i·ness,** *NOUN.*

sleet (slēt),
1 *NOUN.* partly frozen rain. Sleet forms when rain falls through a layer of cold air.
2 *VERB.* to come down as sleet: *It sleeted; then it snowed; then it rained.*
❑ *VERB* **sleets, sleet·ed, sleet·ing.**

sleeve (slēv), *NOUN.* the part of an article of clothing that covers your arm. **—sleeve′less,** *ADJECTIVE.*

sleigh (slā), *NOUN.* a large cart on runners for use on snow or ice. ■ Another word that sounds like this is **slay.**

slen·der (slen′dər), *ADJECTIVE.*
1 long and thin; slim: *He was a slender child.* ■ See the Synonym Study at **thin.**
2 too small: *I had a slender income.*
❑ *ADJECTIVE* **slen·der·er, slen·der·est. —slen′der·ness,** *NOUN.*

slept (slept), *VERB.*
1 the past tense of **sleep:** *The child slept soundly.*
2 the past participle of **sleep:** *I slept well last night.*

slew (slü), *VERB.* the past tense of **slay:** *Jack slew the giant.*

slice (slīs),
1 *NOUN.* a thin, flat piece cut from something: *a slice of bread, a slice of cake.*
2 *VERB.* to cut something into thin, flat slices: *Slice the bread.* ■ See the Synonym Study at **cut.**
3 *VERB.* to cut through or across: *He sliced the apple in two.*
❑ *VERB* **slic·es, sliced, slic·ing. —slic′er,** *NOUN.*

a	hat	ė	term	ô	order	ch	child	⎧a in about
ā	age	i	it	oi	oil	ng	long	⎪e in taken
ä	far	ī	ice	ou	out	sh	she	ə⎨i in pencil
â	care	o	hot	u	cup	th	thin	⎪o in lemon
e	let	ō	open	ù	put	ᴛʜ	then	⎩u in circus
ē	equal	ò	saw	ü	rule	zh	measure	

slick (slik),
1 *ADJECTIVE.* sleek; smooth: *slick hair.* ■ See the Synonym Study at **smooth.**
2 *VERB.* to make something sleek or smooth.
3 *ADJECTIVE.* slippery; greasy: *a road slick with ice.*
4 *NOUN.* a smooth place or spot. Oil makes a slick on the surface of water.
❏ *VERB* **slicks, slicked, slick·ing.**

slid (slid), *VERB.*
1 the past tense of **slide:** *Mud slid down the hill.*
2 the past participle of **slide:** *The runner has slid into third base.*

slide (slid),
1 *VERB.* to move or cause to move smoothly along or over a surface: *The bureau drawers slide in and out.*
2 *VERB.* to move or cause to move quietly or secretly: *I slid behind the curtain.*
3 *NOUN.* the act of sliding: *The children each take a slide in turn.*
4 *NOUN.* a smooth metal or plastic surface for sliding on: *a playground slide, a water slide.*

a water **slide**

5 *NOUN.* a mass of snow and ice or dirt and rocks that has come down from someplace higher up: *The slide cut off the valley from the rest of the world.*
6 *NOUN.* a small, thin sheet of glass or plastic. Objects are put on slides for viewing under a microscope. Slides of photographic film are put in a projector and shown on a screen.
❏ *VERB* **slides, slid, slid·ing.**

slight (slit),
1 *ADJECTIVE.* not serious; not important: *I have a slight headache.*
2 *ADJECTIVE.* not very big around; slender: *a slight child.*
3 *VERB.* to pay too little attention to someone; neglect: *I felt slighted because I was not asked to the party.*
❏ *VERB* **slights, slight·ed, slight·ing.**

slight·ly (slit′lē), *ADVERB.* somewhat; a little: *I knew him slightly.*

slim (slim), *ADJECTIVE.*
1 not fat; slender; thin: *He was very slim, being 6 feet tall and weighing only 160 pounds.* ■ See the Synonym Study at **thin.**
2 small; slight; weak: *We had a slim lead at halftime.*
❏ *ADJECTIVE* **slim·mer, slim·mest. –slim′ness,** *NOUN.*

slim down, *IDIOM.* to make or become slim or slender: *He slimmed down by diet and exercise.*
❏ *VERB* **slims, slimmed, slim·ming.**

slime (slim), *NOUN.* a sticky substance given off by certain animals, such as snails, slugs, and fish. Slime forms a protective coating on these animals.

slim·y (slī′mē), *ADJECTIVE.* covered with slime: *The pond is too slimy to swim in.* ❏ *ADJECTIVE* **slim·i·er, slim·i·est. –slim′i·ness,** *NOUN.*

sling (sling),
1 *NOUN.* a strip of leather or cloth with a string at each end, used for throwing stones.
2 *VERB.* to throw a stone with a sling.
3 *VERB.* to throw; cast; hurl: *I slung the camping equipment into the car trunk.*
4 *NOUN.* a loop of cloth worn around the neck to hold up an injured arm.
5 *VERB.* to hang in a sling and swing loosely: *The bag was slung over her shoulder.*
❏ *VERB* **slings, slung, sling·ing.**

sling·shot (sling′shot′), *NOUN.* a Y-shaped stick with a rubber band fastened to its prongs, used to shoot pebbles.

slink (slingk), *VERB.* to move in a secret, guilty manner; sneak: *After stealing the meat, the dog slunk away.* ❏ *VERB* **slinks, slunk, slink·ing.**

slip¹ (slip),
1 *VERB.* to move or cause to move smoothly, quietly, easily, or quickly: *She slipped out of the room. I slipped the bolt into place and locked the door.*
2 *VERB.* to move out of someone's control: *The knife slipped and cut his finger.*
3 *VERB.* to slide suddenly and lose your balance: *He slipped and fell on the icy sidewalk.*
4 *NOUN.* the act of slipping: *My broken leg was caused by a slip on a banana peel.*
5 *VERB.* to put on or take something off easily or quickly: *Slip off your shoes.*
6 *NOUN.* a sleeveless piece of clothing worn under a dress.
7 *VERB.* to make a mistake or error: *I slipped and mailed the wrong letter.*
8 *NOUN.* a mistake; error: *He makes slips in pronouncing words.* ■ See the Synonym Study at **mistake.**
❏ *VERB* **slips, slipped, slip·ping.**

slip up, *IDIOM.* to make a mistake or error: *I slipped up on that problem and got the answer all wrong.*

slip² (slip), *NOUN.* a narrow strip of paper, wood, or other material.

slip·per (slip′ər), *NOUN.* a light, low shoe worn around the house: *a pair of bedroom slippers.*

slip·per·y (slip′ər ē), *ADJECTIVE.* causing or likely to cause slipping: *A wet street is slippery. The steps are slippery with ice.* ■ See the Synonym Study at **smooth.** ❏ *ADJECTIVE* **slip·per·i·er, slip·per·i·est.**

slit (slit),
1 *VERB.* to make a long, straight cut or tear in something: *Slit the wrapper and open the box.*

2 *NOUN.* a straight, narrow cut or tear in something: *a slit in a bag, the slit in a mailbox.*
❏ *VERB* **slits, slit, slit·ting.**

sloth — between 20 and 27 inches long

slith·er (sliŧн′ər), *VERB.* to go with a slipping, sliding motion: *The snake slithered into the weeds.* ❏ *VERB* **slith·ers, slith·ered, slith·er·ing.**

sliv·er (sliv′ər), *NOUN.* a long, thin piece that has been split off, broken off, or cut off something else; splinter.

slob (slob), *NOUN.* a dirty, untidy, or clumsy person.

slob·ber (slob′ər),
1 *VERB.* to let saliva or liquid food run out of the mouth; drool: *The dog slobbered all over my pants.*
2 *NOUN.* saliva or liquid food running out of the mouth.
❏ *VERB* **slob·bers, slob·bered, slob·ber·ing.**

slo·gan (slō′gən), *NOUN.* a word or phrase used by a business, political party, or any group to advertise its purpose; motto: *"Service with a smile" was the store's slogan.*

slop (slop),
1 *VERB.* to spill liquid on something; spill; splash: *He slopped water on the floor.*
2 *NOUN.* a liquid carelessly spilled or splashed about.
3 *NOUN.* a thin, liquid mud or slush.
❏ *VERB* **slops, slopped, slop·ping.**

slope (slōp),
1 *VERB.* to lie at an angle rather than flat; slant: *The land slopes toward the sea.*
2 *NOUN.* any line, surface, or land that lies at an angle rather than flat. If you roll a ball up a slope, it will roll down again.
3 *NOUN.* the amount of slant: *The floor of the theater has a slope of 4 feet from the back to the front.*
❏ *VERB* **slopes, sloped, slop·ing.**

slop·py (slop′ē), *ADJECTIVE.*
1 untidy; not neat: *She has a very sloppy desk.*
2 careless: *I hate to do sloppy work.*
3 very wet: *We had some very sloppy weather.*
❏ *ADJECTIVE* **slop·pi·er, slop·pi·est. −slop′pi·ness,** *NOUN.*

slop·py joe (slop′ē jō′), half of a hamburger bun covered with a mixture of ground beef and tomato sauce or chili sauce. ❏ *PLURAL* **sloppy joes.**

slosh (slosh), *VERB.* to splash in slush, mud, or water: *The children sloshed through the puddles.* ❏ *VERB* **slosh·es, sloshed, slosh·ing.**

slot (slot), *NOUN.* a small, narrow opening: *I put the letter in the slot that said "out-of-town mail."*

sloth (slȯth *or* slōth), *NOUN.* a very slow-moving animal of South and Central America that hangs upside down from tree branches.

Word Story

Sloth comes from **slow,** as **warmth** comes from **warm.** In old English, **sloth** had the meaning "slowness." It stopped being used that way, probably because it also had the meaning "laziness," and it was easy to confuse the two ideas.

slouch (slouch),
1 *VERB.* to stand, sit, walk, or move in an awkward, bent over manner: *She slouched in her chair.*
2 *NOUN.* the act of bending your head and shoulders forward.
❏ *VERB* **slouch·es, slouched, slouch·ing;** *PLURAL* **slouch·es.**

Slo·va·ki·a (slō vä′kē ə), *NOUN.* a country in eastern Europe. **−Slo·va′ki·an,** *ADJECTIVE or NOUN.*

Slo·ve·ni·a (slō vē′nē ə), *NOUN.* a country in southern Europe. **−Slo·ve′ni·an,** *ADJECTIVE or NOUN.*

slow (slō),
1 *ADJECTIVE.* taking a long time; not fast or quick: *The traffic was very heavy, so it was a slow trip.*
2 *ADJECTIVE.* moving with less speed than others: *The slow runners couldn't keep up.*
3 *ADJECTIVE.* showing time that is earlier than the correct time: *The clock was slow and I was late for school.*
4 *VERB.* to make or become slower: *Cars should slow when they pass a school.*
5 *ADVERB.* in a slow manner or way; slowly: *Go slow!*
6 *ADJECTIVE.* not quick to understand: *a slow learner.*
❏ *VERB* **slows, slowed, slow·ing. −slow′ly,** *ADVERB.* **−slow′ness,** *NOUN.*

sludge (sluj), *NOUN.* a soft, thick, muddy or oily mixture.

slug¹ (slug), *NOUN.*
1 a slow-moving animal like a snail, without a shell or with only a partially developed shell. Slugs live mostly in forests, gardens, and damp places, and feed on plants.
2 a bullet.
3 a round, metal piece or counterfeit coin illegally put into a machine instead of a genuine coin.

slug² (slug),
1 *VERB.* to hit something or someone very hard.
2 *NOUN.* a hard blow with your fist.
❏ *VERB* **slugs, slugged, slug·ging.**

a	hat	ė	term	ô	order	ch	child	(a in about
ā	age	i	it	oi	oil	ng	long	e in taken
ä	far	ī	ice	ou	out	sh	she	ə { i in pencil
â	care	o	hot	u	cup	th	thin	o in lemon
e	let	ō	open	ù	put	ŧн	then	(u in circus
ē	equal	ȯ	saw	ü	rule	zh	measure	

S

slug·gish (slug′ish), *ADJECTIVE.* slow-moving; not active: *When I stay up late, I am sluggish the next day.* —**slug′gish·ly**, *ADVERB.* —**slug′gish·ness**, *NOUN.*

slum (slum), *NOUN.* a run-down, crowded part of a city or town. Poverty and unhealthy living conditions are common in slums.

slum·ber (slum′bər),
1 *VERB.* to sleep lightly; doze: *The baby slumbers away the hours.*
2 *NOUN.* a light sleep: *I awoke from my slumber.*
❑ *VERB* **slum·bers, slum·bered, slum·ber·ing.**

slump (slump),
1 *VERB.* to drop or fall heavily: *I slumped into the chair.*
2 *NOUN.* a sudden fall: *There was a slump in prices.*
3 *VERB.* to slouch: *He slumped down the path.*
4 *NOUN.* a period when things are not going well: *The team was in a slump last month.*
❑ *VERB* **slumps, slumped, slump·ing.**

slung (slung), *VERB.*
1 the past tense of **sling:** *They slung some stones and ran away.*
2 the past participle of **sling:** *She has slung her bag over her shoulder.*

slunk (slungk), *VERB.*
1 the past tense of **slink:** *The dog slunk away ashamed.*
2 the past participle of **slink:** *Has that dog slunk away again?*

slurp (slėrp),
1 *VERB.* to eat or drink something with a noisy, gurgling sound.
2 *NOUN.* a noisy, gurgling sound.
❑ *VERB* **slurps, slurped, slurp·ing.**

slush (slush), *NOUN.* partly melted snow; snow and water mixed together.

sly (slī),
1 *ADJECTIVE.* very clever at doing things without people knowing about it; tricky: *He was very sly in pretending to be friendly.*
2 *ADJECTIVE.* playful or teasing: *Waiting for the surprise party to begin, the children exchanged many sly looks and smiles.*
❑ *ADJECTIVE* **sly·er, sly·est** or **sli·er, sli·est.** —**sly′ly**, *ADVERB.* —**sly′ness**, *NOUN.*
on the sly, *IDIOM.* in secret: *The teacher caught me reading a comic book on the sly.*

smack (smak),
1 *VERB.* to hit something or someone with the open hand; slap: *She smacked the horse on its rump.*
2 *ADVERB.* directly: *He rode the bicycle smack into the hedge.*
3 *VERB.* to make a sharp sound by opening the lips quickly: *He smacked his lips at the thought of cake and ice cream.*
4 *NOUN.* the sharp sound made in this way.
❑ *VERB* **smacks, smacked, smack·ing.**

small (smȯl),
1 *ADJECTIVE.* not large in size, amount, or number; little: *A cottage is a small house.* ■ See the Synonym Study at **little.**
2 *ADJECTIVE.* not very old; young: *Several small children were playing in the yard.*
3 *ADJECTIVE.* not important: *This is only a small matter now, but we should study it further.*

small intestine, the long, winding tube between the stomach and the large intestine. The small intestine receives partly digested food from the stomach, continues the process of digesting the food, and passes the useful parts of it into the blood.

small letter, an ordinary letter, not a capital.

small·pox (smȯl′poks′), *NOUN.* a dangerous disease that causes fever and a rash of blisters on the skin. The rash often leaves permanent scars. Because a vaccine was discovered, no cases of smallpox have been reported since the late 1970s.

smart (smärt),
1 *ADJECTIVE.* having a good mind; clever; bright: *a smart student.*
2 *VERB.* to feel or cause sharp pain: *The wind made her eyes smart.*
3 *VERB.* to feel upset: *She smarted from the unfair criticism.*
4 *ADJECTIVE.* fast; active; lively: *They walked at a smart pace.*
5 *ADJECTIVE.* fresh and neat in style; in good order: *The pilot was wearing a smart uniform.*
❑ *VERB* **smarts, smart·ed, smart·ing.**

Synonym Study

Smart means able to learn easily and solve problems quickly: *The smart puppy figured out how to open the gate.*

Intelligent means able to think clearly and make good decisions: *Your decision to get your work done early so you'll have time left to play shows that you are intelligent.*

Alert can mean very quick to understand and to respond: *The alert bus driver slowed down right away when she saw ice on the road ahead.*

Clever means quick to think of good ideas: *The clever boy had a plan for the Native American Day program.*

Bright can mean smart in an active way: *He is bright, so he enjoys puzzles and riddles.*

Brilliant can mean having extreme intelligence or ability: *My aunt is a brilliant surgeon; she was asked to operate on the President's daughter.*

smash (smash),
1 *VERB*. to break or be broken into pieces with violence and noise: *He smashed the window with a stone. The dish smashed when I dropped it.*
  ■ See the Synonym Study at **break.**
2 *VERB*. to hit something hard; crash: *The car smashed into the tree.*
3 *NOUN*. the sound of a smash or crash: *The smash of broken glass makes Grandmother very nervous.*
  ❑ *VERB* **smash·es, smashed, smash·ing;** *PLURAL* **smash·es.**

smear (smir),
1 *VERB*. to cover or stain something with anything sticky, greasy, or dirty: *He was smeared with mud.*
2 *VERB*. to rub or spread with butter, oil, and so on: *He smeared oil into the palm of his new baseball glove.*
3 *NOUN*. a mark or stain left by smearing: *There are smears of paint on the wallpaper.*
  ❑ *VERB* **smears, smeared, smear·ing.**

smell (smel),
1 *VERB*. to recognize the odor of something by breathing in through your nose: *Can you smell the smoke?*
2 *NOUN*. something that you breathe in and recognize; odor: *The smell of roses is sweet.*
3 *VERB*. to have a smell: *The garden smelled of roses.*
4 *VERB*. to have a bad smell: *That dirty, wet dog smells; take him outside.*
5 *NOUN*. the sense of smelling: *Smell is keener in dogs than in people.*
  ❑ *VERB* **smells, smelled, smell·ing.**

smell·y (smel′ē), *ADJECTIVE*. having a strong or unpleasant smell: *Rotten fish are smelly.* ❑ *ADJECTIVE* **smell·i·er, smell·i·est.**

smelt[1] (smelt), *VERB*. to melt ore in order to get the metal out of it. ❑ *VERB* **smelts, smelt·ed, smelt·ing.**

smelt[2] (smelt), *NOUN*. a small food fish with silvery scales. ❑ *PLURAL* **smelts** or **smelt.**

smelt[2] — up to 8 inches long

smile (smīl),
1 *VERB*. to look happy or amused by turning up the corners of your mouth: *The baby smiled when she saw her mother.*
2 *NOUN*. the act of smiling: *She gave a friendly smile as she came in.*
  ❑ *VERB* **smiles, smiled, smil·ing. –smil′er,** *NOUN*.

smirk (smėrk),
1 *VERB*. to smile in a silly or self-satisfied way.
2 *NOUN*. a silly or self-satisfied smile.
  ❑ *VERB* **smirks, smirked, smirk·ing.**

smith·e·reens (smiтн′ə rēnz′), *NOUN PLURAL*. bits; small pieces: *The glass was smashed to smithereens.*

smock (smok), *NOUN*. a loose outer shirt worn to protect your clothing.

smog (smog), *NOUN*. a brownish haze of pollution, produced by sunlight acting on the exhaust gases from burning gasoline and similar substances: *Exhaust fumes are a major cause of smog.*

smog·gy (smog′ē), *ADJECTIVE*. full of smog: *She breathed in the smoggy air and began to cough.* ❑ *ADJECTIVE* **smog·gi·er, smog·gi·est.**

Smog can cover a whole city.

smoke (smōk),
1 *NOUN*. a mixture of gases and carbon that can be seen rising in a cloud from anything that is very hot or burning.
2 *VERB*. to give off smoke or steam: *The fireplace smokes badly.*
3 *VERB*. to inhale smoke from a pipe, cigar, or cigarette for pleasure or relaxation.
4 *VERB*. to preserve and flavor meat or fish by treating it with smoke.
  ❑ *VERB* **smokes, smoked, smok·ing. –smoke′like′,** *ADJECTIVE*. **–smo′ker,** *NOUN*.

Have You Heard?

You may have heard someone say **"Where there's smoke there's fire"** or **"There's no smoke without fire."** People use these phrases when they want to say that there must be some truth to a rumor, or else no one would be talking about it.

smoke alarm. See smoke detector.

a	hat	ė	term	ô	order	ch	child	(a in about
ā	age	i	it	oi	oil	ng	long	e in taken
ä	far	ī	ice	ou	out	sh	she	ə { i in pencil
â	care	o	hot	u	cup	th	thin	o in lemon
e	let	ō	open	ů	put	тн	then	(u in circus
ē	equal	ò	saw	ü	rule	zh	measure	

S

smoke detector, an electronic device that detects the presence of smoke and sounds an alarm; smoke alarm.

smoke·stack (smōk′stak′), NOUN. a tall chimney above a factory or a large ship.

smok·y (smō′kē), ADJECTIVE.
1 giving off a lot of smoke: *The smoky campfire made us cough.*
2 full of smoke: *a smoky kitchen.*
3 like smoke: *a smoky taste.*
    ❑ ADJECTIVE **smok·i·er, smok·i·est.**

smol·der (smōl′dər), VERB. to burn and smoke without any flame: *The campfire smoldered for hours after the flames died down.* ❑ VERB **smol·ders, smol·dered, smol·der·ing.**

smooth (smüŦH),
1 ADJECTIVE. having an even surface without any bumps, like glass or still water; flat; level: *The table was made of smooth, polished walnut.*
2 ADJECTIVE. free from problems or difficulty: *The mayor praised the smooth handling of the problem by the police.*
3 ADJECTIVE. without lumps: *smooth gravy.*
4 VERB. to make something smooth, flat, even, or level: *I smoothed out the ball of paper and read it.*
5 VERB. to make something easy: *Her willingness to compromise smoothed the way to an agreement.*
6 ADJECTIVE. graceful and polite; elegant: *That salesperson has a smooth manner.*
    ❑ VERB **smooths, smoothed, smooth·ing.**
    —**smooth′ly,** ADVERB.

Synonym Study

Smooth means having a surface with no roughness or uneven spaces: *Is his baseball the new, smooth one?*

Silky means smooth and shiny like silk: *This shampoo promises to make your hair as silky as a baby's.*

Slippery means so smooth that it causes slipping: *When she saw that the floor had just been washed, she knew it would be slippery.*

Slick means smooth. It can also mean slippery: *My father drove slowly because the rain had made the roads slick.*

ANTONYMS: bumpy, rough, uneven.

smoth·er (smüŦH′ər), VERB.
1 to kill someone by keeping air from him or her: *The gas almost smothered the coal miners but they got out in time.*
2 to be unable to breathe freely; suffocate: *We are smothering in this stuffy room.*
3 to cover thickly: *In the fall the grass is smothered with leaves.*

4 to put something out by covering it up completely: *Smother the fire with sand before you leave.*
    ❑ VERB **smoth·ers, smoth·ered, smoth·er·ing.**

smudge (smuj),
1 NOUN. a dirty mark; smear.
2 VERB. to mark something with dirty streaks; smear: *The child smudged her drawing accidentally.*
    ❑ VERB **smudg·es, smudged, smudg·ing.**

smug (smug), ADJECTIVE. too pleased with your own goodness, cleverness, or accomplishments: *Nothing disturbs the smug beliefs of some people.*
    ❑ ADJECTIVE **smug·ger, smug·gest.** —**smug′ly,** ADVERB. —**smug′ness,** NOUN.

smug·gle (smug′əl), VERB.
1 to bring something into or take something out of a country secretly and against the law: *It is a crime to smuggle goods into the United States.*
2 to bring or take something in a secret or hidden way: *I tried to smuggle my puppy into the house.*
    ❑ VERB **smug·gles, smug·gled, smug·gling.** —**smug′gler,** NOUN.

snack (snak),
1 NOUN. a small amount of food eaten between meals: *She had a snack after school.*
2 VERB. to eat a small amount of something between meals: *He snacked on raisins while he watched television.* ■ See the Synonym Study at **eat.**
    ❑ VERB **snacks, snacked, snack·ing.**

snag (snag),
1 NOUN. any sharp or rough point that sticks out, such as a thorn.
2 VERB. to catch on a snag: *I snagged my sweater on a nail.*
3 NOUN. a hidden or unexpected problem: *Our plans hit a snag, and we had to change them.*
    ❑ VERB **snags, snagged, snag·ging.**

snail (snāl), NOUN.
1 a small, slow-moving animal with a soft body. Most snails have shells on their backs into which they can pull back for protection.
2 a lazy, slow-moving person.
    —**snail′like′,** ADJECTIVE.

There are more than 80,000 different kinds of **snails.**

snake (snāk),

1 NOUN. a long, slender, crawling reptile with a dry, scaly skin and no legs. Some snakes are poisonous.
2 NOUN. a sly, treacherous person.
3 VERB. to move, wind, or curve like a snake: *The narrow road snaked through the mountains.*
❑ VERB **snakes, snaked, snak·ing. –snake′like′,** ADJECTIVE.

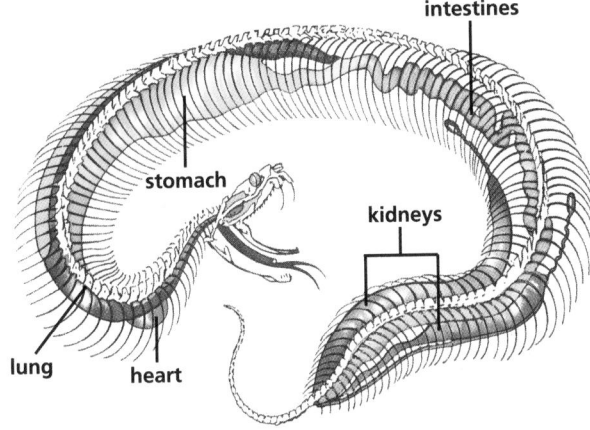

the anatomy of a **snake**

(labels: intestines, stomach, kidneys, lung, heart)

snap (snap),

1 VERB. to break suddenly or sharply: *The violin string snapped because it was fastened too tight.*
2 NOUN. the act of breaking suddenly or the sound of breaking: *A quick snap broke the pencil.*
3 VERB. to make or cause to make a sudden, sharp sound: *The dancer snapped his fingers in time to the music.*
4 NOUN. a quick, sharp sound: *The box shut with a snap.*
5 VERB. to make a sudden, quick bite or snatch at something: *The turtle snapped at the child's hand. The dog snapped up the meat.*
6 VERB. to grab something suddenly: *We snapped up several bargains at the sale.*
7 VERB. to speak quickly and sharply: *"Silence!" snapped the captain.*
8 VERB. to move quickly and sharply: *The soldiers snapped to attention. You better snap it up or you'll never get the job done.*
9 ADJECTIVE. made or done suddenly: *A snap decision is likely to be wrong.*
10 NOUN. something that fastens two things together; fastener: *One of the snaps of your dress is unfastened.*
11 NOUN. a thin, crisp cookie: *We ate a few lemon snaps after school.*
12 NOUN. (informal) an easy job or piece of work: *Building the model was a snap.*
13 in football: **a** VERB. to pass back the ball to begin a play. The center snaps the ball to an offensive back, usually the quarterback. **b** NOUN. a pass from the center to an offensive back, usually the quarterback.
❑ VERB **snaps, snapped, snap·ping.**

snap out of it, IDIOM. to change your attitude or habit suddenly: *He was in a bad mood, but then he snapped out of it and started to laugh.*

snap·drag·on (snap′drag′ən), NOUN. a garden plant with spikes of showy flowers of various colors.

snapping turtle, a large American freshwater turtle that has powerful jaws with which it snaps at its prey.

snap·shot (snap′shot′), NOUN. a photograph taken quickly with a small camera.

snare (snâr),

1 NOUN. a noose for catching small animals and birds: *The boys made snares to catch rabbits.*
2 VERB. to catch something with or as if with a snare; trap: *They snared a rabbit.*
❑ VERB **snares, snared, snar·ing.**

snare drum, a small drum with wires stretched across the bottom to make a rattling sound.

snarl¹ (snärl),

1 VERB. to growl sharply and show the teeth: *The dog snarled at me.*
2 NOUN. a sharp, angry growl.
3 VERB. to say or express something with a snarl: *He snarled out threats.*
4 NOUN. a sharp, angry remark: *She replied with a nasty snarl.*
❑ VERB **snarls, snarled, snarl·ing.**

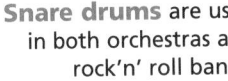

Snare drums are used in both orchestras and rock'n' roll bands.

snarl² (snärl),

1 NOUN. a tangle in a string, in hair, and so on: *He was brushing the snarls out of his hair.*
2 VERB. to tangle or become tangled: *The kitten snarled the yarn by playing with it.*
3 NOUN. a confused situation; confusion: *An accident caused a snarl in traffic.*
4 VERB. to tie up: *The snow snarled traffic for hours.*
❑ VERB **snarls, snarled, snarl·ing.**

snatch (snach),

1 VERB. to seize something suddenly: *The hawk snatched the rabbit and flew away.* ■ See the Synonym Study at **catch.**

a hat	ė term	ô order	ch child		⎧a in about
ā age	i it	oi oil	ng long		e in taken
ä far	ī ice	ou out	sh she	ə⎨ i in pencil
â care	o hot	u cup	th thin		o in lemon
e let	ō open	ů put	ᴛʜ then		⎩u in circus
ē equal	ò saw	ü rule	zh measure		

S

2 NOUN. the act of snatching something: *The boy made a snatch at the ball.*

3 NOUN. a small amount, especially of talk, music, and so on: *We heard snatches of conversation from the next room.*
 ❏ VERB **snatch•es, snatched, snatch•ing;** PLURAL **snatch•es.**

sneak (snēk),
 1 VERB. to move, take, or get something in a sly, secret way: *The children sneaked the puppy into the house.*
 2 VERB. to come or go like a thief or a person who is ashamed to be seen: *She sneaked in the back door.*
 3 NOUN. someone who sneaks; cowardly person.
 4 ADJECTIVE. sly and secret: *a sneak attack.*
 ❏ VERB **sneaks, sneaked** or **snuck, sneak•ing.**

sneak•er (snē′kər), NOUN.
 1 sneakers, light canvas shoes with rubber soles, used for games, sports, and so on.
 2 someone who sneaks; sneak.

sneak•y (snē′kē),
 ADJECTIVE. like someone who is ashamed to be seen. ❏ ADJECTIVE **sneak•i•er, sneak•i•est. —sneak′i•ness,** NOUN.

sneakers

sneer (snir),
 1 VERB. to show scorn or contempt for something or someone by your looks or by what you say: *People sneered at claims that a machine could fly.*
 2 NOUN. a look or an expression that shows your scorn or contempt: *The Wright brothers ignored people's sneers and built an airplane.*
 ❏ VERB **sneers, sneered, sneer•ing.**

sneeze (snēz),
 1 VERB. to blow air suddenly and violently out through your nose and mouth: *The pepper made her sneeze.*
 2 NOUN. the act of sneezing.
 ❏ VERB **sneez•es, sneezed, sneez•ing.**

snick•er (snik′ər),
 1 NOUN. a sly or silly laugh; giggle. ■ See the Synonym Study at **laugh.**
 2 VERB. to laugh in this way: *The children were snickering to each other.*
 ❏ VERB **snick•ers, snick•ered, snick•er•ing.**

sniff (snif),
 1 VERB. to take in air through the nose in short, quick breaths that can be heard: *The man who had a cold was sniffing.*
 2 VERB. to smell something in this way: *The dog sniffed at the stranger.*

3 NOUN. an act or sound of sniffing: *He cleared his nose with a loud sniff.*
 ❏ VERB **sniffs, sniffed, sniff•ing.**

snif•fle (snif′əl),
 1 VERB. to sniff again and again as you do when you have a head cold or when you are trying to stop crying.
 2 NOUN. a loud sniff.
 3 NOUN. **the sniffles,** a slight head cold.
 ❏ VERB **snif•fles, snif•fled, snif•fling.**

snip (snip),
 1 VERB. to cut something off with a small, quick stroke or strokes with scissors: *She snipped the thread.* ■ See the Synonym Study at **cut.**
 2 NOUN. the act of snipping: *With a few snips, she had cut her hair.*
 3 NOUN. a small piece cut off: *a snip of thread.*
 ❏ VERB **snips, snipped, snip•ping.**

snipe (snīp),
 1 VERB. to shoot at an enemy one at a time from a hidden place.
 2 NOUN. a marsh bird with a long bill.
 ❏ VERB **snipes, sniped, snip•ing;** PLURAL **snipe** or **snipes.**

snip•er (snī′pər), NOUN. someone who shoots at other people from a hidden position, usually a high place.

snob (snob), NOUN. someone who cares too much about a person's rank, wealth, or position.

snoop (snüp),
 1 VERB. to go about in a sneaking, prying way; pry.
 2 NOUN. someone who snoops.
 ❏ VERB **snoops, snooped, snoop•ing.**

snooze (snüz),
 1 VERB. to sleep; doze; take a nap: *The dog snoozed on the porch in the sun.*
 2 NOUN. a nap.
 ❏ VERB **snooz•es, snoozed, snooz•ing.**

snore (snôr),
 1 VERB. to breathe during sleep with a harsh, rough sound: *The child had a cold and snored all night.*
 2 NOUN. the sound made this way.
 ❏ VERB **snores, snored, snor•ing. —snor′er,** NOUN.

snor•kel (snôr′kəl),
 1 NOUN. a curved tube which enables swimmers to breathe under water while swimming near the surface.
 2 VERB. to swim using a snorkel.
 ❏ VERB **snor•kels, snor•keled, snor•kel•ing.**

snort (snôrt),
 1 VERB. to force the breath violently through the nose with a loud, harsh sound: *The horse snorted.*
 2 NOUN. the act or sound of snorting: *The horse leaped up with a loud snort.*
 ❏ VERB **snorts, snorted, snort•ing. —snort′er,** NOUN.

snout (snout), NOUN.
 1 the part of an animal's head that sticks forward

and includes the nose, mouth, and jaws. Pigs, dogs, and crocodiles have snouts.

2 anything like an animal's snout.

snow (snō),

1 NOUN. water that freezes high up in the air. Snow falls in soft, white flakes.

2 NOUN. a fall of snow: *We had a heavy snow today.*

3 VERB. to fall in the form of snow: *It is snowing in the mountains, and will start to snow here soon.* ❑ VERB **snows, snowed, snow•ing. −snow′like′,** ADJECTIVE.

snow in, IDIOM. to shut in by snow: *The village was snowed in for three days after the blizzard.*

snow•ball (snō′bȯl′),

1 NOUN. a ball made of snow pressed together.

2 VERB. to grow quickly in size, like a rolling snowball: *The number of signers of the petition for a new school snowballed.* ❑ VERB **snow•balls, snow•balled, snow•ball•ing.**

snow•blow•er (snō′blō′ər), NOUN. a machine that clears snow from sidewalks and driveways by blowing the snow up into the air and off to one side.

snow•capped (snō′kapt′), ADJECTIVE. having its top covered with snow: *a snowcapped mountain.*

snow•drift (snō′drift′), NOUN. a bank of snow that has been piled up by the wind: *Huge snowdrifts blocked the road.*

snow•fall (snō′fȯl′), NOUN.

1 a fall of snow: *There was a snowfall late last night.*

2 the amount of snow falling within a certain time and area: *The snowfall in that one storm was 16 inches.*

snow•flake (snō′flāk′), NOUN. a small, feathery piece of snow.

snow•man (snō′man′), NOUN. a figure something like that of a person made out of snow. ❑ PLURAL **snow•men.**

snowman

snow•mo•bile (snō′mō bēl′),

1 NOUN. a motor vehicle used for traveling on snow. Runners like skis in front are steered by handlebars. Rear treads are powered by an engine.

2 VERB. to travel by snowmobile. ❑ VERB **snow•mo•biles, snow•mo•biled, snow•mo•bil•ing. −snow′mo•bil′er,** NOUN.

snow•plow (snō′plou′), NOUN. a machine for clearing away snow from streets and highways.

snow•shoe (snō′shü′), NOUN. a light wooden frame with strips of leather stretched across it. Snowshoes are worn on your feet to keep you from sinking into deep, soft snow.

snowshoe hare or **snowshoe rabbit,** a hare of northern North America with fur that is white in winter and brown in summer. Its large, furry hind feet are good for running on snow.

snow•storm (snō′stôrm′), NOUN. a storm with a great deal of snow.

snow•y (snō′ē), ADJECTIVE.

1 bringing snow: *It is going to be a snowy day.*

2 covered with snow: *The snowy trees looked lovely.*

3 white as snow: *My grandmother has snowy hair.* ❑ ADJECTIVE **snow•i•er, snow•i•est.**

snub (snub),

1 VERB. to ignore or treat someone rudely: *Ever since we argued, my neighbor snubs me when we meet.*

2 NOUN. an act of snubbing someone: *When she didn't speak to me, I took it as a snub.* ❑ VERB **snubs, snubbed, snub•bing.**

snuck (snuk), VERB. a past tense and past participle of **sneak.**

snuff (snuf), VERB. to put out a candle. ❑ VERB **snuffs, snuffed, snuff•ing.**

snuff out, IDIOM. to end something suddenly and completely; wipe out: *The new dictator snuffed out the people's hopes for freedom.*

snuf•fle (snuf′əl),

1 VERB. to breathe noisily through the nose the way you do if you have a cold in your head.

2 NOUN. the act or sound of breathing like this. ❑ VERB **snuf•fles, snuf•fled, snuf•fling.**

snug (snug), ADJECTIVE.

1 giving warmth and comfort; sheltered: *The cat has found a snug corner behind the stove.* ∎ See the Synonym Studies at **comfortable** and **safe.**

2 fitting your body closely: *That coat is a little too snug.* ❑ ADJECTIVE **snug•ger, snug•gest. −snug′ly,** ADVERB.

Have You Heard?

You may have heard the phrase **"as snug as a bug in a rug."** This phrase means that someone is very warm and comfortable.

S

a	hat	ė	term	ô	order	ch child
ā	age	i	it	oi	oil	ng long
ä	far	ī	ice	ou	out	sh she
â	care	o	hot	u	cup	th thin
e	let	ō	open	ů	put	ᴛʜ then
ē	equal	ȯ	saw	ü	rule	zh measure

ə { a in about / e in taken / i in pencil / o in lemon / u in circus

snug·gle (snug′əl), *VERB.* to lie closely and comfortably together; nestle; cuddle: *The kittens snuggled together in the basket.* ❑ *VERB* **snug·gles, snug·gled, snug·gling.**

snuggling monkeys

so¹ (sō),

1 *ADVERB.* in the same way or degree: *Don't go so soon!*

2 *ADJECTIVE.* true: *Is that really so?*

3 *ADVERB.* very much: *My head aches so.*

4 *ADVERB.* therefore: *The dog was hungry, so we fed it.*

5 *INTERJECTION.* **So** is sometimes used alone to exclaim or to ask a question: *So! Late again! You're late. So?*

6 *PRONOUN.* more or less: *It weighs a pound or so.*

7 *CONJUNCTION.* with the result that; in order that: *Go away so I can rest.*

8 *CONJUNCTION.* with the purpose or intention that: *I did the work so you would not need to.*
  ■ Other words that sound like this are **sew** and **sow**.

and so on, *IDIOM.* a phrase at the end of a list of things to mean that there are other, similar things that could be listed: *The term "vehicles" includes cars, vans, buses, trucks, and so on.*

so that, *IDIOM.* with the result or purpose: *The boy studies so that he will do well.*

so² (sō), *NOUN.* See **sol.** ■ Other words that sound like this are **sew** and **sow**.

soak (sōk),

1 *VERB.* to make or become very wet; wet through: *The rain soaked my clothes.* ■ See the Synonym Study at **wet.**

2 *VERB.* to let something remain in water or other liquid until it is wet clear through: *Soak the jacket all night before you wash it.*

3 *NOUN.* the act or process of soaking: *Give the clothes a long soak.*
  ❑ *VERB* **soaks, soaked, soak·ing.**

soap (sōp),

1 *NOUN.* a substance used for washing, usually made of a fat and a strong chemical called lye.

2 *VERB.* to rub with soap: *Soap the dishes well.*
  ❑ *VERB* **soaps, soaped, soap·ing.**

soap opera, a series of dramatic television shows, usually broadcast during weekdays.

soap·y (sō′pē), *ADJECTIVE.*

1 containing soap: *soapy water.*

2 of or like soap: *The water has a soapy taste.*
  ❑ *ADJECTIVE* **soap·i·er, soap·i·est.**

soar (sôr), *VERB.*

1 to fly at a great height; fly upward: *The eagle soared without flapping its wings.*

2 to rise beyond what is common or usual: *Her spirits soared when she was given the job.*
  ❑ *VERB* **soars, soared, soar·ing.** ■ Another word that sounds like this is **sore.**

sob (sob),

1 *VERB.* to cry or sigh with short, quick breaths: *She sobbed herself to sleep.*

2 *NOUN.* the act of catching short, quick breaths because of grief or some other emotion.
  ❑ *VERB* **sobs, sobbed, sob·bing.**

so·ber (sō′bər),

1 *ADJECTIVE.* not under the influence of alcohol; not drunk: *You should only drive if you are sober.*

2 *ADJECTIVE.* quiet; serious; solemn: *He looked sober at the thought of missing the picnic.*

3 *VERB.* to make or become sober: *The class sobered quickly when the teacher arrived.*
  ❑ *VERB* **so·bers, so·bered, so·ber·ing.** —**so′ber·ly,** *ADVERB.*

so-called (sō′kȯld′), *ADJECTIVE.* called so, but not really so: *Her so-called friend hasn't phoned her.*

soc·cer (sok′ər), *NOUN.* a game played on a field between two teams of eleven players each, using a round ball. The ball is kicked and may be struck with any part of the body except the hands and arms. However, goalies are allowed to use their hands and arms to touch the ball. Players score by hitting the ball into a goal at either end of the field.

playing **soccer**

so·cial (sō′shəl), ADJECTIVE.
1 concerned with human beings as a group: *Schools and hospitals are social institutions.*
2 living or liking to live with others: *People are social beings.*
3 liking company: *She has a social nature.*
4 connected with fashionable society: *The mayor and his wife are the social leaders of our town.*

so·cial·ism (sō′shə liz′əm), NOUN. a system of government in which the means of production and distribution of goods are owned and controlled by the government or by the community as a whole, rather than by private businesses or corporations.

so·cial·ist (sō′shə list), NOUN. someone who favors or supports socialism.

social security, a system of federal insurance for retired people and their dependents, and for people who cannot work. Social security includes a health insurance program for older people.

social studies, the study of people, their activities, and customs. History, economics, geography, and civics are all part of social studies.

so·ci·e·ty (sə sī′ə tē), NOUN.
1 all the people; human beings living together as a group: *Society must work hard for world peace.*
2 a group of people joined together for a common purpose or by common interests. A club, an association, and so on, may be called a society.
3 fashionable, wealthy people or their activities: *His parents are leaders of society.*
❏ PLURAL **so·ci·e·ties.**

sock[1] (sok), NOUN. a short, close-fitting knitted covering of wool, cotton, or other fabric for the foot and ankle, sometimes one that reaches about halfway to the knee.

sock[2] (sok),
1 VERB. to strike or hit someone hard: *He socked me on the jaw.*
2 NOUN. a hard blow: *He gave me a sock on the jaw.*
❏ VERB **socks, socked, sock·ing.**

sock·et (sok′it), NOUN. a hollow part or piece that something fits into. A candlestick has a socket for a candle. Your eyes are set in sockets.

sod (sod), NOUN.
1 any ground thickly covered with grass.
2 a piece or layer of sod containing the grass and its roots. Sod is sold in sections that you lay flat on a bare yard.

so·da (sō′də), NOUN.
1 See **soft drink.**
2 soda water flavored with fruit juice or syrup, and often containing ice cream.
❏ PLURAL **so·das.**

soda fountain, a counter with places for holding soda water, flavored syrups, ice cream, and soft drinks.

soda water, water with carbon dioxide added to it to make it bubble and fizz.

so·di·um (sō′dē əm), NOUN. a soft, silver-white metal that occurs naturally only in combination with other substances. Sodium is a chemical element. Salt and baking soda contain sodium.

so·fa (sō′fə), NOUN. a long, comfortable seat or couch that has a back and arms. ❏ PLURAL **so·fas.**

soft (sȯft), ADJECTIVE.
1 moving when you press into it; tender; not hard: *Feathers, cotton, and wool are soft.*
2 not hard compared with other things of the same sort: *Pine is softer than oak. Lead is softer than steel.*
3 smooth to the touch: *The kitten's fur is soft.*
4 not loud: *a soft voice, soft music.*
5 quietly pleasant; mild: *a soft spring morning, the soft light of candles.*
6 weak; out of condition; not fit: *He became soft from lack of exercise.*
7 free from minerals that keep soap from forming suds: *It is easy to wash clothes in soft water.*
—soft′ly, ADVERB. **—soft′ness,** NOUN.

Synonym Study

Soft means tender, not hard or stiff: *He closed the bread bag so that the bread would stay fresh and soft.*

Fluffy means as soft as fluff: *The young swan has short, fluffy feathers.*

Silky means as soft and smooth as silk: *She showed me her silky new party dress.*

Spongy means soft and absorbent, like a sponge: *He wasn't hurt when he fell on the spongy moss.*

Mushy means as soft and wet as mush: *After the storm, the soccer field will be mushy.*

ANTONYM: **hard.**

soft·ball (sȯft′bȯl′), NOUN.
1 a kind of baseball that is played on a smaller field, with a larger and softer ball. A softball must be pitched underhand.
2 the ball used in this game.

soft drink, a sweetened, flavored drink, made with soda water and containing no alcohol; soda. Root beer and cola are soft drinks.

soft·en (sȯf′ən), VERB. to make or become softer: *Lotion softens the skin.* ❏ VERB **soft·ens, soft·ened, soft·en·ing. —soft′en·er,** NOUN.

S

a	hat	ė	term	ô	order	ch	child	(a in about
ā	age	i	it	oi	oil	ng	long	e in taken
ä	far	ī	ice	ou	out	sh	she	ə ⟨ i in pencil
â	care	o	hot	u	cup	th	thin	o in lemon
e	let	ō	open	u̇	put	ŦH	then	(u in circus
ē	equal	ȯ	saw	ü	rule	zh	measure	

soft·ware (sȯft′wâr′), NOUN. instructions for a computer; programs.

soft·wood (sȯft′wu̇d′), NOUN. any wood that is easily cut. Pine is a softwood; oak is a hardwood.

sog·gy (sog′ē), ADJECTIVE. soaked; thoroughly wet: *The wash on the line was soggy from the rain.*
■ See the Synonym Study at **wet**. ❑ ADJECTIVE **sog·gi·er, sog·gi·est.** —**sog′gi·ness,** NOUN.

soil¹ (soil), NOUN. the top layer of the earth; dirt: *Roses grow best in rich soil.*

soil² (soil), VERB. to make or become dirty: *He soiled his clean clothes.* ❑ VERB **soils, soiled, soil·ing.**

sol (sōl), NOUN. (in music) the fifth tone of a scale.
■ Other words that sound like this are **sole** and **soul**.

so·lar (sō′lər), ADJECTIVE.
1 of or from the sun: *a solar eclipse.*
2 working by means of the sun's light or heat. A **solar cell** traps sunlight and changes it into electrical energy.

solar car, a car that runs on electrical power produced by solar cells built into its roof.

A **solar car** doesn't have to stop for gas.

solar energy, energy from the light or heat of the sun.

solar system, the sun and all the planets, moons, and comets that revolve around it.

solar year, the time it takes for the earth to travel once completely around the sun. It equals 365 days, 5 hours, and 48 minutes.

sold (sōld), VERB.
1 the past tense of **sell**: *She sold her bike a week ago.*
2 the past participle of **sell**: *She has sold it to a friend.*

sol·der (sod′ər),
1 NOUN. a metal that can be melted and used for joining or mending metal surfaces or parts.
2 VERB. to fasten, mend, or join things with this metal: *She soldered the broken wires together.*
❑ VERB **sol·ders, sol·dered, sol·der·ing.**

sol·dier (sōl′jər), NOUN.
1 someone who serves in an army.
2 someone in the army below the rank of lieutenant.

sole¹ (sōl), ADJECTIVE.
1 one and only; single: *He was the sole heir of the fortune when his aunt died.*
2 not shared with others; of or for only one person or group: *That company has the sole right to manufacture this drug.*
■ Other words that sound like this are **sol** and **soul**.

sole² (sōl),
1 NOUN. the bottom or underside of the foot.
2 NOUN. the bottom of a shoe, slipper, or boot.
3 VERB. to put a sole on something: *I must have my shoes soled.*
❑ VERB **soles, soled, sol·ing.** ■ Other words that sound like this are **sol** and **soul**.

sole³ (sōl), NOUN. a flatfish related to the flounder, commonly used for food. ❑ PLURAL **sole** or **soles**.
■ Other words that sound like this are **sol** and **soul**.

sole·ly (sōl′lē), ADVERB.
1 alone: *You will be solely responsible for providing the lunch.*
2 only: *Mangos grow outdoors solely in warm climates.*

sol·emn (sol′əm), ADJECTIVE.
1 serious; dignified; earnest: *He gave his solemn promise to do better. He spoke in a solemn voice.*
2 done with great dignity: *A solemn procession left the cathedral.*
—**sol′emn·ly,** ADVERB.

so·lic·it (sə lis′it), VERB.
1 to ask earnestly; try to get: *The new store is soliciting customers through newspaper advertising.*
2 to make appeals or requests: *to solicit for contributions to a charity.*
❑ VERB **so·lic·its, so·lic·it·ed, so·lic·it·ing.**
—**so·lic′i·ta′tion,** NOUN.

sol·id (sol′id),
1 NOUN. something that takes up space and has its own shape; substance that is not a liquid or a gas.
2 ADJECTIVE. in the form of a solid; not liquid or gaseous: *Water becomes solid when it freezes.*
3 ADJECTIVE. not hollow: *A bar of iron is solid; a pipe is hollow.*
4 NOUN. an object or shape that has height, width, and thickness. A cube is a solid.
5 ADJECTIVE. hard; firm: *They left the boat and put their feet on solid ground.*
6 ADJECTIVE. the same throughout: *The cloth is a solid blue.*
7 ADJECTIVE. unbroken; complete: *I spent a solid hour on my arithmetic.*
8 ADVERB. completely: *The subway was packed solid.*
—**sol′id·ly,** ADVERB.

so·lid·i·fy (sə lid′ə fī), VERB. to make or become solid; harden: *The melted butter solidified as it cooled.* ❑ VERB **so·lid·i·fies, so·lid·i·fied, so·lid·i·fy·ing.** —**so·lid′i·fi·ca′tion,** NOUN.

sol·i·tar·y (sol′ə ter′ē), ADJECTIVE. alone; away from people; lonely: *A solitary rider was seen in the distance. She leads a solitary life in her cabin in the mountains.* ■ See the Synonym Study at **alone**.

a **solitary** horse at sunset

sol·i·tude (sol′ə tüd), NOUN. the condition of being alone: *I like solitude in the evening so that I can read.*

so·lo (sō′lō),
1 NOUN. a piece of music for one voice or instrument: *She sang three solos.*
2 ADJECTIVE. arranged for and performed by one voice or instrument: *He played the solo part.*
3 ADJECTIVE. without a partner, teacher, or associate; alone: *The flying student made her first solo flight.*
4 VERB. to make a flight alone in an airplane.
❑ PLURAL **so·los;** VERB **so·los, so·loed, so·lo·ing.**

so·lo·ist (sō′lō ist), NOUN. someone who performs a solo.

sol·u·ble (sol′yə bəl), ADJECTIVE. capable of being dissolved: *Salt is soluble in water.*

so·lu·tion (sə lü′shən), NOUN.
1 the act or process of solving a problem or explaining a mystery: *That problem was hard; its solution required many hours.*
2 a mixture formed by dissolving a solid in a liquid: *When you put sugar in tea you make a solution.*

solve (solv), VERB. to find the answer to something; clear up; explain: *The detective solved the mystery. He has solved all the problems in the lesson.* ❑ VERB **solves, solved, solv·ing.**

So·ma·li·a (sə mä′lyə), NOUN. a country in eastern Africa. **—So·ma′lian,** ADJECTIVE or NOUN.

som·ber (som′bər), ADJECTIVE.
1 dark; gloomy: *A cloudy winter day is somber.*
2 sad; serious: *His losses made him very somber.*
—som′ber·ly, ADVERB.

som·brer·o (som brer′ō), NOUN. a hat with a broad brim worn in the southwestern United States, Mexico, and Spain. ❑ PLURAL **som·brer·os.**

some (sum),
1 ADJECTIVE. certain or particular, but not known or named: *Some dogs are larger than others.*
2 ADJECTIVE. a number of: *Ask some people to help.*
3 ADJECTIVE. a quantity of: *Drink some milk.*
4 PRONOUN. a certain number or quantity: *She kept some and gave the rest away.*
5 ADJECTIVE. a; any: *Can't you find some person who will help you?*
6 ADVERB. about: *Some twenty people asked for work.*
7 ADJECTIVE. (informal) very big, bad, good, or the like; remarkable of its kind: *That is some dog!*
■ Another word that sounds like this is **sum**.

some·bod·y (sum′bud′ē or sum′bə dē),
1 PRONOUN. a person not known or named; some person; someone: *Somebody has taken my pen.*
2 NOUN. someone of importance: *This restaurant treats you as if you are really somebody.*
❑ PLURAL **some·bod·ies.**

some·day (sum′dā′), ADVERB. at some future time.

some·how (sum′hou′), ADVERB. in one way or another: *I'll finish this work somehow.*

some·one (sum′wun′), PRONOUN. some person; somebody: *Someone has to lock up the house.*

some·place (sum′plās′), ADVERB. in or to some place; somewhere: *They live around here someplace.*

som·er·sault (sum′ər sòlt),
1 NOUN. a movement in which you roll over on the ground, turning your head under your body.
2 VERB. to roll over in a somersault.
❑ VERB **som·er·saults, som·er·sault·ed, som·er·sault·ing.**

three parts of a **somersault**

some·thing (sum′thing′),
1 NOUN. some thing; a particular thing not named or known: *I'm sure I've forgotten something.*
2 NOUN. a part; a certain amount; a little: *There is something of his father in his smile.*

a	hat	ė	term	ô	order	ch	child		a in about
ā	age	i	it	oi	oil	ng	long		e in taken
ä	far	ī	ice	ou	out	sh	she	ə	i in pencil
â	care	o	hot	u	cup	th	thin		o in lemon
e	let	ō	open	ù	put	ŦH	then		u in circus
ē	equal	ò	saw	ü	rule	zh	measure		

645

3 *ADVERB.* to some extent or degree; somewhat: *She and her sister look something alike.*

some·time (sum′tīm′), *ADVERB.*
1 at one time or another: *Come to see us sometime.*
2 at an unknown point of time: *It happened sometime last March or April.*

some·times (sum′tīmz′), *ADVERB.* now and then; at times: *They come to visit sometimes.*

some·what (sum′wät′),
1 *ADVERB.* to some degree; slightly: *My hat is somewhat like yours.*
2 *NOUN.* some part; some amount: *The large gift came as somewhat of a surprise.*

some·where (sum′wâr′), *ADVERB.*
1 in or to some place; in or to one place or another: *It is somewhere around the house.*
2 at some time: *It snowed somewhere around noon.*

son (sun), *NOUN.* a male child. A boy or man is the son of his father and mother. ■ Another word that sounds like this is **sun.**

so·nar (sō′när), *NOUN.* a device for finding the depth of water and locating underwater objects. Sonar sends sound waves into water, which return when they strike the bottom or any object.

Word Story

Sonar comes from the words **so**und **na**vigation **r**anging, which describe what this device does. See the Word Source at **acronym.**

so·na·ta (sə nä′tə), *NOUN.* a piece of music for one or two instruments, having several movements in different tempos but related keys. ❏ *PLURAL* **so·na·tas.**

song (sȯng), *NOUN.*
1 music with words; something to sing: *We learned a new song today.*
2 a sound like music made by a bird: *We heard the song of a nightingale.*

song·bird (sȯng′bėrd′), *NOUN.* a bird that has a musical call.

son·ic (son′ik), *ADJECTIVE.* of or about sound waves.

son-in-law (sun′in lȯ′), *NOUN.* the husband of your daughter. ❏ *PLURAL* **sons-in-law.**

son·net (son′it), *NOUN.* a short poem, especially one of 14 lines with a pattern of rhymes.

So·no·ra (sə nôr′ə), *NOUN.* a state in northwestern Mexico.

soon (sün), *ADVERB.*
1 in a short time; before long: *I hope to see you again soon.*
2 before the usual or expected time; early: *Why have you come so soon?*
3 promptly; quickly: *As soon as I hear, I'll tell you.*

soot (sůt), *NOUN.* a black substance in the smoke from burning coal, wood, oil, or other fuel. Soot makes smoke dark.

soothe (süṯн), *VERB.*
1 to quiet or comfort someone: *The father soothed his crying child.*
2 to make something less painful; ease: *Heat soothes some aches; cold soothes others.*
❏ *VERB* **soothes, soothed, sooth·ing.**

sop (sop), *VERB.* to take up water or other liquid: *Please sop up that water with a cloth.* ❏ *VERB* **sops, sopped, sop·ping.**

sopping wet, *IDIOM.* thoroughly wet; soaking wet: *I stepped in a puddle and my shoes and socks are sopping wet.*

so·phis·ti·cat·ed (sə fis′tə kā′tid), *ADJECTIVE.*
1 knowing how to get along in the world; not simple in your tastes or ideas: *Her sophisticated tastes are the result of world travel.*
2 very complex and advanced in design: *Mom works with sophisticated laboratory equipment.*

soph·o·more (sof′ə môr), *NOUN.* a student in the second year of high school or college.

the outfit of a **sophisticated** gentleman

so·pran·o (sə pran′ō), *NOUN.*
1 the highest singing voice in women and boys.
2 a singer with such a voice.
❏ *PLURAL* **so·pran·os.**

sor·cer·er (sôr′sər ər), *NOUN.* someone who is believed to practice magic with the aid of evil spirits; magician.

sor·cer·ess (sôr′sər is), *NOUN.* a woman who is believed to practice magic with the aid of evil spirits; witch. ❏ *PLURAL* **sor·cer·ess·es.**

sor·cer·y (sôr′sər ē), *NOUN.* magic believed to be performed by the aid of evil spirits; witchcraft: *The prince was changed into a lion by sorcery.*

sore (sôr),
1 *ADJECTIVE.* causing pain; aching: *I have a sore tooth.*
2 *NOUN.* a painful place on your body where the skin or flesh is broken or bruised.
3 *ADJECTIVE.* angry: *She is sore at me for losing her book.* ■ See the Synonym Study at **mad.**
❏ *ADJECTIVE* **sor·er, sor·est.** ■ Another word that sounds like this is **soar.** **—sore′ness,** *NOUN.*

sor·row (sor′ō), *NOUN.*
1 a feeling of grief and sadness: *We felt sorrow at the loss of our kitten.*
2 a cause of grief or sadness; suffering: *His sorrows have aged him.*

sor·row·ful (sor′ə fəl), ADJECTIVE.
1 full of sorrow; feeling sorrow; sad: *He has been sorrowful since his best friend moved away.*
2 causing sorrow: *His death was a sorrowful event.*
—sor′row·ful·ly, ADVERB.

sor·ry (sor′ē), ADJECTIVE.
1 feeling sad about something: *We are sorry that we have to leave.*
2 pitiful: *The hungry, wet, shivering dog was a sorry sight.*
❑ ADJECTIVE **sor·ri·er, sor·ri·est.**

sort (sôrt),
1 NOUN. a group of things that are alike in some way; kind; class: *What sort of work do you do? I like this sort of candy best.*
2 VERB. to arrange things in some order: *Sort these cards according to their colors.*
3 VERB. to separate some things from other things: *The farmer sorted out the best apples for eating.*
❑ VERB **sorts, sort·ed, sort·ing.**

out of sorts, IDIOM. ill, cross, or uncomfortable: *The hot weather made the baby out of sorts.*

sort of, IDIOM. somewhat; rather: *In spite of his faults, I sort of like him.*

SOS (es′ō′es′), NOUN. an urgent call for help used by ships and aircraft.

sought (sȯt), VERB.
1 the past tense of **seek**: *I sought my mother's advice.*
2 the past participle of **seek**: *She has sought a job for weeks now.*

soul (sōl), NOUN.
1 the spiritual part of a human being, believed to be the source of thought, feeling, and action.
2 energy of mind or feelings; spirit: *She puts her whole soul into her work.*
3 a person: *Don't tell a soul.*
■ Other words that sound like this are **sol** and **sole**.

sound¹ (sound),
1 NOUN. something that you hear: *the sound of music, the sound of thunder.*
2 NOUN. energy in the form of waves passing through a substance such as air or water. This energy is heard as sound.
3 NOUN. volume; loudness: *Turn up the sound.*
4 NOUN. one of the simple elements that make up speech: *a vowel sound.*
5 VERB. to make or cause to make a sound or noise: *The wind sounds like an animal howling.*
6 VERB. to pronounce or be pronounced: *"Dough" and "doe" sound just alike.*
7 VERB. to seem: *That answer sounds wrong to me.*
8 VERB. to cause to sound: *He sounded the siren.*
❑ VERB **sounds, sound·ed, sound·ing.**

sound² (sound),
1 ADJECTIVE. free from disease; healthy: *a sound body, a sound mind.*

2 ADJECTIVE. free from injury, decay, or defect: *a sound ship, sound fruit.*
3 ADJECTIVE. dependable; safe; secure: *a sound business firm, sound advice.*
4 ADJECTIVE. deep; heavy: *a sound sleep.*
5 ADJECTIVE. thorough; complete: *a sound defeat.*
6 ADVERB. deeply; thoroughly: *He was sound asleep.*

sound³ (sound), VERB. to measure the depth of water by dropping a weight fastened to the end of a line. ❑ VERB **sounds, sound·ed, sound·ing.**

sound⁴ (sound), NOUN.
1 a long, narrow channel of water that joins two larger bodies of water, or that lies between the mainland and an island: *Long Island Sound.*
2 an inlet or arm of the sea.

sound·ly (sound′lē), ADVERB. deeply; heavily: *The tired child slept soundly.*

sound·proof (sound′prüf′),
1 ADJECTIVE. not letting sound pass through.
2 VERB. to make something soundproof: *The gymnasium has been soundproofed.*
❑ VERB **sound·proofs, sound·proofed, sound·proof·ing.**

sound·track (sound′trak′), NOUN.
1 a recording of the sounds of words, music, and so on, made along one edge of movie film.
2 a recording of the songs or music used in a movie, television show, and so on: *He liked the movie so much that he bought the soundtrack.*

soup (süp), NOUN. a liquid food made by cooking meat, vegetables, or fish in water, milk, or broth.

sour (sour),
1 ADJECTIVE. tasting like vinegar or lemon juice; not sweet: *This green fruit is sour.*
2 ADJECTIVE. spoiled: *Sour milk tastes terrible.*
3 ADJECTIVE. disagreeable; grumpy; cross: *a sour face, a sour remark.*
4 VERB. to make or become sour: *The milk soured while it stood in the hot sun.*
❑ VERB **sours, soured, sour·ing.** **—sour′ness**, NOUN.

source (sôrs), NOUN.
1 someone or someplace from which anything comes or is gotten: *A newspaper gets news from many sources. Mines are the source of diamonds.*
2 the beginning of a brook or river; fountain; spring.

south (south),
1 NOUN. the direction to your left as you face the setting sun; direction just opposite north.
2 ADJECTIVE or ADVERB. toward the south; farther toward the south: *We live on the south side of town. Drive south forty miles.*

a	hat	ė	term	ô	order	ch	child		a in about
ā	age	i	it	oi	oil	ng	long		e in taken
ä	far	ī	ice	ou	out	sh	she	ə<	i in pencil
â	care	o	hot	u	cup	th	thin		o in lemon
e	let	ō	open	ú	put	ŦH	then		u in circus
ē	equal	ȯ	saw	ü	rule	zh	measure		

S

3 ADJECTIVE. coming from the south: *a south wind.*
4 ADJECTIVE. in the south: *the south window of a house.*
5 NOUN. the part of any country toward the south.
6 NOUN. **the South,** the southern part of the United States; the states south of Pennsylvania, the Ohio River, and Missouri. These states formed most of the Confederacy in the Civil War.
south of, IDIOM. further south than: *Oregon is south of Washington.*

South Africa, *Republic of,* a country in southern Africa. **—South African.**

South America, a continent southeast of North America and west of the Atlantic Ocean. Brazil, Argentina, and Peru are countries in South America. **—South American.**

South Car·o·li·na (south′ kar/ə li′nə), one of the southern states of the United States. *Abbreviation:* SC; *Capital:* Columbia. **—South Car·o·li·ni·an** (south′ kar/ə lin′ē ən).

State Story **South Carolina** was named in honor of Charles I, king of England, who lived from 1600 to 1649. His name in Latin is *Carolus.*

South Da·ko·ta (south′ də kō′tə), one of the midwestern states of the United States. *Abbreviation:* SD; *Capital:* Pierre. **—South Dakotan.**

State Story **South Dakota** was named for the Sioux Indians. The Sioux all call themselves **Dakota** or **Lakota.** Their name means "allies" or "friends."

south·east (south′ēst′),
1 ADJECTIVE. halfway between south and east; in the southeast: *the southeast district of town.*
2 NOUN. a southeast direction.
3 NOUN. a place that is in the southeast part or direction.
4 ADVERB. toward the southeast: *Here the road curves southeast.*
5 ADJECTIVE. coming from the southeast: *a southeast wind.*
6 NOUN. **the Southeast,** the southeastern part of the United States, including Alabama, Georgia, Florida, South Carolina, North Carolina, and Virginia.

south·east·ern (south′ē′stərn), ADJECTIVE.
1 toward the southeast: *the southeastern sky.*
2 from the southeast.
3 of or in the southeast: *a southeastern climate.*
4 **Southeastern,** of or in the southeastern part of the United States.

south·er·ly (suŦH′ər lē), ADJECTIVE or ADVERB.
1 facing or toward the south: *We hiked in a southerly direction.*
2 from the south: *a southerly wind.*

south·ern (suŦH′ərn), ADJECTIVE.
1 toward the south: *the southern side of a building.*

2 from the south: *a southern breeze.*
3 of or in the south: *They have traveled in southern countries.*
4 **Southern,** of or in the southern part of the United States. Delaware, Maryland, Virginia, West Virginia, North Carolina, South Carolina, Georgia, Florida, Mississippi, Louisiana, Kentucky, and Tennessee are the Southern states.

south·ern·er (suŦH′ər nər), NOUN.
1 someone born or living in the south.
2 **Southerner,** someone born or living in the southern part of the United States.

South Korea, a country in eastern Asia. **—South Korean.**

south·paw (south′pȯ′), NOUN. (informal)
1 a left-handed baseball pitcher.
2 any left-handed person.

South Pole, the southern end of the earth's axis.

south·ward (south′wərd), ADVERB or ADJECTIVE. toward the south; south: *I walked southward. The orchard is on the southward slope of the hill.*

south·wards (south′wərdz), ADVERB. See southward.

south·west (south′west′),
1 ADJECTIVE. halfway between south and west; in the southwest: *the southwest district of town.*
2 NOUN. a southwest direction.
3 NOUN. a place that is in the southwest part or direction.
4 ADVERB. toward the southwest: *The road from here runs southwest.*
5 ADJECTIVE. coming from the southwest: *a southwest wind.*
6 NOUN. **the Southwest,** the southwestern part of the United States, especially Texas, New Mexico, Oklahoma, Arizona, and sometimes, southern California.

south·west·ern (south′wes′tərn), ADJECTIVE.
1 toward the southwest: *the southwestern sky.*
2 from the southwest.
3 of or in the southwest: *a southwestern climate.*
4 **Southwestern,** of or in the southwestern part of the United States.

sou·ve·nir (sü′və nir′), NOUN. something given or kept as a reminder; keepsake: *She bought a pair of moccasins as a souvenir of her trip out West.*

sove·reign (sov′rən),
1 NOUN. the supreme ruler; king or queen; monarch. Queen Victoria was the sovereign of Great Britain from 1837 to 1901.
2 ADJECTIVE. having supreme rank, power, or authority: *He is our sovereign prince.*
3 ADJECTIVE. independent of the control of other governments: *When the thirteen colonies won the Revolutionary War, America became a sovereign nation.*

So·vi·et (sō′vē et), *ADJECTIVE*. of or about the former Soviet Union.

Soviet Union, a former country reaching from eastern Europe across Asia to the Pacific Ocean; Union of Soviet Socialist Republics; U.S.S.R. It broke up into several countries in 1991.

sow[1] (sō), *VERB*. to scatter seed on the ground; plant seed in: *She sowed grass seed in the yard.* ❏ *VERB* **sows, sowed, sown** or **sowed, sow·ing.** ■ Other words that sound like this are **sew** and **so.** —**sow′er,** *NOUN*.

sow[2] (sou), *NOUN*. a fully grown female pig.

sown (sōn), *VERB*. the past participle of **sow**[1]: *They have sown the field with oats.* ■ Another word that sounds like this is **sewn.**

soy·bean (soi′bēn′), *NOUN*. a bean widely grown in Asia and North America that is an important source of food. Its oil is used in margarine and paints. The meal is fed to livestock or made into flour.

soy sauce, a Chinese and Japanese sauce for fish, meat, and the like, made from soybeans.

space (spās),
1 *NOUN*. the unlimited room or emptiness that exists in all directions: *The earth moves through space.*
2 *NOUN*. room for something to fit in: *Is there space in the car for another person?*
3 *NOUN*. outer space: *the conquest and exploration of space, a rocket launched into space.*
4 *ADJECTIVE*. of or about outer space: *space flight, space vehicles.*
5 *VERB*. to separate things by spaces: *Space your words evenly when you write.*
   ❏ *VERB* **spac·es, spaced, spac·ing.**

space bar, the bar on a typewriter or computer keyboard you use to insert a space.

space·craft (spās′kraft′), *NOUN*. a vehicle used for flight in outer space; spaceship. ❏ *PLURAL* **space·craft.**

space·ship (spās′ship′), *NOUN*. See **spacecraft.**

space shuttle, a spacecraft with wings, which can orbit the earth, land like an airplane, and be used again.

space station, an earth satellite large enough for crew members to live in for months. A space station is used for experiments and observations.

a **space station** with Earth visible below

space·suit (spās′süt′), *NOUN*. an airtight suit that protects travelers in outer space from radiation, heat, and lack of oxygen.

space·walk (spās′wòk′), *NOUN*. the act of moving or floating in space while outside a spacecraft.

spa·cious (spā′shəs), *ADJECTIVE*. having a lot of room or space: *a spacious house, spacious closets.* —**spa′cious·ly,** *ADVERB*. —**spa′cious·ness,** *NOUN*.

spade[1] (spād),
1 *NOUN*. a tool for digging, with an iron blade which can be pressed into the ground with the foot.
2 *VERB*. to dig soil with a spade: *Spade up the garden.*
   ❏ *VERB* **spades, spad·ed, spad·ing.**

spade[2] (spād), *NOUN*.
1 a figure shaped like this: ♠
2 a playing card with a figure shaped like this.

spa·ghet·ti (spə get′ē), *NOUN*. a food made of the same mixture of flour and water as macaroni. Spaghetti is thinner than macaroni and not hollow. Spaghetti is a form of pasta.

S

A space shuttle has two rockets and a large fuel tank that drop off after use in launching the spacecraft.

fuel tank

rockets

space shuttle

Spain (spān), *NOUN.* a country in southwestern Europe.

span (span),
  1 *NOUN.* a space of time, often short or limited: *the span of human life, a five-year span.*
  2 *NOUN.* the part between two supports: *The bridge crossed the river in a single span.*
  3 *NOUN.* the distance between two supports: *The arch had a fifty-foot span.*
  4 *VERB.* to go from one side of something to the other: *A bridge spanned the river.*
  5 *VERB.* to last for a period of time: *The pitcher's sports career spanned three decades.*
  ❑ *VERB* **spans, spanned, span•ning.**

span•gle (spang′gəl), *NOUN.* a small piece of glittering metal used for decoration.

Span•iard (span′yərd), *NOUN.* someone born or living in Spain.

span•iel (span′yəl), *NOUN.* a dog, usually of small or medium size, with long, silky hair and drooping ears.

Span•ish (span′ish),
  1 *ADJECTIVE.* of or about Spain, its people, or their language.
  2 *NOUN PLURAL.* **the Spanish,** the people of Spain.
  3 *NOUN.* the language of Spain, Mexico, most parts of Central America and South America, and many other places.

Word Source

Here are some of the words that have come into English from Spanish. See also the Word Source at **Mexican Spanish.**

alligator	fiesta	mosquito	sierra
armadillo	Florida	Nevada	siesta
burro	hacienda	patio	silo
California	hammock	piñata	sombrero
cargo	lariat	plaza	tornado
castanet	lasso	pueblo	tortilla
Colorado	mesa	ranch	tuna
corral	Montana	rodeo	vanilla

spank (spangk), *VERB.* to slap on the buttocks with an open hand: *She was spanked for telling a lie.*
  ❑ *VERB* **spanks, spanked, spank•ing.**

spare (spâr),
  1 *VERB.* to show mercy to someone; decide not to harm or destroy: *He spared his enemy.*
  2 *VERB.* to make someone free from labor or pain: *They did the work to spare you the trouble.*
  3 *VERB.* to get along without something; do without: *I can't spare the car today, so you'll have to walk.*
  4 *VERB.* to use in small quantities or not at all: *Don't spare the chocolate sauce!*
  5 *ADJECTIVE.* free for other use: *spare time.*
  6 *ADJECTIVE.* extra: *a spare tire, spare parts.*
  7 *NOUN.* an extra thing or part: *We had a spare in the trunk in case of a flat tire.*
  8 *NOUN.* (in bowling) the act of knocking down all the pins with two balls.
  ❑ *VERB* **spares, spared, spar•ing;** *ADJECTIVE* **spar•er, spar•est.**

spar•ing (spâr′ing), *ADJECTIVE.* avoiding waste; economical; frugal: *Dentists recommend a sparing use of sugar.* −**spar′ing•ly,** *ADJECTIVE.*

spark (spärk),
  1 *NOUN.* a small bit of something that is on fire: *The burning wood threw off sparks.*
  2 *NOUN.* the flash given off when electricity jumps across an open space. An electric spark ignites the gasoline vapor in the engine of some vehicles.
  3 *NOUN.* a bright flash; gleam: *We saw a spark of light through the trees.*
  4 *VERB.* to flash; gleam; sparkle.
  5 *NOUN.* a small amount: *I haven't a spark of interest in the plan.*
  6 *VERB.* to send out small bits of fire; produce sparks.
  7 *VERB.* to stir up activity: *Cruelty may spark a revolt.*
  ❑ *VERB* **sparks, sparked, spark•ing.**

spar•kle (spär′kəl),
  1 *VERB.* to send out little sparks: *The fireworks sparkled.*
  2 *NOUN.* a little spark.
  3 *VERB.* to shine; glitter; flash: *The jewels in the crown sparkled.*
  4 *VERB.* to be brilliant; be lively: *This author's wit sparkles.*
  ❑ *VERB* **spar•kles, spar•kled, spar•kling.**

Tiny waves **sparkle** in the sunshine.

spark plug, a device in the cylinder of a gasoline engine that produces an electric spark to ignite a mixture of fuel and air in the combustion chamber.

spar•row (spar′ō), *NOUN.* a small, brownish gray bird. Sparrows are common in North and South America but are also found in Europe, Asia, and Africa.

sparse (spärs), *ADJECTIVE.* thinly scattered; occurring here and there: *a sparse population, sparse hair.*
  ❑ *ADJECTIVE* **spars•er, spars•est.** −**sparse′ly,** *ADVERB.*

spasm (spaz′əm), NOUN. a sudden, abnormal, uncontrollable contraction of a muscle or muscles.

spat[1] (spat), NOUN. a slight quarrel.

spat[2] (spat), VERB.
1 a past tense of **spit**[1]: *The cat spat at me.*
2 a past participle of **spit**[1]: *It hasn't spat at me before.*

spat·ter (spat′ər),
1 VERB. to scatter or splash something in drops: *to spatter mud.*
2 VERB. to fall in drops: *Rain spattered on the walk.*
3 NOUN. the act or sound of spattering: *We listened to the spatter of the rain on the roof.*
❏ VERB **spat·ters, spat·tered, spat·ter·ing.**

spat·u·la (spach′ə lə), NOUN. a tool with a broad, flat, flexible blade, used for spreading, scraping, or stirring soft things such as putty, cake frosting, and so on. ❏ PLURAL **spat·u·las.**

spawn (spȯn),
1 NOUN. the eggs of fish, frogs, shellfish, and other animals growing or living in water.
2 NOUN. the young living things that are newly hatched from these eggs.
3 VERB. to produce eggs.
❏ VERB **spawns, spawned, spawn·ing.**

speak (spēk), VERB.
1 to say words; talk: *A person with a cold often has trouble speaking distinctly.* ■ See the Synonym Study at **talk.**
2 to make a speech: *Who will speak at the meeting?*
3 to say; tell; express; make known: *You should always speak the truth.*
4 to use a language: *Do you speak French?*
❏ VERB **speaks, spoke, spo·ken, speak·ing.**

speak out or **speak up**, IDIOM. to speak loudly, clearly, or freely: *No one dared to speak out against the big bully. The children spoke up in favor of the teacher's suggestion to have a party.*

speak·er (spē′kər), NOUN.
1 someone who speaks.
2 often, **Speaker,** the person who presides over an assembly: *Who is the Speaker of the House of Representatives?*
3 See **loudspeaker.**

spear (spir),
1 NOUN. a weapon with a long shaft and a head with a sharp point.
2 VERB. to pierce something with a spear: *Spear a fish!*
3 VERB. to pierce or stab something with anything sharp: *She speared her string beans with a fork.*
❏ VERB **spears, speared, spear·ing.** —**spear′like′,** ADJECTIVE.

spear·mint (spir′mint′), NOUN. a kind of mint grown for its oil, which is used for flavoring.

spe·cial (spesh′əl),
1 ADJECTIVE. unusual or different in some way: *A bank safe has a special lock.*
2 ADJECTIVE. extraordinary; exceptional: *Snakes are a topic of special interest.*
3 ADJECTIVE. having a particular purpose, function, or use: *Send the letter by a special messenger.*
4 NOUN. something special, such as a sale: *The store advertised a special on raincoats.*
5 NOUN. a television show produced especially for a single broadcast: *I saw a TV special on whales.*
—**spe′cial·ly,** ADVERB.

special effects, pictures and sounds added to a movie or television show. Special effects often show things that cannot be photographed or tape-recorded, such as monsters, space travel, or ghosts.

spe·cial·ist (spesh′ə list), NOUN. someone who has a lot of knowledge about one particular branch of study, business, or occupation. A heart specialist is a doctor who treats diseases of the heart.

spe·cial·ize (spesh′ə līz), VERB. to pursue some special branch of study or work: *Some doctors specialize in children's diseases.* ❏ VERB **spe·cial·iz·es, spe·cial·ized, spe·cial·iz·ing.** —**spe′cial·i·za′tion,** NOUN.

spe·cial·ty (spesh′əl tē), NOUN.
1 a special line of work, profession, or trade: *American history is the specialty of my social studies teacher.*
2 a special product or thing for sale: *This store makes a specialty of children's clothes.*
❏ PLURAL **spe·cial·ties.**

spe·cies (spē′shēz), NOUN. a group of related living things that have the same basic characteristics. Animals of the same species can mate and produce young. ❏ PLURAL **spe·cies.**

spe·cif·ic (spi sif′ik), ADJECTIVE. particular: *There was no specific reason for the quarrel.*

spe·cif·i·cal·ly (spi sif′ik lē), ADVERB. in a definite or positive way: *Mom told her specifically not to go across the busy street.*

spec·i·fy (spes′ə fī), VERB. to mention or name something definitely: *Did you specify any particular time for us to call?* ❏ VERB **spec·i·fies, spec·i·fied, spec·i·fy·ing.**

spec·i·men (spes′ə mən), NOUN.
1 a single example of a group; sample: *He collects specimens of all kinds of rocks.*
2 a sample of blood, urine, and the like, for analysis or examination.

speck (spek), NOUN.
1 a small spot; stain: *Can you clean the specks off this wallpaper?*
2 a tiny bit; particle: *He has a speck in his eye.*

S

a	hat	ė	term	ô	order	ch	child	⎧a in about
ā	age	i	it	oi	oil	ng	long	⎪e in taken
ä	far	ī	ice	ou	out	sh	she	ə⎨i in pencil
â	care	o	hot	u	cup	th	thin	⎪o in lemon
e	let	ō	open	u̇	put	₮H	then	⎩u in circus
ē	equal	ȯ	saw	ü	rule	zh	measure	

speck·le (spek′əl),
1 NOUN. a small spot or mark: *This hen is gray with white speckles.*
2 VERB. to mark with small spots: *He speckled the white frosting with bits of chocolate.*
❏ VERB **speck·les, speck·led, speck·ling.**

spec·ta·cle (spek′tə kəl), NOUN.
1 a public show or display: *The parade was a fine spectacle.*
2 spectacles. See **eyeglasses.**

spec·tac·u·lar (spek tak′yə lər), ADJECTIVE. making a great impression; like a spectacle: *Movies present spectacular scenes like battles, storms, and races.*
—**spec·tac′u·lar·ly,** ADVERB.

spec·ta·tor (spek′tā tər), NOUN. someone who looks on without taking part: *There were many spectators at the game.*

spec·trum (spek′trəm), NOUN. the band of colors formed when a beam of light is passed through a prism or is broken up by other means. A rainbow has all the colors of the spectrum: red, orange, yellow, green, blue, indigo, and violet. ❏ PLURAL

a complete **spectrum**

spec·trums or **spec·tra** (spek′trə).

spec·u·late (spek′yə lāt), VERB.
1 to guess: *She speculated about who would win.*
2 to risk losing money by buying something, hoping to sell it again at a higher price: *He speculates in silver and copper.*
❏ VERB **spec·u·lates, spec·u·lat·ed, spec·u·lat·ing.**
—**spec′u·la′tion,** NOUN.

sped (sped), VERB.
1 a past tense of **speed:** *The car sped down the road.*
2 a past participle of **speed:** *One of the cars has sped away from the scene of the accident.*

speech (spēch), NOUN.
1 the act of speaking; talk: *Human beings express their thoughts by speech.*
2 the power of speaking: *Animals lack speech.*
3 a manner of speaking: *I could tell by their speech that they were from the South.*
4 a formal talk to a group of people: *The President gave an excellent speech.*
❏ PLURAL **speech·es.**

speech·less (spēch′lis), ADJECTIVE. not able to speak: *I was speechless with anger.*

speed (spēd),
1 NOUN. how fast something is going: *The cat pounced on the mouse with amazing speed.*
2 VERB. to go fast: *The boat sped over the water toward the shore.*

3 NOUN. a rate of movement: *The children ran at full speed.*
4 VERB. to go faster than is safe or lawful: *The car was stopped for speeding.*
❏ VERB **speeds, sped** or **speed·ed, speed·ing.**
—**speed′er,** NOUN.

speed up, IDIOM. to go or cause to go faster; increase speed: *I told him he'd better speed up or we'd be late.*

speed·boat (spēd′bōt′), NOUN. a motorboat built to go fast.

speed bump, a raised ridge, often made of asphalt, placed across a street, driveway, or parking lot. A speed bump forces drivers to slow down.

speed·om·e·ter (spē dom′ə tər), NOUN. a device to indicate speed. Motor vehicles have speedometers.

speed·y (spē′dē), ADJECTIVE. happening or working rapidly or quickly: *They hire speedy workers. We came to a speedy decision.*
■ See the Synonym Study at **quick.** ❏ ADJECTIVE **speed·i·er, speed·i·est.**

spell¹ (spel), VERB.
1 to write or say the letters of a word in the right order: *Some words are easy to spell.*
2 to make up or form the letters of a word: *C-a-t spells cat.*
3 to mean: *Her angry frown spells trouble.*
❏ VERB **spells, spelled, spell·ing.** —**spell′er,** NOUN.

spell out, IDIOM. to explain carefully, step by step, and in detail: *We asked him to spell out his plan for raising more money.*

spell² (spel), NOUN.
1 a group of words that some people think has magic power.
2 magic influence; fascination; charm: *A spell of mystery seemed to hang over the old castle.*

spell³ (spel),
1 NOUN. a period or time of anything: *There was a long spell of rainy weather in August.*
2 VERB. to work in place of another person for a while: *I'll spell you at cutting the grass.*
❏ VERB **spells, spelled, spell·ing.**

spell-check·er (spel′chek·ər), NOUN. a computer program for checking spelling in a file: *His spell-checker automatically changes "teh" to "the."*

spell·ing (spel′ing), NOUN.
1 the act or skill of writing or saying the letters of a word in order: *She is poor at spelling.*
2 the way a word is spelled: *"Ax" has two spellings, "ax" and "axe."*

spend (spend), VERB.
1 to use money to buy something: *I spent ten dollars shopping for food today.*
2 to use time to do something: *Spend more time on that lesson.*

3 to pass time somewhere: *We spent last summer at the seashore.*
4 to use up or wear out: *The storm has spent its force.*
❏ *VERB* **spends, spent, spend·ing. –spend'er,** *NOUN.*

spent (spent),
1 *ADJECTIVE.* worn out; tired: *a spent swimmer, a spent horse.*
2 *VERB.* the past tense of **spend:** *We spent the day at the beach.*
3 *VERB.* the past participle of **spend:** *I have spent too much money lately.*

sperm (spėrm), *NOUN.* a cell in a male for producing young when combined with an egg cell. ❏ *PLURAL* **sperm** or **sperms.**

sperm whale, a very large whale with a square head. Sperm whales eat squid.

sphere (sfir), *NOUN.*
1 a round solid object; globe. Every point on the surface of a sphere is the same distance from the center. The sun, moon, earth, and stars are spheres.
2 the place or surroundings in which a person or thing exists, acts, or works: *A teacher's sphere is the classroom.*

sphinx (sfingks), *NOUN.* a statue of a lion's body with the head of a man, ram, or hawk. The **Great Sphinx** is a huge statue with a man's head and a lion's body, near Cairo, Egypt. ❏ *PLURAL* **sphinx·es.**

spice (spīs),
1 *NOUN.* a seasoning used to make food taste better. Pepper, cinnamon, cloves, ginger, and nutmeg are common spices.
2 *VERB.* to put spice in something; season: *spiced pears.*
3 *NOUN.* something that adds flavor or interest to something: *"Variety is the spice of life."*
❏ *VERB* **spic·es, spiced, spic·ing.**

spic·y (spī'sē), *ADJECTIVE.*
1 flavored with spice: *The cookies were rich and spicy.*
2 like spice: *Those carnations have a spicy smell.*
❏ *ADJECTIVE* **spic·i·er, spic·i·est. –spic'i·ness,** *NOUN.*

spi·der (spī'dər), *NOUN.* a very small animal with eight legs, no wings, and a body divided into two parts. Many spiders spin webs to catch insects for food. **–spi'der·like',** *ADJECTIVE.*

Did You Know?

Spiders make their webs from two glands in their abdomens. One gland makes the silk that makes up the structure of the web. Another gland makes the sticky silk to catch insects. Several strands make up each thread of the web for strength.

spied (spīd), *VERB.*
1 the past tense of **spy:** *She spied him in the crowd.*
2 the past participle of **spy:** *Who has spied on us?*

spig·ot (spig'ət), *NOUN.* a faucet.

spike¹ (spīk),
1 *NOUN.* a large, thick nail.
2 *VERB.* to fasten something with spikes: *The work crew laid the track by spiking the rails to the ties.*
3 *NOUN.* a piece of metal or plastic with sharp points on it: *Baseball players wear shoes with spikes.*
4 *VERB.* to drive a volleyball down into the opponent's court by a powerful hit above the net.
5 *VERB.* to pierce or injure someone with a spike.
❏ *VERB* **spikes, spiked, spik·ing.**

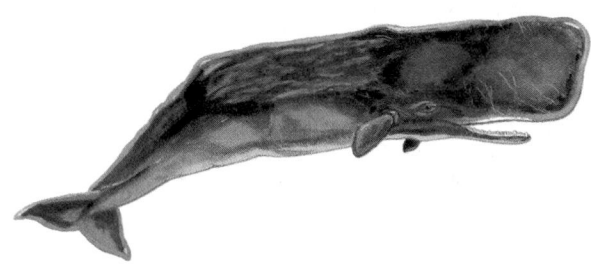

sperm whale — up to 60 feet long

spike² (spīk), *NOUN.*
1 an ear of grain.
2 a long, pointed flower cluster. The flowers of spearmint grow on spikes.

spill (spil),
1 *VERB.* to let something fall out or run out of its container: *to spill milk, to spill salt.*
2 *VERB.* to fall or flow out: *Water spilled from the pail.*
3 *NOUN.* a fall: *He took a bad spill from a horse.*
❏ *VERB* **spills, spilled, spill·ing.**

spilt (spilt), *ADJECTIVE.* spilled: *"Don't cry over spilt milk."*

spider — body up to 3½ inches long

a	hat	ė	term	ô	order	ch	child	⎧a in about
ā	age	i	it	oi	oil	ng	long	⎪e in taken
ä	far	ī	ice	ou	out	sh	she	ə⎨i in pencil
â	care	o	hot	u	cup	th	thin	⎪o in lemon
e	let	ō	open	ù	put	ᴛʜ	then	⎩u in circus
ē	equal	ȯ	saw	ü	rule	zh	measure	

S

spin (spin),
1 *VERB.* to turn or cause to turn around rapidly: *The wheels are spinning. The child spun the top.*
■ See the Synonym Study at **turn.**
2 *VERB.* to twist cotton, flax, or wool fibers into thread.
3 *VERB.* to make a thread, web, or cocoon by giving out from the body sticky material that hardens into thread. *A spider spins a web.*
4 *VERB.* to tell: *We sat around the fire spinning yarns.*
5 *NOUN.* the act of spinning: *The car went into a spin on the icy road.*
6 *NOUN.* a quick ride or drive in a car.
❑ *VERB* **spins, spun, spin·ning.**

spin·ach (spin′ich), *NOUN.* the green leaves of a garden plant, eaten cooked or raw.

spi·nal (spī′nl), *ADJECTIVE.* of or about the spine or backbone: *a spinal injury.*

spinal column, the backbone.

spinal cord, the thick, whitish cord of nerve tissue in the backbone or spine. Nerves to various parts of the body branch off from the spinal cord.

spin·dle (spin′dl), *NOUN.*
1 (formerly) a rod or pin used in spinning to twist, wind, and hold the thread.
2 any rod or pin that turns around or on which something turns. Axles and shafts are spindles.

spin·dly (spind′lē), *ADJECTIVE.* very long and slender; too tall and thin: *a spindly plant.* ❑ *ADJECTIVE* **spin·dli·er, spin·dli·est.**

spine (spīn), *NOUN.*
1 the series of small bones down the middle of the back; backbone.
2 a stiff growth with a sharp point on plants or animals. *A porcupine's quills are spines.*

spine·less (spīn′lis), *ADJECTIVE.*
1 having no spine: *A turtle is spineless.*
2 without courage: *The bully was a spineless coward.*
—spine′less·ness, *NOUN.*

spinning wheel, (formerly) a large wheel with a spindle, arranged for spinning cotton, flax, or wool into thread or yarn.

spin·ster (spin′stər), *NOUN.* a woman who has not married. ★ This word is often considered offensive.

spin·y (spī′nē), *ADJECTIVE.*
1 covered with spines; thorny: *Most cactuses are spiny.*
2 stiff and having a sharp point: *Avoid the spiny quills of a porcupine.*
❑ *ADJECTIVE* **spin·i·er, spin·i·est.**

spi·ral (spī′rəl),
1 *NOUN.* a winding and gradually widening coil. The thread of a screw is a spiral.
2 *ADJECTIVE.* winding; coiled: *a spiral staircase. Some seashells have a spiral shape.*
3 *VERB.* to move in a spiral: *The falling leaves spiraled to earth.*
❑ *VERB* **spi·rals, spi·raled, spi·ral·ing.**

spire (spīr), *NOUN.*
1 the top part of a steeple that narrows to a point.
2 anything tapering and pointed: *The sun shone on the mountain's rocky spires.*

spir·it (spir′it),
1 *NOUN.* the soul: *Some religions teach that at death the spirit leaves the body.*
2 *NOUN.* a human being's moral, religious, or emotional nature.
3 *NOUN.* a supernatural being. Ghosts and fairies are spirits.
4 *NOUN.* **spirits,** a state of mind; disposition; temper: *I am in good spirits.*
5 *NOUN.* a person; personality: *You have been a brave spirit. She is a forceful spirit in the community.*
6 *NOUN.* what is really meant as opposed to what is said or written: *The spirit of a law is more important than its words.*
7 *VERB.* to carry something away secretly: *The gold has been spirited away.*
❑ *VERB* **spir·its, spir·it·ed, spir·it·ing.**

spir·it·ed (spir′ə tid), *ADJECTIVE.* lively; dashing; brave: *a spirited horse, a spirited young girl.*

spir·i·tu·al (spir′ə chü əl),
1 *ADJECTIVE.* sacred; religious: *a spiritual leader.*
2 *NOUN.* a religious song which originated among the African Americans of the southern United States.
3 *ADJECTIVE.* of or about the spirit or spirits.
—spir′i·tu·al·ly, *ADVERB.* **—spir′i·tu·al·ness,** *NOUN.*

spit¹ (spit),
1 *VERB.* to throw out saliva or bits of food from the mouth.
2 *NOUN.* the liquid produced in the mouth; saliva.
3 *VERB.* to make a spitting sound: *The cat spits when it is angry.*
❑ *VERB* **spits, spit** or **spat, spit·ting.**

spit² (spit), *NOUN.* a pointed, slender rod or bar on which meat is roasted.

This shell forms a **spiral.**

spite (spīt),
1 NOUN. mean feelings toward someone: *He broke my new radio out of spite.*
2 VERB. to show mean feelings toward someone: *He broke my new radio just to spite me.*
❏ VERB **spites, spit·ed, spit·ing.**
in spite of, IDIOM. regardless of: *The schools were open in spite of the snowstorm.*

spite·ful (spīt′fəl), ADJECTIVE. full of mean feelings toward someone. —**spite′ful·ly,** ADVERB.

splash (splash),
1 VERB. to cause liquid or wet stuff to fly about and get people wet or soiled: *The swimmers splashed each other with water.*
2 VERB. to cause liquid to splash around: *The baby likes to splash in the tub.*
3 VERB. to fall in scattered masses or drops: *The waves splashed on the beach.*
4 NOUN. the act or sound of something dropping into liquid: *The boat turned over with a splash.*
5 NOUN. a spot of liquid splashed upon something: *She has splashes of grease on her clothes.*
❏ VERB **splash·es, splashed, splash·ing;** PLURAL **splash·es.**

splash·down (splash′doun′), NOUN. the landing of a capsule or other spacecraft in the ocean after reentry into the earth's atmosphere.

splat·ter (splat′ər),
1 VERB. to splash; spatter: *She splattered me with mud.*
2 NOUN. a splash; spatter: *a splatter of paint.*
❏ VERB **splat·ters, splat·tered, splat·ter·ing.**

splen·did (splen′did), ADJECTIVE.
1 brilliant; magnificent: *a splendid sunset, a splendid palace, splendid jewels, a splendid victory.*
2 very good; fine; excellent: *This new job seems to be a splendid opportunity.*
—**splen′did·ly,** ADVERB.

splen·dor (splen′dər), NOUN.
1 great brightness; brilliant light: *The sun set in golden splendor.*
2 a magnificent show; pomp; glory.

splice (splīs), VERB.
1 to join ropes by weaving together the two ends that have been pulled out into separate strands.
2 to join pieces of film, tape, or wire by gluing or cementing their two ends together.
❏ VERB **splic·es, spliced, splic·ing.**

splint (splint), NOUN. an arrangement of wood or metal that holds a broken bone in place so that it will heal properly.

splin·ter (splin′tər),
1 NOUN. a thin, sharp piece of wood, bone, glass, or the like: *I have a splinter in my hand.*
2 VERB. to split or break something into thin, sharp pieces: *He splintered the wood with an ax.*
❏ VERB **splin·ters, splin·tered, splin·ter·ing.**

split (split),
1 VERB. to break or cut something from end to end, or in layers: *We split the logs into firewood.*
■ See the Synonym Studies at **break** and **cut.**
2 VERB. to separate something into parts or to be separated; divide: *The huge tree split when it was struck by lightning. Let's split the cost of the dinner between us.*
3 NOUN. a division in a group: *There was a split in the club for a time, but harmony was soon restored.*
4 NOUN. the act of splitting; break; crack: *Frost caused the split in the rock.*
5 NOUN. often, **splits,** an acrobatic trick of sinking to the floor with one leg straight forward and the other leg straight back.
❏ VERB **splits, split, split·ting.** —**split′ter,** NOUN.

splurge (splėrj), VERB. to spend more money than you should: *We splurged and ate at a fancy restaurant.* ❏ VERB **splurg·es, splurged, splurg·ing.**

splut·ter (splut′ər), VERB. to talk in a hasty, confused way: *She was so excited she spluttered.*
❏ VERB **splut·ters, splut·tered, splut·ter·ing.**

spoil (spoil),
1 VERB. to damage or injure something so that it becomes unfit or useless; ruin; destroy: *Rabbits spoiled our garden's lettuce and spinach. The rain spoiled the picnic.* ■ See the Synonym Study at **destroy.**
2 VERB. to become bad, or not good to eat: *The fruit spoiled because I kept it too long.*
3 VERB. to give a child too much of what he or she asks for: *They spoiled him by always giving him what he wanted.*
4 NOUN. **spoils,** things taken by force: *The soldiers carried the spoils back to their own land.*
❏ VERB **spoils, spoiled, spoil·ing.**

spoke¹ (spōk), VERB. the past tense of **speak:** *She spoke about that yesterday.*

spoke² (spōk), NOUN. one of the bars that runs from the center of a wheel to the outer ring.

spo·ken (spō′kən),
1 VERB. the past participle of **speak:** *She has spoken about coming to visit.*
2 ADJECTIVE. said with the mouth; oral: *There were no written directions for the test, only spoken ones.*

spokes·man (spōks′mən), NOUN. someone who speaks for someone else or for other people: *I am the spokesman for my class in the student council.*
❏ PLURAL **spokes·men.**

spokes·per·son (spōks′pėr′sən), NOUN. someone who speaks for another or others.

a	hat	ė	term	ô	order	ch	child	⎧a in about
ā	age	i	it	oi	oil	ng	long	⎪e in taken
ä	far	ī	ice	ou	out	sh	she	ə⎨i in pencil
â	care	o	hot	u	cup	th	thin	⎪o in lemon
e	let	ō	open	ù	put	ᴛʜ	then	⎩u in circus
ē	equal	ò	saw	ü	rule	zh	measure	

sponge (spunj),
1 *NOUN.* a water animal with a light, elastic skeleton having many holes in it. Most sponges live in large colonies on the bottom of the ocean.
2 *NOUN.* the skeleton of this animal, used for bathing or cleaning.
3 *NOUN.* a similar thing made of rubber or plastic.
4 *VERB.* to live or profit at the expense of someone else in a mean or selfish way: *They are sponging off their relatives instead of working.*
❑ *VERB* **spong·es, sponged, spong·ing.**
–sponge′like′, *ADJECTIVE.*

sponge (definition 1)

Have You Heard?

You may have heard the phrase **"throw in the sponge."** This means that someone is ready to give in and admit defeat. The phrase **"throw in the towel"** means the same thing.

spon·gy (spun′jē), *ADJECTIVE.* like a sponge; soft, light, and full of holes: *spongy moss, spongy dough.* ∎ See the Synonym Study at **soft.**
❑ *ADJECTIVE* **spon·gi·er, spon·gi·est.**

spon·sor (spon′sər),
1 *NOUN.* someone who gives money or other kinds of support to a person or group: *She was the sponsor of two scholarship students.*
2 *NOUN.* someone who stands with the parents at an infant's baptism, agreeing to assist in the child's religious education if necessary; godfather or godmother.
3 *NOUN.* a company, store, or other business firm that pays the costs of a radio or television program that advertises its products: *This show's sponsor is the Clean-Right Mop Company.*
4 *VERB.* to act as sponsor for a person or a group: *The parents' organization at school sponsors our scout troop.*
❑ *VERB* **spon·sors, spon·sored, spon·sor·ing.**
–spon′sor·ship, *NOUN.*

spon·ta·ne·ous (spon tā′nē əs), *ADJECTIVE.* happening in an unplanned, natural way: *Both sides burst into spontaneous cheers at the skillful play.* **–spon·ta′ne·ous·ly,** *ADVERB.*
–spon·ta′ne·ous·ness, *NOUN.*

spook (spük), *NOUN.* a ghost.

spook·y (spü′kē), *ADJECTIVE.* strange and frightening; suggesting the presence of ghosts: *The old house looked spooky.* ❑ *ADJECTIVE* **spook·i·er, spook·i·est.**

spool (spül), *NOUN.* a round piece of wood, plastic, or metal. Thread, tape, fish line, camera film, and so on, are wound onto spools.

spoon (spün),
1 *NOUN.* something to eat with. A spoon has a small, round bowl at the end of a handle. You can eat cereal or soup with a spoon.
2 *VERB.* to lift food up in a spoon: *He spooned great heaps of food onto his plate.*
❑ *VERB* **spoons, spooned, spoon·ing.**

spoon·bill (spün′bil′), *NOUN.* a long-legged, pink wading bird that has a long, flat bill with a spoon-shaped tip.

spoonbill — body about 2½ feet long

spoon·ful (spün′fúl), *NOUN.* as much as a spoon can hold. ❑ *PLURAL* **spoon·fuls.**

spore (spôr), *NOUN.* a special kind of cell. A spore produced by a living thing can grow into a new living thing. Ferns, mosses, and molds produce spores.

sport (spôrt), *NOUN.*
1 a game or contest that requires some skill and usually a certain amount of physical exercise. Baseball and tennis are outdoor sports; bowling and boxing are indoor sports. ∎ See the Synonym Study at **play.**
2 someone who shows sportsmanship when he or she plays.

sport·ing (spôr′ting), *ADJECTIVE.* of, interested in, or engaging in sports: *a sporting event.*

sports (spôrts), *ADJECTIVE.* of, about, or suitable for sports: *sports clothes, sports medicine.*

sports car, a small, fast car, usually with two seats.

sports·cast·er (spôrts′kas′tər), *NOUN.* someone who does the spoken part of a broadcast sporting event.

sports·man (spôrts′mən), *NOUN.*
1 someone who takes part in or is interested in sports, especially hunting or fishing.
2 someone who plays fair.
❑ *PLURAL* **sports·men.**

sports·man·ship (spôrts′mən ship), *NOUN.* the qualities of fairness and respect for your opponent in sports, and the desire to play for the sake of the game, not just to win.

sports·wom·an (spôrts′wủm′ən), NOUN. a woman who engages in or is interested in sports. ❑ PLURAL **sports·wom·en.**

sport utility vehicle, a motor vehicle built and used for ordinary road travel as well as for travel over rough roads and trails.

spot (spot),
1 NOUN. a small mark or stain that you can see on the surface of something: *You have grease spots on your suit. That bluish spot on her arm is a bruise.*
2 NOUN. a small part of a different color: *The shirt is blue with white spots.*
3 NOUN. a place: *From this spot you can see the ocean.*
4 VERB. to find someone or something by using your eyes; locate: *The teacher spotted every mistake in my paper.* ■ See the Synonym Study at **find.**
5 VERB. to make or become spotted: *I spotted my tie.*
❑ VERB **spots, spot·ted, spot·ting.**

hit the spot, IDIOM. (informal) to be just right; be satisfactory: *A cold lemonade really hits the spot on a hot day.*

in a tight spot, IDIOM. in trouble or difficulty: *After the villain tied him to the train tracks, our hero was in a tight spot.*

on the spot, IDIOM.
1 at the very place where needed: *A doctor on the spot gave the injured player first aid.*
2 at once: *His orders were carried out on the spot.*
3 in trouble or difficulty: *He put me on the spot by asking a question I could not answer.*

spot·less (spot′lis), ADJECTIVE.
1 without a spot: *a spotless white shirt.*
2 completely honest: *a spotless reputation.*

spot·light (spot′lit′),
1 NOUN. a strong light thrown upon a particular place or person.
2 NOUN. a lamp that gives a strong beam of light: *a spotlight in a theater.*
3 VERB. to focus public attention on something: *The need for street repairs was spotlighted at the meeting.*

in the spotlight, IDIOM. attracting the attention of an audience, the media, and so on: *Movie stars like to be in the spotlight.*
❑ VERB **spot·lights, spot·light·ed, spot·light·ing.**

spot·ty (spot′ē), ADJECTIVE.
1 having spots; spotted.
2 not of good quality throughout: *The repair job on the car engine was spotty.*
❑ ADJECTIVE **spot·ti·er, spot·ti·est.**

spouse (spous), NOUN. a husband or wife: *Mr. Smith is Mrs. Smith's spouse, and she is his spouse.*

spout (spout),
1 VERB. to throw out a liquid in a stream or spray: *A whale spouts water when it breathes.*
2 VERB. to flow out with force: *Water spouted from a break in the pipe.*
3 NOUN. a pipe for carrying off water: *Rain runs down a spout from our roof to the ground.*
4 NOUN. a tube or lip from which liquid is poured.
❑ VERB **spouts, spout·ed, spout·ing.**

sprain (sprān),
1 VERB. to injure the tissue at a joint by a sudden twist or wrench: *I sprained my ankle.*
2 NOUN. an injury caused by a sudden twist or wrench: *The sprain took a long time to heal.*
❑ VERB **sprains, sprained, sprain·ing.**

sprang (sprang), VERB. a past tense of **spring:** *She sprang from her chair.*

sprawl (sprôl), VERB.
1 to lie or sit with your arms and legs spread out: *The children were sprawled in front of the TV.*
2 to spread out in an irregular or awkward manner: *His large handwriting sprawled across the page.*
❑ VERB **sprawls, sprawled, sprawl·ing.**

spray[1] (sprā),
1 NOUN. a liquid that flies through the air in small drops: *We were wet with the sea spray.*
2 NOUN. a liquid stored under pressure in a container, that can be released as a spray or mist.
3 VERB. to sprinkle small drops of liquid on something: *Spray the apple tree to kill the worms.*
❑ VERB **sprays, sprayed, spray·ing.** –**spray′er,** NOUN.

spray[2] (sprā), NOUN. a small branch or piece of some plant with its leaves, flowers, or fruit: *She cut a spray of lilacs from the bush.*

spread (spred),
1 VERB. to cover or cause to cover a large or larger area; stretch out; unfold: *We spread rugs on the floor.*
2 VERB. to move things farther apart: *Spread your fingers out.*
3 VERB. to affect many people: *Flu has spread rapidly this winter.*
4 NOUN. the act of spreading: *We try to fight the spread of infection.*
5 VERB. to make or become known over a wide area: *News of the storm spread quickly.*
6 NOUN. a covering for a bed or table.
7 VERB. to cover with a thin layer of something: *She spread jam on her bread.*
8 NOUN. a soft food to spread on bread, crackers, or the like. Butter and jam are spreads.
❑ VERB **spreads, spread, spread·ing.** –**spread′er,** NOUN.

spread·sheet (spred′shēt′), NOUN. a computer program designed to process numerical information, especially for financial purposes.

a	hat	ė	term	ô	order	ch	child	(	a in about
ā	age	i	it	oi	oil	ng	long		e in taken
ä	far	ī	ice	ou	out	sh	she	ə {	i in pencil
â	care	o	hot	u	cup	th	thin		o in lemon
e	let	ō	open	ủ	put	ŦH	then		u in circus
ē	equal	ò	saw	ü	rule	zh	measure	(	

spring (spring),
  1 *NOUN.* the season when plants begin to grow; season of the year between winter and summer.
  2 *ADJECTIVE.* of or for spring; coming in spring. Spring wheat is wheat sown in the spring: *Tulips are spring flowers.*
  3 *VERB.* to leap or jump suddenly and lightly: *The dog sprang at the thief. I sprang to my feet.*
  4 *NOUN.* an elastic device in the form of a coil that returns to its original shape after being pulled out of shape. *Many beds have wire springs.*
  5 *VERB.* to move back or away as if by an elastic device: *The door sprang shut.*
  6 *VERB.* to cause to move in this way: *The slightest pressure will spring the trap.*
  7 *NOUN.* a small stream of water that flows naturally from the ground.
  8 *VERB.* to come from some source; arise; grow: *A wind has sprung up. Plants spring from seeds.*
  9 *VERB.* to begin to move, act, or grow suddenly; burst forth: *Towns sprang up along the river.*
  10 *VERB.* to bring out, produce, or make suddenly: *I like to spring surprises on my brother.*
  ❑ *VERB* **springs, sprang** or **sprung, sprung, spring·ing.**

cherry blossoms in the **spring**

Spring·field (spring′fēld′), *NOUN.* the capital of Illinois.

spring·time (spring′tīm′), *NOUN.* the season of spring: *Flowers bloom in the springtime.*

sprin·kle (spring′kəl),
  1 *VERB.* to scatter something in drops or tiny bits: *I sprinkled sand on the icy sidewalk.*
  2 *VERB.* to spray or cover something with small drops: *She sprinkled the flowers with water.*
  3 *VERB.* to rain a little bit: *It's beginning to sprinkle.*
  4 *NOUN.* a sprinkling; small quantity: *a sprinkle of nuts on the cake, a sprinkle of rain.*
  ❑ *VERB* **sprin·kles, sprin·kled, sprin·kling.**

sprin·kler (spring′klər), *NOUN.* a device for sprinkling water on crops, gardens, and lawns.

sprint (sprint),
  1 *VERB.* to run at top speed for a short distance.
  2 *NOUN.* a short race that you run at top speed.
  ❑ *VERB* **sprints, sprint·ed, sprint·ing. −sprint′er,** *NOUN.*

sprock·et (sprok′it), *NOUN.*
  1 one of a set of metal teeth around the rim of a wheel that fit into the links of a chain. The sprockets hold the chain in place.
  2 a wheel made with sprockets, sometimes called a **sprocket wheel.**

sprout (sprout),
  1 *VERB.* to produce new leaves, shoots, or buds; begin to grow: *Violets sprout in the spring.*
  2 *NOUN.* a young plant or a new part of an old plant: *The gardener was setting out sprouts.*
  ❑ *VERB* **sprouts, sprout·ed, sprout·ing.**

spruce (sprüs), *NOUN.* a kind of evergreen tree with leaves shaped like needles. Its soft wood is used in making paper, boxes, and lumber.

sprung (sprung), *VERB.*
  1 a past tense of **spring:** *The mouse sprung the trap.*
  2 the past participle of **spring:** *The trap was sprung.*

spry (sprī), *ADJECTIVE.* lively and active: *The spry old woman traveled all over the country.* ❑ *ADJECTIVE* **spry·er, spry·est** or **spri·er, spri·est.**

spruce

spun (spun), *VERB.*
  1 the past tense of **spin:** *The car skidded and spun on the ice.*
  2 the past participle of **spin:** *This thread is spun from silk.*

spunk (spungk), *NOUN.* (informal) courage; pluck; spirit: *That little girl has lots of spunk.*

spur (spėr),
  1 *NOUN.* a metal point or pointed wheel worn on a rider's heel. It is used to urge a horse forward.
  2 *VERB.* to jab or poke an animal with spurs: *The riders spurred their horses on.*
  3 *VERB.* to urge on: *Cheers spurred the runners on.*
  ❑ *VERB* **spurs, spurred, spur·ring.**
  on the spur of the moment, *IDIOM.* on a sudden impulse, without previous thought or preparation: *We decided to go to the movies on the spur of the moment.*

spurn (spėrn), *VERB.* to refuse to accept something; reject: *The judge spurned the bribe that was offered.* ❑ *VERB* **spurns, spurned, spurn·ing.**

spurt (spėrt),
1 *VERB.* to flow out suddenly in a stream or jet; gush out; squirt: *Water spurted from the fountain.*
2 *NOUN.* a forceful stream of liquid; jet: *There was a spurt of blood from the cut.*
3 *NOUN.* a great increase of effort or activity for a short time: *To win the race he put on a spurt of speed.*
4 *VERB.* to put forth great energy for a short time: *A runner spurted ahead near the end of the race.*
❑ *VERB* **spurts, spurt•ed, spurt•ing.**

sput•ter (sput′ər), *VERB.*
1 to make spitting or popping noises: *Fat sputtered in the frying pan.*
2 to talk in a hasty, confused way: *Embarrassed, he began to sputter and make silly excuses.*
❑ *VERB* **sput•ters, sput•tered, sput•ter•ing.**

spy (spī),
1 *NOUN.* a person who tries to get information about the enemy, especially in time of war, by visiting the enemy's territory in disguise.
2 *NOUN.* someone who secretly watches what other people are doing.
3 *VERB.* to watch secretly: *He saw two men spying on him from behind a tree.*
4 *VERB.* to act as a spy; be a spy.
5 *VERB.* to catch sight of; see: *She spied an old friend across the street.*
❑ *PLURAL* **spies;** *VERB* **spies, spied, spy•ing.**

spy•glass (spī′glas′), *NOUN.* a small telescope.
❑ *PLURAL* **spy•glass•es.**

sq. or **sq,** an abbreviation of **square.**

squab•ble (skwäb′əl),
1 *NOUN.* a noisy quarrel about nothing very important: *Children's squabbles annoy their parents.* ■ See the Synonym Study at **argue.**
2 *VERB.* to take part in a noisy quarrel about nothing very important: *Let's not squabble over a nickel.*
❑ *VERB* **squab•bles, squab•bled, squab•bling.**

squad (skwäd), *NOUN.*
1 a small number of soldiers trained to work or fight together. A squad is the smallest part of an army.
2 any small group of people working together: *A squad of children cleaned up the yard.*

squad•ron (skwäd′rən), *NOUN.*
1 a part of a naval fleet: *a destroyer squadron.*
2 a formation of eight or more airplanes that fly or fight together.

squall (skwȯl), *NOUN.* a sudden, violent gust of wind, often with rain, snow, or sleet.

squan•der (skwän′dər), *VERB.* to use something up in a foolish way; waste: *to squander time and money.*
❑ *VERB* **squan•ders, squan•dered, squan•der•ing.**

square (skwâr),
1 *NOUN.* a figure with four equal sides and four right angles (□).
2 *ADJECTIVE.* having this shape: *a square box. This table is square.*

3 *NOUN.* anything having this shape or nearly this shape: *I gave the child a square of chocolate.*
4 *NOUN.* an open space in a city or town with streets on all four sides, often planted with grass or trees: *There is a fountain in the square opposite the city hall.*
5 *ADJECTIVE.* having a certain length and width. A square meter is the area of a square whose edges are each one meter long.
6 *NOUN.* the sum that results when a number is multiplied by itself. 9 is the square of 3.
7 *ADJECTIVE.* forming a right angle: *This table has four square corners.*
8 *VERB.* to make something straight, level, or even: *He squared the picture on the wall.*
9 *ADJECTIVE.* just; fair; honest: *You will get a square deal at this shop.*
❑ *ADJECTIVE* **squar•er, squar•est;** *VERB* **squares, squared, squar•ing.**

square meal, *IDIOM.* a complete and satisfying meal: *Dad never snacks; he eats three square meals a day.*

square dance, a dance done by groups of four couples in a square formation. The dancers form different patterns according to the directions of a person who calls out the steps of the dances.

square knot, a knot firmly joining two loose ends of rope or cord. Each end is formed into a loop that both encloses and passes through the other.

square root, a number that produces a given number when multiplied by itself. The square root of 16 is 4.

members of a **squadron** flying in formation

squash¹ (skwäsh), *VERB.* to press against something until it is soft or flat; crush: *This package was squashed in the mail.* ❑ *VERB* **squash•es, squashed, squash•ing.**

a	hat	ė	term	ô	order	ch	child		a in about
ā	age	i	it	oi	oil	ng	long		e in taken
ä	far	ī	ice	ou	out	sh	she	ə	i in pencil
â	care	o	hot	u	cup	th	thin		o in lemon
e	let	ō	open	u̇	put	ᴛʜ	then		u in circus
ē	equal	ȯ	saw	ü	rule	zh	measure		

squash² (skwäsh), *NOUN.* the fruit of a garden vine, eaten as a vegetable. There are many kinds of squash, having different shapes and colors, usually yellow, green, or white. ❑ *PLURAL* **squash** or **squash·es.**

squash²

squat (skwät),
1 *VERB.* to crouch on your heels: *She was squatting on the grass watching a caterpillar.*
2 *ADJECTIVE.* short and thick: *a squat teapot.*
❑ *VERB* **squats, squat·ted, squat·ting;** *ADJECTIVE* **squat·ter, squat·test.**

squawk (skwȯk),
1 *VERB.* to make a loud, harsh sound: *Hens and ducks squawk when frightened.*
2 *NOUN.* a loud, harsh sound.
3 *VERB.* (informal) to complain loudly: *They squawked about the large repair bill.* ▪ See the Synonym Study at **complain.**
❑ *VERB* **squawks, squawked, squawk·ing.**

squeak (skwēk),
1 *VERB.* to make a short, sharp, loud sound: *A mouse squeaks.*
2 *NOUN.* this sound: *We heard the squeak of the stairs.*
❑ *VERB* **squeaks, squeaked, squeak·ing.**

squeal (skwēl),
1 *VERB.* to make a long, sharp, shrill cry: *A pig squeals when it is hurt.*
2 *NOUN.* a cry like this.
3 *VERB.* (informal) to give information to the police, a teacher, and so on, about something that another person has done: *One thief squealed on the others.*
❑ *VERB* **squeals, squealed, squeal·ing. −squeal′er,** *NOUN.*

squeeze (skwēz),
1 *VERB.* to push or press hard against something: *Don't squeeze the kitten, or you will hurt it.*
2 *NOUN.* the act of squeezing; a tight pressure: *She gave her sister's arm a squeeze.*
3 *VERB.* to hug: *He squeezed his child.*
4 *VERB.* to force by pressing: *I can't squeeze another thing into my trunk. I squeezed into the crowded meeting room.*
5 *VERB.* to force something out by pressure: *I squeezed the juice from two lemons.*
❑ *VERB* **squeez·es, squeezed, squeez·ing. −squeez′a·ble,** *ADJECTIVE.*

squid (skwid), *NOUN.* a sea animal that looks something like an octopus but having a pair of tail fins and ten arms instead of eight. It is a mollusk. ❑ *PLURAL* **squid** or **squids.**

a **squid** inside a long, curling branch of coral

squig·gle (skwig′əl), *NOUN.* a wiggly twist or curve: *The child drew squiggles on the paper.*

squint (skwint),
1 *VERB.* to look at with your eyes partly closed: *She squinted in the bright sunlight.*
2 *NOUN.* the act of squinting: *The squint she gave me indicated she doubted my story.*
❑ *VERB* **squints, squint·ed, squint·ing.**

squire (skwīr), NOUN.
1 (formerly, in Great Britain) a man who owned most of the land in a district or around a village.
2 (in the Middle Ages) a young man of noble family who attended a knight till he himself was made a knight.

squirm (skwėrm), VERB. to turn and twist your body; wriggle: *The restless girl squirmed in her seat.*
❑ VERB **squirms, squirmed, squirm·ing.**

squir·rel (skwėr′əl or skwėrl), NOUN. a small animal with a bushy tail that usually lives in trees and eats nuts. Squirrels are rodents.
—**squir′rel·like′,** ADJECTIVE.

squirt (skwėrt),
1 VERB. to force liquid out through a narrow opening: *to squirt water through a tube.*
2 VERB. to come out in a jet or stream: *Water squirted from the hose.*
3 NOUN. a jet of liquid: *I put a squirt of oil on the rusty bolt.*
❑ VERB **squirts, squirt·ed, squirt·ing.**

squish (skwish), VERB.
1 to move in a soft, wet oozing way: *The mud squished between my toes.*
2 to make a sound of something soft and wet being pressed: *My wet shoes squished as I walked.*
❑ VERB **squish·es, squished, squish·ing.**

Sr., an abbreviation of **Senior.**

Sri Lan·ka (srē′ läng′kə), an island country in the Indian Ocean. —**Sri Lankan.**

St.,
1 an abbreviation of **Saint.**
2 an abbreviation of **Street.**

stab (stab),
1 VERB. to pierce or wound someone with a pointed weapon: *He was stabbed with a knife.*
2 NOUN. a wound made by stabbing.
3 NOUN. a sudden, sharp feeling: *He felt a stab of pain when he moved his arm.*
❑ VERB **stabs, stabbed, stab·bing.**

take a stab at or **make a stab at,** IDIOM. to try to do something; make an attempt: *I've never skied, but I'd like to take a stab at it.*

a pair of **squirrels**

sta·bil·i·ty (stə bil′ə tē), NOUN. the condition of being stable; firmness: *A brick wall has more stability than a light wooden fence.*

sta·ble¹ (stā′bəl),
1 NOUN. a building where horses and cattle are kept and fed: *She keeps a horse at a local stable.*
2 VERB. to put or keep animals in a stable.
❑ VERB **sta·bles, sta·bled, sta·bling.**

sta·ble² (stā′bəl), ADJECTIVE.
1 not likely to move or change position; steady; firm: *We held the ladder to make it perfectly stable while Mom was changing the light bulb.*
2 not likely to be overturned: *a stable government.*

stack (stak),
1 NOUN. a pile of things lying one upon another: *a stack of wood, a stack of paper.*
2 VERB. to arrange something in a pile: *to stack hay, to stack firewood.*
3 NOUN. a large pile of hay or straw. Stacks of hay are often round and put together so that they will shed water.
❑ VERB **stacks, stacked, stack·ing.** —**stack′a·ble,** ADJECTIVE. —**stack′er,** NOUN.

sta·di·um (stā′dē əm), NOUN. a large building, usually without a roof. A stadium has rows of seats surrounding a playing field.

staff (staf),
1 NOUN. a group assisting a chief; group of employees: *Our school has a staff of twenty teachers.*
2 VERB. to provide a business with employees.
3 NOUN. a stick; pole; rod: *The old man leaned on his staff. The flag hangs on a staff.*
4 NOUN. the five lines and the four spaces between them, on which music is written. See the illustration at **clef.**
❑ VERB **staffs, staffed, staff·ing.**

stag (stag), NOUN. a full-grown male deer.

stage (stāj),
1 NOUN. one step or degree in a process; period of development. Frogs pass through a tadpole stage.
2 NOUN. the raised platform in a theater where the actors perform.
3 NOUN. **the stage,** the profession of acting; the theater: *to write for the stage.*
4 VERB. to present on a stage: *The third grade staged a play last week.*
5 VERB. to plan something and carry it out: *The class staged a surprise party for the teacher's birthday.*
6 NOUN. a section of a rocket or missile having its own engine and fuel. A three-stage rocket has

a	hat	ė	term	ô	order	ch	child		a in about
ā	age	i	it	oi	oil	ng	long		e in taken
ä	far	ī	ice	ou	out	sh	she	ə	i in pencil
â	care	o	hot	u	cup	th	thin		o in lemon
e	let	ō	open	u̇	put	ŦH	then		u in circus
ē	equal	ȯ	saw	ü	rule	zh	measure		

three engines, one in each stage, which separate one after another from the rocket after use.

7 *NOUN.* a short form of **stagecoach.**
❑ *VERB* **stag·es, staged, stag·ing.**

stage·coach (stāj′kōch′), *NOUN.* (earlier) a coach pulled by horses and carrying passengers, mail, and packages over a regular route.

stag·ger (stag′ər),

1 *VERB.* to move or walk unsteadily: *I staggered and fell under the heavy load of books.*

2 *VERB.* to cause someone to almost fall down: *The blow staggered him for a moment.*

3 *NOUN.* a swaying or reeling walk or movement: *She walked with a stagger after spinning around.*

4 *VERB.* to confuse or shock someone greatly; overwhelm: *She was staggered by the news of her friend's death.*
❑ *VERB* **stag·gers, stag·gered, stag·ger·ing.**

stag·nant (stag′nənt), *ADJECTIVE.* not running or flowing; dirty from standing still: *stagnant water.*

stain (stān),

1 *VERB.* to discolor something with dirt, blood, spilled food, and so on; spot: *Spilled grape juice stained the tablecloth.*

2 *NOUN.* a spot: *I have an ink stain on my shirt.*

3 *VERB.* to color or dye something: *She stained the chair green.*

4 *NOUN.* a coloring or dye: *She put a brown stain on the table.*
❑ *VERB* **stains, stained, stain·ing.**

stained glass, pieces of colored glass used to form a picture or design.

a vivid picture in **stained glass**

stain·less steel (stān′lis stēl′), steel containing a certain amount of chromium, making it very resistant to rust. Knives, forks, and spoons are often made of stainless steel.

stair (stâr), *NOUN.*

1 one of a series of steps for walking from one floor to another.

2 stairs, a set of steps: *the top of the stairs.*
■ Another word that sounds like this is **stare.**

stair·case (stâr′kās′), *NOUN.* a flight of stairs with a banister; stairs.

stair·way (stâr′wā′), *NOUN.* a way up and down by stairs; stairs: *the back stairway.*

stake¹ (stāk),

1 *NOUN.* a pointed bar of wood or metal driven into the ground.

2 *VERB.* to fasten something to a stake or with a stake: *to stake down a tent.*

3 *VERB.* to mark the boundaries of something with stakes: *The miners staked out their claims.*
❑ *VERB* **stakes, staked, stak·ing.** ■ Another word that sounds like this is **steak.**

stake² (stāk),

1 *VERB.* to risk money or something valuable on the result of a game or on any chance: *She staked five dollars on the black horse.*

2 *NOUN.* **stakes,** the prize in a race or contest: *The stakes were divided up among the winners.*

3 *NOUN.* something that you can gain or lose; an interest: *Each of us has a stake in the future.*
❑ *VERB* **stakes, staked, stak·ing.** ■ Another word that sounds like this is **steak.**

sta·lac·tite (stə lak′tīt), *NOUN.* a formation of stone, shaped like an icicle, hanging from the roof of a cave. It is formed by minerals in dripping water.

Did You Know?

There is an easy way to remember the difference between **stalactites** and **stalagmites.** Stalactites hang from the top of a cave. The "t" in stalactite stands for "top."

Stalactites and **stalagmites** are usually found in the same places.

sta·lag·mite (stə lag′mīt), *NOUN.* a formation of stone, shaped like a cone, built up on the floor of a cave. It is formed by minerals in dripping water.

stale (stāl), *ADJECTIVE.*

1 not fresh: *stale bread, stale cookies.*

2 no longer new or interesting: *a stale joke.*
❑ *ADJECTIVE* **stal·er, stal·est. −stale′ness,** *NOUN.*

stale·mate (stāl′māt′), *NOUN.*
1 (in chess) the draw that results when you cannot move any of your pieces without putting your own king in check.
2 any contest, argument, and so on, that ends without a clear winner.

stalk¹ (stȯk), *NOUN.*
1 the tall stem of a plant. Corn grows on stalks.
2 any slender, supporting part of a plant or animal. A flower may have a stalk. The eyes of a lobster are on stalks.

stalk² (stȯk), *VERB.*
1 to hunt something or someone by following it silently and carefully: *The hungry lion stalked a gnu.*
2 to walk in a slow, stiff, or proud manner: *She stalked into the room and threw herself into a chair.*
❏ *VERB* **stalks, stalked, stalk·ing.**

stall¹ (stȯl),
1 *NOUN.* a place for one animal in a barn or stable.
2 *NOUN.* a small place for selling things: *At the public market different things were sold in different stalls under one big roof.*
3 *NOUN.* a small enclosed space: *a shower stall.*
4 *VERB.* to put or keep animals in a stall: *The horses were safely stalled.*
5 *VERB.* to stop working or going: *The engine stalled.*
❏ *VERB* **stalls, stalled, stall·ing.**

stall² (stȯl), *VERB.* to act or speak vaguely or uncertainly in order to avoid doing something: *Every time she asks for a raise, her boss stalls.*
❏ *VERB* **stalls, stalled, stall·ing.**

stal·lion (stal′yən), *NOUN.* a male horse.

sta·men (stā′mən), *NOUN.* the part of a flower that contains the pollen. A stamen consists of an anther supported by a slender stem. The stamens are surrounded by the petals.

Each of these flowers has five **stamens.**

stam·i·na (stam′ə nə), *NOUN.* strength or endurance: *He didn't have enough stamina to finish the race.*

stam·mer (stam′ər),
1 *VERB.* to repeat the same sound or pause repeatedly in an effort to speak. People may stammer when they are nervous, embarrassed, or afraid.
2 *VERB.* to say something in this manner: *She stammered an excuse.*
3 *NOUN.* the act of stammering; stuttering: *He has a nervous stammer.*
❏ *VERB* **stam·mers, stam·mered, stam·mer·ing.**

stamp (stamp),
1 *NOUN.* a small piece of paper with glue on the back; postage stamp. You put stamps on letters or packages before mailing them.
2 *VERB.* to put a stamp on: *to stamp a letter.*
3 *VERB.* to bring down your foot with force: *He stamped his foot in anger.*
4 *VERB.* to pound; crush; trample: *Stamp out the fire.*
5 *NOUN.* a device that cuts, shapes, or puts a design on paper, wax, or metal: *The rubber stamp had her name on it.*
6 *VERB.* to make a mark on something: *She stamped the papers with the date.*
❏ *VERB* **stamps, stamped, stamp·ing.**

stam·pede (stam pēd′),
1 *NOUN.* a sudden headlong flight of a frightened herd of cattle or horses.
2 *NOUN.* any headlong flight of a large group: *There was a stampede of people from the burning store.*
3 *VERB.* to scatter or cause to scatter suddenly: *The frightened cattle began to stampede.*
❏ *VERB* **stam·pedes, stam·ped·ed, stam·ped·ing.**

stand (stand),
1 *VERB.* to be on your feet instead of sitting down: *Don't stand if you are tired, but sit down.*
2 *VERB.* to rise to your feet: *The children stood to salute the flag.*
3 *VERB.* to set something upright: *Stand the plant in that sunny corner.*
4 *VERB.* to be in a certain rank or scale: *He stood first in his class in mathematics.*
5 *VERB.* to stay in place; last; remain: *The old house has stood for a hundred years.*
6 *VERB.* to put up with; bear: *This plant cannot stand the cold.*
7 *VERB.* to stop moving; halt; stop: *The cars stood in place, waiting for the green light.*
8 *NOUN.* a stop for defense: *We made a last stand against the enemy.*
9 *NOUN.* a raised place where people can sit or stand: *The mayor sat on the reviewing stand at the parade.*
10 *NOUN.* something to put things on or in: *an umbrella stand, a music stand.*
11 *NOUN.* a place where you can have a small business: *a newspaper stand, a fruit stand.*
❏ *VERB* **stands, stood, stand·ing.**

a	hat	ė	term	ô	order	ch	child	a in about
ā	age	i	it	oi	oil	ng	long	e in taken
ä	far	ī	ice	ou	out	sh	she	ə ⟨ i in pencil
â	care	o	hot	u	cup	th	thin	o in lemon
e	let	ō	open	ů	put	ᴛʜ	then	u in circus
ē	equal	ȯ	saw	ü	rule	zh	measure	

stand by, IDIOM.
1 to side with; help; support: *He stood by his friend when she was in trouble.*
2 to be or get ready for use or action: *The radio operator was ordered to stand by.*

stand for, IDIOM.
1 to mean the same thing as: *The abbreviation "St." stands for "street" or "saint."*
2 to put up with: *The teacher said she would not stand for talking during class.*

stand in for, IDIOM. to take the place of; substitute for: *I stood in for her when she was sick.*

stand out, IDIOM.
1 to stick out; project: *His ears stood out.*
2 to be noticeable or obvious: *Certain facts in the matter stand out.*

take a stand, IDIOM. to state a strong opinion about something: *We took a strong stand against the new garbage dump.*

stan·dard (stan′dərd),
1 NOUN. anything taken as a basis of comparing things; model: *Your work is not up to the class standard.*
2 ADJECTIVE. usual; normal: *Nails come in several standard sizes.*

stand·ing (stan′ding),
1 NOUN. someone's reputation: *He is a person of good standing.*
2 NOUN. the length of time that something has lasted: *We have a friendship of long standing.*
3 ADJECTIVE. permanent: *a standing invitation, a standing army.*
4 ADJECTIVE. not flowing; stagnant: *standing water.*

stand·point (stand′point′), NOUN. a way of thinking about something; point of view: *From my standpoint, you are wrong.*

stank (stangk), VERB. a past tense of **stink:** *The dead fish stank.*

stan·za (stan′zə), NOUN. a group of lines of poetry, usually four or more, arranged according to a fixed plan; a short division of a poem or song: *They sang the first and last stanzas of "America the Beautiful."* ❑ PLURAL **stan·zas.**

sta·ple[1] (stā′pəl),
1 NOUN. a piece of metal with pointed ends bent into a square U shape. Staples are driven into wood to hold hooks, wiring, and insulation.
2 NOUN. a bent piece of wire used to hold together papers or parts of a book.
3 VERB. to fasten paper things together with staples: *I stapled the pages of my report.*
❑ VERB **sta·ples, sta·pled, sta·pling.**

sta·ple[2] (stā′pəl),
1 NOUN. a product, especially a food sold and used all the time. Bread, milk, sugar, and salt are staples in this country.

2 NOUN. the most important or principal product grown or manufactured somewhere: *Cotton is the staple in many Southern states.*
3 ADJECTIVE. most important; principal: *Bread is a staple food.*

sta·pler (stā′plər), NOUN. a device for fastening papers together with wire staples.

star (stär),
1 NOUN. any object appearing as a bright point in the sky at night and shining by its own light. A star is a mass of very hot gas. Some stars are smaller than the earth, while others are many time larger than the sun.
2 NOUN. a shape that has five or more points, like these: ★ ✿
3 NOUN. a very well-known person in some art, sport, or profession, especially one who plays the lead in a performance: *a movie star, a television star, a track star.*
4 ADJECTIVE. chief; best; leading; excellent: *the star player on a football team.*
5 VERB. to act the part of an important character: *She has starred in many movies.*
❑ VERB **stars, starred, star·ring.**

Did You Know?

The closest **star** to the Earth is the Sun, of course! The next closest star is called Proxima Centauri (prok′sə mə sen tôr′ī). It is 25 trillion (25,000,000,000,000) miles away.

star·board (stär′bərd), NOUN. the side of a ship, boat, or aircraft to the right of someone aboard who is facing the front.

starch (stärch),
1 NOUN. a white, tasteless food substance. Potatoes, bread, pasta, and rice contain a lot of starch. Starch is a carbohydrate and is an important nutrient.
2 NOUN. a preparation of this substance used to stiffen clothes.
3 VERB. to stiffen clothes or curtains with starch.
❑ VERB **starch·es, starched, starch·ing.**

starch·y (stär′chē), ADJECTIVE. like starch; containing starch: *Rice is a starchy food.* ❑ ADJECTIVE **starch·i·er, starch·i·est.**

stare (stâr),
1 VERB. to look at someone with your eyes wide open for a long time. A person stares in wonder, surprise, curiosity, or from rudeness: *The little girl stared at the toys in the window.* ■ See the Synonym Study at **look.**
2 NOUN. a long and direct look with the eyes wide open: *The doll's eyes were set in a fixed stare. He gave them an angry stare.*
❑ VERB **stares, stared, star·ing.** ■ Another word that sounds like this is **stair.**

star·fish (stär′fish′),
NOUN. a star-shaped sea animal with a flattened body. Most starfish have five arms, but some kinds have as many as 40 arms. Starfish are not fish.
❑ PLURAL **star·fish** or **star·fish·es.**

starfish — up to 25 inches wide

stark (stärk),
1 ADVERB. entirely; completely: *The boys went swimming stark naked.*
2 ADJECTIVE. barren; bare; desolate: *I love the stark beauty of the desert.*

star·light (stär′līt′), NOUN. the light from the stars.

star·ling (stär′ling), NOUN. a common European and American bird with a plump body and shiny, dark feathers. It flies in large flocks.

star·lit (stär′līt′), ADJECTIVE. lighted by the stars: *a starlit night.*

star·ry (stär′ē), ADJECTIVE. lighted by stars; containing many stars: *a starry sky, a starry night.* ❑ ADJECTIVE **star·ri·er, star·ri·est.**

Our flag is called the **Stars and Stripes.**

Stars and Stripes, the flag of the United States.

Star-Span·gled Ban·ner (stär′spang′gəld ban′ər), the national anthem of the United States.

start (stärt),
1 VERB. to begin to move, go, or act: *The orchestra's performance started on time.*
2 VERB. to begin: *School starts next week.*
3 VERB. to set something going; put into action: *to start a car, to start a fire.*
4 NOUN. the act of setting in motion: *We pushed the car to give the motor a start.*
5 NOUN. the act of beginning to move, go, or act: *We like to see a race from start to finish.*
6 VERB. to move suddenly; move when startled: *I started in surprise.*

7 NOUN. a sudden movement; jerk: *I awoke with a start.*
8 VERB. to put in the original lineup in a contest: *The manager started a left-handed pitcher.*
❑ VERB **starts, start·ed, start·ing.**

Synonym Study

Start means to set something going: *The space shuttle flight starts with the roar of powerful engines.*

Begin means to start something, or to start doing something: *She began her letter, "Dear Grandma." The snow began to fall around midnight.*

Commence means to start. It is a formal word: *My sister's graduation ceremony commences at ten o'clock.*

ANTONYMS: finish, stop.

start·er (stär′tər), NOUN. a small electric motor for starting the engine of a vehicle.

star·tle (stär′tl), VERB. to frighten someone suddenly; surprise: *The dog jumped at the girl and startled her.* ■ See the Synonym Study at **surprise.**
❑ VERB **star·tles, star·tled, star·tling.**

star·va·tion (stär vā′shən), NOUN. the condition of suffering from extreme hunger: *Starvation caused his death.*

starve (stärv), VERB.
1 to suffer from or die of hunger: *People are starving in that country.*
2 to weaken or kill someone with hunger: *The enemy starved the men in the fort into surrendering.*
3 (informal) to feel very hungry: *I'm starving! Let's eat.*
❑ VERB **starves, starved, starv·ing.**

starve for, IDIOM. to suffer or cause to suffer from lack of: *That lonely child is starving for affection.*

stash (stash), VERB. to hide or put something away for protection or future use: *The thieves stashed the money in a cave. I stashed a candy bar in my backpack for later.* ❑ VERB **stash·es, stashed, stash·ing.**

state (stāt),
1 NOUN. the condition a person or thing is in. Ice is water in a solid state: *The crowd was in a state of excitement. The house is in a bad state of repair.*
2 NOUN. a group of people that live in a given area and are organized under a government; nation: *The state of Israel is an independent country.*
3 NOUN. one of the areas that form a federal union: *The state of Alaska is in the United States.*

a hat	ė term	ô order	ch child	(a in about
ā age	i it	oi oil	ng long	e in taken
ä far	ī ice	ou out	sh she	ə i in pencil
â care	o hot	u cup	th thin	o in lemon
e let	ō open	ù put	⟨⟨ then	u in circus
ē equal	ò saw	ü rule	zh measure	

S

4 *VERB.* to say or write something: *The new student stated that she was born in Arizona.* ■ See the Synonym Study at **say**.
❑ *VERB* **states, stat·ed, stat·ing.**

state·ly (stāt′lē), *ADJECTIVE.* grand; majestic: *The Capitol at Washington is a stately building.* ❑ *ADJECTIVE* **state·li·er, state·li·est. –state′li·ness,** *NOUN.*

state·ment (stāt′mənt), *NOUN.*
1 something said or written; account; report: *Her statement was correct.*
2 a summary of an account, showing the amount owed or due: *a bank statement.*

states·man (stāts′mən), *NOUN.* a government leader who is skilled in the management of public or national affairs: *Statesmen from many nations met to discuss possible solutions to serious world problems.* ❑ *PLURAL* **states·men. –states′man·like′,** *ADJECTIVE.* **–states′man·ship,** *NOUN.*

states·wom·an (stāts′wùm′ən), *NOUN.* a woman who is a government leader skilled in the management of public or national affairs. ❑ *PLURAL* **states·wom·en.**

state·wide (stāt′wīd′), *ADJECTIVE.* covering an entire state; over all of a state: *The governor announced a statewide tornado alert.*

stat·ic (stat′ik), *NOUN.* the crackling noise that sometimes comes from radios. Static is produced by electrical disturbances.

static electricity, an electric charge which sometimes builds up on objects that rub against each other. Static electricity often occurs when people comb their hair.

Static electricity makes her hair stick to the balloon.

sta·tion (stā′shən),
1 *NOUN.* a regular stopping place along a route: *a train station, a bus station.*
2 *NOUN.* the place or equipment for sending out or receiving programs or messages by radio or television.
3 *NOUN.* a building or place used for a special reason: *The suspect was taken to the police station. Coast Guard stations are equipped with boats and aircraft to rescue people from the water.*
4 *VERB.* to put someone in a certain place to do a job: *The soldier was stationed at Fort Hays.*
❑ *VERB* **sta·tions, sta·tioned, sta·tion·ing.**

sta·tion·ar·y (stā′shə ner′ē), *ADJECTIVE.* standing still; not moving: *A parked car is stationary.*
■ See the Usage Note at **stationery**.

sta·tion·er·y (stā′shə ner′ē), *NOUN.* writing paper, cards, envelopes, and so on.

Usage Note

Stationery and **stationary** are easy to confuse. One way to remember which is which is to remember that you use a **pen** with **stationery** and both *pen* and *stationery* are spelled with an e. Another memory trick is to remember that a **parked car** is **stationary**. *Parked, car,* and *stationary* are all spelled with an a.

station wagon, a motor vehicle with a rear door for loading and unloading and seats in the rear that can be folded down, for use as a light truck.

sta·tis·tics (stə tis′tiks), *NOUN.* facts in the form of numbers. Statistics are collected to give information about people, weather, businesses, and many other things.

stat·ue (stach′ü), *NOUN.* a figure made from stone, wood, or metal to look like a person or animal. ❑ *PLURAL* **statues.**

stat·ure (stach′ər), *NOUN.* height: *She is a young woman of average stature.*

sta·tus (stā′təs), *NOUN.*
1 someone's social or professional position; rank: *the status of a judge, the status of a factory worker.*
2 condition; state: *Diplomats are interested in the status of world affairs.*
3 high rank or position: *Judges have status.*

stat·ute (stach′üt), *NOUN.* a law: *The statutes for the United States are made by Congress.*

stay (stā),
1 *VERB.* to be in a place for a while: *Stay still. Stay here till I call you. The cat stayed out all night.*
2 *VERB.* to live somewhere for a while; dwell: *She is staying with her aunt for a few weeks.* ■ See the Synonym Study at **live¹**.
3 *NOUN.* a period of time spent somewhere: *Our stay at the seashore was much too short.*
❑ *VERB* **stays, stayed, stay·ing.**

stead·fast (sted′fast′), *ADJECTIVE.* loyal; constant: *The girls were steadfast companions for many years.* **–stead′fast′ly,** *ADVERB.*

stead·y (sted′ē),
1 *ADJECTIVE.* not changing very much; staying as it is: *steady speed, a steady gain in value.*
2 *ADJECTIVE.* not swaying or shaking; firm: *This post is steady as a rock. Hold the ladder steady.*
3 *ADJECTIVE.* not easily excited; calm: *Pilots who test new aircraft must have steady nerves.*
4 *VERB.* to make or become steady; keep steady: *Steady the ladder while I climb to the roof.*
❑ *ADJECTIVE* **stead·i·er, stead·i·est;** *VERB* **stead·ies, stead·ied, stead·y·ing. –stead′i·ly,** *ADVERB.* **–stead′i·ness,** *NOUN.*

steak (stāk), NOUN. a slice of meat (usually beef) or fish for broiling or frying. ■ Another word that sounds like this is **stake.**

steal (stēl), VERB.
1 to take something that does not belong to you: *Robbers stole the money.*
2 to take or get something secretly: *She stole time from her lessons to read a story.*
3 to move secretly or quietly: *She had stolen softly out of the house.*
4 (in baseball) to run to second base, third base, or home plate safely, as the pitcher throws the ball to the catcher.
□ VERB **steals, stole, sto·len, steal·ing.** ■ Another word that sounds like this is **steel.**

stealth·y (stel′thē), ADJECTIVE. done in a secret manner; secret; sly: *The cat crept in a stealthy way toward the bird.* □ ADJECTIVE **stealth·i·er, stealth·i·est. −stealth′i·ly,** ADVERB.

steam (stēm),
1 NOUN. very hot water in the form of vapor or gas. Boiling water gives off steam. Steam is used to produce electricity, and for heating and cooking.
2 VERB. to give off steam: *The coffee was steaming.*
3 VERB. to move by the power of steam: *The ship steamed off to Europe.*
4 VERB. to cook by using steam: *I steam vegetables to cook them.*
5 NOUN. power; energy; force: *I have worked all day and am running out of steam.*
□ VERB **steams, steamed, steam·ing.**

let off steam or **blow off steam,** IDIOM. to get rid of energy or express feelings: *During recess the children ran around the playground to let off steam.*

steam up, IDIOM. to cloud with steam; to cover with condensation: *His long hot shower steamed up the mirrors in the bathroom.*

steam·boat (stēm′bōt′), NOUN. a boat moved by steam. In former times, steamboats carried passengers and cargo on large rivers.

steam engine, an engine that works by the action of steam under pressure. Steam engines were used to drive locomotives, ships, and large machines.

steam·roll·er (stēm′rō′lər), NOUN. a vehicle with a heavy roller, used to crush and level materials in making roads.

steam·ship (stēm′ship′), NOUN. a ship powered by steam.

steel (stēl),
1 NOUN. a very hard, strong, tough metal that is made of iron mixed with carbon. Steel is used to make cars, railroad rails, bridges, buildings, and tools.
2 ADJECTIVE. made of steel: *Steel beams are used in skyscrapers and bridges.*
■ Another word that sounds like this is **steal.**

steel wool, a pad of long, fine steel threads. Steel wool is used to clean or polish surfaces.

steep¹ (stēp), ADJECTIVE.
1 having a sharp slope; almost straight up and down: *The hill is steep.*
2 too high; unreasonable: *a steep price, steep rent.* **−steep′ly,** ADVERB.

steep² (stēp), VERB. to soak: *Let the tea steep in boiling water for five minutes.* □ VERB **steeps, steeped, steep·ing.**

stee·ple (stē′pəl), NOUN. a very tall tower on a church, that usually narrows to a point at the top.

steer¹ (stir), VERB.
1 to cause something to go in a certain direction; guide; control: *She steered the car into the driveway.*
2 to be guided: *This car steers easily.*
3 to direct your way or course: *Steer for the harbor.*
□ VERB **steers, steered, steer·ing.**

steer² (stir), NOUN. a young male of cattle raised for beef, usually two to four years old.

stegosaurus — about 30 feet long, including the tail

steg·o·sau·rus (steg′ə sôr′əs), NOUN. a very large plant-eating dinosaur with bony plates and spikes along the back and tail. □ PLURAL **steg·o·sau·rus·es** or **steg·o·sau·ri** (steg′ə sôr′ī).

Word Story

Stegosaurus comes from two Greek words meaning "roof" and "lizard." The animal was named this because the growths on its back were thought to look or be like parts of the roof of a building.

a hat	ė term	ô order	ch child	⎧a in about
ā age	i it	oi oil	ng long	⎪e in taken
ä far	ī ice	ou out	sh she	ə⎨i in pencil
â care	o hot	u cup	th thin	⎪o in lemon
e let	ō open	ù put	₮H then	⎩u in circus
ē equal	ȯ saw	ü rule	zh measure	

S

stem (stem),

1 *NOUN.* the main supporting part of a plant above the ground. The stem holds up the branches. The trunk of a tree and the stalks of corn are stems.

2 *NOUN.* the part of a flower, a fruit, or a leaf that joins it to the plant or tree.

3 *VERB.* to grow out; come from; develop: *Our difficulties stem from poor planning.*

❏ *VERB* **stems, stemmed, stem·ming.**

stench (stench), *NOUN.* a very bad smell; stink: *the stench of a garbage dump.* ❏ *PLURAL* **stench·es.**

sten·cil (sten′səl),

1 *NOUN.* a thin sheet of metal, paper, or cardboard, with letters or designs cut through it. When it is laid on a surface and ink or color is spread over it, these letters or designs are made on the surface underneath.

2 *VERB.* to mark, paint, or make something with a stencil: *I stenciled my name on the box.*

❏ *VERB* **sten·cils, sten·ciled, sten·cil·ing.**

step (step),

1 *NOUN.* a movement made by lifting your foot and putting it down again in a new position; one motion of your leg in walking, running, or dancing.

2 *NOUN.* the distance covered by one such movement: *I was three steps from the phone when it stopped ringing.*

3 *VERB.* to put the foot down: *Don't step on that bug.*

4 *NOUN.* the sound made by putting the foot down: *I hear steps upstairs.*

5 *NOUN.* a place where you put your foot when you walk up or down stairs. A stair or a rung of a ladder is a step.

6 *VERB.* to move your legs as in walking, running, or dancing: *Please step to the front of the room.*

7 *NOUN.* a short distance; little way: *The school is only a step from our house.*

8 *NOUN.* a way of walking or dancing: *My dance instructor taught me several new steps.*

9 *NOUN.* an action someone takes: *Choosing where to go was the first step in planning our vacation.*

❏ *VERB* **steps, stepped, step·ping.** ∎ Another word that sounds like this is **steppe.**

in step, *IDIOM.* moving the same leg at the same time as another person does: *Band members must learn to march in step.*

step by step, *IDIOM.* little by little; slowly: *You can't just jump in to a big project like that; you have to take it step by step.*

step up, *IDIOM.* to make go faster or higher; increase: *The factory stepped up its production of cars. We stepped up our efforts to start a school newspaper.*

watch your step, *IDIOM.* be careful: *Watch your step when you ride down that steep hill on the bicycle.*

Word Power step-

The prefix **step-** means "related by the remarriage of a parent." A **step**father is the husband in the mother's **remarriage.**

step·fa·ther (step′fä′ᴛʜər), *NOUN.* a man who has married your mother after the death or divorce of your real father.

step·moth·er (step′muᴛʜ′ər), *NOUN.* a woman who has married your father after the death or divorce of your real mother.

steppe (step), *NOUN.* one of the vast, treeless plains in southeastern Europe and in Asia, especially in Russia. ∎ Another word that sounds like this is **step.**

ster·e·o (ster′ē ō *or* stir′ē ō), *NOUN.* a set of connected devices used to produce lifelike sound, usually including speakers, an amplifier, a radio tuner, a CD player, and so on. ❏ *PLURAL* **ster·e·os.**

ster·ile (ster′əl), *ADJECTIVE.* completely free from living germs: *Bandages should be kept sterile.*

ster·i·lize (ster′ə līz), *VERB.* to make something free from living germs: *The water was sterilized by boiling to make it fit to drink.* ❏ *VERB* **ster·i·liz·es, ster·i·lized, ster·i·liz·ing.** **—ster′i·li·za′tion,** *NOUN.*

ster·ling (stèr′ling), *ADJECTIVE.*

1 made of silver that is 92.5 percent pure. *Sterling* is stamped on things made of solid silver.

2 excellent; dependable: *This job requires a person of sterling character.*

stern[1] (stèrn), *ADJECTIVE.* severe; strict; harsh: *The teacher's stern frown silenced the giggling students.* **—stern′ly,** *ADVERB.*

stern[2] (stèrn), *NOUN.* the rear part of a ship or boat.

steth·o·scope (steth′ə skōp), *NOUN.* a medical device used to hear the sounds produced in the lungs, heart, or other parts of the body.

stew (stü),

1 *NOUN.* meat, vegetables, and spices boiled together slowly: *I love beef stew.*

2 *VERB.* to cook something by boiling it slowly: *The cook stewed the chicken for a long time.* ❏ *VERB* **stews, stewed, stew·ing.**

stew·ard (stü′ərd), *NOUN.* a man hired to look after passengers on an airplane or ship.

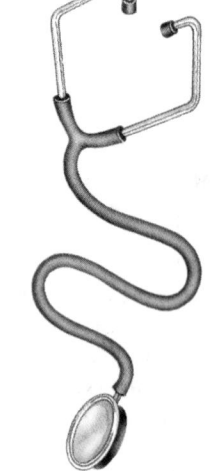

stethoscope

stew·ard·ess (stü′ər dis), *NOUN.* a woman hired to look after passengers on an airplane or ship.

❏ *PLURAL* **stew·ard·ess·es.**

stick¹ (stik), *NOUN.*
1 a long, thin piece of wood: *Put some sticks on the fire.*
2 a piece of wood shaped for a special use: *a walking stick, a hockey stick.*
3 something shaped like a stick: *a stick of candy.*
—**stick′like′**, *ADJECTIVE.*

stick² (stik), *VERB.*
1 to push something sharp into or through an object: *She stuck her fork into the potato.*
2 to fasten by pushing the point or end of something into or through something: *He stuck a flower in his buttonhole.*
3 to put into a position: *Don't stick your head out of the window.*
4 to come out from something: *The sweater shrank so that my arms stick out of the sleeves.*
5 to make things stay tightly together; fasten: *Stick a stamp on the letter.*
6 to be or become fastened together: *Two pages of the book stuck together.*
7 to come to a complete stop; be unable to move: *Our car stuck in the mud.*
8 to keep on; hold fast: *Let's stick to the task until we've finished it.*
❑ *VERB* **sticks, stuck, stick·ing.**
stick by or **stick to**, *IDIOM.* to remain faithful to; be loyal to: *I stick by my friends when they need help.*
stick out, *IDIOM.*
1 to be very obvious or very noticeable: *That red tulip really sticks out among the yellow ones.*
2 to come out from; extend: *His hands stick out from his sleeves. Do my ears stick out?*
stick up for, *IDIOM.* to stand up for; support; defend: *Stick up for your friends when they are in trouble.*

stick·ball (stik′bôl′), *NOUN.* a form of baseball played with a rubber ball and a stick or broom handle for a bat.

stick·er (stik′ər), *NOUN.* a label that has gum or glue on the back of it. A sticker can be fastened onto something else.

stick·y (stik′ē), *ADJECTIVE.*
1 covered with a layer of material that will stick: *Adhesive tape is sticky.*
2 hot and damp: *We have sticky summers here.*
❑ *ADJECTIVE* **stick·i·er, stick·i·est. —stick′i·ness**, *NOUN.*

stiff (stif), *ADJECTIVE.*
1 hard to bend: *He wore stiff work gloves.*
2 not able to move or be moved easily: *My neck is stiff. The hinges on this old door are stiff.*
3 firm: *Beat the egg whites until they are stiff.*
4 strong: *Stiff winds blew us off course.*
5 hard to deal with; hard: *There was stiff competition at the track meet.*
—**stiff′ly**, *ADVERB.* —**stiff′ness**, *NOUN.*

stiff·en (stif′ən), *VERB.* to make or become stiff: *Her muscles began to stiffen in the cold wind.*

I stiffened the cloth with starch. Jelly will stiffen as it cools. ❑ *VERB* **stiff·ens, stiff·ened, stiff·en·ing.**

sti·fle (stī′fəl), *VERB.*
1 to be unable to breathe freely: *I am stifling in this heat.*
2 to keep back; stop: *The conversation was so boring that I had to stifle a few yawns.*
3 to stop someone's breath; smother: *The smoke stifled the firefighters.*
❑ *VERB* **sti·fles, sti·fled, sti·fling.**

still (stil),
1 *ADJECTIVE.* not moving; without motion; quiet: *Please sit still. The lake is still today.*
2 *ADJECTIVE.* without noise; quiet: *The room was so still that you could have heard a pin drop.*
3 *VERB.* to make or become quiet: *The father stilled the crying baby.*
4 *ADVERB.* even; yet: *You can read better still if you try.*
5 *ADVERB.* in spite of; yet; nevertheless: *She has many friends; still, she likes to stay home.*
6 *ADVERB.* up to now; until now: *Is the library still open?*
❑ *VERB* **stills, stilled, still·ing. —still′ness**, *NOUN.*

stilt·ed (stil′tid), *ADJECTIVE.* stiffly dignified: *He had a stilted manner of speaking.*

stilts (stilts), *NOUN.* a pair of poles with pieces fastened on them to hold the feet steady above the ground. Stilts are used by circus clowns or by children for fun.

walking on **stilts**

stim·u·lant (stim′yə lənt), *NOUN.*
1 a food, drug, or medicine that speeds up the activity of the body or some part of the body for a short time. Tea and coffee are stimulants.
2 something that excites, stirs, or stimulates: *Advertising is a stimulant to sales.*

stim·u·late (stim′yə lāt), *VERB.* to make more active; encourage: *The new factory helped to stimulate growth in the town.* ❑ *VERB* **stim·u·lates, stim·u·lat·ed, stim·u·lat·ing. —stim′u·la′tion**, *NOUN.*

stim·u·lus (stim′yə ləs), *NOUN.*
1 something that encourages action or effort: *A lack of money was the stimulus for finding a summer job.*

a hat	ė term	ô order	ch child		a in about
ā age	i it	oi oil	ng long		e in taken
ä far	ī ice	ou out	sh she	ə	i in pencil
â care	o hot	u cup	th thin		o in lemon
e let	ō open	ů put	ᴛʜ then		u in circus
ē equal	ȯ saw	ü rule	zh measure		

2 something that causes a reaction in a living thing: *The stimulus of a bright light makes the pupils of the eyes become smaller.* ❑ PLURAL **stim•u•li** (stim′yə li).

sting (sting),
1 VERB. to pierce or wound with a sharp point: *Bees, wasps, and hornets sting. A bee stung her.*
2 NOUN. a short form of **stinger.**
3 NOUN. a very sore, burning wound: *The wasp sting began to swell.*
4 VERB. to cause someone to suffer sharp pain: *I was stung by the insult.*
5 NOUN. a sharp pain: *Our team felt the sting of defeat.* ❑ VERB **stings, stung, sting•ing. –sting′less,** ADJECTIVE.

sting•er (sting′ər), NOUN. the part of an insect or animal that has a sharp point and pierces or wounds and often poisons; sting.

sting•ray (sting′rā′), NOUN. a large fish that can cause severe wounds with the sharp spine that grows on its tail.

stingray — up to 14 feet long, including the tail

stin•gy (stin′jē), ADJECTIVE. unwilling to spend or share your money; not generous: *He tried to save money without being stingy.* ❑ ADJECTIVE **stin•gi•er, stin•gi•est. –stin′gi•ness,** NOUN.

stink (stingk),
1 NOUN. a very bad smell.
2 VERB. to have a bad smell: *Decaying fish stink.* ❑ VERB **stinks, stank** or **stunk, stunk, stink•ing.**

stir (stėr),
1 VERB. to mix something by moving it around with a spoon, stick, and so on: *Stir the sugar in the lemonade.*
2 VERB. to move something gently: *The wind stirs the leaves.*
3 VERB. to move about: *No one was stirring upstairs.*
4 VERB. to cause strong feelings or actions: *The music stirred her deeply.*
5 NOUN. a movement: *There was a stir in the bushes where the children were hiding.*

6 NOUN. an excitement: *The announcement of the queen's visit caused a great stir.* ❑ VERB **stirs, stirred, stir•ring. –stir′rer,** NOUN.

stir•rup (stėr′əp), NOUN. a loop or ring of metal or wood that hangs from a saddle to support a rider's foot.

Word Story

Stirrup comes from two older English words meaning "a climbing up" and "rope." Originally a stirrup was a loop of rope that hung from the saddle.

stitch (stich),
1 NOUN. one complete movement of a threaded needle through cloth in sewing, or through skin or tissue in surgery.
2 NOUN. one complete movement in knitting, crocheting, or embroidering.
3 NOUN. a loop of thread or yarn made by a stitch: *Rip out these long stitches. The doctor took the stitches out of my cut.*
4 VERB. to sew or fasten something with stitches: *I stitched a patch on my jeans. The doctor stitched the cut.* ❑ PLURAL **stitch•es;** VERB **stitch•es, stitched, stitch•ing.**

in stitches, IDIOM. laughing very hard; out of breath with laughter: *His jokes had us all in stitches.*

Have You Heard?

You may have heard someone say that **"a stitch in time saves nine."** This means that it is better to make a simple fix early than a more complicated one later.

stock (stok),
1 NOUN. things for use or for sale: *This store keeps a large stock of toys.*
2 NOUN. cattle or other farm animals; livestock: *The farm was sold with all its stock.*
3 VERB. to get a supply of something that is needed; supply: *Our camp is well stocked with food.*
4 VERB. to get or keep things regularly for use or for sale: *A toy store stocks toys.*
5 NOUN. the shares owned in a company. The profits of a company are divided among the owners of stock.
6 NOUN. someone's family; ancestry: *The senator is from old New England stock.*
7 NOUN. **the stocks,** (long ago) a framework with holes for the feet, and sometimes for the hands, used as a punishment. ❑ VERB **stocks, stocked, stock•ing.**

in stock, IDIOM. on hand; ready to use or sell: *The store has many brands of canned goods in stock.*

out of stock, IDIOM. not in stock: *That item is out of stock, but we should have some more soon.*

stock·ade (sto kād′), NOUN. a wall made of large, strong posts stuck upright in the ground: *A heavy stockade around the cabins protected them from attack.*

stock car, a standard car, modified for racing.

stock·ing (stok′ing), NOUN. a close-fitting knitted covering of nylon, cotton, or other fabric for your foot and leg.

stock·y (stok′ē), ADJECTIVE. having a solid or sturdy form or build: *a stocky child.* ❑ ADJECTIVE **stock·i·er, stock·i·est.**

stole (stōl), VERB. the past tense of **steal**: *Who stole the money?*

sto·len (stō′lən), VERB. the past participle of **steal**: *A thief has stolen money from our apartment.*

stom·ach (stum′ək),
1 NOUN. the large muscular bag in the body which receives food that is swallowed. The stomach digests some food before passing it on to the intestines.
2 NOUN. the part of the body containing the stomach; abdomen: *The ball hit me in the stomach.*
3 VERB. to put up with; endure: *I cannot stomach violent movies.*
❑ VERB **stom·achs, stom·ached, stom·ach·ing.**

stomp (stomp), VERB. to bring down your foot with force: *He stomped angrily out the door.* ❑ VERB **stomps, stomped, stomp·ing.**

stone (stōn),
1 NOUN. the hard mineral matter of which rocks are made. Stone such as granite and marble is commonly used in building.
2 NOUN. a small piece of rock: *The children threw stones into the pond.*
3 NOUN. a gem; jewel: *The royal rubies are fine stones.*
4 VERB. to throw stones at something or someone: *The cruel children stoned the dog.*
5 NOUN. a hard seed in some fruits: *cherry stones.*
❑ VERB **stones, stoned, ston·ing.**

Stone Age, the earliest known period of human culture, in which people used tools and weapons made from stone.

stood (stud), VERB.
1 the past tense of **stand**: *I stood at the bus stop for 30 minutes before it came.*
2 the past participle of **stand**: *I had stood in line all morning to buy tickets to the game.*

stool (stül), NOUN.
1 a small seat without a back and without arms.
2 a low bench used to rest the feet on, or to kneel on.
–**stool′like′**, ADJECTIVE.

stoop¹ (stüp),
1 VERB. to bend forward at the waist: *I stooped to pick up the money.*
2 NOUN. a forward bend of the head and shoulders: *My uncle walks with a stoop.*
3 VERB. to carry your head and shoulders bent forward: *The old man stoops.*

4 VERB. to do something that people think is bad: *He stooped to cheating.*
❑ VERB **stoops, stooped, stoop·ing.**

stoop² (stüp), NOUN. a porch or platform at the entrance of a house.

stop (stop),
1 VERB. to come to an end; quit: *The rain stopped.*
2 VERB. to stay somewhere for a short time: *She stopped at the bank for a few minutes.*
3 VERB. to keep something or someone from moving or doing something: *She stopped the car. I stopped the child from breaking the toy.*
4 VERB. to close up or block; plug: *Scraps of food have stopped the drain in the sink.*
5 NOUN. the act of coming to a stop: *Her sudden stop startled us. The singing came to a stop.*
6 NOUN. a place where something stops: *a bus stop.*
7 NOUN. a pause somewhere during a trip: *I need to make a stop at the bank.*
8 NOUN. something that blocks or checks: *a door stop.*
❑ VERB **stops, stopped, stop·ping.**

stop by or **stop in,** IDIOM. to visit briefly: *Why don't you stop by after church and say hello?*

stop off, IDIOM. to stop for a short stay: *We just stopped off to return your book.*

stop over, IDIOM.
1 to make a short stay: *I stopped over at his house.*
2 to stop in the course of a trip: *We stopped over in New York on our way to London.*

Synonym Study

Stop means to keep from doing or happening: *"Stop your arguing this minute!" said the baby-sitter. If he wants to stop gaining weight, he has to eat less and exercise more.*

Halt means to force to stop for a time: *The police officer held up his hand and halted traffic.*

Prevent means to stop: *Ropes prevented the crowd from getting too close to the rock group.*

Cease means to stop something that has gone on for a while: *The branch was too high, so he finally ceased his efforts to reach the apple.*

Discontinue means to stop something that has been happening for a long time: *They've discontinued the Happy Harmonica Hour, my favorite TV show!*

See also the Synonym Study at **end.**

ANTONYMS: begin, start.

a	hat	ė	term	ô	order	ch	child		a in about
ā	age	i	it	oi	oil	ng	long		e in taken
ä	far	ī	ice	ou	out	sh	she	ə {	i in pencil
â	care	o	hot	u	cup	th	thin		o in lemon
e	let	ō	open	ù	put	ᴛʜ	then		u in circus
ē	equal	ò	saw	ü	rule	zh	measure		

S

Storms

Storms are what we call weather that brings high winds, rain, hail, snow, sleet, or lightning. We call these storms by many different names: rainstorm, snowstorm, hailstorm, thunderstorm, cyclone, hurricane, and tornado. All storms can be dangerous and cause damage.

Rain falls when water droplets in the clouds combine and fall or when ice falling from a high, cold cloud melts in warmer air.

Snow, sleet, and **hail** are all forms of frozen water. Snowflakes are made up of many tiny ice crystals. As many as 100 of these crystals can make up a one inch snowflake.

Tornadoes, hurricanes, and **typhoons** are all kinds of cyclones. Cyclones are a kind of storm where winds spiral inward. Winds in a tornado can whirl at more than 200 miles an hour.

Lightning and thunder can happen with rain or without. Lightning is a big electrical spark in the air. Some lightning stays in the air and never touches the ground. Lightning that hits the ground can hurt people or start fires.

Thunder happens when air is heated by lightning. The warm air moves very quickly and smashes into the cooler air around it. This smashing makes a big air wave that has the sound of thunder.

Sleet falls when snow or rain falls through cold air and freezes into small pieces of ice. If the pieces of ice collide with water droplets on the way down, they can become much bigger. Then they are called hail. Hailstones that stay in the clouds for a long time can grow very large—bigger than oranges!

stop·light (stop′lit′), NOUN. See **traffic light**.

stop·per (stop′ər), NOUN. a plug or cork for closing the opening of a bottle, tube, or container.

stop sign, a sign that signals motor vehicles to come to a complete stop before moving ahead.

stop·watch (stop′wäch′), NOUN. a watch that can be stopped or started at any instant. A stopwatch is used for timing races and contests. ❑ PLURAL **stop·watch·es**.

stor·age (stôr′ij), NOUN.
1 a place for storing things: *There is storage below the front deck of the boat.*
2 the condition of being stored. *Cold storage is used to keep eggs and meat from spoiling.*
3 the act or fact of storing goods: *She put her fur coat in storage for the summer.*
4 See **memory** (definition 4).

store (stôr),
1 NOUN. a place to buy things: *He opened a children's clothing store.*
2 NOUN. something put away for later use; supply; stock: *We have a large store of food in the freezer.*
3 VERB. to put something away that you will use later: *The squirrel stores away nuts.*
❑ VERB **stores, stored, stor·ing.**

in store, IDIOM. to be expected; waiting to happen: *Lots of new experiences were in store for us.*

store·house (stôr′hous′), NOUN. a place where things are stored: *After the harvest, the storehouses were full.* ❑ PLURAL **store·hous·es** (stôr′hou′ziz).

store·keep·er (stôr′kē′pər), NOUN. a person who has charge of a store.

stork (stôrk), NOUN. a large bird with long legs for wading, a long neck, and a long bill. Storks are found in most warm parts of the world.

storm (stôrm),
1 NOUN. a strong wind, usually with heavy rain, snow, or hail. Some storms have thunder and lightning.
2 VERB. to blow hard; rain; snow; hail: *It stormed all night.*
3 NOUN. a violent outburst or disturbance: *a storm of tears, a storm of angry words.*
4 VERB. to rush violently: *I stormed from the room in anger.*
5 VERB. to attack violently: *They stormed the castle.*
6 NOUN. a violent attack: *The castle was taken by storm.*
❑ VERB **storms, stormed, storm·ing.**

stork — about 3 feet long

storm·y (stôr′mē), ADJECTIVE.
1 having storms; likely to have storms; affected by storms: *stormy weather, a stormy sea, a stormy night.*
2 marked by violence or harsh criticism: *They had stormy quarrels.*
❑ ADJECTIVE **storm·i·er, storm·i·est.** —**storm′i·ness,** NOUN.

sto·ry¹ (stôr′ē), NOUN.
1 an account of some happening or series of happenings: *Tell us the story of your life.*
2 a tale or series of events made up to interest a reader or audience: *fairy stories, stories of adventure.*
3 a falsehood: *That's not true; you're telling stories.*
❑ PLURAL **sto·ries.**

Synonym Study

Story¹ means a set of events, told in words: *My sister told me a scary story. "Do you want me to write a story about you?" she asked.*

Tale means a story, usually of imaginary events: *She loves her grandfather's tales of princesses, treasures, and long voyages.*

Yarn can mean a long story that goes on and on, about unbelievable events: *My little sister believes that Dad's yarn about the pretty mermaid and the blue whale is a true story.*

Narrative means the same as story. It is a formal word: *Every narrative has a beginning, a middle, and an end.*

sto·ry² (stôr′ē), NOUN. all the rooms or space on one level of a building; floor: *That building has nine stories.* ❑ PLURAL **sto·ries.**

sto·ry·book (stôr′ē bůk′), NOUN. a book containing one or more stories, especially for children.

stout (stout), ADJECTIVE.
1 fat and large: *That boy could run faster if he weren't so stout.*
2 strongly built; sturdy; strong: *The fort has stout walls.* ■ See the Synonym Study at **strong**.
3 brave; bold: *Robin Hood was a stout fellow.*

stove (stōv), NOUN. an appliance for cooking or heating. There are electric, gas, oil, wood, and coal stoves.

stow (stō), VERB.
1 to pack: *The cargo was stowed in the ship's hold.*
2 to pack things closely in; fill by packing: *The girls stowed their packs with supplies for the hike.*
❑ VERB **stows, stowed, stow·ing.**

stow away, IDIOM. to hide on a ship, airplane, train, or bus to get a free ride or to make an escape.

stow·a·way (stō′ə wā′), NOUN. someone who hides on a ship, airplane, train, or bus to get a free ride or to make an escape.

St. Paul (sānt′ pȯl′), the capital of Minnesota.

strad·dle (strad′l), VERB. to walk, stand, or sit over something with the legs wide apart: *He straddled the bicycle while waiting for the traffic light to turn green.* ❑ VERB **strad·dles, strad·dled, strad·dling.**

strag·gle (strag′əl), VERB. to wander from or lag behind your group, a leader, or the like: *Several hikers straggled into camp a half hour after the others.* ❑ VERB **strag·gles, strag·gled, strag·gling.** —**strag′gler,** NOUN.

straight (strāt),

1 ADJECTIVE. without a bend or curve: *a straight line, a straight path, straight hair.*
2 ADVERB. in a direct line: *Go straight home.*
3 ADJECTIVE. going in a line; direct: *a straight course, a straight throw.*
4 ADJECTIVE. frank; honest; upright: *a straight answer.*
5 ADJECTIVE. right; correct: *straight thinking, a straight thinker.*
6 ADJECTIVE. in proper order or condition: *Set the room straight. Our accounts are straight.*
▪ Another word that sounds like this is **strait.**

The **straight** road seemed to go on forever.

straight·en (strāt′n), VERB.

1 to make or become straight: *He straightened the bent nail.*
2 to put some place in the proper order or condition: *Straighten your room.*
❑ VERB **straight·ens, straight·ened, straight·en·ing.**

straight·for·ward (strāt′fôr′wərd), ADJECTIVE. honest; frank; direct: *He gave a straightforward answer.* —**straight′for′ward·ly,** ADVERB.

strain (strān),

1 VERB. to draw too tight; stretch too much: *The weight strained the rope.*
2 NOUN. any force or weight that stretches something too much: *The strain on the rope made it break.*
3 VERB. to pull hard: *The dog strained at its leash.*
4 VERB. to injure by too much effort or by stretching: *The runner strained her leg.*

5 NOUN. an injury caused by too much effort or stretching: *The injury to his back was only a slight strain.*
6 NOUN. worry or stress: *The strain of overwork can make you ill.*
7 VERB. to press or pour food through a strainer: *Babies eat food that has been strained.*
❑ VERB **strains, strained, strain·ing.**

strain·er (strā′nər), NOUN. a utensil having holes that let liquids and smaller pieces pass through, but not the larger pieces.

strait (strāt), NOUN.

1 a narrow channel connecting two larger bodies of water. The **Strait of Gibraltar** (jə brȯl′tər) connects the Mediterranean Sea and the Atlantic Ocean.
2 **straits,** difficulty; need; distress: *The family is in desperate straits because of money problems.*
▪ Another word that sounds like this is **straight.**

strand¹ (strand), VERB.

1 to leave someone in a helpless position: *She was stranded a thousand miles from home with a broken-down car and no money.*
2 to run aground: *The ship was stranded on the rocks.*
❑ VERB **strands, strand·ed, strand·ing.**

strand² (strand), NOUN.

1 one of the threads, strings, or wires that are twisted together to make a rope or cable.
2 a thread or string: *a strand of hair, a strand of pearls.*

strange (strānj), ADJECTIVE.

1 hard to explain or understand; unusual; odd; peculiar: *a strange experience, strange clothing, a strange stillness.*
2 not known, seen, or heard of before; not familiar: *She is moving to a strange place. A strange cat is on our steps.*
❑ ADJECTIVE **strang·er, strang·est.** —**strange′ly,** ADVERB. —**strange′ness,** NOUN.

stran·ger (strān′jər), NOUN.

1 someone you have not known, seen, or heard of before: *She is a stranger to us.*
2 someone or something new to a place: *I am a stranger in New York.*
3 someone who is from another country: *The king received the stranger with kindness.*

stran·gle (strang′gəl), VERB.

1 to kill by squeezing the throat to keep someone from breathing.
2 to choke; suffocate: *She almost strangled on a piece of meat that caught in her throat.*
❑ VERB **stran·gles, stran·gled, stran·gling.** —**stran′gler,** NOUN.

a	hat	ė	term	ô	order	ch	child		a in about
ā	age	i	it	oi	oil	ng	long		e in taken
ä	far	ī	ice	ou	out	sh	she	ə	i in pencil
â	care	o	hot	u	cup	th	thin		o in lemon
e	let	ō	open	ů	put	ŧʜ	then		u in circus
ē	equal	ȯ	saw	ü	rule	zh	measure		

S

strap (strap),

1 *NOUN.* a narrow strip of leather, cloth, or other material used for fastening things or holding things together: *Put a strap around the trunk. The strap on my sandal broke.*

2 *VERB.* to fasten something with a strap: *He strapped on a helmet.*

❑ *VERB* **straps, strapped, strap·ping.**

stra·te·gic (strə tē′jik), *ADJECTIVE.*

1 of or based on strategy: *I made a strategic retreat.*

2 important or useful in strategy: *The Air Force is a strategic link in our national defense.*
—**stra·te′gi·cal·ly,** *ADVERB.*

strat·e·gy (strat′ə jē), *NOUN.*

1 planning and directing of military movements and operations.

2 the skillful planning and management of anything: *Strategy helped our team win the game.*
❑ *PLURAL* **strat·e·gies.**

strat·o·sphere (strat′ə sfir), *NOUN.* the region of the atmosphere from about 10 to 30 miles above the earth's surface. —**strat′o·spher′ic,** *ADJECTIVE.*

stra·tus cloud (strā′təs kloud′), a low, horizontal cloud that forms a gray layer over a large area.

straw (strȯ), *NOUN.*

1 the stalks or stems of grain after drying and threshing. Straw is used for bedding for horses and cows, for making hats, and so on.

2 a hollow tube that you drink liquids through. Straws are made of plastic or waxed paper.
—**straw′like′,** *ADJECTIVE.*

Have You Heard?

You may have heard someone say **"That was the straw that broke the camel's back"** or **"That was the last straw."** People say this when they are in a bad situation that has just gotten a tiny bit worse. It means that although they were willing to put up with the situation before, now they are not.

straw·ber·ry
(strȯ′ber′ē), *NOUN.* the small, juicy, red fruit of a plant that grows close to the ground. Strawberries are good to eat. ❑ *PLURAL* **straw·ber·ries.**

ripe **strawberries**

stray (strā),

1 *VERB.* to lose your way; wander; roam: *Our dog has strayed off somewhere.*

2 *ADJECTIVE.* wandering; lost: *A stray cat is crying at the door.*

3 *NOUN.* a wanderer; lost animal: *That cat is a stray that we took in.*

4 *ADJECTIVE.* scattered; here and there: *The beach was empty except for a few stray swimmers.*

❑ *VERB* **strays, strayed, stray·ing.**

streak (strēk),

1 *NOUN.* a long, thin mark or line: *You have a streak of dirt on your face.*

2 *NOUN.* a long flash: *We saw the streaks of lightning before we heard the thunder.*

3 *NOUN.* an element of your character: *She has a streak of humor, although she looks very serious.*

4 *VERB.* to make long, thin marks or lines on something: *The children streaked their faces with watercolors.*

5 *NOUN.* a short period: *a streak of bad luck.*

6 *VERB.* to move very fast; go at full speed: *She streaked past us to win the race.*

❑ *VERB* **streaks, streaked, streak·ing.** —**streak′er,** *NOUN.*

like a streak, *IDIOM.* very fast: *When her dog saw her, it ran like a streak to greet her.*

stream (strēm),

1 *NOUN.* a narrow flow of water across the land. Small rivers and large brooks are both called streams: *Because of the lack of rain many streams dried up.*

2 *NOUN.* any steady flow: *a stream of words, a stream of cars.*

3 *VERB.* to flow steadily: *Rain water streamed down the gutters.*

a **stream** in summer

4 *VERB.* to move steadily; move swiftly: *The crowd streamed out of the theater.*

5 *VERB.* to float or wave: *The flags streamed in the wind.*

❑ *VERB* **streams, streamed, stream·ing.**

stream·er
(strē′mər), *NOUN.*

1 any long, narrow flowing thing: *Streamers of colored paper decorated the gym for the dance.*

2 a long, narrow flag.

stream·line (strēm′līn′), *VERB.* to make something more efficient: *Train service between Boston and Washington, D.C has been streamlined.* ❑ *VERB* **stream·lines, stream·lined, stream·lin·ing.**

stream·lined (strēm′līnd′), *ADJECTIVE.* shaped so as to cause the least possible resistance to motion through air or water. The fastest cars, airplanes, and boats have streamlined bodies.

street (strēt), NOUN.
1 a road in a city or town, usually with buildings along both sides.
2 the people who live in the buildings on a street: *The whole street came to the party.*

street·car (strēt′kär′), NOUN. a vehicle powered by electricity that runs on rails in the streets and carries passengers.

street·light (strēt′līt′), NOUN. a powerful lamp that lights a street or public area of a city or town.

strength (strengkth), NOUN.
1 the quality of being strong; power; force: *I do not have the strength to lift that heavy box. Steel is valued for its strength.*
2 the power to resist force: *the strength of a fort, the strength of a rope.*

strength·en (strengk′thən), VERB. to make or grow stronger: *Exercise strengthens muscles.* ❑ VERB **strength·ens, strength·ened, strength·en·ing.**

stren·u·ous (stren′yü əs), ADJECTIVE.
1 needing much energy or effort: *Running is strenuous exercise.*
2 very active: *We had a strenuous day of gardening.* —**stren′u·ous·ly,** ADVERB.

strep throat (strep′ thrōt′), a very sore throat, caused by an infection.

stress (stres),
1 NOUN. great pressure or force, especially a force that can cause damage to a structure: *The roof collapsed under the stress of the heavy snow.*
2 NOUN. tension, pressure, or strain which affects the mind and body: *A person's blood pressure may increase under stress.*
3 VERB. to cause mental or physical strain in: *Worry can stress a person.*
4 NOUN. importance; emphasis: *That school lays stress upon arithmetic and reading.*
5 VERB. to treat as important; emphasize: *He stressed the value of cooperation.*
6 NOUN. loudness in the pronunciation of syllables, words in a sentence, and so on; accent: *In "zero," the stress is on the first syllable.*
7 VERB. to pronounce a word with stress: *"Accept" is stressed on the second syllable.*
❑ PLURAL **stress·es;** VERB **stress·es, stressed, stress·ing.**

stress·ful (stres′fəl), ADJECTIVE. full of stress; producing stress: *stressful conditions.* —**stress′ful·ly,** ADVERB.

stress mark, a mark (′) written or printed to show the spoken force of a syllable, as in *to·day* (tə dā′); Some words have two stress marks, a stronger stress mark (′) and a weaker stress mark (′), as in *ac·ci·den·tal* (ak′sə den′tl).

stretch (strech),
1 VERB. to make something as long as it can be: *The bird stretched its wings. She stretched the cord until it snapped.*
2 VERB. to reach out your body or arms and legs: *I stretched out on the couch.*
3 VERB. to spread out over a great distance: *The forest stretches for miles.*
4 VERB. to reach out; hold out: *The child stretched out a hand for the candy.*
5 VERB. to pull something out to a greater size: *My brother stretched out my sweater when he wore it.*
6 VERB. to pull something tight; strain: *She stretched the rubber band until it broke.*
7 NOUN. the act of stretching your body, or the condition of being stretched: *I stopped writing and took a big stretch.*
❑ VERB **stretch·es, stretched, stretch·ing;** PLURAL **stretch·es.**

The cat **stretched.**

stretch·er (strech′ər), NOUN. canvas stretched on a frame for carrying a sick or injured person.

stretch·y (strech′ē), ADJECTIVE. able to be stretched: *stretchy elastic.*

strew (strü), VERB. to scatter things around in a disorderly manner: *Please don't strew your clothes all over the house.* ❑ VERB **strews, strewed, strewn** (strün) or **strewed, strew·ing.**

strick·en (strik′ən),
1 ADJECTIVE. affected by disease, trouble, sadness, and so on: *They fled from the stricken city. The stricken man was taken immediately to a hospital.*
2 VERB. a past participle of **strike:** *Disease had stricken the cities of Europe.*

strict (strikt), ADJECTIVE.
1 very careful in following a rule or in making others follow it: *Our teacher is strict but fair.*
2 harsh; severe: *strict discipline, strict rules.*
3 perfect; complete; absolute: *The secret was told in strict confidence.*
—**strict′ly,** ADVERB. —**strict′ness,** NOUN.

stride (strīd),
1 VERB. to walk with long steps: *She strode rapidly down the street.*
2 NOUN. a step, especially a long step: *The child could not keep up with his father's stride.*
❑ VERB **strides, strode, strid·den** (strid′n), **strid·ing.**

S

a	hat	ė	term	ô	order	ch	child		a in about
ā	age	i	it	oi	oil	ng	long		e in taken
ä	far	ī	ice	ou	out	sh	she	ə	i in pencil
â	care	o	hot	u	cup	th	thin		o in lemon
e	let	ō	open	u̇	put	ŦH	then		u in circus
ē	equal	ȯ	saw	ü	rule	zh	measure		

strike (strik),
1 *VERB.* to hit: *Lightning struck the barn.*
2 *VERB.* to give; deal forth or out: *She struck a blow in self-defense.*
3 *VERB.* to set on fire by rubbing: *I struck a match.*
4 *VERB.* to have a strong effect on your mind or feelings: *The plan strikes me as silly.*
5 *VERB.* to tell the time by making a sound: *The clock strikes twelve times at noon.*
6 *VERB.* to find or come upon something suddenly: *After drilling several holes, they finally struck oil.*
7 *NOUN.* an attack: *a strike by bombers on a target.*
8 *VERB.* to stop work to get better pay, shorter hours, or safer working conditions: *The miners struck when the company refused to raise wages.*
9 *NOUN.* the act of stopping work in this way: *The miners were home for six weeks during the strike.*
10 *NOUN.* a baseball pitched through the strike zone and not swung at, any pitch that is swung at and missed, or any pitch that is hit foul under the rules of the game. After three strikes, a batter is out.
11 *NOUN.* (in bowling) the act of knocking down all the pins with the first ball bowled.
   ❏ *VERB* **strikes, struck, struck** or **strick•en, strik•ing.**
strike out, *IDIOM.* (in baseball) to put out or be put out on three strikes: *The pitcher struck out six batters. Two batters struck out.*
strike up, *IDIOM.* to begin: *We struck up a friendship.*
strike•out (strik′out′), *NOUN.* in baseball:
1 an out caused by three strikes.
2 the act of striking out.
strike zone, (in baseball) the zone or area above home plate, between the batter's knees and armpits, through which a pitch must be thrown to be called a strike.

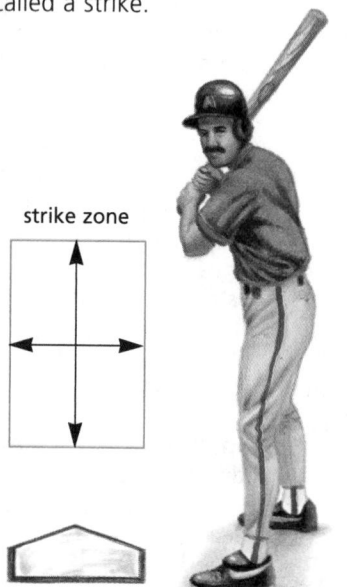

strike zone

The **strike zone** is inside the red box.

strik•ing (stri′king), *ADJECTIVE.*
1 attracting attention; very noticeable: *His tie was a striking shade of bright pink. The soloist gave a striking performance.*
2 on strike: *The striking miners will return to work as soon as the new contract is signed.*
   —**strik′ing•ly,** *ADVERB.*
string (string),
1 *NOUN.* a thick thread, small cord, or very thin rope: *The package is tied with red string.*
2 *NOUN.* a cord or thread with things on it: *She wore a string of beads around her neck.*
3 *VERB.* to put something on a string: *The child is stringing beads to make a necklace.*
4 *NOUN.* one of the wires that make sound on a stringed instrument: *the strings of a violin.*
5 *NOUN.* **strings,** violins, cellos, and other stringed instruments.
6 *VERB.* to provide something with strings: *She had her tennis racket strung.*
7 *VERB.* to tie or hang something up with string or rope: *We dry herbs by stringing them from rafters in the barn.*
8 *VERB.* to stretch something from one point to another: *Telephone wires and cables are strung on telephone poles or placed underground.*
9 *NOUN.* a number of things in a line or row: *The freight train included a long string of boxcars.*
   ❏ *VERB* **strings, strung, string•ing.**
string bean, a long, green or yellow pod containing smooth, somewhat flat seeds; green bean. String beans grow on bushes or vines and are eaten as a vegetable.

three kinds of **stringed instruments**

stringed in•stru•ment (stringd′ in′strə mənt), a musical instrument having strings, played either with a bow or by plucking. The harp, violin, cello, and guitar are stringed instruments.
string•y (string′ē), *ADJECTIVE.* like a string or strings: *When she got out of the pool, her hair was wet and stringy.* ❏ *ADJECTIVE* **string•i•er, string•i•est.**
   —**string′i•ness,** *NOUN.*

strip¹ (strip), VERB.
1 to take the covering off something: *They stripped the wooden table by removing the old paint.*
2 to rob: *Thieves stripped the house of everything valuable.*
3 to take your clothes off; undress.
❏ VERB **strips, stripped, strip·ping.**

strip² (strip), NOUN. a long, narrow, flat piece of cloth, paper, bark, and so on.

stripe (strīp),
1 NOUN. a line or long, narrow part of different color, material, or the like: *A tiger has stripes. The American flag has thirteen stripes.*
2 VERB. to mark something with stripes: *The stick of candy was striped with red.*
❏ VERB **stripes, striped, strip·ing.**

strive (strīv), VERB. to try hard; work hard: *Strive to succeed.* ❏ VERB **strives, strove** or **strived, striv·en** (striv′ən) or **strived, striv·ing.** —**striv′er,** NOUN.

strode (strōd), VERB. the past tense of **stride**: *He strode into the room.*

stroke¹ (strōk), NOUN.
1 the act of hitting something; blow: *I drove in the nail with several strokes of the hammer.*
2 a sudden event or idea that has a powerful effect: *a stroke of good luck, a stroke of genius.*
3 a single complete movement made over and over again: *He rowed with a strong stroke of the oars.*
4 a sudden attack of illness, especially paralysis caused by injury to the brain when a blood vessel breaks or becomes blocked.
5 a movement or mark made by a pen, pencil, or brush: *She writes with a heavy stroke.*

stroke² (strōk),
1 VERB. to move your hand gently over something: *She likes to stroke her kitten.*
2 NOUN. a movement like this: *I brushed the crumbs away with one stroke.*
❏ VERB **strokes, stroked, strok·ing.**

stroll (strōl),
1 VERB. to take a quiet walk for pleasure: *We strolled through the park after dinner.*
2 NOUN. a slow, relaxing walk: *a stroll in the park.*
❏ VERB **strolls, strolled, stroll·ing.**

stroll·er (strō′lər), NOUN. a kind of lightweight baby carriage in which a small child can ride sitting up.

strong (strông), ADJECTIVE.
1 having a great deal of force or power: *A strong person can lift heavy things.*
2 having good bodily strength or health: *Several months after the operation she was strong again.*
3 not easily broken: *She used a strong rope.*
4 having great force or effectiveness; powerful: *a strong argument, strong coffee.*
❏ ADJECTIVE **strong·er** (strông′gər), **strong·est** (strông′gəst). —**strong′ly,** ADVERB.

strong·hold (strông′hōld′), NOUN. a strong place that is easy to defend; fort: *The robbers have a stronghold in the mountains.*

strove (strōv), VERB. a past tense of **strive**: *They strove hard, but did not win the game.*

struck (struk), VERB.
1 the past tense of **strike**: *The clock struck four.*
2 the past participle of **strike**: *The barn was struck by lightning.*

struc·tur·al (struk′chər əl), ADJECTIVE.
1 used in building. Structural steel is steel made into beams and girders.
2 of or about a structure or structures: *Ferns and daisies have structural differences.*
—**struc′tur·al·ly,** ADVERB.

struc·ture (struk′chər), NOUN.
1 a building; something built: *The city hall is a large stone structure.*
2 anything made of parts arranged together: *The human body is a wonderful structure.*
3 the arrangement of parts: *the structure of an atom, the structure of a flower.*

strug·gle (strug′əl),
1 VERB. to try hard; work hard against difficulties: *The poor have to struggle for a living. The swimmer struggled against the tide.*

a hat	ė term	ô order	ch child	ə	a in about
ā age	i it	oi oil	ng long		e in taken
ä far	ī ice	ou out	sh she		i in pencil
â care	o hot	u cup	th thin		o in lemon
e let	ō open	ů put	ᴛʜ then		u in circus
ē equal	ò saw	ü rule	zh measure		

2 *NOUN.* great effort; hard work: *It was a struggle for them to send their six children to college.*

3 *VERB.* to fight: *The dog struggled fiercely with the wildcat.* ■ See the Synonym Study at **fight.**

4 *VERB.* to move or get somewhere with a lot of work: *They struggled the refrigerator up the stairs.*

5 *NOUN.* the act of fighting; conflict: *The struggle between the two enemy countries went on for years.* ❑ *VERB* **strug·gles, strug·gled, strug·gling.** —**strug′gler,** *NOUN.*

strum (strum), *VERB.* to play an instrument by running your fingers lightly across the strings or keys: *to strum a guitar.* ❑ *VERB* **strums, strummed, strum·ming.**

strung (strung), *VERB.*

1 the past tense of **string:** *They strung the beads.*

2 the past participle of **string:** *The vines had been strung on poles.*

strut (strut), *VERB.* to walk about with a proud attitude: *The football player strutted after scoring a touchdown. The rooster struts about the barnyard.* ❑ *VERB* **struts, strut·ted, strut·ting.** —**strut′ter,** *NOUN.*

stub (stub),

1 *NOUN.* a short piece of something that is left after the rest has been used up: *the stub of a pencil.*

2 *NOUN.* the short piece of a ticket, receipt, or check, kept as a record.

3 *VERB.* to strike your toe against something. ❑ *VERB* **stubs, stubbed, stub·bing.**

stub·ble (stub′əl), *NOUN.*

1 the lower ends of grain stalks left in the ground after the grain has been cut: *Walking over the stubble hurt her bare feet.*

2 a short growth of beard: *Since he had not shaved for three days, there was stubble on his face.*

stub·born (stub′ərn), *ADJECTIVE.*

1 not willing to change your opinion: *The stubborn child refused to get in the car.*

2 hard to get rid of: *a stubborn cough, a stubborn stain.* —**stub′born·ly,** *ADVERB.*

stub·by (stub′ē), *ADJECTIVE.* short and thick: *The chubby little baby had stubby little legs.* ❑ *ADJECTIVE* **stub·bi·er, stub·bi·est.**

stuc·co (stuk′ō),

1 *NOUN.* a cement mixture used for covering the outer walls of buildings.

2 *VERB.* to cover an outer wall with stucco: *We had our house stuccoed last year.* ❑ *VERB* **stuc·cos, stuc·coed, stuc·co·ing.**

stuck (stuk), *VERB.*

1 the past tense of **stick²:** *My dog stuck his head out of the car window.*

2 the past participle of **stick²:** *I was stuck in the mud.*

stuck-up (stuk′up′), *ADJECTIVE.* having too high an opinion of yourself; conceited: *We didn't join that group at the party because they seemed stuck-up.*

stud (stud),

1 *NOUN.* a head of a nail, knob, or the like, sticking out from a surface: *The belt was decorated with silver studs.*

2 *VERB.* to decorate with studs or something like studs: *The crown was studded with jewels.* ❑ *VERB* **studs, stud·ded, stud·ding.**

stu·dent (stüd′nt), *NOUN.*

1 someone who is studying in a school, college, or university: *That high school has 3000 students.*

2 someone who studies something: *She is a student of birds.*

Word Story

Student comes from a Latin word meaning "to study." The original meaning of the Latin root was "to be eager." Other English words from the same root include **studio** and **study.**

stu·di·o (stü′dē ō), *NOUN.*

1 the workroom of a painter, sculptor, photographer, or other artist.

2 a place where movies are made.

3 a place that a radio or TV show is broadcast from. ■ See the Word Story above. ❑ *PLURAL* **stu·di·os.**

a painter's **studio**

stud·y (stud′ē),

1 *NOUN.* the effort to learn by reading or thinking: *After an hour's hard study, I knew my lesson.*

2 *VERB.* to make an effort to learn: *She studied her spelling lesson for half an hour.*

3 *NOUN.* a careful look at something: *A careful study of the map showed the best route.*

4 *VERB.* to look at something carefully: *We studied the map to find the shortest road home.*

5 *NOUN.* a room for study, reading, or writing: *The author was at work in her study.*

6 *VERB.* to examine something carefully before you do something; plan: *The mayor is studying ways to cut expenses.*

■ See the Word Story at **student.** ❑ *PLURAL* **stud·ies;** *VERB* **stud·ies, stud·ied, stud·y·ing.**

stuff (stuf),

1 *NOUN.* what something is made of; material: *She bought some white stuff for curtains.*
2 *NOUN.* belongings; possessions: *She was told to move her stuff out of the room.*
3 *NOUN.* worthless material; junk: *Get rid of that old stuff.*
4 *VERB.* to pack something full: *I stuffed the pillow with feathers.* ■ See the Synonym Study at **full.**
5 *VERB.* to stop up or block: *My head is stuffed up by a cold.*
6 *VERB.* to pack something in tightly; cram: *I stuffed my things into a closet.*
7 *VERB.* to prepare meat, fowl, or vegetables by filling with stuffing: *to stuff a turkey, to stuff peppers.*
❏ *VERB* **stuffs, stuffed, stuff·ing.** —**stuff′er,** *NOUN.*

His room was filled with **stuff.**

stuff·ing (stuf′ing), *NOUN.*

1 material used to fill or pack something: *The stuffing is coming out of the pillow.*
2 a seasoned mixture of bread crumbs with chopped nuts, celery, and so on, used to stuff meat, poultry, fish, or vegetables.

stuff·y (stuf′ē), *ADJECTIVE.*

1 lacking fresh air: *a stuffy room.*
2 stopped up: *A cold makes my head feel stuffy.*
❏ *ADJECTIVE* **stuff·i·er, stuff·i·est.** —**stuff′i·ness,** *NOUN.*

stum·ble (stum′bəl), *VERB.*

1 to slip or trip over something by striking your foot against it: *He stumbled over a stool in the dark.*
2 to walk in an unsteady way: *The tired hikers stumbled along.*
3 to speak or act in a clumsy, unsteady way: *The amateur actors stumbled through the play.*
❏ *VERB* **stum·bles, stum·bled, stum·bling.**

stumble on or **stumble upon,** *IDIOM.* to come upon by accident or chance: *We stumbled on some fine antiques at a garage sale.*

stump (stump),

1 *NOUN.* the lower end of a tree or plant left after the main part has been cut down.
2 *NOUN.* anything left after the main or important part of something is removed: *The dog wagged its stump of a tail.*
3 *VERB.* to puzzle someone: *The riddle stumped me.*
❏ *VERB* **stumps, stumped, stump·ing.**

stun (stun), *VERB.*

1 to thoroughly shock or confuse someone: *She was stunned by the news of her friend's death.*
2 to knock someone unconscious: *He was stunned by the fall.*
❏ *VERB* **stuns, stunned, stun·ning.**

stung (stung), *VERB.*

1 the past tense of **sting:** *A wasp stung him.*
2 the past participle of **sting:** *He was stung on the toe.*

stunk (stungk), *VERB.*

1 a past tense of **stink:** *The garbage dump stunk.*
2 the past participle of **stink:** *The rotten eggs had stunk up the kitchen.*

stun·ning (stun′ing), *ADJECTIVE.*

1 excellent; very attractive; good-looking: *a stunning outfit, a stunning painting.*
2 shocking; very surprising: *It was a stunning defeat.*
—**stun′ning·ly,** *ADVERB.*

stunt[1] (stunt), *VERB.* to slow down someone's growth or development: *Lack of proper food stunts a child.*
❏ *VERB* **stunts, stunt·ed, stunt·ing.**

stunt[2] (stunt), *NOUN.* something done to attract attention; unusual performance or trick: *Circus riders perform stunts on horseback.*

stu·pid (stü′pid), *ADJECTIVE.*

1 showing a lack of good sense; not intelligent: *I realized I had just made a stupid remark.*
2 not interesting; boring: *I think it's a stupid book.*
—**stu′pid·ly,** *ADVERB.*

stu·pid·i·ty (stü pid′ə tē), *NOUN.* lack of intelligence.

stur·dy (stėr′dē), *ADJECTIVE.*

1 strong: *She was a very sturdy child.*
2 strongly built: *He built a sturdy table.* ■ See the Synonym Study at **strong.**
❏ *ADJECTIVE* **stur·di·er, stur·di·est.** —**stur′di·ly,** *ADVERB.*

stur·geon (stėr′jən), *NOUN.* a large food fish whose body has a tough skin with rows of bony plates.
❏ *PLURAL* **stur·geon** or **stur·geons.**

This baby **sturgeon** may grow to be 3 feet long.

a	hat	ė	term	ô	order	ch	child	ə	a in about
ā	age	i	it	oi	oil	ng	long		e in taken
ä	far	ī	ice	ou	out	sh	she		i in pencil
â	care	o	hot	u	cup	th	thin		o in lemon
e	let	ō	open	ů	put	ᴛʜ	then		u in circus
ē	equal	ò	saw	ü	rule	zh	measure		

S

stut·ter (stut′ər),
1 *VERB.* to repeat the same sound in an effort to speak. People may stutter when they are nervous, embarrassed, or afraid.
2 *NOUN.* the act or habit of stuttering: *He sometimes speaks with a stutter.*
☐ *VERB* **stut·ters, stut·tered, stut·ter·ing.**

sty¹ (stī), *NOUN.*
1 See **pigpen.**
2 any filthy place.
☐ *PLURAL* **sties.**

sty² (stī), *NOUN.* a painful swelling on the edge of your eyelid. A sty is a small boil. ☐ *PLURAL* **sties.**

style (stīl),
1 *NOUN.* a manner or method of doing something: *She learned several styles of swimming.*
2 *NOUN.* a way of writing or speaking: *Books for children should have a clear, easy style.*
3 *NOUN.* the current custom in dress; fashion: *My clothes are out of style.*
4 *VERB.* to design something according to a fashion: *His suits are styled by a famous designer.*
☐ *VERB* **styles, styled, styl·ing.**

styl·ish (stī′lish), *ADJECTIVE.* in the latest style; fashionable: *stylish clothes.* **–styl·ish·ly,** *ADVERB.*

Sty·ro·foam (stī′rə fōm′), *NOUN.* (trademark) a lightweight, waterproof plastic foam, used to insulate buildings and to make cups, coolers, and so on.

sub¹ (sub),
1 *NOUN.* a short form of **substitute** (definition 2).
2 *VERB.* to act as a substitute: *My mother subbed for our regular teacher in school today.*
☐ *VERB* **subs, subbed, sub·bing.**

sub² (sub), *NOUN.* a short form of **submarine.**

sub³ (sub), *NOUN.* a short form of **submarine sandwich.**

Word Power   sub-

The prefix **sub-** has several meanings. It can mean "under" or "below." A **sub**normal temperature is a temperature that is **below** normal. It can also mean "lower" or "less important." A **sub**committee is a **lower** or **less important** committee.

The prefix **sub-** can mean "further" or "again." **Sub**divide means to divide **again.** It can also mean "near" or "nearly." A **sub**tropical climate is a climate that is **nearly** tropical.

sub·con·ti·nent (sub kon′tə nənt), *NOUN.* an area or region that is very large, but smaller than a continent. India is a subcontinent.

sub·di·vide (sub′də vīd′), *VERB.* to divide something into smaller parts: *The farm was subdivided into lots, and houses were built on them.* ☐ *VERB* **sub·di·vides, sub·di·vid·ed, sub·di·vid·ing.**

sub·due (səb dü′), *VERB.* to control someone or something by the use of force; conquer: *Firefighters fought hard to subdue the flames from the burning warehouse.* ☐ *VERB* **sub·dues, sub·dued, sub·du·ing.**

sub·ject (sub′ jikt *for noun and adjective;* səb jekt′ *for verb*),
1 *NOUN.* something thought about, discussed, or studied; topic: *The subject for our composition was "An Exciting Moment."*
2 *NOUN.* a course of study in some branch of knowledge: *English, science, and arithmetic are some of the subjects we study in school.*
3 *NOUN.* a person who is under the power, control, or influence of another: *He is a subject of the king.*
4 *ADJECTIVE.* under the power or influence of: *We are subject to our country's laws.*
5 *VERB.* to bring a region or country under some power or influence: *Rome subjected all Italy to its rule.*
6 *VERB.* to cause to experience or undergo something: *The school subjected new students to many tests.*
7 *NOUN.* someone or something that is used or studied in an experiment: *Rabbits and mice are frequent subjects of medical experiments.*
8 *NOUN.* (in grammar) the word or group of words about which something is said in a sentence. *I* is the subject of the following sentences: *I saw the deer. I was seen by the deer.*
☐ *VERB* **sub·jects, sub·ject·ed, sub·ject·ing.**

sub·jec·tive (səb jek′tiv), *ADJECTIVE.* influenced by your own thoughts and feelings; not objective: *Subjective judgments are often not fair.* **–sub·jec′tive·ly,** *ADVERB.*

subject pronoun, a pronoun about which something is said in a sentence. In "I slept late," and "He is a good skater," *I* and *He* are subject pronouns.

sub·ma·rine (sub′mə rēn′), *NOUN.* a ship that can go under water; sub. Submarines are used in warfare for attacking enemy ships and launching guided missiles.

submarine sandwich, a large roll cut lengthwise and filled with meat, cheese, lettuce, and so on; hero sandwich; sub.

a very thick **submarine sandwich**

sub·merge (səb mėrj′), VERB.
1 to cover someone or something with water: *A big wave submerged us. At high tide this path is submerged.*
2 to go below the surface of the water: *The submarine submerged to escape enemy attack.*
❏ VERB **sub·merg·es, sub·merged, sub·merg·ing.**

sub·mis·sion (səb mish′ən), NOUN. the act of yielding to the power, control, or authority of someone else: *The defeated general showed his submission by giving up his sword.*

sub·mit (səb mit′), VERB.
1 to surrender to the power, control, or authority of some person or group: *They submitted to the wishes of the majority.*
2 to present something for someone else to read, work on, decide about, and so on: *to submit a report, to submit a request.*
❏ VERB **sub·mits, sub·mit·ted, sub·mit·ting.**

sub·or·di·nate (sə bôrd′n it),
1 ADJECTIVE. lower in rank: *In the army, lieutenants are subordinate to captains.*
2 NOUN. a subordinate person or thing: *Our supervisor usually takes the advice of her subordinates.*

sub·scribe (səb skrib′), VERB. to promise to take and pay for something: *We subscribe to several magazines.* ❏ VERB **sub·scribes, sub·scribed, sub·scrib·ing. –sub·scrib′er,** NOUN.

sub·scrip·tion (səb skrip′shən), NOUN.
1 the right to receive something for a period of time because you have paid for it: *My yearly subscription to the newspaper expired.*
2 the act of subscribing.

sub·set (sub′sət′), NOUN. (in mathematics) a set, each of whose members is a member of a second set: *Fourth graders are a subset of the set that includes all students attending elementary school.*

sub·side (səb sid′), VERB.
1 to become less intense; die down: *The waves subsided when the wind stopped. Her fever subsided after she took the medicine.*
2 to sink to a lower level: *Several days after the rain stopped, the flood waters subsided.*
❏ VERB **sub·sides, sub·sid·ed, sub·sid·ing.**

sub·stance (sub′stəns), NOUN.
1 the material that something is made of; matter: *Ice and water are the same substance in different forms.*
2 the main or important part of anything: *The substance of his letter was advice on how to study.*

sub·stan·tial (səb stan′shəl), ADJECTIVE.
1 solidly made; strong: *That house is substantial enough to last a hundred years.*
2 large; important; ample: *Your work shows substantial improvement.*
–sub·stan′tial·ly, ADVERB.

sub·sti·tute (sub′stə tüt),
1 NOUN. something that is used instead of something else: *Margarine is a common substitute for butter.*
2 NOUN. someone who works in the place of a person who is sick or who is away; sub: *A substitute taught our class today.*
3 VERB. to put something in the place of something else: *We substituted brown sugar for molasses in these cookies.*
4 VERB. to take the place of another person: *The principal substituted for our teacher, who was ill.*
❏ VERB **sub·sti·tutes, sub·sti·tut·ed, sub·sti·tut·ing. –sub·sti·tu′tion,** NOUN.

sub·tle (sut′l), ADJECTIVE.
1 slight; delicate: *There is a subtle odor of burning leaves in the fall air.*
2 not obvious; difficult to perceive: *Subtle jokes are often hard to understand.*
3 working secretly: *a subtle poison.*
4 mysterious: *Her subtle smile interested me.*
5 marked by a quick ability to understand: *He has a subtle mind.*
❏ ADJECTIVE **sub·tler, sub·tlest. –sub′tly,** ADVERB.

sub·tract (səb trakt′), VERB. to take away a number or a part: *Subtract 2 from 10 and you have 8.*
❏ VERB **sub·tracts, sub·tract·ed, sub·tract·ing.**

sub·trac·tion (səb trak′shən), NOUN. the operation of subtracting one number from another: *10 – 2 = 8 is a simple subtraction.*

sub·urb (sub′ėrb′), NOUN. a district, town, or village just outside or near a city: *Many people who work in the city live in the suburbs.*

sub·ur·ban (sə bėr′bən), ADJECTIVE. of or like a suburb; in a suburb: *We do not have good suburban train service.*

sub·way (sub′wā′), NOUN. an underground electric railroad that runs beneath the surface of the streets in a city.

suc·ceed (sək sēd′), VERB.
1 to turn out well: *The plan succeeded.*
2 to accomplish what you intended to do: *She succeeded in completing the project.*
3 to come next after; follow; take the place of: *John Adams succeeded Washington as President.*
❏ VERB **suc·ceeds, suc·ceed·ed, suc·ceed·ing.**

suc·cess (sək ses′), NOUN.
1 a result that you hoped and planned for: *Success in school comes from intelligence and work.*
2 the act or fact of gaining wealth or high position: *She has had success in business.*

a	hat	ė	term	ô	order	ch	child	ə	a in about
ā	age	i	it	oi	oil	ng	long		e in taken
ä	far	ī	ice	ou	out	sh	she		i in pencil
â	care	o	hot	u	cup	th	thin		o in lemon
e	let	ō	open	ů	put	ŦH	then		u in circus
ē	equal	ò	saw	ü	rule	zh	measure		

S

3 someone or something that succeeds: *The circus was a great success.*
❑ PLURAL **suc·cess·es.**

suc·cess·ful (sək ses′fəl), ADJECTIVE.
1 having the success that you hoped and planned for: *The class picnic was very successful.*
2 wealthy: *a successful businessman.*
—**suc·cess′ful·ly,** ADVERB.

suc·ces·sion (sək sesh′ən), NOUN.
1 a group of things happening one after another; series: *A succession of accidents spoiled our trip.*
2 the order or right of someone succeeding to an office, property, or rank: *There was a dispute about the rightful succession to the throne.*
3 the order or arrangement of persons having such a right of succeeding: *The queen's oldest son is next in succession to the throne.*

suc·ces·sive (sək ses′iv), ADJECTIVE. coming one after another; following in order: *It has rained for three successive days.* —**suc·ces′sive·ly,** ADVERB.

suc·ces·sor (sək ses′ər), NOUN. someone who follows or succeeds another person in office, position, or ownership of property: *John Adams was Washington's successor as President.*

suc·cinct (sək singkt′), ADJECTIVE. expressed briefly and clearly: *The principal wrote a succinct one-page memo explaining the new student dress code.*
—**suc·cinct′ly,** ADVERB. —**suc·cinct′ness,** NOUN.

suc·co·tash (suk′ə tash), NOUN. kernels of sweet corn and beans, usually lima beans, cooked together.

suc·cu·lent (suk′yə lənt), ADJECTIVE. juicy: *a succulent peach.* —**suc′cu·lent·ly,** ADVERB.

such (such),
1 ADJECTIVE. of that kind; of the same kind or degree: *We had never seen such a sight.*
2 ADJECTIVE. of the kind already spoken of or suggested: *She does not like doughnuts, waffles, and other such sweet things for breakfast.*
3 ADJECTIVE. so great, so bad, or so good: *They are such liars! Such weather!*
4 PRONOUN. a person or thing of that kind; persons or things of that kind: *There were rowboats, canoes, and such on sale at the store today.*

such as, IDIOM.
1 for example: *He did a report on members of the dog family, such as the wolf and the fox.*
2 similar to; like: *A good friend such as you is rare.*

suck (suk), VERB.
1 to pull liquid into the mouth, using your lips and tongue to create suction: *Lemonade can be sucked through a straw.*
2 to pull or take in; absorb: *Plants suck up moisture from the earth. A sponge sucks in water.*
3 to hold something in your mouth and lick it: *The child sucked a lollipop.*
❑ VERB **sucks, sucked, suck·ing.**

suck·er (suk′ər), NOUN.
1 a piece of hard candy on the end of a small stick; lollipop.
2 a body part of some animals for sucking and holding. An octopus's tentacles have suckers.
3 someone who is easy to fool or to deceive.

the **suckers** of an octopus

suc·tion (suk′shən), NOUN. the process of drawing liquids, gases, dust, and so on, into a space by sucking out part of the air from that space. We draw liquid through a straw by suction. Vacuum cleaners work by suction.

Su·dan (sü dan′), NOUN. a country in northeastern Africa. —**Su·da·nese** (süd′n ēz′), ADJECTIVE or NOUN.

sud·den (sud′n), ADJECTIVE.
1 not expected: *a sudden stop, a sudden storm, a sudden idea.*
2 quick; rapid: *The cat made a sudden jump at the mouse.*
—**sud′den·ly,** ADVERB.

all of a sudden, IDIOM. unexpectedly or quickly: *All of a sudden we were in the middle of the storm.*

sudden death, (in sports) an overtime period played to decide the winner of a game that has ended in a tie. The first team to score wins the game.

suds (sudz), NOUN PLURAL. bubbles and foam on soapy water.

The puppy is covered with **suds.**

sue (sü), VERB. to start a lawsuit against someone: *She sued the driver of the car that hit her.* ❑ VERB **sues, sued, su·ing.**

suede (swād), NOUN. a soft leather that feels like velvet on one or both sides.

suf·fer (suf′ər), VERB.
1 to have or feel pain, grief, or injury: *She suffered a broken leg while skiing.*

2 to experience harm or loss: *Most of the farmers' crops suffered greatly during the dry spell.*
❑ VERB **suf·fers, suf·fered, suf·fer·ing.** —**suf′fer·er,** NOUN.

suf·fer·ing (suf′ər ing), NOUN. pain or great sadness: *Hunger causes suffering.*

suf·fi·cient (sə fish′ənt), ADJECTIVE. as much as is needed; enough: *The family did not have sufficient clothing for the winter.* —**suf·fi′cient·ly,** ADVERB.

suf·fix (suf′iks), NOUN. a letter, syllable, or syllables put at the end of a word to change its meaning or to make another word, as -*ly* in *badly,* -*ness* in *goodness,* and -*ful* in *spoonful.* ❑ PLURAL **suf·fix·es.**

Word Story

Suffix comes from a Latin word meaning "to fasten upon." Suffixes are fastened onto other words.

suf·fo·cate (suf′ə kāt), VERB.
1 to kill someone by stopping his or her breath: *Thick smoke suffocated several people in the burning building.*
2 to keep someone from breathing; choke: *I was suffocating under too many blankets.*
3 to die for lack of air: *The diver suffocated when his air line became twisted.*
❑ VERB **suf·fo·cates, suf·fo·cat·ed, suf·fo·cat·ing.** —**suf′fo·ca′tion,** NOUN.

sug·ar (shùg′ər),
1 NOUN. a sweet substance gotten chiefly from sugar cane or sugar beets, widely used in food products.
2 VERB. to sweeten something with sugar: *I sugared the strawberries before serving them.*
❑ VERB **sug·ars, sug·ared, sug·ar·ing.** —**sug′ar·free′,** ADJECTIVE.

Word Story

Sugar can be traced back to a Sanskrit word meaning "grit." Juice from sugarcane dries in the form of a sandy grit on its stalks.

sugar beet, a large white beet from which sugar is made.

sug·ar·cane (shùg′ər kān′), NOUN. a very tall grass with a strong stem and long, flat leaves, growing in warm regions. Most sugar is made from sugarcane.

sug·ar·less (shùg′ər lis), ADJECTIVE. made with an artificial sweetener; without sugar: *My dentist recommends sugarless chewing gum.*

sug·gest (səg jest′ or sə jest′), VERB.
1 to bring up an idea; propose: *She suggested a swim, and we all agreed.*
2 to bring something to mind; call up the thought of: *The thought of summer suggests swimming, tennis, and hot weather.*

3 to show something in an indirect way; hint: *His yawns suggested that he would like to go to bed.*
❑ VERB **sug·gests, sug·gest·ed, sug·gest·ing.**

sug·ges·tion (səg jes′chən or sə jes′chən), NOUN.
1 something suggested: *The picnic was an excellent suggestion.*
2 the act of suggesting: *The suggestion of a swim made the children jump with joy.*

su·i·cide (sü′ə sīd), NOUN. the act of killing yourself on purpose.

suit (süt),
1 NOUN. a set of clothes to be worn together. A man's suit consists of a jacket, pants, and sometimes a vest. A woman's suit consists of a jacket and either a skirt or pants.
2 VERB. to be convenient or acceptable; please; satisfy: *Which time suits you best? It is hard to suit everybody.*
3 VERB. to be good for; agree with: *A cool climate suits apples and wheat, but not oranges and tea.*
4 VERB. to look good on someone: *That blue sweater suits you.*
5 NOUN. See **lawsuit.**
6 NOUN. one of the four sets of cards (spades, hearts, diamonds, and clubs) that make up a deck.
❑ VERB **suits, suit·ed, suit·ing.**

suit·a·ble (sü′tə bəl), ADJECTIVE. right for the occasion; fitting; proper: *Simple clothes are suitable for school wear.* —**suit′a·bly,** ADVERB.

suit·case (süt′kās′), NOUN. a flat case for carrying clothing and other things while traveling.

suite (swēt), NOUN.
1 a set of connected rooms to be used by one person or family: *She has a suite of rooms at the hotel—a living room, bedroom, and bath.*
2 a set of matching furniture.
■ Another word that sounds like this is **sweet.**

sui·tor (sü′tər), NOUN. (earlier) a man who hopes to marry a woman: *The princess had many suitors.*

sul·fur (sul′fər), NOUN. a light yellow substance that is used in making matches and gunpowder. Sulfur is a chemical element.

sulk (sulk), VERB. to be silent and grouchy: *He sulked all evening.* ❑ VERB **sulks, sulked, sulk·ing.**

sulk·y (sul′kē), ADJECTIVE. silent and grouchy; sullen: *The prince became sulky when he did not get his own way.* ❑ ADJECTIVE **sulk·i·er, sulk·i·est.** —**sulk′i·ly,** ADVERB.

sul·len (sul′ən), ADJECTIVE. silent because of bad temper or anger: *The sullen child wouldn't even speak to me.* —**sul′len·ly,** ADVERB.

a hat	ė term	ô order	ch child	a in about
ā age	i it	oi oil	ng long	e in taken
ä far	ī ice	ou out	sh she	ə i in pencil
â care	o hot	u cup	th thin	o in lemon
e let	ō open	ù put	ᴛʜ then	u in circus
ē equal	ò saw	ü rule	zh measure	

S

sul·tan (sult′n), *NOUN.* a ruler of a Muslim country.

sul·try (sul′trē), *ADJECTIVE.* hot and humid: *We expect some sultry weather during July.* ❏ *ADJECTIVE* **sul·tri·er, sul·tri·est.**

sum (sum), *NOUN.*
1 an amount of money: *The city paid a large sum for street repairs.*
2 a number arrived at by adding two or more numbers together: *The sum of 2 and 3 and 4 is 9.* ■ Another word that sounds like this is **some.**

su·mac (sü′mak *or* shü′mak), *NOUN.* a shrub or small tree which has divided leaves that turn scarlet in the autumn and clusters of red or white fruit. Poison ivy is a kind of sumac.

This kind of **sumac** may grow to be 40 feet high.

sum·ma·rize (sum′ə rīz′), *VERB.* to give only the main points of something; express briefly: *She summarized the story for the class.* ❏ *VERB* **sum·ma·riz·es, sum·ma·rized, sum·ma·riz·ing.**

sum·mar·y (sum′ər ē), *NOUN.* a brief statement giving the main points of something: *This history book has a summary at the end of each chapter.* ❏ *PLURAL* **sum·mar·ies.**

sum·mer (sum′ər),
1 *NOUN.* the warmest season of the year between spring and autumn.
2 *VERB.* to spend the summer: *We hope to summer at the seashore next year.*
❏ *VERB* **sum·mers, sum·mered, sum·mer·ing.**

sum·mit (sum′it), *NOUN.* the highest point; top: *We climbed to the summit of the mountain.*

sum·mon (sum′ən), *VERB.* to order someone to come: *I was summoned to the principal's office.*
❏ *VERB* **sum·mons, sum·moned, sum·mon·ing.**

sum·mons (sum′ənz), *NOUN.* a formal order or notice to appear before a court of law or judge, especially to answer a charge: *I received a summons for speeding.* ❏ *PLURAL* **sum·mons·es.**

sun (sun),
1 *NOUN.* the brightest object in the sky; the star around which the earth and the other planets revolve. The sun supplies the entire solar system with light and heat.
2 *NOUN.* the light and warmth of the sun: *The cat likes to sit in the sun.*
3 *VERB.* to lie or sit in the light and warmth of the sun: *The swimmers sunned themselves on the beach.*
❏ *VERB* **suns, sunned, sun·ning.** ■ Another word that sounds like this is **son.**

Sun., an abbreviation of **Sunday.**

sun·bathe (sun′bāᴛʜ′), *VERB.* to expose yourself to the sun's rays. ❏ *VERB* **sun·bathes, sun·bathed, sun·bath·ing. −sun′bath′er,** *NOUN.*

sun·beam (sun′bēm′), *NOUN.* a ray of sunlight: *A sunbeam brightened the child's hair to gold.*

sun·block (sun′blok′), *NOUN.* See **sunscreen.**

sun·burn (sun′bėrn′),
1 *NOUN.* a redness or blistering of your skin, caused by staying too long in the sun's rays. A sunburn is often red and painful.
2 *VERB.* to burn your skin by staying too long in the sun's rays: *He is sunburned from a day on the beach.*
3 *VERB.* to become burned by the sun: *Her skin sunburns quickly.*
❏ *VERB* **sun·burns, sun·burned** or **sun·burnt, sun·burn·ing.**

sun·burnt (sun′bėrnt′), *VERB.*
1 a past tense of **sunburn:** *A day at the beach thoroughly sunburnt his arms and legs.*
2 a past participle of **sunburn:** *She has been sunburnt since early in June.*

sun·dae (sun′dā), *NOUN.* a dish of ice cream with syrup, crushed fruits, or nuts poured over it.
❏ *PLURAL* **sun·daes.** ■ Another word that sounds like this is **Sunday.**

a fancy **sundae**

Sun·day (sun′dā), *NOUN.* the first day of the week. ■ Another word that sounds like this is **sundae.**

Sunday school,
1 a school held on Sunday for teaching religion.
2 its members.

sun·down (sun′doun′), *NOUN.* See **sunset.**

sun·flow·er (sun′flou′ər), NOUN. a large yellow flower with a brown center that grows on a very tall stalk. Sunflower seeds are used as food and to produce oil for cooking.

sung (sung), VERB.
  1 a past tense of **sing:** *They sung at the concert.*
  2 the past participle of **sing:** *Many songs were sung at the concert.*

sun·glass·es (sun′glas′iz), NOUN PLURAL. eyeglasses that protect the eyes from the glare of the sun. They are made of colored glass or plastic.

sunk (sungk), VERB.
  1 a past tense of **sink:** *The coin sunk to the bottom of the fountain.*
  2 the past participle of **sink:** *The ship had sunk to the bottom of the sea.*

sunk·en (sung′kən), ADJECTIVE.
  1 sunk: *a sunken ship.*
  2 submerged; underwater: *a sunken rock.*
  3 lower than the surrounding level: *We walked down three steps to the sunken garden.*
  4 fallen in; hollow: *After the long illness, his cheeks were pale and sunken.*

sun·light (sun′līt′), NOUN. the light of the sun: *We hung the wash out to dry in the sunlight.*

Did You Know?

Sunlight takes about eight minutes and twenty seconds to reach the Earth. It travels at 186,282 miles per second. This is called the **speed of light.**

sun·lit (sun′lit′), ADJECTIVE. lit by the sun.

sun·ny (sun′ē), ADJECTIVE.
  1 having a lot of sunshine or sunlight: *It was a nice sunny day.* ▪ See the Synonym Study at **bright.**
  2 bright; cheerful; happy: *The baby has a sunny smile.*
  ❏ ADJECTIVE **sun·ni·er, sun·ni·est.**

Did You Know?

Yuma (yü′mə), Arizona, is the **sunniest** place in the United States. It has more than 4000 hours of sunlight every year. That is an average of almost 11 hours a day.

sun·rise (sun′rīz′), NOUN. the first appearance of the sun at the beginning of day; sunup.

sun·screen (sun′skrēn′), NOUN. a lotion or cream containing chemicals that screen out the harmful rays of the sun; sunblock. Sunscreen helps prevent sunburn.

sun·set (sun′set′), NOUN. the last appearance of the sun at the end of day; sundown.

sun·shine (sun′shīn′), NOUN. the light of the sun.

sun·stroke (sun′strōk′), NOUN. a sudden illness with fever and dry skin that is caused by too much exposure to the sun.

The blossoms of the **sunflower** may grow to be 12 inches wide.

sun·tan (sun′tan′), NOUN. the brown color of someone's skin caused by being in the sun.

sun·up (sun′up′), NOUN. See **sunrise.**

su·per (sü′ər), ADJECTIVE.
  1 (informal) excellent: *We thought the movie was super and stayed to see it again.*
  2 special; more than normal: *super heroes.*

Word Power   super-

The prefix **super-** can mean "very large or powerful." A **super**computer is a **very powerful** computer. It can also mean "more than." **Super**human means **more than** human.

su·perb (sů pėrb′), ADJECTIVE. very fine; excellent: *The singer gave a superb performance.*
  —**su·perb′ly,** ADVERB.

su·per·com·put·er (sü′pər kəm pyü′tər), NOUN. a very powerful, high-speed computer that can perform several hundred million operations a second. Supercomputers can work on many parts of a problem at the same time.

su·per·fi·cial (sü′pər fish′əl), ADJECTIVE.
  1 on or at the surface: *His burns were superficial.*
  2 not thorough; shallow: *superficial knowledge.*
  —**su′per·fi′cial·ly,** ADVERB.

sup·er·hu·man (sü′pər hyü′mən), ADJECTIVE. above or beyond ordinary human power, experience, and so on: *With a superhuman burst of speed, the runner set a new Olympic record.*

su·per·in·tend·ent (sü′pər in ten′dənt), NOUN. someone who oversees, directs, or manages: *a superintendent of schools, a police superintendent.*

a	hat	ė	term	ô	order	ch	child		a in about
ā	age	i	it	oi	oil	ng	long		e in taken
ä	far	ī	ice	ou	out	sh	she	ə	i in pencil
â	care	o	hot	u	cup	th	thin		o in lemon
e	let	ō	open	ů	put	ŦH	then		u in circus
ē	equal	ȯ	saw	ü	rule	zh	measure		

su·per·i·or (sə pir′ē ər),
1 *ADJECTIVE.* above average; very good; excellent: *My cousin does superior work in school because she studies very hard.*
2 *ADJECTIVE.* higher in quality; better; greater: *We lost the game to a superior team.*
3 *ADJECTIVE.* higher in position, rank, or importance: *He is my superior officer.*
4 *NOUN.* someone who is superior in rank, position, or ability: *As a violin player, he has no superior.*

Su·per·i·or (sə pir′ē ər), *NOUN.* **Lake,** one of the Great Lakes.

su·per·i·or·i·ty (sə pir′ē ôr′ə tē), *NOUN.* a superior state or quality: *The tennis team showed its superiority by winning all its matches this year.*

su·per·la·tive (sə pėr′lə tiv),
1 *ADJECTIVE.* very good; above all others; supreme: *superlative skills, superlative wisdom.*
2 *NOUN.* a form of a word or combination of words to show the extreme degree or greatest amount. *Fastest is the superlative of fast. Best is the superlative of good. Most quickly is the superlative of quickly.*

su·per·mar·ket (sü′pər mär′kit), *NOUN.* a large store that sells a great variety of groceries and household articles.

su·per·nat·ur·al (sü′pər nach′ər əl), *ADJECTIVE.* above or beyond the forces or laws of nature; of or about God, angels, ghosts, or the like: *The movie was about ghosts, demons, and other supernatural beings.*

su·per·pow·er (sü′pər pou′ər), *NOUN.* a nation so strong and wealthy that its actions and policies greatly affect those of smaller, less powerful nations.

su·per·son·ic (sü′pər son′ik), *ADJECTIVE.* able to move at a speed greater than the speed of sound: *We flew to Europe in a supersonic jet.*

su·per·star (sü′pər stär′), *NOUN.* a person, often an entertainer or athlete, who is exceptionally successful or famous.

su·per·sti·tion (sü′pər stish′ən), *NOUN.* a belief or practice that is based on ignorance, fear, or hope, not on reason or fact: *A common superstition is the belief that 13 is an unlucky number.*

a basketball **superstar**

su·per·sti·tious (sü′pər stish′əs), *ADJECTIVE.* believing in superstitions: *The ancient Romans were a superstitious people.* —**su′per·sti′tious·ly,** *ADVERB.*

su·per·vise (sü′pər vīz), *VERB.* to look after and direct work, workers, or a process; manage: *Morning recess is supervised by teachers.* ❏ *VERB* **su·per·vis·es, su·per·vised, su·per·vis·ing.**

su·per·vi·sion (sü′pər vizh′ən), *NOUN.* management; direction: *The house was built under the careful supervision of an architect.*

su·per·vi·sor (sü′pər vī′zər), *NOUN.* someone who supervises: *a bank supervisor, the music supervisor.*

sup·per (sup′ər), *NOUN.* the evening meal; meal usually eaten sometime between five and eight o'clock.

Word Story

Supper comes from an older French word meaning "soup." When the main meal of the day was eaten earlier, supper was often a light meal of soup and bread.

sup·per·time (sup′ər tīm′), *NOUN.* the time at which supper is served.

sup·ple (sup′əl), *ADJECTIVE.* bending easily: *a supple birch tree, supple leather, a supple dancer.*
❏ *ADJECTIVE* **sup·pler, sup·plest.**

sup·ple·ment (sup′lə mənt *for noun;* sup′lə ment *for verb*),
1 *NOUN.* something added to complete another thing, or to make it better: *Many newspapers have supplements that are included as an extra feature in the weekend edition.*
2 *VERB.* to add to or complete something: *I supplement my diet with vitamin pills.*
❏ *VERB* **sup·ple·ments, sup·ple·ment·ed, sup·ple·ment·ing.**

sup·ply (sə plī′),
1 *VERB.* to provide what someone or something needs: *The school supplies books for the children.*
2 *NOUN.* a quantity that is ready for use: *We have a large supply of vegetables in the freezer.*
3 *NOUN.* **supplies,** the food and equipment necessary for an army, a camping trip, and so on.
❏ *VERB* **sup·plies, sup·plied, sup·ply·ing;** *PLURAL* **sup·plies.** —**sup·pli′er,** *NOUN.*

sup·port (sə pôrt′),
1 *VERB.* to provide money necessary for someone to live: *Parents usually support their children.*
2 *VERB.* to be in favor of something; back: *She supports the proposed law.*
3 *VERB.* to help prove something: *The facts support his claim.*
4 *NOUN.* help; aid: *He needs the financial support of a scholarship.*
5 *VERB.* to keep from falling; hold up: *Walls support the roof.*

6 *NOUN.* someone or something that holds something up; prop: *The neck is the support of the head.*
❏ *VERB* **sup•ports, sup•port•ed, sup•port•ing.** —**sup•port′er,** *NOUN.*

sup•pose (sə pōz′), *VERB.*
1 to consider as possible: *Suppose we are late, what will the teacher say?*
2 to believe; think; imagine: *I suppose she will be late, as usual.*
❏ *VERB* **sup•pos•es, sup•posed, sup•pos•ing.**

supposed to, *IDIOM.* required or expected to do or be something: *I'm supposed to go home right after school.*

sup•press (se pres′), *VERB.*
1 to put an end to something by using force: *The police suppressed the riot.*
2 to hold back; keep from appearing: *She suppressed a yawn.*
❏ *VERB* **sup•press•es, sup•pressed, sup•press•ing.** —**su•pres•sion** (sə presh′ən), *NOUN.*

su•preme (sə prēm′), *ADJECTIVE.*
1 highest in rank or authority: *a supreme ruler.*
2 greatest; extreme: *With supreme effort, we moved the piano.*
—**su•preme′ly,** *ADVERB.*

Supreme Being, God.

Supreme Court, the highest court in the United States, in Washington, D.C. A chief justice and eight associate justices make up the Supreme Court.

sure (shùr),
1 *ADJECTIVE.* free from doubt; certain: *Are you sure you locked the door?*
2 *ADJECTIVE.* to be trusted; safe: *The only sure way of sending a message during the storm was by radio.*
3 *ADJECTIVE.* firm: *I stood on sure ground.*
4 *ADJECTIVE.* certain to come, to be, or to happen: *It is sure to snow this winter.*
5 *ADVERB.* surely: *He sure can run!*
❏ *ADJECTIVE* **sur•er, sur•est.**

Synonym Study

Sure means having no doubt: *She is sure that she saw a strange animal in the forest.*

Confident means sure, with a hopeful feeling: *I am confident that with practice my reading will improve.*

Positive means sure, without any second thoughts: *We are positive that she is the fastest runner in her class, because she wins every race.*

Certain means sure, based on facts: *He was certain that George Washington was the first President of the United States.*

sure•ly (shùr′lē), *ADVERB.* certainly; of course: *Surely you heard that funny noise just now.*

surf (sėrf),
1 *NOUN.* the waves of the sea breaking on the shore.
2 *VERB.* to ride on the crest of a wave, especially with a surfboard.
3 *VERB.* to search or investigate in a rapid, random way: *surfing the Internet, surfing on cable TV.*
❏ *VERB* **surfs, surfed, surf•ing.** ■ Another word that sounds like this is **serf. —surf′er,** *NOUN.*

Surfing takes a lot of practice.

sur•face (sėr′fis),
1 *NOUN.* the outside of anything: *the surface of a golf ball, the surface of a table.*
2 *NOUN.* the top of the ground or soil, or of a body of water or other liquid: *The stone sank beneath the surface of the water.*
3 *NOUN.* outward appearance: *She seems rough, but you will find her very kind below the surface.*
4 *VERB.* to put a smooth top layer on something: *The town must surface this road.*
5 *VERB.* to rise to the surface: *The sub surfaced.*
❏ *VERB* **sur•fac•es, sur•faced, sur•fac•ing.**

surf•board (sėrf′bôrd′), *NOUN.* a long, narrow board for riding the surf.

surge (sėrj),
1 *VERB.* to push forward with force: *A wave surged over us. The crowd surged through the streets.*
2 *NOUN.* a sweeping, upward motion: *Our boat was overturned by a surge of water.*
3 *NOUN.* something like a wave: *I felt a surge of anger.*
❏ *VERB* **surg•es, surged, surg•ing.**

sur•geon (sėr′jən), *NOUN.* a doctor who performs operations: *A surgeon removed my tonsils.*

surge protector, an electronic device that prevents a power surge from reaching and damaging electrical equipment such as a computer or television set.

a	hat	ė	term	ô	order	ch	child		a in about
ā	age	i	it	oi	oil	ng	long		e in taken
ä	far	ī	ice	ou	out	sh	she	ə ⟨	i in pencil
â	care	o	hot	u	cup	th	thin		o in lemon
e	let	ō	open	ù	put	ŦH	then		u in circus
ē	equal	ȯ	saw	ü	rule	zh	measure		

S

sur·ger·y (sėr′jər ē), NOUN. the art and science of treating diseases or injuries by operations and instruments: *Flu can be treated with medicine, but a ruptured appendix requires surgery.*

sur·gi·cal (sėr′jə kəl), ADJECTIVE.
1 of or about surgery: *a surgical patient.*
2 used in surgery: *surgical instruments.*
—**sur′gi·cal·ly**, ADVERB.

Sur·i·na·me (sùr′ə nä′mə), NOUN. a country in northern South America. —**Sur·i·na·mese** (sùr′ə nə mēz′), ADJECTIVE or NOUN.

sur·ly (sėr′lē), ADJECTIVE. grouchy; unfriendly; rude: *They got a surly answer from their grouchy neighbor.* ■ See the Synonym Study at **cross**.
❑ ADJECTIVE **sur·li·er, sur·li·est. —sur′li·ness**, NOUN.

sur·name (sėr′nām′), NOUN. a last name; family name: *Johnson is the surname of Andrew Johnson.*

sur·pass (sər pas′), VERB. to do better at something than someone else does: *He surpasses his sister in music.* ❑ VERB **sur·pass·es, sur·passed, sur·pass·ing.**

sur·plus (sėr′pləs),
1 NOUN. an amount over and above what is needed; extra quantity left over: *The bank keeps a large surplus of money in reserve.*
2 ADJECTIVE. more than is needed: *Surplus wheat is put in storage or shipped abroad.*
❑ PLURAL **sur·plus·es.**

sur·prise (sər prīz′),
1 NOUN. something unexpected: *Our grandparents always have a surprise for us when we visit them.*
2 NOUN. the feeling caused by something that happens suddenly or unexpectedly: *His face showed surprise at the news.*
3 VERB. to cause someone to feel surprise: *The victory surprised us.*
4 ADJECTIVE. surprising; not expected: *a surprise party.*
❑ VERB **sur·pris·es, sur·prised, sur·pris·ing.**

Synonym Study

Surprise means to fill someone with wonder because of something unexpected: *We plan to surprise her with a birthday party.*

Astonish and **amaze** mean to surprise someone greatly: *The magician astonished the children by making the parrot vanish. Next, he amazed them with a card trick.*

Astound means to surprise someone completely, so that the person has trouble understanding what has happened: *It's astounding that a ten-year-old won the chess tournament.*

Startle means to make someone jump in surprise and fright: *The door slammed and startled the teacher.*

sur·ren·der (sə ren′dər),
1 VERB. to stop fighting and give up: *The captain had to surrender to the enemy.*
2 NOUN. the act of surrendering: *The surrender of the fort came at dawn.*
❑ VERB **sur·ren·ders, sur·ren·dered, sur·ren·der·ing.**

sur·round (sə round′), VERB. to shut something in on all sides; encircle; enclose: *A high fence surrounds the field.* ❑ VERB **sur·rounds, sur·round·ed, sur·round·ing.**

sur·round·ings (sə roun′dingz), NOUN PLURAL. everything that is around where someone is: *We enjoyed the peaceful surroundings at the cabin in the mountains.*

sur·vey (sər vā′ for verb; sėr′vā for noun),
1 VERB. to look something over; examine: *The buyers surveyed the goods offered for sale.*
2 NOUN. a general look; examination: *We were pleased with our first survey of the house.*
3 NOUN. a formal or official study, poll, or inspection: *The school board made a survey of public opinion about the new textbooks.*
4 VERB. to measure something very precisely for its size, shape, or boundaries: *The land is being surveyed before it is divided into house lots.*
5 NOUN. a careful measurement of something: *A survey showed that the boundaries were not correct.*
❑ VERB **sur·veys, sur·veyed, sur·vey·ing;** PLURAL **sur·veys.**

sur·vey·or (sər vā′ər), NOUN. someone trained to survey land.

sur·viv·al (sər vī vəl), NOUN.
1 the act or fact of surviving: *The survival of the avalanche victims depended on a quick rescue.*
2 a person, thing, custom, or belief that has lasted from an earlier time: *Many superstitions are survivals from ancient times.*

sur·vive (sər vīv′), VERB.
1 to live longer than someone: *He survived his wife by three years.*
2 to continue to live or exist; remain: *These cave paintings have survived for over 15,000 years.*
❑ VERB **sur·vives, sur·vived, sur·viv·ing.**

sur·vi·vor (sər vī′vər), NOUN. someone or something that survives: *two survivors from the plane crash.*

sus·pect (sə spekt′ for verb; sus′pekt for noun),
1 VERB. to imagine something to be so; suppose: *I suspect that they have been delayed.*
2 VERB. to believe that someone is guilty, false, or bad without proof: *The police suspected them of being thieves.*
3 NOUN. someone believed to be guilty of a crime: *The police have arrested two suspects in connection with the bank robbery.*
❑ VERB **sus·pects, sus·pect·ed, sus·pect·ing.**

sus·pend (sə spend′), VERB.
1 to stop doing something for a while: *We suspended building operations during the winter.*
2 to keep or prevent someone from attending school, being on a team, doing a job, and so on, for a short time: *They were suspended from school for a week for bad conduct.*
3 to cancel something temporarily: *The judge suspended her driver's license.*
4 to hang something by fastening it to something above: *The lamp was suspended from the ceiling.*
5 to stay in place as if hanging there: *We saw the smoke suspended in the still air.*
❏ VERB **sus·pends, sus·pend·ed, sus·pend·ing.**

Word Story

Suspend comes from a Latin word meaning "to hang up." Other English words from the same root include **suspenders, suspense,** and **suspension.**

sus·pend·ers
(sə spen′dərz), NOUN PLURAL. straps worn over the shoulders to hold up your trousers.

sus·pense (sə spens′), NOUN. the condition of being uncertain and anxious about what may happen: *The detective story kept me in suspense until the last chapter.*

sus·pen·sion
(sə spen′shən), NOUN. the act of suspending or the condition of being suspended: *the suspension of a driver's license for speeding.*

Without **suspenders,** this boy might be in big trouble.

suspension bridge, a bridge hung on cables or chains between towers.

sus·pi·cion (sə spish′ən), NOUN.
1 a belief, feeling, or thought: *I have a suspicion that the weather will be very hot today.*
2 a feeling of not trusting someone: *My suspicion of the cook was correct; she turned out to be the murderer.* ■ See the Synonym Study at **doubt.**

above suspicion, IDIOM. not thought to be guilty in any way; completely trusted.

under suspicion, IDIOM. thought to be guilty; not completely trusted.

sus·pi·cious (sə spish′əs), ADJECTIVE.
1 feeling suspicion: *Our dog is suspicious of strangers.*
2 causing someone to suspect something: *She spoke in a suspicious manner.*
—**sus·pi′cious·ly,** ADVERB.

sus·tain (sə stān′), VERB.
1 to give someone strength to keep going: *His cheerfulness sustained us through our troubles.*
2 to suffer: *She sustained a great loss in the death of her husband.*
❏ VERB **sus·tains, sus·tained, sus·tain·ing.**

SW or **S.W.,**
1 an abbreviation of **southwest.**
2 an abbreviation of **southwestern.**

swab (swäb),
1 NOUN. a bit of sponge, cloth, or cotton for cleaning some part of the body or for applying medicine to it.
2 VERB. to clean with a swab: *swab someone's throat.*
3 NOUN. a mop for cleaning decks, floors, and so on.
❏ VERB **swabs, swabbed, swab·bing.**

swag·ger (swag′ər), VERB. to walk, strut, or show off in a conceited or bragging way: *The villain in the play swaggered onto the stage.* ❏ VERB **swag·gers, swag·gered, swag·ger·ing.**

Swa·hi·li (swä hē′lē), NOUN. a Bantu language containing many Arabic and other foreign words, spoken in much of eastern Africa and parts of Zaïre. *Safari* came into English from Swahili.

swal·low¹ (swäl′ō),
1 VERB. to take something into the stomach through the throat: *We swallow all our food and drink.*
2 VERB. to keep from expressing something: *She swallowed her unhappy feelings and smiled.*
3 NOUN. an amount swallowed at one time: *There are only about four swallows of water left in the bottle.*
❏ VERB **swal·lows, swal·lowed, swal·low·ing.**

swal·low² (swäl′ō), NOUN. a small bird that has long, pointed wings and can fly very fast. Some kinds have deeply forked tails.

swam (swam), VERB. the past tense of **swim:** *We swam all afternoon.*

swamp (swämp),
1 NOUN. wet, soft land: *The swamp near the woods has many wild animals living in it.*
2 VERB. to fill something with water and sink it: *The waves swamped the boat.*
3 VERB. to overwhelm someone, as if by a flood: *I was swamped with homework.*
❏ VERB **swamps, swamped, swamp·ing.**
—**swamp′like′,** ADJECTIVE.

swamp·y (swäm′pē), ADJECTIVE.
1 like a swamp; soft and wet: *The front yard is swampy from the heavy rain.*
2 containing swamps: *They live in a swampy region.*
❏ ADJECTIVE **swamp·i·er, swamp·i·est.**

a	hat	ė	term	ô	order	ch	child	⎧a in about
ā	age	i	it	oi	oil	ng	long	⎪e in taken
ä	far	ī	ice	ou	out	sh	she	ə⎨i in pencil
â	care	o	hot	u	cup	th	thin	⎪o in lemon
e	let	ō	open	u̇	put	ŦH	then	⎩u in circus
ē	equal	ò	saw	ü	rule	zh	measure	

S

swan — between 4 and 5 feet long

swan (swän), NOUN. a large, graceful water bird with a long, slender, curving neck. The adult is usually pure white. **−swan′like′**, ADJECTIVE.

Did You Know?

Swans fly very high when they migrate. They have been seen as high as two miles above the ground! They also fly very fast. They can fly as fast as 85 miles per hour.

swap (swäp), VERB. to trade: *The children swapped toys.* ❑ VERB **swaps, swapped, swap·ping.**

swarm (swôrm),
1 NOUN. a group of bees led by a queen that leaves a hive and flies off together to start a new colony.
2 VERB. to fly off together in this way to start a new colony of bees.
3 NOUN. a large group of insects, animals, or people moving about together: *Swarms of children played in the park.*
4 VERB. to fly or move about in great numbers: *The mosquitoes swarmed about us.*
5 VERB. to be crowded: *The lobby of the theater swarmed with people during intermission.*
❑ VERB **swarms, swarmed, swarm·ing.**

swat (swät), VERB. to hit something sharply or violently: *to swat a fly.* ❑ VERB **swats, swat·ted, swat·ting. −swat′ter,** NOUN.

sway (swā),
1 VERB. to swing or cause to swing back and forth; swing from side to side, or to one side: *The dancers swayed to the music.*
2 VERB. to change someone's opinion or feeling: *Nothing could sway him after he had made up his mind.*
3 NOUN. an influence, control, or rule: *Many countries around the world are under the sway of dictators.*
❑ VERB **sways, swayed, sway·ing.**

swear (swâr), VERB.
1 to use bad or offensive language; curse: *The pirates raged and swore when they were captured.*
2 to promise or vow that you will do or not do something: *I swear I will tell no one the secret.* ■ See the Synonym Study at **promise.**
3 to make a solemn statement, appealing to God or some other sacred being or object: *A witness at a trial is asked, "Do you swear to tell the truth, the whole truth, and nothing but the truth, so help you God?"*
❑ VERB **swears, swore, sworn, swear·ing. −swear′er,** NOUN.

swear in, IDIOM. to admit to office or service by giving an oath: *The President of the United States is sworn in on inauguration day, January 20.*

swear off, IDIOM. to promise to give up: *I am going to swear off smoking.*

sweat (swet),
1 NOUN. moisture that comes through the pores of the skin: *After mowing the lawn, she wiped the sweat from her face.*
2 VERB. to give out moisture through the pores of the skin: *We sweated because it was very hot.*
3 NOUN. a fit or condition of sweating: *I was in a cold sweat from fear.*
4 NOUN. moisture given out by something or appearing on its surface.
5 VERB. (informal) to work very hard.
❑ VERB **sweats, sweat or sweat·ed, sweat·ing.**

The bear was chased by a **swarm** of angry bees.

sweat·er (swet′ər), NOUN. a knitted article of clothing made of wool, cotton, nylon, or the like, worn on the upper part of the body.

sweat·pants (swet′pants′), *NOUN*. a pair of baggy pants gathered with elastic at the waist and ankles, often worn to keep warm before and after exercise.

sweat·shirt (swet′shėrt), *NOUN*. a heavy shirt with long sleeves, worn especially to keep warm during exercise.

sweat·suit (swet′süt′), *NOUN*. an exercise suit made of a sweatshirt and sweatpants.

sweat·y (swet′ē), *ADJECTIVE*. covered or wet with sweat: *After moving the boxes we were all sweaty.* ❑ *ADJECTIVE* **sweat·i·er, sweat·i·est.**

hot and **sweaty**

Swede (swēd), *NOUN*. someone born or living in Sweden.

Swe·den (swēd′n), *NOUN*. a country in northern Europe.

Swed·ish (swē′dish),
1 *ADJECTIVE*. of or about Sweden, its people, or their language: *a Swedish movie, Swedish folktales.*
2 *NOUN PLURAL*. **the Swedish,** the people of Sweden.
3 *NOUN*. the language of Sweden.

sweep (swēp),
1 *VERB*. to clean or clear a floor, deck, and so on, with a broom or brush: *The campers swept the floor of their cabin every morning.*
2 *VERB*. to move, brush, or take something away with a broom or as with a broom: *They swept the dust into a pan.*
3 *VERB*. to remove something with a sweeping motion; carry along: *A flood swept away the bridge.*
4 *NOUN*. an act of sweeping: *I need to give the room a good sweep.*
5 *VERB*. to stretch out over a long course or curve: *The shore sweeps to the south for miles.*
6 *NOUN*. a continuous extent; stretch: *The house looks upon a wide sweep of farming country.*
7 in sports: **a** *NOUN*. the act of winning all the games in a series, match, or contest; complete victory. **b** *VERB*. to win all the games in a series, match, or contest.
❑ *VERB* **sweeps, swept, sweep·ing.** —**sweep′er,** *NOUN*.

sweep·ing (swē′ping), *ADJECTIVE*.
1 passing over a wide space: *Her sweeping glance took in the whole room.*
2 having wide range: *a sweeping victory, a sweeping statement.*

sweep·ings (swē′pingz), *NOUN PLURAL*. dust or scraps swept out or up.

sweet (swēt),
1 *ADJECTIVE*. having a taste like sugar or honey: *Pears are much sweeter than lemons.*

2 *ADJECTIVE*. having a pleasant taste or smell: *I took deep breaths of the sweet, fresh air.*
3 *ADJECTIVE*. pleasant; agreeable: *a sweet smile.*
4 *NOUN*. **sweets,** candy or other sweet things.
■ Another word that sounds like this is **suite.**
—**sweet′ly,** *ADVERB*. —**sweet′ness,** *NOUN*.

sweet corn, a kind of corn eaten when it is young and tender.

sweet·en (swēt′n), *VERB*. to make or become sweet: *He sweetened his coffee with sugar.* ❑ *VERB* **sweet·ens, sweet·ened, sweet·en·ing.**

sweet·en·er (swēt′n ər), *NOUN*. a substance that sweetens something: *Do you prefer sugar or an artificial sweetener?*

sweet·heart (swēt′härt′), *NOUN*. a loved one; lover.

sweet pea, a climbing plant with delicate, fragrant flowers of various colors.

sweet potato, the sweet, thick, yellow or reddish root of a vine grown in warm regions. Sweet potatoes are used as a vegetable or in pies.

sweet tooth, a fondness for sweets: *Every time I ask for a second piece of pie, Grandma says I must have inherited her sweet tooth.*

swell (swel),
1 *VERB*. to grow bigger; make bigger: *Bread dough swells as it rises. The bee sting had swelled his finger up.*
2 *VERB*. to increase in amount, degree, or force: *Investments may swell into a fortune.*
3 *NOUN*. a long, unbroken wave or waves: *The boat rocked in the swell.*
4 *VERB*. to grow or make louder: *The sound swelled to a roar. All joined in to swell the chorus.*
5 *ADJECTIVE*. (informal) excellent; very satisfactory.
❑ *VERB* **swells, swelled, swelled** or **swol·len, swell·ing.**

swell·ing (swel′ing), *NOUN*. an increase in size; swollen part: *There is a swelling on her head where she bumped it.*

swel·ter (swel′tər), *VERB*. to suffer from heat: *We sweltered in the humid August evening.* ❑ *VERB* **swel·ters, swel·tered, swel·ter·ing.**

swept (swept), *VERB*.
1 the past tense of **sweep:** *He swept the room.*
2 the past participle of **sweep:** *It was swept clean.*

swerve (swėrv), *VERB*. to turn aside: *The car swerved sharply to avoid hitting the truck.* ❑ *VERB* **swerves, swerved, swerv·ing.**

swift (swift),
1 *ADJECTIVE*. moving very fast; able to move very fast: *a swift car.* ■ See the Synonym Study at **quick.**

a hat	ė term	ô order	ch child	⎧a in about
ā age	i it	oi oil	ng long	⎪e in taken
ä far	ī ice	ou out	sh she	ə⎨i in pencil
â care	o hot	u cup	th thin	⎪o in lemon
e let	ō open	u̇ put	ᵗͪ then	⎩u in circus
ē equal	ȯ saw	ü rule	zh measure	

S

2 *ADJECTIVE.* coming or happening quickly: *She gave me a swift answer.*

3 *NOUN.* a small bird with long wings. A swift looks something like a swallow.
—**swift′ly**, *ADVERB.* —**swift′ness**, *NOUN.*

swim (swim),

1 *VERB.* to move along on or in the water by using arms, legs, or fins: *Fish swim. Most girls and boys like to swim.*

2 *VERB.* to swim across: *He swam the river.*

3 *VERB.* to float in or be covered with: *The roast lamb was swimming in gravy.*

4 *VERB.* to overflow or be flooded with: *His eyes were swimming with tears.*

5 *NOUN.* an act, time, motion, or distance of swimming: *She had had an hour's swim.*

6 *VERB.* to be dizzy; whirl: *The heat and noise made my head swim.*
❏ *VERB* **swims, swam, swum, swim·ming.**
—**swim′mer**, *NOUN.*

swim·suit (swim′süt′), *NOUN.* a bathing suit.

swin·dle (swin′dl),

1 *VERB.* to cheat someone: *Honest storekeepers do not swindle their customers.* ■ See the Synonym Study at **cheat.**

2 *NOUN.* the act of cheating; fraud.
❏ *VERB* **swin·dles, swin·dled, swin·dling.**
—**swin′dler**, *NOUN.*

swine (swin), *NOUN.* a hog or pig. ❏ *PLURAL* **swine.**

swing (swing),

1 *VERB.* to move back and forth, especially with a regular motion: *We swing our arms as we walk.*

2 *VERB.* to move or cause to move in a curve: *I swung the bat. The screen door swung shut with a bang.*

3 *NOUN.* the act or manner of swinging: *With a mighty swing, the batter hit a home run.*

4 *NOUN.* a seat hung from ropes or chains that you can sit and swing on.

5 *VERB.* to ride back and forth on a swing.
❏ *VERB* **swings, swung, swing·ing.**

swipe (swip),

1 *VERB.* (slang) to steal: *Someone swiped her bike.*

2 *NOUN.* (informal) a sweeping stroke: *I made two swipes at the golf ball without hitting it.*

3 *VERB.* (informal) to strike with a sweeping blow: *He swiped at the mosquito, but missed it.*
❏ *VERB* **swipes, swiped, swip·ing.**

swirl (swėrl),

1 *VERB.* to move along with a twisting motion; whirl: *dust swirling in the air, a stream swirling over rocks.*

2 *NOUN.* a twist or curl: *There was a swirl of whipped cream on top of the sundae.*
❏ *VERB* **swirls, swirled, swirl·ing.**

swish (swish), *VERB.*

1 to move with a light hissing or brushing sound: *The whip swished through the air.*

2 *VERB.* to make this sound: *The long gown swished as she danced across the floor.*

3 *NOUN.* a swishing movement or sound: *I love the swish of little waves on the shore.*
❏ *VERB* **swish·es, swished, swish·ing;** *PLURAL* **switch·es.**

Swiss (swis),

1 *ADJECTIVE.* of or about Switzerland or its people: *the Swiss lakes.*

2 *NOUN.* someone born or living in Switzerland.

3 *NOUN PLURAL.* **the Swiss,** the people of Switzerland.

switch (swich),

1 *VERB.* to change or shift something: *We switched places. They switched hats.*

2 *NOUN.* a change; shift: *We were annoyed by the last-minute switch in plans.*

3 *NOUN.* a device for making or breaking a connection in an electric circuit.

4 *VERB.* to turn something on or off by using a switch: *Switch off the light.*

5 *NOUN.* a pair of movable rails by which a train is shifted from one track to another.

6 *NOUN.* a slender stick used to get horses or cattle to move along.

7 *VERB.* to move or swing something like a switch: *The horse switched its tail to drive off the flies.*

8 *VERB.* to whip or strike an animal: *I switched the horse to make it gallop.*

9 *VERB.* to shift by using a switch: *The engineer switched the railroad train to a different track.*
❏ *VERB* **switch·es, switched, switch·ing;** *PLURAL* **switch·es.**

switch·board
(swich′bôrd′), *NOUN.* a panel with electric switches and plugs for connecting telephone lines.

Swit·zer·land
(swit′sər lənd), *NOUN.* a country in central Europe.

swiv·el (swiv′əl),

1 *NOUN.* a fastening that allows something fastened to turn around freely.

2 *VERB.* to turn or spin around on a fastening like this.
❏ *VERB* **swiv·els, swiv·eled, swiv·el·ing.**

an old-fashioned **switchboard**

swol·len (swō′lən),

1 *ADJECTIVE.* swelled: *I couldn't go to the dance because of a swollen ankle.*

2 *VERB.* a past participle of **swell:** *Her ankle has swollen quite a bit since she fell.*

swoon (swün), VERB. to faint: *He swoons at the sight of blood.* ❑ VERB **swoons, swooned, swoon·ing.**

swoop (swüp),
1 VERB. to come down fast on something, as a hawk does when it attacks: *Bats swooped down from the roof of the cave.*
2 NOUN. a fast downward descent or attack: *With one swoop, the hawk seized the chicken and flew away.*
❑ VERB **swoops, swooped, swoop·ing.**

sword (sôrd), NOUN. a weapon, usually metal, with a long, sharp blade fastened to a handle or hilt. **—sword′like′,** ADJECTIVE.

sword·fish (sôrd′fish′), NOUN. a very large sea fish that has a swordlike bone sticking out from its upper jaw. ❑ PLURAL **sword·fish** or **sword·fish·es.**

swordfish — up to 6 feet long, including the upper jaw

swords·man (sôrdz′mən), NOUN. someone who is skilled in using a sword. ❑ PLURAL **swords·men.**

swore (swôr), VERB. the past tense of **swear**: *I swore to keep my friend's secret.*

sworn (swôrn),
1 VERB. the past participle of **swear**: *A solemn oath of loyalty was sworn by all the knights.*
2 ADJECTIVE. stated with an oath: *We have her sworn statement before us.*

swum (swum), VERB. the past participle of **swim**: *I have never swum here before.*

swung (swung), VERB.
1 the past tense of **swing**: *He swung his arms as he walked.*
2 the past participle of **swing**: *The door had swung open.*

syc·a·more (sik′ə môr), NOUN. a kind of shade tree with large leaves and bark that peels off in large patches.

syl·lab·ic (sə lab′ik), ADJECTIVE.
1 of or made up of syllables.
2 forming a separate syllable by itself. The second *l* sound in *little* (lit′l) is syllabic.

syl·la·ble (sil′ə bəl), NOUN.
1 a word or part of a word pronounced as a unit. A syllable is usually made up of a vowel alone

or a vowel with one or more consonants. The word *syllable* (sil′ə bəl) has three syllables. Certain consonant sounds may be used as syllables by themselves, such as the (l) in *bottle* (bot′l), or the (n) in *hidden* (hid′n).
2 a letter or group of letters representing a syllable in writing and printing. *Strength* has only one syllable; *ap·prox·i·mate* has four syllables.

sym·bol (sim′bəl), NOUN. an object, diagram, icon, and so on, that stands for or represents something else: *The olive branch is the symbol of peace. The marks +, −, ×, and ÷ are symbols for add, subtract, multiply, and divide.* ■ Another word that sounds like this is **cymbal.**

sym·bol·ic (sim bol′ik), ADJECTIVE. expressed by a symbol or symbols. **—sym·bol′i·cal·ly,** ADVERB.

sym·bol·ize (sim′bə līz), VERB. to be a symbol of something; represent: *A dove symbolizes peace.* ❑ VERB **sym·bol·iz·es, sym·bol·ized, sym·bol·iz·ing.** **—sym′bol·i·za′tion,** NOUN.

sym·met·ri·cal (si met′rə kəl), ADJECTIVE. having a balanced form or arrangement: *The flowers were planted in a symmetrical pattern. A seesaw is symmetrical.* **—sym·met′ri·cal·ly,** ADVERB.

sym·me·try (sim′ə trē), NOUN. a regular, balanced form or arrangement on opposite sides of a line or around a center.

sym·pa·thet·ic (sim′pə thet′ik), ADJECTIVE. having or showing kind feelings toward other people: *She is an unselfish and sympathetic friend.* ■ See the Synonym Study at **good-natured.** **—sym′pa·thet′i·cal·ly,** ADVERB.

sym·pa·thize (sim′pə thīz), VERB. to feel or show sympathy toward someone: *The boy sympathized with his little sister who had hurt herself.* ❑ VERB **sym·pa·thiz·es, sym·pa·thized, sym·pa·thiz·ing.**

sym·pa·thy (sim′pə thē), NOUN.
1 the act of sharing someone else's sadness or trouble: *We feel sympathy for a person who is ill.*
2 agreement; favor: *We are all in sympathy with your plan.*
❑ PLURAL **sym·pa·thies.**

sym·pho·ny (sim′fə nē), NOUN.
1 a long, complicated musical composition for an orchestra.
2 a large orchestra that plays symphonies, made up of brass, woodwind, percussion, and stringed instruments: *My grandparents attend the local symphony every week.*
❑ PLURAL **sym·pho·nies.**

a	hat	ė	term	ô	order	ch	child		
ā	age	i	it	oi	oil	ng	long		a in about
ä	far	ī	ice	ou	out	sh	she		e in taken
â	care	o	hot	u	cup	th	thin	ə	i in pencil
e	let	ō	open	ù	put	ᴛʜ	then		o in lemon
ē	equal	ȯ	saw	ü	rule	zh	measure		u in circus

S

symp·tom (simp′təm), *NOUN.* a change in someone's condition or appearance that indicates disease or sickness: *Fever is a symptom of illness.* **–symp′tom·less,** *ADJECTIVE.*

syn·a·gogue (sin′ə gog), *NOUN.* a building used by Jewish people for religious instruction and worship. ❑ *PLURAL* **syn·a·gogues.**

syn·drome (sin′drōm), *NOUN.* a group of symptoms thought of together that indicate the presence of a particular disease.

syn·o·nym (sin′ə nim), *NOUN.* a word that means the same or nearly the same as another word. *Keen is a synonym of sharp.*

syn·on·y·mous (si non′ə məs), *ADJECTIVE.* having the same or nearly the same meaning. "Little" and "small" are synonymous. **–syn·on′y·mous·ly,** *ADVERB.*

syn·tax (sin′taks), *NOUN.* the way in which words and phrases are put together to form phrases and sentences.

syn·thet·ic (sin thet′ik), *ADJECTIVE.* not natural; made artificially by chemical processes: *Nylon is a synthetic fiber.*

Syr·i·a (sir′ē ə), *NOUN.* a country in southwestern Asia. **–Syr′i·an,** *ADJECTIVE* or *NOUN.*

sy·ringe (sə rinj′), *NOUN.* a medical instrument that uses a needle to inject medicine under the skin, into a blood vessel, and so on.

syr·up (sir′əp or sėr′əp), *NOUN.* a sweet, thick liquid. Sugar boiled with water or fruit juices makes a syrup. A cough syrup contains medicine to relieve coughing.

sys·tem (sis′tem), *NOUN.*
1 a set of things or parts that make up a whole: *the digestive system, the nervous system.*
2 an ordered group of facts, principles, or beliefs: *a system of education.*
3 a plan; scheme; method: *She has a system for getting the work done in half the time.*
4 an orderly way of getting things done: *Our system of education needs improvement. We have a democratic system of government.*
5 the body as a whole: *Exercise is good for your system.*

sys·tem·at·ic (sis′tə mat′ik), *ADJECTIVE.*
1 according to a system; having a system, method, or plan: *He works in a very systematic way.*
2 orderly in arranging things or in getting things done: *He is a very systematic person.* **–sys′tem·at′i·cal·ly,** *ADVERB.*

toucan

Tt

t. or **t,** an abbreviation of **teaspoon** or **teaspoons.**

T. or **T,** an abbreviation of **tablespoon** or **tablespoons.**

tab (tab), *NOUN.*
1 a small flap. Tabs stick out from caps to cover the ears, from cards used in filing, and from envelopes or cans to make it easier to open them.
2 (informal) a bill or check: *I'll pick up the tab.*

Ta·bas·co (tä bäs'kō *or* tə bas'kō), *NOUN.* a state in southeastern Mexico.

tab·by (tab'ē), *NOUN.* a grayish brown cat with dark stripes. ◻ *PLURAL* **tab·bies.**

ta·ble (tā'bəl), *NOUN.*
1 a piece of furniture with a smooth, flat top on legs.
2 the people seated at a table: *The whole table joined in the conversation.*
3 information arranged in rows or columns; list: *The table of contents is in the front of the book. He is studying the multiplication table.*

turn the tables, *IDIOM.* to reverse conditions or circumstances completely: *They were ahead but we turned the tables on them and won the game.*

under the table, *IDIOM.* in a secret way: *Illegal arrangements were made under the table.*

ta·ble·cloth (tā'bəl klòth'), *NOUN.* a cloth for covering a table: *Spread the tablecloth and set the table for dinner.* ◻ *PLURAL* **ta·ble·cloths** (tā'bəl klòᴛʜz' *or* tā'bəl klòths').

ta·ble·spoon (tā'bəl spün'), *NOUN.*
1 a large spoon used to serve food.
2 a unit of measure in cooking equal to 3 teaspoons or ½ fluid ounce.

tab·let (tab'lit), *NOUN.*
1 a pad made of a number of sheets of writing paper fastened together at one edge.
2 a small, flat surface with something written on it.
3 a small, flat piece of medicine or candy: *That box contains twelve aspirin tablets.*

table tennis. See **Ping-Pong.**

tack (tak),
1 *NOUN.* a short, sharp nail or pin with a broad, flat head: *We bought some carpet tacks.*
2 *VERB.* to fasten something with tacks: *She tacked mosquito netting over the windows.*
□ *VERB* **tacks, tacked, tack·ing.**

tack·le (tak′əl),
1 in football: **a** *VERB.* to seize and stop, or throw to the ground, an opponent who has the ball. **b** *NOUN.* the act of tackling: *The linebacker made a nice tackle.* **c** *NOUN.* an offensive or defensive player next to the end on either side of the line.
2 *VERB.* to try to deal with something: *We have a difficult problem to tackle.*
3 in soccer and field hockey: **a** *VERB.* to strike or kick the ball away from an opponent. **b** *NOUN.* the act of tackling.
4 *NOUN.* equipment; apparatus; gear. **Fishing tackle** is the rod, line, hooks, or other equipment used in catching fish.
□ *VERB* **tack·les, tack·led, tack·ling.**

ta·co (tä′kō), *NOUN.* a tortilla filled with chopped meat, cheese, tomatoes, and other things.
□ *PLURAL* **ta·cos.**

tact (takt), *NOUN.* the ability to say and do the right things without causing anyone to be hurt or angry: *Father's tact kept him from talking about things likely to be unpleasant to his guests.*
—**tact′ful,** *ADJECTIVE.* —**tact′less,** *ADJECTIVE.*

tac·tics (tak′tiks), *NOUN.*
1 *PLURAL.* ways to gain advantage or success; methods: *When coaxing failed, they changed their tactics and began to threaten.*
2 *SINGULAR.* the art or science of arranging military or naval forces, or of putting them in a certain position.

tad·pole (tad′pōl′), *NOUN.* a very young frog or toad, at the stage when it has a tail and lives in water; polliwog.

Word Story

Tadpole comes from old English words meaning "toad" and "head." A tadpole is mostly head at first; eventually, the head grows a toad or a frog behind it.

a young **tadpole**

taf·fy (taf′ē), *NOUN.* a kind of candy made of brown sugar or molasses boiled and pulled back and forth until it is chewy.

tag¹ (tag),
1 *NOUN.* a small card or piece of paper, leather, or plastic, to be tied or fastened to something: *Each coat in the store has a tag with the price on it.*
2 *VERB.* to supply something with a tag or tags: *The saleswomen tagged all the clothing that was on sale.*
□ *VERB* **tags, tagged, tag·ging.**

tag along, *IDIOM.* to follow closely: *The baby tagged along after his brother.*

tag² (tag),
1 *NOUN.* a children's game in which one player who is "it" chases the others and tries to touch them. The first one touched becomes "it" and must chase the others.
2 *VERB.* to touch or tap someone with your hand.
3 in baseball: **a** *VERB.* to touch a runner with the ball to make an out. **b** *NOUN.* the act of touching a runner with the ball to make an out.
□ *VERB* **tags, tagged, tag·ging.**

tail (tāl),
1 *NOUN.* the part that sticks out from the back of an animal's body. Rabbits have short tails. Mice have long tails.
2 *NOUN.* something like an animal's tail: *Rags tied together made the tail of my kite.*
3 *NOUN.* the part at the rear of an airplane.
4 *NOUN.* **tails,** the reverse side of a coin.
5 *VERB.* to follow someone closely and secretly: *The police tailed the suspected killer.*
□ *VERB* **tails, tailed, tail·ing.** ■ Another word that sounds like this is **tale.** —**tail′less,** *ADJECTIVE.* —**tail′like′,** *ADJECTIVE.*

tail·gate (tāl′gāt′),
1 *NOUN.* a gate or board at the rear of a truck, station wagon, and so on, that can be lowered or removed when loading or unloading.
2 *VERB.* to drive a vehicle too close to the one ahead of it.
□ *VERB* **tail·gates, tail·gat·ed, tail·gat·ing.**

tail·light (tāl′līt′), *NOUN.* a warning light, usually red, at the rear end of a vehicle.

tai·lor (tā′lər),
1 *NOUN.* someone whose business is making, altering, or repairing clothes.
2 *VERB.* to make something fit someone exactly: *The suit was well tailored.*
□ *VERB* **tai·lors, tai·lored, tai·lor·ing.**

tail·pipe (tāl′pīp′), *NOUN.* the exhaust pipe at the rear of a motor vehicle or aircraft.

Tai·wan (tī′wän′), *NOUN.* an island country off the coast of eastern Asia.

Ta·jik·i·stan (tä jē′kə stän), *NOUN.* a country in western Asia.

take (tāk), VERB.
1 to hold onto: *I took her hand when we crossed the street.*
2 to carry something to another place: *I think you should take your gloves to school.* ■ See the Usage Note at **bring.**
3 to capture: *The pirates took many prisoners.*
4 to accept: *Take my advice. The dealer won't take a cent less for the car.*
5 to get what someone gives you; receive: *I took the gift with a smile of thanks.*
6 to make use of: *We took a train to go to Boston.*
7 to let yourself have; indulge in: *Are you taking a vacation this year? He took a nap.*
8 to put up with something; stand: *People from the South often find it hard to take cold weather.*
9 to study: *She plans to take art next year.*
10 to need; require: *It takes time and patience to learn how to play the piano.*
11 to choose; select; use: *Take the shortest path.*
12 to subtract one number from another number: *If you take 2 from 7, you have 5.*
13 to go with someone: *I took my friend to the movies.*
14 to make by using a camera: *Please take my photograph.*
❑ VERB **takes, took, tak•en, tak•ing. —tak′er,** NOUN.

take after, IDIOM. to be like; resemble: *She takes after her mother.*

take in, IDIOM.
1 to make smaller: *I took in the waist of my pants.*
2 to understand: *She took in the situation at a glance.*

take off, IDIOM.
1 to rise from the ground or water into the air: *The airplane took off smoothly.*
2 to rush off: *I took off at the first sign of trouble.*

take over, IDIOM. to get control or ownership of: *A big company has taken over our local grocery store.*

take up, IDIOM.
1 to soak up; absorb: *A sponge takes up liquid.*
2 to make shorter: *The tailor took up the hem.*
3 to begin; undertake: *He took up the piano.*

tak•en (tā′kən), VERB. the past participle of **take:** *He has always taken the bus to school.*

take•off (tāk′òf′), NOUN. the act of rising from the ground or water into the air, as in an aircraft.

take•out (tāk′out),
1 NOUN. food that is packaged to be taken away from where it is sold rather than be eaten there; carry-out.
2 ADJECTIVE. of or about such food or the place where it is sold; carry-out.

tal•cum pow•der (tal′kəm pou′dər), a white powder used on the face and body, especially after a bath or shower.

tale (tāl), NOUN. a story, either made-up or true: *We always enjoy hearing grandfather's tales of his boyhood.* ■ See the Synonym Study at **story.**
■ Another word that sounds like this is **tail.**

tal•ent (tal′ənt), NOUN. a special natural ability; ability: *She has a talent for music.*

tal•ent•ed (tal′ən tid), ADJECTIVE. having natural ability: *a talented musician.*

talk (tòk),
1 VERB. to use words; speak: *The baby is learning to talk.*
2 NOUN. a conversation: *The old friends met for a good talk.*
3 NOUN. an informal speech: *The coach gave the team a talk about the need for more team spirit.*
4 VERB. to influence someone by talking to him or her: *We talked her into joining the club.*
5 VERB. to discuss: *They talked politics all evening.*
❑ VERB **talks, talked, talk•ing. —talk′er,** NOUN.

talk back, IDIOM. to answer rudely or disrespectfully: *Don't talk back to the teacher.*

talk over, IDIOM. to speak about; discuss: *We need to talk over this important decision.*

Synonym Study

Talk means to make words with your voice: *The fire chief talked about fire safety.*

Speak means to say words: *She speaks often of how much she liked the class trip to the museum.*

Chat means to talk with others in a light, friendly way: *I often chat with my friends on the phone.*

Discuss means to talk about something, hearing several opinions: *We discussed a plan for collecting glass, tin cans, and newspapers.*

See also the Synonym Studies at **argue** and **say.**

an airplane during takeoff

a hat	ė term	ô order	ch child	a in about
ā age	i it	oi oil	ng long	e in taken
ä far	ī ice	ou out	sh she	ə{ i in pencil
â care	o hot	u cup	th thin	o in lemon
e let	ō open	ù put	ᴛʜ then	u in circus
ē equal	ò saw	ü rule	zh measure	

talk·a·tive (tȯ′kə tiv), *ADJECTIVE.* fond of talking a great deal: *He is shy and not very talkative.*

tall (tȯl), *ADJECTIVE.*
1 high; reaching a long way from top to bottom: *The city is full of tall buildings.*
2 in height: *The tree is 100 feet tall.*
3 hard to believe; exaggerated: *That's a pretty tall story.* —**tall′ness,** *NOUN.*

Tal·la·has·see (tal′ə has′ē), *NOUN.* the capital of Florida.

tal·low (tal′ō), *NOUN.* the fat of sheep and cattle after it has been melted. Tallow is used for making candles and soap.

tal·ly (tal′ē),
1 *NOUN.* a record or count of a number of things: *We are waiting for the final tally of votes in the election for mayor.*
2 *VERB.* to count up: *Will you tally the score?*
❑ *PLURAL* **tal·lies;** *VERB* **tal·lies, tal·lied, tal·ly·ing.**

Tal·mud (tal′məd), *NOUN.* a collection of sixty-three volumes containing the Jewish civil and religious law that interprets the teachings of the Hebrew Scriptures.

tal·on (tal′ən), *NOUN.* the claw of a bird of prey.

ta·ma·le (tə mä′lē), *NOUN.* a food made of cornmeal and minced meat, seasoned with peppers, wrapped in corn husks, and roasted or steamed.

Ta·mau·li·pas (tä′mou′lē′päs), *NOUN.* a state in northeastern Mexico.

tam·bou·rine (tam′bə rēn′), *NOUN.* a small, shallow drum with jingling metal disks around its edge. A tambourine is played by striking it with the knuckles or by shaking it.

tame (tām),
1 *ADJECTIVE.* no longer wild: *The circus had a tame bear.*
2 *ADJECTIVE.* gentle; without fear: *The birds are so tame that they will eat from our hands.*
3 *VERB.* to make or become tame: *The lion was tamed for the circus.*
❑ *ADJECTIVE* **tam·er, tam·est;** *VERB* **tames, tamed, tam·ing.** —**tame′a·ble,** *ADJECTIVE.* —**tame′ly,** *ADVERB.* —**tame′ness,** *NOUN.* —**tam′er,** *NOUN.*

tam·per (tam′pər), *VERB.* to meddle with something, especially without permission: *Do not tamper with the lock.* ❑ *VERB* **tam·pers, tam·pered, tam·per·ing.**

tan (tan),
1 *ADJECTIVE.* yellowish brown: *She has two pairs of tan shoes.*
2 *NOUN.* the brown color of a person's skin caused by being in the sun and air: *He has a dark tan.*
3 *VERB.* to make or become brown by being out in the sun and air: *Sun and wind had tanned her face.*
4 *VERB.* to turn the skin of an animal into leather by taking the hair off and soaking the skin in a special liquid.
❑ *ADJECTIVE* **tan·ner, tan·nest;** *VERB* **tans, tanned, tan·ning.** —**tan′ner,** *NOUN.*

tang (tang), *NOUN.* a sharp or biting taste: *I like the tang of mustard.*

tan·ge·rine (tan′jə rēn′), *NOUN.* a round, reddish orange citrus fruit a little smaller that an orange. Tangerines are very easy to peel and separate into segments.

tangerine

tan·gle (tang′gəl),
1 *VERB.* to twist and twine together in a confused mass: *The kitten had tangled the ball of twine.*
2 *NOUN.* a confused or twisted mass: *I brushed out a tangle in my hair.*
3 *NOUN.* a bewildering confusion; mess: *We tried to sort out the truth from a tangle of lies.*
❑ *VERB* **tan·gles, tan·gled, tan·gling.**

tang·y (tang′ē), *ADJECTIVE.* having a sharp taste.
❑ *ADJECTIVE* **tang·i·er, tang·i·est.**

tank (tangk), *NOUN.*
1 a large container for liquid or gas. A car has a fuel tank. Air tanks are used in scuba diving.
2 a heavily armored combat vehicle carrying machine guns and a cannon, moving on heavy tracks. Tanks can travel over rough ground, fallen trees, and other obstacles. —**tank′like′,** *ADJECTIVE.*

Word Story

Tank (definition 2) comes from a code word. Tanks were invented during World War I, and for a long time they were a secret weapon. They were called "tanks" so that the enemy would not find out about them. When they were finally used, the name stuck.

tank·er (tang′kər), *NOUN.* a ship, airplane, or truck with tanks for carrying oil or other liquid.

tan·trum (tan′trəm), *NOUN.* a sudden, childish outburst of bad temper or ill humor: *Little children sometimes have tantrums when they do not get what they want.*

Tan·za·ni·a (tan′zə nē′ə), *NOUN.* a country in eastern Africa. —**Tan′za·ni′an,** *ADJECTIVE* or *NOUN.*

tap¹ (tap),
1 *VERB.* to hit or strike something lightly: *I tapped on the window.*
2 *NOUN.* a light blow: *There was a tap at the door.*
3 *VERB.* to make or do something by tapping: *to tap a message, to tap a rhythm.*
❑ *VERB* **taps, tapped, tap·ping.**

tap² (tap),
1 *NOUN.* a stopper or plug to close a hole in a barrel containing liquid.

2 *NOUN.* See **faucet.**

3 *VERB.* to make a hole in a tree to let sap flow out: *Sugar maples are tapped to make maple syrup.*

4 *VERB.* See **wiretap.**
❑ *VERB* **taps, tapped, tap·ping.**

tap-dance (tap′dans′), *VERB.* to perform a dance in shoes equipped with hard soles or special metal pieces that make clicking noises as they hit the floor. ❑ *VERB* **tap-danc·es, tap-danced, tap-danc·ing. –tap′-danc′er,** *NOUN.*

tape (tāp),

1 *NOUN.* a long, narrow strip of cloth, paper, or plastic, usually having one side covered with a sticky substance: *Adhesive tape will hold the bandage on for several days.*

2 *NOUN.* a strip something like this. The strip stretched across the finish line in a race is called the tape.

3 See **magnetic tape.**

4 *VERB.* to record sound and images on a tape: *The parade was taped to show on the news in the evening.*

5 *VERB.* to fasten or wrap something with tape: *The players taped their ankles for support.*
❑ *VERB* **tapes, taped, tap·ing.**

tape measure, a long strip of cloth or steel marked in inches and feet for measuring something.

ta·per (tā′pər), *VERB.* to make or become gradually smaller toward one end: *The church spire tapers to a point.* ❑ *VERB* **ta·pers, ta·pered, ta·per·ing.**

tape recorder, a machine that records sound on plastic tape and plays the sound back after it is recorded; recorder.

These two arrows have hit the center of the **target.**

tap·es·try (tap′ə strē), *NOUN.* a fabric with pictures or designs woven into it. A tapestry is used to cover walls or furniture. ❑ *PLURAL* **tap·es·tries.**

tape·worm (tāp′wėrm′), *NOUN.* a long, flat worm that lives in the intestines of people and animals.

tap·i·o·ca (tap′ē ō′kə), *NOUN.* a starchy food obtained from the root of a tropical plant. It is used for puddings.

taps (taps), *NOUN.* a signal on a bugle or drum to put out lights at night. Taps is also sounded at military funerals.

tar (tär),

1 *NOUN.* a black, sticky substance made from wood or coal. Tar is used to cover and patch roads and roofs.

2 *VERB.* to cover something with tar: *The workers tarred our roof last week.*

3 *NOUN.* the poisonous, brownish black residue from the smoke of cigarettes, cigars, or pipes.
❑ *VERB* **tars, tarred, tar·ring. –tar′like′,** *ADJECTIVE.*

ta·ran·tu·la (tə ran′chə lə), *NOUN.* a large, hairy, poisonous spider whose bite is painful but not dangerous. ❑ *PLURAL* **ta·ran·tu·las.**

tarantula — body about 2 inches long

tar·dy (tär′dē), *ADJECTIVE.* not on time; late: *I was tardy for school yesterday.* ❑ *ADJECTIVE* **tar·di·er, tar·di·est. –tar′di·ness,** *NOUN.*

tar·get (tär′git), *NOUN.*

1 a mark for shooting at; thing aimed at. A target is often a circle.

2 any aim you try to achieve; goal: *My target is first place in the long jump.*

Word Story

Target comes from a French word meaning "a shield." Soldiers defended themselves from arrows with their shields, so the shields got a lot of arrows stuck in them. Targets used by people practicing shooting arrows had the same look and got the same name.

tar·iff (tar′if), *NOUN.* any duty or tax on imports or exports: *There is a high tariff on imported jewelry.*

a hat	ė term	ô order	ch child	a in about
ā age	i it	oi oil	ng long	e in taken
ä far	ī ice	ou out	sh she	ə i in pencil
â care	o hot	u cup	th thin	o in lemon
e let	ō open	ů put	ŦH then	u in circus
ē equal	ò saw	ü rule	zh measure	

tar·nish (tär′nish),
1 *VERB.* to dull the luster or brightness of metal things: *Oil from your skin will tarnish silver.*
2 *VERB.* to lose luster or brightness: *Brass candlesticks will tarnish if you do not polish them.*
3 *NOUN.* a dull coating, especially on silver: *Silver polish will remove the tarnish from those spoons.*
❑ *VERB* **tar·nish·es, tar·nished, tar·nish·ing.**

tarp (tärp), *NOUN.* a short form of **tarpaulin.**

tar·pau·lin (tär pȯ′lən *or* tär′pə lin), *NOUN.* a sheet of canvas, plastic, or other strong waterproof material, used as a protective covering over things.

tart¹ (tärt), *ADJECTIVE.* having a sharp taste; sour: *Some apples are tart.*

tart² (tärt), *NOUN.* a pastry filled with cooked fruit, jam, and so on.

tar·tan (tärt′n), *NOUN.* a plaid woolen cloth. Each Scottish clan has its own pattern of tartan.

tar·tar (tär′tər), *NOUN.* a hard, whitish substance that collects on the teeth. Tartar forms deposits of minerals present in saliva that mix with the plaque that forms every day on teeth.

task (task), *NOUN.* work that needs to be done: *His task is to set the table.* ▪ See the Synonym Study at **job.**

tas·sel (tas′əl), *NOUN.* a hanging bunch of threads, small cords, beads, or the like, knotted together at one end.

The special hat worn for graduation has a **tassel.**

taste (tāst),
1 *NOUN.* the particular flavor of something. Sweet, sour, salt, and bitter are the four most important tastes: *This milk is sour; it has a nasty taste.*
2 *VERB.* to find out whether something is sweet, sour, salty, or bitter when you put it in your mouth. You taste things with your tongue.
3 *NOUN.* the power to take in the flavor that different things have. Taste is one of the five senses.
4 *VERB.* to get the flavor of by the sense of taste: *I taste almond in this cake.*
5 *VERB.* to have a particular flavor: *The soup tastes of onion.*
6 *NOUN.* a little bit; sample: *Let me have a taste of that pudding.*
7 *NOUN.* the ability to know and enjoy what is beautiful and excellent: *She has good taste in art.*
❑ *VERB* **tastes, tast·ed, tast·ing.**

taste bud, a very small group of cells on the tongue that let you know how things taste.

taste·less (tāst′lis), *ADJECTIVE.* without taste: *Overcooked vegetables are pretty tasteless.* —**taste′less·ness,** *NOUN.*

tast·y (tā′stē), *ADJECTIVE.* tasting good; pleasing to the taste. ❑ *ADJECTIVE* **tast·i·er, tast·i·est.**

tat·ter (tat′ər), *NOUN.* a torn piece; rag: *After the storm, the flag hung in tatters upon the flagpole.*

tat·tered (tat′ərd), *ADJECTIVE.*
1 torn; ragged.
2 wearing torn or ragged clothes.

tat·tle (tat′l), *VERB.* to tell someone's tales or secrets. ❑ *VERB* **tat·tles, tat·tled, tat·tling.** —**tat′tler,** *NOUN.*

tat·tle·tale (tat′l tāl′), *NOUN.* someone who tells tales on others.

tat·too (ta tü′),
1 *VERB.* to mark your skin with designs or patterns by pricking it and putting in colors: *The sailor had a ship tattooed on his arm.*
2 *NOUN.* the design or pattern made by tattooing.
❑ *VERB* **tat·toos, tat·tooed, tat·too·ing;** *PLURAL* **tat·toos.** —**tat·too′er,** *NOUN.*

taught (tȯt), *VERB.*
1 the past tense of **teach:** *She taught my mother.*
2 the past participle of **teach:** *She has taught science for years.*

taunt (tȯnt),
1 *VERB.* to make fun of someone by saying unkind things to him or her: *My classmates taunted me for being teacher's pet.*
2 *NOUN.* an unkind remark.
❑ *VERB* **taunts, taunt·ed, taunt·ing.**

tav·ern (tav′ərn), *NOUN.*
1 a place where alcoholic drinks can be purchased and consumed.
2 (formerly) an inn.

tax (taks),
1 *NOUN.* money paid by people to support the government.
2 *VERB.* to make people pay taxes. People who own property are taxed in order to provide clean streets, police services, free education, and so on.
3 *VERB.* to put a heavy load on someone: *The work taxed my strength.*
❑ *PLURAL* **tax·es;** *VERB* **tax·es, taxed, tax·ing.**

tax·a·tion (tak sā′shən), *NOUN.* the act or system of taxing: *Taxation is necessary to provide roads, schools, and police.*

tax·i (tak′sē),
1 *NOUN.* a car for hire, usually with an automatic meter to record the fare; taxicab.
2 *VERB.* to ride in a taxi.
3 *VERB.* (of an aircraft) to move slowly on the ground or water: *The airplane taxied off the runway after landing.*
❑ *PLURAL* **tax·is** or **tax·ies;** *VERB* **tax·is** or **tax·ies, tax·ied, tax·i·ing** or **tax·y·ing.**

hailing a **taxicab**

tax·i·cab (tak′sē kab′), *NOUN.* See **taxi.**

TB, an abbreviation of **tuberculosis.**

tbsp., an abbreviation of **tablespoon** or **tablespoons.**

tea (tē), *NOUN.*
1 a dark brown drink made by pouring boiling water over the dried and prepared leaves of a shrub grown chiefly in China, Japan, and India.
2 the leaves themselves.
3 any drink made from some other plant or substance: *peppermint tea.*
■ Other words that sound like this are **tee** and **ti.**

teach (tēch), *VERB.*
1 to help someone learn; show how to do something: *He is teaching his dog to shake hands.*
2 to give lessons in something: *He teaches music.*
3 to give someone lessons: *She teaches for a living.*
❑ *VERB* **teach·es, taught, teach·ing.** —**teach′a·ble,** *ADJECTIVE.*

teach·er (tē′chər), *NOUN.* someone who helps people learn. Most teachers work in schools.

teach·ing (tē′ching), *NOUN.*
1 the work or profession of a teacher.
2 things that are taught: *religious teachings.*

tea·ket·tle (tē′ket′l), *NOUN.* a kettle for boiling water.

teal (tēl), *ADJECTIVE* or *NOUN.* medium bluish green.

team (tēm), *NOUN.*
1 a number of people working or playing together, especially one of the sides in a game: *He is on the football team.*
2 two or more horses or other animals harnessed together to pull a plow or wagon.
■ Another word that sounds like this is **teem.**
team up, *IDIOM.* to join together in a team: *Everybody teamed up to clean the room after the party.* ❑ *VERB* **teams, teamed, team·ing.**

team·mate (tēm′māt′), *NOUN.* a fellow member of a team.

team·work (tēm′werk′), *NOUN.* the combined action of a number of people that makes the work of the group successful and effective: *Football requires teamwork.*

tea·pot (tē′pot′), *NOUN.* a container with a handle and a spout for making and serving tea.

tear¹ (tir), *NOUN.* a drop of salty water that comes from the eye. ■ Another word that sounds like this is **tier.**
in tears, *IDIOM.* shedding tears or crying: *The baby is in tears because he is hungry.*

tear² (târ),
1 *VERB.* to pull something into pieces; pull apart by force: *He tore the box open. I tore the paper in half.*
2 *VERB.* to make a hole in something by pulling it apart: *She tore a hole in her jeans.*
3 *NOUN.* a place where something has been pulled apart: *She has a tear in her jacket.*
4 *VERB.* to pull something violently: *Tear out the page with the phone number on it.*
5 *VERB.* to cut badly; wound: *The jagged stone tore my skin.*
6 *VERB.* to become torn: *Lace tears easily.*
❑ *VERB* **tears, tore, torn, tear·ing.**

tease (tēz),
1 *VERB.* to pester, annoy, or upset someone by jokes, questions, noises, and so on: *The children teased the dog until it snapped at them.*
2 *NOUN.* someone who teases.
❑ *VERB* **teas·es, teased, teas·ing.**

tea·spoon (tē′spün′), *NOUN.*
1 a small spoon often used to stir tea or coffee.
2 a unit of measure in cooking equal to ⅓ of a tablespoon.

tech·ni·cal (tek′nə kəl), *ADJECTIVE.*
1 of or about mechanical or industrial work or applied science: *This technical school trains engineers and chemists.*
2 of or about the special facts of a science or industry: *"Transistor," "thermostat," and "protein" are technical words.*
—**tech′ni·cal·ly,** *ADVERB.*

tech·ni·cian (tek nish′ən), *NOUN.* someone who knows the technical details and methods of a subject or a job.

tech·nique (tek nēk′), *NOUN.*
1 a special method or system used to do something.
2 the method or ability of an artist's performance; technical skill: *The pianist's technique was excellent.*
❑ *PLURAL* **tech·niques.**

tech·nol·o·gy (tek nol′ə jē), *NOUN.* the development and use of scientific knowledge to solve practical problems. ❑ *PLURAL* **tech·nol·o·gies.**
—**tech·nol′o·gist,** *NOUN.*

a	hat	ė	term	ô	order	ch	child		a in about
ā	age	i	it	oi	oil	ng	long		e in taken
ä	far	ī	ice	ou	out	sh	she	ə	i in pencil
â	care	o	hot	u	cup	th	thin		o in lemon
e	let	ō	open	ů	put	ᴛʜ	then		u in circus
ē	equal	ò	saw	ü	rule	zh	measure		

ted·dy bear (ted′ē bâr′), a soft, furry toy bear.

Word Story

Teddy bear comes from President Theodore Roosevelt's nickname, Teddy. A cartoon showed him refusing to shoot a bear cub while hunting. A clever toy maker promptly began to sell a stuffed animal called the Teddy bear, and it was an immediate and lasting success.

te·di·ous (tē′dē əs or tē′jəs), ADJECTIVE. long and tiring; boring: *The tedious movie put me to sleep.* —**te′di·ous·ly**, ADVERB. —**te′di·ous·ness**, NOUN.

tee (tē), NOUN.
1 a short peg that you place a golf ball on before you hit it to start a section of the game.
2 (informal). See **T-shirt**.
❑ PLURAL **tees.** ■ Other words that sound like this are **tea** and **ti**.
tee off, IDIOM. to hit a golf ball from a tee. ❑ VERB **tees, teed, tee·ing.**

teem (tēm), VERB. to be full of; abound; swarm: *The swamp teemed with mosquitoes.* ❑ VERB **teems, teemed, teem·ing.** ■ Another word that sounds like this is **team**.

teen (tēn),
1 ADJECTIVE. teenage: *teen fashions, teen magazines.*
2 NOUN. a short form of **teenager**.

teen·age (tēn′āj′), ADJECTIVE.
1 of or for a teenager or teenagers: *This store has all the latest teenage fashions.*
2 in your teens; being a teenager: *They have two teenage daughters.*

teen·ag·er (tēn′ā′jər), NOUN. someone who is between 13 and 19 years old.

teens (tēnz), NOUN PLURAL. the years of life from 13 to 19.

tee shirt, another spelling of **T-shirt**.

teeth (tēth), NOUN. the plural of **tooth**: *You often show your teeth when you smile.*

teethe (tēŧн), VERB. to grow teeth; cut teeth: *Babies teethe.* ❑ VERB **teethes, teethed, teeth·ing.**

Te·he·ran (te ə ran′), NOUN. the capital of Iran.

Word Power tele-

The prefix **tele-** means "over a long distance." A telescope is device for looking **over a long distance**. It can also mean "television." A telecast is a broadcast over **television**.

tel·e·cast (tel′ə kast),
1 VERB. to broadcast a program over television.
2 NOUN. a television program.
❑ VERB **tel·e·casts, tel·e·cast or tel·e·cast·ed, tel·e·cast·ing.**

tel·e·gram (tel′ə gram), NOUN. a message sent by telegraph: *Dad sent a telegram on my birthday.*

tel·e·graph (tel′ə graf),
1 NOUN. a way of sending coded messages over wires by means of electricity.
2 VERB. to send a message by telegraph: *Mother telegraphed congratulations to the bride and groom.*
❑ VERB **tel·e·graphs, tel·e·graphed, tel·e·graph·ing.**

tel·e·phone (tel′ə fōn),
1 NOUN. a device used to talk to people far away; phone.
2 VERB. to talk to someone by using a telephone; send a message by telephone; phone.
❑ VERB **tel·e·phones, tel·e·phoned, tel·e·phon·ing.**

tel·e·scope (tel′ə skōp), NOUN. a device you look through that makes things far away seem to be nearer and larger. Objects in space are studied by means of telescopes.

The arrows show light coming into the telescope and hitting the curved mirror at the end. This mirror reflects all the light and bends it so that it forms an image on the flat mirror. The flat mirror reflects the image through the eyepiece so that you can look at it.

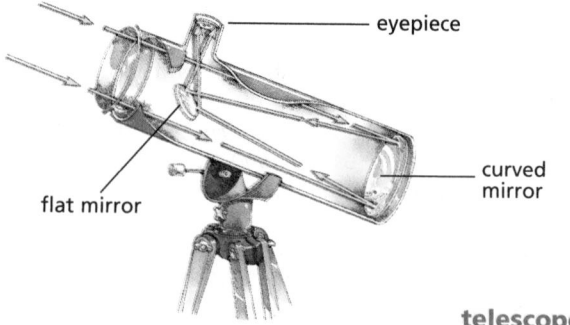

eyepiece

curved mirror

flat mirror

telescope

tel·e·vise (tel′ə vīz), VERB. to broadcast over television: *Will they televise today's game?* ❑ VERB **tel·e·vis·es, tel·e·vised, tel·e·vis·ing.**

tel·e·vi·sion (tel′ə vizh′ən), NOUN.
1 a system of sending and receiving pictures and sounds over wires or through the air by means of electrical signals; TV.
2 a device on which these images and sounds may be seen and heard.

tell (tel), VERB.
1 to put something into words; say: *Tell us a story. Tell the truth.* ■ See the Synonym Study at **say**.
2 to tell to someone; inform: *Tell us about it.*
3 to make known: *Don't tell where the candy is.*
4 to recognize; know: *I can't tell which bike is yours.*
5 to say something to someone as an order or command: *Do as you are told.*
❑ VERB **tells, told, tell·ing.**
tell off, IDIOM. to scold: *She really told me off when she found out I took her book.*

tell on, *IDIOM.* to inform on; tell tales about: *Please don't tell on me.*

tell·er (tel′ər), *NOUN.* a bank cashier who takes in, gives out, and counts money.

tem·per (tem′pər), *NOUN.*
1 an angry state of mind: *He flew into a temper.*
2 a calm state of mind: *He became angry and lost his temper.*

tem·per·a·ment (tem′pər ə mənt), *NOUN.* someone's nature: *a shy temperament.*

tem·per·a·men·tal (tem′pər ə men′tl), *ADJECTIVE.* likely to have sudden changes of mood; easily irritated; sensitive: *A temperamental person can be hard to live with.* **–tem′per·a·men′tal·ly,** *ADVERB.*

tem·per·ate (tem′pər it), *ADJECTIVE.* neither very hot nor very cold: *a temperate climate.*

tem·per·a·ture (tem′pər ə chər), *NOUN.*
1 how hot or cold something is. The temperature of freezing water is 32 degrees Fahrenheit, or 0 degrees Celsius.
2 a body temperature higher than normal (98.6 degrees Fahrenheit, or 37 degrees Celsius): *A sick person may have a temperature.*

tem·pest (tem′pist), *NOUN.* (earlier) a violent storm with a great deal of wind.

tem·ple¹ (tem′pəl), *NOUN.*
1 a building used for the service or worship of a god or gods: *The ancient Greek temples were beautifully built.*
2 any building set apart for worship, especially a Jewish synagogue.

a **temple** in Thailand

tem·ple² (tem′pəl), *NOUN.* the flattened part of your skull, on either side of your forehead.

tem·po (tem′pō), *NOUN.* the speed at which a piece of music is played: *The song was played in a very fast tempo.* ❏ *PLURAL* **tem·pos.**

tem·po·rar·y (tem′pə rer′ē), *ADJECTIVE.* lasting for a short time only: *This is just a temporary job.* **–tem′po·rar′i·ly,** *ADVERB.*

tempt (tempt), *VERB.*
1 to make or try to make someone do something: *Extreme hunger can tempt a person to steal food.*
2 to appeal strongly to; attract: *That cake tempts me.* ❏ *VERB* **tempts, tempt·ed, tempt·ing. –tempt′er,** *NOUN.*

temp·ta·tion (temp tā′shən), *NOUN.*
1 something that tempts: *Money left carelessly lying around is a temptation.*
2 the act of tempting: *No temptation could make her break her promise.*
3 the condition of being tempted: *"Lead us not into temptation."*

ten (ten), *NOUN* or *ADJECTIVE.* one more than nine; 10.

ten·ant (ten′ənt), *NOUN.* someone paying rent for the use of land, a building, or space in a building that belongs to someone else: *That building has apartments for one hundred tenants.*

tend¹ (tend), *VERB.* to be apt; be likely to: *Fruit tends to spoil easily.* ❏ *VERB* **tends, tend·ed, tend·ing.**

tend² (tend), *VERB.* to take care of or look after someone or something: *He tends the store for his parents. The shepherd tends the flock of sheep.* ❏ *VERB* **tends, tend·ed, tend·ing.**

ten·den·cy (ten′dən sē), *NOUN.* a natural inclination to do something: *Wood has a tendency to swell if it gets wet.* ❏ *PLURAL* **ten·den·cies.**

ten·der (ten′dər), *ADJECTIVE.*
1 not hard or tough; soft: *The meat is tender.*
2 delicate; not strong and hardy: *The leaves in spring are green and tender.*
3 kind; affectionate; loving: *She spoke tender words to the baby.*
–ten′der·ly, *ADVERB.* **–ten′der·ness,** *NOUN.*

ten·don (ten′dən), *NOUN.* a tough, strong band of tissue that joins a muscle to a bone.

ten·dril (ten′drəl), *NOUN.* the thin, curling part of a climbing plant that attaches itself to something and helps support the plant.

Ten·nes·see (ten′ə sē′), *NOUN.* one of the southern states of the United States. *Abbreviation:* TN; *Capital:* Nashville. **–Ten′nes·se′an** or **Ten′nes·see′an,** *NOUN.*

State Story **Tennessee** comes from the name of a Cherokee Indian village. The name was used for a stream near the village, for the river the stream ran into, and then for all the country around the river. When Europeans first came to the village, they asked the meaning of the name, but the Cherokee themselves did not know.

a	hat	ė	term	ô	order	ch	child		a in about
ā	age	i	it	oi	oil	ng	long		e in taken
ä	far	ī	ice	ou	out	sh	she	ə {	i in pencil
â	care	o	hot	u	cup	th	thin		o in lemon
e	let	ō	open	ů	put	ŦH	then		u in circus
ē	equal	ò	saw	ü	rule	zh	measure		

T

Temporary Sculptures

When people think of sculptures, they think of large, heavy pieces of solid wood, stone, or metal. But many sculptures are made to exist for only a few days or even a few hours.

Sometimes people let the weather determine the life of their sculpture. **Snow sculptures** can be as simple as a snowman or as complicated as a palace. Competitions are held all over the world—anywhere that there's enough snow to build with. Some places even make snow with special machines to make sure there will be enough.

There are **sandcastle** competitions too, where people sometimes make sandcastles bigger than houses! But all you really need for a great sandcastle are your hands and a good imagination … and a little bit of time before the waves wash your creation away.

You can **carve fruit** and **vegetables** into pretty flowers and baskets.

Ice sculptures and **topiaries** are popular as decorations. Ice sculptures are usually found inside, on banquet tables. Topiaries are bushes and trees cut into fancy shapes. But they are often made the same way—with chain saws! And they both change slowly. Ice sculptures melt and topiaries grow.

topiaries

A sculpture made of **plastic building blocks**, such as this tiger, will last until you take it apart. The most temporary sculpture of all? Try holding very, very still and be a sculpture yourself!

ten·nis (ten′is), NOUN. a game played by two or four players on a special court, in which a ball is hit back and forth over a net with a racket.

ten·or (ten′ər), NOUN.
1 the highest singing voice of a man.
2 a singer with such a voice.

tense¹ (tens),
1 ADJECTIVE. stretched tight: *tense ropes.*
2 VERB. to stretch something very tight: *She tensed her muscles for the leap.*
3 ADJECTIVE. having, showing, or causing strain: *tense nerves, a tense moment.*
   ❑ ADJECTIVE **tens·er, tens·est;** VERB **tens·es, tensed, tens·ing. —tense′ly,** ADVERB.

tense² (tens), NOUN. the form of a verb that shows the time of the action or state expressed by the verb. *I dance* is in the present tense. *I danced* is in the past tense. *I will dance* is in the future tense.

ten·sion (ten′shən), NOUN.
1 the act of stretching or a stretched condition: *The tension of the bow gives speed to the arrow.*
2 mental or nervous strain: *tension from overwork.*

tent (tent), NOUN. a movable shelter made of canvas or nylon held up by a pole or poles.

ten·ta·cle (ten′tə kəl), NOUN. a long, slender, flexible growth on the head or around the mouth of an animal, used to touch, hold, or move something: *Jellyfish have many stinging tentacles.* See the illustration at **sucker.**

tenth (tenth), ADJECTIVE or NOUN.
1 next after the ninth.
2 one of 10 equal parts.

te·pee (tē′pē), NOUN. a tent used by North American Indians, made of hides sewn together. They stretched the tepee over poles arranged in the shape of a cone. ❑ PLURAL **te·pees.**

The Plains Indians lived in **tepees.**

term (tėrm), NOUN.
1 a word or group of words used in connection with some special subject, science, art, or business: *Mom is studying medical terms for her new job.*

2 the length of time that something lasts: *The President's term of office is four years.*
3 one of the periods into which the school year is divided: *Most schools have a fall term and a spring term.*
4 terms, a conditions: *The terms of the peace were hard for the defeated nation.* **b** personal relations: *We are on very good terms with our neighbors.*
5 the numerator or denominator in a fraction: $\frac{4}{12}$ reduced to lowest terms is $\frac{1}{3}$.

ter·mi·nal (tėr′mə nəl), NOUN.
1 a station where you board an airplane, a bus, or a train. Passengers and freight are handled at a terminal.
2 a device for making an electrical connection: *The device is hooked to the terminals of a battery.*
3 a device by which a person and a computer may communicate. A terminal usually has a keyboard like a typewriter and a screen like a television.

ter·mi·nate (tėr′mə nāt), VERB. to bring or come to an end: *The lawyers terminated their partnership and each opened a separate office.* ❑ VERB **ter·mi·nates, ter·mi·nat·ed, ter·mi·nat·ing. —ter′mi·na′tion,** NOUN.

ter·mite (tėr′mīt), NOUN. an insect with a soft, pale body. Termites live in colonies something like ants and eat wood, paper, and other material containing cellulose. They are very destructive to wooden buildings, furniture, and books.

ter·race (ter′is), NOUN.
1 a paved space near a house for outdoor eating or relaxing.
2 a flat piece of land that is cut into a hillside. Terraces create more space for raising crops.

ter·rain (tə rān′), NOUN. an area of land, especially in terms of its natural features: *The hilly, rocky terrain of the island made hiking difficult.*

ter·rar·i·um (tə rer′ē əm), NOUN. a glass enclosure that you can keep plants or small land animals in.

terrarium

ter·res·tri·al (tə res′trē əl), ADJECTIVE.
1 of, about, or living on the planet earth.
2 living on the ground, not in the air, water, or trees: *Cows and elephants are terrestrial animals.*

ter·ri·ble (ter′ə bəl), ADJECTIVE. causing great fear; dreadful; awful: *The terrible storm destroyed a great many lives.*

Synonym Study

Terrible means very bad: *During our camping trip there was a terrible storm.*

Awful can mean very bad or unpleasant: *She stayed home today because of her awful cold.*

Nasty can mean very unpleasant: *He got a nasty scrape when he fell off his bike, but it's not serious.*

Horrible can mean very bad or foul: *A horrible smell came from the garbage truck ahead of us.*

Rotten can mean extremely bad: *I practice, but I'm rotten at video games.*

Horrid can mean extremely bad or unpleasant: *Today the food at school was really horrid.*

See also the Synonym Study at **bad.**

ter·ri·bly (ter′ə blē), ADVERB.
1 in a terrible manner; dreadfully: *The shipwreck survivors suffered terribly before their rescue.*
2 extremely; very: *I am terribly sorry that I stepped on your toes.* ■ See the Synonym Study at **very.**

ter·ri·er (ter′ē ər), NOUN. one of several kinds of small, active, intelligent dogs. Well-known kinds include **Boston terriers, fox terriers,** and **Yorkshire** (yôrk′shər) **terriers.**

ter·rif·ic (tə rif′ik), ADJECTIVE.
1 causing great fear; terrifying: *A terrific earthquake shook Japan.*
2 very great or severe: *A terrific hot spell ruined many of the crops.*
3 very good; wonderful: *She is a terrific tennis player.* **–ter·rif′i·cal·ly,** ADVERB.

ter·ri·fy (ter′ə fi), VERB. to frighten someone very much: *The approach of a large bear terrified the campers.* ■ See the Synonym Studies at **scare** and **afraid.** ❑ VERB **ter·ri·fies, ter·ri·fied, ter·ri·fy·ing.**

ter·ri·to·ry (ter′ə tôr′ē), NOUN.
1 land belonging to or under the rule of a distant government: *Alaska was a territory of the United States until 1958.*
2 land; region: *Much territory in the northern part of Africa is desert.*
3 an area, such as a nesting ground, in which an animal lives, and which it defends from others of its kind. ❑ PLURAL **ter·ri·to·ries.**

ter·ror (ter′ər), NOUN.
1 great fear: *The child has a terror of thunder.* ■ See the Synonym Study at **fear.**
2 a cause of great fear: *Pirates were once the terror of the sea.*

ter·ror·ism (ter′ə riz′əm), NOUN. the use of terror or violence to get what you want.

ter·ror·ist (ter′ər ist), NOUN. someone who uses or favors terrorism.

ter·ror·ize (ter′ə riz′), VERB. to fill someone with terror: *The growling dog terrorized the little child.* ❑ VERB **ter·ror·iz·es, ter·ror·ized, ter·ror·iz·ing.**

test (test),
1 NOUN. a list of questions to find out how much someone knows about something; examination: *a test in arithmetic.*
2 VERB. to put something to a test of any kind; try out: *The doctor tested my eyes.*
3 NOUN. an examination of a substance to see what it is or what it contains: *A test showed that the water was pure.* ❑ VERB **tests, test·ed, test·ing.**

tes·ta·ment (tes′tə mənt), NOUN.
1 written instructions telling what to do with someone's property after he or she dies; will.
2 **Testament,** one of the two parts into which the Christian Bible is divided; the Old Testament or the New Testament.

tes·ti·fy (tes′tə fi), VERB.
1 to declare or give evidence under oath in a court of law.
2 to give evidence; bear witness: *The excellence of Shakespeare's plays testifies to his genius.* ❑ VERB **tes·ti·fies, tes·ti·fied, tes·ti·fy·ing.**

tes·ti·mo·ny (tes′tə mō′nē), NOUN. a statement in a court of law used for evidence or proof: *A witness gave testimony that the accused man was at home all day.* ❑ PLURAL **tes·ti·mo·nies.**

test tube, a thin glass tube closed at one end, used in making chemical tests.

tet·a·nus (tet′n əs), NOUN. a disease caused by certain bacteria entering the body through a wound; lockjaw. Tetanus produces very painful stiffness of muscles,

test tube

a	hat	ė	term	ô	order	ch	child		a in about
ā	age	i	it	oi	oil	ng	long		e in taken
ä	far	ī	ice	ou	out	sh	she	ə	i in pencil
â	care	o	hot	u	cup	th	thin		o in lemon
e	let	ō	open	ů	put	ᴛʜ	then		u in circus
ē	equal	ȯ	saw	ü	rule	zh	measure		

and it sometimes results in death. Vaccinations can prevent tetanus.

teth·er (teᴛʜ′ər),

1 *NOUN.* a rope or chain for fastening an animal so that it can move only within a certain limit: *The cow had broken its tether and was in the garden.*

2 *VERB.* to fasten an animal with a tether: *The horse is tethered to a stake.*

❑ *VERB* **teth·ers, teth·ered, teth·er·ing.**

teth·er·ball (teᴛʜ′ər ból′), *NOUN.* a game played by two people with a ball fastened by a cord to the top of a tall post. The object of the game is to hit the ball so as to wind the cord around the post, in one direction or the other.

playing **tetherball**

Tex·as (tek′səs), *NOUN.* one of the southwestern states of the United States. *Abbreviation:* TX; *Capital:* Austin. **–Tex′an,** *ADJECTIVE* or *NOUN.*

State Story Texas comes from an American Indian word meaning "friends" or "allies." Spanish explorers in this area used the word about the Indians they met there.

text (tekst), *NOUN.*

1 the main body of reading matter in a book: *This book contains 300 pages of text, and a few maps.*

2 the original words of a writer. A text is often changed here and there when it is copied.

3 a short passage in the Bible: *The minister preached on the text "Blessed are the merciful."*

4 a short form of **textbook.**

5 a a topic; subject: *Town improvement was the speakers text.*

text·book (tekst′búk′), *NOUN.* a book for regular study by pupils. Most books used in school are textbooks.

tex·tile (tek′stəl *or* tek′stil), *NOUN.* a woven fabric; cloth: *Beautiful textiles are sold in Paris.*

tex·ture (teks′chər), *NOUN.* the feel that cloth or other things have because of the way they are made: *I love to touch my mother's velvet shirt because of its soft, smooth texture.*

Word Power **-th**

The suffix **-th**[1] means "number ____ in order or position in a series." Sixth means **number** six **in order or position in a series.** The suffix **-eth** is used to form numbers like **fiftieth** and **sixtieth.**

The suffix **-th**[2] means "the act or process of ____ing." Growth means **the act or process of growing.** It can also mean "the quality, state, or condition of being ____." Truth means the **quality, state, or condition of being** true.

Thai (tī),

1 *ADJECTIVE.* of or about Thailand, its people, or their language.

2 *NOUN.* someone born or living in Thailand.

❑ *PLURAL* **Thai** or **Thais.**

Thai·land (tī′land′), *NOUN.* a country in southeastern Asia.

than (ᴛʜan), *CONJUNCTION.*

1 in comparison with: *She is taller than her sister.*

2 compared to that which: *You know better than I do.*

thank (thangk),

1 *VERB.* to tell someone that you are pleased and grateful for what he or she has done or given you: *She thanked her teacher for helping her.*

2 *NOUN.* **thanks, a** I thank you: *Thanks for your good wishes.* **b** a feeling or expression of gratitude: *You have our thanks for everything you have done.*

❑ *VERB* **thanks, thanked, thank·ing.**

thanks to, *IDIOM.* owing to or because of: *Thanks to his efforts, the garden is a great success.*

thank·ful (thangk′fəl), *ADJECTIVE.* feeling pleased about something; grateful: *I am thankful for your help.* **–thank′ful·ness,** *NOUN.*

thank·less (thangk′lis), *ADJECTIVE.*

1 ungrateful: *The thankless child expressed no appreciation for our gift.*

2 not likely to get thanks: *Giving advice can be a thankless act.*

Thanks·giv·ing or **Thanks·giv·ing Day** (thangks giv′ing dā′), a day set apart as a holiday when we give thanks for past blessings. In the United States, Thanksgiving Day is the fourth Thursday in November. In Canada, it is the second Monday in October.

that (ᴛʜat),

1 *ADJECTIVE* or *PRONOUN.* **That** is used to point out some person, thing, or idea. We use *this* for the thing nearer us, and *that* for the thing farther away from us: *Do you know that woman? Shall we buy this book or that one? I like that better.*

2 *PRONOUN.* which: *Bring the box that will hold it all.*

3 *CONJUNCTION.* **That** is used to show purpose: *Study, that you may learn.*

4 *CONJUNCTION.* **That** is used to show result: *I ran so fast that I was five minutes early.*

5 *PRONOUN.* who; whom: *Is he the man that sells dogs? She is the girl that you saw in school.*

6 *CONJUNCTION.* **That** is also used to connect a group of words: *I know that 6 and 4 are 10.*

7 *PRONOUN.* on which; at or in which: *It was the day that school began. The year that we went to England was 1980.*

8 *ADVERB.* to such an extent; to such a degree; so: *The baby cannot stay up that long.*
❏ *ADJECTIVE, PRONOUN PLURAL* **those.**

thatch (thach),
1 *NOUN.* straw, palm leaves, and so on, used as a roof or covering.
2 *VERB.* to make or cover a roof with thatch.
❏ *VERB* **thatch•es, thatched, thatch•ing.**

a house with a **thatched** roof

that's (ᴛʜats), a contraction of **that is.**

thaw (thȯ),
1 *VERB.* to melt ice, snow, or anything frozen: *The sun will thaw the ice on the streets.*
2 *NOUN.* weather above the freezing point (32 degrees Fahrenheit, or 0 degrees Celsius); time when snow and ice melt: *In January we usually have a thaw.*
3 *VERB.* to make or become less cold: *After shoveling snow, I thawed out in front of the fire.*
❏ *VERB* **thaws, thawed, thaw•ing.**

the¹ (ᴛʜə, ᴛʜi, ᴛʜē), *DEFINITE ARTICLE.* a certain; a particular: *The dog I saw had no tail. The girl driving the car is my sister.*

the² (ᴛʜə or ᴛʜi), *ADVERB.* by how much; by that much: *The longer you work, the more you get. The later I sit up, the sleepier I become.*

the•a•ter or **the•a•tre** (thē′ə tər), *NOUN.*
1 a place where people go to see movies or plays.
2 writing, acting in, or producing plays; drama: *She is interested in the theater and is writing a play.*

theft (theft), *NOUN.* the act of stealing: *The prisoner was jailed for theft.*

their (ᴛʜâr), *ADJECTIVE.* of or belonging to them: *I like their house.* ▪ Other words that sound like this are **there** and **they're.**

theirs (ᴛʜârz), *PRONOUN.* the one or ones belonging to them: *Our house is white; theirs is brown.*
▪ Another word that sounds like this is **there's.**

them (ᴛʜem), *PRONOUN.* the people, animals, or things spoken about: *The books are new; take care of them.*

theme (thēm), *NOUN.*
1 a short written composition: *Our school themes must be written in ink and on white paper.*
2 the main subject or idea of a speech, book, play, or movie: *The theme of her speech was equal rights for all Americans.*
3 the principal melody in a piece of music.
4 a melody used to identify a particular radio or television show.

them•selves (ᴛʜem selvz′), *PRONOUN.*
1 *Themselves* is used to make a statement stronger: *The teachers themselves said the test was too hard.*
2 *Themselves* is used instead of *them* in cases like: *They hurt themselves sliding downhill.*
3 their normal or usual selves: *The children are sick and are not themselves this morning.*

then (ᴛʜen),
1 *ADVERB.* at that time: *Father talked of his childhood, and recalled that prices were lower then.*
2 *NOUN.* that time: *By then we will have seen them.*
3 *ADVERB.* soon afterward: *The noise stopped and then began again.*
4 *ADVERB.* next in time or place: *First comes spring, then summer.*
5 *ADVERB.* in that case; therefore: *If she painted the best picture, then she should receive the first prize.*

the•o•ry (thē′ər ē), *NOUN.*
1 an explanation of something, based on observation and reasoning: *According to one scientific theory of life, the more complicated animals developed from the simpler ones.*
2 the principles or methods of a science or art rather than its practice: *Before she began to compose, she studied music theory.*
3 an idea or opinion about something: *I think the fire was started by a careless smoker. What is your theory?*
❏ *PLURAL* **the•o•ries.**

ther•a•pist (ther′ə pist), *NOUN.* someone who specializes in some form of therapy: *The therapist showed me exercises that would strengthen my leg.*

ther•a•py (ther′ə pē), *NOUN.* the treatment of diseases, injuries, or disorders. ❏ *PLURAL* **ther•a•pies.**

there (ᴛʜâr),
1 *ADVERB.* in that place; at that place; at that point: *Sit there. Finish reading the page and stop there.*

a	hat	ė	term	ô	order	ch	child	⎧a in about
ā	age	i	it	oi	oil	ng	long	e in taken
ä	far	ī	ice	ou	out	sh	she	ə⎨i in pencil
â	care	o	hot	u	cup	th	thin	o in lemon
e	let	ō	open	u̇	put	ᴛʜ	then	⎩u in circus
ē	equal	ȯ	saw	ü	rule	zh	measure	

2 ADVERB. to or into that place: *We went there today.*

3 NOUN. that place: *We go from there to Boston.*

4 ADVERB. **There** is also used in sentences in which the verb comes before its subject: *There are three new houses on our street. Is there a drugstore near here?*

5 ADVERB. **There** is used to call attention to some person or thing: *There goes the bell.*

■ Other words that sound like this are **their** and **they're**.

there·a·bouts (ᴛʜâr′ə bouts′), ADVERB.

1 near that place: *She lives in the main part of town, on Front Street or thereabouts.*

2 near that time: *He went home in the late afternoon, at 5 o'clock or thereabouts.*

3 near that number or amount: *It was very cold and the temperature fell to zero or thereabouts.*

there·fore (ᴛʜâr′fôr), ADVERB. for that reason; as a result of that: *She had to work last night and therefore had little time to study.*

there's (ᴛʜârz), a contraction of **there is.** ■ Another word that sounds like this is **theirs.**

ther·mal (thėr′məl), ADJECTIVE. of or about heat.

Word Power   thermo-

The combining form **thermo-** means "heat" or "temperature." A **thermo**stat controls **heat.** A **thermo**meter measures **temperature.**

ther·mom·e·ter (thər mom′ə tər), NOUN. a device to measure temperature. Most thermometers contain mercury or alcohol in a narrow tube. When the temperature outside the tube rises, the liquid rises up the tube by expanding; when the temperature goes down, the liquid drops by contracting.

ther·mos (thėr′məs), NOUN. a container made with a vacuum between its inner and outer walls. A thermos keeps hot foods hot and cold foods cold. ❑ PLURAL **ther·mos·es.**

ther·mo·stat (thėr′mə stat), NOUN. an automatic device that regulates indoor temperature: *Most furnaces and ovens are controlled by thermostats.*

the·sau·rus (thi sôr′əs), NOUN. a reference book in which synonyms, antonyms, and other related words are listed. ❑ PLURAL **the·sau·rus·es** or **the·sau·ri** (thi sôr′ī).

▼ **WORDS AT PLAY** • • • • • • • •
An octopus has many arms
With which to catch its prey—
In all, eight arms
To seize the swarms
Of fish that swim its way.

Catch
verb

Catch means to get hold of someone or something that is moving. *The police tried to catch the man who took the money and ran. Let's catch some fish for dinner.*

Trap means to catch and keep hold of an animal or a person. *Workers at the zoo spent all day trying to trap the escaped leopard.*

Capture means to take by force. *The pirates captured the treasure ship.*

Seize means to take suddenly and by force. *King Richard's soldiers seized the enemy camp and soon won the battle.*

Grab means to seize, especially by hand. *Pablo grabbed the cat before it got out the door.*

Snatch means to grab. *Demaris's hat blew off, but she snatched it out of the air.*

Cheat
verb

Cheat means to do something dishonest while hoping others won't notice. *Susan never cheats at games, and she won't play with anyone else who does.*

Trick means to cheat by misleading or fooling someone. *The villain tricked the cowboy by selling him a good horse and then changing it for another horse that wasn't as good.*

Deceive means to make someone believe something that isn't true. *When the fish hide in the seaweed, their stripes deceive enemies into thinking the fish aren't there.*

Swindle means to cheat someone, usually out of money. *A dishonest roofer swindled the church out of thousands of dollars.*

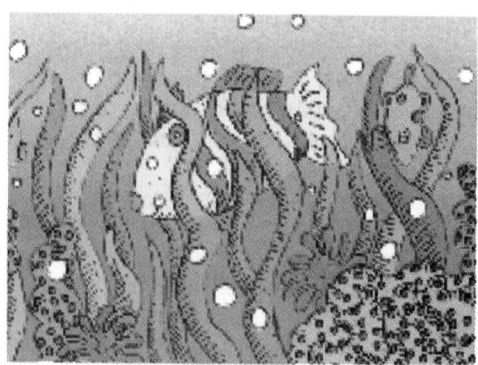

When the fish hide in the seaweed, their stripes **deceive** enemies into thinking the fish aren't there.

This **thesaurus** explains the differences between words with similar meanings. It also gives example sentences.

these (THēz), *ADJECTIVE or PRONOUN PLURAL. These* is used to point out persons, things, or ideas: *These girls helped me. These are my books.* ❏ *SINGULAR* **this.**

they (THā), *PRONOUN PLURAL.*
1 the people, animals, things, or ideas spoken about: *I had three books yesterday. Do you know where they are? They are on the table.*
2 people in general; some people: *They say we should have a new school.*

they'd (THād), a contraction of **they had** or **they would.**

they'll (THāl), a contraction of **they will** or **they shall.**

they're (THâr), a contraction of **they are.** ■ Other words that sound like this are **their** and **there.**

they've (THāv), a contraction of **they have.**

thick (thik),
1 *ADJECTIVE.* big from one side to the other of something; not thin: *The castle has thick stone walls to keep out invaders.*
2 *ADJECTIVE.* measuring between two opposite sides: *This brick is 8 inches long, 4 inches wide, and 2½ inches thick.*
3 *ADJECTIVE.* closely packed together; dense: *a thick forest, thick smoke.*
4 *ADJECTIVE.* like glue or syrup; not flowing easily: *Thick liquids pour more slowly than thin liquids.*
in the thick of, *IDIOM.* in the place where there is the most danger and activity: *They were in the thick of the fight.*
thick and fast, *IDIOM.* rapidly and in large numbers or amounts: *The cars whizzed by thick and fast.*
through thick and thin, *IDIOM.* in good times and bad: *They were friends through thick and thin.*

thick•en (thik′ən), *VERB.* to make or become thick or thicker: *The cook thickens the gravy with flour.* ❏ *VERB* **thick•ens, thick•ened, thick•en•ing.**

thick•et (thik′it), *NOUN.* shrubs, bushes, or small trees growing close together: *We hid in a thicket.*

thick•head•ed (thik′hed′id), *ADJECTIVE.* stupid; dull: *Whose thickheaded idea was it to leave without checking to see if we had the theater tickets?* –**thick′head′ed•ness,** *NOUN.*

thick•ly (thik′lē), *ADVERB.* in a thick manner; densely: *Weeds grow thickly in the rich soil.*

thick•ness (thik′nis), *NOUN.*
1 the quality of being thick: *The thickness of the walls shuts out all sound.*
2 the distance between two opposite sides: *The length of the board is 10 feet, the width 6 inches, the thickness 2 inches.*
3 a layer: *The pad was made up of three thicknesses of cloth.* ❏ *PLURAL* **thick•ness•es.**

thief (thēf), *NOUN.* someone who steals something secretly and without using force: *A thief stole the bicycle from the yard.* ❏ *PLURAL* **thieves** (thēvs).

thigh (thī), *NOUN.* the part of your leg between your hip and your knee.

thim•ble (thim′bəl), *NOUN.* a small metal or plastic cap worn on your finger to protect it when you use a needle while sewing.

thin (thin),
1 *ADJECTIVE.* not big from one side to the other of something; not thick: *thin paper, thin wire. The ice on the pond is too thin for skating.*
2 *ADJECTIVE.* not having much flesh; slender; lean: *His aunt is a thin person.*
3 *ADJECTIVE.* not closely packed together; not dense: *He has thin hair. The air on the tops of high mountains is thin.*
4 *ADJECTIVE.* like water; flowing easily: *This gravy is too thin.*
5 *VERB.* to make or become thin: *She thinned the gravy by adding water.* ❏ *ADJECTIVE* **thin•ner, thin•nest;** *VERB* **thins, thinned, thin•ning.** –**thin′ly,** *ADVERB.*

Synonym Study

Thin means not having much flesh: *He is so thin that he can squeeze easily through the narrow gate.*

Lean² means not fat: *The lost dog was lean and hungry.*

Slender means pleasingly thin: *The slender dancer looked very graceful.*

Slim means slender: *The slim cowgirl mounted her horse.*

Lanky means tall and thin and awkward-looking: *The lanky pitcher struck out ten men.*

Skinny means too thin: *The runner is skinny, but he wins almost every race.*

There was a young lady
  from Lynn,
Who was most
  exceedingly **thin.**
So what do you think?
When she tried to drink,
She slipped through
  the straw and fell in.

a	hat	ė	term	ô	order	ch	child		a in about
ā	age	i	it	oi	oil	ng	long		e in taken
ä	far	ī	ice	ou	out	sh	she	ə	i in pencil
â	care	o	hot	u	cup	th	thin		o in lemon
e	let	ō	open	ù	put	ŦH	then		u in circus
ē	equal	ò	saw	ü	rule	zh	measure		

thing (thing), NOUN.
1 any object or substance; what you can see, hear, touch, taste, or smell: *Put these things away.*
2 whatever is spoken of, thought of, or done: *It was a good thing to do. A strange thing happened. How are things going?*
3 things, personal belongings: *I packed my things and took the train.*

Synonym Study

Thing means any single part of all there is. If it's not a person or a place or an action, it's a thing: *All kinds of things were at their yard sale.*

Object means a thing that can be seen or touched: *She came home from the outing with rocks, leaves, and all sorts of other objects.*

Article can mean a particular thing, and often means a thing of a certain kind: *He has a collection of metal soldiers, model ships, and other military articles.*

Item means a thing that is part of a group or list: *"Will every item on our shopping list fit in the cart?" wondered Mom.*

think (thingk), VERB.
1 to use your mind to form ideas: *I need to think about that problem.*
2 to have an idea in your mind: *He thought that he would go.*
3 to believe something without knowing it for sure; have an opinion: *We thought it might snow.*
4 to consider: *They think their child a genius.*
 ❏ VERB **thinks, thought, think•ing. –think′er,** NOUN.
think of, IDIOM.
1 to imagine: *She doesn't like apple pie. Think of that!*
2 to remember: *I can't think of his name.*

think over, IDIOM. to consider carefully: *He thought it over for days before agreeing to take the job.*

Synonym Study

Think means to use the mind in order to form ideas or understand something: *Grandpa is thinking about living with us.*

Reason means to think carefully in order to make a judgment or solve a problem: *She reasoned her way through the difficult test.*

Concentrate can mean to pay special attention and think really hard: *The acrobat must concentrate to do this trick.*

Meditate means to think about something in a quiet and serious way: *He sat quietly, meditating on the death of his grandmother.*

See also the Synonym Studies at **idea** and **opinion.**

third (thėrd), ADJECTIVE or NOUN.
1 next after the second: *C is the third letter of the alphabet.*
2 one of three equal parts: *We divided the cake into thirds.*

thirst (thėrst),
1 NOUN. a dry, uncomfortable feeling in the mouth or throat caused by a need to have a drink: *The traveler in the desert suffered from thirst. She satisfied her thirst with a glass of water.*
2 NOUN. a strong desire for something: *He has a thirst for adventure.*
3 VERB. to have a strong desire for something: *Some people thirst for power.*
 ❏ VERB **thirsts, thirst•ed, thirst•ing.**

thirst•y (thėr′stē), ADJECTIVE.
1 needing something to drink: *The dog is thirsty; please give it some water.*
2 without water or moisture; dry: *The land was as thirsty as a desert.*
 ❏ ADJECTIVE **thirst•i•er, thirst•i•est.**

thir•teen (thėr′tēn′), NOUN or ADJECTIVE. three more than ten; 13.

thir•teenth (thėr′tēnth′), ADJECTIVE or NOUN.
1 next after the 12th.
2 one of 13 equal parts.

thir•ti•eth (thėr′tē ith), ADJECTIVE or NOUN.
1 next after the 29th.
2 one of 30 equal parts.

thir•ty (thėr′tē), NOUN or ADJECTIVE. three times ten; 30. ❏ PLURAL **thir•ties.**

this (ᴛHis),
1 ADJECTIVE or PRONOUN. **This** is used to point out some person, thing, or idea as present, or near, or spoken of before. We use *that* for the thing farther away from us and *this* for the thing nearer us: *This is my brother. Shall we buy this or that? School begins at eight this year.*
2 ADVERB. to such an extent or degree; so: *I've never seen a sunflower this tall before.*
 ❏ ADJECTIVE, PRONOUN, PLURAL **these.**

this•tle (this′əl), NOUN. a plant with a prickly stalk and leaves and usually with purple flowers. **–this′tle•like′,** ADJECTIVE.

tho or **tho'** (ᴛHō), CONJUNCTION or ADVERB. a short form of **though.**

thong (thong), NOUN.
1 a narrow strip of leather, especially one used as a fastening: *The ancient Greeks laced their sandals on with thongs.*
2 thongs, light rubber sandals held onto the feet by a narrow strip of rubber between the toes and around the sides of the feet.

tho•rax (thôr′aks), NOUN.
1 the part of the body between the neck and the abdomen; chest. It contains the heart and the lungs.

2 the second of the three parts of the body of an insect. It is between the head and the abdomen. ❑ PLURAL **tho·rax·es.**

thorn (thôrn), NOUN. a sharp point on a stem or branch of a tree or other plant. Berries often grow on stems with thorns.

thorn·y (thôr′nē), ADJECTIVE.
1 full of thorns: *I scratched my hands on the thorny bush.*
2 troublesome; annoying: *It took her a long time to solve the thorny problem.* ❑ ADJECTIVE **thorn·i·er, thorn·i·est.**

thor·ough (thèr′ō or thèr′ə), ADJECTIVE. complete and careful: *The doctor was very thorough in her examination.* −**thor′ough·ly,** ADVERB.

thorns on a rose's stem

thor·ough·bred (thèr′ə bred′),
1 ADJECTIVE. of pure breed: *The farmer had a fine herd of thoroughbred cattle.*
2 NOUN. a thoroughbred horse or other animal.

thor·ough·fare (thèr′ə fâr′), NOUN. a main road; highway.

those (ᴛнōz), ADJECTIVE or PRONOUN PLURAL. **Those** is used to point out people, things, or ideas: *Those girls helped me. Those are my library books.* ❑ SINGULAR **that.**

though (ᴛнō),
1 CONJUNCTION. in spite of the fact that: *Though it was pouring, the girls went to school.*
2 CONJUNCTION. even if: *Though we may not finish before the storm, let's keep working in the yard.*
3 ADVERB. however: *I am sorry for our quarrel; you began it, though.*
as though, IDIOM. as if: *You look as though you were tired.*

thought (thȯt),
1 NOUN. something that a person thinks; idea: *Her thought was to have a picnic.* ■ See the Synonym Study at **idea.**
2 NOUN. the process of thinking: *Thought helps us solve problems.*
3 NOUN. concern for the feelings of other people: *Show some thought for others than yourself.*
4 VERB. the past tense of **think:** *We thought it would snow yesterday.*
5 VERB. the past participle of **think:** *They have thought of nothing but the coming holiday.*

thought·ful (thȯt′fəl), ADJECTIVE.
1 thinking hard about something: *He was thoughtful for a while before saying "No."*
2 careful about the feelings of other people; considerate: *She is always thoughtful of her parents' wishes.* ■ See the Synonym Study at **good-natured.** −**thought′ful·ly,** ADVERB. −**thought′ful·ness,** NOUN.

thought·less (thȯt′lis), ADJECTIVE.
1 doing things without thinking; careless: *Thoughtless drivers cause many car crashes.* ■ See the Synonym Study at **careless.**
2 showing little or no care or regard for others: *It is thoughtless of them to keep us waiting so long.* −**thought′less·ly,** ADVERB. −**thought′less·ness,** NOUN.

thou·sand (thou′znd), NOUN or ADJECTIVE. ten hundred; 1000.

thou·sandth (thou′zndth),
1 ADJECTIVE. next after the 999th.
2 NOUN. one of 1000 equal parts.

thrash (thrash), VERB.
1 to hit someone hard and often; beat: *I'd like to thrash whoever broke my camera.*
2 to move violently; toss: *Unable to sleep, I thrashed about in bed.* ❑ VERB **thrash·es, thrashed, thrash·ing.**
thrash out, IDIOM. to settle by thorough discussion: *We thrashed out the details of plan.*

thread (thred),
1 NOUN. a very thin string for sewing. It is made of strands of cotton, silk, wool, nylon, and so on, spun and twisted together.
2 VERB. to put a thread through: *Can you thread a needle?*
3 VERB. to string on a thread: *I threaded beads onto a string.*
4 NOUN. something long and slender like a thread: *The spider hung by a thread.*

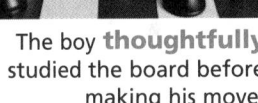

The boy **thoughtfully** studied the board before making his move.

a	hat	ė	term	ô	order	ch	child	ə	a in about
ā	age	i	it	oi	oil	ng	long		e in taken
ä	far	ī	ice	ou	out	sh	she		i in pencil
â	care	o	hot	u	cup	th	thin		o in lemon
e	let	ō	open	u̇	put	ᴛн	then		u in circus
ē	equal	ȯ	saw	ü	rule	zh	measure		

5 NOUN. the main thought that connects the parts of a story or speech: *Something distracted her and she lost the thread of their conversation.*

6 VERB. to make your way carefully through something: *He threaded his way through the crowd.*

7 NOUN. **threads,** the ridges of metal that wind around a bolt, screw, or pipe joint. The threads of a nut fit tightly with the threads of a bolt. ❏ VERB **threads, thread·ed, thread·ing.** –**thread′like′,** ADJECTIVE.

threat (thret), NOUN.

1 a statement of what will be done to hurt or punish someone: *The teacher's threat to keep the class after school stopped the noise.*

2 a sign or cause of possible harm or worry: *Pollution is a threat to our health.*

threat·en (thret′n), VERB.

1 to say what will be done to hurt or punish someone: *The teacher threatened to fail all the students that did no homework.*

2 to give warning of coming trouble: *Black clouds threaten rain.*

3 to be a cause of possible harm or worry to: *A flood threatened the city.* ❏ VERB **threat·ens, threat·ened, threat·en·ing.**

three (thrē), NOUN or ADJECTIVE. one more than two; 3.

thresh (thresh), VERB. to separate the grain or seeds from wheat, rye, or other grain with a **threshing machine.** ❏ VERB **thresh·es, threshed, thresh·ing.** –**thresh′er,** NOUN.

thresh·old (thresh′ōld), NOUN.

1 a piece of wood or stone under a door.

2 the beginning of something important: *The scientist was on the threshold of an important discovery.*

threw (thrü), VERB. the past tense of **throw:** *He threw the ball at me.* ■ Another word that sounds like this is **through.**

thrift (thrift), NOUN. the careful management of your money; habit of saving: *A savings account encourages thrift.*

thrift·y (thrif′tē), ADJECTIVE. careful in spending money; economical; saving: *She is a thrifty shopper.* ❏ ADJECTIVE **thrift·i·er, thrift·i·est.**

thrill (thril),

1 NOUN. a shivering, exciting feeling: *She gets a thrill whenever she sees a parade.*

2 VERB. to give a shivering, exciting feeling to someone: *Stories of adventure thrilled him. She was thrilled to get the movie star's autograph.* ❏ VERB **thrills, thrilled, thrill·ing.**

thrill·er (thril′ər), NOUN. something that thrills people, especially a story, play, television program, or movie that is filled with excitement and suspense.

thrive (thrīv), VERB. to grow strong and healthy: *Flowers will not thrive without sunshine.* ❏ VERB **thrives, thrived** or **throve, thrived** or **thriv·en** (thriv′ən), **thriv·ing.**

throat (thrōt), NOUN.

1 the front part of your neck: *I buttoned the coat up to her throat.*

2 the passage from your mouth to your stomach or your lungs: *A tiny fish bone got stuck in his throat.*

throb (throb),

1 VERB. to beat rapidly or strongly: *Her injured arm throbbed with pain.*

2 NOUN. a rapid or strong beat: *A throb of pain shot through his head.* ❏ VERB **throbs, throbbed, throb·bing.**

throne (thrōn), NOUN.

1 the chair on which a king, queen, bishop, or other person of high rank sits during ceremonies.

2 the power or authority of a king, queen, or other ruler: *The throne of England commands respect.* ■ Another word that sounds like this is **thrown.**

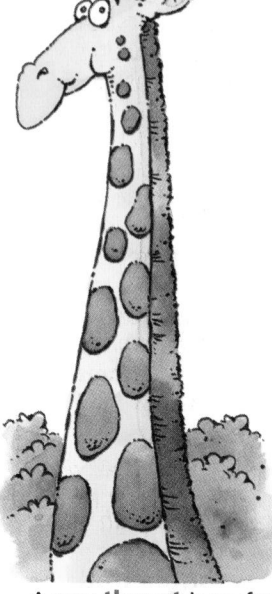

A sore **throat** is no fun for a giraffe.

throng (throng),

1 NOUN. a dense crowd of people.

2 VERB. to go somewhere in large numbers: *People thronged the theater to see the new movie.* ❏ VERB **throngs, thronged, throng·ing.**

throt·tle (throt′l),

1 NOUN. a valve that controls the supply of fuel to an engine.

2 NOUN. a lever or pedal that works this valve. The throttle of a car is called the accelerator.

3 VERB. to choke or strangle: *The thief throttled the dog to keep it from barking.* ❏ VERB **throt·tles, throt·tled, throt·tling.**

through (thrü),

1 PREPOSITION. from end to end of; from side to side of; between the parts of: *They drove through a snowstorm. I bored holes through a board.*

2 ADVERB. from beginning to end; from one side to the other: *She read the book all the way through.*

3 PREPOSITION. here and there in; over: *We traveled through New England and saw many old towns.*

4 PREPOSITION. by means of: *I learned of the new book through my teacher.*

5 ADVERB. completely: *I walked home in the rain and my clothes are wet through.*

6 PREPOSITION. having reached the end of; finished with: *We are through school at three o'clock.*

7 ADJECTIVE. having reached the end; finished: *I will soon be through.*

8 ADJECTIVE. allowing movement or passage through without stopping: *Is this a through street?* ■ Another word that sounds like this is **threw.**

through·out (thrü out′),

1 PREPOSITION. all the way through; through all; in every part of: *The Fourth of July is celebrated throughout the United States.*

2 ADVERB. in every part: *The house is well built throughout.*

throve (thrōv), VERB. a past tense of **thrive:** *The plants throve in the rich soil.*

throw (thrō),

1 VERB. to send something through the air by force of your arm; hurl: *She threw the ball. I threw water on the fire.*

2 NOUN. the act of throwing; toss: *That was a good throw from left field to the catcher.*

3 VERB. to cause someone to fall or fall off: *The wrestler threw his opponent. I was thrown by a horse.*
□ VERB **throws, threw, thrown, throw·ing.** **–throw′er,** NOUN.

throw away, IDIOM.

1 to get rid of; discard: *Throw away those old shoes.*

2 to waste: *Don't throw away your opportunities.*

throw in, IDIOM. to add as a gift: *Our grocer often throws in an extra apple or two.*

throw out, IDIOM.

1 to get rid of; discard: *Let's throw out all this old junk.*

2 to reject: *He threw out my idea.*

throw up, IDIOM. to bring up food from the stomach; vomit.

Synonym Study

Throw means to make something go through the air by moving your arm and hand: *The acrobat's helper throws hoops up for him to juggle.*

Toss means to throw easily or gently: *He tossed the beachball to his little brother.*

Fling means to throw something forcefully without caring just where it goes: *The baby often flings her toys around.*

Hurl means to fling: *The giant picked up a rock and hurled it down the mountainside.*

Pitch[1] means to throw something and try to make it go to a certain place: *I pitched in the softball game yesterday and my friend caught.*

Heave can mean to throw, especially something that is heavy: *He heaved the suitcase into the trunk of his car.*

thrown (thrōn), VERB. the past participle of **throw:** *She has thrown her old toys away.* ■ Another word that sounds like this is **throne.**

thrush (thrush), NOUN. any of a large group of songbirds that includes the robin and the bluebird. □ PLURAL **thrush·es.**

thrush — about 8 inches long

thrust (thrust),

1 VERB. to push something into a place suddenly or violently: *He thrust his hands into his pockets.* ■ See the Synonym Study at **push.**

2 NOUN. a sudden or violent push: *She hid the book behind the pillow with a quick thrust.*
□ VERB **thrusts, thrust, thrust·ing.**

thru·way (thrü′wā′), NOUN. See **expressway.**

thud (thud),

1 NOUN. a dull sound. A heavy blow or fall may cause a thud: *The book hit the floor with a thud.*

2 VERB. to hit, move, or strike with a thud: *The heavy box fell and thudded on the floor.*
□ VERB **thuds, thud·ded, thud·ding.**

thug (thug), NOUN. a rough, violent criminal.

thumb (thum),

1 NOUN. the short, thick finger of the hand.

2 NOUN. the part of a glove or mitten that covers the thumb.

3 VERB. to turn pages rapidly, with your thumb or as if with your thumb: *I didn't read the book; I just thumbed through it.*
□ VERB **thumbs, thumbed, thumb·ing.**

be all thumbs, IDIOM. to be very clumsy or awkward: *I can bat well but when it comes to pitching I'm all thumbs.*

under someone's thumb, IDIOM. under someone's power or influence: *Several members of the club are under the president's thumb.*

thumb·tack (thum′tak′), NOUN. a tack with a broad, flat head, that can be pressed into a wall or board with the thumb.

thump (thump),

1 VERB. to strike with something thick and heavy; pound: *She thumped the table with her fist.*

2 NOUN. a blow with something thick and heavy; heavy knock: *Dad gave the burglar a thump on the head.*

a	hat	ė	term	ô	order	ch child
ā	age	i	it	oi	oil	ng long
ä	far	ī	ice	ou	out	sh she
â	care	o	hot	u	cup	th thin
e	let	ō	open	ù	put	ᵺ then
ē	equal	ò	saw	ü	rule	zh measure

ə { a in about / e in taken / i in pencil / o in lemon / u in circus }

3 NOUN. the dull sound made by a blow, knock, or fall: *We heard a thump when the book fell. What was that thump upstairs?*

4 VERB. to beat violently: *His heart thumped as he walked past the cemetery at night.*
❑ VERB **thumps, thumped, thump·ing.** —**thump′er,** NOUN.

thun·der (thun′dər),
1 NOUN. the loud noise from the sky that comes after a flash of lightning. It is caused by a disturbance of the air resulting from the discharge of electricity.

2 VERB. to make the noise of thunder: *It thundered a few times, but no rain fell.*

3 NOUN. any noise like thunder: *the thunder of a waterfall, a thunder of applause.*

4 VERB. to make a noise like thunder: *The freight train thundered past.*
❑ VERB **thun·ders, thun·dered, thun·der·ing.**

thun·der·bolt (thun′dər bōlt′), NOUN. a flash of lightning and the thunder that accompanies or follows it.

thun·der·cloud (thun′dər kloud′), NOUN. a dark cloud that brings thunder and lightning.

thun·der·ous (thun′dər əs), ADJECTIVE. making a noise like thunder: *The famous actor received a thunderous burst of applause at the end of the play.* ∎ See the Synonym Study at **loud.**

thun·der·storm
(thun′dər stôrm′), NOUN. a storm with thunder and lightning.

thunderstorm

Thurs. or **Thur.,** an abbreviation of **Thursday.**

Thurs·day (thėrz′dā), NOUN. the fifth day of the week; the day after Wednesday.

Word Story

Thursday comes from **Thor** (thôr). The Romans named this day of the week after Jupiter, their god of thunder. The Scandinavians borrowed the idea but used their own god of thunder.

thus (тнus), ADVERB.
1 in this way; in the following manner: *The speaker spoke thus: "Ladies and Gentlemen, welcome."*
2 therefore: *We hurried and thus arrived on time.*
3 to this extent; to this degree; so: *Thus far he is enjoying his studies.*

thwart (thwôrt), VERB. to keep someone from doing what he or she wants to do: *Lack of money thwarted her plans for college.* ❑ VERB **thwarts, thwart·ed, thwart·ing.**

thyme (tīm), NOUN. a small plant with fragrant leaves. The leaves are used for seasoning. ∎ Another word that sounds like this is **time.**

thyme

thy·roid (thī′roid), NOUN. a gland in the neck that affects growth and metabolism.

thy·self (тнī self′), PRONOUN. an old word meaning **yourself.**

ti (tē), NOUN. (in music) the seventh tone of a scale. ❑ PLURAL **tis.** ∎ Other words that sound like this are **tea** and **tee.**

ti·ar·a (tē âr′ə or tē är′ə), NOUN. a band of gold, jewels, flowers, and so on, worn around the head as an ornament. ❑ PLURAL **ti·ar·as.**

Ti·bet (ti bet′), NOUN. a former country in Asia. It is now part of China. —**Ti·bet′an,** ADJECTIVE or NOUN.

tick¹ (tik),
1 NOUN. a short, clicking sound made by a clock or watch.
2 VERB. to make this sound: *The clock ticked.*
❑ VERB **ticks, ticked, tick·ing.**

tick² (tik), NOUN. a tiny animal with eight legs, related to spiders. Ticks live on animals and suck their blood. Some ticks carry disease.

tick·et (tik′it),
1 NOUN. a card or piece of paper that gives you the right to do something or go somewhere: *a ticket to the movies, a concert ticket.*
2 NOUN. a written order to appear in court or to pay a fine, given by a police officer to someone accused of breaking a traffic law or a parking regulation.
3 VERB. to give someone a written order to appear in court or to pay a fine: *The cars were ticketed for illegal parking.*
4 NOUN. the list of candidates to be voted on who belong to one political party: *He ran on the Democratic ticket.*
❑ VERB **tick·ets, tick·et·ed, tick·et·ing.**

tick·le (tik′əl),
1 VERB. to touch someone lightly, causing giggles or little shivers: *He tickled the baby's feet and made her laugh.*
2 VERB. to have a feeling something like a small itch: *My nose tickles from the dust.*
3 NOUN. a tingling or itching feeling.
4 VERB. to amuse or please someone: *The funny story tickled me.*
❑ VERB **tick·les, tick·led, tick·ling.**

tick·lish (tik′lish), ADJECTIVE.
1 sensitive to tickling: *My ribs are very ticklish.*
2 needing to be carefully dealt with; risky: *Telling your friends their faults is a ticklish business.*

tick-tack-toe (tik′tak tō′), NOUN. a game in which two players alternate putting circles or crosses in a figure of nine squares. The object is to be the first to fill three squares in a row with your mark.

tid·al (tī′dl), ADJECTIVE. of or about tides.

tidal wave, a very large, destructive ocean wave that is caused by an earthquake or strong wind.

high and low **tides**

tide (tīd), NOUN. the rise and fall of the ocean about every twelve hours. This rise and fall is caused by the gravitational pull of the moon and the sun.
tide over, IDIOM. to help someone through a hard time: *His savings will tide him over his illness.*
❑ VERB **tides, tid·ed, tid·ing.**

Did You Know?

The place with the highest **tides** in the world is the **Bay of Fundy** (fun′dē) in Canada. Tides there average about 45 feet high. The average high tide in the rest of the world is about 2.5 feet high.

ti·dings (tī′dingz), NOUN PLURAL. news; information: *joyful tidings.*

ti·dy (tī′dē),
1 ADJECTIVE. neat and in order: *a tidy room.* ∎ See the Synonym Study at **neat.**
2 VERB. to make a place neat; put in order: *We tidied the room.*
❑ ADJECTIVE **ti·di·er, ti·di·est;** VERB **ti·dies, ti·died, ti·dy·ing. –ti′di·ness,** NOUN.

tie (tī),
1 VERB. to hold something together by putting string or rope around it; bind: *Please tie this package.*
2 VERB. to arrange something to form a bow or knot: *We tied red ribbons on the party favors.*
3 VERB. to pull shoestrings into a knot in order to fasten them: *She tied her shoes.*
4 NOUN. See **necktie.**

5 NOUN. something that ties; fastening; bond; connection: *family ties, ties of friendship.*
6 NOUN. the condition of having the same number of points in a game: *The game ended in a tie, 3 to 3.*
7 VERB. to make the same score in a game: *The two teams tied.*
8 NOUN. a heavy piece of timber or iron. The rails of a railroad track rest on ties.
❑ VERB **ties, tied, ty·ing.**
tied up, IDIOM. very busy: *I can't go now; I'm all tied up.*

tier (tir), NOUN. one of several rows of seats that are set one above the other: *We sat in the lower tier at the football game.* ∎ Another word that sounds like this is **tear[1].**

ti·ger (tī′gər), NOUN. a large cat of Asia with yellowish orange fur striped with black.

tiger — up to 10 feet long, including the tail

tight (tīt),
1 ADJECTIVE. firmly fastened; not loose: *a tight knot.*
2 ADVERB. firmly: *The rope was tied too tight.*
3 ADJECTIVE. fitting a part of your body closely or too closely: *I don't like to wear tight clothing.*
4 ADJECTIVE. not having much time: *With such a tight schedule, he isn't able to take a vacation this month.*
5 ADJECTIVE. almost even; close: *It was a tight race.*
6 ADJECTIVE. hard to get; scarce: *Money is tight just now.*
7 ADJECTIVE. stingy: *He is tight with his money.*
–tight′ly, ADVERB. **–tight′ness,** NOUN.

tight·en (tīt′n), VERB. to make or become tight: *He tightened his belt. The rope tightened as I pulled it.*
❑ VERB **tight·ens, tight·ened, tight·en·ing.**

tight·rope (tīt′rōp′), NOUN. a rope or wire cable stretched tight on which acrobats perform.

tights (tīts), NOUN PLURAL. a tight-fitting garment, usually covering the lower part of the body and the legs. Tights are worn by gymnasts and dancers.

a	hat	ė	term	ô	order	ch	child		a in about
ā	age	i	it	oi	oil	ng	long		e in taken
ä	far	ī	ice	ou	out	sh	she	ə	i in pencil
â	care	o	hot	u	cup	th	thin		o in lemon
e	let	ō	open	ů	put	ҭH	then		u in circus
ē	equal	ȯ	saw	ü	rule	zh	measure		

ti·gress (ti′gris), *NOUN.* a female tiger. ❏ *PLURAL* **ti·gress·es.**

tile (til),
1 *NOUN.* a thin piece of plastic, baked clay, or stone. Tiles are used for covering roofs, floors, and so on.
2 *VERB.* to put tiles on or in something: *He tiled the bathroom floor.* ❏ *VERB* **tiles, tiled, til·ing.**

Colorful patterns are baked onto the surface of clay **tiles.**

till¹ (til), *PREPOSITION* or *CONJUNCTION.* until; up to the time of; up to the time when: *We stayed outside playing till eight. Walk till you come to a white house, then turn left.*

till² (til), *VERB.* to cultivate land; plow: *Farmers till before planting.* ❏ *VERB* **tills, tilled, till·ing.**

till·er (til′ər), *NOUN.* a bar or handle used to turn the rudder in steering a boat.

tilt (tilt),
1 *VERB.* to tip or cause to tip; slope; slant: *You tilt your head forward when you bow.*
2 *NOUN.* a slope; slant: *the tilt of a wobbly table.* ❏ *VERB* **tilts, tilt·ed, tilt·ing.**
full tilt, *IDIOM.* at full speed; with full force: *The wagon ran full tilt down the hill.*

tim·ber (tim′bər), *NOUN.*
1 wood used for building and making things. Houses, ships, and furniture are made from timber.
2 a large piece of wood used in building. Beams and rafters are timbers.
3 trees or forests that could provide wood for building: *Half their land is covered with timber.*

tim·ber·line (tim′bər lin′), *NOUN.* the line beyond which trees will not grow on mountains and in the polar regions because of the cold.

time (tim),
1 *NOUN.* all the days there have been or ever will be; the past, present, and future. Time is measured in years, months, days, hours, minutes, and seconds.
2 *NOUN.* a part of the past, present, or future: *A minute is a short time. A long time ago people lived in caves.*
3 *NOUN.* a period of history; age: *We are living in the time of space exploration.*
4 *NOUN.* some point in time: *What time is it?*
5 *NOUN.* the right point in time: *It is time to eat dinner.*
6 *NOUN.* an occasion when something happens: *This time we will succeed.*
7 *NOUN.* a way of counting the hours that pass: *standard time, daylight-saving time.*
8 *NOUN.* a period of time and how you felt about what was going on: *Everyone had a good time at the party.*
9 *NOUN.* the rate of beats in music; rhythm: *march time, waltz time.*
10 *VERB.* to measure the speed of someone or something: *I timed the horse at half a mile per minute.*
11 *VERB.* to do something at the time when you want to do it: *They timed their arrival after most tourists had left.*
12 *PREPOSITION.* **times,** multiplied by. The sign for this in arithmetic is ×. *Four times three is twelve. Twenty is five times four.*
❏ *VERB* **times, timed, tim·ing.** ■ Another word that sounds like this is **thyme.**

ahead of time, *IDIOM.* early; before something is supposed to happen: *If he comes to pick you up at six, you should be ready ahead of time.*

at one time, *IDIOM.*
1 at a period in the past: *At one time they lived here.*
2 at the same time; together: *Everyone was interrupting, trying to talk at one time.*

at times, *IDIOM.* now and then; once in a while; sometimes: *At times, I wish I were taller.*

behind the times, *IDIOM.* old-fashioned; out-of-date: *He said I was behind the times for not knowing how to in-line skate.*

for the time being, *IDIOM.* for the present; for now: *The baby is asleep for the time being.*

in no time, *IDIOM.* shortly; before long: *We hurried and arrived home in no time.*

in time, *IDIOM.*
1 after a while: *I think that in time we may win.*
2 soon enough: *Will she arrive in time to have dinner with us?*
3 in the right rate of movement in music, dancing, or marching: *We clapped in time to the music.*

keep time, *IDIOM.*
1 (of a watch or clock) to go correctly: *My watch keeps good time.*
2 to sound or move at the right rate: *The marchers kept time to the music.*

on time, *IDIOM.* at the right time; not late: *We get to school on time each day.*

tell time, *IDIOM.* to know what time it is by the clock.

time after time or **time and again,** *IDIOM.* again and again: *I made the same mistake time after time.*

time·ly (tim′lē), *ADJECTIVE.* happening at exactly the right time: *The timely arrival of the firemen prevented the fire from spreading.* ❏ *ADJECTIVE* **time·li·er, time·li·est. −time′li·ness,** *NOUN.*

time-out (tīm′out′), NOUN.
1 a period when play is stopped during a game.
2 a period of time spent away from others, given to young children as a punishment for bad behavior.

tim·er (tī′mər), NOUN. a device like a clock that tells when a certain amount of time has passed: *The timer rang when the cake had baked for an hour.*

time·ta·ble (tīm′tā′bəl), NOUN. a schedule showing the times when trains, boats, buses, or airplanes come and go.

time zone, a geographical region in which a single standard time is used. The world is divided into 24 time zones. There are six time zones in the United States, including Hawaii and Alaska.

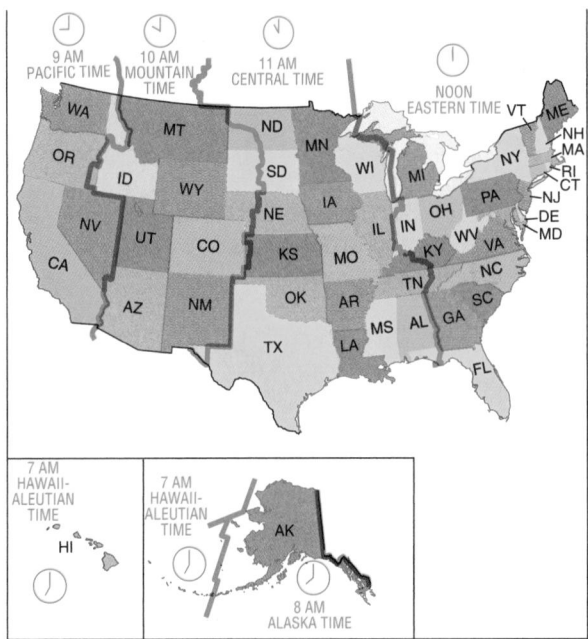

time zones of the United States

tim·id (tim′id), ADJECTIVE. easily frightened; shy: *The timid child was afraid of other children.* ■ See the Synonym Study at **shy.** —**ti·mid·i·ty** (tə mid′ə tē), NOUN. —**tim′id·ly,** ADVERB.

tim·ing (tī′ming), NOUN. the proper control of the time or speed of something to get the greatest effect: *Timing is important when you swing your bat at a baseball.*

tin (tin),
1 NOUN. a soft, silvery white metal. Tin is used to plate other metals and is mixed with other metals to form alloys. Tin is a chemical element.
2 ADJECTIVE. made of or lined with tin: *tin cans.*
3 NOUN. any can, box, or pan made of or lined with tin: *a pie tin, a cookie tin.*

tin·foil (tin′foil′), NOUN. a very thin sheet of aluminum, tin, or tin and lead, used as a wrapping for candy, leftover food, and so on.

tinge (tinj),
1 VERB. to color something slightly: *The dawn sky was tinged with pink.*
2 NOUN. a slight coloring or tint: *There was a tinge of red in the leaves.*
❏ VERB **ting·es, tinged, tinge·ing** or **ting·ing.**

tin·gle (ting′gəl), VERB. to have a feeling of thrills or a prickling, stinging feeling: *He tingled with excitement on his first airplane trip.* ❏ VERB **tin·gles, tin·gled, tin·gling.**

tin·gly (ting′glē), ADJECTIVE. causing a stinging or tingling feeling. ❏ ADJECTIVE **tin·gli·er, tin·gli·est.**

tink·er (ting′kər), VERB. to work on or try to repair something in an unskilled or clumsy way: *He was tinkering with a bicycle in the garage.* ❏ VERB **tink·ers, tink·ered, tink·er·ing.** —**tink′er·er,** NOUN.

tin·kle (ting′kəl),
1 VERB. to make or cause to make short, light, ringing sounds: *Little bells tinkle.*
2 NOUN. a series of short, light, ringing sounds: *We heard the tinkle of sleigh bells.*
❏ VERB **tin·kles, tin·kled, tin·kling.**

tin·sel (tin′səl), NOUN. very thin strips or threads of glittering plastic, used to trim Christmas trees.

tint (tint),
1 NOUN. a shade of a color: *The picture was painted in several tints of blue.*
2 NOUN. a delicate or pale color.
3 VERB. to put a tint on something; color slightly: *The walls were tinted gray.*
❏ VERB **tints, tint·ed, tint·ing.**

ti·ny (tī′nē), ADJECTIVE. very small: *We saw tiny baby chickens at the farm.* ❏ ADJECTIVE **ti·ni·er, ti·ni·est.**

Synonym Study

Tiny means very small: *He wears a tiny hearing aid in his left ear.*

Minute[2] (mī nüt′) means very tiny. : *The gown was covered with thousands of minute, glittering beads.*

Miniature means very much smaller than usual: *The dollhouse in the museum has miniature clocks and miniature furniture.*

Microscopic means so tiny that it can be seen only by using a microscope: *These microscopic living things can be clearly seen when they are magnified.*

See also the Synonym Study at **little.**

ANTONYMS: enormous, gigantic, huge.

a	hat	ė	term	ô	order	ch	child	ə	a in about
ā	age	i	it	oi	oil	ng	long		e in taken
ä	far	ī	ice	ou	out	sh	she		i in pencil
â	care	o	hot	u	cup	th	thin		o in lemon
e	let	ō	open	u̇	put	ᴛʜ	then		u in circus
ē	equal	ȯ	saw	ü	rule	zh	measure		

T

tip¹ (tip),
1 NOUN. the end part of something: *the tips of my fingers, the tip of your nose.*
2 NOUN. a small piece put on the end of something: *We put rubber tips on the legs of our stools.*
3 VERB. to put a tip on something; furnish with a tip: *They carried spears tipped with steel.*
❑ VERB **tips, tipped, tip·ping.**

tip² (tip), VERB.
1 to slope; slant: *She tipped the table toward her.*
2 to turn over: *The boat tipped over, and we fell out.*
❑ VERB **tips, tipped, tip·ping.**

tip³ (tip),
1 NOUN. a small present of money in return for service: *She gave the waiter a tip.*
2 VERB. to give a small present of money to someone: *Did you tip the waiter?*
3 NOUN. a piece of advice that someone gives you; hint: *Someone gave me a tip about pitching tents.*
❑ VERB **tips, tipped, tip·ping.**

tip off, IDIOM.
1 to give secret information to: *They tipped me off about a good bargain.*
2 to warn: *Someone tipped off the criminals and they escaped.*

tip·toe (tip′tō′),
1 NOUN. the tips of your toes: *She stood on tiptoe to watch the parade.*
2 VERB. to walk on the tips of your toes: *She tiptoed quietly up the stairs.*
❑ VERB **tip·toes, tip·toed, tip·toe·ing.**

tire¹ (tīr), VERB. to make or become worn out and sleepy: *The work tires me.* ❑ VERB **tires, tired, tir·ing.**

tire² (tīr), NOUN. the thick, round rubber structure fastened around a wheel of a motor vehicle. Some tires have inner tubes for holding air; others hold the air in the tire itself. Some tires are made of solid rubber.

tired (tīrd), ADJECTIVE. feeling worn out and ready to rest; exhausted: *I'm tired, but I must get back to work.* **–tired′ness,** NOUN.

Synonym Study

Tired means having little energy or strength left: *After working in their garden, the kids were tired.*

Weary means mentally and physically very tired: *Mom was weary after working all day.*

Exhausted can mean having no strength or energy left at all: *At the end of 20 miles, the hikers were too exhausted to go on.*

Worn-out can mean exhausted: *The worn-out runners barely made it to the end of the long race.*

Sleepy means tired and ready to sleep: *She gets sleepy about 9 o'clock.*

tire·less (tīr′lis), ADJECTIVE. never becoming tired; requiring little rest: *She is a tireless worker.*
–tire′less·ly, ADVERB. **–tire′less·ness,** NOUN.

tire·some (tīr′səm), ADJECTIVE. tiring; not interesting: *After dinner we had to listen to a tiresome speech.*

tis·sue (tish′ü), NOUN.
1 a mass of similar cells working together to perform particular functions: *brain tissue, skin tissue.*
2 living matter of any kind: *plant tissue, animal tissue.*
3 a thin, soft paper that absorbs moisture easily.
❑ PLURAL **tis·sues.**

tissue paper, a very thin, soft paper, used for wrapping or covering things.

ti·tle (tī′tl), NOUN.
1 the name of a book, poem, picture, song, and so on: *"Snow White" is the title of a story for children.*
2 a name showing someone's rank, occupation, or condition in life. King, duke, lord, countess, captain, doctor, professor, Mr., and Mrs. are titles.
3 a first-place position; championship: *He won the school tennis title.*

Tlax·ca·la (tlä skä′lä), NOUN. a state in central Mexico.

TN, an abbreviation of **Tennessee.**

to (tü, tu̇, tə), PREPOSITION.
1 in the direction of: *Go to the right.*
2 as far as; until: *This apple is rotten to the core. I will be your friend to the end.*
3 for the purpose of; for: *She came to the rescue.*
4 into: *She tore the letter to pieces.*
5 along with; with: *We danced to the music.*
6 compared with: *The score was 9 to 5.*
7 in agreement with: *Being cold is not to my liking.*
8 on; against: *Fasten it to the wall. They danced cheek to cheek.*
9 about; concerning: *What did he say to that?*
10 *To* is used to show action toward: *Give the book to me. Speak to her.*
11 *To* is used with verbs: *He likes to read. The birds began to sing.*
■ Other words that sound like this are **too** and **two.**

toad (tōd), NOUN. a small animal somewhat like a frog. It lives most of the time on land rather than in water. Toads have a rough, brown skin.
–toad′like′, ADJECTIVE.

The largest kind of **toad** can grow up to 9 inches long. The smallest kind is about 1 inch long.

Did You Know?

Toads can shed their skin as often as every three days. If a toad is well fed, its skin can get too tight and split. The toad rubs it off and rolls it into a ball. Then the toad eats it!

toad·stool (tōd′stül′), *NOUN.* a poisonous mushroom.

toast¹ (tōst),
1 *NOUN.* slices of bread made crisp and brown by heating.
2 *VERB.* to make bread crisp and brown by heating: *We toasted the bread.*
3 *VERB.* to heat something thoroughly: *He toasted his feet before the open fire.*
❑ *VERB* **toasts, toast·ed, toast·ing.**

Word Story

Toast¹ comes from a Latin word meaning "dried by heat." **Toast²** comes from a custom of the Middle Ages. A guest was offered bits of toasted bread in heated wine. The guest would lift the wine goblet and offer thanks to the hosts before drinking.

toast² (tōst),
1 *VERB.* to wish good fortune to someone before drinking; drink to the health of: *We toasted our hosts.*
2 *NOUN.* the act of drinking to someone's health.
❑ *VERB* **toasts, toast·ed, toast·ing.**

toast·er (tō′stər), *NOUN.* an electric appliance for toasting bread.

to·bac·co (tə bak′ō), *NOUN.* the leaves of a plant, dried and cut up. Some people smoke tobacco. Tobacco contains a dangerous, addictive drug called nicotine.

to·bog·gan (tə bog′ən),
1 *NOUN.* a long, narrow, flat, wooden sled without runners. The front of a toboggan curves upwards.
2 *VERB.* to slide downhill on this kind of sled.
❑ *VERB* **to·bog·gans, to·bog·ganed, to·bog·gan·ing.**

to·day (tə dā′),
1 *NOUN.* this day; the present time: *Today is Friday.*
2 *ADVERB.* on or during this day: *What are you doing today?*
3 *ADVERB.* at the present time; now: *Pollution is a problem today.*

tod·dle (tod′l), *VERB.* to walk with short, unsteady steps, as a baby does. ❑ *VERB* **tod·dles, tod·dled, tod·dling.**

tod·dler (tod′lər), *NOUN.* a child who is just learning to walk.

toe (tō), *NOUN.*
1 one of the five parts of your foot that are similar to fingers.
2 the part of a stocking, shoe, or slipper that covers your toes: *She found a hole in the toe of her sock.*
■ Another word that sounds like this is **tow.**

on your toes, *IDIOM.* alert; ready for action: *When I play with him I really have to be on my toes.*

toe·nail (tō′nāl′), *NOUN.* the thin, hard layer that covers the tip of a toe.

Did You Know?

Your **toenails** grow four times more slowly than your fingernails. Your fingernails grow about 0.8 inches a year if they are healthy.

to·fu (tō′fü), *NOUN.* a food something like cheese, made from ground soybeans. Tofu is often pressed into squares.

to·ga (tō′gə), *NOUN.* a loose article of clothing worn in ancient Rome. ❑ *PLURAL* **to·gas.**

to·geth·er (tə geṭH′ər), *ADVERB.*
1 with each other; in cooperation: *Let's work together and get the job done quickly.*
2 into one group, object, and so on: *The principal called the school together. The tailor will sew these pieces together and make a suit.*
3 at the same time: *Rain and snow were falling together.*

To·go (tō′gō), *NOUN.* a country in western Africa. **—To·go·lese** (tō′gə lēz′), *ADJECTIVE* or *NOUN.*

toil (toil),
1 *NOUN.* hard work. ■ See the Synonym Study at **tow.**
2 *VERB.* to work hard: *I toil with my hands for a living.*
3 *VERB.* to move or go somewhere with difficulty or weariness: *Pulling heavy loads, they toiled up the hill.*
❑ *VERB* **toils, toiled, toil·ing. —toil′er,** *NOUN.*

fun on a **toboggan**

toi·let (toi′lit), *NOUN.*
1 a bathroom; washroom.
2 a porcelain bowl with a seat attached and with a drain at the bottom to flush the bowl clean. Waste matter from the body is disposed of in a toilet.
3 *ADJECTIVE.* of or for the toilet: *Combs, brushes, toothpaste, and soap are toilet articles.*

to·ken (tō′kən), *NOUN.*
1 a mark or sign of something; symbol: *I gave her my ring as a token of friendship.*

a	hat	ė	term	ô	order	ch	child	(a in about
ā	age	i	it	oi	oil	ng	long	e in taken
ä	far	ī	ice	ou	out	sh	she	ə ⟨ i in pencil
â	care	o	hot	u	cup	th	thin	o in lemon
e	let	ō	open	u̇	put	ṭH	then	(u in circus
ē	equal	ȯ	saw	ü	rule	zh	measure	

2 a piece of metal shaped like a coin. Tokens are used on some buses and subways instead of money.

To·ky·o (tō′kē ō), *NOUN.* the capital of Japan.

told (tōld), *VERB.*
1 the past tense of **tell:** *You told me that last week.*
2 the past participle of **tell:** *We were told to wait.*

tol·er·ance (tol′ər əns), *NOUN.* a willingness to let people have their own opinions or ways that may be different from our own.

tol·er·ant (tol′ər ənt), *ADJECTIVE.* willing to let other people have their own opinions and ways: *We are tolerant toward all religious beliefs.*

tol·e·rate (tol′ə rāt′), *VERB.*
1 to allow or permit something: *The teacher won't tolerate any disorder.*
2 to put up with; bear; endure: *I cannot tolerate swimming in icy water.*
❏ *VERB* **tol·e·rates, tol·e·rat·ed, tol·e·rat·ing.**

toll¹ (tōl),
1 *VERB.* to sound with single strokes slowly and regularly repeated: *On Sunday all the church bells toll.*
2 *NOUN.* a stroke or sound of a bell being tolled.
❏ *VERB* **tolls, tolled, toll·ing.**

toll² (tōl), *NOUN.*
1 a fee paid to use a road, bridge, tunnel, or ferry: *We pay a toll when we use that bridge.*
2 a charge for a certain service. There is a toll on long-distance telephone calls.
—toll′-free′, *ADJECTIVE.*

tom·a·hawk (tom′ə hȯk), *NOUN.* a light ax used by North American Indians as a weapon and a tool.

to·ma·to (tə mā′tō *or* tə mä′tō), *NOUN.* a juicy, round, red or yellow fruit eaten as a vegetable, either raw or cooked. ❏ *PLURAL* **to·ma·toes.**

There are many kinds of **tomatoes.**

tomb (tüm), *NOUN.* a large grave for a dead body, built above ground.

tom·boy (tom′boi′), *NOUN.* a girl who likes to take part in so-called boys' games and activities.

tomb·stone (tüm′stōn′), *NOUN.* a stone that tells who is buried in a tomb or grave.

tom·cat (tom′kat′), *NOUN.* a male cat.

to·mor·row (tə mor′ō),
1 *NOUN.* the day after today: *Today is Thursday; tomorrow will be Friday.*
2 *NOUN.* the near future: *Houses of tomorrow may all be heated by the sun.*
3 *ADVERB.* on the day after today: *See you tomorrow!*

tom-tom (tom′tom′), *NOUN.* a kind of drum, usually beaten with the hands.

ton (tun), *NOUN.* a unit of weight equal to 2000 pounds in the United States and Canada. A **long ton** is 2240 pounds; a **short ton** is 2000 pounds. A **metric ton** is 1000 kilograms.

tone (tōn), *NOUN.*
1 any sound considered with reference to its quality, pitch, or strength: *angry tones, gentle tones, the deep tone of an organ.*
2 a musical sound, especially one of definite pitch and character.
3 a manner of speaking or writing: *I disliked their disrespectful tone.*
4 normal, healthy physical condition: *Regular exercise will keep your body in tone.*
5 a shade of color: *The room is decorated in tones of brown.*
tone down, *IDIOM.* to soften: *Tone down your voice.*
❏ *VERB* **tones, toned, ton·ing.**

tone-deaf (tōn′def′), *ADJECTIVE.* not able to tell the differences among musical tones. **—tone deafness.**

tongs (tȯngz), *NOUN PLURAL.* a tool with two arms that are joined, used for holding or lifting things.

tongue (tung), *NOUN.*
1 the muscular piece of tissue in the mouth. The tongue is used in tasting. It moves and bends to help you make different sounds.
2 the power of speech: *Have you lost your tongue?*
3 the language of a people: *the English tongue.*
4 the strip of leather under the laces of a shoe.
❏ *PLURAL* **tongues.**
hold your tongue, *IDIOM.* to keep quiet: *Try to hold your tongue while someone else is talking.*
on the tip of your tongue, *IDIOM.*
1 almost spoken: *It was on the tip of my tongue to tell her about the party, when I remembered it was supposed to be a surprise.*
2 almost remembered or thought of: *Her name is on the tip of my tongue.*

tongue-tied (tung′tīd′), *ADJECTIVE.* unable to speak, especially because of shyness, embarrassment, surprise, or shock.

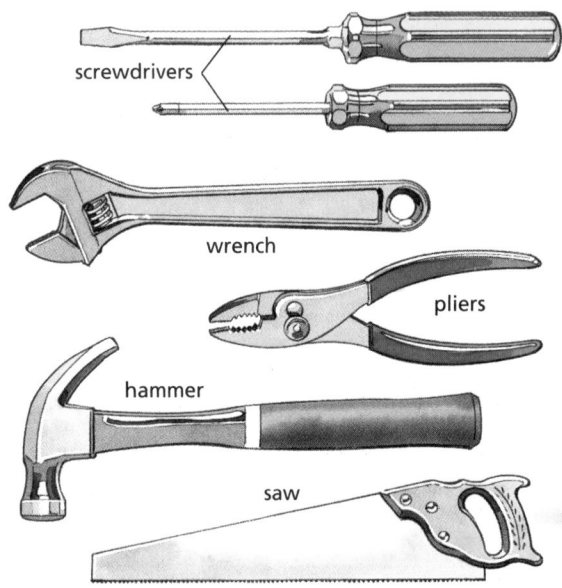

screwdrivers

wrench

pliers

hammer

saw

a variety of **tools**

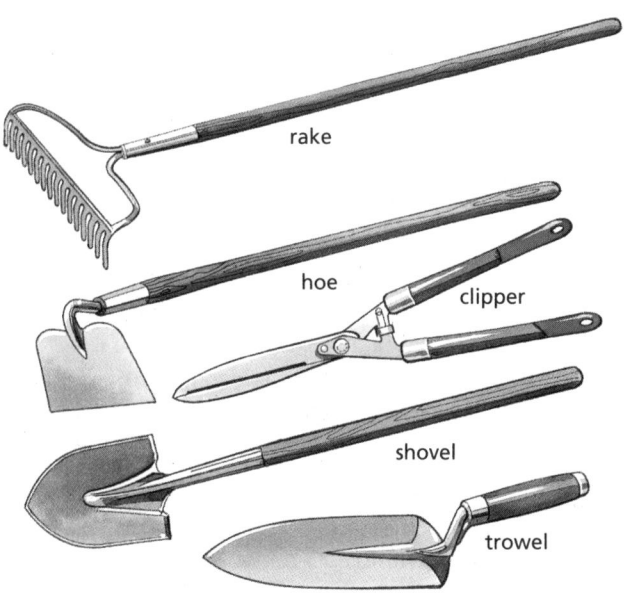

rake

hoe

clipper

shovel

trowel

to·night (tə nīt′),
1 NOUN. the night after today; this night: *I must finish this work by tonight.*
2 ADVERB. on or during this night: *Do you think it will snow tonight?*

ton·sil (ton′səl), NOUN. either of the two small, oval masses of tissue on the sides of your throat, just back of your mouth.

ton·sil·li·tis (ton′sə lī′tis), NOUN. soreness and swelling of the tonsils.

too (tü), ADVERB.
1 also; besides: *The dog is hungry, and thirsty too. We, too, are going away.*
2 more than what is proper or enough: *I ate too much.*
3 very: *I am only too glad to help.*
■ Other words that sound like this are **to** and **two**.

took (tük), VERB. the past tense of **take**: *She took the car an hour ago.*

tool (tül),
1 NOUN. a knife, hammer, saw, shovel, or other device that helps you do work. Gardeners, carpenters, mechanics, and plumbers each have special tools for their work.
2 NOUN. someone or something used like a tool: *Books are a scholar's tools.*
3 VERB. to shape something with a tool: *to tool beautiful designs in leather with a knife.*
❑ VERB **tools, tooled, tool·ing.**

┌ tonsils ┐

tonsil

Synonym Study

Tool means something used to make work easier, especially something used by hand: *The kids picked up their gardening tools and walked home.*

Device means a tool used for a special job: *A tongue depressor is a device a doctor uses to examine your throat.*

Instrument means a tool used for a special job that requires exactness: *The doctor used several instruments when she gave me a complete examination.*

Utensil means a tool, especially one used in cooking: *Which utensil works best for whipping cream?*

Gadget means a small, convenient tool or machine: *My father bought a new gadget to clean his teeth with.*

Appliance means a machine that does a particular job, especially in the home: *She has a business repairing toasters, lamps, and other small appliances.*

tool·box (tül′boks′), NOUN. a box in which tools, small parts, and so on are kept: *I keep my hammer, screwdriver, and drill in my toolbox.*
❑ PLURAL **tool·box·es.**

a hat	ė term	ô order	ch child	(a in about
ā age	i it	oi oil	ng long	e in taken
ä far	ī ice	ou out	sh she	ə ⟨ i in pencil
â care	o hot	u cup	th thin	o in lemon
e let	ō open	ů put	ŦH then	(u in circus
ē equal	ȯ saw	ü rule	zh measure	

T

721

toot (tüt),
1 *NOUN*. the sound of a horn, whistle, or other wind instrument.
2 *VERB*. to give out a short blast of sound: *He heard the train whistle toot three times.*
❏ *VERB* **toots, toot·ed, toot·ing.**

tooth (tüth), *NOUN*.
1 one of the hard, white, bonelike parts in your mouth, used for biting and chewing.
2 something like a tooth. Each sharp point on the edge of a comb, rake, or saw is a tooth.
❏ *PLURAL* **teeth. –tooth′less,** *ADJECTIVE*.

Parts of a Tooth

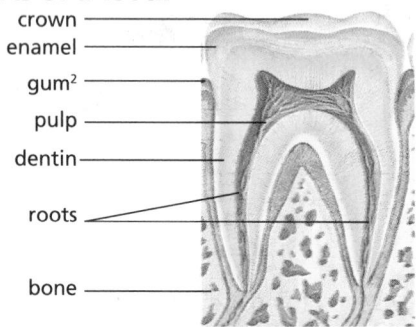

crown
enamel
gum²
pulp
dentin
roots
bone

tooth·ache (tüth′āk′), *NOUN*. a pain in a tooth.
tooth·brush (tüth′brush′), *NOUN*. a small brush used to clean your teeth and gums. ❏ *PLURAL* **tooth·brush·es.**
tooth·paste (tüth′pāst′), *NOUN*. a thick paste used to clean your teeth.
tooth·pick (tüth′pik′), *NOUN*. a small, pointed piece of wood or plastic. A toothpick is used to remove bits of food from between your teeth.

top¹ (top),
1 *NOUN*. the highest point or part of anything: *the top of a mountain, yelling at the top of their voices.*
2 *NOUN*. the upper part, end, or surface: *the top of a table, a shoe top.*
3 *NOUN*. the highest or leading place or rank: *She is at the top of her class.*
4 *NOUN*. the part of a plant that grows above ground: *Beet tops are something like spinach.*
5 *NOUN*. the cover of a bottle, can, and so on.
6 *NOUN*. an article of clothing worn on the upper body: *She wore a blue top.*
7 *ADJECTIVE*. highest; greatest: *The runners set off at top speed.*
8 *VERB*. to be on top of; be the top of: *Whipped cream topped my sundae.*
9 *VERB*. to do better than someone else; outdo; surpass: *His story topped all the rest.*
❏ *VERB* **tops, topped, top·ping.**
on top of, *IDIOM*.
1 in complete control of: *Firefighters were on top of the dangerous situation.*

2 in addition to; along with: *On top of all the rain, there were lightning, thunder, and severe winds.*
3 following right after: *On top of yesterday's bad news comes today's report of an earthquake.*
top off, *IDIOM*. to complete; finish; end, especially in a satisfactory way: *Going out for ice cream topped off a wonderful day.*

top² (top), *NOUN*. a toy that spins on a point.
to·paz (tō′paz), *NOUN*. a hard precious stone that occurs in crystals of various forms and colors. Clear yellow and blue topaz is used in jewelry.
❏ *PLURAL* **to·paz·es.**
To·pe·ka (tə pē′kə), *NOUN*. the capital of Kansas.
top·ic (top′ik), *NOUN*. a subject that people think, write, or talk about: *Newspapers discuss the topics of the day.*
topic sentence, a sentence that expresses the main idea in a paragraph.
top·most (top′mōst), *ADJECTIVE*. highest: *She climbed to the topmost branches of the tree.*
top·ping (top′ing), *NOUN*. something put on top, especially a sauce put on food. Chocolate sauce, chopped nuts, and whipped cream are all toppings for ice cream.
top·ple (top′əl), *VERB*.
1 to fall forward; tumble down: *The chimney toppled over on the roof.*
2 to throw something down; overturn: *The wind toppled the tree.*
❏ *VERB* **top·ples, top·pled, top·pling.**
top·soil (top′soil′), *NOUN*. the upper part of the soil; surface soil: *Farmers need rich topsoil for their crops.*
top·sy-tur·vy (top′sē tėr′vē), *ADVERB* or *ADJECTIVE*. in confusion or disorder: *On moving day everything in the house was topsy-turvy.*
To·rah (tôr′ə), *NOUN*.
1 the entire body of Jewish law and tradition.
2 the first five books of the Old Testament.
torch (tôrch), *NOUN*.
1 a long stick with material that burns at one end of it. A torch can be carried in your hand.
2 See **blowtorch.**
❏ *PLURAL* **torch·es.**
tore (tôr), *VERB*. the past tense of **tear²**: *I tore my new jeans on the fence.*

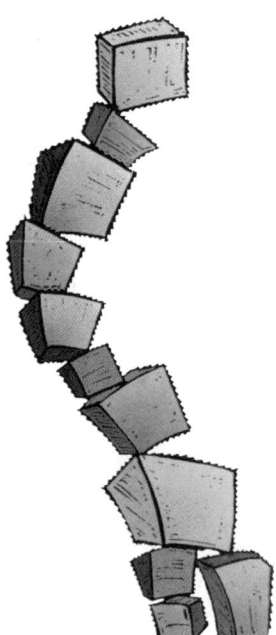

The boxes are beginning to **topple.**

tor·ment (tôr ment′ *or* tôr′ment *for verb;* tôr′ment *for noun*),
1 *VERB.* to cause very great pain to: *Severe headaches tormented him.*
2 *NOUN.* a very great pain: *She suffered torments from her toothache.*
3 *VERB.* to worry or annoy very much: *Don't torment me with silly questions.*
  ❑ *VERB* **tor·ments, tor·ment·ed, tor·ment·ing.**
  —**tor·men′tor** *or* **tor·ment′er,** *NOUN.*

torn (tôrn), *VERB.* the past participle of **tear²**: *The coat was torn at the elbow.*

tor·na·do (tôr nā′dō), *NOUN.* a very violent and destructive windstorm with winds as high as 300 miles per hour; twister. A tornado extends down from a mass of dark clouds as a twisting funnel and moves across the land in a narrow path.
  ❑ *PLURAL* **tor·na·does** *or* **tor·na·dos.**

Did You Know?

More **tornadoes** happened in 1973 than in any other year that records were kept. In that year, 1,102 tornadoes were seen over 46 states. May is supposed to be the month with the most tornadoes in the United States. February has the fewest tornadoes.

tor·pe·do (tôr pē′dō),
1 *NOUN.* a large cigar-shaped bomb that travels through water by its own power. Submarines fire torpedoes at enemy ships to sink them.
2 *VERB.* to attack or destroy a ship with torpedoes: *After the warship was torpedoed, it sank.*
  ❑ *PLURAL* **tor·pe·does;** *VERB* **tor·pe·does, tor·pe·doed, tor·pe·do·ing.**

tor·rent (tôr′ənt), *NOUN.*
1 a violent, rushing stream of water: *The torrent poured down over the rocks.*
2 a heavy downpour.

tor·rid (tôr′id), *ADJECTIVE.* very hot: *In this area, July is usually a torrid month.*

tor·so (tôr′sō), *NOUN.* See **trunk** (definition 4).
  ❑ *PLURAL* **tor·sos.**

tor·til·la (tôr tē′yə), *NOUN.* a thin, flat, round cake made of cornmeal, originally eaten in Latin America but now common in this country. Tortillas are often baked on a flat surface, filled with cheese or meat, and served hot. ❑ *PLURAL* **tor·til·las.**

tor·toise (tôr′təs), *NOUN.* a turtle with a high, arched shell that lives only on land. ❑ *PLURAL* **tor·tois·es** *or* **tor·toise.**

tor·ture (tôr′chər),
1 *NOUN.* the act of causing very severe pain to someone. Torture has been used to make people give evidence about crimes, or to make them confess to having done something.

2 *NOUN.* very severe pain: *You can suffer torture from a toothache.*
3 *VERB.* to cause very severe pain to someone: *It is cruel to torture animals.*
  ❑ *VERB* **tor·tures, tor·tured, tor·tur·ing.**
  —**tor′tur·er,** *NOUN.*

toss (tòs),
1 *VERB.* to throw something lightly with the palm of the hand upward: *She tossed the ball to me.*
  ∎ See the Synonym Study at **throw.**
2 *VERB.* to throw around; pitch around: *The ship was tossed by the waves. He tossed in bed all night.*
3 *VERB.* to throw a coin to decide something by which side falls upward.
4 *NOUN.* a throw; flip: *A toss of a coin decided who should play first.*
5 *VERB.* to lift quickly; throw upward: *She tossed her head and pretended she didn't care.*
  ❑ *VERB* **toss·es, tossed, toss·ing;** *PLURAL* **toss·es.**

tot (tot), *NOUN.* a little child.

to·tal (tō′tl),
1 *NOUN.* the whole amount; sum: *Our expenses reached a total of $108.*
2 *ADJECTIVE.* whole; entire: *The total cost of the house and land will be $250,000.*
3 *VERB.* to add up to an amount of: *The money spent yearly on chewing gum totals millions of dollars.*
4 *ADJECTIVE.* complete: *The lights went out and we were in total darkness.*
  ❑ *VERB* **to·tals, to·taled, to·tal·ing.**

to·tal·ly (tō′tl ē), *ADVERB.* completely: *We were totally unprepared for a surprise attack.*

tote (tōt), *VERB.* to carry; haul. *We toted three enormous suitcases all through Europe.* ❑ *VERB* **totes, tot·ed, tot·ing.**

tortoise — up to 4 feet long

a	hat	ė	term	ô	order	ch	child		a in about
ā	age	i	it	oi	oil	ng	long		e in taken
ä	far	ī	ice	ou	out	sh	she	ə { i in pencil
â	care	o	hot	u	cup	th	thin		o in lemon
e	let	ō	open	ú	put	ŦH	then		u in circus
ē	equal	ò	saw	ü	rule	zh	measure		

tote bag, a large handbag similar to a shopping bag, for carrying bulky objects, groceries, and so on.

to·tem (tō′təm), NOUN.
1 a natural object, often an animal, taken as the emblem of a tribe, clan, or family.
2 the image of such an object. Totems are often carved and painted on poles.

to·tem pole, a pole carved and painted with images of animals, plants, or other natural objects. Totem poles were set up by the Indians of the northwestern coast of North America, especially in front of their houses.

totem pole

tot·ter (tot′ər), VERB. to walk with shaky, unsteady steps: *The baby tottered across the room.* ❑ VERB **tot·ters, tot·tered, tot·ter·ing.**

tou·can (tü′kan), NOUN. a brightly colored bird of warm regions in Central and South America, with a very large beak.

touch (tuch),
1 VERB. to feel something with your hand: *He touched the soft, furry kitten gently.*
2 VERB. to put one thing against another: *He touched the post with his umbrella.*
3 VERB. to be next to; come up against: *Your sleeve is touching the butter.*
4 NOUN. the act of touching or the condition of being touched: *A bubble bursts at a touch.*
5 NOUN. the sense by which a person knows about things by feeling or handling them: *The blind often develop a keen touch.*
6 NOUN. a slight amount; little bit: *a touch of frost.*
7 VERB. to affect with some feeling: *The sad story touched our hearts.*
❑ VERB **touch·es, touched, touch·ing;** PLURAL **touch·es.**

toucan — between 13 and 25 inches long

keep in touch, IDIOM. to stay in communication: *We kept in touch while she was away.*

touch down, IDIOM. to land an aircraft: *The pilot touched down at a small country airfield.*

touch up, IDIOM. to change a little; improve: *The photographer touched up a photograph.*

touch·down (tuch′doun′), NOUN.
1 (in football) a score of six points made by crossing the opponent's goal line with the ball.
2 the landing of an aircraft, especially the moment of first contact with the ground.

touch·ing (tuch′ing), ADJECTIVE. causing tender feeling or sympathy: *a touching story.*

touch·y (tuch′ē), ADJECTIVE. easily hurt or offended; too sensitive: *He is tired and very touchy this afternoon.* ❑ ADJECTIVE **touch·i·er, touch·i·est.**

tough (tuf), ADJECTIVE.
1 bending without breaking: *Leather is tough; cardboard is not.*
2 hard to cut, tear, or chew; not tender: *The steak was so tough I couldn't eat it.*
3 strong; determined: *tough pioneers.* ▪ See the Synonym Study at **strong.**
4 hard to do; not easy; difficult: *Firefighters have a tough job.*
5 rough; disorderly: *That is a tough neighborhood.*
—**tough′ness,** NOUN.

tough·en (tuf′ən), VERB. to make or become tough: *I toughened my muscles by doing exercises.* ❑ VERB **tough·ens, tough·ened, tough·en·ing.**

tour (tùr),
1 VERB. to travel through, or from place to place: *Last year they toured Mexico.*
2 NOUN. a long journey: *The family took a tour through Europe.* ▪ See the Synonym Study at **trip.**
3 NOUN. a short journey; a walk around: *Our class made a tour of the historic old battlefield.*
❑ VERB **tours, toured, tour·ing.**

tour·ist (tùr′ist), NOUN. someone traveling for pleasure: *Each year many tourists go to Canada.*

tour·na·ment (tèr′nə mənt *or* tùr′nə mənt), NOUN.
1 a series of contests testing the skill of many people in some sport: *a golf tournament.*
2 (in the Middle Ages) a contest between two groups of knights on horseback who fought for a prize.

tour·ni·quet (tèr′nə kit), NOUN. something used to stop bleeding by pressing directly against a torn blood vessel, such as a bandage held tightly in place.

tow (tō),
1 VERB. to pull something by a rope or chain: *The tug is towing a barge.* ▪ See the Synonym Study at **pull.**
2 NOUN. the act of towing something: *We phoned for a tow when our car engine stopped running.*
❑ VERB **tows, towed, tow·ing.** ▪ Another word that sounds like this is **toe.** —**tow′a·ble,** ADJECTIVE.

to·ward (tôrd *or* tə wôrd′), PREPOSITION.
1 in the direction of; to: *He walked toward the north.*
2 turned or directed to; facing: *to lie with your face toward the wall.*
3 with regard to; about; concerning: *What is her attitude toward the building of a new library?*
4 near: *Toward morning the storm ended.*

to·wards (tôrdz *or* tə wôrdz′), PREPOSITION. See **toward.**

tow·el (tou′əl), NOUN. a piece of cloth or paper for wiping or drying someone or something that is wet.

tow·er (tou′ər),
1 NOUN. a tall building or part of a building. A tower may stand alone or form part of a church, castle, and so on.
2 VERB. to rise high up: *The new skyscraper towers over the older buildings.*
  ❑ VERB **tow·ers, tow·ered, tow·er·ing.**

a famous **tower** in Paris

tow·er·ing (tou′ər ing), ADJECTIVE.
1 very high: *We climbed the towering peak.*
2 very great: *Making electricity from atomic power is a towering achievement.*

tow·head (tō′hed′), NOUN. someone having very light or pale yellow hair.

town (toun), NOUN.
1 a large group of houses and buildings, smaller than a city: *Do you live in a town or in the country?*
2 any large place with many people living in it: *I hear that Springfield is a fine town.*

town·ship (toun′ship), NOUN. a part of a county that has some governmental responsibilities, such as repair of local roads, school administration, and so on.

tow truck, a truck with the equipment needed to tow away cars.

tow truck

tox·ic (tok′sik), ADJECTIVE. poisonous: *Fumes from a car are toxic.*

toy (toi),
1 NOUN. something for a child to play with; plaything. *Dolls are toys; so are electric trains.*
2 VERB. to amuse yourself; play; trifle: *I toyed with my pencil. Don't toy with matches.*
  ❑ VERB **toys, toyed, toy·ing.**

trace (trās),
1 NOUN. a mark or sign that something used to be present: *The explorer found traces of an ancient city.*
2 VERB. to follow by means of marks, tracks, or clues: *The police trace missing persons.*
3 VERB. to follow the course or history of something: *They traced their family back 300 years to the Pilgrims.*
4 NOUN. a very small amount; little bit: *There was not a trace of gray in her hair.*
5 VERB. to copy by following the lines of something with a pencil or pen: *He put thin paper over the map and traced it.*
  ❑ VERB **trac·es, traced, trac·ing.** −**trace′a·ble,** ADJECTIVE.

tra·che·a (trā′kē ə), NOUN. See **windpipe.** ❑ PLURAL **tra·che·ae** (trā′kē ē′) *or* **tra·che·as.**

trac·ing (trā′sing), NOUN. a copy of something made by putting thin paper over it and following the lines of it with a pencil or pen.

track (trak),
1 NOUN. a pair of parallel metal rails that the wheels of a train run on: *railroad tracks.*
2 NOUN. a mark left by something that has gone by: *The dirt road showed many car tracks.*
3 NOUN. a footprint: *We saw bear tracks near the camp.*
4 VERB. to follow something by means of footprints, smell, or any mark left by anything that has passed by: *We tracked the deer and photographed it.*
5 VERB. to bring snow or mud into a place on your feet: *He tracked mud into the house.*
6 NOUN. a path; trail; rough road: *A track runs through the woods to the house.*
7 NOUN. a place where people or animals can run in a race.
8 NOUN. See **track and field.**
9 NOUN. one of the endless belts of linked steel plates on which a tank or bulldozer moves.
  ❑ VERB **tracks, tracked, track·ing.** −**track′er,** NOUN.

keep track of, IDIOM. to keep within your sight or attention: *There was so much noise it was difficult for me to keep track of what you said.*

lose track of, IDIOM. to fail to keep in your mind or sight: *I often lose track of what time it is.*

a	hat	ė	term	ô	order	ch child		a in about
ā	age	i	it	oi oil	ng long		e in taken
ä	far	ī	ice	ou out	sh she	ə	i in pencil
â	care	o	hot	u cup	th thin		o in lemon
e	let	ō	open	ù put	ᴛʜ then		u in circus
ē	equal	ò	saw	ü rule	zh measure		

track and field, the sports or contests in running, jumping, throwing, and so on, performed around or inside a track. The pole vault, discus, and high jump are track and field events.

track·ball (trak′bȯl′), NOUN. a small ball that can be turned in order to move a cursor on a computer screen. Trackballs are usually built into keyboards and are often used with portable computers.

tract (trakt), NOUN. a stretch of land or water; area: *A tract of desert land has little value.*

trac·tion (trak′shən), NOUN. the ability to grip a surface without sliding or skidding: *Wheels slip on ice because there is too little traction.*

trac·tor (trak′tər), NOUN. a heavy motor vehicle which moves on large rubber wheels. A tractor is used for pulling a wagon, plow, or other vehicle along roads or over fields.

a **tractor** in a field of hay

trade (trād),
1 NOUN. the act or process of buying and selling; exchange of goods; commerce: *The United States has much trade with foreign countries.*
2 VERB. to buy and sell something: *Some American companies trade all over the world.*
3 NOUN. an exchange: *an even trade.*
4 VERB. to exchange; make an exchange: *If you don't like your book, I'll trade with you.*
5 NOUN. a kind of work; business, especially one that requires skilled work: *the carpenter's trade.*
❑ VERB **trades, trad·ed, trad·ing.**

trade in, IDIOM. to give a car, refrigerator, or other article as payment or part payment for something, especially for a newer model.

trade·mark (trād′märk′), NOUN. a mark, picture, name, word, symbol, design, or letters owned and used by a manufacturer or seller. A trademark identifies the product for the buyer.

trad·er (trā′dər), NOUN. someone who trades: *The trappers sold furs to traders.*

trading post, a store or station of a trader, especially on the frontier. Trading posts used to exchange food, weapons, clothes, and other articles for hides and furs.

tra·di·tion (trə dish′ən), NOUN.
1 the process of handing down beliefs, opinions, customs, and stories from parents to children.
2 a custom or belief handed down in this way: *Our family has a tradition of giving half-birthday presents.*
▪ See the Word Story at **treason.**

tra·di·tion·al (trə dish′ə nəl), ADJECTIVE.
1 handed down by tradition: *Shaking hands when you meet is a traditional custom.*
2 made or done according to tradition: *traditional furniture, a traditional festival.*
—**tra·di′tion·al·ly,** ADVERB.

traf·fic (traf′ik), NOUN.
1 people, motor vehicles, ships, and so on coming and going along a way of travel: *Police control the traffic in large cities.*
2 the process of buying and selling; trade: *Governments are trying to stop the illegal drug traffic.*

traffic light, a set of electric lights used to control traffic at a corner or intersection; stoplight. The lights are usually colored red for stop, green for go, and yellow for caution. They flash in sequence automatically every few seconds or minutes.

trag·e·dy (traj′ə dē), NOUN.
1 a serious play with an unhappy ending.
2 a very sad happening: *Her sudden death was a tragedy to her friends.*
❑ PLURAL **trag·e·dies.**

trag·ic (traj′ik), ADJECTIVE. very sad; dreadful: *a tragic death, a tragic accident.* —**trag′i·cal·ly,** ADVERB.

trail (trāl),
1 NOUN. a path across a field or through the woods: *The scouts followed mountain trails for days.*
2 NOUN. a track or natural smell left by a person or animal: *The dogs found the trail of the rabbit.*
3 VERB. to look for an animal by following its track or smell: *The dogs trailed the rabbit across the fields and into the woods.*
4 NOUN. anything that follows along behind something that is moving: *The speeding car left a trail of dust behind it.*
5 VERB. to follow along behind; follow: *The tired children trailed behind their mothers on the walk home from the park.*
6 VERB. to fall or lag behind, as in a race, game, and so on: *Our team trailed by three runs with one turn at bat left.*
❑ VERB **trails, trailed, trail·ing.**

trail·er (trā′lər), NOUN.
1 a large vehicle used for carrying freight. It is usually pulled by a heavy truck called a tractor.

2 a small two-wheeled or four-wheeled vehicle used for hauling something behind a car or truck: *My uncle bought a new boat trailer.*

3 See **mobile home.**

train (trān),
1 *NOUN.* a line of railroad cars hooked together and pulled by a locomotive along a track.
2 *NOUN.* a line of people, animals, wagons, trucks, or the like, moving along together: *The early settlers crossed the continent by wagon train.*
3 *NOUN.* a part that hangs down and drags along: *the train of a wedding gown.*
4 *NOUN.* a continuous series of events or ideas: *I lost my train of thought when I was interrupted.*
5 *VERB.* to bring up someone; rear; teach: *They trained their child to be thoughtful of others.*
6 *VERB.* to make someone skillful by teaching and practice: *to train people as nurses.*
7 *VERB.* to make or become fit by exercise and diet: *The runners trained for the marathon.*
❑ *VERB* **trains, trained, train·ing.**

trai·tor (trā′tər), *NOUN.*
1 someone who betrays his or her country: *The traitor gave the enemy the secret plans for the attack.*
2 someone who betrays a trust, a duty, or a friend. ■ See the Word Story at **treason.**

tramp (tramp),
1 *VERB.* to walk with firm, heavy steps: *They tramped across the snowy field in heavy boots.*
2 *VERB.* to step heavily on something: *He tramped on the flowers.*
3 *NOUN.* the sound of a heavy step: *We could hear the tramp of marching feet.*
4 *NOUN.* a long, steady walk; hike: *The friends took a tramp together over the hills.*
5 *NOUN.* someone who wanders about and lives by begging or doing odd jobs.
❑ *VERB* **tramps, tramped, tramp·ing.**

tram·ple (tram′pəl), *VERB.* to walk or step heavily on something; crush: *The cattle got loose and trampled the farmer's crops.* ❑ *VERB* **tram·ples, tram·pled, tram·pling.**

train

train·er (trā′nər), *NOUN.*
1 someone who trains horses or other animals to take part in competition or other kinds of performances.
2 someone who trains and assists athletes or people in exercise programs.

train·ing (trā′ning), *NOUN.*
1 a practical education in some art, profession, or trade: *The president called for more training for science teachers.*
2 the development of strength and endurance: *Our coach stresses physical training.*
3 good condition maintained by exercise and care: *The athlete kept in training by not overeating and not smoking.*

trait (trāt), *NOUN.* a quality of body, mind, or character; characteristic: *Red hair is a lovely trait. Courage and common sense are desirable traits.*

tram·po·line (tram′pə lēn′), *NOUN.* a piece of canvas or other sturdy fabric stretched on a metal frame, used for jumping or bouncing on.

trance (trans), *NOUN.*
1 a condition something like sleep in which a person no longer responds to his or her surroundings. A person may be in a trance from some illnesses or by being hypnotized. Some people can put themselves into trances.
2 a condition like daydreaming or a trance: *She sat in a trance, watching the flames in the fireplace.*

tran·quil (trang′kwəl), *ADJECTIVE.* calm; peaceful; quiet: *I love tranquil mornings at the lake.*

a hat	ė term	ô order	ch child	a in about
ā age	i it	oi oil	ng long	e in taken
ä far	ī ice	ou out	sh she	ə i in pencil
â care	o hot	u cup	th thin	o in lemon
e let	ō open	ù put	ŦH then	u in circus
ē equal	ò saw	ü rule	zh measure	

T

Word Power   trans-

The prefix **trans-** means "across, over, or through." **Trans**continental means **across** the continent. **Trans-** also means "in or to a different place or position." **Trans**plant means to plant in a **different place.**

trans·con·ti·nen·tal (tran′skon tə nen′tl), *ADJECTIVE*. crossing a continent: *The first transcontinental railroad was completed in 1869.*

trans·fer (tran sfėr′ *or* tran′sfėr′ *for verb;* tran′sfėr′ *for noun*),
1 *VERB*. to change or move from one person or place to another: *The nurse was transferred to another department.* ▪ See the Synonym Study at **move.**
2 *VERB*. to get off one bus, train, subway, and so on, and get on another: *On our way into the city we transferred from a train to a bus.*
3 *NOUN*. a ticket allowing a passenger to change from one bus, train, or the like, to another.
4 *NOUN*. the act of transferring or the condition of being transferred: *a transfer to a different school.*
   ❑ *VERB* **trans·fers, trans·ferred, trans·fer·ring.**

trans·form (tran sfôrm′), *VERB*.
1 to change the form or appearance of something: *The blizzard transformed the trees into mounds of white.*
2 to change in condition, nature, or character: *A tadpole becomes transformed into a frog.*
   ❑ *VERB* **trans·forms, trans·formed, trans·form·ing.**
   –trans·for·ma·tion (tran′sfer mā′shən), *NOUN*.

trans·form·er (tran sfôr′mər), *NOUN*. an electrical device for changing current from one voltage to another.

trans·fu·sion (tran sfyü′zhən), *NOUN*. the act or process of putting blood into someone's body: *The injured driver needed a transfusion.*

tran·sis·tor (tran zis′tər), *NOUN*. a small electronic device used to control or amplify the flow of electrons in an electric circuit. Transistors are used in radios, televisions, computers, and so on.

tran·sit (tran′sit *or* tran′zit), *NOUN*. transportation by trains, buses, and so on: *All systems of transit are crowded during the rush hour.*

tran·si·tion (tran zish′ən), *NOUN*. the process of changing from one condition, place, or thing to another: *Lincoln's life was a transition from poverty to power.*

trans·late (tran slāt′ *or* tranz lāt′), *VERB*. to change something from one language into another: *to translate a book from French into English.* ❑ *VERB* **trans·lates, trans·lat·ed, trans·lat·ing.**
   –trans·la′tor, *NOUN*.

trans·la·tion (tran slā′shən *or* tranz lā′shən), *NOUN*.
1 the result of translating something; version: *She read a Spanish translation of the book.*
2 the act or process of translating something.

trans·lu·cent (tran slü′snt *or* tranz lü′snt), *ADJECTIVE*. letting light through, but not easily seen through: *Frosted glass is translucent.*

trans·mis·sion (tran smish′ən *or* tranz mish′ən), *NOUN*.
1 the part of a car or other motor vehicle that transmits power from the engine to the rear or front axle by the use of gears.
2 the act or process of sending or passing something from one person, thing, or place to another: *Mosquitoes are the only means of transmission of malaria.*
3 the passage through space of radio or television waves from the transmitting station to the receiving station: *When transmission is good, even foreign stations can be heard.*

trans·mit (tran smit′ *or* tranz mit′), *VERB*.
1 to send along; pass along: *Rats transmit disease.* ▪ See the Synonym Study at **send.**
2 to send out signals, voice, music, or pictures by radio or television: *Some stations transmit every hour of the day.*
   ❑ *VERB* **trans·mits, trans·mit·ted, trans·mit·ting.**

trans·mit·ter (tran smit′ər *or* tranz mit′ər), *NOUN*. a device that sends out sounds, or sounds and pictures, by radio waves or by electric current: *Radio stations and television stations have powerful transmitters.*

transfusion

Dr. Charles Richard Drew

Charles Richard Drew did important research about blood banks. During World War II he set up plasma banks, even though the United States government refused to let African Americans donate blood.

trans·par·ent (tran spâr′ənt), *ADJECTIVE*. letting light through so that things on the other side can be clearly seen: *Window glass is transparent.*

trans·plant (tran splant′ *for verb;* tran′splant *for noun*),
1 VERB. to dig something up and replant it in a different place: *We start the flowers indoors and then transplant them to the garden.*
2 VERB. to transfer skin, an organ, and so on, from one person, animal, or part of the body to another: *The surgeon transplanted the kidney.*
3 NOUN. the transfer of skin, an organ, or the like from one person, animal, or part of the body to another: *a heart transplant.*
❑ VERB **trans·plants, trans·plant·ed, trans·plant·ing.**

trans·port (tran spôrt′ *for verb;* tran′spôrt *for noun*),
1 VERB. to carry something from one place to another: *Wheat is transported from the farms to the mills.* ∎ See the Synonym Study at **carry.**
2 NOUN. a ship or aircraft used to carry troops and supplies.
❑ VERB **trans·ports, trans·port·ed, trans·port·ing.**

trans·por·ta·tion (tran′spər tā′shən), NOUN.
1 the business of transporting people or goods: *Railroads, trucks, bus lines, and airlines are all engaged in transportation.*
2 a vehicle used to transport people or things: *When the bus broke down, we had no other transportation to school.*
3 the act of transporting or the condition of a being transported: *The travel agent arranged for our transportation to Mexico.*

trap (trap),
1 NOUN. a device for catching animals: *The mouse was caught in a trap.*
2 NOUN. a trick or other means for catching someone off guard: *The lawyer set traps to make the witness contradict herself.*
3 VERB. to catch an animal in a trap: *We trapped a squirrel in our attic and released it in the woods.*
∎ See the Synonym Study at **catch.**
❑ VERB **traps, trapped, trap·ping.**

tra·peze (trə pēz′), NOUN. a short, horizontal bar hung by ropes like a swing, used by gymnasts and acrobats.

trap·e·zoid (trap′ə zoid), NOUN. a figure having two sides parallel and two sides not parallel.

trap·per (trap′ər), NOUN. someone who traps wild animals for their furs.

trapezoid

trash (trash), NOUN. anything of little or no worth or that is worn out; things to be thrown away; garbage; rubbish: *We cleaned the house, attic, and garage and threw out ten boxes of trash.*

trav·el (trav′əl),
1 VERB. to go from one place to another; journey: *She is traveling in Europe this summer.*
2 NOUN. the act of going in airplanes, trains, ships, cars, and so on, from one place to another: *She loves travel.*
3 VERB. to move or pass: *Sound travels in waves.*
❑ VERB **trav·els, trav·eled, trav·el·ing.** —**trav′el·er,** NOUN.

trawl (trȯl), VERB. to fish or catch fish with a net by dragging it along the bottom of the sea. ❑ VERB **trawls, trawled, trawl·ing.** —**trawl′er,** NOUN.

tray (trā), NOUN. a flat piece of metal or plastic with a rim around it. Trays are used in cafeterias to carry your plates and glasses to your table.

treach·er·ous (trech′ər əs), ADJECTIVE.
1 not to be trusted; not loyal: *The treacherous soldier carried reports to the enemy.*
2 very dangerous while seeming to be safe: *That thin ice is treacherous.*
—**treach′er·ous·ly,** ADVERB.

treach·er·y (trech′ər ē), NOUN. disloyal behavior; treason: *King Arthur's kingdom was destroyed by treachery.*

tread (tred),
1 VERB. to press something underfoot; trample; crush: *In Italy, we watched people tread grapes to make wine.*
2 VERB. to walk; step: *Don't tread on the flower beds.*
3 NOUN. the part of stairs or a ladder that a person steps on: *The stair treads were covered with rubber to prevent slipping.*
4 NOUN. the part of a wheel or tire that touches the ground: *The treads of rubber tires have grooves to improve traction.*
❑ VERB **treads, trod, trod·den** or **trod, tread·ing.**

tread·mill (tred′mil′), NOUN. a device that operates by having a person or animal walk on the moving steps of a wheel or on an endless belt. Treadmills were once used to grind grain. Today a treadmill may be used for walking or jogging exercise.

trea·son (trē′zn), NOUN. a betrayal of your country or ruler. Helping an enemy of your country is treason.

Word Story

Treason comes from a Latin word meaning "to hand over." **Traitor** comes from the same Latin word, and so does **tradition.** When a traitor hands over plans to the enemy, that's treason. When parents or teachers hand over customs to young people, that's tradition.

a	hat	ė	term	ô	order	ch	child		a in about
ā	age	i	it	oi	oil	ng	long		e in taken
ä	far	ī	ice	ou	out	sh	she	ə	i in pencil
â	care	o	hot	u	cup	th	thin		o in lemon
e	let	ō	open	u̇	put	ᴛʜ	then		u in circus
ē	equal	ȯ	saw	ü	rule	zh	measure		

Trees

Trees are essential to life. They make oxygen for the atmosphere and provide a habitat and food for millions of plants and animals. Trees give us building materials and protect the soil from erosion. Trees make the world beautiful and green.

About 1,000 different kinds of trees grow in the United States. Most of our trees can be divided into three main kinds:

Broadleaf trees have thin, flat leaves that change from green to bright yellow, red and orange in the autumn, and fall off in winter.

Needleleaf trees have leaves shaped like needles and stay green all winter long. Their seeds grow in cones.

Palm trees have large leaves that grow at the top of the trunk, but no branches. Palm trees grow only in warm regions.

Food Products

Trees give us food products such as apples, oranges, plums, peaches, nuts, lemons, limes, chewing gum, olives, and maple syrup.

Leaves

The leaves of trees absorb carbon dioxide from the air and use it in photosynthesis to make their own food from sunlight and water. This process helps to clean the air. It also produces much of the oxygen that we breathe.

leaves

Other Products

Products derived from trees include some medicines, soap, paper, wood for houses and furniture, wood for musical instruments, latex rubber, and cork.

old wood

new wood

inner layers

bark

Trunk

Each layer of the trunk has a special function in the life of the tree. The bark of the tree protects it from fire, injury, and disease. One of the inner layers builds new wood. The new wood contains tiny vessels, like veins, that carry sap to the leaves.

Roots

The roots of the tree hold it firmly in the ground and absorb large amounts of water from the soil, which carries vital minerals and provides necessary moisture to the leaves and trunk.

trunk

roots

729B

treas·ure (trezh′ər),
1 NOUN. valuable things, such as gold and jewels: *The pirates buried treasure along the coast.*
2 NOUN. any person or thing that is loved or valued a great deal: *The silver teapot is my parents' chief treasure.*
3 VERB. to value something highly: *She treasures her train more than all her other toys.*
□ VERB **treas·ures, treas·ured, treas·ur·ing.**

treasure

treas·ur·er (trezh′ər ər), NOUN. someone in charge of money. The treasurer of a club pays its bills.
treas·ur·y (trezh′ər ē), NOUN.
1 (earlier) a place where money was kept.
2 money; funds: *We voted to pay for the party out of the club treasury.*
3 **Treasury,** the department of the government that has charge of the income and expenses of a country. The Treasury of the United States collects federal taxes, mints money, supervises national banks, and prevents counterfeiting.
□ PLURAL **treas·ur·ies.**

treat (trēt),
1 VERB. to act a certain way toward someone or something: *The children treat the baby with care.*
2 VERB. to deal with pain or illness in order to relieve or cure it: *The dentist is treating my broken tooth.*
3 VERB. to add a chemical substance to food or water in order to purify it: *to treat drinking water to remove impurities.*
4 VERB. to give food, drink, or amusement to someone: *She treated her friends to ice cream.*
5 NOUN. a gift of food, drink, or amusement: *"This is my treat," she said.*
6 NOUN. anything that gives pleasure: *Being in the country was a treat to the city children.*
□ VERB **treats, treat·ed, treat·ing.**

treat·ment (trēt′mənt), NOUN.
1 a way of treating something: *This cat has suffered from bad treatment.*

2 something done or used to treat a disease or condition: *Doctors are always investigating new treatments for cancer.*

trea·ty (trē′tē), NOUN. a formal agreement, especially one between nations, signed and approved by each nation. □ PLURAL **trea·ties.**

tree (trē),
1 NOUN. a large plant with a woody trunk, usually having branches and leaves at some distance from the ground. Oaks, maples, and elms are some common trees.
2 NOUN. an object often made of wood or resembling a tree, used for some special purpose: *a clothes tree, a hat tree.*
3 NOUN. anything branched like a tree: *a family tree.*
4 VERB. to chase something up a tree: *Several dogs treed my cat.*
□ VERB **trees, treed, tree·ing.** —**tree′less,** ADJECTIVE. —**tree′like′,** ADJECTIVE.

Have You Heard?

You may have heard someone say **"You're barking up the wrong tree."** This means that you are going after the wrong thing or going after something in the wrong way.

trek (trek),
1 VERB. to travel slowly by any means; travel: *The pioneers trekked across the great western plains.*
2 NOUN. a slow, difficult journey: *It was a long trek over the mountains.* ■ See the Synonym Study at **trip.**
□ VERB **treks, trekked, trek·king.**

trel·lis (trel′is), NOUN. a frame of light strips of wood or metal that cross one another, especially one that supports growing vines. □ PLURAL **trel·lis·es.**

a **trellis** supporting a rose bush

trem·ble (trem′bəl),
1 VERB. to shake because you are feeling fear, excitement, weakness, cold, and so on: *The child's voice trembled with fear. My hands trembled from the cold.*

2 *VERB.* to move gently with a quick shaking motion: *The leaves trembled in the breeze.*

3 *NOUN.* the act or fact of trembling: *There was a tremble in her voice as she began to recite.*
❑ *VERB* **trem·bles, trem·bled, trem·bling.**

tre·men·dous (tri men′dəs), *ADJECTIVE.*

1 enormous; very great: *That is a tremendous house for a family of three.*

2 very good; extraordinary: *We had a tremendous time at the party.*
—**tre·men′dous·ly,** *ADVERB.*

trem·or (trem′ər), *NOUN.* a shaking or vibrating movement. An earthquake is sometimes called an earth tremor.

trench (trench), *NOUN.*

1 a ditch; deep furrow: *to dig a trench for a sewer pipe.*

2 a long, deep, narrow area like a valley or canyon in the ocean floor: *The deepest trenches of the Pacific Ocean are much deeper than the Grand Canyon.*

3 a long, narrow ditch with earth piled up in front to protect soldiers from enemy fire.
❑ *PLURAL* **trench·es.**

trend (trend),

1 *NOUN.* a change or tendency toward something new: *One trend of modern living is eating fast food.*

2 *VERB.* to have a general direction; tend; run: *Modern life is trending toward less formal customs.*
❑ *VERB* **trends, trend·ed, trend·ing.**

Tren·ton (tren′tən), *NOUN.* the capital of New Jersey.

tres·pass (tres′pəs or tres′pas), *VERB.* to go onto someone's property without permission: *The farmer put up "No Trespassing" signs to keep hunters off his farm.* ❑ *VERB* **tres·pass·es, tres·passed, tres·pass·ing.**

tress (tres), *NOUN.* usually, **tresses,** *PLURAL.* long, flowing hair: *She had golden tresses.*

tres·tle (tres′əl), *NOUN.* a framework of steel or wood used as a bridge to support railroad tracks.

Word Power   tri-

The prefix **tri-** means "having three ___."
A **triangle** is a shape **having three** angles.
A **triceratops has three** horns.

tri·al (trī′əl), *NOUN.*

1 the act or process of examining and deciding a case in court: *The suspect was brought to trial.*

2 the process of trying or testing something: *The rocket engineers gave the engine another trial to see if it would start properly.*

3 trouble: hardship: *The pioneers suffered many trials.*

on trial, *IDIOM.* being tried in a court of law: *The suspect goes on trial next Monday.*

tri·an·gle (trī′ang′gəl), *NOUN.*

1 a figure having three sides and three angles.

2 something having this shape.

3 a musical instrument made of a steel bar bent into this shape. To play a triangle, you strike the side of it with a steel rod.

tri·an·gu·lar (trī ang′gyə lər), *ADJECTIVE.* shaped like a triangle; having three corners.

trib·al (trī′bəl), *ADJECTIVE.* of a tribe: *tribal customs.*

tribe (trīb), *NOUN.* a group of people who share the same customs, language, and ancestors. A tribe forms a community under one leader or group of leaders.

tribes·man (trībz′mən), *NOUN.* a member of a tribe. ❑ *PLURAL* **tries·men.**

trib·u·tar·y (trib′yə ter′ē), *NOUN.* a stream or river that flows into a larger body of water. ❑ *PLURAL* **trib·u·tar·ies.**

trib·ute (trib′yüt), *NOUN.* something said, done, or given to show thanks or respect; compliment: *Labor Day is a tribute to workers.*

tri·cer·a·tops (trī ser′ə tops), *NOUN.* a dinosaur with a large horn above each eye, a smaller horn on the nose, a bony shield over the back of the neck, and a long and powerful tail.
❑ *PLURAL* **tri·cer·a·tops·es.**

triceratops — about 25 feet long

trich·i·no·sis (trik′ə nō′sis), *NOUN.* a dangerous disease caused by tiny worms most often found in pork that has not been fully cooked. Trichinosis causes fever, nausea, and muscle pain.

trick (trik),

1 *NOUN.* something done to make people laugh or to fool them: *The magician showed us a few amazing tricks with cards.*

2 *VERB.* to play a trick on someone; cheat: *We were tricked into buying a stolen car.* ■ See the Synonym Study at **cheat.**

3 *NOUN.* a clever act of skill that you can teach an animal: *We enjoyed the tricks of the trained animals at the circus.*

a	hat	ė	term	ô	order	ch	child		a in about
ā	age	i	it	oi	oil	ng	long		e in taken
ä	far	ī	ice	ou	out	sh	she	ə ⟨	i in pencil
â	care	o	hot	u	cup	th	thin		o in lemon
e	let	ō	open	ú	put	ᴛʜ	then		u in circus
ē	equal	ò	saw	ü	rule	zh	measure		

4 NOUN. the best way of doing or dealing with something: *She is teaching me the trick of restoring old furniture.*
❏ VERB **tricks, tricked, trick·ing.**

trick·er·y (trik′ər ē), NOUN. the use of tricks; cheating: *He tried to sell me a bike with a broken chain, but I saw through his trickery.*

trick·le (trik′əl),
1 VERB. to flow or fall in drops or in a small stream: *Tears trickled down her cheeks. The brook trickled through the valley.*
2 NOUN. a small flow or stream.
3 VERB. to come, go, or move slowly and unevenly: *An hour before the show started, people began to trickle into the theater.*
❏ VERB **trick·les, trick·led, trick·ling.**

trick·y (trik′ē), ADJECTIVE.
1 full of tricks; apt to deceive or cheat you: *a tricky person.*
2 not doing what is expected; dangerous or difficult to deal with: *The back door has a tricky lock.*
❏ ADJECTIVE **trick·i·er, trick·i·est.**

tri·cy·cle (trī′sə kəl), NOUN. a vehicle used by children. It has one wheel in front worked by pedals, and two wheels in back.

tried (trīd),
1 ADJECTIVE. tested by experience: *a person of tried abilities.*
2 VERB. the past tense of **try:** *I tried to call you.*
3 VERB. the past participle of **try:** *Have you tried calling again?*

tries (trīz),
1 NOUN. the plural of **try:** *After several tries, I gave up.*
2 VERB. a present tense of **try:** *He tries to please.*

tri·fle (trī′fəl), NOUN.
1 something that is not important or of little value.
2 a small amount; little bit: *She was a trifle late.*

trig·ger (trig′ər),
1 NOUN. the small lever that you squeeze with your finger when you fire a gun.
2 VERB. to make something happen: *I broke the glass that triggered the fire alarm.*
❏ VERB **trig·gers, trig·gered, trig·ger·ing.**

tril·lion (tril′yən), NOUN or ADJECTIVE. one thousand billions; 1,000,000,000,000.

trim (trim),
1 VERB. to make something neat by cutting away parts that are not wanted: *The gardener trims the hedge. The barber trimmed my hair.* ∎ See the Synonym Study at **cut.**
2 ADJECTIVE. neat; in good condition or order: *Our whole family works together to keep a trim house.*
3 VERB. to make something beautiful; decorate: *The children were trimming the Christmas tree.*
❏ VERB **trims, trimmed, trim·ming;** ADJECTIVE **trim·mer, trim·mest.**

trim·ming (trim′ing), NOUN.
1 anything used to trim or decorate; ornament: *trimming for a dress.*
2 trimmings, a the parts that are cut away: *trimmings from a hedge.* **b** everything needed to make something complete and festive: *We ate turkey with all the trimmings.*

trin·ket (tring′kit), NOUN. any small fancy article, bit of jewelry, and the like: *The baby played with the trinkets on the bracelet.*

tri·o (trē′ō), NOUN.
1 a piece of music for three voices or instruments.
2 a group of three singers or players performing together.
❏ PLURAL **tri·os.**

trip (trip),
1 NOUN. the act of going from one place to another; journey; voyage: *a trip to Europe.*
2 VERB. to hit your foot against something; stumble: *He tripped on the stairs.*
3 VERB. to cause someone to stumble and fall: *The loose board on the stairs tripped her.*
❏ VERB **trips, tripped, trip·ping.**

Synonym Study

Trip means the act of going some distance: *Her family went on a trip to Long Beach.*

Journey means a long trip: *She spent her vacation on a journey through the desert.*

Tour means a trip, often to see many places: *The zookeeper gave me a tour of the zoo.*

Voyage means a long trip, especially by ship: *He is reading about famous people who made voyages across the Atlantic.*

Cruise means a voyage for pleasure that takes you to several places: *We will visit four islands on our sea cruise.*

Expedition means a trip for some special purpose: *Expeditions into space use special equipment.*

Outing means a short trip for enjoyment: *We have a picnic outing planned for Saturday.*

Trek means a long and difficult trip: *After reaching the peak, the mountain climbers began the hard trek back.*

tri·ple (trip′əl),
1 ADJECTIVE. three times as much or as many: *a triple portion of cake, to get triple pay.*
2 ADJECTIVE. having three parts: *The king wore a triple crown to symbolize the three parts of his country.*
3 VERB. to make or become three times as much or as many: *The number of club members has tripled.*

4 in baseball: **a** NOUN. a hit that allows the batter to reach third base. **b** VERB. to make this kind of hit: *She tripled to start off the inning.*
□ VERB **tri·ples, tri·pled, tri·pling.**

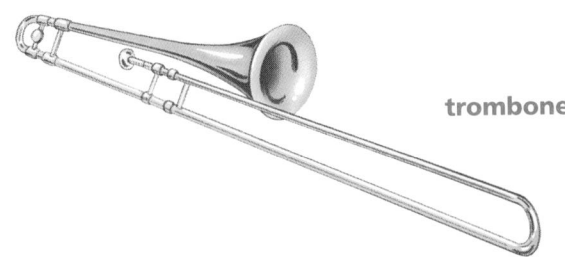

trombone

triple play, (in baseball) a play in which three runners are put out.

tri·plet (trip′lit), NOUN. one of three children born at the same time to the same mother.

tri·pod (trī′pod), NOUN. a three-legged support or stand for a camera, telescope, or the like.

A **tripod** is a very stable support.

tri·umph (trī′umf),
1 NOUN. victory or success after great effort: *The exploration of outer space is a great triumph of modern science.*
2 VERB. to gain victory; win success: *Our team triumphed over theirs.*
3 NOUN. joy because of victory or success: *We welcomed the team home in triumph.* □ VERB **tri·umphs, tri·umphed, tri·umph·ing.**

tri·um·phant (trī um′fənt), ADJECTIVE.
1 victorious; successful: *a triumphant army.*
2 joyful because of victory or success: *The winners spoke in triumphant tones about their skillful play.* —**tri·um′phant·ly,** ADVERB.

triv·i·a (triv′ē ə), NOUN.
1 PLURAL. things of little or no importance; trifles.
2 SINGULAR. a game or quiz involving facts that are not well-known.

triv·i·al (triv′ē əl), ADJECTIVE. not important: *Your composition has only a few trivial mistakes.*

trod (trod), VERB.
1 the past tense of **tread:** *He just trod on my toe.*
2 a past participle of **tread:** *The path has been trod by many feet.*

trod·den (trod′n), VERB. a past participle of **tread:** *The cattle have trodden down the corn.*

troll (trōl), NOUN. (in stories) an ugly giant or dwarf living in caves or underground.

trol·ley (trol′ē), NOUN. See **streetcar.** □ PLURAL **trolleys.**

trom·bone (trom′bōn *or* trom bōn′), NOUN. a brass wind instrument. You move a long sliding tube backward and forward to change the notes as you play it. —**trom·bon′ist,** NOUN.

troop (trüp),
1 NOUN. a group or band of people or animals: *a troop of children, a troop of baboons.*
2 NOUN. **troops,** soldiers: *The king sent more troops.*
3 VERB. to gather and move in a group: *The children trooped after their teacher.*
□ VERB **troops, trooped, troop·ing.** ■ Another word that sounds like this is **troupe.**

troop·er (trü′pər), NOUN. a police officer in some state police forces.

tro·phy (trō′fē), NOUN. an award, often in the form of a statue or cup, given as a symbol of victory. A trophy is often awarded as a prize in a race or contest. □ PLURAL **tro·phies.**

trop·i·cal (trop′ə kəl), ADJECTIVE. of or like the tropics: *Bananas are tropical fruit.*

trop·ics (trop′iks), NOUN PLURAL. regions near the equator. The hottest and wettest parts of the earth are in the tropics.

trop·o·sphere (trop′ə sfir), NOUN. the region of the atmosphere that extends from the earth's surface to a height of about 10 miles. Most weather formations occur in the troposphere.

trot (trot),
1 NOUN. a gait of a horse and some other four-footed animals between a walk and a run. In a trot, the right forefoot and the left hind foot are lifted at the same time.
2 VERB. to ride at a trot: *The riders trotted home.*
3 VERB. to go or cause to go at a trot: *The pony trotted through the field. We trotted our horses through the woods.*
4 VERB. to run, but not fast: *The child trotted after his mother.*
5 NOUN. a slow run.
□ VERB **trots, trot·ted, trot·ting.**

trou·ble (trub′əl),
1 NOUN. problems; difficulty: *The noisy students made trouble for their teacher.*
2 VERB. to upset, bother, or worry someone; disturb: *Lack of business troubled the storekeeper.*
3 NOUN. something that upsets, bothers, or worries you, or that gives you pain: *The trouble began when our car broke down in a storm.*
4 NOUN. extra work: *Take the trouble to do careful work.*

a	hat	ė	term	ô	order	ch	child	a in about
ā	age	i	it	oi	oil	ng	long	e in taken
ä	far	ī	ice	ou	out	sh	she	ə { i in pencil
â	care	o	hot	u	cup	th	thin	o in lemon
e	let	ō	open	u̇	put	ᴛʜ	then	u in circus
ē	equal	ȯ	saw	ü	rule	zh	measure	

5 NOUN. illness; disease: *My grandfather suffers from heart trouble.*

❏ VERB **trou·bles, trou·bled, trou·bling.**

trou·ble·some (trub′əl səm), ADJECTIVE. causing trouble; annoying: *Last year we had noisy, troublesome neighbors.*

trough (trȯf), NOUN. a long, narrow container that holds food or water: *He led the horses to the watering trough.*

troupe (trüp), NOUN. a group of actors, singers, acrobats, and so on. ■ Another word that sounds like this is **troop.**

trou·sers (trou′zərz), NOUN PLURAL. See **pants.**

trout (trout), NOUN. a freshwater food fish that is related to the salmon. ❏ PLURAL **trout** or **trouts.**

There are 10 different kinds of **trout** in North America.

trow·el (trou′əl), NOUN. a tool with a curved blade for digging up plants or loosening dirt.

tru·ant (trü′ənt), NOUN. a student who stays away from school without permission.

truce (trüs), NOUN. an agreement to stop fighting; decision to have peace for a short time: *A truce was declared between the two armies for a week.*

truck (truk),

1 NOUN. a strongly built motor vehicle that can carry heavy loads.

2 VERB. to carry or ship something by truck: *Farmers truck fresh produce to the market.*

❏ VERB **trucks, trucked, truck·ing.**

trudge (truj), VERB. to walk wearily or with effort: *She trudged slowly through the deep snow.* ❏ VERB **trudg·es, trudged, trudg·ing.**

true (trü),

1 ADJECTIVE. based on fact; right; accurate; not false: *The story I told is true; I did not make it up.*

2 ADJECTIVE. real; genuine: *true kindness.*

3 ADJECTIVE. faithful; loyal: *She is a true friend.*

4 ADVERB. in a true manner; truly; exactly: *The batter swung hard and true and hit a home run.*

❏ ADJECTIVE **tru·er, tru·est.**

true bug, an insect with either four wings or none and a mouth made for piercing and sucking.

tru·ly (trü′lē), ADVERB.

1 in a true manner; exactly: *Tell me truly what you think.*

2 really; in fact: *It was truly a beautiful sight.*

trum·pet (trum′pit),

1 NOUN. a brass wind instrument that you play by pressing its keys.

2 NOUN. a sound like that of a trumpet.

3 VERB. to make a sound like that of a trumpet: *An elephant trumpeted in fright.*

❏ VERB **trum·pets, trum·pet·ed, trum·pet·ing.**

trunk (trungk), NOUN.

1 the main stem of a tree. Branches and roots grow out of the trunk.

2 an enclosed compartment usually in the rear of a car: *The spare tire and the jack are in the trunk.*

3 the long, flexible snout of an elephant: *The elephant picked up peanuts with its trunk.*

4 a human or animal body, not including the head, arms, and legs.

5 a big, sturdy box with a hinged lid, to store clothes and other things in, or for use when traveling.

6 trunks, very short pants worn by males for swimming, boxing, and the like.

−**trunk′like′,** ADJECTIVE.

trunk

trust (trust),

1 NOUN. a firm belief in the honesty, truthfulness, justice, or power of a person or thing; faith: *The children put trust in their parents.*

2 VERB. to believe firmly in the honesty, truth, justice, or power of someone or something; have faith in: *They are people you can trust.*

3 VERB. to rely on someone or something; depend on: *If you can't trust your memory, write things down.*

4 VERB. to let someone use or borrow something: *I'll trust you with my favorite sweater for a few days.*

5 VERB. to hope; believe: *I trust you will soon feel better.*

6 NOUN. money or property managed for the benefit of someone else: *They set up a trust for the children.*

❏ VERB **trusts, trust·ed, trust·ing.**

trus·tee (tru stē′), NOUN. someone responsible for the property or affairs of another person or of an institution: *A trustee will manage the children's property until they grow up.* ❑ PLURAL **trus·tees.**

trust·wor·thy (trust′wèr′ᴛʜē), ADJECTIVE. able to be trusted or depended on; reliable: *The class chose a trustworthy student for treasurer.*

trust·y (trus′tē), ADJECTIVE. able to be depended on; reliable: *She left her new car with a trusty friend.* ❑ ADJECTIVE **trust·i·er, trust·i·est.**

truth (trüth), NOUN.
1 something that is true: *Tell the truth.*
2 the quality or nature of being true, accurate, honest, sincere, or loyal: *The jury doubted the truth of the witness's statements.* ❑ PLURAL **truths** (trüᴛʜz or trüths).

Have You Heard?

You may have heard someone say **"Truth is stranger than fiction."** People say this when something really odd happens. It means they think that what has happened is even weirder than the most imaginative writer could think up.

truth·ful (trüth′fəl), ADJECTIVE. telling the truth: *You can count on her for a truthful answer.* —**truth′ful·ly,** ADVERB. —**truth′ful·ness,** NOUN.

try (trī),
1 VERB. to make an effort to do something: *He tried to do the work. Try harder if you wish to succeed.*
2 VERB. to find out about something by using it; experiment with; test: *Try this and see if you like it.*
3 NOUN. a chance to try to do something: *Each girl had three tries at the high jump.*
4 VERB. to judge someone in a court of law: *They were tried and found guilty of robbery.* ❑ VERB **tries, tried, try·ing;** PLURAL **tries.**

try on, IDIOM. to put on to test the fit or looks: *I tried on several coats.*

try out, IDIOM.
1 to test or sample: *Try out this recipe for apple pie.*
2 to perform for a team, band, and so on, in order to become a member: *I tried out for the tennis team.*

try·ing (trī′ing), ADJECTIVE. hard to put up with; annoying: *a long, hot, trying drive.*

try·out (trī′out′), NOUN. a test to determine whether someone is good enough to be on a team, in a play, and so on: *Tryouts for our football team will start a week after school opens.*

T-shirt (tē′shèrt′), NOUN. a light, close-fitting knitted shirt with short sleeves and no collar; tee.

tsp., an abbreviation of **teaspoon** or **teaspoons.**

tub (tub), NOUN.
1 a large, open container that holds water. You can take a bath in a tub or wash clothes in it.
2 a round container for holding butter, honey, or something similar: *a tub of butter.*

tu·ba (tü′bə), NOUN. a large brass wind instrument that has a very deep tone. ❑ PLURAL **tu·bas.**

marching with a **tuba**

tube (tüb), NOUN.
1 a long pipe of metal, glass, rubber, and so on. Tubes are used to hold or carry liquids or gases.
2 a small cylinder made of plastic or thin, flexible metal with a cap. Tubes hold toothpaste, ointment, paint, and so on.
3 a round, inflatable rubber ring inside a tire.
4 **the tube,** (informal) television. —**tube′like′,** ADJECTIVE.

tu·ber (tü′bər), NOUN. the thick part of an underground stem. A potato is a tuber.

tu·ber·cu·lo·sis (tü bèr′kyə lō′sis), NOUN. a disease that destroys various tissues of the body, but most often the lungs. You can catch tuberculosis if you are around someone who has it.

tuck (tuk), VERB.
1 to put something into some narrow space or into some convenient place: *She tucked the book under her arm. He tucked the letter into his pocket.*
2 to put the edge of something into place: *Tuck your shirt in.*
3 to cover snugly: *Tuck the children in bed.* ❑ VERB **tucks, tucked, tuck·ing.**

Tues., an abbreviation of **Tuesday.**

Tues·day (tüz′dā), NOUN. the third day of the week; the day after Monday.

Word Story

Tuesday comes from an earlier English word meaning "Tiw's day." Tiw is the name of the ancient German god of war.

tuft (tuft), NOUN. a bunch of feathers, hair, grass, and so on, held together at one end: *Lions have a tuft of black hair at the end of their tails.*

tug (tug),
1 VERB. to pull hard on something: *We tugged the boat in to shore. The dog tugged at the rope.* ◼ See the Synonym Study at **pull.**
2 NOUN. a hard pull on something: *The baby gave a tug at my hair.*
3 NOUN. a short form of **tugboat.** ❑ VERB **tugs, tugged, tug·ging.**

a	hat	ė	term	ô	order	ch	child		a in about
ā	age	i	it	oi	oil	ng	long		e in taken
ä	far	ī	ice	ou	out	sh	she	ə	i in pencil
â	care	o	hot	u	cup	th	thin		o in lemon
e	let	ō	open	ů	put	ᴛʜ	then		u in circus
ē	equal	ò	saw	ü	rule	zh	measure		

tug·boat (tug′bōt′), *NOUN.* a small, powerful boat used to tow or push other boats; tug.

tug-of-war (tug′əv wôr′ *or* tug′ə wôr′), *NOUN.* a contest between two teams pulling at the ends of a rope. Each team tries to drag the other over a line marked between them. ❑ *PLURAL* **tugs-of-war.**

tu·i·tion (tü ish′ən), *NOUN.* the money paid for being taught: *The college raised its tuition $300.*

tu·lip (tü′lip), *NOUN.* a plant having long, narrow leaves and cup-shaped flowers of various colors. Tulips grow from bulbs.

Word Story

Tulip comes from a Persian word meaning "turban." It was called this because the flower resembles a turban.

tum·ble (tum′bəl),
1 *VERB.* to fall down suddenly headfirst: *The child tumbled down the stairs.*
2 *NOUN.* a fall like this: *The tumble bruised the child.*
3 *VERB.* to roll or toss about: *The clothes dryer tumbled the sheets to dry them.*
4 *VERB.* to perform leaps, somersaults, or other acrobatic tricks.
❑ *VERB* **tum·bles, tum·bled, tum·bling.**

tum·bler (tum′blər), *NOUN.*
1 someone who performs acrobatic leaps or jumps.
2 a drinking glass.

tum·ble·weed (tum′bəl wēd′), *NOUN.* a plant growing in the western United States, that breaks off from its roots and is blown about by the wind.

tum·my (tum′ē), *NOUN.* (informal) the stomach.
❑ *PLURAL* **tum·mies.**

tu·mor (tü′mər), *NOUN.* a lump of cells or tissue in the body that is not normal.

tu·na (tü′nə), *NOUN.* a large sea fish used for food. It sometimes grows to a length of ten feet or more.
❑ *PLURAL* **tu·na** or **tu·nas.**

Did You Know?

Some fishermen believe that the bluefin **tuna** is the fastest swimmer. It has been recorded as swimming as fast as 43 miles per hour. People can swim about five miles per hour.

tun·dra (tun′drə), *NOUN.* a vast, level, treeless plain in the arctic regions. The ground beneath its surface is frozen even in summer. ❑ *PLURAL* **tun·dras.**

tune (tün),
1 *NOUN.* a piece of music; melody: *popular tunes.*
2 *NOUN.* the condition of having proper pitch: *The piano is out of tune. Please sing in tune.*
3 *NOUN.* agreement; harmony: *I hope my ideas are in tune with the times.*
4 *VERB.* to make a musical instrument sound right: *We should have the piano tuned.*
❑ *VERB* **tunes, tuned, tun·ing. –tun′er,** *NOUN.*

tune in, *IDIOM.* to adjust a radio or TV set to hear or see what is wanted: *to tune in an out-of-town station.*

tune up, *IDIOM.* to put an engine or other mechanism into the best working order.

Tulips are a very popular flower.

tu·nic (tü′nik), *NOUN.*
1 an article of clothing like a long shirt, worn by the ancient Greeks and Romans.
2 a short, close-fitting coat, especially one worn by soldiers or police officers.

tuning fork, a small steel device with two prongs. When struck, it makes a musical tone of a certain pitch that can be used to tune musical instruments.

Tu·ni·sia (tü nē′zhə), *NOUN.* a country in northern Africa. **–Tu·ni′sian,** *ADJECTIVE or NOUN.*

tun·nel (tun′l),
1 *NOUN.* an underground road or path: *The railroad passes under the mountain through a tunnel.*
2 *VERB.* to make an underground road or path: *The mole tunneled in the ground.*
❑ *VERB* **tun·nels, tun·neled, tun·nel·ing.**

Word Story

Tunnel comes from a French word meaning "big barrel." If you put a lot of barrels on their sides and took their tops and bottoms off, you'd have a tunnel shape.

tur·ban (tėr′bən), *NOUN.*
1 a scarf wound around the head or around a cap, worn by men in parts of India and in some other countries.
2 any hat or headdress like this.

tur·bine (tėr′bən), *NOUN.* a device containing a wheel with paddles or blades that is caused to rotate by the pressure of rapidly flowing water, steam, or air. Turbines are often used to turn generators that produce electric power.

tur·bu·lence (tėr′byə ləns), NOUN. rough, uneven movement; disturbance: *Severe air turbulence can injure aircraft passengers and crew.*

tur·bu·lent (tėr′byə lənt), ADJECTIVE.
1 causing a disturbance; disorderly: *a turbulent mob.*
2 stormy: *turbulent weather.*

turf (tėrf), NOUN.
1 the upper surface of the soil covered with grass and other small plants, with their roots that hold it all together.
2 See **AstroTurf.**

Turk (tėrk), NOUN. someone born or living in Turkey.

turkey — about 4 feet long

tur·key (tėr′kē), NOUN. a large North American bird with brown or white feathers. A turkey has a bare head and neck. Turkeys are raised for food.
❑ PLURAL **tur·keys.**

Word Story

Turkey, as a name for a bird, comes from a mistake. Actually, two mistakes. When people in Europe first saw turkeys from America, they thought they were seeing other birds. And they thought that those other birds came from Turkey. (They actually come from Africa.) So people called the wrong birds after the wrong place, but the name stuck.

Tur·key (tėr′kē), NOUN. a country in western Asia and southeastern Europe.

Turk·ish (tėr′kish),
1 ADJECTIVE. of or about Turkey, its people, or their language.
2 NOUN. the language of Turkey.

Word Source

Some **Turkish** words that have come into the English language are **coffee, horde, jackal, sherbet, turban,** and **yogurt.**

Turk·men·i·stan (tėrk men′ə stän), NOUN. a country in western Asia.

tur·moil (tėr′moil), NOUN. a condition of confusion and having anxious feelings: *Loss of both electricity and running water in our house has us in a turmoil.*

turn (tėrn),
1 VERB. to face in a new direction: *She turned to the chalkboard and wrote directions for taking the test.*
2 VERB. to give a new direction to: *He turned his flashlight towards the noise in the corner.*
3 VERB. to move or cause to move around as a wheel does; rotate: *The merry-go-round turned as the music played. I turned the key in the lock.*
4 NOUN. a change of direction: *A turn to the left brought him to the park.*
5 NOUN. a time or chance to do something: *It is her turn to bat.*
6 VERB. to take or cause to take a new direction: *The road turns to the north here.*
7 NOUN. a motion like that of a wheel: *At each turn of the screw, it goes in further.*
8 NOUN. a place where there is a change in direction: *Our house is just past the next turn in the road.*
9 VERB. to move part way around; change from one side to the other: *Turn over on your back.*
10 VERB. to change to another condition: *The bitter cold turned his hands blue. He turned pale with fright.*
11 VERB. to move to the other side of; go round; get beyond: *She turned the corner.*
12 NOUN. a change in affairs or conditions: *The patient has taken a turn for the better.*
13 NOUN. a walk, drive, or ride: *We all enjoyed a turn in the park before dinner.*
14 VERB. to pass or get beyond a particular age, time, or amount: *She just turned thirty.*
15 NOUN. time or period of work or action: *We each took a turn at the oars.*
16 VERB. to make or become sick: *The sight of blood turns my stomach.*
❑ VERB **turns, turned, turn·ing.**

in turn, IDIOM. in proper order: *The doctor will see everyone in turn.*

out of turn, IDIOM.
1 not in proper order.
2 without thinking; inappropriately: *He spoke out of turn.*

take turns, IDIOM. to act one after another in proper order: *Take turns on the swings.*

turn down, IDIOM.
1 to fold down: *I turned down the cover on the bed.*
2 to refuse: *They turned down our plan.*
3 to reduce the amount, volume, or brightness of

a	hat	ė	term	ô	order	ch	child		a in about
ā	age	i	it	oi	oil	ng	long		e in taken
ä	far	ī	ice	ou	out	sh	she	ə	i in pencil
â	care	o	hot	u	cup	th	thin		o in lemon
e	let	ō	open	u̇	put	∓H	then		u in circus
ē	equal	ȯ	saw	ü	rule	zh	measure		

T

something by turning a control switch: *Turn down the heat. Turn down the sound on the radio, please.*

turn in, IDIOM.

1 to go to bed: *It's late and I'm going to turn in now.*

2 to give or give back: *to turn in homework, to turn in a library book.*

3 to exchange: *I turned in my old car for a new one.*

turn off, IDIOM. to shut off: *Is the tap turned off or do I hear the water dripping?*

turn on, IDIOM.

1 to start the flow of; put on.

2 to switch something on.

3 to turn around and attack a person or animal that is chasing you.

4 to depend on: *The success of the picnic turns on the weather.*

turn out, IDIOM.

1 to put out; shut off: *Turn out that big spotlight.*

2 to come out; go out: *We turned out for the circus.*

3 to make; produce: *He turns out two novels a year.*

4 to result; end: *How did the game turn out?*

5 to be found or known: *The rumor turned out to be true.*

turn over, IDIOM.

1 to hand over; give: *to turn over a job to someone.*

2 to think carefully about; consider in different ways: *to turn over an idea in the mind.*

turn up, IDIOM.

1 to increase the amount, volume, or brightness of something by turning a control switch: *Turn up the heat. Turn up the sound on the TV, please.*

2 to appear; arrive: *An old friend has turned up.*

Synonym Study

Turn means to go around like a wheel: *When the fan turns, it makes a breeze.*

Revolve means to go in a curve around something or place: *Earth revolves around the sun once every year.*

Rotate means to turn around a central point: *Earth rotates on its axis every day.*

Spin means to turn quickly: *The figure skater spins in a graceful twirl.*

Wheel means to turn quickly and gracefully: *The shortstop wheeled and threw to second base.*

tur·nip (tėr′nəp), NOUN. the large, fleshy, round root of a garden plant, eaten as a vegetable.

turn·out (tėrn′out′), NOUN. a gathering of people: *There was a large turnout at the picnic.*

turn·pike (tėrn′pīk′), NOUN. a highway on which you have to pay a toll; toll road.

turn·stile (tėrn′stīl′), NOUN. a gate with bars that turn, set in an entrance or exit. A turnstile allows one person through at a time.

turn·ta·ble (tėrn′tā′bəl), NOUN. the round, rotating platform of a record player that holds the record being played: *They put a stack of records on the turntable and began to dance.*

tur·pen·tine (tėr′pən tīn), NOUN. a thin oil produced from various trees and used in mixing paints and varnishes.

tur·quoise (tėr′koiz or tėr′kwoiz),

1 NOUN. a clear blue or greenish blue precious stone, used in jewelry.

2 ADJECTIVE or NOUN. greenish blue.

Word Story

Turquoise comes from **Turkey,** because in old times turquoise came from Turkey. It was called "Turkish stone." Large amounts of turquoise were discovered later in parts of America, but the old name stuck.

tur·ret (tėr′it), NOUN.

1 a small tower, often on the corner of a building, such as a castle.

2 any of various low, rotating, armored structures that have guns mounted in them, as on a warship or tank.

tur·tle (tėr′tl), NOUN. a reptile with a hard, rounded shell covering its body. Most turtles can pull their head, legs, and tail into the shell for protection. Turtles live in fresh water, in salt water, and on land. Those living on land are often called tortoises.

There are more than 250 kinds of **turtles.**

tur·tle·neck (tėr′tl nek′), NOUN. a knitted article of clothing with a high, closely fitting collar that is worn turned down over itself.

tusk (tusk), NOUN. a very long, pointed tooth that sticks out of the mouth. Elephants, walruses, and wild boars have tusks.

tus·sle (tus′əl),

1 VERB. to struggle or wrestle; scuffle: *They tussled over the ball.*

2 NOUN. a severe struggle or hard contest: *We thought the game would be easy, but it turned into a long, hard tussle.*

❑ VERB **tus·sles, tus·sled, tus·sling.**

tu·tor (tü′tər),

1 NOUN. a private teacher.

2 VERB. to teach; instruct: *She tutors students in Latin on weekends.*

❑ VERB **tu·tors, tu·tored, tu·tor·ing.**

tu·tu (tü′tü), NOUN. a very short, stiff, full skirt worn by a ballet dancer. ❑ PLURAL **tu·tus.**

tux·e·do (tuk sē′dō), *NOUN.* a formal suit for men. Tuxedos are usually black. ❏ *PLURAL* **tux·e·dos** or **tux·e·does.**

TV, an abbreviation of **television.**

twang (twang),
1 *NOUN.* a sharp ringing sound: *The bow made a twang when I shot the arrow.*
2 *VERB.* to make a sharp ringing sound: *The banjos twanged brightly.*
❏ *VERB* **twangs, twanged, twang·ing.**

tweed (twēd), *NOUN.*
1 a woolen cloth with a rough surface. Tweed usually has two or more colors woven together.
2 **tweeds,** clothes made of tweed.

tweet (twēt),
1 *NOUN* or *INTERJECTION.* the sound made by a bird: *We heard the "tweet, tweet" from a nest in the tree.*
2 *VERB.* to make a tweet or tweets: *Birds tweeted softly.*
❏ *VERB* **tweets, tweet·ed, tweet·ing.**

tweez·ers (twē′zərz), *NOUN PLURAL.* small pincers for pulling out hairs, picking up small objects, and so on: *Pull the splinter from my foot with tweezers.*

twelfth (twelfth),
1 *ADJECTIVE.* next after the 11th.
2 *NOUN.* one of 12 equal parts.

twelve (twelv), *NOUN* or *ADJECTIVE.* one more than 11; 12.

twen·ti·eth (twen′tē ith),
1 *ADJECTIVE.* next after the 19th.
2 *NOUN.* one of 20 equal parts.

twen·ty (twen′tē), *NOUN* or *ADJECTIVE.* two times ten; 20. ❏ *PLURAL* **twen·ties.**

twice (twīs), *ADVERB.*
1 two times: *I have already called you twice.*
2 two times as great, as much, and so on: *You're twice as old as I am.*

twid·dle (twid′l), *VERB.* to flip something back and forth while holding it between your fingers: *twiddle your pencil.* ❏ *VERB* **twid·dles, twid·dled, twid·dling.**

twig (twig), *NOUN.* a very small branch of a tree or bush: *Dry twigs are good for starting fires.*

twi·light (twī′līt′), *NOUN.* the faint light reflected from the sky before sunrise and after sunset.

twin (twin),
1 *NOUN.* one of two human beings born at the same time to the same mother. Twins sometimes look exactly alike.
2 *ADJECTIVE.* being a twin: *Have you met my twin sister?*
3 *NOUN.* one of two things that are exactly alike.
4 *ADJECTIVE.* being one of two things very much or exactly alike: *Twin candlesticks stood on the shelf.*

twine (twīn),
1 *NOUN.* a strong thread or string made of two or more strands twisted together.
2 *VERB.* to twist something together: *We twined holly into wreaths.*

3 *VERB.* to wind: *The vine twines around the tree.*
❏ *VERB* **twines, twined, twin·ing.**

twin·kle (twing′kəl),
1 *VERB.* to shine with quick little flashes of light; sparkle: *The stars twinkled. His eyes twinkled when he laughed.*
2 *NOUN.* a sparkle; gleam; shine: *a twinkle in her eye.*
❏ *VERB* **twin·kles, twin·kled, twin·kling.**

twin·kling (twing′kling), *NOUN.* a very brief period; an instant: *The mouse vanished in a twinkling.*

twirl (twėrl),
1 *VERB.* to turn around rapidly; spin; whirl: *The skater twirled like a top.*
2 *NOUN.* a spin; whirl: *a twirl in a dance.*
❏ *VERB* **twirls, twirled, twirl·ing.**

twist (twist),
1 *VERB.* to turn something with a winding motion: *I twisted the cap off the jar.*
2 *VERB.* to wind together; wind: *This rope is twisted from many threads.*
3 *VERB.* to bend something: *to twist a piece of wire into a loop.* ■ See the Synonym Study at **bend.**
4 *NOUN.* a curve; bend; turn: *The path is full of twists.*
5 *VERB.* to pull or force something out of shape or place with a turning motion: *I fell down the stairs and twisted my ankle.*
6 *NOUN.* the act of twisting: *The toothpaste cap came off with a slight twist.*
❏ *VERB* **twists, twist·ed, twist·ing.**

twist·er (twis′tər), *NOUN.* See **tornado.**

twitch (twich),
1 *VERB.* to move with a quick jerk: *The cat's paw twitched when I touched it.*
2 *NOUN.* a quick movement of some part of the body.
❏ *VERB* **twitch·es, twitched, twitch·ing;** *PLURAL* **twitch·es.**

I love to watch the sky at **twilight.**

a	hat	ė	term	ô	order
ā	age	i	it	oi	oil
ä	far	ī	ice	ou	out
â	care	o	hot	u	cup
e	let	ō	open	ů	put
ē	equal	ò	saw	ü	rule

ch	child
ng	long
sh	she
th	thin
ŦH	then
zh	measure

ə { a in about / e in taken / i in pencil / o in lemon / u in circus }

twit·ter (twit′ər),
1 *NOUN.* a sound made by birds; chirping.
2 *VERB.* to make this sound: *Birds begin to twitter just before sunrise.*
❑ *VERB* **twit·ters, twit·tered, twit·ter·ing.**

two (tü), *NOUN* or *ADJECTIVE.* one more than one; 2.
❑ *PLURAL* **twos.** ■ Other words that sound like this are **to** and **too.**

Have You Heard?

You may have heard the phrase **"put two and two together."** This means that someone can guess at what is going on from the things they already know. However, if they **"put two and two together and get five"** it means that they have reached the wrong conclusion.

TX, an abbreviation of **Texas.**

Word Power   -ty

The suffix **-ty**¹ means "_____ tens." Seven**ty** means seven **tens.**

The suffix **-ty**² means "the quality, condition, or fact of being _____." Safe**ty** means **the condition or quality of being** safe. The form **-ity** is often used instead of **-ty,** as in **timidity.**

ty·coon (tī kün′), *NOUN.* a very rich businessman or businesswoman.

type (tīp),
1 *NOUN.* a kind, sort, or group that is alike in some important way: *three types of groups. She is the type of person I like, kind and friendly.*
2 *NOUN.* a piece of metal or wood having on its upper surface a raised letter, figure, or other character for use in printing.
3 *VERB.* to write with a typewriter or a computer keyboard: *He typed a letter asking for a job.*
❑ *VERB* **types, typed, typ·ing.**

type·writ·er (tīp′rī′tər), *NOUN.* a machine with a keyboard for writing which makes letters, numbers, and other symbols that are similar to printed ones.

Did You Know?

The keyboard of the **typewriter** used to be arranged in alphabetical order. This often caused the keys to jam. In 1872 the **QWERTY** keyboard was developed. It gets its name from the first six keys across the top: Q, W, E, R, T, and Y.

type·writ·ten (tīp′rit′n), *ADJECTIVE.* written with a typewriter or a computer printer: *She received a typewritten letter from her cousin.*

ty·phoid fe·ver (tī′foid fē′vər), an often fatal disease that causes a high fever and soreness and swelling of the intestine. The germs that cause typhoid fever enter the body with impure food or water. People can be protected from typhoid by an injection.

ty·phoon (tī fün′), *NOUN.* a storm with violent wind and, usually, very heavy rain. Typhoons occur in the western Pacific Ocean.

typ·i·cal (tip′ə kəl), *ADJECTIVE.* showing the features or characteristics of a group or kind: *The typical Thanksgiving dinner has turkey and pumpkin pie.*

typ·ist (tī′pist), *NOUN.* someone who types on a typewriter or a computer keyboard.

ty·ran·no·saur (ti ran′ə sôr), *NOUN.* a huge, flesh-eating dinosaur that lived in North America. It walked upright on its hind legs.

ty·ran·no·sau·rus (ti ran′ə sôr′əs), *NOUN.* another form of **tyrannosaur.** ❑ *PLURAL* **ty·ran·no·sau·rus·es.**

tyr·an·ny (tir′ə nē), *NOUN.* government by an absolute ruler: *The colonies escaped from the tyranny of the king.*

typewriter Mark Twain

Mark Twain was the first American writer to give a typewritten manuscript to his publisher. The book, printed in 1883, was Life on the Mississippi. *He paid someone to type it for him.*

ty·rant (tī′rənt), *NOUN.*
1 a cruel or unjust ruler.
2 any person who uses power cruelly or unjustly: *A good coach is never a tyrant.*

unicorn

U or **u** (yü), *NOUN.* the 21st letter of the English alphabet. ❑ *PLURAL* **U's** or **u's.**

U.A.E., an abbreviation of **United Arab Emirates.**

ud·der (ud′ər), *NOUN.* the baglike part that hangs down between the hind legs of a cow, female goat, or other female animal. Milk comes from the udder.

UFO (yü′ef ō′), *NOUN.* an unidentified flying object that people say they have seen in the sky; flying saucer. ❑ *PLURAL* **UFOs** or **UFO's.**

U·gan·da (ü gan′də *or* yü gan′də), *NOUN.* a country in eastern Africa. —**U·gan′dan,** *ADJECTIVE* or *NOUN.*

ugh (ug *or* u), *INTERJECTION.* a word used to express strong dislike, disgust, or horror.

ug·ly (ug′lē), *ADJECTIVE.*
1 very unpleasant to look at: *They have an ugly house.*
2 disagreeable; unpleasant; bad: *What's that ugly smell?*
3 grumpy; cross: *He was in an ugly mood.*
    ❑ *ADJECTIVE* **ug·li·er, ug·li·est.** —**ug′li·ness,** *NOUN.*

uh (u), *INTERJECTION.* a sound expressing hesitation, confusion, and so on.

uh-huh (u hu′), *INTERJECTION.* a sound that means that you are listening or that you agree with what is said.

uh-uh (u′u′), *INTERJECTION.* a sound that means "No."

U.K., an abbreviation of **United Kingdom.**

U·kraine (yü krān′), *NOUN.* a country in eastern Europe. —**U·krain′i·an,** *ADJECTIVE* or *NOUN.*

u·ku·le·le (yü′kə lā′lē), *NOUN.* a small guitar that has four strings.

ul·ti·mate (ul′tə mit), *ADJECTIVE.*
1 last; final: *The ultimate result of driving too fast might be a serious accident.* ■ See the Synonym Study at **last**[1].
2 greatest possible: *To give your life is to pay the ultimate price.*
    —**ul′ti·mate·ly,** *ADJECTIVE.*

Word Power   ultra-

The prefix **ultra-** means "beyond" or "extremely." **Ultrasound is beyond** human hearing. **Ultramodern means extremely** modern.

ul·tra·sound (ul′trə sound′), NOUN. sound waves beyond the limit of human hearing. Ultrasound is used in medicine to form images of parts inside the body: *The ultrasound showed a healthy heart.*

ul·tra·vi·o·let (ul′trə vī′ə lit), ADJECTIVE. of or about invisible rays with wavelengths shorter than those of violet light. Ultraviolet rays cause sunburn.

um·brel·la (um brel′ə), NOUN. something you hold over your head to keep yourself dry when it rains. It is made of cloth or plastic, and can be folded up. ❏ PLURAL **um·brel·las.**

a colorful **umbrella**

ump (ump), NOUN or VERB. (informal) a short form of **umpire.** ❏ VERB **umps, umped, ump·ing.**

um·pire (um′pīr),
1 NOUN. the person who rules on the plays in a game: *The umpire called the player safe.*
2 VERB. to act as umpire.
   ❏ VERB **um·pires, um·pired, um·pir·ing.**

Word Power   un-

The prefix **un-** means "not" or "to do the opposite of." **Unchanged means not** changed. **Unfasten means to do the opposite of** fasten. **Undress means to do the opposite of** dress.

If you look up a word that starts with **un-** and do not find it in the dictionary, you can look up the base word. Then you will know that your word means the opposite.

UN or **U.N.,** an abbreviation of **United Nations.**

un·a·ble (un ā′bəl), ADJECTIVE. not able: *A newborn baby is unable to walk or talk.*

un·ac·cent·ed (un ak′sen tid), ADJECTIVE. not pronounced with force; not accented. In *unanimous* the first, third, and fourth syllables are unaccented.

un·ac·cus·tomed (un′ə kus′təmd), ADJECTIVE.
1 not accustomed: *Polar bears are unaccustomed to hot weather.*
2 not familiar; unusual or strange: *A snowstorm is unaccustomed weather in late spring.*

u·nan·i·mous (yü nan′ə məs), ADJECTIVE.
1 in complete agreement; agreed: *The children were unanimous in their wish to go to the beach.*
2 showing complete agreement: *She was elected by a unanimous vote.*
   —**u·nan′i·mous·ly,** ADVERB.

un·armed (un ärmd′), ADJECTIVE. without weapons: *The police caught the unarmed robber.*

un·a·void·a·ble (un′ə voi′də bəl), ADJECTIVE. not able to be avoided: *The flight had an unavoidable delay.* —**un′a·void′a·bly,** ADVERB.

un·a·ware (un′ə wâr′), ADJECTIVE. not aware; unconscious: *We were unaware of the approaching storm.*

un·bear·a·ble (un bâr′ə bəl), ADJECTIVE. so bad or painful that you cannot stand it: *The pain from a severe toothache is almost unbearable.* —**un·bear′a·bly,** ADVERB.

un·beat·en (un bēt′n), ADJECTIVE. not defeated: *The team was unbeaten all year.*

un·be·com·ing (un′bi kum′ing), ADJECTIVE.
1 not looking very nice; not flattering: *The magazine was full of models in unbecoming clothes.*
2 unsuitable; not proper: *Yelling is unbecoming behavior in school.*

un·be·liev·a·ble (un′bi lē′və bəl), ADJECTIVE. not able to be believed: *He told an unbelievable story.* —**un′be·liev′a·bly,** ADVERB.

un·born (un bôrn′), ADJECTIVE. not yet born: *They had already named their unborn child.*

un·break·a·ble (un brā′kə bəl), ADJECTIVE. not breakable; not easily broken: *Some plastic phonograph records are unbreakable.*

un·bro·ken (un brō′kən), ADJECTIVE.
1 continuous; not interrupted: *He had eight hours of unbroken sleep.*
2 not improved by a higher score; not bettered: *He had an unbroken record in the high jump.*

un·but·ton (un but′n), VERB. to unfasten the button or buttons of something: *He unbuttoned his coat.*
   ❏ VERB **un·but·tons, un·but·toned, un·but·ton·ing.**

un·called-for (un kȯld′fôr′), ADJECTIVE. unnecessary and unkind: *Her classmate made an uncalled-for remark about her low score on the exam.*

un·can·ny (un kan′ē), ADJECTIVE. seeming to have powers or abilities beyond what is normal: *Dogs have an uncanny sense of smell.*

un·cer·tain (un sèrt′n), *ADJECTIVE*.
1 not certain; doubtful: *She was uncertain about how to do several math problems.*
2 likely to change; not be be depended on: *The weather forecast for tomorrow is uncertain.*
   —**un·cer′tain·ly**, *ADVERB*.

un·cer·tain·ty (un sèrt′n tē), *NOUN*.
1 an uncertain condition; doubt: *There was some uncertainty as to our plans.* ■ See the Synonym Study at **doubt.**
2 something uncertain: *When they'll arrive is still an uncertainty.*
   ❑ *PLURAL* **un·cer·tain·ties.**

un·changed (un chānjd′), *ADJECTIVE*. not changed; the same: *They have kept their customs unchanged.*

un·civ·i·lized (un siv′ə līzd), *ADJECTIVE*. not living in a state of civilization: *The cave dwellers were uncivilized people of the Stone Age.*

un·cle (ung′kəl), *NOUN*.
1 a brother of your father or mother.
2 the husband of your aunt.

un·clear (un klir′), *ADJECTIVE*.
1 not clear; confusing; vague: *I gave unclear directions.*
2 uncertain: *We were unclear about the starting time.*
   —**un·clear′ly**, *ADVERB*.

un·com·fort·a·ble (un kum′fər tə bəl), *ADJECTIVE*.
1 not comfortable: *I sat in an uncomfortable chair.*
2 troubled; not relaxed: *I felt uncomfortable when they stared at me.*
   —**un·com′fort·a·bly**, *ADVERB*.

un·con·cerned (un′kən sèrnd′), *ADJECTIVE*. not worried or anxious: *She was quite unconcerned about the cut on her finger.*

un·con·scious (un kon′shəs), *ADJECTIVE*.
1 not able to feel or think; not conscious: *He was knocked unconscious by the blow.*
2 not aware: *Unconscious of the time, she kept on reading and missed her piano lesson.*
   —**un·con′scious·ly**, *ADVERB*. —**un·con′scious·ness**, *NOUN*.

The story was so interesting that she was **unconscious** of the time.

un·con·trol·la·ble (un′kən trō′lə bəl), *ADJECTIVE*. not able to be controlled; beyond your control: *I had an uncontrollable urge to laugh.*
   —**un′con·trol′la·bly**, *ADVERB*.

un·con·trolled (un′kən trōld′), *ADJECTIVE*. not controlled; not restrained.

un·co·op·er·a·tive (un′kō op′ər ə tiv), *ADJECTIVE*. not willing to work or go along with others: *Most of us enjoyed the project, but he was very uncooperative.*

un·couth (un küth′), *ADJECTIVE*. rude; clumsy; crude: *The burglar had uncouth manners.*

un·cov·er (un kuv′ər), *VERB*.
1 to uncover the cover from something: *I uncovered the pot and stirred the stew.*
2 to make something known that has been kept secret: *The reporter uncovered a financial scandal.*
   ❑ *VERB* **un·cov·ers, un·cov·ered, un·cov·er·ing.**

un·de·cid·ed (un′di sī′did), *ADJECTIVE*.
1 not having made up your mind: *I am undecided about which book to buy.*
2 not decided; not settled: *The date for the class picnic is still undecided.*

un·de·ni·a·ble (un′di nī′ə bəl), *ADJECTIVE*. not able to be denied; plain; certain: *The lawyer said that these were undeniable facts.* —**un′de·ni′a·bly**, *ADVERB*.

un·der (un′dər),
1 *ADVERB* or *PREPOSITION*. below; beneath: *The swimmer went under. The book fell under the table.*
2 *PREPOSITION*. below the surface of: *The ancient city had fallen under the sea.*
3 *ADJECTIVE*. lower: *She bit her under lip.*
4 *PREPOSITION*. lower than; lower down than; not so high as: *There was a tiny bruise just under his eye.*
5 *PREPOSITION*. less than: *The coat will cost under twenty dollars.*
6 *PREPOSITION*. according to; because of: *The class learned a great deal under her teaching. The private was acting under orders.*
7 *PREPOSITION*. during the rule or time of: *England under Queen Victoria.*
8 *PREPOSITION*. included in a particular group, category, or class: *In the library, books on the Greek gods are listed under mythology.*

Word Power   under-

The prefix **under-** means "below" or "beneath." It also means "not enough." Underline means to draw a line **below.** Underground means **beneath** the ground. Underfed means **not** fed **enough.**

a	hat	ė	term	ô	order	ch	child	⌠a in about
ā	age	i	it	oi	oil	ng	long	⎪e in taken
ä	far	ī	ice	ou	out	sh	she	ə⎨i in pencil
â	care	o	hot	u	cup	th	thin	⎪o in lemon
e	let	ō	open	ů	put	ᴛʜ	then	⌡u in circus
ē	equal	ȯ	saw	ü	rule	zh	measure	

u

un·der·arm (un′dər ärm′),
1 ADJECTIVE. situated or placed under the arm; found in or near the armpit: *I tested an underarm deodorant.*
2 NOUN. See **armpit**.

un·der·brush (un′dər brush′), NOUN. bushes, shrubs, and small trees growing under large trees in woods or forests; undergrowth.

un·der·clothes (un′dər klōz′), NOUN PLURAL. See **underwear**.

un·der·cur·rent (un′dər kėr′ənt), NOUN. a current below the surface of a body of water.

un·der·de·vel·oped (un′dər di vel′əpt), ADJECTIVE. not normally developed: *The sickly dog had underdeveloped muscles.*

un·der·dog (un′dər dòg′), NOUN. a person or team that people think is apt to lose a game, contest, election, and so on.

un·der·fed (un′dər fed′), ADJECTIVE. fed too little; not well nourished: *The stray cat looked underfed.*

un·der·foot (un′dər fùt′), ADVERB.
1 under your feet; on the ground; underneath: *The leaves crunched underfoot.*
2 in the way: *She complained that the cat was always underfoot.*

un·der·gar·ment (un′dər gär′mənt), NOUN. a piece of underwear.

un·der·go (un′dər gō′), VERB. to go through a difficult or interesting experience; to undergo hardship: *You will undergo many changes as you become a teenager.* ❑ VERB **un·der·goes, un·der·went, un·der·gone** (un′dər gon′), **un·der·go·ing.**

un·der·ground (un′dər ground′ for adverb; un′dər ground′ for adjective and noun),
1 ADVERB. beneath the surface of the ground: *Most miners work underground.*
2 ADVERB. into hiding: *The thief went underground after the robbery.*
3 ADJECTIVE. secret: *The revolt against the government was an underground plot.*
4 NOUN. a secret organization working against an unpopular government, especially during military occupation: *The French underground protected many American fliers shot down over France during World War II.*

Underground Railroad, a system by which people secretly helped fugitives from slavery escape to the free states or Canada before the Civil War.

un·der·growth (un′dər grōth′), NOUN. See **underbrush**.

un·der·hand (un′dər hand′),
1 ADJECTIVE. See **underhanded**.
2 ADJECTIVE or ADVERB. with the hand below the shoulder: *He threw an underhand pitch. I learned to pitch underhand.*

un·der·hand·ed (un′dər han′did), ADJECTIVE. secret; sly; not open or honest: *That was an underhanded trick!* —**un′der·hand′ed·ly,** ADVERB.

un·der·line (un′dər lin′), VERB. to draw a line under: *In writing, we underline titles of books.* ❑ VERB **un·der·lines, un·der·lined, un·der·lin·ing.**

un·der·mine (un′dər min′), VERB.
1 to weaken something by secret or unfair means: *Nasty rumors undermined his reputation.*
2 to weaken or destroy something gradually: *Many severe colds had undermined her health.*
3 to dig under or wear away the foundations of something: *The waves had undermined the cliff.* ❑ VERB **un·der·mines, un·der·mined, un·der·min·ing.**

un·der·neath (un′dər nēth′), PREPOSITION or ADVERB. beneath; below; under: *We can sit underneath this tree. Someone was pushing underneath.*

un·der·nour·ished (un′dər nėr′isht), ADJECTIVE. unhealthy because of a lack of good food: *The advertisement showed an undernourished child.*

un·der·pants (un′dər pants′), NOUN PLURAL. shorts or panties worn as underwear.

un·der·pass (un′dər pas′), NOUN. a road or path that runs under railroad tracks or under another road. ❑ PLURAL **un·der·pass·es.**

un·der·sea (un′dər sē′), ADJECTIVE. being, working, or used beneath the surface of the sea: *an undersea cable, undersea exploration.*

Underground Railroad
Harriet Tubman

Harriet Tubman was the American leader of the Underground Railroad. She made 19 trips to help others to freedom. Neither she nor anyone with her was ever caught.

un·der·shirt (un′dər shėrt′), NOUN. underwear worn next to the skin under a shirt.

un·der·side (un′dər sīd′), NOUN. the bottom side of something: *The underside of the stone was covered with ants. They painted the underside of the table.*

un·der·stand (un′dər stand′), VERB.
1 to get the meaning of something: *Now I understand the teacher's question.*
2 to know something well: *I understand the rules of basketball.*
3 to know about something; have information: *I understand that she is moving to another town.*
4 to know how and why someone feels the way he or she does: *When I have a problem, I know my friend will understand.*
❏ VERB **un·der·stands, un·der·stood, un·der·stand·ing. –un′der·stand′a·ble,** ADJECTIVE.

un·der·stand·ing (un′dər stan′ding),
1 NOUN. the act or fact of knowing something; knowledge: *She has a clear understanding of the problem.*
2 NOUN. intelligence; the ability to learn and know things: *That scholar is a man of understanding.*
3 ADJECTIVE. able to understand and have sympathy for other people's problems: *The teacher made an understanding reply.*
4 NOUN. agreement: *You and I must come to an understanding.*

un·der·stood (un′dər stud′), VERB.
1 the past tense of **understand**: *I understood what she said.*
2 the past participle of **understand**: *Have you understood today's lesson?*

un·der·take (un′dər tāk′), VERB.
1 to agree to do; take upon yourself: *I will undertake the feeding of your dogs while you are away.*
2 to try; attempt: *The class decided to undertake finding a solution to the problem.*
❏ VERB **un·der·takes, un·der·took, un·der·tak·en** (un′dər tā′kən), **un·der·tak·ing.**

un·der·tak·er (un′dər tā′kər), NOUN. someone who prepares the dead for burial and takes charge of funerals.

un·der·tak·ing (un′dər tā′king), NOUN. something undertaken; task; enterprise: *Starting your own business is a large undertaking.* ■ See the Synonym Study at **plan.**

un·der·took (un′dər tuk′), VERB. the past tense of **undertake**: *He failed because he undertook more than he could do.*

un·der·tow (un′dər tō′), NOUN. a strong current below the surface of the water, moving in a direction different from that of the surface current. An undertow is very dangerous to swimmers.

un·der·wa·ter (un′dər wȯ′tər),
1 ADJECTIVE or ADVERB. below the surface of the water: *an underwater current, to swim underwater.*
2 ADJECTIVE. made for use under the water: *A submarine is an underwater boat.*

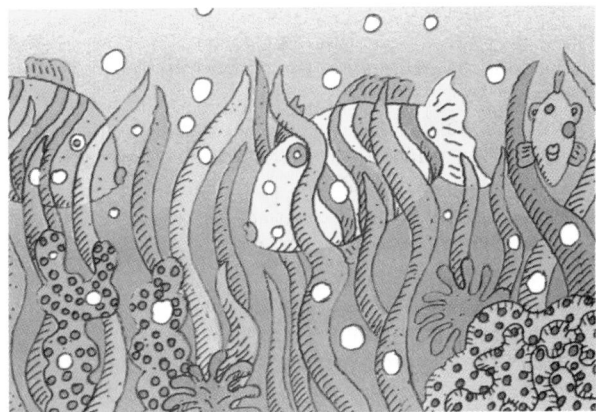
underwater

un·der·wear (un′dər wâr′), NOUN. clothing worn under your outer clothes, especially next to the skin.

un·der·weight (un′dər wāt′), ADJECTIVE. having too little weight; below the normal or required weight.

un·der·went (un′dər went′), VERB. the past tense of **undergo**: *Transportation underwent a great change with the development of the car.*

un·do (un dü′), VERB.
1 to unfasten or untie something: *Please undo the package.*
2 to do away with the effects of something: *Workers repair the road each year, but heavy winter storms undo their work.*
❏ VERB **un·does** (un duz′), **un·did** (un did′), **un·done, un·do·ing.**

un·done (un dun′),
1 ADJECTIVE. not done; not finished: *The scheduled work is still undone.*
2 ADJECTIVE. untied; unfastened: *He noticed his undone shoelaces.*
3 VERB. the past participle of **undo**: *He has undone his boots.*

un·doubt·ed·ly (un dou′tid lē), ADVERB. beyond doubt; certainly: *He is undoubtedly the best speller in class.*

un·dress (un dres′), VERB. to take your clothes off.
❏ VERB **un·dress·es, un·dressed, un·dress·ing.**

un·dy·ing (un di′ing), ADJECTIVE. lasting forever; without ending; not dying: *The actor wanted undying fame.*

a	hat	ė	term	ô	order	ch	child		a in about
ā	age	i	it	oi	oil	ng	long		e in taken
ä	far	ī	ice	ou	out	sh	she	ə {	i in pencil
â	care	o	hot	u	cup	th	thin		o in lemon
e	let	ō	open	ù	put	ŦH	then		u in circus
ē	equal	ȯ	saw	ü	rule	zh	measure		

un·earth (un ėrth′), VERB.
1 to dig up something that was buried: *The scientists unearthed a buried city.*
2 to find out the truth about something: *The police unearthed the evidence.*
 ❏ VERB **un·earths, un·earthed, un·earth·ing.**

un·eas·y (un ē′zē), ADJECTIVE.
1 worried or anxious about something: *They became uneasy when their son didn't come home for dinner.*
2 not relaxed: *The speaker seemed nervous and uneasy.*
 ❏ ADJECTIVE **un·eas·i·er, un·eas·i·est. –un·eas′i·ly,** ADVERB. **–un·eas′i·ness,** NOUN.

un·ed·u·cat·ed (un ej′ə kā′tid), ADJECTIVE. not educated; not taught or trained.

un·em·ployed (un′em ploid′),
1 ADJECTIVE. not having a job; having no work: *Our neighbor is currently unemployed.*
2 NOUN. **the unemployed,** people out of work: *Some of the unemployed sought government aid.*

un·em·ploy·ment (un′em ploi′mənt), NOUN.
1 lack of employment; condition of being out of work.
2 number or percentage of workers that are unemployed: *Unemployment was up last month.*

un·e·qual (un ē′kwəl), ADJECTIVE.
1 not fair; one-sided: *The huge dog racing the tiny mouse was an unequal contest.*
2 not the same in amount, size, number, or value: *unequal sums of money, unequal portions.*
3 not enough; not adequate: *Their strength was unequal to the task.*
 –un·e′qual·ly, ADVERB.

un·e·ven (un ē′vən), ADJECTIVE.
1 not level: *Our playhouse was built uneven ground.*
 ■ See the Synonym Study at **rough.**
2 not always the same or regular; not consistent: *Her work is of uneven quality.*
3 leaving a remainder of 1 when divided by 2; odd: *1, 3, 5, 7, and 9 are uneven numbers.*
 –un·e′ven·ly, ADVERB. **–un·e′ven·ness,** NOUN.

un·ex·pect·ed (un′ek spek′tid), ADJECTIVE. not expected: *We had an unexpected, surprise visit from our grandmother last week.*
 –un′ex·pect′ed·ly, ADVERB.

un·fair (un fâr′), ADJECTIVE. not fair: *It was unfair of you to trick him.* **–un·fair′ly,** ADVERB. **–un·fair′ness,** NOUN.

un·faith·ful (un fāth′fəl), ADJECTIVE. not faithful; not true to duty or your promises; disloyal.
 –un·faith′ful·ly, ADVERB. **–un·faith′ful·ness,** NOUN.

un·fa·mil·iar (un′fə mil′yər), ADJECTIVE.
1 not well-known; unusual; strange: *That face is unfamiliar to me.*
2 not knowing about something: *He is unfamiliar with the Greek language.*

un·fas·ten (un fas′n), VERB. to undo or untie something: *Don't unfasten your seat belt yet.*
 ❏ VERB **un·fas·tens, un·fas·tened, un·fas·ten·ing.**

un·fin·ished (un fin′isht), ADJECTIVE.
1 not finished; not complete: *I can't go out if my homework is unfinished.*
2 not polished or painted; rough: *That store sells unfinished furniture.*

un·fit (un fit′), ADJECTIVE.
1 not fit; not suitable: *This moldy bread is unfit to eat.*
2 not healthy and strong; in poor physical condition: *He was unfit for hard work.*

un·fold (un fōld′), VERB.
1 to spread out something that is folded up: *to unfold a napkin, to unfold your arms.*
2 to tell or explain something to someone else: *The minstrel unfolded the plot of the story.*
 ❏ VERB **un·folds, un·fold·ed, un·fold·ing.**

The dragon **unfolded** its wings before leaping into the air.

un·for·get·ta·ble (un′fər get′ə bəl), ADJECTIVE. so good or so wonderful that you cannot forget it: *Winning the race was an unforgettable experience.*

un·for·tu·nate (un fôr′chə nit), ADJECTIVE. not lucky; having bad luck: *She had an unfortunate accident.*
 –un·for′tu·nate·ly, ADVERB.

un·friend·ly (un frend′lē), ADJECTIVE. not friendly: *The unfriendly dog growled at me.* ❏ ADJECTIVE **un·friend·li·er, un·friend·li·est.**
 –un·friend′li·ness, NOUN.

un·furl (un fėrl′), VERB. to spread out; shake out; unfold: *Unfurl the sail. The flag unfurled.* ❏ VERB **un·furls, un·furled, un·furl·ing.**

un·hap·py (un hap′ē), ADJECTIVE.
1 not happy; sad; depressed: *He seemed to be a very unhappy person.*
2 not pleased with the way something is: *A lot of people were unhappy with the new bus schedule.*
 ❏ ADJECTIVE **un·hap·pi·er, un·hap·pi·est.**
 –un·hap′pi·ly, ADVERB. **–un·hap′pi·ness,** NOUN.

un·health·y (un hel′thē), ADJECTIVE.
1 bad for your health; not healthful: *Smoking is an unhealthy habit.*
2 not having good health; not well: *The unhealthy child ate only candy.*
❏ ADJECTIVE **un·health·i·er, un·health·i·est.**

un·heard-of (un hèrd′uv′), ADJECTIVE.
1 never heard of; unknown; not even imagined: *The electric light was unheard-of 200 years ago.*
2 not known before: *The star was paid an unheard-of sum for making the film.*

un·hitch (un hich′), VERB. to unfasten something: *We unhitched the trailer from our pickup truck.*
❏ VERB **un·hitch·es, un·hitched, un·hitch·ing.**

un·hook (un hùk′), VERB. to undo something by unfastening a hook or hooks. ❏ VERB **un·hooks, un·hooked, un·hook·ing.**

un·hurt (un hèrt′), ADJECTIVE. not hurt; not harmed: *In spite of his fall, he was unhurt.*

U·NI·CEF (yü′nə sef), NOUN. United Nations Children's Fund.

u·ni·corn (yü′nə kôrn), NOUN. (in stories) an imaginary animal like a horse with a single, long horn in its forehead.

a **unicorn** on a tapestry

u·ni·cy·cle (yü′nə sī′kəl), NOUN. a one-wheeled vehicle pedaled like a bicycle.

un·i·den·ti·fied (un′ī den′tə fid), ADJECTIVE. not identified; not recognized.

u·ni·form (yü′nə fôrm),
1 NOUN. the clothes worn by the members of a group that is on duty. Soldiers, police officers, and nurses wear uniforms so that they may be easily recognized.
2 ADJECTIVE. always the same; not changing: *The earth turns at a uniform rate.*
3 ADJECTIVE. all alike; not different: *All the bricks have a uniform size.*

It's hard to keep your balance on a **unicycle.**

u·ni·fy (yü′nə fi), VERB. to combine several things into one: *Several small states were unified into one nation.* ❏ VERB **u·ni·fies, u·ni·fied, u·ni·fy·ing.**

un·im·por·tant (un′im pôrt′nt), ADJECTIVE. not important: *He left out the unimportant details.*

un·in·hab·it·ed (un′in hab′ə tid), ADJECTIVE. not lived in; without inhabitants: *uninhabited land.*

un·in·ter·est·ed (un in′tər ə stid), ADJECTIVE. not interested; paying no attention: *She seemed uninterested in the play.*

un·in·ter·est·ing (un in′tər ə sting), ADJECTIVE. not interesting; boring: *He took the uninteresting book back to the library.* ■ See the Synonym Study at **dull.**

un·ion (yü′nyən), NOUN.
1 a group of workers joined together to protect and and promote their interests; labor union.
2 **the Union,** the United States of America.
3 a joining of two or more people or things into one: *The United States was formed by the union of thirteen former British colonies.*
4 those states that supported the federal government of the United States during the Civil War.

Word Story

Union comes from a Latin word meaning "one." **Onion** probably comes from the same word. Many parts or people together form a union, and many layers together form an onion.

Union of Soviet Socialist Republics. See **Soviet Union.**

u·nique (yü nēk′), ADJECTIVE.
1 being the only one of its kind: *I found a unique specimen of rock. The astronaut described his experience as unique.*
2 very uncommon or unusual; rare; remarkable: *His style of singing is unique.*
—**u·nique′ly,** ADVERB. —**u·nique′ness,** NOUN.

u·ni·sex (yü′nə seks′), ADJECTIVE. suitable for use by either sex: *unisex clothing, a unisex haircut.*

u·ni·son (yü′nə sən), NOUN. **in unison,** together; as one: *The choir sang in unison.*

u·nit (yü′nit), NOUN.
1 any group of things or people considered as one: *The family is a social unit.*
2 a standard quantity or amount by which things are weighed, measured, and so on: *A foot is a unit of length; a pound is a unit of weight.*
3 a special part, division, or section: *We have read some wonderful stories in this unit of our reading class.*

u·nite (yü nīt′), VERB. to join together; make or become one: *Several firms were united to form one company.* ❏ VERB **u·nites, u·nit·ed, u·nit·ing.** ■ See the Synonym Study at **join.**

a	hat	ė	term	ô	order	ch	child		a	in about
ā	age	i	it	oi	oil	ng	long		e	in taken
ä	far	ī	ice	ou	out	sh	she	ə	i	in pencil
â	care	o	hot	u	cup	th	thin		o	in lemon
e	let	ō	open	ù	put	ᴛʜ	then		u	in circus
ē	equal	ò	saw	ü	rule	zh	measure			

U

U·nit·ed Ar·ab Em·ir·ates (yü ni′tid ar′əb em′ər its), a country in eastern Arabia.

United Kingdom, a country in northwestern Europe made up of Great Britain and Northern Ireland.

United Nations, a worldwide organization established in 1945 to promote world peace and economic and social welfare. Its headquarters is in New York City.

United States, a country in North America, extending from the Atlantic to the Pacific and from the Gulf of Mexico to Canada. Alaska, the 49th state, lies northwest of Canada. Hawaii, the 50th state, is an island group in the Pacific.

United States of America, the United States.

u·ni·ty (yü′nə tē), NOUN. the condition of being in agreement: *The group's unity of purpose helped them get results.*

u·ni·ver·sal (yü′nə vėr′səl), ADJECTIVE.
1 of or belonging to everyone; concerning all: *Food is a universal need.*
2 existing everywhere: *The law of gravity is universal.* **–u′ni·ver′sal·ly,** ADVERB.

u·ni·verse (yü′nə vėrs′), NOUN. everything there is, including all space and matter.

u·ni·ver·si·ty (yü′nə vėr′sə tē), NOUN. a school that students may attend after finishing high school. Universities usually have schools of law, medicine, teaching, and business, as well as colleges for general instruction. ❑ PLURAL **u·ni·ver·si·ties.**

un·just (un just′), ADJECTIVE. not fair: *Punishing someone for no reason would be unjust.* **–un·just′ly,** ADVERB.

un·kind (un kīnd′), ADJECTIVE. harsh; cruel: *I didn't like their unkind remarks about my friend.* **–un·kind′ly,** ADVERB. **–un·kind′ness,** NOUN.

un·known (un nōn′),
1 ADJECTIVE. not familiar; strange; unexplored: *He dove into the dark, unknown depths of the sea.*
2 NOUN. someone or something that is unknown: *The diver descended into the unknown.*

un·law·ful (un lò′fəl), ADJECTIVE. against the law; illegal: *Littering is unlawful.* **–un·law′ful·ly,** ADVERB.

un·lead·ed (un led′id), ADJECTIVE. without the addition of a lead compound that reduces engine noise: *My car uses unleaded gasoline.*

un·less (un les′), CONJUNCTION. except if: *I won't go unless you do.*

un·like (un līk′),
1 ADJECTIVE. not like; different: *The two problems are quite unlike.*
2 PREPOSITION. different from: *One kitten was acting unlike the others.*
3 PREPOSITION. not typical of someone: *Giving up easily is so unlike her.*

un·like·ly (un līk′lē), ADJECTIVE.
1 not likely to happen: *She is unlikely to win the race.*

2 not likely to succeed: *Planning a Ferris wheel in the playground is an unlikely undertaking.* ❑ ADJECTIVE **un·like·li·er, un·like·li·est.**

un·load (un lōd′), VERB.
1 to take a load from: *We unloaded the car.*
2 to remove bullets from a gun or film from a camera. ❑ VERB **un·loads, un·load·ed, un·load·ing.**

un·lock (un lok′), VERB.
1 to open the lock of; open anything firmly closed: *I unlocked the door.*
2 to disclose; reveal: *Science has unlocked the mystery of the atom.* ❑ VERB **un·locks, un·locked, un·lock·ing.**

un·luck·y (un luk′ē), ADJECTIVE. not lucky; unfortunate; bringing bad luck. ❑ ADJECTIVE **un·luck·i·er, un·luck·i·est.**

un·manned (un mand′), ADJECTIVE. without a crew: *They planned an unmanned space flight to Mars.*

un·mis·tak·a·ble (un′mə stā′kə bəl), ADJECTIVE. not able to be mistaken or misunderstood; clear; plain: *The artist's talent was unmistakable.* **–un′mis·tak′a·bly,** ADVERB.

un·moved (un müvd′), ADJECTIVE.
1 not moved; firm: *They tried to convince me, but I was unmoved by their arguments.*
2 not disturbed; indifferent: *Their sad tale left me unmoved.*

un·nat·ur·al (un nach′ər əl), ADJECTIVE. not normal: *It is unnatural for someone to have no friends at all.* **–un·nat′ur·al·ly,** ADVERB.

Her hair looked very **unnatural.**

un·nec·es·sar·y (un nes′ə ser′ē), ADJECTIVE. not necessary; not needed: *Our coats were unnecessary on such a warm day.* **–un·nec′es·sar′i·ly,** ADVERB.

un·no·ticed (un nō′tist), ADJECTIVE. not noticed by anyone; not receiving any attention: *I slipped into the room unnoticed.*

un·oc·cu·pied (un ok′yə pīd), ADJECTIVE.
1 empty: *The driver pulled her car into the unoccupied parking space.*

2 not busy; idle: *I enjoy being busy; I don't like being unoccupied.*

un·pack (un pak′), *VERB.* to take things out that were packed in a box, trunk, or other container: *He unpacked his clothes.* ❑ *VERB* **un·packs, un·packed, un·pack·ing.**

un·paid (un pād′), *ADJECTIVE.* not paid: *Their unpaid bills amounted to $2,000.*

un·pleas·ant (un plez′nt), *ADJECTIVE.* not pleasant; disagreeable: *Rotten eggs is an unpleasant odor.* **—un·pleas′ant·ly,** *ADVERB.*

un·plug (un plug′), *VERB.*
1 to remove the plug or stopper from something.
2 to disconnect by removing the plug from an electric outlet.
❑ *VERB* **un·plugs, un·plugged, un·plug·ging.**

un·pre·dict·a·ble (un′pri dik′tə bəl), *ADJECTIVE.* not able to be described or depended on; uncertain: *unpredictable weather, an unpredictable election.*

un·pre·pared (un′pri pârd′), *ADJECTIVE.* not ready: *I was unprepared to answer.* **—un′pre·par′ed·ness,** *NOUN.*

un·ques·tion·a·bly (un kwes′chə nə blē), *ADVERB.* beyond dispute or doubt; certainly: *She is unquestionably the best player on the team.*

un·rav·el (un rav′əl), *VERB.*
1 to separate the threads of; pull apart: *My sweater is unraveling. The cat unraveled the ball of yarn.*
2 to bring out of a tangled or confusing state: *The detective unraveled the mystery.*
❑ *VERB* **un·rav·els, un·rav·eled, un·rav·el·ing.**

Our kitten seems to love **unraveling** Mom's yarn.

un·re·al (un rē′əl), *ADJECTIVE.*
1 not real; imaginary: *In the morning, our fears of last night's storm seemed unreal.*
2 so strange as to be incredible: *He had an unreal, last-minute victory.*

un·rea·son·a·ble (un rē′zn ə bəl), *ADJECTIVE.*
1 not according to reason: *He had an unreasonable attitude about being on time.*
2 too high: *They paid an unreasonable price for the sofa.* **—un·rea′son·a·bly,** *ADVERB.*

un·re·li·a·ble (un′ri lī′ə bəl), *ADJECTIVE.* not able to be depended on: *Old reference books are unreliable.*

un·rest (un rest′), *NOUN.* anger and dissatisfaction about something: *The government's injustices caused political unrest among the people.*

un·roll (un rōl′), *VERB.* to open or become open or spread out flat: *I unrolled my sleeping bag.* ❑ *VERB* **un·rolls, un·rolled, un·roll·ing.**

un·rul·y (un rü′lē), *ADJECTIVE.* hard to rule or control: *The unruly mob stormed the palace.* ■ See the Synonym Study at **wild.** ❑ *ADJECTIVE* **un·rul·i·er, un·rul·i·est.**

un·sat·is·fac·tor·y (un′sat i sfak′tər ē), *ADJECTIVE.* not good enough to meet a need; not satisfactory: *Your work is unsatisfactory because there are too many mistakes.* ■ See the Synonym Study at **bad.**

un·scram·ble (un skram′bəl), *VERB.* to put things back in order: *After the wind died down, I unscrambled the papers that had been scattered.* ❑ *VERB* **un·scram·bles, un·scram·bled, un·scram·bling.**

un·screw (un skrü′), *VERB.* to loosen or take off by turning: *to unscrew a top from a jar, to unscrew an electric light bulb.* ❑ *VERB* **un·screws, un·screwed, un·screw·ing.**

un·seen (un sēn′), *ADJECTIVE.* not seen: unnoticed: *An unseen error caused the plane crash.*

un·self·ish (un sel′fish), *ADJECTIVE.* caring about the needs of other people; generous: *She is an unselfish person.* **—un·self′ish·ness,** *NOUN.*

un·set·tled (un set′ld), *ADJECTIVE.*
1 liable to change; uncertain: *The weather is unsettled.*
2 not inhabited: *Some parts of the world are still unsettled.*

un·sheathe (un shēᴛʜ′), *VERB.* to draw a sword, knife, or the like from a sheath. ❑ *VERB* **un·sheathes, un·sheathed, un·sheath·ing.**

un·sight·ly (un sīt′lē), *ADJECTIVE.* ugly or unpleasant to look at: *The room was an unsightly mess.*

un·skilled (un skild′), *ADJECTIVE.*
1 not skilled; not trained; not expert: *unskilled workers, an unskilled athlete.*
2 not requiring special skills or training: *He hired unskilled labor to dig the ditch.*

un·sound (un sound′), *ADJECTIVE.*
1 not based on truth or fact: *He lost the debate because of his unsound arguments.*
2 not sound; not in good condition: *Don't use those unsound stairs!*

a	hat	ė	term	ô	order	ch	child	ə	a in about
ā	age	i	it	oi	oil	ng	long		e in taken
ä	far	ī	ice	ou	out	sh	she		i in pencil
â	care	o	hot	u	cup	th	thin		o in lemon
e	let	ō	open	ů	put	ᴛʜ	then		u in circus
ē	equal	ò	saw	ü	rule	zh	measure		

U

un·speak·a·ble (un spē′kə bəl), ADJECTIVE.
1 extremely bad: *Murder is an unspeakable crime.*
2 hard to express in words: *The reunited family felt unspeakable joy.*
—**un·speak′a·bly**, ADVERB.

un·sta·ble (un stā′bəl), ADJECTIVE.
1 unsteady; shaky: *That stool with a cracked leg is very unstable.*
2 likely to change or be changed: *The country had an unstable government.*

un·stead·y (un sted′ē), ADJECTIVE. not steady; shaky: *an unsteady voice, an unsteady flame.* ❑ ADJECTIVE **un·stead·i·er, un·stead·i·est.** —**un·stead′i·ly**, ADVERB.

un·stressed (un strest′), ADJECTIVE. said or spoken without stress or accent. In *upward,* the second syllable is unstressed.

un·suc·cess·ful (un′sək ses′fəl), ADJECTIVE. not having the success that you hoped and planned for: *My attempts at juggling were unsuccessful.* —**un′suc·cess′ful·ly**, ADVERB.

un·suit·a·ble (un sü′tə bəl), ADJECTIVE. not right for the occasion or purpose: *That was an unsuitable remark; you should apologize.*

un·tan·gle (un tang′gəl), VERB. to take the knots and twists out of: *Combing will untangle your hair.* ❑ VERB **un·tan·gles, un·tan·gled, un·tan·gling.**

un·think·a·ble (un thing′kə bəl), ADJECTIVE. too awful to be imagined: *The hurricane was an unthinkable disaster.*

un·ti·dy (un tī′dē), ADJECTIVE. not neat; messy: *I have an untidy room.* ❑ ADJECTIVE **un·ti·di·er, un·ti·di·est.** —**un·ti′di·ness**, NOUN.

un·tie (un tī′), VERB. to loosen or unfasten something: *Help me untie this knot. She was untying bundles.* ❑ VERB **un·ties, un·tied, un·ty·ing.**

un·til (un til′),
1 PREPOSITION. up to the time of: *It was cold from November until April.*
2 CONJUNCTION. up to the time when: *We waited until the sun had set.*
3 PREPOSITION. before: *She did not leave until morning.*
4 CONJUNCTION. to the degree or place that: *I worked until I was too tired to do more.*

un·to (un′tü), PREPOSITION. (formerly) **Unto** was used to show action toward someone: *Do unto others as you would have them do unto you.*

un·told (un tōld′), ADJECTIVE.
1 very great: *Wars do untold damage.*
2 too many or too much to be counted: *There are untold stars in the sky.*
3 not told; not revealed: *The king had untold secrets.*

un·true (un trü′), ADJECTIVE. not true to the facts; false: *The story was untrue.*

un·truth·ful (un trüth′fəl), ADJECTIVE. not telling the truth: *An untruthful person tells lies. An untruthful story is a lie.* —**un·truth′ful·ness**, NOUN.

un·used (un yüzd′), ADJECTIVE.
1 not in use; not being used: *We have an unused room in the basement.*
2 never before used: *Get some unused drinking cups from the cabinet.*

unused to (un yüst′ tü), IDIOM. not familiar with something: *The actor's hands were unused to labor.*

un·u·su·al (un yü′zhü əl), ADJECTIVE. not in common use; uncommon; rare: *an unusual adventure, an unusual color.* —**un·u′su·al·ly**, ADVERB.

un·veil (un vāl′), VERB. to remove a veil from; uncover; disclose; reveal: *She unveiled her face. The detective unveiled the criminal's true identity.* ❑ VERB **un·veils, un·veiled, un·veil·ing.**

un·wel·come (un wel′kəm), ADJECTIVE. not welcome; not wanted: *The bees were unwelcome guests at our picnic.*

un·will·ing (un wil′ing), ADJECTIVE. not willing to do something: *They were unwilling to help.* —**un·will′ing·ly**, ADVERB. —**un·will′ing·ness**, NOUN.

un·wind (un wīnd′), VERB.
1 to relax: *After working all day, I needed to unwind.*
2 to unroll or become unrolled: *I had unwound the string from my finger.*
❑ VERB **un·winds, un·wound, un·wind·ing.**

un·wise (un wīz′), ADJECTIVE. not wise; not showing good judgment; foolish: *It is unwise to delay going to the doctor if you are sick.* —**un·wise′ly**, ADVERB.

un·wit·ting·ly (un wit′ing lē), ADVERB. unconsciously; not intentionally.

un·wound (un wound′), VERB.
1 the past tense of **unwind**: *I unwound the string.*
2 the past participle of **unwind**: *She had unwound the bandage before the nurse arrived.*

un·zip (un zip′), VERB. to unfasten a zipper or something held by a zipper. ❑ VERB **un·zips, un·zipped, un·zip·ping.**

up (up),
1 ADVERB. to a higher place or condition; upwards: *Stand up! Prices have gone up.*
2 ADVERB or ADJECTIVE. in a higher place or condition: *We live up in a skyscraper. The sun is up.*
3 PREPOSITION. to a higher place on; at a higher place in: *The cat ran up the tree.*
4 PREPOSITION. along: *They walked up the street.*
5 PREPOSITION. to, near, or at the upper part of: *We sailed up the river.*
6 ADJECTIVE or ADVERB. out of bed: *The children were up at dawn. Please get up before you are late.*
7 ADVERB. completely; entirely: *The house burned up.*
8 ADJECTIVE. at an end; over: *His time is up now.*
9 ADVERB. to or in an even position; not behind: *I tried to catch up in the race. Keep up with the times.*
10 ADJECTIVE. in working condition: *My computer is up after being down all morning.*
11 ADJECTIVE. at bat in baseball: *Who's up first next inning?*

12 *ADJECTIVE.* offered or proposed: *Our car is up for sale.*
up to, *IDIOM.*
1 doing; about to do: *She is up to some mischief.*
2 equal to; capable of doing: *Do you feel up to going out so soon after being sick?*
ups and downs, *IDIOM.* good and bad times.
❑ *PLURAL* **ups.**

Have You Heard?

You may have heard someone say that something is **"on the up and up."** This means that it is honest or legal.

up·bring·ing (up′bring′ing), *NOUN.* the care and training given to a child while he or she is growing up.

up·date (up′dāt′ *or* up dāt′ *for verb;* up′dāt′ *for noun*),
1 *VERB.* to bring something or someone up to date.
2 *NOUN.* the newest, most up-to-date information or data: *a news update, a computer update.*
❑ *VERB* **up·dates, up·dat·ed, up·dat·ing.**

up·heav·al (up hē′vəl), *NOUN.*
1 a sudden change in a situation that causes many problems: *The sale of the company resulted in an upheaval in the plans of many employees.*
2 the action of heaving up, especially of part of the earth's crust.

up·held (up held′), *VERB.*
1 the past tense of **uphold:** *The higher court upheld the lower court's decision.*
2 the past participle of **uphold:** *The judge's decision was upheld by the jury.*

up·hill (up′hil′ *for adjective;* up′hil′ *for adverb*),
1 *ADJECTIVE.* up the slope of a hill; upward: *We had an uphill climb.*
2 *ADVERB.* upward: *We walked a mile uphill.*
3 *ADJECTIVE.* difficult: *Winning this election will be an uphill fight.*

up·hold (up hōld′),
VERB. to give support to something: *The principal upheld the teacher's decision.*
❑ *VERB* **up·holds, up·held, up·hold·ing.**

up·hol·ster
(up hōl′stər), *VERB.*
to provide chairs or sofas with coverings, springs, or stuffing. ❑ *VERB* **up·hol·sters, up·hol·stered, up·hol·ster·ing. –up·hol′ster·er,** *NOUN.*

Pedaling **uphill** can be hard work.

up·hol·ster·y (up hōl′stər ē), *NOUN.*
1 the materials used for covering chairs or sofas: *That chair comes with cloth or leather upholstery.*
2 the business of upholstering.

up·keep (up′kēp′), *NOUN.* the act or process of keeping something in good condition; maintenance: *The upkeep of a large house can be difficult and expensive.*

up·lift (up lift′), *VERB.* to improve someone's moral, emotional, or social condition: *I was uplifted by his encouraging words.* ❑ *VERB* **up·lifts, up·lift·ed, up·lift·ing.**

up·load (up′lōd′), *VERB.* to transfer data or programs to a central computer. ❑ *VERB* **up·loads, up·load·ed, up·load·ing.**

up·on (ə pon′), *PREPOSITION.* on: *I sat upon the rug.*

up·per (up′ər), *ADJECTIVE.* higher: *the upper lip, an upper floor.*

up·per·case (up′ər kās′), in printing:
1 *NOUN.* capital letters.
2 *ADJECTIVE.* in capital letters.
3 *VERB.* to print in capital letters.
❑ *VERB* **up·per·cases, up·per·cased, up·per·cas·ing.**

upper hand, a position of control; advantage: *Get some rest or that cold may get the upper hand.*

up·per·most (up′ər mōst), *ADJECTIVE.*
1 highest: *She climbed to the uppermost branch.*
2 most prominent; having the most force or influence: *Your safety was uppermost in my mind.*

up·right (up′rīt′),
1 *ADVERB.* straight up: *Hold yourself upright.*
2 *ADJECTIVE.* standing up straight; erect: *We need an upright post to support the gate.*
3 *ADJECTIVE.* good; honest: *An upright citizen votes for the best candidate.*

up·ris·ing (up′rī′zing), *NOUN.* a revolt: *A prison uprising was the cause of the guard's death.*

up·roar (up′rôr′), *NOUN.*
1 a confused, disturbed, or excited state: *There was widespread uproar over the large tax increase.*
2 a loud or confused noise: *We heard the uproar following the last-minute touchdown.* ■ See the Synonym Study at **noise.**

up·roar·i·ous (up rôr′ē əs), *ADJECTIVE.* making an uproar; noisy and disorderly: *an uproarious crowd, uproarious laughter.* **–up·roar′i·ous·ly,** *ADVERB.*

up·root (up rüt′), *VERB.*
1 to tear up by the roots: *The storm uprooted the trees.*
2 to remove completely: *The flood uprooted many families from their homes.*
❑ *VERB* **up·roots, up·root·ed, up·root·ing.**

a hat	ė term	ô order	ch child	⎧a in about
ā age	i it	oi oil	ng long	⎪e in taken
ä far	ī ice	ou out	sh she	ə⎨i in pencil
â care	o hot	u cup	th thin	⎪o in lemon
e let	ō open	ů put	ᴛʜ then	⎩u in circus
ē equal	ȯ saw	ü rule	zh measure	

U

up·set (up set′ *for verb;* up′set′ *for adjective and noun*),
1 *VERB.* to make someone feel worried, unhappy, or disappointed: *The bad news upset me.*
2 *ADJECTIVE.* worried, unhappy, or disappointed: *I was upset by the bad news.*
3 *VERB.* to defeat someone unexpectedly in a contest: *She easily upset the mayor in the election.*
4 *NOUN.* an unexpected defeat: *The hockey team suffered an upset.*
5 *VERB.* to tip something over; overturn: *I upset my glass of milk.*
6 *ADJECTIVE.* sick: *He had an upset stomach.*
❑ *VERB* **up·sets, up·set, up·set·ting.**

up·side down (up′sīd′ doun′),
1 with what should be on top at the bottom: *The pie fell upside down on the floor.*
2 in or into complete disorder: *The children turned the house upside down.*

up·stairs (up′stârz′),
1 *ADVERB.* up the stairs: *The boy ran upstairs.*
2 *ADVERB* or *ADJECTIVE.* on or to an upper floor: *She lives upstairs. He is waiting in an upstairs hall.*

up·start (up′stärt′), *NOUN.*
1 someone who has suddenly risen from a humble position to wealth, power, or importance.
2 someone who is very rude, bold, and conceited.

up·stream (up′strēm′), *ADVERB* or *ADJECTIVE.* against the current of a stream; up a stream: *It is hard to swim upstream. We had an upstream campsite.*

swimming **upstream**

up-to-date (up′tə dāt′), *ADJECTIVE.*
1 including the most recent information: *I called for my up-to-date bank balance.*
2 keeping up with modern style or ideas; modern: *She runs an up-to-date store.* ■ See the Synonym Study at **new.**

up·town (up′toun′), *ADVERB* or *ADJECTIVE.* away from the main business section of a town or city: *Let's go uptown. I use an uptown bank.*

up·ward (up′wərd),
1 *ADVERB.* toward a higher place: *She climbed upward until she reached the apple.*

2 *ADJECTIVE.* moving toward a higher place: *I watched the upward flight of a bird.*
−up′ward·ly, *ADVERB.*

up·wards (up′wərdz), *ADVERB.* See **upward.**

u·ra·ni·um (yü rā′nē əm), *NOUN.* a heavy, silvery radioactive metal used as a source of atomic energy. Uranium is a chemical element.

Ur·a·nus (yùr′ə nəs *or* yə rā′nəs), *NOUN.* the third largest planet in the solar system and the seventh in distance from the sun.

Word Story

Uranus was originally called *George.* The British astronomer who discovered the planet named it after King George III. People thought this sounded odd, so another name was chosen later.

ur·ban (ėr′bən), *ADJECTIVE.* of or about cities or towns: *an urban district, urban planning.*

ur·chin (ėr′chən), *NOUN.* (earlier) a small child, especially one who gets into trouble or who is ragged and dirty.

urge (ėrj),
1 *VERB.* to try to persuade; ask earnestly; plead with: *She urged us to stay longer.*
2 *NOUN.* a strong wish to do or have something: *I had an urge to see my old friend again.*
3 *VERB.* to plead or argue earnestly for; recommend strongly: *The doctor urged a change of climate.*
❑ *VERB* **urg·es, urged, urg·ing.**

ur·gent (ėr′jənt), *ADJECTIVE.* very important and needing attention right away: *an urgent duty, an urgent message.* **−ur′gent·ly,** *ADVERB.*

ur·i·nate (yùr′ə nāt), *VERB.* to discharge urine from the body. ❑ *VERB* **ur·i·nates, ur·i·nat·ed, ur·i·nat·ing.**

ur·ine (yùr′ən), *NOUN.* a liquid waste product of the body. Urine is produced by the kidneys, goes to the bladder, and passes out of the body.

urn (ėrn), *NOUN.*
1 a vase with a base. Urns have been used since ancient times to hold the ashes of the dead.
2 a tall metal container with a tap, used for making or serving coffee or tea at the table.
■ Another word that sounds like this is **earn.**

an **urn** from ancient Greece

Ur·u·guay (yùr′ə gwā *or* yùr′ə gwī), *NOUN.* a country in southeastern South America. **−Ur′u·guay′an,** *ADJECTIVE* or *NOUN.*

us (us), *PRONOUN.* We and us mean the person speaking plus the person or persons addressed or spoken about: *Can you help us? Mother went with us to the theater. She gave the book to us.*

U.S., an abbreviation of **United States.**

U.S.A., an abbreviation of **United States of America.**

us·a·ble (yü′zə bəl), *ADJECTIVE.* able to be used; fit for use: *The broken toy was no longer usable.*

us·age (yü′sij), *NOUN.*
1 the usual way of using words: *The actual usage of speakers and writers of English determines what standard English is.*
2 a manner or way of using something; treatment: *This car has had rough usage.*

use (yüz *for verb;* yüs *for noun*),
1 *VERB.* to put into action or service: *We use our legs in walking. We use spoons to eat soup.*
2 *VERB.* to take advantage of someone for your own benefit: *He tends to use people.*
3 *NOUN.* the act of using: *The use of tools is a sign of intelligence.*
4 *NOUN.* the condition of being used: *He brought back methods long out of use in the company.*
5 *NOUN.* a purpose that something is used for; a need: *We found a new use for the empty lot.*
6 *NOUN.* the power of using something; ability to use: *The accident caused him to lose the use of an arm.*
7 *NOUN.* the right or privilege of using something: *I have the use of a friend's boat this summer.*
❑ *VERB* **us·es, used, us·ing.** –**us′er,** *NOUN.*

make use of, *IDIOM.* to use; utilize: *She made use of her Spanish while in Mexico.*

used to (yüst′ tü *or* yüs′ tə), *IDIOM.*
1 accustomed to: *Southerners are not used to cold weather.*
2 formerly did: *I used to have a bicycle, but now I don't.*

use up, *IDIOM.* to consume or expend entirely: *We have used up nearly all of our sugar.*

used (yüzd), *ADJECTIVE.* not new; having belonged to someone else: *I bought a used car.*

use·ful (yüs′fəl), *ADJECTIVE.* of use; giving service; helpful: *They made themselves useful around the house.* –**use′ful·ness,** *NOUN.*

use·less (yüs′lis), *ADJECTIVE.* not usable; worthless: *Snowshoes are useless in the desert.* –**use′less·ly,** *ADVERB.* –**use′less·ness,** *NOUN.*

us·er-friend·ly (yü′zər frend′lē), *ADJECTIVE.* designed to be easy to use, even by people without training or experience: *The computer program is so user-friendly that it fixes your mistakes.*

ush·er (ush′ər),
1 *NOUN.* someone who shows people to their seats in a church, theater, or public hall.
2 *VERB.* to show or lead people where they should go: *We ushered our guests to the door.*
❑ *VERB* **ush·ers, ush·ered, ush·er·ing.**

U.S.S.R. or **USSR,** an abbreviation of **Union of Soviet Socialist Republics.**

u·su·al (yü′zhü əl), *ADJECTIVE.* seen, found, or happening most of the time: *Snow is usual in the Rocky Mountains during winter. His usual bedtime is 8 P.M.* –**u′su·al·ly,** *ADVERB.*

as usual, *IDIOM.* in the usual manner; ordinary; customary: *We met, as usual, very late.*

UT, an abbreviation of **Utah.**

U·tah (yü′tȯ *or* yü′tä), *NOUN.* one of the Rocky Mountain states of the United States. *Abbreviation:* UT; *Capital:* Salt Lake City. –**U′tah·an,** *NOUN.*

State Story Utah got its name from the Ute (yüt), an American Indian tribe that lived in the area. The name of the tribe may have come from a Ute word meaning "person" or "people."

u·ten·sil (yü ten′səl), *NOUN.* a container or implement used for mixing or cooking things. Pots and pans are kitchen utensils. ■ See the Synonym Study at **tool.**

u·ter·us (yü′tər əs), *NOUN.* the part of the body in female mammals that holds and nourishes the young until birth. ❑ *PLURAL* **u·ter·us·es** or **u·ter·i** (yü′tər ī).

u·til·i·ty (yü til′ə tē), *NOUN.*
1 a company that performs a public service. Railroads, bus lines, and gas and electric companies are utilities.
2 usefulness: *I appreciate the utility of my computer.*
❑ *PLURAL* **u·til·i·ties.**

u·ti·lize (yü′tl īz), *VERB.* to make use of something; put to some practical use: *The cook will utilize the leftovers to make soup.* ❑ *VERB* **u·ti·liz·es, u·ti·lized, u·ti·liz·ing.**

ut·most (ut′mōst), *ADJECTIVE.* greatest possible; greatest: *Eating proper food is of the utmost importance to health.*

to the utmost, *IDIOM.* to the greatest possible degree: *He enjoyed himself to the utmost at the circus.*

ut·ter¹ (ut′ər), *ADJECTIVE.* complete; total; absolute: *When the lights went out, we were in utter darkness.*

ut·ter² (ut′ər), *VERB.* to speak or say something: *She didn't utter a word after hearing the news.* ❑ *VERB* **ut·ters, ut·tered, ut·ter·ing.**

ut·ter·ly (ut′ər lē), *ADVERB.* completely; totally; absolutely: *I was utterly delighted with my present.*

U-turn (yü′tėrn′), *NOUN.* a U-shaped turn made by a vehicle in order to go in the opposite direction.

Uz·bek·i·stan (üz′bek′ə stän), *NOUN.* a country in western Asia.

a	hat	ė	term	ȯ	order	ch	child	ə	a in about
ā	age	i	it	oi	oil	ng	long		e in taken
ä	far	ī	ice	ou	out	sh	she		i in pencil
â	care	o	hot	u	cup	th	thin		o in lemon
e	let	ō	open	u̇	put	ᴛʜ	then		u in circus
ē	equal	ȯ	saw	ü	rule	zh	measure		

volcano

V or **v** (vē), *NOUN.* the 22nd letter of the English
alphabet. ❑ *PLURAL* **V's** or **v's.**

V, V., or **v,** an abbreviation of **volt** or **volts.**

VA, an abbreviation of **Virginia.**

va·can·cy (vā′kən sē), *NOUN.*
 1 a job that has not been filled yet: *The retirement
 of two employees created two staff vacancies.*
 2 a room, space, or apartment for rent: *There was
 a vacancy in the motel.*
  ❑ *PLURAL* **va·can·cies.**

va·cant (vā′kənt), *ADJECTIVE.* not occupied or filled;
empty: *a vacant house, a vacant space.* ■ See the
Synonym Study at **empty.**

va·cate (vā′kāt), *VERB.* to go away from a place and
leave it empty: *They will soon vacate the house.*
  ❑ *VERB* **va·cates, va·cat·ed, va·cat·ing.**

va·ca·tion (vā kā′shən),
 1 *NOUN.* a time when you are not at school or at work:
 Our family took three weeks vacation last year.

 2 *VERB.* to take a vacation: *We vacationed at the lake.*
  ❑ *VERB* **va·ca·tions, va·ca·tioned, va·ca·tion·ing.**
  —va·ca′tion·er, *NOUN.*

vac·ci·nate (vak′sə nāt), *VERB.* to give someone
a vaccine by a shot or other means to protect
against a disease. People who are vaccinated
against measles and tetanus will not get these
diseases for several years or longer. ❑ *VERB*
vac·ci·nates, vac·ci·nat·ed, vac·ci·nat·ing.

vac·ci·na·tion (vak′sə nā′shən), *NOUN.* the act of
vaccinating: *Vaccination has wiped out smallpox here.*

vac·cine (vak sēn′), *NOUN.* a preparation of dead or
weakened germs of a particular disease. A vaccine
is given by a shot or other means to prevent or
lessen the effects of a disease. Vaccines are used
against polio, mumps, and other diseases.

vac·u·um (vak′yům *or* vak′yü əm),
 1 *NOUN.* an empty space without any air in it. A
 perfect vacuum has never been found or made.

2 *NOUN.* a space which has almost no air or other matter in it. Outer space is a vacuum of this kind.

3 *VERB.* to clean something with a vacuum cleaner: *I vacuumed the rugs.*

❏ *VERB* **vac·u·ums, vac·u·umed, vac·u·um·ing.**

vacuum cleaner, a machine for cleaning carpets, curtains, floors, and so on. A vacuum cleaner sucks dirt and dust up into a bag.

vague (vāg), *ADJECTIVE.* not definite; not clear; not distinct: *His vague statement confused them.*

❏ *ADJECTIVE* **va·guer, va·guest. –vague′ly,** *ADVERB.*

vain (vān), *ADJECTIVE.*

1 having too much pride in your looks, ability, or achievements: *Some good-looking people are vain.*

2 of no use; unsuccessful: *I made vain attempts to call her.*

■ Other words that sound like this are **vane** and **vein. –vain′ly,** *ADVERB.*

in vain, *IDIOM.* without effect or without success: *They shouted in vain, for no one could hear them.*

val·en·tine (val′ən tīn), *NOUN.* a greeting card or small gift sent on Valentine's Day.

Valentine's Day, February 14, the day on which valentines are exchanged.

val·et (val′it *or* val′ā), *NOUN.*

1 a servant who takes care of a man's clothes and gives him personal service.

2 a hotel worker who helps guests by cleaning their clothes, parking their cars, and so on.

an old-fashioned **valentine**

val·iant (val′yənt), *ADJECTIVE.* very brave; courageous: *A neighbor's valiant efforts saved the children from the burning building.* **–val′iant·ly,** *ADVERB.*

val·id (val′id), *ADJECTIVE.*

1 based on facts or authority; true: *She had valid reasons for her objections to the plan.*

2 having force; effective: *Illness is a valid excuse for being absent from school.*

3 legally acceptable: *A contract made by a minor or a child is not valid.*

val·ley (val′ē), *NOUN.*

1 a region of low land that lies between hills or mountains. Most valleys have rivers running through them.

2 a wide region drained by a great river system: *He has a farm in the Ohio River valley.*

❏ *PLURAL* **val·leys.**

val·or (val′ər), *NOUN.* bravery or courage: *The soldier was given a medal for valor in battle.*

val·u·a·ble (val′yü ə bəl),

1 *ADJECTIVE.* having value; useful; helpful: *valuable information, a valuable friend.*

2 *ADJECTIVE.* worth a lot of money: *I lost a valuable ring.*

3 *NOUN.* **valuables,** articles of value, such as jewelry.

val·ue (val′yü),

1 *NOUN.* the real worth of something in money: *We bought the house for less than its value.*

2 *NOUN.* the usefulness or importance of something: *She appreciated the value of a good education.*

3 *NOUN.* **values,** things or ideas believed to be important and desirable in your life: *The politician supported traditional family values.*

4 *VERB.* to estimate the worth of something: *The land is valued at $5000.*

5 *VERB.* to think highly of something; regard highly: *Since he is an expert, his opinion is valued.*

❏ *PLURAL* **val·ues;** *VERB* **val·ues, val·ued, val·u·ing.**

valve (valv), *NOUN.*

1 a movable part that controls the flow of a liquid or gas through a pipe by opening and closing the passage. A faucet contains a valve.

2 a small flap of tissue that works like a valve. The valves of the heart are membranes that control the flow of blood into and out of the heart.

vam·pire (vam′pīr), *NOUN.* (in stories) a dead body that comes to life at night and sucks the blood of people while they sleep.

a **vampire** from an old movie

van (van), *NOUN.*

1 a large covered truck for moving household goods or animals: *The men loaded our piano into the van.*

2 a motor vehicle with rear and side doors for loading people or freight. A van has several rows of seats that can fold down or be taken out.

a	hat	ė	term	ô	order	ch	child	⎧a in about
ā	age	i	it	oi	oil	ng	long	⎪e in taken
ä	far	ī	ice	ou	out	sh	she	ə⎨i in pencil
â	care	o	hot	u	cup	th	thin	⎪o in lemon
e	let	ō	open	ů	put	ᴛʜ	then	⎩u in circus
ē	equal	ȯ	saw	ü	rule	zh	measure	

V

van·dal (van'dl), NOUN. someone who destroys or damages beautiful or valuable things on purpose: *Vandals had thrown paint on the statues in the park.*

Word Story

Vandal comes from the name of the Vandals, an uncivilized people who invaded parts of Europe and Africa long ago. In A.D. 455 they captured and looted the city of Rome.

van·dal·ism (van'dl iz'əm), NOUN. the act of destroying or damaging beautiful or valuable things on purpose: *They were arrested for breaking windows and other acts of vandalism.*

van·dal·ize (van'dl īz), VERB. to destroy or damage something on purpose. □ VERB **van·dal·iz·es, van·dal·ized, van·dal·iz·ing.**

vane (vān), NOUN.
1 a blade of a windmill, of a propeller, or the like.
2 See **weather vane.**
■ Other words that sound like this are **vain** and **vein.**

va·nil·la (və nil'ə), NOUN. a flavoring used in ice cream, candy, cakes, and cookies. It is made from the bean of a tropical plant.

van·ish (van'ish), VERB. to disappear suddenly: *The sun vanished behind a cloud.* □ VERB **van·ish·es, van·ished, van·ish·ing.**

van·i·ty (van'ə tē), NOUN. too much pride in your looks or ability: *Talent sometimes causes vanity.*

vanilla

va·por (vā'ər), NOUN.
1 moisture in the air that can be seen; fog; mist: *I saw the vapor from my breath in the cool air.*
2 a gas formed from a substance that is usually a liquid or a solid: *We smelled the gasoline vapor as Mom filled the car's gas tank.*

va·por·ize (vā'pə rīz'), VERB. to change a liquid into vapor: *Heat vaporizes water.* □ VERB **va·por·iz·es, va·por·ized, va·por·iz·ing. –va'por·i·za·tion,** NOUN.

va·por·iz·er (vā'pə rī'zər), NOUN. a device that changes a liquid into a vapor. One kind of vaporizer releases steam into a room in order to make breathing easier for someone with a cold.

var·i·a·ble (vâr'ē ə bəl), ADJECTIVE.
1 apt to change; uncertain: *The pilot warned of variable winds.*
2 able to be changed: *The fan's speed is variable.*

var·i·a·tion (vâr'ē ā'shən), NOUN. a change or difference: *There were sudden variations in the temperature during the day.*

var·ied (vâr'ēd), ADJECTIVE. having many different kinds: *The box held a varied assortment of candies.*

va·ri·e·ty (və rī'ə tē), NOUN.
1 the quality of changing frequently; lack of sameness: *Variety in your diet can prevent disease.*
2 a number of different kinds of something: *This store has a variety of toys.*
3 a kind or sort: *Which varieties of fruit are on sale?*
4 a set of living things, all of one species, somehow like each other and different from others of that species: *The store has many varieties of goldfish.*
□ PLURAL **va·ri·e·ties.**

Have You Heard?

You may have heard someone say **"Variety is the spice of life."** This means that they feel that doing many different things makes life better.

var·i·ous (vâr'ē əs), ADJECTIVE. different from one another: *There are various opinions on how to raise children.* **–var'i·ous·ly,** ADVERB.

var·nish (vär'nish),
1 NOUN. a liquid that gives a smooth, glossy appearance to wood, metal, and so on, when it dries. Varnish is often made from resin dissolved in oil or alcohol.
2 VERB. to put varnish on a surface: *They varnished the wood floors of the house.*
□ PLURAL **var·nish·es;** VERB **var·nish·es, var·nished, var·nish·ing.**

var·y (vâr'ē), VERB.
1 to change something; make or become different: *The driver can vary the speed of a car.*
2 to be different; show differences: *Stars vary in brightness.*
□ VERB **var·ies, var·ied, var·y·ing.**

vase (vās), NOUN. a container used to hold flowers. A vase is usually round and tall enough to hold flowers on stems.

vast (vast), ADJECTIVE. very, very large; immense: *Texas and Alaska cover vast territories.* ■ See the Synonym Study at **huge. –vast'ly,** ADVERB. **–vast'ness,** NOUN.

Word Story

Vast comes from a Latin word meaning "empty." A vast space often seems empty because it is so big. **Waste** comes from the same Latin word. Empty land is called wasteland by farmers because it is not used for crops.

vat (vat), NOUN. a very large container for liquids; tank: *The fabric was put into a vat of dye.*

Vat·i·can (vat'ə kən), NOUN.
1 the buildings grouped about the palace of the pope in Rome.
2 the government, office, or authority of the pope.

vault¹ (vȯlt), NOUN.
1 an arched roof or ceiling; series of arches: *The cathedral vault was built hundreds of years ago.*
2 a place for storing valuable things and keeping them safe: *The robber was caught trying to get into the bank vaults.*

vault² (vȯlt),
1 VERB. to jump over something, using your hands or a pole: *She vaulted the fence.*
2 NOUN. a jump like this: *He excels at the pole vault.*
❏ VERB **vaults, vault·ed, vault·ing.**

VCR, videocassette recorder: a machine that records television programs or movies on magnetic tape and can reproduce their sound and pictures.

VDT, video display terminal: a device for communicating with a computer. It has a screen like a television and often a keyboard.

veal (vēl), NOUN. meat from a calf.

veer (vir), VERB. to change direction; shift: *The wind veered to the south.* ❏ VERB **veers, veered, veer·ing.**

veg·e·ta·ble (vej′tə bəl or vej′ə tə bəl),
1 NOUN. a plant that has fruit, seeds, leaves, roots, or other parts used for food: *We grow vegetables such as peas, corn, lettuce, and beets in our garden behind the house.*
2 NOUN. any plant: *Does this substance come from a vegetable or a mineral?*
3 ADJECTIVE. of or like plants: *Radishes are part of the vegetable kingdom.*

delicious, fresh **vegetables**

veg·e·tar·i·an (vej′ə ter′ē ən),
1 NOUN. someone who eats vegetables but no meat.
2 ADJECTIVE. containing or serving no meat: *a vegetarian diet, a vegetarian restaurant.*

veg·e·ta·tion (vej′ə tā′shən), NOUN. plant life; growing plants: *Deserts have little vegetation.*

ve·he·ment (vē′ə mənt), ADJECTIVE. having or showing strong feeling: *Our neighbors often have loud and vehement quarrels.* −**ve′he·ment·ly,** ADVERB.

ve·hi·cle (vē′ə kəl), NOUN. something used to carry people or things. Bicycles and wagons are vehicles. Cars and trucks are motor vehicles. Rockets and satellites are space vehicles.

veil (vāl),
1 NOUN. a piece of very thin material that women sometimes wear to protect or hide the face, or as an ornament.
2 VERB. to cover with a veil: *Some Muslim women veil their faces before going out in public.*
3 NOUN. anything that screens or hides something: *A veil of clouds hid the sun.*
4 VERB. to cover or hide something: *The spy veiled his plans in secrecy.*
❏ VERB **veils, veiled, veil·ing. veil′like′,** ADJECTIVE.

vein (vān), NOUN.
1 one of the blood vessels that carry blood to the heart from all parts of the body.
2 a rib of a leaf or of an insect's wing.
3 a crack or layer in rock filled with a mineral or metal ore: *The miners dug into a vein of gold.*
■ Other words that sound like this are **vain** and **vane.**

ve·loc·i·rap·tor (və los′i rap′tər), NOUN. a very fast, flesh-eating dinosaur with huge claws. It was like a deinonychus, but somewhat smaller.

velociraptor — about 6 feet long, including the tail

ve·loc·i·ty (və los′ə tē), NOUN. the rate of motion in a certain direction; speed: *The velocity of light is 186,282 miles per second.* ❏ PLURAL **ve·loc·i·ties.**

vel·vet (vel′vit), NOUN. a very soft cloth with many short, raised threads on one side. Velvet may be made of silk, rayon, nylon, cotton, or some combination of these.

vel·vet·y (vel′və tē), ADJECTIVE. smooth and soft like velvet: *I love the velvety feel of my baby brother's cheeks.*

vend (vend), VERB. to sell; peddle: *He was vending fruit from a cart.* ❏ VERB **vends, vend·ed, vend·ing.**

vending machine, a machine from which you can get candy, stamps, and so on when you drop coins in.

ven·dor (ven′dər), NOUN. someone who sells something or who provides a kind of service.

a	hat	ė	term	ô	order	ch	child		a in about
ā	age	i	it	oi	oil	ng	long		e in taken
ä	far	ī	ice	ou	out	sh	she	ə {	i in pencil
â	care	o	hot	u	cup	th	thin		o in lemon
e	let	ō	open	u̇	put	ᴛʜ	then		u in circus
ē	equal	ȯ	saw	ü	rule	zh	measure		

Ve·ne·tian blind (və nē′shən blind′), a window shade made of many horizontal slats. The blind can be raised and lowered, or the slats can be tilted to regulate the amount of light let in.

Ven·e·zue·la (ven′ə zwä′lə), NOUN. a country in northern South America. —**Ven′e·zue′lan**, ADJECTIVE or NOUN.

venge·ance (ven′jəns), NOUN. the act of hurting or killing someone in return for what he or she did to you: *She swore vengeance against her enemies.*

with a vengeance, IDIOM. with great force or violence: *It was raining with a vengeance.*

Ven·ice (ven′is), NOUN. a city in Italy. Venice has many canals in place of streets.

ven·i·son (ven′ə sən), NOUN. deer meat used for food.

ven·om (ven′əm), NOUN. the poison of some snakes, spiders, scorpions, lizards, and similar animals.

Word Story

Venom comes from **Venus,** the Roman goddess of love. In ancient times, people believed that love could be caused by giving a person a magic drink. Some of these drinks actually contained poisonous ingredients.

ven·om·ous (ven′ə məs), ADJECTIVE.
1 poisonous: *He killed a venomous snake.*
2 intended to hurt someone's feelings; mean: *I won't listen to your venomous gossip.*
—**ven′om·ous·ly**, ADVERB.

vent (vent),
1 NOUN. a hole or opening, especially one to let out smoke, gas, liquids, and so on: *He cut air vents in the box top so his frog could breathe.*
2 VERB. to express your feelings freely: *Don't vent your anger on the dog.*
3 NOUN. an outlet; way out: *Her great energy found vent in hard work. He gave vent to his grief in tears.*
❏ VERB **vents, vent·ed, vent·ing.**

ven·ti·late (ven′tl āt), VERB. to let fresh air in: *We ventilate a room by opening windows.* ❏ VERB **ven·ti·lates, ven·ti·lat·ed, ven·ti·lat·ing.**
—**ven′ti·la′tion**, NOUN.

ven·ti·la·tor (ven′tl ā′tər), NOUN. a device for letting fresh air into a room, vehicle, or other space. Ventilators may be fans or air conditioners.

ven·tri·cle (ven′trə kəl), NOUN. either of the two lower chambers of the heart. A ventricle receives blood from an upper chamber and pumps it into the arteries.

ven·tril·o·quism (ven tril′ə kwiz′əm), NOUN. the art or practice of speaking with the lips shut or nearly shut. The voice seems to come from some source other than the speaker.

ven·tril·o·quist (ven tril′ə kwist), NOUN. someone who is skilled in ventriloquism.

ven·ture (ven′chər),
1 NOUN. something you do that is exciting but risky: *The explorers hoped to find gold on their venture into the wilderness.*
2 VERB. to go somewhere that is dangerous: *They ventured out on the thin ice and fell through.*
❏ VERB **ven·tures, ven·tured, ven·tur·ing.**

Ve·nus (vē′nəs), NOUN.
1 the sixth largest planet in the solar system and the second in distance from the sun. It is the planet closest to Earth, and appears as the brightest planet.
2 the Roman goddess of love and beauty.

Did You Know?

The planet **Venus** rotates so slowly that there are only two sunrises and sunsets in each of its years. A day on Venus is 243 Earth days long.

Ve·ra·cruz (ver′ə krüz′), NOUN. a state in eastern Mexico.

ve·ran·da (və ran′də), NOUN. a large porch with a roof, built along one or more sides of a house.
❏ PLURAL **ve·ran·das.**

verb (vėrb), NOUN. a word that tells what is or what happens; part of speech that expresses action, condition, or experience. *Do, go, be, sit, know,* and *eat* are verbs.

ver·bal (vėr′bəl), ADJECTIVE.
1 of or created by words: *The paragraph made a verbal picture of the lake.*
2 expressed in spoken words; oral: *I have a verbal promise from him.*
—**ver′bal·ly**, ADVERB.

ver·dict (vėr′dikt), NOUN. the decision of a jury or a judge at the end of a trial: *The jury read a verdict of "Guilty."*

verge (vėrj), NOUN. **on the verge of,** at the point where something begins or happens; brink: *Their business is on the verge of ruin.*

ver·i·fy (ver′ə fī), VERB.
1 to prove something to be true; confirm: *The driver's report of the accident was verified by two women who had seen it happen.*
2 to test the correctness of something: *You can verify the spelling of a word by using a dictionary.*
❏ VERB **ver·i·fies, ver·i·fied, ver·i·fy·ing.**
—**ver′i·fi′a·ble**, ADJECTIVE.

ver·min (vėr′mən), NOUN PLURAL OR SINGULAR. small animals that are troublesome or destructive. Fleas, lice, rats, and mice are vermin.

Ver·mont (vər mont′), NOUN. one of the northeastern states of the United States. *Abbreviation:* VT; *Capital:* Montpelier.
—**Ver·mont′er**, NOUN.

State Story Vermont comes from two French words meaning "green mountain."

ver·sa·tile (vėr′sə təl), *ADJECTIVE.* able to do many things well: *She is a versatile student who is skilled at science, art, mathematics, Spanish, and history. This is a versatile tool that can be used for drilling, sawing, hammering, or scraping.* —**ver′sa·til′i·ty,** *NOUN.*

verse (vėrs), *NOUN.*
1 poetry; a line or lines of words with a regularly repeated accent and often with rhyme.
2 a short division of a chapter in the Bible.

ver·sion (vėr′zhən), *NOUN.*
1 a statement or description given by one person: *Each of the three girls gave her own version of what happened.*
2 a different form of something: *I liked the movie version better than the book.*

ver·sus (vėr′səs), *PREPOSITION.* against: *The best game last week was Los Angeles versus Montreal.*

ver·te·bra (vėr′tə brə), *NOUN.* any of the bones that make up the backbone. ❑ *PLURAL* **ver·te·brae** (vėr′tə brē) or **ver·te·bras.**

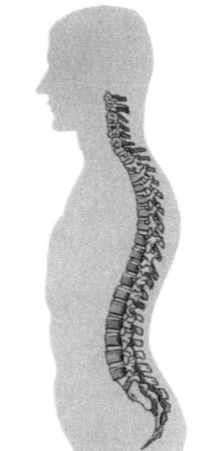

The **vertebrae** make up the spinal column.

Word Story

Vertebra can be traced back to a Latin word meaning "to turn." Having separate vertebrae in the backbone instead of a single, solid bone allows the body to turn or bend easily.

ver·te·brate (vėr′tə brit),
1 *NOUN.* an animal that has a backbone. Fishes, amphibians, reptiles, birds, and mammals are vertebrates. People are vertebrates.
2 *ADJECTIVE.* having a backbone: *Whales, pigeons, lizards, and trout are vertebrate animals.*

ver·tex (vėr′teks), *NOUN.*
1 the point opposite to and farthest away from the base of a triangle, pyramid, or the like.
2 the point where the two sides of an angle meet. ❑ *PLURAL* **ver·tex·es** or **ver·ti·ces** (vėr′tə sēz).

ver·ti·cal (vėr′tə kəl), *ADJECTIVE.* straight up and down; upright. A flagpole is in a vertical position. —**ver′ti·cal·ly,** *ADVERB.*

vertical axis, the main line that runs straight up and down in a graph. An axis has points separated by equal spaces marked on it.

ver·ti·go (vėr′tə gō), *NOUN.* dizziness, especially when looking down from a height; giddiness.

verve (vėrv), *NOUN.* enthusiasm; energy; vigor; spirit; liveliness: *She attacked the project with verve.*

ver·y (ver′ē),
1 *ADVERB.* much; greatly; extremely: *The sunshine is very hot in July.*
2 *ADVERB.* absolute; exactly: *He stood in the very same place for an hour.*
3 *ADJECTIVE.* same: *The very people who supported the plan are against it now.*
4 *ADJECTIVE.* actual: *They were caught in the very act of stealing.*
5 *ADJECTIVE.* absolute; complete: *The storm meant the very end of our hopes for a picnic.*

Synonym Study

Very means much more than usual: *After the storm, it became very hot. With binoculars, you can see very far.*

Awfully and **terribly** can mean truly or deeply: *We walked an awfully long way and were terribly glad to be home!*

Extremely and **exceedingly** mean greatly: *He was extremely happy to have his lost wallet returned. He was exceedingly unhappy about losing it.*

Highly means fully or very: *She is highly pleased with the school's new computer class.*

Mighty can mean very. Used this way, it is an informal word: *We were mighty glad to see land again after four days in a drifting boat.*

ves·sel (ves′əl), *NOUN.*
1 a ship; large boat: *Ocean liners and other vessels are usually docked by tugboats.*
2 a hollow holder or container. Cups, bowls, pitchers, bottles, barrels, and tubs are vessels.
3 See **blood vessel.**

vest (vest), *NOUN.* a short, sleeveless garment usually worn over a shirt or blouse.

vet[1] (vet), *NOUN.* a short form of **veterinarian.**

vet[2] (vet), *NOUN.* a short form of **veteran** (definition 1).

vet·er·an (vet′ər ən), *NOUN.*
1 someone who has served in the armed forces; vet.
2 someone who has had a lot of experience in some position or occupation: *She is a veteran of Congress.*

a **vest** from Guatemala

a	hat	ė	term	ô	order	ch	child	⎧a in about
ā	age	i	it	oi	oil	ng	long	⎪e in taken
ä	far	ī	ice	ou	out	sh	she	ə⎨i in pencil
â	care	o	hot	u	cup	th	thin	⎪o in lemon
e	let	ō	open	ů	put	ᴛʜ	then	⎩u in circus
ē	equal	ò	saw	ü	rule	zh	measure	

V

Veterans Day, November 11, a holiday for honoring all veterans of the armed forces and commemorating the end of World War I and World War II. It was formerly known as **Armistice Day.**

vet·er·i·nar·i·an (vet′ər ə ner′ē ən), NOUN. a doctor or surgeon who treats animals.

A visit to the **veterinarian** can be fun for pets and people.

vet·er·i·nar·y (vet′ər ə ner′ē), ADJECTIVE. of or about the medical or surgical treatment of animals.

ve·to (vē′tō),
1 NOUN. the right of a president, governor, and so on, to reject bills passed by an assembly or congress: *The President has the power of veto.*
2 NOUN. the use of this right or power: *The governor's veto kept the bill from becoming a law.*
3 NOUN. a refusal to allow something: *Our plan met with a veto from the boss.*
4 VERB. to refuse to allow someone to do something: *Her parents vetoed her plan to buy a car.*
❏ PLURAL **ve·toes;** VERB **ve·tos, ve·toed, ve·to·ing.**

Word Story

Veto comes from a Latin word meaning "I forbid." In ancient Rome, the common people were represented in government by officials who could not make laws, but who could forbid new laws by this one word.

vi·a (vī′ə or vē′ə), PREPOSITION. by way of; by a route that passes through: *The plane flew from Boston to Paris via London.*

vi·al (vī′əl), NOUN. a small glass or plastic bottle for holding medicines or the like.

vi·brate (vī′brāt), VERB. to move rapidly back and forth: *A piano string vibrates and makes a sound when a key is struck.* ❏ VERB **vi·brates, vi·brat·ed, vi·brat·ing.**

vi·bra·tion (vī brā′shən), NOUN. a rapid movement back and forth; vibrating: *Passing buses shake the house so much that we feel the vibration.*

vice (vīs), NOUN. an evil habit or tendency: *Lying and cruelty are vices.* ■ Another word that sounds like this is **vise.**

Word Power   vice-

The prefix **vice-** means "substitute" or "assistant." The **vice-president** can be a **substitute** for the the president.

vice-pres·i·dent (vīs′prez′ə dənt), NOUN. a government officer next in rank to the president, who takes the president's place when necessary. If the President of the United States dies or resigns, the Vice-President becomes President.

vice·roy (vīs′roi), NOUN. (formerly) someone who ruled a country, province, or colony, acting as the king's or queen's representative.

vice ver·sa (vī′sə vėr′sə), the other way round: *John blamed Mary, and vice versa (Mary blamed John).*

vi·cin·i·ty (və sin′ə tē), NOUN. the region near or around a place; neighborhood: *There are no houses for sale in this vicinity.* ❏ PLURAL **vi·cin·i·ties.**

vi·cious (vish′əs), ADJECTIVE.
1 very violent or cruel: *He was accused of a terrible, vicious crime.*
2 likely to attack or bite someone; dangerous: *That dog is a vicious animal!*
–**vi′cious·ly,** ADVERB.

vic·tim (vik′təm), NOUN.
1 a person or an animal sacrificed, injured, or destroyed: *victims of war, accident victims.*
2 someone badly treated or taken advantage of: *The swindlers tricked their victims into giving them large sums of money.*

vic·tor (vik′tər), NOUN. a winner; conqueror.

vic·to·ri·ous (vik tôr′ē əs), ADJECTIVE.
1 having won a victory: *Our school welcomed the victorious team.*
2 of or showing victory; ending in victory: *The team gave a victorious shout for the winning run.*
–**vic·to′ri·ous·ly,** ADVERB.

vic·tor·y (vik′tər ē), NOUN. the defeat of an enemy or opponent: *The game ended in a victory for our school.* ❏ PLURAL **vic·tor·ies.**

vid·e·o (vid′ē ō),
1 ADJECTIVE. of or about the picture in television: *The video part of the program was off for several minutes because of problems at the TV station.*
2 NOUN. a short form of **videotape** or **videocassette:** *Do you have that movie on video?*
3 ADJECTIVE. having or using a television screen or a screen like that of a television: *The computer has prepared this information for video display.*
4 NOUN. a movie or television show recorded on videotape: *He rented several videos yesterday.*
❏ PLURAL **vid·e·os.**

vid·e·o·cas·sette (vid′ē ō kə set′), NOUN. a recording on videotape, housed in a cassette.

videocassette recorder. See VCR.

video display terminal. See VDT.

video game, any of many games played on electronic machines that produce changing pictures and sounds, or that use a television set to produce such pictures and sounds. A player uses mechanical devices to control these changes in ways that depend on the rules of the particular game.

vid·e·o·tape (vid′ē ō tāp′),
1 NOUN. a magnetic tape that records and reproduces both sound and picture for television.
2 VERB. to record something on videotape: *The game was videotaped and shown on TV later.*
❑ VERB **vid·e·o·tapes, vid·e·o·taped, vid·e·o·tap·ing.**

Vi·et·nam (vē et′näm′), NOUN. a country in southeastern Asia. —**Vi·et·nam·ese** (vē et′nə mēz′), ADJECTIVE or NOUN.

We had a spectacular **view** of the Grand Canyon.

view (vyü),
1 NOUN. what you can see from a certain place: *The view from the top of the hill is beautiful.*
2 NOUN. the act of seeing; sight: *It was our first view of the ocean.*
3 NOUN. the distance at which the eye can see something: *A ship came into view.*
4 VERB. to see; look at: *They viewed the scene with pleasure.* ■ See the Synonym Study at **look.**
5 NOUN. a way of looking at or thinking about something; opinion: *What are your views on the subject?* ■ See the Synonym Study at **opinion.**
6 VERB. to think about something in a certain way; have an opinion about: *We viewed our design as the best one in the competition.*
❑ VERB **views, viewed, view·ing.**

in view, IDIOM.
1 in sight: *As we waited, the airplane came in view.*
2 under consideration: *Keep the teacher's advice in view as you try to improve your work.*

in view of, IDIOM. considering; because of: *In view of the fact that she is the best player on the team, she should be the captain.*

on view, IDIOM. to be seen; open for people to see: *The exhibit is on view from 9 A.M. to 5 P.M.*

Have You Heard?

You may have heard the phrase **"a bird's eye view."** This means that someone has a clear idea of what is going on, as if they were seeing everything from above, like a bird.

view·er (vyü′ər), NOUN.
1 someone who views something, especially TV.
2 a device that you can use to look at slides, films, and the like.

view·point (vyü′point′), NOUN. a way of thinking about something; point of view: *A heavy rain that is good from the viewpoint of farmers may be bad from the viewpoint of tourists.*

vig·i·lant (vij′ə lənt), ADJECTIVE. paying careful attention to everything that is going on around you; alert: *The dog kept vigilant watch over the sheep.* —**vig′i·lant·ly,** ADVERB.

vig·or (vig′ər), NOUN. great force, strength, or energy: *The principal argued for a new library with great vigor.*

vig·or·ous (vig′ər əs), ADJECTIVE. strong and active; energetic: *The old man is still vigorous and lively.* —**vig′or·ous·ly,** ADVERB.

Vi·king or **vi·king** (vī′king), NOUN. one of the daring seamen from northwest Europe who raided the coasts of Europe during the A.D. 700s, 800s, and 900s. The Vikings were great warriors and explorers. They even came to North America.

Viking

vil·la (vil′ə), NOUN. a house in the country or suburbs, or sometimes at the seashore. A villa is usually a large, elegant residence.
❑ PLURAL **vil·las.**

vil·lage (vil′ij), NOUN.
1 a group of houses, usually smaller than a town.
2 the people of a village: *The whole village turned out to see the circus.*

vil·lag·er (vil′i jər), NOUN. someone who lives in a village.

a	hat	ė	term	ô	order	ch	child		a in about
ā	age	i	it	oi	oil	ng	long		e in taken
ä	far	ī	ice	ou	out	sh	she	ə<	i in pencil
â	care	o	hot	u	cup	th	thin		o in lemon
e	let	ō	open	ů	put	ŦH	then		u in circus
ē	equal	ô	saw	ü	rule	zh	measure		

V

vil·lain (vil′ən), NOUN. a very bad person: *At the end of the story, the villain was punished.*

vine (vin), NOUN. any plant with a long, slender stem that grows along the ground or that climbs by attaching itself to a wall, tree, or other support. Melons and pumpkins grow on vines. Ivy is a vine. —**vine′like′**, ADJECTIVE.

vin·e·gar (vin′ə gər), NOUN. a sour liquid produced from cider or wine. Vinegar is used in salad dressing, in flavoring food, and in preserving food.

vine·yard (vin′yərd), NOUN. a place where grapes are grown.

vin·tage (vin′tij),
1 NOUN. the wine from a certain crop of grapes: *The finest vintages cost much more than others.*
2 ADJECTIVE. of outstanding quality; choice: *That shop has fine vintage wines.*
3 ADJECTIVE. dating from long ago; old-fashioned: *vintage cars, vintage clothing.*

vi·nyl (vī′nl), NOUN. any of various tough plastics, used in floor coverings, toys, and so on.

vi·o·la (vē ō′lə), NOUN. a musical instrument shaped like a violin, but slightly larger, and lower in pitch.

vi·o·late (vī′ə lāt), VERB. to break a law, rule, agreement, or promise: *Speeding violates traffic laws.* ❑ VERB **vi·o·lates, vi·o·lat·ed, vi·o·lat·ing.** —**vi′o·la′tion**, NOUN. —**vi′o·la′tor**, NOUN.

vi·o·lence (vī′ə ləns), NOUN.
1 great force; destructive force: *She slammed the door with violence.*
2 injury and damage caused by forceful acts; brutality: *They protested the violence of war. The dictator ruled with violence.*

images of **virtual reality**

vi·o·lent (vī′ə lənt), ADJECTIVE.
1 acting or done with great force: *He struck a violent blow.*
2 caused by great force: *He suffered a violent death.*
3 showing or caused by very strong feeling: *violent language, a violent rage.*
—**vi′o·lent·ly**, ADVERB.

vi·o·let (vī′ə lit),
1 NOUN. a small plant with purple, blue, yellow, or white flowers. Many violets grow wild and bloom in the early spring.
2 NOUN or ADJECTIVE. bluish purple.

vi·o·lin (vī′ə lin′), NOUN. a musical instrument with four strings played with a bow. The violin is one of the most important instruments in the orchestra because of the variety of sounds it can make.

playing the **violin**

vi·o·lin·ist (vī′ə lin′ist), NOUN. someone who plays the violin.

VIP or **V.I.P.** (informal) very important person.

vi·per (vī′pər), NOUN. a poisonous snake with hollow fangs and a thick body. Rattlesnakes are vipers.

vir·gin (vėr′jən), ADJECTIVE. pure; in its original condition: *virgin snow, a virgin forest.*

Vir·gin·ia (vər jin′yə), NOUN. one of the southern states of the United States. *Abbreviation:* VA; *Capital:* Richmond. —**Vir·gin′ian**, NOUN.

State Story **Virginia** comes from the phrase *the Virgin Queen.* This phrase was used to describe Elizabeth I of England, who never married. English settlers gave this name to the area.

Virgin Islands, a group of islands in the West Indies, several of which belong to the United States.

vir·tu·al (vėr′chü əl), ADJECTIVE. almost something, if not actually or completely so: *The battle was won with so great a loss of soldiers that it was a virtual defeat.*

vir·tu·al·ly (vėr′chü ə lē), ADVERB. nearly: *We are such close friends that we're virtually sisters.*

virtual reality, computer images that are created by interactive software. The images seem like a real environment to the senses of the user.

vir·tue (vėr′chü), NOUN.
1 goodness in thoughts and actions: *She is a person of the highest virtue.*
2 a particular kind of good behavior: *Justice is a virtue.*
3 a good quality: *Consider the virtues of a small car.* ❑ PLURAL **vir·tues.**

vir·tu·ous (vėr′chü əs), ADJECTIVE. good; honest; just: *She led a virtuous life.* —**vir′tu·ous·ly**, ADVERB.

vi·rus (vī′rəs), NOUN. a very tiny particle of protein and other substances that causes a disease. Viruses are so small that they cannot be seen through most microscopes. They can reproduce only inside the cells of living things. Viruses cause rabies, polio, chicken pox, the common cold, and many other infectious diseases of people, animals, and plants. ❑ PLURAL **vi·rus·es.**

vise (vīs), NOUN. a tool with two jaws that are opened and closed by a screw. A vise is used to hold an object firmly. ∎ Another word that sounds like this is **vice. –vise′like′,** ADJECTIVE.

vis·i·bil·i·ty (viz′ə bil′ə tē), NOUN.
1 the distance at which things are visible: *Fog and rain decreased visibility to about 50 feet.*
2 the condition or quality of being visible: *I put reflectors on my bike to increase its visibility.*

vis·i·ble (viz′ə bəl), ADJECTIVE.
1 able to be seen: *The shore was barely visible through the fog.*
2 apparent; obvious: *There has been visible improvement in his work since he changed schools.* **–vis′i·bly,** ADVERB.

vi·sion (vizh′ən), NOUN.
1 the power of seeing; sense of sight: *I have to wear glasses because my vision is poor.*
2 something that is seen: *The vision of the table loaded with food made us very hungry.*
3 the power of using your imagination to see what the future may bring: *The founder of this company was a person of great vision.*

vis·it (viz′it),
1 VERB. to go to see; come to see: *Come visit New York!*
2 VERB. to go to see someone and spend some time there: *I visited my friend last week.*
3 NOUN. an act of visiting someone: *My aunt paid us a visit last week.*
❑ VERB **vis·its, vis·it·ed, vis·it·ing.**

vis·i·tor (viz′ə tər), NOUN. someone who visits; person who is visiting; guest: *Our visitors arrive today.*

vi·sor (vī′zər), NOUN.
1 the part of a helmet that can be raised and lowered to protect the face in a suit of armor.
2 the brim of a cap, which sticks out in front.
3 a stiff shade above a windshield, that can be lowered to shield your eyes from the sun.

vis·u·al (vizh′ü əl), ADJECTIVE. of sight; for sight; by sight: *Nearsightedness is a visual defect.* **–vis′u·al·ly,** ADVERB.

vis·u·al·ize (vizh′ü ə līz), VERB. to form a mental picture of something: *I tried to visualize the face of my old friend.* ❑ VERB **vis·u·al·iz·es, vis·u·al·ized, vis·u·al·iz·ing. –vis′u·al·i·za′tion,** NOUN.

vi·tal (vī′tl), ADJECTIVE.
1 very important; basic; very necessary: *Good government is vital to the welfare of a community.*
2 of or about life: *Vital statistics give facts about births, deaths, marriages, and so on.*
3 necessary to life: *The heart is a vital organ.* **–vi′tal·ly,** ADVERB.

vi·tal·i·ty (vī tal′ə tē), NOUN. strength or vigor of mind or body: *Exercise helps maintain vitality.*

vi·ta·min (vī′tə mən), NOUN. any of a group of special chemical substances necessary for the body in small amounts as nutrients. Vitamins are found especially in milk, butter, raw fruits and vegetables, and the part of grains just inside the husk. Lack of vitamins causes certain diseases as well as generally poor health.

vitamin A, a vitamin found in milk, butter, egg yolk, green and yellow vegetables, and liver. Vitamin A increases the resistance of the body to infection and helps vision at night.

vitamin C, a vitamin found in oranges, lemons, tomatoes, and leafy green vegetables. Vitamin C cannot be stored in the body and must be replaced regularly.

vitamin D, a vitamin found in milk and egg yolk. Vitamin D is necessary for the growth and health of bones and teeth.

viv·id (viv′id), ADJECTIVE.
1 strikingly bright; brilliant; strong and clear: *He paints with vivid colors.*
2 giving clear, detailed ideas of something that happened; lifelike: *Her description of the party was so vivid that I almost felt I had been there.*
3 strong and distinct: *I have a vivid memory of the fire.* **–viv′id·ly,** ADVERB.

vo·cab·u·lar·y (vō kab′yə ler′ē), NOUN.
1 all the words used by a person or group of people: *Reading will increase your vocabulary.*
2 all the words of a language.
3 a list of words, usually in alphabetical order, with their meanings: *There is a vocabulary in the back of our French book.*
❑ PLURAL **vo·cab·u·lar·ies.**

vo·cal (vō′kəl), ADJECTIVE.
1 of or about the voice or speaking: *The tongue is a vocal organ.*
2 made with the voice: *I like vocal music.*
3 speaking forcefully about something that interests you a lot: *She was quite vocal at the recent meeting about summer school hours.*

vocal cords, two bands of elastic tissue in the throat. When they are pulled tight, the passage of breath between them causes them to vibrate, producing the sound of the voice.

V

a	hat	ė	term	ô	order	ch	child	(a in about
ā	age	i	it	oi	oil	ng	long	e in taken
ä	far	ī	ice	ou	out	sh	she	ə { i in pencil
â	care	o	hot	u	cup	th	thin	o in lemon
e	let	ō	open	u̇	put	ᴛʜ	then	(u in circus
ē	equal	ò	saw	ü	rule	zh	measure	

vo·cal·ist (vō′kə list), NOUN. someone who sings, especially a singer of popular songs.

vo·ca·tion (vō kā′shən), NOUN. a particular occupation, business, profession, or trade.

vod·ka (vod′kə), NOUN. a strong alcoholic drink made from potatoes, rye, barley, or corn.

vogue (vōg), NOUN. **in vogue,** in style or fashion: *Hoop skirts were in vogue more than 100 years ago.*

voice (vois),

1 NOUN. a sound made through the mouth, especially by people speaking, singing, or shouting: *The voices of children could be heard next door.*

2 NOUN. the power to make sounds through your mouth: *He was losing his voice because of a cold.*

3 NOUN. ability as a singer: *That child has a very good voice.*

4 VERB. to say with force what you are thinking or feeling: *They voiced their approval.* ▪ See the Synonym Study at **say.**

❏ VERB **voic·es, voiced, voic·ing.**

voice mail, a computer system for recording telephone messages to be played back later. People use their telephones to call the central computer and hear their messages.

voice recognition, the process of analyzing human speech with a computer; speech recognition. Voice recognition is used either to understand speech or to reproduce it.

void (void),

1 NOUN. a feeling of emptiness or great loss: *The death of his dog left an aching void in the boy's heart.*

2 ADJECTIVE. without legal force: *Any contract made by a child is void.*

3 NOUN. an empty space.

4 ADJECTIVE. empty; vacant: *The capsule is a void space.*

vol·can·ic (vol kan′ik), ADJECTIVE.

1 of, about, or caused by a volcano: *They feared a volcanic eruption.*

2 like a volcano; liable to break out violently: *She has a volcanic temper.*

vol·ca·no (vol kā′nō), NOUN.

1 an opening in the earth's crust through which steam, ashes, and lava are sometimes forced out.

2 a cone-shaped hill or mountain around this opening, built up of the material that is forced out.

❏ PLURAL **vol·ca·noes** or **vol·ca·nos.**

Did You Know?

The biggest eruption of a **volcano** happened in 1883. The island of **Krakatoa** (krak′ə tō′ə) exploded and left a hole 1,000 feet deep. It also created a tidal wave that killed more than 36,000 people.

red-hot lava erupting from a **volcano**

vol·ley (vol′ē),
1 NOUN. a shower of stones, bullets, or other missiles: *A volley of arrows rained down upon the attacking knights.*
2 in tennis, volleyball, and so on: a NOUN. the act of hitting a ball while it is still in the air. b VERB. to hit or return a ball while it is still in the air.
❑ PLURAL **vol·leys**; VERB **vol·leys, vol·leyed, vol·ley·ing.**

vol·ley·ball (vol′ē bȯl′), NOUN. a game played by two teams with a large ball and a high net. The players on each side have three hits using only their hands or forearms to return the ball to the other side.

The beach is a perfect place for **volleyball.**

volt (vōlt), NOUN. the unit for measuring the electric force needed to make some amount of current flow through a circuit.

volt·age (vōl′tij), NOUN. electric force, measured in volts. A current of high voltage is used in transmitting electric power over long distances.

vol·ume (vol′yəm), NOUN.
1 the amount of space anything contains or fills. The volume of a cube is found from measurements in three directions: up, across, and toward the back. Thus, all volume is given in cubic inches, cubic meters, and so on.
2 an amount; quantity: *He forecast the volume of business at his store over Christmas.*
3 an amount of sound; loudness: *Please turn the volume down on the stereo.*
4 a book: *We own a library of five hundred volumes.*
5 a book that is part of a set or series: *I found the information in the ninth volume of this encyclopedia.*

vol·un·tar·y (vol′ən ter′ē), ADJECTIVE.
1 acting, done, made, or given of your own choice; not required: *She is a voluntary worker in the school office.*
2 controlled by the will: *Talking is voluntary; hiccupping is not voluntary.*
—**vol′un·tar′i·ly,** ADVERB.

vol·un·teer (vol′ən tir′),
1 NOUN. someone who works without pay. A fire department is often made up of volunteers.
2 VERB. to offer your services: *I volunteered for the job.*
3 NOUN. someone who enters any branch of the armed forces by choice.
❑ VERB **vol·un·teers, vol·un·teered, vol·un·teer·ing.**

Red Cross **volunteers** giving first aid

vom·it (vom′it),
1 VERB. to feel sick and throw up what you have eaten.
2 NOUN. food or liquid that you throw up.
❑ VERB **vom·its, vom·it·ed, vom·it·ing.**

vote (vōt),
1 NOUN. a formal expression of a choice about a proposal, a motion, or a candidate for office. The person receiving the most votes is elected.
2 NOUN. the right to vote: *In this club, only members who have paid all their dues have the vote.*
3 NOUN. a ballot or other means by which a vote is cast or indicated: *A million votes were counted.*
4 NOUN. the act or process of voting: *We took a vote on where to go for vacation.*
5 VERB. to give or cast your vote: *I voted for that senator.*
6 VERB. to decide something or chose someone by voting: *Money for a new school was voted by the board. The new mayor was voted into office.*
❑ VERB **votes, vot·ed, vot·ing.**

vot·er (vō′tər), NOUN.
1 someone who votes.
2 someone who has the right to vote: *Women have been voters in the United States only since 1920.*

vouch (vouch), VERB. to guarantee from your experience that something is so: *I can vouch for his story.* ❑ VERB **vouch·es, vouched, vouch·ing.**

vow (vou),
1 NOUN. a solemn promise: *a vow of secrecy, marriage vows.*
2 VERB. to make a vow: *The knight vowed loyalty to the king.* ■ See the Synonym Study at **promise.**
❑ VERB **vows, vowed, vow·ing.**

vow·el (vou′əl), NOUN.
1 a speech sound that is spelled by the letters *a, e, i, o, u,* and sometimes *y.*

a hat	ė term	ô order	ch child	ə { a in about
ā age	i it	oi oil	ng long	e in taken
ä far	ī ice	ou out	sh she	i in pencil
â care	o hot	u cup	th thin	o in lemon
e let	ō open	u̇ put	ŦH then	u in circus
ē equal	ȯ saw	ü rule	zh measure	

V

2 a letter or combination of letters that stands for a vowel sound.

voy·age (voi′ij),

1 *NOUN.* a journey by water; cruise: *We had a pleasant voyage to England.* ■ See the Synonym Study at **trip.**

2 *NOUN.* a journey through the air or through space: *The earth's voyage around the sun takes 365 days.*

3 *VERB.* to make or take a voyage; go by sea or air: *We voyaged across the Atlantic Ocean.*

❏ *VERB* **voy·ages, voy·aged, voy·ag·ing.**

voy·ag·er (voi′i jər), *NOUN.* someone who makes a voyage; traveler.

vs. or **vs,** an abbreviation of **versus.**

VT, an abbreviation of **Vermont.**

vul·gar (vul′gər), *ADJECTIVE.* showing bad manners or bad taste: *We are forbidden to use vulgar language.*

vul·gar·i·ty (vul gar′ə tē), *NOUN.*

1 lack of good manners or taste; coarseness.

2 a vulgar act or word.

❏ *PLURAL* **vul·gar·i·ties.**

vul·ner·a·ble (vul′nər ə bəl), *ADJECTIVE.*

1 easily harmed; capable of being wounded or injured: *Very old people are vulnerable to some kinds of sickness.*

2 open to attack: *The army's retreat left the city vulnerable to attack by the enemy.*

3 easily hurt by criticism: *Most people are vulnerable to ridicule.*

−**vul′ner·a·bil′i·ty,** *NOUN.*

vul·ture (vul′chər), *NOUN.* a large bird of prey related to eagles and hawks that eats the flesh of dead animals. Vultures usually do not have feathers on their heads and necks.

vultures feeding

well

Ww

W or **w** (dub′əl yü), *NOUN.* the 23rd letter of the English alphabet. ❑ *PLURAL* **W's** or **w's.**

W or **W.,**
1 an abbreviation of **watt** or **watts.**
2 an abbreviation of **west.**
3 an abbreviation of **western.**

WA, an abbreviation of **Washington.**

wad (wäd),
1 *NOUN.* a small, soft ball or chunk of something: *She stepped in a wad of chewing gum. I plugged my ears with wads of cotton.*
2 *VERB.* to roll or press something into a wad: *I wadded up the paper and threw it away.*
❑ *VERB* **wads, wad·ded, wad·ding.**

wad·dle (wäd′l),
1 *VERB.* to walk with short steps and an awkward, swaying motion, as a duck does: *The small child waddled from the house to the playground carrying a large toy.*
2 *NOUN.* an awkward, swaying way of walking: *It made us laugh to see the penguin's waddle.*
❑ *VERB* **wad·dles, wad·dled, wad·dling.**

wade (wād), *VERB.* to walk through water, snow, mud, and so on: *I waded across the brook.*
❑ *VERB* **wades, wad·ed, wad·ing.**

wade through, *IDIOM.* to spend a lot of time doing something hard or boring: *Must I wade through that dull book?*

wa·fer (wā′fər), *NOUN.* a thin, crisp cracker or cookie.

waf·fle (wäf′əl), *NOUN.* a portion of batter cooked in a special griddle that makes a pattern of square holes on both sides. Waffles are usually eaten while hot with butter and syrup.

wag (wag),
1 *VERB.* to move from side to side or up and down: *Dogs often wag their tails.*
2 *NOUN.* a wagging motion: *I saw the wag of its tail.*
❑ *VERB* **wags, wagged, wag·ging.**

wage (wāj),
1 *NOUN.* usually, **wages,** the money paid for work done, especially work paid for by the hour: *He receives a weekly wage of $450.*
2 *VERB.* to fight or be in a struggle with: *Doctors and nurses wage war against disease.*
❏ *VERB* **wag·es, waged, wag·ing.**

wa·ger (wā′jər),
1 *VERB.* to make a bet; bet; gamble: *I'll wager the black horse will win the race.*
2 *NOUN.* the act of betting; bet: *The wager of $10 was promptly paid.*
❏ *VERB* **wa·gers, wa·gered, wa·ger·ing.**

wag·on (wag′ən), *NOUN.*
1 (formerly) a four-wheeled vehicle for carrying loads, usually pulled by a horse: *Milk used to be delivered in a milk wagon.*
2 a child's toy vehicle to ride in that has four wheels and a handle in front.

wail (wāl),
1 *VERB.* to cry aloud for a long time out of grief or pain: *The baby wailed.*
2 *NOUN.* a long, loud cry of grief or pain: *The baby awoke with a wail.*
3 *NOUN.* a sound like this kind of cry: *We heard the wail of a coyote as we sat around the campfire.*
❏ *VERB* **wails, wailed, wail·ing.** ■ Another word that sounds like this is **whale.**

waist (wāst), *NOUN.* the part of the body between the ribs and the hips. ■ Another word that sounds like this is **waste.**

wait (wāt),
1 *VERB.* to stay where you are or stop doing something until someone comes or something happens: *Let's wait in the shade.*
2 *NOUN.* the act or time of staying where you are: *I had a long wait at the doctor's office.*
3 *VERB.* to be left undone; be put off: *This can't wait.*
❏ *VERB* **waits, wait·ed, wait·ing.** ■ Another word that sounds like this is **weight.**
wait on or **wait upon,** *IDIOM.* to serve as a waiter or waitress: *He waited on several tables of diners.*

wait·er (wā′tər), *NOUN.* someone who brings food to people in a restaurant.

waiting room, a room in a doctor's office, railroad station, or the like, for people to wait in.

wai·tress (wā′tris), *NOUN.* a woman who brings food to people in a restaurant. ❏ *PLURAL* **wai·tress·es.**

waive (wāv), *VERB.*
1 to give up a right or claim to something: *The lawyer waived the privilege of cross-examination.*
2 to set aside or not enforce something: *Admission is waived for senior citizens.*
❏ *VERB* **waives, waived, waiv·ing.** ■ Another word that sounds like this is **wave.**

wake¹ (wāk),
1 *VERB.* to stop sleeping: *I usually wake at dawn.*
2 *VERB.* to cause someone else to stop sleeping: *The noise of the traffic always wakes the baby.*
3 *VERB.* to make or become alive or active: *Flowers wake in the spring.*
4 *NOUN.* a watch kept beside the body of a dead person before its burial.
❏ *VERB* **wakes, woke** or **waked, wo·ken** or **waked, wak·ing.**

an old-fashioned **wagon** used for delivering milk

wake² (wāk), *NOUN.* the smooth, white track and waves in the water behind a moving ship.

wake·ful (wāk′fəl), *ADJECTIVE.*
1 not able to sleep: *The wakeful baby wailed.*
2 without sleep: *Her parents spent a wakeful night.*
—**wake′ful·ness,** *NOUN.*

Wake Island, a small island in the northern Pacific. It belongs to the United States.

wak·en (wā′kən), *VERB.* to wake. ❏ *VERB* **wak·ens, wak·ened, wak·en·ing.**

Wales (wālz), *NOUN.* a division of Great Britain in the southwestern part.

walk (wȯk),
1 *VERB.* to move by taking steps. In walking, a person always has one foot on the ground: *Walk down to the post office with me.*
2 *VERB.* to go over, on, or through on foot: *We walked the length of the trail.*
3 *NOUN.* the slowest gait of a four-legged animal, in which at least two feet are always on the ground.
4 *VERB.* to cause an animal to go at a walk: *It's your turn to walk the dog.*
5 *NOUN.* the act of walking, especially for pleasure or exercise: *We went for a walk in the country.*
6 *VERB.* to go with someone while walking: *to walk someone to the corner, to walk a guest to the door.*
7 *NOUN.* a distance to walk: *The library is a twenty-minute walk from our house.*
8 *NOUN.* a manner or way of walking; gait: *We could tell she was happy from her lively walk.*

9 *NOUN.* a place for walking; path: *There are many pretty walks in the park.*

10 *VERB.* in baseball: **a** to go to first base after the pitcher has thrown four balls to one batter: *I walked in the first inning.* **b** to allow a batter to reach first base by pitching four balls to one batter: *The pitcher has walked four batters in a row.*

❑ *VERB* **walks, walked, walk·ing.**

Synonym Study

Walk means to move on foot: *The family spent an hour walking around the mall.*

Step means to walk, especially a short distance: *I stepped over to the fountain for a drink of water.*

Pace means to walk back and forth: *She paced the platform, waiting for the subway train.*

March means to walk steadily, with a regular step: *Bands march to the beat of drums.*

Stride means to take long steps: *The little boy strode along, trying to keep up with us.*

Shuffle means to walk without taking your feet from the ground: *She carefully shuffled her way across the icy bridge.*

walk·er (wȯ′kər), *NOUN.*
1 a lightweight frame with four legs and without wheels, used for support by someone who has difficulty walking.
2 a small framework with wheels in which children support themselves while learning to walk.
3 someone who walks.

walk·ie-talk·ie (wȯ′kē tȯ′kē), *NOUN.* a small, portable radio set, used to receive and send messages. ❑ *PLURAL* **walk·ie-talk·ies.**

walking stick,
1 See **cane** (definition 1).
2 any of several insects with bodies shaped like sticks or twigs.

walking stick — between 2 and 3 inches long, from head to tail

walk·way (wȯk′wā′), *NOUN.*
1 a structure for walking on: *The factory has an overhead steel walkway.*
2 path; walk: *We went down the walkway between the houses.*

wall (wȯl), *NOUN.*
1 the side of a room or building: *to paint a bedroom wall, the brick wall of a house.*
2 a structure of stone, brick, or other material built to enclose, support, or protect something.
3 anything like a wall in looks or use: *The flood came in a wall of water twelve feet high. The mayor met a wall of protesters.*

drive someone up the wall, *IDIOM.* to greatly annoy or irritate: *His singing really drives me up the wall. Stop clicking the pen cap; it's driving me up the wall.*

wall up, *IDIOM.* to enclose, protect, or fill something with a wall: *They walled up the old window.* ❑ *VERB* **walls, walled, wall·ing.**

wal·let (wäl′it), *NOUN.* a small, flat case for carrying paper money or cards in your pocket; billfold.

wal·lop (wäl′əp), *VERB.*
1 to beat someone or something thoroughly; thrash: *I'd like to wallop whoever stole my camera.*
2 to hit very hard: *The batter walloped a home run to win the game.*
3 to defeat thoroughly, as in a game: *Our team walloped them in the finals.* ❑ *VERB* **wal·lops, wal·loped, wal·lop·ing.**

wal·low (wäl′ō), *VERB.* to roll about in mud, water, and so on: *The pigs wallowed in the mud.* ❑ *VERB* **wal·lows, wal·lowed, wal·low·ing.**

wall·pa·per (wȯl′pā′pər),
1 *NOUN.* stiff paper, usually printed with a pattern in color, for pasting on and covering walls.
2 *VERB.* to put wallpaper on: *We are going to wallpaper my bedroom.*
❑ *VERB* **wall·pa·pers, wall·pa·pered, wall·pa·per·ing.**

wal·nut (wȯl′nut), *NOUN.* a large, almost round nut with a very hard shell that forms two halves. The meat of the walnut is eaten by itself or used in cakes and cookies. The wood of some kinds of walnut trees is used in making furniture.

walnut

W

a hat	ė term	ô order	ch child		⎧a in about
ā age	i it	oi oil	ng long		⎪e in taken
ä far	ī ice	ou out	sh she	ə⎨i in pencil
â care	o hot	u cup	th thin		⎪o in lemon
e let	ō open	u̇ put	ᴛʜ then		⎩u in circus
ē equal	ȯ saw	ü rule	zh measure		

walrus — between 8 and 12 feet long

wal·rus (wȯl′rəs), NOUN. a large sea animal of the arctic regions, closely related to the seal. Walruses are hunted for their hides, tusks, and blubber. ❑ PLURAL **wal·rus** or **wal·rus·es**.

Word Story

Walrus comes from two Dutch words meaning "whale" and "horse."

waltz (wȯlts),
1 NOUN. a slow dance with three beats to a measure.
2 NOUN. the music for this dance.
3 VERB. to dance a waltz.
❑ PLURAL **waltz·es**; VERB **waltz·es, waltzed, waltz·ing**.

wam·pum (wäm′pəm), NOUN. beads made from shells, formerly used by eastern North American Indians as money and for ornament.

wan (wän), ADJECTIVE.
1 pale: *Her face looked wan after her long illness.*
2 faint; weak; looking worn or tired: *The sick boy gave the doctor a wan smile.*
❑ ADJECTIVE **wan·ner, wan·nest**.

wand (wänd), NOUN. a thin stick or rod: *The magician waved her wand and a rabbit popped out of the hat.*

wan·der (wän′dər), VERB.
1 to move here and there without any special purpose or goal: *We wandered around the fair.*
2 to leave the right way or path; stray: *The dog wandered off and got lost.*
❑ VERB **wan·ders, wan·dered, wan·der·ing**.

wan·der·er (wän′dər ər), NOUN. a human being or an animal that wanders.

wane (wān), VERB.
1 to gradually become smaller in size: *The moon wanes after it has become full.*
2 to slowly lose power, influence, or importance: *Many great empires have waned.*
❑ VERB **wanes, waned, wan·ing**.

wan·na·be (wän′ə bē′), NOUN. (informal) a person who hopes, often in vain, to become famous.

want (wänt),
1 VERB. to hope to have something, do something, or go somewhere; wish: *We want a new car. I want to become an engineer.*
2 NOUN. a lack of food, clothing, shelter, or something necessary: *The old couple are now living in want.*
❑ VERB **wants, want·ed, want·ing**.

Synonym Study

Want means to have or feel a need for something: *Everyone wants to have friends.*

Wish means to hope for something: *I wish I could find my lost watch.*

Desire means to want very much. It is a formal word: *People all over the world desire peace.*

Crave means to want something greatly: *My sister craves ice cream, and she never gets enough of it.*

war (wôr),
1 NOUN. fighting carried on between nations or parts of a nation. Members of the armed forces fight in wars.
2 NOUN. any fighting or struggle; conflict: *Doctors carry on war against disease.*
3 VERB. to fight; make war: *Germany warred against France.* ■ See the Synonym Study at **fight**.
❑ VERB **wars, warred, war·ring**. ■ Another word that sounds like this is **wore**.

war·ble (wôr′bəl),
1 VERB. to sing in a quick, vibrating way: *Birds warbled in the trees.*
2 NOUN. a bird's song or a sound like it.
❑ VERB **war·bles, war·bled, war·bling**.

war·bler (wôr′blər), NOUN. any of many kinds of small songbirds, often brightly colored.

war·bon·net (wôr′bon′it), NOUN. a ceremonial headdress with feathers and often a long trailing part, worn by certain North American Indians.

an American Indian chieftain wearing a **warbonnet**

ward (wôrd), NOUN.
1 a division of a hospital or prison: *We visited him in the children's ward.*
2 one of the parts a city or town is divided into for purposes of government.
3 someone under the care of a guardian or the legal protection of a court.
ward off, IDIOM. to keep away or turn aside: *He warded off the blow with his arm.*
❑ VERB **wards, ward·ed, ward·ing.**

Word Power   -ward -wards

The suffixes **-ward** and **-wards** mean "toward." Back**ward** means **toward** the back. Home**ward** means **toward** home. West**wards** means **toward** the west.

ward·en (wôrd'n), NOUN.
1 the official in charge of a prison.
2 an official who enforces certain laws and regulations: *a game warden, a fire warden.*
ward·robe (wôrd'rōb'), NOUN.
1 a supply of clothes: *I need a new summer wardrobe.*
2 a closet or piece of furniture for holding clothes.

Word Story

Wardrobe comes from French words meaning "guard" and "garment." A wardrobe that holds clothes keeps them safe from dust and moths. Soon the word came to mean the clothes themselves.

ware (wâr), NOUN.
1 **wares,** things for sale: *Household wares are on the third floor at this store.*
2 a kind of manufactured thing for sale: *This store sells lots of copper ware.*
3 pottery: *He bought some porcelain ware.*
■ Other words that sound like this are **wear** and **where.**
ware·house (wâr'hous'), NOUN. a place where goods are kept; storehouse. ❑ PLURAL **ware·hous·es** (wâr'hou'ziz).
war·fare (wôr'fâr'), NOUN. war; fighting.
war·like (wôr'līk'), ADJECTIVE.
1 ready for war; fond of war: *They are not a warlike nation.*
2 threatening war; hostile: *He made a warlike speech.*
warm (wôrm),
1 ADJECTIVE. more hot than cold; giving forth gentle heat: *She sat in the warm sunshine.*
2 ADJECTIVE. having a feeling of heat: *She was warm from running.*
3 ADJECTIVE. able to keep your body heat in: *We wear warm clothes in winter.*
4 ADJECTIVE. having or showing lively feelings; enthusiastic: *a warm welcome, a warm heart.*

5 ADJECTIVE. (in games, treasure hunts, and the like) getting close to what you are looking for.
6 VERB. to make or become warm: *A fire in the fireplace can really warm a room.*
7 VERB. to cause good, warm feelings: *Their kind words of welcome warmed my heart.*
❑ VERB **warms, warmed, warm·ing.** –**warm'ly,** ADVERB.
warm up, IDIOM.
1 to heat or cook again: *This morning we warmed up yesterday's oatmeal.*
2 to practice or exercise for a few minutes before a game or performance.
warm-blood·ed (wôrm'blud'id), ADJECTIVE. having blood that stays at about the same temperature no matter what the temperature of the air or water around the animal is. Cats are warm-blooded; snakes and fish are cold-blooded.
warmth (wôrmth), NOUN.
1 the condition of being warm: *We enjoyed the warmth of the open fire.*
2 a warm feeling: *We felt the warmth of our host's welcome.*
3 liveliness of feelings or emotions: *She spoke with warmth of the natural beauty of the mountains.*
warm-up (wôrm'up'), NOUN. exercises that you do before a game or performance. A warm-up gets your muscles ready for work or exercise.
warn (wôrn), VERB.
1 to tell someone about danger before it happens; caution: *The clouds warned us of the coming storm.*
2 to tell someone that something is going to happen. A turn signal warns other drivers that you are about to turn right or left.
❑ VERB **warns, warned, warn·ing.** ■ Another word that sounds like this is **worn.**

a sign that **warns** with a symbol and a message

a	hat	ė	term	ô	order	ch	child		a in about
ā	age	i	it	oi	oil	ng	long		e in taken
ä	far	ī	ice	ou	out	sh	she	ə	i in pencil
â	care	o	hot	u	cup	th	thin		o in lemon
e	let	ō	open	u̇	put	ŦH	then		u in circus
ē	equal	ȯ	saw	ü	rule	zh	measure	

W

warn·ing (wôr′ning), NOUN. something that warns; notice given in advance: *That painful experience was a warning to us to be more careful in the future.*

warp (wôrp), VERB. to bend or twist something out of shape: *The heat of the sun had warped the wooden windowsill.* ❑ VERB **warps, warped, warp·ing.**

war·rant (wôr′ənt),
1 NOUN. an official written order that gives the police special authority: *The police had a search warrant for the house.*
2 VERB. to give a good reason for something: *Nothing can warrant such rudeness.*
3 VERB. to give a guarantee for a manufactured product: *The company warranted the quality of their cameras.*
❑ VERB **war·rants, war·rant·ed, war·rant·ing.**

war·ri·or (wôr′ē ər), NOUN. someone experienced in fighting battles.

war·ship (wôr′ship′), NOUN. a ship with guns and armor, used in war.

wart (wôrt), NOUN. a small, hard lump on the skin, caused by a virus.

war·y (wâr′ē), ADJECTIVE. on your guard against danger or being deceived: *They were wary of walking alone at night in that neighborhood.*
❑ ADJECTIVE **war·i·er, war·i·est. —war′i·ly,** ADVERB.

was (wuz or wäz), VERB. a past tense of **be**: *Once there was a queen. I was late. She was going to study. The candy was eaten.*

wash (wäsh),
1 VERB. to clean something with water: *to wash your face, to wash dishes, to wash clothes.*
2 VERB. to remove dirt, stains, paint, or the like by or as by scrubbing with soap and water: *Can you wash that spot out?*
3 VERB. to wash yourself; wash your face and hands: *You should always wash before eating.*
4 NOUN. the act of washing or the condition of being washed: *This floor needs a good wash.*
5 NOUN. a bundle of clothes washed or to be washed: *Take the wash from the dryer.*
6 VERB. to carry or be carried along or away by water or other liquid: *Wood is often washed ashore by waves. The road washed out during the storm.*
❑ VERB **wash·es, washed, wash·ing;** PLURAL **wash·es.**

wash·a·ble (wäsh′ə bəl), ADJECTIVE. able to be washed without damage: *Cotton is a washable fabric.*

wash·cloth (wäsh′klôth′), NOUN. a small cloth for washing yourself. ❑ PLURAL **wash·cloths** (wäsh′klôтHz′ or wäsh′klôths′).

wash·er (wäsh′ər), NOUN.
1 a machine that washes clothes. Washers are electric appliances.

2 a flat ring of metal, rubber, leather, or the like. Washers are used to provide tightness or to prevent friction at joints, especially with nuts and bolts.

washing machine, a machine that washes clothes.

Wash·ing·ton (wäsh′ing tən), NOUN.
1 the capital of the United States, covering the entire District of Columbia. Washington is situated between Maryland and Virginia.
2 one of the Pacific states of the United States. *Abbreviation:* WA; *Capital:* Olympia.
—Wash·ing·to·ni·an (wäsh′ing tō′nē ən), NOUN.

State Story The state and city of Washington were both named in honor of George Washington, the first president of the United States. He lived from 1732 to 1799.

wash·room (wäsh′rüm′), NOUN. a room where people can use the toilet and wash up; restroom.

was·n't (wuz′nt or wäz′nt), a contraction of **was not.**

wasp (wäsp), NOUN. an insect that has narrow sections of the middle of the body and a powerful sting. Hornets and yellow jackets are kinds of wasps. **—wasp′like′,** ADJECTIVE.

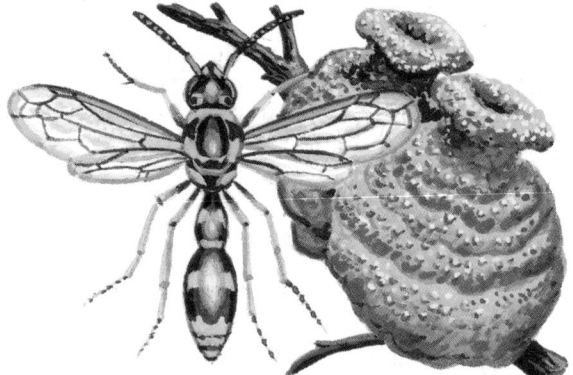

wasp — about 1 inch long

waste (wāst),
1 VERB. to make poor use of something; fail to get full value or benefit from: *Though he had a lot of work to do, he wasted his time watching TV.*
2 NOUN. a use of something in a way that makes no sense: *Buying that suit was a waste of money; it is already starting to wear out.*
3 ADJECTIVE. thrown away because it is useless or worthless: *The construction site had a pile of waste lumber.*
4 NOUN. useless or worthless material; stuff to be thrown away. Garbage or sewage is waste.
5 NOUN. the material which the body gets rid of because it cannot be digested or used.
6 ADJECTIVE. left over; not used: *The restaurant turns its waste food into compost.*
❑ VERB **wastes, wast·ed, wast·ing.** ■ Another word that sounds like this is **waist.**

waste·bas·ket (wāst′bas′kit), *NOUN.* a basket or can where you put wastepaper or trash.

waste·ful (wāst′fəl), *ADJECTIVE.* using or spending too much: *Dad asked us not to be wasteful of water.* —**waste′ful·ly,** *ADVERB.*

waste·land (wāst′land′), *NOUN.* land that is too dry to farm or that lacks topsoil.

waste·pa·per (wāst′pā′pər), *NOUN.* paper thrown away or to be thrown away as worthless.

watch (wäch),
1 *VERB.* to look at something carefully: *The medical students watched while the surgeon and her team performed the operation.* ■ See the Synonym Study at **look.**
2 *VERB.* to look at something: *Are you watching that show on TV? We watched the kittens play.*
3 *VERB.* to look or wait with care and attention; be very careful: *She watched for a chance to cross the street.*
4 *NOUN.* a device for telling time, small enough to be carried in a pocket or worn on the wrist.
5 *NOUN.* the act of being watchful: *There was a tornado watch.*
6 *VERB.* to guard or look after: *Please watch the baby while I make a phone call.*
7 *NOUN.* a person or people hired to guard: *A call for help aroused the night watch.*
8 *NOUN.* a period of time for guarding: *The soldier had the first watch in the night.*
❏ *VERB* **watch·es, watched, watch·ing;** *PLURAL* **watch·es.** —**watch′er,** *NOUN.*

watch out, *IDIOM.* to be careful: *Watch out for cars when you cross the street.*

watch·dog (wäch′dog′), *NOUN.* a dog kept to guard your property.

watch·ful (wäch′fəl), *ADJECTIVE.* wide-awake; very attentive: *Be watchful when you cross the street.* —**watch′ful·ness,** *NOUN.*

watch·man (wäch′mən), *NOUN.* someone hired to guard a building, especially at night: *He is a night watchman for the bank.* ❏ *PLURAL* **watch·men.**

wa·ter (wȯ′tər),
1 *NOUN.* the liquid that fills the ocean, rivers, lakes, and ponds, and falls from the sky as rain. Water is a nutrient necessary for both plant and animal life.
2 *VERB.* to sprinkle with water: *I watered the grass.*
3 *VERB.* to give water to an animal or animals: *After we returned from our ride, we fed and watered the horses.*
4 *VERB.* to fill with water or watery liquid: *Peeling onions can make your eyes water. The cake made my mouth water.*
5 *ADJECTIVE.* done or used in or on water: *Swimming and diving are water sports.*
6 *ADJECTIVE.* growing or living in or near water: *water plants, water insects.*
❏ *VERB* **wa·ters, wa·tered, wa·ter·ing.**

keep your head above water, *IDIOM.* to stay out of trouble or difficulty, especially financial difficulty.

make your mouth water, *IDIOM.* to stir up your appetite or desire: *The smell of that pie is making my mouth water.*

throw cold water on, *IDIOM.* to discourage: *Mom threw cold water on my plan to go camping.*

tread water, *IDIOM.* to keep yourself from sinking by moving your feet up and down.

water down, *IDIOM.*
1 to reduce the strength of something by adding water to it: *She watered down her lemonade.*
2 to reduce the strength or effectiveness of a proposal, law, and so on: *They watered down the regulation by reducing the fine.*

water buffalo, any of several kinds of cattle of Asia. They are often used to pull plows and haul loads.

wa·ter·col·or (wȯ′tər kul′ər), *NOUN.*
1 a paint mixed with water instead of oil.
2 a picture made with watercolors.

wa·ter·cress (wȯt′ər kres′), *NOUN.* a plant that grows in water and has crisp leaves which are used for salad.

water cycle, a cycle in nature by which water evaporates from oceans, lakes, and rivers and returns to them as rain or snow.

The arrows show the way water travels through its cycle. The sun's heat causes water to evaporate. The water vapor then rises to form clouds. When the clouds cool, some of the water returns to earth as rain or snow.

water cycle

a	hat	ė	term	ô	order	ch	child		a in about
ā	age	i	it	oi	oil	ng	long		e in taken
ä	far	ī	ice	ou	out	sh	she	ə {	i in pencil
â	care	o	hot	u	cup	th	thin		o in lemon
e	let	ō	open	u̇	put	ᵺ	then		u in circus
ē	equal	ȯ	saw	ü	rule	zh	measure		

W

wa·ter·fall (wȯ′tər fȯl′), *NOUN.* a stream of water that falls from a high place.

Did You Know?

The world's tallest **waterfall** is **Angel Falls** in Venezuela. It is 3,212 feet high. It is hard to measure waterfalls because many waterfalls have several sections instead of falling straight from the top to the bottom. The longest section of Angel Falls is 2,648 feet high.

wa·ter·front (wȯ′tər frunt′), *NOUN.* land at the water's edge, especially the part of a city beside a river, lake, or harbor.

water lily, a water plant having flat, floating leaves and showy, fragrant, white or pink flowers.

blossoms and leaves of the **water lily**

wa·ter·logged (wȯ′tər lȯgd′), *ADJECTIVE.* so full of water that it will barely float: *The waterlogged boards were no good for our raft.*

wa·ter·mel·on (wȯ′tər mel′ən), *NOUN.* a large, juicy melon with pink pulp and a hard green rind.

water moccasin, a poisonous snake that is found in the southern part of the United States and lives in swamps and along streams.

water pistol, a toy pistol that shoots water.

wa·ter·pow·er (wȯ′tər pou′ər), *NOUN.* the power that comes from flowing or falling water. Waterpower is used to generate electricity.

wa·ter·proof (wȯ′tər prüf′),
1 *ADJECTIVE.* able to keep water from coming through: *An umbrella should be waterproof.*
2 *VERB.* to make something waterproof: *These hiking shoes have been waterproofed.*
❏ *VERB* **wa·ter·proofs, wa·ter·proofed, wa·ter·proof·ing.**

wa·ter·shed (wȯ′tər shed′), *NOUN.*
1 the ridge between the regions drained by two different river systems. On opposite sides of the watershed, rivers and streams flow in two different directions.
2 the region drained by one river system.

water ski, one of a pair of skis for gliding over water while being towed at the end of a rope by a motorboat.

This man has both feet on one **water ski.**

wa·ter·ski (wȯ′tər skē′), *VERB.* to glide over the water on water skis. ❏ *VERB* **wa·ter·skis, wa·ter·skied, wa·ter·ski·ing. —wa′ter·ski′er,** *NOUN.*

wa·ter·tight (wȯ′tər tīt′), *ADJECTIVE.* so tight that no water can get in or out: *The campers had a watertight container for matches.*

wa·ter·way (wȯ′tər wā′), *NOUN.* a river, canal, or other body of water that ships can go on.

wa·ter·wheel, (wȯ′tər wēl′), *NOUN.* (formerly) a wheel turned by water and used to drive machinery.

water wings, two waterproof bags filled with air, put under your arms to hold you afloat while you are learning to swim.

wa·ter·works (wȯ′tər wėrks′), *NOUN PLURAL* or *SINGULAR.* a system of pipes, reservoirs, and pumps for supplying a city with water.

wa·ter·y (wȯ′tər ē), *ADJECTIVE.*
1 full of tears: *Her allergies gave her watery eyes.*
2 containing too much water: *The watery soup was bland.*
3 of water; like water: *A blister is filled with a watery fluid.*
❏ *ADJECTIVE* **wa·ter·i·er, wa·ter·i·est.**

watt (wät), *NOUN.* a unit for measuring electrical power: *My lamp uses a 60-watt bulb.*

wave (wāv),
1 *NOUN.* the water in an ocean or lake that rises and moves forward as it comes near the shore.
2 *NOUN.* any movement like this through air or space. Light, heat, and sound travel in waves.
3 *NOUN.* a sudden increase of a condition or feeling: *A wave of cold weather is sweeping over the country. The news brought a wave of enthusiasm.*
4 *VERB.* to move as waves do; move up and down or back and forth; sway: *The tall grass waved in the breeze.*

5 *VERB.* to move your hand up and down or from side to side.

6 *VERB.* to signal or direct by moving the hand or an object back and forth: *The police officer waved the speeding driver to the side of the road.*

7 *NOUN.* the act of waving: *She said good-bye with a wave of her hand.*

8 *NOUN.* a curve or series of curves: *Her hair has natural waves.*
❑ *VERB* **waves, waved, wav·ing.** ∎ Another word that sounds like this is **waive. –wave′like′,** *ADJECTIVE.*

Did You Know?

Most **waves** are caused by wind. The harder the wind blows, the higher the wave. Tidal waves are caused by earthquakes or volcanoes. These waves can be 100 feet high in shallow water.

wave·length (wāv′lengkth′ or wāv′length′), *NOUN.* the distance between a point on one wave of light, heat, and so on, and a point in the same position on the next wave.

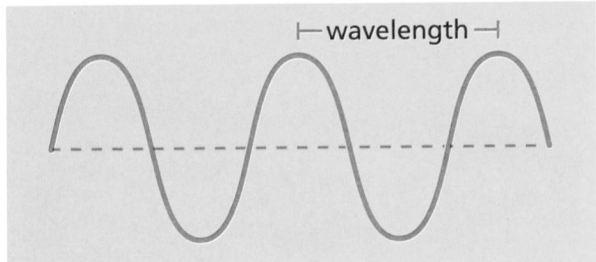

├─wavelength─┤

wavelength

wa·ver (wā′vər), *VERB.*

1 to move back and forth in an unsteady way; flutter: *The curtains wavered in the breeze.*

2 to be undecided about something; hesitate: *We are still wavering between a picnic and a trip to the zoo.*
❑ *VERB* **wa·vers, wa·vered, wa·ver·ing.**

wav·y (wā′vē), *ADJECTIVE.* having waves or curves: *a wavy line, wavy hair.* ❑ *ADJECTIVE* **wav·i·er, wav·i·est.**

wax¹ (waks),

1 *NOUN.* a yellowish substance made by bees for building their honeycomb. Wax is hard when cold, but can be easily shaped when warm.

2 *NOUN.* any substance like this.

3 *NOUN.* a substance containing wax for polishing floors, furniture, cars, or the like.

4 *VERB.* to rub or polish with wax: *We wax that floor every month.*
❑ *PLURAL* **wax·es;** *VERB* **wax·es, waxed, wax·ing. –wax′like′,** *ADJECTIVE.*

wax² (waks), *VERB.* to grow bigger or greater; increase: *The moon waxes till it becomes full, and then it wanes.* ❑ *VERB* **wax·es, waxed, wax·ing.**

wax·y (wak′sē), *ADJECTIVE.*

1 like wax: *The floor had a smooth, waxy surface.*

2 made of wax or containing wax: *Some fruit has a waxy coating.*
❑ *ADJECTIVE* **wax·i·er, wax·i·est.**

way (wā),

1 *NOUN.* a manner; style: *I wear my hair a new way.*

2 *NOUN.* how something is done or can be done; method: *Scientists have found new ways to treat cancer.*

3 *NOUN.* a route that you take from one place to another: *Do you know the way to the library?*

4 *NOUN.* a point; feature; detail: *The plan is bad in several ways.*

5 *NOUN.* a direction: *Look this way, please.*

6 *NOUN.* distance: *The sun is a long way off.*

7 *NOUN.* a road or path: *The scouts found a way through the forest.*

8 *NOUN.* something that people have learned to do, that they do over and over again: *It's Grandma's way to always leave a light on in the hall.*

9 *ADVERB.* at or to a great distance; far: *The cloud of smoke stretched way out to the pier.*
∎ Other words that sound like this are **weigh** and **whey.**

by the way, *IDIOM.* incidentally; in that connection: *By the way, the library has some interesting new books.*

get your own way or **have your own way,** *IDIOM.* to do or get what you want: *He's happy only if he gets his own way.*

give way, *IDIOM.*

1 to retreat: *The enemy gave way and fled when we attacked.*

2 to break down or fail: *The old bridge finally gave way and collapsed.*

3 to abandon yourself to emotion: *The prisoner refused to give way to despair.*

out of the way, *IDIOM.*

1 put where nothing is blocked or stopped: *Get those empty boxes out of the way of the movers.*

2 far from where most people live or go: *They went to a little beach out of the way of most tourists.*

way·side (wā′sīd′), *NOUN.* the edge of a road or path: *We ate lunch on the wayside.*

we (wē), *PRONOUN PLURAL.*

1 the people speaking: *We are glad to see you.*

2 the person speaking. An author, a ruler, or a judge sometimes uses *we* to mean *I.*

weak (wēk), *ADJECTIVE.*

1 not having power; not strong: *After his illness, he was too weak to lift a chair.*

a	hat	ė	term	ô	order	ch	child		a in about
ā	age	i	it	oi	oil	ng	long		e in taken
ä	far	ī	ice	ou	out	sh	she	ə {	i in pencil
â	care	o	hot	u	cup	th	thin		o in lemon
e	let	ō	open	ů	put	ᴛʜ	then		u in circus
ē	equal	ȯ	saw	ü	rule	zh	measure		

2 easily broken or torn: *My foot went through a weak board in the floor.*

3 lacking self-confidence: *A person who is weak can be easily influenced by others.*

4 lacking force or effectiveness: *The weak law was not enforced.*

5 not having much of a particular quality: *Weak tea has less flavor than strong tea.*
■ Another word that sounds like this is **week.**
—**weak′ly,** ADVERB.

weak·en (wē′kən), VERB. to make or become weak or weaker: *You can weaken tea by adding water. My legs weakened near the end of the race.* ❑ VERB **weak·ens, weak·ened, weak·en·ing.**

weak·ness (wēk′nis), NOUN.

1 the condition of being weak; lack of power, force, or vigor: *Weakness kept him in bed.*

2 a weak point; slight fault: *Not trying hard enough is her weakness.*

3 a fondness or liking that is hard to resist: *Our baby-sitter has a weakness for sweets.*
❑ PLURAL **weak·ness·es.**

wealth (welth), NOUN.

1 riches; many valuable possessions; property: *people of wealth, the wealth of a city.*

2 a large quantity; abundance: *The story in the newspaper had a wealth of details.*

wealth·y (wel′thē), ADJECTIVE. having wealth; rich: *She comes from a wealthy family.* ❑ ADJECTIVE **wealth·i·er, wealth·i·est.**

wean (wēn), VERB. to gradually stop nursing a child or young animal and begin to feed it solid foods.
❑ VERB **weans, weaned, wean·ing.**

weap·on (wep′ən), NOUN.

1 any object or tool used to injure, disable, or kill. Swords, clubs, and guns are weapons. Animals use claws, horns, and stingers as weapons.

2 any means of attack or defense: *Drugs are effective weapons against many diseases.*

wear (wâr),

1 VERB. to have something on your body: *to wear a coat, to wear a beard, to wear black, to wear a ring.*

2 VERB. to have a certain expression on your face: *She wore a look of boredom all morning.*

3 NOUN. the act of wearing or the condition of being worn: *Clothing for summer wear is on sale in the stores. This suit has been in constant wear for years.*

4 NOUN. things worn or to be worn; clothing: *The store sells children's wear.*

5 VERB. to last a long time; give good service: *These jeans wear well.*

6 VERB. to use up or damage something by rubbing or scraping part of it away: *This pencil is worn to a stub.*

7 NOUN. damage from being used a lot: *The rug shows wear.*

8 VERB. to make by rubbing or scraping: *Walking wore a hole in my left shoe.*
❑ VERB **wears, wore, worn, wear·ing.** ■ Other words that sound like this are **ware** and **where.**
—**wear′er,** NOUN.

wear off, IDIOM. to become less, slowly and gradually: *The excitement of travel soon wore off.*

wear out, IDIOM.

1 to wear or use until no longer fit for use: *These shoes are worn out.*

2 to tire out; weary: *She is worn out by too much work.*

wear·i·ly (wir′ə lē), ADVERB. in a weary manner: *The tired hikers walked slowly and wearily along the road.*

wear·y (wir′ē),

1 ADJECTIVE. tired: *weary feet, a weary brain.* ■ See the Synonym Study at **tired.**

2 VERB. to make or become tired: *Walking all day wearied the tourists.*
❑ ADJECTIVE **wear·i·er, wear·i·est;** VERB **wear·ies, wear·ied, wear·y·ing.** —**wear′i·ness,** NOUN.

wea·sel (wē′zəl), NOUN. any of various small, quick, furry animals with slender bodies, long tails, and short legs. Otters, ferrets, and wolverines are weasels. —**wea′sel·like′,** ADJECTIVE.

There are more than 65 different kinds of **weasels.**

weath·er (weⱦH′ər),

1 NOUN. the conditions of the air outside at a certain place and time. Weather includes facts about temperature, wind, sun, rainfall, and so on.

2 VERB. to expose something to the weather; change from the effect of the weather: *Wood turns gray if weathered for a long time.*

3 VERB. to go or come through a difficult situation safely: *The ship weathered the storm.*
❑ VERB **weath·ers, weath·ered, weath·er·ing.**
■ Another word that sounds like this is **whether.**

under the weather, IDIOM. sick; ailing: *He felt a little under the weather today so he didn't go to school.*

weath·er-beat·en (weⱦH′ər bēt′n), ADJECTIVE. worn or toughened by the wind, rain, and other forces of the weather: *He took a picture of the weather-beaten old barn.*

weath·er·man (weŧн′ər man′), *NOUN.* a person who forecasts the weather, especially on radio or television. ❏ *PLURAL* **weath·er·men.**

weather vane, a flat piece of metal or wood that shows which way the wind is blowing. Weather vanes are often placed on the tops of buildings and turn with the wind. Weather vanes are often shaped like animals.

a **weather vane** with an arrow and a sailboat

weave (wēv),
1 *VERB.* to form threads or strips into cloth or fabric. People weave fibers from the cotton plant into cloth.
2 *VERB.* to make something out of thread, strips, or strands of the same material: *A spider weaves a web. She is weaving a rug.*
3 *NOUN.* a method or pattern of weaving: *Homespun is a cloth of coarse weave.*
4 *VERB.* to go by twisting and turning: *The police stopped the car that was weaving in and out of traffic.* ★ The past tense of this meaning is **wove** or **weaved.**
❏ *VERB* **weaves, wove, woven, weav·ing.**
■ Another word that sounds like this is **we've.**

weav·er (wē′vər), *NOUN.*
1 someone who weaves.
2 someone whose work is weaving.

web (web), *NOUN.*
1 a woven net of very tiny, sticky threads like silk spun by a spider.
2 anything like a web: *The spy was caught in a web of lies.*
3 the skin joining the toes of swimming birds such as ducks, and the toes of other water animals such as frogs and beavers.

webbed (webd), *ADJECTIVE.*
1 formed like a web or with a web.
2 having the toes joined by a web. Ducks have webbed feet.

web page or **Web page,** a World Wide Web document.

web·site or **web site** (web′sīt′),
1 a place or an address on the Internet where a World Wide Web document can be found.
2 a World Wide Web document.

wed (wed), *VERB.*
1 to marry.
2 to unite: *His art weds painting and sculpture.*
❏ *VERB* **weds, wed, wed·ded** or **wed, wed·ding.**

we'd (wēd),
1 a contraction of **we had.**
2 a contraction of **we should.**
3 a contraction of **we would.**
■ Another word that sounds like this is **weed.**

Wed., an abbreviation of **Wednesday.**

wed·ded (wed′id), *ADJECTIVE.*
1 married.
2 united: *She is wedded to her work.*

wed·ding (wed′ing), *NOUN.*
1 the special happy celebration when a man and a woman get married.
2 an anniversary of this celebration. A golden wedding is the fiftieth anniversary of a marriage.

wedge (wej),
1 *NOUN.* a piece of wood or metal that is thick at one end and tapers to a thin edge at the other. A wedge is driven into something to be split.
2 *NOUN.* something shaped like a wedge: *I ate a wedge of pie.*
3 *VERB.* to force something into a certain position by using a wedge: *We wedged the door open with a piece of wood.*
4 *VERB.* to thrust or force something into a narrow or tight spot: *The hiker's foot was wedged between the rocks.*
❏ *VERB* **wedg·es, wedged, wedg·ing.**

Wednes·day (wenz′dā), *NOUN.* the fourth day of the week; the day after Tuesday.

Word Story

Wednesday comes from an earlier English word meaning "Woden's day." Woden was one of the most important of the old English gods.

weed (wēd),
1 *NOUN.* any plant that tends to grow in great numbers where it is not wanted: *Weeds choked out the vegetables and flowers in the garden.*
2 *VERB.* to take weeds out of a place: *Please weed the garden now.*
❏ *VERB* **weeds, weed·ed, weed·ing.** ■ Another word that sounds like this is **we'd.**

W

a	hat	ė	term	ô	order	ch	child	⎧a in about
ā	age	i	it	oi	oil	ng	long	e in taken
ä	far	ī	ice	ou	out	sh	she	ə⎨i in pencil
â	care	o	hot	u	cup	th	thin	o in lemon
e	let	ō	open	ů	put	ŧн	then	⎩u in circus
ē	equal	ò	saw	ü	rule	zh	measure	

weed out, *IDIOM.* to remove something from a group because it is not wanted: *We weeded out the damaged books when we cleaned the shelves.*

weed·y (wē′dē), *ADJECTIVE.* full of weeds: *We need to work hard or we'll have a weedy garden.*
❑ *ADJECTIVE* **weed·i·er, weed·i·est.**

week (wēk), *NOUN.*
1 seven days, one after another: *My mother has left on a business trip and will be gone a week.*
2 the time from Sunday through Saturday: *He is away most of the week but is home on Sundays.*
3 the working days of a seven-day period: *A school week is usually five days.*
■ Another word that sounds like this is **weak.**

week·day (wēk′dā′), *NOUN.* any day of the week except Saturday or Sunday.

week·end (wēk′end′), *NOUN.* Saturday and Sunday as a time for recreation or visiting: *We plan to spend this weekend in the country.*

week·ly (wēk′lē),
1 *ADJECTIVE.* of or for a week: *Her weekly wage is $500.*
2 *ADJECTIVE.* done or published once a week: *He subscribes to several weekly magazines.*
3 *ADVERB.* once each week; every week: *I play tennis weekly.*
4 *NOUN.* a newspaper or magazine that is published once a week.
❑ *PLURAL* **week·lies.**

weep (wēp), *VERB.* to cry; sob with tears falling: *I wept for joy when I won.* ❑ *VERB* **weeps, wept, weep·ing.**

wee·vil (wē′vəl), *NOUN.* a small beetle whose larvae eat grain, nuts, fruits, or the stems of leaves. Weevils damage grain and cotton crops.

weigh (wā), *VERB.*
1 to find out how heavy something is: *I weigh myself to see if I have gained any weight since last week.*
2 to have as a weight of: *I weigh 110 pounds.*
3 to think about something carefully; consider: *He weighs his words before speaking.*
❑ *VERB* **weighs, weighed, weigh·ing.** ■ Other words that sound like this are **way** and **whey.**

weight (wāt), *NOUN.*
1 how heavy something is; amount something weighs: *The dog's weight is 50 pounds.*
2 the amount of force with which gravity draws an object toward the earth or some other astronomical object. This force is felt as heaviness. An astronaut who weighs 180 pounds on earth has a weight of only 30 pounds on the moon, because the moon draws matter with much less force than the earth does.
3 a unit for measuring how much something weighs, such as a pound or kilogram.
4 a piece of metal having a known heaviness, used in weighing things: *The shopkeeper lost his 2-pound weight.*
5 a heavy object used to hold something in place: *I have a paper weight made of pink marble on my desk.*
6 **weights,** pieces of metal that are lifted for exercise.
■ Another word that sounds like this is **wait.**

weight belt,
1 a wide belt used to support the lower back while lifting weights.
2 a belt loaded with weights used in scuba diving. It keeps the diver from rising to the surface.

weight·less (wāt′lis), *ADJECTIVE.*
1 having little or no weight: *We walked home through the weightless snow.*
2 being free of the pull of gravity.
—**weight′less·ness,** *NOUN.*

An astronaut is **weightless** in outer space.

weird (wird), *ADJECTIVE.*
1 frightening; mysterious; wild: *We were awakened by a weird shriek.*
2 odd; fantastic; strange: *a weird little house, weird shadows on the wall.*
—**weird′ly,** *ADVERB.* —**weird′ness,** *NOUN.*

weird·o (wir′dō), *NOUN.* (slang) a very strange person. ❑ *PLURAL* **weird·os.**

wel·come (wel′kəm),
1 *VERB.* to greet someone kindly: *We always welcome guests at our house.*
2 *NOUN.* a kind greeting: *We got a warm welcome.*
3 *VERB.* to receive something gladly: *We welcome new ideas.*
4 *ADJECTIVE.* gladly received: *a welcome visitor, a welcome letter, a welcome rest from work.*
5 *ADJECTIVE.* gladly or freely permitted: *You are welcome to pick the flowers in my garden, but please don't pick the tomatoes.*
6 *ADJECTIVE.* You say "You're welcome" when someone thanks you for something.
7 *INTERJECTION.* exclamation of friendly greeting: *Welcome, everyone!*
❑ *VERB* **wel·comes, wel·comed, wel·com·ing.**

weld (weld),
1 *VERB*. to join pieces of metal or plastic together by heating the parts that touch to the melting point, so that they flow together and become one piece.
2 *VERB*. to unite closely: *Working together welded them into a strong team.*
3 *NOUN*. a welded joint.
❑ *VERB* **welds, weld·ed, weld·ing.** —**weld′er,** *NOUN*.

wel·fare (wel′fâr′), *NOUN*.
1 health, happiness, and prosperity; being well: *He asked about the welfare of everyone in our family.*
2 money given by the government to poor or needy people.
on welfare, *IDIOM*. receiving aid from the government because of hardship or need.

we'll (wēl),
1 a contraction of **we shall.**
2 a contraction of **we will.**
■ Another word that sounds like this is **wheel.**

well¹ (wel),
1 *ADVERB*. all right; in a fine or good way: *Is everything going well at school? The job was well done.*
2 *ADJECTIVE*. healthy; in good health: *I am very well.*
3 *ADVERB*. thoroughly; completely: *He knew the lesson well. Shake the medicine well before taking it.*
4 *ADVERB*. much; to a considerable degree: *The fair brought in well over a hundred dollars.*
5 *INTERJECTION*. *Well* is sometimes used to show mild surprise or merely to fill in: *Well! Well! Here she is. Well, I'm not sure.*
❑ *ADVERB* **bet·ter, best.**
as well, *IDIOM*.
1 also; besides: *He took them out for ice cream and to the movies as well.*
2 equally: *I like spring, but I like fall as well.*
as well as, *IDIOM*.
1 in addition to; besides: *We're going to go sledding as well as skiing.*
2 as much as: *I like hot dogs as well as you do.*

well² (wel),
1 *NOUN*. a hole dug or bored in the ground to get water, oil, or gas: *I pumped a bucket of water from the well.*
2 *NOUN*. a spring; fountain; source: *This book is a well of ideas.*
3 *NOUN*. a shaft for stairs or elevator, extending through the floors of a building.
4 *VERB*. to flow out suddenly; gush: *Tears welled up in the child's eyes.*
❑ *VERB* **wells, welled, well·ing.**

You have to pump your water from this **well** with the handle.

well-be·haved (wel′bi hāvd′), *ADJECTIVE*. showing good manners or conduct: *The children were well-behaved.*

well-be·ing (wel′bē′ing), *NOUN*. welfare; health and happiness: *Our mayor and city council have concern for the well-being of the citizens.*

well-known (wel′nōn′), *ADJECTIVE*.
1 known by a lot of people; familiar: *It is a well-known fact that the earth is round.*
2 widely known; famous: *She met the well-known actor in the grocery store.*

well-man·nered (wel′man′ərd), *ADJECTIVE*. polite; courteous: *A well-mannered person always remembers to say "please."*

well·ness (wel′nis), *NOUN*. the condition of being well; good health: *Good food promotes wellness.*

well-off (wel′òf′), *ADJECTIVE*. fairly rich: *Her family is well-off but not wealthy.*

well-to-do (wel′tə dü′), *ADJECTIVE*. having enough money to live well; prosperous.

Welsh (welsh *or* welch),
1 *ADJECTIVE*. of or about Wales, its people, or their language.
2 *NOUN PLURAL*. **the Welsh,** the people of Wales.
3 *NOUN*. the language of Wales.

welt (welt), *NOUN*. a streak or ridge made on the skin, often by a blow.

went (went), *VERB*. the past tense of **go:** *I went home promptly after school.*

wept (wept), *VERB*.
1 the past tense of **weep:** *The children wept over the loss of their dog.*
2 the past participle of **weep:** *I have wept at sad movies before.*

were (wėr), *VERB*. a past tense of **be:** *We were cold and hungry after the hike.* ■ Another word that sounds like this is **whir.**

we're (wir), a contraction of **we are.**

weren't (wėrnt), a contraction of **were not.**

were·wolf (wer′wùlf′ *or* wir′wùlf′), *NOUN*. (in stories) someone who changes into a wolf at certain times.
❑ *PLURAL* **were·wolves** (wer′wùlvz′ *or* wir′wùlvz′).

a **werewolf** from the movies

a	hat	ė	term	ô	order	ch	child	⎰a in about
ā	age	i	it	oi	oil	ng	long	e in taken
ä	far	ī	ice	ou	out	sh	she	ə⎨i in pencil
â	care	o	hot	u	cup	th	thin	o in lemon
e	let	ō	open	ù	put	⊤H	then	⎱u in circus
ē	equal	ò	saw	ü	rule	zh	measure	

west (west),

1 *NOUN.* the direction of the sunset.

2 *ADVERB* or *ADJECTIVE.* toward the west; farther toward the west: *Walk west three blocks until you reach the bridge.*

3 *ADJECTIVE.* coming from the west: *Spring brought a warm west wind.*

4 *ADJECTIVE.* in the west: *The kitchen is in the west wing of the house.*

5 *NOUN.* **a the West,** the western part of the United States. **b** the countries in Europe and America as distinguished from those in Asia.

west of, *IDIOM.* farther west than: *Ohio is west of Pennsylvania. The library is three blocks west of the bus stop.*

west·er·ly (wes′tər lē), *ADJECTIVE.*

1 toward the west: *They were heading in a westerly direction.*

2 from the west: *The ship hoped for a westerly wind to carry it into port.*

west·ern (wes′tərn),

1 *ADJECTIVE.* toward the west: *We sailed to the western shore of the island.*

2 *ADJECTIVE.* from the west: *The island was blessed with western breezes.*

3 *ADJECTIVE.* of or in the west: *My ancestors farmed the western prairies.*

4 *ADJECTIVE.* **Western, a** of or in the western part of the United States. **b** of or in the countries in Europe or America.

5 *NOUN.* a movie or TV show about life in the western part of the United States, especially cowboy life: *All of my favorite movies and TV shows are westerns.*

West·ern Sa·mo·a (wes′tərn sə mō′ə), a country made up of several islands in the southern Pacific. **–Western Samoan.**

West Germany, a former country in Europe.

West In·dies (west′ in′dēz), islands in the Atlantic Ocean between Florida and South America.

West Virginia, one of the southern states of the United States. *Abbreviation:* WV; *Capital:* Charleston. **–West Virginian.**

State Story   West Virginia got its name from the state of Virginia. When the Civil War began, the western part of the state withdrew from Virginia because it did not want to withdraw from the United States, as Virginia had. It became a separate state in 1863.

west·ward (west′wərd), *ADVERB* or *ADJECTIVE.* toward the west; west: *I walked westward. The orchard is on the westward slope of the hill.*

west·wards (west′wərdz), *ADVERB.* See **westward.**

wet (wet),

1 *ADJECTIVE.* covered or soaked with water or other liquid; not dry: *wet hands, a wet sponge.*

2 *ADJECTIVE.* not yet dry: *Don't touch wet paint.*

3 *VERB.* to make wet: *Wet the cloth and wipe your face.*

4 *ADJECTIVE.* rainy: *I dislike wet weather.*

5 *NOUN.* wetness; rain: *Come in out of the wet.*
❏ *ADJECTIVE* **wet·ter, wet·test;** *VERB* **wets, wet** or **wet·ted, wet·ting. –wet′ness,** *NOUN.*

Synonym Study

Wet means covered with water or full of water: *It's not safe to go outside in the cold with wet hair.*

Soaked means thoroughly wet from being in water for a while: *Our tent blew over in the storm and we got soaked.*

Soggy means heavy with water: *After I dry the dishes, the towel is all soggy.*

Drenched means completely wet: *The drenched puppy shivered when he came into the house.*

See also the Synonym Study at **damp.**

ANTONYM: dry.

wet·land (wet′land′), *NOUN.* often, **wetlands,** swamp, marsh, or other land that is soaked with water, but where plants continue to grow.

Many forms of life need **wetlands** like this to live in.

wet suit, a closely fitting rubber suit worn by skin divers, surfers, sailors, and so on.

we've (wēv), a contraction of **we have.** ■ Another word that sounds like this is **weave.**

whack (wak),
1 NOUN. a sharp, noisy blow: *She hit the ball with a whack.*
2 VERB. to strike with a blow like this: *The batter whacked the ball out of the park.*
❏ VERB **whacks, whacked, whack·ing.**

whale (wāl), NOUN. a very large animal that lives in the sea. Whales look like fish but are really mammals and breathe air. ■ Another word that sounds like this is **wail.**

Did You Know?

The **blue whale** is the largest animal that has ever lived on the Earth. They can weigh 200 tons and be 100 feet long. There used to be hundreds of thousands of blue whales in the oceans, but now they are an endangered species.

blue **whale**

whal·er (wā′lər), NOUN.
1 someone who hunts whales.
2 a ship used for hunting and catching whales.

whal·ing (wā′ling), NOUN. the hunting and catching of whales.

wharf (wôrf), NOUN. a platform built along the shore or out from it. Ships load and unload at a wharf.
❏ PLURAL **wharves** (wôrvz) or **wharfs.**

what (wät *or* wut),
1 PRONOUN *or* ADJECTIVE. *What* is used in asking questions about people or things: *What is your name? What time is it?*
2 PRONOUN *or* ADJECTIVE. that which: *I know what you mean. Put back what money is left.*
3 PRONOUN *or* ADJECTIVE. whatever; anything that; any that: *Do what you please. What supplies do you need?*
4 ADVERB. how much; how: *What does it matter?*

5 INTERJECTION, ADVERB, *or* ADJECTIVE. *What* is often used to show surprise, liking, dislike, or other feelings: *What a pity! What a catch! What! Are you late again?*

what·ev·er (wät ev′ər *or* wut ev′ər),
1 PRONOUN. anything that: *Do whatever you like.*
2 ADJECTIVE. any person or thing that; any: *Take whatever books you need.*
3 ADJECTIVE *or* PRONOUN. no matter what: *Do it, whatever happens. Whatever excuse you make will not be accepted.*

what's (wäts *or* wuts),
1 a contraction of **what is:** *What's the latest news?*
2 a contraction of **what has:** *What's been going on here lately?*

wheat (wēt), NOUN. the grain of a kind of cereal grass, or the plant that it grows on. The grain is used to make flour, pasta, breakfast food, and so on.

wheel (wēl),
1 NOUN. a round frame or disk turning on an axle or shaft in the center: *bicycle wheels, truck wheels.*
2 NOUN. anything round like a wheel or moving like one. A steering wheel is used in a motor vehicle. Clay is shaped into usable objects on a potter's wheel.
3 VERB. to turn: *She wheeled around when I yelled.* ■ See the Synonym Study at **turn.**
4 VERB. to move on wheels: *I wheeled the load of bricks on the wheelbarrow.*
❏ VERB **wheels, wheeled, wheel·ing.** ■ Another word that sounds like this is **we'll.**

at the wheel, IDIOM. at the steering wheel of a car.

Have You Heard?

You may have heard someone or something called **"a fifth wheel."** This means that the person or thing is unwanted or unimportant.

wheel and axle, an axle on which a wheel is fastened. It is used to lift weights by winding a rope onto the axle as the wheel is turned. A wheel and axle is a simple machine.

wheel·bar·row (wēl′bar′ō), NOUN. a small vehicle with one wheel at the front and two handles at the back. A wheelbarrow holds a small load that one person can push.

wheel·chair (wēl′châr′), NOUN. a chair on wheels, used by people who are sick or unable to walk. A wheelchair can be moved by the person sitting in it, or by battery power.

wheel·ie (wē′lē), NOUN. a stunt in which a moving bicycle, motorcycle, or car is balanced only on its back wheel or wheels. ❏ PLURAL **wheel·ies.**

W

a hat	ė term	ô order	ch child	(a in about
ā age	i it	oi oil	ng long	e in taken
ä far	ī ice	ou out	sh she	ə ⟨ i in pencil
â care	o hot	u cup	th thin	o in lemon
e let	ō open	ů put	ŧн then	(u in circus
ē equal	ò saw	ü rule	zh measure	

wheeze (wēz),
1 *VERB.* to breathe with difficulty and a whistling sound: *He wheezes going up the stairs.*
2 *NOUN.* a whistling sound caused by difficult breathing.
❏ *VERB* **wheez·es, wheezed, wheez·ing.**

whelk (welk), *NOUN.* a sea snail with a spiral shell. One kind is used as food in Europe.

whelk — about 3 inches long

when (wen),
1 *ADVERB.* at what time: *When does school close?*
2 *CONJUNCTION.* at the time that: *Stand up when your name is called.*
3 *CONJUNCTION.* at any time that; if: *The dog comes when it is called.*
4 *CONJUNCTION.* at which time; and then: *We had just started on our walk when it began to rain.*
5 *CONJUNCTION.* although: *We have only three books when we need five.*
6 *PRONOUN.* what time; which time: *Since when have they had a car?*

when·ev·er (wen ev′ər), *CONJUNCTION* or *ADVERB.* when; at whatever time; at any time that: *Come whenever you wish. I'll come whenever I can.*

where (wâr),
1 *ADVERB.* in what place; at what place: *Where do you live? Where is she?*
2 *ADVERB.* to what place: *Where are you going?*
3 *ADVERB.* from what place: *Where did you get that story?*
4 *NOUN.* what place: *Where did it come from?*
5 *CONJUNCTION.* in which; at which: *That is the house where I was born.*
6 *CONJUNCTION.* to which: *I know the place where he is going.*
7 *ADVERB.* in what way; in what respect: *Where is the harm in trying?*
8 *CONJUNCTION.* in the place in which; at the place at which: *Your coat is where you left it.*
9 *CONJUNCTION.* to the place to which: *I will go where you go.*
■ Other words that sound like this are **ware** and **wear.**

where·a·bouts (wâr′ə bouts′),
1 *ADVERB* or *CONJUNCTION.* where; near what place: *Whereabouts are my books?*
2 *NOUN.* a place where a person or thing is: *Do you know the whereabouts of the cottage?*

where·as (wâr az′), *CONJUNCTION.* but; while: *Some children like school, whereas others dislike it.*

wher·ev·er (wâr ev′ər), *CONJUNCTION* or *ADVERB.* where; in or to any place: *Sit wherever you like. Wherever did he go?*

wheth·er (weŦH′ər), *CONJUNCTION.*
1 *Whether* is used in expressing choices or possibilities: *He does not know whether to work or rest. We don't know whether or not it will rain today.*
2 if: *He asked whether he might be excused.*
■ Another word that sounds like this is **weather.**

whew (hwyü), *INTERJECTION.* a word expressing surprise or dismay: *Whew! It's cold!*

whey (wā), *NOUN.* the watery part of milk that separates from the curd when cheese is made. ■ Other words that sound like this are **way** and **weigh.**

which (wich),
1 *ADJECTIVE* or *PRONOUN.* **Which** is used in asking what people or things are indicated, wanted, and so on: *Which is the best plan? Which book do you want to read?*
2 *ADJECTIVE* or *PRONOUN.* **Which** is also used in connecting a group of words with some other word in the sentence: *Read the book, which you should already have. Be careful which way you turn.*
3 *PRONOUN.* the one that; any that: *Here are three boxes. Choose which you like best.*
■ Another word that sounds like this is **witch.**

which·ev·er (wich ev′ər), *PRONOUN* or *ADJECTIVE.*
1 any one; any that: *Take whichever you want. Buy whichever hat you like.*
2 no matter which: *Whichever side wins, I shall be satisfied.*

whiff (wif), *NOUN.*
1 a slight smell; a puff of air having an odor: *I caught a whiff of pizza as I walked into the kitchen.*
2 a slight puff; gust; breath: *A whiff of smoke blew into my face.*

while (wīl),
1 *NOUN.* a period or length of time: *They kept us waiting a long while. The mail came a while ago.*
2 *CONJUNCTION.* during the time that; in the time that; as: *While I was speaking, he said nothing.*
3 *CONJUNCTION.* although: *While I like the color of the car, I do not like its design.*
while away, *IDIOM.* to pass or spend in some pleasant way: *We whiled away the day at the beach.*
❏ *VERB* **whiles, whiled, whil·ing.**
worth your while, *IDIOM.* worth your time, attention, or effort: *If you help me with painting the shed, I'll make it worth your while—I'll pay you ten dollars.*

whim (wim), *NOUN.* a sudden thought or wish: *I had a whim to take a plane somewhere.*

whim·per (wim′pər),
1 *VERB.* to cry with short, low sounds, the way that a sick child or dog does.
2 *NOUN.* a whimpering cry.
❏ *VERB* **whim·pers, whim·pered, whim·per·ing.**

whine (wīn),
1 *VERB.* to make a high, unhappy cry or sound: *The dog whined to go out with us.*
2 *NOUN.* a high, sharp cry or sound: *We heard the whine of the carpenter's drill.*
3 *VERB.* to complain in a cross, childish way: *Some people are always whining about things that don't matter.* ■ See the Synonym Study at **complain.**
❑ *VERB* **whines, whined, whin·ing.** ■ Another word that sounds like this is **wine. –whin′er,** *NOUN.*

Word Story

Whine comes from an old English word meaning "to whiz," used about arrows. It seems that the high whining of dogs sounded to people like an arrow in flight.

whin·ny (win′ē),
1 *NOUN.* the sound that a horse makes sometimes.
2 *VERB.* to make this sound.
❑ *PLURAL* **whin·nies;** *VERB* **whin·nies, whin·nied, whin·ny·ing.**

whip (wip),
1 *NOUN.* something to strike or beat with, usually a stick or handle with a lash at the end.
2 *VERB.* to strike; beat: *The jockey whipped the horse to make it go faster.*
3 *VERB.* to move, put, or pull something quickly and suddenly: *She whipped off her coat.*
4 *VERB.* to defeat someone in a fight or contest: *She whipped her opponent in the election.*
5 *VERB.* to beat cream, eggs, or the like until it becomes stiff and ready for cooking.
❑ *VERB* **whips, whipped, whip·ping.**

whip·lash (wip′lash′), *NOUN.* an injury to the neck caused by a sudden jolt that snaps the head backward and then forward. A driver whose car is hit hard from behind may suffer whiplash.

whip·poor·will (wip′ər wil′), *NOUN.* a North American bird whose call sounds somewhat like its name. It is active at night or twilight.

whir (wėr),
1 *NOUN.* a noise that sounds like something spinning fast: *I like to hear the whir of the sewing machine.*
2 *VERB.* to make this noise: *The motor whirs.*
❑ *VERB* **whirs, whirred, whir·ring.**
■ Another word that sounds like this is **were.**

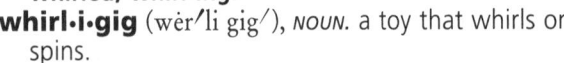

whippoorwill — about 10 inches long

whirl (wėrl),
1 *VERB.* to turn or swing round and round very fast; spin: *The leaves whirled in the wind.*
2 *VERB.* to move something round and round: *The cowboy showed us how to whirl a lasso.*
3 *NOUN.* a whirling movement: *The dancer suddenly made a whirl.*
4 *NOUN.* a dizzy or confused condition: *My thoughts are in a whirl.*
❑ *VERB* **whirls, whirled, whirl·ing.**

whirl

whirl·i·gig (wėr′li gig′), *NOUN.* a toy that whirls or spins.

whirl·pool (wėrl′pül′), *NOUN.* a current of water whirling round and round rapidly.

whirl·wind (wėrl′wind′),
1 *NOUN.* a current of air whirling violently round and round; whirling storm of wind.
2 *ADJECTIVE.* very fast: *They took a whirlwind tour of the city.*

whisk (wisk),
1 *VERB.* to sweep or brush something from a surface: *She whisked the crumbs from the table.*
2 *NOUN.* a quick sweep: *He brushed away the dirt with a few whisks of the broom.*
3 *VERB.* to move quickly: *I whisked the letter out of sight.*
❑ *VERB* **whisks, whisked, whisk·ing.**

whisk broom, a small broom for brushing dust and lint off your clothes.

whisk·er (wis′kər), *NOUN.*
1 one of the hairs that grow on a man's face.
2 **whiskers,** the hair or part of a beard that grows on a man's cheeks.
3 one of the long, stiff hairs that grow near the mouth of a cat, rat, or other animal.

whis·key (wis′kē), *NOUN.* a strong alcoholic drink made from such grains as rye, barley, or corn.
❑ *PLURAL* **whis·keys.**

whis·per (wis′pər),
1 *VERB.* to speak very softly and gently.
2 *NOUN.* a very soft, gentle spoken sound.

a	hat	ė	term	ô	order	ch	child		a in about
ā	age	i	it	oi	oil	ng	long		e in taken
ä	far	ī	ice	ou	out	sh	she	ə	i in pencil
â	care	o	hot	u	cup	th	thin		o in lemon
e	let	ō	open	ù	put	ŦH	then		u in circus
ē	equal	ȯ	saw	ü	rule	zh	measure		

W

3 *VERB.* to make a soft, rustling sound: *The wind whispered in the pines.*

4 *NOUN.* a soft, rustling sound: *The wind was so gentle that we could hear the whisper of the leaves in the trees.*
❑ *VERB* **whis·pers, whis·pered, whis·per·ing.**

whis·tle (wis′əl),

1 *VERB.* to make a clear, high sound by blowing air out through your teeth or through rounded lips: *The girl whistled and her dog ran to her.*

2 *NOUN.* the sound made in this way: *He gave a low whistle to call his dog.*

3 *NOUN.* an instrument for making whistling sounds. Whistles usually consist of a tube through which air or steam is blown.

4 *VERB.* to blow a whistle: *The policeman whistled for the car to stop.*

5 *VERB.* to produce by whistling: *I have never been able to whistle a tune.*
❑ *VERB* **whis·tles, whis·tled, whis·tling. —whis′tler,** *NOUN.*

white (wīt),

1 *NOUN.* the color of snow, salt, or the paper on which this book is printed.

2 *ADJECTIVE.* having this color: *My grandparents have white hair.*

3 *NOUN.* the part of something that is white, pale, or clear: *egg whites, the whites of your eyes.*

4 *ADJECTIVE.* pale: *They turned white with fear.*

5 *ADJECTIVE.* light-colored: *a white wine, white meat.*

6 *ADJECTIVE.* having a light-colored skin.

7 *NOUN.* someone who has light-colored skin.

8 *ADJECTIVE.* snowy: *We were hoping for a white Christmas.*
❑ *ADJECTIVE* **whit·er, whit·est. —white′ness,** *NOUN.*

white blood cell, a colorless cell in the blood that destroys disease germs; white corpuscle.

white·cap (wīt′kap′), *NOUN.* a wave with a foaming white crest.

white-hot (wīt′hot′), *ADJECTIVE.* white with heat; extremely hot: *The molten steel was white-hot.*

White House,

1 the official residence of the President of the United States, in Washington, D. C.

2 the office, authority, or opinion of the President of the United States.

whit·en (wīt′n), *VERB.* to make or become white: *A person's hair whitens with age.* ❑ *VERB* **whit·ens, whit·ened, whit·en·ing.**

white·wash (wīt′wäsh′),

1 *NOUN.* a liquid for whitening walls, woodwork, or other surfaces. Whitewash is usually made of lime and water.

2 *VERB.* to whiten something with whitewash.

3 *VERB.* to cover someone's faults or mistakes: *They tried to whitewash his crime.*

4 *NOUN.* the act or process of covering up someone's faults or mistakes.
❑ *VERB* **white·wash·es, white·washed, white·wash·ing.**

white water, any foaming water, especially in the rapids of a river or stream. **—white′-wa′ter,** *ADJECTIVE.*

whit·ish (wī′tish), *ADJECTIVE.* somewhat white.

whit·tle (wit′l), *VERB.*

1 to cut shavings or chips from wood with a knife, usually for fun.

2 to cut or shape something with a knife: *The class learned how to whittle animals from wood.*
❑ *VERB* **whit·tles, whit·tled, whit·tling.**

whiz (wiz),

1 *VERB.* to move or rush with a humming or hissing sound: *An arrow whizzed past his head.*

2 *NOUN.* a very clever person; expert: *His sister is a computer whiz.*
❑ *VERB* **whiz·zes, whizzed, whiz·zing;** *PLURAL* **whiz·zes.**

who (hü), *PRONOUN.*

1 Who is used in asking questions about persons: *Who goes there? Who is your friend? Who told you?*

2 Who is also used in connecting a group of words with some word that refers to a person in the sentence: *The girl who spoke is my best friend. This is my mother, who works in the hospital.*

whoa (wō), *INTERJECTION.* stop: *"Whoa there!" said the cowgirl to her horse.* ■ Another word that sounds like this is **woe.**

who'd (hüd),

1 a contraction of **who had.**

2 a contraction of **who would.**

the **White House**

who·dun·it (hü dun′it), *NOUN.* (informal) a story, movie, play, and the like, about crime, especially murder, and detectives.

who·ev·er (hü ev′ər), *PRONOUN.*

1 any person who: *Whoever wants the book may have it.*

2 no matter who: *Whoever else may disappoint you, I promise not to.*

whole (hōl),
1 ADJECTIVE. having all its parts; complete: *They gave us a whole set of dishes.*
2 ADJECTIVE. full; entire: *He worked the whole day.*
3 NOUN. all of something; the total: *Three thirds make a whole.*
4 ADJECTIVE. in one piece: *The dog swallowed the meat whole.*
▪ Another word that sounds like this is **hole.**

on the whole, IDIOM.
1 considering everything: *On the whole, it appears that our team is improving rapidly.*
2 generally; mostly: *On the whole, I enjoy sports.*

whole-grain (hōl′grān′), ADJECTIVE. made of grain from which the outer layer of bran has not been removed: *I like whole-grain muffins.*

whole·heart·ed (hōl′här′tid), ADJECTIVE. completely enthusiastic; devoted: *The school gave the team its wholehearted support.* **−whole′heart′ed·ly,** ADVERB.

whole number, a number such as 1, 2, 3, 4, 5, and so on, that is not a fraction or a mixed number. 15 and 106 are whole numbers; ½ and ⅞ are fractions; 1⅜ and 23⅔ are mixed numbers.

whole·sale (hōl′sāl′),
1 NOUN. the sale of goods in large quantities, usually to retail storekeepers or others who will in turn sell them to users.
2 ADJECTIVE. of or about selling in large quantities: *a wholesale merchant, a wholesale price of $20.*

whole·some (hōl′səm), ADJECTIVE.
1 healthful; good for the health: *Milk is a wholesome food.*
2 healthy-looking; suggesting health: *The girl in the advertisement had a clean, wholesome face.* **−whole′some·ness,** NOUN.

whole-wheat (hōl′wēt′), ADJECTIVE.
1 made of the entire wheat kernel including the bran: *The bread is made of whole-wheat flour.*
2 made from whole-wheat flour: *I like whole-wheat bread.*

who'll (hül),
1 a contraction of **who will.**
2 a contraction of **who shall.**

whol·ly (hō′lē), ADVERB. completely; entirely; totally: *The patient was wholly cured.* ▪ Another word that sounds like this is **holy.**

whom (hüm), PRONOUN. what person; which person. *Whom is a form of who. Whom do you like best? He does not know whom to believe. The girl to whom I spoke is my cousin.*

whom·ev·er (hüm′ev′ər), PRONOUN.
1 any person whom.
2 no matter whom.
★ **Whomever** is a form of **whoever.**

whoop (hüp *or* wüp),
1 NOUN. a loud cry or shout: *The winner gave a whoop of joy.*
2 VERB. to shout loudly.
❑ VERB **whoops, whooped, whoop·ing.** ▪ Another word that can sound like this is **hoop.**

whooping cough, a contagious disease most often of children that causes fits of coughing that end with a loud, gasping sound. Vaccination can prevent whooping cough.

whooping crane, a large white crane having a loud, hoarse cry. It is now almost extinct.

whoops (wüps), INTERJECTION. a word used to express surprise, embarrassment, and so on.

whoosh (wùsh *or* wüsh),
1 NOUN. a dull, soft, hissing sound like that of something rushing through the air.
2 VERB. to make a sound like this.
❑ VERB **whoosh·es, whooshed, whoosh·ing.**

whooping crane —
about 5 feet tall

whop·per (wop′ər), NOUN.
1 something very large: *The fish I caught was a whopper.*
2 a big lie: *She was punished for telling such a whopper.*

who's (hüz),
1 a contraction of **who is.**
2 a contraction of **who has.**

whose (hüz), PRONOUN. of or belonging to whom or which: *The girl whose work got the prize is very talented. Whose book is this?*

why (wī),
1 ADVERB or CONJUNCTION. for what reason: *Why did the baby cry? I do not know why they are late.*
2 CONJUNCTION. because of which: *That is the reason why we left.*
3 INTERJECTION. *Why is sometimes used to show surprise or doubt: Why, it's all gone!*

WI, an abbreviation of **Wisconsin.**

wick (wik), NOUN. a cord of twisted thread on an oil lamp or in a candle. When the wick is lit, it draws the oil or melted wax up to be burned.

a	hat	ė	term	ô	order	ch	child		a in about
ā	age	i	it	oi	oil	ng	long		e in taken
ä	far	ī	ice	ou	out	sh	she	ə	i in pencil
â	care	o	hot	u	cup	th	thin		o in lemon
e	let	ō	open	ù	put	ŦH	then		u in circus
ē	equal	ò	saw	ü	rule	zh	measure		

W

wick·ed (wik′id), ADJECTIVE.
1 bad; evil; full of sin: *a wicked person, wicked deeds.*
2 mischievous; naughty: *He smiled a wicked smile.*
3 unpleasant; severe: *A wicked storm hit the state.*
❑ ADJECTIVE **wick·ed·er, wick·ed·est.**
−**wick′ed·ness,** NOUN.

Synonym Study

Wicked means doing wrong things on purpose: *The wicked men forced children to work in dangerous factories.*

Bad can mean wicked: *Hurting an animal is a very bad thing to do.*

Immoral means doing things that people agree are very wrong: *Cheating people to get their money is immoral.*

Evil means wicked and causing great harm: *The evil queen sent many of her people to prison.*

See also the Synonym Study at **naughty.**

ANTONYM: good.

The **wicked** queen's stare could wilt flowers.

wick·er (wik′ər), NOUN. thin twigs or other easily bent material woven together to make baskets and furniture.

Word Story

Wicker comes from a Scandinavian word meaning "a willow branch." Willow branches are commonly used in wicker furniture.

wick·et (wik′it), NOUN. (in croquet) any of several wire arches stuck in the ground to knock the ball through.

wide (wīd),
1 ADJECTIVE. big from one side to the other; not narrow; broad: *a wide street, the wide, blue ocean.*
2 ADJECTIVE. with a certain distance from side to side: *The door is three feet wide.*
3 ADVERB. over a large space or region: *When I am older, I want to travel far and wide.*

4 ADJECTIVE. including many different things: *A healthful diet includes a wide variety of foods.*
5 ADJECTIVE. very open: *The child stared with wide eyes.*
6 ADVERB. to the full extent: *Open your mouth wide. The gates stand wide open.*
❑ ADJECTIVE **wid·er, wid·est.** −**wide′ly,** ADVERB.
wide of, IDIOM. not close to a desired point or object: *The shot was wide of the mark.*

wide-a·wake (wīd′ə wāk′), ADJECTIVE.
1 fully awake; with the eyes wide open.
2 paying close attention to what is going on; alert: *The mountain climber was wide-awake to the dangers of the climb.*

wide-eyed (wīd′īd′), ADJECTIVE. with the eyes wide open: *The children watched the baby rabbits with wide-eyed interest.*

wid·en (wīd′n), VERB. to make or become wide or wider: *We widened the path through the forest. The river widens as it flows.* ❑ VERB **wid·ens, wid·ened, wid·en·ing.**

wide·spread (wīd′spred′), ADJECTIVE.
1 spread over a wide space: *The news reported a widespread flood.*
2 happening in many places or among many people far apart: *There is a widespread belief in UFOs.*

wid·ow (wid′ō),
1 NOUN. a woman whose husband is dead and who has not married again.
2 VERB. to make a widow of someone: *She was widowed in May.*
❑ VERB **wid·ows, wid·owed, wid·ow·ing.**

wid·ow·er (wid′ō ər), NOUN. a man whose wife is dead and who has not married again.

width (width), NOUN. how wide something is; distance across; breadth: *The room is 12 feet in width.*

wield (wēld), VERB. to hold and use something; control: *The worker wielded a hammer. The people wield the power in a democracy.* ❑ VERB **wields, wield·ed, wield·ing.**

wie·ner (wē′nər), NOUN. See **frankfurter.**

wife (wīf), NOUN. a woman who has a husband.
❑ PLURAL **wives.**

wig (wig), NOUN. an artificial covering of natural or false hair for the head.

wig·gle (wig′əl),
1 VERB. to move with short, quick movements from side to side; wriggle: *The puppy wiggled out of my arms.*
2 NOUN. a movement like this.
❑ VERB **wig·gles, wig·gled, wig·gling.**

wig·gly (wig′lē), ADJECTIVE.
1 moving from side to side with quick, short movements: *I couldn't hold the wiggly puppy.*
2 having curves or waves; wavy: *There were wiggly lines on the wallpaper.*
❑ ADJECTIVE **wig·gli·er, wig·gli·est.**

wig·wam (wig′wäm), NOUN. a hut of poles covered with bark, mats, or skins, made by North American Indians of the Eastern Woodlands.

wild (wild),

1 ADJECTIVE. living or growing naturally; not grown or tamed by people: *Tigers are wild animals.*

2 ADJECTIVE. not under control; not disciplined: *The children were wild during the teacher's absence.*

3 ADJECTIVE. violent: *Wild waves pounded the shore.*

4 ADJECTIVE. unreasonable; silly; senseless: *The child had the wild idea that horses could fly.*

5 ADJECTIVE. very eager; enthusiastic: *They were wild about animals.*

6 ADJECTIVE. far from the mark: *The shortstop made a wild throw to first base.*

7 ADVERB. in a wild manner; to a wild degree: *Daisies grew wild in the field.*
—**wild′ly**, ADVERB. —**wild′ness**, NOUN.

Synonym Study

Wild means extremely excited and out of control: *When the athletes came out, the crowd went wild.*

Raging means out of control because of anger: *The raging elephant will not let the zookeepers near her baby.*

Savage can mean fierce and ready to fight: *At night that store is guarded by a savage dog.*

Unruly means hard to control: *If this class gets any more unruly, everyone will get extra homework!*

Disorderly can mean making trouble: *When the team lost a close game, the crowd became disorderly and started yelling at the referee.*

Rowdy means rough, noisy, and disorderly: *If the people at the party get rowdy, the neighbors may call the police.*

Beside yourself is an idiom that means too wild to think: *She is beside herself because she lost a wallet with more than $50 in it.*

See also the Synonym Study at **mad**.

ANTONYMS: calm, peaceful.

wild·cat (wild′kat′), NOUN. a wild animal like a common cat, but larger. A lynx is one kind of wildcat.

wil·de·beest (wil′də bēst′), NOUN. See **gnu**. ❑ PLURAL **wil·de·beest** or **wil·de·beests**.

wil·der·ness (wil′dər nis), NOUN. a wild place; region with few or no people living in it. ❑ PLURAL **wil·der·ness·es**.

wild·fire (wild′fir′), NOUN. a fire that is hard to put out.
like wildfire, IDIOM. very rapidly: *The news spread like wildfire.*

wigwam

wild·flow·er (wild′flou′ər), NOUN. any flowering plant that grows wild in the woods or fields.

wild·life (wild′lif′), NOUN. wild animals and plants: *The campers saw many kinds of wildlife.*

Wild West, the western United States during pioneer days.

will¹ (wil), HELPING VERB.

1 am going to; is going to; are going to: *He will come tomorrow. They will enjoy a visit.*

2 am willing to; is willing to; are willing to: *I will go if you do.*

3 to be able to; can: *The pail will hold four gallons.*

4 must: *Don't argue with me; you will do it at once.* ❑ PAST TENSE **would**.

will² (wil),

1 NOUN. the power of the mind to decide and do something: *A good leader must have a strong will.*

2 VERB. to decide something by using this power: *She willed to stay awake.*

3 NOUN. a purpose; determination: *Although very ill, the patient had a strong will to live.*

4 NOUN. a wish; desire: *Elections express the will of the people.*

5 VERB. to leave someone your property: *They willed all their property to their children.*

6 NOUN. a legal document that says what you want to be done with your property after you die. ❑ VERB **wills, willed, will·ing**.

Have You Heard?

You may have heard someone say **"Where there's a will, there's a way."** This means that if someone really wants to do something, it will get done.

a hat	ė term	ô order	ch child	⎧a in about
ā age	i it	oi oil	ng long	⎪e in taken
ä far	ī ice	ou out	sh she	ə⎨i in pencil
â care	o hot	u cup	th thin	⎪o in lemon
e let	ō open	ů put	ᴛʜ then	⎩u in circus
ē equal	ò saw	ü rule	zh measure	

w

Wild Cats

Cats live in all parts of the world except for the cold polar regions. All cats are hunters by nature. Their bodies and behavior show how they have developed to become successful at finding and killing prey.

The **cheetah** is the fastest animal on land—it can run at a top speed of about 70 miles an hour for short distances. Cheetahs are about 6 feet long and weigh between 70 and 130 pounds.

Lions are 7 to 9 feet long and weigh between 300 and 350 pounds. The lion is the only cat that lives and hunts in groups.

Leopards are about 7 feet long and weigh between 100 and 150 pounds. A few leopards are completely black.

The **lynx** has tufts of hair on its ears and a short tail. Most lynxes are about 4 feet long and weigh between 15 and 30 pounds.

Pumas are about 7 feet long and weigh between 110 and 200 pounds.

Tigers are 8 to 10 feet long from nose to tail, and weigh between 300 and 600 pounds. The tiger is the largest of all cats and is very powerful.

The **house cat** is descended from an African variety of the wildcat. Most house cats weigh between 5 and 15 pounds.

will·ful (wil′fəl), ADJECTIVE. wanting or taking your own way; stubborn. **−will′ful·ly**, ADVERB. **−will′ful·ness**, NOUN.

will·ing (wil′ing), ADJECTIVE.
1 ready or wanting to do something: *He is willing to wait.*
2 cheerfully ready: *She is a willing helper.*
−will′ing·ly, ADVERB. **−will′ing·ness**, NOUN.

wil·low (wil′ō), NOUN. a kind of tree or shrub with tough, slender branches and narrow leaves. The branches of most willows bend easily and are used to make furniture and baskets.

Willows often grow near the water's edge.

will·pow·er (wil′pou′ər), NOUN. strength of will; determination: *She had the willpower not to go along with their silly suggestion.*

wilt (wilt), VERB. to become limp and drooping; wither: *Flowers wilt when they do not get enough water.* ❑ VERB **wilts, wilt·ed, wilt·ing.**

wil·y (wi′lē), ADJECTIVE. using subtle tricks to get something; sly: *The wily thief got away.* ❑ ADJECTIVE **wil·i·er, wil·i·est. −wil′i·ness**, NOUN.

win (win),
1 VERB. to be successful over others; get victory or success: *We all hope our team will win.*
2 VERB. to come in first in a race or contest: *He won the race.*
3 NOUN. a success; victory: *We had five wins and no defeats.*
4 VERB. to get by doing something, such as working hard, answering questions, and so on: *to win fame, to win a prize.*
❑ VERB **wins, won, win·ning. −win′less**, ADJECTIVE.

wince (wins), VERB. to draw back suddenly; flinch slightly: *I winced when the dentist's drill touched my tooth.* ❑ VERB **winc·es, winced, winc·ing.**

winch (winch), NOUN. a machine for lifting or pulling things, powered either by a hand crank or by an engine attached to a rotating bar. A rope or cable wound on the bar raises or pulls the load. ❑ PLURAL **winch·es.**

wind¹ (wind),
1 NOUN. air that is moving. The wind varies in force from a slight breeze to a strong gale: *Winds of ninety miles an hour were blowing.*
2 NOUN. breath; power of breathing: *A runner needs good wind.*
3 VERB. to cause someone to breathe with difficulty: *Walking up the steep hill winded the hiker.*
❑ VERB **winds, wind·ed, wind·ing. −wind′less**, ADJECTIVE.

get wind of, IDIOM. to find out about; get a hint of: *Don't let Mother get wind of our plans for a surprise party on her birthday.*

Have You Heard?

You may have heard the saying **"It's an ill wind that blows nobody any good."** This means that bad situations can often have unexpectedly good results.

wind² (wind), VERB.
1 to move this way and that; change direction; turn: *A brook winds through the woods.* ∎ See the Synonym Study at **bend.**
2 to fold, wrap, or place around something or someone: *She wound her arms around her new puppy.*
3 to roll something into a ball or put it on a spool: *We took turns winding yarn. Thread comes wound on spools.*
4 to twist or turn around something: *The vine winds around a pole.*
5 to make a machine go by turning some part of it: *He winds the clock every night before going to sleep.*
❑ VERB **winds, wound, wind·ing.**

wind up, IDIOM.
1 to bring something to an end: *The committee wound up its meeting in time for dinner.*
2 to finish a process, journey, and so on, in a certain condition or place: *After walking for six hours, we wound up in the place where we had started from.*
3 (in baseball) to swing your arm while twisting your body just before you pitch the ball.

wind·chill fac·tor or **wind·chill** (wind′chil′ fak tər), the combined effect on exposed human skin of cold air temperature and wind speed.

wind·fall (wind′fol′), NOUN.
1 fruit blown down by the wind.
2 an unexpected piece of good luck: *Finding this job was a windfall.*

wind·ing (wīn′ding), ADJECTIVE. bending; turning: *The city was full of narrow, winding streets.*

wind instrument, a musical instrument played by blowing air into it. Horns, tubas, and oboes are wind instruments.

wind·mill (wind′mil′), NOUN. a mill or machine powered by the action of the wind on a wheel of large paddles or sails mounted on a tower.

Windmills are used to pump water, grind grain, and produce electricity.

win·dow (win'dō), NOUN.
1 an opening in an outer wall or roof of a building, or in a vehicle, that lets in air or light.
2 a structure set in such an opening, with glass or plastic panes and a wooden or metal frame.

win·dow·pane (win'dō pān'), NOUN. a piece of glass or plastic in a window.

win·dow·sill (win'dō sil'), NOUN. a piece of wood or stone across the bottom of a window.

wind·pipe (wind'pīp'), NOUN. the passage by which air is carried from the throat to the lungs; trachea.

wind·shield (wind'shēld'), NOUN. a sheet of glass or plastic on the front of a motor vehicle, to keep the wind off the driver or passengers.

4 NOUN. a player on either side of the center in hockey, soccer, and some other games.
5 VERB. to fly: *Modern airplanes wing from continent to continent.*
❑ VERB **wings, winged, wing·ing. —wing'less,** ADJECTIVE. **—wing'like',** ADJECTIVE.

on the wing, IDIOM. in flight.

take wing, IDIOM. to fly away: *The bird took wing when the cat came near.*

under your wing, IDIOM. under your protection: *I took the new kid under my wing.*

winged (wingd), ADJECTIVE. having wings: *A gnat is a winged insect.*

wing·span (wing'span'), NOUN.
1 the distance between the wing tips of an airplane.
2 See **wingspread.**

wingspread

wind·storm (wind'stôrm'), NOUN. a storm with much wind but little or no rain.

wind·surf·ing (wind'sėr'fing), NOUN. surfing on a sailboard.

wind·up (wind'up'), NOUN.
1 the act of winding something up; end; conclusion: *The windup of the movie was very exciting.*
2 a series of swinging and twisting movements of the arm and body made by a baseball pitcher just before pitching the ball.

wind·y (win'dē), ADJECTIVE. with a lot of wind: *The windy weather was bad for a picnic.* ❑ ADJECTIVE **wind·i·er, wind·i·est.**

wine (wīn), NOUN. an alcoholic drink made from the fermented juice of grapes or other fruit.
∎ Another word that sounds like this is **whine.**

wing (wing),
1 NOUN. one of the movable parts of a bird, insect, or bat used in flying, or a similar part in a bird or insect that does not fly. Birds have one pair of wings; insects have usually two pairs.
2 NOUN. one of the long, flat parts of an airplane that help lift it into the air.
3 NOUN. a part that sticks out from the main part of a building: *The house has a wing at each side.*

wing·spread (wing'spred'), NOUN. the distance between the tips of the wings of a bird, insect, and so on, when they are spread out; wingspan.

wink (wingk),
1 VERB. to close your eyes and open them again quickly: *The bright light made me wink.*
2 VERB. to quickly close and open one eye on purpose as a hint or signal: *I winked at my sister to keep still.*
3 NOUN. the act of winking: *I gave them a friendly wink to show I got the joke.*
4 NOUN. a very short time: *I ran upstairs quick as a wink.*
❑ VERB **winks, winked, wink·ing.**

catch forty winks, IDIOM. to have a short nap: *After lunch, I caught forty winks.*

wink at, IDIOM. to pretend not to see: *Mom knew I'd eaten another piece of cake, but she winked at it.*

win·ner (win'ər), NOUN. someone or something that wins: *The winners of the contest got a trip to Washington, D.C., as a prize.*

a	hat	ė	term	ô	order	ch	child	a in about
ā	age	i	it	oi	oil	ng	long	e in taken
ä	far	ī	ice	ou	out	sh	she	ə i in pencil
â	care	o	hot	u	cup	th	thin	o in lemon
e	let	ō	open	ù	put	ŦH	then	u in circus
ē	equal	ò	saw	ü	rule	zh	measure	

W

win·ning (win′ing),
1 ADJECTIVE. victorious; successful: *Everyone wants to be on a winning team.*
2 ADJECTIVE. charming; attractive: *The model had a winning smile.*
3 NOUN. **winnings,** what is won: *The gamblers pocketed their winnings.*

win·ter (win′tər),
1 NOUN. the season of the year between fall and spring. Winter is the coldest season.
2 VERB. to spend the winter: *Robins winter in the South.*
❑ VERB **win·ters, win·tered, win·ter·ing.**

a mountain stream in **winter**

win·ter·green (win′tər grēn′), NOUN. a small evergreen plant with bright red berries. An oil made from its leaves is used in medicine and candy.

win·ter·time (win′tər tīm′), NOUN. the season of winter: *I like to ski in the wintertime.*

win·try (win′trē), ADJECTIVE. of or like winter: *wintry weather, a wintry sky.* ❑ ADJECTIVE **win·tri·er, win·tri·est.**

wipe (wīp),
1 VERB. to rub something in order to clean it or dry it off: *Wipe the dishes. We wipe our shoes on the mat.*
2 VERB. to take something away, off, or out by rubbing: *Wipe away your tears. I wiped off the dust.*
3 NOUN. the act of wiping: *He gave his face a quick wipe.*
❑ VERB **wipes, wiped, wip·ing.**

wipe out, IDIOM. to destroy something completely: *Whole cities have been wiped out by volcanoes.*

wipe·out (wīp′out′), NOUN.
1 complete destruction: *Heavy rain caused the wipeout of our sand castle.*
2 (slang) a fall from a surfboard, skis, and so on.

wip·er (wī′pər), NOUN. a device that wipes a windshield. All cars have windshield wipers.

wire (wīr),
1 NOUN. metal in the form of a long thin rod or thread: *We ran a telephone wire to the back room.*
2 VERB. to supply a building with wiring: *It was expensive to wire the old house for electricity.*

3 VERB. to fasten things with wire: *She wired the two pieces together and placed it gently on the shelf.*
❑ VERB **wires, wired, wir·ing.**

wire·less (wīr′lis), ADJECTIVE. not using wires; sent by radio waves instead of by electric wires.

wire·tap (wīr′tap′),
1 VERB. to make a secret connection with a telephone or telegraph line to hear or record messages sent over it; tap: *They wiretapped the phones of the criminals' headquarters.*
2 NOUN. a secret connection with a telephone or telegraph line; tap.
❑ VERB **wire·taps, wire·tapped, wire·tap·ping.**

wir·ing (wī′ring), NOUN. a system of wires to carry an electric current.

wir·y (wī′rē), ADJECTIVE.
1 like wire: *Our terrier has a wiry coat.*
2 lean, strong, and tough: *The gymnast had a small, wiry body.*
❑ ADJECTIVE **wir·i·er, wir·i·est.**

Wis·con·sin (wi skon′sən), NOUN. one of the midwestern states of the United States. *Abbreviation:* WI; *Capital:* Madison.
—**Wis·con′sin·ite,** NOUN.

State Story **Wisconsin** may have come from *Ouisconsing,* a French form of the American Indian name of the Wisconsin River.

wis·dom (wiz′dəm), NOUN. knowledge and good judgment based on experience: *The leader's wisdom guided the group through difficulties.*

wisdom tooth, the back tooth on either side of each jaw. Wisdom teeth usually appear between the ages of 17 and 25.

wise (wīz), ADJECTIVE.
1 having or showing knowledge and good judgment: *a wise judge, wise advice, wise plans.*
2 knowing a lot about many different things: *The old senator was wise in the ways of politics.*
❑ ADJECTIVE **wis·er, wis·est.** —**wise′ly,** ADVERB.

Word Power -wise

The suffix **-wise** means "in a particular way or direction." Clock**wise** means in the way the hands of a clock go. Length**wise** means in the direction of the length. It can also mean "in connection with" or "about." Publicity**wise** means about publicity.

wish (wish),
1 VERB. to hope to have something, do something, or go somewhere; have a desire; want: *Do you wish to go home? They wished for a new house.*
2 NOUN. the act of wishing or wanting; desire; longing: *I have no wish to be rich. What is your wish?*
3 NOUN. the expression of a wish: *Please give them my best wishes for a happy New Year.*

4 *VERB.* to wish something for someone; have a hope for: *We wish peace for all people. I wish you a happy New Year.*

5 *NOUN.* something wished for: *She got her wish.*
❑ *VERB* **wish·es, wished, wish·ing;** *PLURAL* **wish·es.**

making a birthday **wish**

wish·bone (wish′bōn′), *NOUN.* the Y-shaped bone in the front of the breastbone in poultry and other birds.

Word Story

Wishbone comes from the custom of two people's making wishes while breaking the bone by pulling on the two ends. It is said that the person left with the longer piece of bone will get his or her wish.

wish·ful (wish′fəl), *ADJECTIVE.* having or expressing a wish; desiring: *His boast about winning the race was only wishful thinking.*

wisp (wisp), *NOUN.*
1 a small bit or bunch of something: *She brushed a wisp of hair out of her face.*
2 a tiny puff of smoke, steam, or the like: *Wisps of steam rose from the boiling water.*

wist·ful (wist′fəl), *ADJECTIVE.* longing; yearning. —**wist′ful·ly,** *ADVERB.*

wit (wit), *NOUN.*
1 the power to say things that are unusual, striking, and amusing: *Her wit kept us all smiling.*
2 usually, **wits,** the power of understanding; mind or sense: *People with quick wits learn easily. I was frightened out of my wits.*

witch (wich), *NOUN.* (long ago) a woman that was believed to have magic powers. Witches were generally believed to be evil. ❑ *PLURAL* **witch·es.**
■ Another word that sounds like this is **which.**

witch·craft (wich′kraft′), *NOUN.* the magic power that a witch is believed to have.

with (wiтн *or* with), *PREPOSITION. With* shows that people or things are taken together in some way:
1 in the company of: *Come with me.*
2 among: *They will mix with the crowd.*

3 having: *He is a man with brains. She received a letter with good news.*
4 by means of: *I cut the meat with a knife.*
5 using; showing: *Work with care.*
6 added to: *Do you want sugar with your tea?*
7 in regard to: *We are pleased with the house.*
8 in proportion to: *Her pay increased with her skill.*
9 because of: *The child is shaking with cold.*
10 in the keeping or service of: *Leave the dog with me.*
11 on the side of; for: *They are with us in our plan.*
12 from: *I hate to part with my favorite things.*
13 against: *The English fought with the Germans in two World Wars.*
14 in spite of: *With all his weight, he was not a strong man.*

with·draw (wiтн drȯ′ *or* with drȯ′), *VERB.*
1 to take back; remove: *She withdrew all her savings from the bank.*
2 to go away: *She withdrew from the room.* ■ See the Synonym Study at **leave**[1].
❑ *VERB* **with·draws, with·drew** (wiтн drü′ *or* with drü′), **with·drawn** (wiтн drȯn′ *or* with drȯn′), **with·draw·ing.**

with·er (wiтн′ər), *VERB.* to make or become dry and lifeless; dry up; shrivel: *The hot sun withers the grass. Flowers wither after they are cut.* ❑ *VERB* **with·ers, with·ered, with·er·ing.**

with·held (with held′ *or* wiтн held′), *VERB.*
1 the past tense of **withhold:** *The witness withheld information from the police.*
2 the past participle of **withhold:** *Have you withheld any information?*

with·hold (with hōld′ *or* wiтн hōld′), *VERB.* to refuse to give something to someone: *There will be no school play if the principal withholds consent.* ■ See the Synonym Study at **keep.** ❑ *VERB* **with·holds, with·held, with·hold·ing.**

with·in (wiтн in′ *or* with in′),
1 *PREPOSITION.* not beyond; inside the limits of; not more than: *The task was within their power.*
2 *PREPOSITION.* before a period of time is over: *Within an hour the sunlight had melted all the snow.*
3 *PREPOSITION.* in or into the inner part of; inside of: *By the use of X rays, doctors can see within the body.*
4 *PREPOSITION.* less than a stated distance from something: *We live within an hour of the lake.*
5 *ADVERB.* in or into the inner part; inside: *We heard voices within as we waited by the front door.*

with·out (wiтн out′ *or* with out′), *PREPOSITION.*
1 not having; lacking: *I drink tea without sugar.*

a	hat	ė	term	ô	order	ch	child		a in about
ā	age	i	it	oi	oil	ng	long		e in taken
ä	far	ī	ice	ou	out	sh	she	ə {	i in pencil
â	care	o	hot	u	cup	th	thin		o in lemon
e	let	ō	open	u̇	put	ŦH	then		u in circus
ē	equal	ȯ	saw	ü	rule	zh	measure		

2 leaving out, avoiding, or neglecting: *She walked past us without a smile.*

3 not being with someone: *I won't go without you.*

with·stand (with stand′ or wiᴛʜ stand′), VERB. to stand up to something successfully; endure: *These shoes will withstand hard wear.* ❑ VERB **with·stands, with·stood, with·stand·ing.**

with·stood (with stüd′ or wiᴛʜ stüd′), VERB.
1 the past tense of **withstand**: *The family withstood many hardships.*
2 the past participle of **withstand**: *These shoes have withstood three years of hard wear.*

wit·ness (wit′nis),
1 NOUN. someone who saw something happen, especially an accident or a crime: *There were several witnesses to the collision.*
2 VERB. to see something happen: *He witnessed the accident.*
3 NOUN. someone who takes an oath to tell the truth in a court of law about what he or she saw.
4 NOUN. someone who signs a document to show that he or she saw the writer of the document sign it.
5 VERB. to sign a document as witness: *You usually need two people to witness a will.*
❑ PLURAL **wit·ness·es;** VERB **wit·ness·es, wit·nessed, wit·ness·ing.**

wit·ty (wit′ē), ADJECTIVE. clever and amusing: *"Shut up!" is not a witty remark.* ▪ See the Synonym Study at **funny.** ❑ ADJECTIVE **wit·ti·er, wit·ti·est.** —**wit′ti·ly,** ADVERB.

wives (wīvz), NOUN. the plural of **wife.**

Have You Heard?

You may have heard something called **"an old wives' tale."** This means that it is a belief that was based on old ideas that may have been proved wrong.

wiz·ard (wiz′ərd), NOUN.
1 (long ago) a man that was believed to have magic power.
2 a very clever person; expert: *She is a wizard at mathematics.*

wob·ble (wob′əl), VERB. to move unsteadily from side to side; shake; tremble: *A baby wobbles when it begins to walk alone.* ❑ VERB **wob·bles, wob·bled, wob·bling.**

wob·bly (wob′lē), ADJECTIVE. unsteady; shaky; wavering. ❑ ADJECTIVE **wob·bli·er, wob·bli·est.**

woe (wō), NOUN. great grief, trouble, or distress: *They were helping people overcome the woes of sickness and poverty.* ❑ PLURAL **woes.** ▪ Another word that sounds like this is **whoa.**

woe·ful (wō′fəl), ADJECTIVE. sad; sorrowful; wretched: *The lost child had a woeful expression.* —**woe′ful·ly,** ADVERB.

wok (wok), NOUN. a metal cooking bowl, used for cooking foods quickly by stirring them in a little hot cooking oil.

woke (wōk), VERB. a past tense of **wake**[1]: *I woke before they did.*

wo·ken (wō′kən), VERB. a past participle of **wake**[1]: *She was woken by the sound of bells.*

wolf (wùlf),
1 NOUN. a wild animal similar to the dog and closely related to it. Wolves prey on rodents and other small animals.
2 VERB. to eat greedily: *The starving man wolfed down the food.*
❑ VERB **wolfs, wolfed, wolf·ing;** PLURAL **wolves.** —**wolf′like′,** ADJECTIVE.

wolf — about 2½ feet high at the shoulder

wolf·hound (wùlf′hound′), NOUN. a large dog of any of various kinds once used in hunting wolves.

wol·ve·rine (wùl′və rēn′), NOUN. a fierce, heavily built, meat-eating animal that is a kind of a weasel. It lives in the northern parts of the world.

wolves (wùlvz), NOUN. the plural of **wolf.**

wom·an (wùm′ən), NOUN.
1 a grown-up female person. When a girl grows up, she becomes a woman.
2 See **womankind.**
❑ PLURAL **wom·en.**

Word Story

Woman comes from an earlier English word **wifman.** This was formed from words meaning "woman or wife" and "a human being."

wom·an·hood (wùm′ən hùd), NOUN.
1 the condition or time of being a woman: *The girl was about to enter womanhood.*
2 the character or qualities of a woman.

wom·an·kind (wùm′ən kīnd′), NOUN. women as a group.

wom·an·ly (wùm′ən lē), ADJECTIVE. having qualities that are by tradition admired in a woman: *He* *needed some womanly sympathy and understanding.* **–wom'an•li•ness,** NOUN.

wom•bat (wom'bat), NOUN. either of two kinds of burrowing Australian mammals something like a small bear. A female wombat has a pouch for carrying her young.

wom•en (wim'ən), NOUN. the plural of **woman.**

won (wun), VERB.
1 the past tense of **win:** *Which side won yesterday?*
2 the past participle of **win:** *We have won four games so far this season.*
 ■ Another word that sounds like this is **one.**

won•der (wun'dər),
1 NOUN. a strange and surprising thing or event: *It is a wonder that he refused such a good offer.*
2 NOUN. the feeling caused by what is strange and surprising: *The baby looked with wonder at the snow.*
3 VERB. to be curious about something; wish to know: *I wonder what time it is.*
4 VERB. to be surprised by something: *I wonder why my alarm clock didn't go off this morning.*
 ❑ VERB **won•ders, won•dered, won•der•ing.**

won•der•ful (wun'dər fəl), ADJECTIVE.
1 marvelous; remarkable: *a wonderful adventure, the wonderful creations of nature.*
2 excellent; very enjoyable: *We had a wonderful time at the party.* ■ See the Synonym Study at **nice.**
 –won'der•ful•ly, ADVERB.

won't (wōnt), a contraction of **will not.**

woo (wü), VERB. (earlier)
1 to try to persuade someone to help or support you, vote for you, and so on.
2 (of a man) to spend time with a woman and try to convince her to marry him.
 ❑ VERB **woos, wooed, woo•ing.**

wood (wud), NOUN.
1 the hard substance beneath the bark of trees and shrubs. Wood is used for making houses, boats, boxes, and furniture.
2 trees cut up into logs and boards for use: *The carpenter brought wood to build a playhouse. Put some wood on the fire.*
3 **woods,** a small forest with a large number of growing trees: *We walked through the woods behind the farm.*
 ■ Another word that sounds like this is **would.**

Did You Know?

Out of every tree cut down, only about ⅛ is used as **wood** for building. About a quarter of every tree is lost as sawdust, and another eighth is lost as shavings.

wood•chuck (wud'chuk'), NOUN. a small animal with a thick body, short legs, and a bushy tail; groundhog. Woodchucks grow fat in summer and sleep in their holes in the ground all winter.

wood•ed (wud'id), ADJECTIVE. covered with trees: *The house stood on a wooded hill.*

wood•en (wud'n), ADJECTIVE.
1 made of wood.
2 not showing any feeling; lifeless: *The tired fireman's face had a wooden expression.*

wood•land (wud'lənd), NOUN. land covered with trees.

wood•peck•er (wud'pek'ər), NOUN. a bird with a hard, pointed bill for pecking holes in trees to get insects.

wood•pile (wud'pīl'), NOUN. a pile of wood, especially wood for fuel.

wood•shed (wud'shed'), NOUN. a shed for storing wood.

woods•man (wudz'mən), NOUN. someone used to life in the woods and skilled in hunting, fishing, trapping, and the like. ❑ PLURAL **woods•men.**

woodpecker — about 9 inches long

wood•wind (wud'wind'), NOUN. any of a group of wind instruments which were originally made of wood, but are now often made of metal or plastic. Clarinets, flutes, oboes, and bassoons are woodwinds.

wood•work (wud'werk'), NOUN. things made of wood; wooden parts inside a house, especially doors, stairs, and moldings.

wood•work•ing (wud'wer'king), NOUN. the act or process of making or shaping things out of wood: *She is skilled in woodworking.*

wood•y (wud'ē), ADJECTIVE.
1 covered with trees: *They built the playhouse on a woody hillside.*
2 made up of wood: *It was hard to cut the woody parts of the shrub.*
 ❑ ADJECTIVE **wood•i•er, wood•i•est.**

woof (wuf), NOUN. a dog's bark in a deep voice.

wool (wul), NOUN.
1 the soft curly hair or fur that covers the bodies of sheep and some other animals.
2 yarn, cloth, or garments made of wool: *People in cold climates often wear wool in the winter.*

wool•en (wul'ən),
1 ADJECTIVE. made of wool: *I made a new woolen suit.*
2 NOUN. cloth made of wool.

a hat	ė term	ô order	ch child	⎧a in about
ā age	i it	oi oil	ng long	e in taken
ä far	ī ice	ou out	sh she	ə⎨i in pencil
â care	o hot	u cup	th thin	o in lemon
e let	ō open	ù put	ŦH then	⎩u in circus
ē equal	ò saw	ü rule	zh measure	

3 *NOUN.* **woolens,** cloth or clothing made of wool: *We put away our woolens for the summer.*

4 *ADJECTIVE.* of or about wool or cloth made from wool: *His family owns a woolen mill.*

wool·ly (wul′ē), *ADJECTIVE.* consisting of wool: *The blanket was like the woolly coat of a sheep.*
❑ *ADJECTIVE* **wool·li·er, wool·li·est.**

woolly mammoth, a kind of mammoth having a long, woolly coat. Woolly mammoths lived in Europe, Asia, and North America thousands of years ago.

wool·y (wul′ē), *ADJECTIVE.* another spelling of **woolly.** ❑ *ADJECTIVE* **wool·i·er, wool·i·est.**

word (wėrd),

1 *NOUN.* a sound or a group of sounds that means something. We speak words when we talk.

2 *NOUN.* the written or printed letters that stand for a word: *This page is filled with words.*

3 *NOUN.* a short talk: *May I have a word with you?*

4 *NOUN.* a brief statement: *Can I give you a word of advice?*

5 *NOUN.* a promise: *She kept her word.*

6 *NOUN.* news; information: *I have had no word from them in months.*

7 *VERB.* to put something into words: *He worded the message clearly.*
❑ *VERB* **words, word·ed, word·ing.**

by word of mouth, *IDIOM.* by spoken words; through conversation: *I heard about this new restaurant by word of mouth.*

word for word, *IDIOM.* in the exact words: *Tell me word for word what they said about me.*

Word Source

Many prefixes and suffixes in English come from whole words in Latin or Greek. Because those whole words were used so often combined with other words, they gradually turned into word parts. You can see the same process in English:

-driven	-handed	-less	-proof
extra-	-headed	-like	self-
-footed	-hearted	out-	under-
-free	-legged	over-	

word history, an account or explanation of the origin and history of a word; etymology.

word·ing (wėr′ding), *NOUN.* a way of saying something; choice of words: *Careful wording helps you make clear to others what you really mean.*

word processing, the editing, storage, and reproduction of documents and texts by means of computers, printers, and other electronic machines. **—word processor.**

word·y (wėr′dē), *ADJECTIVE.* using too many words: *He cut the long, wordy description out of the report.* ❑ *ADJECTIVE* **word·i·er, word·i·est.** **—word′i·ness,** *NOUN.*

wore (wôr), *VERB.* the past tense of **wear:** *I wore out my shoes.* ■ Another word that sounds like this is **war.**

woolly mammoth — about 14 feet high at the shoulder

work (wėrk),

1 *NOUN.* effort in doing or making something: *Gardening can be hard work.*

2 *NOUN.* something to do; occupation; employment: *My friend is out of work.*

3 *NOUN.* something made or done; result of effort: *The artist considers that picture to be his greatest work.*

4 *NOUN.* what you put effort into; a piece of work to do: *We carried our work out onto the porch.*

5 *NOUN.* **works,** the moving parts of a machine: *He took apart the watch to look at the works.*

6 *VERB.* to do work or do a job: *We worked together all morning cleaning up the garage.*

7 *VERB.* to work for pay; be employed: *She works at an airplane factory.*

8 *VERB.* to perform or operate properly: *This pump will not work. The plan worked well.*

9 *VERB.* to cause to do work: *That company works its employees hard.*

10 *VERB.* to bring something about; cause: *That medicine works miracles on headaches.*

11 *VERB.* to solve: *Please work all the math problems on this page.*

12 *VERB.* to make; shape: *She worked a piece of copper into a beautiful tray.*

13 *NOUN.* the result of a force moving an object through a distance. In science, work is done only if something moves. Pushing against a wall does no work, but lifting your hand does.
❑ *VERB* **works, worked, work·ing.**

work out, *IDIOM.*

1 to plan; develop: *Each group must work out its own program.*

2 to solve: *I have to work out a few math problems and then I'll be done with my homework.*

3 to turn out; succeed: *Everything worked out fine.*

4 to exercise: *He works out with weights daily.*

Synonym Study

Work means effort in doing or making something: *Washing the car is only an hour's work for the two of us.*

Labor means work that takes a lot of strength: *Building a house requires a lot of human labor and skill.*

Toil means long and tiring work: *After days of toil, the bird completed its nest.*

See also the Synonym Study at **job**.

ANTONYM: **play**.

work·a·ble (wėr′kə bəl), ADJECTIVE. able to be used or put into effect: *He came up with a workable plan.*

work·bench (wėrk′bench′), NOUN. a strong, heavy table used by someone who works with tools and materials. ❏ PLURAL **work·bench·es.**

using a large clamp on a **workbench**

work·book (wėrk′bůk′), NOUN. a book in which a student answers questions and does written work.

work·er (wėr′kər), NOUN.
1 someone who works; workman.
2 a bee, ant, wasp, or other insect that works for its community and usually does not produce young.

work·man (wėrk′mən), NOUN.
1 See **worker**.
2 someone who works with his or her hands or with machines.
❏ PLURAL **work·men.**

work·man·ship (wėrk′mən ship), NOUN. the art or skill in a worker or in the work done: *Good workmanship requires long practice.*

work·out (wėrk′out′), NOUN. a period of doing exercise: *I had a good workout lifting weights today.*

work·room (wėrk′rüm′), NOUN. a room where work is done.

work·shop (wėrk′shop′), NOUN.
1 a shop or building where work is done.
2 a group of people that are working on or studying a special project: *He went to a teachers' workshop.*

work·ta·ble (wėrk′tā′bəl), NOUN. a table to work at.

world (wėrld), NOUN.
1 the earth: *Ships can sail around the world.*
2 all of certain parts, people, or things of the earth: *the insect world, the world of books.*
3 all people; the public: *The whole world knows it.*
4 any planet, especially when thought of as lived on: *The movie showed creatures from another world.*
5 a great deal; a lot of: *Sunshine does a world of good.*
6 all things; everything; the universe.

world-class (wėrld′klas′), ADJECTIVE. of the highest rank or ability in the world: *world-class competition, a world-class scientist.*

world·ly (wėrld′lē), ADJECTIVE. of this world; not of heaven: *He decided to give up his worldly wealth.*

World War I, a war fought from 1914 to 1918. The United States, Great Britain, France, Russia, and their allies were on one side; Germany, Austria, and their allies were on the other side.

World War II, a war fought from 1939 to 1945. The United States, Great Britain, the Soviet Union, and their allies were on one side; Germany, Italy, Japan, and their allies were on the other side.

world·wide (wėrld′wid′), ADJECTIVE. spread throughout the world: *Pollution is becoming a worldwide problem.*

World Wide Web, a system for finding and presenting information files, called documents, over the Internet. World Wide Web documents can include text, images, sound, and hypertext links to other information.

worm (wėrm),
1 NOUN. a small, slender, crawling or creeping animal. Most worms have soft bodies and no legs.
2 VERB. to move like a worm; crawl or creep like a worm: *I wormed my way under the fence.*
3 NOUN. **worms,** a disease caused by parasitic worms in the intestines: *Our dog had a bad case of worms.*
❏ VERB **worms, wormed, worm·ing. –worm′like′,** ADJECTIVE.

W

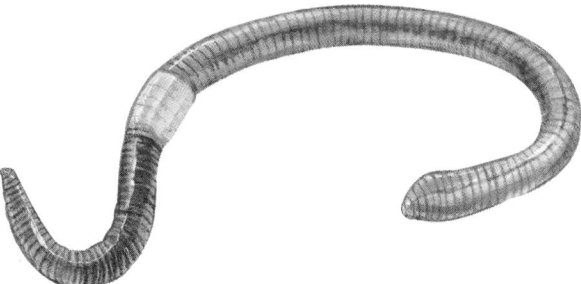

The smallest **worms** can be seen only through a microscope. The largest are about 11 feet long.

a	hat	ė	term	ô	order	ch	child		a in about
ā	age	i	it	oi	oil	ng	long		e in taken
ä	far	ī	ice	ou	out	sh	she	ə	i in pencil
â	care	o	hot	u	cup	th	thin		o in lemon
e	let	ō	open	ů	put	ᴛʜ	then		u in circus
ē	equal	ò	saw	ü	rule	zh	measure		

worm·y (wẻr′mē), ADJECTIVE. having worms; containing many worms: *The basket was full of wormy apples.* ❑ ADJECTIVE **worm·i·er, worm·i·est.**

worn (wôrn),
1 VERB. the past participle of **wear**: *I have worn these jeans all week.*
2 ADJECTIVE. damaged by use: *We gave away the worn rugs.*
▪ Another word that sounds like this is **warn.**

worn-out (wôrn′out′), ADJECTIVE.
1 very worn from long, hard use; worn or used until worthless or in poor condition: *a worn-out lawnmower, worn-out shoes, a worn-out sweater.*
2 very tired; exhausted: *The knight rested his worn-out horse.* ▪ See the Synonym Study at **tired.**

wor·ry (wèr′ē),
1 VERB. to feel uneasy or upset about something: *Don't worry about it. They will worry if we are late.*
2 VERB. to make someone anxious; trouble: *The problem worried him.*
3 NOUN. a feeling of anxiety and sadness caused by things that are on your mind: *Worry kept her awake.*
4 NOUN. a cause of trouble or care: *Parents of a sick child have many worries.*
5 VERB. to annoy someone: *Don't worry me right now with so many questions.*
❑ VERB **wor·ries, wor·ried, wor·ry·ing;** PLURAL **wor·ries.**

worse (wèrs),
1 ADJECTIVE. not as good; not as well; more ill: *The patient seems even worse today.*
2 ADJECTIVE. less good: *That movie was worse than I thought it would be.*
3 ADVERB. in a more severe or evil manner or degree: *It is raining worse than ever today.*
4 NOUN. something worse: *The loss of their property was terrible, but worse followed.*
★ **Worse** is the comparative of **bad.**

wor·ship (wèr′ship),
1 NOUN. great honor and respect: *the worship of God.*
2 VERB. to show great honor and respect to: *to worship God.*
3 NOUN. ceremonies or services in honor of God. Prayers and hymns are part of worship.
4 VERB. to take part in a religious service.
5 VERB. to consider extremely precious; hold very dear; adore: *She worships her mother.*
❑ VERB **wor·ships, wor·shiped, wor·ship·ing.** —**wor′ship·er** or **wor′ship·per,** NOUN.

worst (wèrst),
1 ADJECTIVE. least well; most ill: *This is the worst I've been since I got sick.*
2 ADJECTIVE. least good; most unsatisfactory: *That was the worst movie I've ever seen!*
3 ADVERB. in the worst manner or degree: *The children behave worst when they are tired.*

4 NOUN. something that is the worst: *Today was bad, but the worst is yet to come.*
★ **Worst** is the superlative of **bad.**
if worst comes to worst, IDIOM. if the very worst thing happens: *If worst comes to worst, we'll cancel our vacation this year.*
in the worst way, IDIOM. very badly: *I want that new book in the worst way.*

worth (wèrth),
1 ADJECTIVE. equal in value to: *This book is worth fifteen dollars.*
2 NOUN. how much a certain amount of money will buy: *He bought a dollar's worth of stamps.*
3 NOUN. value: *She got her money's worth out of that coat.*
4 PREPOSITION. good, useful, or important enough for: *That book is worth reading.*
5 PREPOSITION. having property or money that amounts to: *That man is worth millions.*
6 NOUN. merit; usefulness; importance: *We should read books of real worth.*

worth·less (wèrth′lis), ADJECTIVE. useless: *He threw out the worthless, broken toys.* —**worth′less·ness,** NOUN.

worth·while (wèrth′wīl′), ADJECTIVE. worth your time or attention: *This is a worthwhile book; you should read it.*

wor·thy (wèr′ŦHē), ADJECTIVE.
1 having worth or merit: *Helping the poor is a worthy cause.*
2 deserving; meriting: *Her courage was worthy of high praise.*
❑ ADJECTIVE **wor·thi·er, wor·thi·est.** —**wor′thi·ness,** NOUN.

would (wùd), HELPING VERB.
1 the past tense of **will**[1]: *She said that she would come. They would eat with us tonight.*
2 **Would** is also used: **a** to express or report what someone said: *The principal said it would be all right to wear caps in school.* **b** to express action done again and again in the past: *The children would play for hours on the beach.* **c** to express a condition that might have been if something had been done: *It would be cooler by now if we had turned on the air conditioner.* **d** to sound more polite than *will* sounds: *Would you help us, please?*
▪ Another word that sounds like this is **wood.**

would·n't (wùd′nt), a contraction of **would not.**

wound[1] (wünd),
1 NOUN. an injury caused by cutting, stabbing, or shooting: *a knife wound, a bullet wound.*
2 VERB. to injure something or someone by cutting or shooting; hurt: *The hunter wounded the deer.*
3 VERB. to hurt someone's feelings: *Their unkind words wounded me.*
❑ VERB **wounds, wound·ed, wound·ing.**

wound² (wound), *VERB.*
1 the past tense of **wind²**: *I wound the string into a tight ball.*
2 the past participle of **wind²**: *It is wound too tight.*

wove (wōv), *VERB.* the past tense of **weave**: *The spider wove a web in the corner of the room.*

wo·ven (wō′vən), *VERB.* a past participle of **weave**: *This cloth is closely woven.*

wow (wou), *INTERJECTION.* an exclamation of surprise, joy, or wonder: *Wow! I can sure use a gift like that.*

wran·gle (rang′gəl), *VERB.* to argue or dispute in a noisy or angry way; quarrel: *The children wrangled about who should wash the dog.* ❑ *VERB* **wran·gles, wran·gled, wran·gling.**

Spelling Note wr-

Many words beginning with **wr-** come from old English, in which both letters were pronounced in such words. This is not an easy sound to make, and people gradually stopped making it. By about 400 years ago, the **w** had become silent in **wr-**, but the spelling had become familiar, so it lasted.

wran·gler (rang′glər), *NOUN.* someone in charge of horses, cattle, and so on, on a ranch.

wrangler using a lasso to catch horses

wrap (rap),
1 *VERB.* to cover something by winding or folding something around it: *She wrapped herself in a shawl.*
2 *VERB.* to wind or fold as a covering: *Wrap a shawl around yourself.*
3 *VERB.* to cover something with paper and tie it up or fasten it: *Hurry and wrap her presents!*
4 *NOUN.* an outer covering. Shawls, scarfs, coats, and furs are wraps.
❑ *VERB* **wraps, wrapped, wrap·ping.** ■ Another word that sounds like this is **rap.**

wrapped up in, *IDIOM.* devoted to; thinking chiefly of: *She is too wrapped up in her work to join us.*

wrap·per (rap′ər), *NOUN.*
1 a covering or cover: *Pick up those candy wrappers. Some magazines are mailed in plastic wrappers.*
2 someone or something that wraps.

wrap·ping (rap′ing), *NOUN.* paper, cloth, or the like in which something is wrapped: *He saved the pretty wrapping to use again.*

wrath (rath), *NOUN.* very great anger; rage.

wrath·ful (rath′fəl), *ADJECTIVE.* very angry; showing great anger: *His wrathful eyes flashed.* —**wrath′ful·ly,** *ADVERB.*

wreak (rēk), *VERB.* to cause great harm or damage to something: *The tornado wreaked vast damage all across the country.* ❑ *VERB* **wreaks, wreaked, wreak·ing.** ■ Another word that sounds like this is **reek.**

wreath (rēth), *NOUN.*
1 a ring of flowers or leaves that are twisted together: *There are wreaths in the windows at Christmas.*
2 something suggesting a wreath: *a wreath of smoke.*
❑ *PLURAL* **wreaths** (rēTHz or rēths).

We put a **wreath** on our front door at Christmas.

wreathe (rēTH), *VERB.* to decorate something with wreaths: *The inside of the school was wreathed with flowers for the graduation ceremony.* ❑ *VERB* **wreathes, wreathed, wreath·ing.**

wreck (rek),
1 *NOUN.* the destruction of a car, ship, building, train, truck, or aircraft: *Reckless driving causes many wrecks on the highway.*
2 *NOUN.* destruction or serious injury: *Heavy rains will wreck the corn crop.*
3 *VERB.* to completely destroy or ruin something: *A broken rail wrecked the freight train just outside of town.* ■ See the Synonym Study at **destroy.**
❑ *VERB* **wrecks, wrecked, wreck·ing.**

wreck·age (rek′ij), *NOUN.*
1 all that is left of something that has been wrecked: *The shore was covered with the wreckage of the ship.*
2 the act of wrecking: *They felt defeated by the wreckage of their plans.*

wreck·er (rek′ər), *NOUN.*
1 a person, truck, train, or machine that removes wrecked or stalled cars, trucks, and so on.
2 someone whose work is tearing down buildings.

wren (ren), *NOUN.* a small songbird with a slender bill and short, upright tail. Wrens often build nests near houses.

a	hat	ė	term	ô	order	ch	child	⎧a in about
ā	age	i	it	oi	oil	ng	long	⎪e in taken
ä	far	ī	ice	ou	out	sh	she	ə⎨i in pencil
â	care	o	hot	u	cup	th	thin	⎪o in lemon
e	let	ō	open	u̇	put	ŦH	then	⎩u in circus
ē	equal	ȯ	saw	ü	rule	zh	measure	

W

wrench (rench),
1 *NOUN.* a violent twist or twisting pull: *She broke the branch off the tree with a sudden wrench.*
2 *VERB.* to twist or pull something violently: *She wrenched the knob off by turning it too hard.*
3 *VERB.* to injure a part of your body by twisting it: *She wrenched her back doing gymnastics.*
4 *NOUN.* a tool to hold and turn nuts, bolts, pieces of pipe, or the like.
❑ *PLURAL* **wrench•es;** *VERB* **wrench•es, wrenched, wrench•ing.**

wrest (rest), *VERB.*
1 to twist, pull, or tear something away with force: *She bravely wrested the knife from the attacker.*
2 to take by force: *The general wrested control of the nation from the king.*
❑ *VERB* **wrests, wrest•ed, wrest•ing.** ■ Another word that sounds like this is **rest.**

wres•tle (res′əl), *VERB.*
1 to try to throw or force someone to the ground in a contest, usually watched by a referee.
2 to struggle: *I am still wrestling with this problem.*
❑ *VERB* **wres•tles, wres•tled, wres•tling. —wres′tler,** *NOUN.*

wres•tling (res′ling), *NOUN.* a sport or contest in which two opponents try to throw or force each other to the ground.

wretch (rech), *NOUN.*
1 a very unfortunate or unhappy person.
2 a very bad person.
❑ *PLURAL* **wretch•es.**

wretch•ed (rech′id), *ADJECTIVE.*
1 very unfortunate or unhappy.
2 very unsatisfactory; miserable: *a wretched hut, a wretched meal.*
3 very bad: *The king condemned the wretched traitor.* **—wretch′ed•ness,** *NOUN.*

wrig•gle (rig′əl),
1 *VERB.* to twist and turn: *Children wriggle when they are restless.*
2 *VERB.* to move by twisting and turning: *The worm wriggled out of my hand when I tried to grab it.*
3 *NOUN.* a wriggling motion: *He laughed with a wriggle.*
❑ *VERB* **wrig•gles, wrig•gled, wrig•gling.**

wring (ring), *VERB.*
1 to twist with force; squeeze hard: *Wring out your wet bathing suit.*
2 to get by twisting or squeezing; force out: *The boy wrung water from his wet bathing suit.*
3 to get by force, effort, or persuasion: *She really knows how to wring a secret out of someone.*
❑ *VERB* **wrings, wrung, wring•ing.** ■ Another word that sounds like this is **ring.**

wring•er (ring′ər), *NOUN.* a machine for squeezing water from wet clothes.

wrin•kle (ring′kəl),
1 *NOUN.* a fold on the surface of something that is usually flat: *There are many wrinkles in my shirt.*
2 *VERB.* to make a wrinkle or wrinkles in: *She wrinkled her forehead.*
3 *VERB.* to have wrinkles; acquire wrinkles: *This shirt will not wrinkle.*
❑ *VERB* **wrin•kles, wrin•kled, wrin•kling.**

wrist (rist), *NOUN.* the part of the body between the hand and the arm.

wrist•band (rist′band′), *NOUN.* a band worn around the wrist to soak up sweat during exercise.

wrist•watch (rist′wäch′), *NOUN.* a small watch worn on the wrist. ❑ *PLURAL* **wrist•watch•es.**

write (rīt), *VERB.*
1 to make letters or words with pen, pencil, chalk, or the like: *I can read and write. Please write on both sides of the paper.*
2 to put down the letters or words of: *Write your name and address.*
3 to make up stories, books, poems, articles, or the like; compose: *He writes for magazines.*
4 to write a letter: *I write to my friend in England every week.*
5 to write a letter to: *She wrote her parents that she would be home for New Year's.*
❑ *VERB* **writes, wrote, writ•ten, writ•ing.** ■ Other words that sound like this are **right** and **rite.**

write down, *IDIOM.* to put into writing: *I will write down your directions.*

write off, *IDIOM.*
1 to cancel officially: *The bank wrote off the debt.*
2 to state that something now has no value: *After the storm, the insurance company wrote off the boat as a total loss.*
3 to regard as a complete failure: *I finally wrote off my attempts at painting.*

write out, *IDIOM.*
1 to fill in blanks with writing: *He wrote out a check for the whole amount.*
2 to write in full: *He wrote out his speech and memorized it.*

write up, *IDIOM.* to write a description or account of, especially a full or detailed account: *The reporter wrote up his interview with the mayor for the newspaper.*

Word Story

Write comes from an old English word meaning "to scratch." Long ago, Germanic peoples used runes, letters carved into stone or wood, or scratched into coins, jewelry, and weapons. When they began to use the alphabet and ink, their pens were sharpened feathers that made a scratchy sound. If you have an itch to create, writing is a good way to scratch it.

writ·er (rī′tər), *NOUN.*
1 someone who writes.
2 someone whose occupation is writing; author.

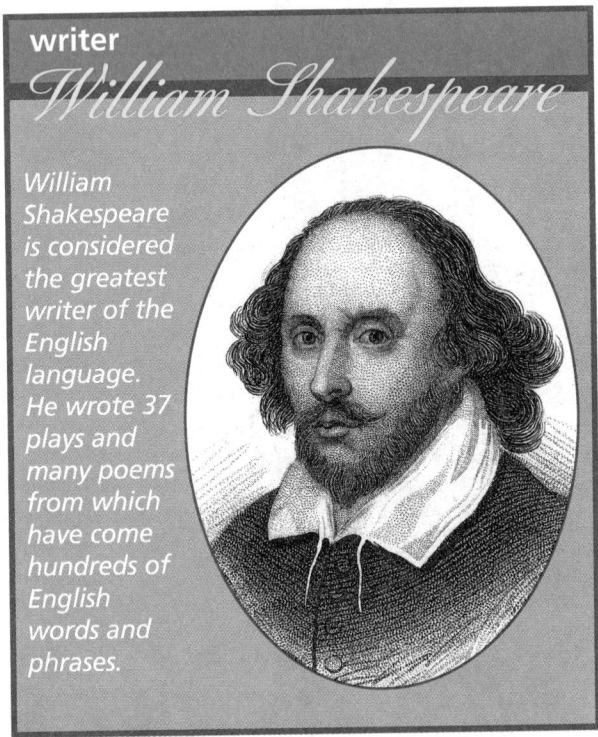

writer

William Shakespeare

William Shakespeare is considered the greatest writer of the English language. He wrote 37 plays and many poems from which have come hundreds of English words and phrases.

writhe (rīтн), *VERB.* to twist and turn; twist about: *The knight saw the wounded dragon writhe in pain.* ❑ *VERB* **writhes, writhed, writh·ing.**

writ·ing (rī′ting), *NOUN.*
1 the act of making letters or words with pen, pencil, chalk, or the like.
2 written form: *Put your ideas in writing.*
3 handwriting: *Your writing is hard to read.*
4 **writings,** a book or other written production: *We read the writings of Benjamin Franklin in class.*

writ·ten (rit′n), *VERB.* the past participle of **write:** *I have written a letter.*

wrong (rŏng),
1 *ADJECTIVE.* not the way it should be; not right; morally bad: *Stealing is wrong.*
2 *ADJECTIVE.* not true; not correct: *She gave the wrong answer.*
3 *ADJECTIVE.* not proper; not suitable: *Heavy boots would be the wrong thing to wear for tennis.*
4 *ADJECTIVE.* not working right; out of order: *Something is wrong with the car.*

5 *ADVERB.* badly; in an incorrect way: *I did my homework wrong and had to do it over.*
6 *NOUN.* anything not right; wrong thing or action: *Two wrongs do not make a right.*
7 *VERB.* to do wrong to someone: *It is often hard to forgive someone who has wronged you.*
❑ *VERB* **wrongs, wronged, wrong·ing. —wrong′ly,** *ADVERB.* **—wrong′ness,** *NOUN.*

go wrong, *IDIOM.* to turn out badly: *Everything went wrong today.*

in the wrong, *IDIOM.* at fault; guilty: *I blamed the fight on my brother, but I was in the wrong.*

wrong·do·er (rŏng′dü′ər), *NOUN.* someone who does wrong.

wrong·do·ing (rŏng′dü′ing), *NOUN.* the act of doing something wrong: *The thief was guilty of wrongdoing.*

wrote (rōt), *VERB.* the past tense of **write:** *He wrote his mother a long letter last week.*

wrought (rŏt), *ADJECTIVE.*
1 made: *The gate was wrought with great skill.*
2 formed by hammering: *The fence was made of wrought iron.*

wrung (rung), *VERB.*
1 the past tense of **wring:** *She wrung out the wet cloth and hung it up.*
2 the past participle of **wring:** *Her heart was wrung with pity for the poor.*
■ Another word that sounds like this is **rung.**

wry (rī), *ADJECTIVE.* twisted; turned to one side: *She made a wry face to show her disgust.* ❑ *ADJECTIVE* **wri·er, wri·est.** ■ Another word that sounds like this is **rye. —wry′ly,** *ADVERB.*

wt., an abbreviation of **weight.**

WV, an abbreviation of **West Virginia.**

WWW, an abbreviation of **World Wide Web.**

WY, an abbreviation of **Wyoming.**

Wy·o·ming (wī ō′ming), *NOUN.* one of the Rocky Mountain states of the United States. *Abbreviation:* WY; *Capital:* Cheyenne. **—Wy·o′ming·ite,** *NOUN.*

State Story **Wyoming** got its name from Wyoming Valley, Pennsylvania. The name *Wyoming* comes from a Delaware Indian word meaning "upon the great plain." It became popular after a poem called "Gertrude of Wyoming" was published. A member of Congress proposed it as the name of the western land that became the state of Wyoming.

W

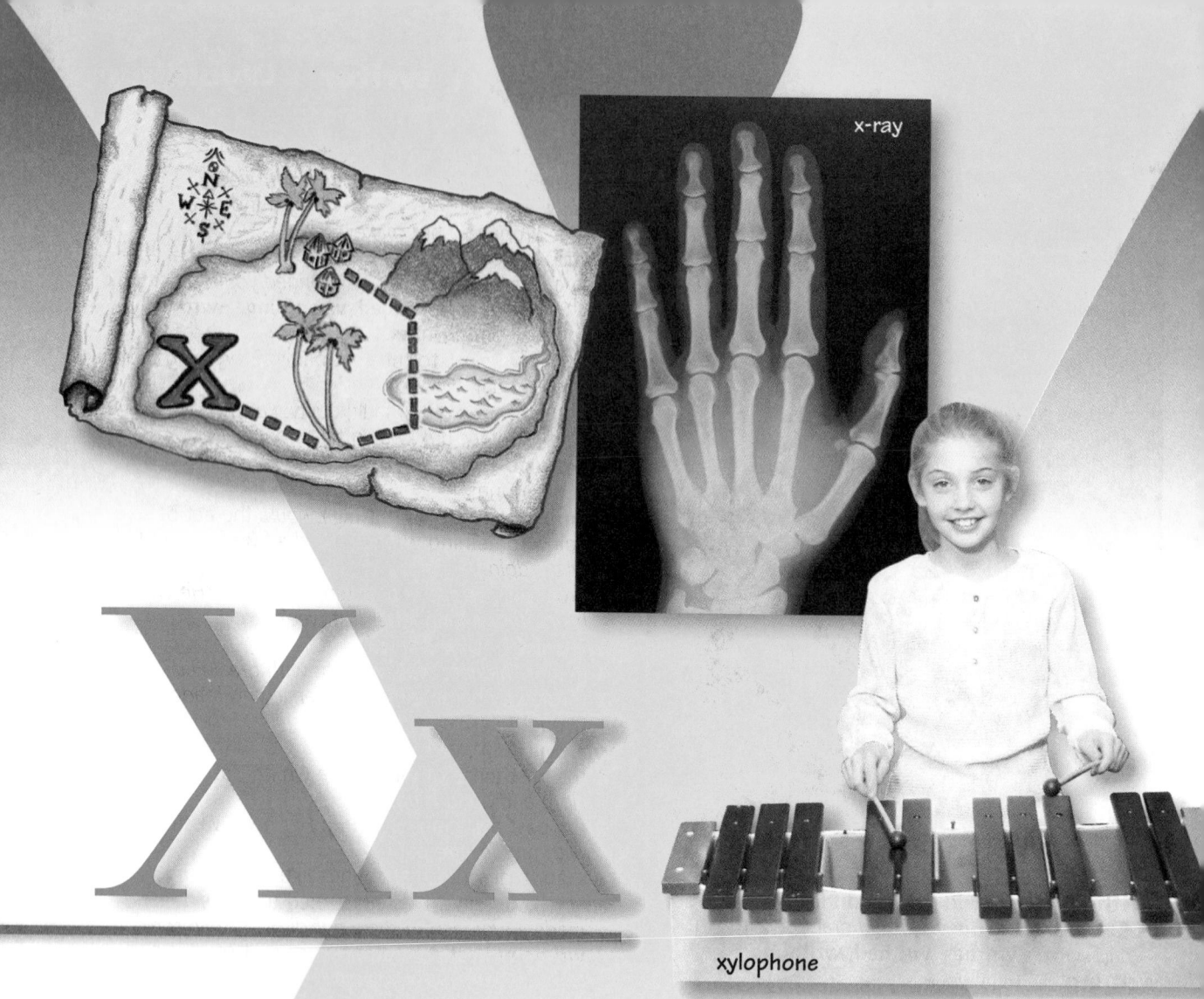

x-ray

xylophone

X or **x** (eks), *NOUN.*
1 the 24th letter of the English alphabet.
2 an unknown quantity in algebra.
❑ *PLURAL* **X's** or **x's.**

xen·o·pho·bi·a (zen/ə fō/bē ə), *NOUN.* fear of foreigners: *Xenophobia made their trip to central Asia difficult.* **–xen/o·pho/bic,** *ADJECTIVE.*

Xer·ox (zir/oks),
1 *NOUN.* (trademark) a process of copying letters or other documents by making photographic prints of them.
2 *VERB.* to make a copy or copies of something by using a Xerox copying machine..
❑ *VERB* **Xer·ox·es, Xer·oxed, Xer·ox·ing.**

XL, an abbreviation of **extra large.**

Xmas (kris/məs *or* ek/sməs), *NOUN.* an abbreviation of **Christmas.**

X ray,
1 a ray which can go through substances that rays of light cannot penetrate. X rays are used to locate breaks in bones or decay in teeth, and to treat certain diseases.
2 a photograph made by means of X rays.

X-ray (eks/rā/),
1 *VERB.* to examine, photograph, or treat someone with X rays.
2 *ADJECTIVE.* of, by, or having something to do with X rays: *The dentist did an X-ray examination of my teeth to look for cavities.*
❑ *VERB* **X-rays, X-rayed, X-ray·ing.**

xy·lo·phone (zī/lē fōn), *NOUN.* a musical instrument made of two rows of wooden bars of different lengths. Sounds are made by striking these bars with wooden hammers.

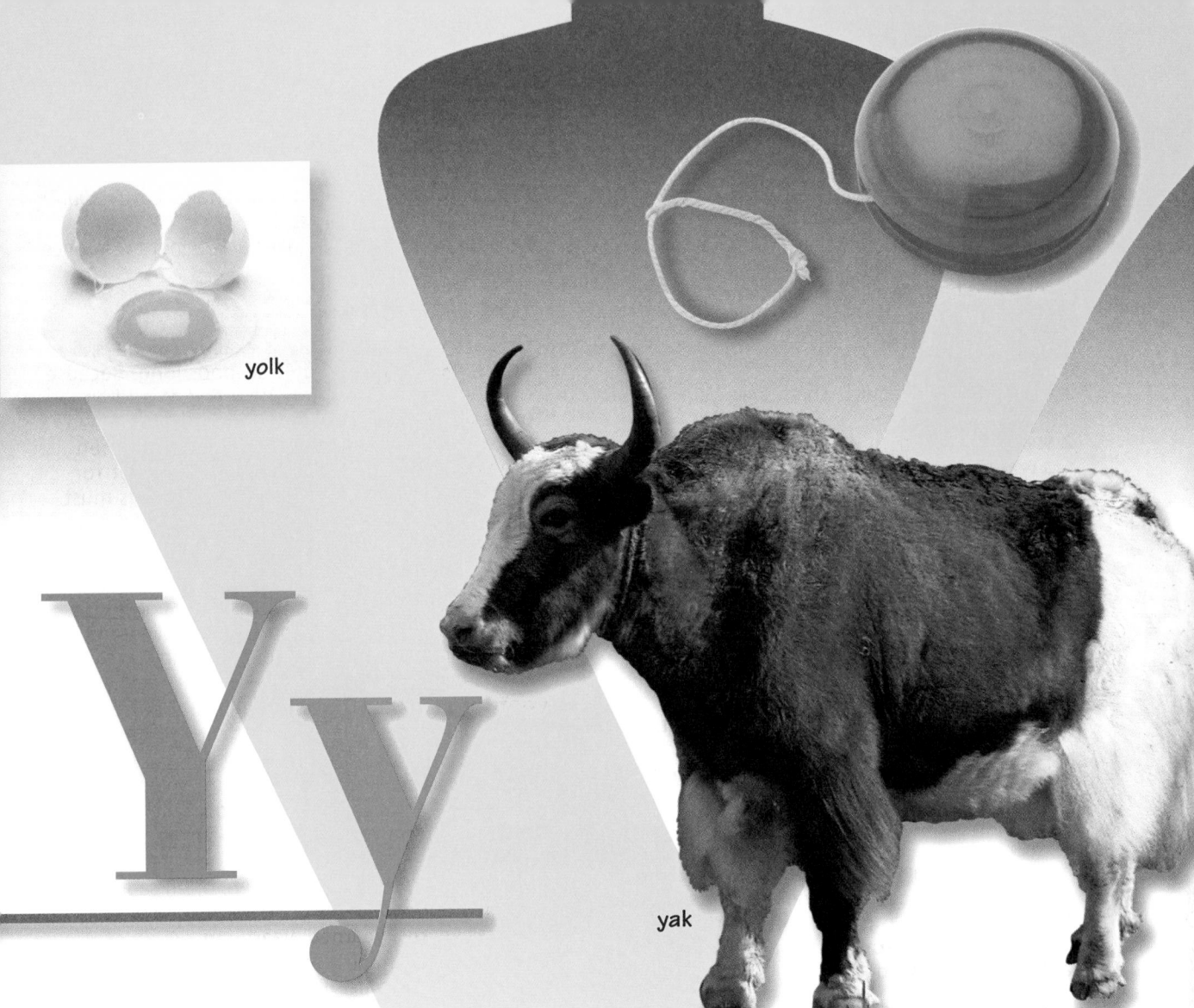

yolk

yak

Yy

Y or **y** (wī), *NOUN.*
1 the 25th letter of the English alphabet.
2 anything shaped like a Y.
❑ *PLURAL* **Y's** or **y's.**

Word Power   -y

The suffix **-y¹** has many meanings. It can mean "full of" or "containing." Bump**y** means **full of** bumps. Salt**y** means **containing** salt. The suffix **-y¹** can mean "having." Wealth**y** means **having** wealth. The same suffix can also mean "inclined to" or "like." Sleep**y** means **inclined to** sleep. Dream**y** means **like** a dream.

The suffix **-y²** means "small" or "dear." A doll**y** is **a small** doll. Dadd**y** means **dear** dad.

yacht (yät), *NOUN.* a boat for pleasure trips or for racing: *The millionaire invited us all to have dinner on his ninety-foot yacht.*

yak¹ (yak), *NOUN.* a large, long-haired animal like an ox that lives in central Asia. It is raised for its meat, milk, and hair.

yak² (yak), *VERB.* (informal) to talk endlessly and foolishly: *We yakked until Mom told me to get off the phone.* ❑ *VERB* **yaks, yakked, yak·king.**

yam (yam), *NOUN.*
1 the sweet potato: *We like candied yams.*
2 the thick, sweet, orange root of a vine of warm regions, eaten as a vegetable.

yam·mer (yam′ər), *VERB.* to talk loudly and constantly: *He yammered to me about his stamp collection.*
❑ *VERB* **yam·mers, yam·mered, yam·mer·ing.**

yank (yangk),
1 *VERB.* to pull something with a sudden motion; jerk; tug: *She yanked the weeds out of the flower bed.*
2 *NOUN.* a sudden pull; jerk; tug: *I gave the door a yank, and it flew open.*
❑ *VERB* **yanks, yanked, yank·ing.**

Yank (yangk), *NOUN.* a short form of **Yankee** (definition 3).

Yan·kee (yang′kē), *NOUN.*
1 someone born or living in New England.
2 someone born or living in the North, especially during the Civil War.
3 someone born or living in the United States; American; Yank.
❑ *PLURAL* **Yan·kees.**

yap (yap),
1 *VERB.* to bark in a quick, sharp way; yelp: *The little dog yapped at me.*
2 *NOUN.* a quick, sharp bark; yelp.
❑ *VERB* **yaps, yapped, yap·ping.**

yard[1] (yärd), *NOUN.*
1 a piece of ground near or around a house, barn, school, or other building: *You must not leave the yard.*
2 a piece of enclosed ground for some special purpose or business: *She works in a lumber yard.*
3 an area with many tracks where railroad cars are stored, shifted around, serviced, or made up into new trains: *My dad works in the railroad yards.*

yard[2] (yärd), *NOUN.*
1 a unit of length equal to 36 inches; 3 feet: *I bought three yards of blue cloth for curtains.*
2 a beam or pole fastened across a mast and used to support a sail.

Have You Heard?

You may have heard talk about **"going the whole nine yards."** This means that someone is doing as much as possible in a certain situation. It can also mean you think that they are doing too much.

yard·stick (yärd′stik′), *NOUN.* a stick one yard long, used for measuring things.

yarn (yärn), *NOUN.*
1 any spun thread, especially thread made for weaving or knitting: *I'm knitting a scarf from this yarn.*
2 a tale; story: *The old sailor made up his yarns as he told them.* ■ See the Synonym Study at **story**[1].

yawn (yòn),
1 *VERB.* to open your mouth wide to get more air. People yawn when they are sleepy, tired, or bored.
2 *NOUN.* the act of opening your mouth in this way.
❑ *VERB* **yawns, yawned, yawn·ing.**

yd., an abbreviation of **yard**[2]. ❑ *PLURAL* **yd** or **yds.**

yea (yā),
1 *ADVERB.* (formerly) yes; indeed.
2 *NOUN.* a vote or voter in favor of something: *The yeas outnumber the nays, so the plan is approved.*
❑ *PLURAL* **yeas.**

yeah (ye, ya, *or* ye′ə), *ADVERB.* (informal). yes.

year (yir), *NOUN.*
1 12 months or 365 days; January 1 to December 31. A leap year has 366 days.
2 12 months counted from any point: *I will see you again a year from today.*
3 the part of a year spent in a certain activity: *Our school year is 9 months.*
4 the amount of time it takes any planet to go once around the sun.

Did You Know?

On Earth, the solar year is exactly 365 days, 5 hours, 48 minutes, and 46 seconds long. Because of those extra five hours, we need to add an extra day in leap years. The extra day is added as February 29. Leap years only happen when the year is exactly divisible by four, except for years that end in two zeroes. Those years must be exactly divisible by 400. So 1900 was not a leap year, but 2000 is.

year·book (yir′bùk′), *NOUN.* a book published every year to report that year's events or facts. The graduating class in a school or college usually publishes a yearbook, with pictures of its members.

year·ling (yir′ling), *NOUN.* an animal that is one year old.

year·ly (yir′lē),
1 *ADVERB* or *ADJECTIVE.* once a year; in every year: *They take a yearly trip to New York.*
2 *ADJECTIVE.* for a year: *She has a yearly salary of $30,000.*

yearn (yern), *VERB.* to feel a deep, often sad longing or desire for something: *He yearns for home.*
❑ *VERB* **yearns, yearned, yearn·ing.**

yearn·ing (yer′ning), *NOUN.* a deep longing or desire: *He felt a deep yearning to see the green mountains of his homeland again.*

year-round (yir′round′), *ADJECTIVE* or *ADVERB.* throughout the year: *She lives here year-round.*

yeast (yēst), *NOUN.* the substance that causes bread dough to rise and beer to ferment. Yeast consists of many tiny fungi that grow quickly in any material containing sugar.

yell (yel),
1 *VERB.* to cry out with a strong, loud sound: *I yelled with pain when the door slammed on my finger.* ■ See the Synonym Study at **shout.**
2 *NOUN.* a loud cry: *Give a yell when you're ready.*
3 *NOUN.* a special shout or cheer used by a school or college at sports events.
❑ *VERB* **yells, yelled, yell·ing.**

yel·low (yel′ō),
1 *NOUN.* the color of gold, butter, or ripe lemons.
2 *ADJECTIVE.* having this color: *Can I borrow your yellow sweater?*
3 *VERB.* to make or become yellow: *Paper yellows with age.*
❑ *VERB* **yel·lows, yel·lowed, yel·low·ing.**

yellow fever, a dangerous disease of warm climates that causes high fever and turns the skin yellow. It is carried by the bite of a certain kind of mosquito.

yel·low·ish (yel′ō ish), ADJECTIVE. somewhat yellow.

yellow jacket, a kind of wasp marked with bright yellow.

Yellow Pages, a telephone book or section of a telephone book that is printed on yellow paper and lists businesses and professional people.

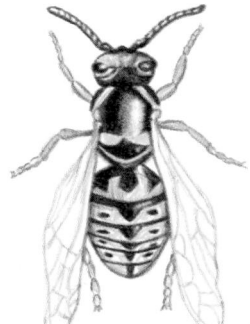

yellow jacket — about ¾ inch long

yelp (yelp),
1 NOUN. the quick, sharp bark or cry of a dog or fox.
2 VERB. to make such a bark or cry.
❑ VERB **yelps, yelped, yelp·ing.**

Yem·en (yem′ən), NOUN. a country in Arabia, in southwestern Asia. –**Yem′en·ite** or **Yem·en·i** (yem′ə nē), ADJECTIVE or NOUN.

yen (yen), NOUN. the unit of money in Japan. ❑ PLURAL **yen.**

yes (yes),
1 ADVERB. a word used to show agreement or consent: *Yes, five and two are seven. When he asked me if I'd go, I said, "Yes."*
2 NOUN. a vote for something: *The yeses won.*
3 ADVERB. and what is more: *"Your work is good, yes, very good," said the teacher.*
❑ PLURAL **yes·es.**

yes·ter·day (yes′tər dā),
1 NOUN. the day before today: *Yesterday was cold and rainy.*
2 ADVERB. on the day before today: *It rained yesterday.*
3 NOUN. the recent past: *We are often amused by the fashions of yesterday.*

yet (yet),
1 ADVERB. up to the present time; thus far: *The work is not yet finished.*
2 ADVERB. now; at this time: *Don't go yet.*
3 ADVERB. then; at that time: *It was not yet dark.*
4 ADVERB. still; even now: *She is doing her homework yet.*
5 ADVERB. sometime: *I may yet get rich.*
6 ADVERB. additionally; again: *Let us try yet one more time.*
7 ADVERB. even: *The judge spoke yet more harshly to the prisoner who had been found guilty.*
8 CONJUNCTION or ADVERB. but: *The work is good, yet it could be better. The story was strange, yet true.*

as yet, IDIOM. up to now: *We have not seen any improvement in your grades as yet.*

yew (yü), NOUN. an evergreen tree of Europe and Asia. Some kinds of yew are grown in the United States as shrubs. Yew leaves and berries are poisonous. ■ Other words that sound like this are **ewe** and **you.**

Yid·dish (yid′ish), NOUN. a language which originally developed from German. Yiddish contains many Hebrew expressions and is written in Hebrew characters. It is spoken mainly by Jews of eastern and central Europe.

yield (yēld),
1 VERB. to produce something: *This land yields good crops. Mines yield ore.*
2 NOUN. the amount that something yields; product: *This year's yield from the silver mine was very large.*
3 VERB. to give up; surrender: *The enemy yielded to our soldiers.*
4 VERB. to allow other traffic to go first: *Traffic on a side street should yield to traffic on a highway.*
❑ VERB **yields, yield·ed, yield·ing.**

yip (yip),
1 VERB. to bark or yelp sharply.
2 NOUN. a sharp, barking sound.
❑ VERB **yips, yipped, yip·ping.**

yo (yō), INTERJECTION. (slang) an expression you use to call to someone, or to greet someone: *Yo, my friend, what's up?*

yo·del (yō′dl),
1 VERB. to sing with frequent changes from the ordinary voice to a forced shrill voice and back again.
2 NOUN. the act or sound of yodeling.
❑ VERB **yo·dels, yo·deled, yo·del·ing**

yo·gurt (yō′gərt), NOUN. a thick, creamy food made from milk, thickened by the action of bacteria. Yogurt is usually sweetened and flavored.

yoke (yōk),
1 NOUN. a wooden frame that fits over the necks of two work animals.
2 NOUN. a pair of animals fastened together with a yoke: *The plow was drawn by a yoke of oxen.*
3 VERB. to put a yoke on; fasten with a yoke: *The farmer yoked the oxen before hitching them to the wagon.*
❑ PLURAL **yokes** for 1, **yoke** or **yokes** for 2; VERB **yokes, yoked, yok·ing.** ■ Another word that sounds like this is **yolk.**

Yo·kuts (yō′kuts), NOUN. a member of a group of American Indians living in north central California and nearby areas. ❑ PLURAL **Yo·kuts.**

yolk (yōk), NOUN. the yellow part of an egg. ■ Another word that sounds like this is **yoke.** –**yolk′like′,** ADJECTIVE.

Y

a	hat	ė	term	ô	order	ch	child		a in about
ā	age	i	it	oi	oil	ng	long		e in taken
ä	far	ī	ice	ou	out	sh	she	ə	i in pencil
â	care	o	hot	u	cup	th	thin		o in lemon
e	let	ō	open	ù	put	ᴛʜ	then		u in circus
ē	equal	ò	saw	ü	rule	zh	measure		

Yom Kip·pur (yom kip′ər or yom ki pùr′), a Jewish holiday. It occurs ten days after Rosh Hashanah, the Jewish New Year. On Yom Kippur, Jewish people fast to show they are sorry for their sins.

yon·der (yon′dər),
1 ADVERB. over there; within sight, but not near: *Look at that wild duck yonder!*
2 ADJECTIVE. situated over there; being within sight, but not near: *On yonder hill stands a castle.*

yore (yôr), NOUN. **of yore,** long past; now long since gone: *Knights in armor and castles belong to the days of yore.*

serenading a fair maiden in times of **yore**

you (yü), PRONOUN SINGULAR or PLURAL.
1 the person or persons spoken to: *Are you ready? Then you may go.*
2 one; anybody: *You never can tell.*
■ Other words that sound like this are **ewe** and **yew.**

you-all (yü′ôl′ or yòl), PRONOUN PLURAL. (informal) you: *You-all come and see us real soon.*

you'd (yüd),
1 a contraction of **you had.**
2 a contraction of **you would.**

you'll (yül),
1 a contraction of **you will.**
2 a contraction of **you shall.**

young (yung),
1 ADJECTIVE. in the early part of life or growth; not old: *A puppy is a young dog.*
2 NOUN. young ones; offspring: *An animal will fight to protect its young.*
3 ADJECTIVE. having the looks or qualities of youth or of a young person: *She seems young for her age.*
❑ ADJECTIVE **young·er** (yung′gər), **young·est** (yung′gist).

young·ster (yung′stər), NOUN.
1 a child: *Those youngsters live next door.*
2 a young person: *The elderly woman was as active as a youngster.*

your (yùr), ADJECTIVE.
1 belonging to you: *Wash your hands.*
2 having to do with you: *We enjoyed your visit.*
3 **Your** is used as part of some titles: *Your Highness, Your Honor.*

you're (yùr), a contraction of **you are.**

yours (yùrz), PRONOUN SINGULAR or PLURAL.
1 the one or ones belonging to you: *This pencil is yours. My hands are clean; yours are dirty.*
2 **Yours** is used at the end of a letter with some other word, *Yours truly, Sincerely yours.*

your·self (yùr self′ or yər self′), PRONOUN.
1 Yourself is used to make a statement stronger: *You yourself know the story is not true.*
2 Yourself is used instead of *you* in cases like: *Did you hurt yourself? Can you teach yourself this song? Try to do it by yourself.*
3 your real self: *Now that your cold is better, you'll feel like yourself again.*
❑ PLURAL **your·selves.**

your·selves (yùr selvz′ or yər selvz′), PRONOUN. the plural of **yourself:** *The two of you will work on the project all by yourselves.*

youth (yüth), NOUN.
1 the fact or quality of being young: *In spite of her youth, she has already traveled widely.*
2 the time between childhood and adulthood.
3 a young man: *a serious youth.*
4 SINGULAR or PLURAL. young people.
❑ PLURAL **youths** (yüths or yüŦHz) or **youth.**

youth·ful (yüth′fəl), ADJECTIVE.
1 young.
2 of, like, or for young people: *youthful energy, youthful pleasures.*
3 lively; fresh; having the looks or qualities of youth: *My grandmother has a very gay and youthful spirit.*

you've (yüv), a contraction of **you have.**

yowl (youl),
1 NOUN. a long, loud, wailing cry; howl.

2 *VERB.* to howl: *That dog is always yowling.*
□ *VERB* **yowls, yowled, yowl·ing.**

yo-yo (yō′yō), *NOUN.* a small wheel-shaped toy made of two wooden or plastic disks joined by a peg. A yo-yo can be spun out and reeled back to the hand by means of a string that is wound around the peg.
□ *PLURAL* **yo-yos.**

yo-yo

yr., an abbreviation of **year.** □ *PLURAL* **yr** or **yrs.**

Yu·ca·tán (yü′kə tan′), *NOUN.* a state in southeastern Mexico.

yuc·ca (yuk′ə), *NOUN.* a plant found in dry, warm regions of North and Central America. It has stiff, narrow leaves and white flowers. □ *PLURAL* **yuc·cas.**

Did You Know?

Most **yucca** plants are short shrubs. But some species of yuccas in the United States and Mexico can become tall trees.

yuck·y (yuk′ē), *ADJECTIVE.* disgusting; very unpleasant; distasteful: *I threw out the yucky old wet rags.* □ *ADJECTIVE* **yuck·i·er,** or **yuck·i·est.**

Yu·go·slav (yü′gō·släv),
1 *NOUN.* someone born or living in Yugoslavia.
2 *ADJECTIVE.* of or about Yugoslavia or its people.

Yu·go·sla·vi·a (yü′gō slä′vē ə), *NOUN.* a former country in southeastern Europe. **—Yu′go·sla′vi·an,** *ADJECTIVE* or *NOUN.*

Yu·kon Ter·ri·to·ry (yü′kon ter′ə tôr′ē), a territory in northwestern Canada.

yule or **Yule** (yül), *NOUN.*
1 Christmas.
2 a short form of **yuletide.**

a **yucca** in bloom

yule·tide or **Yule·tide** (yül′tīd′), *NOUN.* the Christmas season.

yum (yum), *INTERJECTION.* a word used to express pleasure or delight, especially about food: *Yum! Pizza for dinner!*

yum·my (yum′ē), *ADJECTIVE.* very pleasing to the taste; delicious: *The candied yams were yummy. She makes the yummiest pies.* □ *ADJECTIVE* **yum·mi·er, yum·mi·est.**

Y

zinnia

Zeppelin

ZOO

Zz

Z or **z** (zē), *NOUN.* the 26th and last letter of the English alphabet. ❑ *PLURAL* **Z's** or **z's.**

Za·ca·te·cas (sä/kä tä/käs), *NOUN.* a state in north central Mexico.

Za·ïre (zä ir/), *NOUN.* a country in central Africa. **—Za·ïr·e·an** or **Za·ïr·i·an** (zä ir/ē ən), *ADJECTIVE or NOUN.*

Zam·bi·a (zam/bē ə), *NOUN.* a country in southern Africa. **—Zam/bi·an,** *ADJECTIVE or NOUN.*

za·ny (zā/nē), *ADJECTIVE.* foolish or crazy in a playful way: *He had a zany idea about walking backward to school.* ❑ *PLURAL* **za·nies. —za/ni·ness,** *NOUN.*

zeal (zēl), *NOUN.* eager desire or effort: *We worked with zeal to finish the project.*

ze·bra (zē/brə), *NOUN.* a wild animal of Africa that looks something like a horse or a donkey. Zebras have black and white stripes. ❑ *PLURAL* **ze·bras** or **ze·bra.**

ze·bu (zē/bü), *NOUN.* an animal like an ox but with a large hump. The zebu is a farm animal in Asia and eastern Africa. ❑ *PLURAL* **ze·bus** or **ze·bu.**

ze·nith (zē/nith), *NOUN.*
1 the point in the sky directly overhead.
2 the highest point of something: *At the zenith of its power, Rome ruled all of Europe.*

Zep·pe·lin or **zep·pe·lin** (zep/ə lən), *NOUN.* a large, cylinder-shaped aircraft supported by stiff ribs and filled with gas. Zeppelins were mostly used from 1914 to 1937.

ze·ro (zir/ō),
1 *NOUN.* the number 0: *There are three zeros in 40,006.*
2 *NOUN.* the point marked as 0 on the scale of a thermometer.
3 *NOUN.* the temperature that corresponds to 0 on the scale of a thermometer.
4 *NOUN.* nothing; a complete absence of quantity: *One minus zero is one.*
5 *ADJECTIVE.* not any; none at all: *The weather station at the airport announced zero visibility.* ❑ *PLURAL* **zer·os** or **zer·oes.**

zero in on, *IDIOM.*
1 to aim with precision toward a target.
2 to come near from all sides; close in on; surround: *The police zeroed in on the thief.*

Word Story

Zero comes from an Arabic word meaning "empty." A zero shows that a place in a number has no value, and so is empty.

zest (zest), *NOUN.*
1 keen enjoyment; great pleasure: *The hungry children ate with zest.*
2 a pleasant or exciting quality: *Wit gives zest to conversation.*
3 the peel of an orange or lemon.

Word Story

Zest comes from a French word meaning "peel of an orange or lemon." This part of the fruit has a very strong flavor, and is used to make food and drink more appetizing. The word **zest** is now used about many other activities. In olden days, a good meal was probably many people's idea of a good time.

Zeus (züs), *NOUN.* the chief god of the ancient Greeks. The Romans called him Jupiter.

zig·zag (zig′zag′),
1 *ADJECTIVE* or *ADVERB.* with short sharp turns, first to one side, then to the other side: *We traveled in a zigzag direction. The path ran zigzag up the hill.*
2 *VERB.* to move in a zigzag way: *Lightning zigzagged across the sky.*
3 *NOUN.* a zigzag line or course: *Draw a zigzag in red.*
❑ *VERB* **zig·zags, zig·zagged, zig·zag·ging.**

zilch (zilch), *NOUN.* (informal) zero; nothing.

zil·lion (zil′yən), (informal)
1 *NOUN.* any very large, indefinite number.
2 *ADJECTIVE.* very many; a great many: *He knows a zillion jokes.*

Zim·ba·bwe (zim bä′bwe), *NOUN.* a country in southeastern Africa.

zinc (zingk), *NOUN.* a bluish white metal very little affected by air and moisture. Zinc is a chemical element. It is used as a coating for iron, in electric batteries, and in paint.

zin·ni·a (zin′ē ə), *NOUN.* a garden plant grown for its showy flowers of many colors. ❑ *PLURAL* **zin·ni·as.**

zip¹ (zip), *VERB.* to move or act quickly or with much energy: *Cars were zipping along the highway.*
❑ *VERB* **zips, zipped, zip·ping.**

zip² (zip), *VERB.* to fasten or close something with a zipper: *I zipped up my jacket.* ❑ *VERB* **zips, zipped, zip·ping.**

zip³ (zip), *NOUN.* (slang) zero, especially as the score in a game: *We won! The score was three to zip!*

Zip Code,
1 ZIP Code, a system of numbers, each of which identifies one of the postal delivery areas of the United States.
2 a number in this system: *My Zip Code is 60025.*

Word Story

Zip is an acronym. It was formed from the first letters of the words **z**one **i**mprovement **p**lan.

zip·per (zip′ər),
1 *NOUN.* a fastener in which two rows of metal or plastic teeth can be made to hook together or come apart by pulling on a sliding tab. Zippers are used in clothing, boots, luggage, and so on.
2 *VERB.* to fasten or close something with a zipper: *Zipper up your jacket before you go out in the cold.*
❑ *VERB* **zip·pers, zip·pered, zip·per·ing.**

zith·er (zith′ər or ziṯн′ər), *NOUN.* a musical instrument having 30 to 40 strings stretched across a hollow flat board. You play a zither by plucking its strings.

zo·di·ac (zō′dē ak), *NOUN.* an imaginary strip of sky that is divided into 12 equal parts called signs. The signs are named after 12 groups of stars found in them.

Word Story

Zodiac comes from a Greek word meaning "animal." Because so many signs of the zodiac are constellations named for animals, ancient Greeks called this part of the sky the circle of the animals.

zinnia

zom·bie (zom′bē), *NOUN.* (in stories) a dead body brought back to life by supernatural power.
❑ *PLURAL* **zom·bies.**

a	hat	ė	term	ô	order	ch child
ā	age	i	it	oi	oil	ng long
ä	far	ī	ice	ou	out	sh she
â	care	o	hot	u	cup	th thin
e	let	ō	open	ů	put	ṯн then
ē	equal	ò	saw	ü	rule	zh measure

ə { a in about / e in taken / i in pencil / o in lemon / u in circus }

Z

zone (zōn),
1 *NOUN.* any of the five great divisions of the earth's surface, bounded by imaginary lines going around the earth parallel to the equator. Zones differ from each other in climate.
2 *NOUN.* any region or area treated or thought of as different from others. A combat zone is an area where fighting is going on.
3 *VERB.* to divide something into zones: *The city was zoned for factories and residences.*
  ❑ *VERB* **zones, zoned, zon·ing.**
zoo (zü), *NOUN.* a place where animals are kept for people to look at: *There are often many tame animals in a children's zoo.* ❑ *PLURAL* **zoos.**
zoo·keep·er (zü/kē/pər), *NOUN.* someone who takes care of animals in a zoo.

zo·o·log·i·cal (zō/ə loj/ə kəl), *ADJECTIVE.*
1 of or about animals and animal life.
2 of or about zoology.
zo·ol·o·gy (zō ol/ə jē), *NOUN.* the science of animals; the study of animals and animal life. Zoology is a branch of biology. **—zo·ol/o·gist,** *NOUN.*
zoom (züm), *VERB.*
1 to move rapidly upward or downward: *The airplane zoomed up out of sight.*
2 to move very rapidly: *The car zoomed past us, going 80 miles an hour.*
  ❑ *VERB* **zooms, zoomed, zoom·ing.**
zoom in on, *IDIOM.*
1 to adjust a zoom lens to take a close-up shot.
2 to examine closely; concentrate your attention: *She was able to zoom in on the cause of our problem and solve it.*
zuc·chi·ni (zü kē/nē), *NOUN.* a kind of dark green squash shaped like a cucumber. It is eaten as a vegetable. ❑ *PLURAL* **zuc·chi·ni** or **zuc·chi·nis.**
Zu·ñi (zü/nyē), *NOUN.* a member of a tribe of American Indians living in western New Mexico.
  ❑ *PLURAL* **Zu·ñi** or **Zu·ñis.**

A large **zoo** like this one has animals from all over the world.

Reference Section

Table of Contents

The United States

Olympia ★ WASHINGTON

Salem ★

OREGON

Boise ★

IDAHO

★ Helena

MONTANA

C A

NORTH DAK
★ Bism

SOUTH DAK
★ Pierre

WYOMING

PACIFIC
OCEAN

Sacramento ★

NEVADA

★ Carson
City

Salt Lake City ★

Cheyenne ★

NEBRASK

UTAH

CALIFORNIA

Denver ★

COLORADO

KA

ARIZONA

Santa Fe ★

NEW
MEXICO

Oklah

Phoenix ★

T E X

Au

RUSSIA

ARCTIC
OCEAN

M E X I C O

PACIFIC
OCEAN

ALASKA

Kauai

Honolulu ★ Oahu
Molokai
Maui
Lanai

Bering Sea

CANADA

Aleutian Islands

Gulf of
Alaska

Juneau ★

H A W A I I

Hawaii

0   200   400 mi

0   200   400 km

0   100   200 mi

0   100   200 km

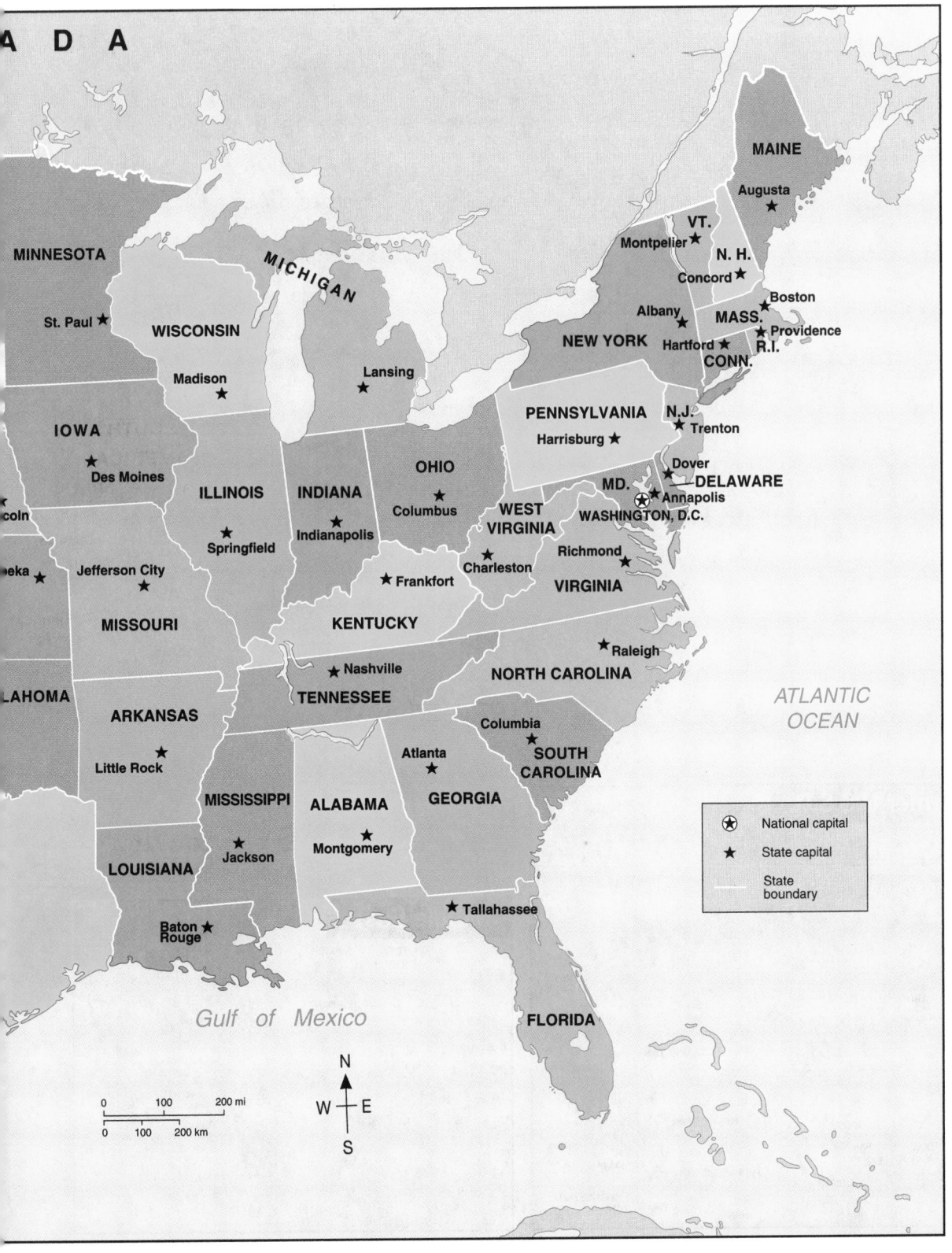

ADA

MAINE
Augusta ★

MINNESOTA

VT. ★
Montpelier ★

N. H.
Concord ★

St. Paul ★

WISCONSIN

Albany ★
MASS. ★ Boston
★ Providence
R.I.

NEW YORK
Hartford ★
CONN.

Madison ★

Lansing ★

MICHIGAN

IOWA

PENNSYLVANIA
Harrisburg ★

N.J.
★ Trenton

Des Moines ★

Dover ★

OHIO

ILLINOIS
INDIANA
Columbus ★

MD. ★ **DELAWARE**
★ Annapolis
⊛ **WASHINGTON, D.C.**

coln

WEST
VIRGINIA

eka ★

Springfield ★
Indianapolis ★

Charleston ★

Richmond ★

Jefferson City ★

★ Frankfort

VIRGINIA

MISSOURI

KENTUCKY

★ Raleigh

LAHOMA

★ Nashville

NORTH CAROLINA

ARKANSAS
TENNESSEE

Columbia ★

ATLANTIC
OCEAN

Little Rock ★

Atlanta ★

SOUTH
CAROLINA

MISSISSIPPI
ALABAMA
GEORGIA

LOUISIANA
Jackson ★
Montgomery ★

⊛ National capital

★ State capital

Baton ★
Rouge

★ Tallahassee

State
boundary

Gulf of Mexico

FLORIDA

0   100   200 mi
0   100   200 km

N
W ✦ E
S

The World

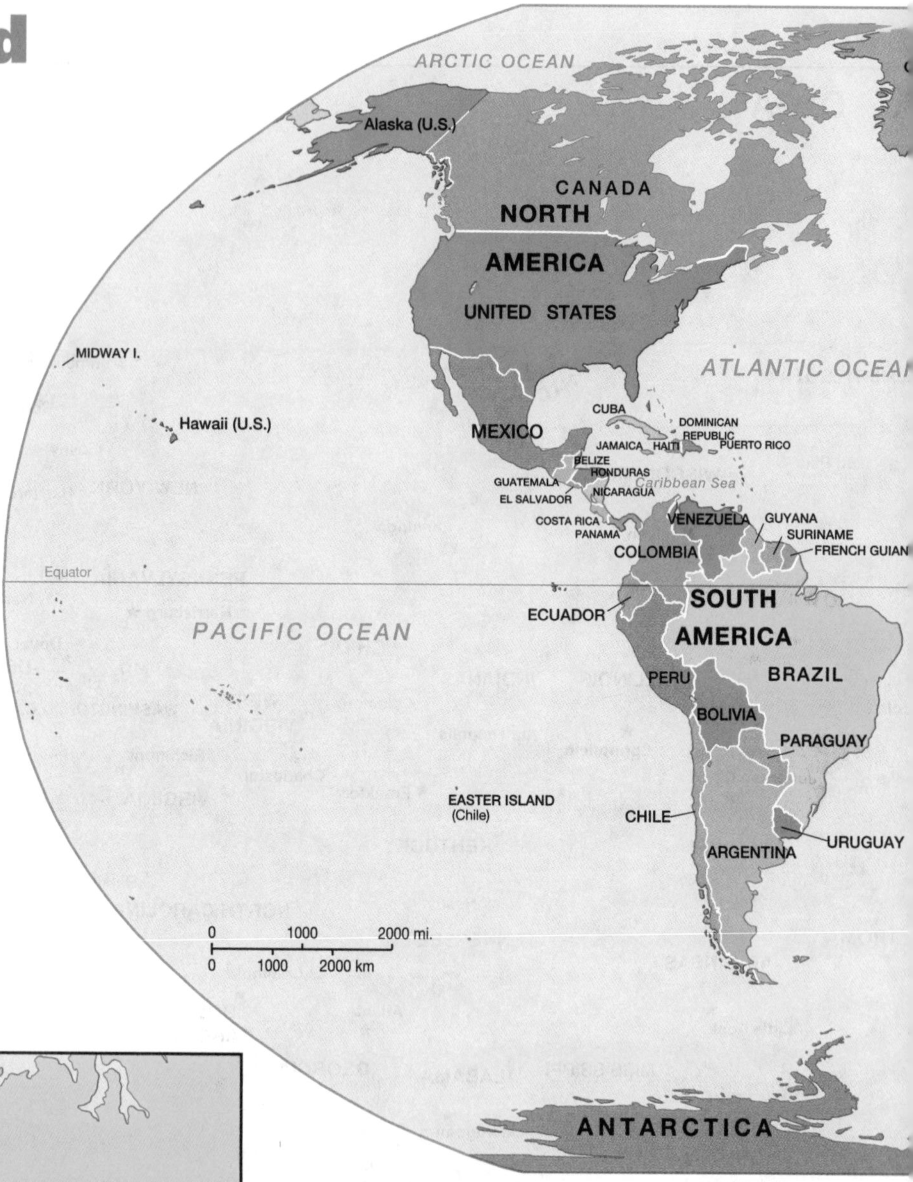

ARCTIC OCEAN

Alaska (U.S.)

CANADA

NORTH

AMERICA

UNITED STATES

ATLANTIC OCEAN

MIDWAY I.

Hawaii (U.S.)

CUBA

DOMINICAN
REPUBLIC

PUERTO RICO

JAMAICA   HAITI

MEXICO

BELIZE

GUATEMALA   HONDURAS

EL SALVADOR   NICARAGUA

Caribbean Sea

COSTA RICA

PANAMA

VENEZUELA   GUYANA

SURINAME

FRENCH GUIANA

COLOMBIA

Equator

ECUADOR

SOUTH

AMERICA

PACIFIC OCEAN

PERU

BRAZIL

BOLIVIA

PARAGUAY

EASTER ISLAND
(Chile)

CHILE

URUGUAY

ARGENTINA

| 0 | 1000 | 2000 mi. |
| 0 | 1000 | 2000 km |

ANTARCTICA

Former U.S.S.R.

FINLAND

RUSSIA

ESTONIA

LATVIA

LITHUANIA

POLAND

BELARUS

N

W   E

S

RUSSIA

UKRAINE

MOLDOVA

ROMANIA

KAZAKHSTAN

Black Sea

Caspian Sea

GEORGIA

UZBEKISTAN   KYRGYZSTAN

TURKEY   ARMENIA

CHINA

| 0 | 500 mi. |
| 0 | 500 km |

AZERBAIJAN   TURKMENISTAN

TAJIKISTAN

SYRIA   IRAQ   IRAN   AFGHANISTAN

PAKISTAN

INDIA

Middle East

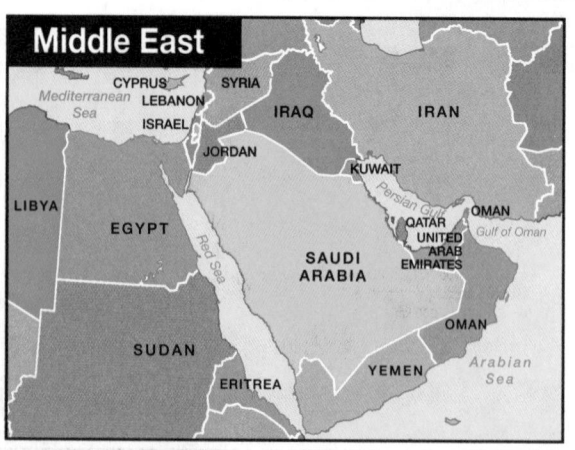

CYPRUS   SYRIA

*Mediterranean
Sea*

LEBANON

ISRAEL

IRAQ

IRAN

JORDAN

KUWAIT

LIBYA

Persian Gulf

OMAN

QATAR

UNITED
ARAB
EMIRATES

Gulf of Oman

EGYPT

Red Sea

SAUDI
ARABIA

OMAN

SUDAN

YEMEN

*Arabian
Sea*

ERITREA

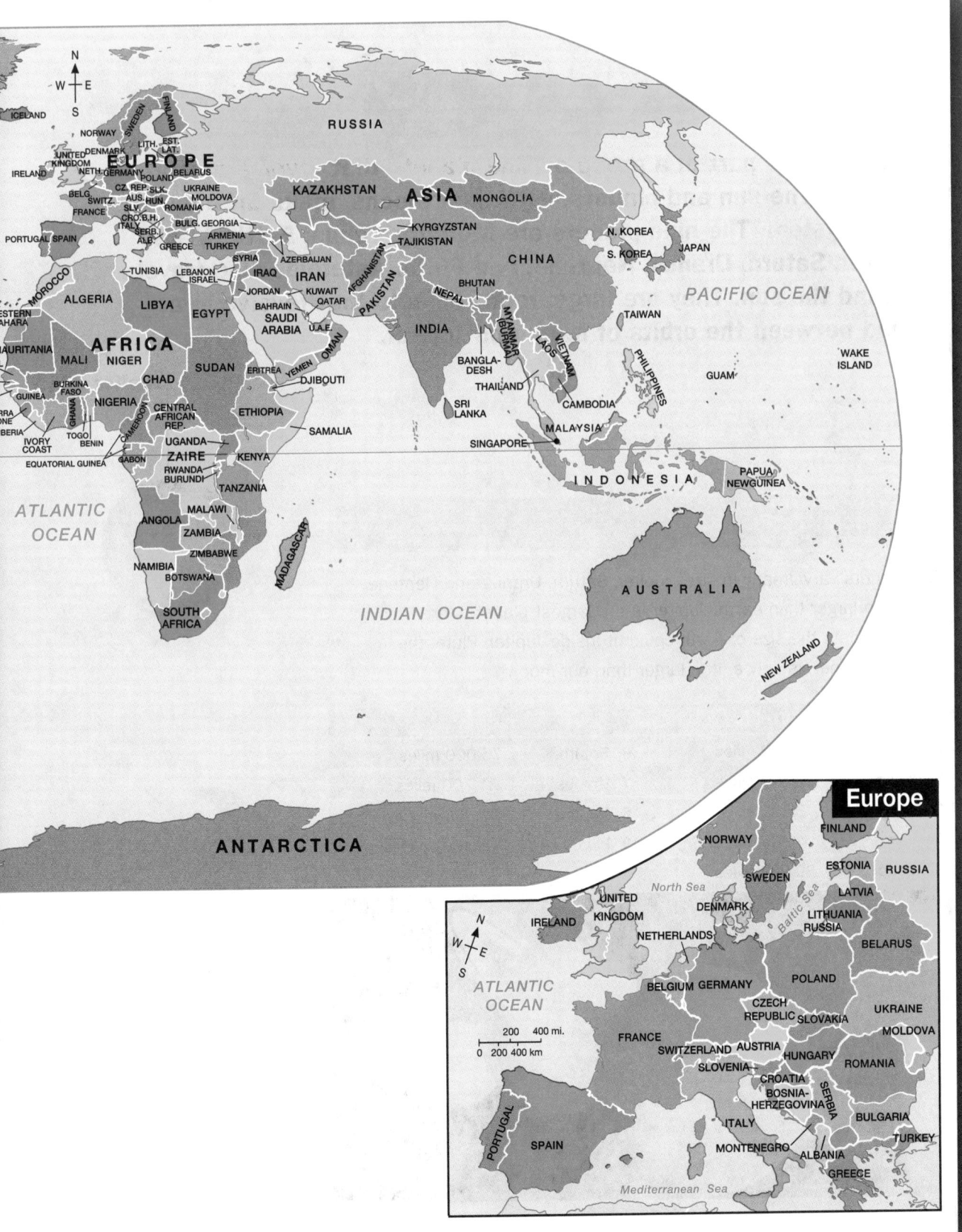

ICELAND

NORWAY

N
W+E
S

SWEDEN
FINLAND

RUSSIA

DENMARK
UNITED
KINGDOM
NETH. GERMANY
IRELAND

EUROPE

LITH. EST.
LAT.

BELG. SWITZ.
AUS. HUN.
POLAND
UKRAINE
MOLDOVA
BELARUS

CZ. REP. SLK.
SLV.
ITAL SERB.
FRANCE
ALB.
CRO. B.H.
ROMANIA
BULG. GEORGIA

PORTUGAL SPAIN

GREECE
ARMENIA
TURKEY

KAZAKHSTAN

ASIA

MONGOLIA

N. KOREA
S. KOREA

JAPAN

MOROCCO

TUNISIA
SYRIA
LEBANON
ISRAEL
IRAQ
JORDAN
IRAN

AZERBAIJAN

KYRGYZSTAN
TAJIKISTAN

CHINA

PACIFIC OCEAN

ALGERIA
LIBYA
EGYPT

BAHRAIN
KUWAIT
QATAR
SAUDI
ARABIA
U.A.E.

AFGHANISTAN
PAKISTAN

NEPAL

BHUTAN

TAIWAN

WAKE
ISLAND

WESTERN
SAHARA

AFRICA

NIGER

CHAD
SUDAN

MALI

ERITREA
YEMEN OMAN

INDIA

BANGLA-
DESH

MYANMAR
(BURMA)

LAOS

VIETNAM

PHILIPPINES

GUAM

MAURITANIA

GUINEA
BURKINA
FASO

NIGERIA

ETHIOPIA

DJIBOUTI

SAMALIA

THAILAND

CAMBODIA

SRI
LANKA

RRA
ONE
GHANA
TOGO
BENIN

CENTRAL
AFRICAN
REP.

MALAYSIA

LIBERIA
IVORY
COAST
CAMEROON

GABON
EQUATORIAL GUINEA

ZAIRE

UGANDA

KENYA

SINGAPORE

INDONESIA

RWANDA
BURUNDI
TANZANIA

PAPUA
NEWGUINEA

ATLANTIC
OCEAN

MALAWI
ANGOLA
ZAMBIA
MADAGASCAR

AUSTRALIA

ZIMBABWE
NAMIBIA
BOTSWANA

INDIAN OCEAN

SOUTH
AFRICA

NEW ZEALAND

ANTARCTICA

Europe

FINLAND

NORWAY

North Sea

ESTONIA
RUSSIA

SWEDEN

Baltic Sea

LATVIA

DENMARK

LITHUANIA
RUSSIA

UNITED
KINGDOM

IRELAND

N
W+E
S

NETHERLANDS

BELARUS

BELGIUM GERMANY

POLAND

ATLANTIC
OCEAN

CZECH
REPUBLIC

SLOVAKIA

UKRAINE

200   400 mi.

0   200 400 km

FRANCE

SWITZERLAND AUSTRIA
SLOVENIA

HUNGARY

MOLDOVA

ROMANIA

CROATIA
BOSNIA-
HERZEGOVINA

SERBIA

PORTUGAL

SPAIN

ITALY

MONTENEGRO

ALBANIA

BULGARIA

TURKEY

GREECE

Mediterranean Sea

The Solar System

Our planet is part of a group of nine planets that revolve around the sun. The sun and planets, with their moons, make up the solar system. The nine planets are Mercury, Venus, Earth, Mars, Jupiter, Saturn, Uranus, Neptune, and Pluto. Asteroids also travel around the sun. They are large, rocky objects that revolve in a band between the orbits of Mars and Jupiter.

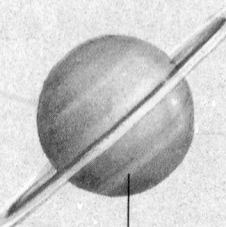

Jupiter

More About the Planets

The planets vary greatly in size. Jupiter, Saturn, Uranus and Neptune are much larger than earth. Jupiter is the largest planet. More than 1,000 planets the size of Earth could fit inside Jupiter. Pluto, the smallest planet, is only a little larger than our moon.

Diameters of the Planets

1	Mercury	3,000 miles	6	Saturn	75,000 miles
2	Venus	7,500 miles	7	Uranus	31,700 miles
3	Earth	8,000 miles	8	Neptune	31,000 miles
4	Mars	4,225 miles	9	Pluto	1,400 miles
5	Jupiter	89,000 miles			

Saturn

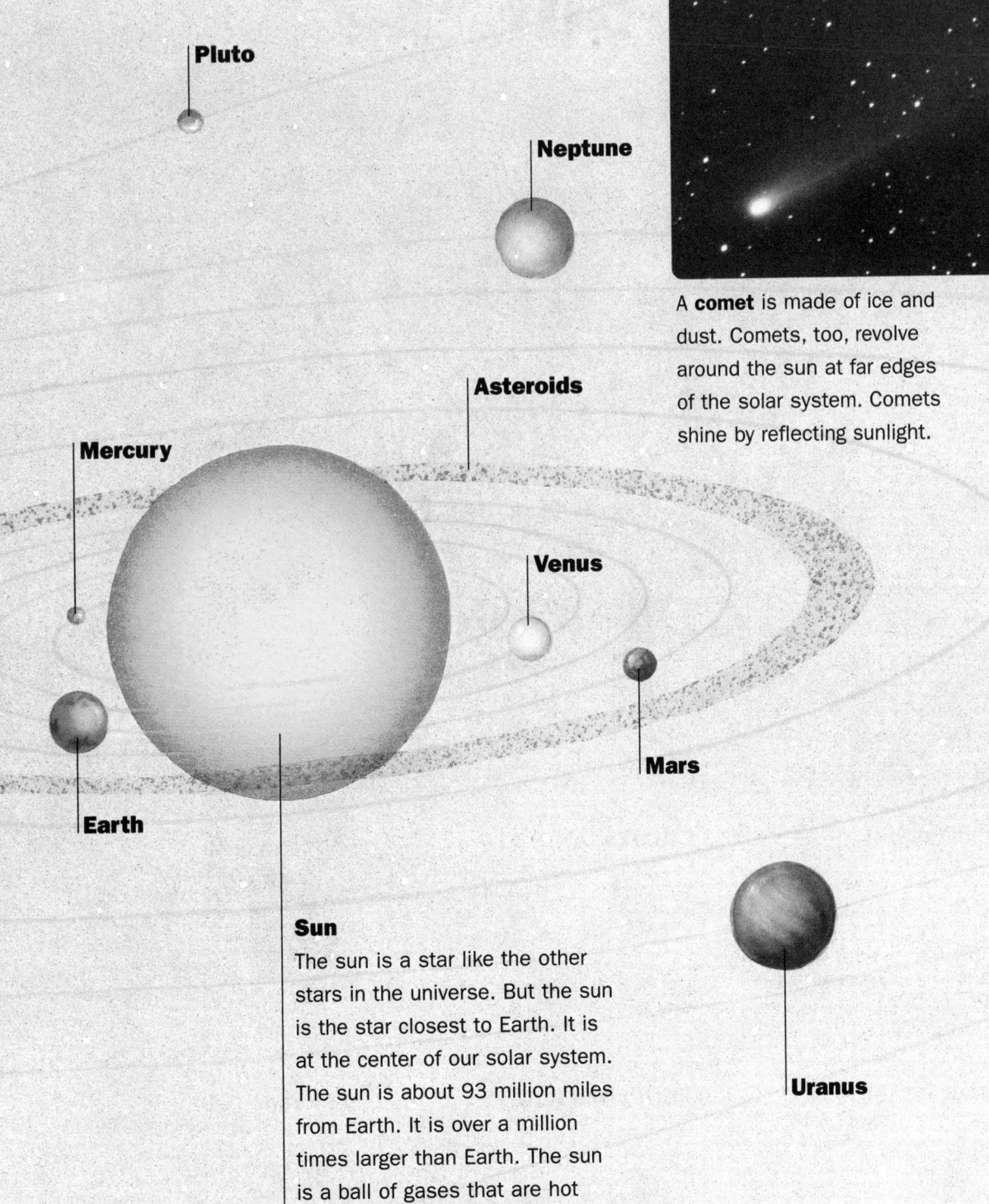

Pluto

Neptune

A **comet** is made of ice and dust. Comets, too, revolve around the sun at far edges of the solar system. Comets shine by reflecting sunlight.

Asteroids

Mercury

Venus

Earth

Mars

Sun
The sun is a star like the other stars in the universe. But the sun is the star closest to Earth. It is at the center of our solar system. The sun is about 93 million miles from Earth. It is over a million times larger than Earth. The sun is a ball of gases that are hot enough to warm the Earth from a great distance.

Uranus

Facts About the 50 States

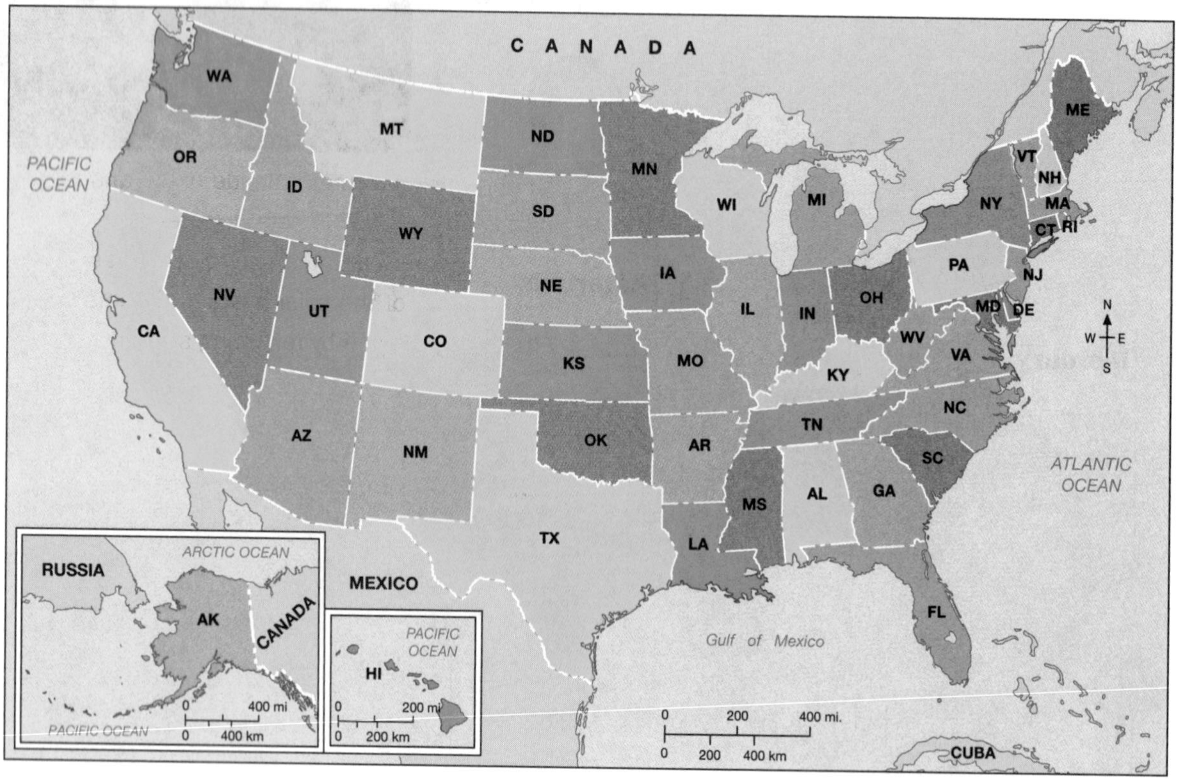

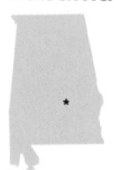

CANADA

PACIFIC OCEAN

ATLANTIC OCEAN

Gulf of Mexico

RUSSIA

ARCTIC OCEAN

MEXICO

PACIFIC OCEAN

CUBA

Alabama (AL)

Capital: Montgomery
Nickname: Heart of Dixie
Bird: Yellowhammer
Flower: Camellia

Alaska (AK)

Capital: Juneau
Nickname: The Last Frontier
Bird: Willow ptarmigan
Flower: Forget-me-not

Arizona (AZ)

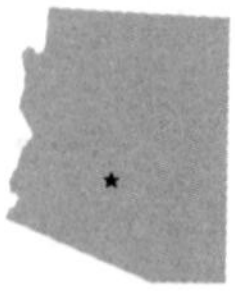

Capital: Phoenix
Nickname: Grand Canyon State
Bird: Cactus wren
Flower: Saguaro (Giant cactus)

Arkansas (AR)

Capital: Little Rock
Nickname: Land of Opportunity
Bird: Mockingbird
Flower: Apple blossom

California (CA)

Capital: Sacramento
Nickname: Golden State
Bird: California valley quail
Flower: Golden poppy

Colorado (CO)

Capital: Denver
Nickname: Centennial State
Bird: Lark bunting
Flower: Rocky Mountain columbine

Connecticut (CT)

Capital: Hartford
Nickname: Constitution State
Bird: Robin
Flower: Mountain laurel

Delaware (DE)

Capital: Dover
Nickname: Diamond State or First State
Bird: Blue hen chicken
Flower: Peach blossom

Florida (FL)

Capital: Tallahassee
Nickname: Sunshine State
Bird: Mockingbird
Flower: Orange blossom

Georgia (GA)

Capital: Atlanta
Nickname: Peach State
Bird: Brown thrasher
Flower: Cherokee rose

Hawaii (HI)

Capital: Honolulu
Nickname: Aloha State
Bird: Nene (Hawaiian goose)
Flower: Hibiscus

Idaho (ID)

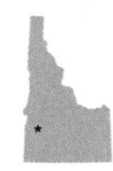

Capital: Boise
Nickname: Gem State
Bird: Mountain bluebird
Flower: Mock orange syringa

Illinois (IL)

Capital: Springfield
Nickname: The Land of Lincoln
Bird: Cardinal
Flower: Native violet

Indiana (IN)

Capital: Indianapolis
Nickname: Hoosier State
Bird: Cardinal
Flower: Peony

Iowa (IA)

Capital: Des Moines
Nickname: Hawkeye State
Bird: Eastern goldfinch
Flower: Wild rose

Kansas (KS)

Capital: Topeka
Nickname: Sunflower State
Bird: Western meadowlark
Flower: Sunflower

Kentucky (KY)

Capital: Frankfort
Nickname: Bluegrass State
Bird: Kentucky cardinal
Flower: Goldenrod

Louisiana (LA)

Capital: Baton Rouge
Nickname: Pelican State
Bird: Brown pelican
Flower: Magnolia

Maine (ME)

Capital: Augusta
Nickname: Pine Tree State
Bird: Chickadee
Flower: White pine cone and tassel

Maryland (MD)

Capital: Annapolis
Nickname: Free State
Bird: Baltimore oriole
Flower: Black-eyed Susan

Massachusetts (MA)

Capital: Boston
Nickname: Bay State
Bird: Chickadee
Flower: Trailing arbutus (Mayflower)

Michigan (MI)

Capital: Lansing
Nickname:
 Wolverine State
Bird: Robin
Flower: Apple
 blossom

Minnesota (MN)

Capital: St. Paul
Nickname: North
 Star State
Bird: Common loon
Flower: Pink and
 white lady's-
 slipper

Mississippi (MS)

Capital: Jackson
Nickname:
 Magnolia State
Bird: Mockingbird
Flower: Magnolia

Missouri (MO)

Capital: Jefferson
 City
Nickname: Show
 Me State
Bird: Bluebird
Flower: Hawthorn

Montana (MT)

Capital: Helena
Nickname: Treasure
 State
Bird: Western
 meadowlark
Flower: Bitterroot

Nebraska (NE)

Capital: Lincoln
Nickname:
 Cornhusker State
Bird: Western
 meadowlark
Flower: Goldenrod

Nevada (NV)

Capital: Carson City
Nickname: Silver
 State
Bird: Mountain
 bluebird
Flower: Sagebrush

New Hampshire (NH)

Capital: Concord
Nickname: Granite
 State
Bird: Purple finch
Flower: Purple lilac

New Jersey (NJ)

Capital: Trenton
Nickname: Garden
 State
Bird: Eastern
 goldfinch
Flower: Violet

New Mexico (NM)

Capital: Santa Fe
Nickname: Land of
 Enchantment
Bird: Roadrunner
Flower: Yucca

New York (NY)

Capital: Albany
Nickname: Empire
 State
Bird: Bluebird
Flower: Rose

North Carolina (NC)

Capital: Raleigh
Nickname: Tar Heel
 State
Bird: Cardinal
Flower: Flowering
 dogwood

North Dakota (ND)

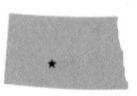
Capital: Bismarck
Nickname: Sioux
 State
Bird: Western
 meadowlark
Flower: Wild prairie
 rose

Ohio (OH)

Capital: Columbus
Nickname: Buckeye
 State
Bird: Cardinal
Flower: Scarlet
 carnation

Oklahoma (OK)

Capital: Oklahoma
 City
Nickname: Sooner
 State
Bird: Scissor-tailed
 flycatcher
Flower: Mistletoe

Oregon (OR)

Capital: Salem
Nickname: Beaver
State
Bird: Western
meadowlark
Flower: Oregon
grape

Pennsylvania (PA)

Capital: Harrisburg
Nickname: Keystone
State
Bird: Ruffed grouse
Flower: Mountain
laurel

Rhode Island (RI)

Capital: Providence
Nickname: Ocean
State
Bird: Rhode Island
Red
Flower: Purple violet

South Carolina (SC)

Capital: Columbia
Nickname: Palmetto
State
Bird: Carolina wren
Flower: Yellow
jessamine
(Carolina
jessamine)

South Dakota (SD)

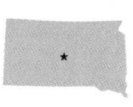

Capital: Pierre
Nickname: The Mt.
Rushmore State
Bird: Ring-necked
pheasant
Flower: American
pasqueflower

Tennessee (TN)

Capital: Nashville
Nickname:
Volunteer State
Bird: Mockingbird
Flower: Iris

Texas (TX)

Capital: Austin
Nickname: Lone
Star State
Bird: Mockingbird
Flower: Bluebonnet

Utah (UT)

Capital: Salt Lake
City
Nickname: Beehive
State
Bird: Sea gull
Flower: Sego lily

Vermont (VT)

Capital: Montpelier
Nickname: Green
Mountain State
Bird: Hermit thrush
Flower: Red clover

Virginia (VA)

Capital: Richmond
Nickname: The Old
Dominion
Bird: Cardinal
Flower: Flowering
dogwood

Washington (WA)

Capital: Olympia
Nickname:
Evergreen State
Bird: Willow
goldfinch
Flower: Coast
rhododendron

West Virginia (WV)

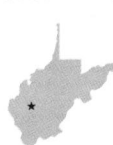

Capital: Charleston
Nickname:
Mountain State
Bird: Cardinal
Flower:
Rhododendron

Wisconsin (WI)

Capital: Madison
Nickname: Badger
State
Bird: Robin
Flower: Wood violet

Wyoming (WY)

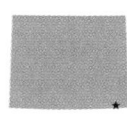

Capital: Cheyenne
Nickname: Equality
State
Bird: Meadowlark
Flower: Indian
paintbrush

Symbols That Make Us Proud

All countries have symbols. The ones you see on these pages are symbols of the United States of America. They stand for the things that make our country great. The American flag stands for the land, the people, the government, and the ideals of the United States.

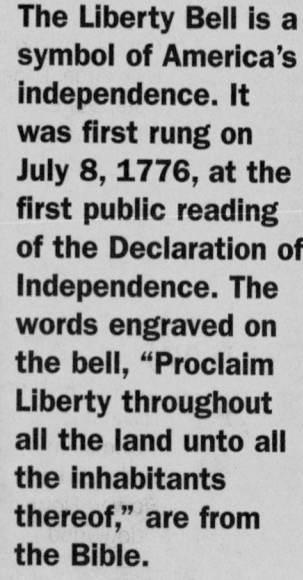

The Liberty Bell is a symbol of America's independence. It was first rung on July 8, 1776, at the first public reading of the Declaration of Independence. The words engraved on the bell, "Proclaim Liberty throughout all the land unto all the inhabitants thereof," are from the Bible.

◀ The Statue of Liberty stands on Liberty Island in New York Harbor. It was a gift of friendship given to the United States by the people of France in 1884. This monument is a symbol of freedom and hope for everyone who comes to America from all over the world.

The Great Seal of the United States is a symbol of America's power. It shows an American eagle with its wings ▶ spread. The olive branch in the eagle's right claw and the arrows in its left means that our country wants to live in peace, but it can wage war.

▲ The bald eagle is the national bird of the United States. It is a symbol of our country's strength and bravery.

Weights and Measures

A guitar is about **1 meter** long.

A crayon is about **8 centimeters** long.

A teaspoon holds about **5 milliliters**.

This bottle contains **1 liter** of water.

One brick weighs about **1 kilogram**.

One small grape weighs about **1 gram**.

Metric Measurements

Length and Width

1 centimeter (cm)	= 10 millimeters (mm)
1 meter (m)	= 1000 millimeters (mm)
	100 centimeters (cm)
1 kilometer (km)	= 1000 meters (m)

Weight

1 gram (g)	= 1000 milligrams (mg)
1 kilogram (kg)	= 1000 grams (g)

Capacity

1 liter (l)	= 1000 milliliters (ml)

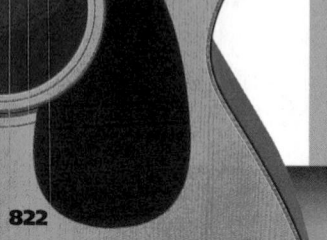

Customary Measurements

Length and Width

1 foot (ft.)	= 12 inches (in.)
1 yard (yd.)	= 36 inches (in.) 3 feet (ft.)
1 mile (mi.)	= 5,280 feet (ft.) 1,760 yards (yd.)

Weight

1 pound (lb.)	= 16 ounces (oz.)
1 ton	= 2000 pounds (lb.)

Capacity

1 tablespoon (tbsp.)	= 3 teaspoons (tsp.)
1 fluid ounce (fl. oz.)	= 2 tablespoons (tbsp.)
1 cup (c.)	= 8 fluid ounces (oz.)
1 pint (pt.)	= 2 cups (c.)
1 quart (qt.)	= 2 pints (pt.)
1 gallon (gal.)	= 4 quarts (qt.)

1 cup

1 pint

1 quart

1 gallon

A quarter is about **1 inch** wide.

A door is about **1 yard** wide.

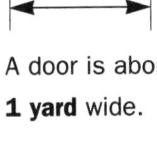

A loaf of bread weighs about **1 pound**.

A small car weighs about **1 ton**.

Full pronunciation key

The pronunciation of each word is shown just after the word, in this way: **ab•bre•vi•ate** (ə brē′vē āt).

The letters and signs used are pronounced as in the words below.

The mark ′ is placed after a syllable with primary or heavy stress, as in the example above.

The mark ′ after a syllable shows a secondary or lighter stress, as in **ab•bre•vi•a•tion** (ə brē′vē ā′shən).

a	hat, cap	p	paper, cup
ā	age, face	r	run, try
â	care, fair	s	say, yes
ä	father, far	t	tell, it
b	bad, rob	th	thin, both
ch	child, much	ᴛʜ	then, smooth
d	did, red	u	cup, butter
e	let, best	u̇	full, put
ē	equal, be	ü	rule, move
ėr	term, learn	v	very, save
f	fat, if	w	will, woman
g	go, bag	y	young, yet
h	he, how	z	zero, breeze
i	it, pin	zh	measure, seizure
ī	ice, five		
j	jam, enjoy		represents:
k	kind, seek	ə	a in about
l	land, coal		e in taken
m	me, am		i in pencil
n	no, in		o in lemon
ng	long, bring		u in circus
o	hot, rock		
ō	open, go		
ȯ	all, caught		
ô	order, board		
oi	oil, voice		
ou	house, out